9. *Callistephus* 'Matsumoto' cut flower.
10. *Dahlia* 'Bon Bini' cut flower.
11. *Echinacea purpurea* 'Ruby Giant.'
12. *Eustoma* 'Cinderella Pink' cut flowers.
13. *Fuchsia* 'Honeysuckle' garden ornamental.
14. Mini *Gerbera* 'Reggea' cut flowers.
15. *Helianthus angustifolia* 'Low Down' garden ornamental.
16. Outdoor planting of *Hippeastrum* 'Red Lion' in Zone 76.

Floriculture
Principles and Species

Second Edition

John M. Dole
Professor, Department of Horticultural Science
North Carolina State University
Raleigh, North Carolina

Harold F. Wilkins
Emeritus Professor, Department of Horticultural Science
University of Minnesota
St. Paul, Minnesota

PEARSON
Prentice
Hall

Upper Saddle River, New Jersey 07458

Library of Congress Cataloging-in-Publication Data

Dole, John M.
  Floriculture : principles and species / John M. Dole, Harold F. Wilkins. -- 2nd ed.
    p. cm.
Includes bibliographical references and index.
  ISBN 0-13-046250-0
  1. Floriculture.   2. Plants, Ornamental.   I. Wilkins, Harold F.   II. Title.

SB405.D58 2004
635.9--dc22

2003026778

Publisher: Stephen Helba
Executive Editor: Debbie Yarnell
Associate Editor: Kimberly Yehle
Production Editor: Lori Dalberg, Carlisle Publishers Services
Production Liaison: Janice Stangel
Director of Manufacturing and Production: Bruce Johnson
Managing Editor: Mary Carnis
Manufacturing Buyer: Cathleen Petersen
Creative Director: Cheryl Asherman
Cover Design Coordinator: Christopher Weigand
Cover Design: Christopher Weigand
Cover Illustrations: Courtesy of John M. Dole
Text Illustrations: John Buettner
Marketing Manager: Jimmy Stephens
Formatting: Carlisle Communications, Ltd.
Printing and Binding: Courier Westford

Pearson Education Ltd.
Pearson Education Singapore Pte. Ltd.
Pearson Education Canada, Ltd.
Pearson Education—Japan
Pearson Education Australia Pty. Limited
Pearson Education North Asia Ltd.
Pearson Educación de Mexico, S. A. de C.V.
Pearson Education Malaysia Pte. Ltd.

10 9 8 7 6 5 4 3 2 1
ISBN: 0-13-046250-0

PEARSON
Prentice Hall

Contents

Part III

Preface

AUDIENCE

Floriculture: Principles and Species is a comprehensive text designed for both industry professionals and academic students and teachers. This text is used by producers to grow their crops, conduct their business operations, and market their products. This book also provides technical information for advisors, suppliers, and sales staff to aid their clientele. Students from all levels of academia, from community colleges to universities, will be able to learn about the diversity and details of floriculture production.

HIGHLIGHTS

This comprehensive book covers all of the major floriculture crop species and many of the minor species being produced today around the world. Diagrams, photographs, and tables illustrate many important concepts and practices. The index is thorough and allows rapid access to all topics. The book is organized into three sections to allow easy use of the information.

The 12 chapters in Part I provide an introduction to floriculture production, postharvest handling, marketing, and greenhouse and business management. Extensive, easy-to-use tables are included on propagation techniques, production temperatures and crop times, photoperiodic requirements for flowering, foliar nutrient levels, effective growth retardants, postharvest storage temperatures, and ethylene sensitivity of hundreds of species.

The chapters in Part II discuss 103 genera or family accounts covering all of the major floriculture crop species being commercially grown in the floriculture industry. These chapters are laid out in a consistent manner to allow easy retrieval of the information. Enough production information is included in each chapter to allow a grower or student to develop a production schedule for the species. Many of the production schedules are presented in tables for easy reference.

Part III contains hundreds of minor crops species and basic production information on bedding plants, field-grown cut flowers, foliage plants, herbs, garden perennials, and forced woody cuts.

CHANGES TO THE SECOND EDITION

We added 19 new chapters, which include hundreds of additional commercially cultivated species. Of these chapters, 14 are on specific genera or families, four are general chapters that include information on hundreds of miscellaneous species, and one chapter is on flowering mechanisms, describing what regulates flowering and how flowering occurs.

We have updated and expanded each chapter with the latest information available. In addition, we have added a Key Points section to each of the chapters, highlighting the most important aspects for both the student and the industry professional.

ORGANIZATION

This book is organized into three sections to assist students and growers. Part I contains general production information and basic plant physiology principles. Common production practices are explained and, in some cases, illustrated.

Chapter 1, *Propagation*, covers taxonomy and nomenclature, cultivar licensing, and various propagation methods.

Chapter 2, *Flowering Control*, discusses flower induction, initiation and development, juvenility, plant habit, and the main environmental stimuli for flowering.

Chapter 3, *Temperature*, focuses on the importance of day, night, and average daily temperatures, DIF, and media temperatures.

Chapter 4, *Light*, explains light saturation and compensation points, acclimatization, and light quality. Methods to increase and decrease light in the greenhouse or field are explained.

Chapter 5, *Water,* covers permanent wilting point, water quality, water treatments, irrigation strategies, irrigation systems, and automation.

Chapter 6, *Nutrition,* explains the essential elements for plant growth, applying fertilizers, pH, soluble salts, monitoring nutrition, correcting problems, and carbon dioxide injection.

Chapter 7, *Media,* covers the physical factors and properties of media, media components, developing the best media for plant production, and controlling media-borne pathogens.

Chapter 8, *Plant Growth Regulation,* lists the endogenous plant growth regulators found within plants and how the growth of floriculture crops is regulated. Specific plant growth regulators have been included because most have been on the market for many years and are likely to remain available in the future.

Chapter 9, *Pest Management,* details integrated pest management, chemical use and safety, insect pests, diseases, and weeds. Specific pest control products have not been included because materials useful for one firm may not be effective for another. In addition, pesticide availability is subject to rapid change.

Chapter 10, *Postharvest,* explains the production and postharvest factors that affect cut flower or potted plant longevity after it leaves the grower's control.

Chapter 11, *Greenhouse Construction and Operations,* covers greenhouse placement, styles, framing, foundations, coverings, benches, beds, production containers, cooling, heating, air circulation, fuels, environmental controls, energy conservation, and alarm systems.

Chapter 12, *Marketing and Business Management,* discusses the fact that production is only part of a successful business—a firm must also sell the crop and make a profit. Growing a quality crop, marketing and sales, and business management and cost accounting are included.

Part II has comprehensive chapters on 103 specific crop genera and families. Virtually all of the potted flowering plants and cut flowers grown in greenhouses are included. The most important bedding and foliage plants also have separate chapters; however, the large number of species used for bedding plants, perennials, outdoor-grown cuts, and potted foliage plants precludes us from covering them all individually. For those segments of floriculture, we trust that the species we have included will serve as representative examples. The species included were chosen due to their current commercial importance or, in a few cases, due to their uniqueness or estimated importance in the future. Note that the Part I and Part III chapters contain information on many species for which there are no individual chapters in Part II.

We have attempted to cover all uses of each species such as potted flowering plant, cut flower, hanging basket, and so forth. Nomenclature follows *The New Royal Horticultural Society Dictionary of Gardening* whenever possible. Dozens to hundreds of cultivars are available for many of the species, the most popular of which change annually. We did not attempt to list cultivars but rather describe the most important attributes of the cultivars that would guide cultivar selection.

One of the keys to producing a crop is the development of a suitable production schedule. Numerous production schedules exist for each crop species because production conditions vary with location, season, cultivar, and desired plant size. One to three sample schedules are included for most species. Because types and quantities of species grown as well as production methods vary from country to country, international references and perspectives are included in many of the chapters.

Specific insect and diseases have been listed for each crop. Refer to Chapter 9, *Pest Management,* in Part I to find more information on methods used to control pests.

Finally, much information from one chapter often overlaps that of another section. For example, photoperiod may be found in both the *Flowering Control* and *Light* chapters. When looking for specific information, it may be helpful to read the entire chapter to find related, useful information.

Part III has six general chapters that cover basic production information on hundreds of minor species. The chapters are grouped into *Bedding Plants, Field-Grown Cut Flowers, Foliage Plants, Garden Perennials, Herbs,* and *Forced Woody Cuts.* We did not include general chapters on potted flowering plants or greenhouse cut flowers because most species grown commercially have already been covered in individual genera chapters in Part II.

FUTURE

At best, textbooks are never finished. New species, cultivars, techniques, materials, and production methods are constantly being introduced and accepted by the industry. In addition, despite the diligence of both authors, numerous assistants, reviewers, and the Prentice Hall and Carlisle Publishers Services staffs, there are no doubt errors. Please send any corrections, suggestions, and additional information to John Dole for inclusion in the next edition.

Acknowledgments

Diversity is the joy and the bane of floriculture. An average retail greenhouse or garden center sells numerous species and cultivars. A typical perennial catalog lists countless species and cultivars. Cut flower wholesalers and foliage plant brokers handle and distribute hundreds of additional cut flower and foliage plant species produced worldwide. These sources do not include the many new plant species being brought into cultivation each day or the thousands of new cultivars waiting to be released from research facilities worldwide. A visit to a grower's conference, large production facility, or Dutch flower auction can leave a person numb with excitement over the great diversity of plant materials. In the floriculture industry, most of us are "plant people" at heart and we revel at the beauty of floriculture plants.

The bane of diversity is that each of those species has different cultural and production requirements, which vary from location to location. Individual cultivars within a species often have unique requirements as well. In addition, a specific species may be grown in several container sizes and styles, at various times of the year, and at varied locations around the world. Production requirements change with each situation.

The excitement and challenge of producing a comprehensive text on floriculture is what led us to write this book. Part I chapters were written by John Dole. Part II chapters were written by Harold Wilkins, except for *Dracaena, Echinacea, Epipremnum, Euphorbia, Lilium* (Easter), *Philodendron, Rumohra,* and *Solidago*, which were written by John Dole, *Heliconia* and *Strelitzia* by Richard Criley, and *Proteaceae* by Audrey Gerber. Part III chapters were written by John Dole, except for *Herbs* and *Forced Woody Cuts*, which were written by Harold Wilkins.

Typing of the first edition was accomplished mainly by Nancy Maness, with assistance from Susie Ruby and Barbie Tiel. First and second drafts were edited by each author. Subsequent editing was done by John Dole, Harold Wilkins, Susie Ruby, and Rhoda Burrows, with assistance from Lee Newell and Linda O'Malley. Final editing of the first edition was performed by John Dole, Harold Wilkins, Prentice Hall, and Carlisle Publishers Services staff, with Chad Thomas as editorial production supervisor. Final editing of the second edition was accomplished by John Dole, Harold Wilkins, Loretta Palagi, and Lori Dalberg of Carlisle Publishers Services. Drawings were made by John Buettner. Many of the chapters have been reviewed by or contributed to by producers and academicians who have specific expertise. Without a doubt this book is much stronger because of the contributions of anonymous reviewers and the following individuals and companies:

Pat Busch, Len Busch Roses—*Lilium* (Asiatic and Oriental)

T. J. Cape, Nurserymen's Exchange—*Anemone, Aquilegia, Astilbe, Campanula, Clematis, Dianthus* (Pot), *Freesia, Lachenalia, Ornithogalum, Oxalis,* and *Ranunculus*

Ray Cloyd, University of Illinois—*Pest Management*

Janet Cole, Oklahoma State University—*Propagation* and *Nutrition*

Pat Edzel, Len Busch Roses—*Rosa*

Bruce Fitzgerald, Alex. R. Masson, Inc.—*Dendranthema, Epipremnum,* and *Hibiscus*

Bill Fonteno, North Carolina State University—*Media*

Terry Gilbertson-Ferriss, University of Wisconsin—Review of Part I and half of Part II chapters of first edition

Fred C. Gloeckner, Inc. Andrew Lee and Associates—*Crocus, Freesia, Hyacinthus, Iris, Narcissus, Oxalis, Ranunculus,* and *Tulipa*

David Hartley, Paul Ecke Poinsettias, Inc.—*Dendranthema* and *Euphorbia*

Royal Heins, Michigan State University—*Cyclamen, Euphorbia, Lilium* (Easter), and *Schlumbergera* and *Hatiora*

Bud Hervey, Abbott-Ipco, Inc.—*Caladium*

Betsy Hitt—*Clarkia, Eustoma, Field-Grown Cut Flowers*

Tim Hooper, Oklahoma State University—*Pest Management* and *Greenhouse Construction and Operations*

Betsy Hudgins, Oklahoma State University—*Pest Management*

Meriam Karlsson, University of Alaska—Review of entire first edition

Judy Laushman, ASCFG—*Liatris*

Rodd Moesel, American Plant Products, Inc.—*Greenhouse Construction and Operations*

Doug Needham, Oklahoma State University—*Propagation*

Steven Newman, Colorado State University—Review of first edition

Geno Picchioni, New Mexico State University—Review of first edition

Erik Runkle, Michigan State University—*Orchidaceae*

Paul Sansone, Here & Now Garden—*Gentiana* and *Paeonia*

Gay Smith, CFX—*Marketing and Business Management*

Vicki Stamback, Bear Creek Farms, Inc.—*Marketing and Business Management, Helianthus*, and *Zinnia*

Rudolf Sterkel, Ernst Benary of America—*Aquilegia*, all *Begonia* chapters, and *Campanula*

Brian Whipker, North Carolina State University—*Plant Growth Regulation*

Finally, the most important acknowledgments are for those who provided moral support, encouragement, and specific information. A great number of colleagues both within our departments and around the world are gratefully acknowledged. A special thanks to Betty Coleman, Rachel McLaughlin, Barb Amos, Diane Mays, Ingram McCall, Aliya Donnell, Frankie Fanelli, Lane Greer, and Megan Weddington here at North Carolina State University.

Harold Wilkins dedicates this book . . .

- To my mother, both grandmothers, and Uncle Samuel, all of whom had wonderful gardens of beauty which sparked me, in my childhood, toward the future.
- To the University of Illinois, Drs. James and Inez Kamp, Dr. and Mrs. Fred Weinard, and Professor John Culbert. Not only was an excellent education given to us, but you also opened my eyes to the world.
- To the Hans and Della Rosacker family and the Carl and Virginia Pearlstein family. You have become my family.
- To my graduate students—you are my greatest pride and happiness.
- Thank you John Martin Dole for telling me this book could be written and for your patience, valuable aid, and contribution.

John Dole dedicates this book . . .

- To John Buettner, Vicki Stamback, Rhoda Burrows, Janette Jacobs, Judy Laushman and Betsy Hitt for your constant support, energy, humor, and encouragement.
- To my father, mother, brother, and sister.
- To Harold Wilkins: advisor, colleague, and friend. Yes, it has been a long road, but this textbook would not have happened without you—twice! What were we thinking when we first decided to write this book!
- To the complex and beautiful natural world around us which constantly inspires me.

John M. Dole
Raleigh, North Carolina

About the Authors

Both John Dole and Harold Wilkins have had a lifelong interest in floriculture. Dole is currently a professor with the Department of Horticultural Science at North Carolina State University. He is a native of West Michigan and received his B.S. degree from Michigan State University. He obtained his Ph.D. degree from the University of Minnesota and served on the Oklahoma State University faculty for 11 years before moving to North Carolina State University. Dole has written hundreds of trade journal articles, scientific journal articles, and book chapters. His research program has focused on specialty cuts, bulbs, Easter lilies, and poinsettias; and on flowering physiology and water and mineral nutrition. As an active member of the Association of Specialty Cut Flower Growers (ASCFG), Dole has served on the board of directors as Southern Region director, treasurer, and executive advisor. He also coordinates the National ASCFG Trial Programs. In addition, Dole teaches greenhouse management and commercial floriculture crop production. Dole has visited floriculture operations in numerous countries in Europe, Asia, and Central and South America. In 1992 he received the Kenneth Post Award for the Outstanding Graduate Student Paper, in 1995 the ASCFG's Outstanding Service Award, and in 2000 the ASCFG's Allan Armitage Award.

Wilkins is an emeritus professor from the University of Minnesota, former D. C. Kiplinger chair holder at The Ohio State University, and former director of research and development for one of the largest potted flowering plant producers in the country. He is a native of southern Illinois and received all three degrees from the University of Illinois, Urbana. He worked as a postharvest physiologist at the University of Florida's Gulf Coast Research Center, Bradenton, before joining the faculty at the University of Minnesota in 1966. Wilkins' research program has spanned a wide range of species including Easter lilies, freesia, alstroemeria, azaleas, tulips, and poinsettias, as well as topics including light quality, branching, and the interaction of cold and light. In 1989 he joined Nurserymen's Exchange in Half Moon Bay, California, as their research and development officer. From 1992 to 1994 he was a visiting professor, D. C. Kiplinger chair of floriculture, at The Ohio State University. Wilkins is recognized as one of the most highly published authors in floriculture. Wilkins is also widely traveled with visits to numerous countries in western and eastern Europe, the Middle East, Asia, South Africa, Australia, New Zealand, Central America, and South America. In 1987 he was awarded a Fulbright Fellowship for study at the University of Norway.

Wilkins career has garnered him and his students numerous awards including Outstanding Floriculture Research Paper from the American Society for Horticulture Science (ASHS) in 1967, 1978, 1980, 1985, and 1992. He has also received the Alex Laurie Award from the Society of American Florists in 1991 and from the Ohio Florists' Association in 1993. He was named a fellow of the ASHS in 1984 and a fellow of *Pi Alpha Xi* in 1992. In 1988 Wilkins was initiated into the Society of American Florist's Hall of Fame.

Note to Readers

In addition to the pesticides mentioned, a variety of chemicals, especially plant growth regulators, are commonly used in floriculture and have been included in this textbook. Chemical use is strictly regulated by federal, state, and, occasionally, other governmental units. Prior to using any chemical, be sure to check the legality of its use. Many experimental chemicals are mentioned in this text but may not be legal to use in your location; in such cases, other related chemicals may be legal and just as effective. Also, note that the status of numerous chemicals may change; some that are currently legal may not be in the future and others currently unregistered may become legal to use in the future. Every person or business bears sole responsibility for understanding and following the laws regarding chemical use in their area.

Part I

Part I contains general production information and basic plant physiology principles. These introductory chapters also include information on many species not covered individually in Parts II and III. Extensive tables on propagation, production temperatures, tissue nutrient analysis, plant growth regulators, postharvest ethylene sensitivity, harvest stage, and storage temperatures for hundreds of species act as easy-to-use reference sections. Specific pesticide recommendations have not been included because materials useful for one firm may not be effective for another. In addition, pesticide availability is subject to rapid change. However, plant growth regulators have been included because most have been on the market for many years and are likely to remain available. Topics covered in Part I are as follows:

Chapter 1

Propagation

INTRODUCTION

At the heart of all commercial floriculture crop production is plant propagation. In the past a floriculture producer often depended on the skill of the staff propagator. Today many businesses purchase liners, plugs, and rooted or un-rooted cuttings from specialists who efficiently propagate species on a large scale. Ultimately, the decision to propagate crops internally or to purchase rooted plants must be based on economics, quality, and dependable delivery. Consideration should also be given to available materials, labor, and greenhouse space. Equally important is the question of whether growers can use their time more profitably if they are not propagating their own plant materials. However, one potential drawback in relying on an outside propagation specialist is that the firm does not have direct control over the crop and must trust the propagator to produce uniformly high-quality plant materials and to deliver them safely to the grower in a timely manner. Ultimately, producers must propagate their own plant materials if they engage in off-season production or are producing species or cultivars not available from a professional propagator.

The various propagation methods can be separated into sexual methods—seeds and spores—and asexual methods—cuttings, layers, divisions, natural reproductive structures such as bulbs, grafting, and *in vitro* micropropagation. Many bedding plants and a signifi-cant number of cut flower, potted flowering plant, and foliage plant species are propagated from seeds. In a number of species, however, sexual reproduction produces plants that are too variable for commercial production or do not reliably replicate desirable traits. In such cases, asexual methods are used to produce *clones*—individual plants propagated from one original plant—which have the same traits as the original plant. Asexual propagation is also used in situations when seed propagation is not possible, too lengthy, or too expensive.

TAXONOMY AND NOMENCLATURE

The goal of propagation is to reproduce a selected plant type, such as a plant species, sub-species, variety, or cultivar. A plant species is defined as having a naturally occurring, unique set of characteristics and is separated from other closely related species by location, flow-ering time, and so on. The unique characteristics of a species are usually transmitted through seeds or spores to the next generation. If cross-pollination between species occurs, the resulting seedlings may be sterile or less suc-cessful in the wild than the parent species.

Exacum affine is an example of a com-mercially cultivated species. Species are desig-nated by two-part, binomial names (epithets). The first epithet is the genus to which the

3

species belongs and the second epithet is the species. The genus is capitalized and the species remains lowercase; both names are italicized. A binomial name is often followed by an abbreviation designating the authority—the person who named the species—such as Isaac Bayley Balfour who named *Exacum affine* Balf. f. The authority is not italicized.

Natural variability in one or more traits often exists among individuals of a species. Populations within a species containing one or more identifiable traits are taxonomically known as *subspecies* or *varieties*. The name for the subspecies or variety is usually preceded by the abbreviation *subsp.* for subspecies or *var.* for variety. Subspecies and variety epithets are usually lowercase and italicized. In the wild, for example, most *Exacum affine* plants have medium blue flowers; however, some plants have dark lavender flowers and thus have been named *Exacum affine* var. *atrocaeruleum*. Characteristics of a subspecies or variety are often passed from one generation to another by seeds or spores.

Cultivars are similar to varieties in that both are variants of species identifiable in some way, but cultivars are usually not naturally occurring and are maintained through cultivation. Unusual individuals of a species that occur in the wild are often asexually propagated and given a cultivar name. The word *cultivar* is a contraction of "cultivated variety." Although *variety* and *cultivar* have distinctive definitions, the two terms are often mistakenly interchanged in commercial horticulture. The epithets for cultivars are capitalized, enclosed in single quote marks, and not italicized (i.e. *Exacum affine* 'Blue Champion'). If naturally occurring subspecies or varieties are brought into cultivation, the epithet is sometimes—erroneously—converted into a cultivar name.

Hybrids are plants produced from genetically distinct parent plants. Although hybrids can occur naturally, they are most commonly produced in cultivation through manipulation by plant breeders. Hybrids can be made between (1) varieties or cultivars of a species, (2) distinct species, or (3) species of two different genera. If individual plants within a hybrid are allowed to cross-pollinate, the resulting offspring are normally quite variable and most offspring will not contain the same set of characteristics that defines the original hybrid. Hybrids between species are usually given a new species epithet that is preceded by an ×, such as the *Delphinium* ×*belladonna*, a hybrid between *D. elatum* and *D. grandiflorum*. In the case of hybrids for which the parentage is unknown, the genus epithet is followed immediately by the cultivar name, such as *Rosa* 'Forever Yours.' Hybrids between species of two genera are usually given a new genus epithet that is also preceded by an ×, such as ×*Fatshedera*, a hybrid between *Fatsia japonica* 'Moseri' and *Hedera hibernica*.

Although definitions of taxonomic terms may appear clear when written, the situation usually is more complex in nature. As more information is learned about specific taxa, the names may be changed. For example, the florist's cineraria is now known as *Pericallis* ×*hybrida* instead of *Senecio* ×*hybrida*. Commercially, further confusion occurs when similar plants are given different names by different companies.

CULTIVAR PROTECTION, LICENSING, AND LEASING

As stated earlier, the goal of plant propagation is to reproduce a plant with a desirable set of characteristics. Although these characteristics may occur through spontaneous mutations (sports), new cultivars are typically produced through a long-term breeding program. Because of the substantial amount of time and money required to produce a new cultivar, plant breeders can choose from a number of processes available in the United States to protect their work and profit from it (Craig, 1993; Darke, 1991; Hutton, 1991; Rogers, 1991). These processes can be involved and typically require the services of a lawyer.

- Plant patents can be obtained on asexually propagated plant materials that are new and unique. Patents are effective for 20 years, after which time the patent expires and cannot be renewed. The plant material can then be freely propagated and marketed. Plant patents are issued in the United States by the U.S. Patent and Trademark Office. Many companies use the acronym *PPAF*, which means "plant patent applied for," at the end of the plant name. This designation is used when a patent application has been filed but not yet granted (Fig. 1-1). It is illegal to use PPAF without actually filing a patent application. In addition, firms that propagate and sell plants marked with PPAF will be liable to the patent holder if

FIGURE 1-1 Plant label showing ®, ™, and PPAF (plant patent applied for).

the application is approved. Plant patents are independent of trademarks.

- Trademarks can be words, symbols, or designs. A trademark "identifies the goods or services of one party as distinct from those of others and indicates the origin of the goods or services" (Hutton, 1991 p. 40). For example, the name of a specific plant or series of plants (such as Sunblaze® roses) can be trademarked. Trademarks are often combined with patents; however, trademarks do not expire. Although a plant can be propagated and marketed after its patent expires, the plant's trademarked name cannot be used unless permission is obtained from the company holding the trademark. Note that the trademarked name of a plant is different from its cultivar name; the latter cannot be trademarked and can be freely used (Darke, 1991). For example, in the name 'Supertunia® Lavender Morn,' the word 'Supertunia' cannot be used by anyone without permission from the trademark holder, but 'Lavender Morn' can be readily used. Unregistered trademarks are noted with the symbol ™ and registered trademarks are noted by ®.

- Plant variety protection provides protection for inbred plant varieties produced from seed. Varieties need to be unique, uniform, and stable.

- Plant utility patents are often used by biotechnology companies to protect unique production processes, genes, plant parts, and physical traits associated with their products.

- Trade secrets are used to commercially protect the parental inbred lines used in the production of many F_1 hybrid seed-propagated cultivars.

- Proprietary rights can be used to control the propagation and marketing of a unique plant without patents, trademarks, or variety protection. Distribution of the plant material is controlled by contractual agreements, making propagation and marketing of a plant by anyone other than those specified in the contract illegal.

Many countries other than the United States have legislation to protect the work of firms and individuals developing new cultivars. For example, European Plant Breeder's Rights are in effect in Europe. The Union for the Protection of New Varieties of Plants (UPOV) is an international agreement among member countries to protect plant developers' work (Fowler, 1994). However, many countries have not joined UPOV and do not recognize plant cultivar protection.

Once a cultivar has been legally protected, propagation by anyone other than the developer requires a license or a sublicense. In effect, propagators may not own the plant material; rather, they lease or rent it from the plant developer. Generally, for each propagule (i.e., cutting or tissue-cultured plantlet) the grower pays a royalty to the plant developer. When a grower buys protected plant materials, the royalty has already been included in the price. Growers cannot legally propagate patented plants without a license from the developer and must appropriately label each plant. Illegal propagation of a protected plant is known as *infringement* and is illegal. Failure to pay royalties for the propagation of protected plants is also illegal. Trademarks can also be licensed.

SEED

Seeds are living plants and must be handled as such to germinate. Seeds need proper temperature, moisture, light, and oxygen to germinate. The optimum conditions will vary with the species and possibly the cultivar. Not only must seeds germinate (viability), they must also germinate rapidly and uniformly (vigor) to be produced cost effectively. Proper seed handling starts with careful storage of the seed.

SEED STORAGE

The best procedure is for the grower to purchase adequate seeds for a season and have none remaining to carry over into the next year. However, this is not realistic, and typically some seeds are stored for sowing the next year.

Optimum seed storage conditions occur when both the humidity and temperature are as low as possible but the temperature is above 35°F (2°C). Primed and pregerminated seeds should be stored at 45°F (7°C). Seeds should be refrigerated in an airtight container with fresh Dryright™ packets to absorb moisture from the air in the container and keep the humidity low. As a general rule, the relative humidity should be 25 to 35% with a temperature of 40 to 50°F (5 to 10°C). Higher temperatures of 59 to 77°F (15 to 25°C) can be used for storage times of less than a year provided that humidity is low (Carpenter et al., 1995). The optimum moisture content of seed is 5 to 8% for most species. However, the moisture content of seed can increase by up to 2% in as short as 2 hours when seed are removed from storage for sowing. Increasing moisture content will decrease germination rate (Carpenter et al., 1995). If the seed moisture content is low enough, 5 to 8%, the seed of many species can be stored below freezing (Styer and Koranski, 1997).

During sowing, remove only enough seed for sowing at one time. Return the seed to the cold storage during lunch or during any other long interruptions. When using the seed, keep it in a cool location with low humidity. Be sure to finish using open seed packets first.

Seeds from many species remain viable for more than 1 year and can be successfully used the following year. However, seeds of a number of species do not store well and if they do germinate, the resulting seedlings will be less vigorous than those from fresh seeds. Seed of species that should not be carried over from one year to the next include *Aquilegia, Callistephus, Catharanthus, Centauria, Cleome, Consolida, Delphinium, Kochia, Linum, Lunaria, Phlox, Salvia, Torenia, Verbena,* and *Viola*.

SEED TESTING

Regardless of the storage method, stored seeds should be tested before the next growing season. A simple method is to count out a specific number of seeds of each cultivar, such as 50,

and place them between two pieces of paper towels. Roll the paper towels up, moisten, place them in plastic bags, and seal. The bags should be kept moist and warm at 70 to 75°F (21 to 24°C). When the seeds germinate, record the number of seeds that germinate promptly—slow to germinate seedlings would probably not be used anyway. Divide the number germinated by the total number of seeds used. Multiplying the resulting number by 100 will yield the germination percentage. If the germination percentage is below 60%, sowing the seeds may be a waste of time and materials. If the germination percentage is less than 100%, overseed to ensure an adequate number of seedlings. To calculate the amount of seeds to be sown, divide the number of seedlings desired by the germination percentage of the seed lot in decimal form. For example, if 3,000 seedlings are needed and the germination percentage is 80%, the amount to sow is 3,000/0.8 = 3,750 seeds.

SEED PRETREATMENTS

Although the seeds of many floriculture crop species, especially bedding plants such as marigold (*Tagetes*), germinate readily when sown in a warm greenhouse, the seeds of other species, especially perennials, require a variety of specific environmental conditions for optimum germination. Some seeds must be subjected to a period of cold temperatures, high moisture, or even the heat or smoke from fires to allow them to germinate (Bell et al., 1993). The seed of other species germinate best in light or in the dark. Some species, such as various orchids, require symbiotic infection with mychorrhizae for proper germination in nature. All of these processes have developed as a way to ensure that seeds germinating in nature have the greatest chance of surviving to maturity.

Several seed treatments can be performed by seed suppliers or growers to improve germination and ease seed handling of many species. These treatments are known as *seed enhancements*. Seed that has not been treated is typically designated as *raw seed*.

Refined seed is produced when raw seed is graded after harvest to produce seed that is uniform in size, weight, shape, color, and density. Refined seed is more likely to germinate uniformly and is available under a number of product names from the seed companies. Several species are available as refined seed including *Impatiens* and *Salvia*.

Stratification is the application of a moist chilling treatment of 32 to 50°F (0 to 10°C) to seeds. The treatment can be applied to seeds already sown in flats or to seeds that have been mixed with moist sand, peat moss, or vermiculite. The duration of the treatment will vary with both the species and the temperature used (Hartmann et al., 1997). Typical storage temperatures are 35 to 45°F (2 to 7°C); higher temperatures may cause premature sprouting, and lower temperatures may increase the required storage duration. A warm water soak may be used prior to stratification to soften seed coats. Stratification requires that the seed be moist but never wet. Excessive moisture may encourage rotting and prevent oxygen from reaching the seeds. If seeds are stratified in airtight containers, they should be opened occasionally for air exchange. Stratification is useful for many perennial species such as *Aconitum* and *Gentiana*.

Scarification is any method of breaking through hard, water-impermeable seed coats to allow water to penetrate. Many members of the pea family such as several lupine (*Lupinus*) and *Baptisia* species benefit from scarification (Hartmann et al., 1997). Small numbers of large seeds can be hand scarified by filing or sandpapering each seed. Large numbers of seeds can be mechanically scarified by equipment designed for the task. Acid scarification can also be used on large amounts of seed and consists of soaking seeds in concentrated sulfuric acid at the rate of one part seed to two parts acid. The seeds should be gently and regularly stirred to produce uniform results; however, stirring will raise the temperature of the acid–seed mixture and vigorous stirring may injure the seeds or cause splattering. Do not leave seeds in the acid too long or they will be damaged; the amount of time required can vary from 10 min to 6 hr for seeds with especially thick coats. At the end of the treatment, remove the seeds and thoroughly wash for up to 10 min to completely remove the acid. The remaining acid should be disposed of properly; dilute by adding it to a large amount of water. Seeds can be planted immediately or dried for later planting. Be sure to experiment first with each seed lot because results can vary depending on the species, cultivar, and seed source.

Chemical soaks can also enhance germination, using substances such as gibberellins, cytokinins, and potassium nitrate. Gibberellins have been effective on several species, such as *Primula*, and can be applied as a 24-hr soak using concentrations ranging from 100 to 10,000 ppm. As with any treatment, test on a small number of seeds first. In addition, seeds can be soaked in Bonzi (paclobutrazol) to decrease elongation after germination (Pasian and Bennett, 2001).

Seed hydration is a technique used by seed suppliers to imbibe the seed and begin germination, but then stop the process before the radicle (root) emerges. When hydrated seeds are planted, the germination process continues. The advantages are faster seedling emergence, improved uniformity of emergence, and greater adaptability to a wider range of germination temperatures (McDonald and James, 1997). Seed hydration can be as simple as placing seeds in four to five times their volume of hot water at 170 to 210°F (77 to 98°C) and allowing the seeds and water to cool for 12 to 24 hr. This treatment works especially well on seeds with a hard seed coat or with germination inhibitors in the coat. Soaking can also speed germination of seeds that are normally slow to germinate. Plant seeds immediately after treatment to allow the germination process to continue. Seeds can be surface dried briefly to allow mechanical sowing.

Seed priming, another hydration method, is more precise, requires specialized equipment, and is usually performed by seed companies. With seed priming, the amount of water that the seeds absorb during the hydration process is controlled by soaking seeds in an aerated salt solution or in a polyethylene glycol (PEG) solution. Both types of solutions restrict the rate of water uptake and provide a more uniform product than hydration with water. Other types of seed priming solutions also exist. The seed of a number of species benefits from priming including *Impatiens*, *Verbena*, and pansy (*Viola*).

Matriconditioning is a form of priming in which seeds are mixed with a moist solid such as granulated clay or vermiculite (McDonald and James, 1997). After hydration, the solid carrier is removed by sieving. After any of the hydration methods are performed, the seeds are surface dried and handled similar to untreated seeds. Hydrated seeds should be used promptly for best results.

Pregermination is similar to seed hydration except the process is allowed to progress further until the seed coat splits and the radicle becomes visible (McDonald and James, 1997). At this point the seeds are sorted, eliminating those that do not have a radicle present.

Pregermination provides even faster seedling production than other hydration methods and results in 100% usable seedlings. Disadvantages are a limited shelf life of 4 to 5 weeks, limited selection, and increased cost. Research continues on pregermination, and products with a longer shelf life are being developed.

Pelleted seeds are produced by encasing them in a coating, allowing them to be used in automated seeders by increasing the size and weight of each seed, such as with the dust-like wax begonia (*Begonia* Semperflorens-Cultorum) seed or smoothing out its shape, such as with tomato (*Lycopersicon esculentum*) seed. The coating can be made of clay, diatomaceous earth, graphite, powdered perlite, or woodflour combined with a binding agent (McDonald and James, 1997). A variety of other substances can be incorporated into the coat to improve germination, such as micronutrients, growth regulators, fungicides, and microbial inoculants. With small seeds, such as alyssum (*Lobularia maritima*) and *Portulaca*, more than one seed is often included in each pellet to ensure at least one plant per plug. Brightly colored dyes color the pellets to make them more visible in the medium.

Coated seed is similar to pelleted seed except the coating is thin and does not obscure the shape of the seed. The primary purpose of a coating is to apply a substance to the seed such as a micronutrient or a fungicide. In film coating, substances to improve germination are applied as liquids in very thin, lightweight coatings. Marigold (*Tagetes*) seed is often coated.

Mechanization treatments are used with some species to facilitate the mechanical sowing of the seeds. For example, projections on marigold seeds, known as *tails*, can be removed in a process known as de-tailing or the wings on *Ageratum* seed can be de-winged. Similarly, tomato and *Gomphrena* seeds can be defuzzed. These processes damage the seed coats, which may shorten the storage life of the seed (Styer and Koranski, 1997).

CONTAINERS

Although seeds can be sown by hand into open flats (Fig. 1-2) or trough flats, the majority are mechanically sown into individual cells of plug flats with automatic seeders (Fig. 1-3). Plug flats vary in the number of cells per flat (50 to 512), the shape of the cell (round, square, octagon), diameter of the cell, and depth of the cell. The larger the cell size, the longer the seedling

FIGURE 1-2 Seedlings sown in rows and germinated in an open flat.

FIGURE 1-3 Automatic seeder. Note vermiculite dispensing on the top of plug flats and behind the operator; flats properly stack to prevent compaction.

can remain before it must be transplanted. The square and octagon-shaped cells are thought to reduce root spiralling around the cell, which can lead to poor establishment of the plant after transplanting. Most plug flats are made of plastic, but some are also made of Styrofoam.

MEDIA

Media for seed germination should be well drained, have a low soluble salt level [electrical conductivity (EC) of less than $1.0 \ dS \cdot m^{-1}$] and fine texture, and contain no pathogens. High soluble salts can damage seedlings easily; EC levels readily tolerated by established plants will damage seedlings. The texture should be fine enough to prevent small seeds from moving too deep into the medium. A pathogen-free medium, of course, is an absolute requirement as fungal damping-off disease can quickly destroy seedlings. Many growers use commercial, premixed germination media, most of which have a low EC but contain a small amount of nutrients. If open or trough flats are used, sterilized sand is frequently added to the medium to facilitate seedling separation during hand transplanting.

TEMPERATURE

Low temperature is often the primary reason for poor seed germination. For most species, optimum media temperature is 70 to 75°F (21 to 24°C), but varies among species (Table 1-1). The temperature should rarely go below 70°F (21°C) or slow, erratic germination will occur. Conversely, the temperature should remain below 80°F (27°C). Note that as the light level increases, the temperature of the flat media will also increase, especially with dark-colored flats (Faust et al., 1997). Medium temperature should be monitored because it can be 5 to 10°F (3 to 6°C) cooler than the air temperature under cloudy conditions, due to water evaporation. Cool water from a mist system can also directly reduce the medium temperature. Eight hours were required for the medium temperature to return to 70°F (21°C) after application of cold water (Ball, 1991). Conversely, several species including foxglove (*Digitalis purpurea*), *Phlox*, and sweet pea (*Lathyrus splendens*) prefer a 60 to 65°F (16 to 18°C) germination temperature rather than a 70 to 75°F (21 to 24°C) media temperature.

There are a number of ways to ensure a warm media temperature without raising the temperature of the entire greenhouse. Electric heating cables laid on the benches are easy to use for small areas. For specific benches, a unit heater with a fanjet tube can be placed below the bench. With either method, line the bench top with plastic to prevent excessive drying, and wrap the bench with plastic to the floor to trap in the heat. For larger areas, bench heating such as Biotherm® microclimate tubing is effective (see Chapter 11, Greenhouse Construction and Operations). Use of a separate germination chamber with multiple shelves can be an efficient way to germinate large numbers of flats. If the chamber does not have fluorescent lights, air circulation for uniform temperatures, or venting, remove the seedlings promptly after they germinate to prevent excessive elongation or overheating.

LIGHT

Small seeds often germinate better with light and should be sown on the top of the medium and not covered (Table 1-1). Generally, relatively low light levels are needed, as little as 0.2 fc (0.04 μmol·m^{-2}·s^{-1}) (Cathey, 1964a, b). The seeds of a few species such as *Dahlia* and marigold (*Tagetes*) require darkness and should be covered or germinated in a dark germination chamber.

Sufficient light for proper growth immediately after germination is also required. Light levels that are too low will cause seedlings to be tall, spindly, and difficult to transplant. In cool or low-light areas, seedlings can be grown in full sun until early spring, with shade applied beginning in April. In southern areas, light shade may be needed starting in late January to prevent excessive heating and drying. Light levels greater than 2,000 fc (400 μmol·m^{-2}·s^{-1}) may cause the media temperature to increase more than 4 to 5°F (2 to 3°C) above the air temperature (Faust et al., 1997). Light levels of 4,000 to 5,000 fc (800 to 1,000 μmol·m^{-2}·s^{-1}) may cause the medium to be 13 to 18°F (7 to 10°C) above the air temperature.

When germination chambers are used, the light levels should be 1,200 fc (240 μmol·m^{-2}·s^{-1}) (Koranski, 1983). For chambers without light or for covered flats, move seedlings as soon as they germinate or they will rapidly elongate, fall over, and be unusable.

WATER

High-quality, low-EC water and uniform application are also critical for proper seed germination. High water EC may prevent seedlings from germinating, cause erratic germination, and increase susceptibility to disease.

Equally important is maintaining uniform media moisture. If seeds begin the germination process but the medium subsequently dries out, the seedlings will be injured or die and germination will be erratic. Media moisture levels can be maintained through mist, fog, or high-humidity enclosures. Fogging and high-humidity enclosures are preferred because excessive misting can leach nutrients from the medium and increase disease problems. If only a few flats are being germinated, they can be enclosed in white or clear plastic bags. A large number of flats can be covered with plastic sheeting or spun-fiber cloths such as Remay® or Vispore®. High-humidity chambers with multiple shelves can also be constructed to hold and germinate large numbers

TABLE 1-1

Lighting and germination temperatures and times for numerous floriculture species (adapted from Nau, 1999).

Scientific Name	Common Name	Lighting	Germination Temperature (°F)	Germination Temperature (°C)	Germination Time (days)	Plug Crop Time (weeks)
Abelmoschus esculentus	Okra	Cover lightly	70	21	4–9	
A. moschatus	Annual hibiscus		72–75	22–24	10–14	
Acanthus mollis	Bear's breech	Cover	65–72	18–22	8–16	
Achillea filipendulina	Fernleaf yarrow	Light	65–70	18–21	11–15	6–7
A. millefolium	Common yarrow					
A. ptarmica	Sneezeweed					
A. tomentosa	Woolly yarrow	Light	65–70	18–21	4–8	
Achimenes hybrids	Achimenes	Light	75–80	24–27	14–27	
Aconitum napellus	Monkshood	Light	65–70	18–21	10–21	
Ageratum houstonianum	Ageratum	Light	75–78	24–25	7–10	5–6
Agrostemma githago	Agrostemma	Light or cover	65–70	18–21	4–8	
Agrostis nebulosa	Cloud grass	Cover lightly	70–72	21–22	3–7	
Alcea rosea	Hollyhock	Cover lightly	70–72	21–22	5–10	
Allium cepa	Onion	Cover	70–75	21–24	9–15	8–9
A. schoenoprasum	Chives	Cover	70	21	7–10	
Amaranthus caudatus	Amaranthus	Cover lightly	70–75	21–24	6–10	
A. tricolor						
Amberboa moschata	Sweet sultan	Cover lightly	65–70	18–21	7–14	
Ammi majus	Lace or bishop's flower	Light	72–75	22–24	12–14	6–7
Anaphalis margaritacea	Pearly everlasting	Light or cover	68–70	20–21	4–8	
Anchusa capensis	Anchusa	Light	68–72	20–21	4–8	
Anemone coronaria	Anemone	Cover	60–65	15–18	7–14	12–13
Anethum graveolens	Dill	Light	65–70	18–21	5–8	
Anthemis tinctoria	Anthemis	Cover lightly	70–72	21–22	3–7	
Antirrhinum majus	Snapdragon	Light	70–75	21–24	5–7	5–6
Apium graveolens						
var. dulce	Celery	Cover	70–75	21–24	14–22	8–9
Aquilegia caerulea	Columbine	Light	70–75	21–24	10–20	
Arabis alpina	Rock cress	Light	65–70	18–21	6–12	
Armeria maritima	Thrift	Light or cover	68–70	20–21	4–10	
Asclepias tuberosa	Butterfly weed	Light	70–75	21–24	21–28	
Asparagus densiflorus	Asparagus	Cover	Day: 85 Night: 75	29 24	21–42	10–12

(continued)

A. setaceus						
Aster alpinus	Michaelmas daisy	Cover	68–70	20–21	11–12	5–6
Astilbe ×arendsii	False spirea	Light	60–70	15–21	14–21	
Aubrieta deltoidea	False rockcress	Light	65–70	18–21	7–14	
Aurinia saxatilis	Alyssum	Light	68–72	20–22	3–8	
Baptisia australis	Wild blue indigo	Cover	70	21	10–18	
Begonia ×heimalis	Heimalis begonia	Light	75–78	24–26	7–14	
B. Semperflorens-Cultorum hybrids	Wax begonia	Light	78–80	26–27	7–14	8–9
B. Tuberhybrida hybrids	Tuberous begonia	Light	75–78	24–26	7–14	8–9
Bellis perennis	English daisy	Light	70–75	21–24	7–14	
Bergenia cordifolia	Heartleaf bergenia	Light	70–75	21–24	4–8	
Beta vulgaris	Beet	Cover lightly	72	22	7–10	
Borago officinalis	Borage	Cover	70	21	5–8	
Brachycome iberidifolia	Swan River daisy	Light	70–72	21–22	4–8	
Brassica oleracea	Flowering cabbage	Cover	65–70	18–21	7–11	4–5
B. oleracea	Flowering kale					
B. oleracea (acephala)	Cole crops	Cover	65–70	18–21	10–11	5–6
B. oleracea var. acephala	Kale					
	Collard					
B. oleracea var. botrytis	Cauliflower					
B. oleracea var. capitata	Cabbage					
B. oleracea var.gemmifera	Brussels sprouts					
B. oleracea var. gongylodes	Kohlrabi					
B. oleracea var. italica	Broccoli					
Briza maxima	Quaking grass	Cover lightly	70	21	4–6	
B. minima	Short quaking grass					
Browallia speciosa	Browallia	Light	75–78	24–25	18–19	6–7
Calceolaria	Calceolaria					
Herbeohybrida group		Light	65–70	18–21	10–14	5–6
Calendula officinalis	Calendula	Cover	70	21	5–10	
Callistephus chinensis	Aster		70	21	8–10	
Campanula isophylla	Campanula	Light	68–72	20–22	14–20	9–10
C. medium	Canterbury bells	Cover lightly	70	21	14–21	
Canna ×generalis	Canna	Cover	70–75	21–24	8–12	
Capsicum annuum	Pepper	Cover	70–75	21–24	10–12	
Carthamus tinctorius	Safflower	Light	68–72	20–22	5–14	7–8
Caryopteris incana	Blue spirea	Cover	70–75	21–24	12	

TABLE 1-1 (continued)

Scientific Name	Common Name	Lighting	Germination Temperature (°F)	(°C)	Germination Time (days)	Plug Crop Time (weeks)
Catananche caerulea	Catananche	Light or cover	70–72	21–22	4–10	
Catharanthus roseus	Vinca	Cover lightly	78–80	25–26	11–16	5–6
Celosia argentea						
Plumosa group	Plume celosia	Cover	75–78	24–25	11–12	5–6
C. argentea Cristata group	Crested celosia	Cover	75	24	8–10	
C. argentea Spicata group	Wheat celosia	Cover	75	24	5–10	
Centaurea americana	Centaurea	Cover lightly	60–65	15–18	7–14	6–7
C. cyanus	Bachelor's buttons	Cover lightly	60–65	15–18	7–14	
C. macrocephala	Golden basket flower	Cover lightly	68–72	20–22	5–10	
C. montana	Perennial cornflower	Cover lightly	68–72	20–22	7–14	
Centranthus ruber	Red valerian	Light or cover	60–65	15–18	14–21	
Cerastium tomentosum	Snow-in-summer	Light	65–68	18–20	7–14	
Chamaedorea elegans	Parlor palm	Cover	75	24	—	
Cirsium japonicum	Japanese thistle	Light or cover	68–72	15–18	12–14	7
Citrullus lanatus	Watermelon	Cover	80–85	27–29	7–11	5–6
Clarkia amoena	Satin flower	Cover	68–72	20–22	7–10	4–7
Cleome hassleriana	Cleome	Light	Day: 80 Night: 70	26 21	8–12	
Cobaea scandens	Cobaea	Light or cover	70	21	4–8	
Coffea arabica	Coffee	Cover	76	24	28–35	
Coix lacryma-jobi	Job's tears	Cover	70	21	10–15	
Coleostephus myconis	Chrysanthemum	Cover lightly	60–65	15–18	10–14	
Consolida ambigua	Larkspur	Cover	55	13	14–27	5–6
Cordyline indivisa	Dracaena	Light	72–78	22–26	56	14–16
Coreopsis grandiflora	Tickseed	Light	65–75	18–24	9–12	
Coriandrum sativum	Coriander	Light or cover	65–70	18–21	7–10	
Cortaderia selloana	Pampas grass	Cover lightly	70	21	4–8	
Cosmos sulphureus	Cosmos	Cover	65–70	18–21	7–11	4–5
C. bipinnatus		Cover	70	21	5–7	
Craspedia uniflora	Craspedia	Cover	72–75	22–24	12–14	8–9
Crossandra infundibuliformis	Crossandra	Cover	Day: 80 Night: 70	26 21	21–28	
Cucumis melo var. *reticulatis*	Muskmelon	Cover	75–80	24–26	7–10	
C. sativus	Cucumber	Cover	75–78	22	7–9	

Scientific name	Common name		°F	°C		
Cucurbita maxima	Pumpkin	Cover	75–78	24–25	5–8	3
C. maxima	Squash	Cover	72	22	5–10	
Cuphea platycentra	Cuphea	Cover lightly	70	21	12–15	
Cyclamen persicum	Cyclamen	Cover	59–68	15–20	28–42	9–10
Cynara scolymus	Artichoke	Light or cover	70–75	21–24	4–8	
Cynoglossum amabile	Cynoglossum	Cover	65–70	18–21	5–8	
Dahlia × hybrida	Dahlia	Cover	68–70	20–21	3–4	4–5
Delphinium grandiflorum	Delphinium	Cover	59–68	15–20	8–15	8–9
D. × belladonna						
D. × cultorum						
Dendranthema × grandiflorum	Chrysanthemum	Light	60–70	15–21	5–10	
Dianthus barbatus	Sweet William	Cover lightly	70–75	21–24	10–12	5–6
D. deltoides	Maiden pinks					
D. plumarius	Cottage pinks					
D. carthusianorum	Pot carnation	Cover lightly	64–68	18–20	5–13	
D. caryophyllus	Cut carnation	Cover lightly	65–70	18–21	12–17	5–6
D. chinensis	Dianthus	Cover lightly	70–75	21–24	10–12	5–6
Digitalis purpurea	Foxglove	Light	65–70	18–21	11–12	7–8
Dolichos lablab	Dolichos	Cover	70–72	21–22	5–8	
Doronicum columnae	Leopard's bane	Light	68–72	20–22	14–21	
Dorotheanthus species	Mesembryanthemum	Light	65–68	18–20	7–15	
Dyssodia tenuiloba	Dahlberg daisy	Light	65–70	18–21	10–16	
Echinacea purpurea	Purple coneflower	Light or cover	64–75	18–24	7–10	
Echinops bannaticus	Globe thistle	Cover lightly	65–70	18–21	14–21	
Emilia javanica	Tassel flower	Cover	68–72	20–22	8–15	
Eschscholzia californica	California poppy		70–72	21–22	4–8	
Euphorbia marginata	Snow-on-the-mountain	Cover	60–68	15–20	10–14+	
E. myrsinites	Myrtle euphorbia	Light	65–70	18–21	7–14	
E. polychroma	Cushion spurge	Light	65–70	18–21	8–15	
Eustoma grandiflorum	Lisianthus	Light	68–77	20–25	10–15	9–11
Exacum affine	Persian violet	Cover lightly	72–77	22–25	14–21	
Fatsia japonica	Fatsia	Light	*Day:* 85 *Night:* 68	29 20	28–40	
Festuca amethystina	Amethyst fescue	Cover lightly	70	21	6–12	
F. ovina var. glauca	Blue fescue				4–6	
Foeniculum vulgare	Sweet fennel	Cover	70	21	7–10	
Fragaria species	Strawberries	Cover lightly	65–70	18–21	10–14	
Freesia species	Freesia	Cover	59–68	15–20	21–25	

(continued)

TABLE 1-1 *(continued)*

Scientific Name	Common Name	Lighting	Germination Temperature (°F)	Germination Temperature (°C)	Germination Time (days)	Plug Crop Time (weeks)
Gaillardia ×grandiflora	Blanket flower	Light	70–75	21–24	5–15	
Gaura lindheimeri	Gaura	Light	70–72	21–22	5–11	
Gazania rigens	Gazania	Cover	68–70	20–21	12–14	5–6
Gentiana species	Gentian	Light or cover	68–77	20–25	20	
Gerbera jamesonii	Gerbera	Light	68–74	20–25	7–14	5–6
Gomphrena globosa	Gomphrena	Cover	72–75	22–24	10–14	6–7
G. haageana						
Goniolimon tataricum	German statice	Light	65–75	18–24	14–21	
Gypsophila elegans	Gypsophila	Light or cover	70–72	21–22	5–15	6–7
G. repens	Creeping baby's breath	Light	70–80	21–26	5–15	
G. paniculata	Baby's breath					
Helenium autumnale	Helenium	Light	72	22	8–12	
Helianthemum nummularium	Rockrose	Light or cover	70–75	21–24	5–15	
Helianthus annuus	Sunflower	Cover	65–75	18–24	2–7	3
Helichrysum bracteatum	Helichrysum	Cover	70–75	21–24	8–12	5–6
Heliconia species	Heliconia		77–95	25–35	Weeks to months	
Heliopsis helianthoides	Oxeye daisy	Light or cover	65–70	18–21	3–10	
Heliotropium arborescens	Heliotropium	Cover lightly	70–72	21–22	4–8	
Helipterum roseum	Acrolinium	Light or cover	70–72	21–22	6–10	
Hesperis matronalis	Sweet rocket	Light	70–72	21–22	5–7	
Heuchera sanguinea	Coral bells	Light	65–70	18–21	21–30	
H. micrantha	Alumroot					
Hibiscus moscheutos	Rose mallow	Cover	70–80	21–26	7–10	
Hordeum jubatum	Squirrel's tail grass	Cover lightly	70–72	21–22	3–5	
Hypericum calycinum	Rose of Sharon	Cover lightly	60–70	15–21	10–21	
Hypoestes phyllostachya	Hypoestes	Light	70–75	21–24	10–11	5–6
Iberis amara	Candytuft	Light or cover	68–72	20–22	7–14	
I. umbellata						
I. sempervirens	Hardy candytuft	Light	60–65	15–18	14–21	5–6
Impatiens balsamina	Balsam	Light	72–77	22–25	13–15	6–7
I. walleriana	Bedding impatiens	Cover lightly	75–80	24–26	15–17	
Ipomoea tricolor	Morning glory	Cover	65–70	18–21	5–7	
Kalanchoe blossfeldiana	Kalanchoe	Light	70	21	10–15	
Kniphofia uvaria	Red hot poker	Light	65–75	18–24	21–28	

Scientific name	Common name		°F	°C	Days	
Koeleria glauca	Koeleria	Cover lightly	70	21	3–7	
Lactuca sativa	Lettuce	Cover	65–70	18–21	7–12	4–5
Lagerstroemia indica	Crape myrtle	Cover	70	21	14–18	
Lagurus ovatus	Hare's tail grass	Cover lightly	70	21	4–8	
Lathyrus splendens	Perennial sweet pea	Cover	62–70	18–21	10–20	
Lavandula angustifolia	English lavender	Light	65–75	18–24	14–21	
L. angustifolia var. munstead		Light	65–75	18–24	14–21	
Lavatera trimestris	Lavatera	Cover	72	22	4–6	
Leea coccinea	Leea	Cover	78	25	28–49	
Leontopodium alpinum	Edelweiss	Light	68–72	20–22	5–11	
Leucanthemum lacustre	Shasta daisy	Cover lightly	65–70	18–21	9–12	
L. paludosum	Chrysanthemum	Cover lightly	60–65	15–18	10–14	
Liatris pycnostachya	Liatris	Light	75–78	24–26	21–28	
L. spicata	Gay feather					
Limonium latifolium	Sea lavender		65–75	18–24	14–21	
L. sinuatum	Statice	Cover	75–77	21–25	7–14	5–6
L. perezii						
Linum perenne	Flax	Light or cover	70–73	21–25	4–8	
Lobelia erinus	Lobelia	Light	75–80	24–26	11–13	5–6
L. ×speciosa		Lightly covered	70–72	21–22	10–14	
Lobularia maritima	Sweet alyssum	Light	78–82	25–28	8–10	
Lonas annua	Lonas	Light	68–72	20–22	3–6	
Lunaria annua	Honesty plant	Light or cover	65–75	18–24	3–7	
Lupinus polyphyllus	Lupine	Cover	70–75	21–24	8–12	4–5
Lychnis chalcedonica	Maltese cross	Light or cover	70	21	5–7	
L. ×haageana						
Lycopersicon esculentum	Tomato	Cover	70–80	21–27	5–7	10
Malva moschata	Musk mallow	Cover	70–72	21–22	3–6	
Marrubium vulgare	Horehound	Cover	70	21	12	
Matthiola incana	Stock	Cover	65–70	18–21	7–14	4–5
Melampodium divaricatum	Melampodium	Cover lightly	65	18	7–10	
Mentha ×piperita	Peppermint	Cover lightly	70–75	21–24	12	
M. spicata	Spearmint	Cover lightly	70–75	21–24	12	
Mimosa pudica	Mimosa	Cover	80	26	12–15	
Mimulus ×hybridus	Monkey flower	Light	60–70	15–21	5–7	
Mirabilis jalapa	Mirabilis	Cover	72	22	4–6	
Moluccella laevis	Bells of Ireland	Light	68–72	20–22	14–20	6–7
Monstera deliciosa	Philodendron	Cover	70–85	21–29	15–20	

(continued)

TABLE 1-1 *(continued)*

Scientific Name	Common Name	Lighting	Germination Temperature (°F)	Germination Temperature (°C)	Germination Time (days)	Plug Crop Time (weeks)
Myosotis sylvatica	Forget-me-not	Light	68–72	20–22	8–14	
Nemesia strumosa	Nemesia	Cover	65	18	10–14	
Nemophila menziesii	Nemophila	Cover	65	18	10–14	
N. maculata						
Nepeta cataria	Catnip	Cover	70	21	5–8	
Nicotiana alata	Nicotiana	Light	75–78	24–26	10–15	5–6
Nierembergia hippomanica var. *violacea*	Nierembergia	Cover lightly	72–75	22–24	17–21	6–7
Nigella damascena	Nigella	Light or cover	65–70	18–21	7–14	
Nolana paradoxa	Nolana	Cover lightly	68–72	20–22	5–8	
Oenothera macrocarpa	Evening primrose	Light	70–80	21–27	8–15	
Ocimum basilicum	Sweet basil	Light or cover	70	21	5–8	
Origanum majorana	Sweet marjoram	Cover lightly	70	21	4–8	
O. vulgare	Oregano	Cover	70	21	4–8	
Papaver nudicaule	Iceland/arctic poppy	Light	65–70	18–21	12–14	6–7
P. orientale	Oriental poppy	Light	65–75	18–24	7–14	
Pelargonium × hortorum	Seed geranium	Cover	75–78	24–26	8–10	5–6
P. peltatum	Ivy geranium	Cover	70–75	21–24	5–10	
Pennisetum setaceum	Fountain grass	Cover lightly	70	21	3–6	
P. villosum	Feathertop					
Pentas lanceolata	Pentas	Light	70–75	21–24	12–17	6–7
Pericallis × hybrida	Cineraria	Light	68–75	20–24	10–14	
Petroselinum crispum	Parsley	Cover	70	21	15–20	
Petunia × hybrida	Petunia	Light	75–78	24–26	10–15	5–6
Phalaris canariensis	Canary grass	Cover lightly	70	21	4–8	
Philodendron domesticum	Philodendron	Cover	75–80	24–27	15–20	
P. bipinnatifidum						
Phlox drummondii	Phlox	Cover	65–68	18–20	12–14	5–6
Physalis alkekengi	Physalis	Light or cover	60–70	15–21	7–14	
Physostegia virginiana	False dragonhead	Light or cover	65–70	18–21	7–14	
Pimpinella anisum	Anise	Light or cover	70	21	10–12	
Platycodon grandiflorus	Balloon flower	Light	68–72	20–22	14–20	9–10
Portulaca grandiflora	Portulaca	Light	78–80	25–26	9–10	5–6
Primula vulgaris	Primula	Light	59–68	15–20	14–24	9–11
P. malacoides						

P. obconica	Primula	Light	59–68	15–20	10–20	
Psylliostachys suworowii	Statice	Light or cover	70–77	21–25	7–15	
Ranunculus asiaticus	Ranunculus	Cover	60–62	15–17	14–28	11–12
Rosmarinus officinalis	Rosemary	Light	70	21	10–15	
Rudbeckia fulgida	Black-eyed Susan	Light or cover	82–88	28–31	7–14	
R. hirta	Black-eyed Susan	Light or cover	70	21	5–10	
Saintpaulia ionantha	African violet	Light	70–75	21–24	18–25	
Salpiglossis sinuata	Salpiglossis	Dark	70–72	21–22	18–25	
Salvia coccinea	Salvia	Cover	75–78	24–26	12–14	5–6
S. farinacea	Salvia	Light	75–78	24–25	12–15	
S. officinalis	Sage	Cover	70	21	6–10	
S. splendens	Salvia	Cover	75–78	24–26	12–14	5–6
S. ×superba	Salvia	Light or cover	72	22	4–8	
Sanvitalia procumbens	Sanvitalia	Cover	70	21	7–10	
Saponaria ocymoides	Rock soapwort	Cover	70	21	4–8	
Satureja hortensis	Summer savory	Light	70	21	12–15	
Scabiosa atropurpurea	Scabiosa	Cover	65–70	18–21	14–17	6–7
S. caucasica	Pincushion flower	Light	65–70	18–21	10–18	
Schefflera actinophylla (Brassaia)	Schefflera	Cover	72–75	22–24	14–21	
S. arboricola	Schefflera	Cover	72–75	22–24	14–21	
S. elegantissima (Dizygotheca)	Aralia	Light	*Day:* 85 *Night:* 68	29 / 20	35–42	
Schizanthus ×wisetonensis	Schizanthus	Light	60–70	15–21	7–14	
Sedum acre	Golden carpet	Light	68–72	20–22	8–14	
S. spurium	Dragon's blood	Light				
Senecio cineraria	Dusty miller	Light	72–75	22–24	10–20	6–7
S. maritimus			21			
Senna angulata	Christmas candle	Cover	*Day:* 85 *Night:* 70	29 / 21	5–8	
Sinningia speciosa	Gloxinia	Light	65–70	18–21	10–12	
Smithiantha zebrina	Smithiantha	Light	65–70	18–21	14–21	
Solanum melongena	Eggplant	Cover	75–78	24–25	10–16	6–7
S. pseudocapsicum	Christmas cherry	Cover lightly	55–86	13–30	7–15	
S. tuberosum	Potato	Cover lightly	60–65	15–18	7–14	
Solenostemon scutellarioides	Coleus	Light	72–75	22–24	14–15	5–6
Solidago species	Goldenrod	Cover lightly	68–72	20–22	14–21	
Stachys byzantina	Lamb's ears	Light	70	21	8–15	
Steirodiscus tagetes	Steirodiscus	Light	60–70	15–21	5–6	

(continued)

TABLE 1-1 (continued)

Scientific Name	Common Name	Lighting	Germination Temperature (°F)	Germination Temperature (°C)	Germination Time (days)	Plug Crop Time (weeks)
Strelitzia reginae	Bird of paradise	Cover	77	25	30–90	
Streptocarpus ×hybridus	Cape primrose	Light	70	21	14	
Syngonium podophyllum	Nephthytis	Cover	75–80	24–26	14–21	
Tagetes erecta	African marigold	Cover lightly	75–80	24–27	2–3	4–5
T. erecta ×patula	Triploid marigold					
T. patula	French marigold					
T. tenuifolia	Signate marigold					
Tanacetum coccineum	Painted daisy	Light	60–70	15–21	5–10	
T. parthenium	Matriacaria	Light	70	21	7–10	
T. ptarmiciflorum	Dusty miller	Light	72–75	22–24	10–15	
Thunbergia alata	Thunbergia	Cover lightly	70–75	21–24	6–12	
Thymus serphyllum	Mother of thyme	Cover	71	21	3–6	
T. vulgaris	Culinary thyme	Cover	70	21	3–6	
Torenia fournieri	Torenia	Light	75–80	24–26	11–13	5–6
Trachelium caeruleum	Throatwort	Light	62–70	17–21	14–21	
Tropaeolum majus	Nasturtium	Cover	65–70	18–21	10–14	
Tweedia caerulea	Oxypetalum	Light	70–72	21–22	6–10	
Vaccaria hispanica	Cow-coddle	Cover	68–72	20–22	4–8	
Verbascum phoeniceum	Purple mullein	Light	70–72	21–22	4–7	
Verbena ×hybrida	Verbena	Cover lightly	75–80	24–26	14–21	5–6
V. bonariensis	Verbena	Cover lightly	75	24	5–10	
V. canadensis						
V. rigida						
Veronica incana	Woolly speedwell	Light	68–72	20–22	12–14	7–8
V. repens	Creeping speedwell					
V. spicata	Spike speedwell					
Viola cornuta	Horned violet	Cover lightly	65–75	18–24	12–14	6–7
V. tricolor	Johnny-jump-up	Cover lightly	55–60	13–16	4–7	
V. ×wittrockiana	Pansy	Cover lightly	62–68	17–20	4–7	5–6
Xeranthemum annuum	Xeranthemum	Light or cover	70–72	21–22	4–8	
Zea mays var. saccharata	Sweet corn	Cover	70–75	21–24	3–5	
Zinnia angustifolia	Zinnia	Cover	75–78	24–26	3–5	3–4
Z. elegans		Cover	68–70	20–21	7–10	3–4

of flats. Regardless of the method, if flats are well watered before placing them in a high-humidity environment, the seeds usually germinate before drying out. However, in areas with low humidity, additional irrigation may be needed. Again, remove seedlings quickly from any type of germination chamber to prevent them from elongating. Chambers should have sufficient cooling to prevent overheating.

NUTRITION

Commercial germination media frequently contain low amounts of nutrients, sufficient for seedlings if they are transplanted within 2 to 3 weeks. Plugs and slow-growing seedlings that take a long time to reach transplant stage will need 25 to 75 ppm N from either a commercial premixed fertilizer, such as 20–10–20, or KNO_3 + $Ca(NO_3)_2$. Liquid fertilizer applications can be applied weekly starting 2 to 3 weeks after germination until transplanting. Be sure to experiment because some species require low fertility and should not be fertilized; others are sensitive to high soluble salts and may be damaged by fertilizer levels that are too high.

DISEASES

The three most prevalent diseases common in seed propagation are damping-off (see later discussion), *Sclerotium* blight, and *Botrytis* blight (see Chapter 9, Pest Management). These diseases are best controlled by prevention, which means strict sanitation and the use of disease-free media. All benches, flats, labels, and other supplies should be clean and sterile. The propagation area should be clean and free of weeds and debris. Promptly removing any flats or plants that may be infected will reduce the level of pathogens in the area. Trying to "save" an infected flat or plant may result in more problems than the value of the original plant material. If a portion of a flat is infected, the safest solution is to discard the entire flat. It is likely that many of the apparently healthy seedlings are infected but not yet showing symptoms.

Damping-off is a general disease usually caused by one or more genera of pathogens, including *Pythium*, *Phytophthora*, and *Rhizoctonia* (Horst, 1990) (see Chapter 9, Pest Management, for additional information). Determining the actual pathogen is difficult because all three are common. Preemergent damping-off occurs when the seedlings are infected before they emerge from the medium, whereas postemergent damping-off occurs after the seedlings have emerged from the medium. In the case of postemergent damping-off, brown or black fungal strands may be visible. Poor germination or lack of germination is often attributed to "bad" seeds, but may be preemergent damping-off. The following factors will increase the likelihood of damping-off:

- Low or excessively high media temperature
- Overwatering or overmisting
- Unpasteurized or contaminated media
- Overfertilization

Although seeds and seedlings can be treated with fungicides, seedlings are especially sensitive to fungicide phytotoxicity. It is best to prevent damping-off and only use fungicides as an emergency treatment.

Sclerotium blight is characterized by distinctive, cottony white growth of *Sclerotium rolfsii*, which can quickly infect a flat of seedlings. *Sclerotium* blight is favored by cool, moist conditions, and because it is a soilborne disease, pasteurized media and sanitation should be effective in controlling the disease.

Botrytis blight (*Botrytis* spp.) is distinguished by gray, fuzzy fungal growth that is usually more profuse than postemergent damping-off. *Botrytis* blight often attacks the seedlings from the top of the plant downward and is more prevalent when seedlings are stressed and when there is insufficient air movement.

TRANSPLANTING

To optimize production, seedlings should be transplanted as soon as possible. Generally, seedlings grown in open flats are transplanted when they have one set of true leaves. Plugs are transplanted at a later stage when the roots are sufficiently developed to allow the root balls to be easily removed intact from the plug cells (see Plug Culture section on page 27). Although seedlings can be held in plugs longer than open flats, in both situations a delay in transplanting will generally cause stem elongation, increase the likelihood of diseases, stunt the seedlings, induce premature flowering, and lower final crop quality. Weather or marketing problems, however, may delay transplanting. Seedlings and plugs can be held in the greenhouse for up to 2 weeks and in the cooler for up to 11 weeks, depending on the species and storage conditions (see Plug Culture section on page 27 for more information).

SPORES

Ferns and other primitive plant species reproduce by spores. Commercially, a number of fern species are grown as indoor foliage plants or ornamental perennials. Initially, fern propagation is similar to seed propagation in that the spores are sown on the media surface and kept warm and moist. However, when spores germinate, they form a small, green leaflike structure known as the *prothallus*. As the prothallus matures, it produces male and female reproductive organs. Under proper environmental conditions—usually high humidity—sexual fertilization occurs and a sporophyte develops. The sporophyte grows into the large plant that we know as a fern. The sporophyte produces the spores, which start the process over again. Additional information can be obtained from Hartmann et al. (1997).

CUTTINGS

Cutting propagation is the most common form of asexual propagation and is the dominant method for many important floriculture species including poinsettias (*Euphorbia pulcherrima*), chrysanthemums (*Dendranthema* ×*grandiflorum*), carnations (*Dianthus*), roses (*Rosa*), and numerous foliage and bedding plant species (Table 1-2). Although cutting propagation often allows a shorter production time than seed propagation, the potential for disease spread is much greater.

DISEASE INDEXING

To reduce disease, commercial propagators have developed a process called *disease indexing*, which allows the production of disease-free cuttings for chrysanthemums, carnations, geraniums (*Pelargonium*), hiemalis begonias (*Begonia* ×*hiemalis*), kalanchoe (*Kalanchoe blossfeldiana*), New Guinea impatiens (*Impatiens* ×*hawkeri*), and streptocarpus (*Streotocarpus* ×*hybridus*) (Klopmeyer, 1991). Plants selected for the process of disease indexing must have the characteristics of the cultivar being propagated, which is known as being *true-to-type*.

Disease indexing involves two disease detection steps: culture indexing and virus indexing. In culture indexing, cuttings are harvested from selected stock plants under strict sanitation and small stem pieces are removed from each cutting and tested for the presence of systemic bacteria and fungi. A cutting and its par-

ent stock plant are eliminated if any disease is noted. Clean cuttings are rooted and the resulting plants are tested for the presence of viruses (virus indexed). If viruses are detected, plants can be heat treated to reduce the virus concentration in the plants. After heat treatment, meristem tissue culture is used to produce plantlets that are likely to be virus free. Plants produced from meristem culture are numbered and tested several times for the presence of viruses. The resulting disease-free plants form a block of mother stock plants from which cuttings are harvested to produce blocks of stock plants for future production. If a diseased stock plant or cutting is found during any of the testing and cutting production, the diseased plant and all plants propagated from it are destroyed.

SANITATION

Most species are not subject to serious systemic diseases that require the plants to be disease indexed. Regardless, care must still be taken to ensure disease-free stock and cuttings. Sanitary conditions must be maintained at all times to prevent cuttings from contracting pathogens. Cleaned and sterilized propagation benches, tools, containers, and hands are essential. For many species, sanitation is the key to successful propagation.

STOCK PLANTS

Stock plants serve as cutting sources. Cuttings can be taken from stock plants or from production plants as part of a pruning and shaping cultural step. If stock plants are used, consider them to be a separate crop with the goal of producing a high-quality cutting. Plan for adequate space and cultural attention. The stock plants may also be sold at the end of the production season as large-size specimens. Poor-quality plants will likely result from cuttings harvested from stock plants that are nutrient deficient, insect or disease infested, or old and woody. Scheduling cutting harvests from stock plants is important, because rooting may be delayed on cuttings not harvested at the optimum number of weeks after the pinch. Poinsettias, for example, show significant differences in rooting ability attributed to the age of the shoot from which the cutting was taken. This trait varies with the cultivar being grown (see *Euphorbia* chapter). For plant species sensitive to photoperiod, care must be taken to ensure that the stock plants do not prematurely initiate flowers, which may negatively affect

TABLE 1-2

Propagation techniques for numerous foliage plants (adapted from Joiner et al., 1981).

Botanical Name	Common Name	Air Layers	Cane Cuttings	Divisions or Offsets	Leaf Cuttings	Seed	Eye Stem Cuttings	Spores	Tip Cuttings	Micropropagation
Adiantum species	Maidenhair fern			X				X		X
Aechmea species	Bromeliad			X						
Aeschynanthus species	Lipstick vine					X	X		X	
Aglaonema species	Aglaonema		X	X		X			X	
Alocasia species	Alocasia			X		X	X			X
Anthurium cultivars	Flamingo flower	X		X					X	X
Aphelandra squarrosa	Zebra plant						X		X	
Araucaria columnaris	Australian pine	X				X			X	
Ardisia crenata	Coral ardisia					X			X	
Asparagus species	Asparagus			X		X				
Aspidistra elatior	Cast-iron plant			X						X
Asplenium nidus	Bird's-nest fern							X		X
Begonia Rex Cultorum hybrids	Rex begonia				X	X	X		X	X
Bromeliaceae species	Bromeliads			X		X				X
Cactaceae species	Cactus			X		X				X
Calathea species	Calathea			X		X	X		X	X
Chamaedorea elegans	Parlor palm					X				
Chlorophytum comosum	Spider plant			X		X				
Cissus antarctica	Kangaroo vine					X	X		X	
C. rhombifolia	Grape ivy						X		X	
Codiaeum variegatum	Croton	X				X			X	
Coffea arabica	Coffee					X			X	
Cordyline terminalis	Ti	X	X			X			X	X
Crassula species	Jade plant				X				X	
Davallia fejeensis	Rabbit's-foot fern			X				X		X
Dieffenbachia species	Dieffenbachia		X						X	X
Dracaena fragrans	Corn plant	X	X						X	X
D. surculosa	Gold-dust dracaena	X							X	X
D. marginata	Marginata	X	X						X	X
D. sanderiana	Ribbon plant	X							X	X
Epipremnum species	Pothos						X		X	
Episcia species	Episcia			X	X	X			X	

(continued)

TABLE 1-2 (continued)

Botanical Name	Common Name	Air Layers	Cane Cuttings	Divisions or Offsets	Leaf Cuttings	Seed	Eye Stem Cuttings	Spores	Tip Cuttings	Micropropagation
×Fatshedera lizei	Fatshedera						X		X	
Fatsia japonica	Japanese fatsia	X				X			X	
Ficus benjamina	Benjamin fig	X							X	X
Ficus elastica	Rubber plant	X					X		X	X
F. lyrata	Fiddle-leaf fig	X					X		X	X
Fittonia verschaffeltii	Nerve plant									
Gynura aurantiaca	Purple passion vine								X	
Hoya carnosa	Wax plant						X		X	
Kalanchoe species	Kalanchoe				X				X	
Maranta species	Maranta								X	X
Monstera deliciosa	Monstera	X				X	X		X	X
Musa species	Banana			X						
Nephrolepis exaltata	Boston fern			X						X
Nolina recurvata	Ponytail palm					X				
Palmae species	Palms			X		X				
Peperomia species	Peperomia				X		X		X	
Philodendron domesticum	Spade-leaf philodendron	X					X		X	X
P. scandens spp. scandens f. micans	Velvet-leaf philodendron						X		X	X
P. scandens spp. oxycardium	Heart-leaf philodendron						X		X	X
P. bipennifolium	Horse-head philodendron						X		X	X
P. bipinnatifidum	Selloum					X				X

Scientific name	Common name							
Pilea cadierei	Aluminum plant						X	
Platycerium species	Staghorn fern		X			X	X	
Plectranthus species	Swedish ivy		X		X		X	
Podocarpus macrophyllus	Podocarpus				X		X	
Polyscias species	Aralia	X						
Pteris species	Pteris fern		X			X	X	X
Radermachia sinica	China doll						X	X
Saintpaulia species	African violet		X	X	X			
Sansevieria trifasciata	Sansevieria		X	X				
S. trifasciata 'Hahnii'	Hahnii sansevieria		X	X				
S. trifasciata 'Laurentii'	Laurentii sansevieria		X	X				
Schefflera actinophylla (Brassaia)	Schefflera	X		X	X		X	
S. elegantissima (Dizygotheca)	False aralia	X		X	X		X	
Schlumbergera species	Christmas cactus		X	X	X		X	
Spathiphyllum species	Spathiphyllum			X			X	
Syngonium species	Nephthytis		X	X			X	
S. species green variegated cultivars	cultivars							
Tolmiea menziesii	Piggyback plant		X	X	X		X	
Tradescantia species	Wandering jew	X						
Yucca elephantipes	Spineless yucca		X	X	X		X	
Zamioculus zamiifolia	ZZ plant	X	X				X	

rooting, delay the crop being propagated, or render cuttings useless. If cutting elongation during propagation is a concern, growth retardants can be applied to the stock plants prior to cutting harvest.

Finally, care must be taken in selecting stock plants to ensure they are true-to-type, vigorous, and healthy. Regularly check stock plants and remove any plants showing mutations or loss in vigor. When carrying over plants from one year to the next, choose the best specimens, not unsold leftover plants. Also, watch for any changes in plant characteristics. Undesirable changes in foliage variegation can often be traced to improper stock plant selection.

ROOTING COMPOUNDS

The need for rooting compounds depends on the species being propagated. Rooting hormones are essential for economical rooting of some species and are not effective or needed with other species. For many species, rooting compounds are not required for rooting, but will accelerate root initiation, increase root uniformity, and increase the number and quality of roots produced. Rooting compounds are most economical on species that are difficult to root or when uniformity is required.

Commercial rooting compounds contain auxins and occasionally fungicides and other materials (see Chapter 8, Plant Growth Regulation). Indole-3-butyric acid (IBA) and naphthaleneacetic acid (NAA) are the most reliable auxins. Typically products containing 0.1% IBA are sufficient for propagation of herbaceous plants. Higher rates may be necessary for difficult-to-root species. The hormone is best applied as a powder dusted on the base of cuttings. Such powders contain auxins mixed with talc and are applied most efficiently to an entire group of cuttings at once. Extra powder should be removed by gently tapping the cuttings. The ends of the cuttings should be moist.

Auxin can also be dissolved in 50% ethanol or isopropyl alcohol and 50% water. The liquid treatments usually provide the most consistent results because application is more uniform than with dusts. However, dusting may be preferable to dipping to avoid spreading disease. Be sure to keep the container tightly sealed to prevent evaporation of the alcohol.

MEDIA

Cuttings can be inserted into foam or rockwool strips (which should be leached and moistened prior to use), expandable peat pellets, or medium-filled pots or flats. Avoid packing the medium around cuttings and avoid hose watering. Both practices compact the medium and reduce the supply of oxygen to the base of the cutting, which inhibits root development and favors pathogen infection. Apply overhead mist to water-in and maintain cutting turgidity. If using flats, the media can contain a low concentration of fertilizer but the medium EC should be below 0.8 $dS \cdot m^{-1}$ using the 2:1 water:medium method.

TEMPERATURE

The optimum medium temperature for rooting varies among species but is generally 72 to 75°F (22 to 24°C). The correct medium temperature will speed rooting. Propagation temperatures that are too high or too low may delay, reduce, or prevent rooting; decrease uniformity of rooting among cuttings; and increase disease incidence. Bottom heating may be needed to maintain proper medium temperature.

LIGHT

Shade the propagation area enough to prevent cuttings from drying and wilting. Light levels generally should be less than 2,000 fc (400 $\mu mol \cdot m^{-2} \cdot s^{-1}$); however, light levels that are too low can slow rooting or cause weak growth. Optimum light levels are generally 1,400 to 1,800 fc (280 to 360 $\mu mol \cdot m^{-2} \cdot s^{-1}$). If possible, slowly increase the light intensity as roots form on the cuttings.

MISTING AND FOGGING

Both misting and fogging apply water directly to cuttings to reduce transpiration and maintain cutting turgidity and thus allow root development. Fog systems produce much smaller water particle sizes than mist systems; hence, they reduce the amount of water applied and the resulting leaching of nutrients from leaves. The mist or fog system should completely cover the bench to ensure that all cuttings are uniformly moistened and free from moisture stress. Cold water can delay rooting substantially, especially during cool weather. Heat the water to 85 to 90°F (29 to 32°C). Nighttime misting or fogging may be required if the air is warm and dry, but can generally be discontinued after a few days. Misting is commonly controlled by time clocks, but time intervals set for sunny conditions will result in overmisting during overcast weather, which can delay rooting and promote the growth of pathogens. Overmisting can also result in leaf nutrient leaching and yellowing. To prevent either from occurring, inject low levels of nitrogen and potassium into the mist water on a constant basis. A mixture of 2 oz (57 g) of KNO_3 and 3 oz (85 g) of $Ca(NO_3)_2$ per 100 gal (379 L) provides approximately 55 ppm N and K. Frequency and duration of the mist or fog can also be controlled by devices that measure solar radiation, evaporation, or vapor pressure deficit (see Chapter 5, Water). Such control systems allow mist or fog application to be tied more directly to the environmental conditions, which will reduce the chance of over- or undermisting the cuttings.

Regardless of the control system, reduce misting frequency as cuttings begin to form roots or during low-light conditions. Mist may be turned off completely if day temperatures can be controlled or if ambient humidity is high.

TENTS

High-humidity tents are generally preferable to misting systems because tenting eliminates overwatering, algae growth on floors, and concerns with malfunctions and ensures a uniform propagation environment (Fig. 1-4). High-humidity tents also reduce leaching of nutrients from the leaves, free moisture on the foliage, and disease incidence compared with misting and fogging. Tenting eliminates the need for a mist or fog system, thus making propagation directly into the final container more feasible. The major drawbacks of tent propagation are the additional labor required to set up, remove, and dispose of the plastic. Tenting may not be feasible in areas with high light intensity or high temperatures due to heat buildup under the tent, even with extra shade to reduce the light intensity. Generally, clear plastic is used in the winter under low-light conditions and white plastic in summer when light levels are greater. To provide short-day photoperiods during propagation, such as with potted *Campanula*, the tents can also be covered at night with an additional layer of black plastic (Fig. 1-5).

To construct a tent, cover a bench with perforated plastic sheeting such that at least one foot hangs over the side of the bench. Next place a capillary mat and perforated black plastic covering over the bench top. Place containers on the capillary mat, which has been watered. Hand mist cuttings once. Cover the bench area with white or clear plastic held above the plants by hoops; the humidity is held in the tent by a water seal between the two plastic sheets. The tent should be totally closed for the first 24 hr, after which time the tent can be opened daily for increasing amounts of time to allow fresh air to enter and harden the cuttings after they have begun to root. Ultimately the plastic is removed.

SPACING

Give cuttings as much space as possible in the propagation area to allow adequate air circulation. Leaves from one cutting should not shade the shoot tip of an adjacent cutting because this may delay rooting of the shaded cutting.

FIGURE 1-4 Hibiscus (*Hibiscus*) cuttings being propagated using high-humidity tents.

FIGURE 1-5 Propagation of *Campanula* cuttings using high-humidity tents. Note the additional layer of black plastic used to provide artificial short days.

DISEASES

A number of diseases are common in the moist and humid cutting propagation areas. Two common diseases are *Botrytis* blight and bacterial soft rot (*Erwinia*), both of which have a wide host range and may infect almost any kind of herbaceous cutting (see Chapter 9, Pest Management). The gray, fuzzy fungal growth of *Botrytis* often begins with injured or necrotic areas and then infects healthy tissue. Bacterial soft rot spreads quickly. The bacteria are spread in splashing water; thus, bacterial soft rot can be especially troublesome during mist propagation.

Sanitation is essential to prevent both of these diseases from becoming established. Quick removal of infected tissue or cuttings can be effective in eliminating limited infections and greater problems can be controlled with fungicides and bactericides. As with chemical applications on seedlings, phytotoxicity can occur and chemicals should be used as a last resort. For chronic pathogen problems, first practice strict sanitation. If problems continue, pesticides can be applied as a preventive measure from one to several days prior to propagation. Be sure to follow label restrictions regarding reentry requirements.

POSTPROPAGATION CARE

After roots begin to form, some species benefit from fertilizer and fungicide drenches. Low concentrations of complete liquid fertilization can begin as soon as rooting is evident. Fertilizer rates should be low to prevent excessive and soft growth from occurring in the low-light environment and to prevent root damage from highly soluble salts. Promptly transplant rooted cuttings to their final containers and avoid drying during the planting process. Cuttings are normally planted at the same level as originally propagated. Care must be taken until the cuttings are totally acclimated to the new environment, well rooted, and starting to grow.

STEM CUTTINGS

Various types of stem cuttings can be taken depending on the species and desired crop time. Terminal cuttings include the stem apex, young leaves, and one or more mature leaves, and they generally produce a finished crop the quickest (Figs. 1-6 and 1–7). The size of the cutting depends on the species being propagated. Old stem tissue is frequently slower to

FIGURE 1-6 Coleus (*Solenostemon scutellarioides*) stem cutting with lower leaves removed, ready for insertion in the propagation medium.

FIGURE 1-7 Rooted poinsettia (*Euphorbia pulcherrima*) cutting ready to plant.

root than young tissue. The stems of some species such as pothos (*Epipremnum aureum*) produce adventitious roots at the nodes, which hastens establishment of the cutting after propagation. Larger cuttings can be taken later in the season with some species, such as poinsettias, to produce a larger plant quicker. Generally, cuttings with thick stems and short internodes will produce the best plants. Normally only the leaves that interfere with inserting the cuttings into the medium are removed, and at least one fully mature leaf should re-

FIGURE 1-8 Single eye *Hydrangea* cuttings consisting of a leaf, bud, and associated stem tissue. Note that the leaf has been trimmed to reduce surface area and transpiration.

main on the cutting. Rooting will be slow if no mature leaves remain on the cuttings to provide a source of photosynthates.

Stem cuttings with one or more axillary buds and leaves, but without the terminal apex, are also used with such species as pothos, hydrangea (*Hydrangea macrophylla*), *Tradescantia*, and *Dracaena*. Single bud (eye) cuttings are those pieces of stems with only one axillary bud (eye) (Fig. 1-8) and double eye cuttings have two axillary buds or eyes. Leaf-bud cuttings are examples of single eye cuttings in which a small amount of stem, including one node and axillary bud, is used and the stem and bud are both inserted below the medium surface. Leaf-bud cuttings are often used when propagation material is limited.

Cane sections without foliage are used with *Dracaena* and other foliage plants (see *Dracaena* chapter). Mature stems are harvested from stock plants, cut into sections of varying length, and inserted into the rooting medium. Care must be taken to ensure that the end of the cutting inserted into the medium was the basal end of the stem closest to the roots (when previously attached to the stock plant).

ROOT CUTTINGS

Some species of plants are propagated by harvesting roots and cutting them into sections which are then planted in the medium. If root cuttings such as that of butterfly weed (*Asclepias tuberosa*) are inserted vertically, be sure the correct orientation is used in planting the cuttings. To avoid confusion, the proximal end (previously closest to the crown) of the cutting can be cut straight across and the distal end (furthest from the crown) can be cut at an angle. Cuttings are planted with the proximal end up. The root cutting of many species such as that of oriental poppy (*Papaver orientale*) can also be planted horizontally 1 to 2 in. (2.5 to 5 cm) below the media surface, which eliminates the problem of orientation.

LEAF CUTTINGS

A number of common floriculture crops can be propagated from leaves including African violet (*Saintpaulia ionantha*), rex begonia (*Begonia* Rex Cultorum), *Sansevieria*, *Peperomia*, *Streptocarpus*, and numerous succulent species. In some cases, such as with *Sansevieria*, the leaves are cut into segments and inserted basipetal end down into the medium. Each segment regenerates shoots and roots. The extreme form of this method is to cut out dozens of begonia leaf disks using a cork borer from a single leaf (Lagerstedt, 1967). The disks are treated with IBA and kinetin and placed on moist filter paper in a petri dish. Other species such as *Peperomia* require that both the leaf blade and the petiole be present for shoot and root regeneration.

PLUG CULTURE

A significant proportion of the floriculture industry is using plug culture in the propagation of plant materials (Fig. 1–9). Plugs can either be purchased from a specialist or grown within the company. Plug production has become a significant business within the field of floriculture.

PLUGS VERSUS OPEN FLATS

There are several advantages to growing or purchasing plugs over open flat propagation. Plugs allow mechanization, automated transplanting, generally shorter production times (little or no transplant shock), longer holding periods until seedlings or cuttings need to be transplanted, reduced disease spread, and increased crop turnover. The disadvantage, however, is that plugs may be more difficult to grow, especially for inexperienced growers. The very small volume of medium in each plug restricts water drainage, yet holds little water, which causes plugs to dry out rapidly. The medium in plugs is also subject to rapid changes in pH and nutrient content. In addition, plug flats require special, often expensive

FIGURE 1-9 Plug production.

seed-sowing equipment and a larger propagation area (approximately four times more space) than open flats. Some species (especially perennials and woody plants) are not well suited to plug culture because of protracted or irregular germination or cutting rooting. The seed of other species may be difficult to sow mechanically because of seed shape or other characteristics. In some cases, specially processed seeds such as de-tailed marigold (*Tagetes*) seeds may be suitable for mechanized sowing.

Efficient, cost-effective plug production requires high-quality seeds that germinate rapidly and uniformly with a high germination percentage and high-quality cuttings that root rapidly and uniformly. Plug production readily integrates with labor-saving technology in the greenhouse including automatic seeders, flat fillers, transplanters, taggers, conveyors, containerized benches, and boom or flood irrigation. The high degree of automation allows total control over the germination and rooting process for uniform propagation.

PURCHASING VERSUS GROWING OWN PLUGS

Of course, problems with plug production can be avoided altogether by purchasing plugs. Another advantage of purchased plugs is that less space is required, which may allow more crops to be produced. Buying plugs may also allow bedding plant and field cut growers to forgo a propagation greenhouse or to start transplant production later in the winter or spring. The disadvantages of purchased plugs include loss of control over quality and timing, potentially higher cost per plug, and insufficient cultivar selection. In particular, firms trying to distinguish themselves from their competitors may need to grow their own plugs of unique varieties not available from plug suppliers. Many firms produce some of their own plugs and purchase others from suppliers.

PLUGS FROM SEED

In plug production, the germination process is divided into four stages:

Stage 1: Radicle (root) emerges.
Stage 2: Root system and cotyledons emerge.
Stage 3: First true leaves develop.
Stage 4: Seedling is almost ready to transplant.

Environmental conditions at each stage will vary with the species. Generally, as the plugs move from stages 1 to 4, the temperature and moisture level should be lowered and the light and nutrition should be increased. Three examples, representing cool (pansy), intermediate (petunia), and warm (impatiens) crops, are listed next (Styer and Koranski, 1997). Temperatures refer to the media.

Pansy (*Viola ×wittrockiana*)
Stage 1: 65 to 75°F (18 to 24°C), 100% relative humidity (RH), 3 to 7 days.
Stage 2: 62 to 75°F (17 to 24°C), 75% RH, 50 to 75 ppm N one time/week, 7 days.
Stage 3: 60 to 75°F (16 to 24°C), 100 to 150 ppm N one time/week, 14 to 21 days.
Stage 4: 55 to 65°F (13 to 18°C), 100 to 150 ppm one time/week, 7 days.

Petunia (*Petunia ×hybrida*)
Stage 1: 75 to 78°F (24 to 26°C), 100% RH, 450 fc (90 μmol·m^{-2}·s^{-1}), 3 to 5 days.
Stage 2: 68 to 75°F (20 to 24°C), 85% RH, 450 fc (90 μmol·m^{-2}·s^{-1}), 50 to 75 ppm N two times/week, 7 to 10 days.
Stage 3: 65 to 70°F (18 to 21°C), 100 to 150 ppm N two times/week, 14 to 21 days.
Stage 4: 60 to 62°F (15 to 17°C), 100 to 150 ppm N two times/week, 7 days.

Impatiens (*Impatiens walleriana*)

Stage 1: 72 to 77°F (22 to 25°C), 100% RH, 450 fc (90 $\mu mol \cdot m^{-2} \cdot s^{-1}$), 3 to 5 days.

Stage 2: 70 to 72°F (21 to 22°C), 75% RH, 450 fc (90 $\mu mol \cdot m^{-2} \cdot s^{-1}$), 50 to 75 ppm N one time/week, 10 days.

Stage 3: 68 to 72°F (20 to 22°C), 100 to 150 ppm N one time/week, 14 to 21 days.

Stage 4: 62 to 65°F (17 to 18°C), 100 to 150 ppm N one time/week, 7 days.

PLUGS FROM CUTTINGS

The cutting propagation process is divided into five stages after cutting harvest (W. Healy, personal communication):

Stage 0: Prior to arrival of cuttings

Stage 1: Arrival to sticking of cuttings

Stage 2: Callusing

Stage 3: Root development

Stage 4: Toning the rooted cutting

During stage 0, the cutting handling and propagation areas should be cleaned, weeded, and disinfected, the environmental controls checked, and clean flats filled with moist, pathogen-free medium. The flat sizes can vary but those with 84 to 105 cells per flat are generally used for cuttings.

During stage 1, open and check boxes for turgid, high-quality, properly labeled cuttings. Cuttings of some species can be stored at 45°F (7°C) for up to 24 hr prior to planting. Begin planting (sticking) cuttings into the media, using rooting hormone if necessary, and turn on the mist system as soon as possible to prevent water stress.

During stage 2, the cuttings form callus. The media should be moist, near 100% relative humidity, but not wet enough to restrict air from reaching the cutting bases.

During stage 3, the roots begin to develop, new top growth may be evident, and cuttings remain turgid more easily. Reduce the amount of moisture in the media by decreasing the amount and frequency of misting or increasing air circulation in tents. Fertilization of 100 to 150 ppm N from nitrate-based fertilizers low in phosphorus can commence. Fertilization can increase to 200 ppm N to maintain a media EC of 1.5 to 1.8 $dS \cdot m^{-1}$. The light intensity can be increased to 1,800 to 2,500 fc (360 to 500 $\mu mol \cdot m^{-2} \cdot s^{-1}$) and the temperatures lowered to 66 to 70°F (19 to 21°C) for the medium and 60 to 65°F (16 to 18°C) for the air. Pesticides and growth retardants can be applied if needed.

During stage 4, the cuttings should be toned for shipping or planting by reducing medium moisture. Although slight wilting is acceptable, severe wilting should not occur. The light intensity can be increased up to 2,500 to 4,000 fc (500 to 800 $\mu mol \cdot m^{-2} \cdot s^{-1}$) and the temperatures lowered to 64 to 66°F (18 to 19°C) for the medium and 58 to 62°F (14 to 17°C) for the air. Pesticides and growth retardants can be applied if needed.

LIGHT

Plug production readily allows the incorporation of supplemental photosynthetic lighting to accelerate plant growth (see Chapter 4, Light). Thousands of plugs can be illuminated by each high-intensity discharge (HID) light fixture. The greatest benefits are gained in the first 4 to 6 weeks after germination, or propagation of the cuttings and the early increase in growth, vigor, and quality is often retained throughout the crop cycle compared with nonlighted plugs. Supplemental lighting may allow more cycles of crops to be produced in the same space per year.

PLUG STORAGE

Plugs can be held in the greenhouse for up to 2 weeks by lowering the temperature to 50 to 60°F (10 to 16°C), increasing the light level greater than 2,500 fc (500 $\mu mol \cdot m^{-2} \cdot s^{-1}$), restricting water applications, switching to nitrate-based fertilizers, reducing fertilization rate, and applying plant growth regulators (Styer and Koranski, 1997). These actions, however, may increase the likelihood of early flowering, especially with sensitive species such as *Celosia*, marigold, larkspur (*Consolida*), lisianthus (*Eustoma*), aster (*Callistephus*), and *Zinnia*. In addition, use plant growth regulators carefully at this stage due to the possibility of carryover growth control after transplanting and the difficulty of making uniform applications on overgrown plug flats.

Long-term storage may be possible by placing the seedlings in a cooler (Heins et al., 1994). Acceptable storage conditions for the plugs of several bedding plant species are listed in Table 1-3. Be sure the plug medium is moist but the foliage dry before placing in the cooler. Good air circulation and fungicide applications may be helpful to prevent *Botrytis*.

TABLE 1-3

Storage conditions and duration for plugs of several bedding plant species (Heins et al., 1994).

Species	Light	Storage Temperature °F(°C)	Storage Duration (weeks)
Ageratum houstonianum	Yes	41–55 (5–13)	6
	No	45 (7)	6
Begonia Semperflorens-Cultorum	Yes	36–45 (2–7)	6
	No	41–45 (5–7)	6
Begonia Tuberhybrida	Yes	41–45 (5–7)	6
	No	41–45 (5–7)	4
Catharanthus roseus	Yes	45–55 (7–13)	6
	No	45–55 (7–13)	3
Celosia argentea	Yes	50 (10)	1
	No	50 (10)	1
Cyclamen persicum	Yes	36–41(2–5)	6
	No	36–41(2–5)	6
Dahlia × hybrida	Yes	41–50 (5–10)	3
	No	41–45 (5–7)	1
Impatiens hawkeri	Yes	55 (13)	3
	No	55 (13)	1
Impatiens walleriana	Yes	45 (7)	6
	No	45 (7)	6
Lobelia erinus	Yes	41 (5)	6
	No	41 (5)	4
Lobularia maritima	Yes	36 (2)	6
	No	36 (2)	2
Lycopersicon esculentum	Yes	45 (7)	3
	No	45 (7)	3
Pelargonium × hortorum	Yes	36 (2)	4
	No	36 (2)	4
Petunia × hybrida	Yes	36 (2)	6
	No	36 (2)	6
Portulaca grandiflora	Yes	50–55 (10–13)	6
	No	41–45 (5–7)	6
Salvia splendens	Yes	45–55 (7–13)	6
	No	45 (7)	4
Tagetes patula	Yes	41 (5)	6
	No	41 (5)	3
Verbena × hybrida	Yes	45–55 (7–13)	4
	No	45–55 (7–13)	1
Viola × wittrockiana	Yes	32–45 (2–7)	16
	No	32–36 (0–2)	16

GEOPHYTES

Geophytes include any species that form modified plant organs for carbohydrate storage including bulbs, corms, tubers, tuberous roots, rhizomes, and pseudobulbs. Many geophytic species reproduce through the natural replication of these storage organs (Fig. 1-10). Some species such as *Gladiolus* produce numerous small cormlets. Propagation can be commercially hastened with corms, tubers, tuberous roots, and rhizomes by cutting these structures into pieces, each containing at least one vegetative meristem (axillary bud or eye), and replanting the pieces. *Caladium, Dahlia, Iris,* and *Narcissus* storage organs can be handled in such a manner. Nontunicate lily (*Lilium*) bulbs can also be propagated by removing individual scales for propagation. Although tunicate bulbs

FIGURE 1-10 Amaryllis (*Hippeastrum*) bulbs with outer scales removed to show bulblet produced at the base of the bulbs through natural replication.

FIGURE 1-11 Scooped hyacinth (*Hyacinthus orientalis*) bulbs with new bulblets forming at the base of the scales.

are generally more difficult to propagate, hyacinth (*Hyacinthus orientalis*) and *Scilla* bulbs can be propagated by "scooping" or "scoring" the basal plate (the basal "stem" of the bulb from which roots develop) (Le Nard and De Hertogh, 1993). In scooping, the entire basal plate is removed and new bulblets form at the base of the scales (Fig. 1-11). In scoring, three crossing knife cuts are made through the basal plate, and bulblets form along these cuts. After propagation or harvest, many geophytes may need to be heat treated to control insects or disease (Dreistadt, 2001).

DIVISION

Division is the process of separating individual shoots clustered in a clump. The clumps are dug and cut into sections with a sharp knife or saw. Each section should have a few roots and one or more growing points to allow for shoot regeneration. Spring and summer flowering species such as coneflower (*Echinacea*) and astilbe (*Astilbe* ×*arendsii*), which produce new growth after flowering, should be divided in fall. Summer and fall flowering plants such as *Aster* and goldenrod (*Solidago*), which produce little growth after flowering, should be divided in the spring. Of course, indoor plants that grow year-round can be divided at any time, although division during the spring and early summer may allow quickest regeneration due to the longer days and greater light intensity. Commercial division is limited in use due to the high labor requirements and slow rate of replication, but can be used with many foliage plant species (Table 1-2).

LAYERING

Layering induces adventitious roots to form on stems while they are still attached to the parent plant. The process of layering can be thought of as rooting a terminal stem cutting while the cutting is still attached to the parent plant. Layering can occur naturally through low-growing branches that root when in contact with the soil, such as with *Forsythia*, or can be induced artificially by burying stems with soil or mounding soil around the base of a multistem plant.

With tip layering, shoot apices are bent into the ground, root, and finally grow upward. Simple layering occurs when the stems are bent to the ground and part of the stem is covered with medium but the shoot tip remains uncovered. Mound layering involves mounding the medium around the base of a multistem plant to induce root development at the base of the stems. In trench layering, the entire plant is bent over and laid flat on the bottom of a trench 3 to 9 in. (8 to 23 cm) deep. The plant is then covered with medium and axillary shoots root and grow upward through the medium.

With air layering, a moistened medium such as sphagnum moss peat is wrapped around a wounded area on the stem and covered with plastic or some other type of water-retentive wrap. In simple mound and air layering, rooting can be promoted by wounding the stem, which involves cutting part of the way through the stem, girdling the stem, or sharply bending the stem. Air layering, in particular, generally requires stem wounding. Rooting powders can be used to increase rooting of difficult-to-root species. In trench layering, rooting is promoted due to the etiolation of the shoots growing through the media. Due to the labor-intensive nature of layering and the large amount of space needed for both the stock plant and layers, layering is rarely done on a large commercial scale in floriculture.

RUNNERS AND OTHER MODIFIED STEMS

Many plant species produce elongated or modified stems terminating in a vegetative meristem that can be easily propagated (Hartmann et al., 1997). Runners arise from leaf axils, which grow horizontally above and along the ground, and produce new plants at each node or the tip. The new plants can be removed and propagated or allowed to form roots while still attached to the original plant. The spider plant (*Chlorophytum*) (Fig. 1-12) and the strawberry geranium (*Saxifraga sarmentosa*), for example, form runners. Red-osier dogwood (*Cornus stolonifera*) and mint (*Mentha*) produce stolons, which are stems that grow at or just below the surface of the soil and produce plants at the nodes. Offsets and suckers are shoots that develop from adventitious or axillary buds at the base of the plant and are removed to form individual plants. Suckers are traditionally defined as those shoots that arise from an adventitious bud on a root; however, the meaning of the term has been blurred in popular usage, and offsets and suckers are often considered synonymous. Runners and stolons are often used in commercial propagation, but suckers and offsets are generally limited to small-scale propagation.

FIGURE 1-12 Young spider plants (*Chlorophytum*) formed at the end of runners.

GRAFTING AND BUDDING

Grafting is the process of uniting two plants or plant parts in such a way that they become one plant after cell division and union occurs. Grafting is used to (1) propagate species or cultivars that cannot be propagated by other methods, (2) enhance vigor, or (3) create a unique plant with improved characteristics compared with the individual plants from which it was created. For example, hybrid tea roses often grow poorly on their own roots but grow better when grafted onto the roots of a vigorous rootstock, which may have inferior flowers. In floriculture, the standard topiary or tree forms of plants such as roses and azaleas (*Rhododendron*) are created by grafting the top cultivar onto an elongated stem and rootstock. Finally, grafting is used in research to study physiological processes or plant diseases. Breeding may also involve grafting seedlings to a rootstock to accelerate maturation and flowering and shorten the time between breeding cycles for species such as crabapple (*Malus*).

Unfortunately, grafting has limitations. The more closely the two plants are botanically related, the more likely the graft will be successful (Hartmann et al., 1997). Grafting is most successful when both plants are of the same species. Grafting between different species of the same genus is also likely to be successful but not guaranteed. Grafting between different genera of the same family and between different families has been successful in some cases, but is rarely commercially significant. Grafting requires that a part of the cambium of both plant parts be in contact. The graft union is wrapped with grafting rubber, plastic, or paraffin to prevent separation and drying. Cell division subsequently occurs that unites the pieces.

Several different types of grafting have been developed including whip (tongue), splice, side, side-tongue, side-veneer, cleft, bark, and approach grafting (Fig. 1-13). Budding is a type of grafting that uses one axillary bud and an associated piece of bark, which is inserted under the bark of a second plant. Budding techniques include T (shield), inverted T, patch budding, flute budding, ring (annular) budding, I budding, and chip budding. Grafting and budding are often described as easy to learn but difficult to master. Detailed procedures can be obtained from Hartmann et al. (1997).

FIGURE 1-13 Approach graft of two poinsettia (*Euphorbia pulcherrima*) plants. Both the basal section of the scion and the acropetal section of the stock have been removed to produce a plant with one shoot and one root system.

MICROPROPAGATION

According to Hartmann et al. (1975), "Micropropagation is the development of new plants on an artificial medium under aseptic conditions from very small pieces of plants, such as embryos, seeds, stems, shoot tips, root tips, callus, single cells and pollen grains" (p. 509). Micropropagation, or *in vitro* propagation, offers the potential to produce a virtually unlimited number of identical plants from one original plant. In practice, however, *in vitro* propagation is elaborate, time-consuming, economically risky, and expensive. Occasionally the resulting plants are not identical to the parent due to somoclonal variation. Regardless, numerous plant species including *Alstroemeria*, hybrid lilies (*Lilium*), *Gerbera*, orchids (Orchidaceae), and numerous foliage plant species (Table 1-2) are commercially propagated through micropropagation. Micropropagation is especially important in the production of disease-free stock plants, such as with geraniums and carnations, new cultivar development, and research.

KEY POINTS

- At the heart of all commercial floriculture crop production is plant propagation.
- The various propagation methods can be separated into sexual methods—seeds and spores—and asexual methods—cuttings, layers, divisions, natural reproductive structures such as bulbs, grafting, and *in vitro* micropropagation.
- Species are designated by two-part, binomial names (epithets). The first epithet is the genus to which the species belongs and the second epithet is the species.
- Cultivars are variants of species identifiable in some way, but cultivars are usually not naturally occurring and are maintained through cultivation.
- Hybrids are plants produced from genetically distinct parent plants.
- A number of processes are available in the United States for plant breeders to protect their work and profit from it, including plant patents and trademarks.
- Plants can be propagated through a variety of methods including seeds, spores, cuttings, geophytic organs, divisions, layering, runners, grafting, and micropropagation.
- Seeds should be stored at 25 to 35% relative humidity with a temperature of 40 to 50°F (5 to 10°C) and germination tested before sowing.
- Several seed treatments can be performed by seed suppliers or growers to improve germination and ease seed handling of many species including refining, stratification, scarification, chemical soaks, hydration, priming, pregermination, pelletizing, coating, de-tailing, de-fuzzing, and de-winging.
- Although seeds can be sown by hand into open flats or trough flats, the majority are mechanically sown into individual cells of plug flats with automatic seeders.
- For most species, optimum media temperature is 70 to 75°F (21 to 24°C).
- Small seeds often germinate better with light and should be sown on the top of the medium and not covered.
- High-quality, low-EC water and uniform application are critical for proper seed germination.
- The three most prevalent diseases common in seed propagation are damping-off

(*Pythium*, *Phytophthora*, and *Rhizoctonia*), *Sclerotium* blight, and *Botrytis* blight.

- To optimize production, seedlings should be transplanted as soon as possible. Generally, seedlings grown in open flats are transplanted when they have one set of true leaves. Plugs are transplanted at a later stage when the roots are sufficiently developed to allow the root balls to be easily removed intact from the plug cells.

- To reduce diseases of cuttings, commercial propagators have developed a process called disease indexing, which allows the production of disease-free cuttings.

- Sanitary conditions must be maintained at all times to prevent cuttings from contracting pathogens.

- Rooting hormones are essential for economical rooting of some species and are not effective or needed with other species.

- The optimum medium temperature for rooting varies among species but is generally 72 to 75°F (22 to 24°C).

- Cutting turgidity can be maintained with misting, fogging, or tenting.

- Types of cuttings include stem cuttings, cane sections, root cuttings, and leaf cuttings.

- A significant proportion of the floriculture industry is using plug culture in the propagation of plant materials.

- In plug production, the seed germination process is divided into four stages and the cutting propagation process into five stages.

BIBLIOGRAPHY

Ball, V. 1991. Seed germination, pp. 219–223 in *Ball RedBook*, 15th ed., V. Ball, editor. Geo. J. Ball Publishing, West Chicago, Illinois.

Bell, D.T., J.A. Plummer, and S.K. Taylor. 1993. Seed germination ecology in southwestern western Australia. *The Botanical Review* 59:24–72.

Carpenter, W.J., E.R. Ostmark, and J.A. Cornell. 1995. Evaluation of temperature and moisture content during storage on the germination of flowering annual seeds. *HortScience* 30:1003–1006.

Cathey, H.M. 1964a. Control of plant growth with light and chemicals. *The Exchange* 141(11):31–33.

Cathey, H.M. 1964b. Control of plant growth with light and chemicals. *The Exchange* 141(12):33–35.

Craig, R. 1993. Intellectual property protection, pp. 389–404 in *Geraniums IV*, 4th ed., J.W. White, editor. Ball Publishing, Geneva, Illinois.

Darke, R. 1991. A curator's viewpoint. *HortScience* 26:362–363.

Dreistadt, S.H. 2001. *Integrated Pest Management for Floriculture and Nurseries*. University of California Division of Agriculture and Natural Resources Publication 3402.

Faust, J.E., R.D. Heins, and J. Shimizu. 1997. Quantifying the effect of plug-flat color on medium-surface temperatures. *HortTechnology* 7:387–389.

Fowler, C. 1994. *Unnatural Selection*. Gordon and Breach, Yverdon, Switzerland.

Hartmann, H.T., and D.E. Kester. 1975. *Plant Propagation: Principles and Practices*, 3rd ed. Prentice Hall, Englewood Cliffs, New Jersey.

Hartmann, H.T., D.E. Kester, F.T. Davies, Jr., and R.L. Geneve. 1997. *Plant Propagation: Principles and Practices*, 6th ed. Prentice Hall, Upper Saddle River, New Jersey.

Heins, R., N. Lange, T.F. Wallace, Jr., and W. Carlson. 1994. *Plug Storage*. Greenhouse Grower. Meister Publishing, Willoughby, Ohio.

Horst, R.K. 1990. *Westcott's Plant Disease Handbook*, 5th ed. Van Nostrand Reinhold, New York.

Hutton, R.J. 1991. New funds for plant breeding. *HortScience* 26:361–362.

Joiner, J.N., R.T. Poole, and C.A. Conover. 1981. Propagation, pp. 284–306 in *Foliage Plant Production*, J.N. Joiner, editor. Prentice Hall, Englewood Cliffs, New Jersey.

Klopmeyer, M. 1991. The importance of disease indexing and pathogen-free production in *Ball RedBook*, 15th ed., V. Ball, editor. Ball Publishing, West Chicago, Illinois.

Koranski, D.S. 1983. Growing annual plugs. *GrowerTalks* 46(11):28, 30, 32.

Lagerstedt, H.B. 1967. Propagation of begonias from leaf disks. *HortScience* 2(1):20–22.

Le Nard, M., and A.A. De Hertogh. 1993. General chapter on spring flowering bulbs, p. 705 in *The Physiology of Flower Bulbs*, A. De Hertogh and M. Le Nard, editors. Elsevier, Amsterdam.

McDonald, M.B., and D.F. James. 1997. Enhancing flower seed performance. *GrowerTalks* 61(7):20, 22, 24–26.

Nau, J. 1999. *Ball Culture Guide, The Encyclopedia of Seed Germination*, 2nd ed. Ball Publishing, Batavia, Illinois.

Pasian, C.C., and M.A. Bennett. 2001. Paclobutrazol soaked marigold, geranium, and tomato seeds produce short seedlings. *HortScience* 36:721–723.

Rogers, O.M. 1991. Germplasm and how to protect it. *HortScience* 26:360–361.

Styer, R.C., and D.S. Koranski. 1997. *Plugs and Transplant Production*. Ball Publishing, Batavia, Illinois.

Chapter 2

Flowering Control

INTRODUCTION

The flowering process is an especially important subject considering that the definition of floriculture is the culture of flowering plants. In this chapter we discuss the processes by which flowers are initiated and develop and the primary environmental stimuli (*flowering stimuli*) required for flowering to occur. The three main environmental control mechanisms for flowering in commercial floriculture crops are photoperiod, light intensity, and temperature. Each species has different environmental requirements for flowering and, occasionally, cultivars within a plant species may vary in their flowering mechanisms.

First, the plants must be *mature* before the flowering stimulus is perceived. The phase before maturity is called the *juvenile period*, and a juvenile plant will not flower even if growing in the proper environment for flowering to occur. For most floriculture crops, the juvenile period is relatively short and defined in various ways. The minimum number of leaves (nodes) is commonly used to indicate the end of juvenility for many nongeophytic plant species such as *Antirrhinum majus* at 18 to 22 leaves (Cockshull, 1985) and *Campanula* 'Champion' at 8 to 9 leaves (Cavins and Dole, 2001). The juvenility period for geophytes is typically determined by minimum storage organ circumference and ranges from approximately 1 year and 1.2 to 1.6 in. (3 to 4 cm) circumference for *Triteleia* Lindl. corms to 4 to 7 years and 2.4 to 4.0 in. (6 to 10 cm) circumference for *Tulipa* bulbs (Fortanier, 1973).

Total plant mass or size must also be considered when inducing plants to flower with photoperiod. Plants need to have sufficient foliage (*photosynthetic capacity*) to support the size and quality of flowers required for commercial production. Although it may be possible to rapidly flower some species, which would reduce production expenses, plant quality may be low. For example, if rooted chrysanthemum (*Dendranthema* ×*grandiflorum*) cuttings are not given 7 to 14 long days (noninductive photoperiod) prior to the start of short days (inductive photoperiod), potted flowering plants will be too short and the flowers too small.

In addition to having the ability to perceive a flowering stimulus, there may be other signs of plant maturity (Hacket 1985). As an example, mature *Hedera helix* plants grow upright, are difficult to cutting propagate, and have flowers, woody stems, and a distinctive leaf shape. However, the more commonly seen juvenile *H. helix* plants are procumbent, easy to cutting propagate, and have flexible stems with a leaf shape different from mature plants.

Other plants may not flower even if they are mature and placed in the proper environmental conditions because they have not received the proper sequence of stimuli. For example, potted azaleas (*Rhododendron*) initiate flower buds during the short days (SD) of fall but require a 4- to 6-week cold treatment at 35 to 45°F (2 to 7°C) before the flower buds will properly open.

The first stage of flower development is known as *flower induction*, during which time the biochemical processes required for flowering commence. During *flower initiation* the first actual microscopic signs of the flowers become apparent. The apical meristem begins to change shape and floral organs are formed. In some plants *flower development* will continue unabated from induction until anthesis once the process commences. In other species flowers will continue to develop as long as the plant remains under the same environmental conditions, but flower development may stop or the flowers may abort if the environmental conditions change. However, for plants such as *Rhododendron*, flower initiation and partial development occur under SD but continued floral development and opening will not occur until the buds have received a cold treatment. In addition, the critical night length for flower development may be longer or shorter than that required for flower initiation. Often the difference between the two critical photoperiods corresponds with the natural sequences that occur outdoors. For example, a SD plant, such as poinsettia (*Euphorbia pulcherrima*), may initiate flowers in late summer under a specific critical night length, but a longer night length, corresponding to the longer nights of fall, is required for further flower development. Further, low light levels, inadequate water, or other plant stresses may cause flower bud abortion.

The definition of *anthesis* or "flowering" varies with the species but typically means the first signs of visible pollen within the flower or when the plant or flowering stem is ready for harvest. The final stage of flowering is senescence, during which time the floral organs wilt and often abscise. Of course, if fruit is desired, then the end of flowering is simply the beginning of fruit development as with ornamental peppers (*Capsicum annuum*).

Photoperiod, light intensity, and cold often have other effects on plants in addition to flower initiation and development including storage organ formation, induction or breaking of quiescence (dormancy), stem elongation, number of nodes formed prior to flowering, axillary bud development, and rooting. For example, with *Dahlia* hybrids tuberous root formation is induced by photoperiods of 11 to 12 hr or less and the dormant tuberous roots do not immediately resume growth unless they have been exposed to 32 to 50°F (0 to 10°C) for 6 weeks (Konishi and Inaba, 1967; Moser and Hess, 1968). Stem elongation and number of nodes are often related—placing *Helianthus annuus* plants under SD not only decreases the number of days to flowering but also decreases the number of nodes and plant height as compared to plants under long days (Pallez et al., 2002). In other cases, stem elongation occurs without any effect on node number such as with dormancy breaking cold treatments on tulips. Increasing duration of cold increases stem elongation but has no effect on node number.

The plant growth habit must also be considered. The apex of determinant plants terminates in an inflorescence, as with poinsettias. Indeterminate plants, such as *Hibiscus rosa-sinensis*, produce inflorescences only in the leaf axils; the main stem remains vegetative and continues to grow indefinitely. With determinant plants, flower initiation ends leaf formation, which then determines the final number of nodes on the plant. For example, poinsettia plants placed under SD 4 weeks after propagation will have fewer nodes and, consequently, be shorter than plants that are placed under SD 8 weeks after propagation due to delayed flower initiation. Thus, flower initiation not only affects flowering date but also plant height and number of leaves on the shoot. However, with indeterminate plants, flowering is a continuous process and the production of axillary flowers is dependent on continued leaf production by the apex. Any factor such as low light or improper temperature that slows the growth rate of the main stem will reduce flower number. Flowering initiation of indeterminant plants does not end vegetative growth and has little effect on node number or height.

With many plants such as poinsettias and chrysanthemum, the cultivars are arranged in *response groups*, which are defined as the amount of time from placement of the plant in the proper environmental conditions for flowering, such as SD for poinsettias, until anthesis occurs. The response groups for poinsettia cultivars range from 6.5 to 10 weeks and for chrysanthemums from 6 to 15 weeks. Familiarity with the response group allows producers to anticipate the flowering date and schedule the crops accordingly.

Producers often use the *week system* to schedule crops. The first week in January (often a partial week) is labeled as week 1 and the last full week in December is week 52. The week system is shorter and easier to use than specifying specific dates such as August 29 to September 4 for week 35. Note that the actual dates indicated by each week will vary with the year.

PHOTOPERIOD

Photoperiodism, the response of plants to night length, regulates many responses in plants, such as flower initiation and development (Table 2–1), plant dormancy, seed germination, storage organ formation, and plant growth habit. Most photoperiodic plant responses can be divided into three basic types: *short day* (SD), *long day* (LD), and *day neutral* (DN). SD plants will flower when the dark period is longer than a critical length (*critical night length*), and LD plants will flower when the dark period is shorter than a critical length. For example, chrysanthemums and poinsettias flower under SD conditions and tuberous begonias under LD. Day neutral plants such as seed geraniums (*Pelargonium ×hortorum*) will flower regardless of the day length.

Many plant species will flower under a wide range of day lengths, but will flower more rapidly under either short or long days and are known as *facultative* SD or LD plants. Increasing the number of SD or LD cycles will generally decrease the time to flower. However, *obligate* SD or LD plants will not develop flowers if placed under incorrect photoperiods. *Salvia* is an example of a facultative SD plant and poinsettia is an obligate SD plant. Photoperiodic responses other than flowering, such as dormancy, may also be termed obligate or facultative. The terms *absolute* and *qualitative* have also been used over the years in place of *obligate*, and *quantitative* has been used in place of *facultative*.

The duration of the critical photoperiod varies with the species. For example, *Calendula* has a critical day length of only 6.5 hr, whereas *Campanula fragilis* has a critical day length of between 14 and 16 hr; both species are LD plants (Kamlesh and Kohli, 1981; Zimmer, 1985). The minimum number of LD or SD required for flower initiation and complete flower development varies considerably from only one inductive cycle for Japanese morning glory (*Pharbitis nil*) to several weeks for poinsettias. If poinsettias are moved from SD to LD after the bracts have begun to form, the bracts will turn green and become leaflike. In fact, SD should continue until anthesis for poinsettias to ensure that the young bracts will not become green (Fig. 2–1).

FIGURE 2-1 Poinsettia (*Euphorbia pulcherrima*) bracts turning green from not being kept under short days long enough.

Some species cannot be simply categorized as SD, LD, or DN plants because they have more complicated photoperiod responses, such as LD followed by SD or SD–LD–SD. For example, *Aster novi-belgii* is considered a LD–SD plant for flower initiation and subsequent development (Schwabe, 1986; Wallerstein et al., 1992). In rare cases, a plant species may be responsive to either LD or SD in that they will flower if the night is longer than one critical night length or shorter than a second, shorter, critical night length. Similarly, a few other plants can be characterized as intermediate day plants that will flower when the night length is shorter than a critical length but longer than a second, shorter critical length. For example, *Stokesia laevis* 'Klaus Jelitto' is a facultative intermediate day plant (Clough et al., 1999).

For many plant species the response to photoperiod interacts with temperature. For example, if night temperatures are above 85°F (29°C), chrysanthemum flower induction and early development is delayed (Whealy et al., 1987). As the night temperature increases from 64 to 75°F (18 to 24°C), shorter photoperiods are required for rapid flowering of chrysanthemums (Will et al., 1997). Eight- to 12-hr day lengths produce acceptable flowering at 64°F (18°C), whereas 8- to 10-hr day lengths are required at 75°F (24°C). For other plants, the photoperiodic response changes with the growing temperature. *Calceolaria* is a facultative LD plant at temperatures of 60 to 68°F (16 to 20°C) and day neutral at 59°F (15°C) or lower.

Photoperiodism is a *phytochrome*-mediated response. The phytochrome molecule is a light-absorbing pigment that exists in

TABLE 2-1

Photoperiodic response for flowering of numerous floriculture plant species. Photoperiodic response listed is primarily for cultivated species and hybrids; individual cultivars within a species and other species not commonly cultivated with a genus may have different responses from that listed. With many species the response listed is for unvernalized plants. Many species can flower under any day length if first given a cold treatment. For several species the photoperiod requirement changes with the production temperature and light level.

Crop Species	Photoperiodic Response
Abutilon × *hybridum*	Day neutral
Achillea species	Day neutral to obligate LD
A. aegyptiaca 'Taygetea'	Facultative LD
A. clypeolata × 'Taygetea' 'Anthea,' 'Moonshine'	Facultative LD
A. filipendulina 'Cloth of Gold'	Obligate LD
A. filipendulina 'Gold Plate'	Facultative LD
A. filipendulina × *clypeolata* 'Coronation Gold'	Facultative LD
A. millefolium × 'Taygetea' 'Appleblossom,' 'Fireland,' 'Galaxy,' 'Hope,' 'Paprika,' 'Terra Cotta'	Facultative LD
A. millefolium × 'Summer Pastels'	Obligate LD
A. ptarmica 'The Pearl'	Facultative LD
A. tomentosa 'King Edward VIII'	Day neutral
Achimenes hybrids	Day neutral
Acroclinium roseum	Obligate LD
Agastache × 'Blue Fortune'	Facultative LD
Ageratum houstonianum	Facultative LD
A. houstonianum 'Blue Danube,' 'Tall Blue Horizon'	Facultative LD
Agrostemma githago	Obligate LD
Alcea rosea	Facultative LD
Alstroemeria hybrids	Facultative LD
Amaranthus caudatus	Facultative SD
A. hybridus 'Pygmy Torch'	Day neutral
Ammi majus	Obligate LD
Anemone coronaria	Day neutral to obligate LD
A. hupehensis	Obligate LD
Anethum graveolens 'Mammoth'	Obligate LD
Anigozanthos species and hybrids	Day neutral to facultative SD or LD
A. flavidus	Facultative LD
A. manglesii	Facultative SD
A. rufus, A. pulcherrimus, A. flavidus × *manglesii*	Day neutral
Anthurium species	Day neutral
Antirrhinum majus	Facultative LD
A. majus 'Floral Showers Crimson,' 'Spring Giants'	Facultative LD
Aquilegia species	Day neutral to facultative LD
Armeria × *hybrida* 'Dwarf Ornament Mix'	Day neutral
A. latifolia	Day neutral
Asclepias tuberosa	Obligate LD
Asperula arvensis 'Blue Mist'	Obligate LD
Aster species	Day neutral to facultative LD followed by facultative SD
A. alpinus 'Goliath'	Day neutral
A. dumosus	Facultative LD followed by facultative SD
A. ericoides	Facultative LD followed by facultative SD
A. novi-belgii	Facultative LD followed by facultative SD
A. pilosus	Obligate SD

Information was collated from Anderson (2002), Armitage (1994), Armitage and Laushman (2003), Cameron et al. (2000), Clough et al. (1999), Dole, unpublished, Erwin et al. (2002), Fausey et al. (1999), Karlsson and Werner (2002), Nausieda et al. (2000), Pallez et al. (2002), Runckle et al. (1996, 1998), and Whitman et al. (1998).

TABLE 2-1 *(continued)*

Crop Species	Photoperiodic Response
Astilbe × *arendsii*	Day neutral to facultative LD
Baptisia australis	Day neutral
Begonia × *hiemalis*	Obligate to facultative SD
B. Semperflorens-Cultorum cultivars	Day neutral
B. Tuberhybrida cultivars	Facultative LD
Bougainvillea spectabilis	Facultative SD
Calceolaria Herbeohybrida cultivars	Facultative LD
Calendula officinalis	Obligate to facultative LD
C. officinalis 'Calypso Orange'	Facultative LD
Calibrachoa 'Colorburst Violet,' 'Liricashowers Rose'	Facultative LD
Callistephus chinensis	Obligate to facultative LD followed by facultative SD
Campanula species	Day neutral to obligate LD
C. 'Birch Hybrid'	Facultative LD
C. isophylla	Obligate to facultative LD
C. medium	Obligate SD followed by obligate LD
C. medium 'Champion'	Obligate LD
C. carpatica 'Blue Clips'	Obligate LD
C. fragilis	Obligate LD
C. grandiflorus 'Sentimental Blue'	Facultative LD
C. leucophylla	Obligate LD
C. persicifolia	Day neutral
C. poscharskyana	Obligate to facultative LD
Capsicum annuum	Day neutral
Carpanthea pomeridiana 'Golden Carpet'	Day neutral
Carthamus tinctorius 'Lasting Yellow'	Facultative LD
Caryopteris incana	Facultative SD
Catananche caerulea 'Blue'	Obligate LD
Catharanthus roseus	Day neutral
Cattleya hybrids	Facultative SD
Celosia argentea	Facultative to obligate SD
C. argentea 'Chief Mix'	Facultative SD
C. argentea plumosa group "Flamingo Feather Purple"	Obligate SD
Centaurea species	Facultative to obligate LD
C. cyanus 'Blue Boy'	Obligate LD
Centranthus macrosiphon	Day neutral
Chrysanthemum coccineum 'James Kelway'	Obligate LD
Cirsium japonicum	Day neutral
Clarkia amoena	Day neutral to obligate LD
Clematis × *jackmanii*	Facultative LD
Cleome hassleriana	Day neutral to facultative LD
C. hassleriana 'Pink Queen'	Facultative LD
C. hassleriana 'Rose Queen'	Day neutral
C. spinosa	Facultative SD
Clerodendrum thomsoniae	Facultative SD
C. × *speciosum*	Facultative SD
Cobaea scandens	Day neutral
Collinsia heterophylla	Facultative LD
Consolida ambigua	Facultative LD
Convolvulus tricolor 'Blue Enchantment'	Day neutral

(continued)

TABLE 2-1 *(continued)*

Crop Species	Photoperiodic Response
Coreopsis grandiflora	Facultative to obligate LD
C. grandiflora 'Early Sunrise'	Obligate LD
C. grandiflora 'Sunray'	Facultative LD
C. verticillata 'Moonbeam'	Obligate LD
Corydalis lutea	Day neutral to facultative LD
Cosmos atrosanguineus	Facultative LD
C. bipinnatus	Facultative to obligate SD
C. bipinnatus 'Early Wonder,' 'Diablo,' 'White Sensation'	Facultative SD
C. sulphureus	Obligate SD
Crossandra infundibuliformis	Day neutral
Cyclamen persicum	Day neutral
Dahlia cultivars	Facultative SD
Delphinium elatum 'Blue Mirror'	Day neutral
Dendranthema ×*grandiflorum*	Obligate to facultative SD
Dianthus species	Day neutral to facultative LD
D. carthusianorum	Day neutral to facultative LD
D. caryophyllus	Facultative LD
D. chinensis 'Ideal Cherry Picotee'	Facultative LD
D. deltoides 'Zing Rose'	Day neutral
Dimorphotheca aurantiaca	Day neutral to obligate LD
D. aurantiaca 'Mixed Colors'	Day neutral
D. aurantiaca 'Salmon Queen'	Obligate LD
Dolichos lablab	Obligate SD
Echinacea purpurea	Facultative to obligate LD
E. purpurea 'Bravado'	Obligate LD
Echinops bannaticus	Facultative LD
Eschscholzia californica 'Sundew'	Facultative LD
Euphorbia marginata	Obligate SD
E. pulcherrima	Obligate SD
Eustoma grandiflorum	Day neutral to facultative LD
Exacum affine	Day neutral
Freesia ×*hybrida*	Day neutral
Fuchsia hybrids	Day neutral to obligate LD
F. 'Dollar Princess'	Obligate LD
F. 'Gartenmeister'	Day neutral
Gaillardia grandiflora 'Goblin'	Obligate LD
Gaura lindheimeri 'Whirling Butterflies'	Facultative LD
Gazania rigens 'Daybreak Red Stripe'	Obligate LD
Geranium dalmaticum	Facultative LD
Gerbera jamesonii	Facultative SD
Gomphrena globosa	Day neutral to facultative SD
G. globosa 'Bicolor Rose'	Facultative SD
Gynura aurantiaca	Facultative LD
Gypsophila elegans, G. paniculata	Facultative to obligate LD
G. paniculata 'Snowflake'	Obligate LD
Hatiora gaertneri	Facultative SD followed by facultative LD
Helianthus annuus	Day neutral to facultative SD
H. annuus 'Big Smile,' 'Elf,' 'Pacino,' 'Sunbright,' 'Sunrich Orange,' 'Sunspot,' 'Teddy Bear'	Facultative SD
H. annuus 'Sundance Kid'	Day neutral
H. debilis 'Vanilla Ice'	Facultative LD

TABLE 2-1 *(continued)*

Crop Species	Photoperiodic Response
Heliconia species	Day neutral, facultative LD or SD
Helipterum roseum	Obligate LD
Heuchera sanguinea 'Bressingham Hybrids'	Day neutral
Hibiscus moscheutos	Obligate LD
H. moscheutos 'Disco Belle Mixed'	Obligate LD
H. rosa-sinensis	Day neutral
Hosta cultivars and species	Obligate LD
H. 'Fortunei Hyacinthina,' 'Francee,' 'Golden Scepter,' 'Golden Tiara,' 'Lancifolia,' 'Royal Standard,' 'Tokudama' gold, 'Tokudama' green, 'Undulata Variegata'	Obligate LD
H. montana	Obligate LD
H. plantaginea	Obligate LD
Hydrangea macrophylla	Day neutral to facultative SD
Hylotelephium (Sedum spectabile × *telephium)* 'Autumn Joy'	Obligate LD
Hypericum species	Facultative LD
Iberis sempervirens 'Snowflake'	Day neutral
Impatiens balsamina	Obligate SD
I. hawkeri	Day neutral
I. walleriana	Day neutral
Ipomoea × *multifida* 'Scarlet'	Facultative SD
I. species	Facultative SD
Ipomopsis rubra 'Hummingbird Mix'	Obligate LD
Kalanchoe blossfeldiana	Obligate SD
Lathyrus odoratus 'Royal White'	Obligate LD
Lavandula angustifolia 'Hidcote Blue'	Obligate LD
Lavatera trimestris 'Silver Cup'	Obligate LD
Legousia speculum-veneris	Obligate LD
Leptosiphon hybrida	Obligate LD
Leucanthemum × *superbum*	Facultative to obligate LD
L. × *superbum* 'Snowlady'	Facultative LD
L. × *superbum* 'Snowcap'	Obligate LD
Lewisia cotyledon	Day neutral
Liatris spicata	Facultative LD
Lilium longiflorum	Facultative LD
L. hybrids	Facultative LD
Limnanthes douglasii	Obligate LD
Limonium sinuatum	Facultative LD
L. sinuatum 'Fortress Deep Rose,' 'Heavenly Blue'	Facultative LD
Linaria maroccana	Day neutral to facultative LD
Linum perenne	Day neutral to obligate LD
L. perenne 'Sapphire'	Day neutral
Lobelia erinus	Day neutral to obligate LD
L. erinus 'Crystal Palace'	Obligate LD
L. × *speciosa*	Facultative LD
L. × *speciosa* 'Compliment Scarlet'	Facultative LD
Lobularia maritima	Day neutral
Lupinus hartwegii 'Bright Gems'	Facultative LD
Lycopersicon esculentum	Day neutral
Lysimachia clethroides	Obligate LD

(continued)

TABLE 2-1 *(continued)*

Crop Species	Photoperiodic Response
Matthiola hybrids	Facultative LD
M. longipetala 'Starlight Scentsation'	Day neutral
Mimulus ×*hybridus* 'Magic'	Obligate LD
Mina lobata	Obligate SD
Mirabilis jalapa	Day neutral to obligate LD
Nemophila maculate 'Pennie Black'	Day neutral
N. menziesii	Day neutral
Nicotiana alata	Day neutral to facultative LD
N. alata 'Domino White'	Day neutral
Nierembergia caerulea	Obligate LD
Nigella damascena 'Miss Jekyll'	Obligate LD
Ocimum basilicum	Facultative SD to facultative LD
Oenothera fruticosa	Facultative LD
O. missouriensis	Obligate LD
O. pallida 'Wedding Bells'	Obligate LD
Orchidaceae, most species	Day neutral
Origanum vulgare	Day neutral
Osteospermum hybrids	Facultative LD
Oxalis crassipes 'Rosea'	Obligate LD
Papaver rhoeas	Day neutral
Pelargonium species	Day neutral
P. ×*domesticum*	Day neutral
P. ×*hortorum*	Day neutral
P. peltatum	Day neutral
Pennisetum setaceum 'Rubrum'	Facultative LD
Penstemon digitalis	Day neutral
P. digitalis 'Husker Red'	Day neutral
Pentas lanceolata	Day neutral
Petunia ×*hybrida*	Facultative SD to obligate LD
P. ×*hybrida* 'White Storm,' 'Cascadia Improved Charlie,' 'Doubloon Blue Star,' 'Marco Polo,' 'Petitunia Bright Dream'	Facultative LD
P. ×*hybrida* 'Fantasy Pink Morn,' 'Purple Wave'	Obligate LD
P. ×*hybrida* 'Cascadie Charme'	Facultative SD
Phacelia campanularia	Day neutral
P. tanacetifolia	Facultative LD
Pharbitis 'Violet'	Facultative SD
Phlox paniculata	Obligate LD
P. subulata	Day neutral
Physostegia virginiana 'Alba'	Facultative LD
Platycodon grandiflorus	Day neutral
Platystemon californicus	Obligate LD
Polemonium viscosum	Obligate LD
Polianthes tuberosa	Day neutral
Primula malacoides	Day neutral to facultative SD
P. obconica 'Libre Light Salmon'	Day neutral to facultative LD
P. veris 'Pacific Giants'	Day neutral
Reseda alba	Facultative LD
Rhododendron hybrids	Facultative SD
Rosa hybrids	Day neutral to facultative LD
Rudbeckia hirta 'Indian Summer'	Obligate LD
R. fulgida 'Goldsturm'	Obligate LD
Saintpaulia ionantha	Day neutral

TABLE 2-1 *(continued)*

Crop Species	Photoperiodic Response
Salpiglossis sinuata	Facultative LD
Salvia farinacea 'Strata'	Facultative LD
S. leucantha	Obligate SD
S. splendens	Day neutral to facultative LD or SD
S. splendens 'Vista Red'	Day neutral to facultative LD
S. ×superba 'Blue Queen'	Facultative LD
Sanvitalia procumbens	Facultative SD
Saxifraga ×arendsii	Facultative LD
S. ×arendsii 'Triumph'	Facultative LD
Scabiosa atropurpurea	Facultative LD
S. caucasica 'Butterfly Blue'	Day neutral
Schlumbergera truncata, S. ×buckleyi	Obligate SD to day neutral
Silene armeria	Obligate LD
S. armeria 'Elektra'	Obligate LD
Sinningia speciosa	Day neutral
Solanum pseudocapsicum	Day neutral
Solenostemon scutellarioides	Facultative SD
Solidago canadensis	Obligate SD
S. graminifolia	Obligate SD
S. nemoralis	Obligate SD
S. rugosa	Obligate LD
×Solidaster luteus	Facultative LD
Stephanotis floribunda	Day neutral
Stokesia laevis 'Klaus Jelitto'	Facultative intermediate
Strelitzia reginae	Day neutral
Streptocarpus ×hybridus	Day neutral
S. nobilis	Day neutral to facultative SD
Tagetes erecta	Day neutral to obligate SD
T. patula	Day neutral
T. tenuifolia	Obligate SD
Thunbergia alata	Day neutral
Tithonia rotundifolia	Facultative LD to SD
T. rotundifolia 'Fiesta Del Sol'	Facultative LD
T. rotundifolia 'Sundance'	Facultative SD
Trachelium caeruleum	Facultative LD
Tweedia caerulea 'Blue Star'	Day neutral
Verbascum phoeniceum	Day neutral
Verbena ×hybridum	Facultative LD
Veronica longifolia 'Sunny Border Blue'	Day neutral
V. spicata 'Blue'	Day neutral
Viguiera multiflora	Facultative LD
Viola ×wittrockiana	Facultative LD
Zantedeschia species	Day neutral
Z. aethiopica	Day neutral
Z. albomaculata	Day neutral
Z. elliotiana	Day neutral
Z. rehmannii	Day neutral
Zinnia species and cultivars	Day neutral to facultative LD or SD
Z. angustifolia	Day neutral
Z. elegans 'Benary Giant Deep Red'	Facultative LD
Z. elegans 'Exquisite Pink,' 'Peter Pan Scarlet,' 'Oklahoma'	Facultative SD

two basic forms: P_{fr} and P_r. The P_r form switches to the P_{fr} form when leaves are irradiated with red light. Similarly, P_{fr} switches to P_r when P_{fr} is struck by far-red light. During the night, P_{fr} slowly reverts to the P_r form. Under the simplest scenarios, high levels of P_{fr} inhibit flowering in long night (SD) plants and promote flowering in short night (LD) plants. Interestingly, using far-red light-blocking filters encourages flower initiation in SD chrysanthemum plants, even under LD photoperiods (McMahon, 1997).

In floriculture, day length is most commonly manipulated by *night interruption lighting* (Fig. 2-2) or by *black cloth* (Fig. 2-3) (see Chapter 4, Light, for procedures). Night interruption divides the dark period into two shorter "nights" and is used to prevent flowering of SD plants. Night interruption can also be used to induce flowering of LD plants. Night interruption lighting is also known as *night breaks* (NB). Long days can also be applied by turning on lamps at sunset or prior to sunrise and extending the day length into the night, which is known as *day continuation* (DC). For many species the light intensity should be at least 10 fc (2 μmol·s⁻¹·m⁻²) measured at the plant apex. The time of the year when the lights are turned on and the minimum intensity required may vary with the species.

The night can be made longer by means of light-excluding fabrics, called *black cloths*, placed over the crops (see Chapter 4, Light, for procedures) (Fig. 2–3). Black cloths are used to induce flowering of SD plants or inhibit flowering of LD plants. The cloths are commonly pulled over the plants from 1700 to 0800 (5 P.M.

FIGURE 2-3 Black cloth for creating artificial short days.

to 8 A.M.) or 1900 to 0700 (7 P.M. to 7 A.M.) if heat buildup is a problem.

Generally, the black cloths are pulled every day, because each day skipped means that flowering will be delayed by the same number of days. In addition, if too many days are skipped, the plants will not flower or flowers will be malformed. For many species, the black cloths do not have to be pulled after the buds or bracts show color; however, some species such as poinsettias require black cloths be used until the first flower buds completely open (Fig. 2–4).

Some plants form reproductive structures under photoperiods normally inductive only to vegetative growth. For example, chrysanthemums form crown buds and poinsettias form splits or prematurely initiated flowers under LD conditions. In both cases, after a specific number of nodes have formed on a shoot, the meristem develops a reproductive structure. As long as the shoots are under LD conditions, the crown buds and splits never develop properly as inflorescences.

FIGURE 2-2 Incandescent long day lighting for photoperiod manipulation.

FIGURE 2-4 Poinsettia (*Euphorbia pulcherrima*) crop ready for market.

LIGHT INTENSITY

The total amount of light (total light integral) is the controlling factor for many day neutral plants. For example, geraniums are DN and will flower more rapidly with increased light energy, that is, the same day length but with increased light energy from supplemental lights. DN plants can often be confused with facultative LD plants in that, as the day length increases in the spring, the total amount of light a plant receives each day and the average daily temperature increase, which hastens flowering. Thus, a DN plant will often appear to be a LD plant. However, DN plants can be separated from LD plants experimentally by providing both types with the same amount of light energy each day but over several different durations. In such situations, LD plants will flower faster under the LD, whereas the DN plants will flower equally fast under all day length durations. DN plants may also flower in response to other stimuli, such as cold temperatures.

TEMPERATURE

The low-temperature promotion of flower initiation and development is often known as *vernalization*. As with photoperiod, the cold requirement can be obligate (i.e., cold is required for flowering) or facultative (i.e., cold hastens flowering). The duration of the cold treatment required varies widely with the species from a few days to several weeks. In some cases, cold can be applied to seeds, while in other cases, only mature plants can perceive the cold temperatures. Many geophytic species have a cold requirement for further floral development and stem elongation, but not for floral initiation (Table 2-2).

The role of low temperatures in the life cycle of a plant varies and plants can be categorized into three groups:

1. Cold is required for growth and development (endodormancy) and the plant cannot complete its life cycle without a cold period. For example, *Tulipa* requires a cold treatment for shoot elongation and flowering (Le Nard and De Hertogh, 1993). With some species such as Easter lilies (*Lilium longiflorum*) cold is required for flower induction and initiation, whereas with other species such as azalea (*Rhododendron*) the flowers are formed prior to the cold treatment and the cold is required only for further development and anthesis of the flowers.

2. Cold is required for continued growth and development if dormancy has been induced (endodormancy); however, the plant can flower and complete its life cycle without a dormancy period. For example, exposure to day lengths of 12 hr or less induces hypocotyl enlargement and dormancy in tuberous begonias (Lewis, 1951) and several weeks of 1 to 5°C are required to break dormancy (Haegeman, 1993). However, when tuberous begonias are grown under 14-hr day lengths without exposure to a cold period, the plants do not develop dormancy and flower (Lewis, 1951).

3. Cold is not required but prevents growth and development and reduces desiccation (ecodormancy). For example, *Hippeastrum* bulbs do not require a cold treatment, but bulbs are stored at 41 to 48°F (5 to 9°C) to delay flower and leaf emergence and allow storage and shipping (Boyle and Stimart, 1987; Rees, 1985).

Devernalization can occur if plants are subjected to periods of high temperature after receiving the cold treatment.

The maximum temperature required for vernalization varies with the species from just above 32°F (0°C) to much higher. Easter lilies will eventually flower if grown at temperatures as high as 68°F (20°C) (Lin and Wilkins, 1973). The minimum temperature for vernalization is

TABLE 2-2

General dormancy breaking protocols for selected geophytic floriculture crops species (De Hertogh, 1996; De Hertogh and Le Nard, 1993).

Species	Storage Organ Type	Cold Temperature and Duration	Comments
Allium aflatunense	Bulb	41°F (5°C) for 16–20 weeks	
A. karataviense	Bulb	32–48°F (0–9°C) for 21–22 weeks	Optimum temperature varies with the stage of plant development[a]
Alstroemeria hybrids	Rhizome	41–61°F (5–16°C) substrate for at least 6 weeks	Temperatures above 70°F (21°C) devernalize rhizomes
Anemone blanda	Tuber	32–48°F (0–9°C) for 15–17 weeks	Optimum temperature varies with the stage of plant development[a]
A. coronaria	Tuber	36–50°F (2–10°C) for 4–6 weeks	Interactions with LD; high temperatures and drought stress occur
A. hupensis	Corm	41°F (5°C) for 6 weeks	
Begonia Tuberhybrida	Enlarged hypocotyl	35–41°F (1–5°C) for 9–13 weeks	Plants go dormant at 12 hr or shorter photoperiods
Convallaria majalis	Rhizome	28–31°F (−2 to −0.6°C) for 2–3 weeks	
Crocus vernus	Corm	32–48°F (0–9°C) for 13–20 weeks	Optimum temperature varies with the stage of plant development[a]
Dahlia hybrids	Tuberous root	32–50°F (0–10°C) for 6 weeks	Plants will not go dormant if grown under 12–14 hr day lengths; tuberization occurs under 11–12 day lengths
Freesia hybrids	Corm	59°F (15°C) or lower substrate for up to 6 weeks	86°F (30°C) pretreatment for minimum of 15–16 weeks may be required; ethylene can replace heat pretreatment
Fritillaria imperialis	Bulb	36°F (2°C) for 18 weeks	
F. meleagris	Bulb	41°F (5°C) for 13–17 weeks	
Gladiolus hybrids	Corm	36–50°F (2–10°C) for 8–22 weeks	100°F (38°C) pretreatment can decrease time required in cold storage; photoperiod influences dormancy and flowering
Hippeastrum hybrids	Bulb	41–48°F (5–9°C) to prevent shoot growth	Cold not required; drought stress prior to storage will decrease days to shoot emergence
Hyacinthus orientalis	Bulb	32–48°F (0–9°C) for 13–18 weeks	Optimum temperature varies with the stage of plant development[a]
Iris danfordiae (Bak.) Boiss	Bulb	32–48°F (0–9°C) for 13–17 weeks	Optimum temperature varies with the stage of plant development[a]
I. germanica	Rhizome	26–39°F (−2–4°C) for 14–16 weeks	LD can substitute for cold ethylene or 86°F (30°C) heat pretreatment may be required

Species	Type	Temperature/Duration	Notes
I. ×hollandica	Bulb	48–59°F (9–15°C) for 6–13 weeks	Optimum temperature varies with the stage of plant development[a]
I. Reticulata hybrids	Bulb	32–48°F (0–9°C) for 14–19 weeks	
Ixia L. species	Corm	48°F (9°C) for 4–6 weeks	Much variation among species
Lachenalia Jacq. f. ex Murray species	Bulb	50–59°F (10–15°C) for 6.5 weeks or 48°F (9°C) for 6 weeks	
Leucocoryne coquimbensis F. Phil.	Bulb	68°F (20°C) for 16 weeks to 11 months	
Leucojum aestivum L.	Bulb	32–48°F (0–9°C) for 15–18 weeks	Optimum temperature varies with the stage of plant development[a]
Liatris spicata	Corm	32–36°F (0–2°C) for at least 10 weeks	GA can partially substitute for cold
Lilium Asiatic hybrids	Bulb	36–41°F (2–5°C) for 6–10 weeks	LD can partially substitute for cold
L. longiflorum	Bulb	36–45°F (2–7°C) for 6 weeks	LD can partially substitute for cold
L. Oriental hybrids	Bulb	36–41°F (2–5°C) for 8–10 weeks	LD can partially substitute for cold
L. speciosum	Bulb	41°F (5°C) for 6 weeks	
Muscari armeniacum	Bulb	32–48°F (0–9°C) for 15–20 weeks	Optimum temperature varies with the stage of plant development[a]
Narcissus pseudonarcissus	Bulb	32–48°F (0–9°C) for 13–24 weeks	Optimum temperature varies with the stage of plant development[a]
Ornithogalum arabicum	Bulb	55°F (13°C) for 4–8 weeks	Cold treatments not required for forcing
O. thyrsoides	Bulb	41°F (5°C) for 6–14 weeks	Use of 86–95°F (30–35°C) pretreatment can reduce the duration of 41°F (5°C) required to break dormancy
Oxalis species	Bulb or rhizome	41°F (5°C) until planted	Some species may require a cold treatment for further growth; with other species the cold treatment prevents desiccation but is not required; drought or nutrient stress or cold temperatures will induce dormancy
O. adenophylla	Tuber	36°F (2°C) for 15–17 weeks	
Ranunculus asiaticus	Tuberous root	39–41°F (4–5°C) for 4–5 weeks or 36°F (2°C) for 2 weeks	
Scilla mischtschenkoana	Bulb	32–48°F (0–9°C) for 15–18 weeks	Optimum temperature varies with the stage of plant development[a]
Sparaxis species	Corm	55°F (13°C) for 2–4 weeks	
Triteleia laxa	Corm	41°F (5°C) for 12 weeks	
Tulipa hybrids	Bulb	32–48°F (0–9°C) for 13–23 weeks	Optimum temperature varies with the stage of plant development[a]

[a]After potting, the cold treatment typically starts at 48°F (9°C) until roots are visible at the bottom of the pot at which time the temperature is lowered to 41°F (5°C). When shoots are of proper length for the species, the temperature is lowered to and held at 32–36°F (0–2°C) until plants are moved to warm temperatures for forcing.

often set by the cold tolerance of the species. If the cold temperatures are applied to seed or storage organs, moisture is often required for the cold to be perceived.

For some species, cold treatments are required after specific environmental stimuli (e.g., high temperatures or drought stress) have been completed (Boyle and Stimart, 1987; Hartsema, 1961; Lewis, 1951). Such pretreatments are imposed to either delay development and allow extended storage of the organs or to accelerate development and allow forcing as quickly as possible after bulb harvest. For example, *Iris* ×*hollandica* bulbs are exposed to warm 86°F (30°C) temperatures to retard further development prior to cool 48 to 59°F (9 to 15°C) temperatures for dormancy release (Hartsema, 1961). Heat treatment for retardation allows the iris to be forced year-round for cut flower production.

Often photoperiod or gibberellic acid (GA) interact with the cold treatment. In some cases SD, LD, or GA may substitute for all or part of the cold treatment. For example, GA has been used on azalea (*Rhododendron*) to completely replace the cold treatment after flower buds have developed (Boodley and Mastalerz, 1959; Larson and Sydnor, 1971). However, in Easter lilies, LD substitute for cold equally on a week-for-week basis only after the plants have received 1 to 2 weeks of cold (Dole and Wilkins, 1994; Weiler and Langhans, 1968, 1972).

KEY POINTS

- Three main environmental control mechanisms for flowering in commercial floriculture crops are photoperiod, light intensity, and temperature.

- Plants must be mature before the flowering stimulus is perceived.

- The phase before maturity is called the juvenile period and a juvenile plant will not flower even if growing in the proper environment for flowering to occur.

- Plants need to have sufficient foliage (photosynthetic capacity) to support the size and quality of flowers required for commercial production.

- The first stage of flower development is known as flower induction, during which time the biochemical processes required for flowering commence.

- During flower initiation the first actual microscopic signs of the flowers become apparent.

- The definition of anthesis or "flowering" varies with the species but typically means the first signs of visible pollen within the flower or when the plant or flowering stem is ready for harvest.

- The apex of determinant plants terminates in an inflorescence, whereas indeterminate plants produce inflorescences only in the leaf axils, and the main stem remains vegetative and continues to grow indefinitely.

- Cultivars can be arranged in response groups, which are defined as the amount of time from placement of the plant in the proper environmental conditions for flowering until anthesis occurs.

- Producers often use the week system to schedule crops. The first week in January (often a partial week) is labeled as week 1 and the last full week in December is week 52.

- Photoperiodism, the response of plants to night length, regulates many responses in plants, such as flower initiation and development, plant dormancy, seed germination, storage organ formation, and plant growth habit.

- Most photoperiodic plant responses can be divided into three basic types: short day (SD), long day (LD), and day neutral (DN). SD plants will flower when the dark period is longer than a critical length (critical night length), and LD plants will flower when the dark period is shorter than a critical length.

- Many plant species will flower under a wide range of day lengths, but will flower more rapidly under either SD or LD days and are known as facultative SD or LD plants.

- Obligate SD or LD plants will not develop flowers if placed under incorrect photoperiods.

- Photoperiodism is a phytochrome-mediated response.

- Day length is commonly manipulated by night interruption lighting or by black cloth.

- The total amount of light (total light integral) is the controlling factor for many day neutral plants.

- The low-temperature promotion of flower initiation and development is often known as vernalization.
- The role of low temperatures in the life cycle of a plant varies and plants can be categorized into three groups: (1) Cold is required for growth and development (endodormancy) and the plant cannot complete its life cycle without a cold period. (2) Cold is required for continued growth and development if dormancy has been induced (endodormancy), however, the plant can flower and complete its life cycle without a dormancy period. (3) Cold is not required but prevents growth and development and reduces desiccation (ecodormancy).

BIBLIOGRAPHY

Anderson, N.O. 2002. New methodology to teach floral induction in floriculture potted plant production classes. *HortTechnology* 12:157–167.

Armitage, A.M. 1994. *Ornamental Bedding Plants*. CAB International, Oxon, United Kingdom.

Armitage, A.M., and J.M. Laushman. 2003. *Specialty Cut Flowers*. Timber Press, Portland, Oregon.

Boodley, J.W., and J.W. Mastalerz. 1959. The use of gibberellic acid to force azaleas without cold temperature treatments. *Proceedings of the American Society for Horticultural Science* 74:681–685.

Boyle, T.H., and D.P. Stimart. 1987. Influence of irrigation interruptions on flowering of *Hippeastrum ×hybridum* 'Red Lion'. *HortScience* 22:1290–1292.

Cameron, A., B. Fausey, R. Heins, and W. Carlson. 2000. Firing up perennials—Beyond 2000. *Greenhouse Grower* 18(8):74–78.

Cavins, T.J., and J.M. Dole. 2001. Photoperiod, juvenility, and high-intensity lighting affect flowering and cut stem qualities of *Campanula* and *Lupinus*. *HortScience* 36:1192–1196.

Clough, E., A. Cameron, R. Heins, and W. Carlson. 1999. Forcing perennials, species: *Stokesia laevis* 'Klaus Jelitto.' *Greenhouse Grower* 17(11):40–46, 48.

Cockshull, K.E. 1985. *Antirrhinum majus*, pp. 476–481 in *Handbook of Flowering*, vol. III, A.H. Halevy, editor. CRC Press, Boca Raton, Florida.

De Hertogh, A.A. 1996. *Holland Bulb Forcers' Guide*, 5th ed. International Flower Bulb Centre, Hillegom, The Netherlands.

De Hertogh, A., and M. Le Nard, editors. 1993. *The Physiology of Flower Bulbs*. Elsevier Science Publishers, Amsterdam.

Dole, J.M., and H.F. Wilkins. 1994. Interaction of bulb vernalization and shoot photoperiods on 'Nellie White' Easter lily. *HortScience* 29:143–145.

Doorenbos, J. 1959. Responses of China aster to daylength and gibberellic acid. *Euphytica* 8:69–75.

Erwin, J., R. Warner, and N. Mattson. 2002. How does daylength affect flowering of spring annuals? *Minnesota Commercial Flower Growers Bulletin* 51(3):6–10.

Fausey, B., A. Cameron, R. Heins, and W. Carlson. 1999. Forcing perennials: Hosta. *Greenhouse Grower* 16(12):84–86, 88, 90.

Fortanier, E.J. 1973. Reviewing the length of the generation period and its shortening, particularly in tulips. *Scientia Horticulturae* 1:107–116.

Hacket, W.P. 1985. Juvenility, maturation and rejuvenation in woody plants, pp. 109–155 in *Horticultural Reviews*, vol. 1, J. Janick editor. AVI Publishing Company, Westport, Connecticut.

Haegeman, J. 1993. Begonia—tuberous hybrids, pp. 227–238 in *The Physiology of Flower Bulbs*, A. De Hertogh and M. Le Nard, editors. Elsevier Science Publishers, Amsterdam.

Hartsema, A.H. 1961. Influence of temperatures on flower formation and flowering of bulbous and tuberous plants, pp. 123–167 in *Handbuch der Pflanzenphysiologie*, vol. 16, W. Ruhland, editor. Springer-Verlag, Berlin.

Kamlesh, S.S., and R.K. Kohli. 1981. *Calendula officinalis* L., a long day plant with an exceptionally low photoperiodic requirement for flowering. *Indian Journal of Plant Physiology* 24:299–303.

Karlsson, M.G., and J.W. Werner. 2002. Photoperiod and temperature affect flowering in German primrose. *HortTechnology* 12:217–219.

Konishi, K., and K. Inaba. 1967. Studies on flowering control of *Dahlia*. VII. On dormancy of crown-tuber. *Journal of the Japanese Society of Horticultural Science* 36:131–140.

Larson, R.A., and T.D. Sydnor. 1971. Azalea flower bud development and dormancy as influenced by temperature and gibberellic acid. *Journal of the American Society for Horticultural Science* 96:786–788.

Le Nard, M., and A.A. De Hertogh. 1993. *Tulipa*, pp. 617–682 in *The Physiology of Flower Bulbs*, A. De Hertogh and M. Le Nard, editors. Elsevier Science Publishers, Amsterdam.

Lewis, C. 1951. Some effects of daylength on tuberization, flowering, and vegetative growth of tuberous-rooted begonias. *Proceedings of the American Society for Horticultural Science* 57:376–378.

Lin, W.C., and H.F. Wilkins. 1973. The interaction of temperature on photoperiodic responses of *Lilium longiflorum* Thunb. cv. Nellie White. *Florists' Review* 153(3965):24–26.

McMahon, M.J. 1997. Chrysanthemum cultivars differ in response to photoperiod when grown under far-red absorbing filters. *HortScience* 32:437. (Abstract)

Moser, B.C., and C.E. Hess. 1968. The physiology of tuberous root development in dahlia. *Proceedings of the American Society for Horticultural Science* 93:595–603.

Nausieda, E., L. Smith, T. Hayahsi, B. Fausey, A. Cameron, R. Heins, and W. Carlson. 2000. Forcing perennials: Achillea. *Greenhouse Grower* 18(5):53, 54, 58, 61–62, 64.

Pallez, L.C., J.M. Dole, and B.E. Whipker. 2002. Production and postproduction studies with potted sunflowers. *HortTechnology* 12:206–210.

Rees, A.M. 1985. *Hippeastrum*, pp. 294–296 in *Handbook of Flowering*, vol. 1. A.H. Halevy, editor. CRC Press, Boca Raton, Florida.

Runckle, E.S., R.D. Heins, A.C. Cameron, and W.H. Carlson. 1996. Manipulating day length to flower perennials. *Greenhouse Grower* 14(6):66, 68–70.

Runckle, E.S., R.D. Heins, A.C. Cameron, and W.H. Carlson. 1998. Flowering of herbaceous perennials under various night interruption and cyclic lighting treatments. *HortScience* 33:672–677.

Schwabe, W.W. 1986. *Aster novi-belgii*, pp. 29–41 in *Handbook of Flowering*, vol. 5, A.H. Halevy, editor. CRC Press, Boca Raton, Florida.

Wallerstein, I., A. Kadman-Zahavi, H. Yahel, A. Nissim, R. Stav, and S. Michal. 1992. Control of growth and flowering of five *Aster* cultivars as influenced by cutting type, temperature, day length. *Scientia Horticulturae* 50:209–218.

Weiler, T.C., and R.W. Langhans. 1968. Determination of vernalizing temperatures in the vernalization requirement of *Lilium longiflorum* (Thunb.) cv. 'Ace.' *Proceedings of the American Society for Horticultural Science* 93:623–629.

Weiler, T.C., and R.W. Langhans. 1972. Growth and flowering responses of *Lilium longiflorum* (Thunb.) 'Ace' to different daylength. *Journal of the American Society for Horticultural Science* 97:176–177.

Whealy, C.A., T.A. Nell, J.E. Barrett, and R.A. Larson. 1987. High temperature effects on growth and floral development of chrysanthemum. *Journal of the American Society for Horticultural Science* 112:464-468.

Whitman, C.M., R.D Heins, A.C. Cameron, and W.H. Carlson. 1998. Lamp type and irradiance level for daylength extensions influence flowering of *Campanula carpatica* 'Blue Clips', *Coreopsis grandiflora* 'Early Sunrise' and *Coreopsis verticillata* 'Moonbeam.' *Journal of the American Society for Horticultural Science* 123:802–807.

Will, E., T.W. Starman, J.E. Faust, and S. Abbitt. 1997. Photoperiodic responses of garden chrysanthemums. *HortScience* 32:502. (Abstract)

Zimmer, K., 1985. *Campanula fragilis*, pp. 117–118 in *Handbook of Flowering*, vol. II, A.H. Halevy, editor. CRC Press, Boca Raton, Florida.

Chapter 3

Temperature

INTRODUCTION

Floriculture literature discusses three types of temperatures: air, leaf, and medium. Generally, air temperature is the easiest to monitor, control, and record, but the actual leaf or plant temperature can differ greatly from the air temperature. For example, when the environment is warm and windy with low humidity, the leaf temperature will be lower than the air temperature because of the cooling effect of transpiration. Conversely, cool and sunny conditions with high humidity and little air movement will result in leaf temperatures higher than the air temperature due to lack of dissipation of the sun's heat from insufficient air movement or transpiration. Medium temperature reflects the actual temperature of the roots. Currently most temperature recommendations refer to air temperatures unless stated otherwise, and most recommendations also refer to night temperature, which is more easily controlled. Advances in environmental monitoring equipment and computer technology are increasingly basing greenhouse production on leaf and medium temperatures rather than on air temperatures.

Temperature can have a general or a specific effect on plant growth. In the former case, plant growth gradually increases or decreases as the temperature changes. Temperature can have a specific effect on plant growth through *vernalization,* or the induction of a specific response such as flowering by cool temperatures.

For example, *Aconitum* tuberous roots require vernalization for flowering (Leeuwen, 1980). For other species, such as purple coneflower (*Echinacea purpurea*), vernalization is not required but results in more rapid flowering and higher quality flowering stems (Armitage, 1993). Many perennial species require vernalization for rapid, economical production. See also Chapter 1, Propagation, regarding stratification, which is a cold treatment applied to seeds to enhance germination.

AIR TEMPERATURE

OPTIMUM AND TOLERABLE TEMPERATURE RANGES

Each plant species has an optimum growing temperature range and a tolerable temperature range. The optimum temperatures produce high-quality plants most rapidly (Table 3–1). Tolerable temperatures allow the plants to continue growing but may result in long production times or low quality. For example, the optimum night temperature range for chrysanthemums (*Dendranthema* ×*grandiflorum*) is 61 to 64°F (16 to 18°C), but chrysanthemums will grow at night temperatures as low as 40°F (4°C) or as high as 80°F (27°C) (Whealy et al., 1987; Wilkins et al., 1990). At the low end of the tolerable temperature range, however, growth will be uneconomically slow and at the high end flower initiation and development temperature

TABLE 3-1

Greenhouse production night temperatures for floriculture species: **cold**: 50°F (10°C) or lower; **cool**: 50 to 58°F (10 to 14°C); **moderate**: 58 to 65°F (14 to 18°C); and **warm**: 65 to 72°F (18 to 22°C). Many species can be grown cooler than the indicated temperature range but crop time may be excessively long. In addition, lowering the temperature at the end of the crop cycle is recommended for some species. Note that higher temperatures might be recommended immediately after planting some species to encourage establishment. In addition, numerous species require specific temperature regimes for flower initiation and development.

Scientific Name	Common Name	Night Temperature
Abelmoschus esculentus	Okra	Moderate
A. moschatus	Annual hibiscus	Moderate
Abutilon × hybridum	Chinese bellflower	Moderate
Acaena microphylla	Scarlet bidi bidi	Warm
Acanthus mollis	Bear's breech	Moderate
Achillea filipendulina	Fernleaf yarrow	Cool to moderate
A. millefolium	Common yarrow	Cool to moderate
A. ptarmica	Sneezeweed	Cool to moderate
A. tomentosa	Woolly yarrow	Cool to moderate
Achimenes hybrids	Achimines	Warm
Aconitum napellus	Aconite	Cool
Acroclinium roseum	Strawflower	Cool
Adenophora liliifolia	Ladybells	Cool
Adiantum species	Maidenhair fern	Warm
Aethionema coridifolium	Stonecress	Cool
Agastache foeniculum	Giant hyssop	Moderate
Ageratum houstonianum	Ageratum	Moderate
Agrostemma githago	Agrostemma	Cool
Agrostis nebulosa	Cloud grass	Cool
Alcea rosea	Hollyhock	Cool
Alchemilla mollis	Lady's mantle	Cool
Allium cepa	Onion	Cool
A. porrum	Leek	Moderate
A. schoenoprasum	Chives	Moderate
A. tuberosum	Garlic	Moderate
Alonsoa warscewiczii	Maskflower	Cool
Aloysia triphylla	Lemon verbena	Moderate
Alstroemeria hybrids	Peruvian lily	Cold to cool
Alternanthera dentata	Alternanthera	Moderate
A. ficoidea		Moderate
Alyssoides uticulata	Bladderpod	Cool
Amaranthus caudatus	Amaranthus	Warm
A. tricolor		Warm
Amberboa moschata	Sweet sultan	Cool
Amethysteya caerulea	Amethysteya	Moderate
Ammi majus	Lace or bishop's flower	Moderate
Ammobium alatum	Everlasting flower	Moderate
Anacyclus depressus	Atlas daisy	Moderate
Anagallis arvensis	Pimpernel	Cool
Anaphalis margaritacea	Pearly everlasting	Cool
Anchusa azurea	Italian bugloss	Cool
A. capensis	Anchusa	Cool
Anemone coronaria	Anemone	Cold
Anethum graveolens	Dill	Cool to moderate
Angelica archangelica	Angelica	Moderate
Angelonia angustifolia	Angelonia	Warm
Anigozanthus hybrids	Kangaroo paw	Cool

TABLE 3-1 *(continued)*

Scientific Name	Common Name	Night Temperature
Anoda cristata	Anoda	Cool
Antennaria dioica	Everlasting	Moderate
Anthemis tinctoria	Hardy marguerite	Cool
A. tinctoria cv. Kelwayi	Anthemis	Moderate
Anthurium species	Anthurium	Warm
Antirrhinum majus	Snapdragon	Cold to cool
Aphelandra squarrosa	Zebra plant	Warm
Apium graveolens var. *dulce*	Celery	Moderate
Aquilegia hybrids	Columbine	Cool
Arabis alpina	Rockcress	Cool
Arctotis fastuosa	African daisy	Moderate
A. venusta	African daisy	Cool
Arenaria montana	Sandwort	Cool
Argeranthemum frutescens	Marguerite daisy	Cold to cool
Armeria maritima	Thrift	Cool
Artemisia dracunculus	Russian tarragon	Cool
A. schmidtiana	Silver mound	Warm
Aruncus dioicus	Aruncus sylvester	Moderate
Asarina scandens	Twining snapdragon	Moderate
Asclepias curassavica	Blood flower	Moderate to warm
A. incarnata	Swamp milkweed	Moderate
A. tuberosa	Butterfly weed	Moderate to warm
Asparagus densiflorus cv. Myers	Asparagus fern	Warm
A. densiflorus cv. Sprengeri		Warm
A. setaceus		Warm
Asperula orientalis		Moderate
Asphodeline lutea	King's spear	Moderate
Aster alpinus	Michaelmas daisy	Moderate
A. novae-angliae	England aster	Moderate
A. novi-belgii	New York aster	Moderate
Astilbe ×*arendsii*	False spirea	Moderate
Astrantia major	Masterwort	Cool
Atriplex hortensis	Salt brush	Warm
Aubrieta deltoidea	False rockcress	Cool
Aurinia saxatilis 'Compacta'	Alyssum	Cool
Banksia species	Banksia	Warm
Baptisia australis	False indigo	Cool to moderate
Bassia scoparia	Burning bush	Moderate
Begonia (Interspecific cross)	Dragon wing	Moderate
B. grandis	Hardy begonia	Moderate
B. ×*hiemalis*	Hiemalis begonia	Moderate to warm
B. Rex Cultorum hybrids	Rex begonia	Moderate
B. Semperflorens-Cultorum hybrids	Wax begonia	Moderate
B. Tuberhybrida hybrids	Tuberous begonia	Moderate
Belamcanda chinensis	Blackberry lily	Moderate
Bellis perennis	English daisy	Cold to cool
Bergenia cordifolia	Heartleaf bergenia	Cool
Beta vulgaris	Beet	Cool
B. vulgaris var. *cicla*	Swiss chard	Cool
Bidens ferulifolia	Tickseed	Moderate to warm
Boltonia asteroides	Boltonia	Cool
Borago officinalis	Borage	Moderate

(continued)

TABLE 3-1 *(continued)*

Scientific Name	Common Name	Night Temperature
Bougainvillea species	Bougainvillea	Cold to cool
Brachycome species	Swan river daisy	Cool
Bracteantha bracteata	Strawflower	Cool to moderate
Brassica oleracea	Flowering cabbage/kale	Cool
B. oleracea	Cole crops	Cool
B. oleracea (acephala)	Kale	Cool
B. oleracea var. *acephala*	Collard	Cool
B. oleracea var. *botrytis*	Cauliflower	Cool
B. oleracea var. *capitata*	Cabbage	Cool
B. oleracea var. *gemmifera*	Brussels sprouts	Cool
B. oleracea var. *gongylodes*	Kohlrabi	Cool
B. oleracea var. *italica*	Broccoli	Cool
Briza maxima	Quaking grass	Moderate
B. minima	Short quaking grass	Moderate
Browallia speciosa	Browallia	Moderate
B. viscosa	Bush violet	Moderate
Brugmansia arborea	Angel's trumpet	Moderate
Buddleia davidii	Butterfly bush	Moderate
Buphthalmum salicifolium	Oxeye daisy	Moderate
Bupleurum rotundifolium	Thoroughwax	Moderate to warm
Caladium bicolor	Caladium	Warm
Calandrinia umbellata	Calandrinia	Moderate
Calathea species	Calathea	Warm
Calceolaria Herbeohybrida group	Calceolaria	Cold to cool
C. integrifolia		Cool
Calendula officinalis	Calendula	Cold
Calibrachoa hybrids	Calibrachoa	Moderate
Callistephus chinensis	Aster	Moderate
Calonyction	Moonflower	Moderate
Camellia japonica	Camellia	Cool to moderate
Camissonia bistorta	Camissonia	Moderate
Campanula carpatica	Carpathian harebells	Cool to moderate
C. elatines	Campanula	Cool
C. glomerata	Clustered bellflower	Cool
C. isophylla	Campanula	Cool to moderate
C. medium	Canterbury bells	Cool to moderate
C. poscharskyana	Campanula	Warm
Canna ×*generalis*	Canna	Moderate to warm
Capsicum annuum	Pepper	Moderate
Carlina acaulis	Carlina	Cool to warm
Carthamus tinctorius	Safflower	Moderate to warm
Caryopteris incana	Blue spirea	Moderate to warm
Cassia alata	Christmas candle	Moderate
Catananche caerulea	Catananche	Moderate
Catharanthus roseus	Vinca	Warm
Cattleya hybrids	Cattleya orchid	Moderate
Celosia argentea Plumosa group	Plume celosia	Warm
C. argentea Cristata group	Crested celosia	Warm
C. argentea Spicata group	Wheat celosia	Warm
Centaurea americana	American basket flower	Cool to moderate
C. cyanus	Bachelor's button	Cool
C. montana	Perennial cornflower	Cool to moderate

TABLE 3-1   *(continued)*

Scientific Name	Common Name	Night Temperature
Centauridia drummondii	Centauridia	Warm
Centranthus ruber	Red valerian	Moderate
Cerastium tomentosum	Snow-in-summer	Cool
Chamaedorea elegans	Parlor palm	Warm
Chenopodium botrys	Feather geranium	Moderate
Chlorophytum comosum	Spider plant	Warm
Chrysalidocarpus lutescens	Areca palm	Warm
Cirsium japonicum	Japanese thistle	Cool to moderate
Citrullus lanatus	Watermelon	Warm
Clarkia amoena	Satin flower	Cool
Clematis species and hybrids	Clematis	Moderate
Cleome hassleriana	Cleome	Warm
Clerodendrum thomsoniae	Tropical bleeding heart	Warm
C. ugandense	Tropical bleeding heart	Warm
Clitoria ternatea	Blue pea	Moderate
Cobaea scandens	Cobaea	Cool
Codiaeum variegatum	Croton	Warm
Coffea arabica	Coffee	Warm
Coix lacryma-jobi	Job's tears	Moderate
Coleostephus myconis	Chrysanthemum	Moderate
Collinsia bicolor	Chinese houses	Moderate
Consolida ambigua	Larkspur	Cool
Convallaria majalis	Lily-of-the-valley	Moderate to warm
Cordyline terminalis	Ti plant	Warm
C. indivisa	Dracaena	Warm
Coreopsis grandiflora	Tickseed	Cool
Coriandrum sativum	Chinese parsley	Cool to moderate
Cortaderia selloana	Pampas grass	Moderate
Cosmos bipinnatus	Cosmos	Moderate
C. sulphureus	Cosmos	Moderate
Cotula barbata	Brass buttons	Moderate
Craspedia uniflora	Craspedia	Moderate to warm
Crepis rubra	Hawk's beard	Moderate
Crocus vernus	Crocus	Cool to moderate
Crossandra infundibuliformis	Crossandra	Warm
Cucumis melo var. *reticulatis*	Muskmelon	Warm
C. sativus	Cucumber	Moderate
Cucurbita maxima	Pumpkin	Moderate
C. maxima	Squash	Moderate
Cuphea hyssopifolia	Mexican heather	Moderate
C. ignea	Cuphea	Moderate
Cyclamen persicum	Cyclamen	Cool to moderate
Cymbidium hybrids	Cymbidium	Cold
Cynara scolymus	Artichoke	Cool
Cynoglossum amabile	Cynoglossum	Moderate
Dahlia hybrids	Dahlia	Cool to moderate
Datura metel	Thorn apple	Moderate
Daucus carota var. *sativus*	Carrot	Cool
Delphinium grandiflorum var. *chinense*	Delphinium	Cool
D. ×*belladonna*		Cool
D. ×*cultorum*		Cool
Dendranthema ×*grandiflorum*	Chrysanthemum	Moderate

(continued)

TABLE 3-1 *(continued)*

Scientific Name	Common Name	Night Temperature
Dendrobium hybrids	Dendrobium	Cool
Dianthus barbatus	Sweet William	Cold to moderate
D. carthusianorum	Pot carnation	Cool to moderate
D. caryophyllus	Cut carnation	Cool
D. chinensis	Dianthus	Cold to cool
D. deltoides	Maiden pinks	Cool
D. plumarius	Cottage pinks	Cool
D. knappii	Yellow flowered pinks	Cool
Diascia hybrids	Diascia	Cool
Dichondra repens	Dichondra	Moderate
Dieffenbachia hybrids	Dumb cane	Moderate to warm
Digitalis purpurea	Foxglove	Cool to moderate
Dimorphotheca sinuata	Rain daisy	Moderate
Dionaea muscipula	Venus' flytrap	Warm
Doronicum columnae	Leopard's bane	Cool
Dorotheanthus species	Mesembryanthemum	Moderate
Dracaena species	Dracaena	Warm
Dyssodia tenuiloba	Dahlberg daisy	Warm
Echinacea purpurea	Purple coneflower	Moderate
Echinops bannaticus	Globe thistle	Moderate
Echium vulgare	Viper's bugloss	Cool
Emilia coccinea	Tassel flower	Moderate to warm
E. javanica cv. Lutea	Tassel flower	Moderate to warm
Epipremnum aureum	Pothos	Warm
Episcia species	Episcia	Warm
Eragrostis tenella	Love grass	Moderate
Eremurus species and hybrids	Foxtail lily	Cool
Erigeron karvinskianus	Fleabane	Moderate
Eryngium planum	Sea holly	Cool
Erysimum cheiri	Wallflower	Cool
E. linifolium	Alpine erysimum	Cool
Eschscholzia caespitosa	Tufted California poppy	Moderate
E. californica	California poppy	Moderate
Eucalyptus species	Gum tree	Moderate
Eucharis ×*grandiflora*	Amazon lily	Moderate to warm
Euphorbia lathyris	Gopher plant	Moderate
E. marginata	Snow-on-the-mountain	Moderate
E. myrsinites	Myrtle euphorbia	Cool
E. polychroma	Cushion spurge	Cool
E. pulcherrima	Poinsettia	Moderate to warm
Eustoma grandiflorum	Lisianthus	Moderate
Evolvulus glomeratus	Evolvulus	Moderate
Exacum affine	Persian violet	Moderate to warm
Fatsia japonica	Fatsia	Warm
Felicia heterophylla	Blue daisy	Cool
Festuca amethystina	Amethyst fescue	Moderate
F. ovina var. *glauca*	Blue fescue	Moderate
Fibigia clypeata	Fibigia	Cool
Ficus species	Fig	Warm
Foeniculum vulgare	Sweet fennel	Cool
Fragaria species	Strawberries	Moderate
Freesia species	Freesia	Cool

TABLE 3-1   *(continued)*

Scientific Name	Common Name	Night Temperature
Fuchsia × hybrida	Fuchsia	Moderate
Gaillardia × grandiflora	Blanket flower	Cool
G. pulchella	Annual gaillardia	Cool
Gardenia jasminoides	Gardenia	Moderate
Gaura lindheimeri	Gaura	Cool
Gazania rigens	Gazania	Cool
Gentiana species	Gentian	Moderate
Geranium sanguineum	Hardy geranium	Moderate
Gerbera jamesonii	Gerbera	Moderate
Geum quellyon	Geum	Cool
Gladiolus hybrids	Gladiolus	Moderate
Gomphrena globosa	Gomphrena	Warm
G. haageneana		Warm
Goniolimon tataricum	German statice	Cool
Gourds	Gourds	Moderate
Gypsophila elegans	Gypsophila	Cool
G. pacifica	Pink baby's breath	Cool
G. paniculata	Baby's breath	Moderate
G. repens	Creeping baby's breath	Cool
Hatiora gaertneri	Easter cactus	Moderate to warm
Hedera helix	English ivy	Warm
Helenium autumnale	Helenium	Cool
Helianthemum nummularium	Rockrose	Cool
Helianthus annuus	Sunflower	Cool to moderate
Helichrysum species	Strawflower	Moderate
Heliconia species	Heliconia	Warm
Heliopsis helianthoides	Oxeye daisy	Moderate
Heliotropium arborescens	Heliotrope	Moderate
Helipterum roseum	Acrolinium	Moderate
Hesperis matronalis	Sweet rocket	Cool
Heuchera micrantha	Alumroot	Cool
H. sanguinea	Coral bells	Cool
Hibiscus acetosella	Red shield	Moderate
H. moscheutos	Rose mallow	Moderate
H. rosa-sinensis	Hibiscus	Warm
Hippeastrum hybrids	Amaryllis	Warm
Hordeum jubatum	Squirrel's tail grass	Cool
Howea forsterianai	Kentia palm	Warm
Humulus lupulus	Hops	Moderate
Hunnemannia fumariifolia	Bush poppy	Cool
Hyacinthus orientalis	Hyacinth	Cool to moderate
Hydrangea macrophylla	Hydrangea	Moderate
Hypericum androsaemum	Hypericum	Warm
H. calycinum	St. John's wort	Cool
Hypoestes phyllostachya	Hypoestes	Moderate
Iberis amara	Candytuft	Cool
I. sempervirens	Hardy candytuft	Cool
I. umbellata	Globe candytuft	Cool
Impatiens balsamina	Balsam	Moderate
I. hawkeri	New Guinea impatiens	Moderate to warm
I. walleriana	Bedding impatiens	Moderate
Incarvillea delavayi	Hardy gloxinia	Moderate

(continued)

TABLE 3-1   *(continued)*

Scientific Name	Common Name	Night Temperature
Ionopsidium acaule	Violet cress	Cool
Ipomoea batatus	Ornamental sweet potato	Moderate
I. lobata	Spanish flag	Moderate
I. tricolor	Morning glory	Moderate
Ipomopsis rubra	Standing cypress	Cool
Iresine herbstii	Gizzard plant	Moderate
Iris × hollandica	Dutch iris	Cool
I. germanica	German iris	Moderate
Isotoma axillaris	Isotoma	Moderate
Jamesbrittania hybrids	Bacopa	Moderate
Kalanchoe blossfeldiana	Kalanchoe	Moderate to warm
Kniphofia uvaria	Red hot poker	Moderate
Koeleria glauca	Koeleria	Cool
Lablab purpureus	Hyacinthus bean	Moderate
Lachenalia species	Lachenalia	Moderate
Lactuca sativa	Lettuce	Cool
Lagerstroemia indica	Crape myrtle	Warm
Lagurus ovatus	Hare's tail grass	Moderate
Lantana hybrids	Lantana	Moderate
Lathyrus odoratus	Sweet pea	Cool
L. splendens	Perennial sweet pea	Cool
Lavandula angustifolia	English lavender	Moderate
L. dentata	French lavender	Moderate
Lavatera trimestris	Lavatera	Moderate
Layia platyglossa	Tidy tips	Cool
Leea coccinea	Leea	Warm
Leontopodium alpinum	Edelweiss	Cool
Leucanthemum lacustre	Shasta daisy	Cool
L. paludosum	Chrysanthemum	Moderate
Levisticum officinale	Lovage	Moderate
Liatris pycnostachya	Liatris	Cool
L. spicata	Gay feather	Moderate
Lilium hybrids	Asiatic/oriental lily	Moderate
L. longiflorum	Easter lily	Moderate
Limnanthes douglasii	Meadow foam	Cool
Limonium latifolium	Sea lavender	Cool
L. sinuatum	Common garden statice	Cool
L. perezii	Seafoam statice	Cool
Linaria maroccana	Toadflax	Cool
Linum grandiflorum	Flowering flax	Cool
L. perenne	Perennial flax	Moderate
Lobelia erinus	Lobelia	Cool to moderate
L. × speciosa		Moderate
Lobularia maritima	Sweet alyssum	Cool
Lonas annua	Lonas	Moderate
Lotus berthelotti	Parrot's beak	Cool
Lunaria annua	Honesty plant	Cool
Lupinus polyphyllus	Lupine	Cool
Lychnis chalcedonica	Maltese cross	Cool
L. coronaria	Rose campion	Cool
L. × haageana	Catchfly	Cool
Lycopersicon esculentum	Tomato	Moderate

TABLE 3-1 *(continued)*

Scientific Name	Common Name	Night Temperature
Lysimachia clethroides	Gooseneck loosestrife	Moderate
Machaeranthera tanacetifolia	Tohoka daisy	Cool
Malva moschata	Musk mallow	Cool
Maranta species	Prayer plant	Warm
Marrubium vulgare	Horehound	Cool
Matthiola incana	Stock	Cold to cool
Melampodium divaricatum	Melampodium	Moderate
Melica ciliata	Pearl grass	Cool
Melissa officinalis	Lemon balm	Cool
Mentha ×piperita	Peppermint	Cool
M. spicata	Spearmint	Cool to moderate
Mimosa pudica	Mimosa	Warm
Mimulus ×hybridus	Monkey flower	Cool to moderate
Mirabilis jalapa	Mirabilis	Moderate
Moluccella laevis	Bells of Ireland	Moderate
Monarda citriodora	Horsemint	Cool
M. didyma	Bee balm bergamot	Cool
Monstera deliciosa	Philodendron	Warm
Myosotis sylvatica	Forget-me-not	Cool
Narcissus pseudonarcissus	Daffodil	Moderate
N. tazetta	Paperwhite	Moderate
Nemesia strumosa	Nemesia	Cool
Nemophila maculata	Fivespot	Cool
N. menziesii	Baby blue eyes	Cool
Nepeta cataria	Catnip	Cool
Nicotiana alata	Nicotiana	Moderate
N. langsdorfii		Moderate
N. ×sanderae		Moderate
N. sylvestris		Moderate
Nierembergia hippomanica	Nierembergia	Moderate
Nigella damascena	Nigella	Cool to moderate
Nolana paradoxa	Nolana	Moderate
Ocimum basilicum	Sweet basil	Moderate
Odontoglossum hybrids	Tooth-tongue orchid	Warm
Oenothera macrocarpa	Evening primrose	Cool
Oncidium hybrids	Dancing lady orchid	Moderate to warm
Origanum majorana	Sweet marjoram	Cool to moderate
O. vulgare	Oregano	Cool
Ornithogalum species	Ornithogalum	Moderate
Osteospermum ecklonis	Cape daisy	Cool to moderate
Oxalis adenophylla	Oxalis	Moderate
O. bowiei		Cool to moderate
O. braziliensis		Cool to moderate
O. corymbosa		Cool
O. hirta		Cool
O. purpurea		Cool
O. regnelli		Moderate
O. tetraphyllua		Cool to moderate
O. versicolor		Cool to moderate
Paeonia lactiflora	Peony	Cool to moderate
Papaver nudicaule	Iceland/arctic poppy	Cool
P. orientale	Oriental poppy	Cool

(continued)

TABLE 3-1 (continued)

Scientific Name	Common Name	Night Temperature
Paphiopedilium hybrids	Lady's slipper orchid	Cool
×*Pardancanda norrisii*	Candy lily	Moderate
Pelargonium ×*domesticum*	Regal geranium	Cool
P. ×*hortorum*	Seed/zonal geranium	Moderate
P. peltatum	Ivy geranium	Moderate
Pennisetum setaceum	Fountain grass	Moderate
P. villosum	Feathertop	Moderate
Penstemon gentianoides	Annual penstemon	Cool
Pentas lanceolata	Pentas	Moderate
Peperomia species	Peperomia	Warm
Pericallis ×*hybrida*	Cineraria	Cool
Perilla frutescens	Perilla	Moderate to warm
Petroselinum crispum	Parsley	Moderate
Petunia ×*hybrida* (single)	Petunia	Cool to moderate
P. ×*hybrida* (double)		Cool to moderate
P. ×*hybrida* (trailing)		Cool to moderate
Phalaenopsis hybrids	Moth orchid	Moderate to warm
Phalaris canariensis	Canary grass	Moderate
Phaseolus coccineus	Scarlet Runner Bean	Moderate
P. vulgaris var. *humilis*	Garden bean	Moderate
Philodendron bipinnatifidum	Philodendron	Warm
P. domesticum		Warm
P. lundii		Warm
Phlox drummondii	Phlox	Cool
P. paniculata	Summer phlox	Moderate
Phragmipedium hybrids	Lady's slipper orchid	Warm
Physalis alkekengi	Physalis	Cool
P. ixocarpa	Tomatillo	Moderate
Physostegia virginiana	Obedient plant	Cool
Pimpinella anisum	Anise	Moderate
Platycodon grandiflorus	Balloon flower	Moderate
Plectranthus species	Plectranthus	Moderate
Plumbago auriculata	Plumbago	Moderate
Polianthes tuberosa	Tuberose	Warm
Polygonum capitatum	Smartweed	Moderate
Portulaca grandiflora	Moss rose	Moderate to warm
P. oleracea	Purslane	Moderate to warm
Potentilla nepalensis	Potentilla	Cool
Primula malacoides	Fairy primrose	Cool to moderate
P. obconica	German primrose	Moderate
P. ×*polyantha*	English primrose	Cool to moderate
P. vulgaris	English primrose	Cool to moderate
Psylliostachys suworowii	Russian statice	Cool
Ranunculus asiaticus	Ranunculus	Cold to cool
Rehmannia angulata	Chinese foxglove	Moderate
Reseda odorata	Evening stock	Cold
Rhodochiton species	Rhodochiton	Moderate
Rhododendron hybrids	Florist azalea	Moderate
Ricinus communis	Castor bean	Moderate
Rosa hybrids	Rose	Moderate
Rosmarinus officinalis	Rosemary	Moderate
Rudbeckia fulgida	Black-eyed Susan	Cool
R. hirta		Cool

TABLE 3-1 *(continued)*

Scientific Name	Common Name	Night Temperature
Rumorha adiantiformis	Leatherleaf fern	Warm
Saintpaulia ionantha	African violet	Warm
Salpiglossis sinuata	Salpiglossis	Cool
Salvia coccinea	Salvia	Moderate
S. farinacea	Salvia	Moderate
S. officinalis	Sage	Cool to moderate
S. patens	Salvia	Moderate
S. pratensis	Meadow clary	Cool
S. splendens	Scarlet sage	Moderate
S. ×superba	Salvia	Cool
S. viridis	Salvia	Moderate
Sanvitalia procumbens	Sanvitalia	Moderate
Saponaria ocymoides	Rock soapwort	Cool
Satureja hortensis	Summer savory	Moderate
Saxifraga ×arendsii	Mossy saxifrage	Moderate
Scabiosa atropurpurea	Scabiosa	Cool
S. caucasica	Pincushion flower	Cool
Scaevola aemula	Fan flower	Warm
Schefflera actinophylla (Brassaia)	Schefflera	Warm
S. arboricola	Schefflera	Warm
S. elegantissima (Dizygotheca)	Aralia	Warm
Schizanthus ×wisetonensis	Schizanthus	Cool
Schlumbergera hybrids	Holiday cactus	Cool to moderate
Sedum acre	Golden carpet	Moderate
S. spurium	Dragon's blood	Moderate
Sempervivum tectorum	Hens and chicks	Moderate
Senecio cineraria	Dusty miller	Moderate
S. maritimus		Moderate
Senna angulata	Christmas candle	Moderate
Sidalcea malviflora	Checkerbloom	Cool
Silene coelirosa	Silene	Cool
Sinningia speciosa	Gloxinia	Warm
Smithiantha zebrina	Smithiantha	Warm
Solanum melongena	Eggplant	Moderate
S. pseudocapsicum	Christmas cherry	Cool
S. tuberosum	Potato	Moderate
Solenostemon scutellarioides	Coleus	Moderate to warm
Solidago species	Goldenrod	Cool to moderate
Spathiphyllum floribundum	Peace lily	Warm
Stachys byzantina	Lamb's ears	Moderate
Steirodiscus tagetes	Steirodiscus	Cool
Stephanotis floribunda	Stephanotis	Warm
Stobilanthes dyerianus	Persian shield	Moderate
Stokesia laevis	Stokes' aster	Moderate
Strelitzia reginae	Bird of paradise	Warm
Streptocarpus ×hybridus	Cape primrose	Moderate
Sutera cordata	Bacopa	Cool to moderate
Syngonium podophyllum	Nephthytis	Warm
Tagetes erecta	African marigold	Moderate
T. erecta ×patula	Triploid marigold	Moderate
T. patula	French marigold	Moderate
T. tenuifolia	Signate marigold	Moderate

(continued)

TABLE 3-1 *(continued)*

Scientific Name	Common Name	Night Temperature
Talinum paniculatum	Jewels of Opar	Moderate
Tanacetum coccineum	Painted daisy	Cool
T. parthenium	Matricaria	Cool
T. ptarmiciflorum	Dusty miller	Moderate
Thalictrum species	Meadow-rue	Cool
Thunbergia alata	Thunbergia	Moderate
Thymophylla tenuiloba	Dahlberg daisy	Moderate
Thymus serphyllum	Mother of thyme	Moderate
T. vulgaris	Culinary thyme	Cool to moderate
Tithonia rotundifolia	Mexican sunflower	Cool
Torenia fournieri	Torenia	Cool
Trachelium caeruleum	Throatwort	Cool to moderate
Trachymene coerulea	Blue lace flower	Cool to moderate
Tradescantia ×andersoniana	Spiderwort	Cool
Tripleurospermum inodorum	Scentless hayweed	Cool
Triteleia laxa	Brodiaea	Cool
Tropaeolum majus	Nasturtium	Warm
T. peregrinum		Warm
Tulipa gesneriana	Tulip	Moderate
Tweedia caerulea	Oxypetalum	Moderate
Vaccaria hispanica	Cow-coddle	Moderate
Verbascum phoeniceum	Purple mullein	Cool
Verbena bonariensis	Verbena	Moderate
V. canadensis		Moderate
V. ×hybrida		Cool
V. rigida		Moderate
V. speciosa		Moderate
V. tenera		Moderate
Veronica incana	Woolly speedwell	Cool
V. repens	Creeping speedwell	Cool
V. spicata	Spike speedwell	Cool
Veronicastrum virginicum	Culver's root	Moderate
Viola cornuta	Horned violet	Cool
V. tricolor	Johnny-jump-up	Cool
V. ×wittrockiana	Pansy	Cold to cool
Wahlenbergia species	Rock bell	Moderate
Xeranthemum annuum	Xeranthemum	Moderate
Yucca elephantipes	Yucca	Warm
Zantedeschia aethiopica	Calla lily	Cool
Z. hybrids		Moderate
Zea mays	Sweet corn	Moderate
Zinnia angustifolia	Zinnia	Moderate
Z. elegans		Moderate
Z. hybrida		Moderate

are delayed and quality reduced. Consequently, chrysanthemums have a relatively narrow optimum temperature range and a wide tolerable temperature range. For many plant species, the temperature is often dropped several degrees from the optimum temperature one to several weeks before the plants are marketed to enhance color and postharvest life.

The economics of greenhouse heating must often be considered when determining the temperature at which to grow a crop. When energy costs become high, producers lower temperatures to reduce heating costs. Unfortunately, lower production temperatures will decrease the average daily temperature and slow plant growth. In some cases, the delay in flowering or harvesting may be more costly due to increased plant care than the extra energy necessary to maintain optimum temperatures. The extent of the delay will depend on the type of crop. Many crop species, such as tulips (*Tulipa*), continue to grow at low temperatures, so lowering the night temperature from 63°F (17°C) to 53°F (12°C) will only delay flowering by a few days. However, reducing the night temperature for a poinsettia (*Euphorbia*) crop from 63°F (17°C) to 53°F (12°C) will virtually stop growth.

Although the focus of energy costs is often on heating, cooling costs in many areas are substantial and growers may increase the day temperature to reduce the electricity necessary to run fans and pads. Excessively high production temperatures may reduce plant quality and postharvest life.

Excessively high or low temperatures can injure plants. Most well-known is frost or freezing injury, which occurs when plant tissues are exposed to temperatures of 32°F (0°C) or lower. Freezing occurs when the air temperature falls below 32°F (0°C) and frost occurs when the air temperature is above 32°F (0°C), but the temperature of the plant tissue falls below 32°F (0°C) due to radiating heat into the atmosphere (Dreistadt, 2001). Frost and freezing damage appears as browning, blackening, or curling of shoots, buds, and flowers. Although younger tissues are most vulnerable, entire plants can be killed. Plants can be protected from cold damage by covering them with cloths, spray irrigating to keep the tissue continuously wet, and providing supplemental heat sources.

Extended periods of low, but nonfreezing temperatures can injure or even kill tropical or subtropical plants, which is known as *chilling injury*. Although temperatures as high as 68°F (20°C) can cause damage to some species, chilling damage increases as temperatures approach freezing. Damage and death to African violets (*Saintpaulia ionantha*) can occur at temperatures of 50°F (10°C) and lower (Brown-Faust and Heins, 1991).

High temperatures can also cause damage, such as yellowing or necrosis of foliage and stunted growth. Damage from high temperatures is closely related to lighting conditions in that the damage from excessively high light levels is often due to high tissue tempera-

tures from insufficient transpiration. In fact, water stress is a key factor in damage caused by both high temperatures and high light. The ability of plants to tolerate high temperatures varies with the specific growing conditions. However, the American Horticulture Society has produced a map of the United States that is divided into 12 heat zones based on climatic conditions. Individual plants are given heat zone ratings indicating their heat tolerance.

AVERAGE DAILY TEMPERATURE

Average daily temperature controls the rate of plant development, often expressed as the *leaf unfolding rate* or as the *flower development rate*. If the average daily temperature is increased (within the tolerable temperature range for a species), most plants will grow faster and flower more rapidly. However, rapid growth often does not mean quality growth. Very warm temperatures result in weak, poor-quality growth that is frequently susceptible to disease. There is often an interaction with light intensity in that low light levels accentuate the poor growth associated with warm production temperatures. Ironically this situation can occur during the summer when heavy shade is used to reduce greenhouse temperatures. Similarly, low daily temperatures may induce premature flower initiation or dormancy. Photoperiod is often involved in these physiological responses to temperature.

Average daily temperature is calculated as an average of temperatures measured each hour (or more frequently if computer monitoring is used), not the average of the high and the low temperatures for a 24-hr period. The latter calculation is likely to be higher than the real average daily temperature, because the night temperature is usually relatively constant, whereas the day temperature often gradually rises during the day to a high in the midafternoon. In addition, brief high temperatures can occur during cloudy days if the sun shines for a short period. Consequently, using the high–low temperature system to calculate average daily temperature will accentuate the day temperature.

DAY AND NIGHT TEMPERATURES

If greenhouse temperatures are included in a publication, they are often the night temperature, unless otherwise specified. Typically, the night temperature is lower than the day temperature and easier to control either by heating or cooling. The heat from sunlight often makes the day temperature difficult to control. For most plants, the night temperature is more important than the day temperature in determining physiological responses, such as flowering (Erwin and Heins, 1993). For example, high night temperatures may cause physiological responses such as delayed flower initiation in chrysanthemums (*Dendranthema* ×*grandiflorum*), poinsettias (*Euphorbia pulcherrima*), and kalanchoes (*Kalanchoe blossfeldiana*) and bolting in petunias (*Petunia* ×*hybrida*) (Grueber, 1985; Whealy et al., 1987). Similarly, low night temperatures may induce premature flower initiation or dormancy (see Chapter 2, Flowering Control). However, with many species it has yet to be determined if night, day, or average daily temperature is most important in obtaining a specific physiological response.

DIF

DIF is the concept of regulating plant height by monitoring the difference between the day and the night temperature (see Chapter 8, Plant Growth Regulation, for additional information). The higher the day temperature relative to the night temperature (day − night = DIF), the greater the stem elongation (Berghage and Heins, 1991; Erwin et al., 1989a, b; Karlsson et al., 1989). Where final plant height is a concern, such as with poinsettias (*Euphorbia pulcherrima*), Easter lily (*Lilium longiflorum*), and many bedding plants, DIF must be taken into consideration. Increasing the day temperature relative to the night will increase internode elongation for many species. Consider three similar greenhouses, for example, where the day and the night are both 12 hr long.

| | Greenhouse | | |
	1 °F (°C)	2 °F (°C)	3 °F (°C)
Day temperature	60 (15.5)	55 (13)	50 (10)
Night temperature	50 (10)	55 (13)	60 (15.5)
DIF	+10 (+5.5)	0	−10 (−5.5)
Plant height	Tall	Medium	Short
Average daily temperature	55 (13)	55 (13)	55 (13)

Greenhouse 1 will produce the tallest plants because the DIF is the greatest (+10), and greenhouse 3 the shortest plants (−10 DIF). Plants from greenhouse 2 will be intermediate in height. All plants will flower simultaneously and have similar leaf numbers because the average daily temperature is the same for each greenhouse. Consequently, for plants where height is a concern, the day temperature should be no more than 0 to 5°F (0 to 3°C) higher than the night regardless of weather. See Chapter 8, Plant Growth Regulation, for additional information on the use of DIF to regulate plant height.

According to actual stem measurements, a large percentage of the daily stem elongation occurs early in the day just prior to and after sunrise, thus cool temperatures (negative DIF) for at least 2 hr starting just before first light in the morning will reduce stem elongation (Cockshull et al., 1995; Erwin et al., 1989c; Grindal and Moe, 1995; Moe et al., 1995). This cool, early morning pulse is known as the *temperature DROP*. However, very warm temperatures during the rest of the day (positive DIF) may negate much of the effects of the temperature DROP.

DIF may also affect other plant responses such as flower size and flower number in some species. Extreme day–night temperature reversals (e.g., DIF ≤−5) may induce chlorosis and leaf curling of Easter lilies (*Lilium longiflorum*), although these effects quickly disappear when DIF is less negative (Erwin et al., 1989a). Plant carbohydrate and nitrogen levels also decrease with extreme negative DIF and may accentuate postharvest leaf yellowing of Easter lilies and bract edge burn and cyathia drop of poinsettias (*Euphorbia pulcherrima*) (Miller, 1997). Some species do not respond to DIF, including most Cucurbitaceae family plants and Dutch bulbs such as *Hyacinthus*, *Tulipa*, and *Narcissus* (Erwin et al., 1989a).

TEMPERATURE RECOMMENDATIONS

General temperature recommendations are based on whether height control is a concern for the crop species. When height control is not a problem, such as with rosette-forming plants or cut flowers, day temperatures are set 0 to 5°F (0 to 3°C) above night temperatures on cloudy days and 10 to 15°F (6 to 8°C) above night temperatures on sunny days to allow maximum photosynthesis during sunny days and reduce respiration during the night. During cold periods, growers generally lower the night temperature as much as possible to reduce fuel costs. When height control is a concern, such as with poinsettias and many other potted and bedding plants, keep the day temperature as close as possible to the night temperature. Specific combinations of day and night temperatures may be required for precise height control (see Chapter 8, Plant Growth Regulation).

MEDIA TEMPERATURE

Monitoring the soil temperature is important in some situations in addition to monitoring the air temperature. Media heating is important for germination or rooting of cuttings of many species (see Chapter 1, Propagation). Generally, media should be at least 70°F (21°C) with 72 to 75°F (22 to 24°C) optimum. Specific species may have a higher or lower optimum medium temperature for propagation. If misting is used during propagation, evaporation of mist may reduce media temperature and additional heat may be required. Heating cables can be placed on the bench, or a heating system may be used under the bench and the bottom of the bench can be enclosed in plastic to trap the heat. Polyethylene tubes can also be used to direct the heat from forced air heaters under the bench, but care must be taken to prevent excess drying of the cuttings or seedlings by covering the bench top with plastic.

Research has been conducted to determine if heating the medium would allow cooler air temperatures to be used during production (Stephens and Widmer, 1976). Root zone heating would allow growers to reduce fuel costs by heating the air immediately around the plant medium and not the entire greenhouse air volume. The heat can be concentrated at the root level by using bench heating systems such as Biotherm™ or by placing heating pipes under the bench and trapping the heat under the bench with plastic. Warm air rises, heating the aboveground portions of the plants.

Root zone heating has proved effective with some plant species such as *Cyclamen* and *Antirrhinum* and may increase plant growth and speed plant development (Stephens and Widmer, 1976; Wai and Newman, 1992). Root zone heating is most effective during the first 6 weeks after transplanting. Potential disadvantages include possible flower bud abortion or blasting and altered watering and nutrition regimes. Generally root zone heating is effective but may not be economically justified.

KEY POINTS

- Three types of temperatures are measured: air, leaf, and medium.
- Floriculture literature usually refers to night air temperature, but leaf temperature is more accurate.
- Temperature can have a general or a specific effect on plant growth: Plant growth gradually increases or decreases as the temperature changes or specific temperatures can cause the induction of a specific response such as flowering by cool temperatures.
- Each plant species has an optimum growing temperature range and a tolerable temperature range, and economics must be considered when determining the temperature at which to grow a crop.
- Excessively high or low temperatures can injure plants.
- Average daily temperature controls the rate of plant development, often expressed as the leaf unfolding rate or as the flower development rate.

- For most plants, the night temperature is more important than the day temperature in determining physiological responses, such as flowering.
- For many plant species the higher the day temperature relative to the night temperature (day − night = DIF), the greater the stem elongation.
- Cool temperatures (negative DIF) for at least 2 hr starting just before first light in the morning will reduce stem elongation. This technique is known as DROP or DIP.
- General temperature recommendations are based on whether height control is a concern for the crop species. When height control is not a problem, day temperatures are set 0 to 5°F (0 to 3°C) above night temperatures on cloudy days and 10 to 15°F (6 to 8°C) above night temperatures on sunny days. When height control is a concern, keep the day temperature as close as possible to the night temperature.
- Media heating is important for germination or rooting of cuttings of many species and should be at least 70°F (21°C) with 72 to 75°F (22 to 24°C) optimum.

BIBLIOGRAPHY

Armitage, A.M. 1993. *Echinacea*, pp. 197–199 in *Specialty Cut Flowers*. Varsity/Timber Press, Portland, Oregon.

Berghage, R.D., and R.D. Heins. 1991. Quantification of temperature effects on stem elongation in poinsettia. *Journal of the American Society for Horticultural Science* 116:14–18.

Brown-Faust, J., and R. Heins. 1991. Cultural notes on African violets. *Greenhouse Grower* 9(2):74, 76–77.

Cockshull, K.E., F.A. Langton, and C.R.J. Cave. 1995. Differential effects of different DIF treatments on chrysanthemum and poinsettia. *Acta Horticulturae* 378:15–25.

Dreistadt, S.H. 2001. *Integrated Pest Management for Floriculture and Nurseries*, University of California Division of Agriculture and Natural Resources Publication 3402.

Erwin, J.E., and R.D. Heins. 1993. Temperature effects on bedding plant growth. *Minnesota Commercial Flower Growers Association Bulletin* 42(3):1–11.

Erwin, J., R. Heins, R. Berghage, and W. Carlson. 1989a. How can temperatures be used to control plant stem elongation? *Minnesota State Florists Bulletin* 38(3):1–5.

Erwin, J.E., R.D. Heins, and M.G. Karlsson. 1989b. Thermomorphogenesis in *Lilium longiflorum*. *American Journal of Botany* 76:47–52.

Erwin, J.E., R.D. Heins, B.J. Kovanda, R.D. Berghage, W.H. Carlson, and J.A. Biernbaum. 1989c. Cool mornings can control plant height. *GrowerTalks* 52(9):75.

Grindal, G., and R. Moe. 1995. Growth rhythm and temperature DROP. *Acta Horticulturae* 378:47–52.

Grueber, K.L. 1985. Control of lateral branching and reproductive development in *Euphorbia pulcherrima* Wild. ex Klotzsch. Ph.D. thesis, University of Minnesota.

Karlsson, M.G., R.D. Heins, J.E. Erwin, R.D. Berghage, W.H. Carlson, and J.A. Biernbaum. 1989. Temperature and photosynthetic photon flux influence chrysanthemum shoot development and flower initiation under short day conditions. *Journal of the American Society for Horticultural Science* 114:158–163.

Leeuwen, V.C. 1980. *Aconitum*, pp. 25–27 in *Annual Report for 1980 of the Aalsmeer Proefstation*, The Netherlands. (In Dutch)

Miller, B. 1997. 1998 Easter lily production. *Southeastern Floriculture* 7(5):43–46.

Moe, R., K. Willumsen, I.H. Ihlebekk, A.I. Stupa, N.M. Glomsrud, and L.M. Mortensen. 1995. DIF and temperature DROP responses in SDP and LDP, a comparison. *Acta Horticulturae* 378:27–33.

Stephens, L.C., and R.E. Widmer. 1976. Soil temperature effects on *Cyclamen* flowering. *Journal of the American Society for Horticultural Science* 101:107–111.

Wai, K.S., and S.E. Newman. 1992. Air and root-zone temperatures influence growth and flowering of snapdragons. *HortScience* 27:796–798.

Whealy, C.A., T.A. Nell, J.E. Barrett, and R.A. Larson. 1987. High temperature effects on growth and floral development of chrysanthemum. *Journal of the American Society for Horticultural Science* 112:464–468.

Wilkins, H.F., W.E. Healy, and K.L. Grueber. 1990. Temperature regime at various stages of production influences growth and flowering of *Dendranthema ×grandiflorum*. *Journal of the American Society for Horticultural Science* 115:732–736.

Chapter 4

Light

INTRODUCTION

Measuring light requires the consideration of three factors: color, intensity, and duration. Color (quality) is the wavelength of the light, intensity (quantity) is the strength of the light, and duration (photoperiod or day length) is the time span of the light or dark episode. All three factors are used to determine the appropriate light requirement of a plant. Light has two functions in plant growth. The first role is to "fuel" plant growth through photosynthesis. Plants convert light energy into chemical energy, which results in plant growth. Secondly, light initiates or modifies specific physiological responses such as seed germination, flowering, senescence, tuber formation, and dormancy.

LIGHT QUALITY

Wavelengths are measured in nanometers (nm) with specific wavelengths corresponding to specific colors; for example, yellow light has a wavelength of approximately 580 nm (Fig. 4-1). Although general plant growth usually requires light with all wavelengths, red (700 nm) and blue (470 nm) wavelengths result in the greatest plant growth response (Fig. 4-2). Conversely, photoperiodism and other specific plant responses involve wavelengths centered around red (660 nm) and far-red (720 nm) light.

Light high in far-red wavelengths will increase internode elongation and leaf size, decrease branching, and reduce leaf and flower color (Runkle and Heins, 2002; Smith, 1986). Plants grown under light high in red wavelengths will be short, dark green, and well branched (Cerny et al., 2003). Light filtered through plant leaves will be high in far-red light because foliage absorbs red light, allowing a greater proportion of far-red light to pass through. Thus, close plant spacing decreases the red to far-red ratio, which results in elongated, poorly branched plants. In addition,

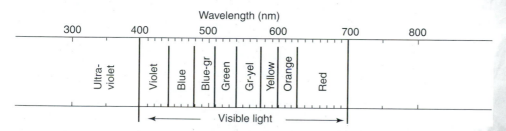

FIGURE 4-1 The colors that various wavelengths produce.

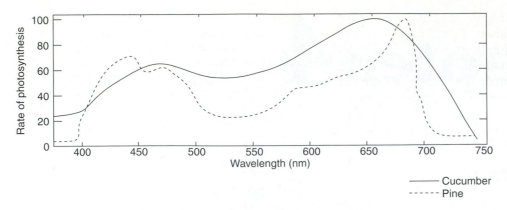

FIGURE 4-2 Response of photosynthesis to various light wavelengths.

incandescent lamps are higher in far-red wavelengths and fluorescent lamps higher in red wavelengths. Light with a high red to far-red light ratio, such as that produced when sunlight is filtered through a copper sulfate solution or through photoselective plastic filters, will reduce elongation (McMahon et al., 1991; Mortensen and Strømme, 1987; Rajapakse and Kelly, 1992; Runkle and Heins, 2002). Even removing the dawn or twilight light, which is high in far-red light, can reduce stem elongation (Blom et al., 1994). However, filtering out blue or red light may produce longer internodes, which would be beneficial during the production of cut flowers (Khattak and Pearson, 1997). Manipulation of light quality by filters is effective in controlling plant height and may be useful in the future, provided that flowering is not delayed.

LIGHT INTENSITY

The footcandle (fc, 1 fc = 10.8 lux) quantifies luminous energy, or light visible to the human eye. This system emphasizes the green-yellow wavelengths (530 to 580 nm), which the human eye sees the best. Photosynthesis, however, is driven by a broader range of wavelengths, with a red-blue emphasis. Light meters that measure footcandles can give an approximation of greenhouse light levels but may have a 45% error compared with the actual photosynthetic energy in radiation (Muckle, 1997). *Photosynthetically active radiation* (PAR) measures the amount of light energy equally in all wavelengths from 400 to 700 nm, without stressing the green-yellow wavelengths most visible to the eye. A third system of measuring light intensity, based on quantum energy, describes light in terms of tiny particles of energy called *photons* or *quanta* and is known as *photosyn-*

thetic photon flux (PPF). The number of photons is measured in moles (mol) or einsteins (E) with 1 mole = 1 einstein = 6.023×10^{23}. Thus, the intensity of light in the quantum system is measured in the number of photons transmitted which is $\mu mol \cdot m^{-2} \cdot s^{-1}$, the preferred unit of measure (Table 4-1). Both PAR and PPF emphasize all wavelengths equally within a specific range such as 400 to 700 nm or 400 to 850 nm without regard to the human eye. PPF meters are available and although most are expensive, low-cost meters have recently been introduced.

The optimum light intensity during production varies greatly with the crop species from low-light-requiring plants such as many indoor foliage plants to high-light-requiring species such as most bedding plants, potted flowering plants, and cut flowers. For example, prayer plants (*Calathea*) are grown under only 1,000 to 2,000 fc (200 to 400 $\mu mol \cdot m^{-2} \cdot s^{-1}$), whereas hydrangeas (*Hydrangea macrophylla*) are grown at

TABLE 4-1

Approximate conversion factors between footcandles (fc) and $\mu mol \cdot m^{-2} \cdot s^{-1}$ (Thimijan and Heins, 1983). Multiply footcandles by the given value to obtain $\mu mol \cdot m^{-2} \cdot s^{-1}$ for wavelengths ranging from 400 to 700 nm.

Light Source	Factor
Daylight (sun and sky)	0.20
High-pressure sodium	0.13
Metal halide	0.15
Mercury deluxe	0.13
Warm white fluorescent	0.14
Cool white fluorescent	0.15
Incandescent	0.22
Low-pressure sodium	0.10

light levels of 7,500 fc (1,500 μmol·m⁻²·s⁻¹) or higher. However, lower light levels, less than 2,000 fc (400 μmol·m⁻²·s⁻¹), are typically used during propagation and often when rooted cuttings are first planted. In addition, lower light levels are occasionally used with some species such as poinsettias (*Euphorbia pulcherrima*) at the end of the crop cycle to prevent burning or bleaching of the petals or bracts.

LIGHT DURATION

Duration refers to the photoperiod or day length and it can affect plant growth two ways: (1) Short photoperiods provide less total light energy to plants than long photoperiods at the same light intensity and (2) the length of the photoperiod may induce specific physiological responses in many plant species independent of the light intensity, which is known as *photoperiodism*. For example, the poinsettia (*Euphorbia pulcherrima*), a short-day plant, is induced to flower by providing long nights and short days. See Chapter 2, Flowering Control, for more information.

DAILY LIGHT INTEGRAL

The total amount of light energy that a plant receives in a day is a combination of the instantaneous intensity measured at one moment (a second) in time with the amount of time that the plant is receiving the light. Of course, light levels change throughout the day. The *daily light integral,* expressed in moles per day, represents the quantity of light that is delivered over the course of a day. Daily light integral is also known as light sum, daily light level, or daily PPF (J. Faust, personal communication). The daily light integral can be estimated, but is best measured using quantum sensors integrated into a datalogger or a computer. The optimum daily light integral varies with the species from

TABLE 4-2

Daily light integral supplied by supplementary high-pressure sodium lights (J. Faust, personal communication).

	Light Intensity (μmol·m⁻²·s⁻¹)	
Hours of Operation	35	75
8	1.0	2.2
12	1.5	3.2
16	2.0	4.3
20	2.5	5.4
24	3.0	6.5

low-light-requiring crops such as African violets (*Saintpaulia ionantha*), which are typically produced at 5 to 10 mol/day, to most bedding, potted, and cut flower species, which are grown at 10 to 20 mol/day. Supplemental lighting can be used to increase the daily light integral (Table 4-2) (see also Supplemental Light section).

PLANT GROWTH

LIGHT SATURATION POINT

The point at which the plant is receiving as much light energy as it can use is the *light saturation point* (Fig. 4-3). Additional light energy cannot be used and may be injurious to the plant. Damage from too much light (sunburning) can appear as yellowing or necrosis of foliage and stunted growth. Plant species vary greatly in their light saturation points. Plant species that require high light, such as cacti, have a much higher light saturation point than low-light-requiring species such as African violets and ferns. The light saturation point can be raised on a particular plant if the leaves are kept cool and the plant is well irrigated. Often the damage from high light levels is due to

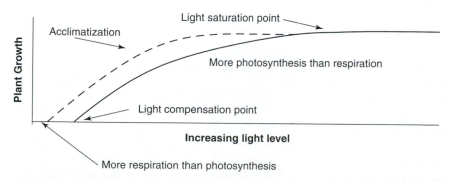

FIGURE 4-3 Effect of acclimatization on the light saturation and light compensation points.

FIGURE 4-4 Damage on poinsettia (*Euphorbia pulcherrima*) foliage due to high light intensity and insufficient water.

insufficient water, which reduces transpiration, allowing the leaf temperature to become dangerously hot (Fig. 4-4).

LIGHT COMPENSATION POINT

The *light compensation point* is the light intensity at which the plant is receiving as much energy from the light during photosynthesis as it is using during respiration (Fig. 4-3). Theoretically, if a plant were placed at the light compensation point, it would neither grow (accumulate dry weight) nor deteriorate. As with the light saturation point, the light compensation point varies with each plant species. Foliage plants intended for use in low-light interiorscapes typically have a low light compensation point. Many bedding plants grown outdoors have a high light compensation point.

ACCLIMATIZATION

Both the light saturation point and the light compensation point in plants can be altered by changing the environment under which the plants are grown (Fig. 4-3). Foliage plants can be grown under high light, near the saturation point, to encourage rapid economical growth, but acclimatized before marketing by reducing light levels (Table 4-3). *Acclimatization* lowers the light saturation point and, more importantly for the consumer, reduces the light compensation point, allowing the plant to survive better in a low-light environment. Acclimatization also lowers the plant's respiration rate, which in turn reduces the amount of carbohydrates that needs to be produced from light (Fonteno and McWilliams, 1978). Some plant

species such as poinsettias are not easily acclimatized, whereas other species such as Benjamin fig (*Ficus benjamina*) acclimatize readily (Milks et al., 1979). Leaves on a poorly acclimatized plant will often yellow and abscise when switched between high- and low-light environments. If the change from a high- to a low-light environment is not too great, the plant will survive and produce new leaves that are acclimatized to the lower light. Leaves grown under low light will tend to be thinner and larger, have a thinner cuticle, and have fewer palisade cells with less organized chloroplasts arranged horizontally within the cell than leaves grown under high light. If the change in environment is too great or if the plant does not acclimatize well, it may slowly deteriorate and die.

Generally, only foliage plants are acclimatized because most potted flowering plants and cut flowers are grown under maximum light levels to maximize carbohydrate accumulation and encourage a long postharvest life (see Chapter 10, Postharvest). Although plants such as chrysanthemums (*Dendranthema*) can be acclimatized, the postharvest life is not extended and may actually be shortened due to decreased carbohydrate accumulations and heavy demand for carbohydrates by the flowers (Nell et al., 1981).

MAXIMIZING LIGHT ENERGY

GREENHOUSE CONSTRUCTION AND MAINTENANCE

Greenhouses should be constructed to allow the maximum amount of light to enter, because reducing light levels in greenhouses is easier and more economical than increasing light. The most important factor will be the type of glazing used; glass is highly transparent, but double-layered polyethylene has one of the lowest light transmission ratings (see Chapter 11, Greenhouse Construction and Operations). Minimize the number of cooling tubes, pipes, and other equipment overhead to allow maximum light transmission. Cleaning the glazing annually in the fall will also improve light levels in the greenhouse during the winter. Paint internal surfaces white to increase the amount of reflected light in the greenhouse.

Above 40° north latitude (below 40° south), single greenhouses should be oriented with the longest side running from east to west to maximize sunlight during the winter when the sun is low in the horizon. Between 40° north and south latitude, greenhouses

TABLE 4-3

Light levels for production and postharvest interiors for numerous foliage plant species (adapted from Conover, 1991; Conover and McConnell, 1981; Vladimirova et al., 1997).

Scientific Name	Common Name	Production Light Intensity (fc)	Production Light Intensity ($\mu mol \cdot m^{-2} \cdot s^{-1}$)	Interior Light Intensity Low	Interior Light Intensity Medium	Interior Light Intensity High
Adiantum species	Maidenhair fern	1200–1800	240–360		x	x
Aechmea fasciata	Silver vase	—	—		x	x
Aeschynanthus pulcher	Lipstick vine	4000–6000	800–1200			x
Aglaonema cultivars	Chinese evergreen	1000–2500	200–500		x	x
Ananas comosus	Pineapple	—	—		x	x
Anthurium species	Flamingo flower	1500–3600	300–720			x
Aphelandra squarrosa	Zebra plant	1000–1500	200–300			x
Araucaria heterophylla	Norfolk Island pine	4000–8000	800–1600		x	x
Ardisia crispa	Coral ardisia	1500–3000	300–600		x	x
Asparagus species	Asparagus fern	2000–4500	400–900		x	x
Aspidistra elatior	Cast-iron plant	2000	400	x	x	x
Asplenium nidus	Bird's-nest fern	1500–3000	300–600	x	x	x
Begonia Rex-Cultorum	Rex begonia	2000–2500	400–500		x	x
Bromeliaccae species	Bromeliads	2500–4000	500–800		x	x
Cactoceae species	Cactus	5000–8000	1000–1600			x
Calathea species	Prayer plant	1000–2000	200–400		x	x
Carissa macrocarpa	Natal plum	—	—			x
Chamaedorea elegans	Parlor palm	1500–3000	300–600	x	x	x
C. erumpens	Bamboo palm	3000–6000	600–1200		x	x
Chlorophytum comosum	Spider plant	1500–2500	300–500		x	x
Chrysalidocarpus lutescens	Areca palm	3500–6000	700–1200		x	x
Cissus species	Grape ivy	1500–2500	300–500		x	x
Citrofortunella microcarpa	Calamondin	—	—			x
Codiaeum variegatum	Croton	3000–8000	600–1600			x
Coffea arabica	Arabian coffee	4000	800			x
Cordyline terminalis	Ti plant	2500–4500	500–900		x	x
Crassula ovata	Jade plant	5000–6000	1000–1200		x	x
Cryptanthus species	Earthstars	—	—		x	x
Cyanotis kewensis	Teddy bear vine	—	—		x	x
Cyrtomium falcatum	Holly fern	—	—		x	x
Davallia fejeensis	Rabbits-foot fern	1200–1800	240–360		x	x
Dieffenbachia species	Dumbcane	1500–3000	300–600		x	x
Dracaena deremensis	Dracaena	2000–3500	400–700	x	x	x
D. fragrans	Corn plant	2000–4000	400–800	x	x	x
D. marginata	Marginata	3000–4000	600–800	x	x	x
D. sanderiana	Ribbon plant	2500–5000	500–1000		x	x
D.—other species	Dracaena	1500–3500	300–700	x	x	x
Episcia species	Episcia	2000–2500	400–500		x	x
Epipremnum aureum	Pothos	1500–3000	300–600	x	x	x
×Fatshedera lizei	Fatshedera	4000–6000	800–1200		x	x
Fatsia japonica	Japanese fatsia	4000–6000	800–1200		x	x
Ficus benjamina	Weeping fig	3000–6000	600–1200		x	x
F. elastica	Rubbertree	4000–6000	800–1200		x	x
F. lyrata	Fiddleleaf fig	4000–6000	800–1200		x	x
F. microcarpa	Cuban laurel	3000–6000	600–1200		x	x
Fittonia spp.	Nerve plant	1000–2500	200–500		x	x
Gynura aurantiaca	Purple passion vine	≤1150	≤230		x	x
Hedera helix	English ivy	1500–2500	300–500	x	x	x

(continued)

TABLE 4-3 *(continued)*

Scientific Name	Common Name	Production Light Intensity		Interior Light Intensity		
		(fc)	($\mu mol \cdot m^{-2} \cdot s^{-1}$)	Low	Medium	High
Howea forsteriana	Kentia palm	2500–6000	500–1200	x	x	x
Hoya carnosa	Wax plant	1500–2500	300–500		x	x
Maranta species	Prayer plant	1000–2500	200–500		x	x
Monstera deliciosa	Swiss cheese plant	3500–4500	700–900		x	x
Neoregelia carolinae	Striped bromeliad	—	—		x	x
Nephrolepis exaltata	Sword fern	1500–3500	300–700		x	x
Nolina recurvata	Ponytail palm	4000–6000	800–1200			x
Palmae species	Palms	1500–6000	300–1200		x	x
Peperomia species	Peperomia	1500–3000	300–600		x	x
Philodendron species	Philodendron	1500–5000	300–1000	x	x	x
Pilea species	Pilea	1500–3000	300–600		x	x
Pittosporum tobira	Japanese pittosporum	—	—		x	x
Platycerium bifurcatum	Staghorn fern	1500–3000	300–600		x	x
Plectranthus species	Swedish ivy	3000–4000	600–800		x	x
Podocarpus macrophyllus	Yew pine	—	—		x	x
Polyscias species	Aralia	1500–4500	300–900		x	x
Pteris ensiformis	Victoria table fern	1200–1800	240–360		x	x
Radermachia sinica	China doll	3000–3500	600–700		x	x
Sansevieria species	Snake plant	3500–5000	700–1000	x	x	x
Scindapsus pictus	Satin pothos	—	—		x	x
Schefflera (Brassaia) species	Schefflera	4000–6000	800–1200		x	x
S. elegantissima (Dizygotheca)	False aralia	2000–4000	400–800		x	x
Schlumbergera ×buckleyi	Christmas cactus	1500–3000	300–600		x	x
Spathiphyllum species	Peace lily	1500–2500	300–500	x	x	x
Synogonium podophyllum	Nephthytis	1500–3500	300–700		x	x
Tolmiea menziesii	Piggyback plant	3500–4000	700–800			x
Tradescantia zebrina	Wandering Jew	3500–4500	700–900		x	x
Yucca elephantipes	Spineless yucca	3500–4500	700–900			x
Zamioculcas zamiifolia	ZZ plant	1500–2500	300–500	x	x	x

should be constructed on the north to south axis. Gutter-connected greenhouses are generally constructed on the north to south axis regardless of the latitude. Also note which shadows from stationary gutters and other overhead objects move with the sun. Mobile shadows present little problem during production other than temporarily reducing the light received by the affected plants. Stationary shadows may require that shade-tolerant plants be grown in the affected areas.

PLANT SPACING

Plants will eventually fill the amount of available space on a bench during production. Therefore, increasing the number of plants on a bench will decrease the amount of light that each plant receives after a solid foliar canopy forms, decrease the amount of dry weight per plant, and may decrease plant quality (Fig. 4-5). Plant quality may be improved by increasing the amount of space per plant if light levels are low, such as during the winter. Unfortunately, increasing the space per plant decreases the number of plants that may be grown in a specific area, and economics typically dictate the final plant spacing.

The number of overhead hanging baskets should also be kept to a minimum because they block light. For example, one line of hanging baskets running the length of a 21-ft-(6.4-m)-wide bay will reduce the amount of light on the benches below by 4%, three lines will reduce light by 11%, and 6 lines by 19% (J. Faust, personal communication). Also,

FIGURE 4-5 Close plant spacing caused stretching and poor quality in these New Guinea impatiens (*Impatiens hawkeri*) plants.

FIGURE 4-6 HID lighting on chrysanthemums (*Dendranthema grandiflorum*) cuttings.

white baskets intercept less light than green baskets and more light is intercepted when baskets are spaced closer together or when the plant size increases.

SUPPLEMENTAL LIGHT

Although supplemental lighting for increasing photosynthesis is generally expensive, it is economical in many situations. In general, northern areas during the winter and cloudy coastal areas will benefit from additional light energy. Supplemental lighting is also important for high-value crops such as roses. Supplemental lighting can also be used on less valuable crops during stages of production when a large number of plants are spaced close together such as with cuttings, seedlings, and plugs (Fig. 4-6). Regardless of the situation, a cost benefit analysis must be completed to determine if the expenses of energy, light fixtures, installation, and maintenance will be offset by increased growth, quality, and reduced crop production times. The heat produced by the lights also may reduce other energy costs in cool areas of the country. While minimum supplemental light requirements vary with each species, 300 to 600 fc (60 to 120 $\mu mol \cdot m^{-2} \cdot s^{-1}$) is a general recommendation for supplementary irradiance. Greater use can be obtained from light fixtures in some situations by installing them on a track system and moving the lights from one section to another. The process is automatically controlled and can be used to light two crops with the same light fixtures.

Various lamp types are available for floricultural use and they can be divided into three basic types: incandescent, fluorescent, and high-intensity discharge (HID) (Table 4-4). Incandescent lamps are most frequently used for photoperiod regulation, fluorescent lamps for propagation, and HID lamps for supplementing sunlight in greenhouse production. HID lighting in greenhouses can be used to supplement the sunlight during the day or to extend the day. Supplemental lighting can be applied during the night to take advantage of low, off-peak electricity rates.

Supplemental lighting not only provides additional light energy but also increases the leaf and media temperature, especially with plugs (Graper and Healy, 1991). The increase in plant growth is due primarily to the additional light energy but is also partially due to the increasing plant temperature.

GROWTH ROOMS

Totally enclosed rooms can be used for starting seedlings and rooting cuttings. Tiers of fluorescent lights (warm white and cool white types combined) stacked 14 to 18 in. (45 to 60 cm) apart provide sufficient light intensity and most of the heat. Supplemental heat may have

TABLE 4-4
Energy efficiency, spectrum, life expectancy, power, and uses for several common lights used in commercial floriculture production.

Lamp Type	Efficiency	Wavelengths Accentuated[z]	Life Expectancy	Power	Use
Incandescent	7%	r, fr	6 mo	Low	Photoperiod
Fluorescent					
Cool white	21%	b, g, y	2 yr	Low	Germination, growth rooms
Warm white	21%	b, g, y	2 yr	Low	Germination, growth rooms
High Intensity Discharge (HID)					
High pressure mercury	13%	b, g, y, o	3 yr	High	Greenhouse
Metal halide	20%	b, g, y, o	2–3 yr	Very high	All purpose, growth rooms, supplemental in greenhouse
Low pressure sodium	27%	g, y, r	4–5 yr	Medium	Supplemental in greenhouse, not sole source
High pressure sodium	25%	y, o, r	3–4 yr	High	Supplemental in greenhouse

[z]b = blue, g = green, y = yellow, o = orange, r = red, fr = far red

to be provided if the room is outside, and fans and ventilation are required to circulate air and exhaust excess heat. The lights are generally on for 16 hr per day, but the duration may vary with each species.

MINIMIZING LIGHT ENERGY

Even though the major concern is often increasing light intensity, too high of light intensity is usually a problem during the summer in most areas of the country. High light levels may damage even the most light-tolerant species, resulting in stunted growth, yellow leaves, and patches of tan necrotic areas on leaves. Equally important for employees is the difficulty of working in high greenhouse temperatures resulting from light energy trapped in the greenhouse. Two common ways to reduce the light intensity in a greenhouse are with shade cloths and shading compounds. Shade cloth is available in a variety of types and can reduce light by 25 to 98%. One common type of shade cloth regulates the amount of shade produced by varying the number of threads per inch used to weave the fabric. This type of shade cloth can be used to cover specific benches or, more commonly, the entire greenhouse. Placing the shade

cloth over the greenhouse also reduces photodegradation of the glazing, such as with polyethylene film or fiberglass, and provides extra protection against wind and hail damage. External shading is more effective than internal shading because in the latter case the light has already entered the greenhouse and is absorbed by the screen, raising the internal greenhouse temperature (Fig. 4-7). However, internal shading can be automated and allows growers to

FIGURE 4-7 External shade system.

FIGURE 4-8 Internal automatic shade system.

regulate light levels by opening the shade cloth during cloudy days and closing it during sunny days (Fig. 4-8). This process is often mechanized by using photosensors to automatically open and close the shade cloth. The cloths are subject to photodegradation and should be stored out of sunlight when not in use.

Another type of shade cloth is made of spun fiber, such as Remay® or Vispore®, that is white and lightweight. Spun-fiber cloths are not strong enough to be used externally and are often used to cover specific benches or beds. The cloth is so lightweight that is can be laid directly on the plants for a temporary light screen such as immediately after transplanting cuttings or after cutting back plants (Fig. 4-9).

Shading compounds can also be used to reduce light intensity. The white compounds can be applied directly to the outside of the glazing in one heavy layer or in two to three diluted layers. Shading compounds specific for greenhouses can be purchased and diluted at 1 part compound to 6 parts water for heavy shade or 1 part compound to 15 to 20 parts water for light shade. Generally, most of the shading compound wears off gradually during the summer, but the remainder may need to be scrubbed off at the end of the season, which is generally not a pleasant job but must be done if any residue remains. Commercial shading compounds designed for greenhouses are easier to remove than diluted latex paint. See Chapter 11, Greenhouse Construction and Operations, for additional details.

PHOTOPERIODISM

Photoperiodism—the response of plants to night length—regulates many responses in plants such as flower initiation and development, plant dormancy, seed germination, and plant growth habit (see Chapter 2, Flowering Control, for more information). Many plant responses can be divided into three basic types: short day (SD), long day (LD), and day neutral (DN). For example, SD plants will flower when the dark period is longer than a critical length, and LD plants will flower when the dark period is shorter than a critical length. Chrysanthemums and poinsettias flower under SD conditions and tuberous begonia (*Begonia* Tuberhybrida) under LD conditions. DN plants will flower regardless of the day length. In the greenhouse photoperiodism is controlled by either natural day lengths or by night interruption lighting and night extension.

NIGHT INTERRUPTION LIGHTING

Night interruption divides the dark period into two or more shorter "nights" and is used to prevent flowering of SD stock plants or to delay flower initiation on SD plants. Night interruption can also be used to induce flowering of LD plants. Night interruption lighting is also known as *night breaks* (NB). Long days can also be applied by turning on lamps at the end of the day and extending the day length into the night, which is known as *day continuation* (DC). Incandescent lights or screw-in fluorescent lights are used because they are inexpensive and easily mounted (de Graaf-van der Zande and Blacquiére, 1992) (Fig. 4-10). Incandescent lights are less expensive than screw-in fluorescent lights but the former use more energy, have a shorter life, and produce a greater stem elongation than incandescent

FIGURE 4-9 Shade cloth used on outdoor cut flower beds to protect transplants and allow them to establish.

FIGURE 4-10 Incandescent light bulbs with reflector used to provide artificial long days.

lights. High-intensity lamps are also effective but are only used when supplemental lighting for photosynthesis is required.

Strings of light bulbs are placed over the plants, and reflectors can be used to direct the light downward and decrease the number of light fixtures needed. The lights are commonly turned on from 2200 to 0200 (10 P.M. to 2 A.M.) when the days are short, generally from mid-September to mid-April. Larger greenhouse operations tailor their night interruption lighting to the season. To save energy, cyclical lighting can be used in which the lights are turned on only 20% of the time during the lighting period. The greenhouse area to be lighted is divided into five zones, with each zone lighted one-fifth of the time during the night. For some plant species the minimum duration the lights need to be on is 1 sec out of each 5-sec period; most greenhouses use 6 min on and 24 min off. For many species the light intensity should be at least 10 fc (2 μmol$\cdot$m$^{-2}\cdot$s^{-1}) measured at the plant apex. The time of the year when the lights are turned on and the minimum intensity required may vary with the species.

NIGHT EXTENSION

The night can be lengthened by means of light-excluding fabrics, or *black cloths*, placed over the crops. Black cloths are used to induce flowering of SD plants or inhibit flowering of LD plants. The cloths are commonly pulled over the plants from 1700 to 0800 (5 P.M. to 8 A.M.) or 1900 to 0700 (7 P.M. to 7 A.M.) if heat buildup is a problem. The cloths can also be pulled over the crop from 1600 to 2100 (4 P.M. to 9 P.M.) or from 1700 to 2200 (5 P.M. to 10 P.M.) and opened for the rest of the night to allow heat to escape. High temperatures under the cloths can be reduced by using cloth with white or aluminum reflective material on the outer side and by installing the cloth from eave to eave in the greenhouse. In the latter case, the pads and fans remain operational under the cloths to provide cooling. The sides of the greenhouse are covered with separate black cloths. Eave-to-eave cloths can also be used as thermal blankets (see Chapter 11) for energy conservation. The opening and closing of black cloths for photoperiod control is often automated. Such cloths require consistent monitoring and maintenance to ensure smooth operation.

Generally, the black cloths are pulled every day, because each day skipped means that flowering will be delayed by the same number of days. In addition, if too many days are skipped, the plants will not flower or flowers will be malformed. For many species, the black cloths do not have to be pulled after the buds or bracts show color; however, some species such as poinsettias require SD until the first flower buds (cyathia) completely open.

KEY POINTS

- Measuring light requires the consideration of three factors: color, intensity, and duration.
- Color (quality) is the wavelength of the light.
- Intensity (quantity) is the strength of the light as expressed as μmol$\cdot$m$^{-2}\cdot$s^{-1}.
- Duration (photoperiod or day length) is the time span of the light episode.

- Light fuels plant growth through photosynthesis and initiates or modifies specific physiological responses such as seed germination, flowering, senescence, tuber formation, and dormancy.
- Duration refers to the photoperiod, which can affect plant growth two ways: (1) Short photoperiods provide less total light energy to plants than long photoperiods at the same light intensity and (2) the length of the photoperiod may induce specific physiolog-

ical response in many plant species independent of the light intensity, which is known as photoperiodism.

- The daily light integral, expressed in moles per day, represents the quantity of light that is delivered over the course of a day.
- The light saturation point is the point at which the plant is receiving as much light energy as it can use.
- The light compensation point is the light intensity at which the plant is receiving as much energy from the light during photosynthesis as it is using during respiration.
- Acclimatization is the process in which both the light saturation point and the light compensation point in plants can be altered by changing the environment under which the plants are grown.
- Light energy could be maximized through proper greenhouse construction and maintenance and maximizing space/plant, minimizing the number of overhead hanging baskets, and providing supplemental light.
- Various lamp types are available for floricultural use and they can be divided into three basic types: incandescent, fluorescent, and high-intensity discharge.

- Totally enclosed rooms can be used for starting seedlings and rooting cuttings.
- High light levels can result in stunted growth, yellow leaves, and occasional patches of tan necrotic areas on leaves.
- Light levels can be lowered to reduce the temperature.
- Two common ways to reduce the light intensity in a greenhouse are with shade cloths and shading compounds.
- Photoperiodic responses can be divided into three basic types: short day (SD), long day (LD), and day neutral (DN). SD plants will flower when the dark period is longer than a critical length, and LD plants will flower when the dark period is shorter than a critical length.
- Night interruption divides the dark period into two or more shorter "nights" and is used to prevent flowering of SD stock plants or to delay flower initiation on SD plants.
- The night can be lengthened by means of light-excluding fabrics, or black cloths, placed over the crops.

BIBLIOGRAPHY

Blom, T.J., M.J. Tsujita, and G.L. Roberts. 1994. Influence of photoperiod and light intensity on plant height of *Lilium longiflorum* Thunb. *HortScience* 29:542. (Abstract)

Cerny, T.A., J.E. Faust, D.R. Layne, and N.C. Rajapakse. 2003. Influence of photoselective films and growing season on stem growth and flowering of six plant species. *Journal of the American Society for Horticultural Science* 128: 486–491.

Conover, C. 1991. Foliage plants, pp. 498–520 in *Ball RedBook*, 15th ed. V. Ball, editor. Ball Publishing, West Chicago, Illinois.

Conover, C.A., and D.B. McConnell. 1981. Utilization of foliage plants, pp. 519–543 in *Foliage Plant Production*, J.N. Joiner, editor. Prentice Hall, Englewood Cliffs, New Jersey.

de Graaf-van der Zande, M.T., and T. Blacquiére. 1992. Light quality during longday treatment for poinsettia and china aster. *Acta Horticulturae* 327:87–93.

Fonteno, W.C., and E.L. McWilliams. 1978. Light compensation points and acclimatization of four tropical foliage plants. *Journal of American Society for Horticultural Science* 103:52–56.

Graper, D.F., and W. Healy. 1991. High pressure sodium irradiation and infrared radiation accelerate *Petunia* seedling growth. *Journal of the American Society for Horticultural Science* 116:435–438.

Khattak, A.M., and S. Pearson. 1997. The effects of light quality and temperatures on the growth and development of chrysanthemum cvs. Bright Golden Anne and Snowdon. *Acta Horticulturae* 435:113–121.

McMahon, M.J., J.W. Kelly, D.R. Decoteau, R.E. Young, and R.K. Pollock. 1991. Growth of *Denranthema ×grandiflorum* (Ramat.) Kitamura under various spectral filters. *Journal of American Society for Horticultural Science* 116:950–954.

Milks, R.A., J.N. Joiner, L.A. Garrard, C.A. Conover, and B.O. Tija. 1979. Effects of shade, fertilizer and media on production and acclimatization of *Ficus benjamina* L. *Journal of American Society for Horticultural Science* 104:410–413.

Mortensen, L.M., and E. Strømme. 1987. Effects of light quality on some greenhouse crops. *Scientia Horticulturae* 33:27–36.

Muckle, E. 1997. Space scientists bring light research down to earth. *Greenhouse Business* 3(5):22–23.

Nell, T.A., J.J. Allen, J.N. Joiner, and L.G. Albrigo. 1981. Light, fertilizer, and water level effects on growth, yield, nutrient composition, and light compensation point of chrysanthemum. *HortScience* 16:222–223.

Rajapakse, N.C., and J.W. Kelly. 1992. Regulation of chrysanthemum growth by spectral filters. *Journal of the American Society for Horticultural Science* 117:481–485.

Runkle, E.S., and R.D. Heins. 2002. Stem extension and subsequent flowering of seedlings grown under a film creating a far-red deficient environment. *Scientia Horticulturae* 96:257–265.

Smith, H. 1986. The perception of the light environment, pp. 187–217 in *Photomorphogenesis in Plants*, R.E. Kendrick and G.H.M. Kronenberg, editors. Martinus Nijoff, Boston.

Thimijan, R.W., and R.D. Heins. 1983. Photometric, radiometric, and quantum light units of measure: A review of procedures for interconversion. *HortScience* 18:818–821.

Vladimirova, S.V., D.B. McConnell, M.E. Kane, and R.W. Henley. 1997. Morphological plasticity of *Dracaena sanderana* 'Ribbon' in response to four light intensities. *HortScience* 32:1049–1052.

Chapter 5

Water

INTRODUCTION

In the past many growers have said that the person at the end of the hose determines plant quality. Today the saying holds true, except that the hose has been replaced or supplemented with a variety of automated systems ranging from flood irrigation to overhead booms. In addition, a variety of factors other than plant quality need to be considered, including cost, water runoff, and nutrition.

Despite the advances in irrigation technology, water still performs the same role in plant growth. Nutrients are absorbed by the roots and transported via transpiration throughout the plants. Water is responsible for the ability of most plants to stand upright because nonlignified cells cannot remain turgid without water. Transpiration of water cools plant tissues. Most importantly, water maintains protoplasm in the cells, allowing enzymes and other cellular processes to occur.

PERMANENT WILTING POINT

Permanent wilting point is the point at which a wilted plant will not recover if watered. At this stage, irreversible damage has occurred to the plant's tissues. Less catastrophic changes occur to plants that have only temporarily wilted. Cells formed during water stress will be small and may have thick walls, resulting in short internodes and a compact plant. Indeed, water restriction is frequently used as a growth retardant with bedding plant crops such as tomatoes (*Lycopersicon esculentum*) (see Chapter 8, Plant Growth Regulation). However, many species do not tolerate water stress or wilting, and plant quality thus declines. Wilting may lead to the yellowing and abscission of flowers, fruits, and lower leaves; reduced photosynthesis due to stomatal closure and nutrient uptake; foliar damage from high sunlight; and increased susceptibility to disease.

WATER QUALITY

The most important consideration in setting up an irrigation plan is water quality (Table 5-1). Water should be tested prior to selecting a site for a new business and then tested periodically because the quality can change seasonally, over time, and among different locations (Argo et al., 1997). Water samples can be commercially tested through the cooperative extension service or a laboratory; the pH and electrical conductivity (EC) can be determined in-house. See Chapter 6, Nutrition, for more information on pH and EC meters.

One of the most important factors is the electrical conductivity, a measure of soluble salts (see Chapter 6, Nutrition). The greater the soluble salt concentration, the more easily an electrical current will pass through a water solution. Water with a low EC, 0.1 to 0.5 deci-Siemens per meter ($dS \cdot m^{-1}$), will give the grower the greatest number of irrigation op-

TABLE 5-1

Desirable characteristics of high-quality irrigation water. Plants can often tolerate much higher levels of some individual ions.

Characteristic	Desired Level	Upper Limit
Soluble salts (EC)	0.2–0.5 dS·m^{-1}	dS·m^{-1} for plugs dS·m^{-1} for general production
Soluble salts (total dissolved salts)	128–320 ppm	480 ppm for plug-grown seedlings 960 ppm for general production
pH	5.4–6.8	7.0
Alkalinity		
$CaCO_3$ equivalent	40–65 ppm (0.8–1.3 meq/L)	150 ppm (3 meq/L)
Bicarbonates	40–65 ppm (0.7–1.1 meq/L)	122 ppm (2 meq/L)
Hardness ($CaCO_3$ equivalent)	<100 ppm (2 meq/L)	150 ppm (3 meq/L)
Sodium (Na)	<50 ppm (2 meq/L)	69 ppm (3 meq/L)
Chloride (Cl)	<71 ppm (2 meq/L)	108 ppm (3 meq/L)
SAR[a]	<4	8
Nitrogen	<5 ppm (0.36 meq/L)	10 ppm (0.72 meq/L)
Nitrate (NO_3)	< 5 ppm (0.08 meq/L)	10 ppm (0.16 meq/L)
Ammonium (NH_4)	<5 ppm (0.28 meq/L)	10 ppm (0.56 meq/L)
Phosphorus (P)	<1 ppm (0.3 meq/L)	5 ppm (1.5 meq/L)
Phosphate (H_2PO_4)	<1 ppm (0.01 meq/L)	5 ppm (0.05 meq/L)
Potassium (K)	<10 ppm (0.26 meq/L)	20 ppm (0.52 meq/L)
Calcium (Ca)	<60 ppm (3 meq/L)	120 ppm (6 meq/L)
Sulfates (SO_4)	<30 ppm (0.63 meq/L)	45 ppm (0.94 meq/L)
Magnesium (Mg)	<5 ppm (0.42 meq/L)	24 ppm (2 meq/L)
Manganese (Mn)	<1 ppm	2 ppm
Iron (Fe)	<1 ppm	5 ppm
Boron (B)	<0.3 ppm	0.5 ppm
Copper (Cu)	<0.1 ppm	0.2 ppm
Zinc (Zn)	<0.2 ppm	0.5 ppm
Aluminum (Al)	<2 ppm	5 ppm
Chlorine (HOCl and OCl$^-$)	<2 ppm	3 ppm
Fluoride (F)	<1 ppm	1 ppm

[a]Sodium adsorption ratio; relates sodium to calcium and magnesium levels.

tions and will reduce future problems from the accumulation of high soluble salts in the root substrate. Plant species vary in their tolerance to high substrate EC, which can stunt plant growth, induce wilting even though the substrate is moist, and cause marginal leaf burn. Plugs are especially sensitive to high EC because of the low media volume. High substrate EC levels can be frequently managed by leaching.

The irrigation water pH should be 6.0 to 7.0 and alkalinity should be between 0.8 and 1.3 millequivalent/liter (meq/L) (40 and 65 ppm). pH is a measure of the concentration of H^+ in a solution and is measured on a scale from 0 to 14 (see Chapter 6, Nutrition). Alkalinity is typically assumed by most laboratories to be equal to the total carbonate and bicarbonate content of the water, expressed as calcium carbonate ($CaCO_3$). Other ions also contribute to alkalinity but are usually present in low concentrations. Carbonates include calcium carbonate and bicarbonates, sodium bicarbonate, and magnesium bicarbonate. Thus, irrigating with water that is highly alkaline is equivalent to applying lime (calcium and magnesium carbonate) to the media.

Typically, water alkalinity determines if media pH will change and how quickly that change will occur. Water that is high in alkalinity usually has a high pH, but moderate to low pH water can have high alkalinity. Thus, *water alkalinity is more important to consider than water pH*. At excessively high or low media pH, some plant nutrients will be unavailable for the roots to absorb. High water pH can also reduce the solubility of some fertilizers, pesticides, and plant growth regulators (Argo and Fisher, 2003).

Water alkalinity can be a problem depending on the crop production time, container size, and crop species (Nelson, 2003). The increase in media pH due to alkalinity will not be a concern for many bedding plants due to short crop times; however, the pH increase will be a problem for the long-term production of many potted and cut flower crops. Although plugs are a short-term crop, they are particularly sensitive to high media pH due to the small container volume. Highly alkaline water can cause the pH of plugs to rapidly rise to unacceptable levels. Finally, some crop species, such as azaleas (*Rhododendron*) or blue hydrangeas (*Hydrangea*), require low media pH (4.5–5.5) and will be difficult to produce with highly alkaline water. Regardless of the level, alkalinity is too high anytime it causes the media pH to rise to an unacceptable level (Nelson, 2003).

Several control options are available for prevention of alkalinity-related problems (Table 5-2). Producers that mix their own media can add less lime to the media. For growers who use basic fertilizers such as calcium nitrate and potassium nitrate, the water pH and alkalinity should be on the low end of the recommended range to prevent the media pH from increasing to unacceptable levels during production (Table 5-1). Growers who use acidic fertilizers, especially in warm climates, can readily use water with the pH and alkalinity in the center or upper part of the recommended range for an individual species.

Producers can rotate among acidic and basic fertilizers. Many premixed fertilizers have relatively high ammonium levels and are acidic, but basic nitrate-based fertilizers are available. In addition, growers can combine potassium nitrate and calcium nitrate to make their own basic fertilizer. Unfortunately, high-ammonium fertilizers are not feasible in some situations, which limits the ability of growers to control media pH through fertilizer choice. High-ammonium fertilizers should not be used when the media temperature is below 55°F (13°C) due to slow conversion of ammonium to nitrates by nitrifying bacteria in the media. Ammonium can also produce excessive growth, which can counteract height control measures for some crops.

For water with high alkalinity levels, acid injection may be required (see Acid Injection section on page 83). If the alkalinity is 8 meq/L or greater, then reverse osmosis may be the only option (see Reverse Osmosis section below).

Although most producers are faced with water that is high in alkalinity, some have water that is too low in alkalinity. In addition, the use of reverse osmosis to treat water (see below) will produce low-alkalinity water. When water that is low in alkalinity is combined with the acidic fertilizers commonly used today, media pH can drop too low. In such cases, higher rates of limestone can be used in media, basic fertilizers can be applied, or potassium bicarbonate can be injected into the water (Table 5-2).

Water that is high in calcium and magnesium is known as *hard water*. Most plant species are tolerant to high calcium and magnesium levels, but overhead irrigation with hard water can leave unsightly white salt deposits on the foliage, especially with mist propagation.

Finally, the nutrient content of the water should be checked. Although low levels of some nutrients can be beneficial, high levels of one or more nutrients may indicate that the nutrition program should be adjusted. If the water has high levels of nitrogen, calcium, or magnesium, less of those nutrients can be added as fertilizers. High nitrogen levels can be especially prevalent in areas with sandy soil, shallow wells, or intensive agriculture. Unfortunately, high levels of calcium, magnesium, and iron can be antagonistic to other nutrients such as manganese or boron and, hence, reduce their uptake. Also, very high boron levels, greater than 1 ppm, can be toxic.

WATER TREATMENTS

A number of options exist if the water quality is poor. The first option is to locate a higher quality water source, such as municipal, well, or surface water from a pond or river. In addition, rainwater can also be collected. If using poor-quality well water, check with a hydrologist to see if another well can be drilled; water quality can vary with the depth of the well. Often it is difficult and expensive to find another water source, and water treatments will need to be considered.

REVERSE OSMOSIS

Reverse osmosis (RO) is the most commonly used method for producing low-EC water. Reverse osmosis forces water through a semipermeable membrane, leaving 90 to 99% of the soluble salts behind. One drawback to RO is

TABLE 5-2

Classification of water alkalinity and associated options for prevention of alkalinity-related problems (Whipker, 2001).

Alkalinity Range (meq/L)	Class	Management Strategies
0–1	Low	• Pure water with little buffering capacity. • Monitor media pH regularly. • Rotate between acidic and basic fertilizers as needed. • If alkalinity is too low, use extra lime in the media or inject potassium bicarbonate at 0.12 g·L^{-1} (0.1 lb/100 gal).
1–3.6 1–1.5 1.6–2.4 2.0–2.8 2.4–3.6	Acceptable for: Plugs Small pots 4- to 5-in. (10- to 13-cm) pots 6-in. (15-cm) or larger pots	• Acceptable rate varies with container size. • Rotate between acidic and basic fertilizers as needed and/or lower rates of lime in the media. • If fertilizer rotation is inadequate, inject phosphoric, sulfuric, or nitric acid. Use sulfuric or nitric acid, if the additional P from phosphoric acid is not desired.
1.5–4	Marginal	• Range depends on pot size. • Use acidic fertilizers and/or lower rates of lime in media. • If the use of acidic fertilizers is inadequate, inject phosphoric, sulfuric, or nitric acid. Use sulfuric or nitric acid if the additional P from phosphoric acid is not desired.
4–8	High	• Inject one or more of the following depending on the desired nutrient rates: phosphoric, sulfuric, or nitric acid.
>8 or greater	Very high	• Use reverse osmosis.

the large quantity of waste water produced, which contains high amounts of salts. Disposal of this brine should be handled carefully due to environmental and regulatory concerns. Also, proper filtration and maintenance is essential for efficient operation of an RO unit. Other pretreatments may be necessary including dechlorination and acid injection. After RO treatment the resulting water has a low pH, around 5, with little or no alkalinity. RO-treated water is usually too pure and too expensive to use directly on crops and is often blended back with untreated water to raise the pH and alkalinity to the desired level. In addition, unblended RO water can be quite corrosive to metal.

Other water treatment systems—deionization, distillation, and electrodialysis—are available for treating water with a high ion content, but are currently more expensive than RO or do not produce the volume of water needed during production (Reed, 1996). With deionization, water flows over ion exchange resins, which remove the ions. The resins are usually solid beads with either positive or negative charges. Deionization is most feasible when highly pure water is required and the water has a low EC. In distillation the water is boiled and the resulting steam is condensed into pure water, which leaves behind the salts, particulates, and nonvolatile compounds. In electrodialysis water is passed between cation-permeable and anion-permeable membranes. When an electrical current is applied, ions migrate through the membranes, leaving pure water. Distillation and electrodialysis are not used on a large commercial scale, but advances in technology may make them more feasible in the future.

If water treatment is not an option for handling water with a high EC, cultural practices can be used to reduce the problem. Increased leaching rates will prevent soluble salts from building up in the substrate and will prevent plant damage. High-EC water is particularly difficult on the production of seedlings and cuttings. Growers may need to buy plugs and rooted cuttings instead of propagating their own plant materials or use high-quality water for propagation. For firms recirculating irrigation water, the use of controlled-release fertilizers can also be used to reduce the nutrient content of water. Generally, proper use of controlled-release fertilizers will allow a greater percentage of the nutrients applied to be taken up by the plant. Consequently, less fertilizer is leached out of the pots with controlled-release fertilizers, which helps to keep the EC of the recirculated water low.

ACID INJECTION

Water with a high alkalinity or high pH can be easily adjusted by injecting phosphoric, nitric, or sulfuric acid into the water. The higher the alkalinity, the more acid needed to reduce the pH. The acid converts the bicarbonates and carbonates to carbon dioxide gas, which allows the pH to decrease. Phosphoric acid is relatively weak, however, and often stronger acids such as nitric or sulfuric acid are needed. If either phosphoric or nitric acid is used, be sure to adjust the nutritional program because of the added nitrogen or phosphorus. The amount of acid required is based on the amount of bicarbonate in the irrigation water (Table 5-3). Citric acid can also be used but is expensive.

Remember, acids are dangerous and proper care and injection equipment must be used. Always pour acid into water—not water into acid! Wear protective clothing and use nonmetal containers and pipes because acid can corrode metals. Acids should be injected into the irrigation water separate from fertilizers using dual-headed injectors.

SPECIFIC NUTRIENTS

Water can occasionally be high in specific nutrients without having a high overall salt content, which would require reverse osmosis. With a few ions, specific treatments are available.

Iron and manganese. Subsurface water can be high in a reduced, soluble form of iron and manganese that oxidizes on contact with air into a less soluble, rust-colored form. The ox-

TABLE 5-3
Amount of acid required to neutralize 1 meq/L of alkalinity in irrigation water. This table will only estimate the amount of acid required; actual amounts will vary with the starting pH and the amount of alkalinity (meq/L) to be neutralized. More exact calculations can be made using the Web site at http://www.ces.ncsu.edu/depts/hort/floriculture/software/alk.html or Whipker et al. (1996).

Acid Type	Fluid Ounces per 1000 Gallons	Milliliters per 1000 Liters
Nitric (67%)	8.6[a]	67
Nitric (61.4%)	9.6	75
Phosphoric (75%)	9.3[a,b]	72
Phosphoric (85%)	7.6	59
Sulfuric (35%)	14.2[a]	111
Sulfuric (93%)	3.6	28

[a]One fluid oz/1000 gal will provide 1.4 ppm N, 2.7 ppm P, and 1.4 ppm S.
[b]Assumes an effective dissociation of 1.1 meq/L H[1] per 3 meq/L of phosphoric acid.

idized form is responsible for the brown- to rust-colored stains on plants and equipment. The iron and manganese can be removed by instigating the oxidation process prior to using the water. The water is sprayed into a tank or pond, which rapidly oxidizes the iron and manganese into insoluble forms that are allowed to settle to the bottom of the tank. The tanks or ponds must be large enough to treat sufficient water to allow the iron and magnesium to settle before the water must be used.

Calcium and Magnesium. The calcium and magnesium in hard water can be replaced by potassium in a process known as *water softening*. The total salt content is not reduced but the potassium can act as a fertilizer and the amount of added potassium can be reduced or eliminated in the fertilizer solution. Water softening should not be confused with home water softening, which replaces the calcium and magnesium with sodium, which can be damaging to plants.

Fluoride. Fluoride can damage many plant species, especially those used as foliage plants, including spider plants (*Chlorophytum*), dracaena (*Dracaena*), peace lily (*Spathiphyllum*), and many in the Marantaceae family. The amount typically added to the water to control tooth decay, 0.5 to 1 ppm, is high enough to damage sensitive plants (Nelson, 2003). Although avoidance of fluorides is generally the best strategy, the use of high-fluoride water may not be avoidable. Activated alumina or activated carbon can absorb fluoride from water. Water must be pH 5.5 for alumina to be effective and an ion exchange system can be used to obtain that pH. In addition, maintaining a substrate pH of 6.0 to 6.5 will make the fluoride relatively insoluble and prevent fluoride toxicity.

Chlorine. Municipal water usually contains 1 to 2 ppm chlorine but can have up to 10 ppm (Nelson, 2003). Although chlorine converts rapidly to chloride in organic-based media, the growth of some potted species, such as begonia (*Begonia*) and geranium (*Pelargonium*), can be inhibited by 2 ppm chlorine in the irrigation water (Frink and Bugbee, 1987). Hydroponically grown crops, however, can be affected by lower chlorine rates. Chlorine can be avoided by not using chlorinated water or can be eliminated by aerating for a day prior to use (Nelson, 2003).

Boron. Anion exchange systems can be used to remove boron, which occurs in water as negatively charged borate. Anion exchange systems act on all anions.

PATHOGEN CONTROL

As recirculatory irrigation systems become more common, many growers are concerned about the possibility of spreading pathogens through irrigation water. Normal sanitation and disease control procedures should prevent problems; however, firms that collect and reuse irrigation water from the entire property are especially prone to problems. Operations that produce long-term crops, such as stock plants, or overhead irrigate foliage plants should be particularly concerned with pathogens in the irrigation water. A number of options are available for controlling pathogens in irrigation water.

Ultraviolet light. Irrigation water flows past high-intensity UV lights, which kills the microorganisms. The system is most effective if the water is filtered to remove 5 µm or smaller particulate matter that might shield the microorganisms from the UV light. Besides normal maintenance, the UV lamps will need to be replaced after 10,000 hr of use. The overall price is moderate compared to other treatment systems.

Ozone. Although complete control of microorganisms is possible with an ozone system and less filtration is needed (120 µm), existing water holding tanks may not be usable. Ozone is a toxic gas that needs to be applied in completely airtight tanks. The ozone is bubbled through the water and collected at the top of the tank. At least two tanks are needed: one for treated water and one for untreated water.

Ultrafiltration. An ultrafiltration system is considered very effective because it physically blocks the microorganisms, but it is relatively expensive, new, and not well tested.

Chlorine. A chlorine system sterilizes the water by pumping low rates (2 to 3 ppm) of chlorine into the water supply such that 1 to 2 ppm chlorine remains during irrigation. The chlorine can be applied in holding tanks or by means of the chlorine generator, through which the water is run, rather than applying the chlorine in the water holding tanks. The system is relatively inexpensive but may not be 100% effective.

Heat treatment. A heat treatment system is considered very effective because it pasteurizes the water. Water is heated to 180°F (82°C) and allowed to cool before use.

FILTRATION

Many automated irrigation systems require water filtration for optimum performance to prevent plugging. Filtration is easier and less expensive than repeatedly cleaning or replacing nozzles and emitters. When purchasing a filtration system, be sure to calculate the price based on the volume of water applied rather than the cost for an individual system. Also, determine the expenses and frequency of maintenance. The efficacy of filtration will be improved if the irrigation system is made of black plastic piping instead of PVC, which allows light to reach the water and encourages microbial algae growth.

IRRIGATION SYSTEMS

Irrigation systems can be divided into two types: *surface irrigation*, such as hand watering, microtube, boom, sprinkler, and drip; and *subirrigation*, including ebb-and-flow, trough, and capillary mat systems. In subirrigation, water is absorbed into the medium through the bottom of the container and distributed throughout the medium by capillary action.

Lower fertilizer rates should be used when subirrigating than when surface irrigating (Barrett, 1991; Dole et al., 1994; Nelson, 2003). Also, soluble salts tend to accumulate in the upper surface of the medium when plants are subirrigated, because salts precipitate out when water evaporates from the medium surface (Argo and Biernbaum, 1995). With surface irrigation these salts redissolve during irrigation and move lower in the medium or leach out of the container. With subirrigation, however, medium EC in the upper 1 in. (2.5 cm) of the medium can easily reach 10 dS·m^{-1}.

Automated systems vary in advantages and disadvantages, but all systems greatly reduce labor costs compared to hand watering (Nelson, 2003; Thorsby, 1994). Although the savings is partially offset by installation expenses, long-term expenses are reduced. For large-scale growers, another benefit will be an increase in crop uniformity. Automated systems work best when the crop is uniform in size and species at planting and maintains the crop uniformity from potting to shipping. Finally, automated irrigation systems can allow growers to conserve water and reduce runoff.

HAND WATERING

Hand watering is the only practical irrigation system to use in some situations, but it is too labor intensive to be economical in many commercial operations (Fig. 5-1). Labor costs will surpass the installation and maintenance costs of automated irrigation systems such as microtubes. Hand watering is the easiest system to install because it requires only a faucet, hose, and nozzle.

Advantages:
- Easiest and least expensive irrigation system to set up.
- Appropriate for retail settings or operations with numerous pot sizes, plant species, and crop schedules.
- Able to check for insects, diseases, and other problems while irrigating.

Disadvantages:
- High ongoing labor costs.
- May produce lower quality plants than microtube or ebb-and-flow systems.
- Compacts the medium and may wash part of the medium out of the pot, resulting in lower medium water retention. Hand watering can reduce the water retention of a media by 10% after only three irrigations (Dole et al., 1994).
- High potential for problems with foliage diseases from splashing water and leaf spotting from dissolved salts.
- Uses large amounts of water and can easily produce excessive runoff.
- Uncomfortable, messy, and tedious to use on overhead hanging baskets.

Hints:
- The amount of wasted runoff can be reduced if the person watering is careful and fast, applies the water directly to the medium, and uses hose shutoffs.
- The use of an automated basket moving system can reduce the hassle of irrigating overhead baskets (Fig. 5-2).

FIGURE 5-1   Hand irrigation of bedding plants.

FIGURE 5-2   Automatic hanging basket irrigation system. Baskets rotate past the watering nozzle.

MICROTUBE

Water is delivered to each pot by means of small tubes (microtubes) originating from a larger plastic pipe (header). The system is also known as spaghetti tubes, capillary tubes, Chapin tubes, trickle tubes, or drip tubes. The microtubes have emitters at the ends to disburse the water into the pot. A variety of plastic and lead weights are available to prevent tubes from slipping out of the pots. Small spray stakes or rings can also be used at the end of each microtube to apply the water to a larger area of the medium (Fig. 5-3). The dimensions of the microtubes and the header pipe are determined by the number of pots that need to be irrigated. In-line drippers can be used in the production of hanging baskets or large containers. In-line drippers provide benefits similar to those of microtubes but are less flexible in that the emitters are attached directly to the supply pipe, thus setting the container spacing and preventing intermediate spacings.

Advantages:
- Produces consistently high plant quality.
- Little medium compaction and washing out of containers, thus the high water and air retention of most media is retained.
- Typically more water efficient than hand watering, using up to 27% less water (Dole et al., 1994; Morvant et al., 1997).

- Low potential for spread of both foliar and root diseases because the foliage does not get wet and water does not splash from one pot to another pot.
- Relatively low installation costs.

Disadvantages:
- Time-consuming to insert the tube into each container. Not practical with pot sizes less than 4 in. (10 cm) in diameter.
- Needs to be checked daily for dry plants, which can result when tubes fall out of the container or has become plugged.
- Header pipe must be level to prevent over- or underwatering at either end of the header.
- Typically less water efficient than recirculating ebb-and-flow and trough systems.

Hints:
- Emitters with adjustable flow rates may be useful when hanging baskets are grown in a multitier system. Emitters are set at a higher flow rate for baskets placed on the lower tiers than for those placed on the higher tiers. Pressure compensators can be attached to each microtube to provide uniform water application to all baskets on the irrigation line.
- Use thinner diameter microtubes for small, high-density pots to minimize the size of the header pipe required.
- With planning, microtube systems can be set up with one tube per pot at a close spacing and two tubes per pot at final spacing. In that case, the intermediate spacing would have to be one-half of the final spacing. For example, an initial spacing of 9 × 9 in. (23 × 23 cm) and a final spacing of 12 × 13 in. (30 × 30 cm) per pot provides 81 and 156 in.^{2} (523 and 1006 cm^2) per pot, respectively.
- Media with excessive drainage will result in channeling, which occurs when water does not spread laterally from the end of the microtube and only waters the medium below the tube. Use spray stakes or ring emitters in those types of media. Most peat or coir-based media are suitable.

FIGURE 5-3 Spray stake attached to a microtube for irrigation of hanging baskets. Note the different sized prongs to provide three different flow rates.

- Media with a high percentage of peat moss (50% or more) tend to contract away from the sides of the pot when excessively dry. In that case, water may run down outside of the root ball without wetting the substrate. If the root ball has shrunk, irrigate for a few minutes, then turn the system off. Repeat as needed until medium is moist and has expanded to refill the container.

SPRINKLER AND BOOM IRRIGATION

Overhead irrigation includes mobile boom systems or sprinkler nozzles placed on pipes originating from the greenhouse floor or from an overhead position (Fig. 5-4). Boom systems are mobile; some sprinkler systems are also portable. Sprinkler systems are divided into high-volume and low-volume (microirrigation) systems. Unfortunately, high-volume irrigation systems are generally unsuitable for most floriculture crops and may produce lower quality plants than microtube or flood systems. Watering with high-volume systems compacts the medium and may wash part of it out of the pot, resulting in lower media water retention.

Low-volume systems can be used to produce a range of droplet sizes from fog (tiny), to mist (intermediate), to large (irrigation) (Fig. 5-5). Fog and mist systems are usually limited to propagation areas. Low-volume systems do not compact the substrate and typically wash less medium from the pots than do high-volume systems. High-volume systems may be necessary, however, to move water through dense foliar canopies.

FIGURE 5-5 Overhead spray nozzle attached to an upright riser.

Advantages:	• Can irrigate large areas at once.
	• Low (sprinklers) to moderate (boom) installation costs.
Disadvantages:	• Difficult to use on some plants, such as foliage plants or poinsettias, which form a heavy foliage canopy, preventing overhead water from reaching the pots.
	• Uses large amounts of water and can easily produce excessive runoff.
	• High potential for problems with foliage diseases from splashing water and leaf spotting from dissolved salts.
	• Generally requires higher fertilizer rates to obtain the same plant quality as with subirrigation.
Hints:	• To achieve optimal uniformity, nozzles need to be carefully spaced and checked often for plugging or wear. Water pressure will need to be maintained within prescribed limits for each type of nozzle used or uneven watering will occur.
	• Sprinkler nozzles placed over the crops should have check valves to shut off the nozzles when the water is turned off to prevent draining of water from the irrigation lines onto plants.
	• Nozzle heads can be easily replaced with some mist systems to convert an area from propagation to production or vice versa.

FIGURE 5-4 Boom irrigation system.

- Low-volume sprinklers work well with subirrigation systems, with the bulk of the irrigation needs provided by subirrigation and occasional leaching provided by sprinklers.
- Water collection saucers or trays can be placed under pots to collect water that would otherwise drain away and be wasted. Square trays can be placed to capture most of the water applied to the crop. These water saucers can increase the amount of time between irrigation by providing a reservoir for longer term water uptake. The collection saucers should have low sides or drain holes on the sides to allow excessive water to drain.

TRICKLE TAPES

Trickle tapes include a variety of slow-release irrigation systems for beds, consisting of soft or hard-walled plastic tubes with built-in emitters or perforations to allow water to trickle out of the tubes (Fig. 5-6). The tubes can be laid in various arrangements and densities for thorough coverage of the bed surface.

FIGURE 5-6 Three lines of drip tape for irrigating a cut flower bed.

Advantages:
- Uniform water application.
- Little medium compaction and medium water retention remains high.
- Low potential for foliar and flower diseases and leaf spotting because the foliage remains dry.

Disadvantages:
- Works best if all plants being irrigated with the system are the same size to prevent over- or underwatering.
- Requires a media with good lateral water movement to ensure moistening of the entire ground bed.

Hints:
- Each bench/bed should be set up with on/off valves to reduce the area that is watered at one time and to provide more flexibility.
- Trickle tapes can be used as a temporary irrigation system for closely spaced pots.

FLOOD (EBB AND FLOW)/TROUGH

Pots are placed on a watertight trough, bench, or floor that is periodically flooded (Fig. 5-7). Water is usually recirculated back to a holding tank for reuse. The tank can be placed underground or made of a light-impermeable material to prevent algae growth. Because no water drains back out of the pots after being subirrigated, the fertilizer concentration in the holding tank changes little after each irrigation. Unfortunately, the EC will increase slightly over time because water remaining on the bench top or floor evaporates, leaving salts behind. These salts dissolve during the next irrigation and drain back into the tank. The higher the EC of the irrigation water, the faster the EC of the tank will rise.

FIGURE 5-7 Trough irrigation.

Advantages:

- Can greatly reduce the amount of water and fertilizer required and the amount lost when used in recirculatory systems because of the solution remaining after the irrigation is reused.
- Excellent plant quality can be obtained using lower fertilizer rates than recommended for surface irrigation methods.
- No medium compaction or loss occurs during irrigation, which allows the water holding capacity to remain high.
- Low potential for foliar and flower diseases and leaf spotting because the foliage remains dry.
- Trough irrigation systems allow air circulation between the pots if the bench top is made of expanded metal or other air-permeable material.

Disadvantages:

- High installation costs; among the highest of all systems.
- Allows salts to accumulate in the upper surface of the substrate, which may have to be removed through overhead irrigation with unfertilized water (leaching).
- Generally not feasible with large pots or tubs because insufficient water is absorbed by capillary action for optimum plant growth.
- The spacing between troughs is usually permanent, which reduces flexibility. However, adjustable trough systems are becoming available.
- Occasionally, high potential exists for root rot pathogens. Proper sanitation, monitoring, and prevention practices will prevent disease spread among plants in a flood system.

Hints:

- High-quality water (low salt) will reduce soluble salt accumulation and reduce the need for leaching.
- Care must be taken to ensure that flood benches have the proper angle of inclination to allow water to rapidly and uniformly cover each area of the bench when flooded, yet drain rapidly.
- Hot water pipes are often incorporated into flood floors to dry them rapidly after irrigation to reduce humidity.

CAPILLARY MAT

Fibrous cloth mats hold water, which is drawn up into the pot substrate by capillary action (Fig. 5-8). The mats are placed on solid bench tops or on plastic sheeting.

Advantages:

- Low installation expense.
- Easy to install and plants can be moved easier than with microtubes.
- Low potential for foliar and flower diseases and leaf spotting because the foliage remains dry.
- Accommodates slightly greater variations in plant age or size than other automated systems, but excessive variations will eventually lead to over- or underirrigation of at least a portion of the crop. Large variations in irrigation requirements can be handled by separating individual crops on the mats and applying water to each crop individually.
- Allows for the use of lower fertilizer rates than top or surface irrigation systems.

Disdvantages:

- Requires good contact between the medium in the pot and the

FIGURE 5-8 Capillary mat irrigation. Note mat for water retention and perforated black plastic cover for algae control.

mat. To ensure this, the first irrigation must be a top watering to establish the connection between the medium and the mat. If the medium dries to the point of plant wilting or if the pots are moved, they will have to be reirrigated again from the top.

- Allows salts to accumulate in the upper surface of the medium. The salts may have to be removed through overhead irrigation with unfertilized water (leaching).

- Allows plant roots to grow out into the mat, making harvest of the plants more difficult and negatively impacting postharvest life. If plants are rooting into the mat, give each pot a turn to break the roots. The problem of rooting into the mats is more prevalent with long-term crops.

- Generally capillary mats are not feasible with large pots or tubs because insufficient water is absorbed by capillary action for optimum plant growth.

- Requires that mats be replaced, leached, or sterilized periodically because of algae, soluble salts, and, potentially, disease organism buildup.

- Occasionally high potential for root rot pathogens. Proper sanitation, monitoring, and prevention practices will prevent spread among plants in a flood system.

Hints:

- Generally, capillary mats are most effective in areas of high humidity and low light levels. In areas of the country with high light and low humidity, capillary mats have generally produced lower quality plants than other irrigation systems due to excessive evaporation (Dole et al., 1994; Morvant et al., 1997).

- Commercially, several types of perforated black plastic coverings are available to reduce algae buildup on the fibrous mat. The perforated plastic may also reduce water loss, but under most conditions this reduction in water use is minimal. The plastic covering can be discarded with each crop to remove precipitated salts, fallen leaves, and other debris.

- Water can be applied to the mats by hand, but adding a water delivery system allows capillary mats to be mechanized. Drip tapes are probably the easiest and can be rolled up when the mats are changed or cleaned. Microtubes can also be used by spreading them evenly over the bench surface but may be more expensive.

- The benches do not have to be perfectly flat, but they *must be reasonably level*. Uneven benches with low spots may cause puddling and lead to uneven plant growth.

AUTOMATION

The use of mechanized irrigation systems can significantly reduce labor requirements. Most systems pay for themselves within a year in labor cost savings. The next step is to automate the process of deciding when and how long to irrigate. The traditional method has been time clocks that irrigate on a set schedule. Time clocks, however, result in over- or underwatering depending on environmental conditions. Other more accurate methods include tensiometers, accumulated light, vapor pressure deficit (VPD), and gravimetric scales. Tensiometers measure the tension (suction) within substrate on a column of water caused by evaporation. Irrigation is triggered when sufficient tension has been reached. In the accumulated light system, irrigation occurs when the sum of light measurements taken at regular intervals reaches a predetermined amount. VPD determines how much water can be absorbed by the air (deficit). Gravimetric scales measure weight loss due to water evaporation, and irrigation is initiated when monitored plants lose sufficient weight. The labor efficiency occurs when the irrigation process is completely automated. Computerized irrigation control systems are available that allow the grower to choose from one of several methods for determining when to irrigate.

IRRIGATION STRATEGIES

Two types of irrigation strategies can be followed: (1) *standard,* which calls for watering only when the medium is "dry"; or (2) *pulse,* in which small amounts of water are applied to each pot one or more times per day.

Standard irrigation. Plants are watered prior to signs of moisture stress. By the time a plant wilts, water stress has already occurred and growth has been reduced. It can be difficult to decide when plants need to be watered before they show any signs of moisture stress. An experienced grower will use many cues to determine when plants need to be watered including pot weight, how moist the substrate feels, time since the last irrigation, weather conditions, and color of the foliage. More precise irrigation decisions can be made when using moisture indicators. One such indicator is a tensiometer, which gauges the moisture tension of the medium.

Pulse irrigation. Plants are irrigated one or more times each day with a small amount of water. The advantages of pulsing are that plant growth is generally greater than with standard irrigation, and lower fertilizer rates can be used. Unfortunately, plants may grow too vigorously, have weak stems, and be more prone to stem breakage. Plants can be hardened and postharvest life improved by switching to standard irrigation the last 3 to 4 weeks before sale. Lower fertilizer rates, a greater percentage of nitrogen as ammonium, and greater spacing will also help to prevent weak growth.

No-leach production. Regardless of the irrigation strategy, water quality determines leaching frequency. Irrigation water with a high EC will require more frequent leaching with unfertilized water than with low-EC irrigation water. When leaching, plants should be irrigated twice within a few minutes with sufficient quantity such that 20 to 30% of the applied water runs out the bottom of the pot. Unless the no-leach production method is used, regular leaching will probably be required during production. Plants can be grown with no leaching, but high-quality water, low fertilizer rates, and an experienced grower are required. Using a no-leach production system on hanging baskets also eliminates water dripping on crops below the baskets. For no-leach production, 25 to 50% lower constant liquid fertilizer rates or controlled-release fertilizers are used.

WATER RETENTION

Plants are prone to drying out rapidly due to warm temperatures or to large canopies transpiring water. The irrigation frequency may become excessive, especially during warm late spring or summer days. One method to reduce irrigation frequency is to use the largest possible pots and baskets, taking into account finished weight and expense. Also, the design of the pot or basket should be considered, because containers of the same diameter may hold different amounts of media. Request samples of various containers from suppliers and measure the amount of medium each will hold.

The medium must retain the maximum amount of water yet retain sufficient aeration. Commercial premixed media vary in water holding capacity. For self-mixed media, the percentage of peat moss can be increased or a water absorbent material can be incorporated to increase water-holding capacity. Water-absorbent polymers or starches expand when placed in water, retaining large amounts of water, but some question their effectiveness.

Reapplication of wetting agents can be especially useful when applied prior to marketing. Although wetting agents are typically used during media mixing to ease the initial wetting, the application of wetting agents prior to marketing will improve postharvest water retention and delay wilting (Barrett, 1997). Remember, increasing the time needed between irrigations will also help customers better maintain the plants in the retail environment or in the home.

INTEGRATED FERTILIZER AND IRRIGATION MANAGEMENT (IFIM)

The integrated fertilizer and irrigation management (IFIM) system is a comprehensive approach to runoff control from container plant production (Table 5-4). IFIM is similar to the integrated pest management (IPM) system already being used by the nursery and greenhouse industries. Through the use of IFIM, runoff from container nurseries and greenhouses can be eliminated while maintaining or increasing plant quality. IFIM methods have been arranged in levels of increasing sophistication of water and nutrition management and runoff control. In addition, higher level practices will often require more experience growing practices or increasing cost.

TABLE 5-4

Integrated fertilizer and irrigation management (IFIM) for reducing water and fertilizer use and runoff. IFIM methods have been arranged in levels of increasing sophistication of water and nutrition management and runoff control. In addition, higher level practices will often require more grower experience or increasing cost.

Level I

- Secure the highest quality water source possible. Water low in soluble salts and alkalinity will give the grower the greatest number of water reduction options.
- Use media with a high available water and nutrient holding capacity.
- Fertilize at or below recommended rates. Use routine media and tissue tests to ensure that the crops are not being over- or underfertilized.
- Reduce water and nutrition at the end of the crop cycle to "harden" plants and increase postharvest life.
- Use mechanized irrigation systems, such as drip or microtube, which deliver water directly to the plants and eliminate runoff between plants.
- Grow cultivars or species that require the least water and nutrients.
- Shade greenhouses promptly in the spring to reduce temperatures and irrigation frequency.
- Repair leaking hoses and water lines promptly.
- Use water shutoffs on all hoses.
- Optimize plant production. Improper production practices may slow plant growth, delay harvest, and increase total water and nutrients applied.

Level II

- Reduce or eliminate leachate.
- Use fertilizers that release lower levels of nutrients in the runoff compared with liquid fertilization.
- Reuse water and nutrients through the use of trough or ebb-and-flow irrigation, which collects and reuses irrigation water.
- Use high-humidity chambers to reduce the amount of water used during propagation.
- Use irrigation indicators to optimize irrigation frequency.

Level III

- Install containment ponds.
- Install artificial wetlands.

KEY POINTS

- High-quality water is a high priority and should be tested periodically for EC, alkalinity, pH, and nutrient content.
- If EC is high, treatment with reverse osmosis may be necessary.
- If alkalinity is high, acid injection can be used.
- Some treatments are available for reducing levels of specific ions such as iron, manganese, calcium, magnesium, fluoride, and boron.
- Water treatments are available for pathogen control in recirculated irrigation water such as ultraviolet light, ozone, ultrafiltration, chlorine, and heat treatment.

- Filtration is required for any automated irrigation system and water treatment processes.
- Irrigation systems can be divided into two types: surface irrigation, such as hand watering, microtube, boom, sprinkler, and drip; and subirrigation, including ebb-and-flow, trough, and capillary mat.
- All automated systems reduce labor costs compared with hand watering and each individual system has various advantages and disadvantages.
- Deciding when to irrigate can also be automated by means of tensiometers, accumulated light methods, vapor pressure deficit, or gravimetric scales.
- Deciding when and how long to irrigate is also influenced by the irrigation strategy

- (standard or pulse) and whether or not leaching is used.
- Water retention of the final container should be considered to prevent excessive irrigation and allow maximum enjoyment by the consumer.
- Water and nutrient use and runoff can be reduced by using the integrated fertilizer and irrigation management (IFIM) system.

BIBLIOGRAPHY

Argo, W.R., and J.A. Biernbaum. 1995. The effect of irrigation method, water-soluble fertilization, preplant nutrient charge, and surface evaporation on early vegetative and root growth of poinsettia. *Journal of the American Society for Horticultural Science* 120:163–169.

Argo, W.R., and P.R. Fisher. 2003. Understanding water quality: Part I—Water pH, alkalinity, and control of media pH. *OFA Bulletin* 878:11–14.

Argo, W.R., J.A. Biernbaum, and D.D. Warncke. 1997. Geographical characterization of greenhouse irrigation water. *HortTechnology* 7:49–55.

Barrett, J. 1991. Water and fertilizer movement in greenhouse subirrigation systems. *Greenhouse Manager* 10(2):89–90.

Barrett, J. 1997. Wetting agents: Do they provide benefits after the first irrigation? *Greenhouse Product News* 7(10):26–28.

Dole, J.M., J.C. Cole, and S.L. von Broembsen. 1994. Growth of poinsettias, nutrient leaching, and water-use efficiency respond to irrigation methods. *HortScience* 29:858–864.

Frink, C.R., and G.J. Bugbee. 1987. Response of potted plants and vegetable seedlings to chlorinated water. *HortScience* 22:581–583.

Morvant, J.K., J.M. Dole, and E. Allen. 1997. Irrigation systems alter distribution of roots, soluble salts, nitrogen and pH in the root medium. *HortTechnology* 7:156–160.

Nelson, P.V. 2003. Watering, pp. 257–301 in *Greenhouse Operation and Management*, 6th ed. Prentice Hall, Upper Saddle River, New Jersey.

Reed, D.W. 1996. Combating poor water quality with water purification systems, pp. 51–67 in *Water, Media, and Nutrition for Greenhouse Crops*, D.W. Reed, editor. Ball Publishing, Batavia, Illinois.

Thorsby, A. 1994. Analysis compares costs of irrigation methods. *Greenhouse Product News* 4(2): 8–10.

Whipker, B.E. 2001. Alkalinity control, pp. 9–12 in *Plant Root Zone Management*, B.E. Whipker, J.M. Dole, T. J. Cavins, J. L. Gibson, W.C. Fonteno, P.V. Nelson, D.S. Pitchay, and D.A. Bailey. North Carolina Commercial Flower Growers' Association, Raleigh, North Carolina.

Whipker, B.E., D.A. Bailey, P.V. Nelson, W.C. Fonteno, and P.A. Hammer. 1996. A novel approach to calculate acid additions for alkalinity control in greenhouse irrigation water. *Communications in Soil Science and Plant Analysis* 27(5–8):959–976.

Chapter 6

Nutrition

INTRODUCTION

Supplying nutrients to floriculture crops is an exact process. The use of well-drained, soilless media and intensive production require growers to supply all the essential plant nutrients with little margin for error. Mineral nutrition programs also tend to be highly individualistic with each grower or greenhouse operation having unique nutrient regimes. A number of variables must be considered when developing a fertilization program for each crop species: total quantity or application rates, proportions of each element, application method, and interactions with media type, pH and soluble salt concentration, light levels, water quality, watering practices, production temperatures, and postharvest life.

One other point to consider is the current three-number method for expressing the concentrations of nitrogen (N), phosphorus (P), and potassium (K) in a fertilizer. Although nitrogen is expressed as the actual percentage of nitrogen in the fertilizer, phosphorus is expressed as percentage of phosphorus pentoxide (P_2O_5) and potassium as the percentage of potassium oxide (K_2O) in the fertilizer. Phosphorus pentoxide is only 44% actual phosphorus and potassium oxide is only 83% actual potassium. Thus, a fertilizer described as 10–10–10 (N–P_2O_5–K_2O) could be written as 10–4.4–8.3 (N–P–K) if the percentages of elemental N, P, and K were used. Most trade journals use the 10–10–10 system, but scientific literature frequently uses percentages of elemental N, P, and K. The rest of the plant nutrients required for proper growth are expressed as a percentage of the actual element present.

ESSENTIAL ELEMENTS

Essential elements are those elements required by plants to complete their growth cycle. Carbon, hydrogen, and oxygen comprise the backbone of all organic matter and are supplied by carbon dioxide (CO_2) and water (H_2O). Although C, H, and O are not considered fertilizers, a crop is sometimes "fertilized" with carbon through supplementary CO_2 injection into the greenhouse atmosphere (see CO_2 Injection section later in this chapter). The three primary *macronutrients*—nitrogen, phosphorus, and potassium—are supplied by most complete fertilizers. Calcium (Ca), magnesium (Mg), and sulfur (S) are considered *secondary macronutrients* because they are used in relatively large amounts but not to the same magnitude as N, P, and K. Most premixed fertilizers contain the secondary macronutrients, but check the fertilizer labels. The remaining essential elements are considered *micronutrients* and include iron (Fe), manganese (Mn), zinc (Zn), copper (Cu), boron (B), molybdenum (Mo), nickel (Ni), and chloride (Cl). Micronutrients are also known as *minor nutrients*, *trace elements*, or *minors*. A number of micronutrients are often combined into various types of micronutrient mixtures. Such mixtures are available as controlled-release formulations, which are incorporated into media prior to planting, or as water-soluble sulfates or chelates, which can be applied through an injector system along with the irrigation water. Micronutrients can frequently be found in significant amounts in water, other fertilizers, media (especially those with soil), and fungicides. Be careful when applying micronutrients, because the difference between deficiency and toxicity is often small.

NITROGEN

Of all the essential elements, nitrogen and potassium are found in the greatest percentage in plant tissue. Fertilizer recommendations are often based on the amount of nitrogen to be supplied, such as 150 ppm N from a 20–10–20 premixed fertilizer, with P and K set in proportion to nitrogen (van Iersel et al., 1998a, b).

Two forms of nitrogen important in floriculture plant growth are ammonium (NH_4^+) and nitrate (NO_3^-). The common fertilizer urea [$CO(NH_2)_2$] is considered an ammonium fertilizer in that it releases amides (NH_2^+), which are converted to ammonium either in the medium by microorganisms or within the plant. Most plant species grow best when both nitrate and ammonium forms of nitrogen are supplied (Ku and Hershey, 1997). Plants receiving only nitrate nitrogen tend to have dark green foliage and compact growth. The presence of ammonium, 25% or more of total nitrogen, tends to encourage lusher growth and greater stem (internode) elongation compared with 100% nitrate fertilizers. Growth can be manipulated in some cases, such as with cut roses (*Rosa*), by controlling the ratio of nitrate to ammonium supplied to the plants.

Nitrate and ammonium also differ in that plants are able to store excessive nitrates but do not store excessive ammonium. Thus, high levels of ammonium can lead to ammonium toxicity. Although 40 to 50% of the nitrogen can be in the form of ammonium, the amount is generally reduced to 25% or less during the winter in cool climates. Cool medium temperatures, especially less than 55°F (13°C), slow the conversion of ammonium to nitrates by nitrifying bacteria in the medium, which results in a buildup of ammonium in the medium. Low pH can also decrease the conversion of ammonium to nitrates. The ammonium level is generally reduced or eliminated at the end of the crop cycle

TABLE 6-1

Common nutrient uptake antagonisms (Nelson, 2003).

Group I

Ca, K, Mg, NH_4, and Na are antagonistic with each other.

High Ca can accentuate B deficiency.

Group II

Fe, Mn, Cu, and Zn are antagonistic with each other. Cu and Zn are less strongly antagonistic than Fe and Mn.

High P_2O_4 accentuates Fe, Mn, Cu, and Zn deficiency.

---

to improve flower development and postharvest life. Excessive ammonium may also accentuate Ca, K, and Mg deficiency (Table 6-1).

Sources

1. Potassium nitrate (KNO_3), soluble and basic
2. Calcium nitrate [$Ca(NO_3)_2$], soluble and basic
3. Ammonium nitrate (NH_4NO_3), soluble and acidic
4. Urea [$CO(NH_2)_2$], soluble and acidic
5. Monoammonium phosphate ($NH_4H_2PO_4$), soluble and acidic
6. Diammonium phosphate [$(NH_4)_2HPO_4$], soluble and acidic
7. Sodium nitrate ($NaNO_3$), soluble, basic; not commonly used
8. Ammonium sulfate [$(NH_4)_2SO_4$], soluble, acidic; not commonly used
9. Nitric acid (HNO_3), liquid, acidic; used to lower water pH and alkalinity
10. Most premixed and controlled-release fertilizers

Deficiency Symptoms (Nelson, 2003)

1. Light-colored chlorotic leaves can develop, especially lower leaves.
2. Older leaves may abscise or turn reddish or purplish on some species.
3. Mobile within the plant, therefore symptoms generally start with the lower leaves.

Ammonium Toxicity Symptoms

1. Yellow margins and necrotic edges can develop, especially on lower leaves.

2. Leaves may curl up or down.
3. Root tips may be necrotic.

PHOSPHORUS

Phosphorus is required in the least amount of the three macronutrients, usually 50% or less of N or K rates. Because many premixed fertilizers contain more phosphorus than is required by plants, fertilizers with lower rates of phosphorus may often be used to reduce nutrient runoff. Phosphorus tends to be relatively immobile in soil-based media, but is readily leached in soilless media, especially under high leaching (irrigation) rates and low pH (Cole and Dole, 1997; Spinks and Pritchett, 1956). The addition of aluminum sulfate to the growing has shown promise as a means to reduce P leaching from the medium (Williams and Nelson, 1996). An interesting relationship exists between mycorrhizae fungi and phosphorus. Mycorrhizae fungi are associated with many plants and are thought to increase nutrient uptake, especially phosphorus, and provide pathogen protection. However, the presence of P suppresses mycorrhizae growth, which has prevented the potential use of mycorrhizae to improve plant growth in commercial operations. Excess P_2O_4 may accentuate Fe, Mn, Cu, or Zn deficiency (Table 6-1).

Sources
1. Triple (treble) superphosphate $[CaH_4(PO_4)_2]$, low solubility, neutral; most commonly used as a preplant medium amendment (Note particle size because smaller particles will release nutrients more quickly than larger ones.)
2. Single superphosphate $[Ca_2H(PO_4)_2]$, low solubility, neutral, also contains gypsum $(CaSO_4)$, which supplies sulfur; most commonly used as a preplant medium amendment; is rarely available (Note particle size because smaller particles will release nutrients more quickly than larger ones.)
3. Monoammonium phosphate $(NH_4H_2PO_4)$, soluble and acidic
4. Diammonium phosphate $[(NH_4)_2HPO_4]$, soluble and acidic
5. Monocalcium phosphate $[Ca(HPO_4)_2]$, soluble and basic
6. Phosphoric acid (H_3PO_4), liquid, acidic; used to lower water pH and alkalinity
7. Most premixed and controlled-release fertilizers

Deficiency Symptoms (Nelson, 2003)
1. Stunting can occur.
2. Dark green foliage is seen first, occasionally developing a purplish color in older leaves.
3. Chlorosis followed by necrosis can also occur in older leaves.
4. Mobile within the plant, therefore symptoms generally start with the lower leaves.

POTASSIUM

Compared to nitrogen, potassium is found in plant tissue in the same or slightly lower level and, consequently, both nutrients are usually supplied in similar amounts. Some species such as azaleas (*Rhododendron*), however, prefer a greater N:K ratio of 3:1 and other species such as cyclamen (*Cyclamen*) prefer a lower N:K ratio of 1:2. Excess K may accentuate Ca and Mg deficiency (Table 6-1).

Sources
1. Potassium nitrate (KNO_3), soluble, basic; the preferred fertilizer because it supplies both K and N
2. Potassium chloride (KCl), soluble and neutral
3. Potassium sulfate (K_2SO_4), soluble and neutral
4. Contained in most premixed and controlled-release fertilizers

Deficiency Symptoms (Nelson, 2003)
1. Margins of older leaves become chlorotic, followed quickly by necrosis.
2. Necrotic spots occur over whole leaf, generally starting with the lower leaves.
3. Older leaves eventually become completely necrotic.
4. Mobile within the plant, therefore symptoms generally start with the lower leaves.

CALCIUM

Calcium is an immobile element that is transported by the movement of water in the transpiration process. Conditions that restrict transpiration can induce temporary Ca deficiency in poinsettia (*Euphorbia pulcherrima*), *Liatris*, and some *Lilium* cultivars. For example, this situation can occur during poinsettia stock plant production when a canopy of leaves forms over the plants, sharply reducing air movement and light levels and increasing the humidity below the canopy. Shoots below the upper canopy develop calcium deficiency symptoms (leaf edge burn), which can be made more severe when the upper layer of cuttings is harvested and the young shoots are exposed to better growing conditions but have insufficient calcium levels to support the new growth. This condition is temporary because the higher transpiration rates will increase calcium levels. Calcium deficiency can be accentuated by high Mg levels and low media pH, which allows faster leaching of calcium from the medium. High levels of ammonium, which may reduce calcium uptake or movement within the plant, can also be a concern with poinsettias. Excess Ca may accentuate K, Mg, or B deficiency (Table 6-1).

Sources

1. Dolomitic limestone ($CaCO_3$ + $MgCO_3$), low solubility; commonly used as a preplant fertilizer to raise media pH; the preferred source of calcium because it contains both Ca and Mg (Note particle size because smaller particles will release nutrients more quickly than larger ones.)
2. Calcitic limestone ($CaCO_3 \cdot 2H_2O$), low solubility; will raise media pH (Note particle size because smaller particles will release nutrients more quickly than larger ones.)
3. Gypsum ($CaSO_4$), low solubility, neutral; used when media pH is not to be increased (Note particle size because smaller particles will release nutrients more quickly than larger ones.)
4. Calcium nitrate [$Ca(NO_3)_2$], soluble, basic; commonly used in premixed fertilizers
5. Irrigation water in many areas may contain high levels of calcium, especially water that has high alkalinity. For most crops, the amount of Ca from both the irrigation water and fertilizers should be approximately 80 to 120 ppm (Biernbaum, 1997)
6. Some premixed fertilizers contain calcium, many controlled-release fertilizers do not. High-nitrate fertilizers usually have more Ca than high-ammonium fertilizers

Deficiency Symptoms (Nelson, 2003)

1. Young leaves become deformed, often straplike, and/or chlorotic.
2. Young leaves curl under, with yellow to tan margins developing into marginal necrosis.
3. Plants become stunted and petals or flowers may collapse.

4. Immobile within the plant, therefore symptoms generally start with the upper leaves.

MAGNESIUM

Magnesium and calcium are often considered together because both are strongly antagonistic with each other in the root medium. High levels of one element can induce a deficiency of the other, even if media levels are considered normal. Nelson (1996) recommends a general ratio of 3 to 5:1 Ca:Mg in irrigation water and media. Biernbaum (1997) recommends a Ca:Mg ratio of 2:1 in plant tissues, but notes that a ratio of 3 to 4:1 may be needed in the media to achieve the proper Ca:Mg ratio in the tissue. Calcitic limestone should be used carefully because it contains only Ca. Poinsettias have a high Mg requirement. Excess Mg may also accentuate K deficiency (Table 6-1).

Sources

1. Dolomitic limestone ($CaCO_3$ + $MgCO_3$), low solubility; commonly used as a preplant fertilizer to raise media pH; contains both Ca and Mg (Note particle size because smaller particles will release nutrients more quickly than larger ones.)
2. Magnesium sulfate (Epsom salts) ($MgSO_4 \cdot 7H_2O$), high solubility and neutral
3. Magnesium ammonium phosphate (Mag-Amp®) ($KMgPO_4$ + NH_4MgPO_4), low solubility and basic
4. Magnesium oxysulfate ($MgO \cdot MgSO_4$), high solubility for up to 8 to 10 weeks, low solubility after 8 to 10 weeks, and neutral (Broschat, 1997)
5. Magnesium oxide (MgO), low solubility and neutral
6. Magnesium nitrate [$Mg(HO_3)_2 \cdot 6H_2O$], soluble and basic
7. Irrigation water in many areas may contain high levels of magnesium, especially water that has high alkalinity. For most crops, the amount of Mg from both the irrigation water and fertilizers should be approximately 20 to 40 ppm (Biernbaum, 1997).
8. Check premixed and controlled-release fertilizers because some have Mg and others do not.

Deficiency Symptoms (Nelson, 2003)

1. Interveinal chlorosis occurs in recently mature or older leaves.

2. Leaves curl downward or become reddish/purplish in some species.

3. Mobile within the plant, therefore symptoms usually start with the lower leaves. However, when sufficient quantities of magnesium are present, the element is present in the highest concentration in the older leaves and the lowest concentration in the younger leaves.

SULFUR

Sulfur deficiency rarely occurs due to the presence of sulfates in many fertilizers.

Sources

1. Gypsum ($CaSO_4 \cdot 2H_2O$), low solubility, neutral; used when media pH is not to be increased (Note particle size because smaller particles will release nutrients more quickly than larger ones.)

2. Single (mono) superphosphate [$Ca_2H(PO_4)_2$], low solubility, neutral; contains gypsum ($CaSO_4$) (Note particle size because smaller particles will release nutrients more quickly than larger ones.)

3. Potassium sulfate (KSO_4), soluble and acidic

4. Magnesium sulfate ($MgSO_4 \cdot 7H_2O$), soluble and acidic

5. Ammonium sulfate [$(NH_4)_2SO_4$], soluble and acidic

6. Iron sulfate ($FeSO_4 \cdot 7H_2O$), soluble and acidic

7. Aluminum sulfate [$Al_2(SO_4)_3$], soluble and acidic

8. Elemental sulfur (S_2), low solubility and acidic

9. Sulfuric acid (H_2SO_4), liquid, acidic; used to reduce water pH and alkalinity

10. Commonly found in premixed and controlled-release fertilizers as sulfates

Deficiency Symptoms

1. Chlorosis occurs over entire plant, similar to N, but starting with younger leaves.

2. Immobile within the plant, therefore symptoms generally start with the upper leaves.

IRON

Iron is a common deficiency problem in greenhouse production. Iron chelates and sulfates can be purchased separately to correct iron deficiency. Iron deficiency is often due to high media pH; check media pH before applying treatments to correct iron deficiency symptoms. Iron toxicity can also occur on several crop species, especially on New Guinea impatiens (*Impatiens hawkeri*), geraniums (*Pelargonium ×hortorum*), and marigold (*Tagetes*). Iron toxicity is usually due to low media pH promoting excessive uptake rather than high levels in the medium; control by raising media pH. Excess Fe may accentuate Mn, Cu, or Zn deficiency (Table 6-1).

Sources

1. Iron sulfate ($FeSO_4 \cdot 7H_2O$), soluble and acidic

2. Iron chelates, soluble and neutral

3. Most commercial micronutrient mixes

Deficiency Symptoms (Nelson, 2003)

1. Interveinal chlorosis occurs on young leaves, sometimes generally chlorotic.

2. In advanced cases, the leaves may appear almost white and then become necrotic.

3. Immobile within the plant, therefore symptoms generally start with the upper leaves.

Toxicity Symptoms

1. Small chlorotic and necrotic spots and edges are seen on older leaves.

2. Spots enlarge and coalesce until entire leaf is necrotic.

MANGANESE

As with iron toxicity, manganese toxicity can also occur on many of the same crop species. Manganese toxicity is usually due to low media pH promoting excessive uptake rather than high levels in the medium; control by raising media pH. Excess Mn can induce Fe, Cu, or Zn deficiency (Table 6-1).

Sources

1. Manganese sulfate ($MnSO_4 \cdot H_2O$), soluble and acidic

2. Manganese chelates, soluble and neutral

3. Most commercial micronutrient mixes

Deficiency Symptoms (Nelson, 2003)

1. Interveinal chlorosis occurs on young leaves.

2. Tan necrotic spots develop on leaves in between the veins.

3. Immobile within the plant, therefore symptoms generally start with the upper leaves.

Toxicity Symptoms

1. Necrotic leaf tips and margins on older foliage occur which may coalesce into patches.
2. Initial symptoms are often similar to iron deficiency due to high manganese restricting iron uptake.
3. Occasionally the foliage has a bronze or reddish color.

ZINC

Zinc is an active component of some fungicides; residues on foliage may inflate Zn levels in tissue tests. Excess Zn may accentuate Mn, Zn, or Fe deficiency (Table 6-1).

Sources

1. Zinc sulfate ($ZnSO_4 \cdot 7H_2O$), soluble and acidic
2. Zinc chelates, soluble and neutral
3. Most commercial micronutrient mixes

Deficiency Symptoms (Nelson, 2003)

1. Stunting and shortened internodes occur.
2. Sometimes general to interveinal chlorosis occurs.
3. Generally immobile, but may be slightly mobile within the plant. Leaves from the middle of the shoot tend to have a lower level of Zn compared with upper or lower leaves.

COPPER

Copper is also an active component of some pesticides; residues on foliage may inflate Cu levels in tissue tests. Excess Cu may accentuate Fe, Mn, or Zn deficiency (Table 6-1).

Sources

1. Copper sulfate ($CuSO_4 \cdot 5H_2O$), soluble and acidic
2. Copper chelates, soluble and neutral
3. Most commercial micronutrient mixes

Deficiency Symptoms (Nelson, 2003)

1. Interveinal chlorosis occurs on young leaves with green edges that may have a blue or gray cast.
2. Leads to veinal chlorosis and sudden necrosis of entire blade of recently mature leaves.
3. Generally immobile, but may be slightly mobile within the plant. Leaves from the middle of the shoot tend to have a lower level of Cu compared with upper or lower leaves.

BORON

Water in some areas of the world can contain high levels of boron and can induce boron toxicity. Be sure to conduct a water analysis. If a plant deficiency is noted, however, apply boron carefully because the difference between deficiency and toxicity is especially narrow for this element.

Sources

1. Sodium tetraborate (borax) ($Na_2B_4O_7 \cdot 10H_2O$), soluble and neutral
2. Boric acid (H_3BO_3), soluble and acidic
3. Most commercial micronutrient mixes

Deficiency Symptoms (Nelson, 2003)

1. Malformations develop in flowers, leaves, leaf petioles, and stems.
2. Witches brooming, which is the development of many axillary shoots and no central shoot due to the repeated death of apices, can occur.
3. Chlorosis of young leaves is seen.
4. Immobile within the plant, therefore symptoms generally start with the upper leaves.

Toxicity Symptoms

1. Lower foliage has marginal necrosis, often reddish brown in color.
2. Symptoms often seen at tips of leaves.

MOLYBDENUM

Molybdenum is rarely a problem, except on poinsettias, which have an unusually high requirement for molybdenum.

Sources

1. Sodium molybdate ($NA_2MoO_4 \cdot 2H_2O$), soluble and neutral
2. Ammonium molybdate [$(NH_4)_2 MoO_4$], soluble and acidic
3. Most commercial micronutrient mixes

Deficiency Symptoms (Nelson, 2003)

1. Only known to occur on poinsettias.
2. Marginal chlorosis develops first on recently mature leaves, leading to marginal necrosis.

3. Upward rolling of leaves may also be present.
4. Older and younger leaves show symptoms in more advanced cases.

NICKEL AND CHLORINE

Nickel and chlorine are required in minute amounts and deficiencies do not occur in floriculture production. Fertilizer and media have nickel and chlorine contaminants so additional sources are not needed.

FERTILIZER APPLICATION

Of the 12 nutrients required by plants, firms must decide whether to apply the nutrients by (1) incorporation into media prior to planting; (2) fertigation, which is defined as dissolving water-soluble nutrients into the irrigation water; or (3) a combination of both. For example, some growers supply most of the micronutrients and secondary macronutrients through the medium and the remaining primary macronutrients though fertigation. Before preparing a nutrition program, be sure to have a complete water analysis to determine the amount of nutrients being obtained through the water supply.

PREPLANT FERTILIZATION

Fertilizers can be supplied through preplant incorporation into media by various controlled-release fertilizers intended to last for the entire crop cycle, or by small amounts of soluble fertilizers intended to serve only as a short-duration starter fertilizer. In the latter case, the nutrients only last about 2 weeks under normal irrigation frequencies and must be followed by a routine fertilization program. Be sure to check premixed media, because many brands contain starter nutrient charges.

Controlled-release fertilizers have the advantage of potentially reducing labor costs and reducing the waste of nutrients through leaching. Controlled-release fertilizers are more nutrient efficient than fertigation because more of the nutrients are absorbed by the plant as opposed to being leached (Hershey and Paul, 1982; Koch and Holcomb, 1983; Mancino and Troll, 1990). Controlled-release fertilizers may also be helpful in providing a low amount of postharvest nutrition for potted or flatted bedding plants that are to remain in the home or on display for a long time.

The main disadvantage of controlled-release fertilizers is that the grower loses control of fertilization. Although this is generally not a problem for the secondary macronutrients or for the micronutrients, it can be a problem with N, P, and K. Levels of the primary macronutrients are often manipulated to regulate quantity and type of growth, and supplying all the nutrients in a controlled-release manner prevents growers from changing the nutritional program. For example, the growth of bedding plants can be slowed by restricting the fertilizer if the weather is poor and sales are slow. Also, if controlled-release fertilizers are the sole source of nutrition, they may not be as effective as constant liquid fertilization (CLF), especially in the winter. Most controlled-release fertilizers are temperature dependent and nutrient release decreases when the temperature is cool. Other disadvantages include the higher cost of some controlled-release fertilizers compared with CLF and the potential difficulty of obtaining an accurate media test when controlled-release fertilizers are incorporated into media. Many media testing labs can accurately test media if they are notified that the media contains controlled-release fertilizers.

TYPES OF CONTROLLED-RELEASE FERTILIZERS

Slowly soluble and plastic-coated fertilizers are most commonly used to provide macronutrients; fritted fertilizers and impregnated clays are typically used to provide micronutrients. Research continues on new controlled-release nutrient sources such as precharged zeolites (Williams and Nelson, 1997).

SLOWLY SOLUBLE. Slowly soluble fertilizers such as limestone, gypsum, superphosphate, and MagAmp® are routinely added to media. MagAmp, which contains magnesium, ammonium, potassium, and phosphorus, should be used with care in cool climates during the winter because the nitrogen is 100% ammonium.

Nutrient release: Slowly soluble fertilizers release nutrients by dissolving; the more finely ground the material, the faster the release rate. Low media pH will allow limestone to dissolve quicker.
Temperature effect: Increasing temperature increases the release rate. Slowly soluble fertilizers can be heat pasteurized.
Moisture effect: Increasing moisture increases the release rate.

PLASTIC COATED. One popular type of complete controlled-release fertilizer (CRF) is the plastic-coated fertilizer, including Osmocote®, Nutricote®, Precise®, and others.

Nutrient release: The hydroscopic fertilizer attracts water through pores in the plastic coat, expanding the capsule and allowing the concentrated fertilizer–water solution to be released. The release rate is controlled by the pore size and thickness of the plastic coat. The longevity of the CRF is specified by the manufacturer and varies from 3 to 14 months. Release rates vary among the different manufacturers depending on the composition of the coating (Cabrera, 1997).

Temperature effect: Increasing temperature increases release rate. Most release rates are based on an average medium temperature of 70°F (21°C). If average daily production temperatures are greater, the CRF will release more quickly and the effective life will be reduced. Similarly, at lower temperatures the fertilizer may remain effective longer than the stated time period. Note that release rates will increase with warm day temperatures, especially for dark colored containers being used outdoors (Husby et al., 2003). The composition of the coating can also influence the temperature sensitivity of the CRF, even for fertilizers with the same longevity rating (Cabrera, 1997). Plastic-coated fertilizers cannot be heat pasteurized because such a process will affect the coating.

Moisture effect: Increasing the moisture level between the permanent wilting point and container capacity will not affect the release rate.

UREA FORMALDEHYDE. Although normally not used in the greenhouse, it does have application in outdoor production.

Nutrient release: Biodegradation by microorganisms releases the urea.
Temperature effect: Increasing temperature increases the release rate. Urea formaldehyde cannot be heat pasteurized.
Moisture effect: Optimum is 50% water saturation of the medium.

SULFUR-COATED FERTILIZERS. Beads of fertilizer are coated with a sulfur and wax coat. Nitrates are not handled in this manner because they could potentially be explosive. Although not normally used in the greenhouse, sulfur-coated urea (SCU) may be useful outdoors.

Nutrient release: Biodegradation by microorganisms converts the elemental sulfur coating to soluble sulfur.
Temperature effect: Increasing temperature increases the release rate. Sulfur-coated fertilizers can be pasteurized.
Moisture effect: Increasing moisture increases the release rate.

FRITTED NUTRIENTS. Nutrients are added to molten glass, which is cooled and ground into a fine powder. The nutrients leach out of the glass. The fine texture of the powder can make it difficult to incorporate into media. The same manufacturing technique can also be used with macronutrients, but is generally too expensive for the volume needed.

Nutrient release: Solubility can be controlled by the type of glass and by altering the size of the particles.
Temperature effect: Increasing temperature increases the release rate. Fritted fertilizers can be pasteurized.
Moisture effect: Increasing moisture increases the release rate.

IMPREGNATED CLAYS. Nutrients are attached to baked clay particles. This type is primarily used for micronutrients. One commonly used product is Esmigran®.

Nutrient release: The nutrients slowly leach out of the clay particles.
Temperature effect: Increasing temperature increases the release rate. Impregnated clays can be pasteurized.
Moisture effect: Increasing moisture increases the release rate.

FERTIGATION

Fertigation is the application of water-soluble fertilizers through the irrigation water. Typically nutrients are applied at every irrigation (constant liquid fertilization) when the plants are actively growing. CLF links the application of fertilizers to the plant's growth rate. Plants that are actively growing and drying quickly are more frequently irrigated and fertilized. Similarly, plants that are growing slowly use less water and fertilizer and are less frequently fertigated. However, when seedlings, cuttings, or plugs are newly potted and have small root systems, the medium may stay moist for long periods and plants may temporarily have insufficient nutrient levels. Also, during cool or cloudy periods, plant nutritional requirements may be greater than the need for water. At these times, fertilizer drenches with high fertilizer rates can be used or the plants may be initially irrigated with a higher CLF rate. Also, occasionally high rates of individual nutrients are applied as a one-time drench via CLF.

The fertilizer concentration depends on a number of variables, the most important of which are the species being grown, the irrigation frequency, and the leaching fraction. Species vary greatly in their fertilizer requirements and can be placed into three general categories: high, medium, and low nutritional requirements. For example, poinsettias require higher levels of nutrients than African violets (*Saintpaulia ionantha*). Many growers are forced to grow a number of crop species using the same fertilizer rate from one injector. In such cases, the nutritional level can be individually tailored to each crop's needs by setting the fertilizer rate for the species requiring the highest fertilizer rate and then combining fertigation with clear water irrigation for the other species. The lower the nutritional requirements of the species, the more frequent the clear water irrigation. The other approach is to set the fertigation rate low and incorporate a CRF into the medium, or top-dress the medium with a CRF for those species that require high nutrition.

Irrigation frequency and leaching fraction (the percentage of water applied that runs out the bottom of the container) are interrelated in that both influence the rate at which nutrients are lost from the medium and must be replaced. Growers who frequently irrigate and use a high leaching fraction will leach more nutrients from the medium and will require higher fertigation rates.

Other variables that influence a plant's nutrient requirements include the season (higher rates in summer compared with winter), the medium (the higher the cation exchange capacity, the lower the fertilizer rate), and the stage of plant growth (higher rates at the beginning of the production cycle and reduced rates or no fertilizer at the end of the production cycle). If a crop species is being grown for the first time, the grower will start with a recommended rate from the literature or from a fellow grower. As the grower gains experience with the crop, the fertilizer rate is adjusted to the grower's individual production environment.

If controlled-release micronutrients have not been incorporated into the medium prior to planting, water-soluble micronutrient mixes must be applied as a water-soluble fertilizer. Micronutrients are also frequently fertigated.

Water-soluble micronutrient mixes usually include iron, manganese, copper, and zinc as sulfates, oxides, or chelates. Boron is usually included in mixes as borax, and molybdenum as molybdate. The sulfates and oxides tend to be the least expensive forms of micronutrients and are suitable for most situations. However, if the medium pH is neutral or higher, the iron, manganese, copper, and zinc sulfates and oxides become less soluble and less available for the plant to absorb. Thus, a variety of deficiency symptoms can occur with high media pH. The best solution is to keep media pH acidic (less than 7.0). If that is not possible or a problem has already occurred, then chelated forms of the micronutrients, which are less influenced by pH, may be used. Controlled-release forms of micronutrients are subject to the same pH concerns unless the product contains chelated forms. Availability of boron and molybdenum is generally not a problem because they remain fairly soluble even at higher pHs.

Chelates are large organic molecules (chelating agents) that bind the iron, copper, zinc, or manganese ions and protect them from forming insoluble compounds. The chelates themselves are soluble and allow the micronutrients to be readily absorbed by the plant. Several chelating agents are available and vary in their reaction to pH. The most pH-resistant chelating agent is EDDHA, with the other agents, DTPA, EDTA, and HEDTA, progressively decreasing in pH resistance. Chelated forms of micronutrients are also more expensive than sulfates and oxides, and chelates are generally used only in certain situations, such as in outdoor beds in areas with high-pH soil or if a specific micronutrient problem develops.

MIXING WATER-SOLUBLE FERTILIZERS

While small quantities of fertilizers can be dissolved and applied by handheld watering cans, injectors or proportioners are used to inject specific amounts of concentrated fertilizer (stock) solution into the irrigation water (Fig. 6-1). Backflow preventers are required

FIGURE 6-1 A fertilizer injector for fertigation.

that stop the siphoning of stock solution back into the general water system, unless a space exists between the water supply line and the stock tank. The space must be equal to twice the diameter of the supply line. Individual states may have different legal requirements.

The ratio of fertilizer concentration to water varies with different injectors from 1:16 to 1:1950. Greenhouses generally use a ratio between 1:16 and 1:200. Some injector models allow the ratio to be adjusted lower for difficult-to-dissolve fertilizers that must be dissolved in a less concentrated solution. Injectors also vary in flow rate and pipe sizes. High flow rates are needed for greenhouses when multiple areas are being fertigated simultaneously. The stock tank should be large enough to prevent the need for constant mixing of the fertilizer concentrate. The electrical conductivity (EC) of fertilized water should be monitored periodically to ensure that the proper ratio is being maintained. An EC meter can be installed in the waterline for constant monitoring or for regulation of the fertilizer level in the irrigation water. EC meters can be equipped with an automated alarm system if the EC becomes too high or too low. Improper functioning of the injectors can lead to serious problems from highly soluble salts or deficiencies from inadequate nutrition.

Several different types of injectors are available and the decision of which type to buy will be based on the amount of fertilized irrigation water needed and on the portability of the injector (Bartok, 1997). The smallest proportioners are the venturi suction devices such as Hozon or Syfonex types, which draw up fertilizer solution by water suction from a small stock bucket. They are easy to set up, inexpensive, and portable.

They have a low ratio of 1:16 and are useful only for small operations since the stock bucket needs frequent refilling. The ratio will vary with the water flow rate and between individual units of the same brand. These injectors are not suitable for precise applications.

Bladder tank injectors such as the GEWA are also portable and moderately priced. The fertilizer stock solution is held in a heavy plastic bag and is forced into the water stream by pressure from water surrounding the bag. GEWAs are available in different stock tank sizes; the larger stock tank sizes have adjustable ratios. The larger tanks also do not need to be refilled with fertilizer concentrate as often as smaller tanks. GEWAs are well suited to medium-sized operations. (GEWA is a contraction of the inventor's name, George Wagner.)

Water motor-controlled injectors such as Dosmatic® injectors insert fertilizer solution into the waterline by means of a piston that moves in response to the water flow. They are moderately priced and at least one model is portable. They are also well suited to medium-sized operations and have a variable dilution ratio.

Water meter-controlled injectors such as Anderson, Smith, and Fert-o-Ject® are capable of handling large volumes of water and inject the stock solution into the water stream by means of an electric or water-powered pump. These injectors have a variable dilution ratio, are usually fixed in place, and are the most expensive.

Depending on the concentration of the injector solution, the fertilizers may be difficult to dissolve into the stock tank solution. In such cases, hot water is required to dissolve the fertilizers. Constant agitation of stock solution may also be required to ensure application of a uniform nutrient solution. Not all fertilizers are compatible with each other in the stock tank and either exhibit reduced solubility or produce insoluble precipitates (Table 6-2). In either case, the nutrients are not reaching the plant materials and the injector may be damaged or plugged. For example, sulfuric acid cannot be directly mixed with calcium nitrate. In such cases, injectors with two or more injecter heads are used to allow the concentrated fertilizer solutions to be diluted in the irrigation water prior to being mixed together.

When using fertigation, growers have the option of using a premixed fertilizer or mixing their own. As with media, premixed fertilizers are usually more expensive than buying indi-

TABLE 6-2

Compatibility and incompatibility of various liquid fertilizer concentrates.

Fertilizer	Reaction with Other Fertilizers Listed	
	Incompatible	Reduced Solubility
Ammonium nitrate	—	—
Ammonium phosphate	Calcium nitrate Magnesium sulfate Sulfates of Fe, Zn, Cu, or Mn	Chelates of Fe, Zn, Cu, or Mn
Ammonium sulfate	Calcium nitrate	Potassium chloride Potassium nitrate Potassium sulfate
Calcium nitrate	Ammonium sulfate Ammonium phosphate Magnesium sulfate Potassium sulfate Sulfates of Fe, Zn, Cu, or Mn Sulfuric and Phosphoric acid	—
Chelates of Fe, Zn, Cu, or Mn	Nitric acid	Ammonium phosphate Phosphoric acid
Magnesium sulfate	Ammonium phosphate	Potassium chloride Potassium nitrate Potassium sulfate
Nitric acid	Chelates of Fe, Zn, Cu, or Mn	—
Phosphoric acid	Calcium nitrate	Chelates of Fe, Zn, Cu, or Mn
Potassium chloride	—	Ammonium sulfate Magnesium sulfate Potassium sulfate Sulfates of Fe, Zn, Cu, or Mn Sulfuric acid
Potassium nitrate	—	Ammonium sulfate Magnesium sulfate Potassium sulfate Sulfates of Fe, Zn, Cu, or Mn Sulfuric acid
Potassium sulfate	Calcium nitrate	Ammonium sulfate Magnesium sulfate Potassium nitrate Potassium chloride Sulfates of Fe, Zn, Cu, or Mn Sulfuric acid
Sulfates of Fe, Zn, Cu, or Mn	Calcium nitrate	Potassium chloride Potassium nitrate Potassium sulfate
Sulfuric acid	Calcium nitrate	Potassium chloride Potassium nitrate Potassium sulfate
Urea	—	—

vidual components, but much of the dollar savings of self-mixed fertilizers can be lost in the labor needed to mix the fertilizer. The production of specialized crop species may dictate that growers mix their own fertilizer or add additional nutrients to a premixed fertilizer. For larger producers, mixing their own fertilizers is often economically justified, although, as with media, the price of premixed fertilizers usually drops with increasing volume purchased.

Small producers generally have many tasks to perform and the higher cost of pre-mixed fertilizers is offset by the convenience. In addition, mixing one's own fertilizer increases the chance of error. With fertilizers, a simple mistake can rapidly damage a crop, especially when micronutrients are being applied.

DEVELOPING A NUTRITIONAL PROGRAM

SELF-MIXED MEDIA. For those firms mixing their own media, it is usually easiest to incorporate fertilizers containing Ca and Mg into the media. The large proportion of sphagnum peat moss used in most media requires the use of slowly soluble calcitic or dolomitic limestone to raise and maintain the medium pH. Dolomitic limestone is preferred because it supplies both Ca and Mg. Due to the variability of peat moss, the exact amount of limestone needed can be difficult to determine. The best method is to mix a small volume of moist medium with limestone, allow to equilibrate for 14 to 21 days, test the pH, and adjust the limestone rate if required. Optimum pH for most crops in soilless media is 5.4 to 6.0, and in soil-based media, 6.2 to 6.8. If the soilless medium pH is 5.2 or higher and the soil-based medium pH is 6.0 or higher, limestone may not be needed if the irrigation water has high alkalinity or high pH. In such cases, the high alkalinity will gradually raise the medium pH. Starting out at the low end of the pH scale will give the grower flexibility to allow the medium pH to naturally increase and still remain acceptable. Limestone will be needed if the water pH (generally 6.0 or lower) or alkalinity is low or if an acidic fertilizer is used. If limestone is not needed, the calcium can be supplied by adding gypsum to the medium or calcium nitrate to the irrigation water. Magnesium can be applied separately through a magnesium sulfate drench.

Superphosphate is used to incorporate phosphorus into media and single superphosphate has the advantage of also supplying sulfur and calcium. Unfortunately, in most soilless media, especially those with low pH, phosphorus ions readily leach out of the media (Cole and Dole, 1997; Spinks and Pritchett, 1956). Growers can still apply most of the phosphorus for short-term crops through the media by using superphosphate, but media should be regularly tested to prevent phosphorus deficiency. If phosphorus levels become low, fertigation with monoammonium and diammonium phosphate can be used to supply additional phosphorus. Most growers, however, use a complete liquid fertilizer containing phosphorus from the beginning of the crop without incorporating superphosphate into the medium.

Growers may add gypsum to prevent sulfur deficiency if gypsum or single superphosphate have not already been incorporated into the medium or if water-soluble fertilizers do not contain sulfates. Sulfur deficiency is rare, however.

Micronutrients are frequently incorporated into the medium and can supply the micronutrients for the entire production cycle in most situations. The micronutrients also can be applied through fertigation. Many firms incorporate one-half of the required amount of micronutrients into the medium and supply the other half through fertigation.

The final decision is how to apply N and K, and most growers use fertigation. Many growers, however, use a combination of controlled-release sources and fertigation. Often the combination of both application types produces better plant quality than either system alone (Simpson et al., 1975). Also, specific situations may require the use of controlled-release sources because of environmental runoff concerns or because the overhead irrigation of containers would waste much of the nutrients in fertigation.

PREMIXED MEDIA. For growers using premixed media, most of the nutrients must be applied using fertigation. Although many premixed media contain a small amount of nutrients, the quantity is sufficient for only a couple of weeks. The medium may contain enough Ca, Mg, S, and micronutrients for the entire crop; however, the nutrient content of the medium must be determined before preparing a nutritional program. Remember that many premixed fertilizers also contain micronutrients, which should be considered. Although N, P, and K are usually applied through fertigation, the media can be top-dressed with controlled-release sources. Application of controlled-release fertilizers to the surface of the medium is as effective as incorporating the controlled-release fertilizers into the medium.

Determining which water-soluble fertilizer to use depends mainly on the desired media pH, which is influenced by the water alkalinity (see Chapter 5, Water). Ammonium- and urea-based fertilizers tend to be acidic and reduce media pH; nitrate-based fertilizers tend to be basic and increase media pH (Argo and Biernbaum, 1997). The fertilizer bag should list the potential acidity, which is expressed as the amount of calcium carbonate required to neutralize the acidity in 1 ton of the fertilizer. The higher the number, the more acidic the fertilizer. Similarly, potential basicity is expressed as the amount of calcium carbonate that would equal the basicity in 1 ton of the fertilizer. Although many premixed fertilizers have relatively high ammonium levels and are acidic, basic nitrate-based fertilizers are available. In addition, growers can combine potassium nitrate and calcium nitrate to make their own basic fertilizer. Unfortunately, high-ammonium fertilizers are not feasible in some situations, which limits the ability of growers to control media pH through fertilizer choice. Producers can rotate among acidic and basic fertilizers as needed to help manage media pH (see below).

pH

In an aqueous solution a certain number of the water molecules (H_2O) are split into the ions H^+ and OH^-. pH is a measure of the concentration of H^+ in a solution, usually the medium water solution, and is measured on a scale from 0 to 14. At pH 7.0 the solution is neutral and the H^+ concentration is equal to the OH^- concentration. A pH of less than 7 is acidic and a pH of greater than 7 is basic or alkaline. pH has a major effect on the availability of nutrients in the medium (Fig. 6-2). The recommended pH for soilless media is 5.4 to 6.0 and for soil-based media containing at least 25% soil, 6.2 to 6.8. Specific crop species may have other pH requirements; a notable example is the azalea (*Rhododendron*), which requires a medium pH of 4.5 to 5.5 (Fig. 6-3). A number of factors affect the medium pH including media components, water, fertilizers, and the plant itself. For example, sphagnum peat moss is acidic, water pH can vary greatly among sources, ammonium-based fertilizers are acidic, and some plants respond to high pH-induced iron deficiency by releasing hydrogen ions, which lowers the pH immediately around the roots and increases iron availability and uptake (Albano and Miller, 1996; Lang et al., 1990).

INCREASING pH

Calcitic or dolomitic limestone is most commonly used to increase media pH prior to planting (see Developing a Nutritional Program section earlier in this chapter). It is more difficult, however, to raise media pH after the crop has been planted. One method is to use basic fertilizers, such as calcium and potassium nitrate, and reduce the use of acidic fertilizers such as ammonium nitrate. Generally, this technique can only moderately alter media pH. Manipulating media pH through fertilizer choice is best done before the medium pH is too low. For faster and greater action, flowable lime, a suspension of lime, can be applied. If faster action is required, hydrated lime (CaOH) can be applied to the medium. Hydrated lime

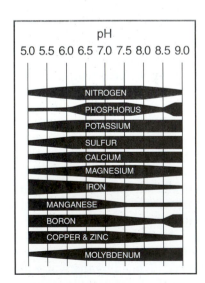
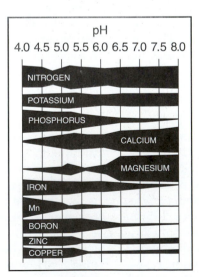

FIGURE 6-2 Nutrient availability chart as related to media pH for (a) soil-based medium and (b) soilless medium (Peterson, 1982a).

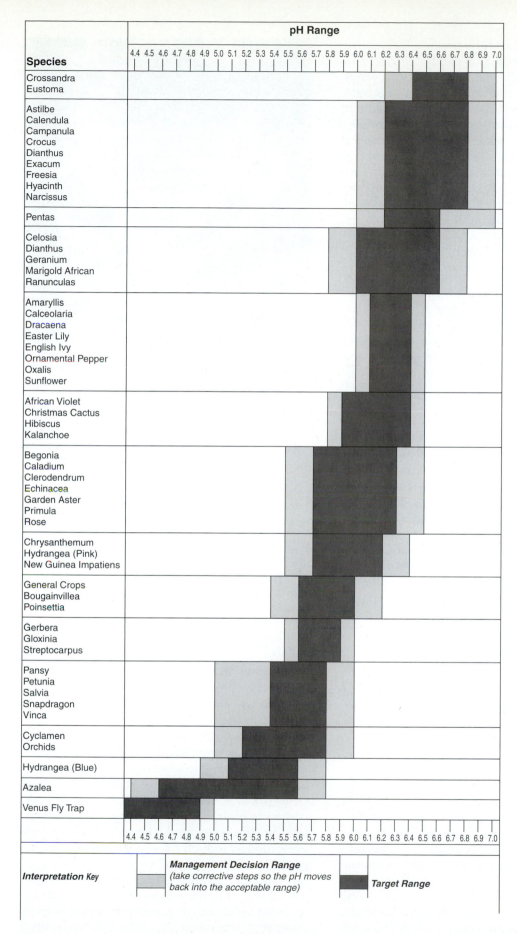

FIGURE 6-3 Suggested media pH ranges for various floriculture crops grown in soilless media (Whipker, 2001).

should be applied carefully because it can burn foliage. Recommendations call for mixing 1 lb (2.2 kg) of hydrated lime in 5 gal (19 L) water and applying only the liquid portion, because not all the hydrated lime will dissolve. Do not use with controlled-release fertilizers containing ammonium or when liquid feed is more than 25% ammonium because ammonia gas may be produced. In cases of chronically low pH, potassium bicarbonate can be injected into the irrigation water to increase alkalinity and media pH (Bailey et al., 1997).

DECREASING pH

Before planting, several options are available for lowering media pH. Elemental sulfur can be incorporated into media and at 5 lb/yd^3 (8.4 kg·m^{-3}) it will reduce media pH about 0.5 point. Iron sulfate can also be used for a quicker action. Of course, adding or increasing the amount of sphagnum peat moss used can create a medium with a lower pH.

After planting, iron sulfate can be used to lower media pH but may produce inconsistent results. At 3 lb/100 gal (0.36 kg/100 L) the pH may be reduced by up to 1.0 point. Apply iron sulfate only to the medium because it is toxic to foliage and be sure to monitor the EC because it can increase media soluble salts. The use of acid fertilizers such as ammonium nitrate can also decrease media pH.

Acid injection to reduce the water pH is a routine practice in many greenhouses (see Chapter 5, Water, for details). Continual acid injection is best used to maintain media pH at the desired level. If the medium pH is already high, such as close to 7.0, acid injection will only slowly decrease the medium pH and may only lower the pH 0.5 to 1.0 point. Phosphoric, nitric, and sulfuric acid are most commonly used, especially in areas with highly alkaline water or by large producers.

SOLUBLE SALTS

The term *soluble salts* refers to the total dissolved ions in medium water solutions. Soluble salts are measured by means of electrical conductivity (EC); the greater the soluble salt concentration, the more easily an electrical current will pass through a medium water solution. Plants require sufficient nutrients to grow, but extremely high levels of soluble salts in the medium can induce *physiological drought*. Physiological drought occurs when the high

FIGURE 6-4 High soluble salt damage on poinsettias (*Euphorbia pulcherrima*).

concentration of salts in media water restricts water from being taken up by the roots due to competitive osmosis. During physiological drought, the plants wilt, even when the medium is moist. More common symptoms of high soluble salt levels include slow growth, necrotic leaf margins (especially on the lower leaves) (Fig. 6-4), reduced or erratic seed germination, reduced or erratic rooting of cuttings, and increased susceptibility to root and crown diseases. In general, optimum root growth is obtained with low media EC (Morvant et al., 1997). Plants with limited root systems, such as seedlings, cuttings, and plugs, are most susceptible to high soluble salt levels. Plant species vary greatly in their sensitivity to high soluble salt levels with some species being particularly susceptible, such as African violets, and others being tolerant, such as poinsettias (Fig. 6-5).

High soluble salt levels can occur either from the overapplication of fertilizers or through inadequate leaching. Many ions, such as NO_3^- or Mg^{2+}, are absorbed by the plant. Other ions, such as Cl^- or Na^+, are not absorbed in high quantities and tend to accumulate in the medium. The problem is best prevented by reducing fertilizer rates or by irrigating with unfertilized water as often as required. For example, many growers routinely use CLF during the week and unfertilized water every weekend, once every 2 weeks, or once every sixth irrigation, depending on the desired

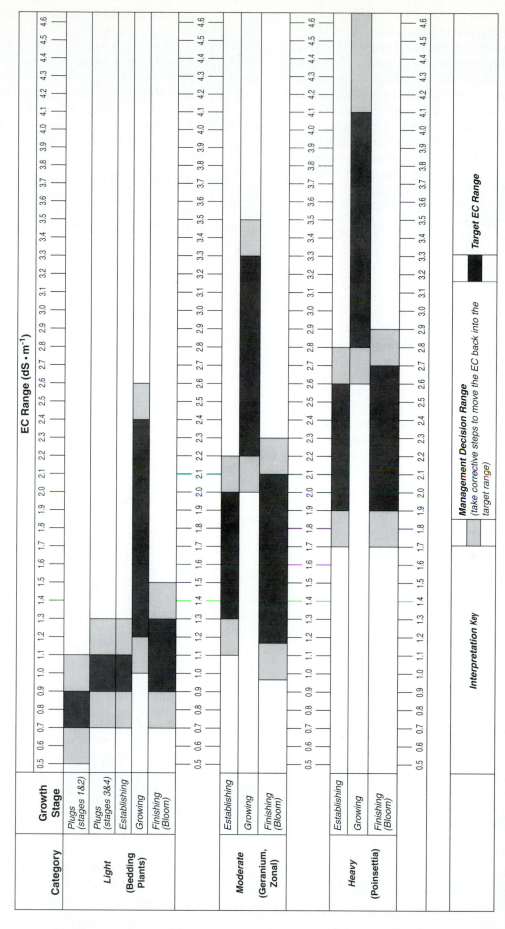

FIGURE 6-5 Suggested media pour-through EC ranges for floriculture crops grown in soilless media, assuming less than 30% of N is ammoniacal. These values are guidelines only and should be based on the actual growing conditions (Whipker, 2001).

medium EC. Growers can also control the problem by regularly overirrigating by 10 to 20%; however, this practice is less desirable due to pollution and the wasted water and fertilizer. Growers with high soluble salt levels in the irrigation water before fertilizers are added will have greater difficulty controlling soluble salts (see Chapter 5, Water). Once the problem has occurred, the only control is through leaching, which is most effective if plants are irrigated with two applications of unfertilized water within 2 to 4 hours of each other.

Not only should total soluble salts be considered, but also the change in soluble salt concentration over time. As the medium dries, the concentration increases. These short-term episodes of high soluble salt levels may reduce plant growth and plant quality. Growers with chronic soluble salt problems should avoid excessive drying of the medium.

MONITORING NUTRITION

Growers always need to vigilantly monitor the nutritional status of their crops. The natural variations in weather, irrigation frequency, leaching, water quality, media nutrient content, and plant growth will combine to make each crop unique.

VISUAL

The simplest monitoring method is to visually assess the crop, which is best done by an experienced grower. Visual monitoring is not effective by itself in the long term. By the time symptoms are noted, damage has already occurred to the crop, reducing quality and sales. For most crops, plant growth slows as the nutrient level drops, but actual deficiency symptoms may not be visible yet. Thus, plant quality may decrease before the grower is aware of any nutritional problems. Visual monitoring of the plants alone may not be adequate to produce the highest plant quality.

pH AND EC TESTS

The next monitoring method is to routinely track media pH and EC levels using pH and EC meters. Although sample pH and EC monitoring charts are provided in Figure 6-6, each firm should develop its own. The best results are obtained when the same person conducts the tests each time. Preferably that person should not be the owner, manager, or grower because they are often unable to regularly perform the tests due to time constraints.

A variety of pH and EC measuring devices are available from greenhouse supply firms. Meters can range from approximately $50 to several hundred dollars. Meters should be calibrated regularly with solutions of a known pH and EC. Such solutions can also be purchased.

Four methods are currently available for testing media pH and EC in-house: (1) dilution, (2) pour-through, (3) press, and (4) saturated media extract.

DILUTION. With the dilution method, the medium is mixed with distilled water in a 1:2 or 1:5 ratio, stirred well, allowed to stand 30 to 60 min, and pH and EC are then recorded (Table 6-3). Filtering to remove media particles will improve the accuracy of the readings but is not necessary. For consistency, the medium should be air dried first and a standard amount of water added to the sample. However, many growers do not do this. When using a moist medium, be sure that it has not been recently watered and is not wet. A greater amount of water in the medium will dilute the ions and reduce the EC reading compared with air-dried samples. This problem is not as great using a 1:5 dilution.

Usually 1/4 to 1/2 cup (50 to 100 mL) of medium is sufficient. A core of medium from top to bottom of the pot should be taken and the upper 0.5 in. (1.8 cm) discarded. Soluble salts are usually high in the upper layer of the medium and roots do not normally grow there. For plugs and bedding plant flats with small cells, it is easiest to harvest the entire root ball because taking a core is impractical. Extra plug flats may need to be grown to provide flats for sampling. In addition, the nutrient content of plug media changes rapidly due to leaching or plant nutrient uptake. Plug media samples should be collected 1 to 2 hr after fertilization to provide the most reliable and accurate assessment of plug media nutrient content (Compton and Nelson, 1997).

Small subsamples should be taken randomly from at least five pots, flats, baskets, or locations in the ground beds and combined. The greater the number of subsamples, the more reliable the results and the more likely the results will accurately reflect the status of the entire crop. Taking subsamples from only a few plants on the edge of the bench may lead to inaccurate results and poor decisions. The samples should be taken from plants that have been similarly produced. Different production conditions such as pot size, nutritional regime, temperature, or even cultivar may result in variable test results.

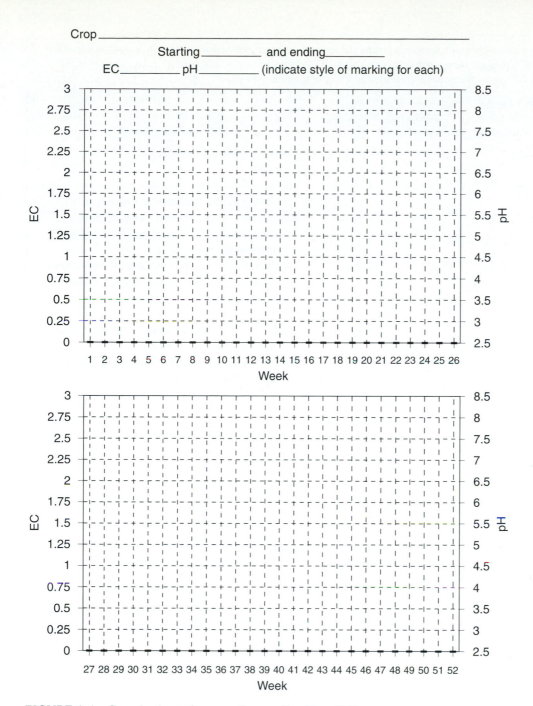

Crop _____

Starting _____ and ending _____

EC _____ pH _____ (indicate style of marking for each)

Week (1–26)

Week (27–52)

FIGURE 6-6 Sample charts for recording media pH and EC.

POUR-THROUGH. The pour-through method is quicker than the dilution and the saturated medium extract methods because no media samples are collected. The pour-through method involves applying sufficient distilled water to the medium surface of a plant to collect enough runoff to test, usually 1/4 to 1/2 cup (50 to 100 mL) (Cavins et al., 2001; Wright, 1986) (Table 6-3). The pot, cell pack, or basket is placed over a water collection tray or saucer.

A saucer with upward projections will allow the pot to drain and allow the person to start another test. The pour-through method has the same precautions about ensuring that the media samples are of similar moisture content as with the dilution method. Generally, 3.0 to 5.2 dS·m^{-1} is suitable for established plants (Lang, 1996). Finally, each reading using the pour-through method is from only one container. Readings from several containers, at least five,

TABLE 6-3

Interpretation of media soluble salt concentrations (EC) using various extraction methods. Values are in dS·m^{-1}; 1 dS·m^{-1} = 1 mS·cm^{-1} (EC meters commonly use this unit) = 1 mmho/cm = 100 mmho × 10^{-5}/cm = 1000 µmho/cm = 640 to 700 ppm. Recommendations for specific species may vary.

1:5 Media: Water Suspension	1:2 Media: Water Suspension	Saturated Media Extract	Pour-Through/ Press	Interpretation/Action
0–0.11	0–0.25	0–0.75	0–1.0	Low—increase nutrient levels for optimum growth.
0.12–0.35	0.26–0.75	0.76–2.0	1.0–2.5	Low to satisfactory—suitable for seedlings, many bedding plants, and salt-sensitive plants.
0.36–0.65	0.76–1.25	2.1–3.5	2.6–4.6	Satisfactory—maintain this range for most established plants; upper limit for species sensitive to soluble salts.
0.66–0.89	1.26–1.75	3.5–5.0	4.7–6.5	High—may be okay for most established plants, but may be damaging to sensitive plants; reduce fertilization rate and/or leach lightly once.
0.9–1.1	1.76–2.25	5.0–6.0	6.6–7.8	Very high—potentially damaging to most plants; leach heavily at least twice.
1.1 +	2.25 +	6.0 +	7.8 +	Extreme-most crops will be damaged; leach heavily at least twice.

within each crop should be taken and averaged to provide accurate results representative of the entire crop.

PRESS. The press method was developed as an easy way to sample plug media (Scoggins et al., 2000, 2001, 2002) (Table 6-3). The surface of the plug is pressed, forcing the media water solution out in a cup. Each plug will produce two to three drops of solution; one row of plugs should provide sufficient solution to measure the pH and EC. Collect separate samples from at least five flats to gauge the status of the crop. For best results, the samples should be collected 1 to 2 hr after fertigation.

SATURATED MEDIA EXTRACT. The saturated media extract (SME) is the most complex test to administer and requires an experienced person to conduct it. The SME is, however, considered to be the most reliable because the moisture content and amount of media have no effect on the results. The SME method is most commonly used by commercial laboratories (Table 6-3). Distilled water is added to 1 pt (470 mL) of medium until the medium is just saturated. There should be little or no water standing on the surface of the medium but the medium is saturated. Determination of when the medium is saturated requires experience, especially with soilless media. The medium is allowed to stand for 30 min and the water is drained using a vacuum filter. Media samples are collected as directed previously.

MEDIA TESTS

At times growers need to know the individual nutrient levels in the medium in addition to the pH and EC. In-house nutrient measuring methods include color reaction or paper test strip kits and ion meters. Color reaction kits can be used to determine the levels of N, P, K, Ca, and Mg in the greenhouse medium water solution. Ion meters, similar in operation to EC meters, are not readily available and are relatively expensive. Ion meters can be used to determine the level of nitrate-nitrogen, potassium, and other ions. At this time the ease and relatively low cost of commercial media testing has restricted widespread use of in-house nutrient testing.

Media testing by a professional laboratory is relatively inexpensive and will provide levels of macronutrients in addition to pH and EC. Some laboratories may also be able to determine certain micronutrient levels. It is important to use the same laboratory for all media testing because results can vary slightly between labs due to different handling and analysis procedures. Also, when choosing a laboratory select one that is prompt in returning results. Media tests are only a "snapshot in time" and the nutrient status of a crop is dynamic. Therefore, the usefulness of tests will diminish if the results are not returned and used promptly to make changes in the nutrient regimes.

Many firms have a routine media testing program and send samples to a laboratory each week. For preventive purposes, samples should be taken (1) when a new medium is being used, (2) halfway through any large crop, and (3) regularly, such as every month or two, if the crop is on a year-round rotation or long term, for example, ground beds or stock plants. For an especially valuable crop, samples should be analyzed every 2 to 3 weeks. Of course, samples can be taken any time visual symptoms indicate that a nutritional problem may be involved. In such cases, a sample taken from a healthy symptomless plant serves as a comparison.

Although most laboratories require at least 1 pt (470 mL) of medium, some request more. Samples are taken in the same manner as described for in-house pH and EC testing. Interpretation of media test results requires guidelines with which to compare the results. The analysis provided by the commercial laboratories will be useful initially, but these are general guidelines and the optimum nutrient levels for a particular crop or production environment may be different. If nutritional problems are suspected, media from healthy plants and from problem plants should be tested to allow comparison. Over time, the results from the healthy plants will allow for the development of specific nutrient level guidelines for a firm.

When studying the results of a medium test, the first datum to check is the pH. The pH strongly affects the availability of nutrients and some nutrient problems may be due to excessively high or low pH. Nutrients may be present in the medium but not available to the plant due to high or low pH. Altering the pH may correct the initial problem. The second datum to check is the EC level (Table 6-3). Again, correcting high or low EC problems by leaching or applying additional fertilizers, respectively, may be all that is needed. Finally, the last data to check are the individual nutrient levels, which should be within acceptable nutrient ranges and should be in balance with each other. For example, Ca levels may be adequate in the medium but the presence of high Mg levels may result in Ca deficiency in the plant.

TISSUE TESTS

Tissue tests have the advantage of being more accurate than media tests. The results indicate nutrient levels actually in the plant versus nutrient levels in the medium. Tissue tests also include most micronutrients and sodium, which can be of concern in areas of the country with high amounts of sodium in the water. However, tissue tests do not include media pH and EC levels and a medium test should be sent with the tissue test. Together the two tests will provide a complete description of the nutritional situation.

Harvest approximately 1 oz (28 g) of leaf tissue, without petioles; up to 60 or 70 leaves may need to be harvested if the leaves are small. With small plugs or cuttings, the entire plant may be harvested. Samples should be randomly harvested from as many plants as possible. If the leaves have media, fertilizer, or pesticide residue, gently wash or dip foliage in distilled water, blot, and air dry. Do not vigorously wash the leaves because nutrients may be leached out. In some cases, a mild detergent may be added to the water to aid in the removal of substances not easily washed off. The commercial lab will have more information on washing or soaking and when it is appropriate. The leaves should not be sent wet because they may rot and deteriorate by the time the lab can handle them.

As with media tests, tissue harvesting and handling need to be consistent from one sampling date to the next. Most tissue test standards are based on the "most recently mature leaf"—the youngest leaf that is fully expanded (Table 6-4). The recommended tissue to harvest may be different for some crops. It is important to properly select the appropriate leaf tissue because nutrient levels can vary greatly depending on the position from which the leaves are harvested (Fig. 6-7). The laboratory can advise which tissue to harvest. If a specific problem is being addressed, harvest tissue from the same location on both symptomatic and healthy plants.

CORRECTING NUTRITIONAL PROBLEMS

DEFICIENCIES

Nitrogen, phosphorus, and potassium deficiencies can be readily corrected by increasing the rate of CLF or by applying a drench of a fertilizer high in the specific nutrient needed. If either a Ca or Mg deficiency is indicated, apply a drench of calcium nitrate or magnesium sulfate, respectively. If the calcium deficiency is related to environmental conditions, increase transpiration by increasing air movement or

TABLE 6-4

Tissue nutrient levels of high-quality plants (Armitage 1994; Armitage and Laushman, 2003; Chase and Poole, 1987; Dole and Wilkins, 1988; Giffith; 1998; Joiner et al., 1981; Mills and Jones, 1996; Peterson, 1982b; Poole et al., 1991; Whipker and Dasoju, 1997). Note that the indicated values are only general recommendations. The optimum values will vary among firms because of different cultural practices, climate, and cultivars.

Species	%					ppm				
	N	P	K	Ca	Mg	Fe	Mn	Zn	Cu	B
Achillea millefolium	2.8–3.1	0.3–0.4	5.1–5.6	0.8–0.9	0.2–0.4	127–135	60–70	40–50	—	25–35
Adiantum	1.5–2.5	0.4–0.8	2.0–3.0	0.2–0.3	0.2–0.4	—	—	—	—	—
Aechmea	1.5–2.0	0.4–0.7	1.5–2.5	0.5–1.0	0.4–0.8	—	—	—	—	—
Aeschynanthus radicans	1.5–2.8	0.2–0.8	2.5–3.3	0.6–1.6	0.2–0.5	50–300	40–300	25–200	9–30	25–50
Aglaonema	2.7–3.5	0.2–0.8	2.7–5.0	1.0–2.0	0.3–0.6	50–300	50–300	25–200	10–100	25–50
Allamanda cathartica	2.0–4.0	0.2–1.0	2.0–4.0	0.7–1.5	0.2–1.0	50–200	50–200	20–200	8–25	25–75
Aloe arborescens	2.3–3.3	0.4–0.6	3.7–5.2	1.5–1.6	0.6–1.2	51–104	72–471	32–59	4–6	26–46
Alpinia purpurata	2.2–2.7	0.3–0.4	2.5–3.3	0.8–1.4	0.4–0.5	30–50	215–530	75–175	10–20	10–20
Alstroemeria	3.8–7.6	0.3–0.7	3.7–4.8	0.6–1.5	0.2–0.6	175–275	60–200	35–110	5–15	5–50
Amsonia tabernaemontana	2.6–2.9	0.2–0.3	2.2–2.4	0.6–1.4	0.1–0.3	50–52	445–896	116–335	3–5	36–108
Antirrhinum	1.0–5.3	0.2–0.6	2.2–4.1	0.5–1.4	0.5–1.0	70–135	60–185	30–55	5–15	20–40
Aphelandra	2.0–3.0	0.2–0.4	1.2–2.0	0.6–2.0	0.5–1.0	50–300	50–300	20–200	10–50	35–45
Artemisia 'Powis Castle'	3.8–4.0	0.4–0.7	3.4–4.0	1.1–1.2	0.1–0.3	72–91	140–244	84–149	9–19	39–49
Asparagus	1.5–2.5	0.3–0.5	2.0–3.0	0.1–0.3	0.1–0.3	—	—	—	—	—
Asplenium nidus	1.4–3.2	0.3–0.5	2.5–4.2	0.5–1.0	0.3–0.5	25–300	25–300	20–100	3–20	15–50
Aster	2.2–3.1	0.2–0.7	3.3–3.7	1.0–1.7	0.2–0.4	162–180	65–273	26–121	—	37–46
Astilbe chinensis	2.9–4.5	0.5–0.7	1.8–2.3	1.9–3.0	0.1–0.3	115–310	90–165	25–40	5–10	20–35
Begonia ×hiemalis	3.4–4.6	0.4–0.8	2.0–3.5	0.7–2.4	0.3–0.8	80–390	35–190	20–30	5–10	35–130
B. Semperflorens-Cultorum hybrids	2.2–5.6	0.3–0.6	3.4–4.2	0.7–4.2	0.4–1.0	100–260	90–355	50–65	10–15	30–40
Bougainvillea	2.5–4.5	0.2–0.8	3.0–5.5	1.0–2.0	0.2–0.8	50–300	50–200	20–200	8–50	25–75
Bouvardia hybrids	4.2–4.9	0.6–1.0	1.9–3.3	2.0–2.4	0.5–0.8	125–225	30–95	40–65	—	30–55
Caladium	3.6–4.9	0.4–0.7	2.3–4.1	1.1–1.6	0.1–0.3	65–90	110–135	125–135	5–10	95–145
Calathea louisae	3.0–3.3	0.3–0.5	2.6–3.4	0.4–0.5	1.1–1.3	—	—	—	—	—
C. makoyana	2.5–4.0	0.2–0.6	2.0–4.5	0.2–1.5	0.2–1.0	30–200	30–200	20–200	6–50	18–50
C. picturata	2.6–3.6	0.2–0.5	2.8–4.3	0.3–0.5	0.7–1.3	—	—	—	—	—
C. roseopicta	2.2–2.6	0.3–0.8	3.2–5.1	0.3–0.4	0.7–1.1	—	—	—	—	—
C. warscewiczii	2.8–3.8	0.3–0.5	3.1–3.4	0.5–0.8	0.9–1.1	—	—	—	—	—
Catharanthus roseus	4.9–5.4	0.4–0.5	2.9–3.6	1.4–1.6	0.4–0.5	95–150	165–300	40–45	5–10	25–40
Cattleya cultivars	1.0–2.5	0.1–0.8	2.0–4.2	0.5–2.0	0.3–0.7	50–200	40–200	25–200	5–20	25–75

Species									
Celosia argentea	3.7–4.1	0.4–1.1	3.9–5.1	2.9–4.1	1.4–4.1	90–190	260–900	180–240	15–25	25–50
Chamaedorea	2.5–3.5	0.1–0.3	1.6–2.8	1.0–2.5	0.2–0.8	50–300	50–250	25–200	6–50	25–60
Chlorophytum	1.5–2.5	0.1–0.3	3.5–5.0	1.0–2.0	0.3–1.0	50–200	50–200	20–200	8–100	20–50
Chrysalidocarpus	2.5–3.5	0.1–0.8	1.3–2.8	1.0–2.5	0.2–0.8	50–300	50–250	25–200	6–50	15–60
Chrysogonum virginianum	1.8–2.1	0.1–0.4	3.8–5.2	1.2–1.5	0.3–0.5	65–271	118–151	24–33	4–20	61–174
Codiaeum variegatum	2.2–5.5	0.2–0.6	2.5–5.5	0.9–2.5	0.4–0.8	50–200	25–315	20–150	5–50	16–75
Coffea	2.5–3.5	0.2–0.3	2.0–3.0	0.5–1.0	0.3–0.5	—	—	—	—	—
Cordyline terminalis	1.8–3.5	0.3–1.0	0.9–4.7	0.8–1.7	0.2–0.5	19–112	20–110	44–131	3–12	9–32
Coreopsis grandiflora	3.1–3.3	0.2–0.3	2.7–3.4	1.1–1.4	0.4–0.5	53–61	74–101	64–75	4–7	26–30
Crassula ovata	1.1–2.1	0.3–0.4	1.4–2.7	1.5–2.6	0.3–0.9	41–45	127–142	45–50	5–11	20–31
Crossandra infundibuliformis	3.0–4.0	0.2–0.4	3.0–4.0	1.2–1.6	0.4–0.6	—	—	—	—	—
Cyclamen	2.9–5.0	0.4–1.0	1.2–4.5	0.3–1.3	0.4–1.3	150–550	100–500	30–100	5–20	70–350
Cymbidium cultivars	1.3–2.5	0.1–0.8	2.0–3.5	0.4–2.0	0.2–0.7	25–200	30–200	20–200	5–25	20–75
Dendranthema	4.0–6.5	0.3–1.0	4.5–6.5	1.0–2.0	0.4–0.7	30–350	60–500	15–50	25–75	50–100
Dianthus	3.2–5.2	0.2–0.3	2.5–6.0	1.0–2.0	0.2–0.5	100–300	50–150	25–75	10–30	30–100
Dicentra eximia	3.7–5.3	0.6–0.7	2.2–3.2	0.3–0.7	0.1–0.4	74–79	891–1504	87–101	4–6	20–24
Dieffenbachia	3.3–5.0	0.2–0.8	2.5–5.5	1.0–2.5	0.2–0.8	60–300	50–300	20–201	8–50	20–50
Dracaena deremensis 'Janet Craig'	2.0–3.0	0.2–0.4	2.5–4.0	1.0–2.0	0.3–0.6	50–300	50–300	20–200	8–300	16–50
D. deremensis 'Warneckii'	2.0–3.0	0.2–0.4	2.5–4.0	1.0–2.0	0.3–0.6	50–300	50–300	20–200	8–300	16–50
D. fragrans 'Massangeana'	2.2–3.5	0.1–0.4	2.0–4.0	1.0–2.5	0.2–0.8	50–300	50–300	20–200	8–50	20–50
D. sanderiana	2.5–3.5	0.2–0.3	2.0–3.0	1.5–2.5	0.5–0.6	—	—	—	—	—
D. surculosa	1.5–2.5	0.2–0.3	1.0–2.0	1.0–1.5	0.3–0.5	—	—	—	—	—
Epipremnum	2.5–3.5	0.2–0.4	3.0–4.5	1.0–1.5	0.3–0.6	50–300	50–300	20–200	6–50	20–50
Euphorbia	4.0–6.0	0.3–0.6	1.5–3.5	0.7–1.8	0.3–1.0	100–300	60–300	25–60	2–10	25–75
E. milii var. *splendens*	2.0–4.0	0.2–1.0	1.5–4.0	1.0–2.5	0.2–1.0	50–200	25–200	20–200	10–50	25–100
Exacum	3.8–5.3	0.3–0.7	2.3–3.4	0.5–0.8	0.4–0.7	55–155	70–165	25–85	5–75	25–60
Ficus benjamina	1.8–2.5	0.1–0.2	1.0–1.5	2.0–3.0	0.4–0.8	—	—	—	—	—
F. elastica	1.3–2.25	0.1–0.5	0.6–2.1	0.3–1.2	0.2–0.5	30–200	20–200	15–200	8–100	20–50
F. lyrata	1.3–2.8	0.1–0.5	0.6–3.1	0.3–2.0	0.2–0.8	30–200	20–200	15–200	8–25	20–50
Foliage plants (general)	1.5–3.5	0.2–0.4	1.0–4.0	0.5–2.0	0.3–0.8	31–300	50–150	16–50	6–20	25–100
Freesia	2.7–5.6	0.4–1.2	3.1–5.9	0.4–1.0	0.3–1.8	80–115	30–540	40–110	5–130	30–100
Fuchsia	2.8–4.6	0.4–0.6	2.2–2.5	1.6–2.4	0.4–0.7	95–335	75–220	30–45	5–10	25–35
Gardenia augusta	1.5–3.0	0.1–0.4	1.0–3.0	0.5–1.3	0.3–1.0	60–250	50–250	20–150	5–40	25–70
Gerbera	2.7–4.1	0.3–0.7	3.1–3.9	0.4–4.2	0.3–2.8	60–130	30–260	19–80	2–10	19–50
Gladiolus hybrids	3.0–5.5	0.2–1.0	2.5–4.0	0.5–4.5	0.1–0.3	50–200	50–200	20–200	5–20	25–100
Gloxinia	3.3–3.8	0.3–0.5	4.5–5.0	1.5–2.2	0.4–0.5	70–150	95–170	20–35	5–20	30–35
Guzmania lingulata	1.9–2.2	0.1–0.5	2.9–3.5	0.5–1.0	0.2–0.4	55–115	45–85	10–25	4–15	30–250

(continued)

115

TABLE 6-4 *(continued)*

Species	%					ppm				
	N	P	K	Ca	Mg	Fe	Mn	Zn	Cu	B
Gynura aurantiaca	3.2–3.8	0.5–0.8	4.1–5.6	1.2–1.6	0.7–1.0	86–168	192–239	34–48	8–14	41–62
Hedera helix	2.5–4.5	0.2–0.9	1.5–4.5	1.0–2.0	0.2–0.7	50–375	50–200	20–100	5–25	20–50
Helianthus annuus	5.0–6.0	0.7–0.8	5.4–6.3	22–25	0.6–0.8	—	67–99	77–115	6–8	43–53
Heliotropium arborescens	3.3–3.8	0.7–0.8	4.6–5.1	2.1–2.4	0.5–0.8	174–314	105–122	77–81	11–13	35–38
Helleborus foetidus	1.8–2.9	0.1–0.4	1.5–2.0	0.7–2.1	0.2–0.6	34–52	47–77	15–33	2–8	19–25
H. hybrids	1.7–3.0	0.2–0.4	2.5–3.1	0.7–2.6	0.2–0.4	31–41	34–103	16–31	1–3	15–20
Hemerocallis cultivars	2.3–3.7	0.2–0.5	2.2–3.0	0.4–1.6	0.1–0.4	41–137	49–494	21–41	3–8	17–35
Heuchera sanguinea	1.2–1.5	0.1–0.3	1.0–1.3	1.4–2.3	0.2–0.3	30–53	13–26	15–32	1–4	21–39
Hibiscus	2.5–3.0	0.2–1.0	1.5–3.0	1.0–2.0	0.2–1.0	50–200	40–200	20–200	6–200	25–100
Hosta fortunei	1.4–2.6	0.2–0.4	1.6–4.5	1.1–2.1	0.1–0.3	57–263	34–179	16–24	2–5	13–19
H. lancifolia	1.8–2.1	0.2–0.4	1.4–2.5	1.0–1.9	0.2–0.4	69–149	91–157	13–20	2–4	15–18
H. plantaginea	1.6–1.7	0.3–0.5	1.9–2.3	0.5–0.6	0.1–0.2	35–39	40–48	14–21	2–4	12–15
H. sieboldii	1.7–2.2	0.2–0.4	1.5–2.0	0.8–1.2	0.2–0.5	117–195	101–176	19–27	3–5	10–15
H. undulata	1.3–3.5	0.2–0.4	1.5–3.3	0.4–1.9	0.2–0.5	62–350	40–441	11–30	2–10	12–17
Hydrangea	2.0–3.8	0.3–2.5	2.5–6.3	0.8–1.5	0.2–0.4	85–115	100–345	50–105	5–10	20–25
Hylotelephium spectabile	0.8–4.1	0.3–0.7	1.3–3.3	1.4–2.7	0.2–0.7	58–69	63–99	47–119	6–10	19–27
H. 'Autumn Joy'	1.7–2.5	0.3–0.5	1.8–3.0	2.7–3.1	0.4–0.5	33–201	51–94	51–94	6–9	24–31
Iberis sempervirens	3.0–3.7	0.4–0.5	3.2–4.5	0.9–1.1	0.3–0.6	98–424	60–113	118–194	6–10	32–41
Impatiens walleriana	3.9–5.3	0.6–0.8	1.8–3.5	2.8–3.3	0.6–0.8	405–885	50–490	65–70	10–15	45–105
I. hawkeri	3.3–4.6	0.3–0.8	1.2–2.7	0.7–2.7	0.3–0.8	75–300	100–250	40–85	5–14	40–80
Iris ensata	1.3–3.6	0.3–0.6	2.3–5.0	0.6–2.0	0.2–0.4	27–48	228–501	37–59	2–9	26–36
I. tectorum	1.0–1.9	0.5–0.6	2.7–3.5	1.2–1.5	0.3–0.4	44–59	81–139	8–12	1–3	13–16
Ixora coccinea	1.8–3.0	0.1–1.0	1.0–2.5	0.8–2.0	0.2–1.0	65–250	20–200	20–200	10–50	25–100
Jasminum	2.0–4.0	0.1–0.5	1.3–2.5	0.7–1.5	0.2–1.0	50–200	40–200	20–200	10–50	25–75
Kalanchoe	2.5–5.0	0.2–0.5	2.0–4.8	1.1–4.5	0.4–1.0	75–200	60–250	25–80	5–20	30–60
Lamium galeobdolon	3.2–3.8	0.2–1.0	3.9–4.2	1.2–2.2	0.4–0.7	70–117	98–225	21–24	5–9	27–58
Leea coccinea	2.2–3.3	0.2–0.6	1.5–2.8	0.6–2.0	0.2–0.8	30–300	20–200	10–100	8–30	15–50
Liatris	2.7–3.3	0.2–0.3	1.2–2.3	1.1–1.5	0.4–0.5	200–230	160–180	85–95	—	20–35
Lilium	2.4–4.0	0.1–0.7	2.0–5.0	0.2–4.0	0.3–2.0	100–250	50–250	30–70	5–25	20–25
Limonium sinuatum	3.4–6.0	0.3–1.0	3.0–7.3	0.5–1.6	0.5–2.1	50–355	35–200	25–90	5–25	20–50
Mandevilla × amabilis	1.9–3.0	0.2–0.5	2.0–4.0	0.8–1.5	0.2–0.5	50–200	25–200	20–200	8–40	25–75
Maranta	2.0–3.0	0.2–0.5	3.0–5.5	0.6–1.5	0.2–1.0	50–300	50–200	20–200	8–50	25–50
Monstera	2.5–3.5	0.2–0.4	3.0–4.5	0.4–1.0	0.3–0.6	—	—	—	—	—

Murraya paniculata	2.0–3.0	0.2–0.5	1.7–3.5	0.8–1.5	0.2–0.4	60–350	50–250	25–200	7–50	25–50
Nephrolepsis exaltata	2.1–3.0	0.3–0.7	1.6–3.8	0.4–2.5	0.3–1.0	25–300	25–200	30–65	5–35	20–70
Nolina recurvata	1.5–2.1	0.1–0.5	1.7–3.0	0.5–2.0	0.2–0.5	40–200	25–200	25–75	3–25	12–35
Oncidium cultivars	1.5–2.1	0.2–0.6	2.2–4.0	0.7–1.1	0.3–0.5	15–65	240–775	20–110	3–65	10–25
Pandanus veitchii	1.0–1.7	0.1–0.3	1.5–2.9	0.6–0.9	0.2–0.4	17–33	27–45	32–46	5–18	13–15
Paphiopedilum cultivars	2.2–3.5	0.2–0.7	2.0–3.5	0.8–2.0	0.2–0.8	50–200	50–200	25–200	5–20	25–75
Pelargonium × domesticum	3.0–3.2	0.3–0.6	1.1–3.1	1.2–2.6	0.3–0.9	120–225	115–475	35–50	5–10	15–45
P. × hortorum, cutting	3.8–4.4	0.3–0.5	2.6–3.5	1.4–2.0	0.2–0.4	110–580	270–325	50–55	5–15	40–50
P. × hortorum seed	3.7–4.8	0.4–0.7	2.5–3.9	0.8–2.1	0.2–0.5	120–200	110–285	35–60	5–15	35–60
P. peltatum	3.4–4.4	0.4–0.7	2.8–4.7	0.9–1.4	0.2–0.6	115–270	40–175	10–45	5–15	30–100
Peperomia argyreia	2.9–3.8	0.8–0.9	3.3–5.3	0.6–0.8	0.3–0.8	63–64	202–275	14–41	5–12	23–25
P. caperata	3.3–3.4	0.5–0.9	2.7–6.0	0.6–0.9	0.5–1.0	40–55	153–160	31–66	5–12	25–42
P. dahlstedtii	2.1–3.6	0.7–1.4	3.6–5.2	0.8–1.1	0.8–1.0	93–171	217–310	38–107	6–14	44–48
P. obtusifolia	2.0–4.5	0.2–1.0	2.0–6.5	1.5–4.0	0.4–1.5	50–300	50–300	25–200	7–40	25–50
Petunia	2.8–5.8	0.5–1.2	3.5–5.5	0.6–4.8	0.3–1.4	40–700	90–185	30–90	5–15	20–50
Phalaenopsis cultivars	2.0–3.5	0.2–0.8	3.9–7.1	1.5–2.8	0.4–1.1	75–200	100–250	20–200	5–25	25–75
Philodendron	2.5–4.5	0.3–0.5	2.0–3.8	1.0–2.5	0.2–0.6	60–200	40–200	26–100	8–100	20–50
Phlox paniculata	3.3–3.9	0.4–0.6	2.4–2.9	1.4–2.4	0.2–0.6	49–142	72–150	81–171	4–10	28–39
Pilea cadierei	2.3–2.5	0.3–0.6	1.8–2.2	2.9–3.8	1.6–1.8	59–66	79–86	39–41	8–12	63–83
P. involucrata	2.0–3.5	0.3–0.5	1.5–3.0	2.0–2.5	1.2–1.4	—	—	—	—	—
Primula	2.5–3.3	0.4–0.8	2.1–4.2	0.6–1.0	0.2–0.4	78–155	50–90	40–45	5–10	30–35
Rhododendron	2.0–3.0	0.2–0.5	1.0–1.6	0.5–1.6	0.2–0.5	50–300	60–150	26–60	5–15	31–100
Rosa	3.5–4.5	0.2–0.3	2.0–2.5	1.0–1.5	0.2–0.4	70–120	80–120	20–40	7–15	40–60
Rumohra adiantiformis	2.0–2.8	0.2–0.4	2.3–3.4	0.3–0.7	0.2–0.4	100–400	40–150	30–150	10–30	25–75
Saintpaulia	2.2–2.7	0.2–0.9	1.5–6.0	0.6–1.7	0.7–1.1	70–320	35–490	20–80	5–30	30–200
Salvia	3.0–4.5	0.3–0.7	3.5–5.0	1.5–2.5	0.3–0.6	60–300	30–280	25–115	10–35	25–75
Sansevieria	1.7–3.0	0.1–0.4	2.0–3.0	1.0–2.0	0.3–0.6	50–300	50–300	25–100	10–100	20–50
Saxifraga stolonifera	2.0–3.7	0.6–1.2	2.1–2.7	1.7–3.7	0.4–0.7	74–177	19–34	33–108	3–10	14–19
Schefflera (Brassaia)	2.5–3.5	0.2–0.5	2.3–4.0	1.0–1.5	0.2–0.8	50–300	50–300	20–200	10–60	20–60
S. (Dizygotheca)	2.0–2.5	0.4–0.3	1.5–2.5	0.5–1.0	0.2–0.3	—	—	—	—	—
Schlumbergera	2.7–3.7	0.5–0.9	6.2–7.0	0.7–0.9	1.6–2.2	105–110	35–130	50–65	10–15	65–70
Sinningia speciosa	3.0–5.0	0.2–0.7	2.5–5.0	1.0–3.0	0.3–0.7	50–200	50–300	20–50	5–25	25–50
Solenostemon scutellarioides	3.0–3.9	1.1–1.3	3.7–4.8	1.5–1.7	1.3–1.5	50–80	310–350	35–50	10–15	29–32
Solidago	2.7–3.6	0.3–0.5	3.8–4.7	0.9–1.2	0.3–0.4	190–210	115–282	25–68	—	24–30
Spathiphyllum	3.3–5.0	0.2–1.0	2.3–6.0	0.8–2.0	0.2–1.0	50–300	40–300	25–200	6–40	20–70
Spigelia marilandica	2.2–2.7	0.2–0.5	2.5–3.0	1.0–2.0	0.5–1.5	88–128	188–394	26–46	4–24	31–49
Stachys byzantina	2.4–5.5	0.3–0.4	2.3–3.4	0.4–0.7	0.2–0.3	108–139	88–271	37–42	2–6	14–26
Strelitzia reginae	1.0–2.5	0.2–0.4	1.5–3.0	0.3–3.0	0.1–0.8	35–200	45–200	20–200	5–30	10–75

(continued)

TABLE 6-4 *(continued)*

Species	%					ppm				
	N	P	K	Ca	Mg	Fe	Mn	Zn	Cu	B
Streptocarpus	2.0–3.5	0.1–0.7	4.8–5.5	1.2–1.9	0.3–0.5	90–260	130–300	85–130	15–20	55–65
Stromanthe amabilis	2.5–3.0	0.2–0.5	3.0–4.0	0.1–0.2	0.3–0.5	—	—	—	—	—
S. sanguinea	2.0–2.2	0.5–1.2	3.2–3.8	0.3–0.5	0.3–0.5	50–59	169–282	23–33	4–6	16–21
Syngonium	2.5–3.5	0.2–0.3	3.0–4.5	0.4–1.0	0.3–0.6	—	—	—	—	—
Tagetes patula	3.3–3.6	0.5–0.6	2.8–2.9	2.4–2.7	1.3–1.4	90–115	275–560	75–100	20–25	35–40
Teucrium chamaedrys	1.7–2.9	0.1–0.4	1.7–2.9	0.2–0.7	0.1–0.2	35–48	92–147	34–103	5–16	26–38
Thalictrum flavum ssp. *glaucum*	3.1–4.3	0.4–0.9	2.2–3.2	0.7–1.6	0.2–0.3	38–54	37–48	48–81	4–8	25–31
Thymus ×citriodorus	2.7–3.1	0.2–0.4	2.3–3.6	0.4–0.9	0.3–0.4	73–134	38–204	50–72	9–12	19–26
T. vulgaris	2.4–2.6	0.2–0.3	2.1–3.2	0.5–1.3	0.2–0.4	85–118	38–98	68–99	6–9	17–28
Torenia fournieri	5.1–5.3	0.5–0.6	2.4–2.9	1.3–1.5	0.9–1.0	150–190	320–350	120–130	10–15	40–50
Tripogandra multiflora	3.7–4.1	0.7–0.8	3.9–4.4	0.9–1.0	0.4–0.5	126–145	142–251	44–64	12–15	29–35
Verbena canadensis	2.7–4.0	0.4–0.8	2.2–4.8	1.1–1.3	0.5–0.8	76–142	59–124	59–141	9–23	37–48
V. ×hybrida	3.6–5.8	0.8–1.2	2.8–4.7	1.6–2.5	0.7–1.6	60–110	55–295	65–130	5–15	45–50
V. tenuisecta	2.2–3.0	0.3–0.5	2.2–2.9	1.1–1.8	0.5–0.7	131–204	66–100	77–285	13–16	25–29
Veronica longifolia	2.9–3.8	0.3–0.9	1.2–3.5	0.5–1.7	0.2–0.6	82–147	30–35	57–59	7	11–25
Viola ×wittrockiana	2.5–4.5	0.3–1.0	2.5–5.0	0.6–3.0	0.3–0.8	30–300	25–300	20–100	5–40	20–80
Yucca elephantipes	1.4–2.5	0.1–0.8	1.2–3.3	1.0–2.5	0.2–1.0	25–200	40–325	20–200	6–25	12–60
Zamia pumila	0.7–1.9	0.1–0.2	0.4–1.4	0.3–0.5	0.2–0.3	43–97	38–104	20–61	3–5	20–55

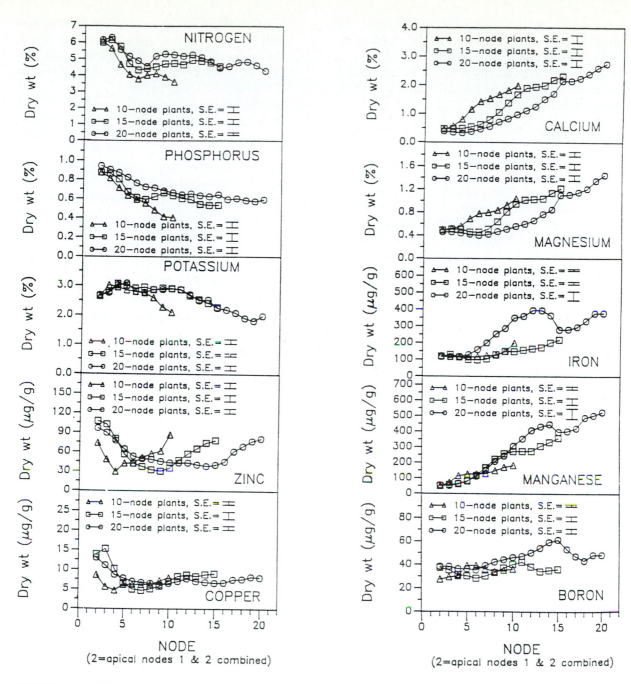

FIGURE 6-7 Effect of nodal position on nutrient levels in poinsettia leaves. Nutrient ion concentrations were found to be distributed within the plant in three patterns: (1) N, P, and K concentrations were higher in upper than lower leaves; (2) Ca, Mg, Fe, Mn, and B concentrations were higher in lower leaves than upper leaves; and (3) Cu and Zn concentrations were higher in both upper and lower leaves than in middle leaves (Dole and Wilkins, 1991).

decreasing humidity. Routine foliar spray of calcium chloride can be used as a preventive practice. Although S deficiency is rare, the deficiency can be readily corrected by drenching with any sulfate-containing compound such as magnesium or potassium sulfate.

With micronutrients, examine the pH first and adjust if needed (see pH section earlier in the chapter). Excessively high or low pH frequently causes micronutrient deficiencies. If the pH is acceptable, water-soluble micronutrient treatments can be applied. Often if only one element is deficient, a complete micronutrient mix can be applied because other micronutrients may also be low. However, do not apply a complete mix at the full rate if one has been used within 2 to 4 months. Consequently, the specific nutrient may need to be applied to correct the deficiency. Remember that micronutrients are usually difficult to leach, and the cure could lead to toxicities that would be more difficult to correct.

TOXICITIES

Toxicity problems rarely occur with the macronutrients and often appear first as soluble salt damage. The solution, of course, is to leach media with unfertilized water (see Soluble Salts section earlier in this chapter). Toxicity problems are most likely to occur with the micronutrients, which can also produce symptoms similar to those seen with high soluble salt levels. Routine monitoring of the media EC will help eliminate the possibility of a high soluble salts problem.

PROBLEM SOLVING

Nutritional problems are often difficult to diagnose because they appear similar to a wide variety of other insect- and disease-related or abiotic problems. The natural reaction of a grower is to act immediately and try to solve the problem as soon as possible. Although time is usually of essence, remember that a hastily made bad decision may cost more time and money than taking the time to logically analyze and solve the problem. Another common reaction is to call someone for help immediately. Again, time and money may be better served by obtaining as much information as possible before seeking outside help. The more information, including digital photographs, you can provide a technical adviser, the more likely that person will be to diagnose the problem correctly and give proper advice. Advice based on limited information can easily lead to the wrong conclusions and will greatly delay solving the problem.

PROBLEM-SOLVING STEPS

The following step-by-step process should be used to diagnose and correct a plant problem. Highly experienced growers who are skilled troubleshooters usually use a similar process intuitively—it just may not be apparent to others.

1. *Describe problem.* Check all parts of the plant including the undersides of leaves, the plant base, and the roots. Take a few notes or a digital picture for your records—if a similar problem occurs in the future, you will have a record to help you decide if it is the same problem. Digital images can also be sent to a technical adviser to help him or her diagnose the problem.
   A. How many plants are affected?
   B. Is there a pattern to the affected plants, such as cultivar, medium used, time planted, etc.?
   C. Are the symptoms changing and, if so, what is the progression?

2. *Compile crop history.* Take a few notes for the record. If a similar problem occurs in the future, the old notes may help you determine the cause of the current problem and remind you of what you did to fix the old problem. Why start over each time?
   A. Any insects or diseases present?
   B. Any chemicals used recently? If so, list.
      Pesticides?
      Plant growth regulators?
      Surfactants?
      Herbicides?
      Neighbors applied any chemicals?
   C. What have been the environmental conditions?
   D. Any extreme weather patterns?
   E. Any air pollutants, such as ozone, around?
   F. Are the heaters malfunctioning?
   G. Is motorized equipment (which could produce ethylene) being used in the area?
   H. Have any changes to normal procedures occurred?

3. *Collect data.* Take samples for in-house testing or external testing. Be sure to file the results with the problem description and crop history for future reference.
   A. Media pH and EC
   B. Water analysis
   C. Media nutrient analysis
   D. Tissue analysis

4. *Determine cause of problem.* Consider all possibilities; see Table 6-5 for assistance. Eliminate the options that obviously do not apply. Select the most likely choice, then try to prove or disprove it. If you disprove your first choice, go back to the table and select the next most likely choice. Repeat until the cause of the problem is determined.

5. *Take action!!* After the problem is solved, decide *now* what you are going to do to prevent the problem from occurring again.

TABLE 6-5

Common floriculture crop problems and possible causes (Dole et al., 2001).

Problems	Possible Causes
Foliage wilting	• Water stress • Root or crown rot • High medium EC • Vascular wilts from pathogens • Poor medium aeration • High levels of fungus gnat larvae • Water transpiration exceeding uptake (temporary condition, high light or warm temperatures after low light or cold temperatures)[a]
Lower/older foliage chlorotic, yellow or reddish	• High medium EC • Low medium pH • Plants spaced too close together • Fe or Mn toxicity • N, P (advanced), K, or Mg deficiency • Spider mites • Root or crown rot • Low light levels[a] • Ethylene damage[a] • Herbicide damage[a] • Root mealybugs[a]
Lower/older foliage purplish	• Cold production temperatures • P, N, or Zn deficiency • Root rot • Excessively wet medium
Lower/older foliage has marginal necrosis	• High medium EC • Fe, Mg, or Mn toxicity • K or P deficiency • Drought stress
Lower/older foliage curled up or down	• High medium EC • P, Mg, K, B, Cu deficiency • Ethylene damage • Drought stress
Lower/older foliage excessively large	• High N (esp. ammonium) or K level • Excessively warm production temperature • Excessive irrigation
Upper/young foliage chlorotic or yellow	• Fe, S, Ca, Mn (recently mature leaves), Zn, or Cu deficiency • High medium pH • Root rot • Excessively wet medium
Upper/young foliage has necrotic spots	• Ca, Cu, or B deficiency
Upper/young foliage curled up or down	• Ammonium toxicity • Ca, Zn, or B deficiency • Thrips or cyclamen mite damage • High medium EC[a] • Excessively high light intensity[a]
Upper/young foliage distorted	• Thrips • Ca or B deficiency • Nutrient toxicity • Cyclamen mite[a] • Ethylene damage[a] • Herbicide damage[a]

(continued)

TABLE 6-5 *(continued)*

Problems	Possible Causes
Foliage (over entire plant) has large yellow or necrotic patches	• Excessive light • S, Mn, or Zn deficiency • Excessive temperature • Wilting from water stress • Chemical phytotoxicity • Ethylene damage[a] • Herbicide damage[a]
Foliage (over entire plant) has necrotic spots	• K, Ca, S, or Zn deficiency • Foliar diseases • Drought stress • Chemical phytotoxicity • Ethylene damage[a] • Herbicide damage[a]
Foliage (over entire plant) has rings	• Diseases (viruses, bacteria, rusts) • Chemical phytotoxicity
Entire plant stunted	• N, P, K, S, Ca, or B deficiency • High medium EC • Low medium EC • Root rot • Poor medium aeration • Excessive plant growth regulator application • Low growing temperature
Slow growth, plant appears okay but is growing slowly	• Nutrient deficiency/insufficient fertilizer • Ca deficiency • High medium EC • Root rot • Production temperatures too cool • Excessive plant growth regulator application • Old plugs with excessive root growth
Excessively long internodes	• Excessive fertilization, esp. ammonium • Excessively high production temperature • Low light intensity • High plant density • Overgrown plugs
Excessive axillary shoot production (witches brooming)	• B or Zn deficiency • Diseases • Florel application • Herbicides • Broad mites[a]
Roots brown/necrotic	• Root rot • High medium EC • P, Fe, Ca, or B deficiency[a] • Excessive irrigation • Excessive medium temperature • Excessive drought stress
Stems/crowns have lesions	• High medium EC • Diseases (esp. fungal and bacterial) • Copper deficiency[a]
Lack of flowering/insufficient flowering	• Excessive watering • Excessive fertilization, especially ammonium • P, Cu, or B nutrient deficiency

TABLE 6-5 *(continued)*

Problems	Possible Causes
	• Improper flowering protocols, i.e., photoperiod, light intensity, cold treatments
	• Florel application
	• Excessive or late plant growth regulator application
	• Drought stress
	• Ethylene damage[a]
	• Plant still juvenile and unable to flower[a]
Flower buds turn brown/dry	• Ethylene damage
	• Excessive production temperature (esp. night temperature)
	• Florel application
	• Phytotoxicity
	• Disease (especially *Botrytis*)
	• Drought stress
	• B or Ca deficiency
Premature flowering	• Excessive fertilization
	• Chronic drought stress
	• N deficiency
	• Improper flowering protocols, i.e., photoperiod, light intensity, cold treatments
	• Plants propagated from stock plants with flowers already initiated or present
Poor seed germination	• High medium EC
	• Temperature too high or too low
	• Improper light level/covered too deep
	• Old, nonviable seed
	• Preemergent diseases
	• Mist too frequent or too infrequent
	• Insufficient medium aeration
Poor cutting rooting	• High substrate EC
	• Temperature too high or too low
	• Improper light level
	• Improper tissue age
	• Diseases
	• Mist too frequent or too infrequent
	• High tissue N content
	• Insufficient medium aeration
	• Presence of fungus gnat larvae
Poor postharvest life	• High medium EC
	• High medium N (esp. ammonium) at end of crop cycle
	• Insufficient medium aeration
	• Insufficient water
	• Low medium nutrient content
	• Ethylene exposure

[a]*Indicates options that occur less frequently or are limited to only a few species.*

CARBON DIOXIDE INJECTION

Many times crops do not reach optimum growth because of limiting factors—any component required for plant growth that is not at the optimum level such as water, light, temperature, nutrients, and carbon dioxide (CO_2). Bringing one factor into the optimum range will increase plant growth until another factor becomes limiting. Eventually all factors are optimum and plant growth is optimum. In greenhouses, CO_2 can become a limiting factor when temperature and light are adequate but the greenhouse is sealed to reduce heat loss, which occurs primarily during the winter. Research has shown that CO_2 levels higher than ambient (approximately 360 ppm) enhance plant growth for some species by increasing plant weight, stem strength, and stem length and decreasing total crop time. The increase in stem length may be partially accounted for by high day temperatures because growers tend to keep the greenhouse tight to prevent loss of the injected CO_2 and allow warmer day temperatures than if they were not injecting CO_2 (see DIF in Chapter 8, Plant Growth Regulation).

Carbon dioxide is injected during daylight when photosynthesis is occurring and during cool weather when vents are kept closed. In fact, plants may reduce the CO_2 levels below ambient in an enclosed environment. CO_2 is generated by the burning of propane or natural gas or by using liquid-solid CO_2 injectors. When using propane or natural gas CO_2 generation, the gas must be low in sulfur dioxide, which can be phytotoxic, and the burner should be periodically inspected to ensure efficient, clean burning. Incomplete combustion results in ethylene and carbon monoxide buildup; the former injures plants and, more importantly, the latter can harm people. Heat from the combustion of propane or natural gas can be used to heat water during the day which can then be used to heat the greenhouse at night. Such systems are generally cost effective only for large producers.

Monitoring of CO_2 injection is important to ensure that proper rates are maintained. Various devices are available ranging from handheld monitoring devices that use disposable indicators to fully automated systems that can be linked to computers.

Before implementing a CO_2 injection and monitoring system, consider the economics. Will the potential advantages of shorter crop times and higher plant quality balance the cost and the occasional need for more growth retardants? In general, the economics are sufficient with high-value crops, such as potted roses, in many parts of the world and with the use of supplemental photosynthetic lighting.

KEY POINTS

- The use of well-drained, soilless growing media has made nutrient management especially critical.
- Essential elements are those required by plants to complete their growth cycle and can be divided into two groups based on the general amounts used by plants: macronutrients—N, P, K, Ca, Mg, and S—and micronutrients—Fe, Mn, Zn, Cu, B, Mo, Ni, and Cl.
- Nitrogen is typically considered the most important of the essential elements and often is the basis for fertilizer recommendations.
- Two forms of nitrogen are important to plant growth: ammonium (NH_4^+) and nitrate (NO_3^-), both of which tend to influence media pH and type of growth obtained.

- Fertilizers are applied through incorporation in the media, fertigation through irrigation water, or a combination of both methods.
- Fertilizers can be incorporated in the media using various types of controlled-release fertilizers such as slowly soluble, plastic coated, urea formaldehyde, sulfur-coated fritted nutrients, and impregnated clays.
- Selection of a water-soluble fertilizer depends mainly on the desired media pH because some fertilizers tend to lower media pH and others tend to raise media pH.
- Concentrated stock solutions of water-soluble fertilizers are blended with irrigation water using various types of injectors.
- Media pH regulates availability of nutrients with high media pH-inducing deficiencies of micronutrients such as Fe, and low media pH-inducing deficiencies of Ca and Mg and toxicities of Fe, Mn, Zn, and Cu.

- Various methods are used to raise or lower media pH.
- Soluble salts are reported as electrical conductivity, EC, and a high EC can damage plants.
- High EC is reduced by lowering the fertilizer application rate or by leaching.
- Growers need to vigilantly monitor the status of their crops using pH and EC meters and water, media, and tissue tests.

- Media samples can be collected and tested using the dilution, pour-through, press, or saturated media extract methods.
- Insufficient carbon dioxide can limit growth in tightly enclosed greenhouses; CO_2 can be injected into the air.

BIBLIOGRAPHY

Albano, J.P., and W.B. Miller. 1996. Iron deficiency stress influences physiology of iron acquisition in marigold (*Tagetes erecta* L.). *Journal of the American Society for Horticultural Science* 121:438–441.

Argo, W.R., and J.A. Biernbaum. 1997. Lime, water source, and fertilizer nitrogen form affect medium pH and nitrogen accumulation and uptake. *HortScience* 32:71–74.

Armitage, A.M. 1994. Growing on, pp. 43–94 in *Ornamental Bedding Plants*. CAB International, Oxon, United Kingdom.

Armitage, A.M., and J.M. Laushman. 2003. *Specialty Cut Flowers*, 2nd ed. Timber Press, Portland, Oregon.

Bailey, D.A., P.V. Nelson, and W.C. Fonteno. 1997. Back to pH basics. *Greenhouse Grower* 15(8):21–22.

Bartok, J.W., Jr. 1997. Know fertigation options. *Greenhouse Management and Production* 17(3):46.

Biernbaum, J. 1997. Selecting blended water-soluble fertilizers. *Greenhouse Product News* 7(3):23–25, 29.

Broschat, T.K. 1997. Release rates of controlled-release and soluble magnesium fertilizers. *HortTechnology* 7:58–62.

Cabrera, R.I. 1997. Comparative evaluation of nitrogen release patterns from controlled-release fertilizers by nitrogen leaching analysis. *HortScience* 32:669–673.

Cavins, T.J., B.E. Whipker, W.C. Fonteno, and J.L. Gibson. 2001. Greenhouse substrate testing, pp. 31–36 in *Plant Root Zone Management*, B.E. Whipker, J.M. Dole, T.J. Cavins, J.L. Gibson, W.C. Fonteno, P.V. Nelson, D.S. Pitchay, and D.A. Bailey. North Carolina Flowers Growers' Association, Raleigh, North Carolina.

Chase, A.R., and R.T. Poole. 1987. Effect of fertilizer rate on growth of fibrous rooted begonia. *Florida Foliage* 13(3):4–5.

Cole, J.C., and J.M. Dole. 1997. Temperature and phosphorus source affect phosphorus retention by a pine bark-based container medium. *HortScience* 32:236–240.

Compton, A.J., and P.V. Nelson. 1997. Timing is crucial for plug seedling substrate testing. *HortTechnology* 7:63–68.

Dole, J.M., and H.F. Wilkins. 1988. University of Minnesota—Tissue analysis standards. *Minnesota State Florists Bulletin* 37(6):10–13.

Dole, J.M., and H.F. Wilkins. 1991. Relationship between nodal position and plant age on the nutrient composition of vegetative poinsettia leaves. *Journal of the American Society for Horticultural Science* 116:248–252.

Dole, J.M., J.L. Gibson, B.E. Whipker, P.V. Nelson, T.J. Cavins, and W.C. Fonteno, 2001. Problem solving, pp. 44–47 in *Plant Root Zone Managment*, B.E. Whipker, J.M. Dole, T.J. Cavins, J.L. Gibson, W.C. Fonteno, P.V. Nelson, D.S. Pitchay, and D.A. Bailey. North Carolina Flowers Growers' Association, Raleigh, North Carolina.

Griffith, L.P. Jr. 1998. *Tropical Foliage Plants*. Ball Publishing, Batavia, Illinois.

Hershey, D.R., and J.L. Paul. 1982. Leaching-losses of nitrogen from pot chrysanthemums with controlled-release or liquid fertilization. *Scientia Horticulturae* 17:145–152.

Husby, C.E., A.X. Niemiera, J.R. Harris, and R.D. Wright. 2003. Influence of diurnal temperature on nutrient release patterns of three polymer-coated fertilizers. *HortScience* 38:387–389.

Joiner, J.N., C.A. Conover, and R.T. Poole. 1981. Nutrition and fertilization, pp. 229–268 in *Foliage Plant Production*, J.N. Joiner, editor. Prentice Hall, Englewood Cliffs, New Jersey.

Koch, G.M., and E.J. Holcomb. 1983. Utilization of recycled irrigation water on marigolds fertilized with osmocote and constant liquid fertilization. *Journal of the American Society for Horticultural Science* 108:815–819.

Ku, C.S.M., and D.R. Hershey. 1997. Growth response, nutrient leaching, and mass balance for potted poinsettia. I. nitrogen. *Journal of the American Society for Horticultural Science* 122:452–458.

Lang, H.J. 1996. Growing media testing and interpretation, pp. 123–139 in *Water, Media and Nutrition for Greenhouse Crops*, D.W. Reed, editor. Ball Publishing, Batavia, Illinois.

Lang, H.J., C.L. Rosenfield, and D.W. Reed. 1990. Response of *Ficus benjamina* and *Dracaena marginata* to iron stress. *Journal of the American Society for Horticultural Science* 115:589–592.

Mancino, C.F., and J. Troll. 1990. Nitrate and ammonium leaching losses from N fertilizers applied to 'Penncross' creeping bentgrass. *HortScience* 25:194–196.

Mills, H.A., and J.B. Jones, Jr. 1996. *Plant Analysis Handbook*. MicroMacro Publishing, Athens, Georgia.

Morvant, J.K., J.M. Dole, and E. Allen. 1997. Irrigation systems alter distribution of roots, soluble salts, nitrogen, and pH in the root medium. *HortTechnology* 7:156–160.

Nelson, P.V. 1996. Macronutrient fertilizer programs, pp. 141–170 in *Water, Media and Nutrition for Greenhouse Crops*, D.W. Reed, editor. Ball Publishing, Batavia, Illinois.

Nelson, P.V. 2003. *Greenhouse Operation and Management*, 6th ed. Prentice Hall, Upper Saddle River, New Jersey.

Peterson, J.C. 1982a. Effects of pH upon nutrient availability in a commercial soilless root medium utilized for floral crop production, pp. 16–19 in *Ohio Agricultural Research and Development Center Research Bulletin 268*.

Peterson, J.C. 1982b. Monitoring and managing nutrition. IV. foliar analysis. *Ohio Florists Association Bulletin 632*.

Poole, R.T., A.R. Chase, and L.S. Osborne. 1991. *Dracaena. Foliage Plant Research Note RH-91-14*. Central Florida Research and Education Center, Apopka, Florida.

Scoggins, H.L., P.V. Nelson, and D.A. Bailey. 2000. Development of the press extraction method for plug substrate analysis: Effect of variable extraction force on pH, EC, and nutrient analysis. *HortTechnology* 10:367–369.

Scoggins, H.L., D.A. Bailey, and P.V. Nelson. 2001. Development of the press extraction method for plug substrate analysis: Quantitative relationships between solution extraction techniques. *HortScience* 36:918–921.

Scoggins, H.L., D.A. Bailey, and P.V. Nelson. 2002. Efficacy of the press extraction method for bedding plant plug nutrient monitoring. *HortScience* 37:108–112.

Simpson, B., A.E. Einert, and H.L. Hileman. 1975. Effects of osmocote application method on soil and plant nutrient levels and flowering of potted chrysanthemums. *Florists Review* 156(4032):27, 28, 68, 69.

Spinks, D.O., and W.L. Pritchett. 1956. The downward movement of phosphorus in potting soils as measured by P^{32}. *Proceedings of the Florida State Horticulture Society* 69:385–388.

van Iersel, M.W., R.B. Beverly, P.A. Thomas, J.G. Latimer, and H.A. Mills. 1998a. Fertilizer effects on the growth of impatiens, petunia, salvia, and vinca plug seedlings. *HortScience* 33:678–682.

van Iersel, M.W., P.A. Thomas, R.B. Beverly, J.G. Latimer, and H.A. Mills. 1998b. Nutrition affects pre- and posttransplant growth of impatiens and petunia plugs. *HortScience* 33:1014–1018.

Whipker, B.E. 2001. pH and EC basics, pp. 4–5 in *Plant Root Zone Management*, B.E. Whipker, J.M. Dole, T.J. Cavins, J.L. Gibson, W.C. Fonteno, P.V. Nelson, D.S. Pitchay, and D.A. Bailey. North Carolina Flowers Growers' Association, Raleigh, North Carolina.

Whipker, B., and S. Dasoju. 1997. Success with pot sunflowers. *GrowerTalks* 51(1):81–82.

Williams, K.A., and P.V. Nelson. 1996. Modifying a soilless root medium with aluminum influences phosphorus retention and chrysanthemum growth. *HortScience* 31:381–384.

Williams, K.A., and P.V. Nelson. 1997. Using precharged zeolite as a source of potassium and phosphate in a soilless container medium during potted chrysanthemum production. *Journal of the American Society for Horticultural Science* 122:703–708.

Wright, R.D. 1986. The pour-through nutrient extraction procedure. *HortScience* 21:227–228.

Chapter 7

Media

INTRODUCTION

A wise grower will invest much thought and money into developing or selecting suitable media. Media provide water, nutrients, and support for the plant. Roots require oxygen, so media must provide adequate gas exchange. Many growers believe the majority of problems that occur during production are linked to the growing medium and the roots. Consequently, growers will test several media to select one that works best for them. Growers should never use an untested medium for an entire crop because switching media often requires changing irrigation frequency and fertilizer regime.

PHYSICAL FACTORS

Growing a plant in the field is different from growing a plant in a container. Plants growing in containers have much less available water and nutrients, and media drainage is restricted. Growers must provide all the water and nutrients for container-grown plants at frequent intervals. Unfortunately, the more shallow the pot size, the more restricted the drainage (Fig. 7-1). This phenomenon is known as a *perched water table*, and in containers the bottom of the container represents the water table. The taller the container, the greater the gravitational pull downward on the water in the medium and the greater the aeration. The shorter the container, the closer the water table is to the medium surface. Very short containers, such as plug flats,

may not adequately drain to allow sufficient air to enter the medium for good plant growth. Media with greater aeration should be used for any containers shallower than 4 in. (10 cm), in particular, plug flats. The problem of reduced drainage is partially alleviated by the use of porous media that drain well and allow ample air movement.

PROPERTIES

MOISTURE RETENTION AND AERATION

A medium must be able to provide plant roots with both water and air. Pores, or spaces of various sizes, allow a medium to accomplish both functions at once. *Total porosity* refers to all of the pore space within the medium (Fig. 7-2). While a plant is being watered from the surface, almost all of the pore space fills with water. After the irrigation is completed, the water filling the large pores (*macro* or *noncapillary pores*) drains out the bottom of the pot by gravitational pull and the pores refill with air. The smaller pores, known as *micro* or *capillary pores*, retain water. The amount of water held in a container by the medium after it has been irrigated and drained is known as the *container capacity*. The water that is held in the medium after irrigation is subdivided into two types: available and unavailable (Table 7-1). The available water is loosely held by the medium

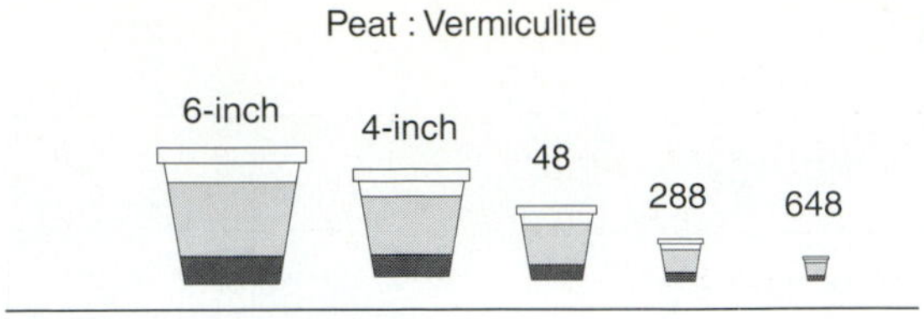

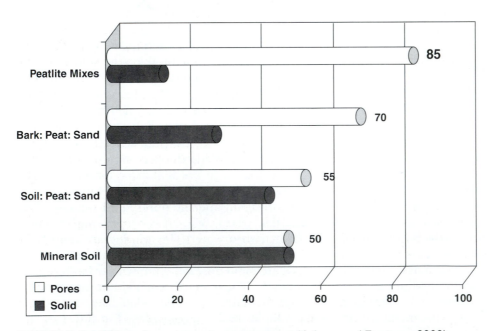

Peat : Vermiculite

	6-inch	4-inch	48	288	648
Air	20	13	8	3	0.5
Water	67	74	79	84	86.5
Solid	13	13	13	13	13

FIGURE 7-1 Effect of container size on percent water retention and aeration of a peat and vermiculite medium (Adams and Fonteno, 2003). Note decrease in percent air and increase in percent water as the container becomes shorter. A 6-in. pot = 15 cm, a 4-in. pot = 10 cm. The '48' is a bedding plant flat and '288' and '648' represent plug flats.

particles and can be absorbed by the plant's roots. The unavailable water is so tightly bound to the surface of the medium particles that the root is not able to absorb the water. When a plant has absorbed all of the available water, the plant has reached the permanent wilting point (see Chapter 5, Water).

A suitable growing medium contains a balance of capillary and noncapillary pores that allows optimal root growth. The same medium in shorter containers retains more water and therefore has less aeration than in taller containers (Fig. 7-1). Do not pack medium into the containers or stack filled containers on top of each other, because air space is decreased

and the percentage of unavailable water is increased (Table 7-1; Fig. 7-3). Overhead irrigation frequently compresses the medium over time, resulting in similar aeration problems. Match the medium to the grower. Growers who grow "on the dry side" can use a medium with greater moisture retention, whereas growers who frequently irrigate will require a medium with better drainage.

Another consideration is the movement of water within the medium. If surface irrigating, water moves down through the medium by gravity and moves laterally by capillary action, which consists of *adhesion*, the ability of water molecules to bind to other materials such as media particles, and *cohesion*, the ability of water to bind to itself. Initially, water molecules bind to the media particles. The layer of water around the media particles attracts additional water molecules, which allows further movement of water through the medium. If the medium has excessive porosity, channeling can occur. In channeling, the water runs downward in a narrow channel with little lateral movement. This action prevents all of the medium in the pot from being moistened, restricting growth and making excessive soluble salts in the medium difficult to leach. Water movement within a medium is an important consideration with subirrigation systems that apply the water to the bottom of the container because the water must move upward by capillary action (see Chapter 5, Water).

FIGURE 7-2 Effect of components on pore space (Adams and Fonteno, 2003).

TABLE 7-1
Effects of filling and packing containers on medium water and air space.

Peat:Vermiculite	6-in. (15-cm) Standard Pot (%)	4-in. (10-cm) Standard Pot (%)	48-Cell Flat (%)
Filled and Brushed			
Available water	43	51	58
Unavailable water	21	21	21
Air space	23	15	9
Filled, Tapped Twice on Bench			
Available water	44	52	56
Unavailable water	26	26	26
Air space	15	9	4
Filled, Pressed, and Refilled			
Available water	45	49	52
Unavailable water	30	30	30
Air space	9	4	2

FIGURE 7-3 Plug trays properly stacked to avoid compaction.

The rate of water uptake by a dry medium can be increased with the incorporation of a wetting agent. *Wetting agents* decrease water surface tension, allowing the water to adhere to the surface instead of becoming a round bead. Wetting agents are especially useful for increasing the amount and rate of water uptake during the first irrigation by media components that can be difficult to wet such as dry peat moss or bark. Applications of wetting agent before marketing of the crop can also increase water re-

tention in retail or home settings when a medium can become quite dry between irrigations (Barrett, 1997). Once a medium is moist, however, wetting agents do not increase total water retention; they increase only the amount retained immediately after a dry medium is irrigated. Wetting agents are typically incorporated into premixed media or can be purchased if a firm is mixing its own media. Follow label recommendations and test wetting agents first, because phytotoxicity can occur.

CATION EXCHANGE CAPACITY

Root media components such as peat moss, vermiculite, and bark have a negative electrical charge that attracts positively charged ions (cations) in the medium water solution. The *cation exchange capacity* (CEC) indicates the strength of that electrical charge for a medium and indicates the capacity of the medium to hold positively charged nutrient ions. The greater the CEC, the more nutrient ions the medium can hold. The CEC is based on volume (meq/100 cm^3) for soilless media and should be high to allow the medium to retain nutrients for the plants. Most of the plant nutrient ions are cations: NH_4^+, K^+, Ca^{2+}, Mg^{2+}, Zn^{2+}, Cu^{2+}, Mn^{2+}, and Fe^{2+}. Anions are negatively charged ions, and include $H_2PO_4^-$, NO_3^-, SO_4^-, and Cl^-, of which the latter two are usually not in limited supply. Components with a high CEC include mineral soil, peat moss, and vermiculite. Components with a low CEC include perlite, Styrofoam, and sand.

pH

pH strongly influences the availability of nutrients to plant roots and is a measure of the concentration of hydrogen ions in media water solution. On a scale of 1.0 to 14.0, pH 7.0 is neutral, above 7.0 is basic (alkaline), and below 7.0 is acidic. The recommended media pH will vary with the species being grown but general recommendations have been developed. For soilless media the pH should be 5.4 to 6.0, and 6.2 to 6.8 for soil-based media (25% or more soil). Media pH often changes over time in response to fertilizers, water alkalinity, and pH (see Chapter 5, Water). If the water alkalinity, is high, the grower may want to begin the crop with a medium pH at the low end of the recommended range and allow the pH to slowly drift upward without causing problems before the crop matures and is sold. However, the grower may want to start the crop at the upper end of the acceptable pH range if the water alkalinity and pH are low, if highly acidic fertilizers are being used, or if the water is acidified.

STABILITY

The properties of a medium continually change from the time the plant is potted until the plant is harvested, marketed, planted outdoors, or disposed of by the consumer. Thus a medium may have the ideal properties at the time of potting, but less than ideal properties later in production or marketing. Medium stability is especially important for the production of long-term crops such as specimen foliage plants, cut flowers in ground beds, or stock plants that will remain in the same medium for a long time.

The main cause of medium instability is biological degradation, the natural decomposition of organic matter. Although all organic matter eventually begins to decompose, not all organic matter decomposes at the same rate. One reason fresh sawdust is not used in media is due to its rapid decomposition rate, which alters the structure of media (see also Carbon:Nitrogen Ratio section that follows). Peat moss and bark, however, decompose more slowly, allowing the medium to retain its original properties much longer.

Vermiculite is also somewhat unstable due to physical compression in media over time. The natural compression from watering and plant root growth can cause the platelike structure of vermiculite to collapse. As a result,

vermiculite particles lose a portion of their excellent moisture retention and aeration capabilities over time. In preparing a medium containing vermiculite, mixing and handling should be kept to a minimum.

BULK DENSITY

Bulk density refers to the dry weight of the medium component relative to the volume. For example, sand has a high bulk density and perlite has a low bulk density. Some components, such as peat moss, are very light when dry but have the ability to absorb a large amount of water and become heavy. For most crops, a medium with a low to medium bulk density of 10 to 30 lb/ft^3 (160 to 480 g·L^{-3}) is generally used to reduce worker fatigue and shipping costs. In addition, hanging baskets should be as lightweight as possible to reduce the weight on the greenhouse frame. Media for bedding plant flats can be especially lightweight because there is no chance the flats will fall over. In some cases, a medium with greater bulk density may be required to prevent tall plants from falling over during production and marketing such as with some foliage plants, Easter lilies (*Lilium longiflorum*), poinsettias (*Euphorbia pulcherrima*), and stock plants.

CARBON:NITROGEN (C:N) RATIO

Any medium with organic components will decompose due to the actions of microorganisms. In the process of decomposition, nitrogen is absorbed by the microorganisms. If a large amount of organic matter is broken down in a short time, nitrogen in the medium is depleted and not available for plant use. Most organic media components, such as peat moss, do not break down rapidly, so nitrogen depletion is minimal. The optimum ratio of organic matter to nitrogen is 30 lb C to 1 lb N. Sawdust has a carbon-to-nitrogen ratio of 1000:1 and decays rapidly, resulting in significant nitrogen depletion. Bark also has a high carbon-to-nitrogen ratio, 300:1, but is slow to decompose and is usually composted prior to use. The composting process results in the rapid breakdown of the small particles of organic matter in the bark, leaving the larger pieces, which do not breakdown rapidly. Thus, the nitrogen depletion occurs during the composting process, and properly processed bark will not deplete nitrogen in a container growing medium during crop production.

MEDIA COMPONENTS

PEAT MOSS

Peat is a natural accumulation of organic matter in bogs or other wetlands that can be divided into four types:

1. Sphagnum peat moss is the partially decomposed remains of various *Sphagnum* moss species. It has a pH range of 3.0 to 4.0, a fiber content of at least 66%, and is the major peat used commercially. Sphagnum peat moss is considered weed, insect, and pathogen free and can suppress fungal growth. Most of the sphagnum peat moss used in North America is mined from bogs in Canada. Europe obtains its peat mainly from Estonia, Finland, and Russia, but other European countries also supply smaller amounts.
2. Hypnum peat moss is the partially decomposed remains of various *Hypnum* moss species. It has a pH range of 5.0 to 7.0 and fiber content of at least 33%.
3. Reed-sedge peat is the partially decomposed remains of reeds and sedges, and has a pH range of 4.0 to 7.5.
4. Peat humus is made of completely decomposed plant material with a pH range of 5.0 to 7.5 and often contains high levels of nitrogen and soil.

The most important type of peat moss is sphagnum peat moss; the other types are used mainly outdoors as soil amendments. Fresh or dried sphagnum moss is also available but should not be confused with sphagnum peat moss. Sphagnum moss is used to line hanging baskets or cover the medium in container gardens for aesthetic reasons, but is not used as a medium component.

The following information applies only to sphagnum peat moss. When purchasing peat moss, check type, degree of decomposition, pH, particle size, and percent moisture if buying by weight. Peat moss is generally consistent within sources but can vary with the age and location of the bog and the harvest method.

Moisture retention and aeration: Excellent water retention and moderate aeration. Sphagnum peat moss can absorb up to 60% of its total volume in water. Peat moss can be difficult to wet if initially dry. The use of a wetting agent and/or warm water can facilitate wetting of dry peat moss

CEC: Medium to high, 7 to 13 meq/100 cm^3

pH: 3.0 to 4.0

Stability: Very stable

Bulk density: Low, 22 lb/ft^3 (352 g·L^{-3}) (Nelson, 2003)

Carbon:nitrogen ratio: 50:1 for sphagnum peat moss, but decomposition is slow, so it does not significantly deplete nitrogen in media

Cost: Moderate

BARK

The type of bark available varies from area to area. The two types are softwood with a pH of 5.0 to 6.0 and hardwood with a higher pH of around 7.0. Bark can be used as the primary medium component for epiphytic plants such as orchids. When purchasing bark, check particle size, species, and degree of decomposition. Bark is more variable than peat moss, especially among sources. Bark can have disease-suppressive properties.

Moisture retention and aeration: Moderate water retention and excellent aeration after composting. Bark can be difficult to wet if allowed to become very dry. The use of a wetting agent and/or warm water can facilitate wetting of bark

CEC: High after composting, 12+ meq/100 cm^3

pH: Softwood, 5 to 6; hardwood, approximately 7

Stability: Very stable. After initial composting, bark does not rapidly decompose

Bulk density: Low to medium, 32.7 lb/ft^3 (523 g·L^{-3}) (Nelson, 2003)

Carbon:nitrogen ratio: High, 300:1, and should be composted or aged prior to use. Bark can be composted rapidly in 4 to 6 weeks by adding nitrogen, usually ammonium nitrate, at the rate of 3 lb actual nitrogen/yd^3 (1.8 kg·m^{-3}) and turning the pile once. Aging involves piling the bark for 3 to 12 months, usually without added nitrogen, and turning it occasionally

Cost: Moderate, assuming the bark is not shipped from a great distance. Beware of exceptionally low priced bark because it may be of poor quality

COIR

Coir is similar in appearance to peat moss and is a by-product of the coconut husk fiber processing industry (Evans et al., 1996; Meerow, 1997). Fibers and dust are removed during processing, composted, graded, dried, and pressed into bricks or bales. The bricks and bales must be rehydrated prior to use. Coir is a relatively recent addition to the list of possible amendments and quality varies with the source (Konduru et al., 1999). In particular, total soluble salt, sodium, chloride, and potassium levels can be injuriously high. Coir dust does not contain weed seeds or pathogens and absorbs water more easily than dry peat moss.

Moisture retention and aeration: Excellent

CEC: Low to medium, 3.9 to 8.4 meq/100 cm^3

pH: 4.5 to 6.9

Stability: Excellent

Bulk density: Low, 22.3 lb/ft^3 (357 g·L^{-3}) (Nelson, 2003)

Carbon:nitrogen ratio: Moderate, 80:1, but decomposes slowly. There may be a slight depletion of nitrogen initially as the small particles decompose

Cost: High, due to shipping and expansion expenses

SELECTED CROP BY-PRODUCTS

Various relatively stable crop by-products are occasionally used, including rice hulls, cocoa hulls, ground peanut hulls, and kenaf (Jacques et al., 2003). Cocoa hulls are also popular as a landscape mulch. Supplies are often local and may be difficult to obtain otherwise.

Moisture retention and aeration: Low to medium water retention and excellent aeration

CEC: Variable depending on the type

pH: Variable, usually 5.0 to 7.0

Stability: Usually stable, but may need to be pasteurized before use

Bulk density: Low

Carbon:nitrogen ratio: High, but usually decomposition is slow. An initial composting, similar to that used for bark, can be used if small, highly degradable particles are present

Cost: Often low, depends on shipping distance

SOIL

Soil generally contains little organic matter (1.5%) and can vary in pesticide and herbicide content, mineral content, and ratio of clay, silt, and sand. It is important to either know the source of the soil or to deal with a reputable supplier. Although the use of soil has decreased due to variable quality, high bulk density, and low aeration, soil may still be useful in reducing water and nutrient runoff because of its high moisture retention, micronutrient content, and CEC.

Moisture retention and aeration: Excellent water retention, but often poor aeration

CEC: Usually very high, up to 40 meq/100 cm^3

pH: Variable and depends on the source of the soil. Test each new source

Stability: Very stable. The low organic content of most soils means that there is little to decay. Soil does not break down during pasteurization

Bulk density: High, 85.3 lb/ft^3 (1364 g·L^{-3}) (Nelson, 2003)

Carbon:nitrogen ratio: Low, in fact, there might be no carbon if there is no organic matter

Cost: Generally low if you have your own source, but can be expensive to purchase and ship

VERMICULITE

Vermiculite is manufactured from ground aluminum-iron-magnesium silicate that is heated to 1400°F (770°C). Water trapped between the fine platelike layers within the ore turns to steam and expands the ore to 15 to 20 times its original volume. The resulting particles have a structure similar to tiny stacks of corrugated cardboard, which results in excellent water retention. There are two sources of vermiculite: African (pH 9.3 to 9.7) and American (pH 6.3 to 7.8).

Vermiculite is also a minor source of calcium, magnesium, and potassium. Vermiculite can be purchased in different particle sizes, ranging from fine to coarse grades. The finer grades are used for propagation and the coarser grades for potted plants.

Moisture retention and aeration: Excellent; do not use with soil that will plug the pores of vermiculite particles

CEC: High, 10 to 16 meq/100 cm^3

pH: African, 9.3 to 9.7; American, 6.3 to 7.8

Stability: Chemically stable and sterile, but the particles compress easily, especially when wet, and should be avoided for long-term crops. Also, avoid overhandling, which will also break down the structure of vermiculite

Bulk density: Low to medium, 31.1 lb/ft^3 (497 g·L^{-3}) (Nelson, 2003)

Carbon: nitrogen ratio: 0:0, no carbon

Cost: High

CALCINED CLAY

Clay particles baked at 1300°F (720°C) can vary with the type of clay used, but are generally very porous. Calcined clays are also used as kitty litter, industrial spill absorbers, and other functions unrelated to floriculture.

Moisture retention and aeration: Excellent

CEC: Typically high, but can be low, 3.4 to 11.8 meq/100 cm^3

pH: Varies from 4.5 to 9.0, usually does not influence pH of medium

Stability: Very stable and already sterile

Bulk density: Medium to high, 30 to 40 lb/ft^3 (480 to 640 g·L^{-3}) (Nelson, 2003)

Carbon:nitrogen ratio: 0:0, no carbon

Cost: High

PERLITE

Aluminosilicate rock is ground and heated to 1800°F (1000°C), resulting in white, popcorn-like pieces. It has many characteristics similar to sand and is commonly used as a low-weight replacement for sand. Dust masks are recommended for the handlers because the mixing of perlite can generate a considerable amount of irritating dust. Perlite has been erroneously reported to contain fluoride. It is actually safe to use with fluoride-sensitive species (Nelson, 2003). Perlite easily floats to the medium surface during overhead irrigation and can create a pollution problem if washed out of the container.

Moisture retention and aeration: Low water retention and excellent aeration

CEC: Very low, 0.15 meq/100 cm^3

pH: Approximately 7.5, but has little influence on media

Stability: Very stable and already sterile

Bulk density: Low and may float to the top of the medium in the container after watering, 20.8 lb/ft^3 (333 g·L^{-3}) (Nelson, 2003)

Carbon:nitrogen ratio: 0:0, no carbon

Cost: High

ROCKWOOL

Rockwool is manufactured by melting basalt rock, steel mill slag, or other minerals at 2900°F (1600°C) and spinning the material into fine fibers similar to fiberglass insulation. Large rectangular slabs of rockwool are used in hydroponic production and smaller cubes can be used in propagation (Sonneveld, 1991). Small pieces of ground rockwool are used in container media for potted plants.

Moisture retention and aeration: Excellent

CEC: Very low, almost none

pH: Neutral to slightly alkaline, but has little effect on media pH

Stability: Very stable and already sterile

Bulk density: Low, 16.5 lb/ft^3 (264 g·L^{-3}) (Nelson, 2003)

Carbon:nitrogen ratio: 0:0, no carbon

Cost: Moderate

SAND

Coarse, concrete-grade sand (0.5 to 2.0 mm) should be used. Fine grade or beach sand and road or driveway sand, which could contain salt, should not be used. For best results, wash the sand to remove any clay particles and pasteurize before use. Sand was once one of the most commonly used components in media but use has declined as low-weight components such as perlite and Styrofoam were developed with characteristics similar to those of sand.

Moisture retention and aeration: Low water retention and low to moderate aeration. If developing a new medium with sand, be certain to test it first because sand can actually reduce aeration when combined with other components, particularly with fine grade sand, which fills the pores in the medium

CEC: Low, up to 2 meq/100 cm^3

pH: Inert and neutral

Stability: Very stable

Bulk density: The heaviest component at 100 to 110 lb/ft^3 (1600 to 1760 g·L^{-3}) (Nelson, 2003)

Carbon:nitrogen ratio: 0:0, no carbon

Cost: Low

STYROFOAM

Styrofoam (polystyrene) is the lightest commonly used component, and the small beads float to the top of the medium with overhead irrigation. The beads often work their way to the medium surface, causing changes in medium properties. In addition, the beads can turn green with algae growth or be washed or blown out of the containers and become a nuisance.

Consequently, legal restrictions may exist regarding the use of Styrofoam.

Moisture retention and aeration: Low water retention and excellent aeration

CEC: Very low, almost none

pH: Inert and neutral

Stability: Very stable and sterile

Bulk density: Very low, 1.6 lb/ft^3 (25 g·L^{-3}) (Nelson, 2003)

Carbon:nitrogen ratio: 0:0, no carbon

Cost: Low

OTHER COMPONENTS

Several other organic and inorganic components are used occasionally in mixing media. Besides bark, sawdust and wood chips are also obtained from wood processing but are generally not suitable for media due to rapid decomposition and a high carbon-to-nitrogen ratio (400:1). Sawdust and wood chips are best used after being composted, after which sawdust and wood chips have the same characteristics as a well-made compost. Wood chips, however, will last longer in media than sawdust due to the larger size of the pieces. When obtaining wood processing by-products, check the tree source because walnut and incense cedar are toxic to plants.

A second type of organic amendment is the various composted products such as composted paper, straw, manures, green wastes (lawn clippings and plant prunings), poultry litter, garden or municipal wastes, spent mushroom composts, and earthworm castings (vermicompost) (Burger et al., 1997; Chen et al., 1999; Cole and Newell, 1996; Geurtal et al., 1997; Hidalgo and Harkess, 2002). The quality of composted products is determined by the ingredients that were used to make the compost. Most composted products continue to decompose after incorporation in the medium, preventing them from being used as the primary component in a growing medium. However, composts may be useful when they make up less than 50% of the growing medium. Composted products usually have excellent moisture retention, good initial aeration, and a high CEC. Compost paper products do not break down as rapidly as other composts and show promise as a medium amendment (Cole and Newell, 1996). Composted manure was once commonly used, but is not recommended because it cannot be pasteurized due to excessive release of NH_4. Some composted products may be more useful as a slow release source of nutrients, especially minor nutrients.

A variety of inorganic materials, such as waste tire components, can be used in growing media and, as with any new medium component, they should be tested first (Bowman et al., 1994; Evans and Harkess, 1997; Newman et al., 1997). When developing a medium with a new component, be certain it will be available for a long time. Lava rock, scoria, and pumice are available in certain areas, especially California, and make excellent additions to a growing medium (Wallach et al., 1992). Scoria has high bulk density, while pumice has low bulk density and can be substituted for perlite. In some cases, ground electrical insulation or plastics have been used. Although the materials are essentially inert, they should be tested first in case of potential contaminants. Commercial greenhouse media also occasionally use cinders.

Water-absorbing polymers and starches are occasionally added to media to reduce the number of irrigations and to delay wilting during marketing. A number of water-absorbent materials are available but some strongly question their effectiveness.

COMBINING COMPONENTS

Combining individual media components into a workable medium requires a number of decisions. First, growers need to decide if they are going to mix their own media or buy premixed media. Although premixed media seem more expensive than buying individual components, much of the financial savings of self-mixed media can be lost in the labor and equipment costs required to mix the media. A wide range of premixed media are available and many media companies will custom blend to a customer's specifications. In addition, an increasing number of specialized premixed media are being offered. For larger producers, mixing their own media is often economically justified, although the price of premixed media usually drops with increasing volume purchased (Fig. 7-4).

Small producers generally have a great many tasks and the higher cost of premixed media compared with self-mixed media is offset by convenience. Small firms or beginning growers should buy and test several premixed media and use the one best suited to their operation. Regardless of the size of the operation, the decision to use premixed or self-mixed media should be periodically reexamined due to changing operating conditions and costs.

FIGURE 7-4 Large bags of premixed medium.

The second consideration is the number of different media types needed in a single firm. Using one basic medium for all crops is the most efficient method; however, one medium may not be optimum for all crop species. The loss in quality for one or more of the crop species can be offset by reduced labor costs. Small firms, especially those producing a large number of crop species, may have no choice but to use only one medium. If a number of media types are needed, efficiency can be improved by limiting the number of media components used and developing the various media with different formulations of the same components. Also, using similar media recipes and only substituting one or more components to create a new medium will help prevent potential mistakes and make media mixing more efficient.

Recipes for self-mixed media can be expressed in actual volumes or ratios. The former method specifies the number of bales or bags of each component required to make an exact volume of medium. The ratio method expresses the components relative to each other based on volume, such as 3:1:1, peat moss:perlite:vermiculite. The recipe can be increased or decreased, depending on the number of containers to be filled. The ratio method also allows easy comparison of different media. The two methods are readily combined when a grower specifies the volume of "one part" of medium. For example, the 3:1:1 could refer to 30 bags of peat moss, 10 bags of perlite, and 10 bags of vermiculite. Nutrient amendments can be expressed in a method similar to that for media components.

Media are often separated into two categories: soil-based media (containing 25% or more soil) and soilless media. Although the majority of producers use soilless mixes, a few growers use soil-based media.

SOIL-BASED MEDIA

Generally, soil-based media have the same characteristics as soil itself, except that the bulk density is reduced and aeration is increased by adding amendments such as perlite, peat moss, bark, or polystyrene. A medium will have the properties of soil if it contains at least 25% soil (Fonteno, 1996). One advantage of soil-based media over soilless media is the high CEC that soil contributes to the mix. Nutrient retention is increased, which makes soil-based media especially useful for long-term crops such as stock plants, cut flowers planted in ground beds, and potted crops that are grown outdoors and subject to heavy leaching from rain, such as perennials, garden chrysanthemums (*Dendranthema ×grandiflorum*), and foliage plants. The soil also provides buffering capacity to withstand pH changes and to reduce the likelihood of micronutrient deficiencies. Of course, the excellent moisture retention of a soil-based medium can be a detriment for crops sensitive to overwatering or situations where the medium does not dry out quickly such as during the winter or at the beginning of the crop cycle before young plants are well rooted. In addition, the high CEC of soil-based media increases the difficulty of reducing high soluble salt or micronutrient levels through leaching.

SOILLESS MEDIA

Soilless media have proven popular with the majority of producers because of their consistency, excellent aeration, reproducibility, and low bulk density, which reduces the shipping and handling costs of the medium itself and of the finished plants. Soilless media, however, generally have a lower CEC than soil-based media, which means that constant attention must be paid to the nutritional program. Micronutrients must be applied to soilless mixes either prior to potting or sometime thereafter. The transition from soil-based to soilless media has resulted in the application of higher fertilizer rates and greater water use and runoff. Soilless media are also harder to wet when dry. Consequently, most premixed soilless media contain a wetting agent to facilitate wetting. Wetting agents can also be added to self-mixed media. The low bulk density of many soilless mixes also means that in some situations a component with high bulk density, such as sand or calcined clay, may be needed for weight.

MEDIA PREPARATION

For testing a new medium or for potting only a few plants, small quantities of medium can be mixed by hand. The proper amount of each component is spread out on a clean floor or bench and mixed with a clean shovel. Be sure to thoroughly mix the components; fertilizers and other amendments should be spread out on the pile as evenly as possible before mixing to ensure uniform distribution of the amendments in the final medium. Many growers and schools use a small cement mixer with a capacity of 1 to 6 ft³ (28 to 170 L), which generally produces a more uniform medium than mixing by hand.

Larger volumes of medium are mixed using a large cement mixer or, more commonly, a commercially manufactured media mixing system. Such systems typically include a number of hoppers linked to a conveyor belt. The hoppers may include grinders to break up large bales of peat moss and to facilitate dropping the media components at the proper rate onto a conveyer belt, which mixes or drops the medium into a storage area or container. Mixing systems are commonly integrated into a pot or flat filling machine for greater efficiency. In turn, the pot filler can also be linked to a conveyer belt for planting, labeling, and the first irrigation. The conveyer can continue into the greenhouse for transportation of containers to the growing benches.

During the mixing process, various amendments can be added to the media. Calcitic or dolomitic limestone can be added to raise the media pH of peat-based media. Superphosphate (containing P and S), controlled-release fertilizers (N, P, and/or K), gypsum (Ca and S), and micronutrient mixes can also be incorporated. Most, if not all, commercial pre-mixed media include wetting agents to allow rapid wetting after planting.

Regardless of the mixing method, it is important to produce a uniform, consistent mixture, especially for plug and bedding plant flats with small volumes of medium in each cell. Nonuniform mixing will lead to a variable crop that will be difficult to water, properly fertilize, and use in machinery such as automatic trans-

planters. However, excessive mixing, such as from rotating mixers, can break down the components and reduce aeration. The use of front-end loaders also leads to excessive medium breakdown from compaction by the wheels.

Media components may need to be moistened prior to or during mixing to reduce dust from perlite and other components. Peat moss should be wet prior to incorporation to facilitate wetting of the mixed medium. If the medium is too dry, excessive shrinkage will occur after planting and irrigation (Adams and Fonteno, 2003). In such situations water should be incorporated prior to planting rather than packing additional medium into the container. In addition, dry media will be difficult to rewet and will require more than one irrigation to saturate the media. For pots and hanging baskets, mix 1:1 water:dry media to obtain 50% moisture before planting. A higher moisture level is preferred for plugs, mix 1:2 water:dry media to obtain 67% moisture. Media can also be moistened during the filling of containers and planting to reduce dust and add water to the medium.

Experience and personal preference are required to determine the optimum amount of medium to fill containers. Too much medium in the container leaves little room for water at the top of the medium if overhead irrigating, causing frequent or lengthy irrigation to saturate the medium. In addition, there may not be enough room for pesticide or plant growth regulator drenches, producing incomplete coverage of the medium. However, if insufficient medium is used, plants will dry out rapidly and pots may be too lightweight and fall over. To maintain proper aeration, never pack media into a container or stack containers directly on top of each other as that will also pack the media (Fig. 7-3). Stagger flats and put pots into carried flats before stacking.

PATHOGEN CONTROL

Modern production of floriculture crops requires that media be free of plant pathogens, insects, and weeds. Many media components such as perlite, vermiculite, rockwool, and calcined clay are sterilized as part of the high-temperature manufacturing process. Other components such as sphagnum peat moss are not sterile but are considered to have few if any pests. The acidic nature of peat moss, the anerobic condition of the bogs, and the remote harvesting locations generally exclude plant pathogens, insects, and weeds from growing, and thus peat moss is considered ready to use without any further treatments for pathogens. Barks are usually considered ready to use because of the aging or composting process. The processing regime for coir also makes it ready to use without pest problems.

Sphagnum peat, bark, and coir also appear to have varying degrees of natural disease suppression properties. Light-colored sphagnum peat moss, which is harvested from the bog surface, suppresses pathogens for about 6 to 12 weeks (Dreistadt, 2001; M. Evans, personal communication). Composted softwood and hardwood barks last 5 to 6 months and up to 2 years, respectively. These components may host beneficial organisms that can compete with or parasitize the pathogenic organisms. Barks also release phenolics, which may suppress pathogens. The disease suppressive properties are influenced by many physical, chemical, and biological factors, which can produce variable results (Dreistadt, 2001). Of course, even properly handled disease suppressive media components may not be completely effective under high disease pressure.

Soil and sand usually contain plant pathogens, weed seeds, and insects and must be pasteurized. If only one or two components require treatment, they should be treated prior to mixing. Also, ground beds that are being replanted with a new crop need to be treated to eliminate any pathogens, weeds, or insects from the previous crop. Many times treatment of the medium is easier and more cost effective than removing, disposing, and replacing the old medium.

PASTEURIZATION

The most common method for pathogen control in greenhouses is to heat media to 140 to 150°F (60 to 65°C) for 30 min. This pasteurization treatment is highly effective in eliminating most pathogens, insects, and nematodes, but unfortunately many nonpathogenic beneficial organisms are also killed. If weed seeds are a problem, heat media to 158 to 176°F (70 to 80°C) (Handreck and Black, 2002). Media can be heated either by electricity or by steam. Electrical pasteurization boxes are available to treat small quantities of soil or sand. Large amounts of soil or sand or ground beds are more economically treated with steam, applied either directly or with aeration. Although direct steam application is rapid, it often results in portions of the medium being overheated at 212°F (100°C) in order that all of it reach 160°F (71°C) for 30 min. Aerated steam can also be used, a process in which the steam is blended with air to 140 to 160°F (60 to 71°C). Aerated steam usually results in a more consistent pasteurization with no overheating and is more energy efficient.

With either steam method, media should be moist, approximately 25 to 40% water by volume, but not wet. Media with excess water will take longer to pasteurize and may lead to incomplete pasteurization in that the moisture must also reach 160°F (71°C). However, media should not be dry because water facilitates the movement of the heat throughout the medium. In addition, pathogens and dormant weed seeds are more resistant to heat in a dry state. Moisten media and store for at least 4 hr, and up to 2 weeks, prior to pasteurization to allow weed seeds to begin germinating and allow resting stages of pathogens and nematodes to become active. The moistening and storing process is especially helpful in controlling weeds. Steam pasteurization is also thought to improve media structure by slightly breaking down some of the organic matter, which then leads to increased bonding between media particles, resulting in greater porosity.

Specially designed carts have a perforated bottom to allow the steam to rise up through the medium (Fig. 7-5). The carts are covered with a tarp, which is tied over the cart to hold in the steam. One side of the cart can usually be lowered horizontally to create a potting bench if needed.

FIGURE 7-5 Steam pasteurization of medium in a cart.

FIGURE 7-6 Steam pasteurization of ground beds.

The media in ground beds should be moist, loose, and slightly mounded to allow for adequate steam penetration (Fig. 7-6). A perforated pipe extends down the length of the bed to carry the steam. The beds are then covered with a tarp, which is anchored to trap the steam.

One obvious disadvantage of steam pasteurization is the cost, which includes not only energy costs but also labor expenses. Other potential problems are manganese and ammonium toxicity. Manganese toxicity can occur if soil is used that contains large amounts of Mn in an unavailable form. The steam converts a portion of the manganese into an available form. Pasteurization at too high of a temperature or for too long can result in high Mn levels that are toxic to plants. Manganese is most available below pH 6.0 in soil-based media and raising the pH can be a temporary solution. Although leaching can also be performed, medium containing soil are more difficult to leach and the process may not be effective.

Ammonium toxicity can occur because the pasteurization process at 160°F (71°C) kills the microorganisms responsible for conversion of ammonium (NH_4^+) to nitrite (NO_2^-) to nitrate (NO_3^{-2}) and ammonium increases in media to a toxic level. If a medium contains high levels of ammonium from composts, urea fertilizer, or highly decomposed peats, ammonium can increase rapidly after pasteurization. The best solution is to avoid components with high ammonium levels and incorporate ammonium-based fertilizers after the medium has been pasteurized. If the problem occurs, the medium can be stored for 3 to 6 weeks to al-

low the proper microorganisms to reestablish. This process can be enhanced by lowering the medium pH to 5.0, which encourages the nitrification bacteria to grow in preference to microorganisms that degrade the organic matter. An amendment with a high carbon-to-nitrogen ratio can also be added to increase bacterial growth and decrease NH_4.

SOLARIZATION

Solarization is slow, but inexpensive and chemical free. Greenhouse or field ground beds or pots of media are watered, drained, and covered tightly with clear, not black, 1.5- to 2-mil plastic (Dreistadt, 2001). The plastic traps heat and increases the temperature of the media. This method is most effective during the summer or in areas of the country with abundant sunshine, warm temperatures, and minimal wind if outdoors. Leave plastic on the media for 4 to 6 weeks. As with heat pasteurization, the media must be moist, but not wet, prior to treatment and clod or lump free. Be sure the plastic is free of holes and tightly sealed, otherwise some of the heat may escape, reducing its effectiveness.

For fields and greenhouse ground beds, the process works best if the plastic is laid close to the soil or medium surface, which should be smooth without protruding vegetation, rocks, and trash (Dreistadt, 2001). Cultivate about 4 in. (10 cm) deep prior to application of the plastic. After solarization avoid cultivating deeper than 3 in. (8 cm), which may bring up weed seeds that have not been killed. Solarization of ground beds in greenhouses is especially effective because higher temperatures can be obtained and there is little wind.

The entire greenhouse can be solarized by shutting down the cooling and venting systems. Clean the glazing, remove any easy-to-handle weeds, and water the aisles and ground under the benches. Monitor temperatures because excessively high heat can damage plastic irrigation pipes.

Containers with media can be solarized by covering with a tent of clear plastic (Dreistadt, 2001). The containers or loose media to a depth of 12 in. (30 cm) can also be sandwiched between a layer of plastic on the ground, which is then folded over the media and sealed. Two layers of plastic, at least 0.5 in. (1.3 cm) apart, are more effective than single layers, resulting in temperatures of up to 50°F (28°C) higher than single layers. Monitor the media temperature. All portions of the media should be 160°F (71°C) for 30 min. Especially effective solarization may reach the indicated temperatures in as little as a week.

Solarization is quite effective against insects and controls most fungi, weeds, and some nematodes (Dreistadt, 2001). Solarization is most effective against winter annual and perennial weed seeds and seedlings and is least effective against summer annuals. With fields, the heat cannot penetrate deep into the soil, which limits its effectiveness against established perennial weeds and other pests deep in the soil.

FUNGICIDES

In an emergency, unpasteurized media can be drenched with fungicides to prevent possible pathogen problems (see the Chapter 9 section on Crown and Root Rot). However, fungicides are expensive and may not be 100% effective in controlling medium-borne pathogens. Using a pasteurized media or using pathogen-free components is more practical and cost effective in the long run.

CHEMICALS

Chemical sterilants are commonly used outdoors to eliminate weeds, insects, and diseases prior to planting. One of the most commonly used chemicals is the gas methyl bromide. Use of methyl bromide in the greenhouse has been limited because the gas is highly toxic to humans and the medium needs to be aerated for 7 to 10 days prior to planting. In addition, some plant species such as carnations (*Dianthus caryophyllus*) are particularly sensitive to methyl bromide. Environmental and toxicological concerns have limited the use of methyl bromide, and it is scheduled to be removed from the market worldwide. Chloropicrin is available and can be used alone as a replacement for methyl bromide or in combination with methyl bromide. Together the two compounds are quite effective against fungi, insects, and nematodes and somewhat effective against weeds. Other chemicals, such as methyl iodide, and sodium azide, and processes are being researched for outdoor soil sterilization and may have an application for greenhouse use as well (Chase, 2003).

KEY POINTS

- A wise grower will invest much thought and money into developing or selecting suitable media.
- Growers should never use an untested medium for an entire crop because changing a medium often requires that the irrigation frequency and fertilizer regime also be adjusted.
- The shorter the container, the less drainage. Very short containers, such as plug flats, may not adequately drain to allow sufficient air to enter the medium for good plant growth.
- Media and media components are evaluated based on several properties or factors including moisture retention and aeration, cation exchange capacity, pH, biological and physical stability, bulk density, carbon-to-nitrogen ratio, and cost.
- Pores, or spaces of various sizes, allow a medium to hold water and air simultaneously. Total porosity refers to all of the pore space within the medium. Large pores

(macro or noncapillary pores) drain after irrigation and refill with air; small pores (micro or capillary pores) retain water.
- Do not pack medium into the containers or stack containers, because air space is decreased and the percentage of unavailable water is increased, resulting in uneven growth.
- Various media components are used to make growing media, including peat moss, bark, coir, soil, calcined clay, vermiculite, perlite, Styrofoam, sand, and rockwool.
- Numerous other organic and inorganic components are used occasionally in mixing media and any new medium component should be tested first.
- Growers need to decide if they are going to mix their own media or buy premixed media.
- Media are often separated into two categories: soil-based media (containing 25% or more soil) and soilless media.
- During the mixing process, various amendments can be added to the media including pH adjusters, nutrients, and wetting agents.

- Media should be moist but not wet prior to planting to prevent excessive shrinkage after planting.
- Modern production of floriculture crops requires that media be free of plant pathogens, insects, and weeds. Many media components such as perlite, vermiculite, rockwool, and calcined clay are sterilized as part of the high-temperature manufacturing process. Other components such as peat moss, bark, and coir are not sterile but are considered to have few if any pests. Soil and sand usually contain plant pathogens, weed seeds, and insects and must be treated.

BIBLIOGRAPHY

Adams, R., and W. Fonteno. 2003. Media, pp. 19–27 in *Ball Redbook*, 17th ed. vol. 1. Ball Publishing, Batavia, Illinois.

Barrett, J. 1997. Wetting agents, do they provide benefits after the first irrigation? *Greenhouse Product News* 7(10):26–28.

Bowman, D.C., R.Y. Evans, and L.L. Dodge. 1994. Growth of chrysanthemum with ground automobile tires used as a container soil amendment. *HortScience* 29:774–776.

Burger, D.W., T.K. Hartz, and G.W. Forister. 1997. Composted green waste as a container medium amendment for the production of ornamental plants. *HortScience* 32:57–60.

Chase, A.R. 2003. Methyl bromide alternatives. *Greenhouse Product News* 13(7):44–46.

Chen, J., C.A. Robinson, R.D. Caldwell, and D.B. McConnell. 1999. Waste composts as components of container substrates for rooting foliage plant cuttings. *Proceedings of the Florida State Horticulture Society* 112:272–274.

Cole, J.C., and L. Newell. 1996. Recycled paper influences container substrate physical properties, leachate mineral content, and growth of rose-of-Sharon and *Forsythia*. *HortTechnology* 6:79–83.

Dreistadt, S.H. 2001. *Integrated Pest Management for Floriculture and Nurseries*. University of California Division of Agriculture and Natural Resources Publication 3402.

Evans, M.R., and R.L. Harkess. 1997. Growth of *Pelargonium ×hortorum* and *Euphorbia pulcherrima* in rubber-containing substrates. *HortScience* 32:874–877.

Evans, M.R., S. Konduru, and R.H. Stamps. 1996. Source variation in physical and chemical properties of coconut coir dust. *HortScience* 31:965–967.

Fonteno, W.C. 1996. Growing media: Types and physical/chemical properties, pp. 93–122 in *Water, Media, and Nutrition for Greenhouse Crops*, D.W. Reed, editor. Ball Publishing, Batavia, Illinois.

Geurtal, E.A., B.K. Behe, and J.M. Kemble. 1997. Composted poultry litter as potting media does not affect transplant nitrogen content or final crop yield. *HortTechnology* 7:142–145.

Handreck, K., and N. Black. 2002. *Growing Media for Ornamental Plants and Turf*, 3rd ed. University of New South Wales Press, Sydney, Australia.

Hidalgo, P.R., and R.L. Harkess. 2002. Earthworm castings as a substrate for poinsettia production. *HortScience* 37:304–308.

Jacques, D.J., N. Morgan, M. Thomas, R. Walden, and R. Vetanovetz. 2003. Regional components could meet your growing media needs. *Greenhouse Management and Production* 23(9): 28–30, 32–34, 36.

Konduru, S., M. Evans, and R.H. Stamps. 1999. Coconut husk and processing effects on chemical and physical properties of coconut coir dust. *HortScience* 34:88–90.

Meerow, A.W. 1997. Coir dust, a viable alternative to peat moss. *Greenhouse Product News* 7(1):17–21.

Nelson, P.V. 2003. Root substrate, pp. 197–236 in *Greenhouse Operation and Management*, 6th ed. Prentice Hall, Upper Saddle River, New Jersey.

Newman, S.E., K.L. Panter, M.J. Roll, and R.O. Miller. 1997. Growth and nutrition of geraniums grown in media developed from waste tire components. *HortScience* 32:674–676.

Sonneveld, C. 1991. Rockwool as a substrate for greenhouse crops, pp. 285–312 in *High-Tech and Micropropagation I*, Y.P.S. Bajaj, editor, *Biotechnology in Agriculture and Forestry*, Vol. 17. Springer-Verlag, Berlin.

Wallach, R., F.F. da Silva, and Y. Chen. 1992. Hydraulic characteristics of tuff (scoria) used as a container medium. *Journal of the American Society for Horticultural Science* 117:415–421.

Chapter 8

Plant Growth Regulation

INTRODUCTION

Plant growth regulation is defined as any chemical process used to produce a specific type of growth response, such as inhibition of internode elongation or acceleration of root development. Growth regulating chemicals or processes usually affect plant growth through alteration of endogenous plant growth regulator (plant hormone) levels. These naturally occurring substances define and direct plant growth. To understand plant growth regulation, we need to understand the five classes of endogenous plant growth regulators.

ENDOGENOUS PLANT GROWTH REGULATORS

AUXINS

Auxins are involved in rooting, axillary shoot growth, shoot elongation, and morphogenic responses of plants to external stimuli (e.g., light and gravity). The most common auxin-type chemical found in plants is indole-3-acetic acid (IAA). Commercially, auxins are most important in enhancing root development during propagation and tissue culture.

GIBBERELLINS

Gibberellins (GAs) are involved in shoot elongation, flower development, and seed germination. Many different forms of GAs occur naturally. Each form is noted with a numbered subscript: GA_3, GA_4, and GA_7 are most commonly used commercially. Some GAs work only on specific plant species and at specific stages of growth. GAs are most commonly used to increase stem elongation and induce flower development. Anti-GA compounds are commonly used to control height.

CYTOKININS

Cytokinins are involved in branching, cell division, and juvenility. Although cytokinins are most commonly used in tissue culture, they are occasionally used to stimulate axillary shoot development and delay leaf senescence during postharvest.

ETHYLENE

Ethylene is involved in senescence, branching, flowering, and ripening. It is the only endogenous growth regulator that is a gas. Ethylene or ethylene-producing compounds are used commercially for height control, branching, leaf and flower abscission, flower induction, and flower inhibition. Anti-ethylene agents are widely used to prolong postharvest life and delay flower, petal, and leaf senescence (see also Chapter 10, Postharvest).

ABSCISIC ACID

Abscisic acid promotes senescence and directs the storage of photosynthates made by the leaves. Currently, there are no commercial uses for abscisic acid in floriculture.

PLANT GROWTH REGULATION

ROOT DEVELOPMENT DURING PROPAGATION

Rapid, uniform root development on cuttings can be hastened by application of auxins. The naturally occurring IAA can be used but is unstable and easily degraded. Fortunately, synthetic auxins, such as indole-3-butyric acid (IBA) and naphthalene acetic acid (NAA), are longer lasting and more reliable than IAA. Since the development of IBA, it has also been found to occur naturally. A number of rooting powders and liquids are available containing a range of auxin concentrations. For example, Hormex® Rooting Powder #1 contains 0.1% IBA in talcum powder, and is used for most greenhouse crops, #2 contains 0.3% IBA, and #3 contains 0.8% IBA. Higher IBA rates are available and generally used on woody plants. Other products, such as Hormodin®, also include IBA. Other rooting compounds contain more than one type of auxin and/or cytokinins, fungicides, and other chemicals. For example, Rootone® contains benzyladenine (BA), NAA, fungicide, and other unspecified chemicals. Rooting compounds are most effective on species when rooting would occur naturally but development is slow, and are least effective on species when rooting is rapid.

Repeatedly dipping cuttings into a bowl of powder or liquid may spread disease organisms on cuttings. To prevent the possibility of disease spread, rooting powders should be applied with dusters.

TISSUE CULTURE

Several natural and synthetic growth regulators are used in the tissue culturing process. Tissue culture is the process of aseptically propagating plants *in vitro* (Hartmann et al., 1997). The amount and ratio of various growth regulators, primarily auxins, cytokinins, and gibberellins, determine the growth and development of roots and shoots *in vitro*.

SEED GERMINATION

Gibberellins (200 to 1000 ppm), cytokinins (100 ppm kinetin), and ethylene (Florel) have been used to stimulate germination of seed in some plant species. Rates will vary with the species and the seed size.

STEM ELONGATION

Gibberellic acid has been used to induce stem elongation for producing tree topiary forms of poinsettia (*Euphorbia pulcherrima*), geranium (*Pelargonium*), and *Fuschia*. The resulting stems may be weak and are staked to prevent breakage. For geraniums, three to five weekly sprays of 250 ppm GA_3 are applied (Whealy, 1993). Gibberellic acid may also have limited effectiveness in reversing the effects of excessive growth retardant application.

CHEMICAL GROWTH RETARDATION

Growth retardants are the most commonly used and important chemical growth regulators in floriculture. Many floriculture crops undergo a triphasic pattern of plant growth: (1) slow initial growth that occurs immediately after propagation or after a pinch, (2) rapid vegetative growth and elongation, and (3) slow final reproductive growth during which time the flowers develop (Fig. 8-1). The effective use of chemical growth retardants requires that the chemicals be applied prior to or during the rapid growth phase to reduce internode elongation. Growth retardants cannot "shrink" plants after they have grown and late application of a growth retardant will have a limited effect on the final plant height. Use graphical tracking (see Graphical Tracking section later in this chapter) to monitor plant height, which will aid in deciding whether or not to apply growth retardants and how much to apply. Multiple applications will often be required.

Chemical growth retardant treatments also result in stockier plants with thickened stems and darker green foliage. These qualities allow plants to survive shipping and handling better than untreated plants. Chemical growth retardants also increase the number of flowers in the inflorescence of azaleas (*Rhododendron*) and can decrease time to flower initiation in seed geraniums (*Pelargonium* ×*hortorum*). The following growth retardants are available.

B-NINE (DAMINOZIDE). B-Nine is one of the most frequently used growth retardant (Norcini et al., 1996) and is used as a spray at the rate of 1250 to 5000 ppm on chrysanthemums (*Dendranthema* ×*grandiflorum*), crossandra (*Crossandra infundibuliformis*), exacum (*Exacum affine*), gardenia (*Gardenia augusta*), hydrangea (*Hydrangea macrophylla*), kalanchoe (*Kalanchoe blossfeldiana*), petunia (*Petunia*

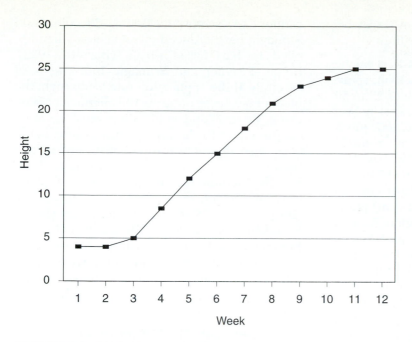

FIGURE 8-1 Triphasic growth pattern typical of many floriculture crops.

×*hybrida*), and numerous other plants. For example, B-Nine is applied to chrysanthemums 1 to 2 weeks after the pinch, when the axillary shoots are 1 to 2 in. (2.5 to 5 cm) long. Granular B-Nine can be stored for at least 2 years as long as it is tightly sealed and dry (Hammer, 2001).

B-Nine is not effective as a drench, but is taken up slowly by the leaves and moves to all parts of the plant. B-Nine is most effective when the foliage remains moist for 8 to 12 hours (Styer, 1997). Do not irrigate overhead during this period or the chemical will be washed off. B-Nine is less effective in warm climates (Barrett, 2001). Because B-Nine is not effective as a medium drench, it eliminates the possibility of additional height control from excessive spray solution draining into the medium. Fortunately, plants that were sprayed with B-Nine during production grew well when planted in the landscape with no long-term residual effects from the B-Nine (Latimer and Oetting, 1998).

CYCOCEL (CHLORMEQUAT). Cycocel is typically used as a spray at the rate of 200 to 5000 ppm, with 1000 to 1500 ppm most commonly used, on *Begonia*, geranium, hibiscus (*Hibiscus rosa-sinensis*), poinsettia, and other crops. Cycocel can also be used as a medium drench at the rate of 2000 to 4000 ppm but is generally less effective as a drench than other chemicals. On poinsettias, Cycocel sprays are

applied approximately 2 weeks after the pinch when the axillary shoots are 1.5 in. (4 cm) long. Cycocel, a liquid, can be stored for at least 2 years under normal storage conditions (Hammer, 2001).

Because foliar uptake is slow, Cycocel will be most effective if the foliage stays moist for 8 to 12 hours (Styer, 1997). Do not irrigate overhead during this period or the chemical will be washed off. Cycocel is less effective in warm climates (Barrett, 2001). Cycocel phytotoxicity typically occurs at rates greater than 1500 ppm and damage appears within 3 to 5 days on leaves that were expanding at the time of application. Symptoms include yellow or light green patches, spots, or rings. A common practice to prevent Cycocel phytotoxicity is to divide the recommended rate in half and make two applications 3 to 4 days apart. Reducing the Cycocel concentration does not affect the amount of initial growth control, but plants grow out of low concentration applications sooner (Fisher et al., 1996).

Cycocel can be tank mixed with B-Nine for a synergistic effect greater than either of the chemicals used alone. This mix is used where additional height control is required, such as in warm climates, or to avoid Cycocel phytotoxicity. The Cycocel rate in the tank mix should be low enough to prevent phytotoxicity from occurring. The tank mix is not effective as a medium drench, thus eliminating the possibility of additional height control from excessive spray solution draining into the medium.

A-REST (ANCYMIDOL). A-Rest can be used either as a media drench or as a foliar spray. Sprays are typically used at the rate of 25 to 50 ppm on Easter lilies (*Lilium longiflorum*), hybrid lilies (*Lilium*), freesia (*Freesia ×hybrida*), tulips (*Tulipa gesneriana*), and numerous other potted species. Lower rates of 3 to 15 ppm are used on plugs. Drenches are applied at 0.15 to 0.5 mg active ingredient (a.i.) per 6-in. (15-cm) pot. On Easter lilies, 0.25 to 0.5 mg/6-in. (15-cm) pot is applied as a drench after flower initiation when shoots are 4 to 6 in. (10 to 15 cm) tall. A-Rest, a liquid, can be stored for at least 3 years under normal storage conditions (Hammer, 2001).

Foliar uptake is fast and A-Rest moves quickly throughout the plant (Styer, 1997). Thus, plants can be irrigated shortly after application, possibly as soon as 5 min (Barrett, 2001). However, this also means that inadvertent applications cannot be removed. A-Rest has reduced effectiveness when applied to bark media (Barrett, 1982). In addition, care should be taken when applying A-Rest to subirrigated plants because spray drift, foliage dripping, and container leachate may contaminate the bench or floor, causing inadvertent applications during the subsequent irrigations (Million et al., 1999).

BONZI (PACLOBUTRAZOL), PICCOLO (PACLOBUTRAZOL), AND SUMAGIC (UNICONAZOLE). Bonzi and Sumagic can be applied either as a drench or as a spray. Bonzi and Piccolo sprays are typically used at the rate of 1 to 90 ppm on miniature pot roses (*Rosa*), calla lilies (*Zantedeschia*), freesias (*Freesia ×hybrida*), hybrid lilies, and numerous other species. Sumagic is generally more effective at the same concentration as Bonzi and is typically applied at 1 to 50 ppm. For chrysanthemums, Bonzi can be applied at 31 to 125 ppm as a spray or at 1 to 4 ppm as a drench (Higgins, 2001). In contrast, Sumagic can be applied at 2.5 to 10 ppm as a spray or as 0.1 to 1 ppm as a drench.

Chemical solution must contact the stem or roots, because it is not readily translocated to the apex through the leaves (Barrett et al., 1994). These chemicals move quickly into and throughout the plant (Styer, 1997). Thus, plants can be irrigated shortly after application, possibly as soon as 5 min (Barrett, 2001). However, this also means that inadvertent applications

cannot be removed. Bonzi, Piccolo, and Sumagic have reduced effectiveness when applied to bark-based media (Barrett, 1982). Bonzi, Piccolo, and Sumagic must be used carefully. If the application rate is too high, the plants may never outgrow the chemical. Measuring, mixing, and application must be done carefully due to the low concentrations being used. Also, do not overapply spray applications because the excess spray solution may drain into the medium, serving as a drench application, and result in excessive height control (Barrett et al., 1994). In addition, care should be taken when applying Bonzi, Piccolo, and Sumagic to subirrigated plants because spray drift, foliage dripping, and container leachate may contaminate the bench or floor, causing inadvertent applications during the subsequent irrigations (Million et al., 1999).

TOPFLOR (FLURPRIMIDOL). Topflor can be applied as a spray or a drench. It is new to the U.S. market but has been available in Europe and other countries for many years. Sprays are typically used at the rate of 10 to 60 ppm on geraniums, petunia, chrysanthemums, and numerous other species (Fig. 8-2). For poinsettias, Topflor sprays can be applied at rates ranging from 2.5 to 40 ppm for low-vigor cultivars to 50 to 80 ppm for vigorous cultivars. Drenches are used at the rate of 0.25 to 4 ppm. Chemical solution must contact the stem or roots, because it is not translocated to the apex through the leaves (SePRO, personal communications).

FIGURE 8-2 Effect of Topflor (flurprimidol) on New Guinea impatiens (*Impatiens hawkeri*). Concentrations applied include 0, 1.25, 2.5, 5, 10, 20, 40, or 80 ppm (from left to right) (photo by Brian Whipker).

FLOREL (ETHEPHON). Florel is typically used as a spray at the rate of 500 to 2000 ppm on narcissus (*Narcissus pseudonarcissus*) and hyacinth (*Hyacinthus orientalis*) and must be applied within 1 to 3 days after bringing potted, cold-treated bulbs into the greenhouse for forcing. Florel is an ethylene-releasing chemical, not an anti-gibberellin, as are the other plant growth retardants just discussed. Premature release of ethylene in the spray tank can occur if the water alkalinity is high (see Branching section on page 156). Florel can be stored indefinitely under normal storage conditions (Hammer, 2001). Besides height control, Florel also has a number of other effects on plant growth, which are listed later in this chapter.

APPLYING CHEMICAL GROWTH RETARDANTS. Plant species vary in their sensitivity to growth retardants (Table 8-1). For a particular species, note which growth retardants are effective and consult the product label to obtain specific application information.

Chemical plant growth regulators are most commonly applied using sprays because of the ease of application. Sprays are typically applied at 2 qt/100 ft² (20 L/100 m²). Higher spray volumes or application to small plants may result in a drench effect, which may produce excessive height control. Be sure your sprayer is accurately calibrated, especially if applying highly effective chemicals to sensitive crop species. Higher chemical concentrations are used for sprays as compared to drenches. Drenches are labor intensive but often more effective than sprays. Drenches are generally applied at 2 to 3 oz/4-in. (60 to 90 mL/10-cm), 3 to 4 oz/5-in. (90 to 120 mL/13-cm), or 4 to 6 oz/6-in. (120 to 180 mL/15-cm) pot. Drench

TABLE 8-1

Effect of A-Rest (ancymidol), Cycocel (chlormequat), B-Nine (daminozide), Florel (ethephon), Bonzi (paclobutrazol), Piccolo (paclobutrazol), Sumagic (uniconazole), and Topflor (flurprimidol) on numerous floriculture crop species (Adriansen, 1985; Gaston et al., 2001; Latimer et al., 2003). A minus (−) indicates the chemical had no effect or a negative effect on the plant species; a plus (+) indicates the chemical is effective, and the number of plus signs refers to how effective, with +++ being most effective. Chemicals marked with + or ++ may require multiple applications to be effective. A blank in the table indicates that information on that species and chemical combination is not available. When trying a new growth retardant, always test it first on a small number of plants. Please check individual chapters for more information on the crop species listed in **bold**. Additional information on plant growth retardant information is available for many species listed in the **Bedding Plants**, **Foliage Plants**, and **Garden Perennials** chapters in Part III.

Species	A-Rest	Cycocel	B-Nine	Florel	Bonzi/Piccolo	Sumagic	Topflor
Abutilon cultivars	−	+++	−		+++		
Abutilon megapotamicum	+++	+++					
Acalypha hispida	++	+++					
A. wilkesiana	++	+++	++				
Achillea cultivars		−	++	+++	++	+++	
Achimenes cultivars	++	++	++		+		
Aechmea araneosa				++			
A. chantinii				++			
A. fasciata				+++			
A. fulgens				++			
Aeschynanthus hildebrandii	++			−			
A. speciosus	++			−			
Agapanthus					++		
Agastache hybrids			++			+++	
Ageratum cultivars	++	+	++	−	+++	+++	++
Aglaonema modestum	+	−	−	−			
Ajuga reptans						++	
Alcea rosea			++		++	+++	
Allamanda cathartica	+	−	+	++			
A. c. var. grandiflora			++				
A. c. var. hendersonii	++						
Alstroemeria hybrids					++		

(continued)

TABLE 8-1   *(continued)*

Species	A-Rest	Cycocel	B-Nine	Florel	Bonzi/Piccolo	Sumagic	Topflor
Alternanthera dentata		−			++		
A. ficoidea var. *amoena*	++		++				
Amberboa moschata		−	+				
Amsonia species					++		
Anagallis monellii		−	−				
Ananas comosus				++			
Anchusa capensis		−	−				
Anemone coronaria	+						
Anigozanthus hybrids					++		
Anisodontea capensis		++	−				
Antirrhinum majus	++	++	−	++	+++	+++	
Aphelandra flava		++					
A. sinclairiana		++					
A. squarrosa	++	−	−				
A. tetragona		++					
Aquilegia cultivars	++	++	++	++	−	−	
Araucaria heterophylla	−		−				
Arctotis venusta		+	++				
Ardisia crenata	−	−	+				
Argyranthemum frutescens		++	+				+++
Asclepias curassavica	++	+	+++				
A. tuberosa			++		+		
Aster novi-belgii			+++		+++	+	
A. ×frikartii			++		++	−	
Astilbe ×arendsii			++			++	
Aucuba japonica	++						
Baptisia species					+		
Barleria cristata			++		+		
Bassia scoparia		+					
Begonia ×hiemalis	+++	+++	−	−	++	++	
B. ×Semperflorens-Cultorum hybrids	++	++		+	+++		
B. ×Tuberhybrida hybrids		+++					
Bidens ferulifolia			++			+++	
Billbergia pyramidalis				++			
Boltonia					++		
Bougainvillea glabra	+	++	+		++		
B. cultivars	+	+	+				
Brassica oleracea (ornamentals)			++		++	++	
Browallia americana		++	+		++	++	
B. speciosa	+	+	+++				
Brugmansia suaveolens	+++	+	++	++			
Brunfelsia pauciflora		+		++			
Buddleia davidii			+		++	−	
Caladium bicolor	++		++		++		
Calceolaria cultivars		++	++	+			
Calendula officinalis		++	++	−	++	++	
Callistephus chinensis	++	+	++	−			
Camellia japonica		++	+	+	++		
Campanula carpatica	++	++	+		+++	+++	
C. isophylla	++	+	++				

TABLE 8-1 *(continued)*

Species	A-Rest	Cycocel	B-Nine	Florel	Bonzi/Piccolo	Sumagic	Topflor
C. persicifolia			++		++		
Canna ×generalis			−	−	++		
Capsicum cultivars (ornamentals)	++	++	++	+		++	
Catalpa bignonioides	++	++	++				
Catharanthus roseus	++	++	+	+		+++	
Celosia argentea	++	++	++		+++	+++	++
Centaurea cyanus	++	−	++				
C. montana			++		++		
Cestrum elegans		−					
Chelone glabra			−		+		
Chlorophytum comosum	−	−					
Chrysanthemum carinatum		++	++				
C. ×spectabile		++	++				
Chrysothemis pulchella		++	+++				
Cissus discolor	+	+					
C. rhombifolia	++	−	+		+		
Citrus cultivars	++		+				
Clarkia amoena	−	++	+++		++	++	
Clematis hybrids					++		
Cleome spinosa	++	++	++		++	++	
Clerodendrum thomsoniae	+++	++	+	+	+++		
Codiaeum variegatum	+	−			+++	+++	
Coffea arabica	++			+			
Columnea species	++	++	++	+			
Conoclinium coelestinum	+		−		+	+	
Convolvulus tricolor	++	++	+				
Cordyline terminalis	++			++			
Coreopsis basalis		++	+				
C. grandiflora	−	−	++		++	++	
C. rosea			++		+	++	
C. tinctoria		−	++				
C. verticillata	−	−	++	−	−	+	
Cortaderia selloana	++				++	+++	
Cosmos bipinnatus		−	+				
Crassula arborescens	++	++					
C. coccinea		+					
Crocosmia species			−				
Crossandra infundibuliformis	++		+++	−			
Cyanotis kewensis	++	+++	+				
Cyclamen persicum	+		++				
Cyperus alternifolius	++	−	−				
Dahlia cultivars	+++	+	++	++	+++	+++	+++
Datura cultivars		−	+				
Delphinium ×cultorum	+++		+			+++	
D. elatum	−	−	−		++	++	
Dendranthema ×grandiflorum	+++	+	+++	+	+++	+++	+++
Dianthus cultivars	++	++	+	+	+++	+++	
Dicentra spectabilis	++	++	+	+			
Dieffenbachia species	++	−	−	−	++	++	

(continued)

TABLE 8-1 *(continued)*

Species	A-Rest	Cycocel	B-Nine	Florel	Bonzi/Piccolo	Sumagic	Topflor
Digitalis cultivars		−	+	−	+	++	
Dimorphotheca cultivars		++					
Dissotis species	+	++	−				
Draceana marginata					+		
Duranta erecta		++			+		
Echinacea purpurea	+	+	+	++	+++	+++	
Echium plantagineum		++	+				
Epipremnum aureum	++	−	+		++	++	
Erica cultivars		++					
Euphorbia fulgens	++	++	++				
E. leucocephala	++	+					
E. pulcherrima	+++	+++	++	+	+++	+++	+++
Eustoma grandiflorum	+++		+++		++	+++	
Exacum affine	++	−	++			++	
×*Fatshedera lizei*	+++	+	+				
Ficus bejamina	++			++			
F. elastica	−	−			+		
F. lyrata					++		
F. microcarpa	++	−	−				
F. retusa	+	−	−				
Freesia hybrids	++				++		
Fuchsia cultivars	+++	++	++	++	+++	+++	
Gaillardia ×*grandiflora*			+		+	+	
Gardenia species	++	++	++		++		+++
Gaura lindheimeri			+++	++	+	+	
Gazania rigens					++	++	
Gentiana species	++		++				
Gerbera jamesonii	++	−	++				
Gladiolus cultivars	++				++		
Gomphrena globosa	−	+	+				
Graptophyllum pictum	++	++	−				
Grevillea robusta	++	++					
Guzmania lingulata				+++			
G. monostachia				+++			
G. zahnii				++			
Gynura procumbens	++	+	+				
Gypsophila cultivars	+++	++	+	+	++	++	
Hebe ×*andersonii*							
Hedera helix	++	+	++				
Helenium autumnale			++		+		
Helianthus annuus	++	+	++		++	++	++
Helichrysum species			++		++	++	
Heliconia species	++				++	++	++
Heliopsis helianthoides			+++	++	+	−	
Heliotropium arborescens	++		++			++	
Hemerocallis cultivars			−		+		
Hemigraphis alternata	++	++	++				
H. exotica	++	−	++				
Heuchera sanguinea			−		+		
Hibiscus moscheutos		++				+	
H. rosa-sinensis	+	+++	+	+	+++	+++	
Hippeastrum cultivars		+			++		

TABLE 8-1 *(continued)*

Species	A-Rest	Cycocel	B-Nine	Florel	Bonzi/Piccolo	Sumagic	Topflor
Hoya carnosa					+		
Hyacinthus cultivars	++			++			++
Hydrangea macrophylla	++	+	++	++	++	++	++
Hylotelephium spectabile		−	++		++	++	
Hypericum calycinum			−		−	+	
Hypoestes phyllostachya	++	++	+				
Iberis amara		++					
I. umbellata		++	++				
Impatiens balsamina	++	++	−	++	++	++	
I. hawkeri	++	+++	++	++	+++	+++	+++
I. walleriana	++	−	++		+++	+++	+++
Ipomoea nil	+	+					
Iresine herbstii		−	+				
I. lindenii		+	++				
Iris germanica					++		
Ixora coccinea	++	++	++				
Jacaranda mimosifolia		+					
Justica species		++			++		
J. brandegeana	++	++	+	++			
Kalanchoe cultivars	+++	++	+++	++	+++	+++	
Kniphofia uvaria		−	−		−	+	
Lamium galeobdolon					++	+	
Lantana camara			++			+	
Lathyrus odoratus	++	++	++				
Lavandula angustifolia	+	−	+		+	+	
Lavatera assurgentiflora		+++	−		+++	+++	
Leonotis leonurus		++					
Leucanthemum paludosum		+	+			++	
L. ×superbum		−	−	++	+	+	
Leucospermum species				++	++		
Liatris spicata	++			+		++	−
Lilium, asiatic hybrids	++	++	−	++	++	++	++
L. longiflorum	++	+		−		+++	
L. oriental hybrids	+++				+++	+++	
L. pumilum		++			++		
L. speciosum	++	−			++		
Limnanthes douglasii		++	−				
Linum perenne			++		+		
Lobelia cardinalis			−		−	+	
L. erinus		+	++		++	++	
L. ×speciosa	+	++	++		+	++	
Lobularia maritima		++	+		++	+++	
Malvaviscus cultivars		++	+				
Mandevilla cultivars	+++	−	+				
Matthiola incana		++	++		++	++	
Mimulus cultivars	++						
Monarda citriodora					++		
M. didyma		−	−	+	+	+	
Monstera deliciosa	++	−	−				
Narcissus cultivars		−	−	+++	+		
Nematanthus strigilosus		+					
Nemesia strumosa	++	++	++				

(continued)

TABLE 8-1 *(continued)*

Species	A-Rest	Cycocel	B-Nine	Florel	Bonzi/Piccolo	Sumagic	Topflor
Neoregelia carolinae				++			
N. cultivars				++			
Nepeta ×faassenii			++		++	++	
Nephrolepis exaltata					−		
Nerium oleander	++	++	+	−			
Nicotiana alata			++		++	++	
N. cultivars			+	−			
Nidularium cultivars				++			
Osteospermum ecklonis		++	++		++		++
***Oxalis* cultivars**	+	++			+++	++	
Pachystachys lutea	++	+++	−	++	+		
***Paphiopedilum* cultivars**	−	−	−	−			
Passiflora species	++	−					
Pavonia ×gledhillii	+	+++	+				
Pelargonium ×domesticum	++	++	+	−			
P. ×hortorum	++	+++	+	++	+++	+++	+++
P. peltatum		+++	+	+++	++		
Pellionia pulchra		++					
Pentas lanceolata		++			+		
Peperomia species	++	−	−		++		
Pericallis ×hybrida	++	−	+++	++			
Perilla frutescens			++				
Perovskia atriplicifolia			+	++	+	+	
***Petunia* cultivars**	++	+	+++	++	+++	+++	+++
Phacelia campanularia		−	++				
P. tanacetifolia		−	+				
***Phalaenopsis* cultivars**					+	+	
Philodendron erubescens		++	++				
P. scandens	++	+	+		−	−	
Phlox drummondii		++	++	+	++	++	
P. paniculata			+	−	+	+	
Physostegia virginiana	−	−	−	+	−		
Pilea species	++	++	−				
Platycodon grandiflorus			++		++		
Plectanthus species					+++	+++	
Plumbago auriculata				++			
P. indica		++	++				
Polemonium caeruleum			++		+		
Polygonum species					+		
Portulaca cultivars	++				++	++	
***Primula* cultivars**		−	++				
Pseuderanthemum cultivars	++	−	+		+		
P. atropurpureum		++	+				
Ranunculus asiaticus	++		++				
Ratibida species					+		
Reseda odorata		+	+				
***Rhododendron* species**	++	++	++	+	++	+++	
***Rosa* species**	+	++	+	+	++	+++	
Rudbeckia hirta		−	+		+	++	
R. triloba		+++	++		+	+	
Salvia greggii			++		+	++	
S. leucantha		++	++	+	++	++	

TABLE 8-1 *(continued)*

Species	A-Rest	Cycocel	B-Nine	Florel	Bonzi/Piccolo	Sumagic	Topflor
S. splendens	++	++	++	++	+++	+++	
S. ×superba			++		+		
S. ×sylvestris			++		+	+	
Sanchezia speciosa		++					
Sanvitalia procumbens		+	++				
Saponaria ocymoides		−			−		
Saxifraga stolonifera	++	−			++		
Scabiosa atropurpurea		+	+				
S. caucasica		−	+		−	+	
Schefflera actinophylla	++	++	+		+	+++	
Schizanthus cultivars	++	++	++				
Scilla peruviana	++	−	−				
Scutellaria costaricana	+	++					
Sedum anglicum	++	++					
S. spurium			−		++		
Senecio cineraria		++	++		++	++	
Silene pendula		++	+				
Sinningia cultivars	++	++	++		++		
S. cardinalis		++					
Solanum pseudocapsicum	−	++	++	−			
Solenostemon scutellarioides	++	++	++	+	++		
Solidago species			++		++	++	
×Solidaster luteus			+		+		
Stephanotis floribunda	−	+++	+++				
Stachys byzantina						++	
Stokesia laevis		−	++		+	−	
Strobilanthes dyerianus	++	++	+				
S. isophyllus		+	++				
Syngonium podophyllum	++	+	+		+	++	
Tagetes erecta	++	+	++	++	+++	+++	+++
T. patula		++	++	−	+++	+++	++
Tanacetum praeteritium		++	++				
T. coccineum			++		+		
Tibouchina grandifolia		++					
Tillandsia lindenii				+++			
Tradescantia species	+++						
T. zebrina	++		++	+	+++		
Tropaeolum majus		++					
Tulipa cultivars	+++	+	−	++	++		++
Vaccaria hispanica			+				
Verbena bonariensis		−	++		+	++	
V. canadensis		++	+	+++	++		
V. elegans	−	++	++		+++	+++	
V. cultivars	−	++	++	−			++
Veronica alpina			++		+	++	
V. peduncularis			++		++		
V. spicata		−	++		++	+++	
Viola ×wittrockiana	++	+	+		+++	+++	+++
Vriesea cultivars				++			
V. splendens				+++			
Zantedeschia species					+++	+	
Zinnia elegans	++	+	+		+++	++	

application rates are usually based on milligrams of active ingredient per container; thus, smaller drench volumes should have higher chemical concentrations. Drenches should be applied to moist but not wet medium. Sprays can also be made to the media prior to or just after planting of plugs or seeds.

In addition to sprays and drenches, selected plant growth regulators can also be effectively applied using subirrigation or spikes into which the chemical has been incorporated (Million et al., 1999). Subirrigation with growth retardants provides a more uniform response, reduces labor expenses, and requires fewer chemicals than typical spray or drench applications (Cox, 2003). Growth retardants can also be applied using other irrigation methods, known as chemigation, in some cases. Growth retardants can be applied to cuttings, seeds, and bulbs or other storage organs by dipping them into the chemical solution (White, 1976). Be sure to check on the legality of applying any chemical growth retardants using novel methods.

NONCHEMICAL HEIGHT CONTROL

Although chemical growth retardants have been used by the floriculture industry for decades, in certain situations their use is limited. Chemical growth retardants are not registered for use on vegetable or other edible bedding plants such as tomatoes (*Lycopersicon esculentum*), peppers (*Capsicum annuum*), and herbs. As with any chemical there are also concerns about both workers' and consumers' safety. In addition, height control using chemical growth retardants is always limited by the fact that the grower must estimate and apply the correct amount of chemical well before the crop is finished growing. Nonchemical height control methods allow day-to-day control of height and allow the grower to monitor the crop as it is growing and alter the final plant height as needed. However, once chemical growth retardants are applied, they cannot be removed and the grower may have to accept a mistake in application rate or an unexpected change in growing conditions.

CULTIVAR SELECTION. The first step in nonchemical height control is to choose the correct cultivar. Some cultivars of many floriculture crop species are genetically short and can be grown with little or no growth retardant. Many new poinsettia cultivars, for example, are short and compact.

LIGHT. Plants should be spaced as far apart as economically possible to allow the maximum amount of light to reach each plant. Similarly, light levels should be as high as possible depending on the appropriate requirements for each species. High-light-requiring crops such as poinsettias should not be grown in greenhouses with low-light-transmitting coverings such as old fiberglass or double polyethylene.

Alteration of light quality can also affect plant height. Light that is high in far-red wavelengths (e.g., from incandescent lamps) encourages stretching, whereas light with a high red–to–far-red light ratio, produced when sunlight is filtered through a copper sulfate solution or from fluorescent lamps, will reduce internode elongation (McMahon et al., 1991; Mortensen and Strømme, 1987; Rajapakse and Kelly, 1992). Manipulation of light quality by filters and greenhouse coverings is effective in controlling plant height and may be useful in the future.

CULTURAL PROCEDURES. Propagation, planting, pinching, and other crop production activities should be executed promptly and on schedule. For example, allowing rooted cuttings or seedlings to remain in propagation for too long or delaying a pinch unnecessarily can increase plant height. The plants of many species can be pinched or cut back if they grow too tall. Flats of bedding plant species such as impatiens (*Impatiens walleriana*), petunias, and wax begonias (*Begonia* Semperflorens-Cultorum) and pots of hibiscus and geraniums can be cut back and allowed to reflower. An additional 2 to 4 weeks will be required before plants are again marketable.

For photoperiodic species height can be controlled by shortening or lengthening the vegetative period before flowers are initiated through photoperiod control. For example, the final height of poinsettia and chrysanthemum plants can be shortened by decreasing the amount of time for vegetative growth (leaf/node initiation) from pinch to the start of SD.

CONTAINER SIZE. Plants generally grow larger in larger containers. Smaller media volume will restrict growth of many species but will also increase the frequency of irrigation. Using plug flats with small cell sizes also tends to produce plants that remain smaller in the final container, especially if plants become slightly stunted in the plug flat. This technique should be used carefully, because excessive stunting and reduced quality can occur if plants are left in the plug flat too long.

NUTRIENT RESTRICTION. Fertilization practices also affect height. Excessive nutritional levels can encourage overall plant growth and stem elongation. Bedding impatiens and petunias, for example, respond well to limiting nutrition in reducing plant height (Barrett and Nell, 1990; Nelson, 2001). Reducing nutrition, especially nitrogen and phosphorus levels, will slow the growth of many plant species. In particular, avoid the overuse of ammonium nitrogen, which tends to encourage rapid, lush growth. The technique of phosphorus restriction is a more specific method of nutrient restriction (Sheldrake, 1991). As with water stress and shaking and brushing, this technique has been used mainly on vegetable bedding plants. No phosphorus is incorporated into the medium prior to planting and transplants are initially watered with a low-phosphorus fertilizer such as 20–1–20 at 100 to 150 ppm nitrogen. Thereafter, plants are fertilized only with a no-phosphorus fertilizer such as 20–0–20 or 15–0–15. The low-phosphorus fertilizer can be applied again if the plants are growing too slowly or showing signs of phosphorus deficiency (lower leaf purpling). All plants should be fertilized with a high-phosphorus fertilizer such as 20–10–20 approximately 4 to 5 days prior to marketing. Plant quality may be reduced and this technique should be used only by an experienced grower. In addition, plants that were grown with low N during production continued to show residual effects in the landscape (Latimer and Oetting, 1998). Potassium restriction is not used because potassium deficiency generally does not stunt growth and there is a narrow margin of safety between growth restriction and obvious damage (Nelson, 2001).

HIGH MEDIA EC. High fertilization levels can also reduce growth (Nelson, 2001). High levels of salts in the medium restrict water uptake and reduce elongation. This process should be used carefully because damage can result from too high of a salt content and excessive growth can occur if the nutrition level is high but too low to restrict growth.

WATER STRESS. The height of some bedding plant species can be restricted by routine wilting (Barrett and Nell, 1990). Plants should not reach the permanent wilting point and are watered regularly for 4 to 5 days before marketing. An experienced grower is usually needed to recognize when plants are sufficiently wilted but not damaged. This technique is commonly used with tomatoes; results may vary with other species and may greatly reduce plant quality. Yellow lower leaves, flower and leaf drop, and increased susceptibility to root rot may result from excessive water stress on some species. In addition, plants that were drought stressed during production continued to show residual effects after planting in the landscape (Latimer and Oetting, 1998).

SHAKING OR BRUSHING. Many plants respond to shaking or light brushing by producing shorter internodes and thicker stems. This process is mainly used to control plant height of vegetable bedding plant species such as tomatoes, eggplants (*Solanum melongena*), cucumbers (*Cucumis sativus*), and watermelons (*Citrullus lanatus*). Shaking and brushing has also been reported to be effective on chrysanthemums, Asiatic lilies, and bedding plants (Baden and Latimer, 1992; Hammer et al., 1974; Jerzy and Krause, 1980; Schnelle et al., 1994; Turgeon and Webb, 1971). One method for bedding plants involves brushing the upper 2 to 4 in. (5 to 10 cm) of the plants lightly once or twice daily for at least 1.5 to 2 min (Latimer, 2001). Increasing the duration or frequency of brushing will generally increase the amount of height reduction. If using one application, it is best applied in the morning (Latimer, 1991). The process can be automated with mechanical booms sweeping over the plants. The process may need to start at the cotyledon stage.

Disadvantages of brushing include potential plant damage and disease spread. Some plant species, such as peppers (*Capsicum annuum*) and cole crops are too heavily damaged by brushing for the technique to be useful. Typically plants with stiff foliage will show the most damage (Latimer, 2001). Damage can be prevented or reduced by not brushing when plants are wet or wilted and when plants are young (Garner and Björkman, 1996). Fortunately, plants that were brushed during production grew well when planted in the landscape with no residual effects from the brushing (Latimer and Oetting, 1998).

DIF. DIF is the concept of controlling plant height by monitoring the difference between day and night temperatures (Berghage and Heins, 1991; Erwin et al., 1989a, b). The greater the DIFference between day and night temperatures (day–night = DIF), the greater the stem elongation (Fig. 8-3) (see also Chapter 3, Temperature). Height can be controlled by minimizing the difference between day and night

FIGURE 8-3 Influence of −29°F (−16°C) DIF from a 57/86°F (14/30°C) day–night temperature and +29°F (+16°C) DIF from an 86/57°F (30/14°C) day–night temperature on Easter lily (*Lilium longiflorum*) shoot elongation (photo by Royal Heins). Note leaf curling due to an extremely negative DIF.

temperatures, reducing +DIF, or growing plants with a day temperature lower than the night temperature, thereby producing a −DIF. The lower the −DIF, the greater the height control.

According to stem measurements, a large percentage of the daily stem elongation occurs early in the day just before and after sunrise, thus cool temperatures (−DIF) for 2 to 4 hr early in the morning starting 30 to 60 min before first light will also reduce stem elongation (Cockshull et al., 1995; Erwin et al., 1989c; Grindal and Moe, 1995; Moe et al., 1995). This cool early morning pulse is known as the temperature DROP or DIP. However, very warm temperatures during the rest of the day (+DIF) may negate many of the effects of the temperature DROP. Fisher and Heins (1997) indicated that for Easter lilies (*Lilium longiflorum*) combining a morning temperature DROP with a zero or slightly negative DIF during the rest of the day is more effective than using a more negative DIF all day.

The use of DIF can be maximized by a number of practices or environmental conditions (Warner and Erwin, 2001):

1. DROP should be at least 5 to 10°F (3 to 6°C) lower than the night temperature starting 30 to 60 min before sunrise.

2. The faster and greater the DROP, the more effective it will be.

3. Water plants or wet the foliage with cold water in the morning. Tissue temperature is most important, not air temperature.

4. DIF becomes more effective as the light intensity increases. Thus, DIF will be more effective when using supplemental HID lighting.

5. DIF is more effective during short days, whether natural or artificial.

6. Other cultural practices can increase the effectiveness of DIF such as adequate spacing and avoiding the use of incandescent lamps for day length extension or night interruption.

Remember, however, that average daily temperature determines the rate of development, and crop timing must be considered in choosing the proper combination of day and night temperatures that not only will reduce excessive stem elongation but will allow the crop to finish on time. This system of 0 DIF during the day plus a negative DROP can be used on many crops without increasing crop time. The process of graphical tracking (see next section) has been developed to enable a grower to monitor plant height and development, determine the proper temperature regime for production, and guide the use of chemical height control agents, if required.

Advantages of DIF include the day-to-day control of plant height. Reducing or eliminating growth retardants may save money, prevent environmental contamination, and eliminate the variability problems associated with chemical applications. As with any new procedure, it is prudent to conduct cost accounting to determine if DIF is economical, because extra heating or cooling may be required. In comparing the two methods, remember to consider not only chemical cost, but also application labor costs.

One major problem associated with DIF is that it can be used only when temperatures can be adequately controlled, which means that it is often not practical in warm climates or during the summer in many locations. Growers need to be wary of unusual warm spells, especially during the spring and fall, which may encourage rapid stem elongation. The use of DROP allows height control when temperatures are warm because it is more practical to reduce temperatures for 2 to 4 hr after sunrise than to maintain cool temperatures all day or warm temperatures all night.

In addition, DIF does not appear to be effective on most Dutch bulb species such as tulips, hyacinths, and daffodils, or Cucurbitaceae family plants. The response also varies among species on which DIF is effective (Warner and Erwin, 2001).

DIF may also affect plant responses other than height such as flower size and flower number in some species. Extreme day–night temperature reversals (i.e., −5 DIF) may induce chlorosis and leaf curling of Easter lilies, although these effects quickly disappear when DIF is less negative (Erwin et al., 1989a). Plant carbohydrate, chlorophyll, and nitrogen levels may also decrease with -DIF, and extremely -DIF may result in postharvest leaf yellowing of Easter lilies, bract edge burn, and cyathia drop of poinsettias (Miller, 1997; Miller et al., 1993; Vågen et al., 2003). Also, the use of -DIF during the day (low day temperatures) will reduce photosynthesis and decrease plant weight. Extensive research has been conducted on only a few species.

GRAPHICAL TRACKING

Graphical tracking is used to monitor plant height regardless of the height control method and can be readily applied to any crop species when height control is a concern. The process can either be done using a pencil and paper or computer software (Heins and Fisher, 1997). Plot the following five points on a piece of paper (Fig. 8-4): (1) minimum desired final plant height (+ pot height), (2) maximum desired final plant height (+ pot height), (3) one-half minimum final plant height (+ pot height), (4) one-half maximum final plant height (+ pot height), and (5) pot height (or initial height of the cutting or seedling). For example, Easter lily plants reach one-half final plant height at the time of visible bud. Connect the minimum final plant height and the maximum final plant height lines to the starting pot height. This will create a window into which the grower will try to maintain the plant height as the crop grows.

The next step in graphical tracking is to monitor the actual height of the crop as it grows. Choose 10 or more plants representative of the crop and record their height every 4 to 7 days. Mark the average height of the sample plants on the graph. If the average height of the crop goes above the maximum height line, height control measures, such as a lower DIF or an application of plant growth retardant, may need to be taken. If the height goes below the minimum height line, increase DIF or hold off applying any plant growth regulators. Other height control methods can be similarly incorporated into graphical tracking.

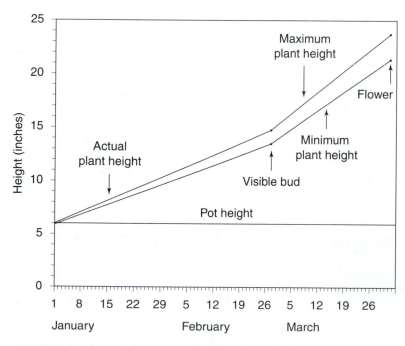

FIGURE 8-4 Sample graphical tracking graph for Easter lily (*Lilium longiflorum*) showing the target height control window (adapted from Heins et al., 1997).

The final step in graphical tracking is to determine normal growth patterns for the crop being tracked. Plant growth curves exist for the Easter lily, Asiatic and Oriental lilies, chrysanthemums, geraniums, and pinched poinsettias, but are not available for most other crops (Heins and Fisher, 1997). However, each firm can create its own plant growth curves by measuring plant height of the desired crop and plotting the results as previously described. Be aware that the curves may differ for the same crop species depending on the cultivar and production method. For example, Heins and Fisher (1997) noted that under the following conditions poinsettia plants elongate more rapidly later than normal: small-size pots, close spacing, very positive DIF, or longer time under LD than recommended. Late elongation is also noted with the cultivar Freedom. Unpinched, single-stem poinsettias also have growth curves that differ from typical pinched poinsettias.

BRANCHING

Several chemical pinching or branching agents are available that operate on different principles. Florel (ethephon) promotes development of the axillary shoots without damaging the apical meristem or growing point. Florel also inhibits flower initiation and aborts young flower buds previously initiated, which encourages branching (Fig. 8-5). Stem elongation may also be reduced (see Chemical Growth Retardation section earlier). Yellowed foliage may occur if Florel is applied to plants that are stressed from drought, high temperatures, or other causes (P. Konjoian, personal communication). Florel can be used on a wide variety of crop species such as chrysanthemum, *Fuchsia*, geranium, New Guinea impatiens (*Impatiens hawkeri*), *Lantana*, and *Verbena* for stock plant, hanging basket, or potted plant production. A typical application rate is 500 ppm; however, split applications or lower rates may be necessary on some crop species. If flowering is desired, cease Florel application 6 weeks prior to marketing. Florel is most stable in the spray solution when the pH is 4 or lower (Barrett, 2001). If spray water has high alkalinity, mix the solution using distilled or reverse osmosis treated water.

Atrimmec (dikegulac sodium) temporarily inhibits shoot elongation, which also induces lateral shoots to develop and has been used on a variety of crops including azalea, hiemalis begonia (*Begonia ×hiemalis*), bougainvillea (*Bougainvillea*), *Clerodendron*, *Fuchsia*, *Gardenia*, English ivy (*Hedera helix*), geranium, kalanchoe, lantana, and schefflera (*Schefflera actinophylla*). Typical application rates vary from 780 to 6250 ppm, which corresponds to 0.5 to 4 fl oz Atrimmec/gal (4 to 32 mL·L^{-1}), respectively.

Accel (10:1 benzyladenine:gibberellic acid) also promotes lateral axillary shoots to develop and is occasionally used to increase lateral branches on lower nodes of cut carnation and rose plants. On roses 200 ppm can be applied to the lower portion of rose bushes after the plants are cut back. A surfactant should be used and be sure to check the label first to determine if Accel is registered for use on the crop species.

Off-Shoot-O (methyl ester of fatty acids) kills the terminal bud, resulting in axillary shoot development. Off-Shoot-O has been used on azaleas to replace one or more manual pinches. Apply 2 to 5 fl oz Off-Shoot-O/qt (63 to 155 mL·L^{-1}) to the shoot tips.

The use of chemical pinching agents may significantly reduce the labor costs associated with hand pinching and flower removal, and increase cutting production, but careful application is needed for uniform results compared with hand pinching.

FLOWER DEVELOPMENT

Exogenous applications of growth regulators affect flowering in two ways: by promoting both flower initiation and development, or by promoting only flower development. In the

FIGURE 8-5 Death of geranium (*Pelargonium ×hortorum*) flowers due to Florel application (photo by Brian Whipker).

first situation, ethylene-releasing chemicals are used to induce flowering of ornamental bromelliads. Plants must be mature and able to perceive the ethylene treatment or flowering will not occur. Similarly, B-Nine or Cycocel can be used to promote earlier flower initiation on vegetative azalea shoots [1 to 2 in. (2.5 to 5 cm)] long. The resulting flower buds still require treatments of cold, gibberellic acid, or LD for further development and anthesis.

Plant growth regulators can promote flower development. For example, gibberellin can substitute for the cold treatment in azaleas with five weekly sprays of 1000 ppm (each weekly spray substitutes for 1 week of cold treatment), which will induce the opening of mature flower buds (see *Rhododendron* chapter) (Larson and Snydor, 1971). Gibberellins can also be used to stimulate flowerscape elongation in cyclamen and increase uniformity of flowering (see *Cyclamen* chapter) (Widmer et al., 1976). After plants are full sized, GA (10 to 25 ppm) is applied below the leaf canopy 8 weeks before the planned flowering date. In calla lily, soaking or spraying tubers with GA will increase flower number and hasten flower development and emergence (Corr, 1988; Corr and Widmer, 1987) (see *Zantedeschia* chapter).

ANTI-ETHYLENE AGENTS

Silver thiosulfate (STS) is used to prevent ethylene action and delay senescence of cut flowers and flowering potted crops. For example, seed geraniums can be sprayed with 1 millimole (mM) STS when the flower buds begin to show color, but before they are open, to prevent petal abscission during marketing (Hausbeck et al., 1987). Many cut flower species are treated with STS to delay senescence and prevent damage from internal ethylene and external ethylene sources such as vehicle exhaust, incomplete combustion of heaters, and ripening fruit and other plant materials. STS for cut flower use is marketed under the name AVB. Be sure to check the legality of using STS on potted plants, because it may not be labeled for such use.

The environmental problems with STS (due to the silver ion) may have led to the development of an organic gas, 1-methylcyclopropene (1-MCP) (Serek et al., 1994). 1-MCP is effective at rates as low as 20 parts per billion. Because 1-MCP is a gas, treatment methods differ from STS, which is usually applied as a spray to potted plants or as an aqueous floral preservative. For example, commercial application of 1-MCP may occur in a closed greenhouse before packing, or after placing in a transportation vehicle, shipping container, or holding or storage area (Serek et al., 1994). 1-MCP is available as a powder, which creates a gas after mixing with water. 1-MCP leaves no residue and is effective on most crops that respond to STS (Shaw, 1997). 1-MCP is marketed under the name EthylBloc for floriculture crops and can be used legally on both cut flowers and potted plants. EthylBloc will also be available as a liquid spray formulation for those operations without proper facilities for using the gaseous form (J. Daly, personal communication). Spray applications should be made under conditions that allow the product to remain on the plant as long as possible.

CHEMICAL GROWTH REGULATOR EFFECTIVENESS

Chemical growth regulators are infamous for producing variable results from one season, environment, or business to another. Although many differences in response can be attributed to human actions, such as improper mixing, improper measuring, and inadequate applicator skill, many other causes of variable results are not personnel related. Always leave one or more plants untreated to determine if the chemical application was effective. Mark the plants to ensure that they can be located later.

ENVIRONMENTAL FACTORS

TEMPERATURE. High temperatures may cause plants to grow more rapidly than expected and require higher chemical concentrations or more frequent applications as compared with production during normal or lower temperatures. Growers in warm climates generally must use higher rates and more frequent applications of growth retardants than growers in cool climates. High temperatures may also cause the foliage to dry faster, which may reduce uptake of chemicals that are slow to be absorbed by the foliage. However, uptake generally increases with warmer temperatures.

LIGHT. Low light, especially from close spacing, results in tall plants that may require more growth retardants. In addition, uptake may increase with higher light levels, possibly due to the warmer tissue temperatures resulting from high light levels.

pH. Very high or low pH of the mixed solution may alter chemical formulation, making it more or less effective. For example, high pH reduces the effectiveness of Florel.

MOISTURE. Uptake from sprays is generally greatest with well-watered, turgid plants in a high-humidity environment. The higher water content of the plant materials may allow the stomates to remain open and increase penetration of the chemical. High humidity, especially in combination with low light levels and minimal air movement, will slow evaporation of foliar sprays and increase absorption of chemicals.

TIME OF YEAR. The time of year combines a number of environmental influences including temperature and light. Generally less chemical is needed in the winter compared with the summer when high light levels and warm temperatures promote vigorous plant growth.

GROWTH MEDIUM. Different media can increase or decrease uptake of chemicals when applied as a drench. Media that retain water well are not irrigated frequently and thus the chemical would not be leached out as rapidly as with well-drained media. More specifically, the nonpolar growth retardants ancymidol, paclobutrazol, and uniconazole are less effective when applied to media containing bark (see Chemical Growth Retardation section earlier in this chapter) (Million et al., 1997). The specific reason for this interaction is not yet known, but is independent of the medium pH (J. E. Barrett, personal communication).

CHEMICAL FACTORS

METHOD OF APPLICATION. Drenches are often more effective than sprays because of the difficulty of spraying uniformly and obtaining complete foliage and stem coverage. Drenches may also remain active longer in the medium by not drying out. However, drenches are more expensive to apply than spray applications due to the increased volume of solution and increased labor costs. Drenches are especially useful on hanging baskets because of the warm temperatures at the top of the greenhouse. This location makes them difficult to spray. Drenches work best when applied in sufficient amounts to produce 10% runoff (Barrett, 1995). Frequently, however, with automated pot or flat filling equipment, insufficient space is allowed to remain to hold the necessary volume of drench solution.

MODE OF APPLICATION. Uptake and application are best with small spray droplets because smaller droplets generally penetrate the plant canopy better and more uniformly cover the foliage and stem than larger spray droplets.

UNIFORMITY. Nonuniform mixing or application of the growth regulator solution may cause irregular results. For spray applications, uniform coverage is a must. This may be one of the most common problems with unsatisfactory plant growth regulator applications.

CONCENTRATION AND TIME COURSE. Several sprays of a lower concentration generally provide better results than one spray of the same total concentration due to the likelihood of more complete coverage. Multiple, low-concentration sprays reduce the chance of phytotoxicity and provide a better plant "picture" with a uniform decrease in internode elongation. Single, high-concentration sprays often cause a cluster of small internodes, which can make some species such as Easter lilies appear palm tree shaped. Multiple sprays are usually applied over a long time, allowing growers to monitor plant height and adjust the amount of growth retardant required accordingly. Graphical tracking can be used in this process.

PLANT FACTORS

CULTIVAR. Cultivars can vary greatly in their response to plant growth regulators. Even cultivars within the same series may also differ in their sensitivity to growth regulators. Be sure to test new cultivars.

AGE AND STAGE OF DEVELOPMENT. Uptake and effectiveness of plant growth regulators decrease as plants age. Mature plant tissue may not absorb as much chemical as younger tissue and the greater mass of larger plants may dilute the effectiveness of the chemical. Many plants reach final height quickly and growth retardants need to be applied early before final height is reached.

WETTABILITY. Uptake decreases if plants are pubescent or the leaf surface is quite waxy, both of which limit absorption of the chemical into the tissue. Wetting agents may increase uptake by reducing surface tension on plant surfaces.

KEY POINTS

- Plant growth regulation is defined as any chemical process used to produce a specific type of growth response.
- Five classes of endogenous plant growth regulators regulate plant growth: auxins, gibberellins, cytokinins, ethylene, and abscisic acid.
- Plant growth regulators are used during propagation, tissue culture, seed germination, flower development, plant production, and postharvest handling.
- Chemical growth regulators are most commonly used to restrict height, which may also darken foliage color, increase stem diameter, and effect flowering.
- Available chemical growth retardants include A-Rest (ancymidol), B-Nine (daminozide), Bonzi (paclobutrazol), Cycocel (chlormequat), Florel (ethephon), Piccolo (paclobutrazol), Sumagic (uniconazole), and Topflor (flurprimidol).
- Chemical growth retardants are not registered for use on vegetable or other edible bedding plants.
- Nonchemical methods of height control include cultivar selection; maximum spacing; minimal use of incandescent lighting; proper propagation, planting, pinching, and photoperiod; small container size; nutrient restriction; high fertilization; water stress; shaking or brushing; and temperature manipulation (DIF and DROP).
- Graphical tracking is used to monitor plant height regardless of the height control method.
- Several chemical pinching or branching agents are available that operate on different principles including Accel (10:1 benzyladenine:gibberellic acid), Atrimmec (dikegulac sodium), Florel, and Off-Shoot-O (methyl ester of fatty acids).
- Anti-ethylene agents such as silver thiosulfate (STS) and 1-methylcyclopropene (-MCP) are used to prevent ethylene action and delay senescence of cut flowers and flowering potted crops.
- Chemical growth regulators often produce variable results from one season, environment, or business to another. Reasons for variations include environmental factors, such as temperature, light, solution pH, moisture, time of year, and type of growth medium; chemical factors, such as method of application, mode of application, application uniformity, and chemical concentration and time course; and plant factors such as cultivar, age and stage of development, and wettability of plant surface.

BIBLIOGRAPHY

Adriansen, E. 1985. Kemisk vækstregulering, pp. 142–162 in *Potteplanter I—Produktion, Metoder, Midler*, O.V. Christensen, A. Klougart, I.S. Pedersen, and K. Wikesjö, editors. GartnerINFO, København, Denmark. (In Danish)

Baden, S.A., and J.G. Latimer. 1992. An effective system for brushing vegetable transplants for height control. *HortTechnology* 2:412–414.

Barrett, J. 1995. The benefits of drench applications. *Greenhouse Manager* 13(10):66–68.

Barrett, J.E. 1982. Chrysanthemum height control by ancymidol, PP333, and EL-500 dependent on medium composition. *HortScience* 17:896–897.

Barrett, J.E. 2001. Mechanisms of action, pp. 32–41 in *Tips on Regulating Growth of Floriculture Crops*, M.L. Gaston, L.A. Kunkle, P.S. Konjoian, and M.F. Wilt, editors. Ohio Florists' Association Services, Columbus, Ohio.

Barrett, J.E., and T.A. Nell. 1990. Factors effecting efficacy of paclobutrazol and uniconazole on petunia and chrysanthemum. *Acta Horticulturae* 272:229–234.

Barrett, J.E., C.A. Bartuska, and T.A. Nell. 1994. Application techniques alter uniconazole efficacy on chrysanthemums. *HortScience* 29:893–895.

Berghage, R.D., and R.D. Heins. 1991. Quantification of temperature effects on stem elongation in poinsettia. *Journal of the American Society for Horticultural Science* 116:14–18.

Cockshull, K.E., F.A. Langton, and C.R.J. Cave. 1995. Differential effects of different DIF treatments on chrysanthemum and poinsettia. *Acta Horticulturae* 378:15–25.

Corr, B.E. 1988. Factors influencing growth and flowering of *Zantedeschia elliottiana* and *Z. rehmanii*. Ph.D. thesis, University of Minnesota, St. Paul.

Corr, B.E., and R.E. Widmer. 1987. Gibberellic acid increases flower number in *Zantedeschia elliottiana* and *Z. rehmanii*. *HortScience* 22:605–607.

Cox, D. 2003. Subirrigating seed geraniums with Bonzi. *Greenhouse Product News* 13(8):30, 32, 34, 35.

Erwin, J., R. Heins, R. Berghage, and W. Carlson. 1989a. How can temperatures be used to control plant stem elongation? *Minnesota State Florists Bulletin* 38(3):1–5.

Erwin, J.E., R.D. Heins, and M.G. Karlsson. 1989b. Thermomorphogenesis in *Lilium longiflorum*. *American Journal of Botany* 76:47–52.

Erwin, J.E., R.D. Heins, B.J. Kovanda, R.D. Berghage, W.H. Carlson, and J.A. Biernbaum. 1989c. Cool mornings can control plant height. *GrowerTalks* 52(9):75.

Fisher, P.R., and R.D. Heins. 1997. Tracking Easter lilies. *Greenhouse Grower* 15(13):65–66.

Fisher, P.R., R.D. Heins, and J.H. Lieth. 1996. Modeling the stem elongation response of poinsettia to chlormequat. *Journal of the American Society for Horticultural Science* 121:861–868.

Garner, C.C., and T.B. Björkman. 1996. Mechanical conditioning for controlling excessive elongation in tomato transplants: Sensitivity to dose, frequency, and timing of brushing. *Journal of the American Society for Horticultural Science* 121:894–900.

Gaston, M.L., L.A. Kunkle, P.S. Konjoian, and M.F. Wilt, editors. 2001. *Tips on Regulating Growth of Floriculture Crops*. Ohio Florists' Association Services, Columbus, Ohio.

Grindal, G., and R. Moe. 1995. Growth rhythm and temperature DROP. *Acta Horticulturae* 378:47–52.

Hammer, A. 2001. Calculations, pp. 42–47 in *Tips on Regulating Growth of Floriculture Crops*, M.L. Gaston, L.A. Kunkle, P.S. Konjoian, and M.F. Wilt, editors. Ohio Florists' Association Services, Columbus, Ohio.

Hammer, P.A., C.A. Mitchell, and T.C. Weiler. 1974. Height control in greenhouse chrysanthemum by mechanical stress. *HortScience* 9:474–475.

Hartmann, H.T., D.E. Kester, F.T. Davies, Jr., and R.L. Geneve. 1997. *Plant Propagation: Principles and Practice*, 6th ed. Prentice Hall, Upper Saddle River, New Jersey.

Hausbeck, M.K., C.T. Stephens, and R.D. Heins. 1987. Variation in resistance of geraniums to *Pythium ultimum* in presence or absence of silver thiosulfate. *HortScience* 22:940–942.

Heins, R.D., and P.R. Fisher. 1997. Tools for the tracking. *Greenhouse Grower* 15(8):131–132.

Heins, R., J. Erwin, M. Karlsson, R. Berghage, W. Carlson, and J. Biernbaum. 1997. Tracking Easter lily height with graphs. *Minnesota Commercial Flower Growers Association Bulletin* 46(2):17–21.

Higgins, E. 2001. Chrysanthemums, pp. 68–70 in *Tips on Regulating Growth of Floriculture Crops*, M.L. Gaston, L.A. Kunkle, P.S. Konjoian, and M.F. Wilt, editors. Ohio Florists' Association Services, Columbus, Ohio.

Jerzy, M., and J. Krause. 1980. The factors controlling growth and flowering of forced lilies 'Enchantment': Light intensity and mechanical. *Acta Horticulturae* 109:111–115.

Larson, R.A., and T.D. Snydor. 1971. Azalea flower bud development and dormancy as influenced by temperature and gibberellic acid. *Journal of the American Society for Horticultural Science* 96:786–788.

Latimer, J.G. 1991. Mechanical conditioning for control of growth and quality of vegetable transplants. *HortScience* 26:1456–1461.

Latimer, J.G. 2001. Mechanical conditioning, pp. 28–31 in *Tips on Regulating Growth of Floriculture Crops*, M.L. Gaston, L.A. Kunkle, P.S. Konjoian, and M.F. Wilt, editors. Ohio Florists' Association Services, Columbus, Ohio.

Latimer, J.G., and R.D. Oetting. 1998. Greenhouse conditioning affects landscape performance of bedding plants. *Journal of Environmental Horticulture* 16:138–142.

Latimer, J., H. Scoggins, and V. Groover. 2003. Lamiaceae response to PGRs. *Greenhouse Product News* 13(7):100, 102, 104–106.

McMahon, M.J., J.W. Kelly, D.R. Decoteau, R.E. Young, and R.K. Pollock. 1991. Growth of *Dendranthema ×grandiflorum* (Ramat.) Kitamura under various spectral filters. *Journal of the American Society for Horticultural Science* 116:950–954.

Miller, B. 1997. 1998 Easter lily production. *Southeastern Floriculture* 7(5):43–46.

Miller, W.B., P.A. Hammer, and T.I. Kirk. 1993. Reversed greenhouse temperatures alter carbohydrate status in *Lilium longiflorum* Thunb. 'Nellie White'. *Journal of the American Society for Horticultural Science* 118:736–740.

Million, J., J. Barrett, D. Clark, and T. Nell. 1997. Influence of several container media components on paclobutrazol efficacy. *HortScience* 32:509. (Abstract)

Million, J.B., J.E. Barrett, T.A. Nell, and D.G. Clark. 1999. Inhibiting growth of flowering crops with ancymidol and paclobutrazol in subirrigation water. *HortScience* 34:1103–1105.

Mortensen, L.M., and E. Strømme. 1987. Effects of light quality on some greenhouse crops. *Scientia Horticulturae* 33:27–36.

Moe, R., K. Willumsen, I.H. Ihlebekk, A.I. Stupa, N.M. Glomsrud, and L.M. Mortensen. 1995. DIF and temperature DROP responses in SDP and LDP, a comparison. *Acta Horticulturae* 378:27–33.

Nelson, P.V. 2001. Nutrition and water, pp. 23–27 in *Tips on Regulating Growth of Floriculture Crops*, M.L. Gaston, L.A. Kunkle, P.S. Konjoian, and M.F. Wilt, editors. Ohio Florists' Association Services, Columbus, Ohio.

Norcini, J.G., W.G. Hudson, M.P. Garber, R.K. Jones, A.R. Chase, and K. Bondari. 1996. Pest management in the U.S. greenhouse and nursery industry: III. Plant growth regulation. *HortTechnology* 6:207–210.

Rajapakse, N.C., and J.W. Kelly. 1992. Regulation of chrysanthemum growth by spectral filters. *Journal of the American Society for Horticultural Science* 117:481–485.

Schnelle, M.A., B.D. McCraw, and T.J. Schmoll. 1994. A brushing apparatus for height control of bedding plants. *HortTechnology* 4:275–276.

Serek, J., E.C. Sisler, and M.S. Reid. 1994. Novel gaseous ethylene binding inhibiter prevents ethylene effects in potted flowering plants. *Journal of the American Society for Horticultural Society* 119:1230–1233.

Shaw, J.A. 1997. The new anti-ethylene: Replacement for STS? *FloraCulture International* 7(3):36.

Sheldrake, R. 1991. Control height with low P. *Greenhouse Grower* 9(10):77–78, 80.

Styer, R.C. 1997. Put the brakes on plug growth. *GrowerTalks* 61(7):40, 42–45.

Turgeon, R., and J.A. Webb. 1971. Growth inhibition by mechanical stress. *Science* 174:961–962.

Vågen, I.M., R. Moe, and E. Ronglan. 2003. Diurnal temperature alternations (DIF/DROP) affect chlorophyll content and chlorophyll a/chlorophyll b ratio in *Melissa officinalis* L. and *Ocimum basilicum* L., but not in *Viola ×wittrockiana* Gams. *Scientia Horticulturae* 97:153–162.

Warner, R.M., and J.E. Erwin. 2001. Temperature, pp. 10–17 in *Tips on Regulating Growth of Floriculture Crops*, M.L. Gaston, L.A. Kunkle, P.S. Konjoian, and M.F. Wilt, editors. Ohio Florists' Association Services, Columbus, Ohio.

Whealy, C.A. 1993. Satisfaction geranium trees, pp. 137–140 in *Geraniums*, J.W. White, editor. Ball Publishing, Geneva, Illinois.

White, J.W. 1976. *Lilium* sp. 'Mid Century Hybrids' adapted to pot use with ancymidol. *Journal of the American Society for Horticultural Science* 101:126–129.

Widmer, R.E., E.C. Stephens, and M.V. Angell. 1976. Giberellin accelerates flowering of *Cyclamen persicum* Mill. *HortScience* 9:476–477.

Chapter 9

Pest Management

INTRODUCTION

The control of greenhouse pests is based on the three basic components required for an insect or disease to become established: (1) the pest organism, (2) a susceptible host, and (3) the proper environment for the pest to develop and reproduce. All three components interact to form a triangle. The goal of pest control is to disrupt or eliminate any one of these three components. For example, *Botrytis* can be controlled by (1) sanitation or chemical applications to eliminate the presence of *Botrytis*, (2) growing *Botrytis*-resistant crops, or (3) reducing humidity to make the environment unsuitable for disease development.

INTEGRATED PEST MANAGEMENT

The focus of *integrated pest management* (IPM) is the integration of all strategies for controlling insects and diseases into one coherent plan (Table 9-1). Effective and efficient pest management requires observant scouting, prompt actions, and follow-through. Please consult a comprehensive pest management text, such as Dreistadt's (2001), for additional information.

PREVENTION

IPM begins with *prevention* to keep pest problems from starting in a crop. New plant material must be inspected and should be isolated from existing crops to prevent infestation of ex-

isting, pest-free crops. Any propagation material with leaves and roots, such as cuttings and liners, is especially prone to harboring pests. Seeds, bulbs, corms, rhizomes, and other storage organs can also be contaminated with pests; various preplanting heat treatments may reduce or eliminate them (Dreistadt, 2001; see also applicable genera chapters).

Pests can be excluded by placing barriers between greenhouses or sections within a greenhouse, by excluding customers and non-essential personnel from key areas, and by using insect-proof screens on pads, fans, and vents. When choosing an insect screen, be certain to consider its effectiveness and its effect on airflow, cost, and longevity. The highest degree of insect exclusion will generally be required for propagation areas where large numbers of plants could be infested. A lesser degree of control may be acceptable for finished crops. Openings within the screen for excluding insects should be less than 0.0075 in. (192 microns, 0.2 mm) for thrips, one of the smallest flying insect pests common in the greenhouse.

When possible, grow pest-resistant species or cultivars, although most crops exhibit little variation in resistance among cultivars. All media should be pasteurized and proper sanitation practices should be implemented including indoor and outdoor weed control, use of clean containers, sterilization of benches, and

TABLE 9-1
Pest control checklist.

Before Production Starts
- Use pasteurized or pathogen-free media.
- Use clean, sterile containers.
- Clean and sterilize benches periodically.
- Clean and sterilize the irrigation system periodically.
- Remove weeds in the greenhouse and within 10 to 30 ft (3 to 9 m) of the outside of the greenhouse.
- Remove fallen plant material, media, and other debris.
- Use insect exclusion screens.
- Remove extra or personal plants.

During Production
- Inspect incoming plant materials carefully.
- Isolate new plant materials, if possible.
- Grow pest-resistant species or cultivars.
- Produce plants at the optimum growing conditions.
- Avoid over- or underirrigation.
- Keep hose ends off the ground.
- Maintain optimum medium pH and EC.
- Avoid water dripping on plants from overhead leaks, condensation, or hanging baskets.
- Irrigate early in the day to allow foliage to dry by evening.
- Reduce humidity by venting/heating in the evening.
- Switch to subirrigation or microtube systems to reduce humidity and decrease water on the foliage.
- Scout regularly and thoroughly.
- Use yellow and/or blue sticky cards for monitoring insect populations.

If a Problem Occurs or Is Likely to Occur
- Decide on the threshold of tolerance for each pest.
- Apply chemical controls when appropriate.
- Rotate between chemical classes.
- Use beneficials when appropriate.
- Remove diseased or heavily insect-infested plants promptly.

prompt removal of all sources of disease inoculum such as dead plants, fallen leaves and other debris, and excess growing medium. Remove extra or personal plants from production areas.

ENVIRONMENTAL AND CULTURAL CONTROLS

The next step in IPM is to implement environmental or cultural control procedures. For example, high humidity can be vented out in the early evening to reduce *Botrytis* and mildew infection. A slight increase in temperature in the early evening will also decrease relative humidity. Proper air circulation and dry foliage reduce foliar diseases. The pH and soluble salt levels (EC) of the media should be regularly tested and maintained near optimum for the crop species, because extremely high or low pH and high EC can predispose plants to root and crown disease problems. Irrigate plants consistently as required by each crop species. Irrigating too frequently or too infrequently can stress plants and increase the likelihood of pest problems. Use a well-drained medium or a naturally disease-suppressive medium, if possible. Root and crown rots are one of the most common disease problems in floriculture production, often due to improper irrigation practices, and can be greatly reduced by media choice and proper management of water, pH, and EC.

BENEFICIALS

The commercial availability of beneficial insects and diseases has greatly expanded pest control options (Gill, 1997; Gill and Sanderson, 1998). Research is taking place around the world and many more pest control options are likely to be available in the future. Beneficial organisms include predators, parasites, and microorganisms. Predators eat the undesirable insect; for example, lacewing larvae (*Chrysoperla rufilabris*) eat aphids. Parasites lay eggs on or in the pest; for example, the parasitic wasp *Encarsia formosa* lays eggs in whitefly pupae. Microorganisms such as viruses, bacteria, fungi, or nematodes directly attack the pest; for example, *Bacillus thuringiensis* bacteria kill caterpillars and fungus gnats, depending on the type applied. Microorganisms also compete with undesired organisms for nutrients and living space; for example, *Agrobacterium radiobacter* is a competitive inhibitor of *Agrobacterium tumefaciens*, the bacterium that causes crown gall. Combinations of two or more beneficials, which draw on the strengths of each species, may be needed for effective pest control. Effective control using beneficials usually requires scheduled releases, proper environment (especially temperature), and receipt of live organisms from reliable suppliers. Generally a pesticide-free environment is required; however, a few pesticides, especially insect growth regulators and botanicals, are compatible with some beneficials.

ECONOMIC THRESHOLD

All commercial crop producers will need to make management decisions regarding the number of pests they can tolerate on a crop before the plant quality is sufficiently reduced to cause a monetary loss. This is known as the *economic threshold*, below which level the pest is thought to be economically unimportant. Unfortunately, the economic threshold is close to zero for potted foliage, potted flowering crops, and cut flowers because they are to be used indoors where the customer readily notices any insect or disease problems. Unlike most vegetable or fruit production, the entire plant is harvested in floriculture and must be unblemished. Even small or isolated insect or disease populations may increase during marketing or in the home. The threshold can be higher for insects on bedding plants because the insects often disappear after the plants are placed outside. In addition, the threshold can occasionally be higher at the beginning of the crop than later in the cycle because there is still time to clean the plants before sale. This strategy can be risky, however, because the pest population may become so great that it cannot be controlled. Regardless, few customers will tolerate the presence of insects on purchased plants.

SCOUTING

Pest scouting and early detection are key components in an effective IPM program. Plants must be checked regularly, at least once a week, for the presence of pests. Set up a regular scouting pattern that allows a uniform and thorough check of the plant materials. Choose up to 10 plants per bench, and select plants from both the outer and inner portions of the bench. Hanging baskets and plants near doors and vents are particularly prone to insects and should be checked accordingly. Examine each plant carefully—check the undersides of old and young leaves, leaf axils, flowers, and buds. Yellow sticky traps can be used to monitor and detect localized adult populations of insect pests such as whiteflies, thrips, fungus gnats, and winged aphids. Blue sticky traps are effective with thrips. Place traps 1 in. (2.5 cm) above the plant canopy and use one card per 1000 ft² (93 m²) for whiteflies or one per 10,000 ft² (930 m²) for other pests. Regardless of the insect being monitored, each production unit, such as a greenhouse section, should have at least one sticky trap. Orient the traps perpendicular to the air flow and raise them as the plants grow taller.

Not only must scouting be done regularly, but the information must be reported and used. Identification of a problem is useless unless prompt and proper action is taken. Although some pest problems may not warrant immediate attention, other problems are easier to treat when populations are low or the infested area is small. The use of routine scouting can result in fewer pesticide applications (Cloyd and Sadof, 2003). Also, the person in charge of scouting should be knowledgeable and keep good records, which will allow the grower to detect patterns and anticipate and plan for future problems.

CHEMICALS

Chemicals have traditionally been one of the main control methods against pest problems. However, problems with cost, pest resistance, availability, and environmental concerns have prompted a focus on the nonchemical pest control methods discussed previously.

PESTICIDE SAFETY

All chemicals, not just pesticides, should be treated with care: plant growth regulators, cleaning supplies, and any organic chemicals. Many countries have regulations designed to protect the safety of workers when chemicals, especially pesticides, are being used. In the United States the federal Worker Protection Standards (WPS) are among the most important of these regulations. Note that most states and some local governments have additional safety and licensing requirements for people who apply pesticides. Anyone who works with chemicals or supervises people who work with chemicals will probably need to obtain a license or be certified. Extension service personnel or the Department of Agriculture in each state should be able to provide additional information. Compliance with the following 10 issues will allow a business to meet most of the requirements for the WPS (Faust, 1995).

1. *Centralized bulletin board.* A bulletin board must be maintained in a centralized location that is accessible to all employees. The bulletin board must contain the following information:

- *WPS safety poster.* Request the "WPS Quick Reference Poster," publication number 055-000-00445-5, through the U.S. Government Printing Office.

- *Emergency medical information.* List the name, address, and phone number of nearest medical facility.
- *Pesticide application list.* The following pesticide application information is to be maintained for 30 days following the application: product name, EPA registration number, active ingredient, amount of chemical applied, location and description of treated area, and time, date, and restricted entry interval (REI) of the pesticide application. The applicator's name and certification number should also be included.
- *Pesticide label and material safety data sheet (MSDS).* EPA requires that growers make pesticide labels available to workers. MSDSs are available through chemical suppliers (see Labels and Material Safety Data Sheets section later in this chapter).

2. *Pesticide safety training.* Pesticide handlers must be trained about pesticide safety and handling prior to performing any handling tasks. Workers must be trained about pesticide safety during their first week of work. Contact your local federal government office concerning assistance in providing the WPS training.

3. *Decontamination sites.* Provide water for routine and emergency eye flushing and whole body washing. Provide clean coveralls, safe drinking water, and 1 pt of eyeflush water for each pesticide handler (Fig. 9-1). The decontamination sites must be within 0.25 mile (400 m) of all employees. Worker decontamination sites cannot be in areas being treated with pesticides or in an REI area, but handler decontamination sites may be within areas being treated with pesticides.

4. *Emergency assistance.* Provide transportation to medical facility and provide pesticide information to the victim and medical personnel.

5. *EPA-approved warning signs.* A 14- × 16-in. (36- × 41-cm) sign must include the wording "Pesticides/Pesticides, Danger/Peligro, Keep Out/No Entre," with an image of a stern face and upraised hand, and be visible at all usual entrances. Contact your government office concerning assistance in obtaining the appropriate signs.

6. *Monitor handlers.* At least once every 2 hours, someone must check by sight or by voice communication any handler who

FIGURE 9-1 Water and eye wash solution readily available to workers.

is handling a pesticide that has a skull and crossbones symbol on its label. Constant voice or visual contact must be made with any handler who is applying or handling a fumigant in a greenhouse. The monitor must be trained as a handler and have immediate access to the required personal protective equipment.

7. *Personal protective equipment.* Personal protective equipment (PPE) includes coveralls, respirators, protective eyewear, chemical-resistant suits, gloves, footwear, aprons, and headgear. Follow PPE requirements as stated on the pesticide label. If you are unsure, use more PPE than required. Be certain that respirators fit correctly. Technically, individuals with beards cannot wear facial respirators. Provide a pesticide-free area for storing personal clothing not in use. Do not allow PPE to be taken or worn home. Wash and store PPE separately from other clothing and laundry. Regularly replace respirators according to respirator manufacturer or pesticide labels.

The respirator can be used separately or in combination with a face shield. The respirator should be cleaned and checked and the filter should be replaced periodically. A fit test may be required by the state before a person is allowed to apply pesticides with a respirator. The fit test determines if any leaks are present when a person is using a respirator.

Gloves should be unlined and made of rubber or vinyl. Be sure to check the label because some chemicals may dissolve gloves. Gloves are worn inside the sleeve if applicators will not be raising their arms, but the gloves should be worn over the sleeves if the person will be spraying tall crops or plants overhead with arms raised.

Boots should also be unlined and made with water-impermeable rubber. Leather or cloth boots should not be used because they will absorb chemicals. Pant cuffs are worn over the boot to prevent spray solution from running into the boot and onto the foot.

Generally, short sleeve shirts, shorts, or sandals are not allowed because they provide no protection for the applicators. Always wear socks and carefully remove clothing while wearing gloves to prevent contamination of the hands. Wash clothes worn during pesticide applications separately from regular clothes. Do not store safety equipment and clothes in the pesticide storage room. Clothes may absorb chemicals and protective clothing may be needed in case of a chemical spill or fire in the room.

8. *Restricted entry interval.* Workers must be kept out of the treated area during the restricted entry interval. Note that all pesticides have an REI, even many *Bacillus thuringiensis* products. In addition, several components of home pesticide formulations such as mineral oil, borax, and diatomaceous earth also have reentry restrictions.

9. *Early entry.* Early entry involving contact with soil, water, air, plants, and so forth is allowed for short-term tasks that last less than 1 hour or for emergencies. The PPE required by the pesticide label must be supplied by the employer. Early entry not involving contact is allowed for less than 1 hour providing at least 4 hours have passed since the pesticide application and WPS ventilation criteria or inhalation exposure criteria listed on the label have been met.

10. *Ventilation criteria for greenhouses.* See the pesticide label for specific requirements; if none, then provide one of the following:

- 10 air exchanges
- 4 hr of passive ventilation with vents
- 2 hr of mechanical ventilation with fans
- 11 hr with no ventilation followed by 1 hr of mechanical ventilation or 2 hr of passive ventilation
- 24 hr without ventilation

This list is only a summary of the WPS standards. For a more complete source of information contact your local federal government office.

CHEMICAL STORAGE AND MIXING AREAS

Chemical storage facilities should be large enough to contain pesticides as well as fertilizers, plant growth regulators, and cleaning supplies. Liquid chemicals should be stored below solid chemicals as a precaution against containers leaking and contaminating lower containers. A chemical absorbent cloth should line the shelf under containers of liquids. Chemicals should not be stored directly on the floor and the room or building should be self-contained such that no chemicals could leak out the door or walls if any containers break. The area should also be as flood and earthquake proof as possible. Although a separate building is best for chemical storage, a room within a headhouse may be allowed in some states. The building or room should be locked with limited access to the key. The room should be well ventilated, heated, and cooled to provide a temperature range of 55 to 65°F (13 to 18°C) (Cloyd, 2003). Although the room should be well lighted, direct sunlight should be avoided. Maintain a relative humidity of 40 to 50%. A list of emergency numbers should be posted in or near the storage area by all telephones and should include police, fire, ambulance, hospitals, poison information centers, and hazardous waste disposal centers. A written or printed inventory of all contents (updated regularly!) should be readily available on site. Other copies should be available at another location in case fire and other emergency personnel need to know the contents of the storage area. The storage area should also be well labeled as a pesticide storage area with government-approved signs (e.g., diamond labels) to warn firefighters in case of fire. Lock doors during chemical mixing and during application in the greenhouse to prevent entry.

Date each chemical container on receipt. Although storage duration will vary with the chemical, many liquid formulations can be safely stored for 2 years and dry formulations for at least 3 to 5 years. Chemicals will show characteristic changes when they begin to break down. Emulsifiable concentrates should not be used if they separate into layers in the original container, have an insoluble sludge on the bottom of the original container, or do not become milky when added to water. Wettable powders should not be used if the powder has lumps prior to or after mixing, if it rapidly clogs the spray nozzle, or if it does not suspend in water.

LABELS AND MATERIAL SAFETY DATA SHEETS

Following the directions on the pesticide container label is the first step toward safe use of a pesticide and complete compliance with environmental regulations. The material safety data sheet is the second source of necessary information for the grower. A notebook with copies of the MSDS for all chemicals on the property should be kept in a location that is accessible at all times. The MSDS and copies of the labels should not be housed with the chemicals because a fire or spill in the chemical room or building would prevent anyone from reaching the information when it is required.

The labels and MSDS contain a variety of information including trade name; chemical name (especially important in case of accidental poisoning); manufacturer's name, address, and phone number; minimum reentry time; application procedures; crop species on which the chemical can be legally used; procedures to follow in case of spills and accidental poisonings; symptoms of accidental poisonings; and toxicity ratings.

The following toxicity ratings indicate the level of danger in using the product and the minimum level of protection required to apply the chemical. The ratings are partially based on the LD_{50} (lethal dose), which is defined as the amount of pesticide necessary to kill 50% of a test population (e.g., rats, mice, rabbits) within 14 days. The lower the LD_{50}, the more toxic the substance and the smaller the quantity of chemical required to kill 50% of the test population. The LD_{50} is expressed in milligrams of chemical per kilogram of the test animal weight used in oral or skin (dermal) exposure studies. The LD_{50} for the toxicity ratings are as follows:

Caution—slightly toxic, LD_{50} = 500 mg and above

Warning—moderately toxic, LD_{50} = 50 to 500 mg

Danger—highly toxic, poison, marked with a skull and crossbones, LD_{50} = 0 to 50 mg

PESTICIDE CONTAINERS

Always keep pesticides in the original container. If the contents are unknown, dispose of them immediately and properly. Containers without labels or with illegible labels can easily lead to accidents endangering workers or damaging crops. Proper disposal is required and a government agency or chemical supplier should be contacted for advice.

SIGNS

All exits and chemical storage and mixing areas should be clearly marked. In addition, the MSDS book and chemical application list (log) should be readily available to all personnel and clearly marked with signs. Areas treated with chemicals must be posted with the chemical used, concentration, and reentry time.

EQUIPMENT

A varity of chemical application equipment is available for growers. Equipment should be labeled according to the class of chemicals used in the equipment (insecticides, fungicides, herbicides, or growth regulators) to prevent accidental contamination. In particular, separate equipment must be used for (1) herbicides due to phytotoxicity and (2) growth regulators due to adverse plant responses. If separate equipment cannot be obtained, be absolutely certain that equipment is washed clean when switching between chemical classes. At minimum, all equipment should be triple rinsed when finished and rinsate handled as described later in the chapter. Specific chemicals for cleaning application equipment are available.

Sprayers can range from handheld spray bottles to large motorized sprayers (Fig. 9-2). Spray bottles have a 0.25- to 0.50-gal (1- to 2-L) capacity and can be used for applications to small areas with a minimum amount of solution. However, the accurate measurement of small amounts of chemicals is difficult.

Hand-pump pressure sprayers have a 2- to 6-gal (8- to 24-L) capacity and are excellent for small greenhouses. However, carrying a large-capacity hand-pump sprayer can easily fatigue the person applying the chemicals. In general, purchasing a quality hand-pump sprayer will be cheaper in the long run because the inexpensive models tend to break easily.

Backpack sprayers have a 4- to 10-gal (12- to 30-L) capacity and are more comfortable to manage. Backpack sprayers are often similar in

FIGURE 9-2 Motorized sprayer.

price to a quality hand-pump sprayer. Gasoline or electric powered sprayers have a large 12- to 100-gal (48- to 400-L) capacity and may be required for large greenhouse and nursery operations. Most powered sprayers are self-agitating and can be adapted with multiple-head spray nozzles or booms. Be careful of exhaust from gasoline powered sprayers as it can damage some crops.

Mist or ultralow-volume (ULV) sprayers apply the spray in very fine, lightweight droplets that penetrate the foliar canopy more readily than the large-sized droplets of regular sprayers. The small droplet size and better coverage generally allow a smaller amount of pesticide solution to cover a larger area than does a regular sprayer.

Another type of sprayer, the electrostatic sprayer, also results in better coverage than a regular sprayer by placing a positive charge on the tiny droplets, which are then attracted to negatively charged plant tissue and thus adhere to all parts of the plant, even the lower sides of the leaves. Electrostatic sprayers also allow less pesticide to be used in covering a specific area than regular sprayers. The efficacy of some pesticides might be improved by using an electrostatic sprayer; other pesticides are equally effective when applied with a conventional sprayer (Tjosvold and Greene, 1997).

Foggers vaporize the pesticide by injecting it into either a hot pipe or a hot airstream. Most foggers use an oil-based carrier, which may cause phytotoxicity. Foggers produce a visible fog, making it easy to estimate complete coverage. The emitting end of the foggers must be aimed at the walkway or under the bench. If the fog comes in direct contact with the plants, excessive pesticide deposits form and the hot exhaust will burn the plants.

Although not often considered greenhouse equipment, sulfur burners can be used to vaporize some pesticides. In particular, sulfur can be vaporized for control of powdery mildew. This method of pesticide application in the greenhouse may not be legal; check with state personnel or suppliers before using sulfur burners.

Granule dispensers are used to drop a measured amount of a granular pesticide in each container. Granule dispensers are labor intensive because each container must be treated. Do not apply granular pesticides with whirlybird fertilizer spreaders because they are wasteful and illegal and increase the chance of phytotoxicity and accidental poisoning.

PESTICIDE ACTION

Pesticides can be divided into two groups based on their method of control: contact or systemic. Contact pesticides require that the chemical actually contact the pest's body or be ingested by the pest. Systemic pesticides are absorbed by the plant, often the roots, and moved throughout the plant. The pest is controlled when it ingests or absorbs plant material, such as leaf tissue or sap, containing the chemical. Although systemic chemicals may be able to control pests that are difficult to control by other means, many plant organs including flowers, woody stems, and old leaves generally do not readily take up systemic chemicals.

TIMING

Pesticides are generally applied as soon as an infestation is apparent. Chemicals are often reapplied, usually three times, 5 to 7 days apart, depending on the residual life of the pesticide, the pest's life cycle, and the method of control—systemic or contact.

PESTICIDE FORMULATIONS

Chemicals are available in a variety of formulations and some chemicals can be obtained in more than one formulation. When considering which formulation to use, the ease of application includes the labor required to apply the pesticide and the amount of time required to clean the equipment. Plant coverage refers to how easy it is to treat an entire plant, especially the lower leaf surfaces.

WETTABLE POWDER (WP). Powdered solid particles are suspended in water; the solution is sprayed on plants. Constant agitation is required to keep the particles suspended in water and a surfactant may be required for better spray coverage on the plant surface. Surfactants decrease the surface tension of water and prevent the pesticide solution from beading and running off the plant. The particles may increase the nozzle opening through abrasion, necessitating regular replacement of the nozzles. Wettable powders can also be used as drenches. Flowable (F) formulations are products containing WPs in a liquid form, eliminating the dust that occurs during preparation. Wettable powders are also available in dissolvable bags for 100-gal (375-L) tanks. The entire packet is dropped in the tank and there is little handling of the chemical.

- *Ease of application*—relatively difficult to keep pesticide solution agitated and to clean equipment
- *Plant coverage*—complete coverage can be obtained with an applicator skilled at applying pesticides
- *Number of pesticides available*—many
- *Residue*—moderate, but variable between different chemicals
- *Potential for phytotoxicity*—among the lowest

EMULSIFIABLE CONCENTRATE (EC). The pesticide is dissolved in an oil, which is emulsified in water; the solution is sprayed on plants. Generally no surfactant is required. This formulation can also be used as a drench.

- *Ease of application*—moderate, considering the mixing of solution and cleaning of equipment
- *Plant coverage*—complete, with an experienced applicator
- *Number of pesticides available*—many
- *Residue*—little
- *Potential for phytotoxicity*—high

DUSTS (D). Pesticide is a powdered solid, mixed with a filler, such as talc, and applied to plant surfaces. Dusts are rarely used in commercial production due to the labor involved, drifting, and heavy residue. Dusts are more commonly used by the general public.

- *Ease of application*—easy, to a small area
- *Plant coverage*—only upper surfaces
- *Number of pesticides available*—few for commercial use
- *Residue*—heavy
- *Potential for phytotoxicity*—among the lowest

AEROSOLS (A). Pesticide is contained in cylinders of compressed gas and available in two types: (1) small handheld containers where a person manually holds down the release button and sprays the plant, or (2) total release containers where the cylinder automatically discharges its contents after being activated. Aerosols should generally be used only when the temperatures are 60 to 85°F (15 to 29°C). Also, the propellant is cold and can freeze nearby plant material. Be sure to have sufficient distance between the cylinder and the plants.

- *Ease of application*—easy
- *Plant coverage*—only upper surface, commonly used to control flying adult insects
- *Number of pesticides available*—few
- *Residue*—little
- *Potential for phytotoxicity*—average; higher if foliage is wet

FOGS. Pesticide is vaporized by injection into either a hot pipe or a hot airstream. Fogs should generally be used only when the temperatures are 60 to 85°F (15 to 29°C).

- *Ease of application*—moderate, considering mixing of solution and cleaning of equipment
- *Plant coverage*—complete
- *Number of pesticides available*—moderate
- *Residue*—little
- *Potential for phytotoxicity*—high (carrier can be phytotoxic); higher if foliage is wet and temperature is above 85°F (29°C)

SMOKES. Pesticide is contained in a combustible carrier, which is ignited. Smokes should be used only when the temperatures are 60 to 85°F (15 to 29°C).

- *Ease of application*—easy
- *Plant coverage*—complete
- *Number of pesticides available*—few

- *Residue*—little
- *Potential for phytotoxicity*—low if plants are dry and temperature is below 85°F (29°C)

GRANULES (G). Pesticide is incorporated into a carrier, such as ground corn cobs, and applied to the root medium surface. Granules are watered in, allowing the pesticide to be released and absorbed by the plant roots. Many granule pesticides are systemic. Little drift occurs and pesticides are safe to handle.

- *Ease of application*—relatively difficult, labor intensive
- *Plant coverage*—complete for systemics
- *Number of pesticides available*—few
- *Residue*—none
- *Potential for phytotoxicity*—average

VOLATILIZATION. Pesticide is heated and volatilizes directly into the air. This method often uses a sulfur burner to heat the chemical. The legality of this method should be checked beforehand.

- *Ease of application*—easy
- *Plant coverage*—complete coverage can be obtained
- *Number of pesticides available*—few
- *Residue*—little
- *Potential for phytotoxicity*—average

A number of other formulations and combinations of formulations are available (Table 9-2) (Oetting and Olson, 1997). One novel method is to cover the inside of containers with paint amended with a systemic insecticide, which would decrease the cost of labor required to apply the pesticide and the amount of pesticide required for effective control (Pasian et al., 1997). This method has not been governmentally approved and disposal problems would have to be considered.

PESTICIDE COMPATIBILITY

Tank mixing two or more chemicals can increase effectiveness, but may lead to more rapid resistance to chemicals. Do not mix pesticides unless you are certain that they are compatible. Consult your chemical supplier or an appropriate government agency to determine which pesticides can be applied together. Mixing in-

TABLE 9-2

Descriptive terms of pesticide formulations (Oetting and Olson, 1997).

Formulation	Abbreviation
Bait	B
Dispersible granules	DG
Dust	D
Emulsifiable	E
Emulsifiable concentrate	EC
Emulsifiable liquid	EL
Flowable	F
Flowable concentrate	FC
Flowable microencapsulated	FM
Granules	G
Liquid	L
Liquid concentrate	LC
Microencapsulated	M
Soluble powder	SP
Sprayable concentrate	SC
Water-based concentrate	WBC
Water-dispersible liquid	WDL
Water miscible	WM
Water-soluble bags	WSB
Water-soluble packets	WSP
Wettable powder	WP

compatible chemicals may result in phytotoxicity, decreased effectiveness of one or both chemicals, formation of insoluble precipitates, and increased human toxicity. To test for compatibility, take a sample from the spray solution in a clear jar after the pesticide has been mixed in water and observe for 15 to 25 min. If the materials are compatible, the solution should appear homogeneous. If the materials are incompatible, they will separate and a noticeable layer will be evident between the pesticides.

DISPOSAL/CLEANING

First of all, calculate as precisely as possible the amount of spray solution required to reduce the amount of excess spray solution. When possible, use all of the pesticide solution. After use, triple rinse equipment and empty containers with a neutralizing cleaning chemical. Dispose of rinsed containers in an approved landfill. Contact government authorities for advice on this matter.

PEST RESISTANCE TO CHEMICALS

Many insects and fungi have become resistant to one or more pesticides. Resistance to a pesticide develops because any one pesticide is rarely 100% effective at controlling an insect or disease. For example, the first application may kill 90 to 95% of individuals in the population. A portion of the surviving 5 to 10% may have come in contact with the pesticide, but survived due to incomplete coverage or inappropriate concentration. When the resistant survivors reproduce, a portion of their offspring will also be resistant. Thus, later applications of the same pesticide may only control 80 to 85% of the next generation. This process continues until the pesticide becomes largely ineffective.

The probability of pest resistance can be reduced by rotating between different chemical classes at each application, because pests resistant to one pesticide may not be resistant to pesticides from an unrelated class. Pest resistance to one pesticide increases the likelihood of resistance to other pesticides in the same class. Examples of different chemical pesticide classes include botanicals, carbamates, chlorinated hydrocarbons, insect growth regulators, inorganics, microbials, oils, pythrethroids, organophosphates, and soaps. The likelihood of resistance can be reduced by applying the correct concentration, completely covering or penetrating the plant, rotating among pesticide classes, and applying a pesticide only when needed. However, if a pesticide appears to be ineffective, be sure to eliminate other causes before deciding that pest resistance is occurring (Table 9-3). When a pest becomes resistant

TABLE 9–3

A number of practices and factors affect how well a pesticide application will work in controlling the target pest. If a pesticide application did not appear to be effective, consider one or more of the following reasons.

- **Coverage inadequate**. In most cases, the pesticide must reach the pests to be effective. Spraying the upper portion of the leaves may not affect the insect underneath the leaves.
- **Incorrect pesticide used**. Be sure the pesticide to be applied actually controls the target pest. Also, be wary of high expectations—some pesticides, such as insect growth regulators, are slow acting and may not exhibit good "knockdown" at first.
- **Pesticide solution required agitation**. Best control is obtained with a uniform solution. A pesticide solution can settle over time, becoming more concentrated at the bottom. Thus, some of the spray area may not have received a high enough concentration. In addition, the chance for phytotoxicity will be greater for the plants that were sprayed with the higher concentration.
- **Timing of application improper**. Pests are more active in the morning or the late afternoon and applications during those times may be more effective. In addition, the pesticide may not be as effective if it dries too fast.
- **Interval between sprays too long**. Too much time between sprays will allow surviving insects to reproduce. In warm weather, many insect pests reproduce faster and spray intervals that worked during the winter may not be effective during the summer. The residue should also be considered because some pesticides last longer before degrading than do others.
- **Pesticide washed away**. Overhead irrigation too soon after application of foliar sprays may wash the pesticide away before it has had a chance to be effective.
- **Water pH too high**. High pH can reduce the effectiveness of some pesticides; a water pH of 4 to 6 is generally safe.
- **Incompatible pesticides mixed together**. Mixing incompatible chemicals may result in decreased effectiveness of one or both chemicals, or formation of insoluble precipitates (see Pesticide Compatibility section).
- **Mixing incorrect**. The pesticide may have been mixed incorrectly at too low of a concentration. Double check calculations and procedures.
- **Pesticides too old**. The cliché "nothing lasts forever" applies to pesticides. Unless otherwise specified, use pesticides within 2 to 3 years, especially if they are not held in temperature-controlled storage.
- **Pesticide required a surfactant**. Some pesticides are more effective when a surfactant is used to improve coverage. Check the label.
- **Pest resistant to pesticide**. Although this is often the first reason used to explain an ineffective pesticide application, be sure none of the above factors apply. The pest resistance can be reduced by rotating between different chemical classes at each application and applying pesticide correctly (see Pest Resistance to Chemicals section).

to all pesticides, radically different measures may be required, such as not growing the susceptible crop, changing to more resistant cultivars, or temporarily closing down and sanitizing the entire greenhouse complex.

PHYTOTOXICITY

Phytotoxicity can occur with the use of any chemical for pest control or growth regulation. Before applying chemicals to a crop, check the label to determine if the chemical is acceptable for use on that species. Symptoms of phytotoxicity include one or more of the following: marginal necrosis, chlorotic or necrotic patches or spots, and blighted or malformed flowers, buds, and young leaves (Fig. 9-3).

A number of factors will increase the likelihood of phytotoxicity. Petals, bracts, and young leaves are most sensitive and more likely to be damaged than mature tissue. Water stress or any other plant stress will also make a plant more sensitive to chemical damage. The chance for phytotoxicity increases sharply with high temperatures; 65 to 80°F (18 to 27°C) is probably the safest temperature range. During warm periods of the year, apply chemicals late in the evening or early in the morning (before 10 A.M., 1000 HR) before the greenhouses become too warm. Phytotoxicity is also likely when foliage is wet and the chemicals are applied through fogging, smokes, aerosols, or volatilization. Do not apply tank mixes of two or more chemicals unless thoroughly tested beforehand. Do not exceed recommended rates and use wetting agents only when necessary. Finally, be sure the application equipment has never been used to apply herbicides and ap-

ply chemicals uniformly to the crop. Luckily, young plants damaged by chemical applications may grow sufficient new foliage to cover up the damaged tissue, but injury sites may allow entry of *Botrytis* at a later date.

INSECTS AND ANIMAL PESTS

Several insects and related organisms that are common pests in the greenhouse are listed in this section. The life cycle of each pest is included. The actual times for each life stage will be determined by the temperature. Generally, the warmer the temperature, the faster each generation or life stage will be completed and the more rapidly the pest population will increase. Outdoor production is subjected to a much greater number of potential pests that normally do not occur in the greenhouse.

APHIDS

Aphids are common insects that can be damaging in high populations. Two of the most common species are the green peach aphid (*Myzus persicae*) and the melon aphid (*Aphis gossypii*). Small populations can occasionally be removed by hand or with a forceful stream of water if detected early. Aphids excrete honeydew, which supports unsightly black sooty mold fungi. Aphids have soft, winged or wingless bodies in a wide range of colors from yellow-green to dark brown to red, depending on the food source. Aphids have become resistant to many pesticides and, consequently, control can be difficult.

- *Host range*—Very wide.
- *Feeding mechanism*—Feed by piercing and sucking shoot tips, buds, and leaves.
- *Damage*—Distortion, curling of shoot tips, buds, and leaves result.
- *Control*—Use aerial contact insecticides, systemic insecticides, and beneficials such as *Aphidius colemani* (parasitic wasp), *Aphidoletes aphidomyza* (aphid midge), *Chrysoperla carnea*, *C. rufilabris* (lacewing), *Harmonia axyridis* (Asian beetle predator), and *Beauveria bassiana* (parasitic fungus).
- *Life cycle*—Aphids normally give birth to live female nymphs, which can mature and begin reproduction in 7 to 10 days. One female aphid can produce 50 to 100 young in a 30-day period. Long-distance movement occurs when winged females are produced

FIGURE 9-3 Phytotoxicity damage from a fungicide application on seed geraniums (*Pelargonium ×hortorum*).

because of overcrowding or low food supplies. Outdoors, both males and females are produced in the fall, then mate and lay eggs for overwintering.

FUNGUS GNAT AND SHORE FLIES

Fungus gnat (*Bradysiai* spp.) adults have antennae longer than the head and are smaller than shore flies. The wings have a Y-shaped vein starting half the way from the end of the wing. Larvae are clear to whitish with black heads. Shore fly (*Scatella stagnalis*) adults have antennae shorter than the head and are larger and more robust than fungus gnats. The wings have 5 to 7 white spots and appear to be mostly parallel veined. Larvae are light tan with no conspicuous heads. Although the adults of both species are annoying and unappealing to consumers, the real damage occurs when fungus gnat larvae feed on roots, stems, and leaf tissue under the medium surface. Shore fly larvae are not thought to damage plant materials, but the adults are considered a nuisance pest due to fecal deposits on the leaves. However, at one time fungus gnats were also considered to be only a nuisance. Fungus gnat populations are favored by growing media containing peat moss and pine bark and abundant moisture, especially in propagation areas where the larvae may initially feed on algae and organic matter under the bench. Not only do fungus gnat larvae cause damage directly, but they are capable of transmitting a variety of disease organisms including *Pythium* and *Thielaviopsis*. Shore flies may also transmit disease.

- *Host range*—Found in the medium of many plants, in algae, fallen plant material, and other debris.
- *Feeding mechanism*—Fungus gnat larvae feed on root tips, bases of unrooted cuttings, and storage organs.
- *Damage*—Young seedlings or cuttings can be seriously injured, killed, or stunted, and leaves may turn yellow. The symptoms are easily confused with root rots.
- *Control*—Pesticide drenches or granules are applied to medium to control larvae, and aerial insecticides can be used to kill adults. Control algae growth with hydrated lime, copper sulfate, or bromine (see Algae, Liverworts, and Moss section later in this chapter). Control measures should be applied to benches, walkways, and underbench areas as well as to plant materials. Remove fallen plant material, media, and other debris. Increase air circulation with horizontal airflow and increase plant spacing. Switch from top irrigation systems, such as hand watering, boom, and spray stakes, to subirrigation systems such as ebb-and-flow or trough, which will reduce algae growth in the greenhouse and decrease the moisture level of the upper surface of the medium. A number of beneficial controls for the larvae are available including nematodes: *Steinernema feltiae* and *Steinernema carpocapsae*; predatory mites, *Hypoaspis miles*; and the bacterium *Bacillus thuringiensis* var. *israelensis*.
- *Life cycle*—The life cycle from adult to adult occurs in 2.5 to 4.0 weeks. Although an adult has a life span of only 7 to 10 days, a female may lay 100 to 150 eggs. The eggs hatch into larvae in 4 to 6 days, and 10 to 14 days later the larvae change into pupae. Three to 4 days later the adults emerge from the pupa. The entire life cycle of the shore fly from egg to adult occurs in 15 to 20 days (Cloyd, 1997). Females lay 300 to 500 eggs that hatch in 2 to 3 days into larvae. Seven to 10 days later larvae pupate, and adults emerge 4 to 5 days later. Adults live 3 to 4 weeks.

LEAF MINERS

Leaf miners are difficult to control if they become established in a greenhouse. The larvae burrow within the leaf tissue and are protected by the upper and lower epidermis of the leaf. All susceptible plant material should be inspected carefully for the distinctive tunnels. The purchase of clean plant material is important. The adults appear as small, dark winged flies.

- *Host range*—Relatively narrow, especially found on chrysanthemums (*Dendranthema* ×*grandiflorum*), kalanchoe (*Kalanchoe blossfeldiana*), and columbine (*Aquilegia*).
- *Feeding mechanism*—Larvae burrow in leaves, eating subcuticular tissue.
- *Damage*—Tunnels lace leaves and high infestations can stunt plants.
- *Control*—Control is difficult, because there are many chemical-resistant strains, and the larvae are encased in leaf tissue. Systemic insecticides are effective against larvae and regular aerial applications of contact pesticides can be used to kill adults. Pesticides that have translaminar (penetrate plant tissue) properties work well on leaf miners.

- *Life cycle*—The life cycle from adult to adult occurs in about 4 to 5 weeks. An adult has a life span of 2 to 3 weeks, during which a female may lay more than 100 eggs. The eggs hatch into larvae in 5 to 7 days and up to 14 days later the larvae change into pupae. Two weeks later the adults emerge from the pupa.

MEALYBUGS

Although mealybugs are rarely a major problem in commercial greenhouses, this insect can build up in large numbers on long-term crops such as stock plants or in conservatories with established plant materials. Some species inject a toxic substance into the plant during feeding which causes chlorosis. Mealybugs excrete honeydew, which supports unsightly black sooty mold fungi. These flat, soft-bodied, wingless insects are distinguished by the waxy white powder on their bodies.

- *Host range*—Wide.
- *Feeding mechanism*—Feed by piercing and sucking shoot tips, leaves, buds, and roots.
- *Damage*—Shoot tips, leaves, and buds become chlorotic and distorted. Heavy infestations may lead to chlorosis of entire plant.
- *Control*—Difficult to kill adults due to waxy coating. Repeated applications of aerial or drench contact insecticides may be required to kill crawlers (vulnerable stage) as they hatch. Systemic pesticides are also effective against adults and larvae. The beneficial insects *Cryptolaemus montrouzieri* (ladybug) and *Leptomastix dactylopii* (parasite) are able to partially control mealybugs.
- *Life cycle*—The life cycle from adult to adult may take anywhere from 6 weeks to 2 months. Females can lay 300 to 600 eggs. The eggs hatch into tiny nymphs 7 to 10 days later, which move around the plant for 6 to 8 weeks before becoming adults. Some types of mealybugs produce live young (Cloyd, 1998).

MITES

The most common mite problem is the two-spotted spider mite (*Tetranychus urticae*), which produces a characteristic webbing when populations are high (Fig. 9-4). Unfortunately, the infestation is quite severe by the time the webbing is noticed. In hot, dry environments, the spider mite population can explode. Sy-

FIGURE 9-4 Characteristic webbing produced by spider mites on marigolds (*Tagetes erecta*).

ringing plants to wash insects off and wetting walkways to raise the humidity were used to prevent spider mite populations from becoming unmanageable before pesticides were widely available. These tiny organisms are not true insects but are related to spiders and scorpions. Mites can be more readily observed by tapping plant parts over a piece of white paper. Leaves may also feel gritty to the touch. Spider mites range in color from red to green to yellow with the two-spotted mites having two, large dark spots after which they are named. Another mite, the Lewis mite (*Eotetranychus lewis*), is similar to the spider mite in appearance and habits but has been a problem on poinsettias, which is not a typical host for the two-spotted spider mite. Cyclamen mites (*Phytonemus pallidus*) are even smaller and cannot be seen with the naked eye. Cyclamen mites differ from spider mites in that they are favored by high humidity (80% or more) and cool temperatures of 60°F (16°C). Though called cyclamen mites, this species can be a problem on other plants.

- *Host range*—Wide.
- *Feeding mechanism*—Feed by piercing and sucking shoot tips and leaves.
- *Damage*—The spider mite attacks the undersides of leaves, causing chlorosis and tiny, necrotic spots (stippling) on the leaves. The cyclamen mite feeds predominantly in bud tissue, thereby distorting young leaves and buds and stunting plants. Cyclamen mite damage is often confused with other problems such as microelement deficiencies. Both types can kill large plants if the infestation is severe.
- *Control*—Difficult, because mites have many pesticide-resistant stages. Mites also

prefer relatively inaccessible locations: The cyclamen mite often burrows deeply within shoot tips and the spider mite prefers the undersides of leaves. Thorough applications of aerial contact pesticides may be effective. Systemic pesticides are not usually effective. Beneficials used to control spider mites include *Neoseiulus californicus* (predatory mite), *Phytoseiulus persimilis* (predatory mite), *P. longipes* (predatory mite), *Neoseiulus fallacis* (predator), *Feltiella acarisuga* (predatory midge), and *Metaseiulus occidentalis* or *Stethorus punctum* (predatory beetles). A low-temperature, high-humidity environment slows spider mite reproduction and spread.

- *Life cycle*—The life cycle from egg to adult can take as little as 7 days during hot, dry weather, but at a temperature of 70°F (21°C) the life cycle is 20 days. Females lay an average of 100 eggs. The eggs hatch into larvae 2 to 8 days later, feed for a short time, and enter into an inactive resting stage of about 1.5 days. This sequence is repeated three more times until the adult is produced from the last resting stage. Female cyclamen mites can produce up to 100 eggs during their 4-week life span. The adults will be produced 4 weeks later.

SCALE

As with mealybugs, scale is rarely a major problem in commercial greenhouses, but can build up in numbers on long-term crops such as foliage plants or in conservatories with established plant materials. Any one of a large number of scale species can occur and soft scale species excrete honeydew, which supports unsightly black sooty mold fungi. Many scale species are inconspicuous and can build up in numbers before they are noticed. Adults of most species have a smooth protective coat ranging in color from black to tan with no wings or legs.

- *Host range*—Very wide.
- *Feeding mechanism*—Feed by piercing and sucking any aerial plant part, especially stems and petioles.
- *Damage*—Includes stunting of plant growth, distortion of new growth, and chlorosis of leaves.
- *Control*—Difficult, due to the hard or waxy coat of many species. Systemic insecticides may control adults. The key is typically to kill nymphs as they hatch with repeated applications of contact insecticides.

- *Life cycle*—The life cycle from egg to adult takes anywhere from 6 weeks to 1 year. A variety of life-cycle patterns can be found among the various scale species. Some species do not have males, and the females give birth to live young or lay eggs under their own shell. Other species may have males with legs, one pair of wings, and no mouthparts and serve only for reproduction. Regardless of whether the young are produced live or from eggs, they have legs, travel around for 2 days looking for suitable feeding areas, and are known as crawlers. After settling into a location, the crawlers begin to form their shell and progress through several molts. Legs are lost after the first molt.

THRIPS

Of the several species that injure plants, the western flower thrips (*Frankliniella occidentalis*) are the most troublesome because they transmit the destructive tomato spotted wilt and impatiens necrotic spot viruses. These tiny insects are less than 0.13 in. (3 mm) long, have two wings, and range in color from yellow to brown or black. Often found in flowers, thrips can be more readily observed by dissecting flowers or tapping plant parts over a piece of white paper.

- *Host range*—Very wide.
- *Feeding mechanism*—Feed by piercing plant parts, especially flowers and young leaves, and sucking the exposed plant sap.
- *Damage*—Includes silvery streaks on flowers and foliage and distortion of new growth. Damage is especially noticeable on dark flower petals.
- *Control*—Aerial applications of contact pesticides applied 3 to 5 days apart; systemics generally do not work well. Beneficial controls include *Orius insidiousus* (predator), *Neoseilus* (*Amblyseius*) *cucmeris* and *N. degenerans* (predatory mites), *Hypoaspis mites* (predatory mites), and *Beauveria bassiana* (parasitic fungus). Heating a greenhouse during the summer by shutting the vents, turning off the cooling system, and allowing the temperature to rise can be used to eliminate thrips populations in the greenhouse. Four days of 104°F (40°C) and 10% relative humidity will kill 100% of

western flower thrips (Will and Faust, 1997).

- *Life cycle*—The life cycle from egg to adult can occur in as little as 2 weeks. Each female can lay 150 to 300 eggs on plant tissue and live from 27 to 45 days (Cloyd and Sadof, 1997). The eggs hatch in 2 to 4 days into small yellowish larvae and molt twice. The larvae then drop off the plant and undergo a pupae stage before emerging as adults.

WHITEFLIES

Whiteflies can quickly build up into large populations. Not only do the whiteflies damage plants but they also are annoying for the customers as they fly. Whiteflies excrete honeydew, which supports unsightly black sooty mold fungi. Two whitefly species are of particular interest, the greenhouse whitefly (*Trialeurodes vaporariorum*) and the silverleaf whitefly (*Bemisia argentifolia*) (Fig. 9-5). Both species are small, white flies covered with a waxy powder. The greenhouse whitefly eggs are bright white when first laid and turn to dark gray. The pupae have parallel sides that are perpendicular to the leaf surface when viewed head-on. The adults have whitish bodies and hold their wings generally flat over the bodies, making the wings parallel to the leaf surface. The color of silverleaf whitefly eggs varies from light brown to gray and the pupae are rounded when viewed from head-on. The adults hold their wings at an angle (roughly 45°) over their bodies, which may have a yellowish cast.

- *Host range*—Very wide, especially poinsettias (*Euphorbia pulcherrima*), cineraria (*Pericallis×hybrida*), gerbera (*Gerbera jamesonii*), tomato (*Lycopersicon esculen-*

tum), and calceolaria (*Calceolaria* Herbeohybrida).

- *Feeding mechanism*—Feed by piercing and sucking leaves.
- *Damage*—Includes stunting of growth and chlorosis of leaves.
- *Control*—Use aerial applications of contact pesticides to undersides of leaves, dip cuttings in insecticide before bringing into the greenhouse, and use systemic insecticides and beneficial controls such as *Encarsia formosa* (parasitic wasps), *Delphastus pusillus* (predator beetle), *Eretmocerus eremicus* (parasitic wasp), and *Beauveria bassiana* (parasitic fungus)
- *Life cycle*—The life cycle from egg to adult takes about 4 to 5 weeks. The females lay up to 250 eggs in batches of up to 20 eggs. The eggs hatch 5 to 14 days later into nymphs, which travel to new feeding areas. The nymphs remain stationary for up to 3 weeks, during which they progress through three molts ending in a pseudopupa. The winged adult emerges 1 week later and can lay eggs in 3 days for silverleaf whiteflies and in 4 days for greenhouse whiteflies. The life cycle for the silverleaf tends to be slightly longer than that for the greenhouse whitefly.

WORMS AND CATERPILLARS

Larvae of moths and butterflies can grow rapidly and devour a large amount of plant tissue. Although few species are problems in the greenhouse, outdoor crops may be attacked regularly. Many caterpillars are green; however, the various species can be almost any color and grow to more than 3 in. (8 cm) long.

- *Host range*—Wide, but individual species are specific to certain crops.
- *Feeding mechanism*—Chews plant parts.
- *Damage*—Includes holes in leaves and removal of buds and shoot tips. In some cases, the entire plant may be eaten to the medium line.
- *Control*—Aerial applications of *Bacillus thuringiensis* var. *kuristaki* (bacterium), insecticides, or beneficial controls such as *Trichogramma* spp. (parasitic wasp).
- *Life cycle*—Larvae stage (caterpillars) of various species of moths and a few butterflies can grow rapidly and usually appear during warm months of the year.

FIGURE 9-5 Whitefly (photo by Janette Jacobs).

SLUGS AND SNAILS

Although slugs and snails are rarely a problem in commercial greenhouses, numbers can build up in moist areas with plant debris, such as propagation areas, and in coldframes. Outdoors, slugs and snails eat young transplants and seedlings, especially if planted into or near mulch in which the animals hide during the day. Snails are similar to the soft-bodied slugs except that snails produce a protective hard shell and are serious pests in California and Florida. Slugs and snails are mollusks, not insects, and produce distinctive shiny slime trails.

- *Host range*—Very wide.
- *Feeding mechanism*—Chews leaves and stems.
- *Damage*—Leaves holes in leaves and may totally consume young plants.
- *Control*—Sanitation is important to remove hiding areas during the day. Slugs and snails can be controlled with baits.
- *Life cycle*—The life cycle from adult to adult occurs in 3 months to 1 year. Slugs and snails lay from 20 to 100 eggs, which hatch in 10 days or less.

NEMATODES

Most nematode species are rarely a problem in commercial greenhouse bedding and potted flowering plant production but can be a major concern in ground beds, perennial plant production, and outdoor cut flower production. Nematodes are tiny worms that are often visible only under a microscope. Root knot nematodes (*Meloidogyne*) are particularly common in fields, and foliar nematodes (*Aphelenchoides*) readily attack container-grown crops as well.

- *Host range*—Narrow for each nematode species, but many species of nematodes may cause problems. Both the root knot and foliar nematodes have broad host ranges; the latter has become a major problem in many perennial plant nurseries.
- *Feeding mechanism*—Burrows into and feeds on root or leaf tissue.
- *Damage*—Depends on the nematode species involved, but includes stunting, wilting, galls on roots, leaf spots, chlorosis, and defoliation. Root knot nematodes produce distorted, stunted roots and swellings (galls) on the roots. Do not confuse with the small nod-

ules that nitrogen-fixing bacteria form on legume roots. The foliar nematodes cause vein-limited, yellowish to dark green or brown lesions and blotches (Dreistadt, 2001).
- *Control*—Purchase nematode-free plants, pasteurize media, sanitize, remove infected plants, solarize soil, apply fumigants, and use hot water dips (see Chapter 7, Media),
- *Life cycle*—Varies greatly among nematode species. Generally, eggs hatch into larvae, of which there may be several stages, and larvae molt into adults.

Unfortunately, a number of other insects and related pests can occur in the greenhouse including beetles, weevils, symphylans, millipedes, springtails, pillbugs, and sowbugs (Gill and Sanderson, 1998). Most only rarely cause significant damage in greenhouse crops. Outdoors many more insects are likely to occur, some of which can cause significant damage, such as Japanese beetles and plant bugs.

VERTEBRATE PESTS

Mice, moles, and rats sometimes feed on seeds, seedlings, and bulbs and are most prevalent in the greenhouse during the fall and early winter. Reduce rodent populations around the greenhouse by removing sources of food (vegetation, garbage, etc.) and cover (vegetation, debris, scrape piles, pallets, etc.). Exclusion, traps, and rodenticides can be used to prevent or control rodent problems in the greenhouse. Two types of rodenticides are available: (1) single dose and fast acting (acute) and (2) multiple dose and slow acting (chronic or anticoagulant). The latter are more readily accepted by the rodents and are safer to use when children, pets, and nontarget wildlife are around.

Outdoor cut flowers, perennials, bedding plants, or other plant materials may be injured or eaten by armadillos, deer, elk, gophers, rabbits, and woodchucks. Exclusion through fencing is usually the best long-term control strategy. Repellants often produce erratic results.

DISEASES

A number of diseases are important and in some cases can completely destroy an entire crop. Generally, prevention is more effective than relying on pesticides. Presently, many reputable propagators carefully index the stock plants of numerous vegetatively propagated crops for diseases (see Chapter 1, Propagation) and produce disease-free cuttings and plugs. A number of common diseases are discussed in this section. Many other diseases are possible, especially with outdoor crops, but most are only locally important.

BACTERIA

Bacterial diseases are most prevalent during propagation when soft rot bacteria such as *Erwinia* can turn cuttings and seedlings into soft, black rotted tissue. Other bacteria cause wilting and yellowing of shoots by plugging the plant's vascular system and cause leaf spots and blights. Many plants are susceptible to bacterial diseases at some point during production.

- *Host range*—Very wide, especially soft rotting bacteria on foliage plants.
- *Damage*—Includes rotting of cuttings, seedlings, bulbs, tubers, corms, and so forth. Other bacterial infections result in leaf spotting with yellow margins, wilting and yellowing of shoots, and crown galls.
- *Control*—Bacteria are spread through human activities, such as propagation, and water movement. Sanitation, eliminating water on the foliage, and prompt removal of infected plant materials will limit the spread of bacteria. Aerial applications of chemicals may help prevent bacterial infections and reduce further contaminations, but control through pesticides is usually marginal.

FUNGI

BOTRYTIS. *Botrytis* can occur at any stage of production, from propagation to marketing. *Botrytis* occurs on fallen leaves, petals, and other debris and on senescing plant tissue still attached to the plant. *Botrytis* is favored by warm temperatures and high humidity and is one of the most common plant diseases in commercial greenhouse production. The gray hyphal growth of the fungus is often visible on infected plant materials, especially deep within the plant canopy where the humidity is high. Numerous *Botrytis* species occur, some of which are specific to certain plant species.

- *Host range*—Very wide.
- *Damage*—*Botrytis* can kill seedlings and cuttings during propagation, which is usually conducted in a warm and humid environ-

ment. On whole plants, *Botrytis* often infects dead tissue but can also infect healthy vigorous leaves, stems, flowers, and buds during production or shipping. *Botrytis* is an especially important problem on flowers and foliage during storage and shipping.

- *Control*—Environmental manipulation with reduced humidity and increased air circulation. Once *Botrytis* is established, aerial fungicide applications may be required. Sanitation is always important to reduce inoculum; clean up fallen plant debris and remove infected plants or plant tissue. Microorganisms showing potential for control or prevention of *Botrytis* include *Gliocladium roseum* (fungus) and *Cryptococcus humicola* (yeast) (Filonow et al., 1996).

CROWN AND ROOT ROT. Crown and root rot is considered to be one of the most important plant diseases in floriculture and typically involves one or more of the following five fungal genera: *Fusarium, Rhizoctonia, Pythium, Phytophthora,* and *Thielaviopsis* (Figs. 9-6 and 9-7). Generally, the specific disease organism is difficult to distinguish without a laboratory diagnosis. Root rot fungi are quite common and often infect plants stressed from high soluble salt levels, inadequate drainage, improper watering, nutritional deficiency, insect damage, or flowering. In some cases,

FIGURE 9-6 Root rot on poinsettias (*Euphorbia pulcherrima*).

FIGURE 9-7 *Fusarium* stem rot on lisianthus (*Eustoma grandiflora*).

pathogens may be systemic in the plant and symptoms may not be visible for many weeks.

- *Host range*—Very wide.
- *Damage*—Plants wilt even though medium may be moist, lower leaves turn yellow, roots turn brown or black. The fungi infect and kill roots and lower stems. Bulbs and other storage organs may also be infected. *Pythium* and *Phytophthora* usually infect roots first. *Pythium* can sometimes be distinguished by pulling off the root tip; the remaining inner root tissue will look like a wire.
- *Control*—Use pasteurized media, clean pots and benches, and good plant care. Fungicides may be used as a preventive measure or after disease is established to prevent spread. Often two chemicals are necessary to treat all genera of fungi causing crown and root rot; some pesticides already contain two of the appropriate chemicals. Be sure to check the label for which fungal genera are controlled. Microorganisms showing potential for control and prevention of *Rhizoctonia* stem and crown rot include *Pseudomonas cepacia* (bacterium) and *Paecilomyces lilacinus* (fungus) (Will and Faust, 1997). *Gliocladium virens* (fungus) and *Trichoderma harzianum* (fungus) can be useful against both *Pythium* and *Rhizoctonia* root rot. *Actinoplanes* (bacterium) has also been effective against

Pythium root rot (A. Filonow, personal communication).

DAMPING-OFF. Damping-off is a general disorder usually caused by *Pythium*, *Phytophthora*, *Rhizoctonia*, and other pathogens. They are difficult to tell apart but are quite common. Preemergent damping-off occurs when the seedlings are infected before they emerge from the medium, and postemergent damping-off occurs after the seedlings have emerged from the medium. Many times growers blame low germination on poor seed quality when preemergent damping-off may be the cause. In the case of postemergent damping-off, white or brown or black fungal strands may be visible. The fungal strands are typically "dull brown to dark brown" with *Rhizoctonia* and "shiny coal-black" with *Pythium* (M. Hausbeck, personal communication).

- *Host range*—Very wide.
- *Damage*—Seedlings are killed before, during, or after emergence from the medium. Seedlings sometimes appear normal at first except for a black area on the stem at or immediately above the medium line.
- *Control*—Use pasteurized media, clean pots and benches, and proper watering practices. Germinate seed under optimum conditions to reduce time in propagation and maintain good air circulation. Seed treated with fungicides can also be helpful. Fungicide drenches may also be used as a preventive measure or to stop the spread of damping-off after it is established. Two chemicals are frequently necessary to treat all genera of fungi causing damping-off; some products already contain two of the appropriate chemicals. Be sure to check the label for which fungal genera are controlled. Microorganisms showing potential for control or prevention of damping-off include *Gliocladium virens* (fungus), *Trichoderma harzianum* (fungus), and *Streptomyces griseoviridis* (fungus) (Will and Faust, 1997).

MILDEW. Two general types of plant pathogenic mildew occur: powdery mildew and downy mildew. Powdery mildew is distinguished by the whitish, powdery growth on plant materials (Fig. 9-8). Although it can occur on old leaves with some species, it is most damaging when it occurs on young leaves, stems, buds, and flowers where it can cause twisting

FIGURE 9-8 Powdery mildew on *Phlox*.

and distortion. On older leaves necrosis and senescense can occur. Powdery mildew should not be confused with downy mildew, a disease that is rarely seen in the greenhouse and is similar in appearance to powdery mildew (Williams, 1997). Downy mildew generally infects the undersides of older leaves, whereas powdery mildew favors the upper sides of younger leaves. Pale green to yellow patches can appear on the upper sides of leaves infected with downy mildew and, frequently, the leaves turn completely brown. Organisms causing downy mildew are related to the "water molds," *Pythium* and *Rhizoctonia*, and are not controlled by the same types of chemicals as powdery mildew.

- *Host range*—Limited to certain species in greenhouses, especially roses (*Rosa*), begonias (*Begonia*), and African violets (*Saintpaulia ionantha*), but can be common on a variety of outdoor crop species. Although mildew species tend to look similar on various plant species, mildew species are usually very host specific (Daughtrey et al., 1997). A strain that infects one plant species is unlikely to infect another plant species.
- *Damage*—Includes reduced plant vigor; new growth may be distorted and curled.
- *Control*—Use systemic fungicides or aerial applications of contact fungicides. Spores will not germinate in free water or below 95% humidity—either frequently spray plants with water or reduce humidity. Powdery mildew is also favored by poor air circulation, which allows areas of high humidity to develop around the leaves. Downy mildew is most prevalent during periods of cool temperatures and high humidity. Biocontrols are being researched, especially those using yeast, which may be available in the future (Ng et al., 1997).

LEAF SPOTS. A large number of fungal diseases cause leaf spots and blights including *Alternaria*, *Septoria*, and *Heterosporium*. The spores of many species are spread by wind or splashing water. Fungal leaf spots tend to be most common and damaging on outdoor production. Leaf spots can also be caused by bacterial pathogens and numerous abiotic disorders such as phytotoxicity, sunburn, and nutrient deficiencies or toxicities.

- *Host range*—Generally limited to certain species in greenhouses, especially roses and azaleas (*Rhododendron*), but can be common on a wide variety of outdoor crop species. Although many fungal leaf spot–causing organisms are often very host specific, numerous species occur.
- *Damage*—Causes irregular or round spots and blotches on leaves, often limited to either the new growth or the older foliage. The spots often have a distinctly lighter or darker margin. Flowers and stems may also be attacked.
- *Control*—Use systemic fungicides or aerial applications of contact fungicides. Sanitation and removal of diseased plants and plant parts can be useful.

PHYTOPLASMAS

Phytoplasmas are small bacteria-like organisms that cause several diseases characterized by stunting and distortion of the plants. Aster yellows is the most common of the phytoplasma diseases to affect ornamentals and is primarily limited to outdoor production but can be devastating when it occurs.

- *Host range*—Wide range of plants species affected, especially common in various *Compositae* family plants such as annual aster (*Callistephus*), for which it is named, and coneflower (*Echinacea*). Annual statice (*Limonium sinuatum*) is also quite susceptible.

- *Damage*—Includes yellowing of flowers and foliage, stunting, and malformed and green flowers.
- *Control*—No pesticides are effective and plants cannot be cured. Remove infected plants as soon as possible. Control leaf hoppers, which are the vectors of the disease. Remove nearby weeds, especially biennial and perennials weeds, that host aster yellows or leafhoppers.

VIRUSES

Although virtually all plants are susceptible to at least one virus, viruses are usually not a problem for most floriculture crop species. The major exceptions are the closely related tomato spotted wilt virus (TSWV) and impatiens necrotic spot virus (INSV), which have broad host ranges and severely damage a wide variety of greenhouse floriculture crops. INSV tends to be more common than TSWV in the greenhouse. Both TSWV and INSV are vectored by the western flower thrips, and they produce symptoms that can mimic a variety of other disease and nutritional problems. The more obvious symptoms include yellow to white rings and spots (Fig. 9-9). Less distinctive symptoms include stunting, leaf distortion, vein clearing, wavy lines on foliage, and mosaics. Both INSV and TSWV can infect plants without showing symptoms for a lengthy period of time and are often introduced into a greenhouse on purchased plugs. Inspect incoming plants carefully. If you suspect plant material may be infected, you should discard.

FIGURE 9-9 INSV damage on gloxinia (*Sinningia speciosa*) foliage (photo by Janette Jacobs). Note diagnostic chlorotic rings.

- *Host range*—Many plant species are susceptible to at least one virus; not all plants show symptoms.
- *Damage*—Wide range, including stunting, yellow mottling, rings, mosaics, and necrotic spots.
- *Control*—Viruses require a vector to transport them from one location to the next. Possible vectors for various viruses include insects, bacteria, fungi, humans (through touching, infected tools, equipment, etc.), and splashing water. Because viruses cannot be eliminated from infected plants (except in a laboratory procedure), the best option is to control the vector and remove (rogue) infected plants. Be especially wary of carrying over plants from one season to the next. Control methods for insect, bacteria, and fungi are listed under their respective sections and sanitation is required to control viruses vectored by humans or human activity.

ALGAE, LIVERWORTS, AND MOSS

Although algae itself is not damaging, it is unsightly and can act as a food source for insects, especially fungus gnats. Algae can be controlled by improving water drainage, not overwatering, and reducing humidity. Hydrated lime at 1 to 2 lb/gal (120 to 240 g/L) can be applied under benches and on bench supports and walkways. Copper sulfate, bromine, and other chemicals can also be used.

Liverworts and mosses occasionally become established on the medium surface of long-term crops, especially in humid climates. Controls include maintaining a dry medium surface by using subirrigation and allowing medium to dry between irrigations.

WEEDS

Although weeds are a greater problem in outdoor production (see Field-Grown Cut Flowers chapter in Part III), they should not be ignored in the greenhouse. Weeds often harbor insects and disease, reducing the effectiveness of pest control on crops. Weeds below the benches or along the walls can be a source of seeds for weeds in container-grown crops, which require expensive hand labor to control.

Because greenhouses are an enclosed environment, prevention should be practiced. Check new plants for weeds and be sure to watch them for the next few weeks for weeds that germinate after the plants have been brought into the greenhouses. The best control is vigilant scouting to locate and remove weeds before they can get established. Weeds are often introduced into the greenhouse with plant materials from other locations. Also, remove weeds from around the outside of the greenhouse to reduce introduction of seeds and insect pests. If large numbers of weeds become established, control measures include solarization and herbicides. *Solarization* is the process of allowing empty, dry greenhouses to heat up and kill weeds through drought and heat.

Herbicides are available that are labeled for greenhouse use; however, careful application is required to prevent damage to crops in the greenhouse. Some herbicides are best applied only when greenhouses are empty because accidental pesticide drift or volatilization can occur. Herbicides are most effective when applied to young, actively growing seedlings (see Field-Grown Cut Flowers chapter in Part III).

KEY POINTS

- The control of a pest is based on three basic components required for it to become established: presence of the pest, a susceptible host, and the proper environment.
- Integrated Pest Management (IPM) combines all strategies for controlling pests into one coherent plan.
- Reduce pest problems by preventing them from entering the production environment, growing pest-resistant species or cultivars, using pathogen-free media, practicing proper sanitation, maintaining stress-free production conditions, and manipulating environmental conditions.
- Beneficial predators, parasites, and microorganisms can be effective.
- Scout for pests to detect their presence early when they can be more easily controlled.
- Chemicals are commonly used to control pests and are available in a number of different formulations.
- Numerous national, state, and local regulations govern the chemicals and their use.
- The pesticide label and material safety data sheet (MSDS) are the sources of pertinent use and safety information and they must be available at all times.

- Pesticides are classified by their toxicity ratings: caution—slightly toxic, LD_{50} = 500 mg and above; warning—moderately toxic, LD_{50} = 50 to 500 mg; danger—highly toxic, poison, marked with a skull and crossbones, LD_{50} = 0 to 50 mg.
- Pesticides are classified into two types: contact or systemic.
- Pest resistance can be reduced by rotating between different chemical classes at each application and applying pesticide correctly.
- Chemical damage to plants, phytotoxicity, can occur.
- A number of insects and animal pests are problems in floriculture production including aphids, fungus gnat and shore flies, leaf miners, mealybugs, mites, scale, thrips, whiteflies, worms and caterpillars, slugs and snails, nematodes, mice, and rats.
- Diseases are classified as viruses, bacteria, phytoplasmas, and fungi.
- Fungal diseases that can be problems include *Botrytis*, crown and root rots, damping-off, and mildew.
- Algae, liverworts, moss, and weeds can also be problems, especially with outdoor production.

BIBLIOGRAPHY

Cloyd, R.A. 1997. Shoreflies: Nemesis or nuisance. *Floriculture Indiana* 11(1):10–11.

Cloyd, R.A. 1998. Citrus mealybug management in greenhouses and interiorscapes. *Ohio Florists' Association Bulletin* No. 827:10–11.

Cloyd, R.A. 2003. Storing pesticides properly. *Greenhouse Management and Production* 23(7):94.

Cloyd, R.A., and C.S. Sadof. 1997. Western flower thrips biology and management. *Floriculture Indiana* 11(3):2–6.

Cloyd, R.A., and C.S. Sadof. 2003. Seasonal abundance and the use of an action threshold for western flower thrips, in a cut carnation greenhouse. *HortTechnology* 13:497–500.

Daughtrey, M., M. Hausbeck, and L. Barnes. 1997. Managing powdery mildew on poinsettias. *Greenhouse Product News* 7(9):26–29.

Dreistadt, S.H. 2001. *Integrated Pest Management for Floriculture and Nurseries*. University of California Division of Agriculture and Natural Resources Publication 3402.

Faust, J. 1995. 10 steps to WPS compliance. *Tennessee Flower Growers' Association Bulletin* 4(2): 1–4.

Filonow, A.B., J.M. Dole, and H.S. Vishniac. 1996. Yeasts that reduce gray mold of geranium flowers. *Biocontrol* 2:47–55.

Gill, S. 1997. TPM Part II: The forward-thinking approach to pest control. *GrowerTalks* 60(13):64, 66, 68, 70, 72.

Gill, S., and J. Sanderson. 1998. *Greenhouse Pests and Beneficials*. Ball Publishing, Batavia, Illinois.

Ng, K.K., L. MacDonald, and Z.K. Punja. 1997. Biological control of rose powdery mildew with the antagonist yeast *Tilletiopsis pallescens*. *HortScience* 32:262–266.

Oetting, R.D., and D.L. Olson. 1997. Explaining chemical formulations. *GrowerTalks* 60(14):76.

Pasian, C.C., R.K. Lindquist, and D.K. Struve. 1997. A new method of applying imidaclorprid to potted plants for controlling aphids and whiteflies. *HortTechnology* 7:265–269.

Tjosvold, S.A., and I.D. Greene. 1997. Evaluations of electrostatic spray application and miticides on the control of two-spotted spider mites infesting commercial greenhouse roses. *Greenhouse Product News* 7(1):8–10.

Will, E., and J. Faust. 1997. Managing thrips with temperature and moisture extremes in the greenhouse. *Bedding Plants International News* 28(8): 22.

Williams, J.L. 1997. Powdery mildew, downy mildew: What's the difference. *Southeastern Floriculture* 7(3):52–53.

Chapter 10

Postharvest

INTRODUCTION

Factors influencing the postharvest life of a crop start well before the crop is marketed. A crop is at its highest quality at the time of harvest and must be properly handled to minimize the loss in quality. To maintain quality during marketing and in the final consumers' location, containerized plants and cut materials must be handled at the correct temperature, have a high carbohydrate level, and be free from water stress and ethylene. Planning for the postharvest process starts during production, and producers must monitor the postharvest life of their crops vigilantly (Nell et al., 1997; Nowack and Rudnicki, 1990).

POSTHARVEST TESTING

Detailed postharvest information is limited to only a few species; consequently, every grower should routinely sample a few potted plants or cut stems of each species or cultivar to observe and determine the postharvest life. In particular, new species or cultivars should be tested as they appear on the market. Dramatic differences in postharvest life can occur among cultivars. Cultural conditions vary from grower to grower and the postharvest life of a crop for one operation often differs from that of another. Knowing the weekly postharvest qualities of your cut flowers, potted flowering plants, or potted foliage plants will allow you to adjust your cultural procedures to improve

postharvest longevity. Proper cultural procedures in combination with postharvest cultivar screening will ensure that a firm is selling high-quality crops with optimum postharvest life. In-house postharvest testing is also valuable in identifying when problems occur within an operation, handling customer complaints, and providing your customers with current postharvest information (Fig. 10-1).

A postharvest testing system does not need to be elaborate and should take only a few minutes to set up and monitor each day. In fact, the simpler the system, the more consistent and use-

FIGURE 10-1 Commercial postharvest testing room for cut flowers.

184

ful the results are likely to be. Testing can be as easy as growing a few plants of several bedding plant species in a display garden. A postharvest test facility for cut flowers, potted flowering plants, or foliage plants can be in the lunchroom or on a countertop in the office. For potted plants, select one to three samples weekly from various crops, label with the date, and record the date the plants are no longer acceptable.

In setting up a testing system for cut flowers or foliage, obtain clean bottles or vases. Use the same preservatives and water as normally used in the operation. For a new species, the easiest test is to place half of the flowers in water as a control treatment and the other half in water plus preservative. For current crops, compare a few untreated flowers to a few flowers after treatment, which will allow you to determine if your handling procedures are effective. If possible, only one stem should be placed in each container because the rotting and senescence of one flower stem may shorten the vase life of other stems in the same container. Place the flowers in an area permanently set aside for the postharvest tests. Check the flowers each day; note which flowers are no longer acceptable and record the number of days from harvest to the end of vase life. The stems can be individually tagged with the harvest date and treatment by using small stickers or paper tags with string.

PRODUCTION FACTORS

The first factor to consider is that different cultivars of the same species vary greatly in their postharvest life. While cultivar selection is difficult with many crop species due to the large number of available cultivars, selecting a cultivar with the maximum postharvest life may reduce customer complaints and rejections and increase profits. For many floriculture crops, breeding and biotech efforts are focused on developing cultivars with a long postharvest life. Whether the plants are to be boxed and shipped should also be considered. For example, some poinsettia (*Euphorbia pulcherrima*) cultivars, typically the dark-leaved cultivars, are better "shippers" than other cultivars.

In production, any cultural factor that "stresses" plants or reduces plant quality is also likely to reduce postharvest life including improper irrigation, temperature, light, or media pH; high media EC; insects or diseases; and poor root systems. In particular, root rots can become evident in potted crops after the stress

of being shipped, sold, transported, and placed in the home. A poor-quality plant will decline quicker after harvest than a high-quality plant.

LIGHT

For potted flowering plants, bedding plants, and cut flowers, the carbohydrate status of the crop should be high to maximize postharvest life. Low light intensity or short duration prior to marketing will reduce the postharvest life of the crop. Each crop species should be produced at the optimum light level for the species to produce a high-quality plant. Low light levels during production may result in premature flower bud and leaf abscission. Low light may also cause less intense flower color (Biran and Halevy, 1974; Kawabata et al., 1995). Of course, foliage plants are the exception where low light acclimatization (see Chapter 4, Light) can greatly extend the life of the plant and increase customer satisfaction (Blessington and Collins, 1993). Unfortunately, acclimatization through low light is not practical on potted flowering plants such as chrysanthemums and poinsettias (Nell et al., 1990).

TEMPERATURE

High temperatures reduce the carbohydrate status of a plant by increasing respiration and may reduce the postharvest life of a floriculture crop. Many crop species benefit from lowering the temperature 2 to 10°F (1 to 6°C) during the last 1 to 3 weeks of the production cycle. Not only will the postharvest life be enhanced, but the flower color may be improved. Temperatures should not be reduced to levels that may cause chilling injury.

NUTRITION

Although good nutritional practices should be followed during the entire production time, the final few weeks have the greatest effect on postharvest life. For many potted flowering plants, such as chrysanthemums and poinsettias, fertilization should be reduced or terminated 1 to 3 weeks prior to sale. For bedding plants such as petunia (*Petunia* ×*hybrida*), marigold (*Tagetes*), and ageratum (*Ageratum houstonianum*), the fertilizer rate should probably be reduced by one-half at visible bud (Armitage, 1993). Completely eliminating fertilizer applications is not advisable for bedding plants because the small amount of media provides little reservoir for the plants. Also, bedding plants often dry out rapidly in the retail areas and are watered frequently, which leads to further nutrient leaching.

For most potted flowering plants, the percentage of nitrogen as ammonium should be reduced to 0 to 40% of the total N in the final weeks of production. With some species, 100% nitrate N is best. In addition, media EC levels should be low and plants should not be given a "shot" of fertilizer prior to sale. High soluble salt concentrations in the medium can cause rapid deterioration if the customer allows the plants to become excessively dry.

WATER

The media of container-grown crops should be moist but the foliage must be dry before packing and shipping. Wet foliage and flowers can be readily damaged by *Botrytis*. Often potted plants can be irrigated in the morning and packed in the afternoon. Remember, however, that water stress during marketing is considered by many to be the major factor limiting potted plant sales. Cut materials should be harvested when fully turgid, usually in the morning, because the water content of the flowers is a major factor in postharvest life (see Harvest Time section later in this chapter). Any wilting of cut materials will reduce vase life.

MEDIUM

A proper medium must balance aeration with nutrient and water retention. Poor water retention will result in excessive drying, whereas too much water retention increases the likelihood of root rot diseases; both reduce postharvest life. Although water-absorbing polymers and starches have proved useful for some growers, other growers have noticed no change in the amount of water needed during postharvest.

CONTAINER SIZE

With bedding plants, the larger the final container size, the better for the retailer and the customer because wilting is delayed (Armitage, 1993). Bedding plant flats, hanging baskets, and pots are often displayed in open, high-light areas, which have the potential to rapidly dry and reduce postharvest life. Large container sizes will reduce the irrigation frequency. Note that the volume of containers with the same diameter can differ. Excessive wilting is especially common with hanging baskets because they are often placed in locations with high air movement. Though small pot sizes for potted plants are popular with consumers and profitable for producers, the rapid drying and wilting limits the distribution and marketing of plants in pots smaller than 4 in. (10 cm) wide.

GROWTH REGULATORS

Application of growth regulators will enhance the postharvest life of many potted and bedding plants by increasing the chlorophyll content, which enhances photosynthesis, and by making plants more compact, which reduces shipping and handling damage. Compact plants also lose less water as compared with taller, untreated plants.

INSECT AND DISEASE DAMAGE

Insects and disease reduce plant vigor and quality, provide entry points for *Botrytis*, induce ethylene production (see next section), and provide cause for rejection of shipments by customers. The latter problem is especially important for cut flower exporters who may need to fumigate their product prior to shipping (Karunaratne et al., 1997). Necrotic leaf edges are sites for *Botrytis* colonization during the warm, humid conditions of shipping. Shipping can also aggravate root rot problems, which can reduce the postharvest life.

ETHYLENE

Most floriculture crops are sensitive to ethylene, an odorless, colorless gas produced naturally by plant materials or by incomplete combustion of heating fuels and engine exhaust. Concentrations as low as 100 parts per billion and exposure times of as little as 2 hours can lead to damage (Nell, 1993). Higher concentrations of ethylene can cause damage in shorter time periods. The ethylene concentration of engine exhaust can be more than 200 ppm for an older car (Hasek et al., 1969). The extent and type of damage will vary with the plant species, duration of exposure, ethylene concentration, and temperature. Numerous symptoms can occur: leaf, flower, and bud abscission; bud abortion; rapid flower senescence; and epinasty (the distinctive curling and drooping of leaves or bracts). Plant ethylene sensitivity varies from high for such species as carnations (*Dianthus caryophyllus*) and tomatoes (*Lycopersicon esculentum*) to low for such species as croton (*Codiaeum variegatum*) (Table 10-1). Ethylene damage can be prevented by

TABLE 10-1

Ethylene sensitivity of numerous floriculture crop species (L. Høyer, personal communication; Redman et al., 2002; Sacalis, 1993; Woltering and van Doorn, 1988).

Scientific Name	Sensitivity	Scientific Name	Sensitivity
Achimenes cultivars	Very sensitive	*E. pulcherrima*	Sensitive
Aconitum napellus	Sensitive	*Eustoma grandiflorum*	Sensitive
Aeschynanthus speciosus	Very sensitive	*Exacum affine*	Slightly sensitive
Alstroemeria cultivars	Sensitive	*Fatsia japonica*	Slightly sensitive
Anemone coronaria	Sensitive	*Ficus benjamina*	Slightly sensitive
Anthurium scherzerianum	Slightly sensitive	*F. deltoidea*	Sensitive
Antirrhinum majus	Very sensitive	*F. pumila*	Slightly sensitive
Asparagus densiflorus	Slightly sensitive	*Freesia* hybrids	Very sensitive
Asplenium nidus	Not sensitive	*Fuchsia* cultivars	Very sensitive
Astilbe × arendsii	Sensitive	*Gerbera jamesonii*	Slightly sensitive
Begonia × hiemalis	Sensitive	*Gladiolus* cultivars	Not sensitive
B. Semperflorens-Cultorum	Very sensitive	*Gypsophila* cultivars	Sensitive
		Hedra helix	Slightly sensitive
Bougainvillea cultivars	Very sensitive	*Helianthus maximilianii*	Sensitive
Browallia speciosa	Very sensitive	*Hibiscus rosa-sinensis*	Very sensitive
Calceolaria Herbeohybrida group	Very sensitive	*Hyacinthus orientalis*	Slightly sensitive
		Impatiens hawkeri	Very sensitive
Campanula carpatica	Sensitive	*I. walleriana*	Very sensitive
C. isophylla	Sensitive	*Iris* hybrids	Sensitive
Capsicum annuum	Sensitive	*Justicia brandegeana*	Very sensitive
Catharanthus roseus	Very sensitive	*Kalanchoe blossfeldiana*	Very sensitive
Cattleya cultivars	Very sensitive	*Kohleria* cultivars	Very sensitive
Chamaedorea elegans	Not sensitive	*Lathyrus odoratus*	Very sensitive
Clerodendrum thomsoniae	Very sensitive	*Lilium* hybrids	Sensitive
Codiaeum variegatum	Not sensitive	*L. longiflorum*	Sensitive
Consolida ambigua	Very sensitive	*Lycopersicon esculentum*	Sensitive
Cordyline terminalis	Not sensitive	*Matthiola incana*	Very sensitive
Cosmos bipinnatus	Not sensitive	*Narcissus pseudonarcissus*	Not to slightly sensitive
Crossandra infundibuliformis	Sensitive	*Nephrolepis exaltata*	Not sensitive
Cyclamen persicum	Sensitive, if pollinated	*Nerine bowdenii*	Not sensitive
Cymbidium species	Very sensitive	*Pachystachys lutea*	Very sensitive
Dahlia cultivars	Sensitive	*Paeonia* cultivars	Not sensitive
Delphinium cultivars	Very sensitive	*Paphiopedilum* cultivars	Very sensitive
Dendranthema × grandiflorum	Slightly or not sensitive	*Pelargonium* cultivars	Sensitive
		Penstemon digitalis	Sensitive
Dendrobium species	Not sensitive	*Pericallis × hybrida*	Not sensitive
Dianthus caryophyllus	Very sensitive	*Petunia* cultivars	Very sensitive
Dieffenbachia species	Slightly sensitive	*Phalaenopsis* cultivars	Very sensitive
Dracaena marginata	Slightly sensitive	*Philodendron scandens*	Sensitive
D. sanderiana	Slightly sensitive	*Phlox paniculata*	Sensitive
Echinacea purpurea	Not sensitive	*Primula vulgaris*	Very sensitive
Epipremnum aureum	Not sensitive	*Radermachera sinica*	Sensitive
Eremurus robustus	Sensitive	*Ranunculus asiaticus*	Slightly sensitive
Eucharis × grandiflora	Slightly sensitive	*Rhododendron simsii*	Sensitive
Euphorbia fulgens	Sensitive	*Rosa* cultivars	Slightly sensitive
E. pseudocactus	Very sensitive	*Saintpaulia ionantha*	Very sensitive

(continued)

TABLE 10-1 *(continued)*

Scientific Name	Sensitivity	Scientific Name	Sensitivity
Schefflera actinophylla (Brassaia)	Sensitive	*Solanum pseudocapsicum*	Very sensitive
		Stephanotis cultivars	Very sensitive
S. *arboricola*	Sensitive	*Streptocarpus* ×*hybridus*	Very sensitive
S. *elegantissima* (Dizygotheca)	Sensitive	*Syringa* cultivars	Sensitive
		Viola ×*wittrockiana*	Sensitive
Schlumbergera cultivars	Very sensitive	*Weigela* cultivars	Sensitive
Scindapsus pictus	Not sensitive	*Yucca elephantipes*	Slightly sensitive
Sinningia cultivars	Not sensitive	*Zantedeschia* cultivars	Not sensitive
S. *cardinalis*	Very sensitive	*Zinnia* cultivars	Slightly sensitive

avoiding exposure to engine exhaust, ripening fruit, senescing plant materials, smoke, welding fumes, and incomplete heating fuel combustion from malfunctioning heaters. Ethylene can also be produced by plant pathogens, which can be especially detrimental during shipping when plant materials are enclosed and air circulation is limited (Qadir et al., 1997).

Endogenous ethylene can be minimized by either lowering the temperature or applying an anti-ethylene agent. Low-temperature storage and shipping greatly reduce the effect of ethylene on cut flowers and potted flowering plants. Of course, crops sensitive to chilling such as African violets (*Saintpaulia ionantha*) or caladiums (*Caladium bicolor*) cannot be shipped at cool temperatures.

Although research continues on a number of anti-ethylene agents, silver thiosulfate (STS) and 1-methylcyclopropene (1-MCP) are currently the most commonly used agents (Fig. 10-2). STS is quite effective at extending

FIGURE 10-2 Effect of silver thiosulfate (center), 1-methylcyclopropene (right), or water (left) on cut sweet pea (*Lathyrus odoratus*) flowers.

the vase life of many cut flowers such as carnation (*Dianthus caryophyllus*), snapdragon (*Antirrhinum majus*), and *Delphinium*. With potted plants STS reduces flower bud abscission on hibiscus (*Hibiscus rosa-sinensis*) and holiday cactus (*Schlumbergera*) and increases the longevity of potted carnation (*Dianthus carthusianorum*). With seed-propagated geraniums (*Pelargonium* ×*hortorum*), STS prevents petal shattering, but makes the plants more susceptible to *Pythium* root rot (Hausbeck et al., 1987). Results can be variable with potted plants, which may be due to the difficulty of making uniform applications on potted plants as compared with the relative ease of treating cut flowers with STS (see Chapter 8, Plant Growth Regulation). Also, be sure to check the legality of using STS on potted plants before application.

Although STS can be mixed from its component chemicals (sodium thiosulfate and silver nitrate), it is more easily obtained commercially as AVB (Cameron et al., 1985). Because the primary component, silver, is a heavy metal, caution should be taken in handling and disposal of STS solutions. In addition, there may be restrictions on its use that vary by state or country.

The environmental problems with STS have led to the development of an organic gas, 1-MCP, which is also an effective anti-ethylene agent (Blankenship and Dole, 2003; Serek et al., 1994). 1-MCP is effective at rates as low as 2.5 parts per billion. Because 1-MCP is a gas, treatment methods will differ from STS, which is usually applied as an aqueous floral preservative. For example, commercial application of 1-MCP may occur in a greenhouse before packing, or placing in a transportation vehicle, shipping container, or holding area (Serek et al., 1994). 1-MCP is available as a powder, which creates a gas after mixing with water and buffer. 1-MCP leaves no residue and is as effective as STS for some crop species such as *Freesia* and wax flower (*Chamelaucium uncinatum*) (Shaw, 1997). However, 1-MCP is not as effective as STS on other species such as carnations, *Bouvardia*, Asiatic lily (*Lilium*), and *Delphinium* (Dole, unpublished data). 1-MCP is marketed under the name EthylBloc and can be legally used on both cut flowers and potted plants. Ethylbloc will also be available as a liquid spray formulation for those operations without proper facilities for using the gaseous form (J. Daly, personal communication). Spray applications should be made under conditions that allow the product to remain on the plant as long as possible.

Research continues on other anti-ethylene agents. Another potential but little studied agent is lysophosphatidylethanolamine (LPE), a naturally occurring phospholipid that delays senescence of cut snapdragon stems (Kaur and Palta, 1997).

HARVESTING

DEVELOPMENTAL STAGE

Crops should be harvested at the optimum stage for maximum postharvest life. Unfortunately, the proper developmental stage varies greatly among species. For example, potted poinsettias should not be sold until the center flowers (cyathia) open, whereas crocus (*Crocus vernus*) should be sold wholesale when the flower color is just beginning to be visible. Fortunately, the marketing window is much greater for bedding plants and foliage plants. However, immature or overgrown bedding plants will be difficult for the consumer to use. For cut flowers, the developmental stage is especially important (Table 10-2). For example, yarrow flowers should be harvested when fully opened and colored, whereas species such as peonies (*Paeonia lactiflora*) and Dutch iris (*Iris ×hollandica*) can be harvested when the buds first show color. For many species, flowers harvested in a tight bud stage can be more easily

TABLE 10-2

Stage of development for harvest of numerous cut flower species (Armitage and Laushman, 2003; Dole and Schnelle, 1991; Redman et al., 2002; Sacalis, 1993). **Optimum harvest stage will vary with type of market.** Flowers for direct retail or florists may be harvested more mature than those harvested for wholesale markets. In most cases, the indicated stage is the earliest that flowers should be harvested.

Name	Stage of Development
Acacia species	From bud stage (green) to ½ florets open (yellow)
Achillea filipendulina	Fully open flowers and pollen visible
A. millefolium	Fully open flowers and pollen visible
A. ptarmica	Fully open flowers
Aconitum napellus	1 to 3 lower florets open
Acroclinum roseum	Before fully open
Agapanthus africanus	¼ florets open
Agastache species	¾ florets open
Ageratum houstonianum	Center floret fully open, lateral florets well colored
Agrostemma githago	1 to 2 flowers open
Alcea rosea	⅓ florets open
Allium cultivars	¼ to ½ florets open
Alstroemeria cultivars	First floret fully colored, lateral buds mostly colored
Amaranthus caudatus	Fresh: ¾ of florets open; dry: allow all flowers to grow seed and inflorescence to become firm
Ammi majus	80% of flowers in umbel open
Ammobium alatum	Buds well colored but before yellow centers are visible
Anemone coronaria	Sepals separated from the center but are not fully open
Anigozanthus cultivars	3 to 4 florets open
Anthurium cultivars	At least ¾ flowers on spadix open
Antirrhinum majus	⅓ flowers open
Aquilegia cultivars	½ flowers open
Argyranthemum frutescens	Most flowers on spray open

(continued)

TABLE 10-2 *(continued)*

Name	Stage of Development
Asclepias tuberosa	½ to ⅔ flowers open
Aster cultivars	¼ florets open
Astilbe cultivars	½ to ¾ florets open
Astrantia major	Uppermost flowers open
Baptisia species	⅓ flowers open
Belamcanda cultivars	Fruit black and covering begins to shed
Bellis perennis	Fully open flowers
Bouvardia hybrids	
White cultivars	Buds fully colored but unopened
Other cultivars	1 to 2 flowers open
Brassica olearaceae	Anytime stems are long enough and center leaves are well colored
Briza species	Soon after heading
Buddleia davidii	25 to 75% of buds open but lower florets not yet fading
Bupleurum rotundifolium	Almost all flowers fully open
Calendula officinalis	Fully open flowers
Callicarpa species	Basal fruit clusters well colored and terminal clusters still green
Callistephus chinensis	Outside ray florets begin to open
Camellia japonica	Fully open flowers
Campanula cultivars	1 to 2 florets well colored and open
Carthamus tinctorius	Most buds opened and well colored
Caryopteris incana	Lower whorl of buds show color or are open
Cattleya cultivars	3 to 4 days after opening
Celastris scandens	Fruit are well colored
Celosia argentea	Inflorescence fully colored but prior to significant seed formation
Centaurea cyanus	Apical flower ¾ to fully open
Centaurea macrocephala	Flower ½ to ¾ open
Centranthus ruber	First flowers in inflorescence open
Cercis canadensis	25 to 75% of buds open
Chasmanthium latifolium	Soon after heading
Chelone species	Lower florets open
Chrysanthemum species	Fully open flowers
Cirsium japonicum	Fully open flowers
Clarkia cultivars	½ or 3 to 6 flowers open
C. amoena	½ florets open
Clivia miniata	¼ florets open
Consolida ambigua	2 to 5 florets open
Convallaria majalis	All florets are white
Coreopsis grandiflora	Fully open flowers
Cornus species	Harvest stems after foliage has fallen and before new growth appears
C. florida	Bracts beginning to open, but pollen not yet visible
Cosmos bipinnatus	Petals on apical flower opening but not yet flat
Costus species	Almost fully open flowers
Cotinus species	Inflorescence is well colored, ignore the tiny flowers
Craspedia globosa	Flowers fully colored
Crocosmia ×crocosmiiflora	First flowers showing color but not yet open
Cyclamen persicum	Flower fully open
Cymbidium cultivars	3 to 4 days after opening
Dahlia cultivars	¾ to fully open flowers
Delphinium cultivars	¼ to ⅓ florets open
Dendranthema ×grandiflorum	
Standard cultivars	Outer petals fully elongated
Spray cultivars:	

TABLE 10-2 *(continued)*

Name	Stage of Development
Singles	Open but before anthesis
Anemones	Open but before disk flowers start to elongate
Pompons and decoratives	Center of the oldest flower fully open
Dendrobium cultivars	1 to 2 days prior to being fully opened
Dianthus barbatus	10 to 20% of florets open
D. caryophyllus	
Standard cultivars	Petals ¼ to ½ in. (0.5 to 1.5 cm) above calyx
Spray cultivars	2 to 3 fully open flowers per spray
Dicentra species	Lower ⅓ flowers fully colored and open
Digitalis purpurea	2 to 3 lower florets open
Doronicum orientale	Almost open flowers
Echinacea purpurea	Petals fully expanded, first ring of disk florets open
Echinops bannaticus	½ to ¾ florets showing color
Emilia coccinea	First flower fully open
Eremurus robustus	Lower three rows of florets open
Erica cultivars	½ florets open
Erigeron cultivars	Fully open flowers
Eryngium cultivars	Entire inflorescence well colored
Erysimum cheiri	½ florets open
Eucharis × *grandiflora*	Just opened flowers
Euonymous alatus	After leaves drop for stems, when foliage is well colored for fall foliage
Eupatorium species	Buds well colored and center florets open
Euphorbia fulgens	Showing enough color to be marketable
E. marginata	Bracts fully colored but flowers not yet open
E. pulcherrima	1 to 2 cyathia showing pollen
Eustoma grandiflorum	One or more open flowers and basal buds showing color
Forsythia × *intermedia*	Buds show color for immediate use, stems with tight buds are harvested for forcing
Freesia cultivars	First floret puffy and beginning to open and at least 2 more buds show color
Fritillaria imperialis	Half open flowers
Gaillardia pulchella	Fully open flowers
Gardenia augusta	Just open flower
Gentiana species	1 to 2 flowers open or ¾ buds well colored
Gerbera jamesonii	Two outer rows of florets showing pollen
Gladiolus cultivars	Lower 2 buds showing color
G. callianthus (Acidanthera)	One flower open
Gloriosa superba	Almost fully open flowers
Gomphrena cultivars	Flower heads large and rounded but not yet elongated
Grains	Seed heads full size but before seeds are mature
Gypsophila cultivars	5 to 30% flowers open for shipping fresh, 80 to 90% flowers open for drying or for local fresh use
Helianthus annuus	Flowers almost fully open
Helichrysum bracteatum	Bracts unfolding and center just visible
Heliconia species	⅔ bracts open
Heliopsis helianthoides	Fully open flowers
Helleborus niger	Well colored flowers
Hemerocallis cultivars	Half open flowers
Hippeastrum cultivars	Colored buds
Hyacinthus orientalis	Colored buds
Hydrangea species	½ florets open
Hypericum species	Fruit are well colored

(continued)

TABLE 10-2 *(continued)*

Name	Stage of Development
Ilex species	Fruit are well colored
Iris germanica	Colored buds
I. × *hollandica*	Before falls reflex, "pencil" stage
Ixia cultivars	Colored buds
Kalanchoe cultivars	10 to 25% florets open
Kniphofia uvaria	Almost all florets showing color
Lagurus ovatus	Plumes fully mature
Lathyrus odoratus	2 to 3 florets showing color
Lavatera trimestris	Petals opening but not yet flat
Leontopodium alpinum	Fully open flowers
Lepidium sativum	Pods fully formed
Liatris spicata	3 to 4 florets open
Lilium cultivars	First bud well colored but not yet open
Limonium perezii	40% flower head open
L. sinuatum	Almost fully open developed bracts, white flower petals visible
Lobelia species and hybrids	⅓ lower flowers open
Lonas annua	Flower clusters fully colored
Lunaria annua	Pods fully developed
Lupinus mutabilis	½ to ⅔ florets open
Lysimachia clethroides	⅓ to ½ florets open
Matthiola incana	6 to 10 florets open
Moluccella laevis	½ flowers open and green
Monarda didyma	One ring of florets open and others fully colored
Muscari botryoides	½ florets open
Myosotis sylvatica	½ florets open
Myrica species	Anytime new foliage is mature
Nandina domestica	Fruit well colored
Narcissus cultivars	Gooseneck stage
Nepeta × *faassenii*	½ florets open
Nerine bowdenii	Oldest bud almost open
Nigella species	Fresh: Flower fully colored but petals not yet totally separated from center; dry: pods mature and well colored
Oreganum species	Flowers are purple and ⅓ open
Ornithogalum cultivars	First flower open and buds colored
Paeonia cultivars	Buds first show color and are medium firm to soft
Papaver cultivars	Calyx cracked and showing petal color (10% may not open) or when first open (cup stage)
Paphiopedilum cultivars	3 to 4 days after opening
Penstemon species	Several florets open
Phalaenopsis cultivars	3 to 4 days after opening
Phlox paniculata	2 or more florets open
Physalis alkekengi	Calyces fully colored
Physostegia virginiana	Spike elongated and 0 to 4 flowers open
Platycodon grandiflorus	2 to 3 opened flowers
Polianthes tuberosa	2 to 4 flowers open
Primula cultivars	½ florets open
Protea cultivars	Flowers fully open, bracts separated but not reflexed from flower head
Pyracantha species	Fruit well colored
Ranunculus asiaticus	Flowers show color and almost fully open
Reseda odorata	½ florets open
Rhodanthe manglesii	Flowers are well colored

TABLE 10-2 *(continued)*

Name	Stage of Development
Rosa cultivars	
Red and pink cultivars	First 1 or 2 petals beginning to unfold, calyx reflexed below a horizontal position
White cultivars	Slighter later than red and pink
Yellow cultivars	Slightly earlier than red and pink
Rudbeckia cultivars	Fully open flowers and first ring of disk florets open
Salix species	Harvest stems after leaves have fallen; some can also be harvested in the spring when catkins or new shoots are first developing
Salvia leucantha	White flower petals visible on lower 3 to 4 flowers
Scabiosa atropurpurea	Half to fully open flowers
S. caucasica	Flower color first visible
S. stellata	Seeds are almost mature
Scilla siberica	Half open flowers
Sedum cultivars	½ to fully open flowers
Solidago cultivars	½ florets open
×*Solidaster* cultivars	⅓ florets open
Stachys species	Inflorescence ½ open
Stephanotis floribunda	Fully open flowers
Strelitzia reginae	Orange tepals first appear, before they emerge from the bract
Syringa cultivars	First florets open
Tagetes erecta	Fully open flowers
Thalictrum species	Most florets open
Trachelium caeruleum	¼ to ⅓ flowers open
Trachymene coerulea	One or more rows of florets open
Tricyrtis species	1 to 2 flowers fully open
Triteleia laxa	4 to 6 flowers open
Trollius species	Half open flowers
Tropaeolum majus	Fully open flowers
Tulipa gesneriana	Half colored buds
Tweedia caerulea	6 cymes present, first one or two cymes showing color
Vaccaria hispanica	¾ to almost all of florets open
Verbena bonariensis	Most florets open
Veronica cultivars	½ florets open
Veronicastrum virginicum	⅓ florets open
Viola odorata	Almost open flowers
V. ×wittrockiana	Almost open flowers
Xeranthemum annuum	Flowers fully open
Zantedeschia cultivars	Just before the edge of the spathe begins to turn downward
Zea mays	Husks are dry
Zinnia elegans	Fully open flowers

shipped than those harvested fully open. Buds of some species respond to postharvest solutions and open into acceptable flowers.

When growing a new species, test a few stems at two or three different stages of flower development. Most species with spike-shaped inflorescences (or other types of flowers with multiple flowers per stem) are harvested when one-third to one-half of the florets are opened. Compositae family flowers (daisy types) are often harvested when the outer petals are fully developed and only one ring of inner disk florets is showing pollen. The use of sucrose in floral preservatives may increase the number of flowers to open on inflorescences and allow the successful opening of flowers harvested as buds (see Floral Preservatives section).

Plants that will be sold immediately to the final consumer can be harvested more mature than plants sold to wholesalers or shipped long distances. Also, some crops can be harvested at a younger stage of development during the summer than the winter because higher light (greater carbohydrate levels in the plant) and warmer temperatures contribute to faster flower development in the marketing chain or in the consumer's home.

HARVEST TIME

Cut flowers are generally harvested in the morning because that is when the plants have the highest water content and tissue is coolest. Although harvesting later in the day would allow for a higher carbohydrate status, the postharvest life of cut flowers and foliage is thought to be influenced to a greater degree by the water status. There is also less "field heat" in the plant material, which must be reduced. In addition, morning harvest saves the rest of the day for grading, packaging, and shipping. Most cut flowers should be immediately placed into buckets of water and hydrating solution in the greenhouse or field. Some cut flower species can remain dry after harvesting. Stems are recut and placed in water or floral preservatives after grading, sorting, and bunching. Ideally, potted plants should be watered in the morning, foliage allowed to dry to reduce disease development during shipping, and packed in the afternoon when the carbohydrate status is the highest (Fig. 10-3). Boxes should be placed in the cooler prior to shipment. Trucks can be either loaded in the evening or early the next morning and should be refrigerated.

SHIPPING AND STORAGE

Potted plants should be watered thoroughly, excess water allowed to drain, and foliage and flowers allowed to dry before packing and shipping (Fig. 10-4). Diseases such as *Botrytis* can develop rapidly in the moist, closed atmosphere of a shipping container. In addition, long-term shipping (2 to 5 days) can allow naturally occurring ethylene to build up. The warmer the shipping temperature, the greater the resulting problems from *Botrytis* and ethylene. Many cut flowers can be shipped dry, but some species need to be shipped with their stem bases in water. Many species with long spike inflorescences, such as *Gladiolus* and snapdragon, need to be shipped upright to prevent the tips from bending upward or treated to prevent bending if shipped in a horizontal position.

Refrigeration after packing and during shipping can significantly increase the postharvest life of crops that are shipped long distances (Table 10-3). Refrigeration reduces the transpiration and respiration rates, which, in turn, slows the depletion of carbohydrates and water and the senescence process. Controlled-atmosphere storage and shipping using low oxygen, elevated carbon dioxide, and low temperature also show potential for

FIGURE 10-3 Carts loaded with plug flats and ready for shipping.

FIGURE 10-4 Potted poinsettia (*Euphorbia pulcherrima*) sleeved and ready for a customer.

TABLE 10-3

Optimum transport and storage temperatures for numerous floriculture crop species (Armitage and Laushman, 2003; L. Høyer, personal communication; Nell and Reid, 2001; Sacalis, 1993).

Name	Form of Plant Material	Temperature °F (°C)
Acacia cultivars	Cut stem	39 (4)
Achimenes cultivars	Potted flowering plant	36–41 (2–5)
Achillea filipendulina	Cut stem	36–45 (2–7)
A. millefolium	Cut stem	40 (4)
A. ptarmica	Cut stem	40 (4)
Acoelorraphe wrightii	Potted foliage plant	50–55 (10–13)
Aconitum napellus	Cut stem	33–35 (1–2)
Adiantum species	Potted foliage plant	54–57 (12–14)
Aeschynanthus cultivars	Potted flowering plant	54 (12)
Agapanthus cultivars	Cut stem	33–35 (1–2)
Ageratum houstonianum	Bedding plant	50–55 (10–13)
A. houstonianum	Plug	41–45 (5–7)
Aglaonema 'Fransher'	Potted foliage plant	55–61 (12–16)
A. 'Silver Queen'	Potted foliage plant	61–64 (16–18)
Agrostemma githago	Cut stem	40 (4)
Allamanda cultivars	Potted flowering plant	54 (12)
Allium cultivars	Cut stem	40–45 (4–7)
Allium sphaerocephalon	Cut stem	32–35 (0–2)
Alstroemeria cultivars	Cut stem	36–39 (2–4)
A. cultivars	Potted flowering plant	39 (4)
Alyssum cultivars	Plug	32–41 (0–5)
Amaranthus caudatus	Cut stem	36–41 (2–5)
Ammi majus	Cut stem	37–40 (3–4)
Anemone coronaria	Cut stem	33–35 (1–2)
Anigozanthos cultivars	Potted flowering plant	50 (10)
A. cultivars	Cut stem	34 (1)
Anthurium cultivars	Potted flowering plant	50–59 (10–15)
A. andraeanum	Cut stem	55 (13)
Antirrhinum majus	Bedding plant	50–55 (10–13)
A. majus	Cut stem	32–36 (0–2)
Aquilegia cultivars	Cut stem	40–45 (4–7)
Ardisia crenata	Potted foliage plant	50–55 (10–13)
Areca cultivars	Potted foliage plant	54–57 (12–14)
Argyranthemum frutescens	Cut stem	32–35 (0–2)
A. frutescens	Potted flowering plant	36–43 (2–6)
Asclepias tuberosa	Cut stem	40–45 (4–7)
Asparagus setaceus	Cut stem	33–35 (1–2)
Aspidistra elatior	Potted foliage plant	50–55 (10–13)
Asplenium species	Potted foliage plant	59–64 (15–18)
Aster cultivars	Potted flowering plant	36–43 (2–6)
A. cultivars	Cut stem	33–35 (1- 2)
Astilbe cultivars	Cut stem	35–40 (2–4)
A. cultivars	Potted flowering plant	37–46 (3–8)
Begonia ×*heimalis*	Potted flowering plant	36–43 (2–6)
B. Rex Cultorum	Potted foliage plant	40 (4)
B. Semperflorens-Cultorum	Bedding plant	58–62 (14–17)
B. Semperflorens-Cultorum	Plug	41 (5)
B. Tuberhybrida	Plug	43–47 (6–8)
B. Tuberhybrida	Potted flowering plant	40 (4)
Bellis perennis	Cut stem	39–41 (4–5)

(continued)

TABLE 10-3   *(continued)*

Name	Form of Plant Material	Temperature °F (°C)
Bougainvillea cultivars	Potted flowering plant	37 (3)
Bouvardia cultivars	Cut stem	33–35 (1–2)
Browallia cultivars	Potted flowering plant	50–61 (10–16)
Brunfelsia species	Potted flowering plant	36–43 (2–6)
Buddleia cultivars	Cut stem	36–41 (2–5)
Buxus sempervirens	Cut stem	36–39 (2–4)
Caladium bicolor	Potted plant	70 (21)
Calceolaria cultivars	Potted flowering plant	36–41 (2–5)
Calendula officinalis	Cut stem	39–41 (4–5)
Callicarpa species	Cut stem	32–36 (0–2)
Callistephus chinensis	Cut stem	32–39 (0–4)
Camellia japonica	Cut flower	45 (7)
C. japonica	Cut foliage	39 (4)
Campanula cultivars	Potted flowering plant	36–43 (2–6)
C. medium	Cut stem	36 (2)
Capsicum annuum	Potted plant	48 (9)
Caryopteris incana	Cut stem	34–40 (1–4)
Catharanthus roseus	Plug	45–54 (7–12)
C. roseus	Potted flowering plant	54 (12)
Cattleya cultivars	Cut stem	46 (8)
C. cultivars	Potted flowering plant	50 (10)
Celosia cultivars	Plug	50–55 (10–13)
C. argentea	Bedding plant	50–55 (10–13)
C. argentea	Cut stem	36–41 (2–5)
Centaurea cyanus	Cut stem	35–41 (2–5)
Centranthus ruber	Cut stem	40 (4)
Cercis canadensis	Cut stem	36 (2)
Chamaedorea elegans	Cut stem	45 (7)
C. elegans	Potted foliage plant	50–55 (10–13)
C. seifrizii	Potted foliage plant	55–61 (13–16)
Chamelaucium uncinatum	Cut stem	33–35 (1–2)
Chrysalidocarpus lutescens	Potted foliage plant	55–61 (13–16)
Chrysothemis cultivars	Potted flowering plant	54–57 (12–14)
Cirsium japonicum	Cut stem	36–41 (3–5)
Cissus cultivars	Potted foliage plant	43–54 (6–12)
Clarkia amoena	Cut stem	36 (2)
C. unguiculata	Cut stem	39(4)
Clerodendrum thomsoniae	Potted flowering plant	46–61 (8–16)
Codiaeum variegatum	Potted foliage plant	61–64 (16–18)
Consolida ambigua	Cut stem	33–35 (1–2)
Convallaria species	Cut stem	31–32 (−1–0)
Cordyline terminalis	Cut stem	45–50 (7–10)
C. terminalis	Potted foliage plant	61–64 (16–18)
Coreopsis cultivars	Cut stem	39–41 (4–5)
Cornus alba	Cut stem	28 (-2)
Cosmos cultivars	Cut stem	36–41 (2–5)
Costus cultivars	Cut stem	55 (13)
Crocosmia hybrids	Cut stem	34–37 (1–3)
Crocus cultivars	Potted flowering plant	33–35 (1–2)
Crossandra infundibuliformis	Potted flowering plant	50–55 (10–13)
Cyclamen cultivars	Plug	32–41 (0–5)
C. cultivars	Potted flowering plant	36–41 (2–5)
C. persicum	Cut stem	34 (1)

TABLE 10-3 *(continued)*

Name	Form of Plant Material	Temperature °F (°C)
Cymbidium cultivars	Cut stem	31–39 (−1–4)
C. cultivars	Potted foliage plant	50–61 (10–16)
Dahlia cultivars	Cut stem	39–41 (4–5)
D. cultivars	Bedding plant	50–81 (10–27)
D. cultivars	Plug	41–55 (5–13)
Delphinium cultivars	Cut stem	33–35 (1–2)
Dendranthema ×*grandiflorum*	Cut stem	32–34 (0–1)
D. ×*grandiflorum*	Cutting with roots	32–37 (0–3)
D. ×*grandiflorum*	Cutting without roots	32–35 (0–2)
D. ×*grandiflorum*	Potted flowering plant	35–40 (2–4)
Dendrobium cultivars	Cut stem	50–55 (10–13)
Dianthus cultivars	Cutting	31–32 (−1–0)
D. cultivars	Potted flowering plant	36–41 (2–5)
D. barbatus	Cut stem	33–35 (1–2)
D. caryophyllus	Cut stem	33–35 (1–2)
Dieffenbachia cultivars	Potted foliage plant	54–59 (12–15)
Dionaea muscipula	Potted plant	50 (10)
Dracaena deremensis	Potted foliage plant	60–65 (16–18)
D. fragrans	Potted foliage plant	60–65 (16–18)
D. marginata	Potted foliage plant	55–61 (13–16)
D. reflexa	Potted foliage plant	61–64 (16–18)
D. surculosa	Potted foliage plant	60–65 (16–18)
Echinacea purpurea	Cut stem	36–45 (2–7)
Echinops bannaticus	Cut stem	40 (4)
Epiphyllum cultivars	Potted flowering plant	50–61 (10–16)
Epipremnum aureum	Potted foliage plant	55–60 (13–16)
Eremurus species	Cut stem	36 (2)
Erica cultivars	Cut stem	36 (4)
Eryngium planum	Cut stem	38–40 (3–4)
Eucalyptus polyanthemos	Cut stem	33–35 (1–2)
Eucharis ×*grandiflora*	Cut stem	45–59 (7–15)
Euphorbia fulgens	Cut stem	48–50 (9–10)
E. marginata	Cut stem	42–55 (6–13)
E. pulcherrima	Cut stem	50–59 (10–15)
E. pulcherrima	Cutting with callus	54–55 (12–13)
E. pulcherrima	Cutting with roots	41 (5)
E. pulcherrima	Cutting without roots	54–55 (12–13)
E. pulcherrima	Potted flowering plant	50–61 (10–16)
Eustoma grandiflorum	Cut stem	33–35 (1–2)
Exacum cultivars	Potted foliage plant	55–60 (13–16)
Ficus benjamina	Potted foliage plant	55–61 (13–16)
F. pumila	Potted foliage plant	43–54 (6–12)
F. microcarpa	Potted foliage plant	55–61 (13–16)
Forsythia ×*intermedia*	Cut stem	41 (5)
Fortunella japonica	Potted foliage plant	50 (10)
Freesia cultivars	Cut stem	32–35 (0–2)
F. cultivars	Potted flowering plant	32–35 (0–2)
Fuchsia cultivars	Potted flowering plant	38 (3)
Gaillardia cultivars	Cut stem	39 (4)
Gardenia augusta	Cut stem	32–34 (0–1)
Gaultheria shallon	Cut stem	32 (0)
Gentiana cultivars	Cut stem	36–41 (2–5)

(continued)

TABLE 10-3 *(continued)*

Name	Form of Plant Material	Temperature °F (°C)
Gerbera jamesonii	Cut stem	32–35 (0–2)
G. jamesonii	Potted flowering plant	54 (12)
Gladiolus cultivars	Cut stem	33–35 (1–2)
Gloriosa superba	Cut stem	34–39 (1–4)
Gomphrena globosa	Cut stem	36–41 (3–4)
Guzmania cultivars	Potted flowering plant	50–54 (10–12)
Gyposphila paniculata	Cut stem	33–35 (1–2)
Hatiora cultivars	Potted flowering plant	50–59 (10–15)
Hedra helix	Potted foliage plant	39–54 (4–12)
H. helix	Cut stem	36–39 (2–4)
Helianthus annuus	Cut stem	33–35 (1–2)
H. maximilianii	Cut stem	36 (2)
Helichrysum bracteatum	Cut stem	36–41 (3–5)
Heliconia cultivars	Cut stem	55–60 (13–16)
Hibiscus rosa-sinensis	Potted flowering plant	50–61 (10–16)
Hippeastrum cultivars	Potted flowering plant	45–50 (7–10)
H. cultivars	Cut stem	40–50 (5–10)
Howea forsteriana	Potted foliage plant	61–64 (16–18)
Hyacinthus orientalis	Potted flowering plant	32–35 (0–2)
H. orientalis	Cut stem	32–35 (0–2)
Hydrangea macrophylla	Potted flowering plant	35 (2)
Hypoestes phyllostachya	Potted foliage plant	43–54 (6–12)
Ilex species	Cut stem	32 (0)
Impatiens hawkeri	Potted flowering plant	60 (16)
I. walleriana	Plug	45–50 (7–10)
I. walleriana	Bedding plant	55–61 (13–16)
Iris cultivars	Cut stem	32 (0)
Jasminum cultivars	Potted flowering plant	36–43 (2–6)
Juniperus cultivars	Cut stem	32 (0)
Kalanchoe blossfeldiana	Potted flowering plant	40–50 (4–10)
Lachenalia cultivars	Potted flowering plant	40–48 (5–9)
Lathyrus odoratus	Cut stem	32–35 (0–2)
Leucanthemum maximum	Cut stem	39 (4)
Leucospermum cordifolium	Cut stem	39 (4)
Liatris cultivars	Cut stem	32–35 (0–2)
Lilium cultivars	Cut stem	32–34 (0–1)
L. cultivars	Potted flowering plant	32–41 (2–5)
Limonium sinuatum	Cut stem	33–35 (1–2)
Lobelia cultivars	Plug	36–45 (2–7)
Lobularia maritima	Bedding plant	39–55 (4–13)
L. maritima	Plug	32–41 (0–5)
Lupinus cultivars	Cut stem	39 (4)
Lycopersicon esculentum	Plugs	45 (7)
Lysimachia clethroides	Cut stem	36–41 (3–5)
Mandevilla cultivars	Potted flowering plant	54–57 (12–14)
Matthiola incana	Cut stem	33–35 (1–2)
Muscari cultivars	Potted flowering plants	36–41 (2–5)
Myosotis sylvatica	Cut stem	39 (4)
Narcissus pseudonarcissus	Cut stem	32–34 (0–1)
N. pseudonarcissus	Potted flowering plant	32–35 (0–2)
Nephrolepis exaltata	Potted foliage plant	50 (10)
Nerine bowdenii	Cut stem	45–50 (7–10)

TABLE 10-3 *(continued)*

Name	Form of Plant Material	Temperature °F (°C)
Nigella damascena	Cut stem	36–41 (2–5)
Ornithogalum cultivars	Cut stem	35–39 (2–4)
Oxalis cultivars	Potted flowering plant	35–39 (2–4)
Paeonia cultivars	Cut stem	32–34 (0–1)
Papaver nudicaule	Cut stem	35–39 (2–4)
P. orientale	Cut stem	39 (4)
Paphiopedilum cultivars	Cut stem	31–39 (−1–4)
Pelargonium cultivars	Potted flowering plant	41 (5)
P. cultivars	Cutting without roots	31 (-1)
P. cultivars	Rooted cutting	41 (5)
P. ×*hortorum*	Plug	36 (2)
Penstemon digitalis	Cut stem	36–45 (2–7)
Pentas lanceolata	Potted flowering plant	36–54 (2–12)
Peperomia bicolor	Potted foliage plant	61–64 (16–18)
Pericallis ×*hybrida*	Potted flowering plant	41–50 (5–10)
Petunia cultivars	Bedding plant	50–55 (10–13)
P. cultivars	Plug	32–50 (0–10)
Phalaenopsis cultivars	Cut stem	45–50 (7–10)
P. cultivars	Vegetative plant	77 (25)
Philodendron bipinnatifidum	Potted foliage plant	55–61 (13–16)
P. scadens oxycardium	Potted foliage plant	55–61 (13–16)
Phlox cultivars	Cut stem	39 (4)
Phoenix roebelinii	Potted foliage plant	54 (12)
Physalis alkekengi	Cut stem	36–41 (3–5)
Physostegia virginiana	Cut stem	34–41 (1–5)
Platycodon cultivars	Potted flowering plant	38–60 (3–16)
Polianthes tuberosa	Cut stem	32–41 (0–5)
Polyscias cultivars	Potted foliage plant	54 (12)
Portulaca cultivars	Plug	41–55 (5–12)
P. cultivars	Potted foliage plant	54–57 (12–14)
Primula cultivars	Potted foliage plant	36–43 (2–6)
Protea cultivars	Cut stem	35–45 (2–7)
Prunus cultivars	Cut stem	41 (5)
Pteris cretica	Potted foliage plant	64 (18)
Radermachera sinica	Potted foliage plant	54 (12)
Ranunculus cultivars	Potted flowering plant	36–43 (2–6)
R. asiaticus	Cut stem	32–34 (0–1)
Rhapis excelsa	Potted foliage plant	50–55 (10–13)
Rhododendron cultivars	Cut stem	32 (0)
R. cultivars	Cutting without roots	31 (−1)
R. cultivars	Potted flowering plant	41–50 (5–10)
Rosa cultivars	Cut stem	32–34 (0–1)
R. cultivars	Potted flowering plant	34–41 (1–5)
Rudbeckia hybrids	Cut stem	36–41 (2–5)
Rumohra adiantiformis	Cut stem	34–40 (1–4)
Saintpaulia ionantha	Potted flowering plant	55–61 (13–16)
Salix species grown for stems	Cut stem	30 (-1)
S. species grown for catkins	Cut stem	35–40 (2–4)
Salvia leucantha	Cut stem	35–40 (2–4)
S. splendens	Plug	41–54 (5–12)
Scabiosa caucasica	Cut stem	36–41 (3–5)

(continued)

TABLE 10-3 *(continued)*

Name	Form of Plant Material	Temperature °F (°C)
Schefflera actinophylla (Brassaia)	Potted foliage plant	50–55 (10–13)
S. arboricola	Potted foliage plant	50–55 (10–13)
Schlumbergera hybrids	Potted flowering plant	50–59 (10–15)
Scilla siberica	Cut stem	32–33 (0–1)
Scirpus cultivars	Potted foliage plant	36–54 (2–12)
Sinningia cultivars	Potted flowering plant	60 (16)
Soleirolia soleirolii	Potted foliage plant	36–43 (2–6)
Solidago hybrids	Cut stem	36–41 (2–5)
Spathiphyllum cultivars	Potted flowering plant	55–61 (13–16)
S. cultivars	Potted foliage plant	55–61 (13–16)
Stephanotis floribunda	Cut stem	39 (4)
S. floribunda	Potted flowering plant	54 (12)
Strelitzia reginae	Cut stem	46 (8)
Streptocarpus cultivars	Potted flowering plant	51–60 (10–16)
Syringa cultivars	Cut stem	41 (5)
Tachelium caeruleum	Cut stem	36–40 (2–4)
Tagetes cultivars	Cut stem	39 (4)
T. patula	Plug	41–45 (5–7)
Tanacetum coccineum	Cut stem	36–39 (2–4)
T. parthenium	Cut stem	39 (4)
Thalistrum species	Cut stem	36–41 (3–5)
Triteleia cultivars	Cut stem	37 (3)
Tropical green plants	Cutting without roots	59–64 (15–18)
Tulipa cultivars	Cut stem	32–35 (0–2)
T. cultivars	Potted flowering plant	32–35 (0–2)
Verbena bonariensis	Cut stem	36–41 (3–5)
Veronica species	Cut stem	36–41 (3–5)
Viola odorata	Cut stem	34–41 (1–5)
V. × wittrockiana	Plug	32–41 (0–5)
Weigela cultivars	Cut stem	36–45 (2–7)
Yucca elephantipes	Potted foliage plant	50–55 (10–13)
Zantedeschia cultivars	Cut stem	33–35 (1–2)
Z. cultivars	Potted flowering plant	37–39 (3–4)
Zinnia cultivars	Cut stem	39 (4)

cut flower handling (Meir et al., 1995; Shelton et al., 1996).

Most, but not all, plant species benefit from cooling. Those species that are intolerant include species sensitive to chilling such as African violet, *Dieffenbachia maculata, Dracaena, Ficus, Heliconia, Spathiphyllum,* and *Strelitzia,* which can be damaged at temperatures below 54 to 60°F (12 to 16°C). Most cut flowers respond to hydration and cooling as soon as possible after harvest, which can be done in a number of ways: (1) Sort and pack flowers in a cold room; (2) cool flowers first, then sort, pack, and return to the cooler (Figs. 10-5, 10-6, and 10-7); or (3) sort and pack flowers and force cooled air through the boxes. With the last method, cool air is forced or removed

FIGURE 10-5 Roses (*Rosa*) being sorted and graded.

FIGURE 10-6 Automatic Dutch iris (*Iris ×hollandica*) bunching machine.

FIGURE 10-7 Sorting, wrapping, and sleeving of cut roses (*Rosa*).

though end flaps or holes in the boxes when in cold storage. For field-grown cut flowers, bring flowers to the cooler frequently during harvest. If no cooler is available, place the flowers in the coldest place possible and ship or sell immediately. Also watch for condensation on the flowers during refrigeration, which can lead to *Botrytis*. If condensation is found, temporarily open boxes and allow to dry before shipping. On the receiving end, all plant materials should be unpacked as soon as possible, because heat can accumulate in the shipping boxes through respiration of the plant materials.

Cold storage is imperative for cut flowers (Table 10-3). With most species, the colder the better—as long as the cooler is above freezing.

The optimum temperature is frequently 33 to 35°F (1 to 2°C) (Nell and Reid, 2001). Many coolers are kept too warm for optimum storage, especially when people are constantly entering the cooler during the day. Field cut growers have noted that some cut flowers, such as *Celosia* and *Zinnia*, are sensitive to cold storage temperatures below 40°F (4°C) when placed into cold storage immediately after harvesting on a hot day. In such cases, rehydrate the flowers and precool at a temperature above 40°F (4°C) before placing them in the cooler.

CUT FLOWER HANDLING

Cut flowers decline after harvest because of numerous factors including lack of water uptake, low carbohydrates, and the presence of ethylene.

WATER UPTAKE

One of the most important factors is lack of water uptake. In general, water uptake can be promoted by using high-quality water which has low soluble salt levels and alkalinity. Avoid water that contains fluoride which can reduce the keeping quality of some cut flowers such as *Gladiolus*, roses, and orchids (V. Stamback, personal communication, Waters, 1968). Be sure to test the pH and EC of the water regularly. Floral preservatives generally contain water acidifiers; however, if the water has high alkalinity and pH, additional acidification will be necessary. The addition of surfactants to the vase may also increase water uptake (Jones et al., 1993; Pak and van Doorn, 1991). Knives and stem cutters must be sharp, because dull blades will crush and tear the stems. Finally, flowers should not wilt. Although any degree of wilting will reduce postharvest life, practical shipping and handling procedures may result in the slight wilting of some flowers.

MICROORGANISMS

The vascular system of stems may be blocked by microorganisms, air plugs, and physiological blockage (van Doorn, 1995). Bacteria and fungi are found naturally on plant tissue and in tap water and can readily build up in large numbers in holding and vase solutions (Hoogerwerf and van Doorn, 1992; van Doorn and de Witte, 1997). The microorganisms are taken up into the stem (xylem tissue) and physically block further water movement. *Sanitation is of utmost importance*. Germicides can greatly increase vase life (Jones and Hill, 1993). All buckets and utensils must be frequently cleaned and disinfected. Buckets should be clean enough to drink from. Decaying plant material provides an important source of microorganisms; therefore, foliage that would remain below the water should be removed. If flowers or foliage are dusty, rinse gently to clean. Flowers grown outdoors in a row system will tend to have more soil splashed on them than flowers grown in a bed system with grass or mulch between the plants.

AIR EMBOLISMS

Another cause of poor water uptake is air embolisms, which form when air is drawn into the xylem cells of the stems. On intact plants, the column of water in stems that extends from the roots to the leaves is under pressure through evapotranspiration; water transpiring through the leaves draws up more water through the roots and stems. When the stems are cut, the column of water recoils and draws air up into the stem's xylem cells. These "air plugs" can reduce or prevent the movement of water through the stems when placed in water. Recut the stems and immediately place in water. Remove at least 1.5 in. (4 cm) of the stem. While recutting under water has been recommended for years, the practice may actually be detrimental if the water is contaminated with bacteria (Haines, 2000). Recutting under water containing disinfectants or under running water may be practical solutions (Knight, 2001). The use of acidified (pH 3.0 to 4.0) and warm 100°F (38°C) water will increase water uptake. Citric acid is commonly used to acidify water. The amount of citric acid required will vary with the water quality and up to 500 ppm may be needed with alkaline water.

PHYSIOLOGICAL BLOCKAGE

No matter how well fresh cut materials are treated, they will eventually stop taking up water. This natural aging process is known as *physiological blockage*.

CARBOHYDRATE LEVEL

Low carbohydrate levels in the stems and leaves will reduce vase life, which can be partially remedied by the presence of sugars (sucrose) in the holding and vase solutions. The best practice is to maximize the endogenous carbohydrates in flowers before harvest and cool as soon as possible to prevent excessive respiration, which will reduce carbohydrate levels. Sugar can also be supplied in concentrations of up to 7% for vase or long-term holding solutions and from 5 to 20% as a 4- to 24-hour pulse.

FLORAL PRESERVATIVES

The efficacy of floral preservatives will vary greatly with the water quality and species. Be sure to test several preservatives to find the ones that are best for your operation. Always follow mixing directions because floral preservatives can be either ineffective or detrimental if supplied to the flowers in the wrong concentration. Flowers will be damaged if the preservative is too concentrated and the biocide will be too dilute to be effective if the floral preservative concentration is too low. Several types of commercial floral preservatives can be used:

- *Hydrators* promote water uptake and typically contain chemicals to reduce water pH. Hydrators usually do not include sugar and, thus, are not used for holding flowers long term. Some flowers may be damaged by keeping cut stems in hydration solution too long. Commercial hydration solutions are available and the amount of time the stems should be kept in the hydration solution varies from a few seconds to 48 hours. The "quick dip"-type solutions primarily reduce the amount of microorganisms on the stems. The long-duration solutions are used for holding flowers 8 to 48 hours until final processing or for shipping in water.

- *Pretreatments/pulses* are short duration treatments, usually 4 to 24 hours, of 100°F (38°C) hot water, 5 to 20% sucrose, antiethylene agents, or other treatments.

- *Processing/holding* solutions usually contain sugar, an acidifying agent, and an antimicrobial compound. These solutions are used for the transport and storage of flowers. Products with a greater percentage of sugar are used to open buds and promote flower development.

- *Consumer preservatives/vase solutions* are intended for the arrangements and bouquets used by the final consumer. Consumer preservatives normally contain sugar, an acidifying agent, and an antimicrobial compound. The preservatives are available in bulk for retailers to use or in individual packets for the customer to mix into the water when the flowers are brought home.

- *Crop-specific preservatives* can be used for species that have special requirements such as to prevent stretch of tulips (*Tulipa*).

A number of chemicals can be added to floral preservatives to extend the postharvest life of cut flowers. Gibberellins, such as GA_4 or GA_7, and cytokinins such as kinetin, zeatin, or 6-benzylaminopurine (PBA), delay leaf yellow of *Alstroemeria* (Hicklenton, 1991; Mutui et al., 2001; van Doorn et al., 1992). Some firms dip *Gerbera* flower heads into a benzyladenine (BA) solution to maintain flower weight and delay senescence. Other non purine cytokinins, such as CPPU [(2-chloro-4-pyridyl)-N-phenylurea] and TDZ (thidiazuron), delay leaf yellowing and floret abscission of cut *Phlox* and *Lupine* (MacKay et al., 2003; Sankhla et al., 2003). The application of calcium chelators (EDTA, EGTA, and CDTA) inhibited the bending of inflorescences that occurs when stems are shipped horizontally in boxes (Philosoph-Hadas et al., 1995). The use of B-Nine (daminozide) in the vase solution of cut snapdragons can also inhibit bending. The vase life of cut *Helianthus* flowers is improved when stems are hydrated after harvest in water with 0.02% detergent such as a dishwashing detergent, Tween-20, or Triton X-100 (Jones et al., 1993).

ETHYLENE AND DISEASES

Other causes of vase life decline include ethylene and disease (see the Ethylene and the Insect and Disease Damage sections earlier in this chapter). Indeed, microorganisms may produce ethylene and stimulate ethylene production from plant tissue.

RETAIL HANDLING

A retailer can take several steps to ensure that the plant materials have maximum longevity in the store and in the customer's home. Unpack all plant materials as soon as possible; inspect for insects, diseases, and damage; and water all potted materials immediately, if needed. Recut the stems of cut materials under running water or water with disinfectants and place them in clean water or preservative solutions. Retailers who do not clean their buckets will shorten the vase life of their flowers (Hoogerwerf and van Doorn, 1992). Place cut materials in a cooler immediately. Many potted flowering plants also can be held in cold storage, such as chrysanthemums (*Dendranthema* ×*grandiflorum*), azaleas (*Rhododendron*), and Dutch bulbs.

Potted flowering plants and foliage plants should be displayed in a well-lighted area with a minimum of 500 to 1000 fc (100 to 200 $\mu mol \cdot m^{-2} \cdot s^{-1}$) light. The postharvest life of bedding plants will also be extended if they are given light to moderate shade (50 to 60%) in display areas when the temperatures are expected to be more than 65°F (18°C) (Armitage, 1993). However, if bedding plants are displayed on stacked shelves, be sure that the light level is not too low for plants on the lowest shelves. Bedding plants need not be shaded in cool areas with temperatures less than 65°F (18°C). Bedding plants that have been shipped for 3 or more days in the dark may benefit from a period of reduced light intensity to reacclimate if displayed in bright sunlight. In areas with high light, high temperatures, and excessive wind, more protection will be needed than in other areas to prevent excessive drying and breakage. Potted foliage plants held indoors for a long time may also benefit from an application of dilute fertilizer at 50 ppm N. Finally, all displays should be kept fresh and dead foliage, flowers, and leaves removed.

KEY POINTS

- A crop is at its highest quality at the time of harvest and must be properly handled to minimize the loss in quality.
- Factors influencing the postharvest life of a crop start well before the crop is marketed.

- To maintain quality during marketing and in the final consumers' location, containerized plants and cut materials must be handled at the correct temperature, have a high carbohydrate level, and be free from water stress and ethylene.
- Every grower should routinely sample a few potted plants or cut stems of each species or cultivar to observe and determine the postharvest life.

- A number of production factors affect postharvest life including cultivar; improper irrigation, temperature, light, or media pH; high media EC; nutrition, container size, plant growth regulators, insects or diseases; and poor root systems.

- High temperatures and low light, in particular, reduce the carbohydrate status of a crop and reduce postharvest life.

- Most floriculture crops are sensitive to internally or externally produced ethylene and two anti-ethylene agents, silver thiosulfate (STS) and 1-methylcyclopropene (1-MCP), are commonly used.

- Crops should be harvested at the optimum stage for maximum postharvest life.

- Plants that will be sold immediately to the final consumer can be harvested when more mature than plants sold to wholesalers or shipped long distances.

- Cut flowers are generally harvested in the morning because that is when the plants have the highest water content and tissue is coolest.

- Potted plants should be watered thoroughly, excess water allowed to drain, and foliage and flowers allowed to dry before packing and shipping.

- Refrigerate after packing and during shipping and keep shipping and storage times as short as possible.

- Cut flowers decline after harvest because of numerous factors including lack of water uptake, low carbohydrates, and the presence of ethylene.

- The vascular system of cut stems may be blocked by microorganisms, air plugs, and physiological blockage.

- Sanitation; clean, high-quality (low EC and pH) water; and cold, 33 to 35°F (0.6 to 2°C) storage are most critical to cut flower longevity.

- Low carbohydrate levels in the stems and leaves will reduce vase life, which can be partially remedied by the presence of sugars (sucrose) in the holding and vase solutions.

- Commercial floral preservatives include hydrators, pretreatments/pulses, processing/holding solutions, consumer preservatives/vase solutions, and crop-specific preservatives.

- Retailers should unpack all plant materials as soon as possible, recut the stems of cut materials, and place them in clean water or preservative solutions and into a cooler immediately.

BIBLIOGRAPHY

Armitage, A.M. 1993. *Bedding Plants, Prolonging Shelf Performance*. Ball Publishing, Batavia, Illinois.

Armitage, A.M., and J.M. Laushman. 2003. *Specialty Cut Flowers*, 2nd ed. Timber Press, Portland, Oregon.

Biran, I., and A.H. Halevy. 1974. Effects of short-term heat and shade treatments on petal colour of 'Baccara' roses. *Physiologia Plantarum* 31: 180–185.

Blankenship, S.M., and J.M. Dole. 2003. 1-Methylcyclopropene: A review. *Postharvest Biology and Technology* 28:1–25.

Blessington, T.M., and P.C. Collins. 1993. *Foliage Plants, Prolonging Quality*. Ball Publishing, Batavia, Illinois.

Cameron, A.C., R.D. Heins, and H.N. Fonda. 1985. Influence of storage and mixing factors on the biological activity of silver thiosulfate. *Scientia Horticulturae* 26:167–174.

Dole, J.M., and M.A. Schnelle. 1991. *The Care and Handling of Cut Flowers*. Oklahoma State University Extension Facts No. 6426. Oklahoma State University, Stillwater, Oklahoma.

Haines, B. 2000. Controversial cutting. *Floral Retailing* 13(9):30, 32, 34, 36.

Hasek, R.F., H.A. James, and R.H. Siaroni. 1969. Ethylene—Its effect on flower crops II. *Florists' Review* 144(3722):16–17, 53–55.

Hausbeck, M.K., C.T. Stephens, and R.D. Heins. 1987. Variation in resistance of geranium to *Pythium ultimum* in the presence or absence of silver thiosulfate. *HortScience* 22:940–944.

Hicklenton, P.R. 1991. GA_3 and benzylaminopurine delay leaf yellowing in cut *Alstroemeria* stems. *HortScience* 26:1198-1199.

Hoogerwerf, A., and W.G. van Doorn. 1992. Numbers of bacteria in aqueous solutions used for postharvest handling of cut flowers. *Postharvest Biology and Technology* 1:295–304.

Jones, R.B., and M. Hill. 1993. The effects of germicides on the longevity of cut flowers. *Journal of the American Society for Horticultural Science* 118:350–354.

Jones, R.B., M. Serek, and M.S. Reid. 1993. Pulsing with Triton X-100 improves hydration and vase life of cut sunflowers (*Helianthus annuus* L.). *HortScience* 28:1178–1179.

Karunaratne, C., G.A. Moore, R.B. Jones, and R.F. Ryan. 1997. Vase life of some cut flowers following fumigation with phosphine. *HortScience* 32:900–902.

Kaur, N., and J.P. Palta. 1997. Postharvest dip in a natural lipid, lysophosphatidylethanolamine may prolong vase life of snapdragon flowers. *HortScience* 32:888–890.

Kawabata, S., M. Ohta, Y. Kusuhara, and R. Sakiyama. 1995. Influences of low light intensities on the pigmentation of *Eustoma grandiflorum* flowers. *Acta Horticulturae* 405: 173–178.

Knight, D. 2001. Don't cut out the cutting. *Floral Management* 17(2):6.

MacKay, W., N. Sankhla, and T. Davis. 2003. Effect of sucrose and CPPU on postharvest performance of cut phlox inflorescences. *HortScience* 38:857. (Abstract)

Meir, S., S. Philosoph-Hadas, R. Michaeli, and H. Davidson. 1995. Improvement of the keeping quality of mini-gladiolus spikes during prolonged storage by sucrose pulsing and modified atmosphere packaging. *Acta Horticulturae* 405:335–342.

Mutui, T.M., V.E. Emongor, and M.J. Hutchinson. 2001. Effect of Accel on the vase life and post harvest quality of alstroemeria (*Alstroemeria aurantiaca* L.) cut flowers. *African Journal of Science and Technology* 2:82–88.

Nell, T.A. 1993. *Flowering Potted Plants, Prolonging Shelf Performance*. Ball Publishing, Batavia, Illinois.

Nell, T.A., and M.S. Reid. 2001. Can't take the heat. *Floral Management* 17(10):33–34.

Nell, T.A., R.T. Leonard, and J.E. Barrett. 1990. Production and postproduction irradiance affects acclimatization and longevity of potted chrysanthemum and poinsettia. *Journal of the American Society for Horticultural Science* 115:262–265.

Nell, T.A., J.E. Barrett, and R.T. Leonard. 1997. Production factors affecting postproduction quality of flowering potted plants. *HortScience* 32:817–819.

Nowack, J., and R.M. Rudnicki. 1990. *Postharvest Handling and Storage of Cut Flowers, Florist Greens and Potted Plants*. Timber Press, Portland, Oregon.

Pak, C., and W.G. van Doorn. 1991. The relationship between structure and function of surfactants used for rehydration of cut astilbe, bouvardia and roses. *Acta Horticulturae* 298:171–173.

Philosoph-Hadas, S., S. Meir, I. Rosenberger, and A.H. Halevy. 1995. Control and regulation of the gravitropic response of cut flowering stems during storage and horizontal transport. *Acta Horticulturae* 405:343–350.

Qadir, A., E.W. Hewett, and P.G. Long. 1997. Ethylene production by *Botrytis cinerea*. *Postharvest Biology and Technology* 11:85–91.

Redman, P.B., J.M. Dole, N.O. Maness, and J.A. Anderson. 2002. Postharvest handling of nine specialty cut flower species. *Scientia Horticulturae* 92:293–303.

Sacalis, J.N. 1993. *Cut Flowers, Prolonging Freshness*, 2nd ed., J.L. Seals, editor. Ball Publishing, Batavia, Illinois.

Sankhla, N., W. MacKay, and T. Davis. 2003. Effect of thidiazuron and abscisic acid on flower abscission and senescence in cut racemes of Big Bend lupine. *HortScience* 38:857. (Abstract)

Serek, M., E.C. Sisler, and M.S. Reid. 1994. Novel gaseous ethylene binding inhibitor prevents ethylene effects in potted flowering plants. *Journal of the American Society for Horticultural Science* 119:1230–1233.

Shaw, J.A. 1997. The new anti-ethylene: Replacement for STS? *FloraCulture International* 7(3):36.

Shelton, M.P., V.R. Walter, D. Brandl, and V. Mendez. 1996. The effects of refrigerated, controlled-atmosphere storage during marine shipment on insect mortality and cut-flower vase life. *HortTechnology* 6:247–250.

van Doorn, W.G. 1995. Vascular occlusion in cut rose flowers: A survey. *Acta Horticulturae* 405:58–66.

van Doorn, W.G., and Y. de Witte. 1997. Sources of the bacteria involved in vascular occlusion of cut rose flowers. *Journal of the American Society for Horticultural Science* 122:263–266.

van Doorn, W.G., J. Hibma, and J. DeWit. 1992. Effect of exogenous hormones on leaf yellowing in cut flower branches of *Alstroemeria pelegrina* L. *Plant Growth Regulation* 11:59–62.

Waters, W.E. 1968. Influence of well water salinity and fluorides on keeping quality of 'Tropicana' roses. *Proceedings of the Florida State Horticultural Society* 81:355–359.

Woltering, E.J., and W.G. van Doorn. 1988. Role of ethylene in senescence of petals—morphological and taxonomical relationships. *Journal of Experimental Botany* 39:1605–1616.

Chapter 11

Greenhouse Construction and Operations

INTRODUCTION

Building and operating greenhouses require much study, information, and assistance from numerous professionals. This chapter provides basic information on the choices that are available in greenhouse operations; specific information should be obtained from reliable suppliers. If the investments are large, several price quotes or bids should be obtained before making a purchase.

GREENHOUSE PLACEMENT

CLIMATE

Climatic differences between and within countries are exploited in floriculture production. In North America, the cool summer temperatures of northern areas and the Pacific Coast allow more precise temperature control than in the south. However, moderate winter temperatures in the south allow more economical production than in the north. The southwest United States not only has the highest light levels in the United States, but the low humidity allows precise temperature control with fan and pad cooling, except during the humid rainy season of mid to late summer. In all areas of the world coastal climates often benefit from moderate temperatures, allowing year-round production of both cool and warm crops, but growers usually have to deal with low light levels under clouds or fog. Mountain areas have the benefit of high light and low humidity compared with

lower elevations, but higher heating expenses. Even in the small country of the Netherlands, the greenhouse industry has shifted to the Westland area from near Amsterdam because the former is 6 to 7°F (2 to 3°C) warmer. However, electricity and fuel costs vary greatly among regions, resulting in widely disparate cooling or heating expenses such that heating expenses in cool climates may be less than cooling expenses in some warm areas.

Any country or area has potential weather disadvantages. For example, in the United States, the East Coast, especially Florida, is subject to hurricanes; the North blizzards; the Midwest and Great Plains tornados; and the West Coast earthquakes. High-elevation areas of Central and South America are subject to unusual cold periods or frosts, which can severely damage or delay cut flower and foliage plant production, most of which is grown without heating systems.

TOPOGRAPHY

The topography must also be considered when selecting a site for a future greenhouse. Level sites are easier to build on and the greenhouses will be easier to operate. Hilly sites or areas with a steep slope can make day-to-day movement of plants and other materials more difficult. Such areas will also need extensive, costly grading to prepare the site for building. In some cases the prevailing winds can be used to cool the greenhouses. For example, the winds off the Pacific Ocean are used to cool greenhouses situated on hills overlooking the ocean in southern California. In windy, cold interior areas of the country, hills can block winds and reduce heating expenses compared with more open areas. If outdoor production is planned, consider that frost pockets can occur in low-lying areas between hills. Finally, inadequate drainage and the potential for flooding needs to be considered in any location. Poor drainage will increase maintenance and disease problems.

ACCESSIBILITY

Accessibility is especially important for retail operations and is exemplified by the cliché "What are the three most important considerations in a business? Location, location, location." A retail business must be easy to find, convenient, and highly visible in the community. Areas for display gardens and other ornamental plantings can be helpful. In addition, there must be sufficient parking to accommodate customers at peak sales times of the year. Accessibility is also an issue for wholesale operations in that sites need to be close to markets, especially large metropolitan areas, to reduce shipping and transportation costs. Potted and bedding plants are especially expensive to ship due to their weight. Being close to expressways and airports also makes it more convenient to receive supplies and ship product, especially cuttings and plugs. Location and accessibility of fuel and other supplies may also be an important consideration. Natural gas is not available in many locations.

WATER

Although water is often a factor forgotten until late in the purchasing process, water rights, availability, and quality should be among the first factors considered. Plentiful, high-quality water will make production much easier. There must be sufficient water to handle peak demand, and more than one source is advisable to prevent problems in case one source is interrupted. Check the history of any wells to ensure that they are reliable in dry weather.

Poor-quality water may prevent the production of some crop species and may limit your production options. The water quality should be tested, preferably more than once, by taking samples at various seasons. The property search and purchase process can be lengthy and often there is time to take two or more water samples.

LAWS

Most communities have a variety of local zoning laws that must be followed. Be sure to check if the property is correctly zoned for your future business. If a new building is going to be erected, then building permits must be obtained and fire and building codes followed. Although the exact building code to follow will vary with the community, three building codes are available as guides: Basic Building Code (BOCA, by Building Officials and Code Administrators), Uniform Building Code (UBC, by International Conference of Building Officials), and Standard Building Code (SBC, by Southern Building Code Congress International). Work is in progress to produce one code, International Building Code, which would replace the three codes in current use (Sray, 1997). Some communities do not have building codes; others have codes that do not apply to greenhouses. Many communities also require stamped engineered calculations in addition to building permits. Most reputable greenhouse manufacturers can provide stamped engineered calculations on their greenhouse frames.

Many communities have specific requirements in regard to parking lot size, amount of landscaping, distance from the road, runoff water retention, entrance sizes, and so forth. Some areas also have special considerations for agricultural industries. Various state and federal regulations may also apply, especially in regard to environmental issues, pesticides, water runoff, light pollution, safety, and wetlands.

NEIGHBORS

As the world becomes increasingly urbanized, the impact of neighbors on a floriculture operation and vice versa must be considered. Light pollution from street, parking lot, and security lights can negatively impact production of short-day crops. Spray drift from herbicide applications can damage both outdoor and greenhouse crops.

EXPANSION

When purchasing land, it is wise to acquire more than is immediately necessary, if sufficient funds are available. A general rule is to buy twice the amount of land needed at the time of the purchase to allow for growth of the business and unexpected needs. Land can often be an investment and the excess land can be sold later. Many businesses in urban or suburban areas find themselves surrounded by development and unable to expand. Expansion may include not only greenhouses for production but also additional service buildings, storage, parking lots, display beds, and so forth.

LABOR SUPPLY

The location of a floriculture firm in relation to the labor supply is increasingly important. Many areas have been unable to find sufficient labor. The seasonal, part-time nature of retail greenhouse work is often well-suited for retired people. A traditional source of seasonal help has been students, but a limited number of students may be interested in floriculture work. To attract additional workers, the business may consider profit sharing, higher wages, and benefits. Remember, one well-trained loyal employee will be worth several temporary, new workers due to the training time, unfamiliarity, and lack of loyalty to the company. The long-term solution to insufficient labor is automation.

GREENHOUSE STYLES

EVEN-SPAN (A-FRAME)

In an even-span or A-frame style of greenhouse, both sides of the roof are equal in length (Figs. 11-1 and 11-2). Even-spans are popular in northern areas because they are not conducive to snow accumulation. Even-span greenhouses are available in two types: American or high profile and Dutch or low profile. The latter have reduced roof and gable areas, which reduce heat loss and construction expenses. Most even-span greenhouses use truss supports rather than columns, which keep the interior free of obstacles and allow the use of thermal blankets, interior ceilings, and other automations.

UNEVEN-SPAN AND SAWTOOTH

In an uneven-span style, one side of the roof is longer than the other and, in some cases (sawtooth), the shorter roof may be completely absent (Fig. 11-3). Uneven-span greenhouses are often used to increase natural cooling, especially on hills or in windy areas. The cool air enters the side vents and rises along the long side

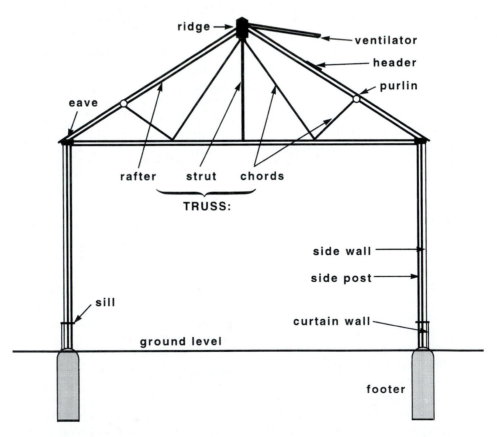

FIGURE 11-1 Components of an even-span greenhouse.

FIGURE 11-2 Even-span greenhouses.

FIGURE 11-4 Quonset-style greenhouses.

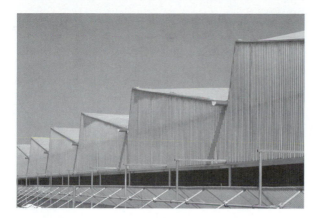

FIGURE 11-3 Uneven-span (sawtooth) greenhouse.

FIGURE 11-5 Gutter-connect greenhouses.

of the roof as the air warms. The warm air exits the top of the greenhouse. Uneven-span greenhouses are also used to accommodate the slant of the ground in hilly areas. When uneven-span greenhouses are oriented with the long side of the roof toward the south, the amount of light entering during the low-light conditions of winter will be greater than that entering comparable even-span greenhouses.

QUONSET

In a quonset-style greenhouse, the roof is rounded and may extend down to the soil level (Fig. 11-4). Sidewalls can also be present. Quonsets are relatively easy and inexpensive to build. Many quonsets are covered in two layers of polyethylene film plastic (known as double poly).

GUTTER-CONNECT

In the gutter-connect style of greenhouse, two or more individual greenhouses are connected together with no interior walls, resulting in a greater percentage of usable production space (Fig. 11-5). The roof shape can be even-span, uneven-span, or quonset style. Even- or uneven-span roofs or gutter-connect greenhouses are also known as ridge-and-furrow or rigid peak greenhouses. A quonset-style roof on a gutter-connect greenhouse is also known as a barrel-vault roof or roundtop and is one of the most popular designs.

Although gutter-connect greenhouses are less flexible than a similar number of individual greenhouses in terms of the growing environment, energy use is reduced by up to 40%, automation and movement of plants between houses become easier, and management of the facility is more convenient. Construction costs for a gutter-connect are less than for an equivalent amount of space in single or detached greenhouses. However, there is increased shading from gutters, insect control is more difficult in the open environment, and carbon dioxide levels can be reduced because of the restricted surface area compared with single detached houses. Temporary walls can be constructed between sections, if needed, with polyethylene film plastic to create individual environments. Gutter-connect greenhouses need to be especially well engineered and constructed if they are to be used in areas with heavy snows because of snow accumulation in the gutters between the roofs. Unlike with a single detached greenhouse, snow removal will be difficult. Heating pipes or cables can be laid in or below the gutters to speed melting of accumulated snow.

RETRACTABLE-ROOF GREENHOUSES

One of the latest advances in greenhouse design is the retractable roof, which allows growers to take advantage of direct sunlight and natural ventilation (Fig. 11-6). Plants are more compact than when grown in conventional greenhouses. The roof can be closed when the temperatures are too high or too low or during inclement weather. Newer designs are improving the heat retention, strength, and wind resistance while reducing the cost. In some styles the roof panels are lifted vertically; in other styles the roof is opened by gathering the polyethylene covering at each truss. Numerous versions are available. Some existing greenhouses can also be retrofitted with retractable roofs. Look for continued advances in this area of greenhouse construction. Opening and closing of the roof can be manual or computer controlled.

OTHER STYLES

Greenhouses can be built in many other configurations and styles than those previously listed, but are rarely used for commercial production. For example, domed greenhouses or curved eave greenhouses are used for conservatories. These types of greenhouses are more architecturally pleasing than typical commercial greenhouses. Also, the large specimens found in many conservatories require much taller greenhouses than those used in commercial operations. A lean-to greenhouse is attached to another building and uses that building as one of its walls. Lean-to greenhouses are small and commonly used by hobbyists, florists, and other small retailers. Lean-to greenhouses are usually not suitable for large-scale production because of reduced light levels, but may be useful as propagation houses.

FRAMING AND FOUNDATIONS

In the past, greenhouses were constructed with wood. Now large commercial greenhouses are constructed of metal. Wood is used for small, inexpensive greenhouses and for hobby greenhouses. Metal has the advantages of long life, high strength, and easy maintenance. The best metal to use is an aluminum alloy that is rust resistant, strong, and lightweight, which reduces the amount of framing components required. Aluminum is the most expensive metal; however, it is the most economical in the long term.

Wood is inexpensive initially but must be well maintained and is subject to rot, termites, and carpenter ants. Only rot-resistant wood should be used. Wood can be painted to help preserve it. Wood can be treated with preservatives such as copper naphthanate or zinc naphthanate to extend the life; creosote and pentachlorophenol must not be used because they produce phytotoxic fumes. Wood is primarily restricted to smaller greenhouses, especially those covered in polyethylene plastic. Wood can be combined with metal in that the trusses and purlins may be metal and the end walls, door frames, and so forth can be made from wood to reduce the cost.

The components of a greenhouse frame are illustrated in Figure 11-1. Not all greenhouses contain all components. For example, quonset greenhouses may not have a side wall, but may have a curtain wall. The height of the side wall from the floor to the eave (Fig. 11-1), also known as the gutter height, should be tall enough to allow workers to move about comfortably, which usually means that the eave should be 7 ft (2 m) or higher. Twelve-foot- (3.7-m)-high gutters are commonly used in

FIGURE 11-6 Retractable-roof greenhouse.

Europe; they are 8 to 8.5 ft (2.4 to 2.6 m) high in the United States. Taller greenhouses are becoming more common in the United States, however. High eaves greatly improve climate control, and allow easier hanging basket production and mechanization. Greenhouses that have to accommodate large foliage plants may need to have a greater eave height. The curtain wall, if used, can be made of poured concrete, concrete blocks, or any other solid material. The curtain wall often supports the heating pipes and should extend 6 in. (15 cm) below the soil level to prevent animals and rhizomatous weeds from entering the greenhouse. The curtain wall should be well insulated and is normally 2 to 3 ft (60 to 90 cm) tall. One or more doors should be located at each end of the greenhouse. For large wholesale greenhouses, one door should be large enough for vehicles and other equipment to enter.

The greenhouse must be constructed strong enough to withstand heavy weight (load). Three types of loads must be considered: (1) *Dead load* is the weight of the greenhouse structure and glazing, (2) *live load* is the weight of snow and water on the greenhouse roof and gutters, and (3) *wind load* is the force due to wind pressure, which is calculated at 20 lb/ft^2 (98 kg/m^2) on a vertical surface. Heavy snowfalls are most common in the fall and late spring. Double polyethylene glazings may need to be deflated to increase heat loss to melt snow. For gutter-connect houses, heating pipes or cables may need to be placed in or below the gutters to melt accumulated snow. In addition, greenhouse operators must consider the weight of hanging baskets and equipment, which may be hung from the greenhouse frame. Greenhouse tomato growers also need to consider the weight of tomato plants if they are supported by wires running off the greenhouse frame. For large or custom-built greenhouses, an engineer should be consulted to verify plans and specifications from greenhouse construction firms. (See also the Laws section earlier in this chapter.)

GLAZINGS

A number of factors are involved in choosing the glazing used to cover a greenhouse. First of all, the type of crops being grown will dictate the minimum light level. High-quality, potted flowering plants and cut flowers require high light transmission, especially during the winter. Darker houses can be used for foliage plants due to their low light requirements and for spring-only bedding plant operations because the crop is being produced at a time of the year when the light levels are naturally increasing. In northern areas heat retention becomes an important factor; in southern or high-altitude areas resistance to ultraviolet light degradation is often more important. A greenhouse can be constructed of more than one glazing. For example, the roof may be covered in corrugated polycarbonate for high light transmission and the end walls in double-layered acrylic for heat retention. Research continues on glazings and new products are continually being released.

GLASS

Glass was the first glazing used in greenhouses and is still considered the premium glazing for greenhouses. One major disadvantage of glass is breakage, especially due to hail. Older structures were often constructed of wood, while newer structures are usually metal. Although most glass panels are relatively small, large panels up to 6.6 × 12 ft (2 × 3.7 m) are available. In the United States the use of the large-size panels has been limited by concerns over hail, heavy snows, and high wind; however, the large panels require fewer roof bars, resulting in increased light transmission compared with greenhouses constructed with smaller panes of glass. Tempered glass should be used overhead because it breaks into numerous small, rounded pieces when struck. In contrast, float glass breaks into large pieces with exceptionally sharp edges and is restricted to the side, end, and interior walls. Low iron glass is available that has a higher light transmission rate (90 to 92%) than float or tempered glass (88%).

Light transmission—High, up to 92%.

Life expectancy—Long; one of the longest lasting glazings. Glass is heat, ultraviolet light, and wind resistant.

Heat retention—Low; usually the lowest.

Thermal contraction—Low; almost no thermal expansion or contraction.

Flammability—Fire resistant.

Flexibility—Rigid and not suitable for quonset-type greenhouses and breaks easily. Tempered glass, which is less prone to breakage, is available, but expensive.

Cost—Expensive, not only due to cost of the glass, but also to the extra construction needed to accommodate the weight of glass. The initial cost is offset by the long life of glass structures.

POLYETHYLENE FILM PLASTIC

Polyethylene film plastic is popular because it is inexpensive. Many types have additives or coatings to prevent ultraviolet light damage, fogging, water condensation, and dripping, as well as to retain heat longer. Colored films, especially pink or blue-green, are being tested for enhanced growth or reduced stem elongation. Plastic is available in standard lengths from 100 to 440 ft (30 to 134 m). Buy plastic film from a reputable supplier who specifically sells plastic for greenhouse coverings, especially with UV protectants. Low-quality film may last only a year and may rip off the greenhouse in a storm. Polyethylene film plastic is relatively easy to install and few support members are needed compared with other glazings, such as glass. Polyethylene film is particularly well suited for glazing quonset and barrel-vault greenhouses. Replacement of the plastic can be difficult in areas with frequent winds. Various systems are available for attachment of the plastic to the frame. Care must be taken when installing plastic to prevent any punctures, because they will serve as locations for future tears, especially if the two-layered inflated design (double poly) is used. Repair any tears in the plastic promptly to prevent further damage. Installation of double poly helps extend the life of the polyethylene by reducing whipping and fatigue against the frame compared with single poly. The outer layer is typically 6 mil (0.15 mm) thick and the inner layer can be 4 mil (0.1 mm) thick.

Light transmission—High for single layers (87%) but low for the more commonly used double-layered (83%) poly systems.

Life expectancy—Up to 5 years in some locations, but usually only 2 to 3 years. Life expectancy is lower in high-light areas. Polyethylene film plastic becomes yellow and brittle with age, making it more susceptible to tearing and wind damage. Using shade cloth over the plastic in the summer will increase the life and will reduce wind damage if the shade cloth is properly secured and does not abrade the plastic.

Heat retention—Single layers of plastic have very low heat retention, but a double-layered,

inflated plastic system has excellent heat retention. Separation between the two layers is maintained by air pressure from a small fan or blower. The dead or static air space created reduces fuel costs by up to 40% compared with glass. The fan should draw in outside air, because it is usually drier than inside air, which will reduce the amount of condensation between the two plastic layers. During heavy snows the plastic can be deflated to allow the internal greenhouse heat to rapidly melt the snow and prevent collapse. Using infrared (IR) plastic on the inside layer of the greenhouse will also improve heat retention during the winter. Infrared plastic reduces the loss of infrared heat radiating from plants, benches, equipment, and the floor.

Thermal contraction—High.

Flammability—Low, compared to fiberglass.

Flexibility—Very flexible, can be used on almost any style of greenhouse; impact resistant and able to tolerate some hail.

Cost—Initially low, but the long-term cost can be high due to the short life and subsequent replacement cost of plastic, especially in high-light areas. Remember the cost of plastic should also include the labor needed to replace the plastic.

OTHER FILM PLASTICS

Polyvinyl fluoride (PVF) films have characteristics similar to those of polyethylene films, but they last up to 10 years and are more resistant to abrasion and weather extremes. PVF plastics are also transparent to ultraviolet light and transmit up to 92% of the available light. However, PVF is more expensive than polyethylene, which has limited the use of PVF.

Ethylene-vinyl acetate copolymer (EVA) film plastic is clear, strong, and reduces radiant heat loss (see Greenhouse Heating section later in this chapter). EVA is also more flexible in cold weather than polyethylene. Although EVA is being used in Japan and Scandinavian countries, it is expensive and not extensively used in North America.

The main advantage of polyvinyl chloride (PVC) is its ability to reduce the transmission of long-wavelength infrared radiation, which reduces heat loss during the night. Houses covered in PVC also intercept radiation from the soil and will be warmer than polyethylene-covered houses. However, PVC attracts particles of dirt and dust, is not available in large widths, and becomes brittle on cold days and soft on warm days. This type is rarely used in North America but is more commonly used in other areas.

FIBERGLASS REINFORCED POLYESTER

Fiberglass reinforced polyester (FRP) was once a popular glazing, but its use has declined in recent years due to the availability of longer lasting corrugated polycarbonate. However, fiberglass is still in use due to its relatively low cost. Fiberglass is easy to fabricate and install and relatively few support members are needed. Although flat sheets are available, corrugated fiberglass is typically used because of its greater strength.

Fiberglass is available in 4 or 5 oz/ft² (1.4 or 1.5 kg/m²) weights; areas with high wind or snow loads should use the heavier weight. Several different surface treatments are available for extending panel life. Greenhouse fiberglass covered with an acrylic or tedlar finish should be used to increase life expectancy.

Light transmission—Initially high, up to 88%, but greatly decreases after a few years.

Life expectancy—Longer than polyethylene film plastic, but much shorter than glass. Fiberglass typically lasts about 20 years, but light transmission can be very low after just 10 years in high-light areas, and fiberglass turns yellow and brittle with age. Panel life can be lengthened by periodically treating the top surface with polyvinyl floride.

Heat retention—Low; corrugated panels have a greater surface area than flat panels, resulting in greater heat loss than flat panels.

Thermal contraction—Moderate.

Flammability—Very high; burns fast and hot.

Flexibility—Wind and hail resistant, suitable for any style of greenhouse; highly impact resistant.

Cost—Moderate.

ACRYLIC

Acrylic is available in single or double layers (twin wall) with two layers separated by small air spaces. Double-layered types provide added stability and heat retention. The dead air space between the sheets serves as insulation. Panels are also lighter and larger than glass, thus reducing construction costs.

Light transmission—Moderate to low (83%).

Life expectancy—Long (25+ years) if properly manufactured and installed. Acrylic is ultraviolet light and wind resistant, but scratches and cracks easily and becomes brittle with age. Initially acrylic has eight times the impact strength of glass, but the strength declines over time, which makes hail a concern in some areas. In addition, expansion and contraction of the panels prevents them from being screwed down. Various systems are available for attaching panels to the frame.

Heat retention—High with double-layered styles; a 50 to 60% reduction in heating fuel compared with glass.

Thermal contraction — High expansion/contraction potential.

Flammability—High, similar to fiberglass.

Flexibility—Easy to fabricate and install, few support members needed; rigid and not suitable for quonset-style greenhouses.

Cost—Expensive, but reduced fuel costs of double-layered types allow quick repayment in cool climates.

POLYCARBONATE

Available in single (corrugated) or double layers (twin wall) with the two layers separated by small air spaces. Double-layered types provide added stability and heat retention. Panels are also lighter and larger than glass, reducing construction costs. The single-layer, corrugated form has become popular because it combines long life with the flexibility of fiberglass.

Light transmission—Low to high (79 to 90%).

Life expectancy—Long (20+ years) if properly manufactured and installed. Polycarbonate is ultraviolet light and wind resistant, but it yellows and becomes brittle with age. Corrugated type may not yellow as readily as double-walled type. Corrugated panels can be attached with screws. Various systems are used to attach double-walled panels to the frame.

Heat retention—High with double-walled styles.

Thermal contraction — High expansion/contraction potential.

Flammability—Low, compared to fiberglass.

Flexibility—Easy to fabricate and install, few support members needed. Corrugated types are suitable for any style of house; double-layered types can also be attached to quonset-style houses if the curvature of the roof is not excessive. Extra purlins or supports will be needed on quonset-style roofs compared with polyethylene film glazing.

Cost—Expensive, but reduced fuel costs of double-layered types allow quick repayment in cool climates.

PURCHASING A GREENHOUSE

The first step in purchasing a greenhouse is determining what exactly it will be used for. For example, the type of house required for a bedding plant producer that needs space only for spring crops is far different than the type of house required by a year-round cut lily grower. The following are several questions that may help determine what is needed in a greenhouse:

- How long will it be used each year? You may be able to forego the use of pad and fan cooling and use inexpensive polyethylene glazings on a ground to ground quonset if the house is to be used only during the spring for bedding plants (Fig. 11-7). However, a cooling system such as pad and fan or roll-up sides will be needed for summer use.

- What crops will be grown in the house? Bedding plants can be grown on the ground in a short house with little problem. Add hanging baskets and the house will need to be taller for the comfort of workers and stronger to support the extra weight. Potted plant production on benches and cut flower production may require a taller house for maximum space usage.

- How much space will be required? Greenhouses are manufactured in standard widths and lengths. If using polyethylene glazing, the standard length ranges from 100 to 150 ft (30 to 46 m). Will a number of low-cost, individual quonset houses be sufficient or will a large, gutter-connect house be best?

- What laws and regulations are in effect for the location where the greenhouse is to be built? Check zoning requirements, building codes, permits required, etc.

- Will you build the house yourself or will you have a company build it for you? The latter is more expensive on paper, but remember that your time is valuable and may be better spent running the business. Do you have the labor to build the house? Many tasks are best handled by a crew of two or more people.

FIGURE 11-7 Quonset-style greenhouse with plastic removed for late spring bedding plant production.

After determining your needs, decide how much money is available for the project. Price is always a consideration. Remember that in addition to purchasing the house and any applicable permits, the utilities will need to be connected and the greenhouse outfitted with supplies. In addition, unexpected expenses will arise and the building suppliers may have useful, but costly, suggestions. One way to take these factors into account is to determine the total amount of money available to be spent. Subtract 10 to 20% for unexpected problems. Subtract an additional 10 to 20% to allow you to take advantage of ideas that your supplier or builder may suggest. Thus, when problems occur or when the builder has a great idea that costs extra, the built-in cushion of 20 to 40% will provide comfort.

- Obtain several bids for the project. Discuss with each company what is included in the price including freight, warranty, blueprints, and follow-up service.

- Ask for references of others who have purchased greenhouses from each supplier. Check with other greenhouse owners about their experiences and recommendations.

- Determine if the greenhouse supplier has its own crew of experienced builders or if the work will be subcontracted to outside crews that may have little experience in constructing greenhouses.

- Finally, be wary of purchasing existing greenhouses. Although the initial cost may be low and attractive, consider the amount of time required to take down and reassemble the greenhouse. The older the house, the more likely it is that major problems will occur and parts will need to be replaced.

BENCHES AND BEDS

BENCHING EFFICIENCY

Bench efficiency is defined as the percentage of greenhouse space that is usable for production:

$$\frac{\text{Area usable for production}}{\text{Area of greenhouse floor}} \times 100 = \% \text{ benching efficiency}$$

A high benching efficiency indicates that a large portion of the space can be used for production and income. The entire greenhouse has to be heated and maintained—the higher the benching efficiency, the greater the area that can be used to cover expenses. Greenhouses with low benching efficiency have less area available to provide income. A wholesale greenhouse with rolling benches can have a benching efficiency up to 90%. A retail greenhouse with island or peninsular benches can have a benching efficiency as low as 40%.

BENCHING ARRANGEMENTS

Although benches can be arranged in many formats within a greenhouse, there are three common arrangements. In the longitudinal or island arrangement, the benches are accessible from all sides. This type is commonly used in retail situations because of easy accessibility, but generally has a low benching efficiency (50 to 60%) and consequently is not commonly used for wholesale production.

Peninsular benching consists of benches jutting out into the middle of the greenhouse from the sides. Three sides of the bench are accessible. This type of arrangement is used for both retail and wholesale situations and can have a low to moderate benching efficiency (60 to 70%).

The rolling bench system consists of bench tops placed on rollers (metal pipes), allowing the bench tops to move back and forth. The benches jut out from the side of the green-

house and there is generally only one aisle per side of the greenhouse or for the entire greenhouse. This system greatly increases the benching efficiency (75 to 90%) by reducing the aisle space. Rolling benches are used only in wholesale production because they limit customer access, and customers are not familiar with rolling the benches. In addition, rolling benches may not be useful in some wholesale production situations where a labor-intensive crop is being grown because only one aisle is accessible at any one time.

BENCH CONSTRUCTION AND AISLES

Almost any type of weight-bearing structure can be used for benches, at least temporarily. Bench tops are often made of expanded metal sheets with the sharp edges covered in metal for safety. Bench tops can also be made of welded wire, treated wood, snow fence, or plastic panels, all of which are prone to warping or bowing. For ebb-and-flow irrigation (see Chapter 5, Water), the bench top consists of a watertight molded plastic or aluminum bench top. The bench top has sides for holding water and channels for quick drainage of the water. Regardless of the bench top, the supports can be made of concrete blocks, metal posts, or treated wood.

The bench width will depend on the crop and ease of accessibility for workers. Retail crops or high labor crops should be grown on benches only 3 to 4 ft (90 to 120 cm) wide to allow easy handling of plant materials. Wholesale production can occur on benches up to 6.5 ft (1.7 m) wide if the bench is accessible from both sides, especially if automated irrigation is used. Benches are generally 2.5 to 3 ft (75 to 90 cm) tall. Main aisles are usually 3 to 4 ft (90 to 120 cm) wide to accommodate carts, and side aisles are 1.5 to 2.5 ft (45 to 75 cm) wide to accommodate people. In some cases, a wide center aisle of 6 to 12 ft (1.8 to 3.7 m) is required to allow large equipment through the greenhouse.

CONTAINERIZED/MOBILE BENCHES

One type of specialized benching system is known as containerized benches. In this situation the plants are placed on the bench, which moves through the greenhouse on rollers. These benches are made of aluminum and plants are generally irrigated by overhead or ebb-and-flow systems. Containerized benches reduce labor costs because large groups of plants can be moved at once instead of individually. Containerized benches can move through a greenhouse linearly from propagation to finish on rollers or by a forklift or computer-directed robots from one section of the greenhouse to another. This system is applicable only for wholesale production.

ROLLOUT BENCHES

Rollout benches are used both in wholesale and retail settings. In this case the bench is placed on rollers and is rolled outside during favorable weather through the side of the greenhouse, which allows the plants to be hardened off and keeps plants short and compact. In some cases two layers of plants can be produced, with the bottom crop moved outside as needed. In bad weather, however, the temperature should be lowered to prevent stretching of the lower crop.

FLOOR PRODUCTION

Many greenhouses do not have benches, but instead the crops are grown directly on the floor. In such cases the floor of the greenhouse is usually concrete or gravel. The concrete may be porous, allowing water to drain, or watertight, allowing the floor to be used for subirrigation (see Chapter 5, Water). In the latter case, the floor is constructed at a slight slant to allow rapid flooding and drainage. With gravel floors, landscape fabric can be installed both under and on top of the gravel to reduce splashing, weeds, and movement of the gravel into the soil. Benching efficiency can be extremely high. Soil floors are not recommended due to increased potential for disease spread and difficulty of controlling weeds and algae. Soil floors also make moving of equipment difficult. To reduce construction expenses, walkways can be made of concrete, and areas under benches covered with gravel and landscape fabric. With labor-intensive crops, the width of production areas may need to be narrow to prevent injury to workers because they are bending down and outward. If drainage is poor, pots and flats can be raised off the ground by placing them on overturned pots, flats, pallets, or other structures.

GROUND BEDS

Ground beds are used to produce cut flowers such as roses (*Rosa*), carnations (*Dianthus caryophyllus*), and lilies (*Lilium*). Usually ground beds are slightly elevated or otherwise separated from the aisle to allow better drainage and pathogen control. Ground beds are usually constructed with sidewalls rising above the medium and walkways to prevent contamination with pathogens from the walkways. The sidewalls are constructed of poured concrete or wood. Decay-resistant wood, such as redwood, coated with copper naphthanate preservative (some preservatives produce toxic fumes) should be used. A "V" is cut into the bottom of the bed and filled with gravel over a drain pipe for proper drainage. The pipe should fall at least 1 in. (2.5 cm) per 100 ft (30 m) of pipe to allow adequate drainage. The beds are filled with a well-drained pasteurized media. The beds are usually 3.5 to 4 ft (105 to 120 cm) wide. Beds should be at least 6 in. (15 cm) deep at the shallowest point, but may be deeper, depending on the crop, such as roses.

Shallow aboveground beds with wooden sides can also be constructed on concrete or gravel floors. The bottom can be landscape fabric or treated wood. The beds should be at least 6 in. (15 cm) deep for adequate root growth of most cut flower crops.

CONTAINERS

The diversity of plant species grown in floriculture is matched only by the variety of containers available. When purchasing containers, be sure to check the thickness and quality of the plastic. Note that containers of the same diameter or apparent size often differ in volume, which affects the quantity of medium required for a crop, the irrigation frequency, and the postharvest life.

POTS

Pots are identified by diameter for greenhouse production and range in diameter from 1.75 to 16 in. (4.4 to 40 cm). Pots for perennial and nursery production are typically round, identified by volume, and range in size from 1 qt (1 L) to 5 gal (19 L) and larger. Note also that pot dimensions may not be accurate. For example, square pots may be measured diagonally and 1-gal (3.8-L) pots may be closer to 3 qt (2.8 L) in volume. Greenhouse pots are available in square or round styles with the latter available in the broadest range of sizes. Square pots contain a larger amount of medium compared with round pots of the same diameter. The depth of the pots often varies with the manufacturer; the two most common depths are "standard" and the slightly shorter "azalea." Plastic pots can be purchased in virtually any color, but dark green is the most common. Black and terracotta are also popular colors. White or other light-colored pots may inhibit root growth of some crop species, such as poinsettias (*Euphorbia pulcherrima*), and allow algae to grow on the medium inside the pot. Pots also vary in the number and configuration of drainage holes in the bottom. A variety of flats are available to hold and carry pots, some of which include their own built-in handle. Some pot styles include detachable saucers. Although clay or terracotta pots are occasionally used for specialty production, most pots are made of plastic. When placing pots on the bench, staggering the rows (such that any three pots make a triangle) increases the number of pots that can be fit into an area by 10 to 12% compared with a square pattern (four pots make a square) (Will and Faust, 1997).

HANGING BASKETS

As with pots, hanging baskets are designated by the diameter, which ranges in size from 6 to 12 in. (15 to 30 cm) in 2-in. (5-cm) increments. Options include style of hanger (wire or plastic), presence of saucer (saucerless or permanent or detachable saucer), volume, and color (green is the most common). Many saucerless baskets contain a disk that is placed in the bottom of the basket to create a reservoir from which water can be reabsorbed later through capillary action. Many growers use baskets with detachable saucers; during production the saucer is removed to allow proper drainage and the saucer is reattached prior to marketing. One style of basket has a flexible saucer that can be folded down during production for drainage and up during marketing.

FLATS AND INSERTS

Flats are identified by the overall dimensions. Currently, the most common size of flats is the standard 1020 flat, which has an actual dimension of 21.5 × 11.13 in. (54.5 × 28.25 cm). Another flat style is the Accurate Dimension (AD) or True Style flat, which is 10 × 20 in. (25 × 51 cm). This flat allows a 6 to 7% increase in the number of flats per area than standard 1020 flats. Many growers for mass market customers have switched to even smaller flats known as Slim Jim (SJ) flats, which measure 8.5 × 20 in. (21.5 × 50 cm). Other types of flats are also more narrow than the standard 1020 flat and are useful for producing more flats in a limited area. The move toward smaller flats with fewer

plants has been caused by the difficulty of raising prices, especially to mass marketers, despite rising production costs. Other factors that vary include the depth, style of bottom (web or solid), and the number and configuration of ribs within the flat. Most flats are black or dark green in color.

The inserts match the dimensions of the flats and are identified by the number of separable cell packs within each flat and the number of cells within each pack. Inserts are designated by a three- or four-digit number indicating the number of cells within each pack (last two digits) and the number of packs within a flat (first one or two digits). For example, an 1803 insert has 18 cell packs, each of which contains three cells, and a 606 insert has six cell packs, each of which contains six cells.

PLUG FLATS

Plug flats are a temporary intermediate container used for propagation of seeds and cuttings. After propagation, the young plants are transplanted into other containers such as pots, hanging baskets, or other flats. Plug flats vary in the number of cells per flat (50 to 512), the shape of the cell (round, square, octagon), diameter of the cell, and depth of the cell. The square- and octagon-shaped cells are thought to reduce root spiraling around the cell, which can lead to poor establishment of the plant after transplanting. Most plug flats are made of plastic, but some are also made of Styrofoam.

SPECIALTY CONTAINERS

A wide range of specialty containers are available including various types of planters, window boxes, and hanging columns. Most of these specialty containers are made of plastic, but terracotta, wood, pressed fiber, metal, and ceramic versions can also be found.

RECYCLING

Containers can be reused by washing and soaking them in a disinfectant. Generally fresh, sterile containers should be used during propagation because of the possibility of disease, even after chemical disinfection. A typical greenhouse, however, will accumulate many damaged or unusable, odd-sized containers, especially flats. In Europe and some areas of the United States and Canada, facilities are available for recycling leftover plastic containers. Contact your local supplier about a recycling program in your area. Flats and inserts are the most commonly recycled containers.

GREENHOUSE COOLING

Greenhouses are large, efficient solar collectors designed to trap much light energy during the day, which turns into heat. Even during days that appear cloudy, greenhouses can readily warm to levels uncomfortable for people and damaging to plants. In addition, in some climates the night temperatures are so high that cooling is required 24 hours a day.

Two different situations exist in regards to cooling. During the cold part of the year, the air outside the greenhouse is colder than that inside and the greenhouse is cooled by bringing in the colder air. This is known as *winter cooling* and utilizes vents and fan-jet tubes to bring in the cold air. In contrast, during the warm season, the outside air temperature might be close to or higher than that inside the greenhouse. This is known as *summer cooling* and the only way to reduce the temperature is through water evaporation by pad-fan or fog cooler or by mechanical air conditioning. When light levels are high, the temperature can be lowered by reducing the amount of light entering the greenhouse. Shade cloth and light-blocking compounds applied to the glazing are used from late spring through early fall in temperate climates and year-round in equatorial or mountainous areas.

NATURAL COOLING

The first step in any cooling system is to take advantage of natural cooling through vents. Ridge or top vents allow the warm air that naturally rises to exit, and sidewall vents allow cooler air to enter. Vents are usually made of hinged sections of greenhouse glazing and are typically automated. Side vents can be made of inflatable polyethylene tubes, which can be raised or lowered as needed to provide cooling (Fig. 11-8). Sidewalls that can be rolled up or down are also common. In some cases the entire sidewall can be hinged and used as a "vent." Greenhouse "tunnels" are available that consist of only a roof with no sides. Natural cooling can be accentuated by greenhouse design as with sawtooth or retractable-roof greenhouses (see Greenhouse Styles section earlier in this chapter). With natural cooling, cool and warm spots can easily form in the winter or summer when using vents. This problem can be corrected by circulating the air within the

greenhouse by horizontal airflow (see Air Circulation section later in this chapter) in conjunction with natural cooling. Of course, the ultimate in natural cooling would be to use retractable-roof greenhouses. Natural and other cooling methods also increase the carbon dioxide levels in greenhouses by bringing in outside air.

SHADE CLOTH

The next step in natural cooling is to use shade cloth, which can reduce light levels by 25 to 98% (see also Chapter 4, Light). The shade cloth can be permanently attached to greenhouses or sections of greenhouses where low light is needed, such as propagation areas. Otherwise shade cloth is installed during the summer when there is excess light, and temperatures can be reduced by decreasing the light levels. Shade cloth is most effective in reducing the temperature when the entire greenhouse is covered from the outside. This task can be especially difficult in windy areas of the country. Covering the entire greenhouse will also reduce photodegradation of coverings, such as polyethylene film or fiberglass and will provide extra protection against wind damage. Shade cloth is typically installed in the spring and removed in the fall, but it can be used year-round if reduced light intensity is required. When the shade cloths are not in use, store them in a dark environment. Continuous exposure to light will cause the fabric to degrade and will shorten the life expectancy of the cloth. See also Chapter 4, Light, for additional information on shade cloth.

Thermal screens or interior ceilings can also be used to shade the production benches

FIGURE 11-8 Roll-up side vents.

(see Energy Conservation section later in this chapter). In such cases the fans and pads are placed below the screen or ceiling. Cooling is facilitated by the shade and by the fact that a smaller volume of air must be cooled. The opening and closing of these ceilings can be automated and connected to light sensors so that the cloths open during cloudy weather.

FAN-TUBE (FAN-JET) SYSTEM

Fan-jet systems consist of a fan blowing air down a long horizontal plastic tube with regularly spaced holes for the forced air to exit and circulate. One or more tubes run the length of the greenhouse. To cool the greenhouses, the fan and tube are connected to a louvered outside vent, which allows cool outdoor air to be pulled into the greenhouse. The fan-tube system is used when the temperature of the outside air is lower than the desired inside temperature, which typically occurs during the winter. These conditions can also occur at other times of the year during cool periods, especially in northern climates. The fan-jet system can also be used to circulate the air without cooling or can be connected to a unit heater and used to distribute heat throughout the greenhouse. During air circulation the fan is on, but the vents are closed and the heater is turned off. Using fan-jet systems for heat distribution is more common in mild climates where the heat demand is not great.

The number, size, and arrangement of the fan-jet tubes and the size of the fan must be accurately calculated prior to installation and are based on a number of factors including difference between inside and outside air temperature, elevation, and light intensity (Aldrich and Bartok, 1989). The smaller the difference between the inside and outside temperatures, the greater the amount of outside air needed to cool the greenhouse. Designing a fan-jet system for a small difference between the inside and outside air temperatures will allow the fan-jet system to be more effective and will reduce the need for pad and fan systems (see below) to be operating in the spring and fall when temperatures can fluctuate widely from day to day. Increasing elevation decreases the amount of water that air can hold and increasing light intensity increases temperatures more rapidly; in both cases more air will need to be pulled through the pads to cool the greenhouse. Formulas and charts for calculating cooling needs can be obtained from greenhouse equipment suppliers.

SHADING COMPOUNDS

White shading compounds are applied to the outside of the glazing in one thick layer or two to three thin layers (see also Chapter 4, Light). Shading compounds specific for greenhouses can be purchased and diluted at 1 part compound to 6 parts water for heavy shade or 1 part compound to 15 to 20 parts water for light shade. Generally, most of the shading compound wears off naturally during the summer but the remainder may need to be scrubbed off at the end of the season. This job is generally not pleasant, but must be done if residue remains. White latex paint can also be diluted and applied but may damage glazing and is not recommended. Check with the glazing manufacturer or supplier before using latex paint. Commercial shading compounds designed for greenhouses are also easier to remove than diluted latex paint due to additives designed to release more easily after a frost or freeze.

FLOWING WATER SHADE

An experimental system involves cooling the greenhouse by running colored water through the glazing. In this system a double-walled acrylic or polycarbonate glazing is used and the liquid flows through the glazing. The colored water absorbs the heat, which is then carried away from the greenhouse. The color of the liquid can be used to control plant growth; for example, the blue-green color from copper sulfate results in short internodes for many plant species by filtering out far-red light.

PAD-FAN SYSTEM

The pad-fan system is used when the outside air temperature is close to or higher than the desired inside temperature, which typically occurs from late spring to early fall. These conditions can also occur in the winter during warm periods or sunny days, especially in warm climates.

Pad-fan cooling relies on the evaporation of water to absorb heat. The water flows downward by gravity through porous pads placed in one wall. Air is pulled through the pads by means of exhaust fans placed in the opposite wall. Unevaporated water is collected in a collection tank or sump for recirculation. The sump can be placed above or below ground. Pad-fan cooling is most effective in climates with moderate to low humidity and least effective in areas where the humidity is high.

The size of the pads and the fans must be calculated prior to installation and are based on a number of factors including elevation, light intensity, acceptable temperature rise from pad to fan, and distance between pads and fans (Aldrich and Bartok, 1989). Increasing elevation decreases the amount of water that air can hold and increasing light intensity increases temperatures more rapidly; in both cases more air will need to be pulled through the evaporation pads to cool the greenhouse. As cool air moves through a greenhouse, it absorbs heat from the plants, benches, walkways, and structure before the air exits the greenhouse. Generally a 7°F (4°C) increase in temperature from the pads to the fans is considered an acceptable amount of heating; however, if less heat gain is desired, then more air must be pulled through the pads. Greenhouse growers frequently use the temperature difference across the greenhouse and grow species that require warm temperatures close to the exhaust fans and species that require cool temperatures close to the pads. Pad-fan cooling is most effective when placed 100 to 200 ft (30 to 60 m) apart; distances greater than 200 ft (60 m) or less than 100 ft (30 m) require expensive, high-volume fans.

The evaporation pads often cover an entire wall. For best air movement, fans should not be more than 25 ft (8 m) apart and should be evenly spaced along the wall opposite the fans at plant height. The size and type of fan needed will vary with the manufacturer. Once you have calculated the amount of airflow required, the manufacturer can give you options regarding the size and number of fans and dimensions and type of pads.

The most commonly used type of pad is the cellulose pad made of heavy, corrugated cardboard, impregnated with insoluble anti-rot salts that prevent deterioration. Cellulose pads that are well maintained should last 4 to 10 years, depending on water quality. Cellulose pads are more expensive than other types but are generally cheaper over time. Pads of varying thickness can be obtained depending on the amount of air that needs to be cooled: 4-in. (10-cm) pads cool 250 cfm/ft^2 (cfm = cubic feet per minute, 1 ft^3/min/ft^2 = 76 m^3·min^{-1}·m^{-2}), and 6-in. (15-cm) pads cool 350 cfm/ft^2 (107 m^3·min^{-1}·m^{-2}). The pads are available in 1-ft-(30-cm)-tall increments, such as 2, 3, 4, 5, or 6 ft (0.6, 0.9, 1.2, 1.5 or 1.8 m).

The pads need to be regularly cleaned of accumulated salts (scale) and algae, both of which reduce airflow and cooling efficiency by plugging pads. Salt buildup can be reduced by continuously draining off high-salt water before it returns to the sump and replacing it with fresh water or by completely replacing the water in the sump every 7 to 14 days with fresh water. In areas with exceptionally high-salt water, the recirculated water may need to be both continuously drained and periodically replaced. Starting with high-quality, low-salt water will reduce salt accumulation.

Anti-algae compounds can also be added to the sump water to reduce algae growth on the pads. Other methods to reduce algae plugging include drying pads once a day, shading as much of the system as possible to reduce algae growth, removing weeds by the pads, and regularly cleaning the entire system. Insect screens on the air inlet side of the pads will also reduce plugging; however, the fan capacity must be increased because the screens will increase air resistance and static pressure.

Other types of pads are made of excelsior (aspen, shredded wood), plastic, aluminum, fiberglass, and hog bristles. Excelsior pads last only 1 year, but are inexpensive. They are thinner than cellulose pads, and cool 150 cfm/ft^2 (47 m^3·min^{-1}·m^{-2}). Excelsior is obtained in bulk and packed into metal frames, which are then placed under the water flow to act as cooling pads. Pads and fans are more efficient when situated so that they work with—not against—prevailing winds. If several houses are close together, be sure that the warm moist air exhausted from one greenhouse does not feed into the pads of the next greenhouse. If two greenhouse ranges are close together, then either the exhaust fans or pads of both greenhouses should face each other. If the fans are faced together, alternate the fans so that each fan does not blow directly against the opposite fan. Fans should always be placed so that they exhaust at least 1.5 times the blade diameter from another building or obstacle.

FOG

Fog is another version of evaporative cooling. A fog of minute water particles is injected into the greenhouse from nozzles located on the roof or sidewalls and cools the air as it evaporates. The droplets must be small enough to evaporate before settling on the foliage or the potential for diseases will be increased. Fog usually provides more uniform cooling across the greenhouse and higher efficiency than pad-fan cooling (Bartok, 1997). A fog system can also be useful in propagation areas where high humidity is required. For fog to be most effective, use high-quality water with a low EC. With poor-quality water, soluble salts precipitate, plug the nozzles, and cause constant maintenance problems. Because a relatively low amount of water is required, it can be treated to remove salts and particulates prior to use (see Chapter 5, Water). As with pad-fan cooling systems, fog cooling is most effective in areas with low humidity.

POSITIVE PRESSURE SYSTEMS

Some research, breeding, and propagation greenhouses are built with positive pressure cooling, which uses large evaporative coolers or fans that blow into pads to push the air into the greenhouse. The air is cooled as it flows through the coolers or pads and is exhausted through pressure-sensitive dampers at the opposite end of the greenhouse. The dampers open in response to increased air pressure. Such systems force air outward through doors and vents, reducing the chance of insects and disease organisms being drawn into the greenhouse. Typical pad-fan cooling exhausts air forcibly, which allows insect and disease organisms to be sucked into the greenhouse when doors or vents are opened.

MECHANICAL AIR CONDITIONING

Although quite expensive, small greenhouses, especially hobby lean-to greenhouses, can be cooled by means of air conditioners. Heavy-duty air conditioners should be used, because the high humidity and warm environment of a greenhouse can be difficult on equipment.

GREENHOUSE HEATING

In cold climates greenhouse heating is frequently the second greatest production expense after labor. Even cool coastal areas that seem quite mild often have high heating expenses because heating may be required year-round. Heat is lost through *air leakage*, *conduction*, and *radiation*. Air leakage occurs through planned openings such as doors, vents, fans, and louvers and unplanned openings such as cracks in the glazings and gaps between the glazing and the frame. Conduction is the process of heat energy moving from the greenhouse glazing and frame to the cooler outside air. For example, the heat from a cup of hot coffee warms the cup, which in turn warms our

hands when we hold the cup. Radiation is the transfer of heat between two objects not in direct contact. For example, we feel the heat of the sun on a sunny day. Heat radiates out of a greenhouse, especially during cool, cloudless nights. The type of heating system used will depend on the maximum amount of heat required, the expense of the equipment, the availability of fuels, and the size and style of greenhouse(s).

CENTRAL HEATING SYSTEM

The central heating system consists of a boiler that can produce either hot water or steam to heat the entire greenhouse range. Boilers are efficient when used on a large scale and can process a wide variety of fuels, including coal, wood chips, gas, and oil. Generally, one boiler is easier to maintain than many individual heating units. However, a boiler system is more expensive than other heating systems.

The boiler is located in the headhouse, which allows the waste heat to warm the headhouse. If the boiler is placed in a separate building, the waste heat is lost. For proper operation, boilers need to be cleaned and inspected every year, usually during the summer when the boiler is not in operation. A small stand-by boiler can be used for heating in late spring, early fall, emergencies, or steam pasteurization. A small boiler is more economical to operate than a large boiler for such tasks.

STEAM. Steam is the most common form of heating in large, northern ranges. Compared with hot water heating, steam uses less water and, because it is a gas, it flows easier. Consequently, with steam heating, a smaller boiler, no circulation pumps, and less plumbing are required. The steam can also be used for pasteurization. Steam is hotter than hot water, which allows the greenhouse temperature to be quickly increased. However, with steam there is no residual water reservoir in the circulation pipes to protect against freezing if the system fails. Thus, steam systems need to be constantly monitored during cold periods. The temperature of steam is always 212 to 215°F (100 to 102°C), which prevents "turning up or down the heat" without turning the system on or off. In addition, insurance expenses and municipal regulations are often greater for steam than for hot water systems. For example, some communities require 24-hour-a-day supervision at facilities with steam boilers. Steam heat systems must also include steam traps to collect the condensed water, which is returned to the boiler.

HOT WATER. Hot water has the advantage of having a reservoir of warm water in the circulation pipes to protect against freezing for a longer period than can steam systems if the system fails. Hot water also allows the temperature of the delivery system to be adjusted and no steam traps are needed. However, the boiler, pumps, and circulation pipes need to be larger for hot water than with steam because hot water carries less heat and must be pumped. In addition, no steam is available for pasteurization and it takes longer to heat a greenhouse with hot water due to the lower water temperature and longer for the greenhouse to cool when heat is not required.

HEAT DELIVERY. In heat delivery, heat is transferred to the greenhouse by pipes. The amount of pipe required will vary with the amount of heat required, the heat source (water or steam), the pipe diameter, the pipe style, and the placement in the greenhouse. More and larger diameter pipes are generally needed with hot water than with steam. The use of fin pipe greatly increases the surface area and reduces the amount of pipe needed by increasing the transfer of heat to the greenhouse air. Fin pipe is more expensive, however. Fin pipe made of galvanized metal can rust, reducing the heat output. Copper pipe is expensive but offers the highest heat output.

A number of locations are used for placement of heating pipes in a greenhouse. Pipes are most commonly placed low along sidewalls with some clearance between the pipes and the sidewall for adequate upward air movement behind the pipes. This location can be used for both steam and hot water. The pipes are out of the way; however, air currents form that can lead to uneven heating of the greenhouse. Heated air rises along the sides of the house and cool air descends from the top of the greenhouse in the center. The air currents can be disrupted by air circulation methods used when the heat is on or by additional heating pipes placed overhead. The heating efficiency of each pipe is reduced when more than one pipe is stacked together. The arrangement of the pipes is determined by the type of heat used (Fig. 11-9). With steam, a trombone coil is used because there is little resistance and steam easily moves through the pipes. There is little difference in temperature from the beginning to the end. With hot water, a box coil is used be-

cause there is greater flow resistance than with steam. Water cools faster and a box coil arrangement reduces the temperature difference from the beginning of the coil to the end.

Pipes can also be placed overhead, but they block light and are inefficient because the heated air is above the plants. This placement can be used with both hot water and steam heat and is occasionally used to disrupt the downward movement of cool air to produce a more uniform distribution of heat within a greenhouse. Overhead pipes can also be placed by gutters to facilitate the melting of accumulated snow.

Pipes can also be placed in the floor under gravel or porous concrete to allow heat to rise. This system is efficient because the heat rises through the plants. This placement is used only with hot water and often cannot supply enough heat during very cold periods in the winter. Frequently floor heating is used in conjunction with pipes placed in other areas of the greenhouse or with unit heaters, which are used only when needed to maintain proper temperature.

Pipes can also be placed directly where the plants are located—adjacent to the sides of ground beds or under the benches. This placement is mainly used with hot water but can also be used with steam. The location is considered to be fuel efficient because the heat is released close to the plants. Bench heating is commonly used in propagation areas because it efficiently maintains a warm media temperature.

UNIT OR FORCED AIR HEATERS

Air is blown over a fire box of thin-walled metal tubes, which is heated by burning nat-

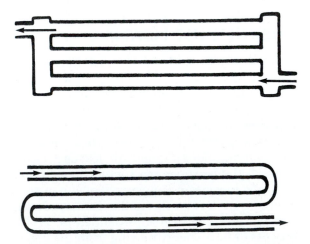

FIGURE 11-9 Box (a) and trombone (b) pipe arrangements for the distribution of hot water and steam in a greenhouse heating system.

ural gas, oil, kerosene, or liquid propane. Greenhouse air is pulled through the tubes and heated. Unit heaters are generally placed above plant level, but they can also be placed at ground level and the heat directed under the benches to provide medium or root zone heating. The latter situation is commonly used in propagation areas. When placed overhead, the air is directed horizontally and the heat is spread by horizontal air flow (HAF) or fan-jets with plastic tubes. It is important to have a routine maintenance program on unit heaters because improper burning or holes in the fire box can lead to air pollution, especially ethylene production, which can damage plants. Adjust the burner setting to produce a clear blue flame; a yellow flame indicates improper burning. Generally the exhaust must be vented. Despite the need for energy conservation, the greenhouse should not be airtight. For each 1 ft³ (0.028 m³) of gas burned, 14 ft³ (0.40 m³) of air is needed. If all of the oxygen is used, the flame extinguishes and the crop may freeze. Also, carbon monoxide will be produced before the flame is extinguished, which can be deadly to people.

MICROCLIMATE TUBING

The microclimate tubing system consists of a network of small, flexible, black rubber tubes that are laid on the bench top, attached underneath the bench top, or installed in or on the floor. Hot water is circulated from water heaters through the tubes, which allows the heat to rise and warm the plants above it. Temperature sensors can be placed in the medium to maintain a proper medium temperature. This places the heat where it is required most and allows the air above the plants to be cooler, resulting in reduced heat loss and energy expenses. With some species, the cooler shoot temperature results in shorter internodes, thicker stems, and more compact growth. Because a microclimate tubing system may not be enough to heat a greenhouse in extremely cold weather, a supplemental heating system may be required.

RADIANT

Radiant heating systems emit infrared radiation, which heats objects such as plants, pots, benches, and walkways, but not the air (Fig. 11-10). The heat from these objects then heats the air. Consequently, the air temperature can be as much as 7°F (4°C) cooler than conven-

tionally heated greenhouses yet it yields similar plant growth. In conventional heating systems the air is heated, which in turn heats the plants. Radiant systems are fuel efficient and estimated to save 30 to 50% over conventional heating systems. The fuel is mixed with air and burned in a pipe, which becomes extremely hot and emits infrared radiation. The pipe is not hot enough to emit visible light. The hot pipes must be placed high over the crops and walkways to avoid contact with plants or people. The upper surface of the tube is covered with a metal reflector that directs the infrared radiation downward. Air circulation equipment is not used when the infrared system is operating because the movement of cool air will cool the plants. Fuel is saved for three reasons: (1) The air is cooler and less heat is radiated or lost to the outside; (2) more heat is extracted from fuel because the exhaust leaves the pipe at 150°F (66°C), not 400 to 600°F (205 to 315°C) as in conventional heaters; and (3) plants are heated, not the air. Radiant heat is expensive to install, however, and cold spots can form in the greenhouse due to shading. Very close plant spacing and dense plant canopies will reduce the penetration of the heat, cause media temperatures to be quite low, and delay crop production. Radiant heat can also be detrimental in retail situations because the radiant energy heats up the upper flowers and foliage, causing plants to senescence more quickly, and increases plant water

FIGURE 11-10 Radiant heating system.

loss. The radiant heating system can also block sunlight. However, during the night radiant heat keeps the foliage several degrees warmer than the surrounding air, which prevents condensation on the foliage and reduces the potential for diseases.

CONVECTION HEATING

Convection heating is similar to forced air heating except that the heat radiates directly from the exhaust pipe to the greenhouse air such as with a wood stove. The pipe is not hot enough to produce infrared radiation, however. Convection heating is too inefficient for large areas, but can be used in display areas or hobby greenhouses. It is important that there are no leaks from the exhaust pipe, because ethylene and carbon monoxide can form with incomplete heating of the fuel.

SOLAR

In the simplest sense, greenhouses are large passive solar heat collectors. The plants, pots, walls, and benches absorb heat during the day, which is subsequently radiated to the air at night. Passive heat collection systems are not sufficient to keep a greenhouse warm throughout an entire night.

With active solar heating, light-collecting equipment traps heat in water or rocks that is later used to heat the greenhouse. Active solar heating is not common, relatively expensive, and requires additional land for placement of the solar collectors. Generally, solar collectors are too large and expensive to meet the needs of a large greenhouse because greenhouses lose heat rapidly at night. Solar heat can be useful for hobby greenhouses or as a supplement to a traditional heating system. Technical advances may lead to more widespread use in future years. In addition, advances in photovoltaic cells may allow them to be economically used to supply greenhouses with electricity. The cells could be placed on the roof of the headhouse.

HEATING SYSTEM CALCULATIONS

The size and type of heating systems are calculated prior to construction by estimating the heat loss of the planned greenhouse. Heat loss calculations include determining the surface area of the greenhouse and determining heat loss from the surface using the following factors: type of greenhouse, construction materials, average wind velocity, and maximum difference between inside and outside temperature (Aldrich and Bartok, 1989). Construction materials lose heat at different rates; for example, a metal greenhouse covered in glass will lose more heat than a wooden greenhouse covered in double-layered polyethylene. Increasing the wind velocity and the difference between the inside and outside temperatures will increase the heat loss and the amount of heat required to keep the greenhouse at the desired temperature. When selecting temperatures to use in these calculations, do not use average monthly low temperatures because these will be too warm. As a result, the heating system will be too small and the inside greenhouse temperature will fall below the desired level when the outside temperature drops below the average monthly temperature. Remember, statistically, 50% of the daily lows will be below the average monthly temperature. It is wisest to use the lowest average daily low temperature of the year, which is usually in mid to late January in North America. However, the greater the difference between the inside and outside temperature, the larger the heating system and the greater the cost. Once the heat loss is estimated, the type and size of the heating system and the quantity of fuel required can be determined. Formulas and charts for calculating heating needs can be obtained from greenhouse equipment suppliers.

FUEL

NATURAL GAS

Natural gas is a versatile, clean-burning fuel that is suitable for both unit heaters and boilers. In many areas of the country, natural gas is the fuel of choice due to ease of use and low pollution. However, natural gas is not available in many areas, especially rural districts.

Cost—Inexpensive to moderately expensive. The price of natural gas is often based on the priority level of the customer, with higher priority customers having to pay more. Greenhouses are naturally high priority because loss of heat in the middle of the winter when temperatures are below freezing would mean death of the crops. The priority level and, consequently, price can be reduced if a backup heating and fuel system, such as oil or propane, is available.

Pollution potential—Burns clean.

Maintenance—Low.

Storage—No storage tanks required.

PROPANE AND BUTANE

As with natural gas, propane and butane are versatile and usable in most heating systems.

Cost—Expensive.
Pollution potential—Burns clean.
Maintenance—Low.
Storage—Storage tanks required.

FUEL OIL

As with natural gas, oil is versatile and usable in all heating systems. Fuel oil thickens (increases in viscosity) in cold weather. Fuel oil is available in grades 1, 2, 4, 5, and 6, with viscosity increasing from grade 1 to 6. Oil may need to be warmed in cold weather to flow properly from the storage tank to the boiler.

Cost—Variable, moderate to expensive.
Pollution potential—Does not burn as clean as natural gas.
Maintenance—More required than with natural gas.
Storage—Storage tanks needed.

COAL

Coal is rarely used except in areas where coal supplies are nearby. The use of coal is limited to centralized boilers.

Cost—Can be cheap, but the extra labor needed to handle coal and ash must be included in the costs.
Pollution potential—High, depending on the type of coal used. High-quality, low-sulfur coal burns the cleanest. Antipollution equipment may be needed.
Maintenance—High; much ash is produced that must be removed and disposed.
Storage—A large storage area is needed.

WOOD

Wood is usually in the form of chips or sawdust from lumber or paper processing mills. The sawdust may be compressed into pellets for easier handling. The use of wood is limited to centralized boilers. Wood is limited to areas where it is readily available.

Cost—Can be cheap, but consider labor needed. At one time waste wood products were a disposal problem for mills. Now waste wood chips and sawdust are valuable and used in a number of products.
Pollution potential—High.
Maintenance—High; produces much ash that must be removed and disposed.
Storage—A large storage area is needed.

GEOTHERMAL

Geothermal energy is a desirable energy source but is geographically limited. Geothermal heating takes advantage of the natural heat contained within the earth, which comes close to the surface in the form of steam or hot water. Iceland is well known for taking advantage of its abundant geothermal heat. Waste hot water from nearby power plants can also be used in a manner similar to geothermal sources. Dumping hot water into surface water disrupts aquatic life, although using the wastewater for heat protects the local environment.

Cost—Heat is "free," but heat exchanging equipment required to extract the heat can be expensive.
Pollution potential—Low, but wastewater from geothermal sites is often high in salts and can be difficult to properly dispose, unless returned to the source.
Maintenance—Low.
Storage—No storage tanks needed, energy "stored" underground.

AIR CIRCULATION

Air movement is often required in a greenhouse, even if heating and cooling are not needed. Air circulation provides a uniform growing temperature that results in a uniform crop. Irrigation, accurate application of growth regulators and pesticides, and marketing are more difficult on an uneven crop. Air circulation is important for the prevention and control of such diseases as *Botrytis* blight, powdery mildew, and bacterial leaf spots. Proper air circulation also improves carbon dioxide distribution and use. Several air circulation methods have already been discussed in the context of heating and cooling. The fan-jet tube system can be used to circulate air without additional heating by operating only the blower of a unit heater. The process of cooling with fan and pads both distributes and circulates the air. The fan and pad system can also be operated without water flowing through it. Of course, natural cooling through side and top vents also promotes air circulation.

HORIZONTAL AIRFLOW

Horizontal airflow (HAF) was developed at the University of Connecticut and treats air as a liquid (Figs. 11-11 and 11-12). Once the air is moving, it takes relatively little energy to maintain movement. Small box fans are used to move the air within a greenhouse and the number and arrangement depend on the size and configuration of the greenhouse. HAF spreads heat and circulates air when cooling from pad-fan or fan-jet tubes is not needed. The total fan capacity in cfm (m³·min⁻¹) for each green-house should be equal to one-quarter of the greenhouse volume. Fans with a 16-in. (40-cm) diameter and a 1/15-hp motor will be adequate (Aldrich and Bartok, 1989).

VERTICAL AIR FANS

Vertical air fans are large, overhead fans situated horizontal to the greenhouse floor. They direct warm air downward from the peak of the greenhouse. Vertical fans circulate heat from the top of the greenhouse, where heat accumulates, to benches or the floor where it is needed. Vertical air fans do not produce uniform heating patterns, cannot be placed over crops, and are not as energy efficient as other air circula-

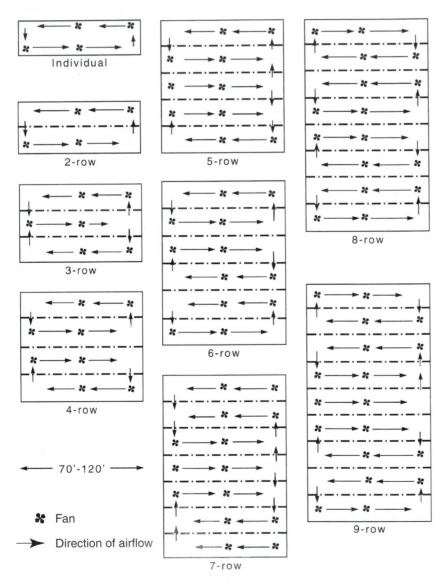

FIGURE 11-11 Diagram showing location of fans for horizontal airflow in various greenhouse sizes and arrangements (Aldrich and Bartok, 1989). One row of fans is added for each additional 50 ft (15 m) of greenhouse length.

FIGURE 11-12 HAF fans and automatic shade cloth.

tion methods. Vertical air fans have been largely replaced by other air circulation methods.

ENVIRONMENTAL MONITORS

THERMOSTATS

Thermostats are temperature monitoring and control devices connected to the heat source. They control when the heating and cooling systems should be activated. Thermostats should be placed where the temperature is average and not in hot or cold locations or else the greenhouse will be chronically over- or underheated. The thermostat must be at plant height because that is the critical heating zone. Thermostats are best placed in a white box to protect them from heating due to sunlight and should be aspirated with a small fan to ensure that heat does not build up and a large air mass is measured over time. Large or gutter-connect greenhouses are divided into individual temperature zones and each zone has its own thermostat and heating/cooling subsystem. This dispersion allows more than one temperature environment within a large, open greenhouse range. However, the temperature variations between zones cannot be too great or the temperatures will not be able to be maintained in each zone. Plastic curtains can be used to temporarily separate zones.

ENVIRONMENTAL CONTROL SYSTEMS

Environmental control systems integrate the methods of heating, cooling, and air circulation into one step-by-step (stage) system. The controls are based on a set point and various equipment in the greenhouse can be turned on or off as the temperature increases or decreases from the set point. For example, a greenhouse environmental control system may work as follows:

Temperature Difference from Set Point	Action
4° below	Both unit heaters turned on
2° below	One of two unit heaters turned on
Set point	Horizontal airflow on
2° above	Top vents are opened
4° above	One of two exhaust fans turned on without pads
6° above	Both exhaust fans turned on
8° above	Both fans and pads turned on

The controllers are located in the headhouse, not greenhouse, because the high humidity and temperatures in a greenhouse increase maintenance problems. The temperature stages can be set close together, but too small of a difference between the settings may lead to equipment rapidly turning on and off, especially during partly cloudy weather. This will increase maintenance and lead to quicker equipment failure.

Computer environmental control systems can also monitor light, humidity, and carbon dioxide levels in addition to temperature. Depending on the system, computers can sense and record environmental conditions every 1 to 10 seconds and adjust greenhouse equipment every few minutes. Computer control systems allow precise environmental regulation and are increasingly important as floriculture crop production becomes more efficient and precise. Computer control systems can also be used to run plant growth modeling programs, which can be used to produce a crop grown to exact specifications, such as height, plant shape, and flowering date. Such systems control greenhouse temperatures, light levels, and CO_2 in response to weather conditions. Computer systems can also be used to control irrigation and fertilization. Although computer control systems may appear to be expensive, the reduction in labor costs and improved environmental control and information will allow a net reduction in costs, as well as increased plant quality. Certainly we can expect to see many advances in this area of greenhouse management.

ENERGY CONSERVATION

Energy conservation is frequently a subject of concern for greenhouse operators. Energy prices, declining profit margins, and increased competition continue to require energy conservation.

DESIGN AND CONSTRUCTION

Energy conservation begins with greenhouse design and construction. Double-layer polyethylene film plastic, acrylic, or polycarbonate retain the most heat. Single-layer polyethylene and glass are among the least energy efficient. The heat loss from glass greenhouses can be reduced by placing double-layer polyethylene film plastic over the glass or by using a single layer attached to the walls from eave to eave over the crop inside the greenhouse. Either method will reduce heat loss but will also reduce light transmission. Quonset-style greenhouses have a low surface-to-volume ratio and thus are more energy efficient than even-span houses. Gutter-connect houses also have a low surface-to-volume ratio because of the reduction in the number of exterior walls.

THERMAL SCREENS AND INTERIOR CEILINGS

Thermal screens are materials drawn over the top and sides of a crop within the greenhouse each night and can reduce heat loss up to 60%. Thermal screens are usually light impermeable and can also be used as black cloths for SD. The upper surface of thermal screens is often white or reflective to reduce heat accumulation under the cloth when used in the late morning or afternoon. Interior ceilings are similar to thermal screens in that they stretch from eave to eave but do not cover the sides of the greenhouse. With both systems the cloth separates the air volume in the eave from the air surrounding the plants and eliminates the need to heat air in the eave during the night, reducing heat loss through the roof. Interior ceilings can also be partially transparent and used as shade cloths during the day to reduce light intensity and aid in temperature control.

Both thermal screens and interior ceilings are automated for ease of use. During heavy snowfall, however, the cloths must remain open to allow the snow to melt and prevent collapse of the structure. Both thermal screens and interior ceilings can also be useful in providing a cool temperature dip (DROP) in the morning (see Chapter 3, Temperature) for plant height control by opening the cloths quickly and allowing the cool upper air to flow down over the plants. In such a case the air

should not be heated, unless it is too cold for the crop, and it should be allowed to naturally warm after cloths are opened. When not using the DROP technique, thermal screens should be opened slowly or remain closed until the sun heats the air.

GREENHOUSE MAINTENANCE

Regular greenhouse maintenance is a necessity for an energy-efficient operation. The covering should be inspected frequently for cracks and openings, especially around the fans and pads. In the winter, fans and pads are frequently sealed tight. Louvers should be able to close tight and fans can be covered with Styrofoam in the winter to reduce heat loss. Remember that not only will leaks allow heat loss, but they will also cause cool areas in the greenhouse, which will affect crop uniformity. The heating system must be inspected and regularly maintained. Remember that improper burning of fuels or venting of gases in the unit heater can release carbon monoxide, which can be toxic to people, and can release ethylene, which will damage plants.

HEATING SYSTEM

Radiant heat is generally the most fuel efficient because it heats the plants and benches, not the air, and more heat units are obtained from the fuel.

CROP SELECTION AND TIMING

Heating costs can be reduced during the winter by growing crops that prefer cool temperatures such as cineraria (*Pericallis* ×*hybrida*), *Calceolaria*, and *Primula*. The success of this strategy depends on being able to market such crops. Within a particular species are cultivar differences, such as between 'Freedom Red' poinsettia (*Euphorbia pulcherrima*), which is more tolerant of low temperatures, and 'Red Velvet' poinsettia, which tolerates higher temperatures. A skilled grower knows the naturally warm or cool spots within a greenhouse and uses these accordingly. Crop species that require warm temperatures, such as vinca (*Catharanthus roseus*) or caladiums (*Caladium bicolor*), should be grown in the warmest areas of the greenhouse, which may eliminate the need for raising the temperature of the entire greenhouse. Other ways to heat specific benches include covering a bench with plastic and trapping in the heat or using unit heaters with fan-jet tubes that run under the bench. This technique is especially helpful with propagation. Purchasing plugs or buying larger plugs for the first crop cycle of bedding plants or hanging baskets in late winter can reduce the amount of space that needs to be heated at one time and delay heating of an entire greenhouse. In some cases, prefinished plants can be purchased, grown for a few weeks, finished, and marketed, greatly reducing the crop time compared to producing a crop from seedlings, cuttings, or other young plants.

COVER NORTH WALL

A layer of white Styrofoam on the north wall will reduce heat loss and will reflect light back onto the nearby plants during winter. During the winter only 5 to 10% of the light enters from the north wall and a white insulated covering will reflect back enough light to compensate for the loss of light coming through the north wall. Transparent bubble plastic can also be used because it allows greater light transmission but has less heat retention than Styrofoam.

WINDBREAKS

Protect greenhouses from wind by planting or installing a windbreak. A windbreak will not only reduce heat loss but also reduce the wear on film plastic coverings. Windbreaks should be placed 2.5 times the height of the windbreak away from the greenhouse to prevent shading. Windbreaks can reduce heat loss by 5 to 10%. If a live windbreak is used, make the distance calculation based on mature height of the trees or shrubs being used. The windbreak should be at least 100 feet (30 m) away from the structure in areas with heavy snow. Windbreaks slow the wind and allow snow to be deposited downwind of the windbreak. Heavy snow drifts can be deposited on structures if windbreaks are placed too close to the structure.

BACKUP AND ALARM SYSTEMS

Due to the high value of greenhouse crops, one or more backup energy, heating, and alarm systems should be considered. Emergency generators can be used in case of electrical power outages to run boilers, heaters, solenoid values, and other equipment. An auxiliary heating system, such as mobile unit heaters, should be available to prevent a total crop loss in case the main heating system fails and outside temperatures are below freezing. If natural gas is used,

a backup oil or propane storage facility will allow the greenhouse to be placed onto nonpriority status and reduce the cost of the natural gas. Remember that backup systems do not need to have the capacity to heat or supply electricity to the entire greenhouse, but only enough to keep emergency systems running and keep temperatures above freezing or above the point of chilling damage.

Regardless of the backup systems, greenhouses should be set up with an alarm system. Large greenhouses employ night patrollers to check temperatures and provide security. Small operations may want to purchase telephone alarm systems that automatically call the grower or the owner if greenhouse temperatures are too high or too low.

AUTOMATION

Floriculture crop production has traditionally been a labor-intensive process. Increasing competition within and among countries requires that extra attention be paid to labor expenses, and automation can be one method of reducing labor expenses. In many areas of the United States, floriculture firms are also having a difficult time finding sufficient employees. Automation can allow current employees to increase output or allow them to accomplish more important tasks. Automation can have a variety of other benefits as well, including reducing employee muscle strain, improving plant quality, and increasing benching efficiency. The counting feature of many machines can even eliminate the annoying distraction of keeping track of the number of plants potted or bouquets made.

Virtually every commercial greenhouse already uses some type of automation, such as environmental controllers to heat and cool greenhouses and switch on/off air circulation equipment. However, greenhouse controllers are only the start of automation. Every business should analyze its operation. The first step is to see what can be done to improve the efficiency of the operation by simplifying layout and decreasing employee movements. For example, are the media and related supplies stored close to the potting area? Do you use an excessive number of container sizes and styles? Harvesting can be notoriously inefficient: Do the employees pack and ship an entire bench or section of bench at once or do they walk the benches selecting specific plants or stems for harvest? Each firm should analyze its operation and make appropriate changes to improve efficiency. The next step is to determine those areas suitable for mechanization.

IRRIGATION

Automated irrigation has become a requirement for large-scale production of any crop. Even small operations can benefit from automated irrigation systems and should install them wherever possible. For potted plants choose from microtube, low-volume sprinkler, boom, flood, trough, or capillary mat systems. The options are fewer for plug and flat production but include low-volume sprinkler, boom, and flood systems. Hanging baskets are particularly demanding to irrigate due to their overhead location, which makes watering difficult and encourages rapid water loss. Even small growers should use microtube or other drip systems on hanging baskets. For cut flower beds, trickle tapes and, in some cases, low-volume sprinklers can be used.

Each irrigation system has specific advantages and disadvantages but all systems are cost effective in the long run. Some systems such as microtube, low-volume sprinklers, and trickle tape will pay for themselves within a year. More expensive systems may have longer payback periods. In addition to labor savings, automated systems may reduce water and fertilizer use and runoff and reduce associated expenses. Some systems such as microtube, flood, capillary mat, and trough can reduce foliar and crown diseases and fungicide use, because there is no wetting of the foliage compared with hand watering or overhead watering systems.

Automated irrigation systems generally increase crop uniformity, which reduces production problems and eases shipping and handling. Automated systems work best when the crop is uniform in size, stage of development, and species at planting and they help to maintain uniformity from potting to shipping.

MEDIA MIXING AND PLANTING

Media mixers, container fillers, and seeders are now used in many greenhouses. Plug dislodgers remove plugs from plug flats and automatic transplanters insert them into the medium. Water is sprayed onto the media during mixing and before or after planting (Fig. 11-13). Taggers insert labels into flats, pots, or hanging baskets after they are filled with media. Although these types of machines usually require

FIGURE 11-13 Watering in newly planted pots.

one or two people to check and correct skips, they can greatly increase employee output.

The next stage of automation may be to integrate video cameras into the transplanting and production process. Video can be used to grade plants prior to planting and to check for skips. Video can also be incorporated during production to grade plants and sort by size. Thus, the smaller plants can be held back, if needed, for additional time to grow and the larger plants moved to the next production stage.

PLANT MOVEMENT

A wide variety of equipment and processes can be used to reduce the number of motions required to produce a crop and reduce employee walking time. For operations that grow on the floor, manual pot grabbers are available allowing one person to pick up, move, and space up to 10 containers at once. Obviously, pot grabbers work best with lightweight containers but grabbers can make the job of moving two thousand 4½-in. pots of geraniums seem a little less daunting.

Carts, conveyers, gantries, and monorails can be used to transport plants within areas of the greenhouse, greatly reducing strain on employees and saving time. Carts work most easily on concrete walkways but carts with large or wide wheels can be used on gravel aisles. Consider carts that can be connected and pulled with an electric vehicle. Conveyors can work well for short-distance movements such as from the potting area to the cooler. Conveyors can be portable and moved around as needed. They can also be used as benches when placed on supports for short-term crops such as potted bulbs or rewholesale plants. Overhead monorails generally work best with an open greenhouse but can also effectively move plants among numerous small greenhouses (Fig. 11-14). Some systems also allow carts to be attached to the

FIGURE 11-14 Hanging cart for moving plants.

monorail, increasing the flexibility of both the monorail and the carts.

A step up in automation is to use mobile benches (bench trays or Dutch trays)—bench tops filled with plants. Mobile trays allow many plants to be handled as one unit rather than handling individual containers separately. The bench trays can be carried by forklift and placed on the bench supports, carried by automatic mechanized trolley, or moved manually on rollers. The most sophisticated systems link each component of the potting, propagation, and production systems via conveyors or mechanized trolleys. In some systems, the trolleys are programmed via a computer to deliver the trays from potting area to an assigned location in the production areas. After moving through production, the trays are emptied for shipping and marketing. The trays are returned to the headhouse for cleaning, storage (if needed), and replanting to complete the cycle. Trays can be loaded or emptied by hand or with automatic pot grippers, which grab, move, and set pots at the proper spacing on the bench tray.

Mobile bench trays are most efficient when used in a first-in, first-out production system. Mobile trays can also allow high benching efficiencies of more than 90% but such systems often have the problem of preventing easy access to plants in the center of the greenhouse. Cranes or robots can be used to access the center trays.

SPRAY APPLICATIONS

The spraying of pesticides, growth regulators, and other chemicals is often a hot and uncomfortable job. Mechanized spraying equipment is available in which robots are programmed to spray specific areas with pesticide or plant growth regulators. The robots can be programmed during regular working hours to perform the work later in the day when employees are not present.

CUTTING HARVESTING

The process of counting and keeping track of the number of cuttings harvested can slow harvesters down. Cutting counters can be constructed that record via electronic eyes the number of cuttings passing through an opening as employees harvest cuttings and drop them into collection containers. Carts can also be designed to make the cutting harvest more efficient by providing easy access to supplies such as knives, disinfectant solution, gloves, and containers.

HARVEST AND POSTHARVEST HANDLING

Video grading systems are available that scan finished plants with cameras; rate them by percent flower color, foliage, height, and diameter; and assign plants to specific grades.

CUT FLOWER HANDLING

Within the floriculture industry, cut flower production, especially harvesting and handling, is the most labor intensive. A wide variety of machines are available to make the handling process easier. Leaf and thorn strippers and bunch binders, cutters, and sleavers can reduce processing time. Machines are also available to assist with bucket cleaning and filling. Bouquet makers should consider bouquet processing machines. One type consists of a conveyor belt that collects stems from workers who place each stem down on the conveyor. After the required number or weight of stems are placed, the flowers and foliage are bound automatically and sleaved.

ECONOMICS

The advantages of automation are obvious, but are they worth the cost? Every operation should compare expenses and potential savings. The less tangible benefits of some machinery such as reduced employee injury or boredom must also be considered. Remember that with the installation of any new equipment it takes time to incorporate the equipment into an operation. Up to 2 years may be required before the full savings are realized.

IMPLEMENTATION

A couple of problems tend to occur when implementing a new handling process or piece of equipment. The first problem is resistance by the employees involved and the second is lack of use or abandonment after a period of time. Try to prevent these problems with these suggestions:

- Make sure that the change solves an actual problem or results in a genuine improvement. If employees don't see the need, they are less likely to implement the change.
- Make sure the new equipment or process flows well with the rest of the system. For example, installing media mixing machinery may not save money if too many different mixes are used. Even a change as simple as buying carts can be ineffective if the carts do not handle well or move easily down the aisles.
- Be sure equipment is easy to operate and maintain. Train and retrain employees periodically on how to operate and troubleshoot the equipment. This will reduce the amount of time the machinery is inoperable.
- Reassure employees that they are not going to be replaced, if that is the case. Many types of labor-saving machinery require a number of people to operate them smoothly. Often the same number of employees is required—they simply get more work done. If positions are going to be eliminated, it may be best to implement the changes when the operation expands, which will reduce the need to hire additional workers and not eliminate current employees.

NONGREENHOUSE STRUCTURES AND PRODUCTION AREAS

HEADHOUSE

The headhouse usually contains the administrative offices, equipment, storage areas, rest rooms, break rooms, and coolers. Media mixing, container filling, potting, and shipping are usually conducted in the headhouse. Pesticide storage can also be included as a separate room in the headhouse or in a separate building (see Chapter 9, Pest Management). If possible, the headhouse should also contain the environmental control systems because the headhouse is dryer, has lower humidity, and has more constant temperatures than greenhouse environments. Control systems placed in the greenhouses are subject to increased degradation and failure. Of course, the thermostats, thermocouples, and other sensors remain in the greenhouses. Generally, the headhouse space is equal to at least 10% of the greenhouse space. The headhouse is connected to the greenhouses to allow easy access and movement of plant materials and equipment. Often the headhouse runs along the north wall of a greenhouse to serve as a windbreak. Large greenhouse complexes with numerous greenhouse ranges may have more than one headhouse or may have one centrally located headhouse.

COOLERS

Coolers are a necessity for cut flower and flowering potted plant producers. Cut flowers need to be cooled prior to being shipped and for storage. Coolers are also required for the production of azaleas (*Rhododendron*), hydrangeas (*Hydrangea macrophyllum*), and potted flowering bulbs to supply the cold treatment. Coolers are also needed when crops have flowered too soon or in excess for marketing and must be stored until sold.

Coolers are a significant expense and must be used as efficiently as possible. Large greenhouse operations have cooler doors large enough to allow small forklifts to move racks or shelves of plants. Often there are many layers of shelves that can extend to the ceiling and a forklift is needed to raise the plants. Air exchange and limited humidity control should be considered. Rapid cooling of plant materials requires good air circulation and that plant materials not be packed too tightly in boxes or carts. A water source should be close to irrigate crops being stored for long periods, and floor drains will be needed. The door opening should have a curtain of hanging plastic straps or a lightweight screen that can be automatically and rapidly opened and closed to maintain temperatures and not waste energy when plant materials are moved in and out.

COLDFRAMES AND HOTBEDS

Coldframes and hotbeds are most commonly used in home gardens and botanical gardens, but they can be valuable for commercial growers as well. Coldframes and hotbeds have solid walls made of treated wood, poured concrete, or concrete blocks, and have a rigid transparent covering that can be opened and closed. The covering is opened during warm days and closed at night to protect plants and retain heat. Hotbeds differ from coldframes by having a heat source, which is usually heating cables, but may be steam or hot water pipes from the main greenhouse heating system. Coldframes and hotbeds can be used for extra storage and hardening of bedding plants, perennials, and cut flower or vegetable transplants, especially when space is limited in the greenhouse. Hotbeds are especially useful for propagation of woody plant materials. Home gardeners may also use coldframes and hotbeds for production of the cool growing crops such as lettuce (*Lactuca sativa*), radishes (*Raphanus salivus*), and some herbs.

CONTAINER PADS

Container pads are outdoor areas for container-grown plants and can either serve as temporary holding areas or as long-term production areas (Fig. 11-15). The pads can be as simple as a level area covered with gravel or as elaborate as a concrete pad with water drains. Many pads have a gravel base for support of the containers and are covered with landscape fabric to prevent weed growth. Another layer of landscape fabric below the gravel will prevent it from being absorbed in the soil. If a great amount of water is going to be applied, be certain to incorporate a drainage system in the site. Plants growing outdoors dry out quickly during hot, sunny weather and a mechanized irrigation system is usually required. Although overhead sprinklers can be used on some crops, microtube systems are usually appropriate for the broadest range of crops. The types of plants typically produced on container pads include garden chrysanthemums (*Dendran-*

thema ×grandiflorum), ornamental cabbage and kale (*Brassica oleracea*), and woody trees, shrubs, and vines. Pads are also commonly used for temporary storage of flatted annuals and potted perennials in the spring or fall prior to marketing.

SHADE AND SARAN HOUSES

Shade houses are open-air structures, without heating or cooling systems. Shade houses are essentially container pads covered with shade cloth (Fig. 11-16). The shade reduces the light level and gives some protection against rain, hail, and wind. Shade houses are used for many of the same purposes as container beds but can be used with a much wider range of crops. For example, much of the foliage plant production occurs in shade houses in warm climates. In general, almost any crop that does not require precise temperature manipulation can be grown in shade houses in moderate climates. One caution with shade houses is that they must be well constructed to prevent the covering from being torn off during high winds. While the shade is partially permeable to the wind, pressure can build up under the coverings during a windstorm.

LATH HOUSES

Lath houses are similar to shade or saran houses, but the shade is provided by wooden lathes laid across the top and sides. Lath houses serve the same purpose as shade houses but are more expensive to construct. They are considered to be more decorative than shade houses and are commonly used in retail situations.

FIGURE 11-15 Outdoor pad for bedding plant production.

FIGURE 11-16 Shade house for cut foliage production.

KEY POINTS

- Placement of greenhouses depends on a variety of factors including climate, topography, accessibility, water, laws, neighbors, labor supply, and the need for future expansion.
- Commercial greenhouses are available in several styles, including even-span (A-frame), uneven-span (sawtooth), quonset, gutter-connect, and retractible-roof styles.
- Greenhouse supports are primarily made from metal, but wood is also used in some cases.
- Greenhouses are covered with glazings such as glass, polyethylene film plastic, fiberglass reinforced plastic, acrylic, or polycarbonate.
- A high benching efficiency is important for cost-effective production and is equal to the area of usable production space divided by the area of greenhouse floor.
- Benches can be arranged in a longitudinal or island, peninsular, or rolling bench system and can be made from wood, plastic, or metal. Expanded metal is commonly used. Plants are also commonly grown on the floor, negating the need for benches.
- Retail benches are typically 3 to 4 ft (90 to 120 cm) wide for convenient reach by the customers, and wholesale production benches can be up to 6.5 ft (2 m) wide.
- Aisles range in width from 3 to 12 ft (0.9 to 3.7 m) for main routes and 1.5 to 2.5 ft (45 to 75 cm) wide for side aisles.
- Two greenhouse cooling situations occur. During the cold part of the year, the air outside the greenhouse is colder than that inside and the greenhouse is cooled by bringing in the colder air (winter cooling) utilizing vents and fan-jet tubes. During the warm season, the outside air temperature is close to or higher than that inside the greenhouse (summer cooling) and the only way to reduce the temperature is through water evaporation by pad-fan or fog cooler or by mechanical air conditioning.
- When light levels are high, the temperature can be lowered by reducing the amount of light entering the greenhouse using shade cloth and compounds.
- Greenhouses are commercially heated using central heating systems (boiler producing hot water or steam), unit or forced-air heaters, microclimate tubing, or radiant heating systems.
- Commonly used fuels include natural gas, propane, butane, and fuel oil; coal, wood, and geothermal are less commonly used.
- Air is circulated in the greenhouses using horizontal airflow (HAF) or fan-jet tubes.
- Energy conservation is accomplished through proper greenhouse design and construction, thermal screens, interior ceilings, greenhouse maintenance, heating system selection, and windbreaks, and by covering north walls.
- Although floriculture crop production has traditionally been a labor-intensive process, most areas of production are becoming increasingly automated, including irrigation, media mixing and planting, plant movement, spray applications, cutting harvesting, finished plant harvest and postharvest handling, and cut flower handling.
- Nongreenhouse structures and production areas include the headhouse, coolers, coldframes and hotbeds, container pads, shade and saran houses, and lath houses.

BIBLIOGRAPHY

Aldrich, R.A., and J.W. Bartok, Jr. 1989. Equipment for heating and cooling, pp. 73–91 in *Greenhouse Engineering*, 2nd ed., NRAES-33. Northeast Regional Agricultural Engineering Service, Cornell University, Ithaca, New York.

Bartok, J.W., Jr. 1997. Keep greenhouses cool, reduce plant stress with fog. *Greenhouse Management and Production* 17(7):64–65.

Sray, A. 1997. Three codes in one. *Greenhouse Grower* 15(4):30.

Will, E., and J.E. Faust. 1997. Comparison of container placement patterns for maximizing greenhouse space use. *HortScience* 32:479. (Abstract)

Chapter 12

Marketing and Business Management

INTRODUCTION

Many people are attracted to the floriculture industry because of their interest in growing plants. However, actual plant production accounts for only a portion of what is required for a successful business:

Grow a quality product $\rightarrow$ Sell the crop $\rightarrow$ Make a profit

Production $\rightarrow$ Marketing $\rightarrow$ Business management

Floriculture businesses must be equally adept at marketing their crops and managing the business to generate a profit and justify the financial investment. Although this book focuses on the production and handling of plants, we also need to emphasize the importance of proper marketing and business management. Without the latter two components, a business will not survive. New businesses should realize that it usually requires 3 to 5 years for the business to show a profit and owners should plan accordingly. Competition in most areas of the world is great enough that a poorly organized business will not be successful. This chapter focuses on a few topics unique to floriculture businesses; general marketing and management information is equally important and can be obtained from a variety of sources.

GROWING A QUALITY PRODUCT

Growing a quality product is required in today's competitive business environment. A grower's attention to the crop must start at the beginning of the production cycle and be diligently maintained until the product is delivered to the customer and the account collected. A company's marketing choices decrease considerably when trying to sell a substandard product. Even if the company is successful in selling the crop, it will lose the confidence of its customers and may have difficulty making another sale to them. If subsequent sales are made, the price obtained may be lower. Opportunities to sell low-quality plant materials are limited and a company will not be able to compete with a competitor selling a higher quality crop for the same or greater price. Management must answer the following questions to define quality for their business:

1. What level of quality do you want to produce?
2. Are you delivering the quality you promised?
3. Are you continuously improving the quality?
4. Do you always deliver above-average products or services?
5. Do you deliver on the date requested?

The first step in growing a quality crop is to understand what constitutes quality. In general terms, a quality crop consists of well-grown, blemish- and pest-free plant material harvested at the proper stage and handled in such a way that it will provide a long postharvest life for the consumer. Potted flowering plants must have sufficient stems, foliage, flowers, and buds to provide an attractive display; cut flowers must have sufficiently long and strong stems, appropriately sized flowers, and enough flowers and foliage. Of course, potted and cut foliage will have similar standards, but without the flowers. Remember that size does not equal quality—large plants may be poor quality.

Unfortunately, beyond these general descriptions, the definition of quality becomes vague and ill defined. Very often the requirements for buying and selling of a crop have little to do with the plant itself and are based on the following factors:

1. Container size—potted flowering and foliage plants, perennials, hanging baskets
2. Number of plants per flat—bedding plant flats
3. Stem length and number of stems in the bunch—fresh cut flowers and foliage
4. Bunch weight, stem number, or a combination of both measurements—fresh cut filler flowers, most cut foliage and dried materials.

The most well-developed grades and standards have traditionally been for cut flowers. Unfortunately, even with cut flowers, no universal grades and standards exist and three general sets are currently followed: European (also followed by Africa), Latin American (also followed by Miami, Florida), and Californian (followed by most of the United States). An example of the three systems using hybrid tea roses is given in Table 12-1. The Society of American Florists has attempted to establish grades and standards for a number of cut flowers and potted flowering plants (Tables 12-2 and 12-3). General acceptance of the grades and standards has been limited.

Growers are in little agreement even on the number of stems per bunch. As a general rule, the European system calls for 10 stems per bunch, but there are many exceptions. The Californian system often relies on the "grower bunch" for many species in which the stem number is determined by the grower. Even grower bunches from one firm may vary in stem number depending on the amount of product that is available. Bunches from one business may be large during peak production and much smaller when product is scarce and prices are high. This variability in bunch size has made it difficult for growers to determine the production costs for each bunch and for buyers to know what they will receive. Certainly, as world trade increases, universal standards will be critical to the survival of local cut flower growers.

Many large buyers and shippers have created their own standards that must be met by the growers from which they buy product. For example, with bedding plants, a buyer may specify the flat insert type (cell number or plants/flat), minimum and maximum plant height, minimum number of flowers, and the minimum flower size. Regardless of the type of plant material, producers and buyers must communicate when selling and purchasing

TABLE 12-1

Specifications of cut hybrid tea roses (*Rosa*) for European, Latin American, or Californian marketing systems. In addition to the indicated specifications, the rose stems should be straight, the flower head in proportion to the stem length, and cut point (degree of openness) the same for all individual flowers within the bunch.

System	European	Latin American	Californian
Number stems/bunch	20	25	25
Flower arrangement	All flower heads even	Flower heads staggered in two rows	All flower heads even
Stem length (grades)	30 cm	30 cm	10–14 inches (short)
	40 cm	40 cm	14–18 inches (medium)
	50 cm	50 cm	18–22 inches (long)
	60 cm	60 cm	22–26 inches (fancy)
	70 cm	70 cm	≥ 26 inches (extra fancy)
	80 cm	80 cm	
Sleeve labeling	Length	Length and variety	–

TABLE 12-2

Society of American Florists' grades and standards for hybrid tea roses (*Rosa*). Stems must also have a stem strength greater than 20° and one flower.

Factors	Grade									
	1	2	3	4	5	6	7	8	9	10
Color:	Blue	Yellow	Red	Green	Orange	Violet	White	Light blue	Gray	Brown
Minimum Length:										
in.	28	26	24	22	20	18	16	14	12	10
cm	70	65	60	55	50	45	40	35	30	25
Stem Deviation/Curvature:										
in.	1	1	1	0.75	0.75	0.75	0.5	0.5	0.5	0.5
cm	2.5	2.5	2.5	2	2	2	1.5	1.5	1.5	1.5

Source: Adapted from PMA/SAF Recommended Grades and Standards for Cut Flowers.

plant materials. The use of digital images, which can be e-mailed, can facilitate communication and prevent misunderstandings.

MARKETING AND SALES

The simplest definition of marketing is the selling of products; however, marketing is much more involved. Marketing involves selecting the right product and developing the correct pricing strategy, promotional programs, and distribution outlets for a particular market. Sales are that part of marketing that involve all the steps required for a customer to buy a product or service. Sales contact with customers can be made in person by a salesperson or by telephone, fax, direct mail, e-mail, or advertising.

The following section covers the basics, but more advanced information should be obtained from university and cooperative extension personnel, consultants, public relations firms, or other firms selling similar products. Conferences, workshops, and conventions are excellent places to meet and discuss marketing with others in the same business who may not be direct competitors.

A beautiful crop is of little value if it cannot be sold. Before production starts, the producer should know where and to whom the crop will be sold. In some cases, the crop can be sold on contract before it is grown. Several options are available for distributing and marketing a crop (Fig. 12-1), as discussed next.

MARKETING OPTION I

The most direct sales path is from the grower to the final consumer, the general public; a large portion of bedding plant and specialty cut flower sales and a small portion of the potted foliage and flowering plant sales are made by this route. Although selling prices should be high when selling directly to the consumers, so too are the marketing costs. Direct marketing costs include maintaining a customer-friendly sales facility, sales personnel, and advertising.

MARKETING OPTION II

The remainder of the bedding plants, most of the potted foliage and flowering plants, and a portion of cut flowers are sold first to a retailer, such as a florist or garden center, before being sold to the general public. Prices paid to the grower tend to be lower than with direct sales to the general public, but marketing costs should also be lower. Because individual retailers typically buy much larger quantities than individuals in the general public, fewer customers are required. Consequently, marketing costs are reduced.

Sales to retailers may be made through a broker who does not take possession of the product but arranges the sale between the grower and the retailer. Brokers usually acquire product from several growers to meet as much of a retailer's needs as possible. Because the broker is usually paid by receiving a percentage of the total sale, the grower receives smaller profits per unit sold. However, the broker incurs the marketing expenses rather than the grower.

In some cases, cooperatives may replace a broker. Although cooperatives can take several different forms, a common type is the grower

TABLE 12-3

Society of American Florists' grades and standards for poinsettias (*Euphorbia pulcherrima*). All plants must have fully pigmented bracts, cyathia present, dark-green foliage, strong stems, healthy root system, moist media, and care tags displayed.

	Grades				
Factors	Small	Medium	Large	Extra Large	Jumbo
Pinched Multibloom Plants					
Height:					
in.	8–12	11–14	14–19	17–23	22–26
cm	20–30	28–36	36–48	43–58	56–66
Width at Top of Plant:					
in.	9	12	15	18	26
cm	23	30	38	46	66
Pot size:					
in.	4–4.5	5–5.5	6–6.5	7–8.5	10
cm	10–11.5	12.5–14	15–16.5	18–21.5	25
Number of Flower Clusters:					
	3	4	5	8	15
Nonpinched Single-Bloom Plants					
Height:					
in.	8–12	14–20	18–22	20–24	22–26
cm	20–30	36–50	46–56	50–60	56–66
Width at Top of Plant:					
in.	6	12	14	16	18
cm	15	30	36	41	46
Pot Size:					
in.	4–4.5	5.5–6	6–7	6.5–8	7–8
cm	10–11.5	12.5–15	15–18	16.5–20	18–20
Number of Flower Clusters:					
	1	2	3	4	5

Source: Adapted from Produce Marketing Association/Society of American Florists' (PMA/SAF) Recommended Grades and Standards for Potted Plants.

cooperative. Cooperatives allow growers to do one or more of the following:

1. Pool their resources to buy larger quantities of supplies at a discount.
2. Coordinate growers to reduce intracooperative competition.
3. Provide customers with a larger quantity and selection of product compared with what a single grower could supply.
4. Reduce the number of items that any one firm produces, which allows individual firms to specialize.

Some cooperatives provide a central shipping area for its members; other cooperatives simply arrange the sales. As with brokers, the cooperative is supported by collecting a percentage of sales.

MARKETING OPTION III

This marketing chain includes another intermediary, the wholesaler or the auction (in some cases, a cooperative may also serve in this capacity). The wholesaler or auction brings in product from numerous growers, allowing re-

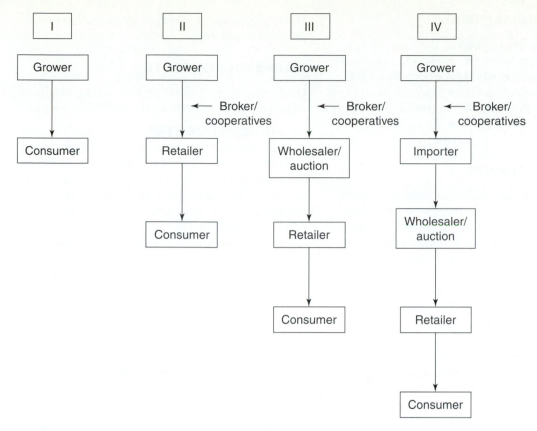

FIGURE 12-1   Marketing options for distribution of floriculture crops.

tailers to obtain all of their plant materials from one location. In North America many of the domestically produced cut flowers and a portion of potted foliage and flowering plants are marketed through wholesalers. Auctions have tended to be small and few in number in North America. However, in Europe, Brazil, and Japan, auctions play an important role in handling both cut flowers and potted plants.

From the grower's point of view, prices received from the wholesaler tend to be low, but so are marketing costs. The price per unit must be recovered by efficiently growing and selling large volumes of plant materials. Wholesalers are also concerned with buying from reputable growers who will be able to deliver a consistent, high-quality product.

MARKETING OPTION IV

The last major marketing chain is the most elaborate and includes an importer who brings in plant material, typically cut flowers, from foreign producers. The most important cut flowers—*Rosa, Dianthus,* and *Dendranthema* and dozens of miscellaneous cut flower species—are handled through importers. The importers sell the product to wholesalers (marketing option III) or directly to mass market retailers. In some countries the auction also acts as the flower importer.

Because this option includes the most steps, prices received by the grower tend to be quite low. Foreign producers are only able to make a profit if they have one or more advantages over domestic producers. While relatively low labor and other production expenses are typically the major advantage of foreign producers, optimum environmental conditions are also important. For example, cut tropicals, such as *Heliconia* and *Protea,* are much more easily produced in tropical countries than in most of the United States and the European Union. In addition, the high mountains in many South American and African countries provide the high light and cool temperatures necessary for high-quality cut *Rosa, Dianthus,* and *Dendranthema* production. However, foreign producers may have problems that domestic producers do not have such as ability to obtain plants and other production materials, high transportation costs, and political changes.

PROPAGATION MATERIALS

Plugs, cuttings, liners, bulbs, dormant plants, and seeds can go through marketing channels similar to those of finished products (Fig. 12-2). Brokers are particularly important in the marketing of plugs, cuttings, liners, bulbs, and dormant plants. Similarly, most seed is sold through wholesale seed distributors.

PREFINISHED PLANTS

Further complicating the marketing process is that some potted crops may be sold prefinished. In this case, the plant materials are purchased partially grown or finished and grown for a short time to allow for flowering or acclimatization before being sold. The producer of the prefinished plants has the responsibility for propagation, early establishment, and, in some cases, flower initiation. In some cases, purchasing prefinished plants allows buyers to obtain small numbers of many species, such as various bedding plants, bypassing the minimum order requirements necessary to pur-

chase plugs, seeds, or other propagative material from suppliers.

MARKETING OUTLETS

Growers use the following marketing methods to sell product directly to the public.

GARDEN CENTER. The garden center has emerged as a primary outlet in the floriculture industry due to recent rapid increases in bedding plant sales (Fig. 12-3). Garden centers typically sell herbaceous and woody plants for outdoor gardens and the associated supplies required by the home gardener. Most garden centers also sell indoor foliage and seasonal potted flowering plants, and a few garden centers include a florist shop for sales of cut flowers, arrangements, and so forth. Garden centers often fill specific niches within a community, such as "the place to go for perennials," "the best spot for gardening advice and service," or "the store that holds great workshops." Some garden centers grow their own product, others buy all their product from wholesale growers, and most do a combination of both.

FARMERS' MARKET. Farmers' markets are a relatively easy marketing method for new growers of bedding plants, perennials, herbs, and cut flowers. Overhead costs are generally low and most, if not all, of the advertising and organization duties are handled by the farmers' market organization. The time spent selling product is usually limited because farmers' markets are only open for a few hours a day for a limited number of days each week. In temperate climates, markets often close after a hard freeze and reopen the following spring.

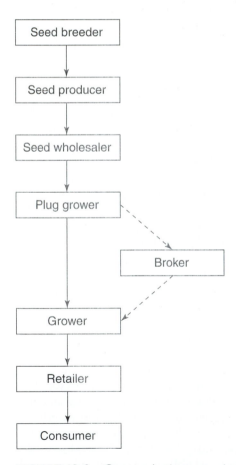

FIGURE 12-2 One marketing scenario for the production of a potted flowering plant from seed breeder to consumer.

FIGURE 12-3 Sign in a garden center indicating "red" plants that prefer full sun.

Customers expect to buy directly from the producer and typically are not as concerned about packaging. Prices can be high because the product is considered fresh from the grower; however, in some cases they may be lower if customers are expecting a "bargain" by buying directly from the grower.

ROADSIDE STAND. As with farmers' markets, the overhead costs on roadside stands are usually low. The stand can be operated directly from the growing location (see also On-Farm Sales below) or can be set up at a highly visible location near or in population centers. Often bedding plants and fresh and dried cut flowers are sold with fruits and vegetables. The floriculture crops are compatible with the edible products in that the bright, eye-catching colors of flowers can bring in customers who might not otherwise stop. As with farmers' markets, prices can be high, depending on customer expectations.

TENTS. Similar to roadside stands, these operations are placed in highly visible and convenient locations in population centers (Fig. 12-4). The overhead costs are low and bedding plants are the main products sold. Prices are typically moderate.

ON-FARM SALES. On-farm sales have been developed more extensively in the fruit and vegetable industries but are readily applicable to floriculture. On-farm sales can range from something as simple as a roadside stand to a pick-your-own field cut flower operation to a fully developed family entertainment center with animals, areas for children, tours, and educational displays. Floriculture crops such as cut flowers or bedding plants are often sold with fruits and vegetables. One appeal of on-farm sales is being able to manage all aspects of the business from the farm. Of course, the drawback is the need to maintain the farm in a highly presentable condition. Location is especially important because the general public must be able to easily locate the business, yet the business should retain a rural image.

MAIL ORDER. Seed, perennials, bulbs, cut flowers, potted plants, and foliage plants are also sold through the mail. Mail order is generally most successful in bringing a large selection of plant materials to customers who are not able to buy them locally. Often a company will cultivate the reputation of having the most complete line of a specific type of plant material such as native plants, shade-loving plants, specialty greenhouse plants, or herbs.

The keys to a successful mail-order business are the catalog (or Web site) and the mailing (e-mail) list. Catalogs or Web sites need not be elaborate but must excite the customer into buying, which can be a daunting task, considering the number of catalogs the typical consumer receives each year or Web sites viewed. Because catalogs are expensive to produce and mail, the mailing list must be directed at those consumers most likely to buy the products without an excess of consumers who are not likely to buy. Internet-based businesses may be able to forgo the catalog.

FLORISTS. Along with garden centers, the traditional florist shop is a major outlet for floriculture products. Florists sell large amounts of cut flowers and foliage, usually in the form of flower arrangements (Fig. 12-5). Florists also sell decorated potted flowering and foliage plants. Much of the florists' sales are based on events such as holidays, birthdays, funerals, anniversaries, and parties. In addition to local sales, florists act as agents for nationwide floral wire services, such as American Floral Services (AFS) or Florist Telegraph Delivery (FTD). To send flowers to a friend or relative in a distant location, customers contact their local florist who wires or sends the order to a florist in the second location.

MASS MARKETS. Mass market outlets are those companies including grocery stores, department stores, farm supply stores, home improvement stores, and hardware stores that sell plant materials as part of a broad range of items. Although the floriculture products are often an important part of the business, they rarely constitute the majority of sales for the

FIGURE 12-4 Tent garden center operating in a parking lot.

FIGURE 12-5 Flowering arrangement in a gourd made by a florist.

FIGURE 12-6 Are butterfly gardens your marketing niche?

business. The commitment to floriculture sales by mass markets ranges from bedding plants sold for a few weeks in the spring to full-service florists or garden centers that operate the entire year. Mass markets often focus on daily or impulse purchases. A large portion of floriculture products are sold through mass market outlets in the United States.

CRAFT STORES. For the dried and preserved segment of the floriculture industry, craft stores are an important source of sales. Products offered range from bunches of single species to mixed bouquets of many flowers to potpourri. Large amounts of arts and crafts using dried and preserved floriculture products are also sold through craft shows, farmers' markets, and other nontraditional outlets.

DEVELOPING A MARKETING PLAN

Marketing and sales also involve how the business will contact customers and the image the business projects. Marketing and sales methods are as numerous and varied as there are businesses in the floriculture industry (Table 12-4 and Figs. 12-6 and 12-7). Each business must develop a marketing plan for the company, which should include the following:

1. Who are your customers (or who will be your customers) and which categories of customers are most important to the business?

FIGURE 12-7 Creative displaying and marketing of plants may be your claim to fame.

2. Why will your customers buy from you (what customer needs are you trying to satisfy)?
3. How will you reach your customers?
4. How will you determine that your marketing plan is effective?
5. What expectations do you have for your marketing plans?
6. What image will the company project?

TABLE 12-4

Marketing and sales techniques and information.

Customer Service		
Routine Information	**Printed Media**	**Electronic Media**
Name of company	Business cards	Radio commercials
Logo	Stationery/envelopes	Television commercials
Hours of operation	Order form/invoice	Audio/video tapes
Days of operation	Inside signs	Telemarketing
Phone number	Outside signs	Phone hold marketing
Personnel demeanor	Price tags on each item	Audiovisual aids
Attire	Classified ads	Internet (web pages)
Enthusiasm	Newspaper display ads	
Smiles	Yellow Pages ads	**Promotional Items/Services**
Greetings	High school yearbook ads	Contests/sweepstakes
Contact time/human bonds	Magazine ads	Samples
Follow-up	Restaurant menu ads	Trade show displays
Shop/garden center/greenhouse	Coupons	Balloons
Location	Circulars	Searchlights
Decor	Brochures	In-store demonstrations
Merchandise displays	Columns in publications	Refreshments
Neatness	Books and articles	Gift baskets
Clean restrooms	Direct mail letters	Bingo prize donations
Company identity	Direct mail postcards	Mall booths
Convenience	Catalogs	Street booths
Speed	Newsletters	Testimonials
Reputation	Billing statement inserts	Publicity contacts
Credibility	School calendars	Seminars/lectures
Competitiveness/pricing	Bag ads	Take-one boxes
Theme	Posters	
Music theme	Research studies	**Miscellaneous**
Window displays	Billboards	Community service
Customer relations	Bus and wind shelters	Tie-ins with other businesses
Brand-name awareness	"Currently available" lists	Credit cards
Assertiveness	Announcements/press releases	Financing
Warranty/guarantees	Gift certificates	Club/association memberships
Customer mailing list/databases	Realtor coupons	Team sponsorships
	Faxes	Consultations
		Sales training
		Sales presentations
		Salespeople

For example, a retail garden center may decide that middle- to upper-income homeowners are their most important customers (question 1) and they will be attracted by the best selection of quality bedding plants in the area (question 2). The customers can be reached through newspaper ads, sport team sponsorships, and direct mail newsletters (question 3). The garden center could include coded coupons in each of its advertisements to determine the effectiveness of the marketing campaign (question 4). The center has decided that a realistic goal for next year's marketing campaign is to increase sales by 5% (question 5). The overall image the company has developed is that of a friendly, helpful merchant who carries the best selection of high-quality bedding plants and unusual perennials in town (question 6).

BUSINESS MANAGEMENT AND COST ACCOUNTING

Other than plant production and handling, floriculture businesses have requirements and problems similar to those of other businesses, and business management and cost accounting information can be obtained from a variety of sources. An important aspect of a successful business is the organization. The simplest business structure is a one-person operation in which the owner performs all functions. Most businesses are considerably more complicated. Regardless of the structure, all floriculture production or retailing businesses have certain responsibilities whether it is a one-person or 1000-person firm:

Overall management and coordination—Could be the owner or a hired manager.

Engineering—Maintains structures and equipment.

Production—Produces crops. Production can be designated by area (e.g., propagation, field, greenhouse A, greenhouse B), by crop (e.g., bulbs, potted flowering plants, bedding plants), by job (media mixing and potting, pest control), or by a combination of these methods. Research and development is often included in this section.

Marketing and sales—Includes sales, packaging, delivery, advertising, and so forth. Shipping and sales are often separate entities.

Financial affairs—Purchasing, accounts payable and accounts receivable, payroll, regulations, cost accounting, and related tasks.

Someone must be responsible for each section and each firm has its own structure for handling those responsibilities. Any number of submanagers may be responsible for more specific areas. The general production employees may be organized by greenhouse or field section or may be part of an overall group whose responsibilities vary with the most pressing needs of the day or week. As with production techniques, management strategies continually change and improve. One recent concept is to use cross-functional teams to improve efficiency, morale, and cost-effective management. Teams of employees monitor, participate in, and are responsible for improving processes within an organization. The manager no longer makes all decisions.

Most firms consider their employees to be the source of their success and maintain a separate personnel management and motivation program. Such a program begins with formally testing a potential employee to determine if the person's skills and personality match the position requirements. After hiring, proper orientation to the organization and discussion of expectations and responsibilities ensures that the employee and the firm have similar expectations. A variety of programs will ensure that the employee continues to prosper and make progress within the firm. Such programs range from annual evaluations to financial rewards such as sales bonuses, attendance bonuses, and profit sharing.

Record keeping is a key to good management. Considering typical time constraints, record keeping should be as convenient and simple as possible. If possible, one or more employees should be designated as record keepers, allowing the owner or grower to focus on other tasks. Records should include the following:

Cultural—Planting dates, pest problems and control, spacing, and so forth.

Environmental—Weather conditions, temperatures.

Production—Quantity and quality of crops produced.

Postharvest—Notes and trials on postharvest life of each species (cultivar) or on the durability and color retention of dried materials.

Financial—All expenses and sales figures (Table 12-5).

Cultural, environmental, production, and postharvest records are needed to determine the amount of product produced and sold and the supplies, energy, and labor needed to produce the product. From these records it is possible to calculate production costs per unit, establish sales prices, and plan future production of crops that are profitable. Accurate, complete records establish a database that can be used to continuously improve production and business processes within the organization. One aspect of management that all businesses have in common is the need for each business to know its expenses and be able to determine the selling prices required to remain in business.

CROP SELECTION

A major consideration of floriculture producers is which crop species to produce. Of course, one of the main reasons should be that the crop is profitable. However, some species may be grown for other reasons, occasionally even when the crop is not profitable:

1. The crop may fill a production void. Fall potted chrysanthemum production for outdoor use may fill production space between the spring bedding plant season and winter

TABLE 12-5

Potential expenses for a floriculture business.

> Labor (wages, benefits, workmen's compensation, payroll taxes):
>   Employee's wages and/or salaries
>   Owner's salary
> Plant materials, such as seed, plugs, liners
> General production materials, including fertilizer, stakes, netting, pesticides, and potting media.
>   Each cost should be attributed to a specific crop.
> Upkeep and repair of equipment, buildings, vehicles
> Purchase of equipment
> Depreciation for buildings and equipment
> Utilities, including electricity, water, sewer, garbage collection
> Office expenses, including telephone, paper, envelopes, stamps, paper clips
> Accountant fees, lawyer fees
> Land expenses:
>   Mortgage
>   Property taxes
> Insurance
> Shipping expenses, including vehicle, mail, packaging
> Interest on business loans
> Marketing expenses, including advertisements, business cards, surveys
> Miscellaneous expenses, including association fees, publications

potted poinsettias. Such crops allow growers to keep key employees working, eliminating the need for temporary layoffs, which may cause valued employees to find permanent positions elsewhere.

2. The crop may be used as a marketing tool. Many specialty cut flowers and bedding plants are produced and sold only in small amounts and often contribute little to the overall sales. However, firms continue to grow these plants because they contribute to their marketing image of having a more complete selection than their competitors. Customers attracted by the specialty items may purchase other more profitable, high-volume products.

3. The customer demands it. For example, potted poinsettias are the major crop species during December in many countries. Some growers grow poinsettias to keep customers for the more profitable spring sales season.

Regardless of the reason to grow a crop species, producers should determine if the crop is profitable. Unprofitable crops should not be produced unless they meet one of the previous criteria.

STARTING YOUR OWN BUSINESS

Many people dream of owning their own business, whether it is a small, high-quality garden center or a large wholesale cut flower operation. Typically businesses are started small, possibly from a hobby such as growing orchids or native plants, and developed into a viable self-sustaining business. Occasionally a thriving business can be purchased. Prior to starting a business, a number of considerations must be made:

1. The first step is to determine if you have the right personality to own and operate your own business. Visit with people who already own their own businesses. Are you ready for the time, responsibility, and commitment required? Analyze your strengths and weaknesses. Are you a natural grower, people manager, or salesperson? Do you dislike managing people or handling customer complaints? Enlist the opinion of family and close friends to help you evaluate your skills and deficiencies. You do not need to be able to do everything well but you must be able to hire or partner with others who have the skills and traits you lack.

2. Obtain sufficient capital to start the business and operate it until it makes a profit. Unless you are quite lucky, your business will not make money the first year and may not for several years. You must not only have enough money to keep the business operating until it is profitable but also to support yourself, and possibly your family, during that time. Even after the business is profitable, it may not make enough money for several more years to allow you to pay yourself enough to live on. There are a number of types of floriculture businesses that do not require much initial capital such as selling bedding plants or cut flowers at a farmers' market or roadside stand. Field cut flower production and marketing to florists, supermarkets, and, possibly, wholesalers is also affordable for many people. Specialty plant producers can use mail order or Web sites to market their plants and slowly increase the size of the business without costly retail facilities. Starting an interior plant care service is feasible for many people.

3. Determine if there is sufficient market for the products or services your business will offer. If you are selling to the general public, are there enough customers within your area to support your business? Define the area you intend to reach. Direct retail will depend on people who can readily drive or walk to your business, which generally means that you must be in or close to a metropolitan area. Selling wholesale may allow you to reach a broader area, such as a 100-mile radius, but will probably require you to deliver the product. Of course, marketing through catalogs and on the Internet will expand your market base to the entire country. See the next point also.

4. Is there demand for the products or services your business will offer? Your potential customer base may be large enough but may not be able to support your business if there are too many competitors already in the market. Analyze your competition. Are there products or services that they do not offer? Define your niche; in other words, why will your customers buy from you rather than from someone else? Remember lower prices will not work in the long run. That strategy only works for large companies who can produce or sell large amounts of products and services and make money through economy of scale.

It may be wise to list out two types of customers. The primary customers are those who you anticipate will buy most of your products or services. They are the ones that you will direct most of your marketing toward. Secondary customers are those who may purchase some of your products and services but not in large enough amounts to support the business. You should always consider your secondary customers, especially in case your primary customers fail to support your business, but do not pay so much attention to secondary customers that you lose your primary customers. For example, a retail garden center may target the residents of nearby upscale neighborhoods as its primary customers and have landscapers as its secondary customers. Similarly, cut flower growers may sell primarily at farmers' markets and secondarily to florists.

After you have addressed these issues, it is time to prepare a business plan (Table 12-6). Typically a business plan is used to raise money from a lending institution or investors. All firms, however, should prepare a business plan, even if they are entirely self-funded, to allow them to be as prepared as possible and increase the likelihood of success.

TABLE 12-6

Business plan outline (Paulson, 2000; V. Stamback, personal communication). Not all sections and statements will apply to each business. In particular, a new business will not have previous financial records, etc.

Executive Summary: Write this section last, so you can provide a 1- to 2-page or paragraph overview of the whole plan.

Industry Analysis: Assume the bankers or investors reading this plan know nothing about the floriculture industry and try to give them a mini-education in this section: what the opportunities are, what's going on in the market, who the major players are, and how they have succeeded.

Market Analysis: After giving a macro view of your industry, talk specifically about what's happening in your geographic market: what the opportunities are, who the competition is, how you can differentiate yourself from them, and how you will succeed, given market demands and trends.

Business Description: Describe your business: how long it has been in operation, what the legal structure is, who the owners are, what your short-term and long-term goals are, and why you need money now—is it for expansion, marketing, equipment purchase, or debt reduction?

Competitive Advantage: To convince potential investors to put money in your business, you need to clearly explain how your business is better than the competition and why it will succeed.

Marketing Plan: Explain who your current customers are, who you would like to have as customers, why they would be interested in buying from you, what your pricing strategy is, how you distribute your product, and how you promote your business.

Organization: After describing how your business operates, describe who is responsible for making it work. Write a brief paragraph about each of your top employees (i.e., manager, grower, salesperson), detailing their expertise and background. Convince the investors that these are the people most capable of making your business a success. Include an organization chart and describe your plans for adding or subtracting staff members.

TABLE 12-6 *(continued)*

Operations: For production firms, describe what will be grown, how it will be grown, and how it will be handled postproduction. Describe land, structures, supplies, and equipment required. For service or wholesale businesses, describe how your business is being run, what the departments are within the business, and how you will be able to expand (by hiring, buying equipment, moving to a new location, outsourcing production, and so on).

Funding Needs: Explain the total amount of money needed, how it will be used (such as for marketing materials, working capital, hiring, equipment purchase), and why that is the right way to spend it.

Financial Statements: This is where you place the past 3 years' balance sheets and income statements. In addition, include 5 years of projections: balance sheets, income statements, and a 5-year cash flow with monthly projections for the first 3 years and quarterly projections thereafter.

Appendix: This section should be used for important reference information that need not appear in the body of the plan. For instance, include a summary of a recent contract you won, a map of planned sites, resumés of key managers, or marketing literature.

KEY POINTS

- Floriculture businesses must be equally adept at producing high-quality plants, marketing their crops, and managing the business to generate a profit and justify the financial investment.

- A quality crop consists of well-grown, blemish- and pest-free plant material harvested at the proper stage and handled in such a way that it will provide a long postharvest life for the consumer. Potted plants must have sufficient stems, foliage, flowers, and buds to provide an attractive display; cuts must have sufficiently long and strong stems, appropriately sized flowers, and enough flowers and foliage.

- A beautiful crop is of little value if it cannot be sold. Marketing involves selecting the right product and developing the correct pricing strategy, promotional programs, and distribution outlets for a particular market. Sales is the part of marketing that involves all the steps required to induce a customer to buy a product or service.

- A number of marketing paths are available by which product moves from the producer to the consumer.

- Some potted and bedding crops may be sold prefinished, in which the plant materials are purchased partially grown or finished and grown by a second firm for a short time to allow for flowering or acclimatization before being sold.

- Numerous marketing outlets are available for floriculture crops to be sold including garden centers, farmers' markets, roadside stands, tents, on-farm sales, mail order, florists, mass markets, and craft stores.

- Each business must develop a marketing plan for the company.

- An important aspect of a successful business is the organization, which must consider a number of functions: overall management and coordination, engineering, production, marketing and sales, and financial affairs.

- Record keeping is a key to good management and typically includes cultural, environmental, production, postharvest, and financial records.

- Various crop species are grown for a number of reasons including profitability, to fill a production void, to serve as a marketing tool, and to fulfill customer demand.

- Producers should determine which products and services are profitable and adjust the business accordingly.

- Many people would like to own their own business. Preparations must be made for a person to start or own a business, including writing a business plan.

BIBLIOGRAPHY

Paulson, E. 2000, *The Complete Idiots Guide to Starting Your Own Business*, Alpha Books, New York, New York.

Part II

Part II has full-length sections on more than 100 specific crop genera. Topics within each genera are arranged in the same order for easy reference. An attempt has been made to cover the various uses of each genera, such as potted flowering plant, cut flower, foliage plant, bedding plant, hanging basket, garden perennial, or patio plant. Nomenclature follows the New Royal Horticultural Society's *Dictionary of Gardening* (1994). One of the keys to producing a crop is the development of a suitable production schedule. Numerous production schedules exist for each crop species since production conditions vary with location, season, cultivar, and desired plant size. One to three sample schedules are included for most species. Because types and quantities of species grown as well as production methods vary from country to country, international references and perspectives are included in many of the sections.

Most of the important potted flowering crop and greenhouse-grown cut flower species currently produced are included in Part II. The large number of species used for bedding plants, perennials, outdoor-grown cuts, and potted foliage prevents all of them from being covered individually. For those segments of floriculture, the species covered in the text may serve as representative examples. In addition, please check the tables in Part I and the general chapters in Part III for information on species not covered in Part II. The species included in Part II were chosen for their current commercial importance or, in a few cases, for their uniqueness or estimated importance in the future. The following species are covered in Part II:

SELECTING WHICH CROP SPECIES TO PRODUCE

Although some crop species, such as potted and cut chrysanthemums, are grown year-round, many crops are seasonal and grown at specific times of the year in each location. For example, in temperate climates, bedding impatiens are grown in the spring and early summer for outdoor planting. In mild climates, however, impatiens can be grown outdoor virtually year-round. Regardless, the following seasonal list reflects when the species is typically grown in the largest amounts in temperate climates.

Achimenes
Aconitum
Antirrhinum
Aquilegia
Asclepias
Aster*
Astilbe
Begonia, Tuberous
Begonia, Wax
Bougainvillea
Caladium
Calendula
Callistephus
Campanula
Capsicum

Centaurea
Convallaria
Cosmos
Dahlia
Delphinium
Dendranthema*
Dianthus, Sweet William
Echinacea
Fuchsia
Gentiana
Gerbera
Gypsophila
Hedera
Hibiscus
Impatiens, Bedding

Impatiens, New Guinea
Liatris
Lilium, Asiatic and Oriental
Lilium, Easter
Limonium
Lycopersicon
Paeonia
Pelargonium
Petunia
Platycodon
Primula*
Solidago
Tagetes
Viola*
Zinnia

BEDDING PLANTS

Bedding plants are those species intended for outdoor use, including flats, pots, hanging baskets, patio plants, and perennials (see list below). Bedding plants are the largest component of floriculture production in North America based on sales. Most are grown in the spring and early summer. A few (*) are typically sold in flower in the late summer and fall. The list does not include cold hardy bulbs, typically planted in the fall for spring flowering, and woody ornamentals. See also Part III chapters on Bedding Plants, Herbs, and Garden Perennials.

POTTED FLOWERING PLANTS

Potted flowering plants are those species intended for indoor use and comprise the second largest component of floriculture production in North America based on sales (see list below). Most species flower and are attractive for only a few days to weeks in the consumer's environment. Other species, such as African violets (*Saintpaulia*) and *Phalaenopsis* orchids, can flower repeatedly indoors (*). Many species can be produced year-round but the majority of the sales are during the indicated season.

Winter/Spring
Achimenes
Anigozanthos
Anthurium*

Begonia, Hiemalis
Calceolaria
Clerodendrum
Convallaria

Crocus
Crossandra*
Cyclamen
Dendranthema

Dianthus, Pot
Eucharis*
Exacum
Freesia
Gerbera
Helianthus
Hibiscus*
Hippeastrum*
Hyacinthus
Hydrangea
Iris
Kalanchoe
Lachenalia
Lilium, Asiatic and Oriental
Lilium, Easter
Narcissus
Orchidaceae*

Ornithogalum
Pericallis
Primula
Rhododendron
Rosa
Saintpaulia*
Schlumbergera*
Sinningia
Solanum
Streptocarpus*
Tulipa
Zantedeschia

Summer/Fall
Anigozanthos
Anthurium*
Begonia, Hiemalis
Crossandra*

Cyclamen
Dendranthema
Eucharis*
Euphorbia
Exacum
Freesia
Gerbera
Kalanchoe
Orchidaceae*
Rhododendron
Rosa
Saintpaulia*
Schlumbergera*
Sinningia
Solanum
Streptocarpus*
Zantedeschia

CUT FLOWERS AND FOLIAGE

Although almost any plant can be cut and used for temporary decoration, most species grown for cut flower production have a vase life of 7 to 10 days. Cut flowers and foliage comprise the fourth largest component in the floriculture industry in North America based on sales (see list below). Cut flowers and fo-liage are produced either under protection or in the field; the latter occurs primarily in the summer in temperate climates but can be year-round in mild climates. See also Part III chapters on Field-Grown Cut Flowers and Woody Cuts, Forced.

Greenhouse
Alstroemeria
Anemone
Anthurium
Antirrhinum
Aster
Callistephus
Campanula
Convallaria
Delphinium
Dendranthema
Dianthus, Cut
Eucharis
Eustoma
Freesia
Gentiana
Gerbera
Helianthus
Hippeastrum
Hyacinthus
Iris
Liatris
Lilium, Asiatic and Oriental
Lilium, Easter
Limonium
Matthiola
Orchidaceae
Polianthes

Ranunculus
Rosa
Rumohra
Solidago
Stephanotis
Tulipa
Zantedeschia

Field
Aconitum
Anigozanthos
Anthurium
Antirrhinum
Aquilegia
Asclepias
Aster
Astilbe
Calendula
Callistephus
Campanula
Capsicum
Centaurea
Clarkia
Convallaria
Cosmos
Dahlia
Delphinium
Echinacea
Eremurus

Eustoma
Gardenia
Gentiana
Gladiolus
Gypsophila
Helianthus
Heliconia
Hydrangea
Iris
Liatris
Lilium, Asiatic and Oriental
Limonium
Matthiola
Narcissus
Ornithogalum
Paeonia
Platycodon
Polianthes
Proteaceae
Ranunculus
Rosa
Rumohra
Solidago
Strelitzia
Tagetes
Zantedeschia
Zinnia

POTTED FOLIAGE PLANTS

Potted foliage plants are intended for indoor use; however, many species are also used as outdoor ornamentals in tropical areas and as patio plants in temperate climates. Foliage plants comprise the third largest component in floriculture production in North America based on sales. Some species may flower, but they are mainly grown for their foliage. Some potted flowering plants also perform well indoors, such as African violets. See also Part III chapter on Foliage Plants.

Anthurium

Dionaea

Dracaena

Epipremnum

Eucharis

Hedera

Philodendron

Spathiphyllum

Achimenes

INTRODUCTION

Common names: achimenes, hot water plant.

Scientific name: *Achimenes* hybrids (Huxley et al., 1992).

Family and related taxa: Gesneriaceae (Dumort.). Several other members of the Gesneriaceae family are important floriculture crops including *Saintpaulia, Streptrocarpus,* and *Sinningia.*

Origin: Northern Mexico to Central America and West Indies (Huxley et al., 1992).

Uses and current status: Flowering potted plant or hanging basket. Achimenes are herbaceous flowering plants popular as potted plants.

The profuse flowers are single, five lobed, and 1 to 2.5 in. (2.5 to 6.3 cm) across. The plants are short stemmed and have three to four pubescent leaves per node (Bailey and Bailey, 1976).

CULTIVARS

Modern hybrids are no doubt derived from crosses made in the early and mid-1800s involving *A. candida* Lindl., *A. erecta* Lam., *A. glabrata* Zucc., *A. grandiflora* Scheide., *A. longiflora* DC (probably the dominant species), and *A. patens* Benth. Currently, rhizomes of hybrids with a wide range of flower colors (blue, violet, pink, rose, and red) can be obtained from Europe (Zimmer and Junker, 1985) and North America (L. Drewlow, personal communication).

PROPAGATION

Achimenes develop from short 0.5- to 1.5-in. (1.3- to 4-cm) rhizomes formed at the base of the shoots. Plants can be propagated from the rhizomes' individual triangular scales or from seed. European production is based on cuttings produced from rhizomes. First, rhizomes for the future stock plants are laid 2 in. (5 cm) apart on a porous medium, then covered with 0.5 in. (1.3 cm) of medium and kept warm and moist until shoots appear. Shoots are pinched when there are two mature leaves (Wikesjö, 1982). Soaking rhizomes in 50 ppm gibberellic acid (GA_3) or 50 ppm benzyladenine (BA) for 8 hr can improve sprouting after 2 to 3 weeks storage at 77°F (25°C) (Kuehny, 2001). The GA_3 soaks may also increase plant height and flower number.

Five to seven flushes, producing 500 to 1000 cuttings/yd² (600 to 1200 cuttings/m²), are taken from February to June (Wikesjö, 1982). Nonterminal leaf cuttings can also be used with two to three nodes per cutting (Wilkins, 1985). One to two pairs of leaves are always left on the mother plant when cuttings are removed (Wikesjö, 1982). As spring advances, cutting quality decreases; hence, three to five cuttings are rooted in a 4-in. (10-cm) pot. Propagation can occur under tents or light mist. Rooting medium should be heated from the bottom and held at 73 to 75°F (23 to 24°C) during propagation. Cuttings root rapidly in 14 to 18 days (Wikesjö, 1982).

Seeds will flower in 5 to 6 months when germinated between December and March. Because the seeds are quite small, 3,000,000/oz (106,000/g), they should be left uncovered after being spread over a well-drained medium. Seeds are germinated at 75 to 80°F (24 to 27°C) (Wiles, 1988). If kept continuously moist, the seeds germinate rapidly in 14 to 21 days. Seedlings are transplanted from seed flats to cell packs and finally to the final pot or basket (Wikesjö, 1982; Wiles, 1988).

FLOWERING CONTROL AND DORMANCY

At the end of the summer growing period and under SD, rhizomes form, plant growth slows, stems dry, and rhizomes become dormant. Depending on the cultivar, dormancy is broken either when freshly harvested rhizomes are placed in a moist medium at 85°F (29°C) or when they are stored at 50 to 60°F (10 to 16°C) for 40 days and then moved to 72°F (22°C) temperature. Pupation, which is the formation of a new and equally dormant rhizome on the top of the old rhizome at the site of the apical-most bud, occurs at 68 to 77°F (20 to 25°C) (Zimmer and Junker, 1985). Dormancy lasts 2 to 5 months when older plants or stock plants are cut back and stored at 50°F (10°C). When such plants are recycled, 2 to 4 months are required for flowering, with production beginning in February to April (Wiles, 1988). Dormancy can be induced by allowing the plants to dry (Zimmer and Junker, 1985).

Flowering will occur regardless of day length after the development of the third or fourth leaf whorl, and achimenes should be considered a DN plant. Long days, however, clearly influence growth rate, flowering, and rhizome development by providing extra energy for photosynthesis (Zimmer and Junker, 1985). The greatest influence on flower number is cultivar, not hours of irradiance; however, LD increase plant height, number of flowers, and accelerate flowering date. Rhizome number and weight are also cultivar, rather than day length, dependent (Vlahos, 1990a).

TEMPERATURE

Force newly planted rhizomes into vegetative growth at 75 to 80/60°F (24 to 27/16°C) day/night temperatures. During early growth or cutting production, lower day temperatures to 68 to 70°F (20 to 21°C) (Wikesjö, 1982). Once propagated, flower initiation and development are most rapid at 68°F (20°C) nights and slower at 59 or 77°F (15 or 25°C). The number of flowers and plant quality are dependent on the number of leaves; vegetative growth was optimal at 68°F (20°C) nights (Wikesjö, 1982; Zimmer and Junker, 1985). An ideal day temperature ranges from 70 to 90°F (21 to 32°C) and night temperature from 65 to 70°F (18 to 21°C) (Wiles, 1988).

Vlahos et al. (1992) reported that a higher constant temperature of 77°F versus 63°F (25°C versus 17°C) produced a taller plant with more nodes and, in some cases, more flowers; flowering was also quite rapid. However, axillary shoot number was higher at 63°F (17°C). Rhizome dry weight was highest at 70°F versus 63°F or 77°F (21°C versus 17°C or 25°C) (Vlahos, 1990b).

LIGHT

Achimenes can be grown in full sun during the winter or in partial shade during the summer. Full summer sun can burn the leaves; the upper limit is 5000 fc (1000 $\mu mol \cdot m^{-2} \cdot s^{-1}$) (Wikesjö, 1982; Wiles, 1988). Stock plants should be grown under LD (Wikesjö, 1982). Plants had greater dry weight of both shoots and rhizomes at an irradiance level of 800 fc (160 $\mu mol \cdot m^{-2} \cdot s^{-1}$) as compared to 410 or 230 fc (82 or 46 $\mu mol \cdot m^{-2} \cdot s^{-1}$) when grown at 70°F (21°C) for 16 hr (Vlahos, 1989). Continuous (24-hr) light, however, is detrimental for growth (Vlahos, 1990b).

WATER

Warm water of 70 to 75°F (21 to 24°C) should be used to irrigate plants (Wikesjö, 1982). Keep plants uniformly moist, but do not overwater (Post, 1949).

CARBON DIOXIDE

No information available.

NUTRITION

Fertilizer rate should be less than 200 ppm N from a 20–20–20 fertilizer (Wikesjö, 1982; Wiles, 1988).

MEDIA

A porous medium such as 1 soil:1 sand:1 peat (by volume) should be used during propagation and production (Post, 1949). In Europe plants are grown in amended peat moss.

HEIGHT CONTROL

Cultivar-dependent plant growth regulators can be used. Both B-Nine (daminozide) at 5000 to 7500 ppm and Cycocel (chlormequat) at 3000 to 5000 ppm are effective. B-Nine can delay flowering and reduce flower size; Cycocel can cause leaf chlorosis (Wikesjö, 1982; Wilkins, 1985). Two spray applications of 100 ppm Bonzi (paclobutrazol) or two spray applications of 50 pm A-Rest (ancymidol) reduced stem elongation by 67 and 48%, respectively (Vlahos and Brascamp, 1989). However, Bonzi delayed flowering and reduced flower number. Adriansen (1985) also noted that A-Rest is effective on achimenes.

SPACING

Rhizomes for stock plants are planted into large pots or into trays with 2-in. (5-cm) spacing if rows are used. Rhizomes are placed end on end and 250 to 300 can be planted in a 16- × 24-in. (40- × 60-cm) tray. Rhizomes are covered with 0.5 in. (1.3 cm) of medium.

Production is most frequently in 4-in. (10-cm) pots. Propagation is pot-to-pot; final spacing is 7 × 7 in. (18 × 18 cm) when appropriate. Specimen plants in hanging baskets or 6-in. (15-cm) pots are also in demand (Wikesjö, 1982; Wilkins, 1985).

PINCHING AND DISBUDDING

None required.

SUPPORT

None required.

SCHEDULE AND TIMING

When rhizomes are planted in January, 2 to 3 weeks are required for new shoots to develop from the dormant rhizomes; another 2 to 3 weeks are required for cutting production to begin in February. Generally, five to seven cycles of cutting propagation can occur. Be certain to leave two nodes behind on the stock plant shoots when cuttings are removed. Cuttings root in 14 to 18 days. During early spring 8 to 9 additional weeks are required to produce a marketable plant by April; later only 7 to 8 weeks are needed (Wikesjö, 1982).

INSECTS

Whitefly outbreaks can occur (Wiles, 1988).

DISEASES

Botrytis can be a problem when ventilation is not adequate. Tobacco mosaic virus has also been noted (Horst, 1990).

PHYSIOLOGICAL DISORDERS

None are known.

POSTHARVEST

Achimenes are tropical plants. Do not store rhizomes or expose plants to temperatures below 41°F (5°C) (Zimmer and Junker, 1985). Chilling damage can occur to the rhizomes and plants at 36 to 41°F (2 to 5°C) (Zimmer and Junker, 1985).

Achimenes are highly sensitive to ethylene; flowers and flower buds abscise within 24 hours when exposed to 1 to 3 ppm. A 0.3 to 0.5 mM spray of silver thiosulfate (STS) was effective in reducing ethylene effects and increasing longevity. Plants should be shipped at the beginning of flowering (Nowak and Rudnicki, 1990).

KEY POINTS

- Achimenes is used as a potted flowering plant or hanging basket plant.
- Plants are propagated by seed or by cuttings from vegetative shoots, which emerge from a rhizome.
- Under SD, plants go dormant and form a rhizome.
- Dormant rhizomes are forced into vegetative growth at 75 to 80/60°F (24 to 27/16°C) day/night temperatures.
- Once propagated, grow plants at 70 to 90/68°F (21 to 32/20°C) day/night temperatures.
- Height is controlled by B-Nine (daminozide), Cycocel (chlormequat), Bonzi (paclobutrazol), or A-Rest (ancymidol).
- Plants are injured if temperatures go below 41°F (5°C).
- Use warm water [70 to 75°F (21 to 24°C)] for irrigation.
- Do not expose plants to ethylene.

BIBLIOGRAPHY

Adriansen, E. 1985. Kemisk vaekstregulering, pp. 142–162 in *Potteplanter I—Produktion, Metoder, Midler,* O.V. Christensen, A. Klougart, I.S. Pedersen, and K. Wikesjö, editors. Gartner-INFO, København, Denmark. (in Danish)

Bailey, L.H., and E.Z. Bailey. 1976. *Achimenes,* pp. 18–19 in *Hortus Third: A Concise Dictionary of Plants Cultivated in the United States and Canada.* Macmillan, New York.

Horst, R.K. 1990. Achimenes, p. 520 in *Westcott's Plant Disease Handbook,* 5th ed. Van Nostrand Reinhold, New York.

Huxley, A., M. Griffiths, and M. Levy. 1992. *Achimenes,* pp. 41–42 in *The New Royal Horticultural Society Dictionary of Gardening,* vol. 1. Stockton Press, New York.

Kuehny, J. 2001. Gloxinias and other gesneriads, pp. 93–95 in *Tips on Regulating Growth of Floriculture Crops,* M.L. Gaston, L.A. Kunkle, P.S. Konjoian, and M.F. Wilt, editors. Ohio Florists' Association Services, Columbus, Ohio.

Nowak, J., and R.M. Rudnicki. 1990. *Postharvest Handling and Storage of Cut Flowers, Florist Greens and Potted Plants,* Timber Press, Portland, Oregon.

Post, K. 1949. *Achimenes,* pp. 317–318 in *Florist Crop Production and Marketing.* Orange Judd Publishing, New York.

Vlahos, J.C. 1989. Effects of GA_3, BA and NAA on dry matter partitioning and rhizome development in two cultivars of *Achimenes longiflora* DC. under three levels of irradiance. *Acta Horticulturae* 251:79–92.

Vlahos, J.C. 1990a. Daylength influences growth and development of *Achimenes* cultivars. *HortScience* 25:1595–1596.

Vlahos, J.C. 1990b. Temperature and irradiance influence growth and development of three cultivars of *Achimenes. HortScience* 25:1597–1598.

Vlahos, J.C., and W. Brascamp. 1989. The influence of the growth retardants paclobutrazol, ancymidol and S-3307 on growth and development of *Achimenes longiflora* DC. 'Viola Michelssen' grown under two light regimes. *Acta Horticulturae* 251:75–77.

Vlahos, J.C., G.F.P. Martakis, and E. Heuvelink. 1992. Daylength, light quality, and temperature influence growth and development of *Achimenes. HortScience* 27:1269–1271.

Wikesjö, K. 1982. Growing hybrid *Achimenes* as a pot plant. *Florists' Review* 168(4357):34, 120, 122.

Wiles, L.S. 1988. Cultural notes—*Achimenes. Grower Talks* 15(12):12.

Wilkins, H.F. 1985. Asexually propagated bedding plants, pp. 471–502 in *Bedding Plants III,* 3rd ed., J.W. Mastalerz and E.J. Holcomb, editors. Pennsylvania Flower Growers, University Park, Pennsylvania.

Zimmer, K., and K. Junker. 1985. *Achimenes,* pp. 391–392 in *Handbook of Flowering,* vol. I, A.H. Halevy, editor. CRC Press, Boca Raton, Florida.

Aconitum

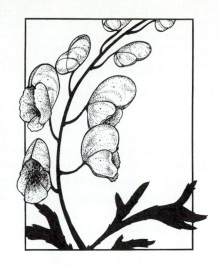

INTRODUCTION

Common names: aconitum, monkshood, helmet-flower, turk's cap.

Scientific name: *Aconitum napellus* L. (Huxley et al., 1992). Other *Aconitum* species are also used occasionally such as *A. ×cammarum* L., *A. carmichaelii* Debeaux., *A. henryi* Pritz., and *A. orientale* Mill. (Armitage and Laushman, 2003).

Family and related taxa: Ranunculaceae Juss. *Aconitum napellus* is one of more than 100 species within the genus. A large and important family in floriculture; other widely used genera include *Anemone, Aquilegia, Clematis, Consolida, Delphinium,* and *Ranunculus.*

Origin: Europe, Asia, and America (Huxley et al., 1992).

Uses and current status: Traditionally used in perennial borders and naturalized areas (Zones 3 to 8); *A. napellus* is also grown as a long-lasting cut flower.

This summer flowering perennial, 36 to 40 in. (90 to 102 cm) tall, is erect and slender. The inflorescence is a raceme and the individual flowers are oppressed by short pedicels to the main stem. The dark blue or violet flowers can be 1.5 in. (4 cm) long and 0.75 in. (2 cm) wide. The upper petaloid sepals form a "hood" or "helmet." The 2- to 4-in.- (5- to 10-cm)-wide leaves are alternate, trilobed with lateral segments (Armitage, 1989; Bailey, 1942; Bailey and Bailey, 1976).

The roots are tuberous (*napellus* means "little turnip"). Aconitum is considered a lethal herb and is reported to have been used to poison arrow tips in ancient China and to poison wolves (Nau, 1996). The Greek word *akoniton* means "dart" (Bailey, 1942; Bailey and Bailey, 1976).

CULTIVARS

Various species and cultivars differ in their date of flower during the growing season, height, and quality (Anonymous, 1981). Pink and white flowering cultivars are available.

PROPAGATION

Aconitum form tubers, and the most common form of propagation is by division (Armitage, 1989). Successive generations of tubers are produced annually. Tubers weighing more than 0.35 oz (10 g) should be used for cut flower production (Luria et al., 1992). Tubers less than this weight should be replanted to increase in size for use the following year.

To grow aconitum from seed, collect the seed while fresh and immediately sow, because the seed develop a deep dormancy if allowed to fully ripen. Armitage and Laushman (2003) recommend placing seed flats at 65 to 70°F (18 to 21°C) for 2 to 4 weeks, followed by 6 to 8 weeks of 20 to 25°F (−7 to −4°C). Do not let media temperatures drop below 16°F (−9°C). After germination, grow at 45 to 55°F (7 to 13°C) until ready to transplant. Two to 3 years are required from seed to flower. Luria (1994) reported optimal germination occurred after a 50-ppm gibberellin treatment. Plants can be *in vitro* propagated (Kochba et al., 1997).

FLOWERING CONTROL AND DORMANCY

When tuberous roots were cold treated at 36°F (2°C) for 10 weeks and thereafter at 28°F (−2°C) for an additional 0, 2, 8, or 15 weeks (for a sum of 10, 12, 18, or 25 weeks), plants flowered in 110, 92, 75, or 68 days, respectively (Leeuwen, 1980). Increasing storage increased inflorescence length and decreased the number of flower buds per inflorescence. Inflorescence weight increased with increasing storage up to 18 weeks, but was decreased by the 25-week treatment. When tubers were stored for 16 weeks at 28, 32, or 36°F (−2, 0, or 2°C), all plants flowered in 86 days. The number of flowering stems produced per tuber was greatest when stored at 28°F (−2°C) compared with 32 or 36°F (0 to 2°C). Tubers can be stored for long durations at 28°F (−2°C) (Leeuwen, 1980).

Israeli workers (Luria et al., 1992; 1997) have reported that GA_3 tuber treatments can substitute for cold to enhance shoot emergence. After emergence, a single GA_3 spray resulted in increased flower yields, stem lengths, and number of daughter tubers. For maximum tuber weight and number, a 16-hr photoperiod was superior compared with an 8-hr photoperiod at 63/54°F (17/12°C) day/night temperatures.

TEMPERATURE

Aconitum prefer cool growing temperatures, both in the greenhouse and outdoors; otherwise, the growth will be weak. Armitage (1989) reports that night temperatures below 70°F (21°C) are essential for quality in the garden environment (see Flowering Control and Dormancy section on previous page). Aconitum are forced at 55°F (13°C) night temperature in greenhouses in the Netherlands (van der Krogt, 1979). Luria et al. (1992; 1997) suggested day temperatures of 63 to 72°F (17 to 22°C).

LIGHT

Aconitum should be grown in full sun in the garden, field, or in the greenhouse. Supplemental photosynthetic lighting under greenhouse conditions in the early spring in the Netherlands did not hasten date of flower nor significantly increase the number of flowering stems; however, stem length was increased (Leeuwen, 1980).

WATER

Keep the medium moist. Commencing 4 weeks after the flowers are harvested, water can be withdrawn so that the plants can dry down and tubers can be harvested and recycled (Luria, 1994). Sufficient foliage must remain for regrowth of tubers.

CARBON DIOXIDE

No information was available on appropriate CO_2 levels when plants are forced in the greenhouse during the winter.

NUTRITION

Prior to planting, incorporate compost to a depth of 0.75 to 1.13 in. (2 to 3 cm). Once growth commenced Luria (1994) used a 7–3–7 fertilizer at 100 ppm N.

MEDIA

A moist, well-drained medium is required. Cover the tubers with 0.75 to 1.13 in. (2 to 3 cm) of soil (Luria, 1994).

HEIGHT CONTROL

None required; grown as a cut flower.

SPACING

For commercial cut flower production in the greenhouse, tubers are planted 3.7 to 4.6/ft² (40 to 50/m²) for 1-year plantings and 5.6 to 7.4/ft² (60 to 80/m²) for 2-year plantings. Outdoors, plants are generally long lived and should be spaced from 18 × 18 to 24 × 24 in. (45 × 45 to 60 × 60 cm) apart in field beds (Armitage and Laushman, 2003). In the home garden, space 12 to 18 in. (30 to 45 cm) apart.

PINCHING AND DISBUDDING

None required.

SUPPORT

Two layers of netting are required to support flowering stems.

SCHEDULE AND TIMING

Total production time requires about 5 to 6 months from dormant tubers (Table II-1 Aconitum). This plant is also commonly grown outdoors under light shade in coastal California from successive plantings of tubers; cold stored at 28°F (−22°C).

TABLE II-I ACONITUM

Sample schedule for forcing *Aconitum* from dormant tubers. Adapted from Luria (1994) and Leeuwen (1980).

Cultural Step	Production Time (weeks)	Temperature °F (°C)
Cold storage		
	10	36 (2)
Cold storage		
	8	28 (−2)
Plant		
	6	Day: 63–72 (17–22) Night: 55 (13)
Flowering		
Total	24	

INSECTS

Aphids and thrips can occur.

DISEASES

Crown rot (*Sclerotinia sclerotiorum* or *S. rolfsii*), mildew (*Plasmopara pygmaea* or *Erysiphe polygoni*), and wilt (*Verticillium albo-atrum* or *Cephalosporium*) can frequently occur and constant care is needed to prevent problems (Horst, 1990). Crown rot produces yellow leaves, wilting, basal stem rot, and black streaks in the stem and root tissue; wilt is noted as green-yellow leaves (often on one side of the plant only) progressing to leaf dieback and black to brown discoloration in the cut stem (Armitage and Laushman, 2003). Other noted diseases include bacterial leaf spot (*Pseudomonas delphinii*), root rot (*Phymatotrichum omnivorum*), rust (*Puccinia recondita* or *Uromyces lycoctoni*), leaf and stem smut (*Urocystis carcinodes* or *U. sorosporioides*), and mosaic virus (Armitage and Laushman, 2003; Horst, 1990). Tubers cannot be hot water treated for pest control.

PHYSIOLOGICAL DISORDERS

Flower abortion occurs when light levels are lower during the winter forcing, particularly if the plant density is high (Luria, 1994).

POSTHARVEST

Stems should be harvested when one to three flowers are open on the raceme (Armitage and Laushman, 2003; Luria, 1994). Flowers are long lasting and frequently no treatments are given (Anonymous, 1981; Barendse, 1979). However, several floral preservatives have been tested and give favorable results (Nowak and Rudnicki, 1990). Flowers should last 7 to 10 days in preservatives (Armitage and Laushman, 2003). Store at temperatures between 33 and 45°F (1 and 7°C). Although temperatures less than 45°F (7°C) have been reported to cause blackening of the flowers due to chilling damage, growers often store at 33 to 41°F (1 to 5°C) with no problems (Armitage and Laushman, 2003).

Flowers are sensitive to ethylene (Barendse, 1979; Nowak and Rudnicki, 1990) and Luria (1994) reports that senescing flowers produce ethylene. Between 0.25 to 0.50 mM of silver thiosulfate (STS) commercial preservative was found to increase vase life by 2.0 to 2.5 days. However, Luria (1994) used 0.75 mM STS, 2% sucrose, and a biocide as a 12-hr pulse to improve vase life. Water uptake of the cut flowers decreases over time and there is little difference in water loss regardless if cut stems are held in light, dark, or light–dark sequences, or held in solutions containing biocides or wetting agents (Kalhman, 1987; Sylsema-Kalhman, 1987, 1988). Interestingly, plants flowering in August lasted an average of 2 days longer than those flowering in June.

KEY POINTS

- This cut flower is grown from a tuber or from seed.
- The plant is reported to be poisonous.
- Tubers require a minimum cold treatment of 36°F (2°C) for 10 weeks.
- For rapid flowering add 8 weeks of 28°F (−2°C) to the above treatment.
- Grow plants at cool day/night temperatures of 63 to 72/55°F (17 to 22/13°C).
- Plants are susceptible to crown and root rot; do not overwater.
- Postharvest life of cut stems is improved with floral preservatives.

BIBLIOGRAPHY

Anonymous. 1981. *Annual Report for 1981 of the Technical University of Weihenstephan. Gartenbauverlag*, pp. 67–68. (in German)

Armitage, A. 1989. *Aconitum*, pp. 12–15 in *Herbaceous Perennial Plants*. Varsity Press, Athens, Georgia.

Armitage, A., and Laushman. 2003. *Aconitum carmichaelii*, pp. 52–57 in *Specialty Cut Flowers*, 2nd ed. Timber Press, Portland, Oregon.

Bailey, L.H. 1942. *Aconitum*, pp. 201–210 in *The Standard Cyclopedia of Horticulture*. Macmillan, New York.

Bailey, L.H., and E.Z. Bailey. 1976. *Aconitum*, pp. 20–22 in *Hortus Third: A Concise Dictionary of Plants Cultivated in the United States and Canada*. Macmillan, New York.

Barendse, L.V.J. 1979. *More Attention to Keeping Quality in Summer Flowers*, pp. 20, 34–35, 37. Proefstation voor de Bloemisterij, Aalsmeer, The Netherlands. (in Dutch)

Horst, R.K. 1990. Monkshood, Aconite, p. 731 in *Westcott's Plant Disease Handbook*, 5th ed. Van Nostrand Reinhold, New York.

Huxley, A., M. Griffiths, and M. Levy. 1992. *Aconitum*, pp. 45–50 in *The New Royal Horticultural Society Dictionary of Gardening*, vol. 1. Stockton Press, New York.

Kalhman, E.Ch. 1987. *Aconitum*, pp. 7–10 in *Internal Report No. 47. Aalsmeer Proefstation*, The Netherlands. (in Dutch)

Kochba, M., V. Gaba, A. Nissim, and A.A. Watad. 1997. An efficient *in vitro* clonal propagation method for *Aconitum napellus*. *Acta Horticulturae* 430:281–287.

Leeuwen, V.C. 1980. Aconitum, pp. 25–27 in *Annual Report for 1980 of the Aalsmeer Proefstation*, The Netherlands. (in Dutch)

Luria, G. 1994. *Aconitum:* Effects of Environmental Conditions on Growth, Flowering and Tub Pro-duction. MS thesis, Hebrew University of Jerusalem, Rehevat, Israel.

Luria, G., A. Borochov, and A.A. Watad. 1992. *Aconitum:* Effect of tuber size, day length and GA$_3$ on growth, flowering and tuber production. *Acta Horticulturae* 325:113–117. (Actual article lists primary author as Lurie)

Luria, G., A. Borochov, and A.A. Watad. 1997. *Aconitum:* Effects of environmental conditions on growth, flowering and tuber production. *Acta Horticulturae* 430:233–240.

Nau, J. 1996. *Aconitum napellus*, pp. 44–46 in *Ball Perennial Manual: Propagation and Production*. Ball Publishing, Batavia, Illinois.

Nowak, J., and R. Rudnicki. 1990. *Postharvest Handling and Storage of Cut Flowers, Florist Greens and Potted Plants*. Timber Press, Portland, Oregon.

Sylsema-Kalhman, E.Ch. 1987. *Aconitum*, pp. 2–3 in *Internal Report No. 3002-3 Exp. Aalsmeer Proefstation*, The Netherlands. (in Dutch)

Sylsema-Kalhman, E.Ch. 1988. *Aconitum*, pp. 5–7 in *Internal Report No. 52. Aalsmeer Proefstation*, The Netherlands. (in Dutch)

van der Krogt, Th.M. 1979. *Aconitum*, pp. 21–23 in *Annual Report for 1979 of the Aalsmeer Proefstation*, The Netherlands. (in Dutch)

Alstroemeria

INTRODUCTION

Common names: alstroemeria, Peruvian lily, Inca lily.

Scientific name: *Alstroemeria* L. hybrids (Huxley et al., 1992).

Family and related taxa: Liliaceae Juss. At least 50 species exist, of which many have been used to produce the present-day hybrids and cultivars (Bailey and Bailey, 1976; Huxley et al., 1992). *Alstroemeria aurea* Graham, *A. haemantha* Ruiz & Pav., *A. ligtu* L., *A. pelegrina*, *A. pulcria* Sims, and *A. violocea* Philippi. have contributed most to the modern commercial hybrids (Healy and Wilkins, 1985; Heins and Wilkins, 1979; Robinson, 1963; Wilkins et al., 1980). The lily family is quite large and contains many commercially important floriculture crops including *Allium*, *Brodiaea*, *Convallaria*, *Eremurus*, *Hyacinthus*, *Lachenalia*, *Lilium*, *Muscari*, *Ornithogalum*, and *Tulipa*.

Origin: South America (Argentina, Chile, Brazil, Peru, Ecuador, Paraguay, and Bolivia). Chile appears to be the center of distribution. Species can be found from dry, warm desert-like regions to moist, cool, high-elevation habitats and from 26° to 40° south latitude. Such diversity of habitats will surely contribute new traits to future hybrids and cultivars (Bridgen, 1993; Tombolata and Matthes, 1998).

Uses and current status: Alstroemeria is a recent introduction into the world's floriculture scene and has become a major cut flower. It is also used as a potted flowering plant for the home

FIGURE II-I ALSTROEMERIA *Alstroemeria* inflorescence.

and as an herbaceous landscape plant in mild climates (Zones 7 to 9). However, plants have routinely survived outdoors in the Netherlands and in Maryland (Zone 6) in the United States. Cultivars are typically patented, and growers must sign agreements. Division is not legal unless authorized.

Flowers are simple or compound. The inflorescence is called a cyme and branches sympodially (Fig. II-1 Alstroemeria). Flower colors range from white to dark yellows to various pinks, violets, purples, and reds. Yellow throats and black dots at the base of the petals and throats are a trademark of alstroemeria (Healy and Wilkins, 1985; Heins and Wilkins, 1979; Robinson, 1963). However, Japanese breeders have developed cultivars with unmarked flowers lacking contrasting throats or spots.

The plants have leaves with parallel veins that twist (180°) close to where the blade joins the stems. Stomates, which are on the true upper surface, are now consequently on the underleaf surface (Healy and Wilkins, 1985; Heins and Wilkins, 1979).

CULTIVARS

The development of new commercial cultivars is common and is occurring at a rapid rate all over the world. The major thrust in breeding is the development of new cultivars that will flower during periods of high temperatures and maintain flower production during the winter under low light stress (Baeure and Bakken, 1997). The development of genetically

dwarf plants for pot plant culture is also being researched (Healy and Klick, 1993a).

PROPAGATION

Alstroemeria grow from seed with ease (King and Bridgen, 1990; Thompson et al., 1979). However, the most common form of propagation for cut flower production is by rhizome division. Rhizomes with three or more vegetative shoots are most commonly sold to growers in 2- to 4-in.- (5- to 10-cm)-deep cells or pots. Plants can be tissue cultured with ease for use in both cut and potted plants, and the method is used to quickly increase new cultivars (Bridgen, 1993; Ziv et al., 1973). Uniform dwarf plants for pot culture are also available from seed, vegetative propagation, or tissue culture (Healy and Klick, 1993a). *In vitro* propagation techniques have been well documented by several researchers (Bond and Alderson, 1993; Lin et al., 1998; Schaik et al., 1996).

All growth activity is subterranean until the new shoots emerge. Aerial shoots develop from a sympodially branching rhizome (Fig. II-2 Alstroemeria). New aerial shoots can also arise from axillary buds at the base of these shoots. These buds can develop into rhizomes (Healy and Wilkins, 1985; Vonk Noordegraaf, 1975). Roots are fibrous, as well as fleshy, and store a tremendous amount of starch (Cox and Mac-Masters, 1947). The terminal growing point of

FIGURE II-2 ALSTROEMERIA Root and shoot system of an *Alstroemeria* plant. Note sympodially branched rhizome growing downward and large fleshy roots.

the rhizome always grows downward by a few degrees. After several years, rhizomes can grow down into a medium profile that is poorly drained, and nutritional problems can easily occur. Consequently, removal and replanting is recommended every 2 to 4 years (Healy and Wilkins, 1985; Wilkins and Heins, 1976).

FLOWERING CONTROL AND DORMANCY

Flowering is controlled by the temperature of the rhizome, which is controlled by the temperature of the medium surrounding it (Cervelli and Zizzo; 1992; Heins and Wilkins, 1979; Vonk Noordegraaf, 1975; Wilkins et al., 1980). Regardless of the air temperature, plants will flower for extended periods if the medium temperature is held at 60°F (16°C). The minimum number of weeks at an optimum temperature has been suggested to be 6 weeks at 41°F (5°C), with forcing at a continuous 55°F (13°C) (Healy and Wilkins, 1981). Another study (Healy and Wilkins, 1982) suggested that reproductive shoots are produced from 48°F (9°C) to 55°F (13°C) up to a continuous 63°F (17°C). At 70°F (21°C) rhizomes were devernalized, and only vegetative shoots were produced. More heat-tolerant cultivars are being developed for summer production (Baeure and Bakken, 1997; Healy and Wilkins, 1981, 1982; Heins and Wilkins, 1979, Vonk Noordegraaf, 1975). At this time, no one knows whether the devernalization signal is slowly accumulative over time or if the temperature must be continuously above a specific level. The same question can be asked about vernalization (Bridgen and Bartok, 1990).

TEMPERATURE

Greenhouse temperatures are maintained at a night temperature of 50 to 55°F (10 to 13°C), whereas day temperatures in the winter are 60 to 65°F (16 to 18°C). During the summer, soil mulches should be used to reduce soil temperature. Monitor soil temperatures and frequently apply short intervals of mist to allow water evaporation off the mulch, which will keep the medium cooler. Some greenhouses have used cold water circulating in pipes buried in their beds in an effort to maintain 63°F (17°C) for rhizome growth and flower production (Bridgen and Bartok, 1990; Healy and Wilkins, 1981; Wilkins and Heins, 1976). The response to temperature and light differs greatly by cultivar (Labeke and Dambre, 1993). 'King Cardinal' and 'Amanda' flower production were higher at 57°F (14°C) media temperature, whereas 'Helios' was higher with 64°F (18°C) and 'Cinderella' at 72°F (22°C) (Baeure and Bakken, 1997).

LIGHT

Photoperiodic incandescent lighting has been reported to induce earlier flowering. These effective incandescent treatments have been given either as a day continuation (natural day + day continuation = 14 or 16 hr) or as a night interruption (natural day + night interruption = 14 or 16 hr). The day continuation and night interruption durations either increase or decrease as the short days of winter lengthen or shorten. Lighting commences in late September and ends in late March. However, continued photoperiods of 14 hr or longer from April to September have resulted in diminished flower production (Powell and Bunt, 1984; Verboom, 1980). The required light intensity for these treatments is at least 3 fc (0.5 μmol $\cdot$ m^{-2} $\cdot$ s^{-1}) from incandescent lights (Healy and Wilkins, 1981, 1985; Heins and Wilkins, 1979; Vonk Noordegraaf, 1975). Cyclic lighting (10 min on, 20 min off) can be used and is equally effective as continuous lighting (Healy and Wilkins, 1981, 1982; Heins and Wilkins, 1979; Vonk Noordegraaf, 1975). Short days (8 hr) delay flowering and reduce yield (Healy et al., 1982).

Photosynthetic lighting has been reported in Minnesota to be ineffective at 45° north latitude. Here the winters are cold, and although the days are short, they are bright and sunny. In the Pacific Northwest, at 50° north latitude, high-intensity lighting has been reported to be effective. However, no low-level-intensity photoperiod treatment was used as a comparison, and this area of the world has poor winter light (Healy et al., 1982; Healy and Wilkins, 1985). In Norway, supplementary lighting of 900 fc (180 μmol $\cdot$ m^{-2} $\cdot$ s^{-1}) from high-pressure sodium lamps is used in the winter (Baeure and Bakken, 1997).

In Northern Europe, alstroemeria plants are photoperiodically lighted only for winter production. Labeke and Dambre (1993) studied the interaction of cultivar, soil cooling, and supplemental lighting in Belgium. There were varied cultivar responses to supplemental lighting, and the economics of cost versus yield must be evaluated. In Columbia, the production sites are essentially on the equator, and natural photoperiods are 12 hr ± 30 min (Healy and Wilkins, 1985; Vonk Noordegraaf, 1975; Wilkins et al., 1980).

Full light should be used for production. Shade plants only in an effort to maintain 55 to 63°F (13 to 17°C) medium temperature (Wilkins and Heins, 1976). Supplementary lighting of potted plants in low-light areas will increase flowers/plant and decrease days to flower (Bridgen, 1997). A minimum of 600 fc (120 μmol $\cdot$ m^{-2} $\cdot$ s^{-1}) for 16 hr should be used.

WATER

Alstroemeria are best grown slightly dry. Too much water will encourage root rot, which is especially true when plants are first planted. In the dense lower foliage, *Botrytis* can develop; avoid overhead watering if possible. When plants are first getting established, overwatering must be avoided until new shoots emerge (Verboom, 1980; Wilkins and Heins, 1976). Potted plants can be irrigated using a variety of automated systems.

CARBON DIOXIDE

Verboom (1980) reported that in the Netherlands supplemental CO_2 slightly increased cut stem yield. In Belgium 900 ppm CO_2 increased production and additional increases were found when supplemental CO_2 was used in combination with 200 fc (40 μmol $\cdot$ m^{-2} $\cdot$ s^{-1}) supplemental lighting (Labeke and Dambre, 1998). Significant differences occur among cultivars. Higher rates of CO_2 at 1400 to 2000 ppm may be useful when plants are growing under high light, but high light would increase greenhouse temperatures and make it difficult to maintain high CO_2 levels due to increased need for ventilation and cooling (Leonardos et al., 1994).

NUTRITION

Alstroemeria are responsive to nitrate nitrogen, which is responsible for dark-green foliage. Weekly applications of nutrients when the medium becomes dry are recommended. Generally, 200 to 280 ppm N have been used from calcium nitrate and potassium nitrate. The medium EC should be 1.3 dS $\cdot$ m^{-1} or lower (Sonneveld, 1988). Edwards and Dixon (1999) found no difference in production when the EC was varied from 1.1 to 2.1 dS $\cdot$ m^{-1}. During the winter, ammonium nitrate should be avoided or greatly reduced (Wilkins and Heins, 1976). Bik

TABLE II-I ALSTROEMERIA

Leaf nutrient content of *Alstroemeria* 'Orchid' grown at a 220 to 330 ppm N and 300 ppm K$_2$O from NH$_4$NO$_3$ and K$_2$SO$_4$, respectively (Bik and van den Berg, 1981).

Nutrient Ion	Range
Nitrogen	4.90–5.14%
Phosphorus	0.31–0.36%
Potassium	3.69–3.90%
Calcium	1.42–1.48%
Magnesium	0.44–0.62%
Iron	175–217 ppm
Manganese	195 ppm
Zinc	84–101 ppm
Copper	6.1–7.1 ppm
Boron	0.6–27.9 ppm

and van den Berg (1981) felt an N:K ratio of 1:1 to 1:4 was proper at pH 5.5. Smith et al. (1998) stated that tissue N should be close to 4.5%, whereas Bik and van den Berg (1981) recommended a slightly higher N level of 4.90 to 5.14% (Table II-1 Alstroemeria). Routine soil and tissue testing regimes should be followed. See Table 6-4 in Chapter 6, Nutrition, for additional foliar nutrient levels.

MEDIA

Alstroemeria rhizomes should be planted in a loose, well-drained medium for both cut and potted flowering plant production. For cut flower production, the parent soil found in beds is amended with peat, perlite, sand, calcine clays, and a variety of organic and inorganic amendments. Beds are normally prepared 12 to 16 in. (30 to 40 cm) or greater in depth because the rhizome grows downward at an ever-increasing angle (Healy and Wilkins, 1985; Verboom, 1980; Wilkins and Heins, 1976).

HEIGHT CONTROL

No height control is needed for cut flowers. While Bridgen (1993) reports that various plant growth regulators currently in use give inconsistent results, Healy and Klick (1993b) stated that one Bonzi spray of 10 to 20 ppm was effective. Genetic dwarfs are available for potted flowering plants.

SPACING

For cut flower production, plants are spaced 5 to 24 in. (12.5 to 60 cm) apart on center, depending on the cultivar and the expected amount of time that the plants are to remain in the production beds. Rhizomes with shoots should not be planted deeper than they are growing in the original containers.

PINCHING AND DISBUDDING

Generally, pinching and disbudding are not needed. However, shoot removal is required because a majority of the stems that emerge are vegetative. They should be thought of as a source of carbohydrates from photosynthesis. Because of branched growth and the presence of an axillary bud on the rhizome in the axil of each stem, stems must be routinely removed to maintain production and to stimulate axillary shoot elongation. Monthly removal or thinning is adequate. Older shoots that are no longer unfolding leaves and weak short stems that are no longer dark green are removed (Wilkins and Heins, 1976).

Cycles of excessively tall, over 5 ft (1.5 m), and thin shoots develop, depending on the cultivar. These cycles are followed by flushes of shoots that are too short for commercial sale. It is recommended that very tall shoots be cut to the appropriate marketing length and the remaining stem left intact for carbohydrate synthesis to help prevent the next cycle of short stems. With short stems, sacrifice the flower head, again leaving the shoot for carbohydrate synthesis. In both cases, remove the stem only when leaf senescence is observed or during the next routine thinning process. Thinning is perhaps the most expensive routine maintenance activity for the crop (Wilkins and Heins, 1976).

Flower stem harvest and thinning is unusual in that stems are not cut; they are instead gently pulled loose from the rhizome. There is a natural abscission layer at the attachment of the shoot to the rhizome (Healy and Wilkins, 1985; Wilkins and Heins, 1976).

For potted plants, 15 to 25% of vegetative shoots should be removed during the winter until flowering begins (Bridgen, 1997). Remove dead or unsightly shoots every 2 to 3 weeks. As with cut flowers, shoots should be pulled, not cut. Care should be taken with young plants not to pull the plant out of the pot.

SUPPORT

A minimum of three and preferably four layers of support are needed for cut flower production, depending on the cultivar. Place supports over the beds at the time of planting.

SCHEDULE AND TIMING

With little information on precision timing, Powell and Bunt (1984) concluded that growth, flower induction, and development are complex and cannot be predicted because of vast differences between cultivars. Some cultivars can be planted any month of the year and will produce flowers year-round as long as soil temperatures do not become excessive.

CUT FLOWERS

Plants can be planted in the spring (February to May), summer (June to July), or fall (September). The date selected will depend on the cultivar, future production cycle, and location in the world. Many producers plant young plants in late summer or early autumn after the major spring and summer production demand has declined. When lighting is used, these plants will commence flowering in late winter to early spring. Most varieties have production peaks in March to May or April to June. Within these two groups, some producers have a good to very modest return flowering 4 months later in the autumn and winter.

POTTED PLANTS

Potted plant production is similar in all cultural aspects to cut flower production. The dwarf cultivars are grown in standard 6- to 7-in. (15- to 18-cm) pots to allow sufficient room for large root systems. Plugs are available from September until March or April. Plants flower from 90 to 120 days after planting as the season advances from winter to spring. These plants are not homozygous, but are generally uniform.

INSECTS

Alstroemeria have few serious insects, but when they are observed, proper chemical treatment is required. Aphids are a rare occurrence. Slugs can be a problem if the lower canopy is not kept clean and open. Thrips are a serious threat, not only to flower quality, but also to plant health because of tomato spotted wilt virus (Bridgen, 1993). Whiteflies, two-spotted mites, and harlequin bug have been reported (Dreistadt, 2001).

DISEASES

Alstroemeria are remarkably free of disease. Routinely drenching the soil with fungicides controls the water mold fungi, such as *Pythium*, and soilborne organisms. If canopies become too thick, thereby reducing air movement and drying, *Botrytis* can become a problem, with new shoots rotting as they emerge. Shoot thinning is required to reduce this problem.

Alstroemeria mosaic virus can be a serious issue (Blank et al., 1994). Tomato spotted wilt virus can also be a problem (Dreistadt, 2001). Phytoplasmas and potyviruses have also been reported (Bertaccini et al., 1996; Bouwen and Vlugt, 1996). Suspect plants must be destroyed immediately (Bridgen, 1993; Wilkins and Heins, 1976).

PHYSIOLOGICAL DISORDERS

Flower abortion can occur when light levels are too low. Leaf scorch from fluoride contaminates in super phosphate or perlite can develop (Verboom, 1980; Wilkins and Heins, 1976).

POSTHARVEST

Alstroemeria as cut flowers have two basic problems: (1) poor flower opening and petal pigment development, and (2) leaf yellowing (Dai and Paull, 1991; Hicklenton, 1991; Sacalis, 1993; Woltering and Harkema, 1981). Problems with flower opening and proper pigment development can be partially alleviated if cymes are not harvested too prematurely. They should have one or two flowers open; however, when shipping long distances, this may not be possible and stems are typically harvested when the first flower is well colored and most of the rest of the florets are showing color. The use of sucrose and 8-hydroxyquinoline citrate (8-HQC) have been reported to increase vase life (Jones and Hill, 1993; Michalczuk et al., 1992). Gibberellins, such as GA_4 or GA_7, and cytokinins such as kinetin, zeatin, or 6-benzylaminopurine (PBA), delay the onset of leaf senescence (Hicklenton, 1991; Jordi et al., 1995; Mutui et al., 2001; van Doorn et al., 1992). GA is used at 50 ppm and PBA at 50 ppm. Use of red light during transport significantly reduces the loss of chlorophyll; far-red light nullified this response (Lieburg et al., 1990).

Long-term storage of 2 weeks in water at 36 to 39°F (2 to 4°C) was reported to be successful if stems were pretreated in a silver thiosulfate (STS) and sucrose solution for 24 hr. These results have been associated with a reduction in ethylene production. The gas 1-MCP is also effective in blocking ethylene action and increasing vase life (Serek et al., 1995). Acidic water (pH 3.5) has been used as a hydrating solution (Paull, 1991; Hicklenton, 1991; Dai and Sacalis, 1993).

Potted plants should be harvested when one to two flowers are open. Stems do not elongate at 50°F (10°C) and plants can be shipped for 4 days. Plants can be shipped at 39°F (4°C) for 6 days. Under home light conditions, plants lasted 16 to 19 days. No responses were seen with STS sprays. The exclusion of hummingbirds in production should be considered because they pollinate flowers, making them rapidly senesce and contributing to potential ethylene problems. Flowers are sensitive to ethylene (Woltering and Harkema, 1981). Frequent contact with *Alstroemeria* foliage and flowers has been reported to cause dermatitis in some individuals (Christensen and Kristiansen, 1995; Sacalis, 1993).

KEY POINTS

- Alstroemeria is an important cut flower grown on every continent and a minor flowering potted plant.
- Plants are propagated by tissue culture, rhizome division, or seed.
- Flowering is mainly controlled by soil temperature; flowering is continuous when the growing point of the rhizome is at 60°F (16°C) or lower.
- Production can be year-round by cooling the medium and with newer, heat-tolerant cultivars.
- Older vegetative shoots are removed to reduce *Botrytis* problems and to allow adequate light to reach newly emerging shoots.
- Stems are pulled loose from the rhizome, not cut, when harvested.
- Postharvest life of cut stems is improved with floral preservatives.

BIBLIOGRAPHY

Baeure, O.A., and A.K. Bakken. 1997. Light intensive production of *Alstroemeria* under different combinations of air and soil temperature. *Scientia Horticulturae* 68:137–143.

Bailey, L.H., and E.Z. Bailey. 1976. *Alstroemeria*, p. 62 in *Hortus Third: A Concise Dictionary of Plants Cultivated in the United States and Canada*. Macmillan, New York.

Bertaccini, A., M. Vibio, M.G. Bellardi, and A. Danielli. 1996. Identification of phytoplasmas in alstroemeria. *Acta Horticulturae* 432:312–319.

Bik, R.A., and Th. J.M. van den Berg. 1981. Nitrogen and potassium fertilization of the *Alstroemeria* cultivars 'Orchid' and 'Carmen' grown on peat. *Acta Horticulturae* 126:287–292.

Blank, C.M. de, A. Van Zaayen, and I. Bouwen. 1994. Towards a reliable detection of alstroemeria mosaic virus. *Acta Horticulturae* 377:199–208.

Bond, S., and P.G. Alderson. 1993. The effect of explant density, temperature and light on rhizome growth *in vitro* of *Alstroemeria*. *Journal of Horticultural Science* 68:855–859.

Bouwen, I., and R.A.A. van der Vlugt. 1996. Identification and characterization of potyviruses of *Alstroemeria* spp. *Acta Horticulturae* 432:72–74.

Bridgen, M.P. 1993. *Alstroemeria*, pp. 201–209 in *The Physiology of Flowering Bulbs*, A. De Hertogh, M. Le Nard, editors. Elsevier, Amsterdam.

Bridgen, M.P. 1997. *Alstroemeria*, pp. 13–16 in *Tips on Growing Specialty Potted Plants*, M.L. Gasten, S.A. Carver, C.A. Irwin, and R.A. Larson, editors. Ohio Florists' Association, Columbus, Ohio.

Bridgen, M.P., and J. Bartok. 1990. Evaluation of a growing medium cooling system and its effects on the flowering of *Alstroemeria*. *HortScience* 25:1592–1594.

Cervelli, C., and G.V. Zizzo. 1992. Effect of rhizome low temperature treatments on stem length, number of leaves and cymes per inflorescence of generative stems of *Alstroemeria*: First results. *Acta Horticulturae* 325:217–222.

Christensen, L.P., and K. Kristiansen. 1995. Identification and quantification of the allergens (tuliposides and tulipalin a) in *Alstroemeria*. *Acta Horticulturae* 420:140–143.

Cox, M.J., and M.M. MacMasters. 1947. Starch from *Alstroemeria*. *Plant Life* 14:71–80.

Dai, J.W., and R.E. Paull. 1991. Postharvest handling of *Alstroemeria*. *HortScience* 26:314.

Dreistadt, S.H. 2001. *Integrated Pest Management for Floriculture and Nurseries*. University of California Division of Agriculture and Natural Resources Publication 3402.

Edwards, D.R., and M.A. Dixon. 1999. Investigation of nutrient fluxes and stem production under nutrient solution recycling and three levels of nutrition in *Alstroemeria*. *HortScience* 34:515. (Abstract)

Healy, W., and S. Klick. 1993a. Potting method improves flowering of alstroemeria. *Acta Horticulturae* 337:19–24.

Healy, W., and S. Klick. 1993b. Controlling shoot elongation of potted alstroemeria. *Acta Horticulturae* 337:25–29.

Healy, W.E., and H.F. Wilkins. 1981. Interaction of soil temperature, air temperature and photoperiod on growth and flowering of *Alstroemeria* 'Regina.' *HortScience* 16:459.

Healy, W.E., and H.F. Wilkins. 1982. The interaction of temperature on flowering of *Alstroemeria* 'Regina.' *Journal of the American Society for Horticultural Science* 107:248–251.

Healy, W.E., and H.F. Wilkins. 1985. *Alstroemeria*, pp. 415–424 in *Handbook of Flowering*, vol. I, A.H. Halevy, editor. CRC Press, Boca Raton, Florida.

Healy, W.E., H.F. Wilkins, and M. Celusta. 1982. The role of light quality, photoperiod, and high intensity supplemental lighting on flowering of *Alstroemeria* 'Regina.' *Journal of the American Society for Horticultural Science* 107:1046–1049.

Heins, R.D., and H.F. Wilkins. 1979. Effect of soil temperature and photoperiod on vegetative and reproductive growth of *Alstroemeria* 'Regina.' *Journal of the American Society for Horticultural Science* 104:359–365.

Hicklenton, P.R. 1991. GA_3 and benzylaminopurine delay leaf yellowing in cut *Alstroemeria* stems. *HortScience* 26:1198–1199.

Huxley, A., M. Griffiths, and M. Levy. 1992. *Alstroemeria*, p. 141 in *The New Royal Horticultural Society Dictionary of Gardening*, vol. 1. Stockton Press, New York.

Jones, R.B., and M. Hill. 1993. The effect of germicides on the longevity of cut flowers. *Journal of the American Society for Horticultural Science* 118:350–354.

Jordi, W., G.M. Stoopen, K. Kelepouris, and W.M. van der Krieken. 1995. Gibberellin-induced delay of leaf senescence of *Alstroemeria* cut flowering stems is *not* caused by an increase in the endogenous cytokinin content. *Journal of Plant Growth Regulation* 14:121–127.

King, J.J., and M.P. Bridgen. 1990. Environmental and genotypic regulation of *Alstroemeria* seed germination. *HortScience* 25:1607–1609.

Labeke, M.-C., van, and P. Dambre. 1993. Response of five *Alstroemeria* cultivars to soil cooling and supplemental lighting. *Scientia Horticulturae* 56:135–145.

Labeke, M.-C., van, and P. Dambre. 1998. Effect of supplementary lighting and CO_2 enrichment on yield and flower stem quality of *Alstroemeria* cultivars. *Scientia Horticulturae* 74:269–278.

Leonardos, E.D., M.J. Tsujita, and B. Grodzinski. 1994. Net carbon dioxide exchange rates and predicted growth patterns in *Alstroemeria* 'Jacqueline' at varying irradiances, carbon dioxide concentrations, and air temperatures. *Journal of the American Society for Horticultural Science* 119:1265–1275.

Lieburg, M.J. van, W.G. van Doorn, and H. van Gelder. 1990. Prevention of phytochrome-related postharvest loss of quality in ornamentals through red light emitted by diodes. *Acta Horticulturae* 272:347–351.

Lin, H.-S., M.J. De Jeu, and E. Jacobsen. 1998. Formation of shoots from leaf axils of *Alstroemeria:* The effect of the position on the stem. *Plant Cell, Tissue and Organ Culture* 52:165–169.

Michalczuk, B., A. Przybyla, D.M. Goszczynska, and R.M. Rudnicki. 1992. Effect of postharvest chemical treatment on longevity of different cultivars of cut *Alstroemeria* flowers. *Acta Horticulturae* 325:199–205.

Mutui, T.M., V.E. Emongor, and M.J. Hutchinson. 2001. Effect of Accel on the vase life and post harvest quality of alstroemeria (*Alstroemeria aurantiaca* L.) cut flowers. *African Journal of Science and Technology* 2:82–88.

Powell, M.C., and A.C. Bunt. 1984. Periodicity of growth in *Alstroemeria* cultivars 'Campfire,' 'Red Sunset' and 'Zebra.' *Scientia Horticulturae* 24:359–367.

Robinson, G.W. 1963. *Alstroemeria. Journal of the Royal Horticultural Society* 88:490–494.

Sacalis, J.N. 1993. *Astroemeria* hybrids, pp. 23–24 in *Cut Flowers, Prolonging Freshness,* 2nd ed., J.L. Seals, editor. Ball Publishing, Batavia, Illinois.

Schaik, C.E, van, A. Posthuma, M.J. De Jeu, and E. Jacobsen. 1996. Plant regeneration through somatic embryogenesis from callus induced on immature embryos of *Alstroemeria* spp. L. *Plant Cell Reports* 15:377–380.

Serek, M., E.C. Sisler, and M.S. Reid. 1995. Effects of 1-MCP on the vase life and ethylene response of cut flowers. *Plant Growth Regulation* 16:93–97.

Smith, M.A., G.C. Elliott, and M.P. Bridgen. 1998. Calcium and nitrogen fertilization of *Alstroemeria* for cut flower production. *HortScience* 33:55–59.

Sonneveld, C. 1988. The salt tolerance of *Alstroemeria* (*Alstroemeria* ×). *Acta Horticulturae* 228:317–326.

Thompson, P.A., P. Newman, and P.D. Keefe. 1979. Germination of species of *Alstroemeria. Gartenbauwissenschaft* 44:97–102.

Tombolato, A.F.C., and L.A.F. Matthes. 1998. Collection of *Hippeastrum* spp., *Alstroemeria* spp. and other Brazilian bulbous species. *Acta Horticulturae* 454:91–98.

van Doorn, W.G., J. Hibma, and J. de Wit. 1992. Effect of exogenous hormones on leaf yellowing in cut flower branches of *Alstroemeria pelegrina* L. *Plant Growth Regulation* 11:59–62.

Verboom, H. 1980. Alstroemeria and some other flower crops for the future. *Scientific Horticulture* 30:33–42.

Vonk Noordegraaf, C. 1975. Temperature and daylength requirements of *Alstroemeria. Acta Horticulturae* 51:267–274.

Wilkins, H.F., and R.D. Heins. 1976. Alstroemeria general culture. *Florists Review* 159(4121):30–31, 78–80.

Wilkins, H.F., W.E. Healy, and T.L. Gilbertson-Ferriss. 1980. Comparing and contrasting the control of flowering in *Alstroemeria* 'Regina,' *Freesia* ×*hybrida* and *Lilium longiflorum*, pp. 51–63 in *Petaloid Monocotyledons, Horticultural and Botanical Research*, C. Brickell, D.F. Cutler, and M. Gregory, editors. Academic Press, London.

Woltering, E.J., and H. Harkema. 1981. Ethylene damage to cut flowers. *Sprenger Institute, Wagenengen, Netherlands: Bedrijfsontwikkeling* 12:193–196.

Ziv, M., R. Kanterovitz, and A.H. Halevy. 1973. Vegetative propagation of *Alstroemeria in vitro. Scientia Horticulturae* 1:271–277.

Anemone

INTRODUCTION

Common names: anemone, blue wood anemone, Greek anemone, lily-of-the-field.

Scientific name: *Anemone coronaria* L. (Huxley et al., 1992).

Family and related taxa: Ranunculaceae Juss. There are approximately 120 perennial herbaceous anemone species. Many other *Anemone* species and hybrids are cultivated, several of which are listed in the *Uses and current status* entry below. Other important genera in this family include *Aconitum, Aquilegia, Clematis, Consolida, Delphinium,* and *Ranunculus*.

Origin: Anemone species are widely distributed in mountainous areas and in the northern temperate zone. *Anemone coronaria* is native to the Mediterranean area and is the biblical lily-of-the-field.

Uses and current status: *Anemone coronaria* is the primary species used in commerce and is used for cut flower and potted plant production. Other species can be grown for cut flowers: *A. ×fulgens* Gay. (*A. pavonina* Lam. ×*A. hortensis* L.), *A. hortensis* L., and *A. hupehensis* Lem. *Anemone blanda* Schott & Kotschy and *A. coronaria* are used for potted flowering plants (Huxley et al., 1992; Leeuwen and Dop, 1990; Meynet, 1993). *Anemone blanda* is an attractive species growing 2 to 8 in. (5 to 20 cm) tall with bright blue flowers, and is excellent for 3-in. (7.5-cm) pots (Bailey and Bailey, 1976; Leeuwen and Dop, 1990). Many species are also used as garden or landscape plants (Bailey and Bailey, 1976; Meynet, 1993).

The showy, poppylike flowers of *A. coronaria* are pink, red, scarlet, blue, and purple to white with numerous black stamens surrounded by 5, 8, or 15 sepals and no corolla (Fig. II-1 Anemone). Double and single forms are available. The leaves are divided or dissected, which is a characteristic of the Ranunculaceae family. Plants form a tuberous root that can last up to 10 years (Bailey and Bailey, 1976; Horovitz, 1985).

CULTIVARS

Most cultivars are propagated by seed from which tubers are produced for forcing (Meynet, 1993). Breeding and selection have resulted in cultivars with short juvenile periods and increased winter hardiness and heat tolerance (Horovitz, 1985).

PROPAGATION

Controlled parental lines are used to produce hybrid seed and tubers of *A. coronaria*. In areas of light frost or mild climates, such as in Israel and southern France, seedlings require two growing seasons for tubers to be of sufficient size for flower initiation and production. If grown under protection or in mild climates, seedlings grow and flower uninterrupted. Propagation by tuber division is not economically acceptable because the multiplication rate is low and disease incidence is high. However, *A. blanda* is propagated by tuber division. *In vitro* propagation is possible but not common (Meynet, 1993).

FIGURE II-I ANEMONE *Anemone* 'Jerusalem' flower.

Israeli seed lines germinate at temperature ranges between 50 and 57°F (10 and 14°C) or 59 and 70°F (15 and 21°C) (Horovitz et al., 1975). With French cultivars, seeds harvested in the fall are immediately germinated at 73°F (23°C), whereas winter and spring harvested seed should be dried first for 10 days at 54°F (12°C) for rapid germination (Meynet, 1993). 'Mona Lisa,' a popular F_1 hybrid, has 56,000 seed/oz (1975/g) and germinates in 7 to 14 days at 59°F (15°C). Germination rates and time are improved when imbibed seeds are first chilled for 2 weeks at 40°F (4°C) (Anonymous, 1985). Germinate seeds in a well-drained peat-based medium. Because anemone develop a long tap root, 4-in.- (10-cm)-deep plug trays should be used.

FLOWERING CONTROL AND DORMANCY

In nature, plants (tubers and seeds) are at rest during the hot, dry summer and become active when temperatures are cool and ample moisture is available in the autumn and winter (Meynet, 1993).

ANEMONE CORONARIA

In France, tuber storage temperature is 4 to 6 weeks at 36°F (2°C) (Maia, 1973). In Japan, 100% of the tubers had initiated flowers after being stored at 41°F (5°C) for 4 weeks and subsequently planted (Ohkawa, 1987). Ohkawa felt that 50°F (10°C) storage for 4 weeks was optimal for good flower quality and high flower production in Japan. In Florida, 7 weeks at 43°F (6°C) was optimal for high flower number (Radspinner and Sheehan, 1963).

Interestingly, Ohkawa (1987) observed that shoots emerged rapidly from hydrated tubers at 68°F (20°C) and emergence slowed as temperatures decreased; however, cold treatment was facultative for floral initiation. Further, Ohkawa felt *A. coronaria* was a facultative LD plant in Japan. With Israeli cultivars, Kadman-Zahavi et al. (1984) observed that the LD response was cultivar dependent in regard to speed of flower initiation, development, quality, and quantity. Long days hastened the onset of dormancy of flowering plants in Israel (Kadman-Zahavi et al., 1984); however, in Japan, this was not observed (Ohkawa, 1987). Ben-Had et al. (1989) found that both LD and high temperatures induced tuber dormancy.

Meynet (1993) suggested moisture stress was also a factor.

OTHER SPECIES

Little information exists on flowering control and dormancy available for other species. Corms of *A. hupehensis,* a native of China, can be cold treated at 40°F (4°C) for 6 weeks and forced at 50°F (10°C). Flower production lasts for 13 or more weeks (January to March). Stems can be 18 in. (45 cm) long (Iverson and Weiler, 1989). The potted plant *A. blanda* requires 15 to 17 weeks of 41°F (5°C) for tuber storage (P. van Leeuwen, personal communication). Flower buds will abort if stored for shorter times. Forcing should be at 54°F (12°C).

TEMPERATURE

Flower yield and quality are highest when night temperatures are 41 to 50°F (5 to 10°C) and day temperatures are 58 to 65°F (14 to 18°C) (Ohkawa, 1987). A temperature of 77°F (25°C) suppresses growth and delays flowering. Albrecht (1987) forced potted anemone plants at 54/45°F (12/7°C) day/night temperatures. Karlsson (1997) noted that flowering was fastest when plants were grown at 61°F (16°C) and 16-hr day lengths.

Mulch beds with straw to keep soil cool during the summer. Use fan and pad cooling in the greenhouse during the summer (Anonymous, 1985). Sakai (1960) and Sakai and Yoshie (1984) noted that *A. coronaria* plants are moderately cold hardy down to 26°F (−3°C), but die at 23°F (−5°C). A well-dried tuber can survive liquid N_2 for 24 hr. With *A. blanda*, a soil temperature of 16°F (−9°C) can be tolerated; plants are best grown at an air temperature of 54°F (12°C) (Meynet, 1993; P. van Leeuwen, personal communication).

LIGHT

In a greenhouse environment, use shade only if summer temperatures must be reduced. Full light intensities are used after September (Anonymous, 1985). In Georgia field production, flower yields and quality were similar, but flower stem length increased as shade was increased from 0 to 55 to 65% (Armitage, 1991).

WATER

Keep anemone plants uniformly moist, but do not overwater. Keep the foliage and growing point (crown) dry (Anonymous, 1985; Meynet, 1993) (see Diseases).

CARBON DIOXIDE

No data are available.

NUTRITION

Fertilizer low in ammonium and urea is recommended because this crop is grown under low temperatures. Using $Ca(NO_3)_2$ as the nitrogen source will encourage compact sturdy growth. A 200-ppm N regime from a 15–16–17 or 20–19–18 fertilizer is suggested. Fertilize every 10 days, and leach every third watering. However, a starter solution high in phosphorus (9–45–15) is suggested when plants are transplanted from the seed flat to the plug tray and then to the final growing environment (beds or pots) (Anonymous, 1985). Albrecht (1987) also used 200 ppm N every 2 weeks, but topdressed the pots with Osmocote (14–14–14).

Under Florida field conditions 460 lb/acre ($515 \text{ kg} \cdot \text{ha}^{-1}$) of 8–8–8 fertilizer was applied monthly during winter production (Meredith and Sheehan, 1965). In another study 5.33 lb/100 ft² (2.6 kg/10 m²) of a 9–9–9 slow-release fertilizer was optimal (Radspinner and Sheehan, 1963).

MEDIA

Never plant anemones too deep or cover the crown. Ground beds should be 24 to 32 in. (60 to 80 cm) deep and should be well prepared. Armitage and Laushman (1990) incorporated composted manure into their Georgia clay loam. For potted seedlings, a peat-based medium should be used with a pH of 6.8 to 7.0 (Anonymous, 1985; Meynet, 1993).

HEIGHT CONTROL

For cut flower production, height control is not needed. For potted plants, compact growth can be encouraged by high light, cool production temperatures, and $Ca(NO_3)_2$ as the nitrogen source. Albrecht (1987) reported that none of the plant growth regulators (used as foliar spray) reduced flower stem length. However, a 21-sec tuber dip of A-Rest (ancymidol) (100 mg a.i./L) reduced peduncle length from 8.75 in. (23 cm) to 5.25 in. (13 cm).

SPACING

When tubers were planted in beds with a 6-in. (20-cm) spacing, production was maximized when compared with 8-in. (15-cm) spacing (Meredith and Sheehan, 1965). Flower diameter or stem length was not influenced by the various spacings used. Armitage and Laushman (1990) used a planting depth three times the tuber diameter with a spacing of 10 × 6 in. (25 × 15 cm) for the 2- to 2.5-in. (5- to 6-cm) tubers. Space 7- or 8-in. (18- to 20-cm) pots 2 in. (5 cm) apart.

PINCHING AND DISBUDDING

None required.

SUPPORT

None required.

SCHEDULE AND TIMING

De Hertogh (1996) has developed greenhouse forcing guides for *A. coronaria* and *A.* ×*fulgens* as cut and potted crops (Tables II-1 and II-2 Anemone). The duration of production depends on climatic temperatures, photoperiod, and moisture (Meynet, 1993). Plants can be produced by seed or tubers. Tuber size has no influence on date of flower—it only influences flower quality and quantity. Tetraploids will flower later than diploids (Meynet, 1993). In Japan, *A. coronaria* plants had 13 to 15 individual flower stems with heights of 14 to 18 in. (40 to 50 cm) when 1-year-old tubers were planted from September 1 to 15 and flowered from early November to April (Ohkawa, 1987).

In Georgia, a November field planting date produced 10 flower stems per plant with lengths of 9.5 in. (24 cm). Harvest commenced in late February and lasted for 65 days (Armitage and Laushman, 1990). Dormant tubers can be planted from October to November. Flowering can be expected in 2 to 4 months (Albrecht, 1987; Armitage, 1991; Ohkawa, 1987; Post, 1949).

INSECTS

Aphids, whiteflies, and thrips are commonly attracted to anemones. Thrips are difficult to control and infested flowers must be harvested and destroyed (Anonymous, 1985). Foliar nematodes (*Aphelenchoides fragariae*) and greenhouse leaftier (*Udea rubigalis*) have also been reported (Dreistadt, 2001).

DISEASES

Keep water off the foliage and crown of the plant. Removing old leaves may enhance venti-

TABLE II-1 ANEMONE

Sample production schedule for cut flowers or potted flowering plants using *Anemone coronaria* tubers.

Cultural Step	Production Time (weeks)	Temperature °F (°C)	Comments
Plant dormant tubers[a]	8[b]–16[c]	Day: 58–65 (14–18) Night: 41–50 (5–10)	Climatic zone dependent, plant from October 1 on, sooner if cool
Flower production	8–16		3 to 15 flower stems/plant; producing for 2 to 4 months
Total	16–32		

[a]Tubers have been previously cooled 4 to 7 weeks at 36 to 50°F (2 to 10°C), cultivar dependent. For potted flowering plants, dip tubers in A-Rest.
[b]In Mediterranean or warmer climates.
[c]In northern or cold climates.

TABLE II-2 ANEMONE

Sample production[a] schedule for cut 'Mona Lisa' *Anemone* from seed.

Cultural Step	Production Time (weeks)	Temperature °F (°C)	Comments
Seed	2	59 (15)	Mid-March to mid-April
Germinate and grow seedlings	6–9	59 (15)	Mid-May to mid-June
Transplant to plugs and grow on	8	59 (15)	Mid-July to mid-August
Transplant plugs to beds or pots[b]	12–13	41–50 (5–10)	November to April
Flowering commences			10 to 12 stems/plants
Total	28–32		

[a]Limited to northern climates.
[b]Plugs from specialty propagators can be purchased and planted at this time.

lation and reduce *Botrytis* (Post, 1949). When stems are harvested, cut the stem as close to the crown as possible. Do not leave a stem stump to rot, which allows disease to enter into the crown of the plant. It is suggested that knives be frequently sterilized (Anonymous, 1985). *Colletotrichum acutatum* can be a problem and can be controlled by 118 to 122°F (47.5 to 50°C) hot water treatments to the tubers (Doornik, 1990; Doornik and Booden, 1990). Other reported diseases include downy mildew (*Plasmopara*), southern blight (*Sclerotium rolfsii*), cottony rot (*Sclerotinia sclerotiorum*), rust (*Puccinia* or *Tranzschelia*), leaf and stem smut (*Urocystis anemones*), and aster yellows (Dreistadt, 2001). Anemones can also be infected with tomato spotted wilt virus, which is spread by thrips (Daughtrey and Chase, 1992).

PHYSIOLOGICAL DISORDERS

If high nutrient levels are used, flower stems may crack (Anonymous, 1985). Foliar necrosis may result from iron deficiency due to high medium pH.

POSTHARVEST

Harvest when sepals have separated from the center but not yet fully opened (Armitage and Laushman, 2003). Flowers last from 3 to 10 days (Anonymous, 1985; Meynet, 1993; Nowak and Rudnicki, 1990; Sacalis, 1993). Meredith and Sheehan (1965) found no difference in postharvest quality among the various nutrient levels used.

Postharvest holding solution should contain a carbohydrate (2 to 4% sucrose), silver thiosulfate (STS), and an antimicrobial agent. Flowers are sensitive to ethylene (Woltering and van Doorn, 1988). Store cut flowers or plants at 33 to 35°F (1 to 2°C) (Nell and Reid, 2001). Long-term storage can be in dry pack. Stems should be sent to market in an upright position or a geotropic response will occur. Bending is apparently controlled by cytosolic calcium (Philosoph-Hadas et al., 1995). The ap-plication of calcium chelators (EDTA, EGTA, and CDTA) inhibited bending, while calcium chloride stimulated bending.

Tubers can be stored at 68 to 77°F (20 to 25°C) until cooling treatments or planting commences (L. Hoyer, personal communication). Marketing of potted plants may be limited by sparse or uneven flowering.

KEY POINTS

- Various species of anemone are used as cut flowers or potted plants because of their vivid blue, red, pink, and purple colors.
- Plants are propagated by tubers or by seed.
- Tubers are stored for 4 to 7 weeks at 36 to 50°F (2 to 10°C).

- Plants are grown cool at 58 to 65/41 to 50°F (14 to 18/5 to 10°C) day/night temperatures.
- Cut flowers are harvested when mature flowers have undergone one to two petal opening–closing cycles.

BIBLIOGRAPHY

Albrecht, M.L. 1987. Growth retardant use with pot-ted anemone and ranunculus. *Journal of the Amer-ican Society for Horticultural Science* 112:82–85.

Anonymous. 1985. Growing *Anemone* 'Mona Lisa' F_1 hybrid culture, in *Notes for Better Growing*. Pan American Seed Company, Elburn, Illinois.

Armitage, A.M. 1991. Shade affects yield and stem length of field-grown cut flower species. *HortScience* 26:1174–1176.

Armitage, A.M., and J.M. Laushman. 1990. Planting date, in-ground time affect cut flower of *Aci-anthera, Anemone, Allium, Brodiaea*, and *Crocos-mia. HortScience* 25:1236–1238.

Armitage, A.M., and J.M. Laushman. 2003. *Anemone coronaria*, pp. 93–99 in *Specialty Cut Flowers*, 2nd ed. Timber Press, Portland, Oregon.

Bailey, L.H., and E.Z. Bailey. 1976. *Anemone*, pp. 75–77 in *Hortus Third: A Concise Dictionary of Plants Cultivated in the United States and Canada*. Macmillan, New York.

Ben-Had, G., J. Kigel, and B. Sternitz. 1989. Photothermal effects on corm and flower devel-opment in *Anemone coronaria* L. *Scientia Horti-culturae* 40:247–258.

Daughtrey, M., and A.R. Chase. 1992. *Anemone*, p. 7 in *Ball Field Guide to Diseases of Greenhouse Or-namentals*. Ball Publishing, Geneva, Illinois.

De Hertogh, A.A. 1996. *Anemone coronaria*, pp. C17–22, D19–22; *Anemone fulgrens*, pp. D23–24, in *Holland Bulb Forcers' Guide*, 5th ed. International Flower Bulb Centre, Hillegom, The Netherlands.

Doornik, A.W. 1990. Hot-water treatment to control *Colletotricum acutatum* on corms of *Anemone coronaria. Acta Horticulturae* 266:491–493.

Doornik, A.W., and E.M.C. Booden. 1990. Decrease in viability of *Colletotricum acutatum* in corms of *Anemone coronaria* during storage. *Acta Horticul-turae* 266:505–507.

Dreistadt, S.H. 2001. *Integrated Pest Management for Floriculture and Nurseries*. University of Califor-nia Division of Agriculture and Natural Re-sources Publication 3402.

Horovitz, A. 1985. *Anemone coronaria* and related species, pp. 455–464 in *Handbook of Flowering*, vol. I, A.H. Halevy, editor. CRC Press, Boca Raton, Florida.

Horovitz, A., S. Bullowa, and M. Negri. 1975. Ger-mination characteristics in wild and cultivated *Anemone coronaria* L. *Euphytica* 24:213–220.

Huxley, A., M. Griffiths, and M. Levy. 1992. *Anemone*, pp. 169–174 in *The New Royal Horti-cultural Society Dictionary of Gardening*, vol. 1. Stockton Press, New York.

Iverson, R.R., and T.C. Weiler. 1989. Forcing the is-sue. *American Nurseryman*, April 15:95–103.

Kadman-Zahavi, A., A. Horovitz, and Y. Ozeri. 1984. Long day induces dormancy in *Anemone coro-naria* L. *Annals of Botany* 53:213–217.

Karlsson, M. 1997. Flowering response of *Anenome coronaria* to photoperiod and temperature. *HortScience* 32:466. (Abstract)

Leeuwen, van P.J., and A.J. Dop. 1990. Effects of storage, cooling and greenhouse conditions on *Anemone blanda, Fritillaria meleagris* and *Oxalis adenophylla* for use as a potplant. *Acta Horticul-turae* 266:101–107.

Maia, N. 1973. *Travaux sur Anémones Rapport d'ac-tivité de la station d'Amélioration des Plantes Flo-rales de Fréjus*, pp. 49–54. (in French)

Meredith, W.C., and T.J. Sheehan. 1965. Anemone fertilization and spacing. *Proceedings of the Florida Horticultural Society* 78:404–405.

Meynet, J. 1993. *Anemone*, pp. 211–218 in *The Physiology of Flowering Bulbs*, A. De Hertogh and M. Le Nard, editors. Elsevier, Amsterdam.

Nell, T.A., and M.S. Reid. 2001. Can't take the heat. *Floral Management* 17(10):33–34.

Nowak, J., and R.M. Rudnicki. 1990. *Postharvest Handling and Storage of Cut Flowers, Florist Greens and Potted Plants.* Timber Press, Portland, Oregon.

Ohkawa, K. 1987. Growth and flowering of *Anemone coronaria* L. 'de Caen'. *Acta Horticulturae* 205:159–168.

Philosoph-Hadas, S., S. Meir, I. Rosenberger, and A.H. Halevy. 1995. Control and regulation of the gravitropic response of cut flowering stems during storage and horizontal transport. *Acta Horticulturae* 405:343–350.

Post, K. 1949. *Anemone coronaria*, pp. 321–324 in *Florist Crop Production and Marketing.* Orange Judd Publishing, New York.

Radspinner, A.L., and T.J. Sheehan. 1963. Effects of fertilization and storage treatments on growth and flowering of Wacabri anemones. *Proceedings of the Florida Horticultural Society* 76:428–531.

Sacalis, J.M. 1993. *Anemone* hybrids, pp. 25–26 in *Cut Flowers, Prolonging Freshness*, 2nd ed., J.L. Seals, editor. Ball Publishing, Batavia, Illinois.

Sakai, A. 1960. The frost-hardiness of bulbs and tubers. *Journal of the Horticultural Association of Japan* 29:233–238. (in Japanese, English summary)

Sakai, A., and F. Yoshie. 1984. Freezing tolerance of ornamental bulbs and corms. *Journal of the Japanese Society of Horticultural Science* 52:445–449. (in Japanese, English summary)

Woltering, E.J., and W.G. van Doorn. 1988. Role of ethylene in senescence of petals–morphological and taxonomical relationships. *Journal of Experimental Botany* 39:1605–1616.

Anigozanthos

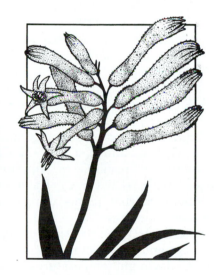

INTRODUCTION

Common name: kangaroo-paw.

Scientific name: *Anigozanthos* (Labill.) hybrids (Huxley et al., 1992).

Family and related taxa: Haemodoraceae R. Br. *Anigozanthos* is the most commercially important member of this family.

Origin: Australia.

Uses and current status: Plants can be grown as a cut flower, a potted plant for the home, or as a garden ornamental in the landscape where temperatures do not go below 32 to 28°F (0 to −2°C). Some cultivars can tolerate temperatures as low as 20°F (−7°C). Outdoor plants do not perform well in areas with high summer rainfall or high humidity.

This herbaceous perennial produces exotic and colorful wooly flowers in various color combinations of yellow, green, red, purple, and near-black (Fig. II-1 Anigozanthos). Sets of linear leaves, known as fans, arise from a thick rootstock, which has been described as a rhizome. Vegetative growing points form fans like those of an iris and terminate in a raceme-type inflorescence. The floral perianth tube is elongated, reflexed, and the underside is split. Flowering stems can vary from 6 to 40 in. (15 to 100 cm) in length, depending on species or cultivar (Bailey, 1914; Bailey and Bailey, 1976; Beard, 1963).

CULTIVARS

There are less than 20 species (Bailey and Bailey, 1976; Beard, 1963; Dixon and Hopper, 1979); Huxley et al. (1992) indicated the existence of only 11 species. The most common species used to produce hybrids are

FIGURE II-I ANIGOZANTHOS *Anigozanthos* inflorescence.

Anigozanthos flavidus DC. (green to deep red flowers), *A. bicolor* Endl. (red and green), *A. manglesii* D. (red and green), and *A. humilis* Lindl. (yellow and orange) (Bailey and Bailey, 1976; Beard, 1963; Dixon and Hopper, 1979). All species apparently hybridize readily and "fascinating" hybrids can be obtained with ease (Grieve and Merchant, 1963; Hopper, 1963, 1977a, 1977b, 1978, 1980; Hopper and Burbidge, 1978; Hopper and Campbell, 1977). Cultivar series are available specifically for cut flower production or for potted plant production.

PROPAGATION

Commercial propagation of hybrids is by *in vitro* propagation (Worrall, 1995). When *in vitro* plantlets arrive, immediately plant and maintain high humidities; however, avoid propagation fog houses and excessive misting. Placing young plantlets in hoop tunnels covered with white plastic in the summer (provided temperatures do not become excessive) or clear plastic in the winter is common in Europe for plant establishment.

Rhizomes can be divided and plants may also be grown from seed (Bailey and Bailey, 1976; Beard, 1963; Dixon and Hopper, 1979; Ellyard, 1978; Hopper, 1963; McComb and Newton, 1981).

FLOWER CONTROL AND DORMANCY

Apparently dormancy does not occur in seeds or plants, other than under hot dry conditions. If not irrigated during dry, hot Mediterranean summer conditions, plants will go dormant until winter rains commence. Once dormant, plants should not be watered until temperatures have decreased to autumn or winter levels, otherwise plants may rot. If kept continuously irrigated, there is no serious problem of summer rhizome rot (Beard, 1963; Dixon and Hopper, 1979; Hopper, 1963; Roh and Lawson, 1987).

A. flavidus is a facultative LD plant, *A. manglesii* is a facultative SD plant, and *A. rufus*, Labill., *A. pulcherrimus* Hook, and *A. flavidus* ×*manglesii* are DN (Motum and Goodwin, 1987a, b). Shade on glass would be used only to reduce temperature (see Temperature, next, for further forcing information).

TEMPERATURE

The original work on flowering was done by Grieve and Merchant in 1963. Cool temperatures are optimal for flowering. *A. manglesii* flowered best at 63/54°F (17/12°C) day/night temperatures; at 73/63°F (23/17°C), plants failed to flower. Plants are seriously stressed at 81°F (27°C) (Motum and Goodwin, 1987a, b). Hagiladi (1983), working with mature *A. manglesii*, found that if night temperatures were from 54 to 59°F (12 to 15°C), plants flowered and responded to watering and nutritional application; at higher temperatures injury and death occurred. With seedlings, a 50°F (10°C) temperature treatment resulted in superior plants compared with 64°F (18°C). Hagiladi (1983) also concluded that plants were day neutral under cool conditions.

In the Netherlands, for early rapid forcing of dormant plants and subsequent flowering, 59/54°F (15/12°C) day/night temperatures were best. After emergence, slightly warmer day/night temperatures of 64/61°F (18/16°C) were optimal for total flower production (van der Krogt, 1978, 1979; van der Krogt and Noordegraaf, 1977). Higher day/night temperatures of 72/68°F (22/20°C) increased vegetative growth. In that experiment, photoperiod was apparently not involved in flowering. Roh et al. (1992) also found that flowering of an *A. man-*

glesii ×*A. flavidus* hybrid was accelerated, with plants producing more fans, at 55°F (13°C) night temperatures, regardless of photoperiod. At 60 or 64°F (16 or 18°C), these hybrids were facultative LD plants. Color and quality was improved at 55 to 61°F (13 to 16°C) (Motum and Goodwin, 1987a). The most vivid coloring was with plants grown at 55°F (13°C); the poorest color was at 82°F (28°C) (Ben-Tal and King, 1997).

LIGHT

Full sun is used in field production and in greenhouses, except when shading is needed for temperature control. Interestingly, ultraviolet-B (UV-B) light influenced flower color, in addition to temperature (Ben-Tal and King, 1997). Because glass blocks out UV light, they suggest plants should be grown under polyethylene films that do not block UV light or use UV-B lamps (302 nm). Regardless, increasing light levels up to 3530 fc (530 μmol · m^{-2} · s^{-1}) improved flower color. Altering the light intensity or color and/or lowering the temperature to improve flower color needs to be done only during the last 1 to 3 weeks of production. Flower color is most intense on plants grown outdoors.

WATER

Plants in the field or in pots need careful watering. They are injured if allowed to wilt, but roots will easily rot if continuously overwatered. Field-grown plants are commonly irrigated by a low-volume trickle water system.

CARBON DIOXIDE

No information is available regarding CO_2 levels in greenhouses during pot plant production.

NUTRITION

In nature, kangaroo-paws grow in low nutrient soils (Beard, 1963). However, Hanger and Brown (1988) discuss various nutrient disorders. In commercial greenhouses, plants are fertilized at every irrigation with 100 to 150 ppm N and 80 to 100 ppm K (Neal, 1987). All species and modern cultivars are tolerant to phosphorus; phosphorus can be added to the medium as superphosphate and not injected into irrigation water.

MEDIA

Kangaroo-paws demand a well-drained, acidic medium (Beard, 1963; Roh and Lawson, 1987).

HEIGHT CONTROL

Not needed for pot or cut flower production when the correct cultivars are selected. Bonzi (paclobutrazol) drenches reduced stem length, with 0.02 g/pot providing the greatest height control, but decreased the number of flowering stems in most of the 10 cultivars tested (Turner, 1987).

SPACING

Field spacing, which is species and cultivar dependent, is 20 to 30 in. (50 to 76 cm) between plants and 40 to 55 in. (100 to 140 cm) between rows. Plants can be forced in 4-in. (10-cm) pots when genetic dwarfs are used or in 6-in. (15-cm) pots. Young plants that have just been potted can be held pot-to-pot until spacing is necessary. Thereafter, 10- × 10-in. (25- × 25-cm) or 15- × 15-in. (37- × 37-cm) spacing can be used for 4- or 6-in. (10- or 15-cm) pots, respectively.

PINCHING AND DISBUDDING

None required.

SUPPORT

None required for cut flower or potted plant production.

SCHEDULE AND TIMING

If species are cultivated or if dominant species' parental traits are known in the cultivars, a flowering schedule can be developed: *A. humilis*, *A. bicolor*, and *A. gabrielae* Domin. flower first in late winter or early spring; then *A. manglesii* and *A. viridis* Endl.; and finally *A. rufus*, *A. flavidus*, and *A. pulcherrimus* flower in the early summer (Motum and Goodwin, 1987b). Total production time for each crop will be up to 7 months (Table II-1 Anigozanthos). Using plugs, production time for potted plants can be reduced to 8 to 15 weeks.

INSECTS

Although kangaroo-paw has few insect pests, thrips may occasionally be a problem.

TABLE II-I ANIGOZANTHOS
Sample production schedule for potted *Anigozanthos*.

Cultural Step	Production Time	Temperature °F (°C)
Planting		
	2.5–3 months	Night: 60 (16)
Flower induction[a]		
	1–2 months	Night: 55 (13)
Flower development to visible bud		
	35 days	Night: 60–65 (16–18)
Flower		
	25 days	Night: 60–65 (16–18)
Total	5.5–7 months	

[a]*An interesting "signal" can be observed when the flower buds are initiated and present—the youngest leaf emerging from the fan will have a hook develop at the tip. From this event to first flower, anthesis is approximately 60 days, or 35 days from hook development to visible bud and 25 days from visible bud to anthesis.*

DISEASES

Black-spot leaf-tip disease has long been a problem and a mystery. The symptoms are terminal black-purple leaf discoloration, which can spread to the lower leaf areas and rhizome areas, causing the plant to collapse and die. The fungus *Mystrosporium adustrum* has been associated with these problems (Beard, 1963), as well as *Dreschleri iridis*, *Alternaria alternala*, and *Puccinia haemodoi* (Fraser, 1963; Smith, 1963). Raabe (1985) has identified a second *Alternaria* species, *A. anigzanthi*. Large populations of nematodes (*Aphelenchoides fragariae*) have also been found in these terminal blackened areas (Raabe, 1990). An oxamyl spray controlled the nematodes and further tip blackening. Further, Raabe (1990) observed that excessive watering and high humidity (fog) are contributing factors to this problem, because terminal leaf guttation and subsequent discoloration are common under these conditions. Consequently, the question arises: Are nematodes swept up and concentrated in the vascular water stream, leading to microorganism invasion? Leaf-tip blackening has also been associated with calcium deficiency (Webb, 1979).

PHYSIOLOGICAL DISORDERS

See Diseases above.

POSTHARVEST

For both cut and potted flowering plants, 3 to 4 flowers should be open prior to harvest. A 3 to 6% sucrose solution increases vase life of cut flowers (Roh and Lawson, 1987). Treatment may vary with species; a 12-hr pulse of 30% sucrose was valuable for *A. rufus*, and 20% sucrose for *A. manglesii* (Manning et al., 1989). Lower sucrose concentrations can also be used with some cultivars; a 5-hr pulse of 2.5% sucrose increased the vase life of 'Gold Fever' from 3.5 to 5 weeks (Teagle et al., 1991). Vase life decreased with increasing 34°F (1°C) storage; 14 days of storage reduced vase life to less than 7 days (Jones and Faragher, 1991). Pulsing stems with 20% sucrose prior to cold storage at 34 to 36°F (1 to 2°C) increased vase life (Teagle et al., 1991). However, the addition of silver thiosulfate to the pulse solution had no effect.

Potted plants ship well in a wide range of temperatures and last in the home for 7 days under moderate light conditions. Long-term shipments should be at or near 50°F (10°C). High water demand and rapid dehydration are problems in the marketplace for potted plants. If plants wilt, injury will occur.

KEY POINTS

- Kangaroo-paw, popular for its unusual flower form and colors, is used primarily as a cut flower, but also as a potted flowering plant and garden plant.
- Field production can occur in mild, near-frost-free areas.
- Potted flowering plants are produced under protection.
- Plants are propagated primarily by *in vitro*; established plants can be divided.
- Cool temperatures of 55°F (13°C) promote flowering and improve plant quality.
- Low nutrient levels are used and, contrary to "oral history," phosphorus can be used.
- Black-spot leaf-tip disease is a problem but the cause is not well defined.
- Pulsing with sucrose increases the vase life of cut stems.

BIBLIOGRAPHY

Bailey, L.H. 1914. *Anigozanthos*, p. 200 in *Standard Cyclopedia of Horticulture*, vol. I. Macmillan, New York.

Bailey, L.H., and E.Z. Bailey. 1976. *Anigozanthos*, pp. 78–79 in *Hortus Third: A Concise Dictionary of Plants Cultivated in the United States and Canada*. Macmillan, New York.

Beard, J.S. 1963. Growing the small kangaroo paws. *Australian Plants* 2:106, 129–131, 135–136.

Ben-Tal, Y., and R.W. King. 1997. Environmental factors involved in colouration of flowers of kangaroo paw. *Scientia Horticulturae* 72:35–48.

Dixon, B., and S. Hopper. 1979. Growing kangaroo paws and related species. *Australian Plants* 10:199–211.

Ellyard, R.K. 1978. *In vitro* propagation of *Anigozanthos manglesii, A. flavidus*, and *Macropidia fuliginosa*. *HortScience* 13:662–663.

Fraser, L.R. 1963. Black disease of kangaroo paws. *Australian Plants* 2:116.

Grieve, B.J., and N. Merchant. 1963. The kangaroo paws of Western Australia. *Australian Plants* 2:107–115.

Hagiladi, A. 1983. Influence of temperature and daylength on growth and flower yield of *Anigozanthos manglesii* D. Don (Haemodoraceae). *HortScience* 18:369–371.

Hanger, B., and A. Brown. 1988. Nutrient disorders in kangaroo paws. *Australian Plants* 14:321–329.

Hopper, S.D. 1963. Hybridizing *Anigozanthos*. *Australian Plants* 10:211–217.

Hopper, S.D. 1977a. The structure and dynamics of a hybrid population of *Anigozanthos manglesii* D. Don. and *A. humilis* Lindl. (Haemodoraceae). *Australian Journal of Botany* 25:413–422.

Hopper, S.D. 1977b. The reproductive capacity of *Anigozanthos maglesii* D. Don., *A. humilis* Lindl. and their hybrids in a wild population. *Australian Journal of Botany* 25:423–428.

Hopper, S.D. 1978. An experimental study of competitive interference between *Anigozanthos manglesii* D. Don, *A. humilis* Lindl. and their F_1 hybrids (Haemodoraceae). *Australian Journal of Botany* 26:807–818.

Hopper, S.D. 1980. A biosystematic study of the kangaroo paws, *Anigozanthos* and *Macropidia* (Haemodoraceae). *Australian Journal of Botany* 28:659–680.

Hopper, S.D., and A.H. Burbidge. 1978. Assortative pollination by red wattlebirds in a hybrid population of *Anigozanthos* Labill. (Haemodoraceae). *Australian Journal of Botany* 26:335–350.

Hopper, S.D., and N.A. Campbell. 1977. A multivariate morphometric study of species relationships in kangaroo paws (*Anigozanthos* Labill and *Macropidia* Drumm. ex. Harv.: Haemodoraceae). *Australian Journal of Botany* 25:523–544.

Huxley, A., M. Griffiths, and M. Levy. 1992. *Anigozanthos*, pp. 181–182 in *The New Royal Horticultural Society Dictionary of Gardening*, vol. 1. Stockton Press, New York.

Jones, R., and J. Faragher. 1991. Cold storage of selected members of the Proteaceae and Australian native cut flowers. *HortScience* 26:1395–1397.

Manning, L.E., D.C. Joyce, and B.B. Lamont. 1989. Postharvest handling of kangaroo paws. Honors Thesis, Curtin University of Technology, Perth Australia.

McComb, J.A., and S. Newton. 1981. Propagation of kangaroo paws using tissue culture. *Journal of Horticultural Science* 56:181–183.

Motum, G.J., and P.B. Goodwin. 1987a. Floral initiation in kangaroo paw (*Anigozanthos* spp.): A scanning electron microscope study. *Scientia Horticulturae* 32:115–122.

Motum, G.J., and P.B. Goodwin. 1987b. The control of flowering in kangaroo paw (*Anigozanthos* spp). *Scientia Horticulturae* 32:123–133.

Neal, K. 1987. Kangaroo paw. *Greenhouse Manager* 6(7):54–58.

Raabe, R.D. 1985. *Alternaria* leaf spot of *Anigozanthos* spp. *Phytopathology* 75:1382. (Abstract)

Raabe, R.D. 1990. Black leaf of *Anigozanthos* hybrids. *Phytopathology* 80:892. (Abstract)

Roh, M.S., and R.H. Lawson. 1987. Kangaroo paws: A classy new floral experience. *Greenhouse Manager* 5(9):87, 107.

Roh, M.S., R. Griesbach, and R. Lawson. 1992. Influence of temperature and photoperiod on flowering of *Anigozanthos* hybrids. *HortScience* 27:575. (Abstract)

Smith, C.W.P. 1963. The ink spot disease of paws. *Australian Plants* 2:115.

Teagle, S., J. White, and M. Sedgely. 1991. Post-harvest vase life of cut flowers of three cultivars of kangaroo paw. *Scientia Horticulturae* 48:277–284.

Turner, M.L. 1987. Flowering response of some kangaroo paws to paclobutrazol. *Acta Horticulturae* 205:137–143.

van der Krogt, T.M. 1978. Invloed van de tempertuur op de bloemproduktie, van *Anigozanthos*. Bloemisterij onderzoek in Nederland over 1977, pp. 20–21. *Proefstation voer de bloemisterij in Nederland (Aalsmeer)*. (in Dutch)

van der Krogt, T.M. 1979. Invloed van de daglengte op de bloemaanleg van *Anigozanthos*, Bloemisterij onderzoek in Nederland over 1978, pp. 28–29. *Proefstation voer de bloemisterij in Nederland (Aalsmeer)*. (in Dutch)

van der Krogt, T.M., and C.V. Noordegraaf. 1977. Invloed van de temperatuur op de bloemproduktie van *Anigozanthos*. Bloemisterij onderzoek in Nederland over 1976, p. 15. *Proefstation voer de bloemisterij in Nederland* (Aalsmeer). (in Dutch)

Webb, J. 1979. Anigozanthos calcium deficiency. *Australian Plants* 10:219.

Worrall, R. 1995. Breeding of dwarf kangaroo pay (*Anigozanthos*) for use as flowering potted plants. *Acta Horticulturae* 397:189–196.

Anthurium

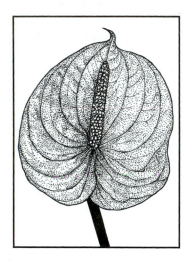

INTRODUCTION

Common names: anthurium, flamingo flower, tail flower, oil cloth flower.

Scientific name: *Anthurium andraeanum* André. is grown as a cut flower; *A. scherzerianum* Schott is grown as a flowering potted plant; and *A. crystallinum* Lind. & André. and *A. leuconeurum* Lemoine. are grown as foliage plants (Bailey and Bailey, 1976; Huxley et al., 1992).

Family and related taxa: Araceae Juss. Five hundred to 600 *Anthurium* species occur in nature (Bailey and Bailey, 1976; Criley, 1985). *Aglaonema, Caladium, Dieffenbachia, Epipremnum, Monstera, Nephthytis, Philodendron, Spathiphyllum, Syngonium,* and *Zantedeschia* are only a few of the important genera in this family.

Origin: *A. andraeanum* and *A. crystallinum* are native to Columbia, South America; *A. leuconeurum* is native to Mexico; and *A. scherzerianum* is native to Costa Rica (Bailey and Bailey, 1976; Huxley et al., 1992).

Uses and current status: Anthuriums are terrestrial herbs, vines, and epiphytes. Anthuriums are used as colorful cut flowers and potted plants in the home or interiorscape (Fig. II-1 Anthurium). They are adapted to low light levels. In frost-free areas anthuriums can be used in the landscape. Hawaii produces one-fifth of the world's cut anthuriums (Chen and Kuehnle, 1996).

A. andraeanum, an epiphyte, is an important parent in numerous cut flower hybrids (Bailey and Bailey, 1976; Huxley et al., 1992). The heart-shaped spathe is showy and is colored from black-red, red, salmon, pink, and green to white (Fig. II-2 Anthurium). Bright red is the most common color produced. The spadix is covered with up to 300 inconspicuous bisexual flowers. Leaves have a prominent central vein

FIGURE II-1 ANTHURIUM   Potted *Anthurium*.

FIGURE II-2 ANTHURIUM   *Anthurium* inflorescence.

and are cordate, 7 to 20 in. (17 to 50 cm) long and 4 to 9 in. (11 to 22 cm) wide. The petiole is 24 in. (60 cm) long and the spathe is 3 to 7 in. (6 to 15 cm) with a 36-in. (1-m)-plus-long scape.

A. crystallinum leaves are 12 to 18 in. (30 to 45 cm) long and 10 to 12 in. (25 to 30 cm) wide. The petiole is 8 in. (20 cm) long and the spathe is 5 in. (14 cm) with a 24-in. (60-cm)-long scape. The leaves are attractive, being described as silky emerald green, veins crystalline white to pink bronze; the spathe is red-purple.

A. leuconeurum has dark-green leaves, which are also cordate, 4 to 6 in. (10 to 15 cm) wide and 4 to 6 in. (10 to 15 cm) long. The scape is 16 to 20 in. (40 to 50 cm) with the spathe 3.5 in (8.5 cm) long.

A. scherzerianum is the common genetic source for potted hybrid flowering plants because this species produces numerous basal shoots, short stems, and clustered leaves. The leaves are elongate, to 9 in. (23 cm), and 2 in. (5 cm) wide. The leaf petiole is up to 10 in. (26 cm) long. The colorful spadix is scarlet to vermillion.

CULTIVARS

New cultivars are developed annually (Henny, 1999; Henny and Hamilton, 1992; Henny et al., 2003). One area of cultivar development is focusing on highly floriferous compact potted flowering plants.

PROPAGATION

Most commercial cultivars for production are *in vitro*-propagated and liners are available year-round from specialty propagators (Henny and Hamilton, 1992; Orlikowska et al., 1995; Wilbret and Sheehan, 1981). Mature *Anthurium* plants can be air layered and cutting propagated. Axillary buds develop into shoots, which can be removed as cuttings and rooted (Post, 1949). Breeding techniques are described by Wilbret and Sheehan (1981).

FLOWER CONTROL AND DORMANCY

Seed-propagated plants produce only axillary vegetative buds in their leaf axils until an apparent juvenile phase has been completed (Christensen, 1971; Criley, 1985; Leffring, 1975). After plants mature and the first reproductive meristems form and reach anthesis, alternating lateral vegetative and reproductive growth occurs. Approximately 30 days elapse between vegetative and reproductive cycles; the exact duration is dependent on temperature and light.

Both *A. andraeanum* and *A. scherzerianum* produce three to eight leaves per shoot per year and, consequently, can produce three to eight flowers per year. Henny and Hamilton (1992) reported that those cultivars suitable for pot plant production have many lateral shoots and tend to require a longer time to flower than the cut flower cultivars, which have a dominant apical shoot and shorter crop time.

Production time can be reduced by a single 500-ppm gibberellic acid (GA_3) spray at 6.8 oz (200 mL) per plant (Henny and Hamilton, 1992). The GA was applied 28 weeks after plants were removed from tissue culture and plants were approximately 4 in. (10 cm) tall in 4-in. (10-cm) pots. The GA treatment increased the number of inflorescences from 0.3 to 5.3 per plant after 3 months. The greatest GA response was noted at a light intensity of 1400 fc ($280 \ \mu mol \cdot m^{-2} \cdot s^{-1}$), whereas at 550 to 850 fc (110 to 170 $\mu mol \cdot m^{-2} \cdot s^{-1}$) the response was commercially insignificant. GA may reduce quality, however, by increasing the spadix angle. A tighter angle allows cut stems to be more easily packed.

Higaki and Rasmussen (1979) reported that adventitious bud break and flower production could also be increased using various chemicals with *A. andraeanum*. Benzyladenine (BA, 1000 ppm), benzylamino (tetrahydropyranyl) purine (PBA, 1500 ppm), or ethephon (1000 ppm) sprays increased axillary shoot production by 3.6, 2.2, or 1.8, respectively, compared with 0 for the control plants.

TEMPERATURE

The cycle between alternating leaf and flower emergence is longer during the cooler season and under lower light intensities than during the warm season. Post (1949) recommended a minimum of 65°F (18°C); several researchers stated that 68 to 72°F (20 to 22°C) was optimum (Criley, 1985; Leffring, 1975; Noordegraaf, 1973). Henny and Hamilton's (1992) GA_3 concentration $\times$ light intensity research on *A. scherzeranum* was conducted outdoors in Florida at 64 to 90°F (18 to 30°C).

In the Netherlands flowering was promoted when plants were held for 6 weeks at 54 or 59°F (12 or 15°C); then moved to 70°F (21°C) (Szendel and Weryszko, 1973). *A. andraeanum* cultivars exist that have higher production at a cooler temperature of 61°F (16°C) compared to 66°F (19°C) (Schenk and Brundert, 1981). However, longer petioles, wider spathes, and better overall quality occurred when plants were grown at 66° and 72°F (19 and 22°C) compared to 55 and 61°F (13 and 16°C). Plants die at 50°F (10°C).

LIGHT

Anthurium are not considered photoperiodic, but Christensen (1971) studied 36 *A. scherzerianum* cultivars in Denmark under greenhouse conditions and observed that most flowered during the spring as light intensity and duration increased.

Light intensity recommendations vary from report to report and between areas of the world. Post (1949) stated that not more than 1500 fc (300 $\mu mol \cdot m^{-2} \cdot s^{-1}$) should be used on *A. andraeanum* or that midsummer light should be reduced to one-fifteenth of the normal intensity.

Early recommendations from the Netherlands were to reduce light by 90% of the normal intensity. However, the optimum light intensity for flower production was determined by Leffring (1975) to be 1440 fc (290 $\mu mol \cdot m^{-2} \cdot s^{-1}$) without leaf cooling or 1730 fc (345 $\mu mol \cdot m^{-2} \cdot s^{-1}$) with leaf cooling from overhead sprinklers.

In Hawaii 3070 to 3650 fc (615 to 730 $\mu mol \cdot m^{-2} \cdot s^{-1}$) (75% shade) is recommended, and commercially full sunlight of 15,000 fc (3,000 $\mu mol \cdot m^{-2} \cdot s^{-1}$) is reduced by 50 to 90% shade. (Criley, 1985; Higaki and Watson, 1973; Nakasone and Kamemoto, 1962). In Florida Henny and Hamilton (1992) stated that 1400 fc (280 $\mu mol \cdot m^{-2} \cdot s^{-1}$) was optimum.

WATER

These species are epiphytes in nature and consequently the medium should be well aerated and never overwatered. Plants grow best at high humidity.

CARBON DIOXIDE

No information was found regarding the use of carbon dioxide.

NUTRITION

For potted flowering plant production, a low nitrogen rate of 126 mg N weekly per pot was the optimum because production decreased with higher or lower N rates; for K 187 mg weekly per pot was optimum for *A. andraeanum*. The N:K ratio recommendation for pot culture was 1:2 (Poole and Greaves, 1969; Poole and McConnell, 1971). For field production a ratio of 2:1 N:K was recommended at 600 to 1000 lb N/acre/year (670 to 1120 kg N/ha/year) (Poole and Greaves, 1969; Poole and

TABLE II-1 ANTHURIUM

Foliar levels of the essential nutrient element found in *Anthurium* for maximum cut flower production (Higaki et al., 1992).

Element	Level
Nitrogen	1.87%
Phosphorus	0.17%
Potassium	2.07%
Calcium	2.93%
Magnesium	0.88%
Sulfur	0.35%
Iron	129 ppm
Manganese	373 ppm
Zinc	181 ppm
Boron	166 ppm
Copper	26 ppm
Molybdenum	5 ppm

McConnell, 1971). Bik (1976), however, stated a ratio of 1:2.5 was best.

For potted flowering plant production a variety of fertilization techniques can be used. Pots can be topdressed with 19–6–12 controlled-release fertilizer at 0.07 oz/pot (2 g/pot) or fertigated at 150 to 200 ppm from 9–3–6 (Henny and Hamilton, 1992). Higaki et al. (1992) also used controlled-release fertilizer at 280N–400P–335K lb/acre/year (312N–448P–375K kg/ha/year) for optimum cut flower production. Table II-1 Anthurium shows the optimum nutrient leaf levels.

Calcium deficiencies result in a color break down in the spathe due to tissue collapse of the middle lamella. The spathe should contain at least 0.32% calcium and the leaves at least 0.88% calcium (Higaki, 1977; Higaki et al., 1980a, b). Calcium can be applied as calcitic or dolomitic limestone at 1000 or 1840 lb/acre/year (1120 or 2060 kg/ha/year), respectively, split into two applications (Higaki et al., 1994). Bik (1976) stated that *A. andraeanum* leaves should contain 2% N and 3% K.

MEDIA

In Europe coarse 100% peat, adjusted to pH 5.0, is most commonly used for potted plant production (Bik, 1976). In Florida, a variety of media have been used for potted plants including peat-lite mixes with additional bark added at 1:1 (v/v) (Henny and Hamilton, 1992). Wood shavings have also been used for cut flower production (Poole and Greaves, 1969). In Hawaii volcanic cinders are used for cut flow-

ering production. However, a wide variety of media can be used including coconut coir, rockwool, and polyphenol foam (R. Criley, personal communication).

HEIGHT CONTROL

None is required.

SPACING

Plants can be spaced at 8 × 10 to 12 × 12 in. (20 × 25 to 30 × 30 cm) in beds, producing 25,000 to 28,000 plants/acre (62,000 to 70,000/ha) (Anthura, 1998; Higaki et al., 1994).

PINCHING AND DISBUDDING

None is required.

SUPPORT

None is required.

SCHEDULE AND TIMING

Approximately 40 weeks (Table II-2 Anthurium) are required to produce a flowering potted plant of *A. scherzerianum* when a GA_3 spray is used to induce flowering (Henny and Hamilton, 1992). Plants for cut flowers remain in production for 4 to 5 years.

INSECTS

Thrips and spider mites can be problems during production (Post, 1949). Nematodes, whiteflies, mealybugs, and scale also occur (Dreistadt, 2001; Goo and Sipes, 1997).

DISEASES

Erwinia carotovera can cause problems during production (Knauss et al., 1981). In the late 1980s, *Xanthomonas campestris* pv. *diffenbachiae*, a bacterium, devastated anthurium worldwide (Norman et al., 1999). The disease problem has been reduced with resistant cultivars developed through *Agrobacterium*-mediated transformation, disease-indexed tissue-cultured stock plants, and sanitation (Chen and Kuehnle, 1996; Norman et al., 1999). Other diseases reported include root rot (*Pythium*), aerial blight (*Rhizoctonia solani*), leaf spot (*Phytophthora*), bacterial leaf spot and blight (*Erwinia chrysanthemi* and *Pseudomonas cichorii*), anthracnose (*Colletotrichum gleosporioides*), and dasheen mosaic virus (Dreistadt, 2001).

TABLE II-2 ANTHURIUM

A sample production schedule for 4-in. (10-cm) potted flowering *A. scherzerianum* plants.

Cultural Step	Production Time (weeks)	Environmental Conditions
Plant liners from *in vitro* plugs		1400 fc (280 μmol · m^{-2} · s^{-1}) light 54 to 59°F (12 to 15°C)
	6	
Increase temperature		Minimum of 70°F (21°C)
	22	
Spray GA$_3$[a]		Minimum of 70°F (21°C)
	12	
Total	40	

[a]*500 ppm at 6.8 oz/plant (200 mL/plant).*

PHYSIOLOGICAL DISORDERS

Calcium deficiencies induce color break down of the spathe (Higaki et al., 1980b).

POSTHARVEST

Potted flowering plants of *A. scherzerianum* are sold when two to three flowers have developed. Plants can be shipped at 55 to 59°F (13 to 15°C) for not more than 3 days in darkness (Nowak and Rudnicki, 1990). Tijskens et al. (1996) found a lower optimum temperature of 52°F (11°C) for long-term storage.

Cut flowers of *A. andraeanum* are harvested when the spathe has unfolded, at least three-quarters of the true flowers on the spadix have opened, and the stem is mature and hardened. Damage can occur if plants or stems are subjected to temperatures lower than 55°F (13°C) (Nowak and Rudnicki, 1990). Flowers can be stored for up to 4 weeks; however, 2 weeks or less in water at 55°F (13°C) is best (Nowak and Rudnicki, 1990). If stems wilt, recut them and place in 77°F (25°C) water (Nowak and Rudnicki, 1990). Flowers can be waxed, which will double shelf life (Paull and Goo, 1982, 1985).

Cut postharvest life can be 14 to 28 days, and flowers respond favorably to preservative solutions (Nowak and Rudnicki, 1990; Paull and Goo, 1982; Sacalis, 1993). Conditioning stems in water containing 170 to 680 ppm AgNO$_3$ for 10 to 40 min at harvest increased longevity by 40 to 60% and prevented wound-generated ethylene from causing basal stem clogging. Flowers are slightly sensitive to ethylene. Paull et al. (1985) have also researched biochemical changes in floral tissue during senescence.

KEY POINTS

- This tropical plant is grown as a cut flower and potted flowering plant.
- The large waxy inflorescence consists of a heart-shaped white, pink, red, or green spathe and an elongated spadix.
- Flower buds are formed in the leaf axils after a juvenile period is complete.
- Production time can be reduced by gibberellic acid applications but tends to increase spadix angle.
- Anthuriums are epiphytic in nature and, thus, require well-aerated, well-drained media.
- Cut flowers are harvested when the spathe has unfolded, the true flowers on the spadix have formed, and the stem is mature and hardened.
- Cut flowers last 14 to 28 days and floral preservatives should be used.

BIBLIOGRAPHY

Anthura. 1998. *Cultivation Guide to Anthurium.* Anthura B.V., Bleiwijk, Holland.

Bailey, L.H., & E.Z. Bailey. 1976. *Anthurium,* pp. 84–86 in *Hortus Third: A Concise Dictionary of Plants Cultivated in the United States and Canada.* Macmillan, New York.

Bik, R.A. 1976. Quality in *Anthurium andreanum* and *Aechma fasciata* grown in peat substrates as affected by nitrogen and potassium nutrition. *Acta Horticulturae* 64:83–91.

Chen, F.-C., and A. R. Kuehnle. 1996. Obtaining transgenic *Anthurium* through *Agrobacterium*-mediated transformation of etiolated internodes. *Journal of the American Society for Horticultural Science* 121:47–51.

Christensen, O.V. 1971. Morphological studies on the growth and flowering of *Anthurium scherzerianum* Schott and *Anthurium andreanum* Lind. *Tidsskrift Planteavl* 75:793–798.

Criley, R.A. 1985. *Anthurium,* pp. 471–475 in *Handbook of Flowering,* vol. 1, A.H. Halevy, editor. CRC Press, Boca Raton, Florida.

Dreistadt, S.H. 2001. *Integrated Pest Management for Floriculture and Nurseries.* University of California Division of Agriculture and Natural Resources Publication 3402.

Goo, M.Y.C., and B.S. Sipes. 1997. Host preference of *Radopholus citrophilus* from Hawaiian anthurium among selected tropical ornamentals. *HortScience* 32:1237–1238.

Henny, R.J. 1999. 'Red Hot' *Anthurium. HortScience* 34:153–154.

Henny, R.J., and R.L. Hamilton. 1992. Flowering of *Anthurium* following treatment with gibberellic acid. *HortScience* 27:1328.

Henny, R.J., D.J. Norman, and J. Chen. 2003. 'Orange Hot' anthurium. *HortScience* 38:133–134.

Higaki, T. 1977. Calcium level in cooler breakdown disorder of anthurium flowers, *Anthurium andreanum* Lind. *Proceedings Tropical Region American Society Horticultural Science* 21:44–45.

Higaki, T., and H.P. Rasmussen. 1979. Chemical induction of adventitious shoot in *Anthurium. HortScience* 14:64–65.

Higaki, T., and D.P. Watson. 1973. *Anthurium Culture in Hawaii.* University of Hawaii Cooperative Extension Service Circular Number 420.

Higaki, T., H.P. Rasmussen, and W.J. Carpenter. 1980a. Calcium deficiency of *Anthurium andreanum* Lind. spathes. *Journal of the American Society for Horticultural Science* 105:438–440.

Higaki, T., H.P. Rasmussen, and W.J. Carpenter. 1980b. Color breakdown in anthurium (*Anthurium andreanum* Lind.) spathes caused by calcium deficiency. *Journal of the American Society for Horticultural Science* 105:441–444.

Higaki, T., J.S. Imamura, and R.E. Paull. 1992. N, P, and K rates and leaf tissue standards for optimum *Anthurium andraeanum* flower production. *HortScience* 27:909–912.

Higaki, T., J.S. Lichty, and D. Moniz. 1994. *Anthurium Culture in Hawaii.* Hawaii Institute for Tropical Agriculture and Human Resources, University of Hawaii, Research-Extension Service 152.

Huxley, A., M. Griffiths, and M. Levy. 1992. *Anthurium,* pp. 190–193 in *The New Royal Horticultural Society Dictionary of Gardening,* vol. 1. Stockton Press, New York.

Knauss, J.F., S.A. Alfieri, Jr., R.B. Marlatt, and F.W. Zettler. 1981. Foliage plants disease, pp. 351–427 in *Foliage Plant Production,* J.N. Joiner, editor. Prentice-Hall, Englewood Cliffs, New Jersey.

Leffring, R.L. 1975. Influence of climatic conditions on growth and flower yield of *Anthurium andreanum. Acta Horticulturae* 51:63–68.

Nakasone, H.Y., and H. Kamemato. 1962. *Anthurium Culture with Emphasis on the Effects of Some Reduced Environments on Growth and Flowering.* Hawaii Agricultural Experimental Station Technical Bulletin Number 50.

Noordegraaf, C.V. 1973. Influence of temperatures on flowering in *Anthurium scherzerianum. Acta Horticulturae* 31:71–76.

Norman, D.J., R.J. Henny, and J.M.F. Yuen. 1999. Resistance levels of pot anthurium cultivars to *Xanthomonas campestris* pv. *dieffenbachiae. HortScience* 34:721–722.

Nowak, J., and R.M. Rudnicki. 1990. *Anthurium andraeanum* (Tailflower), p. 132; *Anthurium scherzerianum* (Flaming Flower, Pigtail Plant), p. 166 in *Postharvest Handling and Storage of Cut Flowers, Florist Greens, and Potted Plants.* Timber Press, Portland, Oregon.

Orlikowska, T., I. Sabala, and E. Nowak. 1995. Adventitious shoot regeneration on explants of *Anthurium, Codiaeum, Dieffenbachia, Gerbera, Rosa* and *Spathiphyllum* for breeding purposes. *Acta Horticulturae* 420:115–117.

Paull, R.E., and T. Goo. 1982. Pulse treatment with silver nitrate extends vase life of *Anthuriums. Journal of the American Society for Horticultural Science* 107:842–844.

Paull, R.E., and T. Goo. 1985. Ethylene and water stress in the senescence of cut *Anthurium* flowers. *Journal of the American Society for Horticultural Science* 110:84–88.

Paull, R.E., N.J. Chen, and J. Deputy. 1985. Physiological changes associated with senescence of cut *Anthurium* flowers. *Journal of the American Society for Horticultural Science* 110:156–162.

Poole, R.T., and B.A. Greaves. 1969. Nitrogen, phosphorus, and potassium fertilization of *Anthurium andraeanum* 'Nitta' and 'Kauana'. *Proceedings Tropical Region American Society Horticultural Science* 13:367–372.

Poole, R.T., and D.B. McConnell. 1971. Effect of shade levels and fertilization on flowering of *Anthurium andraeanum* 'Nitta' and 'Kauana'. *Proceedings Tropical Region American Society Horticultural Science* 15:189–195.

Post, K. 1949. *Anthurium*, pp. 324–325 in *Florist Crop Production and Marketing*. Orange Judd Publishing, New York.

Sacalis, J.N. 1993. *Anthurium × cultorum*, pp. 27–28 in *Cut Flowers, Prolonging Freshness*, 2nd ed., J.L. Seals, editor. Ball Publishing, Batavia, Illinois.

Schenk, M., and W. Brundert. 1981. Temperature influss bei. *Anthurium andraeanum* hybridin. *Deutchen Gartenbau* 35:2064–2065.

Szendel, A.J., and E. Weryszko. 1973. Investigations on structure of flowers and inflorescences of *Anthurium andraeanum* hort. non Linden. *Acta Agrobotanica* 26:261–256.

Tijskens, L.M.M., M. Sloof, E.C. Wilkinson, and W.G. van Doorn. 1996. A model of the effects of temperature and time on the acceptability of potted plants stored in darkness. *Postharvest Biology and Technology* 8:293–305.

Wilbret, G.J., and T.J. Sheehan. 1981. Development of new foliage plant cultivars, pp. 127–136 in *Foliage Plant Production*, J.N. Joiner, editor. Prentice-Hall, Englewood Cliffs, New Jersey.

Antirrhinum

INTRODUCTION

Common name: snapdragon.

Scientific name: *Antirrhinum majus* L. (Huxley et al., 1992).

Family and related taxa: Scrophulariaceae Juss. There are 40 *Antirrhinum* species in the genus, which is found both in the Old and New World. Other important genera in the family include *Calceolaria, Hebe, Penstemon, Verbascum,* and *Veronica.*

Origin: The progenitor of the modern snapdragon is from the Mediterranean area.

Uses and current status: Snapdragons have many uses as cut flowers, garden ornamentals, bedding plants, and potted plants (Figs. II-1 and II-2 Antirrhinum). They can be grown for cut flowers in an open field (Starman et al., 1995) with or without protection depending on climate.

Although the common garden snapdragon is treated as an annual, it is an erect herbaceous perennial. Cultivars in commerce are available with a wide range of genetically controlled heights. Dwarf cultivars are suited for bedding and potted flowering plants; taller varieties with heights of 36 to 72 in. (90 to 180 cm) are suited for cut flowers (Bailey and Bailey, 1976). Although plants are normally upright, trailing cultivars exist. Colors include white, red, rose, pink, yellow, orange, and bicolors, and flower styles include single, double, and open faced ("butterfly"). The inflorescence is a terminal raceme with numerous individual perfect flowers. Each flower is borne on a short pedicel along the stem with five lobed petals; the corolla base is fused into a tube. The three lower lobes or lips are typically spreading, the two upper lobes or lips are erect and form a "mouth"; hence, the name snapdragon. Leaves are lanceolate, entire, dark green to purplish and mainly opposite (Bailey and Bailey, 1976).

FIGURE II-1 ANTIRRHINUM *Antirrhinum*
'Potomac Appleblossom' cut flower.

FIGURE II-2 ANTIRRHINUM *Antirrhinum* cut
flower production.

CULTIVARS

The numerous cut flower cultivars are classified into four flowering response groups, each
suited for different production conditions:
Group I (winter series)—short days, low light,
night temperatures of 45 to 50°F (7 to 10°C);
Group II (late winter to early spring series)—
short days but not as short as Group I, moderate light, night temperatures of 50 to 55°F (10
to 13°C); Group III (spring series)—medium to
long days, moderate to high light, night temperatures of 55 to 60°F (13 to 16°C); and Group
IV (summer series)—high light, long days,
night temperatures higher than 60°F (16°C)

(Tables II-1 and II-2 Antirrhinum). Individual
cultivars are placed into these groups based on
their vegetative and reproductive responses to
seasonal changes of temperature and photoperiod. These response groups are based on climatic conditions in North America and similar
systems are available for Europe (Cockshull,
1985). Snapdragon breed lines also vary considerably in postharvest life, which may be increased by proper breeding (Schroeder and
Stimart, 2001).

PROPAGATION

Although snapdragons can be propagated asexually by tissue culture (Orlikowska et al., 1995;
Pfister and Widholm, 1984; Sangwan and
Harada, 1975; Schroeder and Stimart, 1999),
commercial seed propagation is most commonly used for cut flower production. Both
seed and cutting propagated bedding plant cultivars are available. Seeds germinate within 10
days at 64 to 68°F (18 to 20°C) under light. During the summer, germination in the greenhouse
occurs best under mist to keep the medium
near the correct temperature. Fog is also used
to prevent drying in germination chambers, or
seed flats may be enclosed in plastic or covered
with glass. If hand sowing seed, do not crowd
(Delworth, 1946). Care should be used in preventing water stress (Kumpf et al., 1966). Most
producers buy plugs from specialty propagators (Larson et al., 1985). Light intensities
should be at maximum levels; supplemental
lighting can be used to hasten growth and increase quality (Atwater, 1980).

For plug production the following conditions are used (Ball, 1991; Laughner and Corr,
1996):

- *Stage 1:* Seed uncovered, 70 to 75°F (21 to
  24°C), for 5 to 7 days. Medium pH 5.5 to 5.8
  and EC less than 0.75 dS · m (2:1, water:
  medium). Light level should be 450 to 1500
  fc (90 to 300 μmol · m^{-2} · s^{-1}).
- *Stage 2:* 65 to 70°F (18 to 21°C), for 14
  days. If fertilizer has not already been incorporated into the medium, apply 50 to 75
  ppm from calcium nitrate and potassium
  nitrate.
- *Stage 3:* 60 to 65°F (16 to 18°C), for 14
  days. Apply 100 to 150 ppm N once/week
  and supplement with magnesium sulfate at
  16 oz/100 gal (1.2 g · L^{-1}) or magnesium nitrate. Maintain a ratio of 3:2:1, K:Ca:Mg.

TABLE II-1 ANTIRRHINUM

Sample production schedules for *Antirrhinum* cultivar response groups in the northern and southern United States (Anonymous, 1998).

Cultivar Response Group	North			South		
	Sow	Transplant	Flower	Sow	Transplant	Flower
			Week of the Year			
I	33–35	37–39	50–7	———— Not applicable ————		
II	37–49	40–1	8–19	34–51	38–4	49–17
	30–32	34–38	44–49	———— Not applicable ————		
III	50–11	2–15	20–26	28–33	32–37	40–48
	25–28	28–33	37–43	2–10	5–14	18–24
IV	13–23	16–27	27–36	11–26	15–31	25–39

TABLE II-2 ANTIRRHINUM

The influence of photoperiod (hr) and temperature on the days from snapdragon seed germination to floral initiation, to visible bud and to harvest (average of three seeding dates: 1/15, 1/19, and 2/2). The data in parentheses are the actual days from initiation to visible bud or the days from visible bud to flower (adapted from Maginnes and Langhans, 1961).

Temperature °F (°C)	Days from Germination to:					
	Initiation		Visible Bud		Harvest	
	9 hr	18 hr	9 hr	18 hr	9 hr	18 hr
40 (4.5)	106	85	116 (10)	98 (13)	143 (27)	127 (29)
50 (10.0)	93	75	101 (8)	81 (6)	134 (33)	112 (31)
60 (15.5)	80	65	95 (15)	70 (5)	123 (28)	96 (26)
70 (21.0)	74	51	86 (12)	60 (9)	105 (19)	79 (19)

Light level should be 1000 to 2500 fc (200 to 500 μmol $\cdot$ m^{-2} $\cdot$ s^{-1}).

- *Stage 4:* 60 to 62°F (16 to 17°C), for 7 to 10 days. Fertilize as needed, but avoid ammonium.

Transplant promptly because stunting can occur if plants are held in plug flats for too long. Plugs should be ready for marketing or transplanting within 6 to 7 weeks (see Chapter 1, Propagation, for description of plug stages). Plugs can be stored at 36 to 39°F (2 to 4°C) and 250 fc (50 μmol $\cdot$ m^{-2} $\cdot$ s^{-1}) light from fluorescent lights for up to 6 weeks.

FLOWERING CONTROL AND DORMANCY

The snapdragon is a facultative LD plant in that flowering occurs faster under long photoperiods, but can occur under SD (Cockshull, 1985; Flint, 1960; Hedley, 1974; Hedley and Harvey, 1975; Laurie and Poesch, 1932; Sanderson and Link, 1967). Flower initiation and development has been documented under various light du-

rations, intensities, temperatures, and cultural conditions (Maginnes and Langhans, 1961; Sing and Jain, 1979). A wide variation exists among cultivars in response to LD and temperature (Hedley et al., 1977) (see Cultivars on previous page). Juvenile plants that have less than a specified leaf number will not respond to LD (Cockshull, 1985; Hedley and Harvey, 1975; Maginnes and Langhans, 1961). When plants are mature enough to perceive LD, temperature influences the rate of flower initiation, not development. For example, temperatures between 40 and 70°F (4 to 21°C) had little effect on days to flower once flower initiation occurred (Edwards and Goldberg, 1976; Maginnes and Langhans, 1961) (Table II-2 Antirrhinum).

Vegetative plants grown at 50°F (10°C) or lower become reproductive later and flowering is delayed when compared with plants grown at higher temperatures (Maginnes and Langhans, 1961; Sanderson and Link, 1967). In addition, the time between visible flower bud and anthesis is not influenced by light duration or intensity at any one temperature (Cockshull,

1985; Rabinowitch et al., 1976). The importance of cultivar response to photoperiod and light intensities must be considered.

TEMPERATURE

After propagation Group I cut flower cultivars should be grown at night temperatures of 45 to 50°F (7 to 10°C), Group II at 50 to 55°F (10 to 13°C), Group III at 55 to 60°F (13 to 16°C), and Group IV at 60 to 65°F (16 to 18°C). Larger plants with heavier weights could be grown rapidly if held at warm temperatures during the early growth stage and at low temperatures during the later growth stage (Miller, 1962). Similar results were obtained with temperatures ranging from 80°F (27°C) for small young seedlings to 55 to 61°F (13 to 16°C) for large old plants. Generally, low production temperatures will increase stem length but will also increase crop time (Cavins et al., 2000).

Temperature manipulation can be used if large production blocks are planted at once and temperatures can be lowered as the plants pass through vegetative and reproductive phases. When smaller blocks are planted weekly, plants are usually grown at 50 to 58°F (10 to 14°C) night temperature. Group I and II cultivars are grown at these temperatures in the northern United States and Europe in the winter.

Temperature is also important in controlling the ability of the plant to absorb water. When the medium and roots are at 50°F (10°C) night temperature, moisture stress can occur when day temperatures are 70°F (21°C) or higher because the plant's ability to absorb water is inhibited. This fact explains why snapdragons and many other species commonly wilt on bright sunny winter mornings when the soil temperature is cool (Rutland and Pallas, 1972). McDaniel and Miller (1976) determined that cultivars that did not wilt in the early morning were able to close their stomates, reduce water stress, and produce high-quality flowers.

Seed-propagated bedding plants can be grown at 45 to 55°F (7 to 13°C). Vegetative propagated bedding plants are grown at 50 to 60°F (10 to 16°C).

LIGHT

Floral induction and development are delayed if young plants are grown under low light compared to high light. Hedley (1974) suggested that photosynthates are involved and the ability to fix carbon varies greatly among cultivars and may account for the differences among the cultivar group classifications. Long photoperiods hasten flowering (see Flowering Control and Dormancy, page 286). Supplemental lighting benefits plugs and is normally economical because the plant density is high (Flint, 1960; Peterson, 1955). Although the cost effectiveness of supplemental lighting is questionable on older plants with wide spacing, Dansereau et al. (1998) found that supplementing natural light in Quebec by 460 fc (60 $\mu mol \cdot m^{-2} \cdot s^{-1}$) hastened flowering by 20 to 25 days and improved flower quality. Three weeks of supplemental lighting on newly transplanted seedlings grown at 50°F (10°C) produced results similar to those grown at 60°F (16°C) without lighting (Rogers, 1958, 1959, 1960, 1961). Stefanis and Langhans (1982) used supplemental high-pressure sodium lamps during the winter to decrease flowering time and increase quality. Maximum light intensity during winter is a cultural necessity and greenhouse coverings should be clean. Carpenter (1964) found that even baffles of reflective aluminum foil placed on the north side of benches increased growth.

Snapdragon cultivars are divided into response groups based on their response to light levels and photoperiod. Cultivars recommended for winter flowering are not delayed by low irradiance or SD and flower in an economically reasonable time because they have a short juvenile phase. Summer flowering cultivars have a longer juvenile phase and a higher leaf number under LD and high irradiance (Hedley, 1974; Maginnes and Langhans, 1961; Raulston, 1970; Sing and Jain, 1979). If photoperiodic incandescent lighting is used, the natural day is extended to an 18-hr "day" (Maginnes and Langhans, 1961). Maginnes and Langhans (1967) found that night breaks (2200 to 0200 hr) from either continuous or cyclical lighting (10 or more seconds on per minute) were equally effective.

WATER

Snapdragon plants should never be overwatered. Intervals between irrigation may be long due to low production temperatures. The primary concern in the production of snapdragons is the relationship between overwatering and *Pythium* root rot, especially close to harvest time (Hanan et al., 1963). If *Pythium* can be excluded from the cultural system, snapdragon plants are tolerant of both high and low moisture levels (Hanan, 1965; Hanan and Langhans,

1963; Hanan et al., 1963). In general, ground beds or benches should be 6 in. (15 cm) or greater deep to allow adequate drainage.

CARBON DIOXIDE

Groups I, II, and, to a lesser degree, IV cultivars are highly responsive to CO_2 during the winter. The desired CO_2 level ranges from 750 to 1500 ppm (Duffett, 1968; Koths, 1964; Lindstrom, 1966; Nelson and Larson, 1969; Shaw and Rogers, 1964). Rogers (1980) concluded that under natural light intensities, 800 ppm CO_2 and 60°F (16°C) night temperatures would be appropriate during the low-light periods under northern conditions. With supplemental lighting, the response of snapdragons to CO_2 at various light intensities and growth stages needs to be reevaluated.

NUTRITION

Nutrition of young seedlings and plugs should not be neglected if quality plants and repeat flowering are desired (Larson et al., 1985; Rogers, 1951). Nitrogen levels must be adequate at an early stage of growth to ensure development of strong, thick stems (Boodley, 1962). Hood et al. (1993) compared nutrient uptake of four cultivars during three developmental stages of growth (seedling to flower initiation, initiation to visible flower bud, and visible bud to harvest) and noted that nutritional levels should remain high until harvest and should not be reduced at the final development stage. However, Haney (1961), Rogers (1959), and Sanderson (1975) suggested that fertility levels be reduced during the summer and eliminated during the final stage of flower spike development.

Snapdragon plants have a relatively low nutrient requirement compared to other crops species such as chrysanthemums or poinsettias (Howland, 1946; Rogers, 1951). When the fertilizer rate was increased by two or four times, high soluble salt levels, reduced growth, and injury occurred. Sanderson (1975) believed that if nutrients were applied at each irrigation, 100 ppm N and K were adequate. Major growth differences did not occur when various N, K, or pH levels were tested (Flint and Asen, 1953; Howland, 1946). Rogers (1951) stated that growth varied little among various P and K levels but growth increased when nitrate levels increased from 5 ppm to 25 or 50 ppm. Excessive vegetative growth occurs if N levels are high and nitrate is generally preferred to ammonium (Haney, 1961; Sanderson, 1975). Hood et al. (1993) found that nitrate was taken up at a higher level than ammonium. Snapdragons are sensitive, however, to very low levels of B and growers must be certain adequate levels are present (Furuta, 1960; Mastalerz, 1957). Carmichael (1968) believed that B became deficient when Ca levels were too high.

Hood et al. (1993) found that four cultivars had similar nutrient uptake, except nitrate uptake varied between two of the four cultivars. However, when Arthur and Hedley (1976) and Hedley et al. (1977) compared numerous F_1 hybrid cultivars grown at various nitrogen levels, significant differences were found between each cultivar at any one N level. In summary, the authors felt that it may not be appropriate to formulate one standard nutrient regime for all cultivars.

Oertli (1970a–h) in a series of classic papers described deficiency symptoms and identified both deficiency and optimal levels for N,

TABLE II-3 ANTIRRHINUM
Nutrient tissue content of healthy control of deficient *Antirrhinum* plants (Oertli, 1970a–h).

Element	Healthy	Nutrient Deficiency
Nitrogen	1.1 to 2.0%	<1.0 to 0.3%
Phosphorus	0.17%	0.02%
Calcium	>0.5%	<0.5%
	(at +1% Ca, Fe deficiencies were observed)	
Magnesium	>0.5%	<0.18%
Sulfur	0.5%	<0.14%
Iron	>70 ppm	<30 to 60 ppm
Boron	30 to 40 ppm	10 ppm

P, K, Ca, Mg, S, B, and Fe using a standard Hoagland's solution (Table II-3 Antirrhinum). Data for tissue nutrient levels were also established by Oertli (1970a–h). Additional foliar nutrient levels are listed in Chapter 6, Nutrition, Table 6–4. Similarly, Laurie and Wagner (1940) described nutritional deficiency symptoms.

MEDIA

Seeds are best germinated and planted in a well-aerated medium (Larson et al., 1985). A media pH of 6.0 to 6.5 is optimum for soil-based media and 5.5 to 5.8 for soilless media (Anonymous, 1998). For cut flowers a wide range of media, with or without soil, has been used. Hanan and Langhans (1963) grew excellent crops in peat:perlite (1:1), peat:soil:perlite or sand (1:1:1), or soil:sand (1:1), and Lee et al. (1986) used rockwool. Cut flowers can be grown either in bedding plant flats or in ground beds, which produced the highest quality stems (Sullivan and Pasian, 2000).

HEIGHT CONTROL

Various plant growth regulators can be used including A-Rest (ancymidol), Bonzi (paclobutrazol), B-Nine (daminozide), Cycocel (chlormequat), and Sumagic (uniconazole). For flats, A-Rest sprays at 15 to 20 ppm can be used after transplanting and 15 to 26 ppm at finishing (Bell, 2001). Bonzi sprays are applied at 30 to 90 ppm and Sumagic to 25 to 50 ppm (Barrett and Nell, 1989; Bell, 2001). Sumagic as a 1- to 2-ppm spray can also be applied to the media prior to transplanting plugs. Cycocel and tank mixes of 1250 ppm Cycocel and 1250 ppm B-Nine have also been reported to be effective (Kuehny et al., 2001; Ministry of Agricultural Fisheries and Food, 1970). A-Rest sprays at 6 ppm can be applied within a week to 10 days after sowing to the plug flat media to produce compact, well-branched plugs and subsequent bedding plants (Britten, 1999).

Bonzi drenches at 1.25 or 1.75 mg a.i. per 3.5-in. (9-cm) pot are effective in height control of potted flowering plants (Wainwright and Irwin, 1987). The response to Bonzi is influenced by plant age, and earlier applications are more effective. However, early application also delays flowering and reduces the number of flowering stems produced when plants are pinched. Seasonal and cultivar differences are also observed. With these factors in mind, Wainwright and Irwin (1987) stated that Bonzi and pinching re-

sulted in an acceptable potted flowering plant that could be produced at an affordable price.

DIF is effective on snapdragon (Neily et al., 1997). A positive DIF should be maintained for cut flowers and a 0 or negative DIF for bedding and potted plants. Interestingly, unlike many species, DIF remained equally effective on snapdragons at all stages of growth. Gibberellic acid at 100 ppm is also effective in increasing the stem length of some snapdragon cultivars (Rak and Nowak, 1989).

SPACING

Spacing depends on the season, plant growth habit (single stem or pinched), and supplemental lighting. For cut flowers, plants should be spaced at 3 × 5 to 4 × 5 in. (8 × 13 to 10 × 13 cm) for winter production and 3 × 4 to 3 × 5 in. (8 × 10 to 7.5 × 13 cm) for summer production (Stefanis and Langhans, 1982). The closer spacing of 3 × 4 in. (8 × 10 cm) increased production by 63% when compared with 4 × 5 in. (10 × 13 cm). With potted plants, four to five seedlings are placed in a 6-in. (15-cm) pot and grown pot-to-pot until plants begin to shade each other.

PINCHING AND DISBUDDING

Snapdragon plants can be grown single stem or pinched. Pinched plants require more space per plant and a delay in production will occur. No disbudding is required and the removal of excessive axillary, grassy growth is not commercially practical. Leave four to six leaves (two to three nodes) per plant when pinching, which will produce about four to six stems/plant. Leaving more leaves/plant will produce more stems but they will be short and may not be marketable. For field production pinching can be used to spread out the harvest period; plants that are pinched will flower later than those that are not pinched. After the initial harvest, another harvest can be obtained in some cases but stems will usually be much shorter. Potted flowering plants can be pinched or grown single stem with the appropriate plant growth regulator (Wainwright and Irwin, 1987).

SUPPORT

Two to five tiers of support are sufficient for cut flower production. Any basic netting is acceptable with openings of 4 × 5, 6 × 6, or 6 × 8 in. (10 × 13, 15 ×, 15, or 15 × 20 cm).

TABLE II-4 ANTIRRHINUM

The approximate number of days required for a nonpinched *Antirrhinum* plant to flower as influenced by date of seeding in the southern and northern United States (adapted from Rogers. 1958, 1959).

Location	Month											
	Jan	Feb	Mar	Apr	May	June	July	Aug	Sep	Oct	Nov	Dec
	Approximate Number of Days to Flower											
South	130	120	110	90	90	85	85	85	85	100	110	130
North	140	150	140	145	110	110	110	110	150	160	155	145

SCHEDULE AND TIMING

Scheduling and timing of cut flowers are based on the cultivar and time of the year a producer wishes to harvest a crop (see Cultivars, page 285) (Table II-4 Antirrhinum). The cultivars selected must be suitable for that particular production time span to prevent flowering problems (delayed or accelerated) and plant growth problems (large, vegetative, grassy plants or small, weak plants).

When weekly production timing is viewed year-round, note that season (light duration and intensity) influences the rate of growth. After August 1, the crop time dramatically increases; however, little difference exists in the time required to produce a weekly crop from September or October seeding dates. Because of the increase in production time starting in late August, seeding must occur every 4 or 5 days. If not seeding on this schedule, then there will be 2- or 3-week intervals between harvest dates. The goal of production is to ensure continuous nonstop growth when young plants are placed into the cut flower production bench, pot, or bedding plant flat (Larson et al., 1985).

INSECTS

Aphids, fungus gnats, thrips, and red spider mites are the most common problems; whiteflies and cyclamen mites can also occur. Outdoor caterpillars of several moth and butterfly species and root knot nematodes can be problems (Dreistadt, 2001). All prevention and biological controls must be considered before attempting chemical control.

DISEASES

Slow root degeneration and wilting are related to poor aeration, excess watering, and *Pythium* (Hanan et al., 1963). Rust (*Puccinia antirrhini*), *Botrytis*, powdery mildew (*Oidium*), downy mildew (*Peronospora antirrhini*), and *Pythium* are some of the more common diseases observed (Horst, 1990). Tomato spotted wilt virus and impatiens necrotic spot virus can cause brown or black stem lesions, which often do not appear until just before flowering (Laughner and Corr, 1996). Regionally, leaf spot (*Cercospora antirrhini*) in the southeast and *Alternaria* and *Helminthosporium* in Florida can be major concerns. Sanitation, proper soil treatments before and during production, air movement, humidity control, and the use of protective or control chemical sprays can prevent or reduce disease. A number of other disease organisms have been documented on snapdragons including *Phytophthora* (root rot), *Rhizoctonia solani* (root rot), *Sclerotium rolfsii* (southern blight), *Sclerotinia sclerotiorum* (cottony rot), *Verticillium dahliae* (wilt), *V. alboatrum* (wilt), *Thielaviopsis basicola* (black root rot), *Phyllostica antirrhini* (stem rot), *Phyllostica* (leaf spot), *Colletotrichum* (anthracnose), *Pseudomonas syringae* (bacterial leaf spot), aster yellow phytoplasma, and *Agrobacterium tumefaciens* (crown gall) (Dreistadt, 2001). Disease control has been reviewed by several researchers (Dimock, 1958; Engelhard, 1971; Forsberg, 1958; Nelson, 1962; Porter and Aycock, 1967; Williamson, 1962).

PHYSIOLOGICAL DISORDERS

Hood et al. (1993) questioned if the practice of lowering mineral nutrition during the final stages of production prior to harvest contributed to a tip-breaking problem as snapdragon plants continue to absorb high levels of nutrients up to the time of harvest. Excessive grassy growth can occur with improper cultivar selection and excessive nitrogen application.

POSTHARVEST

Cut flower stems are harvested when one-third of florets (minimum of five to seven) are open. Immature flowers will open small and poorly

TABLE II-5 ANTIRRHINUM

Society of American Florists specifications for *Antirrhinum* standard grades.

Grade Name	Label Color Code	Individual Flower Stem Weight oz (g)		Minimum Flowers Open per Stem (no.)	Minimum Stem Length in. (cm)	Stems per Bunch (no.)
		Min.	Max.			
Special	Blue	2.5 (71)	4.0 (113)	15	36 (91)	12
Fancy	Red	1.5 (43)	2.5 (70)	12	30 (76)	12
Extra	Green	1.0 (29)	1.5 (42)	9	24 (61)	12
First	Yellow	0.5 (14)	1.0 (28)	9	18 (46)	12

colored if the spikes are harvested too soon. Preservatives can increase vase life from 1 week to 2 or more weeks and increase inflorescence length, stem strength, flower pigmentation, and the number of florets that open (Johnson, 1972; Larsen and Scholes, 1966; Marousky and Raulston, 1970; Raulston and Marousky, 1971; Wang et al., 1977). Solutions of 8-hydroxyquinoline citrate (8-HQC, 300 ppm) and sucrose (0.5 to 1.5%) with or without B-Nine were optimal (Johnson, 1972; Larsen and Scholes, 1966; Raulston and Marousky, 1971). Marousky and Raulston (1970) stressed that light and a floral preservative were needed for good pigmentation to develop.

Stem tip curving upward is a common occurrence and B-Nine reduces this geotropic response if cut flower stems are shipped horizontally. Bending is apparently controlled by cytosolic calcium (Philosoph-Hadas et al., 1995). The application of calcium chelators (EDTA, EGTA, and CDTA) inhibited bending, while calcium chloride stimulated bending. Silver thiosulfate (STS) was also effective in reducing bending.

Grades and standards have been developed by the Society of American Florists (Table II-5 Antirrhinum). Cut stems can be stored at 32 to 36°F (0 to 2°C) and bedding plants at 50 to 55°F (10 to 13°C) (L. Høyer, personal communication).

Exogenous or endogenous ethylene can cause floret abscission and senescence of cut snapdragon florets (Wang et al., 1977). Flowers can be treated with a 1-hr pulse of STS at 70°F (21°C) room temperature. Treatment with 1-MCP is also effective at inhibiting ethylene effects (Serek et al., 1995).

KEY POINTS

- Snapdragon is primarily used as a cut flower and garden plant, and occasionally as a potted flowering plant.
- Plants are propagated by seed.
- Cut flower cultivars are classified in four flowering response groups, according to season grown.
- Snapdragon is a facultative LD plant and juvenility exists.
- Optimum quality is obtained when plants are grown cool at 45 to 52°F (7 to 11°C).
- Do not overwater or overfertilize.
- Snapdragons are sensitive to boron deficiencies.
- Root rots and wilting are common problems.
- Cut snapdragons respond dramatically to postharvest floral preservatives and are quite sensitive to ethylene.

BIBLIOGRAPHY

Anonymous. 1998. *Snapdragon Culture Guide*, 4th ed. Pan American Seed, West Chicago, Illinois.

Arthur, A.E., and C.L. Hedley. 1976. The effects of nitrogen on five varieties of *Antirrhinum majus*. *Annals of Botany* 41:627–636.

Atwater, B.R. 1980. Germination, dormancy and morphology of seeds or herbaceous ornamental plants. *Seed Science Technology* 8:523–573.

Bailey, L.H., and E.Z. Bailey. 1976. *Antirrhinum*, L., pp. 86–87 in *Hortus Third: A Concise Dictionary of Plants Cultivated in the United States and Canada*. Macmillan, New York.

Ball, V. 1991. Plugs—The way of the 1990s, pp. 137–153 in *Ball RedBook*, 15th ed., V. Ball, editor. George J. Ball Publishing, West Chicago, Illinois.

Barrett, J.E., and T.A. Nell. 1989. Comparison of paclobutrazol and uniconazole on floriculture crops. *Acta Horticulturae* 251:275–280.

Bell, M. 2001. Bedding plants and seed geraniums, pp. 54–62 in *Tips on Regulating Growth of Floriculture Crops*, M.L. Gaston, L.A. Kunkle, P.S. Konjoian, and M.F. Wilt, editors. Ohio Florists' Association Services, Columbus, Ohio.

Boodley, J. 1962. Fertilization, pp. 28–34 in *Snapdragons: A Manual of Culture, Insect and Diseases and Economics of Snapdragons*, R.E. Langhans, editor. Snapdragon School, New York State Extension Service, and New York State Flower Growers Association, Ithaca, New York.

Britten, A. 1999. PGRs at seeding reduce early stretch. *GrowerTalks* 63(5):46, 48.

Carmichael, O.E. 1968. Boron toxicity of flowering plants. MS thesis, University of Missouri, Columbia.

Carpenter, W.J. 1964. Response of snapdragons and chrysanthemums to supplemental reflective light. *Proceedings of the American Society for Horticultural Science* 84:624–629.

Cavins, T.J., J.M. Dole, and V. Stamback. 2000. Unheated and minimally heated winter greenhouse production of specialty cut flowers. *HortTechnology* 10:793–799.

Cockshull, K.E. 1985. *Antirrhinum majus*, pp. 476–481 in *Handbook of Flowering*, vol. I, A.H. Halevy, editor. CRC Press, Boca Raton, Florida.

Dansereau, B., Y. Zhang, and S. Gagnon. 1998. Stock and snapdragon as influenced by greenhouse covering materials and supplemental light. *HortScience* 33:668–671.

Delworth, C.I. 1946. Fundamentals and details in producing quality snapdragons. *Florists' Review* 99(2559):35–36.

Dimock, A.W. 1958. Snapdragon diseases common in New York. *New York Flower Growers' Bulletin* 145:2–3.

Dreistadt, S.H. 2001. *Integrated Pest Management for Floriculture and Nurseries*. University of California Division of Agriculture and Natural Resources Publication 3402.

Duffett, W.E. 1968. Culture of greenhouse snapdragons. *Ohio Florists' Association Bulletin* 466:5–7.

Edwards, K.J.R., and J.B. Goldberg. 1976. A temperature effect on the expression of genotypic differences in flowering inductions in *Antirrhinum majus*. *Annals of Botany* 40:1277–1283.

Engelhard, A.W. 1971. *Botrytis*-like diseases of rose, chrysanthemum, carnation, snapdragon and king aster caused by *Alternaria* and *Helminthosporium*. *Proceedings of the Florida State Horticultural Society* 83:455–457.

Flint, H.L. 1960. Relative effects of light duration and intensity on growth and flowering of winter snapdragon (*Antirrhinum majus* L.). *Proceedings of the American Society for Horticultural Science* 75:769–773.

Flint, H.L., and S. Asen. 1953. The effects of various nutrient intensities on growth and development of snapdragon (*Antirrhinum majus* L.). *Proceedings of the American Society for Horticultural Science* 62:481–486.

Forsberg, J.L. 1958. Snapdragon diseases. *Illinois State Florists Association Bulletin* 186:5–8.

Furuta, T. 1960. Test boron deficiency in snapdragons at Auburn. *Florists' Review* 126(3244):25.

Hanan, J.J. 1965. Efficiency and effect of irrigation regimes on growth and flowering of snapdragon. *Proceedings of the American Society for Horticultural Science* 86:681–692.

Hanan, J.J., and R.W. Langhans. 1963. Soil aeration and moisture controls snapdragon quality. *New York State Flower Growers Bulletin* 210:3–6.

Hanan, J., R.W. Langhans, and A.W. Dimock. 1963. Pythium and soil aeration. *Proceedings of the American Society for Horticultural Science* 82:574–582.

Haney, W.J. 1961. Snapdragon culture. *Michigan Florist* 366:25–26, 29.

Hedley, C.L. 1974. Response to light intensity and daylength of two contrasting flower varieties of *Antirrhinum majus*. *Journal of Horticultural Science* 49:105–112.

Hedley, C.L., and D.M. Harvey. 1975. Variation in the photoperiod control of flowering of two cultivars of *Antirrhinum majus* L. *Annals of Botany* 39:257–263.

Hedley, C.L., A.E. Arthur, and H.D. Rabinowitch. 1977. The effects of nitrogen level on the performance of *Antirrhinum* cultivars grown in greenhouse conditions. *Euphytica* 26:755–760.

Hood, T.M., H.A. Mills, and P.A. Thomas. 1993. Developmental stage affects nutrient uptake by four snapdragon cultivars. *HortScience* 28:1008–1010.

Horst, R.K. 1990. Snapdragon, p. 816 in *Westcott's Plant Disease Handbook*, 5th ed. Van Nostrand Reinhold, New York.

Howland, J.E. 1946. Foliar dieback of the greenhouse snapdragon *Antirrhinum majus* and a study of the influence of certain environmental factors upon flower production and quality. *Proceedings of the American Society for Horticultural Science* 47:485–497.

Huxley, A., M. Griffiths, and M. Levy. 1992. *Antirrhinum*, pp. 194–195 in *The New Royal Horticultural Society Dictionary of Gardening*, vol. 1. Stockton Press, New York.

Johnson, C.R. 1972. Effectiveness of floral preservative on increasing the vase life of snapdragons. *Florists' Review* 149(3868):47, 95–97.

Koths, J.S. 1964. The effects of CO_2 enriched greenhouse atmosphere on growth of snapdragons. *Michigan Florists* 399:15.

Kuehny, J.S., A. Painter, and P.C. Branch. 2001. Plug source and growth retardants affect finish size of bedding plants. *HortScience* 36:321–323.

Kumpf, J., F. Horton, and R.W. Langhans. 1966. Seedling storage. *New York State Flower Growers Bulletin* 244:1–3.

Larsen, F.E., and J.F. Scholes. 1966. Effects of 8-hydroxyquinoline citrate, *N*-dimethyl amino succinamic acid and sucrose on vase life and spike characteristics of cut snapdragons. *Proceedings of the American Society for Horticultural Science* 89:694–701.

Larson, R.A., C.B. Thorne, and R.R. Milks. 1985. Growth of geranium and snapdragon 'plugs' fertilized with controlled released micro-fertilizer to root-zone heating. *New York Flower Growers Bulletin* 29(3):12–16.

Laughner, L., and B. Corr. 1996. Snapdragons: Formula for success. *GrowerTalks* 60(6):57, 62.

Laurie, A., and G.H. Poesch. 1932. Photoperiodism—the value of supplementary illumination and reduction of light on flowering plants in the greenhouse. *Ohio Agricultural Experiment Station Research Bulletin* 512:8, 31, 35.

Laurie, A., and A. Wagner. 1940. Deficiency symptoms of greenhouse flowering crops. *Ohio Agricultural Experiment Station Research Bulletin* 611:19–21.

Lee, C.W., K.L. Goldsberry, and J.J. Hanan. 1986. Production of cut snapdragons in rockwool. *Colorado Greenhouse Growers Association Bulletin* 438:1–2.

Lindstrom, R.L. 1966. Snapdragons—60°F and CO_2. *Florists' Review* 139(3591):18–19, 51–54.

Maginnes, E.A., and R.W. Langhans. 1961. The effect of photoperiod and temperature on initiation and flowering of snapdragon (*Antirrhinum majus* var. Jack Pot). *Proceedings of the American Society for Horticultural Science* 77:600–607.

Maginnes, E.A., and R.W. Langhans. 1967. Flashing light affects the flowering of snapdragons. *New York State Flower Growers Bulletin* 261:1–3.

Marousky, F.J., and J.C. Raulston. 1970. Enhancement of snapdragon floret color with light and floral preservatives. *HortScience* 5:355. (Abstract)

Mastalerz, J.W. 1957. Boron deficiency of snapdragon. *Pennsylvania Flower Growers Bulletin* 75:3–6.

McDaniel, G.L., and M.G. Miller. 1976. Transpiration of snapdragon under southern summer greenhouse conditions. *HortScience* 11:366–368.

Miller, R.O. 1962. Variations in optimum temperature of snapdragon depending on plant size. *Proceedings of the American Society for Horticultural Science* 81:535–543.

Ministry of Agricultural Fisheries and Food. 1970. Pot plants—inexpensive winter production. *Report for Efford Experimental Horticulture Station* 1969:38–40.

Neily, W.G., P.R. Hicklenton, and D.N. Kristie. 1997. Temperature and developmental stage influence diurnal rhythms of stem elongation in snapdragon and zinnia. *Journal of the American Society for Horticultural Science* 122:778–783.

Nelson, P. 1962. Disease, pp. 70–80 in *Snapdragons: A Manual of the Culture, Insects and Diseases and Economics of Snapdragons*, R.W. Langhans, editor. Snapdragon School, New York State Extension Service, and New York State Flower Growers Association, Ithaca, New York.

Nelson, P.V., and R.A. Larson. 1969. The effects of increased CO_2 concentrations on chrysanthemum (*C. morifolium*) and snapdragon (*Antirrhinum majus*). *North Carolina Agricultural Experiment Station Technical Bulletin* 194:1–15.

Oertli, J.J. 1970a. Nutrient disorders in snapdragon. *Florists' Review* 146(3773):20–21.

Oertli, J.J. 1970b. Phosphorus deficiency in snapdragon. *Florists' Review* 146(3774):28–29.

Oertli, J.J. 1970c. Potassium deficiency in snapdragon. *Florists' Review* 146(3775):29.

Oertli, J.J. 1970d. Calcium deficiency in snapdragon. *Florists' Review* 146(3776):51.

Oertli, J.J. 1970e. Magnesium deficiency in snapdragon. *Florists' Review* 146(3777):23.

Oertli, J.J. 1970f. Sulfur deficiency in snapdragon. *Florists' Review* 146(3778):28.

Oertli, J.J. 1970g. Boron deficiency in snapdragon. *Florists' Review* 146(3779):65.

Oertli, J.J. 1970h. Iron deficiency in snapdragon. *Florists' Review* 146(3780):24.

Orlikowska, T., I. Sabala, and E. Nowak. 1995. Adventitious shoot regeneration on explants of *Anthurium, Codiaeum, Dieffenbachia, Gerbera, Rosa,* and *Spathyphyllum* for breeding purposes. *Acta Horticulturae* 420:115–117.

Peterson, H. 1955. Artificial light for seedlings and cuttings. *New York State Flower Growers Bulletin* 122:2–3.

Pfister, J.M., and J.M. Widholm. 1984. Plant regeneration from snapdragon tissue cultures. *HortScience* 19:852–854.

Philosoph-Hadas, S., S. Meir, I. Rosenberger, and A.H. Halevy. 1995. Control and regulation of the gravitropic response of cut flowering stems during storage and horizontal transport. *Acta Horticulturae* 405:343–350.

Porter, D.M., and R. Aycock. 1967. Snapdragon leafspot caused by *Cercospora antirrhina*. *North Carolina Agricultural Experiment Station Technical Bulletin* 179:1–31.

Rabinowitch, J.D., C.L. Hedley, and A.E. Arthur. 1976. Variation in budding and flowering time of commercial cultivars of *Antirrhinum majus*. *Scientia Horticulturae* 5:287–291.

Rak, J., and J. Nowak. 1989. The effect of gibberellic acid on growth and flowering of snapdragon cuttings. *Acta Horticulturae* 251:67–69.

Raulston, J.C. 1970. Relationships of snapdragon response groups to cultivar performance in Florida field production. *Proceedings of the Florida State Horticultural Society* 83:449–454.

Raulston, J.C., and F.J. Marousky. 1971. Effects of 8–10 day 5°C storage and floral preservatives on snapdragon cut flowers. *Florida Flower Growers* 8(2):4–10.

Rogers, M.N. 1951. *Greenhouse soil fertility analysis and interpretation*. MS thesis, University of Missouri, Columbia.

Rogers, M.N. 1958. Year-round snapdragon culture. 1. Effects of lighting and shading snaps seeded during the summer months. *Missouri State Florists News* 18(3):3–7.

Rogers, M.N. 1959. Year-round snapdragon culture. 2. Summer snapdragons. *Missouri State Florists News* 20(6):3–5.

Rogers, M.N. 1960. Direct benching vs. potting snapdragon seedlings. *Pennsylvania Flower Growers Bulletin* 118:3–5.

Rogers, M.N. 1961. The reactions of varieties of different response groups grown during the winter months at night temperatures of 60°F, 55°F, and 50°F with supplementary lighting. *National Snapdragon Bulletin* 13:1–6.

Rogers, M.N. 1980. Snapdragons, pp. 107–131 in *Introduction to Floriculture*, R.A. Larson, editor. Academic Press, San Diego, California.

Rutland, R.B., and J.E. Pallas, Jr. 1972. Transpiration of *Antirrhinum majus* L. in relation to radiant energy in the greenhouse. *Journal of the American Society for Horticultural Science* 97:34–37.

Sanderson, K.C. 1975. Fertilization, watering, temperature, light and photoperiod. *Florists' Review* 156(4038):17, 59–61.

Sanderson, K.C., and C.B. Link. 1967. The influence of temperature and photoperiod on the growth and quality of winter and summer cultivar of snapdragon, *Antirrhinum majus* L. *Proceedings of the American Society for Horticultural Science* 91:598–611.

Sangwan, R.S., and H. Harada. 1975. Chemical regulation of callus growth, organogenesis, plant regulation, and somatic embryogenesis in *Antirrhinum majus* tissue and cell cultures. *Journal of Experimental Botany* 26:868–881.

Schroeder, K.R., and D.P. Stimart. 1999. Adventitious shoot formation on excised hypocotyls of *Antirrhinum majus* L. (snapdragon) in vitro. *HortScience* 34:736–739.

Schroeder, K.R., and D.P. Stimart. 2001. Genetic analysis of cut flower longevity in *Antirrhinum majus*. *Journal of the American Society for Horticultural Science* 126:200–204.

Serek, M., E.C. Sisler, and M.S. Reid. 1995. Effects of 1-MCP on the vase life and ethylene response of cut flowers. *Plant Growth Regulation* 16:93–97.

Shaw, R.J., and M.N. Rogers. 1964. Interactions between elevated carbon dioxide levels and greenhouse temperatures on the growth of roses, chrysanthemums, carnations, geraniums, snapdragons, and African violets. *Florists' Review* 135(3486):23–24, 88–89.

Sing, V., and D.K. Jain. 1979. Floral organogenesis in *Antirrhinum majus* (Scrophulariaceae). *Proceedings of the Indian Academy of Science Bulletin* 88:183–188.

Starman, T.W., T.A. Cerny, and A.J. MacKenzie. 1995. Productivity and profitability of some field-grown specialty cut flowers. *HortScience* 30:1217–1220.

Stefanis, J.P., and R.W. Langhans. 1982. Snapdragon production with supplemental irradiation from high pressure sodium lamps. *HortScience* 17:601–603.

Sullivan, K.J., and C.C. Pasian. 2000. Evaluation of tow growing systems for cut snapdragon production: Tray vs. ground beds. *HortScience* 35:25–27.

Wainwright, H., and Irwin, H.L. 1987. The effect of paclobutrazol and pinching on *Antirrhinum* flowering pot plants. *Journal of Horticultural Science* 62:401–404.

Wang, C.Y., J.E. Baker, R.E. Hardenburg, and M. Lieberman. 1977. Effects of two analogs of rhizobitoxine and sodium benzoate on senescence of snapdragon. *Journal of the American Society for Horticultural Science* 102:517–520.

Williamson, C.E. 1962. Root diseases and soil sterilization, pp. 62–69 in *Snapdragons: A Manual of the Culture, Insects and Diseases and Economics of Snapdragons*, R.W. Langhans, editor. Snapdragon School, New York State Extension Service, and New York State Flower Growers Association, Ithaca, New York.

Aquilegia

FIGURE II-1 AQUILEGIA Close-up of *Aquilegia* flower structure.

INTRODUCTION

Common name: columbine.

Scientific name: *Aquilegia* L. hybrids (Huxley et al., 1992).

Family and related taxa: Ranunculaceae Juss. Within this family other distinguished ornamentals include *Aconitum, Anemone, Clematis, Consolida, Delphinium,* and *Ranunculus.*

Origin: Temperate and mountainous areas of the Northern Hemisphere (Bailey and Bailey, 1976).

Uses and current status: Columbine are used as perennial garden plants, potted plants, or cut flowers.

Flowers are 1.5 to 4 in. (4 to 10 cm) across and consist of five petal-like sepals, five true petals, five pistils, and numerous stamens (Fig. II-1 Aquilegia). The back of each petal is fused and elongated into a hollow, and frequently exaggerated, spur that is up to 3 in. (8 cm) long. The colors, mostly pastels, include blue, lavender-pink, red, rust, yellow, and white. Sepals and petals may be of similar or contrasting colors. Leaves, as typical of the Ranunculaceae family, are divided two or three times. The name *Aquilegia* is from the Latin *aquila,* meaning "eagle," referring to the clawlike curve of each spur. The common name (columbine) is from *columba,* Latin for "dove," because the spurred flower was thought to resemble the bird (Bailey, 1933).

CULTIVARS

Two major divisions exist within the various species and hybrids: the dwarf alpine types, which are 4 to 12 in. (10 to 30 cm) tall, and the border types, which are 12 to 36 in. (30 to 91 cm) tall (Bailey and Bailey, 1976; White, 1985) (Table II-1 Aquilegia). Present-day hybrids were developed from crosses of *Aquilegia caerulea* James., *A. canadensis* L., *A. chrysantha* A. Gray., *A. longissima* A. Gray., and *A. vulgaris* L. (Cumming and Lee, 1960). Many seed-propagated hybrids are hardy to Zone 4 (McGrew, 1999).

PROPAGATION

Plants are propagated by seed or division (Bailey and Bailey, 1976; Dewolf, 1984; Weiler and Shedron, 1986; White, 1985). Propagation by division is labor intensive and therefore expensive. Seed propagation, being more economical, is most common. There are 15,000 to 20,000 seed/oz (530 to 705 seed/g). Interestingly, freshly harvested seeds will germinate within 1 to 2 weeks, but older or stored seeds will require stratification. Stored seeds should be sown in moist sphagnum moss-peat and allowed to imbibe water for 24 hr at 60°F (16°C), then cold treated at 40°F (4°C) for 3 weeks, followed by germination at 64°F (18°C) under fluorescent lights (White, 1985). Priming was used to bypass stratification for *A. caerulea* and improved germination of stratified seed of *A. canadensis*, but had no effect on *A. hinckleyana* (Finnerty et al., 1992).

Cultivars with low germination rates or old seed may also require scarification (White, 1985). After scarification with 00 sandpaper, seeds are soaked for 2 min in a mild detergent solution and rinsed, and then cold stratified as described.

Germination rates vary among species and cultivars (White, 1985). Nau (1998) states

TABLE II-1 AQUILEGIA

Descriptions of several common *Aquilegia* species found in commerce (Bailey and Bailey, 1976; White, 1985).

Species	Plant Height in. (cm)	Flower Size: in. (cm) Sepal Petal Spur	Color: Sepal Petal Spur	Native Location
Alpine Types				
A. alpina L.	12–24 (30–60)	1.0–2.0 (2.5–5.0)	Bright blue	European Alps
		0.6 (1.5)	Bright blue	
		0.6–1.0 (1.5–2.5)	Bright blue	
A. bertolonii Scott.	12 (30)	0.6–1.3 (1.5–3.3)	Violet blue	S. Europe
		0.5 (1.3)	Violet blue	
		0.5 (1.3)	Violet blue	
A. discolor Levier & Leresche	12 (30)	0.5–0.8 (1.3–2.0)	Blue	
		0.3 (0.8)	White	
		0.3 (0.8)	Blue	
A. flabellata Sieb. & Zucc. (syn. *A. alkitensis*) (numerous cultivars)	12–18 (45)	1.0 (2.5)	Blue, purple, white, pink, lilac	Japan
		0.5 (1.3)	Lilac to pale yellow, white	
		0.3–0.6 (0.8–1.5)	Blue, purple, white, to pink	
A. saxamontana Rydb.	2–10 (5.5–25)	0.5 (1.3)	Blue	Colorado
		0.3 (0.8)	Yellowish	
		0.3 (0.8)	Blue	
A. scopulorum Tidestr.	15 (38)	0.8 (2.0)	Blue to white, rarely red	Wyoming, Utah
		0.5 (1.3)	Yellowish, blue, rose red	
		1.0–1.5 (2.5–4.0)	Yellowish, blue, rose red	
Border Types				
A. caerulea (numerous cultivars)	30 (75)	1.0–1.5 (2.5–3.8)	Blue shades	Rocky Mountains of United States
		0.6–1.0 (1.5–2.5)	White	
		1.4–2.0 (3.6–5.0)	White	
A. canadensis	24 (60)	0.5 (1.3)	Red	Florida to Nova Scotia and west to Minnesota and Tennessee
		0.3 (0.8)	Yellow	
		1.0 (2.5)	Red	
A. chrysantha	42 (106)	1.0–1.5 (2.5–3.8)	Golden yellow	Arizona, New Mexico, and Mexico
		0.3–0.6 (0.8–1.5)	Golden yellow	
		1.5–3.0 (3.8–7.6)	Golden yellow	
A. longissima	36 (90)	1.0 (2.5)	Pale yellow	West Texas, Mexico
		0.6–1.0 (1.5–2.5)	Pale yellow	
		3.5–6.0 (8.9–15.2)	Pale yellow	
A. vulgaris (numerous cultivars)	12–24 (30–60)	0.8–1.0 (2.0–2.5)	White to violet	Europe
		0.5 (1.3)	White to violet	
		0.6–1.0 (1.5–2.5)	White to violet	

that seeds germinate at 70 to 75°F (21 to 24°C) under lights in 21 to 28 days. Seedling plugs of the various cultivars are available from many sources.

FLOWERING CONTROL AND DORMANCY

Although some cultivars such as Songbird will initiate flowers without vernalization under certain photoperiods (Shedron and Weiler, 1982; White et al., 1990; Zhang et al., 1991), 6- to 9-week cold treatments are commonly used to optimize flowering (Table II-2 Aquilegia). Long photoperiods and high temperatures prior to vernalization will accelerate plant development and floral initiation. 'McKana's Giant' and 'Fairyland' developed 1.5 leaves/week at 65°F (18°C) night temperature under a 10- to 12-hr photoperiod, while an 18-hr photoperiod and a 60 to 64°F (15.5 to 18°C) temperature hastened leaf and flower development (White, 1985). Armitage (1996) considered the Songbird cultivars to be facultative LD plants. Garner and Armitage (1998) stated that storing A. flabellata Sieb & Zucc. and A. ×hybrida Sims plants for 8 or 12 weeks of 36±4°F (2±2°C) resulted in rapid flowering under LD or SD. Eight weeks of cooling and LD was the optimal treatment.

Leaf number, optimal 40°F (4°C) cold duration, and cultivar all interact. In general, the greater the leaf number, the shorter the cold treatment required. If plants are too small at the start of vernalization, they will flower poorly regardless of cold treatment. With 12 leaves 100% of 'McKana's Giant' plants flowered; however, 'Fairyland' plants required 15 leaves for 100% flowering (Shedron and Weiler, 1982). Cameron et al. (1996) stated that young plants required at least 15 leaves to flower consistently. 'McKana's Giant' plants with 15 to 18 leaves required 8 weeks of vernalization for floral initiation, compared with only 4 weeks for 'Crimson Star' of the same size. Although leaves are not required to be present during cold treatment (Shedron and Weiler, 1982), the presence of leaves increases both the rate and the percent of plants flowering in production under marginal cooling. However, vernalization of well-developed plants (15 to 16 leaf stage) may decrease flower numbers of some cultivars (Zhang et al., 1991).

The rate of development and flowering after vernalization also depends on cultivar and plant size. Generally, 30 to 60 days are required for development and flowering after the end of vernalization (Shedron and Weiler, 1982; White, 1985; Zhang et al., 1991). Aquilegia flabellata 'Cameo' requires only 3 to 6 weeks cold. Plants stored for longer vernalization durations generally flower more rapidly (Shedron and Weiler, 1982). Regardless of length of vernalization, inflorescence number (Zhang et al., 1991) and rate of flower development (Shedron and Weiler, 1982) increase with longer photoperiod durations. During early forcing, night temperatures should be kept cool. Minimum temperatures greater than 64°F (18°C) reduced percent of plants flowering, compared with night minimums of 55°F (13°C) (Shedron and Weiler, 1982).

Results of gibberellic acid (GA) applications have been varied. Shedron and Weiler (1982) found no practical effect of GA sprays on percent of plants flowering, regardless of photoperiod. On the contrary, Zhang et al. (1991) reported GA reduced the number of days to anthesis, in some cases without increasing plant height, regardless of vernalization duration or supplemental lighting.

TEMPERATURE

During forcing, use 65°F (18°C) maximum day temperature; 55°F (13°C) nights (Shedron and Weiler, 1982). Zhang et al. (1991) used 70/61°F (21/16°C) day/night temperatures. Avoid temperatures in excess of 80°F (27°C), which cause yellow foliage and greatly reduce plant quality.

LIGHT

Plants can be forced into flower in full sun. In the garden they thrive in semishade and flowering is prolonged (Armitage, 1989; Bailey and Bailey, 1976; Cumming and Lee, 1960; Dewolf, 1984). A 12- to 18-hr photoperiod is recommended during forcing at a minimum 300 to 500 fc (40 to 65 μmol $\cdot$ m^{-2} $\cdot$ s^{-1}) light intensity using high-pressure sodium lamps (White, 1985).

WATER

Keep the soil moist, not wet; otherwise, plants may be subjected to root rots (Bailey, 1933).

CARBON DIOXIDE

No information available.

TABLE II-2 AQUILEGIA

Description of several *Aquilegia* species, cultivars, and hybrids suited for forcing (adapted from White, 1985).

Cultivars	Stem Length in. (cm)	Original Flower Color	Flower Color after 12 Days	Postharvest Durability	Comments	Suitability for Forcing
A. skinneri Hook.	32–40 (80–100)	Mixture white and yellow	Fading somewhat	Medium	Light color	Good
Blue Star	32–40 (80–100)	Blue-white	Remains a relatively good blue	Medium	Late development	Good
Cameo	5 (15)	Blue, pink, white		Good	Potted plant	Good
Crimson Star	24–32 (60–80)	Red-white	Somewhat paler	Medium	Good color	Very good
Dynasty (Songbird) series	18–22 (45–55)	Excellent pure colors	Good	Medium		Excellent
Golden Yellow	32–40 (80–100)	Yellow	Color remains	Medium	Flower relatively small, color somewhat pale, late development	Good
Long-spurred Giants	24–40 (60–100)	White	Remains white	Medium	Pleasing color	Very good
McKana's Giant	24–40 (60–100)	Mixture	Somewhat paler	Medium	Good color	Very good
Music series	18–22 (45–55)	Very good individual colors	Good	Medium	Stems quite short but flowers pleasing	Very good
Olympia Blue-White	24–32 (60–80)	Blue-white	Color relatively stable	Medium	Very pleasing color	Very good
Olympia Red-Gold	24–32 (60–80)	Scarlet red	Relatively stable with age	Medium	Pleasing color, small to medium size flower, early	Very good
Red	20–24 (50–60)	Red-white	Color remains stable	Medium	Pleasing color	Very good
Silver Queen	20–28 (50–70)	Creamy	Yellows	Best	Relatively even, early	Very good

Note: A. vulgaris, 'Sky Blue' and 'Libelle' are not suited for forcing because of their low durability.

298

NUTRITION

A 200-ppm nitrogen and potassium fertilizer can be used at each watering (Shedron and Weiler, 1982; Zhang et al., 1991).

MEDIA

A light sandy soil with good drainage is preferred (Bailey, 1933). A potting mix of vermiculite:sphagnum:soil (8:8:5) was used by Zhang et al. (1991). This medium was supplemented with dolomitic lime, superphosphate, potassium nitrate, and fritted trace elements.

HEIGHT CONTROL

Plant height increased as much as two to three times as the photoperiod increased from 10 to 18 hr (Shedron and Weiler, 1982; Zhang et al., 1991). Temperature increases from 55 to 65 to 75°F (13 to 18 to 24°C) resulted in no clear trends on plant heights. Multiple B-Nine (daminozide) or A-Rest (ancymidal) sprays at ± 5,000 ppm or 50 to 100 ppm, respectively, were effective in height control (Shedron and Weiler, 1982). A-Rest drenches at 0.25 to 0.5 mg a.i./6-in. (15-cm) pot (2 to 4 ppm) are also effective. Adriansen (1985) also noted that Cycocel (chlormequat) was effective. Latimer and Oetting (1998) tested a variety of height control measures and noted that B-Nine (5000 ppm), brushing plants with 40 strokes twice daily, drought stress, and low nitrogen reduced plant height.

SPACING

Plants are spaced pot-to-pot until just before leaves touch. Delayed spacing may reduce plant quality.

PINCHING AND DISBUDDING

None required.

SUPPORT

None required.

SCHEDULE AND TIMING

Plants can be programmed to flower for Christmas, Valentine's Day, or Easter (Table II-3 Aquilegia). If plants are forced for Christmas or Valentine's Day, a 12- to 18-hr photoperiod supplemented and extended by high-pressure sodium lamps at 300 to 500 fc (39 to 65 μmol · m^{-2} · s^{-1}) is recommended for high-quality plants. Colors suited for the individual holidays can be selected from the available cultivars (White, 1985).

The longer the greenhouse vegetative growth period is prior to vernalization, the larger the plant will be at the time of flowering. Plant size and pot size are dependent on leaf number. Greater leaf numbers are required as pot sizes increase from 4 to 6 in. (10 to 15 cm) or even up to 8 or 10 in. (20 or 25 cm). The latter size, cultivar dependent, can be used for cut flower production. If 1 to 1.5 leaves are initiated per week, vegetative growth period should be 12 to 15 weeks for 4- or 5-in. (10- or 12.5-cm) pots, 17 to 20 weeks for 6-in. (15-cm) pots, and 22 to 25 weeks for 8-in. (20-cm) pots (White, 1985).

The use of vernalized plugs for potted plant production generally results in poor-quality plants because flowering occurs before plants are sufficiently large.

In nature, seeds sown 1 year normally do not flower until the following season (Cumming and Lee, 1960; Weiler and Shedron, 1986). However, greenhouse plants flower in 15 to 19 weeks or 26 to 36 weeks from seed depending on the cultivars (Shedron and Weiler, 1982; Willmott et al., 2000). At 48 to 55°F (9 to 13°C) Merritt et al. (1997) recorded flowering in 28 to 35 weeks from seed.

INSECTS

Leaf miners are often a major problem and a preventive program will probably be required to prevent damage. Aphids, spider mites, and thrips can also be troublesome. Other pests that have been recorded include ground mealybug, greenhouse whitefly, and caterpillars (Dreistadt, 2001).

DISEASES

Older leaves should be removed during dark cold storage to reduce disease incidence (White, 1985). During production, stem and root rots (*Pythium mamillatum*, *Phymatotrichum omnivorum*, *Phoma*, *Rhizoctonia solani*, or *Sclerotinia sclerotiorum*) can be common, especially if plants are grown outdoors for any length of time (Horst, 1990). Leaf spots (*Ascochyta aquilegiae*, *Cercospora aquilegiae*, and *Septoria aquilegiae*), mildew (*Ersiphe polygoni*), rust (*Puccinia recondita*), verticillium wilt (*Verticillium albo-atrum*), and cucumber mosaic and tomato spotted wilt viruses can also occur (Dreistadt, 2001).

TABLE II-3 AQUILEGIA

Sample production and forcing schedule steps for flowering of 4- to 5-in. (10- to 12.5-cm) potted *Aquilegia* plants for (1) Christmas (market Dec. 11–15), (2) Valentine's Day (market Feb. 7–11), or (3) Easter (market Mar. 27–April 1, for example) (as modified from White, 1985).

Cultural Steps	Production Time (weeks)	Temperature °F (°C)	Date for Each of Three Holidays
Seed germination	2–3	64 (18)[a]	(1) April 22 (2) June 22 (3) Aug. 5
Transplant or growth	12–15	60–64 (15.5–18)	(1) May 19 (2) July 15 (3) Sept. 2
Vernalize	6–8 min; 20 max	35–45 (2–7)	(1) Aug. 15–Oct. 23 (2) Oct. 10–Dec. 19 (3) Nov. 28–Feb. 6
Forcing	8–2 (average 4) season/cultivar dependent	55–64 (13–18)	(1) Oct. 23[b] (2) Dec. 19[b] (3) Feb. 6
Buds visible	5	55–64 (13–18)	(1) Nov. 27 (2) Jan. 24 (3) Mar. 13
Market			(1) Christmas (2) Valentine's Day (3) Easter (Mar. 27 to Apr. 1)
Total	33 (average)		

[a]Under lights.
[b]HID lighting.

PHYSIOLOGICAL DISORDERS

Sulfur in some fungicides can cause phytotoxicity (R. Sterkel, personal communication). Lack of flowering can be due to insufficient cold, immature plants, incorrect growth regulator applications, low light intensity, and SD (Dreistadt, 2001).

POSTHARVEST

Flower inflorescences should have 50% of their flowers open prior to harvest. Individual flowers last 3 to 4 days and inflorescences for 20 days. *Aquilegia chrysantha* 'Silver Queen' ('Mari Star') reportedly has a long postharvest life (Dewolf, 1984; Armitage, 1989; White, 1985) (Table II-2 Aquilegia). Cut flowers can be stored at 40 to 45°F (4 to 7°C).

KEY POINTS

- Columbine is used as a perennial garden plant, potted flowering plant, and cut flower.
- While seed propagation is the most economical method, mature plants can also be divided.
- Cold treatment is used to accelerate plant growth, floral initiation, and development.
- Plants must have a critical leaf number prior to cold treatment; after the critical leaf number is reached, increasing leaf number decreases the amount of cold required.
- LD hastens flower development.
- HID lighting is recommended for midwinter forcing.
- Leaf miners can be a major problem.

BIBLIOGRAPHY

Adriansen, E. 1985. Kemisk vækstregulering, pp. 142–162 in *Potteplanter I—Produktion, Metoder,* Midler, O.V. Christensen, A. Klougart, I.S. Pedersen, and K. Wikesjö, editors. Gartner-INFO, København, Denmark. (in Danish)

Armitage, A. 1989. *Aquilegia,* pp. 51–59 in *Herbaceous Perennial Plants.* Varsity Press, Athens, Georgia.

Armitage, A.M. 1996. Forcing perennials in the greenhouse. *GrowerTalks* 60(3):86, 88, 93, 94, 96, 97.

Bailey, L.H. 1933. *Aquilegia,* pp. 339–343 in *The Standard Cyclopedia of Horticulture.* Macmillan, London.

Bailey, L.H., and E.Z. Bailey. 1976. *Aquilegia,* pp. 93–94 in *Hortus Third: A Concise Dictionary of Plants Cultivated in the United States and Canada.* Macmillan, New York.

Cameron, A., M. Yuan, R. Heins, and W. Carlson. 1996. Juvenility: Your perennial crop's age affects flowering. *GrowerTalks* 60(8):30–32, 34.

Cumming, R.W., and R.E. Lee. 1960. *Contemporary Perennials.* Macmillan, New York.

Dewolf, G. 1984. Columbine. *Horticulture* 62(6): 12–13.

Dreistadt, S.H. 2001. *Integrated Pest Management for Floriculture and Nurseries.* University of California Division of Agriculture and Natural Resources Publication 3402.

Finnerty, T.L., J.M. Zajicek, and M.A. Hussey. 1992. Use of seed priming to bypass stratification requirements of three *Aquilegia* species. *HortScience* 27:310–313.

Garner, J.M., and A.M. Armitage. 1998. Influence of cooling and photoperiod on growth and flowering of *Aquilegia* L. cultivars. *Scientia Horticulturae* 75:83–90.

Horst, R.K. 1990. Columbine, p. 605 in *Westcott's Plant Disease Handbook,* 5th ed. Van Nostrand Reinhold, New York.

Huxley, A., M. Griffiths, and M. Levy. 1992. *Aquilegia,* pp. 205–209 in *The New Royal Horticultural Society Dictionary of Gardening,* vol. 1. Stockton Press, New York.

Latimer, J.G., and R.D. Oetting. 1998. Greenhouse conditioning affects landscape performance of bedding plants. *Journal of Environmental Horticulture* 16:138–142.

McGrew, J. 1999. Aquilegias are looking up. *GrowerTalks* 63(6):51–52.

Merritt, R.H., T. Gianfagna, R.T. Perkins III, and J.R. Trout. 1997. Growth and development of aquilegia in relation to temperature, photoperiod and dry seed vernalization. *Scientia Horticulturae* 69:99–106.

Nau, J. 1998. *Aquilegia* (Columbine), pp. 368–369 in *Ball RedBook,* 16th ed., V. Ball, editor. Ball Publishing, Batavia, Illinois.

Shedron, K.G., and T.C. Weiler. 1982. Regulation of growth and flowering in *Aquilegia* ×*hybrida* Sims. *Journal of the American Society for Horticultural Science* 107:878–882.

Weiler, T.C., and K.G. Shedron. 1986. *Aquilegia* ×*hybrids,* pp. 18–21 in *Handbook of Flowering,* vol. 5, A.H. Halevy, editor. CRC Press, Boca Raton, Florida.

White, J.W. 1985. Try columbine. *Greenhouse Grower* 3(5):96–98, 100.

White, J.W., H. Chen, X. Zhang, D.J. Beattie, and H. Grossman. 1990. Floral initiation and development in *Aquilegia. HortScience* 25:294–296.

Willmott, J., R. Merritt, and T. Gianfagna. 2000. Aquilegias in four months. *GrowerTalks* 64(3):128, 130.

Zhang, X., J.W. White, and D.J. Beattie. 1991. Regulation of flowering in *Aquilegia. Journal of the American Society for Horticultural Science* 116:792–797.

Asclepias

FIGURE II-1 ASCLEPIAS *Asclepias curassavica* 'Silky Gold' dried cut flowers.

INTRODUCTION

Common names: butterfly weed, tuber root.

Scientific name: *Asclepias tuberosa* L. (Huxley et al., 1992).

Family and related taxa: Asclepiadaceae R. Br. The genus *Asclepias* contains 108 species, many of which are also used as cut flowers and garden ornamentals, including *A. curassavica* L., *A. fruiticosa* L., and *A. incarnata* L.

Origin: The butterfly weed is a herbaceous perennial that is widely distributed across North America in fields and prairies.

Uses and current status: Butterfly weed is used as a cut flower and as a long-lived ornamental in the garden landscape (Fig. II-1 Asclepias). *Asclepias tuberosa* is hardy from Zones 4 to 9 (Nau, 1998) and *A. curassavica* is hardy in Zones 9 to 12 but regularly overwinters or reseeds itself in Zones 7 and 8.

Stems can reach up to 39 in. (1 m) tall and the leaves are narrow, lanceolate, and spirally attached to the stem (Bailey and Bailey, 1976). Interestingly, the sap is not milky, but clear. The flower is an umbel with five sepals and five petals (Fig. II-2 Asclepias). The stamens are fused to the stigma. One filament of the stamen develops into a hood, a second into a horn. The hood is "wrapped" around the horn and acts as a block to the nectar (Lyons, 1986). The sap of at least one species, *Asclepias curassavica*, **can cause serious eye injury** and should be handled with care.

FIGURE II-2 ASCLEPIAS *Asclepias tuberosa* inflorescence.

CULTIVARS

Although there are few cultivars of *Asclepias tuberosa*, selections can be made and asexually propagated. Flower color varies from bright yellow to orange to reddish. In Israel, *A. incarnata* 'Cinderella' has pink flowers. Several cultivars of *Asclepias curassavica* are available that range in color from pale orange to bright crimson and grow up to 30 in. (75 cm) tall.

PROPAGATION

Seed and root cuttings are the most common propagation methods (Armitage, 1995; Borland, 1987; Nau, 1998). Freshly harvested seed can be immediately sown at 70°F (21°C) and will germinate in 30 to 90 days. However, Kaspar and McWilliams (1982) reported that 86°F (30°C) was optimum. Seeds are not covered. Older seed require stratification at 36 to 40°F (2 to 4°C) prior to germination (Salac and Hesse, 1975). To produce 1000 seedlings, 0.50 to 0.75 oz (14.2 to 21.3 g) of seed will be required.

For uniform plants, stem or root cuttings can be used (Ecker and Barzilay, 1993), but the process is labor intensive. Three- to 4-in.- (7.5- to 10-cm)-long stem cuttings should be taken prior to flowering. The tap root is cut in sections 2 to 3 in. (5 to 7.5 cm) long. These sections are placed vertically in flats and kept moist at 70°F (21°C). They will root in 3 or 4 weeks under mist (Bhowmilk and Bandeen, 1978). After roots and shoots form, the young plants must be given a cold treatment.

Seedlings and plugs should be transplanted as soon as possible to prevent damage to the tap root that develops rapidly (Armitage and Laushman, 2003). Plants will decline if they become root bound; grow in as large a container as practical. Once production beds are established, flowering shoots arise from adventitious buds on the crown. These shoots will ensure long-term production (Lucansky and Clough, 1986; Wyatt, 1980, 1981). Crown divisions may also be used. Frampton (1994) described both *in vitro* culture and rooting of cuttings.

A. incarnata 'Cinderella' is propagated by stem piece cuttings and *A. curassavica* is propagated by seed.

FLOWERING CONTROL AND DORMANCY

Seedlings will remain vegetative for 1 year (Lyons, 1986; Lyons and Booze, 1983; Shannon and Wyatt, 1986). Both young and mature plants cease to form leaves and shoot elongation stops under SD. This SD response results in a high root-to-shoot dry weight ratio. Basal branching, however, is inhibited under LD (Lyons and Booze, 1983).

Photoperiods of 13 hr or longer must be maintained for both floral induction and development (Armitage, 1996; A.H. Halevy, personal communication). Nordwig (1999) found that 14- to 16-hr day lengths were required. Under short, 9-hr photoperiods, flower bud abortion occurs and "blind shoots" develop. There were no advantages of a 17-hr photoperiod from night break lighting over 13- or 15-hr photoperiods for rapid flower initiation and development. Interestingly, the number of flowering shoots harvested increases if plants are lighted for 13 or 15 hr after being vernalized for 12 or 14 weeks at 39°F (4°C). If plants are vernalized for 16 weeks at 39°F (4°C) and given a 17-hr night break light treatment, the number of flowering stems decreases, but the number of individual flowers per inflorescence doubles (Albrecht and Lehmann, 1991). Shillo (personal communication) reported a 1-hr night break resulted in 100% flowering in Israel. Flowering is perpetual if plants are kept under LD and protection from heat. If crowns become dormant after flowering under natural fall or SD conditions, a cold treatment apparently becomes a requirement for further growth (Albrecht and Lehmann, 1991; A.H. Halevy, personal communication).

TEMPERATURE

Greenhouse-produced dormant crowns stored at 50°F (10°C) for 12 weeks failed to form shoots; however, crowns stored at 39°F (4°C) for 12, 14, or 16 weeks emerged in 16, 16, or 9 days, respectively (Albrecht and Lehmann, 1991). Flower abortion occurs if forcing temperatures go below 61°F (16°C) or above 86°F (30°C). The appropriate forcing temperature is between 63 and 77°F (17 and 25°C) (Albrecht and Lehmann, 1991; A.H. Halevy, personal communication). Fall harvested crowns can be stored successfully for up to 6 months in polyethylene-lined crates at 28 to 36°F (−2 to 2°C) (Maqbool and Cameron, 1994).

LIGHT

High irradiance levels are required (Albrecht and Lehmann, 1991). Even in the winter in Israel's Negev Desert, flower bud abortion occurs during cloudy or rainy periods (A.H. Halevy, personal communication). Flower production from basal shoots is continuous in Israel under LD (A.H. Halevy, personal communication). Either incandescent or high-pressure sodium lighting can be used for photoperiodic control (Nordwig, 1999). Partial shade may increase the height of *A. curassavica*.

WATER

Be careful to not overwater the butterfly weed. It requires a well-drained, sunny location and is very tolerant of drought. However, daily irrigation was used by Ecker and Barzilay (1993) in Israel for *Asclepias tuberosa* with no adverse effect. *Asclepias incarnata*, the swamp milkweed, grows naturally in moist areas (Bailey and Bailey, 1976).

CARBON DIOXIDE

No data available.

NUTRITION

Ecker and Barzilay (1993) used 100 ppm N from a 20–9–16 fertilizer at each irrigation.

MEDIA

A. tuberosa plants naturally grow in well-drained locations. Albrecht and Lehmann (1991) used soil:sphagnum peat:perlite (1:1:1) with dolomitic limestone at 5 lb/yd³ (3 kg · m⁻³). Ecker and Brazilay (1993) grew their root-propagated plants in a "light" sandy soil.

HEIGHT CONTROL

Height of *Asclepias tuberosa* potted plants can be controlled with three to four sprays of 5000 ppm B-Nine (daminozide) or four sprays of 30 ppm Bonzi (paclubutrazol) applied at 10- to 14-day intervals (Latimer, 2001). For potted plant production of *A. curassavica* A-Rest (ancymidol), Cycocel (chlormequat), and B-Nine (daminozide) can be used (Adriansen, 1985). B-Nine is the most effective. However, Nordwig (1999) found no response to these plant growth regulators. DIF is quite effective (Warner and Erwin, 2001).

SPACING

Plants are spaced 18 × 24 in. (45 × 30 cm) apart. Butterfly weeds are long-lived perennials and "clump" size increases annually. *A. curassavica* can be spaced at 5 × 5 to 12 × 12 in. (13 × 13 to 30 × 30 cm).

PINCHING AND DISBUDDING

None required and is detrimental to *Asclepias curassavica* for cut flower production.

SUPPORT

One to three layers of net are required for both field and greenhouse production. Grid openings can be 12 × 18 in. (30 × 45 cm).

SCHEDULE AND TIMING

Plants can be produced from seed, root cuttings, or dormant crowns (Tables II-1, II-2, and II-3 Asclepias). When plants were vernalized at 39°F (4°C) for 12, 14, or 16 weeks and grown at a 77/63°F (25/17°C) day/night temperature under LD, they flowered in 70, 70, or 56 days, respectively. When plants that were vernalized naturally outside and were subsequently forced at 79/63°F (26/17°C) day/night temperatures under 13- or 17-hr photoperiods, plants flowered in 71 and 61 days, respectively (Albrecht and Lehmann, 1991). Once plants are established, replanting or division does not occur for up to 3 to 5 years (Armitage and Laushman, 2003).

TABLE II-I ASCLEPIAS

Sample cultural schedule for production of *Asclepias tuberosa* from seed.

Cultural Step	Production Time (weeks)	Temperature °F (°C)	Photoperiod
Sow seed[a]			
	3–9	36–40 (2–4)	SD
Move to greenhouse			
	2	70–72 (21–22)	SD
Transplant to 4-in. (10-cm) pots[b] and grow seedlings			
	4 minimum	70–72 (21–22)	SD
Plant seedlings in field or greenhouse			
	3–4	60–65 (16–18)	LD
Flowering			
	variable	ambient	LD or natural photoperiods

[a]Seed can be mixed with vermiculite and sown outside in late summer or fall. Germination will occur in late fall or following spring. Flowering may occur in late summer, 1 year later.
[b]Transplant prior to taproot formation (two sets of leaves or less) or quality will be decreased.

TABLE II-2 ASCLEPIAS

Sample cultural schedule for *Asclepias tuberosa* cut flower production from root cuttings.

Cultural Step	Production Time (weeks)	Temperature °F (°C)	Photoperiod
Take cuttings			
	4–6	70 (21)	SD
Roots form			
	2–4	70 (21) or lower to harden	SD
Plant cuttings in field or greenhouse			
	late summer	70 (21)	SD
Check for presence of basal storage organ and buds			
	4	70 (21)	LD
Flowering			
	variable	ambient	LD or natural photoperiods

TABLE II-3 ASCLEPIAS

Sample cultural schedule for *Asclepias tuberosa* cut flower production from cold treated crowns.

Cultural Step	Production Time (weeks)	Temperature °F (°C)	Photoperiod
Cold storage of crowns[a]			
	12 minimum	38 (3)	—
Plant crowns in field or greenhouse			
	1–2	ambient	SD
Shoot emergence			
	2–4	ambient	SD
Rosette formation			
	7–10[b]	ambient	LD or natural photoperiods
Flowering			
Total	22 minimum		

[a]*Cold treat in moist, sphagnum peat moss or sawdust.*
[b]*10 weeks if given 12 to 14 weeks of cold storage, 7 weeks if given 16 weeks of cold storage.*

INSECTS

The butterfly weed is generally free of pests. Aphids can occur, especially on outdoor plantings.

DISEASES

Several diseases can occur on butterfly weed in the field, including stem blight (*Phoma asclepiadea*), leaf spot (*Cercospora asclepiadorae, C. clavata, C. vernturioides,* and *Phyllosticta tuberosa*), root rot (*Phymatotrichum omnivorum*), and rust (*Puccinia bartholomaei* and *Uromyces asclepiadis*) (Horst, 1990).

PHYSIOLOGICAL DISORDERS

Flower abortion occurs under low light intensities or if plants are moved from LD to SD (Albrecht and Lehmann, 1991; A.H. Halevy, personal communication).

POSTHARVEST

Stems are cut when one-half to two-thirds of the florets are open. Harvest early in the morning and place in cold storage as soon as possible as stems are prone to wilting. Flowers last 7 to 8 days (A.H. Halevy, personal communication; Wyatt, 1980). Armitage and Laushman (2003) stated that stems should be placed in a floral preservative solution containing silver thiosulfate (STS) and stored at 40 to 45°F (4 to 7°C). Cut *Asclepias tuberosa* are sensitive to ethylene (Woltering and van Doorn, 1988). Cut *Asclepias curassavica* stems produce latex, which can cause **serious eye injuries.** Use caution with other *Asclepias* species also.

KEY POINTS

- This cut flower and garden ornamental can be propagated by seed, division, or stem or root pieces.
- Once a plant is established and starts to flower, LD stimulates shoot elongation and flowering and SD results in dormancy and basal branching.

- Dormancy is broken if crowns are given 12 or more weeks of 39°F (4°C).
- High light levels are required for forcing during the winter.
- Do not overwater plants, which are susceptible to root rots

BIBLIOGRAPHY

Adriansen, E. 1985. Kemisk vækstregulering, pp. 142–162 in *Potteplanter I—Produktion, Metoder, Midler*, O.V. Christensen, A. Klougart, I.S. Pedersen, and K. Wikesjö, editors. Gartner-INFO, København, Denmark. (in Danish)

Albrecht, M.L., and J.T. Lehmann, 1991. Day length, cold storage, and plant production method influence growth and flowering of *Asclepias tuberosa*. *HortScience* 26:120–121.

Armitage, A.M. 1995. Culture profile *Asclepias tuberosa* butterfly weed. *The Cut Flower Quarterly* 7(2):9–10.

Armitage, A.M. 1996. Forcing perennials in the greenhouse. *GrowerTalks* 60(3):86, 88, 93, 94, 96, 97.

Armitage, A.M., and J.M. Laushman. 2003. *Asclepias tuberosa*, pp. 111–116 in *Specialty Cut Flowers*, 2nd ed. Timber Press, Portland, Oregon.

Bailey, L.H., and E.Z. Bailey. 1976. *Asclepias*, pp. 116–117 in *Hortus Third: A Concise Dictionary of Plants Cultivated in the United States and Canada*. Macmillan, New York.

Bhowmilk, P.C., and J.D. Bandeen. 1978. The biology of Canadian weeds, *Asclepias syriaca* L. *Canadian Journal of Plant Science* 56:579–589.

Borland, J. 1987. Clues to butterfly milkweed germination emerge from a literature search. *American Nurseryman* 165:91–92, 94–96.

Ecker, R., and A. Barzilay, 1993. Propagation of *Asclepias tuberosas* from short root segments. *Scientia Horticulturae* 56:171–174.

Frampton, J.G. 1994. Vegetative Propagation of Butterfly Flower (*Asclepias tuberosa* L.) through Tissue Culture and Stem Cuttings. MS thesis, University of Arkansas.

Horst, R.K. 1990. Butterfly weed, p. 568 in *Westcott's Plant Disease Handbook*, 5th ed. Van Nostrand Reinhold, New York.

Huxley, A., M. Griffiths, and M. Levy. 1992. *Asclepias*, p. 253 in *The New Royal Horticultural Society Dictionary of Gardening*, vol. 1. Stockton Press, New York.

Kaspar, J.J., and E.L. McWilliams. 1982. Effects of temperature on the germination of selected wildflower seeds. *HortScience* 17:595–596.

Latimer, J.G. (2001). Herbaceous perennials, pp. 98–110 in *Tips on Regulating Growth of Floriculture Crops*, M.L. Gaston, L.A. Kunkle, P.S. Konjoian, and M.F. Wilt, editors. Ohio Florists' Association Services, Columbus, Ohio.

Lucansky, T.W., and K.T. Clough. 1986. Comparative anatomy and morphology of *Asclepias perennis* and *Asclepias tuberosa* subspecies *rolfsii*. *Botanical Gazette* 147(3):290–301.

Lyons, R.E. 1986. *Asclepias tuberosa*, pp. 22–28 in *Handbook of Flowering*, vol. V, A.H. Halevy, editor. CRC Press, Boca Raton, Florida.

Lyons, R.E., and J.N. Booze. 1983. Effect of photoperiod on first year growth of two *Asclepias* species. *HortScience* 18(4):575. (Abstract)

Maqbool, M., and A.C. Cameron. 1994. Regrowth performance of field-grown herbaceous perennials following bare-root storage between −10 and +5°C. *HortScience* 29:1039–1041.

Nau, J. 1998. Success with butterfly weed. *Grower Talks* 62(6):71.

Nordwig, G.J. 1999. Evaluation of Floral Induction Requirements and Commercial Potential of *Asclepias* species. MS thesis, University of Minnesota, St. Paul.

Salac, S.S., and M.C. Hesse. 1975. Effects of storage and germination conditions on the germination of four species of wild flowers. *Journal of the American Society for Horticultural Science* 100:359–361.

Shannon, T.R., and R. Wyatt. 1986. Reproductive biology of *Asclepias exaltata*. *American Journal of Botany* 73(1):11–20.

Warner, R.M., and J.E. Erwin (2001). Temperature, pp. 10–17 in *Tips on Regulating Growth of Floriculture Crops*, M.L. Gaston, L.A. Kunkle, P.S. Konjoian, and M.F. Wilt, editors. Ohio Florists' Association Services, Columbus, Ohio.

Woltering, E.J., and W.G. van Doorn. 1988. Role of ethylene in senescence of petals—morphological and taxonomical relationships. *Journal of Experimental Botany* 39:1605–1616.

Wyatt, R. 1980. The reproductive biology of *Asclepias tuberosa*. I. Flower number, arrangement and fruit-set. *New Phytology* 85:119–131.

Wyatt, R. 1981. The reproductive biology of *Asclepias tuberosa*. II. Factors determining fruit-set. *New Phytology* 88:375–385.

Aster

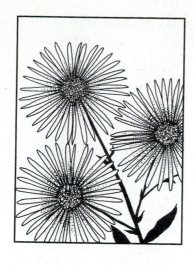

FIGURE II-I ASTER *Aster* 'Lady in Black' garden ornamental and cut flower.

INTRODUCTION

Common names: perennial aster, novi-belgii aster, Michaelmas daisy, New York aster.

Scientific name: *Aster novi-belgii* L. (Huxley et al., 1992).

Family and related taxa: Compositae Giseke. This chapter will deal primarily with *Aster novi-belgii* and its hybrids, and with *A. dumosus* L., *A. ericoides* L., and *A.pilosus* Willd. Relatively little information is known about *A. dumosus* (Zimmer, 1987), *A. ericoides* (Armitage and Laushman, 2003; Johansson, 1990), or *A. pilosus* (Kadman-Zahavi and Yahel, 1986). Compositae is a huge family with many important genera including *Aster, Calendula, Callistephus, Centaurea, Chrysanthemum, Cosmos, Dahlia, Dendranthema, Echinacea, Gerbera, Helianthus, Liatris, Pericallis, Solidago, Tagetes,* and *Zinnia*.

Origin: *A. novi-belgii* is native to eastern North America, from Newfoundland as far south as Georgia (Zones 3 to 9) and can be 4.5 ft (140 cm) tall with blue-violet flowers. *A. dumosus*, another native of southeastern North America (Zones 3 to 9), has flowers of pale lavender, blue, or white on 3-ft (90-cm) stems (Bailey and Bailey, 1976). *A. ericoides* has white to pink or blue flowers on 3-ft (90-cm) stems and is widely distributed from Maine to Georgia, west to Minnesota and South Dakota, and southward to Mexico (Zones 4 to 10) (Bailey and Bailey, 1976). *A. pilosus* is a native of North America (Zones 5 to 9) with white ray flowers. Leaves are spinelike and the 39-in. (1-m) flowering plant produces a cascade of flowers (Kadman-Zahavi and Yahel, 1986).

Uses and current status: These *Aster* species and cultivars are used as potted flowering plants, cut flowers, or garden ornamentals (Fig. II-1 Aster).

Asters are herbaceous perennials with rhizomatous roots. The leaves are alternate, simple, and either entire or toothed. The flowers consist of inner disc florets and outer ray florets, which range in color from white, pink, lavender, and red to blue tints (Bailey and Bailey, 1976).

CULTIVARS

Hybrid cut flower cultivars exist between *A. novi-belgii, A. pilosus,* and *A. ericoides* and flowering responses have been extensively researched (Farina et al., 1994; Wallerstein et al., 1992a,b). Schwabe (1986) researched responses for both tall 12- to 20-in. (30- to 50-cm) cut flower cultivars and 6-in.- (15-cm)-tall genetic dwarfs. Commercially, numerous cultivars and species are available (Armitage and Laushman, 2003; Luczal, 1992; Zimmer, 1987). Eddy and Whipker (1998) described production methods for outdoor pot plant production of five cultivars.

PROPAGATION

Aster propagation is by rhizome division or by rooting vegetative stem cuttings that arise from this rhizome. When a plant has flowered and experienced cool winter temperatures and SD, numerous vegetative rosettes form. These rosettes root with ease at 70°F (21°C) (Armitage and Laushman, 2003; Farina et al., 1994; Schwabe, 1986). Rosette shoots form on outside plantings in late fall, winter, or early spring and can be used as cuttings. However, if cuttings are taken in the summer, rooted, and subsequently pinched, the shoots from these cuttings quickly form an inflorescence with little shoot elongation, regardless of photoperiod. Schwabe (1986), Kadman-Zahavi and Yahel (1986), and Wallerstein et al. (1992a, b) stress that summer-grown axillary shoots are not reliable sources of cuttings, even though they root easily. This type of cutting has been classified as mature, whereas shoots from rosettes are juvenile.

The presence of a rhizome piece was critical for the preservation of juvenility in the rosette form (Wallerstein et al., 1992b). Short days promoted and LD retarded axillary basal bud and rhizome formation (Schwabe, 1986; Wallerstein et al., 1992b). Ethylene (2000 ppm) increased the number of basal buds (Wallerstein et al., 1992b). Tissue culture has been accomplished by Wallerstein et al. (1992b).

Asters are similar to poinsettias and chrysanthemums in that apices go reproductive after a certain number of nodes are formed, regardless of the correct photoperiod for vegetative growth. Consequently, stock plants must constantly be renewed from *in vitro* sources (M. Danziger, personal communication).

Aster novi-belgii stock plants also need to be managed carefully to ensure that vegetative cuttings are available for harvest. Typically, high light and temperatures above 68°F (20°C) are used to maintain vegetative plants. Cuttings that have wide leaves and very short internodes are highly vegetative. Cuttings with narrow leaves, longer internodes, and thin stems are inferior reproductive shoots and should be discarded. Three regimes are used for cutting production:

Type 1—Cut flower crop grown with pinch. Stock plant is produced using *in vitro* propagation and kept under SD at all times. Cuttings are continuously harvested, rooted, and planted in beds for cut flower production.

Type 2—Cut flower crop grown without pinch. Stock plant is produced using *in vitro* propagation and kept under LD. Cuttings are harvested, rooted, and planted in beds under LD for close-spaced cut flower production.

Type 3—Potted plants. Stock plant is kept under LD. Cuttings are harvested, rooted, and planted in pots for potted plant production.

FLOWERING CONTROL AND DORMANCY

The natural sequence of events leading to flowering of perennial asters are vernalization under winter conditions, stem elongation and branching under LD of late spring and early summer, and flowering under the SD of late summer and fall. At the base of flowering stems, rosette growths develop from axillary buds below the soil surface. The formation of these vegetative basal shoots occurs at the same time as autumn flowering. These basal shoots are vernalized by winter temperatures and the growth cycle is repeated (Schwabe, 1986; Wallerstein et al., 1992a, b).

Aster novi-belgii should be considered a LD–SD plant for floral initiation and subsequent development (Kristiansen et al., 1997; Schwabe, 1986; Wallerstein et al., 1992a). *A. dumosus* (Zimmer, 1987) and *A. ericoides* (Johansson, 1990) have similar environmental sequences of cold, LD, and then SD for flowering. *A. ericoides* flowers later in the autumn than *A. novi-belgii* and requires a greater number of SD or shorter day lengths for floral development (Armitage and Laushman, 2003). However, *A. pilosus* does not appear to have a vernalization requirement for shoot elongation to occur and has an obligate SD flowering requirement (Kadman-Zahavi and Yahel, 1986).

Various combinations of cold, LD, and SD sequences were studied for *A. novi-belgii* (Schwabe, 1986). The combinations with the highest number of flowers were LD–cold–SD (10.2 flowers), cold–LD–SD (7.4 flowers), and SD–LD–cold (7.0 flowers). The SD–cold–LD combination resulted in almost no flowers (0.7). In this study, the 41°F (5°C) cold treatment lasted 4 weeks with an 8-hr photoperiod; hence, cold and SD were applied simultaneously as in nature. Regardless, LD as the final treatment was deleterious. Zimmer (1987) found that *A. dumosus* plants had superior flowering when given a cold requirement at 41°F (5°C) for 13 weeks, followed by LD for 15 weeks and SD for 7 weeks. B. Fausey (personal communication), however, suggested 15 weeks or less cold, followed by 8 weeks SD, for *A. dumosus* 'Purple Dome'.

TEMPERATURE

Cold (vernalization) treatments are required for flowering in nature and cannot be totally replaced by LD even with a minor degree of substitution of cold by LD (Schwabe, 1986).

However, under high temperatures and LD, vernalization is eliminated and cold can be replaced by LD, as basal buds below the surface of the soil emerge and elongate (Wallerstein et al., 1992a). Further, rosette-type growth is maintained under 70/63°F (21/17°C) day/night regimes and SD. However, when these mother plants are moved to 81/63°F (27/17°C) day/night or given 36°F (2°C) for 30 days, shoot elongation, shoot branching, and flowering occur (Wallerstein et al., 1992a). Commercially, 41°F (5°C) is used and the duration varies with each cultivar, although 6 to 8 weeks are usually optimal (Schwabe, 1986). Treatments of GA$_3$ at 500 ppm applied to the shoot apex can substitute for both cold or LD, provided plants are under SD (Schwabe, 1986), but not for A. pilosus (Kadman-Zahavi and Yahel, 1986).

Aster novi-belgii plants were not devernalized by 90°F (32°C) after the appropriate cold treatments of 39°F (4°C) for 6 weeks (Schwabe, 1986). However, the highest flower number was at 84°F (29°C) under a 14-hr (SD) photoperiod when following a 4-week, 16-hr LD treatment. Johansson (1990) also reported similar results with A. ericoides (Table II-1 Aster).

In greenhouses, plants are forced at 62 to 68/54 to 57°F (17 to 20/12 to 14°C) day/night temperatures. Oren-Shamir et al. (2000) stated that 65°F (17°C) produced the largest flower diameters, floret number, and flower longevity for A. ericoides ×A. pilosis hybrids.

Fall-harvested crowns of Aster novae-angliae can be stored successfully for up to 6 months in polyethylene lined crates at 28 to 36°F (−2 to 2°C) (Maqbool and Cameron, 1994).

LIGHT

For optimal flower initiation, 14 to 16 hr of light are required, regardless of previous vernalization treatments (Schwabe, 1986). Incandescent lamps at 14 fc (3 μmol · m^{-2} · s^{-1}) were used to extend the natural photoperiod. Three weeks of 12- to 14-hr lighting is the minimum (Schwabe, 1986). Farina et al. (1994) found that 13 hr was optimal. Cyclic lighting was as effective as continuous LD lighting for A. novi-belgii (Schwabe, 1986) and for A. pilosus (Kadman-Zahavi and Yahel, 1986). With A. pilosus, 21 days of 10-hr SD were required for flower initiation and development in the greenhouse; under field conditions 40 days were required.

In greenhouses plants are forced in full light; shading occurs only when temperature control is needed (Oren-Shamir et al., 2000). Supplemental HID lighting will be needed for winter production at most latitudes. Armitage and Laushman (2003) stated that although shade increased stem length in the field with some cultivars, disease incidence also increased and thus shading is not recommended.

WATER

Plants should be maintained at an even moisture level; do not allow to dry out.

CARBON DIOXIDE

No data found.

NUTRITION

Nutrition levels of 150 to 200 ppm N from a balanced N, P, K fertilizer are adequate. High soluble salt levels should be avoided for potted plants. Foliar nutrient levels for high-quality plants are listed in Chapter 6, Nutrition, Table 6–4. Armitage (1993) established tissue nutrient levels for cut flowers.

MEDIA

Any well-drained medium is acceptable with a pH of 5.5 to 6.5 (Luczal, 1992).

TABLE II-1 ASTER

Effects of temperature and day length on days to flower for Aster ericoides 'Monte Casino' (Johansson, 1990).

Temperature °F (°C)	Day Length (hr)				
	8	12	16	24	Average
Days to Flower					
59 (15)	61.7	54.7	135.3	119.7	91.8
64 (18)	42.8	54.7	137.1	128.2	90.7
70 (21)	49.6	58.8	178.6	175.9	115.7
75 (24)	48.3	63.3	180.4	176.7	117.2
Mean	50.6	57.9	157.9	150.1	

HEIGHT CONTROL

For potted flowering plants, B-Nine (daminozide) at 1500 to 5000 ppm can be used shortly after the pinch as axillary buds begin to elongate. Several sprays may be required, depending on the cultivar and season (Faber and McGrew, 1998). To prevent clubby flower formation, do not apply after buds show true color (Humm, 1997). Bonzi (paclobutrazol) foliar sprays at 160 ppm and Sumagic (uniconazole) foliar sprays at 80 to 160 ppm can also be used (Whipker et al., 1995). A 12- to 16-ppm Bonzi drench may also be used (Latimer, 2001). *Aster alpinus* is moderately responsive to DIF (Warner and Erwin, 2001).

SPACING

For a pinched cut flower crop, 14 to 20 plants/yd² (17 to 24 plants/m²) are used; for pink and white cultivars, use 12 to 15 plants/yd² (14 to 18 plants/m²). For unpinched plants, use 40 to 53 plants/yd² (48 to 64 plants/m²).

For potted flowering plants, 4 plants/ft² (43 plants/m²) is a standard final spacing for 4-in. (10-cm) pots with four cuttings/pot. Spacing for fall potted crops ranges from 20 × 20 in. (50 × 50 cm) for plants potted in late May and grown in 8-in. (20-cm) pots to 12 × 12 in. (30 × 30 cm) for plants potted in mid- to late July and grown in 6- to 6.5-in. (15- to 17-cm) pots (Humm, 1997).

PINCHING AND DISBUDDING

For type 1 cuttings (see Propagation), plants are pinched when the shoots are 2.5 to 4 in. (6 to 10 cm) long. When stock plants are grown under LD, the cuttings are not pinched (type 2 cuttings). For potted flowering plants, plants are pinched 7 to 14 days after rooting under LD and moved to SD. Four to five leaves are left on the shoot (Luczal, 1992). Shearing is as effective as hand pinching (Goff et al., 1999). Avoid pinching or cutting back too hard because excessively vigorous shoots that flower late may break from the lower nodes and cause pots to be uneven (Humm, 1997). One or two additional pinches may be used, each 10 to 14 days after the previous pinch. For natural flowering of potted plants, the last pinch date should be prior to July 25 in northern latitudes and prior to August 10 in southern latitudes to prevent delay of flowering (Humm, 1997). Florel (ethephon) may also increase branching if used early in the production cycle.

SUPPORT

Two layers of support will be needed for cut flower production.

SCHEDULE AND TIMING

Various schedules can be devised, depending on type of propagation material, location, and season. Several schedules for potted flowering plants and cut flowers are included (Tables II-2, II-3, and II-4 Aster). Under winter conditions, growth is slow. For outdoor container production, Eddy and Whipker (1998) stated that one to several rooted cuttings planted in early June may be best grown in 1.5-gal (5.7-l) pots, mid-June plantings in 8-in. (20-cm) pots, and July plantings in 6-in. (15-cm) pots.

Farina et al. (1994) rooted cuttings under mist (August 10) from stock plants grown un-

TABLE II-2 ASTER

Proposed schedules for the flowering of *Aster novi-belgii* as a pinched cut flower crop from juvenile type I cuttings.

Cultural Step	Production Time (weeks)	Temperature °F (°C)	Photoperiod
Plant rooted cuttings in beds	1–3	65 (18)	11-hr SD
Pinch[a]	5–6	65 (18)	18-hr LD
Start SD[b]	10	70+ (21+)	11-hr SD
Flower[c]			
Total	16–19		

[a]As soon as plants become established.
[b]Cease 18-hr lighting when shoots are 12 to 20 in. (30 to 50 cm) tall.
[c]In some areas of the world a second crop may be obtained.

TABLE II-3 ASTER

Sample production schedules for the flowering of *Aster novi-belgii* as a nonpinched cut flower crop from type 2 cuttings using close spacing.

Cultural Step	Production Time (weeks)	Temperature °F (°C)	Photoperiod
Plant rooted cuttings in beds			
	5–6	65 (18)	18-hr LD
Start SD[a]			
	7–10	70+ (21+)	11-hr SD
Flower			
Total[b]	12–16		

[a] *Cease 18-hr lighting when plants are 12 to 20 in. (30 to 50 cm) tall.*
[b] *In some areas of the world a second crop may be obtained.*

TABLE II-4 ASTER

Sample production schedules for the flowering of *Aster novi-belgii* as a 4-in. (10-cm) potted flowering plant from type 3 cuttings.

Cultural Step	Production Time (weeks)	Temperature °F (°C)	Photoperiod
Root cutting directly in pot			
	2	70 (21)	20-hr days
Space pot-to-pot			
	1	65 (18)	20-hr days
Pinch[a]			
	1–2	65 (18)	20-hr days
Space and apply growth retardant[b] (B-Nine)			
	4–5	65 (18)	13-hr days
Flower			
Total	8–10		

[a] *After 5 to 7 days move to SD.*
[b] *When shoots are 1-in. (2.5-cm) long.*

der 16-hr photoperiods, and on September 1 plants were placed under greenhouse regimes of 13- to 17.5-hr photoperiods. They flowered within 56 to 57 days in the 13-hr treatment or within 80 to 82 days under the 17.5-hr photoperiod. On January 10, the plants were pruned and reflowered under the same photoperiods in 103 to 108 days. Temperatures ranged from 50°F (10°C) to 77°F (25°C).

Armitage and Laushman (2003) have published cut flower production data for *Aster ericoides*, *A. novae-angliae*, and *A. novi-belgii*. Most cut flower production in North America is outdoors and in Israel under protection. South American production is both outdoors and under protection. Under protection cut flower crops can be cut back after harvest, given 4 to 5 weeks LD, and reflowered 5 to 6 weeks after the start of SD.

INSECTS

Whiteflies and thrips are most prevalent; leaf miner, aphids, and caterpillars may also be problems. Leafhoppers, plant bugs, lace bugs, scale, caterpillars, weevil maggots, and Japanese beetles have also been recorded and may be problems outdoors (Dreistadt, 2001).

DISEASES

Perennial asters are subject to a large number of diseases outdoors (Horst, 1990). Powdery mildew (*Erysiphe cichoracearum*), gray mold (*Botrytis cinerea*), stem rot (*Sclerotinia sclerotiorum*), and root and stem rot (*Rhizoctonia*) can be problems in the greenhouse. A variety of other diseases have been noted including fusarium wilt (*Fusarium*), verticillium wilt (*Verticillium dahliae*), root rot (*Pythium* and

Phytophthora), rust (*Coleosporium asterum* and *Puccinia*), leaf spot (*Septoria*), tomato spotted wilt virus, and aster yellows (Dreistadt, 2001).

PHYSIOLOGICAL DISORDERS

Flower buds fail to develop or abort if LD are not of sufficient duration prior to moving the plants into SD or if the number of SD are not sufficient (Schwabe, 1986).

POSTHARVEST

Plants are harvested when one-quarter of florets are open and the balance of the flowers are beginning to open. Cut flowers respond to 5% sucrose and 5 mM silver thiosulfate (STS) plus an antimicrobial agent. However, *Aster novi-belgii* flowers are not sensitive to ethylene (Woltering and van Doorn, 1988). Plants and cut flowers are best shipped at 33 to 35°F (1 to 2°C) (Nell and Reid, 2001; Nowak and Rudnicki, 1990).

KEY POINTS

- This North American wildflower is used as a cut flower, potted flowering plant, and fall-flowering garden ornamental.
- Plants are propagated by cuttings or rhizome division.

- Asters are considered a LD–SD plant for floral initiation and development.
- In nature, cold is required to break dormancy, but commercially, high temperatures and LD replace vernalization.
- Whiteflies and thrips are common problems.

BIBLIOGRAPHY

Armitage, A.M., and J.M. Laushman. 2003. *Aster*, pp. 116–128 in *Specialty Cut Flowers*, 2nd ed. Timber Press, Portland, Oregon.

Bailey, L.H., and E.Z. Bailey. 1976. *Aster* L., pp. 121–125 in *Hortus Third: A Concise Dictionary of Plants Cultivated in the United States and Canada*. Macmillan, New York.

Dreistadt, S.H. 2001. *Integrated Pest Management for Floriculture and Nurseries*. University of California Division of Agriculture and Natural Resources Publication 3402.

Eddy, R.T., and B.E. Whipker. 1998. Guide to successful outdoor garden aster production. *North Carolina Commercial Flower Growers' Bulletin* 43(3):6–9.

Faber, W., and J. McGrew. 1998. *Aster* (Perennial), pp. 372–385 in *Ball RedBook*, 16th ed. V. Ball, editor. Ball Publishing, Batavia, Illinois.

Farina, E., C.D. Guda, and E. Scordo. 1994. Flowering and morphogenic responses of new *Aster* hybrids to photoperiod. *Physiologia Plantarum* 91:312–316.

Goff, L.M., G. Klingaman, and A.E. Einert. 1999. Evaluation of fifteen perennial garden asters for use in Arkansas, pp. 58–61 in *Horticultural Studies 1998*, J.R. Clark and M.D. Richardson, editors. University of Arkansas, Fayetteville.

Horst, R.K. 1990. *Aster* (Perennial), p. 543 in *Westcott's Plant Disease Handbook*, 5th ed. Van Nostrand Reinhold, New York.

Humm, B. 1997. *Aster* answers: Pot crop success. *GrowerTalks* 60(14):55, 60.

Huxley, A., M. Griffiths, and M. Levy. 1992. *Aster*, pp. 266–272 in *The New Royal Horticultural Society Dictionary of Gardening*, vol. 1. Stockton Press, New York.

Johansson, J. 1990. Flower formation in *Aster ericoides* L. (*A. multiflorus* Ait.), p. 597 in *23rd International Society for Horticultural Science Congress*, Florence, Italy. (Abstract)

Kadman-Zahavi, A., and H. Yahel. 1986. *Aster pilosus*, pp. 42–46 in *Handbook of Flowering*, vol. V, A.H. Halevy, editor. CRC Press, Boca Raton, Florida.

Kristiansen, K., C.W. Hansen, and K. Brandt. 1997. Flower induction in seedlings of *Aster novi-belgii* and selection before and after vegetative propagation. *Euphytica* 93:361–367.

Latimer, J.G. 2001. Herbaceous perennials, pp. 98–110 in *Tips on Regulating Growth of Floriculture Crops*, M.L. Gaston, L.A. Kunkle, P.S. Konjoian, and M.F. Wilt, editors. Ohio Florists' Association Services, Columbus, Ohio.

Luczal, R. 1992. Garden asters: Popular in European market as a potted plant. *Professional Plant Growers Association News* August:20–21.

Maqbool, M., and A.C. Cameron. 1994. Regrowth performance of field-grown herbaceous perennials following bare-root storage between -10 and +5C. *HortScience* 29:1039–1041.

Nell, T.A., and M.S. Reid. 2001. Can't take the heat. *Floral Management* 17(10):33–34.

Nowak, J., and R.M. Rudnicki. 1990. *Postharvest Handling and Storage of Cut Flowers, Florist Greens, and Potted Plants*. Timber Press, Portland, Oregon.

Oren-Shamir, M., L. Shaked-Sachray, A. Nissim-Levi, and D. Weiss. 2000. Effect of growth temperature on *Aster* flower development. *HortScience* 35:28–29.

Schwabe, W.W. 1986. *Aster novi-belgii*, pp. 29–41 in *Handbook of Flowering*, vol. 5, A.H. Halevy, editor. CRC Press, Boca Raton, Florida.

Wallerstein, I., A. Kadman-Zahavi, H. Yahel, A. Nissim, R. Stav, and S. Michal. 1992a. Control of growth and flowering in two *Aster* cultivars as influenced by cutting type, temperature, and day length. *Scientia Horticulturae* 50:209–218.

Wallerstein, I., A. Kadman-Zahavi, A. Nissim, R. Stav, and S. Michal. 1992b. Control by photoperiod and the rhizomatous zone over the production of basal buds and the preservation of the rosette form in *Aster* cultivars. *Scientia Horticulturae* 51:237–250.

Warner, R.M., and J.E. Erwin. 2001. Temperature, pp. 10–17 in *Tips on Regulating Growth of Floriculture Crops*, M.L. Gaston, L.A. Kunkle, P.S. Konjoian, and M.F. Wilt, editors. Ohio Florists' Association Services, Columbus, Ohio.

Whipker, B.E., R.T. Eddy, F. Heraux, and P.A. Hammer. 1995. Chemical growth retardants for height control of pot asters. *HortScience* 30:1309.

Woltering, E.J., and W.G. van Doorn. 1988. Role of ethylene in senescence of petals—morphological and taxonomical relationships. *Journal of Experimental Botany* 39:1605–1616.

Zimmer, K. 1987. Flowering of *Aster dumosus*. *Flowering Newsletter* 4:14.

Astilbe

FIGURE II-1 ASTILBE   Outdoor-grown *Astilbe* for cut flower and perennial plant production.

INTRODUCTION

Common name: astilbe, false spirea.

Scientific name: *Astilbe ×arendsii* Arends. (Huxley et al., 1992).

Family and related taxa: Saxifragaceae Juss. Other important genera in the family include *Saxifraga*, *Bergenia*, and *Tolmiea*.

Origin: Ten of the 12 *Astilbe* species are native to China, Japan, Nepal, and Korea; the remaining two are native to the mountains of Kentucky, Virginia, and Georgia. The *Astilbe ×arendsii* hybrids used in commerce today are from breeding programs in Europe, mainly Germany, between *A. chinensis* (Maxim.) Franch. 'Davidii' and other species.

Uses and current status: Astilbe are grown in gardens, forced in greenhouses as flowering potted plants, or produced in the field or greenhouse as cut flowers (Bailey, 1935; Bailey and Bailey, 1976; Chittendon and Synge, 1956) (Fig. II-1 Astilbe).

FIGURE II-2 ASTILBE   *Astilbe* inflorescence.

Astilbe are semiwoody perennials in Zones 3 to 7. Leaves are dark green, toothed, and pinnately compound. Flowering spikes are composed of numerous feathery flowers on a multibranched panicle (Fig. II-2 Astilbe). Flower colors include white, pink, purple, red, and rose (Armitage and Laushman, 2003; Bailey, 1935; Bailey and Bailey, 1976). Height varies from 15 to 30 in. (38 to 76 cm) (Bailey, 1935; Chittendon and Synge, 1956). Height varies with cultivar, location where plants have been produced, forcing temperature, and photoperiod (Pemberton and De Hertogh, 1994).

CULTIVARS

Numerous cultivars exist. Some are decades old, but still of exceptional quality. Many cultivars are of German origin. Plants range widely in height from 12 to 40 in. (30 to 100 cm). Cultivars can be selected for landscape use or for potted flowering plants (Armitage and Laushman, 2003; De Hertogh, 1996; Smith, 1994).

PROPAGATION

For commercial cut or pot plant production, individual crowns from the Netherlands are cut into pieces. Pieces of the woody underground rhizomatous stem with roots are subsequently sold. Each piece has one to two sites (eyes) for future growth. Crowns with multiple eyes can be purchased in North America. When imported from Europe, however, only pieces with one or two eyes can be brought into the United States for phytosanitary reasons; larger pieces cannot be properly cleaned or heat treated. Larger pieces require longer periods of heat temperature, risking injury to flower buds. Mother plants are lifted in the Netherlands in October to November and divisions are cut apart with a bandsaw. Inspect crowns because damage to eyes commonly occurs when crowns are cut with a bandsaw. Usually four to six eyes are placed in a 6-in. (15-cm) pot (Beattie and Holcomb, 1983; De Hertogh, 1996; Pemberton and De Hertogh, 1994). Three to five single-eye pieces can be used but generally do not force and flower uniformly; crowns with multiple eyes produce higher quality plants. Seed propagation at 60 to 70°F (16 to 21°C) can also be used with certain cultivars or for breeding purposes (Nau, 1993).

FLOWERING CONTROL AND DORMANCY

Fall-harvested crowns have no dormancy and can be immediately replanted in a warm environment; new growth and flowering will take place from reproductive meristems (Pemberton and De Hertogh, 1994). However, if cooled for only 1 week at 41°F (5°C), dormancy is imposed and at least 12 additional weeks at 41°F (5°C) are required (cultivar dependent) before growth and rapid flowering will take place. If stored longer than 12 weeks, use 29 to 32°F (−2 to 0°C) (Beattie and Holcomb, 1983; De Hertogh, 1996; Pemberton and De Hertogh, 1994). Crowns should be stored in nonperforated polyethylene bags in moist or dry peat (Pemberton and De Hertogh, 1994). Long-term storage is common and forcing can occur at any time of the year (Beattie and Holcomb, 1983; De Hertogh, 1996). Some cultivars do not have imposed dormancy (Pemberton and De Hertogh, 1994). Dormancy has also been reported to be broken by a 1-hr moist hot treatment of 109 to 111°F (43 to 44°C) (Lamattre, 1969). Astilbe also respond to etherization (warm water baths) to break dormancy prior to forcing (Chittendon and Synge, 1956). Latta (1939) discovered the effects of etherization when studying insect control treatments.

TEMPERATURE

Plants can be forced at 72/64°F (22/18°C) day/night temperatures to produce flowering plants in 6 to 8 weeks. Higher temperatures do not hasten development, but can decrease quality. Lower night temperatures from 64 to 57°F (18 to 14°C), cultivar dependent, may not increase the number of days to flower (Pemberton and De Hertogh, 1994; Wilkins, 1985). Greenhouse cut flower production is recommended at 46 to 50°F (8 to 10°C) nights for the first 4 weeks after planting and 54 to 59°F (12 to 15°C) thereafter (Bartels Stek, personal communication).

LIGHT

Full light can be used, although light shade (20 to 30%) can improve foliage color and produce broader leaves. Light intensity can be reduced at flowering (De Hertogh, 1996). Plants forced under an artificial 8-hr SD had fewer primary and secondary inflorescences per plant than those grown under a 12-hr photoperiod (8 + 4-hr night interruption) (Pemberton and De Hertogh, 1994). Long-day grown inflorescences were more narrow and taller. Runkle et al. (1998) also noted that plants grown under 13-hr LD (9 + 4-hr night interruption) had longer inflorescences than when grown under 9-hr SD, but photoperiod did not affect time to visible inflorescence or flower number. Lengthening of the inflorescences could be due to the incandescent light used as a night break. In gardens, plants are shade tolerant.

WATER

Astilbe require continuously moist media. The plants use large amounts of water and are easily injured if allowed to dry. High light, warm temperatures, and water stress result in leaf damage. However, excessive moisture during flower development may increase disease incidence.

CARBON DIOXIDE

No data available.

NUTRITION

Low levels of nutrients are required to prevent chlorosis (Pemberton and De Hertogh, 1994). See also Chapter 6, Nutrition, Table 6–4, for foliar nutrient levels.

MEDIA

Smith (1994) stated that the medium should be well drained and slightly acidic for the home landscape. Commercially, peat moss or potting grade pine bark can be used as an amendment or any commercial peatlite medium can be used. The medium pH should be 6.0 to 7.0 (De Hertogh, 1996; Pemberton and De Hertogh, 1994). The medium EC should be 2.0 to 3.5 $dS \cdot m^{-1}$, based on pour-thru testing (H. Scoggins, personal communication). Field production is normally in sandy soils (Beattie and Holcomb, 1983; De Hertogh, 1996; Wilkins, 1985).

HEIGHT CONTROL

B-Nine (daminozide) at 5000 ppm has been reported to reduce inflorescence height on potted flowering plants. Two or more weekly sprays may be required as the inflorescence begins to elongate. It is wise to select only short-growing cultivars (De Hertogh, 1996), although most cultivars will require applications of plant growth regulators. A Bonzi (paclobutrazol) drench at 30 ppm may be used (Latimer, 2001). A 25-ppm Sumagic (uniconazole) drench was effective when applied just prior to flower stem elongation (Holcomb and Beattie, 1990). However, Sumagic applications applied when dormant plants were just beginning to leaf out were either ineffective (0.25 or 2.5 ppm) or resulted in too much height control (25 ppm).

SPACING

During the early phases of greenhouse forcing, plants can be placed pot-to-pot. When leaves begin to overlap, space 4 in. (10 cm) apart for better air circulation and growth. For field cut flower production, plant at 10 × 12 to 12 × 15 in. (25 × 30 to 30 × 38 cm) spacing. Greenhouse spacing can be 1.1 to 1.9 plants/ft^2 (12 to 20 plants/m^2).

PINCHING AND DISBUDDING

No pinching or disbudding needed.

SUPPORT

No support is needed for potted plants. One layer of mesh can be used for outdoor cut flower production of tall-growing cultivars.

SCHEDULE AND TIMING

Plants forced for a November or December market have been in 32 to 35°F (0 to 1.7°C) cold storage since the previous year's harvest. The earliest that freshly harvested (but not cold-treated) roots can be forced into flower is late January. The most common dates for flowering of fall-harvested and cold-treated stock are April, May, and June (Beattie and Holcomb, 1983; De Hertogh, 1996; Pemberton and De Hertogh, 1994). Time to flower after the cold treatment varies with the cultivar from 31 to 41 days for 'Deutschland' to 51 to 70 days for 'Fanal' (Runkle et al., 1998). Days to flower ranged from 49 to 68 for five cultivars in work by Pemberton and De Hertogh (1994) (Table II-1 Astilbe).

One crown is used in a 4- to 6-in. (10- to 15-cm) pot if at least three buds are present. Three single budded pieces can also be used. Four to six eyes are preferred for 6-in. (15-cm) pots. Each eye will produce one major flowering stem.

INSECTS

Spider mites and Japanese beetles are problems on astilbe (Armitage and Laushman, 2003; De Hertogh, 1996). All plants entering the United States from Europe must be given a 110°F (43°C) hot water bath for 2.5 hr to control nematodes.

TABLE II-1 ASTILBE

Sample forcing schedule of *Astilbe* as a potted flowering plant.

Cultural Step	Production Time (weeks)	Temperature F° (C°)
Pot cold-treated crowns	1	60–73 (16–23)
Shoot emergence	2	55–73 (13–23)
Space	2–3	55–73 (13–23)
One or two growth retardant applications	2	55–73 (13–23)
Flower		
Total	7–8	

DISEASES

Powdery mildew (*Erysiphe polygoni*) can occur on the foliage of plants that are not spaced properly (Horst, 1990). *Botrytis* on the inflorescence and *Fusarium* wilting have also been seen.

PHYSIOLOGICAL DISORDERS

No disorders have been described.

POSTHARVEST

Harvest occurs when one-half to three-quarters of the florets are open because little flower development occurs after harvest (Armitage and Laushman, 2003). Young leaves at the base of the plant should not be damaged (Bartels Stek, personal communication). Astilbe flowers are reported to be sensitive to ethylene (Sacalis, 1993). Pulsing cut stems with silver thiosulfate (STS) is recommended (Sacalis, 1993). Stems should be recut after being out of water for any time span. Warm acidified water should be used. Dry stored stems will not rehydrate if pretreated with only water but will rehydrate if pretreated with water plus a surfactant (Pak and van Doorn, 1991; van Doorn et al., 1993). However, some surfactants, such as Tween-20 or Tween-80, caused phytotoxicity while others, such as Triton X-100 or Nonoxynol-8.5, did not. Stems can be stored and shipped at 35 to 40°F (2 to 5°C) (L. Høyer, personal communication).

Pot plants last 10 to 40 days, depending on home conditions. Plants should be shipped at 37 to 46°F (3 to 8°C) for no longer than 4 days (Pemberton and De Hertogh, 1994).

KEY POINTS

- Astilbe, traditionally grown in the garden as a hardy garden perennial, is now a popular cut flower and potted flowering plant.

- For forcing, woody crown pieces with one or two buds (eyes) are used.

- Once crowns are dormant, 12 or more weeks of cold at 41°F (5°C) are required for rapid forcing at 74/64°F (22/18°C) day/night temperatures.

- Do not allow astilbe to become dry as leaf injury will occur.

BIBLIOGRAPHY

Armitage, A.A., and J.M. Laushman. 2003. *Astilbe ×arendsii*, pp. 128–134 in *Specialty Cut Flowers*, 2nd ed. Timber Press, Portland, Oregon.

Bailey, L.H. 1935. *Astilbe*, pp. 422–423 in *The Standard Cyclopedia of Horticulture*. Macmillian, New York.

Bailey, L.H., and E.Z. Bailey. 1976. *Astilbe*, pp. 125–126 in *Hortus Third: A Concise Dictionary of Plants Cultivated in the United States and Canada*. Macmillan, New York.

Beattie, D.J., and E.J. Holcomb. 1983. Effects of chilling and photoperiod on forcing *Astilbe*. *HortScience* 18:449–450.

Chittendon, F.J., and P.M. Synge, editors. 1956. *Astilbe*, pp. 215–216 in *The Royal Horticulture Society Dictionary of Gardening*. Clarendon Press, Oxford Press, Oxford.

De Hertogh, A. 1996. *Astilbe*—(False Spirea)—Potted plants, pp. C23–30 in *Holland Bulb Forcer's Guide*, 5th ed. International Flower Bulb Centre, Hillegom, The Netherlands.

Holcomb, E.J., and D.J. Beattie. 1990. Growth retardants for perennials, pp. 164–170 in *Proceedings for the Plant Growth Regulator Society of America, 17th Annual Meeting*.

Horst, R.K. 1990. *Astilbe*, p. 544 in *Westcott's Plant Disease Handbook*, 5th ed. Van Nostrand Reinhold, New York.

Huxley, A., M. Griffiths, and M. Levy. 1992. *Astilbe*, pp. 273–274 in *The New Royal Horticultural Society Dictionary of Gardening*, vol. 1. Stockton Press, New York.

Lamattre, P. 1969. Nouvellis observations sur le fareage des astilbes. *La Revue Horticole* 2 (287):1631–1635. (in French)

Latimer, J.G. 2001. Herbaceous perennials, pp. 98–110 in *Tips on Regulating Growth of Floriculture Crops*, M.L. Gaston, L.A. Kunkle, P.S. Konjoian, and M.F. Wilt, editors. Ohio Florists' Association Services, Columbus, Ohio.

Latta, R. 1939. Vapor-heat treatment for control of narcissus bulb pests in the Pacific Northwest. *United States Department of Agriculture Technical Bulletin* 672:1–53.

Nau, J. 1993. *Astilbe*, p. 86 in *Ball Culture Guide, The Encyclopedia of Seed Germination*, 2nd ed. Ball Publishing, Batavia, Illinois.

Pak, C., and W. G. van Doorn. 1991. The relationship between structure and function of surfactants used for rehydration of cut astilbe, bouvardia and roses. *Acta Horticulturae* 298:171–176.

Pemberton, G.H., and A.A. De Hertogh. 1994. Influence of harvest date and 2C storage on floral development of Dutch-grown *Astilbe*. *Journal of American Society Horticultural Science* 119:144–149.

Runkle, E.S., R.D. Heins, A.C. Cameron, and W.H. Carlson. 1998. Flowering cold-treated field-grown *Astilbe*. *HortTechnology* 8:207–209.

Sacalis, J.N. 1993. *Astilbe ×arendsii*, p. 34 in *Cut Flowers, Prolonging Freshness*, 2nd ed., J.L. Seals, editor. Ball Publishing, Batavia, Illinois.

Smith, E.M. 1994. Astilbe for the home landscape. *Ohio Florist's Association Bulletin* 774:6–7.

van Doorn, W.G., R.R.J. Perik, and P.J.M. Belde. 1993. Effects of surfactants on the longevity of dry-stored cut flowering stems of rose, *Bouvardia*, and *Astilbe*. *Postharvest Biology and Technology* 1993:69–76.

Wilkins, H. 1985. *Astilbe*, pp. 521–522 in *Handbook of Flowering*, vol. I, A.H. Halevy, editor. CRC Press, Boca Raton, Florida.

Begonia, Hiemalis

INTRODUCTION

Common names: hiemalis begonia, elatior begonia, Rieger begonia, winter-flowering begonia.

Scientific name: *Begonia ×hiemalis* Fotsch (Huxley et al., 1992). This group of hybrids resulted from crosses among *B. socotrana* Hook. and various Andean hybrids (*B.* Tuberhybrida complex) (Fotsch, 1933; Goldschmidt, 1974) and was formerly known as *B. ×elatior*.

Family and related taxa: Begoniaceae Agardh. The Begoniaceae family has more than 1000 species, which are found in tropical and subtropical regions of both hemispheres (Huxley et al., 1992). The genus *Begonia* is valued for many purposes, including bedding plants, potted plants, and hanging baskets, and numerous species have great commercial potential (Bailey and Bailey, 1976; Fotsch, 1933; Wilkins, 1985). Three groups of hybrids and related species are discussed in separate chapters: rex begonia, tuberous begonia, and wax begonia.

Origin: This important group of winter-flowering begonia hybrids combines both the winter-flowering attributes of *B. socotrana* from the hot, sandy island of Socotra off the coast of Yemen with the colorful large double-flowering qualities of *B.* Tuberhybrids from the Andes.

Uses and current status: Hiemalis begonia are used as upright potted flowering plants marketed in various pot sizes or hanging baskets (Fig. II-1 Begonia, Hiemalis).

Begonias are usually perennial and herbaceous to shrublike with stems that can be erect, trailing, or modified into rhizomes or tubers. Leaves are alternate and vary in size, form, texture, substance, and color patterns. The genus is monoecious with unisexual male (staminate) and female (pistillate) flowers appearing within the same inflorescence (Bailey and Bailey, 1976; Fotsch, 1933).

FIGURE II-1 BEGONIA, HIEMALIS *Begonia* ×*hiemalis* plant being grown using capillary mat irrigation.

CULTIVARS

There are numerous breeding efforts and new cultivars are released annually. Breeding is currently aimed at developing cultivars that will flower under LD and will not go dormant or tuberize at temperatures below 65°F (18°C) or under SD.

PROPAGATION

The hiemalis begonia can be propagated by stem or leaf cuttings, seed, or *in vitro* methods (Appelgren, 1978; Goldschmidt, 1974; von Hentig, 1976, 1978). A rooted terminal vegetative stem cutting with one fully expanded leaf is most commonly used in Europe and North America (Karlsson and Heins, 1992; L. Drewlow, personal communication). For cutting production, stock plants are kept vegetative by 16-hr LD and are grown at temperatures of 64 to 68°F (18 to 20°C). Cuttings root within 3 or 4 weeks under LD at a medium temperature of 70 to 72°F (21 to 22°C) with a rooting hormone. Cuttings are best rooted directly in the pot in which they are to be sold. Propagation can be under white plastic tents in the summer, clear plastic in the winter, or intermittent mist. Mist should be used only in areas where temperatures are too high for tents to be used (Goldschmidt, 1974; Karlsson and Heins, 1992; Wikesjö and Schüssler, 1982).

Leaf cuttings are used in Europe and are frequently imported into North America. Better quality plants are produced from leaf cuttings than terminal cuttings because the plants will have more branches and adventitious shoots. However, terminal cuttings will reduce the production time compared with leaf cuttings (L. Drewlow, personal communication), because leaf cuttings must produce both new roots and shoots.

Stock plants should be under SD (12 to 13 hr of light) for 4 weeks, because shoot production is promoted when leaves are used from reproductive stock plants (Hilding, 1982; Karlsson and Heins, 1992; von Hentig, 1976, 1978). Stock plants should be maintained at 60 to 68°F (16 to 20°C) for optimal leaf unfolding and leaf cutting production numbers.

Leaf cuttings require 10 to 13 weeks to form a plantlet with a good root system and three to five shoots (Hilding, 1974, 1975, 1982; Karlsson and Heins, 1992). During root and shoot development, the medium is kept at 64°F (18°C) and supplemental light is used during periods of low irradiance. Although SD hasten shoot formation from leaf cuttings, SD also induce flowering and should not be used for longer than 2 weeks for stem cuttings.

Tissue culture is used only when rapid cultivar multiplication is needed. Techniques have been developed by various researchers (Hilding and Welander, 1976; Reuther, 1980; Simmonds and Werry, 1987).

Seed-propagated cultivars are also available for outdoor use. Seed is germinated uncovered at 75 to 78°F (24 to 26°C) in 7 to 14 days (R. Sterkel, personal communication). There are 1.85 million seed/oz (65,300/g).

FLOWERING CONTROL AND DORMANCY

B. ×*hiemalis* is an obligatory SD plant at temperatures greater than 75°F (24°C); at lower temperatures, flower initiation can slowly occur under LD (Sandved, 1968, 1969, 1971, 1974). For example, at 75°F (24°C) no cultivars flowered under a 16-hr photoperiod and all cultivars flowered under a 10-hr photoperiod (Sandved, 1968, 1969). As temperatures decrease to 64, 61, or 54°F (18, 16, or 12°C), the absolute SD requirement decreases and most cultivars flower under a 16-hr photoperiod at 54°F (12°C). Heide and Rünger (1985) concluded that at 75°F (24°C) the critical maximum photoperiod for floral initiation was 12 to 13 hr for most cultivars. Regardless, all new cultivars in the United States are selected to flower under LD at temperatures greater than 65°F (18°C). Further, in winter plants must be given a 14-hr photoperiod at temperatures greater than 65°F (18°C) or the plants will tuberize and go dormant (Roodenburg, 1952; L. Drewlow, personal communication). However, some cultivars may not be responsive to photoperiod (Karlsson, 1992) and some cultivars may be responsive when young but not after four to six tiers of leaves have formed (Gooder, 2000).

The decision to switch from LD to SD is made when the vegetative plant has formed sufficient foliage to cover the pot. The number of LD for vegetative growth and the number of SD for floral initiation will vary with and depend on the time of year and cultivar.

The critical number of continuous SD is only seven for flower induction, but plants will have low flower numbers (Sandved, 1968). Commercially 2 to 3 weeks of SD are given, followed by LD for normal plant development and abundant flower numbers (Karlsson and Heins, 1992). If SD continue for longer than 3 weeks, plants may become dormant and the number of future flowers would be reduced due to the lower number of leaf axils (Sandved, 1968). This SD response is promoted by 52 or 54°F (11 or 12°C) temperatures (Maatsch and Rünger, 1956). Flowering may also be triggered by moisture stress, low nutrition, sudden temperature changes, and growth retardants (Gooder, 2000).

TEMPERATURE

Temperatures will vary depending on the production stage (see Propagation and Flowering Control and Dormancy sections). Propagation of terminal cuttings is best at 70 to 72°F (21 to 22°C) medium temperature. The optimum temperature for the LD stage prior to and after the pinch is 65°F (18°C) and for the SD stage is 68 to 70°F (20 to 21°C). Plants should be forced at a night temperature of 64°F (18°C) for quality plants with short internodes, appropriately sized leaves, large flower diameters, and bright colors (Hilding, 1975; Sandved, 1968, 1974). Interestingly, Karlsson (1992) determined that the maximum leaf unfolding rate of 0.116 leaves/day occurred at 70°F (21°C) during the LD period. During the SD period, the leaf unfolding rate stayed the same as during the LD period for 'Ballet' but dropped by half for 'Hilda,' indicating that 'Hilda' may be more influenced by photoperiod than 'Ballet.'

LIGHT

Leaf injury can occur under high light levels and an interaction with temperature exists. At 64°F (18°C) and below, high light levels of 3000 fc (600 μmol $\cdot$ m^{-2} $\cdot$ s^{-1}) can be briefly tolerated; at 70°F (21°C), 2000 fc (400 μmol $\cdot$ m^{-2} $\cdot$

s^{-1}) can be tolerated; at 81°F (27°C), 1500 fc (300 μmol $\cdot$ m^{-2} $\cdot$ s^{-1}). Excessively high light can cause slow, hardened growth, cupping of leaf margins, reddening or darkening of the leaf, and sunburned, necrotic areas (Gooder, 2000). Night interruption or day continuation lighting of 12 to 20 fc (2.4 to 4 μmol $\cdot$ m^{-2} $\cdot$ s^{-1}) prior to sunup can be used for artificial LD. The actual length of the LD can increase or decrease as the natural day length fluctuates.

In North America, supplemental high-intensity lighting is not commonly used. In Europe 200 to 600 fc (40 to 120 μmol $\cdot$ m^{-2} $\cdot$ s^{-1}) supplemental lighting is used in the winter. Approximately 20 hr of light/day are used prior to SD to stimulate vegetative growth; during SD 10 to 12 hr/day are used, and after floral initiation, 16 to 24 hr/day are used for rapid flower development (Esberg, 1982; Hilding, 1982; Karlsson and Heins, 1992; Mikkelsen, 1973; Wikesjö and Schüssler, 1982).

WATER

Hiemalis begonias have a fibrous root system and can easily be injured if the peat medium becomes excessively dry or overly moist for long periods. Moisture should be uniformly applied, and water or condensation on foliage should be avoided (Hilding, 1982; Karlsson and Heins, 1992; Mikkelsen, 1973). For these reasons automated watering systems are recommended. Subirrigation, in particular, produces excellent growth compared to overhead irrigation (Son et al., 2002).

CARBON DIOXIDE

The use of supplemental carbon dioxide (300 to 3000 ppm) has resulted in superior plants (more shoots, leaves, and flowers) and in shorter production schedules (Hilding, 1982; Karlsson and Heins, 1992; Lemper, 1980; Mikkelsen, 1973; Mortensen and Ulsaker, 1985). Plants can be shifted into the SD environment sooner when carbon dioxide is used; 600 to 900 ppm is commonly used (Dümmen, USA, personal communication).

NUTRITION

The hiemalis begonia does not require high levels of mineral nutrition. A constant liquid fertilizer of 100 to 125 ppm N is adequate (Nelson et al., 1978). Nutritional programs cease for 1 week in the middle of the SD reproductive treatment to reduce vegetative growth, then resume at 100 ppm N. Excess N has been reported to reduce the flowering response. Ammonium levels in the winter should be monitored and reduced (Karlsson and Heins, 1992; Mikkelsen, 1973). The levels of P and K used in a routine fertilizer regimen will depend on the presence of phosphate and vermiculite in the growing medium. Soil and tissue tests should guide the nutrient program. Media EC should be 1 to 2 dS $\cdot$ m^{-1} based on saturated paste extract (Gooder, 2000). Nelson et al. (1978) described nutrient deficiencies for N, P, K, Ca, Mg, Fe, and B. Foliar nutrient levels for high-quality plants are listed in Chapter 6, Nutrition, Table 6–4.

MEDIA

The growing medium is high in organic matter and should be well drained. Most mixes consist of sphagnum peat moss (45 to 60%) amended with soil for increased cation exchange capacity and coarse perlite, vermiculite, or sand for drainage. The pH should be adjusted to 5.5 to 6.5. Superphosphate can be mixed into the medium because phosphorus deficiencies are common (Nelson et al., 1977). No other slow-release fertilizers, which would increase nutrient levels, should be incorporated into the medium (Karlsson and Heins, 1992; Mikkelsen, 1973).

HEIGHT CONTROL

Cycocel (chlormequat) is commonly used as a spray to reduce internode length (Goldschmidt, 1974; Hilding, 1975, 1982; Karlsson and Heins, 1992; Krauskopf and Nelson, 1976; Mikkelsen, 1973; Sandved, 1972; Wikesjö and Schüssler, 1982). Flower initiation is slightly influenced by Cycocel and flower development can be delayed. The concentration varies from 500 to 3000 ppm and is cultivar related, but 500 to 1000 ppm is commonly used. Foliage is sprayed in the summer 1 week after SD commence and in the winter at the start of SD or when new growth is visible after transplanting. A-Rest (ancymidol), Bonzi (paclobutrazol), and Sumagic (uniconazole) are also effective (Adriansen, 1985; Gooder, 2000). Late applications of plant growth retardants may cause flowers to open up below the foliage canopy (Gooder, 2000).

Hiemalis begonias do not respond to negative DIF during the vegetative phase, but do respond to DIF during the flowering phase of growth. Plants also respond to a 2-hr temperature drop (DROP) at the end of the night or at the beginning of the day (Grindal and Moe, 1995; Moe et al., 1995; Myster et al., 1997). Plant quality is generally better when Cycocel is used compared with DIF-grown plants.

SPACING

Plants are frequently held pot-to-pot until the end of the flower initiation phase. Only during the last 5 to 8 weeks of production are plants spaced. The 4-in. (10-cm) pots are spaced at two plants/ft^2 (22 plants/m^2) and 5- or 6-in. (13- or 15-cm) pots at 10 × 10 in. (25 × 25 cm) (Hilding, 1982; Karlsson and Heins, 1992; Mikkelsen, 1973).

PINCHING AND DISBUDDING

The most vigorous shoots are removed with a soft pinch to improve plant shape and control plant height. This can occur at the end of propagation in the summer or 2 weeks after propagation in the winter. When transplants are purchased, pinching occurs from 2 to 3 weeks after potting. Atrimmec (dikegulac sodium) at 780 to 1560 ppm can be used to increase the number of axillary shoots. During optimal climatic and cultural conditions, large leaves may develop that might have to be removed to open the plant and allow for the proper development of the inflorescences (Esberg, 1982; Hilding, 1982; Karlsson and Heins, 1992; Mikkelsen, 1973; Wikesjö and Schüssler, 1982).

SUPPORT

When 4-in. (10-cm) potted plants are produced, no support is needed. Larger specimens in 6-in. (15-cm) pots require staking and possibly tying.

SCHEDULE AND TIMING

Hiemalis begonias cannot be as precisely programmed as other photoperiodically controlled floriculture crops. Once a plant is out of propagation, 10 to 12 weeks are required for flowering from June to December, and 13 to 16 weeks are required from January to May. Not only is timing and scheduling dependent on climate, but also on pot size, cultivar, and supplemental CO_2 and lighting (Esberg, 1982; Hilding, 1982; Karlsson and Heins, 1992; Lemper, 1980; Mikkelsen, 1973; Mortensen and Ulsaker, 1985; Wikesjö and Schüssler, 1982). Crop time (from sowing to flowering) for seed-propagated plants varies from 16 to 18 weeks for 4-in. (10-cm) pots to 20 to 22 weeks for hanging baskets (Tables II-1 and II-2 Begonia, Hiemalis).

TABLE II-I BEGONIA, HIEMALIS

Sample production schedule for *Begonia* ×*hiemalis* from terminal cuttings for 4-in. (10-cm) pots.

Cultural Step	Production Time (weeks)	Temperature °F (°C)	Photoperiod
Direct rooting of cutting in pot			
	3–4	Medium: 70–72 (21–22)	LD
Removed from propagation[a,b]			
	0–2	Air: 65 (18)	LD
Floral initiation[b,c]			
	2	Air: 68–70 (20–21)	SD
Floral development			
	4–6	Air: 64 (18)	LD
Hardening			
	1	Air: 59–63 (15–17)	LD
Flower			
Total	10–15		

[a]Pinch 0 to 2 weeks after removal from propagation, depending on pot size, season, and cultivar.

[b]SD can start immediately after removal from propagation or wait for 1 to 2 weeks, depending on pot size, season, and cultivar.

[c]Cycocel sprays can be applied beginning immediately at the start of SD or 1 week after SD.

TABLE II-2 BEGONIA, HIEMALIS

Sample production schedule for *Begonia* ×*hiemalis* from leaf cuttings for 4-in. (10-cm) pots.

Cultural Step	Production Time (weeks)	Temperature °F (°C)	Photoperiod
Plant leaf cutting and stimulate shoot formation[a]			
	0–2[b]	Medium: 64 (18)	SD[b,c]
Stimulate root formation			
	10–13	Medium: 64 (18)	LD
Transplant rooted leaf cutting with three to five shoots			
	0–2	Medium: 65 (18)	LD
Removed from propagation[d,e]			
	0–2	Air: 65 (18)	LD
Floral initiation[e,f]			
	2	Air: 68–70 (20–21)	SD
Floral development			
	4–6	Air: 64 (18)	LD
Hardening			
	1	Air: 59–63 (15–17)	LD
Flower			
Total	17–28		

[a]Supplemental lighting may also be required in the winter.

[b]Shoot formation is enhanced by SD during rooting, and should be no longer than 2 weeks because premature reproductive shoots may occur.

[c]Shool formation with leaf cuttings is enhanced if stock plants are under SD for 4 weeks of 12 to 13 hr of light at 60 to 68°F (16 to 20°C).

[d]Pinch 0 to 2 weeks after removal from propagation, depending on pot size, season, and cultivar.

[e]SD can commence immediately after removal from propagation or wait for 1 to 2 weeks, depending on pot size, season, and cultivar.

[f]Cycocel sprays can commence immediately after the start of SD or 1 week after SD.

INSECTS

Thrips, mites, aphids, and foliar nematodes can be encountered during production.

DISEASES

Bacterial soft rot (*Erwinia*) on stems or leaves, *Botrytis* on leaves and flowers, and powdery mildew (*Oidium*) on leaves and flowers are seen during production. Fungal root and stem rots (*Phytophthora*, *Pythium*, *Rhizoctonia solani*, *Sclerotinia sclerotiorum*, *Sclerotium rolfsii*, and *Thielaviopsis basicola*) can be present also. Armillaria root rot (*Armillaria mellea*), powdery mildew (*Erysiphe*), leafspot (*Phyllosticta*), bacterial blight (*Erwinia chrysanthemi*), soft rot (*Erwinia carotovora*), bacterial leaf spot (*Xanthomonas campestris* pv. *begoniae*), and various viruses have also been recorded (Dreistadt, 2001). Disease can be avoided with good sanitation and cultured practices integrated with proper chemical selections (Esberg, 1982; Karlsson and Heins, 1992; Mikkelsen, 1973; Powell, 1973).

PHYSIOLOGICAL DISORDERS

High night temperatures above 75°F (24°C) have been reported to delay flowering (Esberg, 1982; Hilding, 1982; Mikkelsen, 1973). Edema, a rupturing and corking of epidermal cells on the underside of the leaf, is thought to be caused by high medium moisture content and extremely high day and low night temperatures. Edema is also caused when the medium stays warm at night and the air temperature is low, resulting in excessive leaf turgor pressure. Control edema by reducing moisture, maintaining constant temperatures, and reducing humidity (Karlsson and Heins, 1992; Mikkelsen, 1973).

POSTHARVEST

Hiemalis begonias are sensitive to ethylene (Høyer, 1985). Willumsen and Fjeld (1995) found that exposure of only 0.01 ppm for 96 hr resulted in flower and flower bud abscission. A silver thiosulfate (STS) spray (0.5 to 1.0 mM) is effective in preventing ethylene-induced abscission during marketing of a potted flowering plant. Fumigation with 20 ppb 1-methylcyclopropene (1-MCP) for 6 hr or 0.5 mM STS sprays prevented the negative effects of ethylene (Serek et al., 1994). The optimal shipping temperature was listed at 36 to 43°F (2 to 6°C) by L. Høyer (personal communication), but Gooder (2000) recommended that plants not be shipped or stored below 50°F (10°C). Reducing the temperature to 59 to 63°F (15 to 17°F) prior to marketing is recommended for optimal postharvest quality and life (Karlsson and Heins, 1992).

KEY POINTS

- Hiemalis or Rieger begonia is used as a potted flowering plant and hanging basket plant.
- Commercially, propagation is by leaf or terminal cuttings.
- Rooted cuttings are allowed to be vegetative under LD conditions at 65°F (18°C) for 2 weeks, then SD are given for the reproductive phase for only 2 weeks at 68 to 70°F (20 to 21°C), followed by LD until flowering.
- If plants remain under SD, they become dormant and form tubers.
- At 75°F (24°C) or higher, hiemalis begonia is an obligatory SD plant; below 75°F (24°C) it is a facultative SD plant.
- Some cultivars may not be affected by photoperiod.
- Because uniform media moisture is important, plants are best grown using automated irrigation systems.
- Precise height control is frequently more of an art than a science.
- Diseases such as bacterial soft rot, *Botrytis*, and powdery mildew can be troublesome.

BIBLIOGRAPHY

Adriansen, E. 1985. Kemisk vækstregulering, pp. 142–162 in *Potteplanter I—Produktion, Metoder, Midler*, O.V. Christensen, A. Klougart, I.S. Pedersen, and K. Wikesjö, editors. Gartner-INFO, København, Denmark. (in Danish)

Appelgren, M. 1978, Formering av hiemalis begonia *in vitro. Gartneryrket* 32: 911–912. (in Danish)

Bailey, L.H., and E.Z. Bailey. 1976. *Begonia*, pp. 142–154 in *Hortus Third, A Concise Dictionary of Plants Cultivated in the United States and Canada.* Macmillan, New York.

Dreistadt, S.H. 2001. *Integrated Pest Management for Floriculture and Nurseries.* University of California Division of Agriculture and Natural Resources Publication 3402.

Esberg, N. 1982. A complete program for growing Rieger begonias. *Florists' Review* 169(4394):12, 67–68.

Fotsch, K.A. 1933. *Die Begonien.* Eugen Ulmer, Stuttgart, Germany. (in German)

Goldschmidt, H. 1974. *Marktwichtige Blütenbegonien.* Gartnerische Praxis, Paul Parey, Berlin-Hamburg. (in German)

Gooder, M. 2000. How we grow: Hiemalis begonias. *GrowerTalks* 64(5):83, 88.

Grindal, G., and R. Moe. 1995. Growth rhythm and temperature DROP. *Acta Horticulturae* 378:47–52.

Heide, O.M., and W. Rünger. 1985. *Begonia,* pp. 4–23 in *Handbook of Flowering,* vol. II. A.H. Halevy, editor. CRC Press, Boca Raton, Florida.

Hilding, A. 1974. Inverkan av dagslängd och temperatur vid förökning av höstbegonia (*Begonia ×hiemalis*) med bladsticklingar. Lantbrukshögskolans Meddelande A.1:Number 209, Uppsala, Sweden. (in Swedish)

Hilding, A. 1975. Inverkan av temperatur, toppning och retarderande medel på tillväxt och utveckling av höstbegonia, *Begonia ×hiemalis.* Lantbrukshögskolans Meddelande A.252, Uppsala, Sweden. (in Swedish)

Hilding, A. 1982. Production av *Begonia ×elatior.* Trädgård 220. Swedish University of Agricultural Sciences Research Information Center, Alnarp, Sweden. (in Swedish)

Hilding, A., and T. Welander. 1976. Effects of some factors on propagation of *Begonia ×hiemalis in vitro. Swedish Journal of Agricultural Research* 6:191–199.

Høyer, L. 1985. Bud and flower drop in *Begonia elation* 'Sirene' caused by ethylene and darkness. *Acta Horticulturae* 167:387–394.

Huxley, A., M. Griffiths, and M. Levy. 1992. *Begonia hiemalis,* pp. 318–329 in *The New Royal Horticultural Society Dictionary of Gardening,* vol. 1. Stockton Press, New York.

Karlsson, M.G. 1992. Leaf unfolding rate in *Begonia ×hiemalis. HortScience* 27:109–110.

Karlsson, M.G., and R.D. Heins. 1992. *Begonias,* pp. 409–427 in *Introduction to Floriculture,* 2nd ed., R.A. Larson, editor. Academic Press, San Diego, California.

Krauskopf, D.M., and P.V. Nelson. 1976. Chemical height control of Rieger elatior begonia. *Journal of the American Society for Horticultural Science* 101:618–619.

Lemper, J. 1980. *Begonia elatior.* Wirkung von Licht, Temperatur und Kohlendioxid auf Wachstum und Blütenbildung. *Gärtnerbörse und Gartenwelt* 80(11):252–255. (in German)

Maatsch, R., and W. Rünger. 1956. Über den Einfluss der Temperatur auf die Photoperiodische Reak-tion von Knollenbegonien. *Gartenbauwissenschaft* 20:478–488. (in German)

Mikkelsen, J.C. 1973. Production requirements for quality Rieger begonias. *GrowerTalks* 37(6):3–9.

Moe, R., K. Willumsen, I.H. Ihlebekk, A.I. Stupa, N.M. Glomsrud, and L.M. Mortensen. 1995. DIF and temperature drop responses in SDP and LDP, a comparison. *Acta Horticulturae* 378:27–33.

Mortensen, L.M., and R. Ulsaker. 1985. Effects of CO_2 concentrations and light levels on growth, flowering and photosynthesis of *Begonia ×hiemalis* Fotsch. *Scientia Horticulturae* 27: 131–141.

Myster, J., O. Junttila, B. Lindgård, and R. Moe. 1997. Temperature alternations and the influence of gibberellins and indoleacetic acid on elongation growth and flowering of *Begonia ×hiemalis* Fotsch. *Plant Growth Regulation* 21:135–144.

Nelson, P.V., D.M. Krauskopf, and N.C. Mingis. 1977. Visual symptoms of nutrient deficiencies in Rieger Elatior begonia. *Journal of the American Society for Horticultural Science* 102:65–68.

Nelson, P.V., D.M. Krauskopf, and N.C. Mingis. 1978. Nitrogen and potassium requirements of Rieger begonia (*Begonia ×hiemalis* Fotsch). *Journal of the American Society for Horticultural Science* 103:603–605.

Powell, C.C. 1973. Foliar nematode control of rieger begonia. *Ohio Florist Association Bulletin* 530:4–5.

Reuther, G. 1980. Elatiorbegonien I. Weitere Untersuchungen zur Gewinnung von befallsfreien Elitepflanzen durch Gewebekultur. *Gärtnerbörse und Gartenwelt* 80(39):876, 880–881. (in German)

Roodenburg, J.W.M. 1952. Environmental factors in greenhouse culture, pp. 117–126 in *Report of the 13th International Horticultural Congress.*

Sandved, G. 1968. Virkning av daglengde og temperatur på vekst og blomstring hos *Begonia ×hiemalis* Fotsch. *Gartneryrket* (Oslo) 58: 344–349. (in Norwegian)

Sandved, G. 1969. Flowering in *Begonia ×hiemalis* Fotsch, as affected by day length and temperature. *Acta Horticulturae* 14:61–66.

Sandved, G. 1971. Effekt av daglengde og temperature på vekst og blomstring hos *Begonia ×hiemalis* 'Schwabenland' og 'Liebesfeuer.' *Gartneryrket* (Oslo) 61:378–379. (in Norwegian)

Sandved, G. 1972. Effect av CCC til hiemalisbegonia. *Gartneryrket* (Oslo) 62:508. (in Norwegian)

Sandved, G. 1974. Versuche und Erfahrungen mit Elatiorbegonien in Norwegen. *Gartenwelt* 74:379–380. (in German)

Serek, M, E.C. Sisler, and M.S. Reid. 1994. Novel gaseous ethylene binding inhibitor prevents ethylene effects in potted flowering plants. *Journal of the American Society for Horticultural Science* 119:1230–1233.

Simmonds, J.A., and T. Werry. 1987. Liquid-shake culture for improved micropropagation of *Begonia ×hiemalis. HortScience* 22:122–124.

Son, K.-C., H.-J. Kim, Y.-S. Park, and S-C. Chae. 2002. Comparison of the growth and development of elatior begonia as affected by the irrigation method and cultivar. *Journal of the Korean Society for Horticultural Science* 43:639–643.

von Hentig, W.-U. 1976. Zur Vermehrung von Elatiorbegonien 'Riegers Schwabenland' und 'Riegers Aphrodite.' *Gartenwelt* 76:95–100. (in German)

von Hentig, W.-U. 1978. Zur Vermehrung von Weitere Ergebnisse mit Rieger-Sorten. *Gärtnerbörse und Gartenwelt* 78(9):193–195. (in German)

Wikesjö, K., and H. Schüssler. 1982. Growing Rieger begonias year-round. *Florists' Review* 170 (4396):30, 72–74.

Wilkins, H.F. 1985. Begonia, pp. 479–484 in *Bedding Plants III*, 3rd ed., J.W. Mastalerz and E.J. Holcomb, editors. Pennsylvania Flower Growers Publishers, University Park, Pennsylvania.

Willumsen, K., and T. Fjeld. 1995. The sensitivity of some flowering potted plants to exogenous ethylene. *Acta Horticulturae* 405:362–367.

Begonia, Rex

FIGURE II-1 BEGONIA, REX *Begonia* 'Escargot' potted plant.

INTRODUCTION

Common names: rex begonia, king begonia, painted leaf begonia.

Scientific name: *Begonia* Rex-Cultorum hybrids. The species *Begonia rex* Putzeys is probably not in cultivation; consequently, "*Begonia* Rex-Cultorum hybrids" is used because numerous Asiatic species with valuable colorful foliage have been crossed with *Begonia rex* since 1850 (Bailey and Bailey, 1976; Huxley et al., 1992).

Family and related taxa: Begoniaceae Agardh. The Begoniaceae family has more than 1000 species, which are found in tropical and subtropical regions of both hemispheres (Huxley et al., 1992). Begonias are usually perennial and herbaceous to shrublike with stems that can be erect, trailing, or modified into rhizomes or tubers. The genus *Begonia* is valued for many purposes, including bedding plants, potted plants, and hanging baskets (Bailey and Bailey, 1976; Fotsch, 1933; Wilkins, 1985). Three groups of hybrids and related species are discussed in separate chapters: hiemalis begonia, tuberous begonia, and wax begonia.

Origin: Native to India and South China (White, 1923).

Uses and current status: The rex begonias are useful as specimens or as focal points because of their unusual leaf colors and patterns (Fig. II-1 Begonia, Rex). Large specimens are spectacular when mass planted in raised or ground beds. Small plants are used in planters (Henley et al., 1991). They may be grown outdoors in areas of shade or under protection (White, 1923).

Hybrid rex begonias have short stems and fleshy rhizomes. Leaf size and leaf character (spiral or nonspiral) are the basis of group designations. Their leaves are large, 8 to 12 in. (20 to 30 cm) long and 6 to 8 in. (15 to 20 cm) wide, with wrinkled surfaces and frequently with wavy margins. Leaf colors are metallic green, silver gray, green, purple, or reddish brown in various patterns—spotted or blotches. The monoecious flowers are typically inconspicuous (Bailey, 1933; Bailey and Bailey, 1976).

CULTIVARS

More than 500 named cultivars and hundreds of unnamed hybrids are grown for their foliage characteristics.

PROPAGATION

Propagation is accomplished through leaf cuttings, rhizome division, stem cuttings, or seed. Commercially, small plants are best purchased from a specialist. With leaf propagation, which is the most common method of propagation, mature leaves are cut into sections (chips) with a well-developed vein. The chips are placed in the rooting medium at a 45-degree angle. Whole leaves can also be used. Propagation can be in sand or in a peat-lite medium with 75 to 78°F (21 to 24°C) bottom heat (Henley et al., 1991; Thompson and Thompson, 1981; White, 1923). A clump of plantlets develops from each leaf-piece cutting; these are separated and used as transplants (von Hentig and Przyrembel, 1973). Cuttings from rhizomes are possible. Rhizomes can also be divided and rooted. Stem cuttings can be used to propagate cultivars that are not rhizomatous but have upright stems (Thompson and Thompson, 1981). Tissue culture is possible, but typically not used commercially because leaf propagation is easier and more economical. Because most cultivars are hybrids, seed is not true to type and typically used mainly in breeding programs (Thompson and Thompson, 1981). However, a few seed-propagated cultivars are available.

FLOWERING CONTROL AND DORMANCY

This plant is grown exclusively for foliage. However, plants flower in the winter and spring in North America (Post, 1949). Under SD and low temperatures, plants may go dormant.

TEMPERATURE

An average daily temperature of 73°F (23°C) is recommended with slightly lower temperatures of 62°F (17°C) at night and slightly higher, 85°F (29°C), during the day (Henley et al., 1991; Thompson and Thompson, 1981).

LIGHT

Proper light intensity is critical for the most vivid coloration of leaves. Generally, 2000 to 2500 fc (400 to 500 μmol $\cdot$ m^{-2} $\cdot$ s^{-1}) is adequate (Henley et al., 1991). No direct midday sun is desired; plants growing in excessively high light are more compact and color patterns and intensities are reduced. Fluorescent lights, high in red light, are best for the production of the prized velvet textured cultivars. Commercially, plants can even be grown on a shelf under the greenhouse bench where light intensity is low (Thompson and Thompson, 1981).

WATER

Although rex begonias require that the roots be kept continually moist, they do not tolerate overwatering (Thompson and Thompson, 1981). To inhibit leaf spotting and disease, avoid getting any water on the leaves (Henley et al., 1991; White, 1923). Drip irrigation or subirrigation is recommended for controlling foliar disease.

Humidity is the most important factor in growing quality rex begonias. An average of 50% is recommended across all cultivars. More specifically, cultivars with heavy leaf textures require less (40 to 50%) and velvet-like textures require more humidity (50 to 60%). Leaf margins become dry or brown with low humidity levels, whereas excess humidity can cause rotting of leaves and rhizomes (Thompson and Thompson, 1981).

CARBON DIOXIDE

No data available.

NUTRITION

Nutritional requirements are minimal and feeding 100 ppm N every 2 weeks is advised; N:P:K ratios of 3:1:2 or 2:1:2 are suggested (Thompson and Thompson, 1981). Avoid high soluble levels (Henley et al., 1991).

MEDIA

The medium should be light and porous. Various media have been suggested: a peat-lite medium (Henley et al., 1991); a 1 loam:1 leaf mold in the early stages of growth; and a 3 loam:1 well-rotted manure in later stages of growth (White, 1923). Any medium should be at least 50% organic (Post, 1949).

Most rhizomatous cultivars are grown in short azalea-type containers. The upright growing types are best grown in tall, standard-type containers. For older specimens, moss-lined wire baskets can be used (Thompson and Thompson, 1981).

HEIGHT CONTROL

No control required.

SPACING

Plants must be given proper spacing at all stages of development and production, not only for quality plants, but also for disease prevention (Henley et al., 1991).

The range of pot sizes used is from 3 to 10 in. (8 to 25 cm). For the mass market outlets, the greatest number of plants are produced in the 4-, 5-, or 6-in. (10-, 13-, or 15-cm) pot sizes. Specimen plants are grown in 8- or 10-in. (20- or 25-cm) containers (Henley et al., 1991). The number of transplants per pot is one per 4- or 5-in. (10- or 13-cm) pot, two per 6-in. (15-cm) pot, and three per 8- or 10-in. (20- or 25-cm) pot (Henley et al., 1991).

PINCHING AND DISBUDDING

None required.

SUPPORT

Only those cultivars with upright growth may require staking (Thompson and Thompson, 1981).

SCHEDULE AND TIMING

Production schedules are based on cultivar, initial size of the transplant, number of plantlets used, pot size to be produced, and numerous other environmental and cultural conditions (Henley et al., 1991). Rooted plugs are typically purchased from specialty propagators. When six cultivars were compared, crop times varied from 60 to 85 days to market when plugs were used (Poole and Henley, 1989).

INSECTS

Aphids, fungus gnats, mealy bugs, mites, shore flies, thrips, and whiteflies can be found on rex begonias. Prevention and integrated pest control management are essential, rather than depending on chemicals alone (Henley et al., 1991).

DISEASES

Bacterial leaf spot (*Xanthomonas campestris* pv. *begoniae*), botrytis blight (*Botrytis cinerea*), pythium root and stem rot (*Pythium*), fusarium stem rot (*Fusarium*), root and stem rot (*Rhizoctonia solani*), and myrothecium leaf spot (*Myrothecium roridum*) are some of the diseases encountered (Daughtrey and Chase, 1992; Henley et al., 1991; Horst, 1990). Also recorded are root and stem rot (*Phytophthora*), cottony rot (*Sclerotinia sclerotiorum*), black root rot (*Thielaviopsis basicola*), armillaria root rot (*Armillaria mellea*), powdery mildew (*Erysiphe* or *Oidium*), leafspot (*Phyllosticta*), bacterial blight (*Erwinia chrysanthemi*), soft rot (*Erwinia carotovora*), and various viruses (Dreistadt, 2001).

PHYSIOLOGICAL DISORDERS

Dormancy is cultivar dependent and can occur during winter SD. Chilling damage can occur if temperatures are low, 35°F (2°C), but above freezing. Sudden temperature shifts (cold or hot) should also be avoided because dormancy may be induced or leaf injury may occur (Thompson and Thompson, 1981).

POSTHARVEST

Because leaves are brittle and stems are frequently reflexed in baskets, sleeving and boxing and shipping can be difficult. Specimen plants are mainly for local markets. In the indoor plantscape environment, plants do best when light is 150 to 500 fc (30 to 100 μmol $\cdot$ m^{-2} $\cdot$ s^{-1}) and humidity is greater than 30% (Henley et al., 1991). Plants should be shipped at 40°F (5°C).

KEY POINTS

- Rex begonias are grown for their unusual foliage.
- Commercially, leaf pieces or "chips" are used for propagation; seed and tissue culture is also possible.
- Under SD and low temperatures, plants may go dormant.

- Proper light intensity is critical; 2000 to 2500 fc (400 to 500 μmol $\cdot$ m^{-2} $\cdot$ s^{-1}) is optimum.
- Humidity is the most important factor in production; an average of 50% is required.

BIBLIOGRAPHY

Bailey, L.H. 1933. *Begonia*, pp. 469–485 in *The Standard Cyclopedia of Horticulture*. Macmillan, New York.

Bailey, L.H., and E.Z. Bailey. 1976. *Begonia*, pp. 142–154 in *Hortus Third, A Concise Dictionary of Plants Cultivated in the United States and Canada*. Macmillan, New York.

Daughtrey, M., and A.R. Chase. 1992. *Begonia*, pp. 14–15 in *Ball Field Guide to Diseases of Greenhouse Ornamentals*. Ball Publishing, Geneva, Illinois.

Dreistadt, S.H. 2001. *Integrated Pest Management for Floriculture and Nurseries*. University of California Division of Agriculture and Natural Resources Publication 3402.

Fotsch, K.A. 1933. *Die Begonien*. Eugen Ulmer, Stuttgart, Germany. (in German)

Henley, R.W., A.R. Chase, and L.S. Osborne. 1991. Begonia (Foliage types), in *Foliage Plant Research Note RH-91–18*. Central Florida Research and Education Center, Apopka, Florida.

Horst, R.K. 1990. Begonia, pp. 554–555 in *Westcott's Plant Disease Handbook*, 5th ed. Van Nostrand Reinhold, New York.

Huxley, A., M. Griffiths, and M. Levy. 1992. *Begonia*, pp. 318–329 in *The New Royal Horticultural Society Dictionary of Gardening*, vol. 1. Stockton Press, New York.

Poole, R.T., and R.W. Henley. 1989. Production of foliage begonias for interiorscape market. *Proceedings of the Florida State Horticultural Society* 102:280–282.

Post, K. 1949. *Begonia*, pp. 248–342 in *Florist Crop Production and Marketing*. Orange Judd Publishing. New York.

Thompson, M.L., and E.J. Thompson. 1981. Rex cultivars, pp. 172–177 in *Begonias: Complete Review and Guide*. Times Books, New York.

von Hentig, W.-U., and G. Przyrembel. 1973. Einfluss der Ernährung von Rex-Begonien—Mutterpflanzen auf die Entwicklung von Jungflanzen aus Blattstucken. *Gartenwelt* 73(3):49–51. (in German)

White, E.A. 1923. *Begonia*, pp. 326–334 in *The Principles of Floriculture*. Macmillan, New York.

Wilkins, H.F. 1985. Begonia, pp. 479–484 in *Bedding Plants III*, 3rd ed., J.W. Mastalerz and E.J. Holcomb, editors. Pennsylvania Flower Growers Publishers, University Park, Pennsylvania.

Begonia, Tuberous

INTRODUCTION

Common name: tuberous begonia.

Scientific name: *Begonia* Tuberhybrida hybrids (Huxley et al., 1992). Numerous botanical species are designated as tuberous begonias, and they have been used to develop the hybrid cultivars (Huxley et al., 1992). Haegeman (1993) lists only *Begonia boliviensis* DC, *B.* *pearcei* Hook. f., and *B. veitchii* Hook.; whereas Bailey and Bailey (1976) specify an additional three: *B. clarkei* Hook., *B. davisii* hort. Veitch ex. Hook. f., and *B. rosiflora* (now classified as *B. veitchii*); and Weber and Dress (1968) list *B. boliviensis*, *B. baumannii*, *B. froebelii* A. DC, and *B. veitchii*. Because of this variability, it is advisable to use "tuberous begonia hybrids" to designate the large flowered summer blooming begonias.

Family and related taxa: Begoniaceae Agardh. The Begoniaceae family has more than 1000 species, which are found in tropical and subtropical regions of both hemispheres (Huxley et al., 1992). The genus *Begonia* is valued for many purposes, including bedding plants, potted plants, and hanging baskets (Bailey and Bailey, 1976; Fotsch, 1933; Wilkins, 1985). Three groups of hybrids and related species are discussed in separate chapters: hiemalis begonia, rex begonia, and wax begonia.

Origin: Tuberous begonia hybrids are derived from several species (see Scientific Name) from South America and are mainly Andean in origin.

Uses and current status: Plants are used as hanging baskets, specimen plants, or in beds for massive color displays (Anonymous, 1988).

Tuberous begonia hybrids have been described as stemless or with short erect, semierect, or

FIGURE II-1 BEGONIA, TUBEROUS Picotee-style *Begonia* Tuberhybrida flower.

FIGURE II-2 BEGONIA, TUBEROUS *Begonia* Tuberhybrida flower.

trailing stems. Leaves are alternate and change with age from being symmetrical to quite asymmetrical. Flower colors are vivid, in a wide range of colors including pink, rose, red, yellow, orange, and white (Figs. II-1 and II-2 Begonia, Tuberous). The inflorescence consists of one large (single or double) male flower up to 6 in. (15 cm) wide with two smaller female flowers 1 to 2 in. (2.5 to 5 cm) wide on either side (Bailey and Bailey, 1976; Haegeman, 1993).

CULTIVARS

Interspecific hybridization has resulted in the most spectacular and diverse flower types and colors found in the genus since the first native species were collected in 1864 (Thompson and Thompson, 1981). Bailey and Bailey (1976) and Huxley et al. (1992) divide the various tuberous hybrids into 13 groups, depending on their growth habit or form, flower shape, and flower color. The 13 groups do not include hybrid seed

types. Haegeman (1993) also lists 13 groups, but 4 of Haegeman's groups describe hybrid seed groups of recent origin that are primarily used as bedding plant annuals.

Growth of tuberous hybrid begonias is excellent in the cool areas along the west coast of North America and Europe (Post, 1949). Unfortunately, climate restricts both tuber production and specimen plant growth in the Midwest and southern areas of North America, although plants from the newer hybrid seed lines are more tolerant of warmer temperatures (Ewart, 1985).

PROPAGATION

Until 1975, dormant tubers were the primary source of stock for routine greenhouse forcing (Ewart, 1985), although some cultivars were propagated from cuttings (Djurhuus, 1984). Hybrid seed of tuberous begonias has been available since 1975. *In vitro* techniques of propagation from leaves have been reported (Peck and Cummings, 1984; Takayama, 1990).

TUBER (ASEXUAL)

Historically, outstanding seedlings of tuberous hybrids were selected in the field and the tubers harvested, stored, and forced. At best, only 10 rooted cuttings could be obtained for future tuber production from a large plant and six to eight divisions from a large tuber (Haegeman, 1993; Peck and Cummings, 1984). Propagation was slow and expensive. Some tubers could be 25 to 40 years old (Haegeman, 1993).

TUBER (SEXUAL)

For noncultivar-specific tuber production, seeds are sown in January and plants are grown until they naturally become dormant in fall when the days become short and water is withheld (Haegeman, 1993; Laurie et al., 1969). Short days (<12 hr) are required for tuber formation (Lewis, 1951). For production of large specimen hanging baskets, 2-year-old tubers are desired (White, 1923).

Tuber production is limited to specific sites in Europe or along the Pacific Coast in North America with optimal growing conditions. Because seedlings are difficult to handle and the production process is long term, tubers are purchased from European or California production sites. The Ghent, Belgium, area is the world leader in tuber production, followed by the Netherlands (Haegeman, 1993; Laurie et al., 1969). Haegeman (1993) and Langeslag

(1989) give specifics of the tuber production methods used in Belgium and the Netherlands, respectively. The primary site for tuber production in North America is in Santa Cruz County, California, United States.

SEED (SEXUAL)

Historically, seedlings were heterozygous and used only in the development of new cultivars that were increased through asexual means as previously described and distributed as dormant tubers. In the mid-1970s inbred lines became available (Ewart, 1985; Peck and Cummings, 1984). Hybrid seeds (1 million/oz; 35,000/g) are automatically sown onto the surface of a thoroughly moistened peat-lite medium that has been adjusted to a pH of 5.5 to 6.5. Seeds are not covered. Temperatures are held at 75 to 78°F (24 to 26°C) until germination (about 2 weeks), then grown at 64°F (18°C) night and 72°F (22°C) day temperatures (Ewart, 1985; Karlsson and Heins, 1992). Haegeman (1993) found that germination was slow at temperatures under 68°F (20°C), but only 5 to 7 days were required at 73 to 77°F (23 to 25°C). Humidity should be kept high (Haegeman, 1993). Many growers purchase quality plugs from specialty producers.

FLOWERING CONTROL AND DORMANCY

Species that contributed to the modern tuberous begonia hybrids go dormant in nature as a result of reduced rainfall and slight daylength shifts, but not due to temperature. However, with current hybrids under SD and decreasing temperatures, leaf and flower initiation and development cease, shoots senesce, and an abscission zone forms between the stem and tuber (Haegeman, 1993; Heide and Rünger, 1985; Maatsch and Rünger, 1955, 1956; Peters, 1974; Rünger, 1964). Fall-harvested tubers do not sprout again until February. A cold treatment is necessary to break dormancy. Tubers held at 34 to 41°F (1 to 5°C) for 60 to 90 days rapidly formed new shoots, whereas those held at 50 to 86°F (10 to 30°C) failed to sprout (Rünger, 1964). In Belgium, 39°F (4°C) is used to break dormancy (Haegeman, 1993). Storage in 2 to 3% oxygen for up to 20 weeks at 41°F (5°C) increased percent of tubers sprouted compared with those stored in ambient air, without affecting flowering (Prince and Cunningham, 1987).

Flowering is dependent on the continuous formation of new leaves, as flowers are initiated in the leaf axils. At least three nodes are required before floral buds become apparent (Lewis, 1951). Both leaves and flowers are initiated under a 12-hr or longer photoperiod; 14 to 16 hr is highly promotive. If photoperiods are less than 12 hr, leaf and flower initiation slows, finally ceases, and tuber formation is accelerated. After 20 to 30 SD, apical meristem activity ceases, adventitious buds at the stem base develop, and the tuber becomes dormant (Lewis, 1951; Oloomi and Payne, 1982). Most currently available seed-propagated hybrids are not as affected by SD; 4 weeks of 9-hr SD delayed flowering of 'Clips,' 'Musical,' and 'Nonstop' begonias by up to 19 days but did not induce dormancy (Karlsson and Werner, 1999).

TEMPERATURE

With current hybrids both vegetative and reproductive growth as well as tuber formation are temperature controlled. Higher temperatures encourage shoot growth; lower temperatures encourage tuberization and ultimately dormancy (Djurhuus, 1985; Maatsch and Rünger, 1956; Peters, 1974).

At the end of the cold treatment used to break dormancy, tubers are covered in moist peat (or planted in the final pot) and presprouted at 70 to 80°F (21° to 27°C). Once sprouted, the temperature is reduced to 55 to 60°F (13 to 16°C) (Laurie et al., 1969; Post, 1949; White, 1923).

With seed, seedlings are transplanted and grown at 72/65°F (22/18°C) day/night temperatures after germination (Fonteno and Larson, 1982; Prince and Cunningham, 1987). Once flower buds are initiated, quality (flower size and color intensity) is increased under 60/57°F (16/14°C) day/night temperatures (Ewart, 1985).

LIGHT

Light is required for good germination, rapid growth, and flowering (Djurhuus, 1985; Karlsson and Werner, 1999). A 12-hr photoperiod is a minimum for vegetative growth and flowering. For spring bedding plant sales, 800 fc (160 μmol · m^{-2} · s^{-1}) is recommended from November/December to March (Haegeman, 1993). Supplemental lighting (fluorescent tubes or HID lamps) is frequently used on a 24-hr cycle at 500 fc (100 μmol · m^{-2} · s^{-1}) during germination and early growth. Depending on temperature and light, 6 to 10 weeks are required to produce a seedling plug that can be transplanted (Ewart, 1985; Karlsson and Heins, 1992). A 12-hr photoperiod is also a minimum for growth of forced tubers (Haegeman, 1993).

Light extensions at sundown or night interruptions must be used to ensure a total photoperiod of 14 to 16 hr if the natural day length is shorter. Light intensity of 10 fc ($2\ \mu mol \cdot m^{-2} \cdot s^{-1}$) can be used as photoperiodic LD lighting. Cyclic lighting is feasible (6 min on, 24 min off) (Aimone, 1983; Fonteno and Larson, 1982; Oloomi and Payne, 1982).

For rapid tuber production from seed-generated plants, sixty 9-hr SD photoperiods at 72°F (22°C) can be used (Fonteno and Larson, 1982). High light intensity causes injury because tuberous begonia hybrids are not high light tolerant. Light intensity should not exceed 2500 to 3000 fc (500 to 600 $\mu mol \cdot m^{-2} \cdot s^{-1}$) and shade is required for both light and temperature control.

WATER

White (1923) warned ". . . that not too much water be given to plants, for it causes stems to decay at their base." Tuberous hybrid begonias have very fine root systems and can also be easily damaged from high soluble salt and excess drying, as well as excess moisture (Karlsson and Heins, 1992).

CARBON DIOXIDE

Carbon dioxide at 1100 ppm increased cutting production from plants propagated from cuttings in Norway (Djurhuus, 1984). Furthermore, supplemental lighting was more effective when supplemental CO_2 was used. Though there are no reports that CO_2 increases quality or decreases production time with seed propagation hybrids, enrichment is likely to be beneficial.

NUTRITION

A complete fertilizer should be used every 3 to 4 weeks, according to Laurie et al. (1969). Ewart (1985) gave similar recommendations except that nutrient applications were made every 10 days. The N level at each fertilization should not be more than 150 ppm (Karlsson and Heins, 1992). Tuberous hybrid begonias do not require high nutritional levels. Ammonium nitrogen should be avoided or used with care (Aimone, 1983).

MEDIA

It is interesting to review the historic evolution of medium recommendation. In 1923, White recommended ". . . considerable well-rotted manure should be added to a sandy loam. . . ." Presently, a commercial peat-lite media offers good aeration and drainage, promoting excellent root development (Ewart, 1985).

HEIGHT CONTROL

Growth regulators are not usually required. However, Cycocel (chlormequat) at 500 ppm is reported to have given the best height control of seed-propagated hybrids when compared with either 0 or 1000 ppm (Anonymous, 1982). Cycocel may be needed at the end of production to hold plants if sales are slow. Plugs can also be sprayed with 46 ppm Cycocel during propagation stages 1 and 2 and with 92 ppm during stage 3 (Sawaya, 2001). Cycocel sprays (250 ppm) on seedlings during stage 4, while still in the plugs, and a spray (250 ppm) again shortly after transplanting have been reported to result in high-quality 4-in. (10-cm) plants (Anonymous, 1990). Plants have little response to DIF temperature manipulation (Warner and Erwin, 2001).

SPACING

The 4-in. (10-cm) pots can be started at 4 × 5 in. (10 × 13 cm); final spacing should be 8 × 8 in. (20 × 20 cm). The final spacing of 10-in. (25-cm) hanging baskets is 16 × 16 in. (40 × 40 cm). Only one seedling is used per 4-in. (10-cm) pot; three are used for 10-in. (25-cm) pots.

PINCHING AND DISBUDDING

None required for 4-in. (10-cm) pots. Top quality 10-in. (25-cm) pots can be pinched 2 to 3 weeks after transplanting, leaving four nodes with leaves on the plant (Ewart, 1985).

SUPPORT

Normally no support is required. However, the stems can be brittle and care should be taken during handling to avoid breakage.

SCHEDULE AND TIMING

For plants to be produced from tubers, non-dormant stock plants are first sprouted for 2 weeks, then potted and forced from February to May, requiring 14 to 16 weeks (Laurie et al., 1969; Post, 1949). For 4-in. (10-cm) plants to be produced from hybrid seeds, seed germination requires 2 weeks; an additional 7 to 9 weeks are needed until seedlings are ready to be transplanted; then another 8 to 10 weeks until the product can be sold. Larger hanging basket specimens require an additional 4 weeks (Ewart, 1985; Karlsson and Heins, 1992) (Tables II-1 and II-2 Begonia, Tuberous).

TABLE II-1 BEGONIA, TUBEROUS

Sample schedule for 10-in. (25-cm) hanging baskets of *Begonia* Tuberhybrida hybrids from tuberous stock.

Cultural Step	Production Time (weeks)	Temperature °F (°C)	Photoperiod
Sprouting tuber in moist peat[a]			
	2	70–80 (21–27)	LD
Pot tuber and force			
	14–16	55–60 (13–16)	LD
Flower			
Total	16–18		

[a] Tubers have previously been given a dormancy breaking cold treatment for 60 to 90 days at 35 to 41°F (2 to 5°C).

TABLE II-2 BEGONIA, TUBEROUS

Sample schedule for 4-in. (10-cm) *Begonia* Tuberhybrida hybrids from seed.

Cultural Step	Production Time (weeks)	Temperature °F (°C)	Photoperiod
Germination			
	2	75–78 (24–26)	24 hr
Seeding growth			
	7–9	Day: 70 (21)	LD
Transplant to hardening			
	8–10	Day: 72 (22) Night: 57–61 (14–16)	LD
Flower			
Total	17–21		

INSECTS

Cyclamen mites, spider mites, thrips, whiteflies, mealy bugs, and aphids are all problems. Thrips must be controlled because they transmit tomato spotted wilt virus (Daughtrey and Chase, 1992). All pests can be controlled by sanitation, preventive measures, and, when needed, the appropriate chemicals.

DISEASES

The major disease, powdery mildew (*Erysiphe chichoracearum* or *Oidium*), can be controlled by regulating relative humidity, maintaining good air circulation, and keeping foliage dry (Dreistadt, 2001; Horst, 1990). Similarly, *Botrytis* blight (*Botrytis cinerea*) can be controlled with good sanitation. Bacterial leaf spot (*Xanthomonas campestris* pv. *begoniae*) can be avoided by the use of disease-free plants, low humidity, moderate temperatures, and sanitation. Root and stem rots (*Fusarium, Phytophthora, Pythium, Rhizoctonia solani, Sclerotinia sclerotiorum,* and *Thielaviopsis basicola*) are best prevented by appropriate watering practices and constant regulation of the soluble salts. Tomato spotted wilt virus and impatiens necrotic spot virus can also be serious problems (Daughtrey and Chase, 1992). Armillaria root rot (*Armillaria mellea*), leaf spot (*Phyllosticta*), bacterial blight (*Erwinia chrysanthemi*), soft rot (*Erwinia carotovora*), and various viruses have also been recorded (Dreistadt, 2001).

PHYSIOLOGICAL DISORDERS

Poor or abnormal growth of shoots (from tubers or plants from seed) can result from SD photoperiods, because SD induce tuber formation rather than shoot growth. Once tuber formation begins, shoot growth ceases and cannot be renewed (See Flowering Control and Dormancy section).

POSTHARVEST

Begonia flowers from the large flowering hybrid types have been used as corsage flowers (Post, 1949). For potted plants silver thiosulfate (STS) sprays at 0.3 mM prior to shipping resulted in flowers that kept 15 to 20 days (Aimone, 1983). Fumigation with 20 ppb 1-methylcyclopropene (1-MCP) for 6 hr also prevented the negative effects of ethylene (Serek et al., 1994). Flower and flower bud abscission were also reduced. Potted flowering plants should be shipped at 41°F (5°C) and plugs at 43 to 47°F (6 to 8°C) (L. Høyer, personal communication).

Haegeman (1993) discusses harvesting and postharvest handling of tubers. Tuber dormancy and dormancy breaking treatments are discussed in the Propagation section earlier in this chapter.

KEY POINTS

- Tuberous begonias have spectacular flowers and are used as potted flowering plants, hanging basket plants, and bedding plants.
- Commercially tuberous begonias are propagated by cuttings, tubers, or F_1 seed.
- Dormant tubers are given a cold treatment at 34 to 41°F (1 to 5°C), followed by a warm treatment at 70 to 80°F (21 to 27°C) for rapid emergence and a forcing temperature of 55 to 60°F (13 to 16°C).

- Dormancy occurs if photoperiods are less than 12 hr for extended durations, although currently available seed-propagated hybrids are less responsive to SD.
- Plants are not tolerant of warm temperatures and best produced in cool climates.
- Root systems are easily damaged by high soluble salt levels and over- or underwatering.
- Powdery mildew is the major disease.

BIBLIOGRAPHY

Aimone, T. 1983. Non-stop production. *GrowerTalks* 46(11):38, 40, 42.

Anonymous, 1982. Response of tuberous begonias to chemical growth regulator. *Jed's Jottings* April. Jednak Floral Company, Columbus, Ohio.

Anonymous, 1988. Non-stop begonias—vibrant and versatile. *Bedding Plant Incorporated News* 19(4):11.

Anonymous, 1990. Grower research sheds practical light on growth regulators on plugs. *Professional Plant Growers Association News* 21(5):8–9.

Bailey, L.H., and E.Z. Bailey. 1976. *Begonia*, pp. 142–154 in *Hortus Third, A Concise Dictionary of Plants Cultivated in the United States and Canada*. Macmillian, New York.

Daughtrey, M., and A.R. Chase, 1992. Begonia, pp. 17–18 in *Ball Field Guide to Diseases of Greenhouse Ornamentals*. Ball Publishing, Geneva, Illinois.

Djurhuus, R. 1984. The effect of CO_2, daylength and light on the production and subsequent growth of *Begonia ×tuberhybrida* cuttings. *Acta Horticulturae* 162:65–74.

Djurhuus, R. 1985. The effect of photoperiod and temperature on growth and development of *Begonia ×tuberhybrida* 'Karelsk Jomfru.' *Scientia Horticulturae* 27:123–131.

Dreistadt, S.H. 2001. *Integrated Pest Management for Floriculture and Nurseries*. University of California Division of Agriculture and Natural Resources Publication 3402.

Ewart, L.C. 1985. Tuberous rooted begonias, pp. 420–422 in *Bedding Plants III*, 3rd ed. J.W. Mastalerz and E.J. Holcomb, editors. Pennsylvania Flower Growers, University Park, Pennsylvania.

Fonteno, W.C., and R.A. Larson. 1982. Photoperiod and temperature effects on Non Stop tuberous begonias. *HortScience* 17:899–901.

Fotsch, K.A. 1933. *Die Begonien*. Eugen Ulmer, Stuttgart, Germany. (in German)

Haegeman, J. 1993. Begonia-tuberous hybrids, pp. 227–247 in *The Physiology of Flower Bulbs*, A. De Hertogh and M. Le Nard, editors. Elsevier, Amsterdam.

Heide, O.M., and W. Rünger. 1985. *Begonia*, pp. 4–23 in *Handbook of Flowering*, vol. II, A.H. Halevy, editor. CRC Press, Boca Raton, Florida.

Horst, R.K. 1990. Begonia, pp. 554–555 in *Westcott's Plant Disease Handbook*, 5th ed. Van Nostrand Reinhold, New York.

Huxley, A., M. Griffiths, and M. Levy. 1992. *Begonia*, pp. 318–329 in *The New Royal Horticultural Society Dictionary of Gardening*, vol. 1. Stockton Press, New York.

Karlsson, M.G., and R.D. Heins. 1992. *Begonias*, pp. 409–427 in *Introduction to Floriculture*, R.A. Larson, editor. Academic Press, San Diego, California.

Karlsson, M.G., and J.W. Werner. 1999. Photoperiodic control of flowering in seed-propagated *Begonia tuber ×hybrida* Voss. *HortScience* 34:62–63.

Langeslag, J.J.J. 1989. *Teelt en Gebruiksmoglijkheben van bijgoedgewassen*. Tweede uitgave Ministerie Landouw Visserij en Consultschap Algemene Dienst Bloebolenteedt, Lisse, The Netherlands. (in Dutch, English summary)

Laurie, A., D.C. Kiplinger, and K.S. Nelson. 1969. *Begonia*, p. 468 in *Commercial Flower Forcing*. McGraw-Hill Book, New York.

Lewis, C.A. 1951. Some effects of day length on tuberization, flowering and vegetative growth of tuberous-rooted begonias. *Proceedings American Society Horticultural Science* 57:376–370.

Maatsch, R., and W. Rünger, 1955. Über das ober-erdische Wachstum und die Knollenbildung von Knollenbegonien nach Kurz Fristiger Kurztagbehandlung. *Gartenbauwissenschaft* 19:457–464. (in German)

Maatsch, R., and W. Rünger, 1956. Über den Einfluss der Temperatur auf die photoperiod Reaktion von Knollenbegonien. *Gartenbauwissenschaft* 20: 278–484. (in German)

Oloomi, H., and R.N. Payne. 1982. Effects of photoperiod and pinching on development of *Begonia ×tuberhybrida*. *HortScience* 17:337–338.

Peck, D.E., and B.G. Cummings. 1984. *In vitro* propagation of *Begonia ×tuberhybrida* from leaf sections. *HortScience* 19:395–397.

Peters, J. 1974. Einfluss der Temperatur auf das oberirdische Wachstum und die Knollenbildung bie *Begonia ×tuberhybrida* (Voss). *Gartenbauwissenschaft* 39:301–308. (in German)

Post, K. 1949. *Begonia*, pp. 345–348 in *Florist Crop Production and Marketing*. Orange Judd Publishing, New York.

Prince, T.A., and M.S. Cunningham. 1987. Response of tubers of *Begonia ×tuberhybrida* to cold temperatures, ethylene and low-oxygen storage. *HortScience* 22:252–254.

Rünger, W. 1964. *Licht und Temperatur in Zierpflanzenbau.* Paul Parey, Berlin and Hamburg. (in German)

Sawaya, M. 2001. Plugs, pp. 50–53 in *Tips on Regulating Growth of Floriculture Crops*, M.L. Gaston, L.A. Kunkle, P.S. Konjoian, and M.F. Wilt, editors. Ohio Florists' Association Services, Columbus, Ohio.

Serek, M, E.C. Sisler, and M.S. Reid. 1994. Novel gaseous ethylene binding inhibitor prevents ethylene effects in potted flowering plants. *Journal of the American Society for Horticultural Science* 119:1230–1233.

Takayama, S. 1990. *Begonia*, pp. 253–283 in *Handbook of Plant Cell Culture*, P.V. Ammirate, D.A. Evans, W.R. Sharp, and Y.P.S. Bajaj, editors. McGraw-Hill, New York.

Thompson, M.L., and E.J. Thompson. 1981. *Begonias. The Complete Reference Guide*. Time Books, New York.

Warner, R.M., and J.E. Erwin. 2001. Temperature, pp. 10–17 in *Tips on Regulating Growth of Floriculture Crops*, M.L. Gaston, L.A. Kunkle, P.S. Konjoian, and M.F. Wilt, editors. Ohio Florists' Association Services, Columbus, Ohio.

Weber, C., and W.J. Dress. 1968. Notes on the nomenclature of some cultivated begonias (Begoniaceae). *Baileya* 16:42–72, 113–136.

White, E.G. 1923. *The Principles of Floriculture*. Red-Book, New York.

Wilkins, H.F. 1985. Begonia, pp. 479–484 in *Bedding Plants III*, 3rd ed., J.W. Mastalerz and E.J. Holcomb, editors. Pennsylvania Flower Growers Publishers, University Park, Pennsylvania.

Begonia, Wax

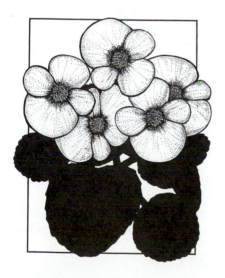

INTRODUCTION

Common names: wax begonia, bedding begonia, fibrous-rooted begonia, ice begonia.

Scientific name: *Begonia* Semperflorens-Cultorum hybrids (Huxley et al., 1992). This group originated from several species including *B. cucullata* var. *hookeri* (A.DC.) L.B. Smi. and Schubert., *B. roezlii* Reg., *B. fuchsioides* Hook., *B. gracilis* HBK., *B. minor* Jacq., and *B. schmidtiana* Reg.

Family and related taxa: Begoniaceae Agardh. The Begoniaceae family has more than 1000 species, which are found in tropical and subtropical regions of both hemispheres (Huxley et al., 1992). The genus *Begonia* is valued for many purposes, including bedding plants, potted plants, and hanging baskets (Bailey and Bailey, 1976; Fotsch, 1933). Three groups of hybrids and related species are discussed in separate chapters: hiemalis begonia, rex begonia, and tuberous begonia.

Origin: Wax begonia seedlings were introduced into Europe at the Berlin Botanical Garden from Brazil by accident as a "weed" in the soil (Ewart, 1985; Thompson and Thompson, 1981).

Uses and current status: Wax begonia is commonly used as a bedding plant, adaptable for shade and sunny areas (Bailey and Bailey, 1976) (Fig. II-1 Begonia, Wax). It is one of the world's most popular bedding plants. The wax begonia is the most widely grown of all begonia species.

The wax begonia has fibrous roots; the stout stems are succulent and well branched; the

FIGURE II-I BEGONIA, WAX *Begonia* 'Ambassador White' flat.

glossy ovate leaves range from green to red, bronze-red, mahogany-red, or even green and white variegated. The monoecious flowers are single or double with colors including red, pink, pale orange, and white. The seed-propagated dragon wing begonias are produced in a manner similar to that of wax begonias but are more vigorous and include some characteristics of angel wing begonias such as a more elongated leaf and a more unidirectional growth habit.

CULTIVARS

Hundreds of seeded hybrids are available from the numerous multinational seed companies.

PROPAGATION

Currently, only a few cultivars with unusual green and white variegated foliage or double flowers are asexually propagated by cuttings. The vast majority of cultivars are sexually propagated. There are 2.5 million seed/oz (90,000/g). The seed is tiny and can be purchased pelleted to allow the use of automated seeding techniques.

Seeds are placed on the surface of a moist medium and the seed flat is kept under high humidity or fog. Some producers place seed flats under clear plastic or in plastic bags. Temperatures should not become excessive on sunny days. Large walk-in lighted growth chambers are commonly used (Ewart, 1985). Light is a requirement for germination and either natural or fluorescent light is effective (Shoemaker and Carlson, 1992). Cool-white fluorescent lamps can be used at a duration of 14 to 24 hr until the first true leaves have developed up to 1.5 in. (1.3 cm) long (Ewart, 1985).

Medium temperature is critical and should be 78 to 80°F (26 to 27°C), because germination rates will decrease with lower temperatures. Air temperature should not exceed 80°F (27°C) (Ewart, 1985; Tayama, 1989). Germination is rapid under light, proper moisture, humidity, and temperatures. After 2 weeks, lower the temperature to 65°F (18°C) nights. For hardening, 60°F (16°C) is acceptable (Ewart, 1985; Tayama, 1989). Heating the media to 80°F (27°C) and supplementing the light increased seedling growth and were most effective when provided for at least 10 days commencing either 5 or 10 days after germination (Graper and Healy, 1990).

For plug production the following conditions are used (Ball, 1991):

- *Stage 1:* Seed uncovered, 78 to 80°F (26 to 27°C), 7 days
- *Stage 2:* 72 to 78°F (22 to 26°C), 21 days, 50 to 100 ppm N one to two times/week
- *Stage 3:* 70 to 75°F (21 to 24°C), 21 days, 150 ppm N two times/week
- *Stage 4:* 62 to 68°F (17 to 20°C), 14 days, fertilize as needed.

Plugs should be ready for marketing or transplanting in 8 to 9 weeks (see Chapter 1, Propagation, for descriptions of stages).

FLOWER CONTROL AND DORMANCY

Wax begonias are day neutral and need no specific photoperiod or temperature. High light is required for rapid flowering. Kessler et al. (1991) noted that flowering was most rapid after 2 weeks of supplemental lighting at 830 fc (125 μmol · m^{-2} · s^{-1}); longer durations or greater intensities did not hasten flowering. Further, Hayashi et al. (1990) stated that the plant simultaneously forms vegetative and flowering structures. Branching is mainly controlled by the available photosynthates, whereas flowering is controlled by temperature.

TEMPERATURE

For optimum growth of the young transplanted seedlings, a 72/65°F (22/18°C) day/night temperature is recommended for the first 2 weeks, after which time, the temperature can be lowered to 60°F (16°C) nights and 67°F (19°C) days (Ewart, 1985).

LIGHT

High light is required for rapid flowering and supplemental light is often beneficial. Kessler et al. (1991) found that when seedlings with one true leaf were exposed to supplemental metal-halide irradiation at 0, 330, 830, or 1300 fc (0, 50, 125, or 200 $\mu mol \cdot m^{-2} \cdot s^{-1}$) for 0, 2, 4, 6, or 8 weeks, plants reached the transplanting stage within 4 weeks at 830 fc (125 $\mu mol \cdot m^{-2} \cdot s^{-1}$) compared with 8 to 6 weeks at 0 or 330 fc (50 $\mu mol \cdot m^{-2} \cdot s^{-1}$). Plants flowered most quickly with fewest nodes after only 2 weeks at 830 fc (125 $\mu mol \cdot m^{-2} \cdot s^{-1}$). Kessler et al. (1991) concluded that supplemental light intensities greater than 830 fc (125 $\mu mol \cdot m^{-2} \cdot s^{-1}$) or durations greater than 2 weeks were not beneficial. Graper and Healy (1990) also noted that 10 days of supplemental lighting was more effective than only 5 days and that increasing supplemental irradiation from 100 to 1800 fc (13 to 233 $\mu mol \cdot m^{-2} \cdot s^{-1}$) increased plant growth. Hershey and Merritt (1987) found little difference in growth between a 9-hr photoperiod and a 9-hr photoperiod plus 4-hr incandescent light extension, except in stem and petiole lengths, which were greatest under the 13-hr treatment.

WATER

High humidity or fog during germination is required for rapid and uniform germination. Care must be taken not to wash seeds or seedlings out of the medium. Young plants should not be water stressed (Ewart, 1985).

CARBON DIOXIDE

Increasing carbon dioxide to 1000 to 1500 ppm increased growth and decreased crop time (Kessler and Armitage, 1993).

NUTRITION

Begonia seedlings initially form shallow roots and care should be taken to ensure that nitrate levels are adequate because nitrates can easily leach away from the root zone (Ewart, 1985). A nutrient regime of 100 to 400 ppm N can be used; 200 ppm N is recommended for 3 weeks after germination. However, at 400 ppm N the number of flowers was reduced (Chase and Poole, 1987b). Using subirrigation James and van Iersel (2001) found the optimum fertilizer concentration to be approximately 225 ppm N from a commercial 20–10–20 fertilizer.

TABLE II-I BEGONIA, WAX

Tissue analysis for *Begonia* Semperflorens-Cultorum hybrids during autumn production in Florida (Armitage, 1994; Chase and Poole, 1987a).

Element	Range for Quality Plants
Nitrogen	2.2–5.6%
Phosphorus	0.3–0.6%
Potassium	3.4–4.2%
Calcium	0.7–4.2%
Magnesium	0.4–1.0%
Iron	100–260 ppm
Manganese	90–355 ppm
Zinc	50–65 ppm
Copper	10–15 ppm
Boron	30–40 ppm
Sodium	0.12–0.18%

Chase and Poole (1987a, b) found that high soluble salts reduced plant quality and that 2.0 to 3.0 $dS \cdot m^{-1}$, using the pour-through method, was appropriate during cool seasonal periods, but was too high in summer. However, James and van Iersel (2001) thought begonias were not sensitive to media EC and grew well with a media EC ranging from 1.7 to 6.1 $dS \cdot m^{-1}$ using the pour-through method. Appropriate tissue analysis levels have been determined (Table II-1 Begonia, Wax). Nelson and Huang (1998) have photographically documented several nutrient deficiency symptoms.

MEDIA

Peat, perlite, and vermiculite (1:1:1) by volume have been used. Many fine-textured commercial mixes are acceptable for seed germination (Ewart, 1985).

HEIGHT CONTROL

Height control is often not required but may be necessary if marketing is delayed. Ewart (1980) reported that 500 ppm Cycocel (chlormequat) could be used on white flowered cultivars and 1000 ppm on other colors. Cycocel should be sprayed at or after the fourth leaf has developed. Ewart (1985) stated that cultivars that are more sun tolerant grow taller and Cycocel improves the appearance of the plants. A-Rest (ancymidol) sprays can be used at 6 to 12 ppm after transplanting plugs and at 10 to 12 ppm for finished plants (Bell, 2001). Tank mixes of 1000 to 1250 ppm Cycocel and 800 to 1250 ppm

B-Nine (daminozide) can also be used (Kuehny et al., 2001).

Bonzi (paclobutrazol) at 5 ppb and A-Rest at 3 ppb are effective when applied through subirrigation (Million et al., 1999). This work also highlights the potential effects of contamination from plant growth regulators on subirrigation benches. Plugs can also be sprayed with 115 ppm Cycocel during propagation stages 1 and 2 and with 230 ppm during stage 3 (Sawaya, 2001). Farthing and Ellis (1990) found that 2 to 4 ppm Bonzi sprays controlled height of begonia plugs and did not delay flowering or root growth when transplanted into the final container. Wax begonias have only a modest response to DIF temperature regimes used for height control (Erwin and Heins, 1993).

SPACING

Seeds are sown in various types of plug trays and transplanted into bedding plant flats spaced flat to flat.

PINCHING AND DISBUDDING

None required. Plants can be cut back and easily regrown if seedlings are not transplanted or plants in packs are not sold on schedule (Ewart, 1985).

SUPPORT

None required.

SCHEDULE AND TIMING

Approximately 6 to 7 weeks are required from sowing to transplanting. Seedlings are ready to transplant when four true leaves have developed (Ewart, 1985). Plugs require 8 to 9 weeks (Ball, 1991). The final crop typically requires an additional 6 to 8 weeks for packs and 8 to 11 weeks for 4-in. (10-cm) pots. Production in warm climates will usually finish 1 week faster than the indicated schedules (Nau, 1999).

INSECTS

Mealy bugs, aphids, fungus gnats, and shoreflies are the most frequent insect pests (Ewart, 1985).

DISEASES

Pythium, *Phytophthera*, and *Rhizoctonia solani* can cause seedlings to rot at the medium surface. Botrytis blight (*Botrytis cinerea*) and powdery mildew (*Oidium*) are common; adequate air movement is a major factor in the control of these problems. Bacterial leaf spot (*Xanthomonas campestris* pv. *begoniae*), fusarium stem rot (*Fusarium*), and tomato spotted wilt virus can also be encountered (Daughtrey and Chase, 1992; Horst, 1990). Cottony rot (*Sclerotinia sclerotiorum*), black root rot (*Thielaviopsis basicola*), armillaria root rot (*Armillaria mellea*), powdery mildew (*Erysiphe*), leafspot (*Phyllosticta*), bacterial blight (*Erwinia chrysanthemi*), soft rot (*Erwinia carotovora*), and various viruses have also been recorded (Dreistadt, 2001).

PHYSIOLOGICAL DISORDERS

None reported.

POSTHARVEST

Seedling plugs can be stored up to 6 weeks at 41 to 45°F (5 to 7°C) (Heins et al., 1994). Plants can be acclimated at 58 to 62°F (14 to 17°C) and transported cool. After 5 or 7 days in darkness at 75°F (24°C), leaves were chlorotic and deteriorating; however, little internode elongation occurred (Armitage, 1989). Increasing nutrition decreased postharvest quality but increasing light intensity during storage increased postharvest quality (Conover et al., 1993). Wax begonias are very sensitive to ethylene (L. Høyer, personal communication).

KEY POINTS

- Wax begonia is one of the world's most important bedding plants.
- Plants are propagated by seed, which are extremely small with 2.5 million/oz (90,000/g).

- Light, 78 to 80°F (26 to 27°C) medium, and uniform moisture are required for proper germination.
- Plants are day neutral.
- Seedlings can be stored up to 6 weeks at 41°F (5°C).

BIBLIOGRAPHY

Armitage, A.M. 1989. Color plants in the garden, increasing longevity of garden plants from seed to sale, pp. 87–100 in *Tips on Growing Bedding Plants*, H.K. Tayama and T.J. Roll, editors. Ohio Cooperative Extension Service Bulletin FP-763, Ohio State University, Columbus, Ohio.

Armitage, A.M. 1994. Growing-on, pp. 43–94 in *Ornamental Bedding Plants*. CAB International, Oxon, United Kingdom.

Bailey, L.H., and E.Z. Bailey. 1976. *Begonia*, pp. 142–154 in *Hortus Third: A Concise Dictionary of Plants Cultivated in the United States and Canada*. Macmillan, New York.

Ball, V. 1991. Plugs, the way of the 1990's, pp. 137–152 in *Ball RedBook*, 15th ed., V. Ball, editor. George J. Ball Publishing, West Chicago, Illinois.

Bell, M. 2001. Bedding plants and seed geraniums, pp. 54–62 in *Tips on Regulating Growth of Floriculture Crops*, M.L. Gaston, L.A. Kunkle, P.S. Konjoian, and M.F. Wilt, editors. Ohio Florists' Association Services, Columbus, Ohio.

Chase, A.R., and R.T. Poole. 1987a. Effect of fertilizer rate on growth of fibrous rooted begonia. *Florida Foliage* 13(3):4–5.

Chase, A.R., and R.T. Poole. 1987b. Effect of fertilizer rate on growth of fibrous rooted begonia. *HortScience* 22:162.

Conover, C.A., L.N. Satterthwaite, and K.G. Steinkamp. 1993. Production fertilizer and postharvest light intensity effects on begonias. *Proceedings of the Florida State Horticultural Society* 106:299–302.

Daughtrey, M., and A.R. Chase. 1992. Begonia, pp. 43–44 in *Ball Field Guide to Diseases of Greenhouse Ornamentals*. Ball Publishing, Geneva, Illinois.

Dreistadt, S.H. 2001. *Integrated Pest Management for Floriculture and Nurseries*. University of California Division of Agriculture and Natural Resources Publication 3402.

Erwin, J.E., and R.D. Heins. 1993. Temperature effects on bedding plant growth. *Minnesota Commercial Flower Growers Association Bulletin* 42(3):1–18.

Ewart, L.C. 1980. A grower's guide to begonias. *American Vegetable Grower and Greenhouse Grower* 28(1):6.

Ewart, L.C. 1985. Shade plants, pp. 413–430 in *Bedding Plants III*, 3rd ed., J.W. Mastalerz and E.J. Holcomb, editors. Pennsylvania Flower Growers, University Park, Pennsylvania.

Farthing, J.G., and S.R. Ellis. 1990. Growth regulants for modules—bedding plants. *Acta Horticulturae* 272:293–297.

Fotsch, K.A. 1933. *Die Begonien*. Eugen Ulmer, Stuttgart, Germany. (in German)

Graper, D.F., and W. Healy. 1990. Synergistic acceleration of *Begonia semperflorens* development using supplemental irradiance and soil heating. *Acta Horticulturae* 272:255–259.

Hayashi, T., H. Kondo, and K. Konishi. 1990. Seasonal variation in plant growth and inflorescence composition in *Begonia semperflorens*. *Journal of Japanese Society Horticultural Sciences* 59:627–633.

Heins, R.D., N. Lang, T.F. Wallace, and W. Carlson. 1994. *Cold Storage of Plug Seedlings*, pp. 1–19. Greenhouse Grower, Meister Publishing Company, Willoughby, Ohio.

Hershey, D.R., and R.H. Merritt. 1987. Influence of photoperiod on crop productivity and form of *Begonia* ×*semperflorens-cultorum* grown as a bedding plant. *Journal of American Society for Horticultural Science* 112:252–256.

Horst, R.K. 1990. Begonia, pp. 554–555 in *Westcott's Plant Disease Handbook*, 5th ed. Van Nostrand Reinhold, New York.

Huxley, A., M. Griffiths, and M. Levy. 1992. *Begonia*, pp. 318–329 in *The New Royal Horticultural Society Dictionary of Gardening*, vol. 1. Stockton Press, New York.

James, E.C., and M.W. van Iersel. 2001. Fertilizer concentration affects growth and flowering of subirrigated petunias and begonias. *HortScience* 36:40–44.

Kessler, J.R., and A.M. Armitage. 1993. Effects of carbon dioxide, light and temperature on seedling growth of *Begonia* ×*semperflorens-cultorum*. *Journal of Horticultural Science* 68:281–287.

Kessler, R., A.M. Armitage, and D.S. Koranski. 1991. Acceleration of *Begonia* ×*semperflorens*-cultorum growth using supplemental irradiance. *HortScience* 26:258–260.

Kuehny, J.S., A. Painter, and P.C. Branch. 2001. Plug source and growth retardants affect finish size of bedding plants. *HortScience* 36:321–323.

Million, J.B., J.E. Barrett, T.A. Nell, and D.G. Clark. 1999. Inhibiting growth of flowering crops with ancymidol and paclobutrazol in subirrigation water. *HortScience* 34:1103–1105.

Nau, J. 1999. *Ball Culture Guide, The Encyclopedia of Seed Germination*, 3rd ed. Ball Publishing, Batavia, Illinois.

Nelson, P.V., and J.-S. Huang. 1998. Photo guide to plug deficiencies. *GrowerTalks* 62(6):32–37.

Sawaya, M. 2001. Plugs, pp. 50–53 in *Tips on Regulating Growth of Floriculture Crops*, M.L. Gaston, L.A. Kunkle, P.S. Konjoian, and M.F. Wilt, editors. Ohio Florists' Association Services, Columbus, Ohio.

Shoemaker, C.A., and W.H. Carlson. 1992. Temperature and light affect seed germination of *Begonia semperflorens-cultorum*. *HortScience* 27:181.

Tayama, H.K. 1989. Seed germination in flats, pp. 4–6 in *Tips on Growing Bedding Plants*, H.K. Tayama and T.J. Roll, editors. Ohio Cooperative Extension Service Bulletin FP-763, Ohio State University, Columbus, Ohio.

Thompson, M.L., and E.T. Thompson. 1981. *Begonia: The Complete Reference Guide*. Time Books, New York.

Bougainvillea

FIGURE II-I BOUGAINVILLEA   Young *Bougainvillea* basket.

INTRODUCTION

Common name: bougainvillea.

Scientific names: *Bougainvillea spectabilis* Willd., *B. glabra* Choisy in DC., and *B. ×buttiana* Holtt. and Standl. (*B. glabra ×B. peruviana*) are the most common commercial species and hybrids (Bailey and Bailey, 1976; Huxley et al., 1992).

Family and related taxa: Nyctaginaceae Juss. The garden ornamental four-o'clocks (*Mirabilis jalapa* L.) is also in the family.

Origin: Tropical and subtropical South America (Brazil, Columbia, Peru).

Uses and current status: Bougainvillea is a prized ornamental shrub-vine in landscapes where heavy frosts or freezes are uncommon, and it is found from hot sunny areas to cool damp coastal regions around the world. This plant has also become an important potted plant and hanging basket in Europe and North America (Bailey, 1933; Bailey and Bailey, 1976; Hackett and Sachs, 1966, 1967, 1968, 1985; Hackett et al., 1972; Kamp-Glass and Ogden, 1991) (Fig. II-1 Bougainvillea).

This genus is noted for the vivid color of the bracts; the tubular flowers are inconspicuous within the colorful bracts. The leaves are alternate and the woody stems, which have thorns, form a vigorous vine with support.

CULTIVARS

Most of the numerous hybrids or cultivars derive from *Bougainvillea spectabilis*, *B. glabra*, or *B. ×buttiana*, of which *B. spectabilis* is more tropical and flowers mostly on older growth, whereas *B. glabra* flowers with ease on younger growth and thrives in cool greenhouses. Cultivars with variegated foliage are also available.

PROPAGATION

Rooting succulent terminal 3- to 3.5-in. (8- to 9-cm)-long cuttings is the most effective propagation method. Removal of the lower leaves and use of a rooting hormone are recommended. Mature green stem sections with three to five nodes are also commonly used. Czekalski (1989) reported that 0.2% naphthaleneacetic acid (NAA) powder with Captan and Benomyl produced a higher percentage of rooted cuttings than 0.2 to 0.4% indole-3-butyric acid (IBA). Higginbotham (1992) used 4000 to 16,000 ppm IBA, depending on the cultivar and time of year. Any well-drained medium or rooting cube can be used; the medium should be held at 75 to 81°F (24 to 27°C). Mist or fog can be used to maintain leaf turgidity (Bailey, 1933; Hackett and Sachs, 1967; Kamp-Glass and Ogden, 1991; Tse et al., 1974). Rooting may be improved by using polyethylene plastic tents or by laying the plastic directly on the cuttings (Higginbotham, 1992; Mudge et al., 1995). Stems up to 6 ft (1.8 m) long and 1.2 in. (3 cm) in diameter can be harvested, and leaves removed, staked, and propagated to produce the trunk of standard bougainvillea plants (Higginbotham, 1992).

FLOWERING CONTROL AND DORMANCY

This plant is a facultative SD plant (Allard, 1935). Plants require 80 days to flower under a 12-hr day length; under a 10-hr photoperiod, only 54 days are needed. Plants will eventually flower under LD, but fewer buds are formed (Allard, 1935). Factors other than photoperiod may induce flowering. High irradiance levels result in the most rapid flowering (Hackett and Sachs, 1966, 1968, 1985). Cool nighttime temperatures may also be a factor with *B. glabra*. Older plants having stem diameters of 0.5 in. (1.25 cm) flower sooner than newly rooted plants with only 0.25-in. (0.5-cm) stem diameters (Hackett and Sachs, 1966).

A-Rest (ancymidol), Cycocel (chlormequat), and B-Nine (daminozide) hasten flowering of plants grown under SD, but are less effective for plants grown under LD (Hackett and Sachs, 1967). Gibberellic acid (GA_3) sprays overcome this response, inhibiting floral initiation and delaying or inhibiting bract initiation altogether (Leapold, 1971). These responses are cultivar and, possibly, location specific. Atrimmec (dikegulac sodium) sprays enhanced flowering in some cultivars and not in others (Norcini et al., 1992, 1993, 1994).

TEMPERATURE

Cool night temperatures promote flowering. Night temperatures of 59°F (15°C) increased flowering under LD conditions, and night temperatures of 79°F (26°C) inhibited flowering under SD conditions. A light/dark temperature regime of 75/70°F (24/21°C) was optimal under SD (Hackett and Sachs, 1966).

LIGHT

High irradiance and inductive 8-hr SD promoted flowering (Criley, 1977). Low irradiance delayed flowering, even under inductive SD cycles and optimal temperatures (Hackett and Sachs, 1966). High light of 4000 to 5000 fc (800 to 1000 μmol $\cdot$ m^{-2} $\cdot$ s^{-1}) encourages rapid compact growth and numerous well-colored flowers.

Far-red light hastens flowering (Sachs and Hackett, 1976). When plants growing under a high red to far-red ratio had their young (most recently unfolded to terminal) leaves removed, flowering was hastened compared with the leafy control. This fact suggests that red light is associated with the development of a translocated flowering inhibitor in the young leaves. Gibberellic acid may be the flowering inhibitor involved, because leaf removal also suppressed internode elongation (Ramina et al., 1979; Sachs and Hackett, 1976).

WATER

In the landscape, plants are drought tolerant when acclimated. While severe water stress may result in abscission of flower bracts, plants are best grown on the "dry" side during greenhouse production.

CARBON DIOXIDE

No data available.

NUTRITION

Bougainvillea responds to constant fertilization of 150 to 200 ppm nitrogen. This plant is reported to have a high magnesium, iron, and manganese requirement (Kamp-Glass and Ogden, 1991). Excess soluble salt levels can cause root damage. Avoid ammonium N if plants are grown cool. However, Broschat (1998) found that using controlled-release urea or ammonium reduced leaf chlorosis and increased flowering in Florida compared with nitrate-based fertilizers. Foliar nutrient levels for high-quality plants are listed in Chapter 6, Nutrition, Table 6-4.

MEDIA

In commercial flowering pot plant production, peat-based media are mainly used. However, any well-drained medium with a pH of 5.5 to 6.0 is acceptable. Medium pH above 6.5 may lead to iron deficiency (Criley, 1997).

HEIGHT CONTROL

Several chemicals are effective on bougainvillea, but all chemicals should be tested carefully on a few plants of each cultivar because wide variations in response among cultivars, season, and geographical location is typical. Neither Cycocel nor A-Rest caused height reduction of 'Raspberry Ice' or 'San Diego Red' in South Carolina, but both growth retardants reduced vegetative growth of 'San Diego Red' in California. A-Rest can be applied as a drench at 50 ppm; Bonzi drenches are applied at 25 to 100 ppm. In addition, Bonzi drenches at 0.38 to 1.17 mg a.i./5-in. (13-cm) pot was effective at reducing the plant height of several cultivars (H.F. Wilkins, unpublished). Adriansen (1985) noted that B-Nine (daminozide) may also be marginally effective.

Atrimmec sprays increased axillary branching and flowering in some cultivars but not in others (Norcini et al., 1992, 1993, 1994). However, Atrimmec drenches at 1600 ppm are generally recognized as the most effective way to reduce shoot elongation (Dierking and Sanderson, 1985; Hackett and Sachs, 1966). Note that Atrimmec at 400 to 1600 ppm may reduce bracteole size during late spring to early summer (increasing temperatures) but not during late summer to midfall (cooler temperatures) when bracteoles were already smaller than during late spring to early summer.

SPACING

Plants are spaced pot-to-pot until the leaves touch. Final spacing for 6-in. (15-cm) pots is 8.5 × 8.5 in. (22 × 22 cm).

PINCHING AND DISBUDDING

Plants can be soft pinched once growth starts, which is approximately 10 days after propagation or when new growth is 3 in. (7.5 cm) long. Plants can be pinched every 4 weeks if needed (Kamp-Glass and Ogden, 1991). Some production schedules, however, do not include any pinching. An increase in branching can be obtained with two spray applications of benzyladenine (BA) at 50 to 100 ppm; the applications are made 24 hr after the first and second pinches. Consumers will want to pinch and prune regularly to keep the plant compact.

SUPPORT

Support is not needed if plants are grown in hanging baskets or if growth is heavily controlled with growth retardants. However, some crops are grown with wire hoops to support the plant.

SCHEDULE AND TIMING

Season and latitude influence growth rate and photoperiod. Plants can be trained on a wire hoop or pinched to form attractive hanging baskets (Tables II-1 and II-2 Bougainvillea).

TABLE II-1 BOUGAINVILLEA

Sample production schedule for *Bougainvillea* as a nonpinched flowering plant trained on a hoop.

Cultural Step	Production Time (weeks)	Temperature °F (°C)	Photoperiod
Root cuttings with 2 to 4 nodes in cubes	2–4	Air: 70–75 (21–24) Medium: 75 (24)	LD[a]
Pot two rooted cuttings in 6-in. (15-cm) pot. space pot-to-pot	4	Air: 70–78 (21–26)	LD
Space at 8.5 × 8.5 in. (22 × 22 cm) and place in wire hoop	4	Air: 70–78 (21–26)	LD
Pinch tip only when two runners meet	1	Day: 60–65 (16–18) Night: 50–55 (10–13)	SD[b]
Apply growth retardant	As needed	Day: 60–65 (16–18) Night: 50–55 (10–13)	SD
Flower	11–15		
Total	22–28		

[a]Long day (normal day + incandescent night break = 16 hr).
[b]Short day (8 hr).

TABLE II-2 BOUGAINVILLEA

Sample production schedule for *Bougainvillea* as a pinched potted flowering plant in an 8-in. (20-cm) hanging basket.

Cultural Step	Production Time (weeks)	Temperature °F (°C)	Photoperiod
Root cutting with 2 to 4 nodes in cubes	2–4	Air: 70–75 (21–24) Medium: 75 (24)	LD[a]
Pot two rooted cuttings in 8-in. (20-cm) basket, space pot-to-pot	4	Air: 70–78 (21–26)	LD
Space at 12 × 12 in. (30 × 30 cm) and pinch when new growth 3 in. (8 cm) long, leave 5 to 6 nodes	2–3	Air: 70–78 (21–26)	LD
Start SD	2–3	Day: 60–65 (16–18) Night: 50–55 (10–13)	SD[b]
Apply growth retardant	As needed	Day: 60–65 (16–18) Night: 50–55 (10–13)	SD
Flower	10–14		
Total	22–28		

[a]*Long day (normal day + incandescent night break=16 hr).*
[b]*Short day (8 hr).*

INSECTS

Aphids, thrips, scale, and mealybugs may appear on isolated plants.

DISEASES

Plants are relatively disease free, but a number of leaf spots (*Cercospora bougainvilleae, Cladosporium arthinioides,* or *Pseudomonas andropogonis*) and blights (*Phytophthora parasitica*) are problems (Daughtrey and Chase, 1992; Higginbotham, 1992; Horst, 1990).

PHYSIOLOGICAL DISORDERS

Iron chlorosis can be a problem when grown in containers and can be the result of high media pH, poor media aeration, high media EC, or root rot (Broschat, 1998) (see also the Nutrition section).

POSTHARVEST

Plants can be shipped up to 6 days at 37°F (3°C); higher temperatures are not advised. Bougainvillea are very sensitive to ethylene and exhibit bract and leaf abscission (Cameron and Reid, 1983; L.Høyer, personal communication; Moe and Fjeld, 1987; Nell, 1993; Nowak and Rudnicki, 1990). A silver thiosulfate (STS) spray (0.5 mM) has also been used to increase shipping quality and prevent bract drop. Experimentally, one 500-ppm spray of NAA applied to fully formed bracts has been used to increase postharvest life (Gago et al., 1997).

KEY POINTS

- Bougainvillea is a common garden shrub-vine in frost-free areas of the world, but is also used as a potted flowering plant or hanging basket.
- The "flowers" are actually a colorful bract; the flowers are inconspicuous.
- Plants are propagated by terminal cuttings.
- Plants are facultative SD plants that flower more quickly when grown under a 10-hr SD photoperiod.

- High irradiance, growth regulators, cool night temperatures of 59°F (15°C), and increased plant age also hasten flowering.

- After initiation, plants can be forced at 75/70°F (24/21°C) day/night temperatures.
- Height control can be difficult; growth retardants are required.

BIBLIOGRAPHY

Adriansen, E. 1985. Kemisk vækstregulering, pp. 142–162 in *Potteplanter I—Produktion, Metoder, Midler.* O.V. Christensen, A. Klougart, I.S. Pedersen, and K. Wikesjö, editors. Gartner-INFO, København, Denmark. (in Danish)

Allard, H.A. 1935. Response of the woody plants *Hibiscus syriacus, Malvavicus conzatti* and *Bougainvillea glabra* to day length. *Journal of Agricultural Research* 51:27–34.

Bailey, L.H. 1933. *Bougainvillea,* pp. 533–534 in *Standard Cyclopedia of Horticulture.* Macmillan, New York.

Bailey, L.H., and E.Z. Bailey. 1976. *Bougainvillea,* p. 174 in *Hortus Third: A Concise Dictionary of Plants Cultivated in the United States and Canada.* Macmillan, New York.

Broschat, T.K. 1998. Nitrogen source affects growth and quality of *Bougainvillea. HortTechnology* 8:346–348.

Cameron, A.C., and M.S. Reid. 1983. Use of silver thiosulfate to prevent flower abscission from potted plants. *Scientia Horticulturae* 19:373–378.

Criley, R.A. 1977. Year round flowering of double bougainvillea: Effect of daylength and growth retardants. *Journal of the American Society for Horticultural Science* 102:775–778.

Criley, R.A. 1997. *Bougainvillea,* pp. 28–31 in *Tips on Growing Specialty Potted Crops,* M.L. Gaston, S.A. Carver, C.A. Irwin, and R.A. Larson, editors. Ohio Florists' Association, Columbus, Ohio.

Czekalski, M.L. 1989. The influence of auxins on the rooting of cuttings of *Bougainvillea glabra* Choisy. *Acta Horticulturae* 251:345–352.

Daughtrey, M., and A.R. Chase. 1992. Bougainvillea, p. 20 in *Ball Field Guide to Diseases of Greenhouse Ornamentals.* Ball Publishing, Geneva, Illinois.

Dierking, C.M., and K.C. Sanderson. 1985. Effect of various chemical spray treatment of *Bougainvillea spectabilis* Willd. *Proceedings of the Southern Nurserymen's Association of Research Conference* 30:220–222.

Gago, C.M., J.A. Monteiro, and H.M. Rodrigues. 1997. Extending potted bougainvillea postproduction: NAA, STS, and ethanol. *HortScience* 32:517. (Abstract)

Hackett, W.P., and R.M. Sachs. 1966. Flowering in *Bougainvillea* 'San Diego Red.' *Proceedings of the American Society for Horticultural Science* 88:606–612.

Hackett, W.P., and R.M. Sachs. 1967. Chemical control of flowering in *Bougainvillea* 'San Diego Red.' *Proceedings of the American Society for Horticultural Science* 90:361–364.

Hackett, W.P., and R.M. Sachs. 1968. Experimental separation of inflorescence development from initiation in *Bougainvillea. Proceedings of the American Society for Horticultural Science* 92:615–621.

Hackett, W.P., and R.M. Sachs. 1985. *Bougainvillea,* pp. 38–47 in *Handbook of Flowering,* vol. II, A.H. Halevy, editor. CRC Press, Boca Raton, Florida.

Hackett, W.P., R.M. Sachs, and J. DeBie. 1972. Growing *Bougainvillea* as a flowering pot plant. *California Agriculture* 26(8):12–13.

Higginbotham, R. 1992. *Bougainvillea* propagation. *Combined Proceedings International Plant Propagators' Society* 42:37–38.

Horst, R.K. 1990. Bougainvillea, p. 561 in *Westcott's Plant Disease Handbook,* 5th ed. Van Nostrand Reinhold, New York.

Huxley, A., M. Griffiths, and M. Levy. 1992. *Bougainvillea,* p. 378 in *The New Royal Horticultural Society Dictionary of Gardening,* vol. 1. Stockton Press, New York.

Kamp-Glass, M., and M.A.H. Ogden. 1991. *Bougainvillea. GrowersTalks* 55(8):17.

Leapold, A.C. 1971. Antagonism of some gibberellin actions by substituted pyrimidine. *Plant Physiology* 48:537–540.

Moe, R., and T. Fjeld. 1987. Keeping quality of potted plants as influenced by ethylene. *Gartner Tidende* 101:1580–1583.

Mudge, K.W., V.N. Mwaja, F.M. Itulya, and J. Ochieng. 1995. Comparison of four moisture management systems for cutting propagation of bougainvillea, hibiscus, and kei apple. *Journal of the American Society for Horticultural Science* 120:366–373.

Nell, T. 1993. *Bougainvillea,* pp. 33–34 in *Flowering Potted Plants, Prolonging Shelf Performance.* Ball Publishing, Batavia, Illinois.

Norcini, J.G., J.M. McDowell, and J.H. Aldrich. 1992. Effect of dikegulac on flowering and growth of *Bougainvillea* 'Rainbow Gold.' *HortScience* 27:35–36.

Norcini, J.G., J.M. McDowell, and J.H. Aldrich. 1993. Dikegulac improves bougainvillea flowering during two production seasons. *HortScience* 28:119–121.

Norcini, J.G., J.H. Aldrich, and J.M. McDowell. 1994. Flowering response of *Bougainvillea* cultivars to dikegulac. *HortScience* 29:282–284.

Nowak, J., and R.M. Rudnicki. 1990. *Postharvest Handling and Storage of Cut Flowers, Florist Greens and Potted Plants*. Timber Press, Portland, Oregon.

Ramina, A., W.P. Hackett, and R.M. Sachs. 1979. Flowering in *Bougainvillea* a function of assimilate supply and nutrient diversion. *Plant Physiology* 64:810–813.

Sachs, R.M., and W.P. Hackett. 1976. Relating gibberellin-induced inhibition of flowering to requirement for far-red radiation and promotion by removal of young leaves, pp. 325–327 in *Proceedings of the 9th International Conference on Plant Growth Substances*, Lausanne, Switzerland, August 30–September 4.

Tse, A.T.Y., A. Ramina, W.P. Hackett, and R.M. Sachs. 1974. Enhanced inflorescence development in *Bougainvillea* 'San Diego Red' by removal of young leaves and cytokinin treatments. *Plant Physiology* 54:404–407.

Caladium

FIGURE II-I CALADIUM Potted *Caladium* plants ready for market.

INTRODUCTION

Common names: caladium, fancy-leaved caladium, angel-wings.

Scientific name: *Caladium bicolor* Ait. (Huxley et al., 1992).

Family and related taxa: Araceae Juss. Present-day hybrids and cultivars are crosses between *Caladium bicolor*, *C. picturatum* C. Kock and Bouche, and *C. marmoratum* Mathieu, which are all now considered the same species (Huxley et al., 1992). Araceae is a large family containing many important genera including *Aglaonema*, *Anthurium*, *Dieffenbachia*, *Epipremnum*, *Monstera*, *Nephthytis*, *Philodendron*, *Spathiphyllum*, *Syngonium*, and *Zantedeschia*.

Origin: All 17 species are found in tropical South America between the equator and 20° south latitude.

Uses and current status: Caladiums are grown for their large colorful leaves as landscape bedding plant specimens and as potted plants (Auman, 1977; Bailey, 1914; Birdsey, 1951; Post, 1949) (Fig. II-1 Caladium). Extensive reviews on caladium history, physiology, and culture are available (Wilfret, 1993; Wilkins, 1985).

CULTIVARS

Presently about 100 cultivars are commercially available. At one time, there were more than 1500 recorded cultivars; many were lost during the 1940s (Birdsey, 1951; Hayward, 1972). Current caladium cultivars can be divided into fancy-leaved and strap-leaved types (Cantwell, 1994). Individual cultivars vary in their suitability for specific pot and hanging basket sizes. De Hertogh (1996) lists numerous cultivars and their forcing requirements. Cultivars also vary in their tolerance to cold temperatures.

PROPAGATION

Commercial caladium tuber production is centered in Florida (Cantwell, 1994). Caladiums are propagated mainly by dividing the tubers,

TABLE II-I CALADIUM

Commercially available *Caladium* tuber sizes.

Grade	Diameter in. (cm)	Numbers of Tubers Used for Various Pot Sizes
Super mammoth	4.5+ (11.5+)	
Mammoth	3.5–4.5 (9.0–11.5)	2 tubers/10-in. (25-cm) basket
Jumbo	2.5–3.5 (6.5–9.0)	1 tuber/6-in. (15-cm) pot, 3 tubers/8-in. (20-cm) pot
No. 1	1.75–2.5 (4.5–9.0)	3 tuber/6-in. (15-cm) pot, 5 to 6 tubers/8-in. (20-cm) pot 1 tuber/4-in. (10-cm) pot, 5 to 6 tubers/10-in. (25-cm basket)
No. 2	1.5–1.75 (4.0–4.5)	5 tubers/6-in. (15-cm) pot, 1 tuber/4-in. (10-cm) pot, 10 to 12 tubers/10-in. (25-cm) hanging basket

making certain each piece has a bud (Bailey, 1914; Poole and Conover, 1977). This is usually done with dormant tubers, prior to replanting. Tubers are available in a number of sizes (Table II-1 Caladium).

Although not used commercially, caladiums can be seed or tissue culture propagated (Hartman, 1974; Hartman et al., 1972; Knauss and Conover, 1975). For maximum seed germination, daily exposure to incandescent light is essential. Seed can be stored for long periods at a wide range of humidity if kept at 59°F (15°C); however, at 77°F (25°C), 100% humidity must be maintained (Carpenter, 1990). Plants can be stimulated to flower for seed production by soaking tubers for 8 to 16 hr in 250 ppm gibberellic acid (GA$_3$) (Harbaugh and Wilfret, 1979; Henny, 2001).

FLOWERING CONTROL AND DORMANCY

Caladiums normally go through an annual rest period, during which leaves are not present. When the leaves begin to wither, moisture is withheld to allow the tuber to dry or "cure." Tubers are then stored for a time before replanting. Tuber dormancy requirements are not well understood. Although the rest period does not seem to be essential, tubers that are stored produce leaves more rapidly than those that are immediately replanted (Poole and Conover, 1977). The required duration of the rest period may depend on the time of year; tubers planted in January take longer for leaf emergence compared with tubers planted in May (Auman, 1977; Post, 1949). Typically at least 6 weeks of storage is recommended (Wilfret, 1997). Forcing should generally not start prior to January 15, because tubers planted later may catch up with tubers planted prior to

January 15. Tubers should never be stored below 70°F (21°C) and the relative humidity should be less than 75%.

TEMPERATURE

Marousky (1974) demonstrated irreversible tuber chilling injury at 41°F (5°C). Tubers tolerated 50°F (10°C) for up to 3 days, but 10 days at 50 to 61°F (10 to 16°C) delayed leaf emergence and reduced leaf number (Marousky, 1974; Marousky and Harbaugh, 1976). Longer durations below 63°F (17°C) damaged tubers. After potting, emergence can be hastened by placing pots on heated benches. Optimum shoot emergence occurs with a medium temperature of 73 to 75°F (23 to 24°C) and high humidity (90%). Pots can be covered with plastic to increase temperature and humidity, but the plastic should be removed at least three times a week for proper ventilation. Other problems can occur with plastic covering, including greening (see Physiological Disorders, page 346), overheating, stretching, and tuber rot (Harbaugh and Evans, 1994).

When plants were forced, Conover and Poole (1975) have shown that 90°F (32°C) resulted in higher quality plants than did 70 or 81°F (21 or 27°C). Marousky and Raulston (1973), however, stated 81°F (27°C) was optimal. Actively growing plants are damaged at temperatures below 63°F (17°C) and plants become dormant. Although not recommended, night temperatures between 63 and 70°F (17 and 21°C) can be balanced with day temperatures of 81 to 86°F (27 to 30°C) (Cantwell, 1994).

LIGHT

Smaller leaves and reduced petiole length and plant quality are the result of insufficient light. Reduced leaf coloration as a result of increased green chlorophyll pigment (greening) occurs under excessively high light. Plants may also be stunted and have smaller leaves under high irradiance (Conover and Poole, 1973). Conover and Poole (1973) stated 5000 fc (1000 μmol · m^{-2} · s^{-1}) of light as found under 40 or 60% shade cloth was optimal. De Hertogh (1996) recommended 3000 to 4000 fc (600 to 800 μmol · m^{-2} · s^{-1}). Less dense shade may be used in northern or coastal areas of the country with low light levels.

WATER

Plants should be kept moist but not wet. If the medium is allowed to dry and plants wilt, irreversible damage occurs and tubers can become dormant (Birdsey, 1951). If overwatered, roots and tubers will rot. Plants can be hardened by reducing irrigation frequency prior to shipment. High soil moisture conditions resulted in optimum growth of caladiums grown for tubers (Stanley and Harbaugh, 2002).

CARBON DIOXIDE

No information is available in regard to the effects of CO_2 on caladiums during greenhouse forcing.

NUTRITION

Caladiums do not require high levels of nutrition and may not need to be fertilized. Harbaugh et al. (2000) showed that field production of caladium tubers in central Florida required no added phosphorus for optimum yield; phosphorus runoff is a concern in that area.

During greenhouse production, superphosphate should be added to the medium; subsequently only nitrogen and potassium are applied (100 to 200 ppm) once a week. Conover and Poole (1973, 1975) have used 14–14–14 controlled-release fertilizer at 10 lb/yd³ (6 kg · m³) or topdressed at 1 tsp/6-in. (4.9 mL/15-cm) pot. Excessive nitrogen may cause excessive chlorophyll formation (greening) and subdued leaf coloration. Harbaugh (1986) developed a key to help identify macro- and micronutritional deficiencies. Foliar nutrient levels for high-quality plants are listed in Chapter 6, Nutrition, Table 6-4.

MEDIA

Caladiums thrive in a wide range of media. A pH of 5.5 to 6.5 is acceptable (De Hertogh, 1996). Tubers should be planted at least 1.5 in. (4 cm) deep. Roots form from the base of the buds at the top of the tuber.

HEIGHT CONTROL

Although B-Nine (daminozide) or Bonzi (paclobutrazol) can be used to control plant height, proper cultural practices can also be used, including increased spacing, reduced shade, reduced irrigation frequency, proper de-eyeing, and selection of smaller tubers (Barrett et al., 1995; De Hertogh, 1996; B. Hervey, personal communication). Bonzi at 0.22 to 1.77 mg a.i./6-in. (15-cm) pot (5 to 15 ppm) is typically used only as a drench and applied when shoot spikes are showing but not yet leafed out. B-Nine at 2500 to 5000 ppm is used as a foliar spray when plants are leafed out and spaced. Up to three sprays of B-Nine may be needed, spaced 5 to 7 days apart. Chemical growth regulators are especially useful for holding back plants in smaller pots.

SPACING

Pot-to-pot spacing is generally used during early forcing, Final spacing is according to pot size and up to 12 × 12 in. (30 × 30 cm) for a 6-in. (15-cm) pot.

PINCHING AND DISBUDDING

Several techniques have been used to attempt to increase the number of axillary buds that break dormancy on the tuber (Auman, 1977; Conover and Poole, 1975; Muzzell and Joiner, 1966; Post, 1949). The most common is de-eyeing or scooping, which is mechanically removing the apical or terminal bud (Figs. II-2 and II-3 Caladium). De-eyeing costs approximately $0.01 per tuber and results in short, compact plants with more and smaller leaves (Cantwell, 1994). Tubers should be de-eyed if planted in 6-in. (15-cm) or smaller pots, while tubers for larger pots or baskets need not be de-eyed. Some cultivars produce multiple dominant eyes known as multitubers, especially strap-leaved types, and do not need to be de-eyed. De-eyeing may delay the finishing date up to 6 days and reduce height and individual leaf area but increase the number of leaves and total leaf area (Cantwell, 1994; Evans and Harbaugh, 1993). As little of the surrounding tissue should be removed as possible when de-eyeing to reduce variability of the response to de-eyeing (Evans and

FIGURE II-2 CALADIUM *Caladium* tubers being de-eyed.

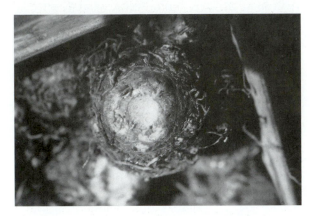

FIGURE II-3 CALADIUM De-eyed *Caladium* tuber.

Harbaugh, 1993). Inverting tubers when planting was reported to produce more shoots, but shoot emergence was delayed and variable (Conover and Poole, 1975).

Various plant growth regulators have been used in efforts to increase bud break and thus shoot numbers. Benzyladenine, benzylamino (tetrahydropyranyl) purine (PBA), ethylene chlorohydrin, ethephon, Promalin (1:1 benzyladenine:gibberellic acid, now available as Fascination), and thidiazuron were ineffective in removing apical dominance (Carter and Mahotiere, 1991; Nixon and Wilfret, 1993). An increase of up to 67% in shoot number resulted from dikegulac-sodium treatments according to Carter and Mahotiere (1991); however, Nixon and Wilfret (1993) found no benefit. GA did not influence bud break, but increased petiole length and stimulated uniform flowering for breeding purposes (Harbaugh and Wilfret, 1979; Marousky, 1974; Marousky and Harbaugh, 1976).

SUPPORT

None required.

SCHEDULE AND TIMING

Caladiums force in 4 to 8 weeks under hot, humid conditions (especially summer) and are considered a fast crop (Post, 1949). Forcing of 6-in. (15-cm) pots can take 8 to 12 weeks under cool conditions (De Hertogh, 1996).

INSECTS

Caladiums are relatively pest free. Post (1949) states that aphids and thrips can be troublesome. Spider mites, mealybugs, and caterpillars can also occur.

DISEASES

Tuber deterioration is associated with temperatures below 50°F (10°C). Even very brief exposures are injurious (Marousky, 1974; Marousky and Harbaugh, 1976; Post, 1949). Several diseases have been noted to occur on caladiums, including bacterial soft rot (*Erwinia carotovora*), southern blight (*Sclerotium rolfsii*), and tuber rot (*Botrytis ricini* or *Fusarium solani*) (Horst, 1990). Southern blight can be controlled in tubers by soaking in 122°F (50°C) water for 30 min plus the time it takes to reach the temperature (Dreistadt, 2001). Cool tubers rapidly in cold water and dry thoroughly with fans or by placing them in sunshine. Polston et al. (1991) reported a possible phytoplasma-caused disease known as grassy tuber, which results in a 10-fold increase in the number of leaves produced, reduced leaf size, and prevented flowering.

PHYSIOLOGICAL DISORDERS

Excessive greening of the foliage can occur from wounds and other plant stresses such as high temperatures, light fluctuations, overwatering, and excessive fertilization (Harbaugh and Evans, 1994). White cultivars are most susceptible to greening and should never be covered with plastic during emergence.

POSTHARVEST

Plants should never be shipped or displayed at temperatures below 63°F (17°C); 70°F (21°C) is best (De Hertogh, 1996). B. Harbaugh (personal communication) stated that 65°F (18°C) was optimum for shipping.

KEY POINTS

- This colorful-leaved foliage plant is used as a bedding plant, potted plant, and perennial garden ornamental in frost-free areas.
- Commercially, caladiums are produced from tubers, which can be divided; seed or *in vitro* propagation can also be used.
- Tuber dormancy or "rest" after harvest is not essential but stored tubers resprout more rapidly than unstored tubers.

- Prior to forcing, corms are "de-eyed," which is the mechanical removal of the apical terminal bud.
- Tubers should never experience temperatures below 70°F (21°C) and plants should not experience temperatures below 63°F (17°C).
- Forcing recommendations vary, but 81 to 90°F (27 to 32°C) is advised.
- At 63°F (17°C) or below, plants become dormant.

BIBLIOGRAPHY

Auman, C.W. 1977. Three years of caladium research. *North Carolina Flower Growers Bulletin* 21(2):3–6.

Bailey, L.H. 1914. *Standard Encyclopedia of Horticulture*, pp. 613–617. Macmillan, New York.

Barrett, J.E., C.A. Bartuska, and T.A. Nell. 1995. Caladium height control with paclobutrazol drench applications. *HortScience* 30:549–550.

Birdsey, M.R. 1951. *The Cultivated Aroids*, p. 42. Gillick Press, Berkeley, California.

Cantwell, T.B. 1994. Caladiums as pot plants. *Professional Plant Growers Association News* 25(11):5, 8, 9.

Carpenter, W.J. 1990. Light and temperature govern germination and storage of caladium seed. *HortScience* 25:71–74.

Carter, J., and S. Mahotiere. 1991. Influence of BA, promalin, and dikegulac-sodium on shoot initiation and vegetative growth of *Caladium*. *HortScience* 26:684. (Abstract)

Conover, C.A., and R.T. Poole. 1973. Influence of shade level and soil temperature on forcing of *Caladium bicolor*. *Proceedings of the Florida State Horticultural Society* 86:369–372.

Conover, C.A., and R.T. Poole. 1975. Influence of fertilizer level, apical bud removal, and tuber orientation on forcing of *Caladium bicolor*. *HortScience* 10:226–227.

De Hertogh, A. 1996. *Caladium*, pp. C31–40 in *Holland Bulb Forcers Guide*, 5th ed. International Flower Bulb Centre, Hillegom, The Netherlands.

Dreistadt, S.H. 2001. *Integrated Pest Management for Floriculture and Nurseries*. University of California Division of Agriculture and Natural Resources Publication 3402.

Evans, M.R., and B.K. Harbaugh. 1993. Method and timing of tuber de-eyeing affects growth and development of caladium. *HortScience* 28:994–996.

Harbaugh, B.K. 1986. Visual nutrient symptoms in *Caladium ×hortulanum* Birdsey. *Journal of the American Society for Horticultural Science* 111:248–253.

Harbaugh, B.K., and J.R. Evans. 1994. Growth inhibition of caladium by high temperature. *HortScience* 14:72–73.

Harbaugh, B.K., and G.J. Wilfret. 1979. Gibberellic acid stimulates flowering in *Caladium hortulanum* Birdsey. *HortScience* 14:72–73. *HortScience* 29:769–770.

Harbaugh, B.K., D.A. DeVoll, and R. Zalewski. 2000. Phosphorus fertilization for caladium tuber production on organic soil. *HortTechnology* 10:169–171.

Hartman, R.D. 1974. Dasheen mosaic virus and other phytopathogens eliminated from caladium, taro, and cocoyam by culture of shoot tips. *Phytopathology* 64:237–240.

Hartman, R.D., R.W. Zettler, J.F. Knauss, and E.M. Hawkins. 1972. Seed propagation of *Caladium hortulanum* and *Dieffenbachia picta*. *Proceedings of the Florida State Horticultural Society* 85:404–409.

Hayward, W. 1972. Fancy-leaved caladium. *Plant Life* 6:131–142.

Henny, R.J. 2001. Foliage plants, pp. 83–87 in *Tips on Regulating Growth of Floriculture Crops*, M.L. Gaston, L.A. Kunkle, P.S. Konjoian, and M.F. Wilt, editors. Ohio Florists' Association Services, Columbus, Ohio.

Horst, R.K. 1990. Caladium, p. 572 in *Westcott's Plant Disease Handbook*, 5th ed. Van Nostrand Reinhold, New York.

Huxley, A., M. Griffiths, and M. Levy. 1992. *Caladiums*, p. 453 in *The New Royal Horticultural Society Dictionary of Gardening*, vol. 1. Stockton Press, New York.

Knauss, J.F., and C.A. Conover. 1975. Field evaluation of caladiums derived from tissue culture. *Proceedings of the American Phytopathology Society* 2:69.

Marousky, F.J. 1974. Influence of curing and low temperature during storage on subsequent sprouting of caladium tubers. *Proceedings of the Florida State Horticultural Society* 87:426–428.

Marousky, F.J., and B.K. Harbaugh. 1976. Influence of relative humidity on curing and growth of caladium tubers. *Proceedings of the Florida State Horticultural Society* 89:284–287.

Marousky, F.J., and J.C. Raulston. 1973. Influence of temperature and duration on curing, storage, shipping and forcing periods on caladium growth. *Proceedings of the Florida State Horticultural Society* 86:363–368.

Muzzell, A.E., Jr., and J.N. Joiner. 1966. Effect of methods of cut, heat treatment and planting on forcing *Caladium* spp. 'Candidum.' *Proceedings of the Florida State Horticultural Society* 79:446–451.

Nixon, S.E., and G.J. Wilfret. 1993. Effect of growth regulators on leaf development of caladium. *Proceedings of the Florida State Horticultural Society* 106:283–286.

Polston, J.E., M.R. Evans, and J.H. Tsai. 1991. Investigation of the etiology of grassy tuber of caladium. *Proceedings of the Florida State Horticultural Society* 104:334–336.

Poole, R.T., and C.A. Conover. 1977. Sprouting of caladiums as influenced by planting date. *Florida Nurseryman*, September: 25.

Post, K. 1949. *Caladium*, pp. 353–354 in *Florist Crop Production and Marketing*. Orange Judd Publishing, New York.

Stanley, C.D., and B.K. Harbaugh. 2002. Water table depth effect on water use and tuber yield for subirrigated caladium production. *HortTechnology* 12:679–681.

Wilfret, G.J. 1993. *Caladiums*, pp. 239–348 in *The Physiology of Flower Bulbs*, A. De Hertogh and M. Le Nard, editors. Elsevier, Amsterdam, The Netherlands.

Wilfret, G.J. 1997. *Caladium*, pp. 33–37 in *Tips on Growing Specialty Potted Crops*, M.L. Gaston, S.A. Carver, C.A. Irwin, and R.A. Larson, editors. Ohio Florists' Association, Columbus, Ohio.

Wilkins, H.F. 1985. *Caladium ×hortulanum*, pp. 101–104 in *Handbook of Flowering*, vol. II, A.H. Halevy, editor. CRC Press, Boca Raton, Florida.

Calceolaria

INTRODUCTION

Common names: calceolaria, pocketbook flower, pouch flower, slipper flower, slipperwort.

Scientific name: *Calceolaria* Herbeohybrida group, developed from the following species: *C. crenatiflora* Cav., *C. corymbosum* Ruiz & Pav., and *C. cana* Cav. (Huxley et al., 1992).

Family and related taxa: Scrophulariaceae L. This genus includes 500 species with growth habits ranging from herbaceous to shrubby. In Europe, *C. Fruticohybrida* group, derived mainly from *C. integrifolia* Murray (formerly known as *C. rugosa*), is also grown for its much smaller and daintier flowers. Other important genera in this family are *Antirrhinum, Hebe, Penstemon, Verbascum,* and *Veronica.*

Origin: The various *Calceolaria* species are natives of the cool, sunny mountains of Argentina and Chile, extending north into Mexico. The species *C. crenatiflora* is a native of Chile and is an herbaceous perennial that can reach 2.5 ft (76 cm) in height.

Uses and current status: The modern hybrids are now used as potted flowering plants and, in cooler areas of the world, as spring and summer bedding plants (Bailey and Bailey, 1976) (Figs. II-1 and II-2 Calceolaria).

The opposite leaves are ovate, and the unique flower is like an inflated pouch. The upper lip is small, and the lower is exaggerated. The colors vary from yellow and orange to red, and flowers can be brown spotted. Although a perennial, it is handled as an annual in North America and Europe (Bailey and Bailey, 1976; White, 1975).

CULTIVARS

There are numerous cultivars from seed companies throughout the world. Seed companies sometimes list 'Multiflora' and 'Grandiflora' to indicate flower number or size, respectively, of pot-

FIGURE II-1 CALCEOLARIA *Calceolaria* potted plant.

FIGURE II-2 CALCEOLARIA *Calceolaria integrifolia* 'Gold Cut' bedding plant and cut flower.

ted plant cultivars (Table II-1 Calceolaria). The epitaphs within these groups for both of these standard sized plants are further broken down to *Multiflora nana* (dwarf) and *Grandiflora primula compacta*. Although the Latin binomial system is used, it is not taxonomically valid. Dwarf cultivars

are available for use as bedding plants and tall cultivars for cut flower production (R. Sterkel, personal communication; White, 2003).

PROPAGATION

The calceolaria is an interesting potted flowering plant that is seed propagated. There are 600,000 to 1 million seed/oz (21,000 to 35,000/g). For every five seeds sown, one seed can be expected to germinate. Seeds are evenly distributed over a fibrous, well-drained pasteurized medium. The seeds are not covered, and mist or fog is used to prevent drying. However, care should be taken to not overwater. Under fluorescent lights at 65 to 70°F (18 to 21°C), germination occurs in up to 2 weeks. After germination, move seedlings to natural light or HID supplemental lighting (Anonymous 1986).

For plug production the following conditions are used (Hamrick, 2003):

- *Stage 1:* Seed not covered, 70 to 75°F (21 to 24°C), 3 to 5 days
- *Stage 2:* 70 to 75°F (21 to 24°C), 7 days, 500 to 1000 fc (100 to 200 μmol $\cdot$ m^{-2} $\cdot$ s^{-1}), and 50 to 75 ppm N once/week
- *Stage 3:* 65 to 70°F (18 to 21°C), 21 to 28 days, 1000 to 1500 fc (200 to 300 μmol $\cdot$ m^{-2} $\cdot$ s^{-1}), and 100 to 150 ppm N once/week
- *Stage 4:* 60 to 62°F (15 to 17°C), 7 days, 1500 to 2500 fc (300 to 500 μmol $\cdot$ m^{-2} $\cdot$ s^{-1}), and 100 to 150 ppm N once/week

Plugs should be ready for marketing or transplanting in 5 to 7 weeks. See Chapter 1, Propagation, for descriptions of stages.

FLOWERING CONTROL AND DORMANCY

Although calceolaria are traditionally sold in late winter and spring for Easter and Mother's Day, year-round flowering is possible through manipulation of photoperiod and temperature (Strømme et al., 1985; White, 1975). Newer

TABLE II-1 CALCEOLARIA
Calceolaria hybrid groups available for potted plant production.

Designation	Flower Size in. (cm)	Plant Height in. (cm)
Grandiflora	1.5 to 2.0 (3.8 to 5.1)	12 to 16 (30 to 40)
Grandiflora primula compacta	1.8 to 2.0 (4.6 to 5.1)	8 (20)
Multiflora	1.2 to 1.6 (3.0 to 4.1)	10 to 12 (25 to 30)
Multiflora nana	0.8 to 1.2 (2.1 to 3.0)	12 (30)

cultivars do not require a cold treatment or LD to flower (Hamrick, 2003).

Older cultivars of calceolaria can be considered facultative LD plants at temperatures below 59°F (15°C) (Poesch, 1931; Post, 1937). Plants must develop four to five pairs of leaves before they are capable of sensing LD treatments. However, temperature interacts with photoperiod, because flowering can occur under SD if temperatures are low (Table II-2 Calceolaria). Photoperiodic lighting or HID lighting can hasten floral induction and development in the winter if temperatures are low. When light durations are long (14 to 15 hr or longer) and intensities are high, low temperatures are not essential for rapid floral induction or flower development.

In the summer, calceolaria is an obligate LD plant when temperatures are above 59°F (15°C). If plants are kept under an 8- to 12-hr photoperiod, a vegetative state is maintained unless a specific cold treatment can be given (Johansson, 1976; Rünger, 1978; Strømme et al., 1985). Under SD, the optimal temperature for floral induction is 46 to 50°F (8 to 10°C), and certainly below 59°F (15°C). Thus, cold overrides photoperiod, and plants will flower under SD. If temperatures are 59°F (15°C) or higher, 10 long photoperiods are required for floral induction.

In the winter, under SD, 70 to 80 days of low temperature are required for floral induction and development (Rünger, 1975, 1978; Strømme et al., 1985). After induction has occurred, flowering takes place rapidly under either LD or SD. If cold treatments are insufficient in the winter, 12- to 18-hr LD will be necessary for floral induction and development. Long-day treatments with incandescent lights are more effective than with cool-white fluorescent lights, but internode elongation occurs with incandescent lights (Rünger, 1975). Day extensions are preferred over night interruptions. Cyclic lighting (4 min on/6 min off) is effective (Rünger, 1978).

TEMPERATURE

For floral induction under SD, a temperature below 59°F (15°C) is required (Johansson, 1976; Rünger, 1978; Strømme et al., 1985). Generally, 46 to 50°F (8 to 10°C) is best for thermofloral induction. For overall plant quality after floral induction, a temperature regime of 50 to 60°F (10 to 16°C) is used during winter forcing (Anonymous, 1986).

Root zone heating was reported to have increased tissue concentrations of most macro- and micronutrients as well as plant weights, flower numbers, and quality (White and Biernbaum, 1984a, b).

LIGHT

In winter, at inductive temperatures, full intensities are best for rapid thermofloral induction. In summer, reduce intensities to 5000 fc (1000 $\mu mol \cdot m^{-2} \cdot s^{-1}$) for temperature control and to prevent flowers from burning. Supplemental high-intensity lighting can be used in winter. If plants are being thermoinduced to flower, the total duration of light should be less than 12 hr; an 8-hr duration is preferable. Under warmer temperatures of 60 to 68°F (16 to 20°C), 12 to 18 hr of light will result in floral induction (Rünger, 1978; Strømme et al., 1985; White, 1975).

WATER

Do not overmist or fog young seedlings. The roots of calceolaria are fine, and plants are grown under cool to mild conditions. Consequently, overwatering and root injury can easily occur (Anonymous, 1986).

CARBON DIOXIDE

Though no data are available, the use of carbon dioxide should be tested because most other species respond favorably to elevated levels.

TABLE II-2 CALCEOLARIA

Flower control response interactions between photoperiod and temperature for *Calceolaria*.

Temperature °F (°C)	Short Day (≤12 hr, optimum = 8 hr)	Long Day (12 to 18 hr)
59 (15) or lower[a]	Flowering	Flowering
60 to 68 (16 to 20)	No flowering	Flowering
[a] Optimum is 46 to 50 (8 to 10).		

NUTRITION

A 300-ppm nitrogen application from a complete fertilizer every 3 to 4 weeks is adequate. Ammonium nitrogen sources should be avoided because of toxicity concerns during cold temperature forcing (Anonymous, 1986).

MEDIA

Peat-lite medium or a peat:sand:perlite (1:1:1 by volume) with a pH of 6.0 to 6.5 is commonly used (Anonymous, 1986). Media pH above 6.2 may cause iron chlorosis (Williams, 2001). Phosphates, trace elements, and a source of calcium are common amendments.

HEIGHT CONTROL

Internode length can be reduced by Cycocel (chlormequat) sprays at 400 to 1000 ppm. The lower concentration can be used twice with a low risk of problems; however, flowering may be delayed or some leaf injury may occur (Johansson, 1976; Strømme et al., 1985). Adriansen (1985) noted that B-Nine (daminozide) may also be effective.

SPACING

Plants can be grown in 4-, 5-, or, rarely, in 6-in. (10-, 13-, or 15-cm) pots. Seedling plugs are transplanted into the final pot and are held pot-to-pot until spacing is required. Final spacing is 8 × 8 in. (20 × 20 cm) for 4-in. (10-cm) pots, 10 × 10 in. (24 × 24 cm) for 5-in. (13-cm) pots, or 12 × 12 in. (30 × 30 cm) for 6-in. (15-cm) pots. Bedding and cut flower cultivars are spaced closer together.

PINCHING AND DISBUDDING

No pinching or disbudding needed.

SUPPORT

Support is not usually required with adequate spacing, light, and use of a plant growth regulator.

SCHEDULE AND TIMING

The production of potted flowering calceolaria is not a short process. Generally, 4.5 to 5 months are required for winter and spring schedules. This time span is reduced to 4 months in the summer under LD and warm temperatures. Short winter schedules are possible if a combination of 18-hr LD for vegetative growth, 8-hr SD for flower initiation, and 55°F (13°C) is used (Williams, 2001). The use of purchased plugs will reduce crop time for 4-in. (10-cm) pots to 12 to 13 weeks. Bedding plant cultivars can be ready for sale in 10 to 12 weeks (White, 2003) (Tables II-3, II-4, and II-5 Calceolaria).

INSECTS

Aphids, leaf miners, thrips, cyclamen mites, and spider mites are observed on calceolaria, and

---

TABLE II-3 CALCEOLARIA

Sample *Calceolaria* production schedule for spring sales of 5-in. (13-cm) pot. Add 3 to 4 weeks if a 6-in. (15-cm) pot is used. Subtract 3 to 4 weeks for a 4-in. (10-cm) pot. Modified from White (1975) and R. Heins (personal communication).

Cultural Step	Production Time (weeks)	Temperature °F (°C)
Seed sown [a]		
	2 to 3	65 to 70 (18 to 21)
Seed germinate and grow in plugs		
	3 to 4	65 to 70 (18 to 21)
Transplant plug to final pot		
	6 to 8	60 (16)
Floral induction		
	6	50 (10)
Increase temperature		
	4 to 6	Days: 65 (18) Nights: 50 to 60 (10 to 16)
Flower		
Total	21 to 27	

[a] Most seeds are sown directly into plugs by specialty propagators and sold as transplants.

TABLE II-4 CALCEOLARIA

A sample *Calceolaria* summer flowering schedule for 4-in. (10-cm) pots commencing in early April for late July sale. Modified from Rünger (1978) and White (1975).

Cultural Step	Production Time (weeks)	Temperature °F (°C)	Photoperiod (hours)
Seed sown[a]			
	2–3	65–70 (18–21)	18
Seed germinate and grow in plugs			
	2–3	65–70 (18–21)	18
Transplant plugs to final pot and provide SD for vegetative growth			
	4–5	59–64 (15–18)	8
LD for rapid floral initiation and development			
	7–8	As cool as possible	18
Flower			
Total	15–19		

[a] *Most seeds are sown directly into plugs by specialty propagators and sold as transplants.*

TABLE II-5 CALCEOLARIA

A sample *Calceolaria* rapid winter flowering schedule for 4-in. (10-cm) pots commencing in late September for late January sale. Modified from Rünger (1975) and White (1975).

Cultural Step	Production Time (weeks)	Temperature °F (°C)	Photoperiod [a] (hours)
Seed sown[a]			
	2–3	65–70 (18–21)	18
Seed germinate and grow in plugs			
	2–3	65–70 (18–21)	18
Transplant plug to final pot			
	2–3	59–64 (15–18)	18
SD for vegetative growth			
	6	55 (13)	8
LD for rapid floral initiation and development			
	4	59–64 (15–18)	18
Flower			
Total	16–19		

[a] *HID lighting would be optimal. Incandescent day extensions cause internode elongation. A plant growth regulator may be used to address this problem.*
[b] *Most seeds are sown directly into plugs by specialty propagators and sold as transplants.*

whiteflies are most commonly seen. Because tomato spotted wilt virus is carried by thrips, this insect is a concern (Zitter et al., 1989). Observation, spot spraying, exclusion, and biological control are basic control considerations.

DISEASES

Calceolaria are most commonly grown under cold temperature regimes. Frequently, low temperature and excess water interact, causing root, crown, and stem rots (*Pythium, Phytophthora, Myrothecium roridum,* or *Sclerotinia*

sclerotiorum) (Dreistadt, 2001; Horst, 1990). Other reported diseases include verticillium wilt (*Verticillium*) and impatiens necrotic spot and tomato spotted wilt viruses (Dreistadt, 2001). Diseases can be prevented by using a well-drained medium, avoiding wet foliage, allowing the soil to dry between irrigations, not planting seedlings or transplants too deeply, avoiding high medium ECs and ammonium, and using good sanitary practices.

Gray mold (*Botrytis cinerea*) on flowers may be a problem during shipping. Pack only plants that are dry and use only paper sleeves.

PHYSIOLOGICAL DISORDERS

Phyllady is a phenomenon that occurs when floral induction is not complete and when the meristem reverts again to vegetative growth (Rünger, 1978). High nutrient levels, alkaline pH, or poor soil aeration may result in chlorosis.

POSTHARVEST

Harvest when 30 to 50% of the buds are mature. Flowers are very sensitive to ethylene; exposure to only 0.1 ppm produces floral abscission (Willumsen and Fjeld, 1995). Plants should be sprayed with 0.2 to 0.5 mM silver thiosulfate (STS) before flowers open. Shipping duration of more than 2 days in darkness is not recommended, even at 36 to 41°F (2 to 5°C), unless plants are treated with STS; then 4 days is acceptable.

Plants do not, unfortunately, hold up well in warm and dark home environments. Advise customers to place the plants in a well-lighted environment—25 to 100 fc (5 to 20 μmol $\cdot$ m^{-2} $\cdot$ s^{-1})—preferably below 68°F (20°C) (Cameron et al., 1981; L. Høyer, personal communication; Nell, 1993; Nowak and Rudnicki, 1990).

KEY POINTS

- This seed-propagated plant is used as a potted flowering plant, bedding plant, and occasional cut flower.
- Plants will flower under either LD or temperatures below 59°F (15°C), regardless of photoperiod.
- Plants must produce four to five pairs of leaves before LD treatments are effective.
- For floral induction, 46 to 50°F (8 to 10°C) is optimum.
- Plants are sensitive to overwatering yet wilt readily if underwatered.
- Whiteflies and root rot are common problems.
- Flowers are sensitive to ethylene.

BIBLIOGRAPHY

Adriansen, E. 1985. Kemisk vaekstregulering, pp. 142–162 in *Potteplanter I—Produktion, Metoder, Midler,* O.V. Christensen, A. Klougart, I.S. Pedersen, and K. Wikesjö, editors. Gartner-INFO, København, Denmark. (in Danish)

Anonymous. 1986. Calceolaria—Pockets for profit. *Bedding Plant Incorporated News* 17(8):6–7.

Bailey, L.H., and E.Z. Bailey. 1976. *Calceolaria,* pp. 199–200 in *Hortus Third: A Concise Dictionary of Plants Cultivated in the United States and Canada.* Macmillan, New York.

Cameron, A.C., M.S. Reid, and G.W. Hickman. 1981. Using STS to prevent flower shattering in potted flowering plants—Progress report in *Flower and Nursery Report: Fall.* Cooperative Extension Bulletin University of California, Davis.

Dreistadt, S.H. 2001. *Integrated Pest Management for Floriculture and Nurseries.* University of California Division of Agriculture and Natural Resources Publication 3402.

Hamrick, D. 2003. *Calceolaria,* pp. 275–277 in *Ball Redbook,* vol. 2, 17th ed. Ball Publishing, Batavia, Illinois.

Horst, R.K. 1990. *Calceolaria,* p. 572 in *Westcott's Plant Disease Handbook,* 5th ed. Van Nostrand Reinhold, New York.

Huxley, A., M. Griffiths, and M. Levy. 1992. *Calceolaria,* pp. 459–461 in *The New Royal Horticultural Society Dictionary of Gardening,* vol. 1. Stockton Press, New York.

Johansson, J. 1976. The regulation of growth and flowering in *Calceolaria* $\times$*speciosa* Lilia. *Acta Horticulturae* 64:239–244.

Nell, T. 1993. *Calceolaria crenatiflora,* p. 31 in *Flowering Potted Plants, Prolonging Shelf Performance.* Ball Publishing, Batavia, Illinois.

Nowak, J., and R.M. Rudnicki. 1990. *Postharvest Handling and Storage of Cut Flowers, Florist Greens and Potted Plants.* Timber Press, Portland, Oregon.

Poesch, G.H. 1931. Forcing plants with artificial light. *Proceedings of the American Society for Horticultural Science* 28:402–406.

Post, K. 1937. Further responses of miscellaneous plants to temperature. *Proceedings of the American Society for Horticultural Science* 34:627–629.

Rünger, W. 1975. Flower formation in *Calceolaria* $\times$*herbeohybrida* Voss. *Scientia Horticulturae* 3:45–64.

Rünger, W. 1978. Influence of temperature and day length after chilling and short day period on flowering of *Calceolaria* $\times$*herbeohybrida* Voss. *Scientia Horticulturae* 9:71–81.

Strømme, E., H.F. Wilkins, and W. Rünger. 1985. *Calceolaria,* pp. 108–111 in *Handbook of Flowering,* vol. II, A.H. Halevy, editor. CRC Press, Boca Raton, Florida.

White, B. 2003. Culture tips for *Calceolaria rugosa* Pita Petit. *GPN* 13(5):80.

White, J.W. 1975. Calceolaria, a year-round crop. *Pennsylvania Flower Growers Bulletin* 383(1):6–9.

White, J.W., and J.A. Biernbaum. 1984a. Effects of root-zone heating on growth and flowering of *Calceolaria. HortScience* 19:289–290.

White, J.W., and J.A. Biernbaum. 1984b. Effects of root-zone heating on elemental composition of calceolaria. *Journal of the American Society for Horticultural Science* 109:350–355.

Williams, K. 2001. Calceolaria: A cool temperature crop to generate cold cash. *Ohio Florists' Association Bulletin* 864:4–5.

Willumsen, K., and T. Fjeld. 1995. The sensitivity of some flowering potted plants to exogenous ethylene. *Acta Horticulturae* 405:362–367.

Zitter, T.D., M.L. Daughtrey, and J.P. Sanderson. 1989. Vegetable/horticulture crops: Spotted wilt virus, p. 107 in *Fact Sheet 735.90*, Cornell Cooperative Extension, Cornell University, Ithaca, New York.

Calendula

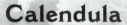

FIGURE II-1 CALENDULA *Calendula* plant being grown as an outdoor bedding plant.

INTRODUCTION

Common names: calendula, pot marigold.

Scientific name: Calendula officinalis L. (Huxley et al., 1992).

Family and related taxa: Compositae Gisete. The genus *Calendula* has only 20 species. The Compositae family is one of the most widely cultivated families in the world and includes *Aster, Centaurea, Chrysanthemum, Cosmos, Dahlia, Dendranthema, Echinacea, Gerbera, Helianthus, Liatris, Pericallis, Solidago, Tagetes,* and *Zinnia.*

Origin: Calendulas are native to southern Europe and the Mediterranean Sea basin (Bailey and Bailey, 1976).

Uses and current status: This species can be grown as a cut flower, bedding plant, or flowering potted plant (Fig. II-1 Calendula).

The plant commonly grows 2 ft (60 cm) tall; cut flower cultivars can grow to 4 ft (120 cm) tall. This annual has oblong leaves and flower heads can reach more than 4 in. (10 cm) wide. The flower color varies from a pale yellow to deep orange with either the same colored or dark brown centers. There are ray and disc florets in the inflorescences (Bailey and Bailey, 1976).

CULTIVARS

The traditional cut flower cultivars are being continually improved. New breeding lines of dwarf calendula are available for potted flowering plants.

PROPAGATION

Calendula is seed propagated with 3000 seed/oz (105/g). Seed can be germinated in plugs and transplanted 4 weeks later or sown directly into beds or pots. Sow under darkness at 70°F (21°C) (Armitage, 1985; Armitage et al., 1987; Holcomb and Mastalerz, 1985; Post, 1949).

FLOWERING CONTROL AND DORMANCY

Kamlesh and Kohli (1981) demonstrated that calendula was a LD plant with a distinctively short critical day of only 6.5 hr. Under a 5.5-hr photoperiod no floral initiation occurred, at 6 hr only 1 plant in 10 initiated floral primordia. No differences appeared in height or leaf number between plants exposed to photoperiods of 6.5 hr or longer and all plants flowered. Plants under only a 4-hr photoperiod were similar in appearance and height to plants under longer photoperiods, except they failed to flower. Plants are not sensitive to photoperiod until four leaves have unfolded (Kamlesh, 1977).

Interestingly, the SD plant *Xanthium stru-marium* L. will flower under LD conditions when shoots of a reproductive *C. officinalis* plant are grafted onto a vegetative *Xanthium* stock plant. However, flowering did not occur when a reproductive *Calendula* plant was the stock (van de Pol, 1971; Wilkins, 1986).

TEMPERATURE

The optimal temperature is 50°F (10°C). Greenhouse production is mainly from October to May. Winter field production is from February to May in frost-free areas; summer production in the north is from June to September (Post, 1949). Armitage (1985) and Armitage et al. (1987) grew 4-in. (10-cm) dwarf potted cultivars at 70°F (21°C) days and 60 to 62°F (16 to 17°C) nights, stating that 55°F (13°C) nights could be used if 2 weeks were added to the production time schedule.

LIGHT

Post (1949) stated that calendula is a profitable summer, field-grown crop, but should be grown under shade which will increase quality, stem length, and flower size. In the winter, maximum light intensities result in quality plants. Armitage et al. (1987) found that 50% shade did not delay flowering.

WATER

The medium should be kept consistently moist. Interestingly, cut flowers grown in benches are shorter with smaller flowers when compared with plants grown in ground beds due to the more constant moisture and cooler temperatures in ground beds (Post, 1949). If plants are grown dry, flowering is delayed (Reger, 1941). Post (1949) reported that some producers withhold water at the end of production to produce sturdy stems and to increase stem strength and vase life.

CARBON DIOXIDE

No data available.

NUTRITION

For field production a soil test should be taken before amending the soil. A standard application of superphosphate of 5 lb/100 ft^2 (0.25 kg · m^{-2}) is common with a source of nitrogen at 1 lb/100 ft^2 (0.05 kg · m^{-2}). For pot plant production, Armitage et al. (1987) used a constant 200 ppm N fertilizer, but leached every fourth irrigation to reduce soluble salts. If irradiance is low, nitrate nitrogen is preferred and should comprise at least 50% of the nitrogen. When flowering commences, nutrition levels should be lowered to 100 ppm N. Reducing nutrition at flowering increases postharvest longevity.

MEDIA

Over the years calendula have been grown in a wide variety of media. Armitage et al. (1987) grew potted plants in 1 peat:1 vermiculite. Certainly bark could be included in a potting mix (Armitage, 1985). The basic requirement for the medium is to be well drained and aerated, with a pH of 6.0 to 7.0.

HEIGHT CONTROL

None is required for cut flowers, which grow to be 3 to 4 ft (0.9 to 1.3 m) tall. For potted plants, even though genetically dwarfed, B-Nine (daminozide) sprays of 3500 ppm are used (Armitage et al., 1987). The first application is 4 to 5 weeks after germination or when three to four mature leaves have developed and again at visible bud, when the terminal bud is the size of a pea. Plugs can also be sprayed with 2500 ppm B-Nine during propagation stage 1 or with 5000 ppm B-Nine, 4 ppm Bonzi (paclobutrazol), or 1 ppm Sumagic (uniconazole) during stages 2 and 3 (Sawaya, 2001). Adriansen (1985) indicated that Cycocel (chlormequat) may also be effective. DIF is strongly effective (Warner and Erwin, 2001).

SPACING

Field spacing is at 10 × 10 in. (25 × 25 cm) and greenhouse spacing can be 8 × 12 in. (20 × 30 cm). For 4-in. (10-cm) pots, final spacing can be 7 × 7 in. (18 × 18 cm).

PINCHING AND DISBUDDING

For field production the terminal bud on some cultivars can be removed to encourage axillary shoot elongation and to increase the number of flowers harvested during a limited time span. For potted plants, two or more flowers will usually open simultaneously; otherwise the terminal bud will flower, followed by three to five axillary flowers (Armitage, 1985).

SUPPORT

Two layers of wire or plastic mesh can be used for cut flowers and layers raised as plants grow.

SCHEDULE AND TIMING

Timing for cut flower production depends not only on the season of the year, but also on location. Crop times can last from 8 to 16 weeks (Post, 1949). The production time for greenhouse-grown potted flowering plants varies from 10 to 12 weeks (Armitage, 1985; Armitage et al., 1987) (Tables II-1 and II-2 Calendula).

INSECTS

Aphids, leaf miners, whiteflies, nematodes, caterpillars, flea beetles, cucumber beetles, plant buds, and mealybugs have been reported (Armitage, 1985; Dreistadt, 2001; Post, 1949).

DISEASES

Aster yellows, transmitted by leaf hoppers, can be a problem for outdoor production. When soils are too wet and foliage is not allowed to dry, root rot (*Phytophthora*, *Pythium*, and *Rhizoctonia solani*), powdery mildew (*Sphaerotheca fuliginea* and *Erysiphe cichoracearum*), and other foliar diseases can occur (Armitage, 1985; Dreistadt, 2001; Horst, 1990; Post, 1949). Other diseases can include leaf spots (*Alternaria* and *Cercospora calendulae*), botrytis blight (*Botryis cinerea*), rust (*Coleosporium*, *Puccinia flaveriae*, and *P. melam-*

TABLE II-I CALENDULA

Sample production schedule for *Calendula* cut flowers.

Cultural Step	Production Time (weeks)	Temperature °F (°C)
Sow seed in plugs		
	2	70° (21°)
Germinate		
	2	70° (21°)
Transplant plugs to field, bench, or pot in:		
September	10–12	45–50° (7–10°)
October	14–16	
May	8–10	
For flowering in: (respectively)		
	November	
	January	
	June/July	

TABLE II-2 CALENDULA

Sample production schedule for *Calendula* for 4-in. (10-cm) potted flowering plants.

Cultural Step	Production Time (weeks)	Temperature °F (°C)
Sow seed in plugs		
	2	70 (21)
Germinate		
	2	Day: 70 (21) Night: 60–62 (16–17)[a]
Transplant to 4-in. (10-cm) pots, apply growth retardant [b] when 3 to 4 leaves are mature		
	4–5	Day: 70 (21) Night: 60–62 (16–17)[a]
Visible bud, apply growth retardant, [b] disbud terminal		
	2–3	Day: 70 (21) Night: 60–62 (16–17)[a]
Flower		
Total	10–12	

[a]If grown at cooler night temperatures of 55°F (13°C) and day temperatures, add 2 weeks to schedule.
[b]B-Nine.

podii), smut (*Entyloma calendulae*), southern blight (*Sclerotium rolfsii*), cottony rot (*Sclerotinia sclerotiorum*), and tomato spotted wilt virus (Dreistadt, 2001; Horst, 1990).

PHYSIOLOGICAL DISORDERS

Small flowers with weak stems may develop when greenhouse light intensities are too low and temperatures are too high (Post, 1949).

POSTHARVEST

Spring-produced flowers have better "keeping" quality than those from winter production (Post, 1949). Flowers should not be harvested prematurely, but rather when the flowers are fully developed. Stems should be placed in warm water with a floral preservative. Shipment of plants or flowers can occur at 39 to 41°F (4 to 5°C) for 3 to 6 days (Nowak and Rudnicki, 1990).

KEY POINTS

- This seed-propagated plant is used as a cool weather bedding plant, potted flowering plant, or most commonly, cut flower.
- Calendula is a LD plant with one of the shortest day length requirements known of only 6.5 hr; plants grown under 4-hr day lengths did not flower.

- Juvenility is present as plants must form four or more leaves before LD start.
- Calendula generally grows best at cool nights of 50°F (10°C) for cut flower production and 60 to 62°F (16 to 17°C) for potted plant production.

BIBLIOGRAPHY

Adriansen, E. 1985. Kemisk vækstregulering, pp. 142–162 in *Potteplanter I—Produktion, Metoder, Midler,* O.V. Christensen, A. Klougart, I.S. Pedersen, and K. Wikesjö, editors. Gartner-INFO, København, Denmark. (in Danish)

Armitage, A. 1985. Georgia takes a look at new crops. *Greenhouse Grower* 3(9):68–69.

Armitage, A.M., B. Bergmann, and E.L. Bell. 1987. Effect of daminozide and light intensity on growth and flowering of *Calendula* as a potted plant. *HortScience* 22:611–612.

Bailey, L.H., and E.Z. Bailey. 1976. *Calendula* L., p. 200 in *Hortus Third: A Concise Dictionary of Plants Cultivated in the United States and Canada.* Macmillan, New York.

Dreistadt, S.H. 2001. *Integrated Pest Management for Floriculture and Nurseries.* University of California Division of Agriculture and Natural Resources Publication 3402.

Holcomb, E.J., and J.W. Mastalerz. 1985. Seedling and seedling production, pp. 87–125 in *Bedding Plants III,* J.W. Mastalerz and J. White, editors. Pennsylvania Flower Growers, University Park, Pennsylvania.

Horst, R.K. 1990. *Calendula,* pp. 572–572 in *Westcott's Plant Disease Handbook,* 5th ed. Van Nostrand Reinhold, New York.

Huxley, A., M. Griffiths, and M. Levy. 1992. *Calendula,* p. 462 in *The New Royal Horticultural Society Dictionary of Gardening,* vol. 1. Stockton Press, New York.

Kamlesh, S.S. 1977. Effect of some regulatory substances on growth and development of *Calendula officinalis* in relation to photoperiod. MS. thesis, G.N.D. University, Amristar, India.

Kamlesh, S.S., and R.K. Kohli. 1981. *Calendula officinalis* L., a long day plant with an exceptionally low photoperiodic requirement for flowering. *Indian Journal of Plant Physiology* 24:299–303.

Nowak, J., and R.M. Rudnicki. 1990. *Postharvest Handling and Storage of Cut Flowers, Florist Greens and Potted Plants.* Timber Press, Portland, Oregon.

Post, K. 1949. *Calendula,* pp. 172, 358–360 in *Florist Crop Production and Marketing.* Orange Judd Publishing, New York.

Reger, M.W. 1941. The relation of soil moisture to the time of bloom of calendulas, larkspurs and geraniums. *Proceedings of the American Society for Horticultural Science* 39:381–383.

Sawaya, M. 2001. Plugs, pp. 50–53 in *Tips on Regulating Growth of Floriculture Crops,* M.L. Gaston, L.A. Kunkle, P.S. Konjoian, and M.F. Wilt, editors. Ohio Florists' Association Services, Columbus, Ohio.

van de Pol, P.A. 1971. The floral hormones of *Helianthus annuus* L., *Calendula officinalis* L. and *Xanthium strumarium* L. *Proceedings Koninklijke Nederlandse Akademie van Wetenschapper* 74:449–454. (in English)

Warner, R.M., and J.E. Erwin. 2001. Temperature, pp. 10–17 in *Tips on Regulating Growth of Floriculture Crops,* M.L. Gaston, L.A. Kunkle, P.S. Konjoian, and M.F. Wilt, editors. Ohio Florists' Association Services, Columbus, Ohio.

Wilkins, H. 1986. *Calendula officinalis,* pp. 53–55 in *Handbook of Flowering,* vol. V, A.H. Halevy, editor. CRC Press, Boca Raton, Florida.

Callistephus

FIGURE II-I CALLISTEPHUS Outdoor-grown *Callistephus* for cut flower production.

INTRODUCTION

Common name: China aster, annual aster.

Scientific name: *Callistephus chinensis* L. Nees. (Huxley et al., 1992).

Family and related taxa: Compositae Giseke. There is only one species in the genus *Callistephus* Cass. The Compositae family contains numerous other extensively cultivated genera including *Aster, Calendula, Centaurea, Chrysanthemum, Cosmos, Dahlia, Dendranthema, Echinacea, Gerbera, Helianthus, Liatris, Pericallis, Solidago, Tagetes,* and *Zinnia.*

Origin: China.

Uses and current status: This species has been used as a summer-flowering bedding plant and as a cut flower (Figs. II-1, II-2, II-3 and II-4 Callistephus). With the development of dwarf cultivars, China asters have also become a potted flowering plant.

The China aster, an herbaceous annual, flowers naturally in late summer and early autumn. The stems are erect and the leaves are alternate, triangularly ovate with dentated margins. The disc flowers in the center of the individual inflorescence are surrounded by the outer ray flowers. The numerous inflorescence classifications are similar to those for *Dendrathema ×grandiflorum,* the chrysanthemum. Flower colors vary from white to yellow to purple, and include violet, blue, red, rose, and pink (Bailey and Bailey, 1976; Honeywell, 1941; Maatsch and Nolting, 1971).

FIGURE II-2 CALLISTEPHUS *Callistephus* 'Daylight Red' spray cut flower.

CULTIVARS

Numerous cultivars are available for cut flower production in the field or in the greenhouse. Dwarf cultivars can be used as a flowering potted plant or bedding plant in the garden.

For plug production the following conditions are used (Hamrick, 2003):

- *Stage 1:* Seed not covered, 68 to 70°F (20 to 21°C), 4 to 5 days, 100 to 400 fc (20 to 80 μmol $\cdot$ m^{-2} $\cdot$ s^{-1})
- *Stage 2:* 68 to 70°F (20 to 21°C), 7 days, 500 to 1000 fc (100 to 200 μmol $\cdot$ m^{-2} $\cdot$ s^{-1}), and 50 to 75 ppm N once/week
- *Stage 3:* 65 to 68°F (18 to 20°C), 21 days, 1500 to 2000 fc (300 to 400 μmol $\cdot$ m^{-2} $\cdot$ s^{-1}), and 100 to 150 ppm N once/week
- *Stage 4:* 60 to 62°F (15 to 17°C), 7 days, 2500 to 3000 fc (500 to 600 μmol $\cdot$ m^{-2} $\cdot$ s^{-1}), and 100 to 150 ppm N once/week

Plugs should be ready for marketing or transplanting in 4 to 5 weeks. See Chapter 1, Propagation, for descriptions of stages.

FLOWERING CONTROL AND DORMANCY

The basic aspects of flowering have been reviewed by Cockshull (1985). The China aster is classified as a facultative LD plant with the critical photoperiod from 12 to 14 hr, although a 16-hr photoperiod is commonly used in commerce. For rapid floral initiation LD at 55 to 68°F (13 to 20°C) is recommended. At 55°F (13°C) or lower, the plant is an obligate LD plant, because it only forms a rosette under SD. However, once floral initiation has occurred, floral development is more rapid under SD and independent of temperature (Doorenbos, 1959; Hughes and Cockshull, 1965; Laurie and Poesch, 1932; Lin and Watson, 1950; Post, 1934). Gibberellic acid (GA) can substitute for LD under SD conditions (Doorenbos, 1959).

Juvenility appears to be present because 3-week-old plantlets did not flower sooner when shifted from SD to LD, whereas 4- to 5-week-old plants did. Apparently once the plant is mature enough to perceive the LD signal, only 7 LD are required for flower initiation (Doorenbos, 1959). A critical number of leaves, four or more, should form under SD before plants are shifted to LD. Increasing the number of SD before LD begins will increase leaf number and subsequently increase flower number and quality (Kofranek, 1954b).

FIGURE II-3 CALLISTEPHUS *Callistephus* 'Matsumoto' cut flower.

FIGURE II-4 CALLISTEPHUS *Callistephus* 'Matsumoto' cut flower production.

PROPAGATION

Propagation is by seed with an optimum germination temperature of 70 ± 4°F (21 ± 2°C) (Thompson and Cox, 1979). Even at 52°F (11°C), 50% of seeds germinate within 3 days. Little difference is noted if seeds are germinated in the light or the dark, although the light treatment had slightly higher numbers of seeds germinating. Seeds should never be allowed to dry out.

TEMPERATURE

Under LD the number of days to floral initiation was increased by 50°F (10°C) when compared with 65°F (18°C) production temperatures. After initiation, flower development under SD is more rapid at 65 than 50°F (18 than 10°C) (Lin and Watson, 1950). Regardless of the photoperiod, temperatures should be above 55°F (13°C) (Biebel, 1936; Lin and Watson, 1950; Post, 1934).

LIGHT

Once plants become established, LD can commence (Kofranek, 1954a, b). In southern California crops were given LD treatments from August 20 to April 20 (Kofranek, 1954b), whereas in Florida, Conover (1969) successfully used a 2- to 3-hr incandescent night break from September 10 to April 20. The LD photoperiod can be 15 hr (natural day + night break) and used for 7 to 13 weeks. Ten weeks of LD appear to be optimal in Florida (Gruis and Joiner, 1960). In New York, Boodley (1961) advised lighting for 4 hr (2200 to 0200) from August 15 to November 30, then for 5 hr from December 1 to January 30 and back to 4 hr February 1 to May 10. Natural days are sufficiently long from May 10 to August 15. Boodley (1961) published a production schedule for mid–North America. In England Cockshull (1966), using only a 1-hr night break in winter, found that this treatment promoted leaf growth and expansion, which in turn caused rapid floral induction. Cyclic lighting (1 min on/1 min off) for 16 hr was as effective as a 1-hr night break (Cockshull and Hughes, 1969). Kofranek (1954a, b) reported that only 1 to 2 fc (0.12 to 0.4 μmol $\cdot$ m^{-2} $\cdot$ s^{-1}) are needed for LD treatments. Zande and Blacquiere (1992) noted that an even lower threshold, 0.5 fc (0.1 μmol $\cdot$ m^{-2} $\cdot$ s^{-1}), was effective and that incandescent, fluorescent, and low-pressure sodium lights were equally effective light sources. Biebel (1936) stated that LD should commence 15 to 45 days after germination. Lighting should cease when the flower buds are 0.88 in. (2.3 cm) in diameter (Conover, 1969). As stated earlier, floral development is hastened by SD.

The highest quality plants are grown in the north under cloth houses, where summer light and temperatures are reduced and plants are protected from wind and direct rain. Cloth houses also reduce the incidence of aster yellows disease transmitted by leaf hoppers (Conover, 1969).

WATER

Asters do not have a deep root system, so plants should not be water stressed (Conover, 1969; Honeywell, 1941). Conover (1969) suggested subirrigation to keep foliage dry for disease prevention and to prevent washing of various protective chemicals from the leaves.

CARBON DIOXIDE

Carbon dioxide (600 to 900 ppm) hastened date of flower by 7 or fewer days and leaf weights were increased by 20 to 30% (Hughes and Cockshull, 1969).

NUTRITION

Supply 100 to 150 ppm N during greenhouse production (Armitage and Laushman, 2003). Conover (1969) suggested that excessive nitrogen reduced the keeping quality and increased *Alternaria* disease problems. When three nutritional levels were compared, 2, 4, or 8 lb/100 ft^2 (98, 195, or 391 g $\cdot$ m^{-2}) of 8–0–8 fertilizer, the lowest and highest levels resulted in reduced stem length and flower number compared with the intermediate rate (Gruis and Joiner, 1960). When plants are actively growing, adequate nutrient levels should be used; if plants are not actively growing (SD), nutrition should be reduced. When salt levels are high or when boron levels are greater than 2.5 ppm, plant height and flower size decrease. Kohl et al. (1957) also determined foliar nutrient levels.

MEDIA

Plants are grown in a wide range of media, which need to be well drained and pasteurized (see Diseases section later).

HEIGHT CONTROL

No height control is needed for cut flower production. Genetically short plants are available for potted flowering production and for bedding plants. A-Rest (ancymidol) sprays at 7 to 26 ppm and B-Nine (daminozide) sprays at 2500 to 5000 ppm may be effective (Bell, 2001). Interestingly, mechanical brushing of plants for an hour each day reduced plant height (Autio et al., 1994). China aster has strong response to DIF (Warner and Erwin, 2001).

SPACING

The most common spacing for cut flowers is 10 × 10 in. (25 × 25 cm) in the greenhouse. In the field, spacing ranges from 4 × 4 to 12 × 18 in. (10 × 10 to 30 × 46 cm) (Honeywell, 1941).

PINCHING AND DISBUDDING

Kofranek (1951) pinched plants when they were 5 to 6 in. (13 to 15 cm) tall; however, no advantage could be seen. No disbudding is needed.

SUPPORT

If grown outside, one or two layers of support may be needed; none may be needed in the greenhouse.

SCHEDULE AND TIMING

Connors (1933) in New Jersey stated that 14 to 18 weeks were required from seed to flower, depending on season and on cultivar chosen, which would allow three crops per year. For field production, seeds are sown in a greenhouse in March, April, and May, then transplanted outside as soon as the danger of frost is over (Connors, 1933). Under LD total floral induction requires 6 weeks (cultivar and season dependent) from date of germination (Doorenbos, 1959). Review the production results of Kofranek's (1951, 1954a) timing and lighting schedules in Table II-1 Callistephus. Two GA sprays of 250 ppm applied 4 and 6 weeks after transplanting decreased crop time but increased stem length and flower diameter (Jayanthi and Narayana-Gowda, 1991).

INSECTS

Aphids, various caterpillars, leafhoppers, leaf miners, spider mites, whitefly, and thrips have been reported as problems (Conover, 1969; Honeywell, 1941; Kofranek, 1954a, b).

DISEASES

Disease control has been a limiting factor in production. Even with *Fusarium*-resistant cultivars, the soil must be pasteurized and not used again for more than 3 years. If nonresistant cultivars are used, one crop every 5 years is recommended. Aster yellow virus is also a serious problem, especially in outdoor production in the central United States. Control aster yellows by removing infected plants and controlling the leaf hopper vector (Horst, 1990). *Alternaria, Ascochyta, Botrytis,* and *Stemphylium* can be controlled by environmental or chemical means. Medium pasteurization should control *Fusarium, Phytophthora, Pythium, Rhizoctonia,* and *Verticillium,* all soilborne diseases. Seed treatments historically were considered necessary because seedborne diseases such as *Ascochyra, Alternaria, Botrytis, Fusarium,* and *Septoria* were found on the seed surface (Gloyer, 1931). Cottony rot (*Sclerotinia sclerotiorum*), powdery mildew (*Erysiphe cichoracearum*), and rusts (*Coleosporium asterum*) have also been reported (Dreistadt, 2001).

PHYSIOLOGICAL DISORDERS

No physiological disorders have been reported.

TABLE II-I CALLISTEPHUS
Year-round flowering schedule for *Callistephus* at minimum temperatures of 13°F (55°C) and 4- or 5-hr incandescent LD night interruptions (during August 15 to May 10 only) applied from seed germination until plants were 24 in. (60 cm) tall (Boodley, 1961; Nau, 1999). Plants grown warmer will flower in a shorter time than indicated.

Proposed Flowering Date	Seed Sown	Seedling Transplanted	Plants Benched
January	July 15	August 10	September 11
February	August 15	September 10	November 1
March	September 10	October 1	December 1
April	October 20	November 15	January 1
May	December 20	January 10	March 1
June	February 1	February 20	April 1
July	March 15	April 1	May 15
August	April 20	May 10	June 15
September	May 20	June 10	July 15
October	June 10	July 1	August 1
November	June 20	July 15	August 20
December	July 10	August 1	September 1

POSTHARVEST

Flowers are harvested when outer ray florets begin to open and are stored at 32 to 39°F (0 to 4°C). Harvested stems were pretreated with various solutions for 17 hr at 72°F (22°C) under 100 fc (15 μmol · m^{-2} · s^{-1}) of fluorescent lamps and then were simulated shipped for 0 or 4 days at 36 or 45°F (1.7 or 7°C). Regardless of temperature during shipping, transportation reduced vase life. Silver nitrate (10-sec dip in 1000 ppm of solution) or Physan-20 (200 ppm), a microorganism inhibitor, increased vase life by two to three times. Because silver nitrate is not available, silver thiosulfate (STS) should be tested and is likely to be effective. Sugar (5%) and citric acid (75 ppm) added to these solutions further increased vase life (Kofranek et al., 1978). Conover (1969) stated that high nitrogen fertilizer will reduce keeping quality and will increase susceptibility to *Botrytis* and *Alternaria*.

KEY POINTS

- This seed-propagated plant is used as a cut flower, potted flowering plant, and summer bedding plant.
- China aster is an obligate LD plant below 55°F (13°C) and a facultative LD plant at 55 to 68°F (13 to 20°C).
- Juvenility is present because plants must form four or more leaves before LD start.
- China aster is susceptible to numerous diseases, the most important of which are *Fusarium* and aster yellows.

BIBLIOGRAPHY

Armitage, A.M., and J.M. Laushman 2003. *Callistephus chinensis*, pp. 151–161 in *Specialty Cut Flowers*, 2nd ed. Timber Press, Portland, Oregon.

Autio, J., I. Voipio, and T. Koivunen. 1994. Responses of aster, dusty miller, and petunia seedlings to daily exposure to mechanical stress. *HortScience* 29:1449–1452.

Bailey, L.H., and E.Z. Bailey. 1976. *Callistephus*, pp. 202–203 in *Hortus Third: A Concise Dictionary of Plants Cultivated in the United States and Canada*. Macmillan, New York.

Bell, M. 2001. Bedding plants to seed geraniums, pp. 54–62 in *Tips on Regulating Growth of Floriculture Crops*, M.L. Gaston, L.A. Kunkle, P.S. Konjoian, and M.F. Wilt, editors. Ohio Florists' Association Services, Columbus, Ohio.

Biebel, J. 1936. Temperature, photoperiod, flowering and morphology in cosmos and China aster. *Proceedings of the American Society of Horticultural Science* 34:635–643.

Boodley, J. 1961. Asters can be grown on a year-round production schedule. *Florists Review* 128(3328):29, 71, 76.

Cockshull, K.E. 1966. Effects of night-break treatment on leaf area and leaf dry weight in *Callistephus chinensis*. *Annals of Botany* 30:791–806.

Cockshull, K.E. 1985. *Callistephus chinensis*, pp. 112–114 in *Handbook of Flowering*, vol. II, A.H. Halevy, editor. CRC Press, Boca Raton, Florida.

Cockshull, K.E., and A.P. Hughes. 1969. Growth and dry-weight distribution in *Callistephus chinensis* as influenced by lighting treatment. *Annals of Botany* 33:367–379.

Connors, C.H. 1933. China asters. *New Jersey Agricultural Experiment Station, Circular 289*, New Brunswick, New Jersey.

Conover, C.A. 1969. Commercial aster production in Florida. *Florida Flower Grower* 6(9): 1–8.

Doorenbos, J. 1959. Responses of China aster to daylength and gibberellic acid. *Euphytica* 8:69–75.

Dreistadt, S.H. 2001. *Integrated Pest Management for Floriculture and Nurseries*. University of California Division of Agriculture and Natural Resources Publication 3402.

Gloyer, W.O. 1931. China aster seed treatment and storage. *New York State Agricultural Experiment Station Technical Bulletin 177*, Geneva, New York.

Gruis, J.T., and J.N. Joiner. 1960. The effect of periods of long days and levels of fertilization on China aster, *Callistephus chinensis*, 'All Saints.' *Proceedings of the Florida State Horticultural Society* 73:378–381.

Hamrick, D. 2003. *Callistephus*, pp. 280–282 in *Ball Redbook*, vol. 2, 17th ed. Ball Publishing, Batavia, Illinois.

Honeywell, E.R. 1941. Aster culture, in *Purdue University Agricultural Experiment Station, Circular 200*, Lafayette, Indiana.

Horst, R.K. 1990. China aster, pp. 542–543 in *Westcott's Plant Disease Handbook*, 5th ed. Van Nostrand Reinhold, New York.

Hughes, A.P., and K.E. Cockshull. 1965. Interrelations of flowering and vegetative growth in *Callistephus chinensis* (variety 'Queen of the Market'). *Annals of Botany* 29:131–151.

Hughes, A.P., and K.E. Cockshull. 1969. Effects of carbon dioxide concentrations on the growth of *Callistephus chinensis* cultivar Johannistag. *Annals of Botany* 33:351–365.

Huxley, A., M. Griffiths, and M. Levy. 1992. *Callistephus*, p. 467 in *The New Royal Horticultural Society Dictionary of Gardening*, vol. 1. Stockton Press, New York.

Jayanthi, R., and J.V. Narayana-Gowda. 1991. Influence of gibberellic acid on flowering and plant sugar content of china aster (*Callistephus chinensis* (L) Nees) cv. 'Heart of France', pp. 389–392 in *Horticulture—New Technologies and Applications*. Kluwer Academic Publishers, the Netherlands.

Kofranek, A.M. 1951. *Lighting China Aster*. Division of Floriculture and Ornamental Horticulture, University of California, Los Angeles.

Kofranek, A.M. 1954a. Fall production of quality king asters grown out of doors. *Southern Florist and Nurseryman* 67(12):76, 78–79.

Kofranek, A.M. 1954b. Artificial light promotes early flowering of asters. *Southern Florist and Nurseryman* 67(43):18.

Kofranek, A.M., E. Evans, J. Kubota, and D.S. Farnham. 1978. Chemical pretreatments for China asters to increase flower longevity. *Florists Review* 162(4206):26, 70–72.

Kohl, H.C., Jr., A.M. Kofranek, and O.R. Lunt. 1957. Response of China aster to high salt and boron concentration. *Proceedings of the American Society for Horticultural Science* 70:437–441.

Laurie, A., and G.N. Poesch. 1932. Photoperiodism—the value of supplementary illumination and reduction of light on flowering of plants in the greenhouse. *Ohio Agricultural Experiment Station Bulletin* 512:1–42.

Lin, L.C., and D.P. Watson. 1950. The influence of daylength and temperature on the growth and flowering of *Callistephus chinensis* Nees. *Proceedings of the American Society of Horticultural Science* 55:441–446.

Maatsch, R., and G. Nolting. 1971. Sortenliste von *Callistephus chinensis* Nees. (Internationale Registerliste). Institut für Zierpflanzenbau der Technische University, Hanover, Germany. (in German)

Nau, J. 1999. *Ball Culture Guide, The Encyclopedia of Seed Germination*, 2nd ed. Ball Publishing, Batavia, Illinois.

Post, K. 1934. The effects of daylength and light intensity on vegetative growth and flowering of the China aster (*Callistephus chinensis*). *Proceedings of the American Society of Horticultural Science* 32:626–630.

Thompson, P.A., and S.A. Cox. 1979. Germination responses of half-hardy annuals. 2. China aster (*Callistephus chinensis*). *Seed Science and Technology* 7:201–207.

Warner, R.M., and J.E. Erwin. 2001. Temperature, pp. 10–17 in *Tips on Regulating Growth of Floriculture Crops*, M.L. Gaston, L.A. Kunkle, P.S. Konjoian, and M.F. Wilt, editors. Ohio Florists' Association Services, Columbus, Ohio.

Zande, de Graff-van der, M.T., and T. Blacquiere. 1992. Light quality during long day treatment for poinsettia and China aster. *Acta Horticulturae* 327:87–93.

Camellia

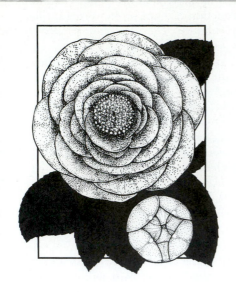

FIGURE II-1 CAMELLIA *Camellia japonica* 'Alba Supreme' flower.

INTRODUCTION

Common name: Camellia.

Scientific name: *Camellia japonica* L. (Huxley et al., 1992).

Family and related taxa: Theaceae D. Don. *Camellia japonica* L. is only one of between 100 and 150 *Camellia* species in the family.

Origin: *Camellias* are native to eastern Asia. *C. japonica* is native to the coastal areas of Japan, southern Korea, and Taiwan (Bailey and Bailey, 1976). Several rare, yellow flowered species exist in southeastern China and were first reported in 1990 (Lifang and Kaiyun, 1990). *C. chrysantha* (Hu) Tuyama can be viewed in the botanical garden at Stellenbosch University, South Africa. *C. sinensis* (L.) Kuntze. leaves are the source of the worldwide beverage English tea.

Uses and current status: *C. japonica* is commonly grown as an outdoor shrub in mild climates (Zones 8 and 9) and the spectacular flowers can be used in corsages or floated in water for decorative purposes. Camellia leaves can be used to cover objects by stapling, taping, gluing or wiring them to the object.

Camellias have dark evergreen elliptical glossy leaves. The large attractive flowers are single or double and colored red, pink, or white (Fig. II-1 Camellia).

CULTIVARS

Hundreds of cultivars of *Camellia japonica* exist. *C. ×williamsii* W. W. Sim. hybrids are popular for their unusually large flowers and can be used as potted plants.

PROPAGATION

Propagation is by seed, mature shoot cuttings [3.25 in. (8 cm) long], air layering, grafting, or *in vitro* (Bailey and Bailey, 1976; Ballester et al., 1997; French and Alsbury, 1989; Kato, 1989; Rünger and Cockshull, 1985). For cutting production, difficult-to-root cultivars benefit from 580 fc (75 μmol $\cdot$ m^{-2} $\cdot$ s^{-1}) HID lighting used during the day (French and Alsbury, 1989). Peat:perlite (1:1) at 70°F (21°C) can be used for propagation.

FLOWERING CONTROL AND DORMANCY

Flower initiation, differentiation, development, and opening is primarily controlled by seasonal variations in temperature and photoperiod. Flower initiation and development occur when temperatures are above 65°F (18°C) and daylengths are long. Rubel (1936) and Post (1949) discussed hastening or delaying flowering to extend the flowering season. Temperature control is critical. Most species initiate flowers in the summer under natural LD or under incandescent day extensions, which result in a 13.5-hr daylength. Afterward, days should become shorter and temperatures lowered, during which time the flower buds develop and become dormant. Flowers will open in late winter or early spring when temperatures increase. Optimum flower initiation, in terms of rapidity and numbers, occurs at temperatures between 75 and 81°F (24 and 27°C). Dormancy is broken by cool temperatures. Forcing should occur at 50 to 60°F (10 to 16°C) (Rünger and Cockshull, 1985).

TEMPERATURE

Flower initiation occurs at temperatures above 65°F (18°C) (Bonner, 1947; McElwee, 1952; Rünger and Cockshull, 1985). Flower buds develop rapidly at temperatures below 60°F (16°C). Flower abscission can occur if temperatures go above 60°F (16°C), which also reduces flower size and pigment intensity. Although the temperature during late fall and winter can range from 32 to 50°F (0 to 10°C), 40 to 50°F (4 to 10°C) is recommended. The low temperatures must be continuously applied for flower opening or flower abscission may occur (Bonner, 1947; Post, 1949).

LIGHT

Plants are usually grown under partial shade in the landscape (Bonner, 1947; McElwee, 1952; Rünger and Cockshull, 1985). Plants can tolerate full winter light; shade reduces flower production. Light is reduced by 35% during propagation. Plants tolerate full sun if the medium is moist.

WATER

The medium should be kept moist. If the medium becomes dry, leaves may have necrotic edges and flowers may abort. High humidity during flowering is desired (Post, 1949).

CARBON DIOXIDE

No data are available. However, most production is outside.

NUTRITION

Nutrition should be high during active vegetative growth, just after flowering, and then reduced (Bonner, 1947; Rünger and Cockshull, 1985; Post, 1949). Post (1949) recommended monthly applications of 360 ppm N from 15–30–15.

MEDIA

The medium should have a 5.5 to 6.0 pH (McElwee, 1952; Post, 1949). A mixture of peat moss and organic soil (1:1) can be used. Good drainage is required.

HEIGHT CONTROL

Several plant growth regulators including Cycocel (chlormequat) and Bonzi (paclobutrazol) have been reported to not only reduce inter-node elongation but also increase flower bud numbers. These chemicals should be applied during early flower initiation and active vegetative growth (Rünger and Cockshull, 1985; Wilkinson and Richards, 1988). B-Nine (daminozide) may also have a slight effect (Adriansen, 1985).

SPACING

Large specimens are spaced enough to prevent overlapping foliage. Post (1949) recommends 3-ft (9-m) spacing between plants.

PINCHING AND DISBUDDING

Pinching and growth regulators can be used to produce compact, well-branched landscape plants. Axillary flower buds can be removed to increase the size of the terminal flower if it is to be used as a cut flower. Flower size and development rate have been reported to be increased by gibberellic acid (GA_3).

SUPPORT

None required.

SCHEDULE AND TIMING

Plants flower naturally during late winter and early spring or when temperatures are held at 40 to 50°F (4 to 10°C). If grown for cut flowers, only large 6-ft (9-m) specimens are used. Camellias for cut flower production were once grown in greenhouses in the north, but they are now grown in the south under shade (Post, 1949). Smaller pot sizes are produced by southern nurseries for landscapes.

INSECTS

Thrips, aphids, scale, spider mites, whiteflies, mealybugs, and various caterpillars can be problems (Dreistadt, 2001; Post, 1949).

DISEASES

Camellias are subject to numerous diseases of which flower blight (*Ciborinia camelliae*) can be particularly devastating (Dreistadt, 2001; Horst, 1990). Because flower blight is typically spread through container-grown plants, one recommendation is to purchase only bare root materials on which all flower buds showing color have been removed. Buds can be removed by application of Florel (ethephon), but results vary greatly with season, cultivar, and concentration (Woolf et al., 1992). Other diseases include leaf spots (*Pestalotia quepini, Phyllosticta camelliae*, and *P. camelliaecola*), canker dieback (*Glomerella cingulata*), gray mold (*Botrytis cinerea*), and nematodes (Horst, 1990). Root and crown rot (*Armillaria, Pythium, Phytophthora, Rhizoctonia*, and *Thielaviopsis*), *Colletotrichum* shoot dieback, and camellia yellow mosaic virus can also be problems (Dreistadt, 2001).

PHYSIOLOGICAL DISORDERS

Flower bud abscission can occur due to high temperatures during flower development and opening.

POSTHARVEST

Cut camellia flowers, without foliage, are harvested when fully open and stored at 45°F (70°C). Flowers last only 2 to 4 days. Camellia foliage can also be cut and stored at 39°F (49°C). Silver thiosulfate (STS) (0.2 mM) can prevent flower abscission on cut stems (Doi and Reid, 1996).

KEY POINTS

- *Camellia* is used as a corsage cut flower, garden shrub, and occasionally as a potted flowering plant.
- Propagation is by seed, cuttings, air layering, grafting, or *in vitro*.
- Flowers are initiated under the LD of summer, become dormant under the SD and cool temperatures of fall, and open during late fall to early spring.
- Growth regulators, pruning, and proper cultivar selection are used for height control in potted plant production.
- Numerous diseases can be a problem.

BIBLIOGRAPHY

Adriansen, E. 1985. Kemisk vækstregulering, pp. 142–162 in *Potteplanter I—Produktion, Metoder, Midler*, O.V. Christensen, A. Klougart, I.S. Pedersen, and K. Wikesjö, editors. Gartner-INFO, København, Denmark. (in Danish)

Bailey, L.H., and E.Z. Bailey. 1976. *Camellia japonica* L., pp. 208–210 in *Hortus Third: A Concise Dictionary of Plants Cultivated in the United States and Canada*. Macmillan, New York.

Ballester, A., L.V. Janeiro, and A.M. Vieitez. 1997. Cold storage of shoot cultures and alginate encapsulation of shoot tips of *Camellia japonica* L. and *Camellia reticulata* Lindley. *Scientia Horticulturae* 71:67–78.

Bonner, J. 1947. Flower bud initiation and flower opening in the camellia. *Proceedings of the American Society for Horticultural Science* 50:401–408.

Doi, M., and M.S. Reid. 1996. Postharvest characteristics of cut *Camellia japonica* L. 'Kumasaka.' *Postharvest Biology and Technology* 7:331–340.

Dreistadt, S.H. 2001. *Integrated Pest Management for Floriculture and Nurseries*. University of California Division of Agriculture and Natural Resources Publication 3402.

French, C.J., and J. Alsbury. 1989. Supplementary lighting and CO_2 mist influence rooting of *Camellia japonica*. *HortScience* 24:452–454.

Horst, R.K. 1990. *Camellia*, p. 576 in *Westcott's Plant Disease Handbook*, 5th ed. Van Nostrand Reinhold, New York.

Huxley, A., M. Griffiths, and M. Levy. 1992. *Camellia*, pp. 479–484 in *The New Royal Horticulture Society Dictionary of Gardening*, vol. 1. Stockton Press, New York.

Kato, M. 1989. Polyploides of camellia through culture of somatic embryos. *HortScience* 24: 1023–1025.

Lifang, X., and Kaiyun, G. 1990. An introduction to yellow camellia. *International Camellia Journal*, Oct.15–23.

McElwee, E.W. 1952. The influence of photoperiod on the vegetative and reproductive growth of the common camellia. *Proceedings of the American Society for Horticultural Science* 60:473–478.

Post, K. 1949. *Camellia japonica*, pp. 369–376 in *Florist Crop Production*. Orange Judge Publishers, New York.

Rubel, R.O., Jr. 1936. *Camellia culture.* Longview, Crichton, Alabama.

Rünger, W., and K.E. Cockshull. 1985. *Camellia japonica,* pp. 115–116 in *Handbook of Flowering,* vol. II, A.H. Halevy, editor. CRC Press, Boca Raton, Florida.

Wilkinson, R.I., and D. Richards. 1988. Influence of paclobutrazol on the growth and flowering of *Camellia* ×*williamsii. HortScience* 23:359–360.

Woolf, A.B., J. Clemens, and J.A. Plummer. 1992. Selective removal of floral buds from *Camellia* with ethephon. *HortScience* 27:32–34.

Campanula

FIGURE II-I CAMPANULA   *Campanula medium* 'Champion Pink' cut flower.

INTRODUCTION

Common names: campanula, bellflower, harebell, bluebell.

Scientific name: *Campanula* L. species (Huxley et al., 1992).

Family and related taxa: Campanulaceae Juss. Several important commercial species are *C. isophylla* Moretti, *C. carpatica* Jacq., *C. elatines* L., *C. fragilis* Cyr., *C. lactiflora* Bieb., *C. medium* L., *C. persicifolia* L., *C. poscharskyana* Degen., and *C. pyramidalis* L. This family includes more than 300 herbaceous species, which are annual, biennial, or perennial. *Lobelia* and *Platycodon* are also members of the Campanulaceae family.

Origin: Northern Hemisphere, especially the Caucasus, between the Black and Caspian Seas, the Balkans and the Mediterranean Sea (Bailey, 1933; Bailey and Bailey, 1976).

Uses and current status: Campanulas are commonly used as bedding plants, potted flowering plants, and cut flowers. Campanulas are an important crop in northern Europe, especially in Scandinavia where they are grown for spring sales in 4-in. (10-cm) pots or in hanging baskets (Adams, 1991; Armitage, 1987; Madson and Madson, 1986; Moe, 1977a; Whitman et al., 1995).

Most *Campanula* species form rosettes before stem elongation and flowering. The leaves are alternate; the flowers are showy and bell-like (hence the common name bellflower) and vary in size and form. The five-lobed corolla can be violet-blue, purple, pink, or white (Bailey, 1933; Bailey and Bailey, 1976; Wellensiek, 1985) (Fig. II-1 Campanula).

CULTIVARS

Bailey's 1953 book, *The Garden of Bellflowers in North America,* describes 140 *Campanula* species for garden use. In commercial floriculture, however, only the species listed under the family section are commonly grown (Adams, 1991; Armitage, 1987; Madson and Madson, 1986; Moe, 1977a, 1981). New interest and demand can be expected with improved selections of vegetatively propagated cultivars, which exhibit compact and uniform growth, and with the new F_1 hybrids (Table II-1 Campanula).

TABLE II-I CAMPANULA

General information on several important perennial greenhouse *Campanula* species and cultivars (Bailey, 1933; Bailey and Bailey, 1976).

Species and Cultivar	Native Location	Common Name	Height in. (cm)	Leaves in. (cm)	Flowers in. (cm) Color
C. carpatica	Carpathians	Tussock bellflower	8–18 (2–45)	2 (5)	1–2 (3–5) Blue-lilac
C. carpatica 'Clips'			8–10 (20–25)	2 (5)	1–2 (3–5) Blue, lilac, white
C. carpatica 'Karl Foerster'			6–18 (15–45)	2 (5)	2 (5) Violet-blue
C. elatines	Adriatic and eastward	Adriatic bellflower	6–8 (15–20)	1 (2.5)	0.5–0.75 (1.5–2) Blue, white
C. isophylla	Italy	Italian bellflower, Star-of-Bethlehem	10–12 (25–30)	1.5 (4)	1–1.5 (2.5–4) Pale to dark blue, white
C. medium	S. Europe	Canterbury bells	24–48 (60–120)	2 (5)	1–2 (2.5–5) Purple, pink, white
C. persicifolia	S. and E. Europe, temperate Asia	Peach-leaf bellflower	12–36 (30–90)	2 (5)	1–1.5 (2.5–4) Purple, white
C. poscharskyana	N. Yugoslavia	none	12 (30)	1–2.5 (2.5–6)	1.25–1.5 (3–4) Bright lilac, white

PROPAGATION

Plants can be propagated by seed, vegetative cuttings, or divisions depending on the species. Historically, the most important species, *C. isophylla,* was propagated from cuttings. However, new vigorous uniform F_1 hybrids are available for both *C. isophylla* and *C. carpatica* (Adams, 1991; Madson and Madson, 1986). Seeds for the perennial species can be sown in the greenhouse at 65 to 70°F (18 to 21°C) in the early spring and moved outdoors after frost. Primed *C. medium* seed germinated faster and more uniformly than unprimed seed (Bosma et al., 2002). Biennial seed can be sown in the summer, then overwintered outside for flowering the following year. Species vary in cold tolerance (Bailey, 1933). All stock plants and juvenile seedlings must be kept vegetative under SD photoperiods of 8 to 12 hr (Adams, 1991; Armitage, 1987; Madson and Madson, 1986; Moe, 1977a, b) (Table II-2 Campanula).

FLOWERING CONTROL AND DORMANCY

Reproductive growth occurs for *C. isophylla, C. carpatica,* and *C. poscharskyana* when the light period is longer than 14 hr (Heide, 1965; Madson and Madson, 1986; Moe, 1977b, 1981; Moe and Heide, 1985; Whitman et al., 1995, 1997). Although the critical day length decreases with increasing temperatures, it is 14 hr at 59 to 70°F (15 to 21°C) (Heide, 1965). Runkle et al. (1996) recommended 16-hr day lengths for *C. carpatica;* cold had no effect on flowering. These LD treatments must be maintained even after the visible bud stage has been reached because shoots revert back to vegetative growth if returned to SD.

C. fragilis, a seed-propagated hanging basket plant, is also an LD plant (Zimmer, 1985a). A 4-hr night interruption was most effective when used in the middle of a 16-hr dark period. The critical day length was between 12 and 14 hr. *C. pyramidalis,* a plant with a 5-ft (152-cm) inflorescence and 100 to 200 flowers, develops rosette offsets from a perennial root. It can be kept vegetative for 5 years at 68°F (20°C) (Zimmer, 1985b). Bolting is regulated by low temperatures of 46°F (8°C) for 6 to 8 weeks and by 14- to 15-hr LDs. The warmer the preinduction temperature, the longer the low-temperature treatment required. Seedlings of this species must be 7 months old be-

TABLE II-2 CAMPANULA

Propagation protocols for selected *Campanula* species (Adams, 1991; Armitage, 1987; Bailey, 1933; Bailey and Bailey, 1976; Madson and Madson, 1986; Moe, 1977a).

Species	Method	Temperature °F (°C)	Light Intensity	Comments
C. carpatica 'Clips'	Seed	65–70 (18–21)	1000–2500 fc (200–500 μmol · m^{-2} · s^{-1})	Uniform flowering
C. Carpatica 'Karl Foerster'		70 (21)		After germination, lower to 65 to 68°F (18 to 20°) and increase light level to 2500 fc (500 μmol · m^{-2} · s^{-1})
C. elatines	Seed	Field	Full sunlight	Plant plugs in spring for garden center sales.
C. isophylla	Cuttings Seed	65 (18) 60–70 (16–21)	Use HID lighting	Roots in 17–18 days; use 1000 to 1500 ppm IBA 5-sec dip. Germinates in 21 days; keep vegetative by SD
C. medium	Seed	60–70 (16–21)	Full sunlight	Germinates in 14–21 days; susceptible to damping-off; keep vegetative by SD
C. persicifolia	Seed	60–70 (16–21)	Full sunlight	Germinates in 14–21 days
C. poscharskyana	Cuttings Seed	70 (21) 68–70 (20–21)	Full sunlight	During October; after germination, lower to 65°F (18°C)

fore they respond to precooling and LD (Zimmer, 1985b).

C. persicifolia requires 12 weeks of 40°F (5°C) cold treatment for flowering (Iversen and Weiler, 1994). A number of other species and cultivars require a 12 to 15 week 41°F (5°C) cold treatment including *C. garganica* Ten., *C. glomerata* L. 'Superba' *C. punctata* Lam. 'Cherry Bells' and *C.* 'Wedding Bells' (B. Fausey, personal communication).

C. medium, "Canterbury Bells," a popular garden biennial, has a complex but remarkable environmental sequence (Wellensiek, 1985). Flowers are initiated only after vernalization under SD followed by LD. Only older seedlings perceive the cold and SD signals. Stem elongation occurs without flowering when treated with gibberellic acid (GA$_3$) under SD. If these elongated plants are cold treated, they flower under LD at the same time as the vernalized plants grown under SD and subsequently placed under LD.

New cultivars of *C. medium* are available that flower rapidly without vernalization and in response to LD. *C. medium* 'Champion' is an obligate LD plant with a critical photoperiod between 8 and 12 hr and plants are not fully mature until they have developed 8 to 9 leaves (Cavins and Dole, 2001).

TEMPERATURE

Various temperature regimes are required during the growth cycle (see Tables II-2, II-3, and II-4 Campanula). Stock plants are grown at 60 to 65°F (16 to 18°C). For the production of cuttings, keep the medium temperature at 70°F (21°C) with an air temperature of 65°F (18°C). For seed propagation, germinate at 65 to 70°F (18 to 21°C) in 14 to 20 days. Growth is fast at 65°F (18°C) during production, but the best quality is obtained at 58 to 62°F (14 to 17°C), which produces floriferous, uniform plants. *C. carpatica* flowered more quickly but with fewer and smaller flowers as the temperature increased from 57 to 79°F (14 to 26°C) (Niu et al., 2001). Cold hardiness and plant regrowth of *Campanula takesimana* Nak. was highest after being acclimated with three alternate freeze–thaw cycles of 27 to 37°F (−3 to 3°C) compared with acclimation at a constant 37°F (3°C) (Herrick and Perry, 1997). *Campanula lactiflora* plants required 20 or more days at 36 to 50°F (2 to 10°C) for quality flowers and acceptable production (K. Ohkawa, personal communication).

LIGHT

The cultivated campanula species are LD plants (Table II-3 Campanula). Plants should

TABLE II-3 CAMPANULA

General information for selected *Campanula* species for potted flowering plants (Adams, 1991; Armitage, 1987; Madson and Madson, 1986; Moe, 1977a; Whitman et al., 1995).

Species	Plant Growth Regulator	Temperature °F (°C)	Forcing Time (weeks)	Forcing Pot Size in. (cm)	Flower Induction Treatment	Cold Treatment
C. carpatica	A-Rest B-Nine Bonzi	46 (8) for first 2 weeks then 59–63 (15–17)	8–10	4.5 (11)	14- to 16-hr LD start 10 days after forcing[a]	8–10 weeks outdoors until mid December[b]
C. carpatica 'Clips'	Same as above	Same as above		4.5 (11)	Same as above	Same as above
C. elatines	None needed	Cool, outside only	15–18 Transplant seedlings 4–6 weeks after germination; flowers 1 year later	4.5 (11)	Occurs naturally in spring; do not force in greenhouse	Overwinter in the field (see *C. carpatica*)
C. isophylla	A-Rest	Air: 64 (18) Medium: 60 (16) until established, then lower to 50 (10) for a slow crop or keep at 60 (16) for a fast crop	10–15 Transplant seedlings 4–6 weeks after germination	4.5 (11)	LD, 14 hr minimum, 16 hr optimum	None
C. persicifolia	B-Nine	60 (16)	8	6 (15)	16 hr	12 weeks or more
C. poscharskyana	A-Rest	72 (22)	8	5 (12) Hanging baskets (prune as needed)	14–16 hr	Yes

[a]*Night break of 3 to 4 hr or extending days at dark and prior to dawn to have 16-hr days.*
[b]*Cold treatment not required; however, flower numbers increase as cold duration increases.*

TABLE II-4 CAMPANULA

A sample forcing schedule for seedlings of *Campanula isophylla* and *C. carpatica* (Adams, 1991).

Cultural Step	Production Time (weeks)	Temperature °F (°C)	Photoperiod
Seed to germination	4–6	70 (21)	SD
Transplant	1–2	46 (8)	SD
Forcing	15–18	58–63 (14–17)	SD for 2 weeks, then LD
Flower			
Total	20–26		

be forced under high natural light (Madson and Madson, 1986). Supplemental HID lighting is used in northern Europe. Reduce light level at the end of the crop cycle to enhance flower color. A variety of lamp types can be used for a 7-hr day extension, including cool-white fluorescent, high-pressure sodium, incandescent, and metal halide, and a minimum of 0.9 to 4.6 fc (0.2 to 0.7 μmol $\cdot$ m^{-2} $\cdot$ s^{-1}) was necessary to influence flowering (Whitman et al., 1995, 1998). However, incandescent lamps (high in far-red light) should be avoided for compact potted plant production because they may result in taller plants than fluorescent lamps (high in red light) (Moe and Heins, 1990). If night interruption is used, the light duration should be at least 2 hr and 6 min on/24 min off was also effective (Runkle et al., 1998).

Although *C. persicifolia* is day neutral, LD from incandescent lights encourages stem elongation, which would be useful for cut flower production (Iversen and Weiler, 1994).

WATER

Most campanula are sensitive to overwatering, which encourages disease, especially on open flowers. The species *C. poscharskyana*, in particular, should be grown on the dry side (Madson and Madson, 1986).

CARBON DIOXIDE

Increased CO_2 (900 ppm) regimes enhance cutting production and quality; the rooting of the cuttings and subsequent growth is also enhanced (Moe, 1977b).

NUTRITION

Nutrient levels should be at 200 ppm N from a complete fertilizer (Adams, 1991; Armitage, 1987; Madson and Madson, 1986; Moe, 1977a). Dinesen et al. (1997) noted that container-grown *C. carpatica* plants grown outdoors in Denmark should not be fertilized after mid-September; later fertilization resulted in fewer shoots and flowers, shorter shoots, and reduced postharvest life when the plants were subsequently forced in a greenhouse.

MEDIA

Any well-drained medium with a pH of 6.0 to 7.0 can be used. A medium EC level of 2.0 to 3.5 ds $\cdot$ m^{-1} using pour-thru is recommended for *Campanula carpatica* (H. Scoggins, personal communication).

HEIGHT CONTROL

If growth is excessive, B-Nine (daminozide) sprays at 2500 to 5000 ppm or Topflor (flurprimidol) sprays at 10 to 60 ppm can be used at visible bud (Adams, 1991; Armitage, 1987; Madson and Madson, 1986; Moe, 1977a; Moe et al., 1991). B-Nine reduces internode length for *C. isophylla* and *C. poscharskyana*, but flowering is delayed by 1 week. Cycocel (chlormequat) has been used on *C. carpatica* (Whitman et al., 1995). A-Rest (ancymidol), Bonzi (paclobutrazol), and Sumagic (uniconazole) are also effective (Latimer, 2001).

Both *C. carpatica* and *C. isophylla* respond to day/night temperature differences. Under positive DIF temperatures, long internodes develop; under negative DIF, short internodes result (Moe et al., 1991; Torre and Moe, 1998; Whitman et al., 1995). A 2- to 3-hr low-temperature drop (DROP) was not as effective as maintaining negative DIF for 9 to 12 hr (Moe et al., 1995).

Best plant quality is obtained by using DIF, rather than B-Nine or A-Rest, for height control. Phytotoxicity often occurs with chemicals, resulting in stunting, leaf curling, and discoloring of foliage. Symptoms may not be readily apparent. GA$_3$ treatments can nullify the inhibition of internode elongation of *C. isophylla* caused by negative DIF temperatures (Moe, 1981). GA$_3$ stimulates shoot elongation, but completely inhibits flower initiation of *C. poscharskyana* (Moe, 1981). Incandescent lamps may need to be avoided for compact potted plant production because they cause excessive internode elongation.

SPACING

After the cuttings and plugs are potted into 4-in. (10-cm) pots, they are kept pot-to-pot for 2 to 3 weeks. Plants are placed at three plants/ft^2 (32/m^2) for production (Madson and Madson, 1986). For cut flower production spacing ranges from 6 × 6 to 12 × 12 in. (15 × 15 to 25 × 25 cm).

PINCHING AND DISBUDDING

Disbudding is not required. *Campanula isophylla* and *C. medium* are usually not pinched, but if needed, it should be done as soon as plants are established. With the other campanulas, plants are routinely cut back after the cold treatment and prior to forcing.

SUPPORT

No support required for potted plants. One to two layers of netting are required for cut flower production.

SCHEDULE AND TIMING

With both *C. carpatica* and *C. isophylla*, 6 to 10 weeks are commonly required from germination to transplanting the plugs, then another 8 to 9 weeks to sales. Be careful, because seedlings damp-off with ease. Long days begin 6 weeks after transplanting, and flowering occurs 8 weeks later. If plants are to be held outside in the field or in coldframes, allow four to six leaves to develop before cold treatments. Cold must be given for 4 to 6 weeks, then plants are cut back and forced (Armitage, 1987; Madson and Madson, 1986) (Table II-4 Campanula).

The cut flower *C. medium* 'Champion' can be grown both in the field and under cover. In the field transplants can be planted either in the fall in mild climates or in early spring in colder climates. Early planting is required because the plants produce the highest quality

stems when newly planted transplants receive 3.5 to 4 weeks of SD prior to LD (Cavins and Dole, 2001). Late planting will result in rapid flowering and short stems. In the greenhouse plants can be produced year-round with photoperiod and temperature control. Plants should be grown in plugs under 8-hr SD until they have formed 5 to 6 leaves (3.4 to 4 weeks after sowing) after which time they can be transplanted to beds or containers and grown under LD. Total crop time will be 18 to 22 weeks (Table II-4 Campanula).

INSECTS

Plants are susceptible to aphids, spider mites, and fungus gnats (Adams, 1991; Armitage, 1987; Madson and Madson, 1986; Moe, 1977a).

DISEASES

Campanula has problems with *Botrytis* (Adams, 1991; Armitage, 1987; Madson and Madson, 1986; Moe, 1977a). Other problems include root and stem rot (*Fusarium, Rhizoctonia solanii,* and *Sclerotinia sclerotiorum*), aster yellows, and powdery mildew (*Erysiphe cichoracearum*) (Horst, 1990). Several leaf spot diseases are also possible when plants are grown outdoors.

PHYSIOLOGICAL DISORDERS

No physiological disorders have been described.

POSTHARVEST

Potted plants should be harvested when more than half of the buds have opened; flowers will not open during marketing if shipped too tight. Cut flowers are harvested when one or two flowers have opened. Flowers are sensitive to ethylene (Willumsen and Fjeld, 1995). Moe and Fjeld (1987) recommended 0.2 to 0.5 mM silver thiosulfate (STS) sprays. 1-methylcyclopropene (1-MCP) is also effective at preventing the effects of exogenous ethylene (Sisler et al., 1996). However, STS produced greater plant and flower postharvest life than 1-MCP (Serek and Sisler, 2001). Interestingly, *C. carpatica* 'Clips' stored at 40°F (4°C) in the dark for 6 days lasted longer than the unstored control and flowers were darker blue. When stored at 60°F (16°C) for 6 days, flowers and foliage were lighter than the control plants. Control plants lasted for 12 days; warm stored plants lasted for 8 days and cold stored plants for 16 days. Plants should be stored at 36 to 43°F (2 to 6°C) (L. Høyer, personal communication).

Cut *C. medium* 'Champion' stems can be stored at 36°F (2°C) either wet or dry for 1 week; increasing storage duration from 1 to 3 weeks decreased vase life (Bosma and Dole, 2002). Stems pretreated with a 1-MCP pulse followed by a 5% sucrose pulse solution produced the longest vase life. Flowers opening after harvest tend to be pale and stems had an average vase life of only 3 days when placed in floral vase foam but lasted 10 days without foam. Optimum sucrose concentration was 1 to 2% for stems used without foam and 4% for stems placed in foam.

KEY POINTS

- *Campanula* is used as a cut flower, potted flowering plant, and bedding plant.
- *Campanula isophylla* and *C. carpatica* are commonly grown as potted flowering plants and *C. medium* is commonly grown as a cut flower.
- Plants are propagated by seed, cuttings, or division.
- Many campanula species are LD plants; some also require a cold treatment for flowering.
- Campanulas are sensitive to overwatering.
- For potted plants, height control is required.

BIBLIOGRAPHY

Adams, R. 1991. "GrowerTalks" on pot culture: Campanula, pp. 50–51 in *GrowerTalks*. George J. Ball Publishing, Geneva, Illinois.

Armitage, A. 1987. Tips of the trade new crops: The present and the future. *Greenhouse Grower* 5(6):122.

Bailey, L.H. 1933. *Campanula*, pp. 642–650 in *The Standard Cyclopedia of Horticulture*, vol. 1. Macmillan, London.

Bailey, L.H. 1953. *The Garden of Bellflowers in North America*. Macmillan, New York.

Bailey, L.H., and E.Z. Bailey. 1976. *Campanula*, pp. 210–215 in *Hortus Third: A Concise Dictionary of Plants Cultivated in the United States and Canada*. Macmillan, New York.

Bosma, T., and J.M. Dole. 2002. Postharvest handling of cut *Campanula* flowers. *HortScience* 37:954–958.

Bosma, T., J.C. Cole, K.E. Conway, and J.M. Dole. 2002. Solid matrix priming hastens canterbury bells seed germination. *HortTechnology* 12: 268–270.

Cavins, T.J., and J.M. Dole. 2001. Photoperiod, juvenility, and high intensity discharge lighting affect flowering response and cut stem quality of *Campanula* and *Lupinus*. *HortScience* 36: 1192–1196.

Dinesen, L.G., A.S. Andersen, and M. Serek. 1997. Influence of late fertilization in the field on forcing and quality of potted *Campanula carpatica*. *Scientia Horticulturae* 71:235–242.

Heide, O.M. 1965. *Campanula isophylla* som långdagsplante. *Gartneryrket* (Oslo) 55:210–212. (in Norwegian, English summary)

Herrick, T.A., and L.P. Perry. 1997. Influence of freeze acclimation procedure on survival and regrowth of container-grown *Campanula takesimana* Nakai. *HortTechnology* 7:43–46.

Horst, R.K. 1990. Campanula, p. 577 in *Westcott's Plant Disease Handbook*, 5th ed. Van Nostrand Reinhold, New York.

Huxley, A., M. Griffiths, and M. Levy. 1992. *Campanula*, pp. 485–495 in *The New Royal Horticultural Society Dictionary of Gardening*, vol. 1. Stockton Press, New York.

Iversen, R.R., and T.C. Weiler. 1994. Strategies to force flowering of six herbaceous garden perennials. *HortTechnology* 4:61–65.

Latimer, J. 2001. Herbaceous perennials, pp. 98–110 in *Tips on Regulating Growth of Floriculture Crops*, M.L. Gaston, L.A. Kunkle, P.S. Konjoian, and M.F. Wilt, editors. Ohio Florists' Association Services, Columbus, Ohio.

Madson, P., and K. Madson. 1986. Campanula—A bright star in the future. *Bedding Plants International News* 16:7.

Moe, R. 1977a. *Campanula isophylla* 'Moretti' culture. *Minnesota State Florist Bulletin* 4:1–2.

Moe, R. 1977b. Effect of light, temperature and CO_2 on the growth of *Campanula isophylla* stock plants and on the subsequent growth and development of their cuttings. *Scientia Horticulturae* 6:129–141.

Moe, R. 1981. Seminar on flower regulation. *Flowering Newsletter* 1:10–11, International Working Group on Flowering.

Moe, R., and T. Fjeld. 1987. Keeping quality of potted plants as influenced by ethylene. *Gartner Tidende* 101:1580–1583. (in Danish)

Moe, R., and O.M. Heide. 1985. *Campanula isophylla*, pp. 119–122 in *Handbook of Flowering*, vol. II, A.H. Halevy, editor. CRC Press, Boca Raton, Florida.

Moe, R., and R. Heins. 1990. Control of plant morphogenesis and flowering by light quality and temperature. *Acta Horticulturae* 272:81–89.

Moe, R., R.D. Heins, and J. Erwin. 1991. Stem elongation and flowering of the long-day plant: *Campanula isophylla* 'Moretti' in response to day and night temperature alternations and light quality. *Scientia Horticulturae* 48:141–149.

Moe, R., K. Willumsen, I.H. Ihlebeck, A.I. Stupa, N.M. Glomsrud, and L.M. Mortensen. 1995. DIF and temperature DROP responses in SDP and LDP, a comparison. *Acta Horticulturae* 378:27–33.

Niu, G., R.D. Heins, A. Cameron, and W. Carlson. 2001. Temperature and daily light integral influence plant quality and flower development of *Campanula carpatica* 'Blue Clips,' 'Deep Blue Clips,' and *Campanula* 'Birch Hybrid.' *HortScience* 36:664–668.

Runkle, E.S., R.D. Heins, A.C. Cameron, and W.H. Carlson. 1996. Effects of cold and photoperiod on flowering of several herbaceous perennial species. *HortScience* 31:581. (Abstract)

Runkle, E.S., R.D. Heins, A.C. Cameron, and W.H. Carlson. 1998. Flowering of herbaceous perennials under various night interruption and cyclic lighting treatments. *HortScience* 33:672–677.

Serek, M., and E.C. Sisler. 2001. Efficacy of inhibitors of ethylene binding in improvement of the postharvest characteristics of potted flowering plants. *Postharvest Biology and Technology* 23:161–166.

Sisler, E.C., M. Serek, and E. Dupille. 1996. Comparison of cyclopropene, 1-methylcyclopropene, and 3,3-dimethylcyclopropene as antagonists in plants. *Plant Growth Regulation* 18:169–174.

Torre, S., and R. Moe. 1998. Temperature, DIF and photoperiod effects on the rhythm and rate of stem elongation in *Campanula isophylla* Moretti. *Scientia Horticulturae* 72:123–133.

Wellensiek, S.J. 1985. *Campanula medium*, pp. 123–126 in *Handbook of Flowering*, vol. II, A.H. Halevy, editor. CRC Press, Boca Raton, Florida.

Whitman, C., R. Heins, A. Cameron, and W. Carlson. 1995. Production guide for *Campanula carpatica* as a flowering plant. *Professional Plant Growers Association News* 26(4):2–3.

Whitman, C., R.D. Heins, A.C. Cameron, and W.H. Carlson. 1997. Cold treatment and forcing temperature influence flowering of *Campanula carpatica* 'Blue Clips.' *HortScience* 32:861–865.

Whitman, C., R.D. Heins, A.C. Cameron, and W.H. Carlson. 1998. Lamp type and irradiance level for daylength extensions influence flowering of *Campanula carpatica* 'Blue Clips,' *Coreopsis grandiflora* 'Early Sunrise,' and *Coreopsis verticillata* 'Moonbeam.' *Journal of the American Society for Horticultural Science* 123:802–807.

Willumsen, K., and T. Fjeld. 1995. The sensitivity of some flowering potted plants to exogenous ethylene. *Acta Horticulturae* 405:362–367.

Zimmer, K. 1985a. *Campanula fragilis*, pp. 117–118 in *Handbook of Flowering*, vol. II, A.H. Halevy, editor. CRC Press, Boca Raton, Florida.

Zimmer, K. 1985b. *Campanula pyramidalis*, pp. 127–130 in *Handbook of Flowering*, vol. II, A.H. Halevy, editor. CRC Press, Boca Raton, Florida.

Capsicum

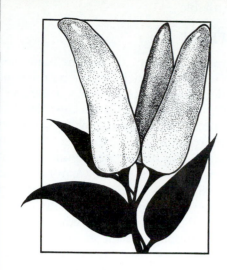

INTRODUCTION

Common name: pepper, Christmas pepper.

Scientific name: *Capsicum annuum* L. (Huxley et al., 1992).

Family and related taxa: Solanaceae Juss. Ornamental peppers, *Capsicum annuum*, are subdivided into three taxonomic groups: the Cerasiforme group (cherry peppers), the Conioides group (cone peppers), and the Fasciculatum group (red or cluster pepper). Other *C. annuum* types include bell (sweet or green) and cayenne (chili, long or red) peppers of culinary fame. Solanaceae also includes important food crops such as tomato (*Lycopersicon*) and potato (*Solanum*) and a number of ornamentals including *Browallia*, *Brugmansia*, *Nicotiana*, *Petunia*, *Salpiglossis*, and *Schizanthus*.

Origin: Peppers are native to Central and South America (Huxley et al., 1992). Although peppers did not become cosmopolitan in distribution until Columbus carried this species into Europe, peppers were being used as early as 7000 B.C. in Mexico and 2000 B.C. in Peru (Bailey and Bailey, 1976; Bosland, 1999; Rylski, 1985).

Uses and current status: Christmas pepper, suited for pot culture, is grown for its bright, colorful fruit (Fig. II-1 Capsicum).

The plants, which can grow to 30 in. (76 cm) tall, can be trained into trees, taking on various ball, cone, or square forms. Leaves are lanceolate. There are one to two flowers per node; the calyx and star-shaped corolla are five lobed. The pungent fruits vary according to cultivar or group, colored yellow to orange to red to purple, shaped elongate to round, and carried upright or pendant (Bailey and Bailey, 1976; Rathmell, 1980). Variegated and purple-colored foliage is also available (Stommel and Griesbach, 1993).

CULTIVARS

Numerous cultivars are available from various countries. Old and new cultivars are evaluated periodically (Armitage and Hamilton, 1987; Christiansen, 1992; Corley and Dempsey, 1971).

PROPAGATION

This annual is generally propagated from seed. The seeds, [9000/oz (320/g)], can be mechanically planted into plugs. Do not let them become overgrown. Germinate seed under mist or fog, in the light or dark (Armitage and Hamilton, 1987; Christiansen, 1992; Love, 1987). For plug production the following conditions are used (Hamrick, 2003):

- *Stage 1:* Seed not covered, 70 to 75°F (21 to 24°C), 5 to 7 days
- *Stage 2:* 70 to 75°F (21 to 24°C), 7 to 10 days, 1000 to 2500 fc (200 to 500 μmol $\cdot$ m^{-2} $\cdot$ s^{-1}), and 50 to 75 ppm N once/week

FIGURE II-I CAPSICUM *Capsicum* 'Medusa' bedding plant in the landscape.

- *Stage 3:* 65 to 68°F (18 to 20°C), 10 to 14 days, 1000 to 2500 fc (200 to 500 μmol · m^{-2} · s^{-1}), and 100 to 150 ppm N once/week
- *Stage 4:* 60 to 62°F (15 to 17°C), 7 days, 1000 to 2500 fc (200 to 500 μmol · m^{-2} · s^{-1}), and 100 to 150 ppm N once/week

Plugs should be ready for marketing or transplanting in 4 to 5 weeks. See Chapter 1, Propagation, for descriptions of stages. Cuttings root with ease (Rathmell, 1980).

FLOWERING CONTROL AND DORMANCY

Flowering of pepper is facultatively controlled by photoperiod (Vince-Prue, 1975). Rylski (1985) reviewed flowering of pepper. The following data are from edible *C. annuum* types, but can serve as a guide. When plants were grown under a photoperiod of 24, 18, 14, 12, 10, 8, or 6 hr, flowers were initiated within 31, 28, 27, 23, 27, or 26 days or failed to flower, respectively (Cochran, 1942). Flowering was most rapid at 77°F (25°C), and no flowers developed at temperatures greater than 86°F (30°C) (Rylski, 1972). Newly emerged plants grown at 54 to 55°F (12 to 13°C) for 3 weeks, then at 64° (18°C), were shorter and produced more flowers due to increased branching and fewer nodes to first flower, compared with plants grown under continuous 64°F (18°C). However, flowering was 8 to 12 days earlier under continuous 64°F (18°C) (Deli and Tiessen, 1969). Buds from basipetal nodes were found to be less "ready" to flower and to root with greater ease than acropetal buds (Rylski and Halevy, 1972).

TEMPERATURE

Recommended forcing temperatures are 64 to 70°F (18 to 21°C) days (Armitage and Hamilton, 1987) or, for Christmas sales, 60 to 64°F (16 to 18°C) (Hammer, 1992) (see Flowering Control and Dormancy section above).

LIGHT

Long days (12 hr) and high irradiance levels induce increased branching and earlier floral induction of lower nodes (Christiansen, 1992; Rylski, 1985; Rylski and Halevy, 1972).

WATER

The medium should be allowed to become "dry" between irrigations, but do not water stress the plants (Love, 1987).

CARBON DIOXIDE

No data available.

NUTRITION

Nutrition rates vary. For example, in Tennessee 200 ppm N was used at each irrigation until fruit set, then decreased to 100 ppm N (Starman, 1993). In Georgia, 200 ppm N was also used at every irrigation, but unamended water was used every third irrigation to prevent soluble salt buildup. The medium salt level should be kept between 0.3 to 0.8 dS · m^{-1} (Armitage and Hamilton, 1987). In North Carolina, 50 ppm of N was used for the first 4 weeks of growth, then increased to 200 ppm, and finally reduced to 100 ppm at the beginning of fruit set (Love, 1987). The three fertilizers used, respectively, were 20–10–20, 15–22–17, or 15–16–17. High nutrition can result in tall plants (Love, 1987).

MEDIA

Several types of media are used for potted ornamental peppers; a primary consideration is drainage. Ten percent additional pinebark increased drainage and was beneficial when added to peat-lite mixes (Armitage and Hamilton, 1987). A pH of 6.0 to 6.5 is recommended (Armitage and Hamilton, 1987; Love, 1987).

HEIGHT CONTROL

If proper cultivars are selected, no plant growth regulators are required for height control (Armitage and Hamilton, 1987; Love, 1987). High light and proper spacing are requirements for short compact growth with maximum branching. According to Sanderson and Martin (1974) in Alabama, several growth regulator treatments failed to effectively reduce plant heights: 5000 ppm B-Nine (daminozide) spray, 100 ppm A-Rest (ancymidol) spray, 200 ppm Florel (ethephon) drench, 1679 ppm Cycocel (chlormequat), and 729 ppm Phosphon drench. Adriansen (1985) in Denmark, however, noted that Cycocel, B-Nine, and Florel may be effective. Regardless, Sumagic (uniconazole) sprays at 10 to 15 ppm control height and increase red coloring of fruit if sprayed 2 weeks after pinching or 10 weeks after seeding. When the higher concentration was used at pinch, excessive retardation occurred (Starman, 1993). Bonzi (paclobutrazol) sprays at 20 ppm are also effective (Whipker et al., 2001). Day/night temperature manipulation (DIF) is effective on *Capsicum annuum* (Si and Heins, 1996).

SPACING

Most *C. annuum* are produced in 4-in. (10-cm) pots with one plant per pot. However, 5- or 6-in. (13 or 15-cm) specimens can be produced with three or four plants per pot, respectively. These latter sizes require more space but can be grown pot-to-pot during early production (Hammer, 1992). For 4-in. (10-cm) pots, spacing of 10 × 10 in. (25 × 25 cm) can be used (Armitage and Hamilton, 1987); for 5- or 6-in. (13- or 15-cm) potted plants, spacing of 15 × 15 or 17 × 17 in. (38 × 38 or 43 × 43 cm) may be required, respectively. Armitage and Hamilton (1987) calculated production costs for a 16-week, 4-in. (10-cm) crop.

PINCHING AND DISBUDDING

No pinching is required for 4-in. (10-cm) pot production; plants in 6-in. (15-cm) pots may be pinched twice; 5-in. plants (13 cm) may be pinched once (Love, 1987). Florel at 300 ppm may increase branching and replace hand pinching (Khademi and Khosh-Khui, 1977). Flowering may be delayed and fruit number decreased, however.

SUPPORT

No support needed.

SCHEDULE AND TIMING

It takes 14 weeks from seeding to sales for 4-in. (10-cm) specimens when seeded in the spring and summer, and 17 weeks when seeded in late winter (Table II-1 Capsicum). Flowering commences 5 to 8 weeks after germination, fruit formation and development require 3 to 4 weeks, and ripening an additional 4 to 6 weeks. Specimens in 6-in. pots require 28 to 32 weeks for production.

Florel sprays will hasten fruit ripening, reducing production time by 2 weeks. Sprays of 150 or 300 ppm at pH 6.3 were most effective when applied 3 to 6 weeks after anthesis. Fruits larger than 1.2 in. (3 cm) long were more sensitive to Florel spray than smaller ones (Armitage, 1989).

INSECTS

Aphids and spider mites are the primary insect concerns.

DISEASES

Phytopthora and *Pythium,* soilborne water molds, can occur as damping-off or root rots; but, if proper preventive precautions are taken, neither is a major threat (Armitage and Hamilton, 1987; Love, 1987). Several diseases can occur if plants are grown outside, but few occur in the greenhouse (Horst, 1990).

PHYSIOLOGICAL DISORDERS

No physiological disorders have been reported.

TABLE II-I CAPSICUM
Sample production schedule for 4-in. (10-cm) potted *Capsicum.*

Cultural Step	Production Time (weeks)	Temperature °F (°C)
Seed into plugs		
	2	70–75 (21–24)
Germination		
	2	65–70 (18–21)
Transplant (plugs), space pot-to-pot		
	2	65–70 (18–21)
Space 10 × 10 in. (25 × 25 cm)		
	6–9	65–70 (18–21)
Flowering and height control[a]		
	Cultivar dependent	65–70 (18–21)
Fruit coloration spray[b]		
	2–3	60–64 (16–18)
Sell when fruit are colored		
Total	18–20	

[a]Sumagic is the plant growth regulator of choice.
[b]Florel (ethephon) spray 3 to 6 weeks after anthesis. May reduce production time of late autumn/early winter crop by 2 weeks.

POSTHARVEST

If plants are shipped prior to 50% of the fruit being in color, the fruits will not color in the low-light home environment (Armitage and Hamilton, 1987). Potted peppers can be stored in the dark for 4 days at 48°F (9°C) (Love, 1987).

Pepper plants are sensitive to ethylene (Høyer, 1990; Kays et al., 1976). The leaves are more sensitive than the fruit; "immature" plants were more sensitive to ethylene than mature plants (Høyer, 1990). However, when Florel sprays were used to stimulate fruit coloring prior to shipping plants in the dark for 4 days, no abscission was observed from any ethylene being emanated (Armitage, 1989). Plants respond to 0.5 mM silver thiosulfate (STS) sprays (Moe and Fjeld, 1987).

KEY POINTS

- This seed-propagated plant is used as a potted plant because of its brightly colored fruit.
- Ornamental pepper is a facultative LD plant with a minimum photoperiod of 8 hr.
- Flowering is inhibited above 86°F (30°C).
- Height control is difficult and best accomplished with proper cultivar selection, prompt spacing, early plant growth regulator applications, and high light intensity.
- Sumagic (uniconazole) sprays may also be effective in controlling height.
- Florel (ethephon) can be used to hasten fruit ripening.

BIBLIOGRAPHY

Adriansen, E. 1985. Kemisk vækstregulering, pp. 142–162 in *Potteplanter I—Produktion, Metoder, Midler,* O.V. Christensen, A. Klougart, I.S. Pedersen, and K. Wikesjö, editors. Gartner-INFO, København, Denmark. (in Danish)

Armitage, A.M. 1989. Promotion of fruit ripening of ornamental peppers by ethephon. *HortScience* 24:962–964.

Armitage, A., and B. Hamilton. 1987. Ornamental peppers: A hot new crop. *Greenhouse Grower* 5(1):92–94.

Bailey, L.H., and E.Z. Bailey. 1976. *Capsicum,* p. 219 in *Hortus Third: A Concise Dictionary of Plants Cultivated in the United States and Canada.* Macmillan, New York.

Bosland, P.W. 1999. Chiles: A gift from a fiery god. *HortScience* 34:809–811.

Christiansen, B. 1992. Ornamental peppers. *GrowerTalks* 56(2):17.

Cochran, H.L. 1942. Influence of photoperiod on the time of flower primordia differentiation in the Perfection pimento (*Capsicum frutescens* L.). *Proceedings of the American Society for Horticultural Science* 40:493–497.

Corley, W.L., and A.H. Dempsey. 1971. Evaluation of new ornamental peppers. *HortScience* 6:491–492.

Deli, J., and H. Tiessen. 1969. Interaction of temperature and light intensity on flowering of *Capsicum frutescens* var. *grossum* cv. California Wonder. *Journal of the American Society for Horticultural Science* 94:349–351.

Hammer, P.A. 1992. *Capsicum* species and *Solanum pseudocapsicum,* pp. 483–484 in *Introduction to Floriculture,* R.A. Larson, editor. Academic Press, New York.

Hamrick, D. 2003. *Capsicum,* pp. 288–290 in *Ball Redbook,* vol. 2, 17th ed. Ball Publishing, Batavia, Illinois.

Horst, R.K. 1990. Pepper, p. 765 in *Westcott's Plant Disease Handbook,* 5th ed. Van Nostrand Reinhold, New York.

Høyer, L. 1990. Developmental stages of *Capsicum annuum* 'Janne' determines the critical ethylene exposure. *Acta Horticulturae* 272:109–114.

Huxley, A., M. Griffiths, and M. Levy. 1992. *Capsicum,* pp. 505–507 in *The New Royal Horticultural Society Dictionary of Gardening,* vol. 1. Stockton Press, New York.

Kays, S.J., C.A. Jaworski, and H.C. Price. 1976. Defoliation of pepper transplants in transit by endogenously evolved ethylene. *Journal of the American Society for Horticultural Science* 101:449–451.

Khademi, M., and M. Khosh-Khui. 1977. Effect of growth regulators on branching, flowering, and fruit development of ornamental pepper (*Capsicum annuum* L.). *Journal of the American Society for Horticultural Science* 102:796–798.

Love, J.W. 1987. Commercial production of potted ornamental peppers, pp. 1–3 in *Horticulture Information Leaflet No. 548,* North Carolina Agricultural Extension Service, Department of Horticultural Science, North Carolina State University, Raleigh.

Moe, R., and T. Fjeld. 1987. Keeping quality of potted plants as influenced by ethylene. *Gartner Tidende* 101:1580–1583. (in Danish)

Rathmell, Jr., J.K. 1980. Ornamental pepper trees, pp. 544–545 in *Introduction to Floriculture*, R.A. Larson, editor. Academic Press, New York.

Rylski, I. 1972. Effect of the early environment on flowering in pepper (*Capsicum annuum* L.). *Journal of the American Society for Horticultural Science* 97:648–651.

Rylski, I. 1985. *Capsicum*, pp. 140–146 in *Handbook of Flowering*, vol. II, A.H. Halevy, editor. CRC Press, Boca Raton, Florida.

Rylski, I., and A.H. Halevy. 1972. Factors controlling the readiness to flower of buds along the main axis of pepper (*Capsicum annuum* L.). *Journal of the American Society for Horticultural Science* 97:309–312.

Sanderson, K.C., and W.C. Martin, Jr. 1974. Effect of various growth retardants on Christmas cherry and Christmas pepper, in *Agricultural Experiment Station, Horticulture Series 20,* March. Auburn University, Auburn, Alabama.

Si, Y., and R.D. Heins. 1996. Influence of day and night temperatures on sweet pepper seedling development. *Journal of the American Society for Horticultural Science* 121:699–704.

Starman, T.W. 1993. Ornamental pepper growth and fruiting response to uniconazole depends on application time. *HortScience* 28:917–919.

Stommel, J.R., and R.J. Griesbach. 1993. New ornamental *Capsicum* germplasm: Lines 90C40, 90C44, and 90C53. *HortScience* 28:858–859.

Vince-Prue, D. 1975. *Photoperiodism in Plants.* McGraw-Hill, London.

Whipker, B.E. J.L. Gibson, T.J. Cavins, and I. McCall 2001. Fall crops, pp. 79–82 in *Tips on Regulating Growth of Floriculture Crops,* M.L. Gaston, L.A. Kunkle, P.S. Konjoian, and M.F. Wilt, editors. Ohio Florists' Association Services, Columbus, Ohio.

Centaurea

INTRODUCTION

Common names: bachelor's button, cornflower.

Scientific name: *Centaurea cyanus* L. (Huxley et al., 1992).

Family and related taxa: Compositea Giseke. The genus *Centaurea* includes approximately 450 species. Closely related species include the annual *C. americana* Nutt., the basket flower; and the perennials *C. montana* L., mountain blue, and *C. macrocephala* Pushk., golden basket flower (Armitage, 1991; Armitage and Laushman, 2003; Cox, 1985, 1987). The Compositea is a large family with many important genera including *Aster, Calendula, Callistephus, Chrysanthemum, Cosmos, Dahlia, Dendranthema, Echinacea, Gerbera, Helianthus, Liatris, Pericallis, Solidago, Tagetes,* and *Zinnia.*

Origin: *Centaurea cyanus* is from northern European and Near East temperate regions; *C. americana* is found from Missouri south to Louisiana and west to eastern Arizona and adjacent Mexico; *C. montana* is from the Caucasus; *C. macrocephala* is from central Europe. It is interesting to note that although species within the genus are widespread, only two species are in North America and one in Australia (Huxley et al., 1992).

Uses and current status: The annual bachelor's button or cornflower, *C. cyanus,* is the *Centaurea* most commonly grown outdoors and is used as a cut flower and garden ornamental and in roadside flower plantings (Harkess and Lyons, 1997) (Fig. II-1 Centaurea). The annual *C. americana* is grown as a cut flower (Fig. II-2 Centaurea). The perennials *C. montana* and *C. macrocephala* are grown as cut flowers and garden ornamentals.

Centaurea cyanus, C. americana, C. montana, and *C. macrocephala* grow from 1.5 to 3.5 ft (45 to 100 cm) tall. Stems are sturdy and terminate in a single flower. *C. cyanus* is often heavily branched, whereas the other species have several unbranched or slightly branched stems. Numerous enlarged, ragged florets occur in a wide range of colors. Plants are grown mainly for the deep blue to purple flowers; however, white, pink, lavender, burgundy, rose, and bicolor flowers are also available (Bailey and Bailey, 1976).

FIGURE II-I CENTAUREA *Centaurea cyanus* cut flower.

FIGURE II-2 CENTAUREA *Centaurea americana* 'Jolly Joker' grown as an outdoor cut flower.

CULTIVARS

Numerous cultivars, which vary in height and flower color, are available for the annual *C. cyanus*. A couple of cultivars that vary in flower color from lavender to white are available for *C. americana*.

PROPAGATION

All *Centaurea* species are commercially propagated from seed and can be directly sown in the field. Seed weights and seeding rates vary between species (Armitage and Laushman, 2003). Seeds can be individually sown in plug trays, germinated rapidly at 65 to 70°F (18 to 21°C), and transplanted within 4 to 6 weeks (Armitage, 1991; Armitage and Laushman, 2003; Cox, 1987; Nau, 1999; Post, 1949). For plug production the following conditions are used (Hamrick, 2003):

- *Stage 1:* Seed covered lightly, 65 to 70°F (18 to 21°C), 5 to 7 days
- *Stage 2:* 62 to 65°F (17 to 18°C), 4 to 7 days, and 50 to 75 ppm N once/week
- *Stage 3:* 62 to 65°F (17 to 18°C), 14 to 21 days, and 100 to 150 ppm N once/week
- *Stage 4:* 60 to 62°F (15 to 17°C), 7 days, and 100 to 150 ppm N once/week

Plugs should be ready for marketing or transplanting in 4 to 6 weeks. Keep plugs under SD. See Chapter 1, Propagation, for descriptions of stages.

The perennial species can also be increased by division. *C. macrocephala* has been tissue culture propagated (Hosoki and Kimura, 1997).

FLOWERING CONTROL AND DORMANCY

Centaurea cyanus, C. montana, and *C. americana* are all LD plants requiring long photoperiods for floral induction. However, seedlings are kept under SD to promote basal branching and increase number of stems. Once plants are induced to flower, floral development is quicker under LD than SD (Cox, 1985; Funke, 1948; Laurie and Poesch, 1932; Post, 1949). Induction is completed within 3 weeks. There does not appear to be a vernalization requirement or juvenile phase for *C. cyanus*, the most commonly grown species (Kadman-Zahavi and Yahel, 1985). Although little research exists on other *Centaurea* species, all appear to be LD plants. Most of the printed research is in Hebrew (Kadman-Zahavi et al., 1973); however, it has been reviewed and summarized in English (Kadman-Zahavi and Yahel, 1985).

TEMPERATURE

A 70/64°F (21/18°C) day/night production temperature was used by Cox (1987). Nau (1999) recommends 50 to 55°F (10 to 13°C) for *C. cyanus* and *C. montana*. Apparently, no vernalization or cold treatments are required for the annual species. The perennial species have not been well researched (Armitage and Laushman, 2003) and may require special treatments.

LIGHT

Under night interruption, LD treatments using incandescent lamps, *C. cyanus* exhibits an intensity × duration interaction for floral induction. For example, at 0.5 fc (0.1 μmol · m^{-2} · s^{-1}), 4 hr of continuous irradiance is required; at 8 fc (1.8 μmol · m^{-2} · s^{-1}), cyclic lighting may be used (2 min light/8 min dark). In Israel during the winter, a 4-hr night break of continuous incandescent irradiance of 10 to 15 fc (2 to 3 μmol · m^{-2} · s^{-1}) is commercially used (Kadman-Zahavi and Yahel, 1985).

Interestingly, various lengths (5 min, 30 min, or 8 hr) of red light used as a night break will also induce flowering in *C. cyanus*. Far-red light treatments or gibberellic acid (GA$_3$) sprays were effective only for shoot elongation but not for floral induction in *C. cyanus* (Kadman-Zahavi and Yahel, 1985). However, GA$_3$ sprays can substitute for LD to induce stem elongation and floral induction in *C. montana* (Cox, 1987).

Under full sun versus 55% shade cloth, *C. americana* yielded 13 versus 7 flowering stems. Although the stems were 7 in. (17 cm) longer under the reduced intensity, this fact could not compensate for the reduction in stem numbers (Armitage, 1991).

WATER

As with most crops, do not overwater. Drought, however, reduces stem elongation.

CARBON DIOXIDE

No data available.

NUTRITION

During the greenhouse production of *C. montana*, Cox (1985) used 200 ppm N (20–10–20). Fertilizer programs should not exceed 200 ppm N; preferably 100 to 150 ppm N from a complete fertilizer should be used (Armitage and Laushman, 2003).

MEDIA

A wide range of media or soil can be used for greenhouse or field production including many commercial premixed media. Cox (1987) used a peat moss and perlite (1:1 v/v) mix that had been amended with dolomitic limestone [5 lb/yd^3 (3 kg · m^{-3})], monosuperphosphate [7.9 lb/yd^3 (4.7 kg · m^{-3})], Esmigram for micronutrients [4.2 lb/yd^3 (2.5 kg · m^{-3})], and chelated iron [0.6 oz/yd^3 (21 g · m^{-3})]. In the field, Armitage (1991) incorporated composted manure into beds of clay loam.

HEIGHT CONTROL

No height control is needed for cut flower production. For bedding plant production, A-Rest (ancymidol) sprays at 10 to 15 ppm applied after transplanting or 15 to 26 ppm for finished plants or B-Nine (daminozide) sprays at 2500 to 5000 ppm applied to finished *C. cyanus* plants are effective (Bell, 2001). Height of *C. montana* can be controlled with up to four sprays of B-Nine at 5000 ppm (Latimer, 2001).

SPACING

Raised ground beds 6 ft (2 m) wide with plants spaced 12 × 12 in. (30 × 30 cm) have been used (Armitage, 1991). Direct seeded plants may be spaced 3 to 4 in. (8 to 10 cm) apart for single stem cut flower production.

PINCHING AND DISBUDDING

No pinching or disbudding is required.

SUPPORT

Two or three layers of support may be required, depending on species or height. *Centaurea cyanus* is often grown without support.

SCHEDULE AND TIMING

For mid-March flowering of *C. cyanus*, sow seeds in mid-September; for May flowering, seed in early January (Armitage and Laushman, 2003). With photoperiodic lighting in the greenhouse during late winter and early spring,

C. montana plants flower 60 to 70 days after being transplanted (Cox, 1985). In Israel, *C. cyanus* plants from seed sown in mid-August elongated toward the end of September, flowered starting in late November, and ceased production in February with 28 flowers/ft² (300/m²). No photoperiod control was used. Plants from seeds sown in early August and lighted September 1 flowered from late January to late March, with 14 flowers/ft² (150/m²) (Kadman-Zahavi et al., 1973).

INSECTS

Aphids and leaf hoppers are concerns, as well as spider mites and leaf rollers (Armitage and Laushman, 2003; Post, 1949).

DISEASES

Aster yellows (spread by leaf hoppers), downy mildew (*Bremia lactucae* or *Plasmopara halstedii*), rusts (*Puccinia cyani* or *P. irrequiseta*), *Botrytis* blight, and several root rots (*Phymatotrichum omnivorum, Pythium,* or *Rhizoctonia solani*) are common problems (Horst, 1990).

Soils should be pasteurized and plants grown in areas with good air movement (Armitage and Laushman, 2003; Post, 1949). Other potential diseases include southern blight (*Sclerotium rolfsii*), powdery mildew (*Erysiphe cichoracearum*), wilt (*Verticillium albo-atrum*), stem rots (*Sclerotinia sclerotiorum, Phytophthora cactorum,* or *Fusarium oxysporum*), and aster yellows (Dreistadt, 2001; Horst, 1990).

PHYSIOLOGICAL DISORDERS

No physiological disorders are known.

POSTHARVEST

Harvest spray types as soon as the apical flower is three-fourths to fully open and single types when the flower is one-half to three-quarters open (Armitage and Laushman, 2003). Cool flowers to 35 to 41°F (2 to 5°C). Flowers have a postharvest life of up to 10 days; a floral preservative should be used (Nowak and Rudnicki, 1990). *Centaurea cyanus* flowers are insensitive to slightly sensitive to ethylene (Woltering and van Doorn, 1988).

KEY POINTS

- *Centaurea* is used as a cut flower and bedding plant and in roadside flower plantings.
- Annual species are propagated by seed and perennials primarily by seed but also occasionally by division or *in vitro*.
- *Centaurea cyanus* is the most commonly grown species and typically used as a field-grown cut flower.
- Commercially grown *Centaurea* species are LD plants.
- Plants should be grown under SD until sufficient leaves and branches have developed to support high numbers of flowering stems.

BIBLIOGRAPHY

Armitage, A.M. 1991. Shade affects yield and stem length of field-grown cut-flower species. *HortScience* 26:1174–1176.

Armitage, A.M., and J.M. Laushman. 2003. *Centaurea*, pp. 183–192 in *Specialty Cut Flowers*, 2nd ed. Timber Press, Portland, Oregon.

Bailey, L.H., and E.Z. Bailey. 1976. *Centaurea*, pp. 242–244 in *Hortus Third: A Concise Dictionary of Plants Cultivated in the United States and Canada*. Macmillan, New York.

Bell, M. 2001. Bedding plants and seed geraniums, pp. 54–62 in *Tips on Regulating Growth of Floriculture Crops*, M.L. Gaston, L.A. Kunkle, P.S. Konjoian, and M.F. Wilt, editors. Ohio Florists' Association Services, Columbus, Ohio.

Cox, D.A. 1985. Production of perennial bachelor's button (*Centaurea montana*) in containers, pp. 98–99 in *Processing Alabama Greenhouse Nursery Seminar*, June 14–15, Auburn, Alabama.

Cox, D.A. 1987. Gibberellic acid induced flowering of containerized *Centaurea montana* L. Acta Horticulturae 205:233–236.

Dreistadt, S.H. 2001. *Integrated Pest Management for Floriculture and Nurseries*. University of California Division of Agriculture and Natural Resources Publication 3402.

Funke, G.L. 1948. The photoperiodicity of flowering under short day with supplemental light of different wave length, pp. 79–82 in *Vernalization and*

Photoperiodism, A.E. Murneek and R.O. Whyte, editors. Lotsya, Waltham, Massachusetts.

Hamrick, D. 2003. *Centaurea*, pp. 295–297 in *Ball Redbook*, vol. 2, 17th ed. Ball Publishing, Batavia, Illinois.

Harkess, R.L., and R.E. Lyons. 1997. A comparison of seeding rate, spacing, and weed control methods in the Virginia Tech transplanted meadow. *HortTechnology* 7:39–41.

Horst, R.K. 1990. *Centaurea*, p. 587 in *Westcott's Plant Disease Handbook*, 5th ed. Van Nostrand Reinhold, New York.

Hosoki, T., and D. Kimura. 1997. Micropropagation of *Centaurea macrocephala* Pushk. ex Willd. by shoot-axis splitting. *HortScience* 32:1124–1125.

Huxley, A., M. Griffiths, and M. Levy. 1992. *Centaurea*, pp. 561–565 in *The New Royal Horticultural Society Dictionary of Gardening*, vol. 1. Stockton Press, New York.

Kadman-Zahavi, A., and H. Yahel. 1985. *Centaurea cyanus*, pp. 169–173 in *Handbook of Flowering*, vol. II, A.H. Halevy, editor. CRC Press, Boca Raton, Florida.

Kadman-Zahavi, A., H. Yahel, and E. Ephrat. 1973. Winter flowering of *Centaurea*. *Hassadeh* 53:1201–1204. (in Hebrew)

Latimer, J. 2001. Herbaceous perennials, pp. 98–110 in *Tips on Regulating Growth of Floriculture Crops*, M.L. Gaston, L.A. Kunkle, P.S. Konjoian, and M.F. Wilt, editors. Ohio Florists' Association Services, Columbus, Ohio.

Laurie, A., and G.H. Poesch. 1932. Photoperiodism—The value of supplementary illumination and reduction of light on flowering plants in the greenhouse, pp. 1–42 in *Ohio Agricultural Experiment Station Bulletin, Number 512*, Wooster, Ohio.

Nau, J. 1999. *Ball Culture Guide, The Encyclopedia of Seed Germination*, 2nd ed. Ball Publishing, Batavia, Illinois.

Nowak, J., and R.M. Rudnicki. 1990. *Postharvest Handling and Storage of Cut Flowers, Florists Greens, and Potted Plants*. Timber Press, Portland, Oregon.

Post, K. 1949. *Centaurea*, pp. 378–381 in *Florist Crop Production and Marketing*. Orange Judd Publishing, New York.

Woltering, E.J., and W.G. van Doorn. 1988. Role of ethylene in senescence of petals—Morphological and taxonomical relationships. *Journal of Experimental Botany* 39:1605–1616.

Clarkia

INTRODUCTION

Common names: godetia, satin flower, farewell-to-spring.

Scientific name: *Clarkia amoena* (Lehm.) Nels & Macbr. (Huxley et al., 1992). Previous scientific names include *Godetia amoena* (Lehm.) G. Dan and *Godetia grandiflora* Lindl. (Bailey and Bailey, 1976; Huxley et al., 1992). *Clarkia* is used to honor the original plant collector, Captain William Clark, of the famous Lewis and Clark expedition, which explored the Louisiana Purchase and traveled to the Pacific Ocean.

Family and related taxa: Onagraceae Juss. *Fuchsia* is the best known floriculture genus in this family.

Origin: There are approximately 33 species in the genus; all are native to the New World from northwestern North America to southern South America. *Clarkia amoena* is native to the cool Mediterranean climate of coastal California, Oregon, Washington, and British Columbia.

Uses and current status: Godetia, an annual, is grown as a greenhouse and field cut flower, potted flowering plant, and garden ornamental (Fig. II-1 Clarkia). Anderson (1998) reported plants can tolerate light frosts if acclimatized. B. Hitt (personal communication) reports that plants can tolerate temperatures as low as 10°F (−12°C).

The leaves are linear to ovate, the inflorescence is a raceme, and the 25 to 40 showy cup shaped

FIGURE II-1 CLARKIA *Clarkia* 'Grace' cut flower.

flowers are held erect. Flowers can be up to 3 in. (8 cm) in diameter and the plant can grow up to 3.5 ft (1.6 m) tall. The flower petal texture is compared to satin, hence, one of the common names. Flower colors include pink, salmon, rose, lavender, and bright red.

CULTIVARS

Numerous F_1 hybrid cultivars have been developed and major breeding work is taking place in Japan, Europe, and the United States. Both single, semi-double, and double flowered cultivars exist. Dwarf cultivars have been developed for flowering pot plant production.

PROPAGATION

Propagation is primarily by seed; terminal cuttings can also be used. Germination is rapid: 6 to 10 days when the medium is held at 70°F (21°C) under mist or high humidity. On the seventh day, move seedlings to high light to accelerate seedling growth. Seeds are best germinated in plug trays with 35 to 50 seedlings/ft² (375 to 535/m²). After week 4 or 5, transplant to beds for cut flower production or after week 5 or 6 to pots for flowering potted plant production (Anderson, 1998; Anderson et al., 1991). One thousand plants can be expected to germinate out of 1/10 oz (2.8 g) of seed with 37,000 seed/oz (1305/g) (Armitage and Laushman, 2003). High-quality plugs ready for transplanting are available from specialty propagators.

For plug production the following conditions are used (Anderson, 1998; Hamrick 2003):

- *Stage 1:* Seed lightly covered, 70°F (21°C) for 7 to 10 days. Do not fertilize and use little or no fertilizer in the medium.
- *Stage 2:* 55 to 60°F (13 to 16°C) for 10 to 14 days. For single-stem cut flower production, use only a starter charge of fertilizer already incorporated into the medium. For potted flowering plants and multistem cut flower production, apply 50 to 100 ppm N (using calcium nitrate-based fertilizers) one time. Do not use constant liquid fertilization or high ammonium or urea-based fertilizers. Begin supplemental HID lighting and continue for 4 to 6 weeks for optimum growth (see Light section later for additional details).
- *Stage 3:* 55 to 60°F (13 to 16°C) for 7 to 18 days. Use B-Nine (daminozide) at 2500 to 5000 ppm or DIF for height control of potted flowering plants. Continue fertilization every 10 to 14 days for potted flowering plants and multistem cut flowers.
- *Stage 4:* 55 to 60°F (13 to 16°C) for 7 days. Transplant promptly. Plugs should be ready for marketing or transplanting within 4 to 7 weeks (see Chapter 1, Propagation, for description of plug stages).

FLOWERING CONTROL AND DORMANCY

Photoperiodic flowering response is temperature dependent. Godetia is a day-neutral plant at 68 to 75°F (20 to 24°C); flowers initiate and develop under both LD or SD (Halevy and Weiss, 1991). However, at the lower temperatures of 54 to 63°F (12 to 17°C) required for high-quality flower production, this species has an obligate LD requirement for floral initiation. At an intermediate temperature of 63 to 72°F (17 to 22°C) some cultivars flowered under either SD or LD, while some cultivars flowered only under LD. At 81 to 90°F (27 to 32°C) all plants died. Halevy and Weiss (1991) used an 8-hr natural day for SD and an 8-hr natural day plus 8 hr of incandescent light [23 fc (5 μmol $\cdot$ m^{-2} $\cdot$ s^{-1})] for LD.

In previous reports, Post (1952) stated godetia was a day-neutral plant, while Allard and Garner (1940) stated it was a long-day plant. Conflicting reports of photoperiodic responses may have been due to differing tem-

TABLE II-1 CLARKIA

The influence of temperature and photoperiod on *Clarkia* (Halevy and Weiss, 1991).

Temperature Day/Night °F (°C)	Photoperiod	Days to Visible Bud[a]	Days to Flower[a]	Height in. (cm)	Observations
90/81 (32/27)	LD	—	—	—	Plants died
81/72 (27/22)	LD	56	—	—	Plants died
72/63 (22/17)	LD	56	77±3	37±3 (94±8)	—
63/54 (17/12)	LD	56	98±4	38±2 (97±4)	—
90/81 (32/27)	SD	—	—	—	Plants died
81/72 (27/22)	SD	56	—	—	Plants died
72/63 (22/17)	SD	56	78±2	29±2 (74±4)	—
63/54 (17/12)	SD	—	—	—	No flower buds formed

[a]*After planting.*

peratures during evaluation (Halevy and Weiss, 1991) (Table II-1 Clarkia). Nomenclature may also play a role in the confusion because Lewis and Went (1945) also stated that godetia was a LD plant but they were referring to *Clarkia purpurea* (Curtis) Nels. & Macbr. rather than *Clarkia amoena*.

TEMPERATURE

Godetia is a cool temperature crop for high-quality cut or potted flowering plants. Commercially, the optimal temperature for highest plant quality is 45 to 55°F (7 to 13°C) night temperature; day temperature may be up to 10°F (5°C) higher (Anderson, 1990, 1998; Halevy and Weiss, 1991; Hamrick, 2003).

LIGHT

Clarkia is a high light-requiring plant. Seedlings in plug trays or plants spaced at high population densities can be given supplemental HID lighting for 24 hr/day for 4 to 6 weeks (Anderson, 1998). Photosynthetic lighting is required in northern areas during the winter under greenhouse conditions (Anderson, 1990, 1998). Supplemental HID photosynthetic lighting resulted in high-quality plants. Incandescent lighting which is high in far-red light resulted in poor-quality plants when used in areas of low light intensity. In Israel, an area of high winter light, low levels of incandescent light [23 to 45 fc (5 to 10 μmol $\cdot$ m^{-2} $\cdot$ s^{-1})] can be used without reducing plant quality (Halevy and Weiss, 1991). In fact, Halevy and Weiss (1991) stated that flower quality and stem length were enhanced by incandescent light, which produced stronger, more erect peduncles with upward-facing flowers.

If the temperature is 63°F (17°C) or lower, HID lighting of 200 to 400 fc (80 to 105 μmol $\cdot$ m^{-2} $\cdot$ s^{-1}) for 18 hr/day or incandescent lighting [23 fc (5 μmol $\cdot$ s^{-1}m^{-2})] for 4 hr/day from 2200 to 0200 (10 p.m. to 2 a.m.) should be used for rapid flowering (Anderson, 1998; Halevy and Weiss, 1991). If lighting is not used, flowering is delayed during midwinter or until days become naturally longer. See also the previous Flowering Control and Dormancy section for temperature and photoperiod interactions.

WATER

Maintain adequate moisture because plants dry quickly and leaves wilt with ease. However, overwatering can result in root and crown rots, especially at cool night temperatures of 50 to 60°F (10 to 16°C). Use microtube or subirrigation to minimize the leaning and curvature of stems from overhead irrigation, especially when in flower, and to reduce potential bacterial wilt problems (Anderson, 1998). In the field, use a drip-type system and avoid overhead irrigation.

CARBON DIOXIDE

No data available.

NUTRITION

Do not overfertilize this species. Young seedlings should not be overfed; 50 to 75 ppm N is sufficient (Armitage and Laushman, 2003). Pot plants have been produced with success with 50 to 100 ppm N and K using an ebb-and-flood irrigation system (Anderson, 1998; Anderson et al., 1991).

TABLE II-2 CLARKIA

Tissue test nutrient levels for *Clarkia*. Leaves were harvested from field-grown plants in California at the visible bud stage (Armitage and Laushman, 2003).

N	P	K	Ca	Mg	Fe	Mn	B	Zn
		(%)[a]				*(ppm)*[a]		
3.2	0.26	4.2	1.0	0.34	189	239	23	36

[a]*Based on dry weight.*

For cut flowers, 200 ppm N from $CaNO_3$ ranges in frequency from every 1 to 2 weeks in California to every 3 to 4 weeks in the midwest. This regime is supplemented with 25 ppm $MgSO_4$. If cut flowers are grown in greenhouses, very low ("almost none") nutrient levels are used (Anderson, 1998).

Overfertilization or high nutrient regimes result in weak stems and flower heads that are not held erect. If nutrition is too low, however, plants are stunted and the leaves have a dull bronze coloration (Armitage and Laushman, 2003). Armitage and Laushman (2003) have sampled nutrient tissue levels (Table II-2 Clarkia). Plants can appear underfertilized during production and can be greened up with a fertilizer application in the last 2 weeks of production (Hamrick, 2003).

MEDIA

Clarkia plants are well adapted to a variety of growing media (Anderson, 1990). A pH between 5.5 and 6.5 is recommended (Anderson, 1998). Media should be well drained to minimize potential root and crown rot diseases. Keep soluble salt levels below 0.6 dS · m^{-1} (Hamrick, 2003).

HEIGHT CONTROL

No height control is required for cut flower production. For potted flowering plants, B-Nine (daminozide) spray or drench at 3000 ppm, Cycocel (chloremequat) drench at 4000 ppm, Bonzi (paclobutrazol) drench at 20 to 30 ppm, or Sumagic (uniconazole) drench at 15 to 25 ppm was effective in internode reduction and resulted in plants 8 to 14 in. (20 to 35 cm) tall (Anderson and Pemberton, 1990). A-Rest was not effective. All the retardants delayed flowering by 2 to 4 weeks. Flower size was not influenced (Anderson, 1990; Anderson and Hartley, 1990; Anderson and Pemberton, 1990).

Up to two or three applications of a plant growth regulator may be required 14 to 18 days apart when plants are grown using HID lighting and 25 to 30 days apart when grown under ambient light (cultivar and season dependent). The first treatment is applied when the plants are 3 to 4 in. (5 to 10 cm) tall; the second when four to six lateral branches have developed and are almost the same height as the main shoot; and the final, 2 to 3 weeks prior to flowering during rapid stem elongation. These recommendations were formulated in Kentucky (38° north longitude) during the winter where HID lighting was used. In 1998, Anderson stated that plant growth regulators may not be needed with newer cultivars grown under cool, dry production conditions and minimum nutrition.

SPACING

Seeds are directly sown in plug trays. Plugs are planted in beds under protection or in the field for cut flower production. For pinched plants rows can be 2 to 2.5 ft (76 cm) apart with a spacing of 8 to 12 in. (20 to 30 cm) between plants. Unpinched plants can be spaced 4 to 6 in. (10 to 15 cm) apart. Close spacing can result in greater plant height. Beds can be up to 5 ft (1.5 m) wide. Cut flowers can also be grown nonpinched in pots with one plant per 4-in. (10-cm) pot or 2 to 4 plants in a 6-in. (15-cm) pot (Anderson, 1998; Armitage, 1992). Pots are spaced at 8 to 10 plants/ft^2 (86 to 108/m^2).

For efficient godetia potted plant production, use a plug from a 1- to 1.5-in. (2.5- to 4-cm) cell and place a single plant in a 4-in. (10-cm) pot. Four plants in a 6-in. (15-cm) pot can also be used. Plants are not pinched and uniformly sized plants should be selected if more than one plant per pot is used. Spacing of pots will depend on cultivar, pot size, and season and on whether photosynthetic lighting is used (Anderson, 1998).

PINCHING AND DISBUDDING

Plants for potted plant production are not pinched. Plants for cut flower production can be pinched, but this will increase production time by 2 to 3 weeks as compared to single stem production. Plants are pinched at transplanting or shortly thereafter leaving 4 to 8 leaves or axillary branches (Anderson, 1998). The center apical flower can be removed to induce elongation of the axillary flowering stems, improve spray development, and improve uniformity of flower opening with the inflorescence (Armitage and Laushman, 2003).

SUPPORT

Two to three layers of support are needed for cut flower production (Anderson, 1998).

SCHEDULE AND TIMING

Plug production for cut flowers requires 28 to 35 days from seeding to planting; plants will be harvested 11 to 18 weeks after planting in a temperature-controlled greenhouse. In Kentucky plugs transplanted in late September flowered in mid-December, in mid-October they flowered in early February, and in early November they flowered in mid-March under incandescent lighting and 50/60°F (10/16°C) day/night temperatures (Anderson, 1998). When pinched, 2 to 3 additional weeks are required as compared to a single-stem plant. For potted plant production, 40 to 49 days are required for plug production and 18 to 19 weeks to finish (Table II-3 Clarkia).

INSECTS

Aphids, leaf miners, thrip, spider mites, and whiteflies are problems (Anderson, 1998).

DISEASES

Root and crown rot from *Fusarium*, *Pythium*, *Phytophthora*, and *Rhizoctonia* are common if the medium is overwatered or not well drained. As stated earlier, use microtube or subirrigation to reduce disease problems. Extreme sanitation measures should be standard. *Botrytis* can occur on both the flowers and leaves during production or in transport (Anderson, 1998; Armitage and Laushman, 2003). Verticillium wilt (*Verticillium albo-atrum* and *V. dahliae*), downy mildew (*Peronospora arthurii*), powdery mildew (*Erysiphe cichoracearum*), rust (*Puccinia*), tomato spotted wilt virus, and aster yellows have also been reported (Dreistadt, 2001).

PHYSIOLOGICAL DISORDERS

Plants do not flower and may die at temperatures greater than 81°F (27°C) (Halevy and Weiss, 1991). Poor flowering and weak stems may result from excessive nutrition or warm production conditions.

TABLE II-3 CLARKIA

Sample production schedule for *Clarkia* as a potted plant in 4-in. (10-cm) pots.

Cultural Step	Production Time (weeks)	Temperature °F (°C)	Light
Plant plug[a] (Jan. 1)		50–55 (10–13) night 60–65 (16–18) day	HID light if possible
	2		
Apply growth retardant[b]		50–55 (10–13) night 60–65 (16–18) day	LD from incandescent lamps
When plants are 3 to 4 in. (5 to 10 cm) tall			
When 4 to 6 axillary branches develop			
Two to 3 weeks prior to flower			
	16-17		
Flower (Mother's Day)			

[a]From a 1- to 1.5-in. (4-cm) cell.
[b]Cultivar dependent; if using DIF, DIP, cool production temperatures, moderate moisture stress, and low nutrition, height control chemicals will not be required.

POSTHARVEST

Harvest when three to six, or up to half, of the flowers are open. The inflorescence can last up to 18 days and each flower up to 6 days; buds will continue to open and color after harvest. Maximizing the number of buds on the stem increases the postharvest life of the stem. Response to postharvest solutions is minimal, increasing vase life by only 1 to 2 days (Armitage and Laushman, 2003), or may be damaging if sucrose in included in the postharvest solution (Anderson, 1998). Shipping should be at 36°F (2°C) in water, if possible. Cold dry storage and long-distance transport should be limited or avoided.

Plants can be dried. Hang the flowering stem in a dry, well-ventilated, dark area. Remove excess lower leaves (Armitage and Laushman, 2003).

KEY POINTS

- Godetia is used primarily as a field and greenhouse cut flower and garden ornamental.
- Godetia is primarily seed propagated.
- Godetia is a day-neutral plant at 68 to 75°F (20 to 24°C) and an obligate LD plant at lower temperatures of 54 to 63°F (12 to 17°C). Intermediate temperatures of 63 to 72°F (17 to 22°C) produce a mixed response.
- Godetia is a cool temperature crop with an optimal night temperature 45 to 55°F (7 to 13°C).
- Flowers are damaged by periods of high humidity and contact with water.
- Cut stems are harvested when up to half of the florets are open.

BIBLIOGRAPHY

Allard, H.A., and W.W. Garner. 1940. Further observations on the response of various species of plants to length of day. *United States Department of Agriculture Technical Bulletin* 727:1–64.

Anderson, R.G. 1990. Satin flower. *GrowerTalks* 54(1):14.

Anderson, R.G. 1998. *Clarkia*, pp. 426–432 in *Ball Redbook*, 16th ed., V. Ball, editor. Ball Publishing, Batavia, Illinois.

Anderson, R.G., and G. Hartley. 1990. Use of growth retardants on satin flower, godetia, for pot plant production. *Acta Horticulturae* 272:285–291.

Anderson, R.G., and G. Pemberton. 1990. Gotta pot godetia. *Greenhouse Grower* 8(13):72–74.

Anderson, R., R. Geneve, and L. Utami. 1991. Gotta cut godetia. *Greenhouse Grower* 9(1):46–48.

Armitage, A.A., and J.M. Laushman. 2003. *Clarkia*, pp. 198–203 in *Specialty Cut Flowers*, 2nd ed. Timber Press, Portland, Oregon.

Bailey, L.H., and E.Z. Bailey. 1976. *Clarkia*, pp. 280 in *Hortus Third: A Concise Dictionary of Plants Cultivated in the United States and Canada*. Macmillan, New York.

Dreistadt, S.H. 2001. *Integrated Pest Management for Floriculture and Nurseries*. University of California Division of Agriculture and Natural Resources Publication 3402.

Halevy, A.H., and D. Weiss. 1991. Flowering control of recently introduced F_1-hybrid cultivars of *Godetia*. *Scientia Horticulturae* 46:295–299.

Hamrick, D. 2003. *Godetia*, pp. 413–416 in *Ball Redbook*, vol. 2, 17th ed. Ball Publishing, Batavia, Illinois.

Huxley, A., M. Griffiths, and M. Levy. 1992. *Clarkia*, pp. 636–637 in *The New Royal Horticultural Society Dictionary of Gardening*, vol. 1. Stockton Press, New York.

Lewis, H., and F.W. Went. 1945. Plant growth under controlled conditions. IV. Responses of California annuals to photoperiod and temperature. *American Journal of Botany* 32:1–12.

Post, K. 1952. *Godetia grandiflora*, pp. 555 in *Florist Crop Production and Marketing*. Orange Judd Publishing, New York.

Clematis

INTRODUCTION

Common name: Clematis.

Scientific names: *Clematis lanuginosa* Lindl., *C. viticella* L., *C. ×eriostemon* Decne., *C. patens* Morr. & Decne., and *C. florida* Thumb. are the primary species involved in the development of commercial cultivars.

Family and related taxa: Ranunculaceae Juss. There are more than 250 species in the genus *Clematis* L. (Huxley et al., 1992). Other important genera in this family include *Aconitum*, *Anemone*, *Aquilegia*, *Consolida*, *Delphinium*, and *Ranunculus*.

Origin: *Clematis* are temperate zone plants found in both hemispheres, but concentrated mainly in the Northern Hemisphere. In particular, China, Japan, Manchuria, Korea, North America, northern and southern Europe, Portugal, and New Zealand have numerous species.

Uses and current status: Clematis are used as specimen climbing plants in the landscape, potted flowering plants, and cut flowers. Clematis potted plants are especially popular in Japan. Garden center plants in flower have instant sales potential and are most successful if sold in pots rather than as bare roots. Plants can also be trained into topiaries and can be sold as flowering potted plants for indoor use; customers are able to plant them outdoors later.

Clematis can be herbaceous, semiwoody, or woody and most can climb (Bailey and Bailey, 1976). Leaves can be simple to compound and are frequently used in climbing by curling their petioles around any means of support. True petals are absent, but the sepals (4, 6, or 8) are colorful and petal-like; the stamens are numerous. Flowers range in size from the inconspicuous up to 10 in. (25.5 cm) in diameter, with colors of pure white to yellow, pink, lavender, various blues, deep purple, and red. Plant height at maturity can be from 6 ft (1.8 m) to 12 ft (3.6 m) (Fig. II-1 Clematis).

CULTIVARS

Many species, hybrids, and cultivars exist. Breeding programs are more common in Europe than in North America. Vining clematis can be divided into three groups: (1) flowers on old wood in summer, (2) flowers on old wood in spring, and (3) flowers on new wood during summer and fall (Lawton, 2002). Some are very cold hardy, to Zone 4.

PROPAGATION

Clematis can be propagated by seed, air layering, grafting, or vegetative cuttings. Bungard et al. (1997) found that *C. vitalba* L. seed germinated best after 12 weeks of 41°F (5°C). Commercially, cutting propagation is most commonly used. Cuttings are propagated in February, March, and April with mist and a rooting hormone and grown for 1 year. Cutting survival and root growth were greatest when cuttings were propagated in sand or perlite compared with peat-based media (Erwin et al., 1997). Propagation should be under 16- to 18-hr incandescent lighting at 80/60°F (27/16°C) day/night temperatures. Stock plants should also be kept under LD (Weyland,

FIGURE II-I CLEMATIS *Clematis* flower.

1978; Leahman Gardens, personal communication). The temperatures are kept at 42 to 45°F (6 to 7°C) during autumn and winter, prior to shipping the dormant liners, which many growers use in producing a flowering crop.

FLOWERING CONTROL AND DORMANCY

Clematis require LD to commence growth and flower after plants have been subjected to the SD and cold temperatures of fall and winter (Table II-1 Clematis). French and Lin (1987) studied dormancy and flowering using plants propagated from spring-rooted cuttings grown in 3-in. (7.5-cm) pots and allowed to go dormant and leafless. On September 21 they were placed under various light intensities and durations. Supplementing natural SD with high-pressure sodium (HPS) lighting failed to induce flowering with 'Comtessie de Bouchard,' but did increase flowering of C. ×jackmanii T. Moore. to 75% from 13% for the unlighted control. Night breaks (8 hr) from incandescent lights were modestly effective; 13 and 53% of plants flowered for 'Comtessie de Bouchard' and C. ×jackmanii, respectively. Similarly, HPS lighting for 16 hr increased flowering of C. ×jackmanii to 87% compared with 27% for 'Comtessie de Bouchard.' Thus, while high irradiance for long durations is recommended for forcing during the winter, effects will depend on the cultivar. Goi et al. (1975) also noted that 16-hr LD hastened and SD inhibited the flower induction and development of C. ×jackmanii plants. No dormancy occurred other than that imposed by low winter temperatures.

TEMPERATURE

French and Lin (1987) used 70 to 79/64°F (21 to 26/18°C) day/night temperatures, but Lin (personal communication) later stated that 60°F (16°C) night and up to 70°F (21°C) day temperatures were more appropriate. Plants flowered 4 to 6 weeks after the start of forcing. Although warm night temperatures of 65°F (18°C) will encourage soft, rapid growth that is easily wrapped around topiary forms, day temperatures should not go above 80°F (27°C).

LIGHT

Though most hybrids thrive in full sun in the landscape, light levels above 2500 fc (500 μmol

TABLE II-I CLEMATIS
Flowering season, origin of flowers, and pruning times of various *Clematis* species and cultivars (Smith, 1995).

Name	Flowering Season	Flowers Occur On:		Date to Prune	Comments
		Old Wood	New Wood		
C. alpine	Spring	X		After flowering	Small flowers, vigorous
C. montana	Spring	X		After flowering	Small flowers, vigorous
C. patens 'Nellie Mosa'	Early summer		X[a]	Late winter to early spring, dead wood only	Large flowers
C. florida 'Belle of Working,' 'Sieboldiana'	Early summer		X	Late winter to early spring, dead wood only	Double flowers
C. lanuginosa 'Henryi'	Spring/summer	X	X	To control size	Large flowers
C. ×jackmanii	Spring/summer		X	Late winter to lowest buds	Flowers continuously
C. viticella 'Comtessie de Bouchard,' 'Jackmanii,' 'Ernest Markham'	Spring/summer		X	Late winter to lowest buds	Flowers continuously
C. mawicziana (C. paniculata)	Mid to late summer	X		Little pruning needed	Controls size, if pruning

[a]New growth originates from axillary buds on old growth.

· m^{-2} · s^{-1}) may cause poor foliage color and hardened growth under greenhouse conditions.

WATER

Plants should not be allowed to dry out. The medium should be kept moist, not wet, at all times. (Lehman Gardens, personal communication).

CARBON DIOXIDE

No data available.

NUTRITION

Nitrate nitrogen should be used in preference to ammonium nitrogen because the latter encourages long internodes and soft growth. French and Lin (1987) fertilized with 100 ppm N from a 20:8:16 N:P:K fertilizer.

MEDIA

Historically, clematis have been thought to require an alkaline medium (6.5 to 7.5 pH). However, some large flowering cultivars tolerate a wide range of media pH from 5.5 upward (Smith, 1995). French and Lin (1987) used peat:pumice:bark (4:3:3) and Leahman Gardens (personal communication) used a standard peat-lite mix. Root (medium) temperatures during growth or in the landscape should be cool; a mulch is recommended and plants frequently thrive on the north side of structures.

HEIGHT CONTROL

Bonzi (paclobutrazol) can be used to reduce internode elongation (Joustra, 1989). A-Rest (ancymidol) sprays at 25 to 132 ppm and drenches at 0.25 to 0.5 mg a.i. (2 to 4 ppm)/6-in. (15-cm) pot are effective (Whipker, 2003). All other commonly used plant growth regulators are also effective (R. Heins, personal communication).

SPACING

Plants are spaced pot-to-pot after transplanting into the final container.

PINCHING AND DISBUDDING

Outdoors, flowering occurs from May to October. For spring flowering cultivars, flowers occur on the old wood that has overwintered and these plants can be pruned soon after flowering. Cultivars that flower later in the season do so on the current season's growth and consequently require pruning late in the autumn or early spring. Some early flowering cultivars also flower later in the season on new growth (Smith, 1995). For topiaries, the terminals can be pinched after a wreath frame has been sufficiently covered to stimulate axillary branching and flowering with suitable cultivars. No disbudding is required. Branching can be increased with both Fascination (formerly known as Promalin, 1:1 benzyladenine: gibberellic acid) sprays at 500 to 1000 ppm and Attrimec (Atrinal, dikegulac sodium) sprays at 250 ppm (Joustra, 1989).

SUPPORT

Support must be given, both during production and in the home landscape. Upright stakes or trellaces may be used, depending on the container.

SCHEDULE AND TIMING

Plants propagated from late winter to early spring will be grown on and allowed to defoliate and go dormant in the fall. Hybrids and cultivars that flower on old wood will flower in the spring or shortly after forcing commences. High-quality topiary plants may require 2 years: one year to develop the plant structure and the second year for flowering.

INSECTS

Spider mites can be a serious problem and aphids can be found on new growth. Outdoors, slugs and snails can cause serious problems.

DISEASES

Mildew (*Ersiphe polygoni*) occurs on the leaves when humidity is high. Sudden wilting and death can be observed if overwatered. A number of leaf spots can also affect clematis including *Ascochyta clematidina*, *Cercospora squalidula*, and *Cylindrosporium clematidis* (Horst, 1990).

PHYSIOLOGICAL DISORDERS

No physiological disorders have been noted.

POSTHARVEST

No information available.

KEY POINTS

- This vine is used as a garden ornamental, potted flowering plant, and cut flower.
- Plants are propagated by seed, air layering, grafting, or, most commonly, cuttings.
- LD are required for growth after the SD and cold temperatures of autumn.

- For topiaries, terminal shoots can be pinched to stimulate axillary shoots after a wreath frame has been sufficiently covered.
- Plants are susceptible to sudden wilting and death if overwatered.

BIBLIOGRAPHY

Bailey, L.H., and E.Z. Bailey. 1976. *Clematis*, pp. 281–284 in *Hortus Third: A Concise Dictionary of Plants Cultivated in the United States and Canada*. Macmillan, New York.

Bungard, R.A., D. McNeil, and J.D. Morton. 1997. Effects of chilling, light, and nitrogen-containing compounds on germination, rate of germination and seed imbibition of *Clematis vitabla* L. *Annuals of Botany* 79:643–650.

Erwin, J.E., D. Schwarze, and R. Donahue. 1997. Factors affecting propagation of *Clematis* by stem cuttings. *HortTechnology* 7:408–410.

French, C.J., and W.C. Lin. 1987. Effects of supplementary lighting on the growth and flowering of clematis. *HortScience* 22:437–439.

Goi, M., Y. Serda, and Y. Ihara. 1975. Studies on the flowering behavior in Clematis: The flowering behavior of *Clematis jackmanii* TH. Moore cv. 'Countess de Bousharld' (sic). *Technical Bulletin of the Faculty of Agriculture, Kayawa University* 26(2):94–100. (in Japanese, English summary)

Horst, R.K. 1990. Clematis, pp. 601–602 in *Westcott's Plant Disease Handbook*, 5th ed. Van Nostrand Reinhold, New York.

Huxley, A., M. Griffiths, and M. Levy. 1992. *Clematis*, pp. 640–652 in *The New Royal Horticultural Society Dictionary of Gardening*, vol. 1. Stockton Press, New York.

Joustra, M.K. 1989. Application of growth regulators to ornamental shrubs for use as interior decoration. *Acta Horticulturae* 251:359–369.

Lawton, B.P. 2002. Pruning clematis a knotty problem. *Perennial Plants* Spring:5–8, 10.

Smith, E. 1995. Clematis for the landscape. *Ohio Florists' Association* 786:10–11.

Weyland, H.B. 1978. The effect of photoperiod on *Clematis* cuttings. *American Nurseryman* 148(11): 13, 48–49.

Whipker, B.E. 2003. Growth regulators for floricultural crops, pp. 439–448 in *2003 North Carolina Agricultural Chemicals Manual*, College of Agriculture and Life Sciences, North Carolina State University, Raleigh.

Clerodendrum

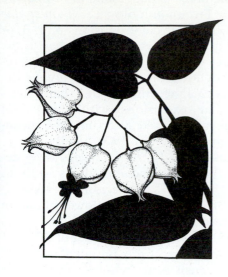

FIGURE II-1 CLERODENDRUM *Clerodendrum thomsoniae* hanging basket.

INTRODUCTION

Common names: clerodendrum, tropical bleeding heart, glory bower.

Scientific names: *Clerodendrum thomsoniae* Balf.f., *C. paniculatum* L., *C. ×speciosum* Dombr., and *C. ugandense* Prain. (Huxley et al., 1992).

Family and related taxa: Verbenaceae Jaume St.-Hil. *Callicarpa, Lantana,* and *Verbena* are important ornamental members of this family. Interestingly, the source of teakwood, *Tectona grandis,* is also in the Verbenaceae family.

Origin: Tropical Africa and Asia (Huxley et al., 1992).

Uses and current status: Spectacular potted or hanging basket plants when in flower. Clerodendrums are especially popular in conservatories for their beautiful floral displays (Fig. II-1 Clerodendrum).

The species seen in commerce are vines, shrubs, or trees and are mostly tropical. Commercial species include *Clerodendrum thomsoniae, C. paniculatum, C. ×speciosum* (*C. splendens* G. Don ex James ×*C. thomsoniae*), and *C. ugandense. Clerodendrum thomsoniae, C. ×speciosum,* and *C. ugandense* are vines and can be grown as flowering potted plants (Bailey and Bailey, 1976; Beck, 1975).

Of the *Clerodendrum* species listed, *C. thomsoniae* is the most common and has been grown for many years. This vigorous twining evergreen shrub is a prized flowering specimen with large [5-in. (13-cm)] ovate shiny green leaves. The flower cymes consist of a pure white calyx with a crimson corolla and long curved stamens (Fig. II-2 Clerodendrum). With age, the white calyx turns pink to purple. A native of west tropical Africa, it is frequently called tropical bleeding heart. In recent years *C. paniculata* from southeastern Asia and *C.×speciosum* have been gaining in popularity. Both species have a red calyx and corolla and are less vigorous than *C. thomsoniae. C. ugandense,* from tropical Africa, has also been used in floriculture because of its unusual flowers. Three lobes of the corolla are pale blue and the fourth is violet-blue; the calyx is crimson, the filaments are purple, and the anthers blue (Anonymous, undated; Bailey and Bailey, 1976).

FIGURE II-2 CLERODENDRUM *Clerodendum thomsoniae* inflorescence.

CULTIVARS

No commercial cultivars are available, but selections have been made for plants that have shorter internodes and are precocious in their flowering (Grandner, 1978; Hildrum, 1972; Koranski et al., 1987).

PROPAGATION

Propagation of *C. thomsoniae* and *C. ugandense* in northern Europe commences in January and continues into spring (Anonymous, undated; Dipner, 1973). Commercial propagation of *C. thomsoniae* is by single node cuttings. Terminal cuttings can be used if the tissue is sufficiently hardened before propagation. Uniform propagation of *C. ugandense* is by terminal cuttings with two nodes (Andersen et al., 1993). Stem cuttings produced thin axillary shoots.

The recommended temperatures for propagation range from 70 to 75°F (21 to 24°C) for the medium and 68 to 77°F (20 to 25°C) for the air. No rooting hormones are needed and two to five cuttings are placed in a 2.75- to 4-in. (7- to 11-cm) pot. Rooting can occur within 3 to 5 weeks under propagation tents or mist. Plants should be slowly acclimated (Anonymous, undated; Bailey and Bailey, 1976; Beck, 1975; Dipner, 1973; von Hentig, 1987).

FLOWERING CONTROL AND DORMANCY

Both *C. thomsoniae* and *C. ×speciosum* can be flowered year-round with day length control. With *C. thomsoniae* flower initiation may be independent of day length but flower development is favored by SD (Beck, 1975). Long days can delay development prior to visible bud (Hildrum, 1972; Koranski et al., 1978, 1979, 1987; Strømme and Hildrum, 1985). An 8-hr natural light treatment not only resulted in 100% flowering of 5-month-old *C. thomsoniae* plants, but also accelerated development from visible bud to anthesis, compared with treatments of high light photosynthetic irradiance or day extensions (Hildrum, 1970, 1973). Short days also promote flowering in *C.×speciosum* and LD promote vegetative growth (Shillo and Engel, 1985). Gibberellic acid (GA_3) sprays promote stem elongation and delay flowering even under SD, LD, or incandescent light (Hildrum, 1973; Koranski et al., 1979).

Red light increases flower numbers under SD or LD (Koranski et al., 1978). A-Rest (ancymidol) further increased the red light flower-

ing response (Koranski et al., 1978). Far-red light, on the other hand, results in little or no flowering. Five-month-old *C. thomsoniae* plants placed under day extensions of 4, 8, or 16 hr with incandescent lamps (higher in the far-red spectrum than fluorescent lamps) responded with flowering delayed to a greater degree, and with longer internodes than plants under similar extensions with fluorescent lamps (higher in the red spectrum than incandescent lamps) (Hildrum, 1970, 1973).

Koranski et al. (1979) followed flower development by histological methods with *C. thomsoniae*. With *C. ×speciosum*, approximately 35 SD are required for flower initiation and early development (Engel, 1983; Shillo and Engel, 1985). Reducing the number of SD to 21 caused flowers that were initiated to abort. High light intensities are required, even under SD. Under 5200 fc (960 μmol $\cdot$ m^{-2} $\cdot$ s^{-1}) 100% of the plants flowered, under 2400 fc (440 μmol $\cdot$ m^{-2} $\cdot$ s^{-1}) 57% flowered, and under 1040 fc (190 μmol $\cdot$ m^{-2} $\cdot$ s^{-1}) none flowered.

Once a flowering panicle is initiated, the terminal growing point ceases growth and becomes dormant (Shillo and Engel, 1985). Terminal growth commences again only when the flowers senesce. Renewed terminal growth is always vegetative, regardless of day length, light level, or temperature. Hence, flowering will subsequently occur on axillary shoots. If very young axillary reproductive shoots are removed as they develop, the terminal shoot remains vegetative. The older the reproductive shoots are prior to removal, the fewer additional reproductive shoots that form. Normally, five to six axillary flowering shoots form. Young leaves apparently perceive the SD signal to flower.

Temperature and photoperiod interact to affect the flowering of *C. ×speciosum* (Engel, 1983). Plants grown at 63/54°F (17/12°C) day/night temperatures initiated, but did not further develop flowers under SD (8 hr) or LD (16 hr). At 72/63°F (22/17°C) day/night temperatures, 80% of the plants initiated flowers under LD and, again, none flowered; under SD, however, 100% initiated and 83% flowered. At 81/72°F (27/22°C) day/night temperatures, no initiation occurred under LD, but under SD 100% of the plants initiated flowers and reached anthesis. At 90/81°F (32/27°C) day/night temperatures, no initiation occurred, regardless of photoperiod. The number of nodes to the first flower initiated increased from 6.5 to 8.3 to 11.3 as day/night temperature increased from 63/54°F (17/12°C) to 72/63°F (22/17°C) to 81/72°F (27/22°C) (Shillo and Engel, 1985).

Clerodendrum ugandense is day neutral and temperature does not influence flower initiation (Andersen et al., 1993). Flower induction occurs after 6 or 7 leaf pairs have formed on a shoot.

TEMPERATURE

Rapid growth of *C. thomsoniae* and *C. ugandense* does not occur at temperatures below 64°F (18°C) and plants can shed their leaves and go dormant (Anonymous, undated; Alvensleben and Steffens, 1989; von Hentig, 1987). Growing temperatures commonly used for *C. thomsoniae* range from 68 to 77/64 to 68°F (20 to 25/18 to 20°C) day/night (Engel, 1983; Shillo and Engel, 1985).

Growth chamber experiments indicate that floral initiation and development of *C. ×speciosum* require day/night temperatures from 72 to 81/63 to 72°F (22 to 27/17 to 22°C); growing at the warmer end of the range would be advisable (Engel, 1983; Shillo and Engel, 1985). At 90/81°F (32/27°C) day/night and low irradiance, no flowers initiated even if under SD. However, when plants were grown under SD and high summer light of 4100 fc (820 μmol · m^{-2} · s^{-1}), 73% of plants flowered even at 102/90°F (39/32°C) day/night temperatures.

LIGHT

All commercially important species require full light; the higher the light intensities the better. When light intensities were decreased, the number of flowers decreased (Anonymous, undated; Engel, 1983; Koranski et al., 1987; Shillo and Engel, 1985, von Hentig, 1987). Under poor light conditions of winter, leaves may abscise and flowering declines (Anonymous, undated).

WATER

Mat irrigation has been successfully used (Alvensleben and Steffens, 1989). Other irrigation systems are also likely to be effective.

CARBON DIOXIDE

No data available.

NUTRITION

High soluble salts can injure roots, and iron deficiencies can occur if pH of 5.5 to 6.5 is not maintained (von Hentig, 1987). A 2:1:2 (N:P:K) fertilizer ratio at 400 ppm N weekly has successfully been used (Sanderson et al., 1990). Other sources alternated between CaNO$_3$ (twice) and 10–12–15 (once) fertilizers at 100 ppm N for research plants (Alvensleben and Steffens, 1989).

MEDIA

The propagation medium should be well aerated. Various combinations of peat, sand, perlite, soil, and compost have been used (Anonymous, undated; Dipner, 1973; Hildrum, 1973; von Hentig, 1987). Sanderson et al. (1990) grew their plants in soil:sphagnum peat:perlite (1:1:1 by volume) amended with dolomitic limestone and superphosphate [5 lb/yd^3 (3.0 kg · m^{-2}) and 2 lb/yd^3 (1.2 kg · m^{-2}), respectively].

HEIGHT CONTROL

Numerous attempts have been made to control internode elongation, because clerodendron are vigorously growing vines. Cycocel (chlormequat) is not effective when used as a spray or as a 10,000-ppm drench (Grandner, 1978). However, a 10,000- to 20,000-ppm Cycocel drench was adequate for Dipner (1973). Differing application methods, media, temperatures, or light intensities may explain the contrasting results between Grandner (1978) and Dipner (1973).

Conversely, A-Rest (ancymidol) sprays or drenches are routinely effective (Adriansen, 1980a; Grandner, 1978; Hildrum, 1972, 1973; Koranski et al., 1978; Kruger, 1979). When 500 ppm A-Rest was used three times, or 750 ppm was used two times, plants were of equal heights (Grandner, 1978). According to Vereecke (1974), A-Rest sprays of 100 to 200 ppm were most effective in reducing internode lengths, but reduced the percent of flowering shoots and number of flowering panicles (Table II-1 Clerodendrum). Sprays of 50 ppm still reduced stem growth by 40% of the control and resulted in vastly superior flowering. When plants are grown into late spring or early summer, repeated applications are required (Kruger, 1979).

A-Rest drench at 0.9 mg a.i./pot not only reduces internode elongation but also dramatically increases flower numbers (Koranski et al., 1978, 1979, 1987). GA stimulates shoot growth and counteracts the enhanced flowering resulting from A-Rest soil drenches (Koranski et al., 1979).

TABLE II-I CLERODENDRUM

The effect of growth retardants on the growth and flowering of *Clerodendrum thomsoniae* 10 weeks after application (modified from Vereecke, 1974).

A-Rest ppm	Shoot Length in. (cm)	Internode Length in. (cm)	Nodes	Shoots Flowering no.	Flower Cluster %	Days to First Visible Flower
50	6.4 (16.3)	1.5 (3.9)	4.7	81.8	54	25
100	4.1 (10.4)	0.5 (1.2)	3.4	66.7	41	26
200	3.3 (8.5)	0.5 (1.3)	3.9	50.0	11	18

Bonzi (paclobutrazol) drenches are equally effective for height control as A-Rest drenches. Concentrations of 750 ppm for A-Rest, 100 ppm for Bonzi, or 0.5 mg a.i./pot for either chemical resulted in similar height control (Alvensleben and Steffens, 1989; Sanderson et al., 1990).

Besides the inhibition of internode elongation, these various plant growth regulators enhance flowering. This enhancement is greater under SD, which is also conducive to flowering. Regardless of photoperiod, A-Rest enhances and hastens both floral initiation and development (Adriansen, 1980a; Hildrum, 1972; Koranski et al., 1978). Adriansen (1980a) recommends 0.5 to 1.5 ppm a.i. in 50 ml A-Rest solution per 4-in. (10-cm) pot at the time of pinching. Bonzi or A-Rest must be used to control internode elongation of *C. ugandense* (Anonymous, undated). DIF and DROP are effective on *C. ugandense* but chemical growth retardants are still required (Andersen et al., 1993).

SPACING

Pots can be grown pot-to-pot until leaves overlap. Spacing will depend on pot size and season.

PINCHING AND DISBUDDING

Roughly nine to eleven nodes of *C. ×speciosum* must develop before flowering occurs. For example, if a shoot is pruned to seven nodes, three additional nodes on the axillary shoot must develop before flowering; if pruned to five nodes, six to seven nodes on the axillary shoot must develop; if pruned to two to three nodes, eight nodes on the axillary shoot develop prior to flowering (Koranski et al., 1987). Atrimmec (dikegulac sodium) can be used at 1000 to 2000 ppm to increase axillary shoots.

Vereecke (1974) rooted *C. thomsoniae* cuttings, potted them, and allowed them to grow for 2 weeks in 4-in. (10-cm) pots before pinching them to one pair or three pairs of leaves. Percent of flowering and number of clusters were greater when plants were pinched to one pair of leaves.

SUPPORT

If growth is not properly controlled, staking may be required.

SCHEDULE AND TIMING

Five months are required for production when propagated in January (Anonymous, undated; Dipner, 1973). The main season for rapid growth and flowering is the spring for summer sales (Table II-2 Clerodendrum).

INSECTS

Mealybugs, spider mites, and whiteflies can be a problem (von Hentig, 1987).

DISEASES

Pythium root rot and mildew can be a problem in the winter, when temperatures are low, humidity is high, and routine fungicidal treatments are not used (von Hentig, 1987). Leaf spots (*Septoria phylctaenioides* and *Cercospora appii*) have also been noted on clerodendrum (Horst, 1990).

PHYSIOLOGICAL DISORDERS

No physiological disorders have been noted.

POSTHARVEST

Shipping can begin when one-quarter to one-third of the flowers are open (Nowak and Rudnicki, 1990). The flowering cyme can last up to 3 months (Strømme and Hildrum, 1985). However, during transport and marketing, leaves and flowers are easily shed and the duration in darkness should be minimal (Adriansen,

TABLE II-2 CLERODENDRUM

Sample production schedule for *Clerodendrum thomsoniae* as a potted flowering plant from cuttings.

Cultural Step	Production Time (weeks)	Temperature °F (°C)
Root 2 to 5 cuttings in 2.75- to 4-in. (7- to 10-cm) pot	3–5	Medium: 70–75 (21–24) Air: 68–77 (20–25)
Pinch	2	Air: 65 (18) minimum
Apply growth retardant (A-Rest or Bonzi)	2	Air: 65 (18) minimum
Growth	8–12	Air: 65 (18) minimum
Flower		
Total	15–17 spring/summer 19–21 autumn/winter	

1980b; Høyer, 1982; Nowak and Rudnicki, 1990; Strømme and Hildrum, 1985). Prior to shipping, plants can acclimate at 61°F (16°C) (von Hentig, 1987). Recommended temperature during the marketing phase ranges from 46 to 54°F (8 to 12°C) (Nowak and Rudnicki, 1990) to 50 to 61°F (10 to 16°C) (Høyer, 1982). Tandler et al. (1989) observed chilling injury after 48 hr at 36°F (2°C).

C. thomsoniae is very ethylene sensitive (Adriansen, 1980b; Høyer, 1982); flowers and flower buds abscise when exposed to 1 to 3 ppm for 24 hr (Nowak and Rudnicki, 1990). Moe and Fjeld (1987) recommend using 0.4 mM silver thiosulfate (STS) sprays. Argylene, a silver-containing compound, is also effective (Anonymous, undated). If plants are not sprayed with STS, flowers will abscise after a dark shipping stress at 70°F (21°C) for 24 hr (Nowak and Rudnicki, 1990). STS is also recommended for *C. ugandense* postharvest handling (Andersen et al., 1993).

KEY POINTS

- This cutting-propagated plant is used as a hanging basket and potted flowering plant.
- *Clerodendrum thomsoniae* is the most commonly grown species.
- Long days, high light intensities, and warm temperatures favor vegetative growth; SD results in rapid flowering initiation and development.
- Plants grow slowly or go dormant below 64°F (18°C).
- High light intensity is required.
- Height control is required; A-Rest (ancymidol) and Bonzi (paclobutrazol) are effective and enhance flowering.

BIBLIOGRAPHY

Adriansen, E. 1980a. The effect of day length and method of ancymidol application on growth and flowering of *Clerodendrum thomsoniae* Balif. *Tidsskrift for Planteavl* 84:399–413. (in Danish)

Adriansen, E. 1980b. Transport and storage of *Clerodendrum*. *Gartner-Tidende* 96:314–315. (in Danish)

Alvensleben, R.V., and M. Steffens. 1989. *Clerodendrum thomsoniae*. *Gärtnerbörse und Gartenwelt* 50:2445–2447. (in German)

Anonymous. Undated. *Clerodendrum thomsoniae. Proceedings from Production of New Ornamental Plants*. Bavarian State Institute for Wine and Horticulture, Veitshochheim, Germany.

Andersen, A.K., T. Wingreen, and L. Andersen. 1993. *Clerodendrum ugandense* Prain. propagation, retardation and post-production performance as an indoor potted plant. *Acta Horticulturae* 337: 31–42.

Bailey, L.H., and E.Z. Bailey. 1976. *Clerodendrum*, pp. 285–286 in *Hortus Third: A Concise Dictionary of Plants Cultivated in the United States and Canada*. Macmillan, New York.

Beck, G.E. 1975. Preliminary suggestions for the culture and production of clerodendrum. *Ohio Florists' Association Bulletin* 547:6–7.

Dipner, M. 1973. *Clerodendron thomsoniae*. *Gärtner Meistner* 81:97. (in German)

Engel, R. 1983. Growth and flowering control of the vine *Clerodendrum speciosum* and its production as a flowering pot-plant. M.S. thesis. Hebrew University of Jerusalem, Rehovot, Israel.

Grandner, U. 1978. Clerodendrum cultivation is still problematical. *Deutcher Gartenbau* 32(43):1788–1789. (in German)

Hildrum, H. 1970. The effect of temperature, day length and growth retardants on growth and flowering of *Clerodendrum thomsoniae* Balif. *Gartneryrket* 60(24):530–533. (in Norwegian)

Hildrum, H. 1972. New pot plant. *New York State Flower Industry Bulletin* 29.

Hildrum, H. 1973. The effect of day length, source of light and growth regulators on growth and flowering of *Clerodendrum thomsoniae* Balif. *Scientia Horticulturae* 1:1–11.

Horst, R.K. 1990. Clerodendrum, p. 605 in *Westcott's Plant Disease Handbook*, 5th ed. Van Nostrand Reinhold, New York.

Høyer, L. 1982. Aethylen og lysmangel. *Gartner Tidende* 96:670–671. (in Danish)

Huxley, A., M. Griffiths, and M. Levy. 1992. *Clerodendrum*, pp. 653–654 in *The New Royal Horticultural Society Dictionary of Gardening*, vol. 1. Stockton Press, New York.

Koranski, D.S., B.E. McCown, B.E. Struckmeyer, and G.E. Beck. 1979. Gibberellin-growth retardant interactions on the growth and flowering of *Clerodendrum thomsoniae*. *Physiologia Plantarum* 45:88–92.

Koranski, D.S., B.E. Struckmeyer, and G. Beck. 1978. The role of ancymidol in *Clerodendrum* flower initiation and development. *Journal American Society Horticultural Science* 103:813–815.

Koranski, D.S., B.E. Struckmeyer, G.E. Beck, and B.H. McCarown. 1987. Interaction of photoperiod, light intensity, light quality and ancymidol on growth and flowering of *Clerodendrum thomsoniae* Balif. 'Wisconsin.' *Scientia Horticulturae* 33:147–154.

Kruger, U. 1979. *Clerodendrum thomsoniae*. *Gärtnerbörse und Gartenwelt* 49: 1189–1190. (in German)

Moe, R., and T. Fjeld. 1987. Keeping quality of potted plants as influenced by ethylene. *Gartner Tidende* 101:1580–1583. (in Danish)

Nowak, J., and R.M. Rudnicki. 1990. *Postharvest Handling and Storage of Cut Flowers, Florist Greens, and Potted Plants*. Timber Press, Portland, Oregon.

Sanderson, K.C., W.C. Martin, Jr., and J. McGuire. 1990. New application methods for growth retardants to media for production of *Clerodendrum*. *HortScience* 25:125.

Shillo, R., and R. Engel. 1985. *Clerodendrum speciosum*, pp. 302–307 in *Handbook of Flowering*, vol. II, A.H. Halevy, editor. CRC Press, Boca Raton, Florida.

Strømme, E., and H. Hildrum. 1985. *Clerodendrum thomsoniae*, pp. 299–301 in *Handbook of Flowering*, vol. II, A.H. Halevy, editor. CRC Press, Boca Raton, Florida.

Tandler, J., A. Borochov, and A.H. Halevy. 1989. Chilling effects on clerodendrum: Interactions of water balance and ethylene. *Acta Horticulturae* 261:333–336.

Vereecke, M. 1974. Chemical control of growth and flowering in *Clerodendrum thomsoniae* Balf. *Mededelingen van de Faculteit Landbouwwetenschappen Rijksuniversita* 39:1597–1602, Gent, Belgium.

von Hentig, W.-U. 1987. *Clerodendrum thomsoniae*, p. C3 in *KulturKartei Zierpflanzenbau*. Verlay Parey, Berlin and Hamburg. (in German)

Convallaria

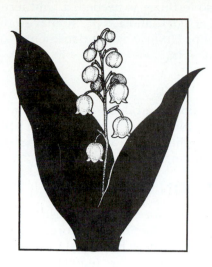

FIGURE II-I CONVALLARIA *Convallaria* cut flowers.

INTRODUCTION

Common name: Lily-of-the-valley.

Scientific name: *Convallaria majalis* L.

Family and related taxa: Liliaceae Juss. The lily family is quite large and contains many commercially important floriculture crops including *Allium, Alstroemeria, Brodiaea, Eremurus, Hyacinthus, Lachenalia, Lilium, Muscari, Ornithogalum,* and *Tulipa.*

Origin: *C. majalis* is native to northern temperate regions including Europe (northern and central to the Ural Mountains), Japan (var. *keiskei*), and the unglaciated mountains of the eastern United States, Virginia, West Virginia, and eastern Tennessee (var. *montana*).

Uses and current status: Lily-of-the-valley has been grown for centuries in the spring garden for its fragrant white 8-in.- (20-cm)-long inflorescences (Huxley et al., 1992). Commercially this plant is forced as a potted flowering plant or as a cut flower (Fig. II-1 Convallaria). Flowers are used in the perfume industry and rhizomes have medicinal value.

The individual bell-shaped flowers nod over on the one-sided raceme. The dark-green leaves are equally attractive and form carpets when naturalized in the garden. The plants survive under a variety of conditions, preferring light shade; yet plants are very stress tolerant and grow from Zones 2 to 5 (Armitage, 1989; Bailey and Bailey, 1976)

CULTIVARS

Cultivars are available with one or more of the following characteristics: yellow variegated leaves, large flowers and foliage, pink flowers, and double flowers. Although little breeding has occurred because there is only one species within the genus and minimal variations, Reimann-Philipp and Reimann-Philipp (1987) documented the use of selection to improve the number of flowers per stems and the yield. *C. keiskei* and *C. montana* are not considered distinct from *C. majalis*. Tetraploids exist (Verron and Le Nard, 1993).

PROPAGATION

Propagation is by divisions of rhizomes. *In vitro* propagation is possible (Verron et al., 1995). Lily-of-the-valley is distributed commercially as a large underground bud with attached roots that form a horizontal growing rhizome. The buds are commonly called *pips*. Three years are required for a new bud to flower, 2 years for the two leaf primordia to form, and 1 year for the flower to form (Pfeiffer, 1935; Post, 1952). The inflorescence is axillary to the leaves.

Pips are commonly supplied from Germany, France, the Netherlands, or Belgium. Holley (1944) demonstrated that pips from North American sources are similar, if not superior, in quality to those from European sources. Three types of pips are available: Plants pips are used for replanting in the field or by perennial growers, #2 pips are intermediate in size and forced in early spring when it is easiest to get sufficiently long flower stems, and #1 pips are the largest and forced in summer when it is most difficult to obtain long stems (A. Rutte, personal communication).

FLOWERING CONTROL AND DORMANCY

Pips are harvested after the foliage has dried in late summer or early autumn, and they require a brief, 3-week cold treatment at 28°F (-2°C) to break dormancy and flower. For pips harvested later in the season, for example November 18 as compared with October 28, fewer weeks (2 weeks) at a warmer temperature of 31°F (-0.6°C) were required. However, pips are commercially stored for 2 months at 25 to 28°F (-4 to -2°C). Pips can be stored for 1 year if kept moist (Hartsema, 1961; Whiteman, 1932). The flowering physiology has also been reviewed by Le Nard and Verron (1993) and Wilkins (1985).

TEMPERATURE

Air temperatures of 75°F (24°C) are used (Whiteman, 1932). Bottom heat at 80°F (27°C) can be used. At 63 to 68°F (17 to 20°C) leaves and flowers develop together while at higher temperatures, the inflorescence elongates more rapidly. Maatsch and Herklotz (1962) demonstrated that 24°F (-4°C) was the best storage temperature when compared to 21 or 14°F (-6 to -10°C)

LIGHT

For cut flower production, plants are kept in darkness for the first 2 weeks to increase stem length; thereafter, light intensity is increased to 1000 fc (200 μmol $\cdot$ m^{-2} $\cdot$ s^{-1}) to green the foliage. With potted plants, full intensity during winter is used, while during the spring light shade may be required (De Hertogh, 1996; Holley, 1944; Whiteman, 1932).

WATER

The media should be kept continuously moist but not wet (De Hertogh, 1996).

CARBON DIOXIDE

Carbon dioxide is not used in forcing.

NUTRITION

Although no fertilizer is needed, a light fertilization of $Ca(NO_3)_2$ and KNO_3, similar to that used for tulips (*Tulipa*), is not detrimental and may be beneficial.

MEDIA

Pips for cut flower production can be planted in sand, peat moss, or any media with a pH of 5.0 to 6.0 that will furnish a constant water supply during forcing (De Hertogh, 1996).

HEIGHT CONTROL

None is required for potted flowering plants. For cut flower production early forcing schedules are kept in the dark for 2 weeks to increase stem length. Cool forcing temperatures and low light intensity will produce the longest stems. Flower stalk length can also be increased by one application of gibberellic acid (GA_3) at 150 ppm (Seo et al., 2002).

SPACING

For potted flowering plants, three to four pips are typically planted in a 4-in. (10-cm) pot and forced pot-to-pot. For cut flower production the pips are spaced 1 × 1 in. (2.5 × 2.5 cm) apart in bulb crates for forcing (De Hertogh, 1996).

PINCHING AND DISBUDDING

None is required.

SUPPORT

None is required.

SCHEDULE AND TIMING

For potted flowering plants 2 to 3 weeks are required for forcing. For cut flowers 3 to 4 weeks are required because the flowers are harvested when more mature than for potted plants (De Hertogh, 1996) (Fig. II-2 Convallaria).

INSECTS

None are usually encountered in the forcing environment.

DISEASES

Botrytis can occur but is not common.

FIGURE II-2 CONVALLARIA *Convallaria* pot showing emerging shoots.

PHYSIOLOGICAL DISORDERS

None have been reported. However, if pips are not properly cooled, flowers may abort. Pips may be blind if they are too small (De Hertogh, 1996; Le Nard and Verron, 1993).

POSTHARVEST

Cut flowers are harvested when all the top bells have turned white. Potted plants are marketed when half of the florets have opened and the terminal flower buds are still green. Flowers are not sensitive to chilling injury and cut flowers can be stored dry at 31 to 32°F (−0.6 to 0°C) for 2 or 3 weeks. Similarly, potted plants can be stored at low temperatures (Nowak and Rudnicki, 1990).

KEY POINTS

- Lily-of-the-valley is used as a garden ornamental, cut flower, and potted flowering plant.
- Plants are propagated by pips, which are the large underground buds with attached roots on the horizontal growing rhizome.
- Pips require a cold treatment for shoot elongation and flowering.
- Flowering occurs in 3 weeks or less after the start of forcing.

BIBLIOGRAPHY

Armitage, A. 1989. *Convallaria*, pp. 150–151 in *Herbaceous Perennial Plants*. Varsity Press, Athens, Georgia.

Bailey, L.H., and E.Z. Bailey. 1976. *Convallaria*, pp. 308–309 in *Hortus Third: A Concise Dictionary of Plants Cultivated in the United States and Canada*. Macmillan, New York.

De Hertogh, A.A. 1996. *Convallaria*, pp. C41–46 in *Holland Bulb Forcer's Guide*, 5th ed. Dutch Bulb Exporters Association, Hillegom, The Netherlands.

Hartsema, A.M. 1961. *Convallaria majalis*, lily-of-the-valley, pp. 156–157 in *Handbach der Pflanzenphysiologie*, W. Ruhland, editor. Springer-Verlag, Berlin.

Holley, W.D. 1944. Domestic lily-of-the-valley pips tested for forcing. *Florists' Review* 94(2443): 21–23.

Huxley, A., M. Griffiths, and M. Levy. 1992. *Convallaria*, pp. 709–710 in *The New Royal Horticulture Society Dictionary of Gardening*, vol. 1. Stockton Press, New York.

Le Nard, M., and P. Verron. 1993. *Convallaria*, pp. 249–256 in *The Physiology of Flower Bulbs*, A. De Hertogh and M. Le Nard, editors. Elsevier, Amsterdam.

Maatsch, R., and A. Herklotz. 1962. A contribution to the storage of lily-of-the-valley. *Gartenwelt* 62:389–390. (in German)

Nowak, J., and R.M. Rudnicki. 1990. *Postharvest Handling and Storage of Cut Flowers, Florist Greens, and Potted Plants*. Timber Press, Portland, Oregon.

Pfeiffer, N.E. 1935. Development of the floral axis and new bud in imported Easter lilies. *Contributions Boyce Thompson Institute* 7:311–321.

Post, K. 1952. *Convallaria majalis*, pp. 426–427 in *Florist Crop Production*. Orange Judd Publishing, New York.

Reimann-Philipp, R., and G. Reimann-Philipp. 1987. *Convallaria majalis* (lily-of-the-valley) improved as ornamental plant after 35 years of breeding work. *Acta Horticulturae* 205:65–69.

Seo, S.Y., C.S. Kim, H.J. Kim, J.M. Kim, D.C. Choi, and Y.G. Choi. 2002. Characteristics of growth and flowering by shading and growth regulators in the lily-of-the-valley (*Convallaria keiskei* M.). *Journal of the Korean Horticultural Society* 43:644–648.

Verron, P., and M. Le Nard. 1993. Characterization of five improved varieties and one wild accession of lily-of-the-valley (*Convallaria majalis* L.) by isozyme analysis and assessment of genetic distance. *Euphytica* 70:21–26.

Verron, P., M. Le Nard, and J. Cohat. 1995. *In vitro* organogenic competence of different organs and tissues of lily of the valley 'Grandiflora of Nantes.' *Plant Cell, Tissue and Organ Culture* 40:237–242.

Whiteman, T.M. 1932. *Commercial forcing of lilies-of-the-valley*, pp. 1–20. United States Department of Agriculture Circular 216.

Wilkins, H. 1985. *Convallaria majalis*, pp. 321–323 in *Handbook of Flowering*, vol. II, A.H. Halevy, editor. CRC Press, Boca Raton, Florida.

Cosmos

INTRODUCTION

Common names: cosmos, lace cosmos.

Scientific names: *Cosmos bipinnatus* Cav., *C. sulphureus* Cav., and *C. atrosanguineus* (Hook.) Voss. (chocolate cosmos) (Huxley et al., 1992).

Family and related taxa: Compositea Giseke. The genus includes approximately 26 species. The Compositea is a large family containing numerous important floriculture genera including *Aster, Calendula, Centaurea, Chrysanthemum, Dahlia, Dendranthema, Echinacea, Gerbera, Helianthus, Liatris, Pericallis, Solidago, Tagetes,* and *Zinnia.*

Origin: Both species are natives of Mexico. All cosmos species are found in the southwestern United States and tropical America (Huxley et al., 1992).

Uses and current status: *Cosmos bipinnatus* and *C. sulphureus* are annuals grown as cut and garden flowers (Starman et al., 1995) (Fig. II-1 Cosmos). *Cosmos sulphureus* is the shorter of the two species and certain cultivars are used for bedding plant purposes (Armitage and Laushman, 2003). Both species are also used in roadside plantings in some states (Harkess and Lyons, 1997). *C. atrosanguineus* is used as a cut flower and is a short-lived perennial.

Both annual species can grow 1 to 10 ft (0.3 to 3.3 m) tall with individual inflorescences 3 to 4 in. (7.5 to 10 cm) across. The ray flowers of *C. bipinnatus* can be white or pink to crimson; those of *C. sulphureus* are red to orange to pale or golden yellow. The disc flowers for both are yellow. The two to three pinnate leaves are lanceolate and alternate (Bailey and Bailey, 1976). The 2-in.- (5-cm)-wide flowers of *C. atrosanguineus* are very dark brownish maroon with a distinctive chocolate fragrance. Plants grow 2 to 3 ft (60 to 90 cm) tall.

FIGURE II-1 COSMOS Outdoor-grown *Cosmos bipinnatus* for cut flower production.

CULTIVARS

There are early, medium, and late flowering cultivars of *C. bipinnatus* (Armitage and Laushman, 2003). Double flowered types exist for both species, and anemone forms of *C. bipinnatus* have been reported. In either case, for the double or anemone types, the disc flowers become petal-like and are the same color as the ray flowers (Bailey and Bailey, 1976). One cultivar of *C. bipinnatus* has a single row of tubular ray petals.

PROPAGATION

Propagation is by seed. Seed can be directly seeded into the field at 0.54 oz/100 ft (50 g/100 m) (Armitage and Laushman, 2003). For *C. bipinnatus* 0.5 oz (14 g) will yield 1000 plants; for *C. sulphureus* 0.7 oz (20 g) will be needed. At 64°F (18°C), germination occurs in 8 to 14 days; at 70 to 72°F (21 to 22°C), germination requires 7 to 10 days (Armitage and Laushman, 2003; Post, 1949). Cosmos is considered to be a facultative SD plant and seedlings should be kept under LD until six pairs of leaves have formed.

FLOWERING CONTROL AND DORMANCY

Flowering of cosmos has been reviewed by Molder and Owens (1985). Flowering occurs during the long days of summer even though *C. bipinnatus* is a facultative SD plant. Seedlings started early in the year under natural or artificial SD will continue to flower in commercially acceptable numbers even under the natural LD of summer. Unless plants were given a SD treatment, however, flowering was irregular or nonexistent with 14 hr or longer days (Post, 1949).

Cultivar differences are seen in response to photoperiod (Peters, 1947). Molder and Owens (1985) classified *C. bipinnatus* as a facultative SD plant in that mature plants will eventually initiate flowers under LD, but floral development is promoted by SD. GA$_3$ sprays (100 ppm) can substitute for SD for *C. bipinnatus*; treated plants flowered under an 18-hr photoperiod (Wittwer and Bukovac, 1959). *C. sulphureus* is an obligatory SD plant and will not flower under LD. Plants are perceptive to photoperiodic control when six to eight leaves have formed (Table II-1 Cosmos). Newer cultivars are more free-flowering and may be facultative SD plants.

C. atrosanguineus, however, is a facultative LD plant (Kanellos and Pearson, 2000). Plants under 17-hr LD flower faster and grew larger than those under 8-hr SD.

TEMPERATURE

Cosmos sulphureus is more temperature sensitive, not flowering under warm 70 to 75°F (21 to 29°C) temperatures, than *C. bipinnatus* (Post, 1949). With *C. sulphureus* a temperature of 60°F (16°C) is as low as production should occur (Biebel, 1936). Under LD, regardless of temperature [68 or 55°F (20 or 13°C)], plants did not flower. Plants flowered rapidly under SD at 68°F (20°C), but failed to flower at 55°F (13°C). If plants were first given SD at 55°F (13°C) for 30 days and then 68°F (20°C), flowering was delayed but flower number was high and stems were long. When 68°F (20°C) was given for 30 days, then 55°F (13°C), flowering was more rapid than the 55/68°F (13/20°C) regime, but flower number was low and stems were short (Biebel, 1936). Newer cultivars may be less sensitive to photoperiods. With *C. atrosanguineus*,

TABLE II-1 COSMOS

The days to flower and number of flowers for pot-grown *Cosmos sulphureus* plants that were seeded October 28, potted on November 11, and placed under one of the following treatments: (1) LD at 68°F (20°C), (2) LD at 55°F (13°C), (3) SD at 68°F (20°C), (4) SD and 30 days at 55°F (13°C) followed by 68°F (20°C), and (5) SD and 30 days at 68°F (20°C) followed by 55°F (13°C) (adapted from Biebel, 1936).

Day Length	Temperature °F (°C)	Days to First Flower[a]	Numbers of Flowers over a 30-Day Period	Stem Length in. (cm)
LD	68 (20)	Plants did not flower	—	—
LD	55 (13)	Plants did not flower	—	—
SD	68 (20)	71	5.2	14.8 (37.5)
SD	55/68 (13/20)[b]	119	12.6	14.0 (37.5)
SD	68/55 (20/13)[b]	95	2.3	3.6 (9.5)

[a] From date of sowing.
[b] Temperature for the first 30 days after sowing/temperature to end of experiment.

increasing the temperature from 54 to 80°F (12 to 27°C) increased height, but decreased flower size (Kanellos and Pearson, 2000).

LIGHT

Plants grow best under full sunlight (Armitage and Laushman, 2003; Post, 1949). Very low light intensities of 2 fc (0.4 μmol · m⁻² · s⁻¹) prevented flowering of *C. sulphureus* when used to create a 16- to 18-hr LD (natural light + night break) (Biebel, 1936). Interestingly, flowering of *C. bipinnatus* was inhibited when incandescent, red, or blue light was used. Red light was the most inhibitory (Zimmer, 1988).

WATER

Maintain a moist medium, but allow for a drying cycle to occur for good root development.

CARBON DIOXIDE

No data available.

NUTRITION

Low levels are used. New transplants can be fertilized with 50 to 75 ppm N from potassium nitrate and increased thereafter to 150 to 200 N (Armitage and Laushman, 2003).

MEDIA

Field soil should be well prepared for direct seeding and the nutrient levels determined prior to seeding. In the greenhouse, any peatlite medium would be acceptable.

HEIGHT CONTROL

B-Nine (daminozide) sprays at 2500 to 5000 ppm serve a dual purpose—reducing internode length and, if used at time of flower peduncle elongation, preventing the drooping of the inflorescence (Samata et al., 1974). For cut flower production in the field, no height control is needed. DIF has a moderate effect on cosmos (Warner and Erwin, 2001).

SPACING

In the field spacing can be 9 × 12 to 12 × 30 in. (23 × 30 to 30 × 76 cm) (Post, 1949). Excessively close spacing will encourage diseases, especially stem cankers.

PINCHING AND DISBUDDING

None is required.

SUPPORT

Two layers of support net are required in the field. Normally no support is required in the greenhouse.

SCHEDULE AND TIMING

Seedlings must be started in early spring when photoperiods are less than 14 hr. If started late in the season, large plants are produced without flowering until the photoperiod is less than 14 hr in the late summer. Days to flower at specific temperatures and photoperiods are listed in Table II-1 Cosmos (Biebel, 1936). Armitage and Laushman (2003) recommended sequential plantings every 2 to 4 weeks.

INSECTS

Tarnish plant bugs, leaf hoppers, aphids, and thrips are problems (Armitage and Laushman, 2003; Post, 1949).

DISEASES

Aster yellows and stem cankers, *Phomopsis stewartic*, have been reported (Post, 1949). Aster yellows can be especially troublesome late in the growing season in the southern United States. Horst (1990) also listed a number of other diseases as potential problems, including bacterial wilt (*Pseudomonas solanacearum*), southern blight (*Sclerotium rolfsii*), leaf spots (*Cercospora* or *Septoria*), powdery mildew (*Erysiphe cichoracearum*), root rots (*Phymatotrichum omnivorum, Macrophomina phaseoli, Pythium*, or *Rhizoctonia solani*), and fusarium wilt (*Fusarium*). Stem blight (*Diaporthe stewartii*) has also been documented (Dreistadt, 2001).

PHYSIOLOGICAL DISORDERS

None reported.

POSTHARVEST

Harvest only flowers that are open but with petals that are not yet flat. The older the flowers on the plant, the shorter the vase life. For ease of harvest, keep malformed and old flowers removed. Plants respond to postharvest solutions and should be shipped or stored at 36 to 41°F (2 to 5°C) for up to 1 week (Armitage and Laushman, 2003; Redman et al., 2002). Vase life ranges from 5 to 9 days (Gast, 1998). Flowers are not sensitive to ethylene and silver thiosulfate (STS) had no effect (Redman et al., 2002).

KEY POINTS

- This seed-propagated plant is used as a cut flower and bedding plant.
- Two species are commonly grown: *Cosmos bipinnatus* and *C. sulphureus*.
- *C. bipinnatus* is a facultative SD plant and *C. sulphureus* is an obligate SD plant.
- Juvenility exists with *C. sulphureus* in that six to eight leaves must form for plants to be receptive to SD.

- Plants exposed to SD in the spring when young will continue to flower under the LD of summer.
- Aster yellows and stem cankers can be a limiting factor in field cut flower production.

BIBLIOGRAPHY

Armitage, A.M., and J.M. Laushman. 2003. *Cosmos bipinnatus*, pp. 220–227 in *Specialty Cut Flowers*, 2nd ed. Timber Press, Portland, Oregon.

Bailey, L.H., and E.Z. Bailey. 1976. *Cosmos*, pp. 321–322 in *Hortus Third: A Concise Dictionary of Plants Cultivated in the United States and Canada*. Macmillan, New York.

Biebel, J. 1936. Temperature, photoperiod, flowering and morphology in cosmos and China aster. *Proceedings of the American Society for Horticultural Science* 34:635–643.

Dreistadt, S.H. 2001. *Integrated Pest Management for Floriculture and Nurseries*. University of California Division of Agriculture and Natural Resources Publication 3402.

Gast, K.1998. *Evaluation of postharvest life of selected fresh-cut flowers*. Report of Progress 840, Kansas State University Agricultural Experiment Station and Cooperative Extension Service.

Harkess, R.L., and R.E. Lyons. 1997. A comparison of seeding rate, spacing, and weed control methods in the Virginia Tech transplanted meadow. *HortTechnology* 7:39–41.

Horst, R.K. 1990. Cosmos, pp. 608–609 in *Westcott's Plant Disease Handbook*, 5th ed. Van Nostrand Reinhold, New York.

Huxley, A., M. Griffiths, and M. Levy. 1992. *Cosmos*, pp. 738–739 in *The New Royal Horticultural Society Dictionary of Gardening*, vol. 1. Stockton Press, New York.

Kanellos, E.A.G., and S. Pearson. 2000. Environmental regulation of flowering and growth of *Cosmos atrosanguineus* (Hook.) Voss. *Scientia Horticulturae* 83:265–274.

Molder, M., and J.M. Owens. 1985. *Cosmos*, pp. 341–349 in *Handbook of Flowering*, vol. II, A.H. Halevy, editor. CRC Press, Boca Raton, Florida.

Peters, J. 1947. Einflus der Tageslänge auf das Blühen einger Sorten von *Cosmos bipinnatus* und *Cosmos sulphureus*. *Gartenbauwissenschaft* 39: 47–50. (in German)

Post, K. 1949. *Cosmos*, pp. 428–430 in *Florist Crop Production and Marketing*. Orange Judd Publishing, New York.

Redman, P.B., J.M. Dole, N.O. Maness, and J.A. Anderson. 2002. Postharvest handling of nine specialty cut flower species. *Scientia Horticulturae* 92:293–303.

Samata, Y., I. Kosei, and E. Hideo. 1974. Effect of B995, succinic acid, 2,2-dimethyl hydrazide application on double cosmos (*Cosmos bipinnatus*) with special reference to the inhibition of peduncle elongation. *Bulletin Faculty Agricultural University of Tamagawa* 14:51–58.

Starman, T.W., T.A. Cerny, and A.J. MacKenzie. 1995. Productivity and profitability of some field-grown specialty cut flowers. *HortScience* 30: 1217–1220.

Warner, R.M., and J.E. Erwin. 2001. Temperature, pp. 10–17 in *Tips on Regulating Growth of Floriculture Crops*, M.L. Gaston, L.A. Kunkle, P.S. Konjoian, and M.F. Wilt, editors. Ohio Florists' Association Services, Columbus, Ohio.

Wittwer, S.J., and M.J. Bukovac. 1959. Effects of gibberellin on photoperiodic response of some higher plants, pp. 373–380 in *Photoperiodism and Related Phenomena in Plants and Animals*, R.B. Withrow, editor. American Association for the Advancement of Science, Washington, D.C.

Zimmer, K. 1988. Photoperidische reaktionen bei *Cosmos bipinnatus*. *Gartenbauwessenschaft* 53: 257–260. (in German)

Crocus

INTRODUCTION

Common names: crocus, Dutch crocus.

Scientific name: *Crocus vernus* Hill. (Huxley et al., 1992).

Family and related taxa: Iridaceae Juss. The genus *Crocus* includes almost 80 species of cormous bulbs. Numerous species flower in the winter, late winter, or early spring and include *C. ancyrensis* (Herb) Maw., *C. augustifolius* Weston., *C. biflorus* Mill., *C. chrysanthus* (Herb) Herb., and *C. flavus* Weston. (Bailey and Bailey, 1976) (Table II-1 Crocus). The autumn flowering saffron crocus, *C. sativus* L., is also well known, especially for the costly saffron spice. Other important ornamentals in the Iridaceae family are *Freesia, Gladiolus,* and *Iris*.

Origin: Crocus species are distributed from Asia Minor for *C. ancyrensis, C. biflorus,* and *C. chrysanthus* to southwestern Russia for *C. augustifolius* and to Austria, France, and Switzerland for *C. vernus. C. sativus,* which has been cultivated for thousands of years, is known only in cultivation from France, Italy, and Iran to India (Bailey and Bailey, 1976).

Uses and current status: Crocus is forced into flower for winter and spring sales in pots or is grown in the garden for winter to early spring color. The various species have a wide range of colors. Unfortunately, fall flowering crocuses have been relatively ignored in the trade for garden center sales or use in the landscape.

Crocus leaves are thin, linear, and seldom more than 4 to 6 in. (10 to 15 cm) long. The flowers are made of six or more equally segmented units that are long, tubular, united at the base, and flared at the top. The corm is tunicated with contractile roots (Bailey and Bailey, 1976; Benschop, 1993).

CULTIVARS

De Hertogh (1996) lists six crocus cultivars that have been researched and the exact programming and forcing schedules. Other cultivars are listed by Benschop (1993) and De Hertogh et al. (1990).

PROPAGATION

Sexual propagation is only used in breeding because 3 to 4 years are required from seed to flower. The 375 million corms produced yearly in the Netherlands are produced through asexual propagation of the cormlets. A new corm is developed annually from the apical-most axillary bud with numerous cormlets arising from the subtending axillary buds. *In vitro* propagation has been used on *C. chrysanthus* but is primarily used on the saffron crocus *C. sativus* (Benschop, 1993).

TABLE II-1 CROCUS

Various *Crocus* species that can be forced in the greenhouse or used in the landscape (Bailey and Bailey, 1976).

Species	Color	Comments
C. ancyrensis	Golden yellow	Flowers in late winter.
C. augustifolius	Bright yellow	Cloth of Gold crocus. Flowers are starlike. Flowers in late winter.
C. biflorus	White to pale purple	Scotch crocus. Flowers in late winter, several cultivars exist.
C. chrysanthus	White, yellow, deep lilac	Several named cultivars. Flowers in winter.
C. flavus	Golden yellow to orange	Flowers in late winter, spring.
C. vernus	White, lilac, purple	Dutch crocus. Many hybrids and cultivars exist. Flowers with feathered or striped petals. Flowers in late winter, spring.

FLOWERING CONTROL AND DORMANCY

Crocus corms for greenhouse forcing must receive a minimum of 13 to 20 weeks of 48°F (9°C) for rooting and shoot development (see Table II-2 Crocus). For early flowering (forcing) schedules, dry bulbs are cooled in August or September and potted in early October. For later schedules, dry corms are held at 63°F (17°C) prior to simultaneously potting and starting the 48°F (9°C) cold treatment (De Hertogh, 1996). Temperatures are reduced to 41°F (5°C) in early November (Rooting Room A) or early December (Rooting Room B) when plants are well rooted (see Table II-3 Crocus). After the first week in January, temperatures are lowered to 32 to 35°F (0 to 2°C). Temperature is reduced to 32 to 35°F (0 to 2°C) when shoots are greater than 1 in. (2.5 cm) tall.

For the spring-flowering species, flower initiation and development occur during late spring and early summer prior to forcing. Corms are harvested in the Netherlands and graded in June and July after vegetative growth has died. Old mother corms are discarded. For *Crocus vernus*, corms should be larger than 2.75 in. (7 cm). For other species, only corms larger than 2 in. (5 cm) in circumference will flower (Benschop, 1993). Flower differentiation and development continue at temperatures between 63 and 72°F (17 and 22°C) (De Hertogh et al., 1990). Corms are then distributed worldwide for greenhouse forcing or for

TABLE II-2 CROCUS

Crocus cultivars are designated by color: by the minimum (Min), optimum (Opt), or maximum (Max) weeks of cold that corms can be stored; and by the presence (PC) or absence of precooling (NP). The approximate days to flower in the forcing greenhouse are denoted by parentheses (Modified from De Hertogh, 1996).

Flower Color: Cultivar	Appropriate Forcing Dates						Weeks of Cold		
	I	II	III	IV	V	VI			
	Dec 15–31	Jan 1–12	Jan 13–25	Jan 26–Feb 9	Feb 10–28	Mar 1–20	Min	Opt	Max
Lavender:									
'Flower Record'	—	PC(21)	PC(18)	NP(18)	NP(12)	NP(8)	13	15	20
'Remembrance'	—	NP(21)	NP(21)	NP(18)	NP(18)	NP(9)	13	15	19
Striped:									
'King of the Striped'	—	—	NP(23)	NP(23)	NP(19)	NP(11)	14	16	19
'Pickwick'	—	NP(23)	NP(23)	NP(21)	NP(16)	NP(10)	13	15	19
White:									
'Joan of Arc'	—	—	PC(21)	NP(21)	NP(18)	NP(11)	14	16	19
Yellow:									
C. flavus	—	—	PC(20)	NP(20)	NP(15)	NP(10)	15	17	19

TABLE II-3 CROCUS

Dates of temperature sequences used in Rooting Rooms A and B (De Hertogh, 1996).

Room	Date	Temperature °F (°C)
A	Potting to Nov. 5–10[a]	48 (9)
	Nov. 5–10 to Jan. 1–5[b]	41 (5)
	Jan. 1–5 to end of cooling	32–35 (0–2)
B	Potting to Dec. 1–5[a]	48 (9)
	Dec. 1–5 to Jan. 1–5[b]	41 (5)
	Jan. 1–5 to end of cooling	32–35 (0–2)

[a] Temperatures are dropped to 41°F (5°C) when plants are well rooted and actual dates may vary from year to year.
[b] On January 1–5, all bulbs are at 41°F (5°C) and either cooler can be used. Temperature may be reduced sooner if shoot elongation is greater than 1 in. (2.5 cm).

use in home gardens. Precise temperature treatments are required for greenhouse forcing. The *Holland Bulb Forcers' Guide* (De Hertogh, 1996) is an essential guide for forcers of crocus. Wilkins (1985) and Benschop (1993) reviewed the vegetative and reproductive cycles for the autumn flowering crocus (*C. sativus*).

TEMPERATURE

Cold treatments for flower development and shoot elongation were previously discussed. The Dutch crocus is forced in a greenhouse at night temperatures of 55 to 60°F (13 to 16°C). Day temperatures can be 3 to 5°F (2 to 3°C) warmer. Forcing is quite rapid, particularly for later schedules (see Table II-4 Crocus).

LIGHT

Full light intensity is used in midwinter for greenhouse forcing. Reduced intensity may be used to elongate plants during the early forcing schedules or to control temperature for late season forcing. Interestingly, high-quality plants with slightly paler green leaves can be produced in growth rooms using only 4 hr of light as low as 19 fc (3 μmol $\cdot$ m^{-2} $\cdot$ s^{-1}) (Jerzy and Krause, 1981).

WATER

During cold storage and forcing, the medium must not be allowed to dry out.

CARBON DIOXIDE

No CO_2 is required.

NUTRITION

Corms are not fertilized during cooling or forcing.

MEDIA

The recommended medium is well drained and low in soluble salts and has a pH of 6.0 to 7.0. Although a wide variety of media mixes can be used, clay should be avoided as a media amendment.

HEIGHT CONTROL

No height control is needed (see Light section earlier).

TABLE II-4 CROCUS

Programming schedules for forcing *Crocus* corms into flower (modified from De Hertogh, 1996). See Table II-3 Crocus for Rooting Room A and B temperature sequences.

Forcing Period	Date of Expected Flowering	Date to Commence Forcing	Date to Pot Corms	Date to Start Precooling	Rooting Room	Total Cold (weeks)
I	Jan. 1	Dec. 12				
	Jan. 7	Dec. 19	Oct. 1–7	August 28–31[a]	A	16
	Jan. 11	Dec. 26				17
II	Jan. 13	Dec. 22	Oct. 1–7	Sept. 1–5[a]	A	17
	Jan. 18	Dec. 29				18
	Jan. 23	Jan. 7				19.5
III	Jan. 13	Dec. 24	Sept. 15–20	None[b]	A	14
	Jan. 18	Dec. 31				15
	Jan. 23	Jan. 7				16
IV	Jan. 25	Jan. 3	Sept. 28–Oct. 2	None[b]	A	13.5
	Jan. 31	Jan. 12				15
	Feb. 7	Jan. 23				16.5
V	Feb. 11	Jan. 25	Oct. 17–20	None[b]	B	14
	Feb. 18	Feb. 6				15.5
	Feb. 24	Feb. 15				17
VI	Mar. 2	Feb. 18	Nov. 5–10	None[b]	B	14.5
	Mar. 9	Feb. 28				19
	Mar. 16	Mar. 8				17.5

[a]Precool at 48°F (9°C).
[b]No precooling required. Hold at 63°F (17°C) until potted.

SPACING

Only corms 3.5 in. (9 cm) and larger in circumference should be planted. Five to six corms are commonly used in a 4-in. (10-cm) pot. Also, short [5-in. (12.5-cm)] crocus pots can be used with seven to nine corms. The pots are placed pot-to-pot in cold storage and forcing.

PINCHING AND DISBUDDING

No pinching or disbudding required.

SUPPORT

No support required.

SCHEDULE AND TIMING

Programming schedules for crocus and numerous other flowering bulbs have been developed by De Hertogh (1996). Both Rooting Rooms A and B are used for exact temperature controls. Forcing schedules have been divided into six forcing or timing schedules. Crocus can be forced from mid-December to early March (see Tables II-2 and II-4 Crocus).

INSECTS

Aphid infestations can develop in storage or in forcing.

DISEASES

Corms must be inspected with care and only healthy corms planted because diseases (*Fusarium* and *Rhizoctonia*) can infect corms prior to forcing and thus impair forcing. Corm dips prior to potting and drenches during and after storage should be done to prevent diseases. *Penicillium* can develop in cold storage and is controllable.

PHYSIOLOGICAL DISORDERS

Flower abortion can occur due to inadequate cooling, excessive temperatures during forcing, or improper cultivar selection for a specific forcing date.

POSTHARVEST

Plants should be shipped and marketed "as soon as the buds' sheaths (not the individual buds) are visible" and can be stored at 33 to 35°F (1 to 2°C) (Ball, 1991). A minimum light intensity of 50 fc (10 μmol $\cdot$ m^{-2} $\cdot$ s^{-1}) can be used. Crocus can be held in the dark for 3 days. Customers should be encouraged to accept "green" plants because flowers develop rapidly and sales of plants with open flowers decrease potential enjoyment (Nell, 1993).

KEY POINTS

- Crocus is used as a potted flowering plant and as a landscape perennial.
- Commercially, propagation is by cormlets but seed or *in vitro* can also be used.
- Corms for greenhouse forcing must receive a minimum of 13 to 15 weeks of 48°F (9°C) or lower for root and shoot development.
- The initial portion of the cold treatment can be applied to the corms either dry and unpotted (known as precooling, PC) for early forcing dates or moist and potted (known as non-precooled, NP) for later forcing dates.
- The final portion of the cold treatment is always applied to moist, potted bulbs.
- After the cold treatment, plants are moved to the greenhouse and forced.
- The forcing season is divided into six periods; recommended cultivars and forcing schedules vary with the period.
- The various forcing schedules are combined into two basic sequences known as Rooting Room A and Rooting Room B.
- Plants are shipped as soon as the buds' sheaths are visible, not when flower color can be seen.

BIBLIOGRAPHY

Bailey, L.H., and E.Z. Bailey. 1976. *Crocus*, pp. 334–335 in *Hortus Third: A Concise Dictionary of Plants Cultivated in the United States and Canada*. Macmillan, New York.

Ball, Vic. 1991. Bulb crops, p. 406 in *Ball Redbook*, 15th ed. Ball Publishing, West Chicago, Illinois.

Benschop, M. 1993. *Crocus*, pp. 257–272 in *The Physiology of Flower Bulbs*, A. De Hertogh and M. Le Nard, editors. Elsevier, Amsterdam.

De Hertogh, A.A. 1996. "Specialty bulbs" for potted plants, pp. B95–118 in *Holland Bulb Forcers' Guide*, 5th ed. International Flower Bulb Centre, Hillegom, The Netherlands.

De Hertogh, A.A., C. Noone, and A. Lutman. 1990. *Geophyte*™ (computer reference listing). North Carolina State University, Raleigh, North Carolina.

Huxley, A., M. Griffiths, and M. Levy. 1992. *Crocus*, pp. 763–768 in *The New Royal Horticultural Society Dictionary of Gardening*, vol. 1. Stockton Press, New York.

Jerzy, M., and J. Krause. 1981. Crocus-forcing in artificial light. *Scientia Horticulturae* 15:263–266.

Nell, T.A. 1993. Crocus, pp. 29–30 in *Flowering Potted Plants, Prolonging Shelf Performance*. Ball Publishing, Batavia, Illinois.

Wilkins, H.F. 1985. *Crocus vernus* and *Crocus sativus*, pp. 350–355 in *Handbook of Flowering*, vol. II, A.H. Halevy, editor. CRC Press, Boca Raton, Florida.

Crossandra

FIGURE II-1 CROSSANDRA Potted *Crossandra* plant (photo courtesy of J and L Plants, Inc.).

INTRODUCTION

Common names: firecracker flower, flame flower, crossandra.

Scientific name: *Crossandra infundibuliformis* (L.) Nees. (Huxley et al., 1992).

Family and related taxa: Acanthaceae Juss. The genus *Crossandra* includes 50 species. Numerous other genera in the Acanthaceae family are cultivated as ornamentals including *Aphelandra, Fittonia, Hypoestes, Justicia, Ruellia,* and *Thunbergia*.

Origin: This species is from southern India and Ceylon. The genus is found in tropical Africa, Madagascar, India, Sri Lanka, and north and west to Arabia.

Uses and current status: Though a minor crop, it is an excellent plant to add variety for major spring holidays, and for large container gardens and baskets. Crossandra is mainly used as a 4- to 5-in. (10- to 13-cm) pot plant or as a heat-tolerant bedding plant for warm climates (Hamrick, 2003; Harthun, 1991). Crossandra is not only grown for its orange, yellow, red, salmon pink, or pink flowers, but also for its smooth dark-green leaves.

The glossy gardenia-like leaves are opposite and 2 to 5 in. (5 to 13 cm) long. Flowers overlap each other and form a dense, erect, raceme-like inflorescence. The individual flowers are a corolla composed of a slender tube that flares and forms a 1.5-in (4-cm)-wide lip with five rounded lobes. Plants can grow to 3 ft (90 cm) tall (Bailey and Bailey, 1976) (Fig. II-1 Crossandra).

CULTIVARS

Cultivars are available as seed or as asexually propagated plants. Asexually propagated cultivars include the 'Florida' series, which is touted as being more cold tolerant than other cultivars and is available in four colors: red, red-orange, yellow, and orange. 'Tropic Flame' is a seed-propagated cultivar with orange flowers.

PROPAGATION

Seed packets contain 4000 seeds/oz (140/g). Seeds should be lightly covered with 0.13 in. (3 mm) of medium. Germination is slow and sporadic even at 80 to 85°F (27 to 29°C) and seedlings emerge over a 3- to 4-week period (Harthun, 1991). Langefeld (1991) recommended 85/70°F (29/21°C) day/night temperatures for optimum germination, which can commence within 10 to 14 days. Nau (1999) recommended a slightly lower day temperature of 80°F (26°C) for germination.

Typically, growers buy 2.5-in. (6.5-cm) liners that have been propagated asexually. Tip cuttings root in 3 to 4 weeks with a rooting hormone when propagated directly into 2.5-in. (6.5-cm) pots. The medium temperature should be 75°F (24°C) with 85/70°F (29/21°C) day/night air temperatures. Light intensity is reduced to 1500 to 1800 fc (300 to 360 μmol · m^{-2} · s^{-1}). Propagation is easier and faster under white plastic tents in the summer or clear plastic in the winter (Harthun, 1991; Langefeld, 1991).

FLOWERING CONTROL AND DORMANCY

Once rooted, high nutrition, warm temperatures, and the long days of summer are conducive to flowering. In Danish greenhouses, flowering occurs naturally from March to September (Wilkins, 1985). Regardless of whether the photoperiod is 8 or 16 hr long, flowering generally occurs 100 to 105 days after liners are planted into final pot sizes (Harthun, 1991).

TEMPERATURE

Though Adriansen (1976) and Pedersen (1975) found that the most rapid flowering occurred when temperatures were 75°F (24°C), Moes (1976) defined the optimum air temperatures as 66/55°F (19/13°C) day/night with a medium temperature of 72°F (22°C). Low forcing temperatures were better when light intensities were low and high plant quality was desired (Moes, 1976; Pedersen et al., 1973a, b). Plants will die at constant temperatures of 45 to 55°F (7 to 13°C) after 6 weeks (Christensen, 1975;

Sandved, 1974). This above-mentioned information was generated in Denmark where light intensity is low in the winter. In the United States temperature recommendations are 78 to 82°F (26 to 28°C) during the day and 70°F (21°C) at night for 6 weeks after propagation, then 65°F (18°C) nights with day temperatures 5°F (3°C) warmer (Harthun, 1991; Langefeld, 1991).

LIGHT

Recommended light intensity during production is 3000 to 3500 fc (600 to 700 μmol · m^{-2} · s^{-1}). Growth is adequate between 2600 and 3000 fc (520 to 600 μmol · m^{-2} · s^{-1}). Below 1800 fc (360 μmol · m^{-2} · s^{-1}) growth is slow. During summer 30% shade is recommended (Harthun, 1991; Langefeld, 1991).

WATER

Do not overwater plants because the roots are susceptible to *Rhizoctonia;* however, do not water stress the plants, because the leaves will burn (Langefeld, 1991). Maintain humidity at 70 to 80% during early growth or for the first 6 weeks, then reduce to 30 to 50% for later growth. Foliar nutrient levels for high-quality plants are listed in Chapter 6, Nutrition, Table 6-4.

CARBON DIOXIDE

No data available.

NUTRITION

After cuttings root, begin a high nutrient regime to stimulate vegetative growth. A constant liquid fertilizer of 200 ppm N from a complete fertilizer is recommended (Harthun, 1991; Langefeld, 1991). Magnesium, iron, and manganese are critical nutrients and should not be overlooked.

MEDIA

A pasteurized medium is essential for propagation and for production. A medium with good water-holding capacity, good drainage, and a pH of 6.2 to 7.0 is acceptable (Langefeld, 1991).

HEIGHT CONTROL

Sprays of B-Nine (daminozide) are routinely used to reduce internode elongation and increase branching without flowering delay

(Adriansen, 1976; Moes, 1976; Veluswamy et al., 1974). A-Rest (ancymidol) has been effectively used in recirculating ebb-and-flow irrigation solution (Adriansen, 1979). The most common plant growth retardant is B-Nine applied as a 2500-ppm spray 2 weeks after plants have been pinched or when the new axillary shoots are 1.5 to 2 in. (4 to 5 cm) long. With high summer irradiance levels, retardants may not be required (Langefeld, 1991).

SPACING

Seedlings and cuttings are transplanted into 2.5-in. (6.25-cm) pots. If commercially propagated as liners, they are held pot-to-pot until shipped. Liners are transplanted into 4-, 4.5-, or 6-in. (10-, 11-, or 15-cm) pots with final spacings of 6.5 × 7, 7 × 7, or 9 × 9 in. (16.5 × 18, 18 × 18, or 23 × 23 cm), respectively. Spacing can be done as needed or after 5 or 6 weeks before leaves overlap. Put one plant per pot for the smaller size pots and three plants per 6-in. (15-cm) pots (Langefeld, 1991).

PINCHING AND DISBUDDING

Plants should be pinched 3 weeks after final potting, allowing five or six leaves to remain on the plant. To prevent a lack of uniformity in plant and shoot development, be sure to (1) start with uniform cuttings (length and node number), (2) grade rooted cuttings for uniformity, and (3) leave uniform node numbers after pinching. No disbudding is required.

SUPPORT

No support required.

SCHEDULE AND TIMING

Only 12 to 14 weeks are required for production from liners; producing liners from rooted cuttings will add an extra 6 to 7 weeks (Table II-1 Crossandra). Production from seed has the disadvantage of requiring up to 31 weeks to get a marketable plant (Table II-2 Crossandra).

INSECTS

Whiteflies, spider mites, and aphids can be problems in production (Langefeld, 1991).

DISEASES

Rhizoctonia and *Thielaviopsis*, or black root rot, can be problems during and after propagation (Daughtrey and Chase, 1992; Langefeld, 1991). Liners purchased from specialists should not be planted too deep, because *Rhizoctonia* and *Pythium* can develop.

PHYSIOLOGICAL DISORDERS

Cold stress occurs at temperatures below 50°F (10°C) and plants will be injured and die. Lack of flowering can occur if light levels fall below 1800 fc (360 μmol $\cdot$ m^{-2} $\cdot$ s^{-1}).

POSTHARVEST

Crossandra must be shipped and stored at 50 to 55°F (10 to 13°C). At low temperatures of 40°F

TABLE II-I CROSSANDRA
Sample production schedule for *Crossandra* as a potted flowering plant from cuttings.

Cultural Step	Production Time (weeks)	Temperature °F (°C)
Root cutting in 2.25-in. (5.7-cm) pots	3–4	Day: 85 (29) Night: 70 (21) Medium: 75 (24)
Growing on	3	Night: 70–75 (21–24)
Transplant to final pot size	3–4	Night: 70–75 (21–24)
Pinch	2–3	Night: 65 (18)
B-Nine application	7	Night: 65 (18)
Flower		
Total	18–21	

TABLE II-2 CROSSANDRA

Sample production schedule for *Crossandra* as a potted flowering plant from seed.

Cultural Step	Production Time (weeks)	Temperature °F (°C)
Germinate seed	2–4	Day: 85 (29) Night: 70 (21) Medium: 75 (24)
Transplant to 2.5-in. (6.3-cm) liners	3	Night: 70–75 (21–24)
Growing on	10	Night: 70–75 (21–24)
Transplant to final pot size	3–4	Night: 70–75 (21–24)
Pinch	2–3	Night: 65(18)
B-Nine application	7	Night: 65 (18)
Flower		
Total	27–31	

(4°C) the leaves turn black; however, shipping temperatures above 65°F (18°C) can also cause damage. A crossandra in flower can last up to a month with adequate light of 1000 fc (200 μmol $\cdot$ m^{-2} $\cdot$ s^{-1}) and care (Nell, 1993). Plants lasted at least 3 months and continued to flower when provided with at least 12 hr or 100 fc (20 μmol $\cdot$ m^{-2} $\cdot$ s^{-1}) of light (Gibbs et al., 1989). Crossandra is sensitive to ethylene and flower buds abscise (Nell, 1993; Nowak and Rudnicki, 1990). Silver thiosulfate sprays of 0.4 to 0.5 mM can be used to extend longevity of the flowers (Moe and Fjeld, 1987).

KEY POINTS

- Crossandra is used as a potted flowering plant and bedding plant.
- Plants are propagated by seed and by cuttings.
- Plants are day neutral and flowering is most rapid with warm night temperatures of 70 to 75°F (21 to 24°C).
- Recommended light intensity is 3000 to 3500 fc (600 to 700 μmol $\cdot$ m^{-2} $\cdot$ s^{-1}).
- Do not overwater because plants are susceptible to *Rhizoctonia* root rot; however, do not water stress because the leaves will burn.
- Cold stress occurs below 50°F (10°C).

BIBLIOGRAPHY

Adriansen, E. 1976. Effect of SADH and ethephon on *Crossandra infundibuliformis* 'Mona Wallhed.' *Tidsskrift for Planteavl* 80:31–40. (in Danish)

Adriansen, E. 1979. Growth retardation of potted plants cultivated in water culture with ancymidol applied to the nutrient solution. *Acta Horticulturae* 91:387–394.

Bailey, L.H., and E.Z. Bailey. 1976. *Crossandra*, pp. 336–337 in *Hortus Third: A Concise Dictionary of Plants Cultivated in the United States and Canada.* Macmillan, New York.

Christensen, O.V. 1975. The influence of low temperature on flowering of *Beloperone, Crossandra, Jacobinia* and *Mackaya. Tidsskrift Planteavl* 79:459–462. (in Danish)

Daughtrey, M., and A.R. Chase. 1992. Crossandra, p. 49 in *Ball Field Guide to Diseases of Greenhouse Ornamentals.* Ball Publishing, Geneva, Illinois.

Gibbs, M.M., T.M. Blessington, J.A. Price, and Y-T. Wang. 1989. Postproduction effects of light level and duration on flowering and quality of *Crossandra. HortScience* 24:705.

Hamrick, D. 2003. *Crossandra*, pp. 321–323 in *Ball Redbook,* vol. 2, 17th ed. Ball Publishing, Batavia, Illinois.

Harthun, E. 1991. Crossandra, pp. 474–475 in *Ball Redbook*, 15th ed., V. Ball, editor. Ball Publishing, West Chicago, Illinois.

Huxley, A., M. Griffiths, and M. Levy. 1992. *Crossandra*, p. 768 in *The New Royal Horticultural Society Dictionary of Gardening*, vol. 1. Stockton Press, New York.

Langefeld, J. 1991. Crossandra, pp. 63–65 in *Growers Talks' on Crop Culture*, D.J. Hamrick, editor. Ball Publishing, Geneva, Illinois.

Moe, R., and T. Fjeld. 1987. Keeping quality of potted plants as influenced by ethylene. *Gartner Tidende* 101:1580–1583.

Moes, E. 1976. Temperature for *Crossandra*. *Gartner Tidende* 11:163–164. (in Danish)

Nau, J. 1999. *Ball Culture Guide, The Encyclopedia of Seed Germination*, 3rd ed. Ball Publishing, Batavia, Illinois.

Nell, T.A. 1993. Crossandra, pp. 31–32 in *Flowering Potted Plants, Prolonging Shelf Performances*. Ball Publishing, Batavia, Illinois.

Nowak, J., and R.M. Rudnicki. 1990. *Postharvest Handling and Storage of Cut Flowers, Florist Greens and Potted Plants*. Timber Press, Portland, Oregon.

Pedersen, A.M. 1975. Standard growing of *Crossandra infundibuliformis* (L.) Nees 'Mona Wallhed.' *Tidsskrift Planteavl* 79:463–473. (in Danish)

Pedersen, A.M., E. Adriansen, and E. Moes. 1973a. Trials at Sørhus with *Crossandra*. *Gartner Tidende* 89(25):307–310. (in Danish)

Pedersen, A.M., E. Adriansen, and E. Moes. 1973b. Trials with *Crossandra*. *Gartneryrket* 63(35): 606–610. (in Danish)

Sandved, G. 1974. Spring flowering of *Crossandra* cultivar 'Mona Wallhed' after overwintering at different temperatures. *Gartneryrket* 64:607–609. (in Danish)

Veluswamy, P., T. Thangaraj, and S. Mathuswamy. 1974. A study on comparative morphology of four cultivars of *Crossandra* (*C. undulaefolia*, Salisb.). *Southern Indian Horticulture* 22:81–83.

Wilkins, H.F. 1985. *Crossandra infundibuliformis*, pp. 356–359 in *Handbook of Flowering*, vol. II, A.H. Halevy, editor. CRC Press, Boca Raton, Florida.

Cyclamen

INTRODUCTION

Common names: cyclamen, florist's cyclamen, Persian violet, alpine violet.

Scientific name: *Cyclamen persicum* Mill. (Huxley et al., 1992).

Family and related taxa: Primulaceae Vent. Although the hybrids and cultivars of *C. persicum* are commercially dominant, several species are suitable for temperate Zones 5 to 9 gardens (*C. coum* Mill., *C. hederifolium* Ait., and *C. purpurascens* Mill.) and for Mediterranean climate gardens (*C. africanum* Boiss. & Reut., *C. cyprium* Kotschy, *C. persicum*, and *C. rohlfsianum* Asch.) (Bailey and Bailey, 1976; Le Nard and De Hertogh, 1993). These species colonize in rock gardens under trees and shrubs, often forming a ground cover. The genus *Primula* is also a member of this family.

Origin: Widmer (1992) wrote a thorough review of the history and taxonomy of cyclamen. The 15 species of cormous cyclamens are found in central Europe and the Mediterranean area and east to Iran. *C. persicum* is a native of the eastern Mediterranean region.

Uses and current status: Common winter and spring flowering potted plant in pot sizes ranging from 2.5 to 7 in. (6.5 to 18 cm) (Fig. II-1 Cyclamen). Occasionally grown as a cut flower and outdoor garden ornamental.

The cordate-shaped leaves are basally attached to a cormlike structure, which can be 6 in. (15 cm) in diameter. The storage organ is difficult to specify as a corm or as a tuber. The leaves have variable green and silver patterns and toothed margins. The leaf petiole and flower scapes are up to 8 in. (20 cm) long. Flowers vary in scent and are colored white, pink, salmon, red, or maroon. Unfortunately, the delicate fragrance of the flowers has been

FIGURE II-1 CYCLAMEN *Cyclamen* plants in 4- and 6-in. (10- and 15-cm) pots showing a range of leaf patterns.

lost in many of the hybrid cultivars. Flowers have five strongly reflexed petals, which can be fluted. Bicolors and double types are available. Petals may have smooth edges or fringes. The union of the petals forms a short tube (Bailey and Bailey, 1976; Le Nard and De Hertogh, 1993; Widmer and Lyons, 1985).

CULTIVARS

Cyclamen growers should test plants from numerous sources or visit cultivar trials hosted by major plug producers to learn which cultivars perform best for their particular environment. The traditional large flowering cyclamen was grown in 6- or 7-in. (15- or 18-cm) pots. Large flowered cyclamens can be either open pollinated or F_1 hybrids and are known as "maxi" types. F_1 hybrid "midi" and "mini" cultivars are also available. Midi types are best suited for 4- to 5-in. (10- to 13-cm) pot production. Some midi types can be grown in 6-in. (15-cm) pots, but plant size may be too small. Mini types are suited for 2.5-, 3-, or 4-in. (6.5-, 7.5-, or 10-cm) pots (Gerritsen, 1998). Heat-tolerant cultivars should be used in warm climates. Cultivars also vary in the amount of silver on the foliage and flower fragrance.

Tetraploid seed lines are now available, which have greater vigor and flower and leaf size. Tetraploids can either be open pollinated (o.p.) or hand pollinated (F_1). The seed for F_1 cultivars is more expensive, but plants are more uniform in flower color, plant habit, and growth rate.

PROPAGATION

Although well-developed cormlike organs form after one growth cycle from seed, they are not commercially used. Frequently, corms are available for the home garden, but should be held suspect because they may have been harvested from a native habitat. Many cyclamen species are endangered due to overharvesting and habitat loss. Farmers in native environments are being encouraged to field-produce the corms. Be sure to check the source of corms before purchasing them.

Seeds germinate in the dark, under 100% humidity (fog) at 59 to 68°F (15 to 20°C) for 3 to 4 weeks. Germination does not occur at 41 or 68°F (5 or 20°C). The seeds are barely indented into the medium by about 0.13 to 0.25 in. (0.2 to 0.5 mm). Very low light inhibits germination (Corbineau et al., 1989). When germination occurs, seedlings are immediately moved to light and humidity reduced to 70% (Corr, 1997). Seeds should be propagated in plugs for ease of transplanting later. A medium pH of 6 to 6.5 is critical for germination (Sumitomo and Kosugi, 1963; Widmer, 1983). Seeds should be used within 1 year but can be stored at 38°F (3°C) in a sealed container for up to 2 years.

Interestingly, this dicot is a pseudomonocot because only one cotyledon is produced. Before and immediately on emergence, the corm begins to form at the base of the cotyledon petiole, and the future storage organ should be thought of as an enlarged hypocotyl. The cormlike storage organ for cyclamen forms best at 59 to 68°F (15 to 20°C). Up to 13 leaves form before flower initiation (Sumitomo and Kosugi, 1963; Sunberg, 1981a, b; Widmer, 1983; Widmer and Lyons, 1985). *In vitro* propagation is possible in the development of new cultivars (Ewald, 1996; Ishizaka, 1998; Takamura et al., 1998).

FLOWERING CONTROL AND DORMANCY

The cyclamen is a day-neutral plant. The plant is vegetative until 10 to 13 leaves have formed, then reproductive apices can be observed in axils of older leaves, beginning with the sixth leaf in many cultivars. Thus, a young plant will initiate up to 13 leaves before the first flowers are formed (Niizu, 1967; Stephens and Widmer, 1976; Sunberg, 1981a, b; Widmer and Lyons, 1985). New cultivars may initiate flowers sooner than older cultivars. Thereafter, flowers alternate with leaves, and this ratio can continue for many months. In nature, flowers eventually begin to abort, and the growth cycle ends after the initiated flowers mature. After this stage, leaves mature and senesce (Sunberg, 1981a, b).

Neuray (1973) divided the growth cycle of the commercial cyclamen into three phases. Phase 1 is vegetative and ends when the first flower is formed in the axils of the leaves. Phase 2 is both vegetative and reproductive. Phase 3 occurs when the growing points begin to abort, and adventitious buds may develop on the corm's surface. Returning to phase 2 is not possible, unless the corm goes through a rest period.

Gibberellic acid (GA_3) can be used to decrease the time to flower after the buds have developed. The GA_3 rate is 25 ppm for open-pollinated cultivars, 10 ppm for F_1 hybrids, and 5 ppm for miniature cultivars. A wetting agent should be added and 0.33 fl oz (2.6 mL) should be applied to each plant. The spray must be directed through the canopy onto the flower buds and not applied overhead to only the leaves. The GA_3 sprays are applied when flower buds are 0.19 to 0.25 in. (0.4 to 0.6 cm) long and when the plant has 10 to 12 leaves (Karlsson, 1997; Widmer et al., 1974, 1976, 1983). Floral development and scape elongation are hastened, not flower initiation. The number of flowers open at one time is increased. If the GA_3 concentration is too high or excessive solution is applied, flower scapes may elongate excessively, become weak, and fall over. Cultivar testing and grower experience are required.

TEMPERATURE

Cyclamen plants were historically grown as a "cold crop" at night temperatures of 50°F (10°C), which required a production period of 13 to 15 months (Post, 1949). Now cyclamen are grown with the fast crop method, which requires only 7 to 9 months (Widmer et al., 1976, 1983). Seeds are germinated and grown until transplanted 16 weeks later at 68°F (20°C), at which time the temperature is lowered to 62 to 64°F (17 to 18°C). When the flower buds are 0.13 to 0.25 in. (3 to 6 mm) long, temperatures are lowered to 60 to 62°F (16 to 17°C) until sales 8 weeks later. Stephens and Widmer (1976) found that medium temperatures of 55 to 65°F (13 to 18°C) hastened flowering by 2

weeks when used during the stage at which the plant had 35 to 40 unfolded leaves. Excessively high summer temperatures can delay flowering for 1 month.

Karlsson and Werner (1998, 2001) have further studied temperature and cyclamen growth using growth chambers in Alaska. Nine-week-old seedlings were placed at 46, 54, 61, 68, or 75°F (8, 12, 16, 20, or 24°C) for 8 weeks, then returned to 61°F (16°C) until plants flowered. The visible bud date was similar: 118 days after sowing or 55 days after completing the intermediate temperature treatment, for plants grown at 54, 61, or 68°F (12, 16, or 20°C). Plants placed at 46 or 75°F (8 or 24°C) were slower and required 60 or 93 days, respectively, to flower. The leaf unfolding rate was greatest and the time to flower was shortest at 68°F (20°C). Leaf and flower number increased from 38 and 18 to 77 and 52, respectively, as the temperature increased from 54 to 75°F (12 to 24°C). M. Karlsson (personal communication) stressed that the longer plants are grown at 68°F (20°C), the more rapid the flowering. The temperature can be lowered to 61°F (16°C) for the last 3 weeks to tone the plant and increase postharvest life without delaying flowering. She further stressed that higher light causes faster development under any temperature or photoperiod. "I used 12 mol · day · m^{-2} with great results. One could go higher if you can keep the temperature below 68°F (20°C)."

LIGHT

Cyclamen plants grown in 10-, 16-, or 20-hr photoperiods of similar intensity had similar leaf number. However, plants form more leaves in the winter prior to the formation of reproductive structures than do those grown in summer. Neuray (1973) concluded that high light intensity and long durations interacted to hasten flower development. Vogelezang and Verbeckt (1990) reduced production time by 6 weeks (from 32 to 26 weeks) by using high-pressure sodium lamps at 270 fc (35 μmol · m^{-2} · s^{-1}) during a Dutch winter. If the light intensity is greater than 4000 fc (800 μmol · m^{-2} · s^{-1}), leaf injury may occur. Shading may be required to prevent both leaf injury and high temperatures, but will slow growth. Higher light levels can be tolerated if temperature remains below 77°F (25°C) (Karlsson, 1997).

WATER

Seed germination occurs at high humidity and is frequently accomplished in fog chambers. Cyclamen quickly form an extensive root system. Plants should be kept moist; wilting often leads to rapid leaf yellowing. Capillary mats are not advised during the winter because excessive growth can occur. Microtube watering is acceptable for larger pot sizes but not practical for sizes smaller than 4 in. (10 cm). Ebb-and-flow and trough systems are commonly used for all pot sizes, especially for small size pots (Widmer, 1992).

CARBON DIOXIDE

Elevated levels of carbon dioxide at 1000 ppm can increase growth during leaf unfolding (Karlsson, 1997).

NUTRITION

There are two critical stages in the nutrition of cyclamen. The first is the correct nutritional level of the medium in which the seeds germinate and develop for the first 16 weeks. This medium must be properly amended, and nutrient levels, pH, and ECs monitored every 2 weeks. The second consideration is medium nutritional level from potting to postharvest, which is during the reproductive phase of plant growth.

- *Stage 1:* If the nutrient-enriched medium is used as devised by Widmer (1983), no additional nutrients are needed for the first 2 months of growth. Thereafter, 100 ppm N can be used at 2- to 3-week intervals, from a 20–20–20 or 20–10–20 fertilizer, before young seedling plants are shifted to their final pot size.
- *Stage 2:* Fertilization begins 4 weeks after young plants are transplanted into a nutrient-amended medium. At this stage, use 100 ppm N until roots are well formed, then increase to 150, and finally 200 ppm N. The potassium level should be 25 to 50 ppm greater than N. Higher potassium results in compact growth, moderate size leaves, rapid flowering, and fewer disease problems.

Micronutrients cannot be neglected. Adequate boron levels in the tissue are critical. Accordingly, tissue tests should be made every 4 to 6 weeks (see Chaper 6, Nutrition, Table 6-4 for foliar nutrient levels). A pH between 5.0 and 6.0 is considered adequate (Widmer, 1983; Widmer et al., 1976).

MEDIA

Media selection is critical at two points in cyclamen production. The first is when seeds are planted into a nutrient-enriched or amended peat moss. The next is when plants are transplanted into the same enriched medium, which eliminates nutrient application for the first 4 weeks after transplanting (Widmer et al., 1976, 1983). Numerous commercial media are also acceptable.

HEIGHT CONTROL

Height control is usually not required, but if needed, A-Rest (ancymidol) and B-Nine (daminozide) are marginally effective (Adriansen, 1985). DIF is also effective in reducing plant height (Karlsson and Werner, 1997). If excessive GA_3 is used to hasten flower scape elongation, leaf petioles become too tall. Excessive nitrogen-to-potassium ratios also cause plants to grow tall and should be avoided. Low light levels, tight plant spacing, and excessively high fertilization can also encourage stretched leaf petioles and flower stems.

SPACING

Seeds are most efficiently planted in plug trays because the roots are not disturbed when transplanted. If germinated in 406-cell plug flats, plants will have to be transplanted relatively quickly into 50-cell plug flats, 1.75- × 1.75-in. (4.5- × 4.5-cm) cells, and then into the final pot. To save space after transplanting, plants are held pot-to-pot until the leaves begin to touch. Similarly, plants must be transplanted when they become crowded in the plugs. In either situation, crowding causes weak growth, elongated leaf petioles, and increased incidence of disease. Ideal spacing for 6-, 5-, or 4-in. (15-, 13-, or 10-cm) pots is 15 × 15, 12 × 12, or 10 × 10 in. (37 × 37, 30 × 30, or 25 × 25 cm), respectively. Typical spacing is generally closer than indicated above.

PINCHING AND DISBUDDING

No pinching or disbudding is required.

TABLE II-I CYCLAMEN

Sample production schedule for 5-in. (13-cm) *Cyclamen* crop.[a]

Cultural Step	Production Time (weeks)	Temperature °F (°C)
Sow seed in plugs 1.75 × 1.75 in. (4.5 × 4.5 cm)		
	2–4	68 (20)
Seed germinate, cotyledon elongates, and move to light immediately		
	12[b]	68 (20)
Transplant plugs to final pot, space pot-to-pot		
	4	62–64 (17–18)
Space		
	4	62–64 (17–18)
Lower temperature[c]		
	8	60–62 (16–17)
Flower		
Total	30–32	

[a]With the correct cultivars for the respective pot sizes, the time to flower will vary with pot size. Production of 7- or 6-in. (17.5- or 15-cm) pots will require 7 to 10 months; 5-in. (12.5-cm) pots will require 7 to 8 months; 4-in. (10-cm) pots, 6 to 7 months.
[b]Weeks to transplant will depend on plug size.
[c]Optional—apply GA_3 when flower buds are 0.19 to 0.25 in. (0.4 to 0.6 cm) long.

SUPPORT

No support required.

SCHEDULE AND TIMING

Post (1949) stated that seeds sown from June to November flowered the December of the next year. Production cycles are now 7 to 9 months for 6-in. (15-cm) pots with proper temperature and nutrition regime sequences, newer cultivars, and GA_3 sprays applied to 0.19- to 0.25-in.- (0.4- to 0.6-cm)-long flower buds (Widmer et al., 1974, 1976, 1983). Crop time is 6 to 7 months for 4-in. (10-cm) pots (Karlsson, 1997) (Table II-1 Cyclamen).

INSECTS

The cyclamen mite results in malformed flowers and leaves. Cyclamen mites are difficult to detect, and a professional entomologist is frequently required to confirm that this tiny mite is present in the tissue. Symptoms are frequently similar to micronutrient deficiencies. Western flower thrips are a major problem, not only because they damage the flowers, but also because they carry the destructive tomato spotted wilt and impatiens necrotic spot viruses. Fungus gnat larvae can be a major problem in propagation and in the early stages of growth when peat is kept moist. Aphids and leaf miners can also cause problems.

DISEASES

Botrytis is the most serious disease, especially because the dense leaf canopy causes poor air circulation and high humidity. Crown, leaf, and flower rot (*Erwinia carotovora* or *Fusarium oxysporum*) can be a problem, which can be decreased by ebb-and-flow or trough irrigation. It is important to keep the crown as dry as possible and maintain good air circulation. *Fusarium* and *Erwinia* are both serious diseases (Horst, 1990). Do not plant the seedling plugs too deeply or cover the young developing cormlike structure. In addition, practice good sanitation, allow an adequate drying cycle between irrigations, and provide adequate venting. Interestingly, low levels of salt (NaCl) have been used experimentally to reduce *Fusarium* infection (W. Elmer, personal communication). In the future, computer environmental controls may allow added control of diseases through environmental manipulation (Lange and Tantau, 1996). Root rots (*Pythium, Phytophthora,* or *Rhizoctonia*) can be avoided by proper irrigation and sanitation. Cyclamen are also susceptible to tomato spotted wilt virus and impatiens necrotic spot virus; both viruses are spread by thrips (Karlsson, 1997). Black root rot (*Thielaviopsis basicola*), corm rot (*Cyclindrocladium*), leaf spot (*Gleosporium cyclaminis*), leaf spots (*Phyllostica cyclaminis* or *Septoria cyclaminis*), stunt (*Ranularia cy-*

claminicola), and soft rot (*Erwinia carotovora*) have also been reported (Dreistadt, 2001).

PHYSIOLOGICAL DISORDERS

High temperatures may delay flowering. Insufficient light and improper spacing of plants can cause leaf petiole elongation, reduced flowering, and delayed timing.

POSTHARVEST

Plants are harvested when four or more flowers are fully open and several buds are evident. The flower and buds of cyclamen are relatively insensitive to ethylene; 1 ppm for 96 hr was required to reduce plant quality (Willumsen and Fjeld, 1995). However, plants can be sprayed with 0.5 to 1.0 mM silver thiosulfate (STS) to increase longevity. Nonpollinated flowers produced little ethylene and are relatively insensitive to external ethylene but become sensitive to ethylene, once pollination occurs (Halevy et al., 1984).

Cyclamen plants lose quality quickly when stored in darkness and are best shipped cool at 35 to 41°F (2 to 5°C). Tijskens et al. (1996) found that 41°F (5°C) was best, but did not test temperatures lower than 41°F (5°C). *Botrytis* is a problem during shipping, and only absorbent paper pot wrap, not plastic, should be used (Nell, 1993; Nowak and Rudnicki, 1990). Cyclamen plugs should be shipped at 32 to 41°F (0 to 5°C). Retailers and customers should be told to immediately unpack and place the plants in a cool 60°F (16°C), well-lighted 100-fc (20 μmol $\cdot$ m^{-2} $\cdot$ s^{-1}) environment.

In Europe, flowers are used as cut flowers, and they respond to postharvest floral preservatives, STS, and 5% ethanol. The latter was superior according to R. Naderi (personal communication). Cut flowers are harvested when fully open and can be stored at 34°F (1°C).

KEY POINTS

- Cyclamen is used mainly as a potted flowering plants, but also as a garden ornamental and occasionally as a cut flower.

- Cyclamen develop a cormlike organ; however, commercially it is propagated by seed.

- Plant sizes vary from the large "standard" to medium-sized "midi" to dwarf "mini."

- Seed should be barely indented into the medium by 1/8 to 1/4 in. (0.2 to 0.5 mm) and germinated in the dark at 65 to 68°F (18 to 20°C) with 100% humidity.

- Cyclamen is a day-neutral plant.

- Plants are vegetative until 10 to 13 leaves have formed, after which flower buds begin to be initiated in the leaf axils.

- Plants are grown at 68°F (20°C) for the first 12 weeks after germination, then 62 to 64°F (17 to 18°C) for 8 weeks, and finally 60 to 62°F (16 to 17°C) until marketing.

- Potassium level should be 25 to 50 ppm higher than nitrogen levels, which results in compact growth, moderate leaf size, and rapid flowering.

- GA$_3$ sprayed onto small flower buds will hasten rate of flower development.

- Plants are susceptible to *Botrytis* and crown rot from *Erwinia* or *Fusarium*, all of which can be major problems.

BIBLIOGRAPHY

Adriansen, E. 1985. Kemisk vækstregulering, pp. 142–162 in *Potteplanter I—Produktion, Metoder, Midler*, O.V. Christensen, A. Klougart, I.S. Pedersen, and K. Wikesjö, editors. Gartner-INFO, København, Denmark. (in Danish)

Bailey, L.H., and E.Z. Bailey. 1976. *Cyclamen*, pp. 351–352 in *Hortus Third: A Concise Dictionary of Plants Cultivated in the United States and Canada*. Macmillan, New York.

Corbineau, F., N. Neveur, and D. Côme. 1989. Characteristics of *Cyclamen persicum* Mill. seed germination. *Acta Horticulturae* 261:337–345.

Corr, B. 1997. The ABC's of plug production. *Greenhouse Product News* 7(2):21–23.

Dreistadt, S.H. 2001. *Integrated Pest Management for Floriculture and Nurseries*. University of California Division of Agriculture and Natural Resources Publication 3402.

Ewald, A. 1996. Interspecific hybridization between *Cyclamen persicum* Mill. and *C. purpurascens* Mill. *Plant Breeding* 115:162–166.

Gerritsen, H. 1998. Cyclamen. *Greenhouse Management and Production* 18(6):23–25.

Halevy, A.H., C.C. Whitehead, and A.N. Kofranek. 1984. Does pollination induce corolla abscission of cyclamen flowers by promoting ethylene production? *Plant Physiology* 75:1090–1093.

Horst, R.K. 1990. Cyclamen, p. 616 in *Westcott's Plant Disease Handbook,* 5th ed. Van Nostrand Reinhold, New York.

Huxley, A., M. Griffiths, and M. Levy. 1992. *Cyclamen,* pp. 792–797 in *The New Royal Horticultural Society Dictionary of Gardening,* vol. 1. Stockton Press, New York.

Ishizaka, H. 1998. Production of microspore-derived plants by anther culture of an interspecific F_1 hybrid between *Cyclamen persicum* Mill. and *C. purpurascens* Mill. *Plant Cell, Tissue and Organ Culture* 54:21–28.

Karlsson, M.G. 1997. Cyclamen, pp. 59–63 in *Tips on Growing Specialty Potted Crops,* M.L. Gaston, S.A. Carver, C.A. Irwin, and R.A. Larsen, editors. Ohio Florists' Association, Columbus, Ohio.

Karlsson, M., and J. Werner. 1997. Growth of cyclamen as affected by day and night temperatures. *HortScience* 32:466. (Abstract)

Karlsson, M., and J. Werner. 1998. Cyclamen flower development in response to temperature. *HortScience* 33:447. (Abstract)

Karlsson, M., and J. Werner. 2001. Temperature affects leaf unfolding rate and flowering of cyclamen. *HortScience* 36:292–294.

Lange, D., and J.J. Tantau. 1996. Climate management for disease control investigations on control strategies, plant densities and irrigation systems. *Acta Horticulturae* 406:105–113.

Le Nard, M., and A. De Hertogh. 1993. General chapter on spring flowering bulbs: *Cyclamen,* pp. 709–712 in *The Physiology of Flowering Bulbs,* A. De Hertogh and M. Le Nard, editors. Elsevier, Amsterdam.

Nell, T.A. 1993. *Cyclamen persicum,* p. 34 in *Flowering Potted Plants, Prolonging Shelf Performance.* Ball Publishing, Batavia, Illinois.

Neuray, G.K. 1973. Bud formation in *Cyclamen persicum. Acta Horticulturae* 31:77–79.

Niizu, Y. 1967. Flower bud differentiation in *Cyclamen. Agriculture Horticulture* 42(8):1269–1270.

Nowak, J., and R.M. Rudnicki. 1990. *Postharvest Handling and Storage of Cut Flowers, Florist Greens and Potted Plants.* Timber Press, Portland, Oregon.

Post, K. 1949. *Cyclamen,* pp. 430–436 in *Florist Crop Production and Marketing.* Orange Judd Publishing, New York.

Stephens, L.C., and R.E. Widmer. 1976. Soil temperature effects on Cyclamen flowering. *Journal of the American Society of Horticultural Science* 101:107–111.

Sumitomo, A., and K. Kosugi. 1963. Studies of *Cyclamen* I. On the germination of seed. *Technical Bulletin of the Faculty of Agriculture Kagawa University* 14(2):137–140.

Sunberg, M. 1981a. Apical events prior to floral evocation in *Cyclamen persicum* 'F-1 Rosemandi' (Primulaceae). *Botanical Gazette* 142:27–35.

Sunberg, M. 1981b. The development of leaves and axillary flowers along the primary shoot axis of *Cyclamen persicum* 'F-1 Rosemandi' (Primulaceae). *Botanical Gazette* 142:214–221.

Takamura, T., T. Sugimura, M. Tanaka, and T. Kage. 1998. Breeding of the tetraploid yellow-flowered cyclamen with "eye." *Acta Horticulturae* 454:119–126.

Tijskens, L.M.M., M. Sloof, E.C. Wilkinson, and W.G. van Doorn. 1996. A model of the effects of temperature and time on the acceptability of potted plants stored in darkness. *Postharvest Biology and Technology* 8:293–305.

Vogelezang, J., and H. Verbeckt. 1990. Supplementary lighting for potplant cultures. *Acta Horticulturae* 272:159–163.

Widmer, R.E. 1983. Cyclamen seed handling and germination. *Minnesota State Florists' Bulletin* 32(5):13–14.

Widmer, R.E. 1992. Cyclamen, pp. 385–407 in *Introduction to Floriculture,* 2nd ed., R.A. Larson, editor. Academic Press, San Diego, California.

Widmer, R.E., and R.E. Lyons. 1985. *Cyclamen persicum,* pp. 382–390 in *Handbook of Flowering,* vol. II, A.H. Halevy, editor. CRC Press, Boca Raton, Florida.

Widmer, R.E., E.C. Stephens, and M.V. Angell. 1974. Gibberellin accelerates flowering of *Cyclamen persicum* Mill. *HortScience* 9:476–477.

Widmer, R.E., R.J. Platteter, and J. Gembis. 1976. Minnesota fast crop cyclamen. *Minnesota State Florists' Bulletin* April 1:3–9.

Widmer, R.E., M.C. Stuart, and R.E. Lyons. 1983. Seven month cyclamen for Christmas. *Minnesota State Florists' Bulletin* 32(2):1–4.

Willumsen, K., and T. Fjeld. 1995. The sensitivity of some flowering potted plants to exogenous ethylene. *Acta Horticulturae* 405:362–367.

Dahlia

INTRODUCTION

Common name: dahlia.

Scientific names: *Dahlia* Cav. hybrids. *Dahlia coccinea* Cav. and *D. pinnata* Cav. are the two species responsible for the modern dahlia (Bailey and Bailey, 1976; Huxley et al., 1992).

Family and related taxa: Compositae Giseke. There are almost 30 species of this tender herbaceous perennial in the genus *Dahlia*, which is highly variable and even includes vine-like species. The Compositae family includes many important genera such as *Aster, Calendula, Callistephus, Centaurea, Chrysanthemum, Cosmos, Dendranthema, Echinacea, Gerbera, Helianthus, Liatris, Pericallis, Solidago, Tagetes,* and *Zinnia*.

Origin: Dahlias are native to the mountains of Mexico, Central America, and Columbia. Hybridization and transport of species from Mexico and South America probably occurred in the early 1700s (De Hertogh and Le Nard, 1993; Rünger and Cockshull, 1985).

Uses and current status: Dahlias are used as bedding plants, garden specimen plants, cut flowers, and occasional potted flowering plants (Armitage and Laushman, 2003).

The stems are hollow, and leaves are opposite and whorled to pinnate with "flowers" consisting of several hundred individual florets in a cyme. Flower morphology is complex and flower size varies from larger than 8.25 in. (25 cm) to less than 4 in. (10 cm) in diameter (De Hertogh and Le Nard, 1993) (Fig. II-1 Dahlia).

CULTIVARS

Cultivars and hybrids are numbered in the thousands and modern cultivars are mainly tetraploids (Crane and Lawrence, 1947). Many of the cultivars have been developed by amateur breeders for the garden. The flowers can be solid, bicolored, or multicolored and include white, yellow, orange, red, and purple (Bailey and Bailey, 1976). Height also varies from 12-in. (30-cm) dwarfs to more than 6 ft (1.8 m) tall (Humm, 1999).

PROPAGATION

Dahlias are propagated by *in vitro* methods, tuberous rooted divisions, stem cuttings, or seed. *In vitro* propagation is possible (Morel and Martin, 1952), but is not commonly used. Dividing tuberous roots is mainly done by home gardeners and each piece must contain at least one terminal adventitious bud. Commercially, stem cuttings are used to increase selected cultivars (De Hertogh and Le Nard, 1993). Stem cuttings are harvested from disease-free tuberous roots that have been stored at 48°F (9°C) over winter and greenhouse forced at 55 to 59°F (13 to 15°C) for 2 to 3 weeks in February and March. Temperatures are increased to 68 to 79°F (20 to 26°C) for rapid shoot elongation. Harvest two to three node cuttings and root in a well-drained rooting medium at 65 to 72°F (18 to 22°C)

FIGURE II-I DAHLIA *Dahlia* 'Bon Bini' cut flower.

(Armitage and Laushman, 2003). When rooted the cuttings are moved outside into cold frames until danger of frost is over and field planted in late May or early June (De Hertogh and Le Nard, 1993; Post, 1949).

Small flowered dahlia cultivars for flats and small pots are seed propagated with 2000 seed/oz (98/g). For plug production the following conditions are used (Hamrick, 2003):

- *Stage 1:* Seed covered, 78 to 80°F (26 to 27°C), 3 to 4 days
- *Stage 2:* 68 to 70°F (20 to 21°C), 5 to 7 days, and 50 to 75 ppm N once/week
- *Stage 3:* 65 to 68°F (18 to 20°C), 14 to 21 days and 100 to 150 ppm N once or twice/week
- *Stage 4:* 60 to 62°F (15 to 17°C), 7 days, fertilize as needed with 100 to 150 ppm N.

Plugs should be ready for marketing or transplanting in 3 to 4 weeks. See Chapter 1, Propagation, for descriptions of stages.

Several series of cultivars for potted plants and for cut flower production are available as unrooted cuttings; heat resistance and rapid production are some of the advantages over seed- or tuber-propagated lines (Humm, 1999).

FLOWERING CONTROL AND DORMANCY

In the northern latitudes with freezing temperatures, the tuberous roots must be dug and stored. Armitage and Laushman (2003) report that in southern areas (Zones 7 to 10) tuberous roots can be left in the ground and divided every 3 years.

Konishi and Inaba (1967a) found that freshly harvested tuberous roots do not immediately regrow (shoot emergence and flower) unless they have 40 days at 32°F (0°C). They later reported that adventitious or axillary shoots from newly planted tubers do not elongate if the photoperiod is less than 12 hr. The impact of cold and photoperiod on dormancy is greatly influenced by cultivar (Konishi and Inaba, 1967b).

Flowering and root tuberization are both influenced by temperature and photoperiod. If plants are kept under 13 to 14 hr of light at 59°F (15°C), they will continuously flower. Most dahlia cultivars flower under a 12- to 14-hr photoperiod. Dahlia is classified as a facultative SD plant, but note that SD will also cause tuberization. Once flowers are initiated, floral development is also slowed under long photoperiods. Photoperiod determines the number of total florets in the inflorescence. For example, flowers under a 14-hr photoperiod had a total of 330 florets, whereas those under an 8-hr photoperiod had only 82 florets (Maatsch and Rünger, 1985). Further information on flowering can be obtained from De Hertogh and Le Nard (1993).

Tuberization is induced by SD (11 to 12 hr) and 5 days are required to induce the formation of tuberous roots. The optimal temperature is 61 to 70°F (16 to 21°C) (Moser and Hess, 1968). Potted dahlia plants for spring sales can be produced from tuberous roots that have been stored at 45 to 48°F (7 to 9°C) over winter after being harvested in the fall. In the Northern Hemisphere the tubers are planted from January to April for greenhouse forcing (De Hertogh, 1996).

TEMPERATURE

Temperature affects the rate of vegetative growth, flower initiation and development, and tuberous root formation. The optimal temperature range for vegetative shoot development is 55 to 77°F (13 to 25°C) (Allen, 1937; De Hertogh and Le Nard, 1993). Flower initiation and development rates, however, are optimum at 50 to 59°F (10 to 15°C). Cutting-propagated types for potted or bedding plants are grown at 65 to 70/63 to 65°F (18 to 21/17 to 18°C) day/night temperatures (Humm, 1999). Post (1949) states, "The greatest profusion of blooms on dahlia is usually in September and October, because the plant responds to short days for bud formation. Highest quality blooms are produced in regions of cool nights" (p. 440).

The shortening days of fall result in tuber formation and frosts terminate the growth cycle. Tuberous roots are best stored at 41 to 50°F (5 to 10°C) in peat (50% water content) to prevent moisture loss. Tuberous roots can also be dipped in paraffin. The lethal freezing point is 28°F (−2°C).

LIGHT

Light duration influences the rate of vegetative growth as well as flower initiation and development. Most cultivars flower with a 12- to 14-hr photoperiod. Seed-propagated plugs should be grown under LD to inhibit tuberous root production and reduce crop time (Legnani and Miller, 2000). Plugs placed under either LD or SD were of equal weights but more of the weight was in the shoots and fibrous roots for LD-grown plugs than the SD-grown plugs. Thus, photoperiod controlled carbohydrate allocation within the plants. For the cultivar 'Royal Dahliette Yellow,' Brøndum and Heins (1993) determined that the optimum production conditions for 4-in. (10-cm) pots were 12- to 14-hr photoperiods and 68°F (20°C). Axillary shoot number and length decreased as photoperiod decreased from 16 to 10 hr. Photoperiods shorter than 12 hr promoted tuberous root formation and inhibited shoot growth.

Low light intensities delay the onset of flowering and reduce the number of flowers. Maximum light of 4500 to 6000 fc (900 to 1200 $\mu mol \cdot m^{-2} \cdot s^{-1}$) is required during all phases of growth (Humm, 1999) and 14 hr of HID lighting at 400 fc (60 $\mu mol \cdot m^{-2} \cdot s^{-1}$) may be useful for the first 6 weeks during winter and early spring. Greenhouse shading should be used only to reduce temperature in midsummer. High-quality field-grown cut flowers can be produced under shade cloth (Armitage and Laushman, 2003; Post, 1949).

WATER

Plants must be kept moist, but not wet (De Hertogh, 1996). Monitor soluble salt levels and leach as necessary. With field-grown crops, a mulch can be used to conserve moisture, control weeds, and reduce soil temperatures (Armitage and Laushman, 2003).

CARBON DIOXIDE

No data available.

NUTRITION

For pot plant production, a standard 200 ppm N solution from 20–10–20 at each watering is adequate. A controlled-release fertilizer can also be used. Always monitor nutrient, pH, and salt levels to ensure proper plant growth (De Hertogh, 1996). For field-grown production a dry fertilizer can be used as a sidedress when shoots first appear. Liquid feed regimes can also be used. The field should be well prepared and annually fertilized and amended with organic matter, especially if clay soils are involved.

MEDIA

In the Netherlands only sandy soil is used; no mineral or peat soils are considered for tuberous root production. For potted plants the medium should be well drained, have a pH of 7.0, and should not contain more than one-third peat (De Hertogh, 1996; De Hertogh and Le Nard, 1993). Dasoju et al. (1998), however, noted that dahlias grew equally well in substrates of 50 to 80% coir or sphagnum peat, with the remainder being perlite.

HEIGHT CONTROL

For cut flower production, no height control is needed. For plugs, A-Rest (ancymidol) sprays at 6 ppm can be applied within a week to 10 days after sowing to the plug flat media to produce compact, well-branched plugs and subsequent bedding plants (Britten, 1999). B-Nine (daminozide) can be applied at 2500 ppm during stage 1 or 2 and at 5000 ppm during stage 3 (Sawaya, 2001).

Numerous chemicals are effective on bedding plants including A-Rest sprays at 15 to 26 ppm, B-Nine sprays at 2500 to 5000 ppm, Bonzi (paclobutrazol) sprays at 15 to 45 ppm, Cycocel (chlormequat) sprays at 800 to 1500 ppm, and Sumagic (uniconazole) sprays at 10 to 20 ppm (Bell, 2001). Sumagic at 0.75 ppm can also be sprayed on the media surface prior to planting.

For potted plants, A-Rest is routinely used to control internode elongation. De Hertogh (1996) stresses that drenches be applied to moist media and must be used when the shoots are 0.25 in. (0.5 cm) long. The A-Rest rate ranges from 0.25 to 0.5 mg a.i. (2 to 4 ppm)/6-in. (15-cm) pot. For Bonzi and Sumagic the recommended rates are 2 to 4 mg and 0.25 to 0.5 mg a.i./6-in. (15-cm) pot, respectively (Whipker and Hammer, 1997; Whipker et al., 1995). Several cultivars require no chemical treatment for height control. DIF has little to no effect on dahlias (Warner and Erwin, 2001).

SPACING

At time of planting, plants can be placed pot-to-pot. After growth begins and foliage begins to touch (3 weeks), space 6 to 12 in. (15 to 30 cm) apart. Tuberous root clumps are spaced 2 ft (60 cm) apart for field-grown cut flowers. For disease prevention and ease of harvest, 36-in. (90-cm) spacing is wiser, but may not be economical (Armitage and Laushman, 2003). Cutting-propagated dahlias can be spaced at 1 plant/ft² (10/m²) in 3 ft (90 cm) wide beds.

PINCHING AND DISBUDDING

Cultivars for potted plants grow at different rates and will require pinching at different times. Pinching is usually practiced when one dominant shoot develops. The appropriate time to pinch is when three or four leaf pairs have fully developed, then "soft prune" the terminal. Leave three to four nodes on the shoot so two to four new axillary shoots will develop. In addition, vigorous dominant shoots should also be pinched on multistem plants (De Hertogh, 1996). Pinching will add 7 to 10 days to production time (Humm, 1999).

Removing the terminal flower should only be done if flowering is too advanced for the date of planned marketing. This step will force the axillary flowers to develop (Humm, 1999).

For field-grown cut flowers, axillary flower buds are removed to increase the size of the terminal flower. However, most growers select cultivars that do not require much disbudding. Pinching of the terminal shoots, when they are 2 ft (60 cm) tall, can increase total production. Some producers prefer to harvest the first (primary) flower, because it is the earliest and largest. A yield of 20 flower stems per plant is possible (Armitage and Laushman, 2003).

SUPPORT

For potted plants, no support is needed. For field-grown cut flowers, support is required and can be accomplished by a variety of methods. Plants can be tied to individual stakes or, if in beds, three levels of horizontal wire or plastic mesh can be used. Three stakes can also be used to form a pyramid into which the individual plant grows and twine used to secure the main stems (Armitage and Laushman, 2003).

SCHEDULE AND TIMING

Tuberous roots require 8 to 12 weeks to flower from date of planting, with most cultivars requiring 11 to 13 weeks (Table II-1 Dahlia). Flowering is possible for Valentine's Day, Easter, Mother's Day, or Memorial Day. Total crop time for bedding plant flats from seed is 11 to 12 weeks in the north and 10 to 11 weeks in the south. For 4-in. (10-cm) pots from seed, add 1 to 3 weeks. Time to flower or marketing for cutting-propagated types ranges from 6 to 8 weeks without a pinch to 8 to 10 weeks with a pinch regardless of pot size (Humm, 1999). However, one cutting is used for 4- to 6-inch (10- to 15-cm) pots and three cuttings for 6.5- to 8-inch (16- to 20 cm) pots.

For outdoor cut flower production, tuberous roots should be removed from cold storage and placed in a warm area to encourage bud growth. Tuberous roots can be planted out-

TABLE II-I DAHLIA

Sample Mother's Day forcing schedule for flowering *Dahlia* plants in 6-in. (15-cm) pots from tuberous roots.

Cultural Step	Production Time (weeks)	Temperature °F (°C)
Pot tuberous root (Feb 15)		
	2	Night: 63–65 (17–18) Day: 73–77 (23–25)
Apply A-Rest when shoots are 0.25 in. (0.5 cm) long (Mar 1)		
	3–4	Night: 63–65 (17–18) Day: 73–77 (23–25)
Space		
	3	Night: 63–65 (17–18) Day: 73–77 (23–25)
Pinch when two fully developed sets of leaves appear[a]		
	3–4	Night: 63–65 (17–18) Day: 73–77 (23–25), drop to 55 (13) to harden after start of flowering
Flowering for Mother's Day Total	11–13[b]	

[a]Pinching can delay flowering by 1 to 2 weeks.
[b]Total time varies with the cultivar.

doors after danger of frost. Dig roots in the fall after the first frost has killed the aboveground foliage and stems. Roots should be stored in a frost-free area at 45°F (7°C) with low humidity or in peat (50% water content).

INSECTS

Insects of concern in the greenhouse are primarily aphids and thrips, but whiteflies and red spider mites can also be a problem. In the field, beetles, worms, and grasshoppers are all major pests (De Hertogh and Le Nard, 1993).

DISEASES

Selecting disease-free cuttings results in high-quality field-grown tuberous roots. Tomato spotted wilt virus has been reported in dahlias (Zitter et al., 1989). *Botrytis* can infect flowers in the greenhouse and during the shipping and marketing process (De Hertogh and Le Nard, 1993). Dahlias are also susceptible to aster yellows, powdery mildew (*Erysiphe cichoracearum*), bacterial soft rot (*Erwinia carotovora*), and root and stem rots (*Pythium, Rhizoctonia solani,* or *Sclerotinia sclerotiorum*) (Horst, 1990). Outdoors a number of leaf spot diseases are also possible. Wilt (*Verticillium dahliae* or *Fusarium oxysporum*), southern wilt (*Sclerotium rolfsii*), root rot (*Armillaria mellea*), and leaf spots (*Alternaria, Cercospora,* or *Phyllosticta*) have also been reported (Dreistadt, 2001).

PHYSIOLOGICAL DISORDERS

Flower abortion and blind terminal meristems can occur, which are usually caused by inappropriate temperature or photoperiod for the cultivar (De Hertogh and Le Nard, 1993).

POSTHARVEST

Cut flowers and flowering plants are harvested when the flowers are three-quarters to fully open. If harvested when buds are too immature, they may fail to open. Shipping or storage for up to 5 days at 39 to 41°F (4 to 5°C) is possible (Nowak and Rudnicki, 1990; L. Høyer, personal communication). For cut flowers, a combination of glucose or sucrose, silver, and 8-hydroxyquinoline sulfate (De Hertogh and Le Nard, 1993) or commercial preservatives are acceptable postharvest treatments (Nowak and Rudnicki, 1990). Flowers are sensitive to ethylene. Water pH should be adjusted to 3.5 to 4.0. Post (1949) and Nowak and Rudnicki (1990) report that dahlia flowers must be quickly placed in 122°F (50°C) water to prevent wilting and encourage water uptake. Arnosky and Arnosky (1997) recommend using 160°F (71°C) water plus a floral preservative. Flowers remain in the solution until it cools. Lack of light results in leaves yellowing during transport of cut flowers or potted plants. Dahlia plugs can be stored at 41 to 45°F (5 to 7°C) and bedding plants at 50 to 81°F (10 to 27°C) (L. Høyer, personal communication).

KEY POINTS

- Dahlias are used as bedding plants, specimen garden ornamentals, cut flowers, and potted flowering plants.
- Plants are propagated by seed, tuberous root divisions, cuttings, or *in vitro*.
- Dahlias are classified as facultative SD plants.
- Once flowers are initiated, flowering will continue under LD but more slowly.
- Tuberization is induced by SD and decreasing temperatures.
- The optimum temperature range for flower initiation and development is 50 to 59°F (10 to 15°C).
- A growth regulator is required for potted plant production.
- Staking is required for cut flower production due to the large heavy flowers.

BIBLIOGRAPHY

Adriansen, E. 1985. Kemisk vækstregulering, pp. 142–162 in *Potteplanter I—Produktion, Metoder, Midler,* O.V. Christensen, A. Klougart, I.S. Pedersen, and K. Wikesjö, editors. GartnerINFO, København, Denmark. (in Danish)

Allen, R.C. 1937. Temperature and humidity requirements for the storage of *Dahlia* roots. *Proceedings of the American Society for Horticultural Science* 35:770–773.

Armitage, A.M., and J.M. Laushman. 2003. *Dahlia* hybrids, pp. 232–238 in *Specialty Cut Flowers,* 2nd ed. Timber Press, Portland, Oregon.

Arnosky, P., and F. Arnosky. 1997. Dahlia are difficult but worth the effort. *Growing for Market* 6(10):11–13.

Bailey, L.H., and E.Z. Bailey. 1976. *Dahlia,* pp. 360–361 in *Hortus Third: A Concise Dictionary of Plants Cultivated in the United States and Canada.* Macmillan, New York.

Bell, M. 2001. Bedding plants and seed geraniums, pp. 54–62 in *Tips on Regulating Growth of Floriculture Crops,* M.L. Gaston, L.A. Kunkle, P.S. Konjoian, and M.F. Wilt, editors. Ohio Florists' Association Services, Columbus, Ohio.

Britten, A. 1999. PGRs at seeding reduce early stretch. *GrowerTalks* 63(5):46, 48.

Brøndum, J.J., and R.D. Heins. 1993. Modeling temperature and photoperiod effects on growth and development of dahlia. *Journal of the American Society for Horticultural Science* 118:36–42.

Crane, M.B., and W.J.C. Lawrence. 1947. Dahlia, pp. 82–90 in *The Genetics of Garden Plants.* Macmillan, London.

Dasoju, S., M.R. Evans, and B.E. Whipker. 1998. Paclobutrazol drench activity in coir- and peat-based root substrates. *HortTechnology* 8:595–597.

De Hertogh, A.A. 1996. *Dahlia*—Potted plants, pp. C47–58 in *Holland Bulb Forcers' Guide,* 5th ed. International Flower Bulb Centre, Hillegom, The Netherlands.

De Hertogh, A.A., and M. Le Nard, 1993. *Dahlia,* pp. 273–283 in *The Physiology of Flower Bulbs.* Elsevier, Amsterdam.

Dreistadt, S.H. 2001. *Integrated Pest Management for Floriculture and Nurseries.* University of California Division of Agriculture and Natural Resources Publication 3402.

Hamrick, D. 2003. *Dahlia,* pp. 329–332 in *Ball Redbook,* vol. 2, 17th ed. Ball Publishing, Batavia, Illinois.

Horst, R.K. 1990. Dahlia, p. 618 in *Westcott's Plant Disease Handbook,* 5th ed. Van Nostrand Reinhold, New York.

Humm, B. 1999. Trendy dwarf dahlias. *GrowerTalks* 63(6):33–34.

Huxley, A., M. Griffiths, and M. Levy. 1992. *Dahlia,* pp. 4–7 in *The New Royal Horticultural Society Dictionary of Gardening,* vol. 2. Stockton Press, New York.

Konishi, K., and K. Inaba. 1967a. Studies on flowering control of *Dahlia.* VII. On dormancy of crown-tuber. *Journal of the Japanese Society of Horticultural Science* 36:131–140. (in Japanese, English summaries)

Konishi, K., and K. Inaba. 1967b. Studies on flowering control of *Dahlia.* VIII. Effect of day-length on dormancy in axillary bud. *Journal of the Japanese Society of Horticultural Science* 36:103–109. (in Japanese, English summaries)

Legnani, G., and W.B. Miller. 2000. Night interruption lighting is beneficial in the production of plugs of dahlia 'Sunny Rose' seedlings. *HortScience* 35:1244–1246.

Maatsch, R., and W. Rünger. 1985. Uber die photoperiodische Reaktion einiger Sorten von *Dahlia variabilis* Desf. *Gartenbauwissenschaft* 1:366–390. (in German)

Morel, G., and C. Martin. 1952. Guérison de dahlias atteints d'une maladie á virus. *Comptes Rendus Academie des Sciences* 235:1324–1325. (in French)

Moser, B.C., and C.E. Hess. 1968. The physiology of tuberous root development in *Dahlia. Proceedings of the American Society for Horticultural Science* 93:595–603.

Nowak, J., and R.M. Rudnicki. 1990. *Postharvest Handling and Storage of Cut Flowers, Florist Greens, and Potted Plants.* Timber Press, Portland, Oregon.

Post, K. 1949. *Dahlia pinnata,* pp. 439–444 in *Florist Crop Production and Marketing.* Orange Judd Publishing, New York.

Rünger, W., and K.E. Cockshull. 1985. *Dahlia,* pp. 414–418 in *Handbook of Flowering,* vol. II, A.H. Halevy, editor. CRC Press, Boca Raton, Florida.

Sawaya, M. 2001. Plugs, pp. 50–53 in *Tips on Regulating Growth of Floriculture Crops,* M.L. Gaston, L.A. Kunkle, P.S. Konjoian, and M.F. Wilt, editors. Ohio Florists' Association Services, Columbus, Ohio.

Warner, R.M., and J.E. Erwin. 2001. Temperature, pp. 10–17 in *Tips on Regulating Growth of Floriculture Crops,* M.L. Gaston, L.A. Kunkle, P.S. Konjoian, and M.F. Wilt, editors. Ohio Florists' Association Services, Columbus, Ohio.

Whipker, B.E., and P.A. Hammer. 1997. Efficacy of ancymidol, paclobutrazol, and uniconazole on growth of tuberous-rooted dahlias. *HortTechnology* 7:269–273.

Whipker, B.E., R.T. Eddy, and P.A. Hammer. 1995. Chemical growth retardant application to tuberous-rooted dahlias. *HortScience* 30:1007–1008.

Zitter, T.A., M.E. Daughtrey, and J.P. Sanderson. 1989. Tomato spotted wilt virus, pp. 107–112 in *Vegetable/Horticulture Crops, Fact Sheet P 735.90.* Cornell Cooperative Extension, Ithaca, New York.

Delphinium and Consolida

FIGURE II-1 DELPHINIUM AND CONSOLIDA
Delphinium cut flowers.

FIGURE II-2 DELPHINIUM AND CONSOLIDA
Consolida cut flowers.

INTRODUCTION

Common names: delphinium (*Delphinium*) and larkspur (*Consolida*) (Huxley et al., 1992).

Scientific name: *D. ×cultorum* Voss., a catchall designation for the various hybrids between *D. elatum* L. and other species; *D. ×belladonna* hort. ex Bergmans, a hybrid between *D. elatum* and *D. grandiflorum* L.; *Consolida ambigua* (L). P.W. Ball & Hey w. (formerly known as *Delphinium ajacis*).

Family and related taxa: Ranunculaceae Juss. *Delphinium* L. includes 250 species and the *Consolida* (DC.) S.F. Gray has 40 species. Other important members of this family include *Aconitum, Anemone, Aquilegia, Clematis,* and *Ranunculus.*

Origin: The original perennial *Delphinium* species are from cold areas of the world such as Siberia, China, and Europe (Bailey and Bailey, 1976). The annual larkspur frequently reseeds itself and is native to the Mediterranean, North Africa, southern Europe, and western Asia.

Uses and current status: Delphiniums and larkspurs are grown for their beautiful spike inflorescences in home gardens, in garden centers as a potted perennial, and in fields or greenhouses as cut flowers.

For all *Delphinium* and *Consolida* species, single or double flowers are borne on long, erect, spike-like racemes. There are five sepals, and one sepal and one petal have spurs. Flower colors are commonly light to dark blue, pink, rose, and white, but red, scarlet, and yellow flowered cultivars are also available. Leaves are divided or have a palmate outline, which is typical of the Ranun-

culaceae family (Bailey and Bailey, 1976) (Figs. II-1 and II-2 Delphinium and Consolida).

CULTIVARS

The tall, stately hybrid perennial delphinium is *D. ×cultorum*. *Delphinium ×belladonna*, also a perennial, is shorter and more heavily branched than *D. ×cultorum* and has flower spurs that can be 1 in. (2.5 cm) long. *Delphinium grandiflorum* is also more informal and shorter than the previously mentioned hybrids and there are dwarf forms. *Delphinium elatum*, however, can grow up to 6 ft (1.8 m), and is no doubt the source of the height in *D. ×cultorum* (Armitage and Laushman, 2003; Bailey and Bailey, 1976). The annual larkspur, *Consolida ambigua*, is commonly associated with delphiniums. Numerous *Delphinium* and *Consolida* cultivars are available and many new cultivars are released annually. Although *Consolida* is generally field planted, cultivars for quick flowering in the greenhouse are available.

PROPAGATION

D. ×cultorum seed stored long term at 41°F (5°C) germinates earlier, more uniformly, and at higher percentages than nonstored seed. The relative humidity should be between 30 and 50% (Carpenter et al., 1995). Prior to germination, seed should be moved to 35°F (2°C) for 3 weeks, then the seed should be hydrated and held at a constant 59 or 68°F (15 or 20°C) temperature in either light or dark. Cultivar differences exist (Carpenter and Boucher, 1992). Germination is within 8 to 15 days. Hybrid delphinium seed (10,000/oz, 350/g) can be sown in the late summer or fall and overwintered. *In vitro*–propagated material is available (Garner et al., 1997). The plants will flower the following spring and fall. Also, seed can be sown in the spring, and the plants will flower in the fall. Perennial root clumps with axillary buds can be divided, but this method is generally not commercially feasible. Established perennial species and cultivars can last for more than a decade in cool climates with proper care. In warm climates, perennial delphiniums are frequently used as annuals (Armitage and Laushman, 2003).

The annual larkspur seed is reported to germinate most rapidly under LD (Schwabe, 1971) after 6 weeks of cold stratification at 35°F (2°C). Germinate seed at 55°F (13°C). Larkspur usually performs better, with more vigorous growth and longer stems, when direct seeded rather than started from plugs. The best results from plugs are obtained if plants are not root bound and planted as soon as possible.

FLOWERING CONTROL AND DORMANCY

With perennials, axillary or dormant buds are still vegetative in the autumn. In the spring, the buds elongate, complete leaf initiation, and initiate and develop inflorescences. When Wilkins (1986) reviewed the literature, it was apparent that most annual and perennial species require cold for shoot elongation and flower initiation and development. The perennial delphinium can be given low temperatures until February, then forced at 50 to 55°F (10 to 13°C) (Post, 1952). However, Holcomb and Beattie (1988, 1990) found that after germination, plants should be kept at 55 to 60°F (13 to 16°C) at night and up to 75°F (24°C) during the day. Under these conditions, flowering was successful if irradiance was high. Wang et al. (1997) noted that visible bud and flowering of *D. grandifolium* 'Blue Mirror' were delayed at temperatures up to 81°F (27°C). B. Fausey (personal communication) noted that flowering protocols vary with the species. *Delphinium × belladonna* 'Volkerfrieden' does not required cold and is day neutral. *D. grandiflorum* 'Summer Blues' also does not require cold but flowering is enhanced by LD. While *Delphinium elatum* 'Magic Fountains' has an obligate cold requirement of 15 weeks or less at 41°F (5°C), *Delphinium grandiflorm* 'Blue Mirror' has a facultative cold response and flowers faster after 5 weeks at 41°F (5°C).

For the annuals, the optimum cold treatment is 6 weeks at 36°F (2°C). Long days are also required because plants rosette at 55°F (13°C) under SD. Elongation occurs with LD incandescent night interruption and 51°F (11°C) temperature. However, when very young annual seedlings are given high temperatures and LD, quality is poor because of premature flower induction. Further, when the annual larkspur was grown in Michigan under the state's naturally short winter days, plants held at 50°F (10°C) failed to flower by the end of the experiment. At 59°F (15°C), 187 days were required for flower buds to appear. With a single gibberellic acid application, 203 or 178 days were required at 50 or 59°F (10 or 15°C), respectively (Lindstrom et al., 1957).

TEMPERATURE

After dormancy requirements are fulfilled, plants should be grown at 50 to 60°F (10 or 16°C) night and up to 75°F (24°C) day temperatures. Stem length is increased by cold night temperatures less than 55°F (13°C) and warm day temperatures (Cavins et al., 2000). Warm summer temperatures reduce quality of outdoor grown crops. White plastic mulch can reduce soil temperatures.

LIGHT

In winter, supplemental HID light must be used, because supplementary light is more important than photoperiod (incandescent night breaks). For example, plants under HID light from 1700 to 0800 hr flowered in 82 days, whereas those under a 2200- to 0200-hr incandescent night break required 152 days. However, Garner et al. (1997) stated that incandescent light night breaks from 1000 to 0200 hr increased yield and reduced days to flower.

WATER

Plants should be kept moist but not wet. Outdoor overwintering success is reduced if plants are too wet.

CARBON DIOXIDE

No data available.

NUTRITION

Young plants grow well under low nutrition, with the irrigation nutrient level increased to 200 ppm N over time. Phosphorus and ammonium nitrogen levels should be kept low. Foliar nutrient analysis values are listed in Table II-1 Delphinium and Consolida.

MEDIA

Plants should be grown in a well-aerated medium. Many cultural problems are due to root/medium problems. The medium pH should be 6.5 to 7.0.

TABLE II-I DELPHINIUM AND CONSOLIDA
Leaf tissue nutrient levels of field-grown *Delphinium* plants prior to flower opening (Armitage and Laushman, 2003).

Nutrient	Level
Nitrogen	3.2%
Phosphorus	0.33%
Potassium	3.52%
Calcium	2.86%
Magnesium	0.80%
Iron	617 ppm
Manganese	59 ppm
Boron	18 ppm
Zinc	35 ppm

HEIGHT CONTROL

If day and night temperatures are kept constant, height of potted plants will be less of a problem because plants respond to DIF and DROP (Hamaker et al., 1996). Both A-Rest (ancymidol) (35- to 132-ppm spray or 2- to 4-ppm drench) and Sumagic (uniconazole) (5-ppm drench) are effective and allow the production of potted flowering plants. B-Nine (daminozide) sprays at 2500 to 5000 ppm and Bonzi (paclobutrazol) sprays at 30 to 60 ppm are also effective (Bell, 2001). Interestingly, night breaks using incandescent light, which is high in far-red light, removed the influence of either A-Rest or Sumagic (Holcomb and Beattie, 1988).

SPACING

Spacing for field-grown delphinium is 9×9 to 12×12 in. (23×23 to 30×30 cm) for 1-year production and up to 12×18 in. (30×45 cm) for multiyear production (Armitage and Laushman, 2003). In the greenhouse plants can be spaced at 1.5 to 1.9 plants/ft^2 (16 to 20 plants/m^2) for 1-year production and at 0.8 plants/ft^2 (9 plants/m^2) for 2-year production (Bartels Stek, personal communication).

With larkspur, 25 oz (709 g) of seed will plant 1 acre (0.4 hectare) in double rows spaced 8 in. (20 cm) apart and seed spaced at 5 to 14 in. (13 to 35 cm) apart within rows (Nau, 1998). The double rows are spaced 3 ft (90 cm) apart.

PINCHING AND DISBUDDING

Delphinium seedlings can be pinched, which delays the harvest, but increases stem length and yields (Garner et al., 1997). Delphinium is usually not pinched, however. Larkspur is not pinched or disbudded.

SUPPORT

Support is required for tall growing cultivars planted in beds. Two rows of netting are common for greenhouse production, and up to four levels of netting are used for outdoor production.

SCHEDULE AND TIMING

In cool northern continental climates, outdoor delphinium plantings flower in late spring or early summer and may flower again with shorter stems in late fall prior to frost. In frost-free areas of the Pacific Northwest and northern California, flowering can occur year-round, but flowering increases as days lengthen in spring and summer. With proper care perennial delphinium plantings can last for many years in cool climates. Leave 2 to 4 in. (5 to 10 cm) of stem on the plant when harvesting stems to allow for axillary shoot development if producing more than one harvest per planting (Bartels Stek, personal communication). In warm climates perennial delphiniums are usually grown as annuals (Armitage and Laushman, 2003).

Under protection perennial delphinium seed are sown in summer or early fall, allowed to rosette, and kept at 34 to 40°F (2 to 4°C) for 6 weeks. Plants are forced at 50 to 60°F (10 or 16°C) night temperatures. Artificial LD from night break lighting improves quality and hastens production. Potted plants are sold; cut flower plants are typically discarded after flowering.

Delphinium seed should be sown in 200-cell plug trays or larger. Plugs do best when transplanted into 5-in. (13-cm) containers for potted plant production or directly into the bed for cut flower production. Larkspur is usually direct sown into the field for cut flower production.

Delphinium and larkspur are planted in the fall or early spring for flowering the following late spring or early summer. While fall planting typically produces longer and higher quality stems, plants may be damaged by severe winter weather. Spring plantings are less subjected to weather problems. In areas with mild winters, seeds can be sown 6 to 7 weeks prior to heavy frost; seed will germinate and the young plants will overwinter. In areas with severe winters, seed can be sown in late fall or early winter and will germinate in the early spring.

Multiple plantings from fall to early spring can extend the harvesting season several weeks, especially in years with cool springs. In warm springs, all plantings tend to flower more quickly and the overall harvesting season tends to be short. The later the planting in spring, the more likely the stem length and quality will be reduced by warm late spring and summer temperatures.

INSECTS

Cyclamen mites, red spider mites, aphids, and thrips are only a few of the pests that must be monitored. The cyclamen mite causes damage that can appear to be a disease: stunting, malformations, and blackening of the buds.

DISEASES

A wide range of diseases are common in delphinium and larkspur, including powdery mildew (*Erysiphe polygoni*, *Sphaerotheca humuli*, and *S. macularis*), crown rot (*Sclerotium rolfsii*), bacteria foot rot (*Erwinia carotovora*), aster yellows phytoplasma, gray mold (*Botrytis cinerea*), stem canker (*Fusarium oxysporum* f. sp. *delphinii*), leaf spots (*Cercospora delphinii*, *Ascochyta aquilegiae*, *Ramularia delphinii*, *Entyloma winteri*, and *Urocystis sorosporioides*), root and stem rot (*Pythium*, *Phytophthora*, *Rhizoctonia solani*, and *Schlerotinia sclerotiorum*), wilt (*Verticillium dahliae*), canker (*Diplodia delphinii*), bacterial leaf spot (*Pseudomonas syringae* pv. *delphinii*), rust (*Puccinia*), and viruses (Dreistadt, 2001; Farnham and McCain, 1982; Horst, 1990; Post, 1952). Disease pressure is often great enough to force growers to handle perennial delphiniums as biennials or annuals.

PHYSIOLOGICAL DISORDERS

Failure to flower in the greenhouse may be related to low light intensities and SD in the winter.

POSTHARVEST

Consolida spikes should be harvested when two to five florets are open and *Delphinium* when one-quarter to one-third of the spike is open. Postharvest pulse treatments of silver thiosulfate (STS) reduce ethylene responses and increase longevity (Awad et al., 1986; Kikuchi et al., 2003). Flowers of both species are very sensitive to ethylene and both 1-methylcyclopropane (1-MCP) and STS are effective at preventing ethylene damage (Serek et al., 1995; Staby et al., 1993). A combination of warm water, pH 3.5 to 4.0, and floral preservatives is beneficial.

Shipping and storage at 33 to 35°F (1 to 2°C) is recommended (Nell and Reid, 2001). Unfortunately, the apical portion of the spike exhibits geotropic upward bending and stems should be shipped in an upright position (Nowak and Rudnicki, 1990; Sacalis, 1993).

KEY POINTS

- The perennial *Delphinium* has larger flower spikes than the similar annual *Consolida*, larkspur, which was once known as *Delphinium ajacis*; both genera are used as cut flowers, potted flowering plants, and garden ornamentals.

- Plants are propagated by seed; mature perennial plants can also be propagated by division.

- A cold treatment is required for flowering of *Delphinium*.

- *Consolida* plants require a cold treatment and/or LD for flowering.

- *Delphinium* and *Consolida* are susceptible to numerous diseases, especially crown and root rots.

- In warm climates, *Delphinium* is usually treated as an annual.

BIBLIOGRAPHY

Armitage, A.M., and J.M. Laushman. 2003. *Delphinium* hybrids, pp. 238–245 in *Specialty Cut Flowers*, 2nd ed. Timber Press, Portland, Oregon.

Awad, A.R.E., A. Meawad, A.K. Dawh, and M. El-Saka. 1986. Cut flower longevity as affected by chemical pre-treatment. *Acta Horticulturae* 181:177–182.

Bailey, L.H., and E.Z. Bailey. 1976. *Delphinium* L., pp. 367–369 in *Hortus Third: A Concise Dictionary of Plants Cultivated in the United States and Canada*. Macmillan, New York.

Bell, M. 2001. Bedding plants and seed geraniums, pp. 54–62 in *Tips on Regulating Growth of Floriculture Crops*, M.L. Gaston, L.A. Kunkle, P.S. Konjoian, and M.F. Wilt, editors. Ohio Florists' Association Services, Columbus, Ohio.

Carpenter, W.J., and J.F. Boucher. 1992. Temperature requirements for storage and germination of *Delphinium* ×*cultorum* seed. *HortScience* 27:989–992.

Carpenter, W.J., E.R. Ostmark, and J.A. Cornell. 1995. Evaluation of temperature and moisture content during storage on the germination of flowering annual seed. *HortScience* 30:1003–1006.

Cavins, T.J., J.M. Dole, and V. Stamback. 2000. Unheated and minimally heated winter greenhouse production of specialty cut flowers. *HortTechnology* 10:793–799.

Dreistadt, S.H. 2001. *Integrated Pest Management for Floriculture and Nurseries*. University of California Division of Agriculture and Natural Resources Publication 3402.

Farnham, D.S., and A.H. McCain. 1982. Delphinium in the greenhouse, growing larkspur as a cut flower. *Florists' Review* 169(4390):16–17.

Garner, J.M., S.A. Jones, and A.M. Armitage. 1997. Pinch treatment and photoperiod influence flowering of *Delphinium* cultivars. *HortScience* 32:61–63.

Hamaker, C., W.H. Carlson, R.D. Heins, and A.C. Cameron. 1996. Diurnal temperature alterations influence final height of herbaceous perennials. *HortScience* 31:678. (Abstract)

Holcomb, E.J., and D.J. Beattie. 1988. Effect of growth retardants on perennials. *Research Report, Bedding Plant Foundation* 32:1–4.

Holcomb, E.J., and D.J. Beattie. 1990. Potted delphiniums. *GrowerTalks* 8:14–15.

Horst, R.K. 1990. Delphinium, pp. 620–621 in *Westcott's Plant Disease Handbook*, 5th ed. Van Nostrand Reinhold, New York.

Huxley, A., M. Griffiths, and M. Levy. 1992. *Consolida*, p. 709, vol. 1; *Delphinium*, pp. 26–33, vol. 2, in *The New Royal Horticultural Society Dictionary of Gardening*. Stockton Press, New York.

Kikuchi, K., K. Kanahama, and Y. Kanayama. 2003. Changes in sugar-related enzymes during wilting of cut delphinium flowers. *Journal of the Japanese Society for Horticultural Science* 72:37–42.

Lindstrom, R.S., S.H. Wittwer, and M.J. Bukovac. 1957. Gibberellin and higher plants, IV. Flowering responses of some flower crops. *Quarterly Bulletin Michigan Agricultural Experiment Station* 39:673–681.

Nau, J. 1998. *Consolida* (Larkspur), pp. 435–436 in *Ball Redbook*, 16th ed., V. Ball, editor. Ball Publishing, Batavia, Illinois.

Nell, T.A., and M.S. Reid. 2001. Can't take the heat. *Floral Management* 17(10):33–34.

Nowak, J., and R. Rudnicki. 1990. *Postharvest Handling and Storage of Cut Flowers, Florist Greens and Potted Plants*. Timber Press, Portland, Oregon.

Post, K. 1952. Delphinium, pp. 446–451 in *Flower Crops Production and Marketing*. Orange Judd Publishing, New York.

Sacalis, J.N. 1993. Delphinium, pp. 45–46 in *Cut Flowers, Prolonging Freshness*, 2nd ed., J.L. Seals, editor. Ball Publishing, Batavia, Illinois.

Schwabe, W.W. 1971. Physiology of reproduction, pp. 258–259 in *Plant Physiology*, vol. VI-A, F.C. Steward, editor. Academic Press, New York.

Serek, M., E.C. Sisler, and M.S. Reid. 1995. Effects of 1-MCP on the vase life and ethylene response of cut flowers. *Plant Growth Regulation* 16:93–97.

Staby, G.L., R.M. Basel, M.S. Reid, and L.L. Dodge. 1993. Efficacies of commercial anti-ethylene products for fresh cut flowers. *HortTechnology* 3:199–202.

Wang, S.-Y., R.D. Heins, W.H. Carlson, and A.C. Cameron. 1997. Effect of forcing temperature on flowering of four herbaceous perennial species. *HortScience* 32:501. (Abstract)

Wilkins, H. 1986. Delphinium, pp. 89–91 in *Handbook of Flowering*, vol. V, A.H. Halevy, editor. CRC Press, Boca Raton, Florida.

Dendranthema

INTRODUCTION

Common names: chrysanthemum, florist's chrysanthemum.

Scientific name: *Dendranthema ×grandiflorum* Kitam. (synonym *Chrysanthemum ×morifolium*) (Huxley et al., 1992).

Family and related taxa: Compositae Giseke. All members of the genus *Chrysanthemum* L. are annuals, of which *C. coronarium* L., the rainbow daisy, is of horticultural interest (Balek and Albrecht, 1988). Several other related species, which were formerly in the genus *Chrysanthemum*, are commonly grown, including feverfew, *Tanacetum parthenium* (L.) Schultz-Bip; pyrethrum, *Tanacetum cinerariifolium* (Trev.) Schultz-Bip; and shasta daisy, *Leucanthemum superbum* (J. Ingram) Bergmans ex Kert. (Anderson, 1987). A brief listing of additional horticultural species and their new current scientific names are included in Table II-1 Dendranthema.

The ancestors of the modern chrysanthemum are *Dendranthema indicum* (L.) Desmoul. and *D. japonicum* (Mak.) Kitam (Anderson, 1987; Bailey and Bailey, 1976; Balek and Albrecht, 1988). Compositae is a huge family with many important genera including *Aster, Calendula, Callistephus, Centaurea, Cosmos, Dahlia, Echinacea, Gerbera, Helianthus, Liatris, Pericallis, Solidago, Tagetes*, and *Zinnia*.

Origin: Chrysanthemum hybrids originated from China and have been cultivated for more than 1200 years in Japan and more than 1400 years in China. Garden chrysanthemums were grown in Europe in the 18th century.

Uses and current status: This herbaceous perennial plant is grown as a cut flower, potted flowering plant, or garden plant for fall color. Potted and cut chrysanthemums are available as lateral disbuds or standards, respectively, with one flower/shoot or as center disbudded or sprays, respectively, with several flowers/shoot. Center disbudded pots and cut sprays are most commonly grown. Currently, little production of cut chrysanthemums is found in North America or Europe; most production has shifted to areas of higher light intensities and more economical labor. Small numbers of cut chrysanthemums are field grown especially in the fall in California. Potted flowering chrysanthemums rank as one of the most popular plants for home use and are widely grown in the Northern Hemisphere. Garden chrysanthemums are either sold in the spring in flower and cut back in the home garden after the flowers have faded to allow for regrowth and fall flowering, or sold as large flowering specimens in the fall for autumn color (Figs. II-1 and II-2 Dendranthema).

CULTIVARS

Over the centuries thousands of cultivars have been developed around the world. The advent of year-round production further encouraged the development of new cultivars primarily for cut or potted flowering plants. Cultivars exist that are suited to specific growing areas around the world such as northern, central, or southern

TABLE II-1 DENDRANTHEMA

Changes in scientific names of several species formerly in the genus *Chrysanthemum* (Anderson, 1987).

Common Name	Former Scientific Name	New Scientific Name
Costmary	*C. balsamita*	*Tanacetum balsamita* L.
Dusty miller	*C. ptarmiciflorum*	*Tanacetum ptarmiciflorum* (Webb and Berlin.) Schultz-Bip.
Feverfew	*C. parthenium*	*Tanacetum parthenium* (L.) Schultz-Bip.
Florist's chrysanthemum	*C. ×morifolium*	*Dendranthema ×grandiflorum* Kitam.
High daisy	*C. serotinum*	*Leucanthemella serotinum* (L.) Tzveleu.
Marguerite daisy	*C. frutescens*	*Argyranthemum frutescens* (L.) Schultz-Bip.
Oxeye daisy	*C. leucanthemum*	*Leucanthemum vulgare* Lam.
Pyrethrum	*C. cinerarifolium*	*Tanacetum cinerariifolium* (Trev.) Schultz-Bip.
Shasta daisy	*C. ×superbum*	*Leucanthemum superbum* (J. Ingram) Bergmans ex Kert.
Tansy	*C. vulgare*	*Tanacetum vulgare* L.
Tansy chrysanthemum	*C. macrophyllum*	*Tanacetum macrophyllum* (Wldst. and Kit.) Schultz-Bip.

FIGURE II-1 DENDRANTHEMA   Greenhouse potted *Dendranthema* production.

FIGURE II-2 DENDRANTHEMA   Outdoor fall *Dendranthema* production.

Europe; North America; Israel; South America; or sections of Africa. Each year new cultivars are released for cut flower, potted flowering plant, or garden use. Unfortunately, as cut flower production has shifted around the world, numerous cultivars have been lost or discarded that were fragile and difficult to transport, such as the spiders and large single daisies.

Modern chrysanthemum cultivars come in an astonishing variety of colors (white, yellow, red, bronze, and pink), color combinations, and petal styles (spoon, quill, and flat) (Figs. II-3, II-4, II-5, II-6, II-7, II-8, II-9, and II-10 Dendranthema). The central disc florets may be numerous to nearly absent; the outer ray florets may also be numerous or have only one or two rows. For the daisy types, consumers prefer the central disc florets be yellow, while growers and wholesalers favor green centers (Anonymous, 2002).

Cultivars for potted plant production can also be grouped by height and vigor: tall, medium, and short. Tall varieties flower naturally on vigorous stems more than 15 in. (38 cm) long after the start of SD. Medium varieties naturally flower on stems no longer than 15 in. (38 cm). Short varieties naturally flower on stems under 15 in. (38 cm) after the start of SD. Knowing the height classification of a cultivar will aid in determining rates and frequency of growth retardant applications (see Height Control, page 438) and pinching date relative to the start of SD (see Pinching and Disbudding, page 440).

PROPAGATION

Plants form stolons in the garden and develop into a multistem clump. Seed propagation is not used other than in breeding programs.

FIGURE II-3 DENDRANTHEMA Daisy, flat petal.

FIGURE II-4 DENDRANTHEMA Daisy, spoon petal.

FIGURE II-5 DENDRANTHEMA Daisy, quill petal.

FIGURE II-6 DENDRANTHEMA Anemone (duet).

FIGURE II-7 DENDRANTHEMA Decorative (cushion).

FIGURE II-8 DENDRANTHEMA Incurved.

FIGURE II-9 DENDRANTHEMA Spider.

FIGURE II-10 DENDRANTHEMA Button.

Seed will germinate in 5 to 10 days when held at 60 to 70°F (16 to 21°C) (Nau, 1993).

Commercially, cuttings are produced by specialty propagators who maintain pathogen-free stock plants. Cuttings are produced in only a few locations around the world and are efficiently distributed by air to growers. Terminal cuttings 2.5 to 3 in. (6.5 to 7.5 cm) long are sold either unrooted or rooted. Cuttings root with ease in 1 to 2 weeks under mist, fog, or plastic (white in the summer and clear in the winter) laid directly over the cuttings. A rooting hormone may be dusted onto the base of the cuttings to speed rooting. Rooted cuttings are directly planted in pots or beds and kept fogged or misted for several days until established. Rooted cuttings are usually purchased directly from specialty propagators. Rooted cuttings of some cultivars can be stored at 32 to 37°F (1 to 3°C) for 4 to 6 weeks, other cultivars can be stored for only 1 week (Rajapakse et al., 1996). The variation among cultivars was related to carbohydrate status. Light intensity of 67 fc (10 μmol · m^{-2} · s^{-1}) from cool-white fluorescent lamps during cold storage improved cutting quality, regardless of the cultivar. Treatment of cuttings with the anti-ethylene agent 1-methylcyclopropene (1-MCP) reduced rooting (Serek et al., 1998).

To maintain vegetative growth, stock plants must be kept under LD (see Flowering Control and Dormancy, next). The use of HID lighting and supplemental CO_2 on stock plants increased the number and quality of cuttings (Eng et al., 1983).

FLOWERING CONTROL AND DORMANCY

Flowering is controlled by the naturally shortening day lengths of late summer and fall with flowering occurring from early fall to winter (Post, 1949). By altering the photoperiod in the greenhouse, flowers are available any day of the year. Long days are used to maintain vegetative growth of stock plants and cuttings prior to placing young plants under SD for flowering (Cockshull, 1985). The critical photoperiod is 12 hr or less for reproductive growth, 14 hr or more for vegetative growth. Floral induction can occur at or below 14 hr but normal flower development does not continue. However, day-neutral breeding lines exist (Anderson and Ascher, 2001).

Juvenility exists because cuttings from older stock become reproductive sooner than those from younger stock, which is thought to be related to the physiological age of the meristem. Conversely, even if stock plants are kept under LD, plants eventually form a terminally reproductive structure called a *crown bud*, which rarely reaches anthesis. For this reason propagators must renew stock plants up to four times a year depending on the cultivar grown (Cathey, 1969; Cathey and Borthwick, 1971; Cockshull and Kofranek, 1985; Seeley and Weise, 1965). Old shoots with a large number of leaves are more likely to produce crown buds than younger shoots.

RESPONSE GROUPS

Cultivars are grouped into response groups, which are based on the required number of weeks from the start of SD to flower. Flower initiation and development are facultative SD responses for the early flowering cultivars found in the shortest response group. These cultivars are primarily garden cultivars and many are never truly vegetative. Cockshull and Kofranek (1992) studied eight garden cultivars and found they were in the 6- to 8-week response groups; all formed flower buds even under LD. Although buds developed slowly under LD, they initiated quickly and were present approximately 13 days after a pinch.

For late flowering cultivars, initiation and development are obligate SD responses; flower initiation may occur under LD, but the flowers never develop. These cultivars are in the longer response groups and include the potted flowering and cut flower cultivars.

The time span from beginning of SD to flower initiation is relatively uniform between cultivars; however, the time from initiation to development of the inflorescence varies among cultivars. Consequently, the total number of weeks from the beginning of SD to harvest or anthesis varies among cultivars. Cultivars that flower 6 to 8 weeks after the start of SD are generally garden types; cultivars that flower 8 to 11 weeks after SD are generally flowering potted plants; and cultivars that flower 8 to 15 weeks after SD are cut flowers.

SHORT DAYS

Regardless of the cultivar response group, floral initiation and development to anthesis are more rapid under an absolute SD. Commercially, black cloths are typically pulled at 1700 hr and removed at 0700 hr. Black cloth must be pulled to maintain SD from March 15 to September 15 in the Northern Hemisphere. To prevent accidents, most growers start the artificial SD sooner than required. Proper application of SD requires a complete blackout of natural and artificial light sources.

LONG DAYS

Commercially, LD are generally created by using incandescent lamps as a night break. As the light intensity or the duration increases, the inhibition of reproductive growth is increased. Often cyclic lighting is used, for example, 6 min on and 24 min off, for the 4-hr night break. Cool-white fluorescent lamps are more efficient in electrical consumption and more effective at floral inhibition than incandescent lamps (Accati-Garibaldi et al., 1977; Cathey and Borthwick, 1961). Regardless, the incandescent lamp is more commonly used because of ease and low cost of installation.

For cyclic night break lighting, the intensity should be at least 10 fc (2.2 μmol $\cdot$ m^{-2} $\cdot$ s^{-1}) at the shoot apex (Mastalerz, 1977). HID lighting can also be used to maintain vegetative growth under LD (Stefanis and Langhans, 1983). If continuous lighting is used, the intensity required is 7 to 10 fc (1.5 to 2.2 μmol $\cdot$ m^{-2} $\cdot$ s^{-1}) (Sachs and Kofranek, 1979).

Duration of the night break in the winter varies with the latitude. Five-hour night breaks are recommended for locations at 40 to 50° latitude, 4 hr at 24 to 40° latitude, and 3 hr at 25° latitude to the equator from August 1 to May 30. Lighting for vegetative growth is necessary year-round from 15° latitude south or north to the equator. Commercial cutting propagators light year-round and many large producers of potted flowering plants also light year-round during the vegetative stage of growth.

FLORAL DEVELOPMENT

At any one time up to 13 leaf primordia exist within a vegetative meristem. When SD begins, 7 to 9 days are required for the first microscopic reproductive changes to be observed in the meristem. Floral initiation is completed after 24 to 30 days. With this information, a producer can predict the number of leaves on future flowering stems by counting the number of visible leaves and adding the proposed number of microscopic leaves (Cockshull, 1985; Popham and Chan, 1950, 1952).

After 28 SD, the terminal bud developmental rate will be similar, without delay, under LD or SD, particularly if the subtending flower buds have been removed (Ben-Jaacov and Langhans, 1969, 1971). After terminal flower buds begin to show petal color, plants can be moved from SD to LD without delay in development (Cathey, 1957; Cockshull, 1985; Kofranek and Halevy, 1974; Seeley and Weise, 1965).

TEMPERATURE

Floral initiation and development are temperature dependent and inappropriate temperatures during SD will delay floral initiation and development. Temperature has a greater influence on initiation and early development during the first weeks of SD. Prior to SD, temperatures ranging from 41 to 81°F (5 to 27°C) had little effect on future flower initiation or development; plants developed similarly at 70/41°F (21/5°C), 81/55°F (27/13°C), or 70/64°F (21/18°C) day/night temperatures. Further, no differences in date of harvest occurred if plants were grown at 63/55°F (17/13°C) or 68/55°F (20/13°C) day/night temperatures from visible bud to flower (Wilkins et al., 1990). These data are for 12/12-hr day/night photoperiods for vegetative growth and 8/16-hr day/night photoperiods for flowering. Cathey (1954a, b) and Vince (1960) both recommended a 61°F (16°C) night temperature from flower initiation and development to visible bud that is then lowered to 50 to 55°F (10 to 13°C) until harvest (Vince and Mason, 1959).

Karlsson et al. (1989a, b) modeled chrysanthemum growth and considered both temperature and light. Leaf unfolding increased linearly from 0.2 to 0.5 leaves/day as temperature increased from 50 to 86°F (10 to 30°C). Most rapid development was at 68/61°F (20/16°C) day/night or a constant 68°F (20°C) from planting to harvest. From (1) start of SD to visible bud, (2) visible bud to disbud, (3) disbud to flower color, or (4) flower color to harvest, the optimum temperatures were 70.5, 68.5, 73.5, and 66.5°F (21.3, 20.3, 23.1 and 19.1°C), respectively. As light intensity increased, one to two fewer leaves were initiated below the flower. Adams et al. (1998) also noted that 68.7°F (20.4°C) was the optimum average daily temperature for the most rapid flowering.

The delay of floral induction and early development is common if temperatures are above 85°F (29°C) during the early portion of the SD period (Whealy et al., 1987). This problem is known as *heat delay* and can be prevented if black cloth is pulled late in the evening as temperatures drop and opened in the middle of the night to release the heat under the cover. Regardless, the cloth must be left covering the plants for 12 or more hours. It is better to leave the cloth on longer in the cool of the morning versus pulling cloth at 1600 hr when workers go home. Automated controls allow the opening and closing of black cloths after workers have gone home. High day/night temperatures of 91/81°F (33/27°C) at the time of pinching or shortly thereafter reduced branching by increasing the number of nonviable axillary buds (Schoellhorn et al., 2001).

For 15 garden chrysanthemum cultivars Will et al. (1997) noted that as the temperature increased from 64°F (18°C) to 75°F (24°C), shorter photoperiods were required for rapid flowering. Eight- to 12-hr day lengths produced acceptable flowering at 64°F (18°C), whereas 8- to 10-hr day lengths were required at 75°F (24°C).

LIGHT

Vegetative growth and floral initiation and development under SD are slower under low light levels and more rapid under high light (Cockshull, 1972; Karlsson et al., 1989a; Mastalerz, 1968; Schoellhorn et al., 1996). In northern latitudes, HID lighting at 175 to 300 fc (35 to 60 μmol $\cdot$ m^{-2} $\cdot$ s^{-1}) is commonly used to supplement natural winter days during the LD vegetative period. The production of high-quality plants requires supplemental HID lighting in the north. Even though the time span from planting unrooted cuttings to shifting plants into the SD is only 4 to 6 weeks, HID lighting greatly increases quality (Carpenter, 1976). HID lighting is rarely used during SD and is of little benefit (Hicklenton, 1984, 1985). HID lighting is effective in providing the LD night interruption (Stefanis and Langhans, 1983). Also, HID lighting is generally economical only for potted flowering plants, not for cut flowers. Potted plants are usually grown pot-to-pot until moved to SD then spaced and pinched. Hence, the cost effectiveness of HID light is high when plant spacing is tight (Hughes and Cockshull, 1972). Shade is used only to reduce greenhouse temperatures in the summer.

WATER

The roots must be in a well-drained environment. Drip irrigation systems are most commonly used for ground beds. Potted chrysanthemums can be irrigated in a variety of ways, including microtubes, capillary mats, and ebb and flow. Interestingly, plants grown with fluctuating media moisture were larger than those grown with constant moisture (Kiehl et al., 1992). Water should be low in salts, which can accumulate and injure the plant. High humidity delayed flowering and reduced flower dry weight by reducing transpiration and nutrient uptake (Hand et al., 1996).

CARBON DIOXIDE

Carbon dioxide enrichment of the atmosphere is used to enhance the growth and quality of *Chrysanthemums*. Supplementary lighting with HID contributes to the effectiveness of supplemental CO_2 in northern greenhouses. Carbon dioxide is used only during daylight with or without supplementary HID lighting. If the HID lights are also used during the night, the intensity is insufficient to make supplemental CO_2

beneficial (Eng et al., 1983; Hughes and Cockshull, 1972). Supplementing CO_2 at 900 ppm enhanced flower number (Mortensen, 1986). Currently, commercial greenhouses use 1000 ppm CO_2 starting 1 hr before sunrise and continuing to 1 hr before darkness. Flowering can be up to 1 week earlier and flowers are larger and are borne on stronger stems when compared with the plants not given the supplemental CO_2 (Heins et al., 1986; Konjoian et al., 1983).

NUTRITION

As soon as cuttings are rooted, fertilization commences and continues until the flowers are in color; fertilization ceases prior to harvest for optimum postharvest life. During the last third of the production period, fertilizer levels can be reduced because vegetative growth is almost completed and only flower development is occurring. Nitrogen uptake is greatest in the first month and then decreases for the next 60 days, which is correlated with the switch from vegetative to reproductive growth (King et al., 1995). Willets et al. (1992) modeled the relationship between growth rate and nutrient uptake, irradiance, and carbon dioxide. Derrig (2000) recommended fertilizing garden mums with an ammonium-based fertilizer for the first 10 to 14 days, alternating it with a calcium and potassium nitrate fertilizer when plants are actively growing, and finishing with a calcium and potassium nitrate fertilizer for compact growth.

Rates not only vary between stages of growth, but also between cut flower crops in beds, where 200 ppm N constant liquid fertilizer is frequently used, and pot culture, where 250 to 400 ppm N is used with a soilless medium. Organic fertilizer sources such as bonemeal and *Brevibacterium lactofermentum*, have been as effective as commercial chemical fertilizers (Williams and Nelson, 1992). Numerous nutrient deficiencies and descriptions have been published (Hammer, 1989; Hershey and Paul, 1981; Huang et al., 1997; Raulston et al., 1972; van Eysinga and Smilde, 1980; Waters, 1964; Woodson and Boodley, 1983) (see Table II-2 Dendranthema). Foliar nutrient levels for high-quality plants are listed in Chapter 6, Nutrition, Table 6-4.

MEDIA

A wide range of media have been successfully used with medium pH ranging from 5.7 to 6.2. When planting potted flowering plants, cuttings should be sorted to ensure uniformity among cuttings in each pot. Also, cuttings should be planted at a 45-degree angle outward, which will make the final plant fuller. Training and retraining employees is a necessity in this matter.

HEIGHT CONTROL

With potted flowering plants, plant growth regulators are required to reduce internode elongation. One or more B-Nine (daminozide) sprays (2500 ppm) are used in most commercial establishments. In summer or with vigorous cultivars, one application of 5000 ppm B-Nine may be used or multiple applications of a lower rate. Typically, treatment commences 2 to 3 weeks after the pinch or when shoots are 1.5 to 3 in. (4 to 8 cm) long. If postponed, inflorescences may be "clubby" as elongation of the stem below each flower is suppressed for "spray" type cultivars. The last application should be made prior to disbudding or center bud removal (Higgins, 2001). B-Nine at 1000 ppm can also be applied as a dip to the foliage of cuttings to prevent stretch during propagation (Higgins, 2001). Unrooted cuttings can be dipped and planted immediately or stored overnight in a 40°F (4°C) cooler before planting. Avoid watering until foliage is dry. Unrooted cuttings are dipped and stored overnight before planting them the next day. Cuttings can also be sprayed with 1250 ppm B-Nine 3 to 5 days after planting.

Bonzi (paclobutrazol) is very effective and can be applied at 31 to 125 ppm as a spray or at 1 to 4 ppm as a drench (Barrett et al, 1986; Higgins, 2001). Sumagic (uniconazole) is also effective and can be applied at 2.5 to 10 ppm as a spray or at 0.1 to 1 ppm as a drench (Tayama and Carver, 1992; Wilfret, 1991). The higher rates of either chemical are used for vigorous cultivars and/or during the summer. Apply when shoots are 2 to 3 in. (5 to 8 cm) long. Multiple applications at low rates can be more effective (Starman, 1990). The presence of bark in the media may reduce the effectiveness of Bonzi or Sumagic drenches (Barrett, 1982).

Topflor (flurprimidol) and A-Rest (ancymidol) are also effective. Apply Topflor sprays at a rate of 7.5 to 15 ppm to sensitive cultivars or use 15 to 25 ppm for vigorous cultivars (SePRO, personal communication). Cycocel (chlormequat) is not effective. Although numerous application methods have been tested including drenches, gels, capsules, and granules, sprays are still favored due to ease of ap-

TABLE II-2 DENDRANTHEMA
Symptoms of nutritional deficiency in *Dendranthema* (Raulston et al., 1972).

Element	Deficiency Symptoms
Nitrogen	1. Reduction in plant vigor and small, light green to yellowish foliage. 2. In severe cases, lower leaves are chlorotic and have reddish veins and margins. 3. Growth and flower size is reduced and flowering date is delayed.
Phosphorus	1. Lower leaves turn reddish to yellow to brown beginning at the leaf apex. 2. Leaf size of newly developed leaves is reduced and lower stem portions may develop a deep purple color.
Potassium	1. Lack of plant vigor; small leaves and weak stems. 2. In severe cases, leaves develop interveinal and marginal chlorosis followed by necrosis with first appearance on lower leaves.
Calcium	1. Small, curled, thickened leaves around growing point. 2. In severe cases, death of growing point and rosetting of leaves. 3. Peduncles break over about time flower color shows and flowers have poor keeping quality. 4. Stubby and brown roots.
Magnesium	1. Appears first as interveinal chlorosis and curling under of older leaves. Veins remain green. 2. Severe cases have reddish colored spots interveinally and along leaf margins, gradually moving to upper leaves.
Iron	Interveinal chlorosis of young leaves becoming a general chlorosis in leaves severely affected. A common deficiency when root substrate pH is high.
Manganese	1. Generally pale green plants with mild interveinal chlorosis of young leaves not as distinctly outlined as in iron deficiency. 2. Severe cases with small necrotic spots in middle leaves, affecting up to one-fourth of the surface. Interveinal areas are first white or gray then tan.
Zinc	1. A rare deficiency. Appears as plant approaches flowering stage. Small chlorotic spots at any position on middle or upper leaves. 2. Chlorotic spots gradually develop necrotic spots in the center.
Copper	1. Dull green leaves, chlorotic veins. Veinal chlorosis produces inverse "netting." Margins remain green. 2. Affected leaves wilt during the day, with outer margins turning upward. 3. Flowers are small, reflex, and soft.
Boron	1. Red pigment in veins with interveinal chlorosis. 2. Corky veins and sides of petioles with brittle, downward-cupped leaves. 3. Terminal bud may die or secondary flower buds fail to develop normally. Larger flowers do not open fully and are more incurved than normal. 4. Roots brown and stubby.

plication and control (Sanderson et al., 1988). Interestingly, Bonzi at 24 ppb and A-Rest at 10 ppb are also effective when applied through subirrigation (Million et al., 1999). This work also highlights the potential effects of contamination from plant growth regulators on subirrigation benches.

As with many crop species, cultivars vary in their sensitivity to growth retardants. Crop timing and plant quality can be greatly affected by improper timing of applications, number of applications, and concentration (Gilbertz, 1992). Proper crop timing is important in meeting precise marketing deadlines.

With the use of computerized plant height models, growers monitor plant heights weekly and can predict rates of growth and height control treatments (Carlson and Heins, 1990; Heins and Carlson, 1990). Further, temperature DIF and DROP techniques can be used to aid in height control (Berghage et al., 1991; Erwin et al., 1989, 1991; Jensen, 1993; Karlsson et al., 1989a, b; Tutty et al., 1994). Fertilizer type is also useful; use ammonium-based fertilizers to increase growth and use calcium and potassium nitrate fertilizers to provide more compact growth (Derrig, 2000). Height control through mechanical stress to release natural pulses of ethylene (Hammer et al., 1974) and through manipulation of light quality by filters (Maki et al., 2002; McMahon et al., 1991; Rajapakse and Kelly, 1992) have been effective and may be useful commercially in the future. The use of light filters to control height may also reduce water and fertilizer use but may impact crop timing (McMahon, 1999; Rajapakse and Kelly, 1993). Genetic engineering may also be a viable, long-term solution to height control (Zheng et al., 2001).

Cut flower cultivars do not require plant growth regulator sprays. For garden cultivars, B-Nine at 2500 ppm, Sumagic at 2.5 to 10 ppm, and Florel (ethephon) at 500 ppm are typically used to control height (see also Pinching and Disbudding).

SPACING

For pinched cut flower production, rooted cuttings are planted in beds at spacings ranging from 6 × 7 in. (15 × 18 cm) in the summer to 7 × 8 or 9 in. (18 × 20 or 23 cm) in the winter. For nonpinched plant production, spacing is 4 × 6 in. (10 × 15 cm) in summer or 5 × 6 in. (13 × 15 cm) in winter.

Potted flowering plants are grown in various pot sizes. Single unrooted cuttings are used for 3- and 4-in. (8- and 10-cm) pots. With the latter pot size, the plant may be pinched. With 5-in. (13-cm) pots, two to three cuttings are used and are pinched. For plants in 6- or 7-in. (15- or 18-cm) pots, three to five cuttings are used and are pinched. Spacing used on the bench will vary with the pot size (Table II-3 Dendranthema).

Garden varieties are typically grown with one cutting/pot, and 8-in. (20-cm) pots are spaced in the field at 18 × 24 in. (45 × 60 cm) (Whipker and Cloyd, 1997). Smaller pots and later plantings are spaced closer together.

TABLE II-3 DENDRANTHEMA
Proposed bench spacing used to produce various sizes of flowering potted *Dendranthema*.

Pot Size in. (cm)	Pot Spacing in. (cm)
3 (7.75)	5 (13) centers
4 (10)	7 (18) centers
5 (13)	10 (25) centers
6 (15)	12 (30) centers
7 (18)	14 (25) centers

PINCHING AND DISBUDDING
PINCHING

For cut flowers, the time span from planting a rooted cutting to pinching varies from winter to summer (see Table II-4 Dendranthema). Excess shoots may need to be removed; only three to four axillary shoots per plant should remain. The time of pinching relative to the start of natural SD and the start of flower initiation is important. If the pinch is too early, the spray becomes too long; if pinched too late, the spray is clubby because of lack of time for vegetative growth before flower initiation (Post, 1950).

When potted flowering plants are pinched to induce axillary branching, a uniform number of nodes must be left on each cutting to ensure uniform plant height. The time from planting rooted cuttings to pinching varies with the type of cultivar and the season.

With garden chrysanthemums, pinching typically occurs between June 12 and July 1, earlier if plants are placed under SD.

If young chrysanthemum shoots are pinched down to woody or "hardened" tissue, axillary shoot development will be slow and the number and quality of shoots will be reduced. If pinched too soft, the number of shoots may be excessive and the apical axillary shoot re-

TABLE II-4 DENDRANTHEMA
Guidelines for amount of time from planting a rooted *Dendranthema* cutting to the pinch for potted plants.

Season and Treatment	Days from Planting to Pinching	
	North	South
Late Spring, Summer, Early Fall:		
Tall treatment	7–10	7–10
Medium treatment	8–11	8–11
Short treatment	10–14	10–14
Early Spring, Late Fall:		
Tall treatment	10–14	10–14
Medium treatment	11–14	11–14
Short treatment	14–17	14–17
Midwinter:		
Tall treatment	14–17	10–14
Medium treatment	15–18	11–15
Short treatment	17–21	14–17

gains dominance too quickly, resulting in an unacceptable inflorescence. Removing the youngest one or two leaves will prevent problems when a soft pinch is used.

DISBUDDING

Potted and cut chrysanthemum cultivars are frequently classified as having a disbud or spray inflorescence. If disbudded, all subtending axillary flower buds are removed as soon as they can be handled by the employees, leaving only the apical or terminal bud to develop into one large flower. Decorative, incurved, fuji, and spider flower types are most commonly disbudded. Some cultivars with large daisy or anemone flowers can also be disbudded.

If a spray inflorescence is desired, only the apical flower bud is removed, which breaks apical dominance and allows all of the subtending axillary flowers to develop. This results in a full inflorescence with all flowers opening at the same time; if the older terminal bud is not removed, it will reach anthesis before the axillary flowers open. The terminal bud is removed when the buds develop some pigmentation. Terminal bud removal is used most commonly on daisy types but occasionally on anemones and decoratives.

CONTROL OF INFLORESCENCE FORM

Inflorescence form can be influenced by adjusting pinching date relative to SD, disbudding, and interrupting the SD flower induction period by LD. The first two methods have already been described, and the last method is used with spray cultivars for cut flower production. To prevent clubby inflorescences or short peduncles below the flower, a SD–LD–SD sequence can be used: 12 SD, 10 LD, and SD until flowering (see Schedule and Timing).

FLOWER FORM

During winter some standard or disbudded cultivar types develop flat inflorescences that may be smaller in diameter and not in the classic globe shape. This problem can be prevented by giving the plants SD for 35 to 42 days, then returning to LD and allowing plants to flower (see Schedule and Timing). The flower bud should be "cracking color" in size when plants are returned to LD.

CHEMICAL PINCHING AND DISBUDDING

Pinching and disbudding are labor-intensive processes. Early research attempts to use chemicals were effective but were difficult to commercially adapt for potted or cut chrysanthemums (Cathey et al., 1966; Garner and Lewis, 1984). However, Florel effectively increases branching in commercial garden chrysanthemum production. Florel can also be used to reduce premature budding or crown bud development, to reduce height, and to increase branching. Florel may result in elimination of a second pinch. Date of flower may be slightly delayed by a few days when using this ethylene-releasing material (Elsburg, 1996; Higgins, 1995; Larson and McCall, 1995). The recommended application rate is 500 ppm sprayed to the point of runoff from the foliage. Applications can be made every 3 to 4 weeks commencing 15 to 17 days after propagating unrooted cuttings, when they are well rooted, and continuing until early July (for natural flowering) or 6 to 7 weeks prior to scheduled flowering date. Later application will delay flowering. When using Florel, adjust or eliminate other height control methods accordingly.

SUPPORT

For cut flower cultivars, a galvanized wire or plastic mesh with 6- × 8-in. (15- × 20-cm) openings is commonly used. Two layers are used and are raised as the plants increase in height. For potted cultivars, no support is required if plants are properly grown with appropriate plant growth regulators. Low irradiance levels and high temperatures, CO_2, NH_4 levels, and moisture can lead to weak, soft growth, which may need support. Potted plants can be wrapped with string around the outer edge, but that process is labor intensive.

SCHEDULE AND TIMING

Chrysanthemums can be scheduled to flower for any day of the year by lighting to keep plants vegetative or by placing plants under SD black cloth to induce flowering. Elaborate schedules are prepared by commercial suppliers of cuttings for all latitudes and climactic conditions. One example for a potted plant is given in Table II-5 Dendranthema and one for a cut flower in Table II-6 Dendranthema. Many garden mum cuttings are in

TABLE II-5 DENDRANTHEMA

Sample *Dendranthema* production schedule for a 6-in. (15-cm) potted 8-week response group cultivar from unrooted cuttings.

Cultivar Step	Production Time (weeks)	Temperature °F (°C)	Photoperiod
Propagate cuttings			
	1–2	Medium: 70–75 (21–23)	LD
Plant rooted cuttings			
	1–2	Day: 65–75 (18–23) Night: 65 (18)	LD
Pinch			
	4	Day: 67–75 (19–23) Night: 62 (16)	SD
Disbud			
	4	Day: 56–62 (13–16) Night: 56 (13)	SD
Flower			
Total	10–12		

TABLE II-6 DENDRANTHEMA

Sample *Dendranthema* production schedule for a cut flower 10-week response group cultivar from unrooted cuttings.

Cultural Step	Production Time (weeks)	Temperature °F (°C)	Photoperiod
Propagate cuttings			
	1–2	Medium: 70–75 (21–23)	LD
Plant rooted cuttings			
	3	Day: 65–75 (18–23) Night: 65 (18)	LD
Pinch			
	5	Day: 67–75 (19–23) Night: 62 (16)	SD
Disbud			
	5	Day: 56–62 (13–16) Night: 56 (13)	SD
Flower			
Total	14–15		

the 6- to 7-week response groups. Most potted flowering chrysanthemums are 8-week cultivars and most cut flower cultivars are 11-week cultivars. The shorter the response time, the shorter the production time and the lower the production costs. However, plants must be sufficiently large to fill the pot or to provide a long enough stem to be used as a cut flower. Regardless of the response group, for all cut flowers 3 or 4 weeks of LD are given to lengthen the stem compared with 2 weeks for many of the pot mum cultivars. Time from planting to pinching can vary with the season and production location (see Pinching and Disbudding, page 440).

Garden chrysanthemums can be produced by planting rooted cuttings directly into the field or into 8-in. (20-cm) pots in the late spring, pinching in midsummer, and allowing plants to naturally flower. The pinch can occur when the vegetative shoot is 3 to 5 in. (8 to 13 cm) long. Depending on season, plants may be pinched twice or Florel can be used. The field-grown items are dug and potted. Pots can be grown in a greenhouse or grown on a container pad outdoors. Pots can also be plunged into the soil, root pruned later, and sold (Elsburg, 1996; Higgins, 1995). The majority of garden chrysanthemums are grown outdoors on container pads. The versatile garden mum can also be grown as a 12-in. (30-cm) hanging basket for summer to fall sales or as a patio plant. Two to three cuttings are used in this system.

Historically, garden mums were allowed to flower naturally. However, with staggered dates of planting, date of flower can be spaced over time. Some producers even use black cloths on garden chrysanthemums for rapid flower induction and development. A fast crop of garden mums can be produced in 9 to 10 weeks by planting one rooted cutting in a 6-in. (15-cm) pot between July 16 and 30 (Higgins, 1995). Plants will have small crowns 10 to 14 in. (25 to 35 cm) wide, allowing for close spacing. No pinching or B-Nine is used. Natural crown bud formation (see Physiological Disorders) stimulates axillary shoot development.

INSECTS

Numerous insects can threaten a chrysanthemum crop. Sanitation, inspection, and treatment of isolated infestations will reduce spraying. Commonly reported insects are aphids, caterpillars, leaf miners, and thrips (Lindquist, 1989; Waters and Conover, 1969). Foliar nematodes are also a problem (Daughtrey and Chase, 1992). Cultivars vary in their resistance to leaf miners, thrips, and aphids (Heinz and Thompson, 1997).

DISEASES

Cuttings from cultured indexed stock plants and the use of pasteurized, well-drained media have eliminated many diseases. *Pythium, Rhizoctonia,* and *Sclerotinia* stem rots can occur. *Botrytis* on foliage and flowers can also occur if moisture and humidity are excessive and air movement is low (Jackson et al., 1966; Powell, 1989). *Fusarium* wilt (*Fusarium oxysporum* f. sp. *chrysanthemi* and *F. oxysporum* f. sp. *tracheiphilum*), stem canker (*F. solani*) bacterial leaf spot and flower blight (*Pseudomonas cichorii*), white rust (*Puccinia horiana*), brown rust (*Puccinia chrysanthemi*), and tomato spotted wilt virus can be found on chrysanthemums (Daughtrey, 2003; Daughtrey and Chase, 1992). Currently, quarantines are being used to prevent the establishment and spread of white rust in the United States. Cultivars vary in their resistance to white rust (Heinz and Thompson, 1997). Outdoor cut flower crops can be more exposed to potential environmental conditions conducive for disease incidence. A number of other diseases that have been reported include verticillium wilt (*Verticillium dahliae*), ray blight (*Didymella ligulicola*), ray speck (*Stemphylium lycopersici*), sclerotinia rot (*Sclerotinia sclerotiorum*), powdery mildew (*Erysiphe cichoracearum*), septoria leaf spot (*Septoria chrysanthemi*), bacterial blight (*Erwinia chrysanthemi*), hollow stem (*Erwinia carotovora*), crown gall (*Agrobacterium tumefaciens*), and aster yellows (Dreistadt, 2001).

PHYSIOLOGICAL DISORDERS

Crown buds form even under LD after a certain number of leaves have developed on a shoot or a number of cuttings have been removed from a stock plant. These crown buds differ from true flower buds and do not develop normally. Frequently, crown buds are removed and discarded at a pinch. However, if single stem plants are grown, crown buds may appear. Crown buds may also form when flower initiation occurs under SD, but the correct conditions for further flower development are not present—day length is too long or the temperature is too high. Regardless of the cause, vegetative shoots frequently develop below the crown buds. Low levels of ethylene have also been known to halt bud development and encourage vegetative bypass shoots.

High night temperatures during the SD phase and insufficient photoperiodic light intensity or duration during the LD phase results in delayed development (heat delay). However, breeding lines are available that are insensitive to heat delay (Anderson and Ascher, 2001). High production temperatures also decrease branching (Schoellhorn et al., 2001). Similarly, during the SD phase, light leaks or inconsistent pulling of black cloth will result in delayed or erratic flowering. Low light levels or temperatures below 60°F (16°C) may result in inappropriate flower development, particularly during the early weeks of SD.

POSTHARVEST

For both cut flowers and potted flowering plants, longevity is enhanced if there is high light during the last 3 to 4 weeks of production [5000 to 6000 fc (1000 to 1200 μmol · m^{-2} · s^{-1})]. Lowering temperatures to 56 to 60°F (13 to 16°C) for 2 to 4 weeks prior to harvest will enhance the flower color of many cultivars. However, white cultivars may develop a pink cast.

Nutrition regimes with 60 to 70% of the nitrogen in the nitrate form are essential; ammonium rates above this level reduce longevity (Roude, 1991a, b). Equal amounts of N and K are also advised. Eliminating fertilizers at the disbud stage 3 to 4 weeks prior to marketing enhances longevity without reducing quality (Nell, 1993; Nell et al., 1989).

L. Høyer (personal communication) considered the chrysanthemum to be sensitive to ethylene and the application of silver thiosulfate (STS) reduced the transpiration rate, which may delay water stress during shipping (Rajapakse et al., 1989). However, Nell (1993) considered potted chrysanthemums to be one of the few species to be completely insensitive to ethylene. Lastly, tremendous differences exist between cultivars in regard to longevity. Wise production firms continuously check the postharvest characteristics of old and new cultivars.

Grades and standards for cut chrysanthemums are summarized by Nowak and Rudnicki (1990). The Society of American Florists has developed standards for potted flowering plants.

CUT FLOWERS

Spray daisy chrysanthemums are harvested when the older flowers are open, but no pollen has been shed. Spray anemone are cut when the older flowers are open but before disc flowers start to elongate, and spray decoratives are harvested when the centers of the older flowers are fully open. Standard chrysanthemums are harvested when the outer petals are fully elongated. Standard chrysanthemums and spray types can be opened in holding or opening solutions. Longevity of leaves is enhanced if flowers are kept under 100 fc (20 μmol $\cdot$ m^{-2} $\cdot$ s^{-1}) of light.

Every time stems are out of water during the marketing process, they should be recut and placed in warm 100°F (38°C) water (Sacalis, 1993). Commercially prepared floral preservatives can be used, but larger firms often find it more economical to prepare their own solutions. Citric acid is used to adjust the water to 3.5 pH; a material that will control the growth of microorganisms [100 to 150 ppm HQC (hydroxyquinoline citrate)] and sucrose (lower than 3%) is also advised (Hussein, 1994). Silver nitrate is beneficial (25 ppm). However, antimicrobial agents had no effect on longevity according to Jones and Hill (1993). Leaf senescence has been reported to be reduced by benzyladenine (10 to 100 ppm).

Once flower stems are hydrated, they should be stored at 32 to 40°F (0 to 4°C). Large flowered standard mums, 5 in. (13 cm) in diameter, can be stored in wax paper-lined boxes dry for 3 weeks; smaller, 3- to 5-in.- (7- to 13-cm)-diameter flowers are stored for only 2 weeks. For opening and hydration, use the same procedure as described, and a wetting agent may aid water uptake.

POTTED FLOWERING PLANTS

Potted plants are marketed when 33 to 50% of the flowers are open and have developed pigmentation characteristic of the cultivar. Eliminating fertilizers at the disbud stage 3 to 4 weeks prior to marketing enhances longevity without reducing quality (Nell, 1993; Nell et al., 1989). Light acclimatization of chrysanthemums is not useful (Nell et al., 1990). Hopefully, the retailer and consumer will place the plant in a minimum of 50 fc (10 μmol $\cdot$ m^{-2} $\cdot$ s^{-1}) and keep it well watered. Plants can be shipped and stored at 35 to 40°F (2 to 4°C).

GARDEN CHRYSANTHEMUMS

Garden chrysanthemums are sometimes grown as a single cutting, spring bedding plant. After flowering, the customer must be told to prune or pinch the plants in mid- to late June in the north or in mid- to late July in the south to encourage branching and produce a large flowering specimen in the autumn garden. Large flowering plants can also be purchased in the fall and immediately planted in the garden.

KEY POINTS

- The chrysanthemum is one of the world's most important floriculture crops and is used as a cut flower, potted flowering plant, and fall-flowering garden ornamental.
- Plants are propagated commercially by cuttings.

- The chrysanthemum is a SD plant and cultivars are classified by their response group, which is the number of weeks required to flower from the beginning of SD.
- Early flowering cultivars (short response group) are facultative SD plants; late flowering cultivars (long response group) are obligate SD plants.

- Floral induction and development are delayed if night temperatures are above 85°F (29°C), which is known as heat delay.
- Height is controlled through cultivar selection, DIF, chemical growth retardants, and graphical tracking.

- Most plants are pinched when young and later disbudded; center bud removal is used to obtain spray inflorescences and lateral disbudding is used to obtain one large flower per axillary shoot.

BIBLIOGRAPHY

Accati-Garibaldi, E., A.M. Kofranek, and R.M. Sachs. 1977. Relative efficiency of fluorescent and incandescent lamps in inhibiting flower induction in *Chrysanthemum morifolium* 'Albatross.' *Acta Horticulturae* 68:51–58.

Adams, S.R., S. Pearson, and P. Hadley. 1998. The effect of temperature on inflorescence initiation and subsequent development in chrysanthemum cv. Snowdon (*Chrysanthemum ×morifolium* Ramat.). *Scientia Horticulturae* 77:59–72.

Anderson, N.O. 1987. Reclassification of the genus *Chrysanthemum* L. *HortScience* 22:313.

Anderson, N.O., and P.D. Ascher. 2001. Selection of day-neutral, heat-delay-insensitive *Dendranthema ×grandiflora* genotypes. *Journal of the American Society for Horticultural Science* 126: 710–721.

Anonymous. 2002. Study reveals chrysanthemum color preferences. *Floral Management* 19(7):60.

Bailey, L.H., and E.Z. Bailey. 1976. *Chrysanthemum* L., pp. 266–269 in *Hortus Third: A Concise Dictionary of Plants Cultivated in the United States and Canada*. Macmillan, New York.

Balek, R.M., and M.L. Albrecht. 1988. Rainbow daisy has bright future as a potted plant. *Greenhouse Grower* 6(10):92, 94, 96.

Barrett, J.E. 1982. Chrysanthemum height control by ancymidol, PP333, and EL-500 dependent on medium composition. *HortScience* 17:896–897.

Barrett, J.E., M.E. Peacock, and T.A. Nell. 1986. Height control of exacum and chrysanthemum with paclobutrazol, XE-1019, flurprimidol and RSW-0411. *Proceedings of the Florida State Horticultural Society* 99:254–255.

Ben-Jaacov, J., and R.W. Langhans. 1969. After lighting of chrysanthemums. *New York State Flower Grower's Bulletin* 285:1–3.

Ben-Jaacov, J., and R.W. Langhans. 1971. Effect of long photoperiods on flower development of chrysanthemum. *Florists' Review* 149(3861):33, 73–75.

Berghage, R.D., J.E. Erwin, and R.D. Heins. 1991. Photoperiod influences leaf chlorophyll content in chrysanthemum grown with negative DIF temperature regime. *HortScience* 26:708. (Abstract)

Carlson, W., and R.D. Heins. 1990. Get the plant height you want with graphical tracking. *GrowerTalks* 53(9):62–68.

Carpenter, W.J. 1976. Photosynthetic supplementary lighting of spray pompon *Chrysanthemum morifolium* Ramat. *Journal of the American Society for Horticultural Science* 101:155–158.

Cathey, H.M. 1954a. Chrysanthemum temperature study. B. Thermal modifications of photoperiods previous to and after flower bud initiation. *Proceedings of the American Society for Horticultural Science* 64:483–489.

Cathey, H.M. 1954b. Chrysanthemum temperature study. C. The effect of night, day, and mean temperature upon the flowering of *Chrysanthemum morifolium*. *Proceedings of the American Society for Horticultural Science* 64:499–502.

Cathey, H.M. 1957. Chrysanthemum temperature study. F. The effect of temperature on the critical photoperiod of *Chrysanthemum morifolium*. *Proceedings of the American Society for Horticultural Science* 69:485–491.

Cathey, H.M. 1969. *Chrysanthemum morifolium* (Ramat.) Hemsl., pp. 268–290 in *The Induction of Flowering*, L.T. Evans, editor. Macmillan, Melbourne.

Cathey, H.M., and H.A. Borthwick. 1961. Cyclic lighting for controlling flowering of chrysanthemums. *Proceedings of the American Society for Horticultural Science* 78:545–552.

Cathey, H.M., and H.A. Borthwick. 1971. Phytochrome control of garden and greenhouse chrysanthemums. *Proceedings of the American Society for Horticultural Science* 87:464–471.

Cathey, H.M., A.H. Yoeman, and F.E. Smith. 1966. Abortion of flower buds in *Chrysanthemum* after application of a selected petroleum fraction of high aromatic content. *HortScience* 1:61–62.

Cockshull, K.E. 1972. Photoperiodic control of flowering in the chrysanthemum, pp. 235–250 in *Crop Processes in Controlled Environments*, A.R. Rees, K.E. Cockshull, D.W. Hard, and R.G. Hard, editors. Academic Press, London.

Cockshull, K.E. 1985. *Chrysanthemum morifolium*, pp. 238–257 in *CRC Handbook of Flowering*, vol. II, A.H. Halevy, editor. CRC Press, Boca Raton, Florida.

Cockshull, K.E., and A.M. Kofranek. 1985. Long-day flower initiation by chrysanthemum. *HortScience* 20:296–298.

Cockshull, K.E., and A.M. Kofranek. 1992. Responses of garden chrysanthemum to day length. *HortScience* 27:113–115.

Daughtrey, M. 2003. Mastering mum maladies. *GrowerTalks* 67(2):94, 96.

Daughtrey, M., and A.R. Chase. 1992. Chrysanthemum, pp. 30–39 in *Ball Field Guide to Diseases of Greenhouse Ornamental*. Ball Publishing, Geneva, Illinois.

Derrig, R. 2000. Feed for the right height. *GrowerTalks* 64(5):134–136.

Dreistadt, S.H. 2001. *Integrated Pest Management for Floriculture and Nurseries*. University of California Division of Agriculture and Natural Resources Publication 3402.

Elsburg, G. 1996. Garden mum production at Elsbury's Greenhouses: An overview. *Ohio Florists' Association Bulletin* 799:1, 8.

Eng, R.Y.N., M.J. Tsujita, B. Grodzinski, and R.G. Dutton. 1983. Production of chrysanthemum cuttings under supplementary lighting and CO_2 enrichment. *HortScience* 18:878–879.

Erwin, J.E., R.D. Heins, B.J. Kovanda, R.D. Berghage, W.H. Carlson, and J.A. Biernbaum. 1989. Cool mornings can control plant height. *GrowerTalks* 52(9):75.

Erwin, J.E., P. Velguth, and R.D. Heins. 1991. Diurnal variations in temperature affect cellular elongation but not division. *HortScience* 26:721. (Abstract)

Garner, J.L., and A.J. Lewis. 1984. Chemical pinching of chrysanthemums. *Florists' Review* 175 (4526):17–19.

Gilbertz, D.A. 1992. Chrysanthemum response to timing of paclobutrazol and uniconazole sprays. *HortScience* 27:322–323.

Hammer, P.A. 1989. Nutrition, pp. 7–12 in *Tips on Growing Potted Chrysanthemums*, H.K. Tayama and T.J. Roll, editors. Ohio Cooperative Extension Service, The Ohio State University, Columbus.

Hammer, P.A., C.A Mitchell, and T.C. Weiler. 1974. Height control in greenhouse chrysanthemum by mechanical stress. *HortScience* 9:474–475.

Hand, D.W., F.A. Langton, M.A. Hannah, and K.E. Cockshull. 1996. Effects of humidity on the growth and flowering of cut-flower chrysanthemums. *Journal of Horticultural Science* 71:227–234.

Heins, R.D., and W. Carlson. 1990. Understanding and applying graphical tracking. *Greenhouse Grower* 8(5):73–80.

Heins, R.D., M.G. Karlsson, J.A. Flore, and W.H. Carlson. 1986. Effects of photosynthetic rate maximization on chrysanthemum growth and development. *Journal of the American Society for Horticultural Science* 111:42–46.

Heinz, K.M., and S. Thompson. 1997. Use resistant varieties for chrysanthemum pest management. *GrowerTalks* 60(13):82, 84, 86.

Hershey, D.R., and J.L. Paul. 1981. Critical foliar levels of potassium in pot chrysanthemum. *HortScience* 16:220–222.

Hicklenton, P.R. 1984. Response of pot chrysanthemum to supplemental irradiation during rooting, long day, and short day production stages. *Journal of the American Society for Horticultural Science* 109:468–472.

Hicklenton, P.R. 1985. Influence of different levels of timing of supplemental irradiation on pot chrysanthemum production. *HortScience* 20:374–376.

Higgins, E.A. 1995. Rewriting the book on garden mum production. *GrowerTalks* 59(2):45, 50.

Higgins. 2001. Chrysanthemums, pp. 68–70 in *Tips on Regulating Growth of Floriculture Crops*, M.L. Gaston, L.A. Kunkle, P.S. Konjoian, and M.F. Wilt, editors. Ohio Florists' Association Services, Columbus, Ohio.

Hughes, A.P., and K.E. Cockshull. 1972. Further effects of light intensity, carbon dioxide concentration, and day temperature on the growth of *Chrysanthemum morifolium* cv. Bright Golden Anne. *Annals of Botany* 36:533–550.

Huang, L., E.T. Paparozzi, and C. Gotway. 1997. The effect of altering nitrogen and sulfur supply on the growth of cut chrysanthemums. *Journal of the American Society for Horticultural Science* 122:559–564.

Hussein, H.A.A. 1994. Varietal responses of cut flowers to different antimicrobial agents of bacterial contamination and keeping quality. *Acta Horticulturae* 368:106–116.

Huxley, A., M. Griffiths, and M. Levy. 1992. *Chrysanthemum*, pp. 33–34 in *The New Royal Horticultural Society Dictionary of Gardening*, vol. 2. Stockton Press, New York.

Jackson, C.R., and L.A. McFadden, revised by R.O. Magie and A.J. Overman. 1966. *Chrysanthemum Diseases in Florida*. Bulletin 637A, Agricultural Experiment Station, Institute of Food and Agricultural Sciences, University of Florida, Gainesville.

Jensen, H.E.K. 1993. Influence of duration and placement of a high night temperature on morphogenesis of *Dendranthema grandiflora* Tzvelv. *Scientia Horticulturae* 54:327–335.

Jones, R.B., and M. Hill. 1993. The effect of germicides on the longevity of cut flowers. *Journal of the American Society for Horticultural Science* 118:350–354.

Karlsson, M.G., R.D. Heins, J.E. Erwin, R.D. Berghage, W.H. Carlson, and J.A. Biernbaum. 1989a. Temperature and photosynthetic photon flux influence chrysanthemum shoot development and flower initiation under short day conditions. *Journal of the American Society for Horticultural Science* 114:158–163.

Karlsson, M.G., R.D. Heins, J.E. Erwin, and R.D. Berghage. 1989b. Development rate during four phases of chrysanthemum growth as determined by preceding and prevailing temperatures.

Journal of the American Society for Horticultural Sciences 114:234–240.

Kiehl, P.A., J.H. Lieth, and D.W. Burger. 1992. Growth response of chrysanthemum to various container medium moisture tension levels. *Journal of the American Society for Horticultural Science* 117:224–229.

King, J.J., L.A. Peterson, and D.P. Stimart. 1995. Ammonium and nitrate uptake thoughout development in *Dendranthema* ×*grandiflorum*. *HortScience* 30:499–503.

Kofranek, A.M., and A.H. Halevy. 1974. Minimum number of short days for production of high quality standard chrysanthemum. *HortScience* 9:543–544.

Konjoian, P.S., G.L. Staby, and H.K. Tayama. 1983. The growth and development of *Chrysanthemum* ×*morifolium* 'Bright Golden Anne' in low-oxygen environments. *Journal of the American Society for Horticultural Science* 108:582–585.

Larson, R.A., and I.F. McCall. 1995. Garden chrysanthemum culture the easy way. *North Carolina Flower Growers' Bulletin* 40(6):1–6.

Lindquist, R.K. 1989. Insects and related pests, pp. 40–49 in *Tips on Growing Potted Chrysanthemums*, H.K. Tayama and T.J. Roll, editors. Ohio Cooperative Extension Service, Columbus, Ohio.

Maki, S.L., S. Rajapakse, R.E. Ballard, and N.C. Rajapakse. 2002. Role of gibberellins in chrysanthemum growth under far red light-deficient greenhouse environments. *Journal of the American Society for Horticultural Science* 127:639–643.

Mastalerz, J.W. 1968. Too much shade delays pot mums. *Pennsylvania Flower Growers* 208:3.

Mastalerz, J.W. 1977. Duration of irradiation, pp. 221–270 in *The Greenhouse Environment*. John Wiley and Sons, New York.

McMahon, M. 1999. Development of chrysanthemum meristems grown under far-red absorbing filters and long or short photoperiods. *Journal of the American Society for Horticultural Science* 124:483–487.

McMahon, M.J., J.W. Kelly, D.R. Decoteau, R.E. Young, and R.K. Pollock. 1991. Growth of *Dendranthema* ×*grandiflorum* (Ramat.) Kitamura under various spectral filters. *Journal of American Society for Horticultural Science* 116: 950–954.

Million, J.B., J.E. Barrett, T.A. Nell, and D.G. Clark. 1999. Inhibiting growth of flowering crops with ancymidol and paclobutrazol in subirrigation water. *HortScience* 34:1103–1105.

Mortensen, L.M. 1986. Effect of intermittent as compared to continuous CO_2 enrichment on growth and flowering of *Chrysanthemum* ×*morifolium* Ramat. and *Saintpaulia ionantha* H. Wendl. *Scientia Horticulturae* 29:283–289.

Nau, J. 1993. Chrysanthemum, p. 88 in *Ball Culture Guide, The Encyclopedia of Seed Germination*, 2nd ed. Ball Publishing, Batavia, Illinois.

Nell, T.A. 1993. *Dendranthema grandiflora*, pp. 35–38 in *Flowering Potted Plants, Prolonging Shelf Performance*. Ball Publishing, Batavia, Illinois.

Nell, T.A., J.E. Barrett, and R.T. Leonard. 1989. Fertilization termination influences postharvest performance of pot chrysanthemums. *HortScience* 24:996–998.

Nell, T.A., R.T. Leonard, and J.E. Barrett. 1990. Production and postproduction irradiance affects acclimatization and longevity of potted chrysanthemum and poinsettia. *Journal of the American Society for Horticultural Science* 115:262–265.

Nowak, J., and R.M. Rudnicki. 1990. *Postharvest Handling and Storage of Cut Flowers, Florist Greens and Potted Plants*. Timber Press, Portland, Oregon.

Popham, R.A., and A.P. Chan. 1950. Zonation in the vegetative stem tip of *Chrysanthemum morifolium* Bailey. *American Journal of Botany* 37: 476–483.

Popham, R.A., and A.P. Chan. 1952. Origin and development of the receptacle of *Chrysanthemum morifolium*. *American Journal of Botany* 39: 329–339.

Post, K. 1949. *Chrysanthemum morifolium* (Chrysanthemum), pp. 385–417 in *Florist Crop Production and Marketing*. Orange Judd Publishing, New York.

Post, K. 1950. Controlled photoperiod and spray formation of chrysanthemum. *Proceedings of the American Society for Horticultural Science* 55: 467–472.

Powell, C.C. 1989. Disease, pp. 50–54 in *Tips on Growing Potted Chrysanthemum*, H.K. Tayama and T.J. Roll, editors. Ohio Cooperative Extension Service, The Ohio State University, Columbus.

Rajapakse, N.C., and J.W. Kelly. 1992. Regulation of chrysanthemum growth by spectral filters. *Journal of the American Society for Horticultural Science* 117:481–485.

Rajapakse, N.C., and J.W. Kelly. 1993. Spectral filters influence transpirational water loss in chrysanthemum. *HortScience* 28:999–1001.

Rajapakse, N.C., D.W. Reed, and J.W. Kelly. 1989. Effects of pre-treatments on transpiration of *Chrysanthemum morifolium* in the dark. *HortScience* 24:998–1000.

Rajapakse, N.C., W.B. Miller, and J.W. Kelly. 1996. Low temperature storage of rooted chrysanthemum cuttings: Relationship to carbohydrate status of cultivars. *Journal of the American Society for Horticultural Science* 121:740–745.

Raulston, J.C., W.E. Waters, S.S. Woltz, and C.M. Geraldson. 1972. Summary of chrysanthemum fertilization programs for field production in Florida. *Florida Flower Grower* 9(10):9.

Roude, N., T.A. Nell, and J.E. Barrett. 1991a. Nitrogen source and concentration, growing medium, and cultivar affect longevity of potted chrysanthemums. *HortScience* 26:49–52.

Roude, N., T.A. Nell, and J.E. Barrett. 1991b. Longevity of potted chrysanthemums at various nitrogen and potassium concentrations and NH$_4$:NO$_3$ ratios. *HortScience* 26:163–165.

Sacalis, J.N. 1993. *Dendranthema grandiflora*, pp. 47–49 in *Cut Flowers, Prolonging Freshness*, 2nd ed., J.L. Seals, editor. Ball Publishing, Batavia, Illinois.

Sachs, R.M., and A.M. Kofranek. 1979. Radiant energy required for the night break inhibition of floral initiation as a function of day time light input in *Chrysanthemum ×morifolium* Ramat. *HortScience* 25:609–610.

Sanderson, K.C., W.C. Martin, Jr., and J. McGuire. 1988. Comparison of paclobutrazol tablets, drenches, gels, capsules, and sprays on chrysanthemum growth. *HortScience* 23:1008–1009.

Schoellhorn, R.K., J.E. Barrett, and T.A. Nell. 1996. Branching of chrysanthemum cultivars varies with season, temperature, and photosynthetic photon flux. *HortScience* 31:74–78.

Schoellhorn, R.K., J.E. Barrett, C.A. Bartuska, and T.A. Nell. 2001. Elevated temperature affects axillary meristem development in *Dendranthema ×grandiflorum* 'Improved Mefo.' *HortScience* 36:1049–1052.

Seeley, J.G., and A.H. Weise. 1965. Photoperiod response of garden and greenhouse chrysanthemum. *Proceedings of the American Society for Horticultural Science* 87:464–471.

Serek, M., A. Prabucki, E.C. Sisler, and A.S. Anderson. 1998. Inhibitors of ethylene action affect final quality and rooting of cuttings before and after storage. *HortScience* 33:153–155.

Starman, T.W. 1990. Whole-plant response of chrysanthemum to uniconazole foliar sprays or medium drenches. *HortScience* 25:935–937.

Stefanis, J.P., and R.W. Langhans. 1983. Photoperiod and continuous irradiation studies of chrysanthemum with high pressure sodium lamps. *HortScience* 18:202–204.

Tayama, H.K., and S.A. Carver. 1992. Residual efficacy of uniconazole and daminozide on potted 'Bright Golden Anne' chrysanthemum. *HortScience* 27:124–125.

Tutty, J.R., P.R. Hicklenton, D.N. Kristie, and K.B. McRae. 1994. The influence of photoperiod and temperature on the kinetics of stem elongation in *Dendranthema grandiflorum*. *Journal of the American Society for Horticultural Science* 119: 138–143.

van Eysinga, J.P.N.L.R., and K.W. Smilde. 1980. *Nutritional Disorders of Chrysanthemums*. Centre for Agricultural Publishing and Documentation, Wageningen, The Netherlands.

Vince, D. 1960. Low temperature effects on flowering of *Chrysanthemum morifolium* Ramat. *Journal of Horticulture Science* 35:161–175.

Vince, D., and D.T. Mason. 1959. Low temperature effects on internode extension in *Chrysanthemum morifolium*. *Journal of Horticulture Science* 34:199–209.

Waters, W.E. 1964. The effects of soil mixture and phosphorus on growth responses and phosphorus content of *Chrysanthemum morifolium*. *Proceedings of the American Society for Horticultural Science* 84:588–593.

Waters, W.E., and C.A. Conover. 1969. *Chrysanthemum Production in Florida*. Bulletin 730, Agricultural Experiment Station, Institute of Food and Agriculture Sciences, University of Florida, Gainesville.

Whealy, C.A., T.A. Nell, J.E. Barrett, and R.A. Larson. 1987. High temperature effects on growth and floral development of chrysanthemum. *Journal of the American Society for Horticultural Science* 112:464–468.

Whipker, B.E., and R.A. Cloyd. 1997. Success with garden mums. *North Carolina Flower Growers Bulletin* 42(3):8–15.

Wilfret, G.J. 1991. Effect of growth regulators on potted chrysanthemums. *Proceedings of the Florida State Horticultural Society* 104:314–316.

Wilkins, H.F., W.E. Healy, and K.L. Grueber. 1990. Temperature regime at various stages of production influences growth and flowering of *Dendranthema ×grandiflorum*. *Journal of the American Society for Horticultural Science* 115:732–736.

Will, E., T.W. Starman, J.E. Faust, and S. Abbitt. 1997. Photoperiodic responses of garden chrysanthemums. *HortScience* 32:502. (Abstract)

Willets, D.H., P.V. Nelson, M.M. Peet, M.A. Depa, and J.S. Kuehny. 1992. Modeling nutrient uptake in chrysanthemum as a function of growth rate. *Journal of the American Society for Horticultural Science* 117:769–774.

Williams, K.A., and P.V. Nelson. 1992. Low, controlled nutrient availability provided by organic waste materials for chrysanthemum. *Journal of the American Society for Horticultural Science* 117:422–429.

Woodson, W.R., and J.W. Boodley. 1983. Accumulation and partitioning of nitrogen and dry matter during the growth of chrysanthemum. *HortScience* 18:196–197.

Zheng, Z.-L., Z. Yang, J.-C. Jang, and J.D. Metzger. 2001. Modification of plant architecture in chrysanthemum by ectopic expression of the tobacco phytochrome *B1* gene. *Journal of the American Society for Horticultural Science* 126:19–26.

Dianthus, Cut

FIGURE II-I DIANTHUS, CUT Greenhouse production of *Dianthus* cut flowers.

INTRODUCTION

Common names: carnation, divine flower, florist carnation.

Scientific name: *Dianthus caryophyllus* L. (Huxley et al., 1992).

Family and related taxa: Caryophyllaceae Juss. Other important cultivated *Dianthus* species include the pot carnation (*D. carthusianorum*) and sweet william (*D. barbatus*). Caryophyllaceae also includes the popular *Gypsophila*.

Origin: *Dianthus caryophyllus* is a native of the Mediterranean area, originally flowering only in the early spring (Bailey and Bailey, 1976).

Uses and current status: The carnation is one of the world's most popular cut flowers (Fig. II-1 Dianthus, Cut). The precise development of the present-day hybrids is not known; however, the original species had single flowers with five petals and a spice-like fragrance. The present carnation flower form originated in the United States as the Sim cultivar group. The "miniature" or "spray" carnation is considered to be more similar to the original specie's branching habit. Colors of *D. caryophyllus* include white, pink, red, purple, yellow, and apricot orange in various combinations (Bailey and Bailey, 1976; Bunt and Cockshull, 1985).

CULTIVARS

Breeders during the past centuries have developed thousands of cultivars, many of which were suited for specific climatic environments. The two basic inflorescence types are the standard and the spray or miniature type. With standard carnations the axillary flower buds below the terminal flower are removed so that only one large flower will develop. With sprays, the axillary buds are on long stems and the terminal bud is removed to encourage their development. The standard types have genetically larger flowers than the spray types. In the early 1900s carnation production in the United States was centered in the New England area and later shifted to Colorado and California in the mid- to late 1950s (Laurie et al., 1969; Post, 1949). Now production in the United States is limited to Colorado and California and the majority of carnations used in North America are imported from Columbia or other nondomestic sources (Whealy, 1992).

The carnation is the subject of much genetic engineering work resulting in strains exhibiting increased branching and cut stem production, improved rooting, delayed senescence, and novel colors, such as mauve and purple (Robinson, 1999; Savin et al., 1995; Zuker et al., 2001). In addition, interspecific hybrids among *Dianthus caryophyllus*, *D. chinensis*, and *D. barbatus* have been created (Guobao et al., 1995).

PROPAGATION

Rooted cuttings are purchased from specialty propagators, who produce culture-indexed, virus-free cuttings (see Chapter 1, Propagation). Unrooted and rooted cuttings can be stored at 31°F (21°C) for 6 or 4 months, respectively, but may delay rooting (Garrido et al.,

1998; Langhans, 1961). Seed of garden cultivars can be germinated at 65 to 70°F (18 to 21°C) (Nau, 1993). *In vitro* propagation is possible (Jeong et al., 1996; Ruffoni et al., 1992; van Altvorst et al., 1992).

FLOWERING CONTROL AND DORMANCY

Axillary vegetative shoots differ in the number of leaves that they will form prior to floral initiation. Shoots from nodes just below the flower will form few leaves prior to flower induction; basipetal shoots will form numerous leaves before flowering. This fact is important in selecting cuttings, pinching plants, and harvesting the flowers. The basal nodes are superior for producing long stems (Bunt and Cockshull, 1985; Hanzel et al., 1955; Harris and Bradbeer, 1966; Powell, 1979).

The modern carnation flowers perpetually under a wide range of photoperiods and climatic conditions. However, *D. caryophyllus* is classified as a facultative LD plant because floral induction is more rapid under LD than under SD conditions. Fewer leaves will subtend the flower under LD, while under SD there will be more leaves. Both the standard and spray carnation cultivars react similarly to LD and SD (Bunt and Cockshull, 1985; Harris and Ashford, 1966; Heins and Wilkins, 1977; Heins et al., 1979; Pokony and Kamp, 1960, 1965). Long days from night interruption lighting are more effective than day extensions; incandescent lamps are more effective than fluorescent lamps, and cyclic lighting is as effective as continuous night break lighting. Floral induction occurs rapidly if irradiance is high; if low, up to 24 to 30 LD are required for floral induction. Shoots become receptive to photoperiod induction when six to eight leaf pairs are formed.

Commercially, alternating 21 days of LD and then 21 days of natural day lengths, if shorter than 12 hr, can be used to time flushes of carnation flowers (Blake and Whitehead, 1961; Bunt and Cockshull, 1985; Bunt et al., 1981; Harris, 1968, 1972; Harris and Harris, 1977; Heins and Wilkins, 1977; Heins et al., 1979; Pokony and Kamp, 1965). Pokony and Kamp (1960, 1965) have shown that SD promote axillary bud activity, which encourages constant vegetative cutting production. Heins and Wilkins (1977) and Heins et al. (1979) proposed that the LD cycle should not be more than 10 days in length if longer axillary buds are induced to flower. Short days should follow

to promote vegetative basal axillary buds for rapid future flower production. Prior to removing old plants for replanting, LD can be applied continuously to induce flowering on every possible shoot for maximum harvest (Koon, 1974). Interestingly, present carnation cut flower production is in areas at cool southern latitudes where the photoperiod is nearly 12 hr light to 12 hr dark year-round. In this situation apical meristems are induced to flower at the same time basal axillary bud activity is encouraged.

TEMPERATURE

Temperature influences the rate of both floral induction and development. The optimal temperature for flower production is 50°F (10°C) night and 55 to 60°F (13 to 16°C) day. A 41°F (5°C) temperature hastens floral induction; 50°F (10°C) temperature delays floral induction as determined by counting leaf pairs below the flower. This "vernalization" effect is an average of the day and night temperatures and is apparent only with the standard carnation, not the spray carnation (Bunt and Cockshull, 1985). Once floral induction has occurred, the rate of flower bud development is temperature controlled (Bunt, 1973). However, flower quality is reduced as temperatures increase to 60°F (16°C) because high temperatures reduce the flower diameter. Cool temperatures and high irradiance are a prerequisite for quality cut carnation flowers. Fan and pad evaporative cooling is essential in many locations of the world if quality flowers are to be grown (Langhans, 1961; Laurie et al., 1969).

LIGHT

Light intensity determines the rate of floral induction. When light levels are low, floral induction is slow and more leaves are produced; with high light, floral induction is more rapid and stems have fewer leaves at harvest. However, rate of flower development is not influenced by light irradiance (Bunt et al., 1981) (see also Carbon Dioxide, on the next page). Low irradiance is responsible for weak stems and, consequently, poor quality or low grades, regardless of flower diameter. Greenhouses are never shaded except to reduce temperatures.

WATER

A variety of bed irrigation systems are available; automation of an irrigation system is essential for efficient production. Reducing available water can result in stronger stems under low light. However, reduced flower diameters can occur if water restriction is carried to an extreme. Soluble salts should be checked because carnation roots are sensitive to high EC and leach medium when needed (Langhans, 1961; Laurie et al., 1969).

CARBON DIOXIDE

Net photosynthesis increases as carbon dioxide is increased up to 1500 ppm. Flower weights and production numbers increase with elevated carbon dioxide levels. With both high light and carbon dioxide, meristematic leaf making activity rate is increased and floral induction is more rapid (Bunt et al., 1981; Enoch and Hurd, 1977).

NUTRITION

Nitrate nitrogen is favored over ammonium in low light areas to avoid soft winter growth and ammonium toxicity under cold temperatures. On the other hand, excess nitrates can cause weak stems. Using hydroponic culture Huett (1994) recommended that 10% of the N should be NH_4. By altering the $NH_4:NO_3$ ratio, Voogt (1995) determined that the optimum pH for maximum production and stem weight should be 5.9 for the nutrient solution and 4.6 for the leachate.

A fertilizer of 200 ppm N and K is recommended in traditional production. The optimal nitrate level in the medium is 25 to 40 ppm, phosphorus 5 to 10 ppm, potassium 25 to 40 ppm, calcium 150 to 200 ppm, and magnesium 30 to 40 ppm (Langhans, 1961). Boron is commonly deficient and media levels should be maintained at 30 to 35 ppm. Regular soil and tissue tests should be taken to determine existing levels (Table II-1 Dianthus, Cut). The optimum tissue to sample is the fifth pair of leaves from the terminal end of shoots until flower buds are visible at which time other shoots should be selected (Nelson and Boodley, 1963). Nutritional regimens and practices will vary according to season and location (Anonymous, 1995; Langhans, 1961). The first nitrogen and potassium deficiency symptoms will appear when the tissue level is below 2% N and 1% K, respectively (Medina, 1992). The deficiency symptoms due to N, P, K, B, and Mg have been well documented (Nelson and Boodley, 1964).

TABLE II-I DIANTHUS, CUT

Tissue nutrient levels for quality *Dianthus caryophyllus* plants (Dole and Wilkins, 1988; Peterson, 1982).

Nutrient	Range
Nitrogen (%)	3.2–5.2
Phosphorus (%)	0.2–0.3
Potassium (%)	2.5–6.0
Calcium (%)	1.0–2.0
Magnesium (%)	0.2–0.5
Iron (ppm)	100–300
Magnesium (ppm)	50–150
Zinc (ppm)	25–75
Copper (ppm)	10–30
Boron (ppm)	30–100

MEDIA

Traditional production used media suitable for long-term production with sufficient aeration and drainage, because the plants are grown for 1 to 2 years. Routine media tests were conducted to maintain proper pH and nutrient levels. The medium had to be free of pathogens, nematodes, and weeds (Langhans, 1961). Hydroponic production is most commonly used now with such substrates as rockwool (Challinor et al., 1995; Huett, 1994; Voogt, 1995).

HEIGHT CONTROL

No height control is required.

SPACING

Spacing is determined by the length of time the bed is to be used before replanting. Cuttings are spaced 4 × 6 in. (10 × 15 cm) for 1-year production and 6 × 6 in. (15 × 15 cm) for 2-year production. A 6- × 8-in. (15- × 20-cm) spacing may also be used for 2-year production (Langhans, 1961).

PINCHING AND DISBUDDING

Pinching of vegetative shoots is an "art" with carnation. Two types of pinches are used for newly planted rooted cuttings: (1) Three to 4 weeks after the cutting has become established and growth has commenced, the young plant is pinched leaving four to five pairs of leaves behind. Although four shoots usually develop, some growers allow only three shoots to develop on the inner rows of plants. (2) Plants are pinched as in method 1 but half of the developing axillary shoots are pinched again. The second pinch can be up to 5 to 7 weeks after the first pinch. Some growers will pinch all the developing axillary shoots from the first pinch.

Proper harvesting of the flowering stems influences future production. With standard cultivars two to three nodes are left on a shoot; four to eight nodes are left on spray carnation shoots. Generally, axillary vegetative shoot development has already occurred at the lower nodes and the next set of flowers will develop rapidly.

With standard carnations, the axillary flower buds are removed as soon as they can be handled, twisted, and removed. All axillary growth, both reproductive and vegetative, must be removed at least 12 to 16 in. (30 to 45 cm) below the terminal flower bud. Buds and shoots should be pulled to the side, not downward, because that can pull the subtending leaf off. With spray carnations the apical or dominant flower bud is removed as soon as feasible, which will encourage axillary flower buds to develop uniformly on equal stem lengths (Langhans, 1961; Laurie et al., 1969; Post, 1949).

SUPPORT

Support is an absolute necessity. Usually four layers of wire or plastic mesh with 6- × 8-in. (10- × 20-cm) openings are used. The first level of support is placed 6 in. (10 cm) above the medium. The remaining layers are spaced 8 in. (20 cm), 10 in. (25 cm), and 12 in. (30 cm) apart, respectively, starting above the previous layer (Laurie et al., 1969).

SCHEDULE AND TIMING

Numerous production schedules have been devised to produce peak production of flowers for specific holidays (Table II-2 Dianthus, Cut). The timing of flower production starts when the rooted cutting is placed in the bench, and the appropriate pinch(es), temperatures, and light intensity and duration are given (Bunt, 1973). Cultivar response is a major factor in timing (Langhans, 1961; Laurie et al., 1969).

INSECTS

The major insects are the spider mites, thrips, and aphids. Other mite species, caterpillars, and slugs can also be a concern. Sanitation and monitoring can help keep these problems under control (Langhans, 1961).

DISEASES

Pathogen control starts with purchasing rooted cuttings from a reliable propagator. Systemic diseases such as *Pseudomonas*, *Corynebacterium*, and *Fusarium* are best controlled by using disease-indexed cuttings, pasteurized medium, and strict sanitation. Be aware that

TABLE II-2 DIANTHUS, CUT

Simplified production schedule for a single-pinched *Dianthus* cut flower crop planted on June 15.

Cultural Step	Production Time	Temperature °F (°C)
Plant rooted cutting		
	3–4 weeks	Day: 55–60 (13–16) Night: 50 (10)
Pinch		
	mid-July	Day: 55–60 (13–16) Night: 50 (10)
Flower		
	September to October[a]	Day: 55–60 (13–16) Night: 50 (10)
Apply LD/natural SD cycles[b] and continue harvesting		
	December to June	Day: 55–60 (13–16) Night: 50 (10)

[a] When a cut flower is harvested in September, 21 to 31 weeks may be required for the axillary shoot to flower. In February, axillary shoots flower in only 15 to 19 weeks.
[b] LD/natural SD sequences of 21 days can commence when the axillary shoots have developed 6 to 8 leaves (see Flowering Control and Dormancy, page 450). Do not use LD until after September 21, when daylength is 12 hr or less; natural day length + night interruption = 14 hr.

pasteurization methods may not penetrate deep enough into the media of the ground bed to kill all of the latent microorganisms from the previous crop. Over the years, new *Fusarium* resistance cultivars have been released into the trade, but this disease is still a threat, particularly when temperatures are above optimal, medium is kept too wet, or when a new crop has been planted.

Alternaria, Botrytis, Phytophthora, Pythium, Rhizoctonia, and various other diseases can be found on the foliage, stems, or flowers (Horst, 1990). These can be frequently controlled by keeping the plants dry. Numerous carnation viruses are known and are fortunately controlled through certified virus-free cuttings from reputable suppliers (Langhans, 1961).

A number of other diseases have been reported including flower rot (*Sclerotinia sclerotiorum*), root rot (*Armillaria mellea*), southern blight (*Sclerotium rolfsii*), charcoal rot (*Macrophomina phaseolina*), greasy blotch (*Zygophiala jamaicensis*), alternaria blight (*Alternaria dianthi* and *A. dianthicola*), leaf spot (*Septoria dianthi* and *Cladosporium*), powdery mildew (*Oidium dianthi*), downy mildew (*Peronospora dianthicola*), phialophora wilt (*Phialophora cinerescens*), calyx rot (*Stemphylium botryosum*), rust (*Uromyces dianthi*), and viruses (Dreistadt, 2001).

PHYSIOLOGICAL DISORDERS

Calyx splitting is the most common non-pathogen problem. The calyx develops under rapid growth conditions, such as high temperatures followed by cool temperatures, which are conducive for optimum petal initiation and development. As a result, the calyx splits under mechanical pressure and individual petals spill out. Uniform night temperatures and reduced variation between day and night temperatures will aid in reducing this problem. Reducing ammonium, using mainly nitrate nitrogen, and applying sufficient boron will also aid in reducing splitting. Cultivars differ widely in the propensity to split and proper cultivars should be selected (Langhans, 1961; Laurie et al., 1969; Post, 1949). One solution is to place a rubber or plastic band ring around each calyx, which many producers automatically do when axillary buds are removed.

POSTHARVEST

Harvesting and grading are major undertakings. Flowers are harvested in the morning when

FIGURE II-2 DIANTHUS, CUT *Dianthus* bud beginning to open after harvest.

turgid, then graded and placed into holding solution under refrigerated 33 to 43°F (1 to 6°C) conditions to reduce tissue temperature. Carnation flowers can be harvested at various stages of development, from very tight buds to when the petals have reflexed over the calyx. For long-distance shipping, standard flower buds are best cut when the petals are 0.25 to 0.5 in. (0.5 to 1.5 cm) above the calyx and the appropriate petal color is visible (Fig. II-2 Dianthus, Cut). Spray carnations are harvested when two or three flowers have opened and petal color is evident on the rest of the buds. When stems are dehydrated, warm 100 to 110°F (38 to 43°C) water should be used (Sacalis, 1993).

Tight flower buds with little or no color showing can be harvested, pulsed with silver thiosulfate (STS), and stored dry for up to 24 weeks with light at 32 to 34°F (0 to 1°C). When typical flowers are "bud harvested" they can be stored for 4 to 5 weeks; open flowers are best stored for 2 to 4 weeks at 32°F (0°C) and 90% relative humidity (Nowak and Rudnicki, 1990; Rudnicki et al., 1989). Buds can be stored for as long as 14 weeks in plastic bags if treated with fungicides, sucrose, and STS prior to storage (Goszczyńska and Rudnicki, 1982). *Botrytis* is a constant potential problem with any stored carnation.

Carnations are very sensitive to external and self-generated ethylene and their response to STS, 1-methylcyclopropene (1-MCP), and

TABLE II-3 DIANTHUS, CUT
Standard *Dianthus* grades and standards used in the United States.

Grade	Description	Minimum Flower Diameter		Minimum Total Stem and Flower Length	
		in.	*cm*	*in.*	*cm*
Fancy (blue)	Tight	2.00	5.0	12.75	5.5
	Fairly tight	2.50	6.2	12.75	5.5
	Open	3.00	7.5	12.75	5.5
Standard (red)	Tight	1.75	4.4	12.50	4.3
	Fairly tight	2.25	5.6	12.50	4.3
	Open	2.75	6.9	12.50	4.3
Short (green)	Tight	none		11.75	3.0
	Fairly tight	none		11.75	3.0
	Open	none		11.75	3.0

other floral preservatives is dramatic (Nichols et al., 1982; Reid et al., 1980; Serek et al., 1995; Sisler et al., 1996; Staby et al., 1993; Uda et al., 1995, 1996). Vase life for an untreated control flowering stem is 6 to 9 days, whereas STS-treated flowers held in a preservative have a vase life of up to 30 days. If a sucrose-based floral preservative is used, vase life is only 12 to 16 days. If flower buds are exposed to very low levels of ethylene, they fail to open; the petals of open flowers turn inward and up-ward, lose turgidity, and become "sleepy" (Nowak and Rudnicki, 1990; Sacalis; 1993). Stems and flowers should be pulsed for 20 hr at 68°F (20°C) with STS, sucrose (10%), and a microorganism inhibitor (8-hydroxyquinoline citrate) in pH 3.5 water. Once pulsed with STS, repeated use of STS is not required and may cause phytotoxicity. 1-MCP is also effective at preventing the effects of exogenous ethylene damage (Serek at al., 1995; Sisler et al., 1996). Interestingly, 8% ethanol as a vase solution extended vase life and inhibited ethylene production (Heins, 1980; Wu et al., 1992). Sucrose-based floral preservatives are best used at all times, whenever flower stems are recut and placed in water.

Much work has been conducted on the senescence of carnations due to their importance in the world market and to their readily visible pattern of senescence. Studies have ranged from the mRNA to the cellular to the phenotypic level (Altman and Solomos, 1995; Brandt and Woodson, 1992; Jiang et al., 1994; Paulin, 1992; Reid and Wu, 1992; Woodson et al., 1992).

TABLE II-4 DIANTHUS, CUT
The United Nations Economic Commission on Europe's standard for cut *Dianthus* flower stem length, including the flower or bud (Anonymous, 1982).

Code	Stem Length	
	in.	*cm*
0	stemless	stemless
5	2.5–5.0	5–10
10	5.0–5.50	10–15
15	5.50–7.75	15–20
20	7.75–12.50	20–30
30	12.50–17.50	30–40
40	17.50–20.00	40–50
50	20.00–27.50	50–60
60	27.50–32.50	60–80
80	32.50–40.00	80–100
100	40.00–47.50	100–120
120	over 47.50	over 120

The grades and standards in the United States were developed jointly by the Society of American Florists and the U.S. Department of Agriculture (Table II-3 Dianthus, Cut). The European standards have been set by the United Nations Economic Commission for Europe (Anonymous, 1982) (Tables II-4 and II-5 Dianthus, Cut). All auctions in Europe require that carnations be pretreated with STS or some other floral preservative.

TABLE II-5 DIANTHUS, CUT

The United Nations Economic Commission on European classifications of cut *Dianthus* flowers with regard to their general appearance (Anonymous, 1982).

Class	Description
Extra	Flowers of best quality; free of extraneous matter; properly developed with strong, rigid stems; fully characteristic of a given species of cultivar; 3% flowers with slight faults allowed.
I-First	Requirements as above but with good quality of flowers and stem rigidity; 5% of flowers with slight faults allowed.
II-Second	Flowers not accepted in higher classes but satisfying minimal requirements and useful for decoration; 10% of flowers with slight faults allowed.

KEY POINTS

- The carnation is one of the world's most popular cut flowers.
- Plants are propagated by cuttings, which are normally purchased from specialty propagators who produce culture-indexed, virus-free cuttings.
- Cut carnation is a quantitative LD plant.
- SD promote axillary bud activity; under LD, branching is reduced.
- Center bud removal is used to obtain spray inflorescences and lateral disbudding is used to obtain one large flower per axillary shoot (standard carnations).
- Numerous diseases are possible, especially *Fusarium*.
- Calyx splitting is a common physiological disorder.
- Cut flowers respond well to floral preservatives.
- Flowers are quite sensitive to ethylene and respond well to anti-ethylene agents.

BIBLIOGRAPHY

Altman, S.A., and T. Solomos. 1995. Differential respiratory and morphological responses of carnations pulsed or continuously treated with silver thiosulfate. *Postharvest Biology and Technology* 5:331–343.

Anonymous. 1982. *Cut flowers document AGRF/ Wp.127/Review 1.* United Nations Economic Commission for Europe. Geneva, Switzerland.

Anonymous. 1995. *Interpretation of Soil Analysis.* Greenhouse Soil Testing Service. University of Minnesota, St. Paul.

Bailey, L.H., and E.Z. Bailey. 1976. *Dianthus*, pp. 276–380 in *Hortus Third: A Concise Dictionary of Plants Cultivated in the United States and Canada.* Macmillian, New York.

Blake, J., and T. Whitehead. 1961. The influence of extended daylength on flower production of carnations. *Experimental Horticulture* 5:1–8.

Brandt, A.S., and W.R. Woodson. 1992. Variation in flower senescence and ethylene biosynthesis among carnations. *HortScience* 27:1100–1102.

Bunt, A.C. 1973. Effect of season on the carnation (*Dianthus caryophyllus* L.) II. Flower production. *Journal of Horticultural Science* 48:315–325.

Bunt, A.C., and K.E. Cockshull. 1985. *Dianthus caryophyllus*, pp. 433–440 in *Handbook of Flowering*, vol. II, A.H. Halevy, editor. CRC Press, Boca Raton, Florida.

Bunt, A.C., M.C. Powell, and D.O. Chanter. 1981. Effects of shoot size, number of continuous light cycles and solar radiation on flower initiation in carnations. *Scientia Horticulturae* 15:267–276.

Challinor, P.F., J.M. Pivert, and M.P. Fuller. 1995. The production of standard carnations on nutrient-loaded zeolite. *Acta Horticulturae* 401:293–299.

Dole, J.M., and H.F. Wilkins. 1988. University of Minnesota. Tissue analysis standards. *Minnesota State Florist Bulletin* 37(6):10–13.

Dreistadt, S.H. 2001. *Integrated Pest Management for Floriculture and Nurseries.* University of California Division of Agriculture and Natural Resources Publication 3402.

Enoch, H.Z., and R.G. Hurd. 1977. Effect of light intensity, carbon dioxide concentration, and leaf temperature on gas exchange of spray carnation plants. *Journal of Experimental Botany* 28:84–95.

Garrido, G., E.A. Cano, M. Acosta, and J. Sánchez-Bravo. 1998. Formation and growth of roots in carnation cuttings: Influence of cold storage period and auxin treatment. *Scientia Horticulturae* 74:219–231.

Goszczyńska, D., and R.M. Rudnicki, 1982. Long-term storage of carnations cut at the green-bud stage. *Scientia Horticulturae* 17:289–297.

Guobao, W., Y. Jingping, and Z. Xiaomei. 1995. Studies on carnation (*Dianthus caryopyllus*) species hybridization. *Acta Horticulturae* 404: 82–90.

Hanzel, R.J., K.S. Nelson, and D.C. Kiplinger. 1955. Floral initiation and development in the carnation var. Northland. *Proceeding America Horticultural Society* 65:455–462.

Harris, G.P. 1968. Photoperiodism in the glasshouse carnation: The effectiveness of different light sources in promoting flower initiation. *Annals of Botany* 32:187–197.

Harris, G.P. 1972. Intermittent illumination and the photoperiod control of flowering in carnation. *Annals of Botany* 36:345–352.

Harris, G.P., and M. Ashford. 1966. Promotion of flower initiation in the glasshouse carnation by continuous light. *Journal of Horticultural Science* 41:397–406.

Harris, G.P., and A.P. Bradbeer. 1966. The flowering behavior of carnation cuttings produced in long and short days. *Journal of Horticultural Science* 41:73–83.

Harris, G.P., and J.E. Harris. 1977. Effects of environment on flower initiation in carnation. *Journal of Horticultural Science* 37:219–234.

Heins, R.D. 1980. Inhibition of ethylene synthesis and senescence in carnation by ethanol. *Journal of the American Society for Horticultural Science* 105:141–144.

Heins, R.D., and H.F. Wilkins. 1977. Influence of photoperiod on 'Improved White Sim' carnation (*Dianthus caryophyllus* L.) branching and flowering. *Acta Horticulturae* 71:69–74.

Heins, R.D., H.F. Wilkins, and W.E. Healy. 1979. The effect of photoperiod on lateral shoot development in *Dianthus caryophyllus* L. cv. Improved White Sim. *Journal of the American Society Horticultural Science* 104:314–319.

Horst, R.K. 1990. Carnation, pp. 580–581 in *Westcott's Plant Disease Handbook,* 5th ed. Van Nostrand Reinhold, New York.

Huett, D.O. 1994. Production and quality of Sim carnations grown hydroponically in rockwool substrate with nutrient solutions containing different levels of calcium, potassium and ammonium-nitrogen. *Australian Journal of Experimental Agriculture* 34:691–697.

Huxley, A., M. Griffiths, and M. Levy. 1992. Dianthus, pp. 50–56 in *The New Royal Horticultural Society Dictionary of Gardening,* vol. 2. Stockton Press, New York.

Jeong, B.R., C.S. Yang, and E.J. Lee. 1996. Photoautotrophic growth of *Dianthus caryophyllus in vitro* as affected by photosynthetic photon flux and CO_2 concentration. *Acta Horticulturae* 440: 611–615.

Jiang, W.B., S. Mayak, and A.H. Halevy. 1994. The mechanism involved in ethylene-enhanced ethylene synthesis in carnations. *Plant Growth Regulation* 14:133–138.

Koon, G. 1974. Timing carnations in Colorado with lights. *Colorado Flower Grower Association Bulletin* 284:3–4.

Langhans, R.W. 1961. *Carnations, A Manual of the Culture, Insects and Diseases, and Economics of Carnation.* New York State and County Agricultural Extension Services, New York State Flower Growers Association, Ithaca, New York.

Laurie, A., D.C. Kiplinger, and K.S. Nelson. 1969. Carnation, pp. 262–282 in *Commercial Flower Forcing.* McGraw-Hill, New York.

Medina, L.A.T. 1992. Study of the effect of some mineral deficiencies on greenhouse carnations (*Dianthus caryophyllus*) in hydroponic culture. *Acta Horticulturae* 307:203–212.

Nau, J. 1993. *Ball Culture Guide, The Encyclopedia of Seed Germination,* 2nd ed. Ball Publishing, Batavia, Illinois.

Nelson, P.V., and J.W. Boodley. 1963. Selection of a sampling area for tissue analysis of carnation. *Proceedings of the American Society for Horticultural Science* 83:745–752.

Nelson, P.V., and J.W. Boodley. 1964. Nutrition of carnations. *New York State Flower Growers Bulletin* 225:1–4.

Nichols, R., A.M. Kofranek, and J. Kubota. 1982. Effect of delayed silver thiosulfate pulse treatments on carnation cut flower longevity. *HortScience* 17:600–601.

Nowak, J., and R.M. Rudnicki. 1990. *Postharvest Handling and Storage of Cut Flowers, Florist Greens and Potted Plants.* Timber Press, Portland, Oregon.

Paulin, A. 1992. New strategies to control cut flowers senescence evolution. *Acta Horticulturae* 307:189–202.

Peterson, J.C. 1982. Monitoring and managing nutrition, Part IV—Foliar analysis. *Ohio Florists' Association Bulletin* No. 632.

Pokony, F.A., and J.R. Kamp. 1960. Photoperiodic control of growth and flowering of carnations. *Illinois State Flower Association Florist Bulletin* 202:6–8.

Pokony, F.A., and J.R. Kamp. 1965. Influence of photoperiod on the rooting response of cuttings of carnations. *Proceedings of the American Society for Horticultural Science* 86:626–630.

Post, E. 1949. *Dianthus caryophyllus*, pp. 451–483 in *Florist Crop Production and Marketing*. Orange Judd Publishing, New York.

Powell, M.C. 1979. Observations on the growth of carnation (*Dianthus caryophyllus* L.) in natural and long days. *Annals of Botany* 43:579–591.

Reid, M.S., and M.-J. Wu. 1992. Ethylene and flower senescence. *Plant Growth Regulation* 11:37–43.

Reid, M.S., D.S. Farnham, and E.P. McEnroe. 1980. Effect of silver thiosulfate and preservative solutions on the vase life of miniature carnations. *HortScience* 15:807–808.

Robinson, K.S. 1999. Violet carnation debuts. *Floral Management* 16(5):44.

Rudnicki, R.M., D.M. Goszczynska, and R. Tomasz. 1989. Bud opening and long term storage of spray carnations. *Acta Horticulturae* 261:265–270.

Ruffoni, B., F. Massabo, and L. Volpi. 1992. Suspension cultures of *Dianthus caryophyllus* cells. *Acta Horticulturae* 307:251–256.

Sacalis, J.M. 1993. *Dianthus caryophyllus*, pp. 52–54 in *Cut Flowers, Prolonging Freshness*, 2nd ed., J.L. Seals, editor. Ball Publishing, Batavia, Illinois.

Savin, K.W., S.C. Baudinette, M.W. Graham, M.Z. Michael, G.D. Nugent, C.-Y. Lu, S.F. Chandler, and E.C. Cornish. 1995. Antisense ACC oxidase RNA delays carnation petal senescence. *HortScience* 30:970–972.

Serek, M., E.C. Sisler, and M.S. Reid. 1995. Effects of 1-MCP on the vase life and ethylene response of cut flowers. *Plant Growth Regulation* 16:93–97.

Sisler, E.C., E. Dupille, and M. Serek. 1996. Effect of 1-methylcyclopropene and methylenecyclopropane on ethylene binding and ethylene action on cut carnations. *Plant Growth Regulation* 18:79–86.

Staby, G.L., R.M. Basel, M.S. Reid, and L.L. Dodge. 1993. Efficacies of commercial anti-ethylene products for fresh cut flowers. *HortTechnology* 3:199–202.

Uda, A., Y. Koyama, and K. Fukushima. 1995. Effect of silver thiosulfate solution (STS) having different ratios of $AgNO_3$ and $Na_2S_2O_3 \cdot 5H_2O$ on Ag absorption and distribution and vase life of cut carnations. *Journal of the Japanese Society for Horticultural Science* 64:185–191.

Uda, A., M. Yamanaka, K. Fukushima, and Y. Koyama. 1996. Effects of various concentrations and durations of treatment with silver thiosulfate complex (STS) solution on Ag absorption, distribution, and the vase life of cut carnations. *Journal of the Japanese Society for Horticultural Science* 64:927–933.

van Altvorst, A.C., T. Bruinsma, H.J.J. Koehorst, and J.J.M. Dons. 1992. Regeneration of carnation (*Dianthus caryophyllus*) using leaf explants. *Acta Horticulturae* 307:109–116.

Voogt, W. 1995. Effect of the pH on rockwool grown carnations (*Dianthus caryophyllus*). *Acta Horticulturae* 401:327–336.

Whealy, C.A. 1992. Carnations, pp. 43–65 in *Introduction to Floriculture*, 2nd ed., R.A. Larsen, editor. Academic Press, San Diego, California.

Woodson, W.R., K.Y. Park, A. Drory, P.B. Larsen, and H. Wang. 1992. Expression of ethylene biosynthesis pathway transcripts in senescing carnation flowers. *Plant Physiology* 99:526–532.

Wu, M.-J., L. Zacarias, M.E. Saltveit, and M.S. Reid. 1992. Alcohols and carnation senescence. *HortScience* 27:136–138.

Zuker, A., T. Tzfira, G. Scovel, M. Ovadis, E. Shklarman, H. Itzhaki, and A. Vainstein. 2001. *RolC*-transgenic carnation with improved horticultural traits: Quantitative and qualitative analyses of greenhouse-grown plants. *Journal of the American Society for Horticultural Science* 126:13–18.

Dianthus, Pot

INTRODUCTION

Common names: miniature carnation, pot carnation, dwarf carnation.

Scientific name: Dianthus carthusianorum L. The name *D. hybriden* is frequently seen in commercial catalogs but has no botanical standing (Huxley et al., 1992).

Family and related taxa: Caryophyllaceae Juss. Numerous species other than *D. carthusianorum* were involved in the development of the present-day hybrids used as potted flowering plants including *D. caryophyllus* L., *D. barbatus* L., *D. chinensis* L., and *D. shinanensis* Mak. (Bailey and Bailey, 1976; Goldsberry, 1979; Moe, 1983). Many other *Dianthus* species are cultivated including the florist carnation (*D. caryophyllus*) and sweet william (*D. barbatus*). Caryophyllaceae also includes the popular *Gypsophila*.

Origin: D. carthusianorum is found from southern to western and central Europe. It is a perennial with a height of 2 ft (60 cm) and has limited flower colors of pink, purple, and white (Bailey and Bailey, 1976).

Uses and current status: Pot carnation is a popular potted flowering plant in Europe and to a lesser extent in North America. Occasionally, pot carnations are grown in hanging baskets and other outdoor containers.

CULTIVARS

Although seed lines are generally true to color, they may not be uniform in height and date of flower; consequently, numerous cultivars are propagated by cuttings or by *in vitro* methods.

Present-day cultivars vary from almost single flowers to doubles. Single-colored or multicolored flowers include white, yellow, pink, red, maroon, and lavender. Some cultivars are also scented (Anonymous, 1983; Goldsberry, 1979; Kuack, 1986).

PROPAGATION

Potted miniature carnations suitable for 4-in. (10-cm) pots can be produced from either seeds or vegetative cuttings. Cuttings and seed can be propagated at 64 to 68°F (18 to 20°C) (Goldsberry, 1979; Wandås, 1989). Only cuttings from disease-indexed sources must be used because carnations are susceptible to a number of diseases.

FLOWERING CONTROL AND DORMANCY

The following data are for vegetatively propagated *Dianthus carthusianorum* 'Napoleon III' (Moe, 1983). Low temperatures of 54 to 59°F (12 to 15°C) promote lateral shoot development, hasten flower initiation, and increase the number of flowering shoots and number of flower buds per shoot. However, temperatures at or above 64°F (18°C) hasten flower development. Short photoperiods at low temperatures promote vegetative axillary shoot development, but delay flower initiation and visible bud. Long days of 14 hr or more from incandescent lights at low temperatures hasten flower initiation, decrease days to visible bud, and increase total number of flowering shoots, but the incandescent light increases internode elongation. After flower initiation development of flower buds is controlled by temperature (Moe, 1983).

TEMPERATURE

For the first 5 weeks cutting-propagated plants should be kept at 54 to 59°F (12 to 15°C) for maximum shoot development and initiation; then 59 to 64°F (15 to 18°C) for rapid floral development (Moe, 1983; Wandås, 1989) (for appropriate photoperiods, see Light, on the next page). For seed-propagated material the night temperature can be 52 to 60°F (11 to 16°C) (Goldsberry, 1979). Increasing temperature up to 70°F (21°C) increases rate of flower development; higher temperatures do not increase rate of flower development. Overwintering is possible with many cultivars up to Zone 5.

LIGHT

Stock plants, cuttings, and young plants should be kept under short photoperiods for the first 5 weeks for maximum shoot development, then 14 hr or longer photoperiods for rapid floral initiation. In Sweden, cuttings from stock plants were given 18 to 20 hr of 290 to 380 fc (60 to 80 μmol $\cdot$ m^{-2} $\cdot$ s^{-1}) of supplemental light (Wandås, 1989). Give full light of 5000 to 6000 fc (1000 to 1200 μmol $\cdot$ m^{-2} $\cdot$ s^{-1}); shade only if excess temperatures occur or to enhance flower color (Goldsberry, 1979; Hasegawa, 1997).

WATER

Do not allow the medium to be continuously moist or plants will have weak stems and grow taller than necessary (Goldsberry, 1979). Allow medium to dry until roots are visible on the edge of the medium; excessive watering during this time will greatly increase crop time. Overhead irrigation should be used carefully because it can spread disease.

CARBON DIOXIDE

Net photosynthesis increases as carbon dioxide is increased up to 1500 ppm. Flower weights and production numbers increase with elevated carbon dioxide levels. With both high light and carbon dioxide, the meristematic leaf-making activity rate is increased and floral induction is more rapid (Bunt et al., 1981; Enoch and Hurd, 1977).

NUTRITION

A constant liquid fertilizer of 200 ppm N and K is recommended. However, nutritional regimes and practices will vary according to season and location (Anonymous, 1995; Langhans, 1961). Nitrate nitrogen is favored over ammonium in low-light areas to avoid soft winter growth and ammonium toxicity under cold temperatures. Even so, excess nitrates can cause weak stems. The optimal nitrate level in the medium is 25 to 40 ppm, phosphorus is 5 to 10 ppm, potassium is 25 to 40 ppm, calcium is 150 to 200 ppm, and magnesium is 30 to 40 ppm. Boron is commonly deficient and should be applied. Soil and tissue tests should be used on a regular basis to determine nutrient levels; foliar nutrient levels for high-quality plants are listed in Chapter 6, Nutrition, Table 6-4 (Dole and Wilkins, 1988).

MEDIA

A well-drained medium should be used. The crown should remain above the medium after planting to prevent disease problems.

HEIGHT CONTROL

Many of the vegetatively propagated plants grow only 5 to 6 in. (13 to 15 cm) tall and do not require any plant growth regulators. Growing plants on the "dry side" is an effective method to obtain short plants with sturdy stems (Goldsberry, 1979). If plants from seed require height control, apply a Cycocel (chlormequat) spray, at 3000 ppm, 50 days after germination (Anonymous, 1983). If plants from cuttings require a Cycocel drench (5000 ppm), do so when shoots are 3.25 to 4 in. (8 to 10 cm) long. Sumagic (uniconizole) and Bonzi (paclobutrazol) at 15 ppm are both effective; Sumagic is preferred because it results in dark foliage and increased axillary shoot number (Goldsberry, 1997). Adriansen (1985) reported that A-Rest (ancymidol) is also effective. Moe (1983) noted that negative DIF can be used to reduce stem elongation.

SPACING

The 4-in. (10-cm) pots are spaced 6 × 6 in. (15 ×15 cm). For 5- or 6-in. (13- or 15-cm) pots, spacings of 2 or 1.5 pots/ft^2 (22 or 16/m^2), respectively, can be used (Goldsberry, 1997).

PINCHING AND DISBUDDING

Only one seedling or rooted cutting is used in a 4-in. (10-cm) pot; three are used in a 6-in. (15-cm) pot. They are pinched only once, regardless of source of plant material. From this pinch four to five breaks will develop. Flowering plants can be severely pruned in the spring and will flower again in 3 weeks (Goldsberry, 1979). Wandås (1989) stated that vegetatively propagated plants should be pinched when repotted. Premature flowers and buds should be removed, but must be done carefully to prevent a second pinch from occurring. A second pinch results in excessive flower number and delayed marketing (Goldsberry, 1997).

SUPPORT

No support required.

SCHEDULE AND TIMING

Twelve to 15 weeks are required from rooting to flower (Kuack, 1986; Wandås, 1989). Sixteen to 18 weeks are required from sowing seed to flower, depending on the cultivar and season (Goldsberry, 1979) (Tables II-1 and II-2 Dianthus, Pot).

INSECTS

Major insects are spider mites, thrips, leafminers, and aphids. Caterpillars and slugs can also be a concern. Sanitation and monitoring can help keep these problems under control (Langhans, 1961).

DISEASES

Pathogenic control commences with purchasing rooted cuttings from a reliable propagator. Systemic diseases such as *Pseudomonas*, *Corynebacterium*, and *Fusarium* can best be controlled by using culture-indexed cuttings, pasteurized media, and strict sanitation. *Alternaria*, *Botrytis*, *Heterosporium*, *Rhizoctonia*, and various other diseases can be found on the foliage, stems, or flowers (Horst, 1990). These can frequently be controlled by keeping the foliage dry, maximizing air circulation, and using fungicides. Numerous carnation viruses are known and are, fortunately, controlled

TABLE II-1 DIANTHUS, POT

Sample production schedules for potted *Dianthus carthusianorum* from seed (Goldsberry, 1979).

Cultural Step	Production Time (weeks)	Temperature °F (°C)
Direct seed in cell packs		
	2	64–68 (18–20)
Seeds germinate. Pinch when plants develop 6 to 7 mature leaves		
	6–8	52–64 (11–18)
Transplant into 4-in. (10-cm) pots when axillary growth commences and plants become crowded[a]		
	8–9	59–64 (15–18)
Flower		
Total	16–19	

[a]Apply Cycocel, if needed, 6 to 8 weeks after germination or after plants are pinched and axillary shoots are 3.75 to 4 in. (8 to 10 cm) long.

TABLE II-2 DIANTHUS, POT

Sample production schedule for flowering 4-in. (10-cm) potted *Dianthus carthusianorum* plants from cuttings (Kuack, 1986).

Cultural Step	Production Time (weeks)	Temperature °F (°C)	Photoperiod
Root cuttings in cubes or plugs			
	2–3	64–68 (18–20)	SD
Plant rooted cuttings in 4-in. (10-cm) pots and pinch same day. Space pot-to-pot			
	3	54–59 (12–15)	SD
Space			
	2	59–64 (15–18)	LD
Apply growth retardants when shoots are 3.25 to 4 in. (8 to 10 cm) long			
	7	59–64 (15–18)	LD
Flower			
Total	14		

Note: Moe (1983) and Wandås' (1989) research plants 'Napolean III' required approximately 100 days to flower.

through certified virus-free cuttings (Langhans, 1961). See also the Dianthus, Cut, chapter for additional diseases that have been reported.

PHYSIOLOGICAL DISORDERS

Poor branching and uneven flower development can be due to low light, low nutrition, high temperatures, and insufficient space (Hasegawa, 1997). Leaf tip burn can be due to water stress, high soluble salts, or pesticide phytotoxicity.

POSTHARVEST

Plants should be shipped at 36 to 41°F (2 to 5°C). If sprayed with silver thiosulfate (STS) at 150 ppm, plants can last 3 weeks and be shipped in the dark for 6 days (L. Høyer, personal communications). Harvest when the apical flowers begin to open. If kept in a cool sunny window, plants should continue to flower for 3 to 4 months. Because plants are not disbudded, axillary buds will continue to flower. Conversely, if sales are slow, the open terminal can be pinched and discarded and plants sold when the axillary buds flower.

KEY POINTS

- Pot carnation is used as a potted flowering plant and occasionally as a hanging basket plant.
- Plants are propagated by seed or cuttings.
- Branching and floral initiation are promoted by low temperatures of 54 to 59°F (12 to 15°C).
- LD hasten flower initiation, decrease days to visible bud, and increase total number of flowering shoots.

- Flower development is hastened at 64°F (18°C) or higher.
- Plants are generally grown on the dry side to prevent weak stems and control height.
- Numerous diseases are possible.
- Flowers are quite sensitive to ethylene and respond well to anti-ethylene agents.

BIBLIOGRAPHY

Adriansen, E. 1985. Kemisk vækstregulering, pp. 142–162 in *Potteplanter I—Produktion, Metoder, Midler*, O.V. Christensen, A. Klougart, I.S. Pedersen, and K. Wikesjö, editors. Gartner-INFO, København, Denmark. (in Danish)

Anonymous. 1983. 'Knight' series mini-carnation popular pot plant. *Greenhouse Management and Production* 2(1):14.

Anonymous. 1995. *Interpretation of Soil Analysis*. Greenhouse Soil Testing Service, University of Minnesota, St. Paul.

Bailey, L.H., and E.Z. Bailey. 1976. *Dianthus*, pp. 376–380 in *Hortus Third: A Concise Dictionary of Plants Cultivated in the United States and Canada*. Macmillan, New York.

Bunt, A.C., M.C. Powell, and D.O. Chanter. 1981. Effects of shoot size, number of continuous light cycles and solar radiation on flower initiation in carnations. *Scientia Horticulturae* 15:267–276.

Dole, J.M., and H.F. Wilkins. 1988. University of Minnesota. Tissue analysis standards. *Minnesota State Florist Bulletin* 37(6):10–13.

Enoch, H.Z., and R.G. Hurd. 1977. Effects of light intensity, carbon dioxide concentration, and leaf temperature on gas exchange of spray carnation plants. *Journal of Experimental Botany* 28:84–95.

Goldsberry, K.L. 1979. *Calceolaria* and *Dianthus* for mini pot program. *Colorado Flower Growers Association* 348:1–3.

Goldsberry, K.L. 1997. Dwarf carnation, pp. 47–53 in *Tips on Growing Specialty Potted Crops*, M.L. Gaston, S.A. Carver, C.A. Irwin, and R.A. Larson, editors. Ohio Florists' Association, Columbus, Ohio.

Hasegawa, M. 1997. Tips for dwarf pot carnations. *Greenhouse Product News* 7(4):8–9.

Horst, R.K. 1990. Carnation, pp. 580–581 in *Westcott's Plant Disease Handbook*, 5th ed. Van Nostrand Reinhold, New York.

Huxley, A., M. Griffiths, and M. Levy. 1992. *Dianthus*, pp. 50–56 in *The New Royal Horticultural Society Dictionary of Gardening*, vol. 2. Stockton Press, New York.

Kuack, W.L. 1986. Mini carnations go to pots in Colorado. *Greenhouse Grower* 4(11):90–92.

Langhans, R.W. 1961. *Carnations, A Manual of the Culture, Insects and Diseases and Economics of Carnation*. New York State and County Agricultural Extension Services, New York State Flower Growers Association, Ithaca, New York.

Moe, R. 1983. Temperature and daylight responses in *Dianthus carthusianorum* cv. Napoleon III. *Acta Horticulturae* 141:165–171.

Wandås, F. 1989. *Dianthus carthusianorum*, pp. 30–32 in *Utplanteringsväxter Trädgård 314*, Swedish University of Agricultural Sciences, Alnarp, Sweden. (in Swedish)

Dianthus, Sweet William

INTRODUCTION

Common name: sweet william.

Scientific name: *Dianthus barbatus* L. (Huxley et al., 1992).

Family and related taxa: Caryophyllaceae Juss. The Pink family has more than 300 species that are annuals, biennials, or perennials. Other notable members of the family include the florist carnation (*D. caryophyllus*), the pot carnation (*D. carthusianorum*), and baby's breath (*Gypsophila*).

Origin: Sweet william is native to the temperate mountains of the Spanish Pyrenees and the Russian Carpathian and down to the Balkan Peninsula. It has become naturalized in areas of North America and China (Bailey and Bailey, 1976).

Uses and current status: Sweet william is used as a cut flower and as a garden ornamental in

FIGURE II-I DIANTHUS, SWEET WILLIAM
Dianthus barbatus 'Messenger Mix' as a garden ornamental (photo by Allan M. Armitage).

FIGURE II-2 DIANTHUS, SWEET WILLIAM
Outdoor hybrid *Dianthus* 'Amazon Neon Duo' cut flower bed.

FIGURE II-3 DIANTHUS, SWEET WILLIAM
Dianthus barbatus 'Electron' cut flower.

Zones 3 to 7 (Figs. II-1, II-2, and II-3 Dianthus, Sweet William).

Sweet william is an herbaceous biennial plant that often reseeds itself each year. If flowers are cut, the plant may perennialize (Armitage and Laushman, 2003). Plants can grow up to 3 ft (90 cm) tall with erect stems and 3- to 6-in.- (7.5- to 15-cm)-long leaves. The inflorescence is multiple flowered, forming a flat "head" or cyme. The flowers are fragrant and in varied colors of white, pink, red, rose, and violet. Bicolors and doubles are common (Bailey and Bailey, 1976; Cockshull, 1985).

CULTIVARS

Numerous cultivars are available from seed companies (Armitage and Laushman, 2003). Both the minimum seedling age needed prior to cold perception and the duration of cold required for flower induction vary among cultivars (Waterschoot, 1957). New cultivars, some of which are actually hybrids, may have little or no cold requirement for flowering and produce high-quality plants first year from seed (Dole, 2003; McGrew, 2001). Some of these cultivars also have excellent heat tolerance.

PROPAGATION

Seeds are sown in July in flats or plugs and germinate at 70°F (21°C) in 1 to 2 weeks under greenhouse conditions. Cover the seed very lightly. Seeds can be sown directly into beds and thinned after germination (Post, 1949). Plants can also be propagated by divisions or by vegetative cuttings (Armitage and Laushman, 2003; Post, 1949).

FLOWERING CONTROL AND DORMANCY

Photoperiod has little influence on flowering regardless of cooling, which makes sweet william different from many other cold-requiring plant species that require a long-day treatment for further floral differentiation and development. Higher temperatures can promote flower development several weeks after the end of the 40 to 45°F (4 to 7°C) cold treatment (Cockshull, 1985; Waterschoot, 1957).

In nature, reproductive meristems can be detected in March and flowering occurs by May to June. Wide variations exist between cultivars in regard to their cold requirements. Typically seedlings or young plants do not become capable of low-temperature perception until they are 12 to 15 weeks old. High temperatures of 95°F (35°C) immediately after the cold treatment can completely or partially devernalize or erase the cold treatment.

TEMPERATURE

Sweet william is a biennial in colder regions, but becomes a perennial in areas of mild climate or if flowers are harvested (Post, 1949). As stated, "mature" plants of many cultivars, 12 or more weeks after transplanting, require a 12-week cold treatment at 40 to 45°F (4 to 7°C) to flower (Waterschoot, 1957). Plants thrive in moderate climates and can be forced at 45 to 50°F (7 to 10°C) night temperatures in the greenhouse (Armitage and Laushman, 2003).

LIGHT

No shade is placed over plants in the fields and plants are grown in full light (Armitage and Laushman, 2003; Post, 1949). HID lighting can accelerate growth at any stage when insufficient light is a problem.

WATER

Sweet william should be watered on demand and allowed to become slightly dry before watering again (Post, 1949).

CARBON DIOXIDE

No data available.

NUTRITION

Sweet william has moderate nutrient requirements, and a complete fertilizer at 100 to 150 ppm N level is adequate (Armitage and Laushman, 2003). Growth will be slightly stunted if only nitrate nitrogen is used (Post, 1949).

MEDIA

Seed germination and plug growth must be in a well-drained, porous medium. Holcomb and Messinger (1986) used soil:peat:perlite (1:1:1) or peat:perlite:vermiculite (1:1:1). The pH should be 6.0 to 7.0. In the field, the beds should be well prepared and fertilizer added as determined by soil test results.

HEIGHT CONTROL

No height control required.

SPACING

Plants can be spaced at 6 × 8 to 12 × 12 in. (15 × 20 to 30 × 30 cm) in beds (Post, 1949).

PINCHING AND DISBUDDING

No pinching or disbudding required.

SUPPORT

Although support is usually not needed, one layer of mesh is occasionally used in the field.

SCHEDULE AND TIMING

For cut flower production, seed can be sown in late summer or autumn in plugs at 70°F (21°C), grown at 55 to 60°F (13 to 16°C), and then planted into the field to overwinter. Plants can also be forced in the greenhouse if vernalization temperature can be given or if non-cold-requiring cultivars are grown (see Tables II-1 and II-2 Dianthus, Sweet William) (Armitage and Laushman, 2003). Plant transplants into the field or greenhouse beds 8 to 10 weeks after germination. After 2 years of production, plants usually die even though they may reseed (Armitage and Laushman, 2003; Post, 1949). For spring perennial plant sales in 4-in. (10-cm) pots, 12 to 14 weeks are required from seed to flower (McGrew, 2001).

INSECTS

Spider mites are the most serious pest.

DISEASES

Fusarium oxysporum and *Rhizoctonia solani* are serious problems; the growing medium must be pasteurized. Aster yellows and various leaf spot diseases can also occur outdoors (Horst, 1990). A number of other diseases have been reported including root rot (*Pythium ultimum*), southern wilt (*Sclerotium rolfsii*), gray mold (*Botrytis cinerea*), leaf spot (*Septoria dianthi* and *Cladosporium*), rust (*Uromyces caryophyllinus*, *U. dianthi*, *Puccinia arenariae*), and anther smut (*Ustilago violacea*) (Dreistadt, 2001).

TABLE II-1 DIANTHUS, SWEET WILLIAM
Sample production schedule for field-grown *Dianthus barbatus* cultivars that require cold treatment for flowering.

Cultural Step	Production Time (weeks)	Temperature °F (°C)
Sow seeds in plugs		
	3–4	65–70 (18–21)
Transplant plugs to fields		
	12	55–60 (13–16)
Growing on and vernalization		
	12 minimum	40–45 (4–7)
Flower in field in late spring as temperatures naturally increase		

TABLE II-2 DIANTHUS, SWEET WILLIAM
Sample production schedule for greenhouse-grown *Dianthus barbatus* cultivars that require cold treatment for flowering.

Cultural Step	Production Time (weeks)	Temperature °F (°C)
Sow seed in plugs		
	3–4	65–70 (18–21)
Transplant plugs into 3-in. (7.5-cm) pots		
	3–4[a]	55–60 (13–16)
Transplant plugs in ground beds		
	8–9[a]	55–60 (13–16)
Lower temperature		
	12	40–45 (4–7)
Flowering		
Total	26–31	

[a] Twelve or more weeks of growth are required prior to the 12 weeks of cold vernalization temperatures after plants have become established in 3-in. (7.5-cm) pots and placed into beds.

PHYSIOLOGICAL DISORDERS

No physiological disorders have been reported.

POSTHARVEST

Stems are harvested when 10 to 20% of the individual flowers on the cyme have opened. Cut stems can be shipped or held in water for 6 to 10 days at 33 to 35°F (1 to 2°C) or dry for 3 to 4 days at 41 to 45°F (5 to 7°C). Quality and longevity are enhanced with the use of commercial preservatives, especially if silver thiosulfate (STS) is included (Nowak and Rudnicki, 1990). Flowers are very sensitive to ethylene (Woltering and van Doorn, 1988). 1-methylcyclopropene (1-MCP) is also effective at preventing the negative effects of exogenous ethylene (Serek et al., 1995). Cut flowers will last for 7 to 16 days (Armitage and Laushman, 2003; Fanelli et al., 2003).

KEY POINTS

- Sweet william is used as an outdoor-grown cut flower and garden ornamental.
- Plants are propagated commercially by seed; may also be cutting propagated.
- Sweet william is typically a biennial, but plants may flower the first year from seed and may perennialize if flowers are cut.
- Generally, 12 or more weeks are required for plants to mature and respond to a 12-week cold treatment of 40 to 45°F (4 to 7°C).

- Many newer cultivars do not require a cold treatment for flowering.
- Numerous diseases are possible, especially crown rot.
- Cut flowers respond well to floral preservatives.
- Flowers are quite sensitive to ethylene and respond well to anti-ethylene agents.

BIBLIOGRAPHY

Armitage, A.M., and J.M. Laushman. 2003. *Dianthus barbatus*, pp. 245–250 in *Specialty Cut Flowers*, 2nd ed. Timber Press, Portland, Oregon.

Bailey, L.H., and E.Z. Bailey. 1976. *Dianthus*, pp. 376–380 in *Hortus Third: A Concise Dictionary of Plants Cultivated in the United States and Canada*. Macmillian, New York.

Cockshull, K.E. 1985. *Dianthus*, pp. 430–432 in *Handbook of Flowering*, vol. II, A.H. Halevy, editor. CRC Press, Boca Raton, Florida.

Dole, J. 2003. The 2002 ASCFG national cut flower seed trials. *The Cut Flower Quarterly* 15(1):7–22.

Dreistadt, S.H. 2001. *Integrated Pest Management for Floriculture and Nurseries*. University of California Division of Agriculture and Natural Resources Publication 3402.

Fanelli, F., J. Dole, B. Harden, B. Fonteno, and S. Blankenship. 2003. Postharvest handling of new cut flowers. *The Cut Flower Quarterly* 15(1):27–29.

Holcomb, E.J., and N.L. Messinger. 1986. Producing dianthus. *Pennsylvania Flower Grower's Bulletin* 365:5–6.

Horst, R.K. 1990. Sweet william, p. 840 in *Westcott's Plant Disease Handbook*, 5th ed. Van Nostrand Reinhold, New York.

Huxley, A., M. Griffiths, and M. Levy. 1992. *Dianthus barbatus*, pp. 50–56 in *The New Royal Horticultural Society Dictionary of Gardening*, vol. 2. Stockton Press, New York.

McGrew, J. 2001. Sweet, easy Noverna dianthus. *GrowerTalks* 65(6):80.

Nowak, J., and N.M. Rudnicki. 1990. *Postharvest Handling and Storage of Cut Flowers, Florist Greens and Potted Plants*. Timber Press, Portland, Oregon.

Post, K. 1949. *Dianthus barbatus*, pp. 483–484 in *Florists Crops Production and Marketing*. Orange Judd Publishing, New York.

Serek, M., E.C. Sisler, and M.S. Reid. 1995. Effects of 1-MCP on the vase life and ethylene response of cut flowers. *Plant Growth Regulation* 16:93–97.

Waterschoot, H.E. 1957. Effects of temperature and day length on flowering in *Dianthus barbatus* L. *Verhandelinger Koninklijke Akademie van Wetenschappen Series C*:60:318–323.

Woltering, E.J., and W.G. van Doorn. 1988. Role of ethylene in senescence of petals—morphological and taxonomical relationships. *Journal of Experimental Botany* 39:1605–1616.

Dionaea

FIGURE II-I DIONAEA *Dionaea* 'Akai Ryu' plants.

INTRODUCTION

Common name: Venus' flytrap.

Scientific name: *Dionaea muscipula* Ellis (Huxley et al., 1992).

Family and related taxa: Droseraceae Salisb. Only one species of *Dionaea* exists; however, a number of other carnivorous species are commercially grown, including the sundew (*Drosera capensis* L.) and the pitcher plant (*Sarracenia flava* L., *S. minor* Walter., *S. psittacina* Michx, and *S. purpurea* L.). The genus *Drosera* contains 90 to 100 species and is in the Droseraceae family. The genus *Sarracenia* contains 8 species total and is in the Sarraceniacea Dumort. family.

Origin: *Dionaea muscipula* is native to a restricted coastal area of North and South Carolina. *Drosera capensis* is a native of South Africa and other members of the genus are found worldwide. *Sarracenia* species are native from eastern North America (Canada to Florida) west to Minnesota and Texas (Bailey and Bailey, 1976).

Uses and current status: Venus' flytrap is one of the most commonly grown carnivorous plants in commerce. Venus' flytrap and the other species listed here are sold in 3- or 4-in. (7.5- or 10-cm) pots. Various *Sarracenia* species and hybrids are grown as novelty cut flowers and potted plants.

Venus' flytrap is a low-growing rosette of distinctive green to reddish-green trap-shaped leaves (Fig. II-1 Dionaea). The traps have two rounded, hinged lobes that are sensitive to movement and snap shut on prey. The petioles are leafy and the rosette grows up to 8 in. (20 cm) wide. The small white flowers are on top of thin stalks up to 12 in. (30 cm) high. Venus' flytrap is hardy in Zones 8 to 10.

Most sundew species produce a rosette of green leaves covered in reddish, glandular sticky hairs that trap and digest tiny insects, but other species are upright or vining in habit. Many species are relatively small, only 2 to 3 in. (5 to 8 cm) across. As species are found all over the world hardiness varies. However, *Drosera anglicae* is one of the cold hardiest, from Zones 4 to 10.

Pitcher plants produce large, hollow, pitcher-shaped leaves topped with a leafy lid (Fig. II-2 Dionaea). The pitchers contain liquids that trap, drown, and digest insects and are up to 48 in. (120 cm) tall. The unusual, nodding flowers have large, floppy sepals and petals surrounding a modified style forming a protective cap over the stamens (Fig. II-3 Dionaea). Most species are hardy only in Zones 7 to 11, but *S. purpurea* is hardy from Zones 4 to 10.

CULTIVARS

Within the three genera of carnivorous plants are wide variations in color and growth habit, which are also observed in nature (Roberts and Oosting, 1958). Several hybrids of *Sarracenia*, both man-made and natural, are grown by plant enthusiasts (Sheridan and Mills, 1998). Cultivars vary in height, leaf pigment color

FIGURE II-2 DIONAEA *Sarracenia leucophylla* pitcher (leaf).

FIGURE II-3 DIONAEA *Sarracenia flava* 'Coppertop' flower.

(red, yellow, white or green), and flower color (red or yellow).

PROPAGATION

Many carnivorous species are under legal protection due to overharvesting from bogs. *Dionaea* at one time was harvested and sold as dormant basal rosette "bulbs" (Bailey, 1933). *Dionaea* and *Drosera* develop rhizomes that can be divided. All species also flower and form seeds that germinate with ease (Roberts and Oosting, 1958). However, 5 to 7 years are required for a plant to reach maturity. *In vitro* propagation is most commonly used to propagate *Dionaea* (Parliman et al., 1982a, b). Many *Drosera* species can also be propagated *in vitro* (Anthony, 1992; Perica and Berljak, 1996).

Venus' flytrap plants from different propagators vary greatly in leaf color, leaf orientation, and vigor. It is unknown whether this variation is due to *in vitro* conditions, parent stock selection, or genetic drift.

FLOWERING CONTROL AND DORMANCY

Vegetative growth and flowering occur under proper temperature, light, and moisture conditions (Roberts and Oosting, 1958). Venus' flytrap becomes dormant with low moisture stress and low temperatures. Naturally shortening photoperiods may also contribute to dormancy. Fall-harvested bulbs quickly form new rosettes if given 4 to 6 weeks of moist cold at 38°F (3°C) (H.F. Wilkins, unpublished).

TEMPERATURE

Appropriate production temperatures are above 72°F (22°C) for Venus' flytrap. In nature, the summer environment is frequently termed "hot and humid" (Roberts and Oosting, 1958). H.F. Wilkins and A.H. Halevy (unpublished) found that 72 to 90°F (22 to 32°C) was acceptable in the greenhouse and Parliman et al. (1982a, b) noted that 73 to 79°F (23 to 26°C) was acceptable for *in vitro* propagation.

LIGHT

For Venus' flytrap in greenhouses, no shade is used except to prevent excessive heating. In nature, a 50% reduction in light was detrimental to growth (Roberts and Oosting, 1958). Sundews and pitcher plants also prefer high light.

A 16-hr photoperiod increased flowering of Venus' flytrap (Roberts and Oosting, 1958). Fluorescent lights were used by Parliman et al. (1982a, b) to supply 16-hr photoperiods in the *in vitro* studies. H.F. Wilkins and A.H. Halevy (unpublished) found that an 8-hr natural day plus 8 hr of incandescent lighting resulted in superior growth when compared with 8-hr natural day lengths in Israel during December to February. Long days encourage long upright "traps."

WATER

The Venus' flytrap, sundews, and pitcher plants are bog plants, which should never be allowed to dry. Plants should be subirrigated, not over-head irrigated. High humidity is also considered a prerequisite for optimal growth. When *in vitro* plugs are newly planted, plants are best placed in a sealed plastic high-humidity chamber, fogged, and checked daily until established. The greenhouse or enclosed environmental area should always be kept at high humidity. High-quality water is a must and should be warmed before irrigation.

CARBON DIOXIDE

No data available.

NUTRITION

Nutritional regimes are not well established for carnivorous plants. H.F. Wilkins (unpublished) used various sources, both organic and inorganic, and rates of N, P, and K with no differences noted. Roberts and Oosting (1958) also had inconclusive results with their various nutritional experiments.

MEDIA

The native medium for Venus' flytrap and pitcher plant in North Carolina has a pH of 3.5 to 4.9 and no calcium, manganese, or nitrate. The ammonium (2 ppm), iron (1 ppm), magnesium (1 ppm), and phosphorus (2 ppm) content was also quite low (Roberts and Oosting, 1958). Commercially, well-shredded acidic peat moss is an accepted medium at a pH of 5.0.

HEIGHT CONTROL

Generally, no height control is needed. Excessive shade can lead to stretching.

SPACING

All plants are grown pot-to-pot.

PINCHING AND DISBUDDING

No pinching or disbudding required.

SUPPORT

No support is needed with the possible exception of *Sarracenia flava,* which can grow to be 4 ft (120 cm) tall.

SCHEDULE AND TIMING

Planting to sales can require 11 to 13 weeks for *in vitro*–propagated Venus' flytrap plantlets, depending on season and transplant size.

INSECTS

Fungus gnats can be a problem.

DISEASES

There are no identified diseases; however, older leaves can turn black and plants may die if growing conditions are not correct.

PHYSIOLOGICAL DISORDERS

No physiological disorders are noted (see Diseases, above).

POSTHARVEST

Venus' flytrap plants should be shipped at cool temperatures of 50°F (10°C). However, plants can be shipped at 60°F (16°C) in the dark for a short time.

KEY POINTS

- *Dionaea muscipula,* Venus' flytrap, and *Drosera,* sundew, are grown as a novelty potted carnivorous plant; *Sarracenia* is grown as a carnivorous potted plant and as a cut flower.
- Commercially, Venus' flytrap plants are propagated by *in vitro*; seed can also be used.

- Plantlets are grown in acidic peat under tents (high humidity) and 50% reduced light.
- Venus' flytrap goes dormant under moisture stress, low temperatures, and SD.
- Venus' flytrap plants are grown warm at 72 to 90°F (22 to 32°C).
- Do not ship Venus' flytrap plants at warm temperatures; optimum is 50°F (10°C).

BIBLIOGRAPHY

Anthony, J.L. 1992. *In vitro* propagation of *Drosera* spp. *HortScience* 27:850.

Bailey, L.H. 1933. *Dionaea*, pp. 1011–1012 in *The Standard Cyclopedia of Horticulture*, vol. I. Macmillan, New York.

Bailey, L.H., and E.Z. Bailey. 1976. *Dionaea*, p. 387; *Drosera*, pp. 400–401; Droseraceae, pp. 401; Sarraceniaceae, p. 1007 in *Hortus Third: A Concise Dictionary of Plants Cultivated in the United States and Canada*. Macmillan, New York.

Huxley, A., M. Griffiths, and M. Levy. 1992. *Dionaea*, pp. 70, 72; *Drosera*, pp. 103–107, vol. 2; *Sarracenia*, pp. 200–203, vol. 4, in *The New Royal Horticultural Society Dictionary of Gardening*. Stockton Press, New York.

Parliman, B.J., P.T. Evans, and E.A. Rupert. 1982a. Tissue culture of single rhizome explants of *Dionaea muscipula* Ellis. ex. L., the Venus fly-trap, for rapid asexual propagation. *Journal of the American Society for Horticultural Science* 107: 305–310.

Parliman, B.J., P.T. Evans, and A.R. Mazur. 1982b. Adventitious bud differentiation and development in leaf cuttings of *Dionaea mascipula* Ellis. ex. L. (Venus fly-trap) cultured *in vitro*. *Journal of the American Society for Horticultural Science* 107:310–316.

Perica, M.C., and J. Berljak. 1996. *In vitro* growth and regeneration of *Drosera spatulata* Labill. on various media. *HortScience* 31:1033–1034.

Roberts, P.R., and H.J. Oosting. 1958. Responses of Venus fly trap (*Dionaea muscipula*) to factors involved in its endemism. *Ecological Monographs* 28:193–218.

Sheridan, P.M., and R.R. Mills. 1998. Genetics of anthocyanin deficiency in *Sarracenia* L. *HortScience* 33:1042–1045.

Dracaena

INTRODUCTION

Common and scientific names: The most commonly grown dracaena, *Dracaena fragrans* (L.) Ker-Gawl., is known as the corn plant. Numerous other species of the genus *Dracaena* are commercially grown, including *D. arborea* (Willd.) Link. (tree dracaena), *D. deremensis* Engl., *D. draco* (L.) L. (dragon tree), *D. fragrans*, *D. goldieana* Bullen ex Mast. & Moore, *D. reflexa* (Decne.) Lam. (song of India), *D. sanderi-*ana hort. Sander ex Mast (ribbon plant), *D. surculosa* Lindl. (gold dust dracaena), and *D. thalioides* hort. Makoy ex E. Morr. *D. marginata* (Madagascar dragon tree) is a commonly used name for either *D. cincta* Bak. or *D. concinna* Kunthi.; the species *D. marginata* is not thought to be in cultivation (Huxley et al., 1992). Because the exact species being grown in cultivation is not yet known, this book will continue to use *D. marginata*, the name commonly used in literature and commerce.

Family and related taxa: Agavaceae Endl. Approximately 40 species of *Dracaena* are found in the wild (Bailey and Bailey, 1976). The Agavaceae family is large and contains several other cultivated ornamental genera such as *Agave, Cordyline, Polianthes, Sansevieria*, and *Yucca*.

Origin: Dracaenas are native to the tropical regions of Asia and Africa (Bailey and Bailey, 1976).

Uses and current status: Dracaenas are popular indoor foliage plants due to their tolerance of low light, low humidity, and erratic watering. All dracaenas are upright growing and range in size outdoors from small 3- to 4-ft (90- to 120-cm) multistem plants to large trees. Dracaenas are grown in a wide variety of containers from 2.25-in. (6-cm) pots for dish gardens to large tubs for interiorscapes. *D. deremensis* and *D. fragrans* are commonly grown with one cutting/6-in. (15-cm) pot or 3 cuttings/10-in. (25 cm) pots. *D. marginata* often are grown with one tip cutting/2.25- to 3-in. (6- to 8-cm) pot or 3 cuttings/8- to 10-in. (20- to 25-cm) pot. A common item has three or more canes of different lengths in a pot, producing an "instant" large tree. Dracaenas are also grown as outdoor ornamentals in tropical regions of the world.

CULTIVARS

Cultivars are available for several of the cultivated species. The species *Dracaena fragrans* has solid, medium green leaves that are up to 3 ft (90 cm) long and 4 in. (10 cm) wide, whereas the popular cultivar 'Massangeana' has a broad yellow stripe down the center of the leaves. Other *D. fragrans* cultivars include 'Lindenii,' which has white marginal stripes, and 'Victoria,' which has golden marginal stripes. *Dracaena fragrans* cultivars are the most commonly produced dracaena types. Cultivars of *D. deremensis* range from 'Warneckii,' with gray-green leathery 2-ft- (60-cm)-long, 2-in-. (5-cm)-wide leaves striped with white, to 'Janet Craig,' with similarly sized leaves that are shiny dark green. *D. marginata* has dark green leaves edged in dark red and are less than 0.75 in. (0.7 cm) wide and up to 2 ft (60 cm) long. *D. marginata* 'Tricolor' has an additional cream-colored stripe down the center of the leaf and 'Colorama' has both cream and red in the center of the leaf.

PROPAGATION

Dracaenas are propagated commercially by terminal cuttings or large cane sections, many of which are imported from Caribbean and Central American countries. Rooted cuttings or liners of many dracaena species are also available from propagation specialists. *Dracaena fragrans* is readily propagated using both terminal cuttings and cane sections. *D. deremensis* is propagated from tip cuttings. *D. marginata* is generally propagated from terminal cuttings, but not cane sections due to the undesirable branching angle of shoots developing from the upper part of the cane (Poole et al., 1991). Stock plants are often grown in full sun for convenience but the best growth rate is obtained when plants are held under 6000 fc (1200 μmol $\cdot$ m^{-2} $\cdot$ s^{-1}).

Leafless *D. fragrans* canes are available in lengths of 1-ft (30-cm) increments ranging from 2 to 8 ft (0.6 to 2.4 m) and are inserted into the media (Figs. II-1 and II-2 Dracaena). The upper end of each cane is dipped in wax to prevent desiccation during shipping and the

lower end of each cane is recut to encourage water uptake (Poole et al., 1974). Success will vary from 50 to 100% depending on the treatment the canes receive after harvest. Canes should root and resprout in 3 to 6 weeks. To keep the tall heavy canes upright, they should be planted deep and the media may have to be slightly compacted (Griffith, 1998).

Canes should be mature but not green, which can lead to rotting, or too old because old sections may not root (Griffith, 1998). Old canes usually have "an elliptical hollow spot on either end, resulting from drying of the woody tissue over time." To increase rooting of canes, 1/8-in. (0.3 cm) cuts can be made on the canes every 2.5 in. (6 cm), starting at the base of the leafless cane (Griffith, 1998). These cuts will form additional roots, especially if indole-3-butyric acid (IBA) is applied.

Although rooting compounds are commonly used, IBA powder is ineffective on *D. deremensis* 'Compacta' and detrimental to *D.*

FIGURE II-1 DRACAENA   Propagation of *Dracaena* through cane sections.

FIGURE II-2 DRACAENA   *Dracaena* cane section sprouting new shoots. Note wax covering on end of cane.

marginata 'Colorama' and *D. surculosa* 'Florida Beauty' (Poole et al., 1991). However, Hata et al. (1994) showed that immersion of *D. fragrans* 'Massangeana,' *D. deremensis* 'Warneckii' and 'Janet Craig,' and *D. marginata* cuttings in 120°F (49°C) hot water for 10 min for insect control followed by 0.8% IBA basal treatment increased rooting and the number of roots produced. In addition, a 50-ppm IBA soak for 18 hr increased bud development on *D. fragrans* 'Massangeana' canes (Poole et al., 1991). A misting regime of 12 sec on out of every 6 min was best for propagation of dracaena (Rauch, 1976).

Although not commercially feasible, dracaenas can be propagated by air layering. Wounding by girdling produces large unbranched roots, whereas wounding by two upward cuts on opposite sides of the stem produces finer, heavily branched roots (Broschat and Donselman, 1983). Plants with the finer root systems are more desirable for propagation.

FLOWERING CONTROL AND DORMANCY

Because the plants are grown for their foliage, flowering is not encouraged and typically occurs only on older plants growing outdoors in tropical areas.

TEMPERATURE

Dracaenas will tolerate a wide range of temperatures, but optimum growth takes place with air temperatures between 65 and 90°F (18 and 32°C), and media temperatures between 75 and 80°F (24 and 27°C). For *D. marginata*, shoot weight was not affected by media temperatures ranging from 82 to 104°F (28 to 40°C); however, root growth was reduced at 104°F (40°C) (Ingram et al., 1986). Growth slows when temperatures are either below 65°F (18°C) or above 90°F (32°C). Nowak and Rudnicki (1990) recommended reducing the temperature when plants are shaded during production.

D. deremensis is sensitive to high temperatures during production (Griffith, 1998). Foliar chlorosis of *D. deremensis* 'Janet Craig' and leaf notching of 'Warneckii' (see Physiological Disorders, page 473) will occur at temperatures above 90°F (32°C). Chilling damage for most species will occur within a week at 55°F (13°C) or 1 to 2 days at 35°F (2°C). Wind protection will reduce chilling damage.

LIGHT

Dracaenas are adaptable to various light levels and are considered sun-shade plants. Dracaenas can be grown entirely under shade or under high light, even full sun, until sufficient plant size is produced and then placed under low light to acclimatize the plants for the interior. Donselman and Broschat (1982) noted that *D. marginata* plants grown in full sun produced more basal shoots and for 5-gal (20-L) pots, recommended 9 months of full sun followed by 3 months of 50% shade for acclimatization. Conover and Poole (1990) suggested light levels of 3000 to 4000 fc (600 to 800 $\mu mol \cdot m^{-2} \cdot s^{-1}$) for *D. marginata* and 'Massangeana' and 2000 to 3500 fc (400 to 700 $\mu mol \cdot m^{-2} \cdot s^{-1}$) for *D. deremensis* 'Warneckii' and 'Janet Craig.' Griffith (1998) suggested that *D. deremensis* should be grown under lower light, 1500 to 1800 fc (300 to 360 $\mu mol \cdot m^{-2} \cdot s^{-1}$), in warm climates to keep temperatures cooler. For *D. fragrans*, 2000 to 4000 fc (400 to 800 $\mu mol \cdot m^{-2} \cdot s^{-1}$) is suggested (Conover, 1998). Vladimirova et al. (1997) recommended 2500 to 5000 fc (500 to 1000 $\mu mol \cdot m^{-2} \cdot s^{-1}$) for *D. sanderiana*. Other dracaenas can be grown under 1500 to 3000 fc (300 to 600 $\mu mol \cdot m^{-2} \cdot s^{-1}$). High light levels will reduce the width of the white stripes on 'Warneckii' and *D. sanderiana* leaves. Light levels above 4000 fc (800 $\mu mol \cdot m^{-2} \cdot s^{-1}$) will reduce performance of dracaenas in the interior under low-light conditions unless plants are properly acclimatized. Large-scale production of dracaenas typically occurs outdoors in large shade houses using 63% or heavier shade. Small plants are often produced in greenhouses with other foliage plants in a crop rotation sequence.

WATER

Although tolerant of drying out, the medium should remain moist for best growth.

CARBON DIOXIDE

No data available.

NUTRITION

General recommendations for constant liquid fertilization are 150 ppm N, 25 ppm P, and 100 ppm K (Conover, 1992). The fertilizer requirement varies with the different species and with the production conditions such as media composition, light levels, growing environment (indoors versus outdoors), and amount of water received either through rain or irrigation

TABLE II-I DRACAENA

Recommended fertilizer rates for *Dracaena* species and their cultivars (Poole et al., 1991).

Species	Nitrogen[a] lb/1000 ft²/month (g/m²/month)	Controlled-Release 19-6-12 g/3 months/pot (in./cm)					
		4(10)	6(15)	8(20)	10(25)	12(30)	14(35)
D. deremensis	2.9 (14)	1.8	4.0	7.2	11.2	16.2	21.8
D. fragrans	2.9 (14)	1.8	4.0	7.2	11.2	16.2	21.8
D. marginata	4.0 (20)	2.5	5.7	10.0	15.7	22.6	30.6
Dracaena spp.	3.4 (17)	2.2	4.8	8.6	13.5	19.4	26.2

[a]Fertilizer source with a N:P:K ratio of 3:1:2.

TABLE II-2 DRACAENA

Tissue nutrient levels from good-quality *Dracaena* plants of several species (Poole et al., 1991).

Species/Cultivar	N	P	K	Ca	Mg
D. deremensis 'Janet Craig'	2.0–3.0	0.2–0.3	3.0–4.0	1.5–2.0	0.3–0.6
D. deremensis 'Warneckii'	2.5–3.5	0.1–0.3	3.0–4.5	1.0–2.0	0.5–1.0
D. fragrans 'Massangeana'	2.0–3.0	0.1–0.3	1.0–2.0	1.0–2.0	0.5–1.0
D. surculosa	1.5–2.5	0.2–0.3	1.0–2.0	1.0–1.5	0.3–0.5
D. sanderiana	2.5–3.5	0.2–0.3	2.0–3.0	1.5–2.5	0.3–0.6

(Conover and Poole, 1990). Table II-1 Dracaena lists fertilizer recommendations for outdoor production in warm climates such as Florida. Tissue nutrient levels for good-quality plants are listed in Table II-2 Dracaena. See also Chapter 6, Nutrition, Table 6-4, for additional foliar nutrient levels. *D. deremensis* have a high requirement for P and Fe and are sensitive to excess B and Fl (Griffith, 1998). In addition, Poole et al. (1991) noted that healthy 'Janet Craig' and 'Warneckii' plant tissue contained 50 and 35 ppm fluoride, respectively, whereas plants with necrotic foliage contained 100 and 75 ppm F, respectively (see Physiological Disorders, page 473). Lang et al. (1990) also showed that *D. marginata* is not tolerant of low iron levels, exhibiting leaf chlorosis and reduced growth with iron deficiency.

MEDIA

Dracaenas are tolerant of a wide range of media as long as they are well drained with a pH of 6.0 to 6.5 (Stamps and Evans, 1999). pH levels above 7.0 may induce iron deficiencies, and pH above 6.0 will prevent fluoride toxicity (see Physiological Disorders, page 473). Media should include a micronutrient mix such as Micromax [1 lb/yd³ (0.6 kg · m⁻³)].

If the cuttings are propagated directly into the final pots, the media must be particularly well aerated, yet retain enough moisture to prevent excessive irrigation when the plants are being grown and finished. A heavy medium component such as sand or calcined clay will probably be needed with large plants to prevent toppling. Small cuttings are usually inserted to the bottom of the pot to provide support, and canes are placed just above the bottom to allow room for rooting.

HEIGHT CONTROL

Height control is generally not needed on dracaenas, which do not appear to be affected by growth retardants (Poole et al., 1991). Bonzi (paclobutrazol) drenches at 0.5 mg a.i./6-in. (15-cm) pot are reported to have a slight effect (Henny, 2001).

SPACING

Newly planted material is spaced pot-to-pot and may remain at that spacing until sale. Plants may need to be spaced further apart if they are not sold immediately and if larger crowns are desired.

PINCHING AND DISBUDDING

Plants are rarely pinched and never need disbudding. When dormant cane sections are used, they produce multiple shoots. Four monthly

TABLE II-3 DRACAENA

Sample production schedule for *Dracaena fragrans* 6-in. (15-cm) cuttings in a 6-in. (15-cm) pot.

Cultural Step	Production Time (weeks)	Temperature °F (°C)
Propagation[a]	3–4	Medium: 75 (24)
Growing on[b]	10+	Night: 75 (24) Day: 85 (29)

[a]*One terminal cutting/6-in. (15-cm) pot; four terminal cuttings/8-in. (20-cm) pot.*
[b]*Large specimens may take many months to produce.*

benzylamino (tetrahydropyranyl) purine (PBA) sprays applied at 250 ppm to the foliage can increase basal branching (Henny, 2001).

SUPPORT

No support needed.

SCHEDULE AND TIMING

A minimum of 13 weeks will be required (Table II-3 Dracaena).

INSECTS

Although dracaenas are considered more pest resistant than many other commercial floriculture crops, a number of insects and related pests can occur including fungus gnats, shore flies, thrips, scales, and mealybugs. The latter two pests can become particularly troublesome under long-term production such as with stock plants or conservatory collections. Caterpillars can also be a problem in warm climates such as Florida, Texas, and California where moths can invade from the outdoors. Hot water immersion has been successfully used to disinfect dracaena cuttings (see Propagation, page 470).

DISEASES

Dracaenas are susceptible to a number of diseases, the most common of which are *Erwinia* leaf and soft rot (*Erwinia carotovora* and *E. chrysanthemi*) and *Fusarium* leaf spot and stem rot (*Fusarium moniliforme*) (Daughtrey and Chase, 1992; Horst, 1990; Poole et al., 1991). Both bacterial soft rot and *Fusarium* stem rot can attack cuttings during propagation. The leaf spot form of *Fusarium* infects the youngest leaves, forming irregularly shaped, tan to reddish brown lesions. Heavy infestations may result in the death of the apical meristem. The

disease is favored by wet foliage and presence of spores. Other diseases noted on dracaenas include bacterial leaf spot (*Pseudomonas*), fungal leaf spots (*Corynespora cassiicola, Gloeosporium polymorphum, G. thuemenii, Glomerella cingulata, Helminthosporium,* and *Phyllosticta dracaenae*), gray mold (*Botrytis cinerea*), stem and leaf rot (*Phytophthora*), southern blight (*Sclerotium roflsii*), and web blight (*Rhizoctonia microsclerotia*) (Dreistadt, 2001; Horst, 1990; McConnell et al., 1981).

PHYSIOLOGICAL DISORDERS

FLUORIDE TOXICITY

The symptoms include mottling, chlorosis, and often necrosis of the leaf tips (Conover and Poole, 1982; Poole and Conover, 1974, 1975). The disorder may also include leaf margins. Fluoride concentrations up to 7 ppm may be found in water and fertilizers. Superphosphates contain up to 2% fluoride. Water should also be checked because 1 ppm fluoride is often added to municipal water to control tooth decay. The fluoride from municipal water is generally not damaging alone, but may be damaging if other sources of fluorides are present. To help prevent the problem, the medium pH should be 6.0 to 6.5, which will tie up fluoride in the media. Also, avoiding high temperatures, high light, low humidity, and wind will reduce evapotranspiration and slow the accumulation of fluoride in the plant tissue. The best long-term solution is to eliminate the source of the fluoride or grow species and cultivars with greater resistance to fluoride injury. Boron accumulation in the tip tissue may also lead to tip burn (Griffith, 1998).

LOOSE CANES

Dracaenas, especially *D. fragrans,* grown from canes often have large crowns and relatively small root systems. During shipping the canes may become loose within the pots, which can be prevented by using foam blocks or other inserts between the canes when shipping. During production the problem can be reduced by using a heavier, more secure medium and by inducing rooting all along the portion of the cane that is below the medium line (see Propagation section, earlier).

SMALL CROWNS

Poor axillary shoot development from the canes results in only one to two shoots per cane. This problem can be prevented by using only high-quality fresh or presprouted canes. Canes that are small and thin or old and thick produce the lowest number of shoots (Poole et al., 1991). In addition, canes that have been stored or shipped too long will also sprout poorly.

CHILLING INJURY

D. marginata will show chilling injury as chlorotic or necrotic bands across several leaves. The symptoms can appear 2 or more weeks after the chilling episode because the young leaves inside the terminal cone of leaves will be damaged and must elongate before the damage will be evident. *D. sanderiana* showed chlorotic and necrotic leaf edges 3 to 4 days after a chilling episode; 1 day of 50°F (10°C) and 2 days of 55°F (13°C) were enough to produce the symptoms (Marousky, 1980). Other dracaenas such as *D. fragrans* initially show water-soaked areas, which later become necrotic.

FLECKING

The youngest leaves of *D. marginata* may show scattered white to yellow spots near the apex under high light and low temperatures (Poole et al., 1991). The spots usually turn green as the leaf matures but salability will be reduced. Plants grown under 2000 fc (400 μmol $\cdot$ m^{-2} $\cdot$ s^{-1}) or less often have no flecking.

TIP CHLOROSIS

The problem of tip chlorosis on *D. deremensis* 'Janet Craig' and 'Warneckii' is typically due to high pH, 7.5 to 8.0, which results in iron deficiency chlorosis (Poole et al., 1991). The new growth is light green to yellow in color. The best long-term solution is to reduce media pH (see Chapter 6, Nutrition), but iron sprays can be used to attempt to correct problems already in progress.

NOTCHING

The base of *D. deremensis* 'Warneckii' leaves are serrated, 0.13 to 0.5 in. (0.3 to 1.3 cm) deep, perpendicular to the long axis of the leaf (Conover and Poole, 1973). This disorder is caused by high temperatures greater than 90°F (32°C), but is also accentuated by high fertilization. Daughtrey and Chase (1992) show a similar notching disorder caused by calcium deficiency.

POSTHARVEST

Properly acclimated draceana plants should have a long postharvest life for the consumer because dracaenas are tolerant of poor interior conditions. Poole et al. (1991) stated that dracaenas can be shipped for at least 2 weeks, and probably up to 4 weeks, at 60 to 65°F (16 to 18°C) with no decrease in quality, except for *D. surculosa* 'Florida Beauty,' which should not be shipped for longer than 2 weeks (Marousky and Harbaugh, 1978). A slightly lower storage or shipping temperature of 55 to 61°F (13 to 16°C) was recommended for *D. marginata* (Conover and Poole, 1983). *D. fragrans* was determined to have an optimum storage temperature of 49°F (9.5°C), but also tolerated up to 2 weeks storage at 50 to 86°F (10 to 30°C) (Tijskens et al., 1996).

D. marginata and *D. sanderiana* are considered to be slightly sensitive to external ethylene concentrations (Nowak and Rudnicki, 1990). However, L. Høyer (personal communication) noted that the same species have low ethylene sensitivity, and Poole et al. (1991) stated that 15 ppm ethylene for 24 hr had no effect on *D. marginata* and *D. sanderiana* and "would probably not affect other dracaenas."

D. deremensis 'Warneckii' and 'Janet Craig' tolerate interior light levels as low as 50 fc (10 μmol $\cdot$ m^{-2} $\cdot$ s^{-1}) but 100 to 150 fc (20 to 30 μmol $\cdot$ m^{-2} $\cdot$ s^{-1}) is preferred (Poole et al., 1991). A light level of 75 to 150 fc (15 to 30 μmol $\cdot$ m^{-2} $\cdot$ s^{-1}) is recommended for *D. marginata* (Conover, 1992).

KEY POINTS

- Dracaena are grown as potted foliage plants and as garden ornamentals in frost-free climates.

- Plants are propagated commercially by terminal cuttings or cane sections; air layering can also be used.

- Cane sections up to 8 ft (2.4 m) long can be used to create instant "trees."

- Optimum light intensity ranges from 1500 to 5000 fc (300 to 1000 μmol $\cdot$ m^{-2} $\cdot$ s^{-1}) depending on the species being grown.

- Plants are susceptible to numerous diseases, especially *Erwinia* leaf and soft rot and *Fusarium* stem rot.

- Foliage tip chlorosis and necrosis can occur because of fluoride toxicity.

- Properly acclimated plants should have a long postharvest life for the consumer.

BIBLIOGRAPHY

Bailey, L.H., and E.Z. Bailey. 1976. *Dracaena*, p. 398 in *Hortus Third: A Concise Dictionary of Plants Cultivated in the United States and Canada.* Macmillan, New York.

Broschat, T.K., and H. Donselman. 1983. Effect of wounding method on rooting and water conductivity in four woody species of air-layered foliage plants, *Ficus benjamina, Ficus elastica, Schefflera arboricola, Dracaena marginata*, propagation. *HortScience* 18:445–447.

Conover, C.A. 1992. Foliage plants, pp. 569–601 in *Introduction to Floriculture*, R.A. Larson, editor. Academic Press, San Diego, California.

Conover, C. 1998. Foliage plants, pp. 273–294 in *Ball Redbook*, 16th ed., V. Ball, editor. Ball Publishing, Batavia, Illinois.

Conover, C.A., and R.T. Poole. 1973. Factors influencing notching and necrosis of *Dracaena deremensis* 'Warneckii' foliage. *Proceedings of the Tropical Region American Society for Horticulture Science* 17:378–384.

Conover, C.A., and R.T. Poole. 1982. Fluoride induced chlorosis and necrosis of *Dracaena fragrans* 'Massangeana.' *Journal of the American Society for Horticultural Science* 107:136–139.

Conover, C.A. and R.T. Poole. 1983. Handling and shipping acclimatized plants in reefers, pp. 149–151 in *Produce Marketing Almanac.* Produce Marketing Association, Newark, Delaware.

Conover, C.A., and R.T. Poole. 1990. *Light and Fertilizer Recommendations for Production of Acclimated Potted Foliage Plants.* Foliage Plant Research Note RH-90-1, Central Florida Research and Education Center, Apopka, Florida.

Daughtrey, M., and A.R. Chase. 1992. *Dracaena*, pp. 69–74 in *Ball Field Guide to Diseases of Greenhouse Ornamentals.* Ball Publishing, Geneva, Illinois.

Donselman, H., and T.K. Broschat. 1982. Light-induced basal branching of *Dracaena marginata* foliage plant. *HortScience* 17:909–910.

Dreistadt, S.H. 2001. *Integrated Pest Management for Floriculture and Nurseries.* University of California Division of Agriculture and Natural Resources Publication 3402.

Griffith, Jr., L.P. 1998. *Tropical Foliage Plants.* Ball Publishing, Batavia, Illinois.

Hata, T.Y., A.H. Hara, M.A. Nagao, and B.K.S. Hu. 1994. Hot-water treatment and indole-3-butyric acid stimulates rooting and shoot development of tropical ornamental cuttings. *HortScience* 4:159–162.

Henny, R.J. 2001. Foliage plants, pp. 83–87 in *Tips on Regulating Growth of Floriculture Crops*, M.L. Gaston, L.A. Kunkle, P.S. Konjoian, and M.F. Wilt, editors. Ohio Florists' Association Services, Columbus, Ohio.

Horst, R.K. 1990. Dracaena, p. 628 in *Westcott's Plant Disease Handbook*, 5th ed. Van Nostrand Reinhold, New York.

Huxley, A., M. Griffiths, and M. Levy. 1992. *Dracaena*, pp. 96–97 in *The Royal Horticultural Society Dictionary of Gardening*, vol. 2. Stockton Press, New York.

Ingram, D.L., C. Ramcharan, and T.A. Nell. 1986. Response of container-grown banana, ixora, citrus and dracaena to elevated root temperatures. *HortScience* 21:254–255.

Lang, H.J., C.L. Rosenfield, and D.W. Reed. 1990. Response of *Ficus benjamina* and *Dracaena marginata* to iron stress. *Journal of the American Society for Horticultural Science* 115:589–592.

Marousky, F.J. 1980. Chilling injury in *Dracaena sanderana* and *Spathiphyllum* 'Clevelandii.' *HortScience* 15:197–198.

Marousky, F.J., and B.K. Harbaugh. 1978. Deterioration of foliage plants during transit, pp. 33–39 in *National Tropical Foliage Short Course.* IFAS Cooperative Extension Service, University of Florida, Orlando.

McConnell, D.B., R.W. Henley, and R.L. Biamonte. 1981. Commercial foliage plants, pp. 544–593 in *Foliage Plant Production*, J. Joiner, editor. Prentice-Hall, Englewood Cliffs, New Jersey.

Nowak, J., and R.M. Rudnicki. 1990. *Postharvest Handling and Storage of Cut Flowers, Florists Greens, and Potted Plants*. Timber Press, Portland, Oregon.

Poole, R.T., and C.A. Conover. 1974. Foliar chlorosis of *Dracaena deremensis* Engler cv. Warneckii cuttings induced by fluoride. *HortScience* 9:378–379.

Poole, R.T., and C.A. Conover. 1975. Floride induced necrosis of *Dracaena deremensis* Engler cultivar Janet Craig. *HortScience* 10:376–377.

Poole, R.T., C.A. Conover, and W.E. Waters. 1974. Bud-break in canes of *Dracaena fragrans* Ker. cv. Massangeana. *HortScience* 9:540–541.

Poole, R.T., A.R. Chase, and L.S. Osborne. 1991. *Dracaena*. Foliage Plant Research Note RH-91-14.

Central Florida Research and Education Center, Apopka, Florida.

Rauch, F.D. 1976. Rooting response of *Dracaena* spp. *University of Hawaii Horticultural Digest* 30:3.

Stamps, R.H., and M.R. Evans. 1999. Growth of *Draceana marginata* and *Spathiphyllum* 'Petite' in sphagnum peat- and coconut coir dust-based growing media. *Journal of Environmental Horticulture* 17:49–52.

Tijskens, L.M.M., M. Sloof, E.C. Wilkinson, and W.G. van Doorn. 1996. A model of the effects of temperature and time on the acceptability of potted plants stored in darkness. *Postharvest Biology and Technology* 8:293–305.

Vladimirova, S.V., D.B. McConnell, M.E. Kane, and R.W. Henley. 1997. Morphological plasticity of *Draceana sanderana* 'Ribbon' in response to four light intensities. *HortScience* 32:1049–1052.

Echinacea

INTRODUCTION

Common names: purple coneflower, purple rudbeckia, black sampson (Still, 1988).

Scientific name: *Echinacea purpurea* (L.) Moench (Huxley et al., 1992).

Family and related taxa: Compositea Giseke. The nine *Echinacea* species are native to North America of which *E. purpurea* is the most commonly cultivated species (Bailey and Bailey, 1976). *E. angustifolia* DC. is shorter and has more narrow petals than *E. purpurea*. *E. pallida* (Nutt.) Nutt. also has narrow, drooping petals. *E. paradoxa* (Norton) Britton has drooping yel-

low petals. The Compositea is a large family containing numerous important genera including *Aster, Calendula, Centaurea, Chrysanthemum, Cosmos, Dahlia, Dendranthema, Gerbera, Helianthus, Liatris, Pericallis, Solidago, Tagetes,* and *Zinnia*.

Origin: *E. purpurea* and *E. pallida* are native to eastern and central North America (Huxley et al., 1992). *E. angustifolia* is native to central North America and *E. paradoxa* to south central North America (Figs. II-1 and II-2 Echinacea).

FIGURE II-1 ECHINACEA *Echinacea purpurea* 'Ruby Giant.'

FIGURE II–2 ECHINACEA *Echinacea pallida.*

Uses and current status: Coneflowers are used as a field-grown specialty cut flower, both fresh and dried, and as a garden perennial. The species is occasionally sold as a fresh cut without the ray petals, which are removed by hand, highlighting the coarse maroon-colored, golden-tipped center disc florets. Coneflower roots are used as an herbal medicine, which has led to excessive and often illegal wild harvesting. *Echinacea* is rapidly becoming rare in many areas due to overharvesting. Fortunately, field production of coneflower for the roots is increasing (Li, 1998).

Native coneflowers are long-lived plants that grow 2 to 4 feet (60 to 120 cm) tall with one to several flowers on each stem. Coneflowers generally flower from late spring to midsummer. The plants tolerate heat, drought, and cold and are hardy from Zones 3 to 9 (Nau, 1996).

CULTIVARS

Numerous cultivars are available in rosy red, pink, and white; many of the cultivars are similar in appearance. Much breeding and selection on coneflower has been taking place recently and many new cultivars have been released or will be released that vary greatly in plant height, flower size, and flower color. Hybridization of *E. purpurea* with *E. paradoxa* has produced a broad range of striking ray colors including orange, gold, and peach (Ault, 2002). Numerous hybrids among other *Echinacea* species are also showing promise.

PROPAGATION

Coneflowers can be propagated from seed, root cuttings, or division. While coneflower seeds germinate readily at 70 to 75°F (21 to 24°C) in

the light (Armitage and Laushman, 2003), stratification for 4 weeks at 32 to 40°F (0 to 4°C) increases the percentage of seeds germinating and germination uniformity and decreases the time to germination (Bratcher et al., 1993; Smith-Jochum and Albrecht, 1987). Li (1998) recommended mixing seed with clean sand (1:1 ratio) in a plastic bag and stratifying the seed for 4 to 6 weeks at 34 to 39°F (1 to 4°C). Maintain 10% moisture in the bag. After stratification, sow seed and hold at 64 to 68°F (18 to 20°C) for germination, which will take place in 7 to 10 days. A quality seed source is important because germination rates among sources can vary considerably (Wartidiningsih and Geneve, 1994).

Seed priming in distilled water or in potassium phosphate decreased time to germination and increased uniformity (Finnerty and Zajicek, 1992). Direct sowing in the field is possible but germination will probably be less uniform than germination under protection (Li, 1998). Soaking seed in 41 to 50°F (5 to 10°C) water for 20 days increased germination (Wartidiningsih et al., 1994).

In early spring, 1- to 3-in. (2.5- to 7.5-cm) root cuttings can be harvested and either inserted upright in propagation medium or laid flat and slightly covered with medium (Armitage and Laushman, 2003). Established plants can be divided every 3 to 4 years. *In vitro* propagation is possible (Li, 1998).

FLOWERING CONTROL AND DORMANCY

Plants may flower the first summer if young plants are started early enough in the spring, indicating that flowering is not cold dependant. However, stem length and yield are greater when plants are given at least 6 weeks of 40°F (4°C) (Armitage and Laushman, 2003). After establishment outdoors, coneflower will flower naturally in May to June in the southern United States and July to August in the northern United States. Long day night interruption lighting of 0.5 to 4 hr/night induced flowering, and cyclical night interruption lighting of 6 min on/24 or 54 min off was also effective (Runkle et al., 1998). Several weeks of SD prior to the LD is beneficial (B. Fausey, personal communication).

TEMPERATURE

After germination, seedlings can be grown at 60 to 65°F (16 to 18°C) night and 70 to 80°F (21 to 27°C) day but will grow better under warmer temperatures. Flowering of container-grown plants for early spring flowering can be enhanced with a minimum of 6 weeks of 40°F (4°C) treatment (Armitage and Laushman, 2003). Nau (1996) recommended growing at 50°F (10°C) or higher unless plants are growing too fast or growth is of poor quality.

LIGHT

Coneflowers prefer full sunlight both in the greenhouse and in the field. Outdoors, light shade may enhance the darker colors and prevent fading of the petals in warm climates.

WATER

Irrigate seedlings and container-grown plants as needed. Established plants are drought tolerant, but the best growth is obtained with regular irrigation prior to water stress.

CARBON DIOXIDE

No data available.

NUTRITION

Seedlings and young plants can be fertilized with 50 to 125 ppm N constant liquid fertilization. Container-grown plants may benefit from use of controlled-release fertilizers. Although field-grown plants for cut flowers have relatively low nutritional requirements, plants may benefit from application of 25 to 30 lb (11 to 14 kg) actual nitrogen per acre from either organic or inorganic sources. The amount of fertilization will vary greatly with native soil fertility, soil type, and rainfall.

For root production, avoid excessive fertilization because that will produce a high amount of shoot tissue but low root growth (Franz, 1983). A nitrogen rate of 196 lb/acre (220 kg $\cdot$ ha^{-1}) is recommended for South Carolina (Dufault et al., 2003). Numerous organic fertilizers are suitable for coneflower production (Li, 1998).

MEDIA

Coneflowers thrive in a wide range of media. A pH of 5.5 to 6.5 is acceptable for container production and 5.0 to 7.5 is acceptable for field production. For retail sales, plants can be grown in cell packs green, one plant per quart (liter) container or two to three plants per gallon (4-liter) container. Outdoor coneflowers tolerate a wide range of soil types as long as the location is well drained.

HEIGHT CONTROL

Height control of container-grown plants is generally not needed, but two B-Nine (daminozide) sprays of 5000 ppm each, one Bonzi (paclobutrazol) spray of 240 ppm, or one Sumagic (uniconazole) spray at 15 to 30 ppm is effective (Latimer and Thomas, 1997). Up to five A-Rest (ancymidol) sprays at 100 ppm or Cycocel (chlormequat) sprays at 1500 ppm are also effective (Latimer, 2001).

SPACING

Generally, spacing of 12 × 12 to 18 × 18 in. (30 × 30 to 45 × 45 cm) is used in the field for both cut flower and root production. Potted plants are spaced pot-to-pot until leaves touch or until sold. Planting *E. pallida* in rows 20 in. (50 cm) apart and spacing plants 12 in. (30 cm) apart within the row produced approximately 1200, 4600, 7300, and 8500 lb/acre (1.3, 5.1, 8.2, and 9.5 t $\cdot$ h^{-1}) of roots 1, 2, 3, and 4 years after planting, respectively (Li, 1998).

PINCHING AND DISBUDDING

No pinching or disbudding needed.

SUPPORT

Although plant stems are generally quite sturdy, field-grown coneflowers usually benefit from one layer of netting for cut flower production.

SCHEDULE AND TIMING

Perry (1989) estimated cut flower production of 15 stems per plant with average lengths of 31 in. (79 cm). Production of a container-grown plant can take 5 to 7 months (Table II-1 Echinacea). Purchasing plugs can reduce production time to 11 to 15 weeks. Plants will flower in summer when seed is sown in winter.

INSECTS

In the greenhouse, coneflowers are usually pest free but may occasionally be susceptible to aphids, whiteflies, and thrips. Outdoors, the coneflower is host to the larvae of numerous moths and butterflies, grasshoppers, and Japanese beetles.

TABLE II-I ECHINACEA

Sample production schedule for *Echinacea* plants grown in I-qt (L) to I-gal (3.8-L) size containers.

Cultural Step	Production Time (weeks)	Temperature °F (°C)
Stratification (optional)		
	4	32–40 (0–4)
Germination		
	1–2	70–75 (21–24)
Growing on seedlings		
	2–3	70–75 (21–24)
Transplant to cell packs[a]		
	7–9	60–65 (16–18)
Finishing		
	4–6	60–65 (16–18)
Total	18–24	

[a]*Cell packs also suitable for transplanting to the field for cut flower production.*

DISEASES

The most common disease problem in the greenhouse is root rot. Do not overwater during cool periods and use a well-aerated medium. Outdoors, the coneflower is susceptible to leaf spots (*Cercospora rudbeckiae, Septoria lepachydis, Ascochyta,* and *Phyllosticta*) (Horst, 1990) and aster yellows phytoplasma. Spacing closer than 15 × 15 in. (38 × 38 cm) increases the potential for foliar diseases (Armitage and Laushman, 2003). Aster yellows phytoplasma can be devastating; the symptoms range from yellowing leaves and flowers to severe stunting and deformed, yellow-green flowers. Rogue infected plants as soon as possible; remove weeds, which are a source of the disease; and control the insect vector, leafhoppers, if possible (Stanosz and Heimann, 1997).

PHYSIOLOGICAL DISORDERS

No physiological disorders are reported.

POSTHARVEST

Flowers are harvested when the petals have expanded and the first ring of disc florets has opened. Vase life is generally 7 to 12 days (Redman et al., 2002). Cut stems can be stored for 1 week at 36 to 45°F (2 to 7°C) and can be shipped in water for up to 5 days. Cut coneflowers are not sensitive to external ethylene concentrations of up to 1 ppm (Redman et al., 2002). Although results can be variable, treatment with silver thiosulfate (STS) and preservatives may extend vase life. Flowers can be sold fresh with or without the ray petals. The centers can also be marketed as a dried flower.

Roots for herbal uses are generally harvested in the fall after the first frost; 3 to 4 years are required for roots to reach harvestable size after sowing (Li, 1998). After harvest, roots are washed and dried with ambient air or with a forced-air dryer. Leaves also contain active ingredients but no information is available on their harvest.

KEY POINTS

- This North American native is used primarily as a cut flower and garden ornamental, but also as an herbal medicine.
- Plants are propagated commercially by seed, but also by root cuttings or division.
- Seeds should be cold treated for 4 weeks at 32 to 40°F (0 to 4°C) prior to germination at 70 to 75°F (21 to 24°C).
- If propagated early enough in the year, plants will flower their first year.
- Aster yellows is an important disease and limits production in many areas.
- Flowers are harvested and sold without or with the ray flowers removed. Roots are dug, washed, and dried for herbal medicine.

BIBLIOGRAPHY

Armitage, A.M., and J.M. Laushman. 2003. *Echinacea purpurea*, pp. 254–259 in *Specialty Cut Flowers*, 2nd ed. Timber Press, Portland, Oregon.

Ault, J. 2002. *Echinacea* evolution. *Nursery Management and Production* 18(11):34–36.

Bailey, L.H., and E.Z. Bailey. 1976. *Echinacea*, pp. 410–411 in *Hortus Third: A Concise Dictionary of Plants Cultivated in the United States and Canada*. Macmillan, New York.

Bratcher, C.B., J.M. Dole, and J.C. Cole. 1993. Stratification improves seed germination of five native wildflower species. *HortScience* 28(9):899–901.

Dufault, R.J., J. Rushing, R. Hassell, B.M. Shepard, G. McCutcheon, and B. Ward. 2003. Influence of fertilizer on growth and marker compound of field-grown Echinacea species and feverfew. *Scientia Horticulturae* 98:61–69.

Finnerty, T., and J.M. Zajicek. 1992. Effects of seed priming on plug production of *Coreopsis lanceolata* and *Echinacea purpurea*. *Journal of Environmental Horticulture* 10:129–132.

Franz, C. 1983. Nutrient and water management for medicinal and aromatic plants. *Acta Horticulturae* 132:203–215.

Horst, R.K. 1990. Echinacea, p. 629 in *Westcott's Plant Disease Handbook*, 5th ed. Van Nostrand Reinhold, New York.

Huxley, A., M. Griffiths, and M. Levy. 1992. *Echinacea*, p. 128 in *The New Royal Horticultural Society Dictionary of Gardening*, vol. 2. Stockton Press, New York.

Latimer, J. 2001. Herbaceous perennials, pp. 98–110 in *Tips on Regulating Growth of Floriculture Crops*, M.L. Gaston, L.A. Kunkle, P.S. Konjoian, and M.F. Wilt, editors. Ohio Florists' Association Services, Columbus, Ohio.

Latimer, J.G., and P.A. Thomas. 1997. Response of perennial bedding plants to three common plant growth regulators. *Southeastern Floriculture* 7(4):16–17.

Li, T.S.C. 1998. *Echinacea*: Cultivation and medicinal value. *HortTechnology* 8:122–129.

Nau, J. 1996. *Echinacea purpurea*, pp. 208–210 in *Ball Perennial Manual*. Ball Publishing, Batavia, Illinois.

Perry, L.P. 1989. Perennial cut flowers, pp. 155–161 in *Proceedings of the 2nd National Conference on Specialty Cut Flowers*, Athens, Georgia.

Redman, P.B., J.M. Dole, N.O. Maness, and J.A. Anderson. 2002. Postharvest handling of nine specialty cut flowers. *Scientia Horticulturae* 92: 293–303.

Runkle, E.S., R.D. Heins, A.C. Cameron, and W.H. Carlson. 1998. Flowering of herbaceous perennials under various night interruption and cyclic lighting treatments. *HortScience* 33:672–677.

Smith-Jochum, C.C., and M.L. Albrecht. 1987. Field establishment of three *Echinacea* species for commercial production. *Acta Horticulturae* 208: 115–118.

Stanosz, G.R., and M.F. Heimann. 1997. Purple coneflower is a host of the aster yellows phytoplasma. *Plant Disease* 81:424.

Still, S.M. 1988. *Echinacea*, p. 174 in *Manual of Herbaceous Ornamental Plants*. Stipes Publishing, Champaign, Illinois.

Wartidiningsih, N., and R.L. Geneve. 1994. Seed source and quality influence germination in purple coneflower [*Echinacea purpurea* (L.) Moench.]. *HortScience* 29:1443–1444.

Wartidiningsih, N., R.L. Geneve, and S.T. Kester. 1994. Osmotic priming or chilling stratification improves seed germination of purple coneflower. *HortScience* 29:1445–1448.

Epipremnum

INTRODUCTION

Common names: pothos, golden pothos, variegated philodendron.

Scientific name: *Epipremnum aureum* Lind. & Andre (formerly known as *Scindapsus aureus* or *Pothos aureus*) (Huxley et al., 1992).

Family and related taxa: Araceae Juss. Several other species of *Epipremnum* are found in the wild. The related *Scindapsus pictus* Hassk. is sometimes known as a pothos and has thick, leathery gray-green leaves with silvery blotches. Araceae is a large family containing many important genera including *Aglaonema, Anthurium, Caladium, Dieffenbachia, Monstera, Nephthytis, Philodendron, Spathiphyllum, Syngonium,* and *Zantedeschia.*

Origin: Originally native to the Solomon Islands, but has naturalized in tropical regions of many parts of the world (Bailey and Bailey, 1976).

Uses and current status: *Epipremnum* is a popular indoor foliage plant due to its waxy variegated foliage, adaptability to the indoor environment, and ease of production. Plants can be grown as a hanging basket, trained on a totem, or produced as a small potted plant for direct sale or incorporation into container gardens (Figs. II-1 and II-2 Epipremnum). In interiorscapes, pothos are also used as ground covers and hanging screens. Pothos are similarly grown as climbing outdoor ornamentals in tropical regions of the world.

When grown indoors, pothos usually exhibit only the heart-shaped juvenile foliage. If grown outdoors in tropical climates, the large, mature leaves with deep indentations appear as the

FIGURE II-1 EPIPREMNUM *Epipremnum* totem.

FIGURE II-2 EPIPREMNUM *Epipremnum* totem. Note stem roots.

plant grows up tree trunks. Because only mature plants flower, flowering plants are not found indoors.

CULTIVARS

Two cultivars commonly grown are 'Golden Pothos' (Hawaiian pothos), which has leaves irregularly splotched with yellow, and 'Marble Queen,' which has leaves heavily splotched with white. Two solid color cultivars are available;

'Jade,' which has medium green leaves and 'Neon' with bright yellowish to chartreuse leaves.

PROPAGATION

Pothos are propagated by tip, single-eye, or double-eye cuttings from stock plants or from the prunings of previous crops (McConnell et al., 1981). Because one of the main features of this species is the coloration, be sure to select cuttings with the best variegation. Stock plants will have more and heavier cuttings when grown under 5000 fc (1000 μmol $\cdot$ m^{-2} $\cdot$ s^{-1}) as compared with 2100 fc (420 μmol $\cdot$ m^{-2} $\cdot$ s^{-1}) (Wang, 1990).

Single-eye cuttings are most commonly used commercially and any adventitious roots should be preserved during cutting harvest. Cuttings should be up to 2 in. (5 cm) long with the stem cut 1.2 in. (3 cm) below the node (Wang and Boogher, 1988). Cuttings root best under 3000 fc (600 μmol $\cdot$ m^{-2} $\cdot$ s^{-1}) light at 80°F (27°C) (Poole et al., 1991). Misting cuttings for 1 week increased plant growth and decreased time to produce the first new leaf (Wang, 1990). Misting for more than 1 week did not have any additional benefits but was not detrimental either. Although cuttings are typically propagated directly into the final container, they can also be rooted in plugs for later planting or for incorporation into container gardens. Cuttings can be stored at 50 to 65°F (10 to 18°C) for later planting, but the best results are obtained when cuttings are planted immediately.

FLOWERING CONTROL AND DORMANCY

Because the plants are grown for their foliage, flowering is not encouraged and typically occurs only on older plants growing outdoors in tropical areas.

TEMPERATURE

Pothos will tolerate a wide range of temperatures, but optimum growth takes place between 70 and 90°F (21 and 32°C). Growth is slowed when temperatures are below 60°F (16°C) or quality is reduced above 90°F (32°C). Temperatures below 55°F (13°C) may cause foliage yellowing (Griffith, 1998). Nowak and Rudnicki (1990) recommended reducing the temperature when plants are shaded during production.

Warm soil temperatures of up to 90°F (32°C) increase plant growth, especially for plants grown with cool air temperatures of 60°F (16°C) (Conover and Poole, 1992b). The optimum medium temperature is 82°F (28°C) (Griffith, 1998). Conover and Poole (1992b) recommend that the air temperature be "at least 65°F (18°C) to get satisfactory growth" with media temperatures of 70°F (21°C). Interestingly, root weight and leaf areas decrease with increasing media temperatures.

LIGHT

Poole et al. (1991) suggest light levels of 1500 to 3000 fc (300 to 600 μmol $\cdot$ m^{-2} $\cdot$ s^{-1}) with 70 to 80% shade for south Florida conditions. Light levels lower than 1000 fc (200 μmol $\cdot$ m^{-2} $\cdot$ s^{-1}) may reduce coloration (Griffith, 1998).

WATER

Although pothos are tolerant of drying out, the media should remain moist for best growth.

CARBON DIOXIDE

No data on carbon dioxide have been reported.

NUTRITION

Conover and Poole (1990) recommended 0.56 oz/ft^2 (172 g $\cdot$ m^{-2}) per year of nitrogen from a fertilizer source with a N:P:K ratio of 3:1:2. Both water-soluble and controlled-release fertilizers have been used successfully. Tissue nutrient levels of quality pothos plants are as follows: N 2.5 to 3.5%, P 0.20 to 0.35%, K 3.0 to 4.5%, Ca 1.0 to 1.5%, and Mg 0.3 to 0.6% of dry weight (Poole et al., 1991).

MEDIA

Pothos are tolerant of a wide range of media as long as the medium is well drained with a pH of 5.0 to 6.5. If the cuttings are propagated directly into the final pots, the medium must be particularly well aerated, yet retain enough moisture to prevent excessive irrigation when the plants are being grown and finished.

HEIGHT CONTROL

The length of the vines can be controlled with growth retardants such as B-Nine (daminozide; 10,000-ppm spray), A-Rest (ancymidol; three 100-ppm sprays or one 0.5- to 5-ppm drench), Sumagic [uniconazole, 0.05 to 0.2 mg a.i. drench/0.5-qt (0.5-L) pot], and Bonzi [paclobutrazol, 4 to 6 mg a.i. drench/8-in. (20-cm) pot] (Conover and Satterthwaite, 1996; Henny, 2001; Poole et al., 1991). Any rate of Bonzi and Sumagic also has the benefit of increasing leaf size and plant quality (Conover and Satterthwaite, 1996; Wang and Gregg, 1994). Bonzi (200-ppm) sprays were less effective than drenches in reducing stem length but did not reduce leaf production rate (Wang and Gregg, 1994). Sumagic (100-ppm) sprays were effective as drenches and also did not reduce leaf production rate.

SPACING

Pots and baskets are spaced pot-to-pot until the foliage touches and the stems begin to vine. Hanging baskets should be either trimmed or spaced out to prevent shoots from becoming intertwined.

PINCHING AND DISBUDDING

Plants are usually shaped up one or two times before sale by trimming the longest shoots. The shoots can then be used to propagate the next production cycle of plants. The trimmed shoots produce multiple axillary shoots, which make the plants fuller.

SUPPORT

Vines can be pinned to totem poles for upright growth.

SCHEDULE AND TIMING

A minimum of 13 weeks is required (Table II-1 Epipremnum).

INSECTS

Although pothos can be considered more pest resistant than many other commercial floriculture crops, several insects and related pests can occur including spider mites, thrips, scale, and

mealybugs. The latter two pests can become particularly troublesome under long-term production such as with stock plants or conservatory collections. Caterpillars can also be a problem in warm climates such as Florida, Texas, and California where moths can invade from the outdoors.

DISEASES

Rhizoctonia root and stem rot (*Rhizoctonia solani*) is one of the most common disease problems and is favored by temperatures between 72°F (22°C) and 86°F (30°C) (Chase and Poole, 1990). Constant temperatures of 86°F (30°C) or maximum daily temperatures above 95°F (35°C) reduce the disease. Unfortunately, plant growth is also reduced above 90°F (32°C).

Pythium splendens is also a major concern and causes the roots and stems to turn black. Lower foliage becomes bright yellow (Griffith, 1998).

A relatively new disease is *Raulstonia solanacearum* (formerly known as *P. solanacearum* or *P. burkholderia*), which causes rotting of cuttings from the base upward and discoloration on the veins of some leaves (Anonymous, 2003). Not only is sanitation critical but infected plant material should be discarded immediately.

Pothos are subject to several other common foliage plant diseases including bacterial leaf spot (*Pseudomonas cichorii, Erwinia carotovora*, and *E. chrysanthemi*), cutting soft rot (*Erwinia carotovora* and *E. chrysanthemi*), and root rot (*Phytophthora*) (Anonymous, 1997; Chase, 1987; Horst, 1990; Poole et al., 1991). Other reported diseases include anthracnose (*Glomerella cingulata*), gray mold (*Botrytis cinerea*), and fungal leaf spot (*Cercospora richardiaecola, Colletotrichum*, and *Phyllosticta*). The strikingly white mycelia of southern blight (*Sclerotium rolfsii*) can also be found on occasion (Chase, 1987).

PHYSIOLOGICAL DISORDERS

EXCESSIVE GREENING OF THE STOCK FOLIAGE

The amount of variegation on the foliage naturally varies from vine to vine; selection and removal of the most variegated vines for propagation from stock plants can favor the less variegated foliage. To maintain proper variegation, discard vines with inadequate variegation and allow one to two leaves with sufficient

TABLE II-1 EPIPREMNUM

Sample production schedule for *Epipremnum* in 8-in. (20-cm) hanging baskets.

Cultural Step	Production Time (weeks)	Temperature °F (°C)
Propagation	3–4	Medium: 80 (27)
Growing on	10–12	Night: 75 (24) Day: 85 (29)
Total	13–16	

variegation to remain after harvesting cuttings. Low light intensities can also encourage excessive greening of the foliage.

DISCOLORED LEAVES

Low temperatures or sudden temperature changes can cause brown patches on the leaves. The disorder is especially prevalent on vigorously growing plants, which produce large soft growth. Be sure to keep temperatures constant between 70 and 90°F (21 and 32°C).

POSTHARVEST

Properly acclimatized pothos plants should have a long postharvest life for the consumer because pothos are tolerant of low-light interior conditions. Plants can be shipped for up to 2 weeks at 55 to 60°F (13 to 16°C) with no decrease in quality (Poole et al., 1991). Pothos plants should survive 6 weeks when given 12-hr days of 125 fc (25 μmol $\cdot$ m^{-2} $\cdot$ s^{-1}) light and have an EC of 1.0 to 6.0 dS $\cdot$ m^{-1}. Plants will produce smaller leaves if the light or fertility levels are too low in the consumer's environment. Self-watering containers work well for pothos (Conover and Poole, 1992a). Although Nowak and Rudnicki (1990) considered pothos to be insensitive to external ethylene concentrations, exposure to high rates of ethylene at 15 ppm for 3 days produced leaf drop (Marousky and Harbaugh, 1978). 1-methylcyclopropene (1-MCP) treatment at 200 ppb reduced leaf drop and yellowing of cuttings stored at 73°F (23°C) for 4 days, but did not affect subsequent rooting of the cuttings (Muller et al., 1997). Silver thiosulfate (STS) at 2 mM, however, injured cuttings.

KEY POINTS

- Pothos is used as a foliage plant grown in a hanging basket or trained on a totem.
- Four cultivars are available: 'Golden Pothos' with yellow variegation 'Marble Queen' with white variegation, 'Jade' with medium green leaves, and 'Neon' with chartreuse leaves.
- Plants are propagated by tip or by single-eye or double-eye cuttings.
- Plants are usually trimmed, shaped, and allowed to regrow before marketing; trimmed shoots are often used for propagation.

- Optimum light intensity is 1500 to 3000 fc (300 to 600 μmol $\cdot$ m^{-2} $\cdot$ s^{-1}).
- Plants are susceptible to numerous diseases, especially root and stem rot, bacterial leaf spot, cutting soft rot, and root rot.
- Properly acclimated plants should have a long postharvest life for the consumer.

BIBLIOGRAPHY

Anonymous. 1997. Pothos disease continues to spread in Florida. *Greenhouse Management and Production* 17(7):12.

Anonymous. 2003. Pothos disease renamed. *Greenhouse Management and Production* 23(5):8.

Bailey, L.H., and E.Z. Bailey. 1976. *Epipremnum*, pp. 431–432 in *Hortus Third, A Concise Dictionary of Plants Cultivated in the United States and Canada*. Macmillan, New York.

Chase, A.R. 1987. *Compendium of Ornamental Foliage Plant Diseases*. American Phytopathological Society Press, St. Paul, Minnesota.

Chase, A.R., and R.T. Poole. 1990. Effect of air and growing medium temperatures on rhizoctonia foot rot of *Epipremnum aureum*. *Journal of Environmental Horticulture* 8:139–141.

Conover, C.A., and R.T. Poole. 1990. *Light and Fertilizer Recommendations for Production of Acclimated Potted Foliage Plants*. Foliage Plant Research Note RH-90-1, Central Florida Research and Education Center, Apopka, Florida.

Conover, C.A., and R.T. Poole. 1992a. Water utilization of six foliage plants under two interior light intensities. *Journal of Environmental Horticulture* 10:111–113.

Conover, C.A., and R.T. Poole. 1992b. Air and soil temperatures and fertilizer level affect growth and quality of *Epipremnum aureum* Bunt. *Journal of Environmental Horticulture* 10:156–159.

Conover, C.A., and L.N. Satterthwaite. 1996. Paclobutrazol optimizes leaf size, vine length and plant grade of golden pothos (*Epipremnum au-*

reum) on totems. *Journal of Environmental Horticulture* 14:44–46.

Griffith, Jr., L.P. 1998. *Tropical Foliage Plants*. Ball Publishing, Batavia, Illinois.

Henny, R.J. 2001. Foliage plants, pp. 83–87 in *Tips on Regulating Growth of Floriculture Crops*, M.L. Gaston, L.A. Kunkle, P.S. Konjoian, and M.F. Wilt, editors. Ohio Florists' Association Services, Columbus, Ohio.

Horst, R.K. 1990. Pothos, p. 785 in *Westcott's Plant Disease Handbook*, 5th ed. Van Nostrand Reinhold, New York.

Huxley, A., M. Griffiths, and M. Levy. 1992. *Epipremnum*, p. 176 in *The New Royal Horticultural Society Dictionary of Gardening*, vol. 2. Stockton Press, New York.

Marousky, F.J., and B.K. Harbaugh. 1978. Deterioration of foliage plants during transit, pp. 33–39 in *National Tropical Foliage Short Course*. IFAS Cooperative Extension Service, University of Florida, Orlando.

McConnell, D.B., R.W. Henley, and R.L. Biamonte. 1981. Commercial foliage plants, pp. 544–593 in *Foliage Plant Production*, J. Joiner, editor. Prentice-Hall, Englewood Cliffs, New Jersey.

Müller, R., M. Serek, E.C. Sisler, and A.S. Andersen. 1997. Poststorage quality and rooting ability of *Epipremnum pinnatum* cuttings after treatment with ethylene action inhibitors. *Journal of Horticultural Science* 72:445–452.

Nowak, J., and R.M. Rudnicki. 1990. *Postharvest Handling and Storage of Cut Flowers, Florists Greens and Potted Plants*. Timber Press, Portland, Oregon.

Poole, R.T., A.R. Chase, and L.S. Osborne. 1991. *Pothos*. Foliage Plant Research Note RH-1991-29, Central Florida Research and Education Center, Apopka, Florida.

Wang, Y.T. 1990. Growth substance, light, fertilizer, and misting regulate propagation and growth of golden pothos. *HortScience* 25:1602–1604.

Wang, Y.T., and C.A. Boogher. 1988. Effect of nodal position, cutting length, and root retention on the propagation of golden pothos. *HortScience* 23:347–349.

Wang, Y.T., and L.L. Gregg. 1994. Chemical regulators affect growth, postproduction performance, and propagation of golden pothos. *HortScience* 29:183–185.

Eremurus

INTRODUCTION

Common names: desert candles, king's spear, and foxtail lily.

Scientific name: *Eremurus* Bieb. species. The genus has 40 or more species and several hybrids and cultivars such as *E.* 'Himrob,' *E.* 'Reiter-hybrids,' and *E.×isabellinus* hort. (Vilm.). *E. stenophyllus* (Boiss. & Buhse) Bak. (formerly known as *E. bungei* Bak.) is a commonly used species in commerce (Bailey and Bailey, 1976; Zimmer, 1985).

Family and related taxa: Liliaceae Juss. The Liliaceae family is quite large and contains many commercially important floriculture crops including *Allium, Alstroemeria, Brodiaea, Convallaria, Hyacinthus, Lachenalia, Lilium, Muscari, Ornithogalum,* and *Tulipa*.

Origin: This geophyte is native to western and central Asia (Huxley et al., 1992).

Uses and current status: Foxtail lilies are used in cut flower production and in perennial gardens (Zones 4 to 7; some species grow in Zone 3) as background plants.

Most foxtail lilies are tall growing plants with flowering racemes up to 7.5 ft (2.5 m) long containing hundreds of individual flowers on a long leafless scape (Fig. II-1 Eremurus). Flower colors include white, cream, pink, rose, pale to dark yellow, brown, copper-orange, and bright orange. Leaves are elongate, form a rosette, and are not attractive (Bailey and Bailey, 1976; Le Nard and De Hertogh, 1993; Zimmer, 1985). Outdoors foliage will die by mid- to late summer.

FIGURE II-1 EREMURUS   Outdoor-grown *Eremurus* plant with approximately 6-ft (1.8-m)-tall inflorescence (photo by Allan M. Armitage).

CULTIVARS

A number of cultivars exist that vary in flower color from white, pink, yellow, and orange to red. Plant height varies from the relatively dwarf 2 to 3 ft (0.6 to 0.9 m) tall *E. stenophyllus* to the 8 ft (2.4 m) tall *E. robustus* (Reg.) Reg. (Armitage, 1989).

PROPAGATION

Propagation is by root divisions, but only one to three new terminal crown buds form on the subtending root system. Two to 3 years are required for production of a high-quality rootstock, which is required to produce an acceptable quantity of flowering stems. The number of flowering stems is dependent on diameter of the terminal crown bud (Bailey and Bailey, 1976; Le Nard and De Hertogh, 1993; Zimmer, 1985). An acorn-like structure (bud) is attached to several tuberous roots that develop fibrous roots during the fall and winter. In the summer, fleshy tuberous roots form with a new terminal growing point and the old storage system disappears (Zimmer, 1985).

Plants can also be produced from seed. Zimmer (1985) reported that freshly harvested *E. robustus* seeds should be pretreated at 86°F (30°C) for 30 to 60 days and 36°F (2°C) for 6 weeks before being sown on a moist medium under darkness. However, seed propagation is slow, requiring up to 4 years to produce a large plant.

When commercial grade size is reached, the underground storage organs can be harvested and immediately replanted or graded and cold stored in a moist medium. However, the flowering meristem must be fully differentiated prior to the 36°F (2°C) treatment, which promotes flower scape elongation (Kamenetsky and Rabinowitch, 1999). Bud abortion will result if this cold treatment is applied prior to total floral development. Early floral differentiation and development is best at 86°F (32°C), followed by 36°F (2°C). Once totally differentiated 68 or 86°F (20 or 30°C) had no influence on further growth. Drying of tuberous roots should be avoided.

FLOWERING CONTROL AND DORMANCY

Axillary floral and vegetative buds are induced to elongate for the next growth cycle during the cold temperature treatment period. Sixteen to 18 weeks of less than 50°F (10°C) are required; Zimmer (1985) and Krebs and Zimmer (1976) stated that 36 to 45°F (2 to 7°C) was optimal for elongation and Kamenetsky and Rabinowitch (1999) stated that 36°F (2°C) was best. After the appropriate cold treatment, the tentacle-like rootstocks can be planted and forced in the greenhouse.

TEMPERATURE

Flower production occurs both in the field and in the greenhouse. Cool greenhouse temperatures of 67°F (16°C) can be used.

LIGHT

Full light is required. Shade only for temperature control.

WATER

The plant is a native of desert conditions; water only when required.

CARBON DIOXIDE

No data available.

NUTRITION

Outdoor beds should be well fertilized, have adequate drainage, and have a pH of 6.0 to 7.0.

MEDIA

The media should be very well drained because the rootstocks are prone to rot in wet soils. In the garden the roots are planted 4 to 6 in. (10 to 15 cm) deep.

HEIGHT CONTROL

None required.

SPACING

Space plants at 75 to 110/ft² (8 to 12/m²) if growing for 1 year and at 55 to 75/ft² (6 to 8/m²) if growing for 2 years (International Flower Bulb Centre, undated). In the garden, plants are spaced 18 in. (45 cm) apart.

PINCHING AND DISBUDDING

None required.

SUPPORT

Although stems are sturdy, some support may be useful in areas prone to high winds or heavy rains.

SCHEDULE AND TIMING

Approximately 17 weeks are required for flowering in the greenhouse at 67°F (16°C). H.F. Wilkins (unpublished) forced *E. stenophyllus* in 18 weeks when potted in late November. Outdoors flowering occurs from May to July. Rootstock are planted outside in September and October, leaves and the inflorescence emerge from the terminal crown buds in the spring, and plants flower in May to July. The crown buds are planted 2 to 3 in. (5 to 8 cm) below the soil surface. Production beds should be mulched in the autumn to prevent frost damage.

INSECTS

Although *Eremurus* appears to be relatively insect free, aphids and thrips can be problems (Armitage and Laushman, 2003).

DISEASES

Pythium is frequently a concern (International Bulb Flower Centre, undated).

PHYSIOLOGICAL DISORDERS

Only leaves may emerge if proper flower initiation and dormancy protocols are not followed (Zimmer, 1985).

POSTHARVEST

Flower stems are harvested when the lowermost three rows of florets have opened and should be held at 36°F (2°C). Lower temperatures may prevent further flower development. Cut stems will generally last at least a week; 3 weeks in a cooler (Armitage and Laushman, 2003). Inflorescences are geotropic and should be shipped upright. Pretreat flowers before shipping for 24 to 48 hr in 8-hydroxyquinoline sulfate and sucrose at 0.05 and 5.4 oz/gal (0.04 and 50 g · L^{-1}), respectively (Nowak and Rudnicki, 1990). Other treatments can be used to prevent geotropic responses (calcium chelators) and ethylene inhibitors such as silver thiosulfate (STS) can be useful (Philosoph-Hadas et al., 1995, 1996). *Eremurus* flowers are sensitive to ethylene (L. Høyer, personal communication).

KEY POINTS

- This cold-hardy perennial is used as a cut flower and garden ornamental for its large spike of unusually colored flowers.
- Plants are propagated by seed or division.

- Sixteen to 18 weeks of less than 50°F (10°C), with 36 to 45°F (2 to 7°C) optimal, is required to break dormancy.
- Cut stems respond very well to floral preservatives.

BIBLIOGRAPHY

Armitage, A.M. 1989. *Herbaceous Perennial Plants*, 2nd ed. Stipes Publishing, Champaign, Illinois.

Armitage, A.M., and J.M. Laushman. 2003. *Eremurus*, pp. 265–269 in *Specialty Cut Flowers*, 2nd ed. Timber Press, Portland, Oregon.

Bailey, L.H., and E.Z. Bailey. 1976. *Eremurus*, pp. 434–435 in *Hortus Third: A Concise Dictionary of Plants Cultivated in the United States and Canada*. Macmillan, New York.

Huxley, A., M. Griffiths, and M. Levy. 1992. *Eremurus*, pp. 181–182 in *The New Royal Horticultural Society Dictionary of Gardening*, vol. 2. Stockton Press, New York.

International Flower Bulb Centre. Undated. *Information on Special Bulbs*. International Flower Bulb Centre, Hillegom, Holland.

Kamenetsky, R., and E. Rabinowitch. 1999. Flowering response of *Eremurus* to post-harvest temperatures. *Scientia Horticulturae* 79:75–86.

Krebs, O., and K. Zimmer. 1976. Über das Kältebedürfnis von *Eremurus stenophyllus var. bungei*. *Gartenbauwissenschaft* 41:44–47.

Le Nard, M., and A.A. De Hertogh. 1993. *Eremurus*, pp. 715–717 in *The Physiology of Flower Bulbs*, A.A. De Hertogh and M. Le Nard, editors. Elsevier, Amsterdam, The Netherlands.

Nowak, J., and R.M. Rudnicki. 1990. *Postharvest Handling and Storage of Cut Flowers, Florist Greens, and Potted Plants*. Timber Press, Portland, Oregon.

Philosoph-Hades, S., S. Meir, I. Rosenberg, and A.H. Halevy. 1995. Control and regulation of the gravitropic response of cut flowering stems during storage and horizontal transport. *Acta Horticulturae* 405:343–350.

Philosoph-Hades, S., S. Meir, I. Rosenberg, and A.H. Halevy. 1996. Regulation of gravitropic responses and ethylene biosynthesis in gravistimulated snapdragon spikes by calcium chelator and ethylene inhibitors. *Plant Physiology* 110:301–310.

Zimmer, K. 1985. *Eremurus*, pp. 466–469 in *Handbook of Flowering*, vol. II, A.H. Halevy, editor. CRC Press, Boca Raton, Florida.

Eucharis

INTRODUCTION

Common name: Amazon lily or Eucharist lily.

Scientific name: *Eucharis amazonica* Linden ex Planchon (Meerow and Dehgan, 1984). Frequently, and apparently erroneously, known as *E. grandiflora* or *E. ×grandiflora* (Huxley et al., 1992).

Family and related taxa: Amaryllidaceae J. St.-Hil. The genus *Eucharis* has 16 species (Meerow, 1987). Other members of the Amaryllidaceae family include *Clivia, Crinum, Hymenocallis, Narcissus,* and *Nerine*.

Origin: This subtropical herbaceous plant is native to the Andean Mountains of Columbia and Peru. Other *Eucharis* species are found from Guatemala to Bolivia (Meerow, 1987).

Uses and current status: The cut flowers are used in high-quality wedding and corsage work. The Eucharist lily also makes a handsome houseplant.

The waxy white flowers are starlike, fragrant, and from 2.5 to 3.25 in. (6 to 8 cm) in diameter. The scape has up to six flowers, grows to 24 in. (60 cm) in length, and emerges from a tunicate bulb. The leaves are handsome, dark green, 12 in. (30 cm) long, and 6 in. (15 cm) broad at the base, tapered, and supported by a 12-in. (30-cm) petiole (Bailey and Bailey, 1976).

CULTIVARS

No cultivars are available. Bailey and Bailey (1976) list the variety Moorei Bak., which has smaller leaves and flowers and a yellow stripe on the toothed stamen cup.

PROPAGATION

Propagation is by bulblet offsets or seed. Plants can be divided after flowering (Bailey and Bailey, 1976). *In vitro* propagation is possible (Pierick et al., 1983).

FLOWERING CONTROL AND DORMANCY

Plants are evergreen and do not go dormant. Flowering is controlled by the slight modulation of temperature change as perceived by the bulb (Adams and Urdahl, 1973; Rees, 1985; van Bragt et al., 1986). For floral induction the medium surrounding the bulbs must be at 85°F (29°C) for 12 days or 67°F (19°C) for 21 days. The plant remains vegetative at 64°F (18°C). After the inductive temperature treatment, plants must be returned to 64°F (18°C) for floral initiation and development. van Bragt et al. (1986) reported that 4 weeks at 80°F (27°C) for flower induction followed by 70°F (21°C) for forcing was best.

Carbohydrate reserves influence the number of bulbs flowering, because bulbs that have not flowered for many months will be more likely to flower compared with recently forced bulbs. Do not use drought stress as a treatment to induce flowering (van Bragt et al., 1986). Frequent division should be avoided (Post, 1952).

TEMPERATURE

As described earlier, a brief period of high temperatures is required for flower induction, followed by a forcing temperature of 64 to 70°F (18 to 21°C) for floral initiation and development.

LIGHT

Shade is required because injury can occur at light intensities above 5000 fc (1000 μmol · m^{-2} · s^{-1}).

WATER

Plants should be kept moist. Do not allow plants to dry; this is not effective or needed to induce flowering (van Bragt et al., 1986).

CARBON DIOXIDE

No data available.

NUTRITION

No information is published. A rate of 200 ppm nitrogen every irrigation has been used by H.F. Wilkins (unpublished).

MEDIA

Any well-drained medium can be used. Post (1952) stated the bulbs grow well in very moist, highly organic soil. van Bragt and Sprenkels (1983) grew their research plants in a mixture of cow manure and clay (1:1 by volume), whereas Bailey and Bailey (1976) stated that a course fibrous soil should be used. Lindstrom (1971) used a more modern media with 1:1:1 coarse peat moss:soil:perlite (by volume).

HEIGHT CONTROL

None required.

SPACING

Plants can be grown in ground or raised beds or in large pots. van Bragt and Sprenkels (1983) grew 40 bulbs per 15- × 19- × 6-in. (37- × 47- × 15-cm) crates. H.F. Wilkins (unpublished) grew bulbs in 6-in. (15-cm) pots (1 bulb/pot) or in beds with a spacing of 12 × 12 in. (30 × 30 cm). Keep root disturbance to a minimum when plants are divided. Plants can remain for up to 3 or more years if planted on 12- or 17-in. (30- or 43-cm) centers in ground beds.

PINCHING AND DISBUDDING

None required.

SUPPORT

None required.

SCHEDULE AND TIMING

Days to flower after the end of the heat treatment are longer in the fall and winter than in the spring and summer. Flowering can be scheduled. Once bulbs were established, 85% of the plants flowered within 94 to 99 days after the end of a 4-week 81°F (27°C) soil treatment (van Bragt and Sprenkels, 1983). The larger the bulb, the greater the flowering percentage. The minimum bulb size that flowered was 1.1 in. (29 mm) with 29% flowering; no bulbs 1 in. (26 mm) or smaller flowered. However, 76 and 90% of the largest bulbs, 1.25 and 1.5 in. (32 and 35 mm) in diameter, respectively, flowered.

Adams and Urdahl (1973) reported that 100% of plants flowered 105 to 110 days after the 3- to 4-week 80 to 83°F (27 to 28°C) heat treatment. Eight weeks of production at 70°F (21°C) were required before plants could be reprogrammed to flower with another 80 to 83°F (27 to 28°C) heat treatment. Flowering will occur 84 days after the end of the heat treatment when forced at 65°F (18°C).

INSECTS

Spider mites are a major concern. Thrips in the flowers may also be a problem.

DISEASES

Gray mold (*Botrytis cinerea*) and leaf scorch (*Stagonospora curtsii*) diseases can cause problems (Horst, 1990). Viruses that cause lesions and yellow mosaic symptoms have also been reported (Jayasinghe and Dijkstra, 1979).

PHYSIOLOGICAL DISORDERS

None reported.

POSTHARVEST

Flowers are harvested just prior to opening or as soon as they open. They are highly sensitive to chilling injury and should be stored at 45 to 59°F (7 to 15°C) (Nowak and Rudnicki, 1990). The individual flowers are stored dry in airtight boxes and misted with water. The longevity is 7 to 10 days. Flowers are slightly sensitive to ethylene (L. Høyer, personal communication).

KEY POINTS

- Amazon lily is used as a potted flowering plant or as a cut flower for fragrant corsages.
- Plants are typically propagated by division of the bulbs in a clump.
- Flower induction occurs at 67 to 85°F (19 to 29°C).
- Plants remain vegetative at 64°F (18°C).
- Plants are injured by light intensities above 5000 fc (1000 μmol $\cdot$ m^{-2} $\cdot$ s^{-1}).
- Plants should not be allowed to dry.
- Spider mites are a major problem.

BIBLIOGRAPHY

Adams, D.G., and W.A. Urdahl. 1973. Temperature controlled floral induction in Amazon lily, *Eucharis grandiflora* Planch. *Journal of the American Society for Horticultural Science* 98:29–30.

Bailey, L.H., and E.Z. Bailey. 1976. *Eucharis*, p. 456 in *Hortus Third: A Concise Dictionary of Plants Cultivated in the United States and Canada*. Macmillan, New York.

Horst, R.K. 1990. Eucharis, p. 637 in *Westcott's Plant Disease Handbook*, 5th ed. Van Nostrand Reinhold, New York.

Huxley, A., M. Griffiths, and M. Levy. 1992. *Eucharis*, pp. 235–236 in *The New Royal Horticultural Society Dictionary of Gardening*, vol. 2. Stockton Press, New York.

Jayasinghe, U., and J. Dijkstra. 1979. Hippeastrum mosiac virus and another filamentous virus in *Eucharis grandiflora*. *Netherlands Journal of Plant Pathology* 85:47–65.

Lindstrom R.S. 1971. Temperature and moisture influence on flowering of *Eucharis grandiflora*. *Acta Horticulturae* 23:106–109.

Meerow, A.W., 1987. Biosystematics of tetraploid *Eucharis* (Amaryllidaceae). *Annuals of the Missouri Botanical Garden* 74:291–309.

Meerow, A.W., and B. Dehgan. 1984. Re-establishment and lectotypification of *Eucharis amazonica* Linden ex Planchon (Amaryllidaceae). *Taxon* 33: 416–422.

Nowak, J., and R.M. Rudnicki. 1990. *Postharvest Handling and Storage of Cut Flowers, Florist Greens, and Potted Plants*. Timber Press, Portland, Oregon.

Pierick, R.I.M., P.A. Sprenkels, and J. van Bragt. 1983. Rapid vegetative propagation of *Eucharis grandiflora in vitro*. *Acta Horticulturae* 147: 179–186.

Post, K. 1952. *Eucharis grandiflora* (Amazon Lily), p. 494 in *Florist Crop Production and Marketing*. Orange Judd Publishing, New York.

Rees, A.R. 1985. *Eucharis grandiflora*, pp. 302–303 in *Handbook of Flowering*, vol. 1, A.H. Halevy, editor. CRC Press, Boca Raton, Florida.

van Bragt, J., and P.A. Sprenkels. 1983. Year-round production of *Eucharis* flowers. *Acta Horticulturae* 147:173–178.

van Bragt, J., W. Luiten, P.A. Sprenkels, and C.J. Keijzer. 1986. Flower formation in *Eucharis amazonica* Linden ex Planchon. *Acta Horticulturae* 177: 157–164.

Euphorbia

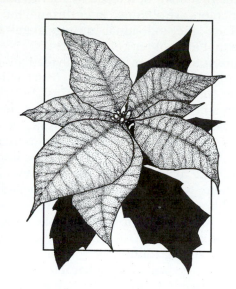

Poinsettias are grown for their large and striking bract clusters, the center of which contains the small true flowers, known as *cyathia*. The cyathia are round to elongate, produce small red stamens, and are subtended by nectaries. Foliage is medium to dark green in color and ranges in shape from entire to lobed, even on the same plant.

FIGURE II-1 EUPHORBIA *Euphorbia* tub.

INTRODUCTION

Common names: poinsettia, Christmas flower, Christmas star, painted leaf, and Mexican flameleaf.

Scientific name: *Euphorbia pulcherrima* Willd. ex Klotzsch (Huxley et al., 1992).

Family and related taxa: Euphorbiaceae Juss. This family is large and diverse with plant forms ranging from leafy annuals to cactus-like succulents to trees. Other commonly grown members of the family include crown of thorns (*E. milii* Desmoul), snow-on-the-mountain (*E. marginata* Pursh), and various garden ornamentals. Crown of thorns is grown as a potted flowering plant. The scarlet plume (*E. fulgens* Karw. ex Klotzsch) is grown as a cut flower and a potted flowering plant (Henrard, 1978, 1981; Runger, 1985; Zhang and Stoltz, 1989a, b). Hybrids between *E. pulcherrima* and *E. cornastra* (Dressler) A. Radcliffe-Smith have been made that show potential as potted flowering plants (Bernuetz, 2001).

Origin: This species originated in southern Mexico and northern Guatemala.

Uses and current status: This species is the number one potted flowering crop in the United States and is sold for the Christmas holiday (Figs. II-1, II-2, II-3 Euphorbia). In North America, the poinsettia sales season extends from early November to Christmas. Poinsettias are a major crop in Europe and Australia and a relatively minor crop in the rest of the world. Poinsettias are also grown as a hanging basket and as a cut flower (Fig. II-4 Euphorbia). Poinsettias are also common as a landscape shrub in Zone 11.

FIGURE II-2 EUPHORBIA *Euphorbia* tree-form.

FIGURE II-3 EUPHORBIA *Euphorbia* hanging basket.

FIGURE II-4 EUPHORBIA *Euphorbia* 'Renaissance Red' cut flower arrangement with *Matthiola*.

CULTIVARS

Red is the most important color (Behe et al., 1997). Other colors and color combinations include pink, white, pink with white margins ("marble"), pink with red flecks, red with pink flecks ("jingle bells"), white with red flecks, purple, and yellow. Several varieties are available with foliage variegated with white or cream. Other varieties have bracts that are curled under or otherwise contorted, providing an unusual look to the poinsettia.

Poinsettia cultivars are often available as a series or family, with each series including red, pink, white, and one or more bicolors such as the marble and jingle bell patterns. Red is usually the first color developed in a series and the other colors are obtained later through mutation. Many other individual cultivars are also available that are not part of a series.

Poinsettia cultivars can be divided into two groups, free-branching and restricted-branching cultivars (Dole and Wilkins, 1991a, 1994). Free-branching cultivars produce numerous axillary shoots when pinched and account for the vast majority of poinsettia cultivars and production. Free-branching plants produce axillary shoots at almost every node when young plants are pinched. Restricted-branching cultivars, however, produce only two to four axillary shoots when pinched, because the axillary shoots quickly reestablish apical dominance over lower shoots. The free-branching characteristic is graft transmissible from free-branching cultivars to restricted-branching cultivars (Dole and Wilkins, 1992, 1994; Dole et al., 1993; Ruiz-Sifre et al., 1997). The cause of the free-branching characteristic has been identified as a phytoplasma, known as poinsettia branch inducing phytoplasma (PoiBI) (Lee et al., 1997). PoiBI increases endogenous cytokinin and decreases endogenous auxin levels after the initial infection (Bernuetz, 2001). In the process of developing new cultivars, grafting is used to transmit PoiBI to seedlings since the phytoplasma is not seed transmissible and seedlings are restricted branching (Dole and Wilkins, 1991a).

Besides bract color and branching, cultivars also vary in height, foliage color (medium versus dark green), time to flowering from start of SD (response group), postharvest life, leaf retention, and flowering date. Many new cultivars tend to be naturally short and may not require growth regulator applications. Some cultivars are quite compact and best suited to 4- to 5-in. (10- to 13-cm) pots. Due to the economic importance of poinsettias, yearly cultivar trials are conducted in many locations. Inquire with your supplier regarding the location of the nearest testing site (Fig. II-5 Euphorbia). Although poinsettias have been produced as field-grown cut flowers since the early 1900s, cut flower product has been minimal in the last 30 years. New breeding efforts with the 'Winter Rose' potted poinsettia have resulted in several colors of cut flower varieties in the 'Renaissance' series. The large, striking flowers are carried on long, strong stems, making them easy to use by the

FIGURE II-5 EUPHORBIA Plants were propagated from approach-grafted, free-branching (BD) and restricted-branching (C-1), *Euphorbia* plants. Note that the C-1/BD (scion/stock) plant is now free branching, while the control C-1/C-1 plant is still restricted branching.

floral industry and the general public (Dole and Aufill, 2000).

PROPAGATION

Commercial propagation is by terminal stem cuttings. Seed is used only in the development of new cultivars; tissue culture has been well documented but is used primarily for research (Preil, 1994; Preil and Beck, 1991). Although many growers produce their own cuttings from stock plants, some growers purchase unrooted cuttings or cuttings rooted in foam blocks from commercial propagators. Growers should annually reevaluate the success and economics of their poinsettia propagation programs.

Rooted cuttings for stock plants can arrive any time from late winter through early summer depending on the individual stock plant program. Factors that determine the arrival date of cuttings include availability of space (e.g., after Easter, Mother's Day, or spring bedding plant sales), number of cuttings desired per stock plant, production location, and dates by which cuttings are needed. Stock plants are sometimes flowered and sold; if large plants are desired, cuttings should arrive in March to April, and if small plants are desired, cuttings can arrive as late as early June. In areas of high light and warm temperatures, such as the southern United States, cuttings can arrive later than in the cooler, lower light areas and still have the same amount of growth. If cuttings arrive before May 5, be sure to provide LD with incandescent lights to prevent premature flower initiation (see Light, page 497).

Growers need to schedule stock plants as any other crop. First, determine the dates by which cuttings are needed. Count back 5 to 7 weeks, depending on the cultivar, to determine the date of the last pinch or cutting harvest. The number of weeks between the last pinch and cutting harvest will vary with the cultivar; most require 6 weeks (Anonymous, 1994). If immature cuttings are harvested, rooting will be slow and uneven. If large stock plants are grown, the first one to two flushes can be timed for major propagations; subsequent cutting production will not be in flushes. Many growers harvest cuttings weekly. Cuttings can be stored at 45 to 50°F (7 to 10°C) for up to 24 hr if kept moist (Gapinski and Yelanich, 1998).

For maximum cutting production, allow the original rooted cutting to develop 7 to 12 nodes before the first pinch (Grueber, 1985). Pinching below 7 nodes forces axillary shoots to develop from axillary buds that originally developed under the stress of propagation and thus are slow to develop. Leaving more than 12 nodes on the original plant results in too much axillary shoot growth, competition between the shoots, and weak cuttings. Generally 9 to 11 nodes should remain on the main stem for optimum cutting production.

If the plants are mature enough, the first pinch can be used as a cutting for another crop of stock plants. Note, however, that such cuttings may form premature flower buds (see Physiological Disorders, page 507). If stock plants are immature, use a soft pinch with young leaf removal (see Pinching and Disbudding, page 501).

After the first pinch, axillary shoots should be pinched or harvested so that two nodes remain on the axillary shoots. If only one node remains, the number of cuttings harvested will not increase in later harvests. If three or more shoots remain, an excessive number of low-quality shoots or cuttings (small stem diameters) will develop, and the timing of successive flushes of cuttings will be less predictable. If weekly harvests are conducted, cutting harvesters should only be concerned about leaving at least two nodes on the remaining shoot. Leaving more than two nodes is not a concern because only the large mature cuttings are harvested and weak cuttings continue to develop until they are large enough to be harvested. However, avoid harvesting older cuttings with more than eight leaves because these may split (see Physiological Disorders section, page 507) (Gapinski and Yelanich, 1998).

Stock plants can also be grown as tree or standard plants. The axillary shoots, which have to be removed to expose the "trunk," are used as propagation material. This system is less efficient for propagation but may result in a more valuable stock plant for retail purposes if allowed to flower.

Regardless of the system for producing stock plants, growers must produce a quality plant. Stock plants that are nutritionally deficient, insect infested, or otherwise improperly managed will produce low-quality cuttings. Such cuttings will be slow to root, uneven in development, and produce a poor-quality final crop. Stock plants should be given sufficient space to properly develop. Stock plants started in March, April, May, or June can be given a final spacing of 18 × 18 in. (45 × 45 cm), 15 × 15 in. (38 × 38 cm), 12 × 12 in. (30 × 30 cm), or 8 × 8 in. (20 × 20 cm), respectively (Ecke et al., 1990). Plants pinched once will produce 8 to 9 cuttings/plant over a 3-week period. Plants pinched twice should produce 15 to 20 cuttings/plant over a 4- to 5-week period. Closely spaced stock plants will not produce the expected number of cuttings per plant; once a foliar canopy forms, only a specific number of cuttings will be produced per square foot per week.

Optimum production temperatures for stock plants are as follows: media 65 to 70°F (18 to 21°C), night air 68 to 72°F (20 to 22°C), and day air 75 to 80°F (24 to 27°C) (Williams, 1993). The temperature for maximum leaf unfolding rate (rate of growth) of poinsettia axillary shoots after the pinch is approximately 79°F (26°C) with day and night temperatures equally important (Berghage et al., 1990). Temperatures should not go above 86°F (30°C) or cutting diameter will become thin and branching may be reduced (Faust and Heins, 1996). Reduced light levels and increased air circulation will allow poinsettia stock plants to tolerate warm temperatures. If needed, night temperatures can be reduced to 64°F (18°C); however, cooler temperatures may increase splitting (see Physiological Disorders, page 507) and leaf mottling and reduce cutting production (Williams, 1993).

Success with poinsettia propagation depends on several factors, which are discussed in the following paragraphs.

SANITATION

Poinsettias are susceptible to several diseases during propagation. Clean and sterilize propagation benches, utensils, containers, and hands before starting to propagate cuttings. Maintain sanitary conditions throughout propagation. If diseased cuttings are found, promptly remove them to avoid pathogen spread to healthy cuttings.

TEMPERATURE

A 70 to 72°F (21 to 22°C) minimum medium temperature must be maintained for rapid rooting with the optimum temperature being 75 to 77°F (24 to 25°C). A temperature that is too low will delay rooting and decrease crop uniformity. Inadequate medium temperature is a common problem in propagation. Even in warm climates, medium temperature must be monitored because the evaporation of mist during propagation reduces media temperatures. Bottom heating is commonly used and will speed rooting if medium temperature is less than 75°F (24°C).

LIGHT

Light levels should be less than 2000 fc (400 μmol · m^{-2} · s^{-1}) to prevent burning and excessive wilting. However, too much shade resulting in less than 1000 fc (200 μmol · m^{-2} · s^{-1}) will slow rooting and increase stem elongation. Increase the light intensity as cuttings root.

MEDIA

Blocks of foam or rockwool are commonly used in commercial cutting propagation. Cuttings can also be directly propagated into the final pot. In such a case, the media should be well drained with a pH of 5.6 to 6.2. Avoid compacting the media during propagation or watering with a hose because reduced oxygen in the media will delay rooting and increase the potential for diseases.

CUTTINGS

Cuttings should be thick [minimum stem diameter of 0.25 in. (0.6 cm)], vigorous, and 1.5 to 3 in. (4 to 7.5 cm) long early in the season. Cuttings are measured from the base of the cutting to the tip of the apex, not to the ends of the leaves. Regardless of length, cuttings should be uniform in size and maturity to provide a uniform finished crop. Cuttings should also have short internodes; a growth retardant can be applied to the stock plants (see Height Control, page 499) to reduce internode elongation and prevent stretched cuttings later in production. Remove only enough leaves to allow easy insertion of the cuttings into the medium; be sure that at least one fully mature leaf remains on the cutting. European growers often use shorter cuttings than North American growers.

ROOTING HORMONES

A rooting hormone is not required for rooting, but using one will speed rooting and increase uniformity. Also, the use of hormones may induce rooting higher up on the stem, providing more support than with non-hormone-treated cuttings (Gapinski and Yelanich, 1998). The hormone can be applied as a powder (0.1% indole-3-butyric acid, IBA) or as a liquid (2500 ppm IBA) using 50% ethanol or isopropyl alcohol and 50% water. Dusting the ends of the cuttings is preferable to dipping the ends in powder or liquid because of the potential for disease spread. However, liquid formulations are more effective (Gapinski and Yelanich, 1998). Liquid IBA solutions should not be stored for more than 2 to 3 weeks when refrigerated at 40°F (4°C) (D. Hartley, personal communication).

TENTING AND MISTING

Cutting turgidity can be maintained with either propagation tents or a mist or fog system. High-humidity tents are generally preferable to misting systems due to reduced leaching of nutrients from the leaves, free moisture on the foliage, and disease incidence. Tenting also eliminates the need for a mist or fog system, which can make propagation directly into the final container more feasible. The major drawbacks of tent propagation are heat buildup and

disposal of the plastic. Tenting may not be feasible in areas with high light intensity or temperatures due to heat buildup under the tent. White plastic is preferred over clear plastic in the summer. High-humidity tents may be needed if water quality is poor, especially if the water EC is over $1.0 \text{ dS} \cdot \text{m}^{-1}$. See Chapter 1, Propagation, for details on constructing propagation tents.

When misting, be sure to not overmist, which can reduce oxygen around the base of the cutting, delay rooting, reduce plant quality, leach nutrients from the foliage, and increase disease. Leaves of overmisted cuttings may appear chlorotic with necrotic edges. Misting may be needed at night during the first few days of propagation if the air is warm and dry. The misting frequency can be reduced during cool, cloudy conditions and when cuttings begin to root, which usually occurs 10 to 14 days after propagation. Rooting is accomplished by 21 days. The mist may be turned off completely if day temperatures can be controlled. Similarly, tents are slowly opened and aeration increased to harden the cuttings. Yellowing from nutrient loss can be prevented by applying 50 to 100 ppm nitrogen and potassium through the mist system. Fertilizer may not be needed if cuttings are not overmisted and were propagated from well-fertilized stock plants.

SPACING

Do not space cuttings too close because this will encourage elongation and increase the potential for disease spread. After propagating a bench of cuttings, be sure that leaves from one cutting are not shading the shoot tip of an adjacent cutting, which will delay rooting.

POSTROOTING CARE

For cuttings propagated in foam or rockwool blocks, fertilizer applications at 100 to 150 ppm N from ammonium nitrate, calcium nitrate, and potassium nitrate can start 10 days after propagation and weekly applications can be made until planting. Growth retardants can be applied to cuttings during propagation to reduce stretching if not previously applied to stock plants. Typically Cycocel (chlormequat) sprays are used at 2000 ppm or a tank mixture of B-Nine (daminozide) at 1250 ppm and Cycocel at 1500 ppm are used together. Growth retardants may not be needed with short cultivars or if an application has been previously made to the stock plants prior to propagation.

Close spacing, high temperatures, low light, and excessive misting will increase the need for growth retardants during propagation. Cuttings should be ready for planting in 4 to 5 weeks. Do not allow propagation blocks to dry out.

DIRECT STICKING

Cuttings can be directly propagated into the final pot, which is known as "direct sticking." This propagation method is becoming increasingly popular because it saves labor, reduces production costs, decreases production time by approximately 1 week, and reduces the potential for foliar disease spread due to the greater amount of space around each cutting. Direct sticking, however, requires four to eight times more propagation space than do foam or rockwool blocks. Media selection is critical in that it must allow sufficient air to prevent root rots, or slow rooting due to waterlogged medium, but still retain enough water later in production to prevent excessive wilting and irrigation.

FLOWERING CONTROL AND DORMANCY

Poinsettias are SD plants that initiate flowers when the night lasts at least 11.75 hr. Flower initiation in most parts of North America occurs naturally around September 25, but can vary from late September to very early October. Some cultivars initiate flowers early in September and may have a shorter critical night length than most other cultivars. Flower development, however, requires a longer night length than that required for initiation, which is usually supplied by naturally lengthening nights in the fall. Night temperatures greater than 70°F (21°C) may delay flower initiation (Grueber, 1985) (Fig. II-6 Euphorbia).

Weeks to flowering from the start of SD vary from 6.5 to 10 (response group) depending on the cultivar. A crop will require a black cloth SD treatment, usually 14-hr nights, to induce flowering earlier than that which occurs under natural photoperiods. The primary cyathium forms after only 4 to 8 SD and is visible under a microscope within 15 days (Berghage et al., 1987). However, SD should be provided until pollen is present on the cyathia (anthesis) to ensure proper bract development. If plants receive LD after flower initiation has occurred but before anthesis, immature bracts will become green and leaflike. Newer cultivars tend to show bract color early and care should be taken to not ship too early or bracts will not develop properly. Shortly after flower initiation, there are usually six to seven young leaves and three primary bracts in the shoot apex. One or more of the young leaves may also develop partial bract coloration in addition to green chlorophyll and are known as *transitional bracts*. From the axils of the primary fully colored bracts, secondary inflorescences (cyathia and bracts) form. Reducing the number of days between pinching and the start of SD can reduce the number of young leaves in the axillary shoot apices and produce a shorter plant with fewer leaves (see Height Control, page 499, and Pinching and Disbudding, page 501).

TEMPERATURE

The optimum media temperature during propagation is 75 to 77°F (24 to 25°C). After propagation, the night temperature used for most poinsettia cultivars is 65 to 68°F (18 to 20°C). Night temperatures higher than 70°F (21°C) may delay flower initiation and temperatures higher than 75°F (24°C) may delay flower development. However, high light intensity and day length may interact with night temperature

FIGURE II-6 EUPHORBIA Effect of temperature and SD or natural days on flowering of *Euphorbia* 'Gutbier V-14 Glory.' Note delayed development of plants grown at 75°F (24°C).

because growers in warm climates are able to produce high-quality plants with no delay in flowering. Note that cultivar selection for warm climates is important because some cultivars branch poorly during high temperatures (Faust and Heins, 1996). Temperatures cooler than 60°F (16°C) will result in slow plant development and small bracts. Temperatures below 55°F (10°C) increase the potential for root rot disease (Berghage et al., 1987).

Temperature and light intensity are related and photothermal ratio, light energy to thermal energy, expresses this relationship as moles of light per degree-day (Liu and Heins, 2002). A high light to low temperature ratio enhances stem strength and increases bract area.

Because DIF is often used for height control, day temperatures are determined by the desired DIF (see Height Control, page 499) (Berghage and Heins, 1991). Generally, a zero DIF is used. Early morning temperature dips (DROP) for height control are also effective on poinsettias (Cockshull et al., 1995; Moe et al., 1995). The temperature can be reduced, usually during the last 1 to 2 weeks of production, to 55 to 60°F (13 to 16°C) to enhance bract color.

LIGHT

High light is necessary for best growth. For both stock plants and the Christmas crop, 3500 to 4500 fc (700 to 900 $\mu mol \cdot m^{-2} \cdot s^{-1}$) is used for cultivars with dark foliage and 5000 to 6000 fc (1000 to 1200 $\mu mol \cdot m^{-2} \cdot s^{-1}$) is used for other cultivars if greenhouse temperatures can be maintained below 90°F (32°C) (Williams, 1993). For the Christmas crop no shading is required in most areas except during propagation and immediately after planting. In warm, high-light areas shading for 1 to 2 weeks after planting rooted cuttings will result in faster plant establishment. Only a slight reduction of light, 10 to 30%, is required and shade should be removed as soon as root growth into the medium is noted. Light levels can be reduced to 2000 ft (400 $\mu mol \cdot m^{-2} \cdot s^{-1}$) after bracts are mature to reduce bract fading and sunburning.

Long days will need to be provided before May 5 for stock plants or after September 15 for late season Christmas crop plants are marketed after December 10. A minimum of 10 fc (2 $\mu mol \cdot m^{-2} \cdot s^{-1}$) measured at plant height will be needed to prevent flower initiation. For early Christmas crops to be marketed prior to Thanksgiving, plants may need to be given SD before September 25.

WATER

Water stress is a concern during poinsettia production. Plants should not be allowed to wilt between waterings; wilting will induce lower leaf drop. Height control through water restriction is not effective and decreases plant quality (Schuch et al., 1995). However, avoid overwatering to prevent root rots, especially with newly planted cuttings. Poinsettias are adaptable to most irrigation systems, which should be used to reduce labor costs because poinsettias have to be frequently irrigated (Dole et al., 1994). Overhead sprinkler irrigation late in the crop cycle can be difficult due to the large canopy, which reduces the amount of water reaching the medium. If water quality is poor and the EC is high, regular leachings will be needed to prevent damage from high medium-soluble salt levels. Bract discoloration may also occur from residue if water quality is poor. Overwatering or using a fertilizer rate that is too high, especially with subirrigated poinsettias, can lead to soft, lush plants that are subject to stem breakage and are difficult to ship. Overhead irrigating poinsettias that had been previously subirrigated increased the EC of the media at the bottom of the pot but had little effect on the plants (van Iersel, 2000).

CARBON DIOXIDE

Carbon dioxide injection has not been shown to be useful in poinsettia production. Any increase in quality is slight and probably not economical (D. Hartley, personal communication).

NUTRITION

Poinsettias have a relatively high nutrient requirement; general recommendations range from 225 to 300 ppm N for overhead-irrigated plants and 100 to 225 ppm N for subirrigated plants (Berghage et al., 1987; Dole et al., 1994; Ecke et al., 1990; Yelanich and Biernbaum, 1990). Dark leaf cultivars should generally be grown with a fertilizer rate that is 25% less than the rate used for light green leaf cultivars. Superphosphate, dolomitic limestone, and micronutrients can be incorporated into the medium prior to planting. Routine medium and tissue tests should be taken (Table II-1 Euphorbia). See Chapter 6, Nutrition, for effect of leaf sampling position on foliar nutrient levels (Dole and Wilkins, 1991b).

Controlled-release fertilizers (CRF) are effective on poinsettias and best combined with

TABLE II-I EUPHORBIA

Critical, normal, and toxic levels of nutrients in *Euphorbia* leaf tissue consisting of the most recently mature leaves and petioles (Ecke et al., 1990).

Nutrient	Critical Level	Normal Levels	Toxic Levels
		%	
Nitrogen	3.5	4.0–6.0	7.3
Phosphorus	0.15	0.3–0.6	0.9
Potassium	1.0	1.5–3.5	4.0
Calcium	0.5	1.0–1.75	—
Magnesium	0.2	0.3–1.0	—
Sulfur	0.05	0.1–0.3	—
Sodium	—	0–0.4	0.5
Chloride	—	0–1.5	3.0
		ppm	
Iron	50	100–300	—
Manganese	40	60–300	650
Zinc	20	25–60	—
Copper	1	2–10	—
Boron	15	25–75	100
Molybdenum	0.5	1–5	—
Fluoride	—	0–4	5
Lithium	—	0–15	20

constant liquid fertilization. A CRF can supply 50 to 75% of the nutrition, and constant liquid fertilization can supply the remainder. The constant liquid fertilization can be replaced with one to several fertilizer drenches, if needed (Smith and Dole, 1993). If plants are propagated directly into the final pots, the CRF will need to be applied after propagation because the warm environment may lead to excessive release of the fertilizer.

Traditionally, growers have assumed that poinsettia nutritional needs are greatest soon after planting of a rooted cutting and during the vegetative growth phase and then decline later in the crop cycle. Fertilizer rates of up to 400 ppm N have been applied if the weather is cool and cloudy immediately after cuttings are planted because irrigation frequency is reduced. Other work, however, indicates that plant nutrient uptake is lowest at potting and highest at flowering (Whipker and Hammer, 1997). Matching nutrient applications to plant nutrient uptake can decrease the total amount of N applied and reduce N lost through leaching without reducing quality (Rose et al., 1994; Whipker and Hammer, 1997). If a CRF is used, a drench of 300 ppm N from ammonium nitrate applied within 1 week of planting can be used to improve plant quality (Smith and Dole, 1993).

NITROGEN

Poinsettias grow best with a combination of both ammonium and nitrate forms of nitrogen (Ku and Hershey, 1997). During the summer and in warm climates, up to 60% of the nitrogen can be supplied with ammonium or urea-based fertilizers. Ammonium nitrogen tends to encourage dark green, lush growth. However, under cool conditions conversion of ammonium into nitrate slows and ammonium can accumulate and cause damage. Ammonium toxicity is characterized by yellow chlorotic bands and downward curling of young leaves, which are dull green. Other symptoms include poor root growth, leaf drop, and stunting. In cool climates, ammonium should not comprise more than 30% of the nitrogen. Regardless of the climate, ammonium should be eliminated 3 to 4 weeks before marketing. Nitrogen deficiency symptoms include yellowing of the foliage starting with the older leaves.

PHOSPHORUS

Phosphorus deficiency causes stunting and also yellowing and necrosis of the older leaves. Phosphorus deficiency should be prevented by applying any complete fertilizer.

POTASSIUM

Potassium deficiency results in lower leaf yellowing and necrosis. Poinsettias are well adapted to extracting K from the medium and deficiencies are rare. If K is deficient, N is also likely to be deficient and the N symptoms may mask K deficiency symptoms.

CALCIUM

Calcium is involved in stem strength and leaf and bract necrosis (Bierman et al., 1990; Hartley, 1992; Lawton et al., 1989; Woltz and Harbaugh, 1986). Although obvious symptoms of calcium deficiency are rare, low calcium levels in the plant are manifested in weak stems and increased potential for bract and leaf necrosis (see Physiological Disorders, page 507). In addition to maintaining adequate calcium levels in the medium and keeping medium pH 5.5 or higher, calcium can be applied through foliar sprays—mix a 200- to 400-ppm solution from calcium chloride and add a spreader sticker. The sprays can be applied weekly starting with bract coloring and continuing until anthesis (pollen shed). Calcium nitrate as a foliar spray is more commonly used on stock plants than flowering plants because the chance for phytotoxicity on bracts is greater than with calcium chloride.

MAGNESIUM

Poinsettias have a high requirement for magnesium. The symptoms for magnesium deficiency include yellow mottling of recently mature leaves that starts at the margin and between veins. In more extreme cases the leaves become highly chlorotic and hardened in appearance. Many growers provide Mg continuously in their constant liquid fertilization at the rate of 40 to 50 ppm; less may be needed depending on the amount of Mg in the water supply.

BORON

Poinsettias are sensitive to both boron deficiencies and boron toxicities. The deficiency symptoms include cessation of terminal growth and leaf and stem distortions. Boron toxicity causes yellowing or necrosis of the foliar margin of older leaves.

MOLYBDENUM

Poinsettias have an usually high requirement for molybdenum and it is often supplied in the constant liquid fertilization program at 0.1 ppm. Deficiency symptoms include marginal chlorosis, upward rolling, and edge burn of recently mature leaves.

SOLUBLE SALTS

Although poinsettias are more tolerant of high media EC than most species, problems can occur. Symptoms include yellowing, abscission and marginal necrosis of lower leaves, stunting, and increased susceptibility to root and stem diseases. In severe cases the lower foliage may show interveinal chlorosis. Lower fertilizer rates and leaching with unamended water will prevent the problem. In general, as root medium EC increases above $3.0 \text{ dS} \cdot \text{m}^{-1}$ (saturated medium extract), plant height, fresh and dry weight, leaf, and bract areas decrease, although plant quality may be visually unaffected (Yelanich and Biernbaum, 1990). Optimum root medium EC should be 2.8 to $4.1 \text{ dS} \cdot \text{m}^{-1}$ using pour-through, 2.0 to $3.5 \text{ dS} \cdot \text{m}^{-1}$ using saturated medium extract, or 0.75 to $1.5 \text{ dS} \cdot \text{m}^{-1}$ using 1:2 medium to water. Dark leaf cultivars are more sensitive to high medium EC than other cultivars and should be grown with a medium EC at the low end of the optimum range. For these cultivars root medium EC should be less than $2.7 \text{ dS} \cdot \text{m}^{-1}$ using pour-through, $3.0 \text{ dS} \cdot \text{m}^{-1}$ using saturated medium extract, or $1.0 \text{ dS} \cdot \text{m}^{-1}$ using 1:2 medium:water from mid-October until flowering.

MEDIA

As with most crops the growing medium must be well drained yet retain water to prevent excessive irrigation or postharvest wilting. Poinsettia prefer approximately 20% free porosity and 50% moisture holding pores (D. Hartley, personal communication). The pH should be 5.8 to 6.3. Considering the value of poinsettias for most growers, it is wise to test several media to determine which is best suited for a specific operation.

HEIGHT CONTROL

Height control options are numerous for poinsettias, including cultural alterations, DIF, and chemicals. High light intensity, clean greenhouse coverings, and maximum plant spacing will prevent excessive stretching. Proper timing of propagation and pinches is also crucial. Increasing the number of days from pinching to the start of SD will increase vegetative growth and node numbers. Tall cultivars may need to be propagated and pinched later in the season than short cultivars.

DIF is quite effective on poinsettias for height control (Berghage and Heins, 1991). The difference between day and night temperatures determines shoot elongation. Plants subjected to the same level of DIF will have similar plant height at flower regardless of the average daily temperature, when grown at temperatures between 60 and 70°F (16 and 21°C). Therefore, temperatures can be altered to stimulate or retard elongation on a daily basis. Graphical tracking can be used to monitor plant height and determine the specific DIF needed (see Chapter 8, Plant Growth Regulation). Note that increasing DIF above zero will have a greater effect on height than a similar reduction below zero DIF. Lowering the temperature in the morning (negative DIF) for 2 to 6 hr (the longer the better) starting at sunrise (DROP) is also effective at reducing height and more practical than maintaining a low DIF all day (Cockshull et al., 1995; Moe et al., 1995). When controlling height with DIF, remember that average daily temperature controls plant development; day/night temperature combinations that reduce average daily temperature will slow plant development.

Several growth retardants are effective on poinsettias including Cycocel, B-Nine, A-Rest (ancymidol), Bonzi (paclobutrazol), Sumagic (uniconazole), and Topflor (flurprimidol). Growth retardants are most commonly applied as sprays early in the season and as drenches late in the season.

Cycocel is the most frequently used growth retardant and is typically used at the rate of 1000 to 1500 ppm, although up to 3000 ppm can be used. Cycocel can cause foliar yellowing and should not be used after October 15 in the northern half of the United States (or after October 21 if temperatures are unusually warm), or after November 1 in the Deep South because of the potential for undesirable reduction in bract size (Barrett, 1996) (Table II-2 Euphorbia). Although mild yellowing of the foliage often turns back to green, permanent symptoms of phytotoxicity can occur (see Physiological Disorders, page 507). Apply early or late in the day to reduce or avoid phytotoxicity; inclusion of a mild surfactant may also help (Hammer and Barrett, 2001). If phytotoxicity is a problem, multiple applications of lower Cycocel rates can be used. Lower Cycocel concentrations do not cause less stem elongation initially but plants resume elongating more quickly; subsequent applications are then used (Fisher et al., 1996b).

B-Nine is not typically used alone but can be applied at 2000 to 3000 ppm. B-Nine is often tank mixed with Cycocel. Typical rates are 750 to 2500 ppm of B-Nine and 1000 to 1500 ppm of Cycocel (Barrett, 1996). Again, multiple applications of lower rates can be used to prevent phytotoxicity. In warm climates 1500 to 2500/1500 ppm B-Nine/Cycocel can be used and in cooler areas only 800/800 ppm B-Nine/Cycocel may be needed. Intermediate regions should try 1000/1250 ppm B-Nine/Cycocel. The B-Nine/Cycocel mix is very active and should not be used after the start of SD (flower initiation).

TABLE II-2 EUPHORBIA

Information for late season *Euphorbia* height control. Do not apply drenches too early or excessive retardation will occur because the indicated rates are intended to stop elongation (Hammer and Barrett, 2001). There is a time period during which no plant growth regulators should be used due to the high risk of delayed flowering and causing small bracts. In cool climates late season drenches are applied when the plants are within 0.5 in. of final desired height and at least two bracts are in color; in warm climates plants should be within 1 in. of final desired height and at least one bract is in color. The following dates and rates are guidelines only; individual firms should always experiment first before making applications to the entire crop.

| | Cutoff Date for Sprays | | Late Drench Rates for Medium or High Vigor Cultivars | |
Chemical	Cool Climates	Warm Climates	Cool Climates (ppm)	Warm Climates (ppm)
Cycocel	Early to mid-October	October 20 to 31	—	—
B-Nine/Cycocel	Start of SD	Start of SD	—	—
A-Rest	Start of SD	Start of SD	1 to 2	2 to 4
Bonzi	Start of SD	October 10 to 25	0.5 to 1	1 to 2–3
Sumagic	Start of SD	October 10 to 25	0.25 to 0.5	0.5 to 1

The mix should be used cautiously because it can delay bract development and reduce bract size. The B-Nine/Cycocel combination is especially effective during situations when height control is difficult such as on stock plants, during propagation, or in warm climates.

Spray applications of Bonzi are typically at 5 to 30 ppm and Sumagic at 2 to 10 ppm in northern climates (Barrett, 1996; Hammer and Barrett, 2001). In warm climates the spray rates can be increased to 15 to 45 ppm for Bonzi and 5 to 10 ppm for Sumagic. Neither chemical should be applied as a spray after the start of SD in northern areas or after October 10 to 25 in the south (Table II-2). Adjust cutoff dates accordingly if black clothing for early production schedules.

Early season Bonzi drenches of 0.25 to 3 ppm or Sumagic drenches of 0.25 to 1 ppm can be used, depending on the cultivar, and often produce more reliable results than spray applications. Generally 0.5 to 0.75 ppm Bonzi is used on 'Eckespoint Freedom' in northern areas and 1 ppm in southern areas. Up to 3 ppm Bonzi can be used in warm climates on more vigorous cultivars. For drenches, apply 4 fl oz of drench solution/6-in. (120 mL/15-cm) pot to moist media.

Late season Bonzi or Sumagic drenches can be applied after the start of SD in cool climates or after October 10 to 25 in warm climates (see Table II-2 Euphorbia). Drench applications applied in early November are less likely to reduce bract size than when applied in October. However, spray applications are more likely to reduce bract size and delay flowering than drench applications when applied any time after flower initiation. Late applications of either Bonzi or Sumagic are less likely to reduce bract size than B-Nine/Cycocel tank mix.

For drenching, A-Rest is applied at rates of 1 to 4 ppm with rates of 1 to 2 ppm in cool areas and 2 to 4 ppm in warmer climates (Barrett, 1996). For late season drenches, see Table II-2. If the medium has pine bark, Bonzi, Sumagic, and A-Rest will be less effective and rates may have to be increased by up to 25%.

The most recent addition to the list of growth regulators is Topflor, which can be applied as a spray at 2.5 to 40 ppm for naturally compact plants, 10 to 60 ppm for moderately vigor plants, and 50 to 80 ppm for vigorous cultivars (SePRO, personal communication). In cool climates applications should be made 5 to 8 weeks after the pinch on compact cultivars, 3 to 4 weeks on moderate vigor plants, and 2 to 3 weeks on vigorous cultivars. In warm climates applications should be made 3 to 5 weeks after the pinch on compact cultivars, 2 to 3 weeks on moderate vigor plants, and 1 to 2 weeks on vigorous cultivars.

Growth retardants are typically applied after the pinch when axillary shoots are 1.5 to 2 in. (4 to 5 cm) long. Actual application time(s) should be based on graphical tracking. In warm climates additional height control can be achieved by applying growth retardants to stock plants before propagation, to cuttings during propagation, and to young plants 3 to 7 days before the pinch. Early applications of growth retardants can reduce the frequency and number of applications later in the growing season. Late application of growth retardants may cause small bracts and will have limited effectiveness.

The timing of DIF and/or growth retardants is critical. Poinsettia growth after pinching is divided into three phases: (1) axillary shoots slowly develop for 1 to 2 weeks after the pinch, (2) stems elongate rapidly, and (3) stem elongation slows as cyathia and bracts develop (see Fig. 7-1, page 128). Loss of temperature control or inadequate application of growth retardants during the second phase will result in tall plants. Fisher et al. (1996a) mathematically modeled the growth curve during each of the three growth phases.

SPACING

For high-quality potted plants, provide the plants the maximum space possible. Delayed or close spacing will result in tall plants with long internodes and increase the chance of stem breakage during marketing (Nell and Leonard, 1996). However, production for mass market customers may require very close spacing. See Table II-3 Euphorbia for recommended spacings. For cut flowers space plants to provide four stems/ft² (43/m²) of bench area, if pinched. This applies whether planting in containers or beds. Closer spacing can be used with unpinched plants.

PINCHING AND DISBUDDING

Poinsettias are produced either as nonpinched, single-stem ("straight up"), or as pinched plants. With nonpinched plants the inflorescences become large and striking but usually more than one cutting is needed per 6-in. (15-cm) or larger pot. Most poinsettias grown are pinched to produce four to seven inflorescences. Generally, plants are pinched when

TABLE II-3 EUPHORBIA

Suggested cutting numbers and spacing for various sizes of potted *Euphorbia* (Ecke et al., 1990). The closer spacing can be used with compact cultivars, delayed planting, high light production areas, and heavy plant growth regulator use. Market frequently determines plant size with large plants grown for direct retail or florists and small plants for mass market.

| Pot Size | | Plants | Pinched/ | Spacing | | Area/Pot | |
in.	cm	(no./pot)	Nonpinched	in.	cm	ft^2	m^2
4	10	1	Pinched	6 × 6 to 9 ×9	15 × 15 to 23 × 23	0.25–0.56	0.02–0.05
4	10	1	Nonpinched	6 × 6 to 9 × 9	15 × 15 to 23 × 23	0.25–0.56	0.02–0.05
5	13	1	Pinched	7 × 7 to 12 × 12	18 × 18 to 30 × 30	0.34–1.00	0.03–0.09
5	13	2	Nonpinched	7 × 7 to 12 × 12	18 × 18 to 30 × 30	0.34–1.00	0.03–0.09
6	15	1	Pinched	10 × 10 to 14 × 14	25 × 25 to 36 × 36	0.69–1.36	0.06–0.13
6	15	2	Pinched	11 × 11 to 15 × 15	28 × 28 to 38 × 38	0.84–1.56	0.08–0.15
6	15	3	Nonpinched	11 × 11 to 15 × 15	28 × 28 to 38 × 38	0.84–1.56	0.08–0.15
7	18	1	Pinched	12 × 12 to 17 × 17	30 × 30 to 43 × 43	1.00–2.00	0.09–0.19
7	18	3	Nonpinched	12 × 12 to 17 × 17	30 × 30 to 43 × 43	1.00–2.00	0.09–0.19
7	18	5	Nonpinched	14 × 14 to 19 × 19	36 × 36 to 48 × 48	1.36–2.51	0.13–0.23

sufficient root growth occurs for roots to be visible on the outer edges of the medium ball, which is within 2 weeks after a rooted cutting is planted in the pot or 4 to 5 weeks after direct sticking a cutting. If pinched too early, there will be insufficient root growth to support the developing axillary shoots and the resulting shoots will be weak and slow to develop. Thus, premature pinching may reduce quality. If the crop is behind schedule prior to the pinch, it is best to raise the temperature if the temperature is not already over 85°F (29°C). See Tables II-4 and II-5 Euphorbia for the recommended number of days from planting to pinching and from pinching to the start of SD.

The number of axillary shoots produced from a pinched plant is usually equal to or one less than the number of nodes or leaves remaining on the plant. For example, leaving five leaves on a plant after a pinch should result in four to five inflorescences. With restricted-branching cultivars, a pinch will usually result in only two to four axillary shoots even if more leaves are left on the plant. If weather or plant quality is poor at the time of the pinch, growers may want to leave one additional leaf to ensure a proper number of quality inflorescences.

The use of Florel may increase the number of branches by one for some cultivars (Bridgen et al., 2003; Hamrick, 2003). Apply two sprays of 350 to 500 ppm; the first one week prior to the pinch and the second one week after the pinch. However, if too many axillary shoots are allowed to remain, stems will be weak and inflorescences will be small. Four

or five large bract clusters can provide as much color as seven or eight small inflorescences.

The four types of pinches are soft, medium, hard, and very hard (Berghage et al., 1987, 1989). With a soft pinch the apex is removed above a young, immature leaf. A medium pinch removes leaves up to 2.8 in. (7 cm) long and associated stem tissue. A hard pinch is made above the first fully expanded mature leaf and a very hard pinch is made in older stem tissue. A soft pinch can result in slow, uneven development of axillary shoots due to inhibition of these shoots by the young leaves. A soft pinch may be needed if propagation and plant establishment are delayed. If a soft pinch is needed, more uniform branching of some cultivars can be promoted by removing one to three young leaves at the time of the pinch, leaving the most recently mature and fully expanded leaves. A hard pinch is the most common pinch and will typically produce uniform, vigorous axillary shoots. Very hard pinches leave only the old, "dormant" axillary buds and will often produce erratic branching results and poor-quality plants.

Lower shoots of tree poinsettias will need to be removed; otherwise poinsettias do not require disbudding. Gibberellic acid (GA$_3$) sprays at 250 to 750 ppm can be applied to increase internode elongation and decrease the amount of time required to produce the "tree trunk" (Mynett and Wilkońska, 1989). However, flowering may be delayed. Stock plants that are to be flowered will have to be thinned; otherwise, too many shoots develop, which are often weak

TABLE II-4 EUPHORBIA

Number of days required for rooted *Euphorbia* cuttings to become established and plant size to be sufficiently large prior to pinching (Williams, 1992).

| Pot Size | | Plants | Days to |
in.	cm	no./pot	Pinch
3	8	1	5
4–4.5	10–11	1	8
5.5–6	14–15	1–2	10–14
6.5	16.5	1–3	14
7	18	1–5	14–17
8	20	1–7	17–20
10	25	1–10	20–25

TABLE II-5 EUPHORBIA

Recommended number of days of vegetative *Euphorbia* growth between pinching and SD (flower initiation) as determined by geographical location and product type (Williams, 1992). South is defined as south of latitude 36°N; central, between 36 and 42°N; and north, north of 42°N.

| Pot Size | | Plants | North American Geographical Location | | |
in.	cm	no./pot	South	Central	North
3	8	1	0	3	5
4–4.5	10–11	1	5	7	9
5.5–6	14–15	1	9	12	15
6.5	16.5	1	12	16	22
7	18	2	18	22	27
8	20	2–3	21	26	31
10	25	3–4	25	30	35

and have small inflorescences. In late August to mid-September all weak shoots should be removed and the remaining shoots cut back, if necessary, leaving four to six nodes on each shoot. If shoots are strong and not too tall after thinning, they can remain unpinched.

For cut flowers, plants can be pinched 1.5 to 2 weeks after planting rooted cuttings, or when roots are visible at the edge of the medium. Generally, two marketable stems can be produced from each cutting. Three weeks after pinching, when the leaves are 1 in. (2.5 cm) long, remove all but two or three of the most vigorous axillary stems. Leave two stems/plant on the inner rows and three stems/plant on the outer rows. Extra stems will probably not produce marketable flowers anyway and will make pest control more difficult. Plants can also be grown unpinched; stem length will be greater and head size will be larger.

SUPPORT

Tree poinsettias must be staked and tied soon after planting. While potted poinsettias often do not need support, many growers use plastic support rings that attach to the pots and prevent stem breakage. Cut flowers will need support. While netting can be used, generally one or two wires or strings around the perimeter of the bench or bed is sufficient.

SCHEDULE AND TIMING

POTTED FLOWERING PLANTS

Numerous schedules have been developed over the years to accommodate a wide range of cultivars, flowering dates, container sizes, plant styles (single stem, pinched, tubs, trees, hanging baskets), and climates. The most commonly grown type of poinsettia is a single pinched plant in a 6-in. (15-cm) pot. As a general rule, approximately 4 weeks are required for propagation, 1.5 to 3 weeks from planting a rooted cutting until pinching to allow plants to establish prior to pinching, and 1.5 to 3 weeks from pinching to start of SD to allow adequate shoot growth before flower initiation (see Tables II-4 through II-6 Euphorbia). All other

TABLE II-6 EUPHORBIA

Sample crop schedule for a medium-vigor *Euphorbia* from receipt of a rooted cutting for stock plant production to sale of a 6-in. (15-cm) pinched plant in central United States.

Cultural Step	Date	Production Time (weeks)	Temperature °F (°C)
Receive and plant rooted cutting	March 21		
		4	Media: 65–70 (18–21) Night: 68–72 (20–22) Day: 75–80 (24–27)
First pinch	April 18		
		4	Media: 65–70 (18–21) Night: 68–72 (20–22) Day: 75–80 (24–27)
Second pinch	May 16		
		4	Media: 65–70 (18–21) Night: 68–72 (20–22) Day: 75–80 (24–27)
Third pinch	June 13		
		6	Media: 65–70 (18–21) Night: 68–72 (20–22) Day: 75–80 (24–27)
Harvest and propagate cuttings[a]	July 24		
		4	Media: 75–77 (24–25)
Transplant rooted cutting[b]	August 21		
		2.5	Night: 65–68 (18–20) Day: 75–80 (24–27)
Pinch[b]	September 8		
		2.5	Constant 65–68 (18–20)
Natural SD commences[b]	September 25		
		1	Constant 65–68 (18–20)
Apply growth retardant based on graphical tracking[c]	October 1		
		5	Constant 65–68 (18–20)
Reduce temperature and eliminate fertilizer	November 3–10		
		2–3	Night: 55–60 (13–16) Day: 70–75 (21–24)
Flowering	Late November		
Total		35–36	

[a]*Several flushes of cuttings can be harvested from mid-July to late August.*
[b]*Plant size can be changed by manipulating dates of planting, pinching, and start of SD.*
[c]*See Chapter 8, Plant Growth Regulation.*

situations are variations of that basic schedule. For example, compact cultivars can be given artificial LD in the fall to delay flower initiation or be propagated up to 2 weeks earlier than some other cultivars to achieve a larger plant.

The poinsettia season is divided into three main periods: (1) early market or pre-Thanksgiving sales; (2) primary market, from Thanksgiving to December 10; and (3) late market, from December 11 to December 24 (Williams, 1992). Although sales in the early marketing period are rapidly increasing, peak demand is generally the first 5 days of December. Proper cultivar selection or photoperiod manipulation will allow growers to have fresh poinsettias for each marketing period. Growers should not anticipate carrying over early flowered poinsettias for the later periods because overmature poinsettias have increased susceptibility to insects, diseases, bract fading, and bract necrosis; increased cyathia abscission; and reduced postharvest life.

The earliest flowering cultivars are generally in flower by mid-November in most parts of North America. If earlier flowering is required, growers will need to use artificial SD during late August and early September.

In the production of tree poinsettias, GA_3 at 250 to 750 ppm can be used to promote rapid elongation of the trunk prior to pinching (Mynett and Wilkońska, 1989). Gibberellic acid should be used after the cutting has become well established in the pot and multiple sprays may be needed. The stem should be staked for support.

CUT FLOWERS

Stem length is determined by the time from pinch to the start of short days. For Christmas sales long stems will be produced by planting rooted cuttings mid- to late July and pinching 1.5 to 2 weeks later (Table II-7 Euphorbia). This will provide 7 to 9 weeks of LD after the pinch and prior to the start of natural SD in late September. A 22-in. (56-cm) long stem can be produced by providing 7 weeks from pinch (pinched) or 4 weeks from transplanting (unpinched) to the start of SD (Njue et al., 2003). Pinching may delay flowering up to 5 days. Flowering date can also be delayed with LD lighting or accelerated with SD black cloth.

For the production of long-stemmed flowers, Pro-Gibb (gibberellic acid) can be applied weekly at 10 ppm and can increase stem length up to 8 in. (20 cm). Start applications 3 weeks after pinching plants or when the leaves are 1 in. (2.5 cm) long. Use 5 to 7 applications and continue them until the start of SD (Njue et al., 2003). GA may delay bract coloring, so do not apply after the start of SD. Of course, do not use growth retardants of any type.

INSECTS

Whiteflies and fungus gnats are the most serious insect problems. Two species of whiteflies are possible, the greenhouse whitefly and the silverleaf whitefly (see Chapter 9, Pest Management). Careful prevention, constant monitoring, and prompt control are essential. Interestingly, Bentz et al. (1995b) noted that silverleaf whiteflies were more attracted to

TABLE II-7 EUPHORBIA

Sample production schedule for 'Renaissance Red' cut *Euphorbia* (J.M. Dole, P.R. Fisher, G. Njue, unpublished).

Cultural Step	Date	Production Time (weeks)	Temperature °F (°C)
Receive and plant rooted cutting	July 7[a]		
		2	Day: 75–80 (24–27) Night: 68–72 (20–22)
Pinch to four nodes per/plant	July 21[b]		
		4	Day: 75–80 (24–27) Night: 68–72 (20–22)
Thin stems to two to three per plant	August 18[c]		
		3	Day: 75–80 (24–27) Night: 68–72 (20–22)
Respace to 12 × 12 in. (30 × 30) if using two plants per 8-in. (20-cm) pot.	September 8		
		2	Day: 75–80 (24–27) Night: 68–72 (20–22)
Natural SD start	September 22–26		
		10	Day: 75–80 (24–27) Night: 64–68 (18–20)
Flower	Dec. 1–5		
			Day: 75–80 (24–27) Night: 64–68 (18–20)
Total		21	

[a]If using Pro-Gibb, plant 2 weeks later.
[b]Or when roots are to the edge of the pot.
[c]Or when stems are large enough to thin.

fertilized vegetative poinsettias than to unfertilized poinsettias and the use of ammonium fertilizer may increase whitefly populations. In addition, whiteflies apparently lay more eggs on older leaves due to their higher leaf nitrogen content (Bentz et al., 1995a). Inspect incoming cuttings carefully, because whitefly eggs and pupae can easily go unnoticed on the undersides of the lower leaves. Dipping cuttings in insecticides may be helpful in reducing egg numbers. Do not depend on seeing flying adults because they are rarely present on recently shipped cuttings.

Fungus gnats are a major problem in many greenhouses; the larvae feed on roots and lower stem tissue of rooted cuttings and prevent root formation. During propagation the medium stays moist for long periods, allowing the larvae to become established. Reduce fungus gnat populations by avoiding overwatering, reducing humidity, removing weeds or decaying plant material, and controlling algae. If insecticidal drenches are used, apply within 6 days of sticking cuttings. Heavy infestations of fungus gnats will delay plant establishment, increase incidence of root rot, and decrease crop uniformity.

Other pests that can occur include Lewis mites, spider mites, mealybugs, and caterpillars. Remember, also, with pest problems that poinsettia bracts are very sensitive to phytotoxicity; if late chemical applications are needed, choose the material carefully.

DISEASES

Poinsettias are susceptible to several diseases from propagation to flowering. Sanitation, pathogen-free media, and optimum cultural practices are particularly important in controlling disease. Poinsettias should be frequently checked and corrective actions taken promptly to prevent widespread outbreaks (Hall, 1993).

ROOT AND STEM ROT

Several organisms can cause root and stem rots on poinsettias including *Pythium, Rhizoctonia solani, Thielaviopsis basicola, Botrytis cinerea, Phytophthora parasitica, Erwinia chrysanthemi,* and *Fusarium. Armillaria mellea* and *Sclerotinia sclerotiorum* have also been reported (Dreistadt, 2001). These organisms are fungi except for *Erwinia,* a bacterium, and can be prevented with a fungicide drench at planting and at 1- to 2-month intervals. Many growers do not use preventive drenches for diseases but carefully monitor the crop and apply chemicals only if

needed. Biocontrol agents are also effective (Gracia-Garza et al., 2003). Because *Erwinia* is a bacterium, chemical controls are limited; sanitation and dry foliage provide the best prevention. *Erwinia* damage during propagation usually occurs within 7 days after sticking cuttings and is most prevalent during hot, sunny weather when cuttings receive heavy misting (R. Heins, personal communication).

BOTRYTIS BLIGHT

Botrytis cinerea can occur on any aboveground part of the plant and symptoms include tan to brown water-soaked lesions. During propagation *Botrytis* can rapidly destroy cuttings. During production the disease symptoms can be stem lesions or spots and blotches on the leaves and bracts. During postharvest the disease often develops on the nectaries and attacks the cyathia clusters. The gray fuzzy fungus, after which the disease is named, can become apparent with humid conditions; keep humidity below 90% and maintain good air circulation to prevent problems. Fungicides can be applied to stock plants prior to cutting harvest and also to cuttings during propagation. The fungus can also be found on dead tissue that has fallen at the base of the plant, which can serve as a reservoir of inoculum for disease on living tissue. Nutrition may be a factor because the incidence of *Botrytis* may be higher on plants with low Ca (Bible and McAvoy, 2000b).

BACTERIAL STEM AND LEAF ROT

Although bacterial rots (*Erwinia caratovora*) are most common during propagation, other bacterial diseases can occur during production, including *Pseudomonas viridiflava* (greasy canker), *Corynebacterium flaccumfaciens* (bacterial canker), *Erwinia chrysanthemi* (bacterial stem rot), and *Xanthomonas campestris* (bacterial leaf spot). As with most bacterial diseases, these are favored by warm, humid conditions and free water. Bacterial leaf spot usually occurs only on outdoor production.

POWDERY MILDEW

Powdery mildew (*Oidium*) is characterized by white powdery growth on foliage. It is favored by mild day temperatures of less than 85°F (29°C), cool nights, reduced light intensities, and no free moisture on the plant. The best control is to lower humidity. Cultivars vary in susceptibility to powdery mildew, but none are resistant (Celio and Hausbeck, 1997).

FUNGAL BLIGHTS AND LEAF SPOTS

Several other fungal disease organisms are known to attack poinsettias including rhizopus blight (*Rhizopus stolonifera*), choanephora wet rot (*Choanephora cucurbitarum*), alternaria blight (*Alternaria euphorbiicola*), poinsettia scab (*Sphaceloma poinsettiae*), leaf spot (*Cercospora*), rusts (*Melampsora* and *Uromyces*), powdery mildew (*Erysiphe* or *Microsphaera euphorbiae*, *Oidium*), and *Corynespora cassiicola* (*Corynespora* bract and leaf spot) (Ecke et al., 1990). Most of these diseases are uncommon and limited to warm climates.

VIRUSES

At least two viruses are known to infect poinsettias—poinsettia mosaic virus (PnMV) and poinsettia cryptic virus (PnCV), but neither shows obvious symptoms in most cases. Mild mottling symptoms can occasionally occur during the cool weather and low light conditions of midwinter, but growers are likely to never see the symptoms on stock plants or Christmas crops.

PHYSIOLOGICAL DISORDERS

BRACT NECROSIS (BURN)

Symptoms include small, submarginal necrotic spots and marginal necrosis of the bracts (Fig. II-7 Euphorbia). The dead areas are prime locations for *Botrytis* infection, which can cause additional damage. The disorder is thought to be related to calcium uptake and is accentuated by any conditions that restrict calcium uptake, including low calcium levels, low medium temperature, high ammonium medium levels, high humidity, and root rot (Bible and McAvoy, 2000a; Hartley, 1992; Woltz and Harbaugh, 1986). Low medium pH also allows rapid leaching of calcium from the medium. High concentrations of other competitive cations such as K and Mg may also accentuate bract necrosis (Strømme et al., 1994; Woltz and Harbaugh, 1985).

Cultivars vary greatly in their sensitivity to bract necrosis, with cultivars having light green leaves being particularly sensitive (Barrett, 1997; R.J. McAvoy, personal communication). The likelihood of bract necrosis increases as the plants mature; be sure to market poinsettias promptly. In general, try to avoid bract necrosis by maintaining low medium EC, using fertilizers with a low percentage of ammonium, reducing fertilizer use and excessive water application during bract formation, avoiding high rates or late applications of controlled-release fertilizers, reducing humidity, and increasing air circulation (Bible and McAvoy, 1997; Hartley, 1992; Nell and Barrett, 1985, 1986). Using plant growth regulators also decreases the incidence of bract necrosis, which may be due to decreasing the size of the bracts, thereby increasing the Ca concentration (Simons and Smith, 1991). Weekly spray applications of 200 to 400 ppm calcium chloride with a spreader sticker can be applied starting with bract coloring and continuing until anthesis (pollen shed) (Hamrick, 1996; Woltz and Harbaugh, 1986). Calcium nitrate is more commonly used on stock plants than flowering plants because the chance for phytotoxicity on bracts is greater than with calcium chloride.

Bract necrosis (Fig. II-7 Euphorbia) may also be influenced by non-nutritive factors other than calcium (McAvoy and Bible, 1996a). In their work, bract necrosis was reduced experimentally by 4 mM sodium silica sprays when applied before anthesis or by one 100 ppm benzyladenine spray applied at anthesis (McAvoy and Bible, 1996a, b, 1998). In addition, low B may also contribute to the problem (Bible and McAvoy, 2000a; McAvoy and Bible, 2000).

LEAF EDGE NECROSIS (BURN)

Leaf edge burn (Fig. II-8 Euphorbia) may start as a downward curling and marginal yellowing to tan coloration of young leaves. Leaf edge burn is associated with low calcium levels in the leaf margins and can be avoided by reducing the ammonium:nitrate ratio and humidity and applying calcium sprays (Bierman et al., 1990). The problem can occur when a canopy of leaves forms over the stock plants, which sharply reduces air movement and light levels

FIGURE II-7 EUPHORBIA Bract necrosis on *Euphorbia*.

FIGURE II-8 EUPHORBIA Leaf edge necrosis on *Euphorbia*.

and increases the humidity around shoots below the canopy. Such shoots develop calcium deficiency symptoms, which can be made more severe when the upper layer of cuttings are harvested; the young shoots are exposed to high light and low humidity but have insufficient calcium levels to support the new growth. The condition is temporary as the higher transpiration rates raise calcium levels, but future cuttings may have necrotic areas on the foliage that can lead to *Botrytis* or bacterial rot during propagation. Calcium sprays or misting with irrigation water containing high levels of calcium can help alleviate the problem (Bierman et al., 1990) (See Bract Necrosis, page 507).

CYCOCEL DAMAGE

Irregular yellow patches or marginal areas on foliage indicate Cycocel phytotoxicity. Marginal necrosis and leaf dropping may occur with severe damage. If damage is slight, yellow areas may regreen. To prevent damage, apply lower concentrations and repeat applications.

LEAF DROP

Once a common problem, the incidence of leaf drop has greatly decreased with improved cultivars and postharvest handling. Loss of the lower leaves can still be an important problem, however, and is accentuated by any type of plant stress including excessive under- or overwatering, root rot, cold temperatures, low light, and high medium EC (see also Postharvest, page 509, for proper postharvest handling).

STEM BREAKAGE

During marketing of finished plants, one or more axillary branches may break off, reducing the value of the plant or making it unsalable. Several preventive measures have been suggested, including using cuttings with thick stems [greater than 0.25 in. (7 mm) wide], reducing the number of lateral shoots to three or four by pinching to four or five nodes, and increasing plant spacing (Faust et al., 1997; Kuehny and Branch, 1997; Nell and Leonard, 1996). Work using susceptibility to sharp impacts as an indicator of stem breakage shows that stock plant management has the greatest effect on stem breakage; specific reasons are still unknown (J. Faust, personal communication). In addition, Faust noted that horizontal growing branches are easily broken when sleaving or transporting. Cultivars vary in their susceptibility to the problem (Dole and Smith, 1997).

PREMATURE FLOWER INITIATION (SPLITTING)

Splitting is the premature initiation and development of terminal flower buds on vegetative or young reproductive plants (Fig. II-9 Euphorbia). The immature flower bud rarely reaches anthesis and is usually surrounded by a whorl of three shoots, each of which is subtended by a leaf. If splitting occurs on vegetative stock plants during LD, the subtending shoots will, in turn, form another terminal flower bud, which is again subtended by a whorl of two to three shoots. The process can continue indefinitely and end cutting production. The entire "inflorescence" should be removed and normal vegetative shoots will grow from subtending axillary buds. If splitting occurs on young plants to be flowered for Christmas, the terminal flower bud may reach anthesis but the inflorescence will be malformed, excessively large, and open. Individual bracts may form in

FIGURE II-9 EUPHORBIA Premature flower initiation (splitting) of *Euphorbia*.

the middle of the flower cluster and grow vertically. In addition, if splitting occurs early in the production schedule, vegetative growth will cease and plants may be too short.

The propensity for splitting increases with the age of the shoot (apex), and the potential for splitting can be reduced by frequent pinching of the stock plants (Evans et al., 1992a). Cultivars vary in their susceptibility to splitting. Splitting can be eliminated by the application of GA_3 at 10 to 25 ppm (Evans et al., 1992b). The application of Florel (ethephon) at 300 to 500 ppm may also reduce splitting if applied within 3 days of planting rooted cuttings (Konjoian, 2000). Splitting can also occur if plants receive enough SD to initiate flowers but insufficient SD for the inflorescence to develop properly. This can especially occur during propagation if LD are not provided.

LEAF CRIPPLING OR DISTORTION

Leaf crippling or distortion can occur either on cuttings just after rooting or on axillary shoots immediately after plants are pinched. The leaves are puckered and often narrow, thickened, curved, and distorted. Although disconcerting at first, plants usually outgrow the problem and the affected leaves are covered by healthy leaves and bracts. When leaf crippling occurs on newly rooted cuttings, the cause may be excessive foliar absorption of phosphorus, which ties up minor elements, causing a transitory minor element deficiency (D. Hartley, personal communication). Phosphorus is present in high amounts in many premixed fertilizers and overhead fertigation may lead to accumulation of phosphorus in young leaves, which are usually "boat shaped" and can retain drops of water and fertilizer after irrigation. The solution is to rinse fertilizer off the foliage after plants are fertigated.

On pinched plants, leaf crippling occurs most frequently on the first one to three leaves that develop on the axillary shoots. The physiological problem may be related to the stress that occurs after cuttings are moved from the low-light, high-humidity environment of the propagation area to the high light, warm temperatures, and low humidity of the production environment. The limited root systems may be unable to take up sufficient water at first to support the new growth. If the problem occurs, try applying light shade and syringing the young plants until roots are well established and axillary shoots begin to develop.

CENTER BUD DROP

Premature abscission of the poinsettia cyathia can make plants appear to be overmature. The disorder is prompted by insufficient carbohydrates to support the flower buds, which can be due to low light levels, close plant spacing, high night temperatures, and water stress (Miller, 1984). The problem is greatest in the low-light areas of the north and coastal areas and less common in southern areas. If growing in a chronically cloudy area, be sure to space plants promptly and sufficiently, maintain a clean glazing to allow as much light transmittance as possible, reduce or eliminate overhead hanging baskets, reduce night temperatures late in the production cycle after bracts have expanded, and avoid water stress. The problem can also occur when bracts and cyathia develop under low-light conditions and readily abscise later when plants are shipped.

RABBIT TRACKS (BILATERAL BRACT SPOTS)

Rabbit tracks are characterized by development of silvery spots on either side of the main vein of bracts, prompting the official name *bilateral bract spots*. This problem has always been erratic in appearance from one year to the next and is rarely seen on newer cultivars. The symptoms occur late in the crop cycle and are associated with high nutritional levels and warm night temperatures. 'Annette Hegg' cultivars tended to be most susceptible to the problem.

POSTHARVEST
POTTED PLANTS

Postharvest life of poinsettia plants can be increased by reducing temperatures to 55°F (13°C) and reducing nutrition during the last 2 to 3 weeks of production. Nitrogen from urea or ammonium should not be used after mid- to late October. High levels of nitrogen, especially ammonium, can enhance leaf and cyathia abscission (ter Hell and Hendriks, 1995). Plants are best harvested when the bracts are fully developed and expanded and the pollen is visible on one or more of the cyathia. Many new cultivars develop excellent bract color before the cyathia mature. However, if plants are shipped before bracts are mature, the young bracts will turn green and not develop proper color. If shipped when too mature or when most of the cyathia are showing pollen, the cyathia may abscise during shipping. Overmature plants are also susceptible to bract necrosis, bract discoloration, leaf drop, and *Botrytis* damage. After bracts have matured, light intensity can be reduced to 2000 fc (400 μmol $\cdot$ m^{-2} $\cdot$ s^{-1}) to prevent fading and sunburning of the bracts. Plants should be shipped at 50 to 61°F (10 to 16°C) but cold temperatures below 50°F (10°C) will cause leaf drop (L. Høyer, personal communication). Optimum storage and shipping temperature is 51°F (10.5°C); lower temperatures may cause chilling damage and shipping temperatures above 68°F (20°C) will reduce postharvest life (Tijskens et al., 1996). Keep storage and shipping times to 3 days or less to reduce leaf and bud drop (Society of American Florists, 1996).

Plants should be sleeved before shipment to prevent damage in transit. Sleeves should be removed promptly, otherwise petiole epinasty may occur due to internal ethylene production. Epinasty is a twisting and curling of the foliage and occurs mainly on the upper foliage and bracts. Poinsettias are sensitive to exogenous ethylene (L. Høyer, personal communication).

Unpack poinsettias immediately and keep display poinsettias watered, cool at about 60°F (16°C), and in 75 to 225 fc (15 to 45 μmol $\cdot$ m^{-2} $\cdot$ s^{-1}) light. With proper care and a cool, well-lighted location, poinsettias can last for many weeks in the consumer's environment. It is not uncommon to see poinsettias purchased in December still look reasonably attractive in March. Postharvest life and sensitivity to epinasty vary with the cultivar (van Dijk and Barendse, 1991). Cultivars with dark green foliage tend to have a longer postharvest life than those with lighter green leaves.

Contrary to popular opinion poinsettias are not toxic. Certainly, poinsettias are not edible and should not be eaten.

CUT FLOWERS

Poinsettias with curled bracts, such as 'Renaissance Red,' work well as cut flowers, cultivars with flat or smooth bracts generally have a much shorter vase life. Harvest cut stems of 'Renaissance Red' when at least 2 of the cyathia are showing pollen (Dole and Aufill, 2000; J.M. Dole, P.R. Fisher, and G. Njue, in press). Cut stems can be harvested up to 4 weeks after anthesis with no decrease in postharvest life, minimizing the need to cold-store stems if too many stems become available for harvest at once. However, buds may drop sooner than if cut when they first flower. All foliage can be removed at the time of harvest or a few leaves can be left on each stem. Removing all foliage increases vase life. Cut stems into clean water with a low EC (0.1 to 0.5) and low pH (less than 5.0).

Contrary to popular opinion, pretreatments with heated floral solution, alcohol dips, or 10% sucrose either have no effect or are detrimental. Recutting stems every 3 days increases vase life and delays leaf abscission. The optimum sucrose concentration was 0 to 1% for holding without foam, or 2% for stems held in foam. The use of floral foam caused leaf yellowing but did not affect vase life. Commercial floral pretreatments and holding solutions delayed leaf abscission but had no other effect.

Stems can be stored or shipped at 34 to 41°F (1 to 5°C) for up to 24 hr. However, long-term storage should be at 50°F (10°C) or higher to prevent cold damage but will decrease vase life. After shipping cut poinsettias can be stored with tropical flowers, which are typically stored at 55 to 59°F (13 to 15°C). Stems can be shipped wet or dry. If shipped dry, keep shipping time to a minimum (24 hr or less), then cut and rehydrate.

KEY POINTS

- Poinsettia is used mainly as a potted flowering plant and to a lesser extent as a cut flower.
- Plants are propagated commercially by cuttings.
- Proper cultivar selection is important for appropriate bract and leaf color, height, and flowering period.
- Proper conditions for rooting of cuttings includes an optimum temperature of 75 to 77°F (24 to 25°C), oxygen at the base of the cutting, sanitation, and proper humidity level or misting frequency.
- Poinsettias are SD plants and cultivars are classified by their response group, which is the number of weeks required to flower from the beginning of SD.
- Poinsettias have an unusually high requirement for calcium, magnesium, and molybdenum.
- Height is controlled through cultivar selection, DIF, chemical growth retardants, and graphical tracking.

- Plants must be properly pinched to leave the appropriate number of axillary buds on reproductive plants.
- Whiteflies, fungus gnats, and root and stem rots are major problems.
- Common physiological disorders are stem breakage and bract edge necrosis.

- Chilling damage occurs at 50°F (10°C) or less.
- Potted and cut poinsettias are harvested when bracts are well colored and one to two cyathia show pollen.

BIBLIOGRAPHY

Anonymous. 1994. Cutting quality. *The Poinsettia* 9:2.

Barrett, J. 1996. Poinsettia height control. 1996. *Greenhouse Product News* 6(8):12–14.

Barrett, J. 1997. Improve the quality of your poinsettias. *Greenhouse Product News* 7(8):12–14, 17.

Behe, B.K., P.M. Redman, and J.M. Dole. 1997. Consumers prefer red poinsettia cultivars. *HortTechnology* 7:438–441.

Bentz, J., J. Reeves III, P. Barbosa, and B. Francis. 1995a. Nitrogen fertilizer effect on selection, acceptance, and suitability of *Euphorbia pulcherrima* (Euphorbiaceae) as a host plant to *Bemisia argentifolii* (Homoptera: Aleyrodidae). *Population Ecology* 24:40–45.

Bentz, J., J. Reeves III, P. Barbosa, and B. Francis. 1995b. Within-plant variation in nitrogen and sugar content of poinsettia and its effects on the oviposition pattern, survival, and development of *Bemisia argentifolii* (Homoptera: Aleyrodidae). *Population Ecology* 24:271–277.

Berghage, R.D., and R.D. Heins. 1991. Quantification of temperature effects on stem elongation in poinsettia. *Journal of the American Society for Horticultural Science* 116:14–18.

Berghage, R.D., R.D. Heins, W.H. Carlson, and J. Biernbaum. 1987. *Poinsettia Production.* Michigan State University Extension Bulletin E-1382, East Lansing.

Berghage, R.D., R.D. Heins, M. Karlsson, and J.E. Erwin. 1989. Pinching technique influences lateral shoot development in the poinsettia. *Journal of the American Society for Horticultural Science* 114:909–914.

Berghage, R.D., R.D. Heins, and J.E. Erwin. 1990. Quantifying leaf unfolding in the poinsettia. *Acta Horticulturae* 272:243–247.

Bernuetz, A. 2001. Studies on breeding dwarf poinsettias (*Euphorbia pulcherrima* Willd.) and the influence of infective agents. Ph.D. dissertation, Plant Breeding Institute, The University of Sydney, Australia.

Bible, B.B., and R.J. McAvoy. 1997. High soluble salts affects water loss and bract necrosis of poinsettia. *HortScience* 32:484. (Abstract)

Bible, B.B., and R.J. McAvoy. 2000a. Calcium-boron regimes effect incidence of postharvest disorders on poinsettia bracts. *HortScience* 35:457. (Abstract)

Bible, B.B., and R.J. McAvoy. 2000b. Differential response of two poinsettia cultivars to calcium stress for postharvest disorders. *HortScience* 35:457. (Abstract)

Bierman, P.M., C.J. Rosen, and H.F. Wilkins. 1990. Leaf edge burn and axillary shoot growth of vegetative poinsettia plants: Influence of calcium, nitrogen form, and molybdenum. *Journal of the American Society for Horticultural Science* 115:73–78.

Bridgen, M., M. Saska, and J. Burns. 2003. Using Florel on poinsettias. *Greenhouse Management and Production* 23(8):40–42.

Celio, G.J., and N.K. Hausbeck. 1997. Evaluation of poinsettia cultivars for susceptibility to powdery mildew. *HortScience* 32:259–261.

Cockshull, K.E., F.A. Langton, and C.R.J. Cave. 1995. Differential effects of different DIF treatments on chrysanthemum and poinsettia. *Acta Horticulturae* 378:15–25.

Dole, J.M., and L. Aufill. 2000. The return of cut poinsettias. *GrowerTalks* 64(2):66, 68, 69.

Dole, J., and R. Smith. 1997. 1996 Oklahoma State University poinsettia cultivar trial. *Combined Newsletter of the Oklahoma and Kansas Greenhouse Growers Association* 1(1):8–16.

Dole, J.M., and H.F. Wilkins. 1991a. Vegetative and reproductive characteristics of poinsettia altered by a graft-transmissible agent. *Journal of the American Society for Horticultural Science* 116:307–311.

Dole, J.M., and H.F. Wilkins. 1991b. Relationship between nodal position and plant age on the nutrient composition of vegetative poinsettia leaves. *Journal of the American Society for Horticultural Science* 116:248–252.

Dole, J.M., and H.F. Wilkins. 1992. *In vivo* characterization of the graft-transmissible agent in poinsettia. *Journal of the American Society for Horticultural Science* 117:972–975.

Dole, J.M., and H.F. Wilkins. 1994. Graft-transmissible free-branching agent, pp. 45–48 in *The Scientific Basis of Poinsettia Production,*

E. Strømme, editor. Agricultural University of Norway, Aas, Norway.

Dole, J.M., H.F. Wilkins, and S.L. Desborough. 1993. Investigations on the nature of a graft-transmissible agent in poinsettia. *Canadian Journal of Botany* 71:1097–1101.

Dole, J.M., J.C. Cole, and S.L. von Broembsen. 1994. Effect of irrigation methods on water use efficiency, nutrient leaching and growth of poinsettias. *HortScience* 29:858–864.

Dole, J.M., P. Fisher, and G. Njue. Optimizing postharvest life of cut 'Renaissance Red' poinsettias. *HortScience*. (in press)

Dreistadt, S.H. 2001. *Integrated Pest Management for Floriculture and Nurseries*. University of California Division of Agriculture and Natural Resources Publication 3402.

Ecke, P., Jr., O.A. Matkin, and D.E. Hartley. 1990. *The Poinsettia Manual,* 3rd ed. Paul Ecke Poinsettias, Encinitas, California.

Evans, M.R., H.F. Wilkins, and W.P. Hackett. 1992a. Meristem ontogenetic age as the controlling factor in long-day floral initiation in poinsettia. *Journal of the American Society for Horticultural Science* 117:961–965.

Evans, M.R., H.F. Wilkins, and W.P. Hackett. 1992b. Gibberellins and temperature influence long-day floral initiation in poinsettia. *Journal of the American Society for Horticultural Science* 117: 966–971.

Faust, J.E., and R.D. Heins. 1996. Axillary bud development of poinsettia 'Eckespoint Lilo' and 'Eckespoint Red Sails' (*Euphorbia pulcherrima* Willd.) is inhibited by high temperatures. *Journal of the American Society for Horticultural Science* 121:920–926.

Faust, J.E., E. Will, X. Duan, and E.T. Graham. 1997. Whole plant and histological analysis of poinsettia stem breakage. *HortScience* 32:509. (Abstract)

Fisher, P.R., R.D. Heins, and J.H. Lieth. 1996a. Quantifying the relationship between phases of stem elongation and flower initiation in poinsettia. *Journal of the American Society for Horticultural Science* 121:686–693.

Fisher, P.R., R.D. Heins, and J.H. Lieth. 1996b. Modeling the stem elongation response of poinsettia to chlormequat. *Journal of the American Society for Horticultural Science* 121:861–868.

Gapinski, J., and M. Yelanich. 1998. Steps for poinsettia propagation. *Ohio Florists' Association Bulletin* 824:10–11.

Gracia-Garza, J.A., M. Little, W. Brown, T.J. Blom, K. Schneider, W. Allen, and J. Potter. 2003. Efficacy of various biological control agents and biorationals against *Pythium* root rot in poinsettia. *HortTechnology* 13:149–153.

Grueber, K.L. 1985. Control of lateral branching and reproductive development in *Euphorbia pulcher-*

rima Willd. ex Klotzsch. Ph.D thesis, University of Minnesota.

Hall, J. 1993. Poinsettia diseases. *The Poinsettia* 7:5–13.

Hammer, A., and J. Barrett. 2001. Poinsettias, pp. 111–116 in *Tips on Regulating Growth of Floriculture Crops,* M.L. Gaston, L.A. Kunkle, P.S. Konjoian, and M.F. Wilt, editors. Ohio Florists' Association Services, Columbus, Ohio.

Hamrick, D. 1996. Calcium sprays eliminate bract edge burn. *GrowerTalks* 60(7):53.

Hamrick, D. 2003. *Euphorbia,* pp. 359–379 *in Ball Redbook,* vol. 2, 17th ed. Ball Publishing, Batavia, Illinois.

Hartley, D. 1992. Bract edge burn. *The Poinsettia* 4:2–7.

Henrard, G. 1978. Le culture de l'Euphorbia fulgens pour la potée fleurie. *Pepiner Hortic Maraich—Revue Horticole* 213:21–26. (in French)

Henrard, G. 1981. Le bouturage estical de l'Euphorbia fulgens. *Pepinier Hortic Maraich—Revue Horticole* 213:21–26. (in French)

Huxley, A., M. Griffiths, and M. Levy. 1992. *Euphorbia,* pp. 245–269 in *The New Royal Horticultural Society Dictionary of Gardening,* vol. 2. Stockton Press, New York.

Konjoian, P. 2000. The effects of florel on the growth and development of poinsettia: A research update. *Ohio Florists' Association Bulletin* 850: 12–14.

Ku, S.M.C., and D.R. Hershey. 1997. Growth response, nutrient leaching, and mass balance for potted poinsettia. I. Nitrogen. *Journal of the American Society for Horticultural Science* 122:452–458.

Kuehny, J.S., and P. Branch. 1997. Poinsettia stem strength. *HortScience* 32:483. (Abstract)

Lawton, K.A., G.L. McDaniel, and E.T. Graham. 1989. Nitrogen source and calcium supplement affect stem strength of poinsettia. *HortScience* 24:463–465.

Lee, I.-M., M. Klopmeyer, I.M. Baroszyk, D.E. Gundersen-Rindal, T.-S. Tau, K.L. Thomson, and R. Eisenreich. 1997. Phytoplasma induced free-branching in commercial poinsettia cultivars. *Nature Biotechnology* 15:178–182.

Liu, B., and R.D. Heins. 2002. Photothermal ratio affects plant quality in 'Freedom' poinsettia. *Journal of the American Society for Horticultural Science* 127:20–26.

McAvoy, R., and B. Bible. 1996a. Benzyladenine and daminozide sprays applied after initial anthesis affect bract necrosis in poinsettia. *HortScience* 31:584. (Abstract)

McAvoy, R.J., and B.B. Bible. 1996b. Silica sprays reduce the incidence and severity of bract necrosis in poinsettia. *HortScience* 31:1146–1149.

McAvoy, R., and B. Bible. 1998. Cytokinin and auxin sprays affect the incidence of poinsettia bract necrosis. *HortScience* 33:485. (Abstract)

McAvoy, R., and B. Bible. 2000. Relationship of bract boron content and boron application to bracts necrosis of poinsettia. *HortScience* 35:457. (Abstract)

Miller, S.H. 1984. Environmental and physiological factors influencing premature cyathia abscission in *Euphorbia pulcherrima* Willd. M.S. thesis, Michigan State University, East Lansing.

Moe, R., K. Willumsen, I.H. Ihlebekk, A.I. Stupa, N.M. Glomsrud, and L.M. Mortensen. 1995. DIF and temperature DROP responses in SDP and LDP, A comparison. *Acta Horticulturae* 378: 27–33.

Mynett, K., and A. Wilkońska. 1989. Growth regulators application in the shape forming of some pot plants. *Acta Horticulturae* 251:311–314.

Nell, T.A., and J.E. Barrett. 1985. Nitrate-ammonium nitrogen ratio and fertilizer application method influence bract necrosis and growth of poinsettia. *HortScience* 20:1130–1131.

Nell, T.A., and J.E. Barrett. 1986. Growth and incidence of bract necrosis in 'Gutbier V-14 Glory' poinsettia. *Journal of the American Society for Horticultural Science* 111:266–269.

Nell, T.A., and R.T. Leonard. 1996. Protecting poinsettias from post production losses. *GrowerTalks* 60(3):98, 100, 103, 104.

Njue, G., P.R. Fisher, and J. Dole. 2003. Optimizing production methods for 'Renaissance Red' poinsettias grown as a cut flower. *HortScience* 38:722. (Abstract)

Preil, W. 1994. *In vitro* culture of poinsettia, pp. 49–55 in *The Scientific Basis of Poinsettia Production*, E. Strømme, editor. Agricultural University of Norway, Aas, Norway.

Preil, W., and A. Beck. 1991. Somatic embryogenesis in bioreactor culture. *Acta Horticulturae* 289: 179–192.

Rose, M.A., J.W. White, and M.A. Rose. 1994. Maximizing nitrogen-use efficiency in relation to the growth and development of poinsettia. *HortScience* 29:272–276.

Ruiz-Sifre, G., J.M. Dole, B.A. Kahn, P.E. Richardson, and J. Ledford. 1997. Correlation of poinsettia graft union development with transmission of the free-branching characteristic. *Scientia Horticulturae* 69:135–143.

Runger, W. 1985. *Euphorbia fulgens*, pp. 483–486 in *Handbook of Flowering*, vol. II, A.H. Halevy, editor. CRC Press, Boca Raton, Florida.

Schuch, U., R.A. Redak, and J. Bethke. 1995. Whole-plant response of six poinsettia cultivars to three fertilizer and two irrigation regimes. *Journal of the American Society for Horticultural Science* 121:69–76.

Simons, B.R., and M.W. Smith. 1991. The influence of gibberellin biosynthesis-inhibiting growth regulators on bract necrosis in 'Gutbier V-14 Glory' poinsettia. *Scientia Horticulturae* 48:117–123.

Smith, R.M., and J.M. Dole. 1993. Effects of supplemental NH_4NO_3 drenches and no-leach production on poinsettias grown with controlled-release fertilizers. *HortScience* 28:549. (Abstract)

Society of American Florists. 1996. Poinsettia care update. *Dateline: Washington* 9(21):4.

Strømme, E., A.R. Selmer-Olsen, H.R. Gislerød, and R. Moe. 1994. Cultivar differences in nutrient absorption and susceptibility to bract necrosis in poinsettia (*Euphorbia pulcherrima* Willd. ex Klotzsch). *Gartenbauwissenschaft* 59:6–12. (in German)

ter Hell, B., and L. Hendriks. 1995. The influence of nitrogen nutrition on keeping quality of pot plants. *Acta Horticulturae* 405:138–147.

Tijskens, L.M.M., M. Sloof, E.C. Wilkinson, and W.G. van Doorn. 1996. A model of the effects of temperature and time on the acceptability of potted plants stored in darkness. *Postharvest Biology and Technology* 8:293–305.

van Dijk, A., and H. Barendse. 1991. Determining keeping quality of pot plants. *Acta Horticulturae* 298:267–273.

van Iersel, M. 2000. Postproduction leaching affects the growing medium and respiration of subirrigated poinsettias. *HortScience* 35:250–253.

Whipker, B.F., and P.A. Hammer. 1997. Nutrient uptake in poinsettia during different stages of physiological development. *Journal of the American Society for Horticultural Science* 122:565–573.

Williams, J.E. 1992. Poinsettia scheduling. *The Poinsettia* 2:2–9.

Williams, J.E. 1993. Stock plant production from the ground up. *The Poinsettia* 5:2–15.

Woltz, S.S., and B.K. Harbaugh. 1985. Effect of nutritional balance on bract and foliar necroses of poinsettia. *Proceedings of the Florida State Horticultural Society* 98:122–123.

Woltz, S.S., and B.K. Harbaugh. 1986. Calcium deficiency as the basic cause of marginal bract necrosis of 'Gutbier V-14 Glory' poinsettia. *HortScience* 21:1403–1404.

Yelanich, M.V., and J.A. Biernbaum. 1990. Effect of fertilizer concentration and method of application on media nutrient content, nitrogen runoff and growth of *Euphorbia pulcherrima* V-14 Glory. *Acta Horticulturae* 272:185–189.

Zhang, B., and L.P. Stoltz. 1989a. Shoot proliferation of *Euphorbia fulgens in vitro* affected by medium components. *HortScience* 24:503–504.

Zhang, B., and L.P. Stoltz. 1989b. Acclimatization systems for *Euphorbia fulgens* microcuttings. *HortScience* 24:1025–1026.

Eustoma

FIGURE II-1 EUSTOMA *Eustoma* 'Cinderella Pink' cut flowers.

INTRODUCTION

Common names: eustoma, lisianthus, prairie gentian, Texas bluebell.

Scientific name: *Eustoma grandiflorum* (Raf.) Shinn (Huxley et al., 1992); formerly known as *Lisianthus russellianus*.

Family and related taxa: Gentianaceae Juss. Although there are currently two *Eustoma* species—*E. exaltatum* (L.) Griseb. and *E. grandiflorum,*—evidence exists for considering all *Eustoma* as only one species (J.S. Pringle, personal communication). Other important genera in this family are *Exacum, Gentiana,* and *Sabatia.*

Origin: *E. grandiflorum* is native from Colorado and Nebraska south to northern Mexico (Huxley et al., 1992). *E. exaltatum* is native from the southern United States to Central America and the West Indies.

Uses and current status: This herbaceous plant is used as a cut flower, potted flowering plant, and bedding plant (Figs. II-1 and II-2 Eustoma). The showy flowers are 2.0 to 3.5 in. (5.0 to 9.5 cm) across; colored white, green, yellow, pale to dark pink, lilac, or blue to purple; and sometimes bicolored or doubled. The opposite leaves are ovate to oblong. Depending on cultural techniques, the plant can be an annual or biennial. Established plants can overwinter in Zone 6, but percentage surviving is often low even in well-drained soil.

CULTIVARS

Numerous cultivars exist and new cultivars are added annually with additional colors, reduced rosetting, improved heat resistance, and fewer

FIGURE II-2 EUSTOMA *Eustoma* 'Piccolo 2 Yellow' cut flowers.

diseases (Harbaugh and Scott, 1996, 1998, 2003; Harbaugh et al., 1996). Breeding efforts are also focusing on increased seed germination, seedling vigor, stem strength, basal branching, uniformity of flowering among plants within a crop, and postharvest life (P. Katz, personal communication). Colchicine induced polyploidy resulted in stronger and shorter stems (Griesbach and Bhat, 1990).

Cut flower cultivars are selected based on petal number (singles or double) and production time (winter, spring, or summer). Double-flowered cultivars are most popular. In addition, short cultivars are being produced for bedding and potted plant use.

PROPAGATION

Seed propagation is the most common propagation method; however, vegetative cuttings or *in vitro* propagation can be used (Griesbach et al., 1988). Seeds are small, 624,000/oz (22,000/g), and germinate within 10 to 15 days at medium temperatures of 68 to 77°F (20° to 25°C). Do not cover the seed and supply a minimum light intensity of 49 fc (10 μmol · m^{-2} · s^{-1}) (Roh et al., 1989). Although seeds germinate best in high humidity or fog, intermittent mist can also be used. Pelleted seeds are available and commonly sown in plug trays. After germination, move seedlings to 70 to 75/60 to 65°F (21 to 24/16 to 18°C) day/night temperatures for 15 to 30 days, after which time temperatures can be reduced to 70/60°F (21/16°C) day/night. Transplant into the field, ground bed, or final container after 2 to 3 months or when four to five pairs of leaves have formed.

FLOWERING CONTROL AND DORMANCY

In nature, plants flower in the early summer and seeds mature, dehisce, and germinate by late autumn. These young plants form a rosette, overwinter, bolt (stems elongate), and flower the following spring and early summer. Commercially, this biennial plant is treated as an annual to reduce flowering time.

Seedlings must form four to five leaf pairs to produce a quality cut flower or potted flowering plant. However, seedlings rosette, that is, form a whorl of leaves with short internodes, when exposed to either (1) 41 to 50°F (5 to 10°C) temperatures and SD or (2) 70°F (21°C) or higher night temperature regardless of photoperiod (Harbaugh et al., 1992; Roh et al., 1989). Seedlings with more than six leaf pairs and not bolted should be considered rosetted and not transplanted because they may not flower or may have excessively long crop times. Harbaugh et al. (1997) noted that cultivars could be grouped based on the minimum temperatures that can induce rosetting based on an average of daytime and nighttime high temperatures [(daytime high + nighttime high)/2]: heat-sensitive cultivars, 70 to 75°F (21 to 24°C); most cultivars, 75 to 82°F (24 to 29°C); and heat-tolerant cul-

tivars, above 88°F (31°C). Gibberellic acid (GA$_3$) can be used to induce bolting in rosetted plants (B. Coward, personal communication; Oka et al., 2001) (see Physiological Disorders section for more information).

Interestingly, Ohkawa et al. (1993) reported that the propensity to rosette and to subsequently require a cold dormancy breaking temperature is based on the temperature under which the mother seed plants form and ripen seed. For example, bolting increased (rosetting decreased) from 20 to 50% when seed maturation day/night temperatures increased from 73/64°F (23/18°C) to 91/82°F (33/28°C), respectively, and seed were subsequently germinated and grown at 73 to 82°F (23 to 28°C). However, if seeds were germinated and grown at a cooler day/night temperature of 73/64°F (23/18°C), regardless of seed maturation temperature, all of the resulting plants bolted.

If plants rosette, then a cold treatment may be required to induce further development. For seedlings of cultivars that do not bolt uniformly, Ohkawa et al. (1994) suggested 4 weeks of 59°F (15°C) or 6 weeks of 50°F (10°C) at 175 fc (35 μmol · m^{-2} · s^{-1}) if previously exposed to 91/82°F (33/28°C) day/night temperatures for 4 or 12 weeks, respectively.

There are two stages of growth during production:

Stage 1 (vegetative): After germination, plants are given SD (less than 12 hr) and 70 to 75/50 to 63°F (21 to 24/10 to 17°C) day/night temperatures for up to 3 months to ensure the development of a young plant having four to five leaf pairs. These plants will eventually bolt uniformly. Night temperatures above 70°F (21°C) may delay bolting and, if elongation has already occurred, may reduce quality.

Juvenility must be considered because four to five leaf pairs must form to produce a quality plant with high flower numbers. If seedlings in plug trays are cooled for 5 weeks at 54°F (12°C), date of flowering is hastened (Roh et al., 1989). Ohkawa et al. (1993, 1994) stated that if hydrated seeds are cooled for 5 weeks at 37 to 50°F (3 to 10°C), bolting is also enhanced.

Stage 2 (reproductive): Floral initiation and bolting occur during the next stage of growth and are favored by higher day/night temperatures of 75/64°F (24/18°C), high light intensity, and 16-hr LD. Long days or the use of HID lighting or artificial LD from incandescent lights may not hasten flowering in natural high-light areas. However, in locations with lower light intensities, 1 month of LD will enhance bolting and HID lighting will enhance plant quality. Consequently, under poor light intensities during winter months, *Eustoma* may be considered a LD plant. With an 8-hr photoperiod, no floral initiation occurred at temperatures from 50 to 68°F (10 to 20°C) (Halevy and Kofranek, 1984; Harbaugh, 1995; Roh et al., 1989). Photoperiodic response is cultivar dependent as Harbaugh et al. (1997) considered most cultivars to be facultative LD plants and a few to be either "almost day-neutral" or obligate LD plants.

TEMPERATURE

Mother seed plants should be grown at close to 73/65°F (23/18°C) day/night in the final weeks prior to harvest for seed that will bolt uniformly (Ohkawa et al., 1993, 1994). Germinate seed at 68 to 77°F (20 to 25°C) in the light. Grow seedlings after germination at 70 to 75/60 to 65°F (21 to 24/16 to 18°C) day/night temperatures. An average daily temperature of 65°F (18°C) is also acceptable during the vegetative period until four to five leaf pairs have developed. Temperatures below 60°F (16°C) will slow growth and increase production time (Harbaugh et al., 1997). Thereafter, force at 65/60°F (18/16°C) day/night for bolting and flowering (Harbaugh, 1995; Harbaugh et al., 1992; Roh and Lawson, 1984; Roh et al., 1989).

LIGHT

Seeds can be germinated under natural light; however, fluorescent light is better. After germination, use natural or artificial 8- to 12-hr photoperiods to reduce rosetting until four to five leaf pairs are formed (Armitage and Laushman, 2003; Roh and Lawson, 1984; Roh et al., 1989). At the four- to five-pair leaf stage, LD can be used from incandescent or HID lamps. Incandescent lighting is applied from 2200 to 0200 (10 p.m. to 2 a.m.), while HID lighting is typically used for 16 hr during the day. Floral induction and bolting is hastened by HID lighting in low-light areas. Light intensities are reduced to lower temperatures and maintain petal color during the summer.

WATER

Do not overwater *Eustoma* plants because they are quite susceptible to root and crown rot. A well-drained medium is a cultural requirement.

CARBON DIOXIDE

No data available.

NUTRITION

Lisianthus requires high nutrient levels. Insufficient nutrients result in small plants, reduced basal axillary shoot development and few flowers, without showing obvious deficiency symptoms (Harbaugh et al., 1997). Once roots are established in the plug trays, plants can be fertilized twice weekly with 250 ppm N and K. When seedlings are transplanted into the final bed or container, fertilize with 250 ppm N and K constant liquid fertilization or up to 500 ppm N and K twice weekly. Lisianthus has a high requirement for potassium and calcium with a recommendation of 1N:1.5K for potted lisianthus (Harbaugh et al., 1997). Calcium nitrate and potassium nitrate can be used as the main fertilizer to help maintain high media pH. Roh and Lawson (1984) found that calcium is not translocated to the apex if plants are asexually propagated.

MEDIA

The medium should be well drained with a pH of 6.5 to 7.5; best growth is obtained with a pH of 6.7 (Harbaugh and Woltz, 1998; Harbaugh et al., 1997). A medium pH of 6.5 or less results in micronutrient toxicity, the symptoms of which include foliar chlorosis, poor root growth, leaf edge and tip necrosis, and stunted growth (Harbaugh et al., 1997, 1998). Harbaugh et al. (1997) noted that zinc toxicity can occur at media pH as high as 5.8 to 6.2. Root systems are never vigorous. A peat-lite medium can be used for potted flowering plant production. For cut flowers, good drainage is essential and raised beds are used.

HEIGHT CONTROL

For potted flowering and bedding plants, genetically short cultivars should be used. If height control is required, A-Rest (ancymidol, 0.5 mg/pot drench), B-Nine (daminozide, 2500 to 5000 ppm spray), Bonzi (paclobutrazol, 4 to

16 ppm drench), or Sumagic (uniconazole, 5 to 10 ppm sprays) can be used (Adriansen, 1989; Starman, 1991; Tjia and Sheehan, 1986; Whipker et al., 1994). Of these chemicals, B-Nine and Bonzi are most commonly used (Harbaugh et al., 1997). Bonzi sprays are ineffective and Cycocel (chlormequat) is not very effective. Late applications of B-Nine may reduce flower size.

Multiple applications may be required, depending on the cultivar, when internode elongation begins. A plant growth curve as with poinsettias can be prepared and used (see Graphical Tracking section of Chapter 8, Plant Growth Regulation). Blue and pink cultivars are reported to be less vigorous than the white cultivars, which require more drenches or higher concentrations (Whipker et al., 1994). Up to four chemical applications may be required for proper height control of vigorous potted plant cultivars, which are shorter than cut flower cultivars (Harbaugh et al., 1997).

SPACING

Commercially, seed are sown in various types of plug trays; the two most commonly used types have (1) 392 plugs per flat with each cell 5/8-in. (1.5-cm) square and (2) 162 plugs per flat with each cell 1 1/6-in. (2.8-cm) square. Cells of the plug flats should be as deep as possible. Never allow young seedlings to become root bound because stunting may occur. For potted flowering plants, use one plug per 4-in. (10-cm) pot and three to five plugs per 5- to 7-in. (13- to 18-cm) pot. Spacing for cut flowers in beds ranges from 6 × 6 to 12 × 12 in. (15 × 15 to 30 × 30 cm) according to season, production site (greenhouse or field), and production method (single stem or pinched crop) (Armitage and Laushman, 2003; Halevy and Kofranek, 1984).

PINCHING AND DISBUDDING

Plants for cut flower or potted plant production can be pinched to induce branching. However, pinching may increase production time by up to 2 weeks (Roh and Lawson, 1984). If plants are pinched, do so when shoots begin to elongate and are 1 to 2 in. (2.5 to 5.0 cm) long or when four to five visible nodes can be left on the plant. On the average, four axillary stems will develop. Do not pinch higher or lower. Many modern cultivars branch naturally and pinching is not necessary.

SUPPORT

Support cut flowers with one to two tiers of support in the field or greenhouse (Armitage and Laushman, 2003). If properly grown with the correct cultivar selection, potted plants do not require support. The use of plant growth regulators will also increase stem quality and strength of potted flowering plants.

SCHEDULE AND TIMING

Lisianthus is a long-term crop of 5 to 7 months (Tables II-1 and II-2 Eustoma). Most producers of cut or potted flowering plants purchase plug-grown seedlings that are approximately 10 to 12 weeks old. Transplant plugs when they have four to five leaf pairs.

INSECTS

Aphids, fungus gnats, whiteflies, thrips, and leaf minor may damage crops if not monitored and treated. Thrips can be especially damaging to dark-colored flowers because the feeding damage is readily apparent. Fungus gnats can inflict enough damage to kill lisianthus plants (Harbaugh et al., 1997). Nematodes have also been reported (Dreistadt, 2001).

DISEASES

Most root and crown rot diseases (*Fusarium, Phytophthora, Pythium,* and *Rhizoctonia*) occur during the long vegetative stage. Do not overwater, and grow plants in a well-aerated medium. Routine preventive drenches for crown, stem, and root rot may be needed. *Botrytis* can be equally damaging by causing tan infection sites on the stem near the medium line (Daughtrey and Chase, 1992). While differences in susceptibility to *Fusarium* were noted in 46 cultivars, none were resistant (Harbaugh and McGovern, 2000). *Curvularia* leaf blotch begins as tiny tan specks that enlarge into blotches and is favored by warm temperatures of 75°F (24°C) (McGovern et al., 1998). Lisianthus is also susceptible to various viruses including impatiens necrotic spot, tomato spotted wilt, bean yellow mosaic, tobacco mosaic, and tomato yellow leaf curl viruses and to downy mildew (*Peronospora*), powdery mildew (*Leveillula taurica*), leaf spot (*Cercospora eustomae*), and *Thielaviopsis* (Dreistadt, 2001; P. Katz, personal communication).

TABLE II-I EUSTOMA

Sample production schedule for *Eustoma* cut flower production.

Cultural Step	Production Time (weeks)	Temperature °F (°C)	Photoperiod	Comments
Sow seed	2	Medium: 68–77 (20–25)	LD, using fluorescent or incandescent lights	Do not cover; germinate in fog or under mist
Grow seedlings to 4 to 5 leaf pair stage	8–10	Medium: 65–73 (18–23)[a] Day: 70–75 (21–24) Night: 59–63 (15–17)	12-hr or shorter day	HID lighting enhances quality
Transplant to beds[b]	6–8	Medium: 65–73 (18–23) Day: 65–75 (18–24) Night: 59–63 (15–17)	16-hr or longer day	Do not allow plugs to become root bound because that will stunt growth after transplanting
Visible bud	4–6	Medium: 65–73 (18–23) Day: 65–75 (18–24) Night: 59–63 (15–17)	16-hr or longer day	Shade may be needed to prevent fading of flowers
Harvest	2	Medium: 65–73 (18–23) Day: 65–75 (18–24) Night: 59–63 (15–17)	16-hr or longer day	Lower temperature if possible to increase postharvest life
Total	22–28			

[a] If day temperatures are warm, 75–80°F (24–27°C), then compensate by reducing night temperature to low end of indicated range.
[b] Plugs can be purchased and planted into beds at this stage.

PHYSIOLOGICAL DISORDERS

Edge or tip leaf burn, a calcium deficiency, occurs after a protracted period of cloudy weather with low transpiration rates, followed by a period of warm bright sunny days. This disorder is seen primarily when flower buds are visible and is also observed in *Liatris*, *Lilium*, and *Euphorbia pulcherrima*. In severe cases, the flower pedicel may collapse (Roh et al., 1989). Calcium nitrate sprays may be used during winter or early spring production (see *Euphorbia* chapter).

Rosetting and nonuniform stem elongation within a population are related to high temperatures at various growth stages from seed development and maturity to the juvenile four- to five-leaf stage. Generally, night temperatures of 70°F (21°C) and higher induce this problem. Gibberellic acid (GA$_3$) sprays at 50 to 100 ppm can be used to induce bolting in rosetted plants (B. Coward, personal communication; Oka et al., 2001). GA can be applied to plants in the plug flat or in the field. In the field, sprays can be made within 30 days to the entire crop or only those plants that are resetted.

Foliar chlorosis, leaf edge and tip necrosis, and poor root and shoot growth are associated with a medium pH of less than 5.5.

Small plants, reduced breaking, and few flowers can result from inadequate nutrition,

TABLE II-2 EUSTOMA
Sample schedule for potted *Eustoma* flowering plant production.

Cultural Step	Production Time (weeks)	Temperature °F (°C)	Photoperiod	Comments
Sow seed	2	Medium: 68–77 (20–25)	LD, using fluorescent or incandescent lights	Do not cover; germinate in fog or under mist
Grow seedlings to 4 to 5 leaf stage	8–10	Medium: 65–73 (18–23)[a] Day: 70–75 (21–24) Night: 59–63 (15–17)	12-hr or shorter day	HID lighting enhances quality
Transplant to beds[b]	6–8	Medium: 65–73 (18–23) Day: 65–75 (18–24) Night: 59–63 (15–17)	16-hr or longer day	Do not allow plugs to become root bound because that will stunt growth after transplanting; apply 1 or 2 growth retardant treatments.[c]
Visible bud	4–6	Medium: 65–73 (18–23) Day: 65–75 (18–24) Night: 59–63 (15–17)	16-hr or longer day	Apply third growth retardant treatment, if required; shade may be needed to prevent fading
Harvest	2	Medium: 65–73 (18–23) Day: 65–75 (18–24) Night: 59–63 (15–17)	16-hr or longer day	Lower temperature if possible to increase postharvest life
Total	22–28			

[a] If day temperatures are warm, 75–80°F (24–27°C), then compensate by reducing night temperature to low end of indicated range.
[b] Plugs can be purchased and planted into pots at this stage.
[c] First application is made when axillary shoots are 2 in. (5 cm) long. Second application can be made 2 to 3 weeks later, if required.

temperatures that are too high during production, and long day lengths. Proper cultivar selection for the specific time of year that the cultivar is produced will reduce this problem.

POSTHARVEST

Longevity of sprays can reach 21 days if properly treated. Halevy and Kofranek (1984) found that pulsing for 24 hr with 5 to 10% sucrose increased longevity up to 13 to 15 days and increased flower opening to 100% compared with untreated flowers. Solutions with 10% sucrose were superior and should include 300 ppm citric acid and 250 ppm 8-hydroxyquinaline citrate. Incorporating a 50-ppm benzyladenine (BA) pulse for 24 hr prior to placing cut stems into 4% sucrose solution was better than just a 4% sucrose pulse (Huang and Chen, 2002).

Flowers that open under low light are paler than those opening in high-light conditions due to decreased anthocyanin biosynthesis (Griesbach, 1992). Kawabata et al.

(1995) also found that cut lisianthus flowers were paler under low light than high light and that shading the leaves and stem reduced flower color. Shading just the flower buds did not change the color but adding 0.5 M sucrose to the vase solution of flowers under low light produced flower color in cut stems similar to potted plants held in high-light conditions.

Cut stems should be shipped and stored at 33 to 35°F (1 to 2°C) (Nell and Reid, 2001). Cut flowers are harvested when one or more flowers are open; flowers for local markets may have up to six flowers open or well colored.

Individual flowers on potted plants last 12 to 14 days and plants last 19 to 25 days (Halevy and Kofranek, 1984). Potted plants can be shipped and sold when one or two flowers per plant are open or opening. Unlike most potted plants, fertilization should continue until harvest for maximum postharvest life (T. Nell, personal communication). Plants should be shipped at 35°F (2°C). Depending on the cultivar, plants may not be shipped for longer than 3 days in the dark. Flowers are sensitive to ethylene, and 0.3- to 0.4-mM silver thiosulfate (STS) spray treatments are advised (Ichimura et al., 1998; Nowak and Rudnicki, 1990).

KEY POINTS

- Lisianthus is used as a cut flower, potted flowering plant, and bedding plant. Primary use is as a cut flower.

- Lisianthus is seed propagated commercially.

- High temperatures during seedling production promote rosetting. Rosetting delays or prevents flowering.

- Plants require high fertilizer rates and high levels of calcium and potassium.

- Media pH should be 6.5 to 7.5, with 6.7 optimum. Lower media pH may cause micronutrient toxicity.

- Flowers are easily damaged by contact with water and rain. Botrytis can be a serious problem on flowers and foliage in storage.

- Sucrose is required for optimum postharvest life of cut stems.

BIBLIOGRAPHY

Adriansen, E. 1989. Eustoma is ideal for pots. *Greenhouse Grower* 7(4):50–51, 54.

Armitage, A.M., and J.M. Laushman. 2003. *Eustoma grandiflorum*, pp. 279–289 in *Specialty Cut Flowers*, 2nd ed. Timber Press, Portland, Oregon.

Daughtrey, M., and A.R. Chase. 1992. *Lisianthus*, pp. 141–142 in *Ball Field Guide to Diseases of Greenhouse Ornamentals*. Ball Publishing, Geneva, Illinois.

Dreistadt, S.H. 2001. *Integrated Pest Management for Floriculture and Nurseries*. University of California Division of Agriculture and Natural Resources Publication 3402.

Griesbach, R.J. 1992. Correlation of pH and light intensity on flower color in potted *Eustoma grandiflorum* Grise. *HortScience* 27: 817–818.

Griesbach, R.J., and R.N. Bhat. 1990. Colchicine-induced polyploidy in *Eustoma grandiflorum*. *HortScience* 25:1284–1286.

Griesbach, R. J., P. Semeniuk, M. Roh, and R.H. Lawson. 1988. Tissue culture in the improvement of *Eustoma*. *HortScience* 23:658, 791.

Halevy, A.H., and A.M. Kofranek. 1984. Evaluation of lisanthus as a new flower crop. *HortScience* 19:845–847.

Harbaugh, B.K. 1995. Flowering of *Eustoma grandiflorum* (Raf.) Shinn. cultivars influenced by photoperiod and temperature. *HortScience* 30: 1375–1377.

Harbaugh, B.K., and McGovern. 2000. Susceptibility of forty-six *Lisianthus* cultivars to fusarium crown and stem rot. *HortTechnology* 10:816–819.

Harbaugh, B.K., and J.W. Scott. 1996. 'Maurine Blue' lisianthus [*Eustoma grandiflorum* (Raf.) Shinn.]. *HortScience* 31:1055–1056.

Harbaugh, B.K., and J.W. Scott. 1998. Six heat-tolerant cultivars of lisianthus. *HortScience* 33:164–165.

Harbaugh, B.K., and J.W. Scott. 2003. 'Maurine Twilight' and 'Maurine Daylight'—heat-tolerant lisianthus with bi-colored flowers. *HortScience* 38:131–132.

Harbaugh, B.K., and S.S. Woltz. 1998. *Eustoma* quality is adversely affected by low pH of root medium. *HortScience* 26:1279–1280.

Harbaugh, B.K., M.S. Roh, R. H. Lawson, and B. Pemberton. 1992. Rosetting of lisianthus cultivars exposed to high temperature. *HortScience* 27:885–887.

Harbaugh, B.K., J.W. Scott, and D.B. Rubino. 1996. 'Florida Blue' semi-dwarf lisianthus [*Eustoma grandiflorum* (Raf.) Shinn.]. *HortScience* 31: 1057–1058.

Harbaugh, B.K., R.J. McGovern, and J.P. Price. 1997. Potted lisianthus: Secrets of success, part 1. *Greenhouse Grower* 15(14):28, 30, 32, 36–37.

Harbaugh, B.K., R.J. McGovern, and J.P. Price. 1998. Potted lisianthus: Secrets of success, part 2. *Greenhouse Grower* 16(1):42, 44, 46, 48, 50, 52.

Huang, K.-L., and W.-S. Chen. 2002. BA and sucrose increase vase life of cut *Eustoma* flowers. *HortScience* 37:547–549.

Huxley, A., M. Griffiths, and M. Levy. 1992. *Eustoma*, p. 271 in *The New Royal Horticultural Society Dictionary of Gardening*, vol. 2. Stockton Press, New York.

Ichimura, K., M. Shimamura, and T. Hisamatsu. 1998. Role of ethylene in senescence of cut *Eustoma* flowers. *Postharvest Biology and Technology* 14:193–198.

Kawabata, S., M. Ohta, Y. Kusuhara, and R. Sakiyama. 1995. Influences of low light intensities on the pigmentation of *Eustoma grandiflorum* flowers. *Acta Horticulturae* 405: 173–178.

McGovern, R.J., B.K. Harbaugh, and J.F. Price. 1998. Potted lisianthus: Secrets of success, part 4. *Greenhouse Grower* 16(3):28, 30, 32, 34, 36.

Nell, T.A., and M.S Reid. 2001. Can't take the heat. *Floral Management* 17(10):33–34.

Nowak, J., and R.M. Rudnicki. 1990. *Postharvest Handling and Storage of Cut Flowers, Florist Greens and Potted Plants*. Timber Press, Portland, Oregon.

Ohkawa, K., M. Korenaga, and T. Yoshizumi. 1993. Influence of temperature prior to seed ripening and at germination on rosette formation and bolting of *Eustoma grandiflorum*. *Scientia Horticulturae* 53:225–230.

Ohkawa, K., T. Yoshizumi, M. Korenaga, and K. Kanematsu 1994. Reversal of heat-induced rosetting in *Eustoma grandiflorum* with low temperatures. *HortScience* 29:165–166.

Oka, M., Y. Tasaka, M. Iwabuchi, and M. Mino. 2001. Elevated sensitivity to gibberellin by vernalization in the vegetative rosette plants of *Eustoma grandiflorum* and *Arabidopsis thaliana*. *Plant Science* 160:1237–1245.

Roh, M.S.M., and R.H. Lawson. 1984. The lure of lisianthus. *Greenhouse Manager* 2(11):103–104, 108, 110, 112–114, 116–121.

Roh, M.S., A.H. Halevy, and H.F. Wilkins. 1989. *Eustoma grandiflorum*, pp. 322–327 in *The Handbook of Flowering*, vol. VI, A.H. Halevy, editor. CRC Press, Boca Raton, Florida.

Starman, T.W. 1991. Lisianthus growth and flowering responses to uniconazole. *HortScience* 26:150–152.

Tija, B., and T.J. Sheehan. 1986. Chemical height control *Lisianthus russellianus*. *HortScience* 21:147–148.

Whipker, B.E., R.T. Eddy, and P.A. Hammer. 1994. Chemical growth retardant application to lisianthus. *HortScience* 29:1368.

Exacum

FIGURE II-1 EXACUM Potted *Exacum* plant.

INTRODUCTION

Common names: exacum, German violet, Persian violet.

Scientific name: *Exacum affine* Balf. f. (Huxley et al., 1992).

Family and related taxa: Gentianaceae Juss. Other important genera in this family are *Eustoma*, *Gentiana*, and *Sabatia*.

Origin: Socotra Islands off the coast of Saudia Arabia.

Uses and current status: Potted flowering plant for summer sales (Fig. II-1 Exacum).

Exacum affine is an annual that grows up to 2 ft (60 cm) tall. The plant is heavily branched, commencing at the base, with ovate, glossy, dark green leaves 1 to 1.5 in. (2.5 to 4 cm) long. Flowers are 0.5 to 0.75 in. (1 to 2 cm) wide, occur in various tints of blue, mauve, or white, may be double, and have golden yellow stamens (Bailey and Bailey, 1976).

CULTIVARS

Various cultivars are available in the commercial trade. Some cultivars are genetically dwarf, only 5 to 6 in. (13 to 15 cm) tall at maturity, and are grown in 4-in. (10-cm) pots. The standard size cultivars grown in 6-in. (15-cm) pots are polyploids. Flower colors include blue, mauve, plum, or white. The double types require 2 to 3 weeks longer to flower. Hybrids with other *Exacum* species may expand the range of characteristics available in the future (Anon and Craig, 1996). Breeders are working to develop consistently double flowers, larger flowers, more colors, dwarf habit, shorter crop time, and improved postharvest life (Rubino, 1991, 1993; Earl J. Small Inc., personal communication).

PROPAGATION

Various cultivars and hybrids are propagated by cuttings or seed. The double flowered cultivars are sterile and must be asexually propagated. Cuttings root easily at 70°F (21°C) media temperature. There are 1 million seeds/oz (35,000/g). Seeds germinate best under light at a temperature range from 60 to 80°F (16 to 27°C), with 72 to 77°F (22 to 25°C) being optimal. Because seeds are quite small, they should be germinated on a fine medium under a high-pressure mist or fog system to keep the seeds moist (Cathey, 1969; Irwin, 1984; Sweet, 1982). *In vitro* propagation has been reported (Torres and Natarella, 1984).

FLOWERING CONTROL AND DORMANCY

Exacum is a day-neutral plant with both vegetative growth rate and rapid reproductive initiation and development dependent on the sum of accumulated light energy photon flux (Wilkins and Halevy, 1989; Williams et al., 1983). Plants grown at three irradiance levels of 425, 915, or 1725 fc (85, 183, or 345 μmol · m^{-2} · s^{-1}) flowered most rapidly at the highest energy level. The number of flowers and plant fresh-weights were also greatest at the highest

energy level (Williams et al., 1983). However, the most commercially acceptable plants were those grown at 915 fc (183 μmol · m^{-2} · s^{-1}).

Double exacum may not completely open or develop a good blue color. Gibberellic acid (GA$_3$) sprays are effective in solving these problems and are applied when the flower buds are 0.5 to 0.75 in. (1.3 to 2 cm) in diameter. One (250- to 500-ppm) spray or two (100-ppm) sprays a week apart can be used (Kofranek et al., 1984). Neumaier et al. (1985) used a 125-ppm GA$_3$ spray. Regardless of the amount applied, flower quality is improved and opening is more rapid with no internode elongation.

TEMPERATURE

Night temperatures are best kept above 60 to 65°F (16 to 18°C) to duplicate exacum's native habitat in a torrid area of the world (Irwin, 1984). Temperatures during production for summer sales can be 86/66°F (30/19°C) day/night (Harbaugh and Waters, 1982; Larson, 1981; Sweet, 1982).

LIGHT

Rapid growth and flowering is light dependent (Williams et al., 1983). Growth of seedlings or young rooted cuttings can be stimulated by a 16-hr day from fluorescent or HID lights (Irwin, 1984). Interestingly, pulse lighting with HID lamps (45 sec off, 90 sec on) from 0600 to 2200 (6 a.m. to 10 p.m.) increased shoot dry weight by 225% over ambient lighting (Tardif and Dansereau, 1993). Full sun is best in the fall, winter, and spring. Shade should be used only to prevent excessive heat buildup in the greenhouse when light levels exceed 4500 to 6000 fc (900 to 1200 μmol · m^{-2} · s^{-1}) (Larson, 1981; Sweet, 1982; Earl J. Small Inc., personal communication).

WATER

Plants should be grown moist but not too wet or dry. Excessive moisture will encourage excessive succulent vegetative growth, which is prone to disease. However, do not allow plants to wilt because they may not recover (Larson, 1981). Excessive wilting will also cause premature flower development and small plant size. Quality plants can be produced when irrigated either by capillary mat or overhead irrigation (Harbaugh and Waters, 1982). Ebb-and-flow irrigation produced superior growth compared to capillary mat irrigation (Willumsen, 1993).

CARBON DIOXIDE

No data on carbon dioxide have been reported.

NUTRITION

A 150- to 200-ppm N, 50-ppm P, and 150-ppm K fertilization regime at each irrigation has been recommended (Larson, 1981). Growers need to exercise caution with fertilization because excessive nutrition can result in soft growth, delayed flowering, and increased susceptibility to disease. Under Florida conditions, Harbaugh and Waters (1982) produced high-quality plants in 4-in. (10-cm) pots with either 3- to 4-month or 8- to 9-month controlled-released fertilizer (Osmocote, 14N–6P–12K or 18N–3P–10K) used at a rate of 5 to 8 lb/yd^3 (3 to 5 kg · m^{-3}). Calcium deficiency can be a problem resulting in death of the apical shoot (Holcomb and Craig, 1983). Foliar nutrient levels for high-quality plants are listed in Chapter 6, Nutrition, Table 6-4.

MEDIA

The medium should be well drained with adequate nutrient and water retention. Various formulations, including commercial premixed media and rockwool and peat-based media, can be used to successfully produce exacum (Hansen et al., 1993; Willumsen, 1993). In Florida, peat, vermiculite, sand, and perlite (5:3:3:1, by volume) have been used when amended with the following: dolomite [10 lb/yd^3 (6 kg · m^{-3})], hydrated lime [5 lb/yd^3 (3 kg · m^{-3})], single superphosphate [2.5 lb/yd^3 (1.5 kg · m^{-3})], and micronutrients (Harbaugh and Waters, 1982). North Carolina growers have used pine bark, peat moss, and sand (3:1:1). A pH of 6.0 to 7.0 is thought to be optimal (Larson, 1981).

HEIGHT CONTROL

A plant growth regulator may need to be used if light is limited. One to three B-Nine (daminozide) spray applications at 2500 ppm each can be used to control internode elongation and improve plant quality (Sweet, 1982). Generally, the first application is applied 7 to 10 days after plugs are transplanted and new growth commences. Bonzi (paclobutrazol) can be used, both as a 75-ppm spray or as a 0.25 to 0.75 mg a.i./ 6-in. (15-cm) pot drench (Hasek et al., 1986). Adriansen (1985) noted that A-Rest (ancymidol) is also effective.

SPACING

If a 4-in. (10-cm) pot plant is being produced from genetic dwarf lines, final spacing ranges from 8 × 8 to 11 × 11 in. (20 × 20 to 28 × 28 cm); for 6-in. (15-cm) pot production, 9 × 9 to 14 × 14 in. (23 × 23 to 36 × 36 cm) can be used. Plants can be placed pot-to-pot for the first 4 weeks after the seedlings or plugs are transplanted (Irwin, 1984). Remember, rapid flowering is dependent on accumulated light energy; hence, do not allow plants to become crowded.

PINCHING AND DISBUDDING

Plants are self-branching and only rarely need to be pinched. Disbudding is unnecessary.

SUPPORT

No support required.

SCHEDULE AND TIMING

If plugs are purchased from a specialist, exacum can be a quick 7-week crop produced in 4-in. (10-cm) pots during summer or up to 22 weeks during winter (Irwin, 1984; Larson, 1981) (see Tables II-1 and II-2 Exacum). Plants can be grown from seed or cuttings.

INSECTS

Exacum is relatively insect free; however, infestations of leaf miners or broad mites can be a major problem. Broad mites cause leaves and the apex to distort and the resulting off-colored flowers fail to develop (Irwin, 1984). Thrips are also a concern because they transmit the tomato spotted wilt virus (see Diseases, below).

DISEASES

Botrytis cinerea has long been a serious problem. This fungus develops in the axils of the lower main axillary branches and results in wilting of the branch or of the entire plant as the vascular system is girdled. Exacum are especially susceptible to *Botrytis* 1 to 2 weeks after transplanting. In the greenhouse *Botrytis* was most severe during cool, damp periods when the temperature was approximately 68°F (20°C) but occurred even when temperatures were up to 86 to 95°F (30 to 35°C) (Ploetz and Engelhard, 1979). Under controlled conditions 90°F (32°C) day temperatures alternating with 73°F (23°C) night temperatures caused rapid development of disease within 4 hr. Environmental and chemical controls are required to prevent losses, especially during conditions of

TABLE II-1 EXACUM

Sample production schedule for *Exacum* from seed for either 4-in. (10-cm) or 6-in. (15-cm) pots.

Cultural Step	Production Time (weeks)	Temperature °F (°C)
Germinate seed in plugs		
	2–3	Medium: 72–75 (22–24)
Move plugs to greenhouse		
	4–5	Day: 72–75 (22–24)
		Night: 60–65 (16–18)
For 4-in. (10-cm) pots:		
Transplant plugs to 4-in. (10-cm) pots, space pot-to-pot		
	3–5	
Space		
	4–9	Day: 72–75 (22–24)
		Night: 60–65 (16–18)
Flower		
Total	13–22[a]	
For 6-in. (15-cm) pots:		
Transplant plugs to 6-in. (15-cm) pots, space pot-to-pot		
	4–10	Day: 72–75 (22–24)
		Night: 60–65 (16–18)
Space pots		
	4–8	Day: 72–75 (22–24)
		Night: 60–65 (16–18)
Flower		
Total	14–26[a]	

[a]Shortest crop times in summer and longest in winter.

TABLE II-2 EXACUM

Sample production schedule for *Exacum* from cuttings for either 4-in. (10-cm) or 6-in. (15-cm) pots.

Cultural Step	Production Time (weeks)	Temperature °F (°C)
Root cuttings in plugs		
	2–3	Medium: 72–75 (22–24)
For 4-in. (10-cm) pots:		
Transplant plugs to 4-in. (10-cm) pots, space pot-to-pot		
	2–3	Day: 72–75 (22–24)
		Night: 60–65 (16–18)
Space pots		
	4–10	Day: 72–75 (22–24)
		Night: 60–65 (16–18)
Flower		
Total	8–16[a]	
For 6-in. (15-cm) pots:		
Transplant plugs to 6-in. (15-cm) pots, space pot-to-pot		
	4–5	Day: 72–75 (22–24)
		Night: 60–65 (16–18)
Space pots		
	4–10	Day: 72–75 (22–24)
		Night: 60–65 (16–18)
Flower		
Total	10–18[a]	

[a]Shortest crop times in summer and longest in winter.

high moisture and humidity (Daughtrey and Chase, 1992; Irwin, 1984; Jones et al., 1981; Pfleger, 1984).

Tomato spotted wilt virus (Daughtrey and Chase, 1992; Zitter et al., 1989) is a serious threat to potted flowering plant production of exacum. Plants die rapidly when this thrips-vectored disease infects the plant.

A number of other diseases have been recorded including fusarium wilt (*Fusarium*), basal stem rot (*Nectria haematococca*), and root rot (*Pythium ultimum*) (Dreistadt, 2001).

PHYSIOLOGICAL DISORDERS

Double exacum may not completely open or develop a good blue pigment (see Flowering Control and Dormancy, page 522, for remedies). Delayed flowering can occur with excessive fertilization or irrigation or low light levels. Premature flowering on plants that are too short can occur with excessive wilting, high light levels, high temperatures, and low nutrition.

POSTHARVEST

Market plants when flowering commences (Nowak and Rudnicki, 1990). Larson (1981) suggested that nutrition should cease 7 to 14 days prior to shipment; however, Harbaugh and Waters (1982) found that foliage deteriorated to a greater degree with low controlled-release fertilizer rates than with high rates.

Though exacum has a low sensitivity to ethylene, abscission of flowers and buds will occur when exposed to ethylene. Sprays of 0.5 to 0.8 mM silver thiosulfate (STS) should be used. Ideal plant shipping temperatures are 55 to 60°F (13 to 16°C). Plants will collapse and die when exposed to temperatures of 40°F (4°C) or lower. Even at 48°F (9°C), the maximum duration is 48 hr or injury will occur (Nowak and Rudnicki, 1990; H.F. Wilkins, personal observations). Plants in retail areas and the home need 50 to 100 fc (10 to 20 μmol $\cdot$ m^{-2} $\cdot$ s^{-1}) (Nell, 1993).

KEY POINTS

- Exacum is used as a potted flowering plant.
- Plants are propagated by cuttings or seed.
- During production, do not overwater or over-fertilize because flowering can be delayed.
- During production, do not water stress because premature flowering can occur on undersized plants.

- Full light is used for rapid flowering and is reduced only for temperature control.
- Plants die at 40°F (4°C) or lower.
- *Botrytis* and tomato spotted wilt virus are major problems.

BIBLIOGRAPHY

Adriansen, E. 1985. Kemisk vækstregulering, pp. 142–162 in *Potteplanter I—Produktion, Metoder, Midler*, O.V. Christensen, A. Klougart, I.S. Pedersen, and K. Wikesjö, editors. Gartner-INFO, København, Denmark. (in Danish)

Anon, K.M., and R. Craig. 1996. Growth and flowering of interspecific hybrids of Sri Lankan *Exacum* species (Gentianaceae): A challenge in domestication. *HortScience* 31:597. (Abstract)

Bailey, L.H., and E.Z. Bailey. 1976. *Exacum*, pp. 468–469 in *Hortus Third: A Concise Dictionary of Plants Cultivated in the United States and Canada*. Macmillan, New York.

Cathey, H.M. 1969. Guidelines for the germination of annual, pot plant and ornamental herb seeds. II. *Florists' Review* 144(3743):18–20, 52–53.

Daughtrey, M., and A.R. Chase. 1992. *Exacum*, pp. 77–79 in *Ball Field Guide to Diseases of Greenhouse Ornamentals*. Ball Publishing, Geneva, Illinois.

Dreistadt, S.H. 2001. *Integrated Pest Management for Floriculture and Nurseries*. University of California Division of Agriculture and Natural Resources Publication 3402.

Hansen, M., H. Grønborg, N. Starkey, and L. Hansen. 1993. Alternative substrates for potted plants. *Acta Horticulturae* 342:191–196.

Harbaugh, B.K., and W.E. Waters. 1982. Influence of controlled-release fertilizer on *Exacum affine* Balf. F. 'Elfin' during production and subsequent simulated home conditions. *HortScience* 17: 605–606.

Hasek, R., R. Sciaroni, and G. Hickman. 1986. New growth regulator tested. *Greenhouse Grower* 4(2):52–53.

Holcomb, E.J., and R. Craig. 1983. Producing *Exacum* profitably. *Greenhouse Grower* 1(11):58, 57.

Huxley, A., M. Griffiths, and M. Levy. 1992. *Exacum*, p. 273 in *The New Royal Horticultural Society Dictionary of Gardening*, vol. 2. Stockton Press, New York.

Irwin, L. 1984. Exacum. *Minnesota State Florists Bulletin* 33(3):8–9.

Jones, R.K., D.L. Strider, and J.C. Trolinger. 1981. Exacum—A new crop with an old disease. *North Carolina Flower Growers Bulletin* 25(4):6–8.

Kofranek, A.M., A.H. Halevy, Y. Mor, and J. Kubota. 1984. Opening double *Exacum affine* flowers with gibberellic acid. *Florists' Review* 174(4506):33–34.

Larson, R.A. 1981. Commercial production of *Exacum*. *North Carolina Flower Growers Bulletin* 25(4):1–5.

Nell, T.A. 1993. *Exacum*, pp. 44–45 in *Flowering Potted Plants, Prolonging Shelf Performance*. Ball Publishing, Batavia, Illinois.

Neumaier, E.E., T.M. Blessington, and J.A. Price. 1985. Effect of gibberellic acid on flowering and quality of double Persian violet. *HortScience* 22:908–911.

Nowak, J., and R.M. Rudnicki. 1990. *Postharvest Handling and Storage of Cut Flowers, Florist Greens and Potted Plants*. Timber Press, Portland, Oregon.

Pfleger, F.L. 1984. *Exacum affine: Botrytis* blight and its control. *Minnesota State Florists Bulletin* 33(6):5–6.

Ploetz, R.C., and A.W. Engelhard. 1979. The botrytis blight of *Exacum affine*. *Proceedings of the Florida State Horticultural Society* 92:353–355.

Rubino, D.B. 1991. Performance of 15 *Exacum affine* genotypes in a low-irradiance environment. *HortScience* 26:1215–1216.

Rubino, D.B. 1993. Genotype × season interaction for time to flowering and flower and plant diameter in *Exacum affine* Balf. *HortScience* 28: 211–212.

Sweet, J. 1982. Latest cultural techniques for gloxinias, exacum, streptocarpus, and begonias. *Minnesota State Florists Bulletin* 31(5):11–13.

Tardif, M., and B. Dansereau. 1993. High R/FR HPS-pulses enhance earliness of flowering of exacum (*Exacum affine* Balf. f.) and geranium (*Pelargonium* ×*hortorum* L.H. Bailey). *Canadian Journal of Plant Science* 73:1163–1167.

Torres, K.C., and N.J. Natarella. 1984. *In vitro* propagation of *Exacum*. *HortScience* 19:224–225.

Wilkins, H.F., and A.H. Halevy. 1989. *Exacum*, pp. 328–330 in *Handbook of Flowering*, vol. VI, A.H. Halevy, editor. CRC Press, Boca Raton, Florida.

Williams, S., S. Wolf, and E.J. Holcomb. 1983. Growth and flowering of *Exacum affine* at three radiant energy levels. *HortScience* 18:366–367.

Willumsen, J. 1993. Assessment of fluctuations in water and air contents of pot substrates during plant growth. *Acta Horticulturae* 342:371–378.

Zitter, T.A., M.E. Daughtrey, and J.P. Sanderson. 1989. Tomato spotted wilt virus, pp. 107–112 in *Vegetable/Horticultural Crops*. Fact Sheet 735.90, Cornell Cooperative Extension, Ithaca, New York.

Freesia

INTRODUCTION

Common name: freesia.

Scientific name: *Freesia* ×*hybrida* Bailey (Huxley et al., 1992).

Family and related taxa: Iridaceae Juss. There are 19 species in the genus *Freesia*. The currently available hybrids are derived from crosses among *F. alba* (G.L. Mey) Gumbl., *F. refracta* (Jacq.) Klatt., *F. corymbosa* (Burmif.) N.E.Br., and *F. leichtlinnii* Klatt. Frequently, *F. refracta* is used in the scientific literature to designate the entire group of hybrids used in the florist industry (Gomans, 1980). Other important genera in this family include *Crocus*, *Gladiolus*, and *Iris*.

Origin: All species are from South Africa.

Uses and current status: Based on number of stems sold, freesia is one of the world's major cut flowers. Attractive and popular potted flowering plants are possible with dwarf cultivars or with the use of plant growth regulators on selected cultivars (De Hertogh, 1991, 1996; De Hertogh et al., 1990; Imanishi, 1993). Freesias can also be used in the garden. They are planted in the fall, flower in the spring, and perennialize in near frost-free zones. Otherwise, precooled corms are planted in the early spring, then flower, and are lifted again in the fall (De Hertogh et al., 1990).

Freesias are tunicated, cormous herbs with long linear leaves. The inflorescence is a spike; the individual flowers are funnel shaped, fragrant, and white, yellow, red, orange, purple, pink, and various shades in between (Bailey and Bailey, 1976).

CULTIVARS

Numerous single- and double-flowered cultivars are available. Genetic dwarfs are available and heat-tolerant cultivars have been reported (De Hertogh, 1996; De Hertogh et al., 1990). The most favored colors of freesia are pink, white, blue, and yellow.

PROPAGATION

The primary source of corms is the Netherlands. As with the related gladiolus, freesias annually form a new corm and numerous cormlets, which normally require an additional year of growth to flower.

Plants can be grown from seed with ease and will flower in approximately 9 months (Gilbertson-Ferriss and Wilkins, 1977, 1978b; Heide, 1965; Smith and Danks, 1985). Seeds germinate at an optimum rate and percentage when covered with vermiculite and held at 59 to 68°F (15 to 20°C). Seeds can be briefly soaked for 24 hr in water before sowing (Gilbertson-Ferriss and Wilkins, 1978b; Kepczynski, 1982; Masuda et al., 1992). Tissue culture is also used to obtain disease-free stock on a limited basis (Pierik and Steegmans, 1976).

FLOWERING CONTROL AND DORMANCY

Freesias have a basic annual thermoperiodic cycle of warm (86°F, 30°C), cool (50°F, 10°C), and warm (86°F, 30°C). Flower production is year-round when night temperatures are 59°F (15°C) or lower. Flowering is induced on seedlings after seven or more leaves are formed by lowering the temperature below 59°F (15°C). Harvested corms are dormant and must be given a minimum of 15 weeks of 86°F (30°C), after which corms can be planted, shoots emerge, and flowering is induced by temperatures of 55 to 59°F (13 to 15°C). However, for potted freesia Startek (2002) recommended 12 to 14 weeks of 82 to 90°F (28 to 30°C) followed by 10 days at 57 to 64°F (14 to 18°C) prior to potting.

To reduce production time in the greenhouse, dry corms can be placed in a cooler at 55 to 58°F (13 to 15°C) for up to 6 weeks for rapid flower initiation and development and shoot elongation. The cold treatment can be applied in various ways. For example, with potted plants, corms can be placed in the cooler dry for 3 weeks, potted, and returned to the cooler for an additional 3 weeks. Roots develop during the last cold treatment prior to forcing.

The decision to cold treat corms depends on the ambient air/media temperature, which must be 55 to 58°F (13 to 14°C) for rapid floral initiation and normal development of the inflorescence. This treatment is especially useful for potted plants because rapid flower initiation reduces the number of leaves formed and plant height. For cut flower production, the cold treatment is used when ambient temperatures are warm and marginal such as in the fall or in the spring before air temperatures are too warm.

If corms are not given a heat treatment of 86°F (30°C) or stored at temperatures near 35°F (2°C), they pupate. Pupation is the formation of a new corm on top of the old corm at the site of the apical-most bud. The new corms are equally dormant and must be heat treated (De Hertogh, 1996; De Hertogh et al., 1990; Gilbertson-Ferriss, 1985; Heide, 1965; Imanishi, 1993; Startek, 2002). Endogenous abscissic acid, indole-3-acetic acid (IAA), and cytokinin have been related to corm development (Gilbertson-Ferriss et al., 1981a, b; Masuda and Asahira, 1978). Ethylene has been used to replace or shorten the heat pretreatment required for *Freesia* corms (Uyemura and Imanishi, 1983, 1984) prior to cold treatment.

Corm treatments are usually done by specialists. Corms are harvested 6 weeks after flowering and stored for 2 weeks at 72°F (22°C). After grading, corms are heat treated for 24 hr at 112°F (44°C) for bulb mite control. Temperatures are lowered to 86°F (30°C) for a minimum of 15 to 16 weeks. Corms can be held for longer periods (retarded) if stored at 35°F (2°C) for 3 or 4 months and then held at 86°F (30°C) for 15 to 16 weeks. During these high-temperature treatments, humidity is kept near 85% with excellent air circulation (De Hertogh et al., 1990). Long-term storage, however, results in some desiccation of the corms and a loss in plant quality.

TEMPERATURE

High-quality freesias grow best at 55 to 60°F (13 to 16°C). Temperatures above 60°F (16°C) should be avoided after corms are first planted. Freesias may be a difficult species to grow if proper temperatures are not maintained. A soil cooling system may be useful for summer cut flower production. To hasten flowering, particularly with potted flowering plants, dry corms can be stored for 2 to 3 weeks at 55°F (13°C) after the initial heat treatment. Floral initiation normally occurs 6 to 9 weeks after planting, or after 5 to 6 weeks if dry stored at 55°F (13°C) before being planted. Corms can be dry stored at 55°F (13°C) for a maximum of 49 days; longer storage may result in pupation (De Hertogh et al., 1990; Imanishi, 1993).

During forcing, Gilbertson-Ferriss et al. (1981b) found that 55°F (13°C) was required for only 8 hr during the day or night when alternated with 75°F (24°C). This time span was sufficient for floral induction and development of an acceptable quality inflorescence.

LIGHT

Floral initiation is enhanced by SD, even though freesia is a day-neutral plant. Vegetative growth is favored by LD and high light levels. Plant and flower quality are best when the light level is greater than 2500 fc (500 $\mu mol \cdot m^{-2} \cdot s^{-1}$); 3000 to 5000 fc (600 to 1000 $\mu mol \cdot m^{-2} \cdot s^{-1}$) is preferred (De Hertogh, 1996; De Hertogh et al., 1990; Gilbertson-Ferriss and Wilkins, 1978b). Although 24-hr supplemental lighting may be deleterious (Blom and Piott, 1992; Doorduin, 1992), Doorduin in the Netherlands recommended 16 hr of supplemental lighting per day during the winter commencing when shoots are 6 in. (15 cm) tall (Doorduin, 1992).

WATER

The medium should be kept moist, but not wet. Freesias have contractile roots and the corm is systematically "pulled" deeper into the medium profile where moisture is more abundant. Consequently, corms are easy to overwater and thus rot. The best irrigation system for cut flower production is drip irrigation laid between the rows of planted corms. Overhead watering is not advised because freesia plants produce a dense leaf canopy and a profusion of flowering spikes. Also, water on the foliage might encourage stem lodging (leaning) and disease (Smith and Danks, 1985).

After flowers are harvested, water is slowly withdrawn for 6 weeks prior to corm and cormlet harvest (De Hertogh et al., 1990). Also, no fluoride should be in the water system (see Nutrition, below).

CARBON DIOXIDE

Photosynthesis can be increased and flower quality enhanced by 560 ppm CO_2 in the Netherlands (Doorduin, 1990). Higher levels may be beneficial if supplemental HID lighting is used.

NUTRITION

Prior to planting corms, growers should perform a soil test. While forcing, 200 ppm N from a balanced N–P–K fertilizer every 14 days is adequate. Ammonium-based nitrogen should be avoided because freesias are a "cold" crop. No superphosphate must be used because it may contain a natural fluoride contaminate, which

TABLE II-1 FREESIA
Freesia leaf nutrient levels from healthy foliar tissue.

Element	Level (Dole and Wilkins, 1988)	Level (Thomas et al., 1998)
Nitrogen	2.7–5.6%	2.2–2.3%
Phosphorus	0.4–1.2%	0.25–0.30%
Potassium	3.1–5.9%	4.0–4.5%
Calcium	0.4–1.0%	0.65–0.80%
Magnesium	0.3–1.8%	—
Iron	80–115 ppm	—
Manganese	30–540 ppm	20–25 ppm
Zinc	40–110 ppm	—
Copper	5–130 ppm	—
Boron	30–100 ppm	—

will cause leaf tip burn (Daughtrey and Chase, 1992; De Hertogh, 1996; Gilbertson-Ferriss and Wilkins, 1978a; Smith and Danks, 1985). Thomas et al. (1998) recommended applying N at 1 to 1.3 lb/yd^3 (600 to 800 g · m^3), P at 0.3 lb/yd^3 (200 g · m^{-3}), and K at 0.5 lb/yd^3 (300 g · m^{-3}) with a media pH of 5.9. Tissue test analysis standards are shown in Table II-1 Freesia.

MEDIA

The medium must be free of fluoride and no super- or treblesuperphosphate added (see Nutrition and Water sections, on previous page). Beds or benches should be at least 10 in. (25 cm) deep and contain pasteurized, well-drained media with a pH of 6.5 to 7.0 (De Hertogh et al., 1990).

HEIGHT CONTROL

Although cut flower producers need not be concerned with reducing stem length, growth regulators should be used on nongenetic dwarf cultivars for potted plants. Soaking corms for 1 hr with A-Rest (ancymidol) or Bonzi (paclobutrazol) will reduce internode elongation and leaf lengths (Gianfagna and Wulster, 1986) (Table II-2 Freesia). Treatments occur after the end of cold storage at 55°F (13°C) prior to planting. A-Rest may be used at 100 to 200 ppm and Bonzi at 50 to 200 ppm (Berghoef and Zevenbergen, 1990; De Hertogh, 1991, 1996; De Hertogh et al., 1990).

The effectiveness of height control measures is dependent on cultivar, season, and ambient temperature. Also, the physiological conditioning and response of the corm to pre-vious temperature treatments are important; for example, 41°F (5°C) storage for up to 4 weeks prior to planting resulted in shorter plants and earlier flowering (Wulster and Gianfagna, 1991).

SPACING

Corms are densely planted, 80 to 100/yd^2 (96 to 120/m^2). Corms are spaced an average of 1.5 in. (4 cm) apart; 1 in. (2.5 cm) during bright weather and 2 in. (5.25 cm) during dark periods. Corms are planted 2 in. (5 cm) deep as measured from the base of the corm.

For potted plants, the planting depth is 1 in. (2.5 cm). Four corms are typically planted per 4-in. (10-cm) pot and five corms per 5-in. (13-cm) pot (De Hertogh, 1991; De Hertogh et al., 1990). Pots can be placed pot-to-pot, but when growth commences use spacing of 10 × 10 in. (25 × 25 cm) for 4-in. (10-cm) pots and 12 × 12 in. (30 × 30 cm) for 5-in. (13-cm) pots.

PINCHING AND DISBUDDING

No pinching or disbudding is required. After harvesting the first stem two to four lateral shoots may develop if temperatures remain cool. Lateral stems will be shorter than the first stems harvested.

SUPPORT

Up to three layers of mesh are required for cut flowers to produce straight stems. For pots no support is required if plants are grown cool. Special plastic or metal rings clamped on the edge of the pot can be used if stems are too long and weak (De Hertogh, 1991, 1996).

TABLE II-2 FREESIA

The effect of A-Rest (ancymidol) or Bonzi (paclobutrazol) treatment[a] on *Freesia* stem length (adapted from Berghoef and Zevenbergen, 1990).

Growth Retardant	Concentration ppm	Stem Length in. (cm)
A-Rest dip	0	35 (88)
A-Rest dip	50	32 (82)
A-Rest dip	100	23 (58)
A-Rest dip	200	18 (46)
Bonzi dip	0	28 (70)
Bonzi dip	40	22 (56)
Bonzi	40 dip + 160 spray	18 (46)

[a]Corms were soaked for 2.5 or 6 hr prior to planting with A-Rest or Bonzi, respectively. Soil drenches can also be used (Wulster and Gianfagna, 1991), but corm soaks are preferred because of the chemical expense, labor application, lack of precision application, and the risk of medium inactivating the regulator associated with soil drenches.

SCHEDULE AND TIMING

When corms are planted after heat treatment, flower initiation occurs in 6 to 9 weeks at 53 to 59°F (12 to 15°C). When corms are planted for cut flowers, a harvest can be expected in 16 to 17 weeks at 50 to 55°F (10 to 13°C) and can last 4 weeks. With potted flowering plants, flowering should occur in 13 to 18 weeks if dry corms are given 3 to 6 weeks of cold treatment prior to planting, respectively (De Hertogh, 1991, 1996; De Hertogh et al., 1990). Growers can purchase heat- and cold-treated corms that are ready for planting.

INSECTS

Aphids and thrips are the most commonly observed insects on freesias (De Hertogh et al., 1990). Miscellaneous leaf chewing insects and fungus gnats may be a problem, with the former being more of a problem with potted plants.

DISEASES

Undoubtedly, viruses are the most serious problem, forcing greenhouse operators to buy selected new stock as frequently as every 3 years. Virus results in streaked flowers with a "withered look" and brown lesions on the leaves (Daughtrey and Chase, 1992). Frequently virus and fluoride damage are similar and difficult to distinguish. *Botrytis* can infect flowers, stems, and leaves. *Fusarium* can infect the corms, so growers should inspect them carefully (De Hertogh et al., 1990; Imanishi, 1993). Any corms showing pinkish lesions should be discarded (Horst, 1990). *Fusarium* is favored during production by warm temperatures and excessively wet medium. Other diseases have been recorded including root and stem rot (*Rhizoctonia*), bacterial soft rot (*Erwinia*), dry rot (*Stromatinia gladioli*), and bean yellow mosaic and cucumber mosaic viruses (Dreistadt, 2001).

PHYSIOLOGICAL DISORDERS

Thumbing is a term used to describe a freesia inflorescence where the lowest two to three flowers are unevenly spaced, separated from the main grouping of flowers along the spike, and the spike is nearly straight (Fig. II-1 Freesia). Normal flowering stems curve at a near 90° angle just below the first floret. Thumbing is caused by marginal flower induc-

FIGURE II-1 FREESIA   Two freesia inflorescences; left is normal and right is of poor quality due to thumbing disorder.

tion temperatures, slightly above 59°F (15°C) (Smith and Danks, 1985). This disorder is avoided if the young growing point can be protected by straw mulches or by shade during borderline temperature regimes (De Hertogh, 1996; Gilbertson-Ferriss et al., 1981).

If light levels are very low or if temperatures are extremely high during flower initiation, flower bud abortion can occur (De Hertogh et al., 1990). During production, plants are highly sensitive to ethylene. Exposures can result in flower bud malformation, abortion, and premature senescence (Nowak and Rudnicki, 1990).

POSTHARVEST

Cut flowers should be harvested, or potted flowering plants should be shipped, when the first floret is puffy and beginning to open and at least two other buds are well colored (De Hertogh et al., 1990; Nowak and Rudnicki, 1990; Sacalis, 1993). Both pots and cuts can be stored at 32 to 35°F (0 to 2°C). Cut flowers can be held dry for brief periods, but should be stored in water with preservative for longer periods. Treating flowers with 0.5 mM silver thiosulfate (STS) or 740 ppb 1-MCP can prevent the decline in vase life due to dry storage (J.M. Dole, unpublished data). Sucrose and other components found in a floral preservative will extend the vase life (Nowak and Rudnicki, 1990; Sacalis, 1993; Spikman, 1986, 1987, 1989; Woodson, 1987). Freesias are very sensitive to ethylene. Fluoride in water can reduce cut flower life.

KEY POINTS

- Freesia is used primarily as a cut flower, but also as a potted flowering plant and garden ornamental.

- Plants are propagated primarily by cormlets or occasionally by seed.

- Freesia corms require a heat treatment after harvest for dormancy release and shoot elongation.

- Flowers will be initiated and develop into a quality crop at 58°F (14°C) or lower, with 55°F (13°C) optimum.

- *Fusarium* and virus corm infections are major problems.

BIBLIOGRAPHY

Bailey, L.H., and E.Z. Bailey. 1976. *Freesia*, p. 487 in *Hortus Third: A Concise Dictionary of Plants Cultivated in the United States and Canada*. Macmillan, New York.

Berghoef, J., and A.P. Zevenbergen. 1990. The effect of precooling environmental factors and growth-regulating substances on plant height of *Freesia* as pot plant. *Acta Horticulturae* 266:251–257.

Blom, T.J., and B.D. Piott. 1992. Assimilative lighting with high-pressure sodium lamps reduces *Freesia* quality. *HortScience* 27:1267–1268.

Daughtrey, M., and A.R. Chase. 1992. Freesia, p. 93 in *Ball Field Guide to Diseases of Greenhouse Ornamental*. Ball Publishing, Geneva, Illinois.

De Hertogh, A. 1991. How to produce potted freesias. *Greenhouse Grower* 9(3):32, 34.

De Hertogh, A.A. 1996. *Freesias*, pp. C59–71 in *Holland Bulb Forcer's Guide*, 5th ed. International Flower Bulb Centre, Hillegom, The Netherlands.

De Hertogh, A., C. Moore, and A. Lutman. 1990. *Freesia*, pp. 1–26 in *Geophyte™*. Department of Horticultural Science, North Carolina State University, Raleigh.

Dole, J.M., and H.F. Wilkins, 1988. University of Minnesota—Tissue analysis standards. *Minnesota State Florist Bulletin* 37(6):10–13.

Doorduin, J.C. 1990. Effects of CO_2 and plant density on growth and yield of greenhouse freesias. *Acta Horticulturae* 268:171–177.

Doorduin, J.C. 1992. Effects of photosynthetic lighting on freesia grown for winter-flowering. *Acta Horticulturae* 325:85–90.

Dreistadt, S.H. 2001. *Integrated Pest Management for Floriculture and Nurseries*. University of California Division of Agriculture and Natural Resources Publication 3402.

Gianfagna, T.J., and G.J. Wulster. 1986. Growth retardants as an aid to adapting freesia to pot culture. *HortScience* 21:263–264.

Gilbertson-Ferriss, T.L. 1985. *Freesia ×hybrida*, pp. 34–37 in *Handbook of Flowering*, vol. III, A.H. Halevy, editor. CRC Press, Boca Raton, Florida.

Gilbertson-Ferriss, T.L., and H.F. Wilkins. 1977. Factors influencing seed germination of *Freesia refracta*. *HortScience* 12:572–573.

Gilbertson-Ferriss, T.L., and H.F. Wilkins. 1978a. Effect of hydrofluosilicic acid, superphosphate, and treblesuperphosphate soil applications on leaf injury in *Freesia hybrida*. *HortScience* 13:298–299.

Gilbertson-Ferriss, T.L., and H.F. Wilkins. 1978b. Flower production of *Freesia hybrida* seedlings under night interruption lighting and short day influence. *Journal of the American Society for Horticultural Science* 103:587–591.

Gilbertson-Ferriss, T.L., M.L. Brenner, and H.F. Wilkins. 1981a. Effects of storage temperatures on endogenous growth substances and shoot emergence in *Freesia hybrida* corms. *Journal of the American Society for Horticultural Science* 106:455–460.

Gilbertson-Ferriss, T., H.F. Wilkins, and R. Hoberg. 1981b. Influence of alternating day and night temperatures on flowering of *Freesia hybrida*. *Journal of the American Society for Horticultural Science* 106:466–469.

Gomans, R.A. 1980. The history of the modern *Freesia*, pp. 161–174 in *Petaloid Monocotyledons*, C.D. Brickell, D.F. Cutler, and M. Gregory, editors. Academic Press, New York.

Heide, O.M. 1965. Factors controlling flowering in seed-raised *Freesia* plants. *Journal of Horticultural Science* 40:267–284.

Horst, R.K. 1990. Freesia, p. 649 in *Westcott's Plant Disease Handbook*, 5th ed. Van Nostrand Reinhold, New York.

Huxley, A., M. Griffiths, and M. Levy. 1992. *Freesia*, pp. 328–329 in *The New Royal Horticultural Society Dictionary of Gardening*, vol. 2. Stockton Press, New York.

Imanishi, H. 1993. *Freesia*, pp. 285–296 in *The Physiology of Flower Bulbs*, A. De Hertogh and M. Le Nard, editors. Elsevier, Amsterdam.

Kepczynski, J. 1982. Hastening of emergence of diploid freesias by means of osmotic conditioning of seeds. *Rosliny Ozdobne Ornamental Plants Tom 7, Series B*, pp. 173–178.

Masuda, M., and T. Asahira. 1978. Changes in endogenous cytokinin-like substances and growth inhibitors in freesia corms during high-temperature treatment for breaking dormancy. *Scientia Horticulturae* 8:371–382.

Masuda, M., Y. Okaba, J. Sekiya, and K. Konishi. 1992. Seed germination of *Freesia* 'Royal Crown' as affected by temperatures. *Journal of the Japanese Society of Horticultural Science* 61:143–149. (in Japanese, English summary)

Nowak, J., and R.M. Rudnicki, 1990. *Postharvest Handling and Storage of Cut Flowers, Florist Greens and Potted Plants.* Timber Press, Portland, Oregon.

Pierik, R.L.M., and H.H.M. Steegmans. 1976. Vegetative propagation of *Freesia* through the isolation of shoots *in vitro. Netherlands Journal of Agricultural Science* 24:274–277.

Sacalis, J.N. 1993. *Freesia* hybrids, pp. 59–60 in *Cut Flowers, Prolonging Freshness, Postproduction Care and Handling,* 2nd ed., J.L. Seals, editor. Ball Publishing, Batavia, Illinois.

Smith, D., and P.N. Danks. 1985. *Freesias, Grower Guide Number 1* (revised). Grower Books, London.

Spikman, G. 1986. The effect of water stress in ethylene production and ethylene-sensitivity of freesia inflorescences. *Acta Horticulturae* 181: 135–140.

Spikman, G. 1987. Ethylene production, ACC and MACC content of freesia buds and florets. *Scientia Horticulturae* 33:291–297.

Spikman, G. 1989. Development and ethylene production of buds and florets of cut freesia inflorescences as influenced by silver thiosulfate, aminoethoxyvinylglycine and sucrose. *Scientia Horticulturae* 39:73–81.

Startek, L. 2002. Growth dynamics and decorative value of 'Easy Pot' potted freesia depending on the growing conditions. *Acta Horticulturae* 570:385–390.

Thomas, M., S. Matheson, and M. Spurway. 1998. Nutrition of container-grown freesias. *Journal of Plant Nutrition* 21:2485–2496.

Uyemura, S., and H. Imanishi. 1983. Effects of gaseous compounds in smoke on dormancy release in freesia corms. *Scientia Horticulturae* 20:91–99.

Uyemura, S., and H. Imanishi. 1984. Effects of duration of exposure to ethylene on dormancy release in freesia corms. *Scientia Horticulturae* 22:383–390.

Woodson, W.R. 1987. Postharvest handling of bud-cut *Freesia* flowers. *HortScience* 22:456–458.

Wulster, G.J., and T.J. Gianfagna. 1991. *Freesia hybrida* respond to ancymidol, cold storage of corms, and greenhouse temperatures. *Hort Science* 26:1276–1278.

Fuchsia

INTRODUCTION

Common name: fuchsia.

Scientific name: *Fuchsia* hybrids. The commonly grown *Fuchsia* hybrids are derived from *F. fulgens* DC ×*F. magellanica* Lam.

Family and related taxa: Onagraceae Juss., which is known as the evening primrose family. *Clarkia* (godetia) also is found in this family.

Origin: Approximately 100 *Fuchsia* L. species are distributed from Mexico to the Patagonia region in Argentina to Tahiti and New Zealand (Huxley et al., 1992). *F. fulgens* and *F. magellanica* are natives of Mexico and southern Chile and Argentina, respectively.

Uses and current status: Fuchsias are grown worldwide as a perennial garden shrub in mild climates and as a potted flowering plant, which is sold in the spring (Bailey and Bailey, 1976). Due to the pendulous nature of the plant and flowers, fuchsias are popular hanging basket plants (Figs. II-1 and II-2 Fuchsia).

The flowers are often showy, pendulous, and colored purple, pink, red, or white. The entire flower may be one color or the sepals and petals may be different colors, resulting in striking color combinations. The calyx is tubular or campanulate; there are four sepals and four petals. Double-flower forms are common. The dark green elliptical leaves are opposite.

FIGURE II-1 FUCHSIA *Fuchsia* hanging basket flowers.

FIGURE II-2 FUCHSIA *Fuchsia* 'Honeysuckle' garden ornamental. Heat tolerant for warm climates.

CULTIVARS

Hundreds of cultivars are available and both commercial and home enthusiasts of fuchsias are found on every continent.

PROPAGATION

Commercial propagation is by 3-in. (7-cm) terminal cuttings, which root under mist or plastic-covered tents within 3 weeks if 68 to 70°F (20 to 21°C) bottom heat is used. Rooting was faster at 88/72°F (31/22°C) day/night than at 73/57°F (23/14°C) (Graves and Zhang, 1996). Although long days increase cutting number and fresh weight, stock plants should be kept under SD of 10 hr or less to ensure vegetative growth of stock plants and cuttings (Hentig et al., 1985). Seed-propagated cultivars are available.

FLOWERING CONTROL AND DORMANCY

The apical meristem always remains vegetative; flowers are axillary. Juvenile plants of most cultivars are obligate LD plants for rapid flowering with a critical day length of approximately 12 hr. Some cultivars require only five consecutive LD to flower; however, increasing the number of LD increases the number of reproductive axillary sites. Once flowers are initiated, floral development will continue regardless of photoperiod. Old flowering plants are essentially day neutral (Roberts and Struckmeyer, 1938; Sachs and Bretz, 1962; Wilkins, 1985).

Four- to 6-hr day continuations of 10 to 20 fc (2 to 4 μmol $\cdot$ m^{-2} $\cdot$ s^{-1}) from incandescent lights starting at sundown are recommended for rapid flower induction. Night breaks are less effective, but can be used. Lighting prior to sunup is not as effective as day continuation or night breaks. Flowering can also be reversed with alternating red/far-red/red light sequences (Holland and Vince, 1968; Sachs and Bretz, 1962; Vince-Prue, 1977; Wilkins, 1985).

TEMPERATURE

Optimal temperatures for vegetative growth vary between 68 and 79°F (20 and 26°C). Little growth occurs below 59°F (15°C) or above 86°F (30°C). Erwin and Kovanda (1990) indicate that 68/61°F (20/16°C) day/night temperatures should provide high quality and maximum flower numbers in a minimum time span. Optimum leaf area production occurred under LD (4-hr night interruptions) when compared with SD (9 hr:15 min) under either 59/50°F (15/10°C) day/night temperatures or 68/59°F (20/15°C) day/night temperatures (Erwin et al., 1991). Flowering ceases when the average daily temperature rises above 76°F (24°C). Internode elongation is reduced at constant temperatures or when negative DIF is used (Erwin et al., 1991).

LIGHT

Both long photoperiods and light intensities of at least 900 fc (180 μmol · m^{-2} · s^{-1}) for 18 hr/day during the winter reduce crop time; however, plants should be shaded in late spring and summer (Erwin et al., 1991; Kofranek et al., 1970; Sachs and Bretz, 1962; Shanks, 1983).

WATER

The media should be kept continuously moist but not wet. Drying will result in lower leaf loss, whereas excess moisture will result in root rot.

CARBON DIOXIDE

No information available. Stock plants and plants grown for spring sales would probably benefit from supplemental carbon dioxide.

NUTRITION

Constant fertilization of 200+ ppm nitrogen and potassium is commonly used. Ammonium should be less than 20% of total nitrogen (Erwin and Kovanda, 1990). Roberts et al. (1990) used Osmocote (14–14–14, 20 g/pot) and fertigated every other week with 240 ppm N from 20–10–20.

MEDIA

A well-drained medium is required. Roberts et al. (1990) used a sandy loam and peat (9:1 by volume) media with a 6.6 pH. Most commercial peat-based media, pH 6.0 to 6.5, are acceptable.

HEIGHT CONTROL

Various plant growth regulators can be used to control internode elongation. B-Nine (daminozide), A-Rest (ancymidol), and Sumagic (uniconizole) hasten and promote floral initiation (Kim, 1995; Sachs et al., 1972). Interestingly, A-Rest sprays (251 ppm) increase the number of flowers, but the flower size is reduced; B-Nine sprays (3000+ ppm) do not produce similar results. Floral initiation is prevented by gibberellic acid (GA$_3$), which also counteracts the influence of plant growth regulators (Sachs et al., 1967, 1972; Shanks, 1983).

Stem elongation is best reduced with drenches of Bonzi (paclobutrazol) at 5 to 10 ppm or Sumagic at 2 to 5 ppm. Cycocel (chlormequat) is also effective in height control (Adriansen, 1985; Roberts et al., 1990).

Stem elongation can also be controlled by DIF (Maas and van Hattum, 1997, 1998). Interestingly, orange light increased stem elongation and negated the effects of DIF. Sprays of various GA's nullified the response to both negative DIF and to Bonzi. Maas and van Hattum (1997, 1998) stated that DIF and light quality influenced endogenous GA levels and stem elongation.

SPACING

Spacing will vary with the size and type of plant produced. Pinched or topiary plants in small 4-in. (10-cm) pots can be produced at 6 × 6 in. (15 × 15 cm). Hanging baskets are spaced sufficiently far enough apart to prevent tangling of the shoots and prevent excessive shading below.

PINCHING AND DISBUDDING

Fuchsia plants respond to pinching and hanging baskets are commonly pinched two or more times. First pinch is 1 to 2 weeks after planting or when roots have reached the edge of the media. Plants are pinched above the fourth or fifth set of leaves. Florel (ethephon) sprays at 500 ppm can be used to increase branching and replace pinching. Atrimmec (dikegulac sodium) sprays at 780 to 2300 ppm are also effective at increasing branching. Topiary trees may be formed using cultivars that have an upright growth habit. Sprays of GA$_3$ (250 to 500 ppm) applied weekly for up to 3 weeks have been used to hasten internode elongation (Mynett, 1985).

SUPPORT

Tree and topiary forms require staking or wire supports; otherwise none is required.

SCHEDULE AND TIMING

Three to five cuttings are used in a 10-in. (25-cm) hanging basket. Generally, 13 to 19 weeks are required to produce a hanging basket, depending on the season, temperature, and geographic location. First flowers occur 52 days after the start of LD (Erwin and Kovanda, 1990). Be sure to allow plants to grow to sufficient size prior to the start of LD.

INSECTS

Aphids, spider mites, whiteflies, and thrips are common pests. Mealybug, scale, and various caterpillars can also occur (Dreistadt, 2001).

DISEASES

Botrytis, Pythium, Phytophthora, Rhizoctonia, Thielaviopsis, Armillaria, Penicillium, Verticillium, and rusts (*Pucciniastrum epilobii* and *Uredo fuchsiae*) occur (Daughtrey and Chase, 1992; Dreistadt, 2001; Horst, 1990). Inspection for insects and diseases is a requirement. Air movement, proper spacing, and dry foliage are major methods to control fuchsia diseases. Tomato spotted wilt virus can also occur.

PHYSIOLOGICAL DISORDERS

Lack of flowering or delayed flowering can be due to incorrect photoperiod, incorrect temperature, low light, excessive Florel application, overfertilization, or overwatering. Leaf scorch can be due to excessively high light or low humidity.

POSTHARVEST

Flower abscission occurs within 24 hr when exposed to ethylene (1 to 3 ppm). Ethylene concentrations as low as 0.01 ppm can cause flower bud and leaf abscission and epinasty (Willumsen and Fjeld, 1995). Plants respond to 0.3 to 0.5 mM silver thiosulfate (STS) sprays. Plants can be shipped at 38°F (3°C) (Nowak and Rudnicki, 1990).

KEY POINTS

- Fuchsia is used as a hanging basket, potted flowering plant, and garden ornamental.
- Plants are propagated by cuttings.
- Flowering is axillary and the terminal meristem is vegetative.
- Fuchsia stock plants should be kept under SD.
- LD rapidly induce flowering.
- If a plant growth regulator is used, B-Nine (daminozide) and A-Rest (ancymidol) will hasten floral initiation.

BIBLIOGRAPHY

Adriansen, E. 1985. Kemisk vækstregulering, pp. 142–162 in *Potteplanter I—Produktion, Metoder, Midler,* O.V. Christensen, A. Klougart, I.S. Pedersen, and K. Wikesjö, editors. GartnerINFO, København, Denmark. (in Danish)

Bailey, L.H., and E.Z. Bailey. 1976. Fuchsia, pp. 489–490 in *Hortus Third: A Concise Dictionary of Plants Cultivated in the United States and Canada.* Macmillan, New York.

Daughtrey, M., and A.R. Chase. 1992. Fuchsia, pp. 94–96 in *Ball Field Guide to Diseases of Greenhouse Ornamentals.* Ball Publishing, Geneva, Illinois.

Dreistadt, S.H. 2001. *Integrated Pest Management for Floriculture and Nurseries.* University of California Division of Agriculture and Natural Resources Publication 3402.

Erwin, J., and B. Kovanda. 1990. Fuchsia production. *Minnesota State Florists Bulletin* 39(5):1–4.

Erwin, J.E., R.D. Heins, and R. Moe. 1991. Temperature and photoperiod effects on *Fuchsia ×hybrida* morphology. *Journal of the American Society for Horticultural Science* 116:955–960.

Graves, W.R., and H. Zhang. 1996. Relative water content and rooting subirrigated stems cuttings in four environments without mist. *HortScience* 31:866–868.

Hentig, W.U. v., M Fischer, and K. Köhler. 1985. Influence of daylength on the production and quality of cutting from fuchsia mother plants. *Combined Proceedings—International Plant Propagators' Society* 34:141–149.

Holland, R.W.K., and D. Vince. 1968. Photoperiodic control of flowering and anthocyanin formation on *Fuchsia. Nature* (London) 219:511–513.

Horst, R.K. 1990. Fuchsia, p. 650 in *Westcott's Plant Disease Handbook,* 5th ed. Van Nostrand Reinhold, New York.

Huxley, A., M. Griffiths, and M. Levy. 1992. *Fuchsia,* pp. 350–357 in *The New Royal Horticulture Society Dictionary of Gardening,* vol. 2. Stockton Press, New York.

Kim, H.Y. 1995. Effects of uniconazole on the growth and flowering of *Fuchsia ×hybrida* 'Coralina.' *Acta Horticulturae* 394:331–335.

Kofranek, A.M., R.M. Sachs, and J. Kubota. 1970. The culture of fuchsia as a pot plant. *Florists' Review* 146(3791):18–21, 61–63.

Maas, F.M., and J. van Hattum. 1997. The role of gibberellins in the thermo- and photocontrol of stem elongation in *Fuchsia. Acta Horticulturae* 435: 93–104.

Maas, F.M., and J. van Hattum. 1998. Thermomorphogenic and photomorphogenic control of stem elongation in *Fuchsia* is not mediated by changes in responsiveness to gibberellins. *Plant Growth Regulation* 17:39–45.

Mynett, K. 1985. Growing tree-like plants of fuchsia by using gibberellic acid (GA₃). *Acta Horticulturae* 167:333–338.

Nowak, J., and R.M. Rudnicki. 1990. *Postharvest Handling and Storage of Cut Flowers, Florist Greens and Potted Plants.* Timber Press, Portland, Oregon.

Roberts, R.H., and B.E. Struckmeyer. 1938. The effects of temperature and other environmental factors upon photoperiodic responses of some of the higher plants. *Journal of Agricultural Research* 56:633–677.

Roberts, C.M., G.W. Eaton, and F.M. Seywerd. 1990. Production of *Fuchsia* and *Tibouchina* standards using paclobutrazol and chlormequat. *HortScience* 25:1242–1243.

Sachs, R.M., and C.F. Bretz. 1962. The effect of daylength, temperature, and gibberellic acid upon flowering in *Fuchsia hybrida*. *Proceedings of the American Society for Horticultural Science* 80:581–588.

Sachs, R.M., A.M. Kofranek, and S.V. Shyr. 1967. Gibberellin-induced inhibition of floral initiation in fuchsia. *American Journal of Botany* 54:921–929.

Sachs, R.M., A.M. Kofranek, J. DeBie, and J. Kubota. 1972. Reducing height of pot grown fuchsia. *Florists' Review* 150(3883):85–87, 99–101.

Shanks, J.B. 1983. Using fuchsias as year-round crops. *Florists' Review* 172(4457):117–118, 120, 122, 124.

Vince-Prue, D. 1977. Photocontrol of stem elongation in light-grown plants of *Fuchsia hybrida*. *Planta* 133:149–156.

Wilkins, H.F. 1985. *Fuchsia×hybrida*, pp. 38–41 in *Handbook of Flowering*, vol. III, A.H. Halevy, editor. CRC Press, Boca Raton, Florida.

Willumsen, K., and T. Fjeld. 1995. The sensitivity of some flowering potted plants to exogenous ethylene. *Acta Horticulturae* 405:362–371.

Gardenia

INTRODUCTION

Common name: gardenia.

Scientific name: *Gardenia augusta* (L.) Merrill., formerly *G. jasminoides*, is the most common species in cultivation because of its large fragrant white flowers (Huxley et al., 1992).

Family and related taxa: Rubiaceae Juss. This family also includes the source of coffee, *Coffea*, and many ornamentals such as *Ixora* and *Pentas*. Approximately 250 tropical or subtropical shrubs and small trees are in the genus *Gardenia*.

Origin: *Gardenia augusta* is a native of China.

Uses and current status: Gardenias are cultivated for the large fragrant white flowers (Huxley et al., 1992) and sold commercially as garden ornamentals, potted flowering plants, and cut flowers for use in corsages or wedding bouquets (Bailey and Bailey, 1976; Post, 1949). Gardenias are mainly grown in Florida and other warm Gulf states in North America by specialty pot plant producers.

The calyx has five elongated stipule-like structures under the pure white, multipetaled flower, which is very fragrant, and can be up to 4 in. (10 cm) in diameter (Fig. II-1 Gardenia). The plant has opposite, thick, dark-green, shiny leaves, which are evergreen and lanceolate to ovate in form.

CULTIVARS

There have been several cultivars in the trade: Belmont, Hadley, McClellan 23, California, and Mystery (Baerdemaeker et al., 1994; Bailey and Bailey, 1976; Rose and Dickey, 1960/1961; Uematsu and Tomita, 1981). At one time the small flowered cultivar Veitchii was grown in North America and in Europe. Many cultivars of the

FIGURE II-I GARDENIA *Gardenia* flower.

gardenia are seen in southern gardens and grow to 6 ft (1.8 m) in height.

PROPAGATION

Propagation is by terminal vegetative cuttings, which are rooted directly in small pots or plugs filled with a well-aerated medium. Cuttings root with ease at 75°F (24°C) and high humidity and are commonly propagated under mist, fog, or plastic tunnels and reduced light. Propagation is from November to February. Although not commercially significant, gardenias can be propagated *in vitro* (Serret et al., 1997).

FLOWERING CONTROL AND DORMANCY

The duration of the flowering period is largely determined by night temperatures; flowering can be continuous if temperatures remain below 65°F (18°C). These conditions can be found in northern Europe and the cool Pacific Coast region. In greenhouses flowering typically starts in December or January and ceases by July; in the South, flowering is in the spring and early summer only (Post, 1949; Wilkins, 1986).

Floral initiation and bud development to 0.25 to 0.50 in. (0.75 to 1.5 cm) in diameter can occur at 70°F (21°C) or higher. Thereafter, lower temperatures of 60 to 61°F (15.5 to 16°C) are required for further development. If temperatures remain over 65°F (18°C), the buds will abort after several months. With proper temperatures, approximately 60 days are required for a 0.25- to 0.50-in. (0.75- to 1.5-cm) bud to develop under LD. High light and LD hasten differentiation and development. Con-

versely, SD hasten flower induction. Although gardenia is a day-neutral plant, SD hasten initiation and early development and LD (natural or supplemental) promote rapid development under cool temperatures (Baird and Laurie, 1942; Davidson, 1941; Hasek, 1948; Joiner and Poole, 1963; Uematsu and Tomita, 1981; Wilkins, 1986). These data were generated in North America, mainly in Ohio, New Jersey, and Florida, and in Japan, which have very warm summers and higher light intensities than northern Europe.

In Belgium, Baerdemaeker et al. (1994) reported that the cultivar Veitchii increasing the natural day length to 16 hr with 300 fc (60 μmol $\cdot$ m^{-2} $\cdot$ s^{-1}) of supplemental light reduced flower bud abortion and increased the number of axillary shoots forming buds. Other flowering responses of the primary bud were similar to the control plants grown under natural day lengths. Plants grown under SD for 4, 6, or 8 weeks and then placed in LD flowered sooner than those kept under SD.

TEMPERATURE

Air temperature should not go below 60°F (16°C); a 70/62°F (21/17°C) day/night temperature is excellent (Baird and Laurie, 1942; Hasek, 1948; Post, 1949; Wilkins, 1986). However temperatures should remain below 65°F (18°C) for flowering. The medium temperature should not go higher than 79°F (26°C). During marketing, night temperature should remain below 65°F (18°C) to maintain flower buds (Nowak and Rudnicki, 1990).

LIGHT

High light (full sun) during the vegetative and induction period increases the number of flower buds that develop (Rose and Dickey, 1960/1961). Supplementary lighting from incandescent or high-intensity discharge lamps reduces flower bud abscisions. Short days and temperatures below 65°F (18°C) result in rapid flower initiation and early development.

WATER

Gardenia grows best when the medium is continuously moist and humidity is high.

CARBON DIOXIDE

No information on carbon dioxide is available; most plants are primarily grown outside.

NUTRITION

High nutrition favors vegetative growth, and sudden shifts in nutrition may increase bud abscission. No treatment or management step should slow plant growth or flower bud development and any plant stress may increase flower bud abscission. Constant liquid fertilization at 150 ppm N from 20–10–20 is acceptable (Hamrick, 2003). Maintain media EC between 1.0 and 2.6 dS · m^{-1} based on pour through testing.

Good growth with high plant and flower quality is obtained at low nutritional levels (Post, 1949). Baerdemaeker et al. (1994) used a 19:6:20 N:P:K ratio and maintained a medium EC of 0.25 dS · m^{-1} using a 1:5 medium:water dilution. In Florida a pH of 5.5 is maintained in the peat medium through constant monitoring. During the reproductive phase 5–20–30 can be used.

MEDIA

Pure peat is typically used and a pH below 6.0 is best or chlorosis can occur. Chlorosis can also occur if the medium temperature falls below 60°F (16°C).

HEIGHT CONTROL

A-Rest (ancymidol), B-Nine (daminozide), Bonzi (paclobutrazol), or Topflor (flurprimidol) can be used to obtain short, compact plants (Baerdemaeker et al., 1994; Banko and Stefani, 1995; Kamoutsis et al., 1999; Whipker, 2003). A-Rest sprays are applied at 50 ppm and drenches at 0.25 mg a.i. (2 ppm)/6-in. (15-cm) pot. B-Nine and Topflor sprays are applied at 5000 ppm and 100 to 200 ppm, respectively. A 12-ppm Bonzi drench could also be used. Bonzi increases flower numbers by decreasing bud abortions. However, Kamoutsis et al. (1999) reported that Bonzi reduced the number of flower buds. Both growth regulators should be used at the start of SD, prior to floral initiation, or 6 weeks after pinching.

SPACING

The most commonly grown pot size is 6 in. (15 cm). Pots are spaced at 12 × 12 in. (30 × 30 cm). Smaller 4-in. (15-cm) pots are spaced at 8 × 8 in. (20 × 20 cm). At no time should foliage overlap.

PINCHING AND DISBUDDING

For 6-in. (15-cm) pots, pinching occurs 8 weeks after rooting. By 3.5 months primary and secondary axillary shoots should be well developed (Baerdemaeker et al., 1994; Joiner and Poole, 1963; Uematsu and Tomita, 1981; Wilkins, 1986). No disbudding occurs with potted plants. Axillary flower buds may be removed with cut flower production for corsages.

SUPPORT

None required except for topiary trees in which the main stem must be staked.

SCHEDULE AND TIMING

In Denmark the gardenia is a 36- to 38-week crop using photoperiod control and temperature manipulation (J. Hansen, personal communication) (Table II-1 Gardenia). In Florida no photoperiodic control is used. Once buds are visible, B-Nine (daminozide) sprays are applied if bypass shoots begin to occur and the night temperatures are not below 65°F (18°C). The B-Nine application will also help prevent flower bud abscission. Schedules in other southern areas are similar with propagation in May and sales the following early spring.

INSECTS

Thrips are common in the large flowers and can be especially difficult to control. Spider mites and scale can also be problems (Post, 1949). Aphids, whiteflies, mealybugs, weevils, and caterpillars have also been documented (Dreistadt, 2001).

DISEASES

Gardenia are susceptible to several diseases, including bud blight (*Botrytis cinerea*), leaf spot (*Phyllosticta, Rhizoctonia, Myrothecium roridum,* and *Xanthomonas campestris* pv. *maculifoliigardeniae*), root and crown rot (*Phytophthora, Rhizoctonia,* and *Armillaria*), and powdery mildew (*Erysiphe polygoni*) (Dreistadt, 2001). Stem canker (*Phomopsis gardeniae*) can be prevalent in greenhouse production and can be minimized by taking cuttings from the tops of plants and using resistant cultivars such as Veitchii (Horst, 1990).

TABLE II-1 GARDENIA

Sample production schedule from Denmark for *Gardenia* flowering in a 4-in. (10-cm) pot (J. Hansen, personal communication).

Cultural Steps	Production Time (weeks)	Temperature °F (°C)	Photoperiod
Cutting propagation in flats (May)[a]	3–4	70 (21)	LD
Plant three cuttings/pot and space pot-to-pot	4–5	70 (21)	LD
Space at 8 × 8 in. (21 × 21 cm)	6	70 (21)	LD
Soft pinch	4	70 (21)	LD
Begin short days[b]	8	61 (16)	SD
Reduce temperature	8	61 (16)	SD
Market	3		
Total	36–38		

[a]Cuttings include one set of mature leaves.
[b]Eight-hour natural or artificial day from incandescent lamps or HID lights in the winter.

PHYSIOLOGICAL DISORDERS

Flower bud abscission can occur if night temperatures remain above 65°F (18°C) or light levels are inadequate. Foliar chlorosis and yellowing due to iron deficiency can occur and are associated with cool media temperatures (Dreistadt, 2001).

POSTHARVEST

Cut flowers should be harvested when buds have just fully opened. Flower buds are reported to have a low sensitivity to chilling injury and can be stored dry at 32 to 34°F (0 to 1°C). Flowers should be handled carefully because they bruise easily, which causes browning. Flowers can be stored on shredded wax paper in tight boxes and misted with water.

For potted plants, well-budded plants can be shipped to market when the first buds begin to "crack" and the white petal color is apparent. The majority of North American budded and flowering gardenia plants are produced in the South for local use or for shipping north. In Europe flowering plants are produced and distributed within the European Community. Buds will continue to develop if night temperatures are below 65°F (18°C) and adequate light is given. Do not allow the plant to dry (Nowak and Rudnicki, 1990).

KEY POINTS

- Gardenia is used as a potted flowering plant and as a cut flower for fragrant corsages.
- Plants are propagated by cuttings.
- Flower buds are initiated and develop up to midsize at 70°F (20°C) or higher; thereafter temperatures of 65°F (18°C) or lower are required for further development.
- Flower buds will often abscise when night temperatures are above 65°F (18°C).
- Although the gardenia is day neutral, SD hasten initiation and early development and LD promote rapid development under cool temperatures.
- Pure peat moss is typically used for the growing medium.

BIBLIOGRAPHY

Baerdemaeker de, C.I., J.M. van Huylenbroeck, and P.C. Debergh. 1994. Influence of paclobutrazol and photoperiod on growth and flowering of *Gardenia jasminoides* Ellis cultivar 'Veitchii.' *Scientia Horticulturae* 58:315–324.

Bailey, L.H., and E.Z. Bailey. 1976. Gardenia, p. 495 in *Hortus Third: A Concise Dictionary of Plants Cultivated in the United States and Canada.* Macmillan, New York.

Baird, E., and A. Laurie. 1942. Studies on the effect of environmental factors and cultural practices on bud initiation, bud abscission and bud development of the gardenia. *Proceedings of the American Horticultural Society* 40:585–588.

Banko, T.J. and M.A. Stefani. 1995. Cutless and Atrimmec for controlling growth of woody landscape plants in containers. *Journal of Environmental Horticulture* 13:22–26.

Davidson, O.W. 1941. Effects of temperature on growth and flower production of gardenia. *Proceedings of the American Society for Horticultural Science* 39:387–390.

Dreistadt, S.H. 2001. *Integrated Pest Management for Floriculture and Nurseries.* University of California Division of Agriculture and Natural Resources Publication 3402.

Hamrick, D. 2003. *Gardenia*, pp. 398–400 in *Ball Redbook*, vol. 2, 17th ed. Ball Publishing, Batavia, Illinois.

Hasek, R. 1948. Observations on gardenia flower production at high air and soil temperatures. *Proceedings of the American Society for Horticultural Science* 51:610–612.

Horst, R.K. 1990. Gardenia, pp. 651–652 in *Westcott's Plant Disease Handbook*, 5th ed. Van Nostrand Reinhold, New York.

Huxley, A., M. Griffiths, and M. Levy. 1992. *Gardenia*, pp. 366–367 in *The New Royal Horticulture Society Dictionary of Gardening*, vol. 2. Stockton Press, New York.

Joiner, J.N., and R.T. Poole. 1963. Variable photoperiod and CCC effects on growth and flowering of *Gardenia jasminoides* 'Veitchii.' *Proceedings of the Florida State Horticultural Society* 75:449–451.

Kamoutsis, A.P., A.G. Chronopoulou-Sereli, and E.A. Paspatis. 1999. Paclobutrazol affects growth and flower bud production in gardenia under different light regimes. *HortScience* 34:674–675.

Nowak, J., and R.M. Rudnicki. 1990. *Postharvest Handling and Storage of Cut Flowers, Florist Greens and Potted Plants.* Timber Press, Portland, Oregon.

Post, K. 1949. *Gardenia jasminoides* (Gardenia), pp. 519–528 in *Florist Crop Production and Marketing.* Orange Judd Publishing, New York.

Rose, S.A. and R.D. Dickey. 1960/1961. The effect of light, plunging medium and fertilization on bud set of *Gardenia jasminoides* 'Veitchii.' *Proceedings of Florida State Horticultural Society* 73:362–363.

Serret, M.D., M.I. Trillas, J. Matas, and J.L. Araus. 1997. The effect of different closure types, light and sucrose concentrations on carbon isotope composition and growth of *Gardenia jasminoides* plantlets during micropropagation and subsequent acclimation *ex vitro*. *Plant Cell, Tissue and Organ Culture* 47:217–230.

Uematsu, L., and H. Tomita. 1981. Studies on gardenia pot plant production. *Bulletin Saitama Horticultural Experimental Station* 10:17–29. (in Japanese)

Whipker, B.E. 2003. Growth regulators for floricultural crops, pp. 439–448 in *2003 North Carolina Agricultural Chemicals Manual*, College of Agriculture and Life Science, North Carolina State University, Raleigh.

Wilkins, H.F. 1986. *Gardenia jasminoides*, pp. 127–131 in *Handbook of Flowering*, vol. V, A.H. Halevy, editor. CRC Press, Boca Raton, Florida.

Gentiana

INTRODUCTION

Common name: gentian or blue gentian.

Scientific name: *Gentiana* L. species. Numerous species can be used in commercial floriculture (Table II-1 Gentiana).

Family and related taxa: Gentianaceae Juss. Other important genera in this family are *Eustoma*, *Exacum*, and *Sabatia*. The genus *Gentiana* has 200 to 350 species.

Origin: The family is distributed worldwide, except in Africa (Huxley et al., 1992). Many Gentiana species are associated with cool mountainous alpine areas; others are found in North America south to Arkansas, Oklahoma, and Florida. There are also species in New Zealand (Bailey and Bailey, 1976; Ohkawa, 1986).

Uses and current status: Gentians are grown as garden ornamentals and as cut flowers and potted plants. Cold-treated plants can be forced into early cut flower production (Bailey and Bailey, 1976; Ohkawa, 1984, 1986).

Gentiana species are mostly perennial with tuberous roots, but annuals and biennial species exist. Though frequently associated with the rich blue to purple colors of their flowers, white, yellow, and red flowered forms and species can be found (Table II-1 Gentiana).

CULTIVARS

Numerous cultivars and selections occur with each species.

PROPAGATION

Although propagation is generally by seed, micropropagation has been used for *G. triflora* Pall. (Tabira, 1994) and *G. makinoi* Kuzn. Pot plant production is by cuttings that root in 10 to 20 days from March to May, respectively, when using 0.1% indole-3-butyric acid. Seed germination may be erratic and often 30% or less. Thompson (1969a, b) has described specific germination temperatures, light, and gibberellic acid treatments for 12 species. Generally, seeds are given 2 to 4 weeks of cold at near freezing temperatures, then 68 to 77°F (20 to 25°C); germination may require 20 days (Ohkawa, 1984). Three years are required from seeding to cut flower production. Seed-propagated *G. makinoi* 'Royal Blue' plants can be highly variable in color (dark blue to white) and flowering time (late July through October) in the field. Vegetatively propagated selections are usually much more uniform than seed-propagated plants.

FLOWERING CONTROL AND DORMANCY

Most gentians are native to cool areas and consequently flower production is normally limited to cool climates such as coastal Oregon and Washington. Flowering in commercial cut flower fields can be sustained up to 4 or 5 years with proper care. Gentian plants have a low temperature requirement to break dormancy. For early forcing, temperatures near 32°F (0°C) are used and the cold duration varies from 60 to 90 days when commenced in August, 30 to 60 days when commenced in September, and 30 days when commenced after October. After October natural cold treatment is used.

For *G. triflora* the optimum forcing temperature is 59 to 64°F (15 to 18°C), depending on the cultivar and season. With early flowering cultivars, LD and 68 to 77°F (20 to 25°C) were optimal for flower development; with late flowering cultivars, development was delayed at these temperatures and development was promoted by SD. Floral initiation occurred when 15 to 17 leaves had unfolded with early cultivars and 24 to 28 leaves with late cultivars (Ohtsuka and Kobayashi, 1972; Yamanaka, 1978; Yamanaka and Kujii, 1978). Cold requirement for *G. scabra* Bunge. is 41°F (5°C) for 30 days (700 hr) commencing in late autumn.

TABLE II-I GENTIANA

Gentiana species used in commerce or in development of hybrids (Bailey and Bailey, 1976; Huxley et al., 1992; Ohkawa, 1984, 1986).

Species	Height in. (cm)	Color	Season	Comments
G. acaulis L.	4 (10)	Dark blue, white	April to May	Potted flowering plant; taller selections exist; easy to cultivate
G. asclepiadea L.	24 (60)	Dark blue, white	August to September	Flowers 1.5 in. (3.75 cm) long
G. dinarica G. Beck	5 (13)	Dark blue, white	April to May	Narrow funnel-form flowers
G. lutea L.	6 (15)	Yellow	June to July	1-in.- (2.5-cm)-long, spathlike flower
G. makinoi	20–50 (50–130)	Blue, purple, white	Late July to October	Flowers cylindrical and never fully open; used in breeding; suitable for forcing; 'Royal Blue' best for cut flower production
G. nipponica Maxim.	4 (10)	Blue-purple	Late August	Wet alpine plant, mini pots
G. purpurea L.	24 (60)	Red, yellow throat	July to August	Rosette, flowers 1.5 in. (3.8 cm) long
G. scabra	4–8 (10–20)	Dark blue	September to October	Mini pot; used in breeding
G. septemfida Pall.	121 (301)	Dark blue	July to August	Mini pots; easy to cultivate; used in breeding
G. septemfida var. *lagodechiana* Kusn.	15 (38)	Blue	Late August to September	Flowers 1.5 in. (3.75 cm) long; easy to cultivate
G. thunbergii (G. Don.) Griseb.	6 (15)	Blue	January	Rosette, mini pots
G. triflora	32–38 (80–100)	Dark to light	Late August to October	Flowers open and face upward; blue, white used in breeding; suitable for forcing
G. verna L.	4 (10)	Dark blue	Late April to May	Rosette growth

TEMPERATURE

As stated, most *Gentiana* species are associated with cool, high elevation climates and are forced at day/night temperatures of 77/59°F (25/15°C). Recommendations vary with the species (see Schedule and Timing section on next page).

LIGHT

Plants are grown in full light. If grown under protection, shade only for temperature control. Photoperiod and temperature interact with many species such as *G. makinoi* (see Table II-2 Gentiana in the Schedule and Timing section on next page).

WATER

Water should never be a limiting factor because most species are associated with cool moist or damp growing conditions.

CARBON DIOXIDE

No information on carbon dioxide is available; most species are primarily grown outside.

NUTRITION

Nutrition should be high during active vegetative growth (Fischer, 1982) and moderate during flower development (Ohkawa, 1984). Additional magnesium may be required (Ohteki, 1982).

MEDIA

The medium pH should be 4.5 to 5.0 (Ohkawa, 1984). However, Fischer (1982) stated that a medium pH of 3.5 was acceptable. Regardless, the medium for ground beds should be acidic, deep, loose, well drained, and highly organic.

HEIGHT CONTROL

Height of potted plants can be controlled with A-Rest (ancymidol) and B-Nine (daminozide) (see Schedule and Timing section for *G. scabra*). Height control is not required for cut flower production.

SPACING

Most plants for cut flower production are spaced in beds 8 to 12 in. (20 to 30 cm) apart. Plants can be grown in 4-in. (10-cm) pots prior to being placed in beds. For potted plants, spacing can be pot-to-pot prior to final spacing. Five-inch (13-cm) pots can be spaced at 8 × 8 in. (20 × 20 cm).

PINCHING AND DISBUDDING

No pinching or disbudding is required. Inflorescences on weak shoots should be removed.

SUPPORT

At least two layers of support netting are needed because some species and cultivars can be 4 ft (120 cm) tall. One layer of support can be used and raised as the plants grow.

SCHEDULE AND TIMING

Plants can be grown in ground beds for cut flower production (Tables II-2 and II-3 Gentiana). Mature plants can be forced for cut flower production by harvesting and cold treating the "clumps." Plastic tunnels can also be placed over the field beds and plants forced after receiving a natural cold treatment. Mature plants in pots can also be forced into flower once cold treated (Fischer, 1982; Ohteki, 1982).

TABLE II-2 GENTIANA

Effect of night temperatures and photoperiods on forced *Gentiana makinoi* (Tsukada, 1984).

Temperature °F (°C)	Days to Flower		Flowering (%) Photoperiod		Number of Flowers/Plant	
	8 hr	16 hr	8 hr	16 hr	8 hr	16 hr
45 (7)	198	182	25	50	8.0	11.0
52 (11)	174	165	76	100	6.5	7.5
59 (15)	161	146	76	100	5.0	7.0

TABLE II-3 GENTIANA

Proposed production schedule for cut flowers of *Gentiana makinoi* (Ohkawa, 1984).

Year 1	Seed March to April. Transplant from seed plugs to 4-in. (10-cm) pots. Hold pot-to-pot. Basal tuber has formed by September or October. Mulch and overwinter.
Year 2	Plant in ground beds. Do not bury crown too deep. Remove flowers when shoots elongate. Mulch and overwinter.
Year 3	Flower in autumn under natural conditions. Properly cold-treated plants can be forced (see Table II-2 Gentiana). Production can be sustained for 4 to 5 years.

To produce potted flowering plants, cuttings with two mature leaves are removed from properly cold-treated *G. scabra* plants in March through May. Four cuttings are used in a 5-in. (13-cm) pot. The bases of cuttings are washed to remove a latex-like substance that is exuded. One stock plant can produce 20 cuttings. Plants are pinched in April, May, and August, leaving two to three nodes per shoot after each pinching. A plant growth regulator such as A-Rest (ancymidol) at 0.05 to 0.4 mg/pot or B-Nine (daminozide) at 2000 to 8000 ppm can be used, depending on the species and date of propagation (Ohkawa, 1984). High light is required for high quality; no shade is used. Photoperiod is secondary to temperature for flower control and days to flower; however, the percent of plants flowering was generally enhanced by LD (Tsukada, 1984).

INSECTS

Thrips can be particularly damaging to dark-petaled flowers. Other insects are likely to be a problem also.

DISEASES

Various fungal leaf and stem diseases (*Asteromella andrewsii*, *Botrytis cinerea*, *Cercopspora gentianae*, or *C. gentianicola*) can occur (Horst, 1990); *Septoria* has been reported to be serious in Japan (Ohteki, 1982). *Fusarium*, virus, and nematodes can also be problems (Ohkawa, 1984). Rogue infected plants promptly.

PHYSIOLOGICAL DISORDERS

None reported.

POSTHARVEST

When stems are harvested, 1 to 2 flowers open or three-fourths of the buds should be in full color. One-fourth of the leaves should be left on the plant for continued photosynthesis. Cut stems with the lower leaves removed should be placed in water for 5 to 6 hr at ambient air temperature, then stored at 36 to 41°F (2 to 5°C). Vase life can be up to 25 days (Ohteki, 1982). A 24-hr pulse of sucrose (87.6 mM) and silver thiosulfate (STS) (0.5 mM) increased vase life (Zhang and Leung, 2001).

KEY POINTS

- Gentian is a very popular cut flower and potted flowering plant in Japan, but is, unfortunately, rarely seen in North America.
- Propagation is generally by seed, but *in vitro* and division of mature plants can be used.

- Plants require a cold treatment of near 32°F (0°C) for flowering.
- Most *Gentiana* species are typically not tolerant of high temperatures and production is found mainly in areas with cool temperatures.
- Water should never be limiting.

BIBLIOGRAPHY

Bailey, L.H., and E.Z. Bailey. 1976. *Gentiana*, pp. 500–503 in *Hortus Third: A Concise Dictionary of Plants Cultivated in the United States and Canada*. Macmillan, New York.

Fischer, P. 1982. *Gentiana* cv. Royal Blue, Influence of pH and fertilizers on flower yield. *Gartenbörse and Gartenwelt* 82(28):652–653.

Horst, R.K. 1990. Gentian, p. 653 in *Westcott's Plant Disease Handbook*, 5th ed. Van Nostrand Reinhold, New York.

Huxley, A., M. Griffiths, and M. Levy. 1992. *Gentiana*, pp. 387–394 in *The New Royal Horticulture Society Dictionary of Gardening*, vol. 2. Stockton Press, New York.

Ohkawa, K. 1984. How to grow gentian, pp. 1–7 in *Horticulture Bulletin*, Shizuoka University, Shizuoka-City, Japan.

Ohkawa, K. 1986. Gentiana, pp. 351–355 in *Handbook of Flowering*, vol. VI, A.H. Halevy, editor. CRC Press, Boca Raton, Florida.

Ohteki, T. 1982. Cut flower production, Japanese techniques. *Technical Bulletin Number 1*. Levin Horticulture Research Center, Levin, New Zealand.

Ohtsuka, F., and T. Kobayashi. 1972. Ecological studies on *Gentiana axillarifolia* (*G. triflora* Pall. var *japonica* Hara). *Bulletin Nagano Experiment Station* 9:91–100. (in Japanese)

Tabira, H. 1994. Development of micropropagation systems in *Gentiana triflora*. Tottori Horticultural Experiment Station, Kurayoshi, Tottori, Japan.

Thompson, P.A. 1969a. Comparative effects of gibberellins A$_3$ and A$_4$ on the germination of seeds of several different species. *Horticulture Research* 9:130–138.

Thompson, P.A. 1969b. Effects of after-ripening and chilling treatments on the germination of species of *Gentiana* at different temperatures. *Journal of Horticultural Science* 44:343–358.

Tsukada, A. 1984. Effect of night temperature and day length on the growth and flowering of gentian, pp. 158–159 in *1984 Annual Report*, Nagano Horticulture Experiment Station. (in Japanese)

Yamanaka, A. 1978. Studies on the nursery stock and forcing culture on cut flower *Gentiana*. *1978 Annual Report, Tochigi Agricultural Experimental Station* 24:13–32. (in Japanese)

Yamanaka, A., and E. Kujii. 1978. Studies on the flowering physiology of *Gentiana*. *1978 Annual Report, Tochigi Agricultural Experimental Station* 24:11–12. (in Japanese)

Zhang, Z.M., and D.W.M. Leung. 2001. Elevation of soluble sugar levels by silver thiosulfate is associated with vase life improvement of cut gentian flowers. *Journal of Applied Bontany—Angewandte Botanik* 75:85–90.

Gerbera

INTRODUCTION

Common names: gerbera, Transvaal daisy, Barberton daisy.

Scientific name: *Gerbera jamesonii* Bol. ex Adlam. (Huxley et al., 1992).

Family and related taxa: Compositae Giseke. The genus *Gerbera* has about 40 species. Present-day cultivars are probably hybrids of *G. jamesonii* and *G. viridifolia* (D.C.) Schultz-Bip. Other species may be involved and natural hybrids may exist in South Africa (Tourjee et al., 1994). The Compositae is a large family containing numerous important genera including *Aster, Calendula, Callistephus, Centaurea, Chrysanthemum, Cosmos, Dahlia, Dendranthema, Echinacea, Gerbera, Helianthus, Liatris, Pericallis, Solidago, Tagetes,* and *Zinnia*.

Origin: *Gerbera jamesonii* is found in South Africa's Transvaal and Natal Provinces and Swaziland; *G. viridifolia* has a much wider distribution between 5°S of the equator and 35°S latitude in Africa. The gerbera was introduced into England as a novelty in 1886. By 1910, the gerbera was well established in commerce as a garden or cut flower along the Riviera in France and by the 1930s as a cut flower in North America (Tourjee et al., 1994).

Uses and current status: Gerbera is most commonly used worldwide as a cut flower; however, dwarf hybrid lines are available for potted plants or bedding plants (Rogers and Tjia, 1990) (Figs. II-1 and II-2 Gerbera).

Leaves are elongated and can be entire or slightly lobed and form an evergreen rosette. The single flowers are born on a nonbranching scape. Flowers are white, yellow, red, pink, orange, or scarlet. The disc flowers may be numerous to almost absent. Disc flowers can be yellow, the same color as the rays, or a vividly contrasting black. Bicolors also exist (Tourjee et al., 1994).

CULTIVARS

Numerous cultivars exist and new releases are a common commercial occurrence. A wide variety of colors are available in various seed mixes. Plant diameters vary from 5 to 6 in. (13 to 15 cm) for pots, 10 to 12 in. (25 to 30 cm) for bedding plants, and up to 20 in. (51 cm) for cut flowers. Potted flowering plants are most commonly 6 to 8 in. (15 to 20 cm) in height; scape length is commonly 28 in. (70 cm) long for cut flowers. Flower size varies from 1.75 to 5 in. (1.3 to 4.5 cm) in diameter.

FIGURE II-I GERBERA   Potted *Gerbera* plant grown with capillary mat irrigation.

FIGURE II-2 GERBERA   Mini *Gerbera* 'Reggea' cut flowers.

TABLE II-I GERBERA
The influence of supplementing natural daylight with high-pressure sodium (HPS) on *Gerbera* germination percentages, seedling dry weight, and days to visible bud from germination (modified from Erwin et al., 1991).

| | Light Treatment | |
Growth Observed	Natural	Natural + HPS
Germination	76%	100%
Seedling dry weight	1.6 oz (45 g)	4.4 oz (125 g)
Germination to visible bud	134 days	113 days

Twelve-month seed storage is possible at 41°F (5°C) if seeds are kept at 4.5 to 5.7% moisture content and held at 32% relative humidity. Reducing seed moisture content to 3.5% is acceptable. Quality is lost at higher humidities regardless of temperatures. However, seed should be brought up to 52% moisture prior to germination for maximum germination (82%). If not, poor germination can result (Carpenter et al., 1995). Alternating day/night temperatures are detrimental, even at the same average daily temperatures.

Seeds are commonly sown in plug trays and should not be covered (Moe et al., 1996). Erwin et al. (1991) presented data indicating that high-pressure sodium lamps supplementing natural light at 500 fc (100 μmol · m^{-2} · s^{-1}) vastly improved germination and seedling dry weight and also decreased days from germination to visible buds (Table II-1 Gerbera). Fluorescent light is also effective. Erwin et al. (1991) felt that 68 to 74°F (20 to 23°C) was optimal, with germination occurring in 7 to 14 days. Germination decreased at temperatures above 75°F (24°C). Flowering can be expected within 16 weeks after germination or 11 to 16 weeks after transplanting *in vitro* propagated plugs. High relative humidity of 85% should be maintained until almost all seedlings are germinated.

PROPAGATION

Historically, propagation was by seed or division; however, division is too slow and impractical (Erwin et al., 1991; Rogers and Tjia, 1990). *In vitro* propagation is now commonly used to quickly increase cultivar selections for both cut and potted flowering plants (Jeong et al., 1996; Pierik et al., 1975; Woltering, 1989).

FLOWERING CONTROL AND DORMANCY

With potted gerberas, the first visible flower buds are observed after 10 to 14 leaves have developed in the primary leaf whorl and after 2 to 6 leaves have developed in the secondary or lateral leaf whorls. Thereafter, 11 days are required for the next flower to become visible under SD conditions or 18 days under LD conditions. Under SD the primary flower required 65 days to reach anthesis after visible bud and 90 days for the secondary flower; under LD 78 and 100 days were required, respectively. Roh and Lawson (1984) speculated that apical dominance is involved in the slower development of the secondary flower, regardless of photoperiod. Photoperiodic response varies among cultivars (Lin and French, 1985). Erwin et al. (1991) found few differences in photoperiodic response among cultivars and stressed that flower initiation and development were mainly affected by light intensity and temperature. High light intensity is most important during seedling growth because flower initiation commences after two to three true leaves are visible. Temperatures above 76°F (24°C) can result in no flowering. Both gibberellic acid and Atrinal (dikegulac sodium) have been used to increase flower numbers and uniformity.

TEMPERATURE

As stated earlier seed germination is best at 68 to 74°F (20 to 23°C). Day/night temperatures of 70/63°F (21/17°C) are optimum for pot plants from potting to visible bud. The rate of development from visible bud to color is most rapid at an average daily temperature of 76°F (24°C). However, leaf area increases with temperature and was greatest at 77°F (25°C). Peduncle length increases as the difference (DIF) between day and night increases. Day/night temperatures of 77/58°F (25/14°C) are optimal for plant dry weight production (Erwin et al., 1991). As a compromise, a day/night temperature of 70 to 75/57 to 66°F (21 to 24/14 to 19°C) is recommended for both cut and pot gerberas (Biotech Plants Pty. Ltd., personal communication). A low temperature of 55°F (13°C), whether in the greenhouse or field, favors vegetative axillary shoots and results in high flower numbers later. Root zone heating of 70°F (21°C) can be used to maintain production (Lin and French, 1985; Rogers and Tjia, 1990).

LIGHT

Rogers and Tjia (1990) indicated gerbera plants are only slightly photoperiodic but dramatically respond to light intensity × duration. As previously stated in the Flowering Control and Dormancy section, high total light integral is essential from germination onward to ensure rapid and uniform flower. Erwin et al. (1991)

recommended supplemental high-pressure sodium lighting of 500 fc (100 μmol · m^{-2} · s^{-1}). During the low-light periods of fall and winter, 300 to 450 fc (60 to 90 μmol · m^{-2} · s^{-1}) light for 16 to 20 hr increased the number of flowers, decreased crop time, and increased plant growth (Gagnon and Dansereau, 1990).

WATER

Native gerbera plants experience very dry conditions during summer and infrequent rain at best during cool winters. Never overwater gerberas during any stages of production, even though plants tend to dry out rapidly due to their large leaf areas. Allowing plants to dry slightly between irrigations will also decrease the need for growth retardants on potted plants.

CARBON DIOXIDE

Carbon dioxide levels of 600 to 800 ppm can be used, but flower yield increases only if supplementary light is used (Tsujita, 1983). However, stem lengths also increase with the use of supplemental CO_2; thus, it may not be useful for potted plants.

NUTRITION

Various nutrient deficiency symptoms have been described (Tjia and Joiner, 1984). During the seedling plug stage, do not allow high soluble salt levels to develop, which can result in malformed leaves and delayed flowering. After transplanting has occurred and new roots begin to form, fertilize with 300 ppm N from a 30–10–30 fertilizer; thereafter, no further phosphorus is needed because little phosphorus is used by the plants. Generally, ammonium should be avoided or should not account for more than 50% of nitrogen. Tjia and Rogers (1984) stated that a 70:30 nitrate:ammonia ratio enhances earliness and flower yields. Magnesium and iron deficiencies are common because gerbera plants have a high requirement for these nutrients. Magnesium sulfate should be applied monthly at 16 oz/100 gal (1.2 g · L^{-1}) and iron chelate constantly at 0.5 oz/100 gal (0.037g · L^{-1}) (Shoemaker and Carlson, 1985). Tissue nutrient content varies with leaf age (see Table II-2 Gerbera).

MEDIA

Medium pH levels above 6.5 and high soluble salt levels are of constant concern and should

TABLE II-2 GERBERA

Mineral nutrient content of gerbera leaves from potted *Gerbera* plants. Leaf sizes or ages were young [less than 1 in. (2.5 cm) long], recently mature [2 to 3.5 in. (5 to 8.75 cm) long], or mature [greater than 4 in. (10 cm) long] (University of Minnesota Soil Testing Service, personal communication).

Nutrient Element	Concentration		
	Young	Recently Mature	Mature
N (%)	2.5	2.7	3.0
P (%)	0.5	0.5	0.5
K (%)	3.2	3.2	3.8
Ca (%)	0.5	0.4	1.3
Mg (%)	0.2	0.4	0.6
Fe (ppm)	62	62	132
Mn (ppm)	17	30	82
Cu (ppm)	2	2	4
Zn (ppm)	19	19	24
B (ppm)	19	19	24

be avoided. Medium pH should be 5.5 to 6.0. Frequent medium monitoring is recommended. Tissue tests during production are also advised. In nature the medium is sandy and well drained. Although plants adapt to most commercial potting materials, good drainage and aeration are essential (Maloupa et al., 1993). In an economic analysis conducted in Greece, soilless perlite bag culture was more profitable than ground beds (Grafiadellis et al., 2000).

HEIGHT CONTROL

Flower scape length and plant diameter are genetically controlled and proper selection of potted plant cultivars is essential. Further, elongation of the scape is controlled by the difference (DIF) between day and night temperature; the greater the difference, the longer the scape. Early morning temperature dips (DROP) for height control are also useful (Erwin et al., 1991).

Plants respond to B-Nine (daminozide), which not only reduces scape length, but also reduces leaf surface and darkens leaf color. B-Nine (4000 ppm) is best applied 8 weeks after transplanting (Armitage et al., 1984). A-Rest (ancymidol) sprays at 25 to 132 ppm are also effective and best applied 6 or 7 weeks after transplanting (Armitage et al., 1984; Bell, 2001). If wide differences exist between high day and low night temperatures, multiple treatments may be required (Erwin et al., 1991). A-Rest drenches at 0.25 to 0.5 mg a.i./6-in. (15-cm) pot can also be used. Cycocel (chlormequat) is not effective (Armitage et al., 1984).

SPACING

At no time during pot plant production should leaves overlap, because this results in lower photosynthesis and reduces and delays flowering. If seedlings are held in plugs, they should be respaced to every other plug cavity. Sorting plugs by size will maintain plant uniformity prior to potting. For cut flower production plants can be grown in beds or large pots spaced 13 × 13 in. to 15 × 15 in. (33 × 33 cm to 38 × 38 cm) apart (Dufault et al., 1990; Rogers and Tjia, 1990). Cut flower production works well in containers rather than ground beds due to the improved drainage, ease of leaf removal and pest management, and less bending to harvest flowers. Growing plants in containers also allows diseased plants to be removed and the remaining plants respaced.

Final spacing for 4-in. (10-cm) pots is 7 to 10 in. (18 to 21.5 cm) apart or 1.4 to 3 plants per square foot (4.2 to 9 plants per square meter). For 5-in. (13-cm) and 6-in. (15-cm) pots, spacing of 11 × 11 in. (28 × 28 cm) and 14 × 14 in. (36 × 36 cm) can be used, respectively.

PINCHING AND DISBUDDING

No pinching or disbudding is required. However, some forcers remove the first flower of potted flowering plants as soon as feasible. They believe this will result in more rapid and uniform elongation of the remaining flower scapes. Lower leaves on established cut flower plants should be removed every 6 to 8 weeks when the foliar canopy closes. Leaves are removed to improve air circulation and allow for easier pest control.

SUPPORT

No support is required for either cut or potted plants.

SCHEDULE AND TIMING

For both cut flowers and potted plants, transplants require similar times to flower regardless of whether the plants were propagated by seed or *in vitro* (see Table II-3 Gerbera). Plants for cut flower production should be replaced after 2 years. Sales of 4-in. (10-cm) pots commence 10 to 11 weeks after transplantation from April to September and 14 to 16 weeks after transplantation from September to April (Erwin et al., 1991; Rogers and Tjia, 1990).

INSECTS

Gerbera are susceptible to aphids, cyclamen mites, fungus gnats, leaf miners, spider mites, thrips, whiteflies, worms, slugs, and snails. However, with proper exclusion and continuous inspection procedures, serious infections and routine chemical treatments can be avoided (Rogers and Tjia, 1990; Short and Tjia, 1985). Thrips and whiteflies are particularly troublesome and have forced some growers to stop production.

DISEASES

Sanitation, venting, proper watering, and continuous plant inspections are required. Monitor nutrition, pH, and soluble salts to avoid root injury and subsequent root rot problems. Powdery mildew (*Erysiphe sclerotiorum*) is the most common disease on gerberas (Barnes et al., 1999). Environmental management of humidity, appropriate chemical applications, scouting, and prompt removal of infected plants are the control strategies. Removal of infected plants is best done in the morning when spores are less likely to be dry and less easily spread.

Other common diseases of gerberas are *Phytophthora, Pythium,* and *Rhizoctonia solani.* An appropriate chemical drench combination for these diseases may be required. *Alternaria, Ascochyta,* and *Botrytis* may be observed on the foliage and flowers (Horst, 1990; Miller and Tjia, 1984; Rogers and Tjia, 1990). Other diseases that have been recorded include cottony rot (*Sclerotinia sclerotiorum*), black root rot (*Thielaviopsis basicola*), verticillium wilt (*Verticillium dahliae*), white rust (*Albugo tragopogonis*), bacterial leaf spot (*Pseudomonas cichorii*), and tomato spotted wilt virus (Dreistadt, 2001).

PHYSIOLOGICAL DISORDERS

Insufficient flower stem hardening or maturation of the stem tissue below the harvested flower can result in stem collapse, which is known as *bent-neck* (see also Postharvest section). Poor winter growing conditions contribute to the problem and the flower head may

TABLE II-3 GERBERA

Sample production schedule for a 4-in. (10-cm) flowering potted *Gerbera* plant from seed.

Cultural Step	Production Time (weeks)	Temperature °F (°C)	Light
Sow seed			
	1–2	Medium: 68–74 (20–23)	HID lighting
Seed germinated			
	4–6	Day: 70 (21) Night: 63 (17)	HID lighting
Transplanted			
	2	Day: 70 (21) Night: 63 (17)	Natural
Visible bud			
	6–9	Day: 77 (25) Night: 57–66 (14–19)	Natural
Flower[a]			
	3–4		
Total	16–23		

[a]*Seed-propagated gerberas do not reach flowering stage uniformly; allow 3 or more weeks to market. In addition, at least 10% of plants may not flower.*

break easily. In the winter, do not harvest flower stems when they are immature (van Doorn et al., 1994). Delayed flowering can be due to close plant spacing.

POSTHARVEST

Both cut and potted gerberas are harvested when the two outer rows of disc florets are open and pollen can be seen. Stems are pulled, not cut, and the "heel" (base of the stem) is then removed to allow hydration. Freshly harvested cut gerbera stems can last from 2 to 3 weeks and cultivar differences in vase life can be extreme. New cultivars should be continually compared to current cultivars because research indicates that breeding and selection can produce cultivars with improved postharvest vase life (van Doorn et al., 1994; Wernett et al., 1996).

Bent-neck, stem break, or *stem bending* is the common cut flower postharvest disorder and it has been related to bacteria contamination, anatomical characteristics, ethylene, and cultivar (Gerasopoulos and Chebli, 1998; Mencarelli et al., 1995; Sacalis, 1993; van Doorn and de Witte, 1994; van Doorn et al., 1994). Commercial floral preservatives specifically formulated for gerbera are available. A variety of hydration, short-term pulses, and long-term holding solutions have also been recommended (Accati and Jona, 1989; Nowak and Rudnicki, 1990; Sacalis, 1993). Pulse cut stems for 10 min with silver nitrate (1000 ppm) or sodium hypochlorite (600 ppm) and Tween 20 surfactant (0.1%) to reduce bacterial stem blockage and increase vase life (Nowak and Plich, 1982; Nowak and Rudnicki, 1990). Sucrose at 6% can be added to increase vase life; however, sucrose will encourage scape elongation immediately below the flower and is often not used.

After long-distance shipping, rehydrate with warm water at 110°F (43°C). For short-term storage either 8-hydroxyquinoline citrate (8-HQC) at 200 ppm or 8-hydroxyquinoline sulfate at 300 ppm can be used to lower water pH and act as an antimicrobial agent (Tjia and Rogers, 1984). Silver nitrate at 25 ppm can also be used for storage and should be adjusted to pH 3.5 with citric acid (Sacalis, 1993). Silver nitrate is more effective than silver thiosulfate (STS) in postharvest treatments, indicating that the silver nitrate may be acting as an antimicrobial agent. *Gerbera* flowers are considered only slightly sensitive to ethylene.

In addition, some firms dip the flower heads into a 0.1 mM benzyladenine solution to maintain flower weight and delay senescence. Flowers are also sensitive to fluoride (1 ppm) in the holding solution (Tjia et al., 1987). Fluoride damage appears as brown spotting (Sacalis, 1993). Ethylene should be avoided for both cut and potted flowering plants because senescence will be hastened.

Precooling flowers at 40°F (5°C) is acceptable for 3 days; shipping and storage should be at 32 to 35°F (0 to 2°C) (Çelikel and Reid, 2002; Sacalis, 1993). Dry cold storage at 39°F (4°C) is preferable to storage in water for long-term storage of 3 to 4 weeks (Rogers and Tjia, 1990; Sacalis, 1993; Tjia and Rogers, 1984; Tjia et al., 1987). Potted flowering plants can be shipped at 54°F (12°C) (L.Høyer, personal communication).

KEY POINTS

- Gerbera is used most commonly as a cut flower but also as a potted flowering plant.
- Plants are propagated by *in vitro* and by seed.
- High light is required for uniform flower initiation and development.
- The growing point must not be covered by anything such as a medium particle or an overlapping leaf that reduces light to the growing point.
- Plugs should be placed under HID lighting, sorted into uniformly sized (stage of development) lots, and placed in every other plug cell.
- Plants are sorted a second time for uniformity when seedling plugs are potted.
- Gerbera have an unusually high requirement for magnesium and iron.
- Insects such as whiteflies and thrips can be major problems and can limit production.
- Cut flowers are susceptible to bent-neck, which is often attributed to harvest of immature flowers.

BIBLIOGRAPHY

Accati, E.G., and R. Jona. 1989. Parameters influencing gerbera cut flower longevity. *Acta Horticulturae* 261:63–68.

Armitage, A.M., B.M. Hamilton, and D. Cosgrove. 1984. The influence of growth regulators on gerbera daisy. *Journal of the American Society for Horticultural Science* 109:629–632.

Barnes, L.W., M.K. Hausbeck, and M. Daughtrey. 1999. Managing powdery mildew on gerberas. *GrowerTalks* 63(3):106–108, 110, 112, 114.

Bell, M. 2001. Bedding plants and seed geraniums, pp. 54–62 in *Tips on Regulating Growth of Floriculture Crops*, M.L. Gaston, L.A. Kunkle, P.S. Konjoian, and M.F. Wilt, editors. Ohio Florists' Association Services, Columbus, Ohio.

Carpenter, W.J., E.R. Ostmark, and J.A. Cornell. 1995. Temperature and seed moisture govern germination and storage of *Gerbera* seed. *HortScience* 30:98–101.

Çelikel, F.G., and M.S. Reid. 2002. Storage temperature affects the quality of cut flowers from the Asteraceae. *HortScience* 37:148–150.

Dreistadt, S.H. 2001. *Integrated Pest Management for Floriculture and Nurseries*. University of California Division of Agriculture and Natural Resources Publication 3402.

Dufault, R.J., T.L. Phillips, and J.W. Kelly. 1990. Nitrogen and potassium fertility and plant populations influence field production of *Gerbera*. *HortScience* 25:1599–1602.

Erwin, J., R. Heins, and W. Carlson. 1991. Pot *Gerbera* production. *Minnesota Flower Growers Association Bulletin* 40(5):1–6.

Gagnon, S., and B. Dansereau. 1990. Influence of light and photoperiod on growth and development of gerbera. *Acta Horticulturae* 272:145–151.

Gerasopoulos, D., and B. Chebli. 1998. Effects of scape-injected one-aminocyclopropane-one-carboxylic acid (ACC) on the vase life of 'Testarossa' cut gerbera. *Journal of the American Society for Horticultural Science* 123:921–924.

Grafiadellis, I., K. Mattas, E. Maloupa, I. Tzouramani, and K. Galanopoulos. 2000. An economic analysis of soilless culture in gerbera production. *HortScience* 35:300–303.

Horst, R.K. 1990. Gerbera, pp. 654–655 in *Westcott's Plant Disease Handbook*, 5th ed. Van Nostrand Reinhold, New York.

Huxley, A., M. Griffiths, and M. Levy. 1992. *Gerbera*, p. 402 in *The New Royal Horticultural Society Dictionary of Gardening*, vol. 2. Stockton Press, New York.

Jeong, B.R., C.S. Yang, and J.C. Park. 1996. Growth of *Gerbera hybrida in vitro* as affected by CO_2 concentration and air exchange rate of the vessel. *Acta Horticulturae* 440:510–514.

Lin, W.C., and C.J. French. 1985. Effect of supplementary lighting and soil warming on flowering of three *Gerbera* cultivars. *HortScience* 20:271–273.

Maloupa, E., I. Mitsios, P.F. Martinez, and S. Bladenopoulou. 1993. Study of substrates use in gerbera soilless culture grown in plastic greenhouses. *Acta Horticulturae* 323:139–144.

Mencarelli, E., R. Agostini, R. Botondi, and R. Massantini. 1995. Ethylene production, ACC content, PAL and POD activities in excised sections of straight and bent gerbera scapes. *Journal of Horticultural Science* 70:409–416.

Miller, J., and B. Tjia. 1984. Diseases of *Gerberas*. *Florists' Review* 174(4496):42–43.

Moe, R., J.E. Erwin, and W. Carlsson. 1996. Factors affecting *Gerbera jamesonii* early seedling branching and mortality. *HortTechnology* 6:59–61.

Nowak, J., and H. Plich. 1982. Ethylene synthesis during senescence of cut gerbera inflorescence as affected by different chemical pretreatments. *Proceedings XXI International Horticultural Congress*, vol. II:1736. (Abstract)

Nowak, J., and R.M. Rudnicki. 1990. *Postharvest Handling and Storage of Cut Flowers, Florist Greens, and Potted Plants*. Timber Press, Portland, Oregon.

Pierik, R.L.M., J.L.M. Jansen, A. Maasdam, and C.M. Binnendijk. 1975. Optimalization of *Gerbera* plantlet production from excised capitulum explants. *Scientia Horticulturae* 3:351–357.

Rogers, M.N., and B.O. Tjia. 1990. Temperature, pp. 32–34 in *Gerbera Production*. Timber Press, Portland, Oregon.

Roh, M.S.M., and R.H. Lawson. 1984. The graces of *Gerbera*. *Greenhouse Manager* 3(8):79, 82, 86–88, 90, 92, 94–95, 98, 100.

Sacalis, J.M. 1993. *Gerbera*, pp. 61–63 in *Cut Flowers, Prolonging Freshness, Postproduction Care and Handling*, 2nd ed., J.M Seals, editor. Ball Publishing, Batavia, Illinois.

Shoemaker, C., and W.H. Carlson. 1985. Don't let iron chlorosis spoil gerbera. *Greenhouse Grower* 3(12):14–15.

Short, D.E., and B. Tjia. 1985. Control those pests bugging your *Gerberas*. *Greenhouse Manager* 3(8):110, 112–113, 116, 118, 120–121.

Tjia, B., and J.N. Joiner. 1984. Mineral deficiency symptoms on gerbera. *Florida Ornamental Growers Association Newsletter* 7(5):1–2.

Tjia, B., and M.N. Rogers. 1984. Growing gerberas. *Greenhouse Manager* 3(6):67, 70, 73–75.

Tjia, B., F.J. Marousky, and R.H. Stamps. 1987. Response of cut gerbera flowers to fluoridated water and a floral preservative. *HortScience* 22:896–897.

Tourjee, K.R., J. Harding, and T.G. Byrne. 1994. Early development of *Gerbera* as a floriculture crop. *HortTechnology* 4:34–40.

Tsujita, M.J. 1983. Greenhouse gerbera production. *Ontario Ministry of Agricultural Fact Sheet* 83–006:1–4.

van Doorn, W.G., and Y. de Witte. 1994. Effect of bacteria on scape bending in cut *Gerbera jamesonii* flowers. *Journal of the American Society for Horticultural Science* 119:568–571.

van Doorn, W.G., M. Veken, and M.-L. Bakker. 1994. Effect of dry storage on scape bending in cut *Gerbera jamesonii* flowers. *Postharvest Biology and Technology* 4:261–269.

Wernett, H.C., T.J. Sheehan, G.J. Wilfret, F.J. Marousky, P.M. Lyrene, and D.A. Knauft. 1996. Postharvest longevity of cut-flower *Gerbera*. I. Response to selection for vase life components. *Journal of the American Society for Horticultural Science* 121:216–221.

Woltering, E.J. 1989. Effect of the gaseous composition on development of gerbera plantlets grown *in vitro*. *Acta Horticulturae* 261:377–383.

Gladiolus

FIGURE II-I GLADIOLUS *Gladiolus* field for cut flower production.

INTRODUCTION

Common name: gladiolus.

Scientific name: *Gladiolus* L. hybrids. The present-day *Gladiolus* cultivars are complex hybrids and include the following species: *G. cardinalis* Curtis., *G. dalenii* van Geel., *G. oppositiflorus* Herb., *G. papilio* Hook. f., *G. carneus* Delaroche, *G. cruentus* Moore., *G. tristis* L., and *G. saundersii* Hook. f. (Bailey and Bailey, 1976; Cohat, 1993; Huxley et al., 1992). The hybrids represent crosses between summer and late winter flowering species from South Africa.

Family and related taxa: Iridaceae Juss. There are between 250 and 300 *Gladiolus* species. Other important genera in this family are *Crocus, Freesia,* and *Iris.*

Origin: The majority of *Gladiolus* species are from Africa, especially South Africa, but a few species are from Europe, the Mediterranean, and the Near East.

Uses and current status: *Gladiolus* is an important cut flower and garden plant and minor potted plant (Fig. II-1 Gladiolus). Dry corm sales are important also.

The inflorescence is called a spike, which consists of numerous florets, each one a tubular corolla with several petals of one or more colors and fluted or smooth edges. The individual flowers open acropetally and consist of two subtending bractlike green structures, six perianth segments, three stamens, and a trilobed stigma. All colors are present except true blue. Flower size varies from 0.75 to 7.75 in. (2 to 20 cm) in diameter.

A flowering plant typically consists of two sheath leaves and eight or more foliage leaves, which are derived from the apical bud on the geophytic corm with contractile roots. The old corm is replaced annually with a new corm, which develops from the apical bud on the old corm (Cohat, 1993).

CULTIVARS

Cultivars are numerous, numbering into tens of thousands worldwide (Cohat, 1993; Wilfret, 1992). Numerous amateur *Gladiolus* hybridizers produce hundreds of new and interesting cultivars annually. Gladiolus cultivars are divided into groups based on floret size, color, and days to flowering after planting (see Table II-1 Gladiolus). In commercial floriculture, the two main groups cultivated are *Gladiolus* "grandiflorum" types, which have large flowers, and *G.* "nanus" types, which have small flowers (Halevy, 1985). These categories have no botanical standing (Huxley et al., 1992). Bailey and Bailey (1976) listed the large flowered type as *Gladiolus ×grandavensis* Van Houtte and the small flowered types as *Babiana* Ker-Gawl., another beautiful South African cormous plant.

The cut flower gladiolus industry has declined since the 1950s as the demand for large flower arrangements and funeral designs diminished. Since the late 1980s many new cultivars have been released with unique flower colors and substance, as well as shorter spike lengths (Wilfret, 1992). The group of miniature cultivars called orchidola gladiolus may be particularly useful for cut flower production due to their short crop time and adaptability to

TABLE II-I GLADIOLUS

North American Gladiolus Council Classification System for *Gladiolus* cultivars.

Category	Characteristic
Floret Size	in. (cm)
Miniature	Under 2.5 (6.3)
Small	2.5–3.5 (6.3–8.9)
Decorative	3.5–4.5 (8.9–11.4)
Large (standard)	4.5–5.5 (11.4–14.0)
Giant	More than 5.5 (14.0)
Flowering Date	(days)
Very early (VE)	Under 70
Early (E)	70–74
Early midseason (EM)	75–79
Midseason (M)	80–84
Late midseason (LM)	85–90
Late (L)	91–99
Very late (VL)	100 or more

winter conditions (Aimore, 1997). The species *G. tritis* and related hybrids and cultivars may also provide new colors and production possibilities (Gonzalez et al., 1998)

Despite the long 2000-year history of the gladiolus, it may be time to rethink the gladiolus plant and flower for the 21st century. The numerous exotic species available in South Africa alone may provide a needed infusion of new characteristics into modern hybrids. Fragrance and a wide range of heights exist (Cohen and Barzilay, 1991) and potted flowering plants are also a possibility (Hwang et al., 1986; Shaw et al., 1991; White and Kling, 1991).

PROPAGATION

Propagation is by cormlets (cormels) derived from stolons developing between the new and old corm, which is discarded annually. Disease-free stock can be derived from tissue culture (Logan and Zettler, 1985; Simonson and Hilderbrandt, 1971; Wilfret, 1992; Ziv et al., 1970). Consequently, disease-free cormlets are possible.

FLOWERING CONTROL AND DORMANCY

The apical bud is vegetative at planting and not all vegetative structures are present. Floral differentiation does not occur until 3 to 8 weeks after planting (weather and cultivar dependent). Depending on the cultivar, macroscopic flowers are generally present when the two first true leaves have emerged and elongated. The number of flowers on the spike depends on the size of the corm, cultivar, and cultural conditions (Cohat, 1993; Halevy, 1985; Hartsema, 1937; Imanishi et al., 2002; Kosugi, 1962).

Emergence and flower development rate are mainly controlled by temperature and light (intensity × duration). Dormancy exists and varies between cultivars and the conditions under which the corms were grown prior to harvest. As an example, plants grown in the winter under SD in Florida, southern California, or Israel are less dormant than those grown in the summer under LD in the northern areas of North America or Europe (Ryan, 1955). Dormancy can be overcome by a 2- to 5-month cold storage treatment at 36 to 50°F (2 to 10°C). Cohen et al. (1990) stated that 41°F (5°C) was better than 36°F (2°C). A high-temperature treatment of 100°F (38°C) for a few days followed by cold is more effective than cold treatments alone for breaking dormancy (Apte,

1962; Cohat, 1993; Halevy, 1985; Tsukamoto and Yagi, 1960). Gibberellic acid is effective in replacing the cold treatment of mature *Gladiolus* corms (Bhattacharjee, 1984; Dua et al., 1984). Ethephon at 400 ppm decreased the number of days to shoot emergence and increased the percentage of cormlets (Ram et al., 2002).

TEMPERATURE

Temperature is the most important factor controlling the rate of development or days to flower. Short days accelerate flowering and reduce days to anthesis under any given temperature with adequate light. However, summer grown crops are harvested after 60 to 80 days and winter grown crops after 140 days due to cooler temperatures (Halevy, 1985). Low temperatures also contribute to reduced floret number and failure to flower (see Light, below).

Corms can be cured immediately after harvest by storing at 95°F (35°C) and 80% relative humidity for 6 to 8 days (Dreistadt, 2001). Be sure to provide air circulation.

LIGHT

Production should be in full light. Reduced numbers of florets and failure to flower can be attributed to low light intensity, SD, low temperature, and poor growing conditions in Florida, Israel, or southern Japan during adverse winter weather conditions (Halevy, 1985; Imanishi and Imae, 1990; Shillo and Halevy, 1976a–d).

WATER

High-quality water is needed for irrigation. Gladiolus plants are sensitive to water stress, which results in reduced flower yields (Halevy, 1985; Wilfret, 1992). Excellent drainage is also required.

CARBON DIOXIDE

No information on carbon dioxide is available; this crop is primarily grown outside.

NUTRITION

Nutrition requirements and nitrogen sources will vary with the soil type, rainfall amounts, and production season (Cohat, 1993; De Hertogh, 1996). Review the literature and develop a nutritional program based on the local soil and environment (see Field Cut-Grown Flowers chapter for field handling procedures). Nitrate nitrogen should be used when ground is cool and wet, whereas ammonium or urea nitrogen can be used when plants are actively growing and soil is warm. See Chapter 6, Nutrition, Table 6-4, for foliar nutrient levels.

MEDIA

Gladiolus are grown in a wide variety of soil types from the white sugar sand of Florida to the black prairie soils of Minnesota. The only requirement is that the soil be well drained. De Hertogh (1996) stated that the soil pH should be between 6.0 and 6.5.

HEIGHT CONTROL

Height control is not required for cut flower production. A-Rest (ancymidol) at 1.5 mg/0.5-gal (2-L) pot or Bonzi (paclobutrazol) drenches at 2.5 to 5.0 mg a.i./pot can be used to control height of potted flowering plants (Hwang et al., 1986; Shaw et al., 1991; White and Kling, 1991).

SPACING

Spacing and planting depth of corms will vary according to season, corm size, and cultivar. De Hertogh (1996) gave a general corm field spacing as 2 in. (5 cm) apart and 4 to 5 in. (10 to 13 cm) deep.

PINCHING AND DISBUDDING

None required.

SUPPORT

None is typically required but some growers may want to provide support in windy areas.

SCHEDULE AND TIMING

Temperature and light (intensity × duration) determine the time from planting to harvest after the appropriate storage treatment (see Flowering Control and Dormancy section). Corms planted under warm summer conditions flower in 60 to 80 days, depending on the cultivar. Time to flower may increase to 140 days for plants grown during the cool winter in frost-free climates. Extended harvest is produced by planting every 1 to 3 weeks and by using cultivars with variable flowering times.

INSECTS

Insects are a concern during production. In particular, various aphid and thrips species are attracted to gladiolus. Nematode and weed control in the field are also problems and expensive to control. Fumigation for nematodes, weeds, and diseases is frequently required if land is reused (Cohat, 1993; Wilfret, 1992). Other problems include mites, plant buds, whiteflies, mealybugs, and caterpillars (Dreistadt, 2001).

DISEASES

Diseases are a constant concern (Forsberg, 1979). Corms, roots, leaves, stems, and flowers are vulnerable. *Fusarium* on the corms is the most serious and destructive disease. Ammonium or urea-based nitrogen may cause more *Fusarium* than nitrate nitrogen (H. Lubbers, personal communication). A number of other organisms can cause wet or dry rots of the corm, including *Stromatinia gladioli, Sclerotium rolfsii, Botrytis gladiolarum, Rhizoctonia solani,* and *Penicillium gladioli* (Dreistadt, 2001; Horst, 1990). Corms may need to be chemically treated after digging, during storage, and/or before planting to prevent losses. Hot water treatments of approximately 131 to 137°F (55 to 58°C) may eradicate *Fusarium, Penicillium, Botrytis,* and *Stromatinia gladioli* in corm (Cohen et al., 1990; Dreistadt, 2001) (see Flowering Control and Dormancy section). After curing corms (see Temperature section), presoak corms for 2 days at 60 to 80°F (16 to 27°C) and discard any that float. Immerse corms in 131°F (55°C) hot water for 30 min. Cool corms rapidly afterward with cold water and dry thoroughly. Dust corms with fungicide and store at 40°F (4°C) and 70 to 80% relative humidity.

The bacteria *Pseudomonas* and *Xanthamonas* cause serious diseases on the leaves and developing spike. Fungal leaf spots include *Curvularia lunata, C. trifolii, Urocystis gladiolicola, Stemphylium,* and *Septoria gladioli* (Dreistadt, 2001). *Botrytis* is destructive on the flowers during shipping, particularly during cold wet harvesting periods, and can develop on the corms as well. Numerous viruses such as cucumber mosaic, bean yellow mosaic, and tobacco ringspot also infect gladiolus (Cohat, 1993; Horst, 1990).

PHYSIOLOGICAL DISORDERS

Fluoride from air pollution can turn leaf tips brown. Fluoride in superphosphate can also cause leaf injury and should not be used as a source of phosphorus (Brewer et al., 1966; Jenkins, 1970). Other possible causes of tip burn include low soil pH, root damage, and nematodes (G. Wilfret, personal communication).

POSTHARVEST

Postharvest care and handling have been well researched (Kofranek and Halevy, 1976; Marousky and Woltz, 1971). Keeping quality varies widely between cultivars. Defined grades and standards exist for marketing the spikes (Fairchild, 1979) (see Table II-2 Gladiolus). Spikes are harvested when the lower two or more flowers are just beginning to show true color. Two to three leaves are left on the plant for photosynthesis and regeneration of the new corm. Individual flowers on the spikes will continue to open after harvest and stems are transported upright because of geotropism. Other treatments can be used to prevent geotropic responses (calcium chelators) and ethylene inhibitors such as silver thiosulfate (STS) can be useful (Philosoph-Hadas et al., 1995).

At time of harvest the cut stems are usually pulsed with a floral preservative prior to or after grading. Flowering spikes respond to floral preservatives in that the flower size increases and the individual flowers last longer. A common opening solution contains sucrose (10%) (Meir et al., 1995) and 8-hydroxyquinoline citrate (300 ppm), which acidifies and acts as a microbial inhibitor. Jones et al. (1994) stressed the benefit of biocides. The stems are recut, placed into this solution, and held for 24 to 72 hr at 70°F (21°C). Afterward, stems are placed in deionized, pH 3.5 water. If stems have been previously pulsed with a preservative by the producer, use only acidified-deionized water for storage (Sacalis, 1993). A 70 to 75°F (21 to 24°C) temperature should be used to

TABLE II-2 GLADIOLUS

Standards used to classify grades for cut *Gladiolus* spikes in the United States (Fairchild, 1979).

Grade	Length	
	Total Stem in. (cm)	Floral Portion of Stem in. (cm)
Fancy	>44 (111)	>18 (45)
Special	37–44 (94–111)	13–18 (32–45)
Standard	32–37 (80–94)	8–13 (20–32)
Utility	<32 (80)	<8 (20)

open the flowers on spikes. Removal of the uppermost stem with a few buds will improve opening of the remaining buds and decrease spike curvature (Sacalis, 1993).

Temperatures of 33 to 35°F (1 to 2°C) are optimum for grading and transport (Nell and Reid, 2001). Stems hydrate best in deionized water with a 3.5 pH. Cut gladiolus spikes are highly sensitive to fluorides (0.25 ppm) in water, which is common in municipal drinking water. The outer margins of the petals become transparent and prematurely wilt. Spikes can be dry stored at 39°F (4°C) for 2 to 3 weeks

when previously pulsed, treated for *Botrytis*, and wrapped to prevent water loss. Gladiolus apparently are not sensitive to ethylene, but longevity is enhanced by STS in the floral preservative (Nowak and Rudnicki, 1990; Serek et al., 1994). Roychowdhury and Sarkar (1995) found that 500 ppm $NiCl_2$ plus 2 to 4% sucrose was superior to various other ions including $AgNO_3$. 1-MCP is also likely to be effective. Modified atmosphere storage of 4 to 7% CO_2 and 10 to 14% O_2 improved floret opening, allowing for long-term transport (Meir et al., 1995).

KEY POINTS

- Gladiolus is a popular field-grown cut flower and is occasionally used as a greenhouse cut flower and potted flowering plant.

- While there are 250 to 300 species of gladiolus, few have been used in the development of modern hybrids.

- Field production begins in the winter in southern climates and moves north with summer.

- Plants are propagated by cormlets.

- Plants are vegetative when the corms are planted, but floral initiation occurs after shoot emergence.

- Fluoride from air pollution, water, or superphosphates can turn leaf tips brown.

- Plants are sensitive to water stress, which reduces flower yield.

- *Fusarium* and thrips are major cultural problems.

- Cut flowers respond very well to floral preservatives.

BIBLIOGRAPHY

Aimore, T. 1997. A cut above. *FloraCulture International* 7(5):22–26.

Apte, S.S. 1962. Dormancy and sprouting in gladiolus corms. *Mededeelingen van de Landbouwhogeschool te Wageningen* 62(5):1–47.

Bailey, L.H., and E.Z. Bailey. 1976. *Gladiolus*, pp. 511–512 in *Hortus Third: A Concise Dictionary of Plants Cultivated in the United States and Canada.* Macmillan, New York.

Bhattacharjee, S.K. 1984. The effect of growth regulating chemicals on gladiolus. *Gartenbauwissenschaft* 49:103–106.

Brewer, R.F., F.B. Guillemet, and F.H. Sutherland. 1966. The effects of atmospheric fluoride on *Gladiolus* growth, flowering and corm production. *Proceedings of the American Society for Horticultural Science* 88:631–634.

Cohat, J. 1993. *Gladiolus*, pp. 297–320 in *The Physiology of Flower Bulbs*, A. De Hertogh and M. Le Nard, editors. Elsevier, Amsterdam.

Cohen, A., and A. Barzilay. 1991. Miniature gladiolus cultivars bred for winter flowering. *HortScience* 26:216–218.

Cohen, A., A. Barzilay, and H. Vigodsky-Haas. 1990. Hot-water treatment tolerance in gladiolus cormels and their state of dormancy. *Acta Horticulturae* 266:495–503.

De Hertogh, A.A. 1996. *Gladiolus*, pp. D25–26 in *Holland Bulb Forcer's Guide*, 5th ed. International Flower Bulbs Centre, Hillegom, The Netherlands.

Dreistadt, S.H. 2001. *Integrated Pest Management for Floriculture and Nurseries.* University of California Division of Agriculture and Natural Resources Publication 3402.

Dua, I.S., O.P. Sehgal, and K.S. Clark. 1984. Gibberellic acid induced earliness and increased production in gladiolus. *Gartenbauwissenschaft* 49:91–94.

Fairchild, L. 1979. *How to Grow Glorious Gladiolus, Bulletin 139.* North American Gladiolus Council, Edgewood, Maryland.

Forsberg, J.L. 1979. *Gladiolus*, pp. 87–104 in *Diseases of Ornamental Plants.* Special Publication Number 3, College of Agriculture, University of Illinois, Urbana-Champaign.

Gonzalez, A., S. Bañon, J.A. Fernandez, J.A. Franco, J.A. Casas, and J. Ochoa. 1998. Flowering response of *Gladiolus tristis* (L.) after exposing to cold treatment. *Scientia Horticulturae* 74: 279–284.

Halevy, A.H. 1985. *Gladiolus*, pp. 63–70 in *Handbook of Flowering*, vol. III, A.H. Halevy, editor. CRC Press, Boca Raton, Florida.

Hartsema, A.M. 1937. Periodieke ontwikkeling van *Gladiolus hybridus* var. *vesuvius*. *Koninklijke Akademie van Wetenschappen Verhandelingen* 36(3):1–35. (in Dutch)

Horst, R.K. 1990. Gladiolus, pp. 657–658 in *Westcott's Plant Disease Handbook*, 5th ed. Van Nostrand Reinhold, New York.

Huxley, A., M. Griffiths, and M. Levy. 1992. *Gladiolus*, pp. 413–422 in *The New Royal Horticultural Society Dictionary of Gardening*, vol. 2. Stockton Press, New York.

Hwang, E.G., J.K. Suh, and B.H. Kwack. 1986. The influence of paclobutrazol on the growth and flowering of potted gladiolus (*G. gandavensis*). *Journal of the Korean Society for Horticultural Science* 27:73–80.

Imanishi, H., and Y. Imae. 1990. Effects of low light intensity and low temperature given at different developmental stages on flowering of gladiolus. *Acta Horticulturae* 266:189–196.

Imanishi, H., Y. Imae, E. Kaneko, and S. Sonoda. 2002. Effect of temperature and daylength on flowering of early flowering gladiolus. *Acta Horticulturae* 570:437–445.

Jenkins, J.M. 1970. Brown tip of *Gladiolus* induced by applications of fertilizer materials. *HortScience* 5:395–396.

Jones, R.B., M., Serek, C.-L. Kou, and M.S. Reid. 1994. The effect of protein synthesis inhibition on petal senescence in cut bulb flowers. *Journal of the American Society for Horticultural Science* 119:1243–1247.

Kofranek, A.M., and A.H. Halevy. 1976. Sucrose pulsing of gladiolus stems before storage to increase spike quality. *HortScience* 11:572–573.

Kosugi, K. 1962. Studies on production and flowering in gladiolus. *Memoirs of Faculty of Agriculture, Kagawa University* 11:1–68. (in Japanese, English summary)

Logan, A.E., and F.W. Zettler. 1985. Rapid *in vitro* propagation of virus indexed gladioli. *Acta Horticulturae* 164:169–180.

Marousky, F.J., and S.S. Woltz. 1971. Effect of fluoride and a floral preservative on quality of cut gladiolus. *Proceedings of the Florida State Horticultural Society* 84:375–380.

Meir, S., S. Philosoph-Hadas, R. Michaeli, H. Davidson, M. Fogelman, and A. Schaffer. 1995. Improvement of the keeping quality of minigladiolus spikes during prolonged storage by sucrose pulsing and modified atmosphere packaging. *Acta Horticulturae* 405:335–342.

Nell, T.A., and M.S Reid. 2001. Can't take the heat. *Floral Management* 17(10):33–34.

Nowak, J., and R.M. Rudnicki. 1990. *Postharvest Handling and Storage of Cut Flowers, Florist Greens and Potted Plants*. Timber Press, Portland, Oregon.

Philosoph-Hadas, S.S. Meir, I. Rosenberger, and A.H. Halevy. 1995. Control and regulation of gravitropic response of cut flowering stems during storage and horizontal transport. *Acta Horticulturae* 405:343–350.

Ram, R., D. Mukherjee, and S. Manuja. 2002. Plant growth regulators affect the development of both corms and cormlets in gladiolus. *HortScience* 37:343–344.

Roychowdhury, N., and S. Sarkar. 1995. Influence of chemicals on vase life of gladiolus. *Acta Horticulturae* 405:389–391.

Ryan, G.F. 1955. Effects of temperature on rest in *Gladiolus* corms. *Proceedings of the American Society for Horticultural Science* 65:463–471.

Sacalis, J.N. 1993. *Gladiolus*, pp. 64–66 in *Cut Flowers, Prolonging Freshness*, 2nd ed., J.L. Seals, editor. Ball Publishing, Batavia, Illinois.

Serek, M., R.B. Jones, and M.S. Reid. 1994. Role of ethylene in opening and senescence of *Gladiolus* sp. flowers. *Journal of the American Society for Horticultural Science* 119:1014–1019.

Shaw, P.M., K.A. Schekel, and V.I. Lohr. 1991. Height control in pot grown 'Wood Violet' *Gladiolus* using ancymidol. *HortScience* 26:1089.

Shillo, R., and A.H. Halevy. 1976a. Inflorescence development of flowering and blasted *Gladiolus* plants in relation to development of other plant parts. *Scientia Horticulturae* 4:79–86.

Shillo, R., and A.H. Halevy. 1976b. The effect of various environmental factors on flowering of *Gladiolus*. I. Light intensity. *Scientia Horticulturae* 4:131–137.

Shillo, R., and A.H. Halevy. 1976c. The effect of various environmental factors on flowering of *Gladiolus*. II. Length of the day. *Scientia Horticulturae* 4:139–146.

Shillo, R., and A.H. Halevy. 1976d. The effect of various environmental factors on flowering of *Gladiolus*. III. Temperature and moisture. *Scientia Horticulturae* 4:147–155.

Simonson, J., and A.C. Hilderbrandt. 1971. *In vitro* growth and differentiation of *Gladiolus* plants from callus cultures. *Canadian Journal of Botany* 49:1817–1819.

Tsukamoto, Y., and M. Yagi. 1960. Dormancy of gladiolus corms. VI. Effects of temperature treatments on breaking dormancy of gladiolus corms stored in a storage room and of those grown under different daylength. *Plant Cell Physiology* 1:221–230.

White, J.W., and G.L. Kling. 1991. Greenhouse culture and cost of production of miniature gladiolus (Pixiolas). *Pennsylvania Flower Growers Bulletin* 405:1–6.

Wilfret, G.J. 1992. *Gladiolus*, pp. 143–157 in *Introduction to Floriculture*, R.A. Larson, editor. Academic Press, San Diego, California.

Ziv, M., A. Halevy, and R. Shillo. 1970. Organs and plantlets regeneration of *Gladiolus* through tissue culture. *Annals of Botany* 34:671–676.

Gypsophila

FIGURE II-1 GYPSOPHILA *Gypsophila* field for cut flower production.

INTRODUCTION

Common names: gypsophila, gyp, baby's breath.

Scientific name: *Gypsophila elegans* Bieb., annual gypsophila, *G. paniculata* L., perennial gypsophila, *G. muralis* L., also known as annual baby's breath, and *G. repens* L., creeping baby's breath. The Latin name means "gypsum loving" (Huxley et al., 1992).

Family and related taxa: Caryophyllaceae Juss. There are more than 125 species of annual, biennial, and perennial *Gypsophila*. The most important genus in the Caryophyllaceae family is the carnation (*Dianthus*).

Origin: *G. elegans* is native to southern Ukraine, the Caucasus, eastern Turkey, and into Iran (Bailey and Bailey, 1976; Huxley et al., 1992). *G. paniculata* is from central and eastern Europe and east into Asia and has naturalized in many areas of the world. *G. muralis* is native to Europe and east into Asia. *G. repens* is native from northwest Spain to the Carpathians.

Uses and current status: *G. elegans* is commonly sold as a summer annual for the home garden. *G. paniculata* is the dominant species grown worldwide, primarily as a commercial filler cut flower (Fig. II-1 Gypsophila). *G. paniculata* is also commonly grown as a garden ornamental and occasionally as a potted flowering plant. *G. muralis* and *G. repens* are grown as garden ornamentals.

Gypsophila elegans is a much-branched plant, 8 to 20 in. (20 to 52 cm) tall, with 1- to 2-in. (3- to 5-cm)-long leaves. The inflorescence is a panicle of cymes with numerous individual flowers up to 1 in. (3 cm) wide and ranging in color from white to red.

G. paniculata, though a perennial, can be grown as an annual and flowers in late spring to fall, with two to three harvest flushes per growing season. Plants can be up to 40 in. (1 m) tall. Leaves are gray green and flowers and branching are similar to *G. elegans*, but flowers are only 1/4 in. (6.5 mm) wide. Flower colors vary from white to reddish and from single to double. *G. paniculata* is hardy from Zones 3 to 7 (Armitage and Laushman, 2003; Bailey and Bailey, 1976).

G. muralis is an annual grown for its light pink, single to double flowers, which tend to close at night. The plants flower most of the summer and reach 7 to 10 in. (18 to 25 cm) tall and 12 to 14 in. (30 to 36 cm) wide (Nau, 1999). The species has a tendency to reseed and should be used accordingly.

G. repens is a mat-forming perennial that grows 4 to 8 in. (10 to 20 cm) tall and up to 12 in. (30 cm) wide. The flowers are white to pink and single or double. *G. repens* is hardy from Zones 3 to 7 and tolerates more acidic soils than other gypsophilas.

CULTIVARS

G. elegans has a limited number of cultivars, which vary in flower size and in color from white to pink, rose, carmine, and red. On the other hand, numerous cultivars of *G. paniculata* exist with colors ranging from white to red (Armitage and Laushman, 2003; Bailey and Bailey, 1976; Huxley et al., 1992). Cultivars vary in height from 12 to 16 in. (30 to 45 cm) for the compact garden cultivars to 40 in. (1 m) for the tall cut flower cultivars. Flower size and doubleness can also vary. 'Million Stars', a small flowered but prolific variety, is quite popular. 'Million Stars,' can be planted more densely than 'Perfecta,' increasing production per acre. The cultivars are asexually propagated to preserve their unique characteristics (Armitage and Laushman, 2003). Wide variations exist in response to temperature and photoperiod treatments between cultivars or selections (Kusey et al., 1981).

Only a limited number of cultivars of *G. muralis* and *G. repens* are available. They vary primarily in flower color, doubleness, and plant vigor.

PROPAGATION

G. elegans, *G. paniculata*, *G. muralis*, and *G. repens* may be propagated by seed sown at 70 to 80°F (21 to 26°C), and 1/16 to 1/8 oz (1.8 to 3.6 g) will yield 1000 plants (Nau, 1993). Germination is rapid and is completed within 5 to 15 days.

Specialty propagators can take cuttings of both *G. elegans* and *G. paniculata* from disease-free stock and root them under mist in 10 to 14 days (Armitage and Laushman, 2003; Danziger, 1993). Kusey and Weiler (1980) noted that rooting of terminal *G. paniculata* cuttings was improved with 3000 to 10,000 ppm indole-3-butyric acid dips for 5 to 30 sec.

G. paniculata is commonly produced *in vitro* to ensure disease-free stock of selected cultivars (Armitage and Laushman, 2003; Danziger, 1998). The elite stock plants are maintained in the same manner as *Pelargonium* or *Dendranthema*. In the summer, stock plants for cuttings are kept under short days to maintain them in a vegetative state (Kusey et al., 1981). Double-flowered clones of *G. paniculata* may be grafted onto vigorous root stock, but this is costly and impractical (Armitage and Laushman, 2003).

FLOWERING CONTROL AND DORMANCY

Gypsophila are LD plants: Flowering does not occur under SD unless the plants are vernalized (Kusey et al., 1981). Flower initiation and development are also influenced by total accumulated photosynthetic irradiance, temperature, and juvenility. The critical day length for nonvernalized plants is 12 to 18 hr (Shillo, 1985). Inflorescences with the longest stems and best quality are obtained with 16- to 18-hr day lengths (Kusey et al., 1981). Juvenility is also critical in that if plants have 12 or fewer leaves, LD are not perceived in a uniform or optimal manner and flowering will be erratic (Shillo et al., 1981). Gibberellic acid is not effective in inducing flowering of plants grown under SD (Kusey et al., 1981; Shlomo et al., 1985).

Total accumulated photosynthetic irradiance is influential (Hicklenton et al., 1993; Shillo, 1985). In summer at 2300 fc (345 μmol · m^{-2} · s^{-1}) 100% of the plants flowered, but total flowers per plant were low. At 7680 fc (1150 μmol · m^{-2} · s^{-1}) 100% of the plants flowered, with vastly increased numbers of flowers per plant. During the winter, at 5570 fc (835 μmol · m^{-2} · s^{-1}) 100% of the plants flowered, but at 2400 fc (360 μmol · m^{-2} · s^{-1}) none flowered. In addition, as photosynthetic photon flux increased, the time to anthesis was shortened.

Night temperature affects flower initiation and development; under LD and 52°F (11°C) 100% of plants flowered, whereas at 45°F (7°C) only 41% of plants flowered (Shillo, 1985). In addition, as the temperature increased, the number of flowering stems increased from 12 to 20, respectively. Optimum night temperatures were 61 to 68°F (16 to 20°C), which produced the maximum flowering percentage and minimum days to flower (Hicklenton et al., 1993). Cultivar differences were noted: 'Bristol Fairy' failed to flower at 46°F (8°C), but almost all 'Bridal Veil' plants flowered.

TEMPERATURE

Temperature not only influences the flowering response of *Gypsophila* to photoperiod and light intensity, but cold temperature also vernalizes the plants. For example, in Israel under high ambient light levels, 80% of the plants flowered

TABLE II-1 GYPSOPHILA

The influence of 7 weeks of cooling at 34°F (1°C) and photoperiod on *Gypsophila paniculata* (Shillo, 1985).

Temperature	Photoperiod	Flowering (%)	Flower Stems (no./plant)
Cooled	LD	97	28
	SD	80	15
Noncooled	LD	71	15
	SD	0	0

under SD when rooted cuttings were stored at 32 to 34°F (0 to 1°C) for 7 weeks under low levels of fluorescent light (480 fc, 72 μmol $\cdot$ m^{-2} $\cdot$ s^{-1}) prior to planting (Table II-1 Gypsophila). On the other hand, 0% of nonvernalized plants flowered under SD (Shillo, 1985). Vernalization also improved percent flowering of plants grown under LD. Kusey et al. (1981), however, did not observe flowering under SD after vernalization for 8 weeks at 41°F (5°C) in Indiana under low light levels. Plants can be vernalized at 52°F (11°C) when subsequent light levels are high. For example, in Florida clumps can be cold stored during the summer and planted in the field in the fall for flowering during the winter (Raulston et al., 1973).

For forcing and flowering in greenhouses, 52°F (11°C) was the minimum night temperature (Shillo, 1985). Hicklenton et al. (1993) found the temperature range for optimal flowering to be 61 to 68°F (16 to 20°C); the higher temperature was best at higher light levels and the lower temperature at lower light levels. At 45°F (7°C) plants remain vegetative even under LD (Shillo, 1985).

LIGHT

Plants should be grown in full light. Plants are most commonly grown outdoors. Dwarf cultivars for potted plants are grown under protection. Sunlight reduction should be used only to control high temperatures. As discussed in the Flowering Control and Dormancy section, high light levels are required for the LD flowering response and influence the number of flowers per inflorescence and the number of stems harvested per plant. If LD treatments are used, they should continue at least until the shoot length is 12 to 16 in. (30 to 40 cm) or, better, until anthesis, when the shoot length is 28 to 32 in. (70 to 80 cm) (Shillo, 1985)

In Israel under high winter light and protection the minimum total photoperiod is 12 hr, and a 4-hr night break provided better re-

sults than a 4-hr day extension (Shillo, 1985; Shillo and Halevy, 1982). However, continuous lighting all night was more effective than either night break or day continuation lighting. Cyclic incandescent lighting can be used (Shillo, 1985; Shillo and Halevy, 1982). Incandescent lights should be on 10 min out of each 30-min cycle. Incandescent lights are most effective because they provide a low red:far red ratio; fluorescent lamps that have a high red:far red ratio are not effective.

WATER

As with most crops, do not overwater; Carlson (1986) suggests growing this crop on the dry side. A well-drained medium is desired.

CARBON DIOXIDE

Supplemental carbon dioxide promotes growth; weight and leaf area are doubled and branching is increased by 50% when plants are grown in plastic hoop houses during the winter in Israel (Shillo, 1985). However, most North American production is outdoors, which prevents the use of supplemental carbon dioxide.

NUTRITION

Gypsophila is sensitive to high soluble salt levels. A pH of 6.5 to 7.0 is optimal (Carlson, 1986; Danziger, 1993). A 150-ppm N nutrient solution can be used with each irrigation. When flowering commences, reduce fertilization to 100 ppm N (Danziger, 1998). Nutrient levels from leaf tissue were reported by Mills and Jones (1996) (Table II-2 Gypsophila).

MEDIA

An artificial medium can be used for propagation and potted plant production. In the field, a wide variety of soil types can be used as long as the pH has been adjusted to 6.5 to 7.0 and drainage is good.

TABLE II-2 GYPSOPHILA

Gypsophila paniculata leaf nutrient levels from healthy foliar tissue based on dry weight (Mills and Jones, 1996).

Element	Level
Nitrogen	3.50–6.00%
Phosphorus	0.25–0.70%
Potassium	2.15–4.50%
Calcium	2.60–6.41%
Magnesium	0.40–1.30%
Iron	50–287 ppm
Manganese	33–286 ppm
Zinc	25–190 ppm
Boron	25–141 ppm

HEIGHT CONTROL

For cut flower production, none is used. For potted plants use dwarf cultivars; Bonsai (paclobutrazol) or Sumagic (uniconazole) are also commonly used (Danziger, 1993). Adriansen (1985) stated that A-Rest (ancymidol) is very effective and was more effective than Cycocel (chlormequat) or B-Nine (daminozide), which is considered ineffective.

SPACING

Field spacing ranges from 12 × 24 to 36 × 48 in. (30 × 60 to 90 × 120 cm) for *G. paniculata*, the perennial species, which can grow up to 3 ft (90 cm) tall. Tight spacing of 12 × 24 in. (30 × 60 cm) is used for crops that are replanted annually, whereas wider spacing is used for crops that are replanted every 2 to 3 years. The spacing is 20 × 30 in. (8 × 12 cm) for *G. elegans*, the annual species, which is typically 18 in. (45 cm) tall (Armitage, 1992; Armitage and Laushman, 2003; Post, 1949). If the appropriate cultivars are grown for 4-in. (10-cm) pot production, spacing is 6 × 8 in. (15 × 20 cm).

PINCHING AND DISBUDDING

None required.

SUPPORT

Generally no support is used, but one layer of support can be used in fields or sites where storms occur.

SCHEDULE AND TIMING

The perennial *G. paniculata* is grown from Zones 3 to 7 and flowers outdoors from late spring through summer if regularly harvested. Plants are primarily field grown but can be produced in the greenhouse. Outdoors after a cold period, plants will flower one to three times from late spring through summer. Flowering can be manipulated by providing temporary hoop houses and LD from incandescent lights. Plants can be kept in production for up to 3 years.

In Florida (Zones 9 and 10) plants can be dug after flowering and cold treated during the summer. They are replanted in September through February for winter and spring production (Armitage and Laushman, 2003; Raulston et al, 1973). Once vernalized, most plants flower regardless of photoperiod. In Florida plants flowered within 104 days when plants were given 6 to 8 weeks of 41°F (7°C) cold treatment. If no cold treatment was given, 124 days were required (Kusey et al., 1981). All plants were grown under natural day lengths during the winter.

In Israel, at higher temperatures, LD (14- to 16-hr) flowering can occur in 50 to 60 days, but quality is low (Danziger, 1998). In northern latitudes *G. paniculata* seedling transplants or rooted cuttings must be planted at least 8 weeks prior to frost and overwintered; plants will flower the following summer. The annual species, *G. elegans*, requires 8 to 12 weeks to flower (Carlson, 1986; Post, 1949).

INSECTS

Leafminers are a major issue in production of *Gypsophila*. Spider mites, aphids, and thrips can become serious if routine scouting is not practiced and control treatments not applied (Armitage and Laushman, 2003; Carlson, 1986; Danziger, 1993). Army worms and leaf miners can also be a problem.

DISEASES

Many diseases are avoided by using *in vitro*-propagated plants or plants originating from elite disease-free stock plants. The use of clean plant material is critical. *Pythium, Phytophthora, Pellicularia,* and *Rhizoctonia* may result in damping-off and death of young plants. Powdery mildew and *Alternaria* leaf spot and flower blight can reduce vigor and quality. *Botrytis* can occur in leaves and flowers during shipping or under cold, moist production environments (Danziger, 1993). Crown gall (*Agrobacterium*) can develop if a few plants are infected and grafting occurs with infected knives (Armitage and Laushman, 2003). *Sclerotinia sclerotiorum* attacks leaves and stems with a characteristic white fungus in moist conditions (Danziger, 1998). Bacteria streak (*Erwinia herbicola*), aster yellows, and tomato spotted wilt virus can also occur (Dreistadt, 2001).

PHYSIOLOGICAL DISORDERS

Low flower numbers can result from low light levels. Plants may return to vegetative growth if plants have been improperly cold treated or placed into LD for an insufficient time period (i.e., until plants flower). If temperatures are too low, improper development of flower stems can also occur (Shillo, 1985). Flower browning can occur, which may be due to overmaturity or *Botrytis* (Sacalis, 1993).

POSTHARVEST

Stems are normally harvested when 5 to 30% of the flowers are open if shipped and 80 to 90% open if sold locally or dried (Armitage and Laushman, 2003). If preservatives are used, stems with 5% open flowers can be harvested. Stems are cold stored at 33 to 35°F (1 to 2°C) (Nell and Reid, 2001). Flowers can be colored by placing stems in dye solutions or they can be air dried.

A variety of postharvest treatments are recommended. First of all, flowers are sensitive to ethylene and either silver or 1-MCP should be used (Doi et al., 1999; Newman et al., 1998). Silver nitrate at 25 ppm plus 10% sucrose can be applied overnight or silver thiosulfate (STS) plus 9.5% sucrose can be applied for 30 min (Sacalis, 1993). Downs et al. (1988) recommended a slightly different regime of a 24-hr STS (25-ppm) treatment in combination with 10 to 15% sucrose.

When stems are shipped dry, rehydrate in deionized water at pH 3.5 (Sacalis, 1993). Stems can be stored for up to 3 weeks at 35°F (2°C), but a shorter duration is recommended. Stems should be held in a preservative during storage.

If stems are harvested with only 5% of buds open, they should be placed in a preservative at 70°F (21°C) and 100 fc (20 μmol $\cdot$ m^{-2} $\cdot$ s^{-1}) light for 2 to 3 days (Sacalis, 1993). A sample preservative solution for continuous use has 5 to 10% sucrose, 200 ppm 8-hydroxyquinoline citrate (8-HQC), and 100 ppm sodium benzoate or 25 ppm silver nitrate. For a 24- to 72-hr pulse, 10% sucrose and 300 ppm 8-HQC can be used. Once flowers are open, cold store. Nowak and Rudnicki (1990) recommended 10% sucrose and 200 ppm Physan 20 (a disinfectant); Farnham et al. (1978) suggested 10% sucrose and 25 ppm silver nitrate. Jones and Hill (1993) noted that the germicides 8-HQC and sodium dichloroisocyanuric acid increased vase life.

KEY POINTS

- Popular filler cut flower and garden ornamental, occasional potted flowering plant.
- Disease-free plant material is critical.
- *G. paniculata* is an obligate LD plant except when plants are vernalized.
- Proper postharvest handling is important for maximum vase life and bud opening.

BIBLIOGRAPHY

Adriansen, E. 1985. Kemisk vækstregulering, pp. 142–162 in *Potteplanter I—Produktion, Metoder, Midler.* O.V. Christensen, A. Klougart, I.S. Pedersen, and K. Wikesjö, editors. GartnerINFO, København, Denmark. (in Danish).

Armitage, A.M. 1992. Specialty cut flowers, pp. 159–192 in *Introduction to Floriculture,* 2nd ed., R.A. Larson, editor. Academic Press, San Diego, California.

Armitage, A.M., and J.M. Laushman. 2003. *Gypsophila paniculata,* pp. 312–319 in *Specialty Cut Flowers,* 2nd ed. Timber Press, Portland, Oregon.

Bailey, L.H., and E.Z. Bailey. 1976. *Gypsophila,* pp. 531–532 in *Hortus Third: A Concise Dictionary of Plants Cultivated in the United States and Canada.* Macmillan, New York.

Carlson, W. 1986. A cultural guide for gypsophila. *Greenhouse Grower* 4(3):12–13.

Danziger, M. 1993. Potted *Gypsophila. GrowerTalks* 56(10):19.

Danziger, M. 1998. Gypsophila, pp. 534–536 in *Ball Redbook,* 16th ed., V. Ball, editor. Ball Publishing, Batavia, Illinois.

Doi, M., T. Saito, T. Nagai, and H. Imanishi. 1999. Occurrence of "flower browning" of cut *Gypsophila paniculata* L. and its prevention by harvesting at bud stage. *Journal of the Japanese Society for Horticultural Science* 68:854–860.

Downs, C.G., M. Reihana, and H. Dick. 1988. Bud-opening treatments to improve *Gypsophila* quality after transport. *Scientia Horticulturae* 34:301–310.

Dreistadt, S.H. 2001. *Integrated Pest Management for Floriculture and Nurseries.* University of California Division of Agriculture and Natural Resources Publication 3402.

Farnham, D.S., A.M. Kofranek, and J. Kubot. 1978. Bud opening of *Gypsophila paniculata* L. cv. Perfecta with Physan-20. *Journal of the American Society for Horticultural Science* 103:382–384.

Hicklenton, P.R., S.M. Newman, and L.J. Davis 1993. Night temperature, photosynthetic photon flux, and long days affect *Gypsophila paniculata* flowering. *HortScience* 28: 888–890.

Huxley, A., M. Griffiths, and M. Levy. 1992. *Gypsophila*, pp. 477–478 in *The New Royal Horticultural Society Dictionary of Gardening*, vol. 2. Stockton Press, New York.

Jones, R.B., and M. Hill. 1993. The effect of germicides on the longevity of cut flowers. *Journal of the American Society for Horticultural Science* 118:350–354.

Kusey, W.E., Jr., and T.C. Weiler. 1980. Propagation of *Gypsophila paniculata* from cuttings. *HortScience* 15:85–86.

Kusey W.E., Jr, T.C. Weiler, P.A. Hammer, B.K. Harbaugh, and G.J. Wilfret. 1981. Seasonal and chemical influences on the flowering of *Gypsophila paniculata* 'Bristol Fairy' selections. *Journal of the American Society for Horticultural Science* 106:84–88.

Mills, H.A., and J.B. Jones, Jr. 1996. *Plant Analysis Handbook II*, MicroMacro Publishing, Athens, Georgia.

Nau, J. 1993. Gypsophila, pp. 72–73, 94–95, in *Ball Culture Guide, The Encyclopedia of Seed Germination*, 2nd ed. Ball Publishing, Batavia, Illinois.

Nau, J. 1999. *Ball Culture Guide, The Encyclopedia of Seed Germination*, 3rd ed. Ball Publishing, Batavia, Illinois.

Nell, T.A., and M.S Reid. 2001. Can't take the heat. *Floral Management* 17(10):33–34.

Newman, J.P., L.L. Dodge, and M.S. Reid. 1998. Evaluation of ethylene inhibitors for postharvest treatment of *Gypsophila paniculata* L. *HortTechnology* 8:58–63.

Nowak, J., and R.M. Rudnicki. 1990. *Gypsophila*, pp. 151–152 in *Postharvest Handling and Storage of Cut Flowers, Florist Greens and Potted Plants.* Timber Press, Portland, Oregon.

Post, K. 1949. *Gypsophila elegans*, pp. 556–557; *Gypsophila paniculata*, p. 558 in *Florist Crop Production and Marketing*, Orange Judd Publishing, New York.

Raulston, J.C., S.L. Poe, F.J. Marousky, and W.T. Witte. 1973. Gypsophila production in Florida. *Florida Flower Grower* 10:1–8.

Sacalis, J.N. 1993. *Gypsophila paniculata*, pp. 68–69 in *Cut Flowers, Prolonging Freshness, Postproduction Care and Handling*, 2nd ed., J.L. Seals, editor. Ball Publishing, Batavia, Illinois.

Shillo, R. 1985. *Gypsophila paniculata*, pp. 83–87 in *Handbook of Flowering*, vol. III, A.H. Halevy, editor. CRC Press, Boca Raton, Florida.

Shillo, R., and A.H. Halevy 1982. Interaction of photoperiod and temperature in flowering-control of *Gypsophila paniculata* L. *Scientia Horticulturae* 16:385–393.

Shillo, R., Shlomo, E., and M. Herman 1981. The effect of termination time of lighting on winter flowering *Gypsophila*, in *Annual Report*. Department of Ornamental Horticulture, Hebrew University. Rehovot, Israel. (in Hebrew)

Shlomo, E., R. Shillo, and A.H. Halevy. 1985. Gibberellin substitution for the high night temperatures required for the long-day promotion of flowering in *Gypsophila paniculata* L. *Scientia Horticulturae* 26:69–76.

Hedera

FIGURE II-1 HEDERA *Hedera* trained on totem poles.

INTRODUCTION

Common names: ivy, English ivy.

Scientific name: Hedera helix L. (Huxley et al., 1992).

Family and related taxa: Araliaceae Juss. The 11 *Hedera* species are all ornamental vines. As *Hedera* plants mature, the leaf shape changes; stems become woody, upright, and difficult to root; and flowering occurs. Root initials are present on juvenile branches and will become attached to any appropriate wall or support system. *Hedera helix* is the most widely grown ivy species in the floriculture industry. Other *Hedera* species in commerce are *H. canariensis* Willd., Algerian or Canary Island ivy; *H. colchica* (K. Koch) Hibb., Persian or fragrant ivy; *H. nepalensis* K. Koch., Nepal ivy; and *H. rhombes* (Miq.) Bean., Japanese ivy (Bailey and Bailey, 1976; Hackett and Srinivasan, 1985). The Araliaceae family also includes *Aralia*, *Fatsia*, and *Schefflera*.

Origin: *H. helix* and the entire genus are found in Europe, northern Africa, and western Asia. *Hedera helix* has become naturalized in areas where the winter is mild and is considered an invasive species in some areas.

Uses and current status: The foliage is evergreen and attractive. Depending on the cultivar, plants are used as indoor plants in hanging baskets, pots, toparies and dish gardens, or as ground, wall, and tree trunk cover in the landscape (Pierot, 1974; Sulgrove, 1982) (Fig. II-1 Hedera). Cut stems also are used as foliage in arrangements.

CULTIVARS

More than 400 English ivy cultivars are known from around the world. Not only does the leaf size vary from 5 to 6 in. (13 to 15 cm) in width to less than 0.5 in. (1.3 cm), but leaf shape and color also vary (see Table II-1 Hedera). Post (1949) stated that greater variation exists among the various ivy cultivars than among the cultivars of any other ornamental. Cultivars also vary greatly in their tolerance to salt (Headley et al., 1992).

PROPAGATION

Ivy plants are propagated by tip cuttings or by leaf/node stem cutting pieces. Cuttings are often directly propagated into the final pot. All ivy cultivars root with ease when juvenile. Adult forms do not root easily. Continuous selection of superior plants for future stock is essential.

FLOWERING CONTROL AND DORMANCY

The ivy is grown as a foliage plant; flowering or dormancy is not considered.

TEMPERATURE

The optimum propagation medium temperature is 70 to 72°F (21 to 22°C); thereafter, 65 to 75°F (18 to 24°C) is adequate. Root zone heating is a common practice. Growth is inhibited at temperatures above 85 to 90°F (29 to 32°C). Some landscape cultivars can survive temperatures down to −10°F (−23°C); most cultivars survive 10 to 20°F (−12 to −7°C) if acclimated

TABLE II-I HEDERA

Classes of *Hedera* species used by the American Ivy Society and examples of cultivars (Pierot, 1974).

Class	Cultivars
Arborescents—plants with stiffly upright stems that frequently produce flowers	Few in cultivation
Bird's foot—leaves with narrow lobes	Brokamp, Green Feather, Irish Lace, Needlepoint, Perfection
Curlies—leaves with ruffles, ripples, or pleats	Big Deal, Ivalace, Manda's Crested
Fans—leaves with lobes of equal length	California Fan, Fan
Heart shapes—leaves shaped like a valentine	My Heart, Sweetheart
Ivy ivies—leaves typical of species with pronounced terminal, lateral, and basal lobes	Hahn, Pittsburgh
Miniatures—leaves less than 0.5 in. (1 cm)	Jubilee
Oddities—plants with unusual form such as fasciated stems or distorted leaves	Few in commercial production
Variegated—leaves multicolored	Glacier, Gold Dust, Gold Heart, Hahn, Kolibri

(Henley et al., 1991). For optimum growth and branching of *H. canariensis,* plants should be grown at 61°F (16°C) with a light intensity of 1400 fc (210 μmol $\cdot$ m^{-2} $\cdot$ s^{-1}) for 8 hr (Al-Juboory et al., 1998).

LIGHT

The solid green landscape cultivars can tolerate full light during some period of the day. Most ornamental types grow better under reduced light levels of 2500 fc (500 μmol $\cdot$ m^{-2} $\cdot$ s^{-1}). All ivies are tolerant of moderate to deep shade in the landscape and in the home. High-quality plants are best produced under protection (Henley et al., 1991; Pierot, 1974; Sulgrove, 1982).

WATER

Plants thrive with moisture, but do not overwater.

CARBON DIOXIDE

No data available.

NUTRITION

A medium pH of near 6.0 should be maintained. A fertilizer N:P:K ratio of 3:1:2 or 2:1:2 should be used. When stock plants are grown in beds for cuttings, 2.5 to 3.0 lb of actual N should be used per 1000 ft^2 (12.2 to 14.6 g $\cdot$ m^{-2}) per month (Henley et al., 1991). See Chapter 6, Nutrition, Table 6-4, for foliar nutrient levels.

MEDIA

Peatlite mixes are commonly used and should be pH 6.0 to 6.5 and well aerated, yet hold adequate water.

HEIGHT CONTROL

A-Rest (ancymidol), Cycocel (chlormequat), and B-Nine (daminozide) are reported to be effective, but are not required (Adriansen, 1985). Conversely, gibberellic acid can be used to elongate internodes to quickly form topiary tree "trunks." Staking of the topiary trees will be required.

SPACING

Numerous sizes of pots, baskets, and other containers are used, which prevents general spacing recommendations. Foliage or branches should not overlap, which is essential for disease control.

PINCHING AND DISBUDDING

No pinching or disbudding required.

SUPPORT

If grown as a potted specimen, the trailing branches are allowed to naturally flow over the container. However, plants are commonly trained onto metal supports producing wreaths, hearts, topiary trees, and other shapes (Fig. II-1 Hedera).

SCHEDULE AND TIMING

With *H. canariensis* Christensen (1973) illustrated the important role of radiant energy. When propagated in early September, production time of a 3.5-in. (9-cm) pot required 290 days; when propagated in January or February, only 140 days were required.

INSECTS

Aphids, caterpillars, fungus gnats, mealybugs, mites, scales, thrips, and whiteflies are but a few of the insects found on ivy. Cyclamen mites cause a "rat tail" symptom and verification must be made by an entomologist with a microscope. Western flower thrips carry tomato spotted wilt virus. Slugs and snails are also found on plants. Clean stock and constant observation are required before a spray program can be effective (Henley et al., 1991; Post, 1949).

DISEASES

Bacterial leaf spot (*Xanthomonas campestris* pv. *hederae*) is the most serious production problem in the greenhouse (Norman et al., 1999). *Botrytis, Phytophthora, Pythium,* and *Rhizoctonia* can also be problems. Several other leaf spot diseases occur outdoors including *Amerosporium trichellum* (anthracnose), *Glomerella cingulata, Phyllosticta concentrica,* and *Sphaceloma hederae* (Horst, 1990). Dry foliage, proper spacing, and good air circulation are of primary importance (Daughtrey and Chase, 1992; Henley et al., 1991; Post, 1949). Tomato spotted wilt virus can also be a problem. Bacterial leaf spot (*Pseudomonas cichorii*) has also been reported (Dreistadt, 2001).

PHYSIOLOGICAL DISORDERS

Stability of a cultivar may be a problem for the grower. Constant selection of stock is required to maintain the desired leaf patterns. Pigmentation or pattern distinction may decrease during winter if the shade is too heavy (Henley et al., 1991). Outdoors, winter injury may cause browning of the foliage.

POSTHARVEST

Plants should be shipped at 39 to 55°F (4 to 13°C). The optimum temperature for long-term storage of *H. canariensis* was 55°F (13°C) (Tijskens et al., 1996). Ivies are moderately sensitive to low levels of ethylene, which causes epinasty in the young growth (Nowak and Rudnicki, 1990).

KEY POINTS

- Ivy is used as a potted foliage plant (especially popular when grown on a variety of topiary forms or totems) and as a garden ornamental.
- Plants are propagated by tip cuttings or by leaf/node cuttings.
- Optimum light intensity is 2500 fc (500 $\mu mol \cdot m^{-2} \cdot s^{-1}$).
- Plants are susceptible to numerous diseases, especially bacterial leaf spot.
- Properly acclimated plants should have a long postharvest life for the consumer.

BIBLIOGRAPHY

Adriansen, E. 1985. Kemisk vækstregulering, pp. 142–162 in *Potteplanter I—Produktion, Metoder, Midler,* O.V. Christensen, A. Klougart, I.S. Pedersen, and K. Wikesjö, editors. Gartner-INFO, København, Denmark. (in Danish)

Al-Juboory, K.H., D.J. Williams, R.M. Skirvin, and D.G. Bullock. 1998. Influence of photoperiod, photosynthetic photon flux, and temperature on growth of Canary Island ivy. *HortScience* 33:237–239.

Bailey, L.H., and E.Z. Bailey. 1976. *Hedera,* pp. 544–545 in *Hortus Third: A Concise Dictionary of Plants Cultivated in the United States and Canada.* Macmillan, New York.

Christensen, O.V. 1973. Seasonal variation in production time of *Hedera canariensis* Willd. 'Gloire de Marengo.' *Tidsskrift for Planteavl* 77:224–231. (in Danish, English summary)

Daughtrey, M., and A.R. Chase. 1992. Hedera, pp. 120–123 in *Ball Field Guide to Diseases of Greenhouse Ornamentals.* Ball Publishing, Geneva, Illinois.

Dreistadt, S.H. 2001. *Integrated Pest Management for Floriculture and Nurseries.* University of California Division of Agriculture and Natural Resources Publication 3402.

Hackett, W.P., and C. Srinivasan. 1985. *Hedera helix* and *H. canariensis*, pp. 89–97 in *Handbook of Flowering*, vol. III, A.H. Halevy, editor. CRC Press, Boca Raton, Florida.

Headley, D.B., N. Bassuk, and R.G. Mower. 1992. Sodium chloride resistance in selected cultivars of *Hedera helix*. *HortScience* 27:249–252.

Henley, R.W., A.R. Chase, and L.S. Osborne. 1991. *English Ivy*. Foliage Research Note RH-91–15, Central Florida Research and Education Center, Apopka, Florida.

Horst, R.K. 1990. Ivy, English, p. 693 in *Westcott's Plant Disease Handbook*, 5th ed. Van Nostrand Reinhold, New York.

Huxley, A., M. Griffiths, and M. Levy. 1992. *Hedera helix*, pp. 510–515 in *The New Royal Horticultural Society Dictionary of Gardening*, vol. 2. Stockton Press, New York.

Norman, D.J., A.R. Chase, R.E. Stall, and J.B. Jones. 1999. Heterogeneity of *Xanthomonas campestris* pv. *hederae* strains from Araliaceae hosts. *Phytopathology* 89:646–652.

Nowak, J.M., and R.M. Rudnicki. 1990. *Postharvest Handling and Storage of Cut Flowers, Florist Greens and Potted Plants*. Timber Press, Portland, Oregon.

Pierot, S.W. 1974. *The Ivy Book—The Growing and Care of Ivy and Ivy Topiary*. Macmillan, New York.

Post, K. 1949. *Hedera helix* (English Ivy), pp. 558–559 in *Florist Crop Production and Marketing*. Orange Judd Publishing, New York.

Sulgrove, S.M. 1982. *The Care of Ivies and the American Ivy Society Ivy Collection*. The American Ivy Society, Dayton, Ohio.

Tijskens, L.M.M., M. Sloof, E.C. Wilkinson, and W.G. van Doorn. 1996. A model of the effects of temperature and time on the acceptability of potted plants stored in darkness. *Postharvest Biology and Technology* 8:293–305.

Helianthus

INTRODUCTION

Common name: sunflower.

Scientific name: *Helianthus annuus* L. is the most commonly grown sunflower species (Huxley et al., 1992).

Family and related taxa: Compositae Giseke. Besides *Helianthus annuus*, *H. augustifolius* L., the swamp sunflower; *H. debilis* Nutt., the cucumber leaf sunflower; *H. decapetalus* L., the thinleaf sunflower; and *H. maximilianii* Schräd., Maximilian's sunflower, are also grown (Armi-

tage and Laushman, 2003; Bailey and Bailey, 1976; Huxley et al., 1992; Post, 1949). *H. tuberosus*, the Jerusalem artichoke, is in the same genus. The Compositea is a large family containing numerous important genera including *Aster, Calendula, Callistephus, Centaurea, Chrysanthemum, Cosmos, Dahlia, Dendranthema, Echinacea, Gerbera, Helianthus, Liatris, Pericallis, Solidago, Tagetes,* and *Zinnia*.

Origin: *Helianthus annuus* is native throughout the United States, from southern Canada to northern Mexico. *H. augustifolius* is found in marshy to swampy areas from Florida to New York, west to Missouri, and southwest into Oklahoma and eastern Texas. *H. debilis* can be found native in southeastern Texas and coastal Florida. *H. decapetalus* is also widely distributed from Maine south to South Carolina, and west to Iowa and Wisconsin. *H. maximilianii* is found in eastern North America from southern Canada to North Carolina, Kentucky, Oklahoma, and Texas (Bailey and Bailey, 1976).

Uses and current status: *Helianthus annuus* is most widely grown in acreage as a field crop for seed and oil. However, *H. annuus* is also grown as a field and greenhouse cut flower and as a potted flowering plant (Figs. II-1 through II-3 Helianthus). Similarly, *H. augustifolius* and *H. decapetalus* are grown for the fresh cut flower market, though they have smaller flowers on heavily branched stems (Fig. II-4 Helianthus).

H. debilis, an annual, can be grown as a cut flower with 3-in. (8-cm)-diameter flowers. This species is heavily branched with deep red-purple disc flowers (Armitage and Laushman, 2003;

FIGURE II-1 HELIANTHUS *Helianthus annus* 'Ring of Fire' harvested cut flower.

FIGURE II-2 HELIANTHUS *Helianthus annuus* 'Lemon Eclair' cut flower.

FIGURE II-3 HELIANTHUS *Helianthus annuus* 'Pacino' potted sunflower.

FIGURE II-4 HELIANTHUS *Helianthus angustifolia* 'Low Down' garden ornamental.

Bailey and Bailey, 1976; Post, 1949). Maximilian's sunflower is a tall perennial with clusters or spikes of flowers and it can be grown as a cut flower or garden perennial. Maximilian's sunflower can be used to extend the field cut flower production season into the fall because the flowers occur late in the season in September and October and are frost tolerant. Flowers of all sunflower species can also be dried.

CULTIVARS

Numerous sunflower cultivars have been developed for ornamental use. The largest selection of cultivars is with *H. annuus*, which ranges in height from 12 in. to 8 ft (30 to 240 cm) tall. The short cultivars are used as potted flower plants. The tall cultivars for cut flower use can be divided into two groups: (1) multifloras (branching), which tend to produce many side shoots and flowers; and (2) grandifloras (upright), which produce one large flower and few side shoots. Although most currently available cultivars are grandifloras, numerous multiflora types are available.

Some cultivars are male sterile and have longer keeping quality (Armitage and Laushman, 2003; Gast, 1995). The absence of pollen also make the flowers less messy for the consumer. Pollen-less cultivars are available for both potted plant and cut flower production.

The ray flowers are typically bright yellow orange, but other colors include lemon to cream, orange, bronze, bicolors, and even pale green or pinkish bronze. Most cultivars have brown to black disc flowers; some cultivars have green centers. Many fully double forms are now available.

Two selections of *Helianthus decapetalus* are available, 'Italian White' with creamy white petals and black centers and the variety multiflorus with light yellow petals. Both selections are heavily branched and produce numerous flowers.

PROPAGATION

Helianthus annuus and *H. debilis* are both annuals and are seeded each production cycle. *H. decapetalus, H. augustifolius,* and *H. maximilianii* are perennials and are propagated by seed or divisions. Both *H. annuus* and *H. decapetalus* can be propagated *in vitro* (Finer, 1987; Hosoki et al., 1995) Sunflower seeds are large [700 to 1600 seed/oz (25 to 56/g)] and rapidly germinate with ease. At 70 to 75°F (21 to 24°C) germination occurs within 2 to 7 days in the greenhouse. Germination percentage of Maximilian's sunflower seed was increased with up to 6 weeks of stratification at 41°F (5°C) (Bratcher et al., 1993). Optimum temperatures for plug production of 'Pacino' are as follows: stage 1, 65 to 70°F (18 to 21°C) for 5 days; stage 2, 70°F (21°C) for 5 to 8 days; stages 3 and 4, 62°F (17°C) for 7 to 14 days (R. Sterkel, personal communication). Transplant at the two true leaf stage. Plants are ready to be transplanted within 2 to 4 weeks. If using greenhouse-grown transplants for field production, do not start transplants too early because overgrown plants do not transplant well (Armitage and Laushman, 2003; Post, 1949). Also, SD cultivars may need to be grown under LD to provide sufficient height if grown during periods of natural SD.

FLOWERING CONTROL AND DORMANCY

Helianthus annuus is considered a facultative SD plant but some cultivars are day neutral (Pallez et al., 2002). Differences also exist among cultivars in the rate of floral induction and flowering with temperatures between 55°F (13°C) and 72°F (22°C) and between a 13- or 17-hr photoperiod. However, flowering is most rapid at 72°F (22°C) regardless of photoperiod (Schuster, 1985).

Although photoperiod may be considered for field specialty crops, it is especially impor-

tant for rapid flower induction and fewer leaves (internodes) on potted flowering plants, which results in shorter plants. Seeds can be germinated in 2- × 2-in. cells or large plugs, held under LD for 10 to 14 days after germination, then transplanted and moved into SD (Armitage and Laushman, 2003; Post, 1949; Schuster, 1985).

TEMPERATURE

Growth is best between 65 to 75°F (18 to 24°C). Growth and development slow at temperatures below 63°F (17°C) and are significantly delayed below 55 to 50°F (13 to 10°C) (Schuster, 1985). Cultivars also exist for cooler climates. Cooler night temperatures, however, increase stem length for cut flower production (Cavins et al., 2000).

LIGHT

Full sun is always preferred. Supplemental lighting will improve quality if grown in the greenhouse in periods of low light (Whipker and Dasoju, 1997).

WATER

Do not overwater; allow the medium to moderately dry, then thoroughly water. However, drought stress will delay floral induction and flowering. Sunflowers use a lot of water because the extensive root system and large leaves cause plants to dry out rapidly.

CARBON DIOXIDE

No data available.

NUTRITION

Sunflowers require high nutritional levels. Beds in the field should be well prepared and adequate nutrients added according to soil tests. Depending on the amount of leaching from rainfall, on irrigation, and on soil type, additional nutrition will frequently be required two to three times as a sidedressing or by liquid feed at 200 ppm N. Generally, a total of 2 to 2.5 lb of actual N/1000 ft^2 (9.8 to 12.2 g · m^2) is used (Stevens et al., 1993).

When growing in the greenhouse during the 2- to 4-week plug production phase, 150 to 200 ppm N is used after roots are established (Armitage and Laushman, 2003). For potted plants, constant liquid fertilizer at 150 ppm N is required (Post, 1949). Pot sunflowers are heavy users of K and the optimal fertilizer ratio

TABLE II-1 HELIANTHUS

Recommended nutrient concentrations for potted *Helianthus* leaf tissue collected from a limited number of plants at flowering (Whipker and Dasoju, 1997).

Nutrient	Recommended Concentration
Nitrogen	5.0–6.0%
Phosphorus	0.7–0.8%
Potassium	5.4–6.3%
Calcium	2.2–2.5%
Magnesium	0.59–0.80 ppm
Boron	43–53 ppm
Copper	6.7–7.2 ppm
Manganese	67–99 ppm
Molybdenum	0.42–1.80 ppm
Zinc	77–115 ppm

of N:P:K:Ca:Mg is 8:1:10:4:2 (Whipker and Dasoju, 1997). Recommended tissue nutrient concentrations are reported in Table II-1 Helianthus. Magnesium and iron deficiencies can occur. In particular, iron deficiency can occur when media pH is higher than 6.8. However, when the media pH drops below 5.5, both magnesium and iron can be toxic.

MEDIA

Any medium that is well drained and has a pH of 6.0 to 6.5 is acceptable. Mixes based on coir and sphagnum peat have been used successfully; plants were taller when grown in coir (Dasoju et al., 1998b). For potted plants, one to three plants are grown in a 6-in. (15-cm) pot, depending on the cultivar (Pallez et al., 2002).

HEIGHT CONTROL

For potted plants, dwarf cultivars are required. Single sprays of B-Nine (daminozide) at 4000 to 8000 ppm or Sumagic (uniconizole) sprays at 16 to 32 ppm provided suitable height control of plants grown in 6-in. (15-cm) pots (Whipker and Dasoju, 1998). Drenches of Bonzi (paclobutrazol) at 2 to 4 mg a.i./6-in. (15-cm) pots and 2 to 8 mg a.i./4-in. (10-cm) pot were also effective (Dasoju et al., 1998a, b; Dole et al., 2002; Whipker and Dasoju, 1997). Higher Bonzi rates, up to 8 mg a.i./pot, may be necessary during the summer. Bonzi sprays up to 80 ppm were not effective (Whipker and Dasoju, 1998). Topflor (flurprimidol) sprays can be applied at 30 to 50 ppm (SePRO, personal com-

munication). A-Rest (ancymidol) sprays at 66 to 132 ppm are effective (Starman et al., 1989). Growth retardants can be applied 3 to 5 weeks after sowing and multiple applications may be needed. Weekly sprays of B-Nine (1500 to 5000 ppm), A-Rest (33 to 66 ppm), or Bonzi (5 to 10 ppm) may also be used, commencing with the first true leaves. The lower rate may be used with the first application; use the higher rate with subsequent applications. Cycocel (chlormequat) at 800 to 1500 ppm may also be effective (Bell, 2001). DIF is effective.

Plant placement under SD immediately after planting the plugs into pots also reduces height. Gibberellic acid hastens floral induction and date of flowering, but is not commercially useful (Schuster, 1985).

SPACING

One seed is placed in a 2- × 2-in. (5- × 5-cm) plug tray cell, peat pot, or plastic pot. Generally, one plant is placed in a 4- or 6-in. (10- or 15-cm) pot; however, two to three plants can be selected for plant uniformity and placed in larger pots (Pallez et al., 2002). Potted plants can be grown pot-to-pot for the first 2 or 3 weeks after transplanting, then spaced 4 to 6 in. (10 to 15 cm) apart as leaves become large.

Field-planted grown plants are spaced 2 to 12 in. (15 to 30 cm) apart. If one-harvest, single flower/plant production is desired, then plants can be spaced relatively close together. If plants are pinched, space further apart (see Pinching and Disbudding, below). Regardless of pinching, close spacing of 2 to 4 in. (5 to 10 cm) will produce small heads and wide spacing of up to 12 in. (30 cm) apart will produce large heads; plant according to the flower size desired (M. Johnson, personal communication). Direct seeding in the field will usually result in thicker stems and larger flowers than transplants planted at the same spacing. Perennial species are spaced up to 3 × 5 ft (0.9 × 1.5 m) apart (Post, 1949). Greenhouse-grown cut sunflowers can be produced in beds, large pots, bulb crates, or bedding plant flats spaced flat-to-flat. Regardless of container, the final plant spacing should range from 2 × 2 to 6 × 6 in. (5 × 5 to 15 × 15 cm).

PINCHING AND DISBUDDING

For cut flower production, the primary flower is the largest and is generally of higher quality with a longer stem than the axillary shoots. If smaller flowers are desired, young plants can be pinched when they have three to six pairs of leaves. Be aware, however, that pinching an older plant will only provide short, unmarketable stems. The multiflora cultivars are especially well suited to being pinched. The resulting side shoots will be long stemmed, but shorter than single-stemmed flowers and will have intermediate size flower heads. Pinching will delay harvest 1 to 2 weeks and can be used to spread out the harvest when used in combination with nonpinched plants. Potted plants are not pinched or disbudded.

SUPPORT

Normally no support is given. Plant height and wind may require that one to two layers of mesh be used in outdoor cut flower plantings. Be sure to secure the mesh well because the flowers are heavy. Dense field plantings reduce axillary shoots and increase stem lengths. Indoor cut flower plantings can usually be grown without support but one layer of netting is usually helpful.

SCHEDULE AND TIMING

For cut flower production, plantings are made every 1 to 3 weeks to provide an uninterrupted harvest schedule. However, height and days to flower decreased as planting dates progressed from May 5 to July 16 (T. Bratcher, unpublished data).

Greenhouse-grown sunflowers can be planted in bedding plant flats, pots, or bulb crates for quick crops. The size of the flower head and the thickness of the stem will vary with the number of plants per flat; 10 to 18 plants per 11- × 22-in. (28- × 56-cm) flat provide 2- to 3-ft (60- to 90-cm) stems with 3- to 4-in. (8- to 10-cm) wide flower heads. The small volume of medium limits the size of the plants and decreases crop time compared with field production but requires that plants be irrigated frequently. Stems are generally harvestable within 8 to 9 weeks from sowing seed.

Actual crop time for potted plants depends on the cultivar and the time of year plants are grown and ranges from 7 to 12 weeks. The fastest crop time for 'Pacino' occurs during warm weather in the late summer and the longest crop time is for plants sown in January or February (R. Sterkel, personal communication). Flowering will occur 5 to 10 days after buds are easily visible.

INSECTS

Unfortunately, sunflowers are subject to numerous insects and diseases outdoors. Grasshoppers and beetles can be prolific in some years and cause extensive damage, especially to the petals. Several caterpillar species prefer sunflowers and can quickly damage and defoliate plants. The larvae of other moths tunnel through flower heads. The female head-clipper weevil is well named; it girdles the stem just below the flower head and lays eggs on the head (Stevens et al., 1993). The heads often fall off, leaving growers to wonder who cut the flower heads off their plants. The weevils are not common but damage can occasionally be significant. Cucumber beetles can be a problem as well.

Aphids, whiteflies, thrips, and spider mites are of primary concern in the greenhouse and may cause flower injury. Thrips can be especially difficult to control in sunflowers. During warm weather when the vents are open for long periods, numerous species of caterpillars may appear and can quickly defoliate a crop. Monitor daily and act immediately to prevent extensive damage.

DISEASES

Do not plant field-grown plants in the same plot of soil for two consecutive years. Rotate annually, because numerous diseases plague sunflowers. Leaf diseases include powdery mildew (*Erysiphe cichoracearum*), downy mildew (*Plasmopara halstedii*), rust (*Puccinia helianthi, Coleosporium helianthi, Uromyces junci,* and *U. silphi*), and leaf spots (*Alternaria, Cercospora helianthi, C. pachypus,* and *Septoria helianthi*) (Horst, 1990).

Several types of wilts and stem rots can be devastating. Cottony rot (*Sclerotinia sclerotiorum*) attacks the base of the plant and may exhibit white cottony mycelium in humid weather. The disease is most severe during cool, wet weather and can also damage flower heads. Another disease, *Sclerotium rolfsii,* southern blight, also attacks the base of the plant and can produce cottony white mycelium. Southern blight, however, is most prevalent during hot weather. *Phoma* causes black stem and head rot with large black lesions on stems, leaves, and flower heads. In dry weather *Macrophomina phaseolina,* charcoal rot, causes stunting, premature flowering, and black cankers or discolorations at the base of the plant. With these diseases, both sanitation and burning of diseased plant materials are important. Pasteurization or fumigation of field soil is possible. Potted sunflowers are especially prone to *Pythium* root rot and growers should avoid overwatering as well as cool air and medium temperatures (Whipker and Dasoju, 1997). Other diseases which have been reported include botrytis (*Botrytis cinerea*), root and stem rot (*Phytophthora*), smut (*Entyloma calendulae*), head rot (*Rhizopus oryzae*), and aster yellows (Dreistadt, 2001).

Leaf edge necrosis can also be a problem. It may not be a fungal or bacterial infection, but a toxic reaction to the whitefly. For pot plants, the dark brown and black irregular marginal symptoms are serious. Also, check media EC to be sure the problem is not due to high soluble salts.

PHYSIOLOGICAL DISORDERS

Premature flowering and stunted plants can occur with SD cultivars (Dole et al., 2001). Be sure to provide sufficient LD after germination to delay flowering enough for plants to reach the required height. Another alternative is to use day-neutral cultivars. See also Diseases, above.

POSTHARVEST

Harvest cut flowers or potted plants when the ray flowers are one-half to fully expanded, usually when the petals are perpendicular to the flower head. Delayed harvest will shorten the vase life because flowers typically develop rapidly on the plant. Gast (1995, 1997) noted that the vase life of 33 cultivars ranged from a high of 13.3 days to a low of 5.5 days; most lasted more than 7 days. Wilting immediately after harvest can be a problem. Be sure plants are well irrigated before harvest; hydrate after harvest with a commercial hydration solution or water with 0.02% detergent such as a dishwashing detergent, Tween-20, or Triton X-100 (Jones et al., 1993). Antimicrobial agents may also be useful (Redman et al., 2002).

Most of the foliage should be removed at harvest and should not be below the water (Armitage and Laushman, 2003; Nowak and Rudnicki, 1990). All foliage is removed in some cases when shipping long distances and weight is an issue. Preservatives are used.

Cold-store flowers at 33 to 35°F (1 to 2°C) for up to 7 days prior to being marketed (Çelikel and Reid, 2002; Nell and Reid, 2001). When transported dry, recut stems and return to water with a wetting agent, which will aid in hydration and increase vase life (Jones et al., 1993). Flowers can also be air or freeze dried.

High fertilizer rates of 200 ppm N can reduce postharvest life of potted sunflowers to 9 days from 11 to 12 days for plants fertilized with 100 ppm N (Whipker and Dasoju, 1997). The best postharvest life for ebb-and-flow irrigated plants is obtained with 100 ppm N and terminating the fertilizer 7 to 10 days prior to flowering. Potted plants tolerated 1 week 41°F (5°C) cold storage without decreased postharvest life, but 2 weeks caused foliar damage (Pallez et al., 2002). Fascination (1:1 benzyladenine:gibberellic acid, formerly known as Promalin) was not commercially useful in extending the postharvest life of potted plants or in delaying foliage yellowing (Pallez et al., 2002).

Silver thiosulfate (STS) is apparently of no value to flowering plants or cut flowers. Although Woltering and van Doorn (1988) reported that *Helianthus annuus* was not sensitive to ethylene, an external ethylene concentration of 1 ppm decreased vase life and caused flower abscission of *Helianthus maximilianii* stems (Redman et al., 2002).

KEY POINTS

- Sunflowers are popular as a cut flower, potted flowering plant, and garden ornamental.

- *Helianthus annuus* cultivars can be divided into two types: multifloras, which have many side shoots and flowers; and grandifloras, which have one large terminal flower and few, short side shoots.

- Annual species are seed propagated; perennial species can be propagated by seed or division.

- *H. annuus* is considered a facultative SD plant, but many cultivars are day neutral.

- While potted plants use large amounts of water and wilt readily, do not overwater and allow medium to dry slightly between irrigations.

- For height control on potted plants, cultivar selection is critical; SD and plant growth regulators are also frequently used.

- Sunflowers are susceptible to a wide range of insects both outdoors and indoors.
- Whiteflies and caterpillar larvae are major problems in the greenhouse; the latter can defoliate plants rapidly.

- Rapid foliage yellowing is a major problem and limits potted flowering plant production.

BIBLIOGRAPHY

Armitage, A.M., and J.M. Laushman. 2003. *Helianthus annuus*, pp. 319–331 in *Specialty Cut Flowers*, 2nd ed. Timber Press, Portland, Oregon.

Bailey, L.H., and E.Z. Bailey. 1976. *Helianthus* L., pp. 549–550 in *Hortus Third: A Concise Dictionary of Plants Cultivated in the United States and Canada*. Macmillan, New York.

Bell, M. 2001. Bedding plants and seed geraniums, pp. 54–62 in *Tips on Regulating Growth of Floriculture Crops*, M.L. Gaston, L.A. Kunkle, P.S. Konjoian, and M.F. Wilt, editors. Ohio Florists' Association Services, Columbus, Ohio.

Bratcher, C.B., J.M. Dole, and J.C. Cole. 1993. Stratification improves seed germination of five native wildflower species. *HortScience* 28:899–901.

Cavins, T.J., J.M. Dole, and V. Stamback. 2000. Unheated and minimally heated winter greenhouse production of specialty cut flowers. *HortTechnology* 19:793–799.

Çelikel, F.G., and M.S. Reid. 2002. Storage temperature affects the quality of cut flowers from the Asteraceae. *HortScience* 37:148–150.

Dasoju, S., M.R. Evans, and B.E. Whipker. 1998a. Paclobutrazol drenches control growth of potted sunflowers. *HortTechnology* 8:235–237.

Dasoju, S., M.R. Evans, and B.E. Whipker. 1998b. Paclobutrazol drench activity in coir- and peat-based substrates. *HortTechnology* 8:595–598.

Dole, J.M., B.E. Whipker, and L. Pallez. 2001. Are potted sunflowers for you? *Grower Product News* 11(9):16, 18–20.

Dole, J., D. Mays, and B. Whipker. 2002. Effect of B-Nine and Bonzi on 'Munchkin' sunflowers. *North Carolina Commercial Flower Growers' Bulletin* 47(6):7.

Dreistadt, S.H. 2001. *Integrated Pest Management for Floriculture and Nurseries*. University of California Division of Agriculture and Natural Resources Publication 3402.

Finer, J.J. 1987. Direct somatic embryogenesis and plant regeneration from immature embryos of hybrid sunflower (*Helianthus annuus* L.) on a high sucrose-containing medium. *Plant Cell Reports* 6:372–374.

Gast, K.L.B. 1995. *1995 Production and Postharvest Evaluation of Fresh-Cut Sunflowers*. Report of Progress 751, Agricultural Experiment Station, Kansas State University.

Gast, K.L.B. 1997. *Evaluation of Postharvest Life of Perennial Fresh-Cut Flowers*. Report of Progress 805, Agricultural Experiment Station, Kansas State University.

Horst, R.K. 1990. Sunflower, pp. 834–835 in *Westcott's Plant Disease Handbook*, 5th ed. Van Nostrand Reinhold, New York.

Hosoki, T., K. Ohta, K. Inaba, and M. Harisaki. 1995. *In vitro* propagation of thin-leaf sunflower (*Helianthus decapetalus* L.). *Acta Horticulturae* 397:125–128.

Huxley, A., M. Griffiths, and M. Levy. 1992. *Helianthus*, pp. 522–525 in *The New Royal Horticultural Society Dictionary of Gardening*, vol. 2. Stockton Press, New York.

Jones, R.B., M. Serek, and M.S. Reid. 1993. Pulsing with Triton X-100 improves hydration and vase life of cut sunflowers (*Helianthus annuus* L.). *HortScience* 28:1178–1179.

Nell, T.A., and M.S. Reid. 2001. Can't take the heat. *Floral Management* 17(10):33–34.

Nowak, J., and R.M. Rudnicki. 1990. *Helianthus*, p. 152 in *Postharvest Handling and Storage of Cut Flowers, Florist Greens and Potted Plants*. Timber Press, Portland, Oregon.

Pallez, L.C., J.M. Dole, and B.E. Whipker. 2002. Production and postproduction studies with potted sunflowers. *HortTechnology* 12:206–210.

Post, K. 1949. *Helianthus* (Sunflower), pp. 559–560 in *Florist Crop Production and Marketing*. Orange Judd Publishing, New York.

Redman, P.B., J.M. Dole, N.O. Maness, and J.A. Anderson. 2002. Postharvest handling of nine specialty cut flower species. *Scientia Horticulturae* 92:293–303.

Schuster, W.H. 1985. *Helianthus annuus*, pp. 98–121 in *Handbook of Flowering*, vol. III, A.H. Halevy, editor. CRC Press, Boca Raton, Florida.

Starman, T.W., J.W. Kelly, and H.B. Pemberton. 1989. Characterization of ancymidol effects on growth and pigments of *Helianthus annuus* cultivars. *Journal of the American Society for Horticultural Science* 114:427–430.

Stevens, S., A.B. Stevens, K.B. Gast, J.A. Mara, N. Tisserat, and R. Bauerfind. 1993. *Sunflowers*. MF-1084, Kansas State University Cooperative Extension Service, Manhattan, Kansas.

Whipker, B., and S. Dasoju. 1997. Success with pot sunflowers. *GrowerTalks* 61(1):81–82.

Whipker, B., and S. Dasoju. 1998. Potted sunflower growth and flowering responses to foliar applications of daminozide, paclobutrazol, and uniconazole. *HortTechnology* 8:86–88.

Woltering, E.J., and W.G. van Doorn. 1988. Role of ethylene in senescence of petals—morphological and taxonomical relationships. *Journal of Experimental Botany* 39:1605–1616.

Heliconia

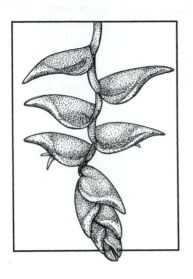

INTRODUCTION

Common names: heliconia, balisier, lobster-claw, parrot flower.

Scientific name: Many species of *Heliconia* are cultivated. Among the most common are *H. angusta* Vell., *H. aurantiaca* Ghiesbr. ex Lem., *H. bihai* (L.) L., *H. bourgaeana* Petersen., *H. caribaea* Lam., *H. champneiana* Griggs., *H. chartacea* Lane ex Barreiros, *H. collinsiana* Griggs., *H. indica* Lam., *H. latispatha* Benth., *H. lingulata* Ruiz & Paz., *H. orthotricha* L. Anderss., *H. platystachys* Bak., *H. psittacorum* L.f., *H. ×rauliniana* Barreiros, *H. rostrata* Ruiz & Pav., *H. stricta* Huber., *H. vellerigera* Poepp., and *H. wagneriana* Petersen. (Criley and Broschat, 1992; Huxley et al., 1992).

Family and related taxa: Heliconiaceae Nakai. Heliconiaceae contains only the genus *Heliconia*, of which there are approximately 250 species (Berry and Kress, 1991).

Origin: New World tropics and Pacific islands. Most of the more colorful species have been collected from Central America, the Caribbean islands, the central Amazon basin, and the mountainous rain forests of Peru, Ecuador, Colombia, and Venezuela. A handful of species with green bracts are found in the Polynesian islands: Fiji, Solomon Islands, Samoa, American Samoa, and New Guinea.

Uses and current status: In the floricultural trade, the principal use is as a cut flower. Some of the smaller species (*H. angusta*, *H. aurantiaca*, *H. psittacorum*, and *H. stricta* 'Dwarf Jamaican') have been grown as potted plants for interior use. A few species with colorful foliage (*H. indica*, *H. stricta*, *H. zebrina*) have been used in conservatories as accent plants and may be useful in interiorscapes. In tropical areas, heliconias are used as landscape plants, helping to convey a tropical ambience in hotel and public settings. Natives use the large leaves to wrap foodstuffs, and the roots of some species may have use as a starchy food. Commercial cut heliconia flower production for export to northern markets exists in Florida and Hawaii in the United States, Central America and to a limited extent in South America, tropical Africa (e.g., Ivory Coast), northern Australia, the Philippines, and Thailand.

Heliconias are grown for their large, leathery, and colorful inflorescences, which are either upright or pendulous. Red, orange, yellow, pink, or green thick bracts surround small and usually inconspicuous flowers. The large leaves are borne on long stalks from a central clump.

CULTIVARS

Most of the named cultivars originated as wild-collected specimens rather than as selections from breeding programs. Two references provide names for the many cultivars among the most popular species (Berry and Kress, 1991; Criley and Broschat, 1992). Interspecific hybrids occur naturally where populations of compatible species overlap. Controlled hybridization has been used to determine compatibilities within some pendent species (Kress, 1983a, b). Self-compatibility was the prevalent condition (Kress, 1987). Limited controlled breeding has been done in botanical gardens (Hirano, 1989).

Most heliconia species are too large for culture in the common pot sizes of 4 to 6.5 in. (10 to 16 cm). *H. stricta* 'Dwarf Jamaican' has been successfully flowered in 6-in. (15-cm) pots (Lekawatana and Criley, 1989), while *H. angusta* 'Holiday' has been flowered in 8- to 10-in. (20- to 25-cm) pots (Ball, 1987b). *H. angusta* and *H. stricta* 'Dwarf Jamaican' tolerate cooler temperatures, down to 60°F (16°C), than the *H. psittacorum* varieties.

H. psittacorum varieties that have been recommended for trial in 6- to 10-in. (15- to 25-cm) pots include 'Tropical Nights Tangerine,' 'Tropical Nights Pink,' 'Andromeda,' and 'Choconiana,' while the interspecific hybrid 'Golden Torch' should be planted in 10- to 14-in. (25- to 36-cm) containers (Ball, 1987b). Many other *H. psittacorum* selections would also be suitable.

Variegated foliage forms of *H. indica* and *H. rubracarpa* are striking in interior plantscapes. Most of these have unattractive bracts and flowers, which can be cut off as they appear. Their culture is similar to the large flowering forms, but high light enhances the whites, yellows, reds, and maroons of the variegation patterns (Criley, 1990).

PROPAGATION

Progeny from seed may be variable (Hirano, 1989), although *H. stricta* 'Dwarf Jamaican' seedlings were uniform and like the parent (Criley, 1988). Seed germination is sporadic and takes place over a period of months—up to 3 years. Temperature requirements for optimum seed germination are unknown, but Carle (1989) recommends 77 to 95°F (25 to 35°C).

Vegetative propagation is used to maintain desirable clonal selections. Clumps can be divided or rhizome systems separated into one or two pseudostem bases. Roots are trimmed off and old leaf bases removed. Cut surfaces should be dusted with a fungicide. A hot water treatment of 118°F (48°C) for up to 1 hr has been recommended to control nematodes (Criley, 1988). The clean propagules are planted in a well-drained, clean medium. Root and shoot development begins in 2 to 3 weeks, and transplanting to the field can take place when sufficient root and shoot development has taken place.

FLOWERING CONTROL AND DORMANCY

Some heliconia species are reportedly sensitive to photoperiod and strongly seasonal flowering patterns suggest that some species are responsive to photoperiod (Criley, 1985, 1999; Criley and Broschat, 1992; Criley et al., 1999; Geert-

sen, 1989, 1990). *H. stricta* 'Dwarf Jamaican' responds to 4 weeks of short photoperiods by initiating inflorescences (Criley and Kawabata, 1986), whereas *H. wagneriana* and *H. rostrata* initiate flowers in December in Hawaii (Criley and Sakai, 1997; Maciel and Criley, 1998). Other species are not sensitive to photoperiod (*H. psittacorum*, *H.* × 'Golden Torch'), and others (*H. angusta*) require long photoperiods to induce flowering (Sakai et al., 1990a, b). An unfurled leaf count of three or four leaves on a stem was usually necessary for any sensitive species to respond to photoperiod. The time to flowering depends on species and the temperature environment. Manipulation of photoperiod could be used to extend the productive season and improve the value per flower for out-of-season production but is not presently a commercial practice.

Heliconia does not go dormant in response to environmental signals, and leaf production continues year-round. Leaf production may slow when plants are subjected to cooler-than-optimum temperatures.

TEMPERATURE

Flower initiation is not affected by temperature, but increasing temperatures enhance the rate at which shoots and flowers develop (Geertsen, 1989). As minimum night temperature increased, shoot and flower production of *H. psittacorum* increased from 6.5 stems/ft² (70 stems/m²) and 2.3 stems/ft² (25 flowers/m²) at 59°F (15°C) to 16 stems/ft² (170 stems/m²) and 5.6 stems/ft² (60 flowers/m²) at 70°F (21°C) during an 8-month production period from June to January in Denmark. Below 50°F (10°C), *H. psittacorum* types do not grow or flower (Broschat and Donselman, 1983a). At 50°F (10°C) the inflorescence develops black spots at the base of the bracts. Early Dutch reports suggested an optimum range of 70 to 95°F (21 to 35°C) for culture of *H. psittacorum* (van Raalte and van Raalte-Wichers, 1973). *H. psittacorum* plants grown under protective cover produced fewer flowers, largely because of reduced light intensities, than plants grown outside (Broschat and Donselman, 1987).

Although most heliconias are considered tender tropicals, some species are reported to survive, if not grow, at temperatures as low as 50°F (10°C) (Broschat and Donselman, 1983b; Donselman and Broschat, 1986; Drysdale, 1987; Hodel, 1985). *H. stricta* 'Dwarf Jamaican' and *H. angusta* are two species that grow and flower at 59°F (15°C). Potted *H. stricta* produced a higher percentage of flowering stems at a 68/59°F (20/15°C) day/night temperature regime than at 79/70 or 86/77°F (26/21 or 30/25°C) (Lekawatana and Criley, 1989).

LIGHT

In their native habitat, heliconias thrive in the clearings where a fallen tree has opened the canopy. As the canopy again encroaches, the number of flowering stalks decreases (Stiles, 1979). In Hawaii, most heliconias are grown under open field conditions. Some species, such as *H. angusta*, seem to perform well under 30% shade. The bract color may be slightly more intense under light shade than full sun for some *H. psittacorum* selections. Reduction of light intensity to 63% shade reduced *H. psittacorum* flower production to 25 to 33% of that in full sun (Broschat and Donselman, 1983a). Low light intensity, whether from shade cloth or excessive crowding, also causes stretching of the pseudostems (Broschat et al., 1984; Lekawatana and Criley, 1989). Potted plants should be grown in high light.

WATER

The broad thin leaves of heliconias are subject to moisture stresses, which is indicated by longitudinal inrolling of the blade. Frequent irrigation is necessary where rainfall is not regular. Overhead sprinklers are recommended because they help to relieve water stress in the foliage. Low level sprinklers and trickle systems are often inefficient because of the density of the pseudostems. Critical studies have not been performed to determine water requirements, but 0.4 in./day (1 cm/day) is recommended in well-drained media (Donselman and Broschat, 1986). In heavier soils, 1 in./week (2.5 cm/week) plus natural rainfall appears to be sufficient (Criley, 1989).

Despite their high water requirement, heliconia plants show chlorosis and develop root rots because of the poor soil aeration in waterlogged soils. Planting the rhizomes too deeply causes similar problems. Irrigation is especially critical in pots because too much water leads to loss of roots, but growing plants require a lot of water.

CARBON DIOXIDE

Because cut flower heliconia are grown in open fields, CO_2 enrichment has not been practiced.

NUTRITION

Heliconias respond to high rates of fertilization (Broschat et al., 1984). In Florida research on *H. psittacorum*, 2.1 oz N/ft²/year (650 g N/m²/year) was recommended (Broschat and Donselman, 1983b). A ratio of 3:1:2 (N:P:K) is recommended in Florida (Broschat and Donselman, 1987), while some Hawaii growers have used a banana fertilizer with a much higher K level (3:1:5), and others use a 1:1:1 fertilizer. Approximately 7 oz (200 g) of the latter is broadcast around the plant three or four times a year. Such a fertilization rate does not have the weight of scientific studies to justify it, but the growers believe the results they obtain are satisfactory.

The levels of essential nutrients contained in healthy, green foliage of several species fertilized by grower practices are shown in Table II-1 Heliconia. Manganese, iron, and magnesium may become deficient in heliconias, as determined by sampling of chlorotic and poorly growing plants.

TABLE II-I HELICONIA
Mean foliar analyses of healthy green leaves of selected *Heliconia* species, and suggested target levels (Criley, 1989).

Heliconia Species	Dry Weight (%)					Dry Weight (ppm)				
	N	P	K	Ca	Mg	Mn	Fe	Cu	Zn	B
H. angusta	3.15	0.14	1.39	0.26	0.26	603	65	10	12	13
H. bihai	2.82	0.20	1.54	0.72	0.37	1087	78	9	17	21
H. caribaea	2.50	0.18	1.68	0.47	0.25	695	53	10	12	25
H. psittacorum	3.11	0.14	1.54	0.50	0.25	654	71	10	15	14
H. stricta	3.05	0.20	2.22	0.37	0.39	574	112	11	20	17
H. wagneriana	2.86	0.23	3.19	0.43	0.29	204	70	16	20	20
Suggested target level	3.00	0.20	1.50	0.35	0.25	>300	75	10	15	20

Manganese levels are often two to four times higher than iron in the same healthy leaf.

Nitrogen deficiency appears as an overall light yellow-green coloration of the foliage and decreased growth rate (Broschat and Donselman, 1983b). Potassium deficiency appears as extensive marginal necrosis on the oldest leaves, often accompanied by a diffuse marginal and/or interveinal chlorosis (Broschat, 1989). Magnesium deficiency appears on the older leaves as broad yellow bands along the leaf margins (Broschat and Donselman, 1983a). Manganese deficiency symptoms occur on new leaves first as interveinal chlorosis developing to transverse necrotic streaks (Donselman and Broschat, 1986). Iron deficiency symptoms appear as uniformly yellow-white foliage with a slightly green midrib. Poor soil aeration, cold soil, high soil pH, and root injury due to disease or nematodes can induce iron deficiency symptoms (Broschat and Donselman, 1983a).

For potted plants moderate amounts of fertilizer should be supplied, such as Osmocote 18–6–12 incorporated into the medium at the label rate, plus minor elements and regular foliar feeding when growing in full sunlight conditions. Fertilizer levels should be reduced if growing under lower light.

MEDIA

Heliconia plants are tolerant of a variety of soil conditions. In Hawaii, heliconias are grown in a variety of media from a'a (volcanic soil) to loose alluvial soils to heavy clay soils. However, a well-drained medium with high fertility is preferred. The media pH should be slightly acidic. Chlorosis develops readily on plants grown in soils with a high pH. The rhizome system of heliconia tends to be relatively shallow and, although the root system will penetrate more deeply, strong winds can topple plants, even in heavy soils.

For pot culture the growing medium should be light and well drained. The rhizomes are planted shallowly with three per 6-in. (15-cm) pot, three or four per 8-in. (20-cm) pot, and four or five per 10- to 14-in. (25- to 36-cm) pot.

HEIGHT CONTROL

The long stems of heliconia are preferred for cut flower use. Thus, growth retardants are not applied for cut flower production. Shading in combination with crowding and copious water and fertilizer can elongate the pseudostems. Gibberellin also causes pseudostem elongation (Ball, 1987a; Broschat and Donselman, 1987). Growth retardants have been used to control pseudostem elongation in potted heliconia, but flowering is often prevented as an adverse side effect (Lekawatana and Criley, 1989).

For potted heliconias growth retardant is applied about 2 to 3 months after planting when the axillary shoots are 4 to 6 in. (10 to 15 cm) high after the primary shoot is removed. The pots are sprayed with 15 to 30 ppm Bonzi (paclobutrazol), although drenches at 0.375 mg a.i./6-in. (15-cm) pot may also be effective (Ball, 1987b). *H. psittacorum* plants treated with 1 to 2 mg Bonzi (paclobutrazol) per gallon (3.75-L) pot were considerably dwarfed, but few plants flowered (R. A. Criley, unpublished research). Other effective growth retardants include A-Rest (ancymidol), Sumagic (uniconazole), and flurprimidol (Criley and Broschat, 1992; Lekawatana and Criley, 1989; Tjia and Jierwiriyapant, 1988).

SPACING

Two growth habits are recognized: clumping and spreading. The spreading types fill in quickly following planting. The clumping types grow more slowly, but some, such as *H. caribaea* and *H. chartacea*, are more upright; yet others, such as *H. stricta* and *H. bihai*, spread at the top and thus require more room. New pseudostems develop mostly on the periphery of the clump and the centers are less productive. Where the clump hollows out, growers will dig and divide at 2- to 3-year intervals. By affecting the rate of growth, irrigation and fertilization will also affect spacing decisions.

Suggested in-row spacings are 2.5 to 3.5 ft (0.75 to 1.0 m) for *H. psittacorum*; 4 to 5 ft (1.2 to 1.5 m) for *H. angusta*, *H. aurantiaca*, *H. hirsuta* L. f., *H. metallica* Plachn. & Lind. Ex Hook., small *H. stricta* forms and *H. vaginalis* Benth.; 5 to 6.5 ft (1.5 to 2 m) for *H. angusta flava*, *H. latispatha*, *H. orthotricha*, *H. rostrata*, tall *H. stricta* forms, and *H.* ×'Golden Torch,' *H.* × 'Yellow Torch', and similarly sized hybrids; and 6.5 to 8 ft (2 to 2.5 m) for *H. bihai*, *H. bourgaeana*, *H. caribaea*, *H. champneiana*, *H. chartacea*, *H. collinsiana*, *H. indica*, *H. platystachys*, and *H. wagneriana*.

PINCHING AND DISBUDDING

Neither pinching nor disbudding are practiced on cut heliconia. A key cultural practice with potted *H. psittacorum* is that the primary shoot is cut off at soil level when daughter shoots are well developed. When these daughter shoots reach 4 to 6 in. (10 to 15 cm) in height, about 2 to 3 months after planting, the plants are sprayed with growth retardant.

SUPPORT

Ordinarily the pseudostems of heliconia are strong enough to stand upright without support. Unfortunately, wire support systems are likely to cause the stems to snap over at the wire in strong winds.

SCHEDULE AND TIMING

The use of photoperiod to flower heliconia out of season has not become a commercial practice (Criley and Kawabata, 1986; Criley and Lekawatana, 1995, 1995; Criley and Sakai, 1997; Criley et al., 1999; Maciel and Criley, 1998; Sakai et al., 1990a, b). Grower records of cut flower production in Hawaii revealed seasonal flowering patterns that may be useful in determining whether species can be manipulated (Criley, 1999; Criley and Broschat, 1992) . Timing control evaluations need to be conducted in other growing environments because it may be easier to import natural season cuts than to manipulate field-grown plants. The time from pseudostem emergence to flower harvest can vary from a few weeks for *H. psittacorum* to 11 months or more for *H. chartacea* (Criley and Lekawatana, 1995). Potted heliconia require 12 to 24 weeks to flower from propagation depending on season (temperature and light).

INSECTS

The principal insect pests are aphids, mealybugs, scale insects, earwigs, and some leaf-eating beetles. Ants frequently tend aphids on the inflorescences and have been observed cutting out tissues from the bracts of some species. The presence of insects in the inflorescence is usually cause for rejection by agricultural inspectors of shipments imported into the mainland United States. In Hawaii, most inflorescences are dipped in insecticidal solutions, then hand washed to remove field debris and dead insects. Mites can affect foliage during hot, dry periods, but they are not usually a problem.

DISEASES

Cucumber mosaic virus has been reported on *H. psittacorum* and *H.* ×'Golden Torch' (Ball, 1986), but its effect is not understood. One of the most important diseases is caused by *Calonectria spathiphylli* (*Cylindrocladium spathiphylli*) (Sewake and Uchida, 1995). *C. spathiphylli* causes root and rhizome rots, and aerial symptoms are expressed as leaf yellowing, drying of the leaf margins, spots on the leaf sheaths, and petiole blights (Uchida et al., 1989). Another soil-borne fungus is *Phytophthora nicotianae*, which causes rotted roots, rhizomes, and basal stems. *Pythium splendens* causes root rot and a slow decline of the plants. Leafspot fungi attacking heliconia include *Bipolaris*, *Exserohilum*, *Pyricularis*, *Cercospora* and *Pseudocercospora*, *Mycosphaerella*, *Phyllosticta*, and *Septoria* (Sewake and Uchida, 1995). A heliconia-infesting pathovar of *P. solanacearum* causes foliar symptoms that include leaf inrolling and wilting as a result of vascular plugging in the roots and rhizomes. The wilt (moko disease) caused by the pathovar of *Pseudomonas solanacearum* that attacks banana does not occur in Hawaii, but banana-growing areas are known to ban importation of heliconias from moko-infested areas.

Plant parasitic nematodes affect heliconia and cause symptoms resembling other factors of plant stress. The principal nematodes that have been associated with heliconias in Hawaii are the burrowing (*Radophilus similis*), lesion (*Pratylenchus coffeae*), reniform (*Rotylenchus reniformis*), spiraling (*Heliotylenchus*), and root-knot (*Meloidogyne*) nematodes. (Holtzmann and Wong, 1986; Sewake and Uchida, 1995). Plants with roots affected by nematodes show water stress and symptoms of nutrient deficiency. Coupled with *Calonectria spathiphylli*, nematode infestations cause toppling of plants due to insufficient anchorage. The burrowing nematode is the most damaging and most common. Fumigation or steam pasteurization of the site where plantings will be made is recommended. In the establishment of new fields, it is important to plant only clean rhizomes.

PHYSIOLOGICAL DISORDERS

Flower bud abortion has been observed in many heliconia species. The cause of bud abortion has not been determined, but it occurs in potted plants in disease-free artificial media as well as in field conditions where environmental stresses may induce it. Bract abscission occurs in some species during shipping and is probably induced by ethylene buildup.

POSTHARVEST

Heliconia inflorescences are usually harvested with about two-thirds of the bracts open. *H. psittacorum* may be cut with one or two bracts open. Bracts will not continue to open, even if bud-opening solutions are employed (Broschat and Donselman, 1983a). The true flowers last about 1 day, and then abscise. Stems are harvested by cutting the pseudostem at ground level. Because water uptake by cut stems is poor, harvests are generally carried out in the morning while the stalk is turgid. Inflorescences last longer if harvested from well-irrigated plants than from water-stressed plants (Broschat and Donselman, 1986). The original Dutch practice of immersing the flowers and foliage in water for 3 hr after cutting (van Raalte and van Raalte-Wichers, 1973) is paralleled by the Hawaii grower practice of placing all cut heliconias in tubs of water soon after cutting. Following harvest, the flowers are transported to a cleaning and packing shed where they are trimmed and washed to remove field debris, dead florets, and insects.

Insects present on the inflorescences are cause for rejection by plant quarantine inspectors. A number of methods have been employed to disinfest heliconia inflorescences of the common insects that inhabit them in the field. Dips in insecticides and insecticidal soaps followed by rinsing have been most commonly used (Criley and Paull, 1993). Hydrogen cyanide fumigation at 2500 ppm was effective on insects and did not cause damage or decrease vase life in comparison to untreated controls, but it is not registered with the Environmental Protection Agency for this purpose (Hansen et al., 1991). Nonchemical disinfestation has been achieved on large-flowered heliconias with vapor heat (water-saturated air) at temperatures of 113 to 115.7°F (45 to 46.5°C) for 60 min (Hansen et al., 1992).

Vase life of heliconia varies considerably, even within a species (Broschat and Donselman, 1983a, 1987; Criley, 1995; Criley and Broschat, 1992; R. E. Paull, unpublished data). Floral preservatives do not improve vase life (Broschat and Donselman, 1983a; Tjia and Sheehan, 1984), but antitranspirants improve postharvest life slightly (Broschat and Donselman, 1987; Ka-ipo et al., 1989; R. E. Paull, unpublished data), probably by conserving internal water. Treatment with silver thiosulfate does not improve vase life or prevent floret abscission (Tjia and Sheehan, 1984). Sprays and dips in 200 ppm benzyladenine improved vase life up to 140% (R. E. Paull, unpublished data). As cut foliage, hydration is necessary to prevent leaf inrolling.

Heliconia inflorescences are sensitive to cold and should be stored at temperatures above 55°F (13°C) in 90 to 95% relative humidity. Cold injury develops as a black spot at the base of the bracts (Broschat and Donselman, 1983b).

The large inflorescences are packed individually, sometimes in a plastic sleeve or in moistened shreds of newsprint. Stems are layered with newspaper to prevent bruising. Often, a leaf petiole is allowed to extend above the inflorescence to prevent it from being damaged at the end of the box. Small inflorescences, usually with one leaf, may be bunched in groups of 5 or 10 and sleeved in plastic film or netting. The small inflorescences are placed on top of the heavier heliconias in shipping cartons.

KEY POINTS

- This tropical plant is grown as a cut flower and occasionally as a potted flowering plant.
- Heliconias are grown for their large, red, orange, yellow, pink, or green inflorescences, which are either upright or pendulous. Thick bracts surround small and usually inconspicuous flowers.
- Plants are commonly propagated by division.
- Some cultivars may be photoperiodic, responding to either SD or LD, and others are day neutral.
- Plants are commonly grown outdoors for cut flower use or in large 6- to 10- in. (15- to 25-cm) pots for potted flowering plants.
- Inflorescences are usually harvested when two-thirds of the bracts have opened because they will not continue to open after harvest.
- Store and ship cut flowers above 55°F (13°C).

ACKNOWLEDGMENT

The authors would like to thank Richard Criley, University of Hawaii, for writing this chapter.

BIBLIOGRAPHY

Ball, D. 1986. Viruses on heliconia. *Bulletin of the Heliconia Society International* 1(3):7.

Ball, D. 1987a. Container culture for *Heliconia augusta* [sic] cv. Holiday. *Bulletin of the Heliconia Society International* 2(1):2.

Ball, D. 1987b. Heliconia as a pot plant. *Proceedings of the Florida State Horticultural Society* 100: 163–165.

Berry, F., and W.J. Kress. 1991. *Heliconia: An identification guide*. Smithsonian Institution Press, Washington, D.C.

Broschat, T.K. 1989. Potassium deficiency in south Florida ornamentals. *Proceedings of the Florida State Horticultural Society* 102:106–108.

Broschat, T.K., and H.M. Donselman. 1983a. Heliconias: A promising new cut flower crop. *HortScience* 18:1–2.

Broschat, T.K., and H.M. Donselman. 1983b. Production and post-harvest culture of *Heliconia psittacorum* flowers in south Florida. *Proceedings of the Florida State Horticultural Society* 96: 272–273.

Broschat, T.K., and H.M. Donselman. 1987. Tropical cut flower research at the University of Florida's Ft. Lauderdale research and education center. *Bulletin of the Heliconia Society International* 2(3–4):5–6.

Broschat, T.K., H.M. Donselman, and A.A. Will. 1984. 'Andromeda' and 'Golden Torch' heliconias. *HortScience* 19:736–737.

Carle, A.W. 1989. Heliconias by seed. *Bulletin of the Heliconia Society International* 4(1):6.

Criley, R.A. 1985. *Heliconia*, pp. 125–129 in *Handbook of Flowering*, vol. III, A.H. Halevy, editor. CRC Press, Boca Raton, Florida.

Criley, R.A. 1988. Propagation of tropical cut flowers: *Strelitzia*, *Alpinia*, and *Heliconia*. *Acta Horticulturae* 226:509–517.

Criley, R.A. 1989. Development of *Heliconia* and *Alpinia* in Hawaii: Cultivar selection and culture. *Acta Horticulturae* 246:247–258.

Criley, R.A. 1990. Production of *Heliconia* as cut-flowers and their potential as new potted plants. *Horticultural Digest* (Univ. Hawaii) 92:1–7.

Criley, R.A. 1995. Culture profile: *Heliconia psittacorum*. *Cut Flower Quarterly* 7(4):7–10.

Criley, R.A. 1999. Seasonal flowering patterns for *Heliconia* shown by grower records. *Acta Horticulturae* 486:323–327.

Criley, R.A., and T.K. Broschat. 1992. Heliconia: Botany and horticulture of a new floral crop. *Horticultural Review* 14:1–55.

Criley, R.A., and O. Kawabata. 1986. Evidence for a short day flowering response in *Heliconia stricta* 'Dwarf Jamaican.' *HortScience* 21:506–507.

Criley, R.A., and S. Lekawatana. 1992. Managing seasonality of flowering in heliconia. The Hawaii Tropical Flower Industy Conference, March 29–31, 1990, 134:167–172. Hawaii Institute for Tropical Agriculture and Human Resources, University of Hawaii, Research-Extension Service.

Criley, R.A., and S. Lekawatana. 1995. Seasonality of flowering in seasonal *Heliconia chartacea* and the potential for its control. *Bulletin of the Heliconia Society International* 7(4):11–15.

Criley, R.A., and R.E. Paull. 1993. Review: Postharvest handling of bold tropical cut flowers—*Anthurium*, *Alpinia purpurata*, *Heliconia*, and *Strelitzia*. *Acta Horticulturae* 337:201–211.

Criley, R.A., and W.S. Sakai. 1997. *Heliconia wagneriana* Petersen is a short day plant. *HortScience* 32:1044–1045.

Criley, R.A., W.S. Sakai, S. Lekawatana, and E. Kwon. 1999. Photoperiodism in the genus *Heliconia* and its effect upon seasonal flowering. *Acta Horticulturae* 486:323–327.

Donselman, H.M., and T.K. Broschat. 1986. Production of *Heliconia psittacorum* for cut flowers in south Florida. *Bulletin of the Heliconia Society International* 1(4):4–6.

Drysdale, W.T. 1987. *Heliconias* in California. *Bulletin of the Heliconia Society International* 3(1):3–4.

Geertsen, V. 1989. Effect of photoperiod and temperature on the growth and flower production of *Heliconia psittacorum* 'Tay.' *Acta Horticulturae* 252:117–122.

Geertsen, V. 1990. Influence of photoperiod and temperature on the growth and flowering of *Heliconia aurantiaca*. *HortScience* 25:646–648.

Hansen, J.D., H.T. Chan, Jr., A.H. Hara, and V.L. Tenbrink. 1991. Phytotoxic reaction of Hawaiian cut flowers and foliage to hydrogen cyanide fumigation. *HortScience* 26:53–56.

Hansen, J.D., A.H. Hara, and V.L. Tenbrink. 1992. Vapor heat: A potential treatment to disinfest tropical cut flowers and foliage. *HortScience* 27:139–143.

Hirano, R.T. 1989. Some observations of *Heliconia* 'Richmond Red' in relation to *H. caribaea* and *H. bihai*. *Bulletin of the Heliconia Society International* 4(1):4–5, 9.

Hodel, D.R. 1985. Status and potential of *Heliconia* in California. *Bulletin of the Heliconia Society International* 1(1):7–8.

Holtzmann, O.V., and M. Wong. 1986. Nematodes in tropical cut flowers and their control. *Horticulture Digest* 80:5–6.

Huxley, A., M. Griffiths, and M. Levy. 1992. *Heliconia*, pp. 529–535 in *The New Royal Horticultural*

Society Dictionary of Gardening, vol. 2. Stockton Press, New York.

Ka-ipo, R., W.S. Sakai, S.C. Furutani, and M. Collins. 1989. Effect of postharvest treatment with anti-transpirants on the shelf-life of H. psittacorum cv. Parakeet cut flowers. Bulletin of the Heliconia Society International 4(3):13–14.

Kress, W.J. 1983a. Crossability barriers in neotropical Heliconia. Annuals of Botany 52:131–147.

Kress, W.J. 1983b. Self-incompatibility in Central America Heliconia. Evolution 37(4):735–744.

Kress, W.J. 1987. Pollination and hybridization of Heliconia. Bulletin of the Heliconia Society International 2(3–4):10–11.

Lekawatana, S., and R.A. Criley. 1989. Pot culture of Heliconia stricta 'Dwarf Jamaican.' Acta Horticulturae 252:123–128.

Maciel, N., and R.A. Criley. 1998. Effecto del fotoperiodo en la floracion de Heliconia rostrata Ruiz & Pavon. 44th Annual Meeting of the Interamerican Society for Tropical Horticulture, p. 106. (abstract).

Sakai, W.S., A. Manarangi, R. Short, G. Nielson, and M.D. Crowell. 1990a. Evidence for long-day flower initiation in Heliconia angusta cv. Holiday—Relationship between time of shoot emergence and flowering. Bulletin of the Heliconia Society International 4(4):1–3.

Sakai, W.S., G. Nielsen, S. Short, R. Ka-ipo, A. Umemoto, and K. Inada. 1990b. Forcing off-season flower production in Heliconia angusta cv. Holiday with artificial long-days. Bulletin of the Heliconia Society International 4(4):10–11.

Sewake, K.T., and J.Y. Uchida. 1995. Diseases of Heliconia in Hawaii. Research-Extension Service Brief No. 159, Hawaii Institute for Tropical Agriculture and Human Resources, University of Hawaii.

Stiles, F.G. 1979. Notes on the natural history of Heliconia (Musaceae) in Costa Rica. Brenesia 15 (Suppl.):151–180.

Tjia, B., and U. Jierwiriyapant. 1988. Growth regulator studies on 'Golden Torch' (Heliconia psittacorum × spathocircinata). Bulletin of the Heliconia Society International 3(3):1, 6.

Tjia, B., and T.J. Sheehan. 1984. Preserving beauty and profits. Longevity, quality studies help prolong life of Heliconia. Greenhouse Manager 2(11): 94–100.

Uchida, J.Y., M. Aragaki, and P.S. Yahata. 1989. Heliconia Root Rot and Foliage Blight Caused by Cylindrocladium. Research-Extension Service Brief No. 85. Hawaii Institute for Tropical Agriculture and Human Resources, University of Hawaii.

van Raalte, D., and D. van Raalte-Wichers. 1973. Heliconia. Vakblad v. Bloemistris 28(3):12–13.

Hibiscus

INTRODUCTION

Common names: hibiscus, Chinese hibiscus, Hawaiian hibiscus, rose of China, China rose, blacking plant.

Scientific name: Hibiscus rosa-sinensis L. (Huxley et al., 1992).

Family and related taxa: Malvaceae Juss. H. rosa-sinensis is one of more than 220 species of herbs, shrubs, or trees in the genus. Though many Hibiscus species are tropical, some species such as H. coccineus (Medik.) Walter., H. grandiflorus Michx., H. lasiocarpus Cav., H. militaris Cav., H. moscheutos L., and H. syriacus L. are native to North America and are very cold hardy, especially H. syriacus. Abelmoschus, Abutilon, Callirhoë, Lavatera, and Malva are also in this family.

Origin: H. rosa-sinensis has been so widely grown in the tropics for centuries that its exact origin is lost, but is probably tropical Asia (Vietnam and southern China).

Uses and current status: Used as a landscape plant in frost-free areas, it can grow up to more than 16 ft (5 m) tall. Outdoors it is adaptable to hot, dry, windy areas. Interestingly, the plant also adapts well to the northern home environment and flowers in winter when acclimatized and grown adjacent to a sunny window. Presently, it is grown as a flowering potted plant

FIGURE II-I HIBISCUS   Flower of potted *Hibiscus.*

in 4- to 10-in. (10- to 25-cm) pots in northern Europe and North America (Fig. II-1 Hibiscus). Stock plants are also popular as large patio specimens. A number of other *Hibiscus* species have been examined for potential commercial value and four were selected: *Hibiscus acetosella* Welw. ex Hiern., *H. cisplatinus* St.-Hil., *H. radiatus* Cav., and *H. trionum* L. (Warner and Erwin, 2001). The future commercial potential of this genus is great. Flowers of *H. rosa-sinensis* are up to 5 in. (13 cm) across and come in a variety of colors. The dark-green glossy leaves are ovate and normally have a serrated margin.

CULTIVARS

Hibiscus rosa-sinensis cultivars are primarily based on flower color, which includes white; numerous shades of red, pink, orange, and yellow; and bicolors. The petal margins can be quite decorative and ruffled; the five-lobed stigma can be deeply divided and petaloid. There are double-flowered forms.

Commercial hybrid seed lines of hardy hibiscus for bedding plant use are available from limited genetic hybridization with *H. moscheutos,* the rose mallow, which is hardy from Zones 5 to 10 and grows 2 to 6 ft (0.6 to 1.8 m) tall. Flowers are from 9 to 11 in. (23 to 28 cm) across. As with *H. rosa-sinensis,* flowers last only 1 day, with new flowers opening each morning. These hybrids are woody, deciduous perennials and survive as far north as Minnesota if properly mulched. Generally, 4 to 5 months are required to flower from seed (Bailey and Bailey, 1976).

PROPAGATION

Hibiscus rosa-sinensis is commercially propagated by soft wood cuttings. Most producers buy unrooted cuttings or grow stock plants, which are later sold as large patio plants. Specialists maintain stock plants for 3 or more years. Seasonal variations in the ability to root occur with some cultivars (Wang and Andersen, 1989). Stock plants that received HID lighting of less than 4500 fc (900 μmol $\cdot$ m^{-2} $\cdot$ s^{-1}) produced cuttings that rooted more rapidly than those receiving higher irradiances (Johnson and Hamilton, 1977; Kelty, 1984). Supplemental lighting may also be beneficial during propagation of cuttings (Wang and Andersen, 1989). Cuttings are 3.5 to 4.75 in. (9 to 12 cm) long with two mature basal leaves. Unrooted cuttings must be protected from direct sunlight, excessive heat, and water stress until planted. If cuttings are allowed to dry prior to sticking in the propagation area or during the early stages of propagation, success is greatly reduced (B. Fitzgerald, personal communication). 1-methylcyclopropene (1-MCP) and silver thiosulfate (STS) retarded storage-induced leaf yellowing of unrooted cuttings but reduced subsequent rooting (Serek et al., 1998).

Cultivars vary widely in rapidity of rooting (Kelty, 1984; Wang and Andersen, 1989). Carpenter and Cornell (1992) found that as the medium temperature increased from 64 to 93°F (18 to 34°C), optimum indole-3-butyric acid (IBA) concentrations and application durations for rooting decreased from 10,000 to 1250 ppm (aqueous solutions) and from 10 to 0.1 min. No definite recommendation can be made regarding the IBA concentration or duration of an aqueous dip, due to seasonal and cultivar variation (Wang and Andersen, 1989). Each cultivar must be individually tested to determine the optimum rooting hormone regime. Carpenter (1989) found the optimum medium temperature to be 79 to 86°F (26 to 30°C) for both difficult and easy-to-root cultivars.

Wikesjö (1981) in Sweden recommended propagation under white plastic tents in the spring and summer and under clear plastic in the autumn and winter instead of using water mist. Carpenter and Cornell (1992) in Florida used a similar system, maintaining 100% relative humidity under polyethylene film. Mist may be successful, however, in climates with low humidity and high light if humidity control is not available. In Kenya, cuttings rooted best when polyethylene film was laid directly over the cuttings as compared to tenting or misting (Mudge et al., 1995). Dead leaves should be removed during propagation to reduce disease spread.

Hibiscus moscheutos seed [2600/oz (92/g)] germinated in 21 days at 70°F (21°C) and plants are handled as bedding plants.

FLOWERING CONTROL AND DORMANCY

Flowers are ephemeral, opening in the morning and senescing by evening. With *H. rosa-sinensis,* flowering is autonomous: The flower number depends on the growth rate of the terminal and axillary shoots, which in turn are dependent on total light energy at the appropriate temperature (Swanson et al., 1975; Wikesjö, 1981; Wilkins, 1986). However, some cultivars flower sooner than others (Karlsson et al., 1991). The reproductive requirements of a number of other *Hibiscus* species have been determined: Five species were day neutral, six were obligate SD plants, six were facultative SD plants, three were obligate LD plants, and one was a facultative LD plant (Warner and Erwin, 2001, 2003). *H. moscheutos* is an obligate LD plant (Runkle et al., 1998; Warner and Erwin, 2001).

TEMPERATURE

Cultivar leaf unfolding rates varied little between nine cultivars grown in similar temperature and natural Florida light conditions. However, when growth rates during week 1 (January 8 to 14) were compared with week 30 (July 24 to 30), significant differences were observed, which were attributed to light (Karlsson et al., 1991). Hibiscus plants have been successfully grown under a wide variety of temperature regimes from 64 to 102°F (18 to 39°C) (Neumaier et al., 1987; Osborne and Chase, 1990; Wang, 1991; Woodson and Raiford, 1986).

Maximum leaf unfolding rate was 0.23 leaves per day at 90°F (32°C) (Karlsson et al., 1991). Growth rate was linear from 52 to 90°F (11 to 32°C); at higher temperatures, leaf development decreased. This study was conducted in growth chambers using 1370 fc (200 μmol $\cdot$ m^{-2} $\cdot$ s^{-1}) of fluorescent light, which was on for 10 hr daily.

LIGHT

In Florida under natural light conditions plants pinched in early January (week 1) unfolded an average of 5.8 leaves in 7 weeks, whereas those pinched in late July (week 30) unfolded 8.3 leaves during 7 weeks. However, all of the leaf unfolding data were based on the development of vegetative shoots prior to visible buds. Once flower buds are visible, the previous data are not accurate. More research is needed to predict flower bud development at various light and temperature regimes.

In Mississippi, Neumaier et al. (1987) reported that the highest quality hibiscus plants were grown under 50% shade in late winter to early spring, reducing light from 4250 fc (850 μmol $\cdot$ m^{-2} $\cdot$ s^{-1}) to 2100 fc (420 μmol $\cdot$ m^{-2} $\cdot$ s^{-1}). Woodson and Raiford (1986) reported a light level of 4000 to 6500 fc (800 to 1300 μmol $\cdot$ m^{-2} $\cdot$ s^{-1}) during their Louisiana experiment commencing in January. Other light intensities reported were 2000 to 5000 fc, 4750 fc, and 1750 fc (400 to 1000, 950, and 350 μmol $\cdot$ m^{-2} $\cdot$ s^{-1}) (Osborne and Chase, 1990; Steinberg et al., 1991; Wang, 1991). These data indicate that hibiscus are tolerant of various temperature and light regimes. However, high quality can be obtained with 75 to 85/65 to 70°F (24 to 29/18 to 21°C) day/night temperatures and high light. In winter, full light is used, whereas shade is used in summer to control temperature. Although shade is used more for human comfort, it can increase plant quality as well (Neumaier et al., 1987).

H. moscheutos plants flowered more rapidly and produced more flowers as the length of the night interruption lighting increased from 1 to 4 hr/night (Runkle et al., 1998). Cyclical night interruption lighting of 6 min on/24 or 54 min off was also effective.

WATER

With a large leaf surface and well-developed roots, adequate water is a constant concern. Hibiscus are readily grown with a variety of irrigation systems including microtube, sprinkler, and ebb-and-flow systems. After pruning, water loss is reduced and care must be taken to not overwater and damage roots during this production period. Prepruning water consumption is quickly restored with new growth (Steinberg et al., 1991). Cycocel (chlormequat) sprays reduce water use by 35%.

CARBON DIOXIDE

Elevated carbon dioxide levels hasten plant growth and plant quality, provided light is not a limiting factor.

NUTRITION

Hibiscus plants are moderate to heavy feeders, requiring 250 ppm N during the summer and only 150 to 200 ppm N during the winter. Regardless, a minimum of ammonium (20:80 ammonium:nitrate) should be used in the winter. In the summer, a higher rate of ammonium:nitrate (80:20) is acceptable. Using hydroponics the optimum rate of K was 156 ppm (Egilla and Davies, 1995).

A variety of water-soluble fertilizers can be used (10–30–10 to 20–10–20). Furthermore, controlled-release fertilizers can be used in combination with water-soluble nutrient programs if plants are watered overhead. Micronutrients can be supplied on a constant basis or incorporated into the medium (Neumaier et al., 1987; Wang, 1991; Woodson and Raiford, 1986). Foliar nutrient levels for high-quality plants are listed in Chapter 6, Nutrition, Table 6-4. Regular drenches of magnesium sulfate at 8 oz/100 gal ($6.6g \cdot L^{-1}$) can prevent the intervenal chlorosis of lower leaves typical of magnesium deficiency. Chlorosis of upper leaves may be due to iron deficiency, which can result from high medium pH or insufficient root development or iron content.

MEDIA

Various media can be used, incorporating different ratios of sphagnum peat, vermiculite, perlite, pine bark, or calcine clays. Dolomitic limestone is frequently used to adjust pH to 5.8 to 6.5 (Neumaier et al., 1987; Wang, 1991; Woodson and Raiford, 1986).

HEIGHT CONTROL

For 4-in. (10-cm) pots, Cycocel has been the most commonly used plant growth regulator. Sprays at 200 ppm are used after the first pinch, when new axillary shoots are 1.5 to 2 in. (3.75 to 5 cm) long. Multiple sprays may be needed depending on the pot size and cultivar. When plants reach the desired height, a 1000-ppm Cycocel spray is used, internode elongation virtually ceases, and uniform flowering occurs. Other Cycocel spray sequences may decrease production time by 4 to 5 weeks if used under propagation tents as rooting begins and a few days before the pinch. Crop schedules need to account for the effect of Cycocel on timing. Leaf coloration is also intensified and axillary branching is increased. Interestingly, Cycocel sprays reduced spider mite numbers 123% over the untreated control (Osborne and Chase, 1990). Bonzi (paclobutrazol) can be used as a 5-ppm spray or 0.5 mg

a.i./pot drench and, depending on the cultivar, higher rates may be needed (Criley, 1980; Shanks, 1972; Wilkins, 1986). Sumagic (uniconazole) sprays at 10 ppm and soil drenches at 0.025 to 0.2 mg a.i./pot were also effective (Newman et al., 1989; Wang and Gregg, 1989). Flowering may be delayed and higher rates may cause foliar distortion. A-Rest (ancymidol) and B-Nine (daminozide) were also reported to be marginally effective (Adriansen, 1985). Multiple spray applications of Cycocel at 1000 ppm or Sumagic at 15 ppm can be used to control the height of *Hibiscus moscheutos* (Latimer, 2001).

SPACING

Cuttings are best rooted in oasis or similar type cubes. When rooted, two to five cuttings are transplanted per 4- to 6-in. (10- to 15-cm) pot. Cuttings can also be propagated directly into the final pot. Although plants can be held pot-to-pot until growth commences, it is best to give full space and light on the bench immediately.

PINCHING AND DISBUDDING

A soft pinch is required to maximize branching, which is also increased by plant growth regulator sprays. Pinching occurs 5 to 6 weeks after propagation when active growth has commenced. Multiple pinches may be required and can occur every 3 to 4 weeks.

One mefluidide spray at 1.3 to 6.6 oz/100 gal (100 to 500 mg $\cdot$ L^{-1}) has been reported to induce axillary branching and decreased internode elongation. No pinching would be required if used (Woodson and Raiford, 1986). No disbudding is required.

SUPPORT

No support required.

SCHEDULE AND TIMING

Wikesjö (1981) formulated production schedules for southern Sweden. From propagation to flowering in the spring required 14 to 19 weeks; in the winter, 27 weeks, even with supplemental lighting. In North America, spring and summer production time is 12 to 15 weeks and up to 24 weeks in the winter (Table II-1 Hibiscus). The main production period runs from February to April for May to July sales.

TABLE II-I HIBISCUS

Sample production schedule for 4-in. (10-cm) pots of *Hibiscus rosa-sinensis* for spring sales.

Cultural Step	Production Time (weeks)	Temperature °F (°C)	Photoperiod
Root cuttings	6	Medium: 72–74 (22–23)	Reduced light intensity
Transplant rooted cuttings,[a] space, and pinch	6	Day: 72–74 (22–23) Night: 68 (20) minimum, 70 (21) optimum	HID, if available
Spray plant with growth regulator	2–3	Day: 72–74 (22–23) Night: 68 (20) minimum, 70 (21) optimum	Natural
Spray plant with growth regulator	2–3	Day: 72–74 (22–23) Night: 68 (20) minimum, 70 (21) optimum	Natural
Spray plant with growth regulator	2–3	Day: 72–74 (22–23) Night: 68 (20) minimum, 70 (21) optimum	Natural
Flower	3	Ambient	Natural
Total	21–24		

[a] *Two cuttings are used per 6-in. (15-cm) pot.*

INSECTS

Commonly encountered insects on hibiscus are aphids, mealybugs, spider mites, scales, thrips, and whiteflies. Inspect cultivar stock plants and production plants to detect isolated infestations (Wilkins, 1998). Aphid populations can build up on lower leaves, which may be difficult to reach with insecticidal sprays.

DISEASES

Two *Pseudomonas* species can occur, one causing an irregular-shaped angular leaf spot (*P. cichorii*) and one causing small circular lesions (*P. syringae*). *Cercospora* and *Xanthomonas* leaf spot are also observed and similar in appearance. The former has a more distinct yellow halo (Daughtrey and Chase, 1992). Discard infected plants. Avoid high soluble salt levels, excess soil moisture, and splashing water on leaves to reduce root rot and most leaf problems. Root rot organisms (*Fusarium* and *Phytophthora*) and viruses can occur (Horst, 1990), especially in stock plants. High media temperatures of 86°F (30°C) or higher may increase the severity of *Phytophthora* root rot (Lyles et al., 1992). Other diseases reported include armillaria root rot (*Armillaria mellea*), gray mold (*Botrytis cinerea*), stem rot (*Mycopsphaerella*), nectria canker (*Nectria*), and bacterial leaf spot (*Pseudomonas*) (Dreistadt, 2001).

PHYSIOLOGICAL DISORDERS

Cold injury can occur at temperatures well above freezing at 50°F (10°C) (see Postharvest, next). Bud drop can occur from water stress, low light, or insect damage (Hamrick, 2003)

POSTHARVEST

At 41 or 52°F (5 or 11°C), plants experience chilling injury or fail to grow (Karlsson et al., 1991). Buds and open flowers will abscise if exposed to water stress or to low light during shipping and marketing (Nell, 1993). Plants are also very ethylene sensitive; 0.05 ppm ethylene for 24 hr can cause extensive bud abscission (Høyer, 1996). Interestingly, 1-MCP and STS had "only a modest effect" in extending the life of individual flowers (Reid et al., 2002). However, bud and flower abscission can be greatly reduced by 4 mM STS sprays 10 days prior to marketing (Høyer, 1986; Nowak and Rudnicki, 1990; Thaxton et al., 1988). Plants are best shipped for no longer than 3 days at 50 to 61°F (10 to 16°C) (Gibbs et al., 1989). Longer storage or higher storage temperature increase bud and flower abscission and lower quality (Gibbs et al., 1989; Thaxton et al., 1988).

Interestingly, exposing plants to red light (2.9 μmol $\cdot$ m^{-2} $\cdot$ s^{-1}) during storage delayed flower bud abscission while far-red light (1.7 μmol $\cdot$ m^{-2} $\cdot$ s^{-1}) accelerated abscission compared to darkness during storage (van Meeteren and van Gelder, 2000). Removing leaves prior to exposing plants to far-red light prevented the abscission. Swanson et al. (1975) associated abscission with increased abscissic acid levels and the leaves may be the source of a flower bud abscission promoting signal.

KEY POINTS

- Hibiscus is used as a potted flowering plant, patio plant, and garden ornamental in frost-free climates.

- Plants are propagated by tip cuttings.

- Flowering depends on the rate of leaf development, which is light and temperature dependent.

- Properly acclimated plants should have a long postharvest life for the consumer and will flower indoors.

- Flower and leaf abscission is a major problem during shipping and marketing.

BIBLIOGRAPHY

Adriansen, E. 1985. Kemisk vækstregulering, pp. 142–162 in *Potteplanter I—Produktion, Metoder, Midler*, O.V. Christensen, A. Klougart, I.S. Pedersen, and K. Wikesjö, editors. Gartner-INFO, København, Denmark. (in Danish)

Bailey, L.H., and E.Z. Bailey. 1976. *Hibiscus*, pp. 560–562 in *Hortus Third: A Concise Dictionary of Plants Cultivated in the United States and Canada*. Macmillan, New York.

Carpenter, W.J. 1989. Medium temperature influences the rooting of *Hibiscus rosa-sinensis* L. *Journal of Environmental Horticulture* 7:79–84.

Carpenter, W.J., and J.A. Cornell. 1992. Auxin application duration and concentration govern rooting of hibiscus stem cuttings. *Journal of the American Society for Horticultural Science* 117:68–74.

Criley, R.A. 1980. Potted flowering hibiscus. *Florists' Review* 165(4290):48–49, 64.

Daughtrey, M., and A.R. Chase. 1992. Hibiscus, pp. 123–125 in *Ball Field Guide to Diseases of Greenhouse Ornamentals*. Ball Publishing, Geneva, Illinois.

Dreistadt, S.H. 2001. *Integrated Pest Management for Floriculture and Nurseries*. University of California Division of Agriculture and Natural Resources Publication 3402.

Egilla, J.N., and F.T. Davies. 1995. Response of *Hibiscus rosa-sinensis* L. to varying levels of potassium fertilization: Growth, gas exchange and mineral element concentration. *Journal of Plant Nutrition* 18:1765–1783.

Gibbs, M.M., T.M. Blessington, J.A. Price, and Y.-T. Wang. 1989. Dark-storage temperature and duration influences flowering and quality retention of hibiscus. *HortScience* 24:646–647.

Hamrick, D. 2003. *Hibiscus*, pp. 434–436 in *Ball Redbook*, 2, 17th ed. Ball Publishing, Batavia, Illinois.

Horst, R.K. 1990. Hibiscus, p. 678 in *Westcott's Plant Disease Handbook*, 5th ed. Van Nostrand Reinhold, New York.

Høyer, L. 1986. Silver thiosulfate can to some extent prevent leaf, bud and flower drop in *Hibiscus rosa-sinensis* caused by ethylene and darkness. *Acta Horticulturae* 181:147–153.

Høyer, L. 1996. Critical ethylene exposure for *Hibiscus rosa-sinensis* is dependent on an interaction between ethylene concentration and duration. *Postharvest Biology and Technology* 9:87–95.

Huxley, A., M. Griffiths, and M. Levy. 1992. *Hibiscus*, pp. 564–567 in *The New Royal Horticultural Society Dictionary of Gardening*, vol. 2. Stockton Press, New York.

Johnson, C.R., and D.F. Hamilton. 1977. Rooting of *Hibiscus rosa-sinensis* L. cuttings as influenced by light intensity and ethephon. *HortScience* 12: 39–40.

Karlsson, M.G., R.D. Heins, J.O. Gerberick, and M.E. Hackmann. 1991. Temperature driven leaf unfolding rate in *Hibiscus rosa-sinensis*. *Scientia Horticulturae* 45:323–331.

Kelty, M.M. 1984. Container grown hibiscus: Propagation and production. *Proceedings of the International Plant Propagators Society* 34:480–486.

Latimer, J. 2001. Herbaceous perennials, pp. 98–110 in *Tips on Regulating Growth of Floriculture Crops*, M.L. Gaston, L.A. Kunkle, P.S. Konjoian, and M.F. Wilt, editors. Ohio Florists' Association Services, Columbus, Ohio.

Lyles, J.L., J.D. MacDonald, and D.W. Burger. 1992. Short- and long-term heat stress effects on phytophthora root rot of *Hibiscus*. *HortScience* 27:414–416.

Mudge, K.W., V.N. Mwaja, F.M. Itulya, and J. Ochieng. 1995. Comparison of four moisture management systems for cutting propagation of bougainvillea, hibiscus, and kei apple. *Journal of the American Society for Horticultural Science* 120:366–373.

Nell, T.A. 1993. *Hibiscus rosa-sinensis*, pp. 48–50 in *Flowering Potted Plants, Prolonging Shelf Performance*. Ball Publishing, Batavia, Illinois.

Neumaier, E.E., T.M. Blessington, and J.A. Price. 1987. Effect of light and fertilizer rate and source on flowering, growth, and quality of hibiscus. *HortScience* 22:902–904.

Newman, S.E., S.B. Tenney, and M.W. Follet. 1989. Use of uniconazole to control height of *Hibiscus rosa-sinensis*. *HortScience* 24:1041.

Nowak, J., and R.M. Rudnicki. 1990. *Postharvest Handling and Storage of Cut Flowers, Florist Greens, and Potted Plants*. Timber Press, Portland, Oregon.

Osborne, L.S., and A.R. Chase. 1990. Chlormequat chloride growth retardant reduces spider mite infestations of *Hibiscus rosa-sinensis*. *HortScience* 25:648–650.

Reid, M.S., B. Wollenweber, and M. Serek. 2002. Carbon balance and ethylene in the postharvest life of flowering hibiscus. *Postharvest Biology and Technology* 25:227–233.

Runkle, E.S., R.D. Heins, A.C. Cameron, and W.H. Carlson. 1998. Flowering of herbaceous perennials under various night interruption and cyclic lighting treatments. *HortScience* 33:672–677.

Serek, M., A. Prabucki, E.C. Sisler, and A.S. Andersen. 1998. Inhibitors of ethylene action affect final quality and rooting of cuttings before and after storage. *HortScience* 33:153–155.

Shanks, J.R. 1972. Chemical control of growth and flowering in hibiscus. *HortScience* 7:574.

Steinberg, S.L., J.M. Zajicek, and M.J. McFarland. 1991. Water relations of hibiscus following pruning or chemical growth regulation. *Journal of the American Society for Horticultural Science* 116: 465–470.

Swanson, B.T., Jr. H.F. Wilkins, C.J. Weiser, and I. Klein. 1975. Endogenous ethylene and abscissic acid relative to phytogerentology. *Plant Physiology* 55:370–376.

Thaxton, D.R., J.W. Kelly, and J.J. Frett. 1988. Control of *Hibiscus rosa-sinensis* L. bud abscission during shipping. *Scientia Horticulturae* 34: 131–137.

van Meeteren, U., and A. van Gelder. 2000. The role of leaves in photocontrol of flower bud abscission in *Hibiscus rosa-sinensis* L. 'Nairobi.' *Journal of the American Society for Horticultural Science* 125:31–35.

Wang, Q., and A.S. Andersen. 1989. Propagation of *Hibiscus rosa-sinensis*: Relations between stock plant cultivar, age, environment and growth regulator treatments. *Acta Horticulturae* 251: 289–309.

Wang, Y.T. 1991. Growth stage and site of application affect efficacy of uniconazole and GA$_3$ in hibiscus. *HortScience* 26:148–150.

Wang, Y.-T., and L.L. Gregg. 1989. Uniconazole affects vegetative growth, flowering, and stem anatomy of hibiscus. *Journal of the American Society for Horticultural Science* 114:927–932.

Warner, R.M., and J.E. Erwin. 2001. Variation in floral induction requirements of *Hibiscus* sp. *Journal of the American Society for Horticultural Science* 126:262–268.

Warner, R.M., and J.E. Erwin. 2003. Effect of photoperiod and daily light integral on flowering of five *Hibiscus* sp. *Scientia Horticulturae* 97: 341–351.

Wikesjö, K. 1981. Odling av *Hibiscus rosa-sinensis*. *Konsulentavdelningens Rapporter, Tradgård 205*, Swedish University of Agricultural Science, Alnarp, Sweden. (in Swedish)

Wilkins, H.F. 1986. *Hibiscus rosa-sinensis*, pp. 142–143 in *Handbook of Flowering*, vol. V, A.H. Halevy, editor. CRC Press, Boca Raton, Florida.

Wilkins, H.F. 1998. *Hibiscus*, pp. 547–551 in *Ball Redbook*, 16th ed., V. Ball, editor. George J. Ball Publishing, Batavia, Illinois.

Woodson, W.R., and R.J. Raiford. 1986. Induction of lateral branching in Chinese hibiscus with mefluidide. *HortScience* 21:71–73.

Hippeastrum

FIGURE II-I HIPPEASTRUM Potted *Hippeastrum* plant.

INTRODUCTION

Common name: amaryllis.

Scientific name: *Hippeastrum* Herb. hybrids (Huxley et al., 1992).

Family and related taxa: Amaryllidaceae J. St.-Hil. *Hippeastrum* hybrids were developed from several species including *H. vittatum* (L'Hérit.) Herb. and *H. reginae* (L.) Herb. (Huxley et al., 1992). Other members of this family include *Clivia, Crinum, Eucharis, Hymenocallis, Narcissus,* and *Nerine.*

Origin: *Hippeastrum* originated in subtropical America, from eastern Brazil to the south-central Andes of Peru, Argentina, and Bolivia (Bailey and Bailey, 1976; Tombolato and Matthes, 1998).

Uses and current status: The bulb is commonly forced in the greenhouse as a flowering potted plant or as a cut flower from fall to late spring (Fig. II-1 Hippeastrum). Bulbs are also sold for home forcing and used as an outdoor perennial in warm climates; in both cases, bulbs may be maintained for years (Bailey and Bailey, 1976; De Hertogh, 1996; Okubo, 1993). While amaryllis are considered cold hardy only in Zones 10 to 11, some cultivars are reliably hardy to Zone 7b (Fig. II-2 Hippeastrum).

The tunicated bulb consists of enlarged leaf bases. Bulbs form four leaves, then a floral stalk. Amaryllis bulbs exhibit sympodial growth in that vegetative growth occurs from a lateral bud at the base of the inflorescence. The flower stalk is always to the side of the four leaves that emerge. Within a typical quiescent, soon-to-be-planted bulb, two sets of four leaves

FIGURE II-2 HIPPEASTRUM Outdoor planting of *Hippeastrum* 'Red Lion' in Zone 7b.

and two flower scapes will be found, all at different stages of development (Okubo, 1993; Rees, 1972, 1985).

CULTIVARS

The genus *Hippeastrum* has more than 60 species. Europe, North America, and Japan have a long history of breeding and introducing numerous cultivars (Meerow, 2000; Meerow and Kane, 1991). The first European hybrids, produced in 1799, were from *H. reginae* and *H. vittatum.* Several categories of flower types are recognized: trumpet, belladonna, regina, Leopoldi, miniatures, doubles, and orchid-flowered types.

PROPAGATION

Specialty producers and home gardeners commonly propagate bulbs by offsets, which is a slow process. Tunic scale propagation is used commercially and 2 years are required from scale propagation to commercial-size bulb (Okubo et al., 1990; Sandler-Ziv et al., 1997a, b). *In vitro* propagation is possible (Tombolato et al., 1994) and seed is normally used only by breeders.

If all environmental factors are favorable and the bulb is large enough, up to three flower scapes can be produced annually (Boyle and Stimart, 1987; Okubo, 1993; Rees, 1972, 1985). Generally the minimum size for a commercial flowering bulb is 8 to 9 in. (20 to 22 cm) in circumference. Most commercial bulbs sold for forcing are 9 to 10 in. (24 to 26 cm) and larger. Universal bulb grades are in increments of 2 cm: 20/22, 24/26, 28/30, and 32/up (De Hertogh, 1996; Okubo, 1993). Commercially, bulbs are produced by Israel, South Africa, and the Netherlands (Okubo, 1993). Israel and South African bulbs are smaller than but equal in quality to Dutch bulbs. The optimal temperature range for bulb production is between 68 and 72°F (20 to 22°C), resulting in the maximum number of flower scapes and buds per bulb (Doorduin and Verkerke, 2002). Bulbs should be shipped and stored in excelsior (shaved wood) in perforated polyethylene bags (De Hertogh and Gallitano, 1998).

FLOWERING CONTROL AND DORMANCY

It is not true that amaryllis requires a rest period before reflowering. For home forcing, the annual flowering of the amaryllis is induced when the dried bulb is potted or brought inside in late fall or early winter and watered. Leaf reemergence and flowering require 3 to 5 weeks.

Flower induction and initiation are autonomous. A flowering scape will emerge with a set of four leaves when a bulb is placed in a favorable environment. The time span between the initiation of each set of vegetative and reproductive structures is 16 to 19 weeks (Doorduin, 1990). The inflorescence that emerges is initiated earlier than the four leaves, and the flower scape requires a longer time span to develop than the leaves (Okubo, 1993; Rees, 1972, 1985). The time span between flower initiation and emergence is 11 to 14 months; for leaves it is 7 to 10 months (Okubo, 1993). Because of this lack of synchrony, flower scapes frequently

FIGURE II-3 HIPPEASTRUM   Three potted *Hippeastrum* plants. Center plant has optimum leaf and flower scape development. Plant on right has insufficient foliage growth. Plant on left has insufficient flower scape development.

emerge without leaves, producing a poor-quality awkward-looking plant (Fig. II-3 Hippeastrum). To ensure that leaves and scapes emerge together for early forcing schedules, only mature bulbs with flower buds greater than 0.75 in. (2 cm) long should be harvested (De Hertogh, 1996). Ideally, leaves on a forced plant should be less than 50% of the flower scape.

When actively growing 'Red Lion' bulbs were allowed to dry for 0, 2, 4, or 8 weeks, a water stress of 4 to 8 weeks resulted in 100% flowering in 140 or 60 days, respectively, compared with 160 days for the 2-week stress (Boyle and Stimart, 1987). Only 83% of the bulbs in the control (0 weeks) treatment flowered in 160 days. T. H. Boyle (personal communication) interpreted these data to mean that drought stress accelerated flower development in 'Red Lion.' After 8 weeks of drought stress, only the older leaves had senesced while the younger leaves were still green.

TEMPERATURE

Bottom heat with temperatures of 68 to 75°F (20° to 24°C) results in rapid root regeneration, leaf emergence, and flowering. Temperatures during forcing may vary from 70 to 81°F (21 to 27°C) (De Hertogh, 1996; Okubo, 1993) (see Schedule and Timing section on next page). If bulbs are stored, hold at 41°F (5°C) if leaves or buds are visible and hold at 48°F (9°C) if no sprouting has occurred.

LIGHT

Force in full light (De Hertogh, 1996; Okubo, 1993). In the home, also keep amaryllis in high light.

WATER

When potting, firm the planting medium around the roots and water thoroughly; then water only when the medium dries and new roots have formed.

CARBON DIOXIDE

Additional CO_2 is not required but 1000 ppm CO_2 has been used to increase bulb size during bulb production in the Netherlands (Silberbush et al., 2003).

NUTRITION

During forcing, amaryllis does not need to be fertilized. For maintaining plants in the home after forcing, additional nutrition is required.

MEDIA

Potting medium should have a pH of 6.0 to 6.5 but not contain any bark. A number of commercial premixed media produced excellent results (De Hertogh and Tilley, 1991). Plant with one-third of the bulb out of the medium. It is important to retain the viable old basal roots during bulb handling and planting (De Hertogh, 1996; Okubo, 1993).

HEIGHT CONTROL

No height control is required, but B-Nine (daminozide) and Bonzi (paclobutrazol) are reported to be marginally effective (Adriansen, 1985).

SPACING

Plants are forced pot-to-pot.

PINCHING AND DISBUDDING

No pinching or disbudding required.

SUPPORT

If marketed in flower, the scape is supported by a stake and secured with an aesthetically pleasing material such as raffia.

SCHEDULE AND TIMING

It is critical to dry newly harvested bulbs as quickly as possible for 2 weeks at 73 to 77°F (23 to 25°C) with excellent ventilation. The bulbs should then be stored for 8 to 10 weeks at 55 to 59°F (13 to 15°C) at 80% relative humidity, followed by 2 weeks at 70 to 73°F (21 to 23°C) for simultaneous flower stalk and leaf growth and development. If a break occurs during the 8- to 10-week 55 to 59°F (13 to 15°C) temperature treatment, flower stalks will prematurely develop. When planted, these stalks will rapidly emerge and the plant will not have leaves until much later (De Hertogh, 1996; Okubo, 1993).

For late forcing schedules, bulbs are treated for 2 weeks at 73 to 77°F (23 to 25°C) for flower development, then 8 weeks at 55°F (13°C). These bulbs can be immediately potted or held for 6 to 9 months at 35 to 41°F (2 to 5°C) (De Hertogh, 1996; Okubo, 1993).

INSECTS

Generally, no major insects present problems during forcing. Spider mites can be a problem, but are usually rare.

DISEASES

The most common disease is leaf scorch or red blotch (*Stagonospora curtisii*), which causes long, dark-red streaks on the leaves and flower stalks and, in severe cases, deformity of foliage and flower stalks (Fig. II-4 Hippeastrum). An appropriate prevention spray on the cut surface of the bulb may be advised (Horst, 1990). The problem may be prevented by not applying water to the top or cut surface of the bulb, which can be more easily done by using microtube or subirrigation. Numerous other diseases have been reported including soft rot (*Erwinia*), gray mold (*Botrytis cinerea*), crown and root rot (*Pythium* and *Rhizoctonia*), armillaria root rot (*Armillaria mellea*), southern blight (*Sclerotium rolfsii*), and hippeastrum mosaic and tomato spotted wilt viruses (Dreistadt, 2001).

PHYSIOLOGICAL DISORDERS

Premature emergence of the flower stalk before the leaves is not desirable (see Flowering Control and Dormancy, page 589, for more information).

POSTHARVEST

Cut flowers are harvested when buds are colored. Splitting and curling up of the stem base

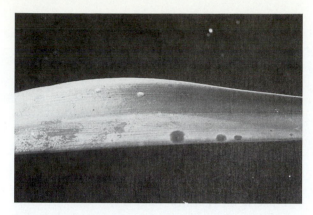

FIGURE II-4 HIPPEASTRUM   Red blotch disease of *Hippeastrum*.

can be prevented by a 24-hr pulse of 0.125 M sucrose at 72°F (22°C) (Halevy and Kofranek, 1984), which will also improve vase life. Vase life is reported to be up to 9 days. Flowers can be stored dry at 40 to 50°F (5 to 10°C), after which stems should be recut and placed in a preservative (Sacalis, 1993).

Potted flowering plants can be stored at 45 to 50°F (7 to 10°C) at various stages of development for 7 to 10 days. Plants are best sold when the flower stalk is 12 in. (30 cm) tall and the leaves are 6 to 12 in. (15 to 30 cm) long (Nell, 1993). Postharvest life should be 14 to 21 days. With proper care amaryllis can make long-lived specimens that can be repeatedly re-flowered in the home.

KEY POINTS

- Amaryllis is used as a potted flowering plant, cut flower, and garden ornamental in warm climates.

- Production is based on the large bulbs, which are propagated commercially by tunic scales or offsets and occasionally by seed.

- In the amaryllis growth cycle, four leaves and a flower scape are initiated; the flower scape frequently emerges first, without the leaves.

- For uniform emergence of both the flower stalks and leaves, store at 55 to 59°F (13 to 15°C) for at least 8 to 10 weeks starting on receipt of bulbs.

- Thereafter, bulbs can be stored for 6 to 9 months at 41°F (5°C).

- Drought stress is not required for flowering but may be useful in timing flower development.

- Leaf scorch or red blotch (*Stagonospora curtisii*) disease is a major problem.

- The base of a cut amaryllis stem sometimes splits and curls upward. This can be prevented with a 24-hr pulse of 0.125 M sucrose at 72°F (22°C).

BIBLIOGRAPHY

Adriansen, E. 1985. Kemisk vækstregulering, pp. 142–162 in *Potteplanter I—Produktion, Metoder, Midler*, O.V. Christensen, A. Klougart, I.S. Pedersen, and K. Wikesjö, editors. Gartner-INFO, København, Denmark. (in Danish)

Bailey, L.H., and E.Z. Bailey. 1976. *Hippeastrum*, pp. 564–565 in *Hortus Third: A Concise Dictionary of Plants Cultivated in the United States and Canada*. Macmillan, New York.

Boyle, T.H., and D.P. Stimart. 1987. Influence of irrigation interruptions in flowering of *Hippeastrum ×hybridum* 'Red Lion.' *HortScience* 22: 1290–1292.

De Hertogh, A.A. 1996. Amaryllis, pp. C7–16 in *Holland Bulb Forcer's Guide*, 5th ed. International Flower Bulb Centre, Hillegom, The Netherlands.

De Hertogh, A.A., and L.B. Gallitano. 1998. Influence of bulb packing systems on forcing of Dutch-grown *Hippeastrum* (*Amaryllis*) as flowering potted plants in North America. *HortTechnology* 8: 175–179.

De Hertogh, A.A., and M. Tilley. 1991. Planting medium effects on forced Swaziland and Dutch grown *Hippeastrum* hybrids. *HortScience* 29: 1168–1170.

Doorduin, J.C. 1990. Growth and development of hippeastrum grown in glasshouses. *Acta Horticulturae* 266:123–131.

Doorduin, J.C., and W. Verkerke. 2002. Effects of bulb temperature on development of *Hippeastrum*. *Acta Horticulturae* 570:313–319.

Dreistadt, S.H. 2001. *Integrated Pest Management for Floriculture and Nurseries*. University of California Division of Agriculture and Natural Resources Publication 3402.

Halevy, A., and A.M. Kofranek. 1984. Prevention of stem-base splitting in cut *Hippeastrum* flowers. *HortScience* 19:113–114.

Horst, R.K. 1990. Amaryllis, p. 526 in *Westcott's Plant Disease Handbook*, 5th ed. Van Nostrand Reinhold, New York.

Huxley, A., M. Griffiths, and M. Levy. 1992. *Hippeastrum*, pp. 570–573 in *The New Royal Horticultural Society Dictionary of Gardening*, vol. 2. Stockton Press, New York.

Meerow, A.W. 2000. 'Rio,' 'Sampra,' and 'Bahia,' three new triploid amaryllis cultivars. *HortScience* 35:147–149.

Meerow, A.W., and K.E. Kane. 1991. Hippeastrum breeding at the University of Florida. *Herbertia* 47:4–10.

Nell, T.A. 1993. *Hippeastrum* × cu., pp. 51–52 in *Flowering Potted Plants, Prolonging Shelf Performance*. Ball Publishing, Batavia, Illinois.

Okubo, H. 1993. *Hippeastrum* (Amaryllis), pp. 321–334 in *The Physiology of Flowering Bulbs*, A.A. De Hertogh and M. Le Nard, editors. Elsevier Science Publishers, Amsterdam.

Okubo, H., C.W. Huang, and S. Uemoto. 1990. Role of outer scale in twin-scale propagation of *Hippeastrum hybridum* and comparison of bulblet formation from single- and twin-scales. *Acta Horticulturae* 266:59–66.

Rees, A.M. 1972. *The Growth of Bulbs*. Academic Press, London.

Rees, A.M. 1985. *Hippeastrum*, pp. 294–296 in *Handbook of Flowering*, vol. I, A.H. Halevy, editor. CRC Press, Boca Raton, Florida.

Sacalis, J.N. 1993. *Hippeastrum* hybrids, p. 72 in *Cut Flowers; Prolonging Freshness*, 2nd ed., J.L. Seals, editor. Ball Publishing, Batavia, Illinois.

Sandler-Ziv, D., A. Cohen, A. Ion, H. Efron, and D. Amit. 1997a. A two-year production cycle of Israeli-grown *Hippeastrum* bulbs from bulb chipping to Christmas flowering. *Acta Horticulturae* 430:361–368.

Sandler-Ziv, D., A. Cohen, A. Ion, M. Kochba, S. Finkelstein, H. Efron, and D. Amit. 1997b. Improving *Hippeastrum* propagation and bulbil yield by cutting and incubation techniques. *Acta Horticulturae* 430:355–360.

Silberbush, M., J.E. Ephrath, C. Alekperov, and J. Ben-Asher. 2003. Nitrogen and potassium fertilization interactions with carbon dioxide enrichment in *Hippeastrum* bulb growth. *Scientia Horticulturae* 98:85–90.

Tombolato, A.F.C., C. Azevedo, and V. Nagai. 1994. Effects of auxin treatments on *in vivo* propagation of *Hippeastrum hybridum* Hort. by twin scaling. *HortScience* 29:922.

Tombolato, A.F.C., and L.A.F. Matthes. 1998. Collection of *Hippeastrum* spp., *Alstroemeria* spp. and other Brazilian bulbous species. *Acta Horticulturae* 454:91–98.

Hyacinthus

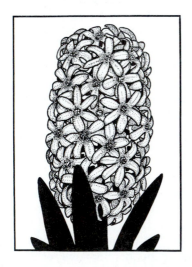

INTRODUCTION

Common names: hyacinth, Dutch hyacinth.
Scientific name: *Hyacinthus orientalis* L.

Family and related taxa: Liliaceae Juss. This genus has only one species according to Bailey and Bailey (1976), but Mathew (1973) and Huxley et al. (1992) believe there are three. The lily family is quite large and contains many commercially important floriculture crops including *Allium, Alstroemeria, Brodiaea, Convallaria, Eremurus, Lachenalia, Lilium, Muscari, Ornithogalum,* and *Tulipa*.

Origin: This tunicated bulbous perennial is native to Mediterranean climates and found in Asia Minor, Greece, North Africa, and Syria. Because 95% of the world's supply of hyacinth bulbs is produced in the Netherlands, the hyacinth is commonly associated with the Dutch.

Uses and current status: Hyacinth is one of several bulbs associated with spring. Plants are grown in gardens or forced as a potted flowering plant for spring sales. Bulbs can also be sold for consumers to easily force in water with specially designed vases. The inflorescence can be harvested and used for cut flowers or the individual florets can be used in corsage and wedding arrangements. Flowers are used by the French perfume industry.

Hyacinth is a herbaceous geophyte with six basally attached narrow leaves arising from the bulb's basal plate. The flowers are numerous and create a formal, cylindrical raceme inflorescence. The individual flowers are bell shaped, six lobed, reflexed, and intensely fragrant. Colors range from pure white to yellow, peach, pink, red, and various shades of blue. Double forms are available. In addition to the common cultivars are Roman hyacinths, which are smaller, flower earlier, and have less formal, more open inflorescences (Bailey and Bailey, 1976; De Hertogh, 1996).

CULTIVARS

Hyacinthus orientalis was first introduced into eastern Europe in 1562, but it had no doubt already been in cultivation for centuries. Cultivars and selections have been developed over the centuries and the process continues today. Commercially, 50 cultivars are commonly produced (Nowak and Rudnicki, 1993). De Hertogh (1996) lists 31 cultivars in his forcing schedules.

PROPAGATION

Seeds are used only for breeding programs because flowering requires 4 to 6 years. Few bulblets are naturally formed. Bulblets can form from leaf scale tissue. Commercially, the two primary processes used for bulblet formation are scoring and scooping mother bulbs (Gude and Dijkema, 1992) (see Fig. 1–11, Propagation, page 31). Scoring involves removing the apical portion of the bulb above the basal plate and making cross cuts through the basal plate. Scooping involves digging out the base of the bulb with a specially curved knife (Rees, 1972a). Afterward, adventitious bulblets form on the surface of the scales. Each method has advantages and disadvantages and typically only professional propagators follow the traditional techniques required for bulblet formation. *In vitro* propagation is also possible (Nowak and Rudnicki, 1993; Rees, 1972b).

FLOWERING CONTROL AND DORMANCY

As with most geophytes from the Mediterranean climate, growth follows a moist cool winter and spring, and a hot dry summer. The meristem is vegetative when bulbs are commercially harvested in June and July. Thereafter, flower formation commences at 68 to 82°F (20 to 28°C) with 78°F (26°C) being the optimum temperature for development.

Specific, often proprietary, temperature treatments are used commercially for forcing of hyacinth bulbs for Christmas and early to mid-January flowering (Vreeburg, 1992). These bulbs are called *prepared bulbs* (Nowak and Rudnicki, 1993; Rees, 1972b). Dormancy is broken and elongation of the leaves and inflorescence scape occurs after a rooting and cooling sequence of 48°F (9°C) for a minimum of 10 weeks; the specific number of weeks depends on the cultivar (De Hertogh, 1996).

Only the rooting room B temperature sequence is used (see *Crocus* chapter, Flowering Control and Dormancy section, and Table II-3 Crocus, p. 407). There are six flowering or forcing periods for potted hyacinths (Table II-1 Hyacinthus). For forcing period 1, prepared bulbs are used; for forcing period 2, either prepared bulbs or regular bulbs are used, depending on the cultivar. Thereafter, regular bulbs are used. Prepared bulbs are kept between 48 and 55°F (9 and 13°C) until planted. Regular bulbs are kept at 63°F (17°C) until the appropriate planting date.

TEMPERATURE

Greenhouse forcing temperatures can be in stages during the forcing process. During the first stage, hold bulbs at 50 to 55°F (10 to 13°C) for 2 days; then place at 73°F (23°C) (De Hertogh, 1996; Nowak and Rudnicki, 1993). This high temperature is used for bulbs to be forced early from December 1 to 26. Thereafter, 65°F (18°C) is used for the forcing dates from December 26 to February 9; and 55 to 60°F (13 to 16°C) for the remaining forcing dates. Hyacinths become easier to force later in the season because scape elongation occurs rapidly and the time span from the beginning of forcing to sales decreases. Care should be taken to not immediately place hyacinths directly from the refrigerated rooting room into a 73°F (23°C) greenhouse temperature. Slowly increase temperature and moisture to prevent flower "spitting" (see Physiological Disorders, page 596).

LIGHT

During the earlier forcing schedules up through January 17, plants may need shade to elongate leaves and flower scapes. Shade can be automated or can be as simple as placing newspaper over the emerging plants. Newspaper, long rows of craft paper, or shade cloth

TABLE II-I HYACINTHUS

Programming schedules for forcing *Hyacinthus* bulbs into flowering; rooting room B is used exclusively (modified from De Hertogh, 1996). See *Crocus*, p. 407, for description of rooting room B temperature sequence.

Date of Expected Flowering	Date to Commence Forcing	Date to Pot Bulb	Type of Bulb to Use	Cold Required (weeks)
I				
Dec 20	Dec 1	Sept 17–22	Prepared[a]	10
Dec 28	Dec 8			11
Jan 3	Dec 15			12
Jan 11	Dec 22			13
II				
Jan 14	Dec 26	Sept 25–30	Prepared or regular[a,b]	13
Jan 21	Jan 5			14
Jan 27	Jan 11			15
Feb 3	Jan 17			16
III				
Feb 9	Jan 26	Oct 24–28	Regular	13
Feb 14	Feb 2			14
Feb 21	Feb 9			15
IV				
Mar 1	Feb 17	Nov 10–15	Regular	15
Mar 7	Feb 24			16
Mar 13	Mar 2			17
V				
Mar 19	Mar 10	Nov 10–15	Regular	18
Mar 25	Mar 16			19
Apr 1	Mar 23			20
VI				
Apr 10	Mar 30	Nov 10–15	Regular	21
Apr 16	Apr 6			22
Apr 20	Apr 13			23

[a]*Prepared bulbs are given special temperature treatment by the bulb supplier. Upon receipt, place at 48 to 55°F (9 to 13°C) until potting.*
[b]*Use of prepared or regular bulbs depends on date of flowering and cultivar.*

should be used with caution because they may act as a heat trap and induce spitting. After January 26, force in full winter light or under 1000 to 2500 fc (200 to 500 $\mu mol \cdot m^{-2} \cdot s^{-1}$) (De Hertogh, 1996).

WATER

During the rooting room process, keep medium moist, not wet. When pots are first brought into the greenhouse forcing environment, allow the forcing medium and bulbs to slowly warm, then increase the temperature and water if needed. Hopefully, pots should be moist, not wet, when they are brought into the greenhouse. Excess available water or rapid water absorption by the roots has been determined to be involved with spitting (see Physiological Disorders, page 596). Keep water off the foliage (De Hertogh, 1996).

CARBON DIOXIDE

No carbon dioxide is needed.

NUTRITION

No nutrients are needed, but 250 ppm N from calcium nitrate can be used.

MEDIA

Any medium that is well drained and pasteurized and has a pH between 6.0 and 7.0 can be used. Other considerations are the weight of a moistened pot in regard to labor considerations and shipping costs. De Hertogh (1996) has evaluated several media. Cut hyacinths can also be forced hydroponically (James, 2002).

Prepared bulbs can be forced in water using specially designed clear glass containers, which allow observers in the home to watch the root system develop. Traditionally, the hyacinth root has been used in university plant anatomy classes to illustrate a root system with a large root cap, root hairs, and contractile roots (De Hertogh, 1996; Nowak and Rudnicki, 1993).

HEIGHT CONTROL

The cultivar and date of forcing will determine whether Florel (ethephon) is needed. Flower scapes of bulbs for late forcing schedules have a greater tendency to elongate than earlier scheduled bulbs. Florel sprays of 500 to 2000 ppm are used and applied to runoff. Only freshly prepared solutions should be used (De Hertogh, 1996). The plant height should be 3 to 4 in. (7.5 to 10 cm) tall, the foliage dry, and the greenhouse temperature set at 60 to 70°F (16 to 21°C). The greenhouse should also be well vented to eliminate any ethylene gas. Do not water for 12 hr after application. If a second application is required, do not spray on any inflorescences that are near maturity or showing color, because premature senescence will occur. Adriansen (1985) noted that A-Rest (ancymidol) might also be effective.

SPACING

When bulbs are potted, one bulb is placed in a 4-in. (10-cm) pot, three in a 6-in. (15-cm) pot, and five to eight in an 8-in. (20-cm) azalea pot. Pots are placed pot-to-pot in the rooting room and in the forcing greenhouse.

PINCHING AND DISBUDDING

No pinching or disbudding required.

SUPPORT

Normally no support is used; however, if the forcer or retailer knows that the plants are to be used in a long-term display at high temperatures under low light, then thin-diameter, round wooden stakes or heavy floral wire can be inserted down the inflorescences' hollow scape. Stem topple is a major problem in the postharvest life of a potted hyacinth. Hopefully, Florel application will reduce the problem of scape elongation.

SCHEDULE AND TIMING

When bulbs arrive, inspect and store at 63°F (17°C) until forcing starts. Complete programming schedules for hyacinth and numerous other geophytes have been developed by De Hertogh (1996). Only rooting room B is used (see *Crocus* chapter, Flowering Control and Dormancy, and Table II-3 Crocus, page 407). Greenhouse forcing schedules have been divided into six forcing or timing schedules. Hyacinths force within 21 days during December and January, but only 4 to 12 days are required during March and April (see Table II-2 Hyacinthus on page 596).

A major drawback in producing hyacinth, however, has been the need for cooler space. The lengthy cold treatment usually means that limited numbers of bulbs can be programmed in the coolers during the high sales period from Valentine's Day to Easter. After bulbs are brought out of the cooler for Valentine's Day, there is not enough time to program additional bulbs for later holidays. However, a delayed potting method has been developed to reduce the amount of cooler time and space needed (Dole, 1996). With this method bulbs are still held in the cooler for the required total number of weeks of cold; however, the first portion is applied to unpotted dry bulbs. At 8 weeks before moving bulbs to the greenhouse, the bulbs are potted, watered, and returned to the cooler. The cooler is held at 41°F (5°C) to allow bulbs to develop roots and shoots at the same time. Thus, a second crop can be programmed in the coolers after the Valentine's Day crop has been moved to the greenhouse for forcing.

Cold, dry storage should not extend beyond 8 weeks or late January, after which time the bulbs must be potted and the remaining 8 weeks of cold applied to bulbs in a moist medium. Cooler temperatures tested for this method included 34, 37, 41, 44.5, and 48°F

TABLE II-2 HYACINTHUS

Representative cultivars of *Hyacinthus* for pot flower forcing; optimum weeks of bulb cold storage; appropriate flowering dates; type of bulb treatment [prepared (PR) or regular (R)]; and the estimated days ( ) required to flower in the forcing greenhouse at 63°F (17°C). Number under type of bulb and days to flower is the recommended Florel (ethephon) spray rate in ppm (modified from De Hertogh, 1996).

Color: Cultivar	Appropriate Dates to Force the Cultivar						Optimum Number of Weeks of Cold	
	I Dec 20– Jan 13	*II* Jan 14– Feb 8	*III* Feb 9– Feb 28	*IV* Mar 1– Mar 18	*V* Mar 19– Apr 9	*VI* Apr 10– Apr 20	*PR*	*R*
Pink:								
Anna Marie[a]	PR (16) (1000)	R (14) (1000)	R (12) (1000)	R (11) (1000)	— —	— —	10–11	13–14
Pink Pearls[a]	PR (20) —	R (13) —	R (11) (1000)	R (9) (1000)	R (7) (1000)	R (4) (1000)	11–12	14–15
Blue:								
Blue Jacket	— —	— —	R (15) (1000)	R (12) (1000)	R (8) (1000)	R (6) (1000)	—	15–17
White:								
Carnegie[a]	— —	PR (19) —	R (16) —	R (13) —	R (7) (1000)	R (4) (1000)	14–15	14–16

[a]*Suited for 4-in. (10-cm) pot plant forcing.*

(1, 3, 5, 7, and 9°C) and the optimum temperature was 41°F (5°C) for both moist and dry treatments. Temperatures cooler than 41°F (5°C) were more detrimental than temperatures greater than 41°F (5°C); flowering percentage generally decreased when temperatures below 41°F (5°C) were used and flower scape height increased at temperatures above 41°F (5°C).

Two turns of a portion of the cooler space can be obtained by holding all or part of the bulbs intended for post–Valentine's Day sales cold and dry. As bulbs for January and Valentine's Day crops are pulled from the cooler, the cooler can be immediately refilled with potted bulbs for later forcing schedules. All bulbs must be potted by the end of January. Although the optimum temperature used was 41°F (5°C), the temperature can be lowered, especially with the later forcing schedules, if excessive shoot or root growth is noted in the cooler.

INSECTS

During forcing, aphids and thrips may become a problem. The latter will only become obvious when plants are in full flower in the home environment.

DISEASES

A variety of diseases are encountered in the forcing process. Always dissect and inspect bulbs on arrival and keep bulbs well vented. Bacterial bulb rot, *Xanthomonas hyacinthi* and *Erwinia carotovora*, can be observed internally and on the bulb surface (Horst, 1990). *Penicillium*, blue mold, can be a serious problem during cold storage. The fungus covers the bulbs and can penetrate and rot the tissue. Rooting rooms must be well vented and bulbs inspected during cooling on a regular basis. *Botrytis* can cause circular blemishes on the florets or foliage if humidity is too high (De Hertogh, 1996; Nowak and Rudnicki, 1993; Post, 1949). Black slime (*Sclerotinia bulborum*) and leaf spot and rot (*Stagonospora*) have also been reported (Dreistadt, 2001). A number of other diseases can occur during bulb production (Nowak and Rudnicki, 1993).

PHYSIOLOGICAL DISORDERS

The papery outer remains of the tunicated scales may result in skin irritation for some people. Moisten bulbs during planting and use gloves and masks to reduce potential skin irritation.

Spitting of the inflorescence is cultivar related and occurs when the flower scape base ruptures at the union with the basal plate. De Hertogh (1996) warned that freezing bulbs may be a cause; rapid water uptake or temperature changes associated with excess moisture may also contribute to the problem. Reduce spitting by allowing media to be on the dry side when moving bulbs to the greenhouse after cooling, slowly increasing the temperature from 50 to 55°F (10 to 13°C) for 2 days to 65 to 70°F (18 to 21°C) for forcing, and by avoiding susceptible cultivars.

Toppling of inflorescence stems should be prevented by using Florel (ethephon) sprays (Shoub and De Hertogh, 1975). Abortion of the uppermost florets is known as *straw-nails* due to the color of the aborted florets. The problem is thought to be due to shipping the bulbs too early at incorrect temperatures or using poorly ventilated storage (Nowak and Rudnicki, 1993).

POSTHARVEST

As soon as the lower florets show color, the plants are only 2 to 4 days from full flower and can be boxed, shipped, or marketed. Plants can be stored for 4 weeks at 32 to 35°F (0 to 2°C) but should be paper sleeved and inspected frequently because *Botrytis* can be destructive.

Advise all customers to keep plants in as high of light as possible and as cool as possible. Advise the homeowner to discard the forced bulbs after flowering. Hyacinth is only slightly sensitive to ethylene (Nell, 1993; Nowak and Rudnicki, 1990).

Cut hyacinth flowers should be marketed when they show color and the basal plate should be attached for maximum water uptake (Swart, 1990). Cash-and-carry customers should be advised to keep the basal plate attached and not recut the stems. Flowers can be stored at 32 to 35°F (0 to 2°C) and the vase life should be 6 to 8 days.

KEY POINTS

- The hyacinth is one of the popular "Dutch bulb" species and is used as a potted flowering plant, cut flower, or garden ornamental.
- Plants are propagated commercially by scoring or scooping of bulbs; naturally occurring bulblets, seed, or tissue culture are possible, but slow and expensive.
- Bulbs for greenhouse forcing must receive a minimum of 9 to 17 weeks of 48°F (9°C) or lower for root and shoot development.
- The initial portion of the cold treatment can be applied to the bulbs either dry and unpotted (known as *prepared*) for early forcing dates or moist and potted (known as *regular*) for later forcing dates.

- The final portion of the cold treatment is always applied to moist, potted bulbs.
- After the cold treatment, plants are moved to the greenhouse and forced.
- The forcing season is divided into six periods; recommended cultivars and forcing schedules vary with the period.
- Height is controlled by Florel (ethephon) sprays, which must be applied quickly after plants are removed from the cooler.
- Spitting is a physiological disorder in which the flower scape separates from the basal plate.
- Potted plants are shipped as soon as the lower florets show color.

BIBLIOGRAPHY

Adriansen, E. 1985. Kemisk vækstregulering, pp. 142–162 in *Potteplanter I—Produktion, Metoder, Midler,* O.V. Christensen, A. Klougart, I.S. Pedersen, and K. Wikesjö, editors. Gartner-INFO, København, Denmark. (in Danish)

Bailey, L.H., and E.Z. Bailey. 1976. *Hyacinthus,* p. 577 in *Hortus Third: A Concise Dictionary of Plants Cultivated in the United States and Canada.* Macmillan, New York.

De Hertogh, A.A. 1996. Cut and pot Hyacinths (*Hyancinthus*), pp. B55–68 in *Holland Bulb Forcer's Guide*, 5th ed. International Flower Bulb Center, Hillegom, The Netherlands.

Dole, J.M. 1996. Spring bulb production: The delayed potting method. *Ohio Florists' Association Bulletin* 806:1, 3–4.

Dreistadt, S.H. 2001. *Integrated Pest Management for Floriculture and Nurseries*. University of California Division of Agriculture and Natural Resources Publication 3402.

Gude, H., and M.H.G.E. Dijkema. 1992. The effects of light quality and cold treatment on the propagation of hyacinth bulbs. *Acta Horticulturae* 325: 157–164.

Horst, R.K. 1990. Hyacinth, p. 687 in *Westcott's Plant Disease Handbook*, 5th ed. Van Nostrand Reinhold, New York.

Huxley, A., M. Griffiths, and M. Levy. 1992. *Hyacinthus*, pp. 604–605 in *The New Royal Horticultural Society Dictionary of Gardening*, vol. 2. Stockton Press, New York.

James, L. 2002. Water works. *FloraCulture International* 12(4):28–34.

Mathew, B. 1973. *Dwarf Bulbs*. B.T. Batsford Limited, London.

Nell, T.A. 1993. *Hyacinthus orientalis*, p. 54 in *Flowering Potted Plants, Prolonging Shelf Performance*. Ball Publishing, Batavia, Illinois.

Nowak, J., and R.M. Rudnicki. 1990. *Postharvest Handling and Storage of Cut Flowers, Florist Greens, and Potted Plants*. Timber Press, Portland, Oregon.

Nowak, J., and R.M. Rudnicki. 1993. *Hyacinthus*, pp. 335–347 in *The Physiology of Flower Bulbs*, A. De Hertogh and M. Le Nard, editors. Elsevier, Amsterdam.

Post, K. 1949. *Hyacinthus orientalis* (Hyacinth), pp. 566–569 in *Florist Crop Production and Marketing*. Orange Judd Publishing, New York.

Rees, A. 1972a. Artificial induction of daughter bulbs, pp. 93–95 in *The Growth of Bulbs*. Academic Press, London and New York.

Rees, A. 1972b. Hyacinth preparation and storage, pp. 134–135 in *The Growth of Bulbs*. Academic Press, London and New York.

Shoub, J., and A.A. De Hertogh. 1975. Floral stalk topple: A disorder of *Hyacinthus orientalis* L. and its control. *HortScience* 10:26–28.

Swart, A. 1990. The effect of basal-plate tissue on the keeping quality of hyacinth cut flowers. *Acta Horticulturae* 266:299–305.

Vreeburg, P.J.M. 1992. Preparation treatment of hyacinth for flowering before Christmas. *Acta Horticulturae* 325:165–173.

Hydrangea

INTRODUCTION

Common names: hydrangea, French hydrangea.

Scientific name: *Hydrangea macrophylla* (Thunb.) Ser. The names *H. hortensis* and *H.* *opuloides* have also been used and are synonyms (Bailey and Bailey, 1976; Huxley et al., 1992; Wallerstein and Rünger, 1985).

Family and related taxa: Hydrangeaceae Dumort. There are 100 species in the genus *Hydrangea*. The ornamental shrubs *Deutzia* and *Philadelphus* are in this family.

Origin: *H. macrophylla* is found in Japan on the Pacific side of Honshu Island (Bailey and Bailey, 1976).

Uses and current status: Most sales occur at Easter and Mother's Day; however, plants could be forced into flower for Valentine's Day or held in storage longer and forced for Memorial Day. Typically, hydrangeas are grown in 6-in. (15-cm) pots and produced from a cutting with two axillary buds and pinched once, resulting in four inflorescences (Fig. II-1 Hydrangea). Plants with one inflorescence are also produced in 4- to 5-in. (10- to 15-cm) pots. Hydrangea is also a common garden ornamental and cut flower. Numerous other hydrangea species are also used as field-grown cut flowers (see Field-Grown Cut Flowers chapter).

H. macrophylla is a woody perennial, growing to 5 ft (1.5 m). Opposite leaves are rounded to

FIGURE II-1 HYDRANGEA Single and multiflowered *Hydrangea* plants.

FIGURE II-2 HYDRANGEA *Hydrangea macrophylla* 'Mariesi Variegata' garden ornamental showing variegated foliage and lacecap inflorescence type.

ovate, toothed, and dark green with a surface luster. Flower colors may be white or various shades of pink, blue, or red. Cultivars are divided into two types: mopheads and lacecaps. With mopheads the terminal inflorescences form a large rounded corymb. The fertile flowers are small, few, and central in the inflorescence. The majority of the inflorescence is sterile and only the large sepals are showy. The lacecaps have a flat inflorescence and a large portion of the inflorescence consists of small, but fertile flowers that do not have large showy sepals and are surrounded by larger sterile flowers with showy sepals (Bailey, 1989a, 1992). The lacecaps are sometimes referred to as *H. macrophylla* var. *normalis*. Mopheads are more commonly used for potted flowering plant production than lacecaps. Some cultivars have variegated leaves and inflorescences (Post, 1949) (Fig. II-2 Hydrangea).

CULTIVARS

There are well over 500 registered varieties. Breeding has occurred mainly in northern Europe (England). The United States is barely acquainted with the numerous exotic types found in Japan. New cultivars and inflorescence forms are continuously being introduced into North America. Miniature cultivars also exist (Vidalie, 1989).

Cultivars are not only grouped by color, but by response group: the number of weeks required to force into flower at 59°F (15°C) nights with 54°F (12°C) for the last 2 weeks of forcing. Bailey (1989a, 1992) compiled an extensive list of commercially available or popular cultivars from many sources.

PROPAGATION

In North America, softwood shoots 5 to 7 in. (13 to 18 cm) long with three or four nodes and a terminal bud are available from propagators in the Pacific Northwest. These shoots are used to make one single terminal cutting with two subtending opposite leaf pairs and two to three "butterfly" cuttings (a cutting with two opposite leaves and axillary buds). Single-eye cuttings can also be made by cutting or dividing a butterfly cutting into two single leaf-node pieces. Single-eye cuttings are usually weaker, require a longer production time, and must be pinched two or more times.

A variety of propagation media can be used; the prerequisite is that the medium must be well aerated and drained during the propagation phase. Mist or fog propagation is used. The medium should be maintained at a temperature of 70 to 74°F (21 to 23°C). Other medium requirements are that it be sterilized and have a pH near 6.0. Rooting hormone (2% IBA) is used. During rooting, shade is used to provide an environment of 2500 to 3000 fc (500 to 600 μmol · m^{-2} · s^{-1}) (Bailey, 1989a; Post, 1949). Rooting occurs within 4 to 5 weeks. Cuttings can be rooted in propagation beds, flats, or directly into 2.25-, 3-, or 4-in. (6-, 8-, or 10-cm) pots. This process begins in April and ends in June. Tissue culture is also possible (Allen and Anderson, 1980; Bailey et al., 1986; Stoltz, 1984).

FLOWERING CONTROL AND DORMANCY

Flowering control during commercial production mimics nature. Spring-rooted vegetative cuttings initiate and develop dormant terminal flower buds by fall under naturally shortening days and cooler temperatures. Plants are defoliated and placed in cold storage and eventually forced into flower in a warm springlike environment. A prerequisite for floral initiation is that a critical vegetative leaf mass must be present to provide adequate photosynthates. For summer growth, plants thrive under moderate night temperatures of 65°F (18°C) and 14-hr photoperiods and are often grown outdoors. Plants can be harmed by several days of 86°F (30°C) or higher temperatures (see Physiological Disorders section later).

Under flower inductive conditions, the apical bud becomes reproductive first, and axillary buds become reproductive later. With night temperatures of 55 to 65°F (13 to 18°C), induction commences regardless of photoperiod (Litlere and Strømme, 1975; Peters, 1975). However, even under 14 hr of light at temperatures between 66 and 70°F (19 and 21°C), floral induction eventually will occur. Above 70°F (21°C) induction is inhibited. A continuous 24-hr photoperiod is also inhibitory. Above 80°F (27°C) night temperature, no flower induction occurs (Bailey and Weiler, 1984).

When temperatures fall below 65°F (18°C) and days become shorter, the plant exhibits no apparent growth. However, development within the apical bud is continuing; microscopic vegetative and reproductive structures will be present. Plants require at least 6 weeks below 65°F (18°C) with leaves present and another 6 weeks of cold storage with the leaves removed before they can be forced (Post, 1949). Leaves are required for flower initiation during the vegetative growth period because the removal of six-leaf pairs prevented flower initiation (Yeh and Chiang, 2001).

Prior to actual flower differentiation, internode elongation slows and ceases, and leaves stop reflexing and commence clasping the apical bud. Leaves within the bud continue to be initiated for another 3 to 4 weeks. The first buds are visible microscopically 2 to 3 weeks after the start of flower induction. Seven leaf pairs will be below the inflorescence. An 8-hr photoperiod results in rapid flower induction, initiation, and development at night temperatures below 65°F (18°C). Prior to defoliation and cold storage, perfect inflorescences with stigmas must have reached G-stage, in that the stigmatic surface must be well indented on all inflorescences (Shanks and Link, 1951; Struckmeyer, 1950). Further floral differ-

entiation and development continue during cold storage.

Plants are moved into dark storage areas. Natural leaf abscission in the dark is aided by using 2-butyne-1,4-diol (7500 to 12,500 ppm) sprays, ethylene (1:1000 ethylene:air, by volume), or ripening apples (1 bu/400 ft³) as a source of ethylene. Application of ethylene gas at 5 ppb for 7 days was effective in defoliating most cultivars (Blom and Smith, 1994). Florel (ethephon) sprays can be used on a trial basis (Blom and Smith, 1994). Vapam and gibberellic acid (GA₃) have also been used (Bailey, 1989a; Shanks, 1985). Defoliation and leaf removal are a major nuisance, but must be done because *Botrytis* will rot the flower buds during cold storage if leaves are not removed (Bailey, 1989a; Shanks, 1985).

The minimum cold treatment is 40 to 45°F (4 to 7°C) for 6 weeks, or 8 weeks at 52°F (11°C). For long-term storage for late forcing production schedules, use 33 to 35°F (0.5 to 2°C) (Shanks, 1985). After cold treatments have been completed, plants can be forced at 60 to 62°F (16 to 17°C). Experimentally, cold treatments can be replaced by using long days (16 hr or longer) or multiple GA₃ sprays (1 to 50 ppm) (Bailey and Weiler, 1984; Shanks, 1985). Hamrick (2003) recommended one or more 2 to 6 ppm GA sprays; if multiple sprays are required, they are applied weekly. Stuart and Cathey (1962) stated that best quality resulted when plants were defoliated and cold treated for 4 weeks followed by two weekly GA₃ sprays (10 ppm). Defoliation is not practiced when LDs are used to stimulate development and flowering after floral initiation.

TEMPERATURE

Dormant budded plants that are ready to be forced can be purchased. Up to this time, plants have been grown in 4-in. (10-cm) pots and are ready to be repotted into 6-in. (15-cm) pots. Two to 3 weeks are required before new root and shoot growth are evident in the forcing greenhouse. A medium temperature of 60 to 62°F (16 to 17°C) supplied by bottom heat and an air temperature of 58°F (14°C) will allow root growth before shoot growth starts (Bailey, 1997).

Forcing temperatures can be increased or decreased above the recommended 60 to 62°F (16 to 17°C) night temperatures to hasten or slow development. The number of weeks to flower at any given temperature varies with the cultivar. Excessively high forcing temperatures will produce small plants and inflorescences, pale color, and poor quality. It is wise to lower the temperature to 54°F (12°C) for 1 to 2 weeks prior to marketing for enhanced pigment coloration and increased postharvest longevity (Bailey, 1989a; Post, 1949).

In the hydrangea Honshu native site, the mean January low is 31°F (20.6°C) and the August high is 85°F (29°C). Plants should not experience severe frosts or freezing for fear of flower bud damage. Plants survive as far north as Zone 7, but flower buds are killed in some years of severe cold temperatures. However, recently a new *H. macrophylla* cultivar was released that requires no vernalization, flowers continuously under LD, and is cold hardy to Zone 4 (Weiland et al., 2003).

LIGHT

Light intensities increase from propagation at 2500 to 3000 fc (500 to 600 μmol $\cdot$ m^{-2} $\cdot$ s^{-1}) to 3000 to 4000 fc (600 to 800 μmol $\cdot$ m^{-2} $\cdot$ s^{-1}) immediately after rooted cuttings are transplanted to 5000 to 7500 fc (1000 to 1500 μmol $\cdot$ m^{-2} $\cdot$ s^{-1}) during vegetative growth. Shading is normally not used during vegetative growth outdoors in northern latitudes (42° and north). In more southerly latitudes, light intensity can be reduced up to 50%. During forcing, full light intensity is preferred until the inflorescences begin to open, then shade to prevent burning and pigment bleaching. Day temperature control may be lost, so shade may also be required for late spring forcing schedules.

WATER

Water loss or stress is a constant concern during hydrangea production and forcing. Hydrangea stomates are reported to never close and with the large leaf surface, abundant amounts of water are required. Marginal leaf and flower necrosis easily occurs if stressed. For this reason, shading is used to reduce temperature and transpiration at high temperatures.

However, excess water is not conducive for good root development and roots must have adequate aeration. This is particularly critical during the time span after the dormant 4-in. (10-cm) liners are shifted into 6-in. (15-cm) pots and forcing commences. Do not overwater, which is particularly common prior to the start of new root and shoot growth.

Automated irrigation systems must be used during the vegetative and forcing period to reduce labor and to ensure rapid irrigation when required. Water quality is a great concern because of the exact pH requirements for proper flower color (see Nutrition, below).

CARBON DIOXIDE

Growth during the vegetative phase most frequently is outdoors and CO_2 cannot be used. When forced under protection, 1500 ppm CO_2 will enhance growth.

NUTRITION

Ample nutrition is required after propagation as cuttings begin to root into the medium. Hydrangea fertilizer regimes of 60 to 100 ppm N are used up to flower initiation. During forcing or after dormancy is broken and new root activity has commenced, 100 to 150 ppm N is adequate. Numerous nutritional regimes are possible (Bailey, 1989a).

Controlling pH is essential to obtain the correct flower color. The appropriate pH must be maintained during both the summer vegetative phase and the subsequent forcing phase of the flowering plant. If the pH regimes for pink or blue inflorescences are switched during forcing, a muddy, purplish color develops due to a residual effect from the vegetative stage in the floral tissue.

The pH is not actually the cause of pink or blue inflorescences, but a low 5.5 pH influences the availability of specific metal ions such as aluminum. When aluminum forms a complex with delphinidin-3-glucoside pigment in the sepals, deep blue inflorescences are produced. If no aluminum is present, the pigment remains pink. Phosphorus is in competition with aluminum, so low-phosphorus fertilizers and no phosphoric acid injection must be used in the production of blue hydrangea cultivars (Okada and Okawa, 1974). To ensure adequate supply of aluminum and to maintain an acidic medium pH of 5.2 to 5.5, aluminum sulfate at 10 to 15 lb/100 gal (12 to 18 g $\cdot$ L^{-1}) is used every 10 to 14 days during forcing. The opposite is true with pink cultivars; superphosphate and ample levels of phosphorus are used and a pH of 6.0 to 6.2 is maintained. Aluminum sulfate is normally applied to blue cultivars one or two times during the summer and at least three times during forcing. However, if plants were not treated with aluminum prior to forcing, aluminum sulfate must be applied within the first 5 weeks of forcing to produce adequate blue color (Blom and Piott, 1992). Apply 12 to

TABLE II-1 HYDRANGEA

A summary of various factors that contribute to the development of deep blue or pink-red pigment in *Hydrangea* flowers.

Contributing Factor	Pigment Color	
	Pink-Red	Blue
pH	6.0–6.2	5.5
Al(SO$_4$)$_3$	None	Use
Fertilizer	25–10–10	25–5–30
P	High	Very low
K	Low	High
Mo	Low	High

16 g aluminum sulfate/pot using subirrigation or more than 20 g/pot using overhead irrigation in four weekly applications. Cultivars that are pink-blue can be either deep blue or pink according to the pH. Pink to red pigment formation can be manipulated if the pH is 6.0 or higher (Asen et al., 1957, 1960, 1963). Other factors essential for good color development are listed in Table II-1 Hydrangea.

Nutrition is also important in shoot and leaf development. Foliar nutrient levels for high-quality plants are listed in Chapter 6, Nutrition, Table 6-4. Nutrient deficiency symptoms have been well documented (Bailey and Hammer, 1988). Good leaf development is essential for flower initiation and development. Roots are sensitive to high salt stress (Ray, 1946; Shanks and Link, 1951).

MEDIA

Plants can be propagated, grown, and forced into flower using a wide variety of media formulated from various components of sand, peat moss, vermiculite, perlite, bark, and soil. For blue flowering cultivars, superphosphate must not be added to the medium and phosphoric acid must not be used to alter pH of the water. The medium should be pasteurized, have an adequate water-holding capacity, but be well drained and aerated. When transplanting dormant plants, slit the bottom of the root ball in an X about one-third of the way up from the bottom (Bailey, 1997). Split open the sections when planting to ensure good contact with the medium in the pot.

HEIGHT CONTROL

Height control is required during both the vegetative and the reproductive forcing phases. A dormant liner with short internodes is required prior to forcing. Final height control will be difficult to achieve if height is not properly controlled earlier in the previous summer. Producers of liners should inform forcers of the plant growth regulator treatments applied because they may have a residual effect (Bailey and Clark, 1992). One to two sprays of B-Nine (daminozide), depending on the cultivar, are used during the vegetative phase at 5000 to 7500 ppm. Two spray applications of 62 ppm Sumagic (uniconazole) are also effective (Bailey and Clark, 1992).

During forcing, two spray applications of B-Nine at 2500 to 5000 ppm are typically used; the first application is made when three to five leaf pairs have begun to unfold (Bailey, 1997). Additional applications can be made as needed. The last application should be before flower buds reach 0.75 in. (2 cm) in size or the flower head will be small. Sumagic can also be used but apply carefully because two 10-ppm sprays caused excessive stunting (Bailey, 1989b).

Other growth retardants can also be used: A-Rest (ancymidol) drenches at 0.25 mg a.i. (2 ppm)/6-in. (15-cm) pot, Topflor (flurprimidol) sprays at 100 to 200 ppm, and Bonzi (paclobutrazol) (Bailey, 1989a; SePro, personal communication; Wilkinson and Hanger, 1992). Cycocel (chlormequat) was effective when applied at 0.3 to 1.6 g a.i./pot but not as a 2000- to 4000-ppm spray (Bailey, 1989a; Kohl and Nelson, 1966).

SPACING

During the vegetative phase, plants can be grown in 4- or 6-in. (10- or 15-cm) pots, which are spaced on 8-in. (20-cm) centers. Plants are pot-to-pot during defoliation. During forcing, the plants with one single stem or three to four inflorescences in a 6-in. (15-cm) pot are commonly spaced on 10-in. (25-cm) or 14-in. (36-cm) centers, respectively.

PINCHING AND DISBUDDING

Butterfly cuttings have one pair of axillary buds. After rooting, these buds break dormancy and, when three nodes have developed, they are pinched, leaving two nodes for a total of four axillary buds. Hopefully, these four buds will break dormancy and will be the site of three to four terminal flower buds. Typically, terminal cuttings are sheared back to allow three leaf pairs (six buds) to remain, which produce premium quality plants with five to six inflorescences. The dates for the last pinch are critical. Sixty days must elapse to produce adequate time for growth prior to temperatures falling below an average of 60°F (16°C) and day lengths shortening for flower induction. At least two fully mature leaves are required on each shoot to ensure flower bud formation. The date for the last pinch is July 1 to 15 in North America (Post, 1949). Bailey (1989a) stated that July 5 was the last date of pinch to ensure adequate time for shoot growth. Annual variation in summer and fall irradiance and temperature can be a concern because these control plant quality, growth rate, date of floral induction, and percentage of shoots that form inflorescences. Thus, selecting the correct pinch date is critical. Weak shoots are removed during the summer or during forcing. Only vigorous shoots are allowed to develop. Do not use weak shoots for future propagation stock. No disbudding is required during forcing.

SUPPORT

Unfortunately, staking and tying with string may be required because of the large inflorescence size, even with the proper use of plant growth regulators.

SCHEDULE AND TIMING

After propagation, plants in 4-in. (10-cm) pots are plunged into ground beds outdoors. If growing in areas where temperatures frequently fall below 65°F (18°C), premature budding may occur and production should be done in greenhouses.

The first pinch is 2 to 3 weeks after cuttings have become established (Table II-2 Hydrangea). Schedule and timing are based on type of cutting (terminal, butterfly, or single eye), date of propagation, and date of pinching. These three factors are under the control of the producer and are in turn based on market demand regarding the desired number of inflorescences per plant and size of pot being produced for sale. Cultivars also vary in vigor and appropriate pot size required for their culture.

Many growers bypass propagation and purchase dormant plants in 4- to 6-in. (10- to 15-cm) pots or bare root plants. Dormant plants in 4-in. (10-cm) pots are repotted into 6-in. (15-cm) pots.

Schedules are further complicated by the type of dormancy release treatments used: the traditional 6 weeks of cold or LD photoperiods along with GA_3. An alternative method is to root budded terminal cuttings in 3-in. (8-cm) pots in mid-October and force these single-stem plants in 5-in. (12-cm) pots as a single specimen or combined in various numbers in larger pots (see Table II-3 Hydrangea). After cold treatments, the rate of flower bud development is highly dependent on night temperatures, production method, and forcing date (Table II-4 Hydrangea). Days to force can vary from as little as 88 days for 'Merritt's Supreme' to 103 days for 'Rose Supreme' (Bailey, 1992; Litlere and Strømme, 1975). Note also that the higher the light level, the more rapid the development at any one temperature (Mortensen et al., 1995).

INSECTS

Aphids, spider mites, whiteflies, snails, and slugs may be problems. Constant surveillance is required. During greenhouse forcing, practice biological control before using chemical control (Bailey, 1989a; Post, 1949).

DISEASES

Powdery mildew (*Ersiphe polygoni*) on leaves is the major problem on outdoor vegetative growth (Bailey, 1989a; Horst, 1990). *Botrytis* during propagation and cold storage is also a concern. Botrytis during forcing can ruin inflorescences if humidity control and air circulation are not practiced.

Virus contamination and selecting of clean stock are issues for the supplier of

TABLE II-2 HYDRANGEA

Sample production schedule from propagation of cuttings to flowering of *Hydrangea* for April I (Easter).

Cultural Step	Production Time (weeks)	Temperature °F (°C)	Photoperiod
Propagation by cuttings			
	3–4	70 (21)	LD
Pot into 4-in. (10-cm) pots			
	6+	65 (18)	LD
Pinch by July 1 to 15			
	4–8	65 (18)	LD
Plant growth regulator			
	3–5	65 (18)	Natural day
Flower induction starts Sept. 1			
	6	65 (18)	SD
Defoliate Oct. 15			
	6	Below 40–45 (4–7)	Dark
Forcing starts Dec. 20–31			
	2–3	60–65 (16–18)	Natural or LD
Apply growth regulator, Jan. 7			
	2–3	60–65 (16–18)	Natural or LD
Apply growth regulator, Jan. 15			
	1	60–65 (16–18)	Natural or LD
Visible buds May 1			
	6	60–65 (16–18)	Natural or LD
Lower temperature			
	2	54–60 (12–16)	Natural or LD
Flower Apr. 1			
Total	41+		

unrooted cuttings because a number of viruses can occur. Obviously infected plants should be discarded during production and forcing. Leaf spots (*Cercospora arborescentis, C. hydrangeae, Phyllosticta hydrangeae,* and *Septoria hydrangeae*) can also occur on outdoor grown plants. Other diseases recorded include root and stem rot (*Pythium* and *Rhizoctonia solani*), southern blight (*Sclerotium rolfsii*), armillaria root rot (*Armillaria mellea*), rust (*Pucciniastrum hydrangeae*), and tomato spotted wilt virus (Dreistadt, 2001).

PHYSIOLOGICAL DISORDERS

Weak shoots with or without a flower bud are considered to be the result of insufficient irradiance by overcrowding during the summer. Premature budding in late summer and fall results in small flower heads due to inadequate photosynthate/leaf numbers. Total failure to form flower buds can be attributed to temperatures too warm for floral initiation and development, defoliation by mildew or other causes

prior to flower formation, or insufficient time for vegetative growth prior to floral induction because of late pinching.

Insufficient cooling (duration or correct temperature) or premature cooling prior to development of G-stage results in slow forcing and an inflorescence that is not morphologically correct and will not form the proper pigment (Bailey and Hammer, 1990; Post, 1949). Various viruses also result in abnormal flower and pigment coloration. Foliar malformations can also occur during the summer; the leaves are thickened, leathery, puckered, straplike, and occasionally mottled (Bailey and Hammer, 1988). These malformations are not due to nutrient deficiencies but occur when temperatures are 91/82°F (31/28°C) or greater (Bailey and Hammer, 1989). High light levels of 2500 fc (500 μmol $\cdot$ m^{-2} $\cdot$ s^{-1}) accentuate the malformations and some cultivars are not susceptible to the problem.

Occasionally the roots of dormant plants do not grow out into the new media when repotted, resulting in stunted, poor quality

TABLE II-3 HYDRANGEA

Experimental *Hydrangea* production schedule for late May flowering using cuttings from reproductive plants.

Cultural Step	Production Time (weeks)	Temperature °F (°C)	Photoperiod
Propagation by cuttings in 3-in. (8-cm) pots on Oct. 15			
	4	65 (18)	Natural day
Establish plants on Nov. 15			
	2	60–65 (16–18)	Natural day
Lower temperature			
	4	50 (10)	Natural day
Defoliate			
	6	40–45 (4–7)	Dark
Forcing starts			
	2	60–65 (16–18)	Natural to LD
Pot three plants per 6-in. (15-cm) pot			
	2	60–65 (16–18)	Natural to LD
Apply growth regulator, if needed			
	2	60–65 (16–18)	Natural to LD
Visible buds			
	6	60–65 (16–18)	Natural to LD
Lower temperature			
	2	54–60 (12–16)	Natural to LD
Flower			
Total	30+		

TABLE II-4 HYDRANGEA

Influence of various night temperatures on the rate of flower bud development from the transplanting of a dormant *Hydrangea* plant into a 6-in. (15-cm) pot to flowering.

Development Stage	Night Temperature °F(°C)		
	54 (12)	60 (16)	66 (19)
	Weeks to Flower		
Transplant to flower	16	12	10
Transplant to visible bud	6	4	3
Flower diameter in. (cm):			
0.19 (0.5) (pea size) to flower	10	8	7
1.19 (2.0) (nickel size) to flower	7.5	6	5
1.56 (4.0) (silver dollar size) to flower	5	4	3
First pigment evident to flower[a]	2.6	2.6	2.6

[a]Lower temperature to 54°F (12°C), if possible, to intensify color.

plants. The problem is especially common during early forcing and in the north (Hamrick, 2003). Avoid the problem by cutting the root ball (see Media section), using a media with low nutrient content, and if using microtube irrigation, placing the emitter directly over the original media ball. If the problem has already occurred, a gibberellic acid (GA) spray of 5 ppm can be applied when the inflorescences are less than 0.75 in. (2 cm) wide (Dahlstrom and Watt, personal communication). Later application will cause the inflorescences to be open and unsalable. Occasionally a second application may be helpful.

A variety of other problems can occur. Various insects can injure immature leaves and buds and can cause malformed leaves. Nutrient deficiencies can occur at a pH below 5.2 or above 6.5. Pigmentation that is not appropriate for the cultivar is the result of inappropriate pH not being maintained throughout the production and forcing. In addition, hydrangeas are especially prone to phytotoxicity from pesticide applications.

POSTHARVEST

Postharvest longevity is excellent, lasting up to a month. Ship at 3°F (2°C) when plants have reached maximum coloration. Retailers and customers must be informed regarding the high demand for water. Keep plants in a well-lighted environment at the market and home environments at 250 fc (50 μmol · m^{-2} · s^{-1}) (Nell, 1993). Inflorescence color frequently fades to green with time in the postharvest environment. Reduce fertilization by half when color begins to show on inflorescenses.

KEY POINTS

- Hydrangea is used as a potted flowering plant, cut flower, and garden ornamental.
- Plants are propagated by terminal, double-eye (butterfly), or single-eye cuttings.
- Floral initiation and development occur when temperatures fall below 65°F (18°C) and day lengths shorten.
- At least 6 weeks of 65°F (18°C) or lower and high light are required for a properly mature inflorescence to form.
- After the inflorescence is mature, at least 6 weeks of cold at 40 to 45°F (4 to 7°C) is commonly used to break dormancy and allow rapid flowering.
- The leaves are typically removed prior to cold storage to prevent *Botrytis* rot.
- pH controls the pigment color of the bracts by controlling the availability of aluminum (Al) ions.

- Acidic pH (5.5) and high aluminum (Al) levels result in blue flowers, while a higher pH (6.2 to 6.5) and no Al results in pink and red flowers.
- Low-phosphorus (P) levels are used in producing blue hydrangeas because P competes with Al for binding sites in the medium and Al is less available.
- If exact cultural requirements for the colors are not followed, a muddy, purplish color will result.
- If using dormant plants, slit the bottom of the root ball in an X about one-third of the way up from the bottom when transplanting.
- Weak shoots with or without a flower bud can result from low light levels during the previous summer and fall or from crowding.
- Postharvest life for the consumer can be long if plants are kept well watered.

BIBLIOGRAPHY

Allen, T.C., and W.C. Anderson. 1980. Production of virus-free ornamental plants in tissue culture. *Acta Horticulturae* 110:245–251.

Asen, S., N.W. Siegelman, and N.W. Stuart. 1957. Anthocyanin and other phenolic compounds in red and blue sepals of *Hydrangea macrophylla* var. Merveille. *Proceedings of the American Society for Horticultural Science* 69:561–569.

Asen, S., N.W. Stuart, and A.W. Specht. 1960. Color of *Hydrangea macrophylla* sepals as influenced by the carry-over effects from summer applications of nitrogen, phosphorous, and potassium. *Proceedings of the American Society for Horticultural Science* 76:631–636.

Asen, S., N.W. Stuart, and E.L. Cox. 1963. Sepal color of *Hydrangea macrophylla* as influenced by

the source of nitrogen available to plants. *Proceedings of the American Society for Horticultural Science* 82:504–507.

Bailey, D.A. 1989a. *Hydrangea Production*. Timber Press, Portland, Oregon.

Bailey, D.A. 1989b. Uniconazole effects on forcing of florists' hydrangeas. *HortScience* 24:518.

Bailey, D.A. 1992. *Hydrangea*, pp. 365–383 in *Introduction to Floriculture*, R.A. Larson, editor. Academic Press, San Diego, California.

Bailey, D.A. 1997. Commercial hydrangea forcing. *Bedding Plants International News* 28(10):1, 6–8.

Bailey, L.H., and E.Z. Bailey. 1976. *Hydrangea*, pp. 578–579 in *Hortus Third: A Concise Dictionary of Plants Cultivated in the United States and Canada*. Macmillan, New York.

Bailey, D.A., and B. Clark. 1992. Summer applications of plant growth retardants affect spring forcing of hydrangeas. *HortTechnology* 2:213–216.

Bailey, D.A., and P.A. Hammer. 1988. Evaluation of nutrient deficiency and micronutrient toxicity symptoms in florists' hydrangea. *Journal of the American Society for Horticultural Science* 113:363–367.

Bailey, D.A., and P.A. Hammer. 1989. Stimulation of "hydrangea distortion" through environmental manipulations. *Journal of the American Society for Horticultural Science* 114:411–416.

Bailey, D.A., and P.A. Hammer. 1990. Possible nonpathogenic origin of hydrangea distortion. *HortScience* 25:808.

Bailey, D.A., and T.C. Weiler. 1984. Control of floral initiation in florists' hydrangea. *Journal of the American Society for Horticultural Science* 109:785–791.

Bailey, D.A., G.R. Seckinger, and P.A. Hammer. 1986. *In vitro* propagation of florists' hydrangea. *HortScience* 21:256–257.

Blom, T.J., and B.D. Piott. 1992. Florists' hydrangea blueing with aluminum sulfate applications during forcing. *HortScience* 27:1084–1087.

Blom, T.J., and R.B. Smith. 1994. Ethylene gas for defoliation of hydrangeas. *HortScience* 29:636–637.

Dreistadt, S.H. 2001. *Integrated Pest Management for Floriculture and Nurseries.* University of California Division of Agriculture and Natural Resources Publication 3402.

Hamrick, D. 2003. *Hydrangea,* pp. 442–449 in *Ball Redbook,* vol. 2, 17th ed. Ball Publishing, Batavia, Illinois.

Horst, R.K. 1990. Hydrangea, p. 688 in *Westcott's Plant Disease Handbook,* 5th ed. Van Nostrand Reinhold, New York.

Huxley, A., M. Griffiths, and M. Levy. 1992. *Hydrangea,* pp. 606–611 in *The New Royal Horticultural Society Dictionary of Gardening,* vol. 2. Stockton Press, New York.

Kohl, H.C., Jr., and R.L. Nelson. 1966. *California Agriculture* 20(2):5.

Litlere, B., and E. Strømme. 1975. The influence of temperature, day length, and light intensity on flowering of *Hydrangea macrophylla* Thumb. Ser. *Acta Horticulturae* 51:285–298.

Mortensen, L.M., E. Braut, and R.L. Rosland. 1995. Lys og temperatur til hortensia. *Gartneryrket* 17:15–16.

Nell, T.A. 1993. *Hydrangea,* pp. 55–56 in *Flowering Potted Plants, Prolonging Shelf Performance.* Ball Publishing, Batavia, Illinois.

Okada, M., and K. Okawa. 1974. The quantity of aluminum and phosphorus in plants and its influence on the sepal color of *Hydrangea macrophylla* DC. *Journal of the Japanese Society for Horticultural Science* 42:361–370.

Peters, J. 1975. Flower formation in some cultivars of *Hydrangea macrophylla.* *Gartenbauwissenschaft* 40:63–65. (in German)

Post, K. 1949. *Hydrangea macrophylla* (Hydrangea), pp. 569–580 in *Florist Crop Production and Marketing.* Orange Judd Publishing, New York.

Ray, S. 1946. Reduction of blindness in hydrangeas. *Proceedings of the American Society for Horticultural Science* 47:501–502.

Shanks, J. 1985. *Hydrangea,* pp. 535–558 in *Ball Redbook,* 14th ed., V. Ball, editor. Reston Press, Reston, Virginia.

Shanks, J.B., and C.B. Link. 1951. Effect of temperature and photoperiod on growth and flower formation in hydrangeas. *Proceedings of the American Society for Horticultural Science* 58:357–366.

Stoltz, L.P. 1984. *In vitro* propagation and growth of hydrangea. *HortScience* 19:717–719.

Struckmeyer, B.E. 1950. Blossom bud induction and differentiation in *Hydrangea. Proceedings of the American Society for Horticultural Science* 56:410–414.

Stuart, N.W., and H.M. Cathey. 1962. Control of growth and flowering of *Chrysanthemum morifolium* and *Hydrangea macrophylla* by gibberellin. *Proceedings of the International Horticulture Congress* 15(2):391–399.

Vidalie, H. 1989. Behaviour of miniature *Hydrangea macrophylla* (quality and duration of forcing) after various cold treatments before forcing. *Acta Horticulturae* 261:355–358.

Wallerstein, I., and W. Rünger. 1985. *Hydrangea macrophylla,* pp. 173–177 in *Handbook of Flowering,* vol. III, A.H. Halevy, editor. CRC Press, Boca Raton, Florida.

Weiland, J., N. Anderson, W. Gagne, E. Janiga, and M.J. Rosenow. 2003. Comparative forcing of *Hydrangea macrophylla* 'Endless Summer' as a florist's hydrangea. *HortScience* 38:721. (Abstract)

Wilkinson, R.E., and B. Hanger. 1992. Paclobutrazol in hydroponic solution advance inflorescence development of hydrangea 'Merritt's Supreme.' *HortScience* 27:1195–1196.

Yeh, D.M., and H.H. Chiang. 2001. Growth and flower initiation in hydrangea as affected by root restriction and defoliation. *Scientia Horticulturea* 91:123–132.

Impatiens, Bedding

FIGURE II-1 IMPATIENS, BEDDING *Impatiens* 'Fiesta Olé Frost' hanging baskets.

INTRODUCTION

Common names: bedding impatiens, patience plant, sultana impatiens.

Scientific name: *Impatiens walleriana* Hook. f. (Huxley et al., 1992).

Family and related taxa: Balsaminaceae A. Rich. The genus *Impatiens* has approximately 8500 species. Two other species commonly seen in horticulture are *I. hawkeri* Bull., the progenitor of the wonderful New Guinea impatiens, and *I. balsamina* L., whose seed outwardly explode when the fruit is touched (Bailey and Bailey, 1976; Cathey, 1995). *I. balsamina* is a summer annual, native to the tropical latitudes of China, India, and the Malay Peninsula and commonly called rose balsam or garden balsam. *I. balsamina* is not discussed in this text and *I. hawkeri*, the New Guinea impatiens, is discussed in the next chapter, page 613.

Origin: *I. walleriana* is a succulent perennial herb native from Mozambique to Tanzania on the east coast of equatorial Africa.

Uses and current status: Along with geraniums, the bedding impatiens is the most important bedding plant in North America (Voigt, 1994). Bedding impatiens cultivars are sexually propagated except for the variegated-leafed and many of the double-flowered types, which are cutting propagated. Plants thrive in open locations to almost deep shade and plants can be grown in beds, pots, or hanging baskets (Fig. II-1 Impatiens, Bedding).

CULTIVARS

Hundreds of cultivars are available from numerous international seed companies. Colors in-

FIGURE II-2 IMPATIENS, BEDDING Double-flowered *Impatiens* bedding plant.

clude white, pink, rose, scarlet, and violet and all possible shades in between (Fig. II-2 Impatiens, Bedding). There are flowers with white markings and darker flecks and those whose margins are darker in color than the center (picotee). Disease-resistant cultivars developed via transgenic production may be available in the future (Knapp and Brand, 2003).

PROPAGATION

There are on average 50,000 seed/oz (1760/g). If seeds are stored, hold at approximately 40°F (4°C) and low, 25 to 30%, humidity (Corr, 1997). Keep packets unopened until sowing;

seal and return the remaining seeds to low temperatures as soon as possible. Germination is rapid (15 days) with fresh seeds at 70 to 78°F (21 to 26°C). Water may have to be warmed to 78°F (26°C) to ensure proper medium temperature. Germination should be under high-pressure sodium, fluorescent, or incandescent lights. An intensity × duration interaction exists. At 10 fc (2 $\mu mol \cdot m^{-2} \cdot s^{-1}$), 3 continuous days of irradiance are required for 86% germination; at 100 fc (20 $\mu mol \cdot m^{-2} \cdot s^{-1}$), 2 days are required; and at 500 fc (100 $\mu mol \cdot m^{-2} \cdot s^{-1}$), only 1 day is required. Do not light continuously; lighting should stop when the root begins to elongate (Ball, 1991, 1995; Carpenter, 1994; Carpenter et al., 1994; Corr, 1998).

The pH of the germination medium should be 6.0 to 6.5. A well-drained medium with adequate water retention is desired. Most seeds are germinated in plug containers in germination rooms with fog or high humidity. Seeds may be lightly covered with vermiculite to keep them moist but allow light to filter through. Germination is completed within 21 days and the young seedlings are moved into the greenhouse (Kaczperski and Carlson, 1988).

For plug culture the following conditions are used (Ball, 1991):

Stage 1: 75 to 78°F (24 to 26°C), 100% RH, 100 to 400 fc (20 to 80 $\mu mol \cdot m^{-2} \cdot s^{-1}$), no fertilizer

Stage 2: 72 to 75°F (22 to 24°C), 75% RH, 450 to 700 fc (90 to 140 $\mu mol \cdot m^{-2} \cdot s^{-1}$), 50 to 75 ppm N one time/week

Stage 3: 68 to 72°F (20 to 22°C), 1000 to 1500 fc (200 to 300 $\mu mol \cdot m^{-2} \cdot s^{-1}$), 100 to 150 ppm N one time/week

Stage 4: 60 to 62°F (16 to 17°C), fertilize as needed

Slightly higher temperatures may be beneficial during stages 2 and 3: 75 to 77°F (24 to 25°C) for stage 2 and 73 to 75°F (23 to 24°C) for stage 3 when grown at approximately 1500 fc (300 $\mu mol \cdot m^{-2} \cdot s^{-1}$) (Dreesen and Langhans, 1992). Plugs should be ready for marketing or transplanting within 5 to 6 weeks (Ball, 1991).

Double impatiens are propagated by cuttings at a media temperature of 70 to 75°F (21 to 24°C) and 500 to 1000 fc (100 to 200 $\mu mol \cdot m^{-2} \cdot s^{-1}$) (Hamrick, 2003). Root cuttings under mist or humidity chambers. Begin foliar fertilizing at 50 to 75 ppm N once root initials

are visible. Increase fertilizer rate to 100 ppm and then to 200 ppm as roots develop. Cuttings will be ready to transplant after 21 to 25 days.

FLOWERING CONTROL AND DORMANCY

Impatiens is a day-neutral plant. The rate of flowering depends on total irradiance (energy accumulated) at an appropriate temperature. Little research has been conducted on bedding impatiens; Nanda and Sood (1985) reviewed flowering mechanisms.

TEMPERATURE

Greenhouse temperatures are lower than the germination environment. For production, recommended day temperatures are 70 to 75°F (21 to 24°C) and night temperatures are 60 to 65°F (16 to 18°C). Leaf damage can occur if temperatures are too high in combination with high light (Armitage and Vines, 1982; Kaczperski and Carlson, 1988). High temperatures, such as 95/86°F (35/30°C), can produce greater shoot dry weights than lower temperatures but can cause leaf curling, excessive stem elongation, and small, cupped flowers (Lee et al., 1990).

LIGHT

Little or no shade is used during greenhouse production, season dependent. High temperature may reduce growth if too bright. However, internode elongation occurs with too much shade (Kaczperski and Carlson, 1988). Armitage and Vines (1982) compared *Pelargonium* and *Impatiens* CO_2 fixation at similar light intensities. *Impatiens* fixed similar amounts of carbon at low light intensities of 150 fc (30 $\mu mol \cdot m^{-2} \cdot s^{-1}$) as *Pelargonium* did at high irradiance of 2650 fc (530 $\mu mol \cdot m^{-2} \cdot s^{-1}$). Impatiens were more efficient at the low irradiance than at the high level.

WATER

Internode elongation is maximized when plants are kept continually moist. Moderate water stress results in short plants (Kaczperski and Carlson, 1988).

CARBON DIOXIDE

No data were found for supplemental CO_2 injection. Most likely, an enriched CO_2 atmosphere would be a factor for maximized growth.

TABLE II-I IMPATIENS, BEDDING

Nutrient values found in healthy *Impatiens walleriana* leaves (Nelson, 1994).

Dry Weight (%)					ppm		
N	P	K	Ca	Mg	Fe	Mn	B
3.90	0.71	3.47	2.86	0.71	495	56–282	103

NUTRITION

A rate of 100 ppm N is adequate at every second or third irrigation. Excess nitrogen results in long internodes, delayed flowering, and numerous leaves (Kaczperski and Carlson, 1988). However, van Iersel et al. (1998b) obtained the most rapid growth with 336 or 448 ppm N during plug production and 224 to 448 ppm N after transplanting to the final flat. Nitrogen was the primary influence on plant growth indicating the plants can be grown with greatly reduced amounts of K and P (van Iersel et al., 1998a). The NO_3:NH_4 ratio should be 75:25 to 50:50 for maximum growth (Nelson, 1994). Whipker et al. (1998) recommended using 100 ppm N on subirrigated cutting-propagated variegated impatiens.

Plants respond quickly to nutrient applications. Nutrient deficiencies should not occur if routine media and tissue tests are taken and proper foliar nutrient levels maintained (see Table II-1 Impatiens, Bedding). Color photographs of nutritional deficiencies have been published (Nelson and Huang, 1998).

MEDIA

A light, well-drained medium at a pH of 6.0 to 6.2 is desired (Kaczperski and Carlson, 1988). Armitage and Vines (1982) used a 50:50 peat moss and vermiculite medium for their research.

HEIGHT CONTROL

Plant growth regulators are generally not required if plants are not overwatered or overfertilized. However, 5000-ppm B-Nine (daminozide) sprays can be used (Kaczperski and Carlson, 1988). Bonzi (paclobutrazol) is effective at 5 to 18 ppm, but excess concentrations delay flowering. Sprays of Sumagic (uniconazole) are also effective at 5 ppm, Topflor (flurprimidol) at 20 to 60 ppm, and A-Rest (ancymidol) at 10 to 44 ppm (Barrett, 1994; SePRO, personal communication; Whipker, 2003). Plants respond moderately to negative temperature differences (DIF) (Barrett and Erwin, 1994).

Bonzi at 17 ppb and A-Rest at 98 ppb are also effective when applied through subirrigation (Million et al., 1999). This work also highlights the potential effects of contamination from plant growth regulators on subirrigation benches.

Application of Sumagic increased drought stress tolerance but also reduced plant size after transplanting into the landscape (Keever and Foster, 1991). Plants eventually grew out of the Sumagic treatment; plants treated with 10 ppm or less were the same height as untreated plants by 5 to 7 weeks after transplanting.

Plant growth regulators such as Bonzi may also be used on cuttings after rooting to prevent elongation. Application of Bonzi at 30 ppm to the media at sowing could also be used to produce compact plugs (Barrett et al., 1999). During plug production 4 ppm Bonzi or 1 ppm Sumagic can be applied during stage 1, stage 2, or stage 3 (Sawaya, 2001).

SPACING

Seedlings are usually germinated in plug trays or transplanted into a variety of cell pack types, pots, or hanging baskets prior to being sold in garden centers. Bedding flats are spaced flat to flat. In landscape beds, space 8 to 10 in. (20 to 25 cm) apart (Arent and Voigt, 1994).

PINCHING AND DISBUDDING

No pinching or disbudding required. If plants become overgrown in packs, they can be pruned and regrowth is rapid, although plant quality may be reduced. Monthly Florel (ethephon) can be used on double impatiens stock plants to keep plants vegetative and promote branching.

SUPPORT

No support needed.

SCHEDULE AND TIMING

After plants are 5 weeks old, plugs are transplanted into packs (Corr, 1998). An additional 5 weeks are required for plants to reach marketable size (see Table II-2 Impatiens, Bedding). Four weeks may be required later in the spring when day lengths are longer and temperatures are warmer. However, if grown cold for early spring schedules, 7 weeks production time span could result. Hanging baskets and pots will require 2 to 3 additional weeks (Kaczperski and Carlson, 1988).

TABLE II-2 IMPATIENS, BEDDING

Sample production schedule for *Impatiens walleriana* flats from seeding to sales (see Chapter 1, page 28, for description of plug stages).

Cultural Step	Production Time	Temperature	Environment	Comments
Plug stage 1	3–5 days	75–80 (24–27)	Growth room	
Plug stage 2	10 days	72–75 (22–24)	Growth room	50–100 ppm N after 7 days
Plug stage 3	14 days	65–70 (18–21)	Greenhouse	150 ppm N after 14 days
Plug stage 4	7–14 days	60–62 (16–17)	Greenhouse	Fertilize as needed
Total time for plugs:	**5–6 weeks**			
Transplant to flats	5 weeks	65–70 (18–21)	Greenhouse	Feed 100–150 ppm N weekly
Flower				
Total time from seed: 10–11 weeks				

Cuttings of vegetatively propagated plants will be ready to transplant in 3 to 3.5 weeks (Hamrick, 2003). An additional 6 to 8 weeks will be required for a 6-in. (15-cm) pot. Plants can be pinched 1 to 2 weeks after planting, but that will add 1 to 2 weeks to the crop time.

INSECTS

Aphids, spider mites, and thrips can be a problem in production or in the landscape. Proper management and inspections are required (Baker, 1994; Linquist, 1994; Post, 1949). Cyclamen mite injury is sometimes mistaken for a virus infection (Daughtrey and Chase, 1992).

DISEASES

Unfortunately, impatiens, especially vegetatively propagated material, is highly susceptible to impatiens necrotic spot and tomato spotted wilt viruses and exhibits a variety of symptoms (Daughtrey and Chase, 1992). Thrips control is an absolute requirement. A variety of other diseases such as *Rhizoctonia* stem rot and damping-off, *Pseudomonas syringae* leaf spot, and *Botrytis cinerea* on the flowers can occur. Moisture and humidity control are major factors in disease management (Moorman, 1994; Powell, 1994). A number of other diseases have been reported including root and crown rot (*Pythium*), verticillium wilt (*Verticillium dahliae*), black root rot (*Thielaviopsis basicola*), southern wilt (*Sclerotium rolfsii*), leaf spots (*Cercospora Phyllosticta, Ra-*

mularia, or *Septoria*), and soft rot (*Erwinia carotovora*) (Dreistadt, 2001).

PHYSIOLOGICAL DISORDERS

Various seed germination problems can occur, which were reviewed by Ball (1995) and Khademi and Karlovich (1995) who suggested a medium pH of 6.2, low water EC, light provided up to root radical emergence, and 68 to 72°F (20 to 22°C) temperatures for optimum germination. Ethylene can abort meristems (Daughtrey and Chase, 1992). Delayed or inadequate flowering and excessive height are often due to excessive fertilization and/or irrigation.

POSTHARVEST

L. Høyer (personal communication) and Heins et al. (1994) suggested that seedlings can be stored for 6 weeks at 45°F (7°C). Flowering plants should be shipped at 55 to 61°F (13 to 16°C). Ethylene causes flower abscission and 0.3 to 0.5 mM silver thiosulfate (STS) increases postharvest quality (Nowak and Rudnicki, 1990). Doi et al. (1992) reported that under low-light conditions flower retention was increased by 60 to 80% with STS sprays over a 30-day period.

Unfortunately, various materials added to the medium to reduce water loss during the marketing process are of limited value (Blodgett et al., 1995). Large hanging baskets in the summer are difficult to keep sufficiently watered.

KEY POINTS

- Bedding impatiens is one of the most important seeded bedding plants in North America.
- Most cultivars are seed propagated; some variegated-leafed and double-flowered cultivars are cutting propagated.
- Bedding impatiens are day neutral.

- Do not overwater because moderate water stress produces more compact plants and rapid flowering.
- Excessive nitrogen and/or irrigation results in long internodes and delayed flowering.
- Impatiens are highly susceptible to impatiens necrotic spot and tomato spotted wilt viruses.

BIBLIOGRAPHY

Arent, G.L., and M.L. Voigt. 1994. Landscaping, pp. 75–91 in *Bedding Plants IV*, E.J. Holcomb, editor. Ball Publishing, Batavia, Illinois.

Armitage, A.M., and H.M. Vines. 1982. Net photosynthesis, diffusive resistance, and chlorophyll content of shade and sun tolerant plants growth under different light regimes. *HortScience* 17:342–343.

Bailey, L.H., and E.Z. Bailey. 1976. *Impatiens* L., pp. 594–595 in *Hortus Third: A Concise Dictionary of Plants Cultivated in the United States and Canada.* Macmillan, New York.

Baker, J.R. 1994. Insects and mites, pp. 257–271 in *Bedding Plants IV*, E.J. Holcomb, editor. Ball Publishing, Batavia, Illinois.

Ball, V. 1991. Plugs—The way of the 1990s, pp. 137–153 in *Ball Redbook*, 15th ed., V. Ball, editor. Geo. J. Ball Publishing, West Chicago, Illinois.

Ball, V. 1995. Impatiens germination. *GrowerTalks* 58(11):8.

Barrett, J.E. 1994. Chemical growth regulators, pp. 99–105 in *Tips on Growing Bedding Plants*, 3rd ed., H.K. Tayama, T.J. Roll, and M.L. Gaston, editors. Ohio Florists Association, Columbus, Ohio.

Barrett, J.E., and J.E. Erwin. 1994. Height control, pp. 197–213 in *Bedding Plants IV*, E.J. Holcomb, editor. Ball Publishing, Batavia, Illinois.

Barrett, J.E., C.E. Wieland, T.A. Nell, and D.G. Clark. 1999. Early applications of growth regulators to bedding plants. *HortScience* 34:528. (Abstract)

Blodgett, A.M., D.J. Beattie, and J.W. White. 1995. Growth and shelf life of Impatiens in media amended with hydrophyllic polymer and wetting agent. *HortTechnology* 5:38–40.

Carpenter, W.J. 1994. Germination, pp. 10–14 in *Tips on Growing Bedding Plants*, 3rd ed., H.K. Tayama, T.J. Roll, and M.L. Gaston, editors. Ohio Florists' Association, Columbus, Ohio.

Carpenter, W.J., E.R. Ostmark, and J.D. Cornell. 1994. Light governs the germination of *Impatiens wallerana* Hook. f. seed. *HortScience* 29:854–857.

Cathey, H.M. 1995. History of commercialization, pp. 110–120 in *New Guinea Impatiens*, W. Banner, and M. Klopmeyer, editors. Ball Publishing, Batavia, Illinois.

Corr, B. 1997. The ABC's of plug production. *Greenhouse Product News* 7(2):21–23.

Corr, B. 1998. *Impatiens* (bedding plant), pp. 567–575 in *Ball Redbook*, 16th ed., V. Ball, editor. Ball Publishing, Batavia, Illinois.

Daughtrey, M., and A.R. Chase. 1992. *Impatiens*, pp. 125–131 in *Ball Field Guide to Diseases of Greenhouse Ornamentals*. Ball Publishing, Geneva, Illinois.

Doi, M., T. Mizuno, and H. Imanishi. 1992. Postharvest quality of potted *Impatiens walleriana* Hook. f. ex. D. Oliver as influenced by silver thiosulfate applications and light conditions. *Journal of Japanese Society of Horticulture Science* 61:643–649 (in Japanese, English summary)

Dreesen, D.R., and R.W. Langhans. 1992. Temperature effects on growth of impatiens plug seedlings in controlled environments. *Journal of the American Society for Horticultural Science* 117:209–215.

Dreistadt, S.H. 2001. *Integrated Pest Management for Floriculture and Nurseries.* University of California Division of Agriculture and Natural Resources Publication 3402.

Hamrick, D. 2003. *Impatiens*, pp. 461–463 in *Ball Redbook*, vol. 2, 17th ed. Ball Publishing, Batavia, Illinois.

Heins, R.D., N. Lange, T.F. Wallace, Jr., and W. Carlson. 1994. *Cold Storage of Plug Seedlings.* Meister Publishing, Willoughby, Ohio.

Huxley, A., M. Griffiths, and M. Levy. 1992. *Impatiens*, pp. 649–651 in *The New Royal Horticultural Society Dictionary of Gardening*, vol. 2. Stockton Press, New York.

Kaczperski, M.P., and W.H. Carlson. 1988. Production pointers for Impatiens—#1 bedding plant crop. *Bedding Plants Incorporated* 19(1):6–7.

Keever, G.J., and W.J. Foster. 1991. Production and postproduction performance of uniconazole-treated bedding plants. *Journal of Environmental Horticulture* 9:203–206.

Khademi, J., and P. Karlovich. 1995. How can you avoid impatiens tip abortion? *Greenhouse Management and Production* 14(2):32, 37.

Knapp, J.E., and M.H. Brand. 2003. Transgenic production of disease-resistant *Impatiens walleriana*. *HortScience* 38:748.

Lee, W.-S., J.E. Barrett, and T.A. Nell. 1990. High temperature effects on the growth and flowering of *Impatiens walleriana* cultivars. *Acta Horticulturae* 272:121–127.

Linquist, R.K. 1994. Insect management, pp. 117–121 in *Tips on Growing Bedding Plants*, 3rd ed., H.K. Tayama, T.J. Roll, and M.L. Gaston, editors. Ohio Florists' Association, Columbus, Ohio.

Million, J.B., J.E. Barrett, T.A. Nell, and D.G. Clark. 1999. Inhibiting growth of flowering crops with ancymidol and paclobutrazol in subirrigation water. *HortScience* 34:1103–1105.

Moorman, G.W. 1994. Bedding plant diseases, pp. 245–255 in *Bedding Plants IV*, E.J. Holcomb, editor. Ball Publishing, Batavia, Illinois.

Nanda, K.K., and V. Sood. 1985. *Impatiens balsamina*, pp. 187–199 in *Handbook of Flowering*, vol. III, A.H. Halevy, editor. CRC Press, Boca Raton, Florida.

Nelson, P.V. 1994. Fertilization, pp. 151–175 in *Bedding Plants IV*, E.J. Holcomb, editor. Ball Publishing, Batavia, Illinois.

Nelson, P.V., and J.-S. Huang. 1998. Photo guide to plug deficiencies. *GrowerTalks* 62:32–37.

Nowack, J., and R.M. Rudnicki. 1990. *Postharvest Handling and Storage of Cut Flowers, Florist Greens and Potted Plants*. Timber Press, Portland, Oregon.

Post, K. 1949. *Impatiens*, p. 582 in *Florist Crop Production and Marketing*. Orange Judd Publishing, New York.

Powell, C.P. 1994. Disease management, pp. 122–129 in *Tips on Growing Bedding Plants*, 3rd ed., H.K. Tayama, T.J. Roll, and M.L. Gaston, editors. Ohio Florists' Association, Columbus, Ohio.

Sawaya, M. 2001. Plugs, pp. 50–53 in *Tips on Regulating Growth of Floriculture Crops*, M.L. Gaston, L.A. Kunkle, P.S. Konjoian, and M.F. Wilt, editors. Ohio Florists' Association, Columbus, Ohio.

van Iersel, M.W., R.B. Beverly, P.A. Thomas, J.G. Latimer, and H.A. Mills. 1998a. Fertilizer effects on the growth of impatiens, petunia, salvia, and vinca plug seedlings. *HortScience* 33:678–682.

van Iersel, M.W., P.A. Thomas, R.B. Beverly, J.G. Latimer, and H.A. Mills. 1998b. Nutrition affects pre- and posttransplant growth of impatiens and petunia plugs. *HortScience* 33:1014–1018.

Voigt, A.O. 1994. Marketing trends, pp. 17–33 in *Bedding Plants IV*, E.J. Holcomb, editor. Ball Publishing, Batavia, Illinois.

Whipker, B.E. 2003. Growth regulators for floricultural crops, pp. 439–448 in *2003 North Carolina Agricultural Chemicals Manual*, College of Agriculture and Life Science, North Carolina State University, Raleigh.

Whipker, B.E., S.K. Dasoju, M.S. Dosmann, and J.K. Iles. 1998. Effect of fertilizer concentration on growth of variegated and non-variegated double impatiens. *HortScience* 33:466. (Abstract)

Impatiens, New Guinea

INTRODUCTION

Common name: New Guinea impatiens.

Scientific name: *Impatiens hawkeri* Bull. (Huxley et al., 1992).

Family and related taxa: Balsaminaceae A. Rich. The New Guinea impatiens and the bedding impatiens (*Impatiens Walleriana*) constitute an important segment of the world's bedding plant industry. The bedding impatiens is covered in the preceding chapter (see page 608).

Origin: The species involved in the present hybrids are all natives of New Guinea, Java, and the Celebres (Bailey and Bailey, 1976). The impatiens has a fascinating history, documented by Cathey (1995) and others (Arisumi and Cathey, 1976; Armstrong, 1974; Winters, 1973), from when it arrived in Kew Gardens in 1884 to the 1970 collection trip by John Creech, Agricultural Research Service, and Russell Siebert, Longwood Gardens. Internationally, few floriculture crops have had such rapid economic success as the New Guinea impatiens (Larson, 1995) (Fig. II-1 Impatiens, New Guinea).

Uses and current status: New Guinea impatiens can be used in a wide variety of ways. Originally considered a spring bedding plant and a hanging basket, many plants are now

FIGURE II-1 IMPATIENS, NEW GUINEA
Impatiens hawkeri 'Paradise Lilac' potted plant.

sold year-round as potted flowering plants. Breeding and cultivar cutting production and distribution are truly international. Annually, superior new cultivars are released with stunning new colors and increased flower size, foliage variegation, and environmental tolerances (Larson, 1995; Strefeler, 1995; Strefeler and Quené, 1995; Trees, 1995).

CULTIVARS

In 1985 17 cultivars were listed by Christensson; in 1988 Carlson listed 23, and by 1995 more than 90 had been described by Whealy. Annually numerous cultivars are released worldwide from intensive breeding programs. Whealy (1995) divided the various cultivars according to colors: (1) fuchsia; (2) lavender; (3) orange, bicolor orange, dark orange; (4) pink, bicolor pink, hot pink, light pink, medium pink; (5) purple, bicolor purple, blue-toned purple, red-toned purple; (6) bicolor red, cherry red, scarlet red; (7) salmon, dark coral, light salmon; and (8) white, blush white.

Cultivar improvements include disease and insect resistance, drought tolerance, heat tolerance, and high or low irradiance tolerance (Shaw, 1997; Strefeler, 1995; Strefeler and Quené, 1995; Strope and Strefeler, 1997; Whealy, 1995).

PROPAGATION

The primary method of propagation is asexual with specialists supplying unrooted or rooted cuttings in plugs. Seed availability of commercially acceptable cultivars occurred in 1989 and improved cultivars can be expected. Seedlings in plugs are available from specialists.

CUTTINGS

Cuttings are rooted at an air and medium temperature of 68°F (20°C). Leaf turgidity can be maintained under mist, fog, or plastic tunnel tents (clear in the winter, white in the summer). Cuttings comprise one pair of fully expanded leaves, one pair of expanding leaves, and the growing point. Rooting hormones are used. Light levels below 2000 fc (400 μmol · m^{-2} · s^{-1}) are advised. Cuttings can be rooted in plug trays or directly into the final pots. A medium pH of 5.8 to 6.5 is preferred (Mikkelsen, 1995). Callus develops by day 7, roots are visible by days 10 to 12, and a transplantable cutting is ready by weeks 3 to 4.

SEEDS

There are 11,000 to 17,000 seed/oz (400 to 600/g), cultivar dependent. A medium temperature of 78°F (26°C) is required for at least 10 days or after the root radical has emerged (stage 1). Thereafter, temperature can be reduced to 75°F (24°C) and later to 70°F (21°C). Seeds can be directly sown into plug trays and seedlings are ready to transplant in 6 weeks.

Light is critical for rapid and uniform seed germination, as well as high germination percentages. Low light levels of 100 fc (20 μmol · m^{-2} · s^{-1}) are adequate until the first true leaves develop; thereafter use 4000 to 5000 fc (800 to 1000 μmol · m^{-2} · s^{-1}) until seedlings are transplanted.

Moisture during germination can be maintained by fog or mist. Seed can be lightly covered with large-size vermiculite to maintain moisture uniformity and improve germination. Light is capable of filtering through the vermiculite (Corr, 1995). For both cutting and seed propagation, nutrient application can commence when rooted plants can withstand wilting or the cotyledons are fully expanded.

FLOWERING CONTROL AND DORMANCY

Plants are day neutral. Flowering control is based on total light and temperature because these influence total carbohydrates through photosynthesis (Erwin et al., 1992).

TEMPERATURE

Temperature is a major factor influencing the rate of leaf initiation, development and unfolding, and net photosynthesis. At optimal light, temperature controls days to flower, number of flowers, and overall growth. New Guinea impatiens have a very narrow optimum temperature range of 77 to 80°F (25 to 27°C) (Erwin, 1995; Erwin et al., 1992). Growth is inhibited above 80°F (27°C) and below 63°F (17°C). Erwin (1995) stressed leaf temperature as important because it can be 4 to 8°F (2 to 5°C) warmer than the air when plants are in direct light; hence, an air temperature of 75°F (24°C) may be appropriate.

LIGHT

Light intensity below 3000 fc (600 $\mu mol \cdot m^{-2} \cdot s^{-1}$) results in increased internode elongation and increased days to flower. Intensities above 5000 fc (1000 $\mu mol \cdot m^{-2} \cdot s^{-1}$) can result in reduced growth (Erwin et al., 1992). Erwin (1995) reviewed the influence of light quality and stressed the importance of adequate spacing as overlapping leaves filter out red light, decrease branching, and increase internode lengths due to the accentuated levels of far-red light.

WATER

Once established, New Guinea impatiens transpire large quantities of water, which can be related to their large leaf canopy mass and warm production temperatures. One breeding objective is to increase drought tolerance (Hartley, 1995; Strefeler, 1995). On the other hand, overwatering newly transplanted plugs can have serious consequences before new roots adequately develop. Roots form better in moist than wet medium.

Plants can be irrigated by a variety of methods including microtube, capillary mat, or ebb-and-flow (Hartley, 1995). Plants kept constantly moist may be large, vigorous, slow to flower, and not well adapted to the marketing channels or the homeowner's environment. Consequently, plants should be grown on the dry side, but not routinely stressed because leaf abscission or marginal burning could occur (Carlson, 1988; Carlson and Klien, 1985; Mikkelsen Inc., 1989).

CARBON DIOXIDE

During the winter when vents are closed, a concentration of 1000 ppm CO_2 results in superior plants compared with plants without supplemental CO_2 (Christensson, 1985; Mikkelsen Inc., 1989). Carlson and Klien (1985) stated that 1500 to 2000 ppm CO_2 was appropriate and temperatures should be increased by 5 to 10°F (3 to 6°C) if CO_2 is used.

NUTRITION

New Guinea impatiens are highly sensitive to excessive soluble salts; maintain the EC less than 1.5 dS $\cdot m^{-1}$ using 1:2 media:water dilution (Judd and Cox, 1992b). However, fertilizer at 50 to 75 ppm should be applied early in cutting or seed plug production. After transplanting to the final container, irrigate with either 0 to 100 ppm N for up to 3 weeks (Fischer, personal communication; Judd and Cox, 1992a). Thereafter, a range of 100 to 200 ppm N from a balanced fertilizer is adequate for finished plant production. According to Lang and Pannkuk (1998) 168 ppm N was optimum and, at that rate, no differences were found between standard and minimal leaching practices using drip irrigation. With ebb-and-flow irrigation the optimum rate was 112 ppm N (Kent and Reed, 1996). A lower level of P can be used if superphosphate has been added to the medium. Controlled-release fertilizers can be used if the medium moisture level remains high (Haver and Schuch, 1996). Micronutrients are essential if they have not been previously added to the medium (Erwin et al., 1992; Hartley, 1995; Judd and Cox, 1992a, b). Typical tissue nutrient levels found in healthy, newly expanded leaves are listed in Table II-1 Impatiens, New Guinea.

New Guinea impatiens are susceptible to iron and manganese toxicity, which is often a result of low medium pH. Symptoms include

TABLE II-I IMPATIENS, NEW GUINEA

Tissue level ranges for nutrients found in leaf tissue of *Impatiens hawkteri* (Dole and Wilkins, 1988; Erwin et al., 1992).

Nutrient	University of Minnesota	Soil and Plant Laboratory
N (%)	3.3–4.9	3.4–4.6
P (%)	0.3–0.8	0.4–0.6
K (%)	1.9–2.7	1.2–2.4
Ca (%)	1.9–2.7	0.7–1.0
Mg (%)	0.3–0.8	0.3–0.8
Fe (ppm)	160–300	75–300
Mn (ppm)	140–245	100–250
Zn (ppm)	40–85	60–86
Cu (ppm)	5–10	8–14
B (ppm)	50–60	40–80

stunting and twisting or malformations of the upper leaves. Foliar levels of these elements should not exceed 500 ppm (Erwin, 1997). If toxicity occurs, raise medium pH above 6.0 to make iron and manganese less available to the plant.

MEDIA

Selection of a well-aerated medium that still retains moisture is critical but challenging. Peat moss is a basic ingredient for most mixes as are a variety of other materials such as barks, vermiculite, and perlite. The pH should be 5.8 to 6.5 with 5.9 to 6.1 optimum (Carlson, 1988; Fischer, personal communication; Hartley, 1995; Judd and Cox, 1992a).

HEIGHT CONTROL

Most cultivars are compact, well branched, and require little or no plant growth regulator applications. Height control begins in plug production, regardless of whether the propagule source is a cutting or seed. Proper spacing and growing plants dry, but not stressed to wilting, is one step. High light and zero to negative DIF are also important. Constant day/night temperature or early morning temperature dips (DROP) can be used to deliver the needed DIF (Mikkelsen, 1995). All commonly used plant growth regulators are effective as sprays including A-Rest (ancymidol) at 67 ppm, B-Nine (daminozide) at 1500 ppm, Bonzi (paclobutrazol) at 0.5 to 5 ppm, Cycocel (chloremequat) at 500 ppm, Sumagic (uniconazole) at 2 ppm, and Topflor (flurprimidol) at 2.5 to 7.5 ppm (Corr, 1995; Pasutti and Weigle, 1980; SePRO, personal communication). Plant growth regulators should be used carefully because they can have long-term effects in the landscape (Latimer and Oetting, 1998).

SPACING

New Guinea impatiens are commonly grown in 4- to 6-in. (10- to 15-cm) pots or in 8- to 10-in. (20- to 25-cm) hanging baskets. One or two plants are used in a 4- to 6-in. (10- to 15-cm) pot, whereas two to three plants are used in hanging baskets. Plants can be grown pot-to-pot until spaced. Plants should never become crowded during plug production or on the production bench. Adequate spacing, light, and air circulation are absolutes for disease-free, short, well-branched plants (Table II-2 Impatiens, New Guinea).

TABLE II-2 IMPATIENS, NEW GUINEA
Proposed final spacing for *Impatiens hawkeri*.

Pot Size in. (cm)	Number of Cuttings per Pot	Space on Centers in. (cm)
4 (10)	1–2	7–8 (18–20)
5 (13)	1–2	8–9 (20–23)
6 (15)	1–2	10–12 (25–30)
8 (20)[a]	2–3	16+ (41)
10 (25)[a]	3–4	22+ (56)

[a]*Commonly hung on racks.*

PINCHING AND DISBUDDING

No pinching or disbudding is required if plants are spaced and grown in adequate light. A soft pinch may be required in midwinter (January and February). Pinching will delay flowering (Fischer, personal communication; Starman, 1991). Florel (ethephon) at 250 to less than 500 ppm aborts flower buds and increases branching of stock plants (Yoder Brothers, personal communication). Treatments should stop 8 weeks prior to sales to allow for flower development.

SUPPORT

No support required.

SCHEDULE AND TIMING

Scheduling is based on the size of the pot being produced, time of year, and correct temperatures (Erwin et al., 1992). Cultivars vary in the number of days to flower. The crop time is 10 to 14 weeks from transplanting a rooted plug (Table II-3 Impatiens, New Guinea). Large 6-, 8-, 10- or 12-in. (15-, 20-, 25-, or 30-cm) pots require 2 or more weeks longer to produce than 5-in. (13-cm) pots.

INSECTS

Aphids, fungus gnats, mealybugs, shore flies, spider mites, and thrips have been listed by both Erwin et al. (1992) and Lindquist (1995) as potential pest problems. Chemical control (Erwin et al., 1992), understanding the insects' life cycles (Lindquist, 1995), and integrated pest management (Hall, 1995) are essential for their control. Of major concern is the spread of impatiens necrotic spot and tomato spotted wilt virus disease by thrips. Insect screening to keep out thrips is necessary for stock plant and

TABLE II-3 IMPATIENS, NEW GUINEA

Sample production schedule of 5-in. (13-cm) potted *Impatiens hawkeri* from two cuttings.

Cultural Step	Production Time (weeks)	Temperature °F (°C)
Root cutting in plug		
	3–4	Medium: 68 (20)
Transplant plug to final pot size, space pot-to-pot		
	2	Air: 77–80 (25–27)
Space		
	10	Air: 77–80 (25–27)
Flower		
Total	15–16	

cutting production to produce virus-free plants (Baker et al., 1995).

DISEASES

The most serious diseases are impatiens necrotic spot and tomato spotted wilt viruses, which can be controlled by screening the greenhouse and providing positive airflow to exclude other insects (Baker et al., 1995). The viruses display numerous symptoms (Daughtrey and Chase, 1992) that can be confused with fungal leaf problems or micronutrient deficiencies. All major breeders have patented cultivars and licensed propagators have elaborate procedures to maintain disease-free stock plant programs. The major fungus diseases of *Rhizoctonia* (damping-off and crown rot), *Pythium* (root rot), and *Botrytis* (leaf spot and cutting dieback) can be serious (Daughtrey, 1995; Daughtrey and Chase, 1992). Bacterial diseases *Pseudomonas* and powdery mildew have also plagued production. Other reported diseases include verticillium wilt (*Verticillium dahliae*), black root rot (*Thielaviopsis basicola*), southern wilt (*Sclerotium rolfsii*), leaf spots (*Cercospora, Phyllosticta, Ramularia,* or *Septoria*), and soft rot (*Erwinia carotovora*) (Dreistadt, 2001).

PHYSIOLOGICAL DISORDERS

Cold damage leading to plant death can occur with extended temperatures of 42 to 47°F (6 to 8°C). Delayed or lack of flowering can be due to light levels lower than 2500 fc (500 μmol · m^{-2} · s^{-1}), night temperatures higher than 68°F (20°C), Florel application, and/or N levels higher than 200 ppm (Fischer, personal communication). Slow root development after planting could be due to root rot, medium that is too wet, or high medium EC. Dark green, cupped or wavy leaves with a bluish tinge may be due to overfertilization.

POSTHARVEST

New Guinea plants are sensitive to low temperatures and cannot tolerate temperatures below 42°F (6°C). Suggested shipping duration is 4 days at 60°F (16°C). Plants are also quite sensitive to ethylene (L.Høyer, personal communication). Silver thiosulfate (STS) pretreatment sprays (1.0 mM) reduce ethylene-induced flower abscission and prolong postharvest life (Dostal et al., 1991).

KEY POINTS

- New Guinea impatiens is one of the few new species to enter the world floriculture industry in the past 25 years and become a major potted flowering plant and bedding plant.
- Plants are primarily propagated by cuttings; seeded cultivars are available.
- New Guinea impatiens are day neutral.

- Temperature is the controlling factor in flowering.
- Optimum light intensity is 3000 to 5000 fc (600 to 1000 μmol · m^{-2} · s^{-1}).
- Once established, plants require large quantities of water, but should be grown on the dry side to prevent excessive growth and delayed flowering.

- Maintaining an adequate moisture supply in hanging baskets or in landscape plantings is a major postharvest concern because plants are not tolerant of water stress.
- Plants are sensitive to high soluble salt levels and to iron and manganese toxicity, especially when the medium pH is low.

- Impatiens are highly susceptible to impatiens necrotic spot and tomato spotted wilt viruses.
- Cold damage can occur if exposed to 47°F (8°C) or lower for an extended duration.

BIBLIOGRAPHY

Arisumi, T., and H.M. Cathey. 1976. The New Guinea impatiens. *HortScience* 11:2.

Armstrong, R.J. 1974. An impatiens circus, the Longwood New Guinea hybrid impatiens. *American Horticulture* 53(1):14–18.

Bailey, L.H., and E.Z. Bailey. 1976. *Impatiens*, pp. 594–595 in *Hortus Third: A Concise Dictionary of Plants Cultivated in the United States and Canada*. Macmillan, New York.

Baker, J.R., J.A. Bethke, and E.A. Shearin. 1995. Insect screening, pp. 155–170 in *New Guinea Impatiens*, W. Banner and M. Klopmeyer, editors. Ball Publishing, Batavia, Illinois.

Carlson, W.H. 1988. New Guinea impatiens—Exotic new relative of an old garden favorite. *Bedding Plant Incorporated News* 19(5):6–7.

Carlson, W., and M. Klien. 1985. Try New Guinea impatiens. *Greenhouse Grower* 3(8):12–13.

Cathey, H.M. 1995. History of commercialization, pp. 10–20 in *New Guinea Impatiens*, W. Banner and M. Klopmeyer, editors. Ball Publishing, Batavia, Illinois.

Christensson, H. 1985. *Odling av Nya Guinea—Impatiens*. Swedish University of Agricultural Sciences, Trädgård 288, Alnarp, Sweden. (in Swedish)

Corr, B. 1995. Seed New Guinea impatiens: Seed to plug to finish, pp. 105–111 in *New Guinea Impatiens*, W. Banner and M. Klopmeyer, editors. Ball Publishing, Batavia, Illinois.

Daughtrey, M. 1995. Other diseases and their control, pp. 133–140 in *New Guinea Impatiens*, W. Banner and M. Klopmeyer, editors. Ball Publishing, Batavia, Illinois.

Daughtrey, M. and A.R. Chase. 1992. *Impatiens*, pp. 132–134 in *Ball Field Guide to Diseases of Greenhouse Ornamentals*. Ball Publishing, Geneva, Illinois.

Dole, J.M., and H.F. Wilkins. 1988. University of Minnesota—Tissue analysis standards. *Minnesota Commercial Flower Growers Association Bulletin* 37(6):10–13.

Dostal, D.L., N.H. Agnew, R.J. Gladon, and J.L. Weigle. 1991. Ethylene, simulated shipping, STS, and AOA affect corolla abscission of New Guinea impatiens. *HortScience* 26:47–49.

Dreistadt, S.H. 2001. *Integrated Pest Management for Floriculture and Nurseries*. University of California Division of Agriculture and Natural Resources Publication 3402.

Erwin, J. 1995. Light and temperature, pp. 41–54 in *New Guinea Impatiens*, W. Banner and M. Klopmeyer, editors. Ball Publishing, Batavia, Illinois.

Erwin, J. 1997. Irrigation water considerations. *Minnesota Commercial Flower Growers Association Bulletin* 45(6) and 46(1):1–10.

Erwin, J., M. Ascerno, F. Pfleger, and R. Heins. 1992. New Guinea impatiens production. *Minnesota Commercial Flower Growers Association Bulletin* 41(3):1–15.

Hall, J. 1995. IPM programs, pp. 171–185 in *New Guinea Impatiens*, W. Banner and M. Klopmeyer, editors. Ball Publishing, Batavia, Illinois.

Hartley, D.E. 1995. Feeding and watering, pp. 31–39 in *New Guinea Impatiens*, W. Banner and M. Klopmeyer, editors. Ball Publishing, Batavia, Illinois.

Haver, D.L., and U.K. Schuch. 1996. Production and postproduction performance of two New Guinea impatiens grown with controlled-release fertilizer and no leaching. *Journal of the American Society for Horticultural Science* 121:820–825.

Huxley, A., M. Griffiths, and M. Levy. 1992. *Impatiens*, pp. 649–651 in *The New Royal Horticultural Society Dictionary of Gardening*, vol. 2. Stockton Press, New York.

Judd, L.K., and D.A. Cox. 1992a. New Guinea impatiens: Watch out for soluble salts. *Greenhouse Grower* 10(2):68, 70–71.

Judd, L.K., and D.A. Cox. 1992b. Growth of New Guinea impatiens inhibited by high growth—medium electrical conductivity. *HortScience* 27:1193–1194.

Kent, M.W., and D.W. Reed. 1996. Nitrogen nutrition of New Guinea impatiens 'Barbados' and *Spathiphyllum* 'Petite' in a subirrigation system. *Journal of the American Society for Horticultural Science* 121:812–819.

Lang, H.J., and T.R. Pannkuk. 1998. Effects of fertilizer concentration and minimum-leach drip irrigation on the growth of New Guinea impatiens. *HortScience* 33:683–688.

Larson, R.A. 1995. Status of the industry, pp. 1–10 in *New Guinea Impatiens*, W. Banner and M. Klopmeyer, editors. Ball Publishing, Batavia, Illinois.

Latimer, J.G., and R.D. Oetting. 1998. Greenhouse conditioning affects landscape performance of bedding plants. *Journal of Environmental Horticulture* 16:138–142.

Lindquist, R.K. 1995. Other insects, mites and their control, pp. 141–153 in *New Guinea Impatiens*, W. Banner and M. Klopmeyer, editors. Ball Publishing, Batavia, Illinois.

Mikkelsen, E.P. 1995. Rooting, pp. 81–86 in *New Guinea Impatiens*, W. Banner and M. Klopmeyer, editors. Ball Publishing, Batavia, Illinois.

Mikkelsen Incorporated. 1989. *Cultural Information for Mikkel Sunshine New Guinea Impatiens*. Mikkelsens Incorporated Publication, Ashtabula, Ohio.

Pasutti, D.W., and J.L. Weigle. 1980. Growth-regulated effect on New Guinea impatiens hybrids. *Scientia Horticulturae* 12:293–298.

Shaw, J.A. 1997. Virus-resistant New Guinea impatiens. *FloraCulture International* 7(11):38.

Starman, T.W. 1991. Response of Kientzler New Guinea impatiens to manual and chemical pinching. *HortScience* 26:856–857.

Strefeler, M.S. 1995. Genetics, pp. 227–247 in *New Guinea Impatiens*, W. Banner and M. Klopmeyer, editors. Ball Publishing, Batavia, Illinois.

Strefeler, M.S., and R.-J.W. Quené. 1995. Variability in water loss patterns of New Guinea Impatiens cultivars and breeding selections. *Journal of the American Society for Horticultural Science* 120: 527–531.

Strope, K.M., and M.S. Strefeler. 1997. Analysis of heat tolerance in New Guinea impatiens (*Impatiens hawkeri*) utilizing diallel analysis. *HortScience* 32:499. (Abstract)

Trees, S. 1995. Breeding for the future, pp. 249–265 in *New Guinea Impatiens*, W. Banner and M. Klopmeyer, editors. Ball Publishing, Batavia, Illinois.

Whealy, C.A. 1995. Commercial varieties, pp. 213–226 in *New Guinea Impatiens*, W. Banner and M. Klopmeyer, editors. Ball Publishing, Batavia, Illinois.

Winters, H.F. 1973. New impatiens from New Guinea. *American Horticulture* 52(3):16–22.

Iris

INTRODUCTION

Common name: iris.

Scientific names: Numerous *Iris* species and hybrids are important in the floriculture world: (1) *I. danfordiae* (Bak.) Boiss. and *I. reticulata* Bieb. (dwarf iris), (2) *I. ensata* Thunb. (Japanese iris), (3) *I. germanica* L. (bearded iris), (4) *I. ×hollandica* hort. (Dutch iris), (5) *I. pumula* L. (dwarf bearded iris), (6) *I. siberica* L. (Siberin iris), (7) *I. spuria* L. (spuria iris), and (8) *I. xiphioides* J.F. Ehrh. (English iris) (Bailey and Bailey, 1976; Huxley et al., 1992; Post, 1949).

Family and related taxa: Iridaceae Juss. The 300 or more species of *Iris* can be divided into two groups: bulbous or rhizomatous geophytes. The bulbous iris are divided into two subgenera: *Xiphium* or *Scorpiris*. The *Xiphium* type iris have large erect standards and either smooth bulbs or reticulated netlike bulb coverings. The *Scorpiris* types have small spreading, reflexed standards and fleshy bulbs. The rhizomatous iris may be divided into three types based on the structure of the "falls": bearded, nonbearded, or crested. Other genera in the Iridaceae family are *Crocus*, *Freesia*, and *Gladiolus*.

Origin: Iris are native primarily to northern temperate zones. Many of the horticulturally important iris are native to Mediterranean and European countries. *Iris ×hollandica*, the Dutch iris, is not a true species, but a complex of several species including *I. filifolia* Boiss., *I. tingitana* Boiss. & Reut., *I. xiphium* L., and others. These species are all native to southern France, Portugal, Spain, northern and northwestern Africa, and Morocco. The two dwarf iris, *Iris danfordiae* and *I. reticulata*, are native to the Caucasus Mountains and east Asia Minor, respectively. *Iris xiphioides*, English iris, is found in the French and Spanish Pyrenees

Mountains. *Iris siberica*, the Siberian iris, is native from central Russia west to central Europe. *Iris spuria*, the butterfly or spuria iris, is native to central and southern Europe, Algeria, and Iran. *Iris ensata*, the Japanese iris, is found in Japan, Korea, and China (Fig. II-1 Iris). *Iris pumila*, dwarf bearded iris, occurs in central and eastern Europe and Turkey. The exact origin of *Iris germanica*, the bearded iris, is unknown—it may be a Mediterranean native or an ancient fertile hybrid (Bailey and Bailey, 1976; De Munk and Schipper, 1993; Huxley et al., 1992) (Fig. II-2 Iris).

Uses and current status: Iris are grown in greenhouses as cut or potted flowering plants, in fields as cut flowers, or in gardens as common and beloved perennials (Armitage, 1989; Bailey, 1933; Bailey and Bailey, 1976; De Munk and Schipper, 1993). *I. ×hollandica* bulbs are forced by the millions worldwide as cut flowers. In the hot dry areas of Zones 7 to 10 where soils do not freeze deeply, they may become perennials in the garden. *I. reticulata* and *I. danfordiae* bulbs are commonly forced in the greenhouse as potted specimens and can perennialize in Zones 4 to 7. *I. siberica* is also grown outdoors as a commercial cut flower in Zones 3 to 9. In the garden, *I. xiphioides* may be grown in Zones 6 to 9, *I. spuria* in Zones 4 to 9, and *Iris siberica* in Zones 3 to 9. *I. ensata* grows in Zones 4 to 9, and is a prized cut flower for Children's Day in Japan. *I. pumila* is a garden ornamental in Zones 4 to 9 and a potential potted plant (Holcomb et al., 1993). *I. germanica* is the ever popular and prized garden bearded iris for

FIGURE II-2 IRIS *Iris germanica* garden ornamental.

Zones 3 to 10. Many firms pot and force the rhizomes of early flowering bearded iris for spring sales (Buxton and Mohr, 1969; Holcomb, 1990).

Leaves are parallel veined, linear, and sword shaped. Flowers consist of three outer or basal petals known as "falls," which can be bearded. The inner three standard petals are upright, spreading, or reflexed. Flower colors range from white to various tints of pink, blue, lilac, purple, red, orange, and yellow. Two unusual species *I. susiana* L. and *I. nigricans* Dinsm. in Iran and Israel are almost purple-black and brown-purple (Bailey, 1933; Bailey and Bailey, 1976; De Munk and Schipper, 1993).

CULTIVARS

The Dutch hybrids, *I. ×hollandica*, are widely grown as cut flowers around the world. The primary field production sites for bulb forcing stock are in the Netherlands, followed by lesser production in the United States, Japan, France, Israel, and the United Kingdom. Unfortunately, few new cultivars are introduced and quality is limited. Some cultivars have been in existence for generations. Eighteen Dutch iris cultivars are commonly forced in greenhouses (De Hertogh, 1996b). Work is progressing on developing new hybrids between Dutch iris and other species (Eikelboom and van Eijk, 1990). De Hertogh (1996a) listed only three cultivars for *I. reticulata* and one for *I. danfordiae*. Some commercial catalogs list 200 or more cultivars

FIGURE II-I IRIS *Iris ensata* 'Strut & Flourish' garden ornamental.

of *Iris xiphioides*, *I. spuria*, and *I. siberica*. Annually, hundreds of new cultivars of *I. germanica* are introduced worldwide.

PROPAGATION

Propagation, with rare exceptions, is done by specialty producers who distribute bulbs and rhizomes worldwide. Rhizomatous iris are propagated by simple division; *in vitro* propagation is possible (Anderson et al., 1990; Meyer, 1984; De Munk and Schipper, 1993; Wang et al., 1999a, b). *I. ×hollandica* bulbs are propagated asexually for commercial sales. Annually, two to four axillary buds form bulblets. *In vitro* propagation of Dutch iris is possible and pathogen-free stock is available from specialty growers. This elite disease-free bulbous stock is increased by "chipping," a procedure similar to that used with narcissus (see *Narcissus* chapter, Propagation section, p. 689). Commercial quantities of bulbs are dependent on natural propagation from bulb offsets (De Munk and Schipper, 1993; Jones and Hanks, 1988).

FLOWERING CONTROL AND DORMANCY

Dutch iris bulbs are available every day of the year for immediate cut flower forcing. The limiting factor for forcing in most areas of the world is excessive summer temperatures, except in northern Europe and along the Pacific coast of North America. Bulbs are forced in greenhouses worldwide when temperatures are appropriate. Cut flowers are field grown in summer in northern Europe and year-round along the Pacific coast of North America. The programming of bulbs for floral initiation and development and holding (retarding) for long durations is a sophisticated and highly organized international process. The exacting process of precision forcing and propagation explains why few new cultivars of Dutch iris survive the selection process and become new standard commercial cultivars (De Hertogh, 1996b; De Munk and Schipper, 1993).

Dutch iris bulbs must reach a minimum size, cultivar dependent, before they can be programmed to flower by a high-temperature treatment. This treatment emulates the long dry and hot summers of the areas from which the various species originated. Bulbs have initiated three or more leaves at the time of harvest, when the old leaves begin to senesce; thereafter, the commercial heat treatment commences.

Heat greater than 68°F (20°C) results in the termination of the leaf initiation process and commences the floral induction process. Heat treatment for the maturation of Dutch iris bulbs can be partially substituted by use of ethylene gas or by Florel (ethephon) bulb dips (Cascante and Doss, 1988; De Munk and Schipper, 1993; Imanishi and Fortanier, 1982). Ethylene also reduces bud blasting by decreasing the number of leaves formed (Kamerbeek et al., 1980). The optimum temperature for floral induction is 86°F (30°C) or greater. After the high-temperature treatment, a cold treatment of 48 to 59°F (9 to 15°C) must be applied, which results in elongation of leaves and flowers when the bulbs are planted (Halevy and Shoub, 1964). After a cold treatment of 6 to 13 weeks, bulbs are ready to force into flower. The standard greenhouse forcing temperature is 55 to 60°F (13 to 16°C).

Microscopic floral initials are not present until after bulbs have been planted. However, bulbs can be held for long durations at high temperatures of 86°F (30°C) and high humidity prior to the cold treatment. These bulbs are called *retarded* bulbs; however, these retarded bulbs may start forming floral structures prior to the cold treatment.

Typical plants will have eight leaves once the plants are forced into flower. The basal leaf may not be more than 2 to 3 in. (5 to 8 cm) in length. The upper two leaves are "sheaths" surrounding the inflorescence. The inflorescence should be positioned well above the sheath leaves and subtending foliage, which should be abbreviated as well. The middle four leaves should not be over 6 in. (15 cm) long. In addition to the obvious terminal flower, there are one to two axillary flowers, which only occasionally develop or are seen in the cut flower postharvest environment, but do develop if plants are left in the field or greenhouse.

The year-round availability of bulbs is possible due to the ability to store bulbs for long durations prior to cold treatment. In addition, bulbs are also available for long durations due to seasonal differences. Bulbs are harvested from south to north as the season progresses, starting in Israel, the south of France, and North America (Washington State) and ending in the Netherlands and the United Kingdom. Thus, totally programmed iris bulbs are available year-round to iris bulb forcers.

Rhizomes of *Iris pumila* flowered best when cold treated at 37 to 39°F (3 to 4°C) for 4 to 8 weeks (Holcomb et al., 1993). Some cultivars flowered without cold treatment and most flowered slowly or not at all under SD if bulbs were not previously cold treated.

Rhizomes of *Iris germanica* should be planted, cooled at 36 to 40°F (2 to 4°C) for a minimum of 6 to 8 weeks, and forced under night interruption lighting or supplemental HID lighting. Long days can substitute for cold. With only 6 to 8 weeks of cold, flowering did not occur under SD, depending on the cultivar. To ensure adequate flowering, rhizomes are cold-stored for 14 to 16 weeks (Buxton and Mohr, 1969; Holcomb, 1990; Stephenson Preston et al., 1983). Imanishi (1989) reviewed the control of floral initiation and development for *I. ensata*.

TEMPERATURE

Bulbs of the Dutch iris perform best when greenhouse forced at 55 to 60°F (13 to 16°C). Plants scarcely grow at 43°F (6°C). Temperatures above 70°F (21°C) should be avoided to prevent bud abortion, particularly during the winter. Forcing duration is 6 to 9 weeks, depending on the temperature and cultivar.

When nonprecooled Dutch iris bulbs are grown outdoors in the cool coastal areas of California, 4 to 9 months may be required to produce flowers after the bulbs are planted. Bulbs of Dutch iris are used only once and not allowed to perennialize. Some field cut growers in warm climates treat Dutch iris as a perennial and grow individual plantings for two or more years.

Dwarf iris planted for potted flowering plants need greenhouse forcing temperatures of 60 to 63°F (16 to 17°C) during the day and 55 to 60°F (13 to 16°C) at night. Dwarf iris bulbs require 15 to 16 weeks of cold treatment after flowers are initiated in late summer (mid-August to mid-September) (Table II-1 Iris). The optimum temperature for initiation is 68 to 77°F (20 to 25°C). Dwarf iris flower very early in February and March in the Netherlands and the bulbs are harvested in late June and stored at 68 to 73°F (20 to 23°C). For forcing as potted flowering plants, both Rooting Room A and B are used (see *Crocus* chapter, Flowering Control and Dormancy section, Table II-3 Crocus, p. 407). Dwarf iris bulbs used for early forcing schedules are designated as precooled and are potted and placed immediately into 48°F (9°C) storage. For later forcing schedules, bulbs are stored at 63°F (17°C) before being potted and are designated as nonprecooled bulbs. *Iris danfordiae* can be forced for Christmas (De Hertogh, 1996a, b).

For *Iris germanica*, forcing quality was superior at 60°F (16°C) when compared with 65°F (18°C) (Buxton and Mohr, 1969; Holcomb, 1990).

LIGHT

During winter, Dutch iris flower buds abort under periods of low irradiance levels of short duration. Clean glass, adequate plant spacing, large bulb sizes, and supplemental lighting can prevent this physiological problem. The optimal light intensity is greater than 2500 fc (500 $\mu mol \cdot m^{-2} \cdot s^{-1}$) in a forcing greenhouse. Flower bud abortion is reduced if bulbs have been treated with ethylene instead of heat (De Munk and Schipper, 1993; Kamerbeek et al., 1980). H.F. Wilkins (unpublished) noted that night breaks of incandescent light reduced bud abortions and resulted in more uniform flowering in northern climates.

Regardless of species, all iris require high light during winter forcing. Shade would only be used to control temperature during bright sunny days. With early forcing schedules, potted iris may have to be shaded or have paper placed over them to stretch the emerging plants. Beware of excess heat under the coverings (De Hertogh, 1996a, b). Late spring plantings of Dutch iris benefit from shade to reduce temperature and increase stem length. Potted *Iris pumila* plants flowered earlier and were of higher quality when grown under supplementary HID lighting than under ambient light (Holcomb et al., 1993).

WATER

Most iris do not tolerate poor drainage (Bailey, 1933). Some exceptions include Japanese iris, *I. ensata*; the yellow water iris, *I. pseudacorus* L.; and *I. fulva* Ker-Gawl., the copper-colored swamp iris, which thrives in standing water. After planting Dutch iris bulbs, water medium thoroughly. Thereafter, keep the medium moist, but do not overwater (De Hertogh, 1996a, b). Avoid using water with an EC greater than 0.5 dS $\cdot$ m^{-1} (Buschman, undated).

CARBON DIOXIDE

No data available.

NUTRITION

Bulbous Dutch iris can be fertilized weekly with 250 ppm of calcium nitrate once growth has commenced. When the medium is reused

TABLE II-1 IRIS

Programming schedules for forcing dwarf potted *Iris* bulbs into flower using precooled (PC) or nonprecooled (NP) corms (modified from De Hertogh, 1996a).

Date of Expected Flowering	Date to Commence Forcing	Date to Pot Bulb	Date to Start Precooling	Rooting Room[a]	Cold Required (weeks)
I. Use *Iris danfordiae* only for Christmas forcing (PC bulbs).[b]					
Dec.15	Dec. 5	Oct. 1–7	Aug. 28–31	A	14
Dec. 20	Dec. 12				15
Dec. 26	Dec. 19				16
Dec. 31	Dec. 26				17
II. A. *I. reticulata* and *I. danfordiae* (PC bulbs)[b]					
Jan. 1	Dec. 12	Oct. 1–7	Aug. 28–31	A	15
Jan. 7	Dec. 19				16
Jan. 11	Dec. 26				17
II. B. *I. reticulata* and *I. danfordiae* (NP bulbs)[c]					
Jan. 13	Dec. 22	Oct. 1–7	Sept. 1–5	A	17
Jan. 18	Dec. 29				18
Jan. 23	Jan. 7				19.5
III. *I. reticulata* and *I. danfordiae* (NP bulbs)[c]					
Jan. 13	Dec. 24	Sept. 15–20	None	A	14
Jan. 18	Dec. 31				15
Jan. 23	Jan. 7				16
IV. *I. reticulata* and *I. danfordiae* (NP bulbs)[c]					
Jan. 25	Jan. 3	Sept. 28–Oct. 2	None	A	13.5
Jan. 31	Jan. 12				15
Feb. 7	Jan. 23				16.5
V. *I. reticulata* and *I. danfordiae* (NP bulbs)[c]					
Feb. 11	Jan. 25	Oct. 17–20	None	B	14
Feb. 18	Feb. 6				15.5
Feb. 24	Feb. 15				17
VI. *I. reticulata* and *I. danfordiae* (NP bulbs)[c]					
Mar. 2	Feb. 18	Nov. 5–10	None	B	14.5
Mar. 9	Feb. 28				16
Mar. 16	Mar. 8				17.5

[a]See Crocus chapter, Flowering Control and Dormancy section, Table II-3 Crocus, p. 407.
[b]Precool at 48°F (9°C).
[c]No precooling required; hold at 63°F (17°C) until potted.

for cut flower production, a medium test should first be taken to determine pH, EC, and nutrient levels. Rooting can be delayed if the media EC is too high, 1 to 1.5 dS · m^{-1} (Buschman, undated).

Field-grown Dutch iris need a balanced 10–20–10 fertilizer. De Hertogh (1996b) suggested 2 lb/100 row ft (1 kg/33 m). Similar fertilizer regimes may be used for field-grown perennial species. No fertilization is required during the forcing of potted dwarf iris.

MEDIA

A well-drained loose medium is required for ground beds or forcing flats. The pH should be near 7.0. A minimum depth of 10 in. (25 cm) is suggested for flats. Bulbs are planted 1 in.

(2.5 cm) deep. Bulbous iris have contractile roots. In the field, bulbs are planted 4 in. (10 cm) deep (De Hertogh, 1996b; De Munk and Schipper, 1993). Do not contaminate the monocotyledonous iris with fluoride from inadvertent use of superphosphates in the medium. Iris can be forced hydroponically (James, 2002).

HEIGHT CONTROL

No height control is required for either cut flowers or potted plants. Dwarf potted iris may be too short during the early forcing schedules (see Light section, on page 622). Height of German iris can be controlled by applying a 30-ppm Bonzi (paclobutrazol) drench (Uniroyal Chemical, personal communication).

SPACING

Dutch iris bulbs should be given greater planting space in late autumn, winter, and early spring than in the late spring or early summer (see Table II-2 Iris). Lack of light is a primary reason for flower abortion during winter. Field-grown iris are spaced in a row at 45 bulbs/yd (49/m) or 200 to 250 bulbs/yd² (240 to 300/m²). Lower planting densities may be required for low-light climates (Buschman, undated).

Plant five to six 2.3-in. (6-cm)-diameter dwarf iris bulbs in a 3-in. (8-cm) pan or 9 to 12 bulbs in a 4-in. (10-cm) pan. Larger pans can be used, and combination bulb gardens using iris, crocus, hyacinths, narcissus, and tulips are common (De Hertogh, 1996a).

PINCHING AND DISBUDDING

No pinching or disbudding required.

SUPPORT

Field-grown Dutch iris typically do not require support, but a single layer of mesh can be used in the greenhouse. Perennial iris species do not require support.

SCHEDULE AND TIMING

Dutch iris bulbs are given a 48°F (9°C) cold treatment of 6 to 13 weeks for rapid shoot elongation after the required heat treatment for floral induction. Bulbs are then shipped to bulb forcers. When received, bulbs should be planted immediately; store bulbs only briefly at 41 to 48°F (5 to 9°C). Bulbs flower within 6 to 8 weeks in a greenhouse. In coastal California, bulbs are generally planted from August to December, or when soil temperatures are below 60°F (16°C) (Armitage and Laushman, 1990; De Hertogh, 1996b). However, *Iris xiphioides, I. spuria,* and *I. siberica* are grown as perennial cut flower crops and are harvested and sold as the season advances from south to north. Dutch iris is also treated as a perennial by some field cut flower growers in warm climates.

Programming schedules for potted dwarf iris have been developed by De Hertogh (1996a). Both Rooting Room A and B are used for exact temperature control (see *Crocus* chapter, Flowering Control and Dormancy section, Table II-3 Crocus, page 407). Forcing schedules have been divided into six periods (see Tables II-1 and II-3 Iris). Forcing in the greenhouse can vary from 6 to 20 days for potted *Iris reticulata*. Forcing is quite rapid—only 4 to 10 days for *I. danfordiae. Iris germanica* rhizomes are forced into flower in 33 to 39 days in late January under night interruption or HID lighting at 60°F (16°C); if not lighted, most cultivars fail to flower. In late March, only 12 days are required for flowering (Buxton and Mohr, 1969; Holcomb, 1990).

INSECTS

Aphids and thrips may be seen during forcing, but are usually not serious (De Hertogh, 1996b). Bulbs can be heat treated to eliminate some insects (Dreistadt, 2001). After soaking Dutch iris bulbs for 2 or 3 hr or overnight in 75°F (24°C) water containing a wetting agent, place in 111°F (44°C) water for 1.5 hr. Cool and dry bulbs after

---

TABLE II-2 IRIS

Suggested spacing of bulbs/yd² (m²) for forcing cut *Iris* flowers under glass (De Hertogh, 1996b).

Season	Bulb Size—in. (cm)		
	4+ (10+)	3.5–4 (9–10)	3.1–3.5 (8–9)
Low light	180 (220)	200 (240)	225 (270)
High light	200 (240)	225 (270)	250 (300)

TABLE II-3 IRIS

Forcing of dwarf *Iris* from either precooled (PC) or nonprecooled (NP) corms (modified from De Hertogh, 1996a). Days to flower are indicated in parentheses following type of bulb.

Cultivar: (Color)	Appropriate Forcing Dates						Weeks of Cold		
	I Dec. 15–31	II Jan. 1–12	III Jan. 13–25	IV Jan. 26– Feb. 9	V Feb. 10–28	VI Mar. 1–20	Min.	Opt.	Max.
Iris reticulata									
Harmony (deep blue)	—	PC (18)	NP (18)	NP (17)	NP (12)	NP (7)	14	15	19
J.S. Dyt (lavender)	—	—	PC (15)	NP (15)	NP (13)	NP (7)	14	16	19
Cantab (light blue)	—	PC (20)	NP (20)	NP (18)	NP (11)	NP (6)	13	15	19
Iris danfordiae (yellow)	PC (10)	PC (8)	NP (10)	NP (8)	NP (4)	—	13	15	17

treatment. Iris borers may be a problem in the home garden on rhizomatous iris.

DISEASES

Bulbs can be infected with *Fusarium*. Growers are dependent on obtaining clean stock from suppliers. During bulb cold storage, *Penicillium* can be a concern. *Rhizoctonia* is rarely seen in forcing stock. Disease is not a serious problem provided humidity is controlled, proper temperatures are maintained, and air is circulated during storage, forcing, and marketing (De Hertogh, 1996a, b; Gould and Byther, 1979).

Several diseases can infect bearded and Siberian irises growing outdoors (Dreistadt, 2001; Horst, 1990). Bacterial soft rot (*Erwinia*) is common in the rhizomes and often follows attacks by iris borers. Controlling iris borers will help to prevent the disease. Other problems include root and crown rot (*Pythium irregulare, Phytophthora cryptogea, Rosellinia necatrix*), southern blight (*Sclerotium rolfsii*), leaf spot (*Didymellina macrospora*), botrytis rhizome rot (*Botrytis convoluta*), black slime (*Sclerotinia bulborum*), ink spot (*Drechslera* or *Bipolaris iridis*), gray mold (*Botrytis cinerea*), black storage mold (*Rhizopus* and *Aspergillus*), leaf spot (*Heterosporium gracile* or *Mycosphaerella macrosphora*) rust (*Puccinia iridis*), bacterial blight (*Xanthomonas campestris* pv. *tardicrescens*), and various viruses (Dreistadt, 2001). Southern blight can be controlled in iris rhizomes by placing them in 122°F (50°C) wa-

ter for 30 min plus the time necessary to reach this temperature (Dreistadt, 2001). Cool and dry rhizomes after treatment.

PHYSIOLOGICAL DISORDERS

Numerous disorders are encountered with bulbous Dutch iris, the causes of which are frequently difficult to determine. Categories of problems encountered are (1) blindness (no flower buds formed), (2) abortion (flower buds form, but cease to develop), (3) formation and development of abnormal flowers, (4) flowering stems that are too short, and (5) leaves and flower sheaths that are too long. Table II-4 Iris lists possible causes of each disorder. It is not surprising that physiological disorders occur considering all the steps involved in bulb curing, heat treating, retardation, cooling, shipping, and forcing (De Munk and Schipper, 1993).

POSTHARVEST

Dutch iris flowers should be harvested before the falls reflex and the standards expand (Fig. II-3 Iris). Open flowers are easily damaged and tight, colored buds open quickly in postharvest solutions. For most cultivars, flowers are best harvested in the summer in the "pencil stage" of development or when the flower tip is 0.25 in. (0.5 cm) above the green clasping sheath. In the winter, wait until the bud is 0.38 in. (1.0 cm) above the sheath. However, flowers of 'Professor Blaauw' should be more open when harvested, 0.75 in.

TABLE II-4 IRIS

Possible causes of disorders seen in *Iris* ×*hollandica* (De Munk and Schipper, 1993; Gould and Byther, 1979).

1. Plants blind:	Undersized bulbs used; heat treatment ineffectual (too short and/or temperature too low); temperature of cooling treatment too low, 32 to 41°F (0 to 5°C); ethylene treatment, if used, failed to be effective; and various pathological problems.
2. Flower abortion:	Undersized bulbs used (insufficient carbohydrate reserves); poor root development: medium too wet; plants experienced severe water deficiency (wilted); forcing temperatures too high; low light (winter) stress; bulb/plant population too dense; and various pathological problems.
3. Abnormal flowers:	Additional organs form during flower formation if temperature too cold, such as 32°F (0°C); lack of oxygen during transport after cold treatment; and "floral skips" can occur if bulbs retarded too long.
4. Short flowering stem:	Bulbs given inadequate cold; flowering delayed; and flowers have difficulty emerging from the sheath.
5. Excessive leaf extension:	Leaf making process not halted by high temperature treatment (too short or at inadequate temperatures) and/or ethylene treatment; forced at too cool temperatures; and programming not correct for the cultivar.

FIGURE II-3 IRIS   Dutch iris flowers at various stages of opening.

(2.0 cm) in the summer; 1.5 to 2 in. (4 to 5 cm) in the winter. Flowering stems may need to be harvested twice and sometimes three times a day (Buschman, undated).

Unfortunately, Dutch iris last only 2 to 5 days, depending on room temperature. Using a floral preservative is essential to increase postharvest life. Flowers can be stored up to 5 days at 32°F (0°C). Slightly warmer storage temperatures, 36 to 41°F (2 to 5°C), can also be used (Buschman, undated). Dry storage, long-duration dry shipping, and wilting should be avoided. Rehydration may be difficult and vase life further reduced. Always recut the stems when hydrating. Deionized water (pH 3.5) is preferred (Kosugi et al., 1976; Sacalis, 1993). Gibberellic acid pulses induced flower opening of stems that had been harvested with tepal tips just visible and dry stored for 2 days at 68°F (20°C) (Çelikel and van Doorn, 1995). Untreated flowers did not open.

Siberian iris flowers are cut when the color is visible at the tip. If the first flower is removed after it senescences, a second and possibly third flower will open.

Other than using ethylene for maturation of the bulb (see Flowering Control and Dormancy section, earlier in the chapter), ethylene should be avoided because Dutch iris bulbs, plants, and cut stems are sensitive to ethylene.

Potted iris plants should also be marketed in an immature stage of development and kept at low temperatures. Fortunately, with potted plants the subtending secondary and tertiary flowers frequently develop. Nell et al. (1992) reported that *I. reticulata* 'Harmony' had a shelf life of 6 days at 64°F (18°C) when pots were marketed just as flowers emerged from tight shoots.

Bearded iris can be shipped at 48°F (9°C). Little postharvest information is available on flowers cut from perennial outdoor-grown species. Flowers probably should be handled the same as Dutch iris.

KEY POINTS

- This genus *Iris* includes many species of floriculture interest as cut flowers, potted flowering plants, and garden ornamentals.
- The Dutch iris (*I. ×hollandica*) is a major worldwide cut flower.
- *I. reticulata* and *I. danfordiae*, dwarf potted iris, are commonly forced as potted flowering plants.
- *I. germanica*, the rhizomatous bearded or German iris, is grown worldwide as a garden ornamental.
- *I. pumila*, the dwarf bearded iris, is grown as a garden ornamental and possible potted flowering plant.
- Plants are produced from bulbs or rhizomes, which are propagated by bulblets, scale cuttings, or *in vitro*.
- Dutch iris bulbs can be held "dormant" or retarded for months at 86°F (30°C) or higher; the high-temperature treatment is also required for floral initiation.
- A cold treatment of 48 to 59°F (9 to 15°C) is required after the heat treatment for elongation and development of Dutch iris leaves and flowers.

- Dwarf potted iris bulbs for greenhouse forcing must receive a minimum of 13 to 15 weeks of 48°F (9°C) or lower for root and shoot development.
- The initial portion of the cold treatment can be applied to the dwarf iris bulbs either dry and unpotted (known as precooled) for early forcing dates or moist and potted (known as nonprecooled) for later forcing dates.
- The final portion of the cold treatment is always applied to moist, potted dwarf iris bulbs.
- After the cold treatment, dwarf iris plants are moved to the greenhouse and forced.
- The forcing season for dwarf potted iris is divided into seven periods; recommended cultivars and forcing schedules vary with the period.
- *I. germanica* rhizomes require 36 to 40°F (2 to 4°C) for at least 6 to 8 weeks for flowering.
- *Fusarium* can be a major disease and limit production, especially during warm temperatures.
- Iris cut flowers and plants tend to be short lived and must be marketed promptly.

BIBLIOGRAPHY

Anderson, W.C., K.A. Mielke, P.N. Miller, and T. Allen. 1990. *In vitro* bulblet propagation of virus-free Dutch iris. *Acta Horticulturae* 266:77–81.

Armitage, A.M. 1989. *Iris,* pp. 301–321 in *Herbaceous Perennial Plants.* Varsity Press, Athens, Georgia.

Armitage, A.M., and J.M. Laushman. 1990. Planting date and in ground time affect cut flowers of *Liatris, Polianthes,* and *Iris. HortScience* 25: 1239–1241.

Bailey, L.H. 1933. *Iris,* pp. 1663–1682 in *The Standard Cyclopedia of Horticulture,* vol. II. Macmillan, New York.

Bailey, L.H., and E.Z. Bailey. 1976. *Iris,* pp. 598–606 in *Hortus Third: A Dictionary of Plants Cultivated in the United States and Canada.* Macmillan, New York.

Buschman, J.C.M. undated. *The Iris as Cut Flower.* International Flower Bulb Centre, Hillegom, Holland.

Buxton, J.W., and H.C. Mohr. 1969. The effect of vernalization and photoperiod on flowering of tall bearded iris. *HortScience* 4:53–55.

Cascante, X.M., and R.P. Doss. 1988. Ethephon dip concentration and heat curing duration influence forcing performance of Dutch iris. *HortScience* 23:1006–1008.

Çelikel, F.G., and W.G. van Doorn. 1995. Effects of water stress and gibberellin on flower opening in *Iris ×hollandica. Acta Horticulturae* 405:246–252.

De Hertogh, A. 1996a. "Specialty bulbs" for potted plants, pp. B95–103 in *Holland Bulb Forcer's Guide,* 5th ed. International Flower Bulb Centre, Hillegom, The Netherlands.

De Hertogh, A. 1996b. *Iris ×hollandica,* pp. C73–77 and D27–28 in *Holland Bulb Forcer's Guide,* 5th ed. International Flower Bulb Centre, Hillegom, The Netherlands.

De Munk, W.J., and J. Schipper. 1993. *Iris*—Bulbous and rhizomatous, pp. 349–379 in *The Physiology of Flower Bulbs,* A. De Hertogh and M. Le Nard, editors. Elsevier, Amsterdam.

Dreistadt, S.H. 2001. *Integrated Pest Management for Floriculture and Nurseries.* University of California Division of Agriculture and Natural Resources Publication 3402.

Eikelboom, W., and J.P. van Eijk. 1990. Prospects of interspecific hybridization in Dutch iris. *Acta Horticulturae* 266:353–356.

Gould, C.J., and R.S. Byther. 1979. *Diseases of Bulbous Iris*. Washington State University Extension Bulletin 710, Puyallup.

Halevy, A.H., and J. Shoub. 1964. The effect of cold storage and treatment with gibberellic acid on flowering bulb yield of Dutch iris. *Journal of the American Society for Horticultural Science* 39: 120–129.

Holcomb, E.J. 1990. Forcing reblooming iris as a potted plant. *The Reblooming Iris Recorder* 31:4.

Holcomb, E.J., V.E. Anjichi, and D.J. Beattie. 1993. Cultivar evaluation of dwarf irises as potted plants. *Acta Horticulturae* 337:115–119.

Horst, R.K. 1990. Iris, pp. 691–692 in *Westcott's Plant Disease Handbook*, 5th ed. Van Nostrand Reinhold, New York.

Huxley, A., M. Griffiths, and M. Levy. 1992. *Iris*, pp. 665–679 in *The New Royal Horticultural Society Dictionary of Gardening*, vol. 2. Stockton Press, New York.

Imanishi, H. 1989. *Iris ensata*, pp. 375–378 in *Handbook of Flowering*, vol. VI, A.H. Halevy, editor. CRC Press, Boca Raton, Florida.

Imanishi, H., and E.J. Fortanier. 1982. Effects of an exposure of bulbs to ethylene and smoke on flowering of Dutch iris. *Bulletin of the University of Osaka Prefecture* 34:1–5.

James, L. 2002. Water works. *FloraCulture International* 12(4):28–34.

Jones, S.K., and G.R. Hanks, 1988. Bulking up bulbous iris. *The Plantsman* 9:247–251.

Kamerbeek, G.A., A.J.B. Durieux, and J.A. Schipper. 1980. An analysis of the influence of ethrel on flowering of iris 'Ideal': An associated morphogenetic physiological approach. *Acta Horticulturae* 109:235–240.

Kosugi, K., M. Yokoi, A. Muto, and N. Harada. 1976. *The Keeping Quality of Cut Flowers as Influenced by Growth and Storage Temperatures. II. Dutch Iris*. Technical Bulletin Number 24, Faculty of Horticulture, Chiba University, Chiba, Japan.

Meyer, M.M. 1984. *In vitro* propagation of Siberian iris from flower stalks. *HortScience* 19:575.

Nell, T., J. Barrett, and A.A. De Hertogh. 1992. *Post-Greenhouse (Consumer) Requirements for Rooting Room Bulbs Forced as Potted Plants*. Holland Flower Bulb Technical Service Bulletin 34, International Flower Bulb Centre, Hillegom, The Netherlands.

Post, K. 1949. *Iris*, pp. 582–589 in *Florist Crop Production and Marketing*. Orange Judd Publishing, New York.

Sacalis, J.N. 1993. *Iris* hybrids, pp. 73–74 in *Cut Flowers, Prolonging Freshness*, 2nd ed., J.L. Seals, editor. Ball Publishing, Batavia, Illinois.

Stephenson Preston, M.A., J.W. Buxton, R.G. Anderson, and H.C. Mohr. 1983. Effect of vernalization duration and storage method on forcing of tall bearded irises. *HortScience* 18:455–456.

Wang, Y., Z. Jeknić, R.C. Ernst, and T.H.H. Chen. 1999a. Efficient plant regeneration from suspension-cultured cells of tall bearded iris. *HortScience* 34:730–735.

Wang, Y., Z. Jeknić, R.C. Ernst, and T.H.H. Chen. 1999b. Improved plant regeneration from suspension-cultured cells of *Iris germanica* L. 'Skating Party,' *HortScience* 34:1271–1276.

Kalanchoe

FIGURE II-I KALANCHOE   Potted *Kalanchoe* plant.

INTRODUCTION

Common name: kalanchoe.

Scientific name: *Kalanchoe blossfeldiana* Poelln. (Huxley et al., 1992).

Family and related taxa: Crassulaceae DC. This genus has approximately 125 species. Though *K. blossfeldiana* is used extensively as a flowering potted plant, other species are considered foliage plants and grown for their large, colorful, glossy to pubescent, succulent leaves. *Kalanchoe porphyrocalyx* (Bak.) Baill. is also seen as a flowering plant in hanging baskets (Zimmer, 1985). Other kalanchoe species grown commercially include *K. beharensis* Drake., velvetleaf; *K. daigremontiana* Hamet & Perrier., devil's backbone; *K. dalogonensis* Ecklon & Zeyh., chandelier plant; *K. fedtschenkoi* Hamet & Perrier., lavender scalped air plant; *K. marmorata* Bak., pen wiper kalanchoe; *K. pinnata* (Lam.) Pers., air plant; and *K. tomentosa* Bak., plush or panda plant. *Kalanchoe* species may be found in plant collections and specialty garden centers (Bailey and Bailey, 1976; Graf, 1978). Other Crassulaceae genera include the garden ornamentals *Echeveria* and *Sedum*.

Origin: Most species, including *K. blossfeldiana*, are from Madagascar (Bailey and Bailey, 1976).

Uses and current status: *Kalanchoe blossfeldiana* is an internationally produced flowering potted plant. In Europe, kalanchoe is one of the leading potted plants (Fig. II-1 Kalanchoe). The plant is prized for its longevity in the home environment and a host of colors has increased its popularity. Kalanchoes can also be used in hanging baskets, dish gardens, and the outdoor garden. Kalanchoe are occasionally used as cut flowers. *Kalanchoe porphyrocalyx* is also used as a potted flowering plant. It is native to Madagascar and has interesting bell-shaped individual flowers 1 in. (2.5 cm) in diameter and 1.25 in. (3.2 cm) in length. The calyx is greenish purple, and the corolla is purplish and reflexed to reveal yellow. There can be up to 35 flowers per inflorescence (Zimmer, 1985). Unfortunately, the long production times make this species expensive to produce.

CULTIVARS

Scores of *K. blossfeldiana* cultivars are available in Europe, Japan, and North America with new improvements released annually. In the 1950s, only orange and red flowering plants were available. Now pastel pink, yellow, pure white, and bicolored flowers exist. The currently available cultivars may be hybrids of *K. blossfeldiana* with *K. flammea* Stapf., *K. pumila* Bak., and other species (Huxley et al., 1992).

PROPAGATION

Plants can be propagated from cuttings, seed, or *in vitro* methods. The latter two methods are only used by breeding firms or for special purposes. Seeds are quite small and germinate with ease at 70°F (21°C) under light; far-red light is inhibitory and red light is stimulatory (Schwabe, 1985). Seedling production from germination to flower requires 6 to 10 months, whereas flowering plants from cuttings require 17 weeks maximum with 14 weeks most common. Stock plants are maintained by specialty propagators and unrooted cuttings are internationally distributed to customers year-round. Use artificial LD to maintain vegetative growth of stock plants during the winter.

Terminal cuttings are rooted directly into the final pots. Cuttings will vary in length because various cultivars have different internode lengths. Typically, cuttings have one pair of mature leaves. Rooting hormone is not required because roots form with ease. In Europe, propagation tents are used and made with clear plastic in the winter and white plastic in the summer. This technique can be used in North America, except perhaps in summer when intermittent mist must be used due to summer heat buildup under the tents. A minimum amount of mist will be required. Some producers lay lightweight white Remay® or Vispore® over the cuttings and mist a few times a day. Do not oversaturate the medium with water. A medium temperature of 70 to 77°F (21 to 25°C), with 72°F (22°C) optimum, is required for rapid callus formation and rooting within 14 to 21 days (Miller, 1991; Schwabe, 1985).

FLOWERING CONTROL AND DORMANCY

Kalanchoe blossfeldiana is a SD plant, requiring only two short days/long nights (SD/LN) for the beginning of floral induction. However, increasing the number of SD results in greater numbers of individual flowers in the inflorescence, which is a cyme. There can be several hundred flowers per inflorescence (Schwabe, 1985). While maximum flower numbers were obtained in one study after 14 SD/LN cycles, another study found that some cultivars required 14 SD/LN cycles and others required up to 28 SD/LN cycles for complete development (Nell et al., 1982; Schwabe, 1985). Commercially, plants are typically kept under SD conditions for induction, initiation, and development until sold. Seeley (1952) reported that 21 SD cycles were sufficient for induction and initiation with continued development and anthesis under LD. The advantage was that the inflorescence was more compact under LD than an inflorescence developed under continuous SD. Commercially, 40 SD are the minimum number with many cultivars; afterward plants can be returned to natural LD during the summer. If LD are applied during the earlier SD period, each day of LD will result in a 1-day delay in flowering.

Eleven to 11.5 hr of light, 13 to 12.5 hr of dark is the minimum for flowering, because the critical night length is 12.5 hr. Commercially, most establishments pull black cloth over the crop at 1630 hr and remove it at 0730 or 0800 hr. Cyclic night interruption lighting can be used to prevent flowering of stock plants and cuttings during the short days of fall, winter, and early spring.

Floral induction and development are temperature related. During the SD/LN flower induction period, temperatures 80°F (27°C) and higher must be avoided, particularly if this temperature is experienced during the first 3 hr of dark. Commercially, SD should commence as late as possible during hot summer days to avoid heat buildup, and the black cloth should remain closed in the morning until sufficient dark duration has been reached. Warm 80°F (27°C) temperatures for the last 3 hr prior to the light cycle will not delay flowering. A night temperature of 70°F (21°C) is recommended for the most rapid flower initiation (Hillman, 1962; Pertuit, 1977).

Several factors are involved in the decision to end LD and commence SD: (1) the market date, (2) the response group (number of weeks from start of SD to anthesis), (3) the season, (4) the pot size (the larger the volume of medium, the slower the plant flowers), and (5) the need to pinch. Interestingly, under LD, leaves become thick, succulent, and turgid with 2400% more water than dry matter, whereas under SD the leaves have only 900% more water than dry matter (Zabka and Chaturvedi, 1975).

Kalanchoe porphyrocalyx is also a SD plant and will flower at 11 hr light, but not at 12 hr. Plants reach visible bud stage most rapidly at 9- to 10-hr day lengths. The optimum temperature appears to be 55 to 57°F (13 to 14°C), which is cooler than for *K. blossfeldiana*, and a minimum of 40 to 45 days is necessary for maximum floral induction. After this induction, plants develop visible flowers within 17 to 20 days at 64°F (18°C) or 72°F (22°C) under an 8- or 16-hr photoperiod.

TEMPERATURE

The optimum temperature for growth is between 64 and 68°F (18 to 20°C). Delay in flowering is observed at temperatures below 61°F (16°C). Above 72°F (22°C), the growth rate increases for some cultivars while others may be delayed. At 80°F (27°C) flowering is delayed for all cultivars (Anonymous, 1988; Miller, 1991;

Schwabe, 1985). Heat delay is caused by high temperatures during the first part of the night (dark period).

LIGHT

In winter during propagation, LD must be provided to maintain vegetative growth and supplemental lighting can advance the rate of rooting. Natural day length must be 11.5+ hr for vegetative growth to be maintained. Artificial lighting is used from September 15 to April 1 in northern areas of production. Incandescent light can be used between 2300 and 0200 hr and can be continuous or cyclic (8 to 10 min on/22 to 20 min off).

If supplemental HID lighting is used during rooting and during LD, 200 fc (40 $\mu mol \cdot m^{-2} \cdot s^{-1}$) are beneficial for "summer quality light" during winter. Additional supplemental lighting during the winter when plants are under SD has limited influence, particularly if supplemental HID lighting was used during LD.

During winter, the glazing must be clean. From mid-April to mid-September, however, the light level must be reduced to 5800 fc (1160 $\mu mol \cdot m^{-2} \cdot s^{-1}$) or leaf anthocyanin dramatically increases and the foliage develops an undesirable red cast. Shading also aids in summer temperature control (Anonymous, 1988; Miller, 1991; Schwabe, 1985). High light increases number of flowers in *K. porphyrocalyx* (Zimmer, 1985).

WATER

In the native environment of southern and southwestern Madagascar, the rainfall is only 10 to 15 in. (25 to 38 cm) per year. Do not overirrigate kalanchoe during the rooting process. Excess water enhances root rot problems during growth. Conversely, salt buildup must be avoided when too little water is used at each irrigation. Kalanchoe requires evenly moist medium with little fluctuation in the moisture level. Regardless, the irrigation system should be automated. The vast majority of kalanchoe grown in the world are produced with ebb-and-flow systems.

CARBON DIOXIDE

Though *Kalanchoe* belongs to the Crassulaceae family, where plant stomates open and CO_2 is absorbed during the night, modern cultivars do not open stomates at night. During the day use up to 900 ppm CO_2 for more vigorous growth (Anonymous, 1988; Miller, 1991; Mortensen and Moe, 1992; Zabka and Chaturvedi, 1975). High CO_2 levels cause excess stem elongation, leaf growth, and pigment formation.

NUTRITION

Nutritional levels should slowly increase during production (see Tables II-1 and II-2 Kalanchoe). Prior to anthesis, the level should decrease for maximum postharvest life. Medium and leaf tissue nutritional levels and medium pH and EC should be monitored on a regular basis (Anonymous, 1988; Miller, 1991; Nelson et al., 1980). Foliar nutrient levels for high-quality plants are listed in Chapter 6, Nutrition, Table 6-4.

MEDIA

The medium pH should be 5.8 to 6.5 (Table II-2 Kalanchoe). The medium should consist of at least 50% peat moss and be well aerated because the root system is quite fibrous (Anonymous, 1990; Ball, 1998; Laurie et al., 1968). The peat moss can be amended with various amounts of perlite, vermiculite, rock wool, or scoria.

HEIGHT CONTROL

A plant growth regulator may have to be applied to control internode elongation (Anonymous, 1988; Carlson et al., 1977; Hasek et al., 1986; Lyons and Hale, 1987; Miller, 1991; Pertuit, 1997). B-Nine (daminozide) sprays are used weekly in summer, every 10 to 15 days in fall and spring, and every 14 to 21 days in winter. The timing of sprays can be more accurate and predictable with the use of weekly height control measurements and estimated growth curves. B-Nine rates vary from 2500 to 5000 ppm, depending on the season and cultivar and are typically applied commencing 2 weeks after pinching. B-Nine can also be applied to cuttings during propagation starting 10 days after sticking.

A-Rest (ancymidol) sprays at 50 ppm can also be used when axillary growth is observed and again 20 to 30 days after short days commence. Florel (ethephon) at 250 to 500 ppm, Sumagic (uniconazole), and Bonzi (paclobutrazol) at 2 to 4 ppm are very effective, but are less utilized due to lack of research or experience with these chemicals. Adriansen (1985) noted that Cycocel (chlormequat) is also effective. With *K. porphyrocalyx*, only one B-Nine spray applied after 65 SD is required to reduce plant height by 50%.

TABLE II-1 KALANCHOE

Four basic nutritional periods that must be considered for the propagation, production, and marketing of *Kalanchoe*.

Period	Description of Period
1	Long-day vegetative period
2	Beginning of short day to flower bud initiation (after 6–7 weeks of SD)
3	Flower bud initiation to early flower color
4	Early flower color to marketing (7–10 days)

TABLE II-2 KALANCHOE

Suggested medium pH, EC, and nutrient levels for *Kalanchoe* during the various periods of production (Anonymous, 1988).

Period	pH	EC $dS \cdot m^{-1}$	N:P:K	NO_3	NH_4	PO_4 (ppm)	K	Ca	Mg	Fe
1	5.5	0.5	1:1:1	155	2	50	40	80	15	25
2	5.8	1.2	3:1:3 4:1:4	280	2	60	80	120	40	25
3	5.8	1.5	2:1:4 3:1:4	410	2	60	120+	120	40	20
4	6.0	1.0	1:1:1	150	2	50	160	120	20	20

Growers attempt to maintain a constant 68/68°F (20/20°C) (zero DIF) or 64/68°F (18/20°C) (-4 DIF) day/night temperature to reduce internode elongation. This procedure is economical if thermoblankets are also used as a black cloth system. Temperature dips for 2 to 3 hr prior to sunrise (DROP) have not been effective in reducing internode elongation (Mortensen and Moe, 1992). Graphical tracking to monitor plant height may be useful.

SPACING

Cuttings are directly rooted into the final pots during propagation and pots are kept pot-to-pot until they are moved to SD. The kalanchoe is most commonly grown in 4-in. (10-cm) pots spaced 5 × 5 in. (13 × 13 cm) apart. Five- or 6-in. (13- or 15-cm) pots can be spaced 9 × 9 or 10 × 10 in. (23 × 23 or 25 × 25 cm) apart, respectively.

PINCHING AND DISBUDDING

Modern kalanchoe cultivars freely branch and often do not need to be pinched. With 4-in. (10-cm) production, plants are typically not pinched. Larger pot sizes are pinched and only 0.5 to 0.75 in. (1 to 2 cm) of young growth is removed. Plants are pinched any time from just prior to the start of SD, when lateral shoots are less than 0.2 in. (0.5 cm) long, to 1 week after

the start of SD. If pinched, an additional 2 or 3 weeks of LD is needed for the 5- or 6-in. (13- or 15-cm) pots, respectively.

Atrinal sprays of 0.25 oz/gal (1.9 g · L⁻¹) are commonly used by large year-round specialty growers, especially on 2.25-in. (6-cm) mini pots. Excess application can cause crop delay. When appropriately used, maximum axillary shoot and flower development occur (Anonymous, 1988).

SUPPORT

No support required.

SCHEDULE AND TIMING

Most cultivars require 9 or more weeks for flowers to reach anthesis from the beginning of SD (see Table II-3 Kalanchoe). For a typical 10-week response cultivar, however, this time span can be as long at 12 to 13 weeks from November to April. Scheduling can be influenced not only by cultivar and season, but also by the use of HID lighting under LD and the use of CO_2 during production.

"Mini" kalanchoes in 2.25- to 3-in. (6- to 8-cm) pots are popular and profitable to produce. If 1 week of LD is given prior to SD, no pinching is needed. Atrinal is used and B-Nine sprays are used at 3 (5000 ppm), 6 (5000 ppm), and 9 (2500 ppm) weeks after SD commence (Miller,

TABLE II-3 KALANCHOE

Sample production schedule for 4-in. (10-cm) flowering potted *Kalanchoe*.

Cultural Step	Production Time (weeks)	Temperature °F (°C)	Photoperiod
Propagate cuttings	2–3	Medium: 70–77 (21–25)	LD
Moved to SD	2	Constant: 64 (18) or Day: 64 (18) Night: 68 (20)	SD
Normal photoperiod[a]	5–6	Constant: 64 (18) or Day: 64 (18) Night: 68 (20)	Natural or SD
Flower	4–6	Constant: 64 (18) or Day: 64 (18) Night: 68 (20)	Natural or SD
Total	13–17		

[a]*Because most production facilities have only one LD and one SD environment, most plants remain continually under SD until flowering.*

1991). *K. porphyrocalyx* requires 67 days to visible bud after SD commence and will flower 30 days later.

INSECTS

Aphids, cyclamen mites, mealybugs, and various leaf-chewing larvae can be a problem (Baker, 1978). With exclusion and rigid inspection, control generally requires minimal chemical use. Thrips are especially important because they can spread the tomato spotted wilt virus (Hausbeck et al., 1992). Kalanchoes, especially flower buds and flowers, are prone to phytotoxicity from many chemicals. Test all new chemicals on a few plants before applying to the entire crop. Wettable powders are least likely to cause phytotoxicty (Pertuit, 1997).

DISEASES

The three most prevalent diseases are powdery mildew (*Sphaerotheca fuliginea*), *Botrytis*, and *Phytophthora* crown rot. These may be controlled environmentally by monitoring humidity, temperature, and water. *Rhizoctonia* stem blight and *Rhizopus* stem canker can also be observed (Daughtrey and Chase, 1992). Tomato spotted wilt virus is a disastrous disease spread by thrips (Hausbeck et al., 1992). Other reported diseases include stem rot (*Myrothecium roridum*), black root rot (*Thielaviopsis basicola*), leaf spots (*Stemphylium* and *Cercospora*),

gray mold (*Botrytis cinerea*), and kalanchoe virus 1 (Dreistadt, 2001). A number of other viruses may cause problems.

PHYSIOLOGICAL DISORDERS

Failure to flower, malformed flowers, or reduced individual flower numbers per inflorescence can frequently be related to temperatures that are too high or too low during induction and initiation. High light causes abnormal leaf coloration (see Light section earlier in chapter). Ethylene exposures at any stage of growth can cause a wide range of symptoms (see Postharvest section next).

The unsightly corkiness of edema can disfigure foliage. Edema is caused by the rupture of stomatal cells from excessive water pressure and is accentuated by high humidity, low light, and wet medium (Pertuit, 1997).

Excessive growth of the axillary shoots can cover up the central florets due to reversion of growth from reproductive to vegetative (Hamrick, 2003). This can be due to low or high temperatures during SD, too few SD, or light contamination during the dark period.

POSTHARVEST

Kalanchoe plants or cut flowers should be marketed when 10 to 25% of the individual flowers are open on an inflorescence (Leonard and Nell, 1998). Cultivar selection is important because postharvest longevity can vary from 5 to 9 weeks. Because fertilizer rate has little effect on postharvest life, fertilization can be terminated 2 to 4 weeks prior to marketing.

Plants are very sensitive to ethylene; 0.1 ppm was sufficient to produce a response (Willumsen and Fjeld, 1995). When plants are exposed to ethylene, unopened flowers will not develop any further and open flowers senesce and become sleepy (partially closed). Both 1-methylcyclopropene (1-MCP, 20 ppb) gas and silver thiosulfate (STS, 0.5 mM) sprays are effective at preventing the effects of exogenous ethylene (Serek and Reid, 2000; Serek et al, 1994; Sisler et al., 1999). However, STS sprays may cause leaf necrosis (H.F. Wilkins, unpublished data).

Plants can be transported or held in the dark for up to 2 weeks at 50°F (10°C) and 3 weeks at 40°F (4°C). However, this long duration is not advised; market as soon as possible (Nell, 1993; Nowak and Rudnicki, 1990). In the home plants lasted longest when placed in cool, 65°F (18°C), and bright locations, 100 fc (15 μmol · m^{-2} · s^{-1}) (Leonard and Nell, 1998).

KEY POINTS

- Kalanchoe is used primarily as a potted flowering plant, but also occasionally as a cut flower and hanging basket plant.
- Producers must continuously test new cultivars for new colors and postharvest qualities.
- Propagation of cuttings is best under plastic tents or lightweight Remay® or Vispore® cloths.
- Kalanchoe is a SD plant requiring only 2 SD/LN to start flower induction but up to 28 SD/LN cycles are required for maximum flower development of some cultivars.

- Flowering can be delayed at night temperatures above 80°F (27°C) or below 61°F (16°C).
- Height is controlled through cultivar selection, DIF, chemical growth retardants, and graphical tracking.
- Plants are susceptible to powdery mildew, *Botrytis,* and *Phytophthora* crown rot.
- Plants are very sensitive to ethylene and 1-methylcyclopropene (1-MCP) and silver thiosulfate (STS) are effective in preventing the effects of exogenous ethylene.

BIBLIOGRAPHY

Adriansen, E. 1985. Kemisk vækstregulering, pp. 142–162 in *Potteplanter I—Produktion, Metoder, Midler,* O.V. Christensen, A. Klougart, I.S. Pedersen, and K. Wikesjö, editors. Gartner-INFO, København, Denmark. (in Danish)

Anonymous. 1988. *Kalanchoe,* pp. 1–23. Fides Beheer B.V. DeLier, Holland.

Anonymous. 1990. *Mikkelsens 'Bonanza' Hybrid Kalanchoe.* Mikkelsen, Inco., Astabula, Ohio.

Bailey, L.H., and E.Z. Bailey. 1976. *Kalanchoe,* pp. 620–623 in *Hortus Third: A Concise Dictionary of Plants Cultivated in the United States and Canada.* Macmillan, New York.

Baker, R. 1978. *Insects and Related Pests of Flower and Foliage Plants.* North Carolina Agricultural Extension Service, North Carolina State University, Raleigh.

Ball, V. 1998. *Kalanchoe,* pp. 586–591 in *Ball Redbook,* 16th ed., V. Ball, editor. Ball Publishing, Batavia, Illinois.

Carlson, W.H., S. Schnabel, J. Schnabel, and C. Turner. 1977. Concentration and application time of ancymidol for growth regulation of *Kalanchoe blossfeldiana* Poellniz. cv. Mace. *HortScience* 12:568.

Daughtrey, M., and A.R. Chase. 1992. *Kalanchoe,* pp. 135–137 in *Ball Field Guide to Disease of Greenhouse Ornamentals.* Ball Publishing, Geneva, Illinois.

Dreistadt, S.H. 2001. *Integrated Pest Management for Floriculture and Nurseries.* University of California Division of Agriculture and Natural Resources Publication 3402.

Graf, A.B. 1978. Crassulaceae (*Kalanchoe*), pp. 372–378 in *Tropica.* Roehrs Publishers, East Rutherford, New Jersey.

Hamrick, D. 2003. *Kalanchoe,* pp. 471–476 in *Ball Redbook,* vol. 2, 17th ed. Ball Publishing, Batavia, Illinois.

Hasek, R., R. Sciaroni, and G. Hickman. 1986. New growth regulator tested. *Greenhouse Grower* 4(2): 52–53.

Hausbeck, M.K., R.A. Welliver, M.A. Derr, and F.E. Gildow. 1992. Tomato spotted wilt virus survey among greenhouse ornamentals in Pennsylvania. *Plant Disease* 76:795–800.

Hillman, W.S. 1962. *The Physiology of Flowering*. Holt, Rinehart, and Winston, New York.

Huxley, A., M. Griffiths, and M. Levy. 1992. *Kalanchoe*, pp. 728–730 in *The New Royal Horticultural Society Dictionary of Gardening*, vol. 2. Stockton Press, New York.

Laurie, A., D.C. Kiplinger, and K.S. Nelson. 1968. *Kalanchoe*, pp. 413–414 in *Commercial Flower Forcing*. McGraw-Hill, New York.

Leonard, R.T., and T.A. Nell. 1998. Kalanchoes: Grow, ship right for long life. *GrowerTalks* 62(10): 78, 80, 82, 84.

Lyons, R.E., and C.L. Hale. 1987. Comparison of pinching methods on selected species of *Columnea, Kalanchoe,* and *Crassula*. *HortScience* 22:72–74.

Miller, R. 1991. New potted plants. *GrowerTalks* 54(11):51, 53, 55.

Mortensen, L.M., and R. Moe. 1992. Effects of CO_2 enrichment and different day/night temperature combinations on growth and flowering of *Rose* L. and *Kalanchoe blossfeldiana* v. Poelln. *Scientia Horticulturae* 51:145–153.

Nell, T.A. 1993. *Kalanchoe*, pp. 57–58 in *Flowering Potted Flowering Plants, Prolonging Shelf Performance*. Ball Publishing, Batavia, Illinois.

Nell, T.A., J.M. Fischer, T.J. Sheehan, and J.E. Barrett. 1982. Relationship of number of long nights to meristem development and flowering in kalanchoe. *Journal of the American Society for Horticultural Science* 107:900–904.

Nelson, P.V., G.C. Elliott, and N.C. Mingis. 1980. Sampling procedure for foliar analysis of *Kalanchoe blossfeldiana* 'Feuerzauber.' *Journal of the American Society for Horticultural Science* 105:599–603.

Nowak, J., and R.M. Rudnicki. 1990. *Postharvest Handling and Storage of Cut Flowers, Florist Greens and Potted Plants*. Timber Press, Portland, Oregon.

Pertuit, A.J., Jr. 1977. Influence of temperatures during long-night exposures on growth and flowering of 'Mace,' 'Thor,' and 'Telstar' *Kalanchoes*. *HortScience* 12:48–49.

Pertuit, A.J., Jr. 1997. *Kalanchoe*, pp. 94–101 in *Tips on Growing Specialty Potted Crops*, M.L. Gaston, S.A. Carver, C.A. Irwin, and R.A. Larson, editors. Ohio Florists' Association, Columbus, Ohio.

Schwabe, W.W. 1985. *Kalanchoe blossfeldiana*, pp. 217–235 in *Handbook of Flowering*, vol. III, A.H. Halevy, editor. CRC Press, Boca Raton, Florida.

Seeley, J.G. 1952. Long days after budding improve kalanchoes. *Pennsylvania Flower Growers Bulletin* 15:1–3.

Serek, M., and M.S. Reid. 2000. Ethylene and postharvest performance of potted kalanchoë. *Postharvest Biology and Technology* 18:43–48.

Serek, M., E.C. Sisler, and M.S. Reid. 1994. Novel gaseous ethylene binding inhibitor prevents ethylene effects in potted flowering plants. *Journal of the American Society for Horticultural Science* 119:1230–1233.

Sisler, E.C., M. Serek, E. Dupille, and R. Goren. 1999. Inhibition of ethylene responses by 1-methylcyclopropene and 3-methylcyclopropene. *Plant Growth Regulation* 27:105–111.

Willumsen, K., and T. Fjeld. 1995. Ethylene sensitivity of some flowering potted plants to exogenous ethylene. *Acta Horticulturae* 405:362–371.

Zabka, G.G., and S.N. Chaturvedi. 1975. Water conservation in *Kalanchoe blossfeldiana* in relation to carbon dioxide dark fixation. *Plant Physiology* 55:532–535.

Zimmer, K. 1985. *Kalanchoe porphyrocalyx*, pp. 236–239 in *Handbook of Flowering*, vol. III, A.H. Halevy, editor. CRC Press, Boca Raton, Florida.

Lachenalia

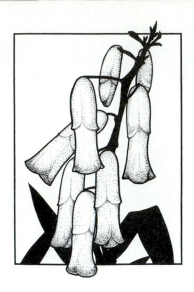

INTRODUCTION

Common name: Lachenalia.

Scientific name: *Lachenalia aloides* (L.f.) Engl., *L. bulbifera* (Cyr.) Engl., and *L. viridiflora* (W. Barker).

Family and related taxa: Liliaceae Juss. The lily family is quite large and contains many commercially important floriculture crops including *Allium*, *Alstroemeria*, *Brodiaea*, *Convallaria*, *Eremurus*, *Hyacinthus*, *Lilium*, *Muscari*, *Ornithogalum*, and *Tulipa*.

Origin: There are approximately 90 species of this South African bulbous plant in the family (Bailey and Bailey, 1976; Duncan, 1988; Huxley et al., 1992).

Uses and current status: Lachenalia can be used as handsome potted plants, cut flowers, or landscape plants.

The inflorescence of *Lachenalia* can be a spike or raceme, depending on the species. The individual flowers are bell shaped and colored blue, yellow, red, orange, or green. The flowers can also be bicolored and scented. The scape can be 12 to 16 in. (30 to 40 cm) tall. Both leaves and flower scape may be spotted or banded with brown or near black (Duncan, 1988, 1998; Le Nard and De Hertogh, 1993).

The striking flowers of this genus have been known to the Western world in the Northern Hemisphere for more than 300 years; however, widespread acceptance has been limited by sensitivity to frost and virus infections of stock apparently transmitted by aphids. In addition, variations in growth rate and flowering date have made scheduling and commercialization difficult. *Lachenalia* can be seen in gardens in Australia and California as well in world-renowned South African plant collections.

CULTIVARS

The *Lachenalia* species and cultivars seen in the trade include *L. aloides* var. *aurea* (Lindl.) Engl. with golden yellow flowers, *L. aloides* 'Pearsonii' with yellow-orange flowers tipped in maroon, *L. bulbifera* (Cyr.) Engl. with bright red to orange flowers, and *L. viridiflora* W. Barker with green flowers. Genetic improvements have been made for both cut flowers and potted flowering plants. These hybrids and cultivars have been released primarily through firms in the Netherlands and Israel. An active breeding program has been in existence for several years in South Africa (Hancke and Coertze, 1988).

PROPAGATION

Propagation is by seed, bulblets, leaf cuttings, or *in vitro* (Duncan, 1988; Le Nard and De Hertogh, 1993; Niederwieser and Ndou, 2002; Niederwieser and Vcelar, 1990; Perrignon, 1992; Suh et al., 1997). Commercially, the primary source of plant material is from bulblets and leaf cuttings. If using *in vitro*, care must be taken when removed from culture (Ault, 1995).

FLOWERING CONTROL AND DORMANCY

Most species are from areas with winter rain, cool winter and spring temperatures, and hot, dry summers. A few species are found in areas where rain is more or less consistent throughout the year. Regardless, all species are spring flowering and are dormant during the summer. High summer temperatures are thought to be required to break physiological rest (Du Plessis and Duncan, 1989; Duncan, 1988).

A. Halevy (personal communication) felt that *Lachenalia* bulbs should be treated with 12 weeks at 68 to 77°F (20 to 25°C) after harvest, followed by 3 weeks at 63°F (17°C) and 6 weeks at 48°F (9°C). Flowering was advanced by 6 to 8 weeks and occurred within 63 to 112 days after planting. However, Roh et al. (1995) stated that floral initiation was promoted by 73 to 81°F (23 to 27°C) temperatures prior to and after bulb harvest. At 77°F (25°C) bulbs became reproductive within 90 days; at 59°F (15°C)

TABLE II-1 LACHENALIA

The influence of temperature treatment on Israeli-grown *Lachenalia* bulbs potted July 28. Subsequent forcing occurred in an unheated polyethylene covered greenhouse in Israel.

Treatment (weeks)		Days to Flower after Termination of Treatment (date)	
Warm 75°F (24°C)	Cold 48°F (9°C)	L. aloides 'Pearsonii'	L. bulbifera
0	0	103 (Nov. 8)	138 (Dec. 13)
0	4	82 (Nov. 15)	92 (Nov. 21)
0	6	78 (Nov. 25)	—[a]
0	8	—	—
10	0	78 (Dec. 23)	93 (Jan. 7)
10	4	60 (Jan. 2)	65 (Jan. 3)
10	6	20 (Dec. 7)	—
10	8	—	—

[a]Unacceptable quality, flower aborted.

bulbs were vegetative 150 days (Roh et al., 1998). After floral initiation 45 days of 50 to 59°F (10 to 15°C) was required for rapid forcing at 59°F (15°C).

With *L. aloides* 'Pearsonii' and *L. bulbifera*, H.F. Wilkins (unpublished data) noted that when the initial heat treatment was given in Israel, neither an additional 10 weeks of 75°F (24°C) nor 4 to 8 weeks of 48°F (9°C) had a great impact on date of flowering (see Table II-1 Lachenalia). However, days to flowering after treatment decreased with both the additional heat and cold treatments. Thus, heat and cold treatments greatly reduced greenhouse forcing time. Similar data were obtained with *L. aloides* var. *aurea* and *L. viridiflora*.

TEMPERATURE

After corms are treated with the appropriate temperature (see Table II-1 Lachenalia), forcing occurs at cool night temperatures between 50 and 59°F (10 and 15°C), with 50 to 53°F (10 to 12°C) being optimum. Day temperatures are 63 to 77°F (17 to 25°C) .

LIGHT

Full light is required for production.

WATER

Do not overwater this desert species and use a well-drained medium.

CARBON DIOXIDE

No information available.

NUTRITION

Plants respond well to 200 ppm N and 175 K. No superphosphate should be used for fear of fluoride leaf damage with this monocot.

MEDIA

Duncan (1988) stated that the various species are found in a variety of soil types and pH ranges. In commerce, plants thrive in a peat medium with redwood bark and sand (4:2:1). Regardless, the media must be well drained.

HEIGHT CONTROL

Growth retardants may not be necessary if plants are grown in full light at the proper temperature. However, if necessary, Bonzi (paclobutrazol) drenches at 1 to 2 mg a.i./4-in. (10-cm) pot or sprays at 100 to 200 ppm may reduce leaf length (Ogutu and Miller, 2003). Sumagic (uniconazole) corm dips at 20 ppm may also be effective.

SPACING

One to four bulbs are planted in a 3- to 4-in. (8- to 10-cm) pot and five bulbs in a 6-in. (15-cm) pot. Plants grow upright, and not more than 2 to 3 in. (5 to 7.5 cm) is required between pots.

PINCHING AND DISBUDDING

No pinching or disbudding required.

SUPPORT

No support required.

SCHEDULE AND TIMING

Pretreated corms that have received the appropriate warm temperature treatment are received from suppliers. The bulbs can be forced within 60 days at 70/65°F (18/21°C) day/night temperatures (Roh et al., 1995; unpublished data).

INSECTS

Pests include mealybugs, slugs, and snails (Du Plessis and Duncan, 1989).

DISEASES

Plants are susceptible to *Erwinia* infections. Reduction of vigor and quality caused by viruses is a serious issue (Du Plessis and Duncan, 1989).

PHYSIOLOGICAL DISORDERS

Corms will not produce flowers (blind) if not given the appropriate temperature treatments.

POSTHARVEST

Harvest when the lower three to four florets are open. Potted plants can flower for up to 6 weeks (Hancke and Coertze, 1988). Plants or cut flowers should be shipped at 40 to 48°F (5 to 9°C).

KEY POINTS

- *Lachenalia* is a long neglected garden ornamental that can be used as a potted flowering plant and cut flower.
- Plants are propagated by seed, bulblets, leaf cuttings, or *in vitro*.

- High-temperature treatments are required for floral initiation and development, after which cold treatment allows rapid forcing.

BIBLIOGRAPHY

Ault, J.R. 1995. *In vitro* rooting and greenhouse acclimatization of *Lachenalia* shoots. *HortScience* 30:1304–1306.

Bailey, L.H., and E.Z. Bailey. 1976. *Lachenalia*, p. 630 in *Hortus Third: A Concise Dictionary of Plants Cultivated in the United States and Canada.* Macmillan, New York.

Du Plessis, P., and G. Duncan. 1989. *Bulbous Plants of South Africa—A Guide to Their Cultivation and Propagation.* Tafelberg Publishers, Cape Town, South Africa.

Duncan, G.D. 1988. *The Lachenalia Handbook.* CIP Book Printers, Cape Town, South Africa.

Duncan, G. 1998. Notes on the genus *Lachenalia. Herbertia* 53:40–48.

Hancke, F.L., and A.F. Coertze. 1988. Four new *Lachenalia* cultivars with yellow flowers. *HortScience* 23:923–924.

Huxley, A., M. Griffiths, and M. Levy. 1992. *Lachenalia*, pp. 2–4 in *The New Royal Horticulture Society Dictionary of Gardening*, vol. 3. Stockton Press, New York.

Le Nard, M., and A.A. De Hertogh. 1993. *Lachenalia*, pp. 728–729 in *The Physiology of Flower Bulbs*, A.A. De Hertogh and M. Le Nard, editors. Elsevier, Amsterdam.

Niederwieser, J.G., and A.M. Ndou. 2002. Review on adventitious bud formation in *Lachenalia. Acta Horticulturae* 570:135–140.

Niederwieser, J.G., and B.M. Vcelar. 1990. Regeneration of *Lachenalia* species from leaf explants. *HortScience* 25:684–687.

Ogutu, R., and W.B. Miller. 2003. Growth regulation of *Lachenalia aloides* cultivars. *HortScience* 38: 727. (Abstract)

Perrignon, R.J. 1992. Bulblet production in vivo from leaves of *Lachenalia* (Jacq.). *Acta Horticulturae* 325:341–347.

Roh, M.S., R.H. Lawson, C.-Y. Song, and E. Louw. 1995. Forcing *Lachenalia* as a potted plant. *Acta Horticulturae* 397:147–153.

Roh, M.S., A. Grassotti, and L. Guglieri. 1998. Storage and forcing temperatures affect inflorescence initiation, flowering, and floret blast of *Lachenalia aloides* 'Pearsonii.' *Acta Horticulturae* 454: 213–221.

Suh, J.K., M.S. Roh, and J.S. Lee. 1997. Leaf cutting propagation, growth and flowering of *Lachenalia. Acta Horticulturae* 430:369–376.

Liatris

FIGURE II-1 LIATRIS *Liatris spicata* 'Floristan' garden ornamental and cut flower.

INTRODUCTION

Common names: liatris, gay-feather, blazing-star.

Scientific names: *Liatris spicata* (L.) Willd. is the most common species grown in commerce (Huxley et al. 1992). *L. aspera* Michx., *L. microcephala* (Small) K. Schum., *L. pycnostachya* Michx., and *L. scariosa* (L.) Willd. are less commonly grown. *L. callilepis,* a name commonly seen in the literature, has no botanical standing and should be considered *L. spicata.*

Family and related taxa: Compositae Giseke. Approximately 35 species occur in this genus, all of which are native to North America. These perennial herbs develop a corm or an enlarged root structure. Related genera include *Aster, Calendula, Callistephus, Centaurea, Cosmos, Dahlia, Dendranthema, Echinacea, Gerbera, Helianthus, Pericallis, Solidago, Tagetes,* and *Zinnia.*

Origin: *L. spicata* is widely distributed in the United States from northern Minnesota to Michigan, south to Florida and Louisiana, and is hardy from Zones 3 to 8 (Bailey and Bailey, 1976). *L. pycnostachya* and *L. spicata* are found from Indiana to South Dakota, south to Texas and east to Louisiana, South Carolina, and Florida. *L. scariosa* is found in the mountains of Pennsylvania south to South Carolina and Georgia. *L. aspera* is broadly distributed in eastern and central North America, while *L. microcephala* is native only to southeast United States (USDA–NRCS, 2002).

Uses and current status: At one time this genus was relegated to the perennial garden; in the late 1970s and early 1980s, however, *L. spicata* quickly became an important greenhouse and field-grown cut flower (Starman et al., 1995) (Fig. II-1 Liatris). The early development of *Liatris* commenced in Israel and Europe and spread to North America, the origin of the genus. Other species are also used as cut flowers and garden ornamentals. Plants can also be grown in containers as a potted flowering plant, but height control is difficult.

The inflorescence is a long slender spike with numerous individual flowers 1/2 to 3/4 in. (1.3 to 2.0 cm) across. The individual flowers can be closely attached (sessile) to the stem or have a peduncle. The terminal or apical buds always open first and the remaining buds mature downward. Leaves are opposite, linear, and frequently form a basal rosette prior to the elongation of the floral spike (Armitage, 1987, 1989; Bailey and Bailey, 1976; Dress, 1959).

CULTIVARS

Heights of the flowering spikes vary from 10 to 20 in. (25 to 51 cm) up to 5 ft (1.5 m), of which the upper third has flowers and the lower two-thirds linear leaves (Bailey and Bailey, 1976). 'Kobold' is short, 1.5 to 2 ft. (45 to 60 cm) tall, and may also be called 'Goblin' or 'Gnome' (Armitage, 1989; Nau, 1998).

Many cultivated species have white forms. For *L. spicata* there are several cultivars whose colors vary from the natural medium blue color to deep purple-blue, as well as creamy white (Armitage and Laushman, 2003; Bailey and Bailey, 1976; Dress, 1959).

PROPAGATION

Plants can be propagated by corm divisions or from seed, which eventually produce corms. Cuttings can be made from young shoots (Salac and Fitzgerald, 1983). Typically, the underground storage organs are commercially harvested and graded in the fall and cold stored for subsequent forcing. After corms are harvested and divided, they are air cured at ambient temperatures for 3 to 7 days. Smaller corms are replanted in the field or garden for summer flowering the following year (Armitage and Laushman, 2003).

Seed is available for heterozygous planting stock [9400 seed/oz (332/gm)]. Seed germinates in 21 to 28 days at 65 to 70°F (18 to 21°C) (Nau, 1998). Armitage and Laushman (2003) stated that 75 to 78°F (24 to 26°C) was best and high humidity should be maintained. Salac and Hesse (1975) reported that the best results for *L. pycnostachya* and *L. aspera* were stratification at 39°F (4°C) for 105 days and then germination at 91/66°F (33/19°C) light/dark regimes under 12-hr light from cool white fluorescent lamps.

Seed can be sown in the spring for immediate germination or in the autumn for germination the following growing season after being overwintered (Post, 1949). Seed germination is enhanced by stratification for 10 weeks, benzyladenine at 10 or 100 ppm, and thiourea at 0.76 or 7.61 ppm (Parks and Boyle, 2002). *L. pycnostachya* corms will produce high-quality flowers in the first year, whereas seedlings will not produce similar cut flower yields until at least the second year (Salac and Fitzgerald, 1983). *In vitro* propagation has been reported by Stimart and Harbage (1989) and Stimart and Mather (1996).

FLOWERING CONTROL AND DORMANCY

Flowering in nature occurs in late July, August, and into September, depending on the species. Dormant corms are harvested in the fall at the end of the warm summer and under shortening day lengths. Dormancy is greater in November and decreases with time (Keren-Paz et al., 1989). Ethylene may be involved in dormancy and the greater the degree of dormancy, the less ethylene that is produced. Ethrel (ethylene) treatment resulted in rapid shoot elongation.

Corms do not flower unless they receive a cold vernalization treatment (Zieslin, 1985). Moe (1993) and Moe and Berland (1986) have shown that the longer the cold treatment, the more rapidly flowering occurs. Little difference existed in days to flower between corms stored for 9 or 12 weeks (90 versus 84 days to flower); however, the number of flowering stems decreased from 240 to 167. When 41 versus 32°F (5 versus 0°C) storage temperatures were compared, days to flower were not different, but 32°F (0°C) reduced the number of flowering stems. The cold requirement for flowering can be partially substituted by dipping the corms in a 500-ppm gibberellic acid (GA$_3$) solution for 1 hr.

The apparent dormancy in *Liatris* can be complicated. Corms from late spring and early summer production schedules grown in subtropical areas, such as Kenya or Israel, do not develop dormancy in the field if plants are kept irrigated. Plants form vegetative rosettes of foliage in late summer and early autumn, but never flower. However, when corms are harvested in Israel during the cold winter, little or no dormancy exists and emergence occurs (Waithaka, 1985; Waithaka and Wanjao, 1982; Wanjao and Waithaka, 1983; Zieslin and Geller, 1983a).

If corms are cold treated, floral tissue initiates and develops under both SD and LD. However, rate of development is enhanced under LD conditions (Zieslin, 1985; Zieslin and Geller, 1983b).

TEMPERATURE

Corms must be cold treated for rapid flowering when harvested in the summer. In Israel, only 1 week of 36°F (2°C) cooling will result in 30% of the corms flowering; flowering percentage increased with increasing cold storage duration (Zieslin, 1985; Zieslin and Geller, 1983a). However, the flowering percentage of corms cold stored for 1 week increased to 50% if they received a 500-ppm GA$_3$ treatment. After 5 weeks of 36°F (2°C), 60% flowered without GA; 100% flowered with the additional GA$_3$ treatment. Keren-Paz et al. (1989), also from Israel, state that 9 weeks at 37°F (3°C) resulted in dormancy release. In Kenya, only 90% of corms flowered after 8 weeks of cooling at 37 to 41°F (3 to 5°C); increasing the duration of cold up to 12 weeks had no effect on percent of corms flowering (Waithaka and Wanjao, 1982; Wanjao and Waithaka, 1983). Wanjao and Waithaka (1983) found that GA_3 corm dips were beneficial even with corms cooled for 8 weeks. Moe and Berland (1986) stated that the optimum corm treatment was 41°F (5°C) for 9 weeks followed by a 1-hr 500-ppm GA_3 dip.

After corms have been cold treated, soil temperature for forcing should be held below 68°F (20°C) for the first 4 weeks (De Hertogh, 1996). Espinosa et al. (1991) reported that shoots emerged most rapidly at 68°F (20°C) when compared to 59, 77, or 86°F (15, 25, or 30°C). Forcing temperatures that have been reported are 63°F (17°C) in Norway and 70 to 77°F (21 to 25°C) outdoors in Kenya (Moe and Berland, 1986; Waithaka and Wanjao, 1982; Wanjao and Waithaka, 1983).

LIGHT

Liatris spicata is a facultative LD plant in that fewer leaves are formed under LD treatments than under SD (88 versus 156 leaves) (Berland, 1983; Moe, 1993). However, plants will flower under either LD or SD. Long photoperiods will also hasten the rate of elongation. When LD are applied using incandescent lights, plants are taller and the number of flowering stems is reduced. On the other hand, under SD plants are slower to flower, shorter, and produce more flowering stems. Temperature interacts with photoperiod such that cool temperatures and LD hasten flowering, but there is little response to both LD and warm temperatures. If used, LD (natural day lengths plus 4-hr night breaks) treatments are applied during the first 5 weeks of the forcing process (Espinosa and Healy, 1990; Espinosa et al., 1991; Zieslin, 1985; Zieslin and Geller, 1983b).

Plants are grown in full sun outdoors; when grown under protection, shade only for temperature control.

WATER

Although *L. spicata* originated from moist situations and *L. pycnostachya* from dry sites, well-drained soil is used for commercial outdoor-grown *Liatrus*. An open porous medium is used for good water drainage in containers. Do not overwater. On the other hand, *Liatrus* will not have high flower yields unless properly irrigated, particularly during the early stages of growth when flowers are initiating and developing (Anonymous, 1988).

CARBON DIOXIDE

No information available.

NUTRITION

Armitage and Laushman (2003) recommended 100 to 150 ppm N after shoots emerge when forced in a greenhouse; however, a major source of corms, Agrexco-Agriculture Export Company from Israel, recommends 100 ppm N, 20 ppm P, and 150 ppm K (Anonymous, 1988). Tissue nutrient levels are listed in Table II-1 Liatris. With field-grown *L. pycnostachya* in Nebraska, United States, 5.5 lb/yd² (3 kg/100 m²) of 10–10–10 fertilizer was sufficient for superior production and yields (Salac and Fitzgerald, 1983).

MEDIA

With seed germination and potted plant production, a variety of commercial peat-based media are commonly used. As stated in the Water section, the medium should be well drained. A medium pH of 6.5 to 7.0 was recorded by Salac and Fitzgerald (1983); 6 to 7 was recommended by De Hertogh (1996).

HEIGHT CONTROL

Little information is available on height control for flowering potted plant production. For potted plant production, cultivar selection is of primary importance. *L. spicata* 'Kobold' is one of the shortest cultivars available and best suited for potted plant production (Nau, 1998). Note that LD produce longer stems with both *L. spicata* and *L. pycnostachya* (Salac and Fitzgerald, 1983; Zieslin and Geller, 1983b).

TABLE II-I LIATRIS
Tissue nutrient levels found in *Liatris spicata* (Armitage and Laushman, 2003).

Location	N	P	K	Ca	Mg	Fe	Mg	B	Zn
			%					ppm	
Georgia	2.7	0.20	1.16	1.49	0.45	207	163	24	94
California	3.3	0.19	2.31	1.12	0.41	207	178	31	86

Holcomb and Beattie (1988) reported that one 25-ppm Sumagic (uniconazole) drench produced the best height control; treated plants were 13 in. (33 cm) tall and untreated control plants were 29 in. (74 cm) tall. However, the flower spikes were too short with Sumagic treatment and some flowers aborted. A 100-ppm A-Rest (ancymidol) spray resulted in 18-in. (56-cm)-tall plants. A-Rest drenches at 0.25 to 0.5 mg a.i. (2 to 4 ppm)/6-in. (15-cm) pot may also be effective (Whipker, 2003). Lower rates of Sumagic, corm soaks, combinations of application methods (corm soaks, medium drenches, and foliar sprays), and multiple applications may also be useful. Bonzi (paclobutrazol) sprays at 160 ppm were not effective (Latimer, 2001).

SPACING

Commercially available corm sizes vary in circumference from 2.0 to 2.4 in. (5 to 6 cm), 2.4 to 3.1 in. (6 to 8 cm), 3.1 to 4.0 in. (8 to 10 cm), 4.0 to 4.7 in. (10 to 12 cm), to 4.7+ in. (12+ cm). Larger corms produce a greater number of stems per corm (Salac and Fitzgerald, 1983) (Table II-2 Liatris). Corms are planted 2 to 3 in. (5 to 7.5 cm) deep (Armitage and Laushman, 2003; De Hertogh, 1996).

Cut flowers can be grown in rows 3 ft (1 m) apart or in beds. Corms are spaced 2 to 4 in. (5 to 12 cm) apart in rows, depending on the corm size (Armitage and Laushman, 2003; Salac and Fitzgerald, 1983). In beds, 80 to 100 small-sized corms, less than 3.1 in. (8 cm) diameter, are planted/yd² (96 to 120/m²) and 36 to 60 large corms, greater than 3.1 in. (8 cm) diameter, are planted/yd² (42 to 72/m²) (Anonymous, 1988; Salac and Fitzgerald, 1983). For field plantings grown for more than one season wider spacings may be used; increasing the space per plant from 1 to 4 ft² (0.09 to 0.37) increased the number of flowers harvested per

TABLE II-2 LIATRIS

Influence of corm size of *Liatris pycnostachya* 'Eureka' on yield (Salac and Fitzgerald, 1983).

Corm Diameter in. (cm)	Flowering Stems (no.)	Stem Length in. (cm)
0.4–0.6 (1.0–1.4)	2.0	36 (90)
0.9–1.3 (2.4–3.4)	5.5	42 (106)
1.8–2.1 (4.5–5.4)	9.0	42 (105)
2.8–3.1 (7.0–7.9)	18.4	39 (98)

plant but decreased the number of flowers harvested per square foot or square meter (Armitage, 1987).

In a 6-in. (15-cm) azalea pot, use only the smallest size corms and plant five corms per pot. Plants are grown pot-to-pot, then spaced on 10-in. (25-cm) centers when leaves begin to overlap.

PINCHING AND DISBUDDING

None is required or practiced. However, each individual inflorescence is capable of developing a smaller but elongated inflorescence if apical dominance is broken either by horizontally orienting the stem or by soft pinching the inflorescence when it is 3 to 4 in. (8 to 10 cm) long (Zieslin, 1985; H.F. Wilkins and J. Erwin, personal communication). Commercially sprayed liatris can be produced by pruning developing inflorescences.

Moe (1993) and Moe and Berland (1986) illustrated that 500-ppm GA$_3$ corm soaks for 1 hr increased axillary bud activity and the number of harvested flowering stems. The most pronounced GA$_3$ activity was with corms cooled at 32°F (0°C) for 7 weeks. However, 9 weeks of cold is the optimal cold duration for the maximum number of flowering stems (see Flower Control and Dormancy and Temperature sections earlier in chapter).

SUPPORT

For greenhouse cut flower production, one to two layers of netting may be helpful. In the field, usually one layer is sufficient to prevent damage from wind.

SCHEDULE AND TIMING

Flowering typically occurs 10 to 12 weeks after planting in a greenhouse (Bartels Stek, personal communication). Moe and Berland (1986) forced corms under cover in Norway in 96, 94, 90, 84, 80, or 80 days when corms were cold stored for 3, 6, 9, 12, 15, or 18 weeks, respectively, at 41°F (5°C).

Outdoors Armitage and Laushman (1990) planted corms monthly in Georgia from November through March and the first date of harvest ranged from July 1 for the November and December plantings to July 21 for the March planting. Little difference existed among the planting dates in time from the first to last harvested stem, stem length, and stem diameter. However, flower yield was dramati-

TABLE II-3 LIATRIS

The influence of years of production of *Liatris spicata* corms on survival and production (Armitage and Laushman, 1990).

Year	Survival (%)	Stems/Plant (no.)	Stem Length in. (cm)
1	100	2.7	24.6 (61.6)
2	95	8.0	30.0 (74.9)
3	93	15.0	39.2 (98.0)

cally greater for the February and March planting dates and increased annually (Table II-3 Liatris). In Kenya, corms flowered an average of 90 days after being planted (Waithaka, 1985).

In Minnesota outdoors, *L. pycnostachya* is the first species to flower, then *L. aspera* and *L. spicata. L. punctata* Hook. is the last to flower (Sallee, 1991).

Corms are frozen in moist peat at 28 to 30°F (−2 to 1°C) by commercial firms, allowing corms to be available throughout the year. When corms are thawed, do not refreeze. Thawed corms can be stored at 45°F (7°C) for up to 2 weeks after they are received (De Hertogh, 1996; J. Vanderberg, personal communication).

INSECTS

Aphids, spider mite, thrips, and nematodes can reduce quality. However, *Liatris* have few serious pest problems (Moe, 1993).

DISEASES

Moe (1993) listed *Botrytis, Sclerotinia, Rhizoctonia,* and *Verticillium* as potential problems. Nematodes are a serious issue if not detected and controlled. Postharvest treatment of corms with 120°F (49°C) hot water for 40 min destroyed verticillium spores in liatris tubers but damaged buds (Gilad and Borochov, 1993). Leaf spots (*Phyllosticta liatridis* and *Septoria liatridis*) and rust (*Coleosporium laciniariae* and *Puccinia poarum*) have also been reported (Dreistadt, 2001).

PHYSIOLOGICAL DISORDERS

Leaf scorch or tip burning of the foliage is a problem (Moe, 1993). This disorder is frequently limited to the foliage along specific sections of the stem. The leaves are often normal above or below the affected area. Leaf scorch has been attributed to a transitory calcium deficiency due to periods of rain, high humidity, and low water transpiration that combine to produce insufficient calcium uptake into young developing leaves (see Physiological Disorders sections in the *Lilium* and *Euphorbia* chapters). Moe (1993) stated that leaf scorch may be related to wide temperature shifts. Plants in both the greenhouse or field are susceptible.

POSTHARVEST

Nowak and Rudnicki (1990) recommended that stems should be harvested when 50% of the florets are open if a floral preservative is not used. Only three to four flowers should be open prior to harvest if a preservative is used. Lower foliage that would be below water should be removed. If stems are treated with a floral preservative, a vase life of up to 12 days can be expected.

Preservatives can be used as a 24- to 72-hr pulse with 5% sucrose and 200 ppm 8-hydroxyquinoline citrate, a common biocide, or a continuous supply of 2.5 to 5% sucrose can be used (Han, 1992; Nowak and Rudnicki, 1990; Sacalis, 1993). Han (1992), however, recommended pulses of 10% or greater sucrose for 20 hr. A biocide must be used in conjunction with sucrose; Borochov and Keren-Paz (1984) used 0.2% 8-HQC. Liatris are not sensitive to ethylene (Woltering and van Doorn, 1988).

Harvested stems can be stored at 32 to 35°F (0 to 2°C) for 5 days if dry or 7 days if in water. In both cases, stems had been pulsed with a preservative (Armitage and Laushman, 2003).

Flowering stems can be air dried after the foliage has been removed. Purple-flowered stems retain color well after drying.

KEY POINTS

- This hardy perennial is grown for its tall spikes of purple or white flowers and is used primarily as a cut flower and garden ornamental.

- *Liatris* is native to North American grasslands.

- *Liatris* is commercially propagated from corms or seed.

- Corms should be cold treated at 41°F (5°C) for 9 weeks for rapid emergence and flowering.
- The cold requirement can be partially replaced with a 500-ppm GA$_3$ dip for 1 hr.

- Stems are harvested when only three to four florets are open if a floral preservative is used. Otherwise stems should be harvested when 50% open.
- Cut purple-flowered stems air dry well.

BIBLIOGRAPHY

Anonymous. 1988. *Liatris callilepis Corms Storing & Growing Instructions.* Agrexco-Agricultural Export Co., Israel.

Armitage, A.M. 1987. The influence of spacing on field-grown perennial crops. *HortScience* 22:904–907.

Armitage, A.M. 1989. *Liatris,* pp. 333–334 and 359 in *Herbaceous Perennial Plants.* Varsity Press, Athens, Georgia.

Armitage, A.M., and J.M. Laushman. 1990. Planting date and in-ground time affect cut flowers of *Liatris, Polianthes,* and *Iris. HortScience* 25:1239–1241.

Armitage, A.M., and J.M. Laushman. 2003. *Liatris spicata,* pp. 373–380 in *Specialty Cut Flowers,* 2nd ed. Timber Press, Portland, Oregon.

Bailey, L.H., and E.Z. Bailey. 1976. *Liatris,* p. 655 in *Hortus Third: A Concise Dictionary of Plants Cultivated in the United States and Canada.* Macmillan, New York.

Berland, M. 1983. Growth and flowering in *Liatris spicata* (L.) Willd. M.S. thesis, Agricultural University of Norway, Ås. (in Norwegian)

Borochov, A., and V. Keren-Paz. 1984. Bud opening of cut liatris flowers. *Scientia Horticulturae* 23:85–89.

De Hertogh, A. 1996. Liatris, pp. D31–32 in *Holland Bulb Forcers' Guide,* 5th ed. International Flower Bulb Centre, Hillegom, The Netherlands.

Dress, W.J. 1959. Notes on the cultivated Compositae. 3. Liatris. *Baileya* 7:23–32.

Dreistadt, S.H. 2001. *Integrated Pest Management for Floriculture and Nurseries.* University of California Division of Agriculture and Natural Resources Publication 3402.

Espinosa, I., and W. Healy. 1990. Influence of photoperiod on *Liatris spicata* generative shoot growth. *HortScience* 25:764–766.

Espinosa, I., W. Healy, and M. Roh. 1991. The role of temperature and photoperiod on *Liatris spicata* shoot development. *Journal of the American Society for Horticultural Science* 116:27–29.

Gilad, Z., and A. Borochov. 1993. Hot-water treatment of liatris tubers. *Scientia Horticulturae* 56:61–69.

Han, S.S. 1992. Role of sucrose in bud development and vase life of cut *Liatris spicata* (L.) Willd. *HortScience* 27:1198–1200.

Holcomb, E.J., and D.J. Beattie. 1988. Can perennials be indoor/outdoor plants? *Greenhouse Grower* 6(9):104, 107–108.

Huxley, A., M. Griffiths, and M. Levy. 1992. *Liatris,* pp. 63 in *The New Royal Horticultural Society Dictionary of Gardening,* vol. 3. Stockton Press, New York.

Keren-Paz, V., A. Borochov, and S. Mayak. 1989. The involvement of ethylene in liatris corm dormancy. *Plant Growth Regulation* 8:11–20.

Latimer, J. 2001. Herbaceous perennials, pp. 98–110 in *Tips on Regulating Growth of Floriculture Crops,* M.L. Gaston, L.A. Kunkle, P.S. Konjoian, and M.F. Wilt, editors. Ohio Florists' Association Services, Columbus, Ohio.

Moe, R. 1993. *Liatris,* pp. 381–390 in *The Physiology of Flower Bulbs,* A. De Hertogh and M. Le Nard, editors. Elsevier, Amersterdam.

Moe, R., and M. Berland. 1986. Effect of various corm treatments on flowering of *Liatris spicata* Willd. *Acta Horticulturae* 177:197–201.

Nau, J. 1998. *Liatris,* pp. 598–599 in *Ball Redbook,* 16th ed., V. Ball, editor. Ball Publishing, Batavia, Illinois.

Nowak, J., and R. Rudnicki. 1990. *Postharvest Handling and Storage of Cut Flowers, Florist Greens and Potted Plants.* Timber Press, Portland, Oregon.

Parks, C.A., and T.H. Boyle. 2002. Germination of *Liatris spicata* (L.) Willd. seed is enhanced by stratification, benzyladenine, or thiourea but not gibberellic acid. *HortScience* 37:202–205.

Post, K. 1949. *Liatris,* p. 611 in *Florist Crop Production and Marketing.* Orange Judd Publishing, New York.

Sacalis, J.N. 1993. Liatris spp., pp. 77–78 in *Cut Flowers, Prolonging Freshness,* 2nd ed., J.L. Seals, editor. Ball Publishing, Batavia, Illinois.

Salac, S.S., and J.B. Fitzgerald. 1983. Influence of propagation method and fertilizer rate on growth and development of *Liatris pycnostachya. HortScience* 18:198–199.

Salac, S.S., and M.C. Hesse. 1975. Effects of storage and germination conditions on the germination of four species of wild flowers. *Journal of the American Society for Horticultural Science* 100:359–361.

Sallee, K. 1991. How a Minnesota operation propagates liatris from seed. *Nursery Manager* 174(12):14, 16, 18.

Starman, T.W., T.A. Cerny, and A.J. MacKenzie. 1995. Productivity and profitability of some field-grown specialty cut flowers. *HortScience* 30: 1217–1220.

Stimart, D.P., and J.F. Harbage. 1989. Shoot proliferation and rooting *in vitro* of *Liatris spicata*. *HortScience* 24:835–836.

Stimart, D.P., and J.C. Mather. 1996. Regenerating adventitious shoots from *in vitro* culture of *Liatris spicata* (L.) Willd. cotyledons. *HortScience* 31: 154–155.

USDA–NRCS. 2002. The PLANTS Database, Version 3.5 (http://plants.usda.gov). National Plant Data Center, Baton Rouge, Louisiana.

Waithaka, K. 1985. Growth and flowering patterns of *Liatris* corms in Kenya. *Acta Horticulturae* 158:249–253.

Waithaka, K., and L.W. Wanjao. 1982. The effect of duration of cold treatment on growth and flowering of liatris. *Scientia Horticulturae* 18:153–158.

Wanjao, L.W., and K. Waithaka. 1983. The effect of GA$_3$-application on growth and flowering of *Liatris*. *Scienta Horticulturae* 19:343–348.

Whipker, B.E. 2003. Growth regulators for floricultural crops, pp. 439–448 in *2003 North Carolina Agricultural Chemicals Manual*. College of Agriculture and Life Science, North Carolina State University, Raleigh.

Woltering, E.J., and W.G. van Doorn. 1988. Role of ethylene in senescence of petals—morphological and taxonomical relationships. *Journal of Experimental Botany* 39:1605–1616.

Zieslin, N. 1985. *Liatris*, pp. 287–291 in *Handbook of Flowering*, vol. III, A.H. Halevy, editor. CRC Press, Boca Raton, Florida.

Zieslin, N., and Z. Geller. 1983a. Studies with *Liatris spicata* Willd. 1. Effect of temperature on sprouting, flowering and gibberellin content. *Annals of Botany* 52:849–853.

Zieslin, N., and Z. Geller. 1983b. Studies with *Liatris spicata* Willd. 2. Effects of photoperiod on stem extension, flowering and gibberellin content. *Annals of Botany* 52:855–859.

Lilium, Asiatic and Oriental

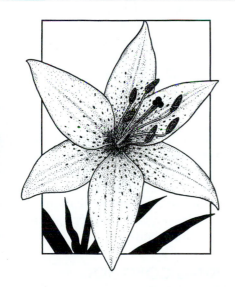

INTRODUCTION

Common names: Asiatic lily, oriental lily, colored lily, hybrid lily.

Scientific name: *Lilium* L. hybrids (Huxley et al., 1992).

Family and related taxa: Liliaceae Juss. Other important lilies include the Easter lily (*Lilium longiflorum* Thunb.) and many garden species and hybrid lilies. The lily family is very large and contains many commercially important floriculture crops including *Allium*, *Alstroemeria*, *Brodiaea*, *Convallaria*, *Eremurus*, *Hyacinthus*, *Lachenalia*, *Muscari*, *Ornithogalum*, and *Tulipa*.

Origin: The genus *Lilium* includes almost 100 species, most of which are distributed between 10° and 60° north latitude. Asia has 50 to 60 species, North America has 24 species, and Europe has 12 species (Anderson, 1986; Beattie and White, 1993; Daniels, 1986; Haw, 1986; Shimizu, 1973).

Uses and current status: Numerous hybrids and cultivars exist and are grown as garden perennials for summer color, as field- and greenhouse-grown cut flowers, and as potted flowering plants. Cut flowers and potted plants are grown either for specific holidays or for regular production year-round (Fig. II-1 Lilium, Asiatic and Oriental).

Although collectively referred to as "hybrid" or "colored lilies," lilies are often referred to by the hybrid group to which they belong such as "Asiatic," "Oriental," or "LA" (Beattie and White, 1993). Asiatic hybrids include such flower colors as orange, red, yellow, tan, and white; the flowers are usually orientated upward with little or no fragrance. Oriental hybrids have various shades of red, pink, and white with strongly fragrant flowers oriented horizontally. The leaves of commercial hybrids

FIGURE II-1 LILIUM, ASIATIC AND ORIENTAL
Asiatic *Lilium* for cut flower production.

and most species are evenly spaced along the stem, but the leaves of some species are in distinct whorls.

Crosses between *Lilium longiflorum* and Asiatic lilies have resulted in "LA hybrids," while crosses between *L. longiflorum* and Oriental types have produced "LO hybrids." The incorporation of *L. longiflorum* genes into these complex gene pools was intended to provide the long, graceful *L. longiflorum* leaves and to enhance lower leaf characteristics. In addition, the individual flowers of LA hybrids are oriented outward rather than upward as with the typical Asiatic hybrid (Van Tuyl et al., 1988). Many more hybrid groups are being developed, further blurring the lines between Asiatic, Oriental, and Easter lilies.

The species contributing to these hybrids as well as to the taxonomic and botanical classification have been reviewed by several authors (Anderson, 1986; Bailey and Bailey, 1976; Beattie and White, 1993; Daniels, 1986). Corr and Wilkins (1984) listed the species thought to have gone into the two major hybrid categories, Asiatic and Oriental.

CULTIVARS

Numerous hybrids are available and more are introduced yearly for the home garden or for commercial forcing as a cut flower or potted flowering plant (Beattie and White, 1993; De Hertogh, 1996, 2000). Genetically determined heights range from tall for cultivars used exclusively for cut flowers, to medium for cultivars used either for cut flowers or for potted flowering plants (if plant growth regulators are used), to short for true genetic dwarfs used exclusively for potted flowering plants (De Hertogh, 1996). In addition, double flowered Oriental cultivars

have been developed. Lily production has increased dramatically during the last few decades (De Hertogh, 2000).

Breeding efforts have targeted specific height and leaf characteristics, as well as a wide color range, improved root development during forcing, disease resistance in the field and greenhouse, increased flower number from small bulb sizes, tolerance to a wide variety of potential forcing and climate conditions (specifically for poor irradiance conditions, which result in flower bud abortion), rapid and uniform forcing, decreased flower fragrance in the Oriental hybrids, improved flower substance, and, especially, postharvest performance (Lim et al., 2002; van der Meulen-Muisers et al., 1997). An additional goal is to provide lily flowers with little or no pollen, which would eliminate stained clothing (Yamagishi, 2003). For the home garden, additional desired characteristics include winter hardiness and a wider range of flowering times, from early spring to late fall (Beattie and White, 1993). Van Tuyl and Kwakkenbos (1986) are breeding and selecting for hybrids that can be forced under low irradiances.

PROPAGATION

The storage organ is an imbricated bulb that consists of numerous fleshy scales, which are modified leaves attached to a compacted stem (basal plate) (Bailey and Bailey, 1976; Daniels, 1986). Commercially, scale propagation or *in vitro* propagation are most common (Park et al., 2002; Marinangeli and Curvetto, 1997). Plants can also be propagated by seed, aerial axillary stem bulbils, underground stem bulblets, or bulb divisions (Beattie and White, 1993; Van Aartrijk et al., 1989). Larger bulbs generally produce more flowers/stem than smaller bulbs (V. Kuyvenhoen, personal communication). Never allow bulbs to dry out during shipping, storage, programming, and planting.

FLOWERING CONTROL AND DORMANCY

The time of floral initiation and development of 35 *Lilium* species has been categorized as follows: (1) Flowers initiate in late summer and are well developed by fall, (2) flower initiation commences in late summer but development is not completed until the following spring, (3) flowers initiate and develop in spring prior to shoot emergence, and (4) flowers initiate in spring but not until after the shoot has emerged (Baranova, 1972). In 18 native Asiatic and Oriental type species, three flower initiation and development patterns were found, which were similar to types 1, 2, and 3 as previously described (Ohkawa, 1989). For example, *Lilium rubellum* Bak. can be classified as type 2 (Niimi and Oda, 1989). Apparently, no single flower initiation pattern exists with Asiatic hybrids; out of 85 cultivars studied, 27 (31%) were type 1 and 58 (69%) were type 4. Generally, the former species flower early and the latter species flower later in the season (Ohkawa et al., 1990).

For the entire *Lilium* genus, the primary responses to temperature (cold) are rapid stem elongation, flower initiation, and flower development. When bulbs of two Asiatic hybrids were harvested on July 15, August 1, August 15, September 1, or September 15 and given 6 weeks of 40°F (4.5°C), all bulbs developed shoots and elongated stems. Bulbs from the first two harvest dates had no detectable floral meristems and the stems had few leaves; bulbs from the August 15 harvest date developed shoots with more leaves and detectable but aborted floral meristems. Flowers developed, flower number increased, and leaf number increased further with the September 1 and 15 harvest dates (H.F. Wilkins, unpublished). The respiration rate of several Asiatic cultivars during cold treatment increases and then declines; the decrease in respiration could be used by commercial jobbers to determine when floral initiation is complete (Pergola and Roh, 1987).

Light influences flowering both photoperiodically and photosynthetically. Plant quality is increased and height is usually reduced with natural high light levels or with supplemental high-intensity lighting (Boontjes, 1973; Boontjes et al., 1975). Long photoperiods enhance floral initiation, making lilies a facultative LD plant (Grueber and Wilkins, 1984; Roh, 1989). Night interruptions of low light intensity from incandescent lamps can induce flowering of the appropriate species or hybrid; natural LD can serve the same purpose.

Increasing light intensity increases photosynthesis, which increases the rate of flower development (see Light, on the next page) and the number of flowers formed, reduces bud abortion, and enhances the total flower potential (see Physiological Disorders section later in chapter).

TEMPERATURE

Asiatic hybrids are cooled at 36 to 41°F (2 to 5°C) for 6 to 10 weeks, cultivar dependent, prior to greenhouse forcing (Beattie and White, 1993; De Hertogh, 1996). Oriental and LA hybrids are cooled at 36 to 39°F (2 to 4°C) for at least 8, preferably 9 to 10, weeks prior to greenhouse forcing (Beattie and White, 1993; De Hertogh, 1996; Holcomb et al., 1989). Moving bulbs from cold storage too early will extend the forcing period.

Bulbs can be held in moist peat for many months if temperatures are lowered from 30 or 28 to 25°F (−1 or −2 to −4°C) (Beattie and White, 1993; De Hertogh, 1996; Zhang et al., 1990b). Asiatic and LA bulbs are typically stored at 28°F (−2°C) and Orientals and LO bulbs are stored at 29°F (−1.5°C) (A. Rutte, personal communication). Consequently, year-round forcing is possible. However, prolonged storage lowered the number of flower buds (Lee and Roh, 2001). Prior to freezing, bulbs are first cooled for 9 to 12 weeks and then frozen. During freezing, high humidity must be maintained to prevent sprouting. The duration of the precooling depends on the hybrid type and cultivar (Beck, 1984; McKenzie, 1989). The freezing tolerance of numerous *Lilium* species and hybrids has been researched (Sakai and Yoshie, 1984; Zhang, 1991).

Mid-Century hybrids, an Asiatic type, required at least 6 weeks of cold at 41°F (5°C) for rapid flowering, and days to flower were not affected by SD or LD (Roh, 1985). LD did not substitute for cold. Conversely, 'San Souci,' an Oriental hybrid, flowered at the same time (118 to 120 days) regardless of whether bulbs were given either 9 weeks of cold at 40°F (4.5°C) or 6 weeks of cold followed by 3 weeks of incandescent lighting on shoot emergence (Grueber and Wilkins, 1984). However, partial substitution of the bulb cold treatment by long photoperiods reduced flower numbers and increased plant height. Long photoperiods can also partially substitute for cold with *L. speciosum rubrum* Mast. ex Bak. and with *L. lancifolium* Thunb., but a cold treatment is still required (Ohkawa, 1977; Roh, 1989; Weiler, 1973). *Lilium speciosum* bulbs had 100% shoot emergence but did not flower without cold treatment; flowering required exposure to 6 weeks at 41°F (5°C) (Weiler, 1973). Cold treatments were required for both shoot elongation and flower induction of *Lilium speciosum rubrum* bulbs (Ohkawa, 1970, 1977, 1979).

Increasing the duration that bulbs are cold stored decreases days to flower, flower number, plant height, and general quality and increases flower bud abortion (seasonally adjusted) (Boontjes, 1981; Roh, 1990b). However, flower bud numbers of 'San Souci' increased from 7 to 11 when weeks of cooling increased from 6 to 9.

It appears that gibberellic acid (GA_3) is involved in flower development, but not in floral differentiation. The bulb scales may be the site of the plant growth regulators (Ohkawa, 1977). Exogenously applied GA_3 enhanced only shoot emergence (Ohkawa, 1976).

During greenhouse forcing 50 to 63°F (10 to 17°C) night and 70°F (21°C) maximum day can be used for hybrid lilies (Boontjes, 1982; Boontjes and Van der Rotten, 1983; Holcomb et al., 1989; Seeley, 1982; White, 1976). More specifically, 55 to 60°F (13 to 16°C) is suggested for Asiatic lilies and 60 to 62°F (16 to 17°C) for Oriental and LA lilies.

If possible, commence greenhouse forcing of the Oriental hybrids at 59°F (15°C) for 4 weeks; then increase the temperature to 63 to 64°F (17 to 18°C), which is higher than the standard night temperature for Asiatic types (De Hertogh, 1996). For premium quality potted plants with long lower leaves, cool temperatures of 45 to 55°F (7 to 13°C) may be useful for root formation for 2 to 3 weeks prior to higher forcing temperatures.

For maximum stem strength and minimum bud abortion, avoid warm temperatures. During hot weather, try to keep the soil and air below 68°F (20°C) and use a soil mulch, if possible (De Hertogh, 1996).

LIGHT

Once flower initiation occurs in Asiatic hybrids, light intensity and duration have little influence on rate of flower development, which is temperature dependent (Beattie and White, 1993; Corr and Wilkins, 1984; Grueber and Wilkins, 1984; Zhang, 1991; Zhang et al., 1990a). However, in several cultivars of *Lilium speciosum* Thunb. (an Oriental type), LD incandescent or fluorescent treatments hastened flowering by 25 days. Similar results were recorded whether bulbs were minimally cooled or frozen for long periods. Up to 40 to 50% shade can be used on Oriental lilies to increase stem length of cut lilies; remove when buds are well developed. However, in Northern Europe supplemental HID lighting of 460 fc (60 μmol $\cdot$ m$^{-2} \cdot$ s^{-1}) reduced flower bud abortion and ac-celerated flowering (Treder, 2003). The influence of light on prevention of flower abortion and abscission is discussed under the Physiological Disorders section on page 651).

WATER

The packing material must be moist for the cold storage of bulbs because (1) both cold and moisture are required for physiological processes to occur and (2) lily bulbs lose water and desiccation must be prevented particularly during long-term storage (Beattie and White, 1993; Corr and Wilkins, 1984; Hartsema, 1961). The growing medium should be kept moist but not saturated, because root rot problems can be intensified by poor aeration. Water stress and wilting can cause bud abortion or abscission (Aimone, 1986; Beck, 1984).

CARBON DIOXIDE

Days to flower and flower bud abortion of 'Enchantment' were reduced and plant quality improved when 1000 ppm CO_2 was used in conjunction with supplemental lighting at 460 fc (90 μmol $\cdot$ m$^{-2} \cdot$ s^{-1}). Forcing temperature could be increased from 64 to 68°F (18 to 20°C) when CO_2 was used (Hendriks, 1986).

NUTRITION

With cut lilies, excessively high nutrient levels can reduce plant height. Because the bulb has nutrient reserves, it is suggested that fertilization is not needed during forcing (McKenzie, 1989), that fertilization should commence only after shoot emergence (Aimone, 1986), or that fertilization should start at the visible bud stage of development if the medium has nutrient reserves (Beck, 1984). Experimental results from Gamez (1990) were inconclusive regarding nutritional levels and plant quality. De Hertogh (1996) stated that a nutrition program should commence at shoot emergence, using calcium nitrate and potassium nitrate at a 2:1 ratio on a weekly basis, assuming that the medium has been amended with phosphorus. Slow-release fertilizers can also be used. Others have suggested using a constant 200- to 500-ppm N fertilization (Aimone, 1986; Lewis and Gilbertz, 1987; McKenzie, 1989).

With potted lilies, constant liquid fertilization should be used in conjunction with routine medium and tissue analysis. Foliar nutrient levels for high-quality plants are listed in Chapter 6, Nutrition, Table 6-4.

MEDIA

Lily bulbs are grown around the world in an amazingly wide range of soil and media types both in the field or under protection in ground beds, bulb crates, or pots (Bent, 1999). De Hertogh (1996) recommended a well-drained, fluoride-free, sterilized planting medium. Adzima (1986) used a 1:1:1 soil mix of "composted soil, coarse peat, and coarse perlite." Various other media have been used: a commercial "peatlite" medium (Holcomb et al., 1989; White et al., 1989), "ordinary" garden soil (Berghaef, 1985), and peat and sand (Hanks and Menhenett, 1980). The pH of the growing medium is extremely important, with pH 6.0 optimum.

HEIGHT CONTROL

Although cultivars with stem lengths 20 in. (50 cm) and longer are appropriate for cut flowers, potted flowering plants generally require a height between 8 and 20 in. (20 and 50 cm). The height depends on the pot size. Much has been written about height control of potted lilies, but the ultimate solution will be the use of genetically dwarf hybrid cultivars. Chemical plant growth regulators can produce erratic results and potentially injure leaves (Nell et al., 1998). Plant heights can vary even for the same cultivar if it is obtained from two or more sources. Further, length of storage, bulb size, and environmental conditions such as temperature, light intensity, and light duration all impact height. Bulbs propagated from virus-free stock also will produce taller plants.

Forcing plants at high night and low day temperatures (-DIF), dropping temperatures for 2 hr or longer after sunrise (DROP), or holding day and night temperatures constant (0 DIF) are all commonly used to reduce stem elongation (Boontjes and Van der Rotten, 1983; Erwin et al., 1989; Heins et al., 1987; Malorgio et al., 1987; Moore, 1979). Shaking the plants twice daily also reduced height nonchemically (Jerzy and Krause, 1980). Graphical tracking should be used to monitor plant height and assist growers with height control decisions.

Chemical height control is difficult and is more of an art than a science. De Hertogh (1996) indicated in his forcing guide which cultivars require a plant growth regulator drench. Several growth regulators are effective including A-Rest (ancymidol), Bonzi (paclobutrazol), and Sumagic (uniconizole). B-Nine (daminozide) is not effective (Choi et al., 2002).

When using A-Rest, it is wise to divide the application into two or more drenches. After the first application, observe growth and determine if additional applications are needed. The first drench is usually applied at shoot emergence and additional drenches every 10 to 14 days as required. This method produces uniform internode lengths rather than long, short, long internodes. If more than one bulb is used per pot, apply growth retardants when the first shoots are 0.5 in. (1.3 cm) tall, not when all shoots have emerged. A-Rest is used at 2 to 4 ppm [0.25 to 0.5 mg a.i./6-in. (15-cm) pot] for Oriental lilies, at 1 to 2 ppm (0.25 to 0.5 mg a.i./pot) for Asiatic lilies, and at 1 to 4 ppm (0.25 to 0.5 mg a.i./pot) for LA lilies (Miller, 2001). Bark in the medium may reduce the effectiveness of A-Rest (De Hertogh, 1996). Foliar sprays are less effective but 20 to 40 ppm can be used. A-Rest bulb dips are effective (Lewis and Gilbertz, 1987).

Sumagic and Bonzi are also effective in reducing internode elongation as a spray, media drench, or bulb soak (Bailey and Miller, 1989; Holcomb et al., 1989; Jiao et al., 1990; Miller, 2001; White, 1976; White et al., 1989). Sumagic sprays of 1 to 10 ppm can be used on all types of lilies. Drenches of 0.05 mg a.i./pot of Sumagic were effective on Oriental lilies. Bulb dips for 1 min with Sumagic at 2.5 to 10 ppm or Bonzi at 100 to 300 ppm are recommended for Oriental lilies. Sumagic dips at 1 to 5 ppm will work on both Asiatic and LA lilies with 25 to 75 ppm Bonzi suggested for Asiatic lilies and 50 to 200 ppm for LA lilies. Variation in the response of lilies to bulb dips may be due to the moisture content of the bulbs. Bulbs that are drier absorb more of the plant growth regulator dip solution than bulbs that are more moist (Damayanthi Ranwala et al., 2003). However, sequentially dipping multiple batches of bulbs in plant growth regulator dip solution did not change the effectiveness of the dip solution.

SPACING

Bulb size and type of hybrid dictate spacing for cut flower production. Due to the smaller plant circumference of Asiatic hybrids, more bulbs per square meter can be planted compared with Oriental hybrids. Generally, 45 to 72 bulbs can be planted/yd^2 (54 to 86/m^2) with the Asiatics and 27 to 36/yd^2 (32 to 43/m^2) with the Orientals when using 6- to 7-in. (15- to 17.5-cm) bulbs. The bulbs should be planted at least 2 in. (5 cm) below the surface of the medium to encourage stem roots (De Hertogh, 1996).

Bulbs for cut flower production are commonly grown in plastic crates, which are placed crate-to-crate on the ground. Crates allow easy handling of large numbers of bulbs.

Potted plants can be grown pot-to-pot until flowering but excessive elongation can occur. For 6-in. (15-cm) pots, a final spacing of 7 × 8 to 9 × 9 in. (18 × 20 to 23 × 23 cm) can be used.

PINCHING AND DISBUDDING

No pinching or disbudding required.

SUPPORT

Some cut flower cultivars require one or two layers of netting for support. It is wise to place the net on the beds at planting and then slowly raise it as the shoots elongate (De Hertogh, 1996).

SCHEDULE AND TIMING

Bulbs can be forced any week of the year from frozen bulbs or from bulbs produced in the other hemisphere. De Hertogh (1996) compiled elaborate flowering schedules for numerous cultivars of both Asiatic and Oriental types used for cut or potted flowering production. These schedules are for March to June forcing in the Northern Hemisphere. Precise timing is complicated because the forcing time varies greatly with each cultivar. The leaf numbers at any particular forcing date and flower develop-

ment rate also depend on the cultivar. Days to shoot emergence vary from 2 to 3 weeks in midwinter to 3 to 4 days for bulbs planted in April or later (B. Miller, personal communication). Generally Asiatics require 60 to 85 days of total greenhouse forcing time with 30 to 35 days to flower from visible bud, and Orientals require 85 to 120 days of greenhouse forcing time with 50 to 55 days to flower from visible bud (De Hertogh, 1996; Lee and Roh, 2001). As the forcing season changes, temperatures influence leaf unfolding rate, flower bud development, and, ultimately, flowering date (Lee and Roh, 2001; Roh, 1990a; Zhang et al. 1990b). Keep in mind that a high day temperature relative to the night temperature is acceptable for cut flower production, but not for potted plant production. See Table II-1 Lilium, Asiatic and Oriental for a sample forcing schedule for potted Asiatic lilies and Table II-2 Lilium, Asiatic and Oriental for a sample forcing schedule for cut Oriental lilies.

INSECTS

Although a variety of insect pests can infest lilies, including aphids, fungus gnats, bulb mites, and thrips, the most serious are aphids and fungus gnats. The lily leaf beetle (*Lilioceris lilii*) is a recent invader from Europe, which may become a serious pest of outdoor-grown lilies (R. Casagrande, personal communication).

TABLE II-1 LILIUM, ASIATIC AND ORIENTAL

Sample forcing schedule for 'Harmony,' a potted Asiatic *Lilium* for Mother's Day.

Cultural Step	Production Time (weeks)	Temperature °F (°C)
Receive bulbs from jobber[a] and plant four bulbs in a 6-in. (15-cm) pot	1	Day: Within 5 (3) of night Night: 55–63 (13–17)
Shoots emerge[b] and increase temperature[c]	1–2	Constant: 68 (20) or Day: Within 5 (3) of night Night: 63–65 (17–18)
Visible bud	5–6	Constant: 68 (20) or Day: Within 5 (3) of night Night: 63–65 (17–18)
Flower		
Total	7–9	

[a]Bulbs must have 6+ weeks of precooling, which is given prior to freezing at 28 to 30°F (−2 to −1°C).
[b]Drench plants with growth regulator shortly after shoot emergence, if needed.
[c]Control height through DIF, if possible.

TABLE II-2 LILIUM, ASIATIC AND ORIENTAL
Sample forcing schedule for 'Star Gazer,' a cut Oriental *Lilium* for Mother's Day.

Cultural Step	Production Time (weeks)	Temperature °F (°C)
Receive bulbs from jobber[a] and plant in crates or beds	7–8	Day: Within 5 (3) of night Night: 59 (15)
Visible bud, increase temperature	7–8	Day: Within 5 (3) of night Night: 63–65 (17–18)
Flower		
Total	14–16	

[a]Bulbs must have 8 weeks of precooling, which is given prior to freezing at 28 to 30°F (−2 to −1°C).

DISEASES

Plant disease is a major concern. The root rot complex of diseases (*Fusarium oxysporum* f. sp. *lilii*, *Pythium*, *Rhizoctonia solani*, *Phytophthora cactorum*, and *P. parasitica*) (Dreistadt, 2001; Horst, 1990) should first be prevented by using reliable bulb sources, pasteurizing the media, and sanitizing the growing area. If necessary, both preplant chemical bulb dips and routine media drenches can be used (De Hertogh, 1996). Gray mold (*Botrytis cinerea*) can occur on flowers and leaves if air circulation and humidity control are not practiced. Gray mold can be especially troublesome during shipping if open flowers are present; the fungus finds a suitable environment in the sugar-laden nectar at the end of the stigma. Various viruses can be present, but the control of these diseases is in the hands of the bulb producer. A number of other diseases can be found, especially on lilies grown outdoors in perennial gardens, including scale rot (*Colletotrichum*), bulb rot (*Rhizopus stolonifera* or *Penicillium*), rust (*Uromyces*), leaf spots (*Cercospora*, *Cercosporella*, *Heterosporium*, and *Ramularia*), and cottony rot (*Sclerotinia sclerotiorum*) (Dreistadt, 2001).

PHYSIOLOGICAL DISORDERS

Flower bud abortion at an early stage of development or abscission at a later stage is a low-light and ethylene-mediated phenomenon (Fig. II-2 Lilium, Asiatic and Oriental). High temperatures may accentuate bud abortion and abscission (Durieux, 1975; Kamerbeek and Durieux, 1971), perhaps due to depletion of the carbohydrate supply (Roh, 1990a, b). Night interruption LD lighting reduces bud abortion,

FIGURE II-2 LILIUM, ASIATIC AND ORIENTAL
Blasted bud on Asiatic *Lilium* plant.

and higher intensity supplemental lighting from various lamp types also prevents abortion during the winter and accelerates flowering (Treder, 2003). Interestingly, mechanical stress (shaking plants twice daily), which tends to cause the release of ethylene, also reduced abortion (Jerzy and Krause, 1980).

Leaf or leaf tip burn, also known as upper leaf necrosis, is a common problem, which occurs when the palisade parenchyma cells under the epidermis collapse. These areas turn a white-gray approximately 0.75 in. (2 cm) back from the tip, while the tip remains green. The typical developmental sequence of the symptoms from bottom to top of the plant is normal leaves, injured leaves, and then normal leaves and flowers. These symptoms occur shortly before or at visible bud (Berghaef, 1985). Leaf burn is thought to be due to insufficient translocation of calcium (Chang and Miller, 2003). Culturally, leaf burn is associated with high relative humidity and little or no stem root development. The problem can be reduced experimentally by removing the lower leaves or commercially by routinely spraying calcium chloride or calcium nitrate (68 to 136 mM). The disorder developed with low calcium levels in hydrocultured plants (Berghaef, 1985). With other crop species, ammonium was found to reduce calcium uptake and translocation. Along with eliminating ammonium, good air movement to encourage high transpiration rates was suggested (Bierman et al., 1990). Leaf burn can be reduced by multiple sprays of calcium chloride at 400 ppm commencing at the first time symptoms appear and continuing until visible bud or beginning at least 1 week prior to the time when the first plants reach visible bud and continuing until 1 week after all plants have reached visible bud (Leonard et al., 1998; E. Runkle, personal communication). Sprays can be applied every 3 to 4 days and it is particularly important to spray at the end of a cloudy period before sunny weather returns.

Another foliar problem, leaf scorch, appears as a burned-looking, crescent-shaped area on the margins of the leaves, or as an actual tip burn. The cause is fluoride, which is a natural contaminant of phosphate or is injected into municipal water sources (De Hertogh, 1996; Wilkins, 1980). De Hertogh (2000) documented numerous other forcing problems and their possible causes.

POSTHARVEST

Cut stems are generally harvested when buds are well colored but not yet open. Each cultivar, however, has an optimal stage of development (number of flowers showing color) for harvest (Schenk, 1987; Swart, 1980). There are also major differences in postharvest life among cultivars (Lim et al., 2002).

Various types of postharvest preservatives can be used to allow all buds of cut Asiatic hybrid flowers to open and to prevent leaf yellowing. The lily is considered sensitive to ethylene, and silver thiosulfate (STS) treatments increase longevity (Song et al., 1996; Swart, 1979). However, Elgar et al. (1999) considered most cultivars to be unaffected by ethylene and

only a few slightly sensitive to ethylene. Postharvest life was improved even when bulbs were soaked in STS. The soaking treatment protected flowers from exogenous ethylene, resulting in a similar improvement to vase life as placing the stems in STS solutions (Swart, 1980). Flower bud abscission under low light stress results in increased ethylene evolution and action. Experimentally, abscission was prevented by injection of STS (0.2 mM) into the flower buds (Van Meeteren and De Proft, 1982). 1-Methylcyclopropene is also effective at preventing bud and flower abscission and vase life decline due to exogenous ethylene (Çelikel et al., 2002).

Cut stems can be stored for 4 weeks at 34°F (1°C) if stems are first treated for 24 hr in silver nitrate at 50 ppm (Nowak and Mynett, 1985). After cold storage, recut the stems and place in 30 ppm sucrose and 200 ppm 8-hydroxyquinolin citrate (8-HQC). Antimicrobial agents other than 8-HQC are also effective (Jones and Hill, 1993). Cold storage decreases longevity by increasing leaf yellowing and bud blasting and reduced vase life (Han, 2001).

Leaf yellowing can also be prevented by spraying Fascination [1:1 benzyladenine:gibberellic acid (BA:GA)] at 25:25 ppm BA:GA on the cut stems prior to or immediately after cold storage. The chemical cannot reverse leaf yellow so it must be applied when the leaves are still green. Application of Fascination as a pulse or vase solution treatment prevented leaf yellowing but increased bud blasting. At 100 ppm GA_{4+7} was more effective than GA_3 and spray treatments were as effective as pulse solutions (Ranwala and Miller, 2002). Placing cold-stored Oriental lilies in a vase solution containing 2% sugar increased the number of buds opening and darkened flower color (Han, 2003). However, sugar in the vase solution had little effect on unstored cut lilies.

Potted plants are generally sold wholesale when buds are well colored and retail when one flower is open. Plants can be stored and shipped at 32 to 41°F (0 to 5°C) (Nell et al., 1995). The shorter the storage duration, the longer the postharvest life. In particular, Oriental hybrids generally do not store well because the lower foliage yellows and drops soon after removal from the cooler. Cold storage also decreases postharvest life of the flowers and increases flower bud abortion. However, the use of fluorescent lamps providing 260 fc (40 μmol · m^{-2} · s^{-1}) in the cooler will greatly improve poststorage plant quality (Ranwala and Miller,

1998). Leaf yellowing can also be prevented by spraying Fascination at 100:100 to 250:250 ppm BA:GA on the entire plant (Funnell and Heins, 1998; Ranwala and Miller, 1998). Combining light in the cooler with Fascination sprays provided even greater benefits.

Sales of packaged lily bulbs in garden centers are a major source of income. However, the bulbs frequently sprout in the package, reducing plant quality. Using low-O_2 atmospheres (1%) during distribution can reduce shoot elongation (Legnani et al., 2002).

KEY POINTS

- Lilies are used as cut flowers, potted flowering plants, and garden ornamentals.
- Cultivars can be separated into two main groups: Asiatic lilies with upward facing flowers and no fragrance and Oriental lilies with outward facing flowers and strong fragrance.
- Cultivars from interspecific hybrids between *Lilium longiflorum* and the Asiatic and Oriental cultivar groups are available, increasingly popular, and blurring the lines between cultivar groups.
- Production is based on bulbs that are commercially propagated by scales or *in vitro;* seed, aerial stem bulbils, underground stem bulblets, or bulb divisions can also be used.
- Typically flower induction occurs after bulbs receive a cold moist treatment of 36 to

41°F (2 to 5°C) for 6 to 10 weeks for Asiatic lilies and 36 to 39°F (2 to 4°C) for at least 8 weeks for Oriental lilies.
- Increasing the duration of the cold treatment decreases days to flower, flower number, final plant height, and plant quality.
- Bulbs can be stored (frozen) at 28°F (−2°C) for months allowing year-round forcing.
- For potted plants height control is a concern and best accomplished by cultivar selection, DIF, and chemical growth retardants.
- Root rots are a major problem.
- Cut stems and pots are harvested wholesale when the buds are well colored and retail when one flower is open.

BIBLIOGRAPHY

Adzima, R. 1986. The influence of bulb dips on the hybrid lilies grown in warm temperatures. *Connecticut Greenhouse Newsletter* 135:15–18.

Aimone, T. 1986. Culture notes. *GrowerTalks* 50:16.

Anderson, N. 1986. The distribution of the genus *Lilium* with reference to its evaluation. *The Lily Yearbook of the North American Lily Society* 42: 1–18.

Bailey, D.A., and W.B. Miller. 1989. Response of Oriental hybrid lilies to ancymidol and uniconazole. *HortScience* 24:519.

Bailey, L.H., and E.Z. Bailey. 1976. *Lilium,* pp. 658–664 in *Hortus Third: A Concise Dictionary of Plants Cultivated in the United States and Canada.* Macmillan, New York.

Baranova, M.A. 1972. Biological peculiarities of lilies. *The Lily Yearbook of the North American Lily Society* 25:7–20.

Beattie, D.J., and J.W. White. 1993. *Lilium*—Hybrids and species, pp. 423–454 in *The Physiology of Flower Bulbs,* A. De Hertogh and M. Le Nard, editors. Elsevier, Amsterdam.

Beck, R. 1984. The "hows" and "whys" of hybrid lilies; establishing a multicolored lily program for cuts or pots. *Florist's Review* 175(4529):22, 24, 27.

Bent, E. 1999. Growing flowers in boxes and pots. *FloraCulture International* 9(8):38.

Berghaef, J. 1985. Effect of calcium on tip burn of *Lilium* 'Pirate.' *Acta Horticulturae* 177:433–438.

Bierman P., C. Rosen, and H.F. Wilkins. 1990. Leaf edge burn and axillary shoot growth of vegetative poinsettia plants: Influence of calcium, nitrogen form, and molybdenum. *Journal of the American Society for Horticultural Science* 115(1):73–78.

Boontjes, J. 1973. The regulation of the forcing period in *L. speciosum* by glasshouse temperature and long-day treatment. *The Lily Yearbook of the North American Lily Society* 26:63–68.

Boontjes, J. 1981. Can't 'Rubrum' lilies also be frozen? *Weekblad voor Bloembollencultuur* 92:364–365. (in Dutch, English summary)

Boontjes, J. 1982. 'Blinden' bij 'Connecticut King,' nog steeds een probleem. *Weekblad voor Bloembollencultuur* 92:1230–1231. (in Dutch)

Boontjes, J., and L.A.J.M. Van der Rotten. 1983. Is it possible to grow lilies for cut flower production by lowering the night temperature and raising the temperature at which the air is changed? *Revue Horticole* 240:53–57. (in French, English summary)

Boontjes, J., A.J.B. Durieux, and G.A. Kamerbeek. 1975. Progress in the promotion of flowering in lilies by supplementary illumination. *Acta Horticulturae* 51:261–262.

Çelikel, F.G., L.L. Dodge, and M.S. Reid. 2002. Efficacy of 1-MCP (1-methylcyclopropene) and Promalin for extending the post-harvest life of Oriental lilies (*Lilium* × 'Mona Lisa' and 'Stargazer'). *Scientia Horticulturae* 93:149–155.

Chang, Y.-C., and W.B. Miller. 2003. Effects of solution calcium level and bulb calcium level on the development of upper leaf necrosis on *Lilium* cv. Star Gazer. *HortScience* 38:848. (Abstract)

Choi, J.J., J.S. Lee, J.M. Choi, and K.H. Kwon. 2002. Effects of foliar spray of growth retardants on growth and flowering of potted *Lilium* species. *Journal of the Korean Society for Horticultural Science* 45:633–638.

Corr, B.E., and H.F. Wilkins. 1984. Hybrid lily forcing. *Minnesota State Florist's Bulletin* 33:1–4.

Damayanthi Ranwala, N.K., A.P. Ranwala, and W.B. Miller. 2003. Studies on plant growth regulator (pgr) uptake by lily bulbs. *HortScience* 38:727. (Abstract)

Daniels, L.H. 1986. The lily plant. *The Lily Yearbook of the North American Lily Society* 39:6–17.

De Hertogh, A.A. 1996. Lilies (Asiatic and Oriental hybrid lilies), pp. C95–121 in *Holland Bulb Forcer's Guide*, 5th ed. International Flower Bulb Centre, Hillegom, The Netherlands.

De Hertogh, A.A. 2000. Growing hybrid lilies. *GrowerTalks* 18(1):72, 74, 76, 78, 80.

Dreistadt, S.H. 2001. *Integrated Pest Management for Floriculture and Nurseries*. University of California Division of Agriculture and Natural Resources Publication 3402.

Durieux, A.J.B. 1975. Additional lighting of lilies (cv. Enchantment) in the winter to prevent flower-bud abscission. *Acta Horticulturae* 47:237–240.

Elgar, H.J., A.B. Woolf, and R.L. Bieleski. 1999. Ethylene production by three lily species and their response to ethylene exposure. *Postharvest Biology and Technology* 16:257–267.

Erwin, J.E., R.D. Heins, and M. Karlsson. 1989. Thermomorphogensis in *Lilium longiflorium*. *American Journal of Botany* 76:47–52.

Funnell, K.A., and R.D. Heins. 1998. Plant growth regulators reduce postproduction leaf yellowing of potted asiflorum lilies. *HortScience* 33:1036–1037.

Gamez, S.E. 1990. Effect of fertilizer treatment on *Hedra helix* and Asiatic hybrid lily growth with ebb and flow and overhead drip irrigation. M.S. thesis, The Pennsylvania State University, University Park.

Grueber, K.L., and H.F. Wilkins. 1984. Forcing 'San Souci' lilies. *Minnesota State Florist's Bulletin* 33(5):17–18.

Han, S.S. 2001. Benzyladenine and gibberellins improve postharvest quality of cut Asiatic and Oriental lilies. *HortScience* 36:741–745.

Han, S.S. 2003. Role of sugar in the vase solution on postharvest flower and leaf quality of Oriental lily 'Stargazer.' *HortScience* 38:412–416.

Hanks, G.R., and R. Menhenett. 1980. An evaluation of new growth retardants on Mid-Century hybrid lilies. *Scientia Horticulturae* 13:349–359.

Hartsema, A.M. 1961. Influence of temperature on flower formation and flowering of bulbous plants, pp. 123–167 in *Encyclopedia of Plant Physiology*, vol. 16. Springer-Verlag, Berlin.

Haw, S.G. 1986. *The Lilies of China*. Timber Press, Portland, Oregon.

Heins, R.D., M. Karlsson, and J. Erwin. 1987. The control of plant height by innovative temperature control. *GrowerTalks* 50:58.

Hendriks, C.H.M. 1986. Longer days for lilies. Flowering of the Oriental hybrids can be advanced. *Weekblad voor Bloembollencultuur* 97:12–13. (in Dutch, English summary)

Holcomb, E.J., J.W. White, and D.J. Beattie. 1989. Adaption of 'San Souci' lilies to potted plant culture. *Herbertia* 45:81–90.

Horst, R.K. 1990. Lily, pp. 707–708 in *Westcott's Plant Disease Handbook*, 5th ed. Van Nostrand Reinhold, New York.

Huxley, A., M. Griffiths, and M. Levy. 1992. *Lilium*, pp. 68–80 in *The New Royal Horticultural Society Dictionary of Gardening*, vol. 3. Stockton Press, New York.

Jerzy, M., and J. Krause. 1980. The factors controlling growth and flowering of forced lilies 'Enchantment': Light intensity and mechanical. *Acta Horticulturae* 109:111–115.

Jiao, J., X. Wang, and M.J. Tsujita. 1990. Comparative effects of uniconazole drench and spray on shoot elongation of hybrid lilies. *HortScience* 25:1244–1246.

Jones, R.B., and M. Hill. 1993. The effects of germicides on the longevity of cut flowers. *Journal of the American Society for Horticultural Science* 118:350–354.

Kamerbeek, G.A., and J.B. Durieux. 1971. Influence of light on flower bud abscission in plants of the lily 'Enchantment.' *Acta Horticulturae* 23:71–74.

Lee, J.S., and M.S. Roh. 2001. Influence of frozen storage duration and forcing temperature on flowering of Oriental hybrid lilies. *HortScience* 36:1053–1056.

Legnani, G., C.B. Watkins, and W.B. Miller. 2002. Use of low-oxygen atmospheres to inhibit sprout elongation of dry-sale Asiatic lily bulbs. *Acta Horticulturae* 570:183–189.

Leonard, R.T., T.A. Nell, A.A. De Hertogh, and L. Gallitano. 1998. Lilies your customers will love. *GrowerTalks* 62(1):80, 82, 87–89.

Lewis, A.J., and D.A. Gilbertz. 1987. Hybrid lily response to various methods of ancymidol application. *Acta Horticulturae* 205:237–247.

Lim, K.-B., J.J.M. van der Meulen Muisers, and J.M. van Tuyl. 2002. Breeding for flower longevity enhancement of Asiatic hybrids lilies. *Acta Horticulturae* 570:409–413.

Malorgio, F., E. Moschini, and B. Lercari. 1987. The adaptation to forced culture of some cultivars of *L. longiflorum, L. speciosum,* and Mid-Century hybrids. *Colture Protette* 16:75–79. (in Italian, English summary)

Marinangeli, P., and N. Curvetto. 1997. Bulb quality and traumatic acid influence bulblet formation from scaling in *Lilium* species and hybrids. *HortScience* 32:739–741.

McKenzie, K. 1989. Potted lilies made easy: The new, naturally short Asiatic lily varieties. *GrowerTalks* 52:48–58.

Miller, W.B. 2001. Bulb crops, pp. 63–67 in *Tips on Regulating Growth of Floriculture Crops,* M.L. Gaston, L.A. Kunkle, P.S. Konjoian, and M.F. Wilt, editors. Ohio Florists' Association Services, Columbus, Ohio.

Moore, T.C. 1979. *Biochemistry and Physiology of Plant Hormones.* Springer-Verlag, New York.

Nell, T.A., R.T. Leonard, A.A. De Hertogh, and J.E. Barrett. 1995. Postproduction evaluations of potted Asiatic and Oriental hybrid lilies. *HortScience* 30:1433–1435.

Nell, T.A., R.T. Leonard, A.A. De Hertogh, and L. Gallitano. 1998. Boosting lily performance. *GrowerTalks* 61(11):62, 64, 66, 68, 72.

Niimi, Y., and M. Oda. 1989. Time of initiation and development of flower buds in *Lilium rubellum* Baker. *Scientia Horticulturae* 39:341–348.

Nowak, J., and K. Mynett. 1985. The effect of sucrose, silver thiosulfate and 8-hydroxyquinoline citrate on the quality of *Lilium* inflorescences cut at the bud stage and stored at low temperature. *Scientia Horticulturae* 25:299–302.

Ohkawa, K. 1970. Studies on dormancies of *Lilium speciosum rubrum. Kanagawa Horticulture Experimental Station Bulletin* 18:160–170. (in Japanese, English summary)

Ohkawa, K. 1976. The role of gibberellins in shoot emergence and elongation, flower differentiation and development of *Lilium speciosum rubrum. Journal of the Japanese Society for Horticultural Science* 45:289–299. (in Japanese, English summary)

Ohkawa, K. 1977. *Studies on the Physiology and Control of Flowering of Lilium Speciosum Rubrum.* Special Bulletin No. 73, Kanagawa Horticulture Experimental Station, Kanagawa, Japan. (in Japanese, English summary)

Ohkawa, K. 1979. Effects of gibberellins and benzladenine on dormancy and flowering of *Lilium speciosum. Scientia Horticulturae* 10:255–260.

Ohkawa, K. 1989. Time of flower bud differentiation in lilies native of Japan. *Journal of the Japanese Society for Horticultural Science* 57:655–661. (in Japanese, English summary)

Ohkawa, K., A. Kana, and A. Kukaya. 1990. Time of flower bud differentiation in Asiatic hybrid lilies. *Acta Horticulturae* 266:200–211.

Park, K.I., J.D. Choi, S.J. Eum, and K.W. Kim. 2002. Effects of MS medium strength, nitrogen concentration, culture temperature and daylength on callus proliferation and plant regeneration from calli of *Lilium* Oriental hybrids 'Casa Blanca.' *Journal of the Korean Society of Horticultural Society* 43:628–632.

Pergola, G., and M.S. Roh. 1987. The relationship between flower bud initiation and respiration in Asiatic hybrid lily bulbs. *Acta Horticulturae* 205:241–247.

Ranwala, A.P., and W.B. Miller. 1998. Gibberellin$_{4+7}$, benzyladenine, and supplemental light improve postharvest leaf and flower quality of cold-stored 'Stargazer' hybrid lilies. *Journal of the American Society for Horticultural Science* 123:563–568.

Ranwala, A.P., and W.B. Miller. 2002. Effects of gibberellin treatments on flower and leaf quality of cut hybrid lilies. *Acta Horticulturae* 570:205–210.

Roh, S.M. 1985. Flowering responses of Mid-Century hybrid lilies to bulb vernalization and shoot photoperiod treatments. *HortScience* 20:710–713.

Roh, S.M. 1989. Control of flowering in *Lilium*—A review. *Herbertia* 45:65–69.

Roh, S.M. 1990a. Effect of high temperature on bud blast in Asiatic hybrid lily. *Acta Horticulturae* 266:142–146.

Roh, S.M. 1990b. Bud abnormalities during year-round forcing of Asiatic hybrid lilies. *Acta Horticulturae* 266:147–154.

Sakai, A., and F. Yoshie. 1984. Freezing tolerance of ornamental bulbs and corms. *Journal of the Japanese Society for Horticultural Science* 52:445–449. (in Japanese, English summary)

Schenk, P.C. 1987. New directions with polyploids in Asiatic and Oriental lilies. *The Lily Yearbook of the North American Lily Society* 40:7–12.

Seeley, J.G. 1982. Tailoring garden lilies as potted plants. *Florists Review* 169(4392):21–24, 75–78.

Shimizu, M. 1973. Lilies in Japan. *Japan Agricultural Research Quarterly* 7(2):116–121. (in Japanese, English summary)

Song, C.Y., C.S. Bang, J.S. Lee, and D.C. Lee. 1996. Effects of postharvest pretreatments and preservative solutions on vase life and flower quality of Asiatic hybrid lily. *Acta Horticulturae* 414:277–285.

Swart, A. 1979. The quality of the lily 'Enchantment' as a cut flower. *Weekblad voor Bloembollencultuur* 89:902–903. (in Dutch, English summary)

Swart, A. 1980. Quality of *Lilium* 'Enchantment' flowers as influenced by season and silver thiosulfate. *Acta Horticulturae* 113:45–49.

Treder, J. 2003. Effects of supplementary lighting on flowering, plant quality and nutrient requirements of lily 'Laura Lee' during winter forcing. *Scientia Horticulturae* 98:37–47.

van Aartrijk, J., G.J. Blom-Barnhoorn, and P.C.G. van der Linde. 1989. Lilies, pp. 535–576 in *Handbook of Plant Cell Culture, Ornamental Species,* vol. 5, P.V. Amirato, editor. McGraw-Hill, New York.

van der Meulen-Muisers, J.J.M., and J.C. van Oeveren. 1997. Influence of bulb stock origin, inflorescence harvest stage and postharvest evaluation conditions on cut flower longevity of Asiatic hybrid lilies. *Journal of the American Society for Horticultural Science* 122:368–372.

van Meeteren, U., and M. De Proft. 1982. Inhibition of flower bud abscission and ethylene evaluation by light and silver thiosulfate in *Lilium. Physiologia Plantarum* 56:236–240.

van Tuyl, J.M., and T.A.M. Kwakkenbos. 1986. Effect of low light intensity on flowering of Asiatic lilies. *Acta Horticulturae* 177:607–611.

van Tuyl, J.M., C.J. Keijzer, H.J. Wilms, and T.A.M. Kwakkenbos. 1988. Interspecific hybridization between *Lilium longiflorium* and the white Asiatic hybrid 'Mont Blanc.' *The Lily Yearbook of the North American Lily Society* 41:103–109.

Weiler, T.C. 1973. Cold and daylength requirements for flowering in a *Lilium speciosum* Thunb. cultivar. *HortScience* 8:185.

White, J.W. 1976. *Lilium* sp. 'Mid-Century Hybrids' adapted to pot use with ancymidol. *Journal of American Society for Horticultural Science* 101:126–129.

White, J.W., E.J. Holcomb, K. Shumae, M. Rose, and T. Margard. 1989. Oriental hybrid lilies as pot plants. *Pennsylvania Flower Growers* 395(7):1–5.

Wilkins, H. 1980. Easter lilies, pp. 327–352 in *Introduction to Floriculture,* R.A. Larson, editor. Academic Press, New York.

Yamagishi, M. 2003. A genetic model for a pollenless trait in Asiatic hybrid lily and its utilization for breeding. *Scientia Horticulturae* 98:293–297.

Zhang, X. 1991. Flower initiation and regulation of flowering in genetically dwarf Asiatic hybrid lilies. Ph.D. thesis, The Pennsylvania State University, University Park.

Zhang, X., D.J. Beattie, and J.W. White. 1990a. Flower initiation in three Asiatic hybrid lily cultivars. *Acta Horticulturae* 266:183–188.

Zhang, X., D.J. Beattie, and J.W. White. 1990b. Year-round scheduling of dwarf Asiatic hybrid lily. *Acta Horticulturae* 272:267–272.

Lilium, Easter

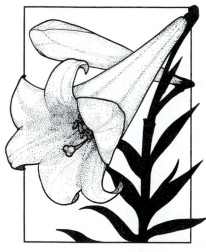

INTRODUCTION

Common names: Easter lily, trumpet lily, white lily.

Scientific name: *Lilium longiflorum* Thunb. (Huxley et al., 1992).

Family and related taxa: Liliaceae Juss. Other important lilies are the Asiatic and Oriental lilies and related hybrid groups used for flowering potted plants and cut flowers and the numerous garden lilies. The lily family is quite large and contains many commercially important floriculture crops including *Allium, Alstroemeria, Brodiaea, Convallaria, Eremurus, Hyacinthus, Lachenalia, Muscari, Ornithogalum,* and *Tulipa.*

Origin: Tropical islands of southern Japan, including Okinawa, Amami, and Erabu (Wilson, 1925).

Uses and current status: Easter lilies are a major flowering potted crop in the United States and primarily a cut flower in Europe and Japan. They are also grown as outdoor garden ornamentals in many parts of the world and have become naturalized in southern South Africa.

CULTIVARS

The major cultivar grown for potted Easter lily production in the United States is 'Nellie White.' Several cultivars are also available specifically for cut flower production in Europe, Israel, and Japan. Cut flower cultivars have fewer flowers and are taller, at least 3 ft (90 cm), than potted plant cultivars.

PROPAGATION

The principal means of propagating is by scale bulblets (Marinangeli and Curvetto, 1997). The Easter lily bulb is an imbricated or nontunicate bulb composed of scales, a basal plate, an apical meristem, and roots. Superior mother bulbs are carefully selected annually and mother block propagation stock is developed from their scales.

Two to 3 years are required to produce a commercial-size bulb from a scale for potted plant production. In southern Oregon and northern California, bulb harvest starts in September and ends by early October, the warmest and driest part of the year. Bulbs are graded according to bulb circumference. Commercial grades in the United States are presently known as 7–8, 8–9, or 9–10 in. (18–20, 20–23, or 23–25 cm). The most popular is the 8–9-in. (20–23-cm) grade. All bulbs are packed in crates of moist peat for shipment with 250 bulbs per crate for the 7–8 size, 200 for the 8–9 size, 150 for the 9–10 size, and 100 for the 10+ size (Blaney and Roberts, 1967).

The larger the bulb size, the greater the leaf and flower number (De Hertogh et al., 1969, 1976). Larger bulbs also have a more rapid leaf unfolding rate (Lange and Heins, 1990). Easter lily bulbs will produce either one shoot (single-nosed bulb) or two shoots (double-nosed bulb). The proportion of double-nosed bulbs is normally less than 5% and the two types are generally sold together (Erwin et al., 1987). Each of the two individual plants produced from a double-nosed bulb will be smaller and have a lower leaf and flower number than plants from single-nosed bulbs.

Roots are present and attached to the basal plate when the greenhouse forcer receives the bulbs. These roots should not be removed or allowed to dry out. The apical meristem continues to produce leaves during harvesting, packing, shipping, cold storage programming, planting, emergence, and up to flower initiation in January. Bulbs do not have a distinct dormancy period (De Hertogh and Wilkins, 1971a, b). The environmental conditions during bulb production can have a great effect on subsequent forcing by affecting the maturity and level of dormancy of the bulbs at harvest, leaf number, and emergence rate (Roberts et al., 1985). Great variability in plant characteristics for the same cultivar often exists between sources and within the same source. Forcing characteristics, such as days to shoot emergence and visible bud, node number, and leaf number varies with the producer of the bulbs (Zlesak and Anderson, 2003).

Plants can also be propagated by rooting stem leaves, which produce approximately two bulblets per leaf (Tammen et al., 1986). The production of flowering plants grown from leaf cutting-propagated or tissue culture bulblets in less than 1 year is possible but not commercially practiced (Holcomb and Berghage, 2001; Takayama et al., 1982; Tammen et al., 1986) (see Schedule and Timing on page 663).

FLOWERING CONTROL AND DORMANCY

Historically, flower induction has been controlled by subjecting bulbs to a cold moist treatment of 35 to 45°F (2 to 7°C) for 1000 hr or 6 weeks (Miller, 1993; Stuart, 1954; Wilkins, 1980). Bulbs may be packed in cases or planted in pots during the cold treatment. If bulbs are harvested, never cooled, and always exposed to 70°F (21°C) or above during forcing, plants will not flower regardless of photoperiod (Lin and Wilkins, 1973). Bulbs or shoots subjected to temperatures below 70°F (21°C) will eventually flower. The duration of the cold determines final plant quality. Increasing the duration of the cooling treatment (De Hertogh and Wilkins, 1971a, b) does the following:

1. Reduces the number of days to shoot emergence.
2. Increases uniformity of shoot emergence.
3. Reduces the number of days from shoot emergence to flowering.
4. Increases uniformity among plants in the time from shoot emergence until flower.
5. Reduces leaf and flower number.
6. Reduces lower leaf length.
7. Lengthens internodes.
8. Decreases (up to 6 weeks of cold storage) or increases final plant (more than 6 weeks of cold storage) height.

Cooling longer than 6 weeks (overcooled) generally results in fewer flowers and leaves, longer internodes, and shorter lower leaves. Plants cooled less than 6 weeks (undercooled) have more leaves and flowers, longer lower leaves, and shorter internodes, and may not flower by Easter

(Fig. II-1 Lilium, Easter). The cold storage temperature is normally 40 to 45°F (4.5 to 7°C) for 'Nellie White' and 35 to 40°F (2 to 4.5°C) for 'Ace.' Temperatures over 70°F (21°C) can result in devernalization if given to plants immediately after bulb storage (Miller and Kiplinger, 1966).

Three methods are used to commercially cool lilies from the arrival of bulbs to the end of the cooling period: natural cooling, controlled temperature forcing (CTF), and case cooling (De Hertogh and Wilkins, 1971a, b). Long days can also reduce time to flower initiation. Methods can be combined, such as 3 weeks of natural cooling and 3 to 4 weeks of CTF cooling or 4 weeks of CTF cooling and 2 weeks of LD. Moist media and strict temperature control/measurement must be used in all methods. Advantages and disadvantages for the methods are listed in Table II-1 Lilium, Easter.

NATURAL COOLING

Uncooled bulbs are received in October, potted, rooted, and cold treated using natural temperatures in the field, unheated greenhouse, or coldframes. Media temperatures are recorded twice daily and used to calculate the number of hours between 33 and 48°F (1 and 9°C). Hours above 48°F (9°C) are not counted as cooling temperatures. Bulbs should be cooled for 1000 hr. In cold climates, the structure can be heated if necessary to keep the temperature above 33°F (1°C) and prevent bulbs from freezing.

CONTROLLED TEMPERATURE FORCING

Uncooled bulbs are potted in October in a moist medium, rooted at 63 to 65°F (17 to 18°C) for 1 to 3 weeks, and cold treated at 35 to 40°F (2 to 5°C) in a cooler for 6 weeks. If shoots emerge while the bulbs are in the cooler, the temperature should be decreased to 33 to 35°F (1 to 2°C) and the shoots exposed to light. The purpose of the 63 to 65°F (17 to 18°C) temperature is to develop a root system before cooling, which leads to higher flower bud count. The precooling phase lasts from 1 to 3 weeks and is determined by the arrival date of the bulbs and the date of Easter; the precooling (rooting) phase will be short if bulbs arrive late or Easter is early.

CASE COOLING

Bulbs may be received uncooled by the forcer in mid-October to late November and placed in a cooler at 41°F (5°C) for 5 to 6 weeks for home case cooling or from the supplier in early December after being commercially case cooled (Fanelli and De Hertogh, 2002). In both situations, the forcer plants the bulbs in the first half of December and grows the plants at 55 to 59°F (13 to 15°C) for approximately 2 weeks to encourage root development.

PHOTOPERIOD

Long-day photoperiods applied using incandescent lamps to a shoot from a bulb can also program plants to flower and can substitute for cold treatments (Waters and Wilkins, 1967). The ultimate growth responses to bulb cold treatments or shoot light treatments are similar (Dole and Wilkins, 1994; Kohl and Nelson, 1963; Roh and Wilkins, 1973). Long photoperiods and cold treatments can substitute equally

TABLE II-1 LILIUM, EASTER

Advantages and disadvantages of various *Lilium longiflorum* programming methods (De Hertogh and Wilkins, 1971a, b).

Programming Method	Advantages	Disadvantages
Case cooling (CC)	1. Requires only limited refrigeration space 2. Can be performed by supplier or forcer	1. Reduces number of leaves and flowers produced 2. Shorter basal leaves than NC or CTF 3. Greenhouse bench space and labor requirements overlap with poinsettias
Natural cooling (NC)	1. Higher leaf and flower numbers than CC 2. Longer basal leaves 3. Greenhouse time does not compete with poinsettias 4. Shorter plants 5. More labor is generally available in October than later November and early December	1. Must be performed by forcer 2. Takes additional labor to move to field/coldframe and back to greenhouse 3. Dependent on prevailing weather conditions 4. If cold treatment insufficient, must have LD
Controlled temperature forcing (CTF)	1. Control of rooting and flowering process 2. Standard conditions every year 3. High leaf and flower number 4. Long basal leaves 5. Greenhouse time does not overlap with poinsettias 6. More labor available in October than late November and early December	1. Requires large amount of cooler space, which can be set at both warm and cool temperatures 2. Must be performed by forcer 3. Additional labor needed to move plants to and from cooler

on a week-for-week basis after bulbs are treated with 1 to 2 weeks of cold (Dole and Wilkins, 1994; Weiler and Langhans, 1968, 1972) (Fig. II-2 Lilium, Easter). For example, plants given 6 weeks of cold treatment will flower at the same time as those plants given 2 weeks of cold (to bulbs) and 4 weeks of LD (to shoots). As the photoperiod decreased from 16 to 12 hr day lengths, flowering was delayed and leaf number increased (Holcomb and Berghage, 2001). As with cold treatments, increasing the duration of LD lighting from 0 to 6 weeks reduced the number of leaves; primary, secondary, and tertiary flowers; and time to flower. Two pathways or methods may exist by which a lily can be programmed to flower rapidly, either by a bulb cold treatment or by a shoot long photoperiod treatment (Roh and Wilkins, 1973). At temperatures greater than 70°F (21°C), the long photoperiod treatment cannot be perceived by the shoot (Lange and Heins, 1988; Roh and Wilkins, 1973; Weiler

and Langhans, 1972). If bulbs have been given sufficient cold treatment, photoperiodic lighting has little or no effect on rate of flowering, but does increase height and decrease bud count (Smith and Langhans, 1962). Interestingly, in the Easter lily's natural Japanese environment, the average temperature is near 70°F (21°C) and Easter lilies are probably induced to flower by LD after plants are subjected to a short duration of temperatures below 70°F (21°C) (Wilkins, 1973).

Commercially, long days alone are not used to induce flowering due to uneven emergence of uncooled lily shoots and to the longer time the plants are in the greenhouse. Economical production of Easter lilies requires rapid and uniform shoot emergence, which is the result of a cold treatment.

Supplementing cold treatments with LD has been called the "Insurance Policy" (Wilkins et al., 1968). The procedure is to light lily shoots for 1 or 2 weeks, starting at emergence.

FIGURE II-2 LILIUM, EASTER
Effect of 6 weeks of 40°F (4.5°C) cold and/or LD on potted *Lilium longiflorum* plants. Note uniform flowering, leaf numbers, and internode elongation on plants receiving 2 or more weeks of cold plus LD.

Photoperiodic lighting is most effective if given as a night interruption for 4 hr from 2200 to 0200 hr with a minimum of 10 fc (2 μmol · m⁻² · s⁻¹) (Wilkins and Roh, 1970). This procedure will ensure that the plant is totally programmed and rapid flowering will occur (Wilkins et al., 1968). Although lighting should be a standard practice with early Easters, it can be especially important if bulbs have not received a total of 1000 hr of cold. Note, however, that long photoperiods after cooling can increase plant height (Dole, 1993; Smith and Langhans, 1962; Weiler and Langhans, 1968). In addition, although the "Insurance Policy" is often considered important for late emerging bulbs to ensure prompt flowering, bulbs emerging 1 to 3 weeks late will still flower within a few days of early emerging bulbs, regardless of photoperiod treatment (Dole, 1993). Flower initiation typically occurs after shoot emergence during the last 2 weeks of January and is normally complete when the plants are approximately 4 to 6 in. (10 to 15 cm) tall.

TEMPERATURE

Temperature is a critical factor in Easter lily production, and is often divided into the following stages:

1. Production of bulbs in field to receipt of bulbs
2. Receipt of bulbs to end of cold treatment
3. End of cold treatment to shoot emergence
4. Shoot emergence to flower initiation
5. Flower initiation to visible bud
6. Visible bud to flowering

Temperatures to which the bulbs are subjected during production in the field, stage 1, influence the degree of dormancy (Roberts et al., 1985). If the summer prior to bulb harvest is warm, bulbs will acquire little cold, be highly dormant, and be slow to emerge even after a typical 6-week cold treatment. However, if the summer is cool, bulbs will emerge faster the following forcing season. In addition, if the bulbs are larger than average, they are more dormant due to an increased number of inner scales, which inhibit growth the next season. If the growing season is poor, bulbs will be less dormant.

Stage 2 temperatures were discussed earlier under Flowering Control and Dormancy, page 657. During stage 3, optimum root media temperatures of 60 to 62°F (16 to 17°C) are typically used in years with a late Easter and 63 to 65°F (17 to 18°C) in years with an early Easter. Warmer temperatures are used for early Easters to hasten plant development. Media temperatures above 70°F (21°C) reduce flower bud number (H.F. Wilkins, unpublished) and if temperatures above 70°F (21°C) occur for an extended duration immediately after cold storage, the cold treatment may be erased (devernalized) and flowering delayed (Miller and Kiplinger, 1966). Temperatures lower than 60°F (16°C) slow root development. During stage 4, shoots emerge and become reproductive in mid- to late January.

Once flower initiation has occurred, plant development is controlled by temperature. During stage 5, the leaf unfolding rate increases linearly with increasing average daily temperature (Karlsson et al., 1988) and after flower initiation, leaf counting can begin (see Schedule and Timing, page 663). Increasing the temperature from 60 to 65°F (16 to 19°C) will increase the leaf unfolding rate the same as increasing the temperature from 70 to 75°F (21 to 24°C). However, in stage 6, increasing the temperature from 60 to 65°F (16 to 19°C) will decrease time from visible bud to flower more than increasing the temperature from 70 to 75°F (21 to 24°C) (Erwin and Heins, 1990; Healy and Wilkins, 1984). In stage 6, temperatures greater than 75°F (24°C) will only slightly decrease time to flower and flower bud blasting might occur (see Physiological Disorders, page 666). During stages 3 to 6, from emergence to visible bud, height control will need to be considered in choosing day and night temperatures (see Height Control, page 662) (De Hertogh, 1996; Karlsson et al., 1988). The timing of the crop will determine the average daily temperatures needed (see Schedule and Timing, page 663).

LIGHT

During forcing, maximum sunlight is desired for high-quality plants. As light intensity decreases, final plant height increases, and at very low light levels, flower bud abortion might occur (Fig. II-3 Lilium, Easter). Excessive use of incandescent lighting for LD, such as during the "Insurance Policy" period, may increase plant height as well (Dole, 1993; Smith and Langhans, 1962; Weiler and Langhans, 1968).

WATER

Easter lilies are more tolerant of dry media than many other floriculture crops; however, excessive drying will cause the lower leaves to yellow and flower buds to abort. Conversely, too frequent irrigation may lead to root rots (see Diseases, page 666). Water high in fluoride may cause leaf scorch (see Physiological Disorders, page 666).

CARBON DIOXIDE

Supplemental carbon dioxide injection is not used in commercial forcing because it does not increase quality or decrease crop time although it will increase height.

NUTRITION

If overhead irrigation is used, constant liquid fertilization of 200 ppm N and K can be used.

FIGURE II-3 LILIUM, EASTER Two *Lilium longiflorum* plants grown at 64°F (18°C) either in total darkness (left) or in 24-hr HID lighting (right) after flower initiation. Note that both plants are in flower (photo by Royal Heins).

Lower fertilization rates should be used with subirrigation or reduced leaching methods. Another fertilization regime uses 100 ppm N during the early stages of growth, 200 ppm N during the middle of forcing, and 400 ppm N when the roots are well developed during the final stage of growth. Another strategy is to fertilize with 400 to 600 ppm N the first two irrigations to encourage rapid initial growth and reduce fertilizer rate later. Forcers may also top-dress with controlled-release fertilizers to ensure adequate nutrition as the plant begins to flower. Monitor medium electrical conductivity (EC) carefully, especially from visible bud to flowering, because roots are highly sensitive to root rot during this stage. Foliar nutrient levels for high-quality plants are listed in Chapter 6, Nutrition, Table 6-4.

MEDIA

A well-drained and aerated medium is a prerequisite for top-quality plants with good root growth. Medium pH should be between 6.5 and 7.0 for soil-based media and 6.0 and 6.5 for soilless media (Seeley, 1950). The EC should be low, because a high EC of 3.5 dS · m^{-1} (saturated paste extract) or 2.0 dS · m^{-1} (2:1, water: medium) increases the susceptibility of lilies to root rots. Superphosphate should be avoided because it contains fluoride, which can cause leaf scorch (see Physiological Disorders, page 666). Phosphorus can be applied through constant liquid fertilization or through controlled-release fertilizers.

Unlike most bulb species which form roots only from the base of the bulb, lily bulbs are placed deep in standard size pots, about 0.5 in. (1.3 cm) from the bottom, to allow for maximum stem root development. A large number of stem roots will increase the vigor of the plant, and supplement roots from the basal plate which tend to rot easily (see Diseases, page 666). Stem root development is essential for the production of a high-quality crop.

HEIGHT CONTROL

The height of potted Easter lily plants can be controlled through the use of A-Rest (ancymidol), Sumagic (uniconazole), or DIF (Erwin et al., 1989; McAvoy, 2001). Do not apply growth regulators during flower initiation in mid January because a reduction in flower number may occur. Height control through water restriction is ineffective. However, high light, blackclothing, and cold water irrigation can prevent excessive stem elongation. Blackclothing at the end of the day excludes the evening light which is high in far-red and can reduce plant height by 20 to 30% (B. Miller, personal communication). Frequent irrigation with 40°F (5°C) cold water to the upper leaves is also effective (T. Blom, personal communication).

A-Rest can be applied as a drench at 2 to 4 ppm [0.25 to 0.5 mg a.i./6-in. (15-cm) pot] or as a spray at 30 to 132 ppm, with 50 ppm most commonly used (McAvoy, 2001). Applications are made when plants are 2 to 6 in. (5 to 15 cm) tall. If using sprays, multiple applications can be made using low to moderate concentrations. Effectiveness of A-Rest drenches is greatly decreased in bark media or when media pH is low (Larson et al., 1987).

Sumagic is applied as a drench at 0.25 to 1.25 ppm [0.03 to 0.15 mg a.i./6-in. (15-cm) pot] or as a spray at 2.5 to 15 ppm (Bailey and Miller, 1989; McAvoy, 2001; Wilfret, 1987). Plants are typically treated when they are 3 in. (8 cm) tall and multiple applications are not recommended. Sumagic may slightly delay flowering (Bailey and Miller, 1989; Wilfret, 1987). Uniform application of Sumagic is critical; excessive spray application [more than 1 gal/200 ft² (0.2 L · m⁻²)] will run off the leaves

into the medium, produce a drench in addition to a spray, and may cause excessive stunting. The effectiveness of Sumagic drenches is decreased when the media contains more than 20% bark. Use Sumagic at low rates if combining with DIF or plants may be too short. Adriansen (1985) indicated that Cycocel (chlormequat) is also marginally effective in controlling height.

The effectiveness of DIF can be monitored through graphical tracking (see Chapter 8, Plant Growth Regulation) and proper temperatures can be selected (Fisher and Heins, 1996; Heins et al., 1987) (Fig. II-4 Lilium, Easter). The use of DIF can have other effects. For example, with negative DIF, the leaves curl downward. As DIF becomes more positive, the leaves quickly become horizontal again (Erwin et al., 1989). In addition, temporary leaf chlorosis may occur when night temperature is greater than the day temperature (Erwin et al., 1987). This chlorosis rapidly disappears when night temperatures are equal or below day temperatures. Negative DIF for 2 to 4 hr commencing just after sunrise (DROP) is commonly used to control height. Interestingly, misting plants for 30-min intervals over a 3-hr period after sunrise reduced leaf temperature, which reduced

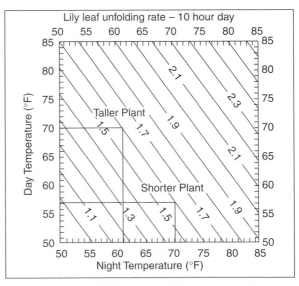

FIGURE II-4 LILIUM, EASTER Plot used to select the appropriate day and night temperature for forcing *Lilium longiflorum* based on desired leaf unfolding rate (Erwin et al., 1987). Pick a day temperature and draw a horizontal line from it to the diagonal line with the desired leaf unfolding rate. Draw a vertical line downward from the intersection to find the night temperature. Change the day/night temperature as needed to maintain the proper DIF.

stem elongation more than a negative DROP of 7°F (4°C) for 3 hr (Faust et al., 1994).

SPACING

If using CTF cooling, stack pots so that they can be watered and monitored for shoot emergence. In the greenhouse, plants can be placed pot-to-pot until leaves touch. Final pot spacing ranges from 8 × 8 to 12 × 12 in. (20 × 20 to 30 × 30 cm). Close spacing contributes to lower quality, lower leaf yellowing, and increased height.

PINCHING AND DISBUDDING

No pinching or disbudding required.

SUPPORT

No support required.

SCHEDULE AND TIMING

Timing of Easter lilies in North America is critical because the narrow sales window is only 1 to 2 weeks prior to Easter (Tables II-2, II-3, and II-4 Lilium, Easter). Two techniques are used to estimate flowering times and adjust temperatures: leaf counting and bud development meter. Leaf counting is used from flower initiation to visible bud and the bud development meter is used from visible bud to flowering (Fig. II-5

Lilium, Easter). Computer programs allow the integration of timing practices with height control practices.

The production of flowering plants grown from leaf cutting-propagated or tissue culture bulblets in less than 1 year is possible (Holcomb and Berghage, 2001; Takayama et al., 1982; Tammen et al., 1986). The bulblets remain vegetative when grown under short photoperiods at 70°F (21°C) (Stimart et al., 1982; Tammen, 2003). Under these conditions the plants form a leafy rosette and remain vegetative. When plants are placed under lower temperatures of 65°F (18°C) and LD, the stem elongates and flowers are initiated, both of which occur approximately 75 days after start of LD (Tammen et al., 1986). This process has been patented by Oglevee et al. (1986). Optimum plant quality is obtained if the plants receive 4800 cool temperature units (CTU), defined as 1.8°F below 70°F (1°C below 21°C) for 1 hr (Tammen, 2003).

LEAF COUNTING

Leaf counting is based on the fact that a set number of leaves are formed annually. This leaf number can be determined early in the forcing period, late January, and no more leaves are formed after flower initiation (Blaney et al., 1967; Wilkins and Roberts, 1969). At visible

TABLE II-2 LILIUM, EASTER

A general production schedule for controlled temperature forcing of 'Nellie White' *Lilium longiflorum* for an April 15 Easter.

Cultural Step	Date	Production Time (weeks)	Temperature °F (°C)
Bulbs arrive and are potted, root development	Oct. 14	3.5	62–65 (17–18)
Lower temperature	Nov. 8	6	40 (4)
Move plants to greenhouse	Dec. 20	6	60–62 (16–17)
Check for flower initiation and count leaves	Jan. 18–31	—	60–62 (16–17)
Adjust temperature for optimum leaf unfolding rate and height	Feb. 1	4	Variable
Visible bud, adjust temperatures for optimum bud development	Mar. 2	5.5	Variable
Flower	Apr. 8		
Total		25	

TABLE II-3 LILIUM, EASTER

Range of Easter dates and key forcing dates.

| Classification of Easter Dates | Initial Leaf Count | Date of | |
		First Sunday of Lent (visible bud)	Palm Sunday (market)
Early			
Mar. 23	Jan. 28–31	Feb. 10	Mar. 16
Apr. 1	Jan. 28–31	Feb. 19	Mar. 25
Medium			
Apr. 7	Jan. 28–31	Feb. 25	Mar. 31
Apr. 13	Jan. 28–31	Mar. 2	Apr. 6
Late			
Apr. 18	Jan. 28–31	Mar. 7	Apr. 11
Apr. 25	Jan. 28–31	Mar. 13	Apr. 18

TABLE II-4 LILIUM, EASTER

Date of the Easter holiday in the United States from 2004 to 2023.

Year	Date of Easter Holiday
2004	April 11
2005	March 27
2006	April 16
2007	April 8
2008	March 23
2009	April 12
2010	April 4
2011	April 24
2012	April 8
2013	March 31
2014	April 20
2015	April 5
2016	March 27
2017	April 16
2018	April 1
2019	April 21
2020	April 12
2021	April 4
2022	April 17
2023	April 19

timum greenhouse temperatures. The leaf counting method is as follows (Wilkins and Roberts, 1969):

1. Start leaf counting in late January or when plants are 4 to 6 in. (10 to 15 cm) tall. Harvest several plants to determine if flower initiation has occurred. If the first plants are still vegetative, examine a new set of plants 4 to 5 days later. The apical meristem will be round if it is still vegetative.

2. Select a minimum of three to five plants for every bulb source and bulb size to estimate the average leaf number of the crop. Count the number of leaves that have unfolded and the number yet to unfold on each plant. Unfolded leaves are defined as those at a 45° or greater angle with the plant stem. Leaves yet to unfold are those that have an angle of less than 45° to the plant stem. A large needle and a magnifying glass can be used to remove small, scalelike leaves near the shoot apex. The developing flower buds should be visible on reproductive plants using a magnifying glass. The future bud count can be estimated from these plants.

3. Divide the number of leaves already unfolded by the number of days from emergence until the present date to determine the number of leaves that have unfolded each day to date.

4. Determine the visible bud date. The visible bud date is normally set at 30 to 35 days prior to the expected market date (often Palm Sunday). It takes 28 days from visible

bud, all leaves have unfolded. The crop can be timed to flower on schedule by determining the total number of leaves and controlling the leaf unfolding rate by temperature from flower initiation to visible bud (Wilkins and Roberts, 1969). Fisher and Heins (1996) presented a convenient chart system to allow growers to monitor leaf unfolding rate and choose the op-bud to puffy bud stage at 70°F (21°C) and 35 days at 63°F (17°C) (see Temperature, page 660).

5. Divide the number of leaves that have yet to unfold by the number of days from the day of leaf counting until the expected visible bud date. This figure determines the number of leaves that must unfold each day to achieve visible bud at the desired time.

6. If the calculated number of leaves to unfold each day is greater than the actual unfolding rate, then increase the average daily greenhouse air temperature to speed development. In contrast, if the calculated number of leaves to unfold each day is less than the actual number of leaves unfolded each day prior to leaf counting, decrease the average daily air temperature to slow development.

7. In the greenhouse, mark the last unfolded leaves (those at a 45° angle) on several representative plants of each lot and bulb size. Mark each unfolded leaf by placing a wire hoop above all expanded leaves on the shoot but below the unexpanded leaves.

8. Determine the leaf unfolding rate twice per week. Compare the actual number of leaves unfolding per day with the calculated number to determine if the leaf unfolding rate was higher or lower than that necessary for proper timing. Adjust greenhouse temperatures accordingly. Average daily temperature affects leaf unfolding but since day–night temperature (DIF) determines rate of stem elongation, the actual day and night temperatures must also be considered. Use Figure II-4 Lilium, Easter to select the proper day and night temperature combination that will produce both the desired leaf unfolding rate and the desired stem elongation (Karlsson et al., 1988).

LILY BUD METER

The lily bud meter was developed to assist growers with determining greenhouse temperatures from visible bud to flowering (Grueber et al, 1986; Healy and Wilkins, 1984). Place the end of the meter at the base of the largest bud. Choose the temperature closest to the greenhouse average daily temperature and note the number of days until the bud is expected to open. Raise or lower temperatures accordingly. Fisher and colleagues (1996) updated and refined the bud meter (see Fig. II-5 Lilium, Easter). Be careful when using night temperatures greater than 70°F (21°C) because quality

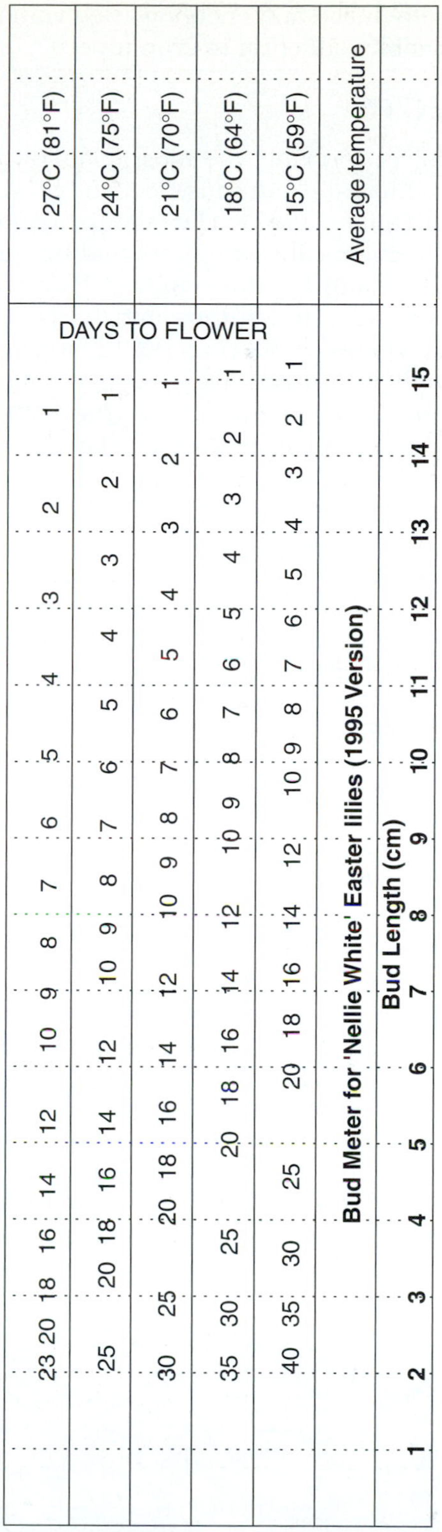

FIGURE II-5 LILIUM, EASTER Place end of meter at the base of the *Lilium longiflorum* flower bud. Observe where the tip of the bud falls on the meter, which corresponds to the number of days to flower at the specified temperatures (Fisher et al., 1996).

Bud Meter for 'Nellie White' Easter lilies (1995 Version)

DAYS TO FLOWER

Average temperature	27°C (81°F)	24°C (75°F)	21°C (70°F)	18°C (64°F)	15°C (59°F)
	1	1	1	1	1
				2	2
	2	2	2	3	3
	3	3	3	4	4
		4	4	5	5
	4	5	5	6	6
	5	6	6	7	7
	6	7	7	8	8
	7	8	8	9	9
	8	9	9	10	10
	9	10	10	12	12
	10	12	12	14	14
	12	14	14	16	16
	14	16	16	18	18
	16	18	18	20	20
	18	20	20	25	25
	20	25	25	30	30
	23 20		30	35	35
					40

Bud Length (cm): 1 2 3 4 5 6 7 8 9 10 11 12 13 14 15

may be reduced and energy wasted without an appreciable reduction in crop time.

INSECTS

Aphids are probably the most common insect pest on lilies and can cause leaf and flower distortion (Miller, 1997). They can be controlled through chemical insecticides and through biological controls. Bulb mites, *Rhizoglyphus echinopus*, are ubiquitous and feed on dead tissue (Wilkins, 1980) (Fig. II-6 Lilium, Easter). Although their effect varies greatly from year to year and cannot be predicted, they can enter stem tissue and cause extensive damage. Plants may appear to be weak, stunted, and frequently have injured leaves. Bulbs should be soaked with the appropriate miticide prior to planting. Fungus gnats are a major problem and the larvae can cause plant stunting and foliar chlorosis by damaging the roots. Chemical and biological controls are available.

DISEASES

Plant disease is a major concern and root rots are among the most common. The root rot complex of diseases includes *Cylindrocarpon radicicola*, *Fusarium oxysporum*, *Pythium*, *Rhizoctonia solani*, *Phytophthora cactorum*, and *P. parasitica* (Horst, 1990; Linderman, 1985). Preventive fungicides can be applied as a bulb dip prior to potting and/or as a drench immediately after potting (De Hertogh, 1996). If bulbs are programmed by CTF, a second fungicide drench is applied immediately on placement of the plants in the greenhouse. All bulbs can be treated every 3 to 4 weeks thereafter. Low media EC from proper fertilization and irrigation, sufficient medium aeration, and avoidance of overwatering will reduce the chance of root rot.

FIGURE II-6 LILIUM, EASTER Bulb mite (*Rhizoglyphus echinopus*) on *Lilium longiflorum* bulb tissue.

Consider root rot-causing organisms to always be present and able to cause problems. Damage from root rots can be especially prevalent at the time of visible bud.

Gray mold (*Botrytis cinerea*) can occur on flowers and leaves if air circulation and humidity control are not practiced. Well-aerated greenhouses, ventilation of humid air before dark, and sanitary conditions will normally prevent this disease. Gray mold can be especially troublesome during shipping if open flowers and dead leaves are present; the fungus finds a suitable environment in the sugar-laden nectar at the end of the stigma. Reduce cooler humidity and use preventive fungicides, if necessary.

Various viruses are normally present, but the control of these diseases is the responsibility of the bulb producer. A number of other diseases can be found, especially on lilies grown outdoors in perennial gardens, including scale rot (*Colletotrichum*), bulb rot (*Rhizopus stolonifera* or *Penicillium*), rust (*Uromyces*), leaf spots (*Cercospora*, *Cercosporella*, *Heterosporium*, and *Ramularia*), and cottony rot (*Sclerotinia sclerotiorum*) (Dreistadt, 2001).

PHYSIOLOGICAL DISORDERS

YELLOWING OF LOWER LEAVES

Chlorosis and death of lower leaves are caused by numerous factors and are common problems in Easter lily production. A few causes during production include root injury, root loss (due to high soluble salt levels, insufficient medium aeration, overwatering, or root rot), inadequate or excessive fertilizer, moisture stress (insufficient water), or plant crowding (insufficient light at the base of the plant). Leaf yellowing can also occur after excessively long cold storage of budding plants.

Leaf yellowing during production can be prevented by spraying Fascination [(1:1 benzyladenine:gibberellic acid (BA:GA)] on the lower foliage (Franco and Han, 1997; Han, 1995, 1997; Heins et al., 1996; McAvoy, 2001). The first spray is made at 5:5 to 25:25 ppm (BA:GA) 7 to 10 days before visible bud and a second application at the same rates can be applied 7 to 10 days after visible bud. Apply Fascination carefully to the lower leaves because inadvertent application to young leaves will cause excessive shoot elongation. The earlier the applications, the greater the stem elongation (Han, 2000). Do not apply too much volume because the excess will run off in the media and cause stem elongation. On the other hand, coverage must be complete because leaves not directly sprayed will not be protected. Note that A-Rest application and negative DIF during production can aggravate lower leaf chlorosis and cause death (Ranwala et al., 2000).

Leaf yellowing after cold storage can be prevented by spraying Fascination at 100:100 ppm over the top of plants when the buds are about 3 in. (8 cm) long. Applications should be made 2 weeks or less prior to cold storage. Little stem elongation occurs with late applications (Ranwala and Miller, 1999).

LEAF SCORCH/TIP BURN

Leaf tips and areas on the leaf margins turn yellow and later brown. The problem is mainly due to high fluoride levels and has been reduced by the selection of resistant cultivars and reduction of fluoride contaminants (Widmer et al., 1976). The cultivar 'Ace' is much more susceptible to leaf scorch than 'Nellie White.' Fluoride is found in superphosphate and irrigation water (Marousky and Woltz, 1977). Contrary to previous reports, perlite does not contain fluoride and can be used (Nelson, 2003). The problem may be more severe one year than another even though forcing techniques appear to be the same in both years.

FLORAL BUD ABORTION AND BLASTING

Flower buds can die when they are very young (abortion) or later when they are well developed and easily visible (blasting). Both types can occur due to root loss (from high-medium soluble salt accumulation, water stress, or root rots), low light levels (from close plant spacing or greenhouse shading), ethylene, or high temperatures during greenhouse forcing. A-Rest application (see Height Control, page 662) can aggravate bud abortion and blasting. The application of benzylamino (tetrahydropyranyl) purine (PBA) at 500 ppm did not prevent flower bud abortion (Wang, 1996).

POSTHARVEST

Plants are generally sold wholesale when buds are puffy white and retail when one flower is open, although plants can be adequately stored in the dark at 32°F (0°C) for up to 14 days when buds are white and puffy. Warmer storage temperatures of 35 to 50°F (2 to 10°C) can be used if 50 fc (10 μmol $\cdot$ mol$^{-2} \cdot$ s^{-1}) light is provided (Nell, 1993). Bud blasting and foliar chlorosis will increase and postharvest floral longevity will decrease with increasing storage time (Prince et al., 1987; Staby and Erwin, 1977). Be sure plant foliage is dry and medium is moist when placing plants in the cooler.

Fascination spray can be applied to the lower foliage to greatly reduce postproduction leaf yellowing (see Physiological Disorders, page 666). Fascination was effective even when applied to foliage already starting to yellow (Han, 1997). Pemberton et al. (1997) also used 500-ppm sprays of PBA, applied to the flower buds, to experimentally increase postharvest life of the flowers. Extremely negative DIF may contribute to postharvest leaf yellowing by reducing plant carbohydrate and nitrogen levels during production (Miller, 1997).

Easter lilies are sensitive to ethylene, which will cause various problems depending on concentration, length of exposure, temperature, and the developmental stage of the lily bulb or plant (H.F. Wilkins, unpublished). Exposure of bulbs to ethylene may prevent or delay emergence and cause leaf abnormalities. If shoots are exposed to ethylene during flower bud initiation, malformations and reductions in bud numbers result, and if exposed at or near flower bud opening, anthesis of the older buds will be hastened and the younger buds will be aborted. The anti-ethylene agent 1-methylcyclopropene (1-MCP) is effective at preventing damage due to exogenous ethylene on cut Easter lilies (Elgar et al., 1999).

Pollen is frequently removed by the grower or retailer to prevent discoloration of the petals.

KEY POINTS

- Easter lily is used as a potted flowering plant, cut flower, and garden ornamental.
- Plants are produced from bulbs that are propagated commercially by scale bulblets.

- Typically flower induction occurs after bulbs receive a cold moist treatment of 35 to 45°F (2 to 7°C) for 6 weeks.

- Increasing the duration of the cold treatment above 6 weeks reduces leaf and flower number, increases final plant height, and reduces lower leaf length.
- Easter lilies are facultative LD plants and LD can substitute for cold on a week-for-week basis after bulbs have received 1 to 2 weeks of cold treatment.
- Timing of the Easter lily crop is a major concern in North America due to the narrow marketing window; leaf counting and the leaf development meter are used to estimate flowering time and adjust production temperatures.
- Yellowing or loss of lower leaves is a frequent problem and can be due to root rot, high medium EC, under- or overwatering, insufficient medium aeration, inadequate or excessive fertilization, or plant crowding. Leaf yellowing can be prevented with the use of Fascination.
- Root rots are a major problem.

BIBLIOGRAPHY

Adriansen, E. 1985. Kemisk vækstregulering, pp. 142–162 in *Potteplanter I—Produktion, Metoder, Midler*, O.V. Christensen, A. Klougart, I.S. Pedersen and K. Wikesjö, editors. Gartner-INFO, København, Denmark. (in Danish)

Bailey, D.A., and W.B. Miller. 1989. Whole-plant response of Easter lilies to ancymidol and uniconizole. *Journal of the American Society for Horticultural Science* 114:393–396.

Blaney, L.T., and A.N. Roberts. 1967. Bulb production, pp. 23–36 in *Easter Lilies: The Culture, Diseases, Insects and Economics of Easter Lilies*, D.C. Kiplinger and R.W. Langhans, editors. Cornell University Press, Ithaca, New York.

Blaney, L.T., A.N. Roberts, and P. Lin. 1967. Timing Easter lilies. *Florists' Review* 140(3624):19.

De Hertogh, A. 1996. *Lilium longiflorum*, pp. C79–94 in *Holland Bulb Forcer's Guide*, 5th ed. International Flower Bulb Centre, Hillegon, The Netherlands.

De Hertogh, A.A., and H.F. Wilkins. 1971a. The forcing of northwest-grown 'Ace' and 'Nellie White' lilies, Part 1. *Florists' Review* 149(3857):29–31.

De Hertogh, A.A., and H.F. Wilkins. 1971b. The forcing of northwest-grown 'Ace' and 'Nellie White' lilies, Part 2. *Florists' Review* 149(3858):57, 104–111.

De Hertogh, A.A., W.H. Carlson, and S. Kays. 1969. Controlled temperature forcing of planted lily bulbs. *Journal of the American Society for Horticultural Science* 94:433–436.

De Hertogh, A.A., H.P. Rasmussen, and N. Blakely. 1976. Morphological changes and factors influencing shoot apex development of *Lilium longiflorum* Thunb. during forcing. *Journal of the American Society for Horticultural Science* 101:463–471.

Dole, J.M. 1993. Interaction of shoot emergence date and long days after controlled-temperature forcing of 'Nellie White' Easter lilies. *Journal of the American Society for Horticultural Science* 118:741–746.

Dole, J.M., and H.F. Wilkins. 1994. Interaction of bulb vernalization and shoot photoperiod on 'Nellie White' Easter lily. *HortScience* 29:143–145.

Dreistadt, S.H. 2001. *Integrated Pest Management for Floriculture and Nurseries*. University of California Division of Agriculture and Natural Resources Publication 3402.

Elgar, H.J., A.B. Woolf, and L. Bieleski. 1999. Ethylene production by three lily species and their response to ethylene exposure. *Postharvest Biology and Technology* 16:257–267.

Erwin, J.E., and R.D. Heins. 1990. Temperature effects on lily development rate and morphology from the visible bud stage until anthesis. *Journal of the American Society for Horticultural Science* 115:644–646.

Erwin, J., R. Heins, M. Karlsson, W. Carlson, and J. Biernbaum. 1987. *Producing Easter lilies*. Extension Bulletin E-1406, Michigan State University Cooperative Extension Service, East Lansing.

Erwin, J.E., R.D. Heins, and M.G. Karlsson. 1989. Thermomorphogenesis in *Lilium longiflorum*. *American Journal of Botany* 76:47–52.

Fanelli, F.L., and A.A. De Hertogh. 2002. The effects of precooling temperatures and durations on forcing of *Lilium longiflorum*, 'Nellie White.' *Acta Horticulturae* 570:147–152.

Faust, J.E., S. Verlinden, and R.D. Heins. 1994. Pulsing temperatures and syringing stem elongation of Easter lily. *HortScience* 29:544. (Abstract)

Fisher, P.R., and R.D. Heins. 1996. A graphical control chart for monitoring leaf count of Easter lily to support crop timing decisions. *HortTechnology* 6:68–70.

Fisher, P.R., J.H. Lieth, and R.D. Heins. 1996. Modeling flower bud elongation in Easter lily (*Lilium longiflorum* Thunb.) in response to temperature. *HortScience* 31:349–352.

Franco, R.E., and S.S. Han. 1997. Respiratory changes associated with growth-regulator-delayed leaf yellowing in Easter lily. *Journal of the American Society for Horticultural Science* 122:117–121.

Grueber, K.L., W.E. Healy, H.B. Pemberton, and H.F. Wilkins. 1986. Easter lily unfolding rate as influenced by temperature. *Minnesota State Florists Bulletin* 35(6):1–4.

Han, S.S. 1995. Growth regulators delay foliar chlorosis of Easter lily leaves. *Journal of the American Society for Horticultural Science* 120:254–258.

Han, S.S. 1997. Preventing post-production leaf yellowing in Easter lily. *Journal of the American Society for Horticultural Science* 122:869–872.

Han, S.S. 2000. Growth regulators reduce leaf yellowing in Easter lily caused by close spacing and root rot. *HortScience* 35:657–660.

Healy, W.E., and H.F. Wilkins. 1984. Temperature effects on 'Nellie White' flower bud development. *HortScience* 19(6):843–844.

Heins, R., J. Erwin, M. Karlsson, R. Berghage, W. Carlson, and J. Biernbaum. 1987. Tracking Easter lily height with graphs. *GrowerTalks* 51(8):64, 66, 68.

Heins, R.D., T.F. Wallace, and S.S. Han. 1996. GA_{4+7} plus benzyladenine reduce leaf yellowing of greenhouse Easter lilies. *HortScience* 31:597. (Abstract)

Holcomb, E.J., and R. Berghage. 2001. Photoperiod, chilling, and light quality during daylight extension affect growth and flowering of tissue-cultured Easter lily plants. *HortScience* 36:53–55.

Horst, R.K. 1990. Lily, pp. 707–708 in *Westcott's Plant Disease Handbook*, 5th ed. Van Nostrand Reinhold, New York.

Huxley, A., M. Griffiths, and M. Levy. 1992. *Lilium*, pp. 68–80 in *The New Royal Horticultural Society Dictionary of Gardening*, vol. 3. Stockton Press, New York.

Karlsson, M.G., R.D. Heins, and J.E. Erwin. 1988. Quantifying temperature-controlled leaf unfolding rates in 'Nellie White' Easter lily. *Journal of the American Society for Horticultural Science* 113:70–74.

Kohl, H.C., Jr., and R.L. Nelson. 1963. Daylength and light intensity as independent factors in determining height of Easter lily. *Proceedings of the American Society for Horticultural Science* 83:808–810.

Lange, N.E., and R.D. Heins. 1988. Interaction of photoperiod and temperature in promoting flowering of *Lilium longiflorum*. *HortScience* 23:749. (Abstract)

Lange, N., and R. Heins. 1990. The lowdown on how bulb size influences lily development. *GrowerTalks* 53(10):52–54.

Larson, R.A., C.B. Thorne, R.R. Milks, Y.M. Isenberg, and L.D. Brisson. 1987. Use of ancymidol bulb dips to control stem elongation of Easter lilies grown in a pine bark medium. *Journal of the American Society for Horticultural Science* 112:769–773.

Lin, W.C., and H.F. Wilkins. 1973. The interaction of temperature on photoperiodic responses of *Lilium longiflorum* Thunb. cv. 'Nellie White.' *Florists' Review* 153(3965):24–26.

Linderman, R.G. 1985. Easter lilies, pp. 9–40 in *Diseases of Floral Crops*, 2nd ed. New York, Praeger.

Marinangeli, P., and N. Curvetto. 1997. Bulb quality and traumatic acid influence bulblet formation from scaling in *Lilium* species and hybrids. *HortScience* 32:739–741.

Marousky, F.J., and S.S. Woltz. 1977. Influence of lime, nitrogen and phosphorus sources on the availability and relationship of soil fluoride to leaf scorch in *Lilium longiflorum* Thunb. *Journal of the American Society for Horticultural Science* 102:799–804.

McAvoy, R. 2001. Easter lilies, pp. 74–78 in *Tips on Regulating Growth of Floriculture Crops*, M.L. Gaston, L.A. Kunkle, P.S. Konjoian, and M.F. Wilt, editors. Ohio Florists' Association Services, Columbus, Ohio.

Miller, B. 1997. 1998 Easter lily production. *Southeastern Floriculture* 7(5):43–46.

Miller, R.O., and D.C. Kiplinger. 1966. Reversal of vernalization in northwest Easter lilies. *Proceedings of the American Society for Horticultural Science* 88:646–650.

Miller, W.B. 1993. *Lilium longiflorum*, pp. 391–422 in *Physiology of Flower Bulbs*, A. De Hertogh and M. Le Nard, editors. Elsevier, Amsterdam.

Nell, T.A. 1993. *Lilium longiflorum*, pp. 59–61 in *Flowering Potted Plants: Prolonging Shelf Performance*. Ball Publishing, Batavia, Illinois.

Nelson, P.V. 2003. Root substrate, pp. 197–236 in *Greenhouse Operation and Management*, 6th ed., Prentice Hall, Upper Saddle River, New Jersey.

Oglevee, J.R., J.F. Tammen, and W. O'Donnovan. 1986. Lily process. United States patent number 4,570,379a.

Pemberton, H.B., Y.-T. Wang, and G.V. McDonald. 1997. Increase of Easter lily postharvest flower longevity with PBA application to young flower buds. *HortScience* 32:458–459. (Abstract)

Prince, T.A., M.S. Cunningham, and J.S. Peary. 1987. Floral and foliar quality of potted Easter lilies after STS or phenidone application, refrigerated storage, and simulated shipping. *Journal of the American Society for Horticultural Science* 112:469–473.

Ranwala, A.P., and W.B. Miller. 1999. Timing of gibberellin$_{4+7}$ + benzyladenine sprays influences efficacy against foliar chlorosis and plant height in Easter lily. *HortScience* 34:902–903.

Ranwala, A.P., W.B. Miller, T.I. Kirk, and P.A. Hammer. 2000. Ancymidol drenches, reversed greenhouse temperatures, postgreenhouse cold storage, and hormone sprays affect postharvest leaf chlorosis in Easter lily. *Journal of the American Society for Horticultural Science* 125:248–253.

Roberts, A.N., J.R. Stang, Y-T. Wang, W.R. McCorkle, L.L. Riddle, and F.W. Moeller. 1985. *Easter lily growth and development.* Oregon State University Agricultural Experiment Station Technical Bulletin 148, Corvallis.

Roh, S.M., and H.F. Wilkins. 1973. The influence and substitution of long days for cold treatments on growth and flowering of Easter lilies (*Lilium longiflorum* Thunb. 'Georgia' and 'Nellie White'). *Florists' Review* 153(3960):19–21, 60–63.

Seeley, J.G. 1950. Mineral nutrient deficiencies and leaf burn of Croft Easter lilies. *Proceedings of the American Society for Horticultural Science* 56:439–445.

Smith, D.R., and R.W. Langhans. 1962. The influence of photoperiod on the growth and flowering of the Easter lily (*Lilium longiflorum* Thunb. var. Croft). *Proceedings of the American Society for Horticultural Science* 80:599–604.

Staby, G.L., and T.D. Erwin. 1977. The storage of Easter lilies. *Florists' Review* 161(4162):38.

Stimart, D.P., P.D. Ascher, and H.F. Wilkins. 1982. Overcoming dormancy in *Lilium longiflorum* bulblets produced in tissue culture. *Journal of the American Society for Horticultural Science* 107:604–1007.

Stuart, N.W. 1954. Moisture content of packing medium, temperature and duration of storage as factors in forcing lily bulbs. *Proceedings of the American Society for Horticultural Science* 63:488–494.

Takayama, S., M. Misawa, Y. Takashige, and H. Tsumori. 1982. Cultivation of *in vitro*-propagated *Lilium* bulbs in soil. *Journal of the American Society for Horticultural Science* 107:830–834.

Tammen, J.F. 2003. Quantifying the cooling period for flowering of 'Nellie White' Easter lily. *HortScience* 38:21–25.

Tammen, J.F., J.R. Oglevee, E.J. Oglevee, and L. Duffy. 1986. A new process for producing pathogen-free Easter lilies. *GrowerTalks* 50(3):62, 65–66.

Wang, Y.-T. 1996. Cytokinen and light intensity regulate flowering of Easter lily. *HortScience* 31:976–977.

Waters, W.E., and H.F. Wilkins. 1967. Influence of intensity, duration and date of light on growth and flowering of uncooled Easter lily (*Lilium longiflorum* Thunb. 'Georgia'). *Proceedings of the American Society for Horticultural Science* 90:433–439.

Weiler, T.C., and R.W. Langhans. 1968. Determination of vernalizing temperatures in the vernalization requirement of *Lilium longiflorum* (Thunb.) cv. 'Ace.' *Proceedings of the American Society for Horticultural Science* 93:623–629.

Weiler, T.C., and R.W. Langhans. 1972. Growth and flowering responses of *Lilium longiflorum* Thunb. 'Ace' to different daylengths. *Journal of the American Society for Horticultural Science* 97:176–177.

Widmer, R.E., R. Mugaas, and H.F. Wilkins. 1976. Lime and phosphate effects on Easter lilies, *Lilium longiflorum* Thunb. *Minnesota State Florists' Bulletin* Dec.:1–7.

Wilfret, G.J. 1987. Height retardation of Easter lilies grown in containers. *Proceedings of the Florida State Horticultural Society* 100:379–382.

Wilkins, H.F. 1973. Our Easter lily: Where did it come from, why does it flower at Easter time; chasing the wild lily. *Minnesota Horticulture* 101:36–38.

Wilkins, H.F. 1980. Easter lilies, pp. 327–352 in *Introduction to Floriculture*, R.A. Larson, editor. Academic Press, New York.

Wilkins, H.F., and A.N. Roberts. 1969. University of Minnesota's Easter Lily Research Report: Paper No. IV. Leaf counting—A new concept in timing Easter lilies. *Minnesota State Florists' Bulletin* Dec.:10–13.

Wilkins, H.F., and S.M. Roh. 1970. University of Minnesota's Easter Lily Research Report: Paper No. IX. Lighting lilies at shoot emergence. Night interruption shown to be most effective. *Minnesota State Florists' Bulletin* Dec.:10–12.

Wilkins, H.F., W.E. Waters, and R.E. Widmer. 1968. University of Minnesota's Easter Lily Research Report: Paper No. II. An insurance policy: Lighting lilies at shoot emergence will overcome inadequate bulb precooling. *Minnesota State Florists' Bulletin* Aug.:6–11.

Wilson, E.H. 1925. Subgenera, sections, and species (*Lilium longiflorum*), pp. 23–28 in *Enumeration of the lilies of Eastern Asia*, E.H. Wilson, editor. Dunlan and Company, London.

Zlesak, D., and N. Anderson. 2003. Somaclonal variation among *Lilium longiflorum* 'Nellie White' bulb growers sources. *HortScience* 38:679. (Abstract)

Limonium

INTRODUCTION

Common names: statice, sea lavender.

Scientific names: Botanically, commercially grown statice are divided among three genera: (1) *Limonium bellidifolium* (Gouan) Dumort., *L. gmelinii* (Willd.) Kuntze, *L. latifolium* (Sm.) Kuntze, *L. peregrinum* (Bergius) R.A. Dyer, *L. perezii* (Stapf) Hubb., *L. sinuatum* (L.) Mill., annual statice, and *L. tetragonum* (Thumb) Bullocki (formerly *L. sinense*); (2) *Psylliostachys suworowii* (Reg.) Roshk. (formerly *L. suworowii*), rat's tail statice; and (3) *Goniolimon tataricum* (formerly *L. tataricum*) (Bailey and Bailey, 1976; Harada, 1998; Huxley et al., 1992) (Table II-1 Limonium). In addition, several hybrids have been developed and three names are often listed in the horticultural literature but are not of botanical standing: *Limonium altaica* (similar to *G. tataricum*), *L. bonduellii* (considered to be part of *L. sinuatum*), and *L. dumosum* (most likely *G. tataricum*).

Family and related taxa: Plumbaginaceae Juss. More than 170 annual, biennial, and perennial species are found within the *Goniolimon*, *Limonium*, and *Psylliostachys* genera. Within the family, the genera *Armeria* and *Plumbago* are useful in ornamental horticulture.

Origin: Statice are found worldwide. Most of the commercially important species or hybrids are originally from the Mediterranean and Europe west into China. *L. peregrinum*, a near shrub, occurs in South Africa.

Uses and current status: Depending on the genus, species, or hybrid, plants are grown worldwide in the field or under protection as fresh or dried cut flowers. *L. sinuatum* is one of the world's most commonly grown and recognized cut flowers (Fig. II-1 Limonium). Genetically dwarf types are available and are used as potted flowering plants and bedding plants.

Statice typically have a low basal rosette of foliage from which large panicle inflorescences arise on slender stems. *Goniolimon* are perennial species that become woody at the base and have white, pink, blue, or purple inflorescences. *Limonium* may be annual, biennial, or perennial, but are most commonly perennial, and exhibit a broad range of colors including white, pink, blue, purple, yellow, and many intermediate shades. *Psylliostachys* are annuals with long, thin upright inflorescences of white to pink or rose-colored flowers.

CULTIVARS

Statice cultivars developed for cut flower production can be divided into those that are annual, biennial, or perennial (Bailey and Bailey, 1976; Huxley et al., 1992). For example, *L. sinuatum*, the annual statice, is a tender perennial that is typically handled as an annual. Harada (1998) has also divided statice into Type I and Type II flowering requirements. Type I plants require a cold treatment and flowering occurs only once during late spring or summer. Type II will flower any time of the year if temperature and light intensity and

FIGURE II-I LIMONIUM *Limonium sinuatum* 'Friendly Yellow' cut flower.

TABLE II-I LIMONIUM

Genera, species, and hybrids of statice which are useful in floriculture.

Species or Hybrid	Common Name	Annual (a) Biennial (b) Perennial (p)	Flower Color	Height in. (cm)	Cold Hardiness Zone
Goniolimon tataricum (formerly *Limonium tataricum*)	German or seafoam statice	p	Blue, white, ruby red	10–18 (25–45)	4–11
Limonium altaica (of no botanical status)	'Emile' series	p Type II	Lavender, light blue	12–24 (30–60)	7
L. bellidifolium	Caspian statice	p	Blue, violet	4–12 (10–30)	8
L. bonduellii (see *L. sinuatum*)					
L. dumosum (of no botanical status)	'Tres Bien'	Type I	Rose	24+ (60+)	—
L. gmelinii	Siberian statice	p Type I	Lilac, blue, red	20–30 (50–76)	4
L. latifolium	'Avignon' series	p Type I	White, blue, violet	18–32 (46–80)	5–9
L. peregrinum	'Bellarina' series	p Type II	Rose pink	36 (90)	9, tender
L. perezii	Perezii statice	p Type II	Deep colors, violet	18–28 (46–70)	8, tender
L. sinuatum	Annual statice	p (treated as an annual)	White, blue, purple, pink, yellow	12–36 (30–90)	9
L. sinense (see *L. tetragonum*)					
L. tetragonum	Star dust	b	White, yellow center	8–24 (20–60)	6 to 7
L. bellidifolium x *L. latifolium*	'Misty' series	p	Light-purple blue	20–30 (50–75)	7
L. caspium x *L. latifolium*	'St. Pierre,' 'Beltlaard'	p Type II	Dark purple-blue	20 (50)	7
L. gmelinii x *L. latifolium*	'Charm' series	p Type I	Blue	31 (80)	6
L. aurea x *L. sinensis*	'Lemon Star'	p Type II	Yellow	10+ (25+)	9, tender
Psylliostachys suworowii (formerly *L. suworowii*)	Rat tail, Russian statice	a	Pink	10–24 (25–60)	—

duration are appropriate. Cultivars for potted flowering plants and for bedding plants are raised from seed and treated as annuals.

PROPAGATION

ANNUALS

There are approximately 10,000 seeds/oz (350/g) for *L. sinuatum* and 195,000 seeds/oz (6900/g) for *P. suworowii*. However, only 4000 *L. sinuatum* seedlings/oz can be expected to

germinate and be transplanted (Armitage and Laushman, 2003). Seed should be "just covered" or distributed on the medium surface and allow misting to "bury" the seed. Germinate seed at 70 to 77°F (21 to 25°C); seedlings emerge within 7 to 14 days and can be transplanted within 3 weeks. Seed of *L. sinuatum* can be vernalized at 36°F (2°C) for 30 to 40 days to reduce time to flower (Azuma et al., 1983). Plugs can be field planted 6 to 8 weeks after seeding.

PERENNIALS

Perennials can be propagated by seed, if available, plant division, root cuttings, or *in vitro*.

SEED. Germinate seed at 70 to 77°F (21 to 25°C), which occurs in 10 to 14 days.

PLANT DIVISION. Individual plantlets are removed from the basal area of the old plant with care and with as many roots as possible. Spring is the most appropriate time to divide plants. Little flower production occurs during the first year.

ROOT CUTTINGS. The largest diameter roots are best used and cut into 1- to 3-in. (2.5- to 7.5-cm) lengths. The roots are planted upright in a well-aerated medium. If thinner roots must be used, place them horizontally on the well-aerated medium and do not cover too deep. Root propagation can be done any time of the year; a greenhouse or growth room may be required to maintain temperatures of 70°F (21°C).

IN VITRO. *L. altaica* ×*L. caspium* plants are *in vitro* propagated (Matsumoto et al., 1997). *L. latifolium* can be propagated by *in vitro* or seed (Clemens and Welsh, undated). *L. latifolium* ×*L. bellidifolium* hybrid series are widely *in vitro* propagated (Anonymous, undated; Meyer, 1991). When *in vitro* plants are received, plant and acclimate by placing under 75% light reduction, a light mist or fog applied several times a day, and 65 to 75°F (18 to 24°C) temperatures. After at least 2 weeks, reduce shade to 20% and commence nutrition at a low rate (Meyer, 1991).

FLOWERING CONTROL AND DORMANCY

Flowering control is still being researched for the various genera, species, and hybrids and is not well understood for some taxa. Most of the research has been with *L. sinuatum*, which is typically treated as an annual. Harada (1992, 1998) divided statice into two groups. *Type I* plants require a seed or plant vernalization treatment. Type I plants must reach "maturity," which is defined as a specific plant size/leaf number, before the cold treatment will induce flowering. In addition, Type I has three growth and temperature phases: (1) high temperature for germination, (2) low temperature for vernalization (floral induction and initiation), and (3) high temperature for floral development and stem elongation. *Type II* plants will flower throughout the year as long

as light intensity and duration and temperatures are appropriate.

Gibberellic acid (GA$_3$) sprays have been reported to accelerate date of flower and to increase yields (Wilfret and Raulston, 1975). With *L. sinuatum*, a single GA$_3$ spray (500 ppm) 87 days after sowing reduced the days to flower by 90 days. If plants were sprayed 129 days after seeding, no response was seen. With *L.* 'Misty Blue' (*L. latifolium* ×*L. bellidifolium*) a single GA$_3$ (400 ppm) spray hastened date of flower by 20 days if treated 9 to 33 days after transplanting (Garner and Armitage, 1996). If applied later, the response was reduced.

TEMPERATURE

Germination of *L. sinuatum* is accomplished within 7 to 14 days at 70 to 77°F (21 to 25°C) and plants can remain at this temperature until two or more true leaves are produced. If seed are vernalized, use cultural temperatures well below 77°F (25°C) to prevent devernalization at 86°F (30°C) (Azuma et al., 1983).

Floral induction and initiation of *L. sinuatum* occur at low temperatures, which should be considered a vernalization treatment. Cold treatments hasten flower initiation. At least 3 to 6 weeks of 52 to 55°F (11 to 13°C) was a prerequisite for *L. sinuatum* floral initiation and seedlings were most sensitive to the low temperature from when the cotyledons were present up to the fifth or sixth true leaf (Krizek and Semeniuk, 1972; Shillo, 1976; Shillo and Zamski, 1985). Five leaves are best formed on the rosette plants during this treatment or stage of development for future maximum flower stem production (Armitage and Laushman, 2003). High night temperatures of 72°F (22°C) promote leaf production and stem elongation but inhibit flowering (Shillo and Zamski, 1985). Nau (1988) recommended that field night temperatures should be below 60°F (16°C).

Continued leaf development and stem elongation and flower development of *L. sinuatum* is promoted by high temperatures. The optimum production temperature is 68 to 77/54 to 61°F (20 to 25/12 to 16°C) day/night (Espinosa and Healy, 1988; Shillo, 1976).

Limonium can be field grown or forced under protection with a day temperature up to 68 to 77°F (20 to 25°C). As an example, *L. sinuatum* can be grown for 1 to 2 weeks at 60 to 62°F (16 to 17°C) night temperature after germination, then lower the night temperature to 50 to 55°F (10 to 13°C) for a minimum of 4 to

5 weeks. A rosette with 6 to 10 leaves will form (Nau, 1988). Temperatures are increased for flower stem development.

Psylliostachys suworowii will flower in February when seeded in September and forced in a 55°F (13°C) greenhouse. In warmer areas, flowering may be earlier. Incandescent lighting may hasten flowering in the north (Nau, 1988).

LIGHT

Statice thrive in full sun. Reduce light in the greenhouse only to reduce temperatures. Supplemental lighting is required during the winter in northern climates for quality plants.

The optimum photoperiod for *L. sinuatum* appears to be 13 hr (Shillo and Zamski, 1985). If seedlings are grown under LD, the duration of cold required is decreased. LD does not substitute for cold, but LD hasten floral development after floral initiation (Semeniuk and Krizek, 1972). However, LD are not effective at high temperatures. LD promote earlier flowering and increase flowering percentage and yields when applied to plants that have been cooled (Armitage and Laushman, 2003). Short days reduce the percent of flowering *L. sinuatum* plants (Semeniuk and Krizek, 1972).

If HID lighting is used with Type II plants, winter temperatures can be lowered to 55 to 57°F (13 to 14°C) (Harada, 1992). Without HID lighting, 61 to 64°F (16 to 18°C) temperatures are required for flowering.

WATER

Water stress is not acceptable when young plants are first being established in the field. Adequate moisture is also imperative during the vegetative phase of growth. However, never overwater and reduce water once flower stem harvest commences. Mature, established flowering plants, especially newer hybrids, require little water (Harada, 1992). Meyer (1991) and Whipker and Hammer (1994) suggested that a drip tube or trickle irrigation system be used.

CARBON DIOXIDE

No data available.

NUTRITION

In a classic paper on cultural technique for the commercial production of *Limonium* in Florida, Wilfret et al. (1973) suggested one of three methods: (1) Apply N and K periodically every 3 to 4 weeks at approximately 30 lb/acre (34 kg · ha^{-1}) each of N and K. The actual amount of fertilizer applied will depend on rainfall and soil type; in Florida, the soil is frequently highly porous "sugar sand." (2) Apply a single nutrient application under a water-tight plastic cover or mulch, using a 6–6–6 fertilizer at 600 lb/acre (670 kg · ha^{-1}). (3) Apply a controlled-release fertilizer (i.e., 18–6–12 Osmocote) with a 6- to 9-month release rate at 300 lb N/acre (335 kg · ha^{-1}). Whipker and Hammer (1994), in Indiana, fertigated for the first 3 weeks after planting with a 100 ppm N–P–K (20–10–20) solution through a trickle irrigation system. In both systems from Florida and Indiana, the soil was amended with superphosphate, dolomite, fritted trace elements, and lime according to soil test recommendations.

Paparozzi and Hatterman (1988) in Nebraska found that different cultivars responded to various levels of nutrients differently. Total N recommended was 40.5 to 60.8 lb/acre (45.4 to 68.1 kg · ha^{-1}). At least half of this amount should be used at planting date and then the balance applied at one or two later applications.

Armitage and Laushman (2003) published data on leaf tissue nutrient analysis for two statice species (Table II-2 Limonium). Leaf tissue was harvested from healthy plants at the visible bud stage of development. See also Chapter 6, Nutrition, Table 6-4, for additional foliar nutrient levels.

TABLE II-2 LIMONIUM

Nutrient tissue analysis for *L. perezii* and *L. sinuatum* foliage from healthy plants when buds were visible but not yet open (Armitage and Laushman, 2003).

Species	N	P	K	Ca	Mg	Fe	Mn	B	Zn
			(%)^a				(ppm)^a		
L. perezii	3.28	0.29	2.27	0.61	0.55	105	78	17	181
L. sinuatum	3.50	0.66	3.11	0.57	0.92	159	117	20	70
^{a} Based on dry weight analysis.									

MEDIUM

Seeds are germinated in a peat-based medium and transplanted into any well-drained medium. The genus is adapted to many soil types as long as it is well drained, with a pH of approximately 6.5 and an EC of 0.5 dS · m^{-1} (Harada, 1998).

HEIGHT CONTROL

No height control is required for cut flower cultivars. With pot flower cultivars, genetic dwarfs are used, which grow 10 to 14 in. (26 to 40 cm) tall.

SPACING

A wide variety of spacings have been used in *Limonium* field production. Paparozzi and Hatterman (1988) used 12 in. (30 cm) between plants and 27 in. (69 cm) between rows. Whipker and Hammer (1994) used 12- × 12-in. (30- × 30-cm) spacing between plants and rows. Wilfret et al. (1973) used two rows of plants with 12 in. (30 cm) between plants and 12 in. (30 cm) between rows. Plants were grown on raised beds 30 to 36 in. (76 to 90 cm) wide and 54 in. (135 cm) between bed centers, resulting in approximately 20,000 plants/acre (50,000/ha). Increasing plant density to 40,000 plants/acre (100,000/ha) will increase total yields but decrease yield per plant (Wilfret et al., 1973). Potted plants in 6-in. (15-cm) pots can produce a foliage rosette 12 in. (30 cm) wide and must be spaced accordingly (Jelitto Staudensammen GmbH, 1992).

PINCHING AND DISBUDDING

None required.

SUPPORT

None required.

SCHEDULE AND TIMING

As stated earlier there are two basic flowering response types. Type I requires cold and flowers once a year; Type II flowers throughout the year if temperature and light are appropriate (Harada, 1992). The average time from seed to flower for *L. sinuatum* is 3 to 5 months in the south and 4 to 6 months in the north (Armitage and Laushman, 2003) (Tables II-3, II-4, and II-5 Limonium). Date of flower and yields varies widely among cultivars of *L. sinuatum* (Semeniuk and Krizek, 1972, 1973; Whipker and Hammer, 1994; Wilfret and Harbaugh 1978; Wilfret et al., 1973). With *L. altaica*, a cold requiring perennial, field production has been sustained for four or more years without a yield decline.

TABLE II-3 LIMONIUM

Sample production schedule for *Limonium sinuatum* from seed in a northern area with a frost-free date of early May or later.

Cultural Step	Production Time (weeks)	Temperature °F (°C)
Germinate seed in March or April in greenhouse		
	3–4	65–70 (18–21)
Apply vernalization treatment and place under a 16-hr photoperiod at an irradiance of 2375 fc (475 µmol · m^{-2} · s^{-1}) until plants develop five to six true leaves[a]		
	2	52–55 (11–13)
Transplant seedlings in greenhouse, place under 12-hr photoperiod[a]		
	3	Day: 68–77 (20–25) Night: 54–61 (12–16)
Planted in field	May–June	
Flower	Mid-July to September or first frost	Ambient

[a]If long photoperiods cannot be given, cool seedlings for 5 to 8 weeks at 50 to 55°F (10 to 13°C).

TABLE II-4 LIMONIUM

Sample production schedule for *Limonium sinuatum* from seed in a warm climate without frost.

Cultural Step	Production Time (weeks)	Temperature °F (°C)
Germinate seed June–August in greenhouse		
	3–4	65–70 (18–21)
Plant in field August–November		
	2	Ambient
Spray with GA₃ (500 ppm) two times, 1 month apart		
	8 weeks after transplant	Ambient
Flower[a]	23–24	Ambient

[a]*Ranges from 168 to 219 days from seed, depending on the cultivar (Wilfret et al., 1973).*

TABLE II-5 LIMONIUM

Sample production schedule for *Limonium sinuatum* 'Biedermeier' series, a dwarf flowering potted plant, in 4- or 6-in. (10- or 15-cm) pots.

Cultural Step	Production Time (weeks)	Temperature °F (°C)
Seed in plugs		
	2	65–70 (18–21)
Growing or transplanted		
	5	61–55 (16–13)
Flower	12	65–70 (18–21)

INSECTS

Numerous insects can attack *Limonium*, including Southern armyworm, cut worms, and cabbage loopers. Thrips and aphids rarely are a problem, but spider mites can be devastating. Constant inspection and appropriate controls are required, which is particularly true for open field production (Wilfret et al., 1973).

DISEASES

Colletotrichum is particularly serious, causing leaf and flower spots and crown rot. *Cercospora* leaf spot can also cause crown rot, severe leaf spots, defoliation, and total crop loss. *Botrytis* is an ever present problem, as is *Pythium*, *Phytophthora*, *Sclerotium*, and *Rhizoctonia*. Wilfret et al. (1973) have described the previous diseases as they exist under conditions in Florida. Aster yellows disease can also be devastating in areas where it occurs (Dreistadt, 2001). Appropriate sanitation and control procedures must be followed with this crop (Armitage, 1992). Other diseases include rust (*Uromyces*), verti-cillium wilt (*Verticillium dahliae* and *V. albo-atrum*), bacterial blight (*Corynebacterium*), powdery mildew (*Erysiphe polygoni*), downy mildew (*Peronospora statices*), bacterial soft rot (*Erwinia chrysanthemi*), bacterial crown rot (*Pseudomonas*), and tomato spotted wilt and turnip mosaic virus (Dreistadt, 2001).

POSTHARVEST

For all *Limonium*, harvest the flowering stems when at least 40% of the individual flowers are open. With hybrid *L. bellidifolium* ×*L. latifolium*, continued bud opening occurred when stems were held continuously in a solution of Physan (200 ppm) and sucrose (20 g · L⁻¹). Vase life increased from 4 to 5 days for untreated stems to 17 days for stems treated with Physan and sucrose. Short-term stem pulsing with Physan (200 ppm) and sucrose (100 g · L⁻¹) for 12 hr and then into water resulted in a vase life of 10 days; but vase life was 15 days if stems were placed in the water first for 12 hr and then into the above solution (Doi and Reid, 1995). Steinitz and Cohen (1982) found GA₃ to aid in promoting petal expansion with *L. sinuatum*; however, Doi and Reid (1995) did not observe this response with hybrid *L. bellidifolium* ×*L. latifolium*. Steinitz and Cohen (1982) found that GA$_3$ increased flower opening (195 open flowers) as compared to untreated control flowers (94 open flowers). Statice should be shipped and stored at 33 to 35°F (1 to 2°C) (Nell and Reid, 2001).

Many statice types are important dry flowers. Bundle stems loosely and hang upside down in a dark, well-vented area with low humidity.

KEY POINTS

- Three genera of statice are grown: *Goniolimon*, *Limonium*, and *Psylliostachys*. All were formerly known as *Limonium*.

- Statice is a common fresh or dried cut flower grown worldwide.

- Type I species and cultivars require a cold treatment for flowering; Type II do not.

- For *L. sinuatum* 3 to 6 weeks of 52 to 55°F (11 to 13°C) was optimum for flower initiation. Optimum period of application was from when cotyledons were present up to the presence of the fifth or sixth leaf.

- Flowers are typically harvested when 40% of the florets are open in the inflorescence.

- Floral preservatives are useful for fresh statice and the hybrid *L. bellidifolium* ×*L. latifolium* responds to GA$_3$ by opening more florets.

BIBLIOGRAPHY

Anonymous. Undated. Cultural recommendation of *Limonium* Misty variety. Dai-Ichi Seed Holland, Rijsenhout, Holland.

Armitage, A.A. 1992. Specialty cut flowers, p. 159–192 in *Introduction to Floriculture*, 2nd ed., R.A. Larson, editor. Academic Press, San Diego, California.

Armitage, A.A., and J.M. Laushman. 2003. *Limonium* hybrids, pp. 387–403 in *Specialty Cut Flowers*, 2nd ed. Timber Press, Portland, Oregon.

Azuma, A., J. Shimasake, and S. Inubushi. 1983. Acceleration of flowering of statice (*Limonium sinuatum Mill.*) by seed vernalization. *Journal of the Japanese Horticulture Society* 51:466–473. (in Japanese, English summary)

Bailey, L.H., and E.Z. Bailey. 1976. *Limonium*, pp. 664–666 in *Hortus Third: A Concise Dictionary of Plants Cultivated in the United States and Canada*. Macmillan, New York.

Clemens, J., and T.E. Welsh. Undated. *Statice Status*. Report for New Zealand Nursery Research Centre, Massey University, Palmerston North, New Zealand.

Doi, M., and M.S. Reid. 1995. Sucrose improves the postharvest life of cut flowers of a hybrid *Limonium*. *HortScience* 30:1058–1060.

Dreistadt, S.H. 2001. *Integrated Pest Management for Floriculture and Nurseries*. University of California Division of Agriculture and Natural Resources Publication 3402.

Espinosa, I., and W. Healy. 1988. Statice production. *Greenhouse Grower's News* 3(5):1–4.

Garner, J.M., and A.M. Armitage. 1996. Gibberellin applications influence the scheduling and flowering of *Limonium* ×'Misty Blue.' *HortScience* 31:247–248.

Harada, D. 1992. How to grow limonium. *FloraCulture International* 2(6):22–25.

Harada, D. 1998. *Limonium* (Statice, sea lavender), pp. 630–633 in *Ball Redbook*, 16th ed. V. Ball, editor. Ball Publishing, Batavia, Illinois.

Huxley, A., M. Griffiths, and M. Levy. 1992. *Goniolimon*, pp. 432–433, vol. 2; *Limonium*, pp. 83–85, vol. 3; *Psylliostachys*, p. 752, vol. 3, in *The New Royal Horticultural Society Dictionary of Gardening*. Stockton Press, New York.

Jelitto Staudensammen GmbH. 1992. Limonium, p. 46. Postfach 560–127, Hamburg, Germany.

Krizek, D.T., and P. Semeniuk. 1972. Influence of day/night temperature under controlled environments on the growth and flowering of *Limonium* 'Midnight Blue.' *Journal of the American Society for Horticultural Science* 97:597–599.

Matsumoto, T., Y. Nako, C. Takahashi, and A. Sakai. 1997. Induction of *in vitro* cultured masses of shoot primordia of hybrid statice and its cryopreservation by vitrification. *HortScience* 32:309–311.

Meyer, F. 1991. Culture notes: Statice—Misty series. *GrowerTalks* 54(12):17.

Nau, J. 1988. Culture notes: Statice. *GrowerTalks* 52(2):12, 14, 16, 18.

Nell, T.A., and M.S Reid. 2001. Can't take the heat. *Floral Management* 17(10):33–34.

Paparozzi, E.T., and H.M. Hatterman. 1988. Fertilizer applications on field-grown statice. *HortScience* 23:157–160.

Semeniuk, P., and D.T. Krizek. 1972. Long days and cool night temperature increase flowering of greenhouse grown *Limonium* cultivars. *HortScience* 7:293.

Semeniuk, P., and D.T. Krizek. 1973. Influence of germination and growing temperature on flowering of six cultivars of annual statice (*Limonium* cv.). *Journal of the American Society for Horticultural Science* 98:140–142.

Shillo, R. 1976. Control of flowering initiation and development of statice (*Limonium sinuatum*) by temperature and daylength. *Acta Horticulturae* 64:197–203.

Shillo, R., and E. Zamski. 1985. *Limonium sinuatum*, p. 292–301 in *The Handbook of Flowering*, vol III, A.H. Halevy, editor. CRC Press, Boca Raton, Florida.

Steinitz, B., and A. Cohen. 1982. Gibberellic acid promotes flower bud opening on detached flower stalks of statice (*Limonium sinuatum* L.). *HortScience* 17:903–904.

Whipker, B.E., and P.A. Hammer. 1994. Growth and yield characteristics of field-grown *Limonium sinuatum* (L.). *HortScience* 29:638–640.

Wilfret, G.J., and B.K. Harbaugh. 1978. *Annual Statice Production Guide*. Institute of Food and Agricultural Science, Agriculture Research and Education Center, University of Florida, Bradenton.

Wilfret, G.J., and J.C. Raulston. 1975. Acceleration of flowering of statice (*Limonium sinuatum* Mill.) by gibberellic acid (GA$_3$). *HortScience* 10:37–38.

Wilfret, G.J., J.C. Raulston, S.L. Poe, and A.W. Engelhard. 1973. Cultural techniques for the commercial production of annual statice (*Limonium* spp. Mill.) in Florida. *Proceedings of the Florida State Horticultural Society* 86:399–404.

Lycopersicon

INTRODUCTION

Common name: tomato.

Scientific name: *Lycopersicon esculentum* Mill. (Huxley et al., 1992).

Family and related taxa: Solanaceae Juss. The *Lycopersicon* genus has seven species, of which the most familiar is *L. esculentum*, the prized garden tomato. Though botanically a fruit, tomatoes are commonly referred to as a vegetable (Bailey and Bailey, 1976). Solanaceae also includes other important food crops such as pepper (*Capsicum*) and potato (*Solanum*) and a number of ornamentals including *Browallia*, *Brugmansia*, *Nicotiana*, *Petunia*, *Salpiglossis*, and *Schizanthus*.

Origin: Grown throughout the world, the tomato's origin is the Andean Mountains of South America.

Uses and current status: The tomato is grown for its fruit for home or local fresh market consumption; numerous acres (hectares) of tomatoes are grown for shipping and processing into a variety of food products. During the winter, production occurs under glass or plastic structures in many places around the world. The tomato is the most important vegetable bedding plant for the floriculture industry.

CULTIVARS

Hundreds of tomato cultivars exist for specific uses, including home garden, local commercial fresh production in the field or in the greenhouse, winter shipment from warm production sites for fresh use, and food processing. New cultivars are introduced annually.

The fruit of various cultivars varies in size from 0.5 to 7 in. (1 to 18 cm); mature color from green to yellow, orange, red, or purple; and shape from round to pear. Multicolor fruit are also available. Fruit acidity and date of maturity vary among cultivars. Plant height ranges from 1 to 6 ft (30 to 180 cm) and occasionally taller. Plant growth habit may be determinate or indeterminate. The apex of determinate cultivars eventually terminates in an inflorescence, whereas indeterminate cultivars produce inflorescences only in leaf axils and the main stem can grow indefinitely. Determinate cultivars will be shorter and more compact than indeterminate cultivars. Cultivars also vary greatly in disease resistance (see Diseases, page 680).

PROPAGATION

Though a perennial, tomatoes are treated as an annual in the home garden and in commercial production. While tomatoes are mainly seed propagated, terminal cuttings root easily. Seeds germinate quickly in 5 to 7 days at 70 to 80°F (21 to 27°C) in the light or dark. There are 10,000 seeds/oz (353/g). Lightly cover seed with 0.25 to 0.5 in. (0.6 to 1.2 cm) of medium (Ball, 1991b; Ferretti, 1985).

For plug production the following conditions are used (Ball, 1991a):

Stage 1: Seed covered, 70 to 72°F (21 to 22°C), for 2 days

Stage 2: 68 to 72°F (20 to 22°C), for 7 days, no fertilizer

Stage 3: 60 to 65°F (16 to 18°C), for 7 days, 100 ppm N once/week

Stage 4: 60 to 62°F (16 to 17°C), for 7 days, fertilizer as needed.

Plugs should be ready for marketing or transplanting within 3 to 4 weeks. See Chapter 1, Propagation, for description of plug stages.

FLOWERING CONTROL AND DORMANCY

Pickens et al. (1985) conducted an extensive literature review on the influence of temperature, light (intensity, duration, and quality), carbon dioxide, water, nutrition, and plant growth regulators on tomato flowering. This review has been the primary reference used in this chapter instead of citing all of the numerous contributors. Rate of growth, flowering, and fruit production are primarily dependent on light. As irradiance and duration (intensity × time) increase, the ratio of the number of leaves prior to the first inflorescence decreased and anthesis date and fruit ripening were hastened.

TEMPERATURE

Optimum production or growth occurs between 59 and 68°F (15 to 20°C) night temperature. Day temperatures of 75°F (24°C) are acceptable on sunny days. Fruit set is reduced or inhibited if temperatures are above 81°F (27°C) or below 41 to 50°F (5 to 10°C) (Ball, 1991b; Ferretti, 1985; Pickens et al., 1985).

LIGHT

Seeds are frequently germinated in growth rooms with fluorescent lights. Seedlings are moved into full light upon germination. If production is under glass or plastic protection, shade is used only to reduce excessive temperatures (Ball, 1991b; Ferretti, 1985).

Supplemental lighting during transplant production can increase future fruit yield (Masson et al., 1991).

WATER

Water restrictions appear to result in the continued development of a greater percentage of inflorescences. The appearance of an inflorescence is used as a marker by commercial growers to indicate that tomato plants are ready to be transplanted into beds. Flower and fruit development are reduced by excessive watering, unrestricted growth, or high levels of nitrogen (Pickens et al., 1985).

CARBON DIOXIDE

CO_2 is rarely used for the production of seedling plants. Increased CO_2 levels (1000 ppm) are commonly used for fruit production under protection. Adequate light must be present to enhance photosynthesis in the presence of supplemental CO_2 (Pickens et al., 1985).

NUTRITION

Kraus and Kraybill's (1918) experiments with tomatoes have long been used by academics to illustrate to students how excessive nitrogen slows flowering and fruiting and how a proper balance between carbohydrates and nitrogen must exist (Pickens et al., 1985). Although 100 ppm N is commonly used, reduced nutrition can be used to slow tomato internode length and control height in bedding flats. Nutrient restriction must be used carefully because low nutrition during transplant production may reduce future fruit production (Nicola and Basoccu, 1994). High N rates of 300 to 400 ppm during transplant production increased future fruit yields in the field (Masson et al., 1991).

MEDIA

Any sterilized medium that is well drained with a reasonable water-holding capacity is acceptable. Typical peat-lite mixes used with other bedding plants are suitable as well as media containing coir (Arenas et al., 2002).

HEIGHT CONTROL

Chemical growth retardants are illegal on all vegetable plants in the United States. To restrict growth, tomato plants are grown cool and dry with reduced nutrition. Low day and high night temperatures (DIF) and early morning low-temperature pulses (DROP) are

FIGURE II-I LYCOPERSICON Wilting of *Lycopersicon* flats to control height.

also effective in reducing internode length (De Konig, 1988; Grimstad, 1993). Many bedding plant producers overcome height concerns and maintain a ready supply of young, short plants by sowing seed every 1 to 3 weeks.

Vibrating the plants and shaking or brushing the leaves have also been used to reduce internode elongation (Baden and Latimer, 1992; Garner and Björkman, 1997; Hammer et al., 1974; Schnelle et al., 1994; Turgeon and Webb, 1971). Brushing should begin when plants are 2.4 to 3.1 in. (6 to 8 cm) tall; starting later may cause leaf damage (Garner and Björkman, 1996). One or two brushing treatments per day should be made; if using one treatment, it is best applied in the morning (Latimer, 1991).

Many growers also use water stress to control plant height (Fig. II-1 Lycopersicon). This method is effective, but it requires an experienced grower and careful monitoring to prevent plant injury or death, especially during warm sunny weather. Interestingly, the application of cold water, 41 to 59°F (5 to 15°C), in the morning also reduced stem length by 28 to 32% (Chen et al., 1999).

SPACING

Flats and pots are often spaced container-to-container in the garden center (Ball, 1991b). Larger size containers will need more space if plants are to be sold in flower and fruit.

PINCHING AND DISBUDDING

No pinching or disbudding required.

SUPPORT

No support is required for tomatoes grown for bedding plant sales. The cultivar's growth habit determines whether support is needed in the home garden or in the field. Indeterminant plants may become very large and should be trellised, staked, or otherwise supported in the garden.

SCHEDULE AND TIMING

Germination occurs rapidly in 5 to 7 days. Because plants are sold in numerous formats, it is difficult to develop a timing schedule. To produce a sufficient number of plants needed during the brief garden center sales season, some plants are seeded early, transplanted, and hardened by slowing growth through temperature, water, and nutrient manipulation. Later crops are seeded and given optimal environmental conditions until sold. Five to 7 weeks will be required to produce quality garden transplants when plants are grown at temperatures of 75°F (24°C) days and 60°F (16°C) nights (Ferretti, 1985). Vigorous vegetative transplants can be sold within 30 days from sowing.

A wide variation exists in the amount of time needed to produce mature fruit (50 to 80 days) (Ball, 1991b). At high light, long photoperiods, and 64°F (18°C) night temperatures, the first visible flower cluster could be seen in an average of 40 days from seeding.

INSECTS

In the greenhouse, constantly inspect for local infestations of aphids. Whiteflies, spider mites, and thrips can also be serious pests. Regardless of the pest, follow pesticide label directions carefully when treating plants being sold for food production.

DISEASES

Numerous diseases infect tomato plants. Many newer cultivars are more resistant than older cultivars to *Alternaria* (A), *Fusarium* race 1 (F), *Fusarium* races 1 and 2 (FF), *Septoria* leaf spot (L), nematodes (N), *Stemphylium* (St), tobacco mosaic virus (T), and *Verticillium* (V) as indicated by the appropriate letter following the cultivar name. For example, a cultivar resistant to *Verticillium* would have a V after its name (Ball, 1991b). Several viruses can cause problems. Tobacco mosaic virus can be transmitted to seedlings by individuals who use tobacco products and transplant seedlings. Tomato spotted wilt virus is more serious and can destroy a crop. This virus is spread by thrips.

The total number of potential diseases and nematodes that can affect tomatoes in the field is staggering (Horst, 1990), but few diseases attack plants in the greenhouse. One of the more damaging outdoor diseases is late blight (*Phytophthora infestans*); commercial field growers monitor environmental conditions carefully and spray prophylactically.

PHYSIOLOGICAL DISORDERS

Tomato plants are sensitive to ethylene. Epinasty of the leaves occurs quickly and the plants' response to very low levels of ethylene make the tomato an ideal detection device for ethylene contamination in the greenhouse.

POSTHARVEST

Seedling plugs can be stored in the dark at 45°F (7°C); however, do not store for more than 3 weeks (Heins et al., 1994). Chilling injury occurs at 41°F (5°C) or lower (Nishina et al., 1996). Plugs could be stored for up to 20 days at 43 to 54°F (6 to 12°C) if supplied with 6 to 60 fc (1to 10 μmol $\cdot$ m^{-2} $\cdot$ s^{-1}) (Nashina et al., 1996). There appears to be no lasting influence of cold storage after the plants are removed and placed at optimal growing temperature. As indicated under Physiological Disorders, above, tomato plants are very sensitive to ethylene.

KEY POINTS

- Tomato is the most commonly produced vegetable transplant sold as a spring bedding plant.
- Plants are propagated by seed.
- Height control is the major problem because chemical plant growth regulators cannot be legally used.

- Height control is not required if multiple crops are seeded weekly as markets demand the product.
- Height control can be accomplished by growing cool, restricting water and nutrition, applying DIF, or brushing and shaking.
- Plants are quite sensitive to ethylene.

BIBLIOGRAPHY

Arenas, M., C.S. Vavrina, J.A. Cornell, E.A. Hanlon, and C.J. Hochmuth. 2002. Coir as an alternative to peat in media for tomato transplant production. *HortScience* 37:309–312.

Baden, S.A., and J.G. Latimer. 1992. An effective system for brushing vegetable transplants for height control. *HortTechnology* 2:412–414.

Bailey, L.H., and E.Z. Bailey. 1976. *Lycopersicon* Mill., pp. 688–689 in *Hortus Third: A Concise Dictionary of Plants Cultivated in the United States and Canada*. Macmillan, New York.

Ball, V. 1991a. Plugs—The way of the 1990s, pp. 137–153 in *Ball Redbook*, 15th ed., V. Ball, editor. George J. Ball Publishing, West Chicago, Illinois.

Ball, V. 1991b. Tomato—For bedding, pp. 776–779 in *Ball Redbook*, 15th ed., V. Ball, editor. George J. Ball Publishing, West Chicago, Illinois.

Chen, J.-J., Y.-W. Sun, and T.-F. Sheen. 1999. Use of cold water for irrigation reduces stem elongation of plug-grown tomato and cabbage seedlings. *HortScience* 34:852–854.

De Konig, A.N.M. 1988. The effect of different day/night temperature regimes on growth, development and yield of glass house tomatoes. *Journal of Horticultural Science* 63:465–471.

Ferretti, P.A. 1985. Vegetable transplants, pp. 459–470 in *Bedding Plants III*, 3rd ed., J.W. Mastalerz and E.J. Holcomb, editors. Pennsylvania Flower Growers, University Park, Pennsylvania.

Garner, L.C., and T.B. Björkman. 1996. Mechanical conditioning for controlling excessive elongation in tomato transplants: Sensitivity to dose, frequency, and timing of brushing. *Journal of the American Society for Horticultural Science* 121:894–900.

Garner, L.C., and T. Björkman. 1997. Using impedance for mechanical conditioning of tomato transplants to control excessive stem elongation. *HortScience* 32:227–229.

Grimstad, S.O. 1993. The effect of a daily low temperature pulse on growth and development of greenhouse cucumber and tomato plants during propagation. *Scientia Horticulturae* 53:53–62.

Hammer, P.A., C.A. Mitchell, and T.C. Weiler. 1974. Height control in greenhouse chrysanthemum by mechanical stress. *HortScience* 9:474–475.

Heins, R.D., N. Lang, T.F. Wallace, Jr., and W. Carlson. 1994. *Plug Storage, Cold Storage of Plug Seedlings*. Meister Publishing, Willoughby, Ohio.

Horst, R.K. 1990. Tomato, pp. 845–848 in *Westcott's Plant Disease Handbook*, 5th ed. Van Nostrand Reinhold, New York.

Huxley, A., M. Griffiths, and M. Levy. 1992. *Lycopersicon*, p. 138 in *The New Royal Horticultural*

Society Dictionary of Gardening, vol. 3. Stockton Press, New York.

Kraus, E.J., and H.R. Kraybill. 1918. Vegetation and reproduction with special reference to the tomato. *Oregon Agricultural Experiment Station Bulletin* 149:1–90.

Latimer, J.G. 1991. Mechanical conditioning for control of growth and quality of vegetable transplants. *HortScience* 26:1456–1461.

Masson, J., N. Tremblay, and A. Gosselin. 1991. Effects of nitrogen fertilization and HPS supplementary lighting on vegetable transplant production. II. Yield. *Journal of the American Society for Horticultural Science* 116:599–602.

Nashina, H, K. Yoshida, N. Masui, and Y. Hashimoto. 1996. Storage of tomato seedling plant plugs under faint irradiation and low temperature. *Acta Horticulturae* 440:268–273.

Nicola, S., and L. Basoccu. 1994. Nitrogen and N, P, K relation affect tomato seedling growth, yield and earliness. *Acta Horticulturae* 357:95–102.

Pickens, A.J.F., R.G. Hurd, and D. Vince-Prue. 1985. *Lycopersicon esculentum*, pp. 330–346 in *Handbook of Flowering*, vol. III, A.H. Halevy, editor. CRC Press, Boca Raton, Florida.

Schnelle, M.A., B.D. McCraw, and T.J. Schmoll. 1994. A brushing apparatus for height control of bedding plants. *HortTechnology* 4:275–276.

Turgeon, R., and J.A. Webb. 1971. Growth inhibition by mechanical stress. *Science* 174:961–962.

Matthiola

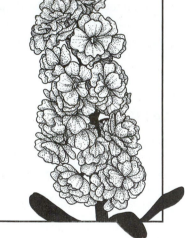

INTRODUCTION

Common names: stock, gillyflower, Brampton stock, imperial stock.

Scientific names: Matthiola R. Br. hybrids. *M. incana* (L.) R. Br. and *M. sinuata* R. Br. are the two species from which the modern hybrids are largely derived (Huxley et al., 1992; Griffiths, 1994).

Family and related taxa: Cruciferae. The genus *Matthiola* includes approximately 50 species of annuals, biennials, and perennial herbs. Other members of the Cruciferae family include *Lunaria* and some of the most important vegetable crops in the world including broccoli, Brussels sprouts, cabbage, horseradish, kale, kohlrabi, mustard, radish, rutabaga, turnip, and water cress (Bailey and Bailey, 1976).

Origin: *Matthiola incana* is native to southern and western Europe (Bailey and Bailey, 1976).

Uses and current status: Stock is most commonly grown as a field cut flower but also is grown under protection (Fig. II-1 Matthiola). At one time stock was a major cut flower in cool areas of North America. Presently stock is mainly produced outdoors in California and Arizona. Genetically dwarf plants are used as bedding plants or potted flowering plants (Fig. II-2 Matthiola).

The leaves are lightly pubescent and elliptic in shape. Stems are erect and frequently woody, growing up to 3 ft (90 cm) tall. Flower colors range from pure white to lavender, purple,

FIGURE II-1 MATTHIOLA *Matthiola* 'Iron Rose' cut flower.

FIGURE II-2 MATTHIOLA *Matthiola* bedding planting.

blue, red, and pale yellow. Flowers are distinctly fragrant and single or double. The singles are fertile and can produce seed; the doubles are sterile (Bailey and Bailey, 1976).

CULTIVARS

Height can range from 3 ft (90 cm) for cut flower cultivars to 8 to 10 in. (15 to 25 cm) for bedding cultivars. The columnar stock (non-branching) is the most commonly grown cut flower type. The percent of double flowers varies widely among cultivars, ranging from 50 to 95% double flowers (Armitage and Laushman, 2003; Cockshull, 1985). Three types of cut flower cultivars are available: mostly doubles, which are 95% double flowered; nonselectables, which are 50 to 60% double; and selectables, which are also 50 to 60% double but the single-flowered plants have distinct leaf characteristics and can be discarded. The mostly double cultivars currently have a limited color range of white to ivory or pale yellow but tend to initiate flowers at warmer temperatures than the other types of cultivars. The selectables and nonselectables are available in a broad range of colors. Some commercial hybrids boast of having up to 14 commercial colors (Healy, 1998). Seedling plugs of selectable cultivars for cut flower production are frequently purchased from specialty producers to ensure a specific percentage of doubles (Healy, 1998). Cultivars also differ in their temperature and photoperiod requirements for flowering and days to flower (response group) (Healy, 1998).

PROPAGATION

This biennial is typically treated as an annual and is propagated by seed, which germinates within 7 to 14 days when placed in a temperature of 65 to 70°F (18 to 21°C). Seeds can be germinated in plug trays or directly field sown. Seed should be lightly covered. There are 18,000 to 19,000 seeds/oz (635 to 670 seeds/g). After germination the temperature should be reduced to 60 to 62°F (16 to 17°C) until transplanting.

The single-flowered forms of selectable cultivars have darker green leaves, slower germination, and less vigorous growth than the double-flowered forms. The single-flowered plants are often manually removed because they are of little commercial value. Leaf color differences are to be more easily seen when seedlings are grown at 50°F (10°C) or lower (Armitage and Laushman, 2003; Healy, 1998). Consequently, reduce temperatures to 39 to 46°F (4 to 8°C) for 8 days after the cotyledons are fully developed (R. Sterkel, personal communication). The culling process is expensive and a person with experience should be given this task because seedling differences are often not obvious. If field seeded, the single flowering plants are not culled and are usually allowed to flower.

FLOWERING CONTROL AND DORMANCY

Most cultivars have a juvenile growth phase in that a specific number of leaves must form prior to floral initiation even when plants are grown at inductive temperatures (see Temperature, next) and light conditions. The number of leaves that are required to form prior to maturity is cultivar dependent and ranges from 16 to 60 leaves for early to late flowering cultivars, respectively (Cockshull, 1985). Using a nonselectable cultivar, Emsweller and Borthwick (1937) showed that as little as 2 days of 55°F (13°C) could induce flower initial; however, 100% flowering required 3 days of 55°F (13°C).

TEMPERATURE

Temperature is the primary factor controlling flower initiation. With late flowering cultivars 55°F (13°C) or lower is required. Early flowering cultivars have a higher temperature threshold for flower induction, forming flowers at temperatures less than 64°F (16°C). Early flowering cultivars require 10 or more days of cool temperatures for flowering; late flowering cultivars require 21 or more days (Armitage and Laushman, 2003). The optimum flower induction temperature and duration is 50 to 55°F (10 to 12°C) for 3 to 6 weeks. In addition, older plants with greater leaf numbers require fewer days of cold treatment when compared to younger plants (Cockshull, 1985). If the temperature rises above 64°F (19°C), a noninductive temperature, at least 18 hr out of 24, must be at 50°F (10°C) for floral induction (Cockshull, 1985; Post and Bell, 1936).

A temperature of 55 to 60°F (13 to 16°C) is optimal for further differentiation and development after floral initiation (Armitage and Laushman, 2003; Cockshull, 1985; Heide, 1963). Night temperatures during production can be as low as 40°F (5°C) but will extend crop time. Cool night temperatures will greatly increase stem length (Cavins et al., 2000). One week of 60 to 62°F (16 to 17°C) can be used immediately after transplanting and prior to the cold treatment to enhance plant establishment. Stock can tolerate light frost and may be able to tolerate colder temperatures if plants are acclimated.

In summary, increasing the air temperature after planting in the production beds generally delays flower initiation, increases leaf number, and decreases quality but may also decrease crop time. Decreasing the temperature increases rate and percentage of plants initiating flowers and plant quality and increases total crop time.

LIGHT

Flower induction for most cultivars occurs more quickly under LD during and after the cold treatment because plants flower with fewer leaf numbers than those under SD. LD can only partially substitute for cold if temperatures are not optimal (Heide, 1963; Post, 1949).

Increasing supplemental HID lighting causes earlier flowering (Biswas and Rogers, 1963). Supplemental HID lighting for 15 to 16 hr is required for seedlings and the first 3 to 5 weeks after transplanting in areas of the world with low light levels and short winter days, as in Europe or northern North America (Healy, 1998).

No shade cloth is used in field planting or when plants are grown under protection. Air venting or a pad and fan system are required for cooling.

WATER

Young plants can be watered overhead, but once the leaves begin to expand and form a canopy, drip irrigation is best to reduce diseases.

CARBON DIOXIDE

No data available.

NUTRITION

Field or greenhouse medium should have a soil analysis prior to planting. Liquid fertilization is better than placing a high level of fertilizer into the medium at planting (Healy, 1998). Stock have a high K requirement and potassium sulfate has been associated with excellent stem quality. Stock have a modest total nutrient requirement, which can be supplied with 150 ppm N from fertigation. Excessive nitrogen can produce soft growth.

MEDIA

Any medium that is well drained, aerated, and pH 5.5 to 6.5 is acceptable. Hydroponic culture is possible and stock can tolerate up to 8 ds · m^{-1} EC (Grieve et al., 2003). Higher soluble salt levels will decrease stem length.

HEIGHT CONTROL

For field cut flowers, no height control is required. For potted flowering plants or bedding annuals, genetic dwarfs are available. However, paclobutrazol (Bonzi) drenches have been reported to reduce internode length (Ecker et al., 1992). Tank mixes of Cycocel (chlormequat) at 1000 to 1500 ppm and B-Nine (daminozide) at 800 to 5000 ppm are effective (Kuehny et al., 2001). The height of plugs can be controlled with 2500-ppm B-Nine sprays during stage 1 or 5000-ppm B-Nine, 4-ppm Bonzi, or 1-ppm Sumagic (uniconazole) sprays during stages 2 and 3 (Sawaya, 2001).

SPACING

If seeding plugs are hand transplanted into beds, spacing can be 3 × 6 in. (8 × 15 cm) under high light and 6 × 10 in. (15 × 25 cm) under low light. Closer spacing increases the disease potential. When direct sowing, seeds can be placed every 3 in. (8 cm). However, thinning by removing the single plants can be done to decrease population density and to increase the percent of double-flowering plants (Armitage and Laushman, 2003; Healy, 1998).

PINCHING AND DISBUDDING

None is required because the markets desired the columnar (nonbranching) inflorescences.

SUPPORT

None is required in field production and only occasionally in the greenhouse. However, one to two layers can be used if necessary. Cultivars intended for greenhouse production tend to not produce strong enough stems to be useful outdoors.

SCHEDULE AND TIMING

Nau (1990) listed several sample greenhouse production durations for the Chicago, Illinois, area (Table II-1 Matthiola). A general schedule is listed in Table II-2 Matthiola. Supplementary HID or incandescent lighting at 15 to 16 hr per day should be used for the fall and winter schedules.

Seeds are commonly direct sown for field production during the winter in Arizona, Florida, or year-round in coastal California. Crop time varies from year to year, but generally 6.5 months is required from sowing to flowering in midwinter.

In cold climates, stock seed can be sown in winter in plugs and transplanted to the field in late winter/early spring for spring flowering (B. Wollam, personal communication).

INSECTS

Field and glasshouse production can be troubled with thrips, aphids, and leaf rollers (Post, 1949). Armitage and Laushman (2003) also listed

TABLE II-1 MATTHIOLA

Effect of sowing date on flowering date of greenhouse-grown *Matthiola* near Chicago, Illinois, using 55 to 60/45 to 50°F (13 to 16/7 to 10°C) day/night temperatures (Nau, 1990).

Proposed Harvest Date	Sowing Date[a]	Expected Time to Harvest (weeks)
January 15	August 1	24
February 7	September 1	23
Easter (late March)	October 1	23
May 1–10	December 15	20
June	February 26	16
December 25	July 15–20	23

[a]Allow 7 to 10 days to germinate in plugs at 65 to 70°F (18 to 21°C); grow plugs for 4 to 6 weeks at 50°F (12°C) then transplant seedlings to greenhouse beds.

TABLE II-2 MATTHIOLA

Sample production schedule for greenhouse-grown *Matthiola*.

Cultural Step	Production Time (weeks)	Temperature °F (°C)
Sow seed in plugs		
	1–2	65–70 (18–21)
Reduce temperature[a]		
	4–5	60–62 (16–17)
Transplant to beds		
	1	60–62 (16–17)
Reduce temperature for flower initiation		
	3–6	50 (10)
Raise temperature		
	4–10	55–60 (13–16)
Flower and begin harvesting		
	2–3	
Total	13–24	

[a]If growing selectable cultivars, lower temperature to 50°F (10°C) or lower for 8 days when cotyledons are well developed. Temperature can be raised after single-flowering seedlings have been removed.

diamondback moth larvae, flea beetles, and springtails as potential problems in the field.

DISEASES

Post (1949) and Healy (1998) stated that two fungi, *Rhizoctonia* and *Phytophthora*, and a bacterium, *Xanthomonas campestris* pv. *incanae*, are concerns. The two fungi are controlled by following standard sanitation and soil pasteurization. However, the bacterium is seed-borne and seed should have been heat treated in water at 122 to 131°F (50 to 55°C) for 10 min and cooled immediately. Virus streaking has also been observed. Armitage and Laushman (2003) listed *Verticillium* wilt, *Plasmodiophora brassicae* club rot, and downy mildew (*Peronospora arthurii*). Dreistadt (2001) also reported root and stem rot (*Pythium*), wilt (*Fusarium*), powdery mildew (*Erysiphe cichoracearum*), rust (*Puccinia*), tomato spotted wilt virus, and aster yellows.

PHYSIOLOGICAL DISORDERS

Short plants develop if seedling cold treatments begin too soon—the plants initiate flowers too quickly and produce few leaves and short internodes. However, if cold-treatment temperatures are too brief or too high, plants do not become reproductive, are blind, or produce poor-quality spikes. The absence of flowers or "skips" along the spike may be attributed to low light levels in the north during the winter (Cockshull, 1985; Healy, 1998; Post, 1949). Potassium deficiency may appear as marginal necrosis of the lower leaves, which later moves upward.

POSTHARVEST

Flower stems are harvested when 6 to 10 flowers are open along a spike. Floral preservatives should be used. Storage and shipping should be at 33 to 35°F (1 to 2°C) and stems should remain vertical because the geotropic response is rapid (Nell and Reid, 2001; Nowak and Rudnicki, 1990). The basal part of the flowering stem can become quite woody, restrict water uptake, and be removed (Sacalis, 1993). Many florists, however, crush the stem in a mistaken belief that this will aid in water uptake (Nowak and Rudnicki, 1990). Stock is quite sensitive to ethylene and both silver thiosulfate (STS) and 1-methyl-cyclopropene (1-MCP) are effective at preventing the negative effects of ethylene (Çelikel and Reid, 2002; Serek et al., 1995). However, STS-treated flowers lasted longer than 1-MCP-treated flowers. Foliage tends to turn yellow readily on stems that have been shipped dry.

KEY POINTS

- This fragrant species is grown primarily as a cut flower but also makes a great bedding plant.
- Three types of cut flower cultivars are available: mostly doubles, which are 95% double flowered; nonselectables, which are 50 to 60% double; and selectables, which are also 50 to 60% double but the single-flowered plants have distinct leaf characteristics and can be removed.
- The single-flowered plants are often manually removed because they are of little commercial value.

- Cool temperatures are required for flowering; 55°F (13°C) or below for late flowering cultivars to 64°F (18°C) or lower for early flowering cultivars.
- Short plants develop if seedling cold treatments begin too soon—the plants initiate flowers too quickly and produce few leaves and short internodes.
- Flower stems are harvested when 6 to 10 flowers are open along a spike and floral preservatives should be used.

BIBLIOGRAPHY

Armitage, A.A., and J.M. Laushman, 2003. *Matthiola incana*, p. 415–424 in *Specialty Cut Flowers*, 2nd ed. Timber Press, Portland, Oregon.

Bailey, L.H., and E.Z. Bailey. 1976. *Matthiola*, pp. 718 in *Hortus Third: A Concise Dictionary of Plants Cultivated in the United States and Canada*. Macmillan, New York.

Biswas, P.K., and M.N. Rogers. 1963. The effects of different light intensities applied during the night on the growth and development of column stocks

(*Mathiola* [sic] *incana*). *Proceedings of the American Society for Horticultural Science* 82:586–588.

Cavins, T.J., J.M. Dole, and V. Stamback. 2000. Unheated and minimally heated winter greenhouse production of specialty cut flowers. *HortTechnology* 19:793–799.

Çelikel, F.G., and M.S. Reid. 2002. Postharvest handling of stock (*Matthiola incana*). *HortScience* 37:144–147.

Cockshull, K.E. 1985. *Matthiola incana*, pp. 363–367 in *Handbook of Flowering*, vol. III. A.H. Halevy, editor. CRC Press, Boca Raton, Florida.

Dreistadt, S.H. 2001. *Integrated Pest Management for Floriculture and Nurseries*. University of California Division of Agriculture and Natural Resources Publication 3402.

Ecker, R., A. Barzilay, L. Afgin, and A.A. Watad. 1992. Growth and flowering responses of *Matthiola incana*. L.R. B.R. to paclobutrazol. *HortScience* 27:1330.

Emsweller, S.L., and H.A. Borthwick. 1937. Effects of short periods of low temperature on flower production in stocks (*Matthiola*). *Proceedings of the American Society for Horticultural Science* 35:755–757.

Gaston, L.A., Kunkle, P.S. Konjoian, and M.F. Wilt, editors. 'Ohio Florists' Association Services, Columbus, Ohio.

Grieve, C., J. Poss, and J. Draper. 2003. Response of *Matthiola incana* to saline wastewaters. *HortScience* 38:814.

Griffiths, M. 1994. *Matthiola*, pp. 730 in *Index of Garden Plants*. Timber Press, London.

Healy, W. 1998. *Matthiola* (Stock), pp. 641–645 in *Ball Redbook*, 16th ed., V. Ball, editor. Ball Publishing, Batavia, Illinois.

Heide, O.M. 1963. Juvenile phase and flower initiation in brilliant stocks *Matthiola incana* B.Br. *Journal of Horticultural Science* 38:4–18.

Huxley, A., M. Griffiths, and M. Levy. 1992. *Matthiola*, pp. 200–201 in *The New Royal Horticultural Society Dictionary of Gardening*, vol. 3. Stockton Press, New York.

Kuehny, J.S., A. Painter, and P.C. Branch. 2001. Plug source and growth retardants affect finish size of bedding plants. *HortScience* 36:321–323.

Nau, J. 1990. Stock growing comments, pp. 119–123 in *Proceedings of 3rd National Conference on Speciality Cut Flowers, Ventura, California*. Association of Specialty Cut Flower Growers.

Nell, T.A., and M.S. Reid. 2001. Can't take the heat. *Floral Management* 17(10):33–34.

Nowak, J., and R.M. Rudnicki. 1990. *Matthiola incana* (Stock), p. 154 in *Postharvest, Handling and Storage of Cut Flowers, Florist Greens and Potted Plants*. Timber Press, Portland, Oregon.

Post, K. 1949. *Mathiola* [sic] *incana*, pp. 636–644 in *Florist Crop Production and Marketing*. Orange Judd Publishing, New York.

Post, K., and R.S. Bell. 1936. Effect of alternating temperature on the flowering of lavender column stock. *Proceedings of the American Society for Horticultural Science* 34:630–634.

Sacalis, J.N. 1993. *Matthiola incana*, pp. 84–85 in *Cut Flowers, Prolonging Freshness*, 2nd ed., J.L. Seals, editor. Ball Publishing, Batavia, Illinois.

Sawaya, M. 2001. Plugs, pp. 50–53 in *Tips on Regulating Growth of Floriculture Crops*, M.L.

Serek, M., E.C. Sisler, and M.S. Reid. 1995. Effects of 1-MCP on the vase life and ethylene response of cut flowers. *Plant Growth Regulation* 16:93–97.

Narcissus

FIGURE II-1 NARCISSUS *Narcissus tazetta* potted plant.

INTRODUCTION

Common names: *Narcissus pseudonarcissus* L., trumpet narcissus, is also called daffodil, Easter flower, and Lent daffodil. *N. tazetta* L., paperwhites, is also called Lent lily or polyanthus narcissus (Huxley et al., 1992). Some cultivars of *N. tazetta* with pseudo-Latin designations of "polyanthus" are called Chinese sacred lilies (Bailey and Bailey, 1976).

Scientific names: *Narcissus* L. species (Huxley et al., 1992). The two primary species used in horticulture are *N. pseudonarcissus*, trumpet narcissus, and *N. tazetta*, paperwhites. *N. pseudonarcissus* usually has one flower per scape and requires cold for further flower development and elongation. *N. tazetta* has several flowers on the scape and does not require cold (Bailey and Bailey, 1976) (Fig. II-1 Narcissus).

Family and related taxa: Amaryllidaceae J. St.-Hil. The genus *Narcissus* is taxonomically complex with 50 species and three subgenera: *Ajax*, *Corbularia*, and *Narcissus*. The *Narcissus* subgenus is further divided into six sections. *N. pseudonarcissus* belongs to the *Ajax* subgenus, and *N. tazetta* to the Narcissus subgenus (Bailey and Bailey, 1976; Hanks, 1993). A lifetime could be spent reflecting on the narcissistic *Narcissus*, which is named after a Greek lad who drowned while admiring his own reflection and was changed into a flower. Other members of this family include *Clivia*, *Crinum*, *Eucharis*, *Hippeastrum*, *Hymenocallis*, and *Nerine*.

Origin: The genus is primarily found in the Mediterranean area and the center of origin is Spain, Portugal, and the Iberian Peninsula. Species are also found in northern Africa, France, and Greece. *Narcissus pseudonarcissus* is European and *N. tazetta* is Mediterranean in origin. Interestingly, a narrow band of *N. tazetta* grows naturally into China and Japan. It is postulated these were distributed, planted, and spread along ancient trade routes (Bailey and Bailey, 1976; Hanks, 1993; Meyer, 1966).

Uses and current status: *Narcissus* is a major horticulture crop. Species and cultivars are found growing in every corner of the world, except the tropics. R. Criley (personal communications) stated that *N. tazetta* 'Chinese Sacred Lily' grows at high elevations in Hawaii.

Annually, tons of bulbs are grown, harvested, and distributed for dry bulb sales, destined for landscape and home gardens where they perennialize with ease and survive for decades (Fig. II-2 Narcissus). Perennialization is cultivar dependent in warm climates (Cavins and Dole, 2002). Bulbs may also be temperature programmed for early forcing as potted flowering plants or cut flowers, sold with or without leaves.

For many people, this early flowering flower is a welcome sign of spring after winter in the temperate areas of the world. England, Wales, and Scotland, followed by the Netherlands, grow well over half of the worldwide production of *N. pseudonarcissus* bulbs. All locations are increasing production. The United States is a distant third, with the bulb production in Washington and Oregon significantly decreasing annually. At one time, out-

FIGURE II-2 NARCISSUS Field production of *Narcissus* for dry bulb production.

door cut flower production of cut narcissus stems was important. This practice has virtually disappeared in North America but still occurs in Europe (Hanks, 1993). Israel dominates the world market production of *N. tazetta* bulbs with new cultivars in development, including some with less powerful fragrance.

All *Narcissus* are herbaceous, with species flowering in the spring or fall. The monocot leaves are parallel veined. Plant heights are 6 to 18 in. (15 to 46 cm). Flower form is a six-lobed corolla (three modified sepals and three petals) fused at the base with an extended central trumpet or crown, or corona, of various lengths, colors, and configurations. All form tunicated bulbs by which this geophyte is propagated (Armitage, 1989; Bailey and Bailey, 1976; De Hertogh, 1996; Hanks, 1993).

CULTIVARS

Horticulturally, various descriptive divisions have been developed to accommodate the hundreds of cultivars, hybrids, and species: trumpet; large-cupped; small-cupped; double; triandrus; cyclamineus; jonquilla; tazetta; poeticus; species, wild forms, and their hybrids; split-coronas; and miscellaneous narcissus (Bailey and Bailey, 1976; Hanks, 1993). More than 5000 cultivars and species are listed by the American Daffodil Society. Commercially, fewer than 150 cultivars are produced on a large scale. Six cultivars alone represent 65% of the production area for the trumpet types. The colors can vary from pure white, pale lemon, yellow, to bright orange. Pink and various tints of yellow are also popular. The flowers of many pink-colored cultivars tend to fade in warm temperatures and are not well suited to warm climates. Double forms exist with the corona

(trumpet) totally petaloid. *N. cyclamineus* DC 'Tête-à-tête,' a multiple flowered type, which is 8 in. (20 cm) tall with bright yellow flowers, has become an important species in recent years. There are vastly fewer paperwhite cultivars, with fewer than 10 cultivars dominating the commercial market. The fall flowering narcissus species have sadly been neglected.

PROPAGATION

Narcissus can be propagated by seed, natural bulb division, scales (twin scale or chipping), or *in vitro*. Seed is only used in breeding programs. With the twin-scale propagation method, a mature bulb is cut into 8 to 16 longitudinal individual units or wedges, which are attached at the base. These wedges are in turn divided into 60 to 100 twin-scale units, which are still attached by a piece of the basal plate. Twin scales are placed at 68°F (20°C) and covered with moist vermiculite; a bulblet forms within 90 days. Commonly, 90% of these twin scales survive and generally form a single uniform round bulb, which flowers within 3 to 4 years. Chipping, a similar process using only one scale, has been found to be more efficient and consequently is preferred for some species and cultivars. Natural division by slabs (offsets) results in an average of three new flowering size bulbs within 4 years (Hanks, 1993). During bulb shipping, external ethylene sources from diseased bulbs, apples, or combustion products abort flower buds or result in abnormal flowering.

Bulbs originating from *in vitro* propagation techniques can be developed from a variety of tissue types: leaves, scapes and ovary tissue, or bulb scale. The expense involved and the losses accrued after the tissue or bulblets are removed from culture make this method mostly of academic interest. Hanks (1993) summarized propagation with numerous references.

FLOWERING CONTROL AND DORMANCY

The annual *Narcissus* growth cycle follows seasonal temperature and moisture cycles. This geophyte emerges quickly in the spring, flowers, senesces its leaves, and survives for lengthy time spans during a hot dry summer and a cold winter as a dormant bulb.

N. pseudonarcissus and *N. cyclamineus* require an absolute cold treatment for further floral differentiation, development, and rapid emergence. *N. tazetta* does not require cold. All three narcissus species, however, require warm temperatures for floral initiation and differentiation, which occur prior to harvest and continue afterward (Hanks, 1993; Rees et al., 1972).

The bulb cold treatment must be sufficiently long so that when bulbs are placed at a forcing temperature of 61°F (16°C), flowering occurs quickly, within 21 days. The cold duration for various commercial cultivars varies, with the minimum being 13 to 15 weeks, the maximum being 17 to 24 weeks before unacceptable quality results. *Narcissus* cultivars are divided into seven forcing periods for potted plants and five for cut flower production (Tables II-1 and II-2 Narcissus). The appropriate cultivar must be selected for each forcing period, depending on the cultivar's cold temperature and forcing responses (De Hertogh, 1996).

N. tazetta bulbs have no obligate cold treatment requirement, but growth (emergence and elongation of leaves and scapes) can be inhibited by 41°F (5°C) temperatures. Long durations of 41°F (5°C) can reduce quality, decrease number of flowers per scape, and lengthen scapes (Hanks, 1993; Roh and Lee, 1981).

Lifting of *N. pseudonarcissus* and *N. cyclamineus* bulbs in June and storing at 95°F (35°C) for 5 days result in early forcing and rapid floral development. These bulbs will flower up to 2 weeks sooner than bulbs not treated with 95°F (35°C) storage (Hanks, 1993). Similarly, *N. tazetta* can be heat treated and stored at 77 to 86°F (25 to 30°C) for 5 months and will flower rapidly when forced (Vreeburg and Dop, 1990; Vreeburg and Korsuize, 1989). High humidity during heat treatment is used to prevent bulb weight loss for all cultivars of *N. tazetta*. Not only can early flowering *N. tazetta* be accomplished by heat, but also by burning straw or other plant debris over the planting rows. This advance in flowering is thought to occur due to ethylene in the smoke as similar responses are observed with bulbs treated with ethylene in chambers (Haber, 1927; Hanks, 1993; Imanishi and Yue, 1987; Tompsett, 1985).

For the cold-requiring species, floral initiation occurs in early May and differentiation is completed by July or August depending on the cultivar and country. If bulbs are harvested early for special early forcing schedules, heat treatments are given as described. The flower

TABLE II-I NARCISSUS

Representative cultivars of trumpet *Narcissus* for pot flower forcing; minimum, optimum, and maximum bulb cold storage; appropriate flowering dates; type of bulb [precooled (PC) or nonprecooled (NP)]; and the estimated days () required to flower in the forcing greenhouse (modified from De Hertogh, 1996). Number under type of bulb and days to flower is the recommended Florel (ethephon) rate in ppm.

Flower Type Cultivar (color)	Appropriate Date to Force Cultivar							Weeks Cold		
	I 12/22 12/31	II 1/1 1/16	III 1/17 2/2	IV 2/3 2/24	V 2/25 3/21	VI 3/22 4/9	VII 4/10 4/20	Min.	Opt.	Max.
Trumpet:										
'Dutch Master,' (yellow)	—	PC(23) —	PC(21) —	NP(18) —	NP(15) 2000	NP(11) 2000	NP(7) 2000	13	16	24
Large Cup: 'Carlton' (all yellow)	—	PC(23) 2000	PC(17) 2000	NP(16) 2000	NP(14) 2000	—	—	14	15	20
Small cup: 'Barret Browning' (orange cup, white perianth)	—	PC(21) 2000[a]	PC(18) 2000[a]	NP(15) 2000[a]	NP(15) 2000	NP(11) 2000	NP(7) 2000	14	16	24
Cyclamineus (small yellow trumpet) 'Tête-a-Tête'	PC(22) —	PC(17) —	PC(12) —	NP(12) —	NP(9) —	NP(8) —	NP(5) —	13	15	22

[a] *Two applications required.*

TABLE II-2 NARCISSUS

Programming schedules for forcing cold-requiring potted *Narcissus* bulbs into flower (modified from De Hertogh, 1996).

Date of Expected Flowering	Date to Commence Forcing	Date to Pot Bulbs	Date to Start Precooling	Rooting Room to Use[a]	Cold Required (weeks)
I					
Dec. 22	Dec. 1	Oct. 1–7	Aug. 26–31[b]	A	13.5
Dec. 27	Dec. 8				14.5
II					
Jan. 1	Dec. 10	Oct. 1–7	Aug. 26–31[b]	A	15
Jan. 7	Dec. 17				16
Jan. 13	Dec. 24				17
III A					
Jan. 17	Dec. 31	Oct. 1–7	Sept. 1–5[b]	A	17.5
Jan. 23	Jan. 7				18
Jan. 28	Jan. 13				19
III B					
Jan. 17	Dec. 31	Sept. 25–30	None[c]	A	13.5
Jan. 23	Jan. 7				14.5
Jan. 28	Jan. 13				15.5
IV					
Feb. 3	Jan. 16	Oct. 1–5	None[c]	A	15
Feb. 11	Jan. 26				16.5
Feb. 18	Feb. 4				17.5
V[a]					
Feb. 25	Feb. 12	Oct. 28–	None[c]	B	15
Mar. 5	Feb. 20	Nov. 2			16
Mar. 15	Mar. 2				17
VI					
Mar. 22	Mar. 10	Nov. 8–12	None[c]	B	17
Mar. 29	Mar. 17				18
Apr. 5	Mar. 25				19
VII					
Apr. 10	Apr. 2	Nov. 8–12	None[c]	B	22
Apr. 15	Apr. 7				22.5
Apr. 20	Apr. 14				23.5

[a]See Crocus, Flowering Control and Dormancy, Table II-3 Crocus, p. 407, for rooting room schedules.
[b]Precool at 48°F (9°C).
[c]Nonprecooling required, hold at 63°F (17°C) until potted.

initials must have reached the G-stage of development (the gynoecium's three carpels are visible and the trilobed stigma is well divided) before bulbs can be placed into cold treatments (De Hertogh, 1996; Hanks, 1993).

In Israel, *N. tazetta* flower initiation naturally occurs in July and August. High summer temperatures retard further differentiation and development. Continued development and elongation occur only when temperatures are lower and water (rain during the winter in nature) is applied to the planted bulb (Yahel and Sandler, 1986; Yahel et al., 1990). Similarly, G-stage must be reached for early forcing schedules. If bulbs for the early forcing schedules have been given a cold holding treatment of 35°F (2°C), it is wise to warm the bulbs at 63°F (17°C) for 2 to 3 days.

TEMPERATURE

High temperatures control floral initiation and development for all species that require cold for further floral development and differentiation (*N. pseudonarcissus* and *N. cyclamineus*) and for the noncold requiring species (*N. tazetta*) for flower scape and leaf elongation.

Cold temperature treatments required for flowering vary between cultivars (see Flowering Control and Dormancy, page 689). Paperwhite bulbs are best held at ambient temperatures of 75 to 86°F (24 to 30°C). Weekly inspections should be made to determine if root initials are developing or shoots (leaves) are emerging. If roots or shoots are developing, hold the bulbs at 35°F (2°C). Heat or cold treatment usually does not commence until after November 1 to be certain floral development is completed (De Hertogh, 1996). If cold is used, warm bulbs at 63°F (17°C) for 2 to 3 days prior to forcing. Greenhouse forcing is at 60 to 63°F (16 to 17°C) for *N. pseudonarcissus*, *N. cyclamines*, and *N. tazetta*.

LIGHT

Full light is required for maximum bulb production and field production of cut flowers. During forcing, a medium light intensity of 1000 to 2500 fc (200 to 500 μmol $\cdot$ m^{-2} $\cdot$ s^{-1}) is necessary for the trumpet species and 5000 fc (1,000 μmol $\cdot$ m^{-2} $\cdot$ s^{-1}) for paperwhite narcissus. A low light intensity is used for early forcing schedules to etiolate stems if length is not sufficiently long (De Hertogh, 1996).

WATER

Keep potted bulbs moist, not overwatered, for good root formation. Similarly for bulb production, constant moisture is required (De Hertogh, 1996).

CARBON DIOXIDE

Carbon dioxide is not used in forcing.

NUTRITION

No fertilizer is used during the rooting or forcing stages (De Hertogh, 1996).

MEDIA

Field soil is still used occasionally in media along with bark, peat, perlite, sand, vermiculite, or other available components. Regardless of the formula, the medium must be well drained, pasteurized, and have a low EC and a pH of 6.0 to 7.0 (De Hertogh, 1996). Paperwhite narcissus can also be grown hydroponically.

HEIGHT CONTROL

For potted *Narcissus* requiring a cold treatment, Florel (ethephon) sprays at 1000 to 2000 ppm are commonly used (Fig. II-3 Narcissus). Generally, a 2.5-gal (9.5-L) volume should cover 500 pots to the point of runoff. The first application is applied when the leaves and flowering scape have reached 3 to 4 in. (8 to 10 cm). Not all cultivars require Florel treatment, while some require two applications. Bonzi (paclobutrazol) is also reported to be marginally effective in controlling height (Adriansen, 1985). With paperwhite narcissus, 2000 ppm is the most common Florel spray rate and it is used when plants are 4 to 5 in. (10 to 13 cm) tall (De Hertogh, 1996).

Preforce several pots prior to a major crop to determine the bulbs' response and plan accordingly. Remove sample pots 10 days prior to the main crop and test applications of 0, 500, 1000, 2000, and 4000 ppm Florel. Thus, a forcer can determine the appropriate concentration for that date, cultivar, and bulb source. Height will increase from the early forcing dates to the later forcing dates. The final height varies annually between cultivars from a source and between cultivars from different sources at any one forcing date.

SPACING

Wooden flats or plastic trays filled with an open porous medium are used for forcing cut narcissus flowers. Twenty-five large, double-nose grade bulbs are placed in a 16- $\times$ 14- $\times$ 4-in. (40- $\times$ 35- $\times$ 10-cm) flat. Generally, 48 flowers can be expected from these 25 bulbs. The 6- to 6.25-in. (15- to 16-cm) grade or larger of paperwhite narcissus is most commonly used. For paperwhite bulbs, 35 to 50 bulbs are used per flat (bulb-to-bulb) resulting in 70 or more flowers.

The number of bulbs per pot depends on bulb size and whether standard or miniature cultivars are used. For standard narcissus cultivars, three bulbs are used in a 6-in. (15-cm)

FIGURE II-3 NARCISSUS Comparison of Florel (ethephon) with A-Rest (SADH–ancymidol), B-Nine (daminozide), and Cycocel (CCC–chlormequat) for height control of *Narcissus*.

pot and five to six bulbs in an 8-in. (20-cm) pot. For the miniature cultivars, two, three, five, and seven bulbs are used in 4-, 5-, 6-, and 7-in. (10-, 13-, 15-, 18-cm) pots, respectively. Cold storage and forcing is done pot-to-pot (De Hertogh, 1996).

PINCHING AND DISBUDDING

No pinching or disbudding required.

SUPPORT

No support is required if adequate light is present.

SCHEDULE AND TIMING

The indispensable *Holland Bulb Forcer's Guide* (De Hertogh, 1996) divides narcissus forcing

and cultural information into potted and cut flower sections for both the cold-requiring species and for the non-cold-requiring paperwhite narcissus. There are also outdoor cut flower guidelines for seasonal production. Under each division, suitable cultivars are listed for specific forcing dates. De Hertogh (1996) further divides information for *N. pseudonarcissus* into trumpets, large cupped, small cupped, and double types; *N. cyclamineus; N. tazetta;* the split-corona types; and *N. jonquilla.*

For the paperwhites there are five or six schedules for the respective cultivars used in pot or cut flower forcing. Forcing guides for potted cold-requiring narcissus and for cut non-cold-requiring narcissus are given in Tables II-1, II-2, and II-3 Narcissus.

One major drawback in producing narcissus, however, has been the need for cooler

TABLE II-3 NARCISSUS

Program schedule for forcing non-cold-requiring paperwhite narcissus bulbs as a flowering potted plant (De Hertogh, 1996, modified).

Average Flower Bud Date		Average Days to Bud		Date to Pot Bulbs	
'Galil'	*'Ziva'*	*'Galil'*	*'Ziva'*	*'Galil'*	*'Ziva'*
Nov. 25–30	Nov. 12–17	40	33	Oct. 15–20	Oct. 10–20
Dec. 20–25	Dec. 6–11	35	26	Nov. 15–20	Nov. 10–20
Jan. 12–17	Dec. 30–Jan. 4	28	20	Dec. 15–20	Dec. 10–20
Feb. 1–5	Jan. 25–30	20	15	Jan. 15–20	Jan. 10–20
Mar. 1–5	Feb. 20–Mar. 3	15	10	Feb. 15–20	Feb. 10–20

space. The lengthy cold treatment usually means that limited numbers of bulbs can be programmed in coolers during the high sales period from Valentine's Day to Easter. After bulbs are brought out of the cooler for Valentine's Day, there is no time to program additional bulbs for later holidays. However, a delayed potting method has been developed to reduce the amount of cooler time and space needed (Dole, 1996). With this method bulbs are still held in the cooler for the required total number of weeks of cold; however, the first portion is applied to unpotted bulbs. At 8 weeks before moving bulbs to the greenhouse, the bulbs are potted, watered, and returned to the cooler. The cooler is held at 41°F (5°C) to allow bulbs to develop roots and shoots simultaneously. Thus a second crop can be programmed in the coolers after the Valentine's Day crop has been moved to the greenhouse.

Cold, dry storage should not extend beyond 8 weeks or late January, after which time the bulbs must be potted and the remaining 8 weeks of cold applied to bulbs in a moist medium. Cooler temperatures tested for this method included 34, 37, 41, 44.5, and 48°F (1, 3, 5, 7, and 9°C) and the optimum temperature was 41°F (5°C) for both moist and dry treatments. Temperatures cooler than 41°F (5°C) were more detrimental than temperatures greater than 41°F (5°C); flowering percentage generally decreased when temperatures below 41°F (5°C) were used and shoot height increased at temperatures above 41°F (5°C).

Two turns of a portion of the cooler space can be obtained by holding all or part of the bulbs intended for post–Valentine's Day sales cold and dry. As bulbs for January and Valentine's Day crops are pulled from the cooler, it can be immediately refilled with potted bulbs for later forcing schedules. All bulbs must be potted by the end of January. While the optimum temperature used was 41°F (5°C), the temperature can be lowered, especially with the later forcing schedules if excessive shoot elongation is noted in the cooler.

INSECTS

Numerous insects and nematodes are serious problems in bulb production (Hanks, 1993). Bulbs may be heat treated to eliminate some insects (Dreistadt, 2001). After soaking bulbs for 2 or 3 hr or overnight in 75°F (24°C) water containing a wetting agent, place in 111°F (44°C) water for 1.5 hr. Cool and dry bulbs after treatment. Aphids may be the only pest observed during forcing.

DISEASES

Numerous diseases are present in bulb production fields (Hanks, 1993). When bulbs arrive, they should be inspected for *Fusarium* basal rot. Infected bulbs should be discarded because they will not produce salable flowers, and will affect adjacent bulbs through ethylene production. Numerous other types of neck and bulb rot can occur, usually outdoors, including smoulder (*Sclerotinia narcissicola*), blue mold (*Penicillium*), bacterial streak (*Pseudomonas*), soft rot (*Rhizopus stolonifer* and *Erwinia carotovora*), bulb rot (*Rhizoctonia solani*), dry rot (*Stromatinia gladioli*), black slime (*Sclerotinia bulborum*), rust (*Puccinia schracteri*), scorch (*Stagonospora curtisii*), white mold (*Ramularia vallisumbrosae*), root rot (*Armillaria mellea* and *Cylindrocladium destructans*), and crown rot (*Sclerotium rolfsii*) (Dreistadt, 2001; Horst, 1990). During forcing, *Botrytis* may develop if air circulation is not adequate. Various diseases can be reduced or eliminated by heat treatments, which differ from those used for insects (Dreistadt, 2001). Pre-soak bulbs in 60 to 64°F (16 to 18°C) water prior to holding for 2 or 3 hr or overnight in 75°F (24°C) water containing a wetting agent. After presoaking, place in 109 to 111°F (43 to 44°C) water and hold for 3 to 4 hr after temperature reaches 109°F (43°C). Cool and dry bulbs after treatment.

PHYSIOLOGICAL DISORDERS

If trumpet narcissus are forced at temperatures of 65°F (18°C) or higher, bull nosing can occur, a symptom in which the flower fails to expand and open in a proper manner (De Hertogh, 1996). Flower distortion is attributed to boron deficiency (Tompsett, 2002).

POSTHARVEST

Potted trumpet narcissus are best shipped when buds are in the pencil stage of development, which is defined as the scape standing totally erect and not bent over as in the gooseneck stage. Flowers are only 3 to 4 days from opening in the pencil stage. However, cut narcissus are best harvested when they are in the gooseneck stage (Fig. II-4 Narcissus). Stems

FIGURE II-4 NARCISSUS Cut *Narcissus* should be harvested at the gooseneck stage of flower development.

can be stored dry or hardened for 2 hr in water. Do not place narcissus in the same water as other cut flowers, because narcissus cut stems exude sap, which is not conducive for water uptake by other species. All *Narcissus* species can be stored or shipped at 32 to 35°F (0 to 2°C).

Market paperwhite potted flowering plants when the leaves and flowering scape are 8 to 10 in. (20 to 25 cm) long. Harvest both trumpet and paperwhite narcissus cut flowers with leaves. Harvest paperwhite narcissus cut flowers when the first flowers are showing color (De Hertogh, 1996). Longevity in the marketplace is decreased if plants are allowed to show color.

Use a commercial preservative or 8-hydroxyquinoline citrate (8-HQC) at 200 ppm and sucrose at 2% for cut flowers. Germicides other than 8-HQC may also be effective (Jones and Hill, 1993). Cut stems can be held up to 2 weeks at 33 to 35°F (1 to 2°C) in 90% humidity. Stems are rehydrated in warm water (Sacalis, 1993). Silver thiosulfate (STS) at 0.1 mM increased the vase life of paperwhite narcissus (Ichimura and Goto, 2002).

Both cut flowers and potted flowering plants are short lived. Educate customers to accept *Narcissus* at the appropriate stage of development and keep at cold temperatures. In the home, keep potted plants in a cold environment when not in use or on display. When home owners want to replant potted material that has been forced, they should know it may take 2 years to reestablish the bulbs. Paperwhites in commerce are not cold hardy and tolerate Zones 8 to 10 with only moderate winter conditions.

KEY POINTS

- Daffodil is used as a potted flowering plant, cut flower, and garden ornamental.

- Plants are propagated by natural bulb division, seed, scales, or *in vitro*.

- Narcissus can be divided into those genera that require a cold treatment (i.e., *N. pseudonarcissus*) for further floral differentiation and development and those that do not (i.e., *N. tazetta*, the paperwhite narcissus).

- *N. pseudonarcissus* bulbs for greenhouse forcing must receive a minimum of 13 to 16 weeks of 48°F (9°C) or lower for root and shoot development.

- The initial portion of the cold treatment can be applied to the corms either dry and unpotted (known as precooling) for early forcing dates or moist and potted (known as nonprecooled) for later forcing dates.

- The final portion of the cold treatment is always applied to moist, potted bulbs.

- After the cold treatment, plants are moved to the greenhouse and forced.

- The forcing season is divided into seven periods; recommended cultivars and forcing schedules vary with the period.

- The various forcing schedules are combined into two basic sequences known as Rooting Room A and Rooting Room B.

- *N. tazetta* are retarded for late forcing schedules by heat at 77 to 86°F (25 to 30°C).

- Height is controlled by Florel (ethephon) sprays, which must be applied quickly after removal from the cooler.

- Bulbs are susceptible to *Fusarium* basal rot.

- Cut flowers are harvested in the gooseneck stage of development; for potted flowering plants, harvest and ship in the pencil stage of development.

BIBLIOGRAPHY

Adriansen, E. 1985. Kemisk væstregulering, pp. 142–162 in *Potteplanter I—Produktion, Metoder, Midler*, O.V. Christensen, A. Klougart, I.S. Pedersen, and K. Wikesjö, editors. GartnerINFO, København, Denmark. (in Danish)

Armitage, A.M. 1989. *Narcissus*, pp. 418–424 in *Herbaceous Perennial Plants*. Varsity Press, Athens, Georgia.

Bailey, L.H., and E.Z. Bailey. 1976. *Narcissus*, pp. 754–756 in *Hortus Third: A Concise Dictionary of Plants Cultivated in the United States and Canada*. Macmillan, New York.

Cavins, T.J., and J.M. Dole. 2002. Precooling, planting depth, and shade affect cut flower quality and perennialization of field-grown spring bulbs. *HortScience* 37:79–83.

De Hertogh, A. 1996. *Narcissus*, pp. B69–93, C123–132 in *Holland Bulb Forcer's Guide*, 5th ed. International Flower Bulb Information Centre, Hillegom, The Netherlands.

Dole, J.M. 1996. Spring bulb production: The delayed potting method. *Ohio Florists' Association Bulletin* 806:1, 3–4.

Dreistadt, S.H. 2001. *Integrated Pest Management for Floriculture and Nurseries*. University of California Division of Agriculture and Natural Resources Publication 3402.

Haber, E.S. 1927. A preliminary report on the stimulation of growth of bulbs and seeds with ethylene. *Proceedings of the American Society for Horticultural Science* 23:201–203.

Hanks, G.R. 1993. *Narcissus*, pp. 463–558 in *The Physiology of Flower Bulbs*, A. De Hertogh and M. Le Nard, editors. Elsevier, Amsterdam.

Horst, R.K. 1990. *Narcissus*, pp. 737–738 in *Westcott's Plant Disease Handbook*, 5th ed. Van Nostrand Reinhold, New York.

Huxley, A., M. Griffiths, and M. Levy. 1992. *Narcissus*, pp. 285–294 in *The New Royal Horticultural Society Dictionary of Gardening*, vol. 3. Stockton Press, New York.

Ichimura, K., and R. Goto. 2002. Extension of vase life of cut *Narcissus tazetta* var. *chinensis* flowers by combined treatment with STS and gibberellin A$_3$. *Journal of the Japanese Society for Horticultural Science* 71:226–230.

Imanishi, H., and D. Yue. 1987. Effect of ethylene exposure on flowering of *Narcissus tazetta* 'Grand Soleil d'Or.' *Acta Horticulturae* 201:29–35.

Jones, R.B., and M. Hill. 1993. The effect of germicides on the longevity of cut flowers. *Journal of the American Society for Horticultural Science* 118:350–354.

Meyer, F.G. 1966. Narcissus species and wild hybrids, pp. 47–76 in *Daffodil Handbook*, G. Lee, Jr., editor. *American Horticultural Magazine* 45(1).

Rees, A.R., L.W. Wallis, E.D. Turguand, and J.B. Briggs. 1972. Storage treatments for early flowering of narcissus. *Experimental Horticulture* 23:64–71.

Roh, S.M., and J.S. Lee. 1981. The study of the forcing of bulbous floricultural crops. *Journal of the Korean Society of Horticultural Science* 22:121–130. (in Korean, English summary)

Sacalis, J.N. 1993. *Narcissus pseudonarcissus*, pp. 86–87 in *Cut Flowers, Prolonging Freshness*, 2nd ed., J.L. Seals, editor. Ball Publishing, Batavia, Illinois.

Tompsett, A.A. 1985. Isles of Scilly Experimental Substation. *Rosewaine and Isles of Scilly Experimental Station's Annual Review* 1984:43–50.

Tompsett, A. 2002. *Narcissus tazetta*: Boron deficiency as a cause of flower distortion. *Acta Horticulturae* 570:141–144.

Vreeburg, P.J.M., and A.J. Dop. 1990. Culture of *Narcissus tazetta* 'Ziva' in The Netherlands. *Acta Horticulturae* 266:267–272.

Vreeburg, P.J.M., and C.A. Korsuize. 1989. Teelt en broei van tazetta-narcis. Ziva geeft narcisseteelt nieuw impula. *Bloembollenculture* 100(13):30–31. (in Dutch, English summary)

Yahel, H., and D. Sandler. 1986. Retarding the flowering of *Narcissus tazetta* 'Ziva.' *Acta Horticulturae* 177:189–195.

Yahel, H., D. Sandler Ziv, and M. Ron. 1990. Growth retardants for flowering pot plant production of *Narcissus* 'Grand Soleil d'Or.' *Acta Horticulturae* 266:205–210.

Orchidaceae

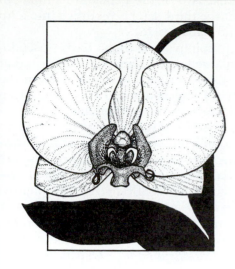

FIGURE II-I ORCHIDACEAE *Cattleya* flower.

FIGURE II-2 ORCHIDACEAE *Phalaenopsis* flower.

INTRODUCTION

Common and scientific names (Huxley et al., 1992):

1. *Cattleya* Lindl., cattleya orchid
2. *Cymbidium* Sw., cymbidium orchid
3. *Dendrobium* Sw., dendrobium orchid
4. *Odontoglossum* HBK, tooth-tongue orchid
5. *Oncidium* Swatz, dancing lady orchid
6. *Paphiopedilium* Pfitz., Venus' slipper or lady's slipper orchid
7. *Phalaenopsis* Bl., moth orchid

Family and related taxa: Orchidaceae Juss. The orchid family is huge, the largest in the plant kingdom with almost 800 genera, 17,500 species, and a worldwide distribution (Huxley et al., 1992). Most orchids are tropical ephiphytes, but numerous terrestrial species are found as far north as Zone 3. One such species is the showy lady slipper orchid, *Cypripedium reginae* Walter, the state flower of Minnesota.

Origin: (1) *Cattleya* (60 species) is native to the tropical Americas. (2) *Cymbidium* (40 species) is from tropical Asia and Australia. (3) *Dendrobium* (900 species) is native to tropical and subtropical Asia, Australia, and various Pacific Islands. (4) *Odontoglossum* (250 species) occurs in the cooler highlands of tropical America. (5) *Oncidium* (400 species) is found in Central and South America. (6) *Paphiopedilium* (60 species) is native to tropical Asia. (7) *Phalaenopsis* (55 species) is native to Asia, the Malaysian Archipeligo, and Oceania (Bailey and Bailey, 1976) (Figs. II-1 and II-2 Orchidaceae).

Uses and current status: Orchids are used mainly as cut flowers for corsages and floral arrangements, as potted flowering plants, and as bedding plants in tropical areas. Of the hundreds of genera only a few are produced on a commercial scale. (1) *Cattleya* orchids were at one time popular for corsages. New hybrids are available in a wide variety of flower sizes and colors from white to the typical "orchid purple," which make attractive potted plants. *Cattleya* are generally not successful in a typical home environment, but grow well in home greenhouses. (2) *Cymbidium* are mainly used as cut flowers, but standard and dwarf cultivars are widely used for potted flowering plants. *Cymbidium* can be overwintered in a cool southern window, but must be moved outdoors in summer for best growth. (3) *Dendrobium* are used both as cut flowers and as a potted plant. *Dendrobium* can be grown in the home if provided with relatively high light and warm temperatures. (4) *Odontoglossum* is used as a potted flowering plant for cool growing areas.

(5) *Oncidium* are useful for both cut flowers and potted flowering plants that can be grown in cool areas. (6) *Paphiopedilium* are used primarily as a potted flowering plant and will do well in the home especially in a cool, humid area. (7) *Phalaenopsis* orchids are used as potted plants and as cut flowers in design work, particularly for weddings because of the pure white flowers. Other colors are available, varying from various pink tints to yellows. Of all the orchids, this orchid is easiest to maintain in the home in a sunny window and will flower annually with reasonable care and is one of the most widely produced potted flowering plants in the world.

Orchid production is expensive due to the long time needed to produce a plant, traditionally several years (Table II-1 Orchidaceae). On the other hand, if grown for cut flowers, the long-lived plants are typically grown for many years. Frequently, flowering is annual and seasonal. Thus, a large number of flowers of the same species are on the market at the same time, which often drives prices down. Orchids require specific cultural details; experienced growers are needed to produce this crop. These factors contribute to limited production in northern latitudes.

Potted plant production systems have been developed where tissue-cultured seedlings are grown in countries with low labor cost and appropriate climates for the slowly developing vegetative plant. Adult plants are sent to the final production sites, potted, spaced, and forced into flower. Some firms also purchase flasks of tissue cultured plantlets, grow them for 6 to 18 months, and sell mature or nearly mature plants ready to force.

Orchidaceae plants have elongated leaves with parallel veins. The leaves range from quite thick to almost grasslike. Flower form, color, size, and texture are extremely varied. Most commonly the flower has three sepals and three petals. Two of the petals are similar in shape, but the third petal is modified into a lip (Bailey and Bailey, 1976).

Most epiphytic orchids have "pseudobulbs," enlarged aerial stemlike structures that serve as storage organs. Roots arise from the axils of basal internodes and the leaves clasp the upper portions of the pseudobulb. Vegetative buds arise from the basal axillary bud on the pseudobulb and form new leaves and flowers (sympodia growth). Some orchids are monopodial and always have a dominant apical meristem. Roots are fleshy and the outer tissue, called the *velamen*, quickly absorbs water and nutrients. Of the seven commercial orchid genera covered in this chapter, *Cattleya*, *Dendrobium*, *Odontoglossum*, *Oncidium*, and *Phalaenopsis* are primarily epiphytic and *Cymbidium* and *Paphiopedilium* are primarily terrestrial.

CULTIVARS

Orchid breeding occurs internationally with both commercial and hobbyist breeders developing hundreds of new hybrids and cultivars annually. Interspecific hybridization is common and easy to accomplish. In the northern latitudes cut flower production has drastically decreased over the decades, with the exception of *Cymbidium*. On the other hand, potted flowering plant production is expanding. The breeding goals for new cultivars are generally smaller plant sizes for more economical spacing and ease of marketing, new colors, improved keeping quality, easier cultural procedures, and pest resistance. *Dendrobium* breeding in Hawaii has occurred for both cut and potted flowering plants (Kamemoto and Kam, 1985).

PROPAGATION

Commercial orchid production is based on asexual mericlonal techniques or sexual methods (Nagashima, 1993). With asexual techniques thousands of identical plants can be produced in a brief time span. Seeds are extremely small, with a rudimentary seed coat, no nurse tissue (endosperm), and a naked embryo. Both sexual and asexual propagation methods require aseptic conditions, specific nutrient media (solid or liquid), and exact environmental conditions for growth (Keithly et al., 1991). For these reasons, specialists are needed for propagation (Post, 1949; Sheehan, 1992). Orchid seedlings or explants must be

TABLE II-I ORCHIDACEAE
The average time required for various orchids to flower from seed (Goh and Arditti, 1985; Kerbauy, 1984; Wang and Lee, 1994a).

Species	Time to Flower
Cattleya	4 to 7 years
Cymbidium	5 years
Dendrobium	5+ years
Odontoglossum	3 years
Oncidium	3 years
Paphiopedilium	3 to 6 years
Phalaenopsis	2 to 6 years

transferred carefully from the aseptic culture flask to a greenhouse environment and the light intensity is critical at each stage (Konow and Wang, 1998). A number of terrestrial hardy orchids have also been propagated *in vitro* (Jørgensen and Andersen, 1998).

Commercially, some monopodial orchids can also be propagated by tip cuttings (*Phalaenopsis*). Other propagators use flower stalk cuttings (*Phalaenopsis*) or division (*Cattleya, Cymbidium, Dendrobium, Paphiopedilium*). *Dendrobium*, especially *D. nobile*, can be propagated by dividing the elongated pseudobulbs into sections of two to three nodes (E. Runkle, personal communication).

FLOWERING CONTROL AND DORMANCY

Little scientific information exists regarding how to precisely flower the numerous commercial species, hybrids, and interspecific hybrids (Table II-2 Orchidaceae). This is not surprising considering the broad range of species and hybrids within each genera. For example, the 400 species of the genus *Oncidium* are found from the cool mountains to humid tropical areas, undoubtably resulting in many environmental factors that relate to flowering.

A juvenile phase exists within orchids, the duration of which is highly variable between species and cultivars. For example, *Phalaenopsis*

hybrid seedlings from the same cross have been reported to flower within 15 months, while others required 2 or more years. The appropriate temperature for rapid juvenile growth is 77 to 86°F (25 to 30°C) (Lee and Lin, 1984). Typically 4 to 7 years are required for many orchids to flower from seed (Goh and Arditti, 1985). After the juvenile period is passed, the two primary environmental factors used to control flowering are low temperature and light (photoperiod and intensity) (see Temperature, next, and Light, page 701). Interestingly, injections of benzyladenine (BA) and gibberellic acid (GA_3) into 1- or 2-year-old pseudobulbs greatly increased flowering of tropical *Dendrobium* in Hawaii (Sakai et al., 2000). Also, *Oncidium* and *Dendrobium* plantlets flowered as very small explants after 8 to 9 months or 5 months, respectively, in culture, which may have been due to the origin of the explants, micro-inflorescences, or the culture conditions (Goh and Yu, 2000; Kerbauy, 1984).

TEMPERATURE

Flower initiation is low temperature dependent for *Cymbidium, Dendrobium, Paphiopedilium,* and *Phalaenopsis*. This cold temperature ranges from 41 to 54°F (5 to 12°C) for *Cymbidium;* 55 to 65°F (13 to 18°C) for *Dendrobium;* 55 to 60°F (13 to 16°C) for *Paphiopedilium;* and 59 to 68°F (15 to 20°C) for *Phalaenopsis*. *Cymbidium* plants respond to day/night

TABLE II-2 ORCHIDACEAE

A summary of factors reported to be involved in the control of flowering of various species and hybrid orchids (Goh and Arditti, 1985; Rotor, 1952; Wang and Lee, 1994b; Yoneda et al., 1991).

Species	Factor
Cattleya	Temperatures close to 63°F (17°C); LD may delay flowering; 8-hr days result in earlier flowering; use 16+-hr days and discontinue 4 months prior to date of flower. Cultivar variations exist. High light aids in flower induction.
Cymbidium	Summer—bright sun and 70/57°F (21/14°C) day/night temperature; winter—63°F (17°C). For best flower induction, use 41 to 46°F (5 to 8°C). Temperature can be raised to 77°F+ (25°C+) after spikes are visible.
Dendrobium	Low temperature 55 to 65°F (13 to 18°C) nights; probably LD. Duration of cold is brief. Grow at 65°F (18°C) for vegetative growth.
Odontoglossum	LD enhance flower initiation and formation, 8-month cycle.
Oncidium	Flowers are initiated under cool SD (late December); diurnal variation ±68°F (20°C).
Paphiopedilium	Night temperatures of 55°F (13°C) for 2 to 3 weeks. Grow at 60°F (16°C) for vegetative growth. Not photoperiodic.
Phalaenopsis	Floral induction at 77/68°F (25/20°C) day/night or an average night temperature of 59 to 68°F (15 to 20°C) for 2 to 6 weeks, depending on the cultivar. Although not photoperiodic, SD may stimulate spiking and decrease crop time. Vegetative growth occurs at 75+°F (24°C) constant.

temperature fluctuations of 77/54°F (26/12°C) for most rapid flower initiation (Powell et al., 1988) and 55°F (18°C) was best for vegetative growth (Rotor, 1952). Goh and Arditti (1985) use the word *vernalization*. These lower temperatures are related to their native habitats, many of which are mountainous.

Optimum production temperatures for vegetative growth of *Dendrobium* and *Phalaenopsis* seedlings are 82 ± 7°F (28 ± 4°C) day/night and 68 ± 3°F (20 ± 2°C) (Keithly et al., 1991). At constant 82°F (28°C) no flowering occurs with juvenile or adult *Phalaenopsis* plants (Yoneda et al., 1991). At these temperatures leaf production is enhanced; the greater the number of leaves, the greater the number of spikes and flowers. A constant 68°F (20°C) was optimum for CO_2 uptake with *Phalaenopsis* (Ota et al., 1991), which correlates with data that the optimum temperature for reproductive growth and development after flower initiation is 77/68°F (25/20°C) day/night (Wang and Lee, 1994b) (see Table II-3 Orchidaceae). Economically, 65 to 82/59 to 68°F (18 to 28/15 to 20°C) day/night temperatures can be used for energy conservation (Wang and Lee, 1994b).

With *Phalaenopsis* any temperature below 77°F (25°C) day or night results in initiation; however, 68 to 77/59 to 68°F (20 to 25/15 to 20°C) day/night is optimum for initiation, which occurs in 4 to 5 weeks (Lee and Lin,

1984). Newly mature plants appear to require lower temperatures or longer durations to become reproductive compared to older plants (Wang and Lee, 1994b). After flower initiation, time to flower is based on temperature. With a day of 77°F (25°C), each 1.8°F (1°C) drop in night temperature between 59 and 77°F (15 and 25°C) delayed flowering 1 day (Wang and Lee, 1994b). Similarly, using constant day and night temperatures, time to flower decreased from 26 to 10 weeks as the temperature increased from 57 to 79°F (14 to 26°C) (Robinson, 2002). At 84°F (29°C) plants did not flower.

Cattleya hybrids are best grown at 60 to 65°F (16 to 18°C) days, 60°F (16°C) nights (Table II-4 Orchidaceae). However, Hagar (1957) used 80/65°F (27/18°C) day/night temperatures for two species (Table II-5 Orchidaceae). With *Cymbidium* 79°F (26°C) day or night temperatures were optimum for maximum flower number per inflorescence after flower initiation (Powell et al., 1988). *Dendrobium* vegetative growth is best at 68°F (20°C) nights; for flower initiation, lower temperature to 63°F (17°C). *Odontoglossum* hybrids produced optimum growth at 64°F (18°C) but flowered the fastest at 77°F (25°C) (Yoneda and Suzuki, 1998). *Oncidium* is considered a warm-growing species with day/night temperatures of 80 to 85/55 to 60°F (27 to 29/13 to 16°C) (American Orchid Society, undated). With *Paphiopedilium* during ac-

TABLE II-3 ORCHIDACEAE

Effect of day/night air temperatures on *Phalaenopsis* flowering from flower spike appearance to anthesis (Lee and Lin, 1984).

Day/Night Temperature °F (°C)	Plant Spiking		
	Weeks	(%)	Days from Spike Appearance to Flowering
86/72 (30/25)	13	39	67
77/68 (25/20)	4	100	104
68/59 (20/15)	5	100	205

TABLE II-4 ORCHIDACEAE

The influence of day/night temperature on the rate of development of *Cattleya labiata* orchid flowers (Hager, 1957).

Flower Bud Size in. (cm)	Day/Night Temperature °F(°C)		
	70/55 (21/13)	78/60 (26/16)	85/70 (29/21)
	Days to Flower		
0.75 (1.8)	67	50	36
1–2 (2.5–5)	53	38	28
2–3 (5–7.5)	42	24	18
3–4 (7.5–10)	30	20	12–14

TABLE II-5 ORCHIDACEAE

Production schedules for flowering *Cattleya trianae* Lind. & Rchb. f., *C. labiata* Lindl., and their hybrids twice each year in Santa Cruz, California (Hagar, 1957).

Cultural Step	Dates	Day/Night Temperature °F (°C)
LD[a]	June 5–Oct. 12	80/65 (27/18)
Natural day length	Oct. 12–Dec. 15	80/65 (27/18)
Flower	Dec. 15–20	80/65 (27/18)
LD	Dec. 15–Apr. 1	85/65 (29/18)
SD[b]	Apr. 1–June 5	85/65 (29/18)
Flower	June 5–10	85/65 (29/18)

[a]LD provided by natural day length plus incandescent lights [100- or 150-watt bulbs spaced 6 ft (1.8 m) apart] or natural long days of summer.
[b]SD provided by black cloth or natural short days of winter.

tive vegetative growth, use 65 to 70°F (18 to 21°C) day temperature, then lower to 55°F (13°C) for rapid flower induction (Goh and Arditti, 1985; Rotor, 1952). *Phalaenopsis* are typically finished at 82/65°F (28/18°C).

LIGHT

The standard commercial orchids are generally day neutral. This is not true with many of the tropical species close to the equator, which respond not only to small changes in day length, but also to temperature.

Proper light intensity is needed for quality vegetative growth and for floral induction and development. Many orchids require low light levels during their entire growth cycle (*Cattleya* and *Phalaenopsis*) or high light in the winter and reduced light in the summer (*Cymbidium*) (Poole and Seeley, 1978).

Fluorescent lamps are used in aseptic cultural conditions during propagation. Both fluorescent and incandescent lamps (70:30, based on wattage) can be used in growth rooms. Young seedlings of *Phalaenopsis* and *Dendrobium* were produced under 40% shade cloth and a 12-hr photoperiod was provided by HID lighting to supplement natural day lengths (Keithly et al., 1991).

Cattleya and *Phalaenopsis* growth was compared at 1500 and 3000 fc (300 to 600 μmol · m^{-2} · s^{-1}). The higher level was better for *Cattleya*, the lower for the *Phalaenopsis* (Krizek and Lawson, 1974; Wang, 1995b). The maximum CO_2 uptake (day and night) with *Phalaenopsis* was with 650 fc (130 μmol · m^{-2} · s^{-1}). There were no differences in CO_2 uptake between juvenile or older leaves (Ota et al., 1991). Light is reduced in greenhouses to 1200

to 2000 fc (240 to 400 μmol · m^{-2} · s^{-1}) to control temperatures (Wang and Lee, 1994a). Plant shoot growth is better by two to four times in controlled-growth rooms than in greenhouses for *Cattleya* and *Phalaenopsis*.

Recommended light levels are 1500 to 3000 fc (300 to 600 μmol · m^{-2} · s^{-1}) for *Cattleya*, 1200 to 2000 fc (240 to 400 μmol · m^{-2} · s^{-1}) for *Phalaenopsis*, and 700 fc (140 μmol · m^{-2} · s^{-1}) for *Paphipedilium*. Post (1949) recommended 1800 to 2400 fc (360 to 480 μmol · m^{-2} · s^{-1}) for *Cymbidium* and 2400 to 3600 fc (480 to 720 μmol · m^{-2} · s^{-1}) for *Dendrobium*.

WATER

Cattleya are watered every 5 days, *Cymbidium* once every 3 days, *Dendrobium* every 7 days, *Paphiopedilium* every 2 days, and *Phalaenopsis* every 5 to 7 days in summer and 2 to 3 weeks in winter (Wang and Lee, 1994a). Of course, these are rough estimates and depend on temperature, season, and plant size. Water stress results in decreased CO_2 uptake (Goh and Arditti, 1985). Although water EC should generally be very low, Wang (1998b) obtained maximum leaf area of *Phalaenopsis* with 1.1 dS · m^{-1} water.

CARBON DIOXIDE

Little work has been conducted on the influence of CO_2 in greenhouses or environments where structures are enclosed (see Light section). One report appearing in the November 1941 issue of *Orchid Digest* said that growing 3-month-old seedlings using 1000 or 10,000 ppm CO_2, the higher concentration resulted in "very stout appearance, the leaves became very thick, and dark green . . ." with the control plants inferior. Daily CO_2 uptake increased by 82% when *Phalaenopsis*, a CAM plant, was grown under 950 ppm versus 380 ppm CO_2 at 68/59°F (20/15°C) day/night temperature (Lootens and Heursel, 1998).

NUTRITION

For *Cattleya*, 50 ppm each of N, K, and Mg was optimum and the ratio of NH_4:NO_3 was 1:3. The levels of P, Ca, Fe, Mn, B, Zn, Cu, and Mo were 20, 200, 3, 1, 0.25, 0.20, 0.025, and 0.0001 ppm, respectively (Poole and Seeley, 1978).

A fertilizer rate of 100 ppm N, 50 to 100 ppm K, and 25 ppm Mg were best for *Cymbidium* (Poole and Seeley, 1978). Daily nutrient applications of 17 or 170 ppm N failed to influence flower number per *Cymbidium* inflorescence (Powell et al., 1988). However, excessive ammonium fertilizer can delay *Cymbidium* flowering.

Dendrobium seedlings were fed every 10 days with 50 ppm N, 4.5 P, and 8.2 K plus iron chelate and micronutrients (Keithly et al., 1991).

Young *Phalaenopsis* plants are heavy feeders and 200 ppm N from 20–20–20 fertilizer with each irrigation was acceptable; older plants can be given 10–30–20 (Wang and Lee, 1994a). Poole and Seeley (1978) reported that 100 ppm N, 50 to 100 ppm K, and 25 ppm Mg were best for *Phalaenopsis*. Increasing the N rate from 50 to 200 ppm increased *Phalaenopsis* flower count, stalk length, and leaf production after flowering and decreased crop time (Wang and Gregg, 1994; Wang and Lee, 1994a). A high nitrogen level is particularly important from before floral initiation until after spiking (Wang, 2000). Fertilizers with urea as a nitrogen source produced greater growth than fertilizers without urea (Wang and Konow,

2002). A medium EC of less than 2.0 dS · m^{-1} is recommended (Wang and Lee, 1994a).

Numerous inorganic and organic fertilizer combinations and ratios have been used successfully. For orchids in osmunda fiber use a 1:1:1 N:P:K ratio; for plants in bark or various bark mixes, use a 3:1:1 ratio (Sheehan, 1992). Usually calcium, magnesium, and micronutrients are natural contaminants in the water supply and fertilizers and are not added to the standard fertilizer solutions. Slow-release fertilizers such as various organics (fish emulsion, hoof and horn, and dried bone meal) or Osmocote can be used as a supplement or as a main source of nutrients.

Foliar analyses are commonly taken by commercial firms and used as guides for their nutritional programs. See Chapter 6, Nutrition, Table 6-4, for foliar nutrient levels. Tissue sample location is important (Table II-6 Orchidaceae).

MEDIA

Numerous media or mixes are used in seedling and flowering plant production. Cost and longevity of the medium prior to breakdown and loss of drainage capacity are considerations. The media should also have a pH of 5.0 to 6.0 (Griesbach, 1985). Osmunda fern root fiber was frequently used for the epiphytes (Post, 1949). Currently, redwood or fir bark chips of various sizes are used for both epiphytes and terrestrial types (Wang and Lee, 1994a). *Cymbidium* orchids are routinely grown in an oasis or rockwool medium (Boodley, 1988; Thomas, 1989). Coconut husk chips (coir chunks) are also commonly used (E. Runkle, personal communication).

Wang (1995a) reported that with *Dendrobium* neither medium nor fertilizer frequency

TABLE II-6 ORCHIDACEAE

Suggested location of orchid leaf tissue for analysis (Seeley, 1978; H.F. Wilkins, unpublished data). Always use same maturity stage and location. If a problem exists, attempt to get tissue from source with normal tissue for comparison.

Species	Leaf Tissue
Cattleya	Terminal half of young mature leaf
Cymbidium	Terminal half of recently mature leaf tissue
Dendrobium	The upper two or three mature leaves
Odontoglossum	Terminal 3 in. (8 cm) of recently mature leaf
Oncidium	Terminal 3 in. (8 cm) of recently mature leaf
Paphiopedilium	Entire mature leaf
Phalaenopsis	Fourth or fifth leaf from growing point; on younger plants use second leaf

affected flowering date of young pseudobulbs. However, return flowering was hastened and flower numbers increased when plants were grown in fir bark (small or large grades) amended with peat moss (30% by volume) and constant liquid fertilizer with 200 ppm N from 20–10–20 N fertilizer. Leaf area, lateral inflorescence number, and flower spike number of *Phalaenopsis* plants was superior when grown in 1:1:1 perlite:Metromix 700:charcoal or 4:2:1:1:1:1 medium grade fir bark:peat moss:No. 3 grade perlite:No. 2 grade perlite:vermiculite:rockwool than in 100% fir bark. In later studies, 80:20 or 70:30 fir bark:peat were superior to 100% fir bark (Wang, 1998b; Wang and Konow, 2002).

HEIGHT CONTROL

No height control is needed for cut flower production. For potted flowering plants, growth retardants can be used to keep the inflorescence from getting too tall and are used only if transporting and marketing the flowering plants are too difficult without height control (Wang and Lee, 1994b). With *Phalaenopsis*, Bonzi (paclobutrazol) at 250 ppm or Sumagic (uniconazole) at 100 to 200 ppm can be used as a spray when the flower spike is 1 in. (3 cm) in length. The longer spraying is delayed, the less effective the treatment (Wang and Hsu, 1994). The use of DROP may decrease spike length of *Phalaenopsis* and *Odontoglossum*.

SPACING

Spacing will vary with the production stage. Space plants when leaves begin to overlap at all production stages. Also, good air circulation between plants is a necessity for disease control.

PINCHING AND DISBUDDING

No pinching or disbudding is required. If an inflorescence is too small to be sold, it can be removed. After *Phalaenopsis* plants flower, the spike can be cut above the second node to encourage reflowering.

SUPPORT

For potted plants all inflorescences are normally staked and tied into position when harvested to avoid damage. Frequently this is done with an aesthetically pleasing material such as raffia.

SCHEDULE AND TIMING

Post (1949) listed the flowering period for numerous species. Sheehan (1992) listed dates of flowering for *Cattleya* orchid.

CATTLEYA

By selecting the proper species and cultivars, flowers can be harvested every day of the year (Hager, 1957). Some cultivars will flower twice in one year if photoperiod treatments are given (see Tables II-4 and II-5 Orchidaceae). Once flower buds are present, their development can be hastened or slowed by adjusting temperature. In Hager's publication (1957) numerous tables are presented on the influence of temperature and photoperiod on numerous *Cattleya* species.

CYMBIDIUM

Presently this orchid is mainly grown outdoors in areas of the world with cool, frost-free winters and warm sunny summers. Plants for cut flowers are typically grown in 18-in. (45-cm) containers. These plants traditionally flower between late December and May in the northern latitude and the primary demand is for Easter and Mother's Day. Plants in flower can be brought into temperature-controlled environments for forcing or placed in 40°F (4°C) cold storage for up to 1 month.

Cymbidium plants at the tight bud stage, puffy bud stage, or at the first open flower stage can be cold-stored at 40°F (4°C) for 30 days and then returned to growing temperatures with no detrimental effect (H.F. Wilkins, unpublished data). One treatment included placing plants with tight buds into storage for 30 days, returning them to the greenhouse to allow the first open flower to develop, and storing them again for 35 days without injury. Production can be more evenly distributed throughout the year with selection of early, medium, and late cultivars and the above-mentioned storage techniques.

DENDROBIUM

Dendrobium flower in late fall to early spring in northern latitudes. Date of flower is dependent on the cultivar and production schedule (Kamemoto and Kobayashi, 1985). *D. nobile* can be timed by maintaining temperatures at 65°F (18°C) or above; then applying LD and 55°F (13°C). Flowering occurs 4 months after temperatures are lowered (Rotor, 1952).

ONCIDIUM

The annual growth cycle in North America is as follows: Vegetative growth commences February to March, growth ceases August to September, flowering occurs October to December, and quiescence occurs December to February (Jessup, 1985). In Japan early meristem formation was observed in early May and flowering in early October (Tanaka et al., 1986).

PHALAENOPSIS

Production involves three phases: vegetative leaf making at 82/65°F (28/18°C), floral initiation at 77/68°F (25/20°C), and finishing at 82/65°F (28/18°C). *Phalaenopsis* forms a primary inflorescence, which elongates and flowers within 104 days after 4 weeks of 77/68°F (25/20°C) day/night followed by 82/65°F (28/18°C) until flowering (Wang and Lee, 1994a, b). Flowering occurs in approximately 18 months from tissue culture. The presence of the spike can be first seen 4 to 5 weeks after flower initiation (Wang, 1995b). The time to visible bud represents 60% of the total production time from spiking to flowering (Robinson, 2002). The time to flower from appearance of the flower spike can be predicted; 769 degree days are required using a base temperature of 51.4°F (10.8°C).

Most species and hybrids flower naturally from fall to February. To delay production into the high market demand periods, Wang (1995b, 1997b, 1998a) placed plants in alternating periods of total darkness and light of 5 days dark and 2 days light. Another option is to grow plants at 82°F (28°C) or higher and provide a 77/68°F (25/20°C) day/night chilling temperature later in the year to induce flowering.

P. amabilis, the traditional white butterfly orchid, can be kept in flower continuously by removing the primary inflorescence just below the basal flower. Within approximately 8 weeks, a secondary inflorescence develops from an axillary bud and flowering will be repeated. If the first or primary inflorescence is not salable on potted plant, the spike can be pruned for later flowering. The secondary spike will be of better quality.

Individual flowers can have a longevity on the plant of 30 (*P. violacea*) to 120 (*P. amabilis*) days (Goh and Arditti, 1985). With cut flower production, either individual flowers or the entire inflorescence can be harvested.

PAPHIOPEDILUM

Plants initiate flowers naturally in the fall (September to October) and flower 6 months later in the spring. If grown at a minimum of 65°F (18°C), flower initiation will not occur. At 55°F (13°C) flowers will initiate and develop, which requires 6 months. Photoperiod has no effect (Rotor, 1952). Development can be hastened after the inflorescence is visible by forcing at 65°F (18°C).

INSECTS

Mealybugs, scale, and thrips can be difficult to control and eradicate once established. One thrips feeding site will make a flower worthless. Aphids can occur and must be destroyed before a colony develops. Slugs and snails are particularly troublesome with plants grown outdoors (Griesbach, 1985; Post, 1949; Sheehan, 1992).

DISEASES

Constant air circulation and venting are primary methods for disease control. Plants should never be spaced too closely. *Botrytis* petal blight can disfigure open flowers and *Pythium* and *Phytophthora* can result in serious stem and leaf rots. *Erwinia* and *Pseudomonas* soft rots are bacterial; sanitation is required and no splashing of water will aid in the control of these diseases. Dozens of leaf spot diseases attack orchids and rusts can be serious in semitropical areas such as Florida and Taiwan (Chen and Wang, 1996; Horst, 1990). Numerous viruses infect orchids (Dreistadt, 2001). Suspected plants must be immediately destroyed because viruses are easily spread by knives when flowers are harvested (Daughtrey and Chase, 1992; Post, 1949; Wang and Lee, 1994b). Use a hot knife or disinfest between cuts to prevent the spread of diseases (Horst, 1990). Leaf spot (*Gloeosporium*) has also been reported on *Cattleya* and bulb and root rot (*Fusarium oxysporum*), root and crown rot (*Rhizoctonia*), black root rot (*Thielaviopsis basicola*), southern wilt (*Sclerotium rolfsii*), and leaf spots (*Colletotrichum* and *Glomerella*) on *Cymbidium* (Dreistadt, 2001).

PHYSIOLOGICAL DISORDERS

With *Phalaenopsis*, the plant may become vegetative again if temperatures are not maintained at or below 77°F (25°C) after inflorescences are formed or if temperatures go over

86°F (30°C) (Chen et al., 1997; Wang and Lee, 1994b). Water and high-temperature stress will cause flower bud abortion for all species. Cold, even temperatures well above freezing can result in malformed flowers, internodes that do not elongate, and flower bud abortion. These symptoms may not be observed until weeks after the adverse cold temperature occurred. *Cymbidium* flowers abort at day/night temperatures of 86/77°F (30/25°C) or greater (Ohno, 1991a).

POSTHARVEST

Cattleya, Cymbidium, Paphiopedilium, and *Phalaenopsis* flowers should not be harvested until 3 to 4 days after they have opened. Orchids frequently do not open properly even in floral preservatives. *Dendrobium* can be harvested 1 or 2 days prior to being fully open.

The flowers of many orchid species are very sensitive to low levels of ethylene, whether it be endogenous or exogenous. Anti-ethylene agents such as silver thiosulfate (STS) or 1-methylcyclopropene (1-MCP) should be used prior to marketing (Porat et al., 1995; Wang and Wang, 2000). Air contamination from faulty heaters can be a disaster in production. Pollination also induced ethylene production and rapid senescence (Halevy, 1995).

Individual flowers or spikes are usually placed in water tubes and shipped in shredded wax paper. Most firms have a special refrigerator to hold orchid flowers above 50°F (10°C) to prevent cold injury. Exceptions are *Cymbidium* and *Paphiopedilium*, which tolerate storage temperatures as low as 31°F (20.5°C). There is tremendous variation in longevity of potted plants between genera species and cultivars (Goh and Arditti, 1985) (Table II-7 Orchidaceae).

CATTLEYA

Pollination and temperatures below 46°F (8°C) must be avoided. Flowers can last up to 3 or 4 weeks on the mother plant. Flowers and plants can be stored at 50°F (10°C) (Nowak and Rudnicki, 1990); Sacalis (1993) recommended 60°F (16°C).

CYMBIDIUM

Flowers are very sensitive to ethylene—they abort or quickly senesce. Interestingly, applications of either STS or GA$_3$ prevented the action of ethephon, a synthetic ethylene agent

TABLE II-7 ORCHIDACEAE
The longevity of potted orchid inflorescences (Goh and Arditti, 1985; Hew, 1987).

| Species | Longevity (days) | |
	Minimum	Maximum
Cattleya	9	60
Cymbidium	15	90
Dendrobium	19	55
Odontoglossum	30	48
Oncidium	13	21
Paphiopedilium	30	120
Phalaenopsis	30	120

(Ohno, 1991b). If flowers are pollinated, senescence occurs and this response will travel to adjacent flowers (Woltering et al., 1991). *Cymbidium* flowers are tolerant to temperatures of 31 to 39°F (−1 to 4°C). Sacalis (1993) says 50°F (10°C) is best. Entire spikes are harvested when the apical flower matures. Flowers last for 7 or more days and respond to floral preservatives.

DENDROBIUM

Cultivars vary greatly in their postharvest longevity (Dai and Paull, 1991). Flowers from tetraploid plants last longer than those from diploid plants (Ketsa et al., 2001). *Dendrobium* is very sensitive to water stress and chilling injury. Floral preservatives and STS treatments were of no value and apparently ethylene is not a major factor in postharvest fading. However, silver nitrate was more effective than STS in extending vase life, which was due to the antimicrobial action of silver nitrate (Ketsa et al., 1995). Microbial blocking of water in the xylem appears to be a major cause of poor vase life (Dai and Paull, 1991). The use of either sucrose (4%) or aminooxyacetic acid had no effect on vase life but both together greatly enhanced vase life primarily due to the fact that the solution pH remained low (approximately 3), reducing microbial growth and allowing sucrose uptake (Rattanawisalanon et al., 2003). Immediately after harvest, place the newly cut stem in hot water. Flowers should be shipped at 50 to 55°F (10 to 13°C).

ODONTOGLOSSUM

The plants are shipped when three to four flowers are open.

ONCIDIUM

This flower should be cut at the bud stage and is less susceptible to ethylene (Hew, 1987). A floral preservative should be used. Sucrose and 8-hydroxyquinoline sulfate were effective.

PAPHIOPEDILIUM

Flowers are very sensitive to ethylene. Flowers can be stored for 3 weeks in water at 31 to 39°F (-1 to 4°C). Flowers on potted plants can last for 3 months.

PHALAENOPSIS

Cut stems should be quickly dipped for 10 min in 1000 ppm STS as flowers are very sensitive to ethylene. Flowers can be stored for 14 days at 45 to 50°F (7 to 10°C). Postharvest solutions should be used. Vegetative plants can be shipped and stored at 77°F (25°C) for up to 2 weeks (Wang, 1997a). Shipping and storage at 59°F (15°C) increases the likelihood of chilling injury. Plants in the home require at least 250 fc (38 μmol $\cdot$ m^{-2} $\cdot$ s^{-1}) for flowering but plants already in flower will continue at light levels as low as 50 fc (8 μmol $\cdot$ m^{-2} $\cdot$ s^{-1}) (Wang, 1997b).

KEY POINTS

- The orchid family is the largest plant family in the world and contains hundreds of species, hybrids, and cultivars that are grown horticulturally as cut flowers and potted flowering plants.
- The most important genera commercially are *Cattleya*, *Cymbidium*, *Dendrobium*, *Odontoglossum*, *Oncidium*, *Paphiopedilium*, and *Phalaenopsis*.
- Commercially, orchids are most commonly propagated by *in vitro* or seed; division or cuttings can also be used.
- Propagation of orchids is typically highly specialized and performed mainly by speciality firms.
- Production times from seed are very long, as much as 4 to 7 years.

- Most firms that produce potted orchid plants on a large scale buy prefinished plants or young plants that require an additional 5 to 6 months to flower.
- Flower induction requirements vary greatly with the various taxa and are often not well known.
- Most orchid species require a coarse, very well-drained medium.
- Flower longevity is excellent, both for cut flowers and potted flowering plants.
- Many species of potted flowering orchids adapt well to the home environment, re-flower with modest care, and are long-lived plants.

BIBLIOGRAPHY

American Orchid Society. Undated. *Oncidium alliance*. West Palm Beach, Florida.

Bailey, L.H., and E.Z. Bailey. 1976. *Hortus Third: A Concise Dictionary of Plants Cultivated in the United States and Canada*. Macmillan, New York.

Boodley, J.W. 1988. *Directions for Growers Use of Oasis Orchid Medium*. Smithers Oasis, Kent, Ohio.

Chen, W.H., and Y.T. Wang. 1996. *Phalaenopsis* orchid culture. *Taiwan Sugar* 43(5):11–16.

Chen, W.-S., H.-W. Chang, W.-H. Chen, and Y.-S. Lin. 1997. Gibberellic acid and cytokinin affect *Phalaenopsis* flower morphology at high temperature. *HortScience* 32:1069–1073.

Dai, J., and R.E. Paull. 1991. Effect of water status on *Dendrobium* flower spray postharvest life. *Journal of the American Society for Horticultural Science* 116:491–496.

Daughtrey, M., and A.R. Chase. 1992. *Ball Field Guide to Diseases of Greenhouse Ornamentals*. Ball Publishing, Geneva, Illinois.

Dreistadt, S.H. 2001. *Integrated Pest Management for Floriculture and Nurseries*. University of California Division of Agriculture and Natural Resources Publication 3402.

Goh, C.-J., and J. Arditti. 1985. Orchidaceae, pp. 309–336 in *Handbook of Flowering*, vol. I, A.H. Halevy, editor. CRC Press, Boca Raton, Florida.

Goh, C.-J., and H. Yu. 2000. Gene expression during flowering in orchids. *Flowering Newsletter* 30: 8–16.

Griesbach, R.J. 1985. An orchid in every pot. *Florists' Review* 176 (4548):26–30.

Hager, H. 1957. Control of flowering in cattleya, pp. 130–132 in *Proceedings of the Second World*

Orchid Conference, Honolulu Orchid Society, Honolulu, Hawaii.

Halevy, A.H. 1995. The role of sensitivity to ethylene in pollination-induced corolla senescence syndrome. *Acta Horticulturae* 405:210–215.

Hew, C.S. 1987. The effect of 8-hydroxyquinoline sulphate, acetylsalicylic acid and sucrose on bud opening of *Oncidium* flowers. *Journal of Horticultural Science* 62:75–78.

Horst, R.K. 1990. Orchids (imported species), p. 747 in *Westcott's Plant Disease Handbook*, 5th ed. Van Nostrand Reinhold, New York.

Huxley, A., M. Griffiths, and M. Levy. 1992. in *The New Royal Horticultural Society Dictionary of Gardening*, vols. 1, 2, and 3. Stockton Press, New York.

Jessup. H.P. 1985. The culture of *Oncidium varicosum*, its relatives and hybrids. *American Orchid Society Bulletin* 54(6):719–725.

Jørgensen, B.I., and T.F. Andersen. 1998. Hardy and half hardy terrestrial orchids as potential new potplants. *Acta Horticulturae* 454:195–205.

Kamemoto, J., and J. Kam. 1985. Evaluation of dendrobium selections under test with cooperators. *Hawaii Cooperative Extension Service Flower and Nursery Information* 76:1–2.

Kamemoto, J., and R. Kobayashi. 1985. *Dendrobium* Lynne Horiuchi—A seed propagated, flowering potted plant cultivar. *Hawaii Cooperative Extension Service Flower and Nursery Information* 76: 3–4.

Keithly, J.H., D.P. Jones, and H. Yokoyama. 1991. Survival and growth of transplanted orchid seedlings enhanced by DCPTA. *HortScience* 26:1284–1286.

Kerbauy, G.B. 1984. *In vitro* flowering of *Oncidium varicosum* mericlones (Orchidaceae). *Plant Science Letters* 35:73–75.

Ketsa, S., Y. Piyasaengthong, and S. Prathuangwong. 1995. Mode of action of $AgNO_3$ in maximizing vase life of *Dendrobium* 'Pompadour' flowers. *Postharvest Biology and Technology* 5: 109–117.

Ketsa, S., A. Uthairatanakij, and A. Prayurawong. 2001. Senescence of diploid and tetraploid cut inflorescences of *Dendrobium* 'Caesar.' *Scientia Horticulturae* 91:133–141.

Konow, E.A., and Y.-T. Wang. 1998. Effects of irradiance levels during flasking and greenhouse production on growth and flowering of the phalaenopsis orchid. *HortScience* 33:537. (Abstract)

Krizek, D.T., and R.H. Lawson. 1974. Accelerated growth of cattleya and phalaenopsis under controlled-environment conditions. *American Orchid Society Bulletin* 43:503–510.

Lee, N., and G.-M. Lin. 1984. Effect of temperature on growth and flowering of *Phalaenopsis* white hybrid. *Journal of the Chinese Society for Horticultural Science* 30:223–231. (in Chinese, English summary)

Lootens, P., and J. Heursel. 1998. Irradiance, temperature, and carbon dioxide enrichment affect photosynthesis in *Phalaenopsis* hybrids. *HortScience* 33:1183–1185.

Nagashima, T. 1993. Studies on relationship between embryogenesis and germination in Orchidaceae. *Journal of the Japanese Society for Horticultural Science* 62:581–594.

Nowak, J., and R.M. Rudnicki. 1990. *Postharvest Handling and Storage of Cut Flowers, Florist Greens, and Potted Plants*. Timber Press, Portland, Oregon.

Ohno, H. 1991a. Microsporogenesis and flower bud blasting as affected by high temperature and gibberellic acid in *Cymbidium* (Orchidaceae). *Journal of the Japanese Society for Horticultural Science* 60:149–157.

Ohno, H. 1991b. Participation of ethylene in flower bud blasting induced by high temperature in *Cymbidium* (Orchidaceae). *Journal of the Japanese Society for Horticultural Science* 60:415–420.

Ota, K., K. Morioka, and Y. Yamamoto. 1991. Effects of leaf age, inflorescence, temperature, light intensity, and moisture conditions on CAM photosynthesis in *Phalaenopsis*. *Journal of the Japanese Society for Horticultural Science* 60:125–132.

Poole, H.A., and J.G. Seeley. 1978. Nitrogen, potassium and magnesium nutrition of three orchid genera. *Journal of the American Society for Horticultural Science* 103:485–488.

Porat, R., A.H. Halevy, M. Serek, and A. Borochov. 1995. An increase in ethylene sensitivity following pollination is the initial event triggering an increase in ethylene production and enhanced senescence of *Phalaenopsis* orchid flowers. *Physiologia Plantarum* 93:778–784.

Post, K. 1949. Orchids, pp. 663–719 in *Florist Crop Production and Marketing*, Orange Judd Publishing, New York.

Powell, C.L., K.I. Caldwell, R.A. Littler, and I. Warrington. 1988. Effect of temperature regime and nitrogen fertilizer level on vegetative and reproductive bud development in *Cymbidium* orchids. *Journal of the American Society for Horticultural Science* 113:552–556.

Rattanawisalanon, C., S. Ketsa, and W.G. van Doorn. 2003. Effect of aminooxyacetic acid and sugars on the vase life of *Dendrobium* flowers. *Postharvest Biology and Technology* 29:93–100.

Robinson, K.A. 2002. Effects of temperature on flower development rate and morphology of *Phalaenopsis*. M.S. thesis, Department of Horticulture, Michigan State University, East Lansing.

Rotor, G.B., Jr. 1952. *Day Length and Temperature in Relation to Growth and Flowering of Orchids*. Bulletin 885, Cornell University Agricultural Experiment Station, Ithaca, New York.

Sacalis, J.N. 1993. *Cattleya* hybrids, pp. 39–40; *Cymbidium* hybrids, pp. 41–42; in *Cut Flowers, Prolonging Freshness*, 2nd ed., J.L. Seals, editor. Ball Publishing, Batavia, Illinois.

Sakai, W.S., C. Adams, and G. Braun. 2000. Pseudobulb injected growth regulators as aids for year around production of Hawaiian dendrobium orchid cutflowers. *Acta Horticulturae* 541:215–220.

Seeley, J.G. 1978. Orchid nutrition, pp. 12–16 in *Proceedings of the 23rd Orchid Congress*, Long Island, New York.

Sheehan, T.J. 1992. Orchids, pp. 113–142 in *Introduction to Floriculture*, R.A. Larson, editor. Academic Press, San Diego, California.

Tanaka, M., S. Yamada, and M. Goi. 1986. Morphological observation on vegetative growth and flower bud formation in *Oncidium* Boissiense. *Scientia Horticulturae* 28:133–146.

Thomas, W. 1989. Growing orchids in rockwool. *American Orchid Society Bulletin* 58:1212–1218.

Wang, Y.-T. 1995a. Medium and fertilization affect performance of potted *Dendrobium* and *Phalaenopsis*. *HortTechnology* 5:234–237.

Wang, Y.-T. 1995b. *Phalaenopsis* orchid light requirement during induction of spiking. *HortScience* 30:59–61.

Wang, Y.-T. 1997a. Effect of postharvest temperature and storage duration on growth and flowering of the phalaenopsis orchid. *HortScience* 32:517. (Abstract)

Wang, Y.-T. 1997b. Phalaenopsis light requirements and scheduling of flowering. *Orchids* 69:934–939.

Wang, Y.-T. 1998a. Deferring flowering of greenhouse-grown *Phalaenopsis* orchids by alternating dark and light. *Journal of the American Society for Horticultural Science* 123:56–60.

Wang, Y.-T. 1998b. Impact of salinity and media on growth and flowering of a hybrid *Phalaenopsis* orchid. *HortScience* 33:247–250.

Wang, Y.-T. 2000. Impact of a high phosphorus fertilizer and timing of termination of fertilization on flowering of a hybrid moth orchid. *HortScience* 35:60–62.

Wang, Y.-T., and L.L. Gregg. 1994. Medium and fertilizer affect the performance of *Phalaenopsis* orchids during two flowering cycles. *HortScience* 29:269–271.

Wang, Y.-T., and T.Y. Hsu. 1994. Flowering and growth of *Phalaenopsis* orchids following growth retardant applications. *HortScience* 29:285–288.

Wang, Y.-T., and E.A. Konow. 2002. Fertilizer source and medium composition affect vegetative growth and mineral nutrition of a hybrid moth orchid. *Journal of the American Society for Horticultural Science* 127:442–447.

Wang, Y.-T., and N. Lee. 1994a. Potted blooming orchids. *Greenhouse Grower* 12(1):79–80.

Wang, Y.-T., and N. Lee. 1994b. Potted blooming orchids, Part 2. *Greenhouse Grower* 12(2):36–38.

Wang, M., and Y.-T. Wang. 2000. 1-MCP and STS counteract ethylene effects on cut orchid flowers. *HortScience* 35:349.

Woltering, E.J., H. Overbeek, and F. Harren. 1991. Ethylene and ACC: Mobile wilting factors in flowers. *Acta Horticulturae* 298:47–59.

Yoneda, K., and N. Suzuki. 1998. Effect of temperature and light intensity on the growth and flowering of *Odontoglossum* intergeneric hybrids. *Journal of the Japanese Society for Horticultural Science* 67:619–625.

Yoneda, K., H. Momose, and S. Kubota. 1991. Effects of daylength and temperature on flowering in juvenile and adult *Phalaenopsis* plants. *Journal of the Japanese Society for Horticultural Science* 60:651–657. (in Japanese, English summary)

Ornithogalum

INTRODUCTION

Common name: ornithogalum.

Scientific name: The primary species used in commerce are *Ornithogalum arabicum* L., *O. dubium* Houtt., and *O. thyrsoides* Jacq.

Family and related taxa: Liliaceae Juss. The Liliaceae family is quite large and contains many commercially important floriculture crops including *Allium, Alstroemeria, Brodiaea, Convallaria, Eremurus, Hyacinthus, Lachenalia, Lilium, Muscari,* and *Tulipa*.

Origin: The genus consists of approximately 80 species, which are widely distributed in Africa, Europe, and western Asia. *Ornithogalum arabicum* is native to the Mediterranean area,

while both *O. dubium* and *O. thyrsoides* are from South Africa.

Uses and current status: Species such as *O. arabicum* and *O. thyrsoides* are produced as greenhouse or outdoor cut flowers. *O. dubium* can also be used as a potted plant. These species and others can be grown as garden ornamentals. The species previously described above are hardy to Zone 9. *O. dubium* can be planted outdoors after soil temperatures reach 63°F (17°C) (G. Luria, personal communication).

The genus consists of 80 species with tunicate bulbs and flowers varying in color from white to yellow to orange to orange-red (Huxley et al., 1992) (Table II-1 Ornithogalum). Date of flowering and hardiness vary according to the species (Bailey and Bailey, 1976; De Hertogh and Le Nard, 1993).

CULTIVARS

Although breeding efforts on *Ornithogalum* have not been extensive, selections have been made (Griesbach and Meyer, 1998). For example, with *O. dubium* the flower scape can be up to 16 in. (40 cm) tall but selections are available with a scape length of only 8 in. (20 cm). Bailey and Bailey (1976) listed two variants for *O. thyrsoides*. However, the potential for *Ornithogalum*, especially the creation of new flower colors, is great because of inter- and intraspecific hybridization, the large number of species, and the wide geographical and climate diversity of the genus (Griesbach and Meyer, 1998; Griesbach et al., 1993; Littlejohn and Blomerus, 1992; Littlejohn et al., 1992; Meyer et al., 1990) (Fig. II-1 Ornithogalum).

TABLE II-1 ORNITHOGALUM

General information on the most commonly produced *Ornithogalum* species in commerce.

Species	Native Area	Flower Color	Height in. (cm)	Flower Number	Hardiness Zone	Flowering Season
O. arabicum[a]	Mediterranean	White	12–32 (30–80)	6–12	8–10	Late spring/ early summer
O. dubium	Cape Province, South Africa	Yellow to orange	8–12 (20–30)	25+	9–11	Late spring
O. nutans[b]	Europe, south-western Asia	White, green stripe	12–24 (30–60)	3–12	5–9	Late spring
O. thyrsoides[c]	South Africa	White	12+ (30+)	12–30	7–9	Early spring

[a]*Plant bulbs 6 in. (15 cm) deep; leaves are damaged by late frost; best for West Coast gardens.*
[b]*Has become naturalized in eastern United States.*
[c]*Not cold hardy; most commonly seen in florist shops; bulbs can be treated as an annual, being lifted each autumn.*

FIGURE II-1 ORNITHOGALUM *Ornithogalum saundersiae Bak.*, a little used tall species with a long postharvest life suitable for cut flower production.

PROPAGATION

Propagation methods are numerous. Bulblets form around the bulb, which can also be divided. Bulblets and divided bulbs are graded and replanted; 2 to 3 years are required to reach commercially salable size for the former method, 1 to 2 years for the latter. Seed propagation is common but the resulting plants are highly variable, which reduces plant uniformity. Young juvenile leaf sections root easily under mist or high-humidity propagation tents (Blomerus and Schreuder, 2002). *In vitro* propagation is also possible (Blomerus and Schreuder, 2002; De Hertogh and Le Nard, 1993; Halaban et al., 1965; Niederwieser et al., 1990; van Rensburg et al., 1989).

FLOWERING CONTROL AND DORMANCY

Bulb temperature treatments vary with the species, country, and climate (Table II-2 Ornithogalum). In Israel plants flower from late March to early April, foliage senesces, bulbs are harvested in midsummer, and stock is replanted in the field by mid-September (Shimada et al., 1995; Shoub and Halevy, 1971). Floral initiation commences after leaf senescence. There are several reported temperature sequences in the literature for floral initiation and development for *O. arabicum*. Bulbs can be either programmed for immediate flower development or can be placed at 86 to 91°F (30 to 33°C) to retard development for several months (see Table II-2). The use of nonretarded and retarded bulbs provides an extended production season. Treatments are most effective if bulbs

are stored in a moist medium. Forcing temperature regimes have been developed for *O. thyrsoides, O. dubium,* and *O. nutans* L.

TEMPERATURE

In the greenhouse, *Ornithogalum arabicum* and *O. dubium* require 20 to 22 weeks from planting to flowering at forcing temperatures of 70/50°F (21/10°C) day/night (H.F. Wilkins, unpublished data); 13 to 14 weeks at 72/64°F (22/18°C) day/night temperatures; and 10 to 11 weeks at 79/72°F (26/22°C) day/night temperatures (De Hertogh and Gallitano, 1997). For cut flower production of *O. arabicum,* keep the day and night temperatures below 75°F (24°C) and 60°F (16°C), respectively, or plants will be short and of low quality (S. Houck, personal communication). Plants of *O. dubium* continue to flower at 72/64°F (22/18°C) day/night temperatures if kept moist. With *O. thyrsoides* 16 to 20 weeks are required to flower at 50 to 63°F (10 to 17°C) night temperature. In the Netherlands, *O. nutans* are planted outdoors from October to early November and flower in mid-May. In the United States outdoor production of *O. arabicum* is primarily limited to the West Coast due to lack of heat tolerance and cold hardiness (Armitage and Laushman, 2003).

LIGHT

Full light is required in all environments, during forcing or outdoors. For summer production in Israel up to 40% shade was suggested, while no shade is used in Europe or North America. In the winter, LD (day extension from incandescent lamps) are recommended for year-round cut flower production (Luria et al., 2002). *O. dubium* flower scape lengths were longer under natural 8-hr days plus 8-hr incandescent light when compared with natural 8-hr days alone. LD tended to hasten flowering (Luria et al., 2002).

WATER

In nature *Ornithogalum* are found in areas with dry summers and plants go dormant after flowering. In commerce plants should be kept moist, but not wet. *O. dubium* will continue to form leaves and flower for weeks if kept moist and in adequate light (R. Shillo, personal communication). G. Luria (personal communication) also stated that *O. dubium* would flower year-round if grown at 64°F (18°C) and LD.

TABLE II-2 ORNITHOGALUM

Bulb storage temperatures favorable for flowering of four commercial *Ornithogalum* species.

Species	Temperature °F (°C) and Bulb Storage Durations
O. arabicum	1. Three possible nonretarding schedules for production in the fall and early winter: a. 68°F (20°C) after bulb harvest until Nov. 1, then hold at 55°F (13°C) for 30 days prior to planting.[a] b. 77°F (25°C) after bulb harvest until Nov. 1, then hold at 63°F (17°C) for 30 days prior to planting.[b] c. For rapid flower initiation and development, store at 86°F (30°C) for 12 weeks, then store for 4 weeks at 68°F (20°C) and finally hold at 55°F (13°C) for 8 weeks prior to planting.[c] 2. For delayed production of cut flowers from late fall to early winter, retard bulb development at 86 to 91°F (30 to 33°C) for several months.[a] Follow with temperature regime *a.* or *c.* prior to planting.
O. dubium	77°F (25°C) after bulb harvest until Nov. 1, then hold at 63°F (17°C) for 30 days prior to planting.[d]
O. nutans	68°F (20°C) after bulb harvest until September 1, then hold at 63°F (17°C) for 30 days until planting.[b]
O. thyrsoides	1. Two possible nonretarding schedules for production in the fall and early winter: a. 86°F (30°C) for 8 weeks after bulb harvest, provide an end treatment of 73°F (23°C) after bulb harvest, then hold at 63°F (17°C) for 30 days prior to planting.[d] b. 41°F (5°C) for 14 weeks after bulb harvest and prior to planting.[e] 2. For delayed production of cut flowers from late fall to early winter, retard bulb development at 86–95°F (30–35°C) for several months.[a] Follow with 41°F (5°C) for 6 to 14 weeks prior to planting. Duration of cold treatment decreases with increasing duration of heat retardation.[e]

[a]*Shoub and Halevy, 1971; Shoub et al., 1971.*
[b]*De Hertogh and Le Nard, 1993.*
[c]*Shimada et al., 1995.*
[d]*De Hertogh and Gallitano, 1997.*
[e]*van Vuuren, 1997; van Vuuren and Holtzhausen, 1992.*

CARBON DIOXIDE

No data available.

NUTRITION

For *O. arabicum* in the greenhouse, S. Houck recommended using 250 ppm N from a 20–10–20 fertilizer for the first month and switching to calcium nitrate until flowering. A N:P:K ratio of 2:1:2 should be used with 70 to 130 ppm N for *Ornithogalum dubium* (G. Luria, personal communication).

MEDIA

A variety of well-drained commercial premixed media with pH 5.5 to 6.0 may be used in the greenhouse (Armitage and Laushman, 2003). For *Ornithogalum dubium* G. Luria (personal communication) recommended a well-drained media with a 6.0 to 6.5 pH, and De Hertogh et al. (1997) stated 5.5 to 6.0 should be used. In the field, soil should be well drained because bulbs have a tendency to rot.

HEIGHT CONTROL

No height control is required for cut flower species. In fact, a 3-week preplanting temperature of 55°F (13°C) produced longer *O. dubium* stems than 36, 48, or 77°F (2, 9 or 25°C) (Luria et al., 2002). Other treatments that increased stem length include a 100-ppm gibberellic acid dip for 20 min prior to planting or a spray approximately 30 days after planting, 20 to 40% shade during production, and 100 ppm ethylene application for 24 hr prior to planting.

SPACING

In Israel G. Luria (personal communication) spaced *Ornithogalum dubium* bulbs at 70 to 100 per 3 ft^2 (m^2) for cut flower production. For *O. arabicum* S. Houck (personal communication) recommended 8 to 9 bulbs/ft^2 (86 to 96 bulbs/m^2) for greenhouse cut flower production. For field production, space *O. arabicum* bulbs 6 to 9 in. (15 to 23 cm) apart (Armitage and Laushman, 2003). Plantings can remain for 2 years, but are generally treated as annuals.

For potted plant use 1 bulb/4-in. (10-cm) pots and 5 bulbs/8-in. (25-cm) pots if using 2- to 2.5-in. (5- to 6-cm)-diameter bulbs (De Hertogh et al., 1997). Plant bulbs such that the tip of the bulb is 1 in. (2.5 cm) below the media surface. Potted plants can be grown pot-to-pot and spaced before leaves overlap.

PINCHING AND DISBUDDING

No pinching or disbudding is required.

SUPPORT

No support is required but netting may be helpful for field cut flower production.

SCHEDULE AND TIMING

After bulbs are planted, *O. arabicum* and *O. dubium* flower in 20 to 22 weeks at 70/50°F (21/10°C) day/night temperatures. At 79/72°F (26/22°C) day/night temperatures, only 10 to 11 weeks are required. However, for cut flower production of *O. arabicum* the night temperature should remain below 60°F (16°C) for highest quality (S. Houck, personal communication); November greenhouse plantings will flower 4 months later and February plantings will flower 3 months later. With *O. thyrsoides* 16 to 20 weeks are required to flower at 50 to 63°F (10 to 17°C) (De Hertogh and Gallitano, 1997). For potted *O. dubium* plant production, plants will flower in 12 to 15 weeks.

INSECTS

Aphids and thrips can be a problem.

DISEASES

Viruses are the most serious problem in large-scale production and long-term use of bulbs. Several approaches have been researched to solve this problem (Vcelar et al., 1992). *Erwinia* is also a major problem and can cause heavy losses. Other potential diseases are *Penicillium*, *Sclerotium rolfsii*, and *Sclerotinia* (Horst, 1990). Leaf spots from *Mycosphaerella ornithogali* and *Septoria ornithogali* and ornithogalum mosaic virus have also been reported (Dreistadt, 2001).

PHYSIOLOGICAL DISORDERS

De Hertogh et al. (1997) reported flower abortion due to very high forcing temperatures, leaf chlorosis due to very low forcing temperatures, and leaf tip scorch. Tip scorch has been associated with a variety of causes including high soluble salt levels, excessive media drying, poor air movement, and high forcing temperatures. In addition, high boron levels have been found in the tip scorched areas when compared to symptomless leaf tips (H.F. Wilkins, personal communication).

POSTHARVEST

Flower spikes should be harvested when the first flower is open and the buds are colored. Stems can be stored dry for 4 to 6 weeks at 35 to 39°F (2 to 4°C). Vase life is up to 4 weeks (Nowak and Rudnicki, 1990). Stems should be transported upright because of geotropism. Ethylene inhibitors such as silver thiosulfate (STS) and calcium chelators can be used to prevent geotropic responses (Philosoph-Hadas et al., 1995). *Ornithogalum* is considered to be only slightly sensitive to ethylene (Woltering and van Doorn, 1988).

Pots are shipped at 35 to 39°F (2 to 4°C) when three florets are fully open but do not store well. Potted *Ornithogalum dubium* plants can last up to 7 weeks if given high light and fertilized (De Hertogh et al., 1997). Plants can be reflowered by ceasing irrigation in the summer and placing pots at 70 to 80°F (21 to 27°C) in a dry dark area until fall. At that time, move the plant to a high light area and resume watering and fertilizing.

KEY POINTS

- The numerous species can be used as cut flowers, potted flowering plants, and garden ornamentals.
- Plants are propagated by bulblets, bulb division, seed, leaf cuttings, or *in vitro*.
- A number of different temperature regimes can be used for bulb storage and forcing, depending on the species being grown.
- Production can be spread out over time by holding bulbs at specific temperature regimes.
- Many species grow best in cool climates.
- Viruses and foliar tip burn are major limitations.

BIBLIOGRAPHY

Armitage, A.A., and J. M. Laushman. 2003. *Ornithogalum arabicum*, pp. 432–437 in *Specialty Cut Flowers*, 2nd ed. Timber Press, Portland, Oregon.

Bailey, L.H., and E.Z. Bailey. 1976. *Ornithogalum*, pp. 800–801 in *Hortus Third: A Concise Dictionary of Plants Cultivated in the United States and Canada*. Macmillan, New York.

Blomerus, L.M., and H.A. Schreuder. 2002. Rapid propagation of *Ornithogalum* using leaf cuttings. *Acta Horticulturae* 570:293–296.

De Hertogh, A.A., and L. Gallitano. 1997. Basic forcing requirements for Israeli-grown *Ornithogalum dubium*. *Acta Horticulturae* 430:227–232.

De Hertogh, A.A., and M. Le Nard. 1993. *Ornithogalum*, pp. 761–764 in *The Physiology of Flower Bulbs*, A.A. De Hertogh and M. Le Nard, editors. Elsevier, Amsterdam.

De Hertogh, A. A., L. Gallitano, T. Nell, and R.T. Leonard. 1997. Forcing South Africa's "doubtful lily." *GrowerTalks* 61(8):84, 85, 87.

Dreistadt, S.H. 2001. *Integrated Pest Management for Floriculture and Nurseries*. University of California Division of Agriculture and Natural Resources Publication 3402.

Griesbach, R.J., and F. Meyer. 1998. Three new cultivars of *Ornithogalum*: 'Chesapeake Blaze,' 'Chesapeake Sunset,' and 'Chesapeake Sunshine.' *HortScience* 33:345–347.

Griesbach, R.J., F. Meyer, and H. Koopowitz. 1993. Creation of new flower colors in *Ornithogalum* via interspecific hybridization. *Journal of the American Society for Horticultural Science* 118: 409–414.

Halaban, R., E. Galun, and A.H. Halevy. 1965. Experimental morphogenesis on stem tips of *Ornithogalum arabicum* L. cultured *in vitro*. *Phytomorphology* 15:379–387.

Horst, R.K. 1990. Star-of-Bethlehem, p. 828 in *Westcott's Plant Disease Handbook*, 5th ed. Van Nostrand Reinhold, New York.

Huxley, A., M. Griffiths, and M. Levy. 1992. *Ornithogalum*, pp. 408–409 in *The New Royal Horticultural Society Dictionary of Gardening*, vol. 3. Stockton Press, New York.

Littlejohn, G.M., and L.M. Blomerus. 1992. Breeding with indigenous South African *Ornithogalum* species. *Acta Horticulturae* 325:549–553.

Littlejohn, G.M., L.M. Blomerus, R. de V. Pienaar, and H.A. van Niekerk. 1992. Cytogenetic studies in the genus *Ornithogalum*. *Acta Horticulturae* 325:879–882.

Luria, G., A.A. Watad., Y. Cohen-Zhedek, and A. Borochov. 2002. Growth and flowering of *Ornithogalum dubium*. *Acta Horticulturae* 570: 113–119.

Meyer, F., R.J. Griesbach, and H. Koopowitz. 1990. Inter- and intraspecific hybridization in the genus *Ornithogalum*. *Herbertia* 46:129–138.

Niederwieser, J.G., H.A. van de Venter, and P.J. Robbertse. 1990. Embryo rescue in *Ornithogalum*. *HortScience* 25:565–566.

Nowak, J., and R.M. Rudnicki, 1990. *Postharvest Handling and Storage of Cut Flowers, Florist Greens and Potted Plants*. Timber Press, Portland, Oregon.

Philososoph-Hadas, S.S. Meir, I. Rosenberger, and A.H. Halevy. 1995. Control and regulation of gravitropic response of cut flowering stems during storage and horizontal transport. *Acta Horticulturae* 405:343–350.

Shimada, Y., G. Mori, and H. Imanishi. 1995. Effect of temperature on the flowering of *Ornithogalum arabicum* L. *Journal of Japanese Society of Horticultural Science* 64:617–623. (in Japanese, English summary)

Shoub, J., and A.H. Halevy. 1971. Studies in the developmental morphology and the thermoperiodic requirement for flower development in *Ornithogalum arabicum* L. *Horticultural Research* 11: 29–39.

Shoub, J., A.H. Halevy, R. Maatsch, A. Herklotz, J. Bakker, and G. Papandrecht. 1971. Control of flowering in *Ornithogalum arabicum* L. *Horticultural Research* 11:40–51.

van Rensburg J.G.J., B.M. Vcelar, and P.A. Landby. 1989. Micropropagation of *Ornithogalum maculatum*. *South African Journal of Botany* 55: 137–139.

van Vuuren, P.J.J. 1997. Predicting the flowering date of *Ornithogalum thyrsoides* (Jacq.). *Acta Horticulturae* 430:167–173.

van Vuuren, P.J.J., and L.C. Holtzhausen. 1992. The influence of temperature on phenological dating of *Ornithogalum thyrsoides* Jacq. as a commercial cut flower. *Acta Horticulturae* 325:119–129.

Vcelar, B.M., D.I. Ferreira, and J.G. Niederwieser. 1992. Elimination of ornithogalum mosaic virus in the *Ornithogalum* cv. Rogel through meristem tip culture and chemotherapy. *Plant Cell, Tissue and Organ Culture* 29:51–55.

Woltering, E.J., and W.G. van Doorn. 1988. Role of ethylene in senescence of petals—Morphological and taxonomical relationships. *Journal of Experimental Botany* 39:1605–1616.

Oxalis

INTRODUCTION

Common names: oxalis, four-leaved clover, good luck plant, shamrock, wood sorrel, lady sorrel.

Scientific name: *Oxalis* L. spp. (Huxley et al., 1992).

Family and related taxa: Oxalidaceae R. Br. The *Oxalis* genus contains almost 600 species, including several weedy species, which are problems in greenhouse production.

Origin: *Oxalis* species are distributed on every continent, but most are concentrated along coastal South Africa and from southern Peru to the southern tip of South America.

Uses and current status: Commercially grown as potted plants for their clover-like leaves and colorful flowers (Fig. II-1 Oxalis). In North America, this plant is commonly grown for the

FIGURE II-I OXALIS   *Oxalis regnelli* potted plant.

St. Patrick's Day holiday. The tubers and roots of some species are eaten in Mexico and the Andes. Some species are woody to treelike (Bailey, 1935; Bailey and Bailey, 1976; Schauenberg, 1965; Synge, 1956).

CULTIVARS

Unfortunately, only a few of the 600 species are used for greenhouse forcing or in gardens (Table II-1 Oxalis). The various species and selections have a wide range of leaf and flower colors. Leaf colors vary from green to purple; leaf patterns range from uniform to dotted with rust-colored spots on the undersurface to various colored markings at the leaflet axils. Flower colors include white, pink, purple, and yellow; some flowers have red, purple, or yellow veins or are dotted with red. Flowers are five petaled, with one to several flowers on a single scape. The most commonly grown species is *O. regnellii* Miq. (Miller, 1997).

Nomenclature of species varies between countries, commercial firms, and researchers. For example, *O. triangularis* is often considered to be a separate species from *O. regnellii* (Miller, 1997), while at other times the two taxa are considered to be *O. regnellii* (Huxley et al., 1992).

PROPAGATION

South African *Oxalis* species form bulbs, but many South American species do not and are propagated from tubers or rhizomes. Propagation may be from seed, division, or natural offsets of bulbs, rhizomes, roots, or root-stem pieces. De Hertogh and Le Nard (1993) reviewed commercial bulb production.

Bulbing of *O. pes-caprae* L., *O. bowiei* Lindl., *O. purpurea* L., and *O. versicolor* L. has been induced by exposing the seedlings or bulbs to either 41 or 50°F (5 or 10°C) for 30 days, after which plants were moved to 68°F (20°C) and a 16-hr photoperiod (Aoba, 1972). Low temperature is an absolute requirement for bulbing of *O. bowiei*, *O. purpurea*, and *O. versicolor*.

FLOWER CONTROL AND DORMANCY

Dormancy can be induced by moisture stress, cold temperatures, inadequate nutrients, or other unfavorable environmental conditions. Commercially, the plants are allowed to drydown after flowering. Once dormant, the storage organs are lifted and graded for sale, or the plants are left potted and placed in a cool

TABLE II-I OXALIS

Origin and plant characteristics of various *Oxalis* species (Bailey, 1935; Bailey and Bailey, 1976; Huxley et al., 1992; Schauenberg, 1965; Synge, 1956).

Species	Origin	Flower Color	Leaf Color	Leaflet Number	Storage Organ
O. adenophylla	Chile, Argentina	Lilac-pink	Gray to silver green	9–22	Bulblike tuber
O. bowiei	S. Africa	Pink to red, purple to violet	Green, underneath purple	3	Scaly-bulb (tunicated)
O. braziliensis	Brazil	Reddish rose to purple	Dark green	3	Bulb
O. corymbosa	S. America, spread to S. & E. Asia, Pacific Is. (tropical)	Bluish, rose-pink, purple, violet	Green, hairy	3	Bulb (tunicated)
O. deppei— synonym to *O. tetraphylla*					
O. hirta	S. Africa	Violet, yellow tube	Green, hairy	3	Bulb (nontunicated)
O. martiana— synonym to *O. corymbosa*					
O. purpurea	S. Africa (Cape of Good Hope)	Yellow tube, other parts colored pink, purple, white or lavender; 'Grand Duchess' series: 1. 'Lavender' 2. 'Pink' 3. 'White'	Green, smooth, purplish beneath	3	Bulb (tunicated)
O. regnellii	S. America	White to pale pink	Bright green to burgundy to purple	3	Scaly-rhizome
O. tetraphylla	Mexico	Rose to red, purplish to violet, white	Dark green	4	Scaly-bulb
O. triangularis— synonym to *O. regnellii*					
O. varabilis— synonym to *O. purpurea*					
O. versicolor	S. Africa	Tube yellow, white or purplish, violet, rarely yellow	Lime green	3	Bulb (tunicated)

location for reforcing and flowering when watered and returned to warm temperatures (Aoba, 1972; Jackson, 1960; Wikesjö and Schüssler, 1981).

Specific storage requirements vary for the different commercial species (Table II-2 Oxalis). Storage temperatures from 33 to 40°F (1 to 4°C) have been used for *Oxalis tetraphylla* Cav. (synonym with *O. deppei*), *O. pes-caprae*, and *O. adenophylla* Gillies. Armitage et al. (1996) found moist cold treatment better than dry and that 41°F (5°C) for 10 weeks was best for regrowth of *O. adenophylla*. However, P. van Leeuwen (personal communication) stated that 36°F (2°C) for 13 to 17 weeks was optimum for *O. adenophylla*. Storage temperature and

TABLE II-2 OXALIS

Cold storage temperatures and durations required to force *Oxalis* plants into flower when potted from October 1 to January 2 (Armitage et al., 1996; De Hertogh, 1996; De Hertogh and Le Nard, 1993; Schauenberg, 1965; van Leeuwen, personal communication; Wikesjö and Schüssler, 1981) (see Table II-1 for synonyms of species listed).

Species	Temperatures °F(°C)	Weeks to force
O. adenophylla	48 (9) preplant, pot, place at 36–41 (2–5) for 10 to 15 weeks. May need 2 years' growth to fill the pot.	4–5
O. bowiei	77 (25) from receipt of bulbs to Dec. 13, then 41 (5) constant for 8–10 weeks until planted.	
O. braziliensis	41 (5) for 4 weeks, plant, do not allow to dry out.	6–8
O. cosymbosa	41 (5) constant until planted.	5–7
O. hirta	41 (5) constant until planted.	6–8
O. purpurea 'Grand Duchess'	77 (25) until 2 weeks prior to potting, then 41 (5) for 2 weeks, pot.	6–8 / 6–8
O. regnellii	77 (25) until 2 weeks prior to pot, then 41 (5) constant, pot. Can hold at 33–36 (1–2) for 10+ months if stored in moist peat moss to prevent drying.	5–10
O. tetraphylla	36–39 (2–4) until planting, use only 8- to 10-week stored bulbs for quality plants.	5–7
O. versicolor	41 (5) until 2 weeks prior to pot; then 77 (25), pot.	7–9

duration influence rate of emergence, uniformity, and weeks to force. For example, freshly harvested *O. tetraphylla* bulbs will produce poor-quality plants, having few leaves on long petioles, whereas bulbs stored long term will produce plants with numerous leaves on short petioles. Production from freshly harvested bulbs is also very slow, while properly stored bulbs will result in salable plants in 5 to 7 weeks. Some bulbs can be devernalized by 10 to 20 days of 86 to 95°F (30 or 35°C) after cold treatments.

TEMPERATURE

Forcing temperatures are species and cultivar dependent, but generally the early forcing temperatures are cool and are slowly increased as the plants mature (De Hertogh, 1996). European recommendations usually suggest that plants be forced at 57 to 59°F (14 to 15°C) to increase leaf and flower numbers; temperature is increased by 5°F (3°C) after shoot emergence and formation of a rosette-like clump of leaves and flowers. For *O. regnellii*, however, Miller (1997) recommended 70 to 75°F (21 to 24°F) medium temperatures after repotting until plants are well rooted, after which 65°F (18°C) can be used. *Oxalis tetraphylla* and *O. adenophylla* are commonly forced in Sweden and have defined forcing schedules (see also Flowering Control and Dormancy, page 714).

LIGHT

Photoperiod effects are species dependent. A Swedish study found that LD with *O. articulata* Savigny (12 to 16 hr) promoted earlier flowering, decreased leaf number, and increased flower numbers; however, leaf and flower petiole length increased. A 24-hr photoperiod, however, resulted in closed flowers, particularly at 59°F (15°C) (Wikesjö and Schüssler, 1981). Long-day night breaks should be avoided during forcing, especially with *O. purpurea* 'Grand Duchess' (De Hertogh and Le Nard, 1993). With *O. triangularis*, however, LD night breaks enhanced flowering (De Hertogh et al., 1995).

Flowering of *O. latifolia* HBK occurs regardless of whether it is grown under an 8- or 16-hr photoperiod. Supplemental lighting, provided by high-energy photosynthetic lamps, increased early forcing quality (Jackson, 1960).

Required light intensities are also species or cultivar dependent. During early and late winter, full sun is generally required (Wikesjö and Schüssler, 1981). *Oxalis bowiei* 'Grand Duchess,' *O. hirta* L., *O. corymbosa* DC., *O. regnellii*, and *O. purpurea* should be forced at 2500 to 5000 fc (500 to 1000 μmol $\cdot$ m^{-2} $\cdot$ s^{-1}) and *O. tetraphylla* at 1000 to 1500 fc (200 to 300 μmol $\cdot$ m^{-2} $\cdot$ s^{-1}) (De Hertogh, 1996; De Hertogh et al., 1995; Wikesjö and Schüssler, 1981).

WATER

The bulb or rhizome should be watered at the time of planting. During early forcing stages, the medium should be allowed to dry between waterings. During flowering, however, the medium must be kept moist to prevent yellowing of the foliage. Overwatering can cause serious root problems.

CARBON DIOXIDE

No data have been found regarding supplemental carbon dioxide on oxalis.

NUTRITION

Refer to Table II-3 Oxalis for limited foliar analysis level data. Dormancy levels can be affected by fertility; greater dormancy levels developed when *O. latifolia* was grown under low-nutrient regimes. Only *O. regnellii* requires a moderate to heavy fertilization of 200 ppm N, starting when plants are well established. Recently, *O. regnellii* plants have developed inter-veinal chlorosis during forcing in some locations. A micronutrient or virus may be involved (De Hertogh, 1996) (see also Physiological Disorders section).

MEDIA

Any medium that is well drained, with a pH of 6.0 to 7.0, is satisfactory. Many crops in Europe are grown in amended peat moss. The storage organs are shallowly planted with the number of storage organs for forcing in a 4-in. (10-cm) pot determined by the species (Table II-4 Oxalis).

HEIGHT CONTROL

Drenches or sprays of Cycocel (chlormequat) can reduce leaf petiole length. Workers in Sweden report that as the season progressed from winter to summer, fewer treatments were needed. During the winter, two to four applications were required at 7-, 10-, or 12-day intervals. When LD incandescent lighting was used,

TABLE II-3 OXALIS
Nutrient levels in leaves of *Oxalis regnellii* (unpublished data).

N	P	K	Ca	Mg	Fe	Mn	Zn	Cu	B
	(%)				(ppm)				
—	0.53	2.33	0.71	0.30	84	64	35	4.7	67

TABLE II-4 OXALIS
The common name and number of *Oxalis* bulbs per 4-in. (10-cm) standard pot (Aoba, 1972; Armitage et al., 1996; Bailey and Bailey, 1976; De Hertogh and Le Nard, 1993; Jackson, 1960; Schauenberg, 1965; Synge, 1956; Wikesjö and Schüssler, 1981) (see Table II-1, for synonyms of species listed).

Species	Common Name	Number of Bulbs
O. adenophylla	Surelle (French)	4
	Sauerklee (German)	
O. bowiei	—	3–4
O. braziliensis	—	3–4
O. corymbosa	—	4–6
O. hirta	Fern shamrock	3–4
O. purpurea 'Grand Duchess'		–
O. regnellii	Evergreen shamrock	3–5
'Purple leaf'	Purple leaf oxalis	5
'Pink leaf'	Pink leaf oxalis	5
'Emerald green'	Green oxalis	3
O. tetraphylla	Good-luck leaf,	4–6
	Lucky clover, 'Iron Cross'	

Cycocel was needed to produce commercially acceptable short plants. Spraying in the evening was advised.

Bonzi (paclobutrazol) can be applied as a drench at 0.05 to 0.1 mg a.i./4.5-in. (11-cm) pot or as a spray at 10 to 25 ppm with *O. regnellii* (Miller, 1997). Later, however, Miller (2001) recommended lower Bonzi rates of 1- to 4-ppm sprays and 1- to 10-ppm preplant dips for 5 min. Sumagic can be applied at 0.10 mg a.i./4.5-in. (11-cm) pot. Wikesjö and Schüssler (1981) noted that A-Rest (ancymidol) can also reduce petiole length and Miller (2001) suggested 33-ppm sprays.

SPACING

Oxalis are mainly grown in 4-in. (10-cm) pots. Plants can be spaced pot-to-pot early in production; thereafter, 3 in. (8 cm) should be allowed between pots.

PINCHING AND DISBUDDING

No pinching or disbudding required.

SUPPORT

No support required.

SCHEDULE AND TIMING

See Flowering Control and Dormancy, page 714; and Temperature, page 716; and Tables II-5 and II-6 Oxalis.

INSECTS

Oxalis are generally insect free; however, fungus gnat larvae have been reported to feed on the roots early in forcing when media are less likely to dry quickly. Spider mites can also be a problem. Pesticides should be tested prior to widespread application because the species or cultivars may respond differently.

TABLE II-5 OXALIS

Appropriate forcing temperatures for various *Oxalis* species (Armitage et al., 1996; De Hertogh and Le Nard, 1993; Schauenberg, 1965; J.P. van Leeuwen, personal communication; Wikesjö and Schüssler, 1981) (see Table II-1 for synonyms).

Species	Temperatures of (°C)
O. adenophylla	54–59 (12–15) early then increase to 64 (18)
O. bowiei	50–61 (10–16); avoid temperatures above 61 (16), if possible
O. braziliensis	55 (13) early, then increase to 59–64 (15–18)
O. corymbosa	50–61 (10–16); avoid temperatures above 61 (16)
O. hirta	50–61 (10–16); avoid temperatures above 61 (16)
O. purpurea 'Grand Duchess'	50–61 (10–16); avoid temperatures above 61 (16)
O. regnellii	70–75 (21–24) until plants are well rooted, decrease to 61–64 (16–18); if high light, use 71 (22)
O. tetraphylla	55–61 (13–16)
O. versicolor	50–61 (10–16); avoid temperatures above 61 (16)

TABLE II-6 OXALIS

Sample forcing schedule for *O. adenophylla* (modified from Wikesjö and Schüssler, 1981).

Cultural Step	Production Time Required (weeks)	Temperature °F (°C)	Photoperiod
Plant into 4-in. (10-cm) pot			
	3–6[a]	56 (13)	LD
Increase temperature			
	4–5[b]	64 (18)	LD
Flowering		64 (18)	Natural
Total	7–11		

[a]Three weeks when planted in early February and 6 weeks when planted in early November.
[b]Four weeks when planted in early February and 5 weeks when planted in early November.

DISEASES

The major disease problem is *Penicillium* on the storage organs during storage and transport. Nematodes are also a concern (De Hertogh and Le Nard, 1993). Powdery mildew (*Microsphaera russellii*) and rust (*Puccinia andropogonis, P. oxalidis,* and *P. sorghi*) can also occur, especially on outdoor plantings (Horst, 1990).

PHYSIOLOGICAL DISORDERS

Leaf chlorosis, mottling, wrinkling, and bronzing of *O. regnellii* and *O. triangularis* are possible under cool temperatures, unless grown at 70 to 79°F (21 to 26°C) and under 3-hr night interruption lighting during the winter (De Hertogh et al., 1995). This problem has been related to a virus as symptoms are not apparent with heat-treated bulbs (H.F. Wilkins, unpublished data).

POSTHARVEST

After 6 days of shipping at 55°F (13°C) plants arrived etiolated and in need of immediate irrigation, whereas plants shipped at 48°F (9°C) maintained their quality. L. Høyer (personal communication), however, recommended 36 to 41°F (2 to 5°C) for transport and storage. *O. adenophylla* can continue to flower for 5 to 6 weeks. *O. regnellii* and other species can make long-lived indoor plants with proper care.

KEY POINTS

- Oxalis is used as a potted flowering plant or foliage plant.
- In the United States oxalis is commonly grown for St. Patrick's Day.
- Plants are propagated by seed, division, or natural offsets of tubers, rhizomes, or root-stems.
- The tubers, rhizomes, or roots are cold treated for various durations prior to forcing, depending on the species.
- Dormancy can be induced by moisture stress, cold temperatures, inadequate nutrients, or other environmental stress.

BIBLIOGRAPHY

Aoba, T. 1972. Effect of temperature on bulb- and tuber-formation in bulbous and tuberous plants. II. On bulb formation in bulbous *Oxalis. Journal of the Japanese Society for Horticultural Science* 41:393–397. (in Japanese, English summary)

Armitage, A.M., L. Copeland, P. Gross, and M. Green. 1996. Cold storage and moisture regime influence flowering of *Oxalis adenophylla* and *Ipheion uniflaum. HortScience* 31:1154–1155.

Bailey, L.H. 1935. *Oxalis,* pp. 2417–2419 in *The Standard Cyclopedia of Horticulture.* Macmillan, London.

Bailey, L.H., and E.Z. Bailey. 1976. *Oxalis,* pp. 805–806 in *Hortus Third: A Concise Dictionary of Plants Cultivated in the United States and Canada.* Macmillan, New York.

De Hertogh, A.A. 1996. *Oxalis,* pp. C133–145 in *Holland Bulb Forcer's Guide,* 5th ed. International Flower-Bulb Centre, Hillegom, The Netherlands.

De Hertogh, A.A., and M. Le Nard. 1993. *Oxalis,* pp. 764–767 in *The Physiology of Flower Bulbs,* A.A. De Hertogh and M. Le Nard, editors. Elsevier Science Publisher, Amsterdam.

De Hertogh, A.A., L. Gallitano, and K. Kim. 1995. The effects of photoperiod and temperature on forcing of *Oxalis regnellii* and *O. triangularis. HortScience* 30:432. (Abstract)

Horst, R.K. 1990. Oxalis, pp. 748–749 in *Westcott's Plant Disease Handbook,* 5th ed. Van Nostrand Reinhold, New York.

Huxley, A., M. Griffiths, and M. Levy. 1992. *Oxalis,* pp. 421–424 in *The New Royal Horticultural Society Dictionary of Gardening,* vol. 3. Stockton Press, New York.

Jackson, D.I. 1960. A growth study of *Oxalis latifolia* HBK. *New Zealand Journal of Science* 3:600–609.

Miller, B. 1997. Production tips and height control techniques for oxalis. *Greenhouse Product News* 7(8):8–10.

Miller, W.B. 2001. Bulb crops, pp. 63–67 in *Tips on Regulating Growth of Floriculture Crops,* M.L.

Gaston, L.A. Kunkle, P.S. Konjoian, and M.F. Wilt, editors. Ohio Florists' Association Services, Columbus, Ohio.

Schauenberg, P. 1965. *Oxalis*, pp. 237–239 in *The Bulb Book*. F. Warne and Company Limited, London.

Synge, P.M. 1956. *Oxalis*, pp. 1458–1461 in *The Royal Horticulture Society Dictionary of Gardening*. Oxford Clarendon Press.

Wikesjö, K., and H. Schüssler. 1981. Growing of oxalis as a pot plant. *Florists' Review* 168(4367):14, 16–17.

Paeonia

INTRODUCTION

Common name: peony.

Scientific name: *Paeonia lactiflora* hybrids. The present-day herbaceous peonies are derived primarily from *P. officinalis* L. and from *P. lactiflora* Pall. (Huxley et al., 1992).

Family and related taxa: Paeoniaceae F. Rudolphi. *Paeonia* is the only genus of ornamental value in the family.

Origin: *P. officinalis* is native to southern Italy and France and *P. lactiflora* is native to China, to Tibet, and Siberia. *P. officinalis* is hardy to Zone 8, *P. lactiflora* to Zone 6, and their hybrids to Zone 3. *P. suffruticosa* Andrews., the tree peony, is a semiwoody species from China (Zone 4).

Uses and current status: *Paeonia lactiflora*, the common and popular garden plant, was once a highly valued cut flower in the United States, used primarily for Memorial Day (late May). At one time more than 4000 acres were in production in the Midwest, primarily in Indiana (Post, 1949). Today, the peony has returned as a specialty cut flower with production from the East Coast to Oregon and south to northern California, Kansas, and North Carolina.

The peony (*P. lactiflora* hybrids) is a cold hardy (up to Zone 3), easily maintained, and long-lived herbaceous perennial and is primarily used in gardens and commerce. *Paeonia suffruticosa*, the tree peony, is popular in Japan, and numerous areas have been extensively researched including morphological characteristics (Hamada et al., 1989), identification of possible hybrid ancestry (Hosoki et al., 1991), anatomical studies on flower bud differentiation and development (Hosoki et al., 1988), temperature effects on dormancy release and forcing quality (Aoki, 1992; Aoki and Yoshino, 1984a, b), chemical use to break dormancy (Hosoki, 1983; Hosoki et al., 1985), forcing (Aoki and Yoshino, 1989; Hosoki et al., 1983; Hosoki et al., 1984; Hosoki et al., 1992), and control of shoot length by plant growth regulators (Hamada et al., 1990). Armitage (1989) also reviewed cultural aspects of the tree peony as it pertains to the home landscape.

CULTIVARS

The 33 *Paeonia* species are divided into three sections, four subsections, 16 groups, and 12 botanical varieties (Bailey and Bailey, 1976). The cultivated species and cultivars can also be distinguished by date of flowering (early, mid, or late) and flower types (single, semidouble, double, or Japanese) (Armitage, 1989; Bailey and Bailey, 1976; Post, 1949; Wister, 1962). Hundreds, if not thousands, of cultivars have been developed in the 1400 years of known cultivation in China and are still being developed today. At the southern limit of its range, a few cultivars do well including 'Festiva Maxima,' 'Sarah Bernhardt,' and 'Karl Rosenfeld,' but stems will be shorter than when the same cultivars are grown further north.

PROPAGATION

Peonies are propagated by root divisions with two to five buds (eyes) and one to two large roots per unit. Three to 4 years are required for peony plants to grow large enough to be divided. If cut flowers are harvested, 5 to 6 years will be needed (P. Sansone, personal communication). Plants should be divided in August or

September after foliage has changed to yellow, brown, or red.

During the division process, small pieces with eyes (planters) or without eyes are produced. Planters are replanted and will grow into marketable roots in 1 to 2 years. Pieces without eyes can also be replanted; however, most pieces will not produce adventitious shoots. A few pieces may produce shoots, which generally take 2 years to form. Additional time will be needed to produce a marketable root. Some cultivars are more prone to producing adventitious shoots than other cultivars (P. Sansone and A. Rogers, personal communication).

Seeds can be used but are primarily for breeding programs (Post, 1949). Tissue culture has been accomplished (Habib et al., 2000; Hansen et al., 1995), but is not economically feasible at this time.

FLOWERING CONTROL AND DORMANCY

Flower bud initiation commences after the old flowers senesce and development continues until autumn dormancy (Byrne and Halevy, 1986). Apical buds initiate flowers first, followed by lateral buds (Halevy et al., 2002). Flowering of the herbaceous peony is mainly limited to colder climates, north or south of the 35° parallel. However, Armitage (1989) reported that some early and midseason single and Japanese cultivars do well in Athens, Georgia (Zone 7). Peonies thrive in cold climates. Although flower initiation and development do not require low temperatures, a cold treatment is required to break dormancy and promote further flower development (Barzilay et al., 2002). The optimum number of days at 42°F (6°C) (chilling unit) was 40 for most cultivars for shoot elongation and further flower development (Halevy et al., 2002). Byrne and Halevy (1986) reported that the peony required a minimum of 4 weeks of 42°F (6°C) to break dormancy and flower, while 6 weeks at 42°F (6°C) or 34°F (1°C) maximized the number of flowering shoots. Kamenetsky et al. (2003) suggested that 10 weeks at 42°F (6°C) or 8.6 weeks at 36°F (2°C) was optimum.

Dormancy can be broken and flowering occurs if "clumps" are removed from the field and greenhouse and forced into flower after early December in Urbana, Illinois, or after December 15 in St. Paul, Minnesota (Shannon and Kamp, 1959; Wilkins and Halevy, 1985).

Evans et al. (1990) prerooted freshly harvested divisions at 61°F (16°C) and then cold treated them at 42°F (6°C) for 0, 6, 8, 10, 14, and 20 weeks. Control plants not treated with cold failed to emerge. All plants receiving 6 weeks or more of cold flowered and 10 weeks appeared to be optimal for rapid flowering and flower numbers. Plants aborted flowers after 20 weeks, but this could have been due to high greenhouse temperatures during late spring forcing. When gibberellic acid (GA_3) at 2000 ppm or 118 mg a.i./pot was applied as a drench onto potted noncooled roots, all plants had shoots that emerged, but flowers aborted (Evans et al., 1990).

However, in Israel 100 ppm GA_3 [0.25 gal (1 L) per plant] soil drenches are effective in producing shoot elongation and flowering after plants are partially vernalized with cold in the field (Halevy et al., 2002). Plants are subsequently forced and harvested under plastic greenhouses for European market sales. GA_3 also increased the number of flowering stems. GA_3 rates higher than 100 ppm or application volumes greater than 9 fl oz (250 mL) tended to induce the sprouting of more shoots but many had aborted flower buds. First harvest occurs in the second year and maximum production is obtained from 4-year-old plants (A.H. Halevy, personal communication). Photoperiod treatments to plants prior to cold treatments or during forcing did not influence flowering in any way (Byrne and Halevy, 1986).

Regardless of production method, keep the foliage active as long as possible to maximize photosynthate accumulation, which will maximize flower production the following year. Do not remove foliage until after it has senesced.

TEMPERATURE

Greenhouse forcing of properly cold treated plants can occur at 54 to 65°F (12 to 18°C) (Bailey, 1916). Byrne and Halevy (1986) used 70 to 79°F/63°F (21 to 26°C/17°C) day/night greenhouse temperatures. Evans et al. (1990) used 64°F (18°C) night temperatures. In Israel 72/50°F (22/10°C) was best for enhancing stem length; higher temperatures increased flower bud abortion (Kamenetsky et al., 2003).

LIGHT

Full sun is a prerequisite for good growth, quality flowers, and high yields.

WATER

Outdoors adequate water is a necessity during the summer, which may require an irrigation system. For artificially cooled plants be sure that the media stays moist for plants to perceive the cold. During production, especially under protection, avoid wetting the foliage and flowers to prevent *Botrytis*.

CARBON DIOXIDE

No data available.

NUTRITION

Although Decker and Weinard (1931) found yield differences due to different fertilizer rates, cut stem production varied with the cultivar. The American Peony Society states that too much nitrogen may reduce the flowering capacity (Armitage, 1989). Test soil fertility annually.

MEDIA

Peony plants thrive in any well-drained media. Outdoors the soil should be well aerated with plenty of organic matter for rapid establishment. Flowering is reduced if the underground storage roots and buds are planted too deep. The number of flowers produced per plant was 24, 21, 15, 4, or 0 when planted at ground level or 2, 4, 6, or 8 in. (5, 10, 15, or 20 cm) below the soil surface, respectively (Howard, 1968). Plants survive and produce foliage, but shoots do not flower when planted too deep.

HEIGHT CONTROL

None required.

SPACING

Spacing in the field is critical for adequate light and air movement. In the field dormant roots are spaced 2 × 2 to 2 × 3 ft (60 × 60 to 60 × 90 cm) between plants in 4-ft (1.2-m)-wide beds (Armitage, 1989). Economical production is obtained with plants spaced on 16-in. (40-cm) centers in 3-ft (90-cm)-wide beds. Dormant roots should have five buds (eyes) for rapid production. Roots with three are acceptable but will take longer to reach maximum production.

In the greenhouse, two dormant roots with five buds are used per plastic bulb box [9 × 14 × 22 in. (23 × 37 × 56 cm)]. After forcing for 3 years, it may be useful to replant in fresh medium after plants go dormant. In ground beds, 0.4 plants/ft² (4/m²) can be used (Bartels Stek, personal communication).

PINCHING AND DISBUDDING

Larger flower sizes are typically obtained if axillary flower buds are removed. Axillary flower buds are best removed when they are pea size, approximately 0.25 in. (0.6 cm) in diameter, and the pedicel is 0.5 to 1 in. (1.3 to 2.5 cm) long. The process is easiest in the early morning when plants are turgid and covered with dew, which prevents the sticky sugars on the buds from sticking to the disbudder's hands (P. Sansone, personal communication). Spray peonies can be obtained by leaving the side buds or by removing the main bud on some cultivars. For dried peonies, do not disbud because the extra flowers add many additional petals.

SUPPORT

Support in the home garden is often required because double-flowered types become heavy when rain water collects in the petals causing the flowering stem to bend to the soil. Placing circular fences around the plant at emergence or shortly afterward is encouraged. Commercially, flowering stems are removed when the bud is just showing color and support is not required.

SCHEDULE AND TIMING

In the field, flowering progresses as spring advances. Peony flowers open in April in North Carolina but not until July in northern Minnesota. The time of field flowering naturally varies from year to year. Warm temperatures, especially night temperature, can compress the flowering period and cause excessive numbers of flowers to be harvested in a short period (P. Sansone, personal communication). Flowering can be staggered by planting cultivars with different flowering dates and storing harvested flowers. Once plants have flowered, keep foliage green and photosynthetically active as long as possible with adequate irrigation and nutrition.

In Israel early harvests can be produced up to 3 months before natural outdoor flowering by cold treating roots and applying 100 ppm GA_3 (Halevy et al., 2002). Plants in the field can also be covered with plastic tunnels and treated with 100 ppm GA_3, which will produce flowering 1 month before natural outdoor flowering.

Herbaceous peonies are commonly forced for flower shows or occasionally for potted plant production. Plants of 'Scarlet O'Hara' flowered in 72, 59, 52, or 29 days after being given 6, 8, 10, 14, or 20 weeks of cold, respectively, at 42°F (6°C) and forced at 64°F (18°C) under natural day length commencing December 15. 'Krenkeld White' flowered in 72 days when given either 4 or 6 weeks of cold (Evans et al., 1990). Byrne and Halevy (1986) found the mean forcing time across cultivars in California to be 67, 67, and 69 days for plants cooled for 4, 6, or 8 weeks, respectively, at 42°F (6°C) and forced at a minimum day temperature of 70 to 79°F (21 to 26°C) and 63°F (17°C) at night. Bud abortion is a common problem with forced plants if the temperature is too high, light level too low, or plants are insufficiently cooled.

INSECTS

Insects are generally of little concern; however, flea beetles can be a problem, especially during warm weather. Thrips, mites, mealybugs, and scale have also been reported (Dreistadt, 2001). Ants are frequently seen feeding on the buds's sweet exudate, but are not detrimental. Nematodes can occur and heat treating roots in 110 to 111°F (43 to 44°C) water for 1 hr may disinfect roots (A. Hommes, personal communication).

DISEASES

Unfortunately, there are numerous diseases, of which *Botrytis* is the primary concern and causes stem, flower, and bud rot during production and marketing (Horst, 1990). Sanitation, removal of infected buds, removal of all debris from the previous year's growth, and appropriate sprays, if needed, are suggested. Cultivars vary in susceptibility. Similarly, *Phytophthora*, *Sclerotinia* stem rot, and *Verticillium* wilt are also problems and should be controlled in the same manner as *Botrytis*. Several leaf spot diseases (*Cladosporium paeoniae*, *Cercospora paeoniae*, and *Septoria paeoniae*) and root rots (*Armillaria mellea* and *Rosellinia necatrix*) also occur (Dreistadt, 2001). Powdery mildew (*Erysiphe polygoni*) and viruses can be a problem. Destroy any suspected plant because the infection agent will be carried on knife blades. Nematodes can be controlled by hot water treatments.

PHYSIOLOGICAL DISORDERS

Lack of flowering may occur if plants are immature or insufficiently cooled, roots are planted too deep, clumps are too large or old,

or insufficient photosynthates were produced the previous year due to low light, crowding, or foliage removal. Bud abortion is a common problem with forced plants if the temperature is too high, light level is too low, nutrition is too low, or plants are insufficiently cooled. *Botrytis* may also kill flower buds before they open.

POSTHARVEST

Postharvest grades and standards have been established (Post, 1949). Flower buds should be harvested at the first signs of color when the buds are "medium firm to soft" at 1.25 to 1.63 in. (3.2 to 4.2 cm) (Fig. II-1 Paeonia). The degree of softness for optimum postharvest life varies with the cultivar. The flowers of red cultivars open the slowest, pinks intermediate, and whites the fastest (P. Sansone, personal communication). Generally the less mature the flower bud, the longer the vase life (Eason et al., 2002).

Gast (2000) has conducted annual production and postharvest evaluations since 1992 and noted that the vase life of freshly harvested flowers from 28 cultivars ranged from a low of 4.4 days to a high of 8.7 days. Large variations in vase life can occur from one year to the next, however (Gast, 1995, 2000). Many cultivars also produced flowers suitable for freeze-drying.

Flowers should be picked early in the morning and stored dry by the grower; flowers hydrated by the grower are more likely to open during shipping. Cool flowers to 34°F (1°C) as

FIGURE II-1 PAEONIA   *Paeonia* bud ready to harvest.

quickly as possible; later grade and bunch rapidly without allowing flowers to warm up. To reduce *Botrytis* problems during storage and shipping, foliage should be dry and sleeves should not be used (P. Sansone, personal communication).

The season can be extended by long-term cold storage of buds at 32 to 34°F (0 to 1°C) in plastic lined boxes for up to 3 to 4 weeks (Eason et al., 2002; Gast, 2000). Cut peonies still had a vase life of 4.7 to 8.6 days, depending on the cultivar, after 4 weeks of storage (Gast, 2000). Longer storage of up to 12 weeks is possible but vase life will be reduced. Peony buds are relatively insensitive to ethylene. Opening floral preservative solutions should be used. After long-term dry storage, stems should be recut and held in a warm water (pH 3.5 using citric acid) hydrating solution at 70°F (21°C). After hydration move flower stems to a floral preservative (Heuser and Evensen, 1986; Nowak and Rudnicki, 1990).

KEY POINTS

- The peony is one of the oldest cultivated ornamental plants with records in China dating back 1400 years.
- Peony is used as a cut flower, potted flowering plant, and garden ornamental.
- Plants are propagated commercially by root divisions with two to five buds (eyes).
- Flower bud initiation starts after the old flowers senesce.
- A cold treatment lasting at least 4 weeks is required for shoot elongation and flower development.

- Full sun is required for good growth, quality flowers, and high yields.
- Flowering is reduced if the fleshy roots and buds are planted too deep.
- Axillary buds are typically removed on stems for cut flower production.
- *Botrytis* can be a major problem.
- Peony flowers can be dry stored at 32 to 34°F (0 to 1°C) for up to 3 to 4 weeks and rehydrated in warm 70°F (21°C) water after stems are recut.

BIBLIOGRAPHY

Aoki, N. 1992. Effects of pre-chilling and pre- and post-budbreak temperature on the subsequent growth and cut flower quality of forced tree peony. *Journal of the Japanese Society for Horticultural Science* 61:127–133. (in English)

Aoki, N., and S. Yoshino. 1984a. Effects of precooling and the temperature of cold storage on the growth and the quality of cut flowers of forced tree peony (*Peony suffruticosa* Andr.). *Journal of the Japanese Society for Horticultural Science* 53:338–346. (in English)

Aoki, N., and S. Yoshino. 1984b. Effects of the duration of cold storage on the growth and the quality of cut flowers of forced tree peony (*Peony suffruticosa* Andr.). *Journal of the Japanese Society for Horticultural Science* 52:450–457. (in Japanese, English summary)

Aoki, N., and S. Yoshino. 1989. Effects of summer cultural conditions on the growth and development of flower buds and cut flower quality of forced tree peony (*Paeonia suffruticosa* Andr.). *Journal of the Japanese Society for Horticultural Science* 58:415–420. (in Japanese, English summary)

Armitage, A.M. 1989. *Paeonia*, pp. 437–443 in *Herbaceous Perennial Plants*. Varsity Press, Athens, Georgia.

Bailey, L.H. 1916. *Paeonia*, pp. 2432–2433 in *The Standard Cyclopedia of Horticulture*. Macmillan, New York.

Bailey, L.H., and E.Z. Bailey. 1976. *Paeonia*, pp. 810–811 in *Hortus Third: A Concise Dictionary of Plants Cultivated in the United States and Canada*. Macmillan, New York.

Barzilay, A., H. Zemah, and R. Kemenetsky. 2002. Annual life cycle and floral development of 'Sarah Bernhardt' peony in Israel. *HortScience* 37: 300–303.

Byrne, T.G., and A.H. Halevy. 1986. Forcing herbaceous peonies. *Journal of the American Society for Horticultural Science* 111:379–383.

Decker, S.W., and F.F. Weinard. 1931. Peony fertilizers and cutting. *Proceedings of the American Society for Horticultural Science* 28:423–426.

Dreistadt, S.H. 2001. *Integrated Pest Management for Floriculture and Nurseries*. University of California Division of Agriculture and Natural Resources Publication 3402.

Eason, J., T. Pinkney, J. Heyes, D. Brash, and B. Bycroft. 2002. Effect of storage temperature and harvest bud maturity on bud opening and vase life of *Paeonia lactiflora* cultivars. *New Zealand*

Journal of Crop and Horticultural Science 30: 61–67.

Evans, M.R., N.O. Anderson, and H.F. Wilkins. 1990. Temperature and GA$_3$ effects on emergence and flowering of potted *Paeonia lactiflora*. *HortScience* 25:923–924.

Gast, K.L.B. 1995. *Production, Postharvest, Freeze-Drying Evaluation of Fresh-Cut Peonies*. Report of Progress 767, Agricultural Experiment Station, Kansas State University.

Gast, K.L.B. 2000. *Production and Postharvest Evaluations of Fresh-Cut Peonies*. Report of Progress 866, Agricultural Experiment Station, Kansas State University.

Habib, A., L. D'Aoust, and D. Donnelly. 2000. Micropropagation of herbaceous peony. *HortScience* 35:447. (Abstract)

Halevy, A.H., M. Levi, M. Cohen, and V. Naor. 2002. Evaluation of methods for flowering advancement of herbaceous peonies. *HortScience* 37: 885–889.

Hamada, M., T. Hosoki, and K. Inaba. 1989. Morphological peony cultivars classification based on multivariate analysis. *Journal of the Japanese Society for Horticultural Science* 58:697–704. (in Japanese, English summary)

Hamada, M., T. Hosoki, and T. Maeda. 1990. Shoot length control of tree peony (*Paeonia suffruticosa*) with uniconazole and paclobutrazol. *HortScience* 25:198–200.

Hansen, C., L. Stephens, and H. Zhang. 1995. *In vitro* propagation of fern-leaf peony. *American Peony Society Bulletin* 296:7–10.

Heuser, C.W., and K.B. Evensen. 1986. Cut flower longevity of peony. *Journal of the American Society for Horticultural Science* 111:896–899.

Horst, R.K. 1990. Peony, pp. 764–765 in *Westcott's Plant Disease Handbook*, 5th ed. Van Nostrand Reinhold, New York.

Hosoki, T. 1983. Breaking dormancy with ethanol and storage. *HortScience* 18:876–878.

Hosoki, T., M. Hamada, and K. Inaba. 1983. Forcing tree peony by chemicals, low temperature treatment, and retarding by long-term cold storage. *Bulletin of the Faculty of Agriculture, Shimane University* 17:8–12. (in Japanese, English summary)

Hosoki, T., M. Hamada, and K. Inaba. 1984. Forcing of tree peony for December shipping by pre-chilling and chemical treatments. *Journal of the Japanese Society for Horticultural Science* 53: 187–193. (in Japanese, English summary)

Hosoki, T., H. Hiura, and M. Hamada. 1985. Breaking bud dormancy in corms, tubers, and trees with sulfur containing compounds. *HortScience* 20:290–291.

Hosoki, T., M. Hamada, and K. Inaba. 1988. Flower bud differentiation and development of tree peony. *Bulletin of the Faculty of Agriculture, Shimane University* 22:16–21. (in English)

Hosoki, T., M. Hamada, T. Kaudo, R. Moriwaki, and K. Inaba. 1991. Comparative study of anthocyanins in tree peony flowers. *Journal of the Japanese Society for Horticultural Science* 60: 395–403. (in English)

Hosoki, T., M. Hamada, T. Maeda, and T. Gotoh. 1992. Forcing of tree peony for December shipping using spring and winter blooming cultivars. *Journal of the Japanese Society for Horticultural Science* 61:121–126. (in English)

Howard, G.S. 1968. How depth of planting affects the garden peony. *HortScience* 3:279–280.

Huxley, A., M. Griffiths, and M. Levy. 1992. *Paeonia*, pp. 434–440 in *The New Royal Horticultural Society Dictionary of Gardening*, vol. 3. Stockton Press, New York.

Kamenetsky, R., A. Barzilay, A. Erez, and A.H. Halevy. 2003. Temperature requirements for floral development of herbaceous peony cv. 'Sarah Bernhardt.' *Scientia Horticulturae* 9:309–320.

Nowak, J., and R.M. Rudnicki. 1990. *Postharvest Handling and Storage of Cut Flowers, Florist Greens and Potted Plants*. Timber Press, Portland, Oregon.

Post, K. 1949. *Paeonia albiflora* or *P. officinalis*, pp. 720–727 in *Florist Crop Production and Marketing*. Orange Judd Publishing, New York.

Shannon, J., and J.R. Kamp. 1959. Trials of various possible propagation methods on herbaceous peonies. *Illinois State Florists' Association Bulletin* 197:4–7.

Wilkins, H.F., and A.H. Halevy. 1985. *Paeonia*, pp. 2–4 in *Handbook of Flowering*, vol. IV, A.H. Halevy, editor. CRC Press, Boca Raton, Florida.

Wister, J.C. 1962. *The Peonies*. American Horticultural Society, Alexandria, Virginia.

Pelargonium

INTRODUCTION

Common names: geranium, pelargonium, storksbill, also see the following.

Scientific names: *Pelargonium* L'Hérit. species and hybrids (Bailey and Bailey, 1976; Huxley et al., 1992). This important genus has six commercially distinct species and hybrid groups, which have unique production regimes.

1. *P. ×hortorum* L.H. Bail., the zonal or common house geranium, propagated by cuttings. This group originated from *P. inquinaus* (L.) L'Hérit. ×*P. zonale* (L.) L'Hérit. crosses (Fig. II-1 Pelargonium).

2. *P. ×hortorum*, the seed geranium, propagated by hybrid seed (Figs. II-2 and II-3 Pelargonium).

3. *P. peltatum* (L.) L'Hérit., the ivy or hanging basket geranium, propagated primarily from cuttings. A few cultivars are seed propagated.

4. *P. ×domesticum* L.H. Bail., the most beautiful of the flowering geraniums, is known as the regal geranium, the queen of the garden geranium, the fancy geranium, the Martha Washington geranium, or the Lady Washington geranium, and is cutting propagated.

5. Scented geraniums, various species or hybrids with distinct leaf fragrances, leaf form, and flower types. They are frequently lumped under the common name "scented" geraniums. Bailey and Bailey (1976) listed 13 scented species and approximately 35 hybrids or cultivars between the various species. The majority of cultivars are propagated by cuttings and a few by seed.

FIGURE II-1 PELARGONIUM *Pelargonium ×hortorum* 'Happy Thought.'

FIGURE II-2 PELARGONIUM *Pelargonium ×hortorum* 'Starburst Red.'

6. *P. floribunda* (name has no botanical standing), a new hybrid group that resulted from a cross between *P. ×hortorum* and *P. peltatum*; also referred to as "cascade" geraniums. These cutting-propagated geraniums are less susceptible to decline or deterioration in vigor during high summer temperatures as with *P. peltatum* and are excellent

FIGURE II-3 PELARGONIUM *Pelargonium* ×*hortorum* greenhouse production.

for hanging baskets, balcony flower boxes, and planter box specimens.

Family and related taxa: Geraniaceae Juss. species. Within the genus *Pelargonium* are more than 250 species (Huxley et al., 1992). Geraniaceae also contains the genus *Geranium*, which includes many garden ornamentals.

Origin: Most *Pelargonium* species are from South Africa in the Mediterranean climate of Cape Province. In nature, they are found growing in ". . . dry, hot habitats, fissures of rocky outcrops, sandy soil, rocky soil, sand dunes . . ." (Van der Walt, 1977).

Uses and current status: Geraniums have been one of the most important species in the bedding plant business for decades (Berninger, 1993). Hybrid seed and zonal geraniums are the most important *Pelargonium* types and are primarily planted in porch (balcony) boxes, ground beds, or in large pots or tubs. The ivy geranium, *P. peltatum*, and cascade geranium, *P. floribunda*, are used in hanging baskets and balcony or porch boxes where the stems can trail naturally downward.

Unfortunately, the beautiful, showy Regal types flower only when temperatures are near 50°F (10°C). Hence, in most areas of the world where they are sold in the spring, flowering ceases in the summer due to high temperatures. Frequently, they are sold as gift or specimen potted flowering plants. Plants can be planted directly in the garden in cooler climates such as along the coastal area of western North America.

Scented geraniums are used most frequently as potted plants or in patio or porch boxes. Essential oils used in the perfume industry may be extracted from this group. Most selections are not cold or winter hardy, but they do well in the home during the winter in a sunny southern window.

All *Pelargoniums* in commerce are perennial herbs with leaves that range from obscurely lobed (*P.* ×*domesticum*) to highly dissected (scented geraniums). The foliage occurs in various combinations of green, white, ivory, bronze, yellow, and red. Flowers are an umbel inflorescence and colors include shades of red, pink, salmon, or white. Flowers can be solid colored or various combinations of all colors. Near black coloration can occur with *P.* ×*domesticum*. Flowers can be single or double. The individual petals may be round to serrate and wide to narrow.

CULTIVARS

International breeding programs in North America, Europe, and Japan are being conducted on the zonal and seeded geranium. In 1966, the first hybrid seed cultivars were released and they required more than 160 days to flower from germination and were taller than 18 in. (46 cm). Presently, breeding and cultural techniques have reduced days to flower and height by one-half to two-thirds. Breeding efforts are also focusing on leaf and flower resistance to *Botrytis* blight (Uchneat et al., 1999). New hybrid lines and new cultivars of cutting-propagated geraniums are being bred from *P.* ×*hortorum*, *P. peltatum*, and *P.* ×*domesticum*, blurring the distinctions among the groups.

Although *P. peltatum* has long been popular as a balcony plant in cool northern Europe, new cultivars and selections are being released annually for portions of North America with warm summers. *P.* ×*domesticum* cultivars vary in temperature sensitivity, branching, edema resistance, shattering resistance, and days to flower. Scented geraniums remain popular for garden enthusiasts with new species and hybrids being introduced. Some cultivars, however, are decades old.

PROPAGATION

Until the late 1960s, geraniums were exclusively asexually propagated, except for professional breeding programs. Since then, seed or sexually propagated plants have become a commercial reality for *P.* ×*hortorum*. Tissue culture propagation is possible and used in the maintenance of disease-free nuclear stock blocks from certified stock plants by certain cutting distributors (see Diseases, page 735) (Larson, 1993; Oglevee-O'Donovan, 1993). Tissue culture of *P. graveolens* L'Hérit., a species used for essential oil production, has been reported (Gupta et al., 2002).

ASEXUAL PROPAGATION—STOCK PLANTS

In the past, most greenhouses propagated their own cuttings from stock plants started in July or August of the previous year. Today, cutting-propagated geraniums are primarily grown from unrooted or rooted cuttings received directly from cutting distributors and propagators in early spring. Stock plants grown in an ideal environment can produce up to 80 cuttings when planted in August and grown in a 7-in. (18-cm) or larger container (Rogers, 1982) (Table II-1 Pelargonium). Stock plants of the cascading types, *P. peltatum* and *P. floribunda*, are grown in hanging baskets. Ideally, supplemental lighting should be used in the winter, which increases cutting production 20 to 50%. Shade plants in the summer and fall to a maximum light intensity of 5000 to 6000 fc (1000 to 1200 μmol $\cdot$ m^{-2} $\cdot$ s^{-1}).

Stock plants can be trained in a variety of methods (Carlson, 1993; O'Donovan, 1993; Oglevee, 1991; Whealy, 1993). For the "natural bush" method, plants are allowed to branch naturally. When young stock plants are an average of 5 in. (13 cm) tall, they are pinched leaving at least four nodes. Thereafter, two nodes on each stem are left behind when a cutting is removed.

For upright growing geraniums, a variation to the natural bush method is to leave the terminal shoot unpinched and pinch only the side shoots when they are 6 in. (15 cm) long.

TABLE II-I PELARGONIUM

Cutting yield relative to that of stock plants established in June. For example, planting stock cuttings in October will provide only 50% of the cutting numbers obtained from planting stock cuttings in June. (O'Donovan, 1993).

Month Cutting Planted	Cutting Yield (%) of June Yield
June	100
July	90
August	80
September	65
October	50
November	40
December	30
January	20

Thereafter, cuttings are removed. A tall, well-branched stock plant can be grown for sale in May and June, yet produce a maximum number of cuttings in January and February. Plants are supported with a 3- to 4-ft stake. Large older leaves can be removed to allow for light to penetrate to the plant's interior, which also helps to prevent *Botrytis* and increase production. Plants can also be trained against a board for aesthetics and sold later to retail customers.

Finally, a *P. ×hortorum* topiary tree can be formed by gibberellic acid (GA$_3$) sprays at 250 ppm to quickly elongate single stem cuttings. Four to five applications are made every 7 to 10 days. When the "trunk" is 24 to 30 in. (61 to 76 cm) tall, pinch the plant and start harvesting cuttings. Plants must be staked. The numbers of cuttings produced by this method are reduced, but the stock plants are of greater retail value.

ASEXUAL PROPAGATION—ROOTING CUTTINGS

Cuttings are rooted in a variety of containers: oasis strips, rockwool, "peat-pellets," or final pots filled with a well-aerated medium. Rooting hormone is not required. If used, dust the base of the cutting; do not dip the base of cuttings in the hormone, which can spread disease. Use bottom heat or maintain the medium at 70 to 75°F (21 to 24°C) for rapid callus and rooting for all geranium types. Mist propagation can be used with present-day pathogen-free cuttings. Use the absolute minimum amount and duration of mist to maintain leaf turgidity. Do not overmist! Light also ensures rapid rooting; full light can be used after the danger of wilting has passed during fall, winter, and early spring. Rooting occurs within 12 to 21 days.

SEXUAL PROPAGATION

There are approximately 6000 seeds/oz (212/g). Seeds are automatically placed into plug trays for germination under "as needed" mist or fog. Seeds are very lightly covered; vermiculite is recommended. Light enhances germination. Germination and early plug growth occur in four stages, each with its unique optimal conditions (see Table II-2 Pelargonium). Seedlings are transplanted 31 to 50 days after sowing or 23 to 37 days after removal from the germination room (Aimone, 1985; Armitage, 1993, 1994; Bethke and Carlson, 1985; Koranski and Khademi, 1993).

TABLE II-2 PELARGONIUM

Suggested optimal conditions for germination and production of hybrid seed *Pelargonium ×hortorum* plugs. Total production time is 31 to 50 days to transplant, depending on plug cell size. Stage I: water imbibition to root radical emerges; stage II: elongation of radical to cotyledon expansion and evidence of true leaf, move to greenhouse; stage III: true leaves develop; and stage IV: harden plants (Koranski and Khademi, 1993).

Growth Stage	Time (Days)	Temperature °F (°C)	Moisture (Humidity)	Light (fc)	Nutrition (ppm)	Cycocel Application
I	1–3	75–78 (24–26)	100%	50[a]	25[b,c]	–
II	7–10	70–72 (21–22)	95%	350–450	–	–
III	16–23	68–72 (20–22)[d]	Water as needed	Supplement ambient light with HID	Each watering based on medium analysis[b,c]	2 to 4 leaf stage, 750 ppm
IV	7–14	62 (17)	Water as needed	Supplement ambient light with HID	Each watering, based on medium analysis[b,c]	6 to 8 leaf stage, 750 ppm

[a]*Fluorescent lamps, 16 to 18 hr. can be 24 hr.*
[b]*Ca(NO₃)₂ and KNO₃, when radical emerges.*
[c]*EC of 0.75 to 1.0, no NH₄.*
[d]*Uniform air and medium temperature: warm the water, if needed.*

FLOWERING CONTROL AND DORMANCY

All commercial geranium cultivars are considered day neutral and the rate of floral initiation and subsequent development is dependent on total light energy received (intensity × duration) at any appropriate temperatures (Langton and Runger, 1985).

Juvenility may exist with some cultivars of seed geraniums (Bethke and Carlson, 1985). After this juvenility phase is completed, light intensity and duration become critical. With seed geraniums the plant growth regulator Cycocel (chlormequat) can hasten floral initiation in some cultivars (Quatchak et al., 1986). Timing of the Cycocel spray is critical to hasten the floral initiation of seed geraniums. Cycocel spray should be applied 2 weeks after germination commences. After 40 days elapse, no response may be observed (Miranda and Carlson, 1980; White and Warrington, 1984).

Timing of seed geraniums can be divided into different growth phases: (1) from germination to the formation of a microscopic flower bud, (2) from microscopic to a macroscopic visible bud, and (3) from visible bud to the opening of the first floret on the inflorescence. Wetzstein and Armitage (1983) described in detail the microscopic stages of floral and inflorescence development. The rate at which these stages occur is based on the speed at which plants can develop the first six to eight leaves. Leaf area determines rate of floral initiation. The photosynthetic capacities of these first leaves are directed to the primary flower. A minimum of 15 nodes must form prior to flowering (Armitage and Wetzstein, 1984). Upon flowering, the photosynthetic energy of the plant is directed to axillary shoots and secondary flowers (Armitage and Tsujita, 1979).

Low temperatures are critical with *P. ×domesticum*, because flower initiation occurs only when temperatures are less than 62°F (17°C) (Erwin, 1991). This temperature response varies among cultivars and is dependent on total light energy (Post, 1942, 1949). Initiation requires 4 weeks. Cold treatments can occur in the greenhouse or in lighted (fluorescent or incandescent) coolers at greater than 1950 fc (390 μmol · m⁻² · s⁻¹) for 3 to 6 weeks at 45 to 58°C (7 to 14°C) (Batschke, 1999; Erwin and Engelen, 1992), with 54 to 55°F (12 to 13°C) most commonly used (Table II-3 Pelargonium). Under lower irradiance, the required cold treatment may be longer or colder. The higher the light level during flower initiation, the greater the number of petals in the inflorescence (Batschke, 1999). Craig (1986) reported that 35°F (2°C) can also be used. Increasing the average daily temperature of the cooling treatment from 36 to 57°F (2 to 14°C) delayed floral induction, but increasing the night temperature from 36 to 43°F (2 to 6°C)

TABLE II-3 PELARGONIUM

The influence of 12-hr day/12-hr night temperatures and a 3-hr day length extension using fluorescent lights (10 μmol · m^{-2} · s^{-1}) to the main 8-hr photoperiod on date of flowering (days to flower) of *Pelargonium ×domesticum* 'Vicki.' Plants were previously vernalized and treatments commenced on January 24 (Erwin, 1991; Erwin and Engelen, 1992).

Night Temperature °F (°C)	Photoperiod	Day Temperature °F(°C)		
		54 (12)	63 (17)	76 (24)
54 (12)	8 hr	Mar. 31 (72)	Mar. 24 (69)	Apr. 18 (90)
	8 hr + 3 hr	Mar. 23 (64)	Mar. 24 (64)	Apr. 18 (90)
Average temperature		54 (12)	57 (14)	61 (16)
63 (17)	8 hr	Apr. 25 (97)	Aborted	Aborted
	8 hr + 3 hr	Apr. 13 (85)	Aborted	Aborted
Average temperature		60 (16)		
76 (24)	8 hr	Aborted	Aborted	Aborted
	8 hr + 3 hr	Aborted	Aborted	Aborted
Average temperature		69 (21)		

increased total number of flowers (Erwin and Engelen, 1992). During forcing, average daily temperature should not go over 63°F (17°C) because flower bud abortion can occur.

TEMPERATURE

Carpenter and Carlson (1970) found that zonal geraniums initiated and developed flowers under a wide range of temperatures. If growth occurred, flowering occurred with time. A 70°F (21°C) night temperature promoted flowering over 59°F (15°C) or 50°F (10°C) with plants grown from cuttings (Mastalerz, 1967; Post, 1942).

With seed geraniums, as temperatures increased from 50 to 75°F (10 to 24°C), the rate of growth and flowering progressively increased. However, when economics and plant quality are concerned, temperature regimes of 68/63°F (20/17°C) day/night are optimal. When node numbers were considered, 17, 16, or 14 nodes were formed prior to floral initiation at 50, 60, or 70°F (10, 16, or 21°C), respectively (Carpenter and Rodriguez, 1971; Erwin and Heins, 1992, 1993). For each 1°F (0.6°C) increase in temperature, the rate of inflorescence development was hastened by 0.5 to 1.0 days. At 90°F (32°C), the rate of development slowed. According to Erwin and Heins (1992, 1993), leaf unfolding rate peaks at 76°F (24°C).

For ivy geraniums, an average daily temperature of 68°F (20°C) is best according to Trellinger (1997) and can be supplied by constant 68°F (20°C) for compact growth or by 75/61°F (24/16°C) day/night for greater stem elongation. Increasing daily average temperature from 50 to 76°F (10 to 24°C) will increase the growth rate but decrease the number of florets per inflorescence (Erwin, 1999). See Flowering Control and Dormancy, on page 729, for a discussion of temperature effects on regal geraniums.

LIGHT

Floral initiation is dependent on total cumulative light energy for *P. ×hortorum*. Supplemental lighting hastens flowering during periods of low light in winter. Supplemental lighting has been found to accelerate floral initiation only when used during the early stages of seedling growth (Armitage and Tsujita, 1979; Carpenter and Rodriguez, 1971). Consequently, supplemental lighting of at least 350 fc (70 μmol · m^{-2} · s^{-1}) is most important for the first 4 to 6 weeks after germination for at least 4 weeks (Bethke and Carlson, 1985). Supplemental lighting after transplanting also hastened flowering (Quatchak et al., 1986). Kaczperski and Heins (1995) found that 28- to 35-day-old seedlings were more responsive to supplemental irradiance than 7- to 21-day-old seedlings. For every 1% increase in irradiance, expect a 1% growth increase (Aimone, 1985). Certainly, optimum temperatures are required for optimal growth response from supplemental lighting. White and Polys (1987) suggested the best combination was a daily mean temperature of 70°F (21°C) and an irradiance of 17.3 μmol · m^{-2} · day^{-1}. In production, zonal geraniums are best grown at 3500 to 5000 fc (700 to 1000 μmol · m^{-2} · s^{-1}).

Plants grown under 60% shade developed 22 to 24 nodes prior to floral initiation; only 16 to 18 nodes developed when plants were grown at full ambient light. The shaded plants flowered in 110 days and the full sun plants flowered in only 37 days. However, only 8 days difference existed between the shade and full sun treatments from floral initiation to visible flower buds even though both were grown at 75°F (24°C), which illustrates again that floral initiation is a light-driven process and floral development is a temperature-driven process (Armitage and Wetzstein, 1984). In summary, the time from visible bud to opening of the first floret of the inflorescence is less dependent on light and more dependent on temperature (Armitage et al., 1981).

Ivy geraniums are best grown at 2500 to 3500 fc (500 to 700 μmol $\cdot$ m^{-2} $\cdot$ s^{-1}) (Aimone, 1985; Erwin, 1999). *P. peltatum* is frequently grown at a light intensity and temperature that are too high because this type is commonly hung high in the greenhouse in the high-light areas where temperatures are apt to be well over 80°F (27°C) (Craig, 1986). Indeed, this is the location where *P. ×hortorum* should be produced.

WATER

As noted earlier, geraniums are genetically adapted to dry conditions and to well-drained soils. Many root rot problems can be traced to excess water, low oxygen, improper leaching, and excess soluble salt accumulation.

Economically, the irrigation system should be automated and water splashing must be avoided to reduce disease spread. Ebb-and-flow irrigation is the most water and nutrient efficient method (Morvant et al., 2001). Many producers use water stress as a method to slow growth, control plant height, and harden plants

prior to marketing. In fact, regal geraniums grown with no moisture stress and high humidity may remain vegetative (Batschke, 1999).

CARBON DIOXIDE

Carbon dioxide (800 to 1500 ppm) is used when vents are closed during stock plant production, cutting propagation, and seed geranium production (Shaw and Rogers, 1964).

NUTRITION

Constantly monitor soluble salt levels, pH, and nutrient content of the medium and tissue (Kang and van Iersel, 2000). Stock plants especially need constant monitoring of tissue and medium nutrient status because they are frequently in production more than 6 months. Geraniums have a high requirement for magnesium and calcium. Many nutrient regimes are based on KNO_3 and $Ca(NO_3)_2$ combinations, provided phosphorus is added to the medium as superphosphate or in the water as phosphoric acid to maintain proper pH. Nutrients can also be provided by means of controlled-release fertilizers (Morvant et al, 2001; Tayama and Carver, 1992). Certainly, micronutrients cannot be ignored. However, excess levels of micronutrients can also cause problems (Lee et al., 1996).

Hybrid *P. ×hortorum* seedlings in the plug trays are sensitive to high soluble salt levels due to restricted drainage of plug flats; however, adequate nutrition is required for maximum growth. Nutrient concentrations vary between the different production stages (see Table II-4 Pelargonium). Seedlings should be fertilized with 100 to 150 ppm N until transplants are well rooted, then increased to 250 ppm N. When the

TABLE II-4 PELARGONIUM

Leaf foliar analyses levels from healthy leaves of zonal, seed, ivy, and regal *Pelargoniums*. Tissue was from the first fully expanded mature leaf (adapted from Armitage, 1994; Dole and Wilkins, 1988).

Nutrient	Zonal	Seed	Ivy	Regal
Nitrogen (%)	3.8–4.4	3.7–4.8	3.4–4.4	3.0–3.2
Phosphorus (%)	0.3–0.5	0.4–0.7	0.4–0.7	0.3–0.6
Potassium (%)	2.6–3.5	2.5–3.9	2.8–4.7	1.1–3.1
Calcium (%)	1.4–2.0	0.8–2.1	0.9–1.4	1.2–2.6
Magnesium (%)	0.2–0.4	0.2–0.5	0.2–0.6	0.3–0.9
Iron (ppm)	110–300	120–200	115–270	120–225
Manganese (ppm)	270–325	110–285	40–175	115–475
Zinc (ppm)	50–55	35–60	10–45	35–50
Copper (ppm)	5–15	5–15	5–15	5–10
Boron (ppm)	40–50	35–60	30–100	15–45

FIGURE II-4 PELARGONIUM Iron/manganese toxicity on *Pelargonium* ×*hortorum* due to low medium pH.

inflorescence begins to color, decrease concentrations to 150 ppm N. Reduce to 50 ppm N during the final weeks prior to shipping when plants are grown at 55°F (13°C). A similar regime is appropriate for cutting-propagated zonal geraniums. Hammer (1991) reviewed fertilizer and nutrient considerations for the zonal or vegetatively propagated geraniums and Biamonte et al. (1993) reviewed the various essential elements.

While some recommend that *P. peltatum* and *P.* ×*domesticum* should not be fed over 200 ppm N (Craig, 1986), others recommend 224 to 364 ppm N (Jonas and Williams, 2000; Trellinger, 1997). Tissue nutrient levels ranged from 2.8 to 3.9% N for plants of similar size.

Seed geraniums are susceptible to iron and manganese toxicity, which is often due to accentuated uptake of those elements at low medium pH. Symptoms include stunting and necrotic spots, necrotic leaf edges, and chlorosis or reddening on lower leaves (Fig. II-4 Pelargonium). Foliar tissue levels of iron and manganese should not exceed 500 ppm (Erwin, 1997). If toxicity occurs, raise medium pH above 6.0 to make iron and manganese less available to the plant.

MEDIA

Geraniums require a pasteurized, well-drained medium for adequate root aeration. Selection and construction of a proper medium are critical for the success of all production stages. Hammer (1991) and Bethke (1993) reviewed various factors involved in the selection of a medium for the seed geraniums. Numerous materials have been successfully used including clay (Ehret et al., 1998), coir dust (Evans and Stamps, 1996), and rockwool (Hansen et al., 1993).

Optimum pH is 5.6 to 6.0, unless iron or manganese toxicity is a problem, in which case a higher pH, up to 6.2, should be used. Use a slightly lower pH of 5.3 to 5.5 for ivy geraniums (Trellinger, 1997). Media EC should be maintained at 3 to 4 dS · m^{-1} for optimum growth of seed geraniums. With regal geraniums the pH should be 5.6 to 6.0 and an EC of 0.9 to 1.1 dS · m^{-1} (Batschke, 1999).

HEIGHT CONTROL

STOCK PLANTS

While Florel (ethephon) is often used on stock plants to increase branching and prevent flowering, it also controls height (Lang and Trellinger, 2001) (see Pinching and Disbudding section). Cycocel (chlormequat) sprays (1500 ppm) are used to improve cutting "substance," particularly during winter and low light. Shorter cuttings with thicker and darker green leaves are less prone to wilting. However, some producers spray with GA$_3$ to encourage internode elongation and facilitate ease of cutting harvest.

CUTTINGS

Cycocel can also be applied during the rooting process or prior to shipping cuttings. Application at this time can reduce the etiolation frequently observed during rooting and shipping. Florel at 150 ppm can also be used on rooting cuttings destined for small containers (Lang and Trellinger, 2001). Florel should only be applied to healthy, well-rooted cuttings.

SEEDLINGS PRIOR TO TRANSPLANTING

The use of plant growth retardants on hybrid seed geraniums during this stage of production is critical and several growth modifications are observed (Koranski and Khademi, 1993). Besides the reduction of internode elongation, increased axillary branching and hastening of flower initiation are commercially beneficial. Cycocel sprays at 750 to 1500 ppm can be used.

FINISHING *P.* ×*HORTORUM* PLANTS

Cycocel spray at 750 to 1500 ppm is the most common chemical used to reduce plant height, particularly if space or light is limited. Multiple applications may be required on vigorous cultivars. Phytotoxicity can occur at the higher application rates; yellow bands and patches will appear, but if they are not too severe, they should turn back to green in 3 to 4 weeks. A lower concentration applied more frequently may reduce this problem. Cycocel at 750 ppm can be tank mixed with B-Nine (daminozide) at 750 to 4000 ppm to reduce the possibility of phytotoxicity. Cycocel at 750 ppm can also be tank mixed with Bonzi (paclobutrazol) at 2 to 4 ppm.

Florel sprays at 250 to 350 ppm can be used, but flower abortion and lower leaf yellowing can occur if overdosed or if plants are water stressed. The first application can occur 10 to 14 days after planting when roots are visible at the edge of the medium and new foliar growth is evident. Multiple applications may be necessary with vigorous cultivars. The last application of Florel should take place 6 to 8 weeks before marketing.

A-Rest (ancymidol) sprays at 5 to 10 ppm, Bonzi sprays at 1 to 4 ppm or drenches at 0.01 to 0.1 ppm, Topflor (flurprimidol) sprays at 15 to 25 ppm, and Sumagic (uniconazole) sprays at 0.5 to 2 ppm or drenches at 0.025 mg a.i./pot can also be used (Lang and Trellinger, 2001; Se-PRO, personal communication; Starman et al., 1994). Care must be taken not to overdose plants with Bonzi or Sumagic; however, they are reported to not cause leaf chlorosis as with Cycocel. Gibberellic sprays at 100 ppm have been used to reverse the effects of excessive Bonzi applications; however, results can be variable (Cox, 1991). Higher Bonzi drench rates of 0.03 to 0.3 ppm can be used once plants reach the desired size and flower number to hold the plants until marketing. Application of A-Rest, Bonzi, and Sumagic through a subirrigation system can be effective but problematic due to contamination of subsequent irrigation water (Adriansen, 1989).

Temperature can be manipulated to control height. The greater the difference in day and night temperatures (DIF), the greater the internode elongation (see Chapter 8, Plant Growth Regulation). High day and low night temperatures result in elongated internodes. Low day and high night temperatures result in short internodes. Lowering day temperatures for 2 to 4 hr to below the night temperature commencing at sunrise (DROP) will also aid in height control (Erwin and Heins, 1992, 1993; Erwin et al., 1989).

FINISHING IVY AND REGAL GERANIUMS

Ivy geraniums can also be sprayed with Cycocel (750 to 1500 ppm), resulting in a more compact, branched plant (Barrett and Holcomb, 1993;

Larson, 1991; Trellinger, 1997). B-Nine (1000 ppm) and Cycocel (750 ppm) tank mixes or Bonzi (1 to 4 ppm) can be used in warm climates. Multiple applications of growth retardants may be required. DIF and DROP (negative DIF for 2 to 4 hr after sunrise) are effective. Cycocel sprays at 1500 to 3000 ppm or Bonzi sprays at 8 ppm can be used on regal geraniums during forcing (Batschke, 1999). Multiple applications may be necessary. If HID lights are used, Cycocel is not needed (Craig, 1986).

SPACING

Geranium species and hybrids require high light to produce quality plants. Generally, economic pressures in spring result in a lack of space for growers. Improper spacing results in poor-quality plants exhibiting elongated internodes and reduced branching and flowering. Improperly spaced plants are subject to disease problems and lose lower leaves. The majority of final *P. ×hortorum* plants sold are produced in 4- or 6-in. (10- or 15-cm) pots. Plants can be grown pot-to-pot until leaves overlap and a growth retardant is required. Final spacing is on 6- to 7-in. (15- to 18-cm) centers for 4-in. (10-cm) pots and 8- to 9-in. (21- to 23-cm) centers for 6-in. (15-cm) pots.

Regal geranium production in 6-in. (15-cm) pots requires 12- × 12-in. (31- × 31-cm) final spacing (Tayama and Klesa, 1991). Small 4-in. (10-cm) pots can be grown at 6- × 6-in. (15- × 15-cm) spacing.

With the ivy geranium, be sure to plant ample cuttings per basket with four to five cuttings per 10-in. (25-cm) basket and seven per 12-in. (30-cm) basket (Trellinger, 1997). Place one to two cuttings in the center. Fewer cuttings will be needed if a longer crop time is used.

PINCHING AND DISBUDDING

Hybrid seed geraniums do not require pinching because they are self-branching. Zonal geraniums are often pinched during production, more to obtain a cutting than to stimulate axillary branching. This is true for stock plants as well as for high-quality potted specimens that are in 4-, 4.5-, 6-, or 6.5-in. (10-, 12-, 15-, or 17-cm) or larger pots.

Axillary branching of stock plants can be stimulated by the use of Florel sprays (350 to 500 ppm). Cutting production can be increased by 30% when Florel is sprayed on newly planted stock plants 2 weeks prior to pinching when they are 6 to 8 in. (15 to 21 cm) tall. Repeat sprays can be applied to stock plants until midwinter. This ethylene-releasing chemical can cause flower abortion and has been used in commercial propagation to reduce the labor needed to remove flowers to control disease and improve sanitation (Barrett and Holcomb, 1993; Larson, 1991). Multiple applications of Florel at 350 ppm can be used on ivy geranium plants to encourage branching and reduce elongation (Trellinger, 1997). Do not use Florel within 6 weeks of shipping cuttings or finished plants. Branching can also be enhanced by removing large outer leaves to allow more light to penetrate the canopy.

SUPPORT

Staking is required only when topiary geranium trees are produced.

SCHEDULE AND TIMING

There are numerous production and timing schedules, which vary with the propagation method, cultivar, latitude, and climatic conditions (Tables II-5 and II-6 Pelargonium). Tayama and Klesa (1991) proposed and discussed several schedules for zonal geraniums and Armitage (1993) for seed geraniums in 4-in.

TABLE II-5 PELARGONIUM

Optimal schedule for the production of a seed *Pelargonium* ×*hortorum* from transplanting a plug to flower in a 4-in (10-cm) pot (see Table II-1 for plug production information).

Cultural Step	Production Time (weeks)	Temperature °F (°C)	Light
Transplant plug			
	2	Day: 70 (21)	Supplemental
Spray Cycocel			
	1	Day: 70 (21)	Supplemental until spaced
Spray Cycocel			
	4–5	Day: 70 (21)	Supplemental/ambient
Visible bud			
	2–3	Day: 70 (21)	Ambient
Color			
	1	Night: 55 (13)	Ambient
Flower			
Total	10–12		

TABLE II-6 PELARGONIUM

Sample schedule for the production of a zonal *Pelargonium* ×*hortorum* from transplanting a cutting to flower in a 4-in. (10-cm) pot.

Cultural Step	Production Time (weeks)	Temperature °F (°C)	Light
Transplant rooted cutting			
	3	Day: 70 (21)	Supplemental until spaced
Space			
	1	Day: 70 (21)	Ambient
Spray Cycocel			
	2	Day: 70 (21)	Ambient
Spray Cycocel			
	2	Day: 70 (21)	Ambient
Spray Cycocel			
	3	Night: 55 (13)	Ambient
Flower			
Total	11[a]		

[a] If pinched, add 2 weeks.

(10-cm) pots. Generally, in cool climates one rooted cutting in a 4-in. (10-cm) pot will finish in 7 to 8 weeks, a 5-in. (13-cm) pot in 9 to 10 weeks, a 6-in. (15-cm) pot in 11 to 12 weeks, and a 7-in. (18-cm) pot in 14 to 15 weeks. Plants in warm climates will finish 1 to 2 weeks quicker.

With regal geraniums the 4-week cold treatment can commence 4 weeks after rooted cuttings have become established. Forcing requires 7 to 10 weeks at 58 to 68°F (15 to 20°C) during midwinter (January to April) and LD night breaks are implemented from 2200 to 0200 HR using incandescent lamps (Batschke, 1999; Craig, 1986). Precooled liners with flowers already initiated can be used and will flower in 7 to 10 weeks.

Ivy geranium propagation and production commence in December, January, and February for April, May, and June hanging basket sales (Craig, 1986). Unpinched plants grown at optimum light intensities of 2000 to 3000 fc (400 to 600 μmol $\cdot$ m^{-2} $\cdot$ s^{-1}) and temperatures of 65 to 80°F (18 to 27°C) can be produced in as little as 8 to 9 weeks. Generally, in cool climates a 4-in. (10-cm) pot will finish in 11 to 12 weeks, a 5-in. (13-cm) pot or 10-in. (25-cm) basket in 13 to 14 weeks, a 6-in. (15-cm) pot in 15 to 16 weeks, and a 7-in. (18-cm) pot in 17 to 18 weeks. Plants in warm climates will finish 1 to 2 weeks quicker. Reduce crop time by 2 to 3 weeks if Florel is applied. Use one rooted cutting/4- to 5-in. (10- to 13-cm) pot, 2 cuttings/6- to 7-in. (15- to 18-cm) pot, and 4 to 5 cuttings/10-in. (25-cm) hanging basket.

INSECTS

Geraniums are relatively insect free. Aphids, spider mites, cyclamen mites, and caterpillars can cause damage. Significant variation in resistance to spider mites exists in *P.* ×*hortorum*; resistance is related to the type of exudates from glandular hairs on geranium foliage (Grazzini et al., 1997). Fungus gnats and shoreflies can also be pests. Sound pest control techniques such as exclusion, inspection, and chemical control will reduce major problems (Lindquist, 1993).

DISEASES

The single factor that limits stock production success is disease (O'Donovan, 1993). This quote can only relate the seriousness of the numerous diseases which both historically and currently plague the geranium industry. *Xanthomonas campestris* pv. *pelargonii* is the most serious disease of geraniums because it is easily spread by propagation or irrigation, often difficult to detect, symptomless for many months after infection, and difficult to control with chemicals (Roberts, 1997). Biological controls are being investigated (Flaherty et al., 2001). Symptoms of *Xanthomonas* include small dark brown water-soaked appearing spots generally surrounded by a yellow ring, yellow to tan areas between the veins, and wilting of plants or branches.

Other systemic diseases include vascular bacterial blights [(*Raulstonia* (formerly *Pseudomonas*) *solanacearum*], verticillium wilt (*Verticillium albo-atrum*), root and stem rots (*Pythium*, *Rhizoctonia*, *Phytophthora*, *Fusarium*, and *Thielaviopsis*), bacterial stem fascination (*Clavibacter fascians*), and viral diseases (Daughtrey and Chase, 1992; Horst, 1990). *Raulstonia* is of particular importance because it has a broad host range and one type, known as Race 3, Biovar 2, is cold tolerant and can infect potatoes with the potential to cause serious crop losses if it were to escape the greenhouse (M. Daughtrey and S. Nameth, personal communications). Race 3, Biovar 2, is not normally found in the United States and Canada but occurs in many areas of the world and, consequently, its presence is regulated by U.S. federal quarantine. Race 1 already occurs in the southern United States. Symptoms include wilting and yellowing of the foliage, but without the foliar spots indicative of *Xanthomonas* (Hammer and Rane, 1999). High fertilizer rates tend to increase *Pythium* root rots (Gladstone and Moorman, 1990).

Foliar and flower diseases include *Botrytis*, bacterial leaf spots and blights (*Pseudomonas cichorii*, *P. syringae*), fungal leaf spots (*Cercospora brunkii*), and rust (*Puccinia pelargonii-zonalis*) (Horst, 1990; Simone, 1997). *Botrytis*-resistant cultivars exist and should be investigated if *Botrytis* is a problem (Uchneat et al., 1999). Other reported diseases include bacterial leaf spot (*Pseudomonas cichorii*), leaf spot (*Alternaria alternata*), gray mold (*Botrytis cinerea*), and armillaria root rot (*Armillaria mellea*) (Dreistadt, 2001).

Fortunately, today, indexing and maintenance of elite nuclear stock free from vascular systemic diseases and viruses have occurred (Tammen, 1960; Oglevee-O'Donovan, 1993; White, 1993). Cuttings from these culture-indexed plants are distributed by international firms; however, serious sanitation precautions must still be maintained in the greenhouse during cutting production (White, 1993).

The most tragic situation involves serious vascular systemic blights and wilts, symptoms of which are frequently not visually evident until after cuttings and plants have been distributed to wholesale and retail customers. These diseases become evident with warm spring and summer temperatures, frequently when the plants are in the hands of the consumer.

PHYSIOLOGICAL DISORDERS

P. peltatum has a common disorder called *edema*, where areas of stomatal cells on the underside of the leaves rupture and form corky abnormalities (Freeman, 1993). This problem is species and cultivar dependent. Rarely has this problem been seen on zonal or seed geraniums. Edema is thought to be related to excessive turgor pressure at night when the stomates close. Water loss is reduced, but an active, well-developed root system with an adequate water supply and warm medium temperatures continues to translocate water to the leaves. As the disorder progresses, the numbers of "blisters" increase. As noted under Temperature, page 730, ivy geraniums prefer to be grown in cooler temperatures than *P. ×hortorum* types, but the former are commonly hung high in the greenhouse in very warm temperatures. Consequently, proper temperatures and possibly reduction of water supply, lower humidity, and cultivar selection can reduce edema.

Chlorotic or reddish lower foliage may be due to iron or manganese toxicity (see Nutrition section). Reddish foliage may also be due to low temperatures or severe P deficiency.

POSTHARVEST

Seedling plugs can be stored up to 4 weeks at 36°F (2°C) (Heins et al., 1994). Using fluorescent light is better than storing plugs in the dark. Incandescent lamps can also be used, but are less desirable. Disease can be a concern (Armitage, 1993). Plugs tolerate shipping and storage best when previously irrigated with 150 ppm N for 2 weeks (Kaczperski et al., 1996a).

Geranium cuttings have a relatively short postharvest life and low tolerance to long-distance shipping at warm temperatures. The rapid decline in quality was attributed to ethylene (Arteca et al., 1996; Cheng et al., 1998). Unrooted cuttings can be stored for 4 to 6 weeks at 31°F (20.5°C) (Eisenberg et al., 1978). Rooted cuttings could be stored for up to 56 days at 41°F (5°C) and 250 fc (50 μmol $\cdot$ m^{-2} $\cdot$ s^{-1}) light for 9 hr/day (Kaczperski et al., 1996b). The anti-ethylene agents, silver thiosulfate (STS) and 1-methylcyclopropene (1-MCP), have been used experimentally to prevent storage-induced leaf yellowing of unrooted cuttings but also reduced rooting (Paton and Schwabe, 1987; Serek et al., 1998).

All geranium species are sensitive to ethylene as low as 0.01 ppm and exhibit a variety of responses depending on concentration, duration of exposure, temperature, and stage of development (Willumsen and Fjeld, 1995). Apical meristems can become totally aborted, leaves can become thickened and cupped, veins exaggerated, stems thickened and swollen, and flower buds aborted or abnormally developed.

Seed geranium plants in flower have a propensity to shatter their petals during transport and are sensitive to stress ethylene. Sprays of STS can be used 14 to 21 days prior to shipping, but predispose the plants to *Pythium*, which can devastate a crop unless a prophylactic fungicide drench is used (Hausbeck et al., 1987). In addition, STS sprays (175 ppm) can be used on zonals and regal geraniums. 1-methylcyclopropene (1-MCP) is also very effective in preventing petal drop of both seed and ivy geraniums, even without the presence of exogenous ethylene (Cameron and Reid, 2001; Jones et al., 2001).

During the marketing process both wholesale and retail customers must be urged to unpack as soon as possible, maintain adequate water, and provide adequate light. Shipping can occur at 41°F (5°C) (Deneke et al., 1990).

KEY POINTS

- Geranium is used as a bedding plant, potted flowering plant, hanging basket plant, and garden ornamental.
- Six commercially distinct species and hybrid groups are produced: *P. ×hortorum*, the zonal geranium, is cutting propagated; *P. ×hortorum*, the seed geranium, is seed propagated; *P. peltatum*, the ivy geranium, is primarily cutting propagated; *P. ×domes-* *ticum*, the regal geranium, is cutting propagated; the scented geranium, which includes numerous species, is both cutting and seed propagated; and *P. floribunda*, the cascade geranium, is cutting propagated.
- The development of certified disease-free geranium cuttings from specialty propagators was a major event in floriculture history.

- All commercial geraniums are considered day neutral with initiation and development dependent on light and temperature.
- Regal geraniums require a temperature below 62°F (17°C) for floral initiation; the optimum is 45 to 58°F (7 to 14°C) for 4 to 6 weeks.
- Growth retardant sprays, especially Cycocel, are required for height control and also increase branching and hasten flower initiation.
- Geraniums are susceptible to many diseases, which at one time limited production.
- Flowers are sensitive to ethylene and flower petal abscission is a problem; anti-ethylene agents are useful.

BIBLIOGRAPHY

Adriansen, E. 1989. Growth and flowering in pot plants soaked with plant growth regulator solutions in ebb and flood benches. *Acta Horticulturae* 251:319–327.

Aimone, T. 1985. New geranium technology. *GrowerTalks* 48(11):128, 130, 132, 134.

Armitage, A.M. 1993. Growing from seedlings, pp. 125–134 in *Geraniums IV*, 4th ed., J.W. White, editor., Ball Publishing, Geneva, Illinois.

Armitage, A.M. 1994. Growing on, pp. 43–94 in *Ornamental Bedding Plants*. CAB International, Oxon, United Kingdom.

Armitage, A.M., and M.J. Tsujita. 1979. The effect of supplemental light source, illumination and quantum flux density on the flowering of seed-propagated geranium. *Journal of Horticultural Science* 54:195–198.

Armitage, A.M., and H.Y. Wetzstein. 1984. Influence of light intensity on flower initiation and differentiation in hybrid geranium. *HortScience* 19:114–116.

Armitage, A.M., W.H. Carlson, and J.A. Flore. 1981. The effect of temperature and quantum flux density on the morphology, physiology, and flowering of hybrid geraniums. *Journal of the American Society for Horticultural Science* 106:643–647.

Arteca, R.N., J.M. Arteca, T.-W. Wang, and C.D. Schlagnhaufer. 1996. Physiological, biochemical, and molecular changes in *Pelargonium* cuttings subjected to short-term storage conditions. *Journal of the American Society for Horticultural Science* 121:1063–1068.

Bailey, L.H., and E.Z. Bailey. 1976. *Pelargonium*, pp. 832–836 in *Hortus Third: A Concise Dictionary of Plants Cultivated in the United States and Canada*. Macmillan, New York.

Barrett, J.E., and E.J. Holcomb. 1993. Growth regulating chemicals, pp. 65–74 in *Geraniums IV*, 4th ed., J.W. White, editor. Ball Publishing, Geneva, Illinois.

Batschke, K., 1999. The regal details. *GrowerTalks* 63(6):57, 58, 60.

Berninger, L.M. 1993. Status of the industry, pp. 1–2 in *Geraniums IV*, 4th ed., J.W. White, editor. Ball Publishing, Batavia, Illinois.

Bethke, C.L. 1993. Growing media, pp. 3–23 in *Geraniums IV*, 4th ed., J.W. White, editor. Ball Publishing, Geneva, Illinois.

Bethke, C.L., and W.H. Carlson. 1985. Seed geraniums—18 years of research. *GrowerTalks* 49(6):58, 60, 62, 64, 66.

Biamonte, R.L., E.J. Holcomb, and J.W. White. 1993. Fertilization, pp. 39–54 in *Geraniums IV*, 4th ed., J.W. White, editor. Ball Publishing, Geneva, Illinois.

Cameron, A.C., and M.S. Reid. 2001. 1-MCP blocks ethylene-induced petal abscission of *Pelargonium peltatum* but the effect is transient. *Postharvest Biology and Technology* 22:169–177.

Carlson, W.H. 1993. Tree geraniums, pp. 135–137 in *Geraniums IV*, 4th ed., J.W. White, editor. Ball Publishing, Geneva, Illinois.

Carpenter, W.J., and W.H. Carlson. 1970. The influence of growth regulators and temperature on flowering of seed propagated geraniums. *HortScience* 5:183–184.

Carpenter, W.J., and R.C. Rodriguez. 1971. Earlier flowering of geranium cv. Carefree Scarlet by high intensity of supplemental light treatment. *HortScience* 6:206–207.

Cheng, G.W., S.S. Sargent, and D.J. Huber. 1998. Effects of ethylene scrubber and light on yellowing of geranium transplants. *HortScience* 33:486. (Abstract)

Cox, D.A. 1991. Gibberellic acid reverses effects of excess paclobutrazol on geraniums. *HortScience* 26:39–40.

Craig, R. 1986. Regal and ivy leaved geraniums. *Bedding Plant News* 17(6):6–10.

Daughtrey, M., and A.R. Chase. 1992. Geranium, pp. 97–113 in *Ball Field Guide to Diseases of Greenhouse Ornamentals*. Ball Publishing, Geneva, Illinois.

Deneke, C.F., K.B. Evensen, and R. Craig. 1990. Regulation of petal abscission in *Pelargonium ×domesticum*. *HortScience* 25:937–940.

Dole, J.M., and H.F. Wilkins. 1988. University of Minnesota—Tissue analysis standards. *Minnesota State Florists Bulletin* 37(6):10–13.

Dreistadt, S.H. 2001. *Integrated Pest Management for Floriculture and Nurseries*. University of California Division of Agriculture and Natural Resources Publication 3402.

Ehret, D.L., B.J. Zebarth, J. Portree, and T. Garland. 1998. Clay addition to soilless media promotes growth and yield of greenhouse crops. *HortScience* 33:67–70.

Eisenberg, B.A., G.L. Staby, and T.A. Fretz. 1978. Low pressure and refrigerated storage of rooted and unrooted ornamental cuttings. *Journal of the American Society for Horticultural Science* 103: 732–737.

Erwin, J. 1991. Cool temperatures are still critical on regals. *Minnesota Commercial Flower Growers Association Bulletin* 40(3):3–4.

Erwin, J. 1997. Irrigation water considerations. *Minnesota Commercial Flower Growers Association Bulletin* 45(6) and 46(1):1–10.

Erwin, J. 1999. Ivy geranium production. *Ohio Florists' Association Bulletin* 831:1, 15–20.

Erwin, J., and G. Engelen. 1992. Regal geranium production. *Minnesota Commercial Flower Growers Association Bulletin* 41(6):1–9.

Erwin, J.E., and R.D. Heins. 1992. Environmental effects on geranium development. *Minnesota Commercial Flower Growers Association Bulletin* 41(1):1–9.

Erwin, J.E., and R.D. Heins. 1993. Light and temperature, pp. 55–63 in *Geraniums IV*, 4th ed., J.W. White, editor. Ball Publishing, Geneva, Illinois.

Erwin, J.E., R.D. Heins, B.J. Kovanda, R.D. Berghage, W.H. Carlson, and J.A. Biernbaum. 1989. Cool mornings control plant height. *GrowerTalks* 52(9):75.

Evans, M.R., and R.H. Stamps. 1996. Growth of bedding plants in sphagnum peat and coir dust-based substrates. *Journal of Environmental Horticulture* 14:187–190.

Flaherty, J.E., B.K. Harbaugh, J.B. Jones, G.C. Somodi, and L.E. Jackson. 2001. H-mutant bacteriophages as a potential biocontrol of bacterial blight of geraniums. *HortScience* 36:98–100.

Freeman, R.N. 1993. Physiological and environmental disorders, pp. 351–362 in *Geraniums IV*, 4th ed., J.W. White, editor. Ball Publishing. Geneva, Illinois.

Gladstone, L.A., and G.W. Moorman. 1990. Pythium root rot of seedling geraniums associated with high levels of nutrients. *HortScience* 25:982.

Grazzini, R., D. Walters, J. Harmon, D.J. Hesk, D. Cox-Foster, J. Medford, R. Craig, and R.O. Mumma. 1997. Inheritance of biochemical and morphological characters associated with two-spotted spider mite resistance in *Pelargonium ×hortorum*. *Journal of the American Society for Horticultural Science* 122:373–379.

Gupta, R., S. Banerjee, G.R. Mallavarapu, S. Sharma, S.P.S. Khanuja, A.K. Shasany, and S. Kumar. 2002. Development of a superior somaclone of rose-scented geranium and a protocol for inducing variants. *HortScience* 37:632–636.

Hammer, P.A. 1991. Nutrition, pp. 18–22 in *Tips on Growing Zonal Geraniums*, 2nd ed., H.K. Tayama and T.J. Roll, editors. Ohio Cooperative Extension Service, Ohio State University, Columbus.

Hammer, P.A., and K. Rane. 1999. Southern bacterial wilt found in geraniums. *GrowerTalks* 63(3): 80, 82.

Hansen, M., H. Grønborg, N. Starkey, and L. Hansen. 1993. Alternative substrates for potted plants. *Acta Horticulturae* 342:191–196.

Hausbeck, M.K., C.T. Stephens, and R.D. Heins. 1987. Variation in resistance of geraniums to *Pythium ultimum* in presence or absence of silver thiosulfate. *HortScience* 22:940–943.

Heins, R., N. Lange, T.F. Wallace, Jr., and W. Carlson. 1994. *Plug Storage, Cold Storage of Plug Seedlings*. Meister Publishing, Willoughby, Ohio.

Horst, R.K. 1990. Geranium, pp. 653–654 in *Westcott's Plant Disease Handbook*, 5th ed. Van Nostrand Reinhold, New York.

Huxley, A., M. Griffiths, and M. Levy. 1992. *Pelargonium*, pp. 498–504 in *The New Royal Horticultural Society Dictionary of Gardening*, vol. 3. Stockton Press, New York.

Jonas, V.M., and K.A. Williams. 2000. Optimum irrigation and fertilization regimes for ivy geranium (*Pelargonium peltatum*). *HortScience* 35:508. (Abstract)

Jones, M.L., E.-S. Kim, and S.E. Newman. 2001 Role of ethylene and 1-MCP in flower development and petal abscission in zonal geraniums. *HortScience* 36:1305–1309.

Kaczperski, M.P., and R.D. Heins. 1995. The effect of timing and duration of supplemental irradiance or flower initiation of plug grown geraniums. *HortScience* 30:760. (Abstract)

Kaczperski, M.P., A.M. Armitage, and P.M. Lewis. 1996a. Performance of plug-grown geranium seedlings preconditioned with nitrogen fertilizer or low-temperature storage. *HortScience* 31: 361–363.

Kaczperski, M.P., R.D. Heins, and W.H. Carlson. 1996b. Using temperature, light, and fungicides to prolong the storage life of rooted geraniums cuttings. *HortScience* 31:656. (Abstract)

Kang, J.-G., and M. van Iersel. 2000. Interaction of temperature and fertilizer concentration affect growth of petunia and geranium. *HortScience* 35:457. (Abstract).

Koranski, D.S., and M. Khademi. 1993. Plug culture, pp. 113–123 in *Geraniums IV*, 4th ed., J.W. White, editor. Ball Publishing. Geneva, Illinois.

Lang, H., and K. Trellinger. 2001. Geraniums, pp. 88–92 in *Tips on Regulating Growth of Floriculture Crops*, M.L. Gaston, L.A. Kunkle, P.S. Konjoian, and M.F. Wilt, editors. Ohio Florists' Association Services, Columbus, Ohio.

Langton, F.A., and W. Runger. 1985. *Pelargonium*, pp. 9–21 in *Handbook of Flowering*, vol. IV, A.H. Halevy, editor. CRC Press, Boca Raton, Florida.

Larson, R.A. 1991. Growth regulators, pp. 37–39 in *Tips on Growing Zonal Geraniums*, 2nd ed., H.K.

Tayama and T.J. Roll, editors. Ohio Cooperative Extension Service, Ohio State University, Columbus.

Larson, R.A. 1993. Vegetative propagation—Tissue culture, pp. 87–95 in *Geraniums IV*, 4th ed., J.W. White, editor. Ball Publishing, Geneva, Illinois.

Lee, C.W., J.-M. Choi, and C.-H. Pak. 1996. Micronutrient toxicity in seed geraniums (*Pelargonium ×hortorum* Bailey). *Journal of the American Society for Horticultural Science* 121:77–82.

Lindquist, R.K. 1993. Insects and other pests—Integrated insect and mite management, pp. 313–315 in *Geraniums IV*, 4th ed., J.W. White, editor. Ball Publishing, Geneva, Illinois.

Mastalerz, J.W. 1967. Geraniums in six weeks. *Pennsylvania Flower Growers' Bulletin* 193:1–9.

Miranda, R.M., and W.H. Carlson. 1980. The effect of timing and number of applications of chlormequat and ancymidol on the growth and flowering of seed geraniums. *Journal of the American Society for Horticultural Science* 105:273–277.

Morvant, J.K., J.M. Dole, and J.C. Cole. 2001. Fertilizer source and irrigation system affect geranium growth and nitrogen retention. *HortScience* 36:1022–1026.

O'Donovan, E.J. 1993. Stock plants, pp. 75–85 in *Geranium IV*, 4th ed., J.W. White, editor. Ball Publishing, Geneva, Illinois.

Oglevee, J.R. 1991. Stock plant management, pp. 2–11 in *Tips on Growing Zonal Geraniums*, 2nd ed., H.K. Tayama, editor. Ohio Cooperative Extension Service, Ohio State University, Columbus.

Oglevee-O'Donovan, W. 1993. Clean stock production—Culture—Indexing for vascular wilts and viruses, pp. 277–286 in *Geranium IV*, 4th ed., J.W. White, editor. Ball Publishing, Geneva, Illinois.

Paton, F., and W.W. Schwabe. 1987. Storage of cuttings of *Pelargonium ×hortorum* Bailey. *Journal of Horticultural Science* 62:79–87.

Post, K. 1942. *Effects of Daylight and Temperature on Growth and Flowering of Some Florist Crops*. Cornell Agricultural Experimental Station Bulletin.

Post, K. 1949. *Pelargonium*, pp. 730–737 in *Florist Crop Production and Marketing*, Orange Judd Publishing, New York.

Quatchak, D.J., J.W. White, and E.J. Holcomb. 1986. Temperature, supplemental lighting and chlormequat chloride effects on flowering of geranium seedlings. *Journal of the American Society for Horticultural Science* 111:376–379.

Roberts, D.L. 1997. Major geranium diseases. *Professional Plant Growers Association News* 28(1):21–22.

Rogers, M.N. 1982. Stock plants, pp. 114–133 in *Geraniums III*, 3rd ed., J.W. Mastalerz and E.J. Holcomb, editors. Pennsylvania Flower Growers, University Park, Pennsylvania.

Serek, M., A. Prabucki, E.C. Sisler, and A.S. Andersen. 1998. Inhibitors of ethylene action affect final quality and rooting of cuttings before and after storage. *HortScience* 153–155.

Shaw, R.J., and M.N. Rogers. 1964. Interactions between elevated carbon dioxide levels and greenhouse temperatures on the growth of roses, chrysanthemums, carnations, geraniums and African violets. Part 5. Various flowers. *Florists' Review* 135(3491):19, 37–39.

Simone, O. 1997. And now there are four: Foliar bacterial diseases of geranium. *Greenhouse Product News* 7(6):38–41.

Starman, T.W., T.A. Cerny, and T.L. Grindstaff. 1994. Seed geraniums growth and flowering responses to uniconazole. *HortScience* 29:865–867.

Tammen, J.F. 1960. Disease-free geraniums from cultured cuttings. *Pennsylvania Flower Growers' Bulletin* 117:1, 6–9.

Tayama, H.K., and S.A. Carver. 1992. Comparison of resin-coated and soluble fertilizer formulations in the production of zonal geranium, potted chrysanthemum and poinsettia. *HortTechnology* 2:476–479.

Tayama, H.K., and J.M. Klesa. 1991. Scheduling, pp. 34–36 in *Tips on Growing Zonal Geraniums*, 2nd ed., H.K. Tayama and T.J. Roll, editors. Ohio Cooperative Extension Service, Ohio State University, Columbus.

Trellinger, K. 1997. Top 10 tips for perfect ivy geraniums. *GrowerTalks* 61(8):73, 75.

Uchneat, M.S., K. Spicer, and R. Craig. 1999. Differential response to floral infection by *Botrytis cinerea* within the genus *Pelargonium*. *HortScience* 34:718–720.

Van der Walt, J.J.A. 1977. *Pelargoniums of Southern Africa*. Purnell and Sons, S.A. Limited, Cape Town.

Wetzstein, H.Y., and A. Armitage. 1983. Inflorescence and floral development in *Pelargonium ×hortorum*. *Journal of the American Society for Horticultural Science* 108:595–600.

Whealy, C.A. 1993. Tree geraniums—Satisfaction geranium trees, pp. 137–140 in *Geraniums IV*, 4th ed., J.W. White, editor. Ball Publishing, Geneva, Illinois.

White, J.W. 1993. pp. 215–298 in *Geraniums IV*, 4th ed. Ball Publishing, Geneva, Illinois.

White, J.W., and S.M. Polys. 1987. Photon flux and leaf temperature effects on flower initiation and early development of 'Red Elite' geraniums. *Journal of the American Society for Horticultural Science* 112:945–950.

White, J.W., and I.J. Warrington. 1984. Effects of split night temperatures, light and chlormequat on growth and carbohydrate status of *Pelargonium ×hortorum*. *Journal of the American Society for Horticultural Science* 109:458–463.

Willumsen, K., and T. Fjeld. 1995. The sensitivity of some flowering potted plants to exogenous ethylene. *Acta Horticulturae* 405:362–371.

Pericallis

INTRODUCTION

Common name: cineraria.

Scientific name: *Pericallis* ×*hybrida* R. Nordenstam (Huxley et al., 1992).

Family and related taxa: Compositae Giseke. The florists' cineraria is thought to be developed from *P. lanata* (L'Herit.) R. Nordenstam, *P. cruenta* (L'Herit.) R. Nordenstam, and possibly other species. There are approximately 14 species of *Pericallis* and the genus was formerly considered part of the genus *Senecio*. The Compositae family contains many important ornamental crops including *Aster, Calendula, Callistephus, Centaurea, Chrysanthemum, Cosmos, Dahlia, Dendranthema, Echinacea, Gerbera, Helianthus, Liatris, Pericallis, Solidago, Tagetes,* and *Zinnia.*

Origin: The parent species are natives of the Canary Islands (Bailey and Bailey, 1976).

Uses and current status: An attractive spring potted flowering plant whose height can range from less than 12 in. up to 3 ft (30 to 90 cm) (Fig. II-1 Pericallis).

The terminal inflorescence is a corymb made up of numerous individual flowers. The outer ray floret colors include white, pink, red, deep to pale blue, purple, or violet. The ray flowers can also be bicolored with the base usually white; the disc flowers are yellow. The leaves are ovate and can become large and form a rosette (Bailey and Bailey, 1976). The cineraria is a perennial; however, it is treated as an annual in commercial production.

CULTIVARS

Two dwarf types are common: the grandiflora with large flowers and the multiflora with small flowers (Nau, 1984). Cultivars vary in regard to the duration of cold temperature required for floral induction (Hildrum, 1967, 1969; Larsen, 1985; Strømme and Hildrum, 1985). Early flowering cultivars are available that flower in January if seeded in August (Strømme and Hildrum, 1985).

PROPAGATION

This colorful potted plant is universally propagated from seed. The germination temperature ranges from 68 to 81°F (20 to 27°C), though 68 to 72°F (20 to 22°C) was deemed optimal (Kaukovirta, 1973). *In vitro* propagation has been achieved (Cockrel et al., 1986).

FLOWERING CONTROL AND DORMANCY

Cineraria is a facultative cold requiring plant; flowering is promoted by cold temperatures and delayed by warm temperatures (Yeh et al., 1997a). A 5- to 6-week cold treatment of 50 to 55°F (10 to 13°C) is suggested for flower initiation and development, although induction can occur in as little as 2 weeks (Hildrum, 1969; Post, 1942; Strømme and Hildrum, 1985). Vernalization occurs between the temperatures of 32 and 60°F (0 and 16°C) with the optimum vernalization temperature being 43°F (6°C) (Yeh et al., 1997a). Plants must be old enough to respond to a 54°F (12°C) cold treatment; plants 8 to 10 weeks old are capable of perceiving the cold temperature. Yeh and Atherton

FIGURE II-I PERICALLIS Potted *Pericallis* plants.

(1997b) reported that six or more leaves must be formed by the plant for rapid flower initiation when cold treated at 41 to 45°F (5 to 7°C). Interestingly, chilling imbibed seed at 39°F (4°C) for 4 weeks resulted in faster flower initiation when plants were subsequently grown at 68°F (20°C). The effect of chilling on imbibed seed was not apparent when plants were grown at 50 or 59°F (10 or 15°C).

Gibberellic acid (GA_3) at 100 ppm can substitute for cold treatment, but plants elongate (Strømme and Hildrum, 1985). Larsen (1985) documented the floral development and suggested that with proper cultivar selection, cineraria could be flowered year-round.

TEMPERATURE

In 1942, Post found that a temperature of 59°F (15°C) or lower was required for flowering. There are cultivar differences and this critical temperature can range from 54 to 64°F (12 to 18°C) (Hildrum, 1967, 1969; Strømme and Hildrum, 1985). At a constant temperature, plants flowered the quickest at 54°F (12°C) (Hildrum, 1969). After flower initiation, which requires 4 to 6 weeks, temperatures can be increased for rapid development. The suggested production temperature is 59°F (15°C), certainly below 64°F (18°C) for quality plants (Hildrum, 1967). Mature plants with 6 to 8 leaves can be devernalized if subjected to 68 or 77°F (20 or 25°C) after receiving only 1 or 2 weeks of 43°F (6°C) (Yeh et al., 1997b). However, devernalization did not occur with plants that have been cold treated for 4 weeks at 43°F (6°C).

LIGHT

Day lengths of 8 to 12 hr accelerated floral initiation and LD delayed flower initiation when plants were grown at 57 to 64°F (14 to 18°C) (Yeh and Atherton, 1997a). The optimum photoperiod was 12 hr and 15 to 20 SD accelerated flowering, depending on the cultivar.

Cineraria can be grown at light levels as low as 1000 fc (200 μmol $\cdot$ m^{-2} $\cdot$ s^{-1}); it is one of the few plants that can grow in Norway during the winter without supplemental lighting (Hildrum, 1969). After floral induction, 223 and 1090 fc (49 and 163 μmol $\cdot$ m^{-2} $\cdot$ s^{-1}) from incandescent or fluorescent lamps decreased crop time by 10 to 14 days (Hildrum, 1967). However, plant height increased to an unacceptable degree by incandescent light (Hildrum, 1967; Post, 1942; Wasscher, 1950); fluorescent does not have the same effect (Hildrum, 1967; Wasscher, 1950). Young plants given high light for 12 weeks, followed by lower light levels, flowered faster than when the sequence was reversed (Kaukovirta, 1973).

WATER

Cineraria should not be allowed to wilt, which is no easy task because the leaves frequently become large and the plants readily wilt. However, if grown too moist, plants have the tendency to become too large.

CARBON DIOXIDE

It is not known whether increasing CO_2 levels over ambient is beneficial.

NUTRITION

Cineraria do not require high levels of nutrition. Weekly applications of 150 ppm N or constant liquid fertilization of 100 ppm are adequate. The use of nitrate rather than ammonium or urea nitrogen is a must. With soilless media, minor elements must be added (Nau, 1984) (see Physiological Disorders, page 742).

MEDIA

Most commercial premixed media should be adequate. Various media have been used: Finnish peat (Kaukovirta, 1973); peat compost (Larsen, 1985); or loam, sand, and peat (Potter, 1962).

HEIGHT CONTROL

Cycocel (chlormequat) has no effect on stem height, whereas B-Nine (daminozide) controls it (Strømme and Hildrum, 1985). Nau (1984) suggested two B-Nine sprays (2500 ppm), the first at 14 to 21 days after placing the plug in the final pot size, and the second 10 days later. Adriansen (1985) noted that A-Rest (ancymidal) was also effective in controlling height.

SPACING

Spacing will vary depending on whether plants are grown in 4-, 5-, or 6-in. (10-, 13-, or 15-cm) pots. Economics dictate whether pots are set pot-to-pot after transplanting and then later spaced. Do not allow plants to become crowded. Plants thrive if air movement is good; this is a must for powdery mildew disease control. Regardless, final spacing of 8 × 8 or 10 × 10 in. (20 × 20 or 25 × 25 cm) is ample for 4- or 6-in. (10- or 15-cm) pot production, respectively (Potter, 1962).

PINCHING AND DISBUDDING

No pinching or disbudding required.

SUPPORT

No support required unless plants become too tall.

SCHEDULE AND TIMING

Valentine's Day and Mother's Day are common production targets. When seeded in July, plants flower shortly after Christmas; in early September, plants flower in early March. Seeding dates can be staggered; 20 to 27 weeks are required to flower. Transplant young plants within 3 to 4 weeks from seed flats into cell packs or, better, seed directly into the plugs. Temperatures at this stage can be 68 to 77°F (20 to 25°C) for maximum growth (Kaukovirta, 1973; Potter, 1962). When using cell packs, shift plants into the final pot after 4 to 5 weeks. To induce floral initiation at this time, temperatures are lowered for 4 to 6 weeks to 43 to 54°F (6 to 12°C). After floral initiation, temperatures are increased to 55°F (13°C) (Nau, 1984). Most plants sold are in 4.5- to 6-in. (12- to 15-cm) pots.

Strømme and Hildrum (1985) recommend favorable growing conditions of high light and 68 to 77°F (20 to 25°C) for 8 to 10 weeks, then 48 and 55°F (9 and 13°C) for 6 weeks, then 59°F (15°C). Potter (1962) stated 22 weeks are required for production (Table II-1 Pericallis).

INSECTS

Aphids, thrips, red spider mites, and whiteflies can occur. Thrips spread tomato spotted wilt and impatiens necrotic spot viruses and should be controlled (Nau, 1984).

DISEASES

Alternaria leaf spot, *Botrytis*, and powdery mildew (*Erysiphe cichoracearum*) can occur on flowers and foliage. The best means of control is to keep the foliage dry (Nau, 1984). Various root and stem rots can occur if plants are overwatered or plugs are planted too deeply (*Fusarium*, *Phytophthora*, *Pythium ultimum*, *Rhizoctonia solani*, *Schlerotinia sclerotiorum*, or *Thielaviopsis basicola*) (Horst, 1990). Verticillium stem wilt can occur. Tomato spotted wilt and impatiens necrotic spot viruses can be serious and cause various leaf and petiole symptoms (Daughtrey and Chase, 1992). Downy mildew (*Plasmopara halstedii*) has also been reported (Dreistadt, 2001).

TABLE II-1 PERICALLIS

Sample schedule for production of 5-in. flowering *Pericallis* potted plants using direct seeding into plugs. Plants grown in 6-in. (15-cm) pots require an additional 2 weeks (Nau, 1984).

Cultural Step	Production Time (weeks)	Temperature °F (°C)	Photoperiod
Sow seed in plugs			
	1–2	68–72 (20–22)	Ambient
Germinate			
	2	65–68 (18–20)	Ambient
Transplant and space pot-to-pot			
	3–4	65–68 (18–20)	Ambient
Space			
	2	65–68 (18–20)	Ambient
Lower temperature for flower initiation			
	4–6	43–54 (6–12)	12 hr
Increase temperature for flower development			
	7–9	55–59 (13–16)	Ambient
Flower and clear bench			
	1–2	55–59 (13–16)	Ambient
Total	22–27		

PHYSIOLOGICAL DISORDERS

If the cold treatment is too short or too warm, small inflorescence size or malformed flower development can occur (Wilkins, 1974). If high levels of ammonium are used, leaves roll up and turn silvery green (Nau, 1984) (see Nutrition, page 741). Foliar chlorosis from iron deficiency can occur if medium pH is too high.

Leaf burning may be due to high light levels, especially in combination with warm temperatures (Hamrick, 2003). Boron deficiency can appear as stunting and distorted and mottled leaves. The problem is accentuated during warm weather due to frequent irrigation. Excessively large leaves can be due to overfertilization or low light in combination with high temperatures.

POSTHARVEST

Customers should be informed to keep this plant as cool as possible, 55°F (13°C) would be ideal, and in a sunny location for maximum life. Postproduction life is 10 days versus 20 if kept at 50 fc (10 μmol $\cdot$ m^{-2} $\cdot$ s^{-1}) versus 250 fc (50 μmol $\cdot$ m^{-2} $\cdot$ s^{-1}). Plants apparently have a low sensitivity to ethylene; however, 2 mM silver thiosulfate (STS) can be used as a spray to prolong shelf life. Transport at 41 to 50°F (5 to 10°C) (Nowak and Rudnicki, 1990; Tijskens et al., 1996).

KEY POINTS

- Cineraria is used as a potted flowering plant.
- Plants are propagated by seed.
- Temperatures below 64°F (18°C) are required for flower initiation; a 4- to 6-week cold treatment of 43 to 55°F (6 to 13°C) is recommended.
- Juvenility must be considered because plants must be 8 to 10 weeks old, and have six or more leaves, to respond to the cold treatment.

- Although plants use a large amount of water, they should not be allowed to wilt.
- Plants should also not be grown too moist or plants will become excessively large.
- Whiteflies and thrips are major insect problems.
- Impatiens necrotic spot and tomato spotted wilt viruses can be major concerns.

BIBLIOGRAPHY

Adriansen, E. 1985. Kemisk vækstregulering, pp. 142–162 in *Potteplanter I—Produktion, Metoder, Midler*, O.V. Christensen, A. Klougart, I.S. Pedersen, and K. Wikesjö, editors. GartnerINFO, København, Denmark. (in Danish)

Bailey, L.H., and E.Z. Bailey. 1976. *Senecio*, pp. 272, 1034–1038 in *Hortus Third: A Concise Dictionary of Plants Cultivated in the United States and Canada*. Macmillan, New York.

Cockrel, A.D., G.L. McDaniel, and E.T. Graham. 1986. *In vitro* propagation of florists' cineraria. *HortScience* 21:139–140.

Daughtrey, M., and A.R. Chase. 1992. *Cineraria*, pp. 39–42 in *Ball Field Guide to Diseases of Greenhouse Ornamentals*. Ball Publishing, Geneva, Illinois.

Dreistadt, S.H. 2001. *Integrated Pest Management for Floriculture and Nurseries*. University of California Division of Agriculture and Natural Resources Publication 3402.

Hamrick, D. 2003. *Pericallis*, pp. 564–565 in *Ball Redbook*, vol. 2, 17th ed. Ball Publishing, Batavia, Illinois.

Hildrum, H. 1967. The effect of temperature and day length on growth and flowering of cineraria (*Senecio cruentus* L.). *Gartneryrket* 57:849–851. (in Norwegian)

Hildrum, H. 1969. Factors affecting flowering in *Senecio cruentus* D.C. *Acta Horticulturae* 14: 117–123.

Horst, R.K. 1990. Cineraria, p. 598 in *Westcott's Plant Disease Handbook*, 5th ed. Van Nostrand Reinhold, New York.

Huxley, A., M. Griffiths, and M. Levy. 1992. *Pericallus*, p. 525 in *The New Royal Horticultural Society Dictionary of Gardening*, vol. 3. Stockton Press, New York.

Kaukovirta, E. 1973. Effects of temperature and light intensity on the growth of *Senecio ×hybridus* Hyl. seedlings. *Acta Horticulturae* 31: 63–69.

Larsen, R. 1985. Temperature and flower induction of *Senecio ×hybridus* Hyl. *Swedish Journal of Agricultural Research* 15:87–92.

Nau, J. 1984. Cineraria: Sow now for late-winter sales. *Florists' Review* 175(4528):8–9.

Nowak, J., and R.M. Rudnicki. 1990. *Postharvest Handling and Storage of Cut Flowers, Florist Greens, and Potted Plants.* Timber Press, Portland, Oregon.

Post, K. 1942. Effect of daylength and temperature on growth and flowering of some florist crops. *Cornell Agriculture Experiment Station Bulletin* 787:1–10.

Potter, C.N. 1962. Flowering pot plants: Cinerarias for color. *Florists' Review* 129(3352):23–24, 53.

Strømme, E., and H. Hildrum. 1985. *Senecio cruentus,* pp. 306–308 in *Handbook of Flowering,* vol. IV, A.H. Halevy, editor. CRC Press, Boca Raton, Florida.

Tijskens, L.M.M., M. Sloof, E.C. Wilkinson, and W.G. van Doorn. 1996. A model of the effects of temperature and time on the acceptability of potted plants stored in darkness. *Postharvest Biology and Technology* 8:293–305.

Wasscher, J. 1950. Belichtingsproeven, p. 72. *Jaarverslag, Proefsation voorde Bloeminstreij*; Aalsmeer. (in Dutch)

Wilkins, H.F. 1974. Cineraria (*Senecio cruentus*). *Minnesota State Florist Bulletin,* Dec.:13–14.

Yeh, D.M., and J.G. Atherton. 1997a. Manipulation of flowering in cineraria. I. Effects of photoperiod. *Journal of Horticultural Science* 72:43–54.

Yeh, D.M., and J.G. Atherton. 1997b. Manipulation of flowering in cineraria. II. Juvenility. *Journal of Horticultural Science* 72:55–66.

Yeh, D.M., J.G. Atherton, and J. Craigon. 1997a. Manipulation of flowering in cineraria. III. Cardinal temperatures and thermal times for vernalization. *Journal of Horticultural Science* 72:379–387.

Yeh, D.M., J.G. Atherton, and J. Craigon. 1997b. Manipulation of flowering in cineraria. IV. Devernalization. *Journal of Horticultural Science* 72: 545–551.

Petunia

INTRODUCTION

Common name: petunia.

Scientific name: *Petunia* ×*hybrida* hort. Vilm.-Andr. (Huxley et al., 1992).

Family and related taxa: Solanaceae Juss. There are 35 species in the genus *Petunia*. *P.* ×*hybrida* is derived from crosses between *P. axillaris* (Lam.) BSD and *P. integrifolia* (Hook.) Schinz and Thell. Solanaceae also includes important food crops such as tomato (*Lycopersicon*) and potato (*Solanum*) and a number of ornamentals including *Browallia, Brugmansia, Capsicum, Nicotiana, Salpiglossis,* and *Schizanthus*.

Origin: All petunia species are natives to Argentina, Brazil, or Uruguay.

Uses and current status: Petunias are grown for their showy flowers, making them a popular summer bedding plant. In warm climates petunias are perennial but are used as annuals in temperate zones (Armitage, 1985; Bailey and Bailey, 1976). Many of the vegetatively propagated petunias can tolerate temperatures below freezing (Weidner, 1994). Petunias are used in mass plantings, porch boxes, tubs, and hanging baskets (Figs. II-1, II-2, and II-3 Petunia).

CULTIVARS

Historically, the six classifications of hybrid seed petunias were grandiflora doubles, multiflora doubles, California giants, single grandifloras, single multiflora, and single floribunda. New types of petunias have been released: "millifloras" with numerous small flowers and vegetatively propagated petunias with vigorous, trailing growth (Weidner, 1994). The latter are

FIGURE II-1 PETUNIA Close-up of seed-propagated *Petunia* flowers.

FIGURE II-2 PETUNIA Vegetatively propagated *Petunia* 'Doubloon Blue Star' bedding plant.

FIGURE II-3 PETUNIA Seed-propagated *Petunia* 'Wave' hanging baskets.

the result of the reintroduction of *P. axillaris* genes into the seed-propagated hybrids (*P. axillaris* × *P. integrifolia*). The single grandifloras have been the most common or popular group on the market; however, new cultivar releases of vegetatively propagated petunias have dramatically increased interest in the petunia. Vegetatively propagated petunias are asexually propagated by cuttings because this group produces few or no seed. The first series released were the "Supertunias." Numerous series of cutting-propagated petunias are now available with single or double flowers. The seed-propagated 'Wave' series has similar characteristics to cutting-propagated petunias but a more restricted color range. Numerous cultivars are available in a wide range of colors and color combinations in all classifications.

PROPAGATION

Propagation is primarily by seed with 245,000 to 285,000/oz (8600 to 10,000/g). Uncovered seeds germinate within 10 to 12 days when at 75 to 78°F (24 to 26°C). Some cultivars required light, others dark (Holcomb and Mastalerz, 1985). Numerous cultivars are propagated by terminal cuttings.

For plug production the following conditions are used (Ball, 1991; Britten, 1999; Sawaya, 2001):

Stage 1: Seed uncovered, 75 to 78°F (24 to 26°C), for 3 to 5 days; 2500-ppm B-Nine (daminozide) or 8-ppm A-Rest (ancymidol) sprays can be applied.

Stage 2: 72 to 78°F (22 to 26°C), for 14 days, 50 to 75 ppm N once or twice/week; 5000-ppm B-Nine, 4-ppm Bonzi (paclobutrazol), 1-ppm Sumagic (uniconazole), or 8-ppm A-Rest sprays can be applied.

Stage 3: 62 to 68°F (16 to 20°C), for 14 days, 150 ppm N once or twice/week; 5000-ppm B-Nine, 4-ppm Bonzi, or 1-ppm Sumagic sprays can be applied.

Stage 4: 62 to 65°F (17 to 18°C), for 7 to 10 days, fertilizer as needed.

Plugs should be ready for marketing or transplanting within 5 to 6 weeks (see Chapter 1, Propagation, for description of plug stages).

FLOWERING CONTROL AND DORMANCY

Petunias become reproductive at the sixth leaf stage. The rate of vegetative and reproductive development is dependent on light duration, intensity, and quality interacting with temperature. Flowering will occur under LD or SD; however, plants will flower earlier with longer photoperiods and higher light intensities (Karlsson, 1996). Consequently, petunias are a facultative LD plant with the critical night length for flowering between 13 and 10 hr (Wilkins and Pemberton, 1981). However, many newly released cultivars of cutting-propagated petunias appear to be DN or SD plants (Dole et al., 2002). High light intensity can overcome photoperiod in that some cultivars are LD plants under ambient light and DN under supplemental HID lighting. Adams et al. (1998) found that time to first flower decreased as day length increased from 8 to an optimum day length of 14.4 hr; no increase in growth occurred at longer day lengths.

Photoperiod has a distinctive effect on the plant morphology of seed-propagated petunias

(Adams et al., 1998; Merritt and Kohl, 1982; Piringer and Cathey, 1960). Under SD plants are well branched with a compact to trailing habit, and under LD plants are strongly upright with fewer axillary shoots.

TEMPERATURE

Temperature influences rate of flowering and the number of axillary branches and interacts with photoperiod. Flowering is rapid at 70 to 79°F (21 to 26°C) and slow at 50 to 59°F (10 to 15°C). The optimum temperature for rapid flowering was 77°F (25°C) (Kaczperski et al., 1991). Branching is enhanced by the cooler temperatures, even under LD, and increasing temperature decreases branching and increases height (Kaczperski et al., 1991). Rate of flower development is most rapid at warmer temperatures even under SD (Piringer and Cathey, 1960; Wilkins and Pemberton, 1981). Adams et al. (1998) found that the growth rate linearly increased from 43 to 79°F (6 to 26°C).

LIGHT

Light intensity interacts with duration in that as total light energy increases, photosynthesis is enhanced, which hastens the transition from the juvenile or vegetative stage to the reproductive stage. At any one photoperiod, higher light intensity will result in more rapid flowering (Adams et al., 1998). Supplemental HID lighting speeds the transition from vegetative to reproductive, even if HID lighting is for only 15 days, commencing immediately after germination (Carpenter and Carlson, 1973). Supplemental lighting for 5 days from the 10th to 15th day after germination or for 10 days from the 10th to the 20th day after germination was most effective (Graper et al., 1990). For cutting-propagated petunias, HID lighting during propagation is beneficial (Dole et al., 2002).

Likewise, light quality influences rate of flowering. As with most LD species, far-red (incandescent) light sources promote flowering when compared with red (fluorescent) light sources (Lane et al., 1965; Piringer and Cathey, 1960).

WATER

Water is a critical aspect of growth. Water restriction is frequently used to slow growth rates and thus prevent rapid flowering, but may reduce plant quality (Flohr and Conover, 1994).

CARBON DIOXIDE

Supplemental carbon dioxide (1000 ppm) for only 2 weeks during the early juvenile phase of growth hastens flowering (Krizek et al., 1968). The effect of supplemental carbon dioxide varies with the photoperiod (Reekie et al., 1997). Higher CO_2 rates increased number of buds, open flowers, and height but decreased branching and time to flowering, with a greater effect under 9-hr SD than 13-hr LD.

NUTRITION

Petunias generally require relatively high levels of nitrogen during production with constant liquid fertilization rates of approximately 200 ppm for seed-propagated petunias and 250 to 350 ppm for cutting-propagated types (Dole et al., 2002; Konjoian, 2001; Shaw, 1998; van Iersel et al., 1998). Lower rates of up to 100 ppm are used during plug production for seed-propagated petunias. During plug production P and K rates have relatively little effect on seedlings (van Iersel et al., 1998). Recommendations call for reducing the routinely high rates of P and K typically used in petunia production (Cox, 2000; van Iersel et al., 1998). Even during finished plant production rates of 50 ppm P are adequate (James and van Iersel, 1998).

Nutrition may be used to control growth rate. Low nitrogen rates can be used to reduce growth for both seed and cutting-propagated types. After planting plugs, nitrogen rates of 150 ppm for cutting-propagated petunias produced large plants with light-green foliage, whereas 0 ppm N was required to control growth (Dole et al., 2002). Higher N rates can be used for 1 to 2 weeks prior to marketing to make the foliage greener.

Ammonium should be avoided if cold production temperatures are used to prevent ammonium toxicity. Petunia nutrition is reviewed by Nelson (1985). Foliar nutrient levels for high-quality plants are listed in Chapter 6, Nutrition, Table 6-4. The levels of several micronutrients that can cause foliar toxicity symptoms and reduce growth are 5.4 ppm B, 32 ppm Cu, 28 ppm Mn, 24 ppm Mo, and 16 ppm Zn (Lee et al., 1992).

MEDIA

Various media are used but peat-based mixes are most common (White, 1985). Coir-based media are also effective (Evans and Stamps, 1996).

HEIGHT CONTROL

Height control, short internodes, and high numbers of axillary shoots are the primary horticultural challenges during production. When plants are started in early spring under natural SD and brief durations of twilight (which is high in far-red light), growth is slow and branching or rosetting occurs. When spring advances with longer days and twilight periods, growth and flowering is very rapid, but branching is poor and internodes are long. Light quality influences internode length (Karlsson and Nilsen, 1995; Wilkins and Pemberton, 1981).

Several plant growth regulators can be used to control height during production of seed-propagated petunias: B-Nine sprays at 2500 to 5000 ppm, A-Rest sprays at 15 to 26 ppm , Bonzi sprays at 15 to 45 ppm, or Sumagic sprays at 25 to 50 ppm (Armitage, 1985; Bailey, 1995; Barrett and Nell, 1990; Bell, 2001). Topflor (flurprimidol) sprays can be used at 20 to 60 ppm (SePRO, personal communication). Bonzi at 390 ppb and A-Rest at 80 ppb are also effective when applied through subirrigation (Million et al., 1999). This work also highlights the potential effects of contamination from plant growth regulators on subirrigation benches. Bonzi at 20 to 60 ppm and Sumagic at 5 to 7.5 ppm can also be sprayed on the media surface immediately prior to planting (Barrett et al., 1999; Bell, 2001). Adriansen (1985) noted that Cycocel (chlormequat) is also effective on petunias. A tank mix of 1000 ppm Cycocel and 800 ppm B-Nine can be used (Kuehny et al., 2001). See Propagation section for the application of growth retardants during plug production.

Cutting-propagated petunias require higher plant growth regulator application rates or more frequent applications than seed-propagated petunias. Recommendations include single Sumagic sprays at 20 to 30 ppm or two sprays with the first application at 20 ppm and the second at 10 ppm (Dole et al., 2002; Starman, 2001). Two spray applications of B-Nine at 7500 ppm, single A-Rest sprays at 100 ppm, or one Bonzi drench at 5 ppm or spray at 40 to 60 ppm can be used (Dole et al., 2002; Wang, 1999).

Use of N or P restriction and water stress is effective (Cox, 2000; Dole et al., 2002). Higher N rates can be applied 1 to 2 weeks prior to marketing to green the foliage. DIF is effective but DROP may not be (Moe et al., 1995). Mechanical stress from brushing also reduces height (Autio et al., 1994).

SPACING

Spacing must be considered on three occasions: seeding, transplanting, and planting in the garden. Historically, seeds were hand sown onto the medium in flats and then transplanted into packs or baskets. Presently, individual seeds are sown directly into plug trays and then transplanted into the final sales container. Generally, final spacing for the container, hanging basket, tub, or garden is 10 in. (25.5 cm) for seed-propagated petunias (Nau, 1991). Flats are placed flat-to-flat.

Cutting-propagated petunias are quite vigorous and readily intertwine, which makes marketing difficult. Provide as much space as possible for pots and baskets. Cutting-propagated petunias are not sold in flats.

PINCHING AND DISBUDDING

Pinching is not required; however, if plants become too tall in the flat, they can be cut back. Disbudding is neither practiced nor practical. The long vines of many cutting-propagated cultivars can be pinched at any time to increase axillary branching and control growth. Florel (ethephon) at 500 ppm increases branching but greatly delays flowering (Dole et al., 2002; Wang, 1999).

Flowers can be removed by the home gardener to aid in *Botrytis* control for the large-flowered single or double grandiflora types. Overgrown, lanky plants in the garden can be sheared back to allow for vigorous regrowth and renewed flowering later in the season.

SUPPORT

No support needed.

SCHEDULE AND TIMING

Scheduling and timing vary with the latitude as spring advances. As indicated, short, well-branched, rosette-type plants are desired. Though Krizek and colleagues (1968) were able to produce a flowering plant from seed in only 35 days, the quality was undesirable. On the other hand, numerous producers start weeks or months too early and hold the plant under cold, dry, and low-nutrient conditions. This may be uneconomical and may result in a plant that does not perform well for the customer. This long production process may be due to lack of understanding of the physiology of this plant or lack of greenhouse automation as large numbers of plants must frequently be produced for sales during a brief 2- to 3-week time span.

Production of seed-propagated petunias requires 13 weeks in the winter and 8 weeks in the spring (Armitage, 1985). Generally, plugs are ready for transplanting in 5 to 6 weeks after sowing and buds are visible 2 to 3 weeks before plants are marketable.

Vegetatively propagated petunias in 4- to 6-in. (10- to 15-cm) pots will be marketable in 5 to 7 weeks without a pinch; add 2 more weeks if pinching (Dole et al., 2002). Generally one rooted cutting is used per pot; however, crop time can be reduced by using two cuttings/6-in. (15-cm) pot. Plant three to four cuttings per hanging basket, which will finish in 6 to 11 weeks. Winter production will take 1 to 2 weeks longer than late spring production due to lower light levels and cooler temperatures.

INSECTS

Petunias are more insect resistant than many bedding plants, but thrips, aphids, whiteflies, fungus gnats, and caterpillars can be a problem.

DISEASES

Rhizoctonia and *Schlerotinia* result in basal stem canker and lower leaf collapse and yellowing (Daughtrey and Chase, 1992). *Botrytis* is a common problem on open flowers and can quickly eliminate summer floral displays after a rain or periods of high humidity. Cultivars vary considerably in their resistance to *Botrytis* (Krahl and Randle, 1999). Root knot nematodes (*Meloidogyne*) may cause problems outdoors (Horst, 1990). Numerous other diseases have been reported including crown and root rot (*Pythium*

and *Phytophthora*), verticillium wilt (*Verticillium dahliae*), black root rot (*Thielaviopsis basicola*), cottony rot (*Sclerotinia sclerotiorum*), leaf spot (*Mycocentrospora acerina*), powdery mildew (*Oidium*), aster yellows and petunia mosaic, beet curly top, impatiens necrotic spot, and tomato spotted wilt viruses (Dreistadt, 2001). Tobacco mosaic and tomato mosaic viruses have also been documented on cutting-propagated petunias (Cohen et al., 1999).

PHYSIOLOGICAL DISORDERS

Chlorosis can occur with iron deficiency (low pH), nitrogen deficiency, or low temperatures. Excessive vegetative growth of cutting propagated petunias can be due to overfertilization, high ammonium levels, too low of light intensity, or improper photoperiod, especially SD (Hamrick, 2003).

POSTHARVEST

Plugs can be stored at 32 to 50°F (0 to 10°C); the optimum is 36°F (2.2°C). Storage can be in the dark or under 5 fc (1 μmol $\cdot$ m^{-2} $\cdot$ s^{-1}) for 6 weeks (Heins et al., 1994; Kaczperski and Armitage, 1992). Botrytis infections can be a major problem in storage.

Marketable plants should be stored or shipped at 50 to 55°F (10 to 13°C). If long-duration storage is needed, 3000 fc (600 μmol $\cdot$ m^{-2} $\cdot$ s^{-1}) should be used (Armitage, 1985; Armitage and Kowalski, 1983).

Petunia flowers are highly sensitive to ethylene and exposure results in rapid wilting (Nowak and Rudnicki, 1990), but flowers do respond to 0.2 to 0.5 mM silver thiosulfate sprays and to 1-methylcyclopropene (Moe and Fjeld, 1987; Serek et al., 1995).

KEY POINTS

- Petunia is one of the leading bedding plants worldwide and also is grown as a hanging basket plant.
- Commercially plants are seed and cutting propagated.
- The introduction of cutting-propagated vigorous trailing petunia cultivars dramatically increased interest in the petunia.
- Petunia is generally considered a facultative LD plant, but newer cultivars, especially

of cutting-propagated types, are SD to DN plants.
- Flowering and branching are subject to a temperature $\times$ light interaction; SD and cool temperatures of 50 to 59°F (10 to 15°C) promote axillary branching and delay flowering, while LD and high temperatures results in rapid flowering and poor branching.

BIBLIOGRAPHY

Adams, S.R., P. Hadley, and S. Pearson. 1998. The effects of temperature, photoperiod, and photosynthetic photo flux on the time to flowering of petunia 'Express Blush Pink.' *Journal of the American Society for Horticultural Science* 123: 577–580.

Adriansen, E. 1985. Kemisk vækstregulering, pp. 142–162 in *Potteplanter I—Produktion, Metoder, Midler*, O.V. Christensen, A. Klougart, I.S. Pedersen, and K. Wikesjö, editors. GartnerINFO, København, Denmark. (in Danish)

Armitage, A.M. 1985. *Petunia*, pp. 41–46 in *Handbook of Flowering*, vol. IV, A.H. Halevy, editor. CRC Press, Boca Raton, Florida.

Armitage, A.M., and T. Kowalski. 1983. Effects of light intensity and air temperature in simulated postproduction environment on *Petunia hybrida* Vilm. *Journal of the American Society for Horticultural Science* 108:115–118.

Autio, J., I. Voipoi, and T. Koivunen. 1994. Responses of aster, dusty miller, and petunia seedlings to daily exposure to mechanical stress. *HortScience* 29:1449–1452.

Bailey, D.A. 1995. Growth regulators for floricultural crops. *North Carolina Flower Growers Bulletin* 40(6):4–10.

Bailey, L.H., and E.Z. Bailey. 1976. *Petunia*, pp. 850–851 in *Hortus Third: A Concise Dictionary of Plants Cultivated in the United States and Canada*. Macmillan, New York.

Ball, V. 1991. Plugs—The way of the 1990s, pp. 137–153 in *Ball Redbook*, 15th ed. George J. Ball Publishing, West Chicago, Illinois.

Barrett, J.E., and T.A. Nell. 1990. Factors affecting efficacy of paclobutrazol and uniconizole on petunia and chrysanthemum. *Acta Horticulturae* 272:229–234.

Barrett, J.E., C.E. Wieland, T.A. Nell, and D.G. Clark. 1999. Early applications of growth regulators to bedding plants. *HortScience* 34:528. (Abstract)

Bell, M. 2001. Bedding plants and seed geraniums, pp. 54–62 in *Tips on Regulating Growth of Floriculture Crops*, M.L. Gaston, L.A. Kunkle, P.S. Konjoian, and M.F. Wilt, editors. Ohio Florists' Association Services, Columbus, Ohio.

Britten, A. 1999. PGRs at seeding reduce early stretch. *GrowerTalks* 63(5):46, 48.

Carpenter, W.J., and W.H. Carlson. 1973. Comparison of photoperiodic and high intensity lighting on the growth and flowering of *Petunia hybrida* Vilm. *Florists' Review* 154(3998):27–28, 68–71.

Cohen, J., N. Sikron, S. Shuval, and A. Gera. 1999. Susceptibility of vegetatively propagated petunia to tobamovirus infection and its possible control. *HortScience* 34:292–293.

Cox, D. 2000. Low phosphorus controls bedding plant growth. *HortScience* 35:457. (Abstract)

Daughtrey, M., and A.R. Chase. 1992. Petunia, pp. 153–154 in *Ball Field Guide to Diseases of Greenhouse Ornamentals*. Ball Publishing, Geneva, Illinois.

Dole, J.M., B.E. Whipker, and P.V. Nelson. 2002. Producing vegetative petunias and calibrachoa. *Greenhouse Product News* 12(2):30–31, 33, 34.

Dreistadt, S.H. 2001. *Integrated Pest Management for Floriculture and Nurseries*. University of California Division of Agriculture and Natural Resources Publication 3402.

Evans, M.R., and R.H. Stamps. 1996. Growth of bedding plants in sphagnum peat and coir dust-based substrates. *Journal of Environmental Horticulture* 14:187–190.

Flohr, R.C., and C.A Conover. 1994. Production and postproduction watering schedule effects on plant growth, quality and blooming of pansies and petunias. *Proceedings of the Florida State Horticultural Society* 107:414–416.

Graper, D.F., W. Healy, and D. Lang. 1990. Supplemental irradiance control of petunia seedling growth at specific stages of development. *Acta Horticulturae* 272:153–157.

Hamrick, D. 2003. *Petunia*, pp. 567–574 in *Ball Redbook*, vol. 2, 17th ed. Ball Publishing, Batavia, Illinois.

Heins, R., N. Lange, T.F. Wallace, Jr., and W. Carlson. 1994. *Plug Storage, Cold Storage of Plug Seedlings*. Meister Publishing, Willoughby, Ohio.

Holcomb, E.J., and J.W. Mastalerz. 1985. Seedling and seedling production, pp. 87–125 in *Bedding Plants III*, J.W. Mastalerz and E.J. Holcomb, editors. Pennsylvania Flower Growers, University Park, Pennsylvania.

Horst, R.K. 1990. Petunia, pp. 768–769 in *Westcott's Plant Disease Handbook*, 5th ed. Van Nostrand Reinhold, New York.

Huxley, A., M. Griffiths, and M. Levy. 1992. *Petunia*, pp. 533–534 in *The New Royal Horticultural Society Dictionary of Gardening*, vol. 3. Stockton Press, New York.

James, E., and M. van Iersel. 1998. Phosphorus fertilization in ebb and flower production of bedding plants. *HortScience* 33:522. (Abstract)

Kaczperski, M.P., and A.M. Armitage. 1992. Short-term storage of plug-grown bedding plant seedlings. *HortScience* 27:798–800.

Kaczperski, M.P., W.H. Carlson, and M.G. Karlsson. 1991. Growth and development of *Petunia ×hybrida* as a function of temperature and irradiance. *Journal of the American Society for Horticultural Science* 116:232–237.

Karlsson, M. 1996. Control of flowering in petunia by photoperiod and irradiance. *HortScience* 31:681. (Abstract)

Karlsson, M., and J. Nilsen. 1995. Light quality initiating or ending the day affects internode length in petunia. *HortScience* 30:861. (Abstract)

Konjoian, P. 2001. Production pointers for petunias: Seed and vegetative. *Ohio Florists' Association Bulletin* 855:1, 8–10.

Krahl, K.H., and W. M. Randle. 1999. Resistance of petunia phenotypes to *Botrytis cinerea*. *HortScience* 34:690–692.

Krizek, D.T., W.A. Bailey, H.H. Klueter, and H.M. Cathey. 1968. Control environments for seedling production. *Proceedings of International Plant Propagators Society* 18:273–280.

Kuehny, J.S., A. Painter, and P.C. Branch. 2001. Plug source and growth retardants affect finish size of bedding plants. *HortScience* 36:321–323.

Lane, H.C., H.M. Cathey, and L.T. Evans. 1965. The dependency of flowering in several long-day plants on the spectral composition of light extending the photoperiod. *American Journal of Botany* 52:1006–1014.

Lee, C.W., C.-H. Pak, J.-M. Choi, and J.R. Self. 1992. Induced micronutrient toxicity in *Petunia hybrida*. *Journal of Plant Nutrition* 15:327–339.

Merritt, R.H., and J.C. Kohl, Jr. 1982. Effect of root temperature and photoperiod on growth and crop productivity efficiency of petunia. *Journal of the American Society for Horticultural Science* 107:997–1000.

Million, J.B., J.E. Barrett, T.A. Nell, and D.G. Clark. 1999. Inhibiting growth of flowering crops with ancymidol and paclobutrazol in subirrigation water. *HortScience* 34:1103–1105.

Moe, R., and T. Fjeld. 1987. Keeping quality of potted plants as influenced by ethylene. *Gartner Tidende* 101:1580–1583. (in Danish)

Moe, R., K. Willumsen, I.H. Ihlebekk, A.I. Stupa, N.M. Glomsrud, and L.M. Mortensen. 1995. DIF and temperature drop responses in SDP and LDP, a comparison. *Acta Horticulturae* 378:27–33.

Nau, J. 1991. *Petunia*, pp. 690–692 in *Ball RedBook*, 15th ed., V. Ball, editor. George J. Ball Publishing, West Chicago, Illinois.

Nelson, P. 1985. Fertilization, pp. 182–211 in *Bedding Plants III*, J.W. Mastalerz and E.J. Holcomb, editors. Pennsylvania Flower Growers, University Park, Pennsylvania.

Nowak, J., and R.M. Rudnicki. 1990. *Postharvest Handling and Storage of Cut Flowers, Florist Greens and Potted Plants*. Timber Press, Portland, Oregon.

Piringer, A.A., and H.M. Cathey. 1960. Effect of photoperiod, kind of supplemental light and temperature on the growth and flowering of petunia plants. *Proceedings of the American Society for Horticultural Science* 76:649–660.

Reekie, J.Y.C., P.R. Hicklenton, and E.G. Reekie. 1997. The interactive effects of carbon dioxide enrichment and daylength on growth and development in *Petunia hybrida*. *Annuals of Botany* 80:57–64.

Sawaya, M. 2001. Plugs, pp. 50–53 in *Tips on Regulating Growth of Floriculture Crops*, M.L. Gaston, L.A. Kunkle, P.S. Konjoian, and M.F. Wilt, editors. Ohio Florists' Association Services, Columbus, Ohio.

Serek, M., G. Tamari, E.C. Sisler, and A. Borochov. 1995. Inhibition of ethylene-induced cellular senescence symptoms by 1-methylcyclopropene, a new inhibitor of ethylene action. *Physiologia Plantarum* 94:229–232.

Shaw, J.A. 1998. Growing today's cutting petunias. *GrowerTalks* 62(9):49.

Starman, T.W. 2001. Vegetative crops, pp. 117–122 in *Tips on Regulating Growth of Floriculture Crops*, M.L. Gaston, L.A. Kunkle, P.S. Konjoian, and M.F. Wilt, editors. Ohio Florists' Association Services, Columbus, Ohio.

van Iersel, M.W., R.B. Beverly, P.A. Thomas, J.G. Latimer, and H.A. Mills. 1998. Fertilizer effects on the growth of impatiens, petunia, salvia, and vinca plug seedlings. *HortScience* 33:678–682.

Wang, S.-Y. 1999. Effects of plant growth regulators on plant size, branching, and flowering in *Petunia ×hybrida*. *HortScience* 34:528. (Abstract)

Weidner, E. 1994. Supertunias™—More than just a petunia. *Ohio Florists' Association Bulletin* 777: 4–5.

White, J. 1985. Growing media, pp. 151–172 in *Bedding Plants III*, J.W. Mastalerz and E.J. Holcomb, editors. Pennsylvania Flower Growers, University Park, Pennsylvania.

Wilkins, H.F., and H.R. Pemberton. 1981. Interaction of growth regulators and light. *Proceedings 14th International Bedding Plant Conference*, Seattle, Washington, 14:182–188.

Philodendron

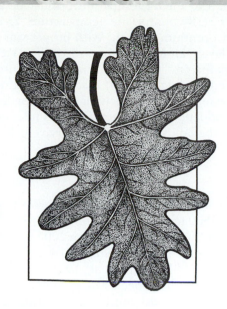

FIGURE II-1 PHILODENDRON Potted *Philodendron scandens oxycardium* being grown on a totem pole.

INTRODUCTION

Common and scientific names: Vining philodendrons: (1) *Philodendron scandens oxycardium* C. Koch & Sello (formerly known as *P. oxycardium* or *P. cordatum*), heart-leaf philodendron, parlor ivy, or common philodendron; (2) *P. erubescens* K. Koch. & Augustin., red-leaf philodendron, or blushing philodendron; and (3) *P. cordatum* (Vell. Conc.) Kunth., heart-leaf philodendron (Huxley et al., 1992). Self-heading philodendrons include (1) *P. cannifolium,* Kunth. and (2) *P. wendlandii* Schott. (Huxley et al., 1992). Erect-arborescent philodendrons include *P. bipinnatifidum* Endl. (formerly known as *P. selloum*), horse-head philodendron, fiddle-leaf philodendron, or lacy-tree philodendron, which appears self-heading when young but becomes more erect and woody when mature (Griffiths, 1998). Numerous other species and hybrids are grown.

Family and related taxa: Araceae Juss. This plant family has contributed a number of important foliage plant species to the industry including *Aglaonema, Anthurium, Caladium, Dieffenbachia, Epipremnum, Monstera, Nephthytis, Spathiphyllum, Syngonium,* and *Zantedeschia.* Another aroid, the calla lily (*Zantedeschia*), is also an important cut flower and potted flowering plant.

Origin: Philodendrons are native to the tropical regions of Central and South America, but have been naturalized in tropical regions of many parts of the world (Bailey and Bailey, 1976).

Uses and current status: Philodendrons are popular foliage plants due to their glossy green foliage, adaptability to the indoor environment, and ease of production. Several cultivars also have reddish leaves and stems or yellow foliage.

P. scandens oxycardium is probably one of the most tolerant foliage plants for low light and low humidity in the interior (Fig. II-1 Philodendron). Vining philodendrons are usually grown in hanging baskets but can also be grown on totems or in small pots for direct sale or for incorporation into container gardens. Self-heading or erect-arborescent philodendrons are sold as potted plants in pot sizes ranging from 3 in. (7.5 cm) to 17 in. (43 cm). Philodendrons can also be used as landscape ornamentals in warm regions.

CULTIVARS

Philodendrons can be divided into three types: vining philodendrons, of which *P. scandens oxycardium* is the most commonly grown; self-headed philodendrons, which have short internodes and form self-supporting plants; and erect-arborescent philodendrons, which appear self-heading when young but become more erect and woody when mature. In the low light of the interior environment, the stems of some self-headed philodendrons may elongate and become more vinelike. Numerous cultivars and hybrids of self-headed and erect-arborescent types are available.

PROPAGATION

Vining philodendrons are propagated by tip, single-eye, or double-eye cuttings taken from stock plants or from the prunings of previous crops (McConnell et al., 1981). Cuttings root best under 3000 fc (600 μmol $\cdot$ m^{-2} $\cdot$ s^{-1}) light at 80°F (27°C) (Henney et al., 1991). Little or no mist is used and tent propagation works well (Griffith, 1998). Rooting hormone is not required. Although cuttings are typically propagated directly into the final container, they can also be rooted in plugs for later planting or for incorporation into container gardens. Optimum light level for stock plants is 3000 fc (600 $\mu mol \cdot m^{-2} \cdot s^{-1}$).

Self-headed and erect-arborescent philodendron species are typically propagated by seed and hybrids by tissue culture. Cutting propagation is impractical due to the large leaves and short internodes. Tissue-cultured philodendrons are especially desirous because they have numerous basal branches, which produce compact plants, while seed- or cutting-propagated plants are poorly branched. Tissue-cultured plants can be purchased as nonestablished microcuttings or as rooted plugs. The microcuttings require rooting, while the plugs are established and are much easier to use.

Philodendron seeds are tiny and best germinated at 75 to 80°F (24 to 27°C) on a media with a low EC (Henley et al., 1991). Germination can be done in the propagation house or in germination rooms. Light levels of 300 to 600 fc (60 to 120 $\mu mol \cdot m^{-2} \cdot s^{-1}$) are used during germination and 1500 to 2500 fc (300 to 500 $\mu mol \cdot m^{-2} \cdot s^{-1}$) after the seedlings have developed two leaves. As with tissue-cultured plants, many producers buy plugs and avoid the problems with seed propagation.

FLOWERING CONTROL AND DORMANCY

Because plants are grown for their foliage, flowering is not encouraged and typically occurs only on older plants growing outdoors in tropical areas.

TEMPERATURE

Philodendrons are tolerant of a wide range of temperatures but optimum growth takes place between 70 and 85°F (21 and 29°C) (Henley et al., 1991). The media temperature must be at least 65°F (18°C) and air temperature 75°F (24°C) for optimum growth. With proper water and light levels, air temperatures of 105°F (41°C) are not damaging to *P. scandens oxycardium.* Nowak and Rudnicki (1990) recommended reducing the temperature when plants are shaded during production. *P. bipinnatifidum* is tolerant of cold in the landscape and can survive below freezing temperatures (Griffith, 1998).

LIGHT

Heart-leaf and hybrid philodendrons grow best at 1500 to 2500 fc (300 to 500 $\mu mol \cdot m^{-2} \cdot s^{-1}$), with the optimum light level being 2000 fc (400 $\mu mol \cdot m^{-2} \cdot s^{-1}$) for *P. scandens oxycardium* (Henley et al., 1991; Henny et al., 1991). *P. bipinnatifidum* and other species of philodendrons can be grown in full sun outdoors in Florida; the most attractive foliage is obtained at 3000 to 5000 fc (600 to 1000 $\mu mol \cdot m^{-2} \cdot s^{-1}$).

WATER

Although philodendrons are tolerant of drying out, the media should remain moist for best growth.

CARBON DIOXIDE

No data available.

NUTRITION

Constant liquid fertilization rates of 200 ppm N and controlled-release or granular fertilizers at 0.56 oz/ft²/year (170 g $\cdot m^{-2} \cdot year^{-1}$) N can be used (Griffith, 1998; Henny et al., 1991). For both types of fertilization a 3:1:2 N:P:K ratio fertilizer should be used (Table II-1 Philodendron). Marginal necrosis of older foliage can occur with magnesium deficiency. Extra magnesium should be included in the fertilizer program. Calcium deficiency in *P. scandens*

TABLE II-1 PHILODENDRON

Recommended fertilizer rates for *Philodendron* species and their cultivars (Conover and Poole, 1990).

Species	Controlled Release 19–6–12 g/3 Months/Pot [in. (cm)]					
	4 (10)	6 (15)	8 (20)	10 (25)	12 (30)	14 (35)
P. scandens oxycardium	1.8	4.0	7.2	11.2	16.2	21.8
P. bipinnatifidum	2.2	4.8	8.6	13.5	19.4	26.2
Other *Philodendron* species and hybrids	1.8	4.0	7.2	11.2	16.2	21.8

oxycardium produced death of the root tips, chlorotic spots on young foliage, and distortion of expanding leaves (Hershey and Merritt, 1987). Calcium foliar sprays may be useful (Griffith, 1998). Foliar nutrient levels for high-quality plants are listed in Chapter 6, Nutrition, Table 6-4.

MEDIA

Philodendron media should be well drained with a pH of 5.5 to 6.0 (Griffith, 1998). If the cuttings are propagated directly into the final pots, the media must be particularly well aerated, yet retain enough moisture to prevent excessive watering when plants are ready to market.

HEIGHT CONTROL

Height control is generally not needed on philodendrons; however, the length of the vines has been controlled with growth retardants. Results are often mixed but the following chemicals and rates have been used with varying degrees of success: B-Nine (daminozide) (10,000-ppm spray), Cycocel (chlormequat) (3000-ppm spray), and A-Rest (ancymidol) [50- to 100-ppm spray or 0.25 to 1.0 mg a.i. drench per 6-in. (15-cm) pot] (Henny, 2001). Adriansen (1985) noted that Cycocel and B-Nine are effective on *P. erubescens* and A-Rest is effective on *P. scandens oxycardium*.

SPACING

Pots and baskets are spaced pot-to-pot until the foliage touches and the stems begin to vine. Hanging baskets should be either trimmed or spaced out to prevent shoots from becoming tangled. Final spacing on self-headed philodendrons will depend on pot size.

PINCHING AND DISBUDDING

Vine philodendron plants are often shaped one or two times before sale by trimming the longest shoots. The shoots can then be used to propagate the next cycle of plants. The trimmed shoots produce multiple axillary shoots, which make the plants fuller. Self-headed and erect-arborescent philodendrons generally do not require pinching.

SUPPORT

Vines can be attached mechanically or by natural root growth to totem poles for upright growth. Self-headed philodendrons generally do not need support.

SCHEDULE AND TIMING

Cuttings usually require 3 to 4 weeks for rooting at 80°F (27°C). Production of a hanging basket can take an additional 10 to 12 weeks at night temperatures of 75°F (24°C) and day temperatures of 85°F (29°C). Large-size potted specimens can take many months from propagation to finish.

INSECTS

Several insects and related pests can infest the greenhouse including aphids, mealybugs, scale, thrips, fungus gnats, and shoreflies. Mealybugs and scale can become particularly troublesome under long-term production such as with stock plants or conservatory collections. Caterpillars can also be a problem in warm climates such as Florida, Texas, and California. Because caterpillars can cause much damage in a short time, frequent checks are required to find and control outbreaks before major damage occurs.

DISEASES

Philodendrons are subject to several common foliage plant diseases including bacterial leaf spot (*Xanthomonas camperstris* pv. *dieffenbachiae, Pseudomonas cichorii, Erwinia carotovora,* and *E. chrysanthemi*), cutting soft rot (*Erwinia carotovora* and *E. chrysanthemi*), and root rot (*Pythium splendens, Phytophthora,* and *Rhizoctonia solani*) (Chase, 1987; Horst, 1990; Henley et al., 1991; Henny et al., 1991). Free moisture on leaves and wounding increases disease severity of *Erwinia chrysanthemi* on *Philodendron bipinnatifidum* (Haygood and Strider, 1981). Once *Erwinia chrysanthemi* becomes established in a production area, the pathogen can remain in fallen leaves and rooting medium and on symptomless leaves and seeds for at least 11 months (Haygood et al., 1982a). Interestingly, increased N applications reduced the severity of *Erwinia chrysanthemi* on *P. bipinnatifidum,* but the effective N levels also reduced plant growth (Haygood et al., 1982b).

Other reported diseases include fungal leaf spot (*Cercospora, Colletotrichum, Dactylaria humicola, Myrothecium roridum, Phyllosticta,* and *Phytophthora parasitica*), anthracnose (*Gloeosporium*), and gray mold (*Botrytis cinerea*) (Horst, 1990). Of these, *Dactylaria humicola* and *Phytophthora parasitica* are particularly common (Griffith, 1998). The striking white mycelia of southern blight

(*Sclerotium rolfsii*) can also be found on occasion. Dasheen mosaic virus can also occur causing foliar mosaic, stunting, and leaf distortions (Griffith, 1998). Outdoor production areas may be subject to one or more nematode species as well (Horst, 1990).

PHYSIOLOGICAL DISORDERS

High fertilizer rates can also cause large foliage; rapid, weak growth; and increased susceptibility to root rot if the medium EC is equally high. Light that is too intense during production can cause foliage to bleach and become pale green. Conversely, light that is not intense enough can cause slow growth, weak stems, poor rooting of cuttings, and excessive stretching of stems and petioles. Low nutrition and low temperatures can also cause light-green foliage color. *P. scandens oxycardium* is subject to two types of foliar chlorosis according to Henny et al. (1991): (1) Chlorosis appears on the outer lobe margins near the petiole attachment and is due to magnesium deficiency. (2) Chlorosis appears on the lower margins opposite the petiole with some streaks extending upward and occasionally margin chlorosis. The cause of this latter symptom is unknown but may be due to a micronutrient imbalance.

POSTHARVEST

Properly acclimated philodendron plants should have a long postharvest life for the consumer because philodendrons are tolerant of poor interior conditions. Plants will produce smaller leaves if the light or fertility levels are too low in the consumer's environment.

P. scandens oxycardium can be shipped for up to 2 weeks and *P. bipinnatifidum* for up to 4 weeks at 55 to 61°F (13 to 16°C) with no decrease in quality (Conover, 1991). *P. scandens oxycardium* plants tolerated up to 24 days in the dark at 72°F (22°C), but some of the young leaves failed to expand (Biran and Kofranek, 1981). The optimum temperature for long-term storage of *P. erubescens* was 57°F (14°C) (Tijskens et al., 1996). Philodendrons are sensitive to external ethylene concentrations, with leaf abscission occurring after exposure to 5 ppm ethylene for 3 days (L. Høyer, personal communication; Marousky and Harbaugh, 1978; Nowak and Rudnicki, 1990).

KEY POINTS

- Philodendron is used as a potted foliage plant, grown with or without a totem, and a hanging basket plant.
- Numerous species, cultivars, and hybrids are grown and can be separated into three groups: vining, self-heading, and erect-arborescent.
- The most popular vining type is *Philodendron scandens oxycardium*.
- Plants are propagated by tip, single-eye, or double-eye cuttings seed, or *in vitro*.
- Vining plants are usually trimmed, shaped, and allowed to regrow before marketing; trimmed shoots are often used for propagation.
- Optimum light intensity is 1500 to 2500 fc (300 to 500 μmol $\cdot$ m^{-2} $\cdot$ s^{-1}) for most species.
- Plants are susceptible to numerous diseases, especially bacterial leaf spot, cutting soft rot, and root rot.
- Properly acclimated plants should have a long postharvest life for the consumer.

BIBLIOGRAPHY

Adriansen, E. 1985. Kemisk vækstregulering, pp. 142–162 in *Potteplanter I—Produktion, Metoder, Midler*, O.V. Christensen, A. Klougart, I.S. Pedersen, and K. Wikesjö, editors. Gartner-INFO, København, Denmark. (in Danish)

Bailey, L.H., and E.Z. Bailey. 1976. *Philodendron*, pp. 856–860 in *Hortus Third: A Concise Dictionary of Plants Cultivated in the United States and Canada*. Macmillan, New York.

Biran, I., and A.M. Kofranek. 1981. The influence of sustained and alternating dark periods on the growth of three foliage plants. *Journal of the American Society for Horticultural Science* 106:64–68.

Chase, A.R. 1987. *Compendium of Ornamental Foliage Plant Diseases*. American Phytopathological Society Press, St. Paul, Minnesota.

Conover, C. 1991. Foliage plants, pp. 498–523 in *Ball Redbook*, 15th ed., V. Ball, editor. George J. Ball Publishing, West Chicago, Illinois.

Conover, C.A., and R.T. Poole. 1990. *Light and Fertilizer Recommendations for Production of Accli-*

mated *Potted Foliage Plants*. Research Report RH-90-1, Central Florida Research and Education Center, Apopka, Florida.

Griffith, Jr., L.P. 1998. *Tropical Foliage Plants*. Ball Publishing, Batavia, Illinois.

Haygood, R.A., and D.L. Strider. 1981. Influence of moisture and inoculum concentration on infection of *Philodendron selloum* by *Erwinia chrysanthemi*. *Plant Disease* 65:727–728.

Haygood, R.A., D.L. Strider, and E. Echandi. 1982a. Survival of *Erwinia chrysanthemi* in association with *Philodendron selloum*, other greenhouse ornamentals, and in potting media. *Phytopathology* 72:853–859.

Haygood, R.A., D.L. Strider, and P.V. Nelson. 1982b. Influence of nitrogen and potassium on growth and bacterial leaf blight of *Philodendron selloum*. *Plant Disease* 66:728–730.

Henley, R.W., A.R. Chase, and L.S. Osborne. 1991. *Philodendron—Self-Heading Types*. Foliage Plant Research Note RH-1991-27, Central Florida Research and Education Center, Apopka, Florida.

Henny, R.J. 2001. Foliage plants, pp. 83–87 in *Tips on Regulating Growth of Floriculture Crops*, M.L. Gaston, L.A. Kunkle, P.S. Konjoian, and M.F. Wilt, editors. Ohio Florists' Association Services, Columbus, Ohio.

Henny, R.J., L.S. Osborne, and A.R. Chase. 1991. *Philodendron—Vining*. Foliage Plant Research

Note RH-1991-26, Central Florida Research and Education Center, Apopka, Florida.

Hershey, D.R., and R.H. Merritt. 1987. Calcium deficiency symptoms of heartleaf philodendron. *HortScience* 22:311.

Horst, R.K. 1990. Philodendron, p. 769 in *Westcott's Plant Disease Handbook*, 5th ed. Van Nostrand Reinhold, New York.

Huxley, A., M. Griffiths, and M. Levy. 1992. *Philodendron*, pp. 546–549 in *The New Royal Horticultural Society Dictionary of Gardening*, vol. 3. Stockton Press, New York.

Marousky, F.J., and B.K. Harbaugh. 1978. *Deterioration of Foliage Plants during Transit*. National Tropical Foliage Short Course, 33-39, IFAS Cooperative Extension Service, University of Florida, Orlando.

McConnell, D.B., R.W. Henley, and R.L. Biamonte. 1981. Commercial foliage plants, pp. 544–593 in *Foliage Plant Production*, J. Joiner, editor. Prentice-Hall, Englewood Cliffs, New Jersey.

Nowak, J., and R.M. Rudnicki. 1990. *Postharvest Handling and Storage of Cut Flowers, Florists Greens, and Potted Plants*. Timber Press, Portland, Oregon.

Tijskens, L.M.M., M. Sloof, E.C. Wilkinson, and W.G. van Doorn. 1996. A model of the effects of temperature and time on the acceptability of potted plants stored in darkness. *Postharvest Biology and Technology* 8:293–305.

Platycodon

INTRODUCTION

Common name: platycodon, balloon flower.

Scientific name: *Platycodon grandiflorus* (Jacq.) A. DC. (Huxley et al., 1992).

Family and related taxa: Campanulaceae Juss. This family also contains the popular ornamentals *Campanula* and *Lobelia*.

Origin: The *Platycodon* is a native of China, Manchuria, and Japan.

Uses and current status: The species is used as a potted flowering plant, bedding plant, or cut flower (Halevy et al., 2002; Starman et al., 1995) (Figs. II-1and II-2 Platycodon).

Platycodon grandiflorus, a hardy herbaceous perennial, is the only species in this genus. The unopened flower buds resemble inflated balloons and open into five lobed star-shaped flowers, which can be 2 to 3 in. (5 to 8 cm) across. With time this perennial will develop a carrot-like taproot (Bailey, 1935; Bailey and Bailey, 1976). Plants thrive from Zones 3 to 8 (Armitage, 1989). When used as a bedding plant, a blue color show can be expected throughout the summer, even during hot weather.

FIGURE II-I PLATYCODON Potted *Platycodon* plant.

FIGURE II-2 PLATYCODON Balloon-shaped *Platycodon* bud, from which the common name is derived.

CULTIVARS

Single blue flowers are the most common, however, white, pink, and double-flowered types exist (Bailey, 1935; Bailey and Bailey, 1976; Evensen, 1987). Plant height varies according to cultivar from 4 to 36 in. (10 to 90 cm) (Armitage, 1989; Bailey, 1935; Bailey and Bailey, 1976).

PROPAGATION

Plants can be divided in the spring or, more commonly, propagated by seed (Bailey and Bailey, 1976; Evensen, 1987). At 70°F (21°C), seed germinates in 10 to 12 days. Imbibition of seed at 39°F (4°C) had no effect on germination (Park et al., 1998). Seedlings should be transplanted 4 weeks after sowing (Evensen, 1987; Holcomb and Beattie, 1991).

FLOWERING CONTROL AND DORMANCY

Seed-grown plants flower with six to eight nodes (Holcomb and Beattie, 1991). Seed-grown, noncooled material will flower the first year without a cold treatment; however, plants will be short and may be prostrate. Plants initiate flowers more rapidly at 68°F (20°C) than at 50°F (10°C) (Park et al., 1998). Platycodon is a day-neutral plant (Halevy et al., 2002).

A cold treatment of 6 weeks at 40°F (4°C) is required to break dormancy of underground storage organs (Armitage, 1989; Evensen, 1987; Iversen and Weiler, 1994). Increasing duration of cold treatment from 6 to 12 weeks decreased days to flower by about 2 weeks (Iversen and Weiler, 1994). In Israel 12 weeks of 36 to 39°F (2 to 4°C) cold resulted in the highest cut flower yield when forced at 54 to 57°F (12 to 14°C) (Halevy et al., 2002).

TEMPERATURE

A night temperature of 60°F (16°C) was recommended for winter forcing. However, summer flower quality is also excellent (Holcomb and Beattie, 1991). Increasing temperature from 57 to 84°F (14 to 29°C) decreased plant fresh and dry weight; however, plants were tallest at 66°F (19°C) and most heavily branched at 72°F (22°C) (Park et al., 1998).

LIGHT

There apparently is no true photoperiodic effect because both control and 20-hr light treated [500 fc, (100 μmol $\cdot$ m^{-2} $\cdot$ s^{-1})] plants flowered (Holcomb and Beattie, 1991). However, lighted plants flowered earlier, were of better quality, and had more compact inflorescences. LD also provided better quality cut stems (Halevy et al., 2002). Bailey and Bailey (1976) recommended full sunlight for production.

WATER

Use a well-drained medium and do not overwater. Many cultural problems are related to poor medium aeration.

CARBON DIOXIDE

No data on carbon dioxide were found, but supplemental CO_2 is not likely to be harmful.

NUTRITION

When grown in a peat-lite mix, a 15–16–17 fertilizer at 200 ppm N can be used (Evensen, 1987; Holcomb and Beattie, 1990, 1991).

MEDIA

A well-drained medium with a pH of 6.0 is optimum (Holcomb and Beattie, 1991).

HEIGHT CONTROL

Most cultivars for pot plant production do not need to be pinched nor do they require a plant growth regulator. However, B-Nine (daminozide) sprays at 1500 to 5000 ppm and A-Rest (ancymidol) sprays at 100 ppm can be used to reduce height (Holcomb and Beattie, 1991). Platycodon has a moderate response to DIF (Warner and Erwin, 2001).

SPACING

Production is in 4-in. (10-cm) pots, with three seedlings in each pot (Evensen, 1987; Holcomb and Beattie, 1991). For field cut flower production, space plants 12 × 12 in. (30 × 30 cm).

PINCHING AND DISBUDDING

Most cultivars do not require pinching.

SUPPORT

No support is required for potted flowering or bedding plants. If grown outside as a cut flower, then one to two layers of support should be used.

SCHEDULE AND TIMING

SEEDLINGS

Plants seeded in mid-January flowered in 90 days (Sakata Seed, personal communication).

If seeded in late summer (August 25), plants flowered January 1 to 9; if seeded in winter (January 11), plants flowered June 5 to 12; if seeded in the early spring (April 6), plants flowered July 15 to 31; this is 129, 145, or 100 days from seed to flowering, respectively. Park et al. (1998) found that 'Astra Blue' flowered in 45 to 108 days at temperatures ranging from 84°F (29°C) to 57°F (14°C), respectively.

DORMANT ROOTS

'Mariesii' dormant roots flowered in 13 weeks at 60°F (16°C) when grown under a 16-hr photoperiod, after receiving a 6-week 40°F (4°C) cold treatment (Iversen and Weiler, 1994). Precooled material planted in February flowered in 80 days when forced at 68°F (20°C) (Evensen, 1987). In these trials, cool white fluorescent lights were placed 3 ft (90 cm) above the plants, lighting from 2200 to 0200 (10 P.M. to 2 A.M.). A chilling period was required for repeat flowering and upright growth; chilling was also necessary for high-quality cut flower production (Evensen, 1987).

INSECTS

No major insect problems have been reported.

DISEASES

Root rots (*Rhizoctonia solani*) are a result of overwatering (Horst, 1990).

PHYSIOLOGICAL DISORDERS

No physiological disorders have been reported.

POSTHARVEST

Plants ship well for 5 days at 38°F (3°C) or 60°F (16°C) and continue to flower for 10 days thereafter. However, cold shipping is recommended because some etiolation occurs at 60°F (16°C).

Individual flowers last for 2 to 3 days from opening to senescence. Provided an appropriate floral preservative was used, an inflorescence with two to three opened flowers and six to eight unopened buds will continue development with an aesthetic vase life of 8 to 10 days (Evensen, 1987).

KEY POINTS

- Balloon flower is used as a cut flower, flowering potted plant, and hardy garden perennial.
- The large balloon-shaped bud opens into white, blue, or pink flowers.
- Plants can be propagated by seed or division.

- A 6-week cold treatment at 40°F (4°C) is required to break dormancy of underground storage organs.
- Seed-grown plants will flower without a cold treatment but the stems will be short and may be prostrate.

BIBLIOGRAPHY

Armitage, A. 1989. *Platycodon*, pp. 466–467 in *Herbaceous Perennial Plants: A Treatise on Their Identification, Culture, and Garden Attributes.* Varsity Press, Athens, Georgia.

Bailey, L.H. 1935. *Platycodon*, pp. 2710–2711 in *Standard Cyclopedia of Horticulture.* Macmillan, New York.

Bailey, L.H., and E.Z. Bailey. 1976. *Platycodon*, p. 884 in *Hortus Third: A Concise Dictionary of Plants Cultivated in the United States and Canada.* Macmillan, New York.

Evensen, K.B. 1987. Lift sales with balloon flowers. *Greenhouse Grower* 5(1):26.

Halevy, A.H., E. Shlomo, and O. Ziv. 2002. Improving cut flower production of balloon flower. *HortScience* 37:759–761.

Holcomb, E.J., and D.J. Beattie. 1990. Growth retardants for perennials, pp. 164–170 in *Proceedings for the Plant Growth Regulator Society of America, 17th Annual Meeting.*

Holcomb, E.J., and D. Beattie. 1991. Perennials in pots could expand your crop line-up for spring. *GrowerTalks* 54(9):83, 86, 90.

Horst, R.K. 1990. Platycodon, p. 777 in *Westcott's Plant Disease Handbook,* 5th ed. Van Nostrand Reinhold, New York.

Huxley, A., M. Griffiths, and M. Levy. 1992. *Platycodon*, p. 651 in *The New Royal Horticultural Society Dictionary of Gardening,* vol. 3. Stockton Press, New York.

Iversen, R.R., and T.C. Weiler. 1994. Strategies to force flowering of six herbaceous garden ornamentals. *HortTechnology* 4:61–65.

Park, B.H., N. Oliveira, and S. Pearson. 1998. Temperature affects growth and flowering of the balloon flower [*Platycodon grandiflorus* (Jacq.) A. DC. cv. Astra Blue]. *HortScience* 33:233–236.

Starman, T.W., T.A. Cerny, and A.J. MacKenzie. 1995. Productivity and profitability of some field-grown specialty cut flowers. *HortScience* 30: 1217–1220.

Warner, R.M., and J.E. Erwin. 2001. Temperature, pp. 10–17 in *Tips on Regulating Growth of Floriculture Crops,* M.L. Gaston, L.A. Kunkle, P.S. Konjoian, and M.F. Wilt, editors. Ohio Florists' Association Services, Columbus, Ohio.

Polianthes

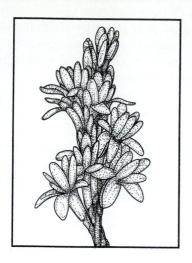

INTRODUCTION

Common name: tuberose.

Scientific name: *Polianthes tuberosa* L. (Huxley et al., 1992).

Family and related taxa: Agavacea Endl. In addition to the well-known *Agave* and *Yucca* desert plants, *Cordyline*, *Dracaena*, and *Sansevieria* are important ornamental genera in the family. The *Polianthes* genus contains 13 species (Huxley et al., 1992).

Origin: *Polianthes tuberosa* has never been found or seen in nature and is only known from cultivation in pre-Columbian Mexico. The species was first seen in cultivation by the Spanish in 1522.

Uses and current status: The spikes inflorescences bear fragrant single or double tubular waxy flowers and are harvested commercially as a summer cut flower. In France and India, flowers are grown for perfume fragrances and in India and Hawaii, flowers are commonly used in garlands and leis, respectively (Bailey and Bailey, 1976; Sadhu and Bose, 1973; Wilkins, 1985). Plants are also grown in the home garden as a cut flower.

Polianthes are herbaceous perennials with a basal whorl of leaves that are succulent and linear. The spike can be up to 3 ft (90 cm) tall with 30 or more white flowers. Plants are grown from a thickened bulb with basal roots (Bryan, 1989).

CULTIVARS

Single-flowered ('Single Mexican') and double-flowered ('The Pearl,' 'Excelsior Double Pearl')

forms exist (Bailey and Bailey, 1976; Huxley et al., 1992). The double types are more common in commerce. Red and orange rose-colored forms occur with *P. geminiflora* (Bailey and Bailey, 1976), but as far as the authors know, no active breeding has occurred between species.

PROPAGATION

At the end of the growing season, the bulbs must be lifted north of Zone 8 in North America because they are tender (Armitage and Laushman, 2003; Post, 1952). The bulbs are graded and stored dry over winter at 40°F (4°C). In the spring, axillary rhizomes are removed, allowed to callus for 24 hr, and replanted. These offsets are produced in large numbers; 15 to 20 offsets develop from a larger bulb in a single season in India (Sharga, 1980). Two to 3 years are required for a bulblet offset to reach flowering size, which is between 2.5 and 4.25 in. (6.5 and 11 cm) in diameter (Benschop, 1993). In addition, plants can be propagated by seed or *in vitro* techniques (Benschop, 1993; Sharga, 1980).

A 1000- to 2000-ppm Cycocel (chlormequat) dip increased axillary bulblet formation (Cirrito and De Vita, 1982). A table of responses to numerous plant growth regulators has been compiled by Benschop (1993).

FLOWER CONTROL AND DORMANCY

The capacity of a bulb to flower is dependent on the supply of carbohydrates (Makhopadhyay and Nagaraju, 1988). However, Kosugi and Kimura (1961) concluded that high temperatures are required for flower initiation, differentiation, and development. Kosugi and Kimura (1961) describe 14 distinct stages of development. A minimum production temperature of 70°F (21°C) was recommended by Post (1952). Bailey and Bailey (1976) stated 75 to 85°F (24 to 29°C) was optimum for growth and flowering. Shoots are slower to emerge but flower faster from large bulbs than from smaller ones (Armitage and Laushman, 2003).

After flowering, the bulb apparently enters a period of dormancy, the onset of which is hastened by water restriction and cooler temperatures. Imposed dormancy can be maintained by low temperature; internal dormancy is broken by up to 6 weeks at 68°F (20°C) (Benschop, 1993; Howard, 1985; Sadhu and Bose, 1973).

TEMPERATURE

Plants are not frost hardy and thrive at high temperatures from 70 to 85°F (21 to 29°C) (Bailey and Bailey, 1976; Post, 1952). Tuberose can perennialize from Zones 8 to 10 (Armitage and Laushman, 2003). Optimum soil temperature should be above 68°F (20°C) for maximum root growth (Steenstra and Brundell, 1986) and the air temperature should be between 68 and 86°F (20 and 30°C) for maximum bulb production (Makhopadhyay, 1987). Flower production is best when the climate is neither too hot [greater than 86°F (30°C)] nor too cool [less than 65°F (13°C)]. Kosugi and Kimura (1961) and Zizzo et al. (1986) agree that the minimum temperature for spike formation was 55°F (13°C) and for individual flower formation 67°F (19°C). Bulbs can be forced into flower in 130 or more days in the greenhouse, but it is not economical because a minimum of 68°F (20°C) is required (Benschop, 1993). Bailey (1933) reported that freshly harvested bulbs were heat cured for 4 to 8 weeks at 80 to 100°F (27 to 38°C) prior to being distributed to dealers for sale.

LIGHT

Plants are field grown in full light. Howard (1985) stated that full sun is acceptable; however, when temperatures near 86°F (30°C), Sadhu and Bose (1973) recommended shading if possible. While *Polianthes* is a day-neutral plant, vegetative growth and flowering were advanced by 10 days under 16-hr photoperiods (Sadhu and Bose, 1973).

WATER

Good drainage is a requirement (Armitage and Laushman, 2003). Plants should not be water stressed (Steenstra and Brundell, 1986). The amount of irrigation water required varies with the stage of plant growth, soil type, and climate (Benschop, 1993).

CARBON DIOXIDE

This is a field-grown crop and supplemental carbon dioxide is not used.

NUTRITION

Various nutrient levels and formulations have been used and vary from country to country. Bailey (1933) reported that adequate potassium was required. Steenstra and Brundell (1986) stated that tuberose had a high nutrient requirement of 89 lb/acre N (100 kg · ha^{-1}). The balance among N–P–K varied if bulb/bulblet formation was desired or if flower production was the main concern. Benschop (1993) reviews these variations in detail.

MEDIA

While tuberoses thrive from the south of France and Italy to India, Hawaii, and North America in a wide array of field soil types, good drainage is essential. Steenstra and Brundell (1986) stated that a light sandy soil made bulb harvesting easier. The reported optimum medium pH ranges from 6.5 to 7.5 (El-Rouni, 1981) to 8.1 to 8.4 (Cirrito and Zizzo, 1981).

HEIGHT CONTROL

None is required for this cut flower.

SPACING

Bulbs can be planted in rows 6 to 12 in. (23 to 30 cm) apart at a depth of 2 to 3 in. (5 to 8 cm). Bulbs are planted 4 to 6 in. (10 to 15 cm) apart within the rows. Smaller axillary bulbs, which are removed in spring, can be planted in a nursery bed for 1 year. Bulbs can be up to 8 in. (20 cm) in diameter; smaller bulbs 3 to 4 in. (8 to 10 cm) in diameter are available and quickly increase in size if grown at 68°F (20°C) or higher in the summer (Armitage and Laushman, 2003; Kosugi and Kimura, 1961).

PINCHING AND DISBUDDING

None required.

SUPPORT

None required.

SCHEDULE AND TIMING

Bulbs are planted after the danger of frost. Bulbs can safely remain in the fields in areas of mild winter, Zones 8 to 10 (Armitage and Laushman, 2003). Approximately 5 months are required for annual plantings to flower. Flower harvest can extend over a 2-month time span. Yields per bulb increase with perennialized plantings (Armitage and Laushman, 1990, 2003).

Bulbs can be forced in the greenhouse to protect the crop from cold, to presprout bulbs prior to planting outdoors, or to extend the season in the fall. These procedures are summarized by Benschop (1993). Greenhouse forcing has occurred in Japan and 132 days were required for the double cultivars to flower at 68°F (20°C) (Kosugi and Kimura, 1961). Single cultivars require 21 to 28 days longer to flower. Post (1952) stated that January bulbs forced in a 70°F (21°C) greenhouse flowered in May in Ithaca, New York.

INSECTS

Nematodes, thrips, and spider mites are reported to be problems (Armitage and Laushman, 2003; Dreistadt, 2001; Sadhu and Bose, 1973).

DISEASES

Although the tuberose is quite disease free, problems can occur. Bulbs will rot during the winter if left in fields that are too wet and poorly drained (Armitage and Laushman, 2003). *Botrytis* can be a problem on the flowers if the climate is cool (Steenstra and Brundell, 1986). *Erwinia*, *Fusarium*, and *Sclerotinium* have been reported in India (Benschop, 1993; Sadhu and Bose, 1973). Virus has been reported in New Zealand (Horner and Pearson, 1988). Root and crown rot (*Pythium* and *Rhizoctonia*), southern wilt (*Sclerotium rolfsii*), and various leaf spots (*Cercospera*, *Curvularia*, and *Helminthosporium*) also occur (Dreistadt, 2001).

PHYSIOLOGICAL DISORDERS

None reported.

POSTHARVEST

The spikes are harvested when two to four flowers have opened. Unfortunately, the lower flowers may senesce by the time that half of the flowers on the spike are open (Armitage and Laushman, 2003). For long-distance shipping, spikes should be harvested when only two florets are open; for local domestic markets, more flowers can be open on the spikes. Stems should be harvested in the cool of the morning or very late in the evening. The former is better and stems should be placed immediately in water. Benschop (1993) reviewed various articles on harvesting, shipping, and storage which are summarized here.

Each floret lives for approximately 3 days. The average life of a spike is 10 to 14 days. Single flowers last longer than double flowers (Vaughn, 1988). A floral preservative or a 1.5% sugar vase solution is recommended (Naidu and Reid, 1989). Pulsing with a 20% sugar solution for 15 to 24 hr prior to storage greatly increased vase life (Naidu and Reid, 1989; Waithaka et al., 2001). Little effect on vase life was observed with silver thiosulfate (STS) treatment. Ethylene reduced floret opening (Waithaka et al., 2001).

A 32 to 41°F (0 to 5°C) temperature is recommended for shipping and storage (Armitage and Laushman, 2003; Nell and Reid, 2001; Waithaka et al., 2001). Bulb storage data are conflicting: (1) Post (1952) recommended 40°F (4.5°C) storage. (2) Rockwell and Grayson (1953) recommended 64 to 70°F (18 to 21°C). (3) Makhopadhyay and Sadhu (1987) stated that 6 weeks at 86°F (30°C) resulted in the production of larger bulbs; if bulbs were held longer than 6 weeks, flowering was quicker, but quality of spikes and axillary bulb numbers decreased. Further, 50°F (10°C) storage for more than 30 days decreased bulb yields. (4) Dhua et al. (1987) stated that 30 days at 50°F (10°C) increased flower production yields.

KEY POINTS

- Tuberose (*Polianthes*) is a bulbous plant grown for its tall spikes of fragrant flowers.
- Tuberose can perennialize from Zones 8 to 10.
- Flower production is best when the climate is neither too hot [greater than 86°F (30°C)] nor too cool [(less than 65°F (13°C)].

- The spikes are harvested when two to four flowers have opened.
- The vase life of cut stems averages 10 to 14 days. Floral preservatives are recommended.

BIBLIOGRAPHY

Armitage, A.M., and J.M. Laushman. 1990. Planting date and in-ground time affect cut flowers of *Liatris, Polianthes,* and *Iris. HortScience* 25: 1239–1241.

Armitage, A.M., and J.M. Laushman. 2003. *Polianthes tuberosa,* pp. 470–475 in *Specialty Cut Flowers,* 2nd ed. Timber Press, Portland, Oregon.

Bailey, L.H. 1933. *Polianthes,* pp. 2731–2733 in *The Standard Cyclopedia of Horticulture,* vol. 3. Macmillan, New York.

Bailey, L.H., and E.Z. Bailey. 1976. *Polianthes,* p. 893 in *Hortus Third: A Concise Dictionary of Plants Cultivated in the United States and Canada.* Macmillan, New York.

Benschop, M. 1993. *Polianthes,* pp. 589–601 in *The Physiology of Flower Bulbs,* A. De Hertogh and M.L. Nard, editors. Elswith, Amsterdam.

Bryan, J.J. 1989. Tuberose, *Polianthes,* p. 78 in *Bulbs,* vol. II. Timber Press, Portland, Oregon.

Cirrito, M., and M. De Vita. 1982. Prova orietativa per inibire lo sviluppo dei bulbetti laterali del cespo della tuberosa *(Polianthes tuberosa)* per l'ingrossamento dei bulbi. *Annali Instituto Sperimentale per la Floricultura* 13:43–51. (in Italian, English summary)

Cirrito, M., and G.C. Zizzo. 1981. Fertilizzazione della tuberosa coltivata per l'ingrossamento dei bulbi. *Annali Instituto Sperimentale per la Floricultura* 12:67–77. (in Italian, English summary)

Dhua, R.S., S.K. Ghosh, S.K. Mita, L.P. Yadav, and T.K. Bose. 1987. Effect of bulb size, temperature treatment of bulbs and chemicals on growth and flower product in tuberose *(Polianthes tuberosa L.). Acta Horticulture* 205:121–125.

Dreistadt, S.H. 2001. *Integrated Pest Management for Floriculture and Nurseries.* University of California Division of Agriculture and Natural Resources Publication 3402.

El-Rouni, M.K. 1981. Effect of irrigation frequency on growth and flowering of tuberose *Polianthes tuberosa L. Agricultural Research Review* 59: 305–311.

Horner, M.B., and M.N. Pearson. 1988. Purification and electron microscopy studies of a probable polyvirus from *Polianthes tuberosa L. Journal of Phytopathology* 122:261–266.

Howard, T.M. 1985. Mexican field trip 1984. Stalking the *Polianthes* of Mexico, Part I (1985). *Herbertia* 41:98–117.

Huxley, A., M. Griffiths, and M. Levy. 1992. *Polianthes,* pp. 672 in *The New Royal Horticultural Science Dictionary of Gardening,* vol. 3. Stockton Press, New York.

Kosugi, K., and Y. Kimura. 1961. *On the Flower Bud Differentiation and Flower Bud Development of Polianthes tuberosa L. Technical Bulletin of the Faculty of Agriculture,* Kagawa University 12:230–234. (in Japanese, English summary)

Makhopadhyay, A. 1987. Importance of nitrogen nutrition for *Polianthes tuberosa L.* in India. *Herbertia* 43:33–39.

Makhopadhyay, A., and H.T. Nagaraju. 1988. Changes in growth, flowering and chemical composition of tuberose 'Single.' *Herbertia* 44:61–67.

Makhopadhyay, A., and M.K. Sadhu. 1987. Growth and flowering responses of *Polianthes tuberosa L.* to storage temperature and duration of treatments. *Herbertia* 43:30–32.

Nell, T.A., and M.S. Reid. 2001. Can't take the heat. *Floral Management* 17(10):33–34.

Naidu, S.N., and M.S. Reid. 1989. Portharvest handling of tuberose *(Polianthes tuberosa L.). Acta Horticulturae* 261:313–317.

Post, K. 1952. *Polianthes tuberosa,* pp. 745–746 in *Florists Crop Production.* Orange Judd Publishing, New York.

Rockwell, F.I., and E.C. Grayson. 1953. *Polianthes,* p. 252 in *The Complete Book of Bulbs.* The American Garden Guild and Doubleday and Company, Garden City, New York.

Sadhu, M.K., and T.K. Bose. 1973. Tuberose for more artistic garlands. *Indian Horticulture* 18:17, 19–20.

Sharga, A.M. 1980. Maximizing tuberose *(Polianthes tuberosa* Linn) multiplication by using bulb segments. *Progressive Horticulture* 12:71–77.

Steenstra, D.R., and D.J. Brundell. 1986. *Tuberose: Cultivation, Cut-Flower Production.* Ministry of Agriculture and Fisheries Information Bulletin 187, Wellington, New Zealand.

Vaughn, M.J. 1988. *Polianthes,* p. 78 in *Complete Book of Cut Flower Care.* Timber Press, Portland, Oregon.

Waithaka, K., M.S. Reid, and L.L. Dodge. 2001. Cold storage and flower keeping quality of cut tuberose *(Polianthes tuberosa L.). Journal of Horticultural Science and Biotechnology* 76:271–275.

Wilkins, H.F. 1985. *Polianthes tuberosa,* pp. 127–129 in *Handbook of Flowering IV,* A.H. Halevy, editor. CRC Press, Incorporated, Boca Raton, Florida.

Zizzo, G.V., M.G. Provenzale, M. De Vita, and S. Agnello. 1986. Influenza della epoche d'impionto sulla floritura della tuberosa *(Polianthes tuberosa). Annali Instituto Sperimentale per la Floricultura* 17:161–172. (in Italian, English summary)

Primula

FIGURE II-1 PRIMULA Potted *Primula vulgaris* plants.

FIGURE II-2 PRIMULA Potted *Primula obconica* inflorescence.

INTRODUCTION

Common and scientific names:
1. *Primula malacoides* Franch, fairy primrose, baby primrose
2. *Primula obconica* Hance, German primrose, poison primrose
3. *Primula ×polyantha* Hort [*Primula veris ×P. elatior* (L.) Hill. *×P. vulgaris*], polyantha primrose
4. *Primula sinensis* Sab. ex Lindl, Chinese primrose
5. *Primula veris* L. cowslip primrose
6. *Primula vulgaris* Huds, English primrose (synonym: *P. acaulis*) (Huxley et al., 1992)

Family and related taxa: Primulaceae Vent. The family consists of 22 genera, including the popular *Cyclamen*. Of the 800 species in the family, more than 400 are in the genus *Primula*. Several *Primula* species are important to the floriculture industry, and numerous species are used in the garden including *P. japonica* A. Gray, *P. juliae* Kuzn., *P. ×pubescens* Jacq., *P. rosea* Royle., and *P. sieboldii* E. Morr. These can also be forced into flowering in January at temperatures between 43 and 46°F (6 and 8°C) (Bailey and Bailey, 1976; Zimmer, 1985).

Origin: Most *Primula* species are native to the Northern Hemisphere in cool temperate climates. In North America, this genus is particularly well adapted to the West Coast from San Francisco north, and in northern Europe as a winter to midsummer bedding plant and garden specimen.

Uses and current status: *Primula malacoides, P. obconica, P. sinensis,* and *P. veris* are grown primarily as flowering potted plants for the home and are popular in Europe (Fig. II-1 Primula). *P. obconica* can cause a skin rash with some people due to the presence of the allergen primin; this problem is eliminated with newer cultivars, which are primin free (Gray, 2000; Karlsson, 2001) (Fig. II-2 Primula). *P. ×polyantha* and *P. vulgaris* are world famous for their vivid colors as bedding plants, potted indoor plants, and baskets. *P. ×polyantha* and *P. vulgaris* are hardy from Zones 5 to 9 and can be used as outdoor perennials.

Most of the horticulturally important species are short-lived, herbaceous plants. The leaves are basal, rosette, and simple. Flowers come in many fascinating colors and combinations of colors. The flower is five lobed and frequently funnel shaped (Bailey and Bailey, 1976) (see Table II-1 Primula).

TABLE II-I PRIMULA

Descriptive information on various *Primula* species commonly used in the floriculture industry as bedding plants or flowering potted plant.

Species	Origin	Leaves	Flower	Height in. (cm)	Color	Comments
P. malacoides	China, Yunnan Province, and North Burma Mountains	Ovate to elliptical, hairy	Scape with up to 12 flowers, each is up to 1.5 in. (3.8 cm) across	4–18 (10–46)	White, rose, lavender	Flowers in spring and winter in greenhouses, an annual
P. obconica	China	Ovate to elliptical	Up to 13 flowers, each is 1.5 in. (3.8 cm)	12 (30)	White to pink	Hairs can irritate skin, new cultivars are primin free
P. ×polyantha	Hybrid	Obovate	Numerous, each is 1.5 in. (3.8 cm) across	12 (30)	Many colors	A hybrid group, parents are *P. veris, P. elatior, P. vulgaris;* an old garden plant
P. sinensis	China	Broad ovate to cordate, pubescence both sides	Each flower is 1.5 in. (3.8 cm) across	12 (30)	Many colors	Flowers in winter in the greenhouse
P. veris	Europe	Ovate to oblong	Each flower is 0.5 in. (1.3 cm) across	12 (30)	Bright yellow in nature, but white, crimson, apricot, lilac, and orange cultivate are available	Fragrant
P. vulgaris	Southeastern Europe	Obovate	Each flower is 0.5 in. (1.3 cm) across	6 (15)	Yellow, purple, blue, white, lilac, red, and crimson	Most commonly used species

CULTIVARS

Each of the species listed in Table II-1 has numerous cultivars. Annually, international seed companies and regional greenhouse firms conduct cultivar tests and demonstrations (Anonymous, 1994; Hartnett, 1993; Markham, 1994). Karlsson (2001) reviewed the many cultivars that are available.

PROPAGATION

Commercially, primula are propagated by seed, although *in vitro* propagation of *P. obconica* has been reported (Coumans et al., 1979). Seed numbers range from 360,000 seed/oz (12,800/g) for *P. malacoides* to 28,000 seed/oz (990/g) for *P. veris* and *P. vulgaris*. Germination of primula seed has been reported to be difficult and erratic (Atwater, 1980; Heydecker, 1975; Thompson, 1970). Seed germination rates and uniformity have improved due to breeding efforts (Karlsson, 2001). Germination treatments that have been tested are listed in Table II-2 Primula.

Light is not necessary for most primula species but does help to control seedling height after germination (Karlsson, 2001). However, for 12 Asian *Primula* species tested, all were at least partially light dependent for maximum germination (Tod, 1958). The total light intensity was not critical and either natural or fluorescent light was acceptable (Thompson, 1969a, b). Regardless of light, proper moisture is critical (Cathey, 1969a, b; Karlsson, 2001; Wikesjö, 1975). Thus, seeds may be covered with a thin layer of vermiculite or other media to improve moisture retention without blocking light.

TABLE II-2 PRIMULA

The influence of indole-3-acetic acid (IAA), nicotinic acid (NA), potassium nitrate (KNO$_3$), and various gibberellins (GA$_3$, GA$_4$, GA$_7$) on seed germination of several *Primula* species.

Species	Chemical	Optimal Concentration and Duration
Asian species	GA$_3$	25 or 50 ppm, 20 hr (Tod, 1958)
P. auricula L.	GA$_3$	100 or 1000 ppm (Thompson, 1971)
P. elatior (L.) Hill.	GA$_7$	2.5 or 25 ppm (Thompson, 1970)
P. elatior 'Columnae'	GA$_7$	2.5 or 25 ppm (Thompson, 1970)
P. elatior 'Intricata'	GA$_7$	2.5 or 25 ppm (Thompson, 1970)
P. japonica	GA$_3$, GA$_4$	100 or 50 ppm, 12 hr (Thompson, 1970)
P. japonica	GA$_3$	500 to 1000 ppm (Maurer and Ohm, 1978)
P. japonica	KNO$_3$	2% (Maurer and Ohm, 1978)
P. juliae	GA$_7$	0.25 or 2.5 ppm (Thompson, 1970)
P. obconica	IAA + NA	500 ppm, 12 hr (Hieke, 1964)
P. ×*polyantha*	GA$_3$	250 ppm, 24 hr (Miller and Holcomb, 1982)
P. reidii Duthie.	GA$_3$	100 or 1000 ppm (Thompson, 1971)
P. vulgaris	GA$_3$	500 ppm, 24 hr (McNertney et al., 1991)
P. vulgaris	GA$_3$	No effect at 0 to 1000 ppm, 24 hr (Miller and Holcomb, 1982)

Seeds should be germinated at 59 to 68°F (15 to 20°C) (Cathey, 1969a, b; Chavagnat and Jeudy, 1981). Temperatures should be lower than 68°F (20°C) (Hammer, 1992; Hamrick, 2003; Houghton, 1940). However, Rohde and Albert (1972) reported that *P. sinensis* germinated equally well at temperatures ranging from 66 to 80°F (19 to 27°C).

Seed soaks of indole-3-acetic acid (IAA), nicotinic acid, GA$_3$, GA$_4$, and GA$_7$ have been reported to hasten germination of several primula species (Hieke, 1964; Kuze et al., 1979; Miller and Holcomb, 1982; Thompson, 1969a, b, 1970, 1971; Tod, 1958) (see Table II-2 Primula). *P. japonica* H. Gray. benefitted from stratification at 32 to 48°F (0 to 9°C) for 1 to 12 weeks (Maurer and Ohm, 1978).

A well-aerated peat-based media with a pH of 5.5 to 6.0 should be used (Karlsson, 2001). The media EC should be less than 0.75 dS · m^{-1} (McNertney et al., 1991). Plants are ready to transplant when two to three true leaves have developed (Karlsson, 2001).

FLOWERING CONTROL AND DORMANCY

PRIMULA MALACOIDES

Historically, *Primula malacoides* was considered either a SD plant or a DN plant depending on the temperature (Post, 1936, 1942, 1949; Zimmer, 1985). Plants flowered under SD or were DN when temperatures were from 50 to 60°F (10 to 16°C). However, *P. malacoides* plants were obligate SD plants at temperatures from 60 to 76°F (16 to 24°C). Plants grown under LD at 60 to 70°F (16 to 21°C) never flowered and LD delayed flowering even at 50 to 60°F (10 to 16°C). Zimmer (1969) also stated that the number of inflorescences per plant decreased as the day length increased from 8 to 16 hr.

Recently developed cultivars, however, initiated flowers independent of photoperiod at 61 or 68°F (16 or 20°C) and LD actually reduced crop time compared with SD (Karlsson and Werner, 1999a).

While 45 to 50°F (7 to 10°C) is commonly used for flower initiation (see Table II-3 Primula), flower initiation is most rapid at 59°F (15°C) (Rünger and Wehr, 1971; Zimmer, 1969). Flowering can occur without a low-temperature treatment, but plant and flower quality will be reduced. At temperatures above 55°F (13°C) flower stalks were elongated and weak (Hammer, 1992; Zimmer, 1969). Rünger and Wehr (1971) noted that after flower induction at 50°F (10°C) under LD, subsequent flower development ceased at 77°F (25°C). In addition, some flowers opened and some aborted at 68°F (20°C). At 86°F (30°C), plants died 4 weeks after being induced to flower at 50°F (10°C).

PRIMULA OBCONICA

Primula obconica does not require a cold treatment or a specific photoperiod for flowering (Karlsson, 1997). Production temperatures of 65 to 68°F (18 to 20°C) are typically used and 59 to 65°F (15 to 18°C) temperatures are used

TABLE II-3 PRIMULA

Recommended production temperatures and light levels for various primula species as summarized by Karlsson (2001).

Production Stage	Temperature °F (°C)	Light Photoperiod	Light Intensity	Comments
P. vulgaris and P. ×polyantha				
Germination	60 (16)	Light not required[a]		10–14 days
Early plant development	60–65 (16–18)	LD	Opt. 10 mol · m^{-2} · day^{-1}	6–8 weeks
Flower initiation	55–60 (13–16)	LD	>10 mol · m^{-2} · day^{-1}	Peak light intensity should be below 3000 fc (600 µmol · m^{-2} · s^{-1}); new cultivars do not require a cold treatment
Flower development	55–60 (13–16)	LD	≥10 mol · m^{-2} · day^{-1}	Peak light intensity should be below 3000 fc (600 µmol · m^{-2} · s^{-1})
Finish to marketing	55–60 (13–16)	Ambient	≥5 mol · m^{-2} · day^{-1}	—
P. malacoides				
Germination	60–65 (16–18)	Light not required[a]		2 weeks
Early plant development	60–65 (16–18)	Ambient	Opt. 10 mol · m^{-2} · day^{-1}	6–8 weeks
Flower initiation	45–50 (7–10)	DN	Opt. 10 mol · m^{-2} · day^{-1}	6 weeks
Flower development	57–65 (14–18)	LD	Opt. 10 mol · m^{-2} · day^{-1}	Photoperiod applies to 'Prima'
Finish to marketing	57–60 (14–16)	Ambient	≥5 mol · m^{-2} · day^{-1}	—
P. obconica				
Germination	65–68 (18–20)	Light not required[a]		10–14 days
Early plant development	60–68 (16–20)	LD	Opt. 10 mol · m^{-2} · day^{-1}	6–8 weeks
Flower initiation	65–68 (18–20)	LD	Opt. 10 mol · m^{-2} · day^{-1}	Photoperiod applies to 'Libre'
Flower development	65–68 (18–20)	LD	Opt. 10 mol · m^{-2} · day^{-1}	Photoperiod applies to 'Libre,' DN at 60°F (16°C)
Finish to marketing	60–65 (16–18)	Ambient	≥5 mol · m^{-2} · day^{-1}	—

[a]Light is beneficial immediately on germination.

prior to marketing to improve flower color and plant quality.

PRIMULA ×POLYANTHA AND P. VULGARIS

Traditionally, *Primula ×polyantha* and *P. vulgaris* have been considered cool crops requiring a 6-week cold period of 45 to 50°F (4 to 10°C) for flower initiation. Several studies indicate that *Primula ×polyantha* and *P. vulgaris* do not require a cold treatment for flower initiation (Armitage and Billingsley, 1983; Karlsson, 2001; Welander and Selander, 1981) (see Table II-3 Primula). Armitage and Billingsley (1983) in Georgia noted that plants grown at either 50 or 68°F (10 or 20°C) night temperature flowered at the same time. Karlsson (1997) in Alaska estimated the optimum flower initiation temperature to be 55°F (13°C).

Light intensity and duration interact with temperature in flower initiation and development. Optimum light intensity decreases with increasing temperature (Armitage and Billingsley, 1983; Karlsson, 2001). Under cool temperatures of 49 to 61°F (9 to 16°C), however, high light and LD result in fastest flower initiation. At temperatures of 48°F (9°C) or less, flower initiation and development are delayed and production is slow compared with warmer temperatures regardless of photoperiod; however, high light intensity and LD will decrease the time to flower initiation.

TEMPERATURE

Producers of *Primula ×polyantha* and *P. vulgaris* need to consider the two stages of growth: floral initiation and floral development (see Table II-3 Primula). Traditionally, floral induction was thought to occur naturally at a lower temperature and floral development at a warmer temperature, but floral development is very slow at the suboptimal temperatures commonly used in production. Efficiency and quality could be improved if proper temperatures are applied at both stages. Low temperature during production, however, is one reason for the increased interest in primula (Anonymous, 1977; Goldsberry, 1980; Perry, 1981). There are wide discrepancies in recommended temperatures. Holcomb (1983) stated 39 to 45°F (4 to 7°C) is optimal, while Hammer (1992) recommended 41 to 45°F (5 to 7°C) from transplanting until two to three flower buds are visible, then force at 55°F (13°C) until flower. However, Goldsberry (1980) and others recommended warm temperatures, up to 68°F (20°C), for faster development (Armitage and Billingsley, 1983; Karlsson, 2001; Post, 1949; Smith, 1969). Forcers must calculate the cost of production and effect on plant quality: low temperatures and slow growth versus warmer temperatures and rapid growth. See Flowering Control and Dormancy, page 765, and Table II-3 Primula for *P. malacoides* and *P. obconica* production temperatures.

LIGHT

PRIMULA MALACOIDES

During production, no shade is used except for temperature control in the late spring and summer (see Table II-3 Primula, page 766). Use full light in the winter. Modern cultivars are DN for flower initiation and may be facultative LD for development (Karlsson and Werner, 1999a).

PRIMULA OBCONICA

LD favor faster flower development and shorter crop times (Karlsson and Werner, 1999b) (see Table II-3 Primula, page 766). A high daily light integral of at least 10 mol · m^{-2} · day^{-1} promotes rapid growth (Karlsson, 1997). However, shade may be required to prevent burning and control temperatures.

PRIMULA ×POLYANTHA AND P. VULGARIS

During production, no shade is used except for temperature control in the late spring and summer, when light levels should be kept below 3000 fc (600 μmol · m^{-2} · s^{-1}) (Karlsson, 1997) (see Table II-3 Primula, page 766). Use full light in the winter. Karlsson (2001) noted that high light is beneficial for *Primula ×polyantha* and *P. vulgaris* when production temperatures are low; however, optimum light level decreases from 10 to 2 mol · m^{-2} · day^{-1} with increasing temperature from 54 or 60 (12 or 16°C) to 68°F (20°C). A 2 mol · m^{-2} · day^{-1} light integral is equal to approximately 350 fc for 8 hr or 200 fc for 14 hr, and 10 mol · m^{-2} · day^{-1} is equal to approximately 1700 fc for 8 hr or 1000 fc for 14 hr.

WATER

Overwatering can occur, especially at low temperatures. Frequently, loss of leaf turgidity is observed after several days of dark weather and cold soil temperature. Do not water if medium is moist; use a shade cloth to be safe until soil temperatures rise. Poor growth and chlorotic foliage are often attributed to overwatering. These problems can be corrected by iron chelate sprays and more careful irrigation (Anonymous, 1971). Goldsberry (1979a, b, 1980) stressed not to overwater, particularly after transplanting. On the other hand, uniform moisture is necessary for optimum seed germination for all species and underwatering during production will lead to necrotic leaf edges on *P. malacoides* and *P. obconica*. Dipner (1979) stated that since *Primula sinensis* plants are grown at low temperatures of 54°F (12°C), they have low water and low fertilizer requirements.

CARBON DIOXIDE

Increasing CO_2 from 350 to 800 ppm increased fresh and dry weight and plant quality; however, increasing light levels were more important than elevated CO_2 levels

(Combe et al., 1990, 1993). Karlsson (1997), however, recommended 900 to 1000 ppm during production.

NUTRITION

Fertilization of *P. ×polyantha* and *P. vulgaris* at 60 ppm N and K should commence when the cotyledons develop and can be increased to 200 ppm N just before transplanting (Karlsson, 2001). During production 90 to 100 ppm N and K are acceptable. *P. obconica* generally requires 250 ppm N with equal or greater levels of potassium (Karlsson, 1997).

Holcomb (1983) stated that mineral nutrition of primula is complicated because of the cool forcing temperatures. The conversion of ammonium to nitrate nitrogen by soil microorganisms is reduced, and the release of other medium nutrients is slowed by cool production temperatures. Ammonium-based fertilizers should not be used at these cool temperatures, especially during the winter, to prevent excessive ammonium accumulation.

Primula are injured by high nitrogen levels, are very sensitive to high salt levels, and prefer a medium pH range of 5.5 to 6.5 (Penningsfeld, 1972, 1973; Robert et al., 1982; Straver, 1970). High nitrogen, especially from ammoniacal nitrogen, can produce excessive foliage growth. High soluble salt levels will result in necrotic leaf edges (Karlsson, 2001). Iron chelate can correct high-pH, lime-induced leaf chlorosis with *Primula obconica* and *P. vulgaris* (Anonymous, 1971).

Bowden (1944) did comprehensive research in establishing that supplemental magnesium application of $MgSO_4$ at 3.7 oz/ft³ (3.7 kg · m⁻³) would eliminate chlorosis and in-crease the growth rate. Symptoms of severe cases of magnesium deficiency included severe plant dwarfing, leaf canker, marginal burning, and finally root rot and death. Bowden (1944) also stated that *P. obconica* was more susceptible to low Mg levels than *P. malacoides*. Other nutrient deficiency symptoms are listed in Table II-4 Primula. Holcomb (1983) established appropriate foliar ranges of essential nutrient ions for primula (see Table II-5 Primula).

MEDIA

Primula are grown in a wide variety of media, all of which are well drained with a pH of 5.5 to 6.0. For *P. vulgaris* and *P. obconica*, a slightly acidic pH (5.5 to 5.7) is optimal for production (Straver, 1970). Most media are high in peat moss.

HEIGHT CONTROL

No height control is normally needed; however, B-Nine (daminozide) sprays at 1000 to 2000 ppm can be used if flower stem elongation of *P. vulgaris*, *P. ×polyantha*, *P. sinensis*, and *P. malacoides* is excessive. B-Nine is ineffective on *P. obconica* (Karlsson, 1997). Height is best controlled through proper spacing, temperature, and irrigation. DIF temperature manipulation is also effective (Hartnett, 1993).

SPACING

Seedlings develop in plugs and are transplanted to 4-in. (10-cm) pots. Potted plants can remain pot-to-pot for space efficiency until leaves touch; the plants are then spaced at 6 × 6 in. (15 × 15 cm). Some growers prefer 7- × 7-in. (18- × 18-cm) spacing.

TABLE II-4 PRIMULA

Primula foliar nutrient deficiencies descriptions (Holcomb, 1983).

Nutrient	Description
Nitrogen	Leaves chlorotic, leaf veins discolored and become black with time. New growth pale; old growth becomes chlorotic with marginal necrosis.
Phosphorus	Lower leaves become bronzed; new growth curls inward with necrosis at tip; veins become brown and eventually die.
Potassium	Lower leaves become chlorotic and eventually necrotic, wilt and die. New leaf expansion is reduced and new growth curls inward. Leaf margins are severely curled or rippled.
Calcium	Leaves are pale green.
Magnesium	Older leaves have interveinal chlorosis which develops into a tip and marginal necrosis. New leaves curl under and arch backward.
Iron	New leaves chlorotic to completely white to necrotic over time. Older leaves developed chlorosis at margins which moves to midvein.

TABLE II-5 PRIMULA

Foliage analysis values of deficient and optimal ranges for *Primula* ×*polyantha* plants grown in nutrient solution cultures (Holcomb, 1983).

Nutrient	Deficient	Optimum	Highest Observed Values	Commercial Sample
Nitrogen (%)	1.51	2.50–3.30	3.30	2.84
Phosphorus (%)	0.22	0.36–0.81	0.97	0.67
Potassium (%)	1.56	2.11–4.20	4.73	5.26
Calcium (%)	0.18	0.62–1.01	1.66	0.80
Magnesium (%)	0.09	0.20–0.42	0.54	0.34
Iron (ppm)	0.60	78–155	211	249
		Other elements were averaged (ppm):		
Manganese		49.70		87.67
Copper		6.45		8.67
Boron		35.90		28.33
Aluminum		80.15		221
Zinc		38.55		42.00
Strontium		12.80		16.00
Lead		5.90		10.70
Silicon		40.35		269

TABLE II-6 PRIMULA

Sample production schedule for *Primula* ×*polyantha* and *P. vulgaris*.

Cultural Step	Production Time (weeks)	Temperature °F (°C)
Seeds sown in light		
	2	65 (18)
Seeds germinate		
	4–6	60 (16)
Plugs transplanted size to 4-in. (10-cm) pots. Space pot-to-pot		
	2–3	60 (16)
Commence reproduction temperature, space when 6 to 10 leaves developed		
	6	54–60 (12–16)
Visible buds		
	2–4	60 (16)
Buds with color		
	2	60 (16)
Flower		
Total	18–23	

PINCHING AND DISBUDDING

No pinching or disbudding required.

SUPPORT

No support required.

SCHEDULE AND TIMING

Total crop time for primula will be 3 to 5 months, depending on production temperatures. See Flowering Control and Dormancy, page 765, for specific temperatures, day lengths, and light intensities, and Table II-6 Primula for a production schedule of *P.* ×*polyantha* and *P. vulgaris*.

INSECTS

Aphids are a common problem, and thrips, caterpillars, fungus gnats, and mites can also occur. Unfortunately, the western flower thrips carry tomato spotted wilt virus.

DISEASES

Tomato spotted wilt virus causes the leaves to form interveinal brown spots similar to spray injury. Some cultivars develop yellow leaves and marginal browning (Daughtrey and Chase, 1992). *Pythium* root rot and *Botrytis* can develop during periods of high humidity and cold production temperature. *Ramularia primulae* leaf spot produces brown, necrotic leaf spots (Karlsson, 1997). Keep leaves and flowers dry and do not overwater. Numerous other diseases have been reported including black root rot (*Thielaviopsis basicola*), rusts (*Uromyces apiosporus*), bacterial leaf spot (*Pseudomonas syringae*), aster yellows phytoplasma, and impatiens necrotic spot, tomato spotted wilt, and primula mosaic viruses (Dreistadt, 2001).

PHYSIOLOGICAL DISORDERS

A variety of leaf problems including chlorosis, marginal necrosis, and tip burn can be caused by overwatering, underwatering, high medium EC, high pH (iron chlorosis), and magnesium deficiency. Ammonium toxicity, excess nitrogen, and high EC cause root injury, which also produces leaf problems. Excessively large leaves can be attributed to high nitrogen levels or production temperatures (Karlsson, 1997). Premature flowering on small plants can be due to cold production temperatures or low nutrition (Hamrick, 2003).

POSTHARVEST

Harvesting should commence when the first five to seven florets are open. Ethylene results in wilting flowers and primula are considered to be highly sensitive to ethylene with negative effects apparent from 0.05 ppm (Willumsen and Fjeld, 1995). Silver thiosulfate (STS) sprays of 0.2 to 0.5 mM increase longevity (Nowak and Rudnicki, 1990). Ship at 36 to 43°F (2 to 6°C) and do not allow media to dry because foliage will deteriorate (L. Høyer, personal communication). With proper care plants should last 2 to 4 weeks in the home (Hartnett, 1993). Although rarely used as a cut flower, stems of some species or cultivars can be cut when one-half of florets are open.

KEY POINTS

- The numerous primrose species are used as potted flowering plants, bedding plants, and garden ornamentals.
- Seed propagation is most common; *in vitro* propagation is possible.
- *Primula malacoides* was formerly considered a day-neutral plant below 60 to 63°F (16 to 17°C) and an obligate SD plant above 60 to 63°F (16 to 17°C). Currently available cultivars are considered day neutral regardless of temperature.
- While *P. ×polyantha* and *P. vulgaris* have traditionally been given a 6-week cold period of 45 to 50°F (4 to 10°C) for flower initiation, initiation occurs under a wide range of temperatures for currently available cultivars.
- The best quality primula plants are usually produced under cool production temperatures of 40 to 65°F (4 to 18°C).
- Be careful to not overwater plants, especially after transplanting.
- Foliar chlorosis, marginal necrosis, and tip burn is common and can be due to overwatering, high pH, magnesium deficiency, ammonium toxicity, excessive nitrogen, and high EC.

BIBLIOGRAPHY

Anonymous. 1971. *Primula,* pp. 98–99. Netherland, Proefstation voor de Bloemisteru in Nederland te Aalsmeer Jaarverslag.

Anonymous. 1977. Strong future seen for primrose sales. *The Grower* 87(14):794–795.

Anonymous. 1994. Growing basics for *Primula. Professional Plant Growers Association News* 25(10):5.

Armitage, A.M., and J.W. Billingsley. 1983. Influence of warm night temperatures on growth and flowering of *Primula ×polyanthus. HortScience* 18: 882–883.

Atwater, B.R. 1980. Germination, dormancy and morphology of the seeds of herbaceous ornamental plants. *Seed Science and Technology* 8:523–573.

Bailey, L.H., and E.Z. Bailey. 1976. *Primula*, pp. 907–912 in *Hortus Third: A Concise Dictionary of Plants Cultivated in the United States and Canada.* Macmillan, New York.

Bowden, R.A. 1944. Experiments show effect of magnesium on primula plants. *Florists Review* 93(2412):23–24.

Cathey, H.M. 1969a. I. Guidelines for the germination of annual pot plant and ornamental herb seed. *Florists Review* 144(3742):21–23, 58–60.

Cathey, H.M. 1969b. II. Guidelines for the germination of annual pot plants and ornamental herb seed. *Florists Review* 144(3743):18–20, 52–53.

Chavagnat, A., and B. Jeudy. 1981. Study of the germination in the laboratory of *Primula obconica. Seed Science and Technology* 9:577–586.

Combe, L., J.M. Bertolini, P. Quétin, and P. Locher. 1990. Growth and photosynthesis of CO_2-enriched primrose. *Acta Horticulturae* 268:55–62.

Combe, L., J.M. Bertolini, and P. Quétin. 1993. Photosynthése de la primevére (*Primula obconica* Hance): Effets du gaz carbonique et de l'éclairement. *Canadian Journal of Plants Science* 73: 1149–1161. (in French, English summary)

Coumans, M., M.F. Coumans-Gilles, J. Delhez, and T. Gaspar. 1979. Mass propagation of *Primula obconica. Acta Horticulturae* 91:287–293.

Daughtrey, M., and A.R. Chase. 1992. Primula, p. 176 in *Ball Field Guide to Diseases of Greenhouse Ornamentals.* Ball Publishing, Batavia, Illinois.

Dipner, H. 1979. Sind die Chinesen-Primeln vergessen? *Deutscher Gartenbau* 33:774–775. (in German, English summary)

Dreistadt, S.H. 2001. *Integrated Pest Management for Floriculture and Nurseries.* University of California Division of Agriculture and Natural Resources Publication 3402.

Goldsberry, K.L. 1979a. Mini pots—Colorado State University style. *Colorado State Greenhouse Growers Association Bulletin* 346:1–3.

Goldsberry, K.L. 1979b. *Calceolaria* and *Dianthus* for mini-pot plants. *Colorado Greenhouse Growers Association Bulletin* 348:1–3.

Goldsberry, K.L. 1980. Primula: A flowering mini-pot plant. *Colorado Greenhouse Growers Association Bulletin* 359:1–2.

Gray, D. 2000. Global notes. *FloraCulture International* 10(4):6.

Hammer, P.A. 1992. Other flowering pot plants, I. *Primula*, pp. 492–493 in *Introduction to Floriculture*, 2nd ed., R.A. Larson editor. Academic Press, New York.

Hamrick, D. 2003. *Primula*, pp. 589–591 in *Ball Redbook*, vol. 2, 17th ed. Ball Publishing, Batavia, Illinois.

Hartnett, G. 1993. Focus on *Primula* production. *Professional Plant Growers Association News* 24(7): 4–7, 10–11, 14.

Heydecker, W. 1975. "Seed priming"—the treatment of the future? *The Grower* 84:554–555.

Hieke, K. 1964. The effect of some stimulants of seed germination in *Primula obconica. Horticulture Abstracts* 35:881. (Abstract)

Holcomb, E.J. 1983. The primrose path to nutrition. *Greenhouse Grower* 1(10):224–225.

Houghton, K.W. 1940. Growing primroses from seed. *Horticulture* 18:204.

Huxley, A., M. Griffiths, and M. Levy. 1992. *Primula*, pp. 708–724 in *The New Royal Horticultural Society Dictionary of Gardening*, vol. 3. Stockton Press, New York.

Karlsson, M.G. 1997. *Primula*, pp. 107–111 in *Tips on Growing Specialty Potted Crops*, M.L. Gaston, S.A. Carver, C.A. Irwin, and R.A. Larson, editors. Ohio Florists' Association, Columbus, Ohio.

Karlsson, M.G. 2001. Primula culture and production. *HortTechnology* 11:627–635.

Karlsson, M.G., and J.W. Werner. 1999a. Rate of flower formation in *Primula malacoides* varied with photoperiod and temperature conditions. *HortScience* 34:476. (Abstract)

Karlsson, M.G., and J.W. Werner. 1999b. Daylength and temperature affect rate of flowering in *Primula obconica. HortScience* 34:476. (Abstract)

Kuze, S., M. Ushijima, and H. Tanaka. 1979. *Dormancy and Changes in the Levels of Endogenous Gibberellin-Like Substances in Primula sieboldi.* Bulletin, Faculty of Agriculture, Tamagawa University, Tokyo.

Markham, E. 1994. Primulas on parade. *Greenhouse Growers* 12(4):34–35.

Maurer, M., and E. Ohm. 1978. *Primula japonica.* Samen stratifizieren und mit Gibberelline behandeln (aber wie?). *Gartenbauwissenschaft* 78:348–350. (in German)

McNertney, D., M. Khademi, and D. Koranski. 1991. Raise your primula germination rates. *GrowerTalks* 55(8):43, 45.

Miller, E.A., and E.J. Holcomb. 1982. Effect of GA_3 on germination of *Primula vulgaris* Huds. and *Primula ×polyantha* Hort. *HortScience* 17:814–815.

Nowak, J., and R.M. Rudnicki. 1990. *Postharvest Handling and Storage of Cut Flowers, Florist Greens and Potted Plants.* Timber Press, Portland, Oregon.

Penningsfeld, F. 1972. Macro and micro nutrient requirements of pot plants in peat. *Acta Horticulturae* 26:81–102.

Penningsfeld, F. 1973. Boden—und Düngungsfragen der Staudenkultur. *Neue Landschaft* 18:436–446. (in German)

Perry, L.P. 1981. Primulas make a comeback as a 5-month cool crop. *Florists Review* 168(4344):22, 55.

Post, K. 1936. Further responses of miscellaneous plants to temperature. *Proceedings of the American Society for Horticultural Science* 34:627–629.

Post, K. 1942. Effects of daylength and temperature on growth and flowering of some florist's crops. *Cornell University Agriculture Experiment Station Bulletin*, 787:1–70.

Post, K. 1949. *Primula* (Primrose), pp. 746–748 in *Florists Crop Production and Marketing.* Orange Judd Publishing, New York.

Robert, R., P. Fischer, and G. Fritzsche. 1982. Water treatment and irrigation experiment. Effect on the growth of pelargoniums and primulas. *Deutscher Gartenbau* 36:1058–1061. (in German, English summary)

Rohde, J., and G. Albert. 1972. Keimung bei *Primula sinensis fimbriata* 'Helle Zukunft.' *Gartenwelt* 72:146. (in German)

Rünger, W., and B. Wehr. 1971. Einfluss von Tageslänge und Temperatur auf die Blütenbildung und—entwicklung von *Primula malacoides. Gartenbauwissenschaft* 36:51–62. (in German)

Smith, D.R. 1969. Controlled flowering of *Primula malacoides. Experimental Horticulture* 20:22–34.

Straver, N. 1970. Een proef met verschillended zaaigronden bij primula. *Proefstation Vakblai Bloemisterij (Aalsmeer)* 25:1758. (in Dutch)

Thompson, P.A. 1969a. Germinating primula seed. *Journal of Royal Horticulture Society* 93:133–138.

Thompson, P.A. 1969b. Comparative effects of gibberellins A$_3$ and A$_4$ on the germination of seeds of several different species. *Horticulture Research* 9:130–138.

Thompson, P.A. 1970. Effect of temperature, chilling and treatment with gibberellins on the germination of *Primula* species. *Journal of Horticultural Science* 45:175–186.

Thompson, P.A. 1971. Research into seed dormancy and germination. *Proceedings of International Plant Propagators Society* 21:211–228.

Tod, H. 1958. Effect of gibberellic acid on seed germination. *Gardeners Chronicle* 144:257, 260.

Welander, T., and C. Selander. 1981. Flower formation in *Primula vulgaris. Swedish Journal of Agricultural Research* 11:41–47. (in Swedish, English summary)

Wikesjö, K. 1975. *Production Programs for Pot Plants and Cut Flower in Sweden.* Horticultural Advisors Bulletin 89, Agriculture College, Alnarp, Sweden. (in Swedish)

Willumsen, K., and T. Fjeld. 1995. The sensitivity of some flowering potted plants to exogenous ethylene. *Acta Horticulturae* 405:362–367.

Zimmer, K. 1969. Zur Blütenbildung bei *Primula malacoides. Gartenwelt* 69:137–138. (in German)

Zimmer, K. 1985. *Primula*, pp. 137–138 in *Handbook of Flowering*, vol. IV, A.H. Halevy, editor. CRC Press, Boca Raton, Florida.

Proteaceae

INTRODUCTION

Common and scientific names (Huxley et al., 1992; Olde and Marriott, 1994; Vogts, 1982; Wrigley and Fagg, 1991):

1. *Banksia* L. f., banksia
2. *Grevillea* R. Br. ex Knight, grevillea, spider flower
3. *Leucadendron* R. Br., conebush
4. *Leucospermum* R. Br., pincushion, sunburst protea
5. *Protea* L., protea, sugarbush
6. *Telopea* R. Br., waratah.

Family and related taxa: Proteaceae. There are two subfamilies: *Proteoideae* including *Leucadendron* (79 species), *Leucospermum* (48 species), and *Protea* (117 species) and *Grevilleoideae* including *Banksia* (50 species), *Grevillea* (250 species), and *Telopea* (4 species). According to a ruling by the International Protea Association the term *protea* can be applied to any member of the Proteaceae, generally with reference to the ornamental flower.

Origin: *Banksia, Grevillea,* and *Telopea* are indigenous to Australia. *Leucadendron* and *Leucospermum* are restricted to South Africa. *Protea* is the largest and most widespread genus with 82 species occurring in South Africa and an additional 35 species occurring in tropical Africa (Vogts, 1982). The scientific name *Protea* arises from the great variation within the genus, leading Linnaeus to liken the genus to the sea god Proteus who was capable of appearing in many diverse forms.

Uses and current status: Proteaceae are used mainly as fresh cut flowers or foliage with commercial production in South Africa, Australia, New Zealand, Zimbabwe, United States (primarily Hawaii and California), Israel, and parts of Europe. The majority of high-quality Proteaceae are cultivated in plantations, but some wild harvesting still occurs. *Banksia* flowers are also sold dyed or dried. *Banksia*, *Leucadendron*, and *Leucospermum* may be useful as potted flowering plants; *Leucadendron discolor* Buek. can be produced in 3 to 5 months (Ben-Jaacov et al., 1986). Various Proteaceae are also grown as garden ornamentals.

The growth habit of Proteaceae plants varies from trees 26 ft (8 m) tall (*P. nitida* Mill.) to medium-sized shrubs and prostrate, creeping, woody plants, often with underground stems. Most species have evergreen foliage. *Leucadendron* are dioecious, and male and female plants are commonly very distinct.

CULTIVARS

BANKSIA

Present production is based on seedling material and few cultivars are available. Breeding and selection programs for cut flowers have focused on *B. coccinea* R. Br., *B. menziesii* R. Br., *B. hookeriana* Meissner, and *B. prionotes* Lindl., which produce showy, terminal flowers on long, straight stems (Sedgley, 1997). *B. ashbyii* E.G. Baker, *B. burdettii* E.G. Baker, and *B. speciosa* R. Br. can also be used as cut flowers (Webb, 1996a). Selection criteria include rooting ability and tolerance to the root rot fungus *Phytophthora cinnamomi*, in addition to typical cut flower criteria of good color, high productivity, and stem length. Color variation in banksia ranges from scarlet and dark red to yellow, pink, and orange. The banksia inflorescence comprises many individual florets arranged in a spiral pattern on a woody receptacle. Flowers open acropetally.

Cultivars are few. Of the seven landscape cultivars three are prostrate and one ('Birthday Candles') is suitable for pot production. Two of the three cut flower cultivars are selections of *B. coccinea* ('Waite Crimson' and 'Waite Flame') and the third ('Waite Orange') is a natural interspecific hybrid between *B. hookeriana* and *B. prionotes* (Sedgley, 1997).

GREVILLEA

Numerous grevillea cultivars have been registered, with the majority used as landscape plants. The best known is *G. robusta* A. Cunningham ex R. Br., an attractive flowering tree commonly known as the silver, or silky, oak. Species suitable for cut flower production have large, prominent, colorful flowers or attractive, often silvery, foliage. The flowers have a short vase life, which limits the use of grevillea as a cut flower. However, Dupee (1986) discussed *G. longistyla* W.J. Hooker and *Grevillea* 'Poorinda Peter' as cut flowers. New cultivars are registered with the Australian Cultivar Registration Authority (ACRA) and short descriptions have been published in *Australian Plants* (Anonymous, 1993; Costin and Costin, 1988a; Payne, 1995, 1997).

Flower colors vary from cream and white to yellow, orange, pink, and all shades of red. All inflorescences are composed of many individual florets and occur in a variety of flowering habits. In most species flowers open acropetally and many are fragrant.

LEUCADENDRON

Leucadendron are grown for their attractive foliage ranging from silvery, such as *L. argenteum* (L.) R. Br., *L. floridum* R. Br., and *L. album* (Thunb.) Fourc., to yellow, such as *L. platyspermum*, R. Br. and *L. laureolum* am. Fourc., and red, such as *L. salignum* Berg. Intense foliage color generally occurs when shoot growth stops and flowering starts. The most popular cut flower species have large, showy bracts surrounding the flower head (Van den Berg and Brits, 1995). The female flower is a cone composed of floral bracts, each subtending individual small florets, forming attractive, showy heads. Although the male flower is generally unattractive, *L. discolor* male plants show striking contrast between yellow bracts and red florets. Male plants have limited commercial potential due to the tendency of the flowers to blacken rapidly, although many have merit as cut foliage. Fine-leaved foliage varieties are also grown commercially. Cultivars are both selections of pure species and interspecific hybrids. Seedling populations vary, indicating potential for development of new products.

LEUCOSPERMUM

Species with large, single flowers are used for both cut flower and pot plant production, while those with smaller, multiple-headed flowers (conflorescences) are more suited to pot plant production. Cultivars are selections of pure species and hybrids. Flower color is mainly yellow and orange, with some deep orange and red selections.

Breeding is directed at increasing productivity, long stems, color, and resistance to *Phytophthora*. Research has identified lines which are tolerant to *Phytophthora cinnamomi* and can be used as rootstocks.

PROTEA

Protea in commerce have large, showy terminal flowers produced on shrubby plants with an upright growth habit, ensuring long, straight stems. A few creeping forms are harvested for foliage or bouquets. The inflorescence consists of many individual florets surrounded by a crown of colored, often hirsute, involucral bracts. The color of involucral bracts varies from white, green-white to creamy, light to dark pink, and red. Hairs on the involucral bracts may be absent or colored white, brown, or black, as are the hairs on the tips of individual florets. The most commonly produced cut flowers are hybrids and selections of *P. cynaroides* (L.) L., *P. magnifica (barbigera)* Link, *P. compacta* R. Br., *P. eximia* (Salisb. ex Knight) Fourc., *P. repens* (L.) L., *P. neriifolia* R. Br., and *P. grandiceps* Tratt.

TELOPEA

Telopea speciosissima (Sm.) R. Br. is the main species of waratah grown as a cut flower. Flower color ranges from red through pink to white, and flower size, plant vigor, and productivity vary greatly. The inflorescence is composed of individual florets arranged spirally in pairs on a receptacle. Both florets and involucral bracts surrounding the floret mass have intense color. Bracts are susceptible to browning and flowers with small or insignificant involucral bracts are generally superior. Cultivars suitable as landscape plants or for cut flower production are available. Names and short descriptions of new cultivars are published in *Australian Plants* (Nixon and Payne, 1995).

PROPAGATION

ASEXUAL PROPAGATION—CUTTINGS

BANKSIA. Both terminal and subterminal cuttings are used (Sedgley, 1998, 1995). For difficult-to-root cultivars, use higher rates of IBA or soak (Sedgley, 1995) (Table II-1 Proteaceae).

GREVILLEA. With difficult species use higher concentration of indole-3-butyric acid (IBA) (Olde and Marriott, 1994) (Table II-1 Proteaceae). Cuttings should be treated with both soil and foliage fungicides during rooting, which takes 3 to 6 weeks (Costin and Costin, 1988a).

LEUCADENDRON. Cuttings taken in late summer will be rooted and ready for planting in late winter/early spring (Rodríguez-Pérez, 1992; Rodríguez-Pérez et al., 1997. (Table II-1 Proteaceae).

LEUCOSPERMUM. The majority of production is from cutting propagation, although seed is still used rarely (Criley, 1998). Propagation information from various sources has been summarized in Table II-1 Proteaceae. (Brown et al., 1998; Criley, 1998; Jacobs and Steenkamp, 1975, 1976; McKenzie, 1973).

PROTEA. Most commercial plantations are established from rooted cuttings (Table II-1 Proteaceae). The exceptions are *P. cynaroides* and *P. magnifica*, which are grown from seed. Propagation information from various sources has been summarized in Table II-1 Proteaceae (Brown et al., 1996; Dawson and King, 1994; Harre, 1988; Jacobs and Steenkamp, 1975; McKenzie, 1973; Rodríguez-Pérez, 1990). *P. neriifolia, P. magnifica,* and *P. grandiceps* are slow to root while others, such as *P. repens, P. cynaroides, P. compacta,* and *P. eximia* root more quickly. Plants should be hardened off under 50% shade for 2 weeks before planting in the field.

TELOPEA. Waratah is susceptible to toxic uptake of IBA if high concentrations are used (Worrall, 1983) (Table II-1 Proteaceae). Rooting takes 4 to 5 weeks. Both cuttings and seedlings should be given a 6-month establishment phase in pots before transplanting to improve survival. If plant material is limited, waratah can be propagated using leaf bud cuttings, consisting of a leaf blade, petiole, and a short piece of stem with the axillary bud attached (Ellyard and Butler, 1985).

ASEXUAL PROPAGATION—GRAFTING

BANKSIA. Grafting of banksia have been investigated but has produced inconsistent and inconclusive results (Sedgley, 1998).

GREVILLEA. Grevillea are grafted to improve their aesthetic appeal or to overcome intolerance to soil conditions. Weeping standards can be produced by grafting ground cover and decumbant species such as *G. laurifolia*

TABLE II-1 PROTEACEAE

Propagation methods used for rooting cuttings of *Banksia*, *Grevillea*, *Leucadendron*, *Leucospermum*, *Protea*, and *Telopea* under intermittent mist.

Tissue Type	Cutting Length in. (cm)	Leaf Removal	Hormone Application	Rooting Media[a]	Temperature °F (°C)
Banksia					
Semi-hard, after spring growth flush	4 (10)	Yes, lower ½	IBA dip, 3500–12,000 ppm, 5 sec	1:1:1 P:CS:Pr	77 (25)

Comments: Two longitudinal cuts 0.4 to 0.8 in. (1 to 2 cm) long are made on stem prior to IBA application. Soak difficult-to-root cuttings (5 hr) in water with ascorbic acid (13.4 oz/100 gal., 1 g · L^{-1}) and citric acid (20 oz/100 gal, 1.5 g · L^{-1}) to remove tissue phenols.

Tissue Type	Cutting Length in. (cm)	Leaf Removal	Hormone Application	Rooting Media[a]	Temperature °F (°C)
Grevillea					
Semi-hard, in fall or in in never winter	2–4 (6–10)	Yes, lower ½ to ⅓	IBA, 4000–10,000 ppm powder, 500–1200 ppm dip	3:1 S:P, 1:1 Pr:V 3:2:1 S:Pr:P 3:1:0.5 S:P:L	Ambient, use bottom heat

Comments: Basal end of cutting should be made below a leaf node on a lateral shoot (remove shoot to form a heel for maximum cambium area). Wound stem if difficult to root.

Tissue Type	Cutting Length in. (cm)	Leaf Removal	Hormone Application	Rooting Media[a]	Temperature °F (°C)
Leucadendron					
Semi-hard, current year's growth	6–8 (15–20)	Yes, lower ⅓	IBA dip, 2000–4000 ppm in 50% ethanol or acetone, 5–10 sec	1:2 P:Pr, 1:1 P:S 1:1:1 P:S:Ps 1:1 Ps:S 3:1 Ps:S	72–77 (22–25)

Comments: For *L. discolor* wound stem, L. 'Safari Sunset' can be propagated by leaf-bud cuttings.

Tissue Type	Cutting Length in. (cm)	Leaf Removal	Hormone Application	Rooting Media[a]	Temperature °F (°C)
Leucospermum					
Semi-hard	6–8 (15–20)	Yes, lower ⅓	IBA dip, 2000 to 4000 ppm, 5 sec	1:2 P:Pr, 1:1 P:S 2:1 P:Ps 1:1 P:Ps	72–77 (22–25)

Comments: Ethanol or acetone dips are more effective than IBA in talc.

Tissue Type	Cutting Length in. (cm)	Leaf Removal	Hormone Application	Rooting Media[a]	Temperature °F (°C)
Protea					
Semi-hard	6–8 (15–20)	Yes, lower ⅓	IBA dip, 2000 to 4000 ppm, 5–10 sec	1:1 P:S, 2:1 P:Ps 1:1 P:Ps	68–77 (20–25)

Comments: Hardwood cuttings should not be used.

Tissue Type	Cutting Length in. (cm)	Leaf Removal	Hormone Application	Rooting Media[a]	Temperature °F (°C)
Telopea					
Terminal or subterminal stem in spring	6 (15)	No	IBA, dip basal 2 in. (5 cm) of cutting in 2000 ppm or use 0.3% dust	100% peat moss for cuttings, 1:1:1 S:P:Pr for leaf bud	81 (27)

Comments: Cuttings with four to five leaves are used, IBA dissolved in ethanol, excess leaf trimming can result in death of cutting.

[a]CS = course sand, L = pasteurized loam, P = peat moss, Pr = perlite, Ps = polystyrene, V = vermiculite.

F.W. Sieber ex CPJ Sprengel, *G. tenuiloba* C.A. Gardner, and *G. gaudichaudii* R. Br. ex C. Gaudichaud-Beaupré onto a vigorous root-stock, such as *G. robusta*, using wedge, splice, or approach grafting. Grafting should be performed after rooting. The leaves of large-leafed varieties should be trimmed to minimize desiccation and save nursery space. Grafting is best performed just before vigorous growth starts in spring. Potential rootstock have been evaluated for summer and winter rainfall areas (Olde and Marriott, 1994).

LEUCADENDRON. Production of *Leucadendron* is often limited by soil-root problems, such as high pH, *Phytophthora*, and nematodes, and can be overcome by the use of suitable root-stocks. Wedge grafting, top-cleft grafting, and side grafting techniques are successful, both before or after rooting of the rootstock cutting (Ackerman et al., 1997).

LEUCOSPERMUM. Grafting can be used to overcome root problems with high pH, salinity, or soil-borne diseases (Moffat and Turnbull, 1993). Fall to late winter is the best time for grafting, allowing wound healing before resumption of shoot growth in spring (Brits, 1990b). Wedge grafting is a convenient, cost effective, and successful method. Reduce scion desiccation by limiting the size of the scion to two buds and trimming the subtending leaves. Chip budding is also successful, provided leaves remain above the bud, and the distal rootstock portion is removed only after the bud union has healed and vegetative growth has begun.

Rootstock cuttings may be grafted prior to rooting, which allows simultaneous rooting and graft union formation in the mist bed and the production of a grafted rooted plant in 7 to 8 weeks (Ackerman et al., 1997). Alternatively, rooted cuttings may be grafted and the union allowed to form before transplanting.

PROTEA. Wedge grafting techniques suitable for other Proteaceae were not very successful with *Protea* (Brits, 1990b). Some success was achieved grafting *P. cynaroides* and *P. neriifolia* onto the lime-tolerant *P. obtusifolia* Buek. ex Meisn. by top-cleft grafts and side grafts (Ben-Jaacov et al., 1992). Development of rootstocks tolerant to high soil pH, nematodes, and *Phytophthora* has been occurring concurrently with research to improve grafting techniques (Moffat and Turnbull, 1993).

ASEXUAL PROPAGATION— MICROPROPAGATION

Micropropagation of *Banksia*, *Leucadendron*, and *Leucospermum* has yielded inconsistent and inconclusive results (Pérez-Francés et al., 1995; Rugge and Jacobs, 1990; Sedgley, 1998; Tal et al., 1992a, b). Rapid multiplication of *Grevillea*, *Telopea*, and some species of *Protea* is possible (Malan, 1992; Offord et al., 1990; Rugge, 1995; Seelye et al., 1986; Tal et al., 1992a, b; Watad et al., 1992).

SEXUAL PROPAGATION

BANKSIA. Banksia seeds need no pregermination treatment and the optimum temperature for germination varies with species. Seed of *B. integrifolia* L.f. germinates at a temperature range of 64 to 73°F (18 to 23°C), *B. aemula* R.Br. at 82 to 90°F (28 to 32°C), and *B. coccinea* at 50 to 77°F (10 to 25°C). Germination of *B. coccinea*, *B. ornata* F. Meull. ex Meissner, and *B. aculeata* A.S. George was successful at 59°F (15°C) (Sedgley, 1998). Germination takes 3 weeks to 3 months on a well-drained, acidic medium. Seedling grow most rapidly at 77°F (25°C).

GREVILLEA. Grevillea seed varies greatly in shape, structure, and ease of germination. Large, fleshy seeds or seeds with a papery fringe require no pretreatment, and germination occurs within a couple of weeks. However, the impermeable barrier surrounding some seeds must be broken, allowing water and oxygen to penetrate, before germination will occur. Nicking a small piece of the seed coat off with the fingernail, or peeling the entire outer skin away, are effective but time-consuming methods. Large quantities of seed can be soaked for 24 to 48 hr in warm to hot water. Seed from alpine species, such as *G. victoriae* F. Mueller and *G. australis* R. Br., require stratification for a few months before scarification. With *G. annulifera* F. Mueller and *G. nana* C.A. Gardner, the corky layer surrounding the seeds must be carefully removed by hand to allow germination (Olde and Marriott, 1994).

Seed is sown onto a well-drained, sterile medium, such as 3 to 5:1 washed river sand:peat and various combinations of peat and sand, peat and perlite, sand and gravel, or sand and vermiculite. Seed should be covered to approximately its own depth, or deeper, and kept moist. As with other Proteaceae native to temperate regions, seed germination is best during late autumn or early spring with cool 43 to 54°F (6 to12°C) nights and warm 64 to 72°F (18 to 22°C) days. However, grevillea native to tropical and arid regions of Australia will germinate at any time of year. Seedlings should, ideally, be transplanted when the first pair of true leaves are present.

LEUCADENDRON. *Leucadendron* is divided into two subgenera on the basis of seed morphology: *Alatosperma*, in which seeds are flat, and *Leucadendron*, in which seeds are round nuts (Rebelo, 1995). Flat seeds require no pregermination treatment. However, the hard coating of round nutlike seeds must be removed. Seeds are soaked in 1% hydrogen peroxide for 24 hr to soften the outer coat (pericarp), which is then manually removed. After the seeds have dried, they are dusted lightly with fungicide before planting.

Seed germinate best when sown in fall with 59 to 68/39 to 50°F (15 to 20/4 to 10°C) day/night temperatures (Brown et al., 1998). The medium should be well drained, such as 1:1 peat:sand or 1:1:1 peat:coarse sand:loam (Vogts, 1982). Seed is placed on the moist medium, covered lightly, and watered.

LEUCOSPERMUM. Seed is broadcast onto beds for field cut flower production. For use in a breeding program or a commercial nursery, seeds are germinated then transplanted. The seed is a nutlike achene enclosed by a pericarp, which may have to be removed for germination. Approximately 60% germination is obtained by first soaking the dry seeds in a 1% hydrogen peroxide solution for 24 hr (Brits, 1986a). The gelatinous pericarp is manually removed and the seeds sown in seed beds. Other treatments include sulfuric acid scarification, whereby seeds are soaked in concentrated acid for 8 min at 72°F (22°C) and washed before sowing, or soaked in hot water 140°F (60°C) for 30 min (Brits, 1990a; Harre, 1986). Germination of seeds can be improved by presoaking in a solution of gibberellic acid (GA$_3$, 25 ppm) or Fascination (1:1 benzyladenine:gibberellic acid) at 200 ppm (Brits, 1990a; Brown, 1986). For all of these treatments the best results are obtained by sowing seeds in fall when temperatures fluctuate between 59 and 68°F (15 to 20°C) during the day, followed by 39 to 50°F (4 to 10°C) at night (Brown et al., 1998).

Seeds should be dusted with a fungicide. Recommended media are well drained, consisting of 1:1 sand:peat or leaf mold or 1:1:1 peat:coarse sand:loam (Vogts, 1982). After sowing onto a moist seedbed, they are covered by a thin layer of dry sand and watered. For large-scale seedling production, seeds are placed between two layers of moist hessian (burlap) and transplanted after the radicle appears.

PROTEA. *Protea* seed are flat or cylindrical in shape and covered densely, with long, straight hairs. Some *Protea* are reported to have a low-temperature requirement for germination of 34 to 52°F (1 to 11°C) (Brown et al., 1998; Malan, 1992; Mitchell et al., 1986). For example, germination of *P. compacta* seed was significantly improved by stratification at 41°F (5°C) for 30 to 60 days (Mitchell et al., 1986). Since the seed are adapted to fire (serotinous), germination is stimulated by plant-derived smoke or commercially available aqueous smoke extracts, and such pretreatment may break dormancy. Commercial seed suppliers recommend soaking *Protea* seed in hot water [122°F (50°C)] for 30 min, drying them, and dusting them with a fungicide before sowing. GA$_3$ soaks (24 hr) significantly improved *P. eximia* and *P. neriifolia* germination, but results were undefined for *P. cynaroides* and *P. repens* (Rodríguez–Pérez, 1995). For large-scale seedling production, seeds are placed between two layers of moist hessian and transplanted after the radicle appears.

The germination media should be well drained, such as 1:1 sand:peat or leaf mold or 1:1:1 peat:coarse sand:loam (Vogts, 1982). After sowing seed onto moist media, the seed should be covered by a thin layer of sand and then watered. A day/night temperature difference of 22°F (12°C) will give optimum germination; ideal day/night temperatures are 59 to 68/39 to 50°F (15 to 20/4 to 10°C) (Brown et al., 1998).

TELOPEA. Fresh (less than 6-months-old) waratah seed germinates easily without any treatments in a well-drained, sterile medium such as perlite. Cover with 0.2 in. (5 mm) of medium and drench with a fungicide. After germination, which occurs in 2.5 to 4 weeks, seedlings are transplanted into individual containers filled with 1:2 peat:coarse sand or perlite. Seedlings can be transplanted into the field when they are 6 in. (15 cm) high, but will benefit from a 6-month establishment phase in large containers [1 quart (1:1) or larger] filled with 1:1:1 composted hardwood sawdust:aged bark:coarse sand, adjusted to pH 5.5 (Worrall, 1983). The addition of a controlled-release fertilizer will improve growth. Seedlings are best transplanted in spring or fall.

FLOWERING CONTROL AND DORMANCY

BANKSIA

Flower initiation occurs in late spring and early summer for *B. coccinea, B. menziesii, B. hookeriana,* and *B. baxteri,* possibly due to increasing temperature and day length (Rieger and Sedgley, 1996). Flower initiation with *B. ashbyi* may be controlled by a long–short day sequence (Wallerstein and Nissim, 1992). A minimum shoot diameter must occur before flowering will occur. The critical stem diameter, measured at the junction between the previous and current growth, is 0.18 in. (4.5 mm) for *B. coccinea,* 0.24 in. (6 mm) for *B. menziesii,* 0.31 in. (8 mm) for *B. hookeriana,* and 0.43 in. (11 mm) for *B. baxteri* (Sedgley, 1998).

Although flower initiation in different species occurs at a similar time, the time of flowering varies, due to different rates of flower development, ranging from 3 to 12 months (Röhl et al., 1994; Sedgley, 1998).

GREVILLEA

Little information is available for *Grevillea.* Some species flower in winter and spring, while others, such as *G.* 'Sylvia,' have a long flowering period or flower year-round. References are made to a winter dormant period, but whether this is semiquiescence during cooler temperatures (as seen in *Protea*) or is true dormancy is unclear (Olde and Marriott, 1994).

LEUCADENDRON

Control of flowering in *Leucadendron* has received little attention because they are mainly grown for the attractive foliage rather than the flower. Control of flowering of *L.* 'Safari Sunset' may be similar to *Leucospermum,* where flower initiation occurs only after cessation of shoot growth and in response to shortening day length (Wallerstein and Nissim, 1992). *L. discolor* initiates flowering in fall, but the shoot is not committed to flowering until all florets of the inflorescence have been initiated. Stress results in abortion of all or some florets and can cause reversion, producing compressed, leafy growth (Ben-Jaacov et al., 1986). *L. cordatum* and *L.* 'Safari Sunset' are reported to flower in August/September and November/December, respectively, in the Southern Hemisphere, but no information on flower initiation is offered (Brits et al., 1992).

LEUCOSPERMUM

Leucospermum are short-day plants that initiate flowers in the fall, following cessation of shoot growth in late summer. The inflorescence with many individual florets arises from a lateral bud, which appears to be terminal, due to developmental dominance. The critical day length and number of days essential for flowering are cultivar and species dependant. For flower initiation in *L. cordifolium* (Salisb. ex Knight) Fourc. ×*L. lineare* R. Br. 'Red Sunset,' the day length must be shorter than 12 hr, and at least 42 inductive cycles are required for normal flower development (Malan and Jacobs, 1990). Flower development occurs through winter with flowering in late winter to early summer.

Under inductive conditions the top 5 to 10 lateral buds on a shoot initiate flowers but only the most apical primary bud develops. Removal of this primary bud about 2 months prior to flowering enables the secondary bud to develop, delaying flowering (Jacobs and Honeyborne, 1978). The later the shoot is disbudded, the greater the delay in flowering, up to a point after which flowers will no longer develop under natural conditions. Cultivars vary in their response to disbudding, and interaction with local conditions should be evaluated to determine the suitability of disbudding. The delay in flowering of 13 cultivars due to disbudding has been reported under South African conditions (Criley, 1998; Gerber, 1999). Florel (ethephon) sprays are effective in disbudding the primary flower but are not used commercially, mainly due to crucial timing of application necessary to avoid loss of yield and a decrease in flower quality (Brits, 1986b).

PROTEA

The factors controlling flower initiation in *Protea* are not understood. The great variation in flowering time between species suggests that, unlike *Leucospermum* (SD plant), no single controlling mechanism is likely (Jacobs, 1983; Malan and Brits, 1990).

Many species initiate flowers in spring and environmental factors, such as low temperature and short photoperiod, may play an inductive role (Gerber et al., 2001a, 2002). South African Protea species can be classified broadly into three categories according to flowering times. The first category contains the summer to autumn flowering types, and includes *P. compacta ×P. neriifolia* 'Carnival.' Flowers develop terminally on the spring shoot growth flush. Development continues during spring and summer, and flowers reach anthesis from January to May.

Proteas in the second category also initiate flowers on the spring flush, but development does not start until January. Inflorescence development occurs during summer and winter and anthesis is reached from late winter to early summer. The hybrid *P. magnifica ×P. compacta* 'Lady Di' belongs in this category.

The third category, to which *P. eximia ×P. susannae* 'Sylvia' belongs, includes those proteas that can initiate inflorescences at any time of year. Inflorescence development directly follows initiation and the time of anthesis is dependent on the time of initiation. 'Sylvia' has, in effect, an open window for inflorescence initiation, whereas 'Carnival' and 'Lady Di' have a limited window for inflorescence initiation. Inflorescence initiation in 'Carnival' and 'Lady Di' is restricted to the spring flush due to the obligate requirement for the presence of mature, overwintering leaves (Gerber, 2000). In 'Sylvia' a facultative requirement for mature overwintering leaves is apparent. Although inflorescences can be initiated at any time of year, inflorescences are initiated more readily on the spring flush of growth.

TELOPEA

The first signs of flowering of *Telopea* were microscopically visible in mid-December (Southern Hemisphere), suggesting that flower initiation occurs in spring and early summer, during high light intensity and increasing day length (Dupee and Goodwin, 1990). Whether these factors promote flower initiation directly, or indirectly via increased assimilate supply, has yet to be established. With *T. speciosissima* and *T. mongaensis* Cheel, flowers open acropetally. In *T. truncata* (Labill) R. Br. and *T. oreades* F. Muell., flowers open simultaneously, not sequentially (Faragher, 1989).

TEMPERATURE

BANKSIA

Flower initiation of *B. hookeriana* occurred under day/night temperatures of 77/68°F (25/

20°C), but not at 59/50°F (15/10°C) (Rieger and Sedgley, 1996), suggesting a flowering response to temperature, although at high temperatures flower development may be inhibited (Fuss and Sedgley, 1991). However, warm temperatures hasten flower development of *B. ashbyi*, and the 6-month spread of flowering that occurs with this species is due to different rates of flower development following flower initiation during winter (Wallerstein and Nissim, 1992).

GREVILLEA

No information is available.

LEUCADENDRON

No verified information is available. Anecdotal reports that leaf color is related to temperature have yet to be scientifically confirmed.

LEUCOSPERMUM

No direct interaction between vegetative growth and temperature has been demonstrated in *Leucospermum*, apart from susceptibility to frost. Shoot growth ceases in late summer, but it is unclear whether this is related to temperature or photoperiod or is independent of environmental conditions.

A relationship exists between heat unit accumulation and flower development. Using a base temperature of 43°F (6°C), 925 units (degree-days) are required for 90% of flowers of *L.* 'Golden Star' to mature (Jacobs and Honeyborne, 1979). With *L.* 'Vlam' heat unit accumulation is not a linear process, with one-quarter of the total heat units being accumulated during the last month of the 3.5-month development period, coinciding with rapid flower growth (Criley et al., 1990).

PROTEA

No interaction between temperature and growth or flowering of *Protea* has been established. The rate of flower development is slower in cooler regions (Dupee and Goodwin, 1992) and during cooler conditions in fall compared with summer (Gerber et al., 2001b) but this response has yet to be quantified.

TELOPEA

Flower development occurs at a slower rate in cool areas of Australia compared with warm areas and flowering can be delayed by 2 to 4 weeks (Worrall, 1995).

LIGHT

BANKSIA

A SD requirement for flower initiation is postulated for *B. coccinea* (Rieger and Sedgley, 1996), and as is a LD–SD requirement for *B. ashbyi* (Wallerstein and Nissim, 1992). High light intensity is suggested to be necessary for flowering of all banksia (Sedgley, 1998).

GREVILLEA

No specific information is reported. Shaded plants fail to thrive and do not flower.

LEUCADENDRON

Apart from a possible SD requirement for flowering in some *Leucadendron*, no information is available on the effect of light intensity or quality on growth and flowering.

LEUCOSPERMUM

Low light intensity decreases the number of flowering shoots, which was observed when plants were shaded during vegetative growth (midsummer). Shading plants during the reproductive phase caused a rapid loss in responsiveness to inductive short days following decapitation (Jacobs, 1983; Napier and Jacobs, 1989). Whether the effect of shading on flowering is due to changes in carbohydrate accumulation and allocation remains unclear.

The rate of flower development is not affected by up to 50% light intensity reduction, although flower quality is compromised, with a decrease in the number of styles per flower, receptacle length and diameter, and flower diameter (Jacobs and Minaar, 1980).

PROTEA

Shoot growth of *P. lacticolor* Salisb. 'Ivy' continued in winter when long days were simulated with artificial lighting (D.C. de Swardt, unpublished results).

TELOPEA

High light intensity is essential for flowering. Plants grown in the shade fail to flower. Low light intensity during the early stages of flower development results in abnormal blooms, with individual florets aborting or reverting to the vegetative state, or complete inflorescence abortion (Faragher, 1989).

WATER

All Proteaceae are extremely susceptible to root diseases and good drainage is essential. Overhead irrigation is not recommended due to risk of fungal leaf diseases. Drip irrigation is preferred in commercial plantations to keep the foliage dry.

BANKSIA

Irrigation, when necessary, is supplied by drip at 0.5 to 1.0 gal (2 to 4 L) per plant per day, based on 40% replacement of evaporation (Röhl et al., 1994; Webb, 1996a).

GREVILLEA

No detailed information is available. In general, free water on foliage should be avoided due to fungal diseases.

LEUCADENDRON

Leucadendron are less susceptible to fungal leaf diseases than other members of Proteaceae and overhead watering can be used. Optimum field irrigation rates have not been established.

LEUCOSPERMUM

Optimum irrigation requirements for *Leucospermum* have yet to be determined. In their natural habitat in South Africa, rainfall occurs mainly during winter and varies from 16 to 39 in. (400 to 1000 mm) per year. In field cultivation, irrigation rates of 1.5 to 2 gal (5.5 to 7.5 L) per plant per day and 9 gal (35 L) per week are reported (Criley, 1998).

Avoid water stress during shoot growth (midsummer) for cut flower production. Under water stress, shoot growth stops, apical dominance is lost, and lateral shoots grow, resulting in a branched, unmarketable shoot.

PROTEA

Protea are adapted to hot, dry conditions and do not readily wilt. However, water stress leads to crop losses and plant death. Optimum drip irrigation rates for *Protea* have yet to be established and can vary from 0.5 to 3 gal (2 to 12 L) per plant per day, depending on soil type, weather conditions, and plant size (Webb, 1996b).

TELOPEA

No drip irrigation rates or frequencies are recommended, but it is essential for deep soil to be continuously moist (Nixon and Payne, 1995).

CARBON DIOXIDE

No information available. All crops are field grown.

NUTRITION

BANKSIA

Banksia, in nature, grow in acidic, nutrient-poor soils and, like other Proteaceae, possess roots specialized for mineral absorption. High levels of P are toxic, with symptoms becoming apparent when soil P levels exceed 40 ppm. In pot trials using soilless media, the incidence of iron deficiency symptoms increased with increasing P, indicating preferential translocation of P over Fe (Handreck, 1991). Recommendations for fertilizer rates are not available, but the use of controlled-release, low-P fertilizers (Webb, 1996a) or N and K fertigation is suggested (Sedgley, 1998). It is not known if *Banksia* is sensitive to NO_3-N as are some other Proteaceae, where NH_3 is the preferred form of N.

GREVILLEA

Grevillea naturally grow on acidic, nutrient-poor soils and, as with other Proteaceae, show a toxicity to high-P concentrations. Symptoms include poor growth, necrotic and brown edges to foliage, and yellowing and death of new growth. However, yellowing of new growth, the early signs of P toxicity, are often observed as iron deficiency due to a nutrient interaction resulting in low availability of iron even on low pH soils. To prevent iron chlorosis, a soil drench containing iron chelate is necessary—in extreme cases three to four treatments per year. In a soilless medium, a higher P content was tolerated when levels of available iron were higher (Leake, 1996). A controlled-release fertilizer containing N:P:K at 18:1.8:10 is most suitable, applied after flowering and before active growth starts in spring (Olde and Marriott, 1994). No mention is made of sensitivity to NO_3-N apparent in some other Proteaceae, where NH_4 is the preferred form of N.

LEUCADENDRON

As with some other Proteaceae, *Leucadendron* are sensitive to nitrate-nitrogen, but are less susceptible to P toxicity. In water culture NH_4 applied at relatively high levels promoted growth, whereas NO_3 was toxic at a concentration of 2.5 mM. Optimum growth of *L. salignum* occurred with a solution of greater than 3 mM NH_4, 0.08 to 0.31 mM K, and 0.008 to 0.125 mM P (Heinsohn and Pammenter, 1986). 'Safari Sunset' showed no signs of toxicity with the addition of 20 or 25 ppm P (Prasad and Dennis, 1986; Silber et al., 1997).

In the field tissue samples should be taken in June (midwinter, Southern Hemisphere) because overall plant nutrient status fluctuates seasonally. Based on estimates of nutrients removed by the harvesting of flowers, annual fertilizer applications of N and Ca at 0.7 to 1.1 oz (20 to 30 g)/plant and Mg and K at 0.4 to 0.5 oz (10 to 15 g)/plant are recommended for *Leucadendron* 'Silvan Red' and 'Safari Sunset' on acid sands (Cecil et al., 1995).

LEUCOSPERMUM

Liquid foliar spray, such as commercial seaweed preparations applied at one-half the recommended strength, are suitable for fertilizing rooted cuttings before they are transplanted. Drip fertigation is the preferred method of fertilizing field-grown *Leucospermum*. Plants are sensitive to phosphates and nitrogen applied in the nitrate form (Claasens, 1986). Fertigation solutions are commonly composed of 1:1 N:K from ammonium sulfate and potassium chloride. Soil acidification is corrected with gypsum. For pot culture controlled-release, low-phosphate fertilizers are suitable.

PROTEA

In nature *Protea* grow in acidic, nutrient-deficient soils. In cultivation plants exhibit sensitivity to nitrogen supplied in the nitrate form and show toxicity to relatively low levels of phosphate (Claasens, 1986). Typical P toxicity symptoms in *Protea* are marginal redness on young and old leaves, interveinal chlorosis on young leaves, and poor vigor and flowering (Leake, 1996).

In soilless culture a nutrient solution containing 1:0.1:0.7 N:P:K with a NH_4:NO_3 ratio of 1:1, and total salt content of 0.8 meq $\cdot$ L^{-1}, was suitable (Montarone and Allemand, 1995). This nutrient ratio corresponds well with the 1:0:1 N:P:K fertigation commonly used in commercial *Protea* plantations. Analysis of the flowering shoot is recommended to estimate total nutrient removal by harvest. Timing of application for nutrient replacement should coincide with the growth stage of the plant. Nitrogen is essential for vegetative flushing and, in *P. cynaroides,* an increase in N uptake corresponded with lignotuber formation (Montarone and Ziegler, 1997). Potassium uptake increased in *P. cynaroides* and *P. eximia* during flowering, and with *P. compacta* ×*P. susannae* Phill. 'Pink Ice' K concentration was higher in the flower than in leaves and stem, indicating that the flower is a K sink (Maier et al., 1995; Montarone and Ziegler, 1997).

TELOPEA

Telopea are not as sensitive to high nutrient rates as other Proteaceae. Generally the use of a controlled-release fertilizer is recommended. The addition of 0.12 to 0.24 oz/1000 lb P (1.6 to 3.1 mg · kg^{-1}) to the medium improved growth in phosphate-deficient sand. At lower P levels growth was stunted and plants had thick leaves with purpling of leaf tips. At higher P levels toxicity symptoms occurred, including severe necrosis of leaf tips and plant death (Grose, 1989). Worrall recommends the application of 8 lb/acre/year (9 kg · ha^{-1} · yr^{-1}) single superphosphate. Young plants are particularly sensitive to high levels of available NO$_3$ nitrogen (Worrall, 1995).

MEDIA

BANKSIA

All banksia species grow best in well-drained, sandy soil of low pH. Container trials used a medium of 1:1:1 sand:peat:perlite, with a controlled-release, low-P fertilizer added (Rieger and Sedgley, 1996).

GREVILLEA

Soils must be well drained, low in P content, and with a pH of 6 to 6.5. However, *G. variifolia* C.A. Gardner and A.S. George, *G. crithmifolia* R. Br., and *G. preisii* C.F. Meissner are tolerant of alkaline conditions. In containers a porous medium is suitable, such as 60% pine bark; 20% coarse, washed river sand; 10% fine, washed river sand; and 10% sterilized loam (Olde and Marriott, 1994).

LEUCADENDRON

Leucadendron require a well-drained acidic medium. High pH greater than 6 inhibits root growth and subsequent shoot growth of *L.* 'Safari Sunset' (Ganmore-Neumann et al., 1997).

LEUCOSPERMUM

For *Leucospermum* the media must be well drained with a low pH. In commercial plantations deep, sandy soil is ideal. For pot culture the medium must be lightweight, yet have sufficient water and nutrient retention capacity, for example, 1:4:5 peat:pine bark:river sand (Ackerman et al., 1995; Brits et al., 1992).

PROTEA

In commercial plantations a deep, well-drained sandy soil is ideal. Some *Protea* species are tolerant of alkaline soils (*P. obtusifolia, P. susannae,* and *P. burchellii* Stapf) (Vogts, 1982), but in general pH must be 4.5 to 6. In pots a well-drained, acidic medium is suitable (see Propagation section, earlier).

TELOPEA

Telopea grow in a wide range of soils, provided the soil is deep, well aerated, and well drained. A 5.0 to 6.0 pH is ideal, although some success has been achieved in alkaline soils (Loffler, 1995; Nixon and Payne, 1995).

HEIGHT CONTROL

No height control is necessary for cut flower production. For pot plant production of *Leucospermum,* Florel (ethephon) and Bonzi (paclobutrazol) are used to induce branching and improve compactness (Brits, 1995). These treatments can be performed on *Leucospermum* stock prior to removal of branched cuttings and on plants in containers.

SPACING

Generally single rows are used in plantations, with the in-row distance varying from 3 to 11 ft (1 to 3.5 m) according to the compactness of plant growth. Between-row spacing ranges from 6.5 to 21 ft (2 to 6.5 m) depending on species, equipment used, and management practices.

Double rows with 5 to 6.5 ft (1.5 to 2 m) of pedestrian access between allows denser planting of *Protea,* but necessitates extra attention to spray penetration. *P. cynaroides* is grown intensively at a density of 1620 to 2020 plants/acre (4000 to 5000/h). Plant height of this species remains low and plants are sprayed with an overhead boom or adapted mistblower (air-assisted sprayer). For pot culture plants are provided as much space as possible to supply high light intensity for flower initiation and reduce fungal leaf diseases.

PINCHING AND DISBUDDING

BANKSIA

Young plants are pinched at a height of 24 to 28 in. (60 to 70 cm) to develop a framework of four to five main branches on a single trunk. Pruning banksia must be done with care because some species only produce flowers on 2-year-old wood, which annual pruning would remove (Fuss, 1994). Application of benzyladenine (BA) at 100 to 500 ppm to *B. ashbyi* in pots hastened sprouting of axillary shoots and increased the number of new shoots (Wallerstein and Nissim, 1992).

GREVILLEA

Young plants are pinched regularly to encourage branching. Pruning immediately after flowering rejuvenates vegetative growth and prolongs plant life. Fall and winter flowering species should only be pruned when the danger of frost has passed, and prior to active growth resuming.

LEUCADENDRON

In field production plants are pinched after transplanting to encourage branching and enhance production potential. For pot plant production repeated pinching induces branching and improves compactness.

LEUCOSPERMUM

Rooted cuttings are pinched after transplanting and pruned after the first season's growth to develop a highly branched, balanced framework. For cut flower production flowering shoots are disbudded to delay flowering (see Flowering Control and Dormancy section, earlier) and to prevent unmarketable multiple headed shoots.

After harvest plants are pruned to develop a framework to support subsequent production. The 4- to 6-in. (10- to 15-cm) stumps (bearers) that remain following harvest of flowering stems are thinned out and nonflowering shoots are removed. Cultivars differ in bearing capacity and care must be taken to achieve suitable branching structure, thus optimizing yield, while avoiding short flowering stems.

Development of plant branching in pot culture is achieved by pinching. Multiple-headed stems are generally desirable.

PROTEA

Young *Protea* plants are pinched after transplanting and after each subsequent growth flush to rapidly increase branching and enhance production potential (Hettasch et al., 1997). Lateral shoots arising below the developing flower bud, known as bypass shoots, must be removed while the tissue is still soft and can be easily removed.

Pruning after harvesting entails removal of thin shoots (thinner than a pencil) to increase air movement within the plant and facilitate light and spray penetration. The flowering capacity of *Protea* is largely self-regulated and thinning of bearers, the 4- to 6-in. (10- to 15-cm) stumps that remain following harvest of flowering stems, is unnecessary.

TELOPEA

Weak, short shoots are removed during or immediately after harvesting. Heavy annual pruning will weaken the plant; however, plants are severely cut back to rejuvenate growth at intervals of about 10 years. The yield is reduced for 2 to 3 years following severe cutbacks.

SUPPORT

No support required.

SCHEDULE AND TIMING

The lack of knowledge of factors controlling flowering in Proteaceae hinders the development of exact scheduling.

BANKSIA

Manipulation of banksia flowering to induce early or late flowering or prolong production is not currently practiced. Nevertheless, the possibility exists to induce early flowering by supplemental lighting of species such as *B. coccinea* and *B. ashbyi*, which appear to initiate flowers under decreasing day length (Sedgley, 1998).

GREVILLEA

Control of scheduling is not possible due to lack of flowering control information.

LEUCADENDRON

With the exception of those species harvested while in flower (e.g., *L. discolor*), most *Leucadendron* are grown for their foliage and have a long harvest period. The protocols for scheduling of either flowering or color development have yet to be developed.

LEUCOSPERMUM

Day length manipulation to schedule cut flower production of *Leucospermum* is not economically feasible due to the slow growth and large, shrubby nature of the plants. Flowering can be delayed for several weeks by disbudding (see Flowering Control and Dormancy section, earlier). Day length control to force flowering of potted plants is theoretically possible, but the high light intensity required for flower initiation makes it impractical. Producing plants in both the Northern and Southern Hemispheres is a more feasible method to supply flowering pot plants year-round (Brits et al., 1992).

PROTEA

Within some species, such as *P. cynaroides*, variants exist with different flowering times and selective planting, which provides some control over harvesting. In cooler areas flower development of *P. magnifica* is retarded, which is exploited to produce flowers in the pre-Christmas peak. *P. eximia* can produce flowers at any time of year and this characteristic is used, through judicious pruning, to schedule harvests of *P. eximia* ×*P. susannae* 'Sylvia' (Gerber et al., 2001b). In many species more than 1 year is required to produce a long, marketable shoot and a flower. A biennial flowering cycle was determined for *P. compacta* ×*P. neriifolia* 'Carnival,' which increases the shoot length and the percentage of flowering shoots, and improves timing of flowering for peak marketing periods (Gerber et al., 1995; Hettasch et al., 1997). Flowering of 'Carnival' can be delayed by defoliation applied after induction has occurred.

TELOPIA

Flower development is slower in cool production areas (Worrall, 1995). Site selection can be used to regulate flowering.

INSECTS

BANKSIA

Most of the insects associated with banksia are seed predators and not a threat to cut flower production. However, tunneling moth larvae (*Arthrophora*) and other *Lepidoptera* can damage flowers. Leaf damage can be caused by a number of insects, including grasshoppers and snout beetles (*Catasarcus*) (Webb, 1996a, b; Sedgley, 1998).

GREVILLEA

Aesthetic damage to leaves is caused by the grevillea leaf-miner (*Peraglyphis atimana*), grevillea looper (*Oenachroma vinaria*), sap sucking insects (psyllids, aphids, and whiteflies), and other leaf feeders. Plants are susceptible to scale infestation when grown under stress. Plant death can be caused by severe infestation of borers and Macadamia twig girdlers (*Neodrepta luteotactella*). Flower damage is caused by the macadamia flower caterpillar (*Homeosoma vagella*) (Olde and Marriott, 1994). Deformation of shoot tips is caused by mites, which attack new growth (Costin and Costin, 1988b).

LEUCADENDRON

Leaf feeders, leaf miner (*Phyllocnistis*), and sap sucking insects are major problems, causing aesthetic damage on the foliage. Devastating crop losses can be caused by unchecked infestation of carnation worm (*Epichoristodes acerbella*) (Wright, 1999). Developing cones are susceptible to damage by the flat-headed borer (*Sphenoptera*) (Coetzee, 1986).

LEUCOSPERMUM

Flower damage due to insects is infrequent but the presence of insects within the flower head is a phytosanitary problem. Leaf feeders, leaf miners (*Phyllocnistis*), and sap sucking insects pose the major problem, causing aesthetic damage to the foliage. Crop losses and plant death can occur due to borers (*Sphenoptera*). Tip fly (*Resseliella proteae*) can result in major crop losses by causing malformed leaves and twisted, branched shoots (Wright, 1999).

PROTEA

Aesthetic damage to foliage is caused by channel leaf miner (*Phyllocnistis*), leaf feeders, and sap sucking insects. Significant crop losses occur due to flower damage by various borers

(*Argyroploce*, *Capys alphaeus*, *Erioderes candezei*, and *Sphenoptera*) and protea bud weevil (*Euderes lineicollis*) (Wright, 1999). Monitoring plants for the presence of eggs is an essential part of control. Witches broom, a dense proliferation of shoots with malformed leaves, is caused by a phytoplasma that may be transmitted by mites (Wright, 1999).

TELOPEA

Information on insect damage of waratah is scarce. Flower damage caused by borers is reported, and, presumably, common leaf feeders, leaf miners, and sap sucking insects need to be controlled.

DISEASES

Many Proteaceae plants are extremely susceptible to root rot caused by the soil- and water-borne pathogen *Phytophthora cinnamomi*. The best method of control is prevention, which is achieved by maintaining good root drainage and minimal root disturbance; although foliar phosphonic acid sprays have a preventive effect on *Grevillea* (Olde and Marriott, 1994). In the nursery both water and growth medium must be disease free and the use of tolerant cultivars or rootstocks is effective with *Leucospermum*.

BANKSIA

Species vary in their susceptibility to *Phytophthora cinnamomi* (Tynan et al., 1998) and the search continues for tolerant plants that could be used as rootstocks. Fungal leaf diseases on banksia are not reported.

GREVILLEA

Small black patches appear on leaves infected by grevillea leaf spot (*Placoasterella baileyi*). Red-brown blotching of the leaves is caused by *Verrucispora* and occurs mainly in humid and tropical climates. Several fungal pathogens (e.g., *Cystospora*, *Epicoccum*, and *Phomopsis*) cause branch dieback. Grevillea are also susceptible to *Phytophthora cinnamomi*.

LEUCADENDRON

Leucadendron are less prone to fungal leaf diseases than other members of Proteaceae. Aesthetic leaf damage can be caused by *Batcheleromyces leucadendri*, *Cercostigmina protearum* var. *leucadendri*, *Coleroa senniana*, *Vizella interrupta*. Stem and shoot tip damage result from infection by *Botrytis cinerea* and *Elsinoë*. *Leucadendron* are less susceptible to *Phytophthora cinnamomi* than *Leucospermum*, but more so than *Protea* (Swart, 1999).

LEUCOSPERMUM

Blight, caused by *Dreschlera dematioidea*, attacks current season's shoots producing brown, irregular lesions. A dieback or canker develops if the infection moves into the stem and young plants may die. Scab lesions on the stem, resulting from infection by *Elsinoë*, can cause twisting and abnormal growth. Other leaf spot diseases include *Cercostigmina protearum* var. *protearum*, *Cleroa senniana*, and *Vizella interrupta* (Swart, 1999). To prevent infection by these diseases, obtain disease-free material and avoid conditions leading to moisture retention on the foliage, such as overhead watering and inadequate air movement. *Botryosphaeria* causes canker and dieback. Infection spreads easily with lack of sanitation/disinfection of pruning and harvesting equipment (Knox-Davies et al., 1986). Young plants are susceptible to wilt caused by *Verticillium dahliae* (Criley, 1998). Media should be sterilized before planting cuttings. *Leucospermum* is extremely susceptible to *Phytophthora cinnamomi* and most losses occur during the first 2 years after establishment in the field.

PROTEA

Fusarium wilt (*Fusarium oxysporum*) causes stem die-off in some *Protea* species and, eventually, death of the entire plant, but the disease tends to be limited to summer rainfall regions (Swart, 1999). *Protea* leaf diseases showing characteristic lesions that assist in identification are caused by the following pathogens: *Batcheloromyces proteae* (particularly *P. cynaroides*), *Cercostigmina protearum* var. *protearum*, coleroa leaf spot (*Coleroa senniana*), anthracnose (*Colletotrichum gleosporioides*), *Leptosphaeria protearum* (particularly *P. magnifica*), *Teratosphaeria maculiformis*, and *Vizella interrupta*. Young tip dieback is caused by anthracnose and flower head blight (*Botrytis cinerea*) (Swart, 1999; von Broembsen, 1989). A regular preventive spray program is recommended, especially during warm, moist conditions that favor disease incidence. Plant death occurs due to canker (*Botryosphaeria*). Most *Protea* species are fairly tolerant of *Phytophthora* provided root drainage is adequate (Swart, 1999).

TELOPEA

Young plant death can be caused by *Pythium, Phytophthora,* and *Rhizoctonia.* Most losses occur in the first 3 months.

PHYSIOLOGICAL DISORDERS

BANKSIA

Flower abortion, either of individual florets or of the entire inflorescence, causes truncated or abnormal flowers and is often associated with unseasonably cold temperatures during flower initiation (Fuss and Sedgley, 1991; Fuss et al., 1992).

GREVILLEA

The cause of flower fasciation is unknown. Affected branches must be removed. The term *slippers* refers to abnormal style extension where the perianth remains intact, clasping the distal end of the style, and occurs when the plant is subjected to water stress or high humidity. Slippers can also occur postharvest.

LEUCADENDRON

Old, lower leaves show chlorosis followed by abscission in response to water or nutritional stress. The production of abnormally small leaves with or without interveinal chlorosis may be physiological, although the possibility of a viral pathogen has yet to be eliminated (Malan, 1999).

LEUCOSPERMUM

On mature plants lower leaf yellowing and senescence are generally a sign of nutritional stress.

PROTEA

Older lower leaves yellow before abscising under stress conditions, particularly water and nutrition. Many physiological disorders arise due to the strong sink strength of the developing flower. Blackening of subtending leaves below the flower bud occurs preharvest under conditions of low light intensity and rapid daily temperature fluctuations. The initial stages with *P. eximia* ×*P. susannae* 'Cardinal,' apparent as leaf yellowing, may be reversed by foliar potassium sprays. Postharvest leaf blackening is discussed in the Postharvest section. The cause of leaf tip scorch, resulting in aesthetic damage, is unclear but may be associated with nutritional imbalance.

TELOPEA

Bract burn, browning of the involucral bract tips, is related to environmental conditions, particularly water stress, and often occurs after hot, dry, windy conditions.

POSTHARVEST

BANKSIA

Banksia flowers are harvested when 5 to 10% of the florets are open. Because the flowers have a long vase life, little research has been required. Sucrose pulsing had no beneficial effect on the vase life of *B. coccinea,* which lasted for 15 days in water treated with 0.01% chlorine. Flowers still had a poststorage vase life of 10 days if stored in the dark for 14 days at 36°F (2°C) and 100% humidity (Sedgley, 1998). Prolonged storage at low temperatures of 34°F (1°C) for 10 to 14 days is an effective technique for insect disinfestation of flowers, which is an essential postharvest treatment for international shipments. Storage can be reduced to 7 days when combined with 45 to 60% CO_2, resulting in insect removal while retaining an acceptable vase life (Seaton and Joyce, 1993).

GREVILLEA

The harvest stage of grevillea is determined by the degree of "looping" of the styles. Styles form a loop as they extend and straighten, then reflex as the flower matures. Generally the best vase life is attained when flowers are harvested slightly immature, at the early looping stage (loops one-quarter to one-half the length of floret) (Ligawa et al., 1997).

Vase life of grevillea cut flowers can be short, ranging from 3 to 9 days (Joyce et al., 1996). Adding 3% sucrose to the vase solution increased the vase life of *G.* 'Sylvia' from 7 to 12 days, but a 10% sucrose pulsing solution for 6 to 24 hr gave inconsistent results (Ligawa et al., 1997). Ethylene-induced floral abscission can be reduced by a 15-min pulse with 4 mM silver thiosulfate (STS) at 70°F (21°C) or by 10 ppb 1-methylcylcopropene (1-MCP) (Joyce et al., 1993; Macnish et al., 2000).

Cut *Grevillea* foliage has a longer vase life, ranging from 14 to 30 days, which can be extended by using commercial floral preservatives. During these vase life trials, stems were kept at minimum/maximum temperatures of 55/73°F (13/23°C) and given 8 hr of light from fluorescent fixtures. Foliage harvested in midsummer had a shorter vase life than that harvested in midwinter (Criley and Parvin, 1993).

LEUCADENDRON

Leucadendron stems are harvested when leaves are of the desired color and hardened off. Immature tissue wilts rapidly. *L.* 'Silvan Red' had a vase life of 19 days following 49 days of 34°F (1°C) storage (Jones and Faragher, 1991). Prestorage pulsing with 20% sucrose for 24 hr prevented leaf desiccation (Jones, 1995). Isotope studies indicated that sucrose was distributed primarily to the leaves. Sorbitol and mannitol pulses accelerated leaf desiccation during storage.

LEUCOSPERMUM

Flowers are harvested when 50% of the styles are open. Vase life is prolonged by cooling shortly after harvest and during air shipment. Pulsing solutions are not routinely used due to variable results. Fungal dips are effective against postharvest flower rot, specifically *Botrytis cinerea*.

Cultivars vary in postproduction conditions of pot plants. Cold storage for 4 to 8 days in darkness caused blackening of buds and discoloration of leaves in *L. oleifolium* (Berg.) R. Br. and *L. mundii* Meisn., but produced high-quality, long-lasting flowering pot plants in *L. lineare* ×*L. tottum* (L.) R. Br. 'Ballerina' (Ackerman et al., 1995).

PROTEA

Flowers are harvested when the involucral bracts begin to loosen but before they start to reflex. The time between harvest, hydration, and cooling must be short to ensure maximum vase life. Leaf blackening, caused by carbohydrate depletion in the leaves directly below the flower, is a major postharvest problem, often occurring only during air shipment (McConchie et al., 1991). The effectiveness of carbohydrate-containing pulsing solutions to prolong vase life or prevent leaf blackening is debatable. Biocidal pulsing solutions may be more effective (Paull and Dai, 1990). STS has no effect on vase life of *Protea* (Newman et al., 1990). Girdling below the flower bud inhibits movement of photosynthates from the leaves to the flower and significantly reduces leaf blackening (Jones et al., 1995; Reid et al., 1989). Reducing respiration by lowering the cold storage temperature to 34°F (1°C) dramatically reduces leaf blackening, and the effect is enhanced when combined with girdling (I.A. Stephens, personal communication). Postharvest fumigation is necessary to disinfest flowers to comply with phytosanitary regulations (Karunaratne et al., 1997a, b; Wright, 1999).

TELOPEA

The optimum harvest stage of *Telopea* is when 0 to 5% of the florets are open (Joyce et al., 1993). A vase life of about 7 to 13 days at 68°F (20°C) can be expected. Flowers can be stored for 2 weeks at 34°F (1°C), with relative humidity maintained at 100%, without a reduction in vase life (Faragher, 1986). Floral preservatives, STS, or sucrose do not consistently improve vase life (Lill and Dennis, 1986).

ACKNOWLEDGMENT

The authors would like to thank Audrey Gerber, Department of Primary Industries, Primary Industries Research Victoria, Myrtleford, Victoria, Australia, for writing this chapter.

KEY POINTS

- Members of the Proteaceae family are used mainly as field-grown fresh cut flowers or foliage and occasionally as potted flowering plants.

- Proteaceae are grown for their unusual and often spectacular inflorescences or for their colorful foliage.

- The shrub to tree size *Banksia*, *Grevillea*, and *Telopea* are indigenous to Australia, and *Leucadendron* and *Leucospermum* are restricted to South Africa.

- While cutting propagation is most common, seed, grafting, and tissue culture are also used.

- Many Proteaceae species grow in acidic, nutrient-poor soils in nature, possess roots specialized for high mineral absorption, and are sensitive to high levels (greater than 40 ppm) of soil P.
- All Proteaceae are extremely susceptible to root diseases and good drainage is essential. Overhead irrigation is not recommended due to risk of fungal leaf diseases. Drip irrigation is preferred in commercial plantations to keep the foliage dry.
- *Banksia* flowers are harvested when 5 to 10% of the florets are open and have a long vase life.
- *Grevillea* flowers are picked slightly immature, at the early looping stage, and vase life is short.
- *Leucadendron* stems are harvested when leaves are of the desired color and hardened off.
- *Protea* flowers are harvested when the involucral bracts begin to loosen but before they start to reflex.
- *Telopea* flowers are harvested when 0 to 5% of the florets are open.

BIBLIOGRAPHY

Ackerman, A., J. Ben-Jaacov, G. J. Brits, D. G. Malan, J.H. Coetzee, and E. Tal. 1995. The development of *Leucospermum* and *Serruria* as flowering pot plants. *Acta Horticulturae* 387:33–46.

Ackerman, A., S. Gilad, B. Mechnik. Y. Shchori, and J. Ben-Jaacov. 1997. "Cutting-grafts" for *Leucospermum* and *Leucadendron*—A method for quick propagation for simultaneous rooting and grafting. *Acta Horticulturae* 453:15–28.

Anonymous. 1993. Australian plant cultivars. *Australian Plants* 17(134):53–62.

Ben-Jaacov, J., R. Shillo, and M. Avishai. 1986. Technology for rapid production of *Leucadendron discolor* E. Phillips, S. Hutch. *Scientia Horticulturae* 28:379–387.

Ben-Jaacov, J., A. Ackerman, S. Gilad, R. Carmeli, A. Barzilay, and Y. Shchori. 1992. Grafting techniques and the use of rootstocks in *Leucadendron*, and other Proteaceous plants. *Acta Horticulturae* 316:69–80.

Brits, G.J. 1986a. The effect of hydrogen peroxide treatment on germination in Proteaceae species with serotinous and nut-like achenes. *South African Journal of Botany* 52(4):291–293.

Brits, G.J. 1986b. Extension of harvesting period in *Leucospermum* by means of manual and chemical pruning methods. *Acta Horticulturae* 185:237–240.

Brits, G.J. 1990a. Techniques for maximal seed germination of six commercial *Leucospermum* R. BR. species. *Acta Horticulturae* 264:53–60.

Brits, G.J. 1990b. Rootstock production research in *Leucospermum* and *Protea*: I. Techniques. *Acta Horticulturae* 264:9–25.

Brits, G.J. 1995. Selection criteria for protea flowering pot plants. *Acta Horticulturae* 387:47–54.

Brits, G.J., E. Tal, J. Ben-Jaacov, and A. Ackerman. 1992. Co-operative production of protea flowering pot plants selected for rapid production. *Acta Horticulturae* 316:107–118.

Brown, N.A.C. 1986. Germination of achenes of *Leucospermum cordifolium*. *Acta Horticulturae* 185:53–59.

Brown, N.A.C., J. van Staden, and G. Brits. 1996. Propagation of Cape Proteaceae, Ericaceae and Restionaceae from seed. *International Plant Propagators Society Combined Proceedings* 46:63–67.

Brown, N.A.C., D. Kotze, and P. Botha. 1998. *Grow Proteas. A Guide to the Propagation and Cultivation of Some South African Proteaceae*. Kirstenbosch Gardening Series, National Botanical Institute, Cape Town.

Cecil, J.S., G.E. Barth, N.A. Maier, W.L. Chvyl, and M.N. Bartetzko. 1995. Leaf chemical composition and nutrient removal by stems of *Leucadendron* cv. Silvan Red and Safari Sunset. *Australian Journal of Experimental Agriculture* 35:547–555.

Claasens, A.S. 1986. Some aspects of the nutrition of proteas. *Acta Horticulturae* 185:171–179.

Coetzee, J.H. 1986. Insects—A hazard to the protea industry. *Acta Horticulturae* 185:209–215.

Costin, R., and S. Costin, 1988a. Tropical *Grevillea* hybrids. *Australian Plants* 14:335–343.

Costin, R., and S. Costin. 1988b. Growing the *Grevillea* hybrids. *Australian Plants* 14:372.

Criley, R.A. 1998. *Leucospermum*: Botany and Horticulture. *Horticultural Reviews* 22:27–90.

Criley, R.A., and P.E. Parvin. 1993. New cut foliages from Australia, New Zealand, and South Africa. *Acta Horticulturae* 337:95–98.

Criley, R.A., P.E. Parvin, and S. Leketwana. 1990. Flower development in *Leucospermum cordifolium* cv. Vlam. *Acta Horticulturae* 264:71–78.

Dawson, I.A., and R.W. King. 1994. Propagation of some woody Australian plants from cuttings.

Australian Journal of Experimental Agriculture 34:1225–1231.

Dupee, S. 1986. The production of Australia's major Proteaceae as florist crops. *Acta Horticulturae* 185:259–264.

Dupee S.A., and P.B. Goodwin. 1990. Flower initiation in *Protea* and *Telopea*. *Acta Horticulturae* 264:71–77.

Dupee, S.A., and P.B. Goodwin. 1992. Flowering and vegetative growth of *Protea neriifolia* and *Protea cynaroides*. *Acta Horticulturae* 316:81–98.

Ellyard, R.K., and G. Butler. 1985. Breakthrough in waratah propagation. *Australian Horticulture* 83:27–31.

Faragher, J.D. 1986. Effects of cold storage methods on vase life and physiology of cut waratah inflorescences (*Telopea speciosissima*). *Scientia Horticulturae* 29:163–171.

Faragher, J.D. 1989. *Telopea*, pp. 593–597 in *Handbook of Flowering*, vol. VI, A.H. Halevy, editor. CRC Press, Boca Raton, Florida.

Fuss, A. 1994. *Pruning Banksias*. Western Australian Department of Agriculture Farmnote Number 100/94.

Fuss, A.M., and M. Sedgley. 1990. Floral initiation and development in relation to the time of flowering in *Banksia coccinea* R. Br. and *B. menziesii* R. Br. (Proteaceae). *Australian Journal of Botany* 38:487–500.

Fuss, A.M., and M. Sedgley. 1991. Variability in cut flower production of *Banksia coccinea* R. Br. and *Banksia menziesii* R. Br. at six locations in southern Australia. *Australian Journal of Experimental Agriculture* 31:853–858.

Fuss, A.M., S.J. Pattison, D. Aspinall, and M. Sedgley. 1992. Shoot growth in relation to cut flower production of *Banksia coccinea* and *Banksia menziesii* (Proteaceae). *Scientia Horticulturae* 49:323–334.

Ganmore-Neumann, R., A. Silber, B. Mitchnick, S. Gilad, and J. Ben-Jaacov. 1997. Effect of pH on the development of *Leucadendron* 'Safari Sunset.' *Acta Horticulturae* 453:47–52.

Gerber, A.I. 1999. *Manipulation of Flowering Time of Leucospermum by Disbudding*. SAPPEX Fynbos Research Pamphlet Number 29.

Gerber, A.I. 2000. Inflorescence initiation and development, and the manipulation thereof, of selected cultivars of the genus *Protea*. Dissertation, University of Stellenbosch, Stellenbosch, South Africa.

Gerber, A.I., E.J. Greenfield, K.I. Theron, and G. Jacobs. 1995. Pruning of *Protea* cv Carnival to optimise economic biomass production. *Acta Horticulturae* 387:99–106.

Gerber, A.I., K.I. Theron, and G. Jacobs. 2001a. The role of leaves and carbohydrates in flowering of *Protea* cv. Lady Di. *HortScience* 36:905–908.

Gerber, A.I., K.I. Theron, and G. Jacobs. 2001b. Manipulation of flowering time by pruning of *Protea* cv. Sylvia (*P. eximia* × *P. susannae*). *HortScience* 36:909–912.

Gerber, A.I., K.I. Theron, and G. Jacobs. 2002. Defoliation alters spring growth flush characteristics and inhibits flowering in *Protea* cv. Carnival. *Scientia Horticulturae* 94:345–350.

Grose, M.J. 1989. Phosphorous nutrition of seedlings of the waratah, *Telopea speciosissima* (Sm.) R. Br. (Proteaceae). *Australian Journal of Botany* 37:313–320.

Handreck, K.A. 1991. Interactions between iron and phosphorous in the nutrition of *Banksia ericifolia* L.f. var. *ericifolia* (Proteaeceae) in soil-less potting media. *Australian Journal of Botany* 39:373–384.

Harre, J. 1986. Propagation of South African Proteaceae by seed. *International Plant Propagators Society Combined Proceedings* 36:470–476.

Harre, J. 1988. *Proteas, the Propagation and Production of Proteaceae*. Riverlea Promotions, Fielding, New Zealand.

Heinsohn, R.D., and N.W. Pammenter. 1986. A preliminary study of interactions between nitrogen, potassium and phosphorous in the mineral nutrition of seedlings of *Leucadendron salignum* Berg. (Proteaceae). *Acta Horticulturae* 185:137–143.

Hettasch, H.B., A.I. Gerber, K.I. Theron, and G. Jacobs. 1997. Pruning *Protea* cv. Carnival for biennial crops of improved yield and quality. *Acta Horticulturae* 453:127–133.

Huxley, A., M. Griffiths, and M. Levy. 1992. *Banksia*, pp. 303–305, vol. 1; *Grevillea*, pp. 461–464, vol. 2; *Leucadendron*, pp. 54–55, vol. 3; *Leucospermum*, pp. 58–59, vol. 3; *Protea*, pp. 728–729, vol. 3; *Telopea*, p. 444, vol. 4 in *The New Royal Horticultural Society Dictionary of Gardening*. Stockton Press, New York.

Jacobs, G. 1983. Flower initiation and development in *Leucospermum* cv. Red Sunset. *Journal of the American Society for Horticultural Science* 108(1):32–35.

Jacobs, G., and G.E. Honeyborne. 1978. Delaying the flowering time of *Leucospermum* cv. Golden Star by deheading. *Agroplantae* 10:13–15.

Jacobs, G., and G.E. Honeyborne. 1979. The relationship between heat unit accumulation and the flowering date of *Leucospermum* cv. Golden Star. *Agroplantae* 11:83–85.

Jacobs, G., and H.R. Minnaar. 1980. Light intensity and flower development of *Leucospermum cordifolium*. *HortScience* 15(5):644–645.B.7.

Jacobs, G., and J.C. Steenkamp. 1975. Studies on the rooting of Proteaceae stem cuttings, pp. 48–49 in *Annual Report of the Department of Horticultural Science*. University of Stellenbosch, Stellenbosch, South Africa.

Jacobs, G., and J.C. Steenkamp. 1976. Rooting of stem cuttings of *Leucospermum cordifolium* and some of its hybrids under mist, *Series: Flowers, Ornamental Shrubs, and Trees Proteas*. Department of Agricultural Technical Services, Pretoria, South Africa.

Jones, R.B. 1995. Sucrose prevents foliage desiccation in cut *Leucadendron* 'Silvan Red' during cool storage. *Postharvest Biology and Technology* 6: 293–301.

Jones, R.B., and J. Faragher. 1991. Cold storage of selected members of Proteaceae and Australian native cut flowers. *HortScience* 26(11):1395–1397.

Jones, R.B., R. McConchie, W.G. van Doorn, and M.S. Reid. 1995. Leaf blackening in cut *Protea* flowers. *Horticultural Reviews* 17:173–201.

Joyce, D., R. Jones, and J. Faragher. 1993. Postharvest characteristics of native Australian flowers. *Postharvest News and Information* 4(2):61–67.

Joyce, D.C., P. Beal, and A.J. Shorter. 1996. Vase life characteristics of selected grevillea. *Australian Journal of Experimental Agriculture* 36:379–382.

Karunaratne, C., G.A. Moore, R.B. Jones, and R. Ryan. 1997a. Phosphine and its effect on some common insects in cut flowers. *Postharvest Biology and Technology* 10:255–262.

Karunaratne, C., G.A. Moore, R.B. Jones, and R.F. Ryan. 1997b. Vase life of some cut flowers following fumigation with phosphine. *HortScience* 32:900–902.

Knox-Davies, P.S., P.S. van Wyk, and W.F.O. Marasas. 1986. Diseases of proteas and their control in the South Western Cape. *Acta Horticulturae* 185:189–200.

Leake, S.W. 1996. *Soil Conditions and Fertilizers for Phosphorous Sensitive Plants*. Australian Flora and Protea Growers Association Conference.

Ligawa, J.K., D.C. Joyce, and S.E. Hetherington. 1997. Exogenously supplied sucrose improves the postharvest quality of *Grevillea* 'Sylvia' inflorescences. *Australian Journal of Experimental Agriculture* 37:809–816.

Lill, R.E., and D.J. Dennis. 1986. Post harvest studies with NSW waratah. *Acta Horticulturae* 185:267–271.

Loffler, T.G. 1995. Waratahs grown in alkaline soils. *Australian Plants* 18:365.

Macnish, A.J., D.H. Simons, D.C. Joyce, J.D. Faragher, and P.J. Hoffman. 2000. Responses of native Australian cut flowers to treatment with 1-methylcyclopropene and ethylene. *HortScience* 32:254–255.

Maier, N.A., G.E. Barth, J.S. Cecil, W.L. Chvyl, and M.N. Bartetzko. 1995. Effect of sampling time and leaf position on leaf nutrient composition of *Protea* 'Pink Ice.' *Australian Journal of Experimental Agriculture* 35:275–283.

Malan, D.G. 1992. Propagation of Proteaceae. *Acta Horticulturae* 316:27–34.

Malan, D.G. 1999. *Leucadendron* 'disease' problems. *SAPPEX News* 104:6–7.

Malan, D.G., and G.J. Brits. 1990. Flower structure and the influence of daylength on flower inititation of *Serruria florida* Knight (Proteaceae). *Acta Horticulturae* 264:87–92.

Malan, D.G., and G. Jacobs. 1990. Effect of photoperiod and shoot decapitation on flowering of *Leucospermum* 'Red Sunset.' *Journal of the American Society for Horticultural Science* 115(1): 131–135.

McConchie, R., N.S. Lang, and K.C. Gross. 1991. Carbohydrate depletion and leaf blackening in *Protea neriifolia*. *Journal of the American Society for Horticultural Science* 116:1019–1024.

McKenzie, B.L. 1973. Propagation of Proteaceae by cuttings. *International Plant Propagators Society Combined Proceedings* 23:380.

Mitchell, J.J., J. van Staden, and N.A.C. Brown. 1986. Germination of *Protea compacta* achenes: The relationship between incubation temperature and endogenous cytokinin levels. *Acta Horticulturae* 185:31–37.

Moffat, J., and L. Turnbull. 1993. *Grafting Proteas*. Nanju Protea Nursery, Queensland, Australia.

Montarone, M., and P. Allemand. 1995. Growing Proteaceae soilless under shelter. *Acta Horticulturae* 387:73–84.

Montarone, M., and M. Ziegler. 1997. Water and mineral absorption for two protea species (*P. eximia* and *P. cynaroides*) according to their development stage. *Acta Horticulturae* 453:135–144.

Napier, D.R., and G. Jacobs. 1989. Growth regulators and shading reduce flowering of *Leucospermum* cv. Red Sunset. *HortScience* 24(6):966–968.

Newman, J.P., W. van Doorn, and M.S. Reid. 1990. Carbohydrate stress causes leaf blackening in proteas. *Acta Horticulturae* 264:103–108.

Nixon, P., and W.H. Payne. 1995. Waratahs—The new breed to the year 2000. *Australian Plants* 18:303–311.

Offord, C.A., P.B. Goodwin, and P. Nixon. 1990. Clonal selection and micropropagation of waratah. *Acta Horticulturae* 264:49–52.

Olde, P., and N. Marriott. 1994. *The Grevillea Book*, vol. 1. Kangaroo Press, Kenthurst, New South Wales, Australia.

Paull, R.E., and J.-W. Dai. 1990. *Protea* postharvest leaf blackening: A problem in search of a solution. *Acta Horticulturae* 264:93–101.

Payne, W.H. 1995. Wildflowers developed for horticulture. *Australian Plants* 18(142):87–88.

Payne, W.H. 1997. Wildflowers as garden plants. *Australian Plants* 19(150):79, 81.

Pérez-Francés, J.F., A.J. Expósito, and J.A. Rodríguez. 1995. Effect of different factors on *in vitro* multiplication of *Leucadendron* 'Safari Sunset' (Proteaceae). *Acta Horticulturae* 387:115–120.

Prasad, M., and D.J. Dennis. 1986. Phosphorous nutrition of *Leucadendron* 'Safari Sunset.' *Acta Horticulturae* 185:155–162.

Rebelo, A. 1995. *Sasol Proteas, A Field Guide to the Proteas of Southern Africa.* Fernwood, Cape Town.

Reid, M.S., W. van Doorn, and J.P. Newman. 1989. Leaf blackening in proteas. *Acta Horticulturae* 261:81–84.

Rieger, M.A., and M. Sedgley. 1996. Effect of daylength and temperature on flowering of the cut flower species *Banksia coccinea* and *Banksia hookeriana. Australian Journal of Experimental Agriculture* 36:747–753.

Rodríguez-Pérez, J.A. 1990. A technique to improve the propagation by stem cuttings of *Protea obtusifolia. Acta Horticulturae* 264:41–44.

Rodríguez-Pérez, J.A. 1992. Propagation by leaf bud cuttings of *Leucadendron* 'Safari Sunset,' *Leucospermum cordifolium, L. patersonii* and *Protea obtusifolia. Acta Horticulturae* 316:35–45.

Rodríguez-Pérez, J.A. 1995. Effects of treatment with gibberellic acid on germination of *Protea cynaroides, P. eximia, P. neriifolia* and *P. repens* (Proteaceae). *Acta Horticulturae* 387:85–89.

Rodríguez-Pérez, J.A., A.M. de León Hernández, M.C. Vera Batista, and M.C. Hoyos Rodríguez. 1997. Influence of cutting position, wounding and IBA on the rooting of *Leucadendron discolor* stem cuttings. *Acta Horticulturae* 453:29–34.

Röhl, L.J., A.M. Fuss, J.A. Dhaliwal, M.G. Webb, and B.B. Lamont. 1994. Investigation of flowering in *Banksia baxteri* R. Br. and *B. hookeriana* Meissner for improving pruning practices. *Australian Journal of Experimental Agriculture* 34:1209–1216.

Rugge, B.A. 1995. Micropropagation of *Protea repens. Acta Horticulturae* 387:121–127.

Rugge, B.A., and G. Jacobs. 1990. Factors affecting bud-sprouting in multinodal stem segments of *Leucospermum* cv. Red Sunset *in vitro. Journal of Horticultural Science* 65(1):55–58.

Seaton, K.A., and D.C. Joyce. 1993. Effects of low temperature and elevated CO_2 treatments and of heat treatments for insect disinfestation on some Australian cut flowers. *Scientia Horticulturae* 56:119–133.

Sedgley, M. 1995. *Cloning and Selection of Banksias.* Australian Flora and Protea Growers Association Conference.

Sedgley, M. 1997. New *Banksia* cultivars for cut flower production. *Acta Horticulturae* 453:77–79.

Sedgley, M. 1998. *Banksia*: New Proteaceous cut flower crop. *Horticultural Reviews* 22:1–25.

Seelye, J.F., S.M. Butcher, and D.J. Dennis. 1986. Micropropagation of *Telopea speciosissima. Acta Horticulturae* 185:281–285.

Silber, A., R. Ganmore-Neumann, J. Ben-Jaacov, and A. Ackerman. 1997. Effects of phosphorous and nitrogen concentration on *Leucadendron* 'Safari Sunset' development. *Acta Horticulturae* 453: 35–46.

Swart, L. 1999. *Proteaceae Disease Control.* SAPPEX Fynbos Research Pamphlet Numbers 14–28.

Tal, E., J. Ben-Jaacov, and A.A. Watad. 1992a. Hardening and *in vivo* establishment of micropropagated *Grevillea* and *Leucospermum. Acta Horticulturae* 316:63–67.

Tal, E., H. Solomon, J. Ben-Jaacov, and A.A. Watad. 1992b. Micropropagation of selected *Leucospermum cordifolium*: Effect of antibiotics and GA_3. *Acta Horticulturae* 316:55–58.

Tynan, K.M., E.S. Scott, and M. Sedgley. 1998. Evaluation of *Banksia* species for response to *Phytophthora* infection. *Plant Pathology* 47:446–455.

Van den Berg, G.C., and G.J. Brits. 1995. Development of *Leucadendron* single stem cut flowers. *Acta Horticulturae* 387:191–198.

Vogts, M. 1982. *Protea*, pp. 82–125; *Leucospermum*, pp. 126–150, *Leucadendron*, pp. 156–209, in *South Africa's Proteaceae, Know Them and Grow Them.* C. Struik, Cape Town.

Von Broembsen, S.L. 1989. *Handbook of Diseases of Cut-Flower Proteas.* International Protea Association, Monbulk, Victoria, Australia.

Wallerstein, I., and A. Nissim. 1992. Control of growth and flowering in *Banksia ashbyi, Leucospermum patersonii* and *Leucadendron* 'Safari Sunset.' *Acta Horticulturae* 316:73–80.

Watad, A.A., J. Ben-Jaacov, E. Tal, and H. Solomon. 1992. *In vitro* propagation of *Grevillea* species. *Acta Horticulturae* 316:51–53.

Webb, M. 1996a. *Banksias for Cutflower Production.* Western Australian Department of Agriculture Farmnote Number 23/96.

Webb, M. 1996b. *Growing Proteas.* Western Australian Department of Agriculture Farmnote Number 79/96.

Worrall, R.J. 1983. Growing waratahs commercially. *Australian Horticulture.* 81(8):101, 103.

Worrall, R.J. 1995 Growing waratahs. *Australian Plants.* 18:17–21.

Wright, M.G. 1999. *SAPPEX Fynbos Research Pamphlet* Numbers 1–13.

Wrigley, J.W., and M. Fagg. 1991. *Banksias, Waratahs and Grevilleas, and all Other Plants in the Australian Proteaceae Family.* Collins, Angus & Robertson Publishers: North Ryde, New South Wales, Australia.

Ranunculus

FIGURE II-1 RANUNCULUS Bench of potted *Ranunculus* plants.

INTRODUCTION

Common names: ranunculus, Persian ranunculus, French ranunculus, turban ranunculus, peony-flowered ranunculus.

Scientific name: *Ranunculus asiaticus* L. (Huxley et al., 1992).

Family and related taxa: Ranunculaceae Juss. Bailey and Bailey (1976) stated that 250 species of *Ranunculus* exist and the Royal Horticultural Society Dictionary of Gardening lists 400 species (Huxley et al., 1992). The Ranunculaceae family also includes other important genera such as *Aconitum, Anemone, Aquilegia, Clematis, Consolida,* and *Delphinium.*

Origin: Generally found in the eastern Mediterranean area: southern Europe, Asia Minor, Syria, Iran, and the Greek Islands.

Uses and current status: *R. asiaticus* is the most common species with worldwide distribution as a garden plant, cut flower, perennial, and flowering potted plant (Figs. II-1 and Figs. II-2 Ranunculus).

R. asiaticus is a perennial geophyte that can have a tuberous root up to 1.5 ft (45 cm) long when mature. Segmented leaves form a rosette and easily distinguish the plant as a member of the crowfoot or buttercup family. The flower stem length determines which cultivars are used for cut flower or potted plant production. The vividly colored flowers can be white, red, vermillion, orange, violet, yellow, pink, or rose. Most cultivars are double; however, single-flower types with only five petals exist (Bailey and Bailey, 1976; Meynet, 1993). Roots consist of short, cylindrical

FIGURE II-2 RANUNCULUS *Ranunculus* 'LaBelle' cut flowers.

tuberous root structures, which are branched and apically unite to form a crown. The storage organ in active growth is not frost tolerant (Armitage, 1989; Horovitz, 1985; Meynet, 1993). The plant requires mild climates or temperatures; flowering occurs in the spring and early summer in outdoor gardens or in the winter and spring in greenhouses. Tuber production for the home garden or for forcing occurs worldwide. Once harvested, the tuberous roots are dried to 15% moisture (Horovitz, 1985; Meynet, 1993).

CULTIVARS

Ranunculus has been in cultivation for more than 300 years. In 1665, 20 cultivars were known, and by 1775 some 800 were listed. By 1820, however, the number had fallen to 400. Certain strains are used for cut flowers and others for potted flowering plant production.

PROPAGATION

Although tubers can be divided in the fall, ranunculus are more easily and commonly propagated from seed. In the first year, flower yield is limited and flowering is late when grown from seed. In California seeds are directly sown in the field for sustained flower production. In the greenhouse seeds germinate in 6 to 8 weeks at 60 to 62°F (16 to 17°C) and plants do not require a cold treatment to flower (Armitage, 1989; Meynet, 1993; Post, 1949). Tubers are easily transportable and vernalized for rapid flowering. *In vitro* propagation is possible and the resulting liners are mainly used for cut flower production (Lercaria et al., 1984; Maia et al., 1973; Meynet and Duclos, 1990a, b; White, 2002).

Seed-propagated plugs are commonly used by producers. For plug production the following conditions are used (White, 2002):

Stage 1: Seed uncovered, 50 to 68°F (10 to 20°C), for 7 to 14 days, light not needed

Stage 2: 50 to 68°F (10 to 20°C), for 7 to 14 days, 500 to 1500 fc (100 to 300 μmol $\cdot$ m^{-2} $\cdot$ s^{-1}), 50 to 75 ppm N once/week

Stage 3: 55 to 75°F (13 to 14°C), for 28 to 35 days, 1500 to 2500 fc (300 to 500 μmol $\cdot$ m^{-2} $\cdot$ s^{-1}), 100 to 150 ppm N once/week

Stage 4: 62 to 65°F (17 to 18°C), for 7 days, 2000 to 3000 fc (400 to 600 μmol $\cdot$ m^{-2} $\cdot$ s^{-1}), 100 to 150 ppm N once/week, B-Nine (daminozide) at 2500 ppm can be applied for potted plant production.

FLOWERING CONTROL AND DORMANCY

Shoots emerge from vegetative buds located on the crown of the tuberous root during the cool moist winter. Each shoot has its individual root system. Shoots initiate flowers after 60 days with medium to large tubers, while seedlings require 120 days. With tubers, seven or more leaves are formed before flower initiation occurs; with seedlings, 8 to 15 leaves must form. Naturally, the larger the tuberous root, the greater the number of flowering shoots (Horovitz, 1985; Meynet, 1974, 1993).

High temperatures and LD (13 hr or longer) promote the development of tuberous roots on *in vitro*–derived material and promote dormancy in seedlings and mature plants. The critical temperature for tuberous root formation is 77°F (25°C) for young plants and 64°F (18°C) for mature plants (Meynet, 1993).

Rapid shoot emergence and floral initiation can occur by soaking the tuberous roots for 12 to 48 hr after a 4- to 5-week cold treatment at 39 to 41°F (4 to 5°C) (Elber, 1970; Ohkawa, 1986). Meynet (1974) found that 36°F (2°C) was acceptable for no more than 2 weeks for a cold treatment; longer than this, plant quality decreased.

TEMPERATURE

Ranunculus can be forced at 45 to 50°F (7 to 10°C) night temperature, allowing it to be produced in energy-efficient greenhouses in the winter (Post, 1949). Temperatures of 54 to 60°F (12 to 16°C) result in rapid growth and high leaf numbers (Karlsson, 1998). Increasing temperature from 46 to 68°F (8 to 20°C) decreased time to flower but also decreased flower number and quality and increased height (F. Arnoskey, personal communication; Karlsson, 1998). In Georgia, Natarella and Kays (1979) forced potted tubers at 50 to 54°F (10 to 12°C) nights with 64 to 68°F (18 to 20°C) days.

Temperatures above 60°F (16°C) are detrimental (Albrecht, 1985, 1987; De Hertogh, 1996; Ohkawa, 1986). Above 80°F (27°C) lower foliage will turn yellow. Ranunculus can survive at 23°F (25°C); dormant tubers with 15% moisture can survive liquid N$_2$ for 24 hr (Sakai, 1960).

LIGHT

Short-day conditions and cool nights are optimal for high-quality flower production and high yields (Ohkawa, 1986). Long days accelerate floral development and increase plant height but reduce flower quality (Karlsson, 1998). Also, LD and high temperatures result in tuberous root formation, plant senescence, and tuberous root dormancy (Armitage, 1987). Ranunculus force best at a light intensity of 2400 fc (480 μmol $\cdot$ m^{-2} $\cdot$ s^{-1}) or higher (De Hertogh, 1996). For compact growth and rapid establishment, use 3500 to 4000 fc (700 to 800 μmol $\cdot$ m^{-2} $\cdot$ s^{-1}) initially and reduce to 2000 fc (400 μmol $\cdot$ m^{-2} $\cdot$ s^{-1}) when flowers are visible. Increasing the daily light integral from 8 to 16 mol $\cdot$ m^{-2} $\cdot$ day^{-1} decreased crop time (Karlsson, 1998).

WATER

Ranunculus require well-drained media. Overwatering or anaerobic medium conditions increase disease incidence (Meynet, 1993).

CARBON DIOXIDE

No data available.

NUTRITION

Armitage (1987) believed that the stored food in the tuberous roots was sufficient with a starter solution at planting; after establishment, a nitrogen level of approximately 100 ppm can be used. However, De Hertogh (1996) noted that ranunculus require a good fertilizer program. Plants can be fertilized twice a week with 300 ppm N and 280 ppm K from $Ca(NO_3)_2$ and KNO_3. High fertilizer rates will deepen foliage color. An N:P:K ratio of 1:0.5:1.5 is acceptable. Ammonium and urea should be avoided or used only at low rates (Meynet, 1993). Micronutrients should also be used (Natarella and Kays, 1979). Albrecht (1985, 1987) top-dressed pots with controlled-release fertilizers (14–14–14) at 0.08 oz (2.2 g)/pot and used 200 ppm N every 2 weeks. Albrecht also stated that excessive root growth can occur and will force the plant out of the pot if overfertilized.

MEDIA

Ranunculus require a well-drained medium (De Hertogh, 1996; Meynet, 1993). Ranunculus are tolerant to a wide pH range from 5.8 to 7.5; however, a low soluble salt level is required. Natarella and Kays (1979) forced tubers in a 1:1 vermiculite:milled pine bark medium amended with dolomitic limestone and superphosphate at 10 and 5 lb/yd^3 (6 and 3 $kg \cdot m^{-3}$), respectively.

HEIGHT CONTROL

No height control is needed for cut flower production; however, potted plants grown in greenhouses under poor light conditions may produce flowers with excessively long peduncles. Foliar application of A-Rest (ancymidol) (0.5 mg a.i./plant) or B-Nine (daminozide) (5000 ppm) reduced peduncle lengths (Albrecht, 1985, 1987). Armitage (1987) suggested that B-Nine sprays (5000 ppm) be used after 6 to 10 leaves have unfolded. Three or more applications of 2500-ppm B-Nine foliar sprays may also be effective with the first application 4 weeks after beginning greenhouse forcing

and subsequent applications every 2 weeks (Fred C. Gloeckner, Inc., personal communication). DIF is effective on ranunculus; maintain a positive DIF for cut flower production and a negative DIF for potted and bedding plant production (Karlsson, 1998).

SPACING

One presprouted tuberous root or plug is potted in a 4-in. (10-cm) pot and two to three in a 6-in. (15-cm) pot (Albrecht, 1987; White, 2002). Top-grade, 0.75- to 2.4-in. (2- to 6-cm)-diameter tuberous roots should be used. Pots are kept pot-to-pot until foliage touches. Space promptly or stems and foliage petioles will elongate excessively.

For cut flower production, plant 4 to 6 tubers/ft^2 (45 to 65/m^2) (Houck, 1994). Tubers can also be presprouted in 32- to 50-cell trays. Use tubers that are 1.2 to 2.0 in. (3 to 5 cm), 2.0 to 2.4 in. (5 to 6 cm), or 2.4+ in. (6+ cm) in size (De Hertogh, 1996).

PINCHING AND DISBUDDING

No pinching or disbudding is required. However, the first flower can be removed if potted plants flower too soon or if the flower stem is too tall. The next flower stems are usually not as tall and several may be open at one time.

SUPPORT

No support required.

SCHEDULE AND TIMING

Ranunculus are typically sold in late winter through spring as cut flowers and potted flowering plants. Ranunculus can also be sold as fall bedding plants for outdoor areas with a Mediterranean climate (White, 2002) (Table II-1 Ranunculus).

TUBERS

Three months are allowed to elapse between harvest and beginning of cold treatments. Vernalization is required. Various tuberous rooted temperature treatment regimes are reported to be used in Europe (Horovitz, 1985). Most forcers in North America receive precooled tuberous roots.

Dry tubers are presprouted for 2 to 3 weeks in moist perlite or other media at 61 to 65°F (16 to 18°C). Flats are used and approximately 50 tubers are placed in each flat. It is essential that

TABLE II-I RANUNCULUS

Ranunculus production schedule for flowering potted plants or bedding plants from dormant tubers (modified from Albrecht, 1985).

Cultural Step	Production Time (weeks)	Temperature °F (°C)
Presprout tubers[a]		
	3	65 (18)
Pot[b] and develop roots		
	1	Night: 60 (16)
Lower temperature		
	7	Night: 45 (7) Day: 55 (13)
Apply B-Nine		
	7–8	Night: 45 (7) Day: 55 (13)
Flower		
Total	18–19	

[a]Use a flat filled with perlite and kept moist, growing point exposed.
[b]One tuber/4-in. (10-cm) pot; three tubers/6-in. (15-cm) pot.

the crowns of the tuber are just above the perlite (Albrecht, 1987; Meynet, 1993). Direct planting of presprouted tubers typically occurs on week 29 (approximately July 16 to 22). If temperatures are too high, planting can be delayed until week 34 (approximately August 20 to 26). Sprouted tubers must be stored at 36°F (2°C), but for no more than 2 weeks. Flowering can occur in 11 to 17 weeks with presprouted tubers, depending on the temperature (Albrecht, 1987). Armitage (1989), however, stated only 49 to 70 days are needed for flowering. When tubers were planted monthly from July to October, the last planting date produced superior quality plants under Mediterranean conditions (Mohamed et al., 1974).

To reduce the amount of time in the cut flower bed, tubers can be grown in 32- to 50-cell plug trays for 4 to 6 weeks prior to planting (Houck, 1994). For cut flower production, 10 to 15 stems will be produced per plant (F. Arnoskey, personal communication).

SEED

Seed to sale required 20 to 28 weeks; 13 to 21 weeks from plugs or tubers to finish (Armitage, 1989; White, 2002). In the Netherlands seeds are sown in May for November flower production. Consequently, only vernalized tuberous roots permit early flowering (Horovitz, 1985; Meynet, 1993). Karlsson (1998) reported that when potted plants were grown at 46°F (8°C) under 8-, 12-, or 16-hr day lengths, flowering oc-

curred in 83, 72, or 65 days, respectively; at 54°F (12°C) in 70, 58, or 50 days, respectively; and at 60°F (16°C) in 58, 43, or 38 days, respectively.

INSECTS

Leaf miners, caterpillars, and thrips are listed by Meynet (1993) as problems. Leaf miners are probably the most serious and thrips can vector the tomato spotted wilt virus.

DISEASES

Pseudomonas (bacterial leaf spot), *Rhizoctonia,* and several viruses are of primary concern in tuberous root production and forcing (De Hertogh, 1996). Southern blight (*Sclerotium rolfsii*) can also be a major problem (F. Arnosky, personal communication). Tubers are frequently soaked in a fungicide solution prior to planting and presprouting treatments. Tomato spotted wilt virus is a serious threat and is spread by thrips. The diseases that occur in production and forcing are summarized by Meynet (1993). Horst (1990) noted that powdery mildew (*Ersiphe polygoni*), downy mildew (*Peronospora ficariae*), aster yellows, gray mold (*Botrytis cinerea*), and stem rot (*Pythium*) can be problems. Other diseases reported include cottony rot (*Sclerotinia sclerotiorum*), rust (*Puccinia* and *Uromyces*), smut (*Entyloma* and *Urocystis*), leaf spot (*Ramularia*), and bacterial blight (*Xanthomonas campestris*) (Dreistadt, 2001).

PHYSIOLOGICAL DISORDERS

Freshly harvested tuberous roots may be slow and erratic in emergence. The lack of uniformity of plants from F_1 seed lines prevents rapid and efficient clearing of the production area and accurate scheduling. Cold temperature requirements for forcing and production during SD periods limit production to the winter in temperate areas (Armitage, 1987). Overcooling of tuberous roots results in early flowering (Meynet, 1993).

POSTHARVEST

Harvest cut flowers when buds show color and are almost fully open. Flowers close at night and harvesting, grading, and packing are best done early in the morning when flowers are still closed. Flowers are stored and shipped at 34 to 36°F (1 to 2°C). If stored for long periods, the temperature should be 32 to 34°F (0 to 1°C) and good-quality water should be used. At 50°F (10°C), deterioration is rapid. Results regarding the use of silver thiosulfate (STS) are variable in that Houck (1994) recommended the use of STS, but Kenza et al. (2000) stated that it was not effective.

With potted plants, commence shipping when the first flowers are open (Meynet, 1993; Natarella and Kays, 1979). Ranunculus are reported to have low sensitivity to ethylene (Nowak and Rudnicki, 1990). Armitage (1987) stated that potted plant survival in the average home is "fair;" if kept in a cool area, plants should last up to 14 days.

KEY POINTS

- *Ranunculus* is used as a cut flower, potted flowering plant, and garden ornamental.
- Flowering plants are commercially grown from tubers or seed; *in vitro* is possible.
- Young seedlings do not need to be vernalized.
- Mature tubers require a 4- to 5-week cold treatment at 39 to 41°F (4 to 5°C).
- High temperatures and LD promote dormancy.

- Growth in the greenhouse or in the field is best at night temperatures of 45 to 50°F (7 to 10°C), but 54 to 60°F (12 to 16°C) results in rapid growth and high leaf numbers. Temperatures above 60°F (16°C) are detrimental.
- Overwatering or poor medium aeration promotes diseases.
- Leaf miners, bacterial leaf spot, and *Rhizoctonia* can be serious problems.

BIBLIOGRAPHY

Albrecht, M.L. 1985. Cool it with anemone and ranunculus. *Greenhouse Grower* 3(12):30–31, 34.

Albrecht, M.L. 1987. Growth retardant use with potted *Anemone* and *Ranunculus*. *Journal of the American Society for Horticultural Science* 112: 82–85.

Armitage, A. 1987. New crops: The present and the future. *Greenhouse Grower* 5(10):50.

Armitage, A.M. 1989. *Ranunculus*, pp. 495–499 in *Herbaceous Perennial Plants*. Varsity Press, Athens, Georgia.

Bailey, L.H., and E.Z. Bailey. 1976. *Ranunculus*, pp. 938–940 in *Hortus Third: A Concise Dictionary of Plants Cultivated in the United States and Canada*. Macmillan, New York.

De Hertogh, A.A. 1996. *Ranunculus asiaticus*, pp. C147–151 in *Holland Bulb Forcer's Guide*, 5th ed. International Flower Bulb Centre, Hillegom, The Netherlands.

Dreistadt, S.H. 2001. *Integrated Pest Management for Floriculture and Nurseries*. University of California Division of Agriculture and Natural Resources Publication 3402.

Elber, Y. 1970. Cold storage treatment for earlier bloom of *Ranunculus* tubers, p. 145 in *Proceedings of the 18th International Horticultural Congress*, vol. I. Tel Aviv, Israel.

Horovitz, A. 1985. *Ranunculus*, pp. 155–161 in *Handbook of Flowering*, vol. IV, A.H. Halevy, editor. CRC Press, Boca Raton, Florida.

Horst, R.K. 1990. Ranunculus, pp. 791–792 in *Westcott's Plant Disease Handbook*, 5th ed. Van Nostrand Reinhold, New York.

Houck, S. 1994. Ranunculus. *Greenhouse Manager* 13(2):45, 46, 48, 49.

Huxley, A., M. Griffiths, and M. Levy. 1992. *Ranunculus*, pp. 3–8 in *The New Royal Horticultural Society Dictionary of Gardening*, vol. 4. Stockton Press, New York.

Karlsson, M. 1998. *Temperature and Light Requirements for Flowering and Development of Ranunculus.* Bedding Plants Foundation Research Report No. F-9803.

Kenza, M., N. Umiel, and A. Borochov. 2000. The involvement of ethylene in the senescence of ranunculus cut flowers. *Postharvest Biology and Technology* 19:287–290.

Lercaria, G., E. Accati-Garibaldi, and M. Littardi. 1984. Primi risultati sull'impiego della coltural in vitro del ranuncolo. *Culture Protette* 10:73–74. (in Italian, English summary)

Maia, E., B. Bettachini, D. Beck, and A. Marais. 1973. Régénération de renoncules par culture d'apex in vitro. *Annales de Phytopathologie* 5:125–129. (in French, English summary)

Meynet, J. 1974. Travaux d'amelioration de la renoncule. Eucarpia, *Reunion sur les plantes ornamentales, Fréjus,* France:4–17. (in French, English summary)

Meynet, J. 1993. *Ranunculus,* pp. 603–610 in *The Physiology of Flower Bulbs,* A. De Hertogh and M. Le Nard, editors. Elsevier, Amsterdam.

Meynet, J., and A. Duclos. 1990a. Culture *in vitro* de la renoncule des fleuristes (Ranunculus asiaticus L.). *Agronomie* 10:157–162. (in French, English summary)

Meynet, J., and A. Duclos. 1990b. Production des plantes par culture d'antheres in vitro. *Agronomie* 10:213–218. (in French, English summary)

Mohamed, B.R., H. Kamel, and A. Nabib. 1974. The effect of storage and planting date on *Ranunculus asiaticus* flowering. *Gartenbauwissenschaft* 39:155–160.

Natarella, N.J., and S.J. Kays. 1979. Effect of storage temperature on cut flowers of *Ranunculus asiaticus* L. *HortScience* 14:504–505.

Nowak, J., and R.M. Rudnicki. 1990. *Postharvest and Storage of Cut Flowers, Florist Greens, and Potted Plants.* Timber Press, Portland, Oregon.

Ohkawa, K. 1986. Grown and flowering of *Ranunculus asiaticus. Acta Horticulturae* 177:165–172.

Post, K. 1949. *Ranunculus asiaticus* hybrids, p. 749 in *Florist Crop Production and Marketing.* Orange Judd Publishing, New York.

Sakai, A. 1960. The frost hardiness of bulbs and tubers. *Journal of the Horticultural Association of Japan* 29:233–238. (in Japanese, English summary)

White, J.D. 2002. How to grow *Ranunculus. GrowerTalks* 66(5):81, 86.

Rhododendron

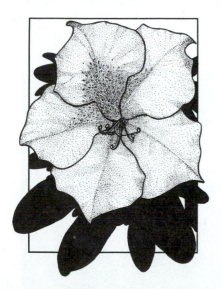

INTRODUCTION

Common names: florists' azalea, evergreen azalea, azalea.

Scientific names: *Rhododendron* hybrids. The following species and hybrids have made major genetic contributions to the present-day azalea hybrids: *Rhododendron indicum* (L.) Sweet, *R. linearifolium* Sieb. & Zucc., *R. mucronatum* G. Don., *R. ×obtusum* Planch., *R. ×pulchrum* Sweet, *R. scabrum* G. Don., *R. simsii* Planch., *R. tschonoskii* Maxim., and *R. yedoense* variety *poukhanense* Nak. (Bailey and Bailey, 1976; Huxley et al., 1992).

Family and related taxa: Ericaceae Juss. There are at least 103 genera and more than 3350 species in the family; the genus *Rhododendron* alone contains 700 to 800 species. *Rhododendron* species have been divided into at least 44 series, one of which is the Azalea series. The Azalea series has been subdivided into the following subseries: *canadense, luteum, nipponicum, obtusum, schlippenbachii,* and *tashiroi.* The evergreen florists' forcing azalea is primarily derived from the subseries *obtusum.* The species and hybrids within the *obtusum* subseries are listed in the preceding Scientific Names section (Bailey and Bailey, 1976; Leiser, 1975). The Ericaceae family also includes blueberries and cranberries (*Vaccinium*) and numerous garden ornamentals such as *Calluna, Erica, Kalmia,* and *Pieris.*

Origin: The species used to develop the florists' azalea are from east Asia. *Rhododendron indicum* (Zone 6), *R. linearifolium* (Zone 7), and *R. ×obtusum* (Zone 7) are from southern Japan. *R. mucronatum* is from northern Japan

(Zone 5) and *R. ×scabrum* is from the tropical southern Japanese Ryukyu Islands (Zone 8). *R. ×pulchrum*, possibly a hybrid long in cultivation, is from China, and *R. simsii* is from China and Taiwan (Zone 8). Both *R. tschonoskii* and *R. yedoense* are from southern Korea (Zone 6); the former is also found in Japan (Bailey and Bailey, 1976). Since the species used to develop the florists' azalea are mainly from Zones 6, 7, or 8, the florists' azalea has only moderate winter or frost hardiness.

Uses and current status: Potted plants are most commonly forced into flower from Christmas to Mother's Day, although they can be programmed to flower by controlling temperature and photoperiod on a year-round basis. Historically, the most common pot size was a 6- to 7-in. (15- to 18-cm) azalea pan; now pot sizes of 5, 4, and 2 in. (13, 10, and 5 cm) are used and have increased sales of azaleas. Known to be an expensive plant because of its long-term production cycle, sales have generally been static. However, recent sales seem to be increasing.

The florists' azalea is characterized by small 1.5-in. (4-cm) evergreen glossy leaves, a short 12-in. (30-cm) height, and two or more 1- to 3-in. (2- to 8-cm)-wide flowers per terminal bud. Plants are very well branched and stems are thin. Individual flowers can be single or double with smooth or ruffled edges; colors vary from pure white through pale to dark pinks, rose, orange, salmon, and various reds (scarlet, carmine, crimson) (Stadtherr, 1975).

Other members of the genus *Rhododendron* also show potential as potted flowering plants including a group of tropical rhododendrons, the Vireyas, which have a broad range of vibrant colors and some fragrant species (Criley, 2001). The evergreen rhododendrons with large flower clusters also have potential (French and Alsbury, 1988; Wilkinson and Richards, 1991).

CULTIVARS

Frequently hybrid azalea cultivars are grouped under the name of the individual hybridizer, location of origin, or primary species used in the hybrid. For example, a few better known cultivar groups are Kurume, Indian (Indica), Kaempfrei, Gable, Glen Dale, Pericat, and Rutherfordiana (Leiser, 1975). Hundreds of cultivars are found worldwide. Stadtherr (1975) listed well over 200, and Larson (1992) mentioned several additional popular cultivars that should be added to the list and stated that Europe still has a wider cultivar base than

North American. Japan, Korea, and China have additional cultivars and species. Regardless, few new cultivars are introduced for greenhouse production each decade.

PROPAGATION

Azaleas are mainly propagated in the spring by semihardwood cuttings 3 to 4 in. long (7.5 to 10 cm) using indole-3-butyric acid (IBA) and rooted at 70°F (21°C) medium temperature in peat moss. For tree-form topiary plants, the desired cultivar is grafted on the rootstock *R. concinnum* Hemsl. (Fig. II-1 Rhododendron). Propagation in North America is usually done by specialists in Oregon, California, Florida, and Alabama. Plants can be *in vitro* propagated to quickly build up new cultivars or to acquire disease-free material (Anderson, 1978; Blazich and Acedo, 1988; Brand et al., 2000; McCulloch, 1984; Mertens et al., 1996).

Up to 2 years or longer are usually required to produce a 6-in. (15-cm) potted flowering plant from a cutting; shorter time spans are required for smaller plants. Commercially, local producers often buy young plants (liners) that have already been sheared one to three times to induce branching. The producer needs only to plant them in 6-in. (15-cm) pots, grow them, pinch one additional time, induce flower buds, treat with cold and/or gibberellic acid (GA), and force. Some forcers buy "budded

FIGURE II-I RHODODENDRON *Rhododendron* potted plant in tree form.

plants" with fully initiated flowers ready to be forced into flower after a cold treatment.

FLOWERING CONTROL AND DORMANCY

The vegetative and reproductive growth cycles used in commerce mimic nature (Fig. II-2 Rhododendron). When plants (shoots) reach the size required for sale, pinching ceases and flower buds are allowed to form. The maturity of the shoot influences the rate and capacity of the apex to form flowers. Older shoots form flowers more rapidly under a wider range of environmental conditions. Juvenile shoots only respond to precise vegetative or reproductive conditions (Criley, 1969; Pemberton and Wilkins, 1985; Petterson, 1972; Shanks and Link, 1968).

Vegetative growth is maintained by LD using night interruption from incandescent lamps. A 16- to 18-hr total photoperiod (normal day plus night break) is used from fall to spring after a pinch to maintain or promote vegetative growth. A night temperature of 64 to 72°F (18 to 22°C) with 10°F (6°C) or warmer day temperature also promotes vegetative growth (Cathey, 1965; Criley, 1985; Skinner, 1939).

Floral initiation and development are under the control of natural shortening days or 8-hr SD provided with black cloth. Warm night temperatures of 64 to 72°F (18 to 22°C) also promote rapid and uniform initiation with the greatest number of flower buds formed under SD. Six to 8 weeks must be allowed after the last pinch to the beginning of SD. A dormant flower bud is present after 12 to 16 weeks of SD (Jorgensen, 1969; Kiplinger, 1944; Kiplinger and Bresser, 1951; Petterson, 1972).

Plant growth regulators such as B-Nine (daminozide) sprays at 1500 to 2500 ppm and Cycocel (chlormequat) sprays at 1000 to 4000 ppm are used to reduce internode elongation and synergistically interact with SD to promote earlier floral initiation and development (Cathey, 1965; Jorgensen, 1969; McDowell and Larson, 1966; Stuart, 1964). Plants treated with growth retardants also have more flowers per bud and leaves are darker green. Plants given SD and plant growth regulator treatments force and break dormancy after a cold treatment more uniformly and rapidly than untreated plants (Criley, 1985; Schneider, 1967).

Dormancy breaking and rapid development of flower buds can be accomplished by several methods. Cold treatments for 4 to 6 weeks in the dark at 35 to 40°F (2 to 4°C) or at 40 to 50°F (4 to 10°C) if lighted with 125 fc (25 μmol $\cdot$ m^{-2} $\cdot$ s^{-1}) for 12 hr are the most common methods. Womack et al. (1995) noted that cooling dormant plants at temperatures less than 45°F (7°C) increased days to marketability by up to 7 days compared with plants cooled at 55 or 65°F (13 or 18°C). Cooling for greater than 6 weeks at temperatures greater than 45°F (7°C) increased bypass shoot development and bud abortion and decreased percentage of marketable plants. Plants artificially cooled at temperatures warmer than 45°F (7°C) force more rapidly (Criley, 1985; Larson and Sydnor, 1971). Cold treatments can also be given in

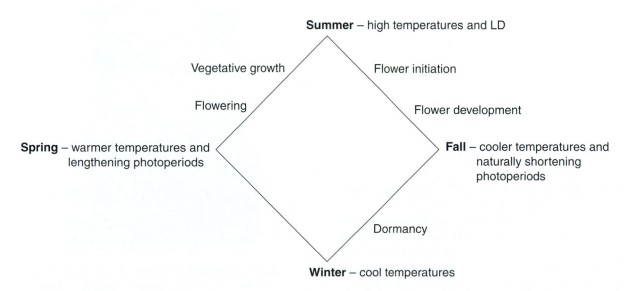

FIGURE II-2 RHODODENDRON   The schematic representation of the annual growth cycle for the florists' evergreen *Rhododendron.*

glass or plastic-covered structures where temperatures can be held above freezing. Shade must be used because the temperature on sunny days can go above 50° (10°C) even in very cold climates. In many areas refrigerated cooling must be used; however, coolers are expensive to construct, maintain, and operate, and thus other methods have been devised to eliminate cooling.

Sprays of GA_3, GA_7, and GA_{4+7} can substitute for cold. Benzyladenine (BA) and kinetin alone are not effective, but rather are additives in combination with GA in breaking dormancy. The basic treatment is a weekly spray of GA at 130 to 1000 ppm; the rate and number of sprays depend on the cultivar (Heins et al., 1978). Flower buds must be at the correct stage of development or maturity. Combination treatments of 3 weeks of cold and 3 weekly GA sprays are also possible. Combination treatments use the cold storage facility more efficiently, but part of the savings is offset by the labor of moving plants into and out of the cold facility (Boodley and Mastalerz, 1959; Larson and Sydnor, 1971).

Plants with mature flower buds can also be flowered without prior cold treatment by the use of LD lighting for 4 to 6 weeks. Night interruptions can be supplied by high-intensity lights or low-intensity photoperiod lighting. One to 2 weeks of cold prior to LD or LD in combination with GA_3 can also be used to substitute for 6 weeks of cold treatment (Brown and Box, 1971; Pemberton and Wilkins, 1985).

High temperatures of 86 to 100°F (30 to 38°F) for 12 to 40 hr may cause flower bud abortion unless plants were previously cold treated for 4 weeks. However, rapid flowering occurred if plants were cold treated and then briefly treated with high temperatures (Wilkins, 1980).

Although GA sprays hasten floral differentiation and development after flower bud dormancy, they are inhibitory to floral initiation during the vegetative stage. Further, indole-3-acetic acid (IAA) and naphthaleneacetic acid (NAA) sprays had no influence on number of flower buds (Ballantyne and Link, 1961; Criley, 1969).

Flower bud initiation and development have been studied in relation to temperature and timing after the last pinch (Adams and Roberts, 1968; Bodson, 1983; Johnson and Roberts, 1968) and reviewed by Criley (1985). Pemberton et al. (1985, 1998) followed the en-

dogenous abscissic acid levels during the various stages of development and during the 48°F (9°C) cold treatment and modeled plant growth.

TEMPERATURE

A night temperature of 65°F (18°C) is needed for both optimal vegetative growth and rapid floral initiation and development. For optimum flower bud dormancy release, 4 to 6 weeks of lighted 40 to 50°F (4 to 10°C) storage is commonly used (see Flowering Control and Dormancy, page 799, and Physiological Disorders, page 803) (Fig. II-3 Rhododendron). For greenhouse forcing into flower, an acceptable temperature is 60 to 65°F (16 to 18°C) (Criley, 1975; Love, 1975).

LIGHT

Light intensity is critical during the vegetative growth period. During the summer, light levels are reduced by shading to 3000 to 4000 fc (600 to 800 μmol $\cdot$ m^{-2} $\cdot$ s^{-1}). In the winter, full light intensity is required for growth or forcing. During cold storage, if temperatures are above 40°F (4°C), light is needed for 12 hr at 125 fc (25 μmol $\cdot$ m^{-2} $\cdot$ s^{-1}).

Long days of 16 hr are required during vegetative growth and up to 6 to 8 weeks after the last pinch. Thereafter, 8-hr SD hasten flower initiation (Criley, 1975; Love, 1975).

FIGURE II-3 RHODODENDRON Rack of potted *Rhododendron* plants after being cooled for 6 weeks at 40°F (4°C).

WATER

A peat moss medium is not easy to water properly. It is easily overwatered, which leads to root rot problems. Conversely, if allowed to become too dry, the peat shrinks away from the pot and rehydration is a problem that causes plant water stress, root injury, and leaf loss.

When grown outdoors, overhead irrigation is a common form of watering. However, water quality must be good to avoid leaf residue and constant monitoring for foliar diseases is required. Other irrigation methods such as ebb-and-flow and microtube can be used (Kofranek and Lunt, 1975). During cold storage, the moisture of the medium must be monitored. A humidity of 90% is suggested in the cooler.

CARBON DIOXIDE

If plants are grown in an environment where CO_2 can be used, 800- to 1000-ppm levels are used during vegetative growth and greenhouse forcing.

NUTRITION

Kofranek and Lunt (1975) characterized the unique nutritional requirements of azaleas. Plants must be grown in an acid medium, they have a low requirement for nutrients (Table II-1 Rhododendron), and roots are easily injured by excessive EC. Larson (1992) recommended 315 ppm N from a neutral 21–7–7 soluble fertilizer at one application every 1 to 2 weeks. Various descriptions of nutrient deficiencies have been published (Kofranek and Lunt, 1975; Larson, 1992; Oertli, 1964a, b, c; Twigg and Link, 1951). Frequent medium and tissue tests should be taken (Dole and Wilkins, 1988).

MEDIA

Azaleas are always grown in a 100% peat moss medium with the pH adjusted at 4.5 to 5.5 (Kofranek and Lunt, 1975).

HEIGHT CONTROL

A-Rest (ancymidol), B-Nine, Cycocel, Bonzi (paclobutrazol), or Sumagic (uniconazole) can be used to control internode elongation (Adriansen, 1985; Keever and Foster, 1991; Nell, 2001) (Fig. II-4 Rhododendron). Growth regulators are usually applied 3 to 6 weeks after the last pinch or when shoots are 1.5 to 2 in. (4 to 5 cm) long. B-Nine foliar sprays are used at the rate of 1500 ppm to 3500 ppm. Cycocel foliar sprays are used at the rate of 1000 to 4000 ppm; two applications at a half rate 1 week apart are frequently practiced to avoid leaf chlorosis. Multiple applications of B-Nine or Cycocel are often used. A-Rest (26-ppm spray), Bonzi (100- to 200-ppm spray or 0.6 to 1.77 mg a.i./pot drench), and Sumagic (10- to 15-ppm spray) are usually applied only once or twice (Whipker, 2003). Rates vary with the cultivar, season, location, and production site. All growth regulators hasten flower bud initiation under SD, enhance flowering uniformity, and increase number of flower buds formed in the terminal flower cluster bud (Heins et al., 1978; Stuart, 1961, 1964, 1975).

TABLE II-I RHODODENDRON
Macro- and micronutrient levels found in normal leaf tissue from the first mature leaf on a florist *Rhododendron* (Peterson, 1982).

Element	Level
Nitrogen	2.0–3.0%
Phosphorus	0.2–0.5%
Potassium	1.0–1.6%
Calcium	0.5–1.6%
Magnesium	0.2–0.5%
Iron	50–300 ppm
Manganese	60–150 ppm
Zinc	26–60 ppm
Copper	5–15 ppm
Boron	30–100 ppm

FIGURE II-4 RHODODENDRON   Azalea plant that has not been sprayed with B-Nine (daminozide) to inhibit excessive shoot elongation.

SPACING

Vegetative plants should be adequately spaced for maximum light and growth prior to shearing. Crowding is one cause of poor flower bud formation on lower branches and uneven flowering after the cold or LD/GA treatment. Spacing is also essential for air circulation, disease control, and adequate spray penetration. A spacing of 10 × 10 in. (25 × 25 cm) is minimal, 12 × 12 in. (30 × 30 cm) is preferable.

PINCHING AND DISBUDDING

The number of pinches determines the size of the final plant. Azaleas produced in 6-in. (15-cm) or larger pots are often grown from "liners." These liners have been sheared up to three times to produce a well-branched plant. The time span between shearing is normally 6 to 8 weeks. Generally, three to four nodes are left on the shoot and a 3- to 4-in. (7.5- to 10-cm) shoot tip is removed. These shoots can be trimmed and used as cuttings (Criley, 1975; Love, 1975). Chemicals such as Atrimmec (dikegulac sodium), Off-Shoot-O (methyl ester of fatty acids), Florel (ethephon), or Embark can be used (Heins et al., 1978; Nell, 2001; Stuart, 1975; Whipker, 2003). Chemical pinching is more labor efficient and produces more axillary shoots. However, irregular results from chemical pinching have limited its use, because plants must be individually inspected and pruned again by hand if needed.

SUPPORT

No support is needed, unless topiary trees are produced, which should be staked.

SCHEDULE AND TIMING

Azaleas are available on a year-round basis, which is accomplished by manipulating photoperiod or long-term storage of budded plants for up to 6 to 8 months at 35 to 37°F (2 to 3°C). During storage, the root medium must be kept moist. The production of a liner commonly used by most nonspecialist producers requires 1 year. The production time from potting a liner to the earliest possible sale of a 6-in. (15-cm) pot is 7 months (Tables II-2 and II-3 Rhododendron). Small 2- to 3-in. (5- to 7.5-cm) pots are useful for dish gardens and for color in baskets (Table II-4 Rhododendron).

INSECTS

A complete review of insects, mites, and nematodes was made by Streu (1975). Lace bugs, thrips, leaf miners, spiders, cyclamen mites, and several species of nematodes are seen on azaleas. Monitoring, sanitation, and chemical treatments are all necessary for control of these pests.

DISEASES

Several diseases can cause serious problems during production, cold storage, and forcing. In storage, *Botrytis* can infect flower buds or open flowers. Frequent air exchanges are required. The most important disease is *Cylindrocladium*, which is systemic and causes wilting, root deterioration, and necrotic leaf spotting during any stage of production. *Phytophthora* root rot can be a serious problem and symptoms are frequently expressed as a slow deterioration of the plant. *Phomopsis* and *Rhizoctonia* are also listed

TABLE II-2 RHODODENDRON

Sample production schedules for liners of the florists' *Rhododendron* from cutting propagation to shipment of vegetative liners.

Cultural Step	Production Time (weeks)	Temperature °F (°C)	Photoperiod
Cuttings propagated in beds or flats			
	6–8+	70 (21)	LD
Remove from propagation			
	6–8+	65 (18)	LD
Transplant to 2.5- to 3-in. pot (6.25- to 7.75-cm), first pinch			
	6–8+	65 (18)	LD
Transplant to 4-in. (10-cm) pot, second pinch			
	6–8+	65 (18)	LD
Third pinch			
	6–8+	65 (18)	LD
Liners shipped to producers			
	6–8+	65 (18)	LD
Total	30–40+		

TABLE II-3 RHODODENDRON

Sample production schedules of florists' *Rhododendron* from vegetative liners to flowering 6-in. (15-cm) potted plants.

Cultural Step	Production Time (weeks)	Temperature °F (°C)	Photoperiod
Pot liners in 6-in. (15-cm) pots			
	1–2	65 (18)	LD
Pinch			
	4–6	65 (18)	LD
Apply growth regulator			
	1	65 (18)	LD
Repeat growth regulator application			
	4+	65 (18)	LD
SD commence			
	5+	65 (18)	SD
Plant with flower buds, cold treatment commences[a]			
	6	35–50 (2–10)	Apply light if 40–50 (4–10)
Force to flower			
	4–6	65 (18)	Natural
Flower			
Total	25–30+		

[a]Plants can also be treated with GA, LD, or any combinations of cold, GA, and LD (see Flowering Control and Dormancy, page 799).

TABLE II-4 RHODODENDRON

Sample production schedule of florists' *Rhododendron* from cuttings to 3-in. (7.75-cm) flowering potted plant.

Cultural Step	Production Time (weeks)	Temperature °F (°C)	Photoperiod
Cuttings propagated in pots			
	5	73 (23)	LD
Remove from propagation			
	5	65 (18)	LD
Pinch			
	6+	65 (18)	LD
Apply growth regulator			
	1	65 (18)	LD
Second growth regulator application			
	2	65 (18)	LD
Third growth regulator application			
	1	65 (18)	LD
Fourth growth regulator application			
	1	65 (18)	LD
SD commence			
	1	65 (18)	SD
Fifth growth regulator application			
	4	65 (18)	SD
Cold treatment commences			
	2	35–50 (2–10)	—[a]
Forcing commences			
	4	65 (18)	HID
Flower			
Total	32+		

[a]Use low-intensity lighting in the cooler if 40 to 50°F (4 to 10°C) temperatures are used.

by Aycock and Daughtry (1975), Coyier and Roane (1986), and Striden et al. (1985). Horst (1990) mentioned that numerous leaf spots can occur on outdoor grown plants including *Pseudocercospora handelii*, *Septoria azaleae*, *S. solitaria*, and *Pestalotia*. Other diseases have been reported including leaf rust (*Chrysomyxa*), petal blight (*Ovulinia azaleae*), and powdery mildew (*Erysiphe polygoni* and *Microsphaera penicillata*) (Dreistadt, 2001).

PHYSIOLOGICAL DISORDERS

Chlorotic foliage because of high or alkaline pH is common (see Media, page 801). Nonuniform flowering can be the result of placing plants with immature flower buds into cold or other dormancy-breaking treatments. Immature flower buds can result from late pinching. If the dormancy-breaking treatments are inadequate, forcing will be slow or flowering will be nonuniform. Reduced flower numbers, particularly on lower branches, is the result of growing plants too close or inadequate light.

Leaf defoliation can occur if light intensity is not adequate during 41 to 50°F (5 to 10°C) cold storage. Also, defoliation can be serious if there is not a careful transition after plants are removed from cold storage until the roots become active and the root ball is rewarmed to allow for water uptake. Plants can be watered with warm water or can be well misted, temporarily shaded, and held at moderate temperatures to reduce leaf water stress and transpiration. Leaf defoliation may also be due to ethylene or low humidity, less than 70%, in the cooler (Hamrick, 2003). Water stress at any time during production can encourage leaf drop.

Bypass shoots are vegetative shoots that develop below the flower buds during floral differentiation (Fig. II-5 Rhododendrun). These shoots reduce the quality of the plant by covering up the flowers and possibly causing flower bud abortion if the shoots are especially vigorous. The problem is accentuated by late forcings and by cooling for greater than 6 weeks at temperatures greater than 45°F (7°C). It is labor intensive to manually remove the shoots which are twisted sideways when 0.5 in. (0.13 cm) long. To control bypass shoots, Bonzi can be applied at 100 ppm 6 to 7 weeks prior to placing plants in cold storage (Nell, 2001; Whealy et al., 1988). A higher Bonzi rate of 200 ppm is used in Texas and Florida. Sumagic is also effective at 5 to 25 ppm (Keever and Foster, 1991).

During the summer in warm climates, dormant budded azaleas directly shipped from the supplier should be unpacked and held in the greenhouse for 1 week prior to placement in the cooler. This process will allow plants to increase carbohydrate levels and will reduce foliage loss.

POSTHARVEST

Plants should be marketed when they are beginning to show flower color or flowers are in the "candle stage" (Fig. II-6 Rhododendron). Flowers quickly open and are easily injured if shipped too mature. Black et al. (1990, 1991a) found that when bud dormancy was broken by cold and GA, flower life was 2 days shorter than those of cold-treated plants. Optimum postharvest life resulted from high light of 4500 to 5550 fc (900 to 1110 μmol $\cdot$ m^{-2} $\cdot$ s^{-1}) during forcing to enhance flower color, day/night temperatures of 64 to 73/61 to 70°F (18 to 23/16 to 21°C) forcing temperatures, and no fertilizer (Black et al., 1991b).

L. Høyer (personal communication) found that azaleas are only moderately sensitive to

FIGURE II-5 RHODODENDRON Bypass shoots on a potted *Rhododendron* plant.

FIGURE II-6 RHODODENDRON Potted *Rhododendron* plant ready for marketing with most of the buds in the candle stage.

ethylene, which will cause defoliation. He has also found that postharvest life is extended when silver thiosulfate (STS) sprays are used.

Customers should be educated to buy plants on the "immature" side of floral development. Though all cultivars are not equal in keeping quality, most can last for 3 to 4 weeks, particularly if held cool at night (Nell, 1993; Nell and Barrett, 1986). Plants can tolerate up to 7 days of dark storage at 35 to 40°F (2 to 4°C) when in flower; but the medium must not be allowed to dry. Plants should be shipped at 41 to 50°F (5 to 10°C). Unrooted cuttings can be held at 31°F (21°C) and cut stems at 32°F (0°C) (L. Høyer, personal communication). Light at the store or home level should be above 35 fc (7 μmol · m^{-2} · s^{-1}); 100 fc (20 μmol · m^{-2} · s^{-1}) is preferred (Nell, 1993).

KEY POINTS

- This woody shrub can be used as a potted flowering plant and garden ornamental.

- Plants are propagated by semiwoody cuttings; *in vitro* is possible.

- The production of the florists' azalea is a long process with part of the production typically performed by specialists who produce "liners," which are 1.5- to 2-year-old plants.

- Flower initiation and development occur under SD and 64 to 72°F (18 to 22°C).

- A 4- to 6-week cold treatment at 35 to 50°F (2 to 10°C) is required for dormancy breaking and rapid flower opening; 35 to 40°F (2 to 4°C) without light in the cooler; and 40 to 50°F (4 to 10°C) if light is supplied in the cooler.

- LD and/or gibberellic acid (GA) can also be used to replace the cold treatment but are not as effective.

- Several different production methods can be used to produce flowering azalea plants: (1) purchase mature plants in bud, cold treat, and force; (2) purchase vegetative liners, shear one or two times, initiate flower buds, cold treat, and force; and (3) propagate own plants and perform all of the previous steps.

- Forcing requires approximately 4 to 6 weeks at 60 to 65°F (16 to 18°C).

- A plant growth regulator must be used to reduce internode elongation. It also hastens floral initiation and development, increases flower numbers per terminal bud, and darkens foliage color.

- Azaleas must be grown with acidic medium pH of 4.5 to 5.5 and is usually grown in peat moss.

- Plants must not be overwatered, but underwatering leads to shrinkage of the peat medium and difficulty in rewetting the peat moss.

- Leaf defoliation can occur if light intensity is inadequate during cold treatment or if plants are moved too abruptly from cold storage to the warm greenhouse.

- Reduced flower numbers, especially on the lower branches, occur if light intensity is too low during flower initiation or plants are spaced too close together.

BIBLIOGRAPHY

Adams, D.G., and A.D. Roberts. 1968. Time of flower initiation in *Rhododendron* 'Roseum Elegans' as related to shoot and leaf elongation. *HortScience* 3:278–279.

Adriansen, E. 1985. Kemisk vækstregulering, pp. 142–162 in *Potteplanter I—Produktion, Metoder, Midler*, O.V. Christensen, A. Klougart, I.S. Pedersen, and K. Wikesjö, editors. GartnerINFO, København, Denmark. (in Danish)

Anderson, W.C. 1978. Rooting of tissue cultured rhododendron. *Proceedings of the International Plant Propagators Society* 28:135–139.

Aycock, R., and B.I. Daughtry. 1975. Major diseases, pp. 78–88 in *Growing Azaleas Commercially* (Number 4058), A.M. Kofranek and R.A. Larson, editors. University of California Cooperative Extension Service, Davis.

Bailey, L.N., and E.Z. Bailey. 1976. *Rhododendron* L. pp. 949–965 in *Hortus Third, A Concise Dictionary of Plants Cultivated in the United States and Canada*. Macmillan, New York.

Ballantyne, D.J., and Link, C.B. 1961. Growth regulators and the flowering of evergreen azaleas (*Rhododendron* cv.). *Proceedings of the American Society for Horticultural Sciences* 78:521–531.

Black, L.A., T.A. Nell, and J.E. Barrett. 1990. Dormancy-breaking methods effect on azalea longevity. *HortScience* 25:810.

Black, L.A., T.A. Nell, and J.E. Barrett. 1991a. Post-production performance of 'Gloria' azalea in response to flower maturity and simulated transport. *HortScience* 26:571–574.

Black, L.A., T.A. Nell, and J.E. Barrett. 1991b. Forcing irradiance, temperature, and fertilization affect quality of 'Gloria' azalea. *HortScience* 26:1397–1400.

Blazich, F.A., and J.R. Acedo. 1988. Micropropagation of 'Flame' azalea. *Journal of Environmental Horticulture* 6:45–47.

Bodson, M. 1983. Effects of photoperiod and irradiance on floral development of young plants of a semi-early and a late cultivar of azalea. *Journal of the American Society for Horticultural Science* 108:382–386.

Boodley, J.W., and J.W. Mastalerz. 1959. The use of gibberellic acid to force azaleas without cold temperature treatments. *Proceedings of the American Society for Horticultural Science* 74:681–685.

Brand, M.H., Y. Ruan, and R. Kiyomoto. 2000. Response of *Rhododendron* 'Montego' with "tissue proliferation" to cytokinin and auxin *in vitro*. *HortScience* 35:136–140.

Brown, W.L., and C.O. Box. 1971. Effects of succinic acid-2, 2-dimethyl-hydrazide, and photoperiod temperature manipulation on flowering and vegetative bypassing in azalea cvs. Red Wing and Alaska. *Journal of the American Society for Horticultural Science* 96:823–825.

Cathey, H.M. 1965. Initiation and flowering of *Rhododendron* following regulation by light and growth retardants. *Proceedings of the American Society for Horticultural Science* 86:753–760.

Coyier, D.L., and M.K. Roane. 1986. *Compendium of Rhododendron and Azalea Diseases*. American Phytopathogical Society Press, St. Paul, Minnesota.

Criley, R.A. 1969. Effect of short photoperiods, Cycocel, and gibberellic acid upon flower bud initiation and development of azalea 'Hexe.' *Journal of the American Society for Horticultural Science* 94:392–396.

Criley, R.A. 1975. Effects of light and temperature on flower initiation and development, pp. 52–61 in *Growing Azaleas Commercially* (Number 4058), A.M. Kofranek and R.A. Larson, editors. University of California, Davis.

Criley, R.A. 1985. *Rhododendron* and *Azalea*, pp. 180–197 in *Handbook of Flowering*, vol. IV, A.H. Halevy, editor. CRC Press, Boca Raton, Florida.

Criley, R. 2001. Vireyas: New rhododendron variants for use as potted plants. *Ohio Florists' Association Bulletin* 855:4–6.

Dole, J.M., and H.F. Wilkins. 1988. University of Minnesota—Tissue analysis standards. *Minnesota State Florists' Bulletin* 37(6):10–13.

Dreistadt, S.H. 2001. *Integrated Pest Management for Floriculture and Nurseries*. University of California Division of Agriculture and Natural Resources Publication 3402.

French, C.J., and J. Alsbury. 1988. Effect of pre-force storage conditions on early flowering of *Rhododendron*. *HortScience* 23:356–358.

Hamrick, D. 2003. *Rhododendron*, pp. 595–601 in *Ball Redbook*, vol. 2, 17th ed. Ball Publishing, Batavia, Illinois.

Heins, R.D., R.W. Widmer, and H.F. Wilkins. 1978. Growth regulators effective on floricultural crops. *Minnesota State Florists' Bulletin*, Aug.:1–4.

Horst, R.K. 1990. Azalea, pp. 545–546 in *Westcott's Plant Disease Handbook*, 5th ed. Van Nostrand Reinhold, New York.

Huxley, A., M. Griffiths, and M. Levy. 1992. *Rhododendron*, pp. 30–78 in *The New Royal Horticultural Society Dictionary of Gardening*, vol. 4. Stockton Press, New York.

Johnson, C.R., and A.N. Roberts. 1968. The influence of terminal bud removal at successive stages of shoot development on rooting of rhododendron leaves. *Proceedings of the American Society for Horticultural Science* 93:673–678.

Jorgensen, S. 1969. The effect of storage temperature, short day treatment, and B-Nine on the flowering of thirteen cultivars of greenhouse azalea. *Acta Horticulturae* 14:17–26.

Keever, G.J., and W.J. Foster. 1991. Uniconazole suppresses bypass shoot development and alters flowering of two forcing azalea cultivars. *HortScience* 26:875–877.

Kiplinger, D.C. 1944. The effects of cooling and shading the azalea 'Coral Bells' on early forcing for Christmas flowering. *Proceeding of the American Society for Horticultural Science* 44:542–544.

Kiplinger, D.C., and H. Bresser. 1951. Some factors affecting multiple bud formation on azaleas. *Proceedings of the American Society for Horticultural Science* 57:393–394.

Kofranek, A.M., and O.R. Lunt. 1975. Mineral nutrition, pp. 36–46 in *Growing Azaleas Commercially* (Number 4058), A.M. Kofranek and R.A. Larson, editors. University of California Cooperative Extension Service, Davis.

Larson, R.A. 1992. Azaleas, pp. 223–248 in *Introduction to Floriculture*, R.A. Larson, editor. Academic Press, San Diego, California.

Larson, R.A., and T.D. Sydnor. 1971. Azalea flower bud development and dormancy as influenced by temperature and gibberellic acid. *Journal of the American Society for Horticultural Science* 96: 786–788.

Leiser, A.T. 1975. Taxonomy and origin of azaleas used for forcing, pp. 9–16 in *Growing Azaleas Commercially* (Number 4058), A.M. Kofranek and R.A. Larson, editors. University of California Cooperative Extension Service, Davis.

Love, J. 1975. Vegetative growth, pp. 47–51 in *Growing Azaleas Commercially* (Number 4058), A.M. Kofranek and R.A. Larson, editors. University of California Cooperative Extension Service, Davis.

McCulloch, S. 1984. Micropropagation of rhododendron. *American Rhododendron Society* 38(2): 72–73.

McDowell, T.C., and R.A. Larson. 1966. Effects of (2-chloroethyl) trimethyl ammonium chloride (CYCOCEL), N–dimethyl succinamic acid (B-NINE), and photoperiod on flower bud initiation and development in azaleas. *Proceedings of the American Society for Horticultural Science* 88: 600–605.

Mertens, M., S. Werbrouck, G. Samyn, H. Botelho dos Santos Moreira da Silva, and P. Debergh. 1996. *In vitro* regeneration of evergreen azalea from leaves. *Plant Cell, Tissue and Organ Culture* 45:231–236.

Nell, T.A. 1993. *Rhododendron* spp., pp. 71–73 in *Flowering Potted Plants, Prolonging Shelf Performance.* Ball Publishing, Batavia, Illinois.

Nell, T. 2001. Azaleas, pp. 48–49 in *Tips on Regulating Growth of Floriculture Crops,* M.L. Gaston, L.A. Kunkle, P.S. Konjoian, and M.F. Wilt, editors. Ohio Florists' Association Services, Columbus, Ohio.

Nell, T.A., and J.E. Barrett. 1986. Chrysanthemum and azalea varieties for the interiorscape. University of Florida, Staff Report Series, *Ornamental Horticulture* 86:1.

Oertli, J.J. 1964a. Azalea nutrition disorders. I. Nitrogen, phosphorus and potassium deficiencies. *Florists' Review* 134(3482):20, 62.

Oertli, J.J. 1964b. Azalea nutrition disorders. II. Calcium, magnesium and sulphur deficiencies. *Florists' Review* 134(3483):21, 62.

Oertli, J.J. 1964c. Azalea nutrient disorders. III. Chlorosis, tipburn, results of iron and boron deficiencies. *Florists' Review* 134(3484):31, 80.

Pemberton, H.B., and H.F. Wilkins. 1985. Seasonal variation on the influence of low temperature, photoperiod, light source, and GA in floral development of the evergreen azalea. *Journal of the American Society for Horticultural Science* 110: 730–737.

Pemberton, H.B., M.L. Brenner, and H.F. Wilkins. 1985. Endogenous ABA levels in floral bud parts of evergreen azalea during floral development. *Journal of the American Society for Horticultural Science* 110:737–742.

Pemberton, H.B., H.F. Wilkins, and J.S. Hodges. 1998. Growth relationships of individual flowers during late stages of floral development of *Rhododendron* L. 'Prize' and 'Gloria.' *Canadian Journal of Botany* 76:1350–1358.

Peterson, J.C. 1982. Monitoring and managing nutrition, part IV—Foliar analysis. *Ohio Florists' Association Bulletin,* No. 632.

Petterson, H. 1972. The effect of temperature and daylength on shoot growth and bud formation in azaleas. *Journal of the American Society for Horticultural Science* 97:17–24.

Schneider, E.F. 1967. The flowering response of azaleas as influenced by photoperiod. *Canadian Journal of Plant Science* 47:112–113.

Shanks, J.B., and C.B. Link. 1968. Some factors affecting growth and flower initiation of greenhouse azaleas. *Proceedings of the American Society for Horticultural Science* 92:603–614.

Skinner, H.F. 1939. Factors affecting shoot growth and flower bud initiation in rhododendron and azalea. *Proceedings of the American Society for Horticultural Science* 37:1007–1011.

Stadtherr, R.T. 1975. Commercial cultivars, pp. 17–29 in *Growing Azaleas Commercially* (Number 4058), A.M. Kofranek and R.A. Larson, editors. University of California Cooperative Extension Service, Davis.

Streu, H.T. 1975. Insects, mite and nematode control on azaleas, pp. 89–96 in *Growing Azaleas Commercially* (Number 4058), A.M. Kofranek and R.A. Larson, editors. University of California Cooperative Extension Service, Davis.

Striden, D.L., D.M. Benson, R.K. Jones, and R. Aycock. 1985. Major infectious diseases of hybrid evergreen azaleas. *North Carolina Growers' Bulletin* 29(2):9–12.

Stuart, N.W. 1961. Initiation of flower buds in rhododendron after application of growth retardants. *Science* 134:50–52.

Stuart, N.W. 1964. Report of cooperative trials on controlling flowering of greenhouse azaleas with growth retardants. *Florists' Review* 133(3477): 37–39, 74.

Stuart, N.W. 1975. Chemical control of growth and flowering, pp. 62–71 in *Growing Azaleas Commercially* (Number 4058), A.M. Kofranek and R.A. Larson, editors. University of California Cooperative Extension Service, Davis.

Twigg, M.C., and C.B. Link. 1951. Nutrient deficiency symptoms and leaf analysis of azaleas grown in sand culture. *Proceedings of the American Society for Horticultural Science* 57:369–375.

Whealy, C.A., T.A. Nell, and J.E. Barrett. 1988. Plant growth regulator reduction of bypass shoot development in azalea. *HortScience* 23:166–167.

Whipker, B.E. 2003. Growth regulators for floricultural crops, pp. 439–448 in *2003 North Carolina Agricultural Chemicals Manual.* College of Agriculture and Life Science, North Carolina State University, Raleigh.

Wilkins, H.F. 1980. Azaleas may be forced into flowering by using high light or high temperature. *Minnesota State Florists' Bulletin* 29(1):10.

Wilkinson, R.I., and D. Richards. 1991. Influence of paclobutrazol on growth and flowering of *Rhododendron* 'Sir Robert Peel.' *HortScience* 26:282–284.

Womack, W.M., J.E. Barrett, and T.A. Nell. 1995. A model describing release of flower bud dormancy in 'Prize' and 'Gloria' azaleas. *HortScience* 30:760. (Abstract)

Rosa

INTRODUCTION

Common name: rose.

Scientific name: *Rosa* L. hybrids (Huxley et al., 1992).

Family and related taxa: Rosaceae Juss. This family is huge with more than 100 genera and 2000 herbaceous to woody species. Many important food and ornamental plants are in the Rosaceae family including *Fragaria*—strawberry; *Malus*—apple; *Prunus*—almond, apricot, cherry, peach, and plum; *Pyrus*—pear; and *Rubus*—blackberry, loganberry, and raspberry.

Origin: The exact species involved in the development of the present-day rose is not known. Most rose species are found in the temperate parts of the Northern Hemisphere, especially from southern China and the Far East, the Indian Himalayas and Bengal into Ethiopia and west to North America from the Arctic Circle to New Mexico (Bailey and Bailey, 1976; Zieslin and Moe, 1985). Recurrent or perennial flowering rose plants were introduced into Europe from the Far East at the end of the 18th century and were the results of countless generations of breeding in China, India, and Japan. *Rosa chinensis* Jacq. and *R. gigantea* Collet ex Crepin. were major contributors to recurrent roses (Zieslin and Moe, 1985). *Rosa* ×*centifolia* L., *R. gallica* L., *R. damascena* Mill., and *R.* ×*borboniana* Desp. are commonly believed to also be involved in the evolution of modern hybrids (Post, 1949). For those interested in the history of cut roses, Zieslin and Moe (1985) reviewed the history with numerous reference citations.

Uses and current status: The rose is one of the world's most popular flowers. Roses are commonly grown as cut flowers, potted plants, or specimen plants in home gardens. There are numerous types of cut roses: long stem standards, short stem standards, small flowered sweethearts, multiflowered bunch roses, and outdoor-grown "garden" or "antique" roses. Cut flower production has shifted from northern latitudes to areas near the equator, which have a higher altitude, equal day/night durations, high light intensities, uniformly cool temperatures, and economical labor. Such areas include the South American countries of Columbia and Ecuador and the African country of Kenya. In particular, the high light and cool temperatures result in high quality. The shift in production away from northern climates has been dramatic. For example, North America is estimated to produce only 10 to 15% of the roses it uses each year (L. Busch, personal communication).

Potted plant sizes can range from small plants in 3-in. (7.5-cm) pots to 36-in. (90-cm) tall topiary tree roses. Genetically dwarf miniature roses originated from Chinese breeding efforts. They were for garden use and one is reported to be pictured in an 1815 Curtis Botanical Magazine. In 1917 a Swiss nursery became interested in dwarf cultivars and discovered that many individual dwarf plants were more than 100 years old. The 1930s saw a flurry of activity in miniature rose breeding, with crosses including dwarf *R. multiflora* Thunb. ex Murray. in the Netherlands. Interest in miniature roses continues today with many cultivars patented in Denmark, the Netherlands, the United States, and Canada (Fitch, 1977; Pinney, 1964).

Garden roses can be forced into flower for spring sales. Breeding programs on modern garden rose cultivars and cut flower cultivars have been similar, but genetically distinct. Both breeding programs stressed long postharvest life and disease and insect resistance. Although outdoor cultivars are seldom used for indoor forcing, cut flower varieties have become popular as garden plants (P. Klement, personal communication).

All species in the genus *Rosa* are woody and noted for their thorns, spines, or prickly stems. Plants can be upright, forming a shrub, or can be trailing and climbing. The leaves are alternate and may be deciduous or persistent. Flowers may be solitary, corymbose, or panicled. Many native species have five petals and numerous stamens. The ovary is inferior and develops into a fleshy fruit or "hip," which can become a colorful yellow to red when ripe. The prominent five-part sepals (calyx) are leaflike, cover the flower bud, and become reflexed at flowering to expose the petals. Petal colors range from white to pink, yellow, orange, or red with an unbelievable variety of shades and color combinations. Rose fragrance is world renown, but unfortunately is absent in many modern cultivars (Bailey and Bailey, 1976).

CULTIVARS

Zieslin and Moe (1985) estimated that more than 10,000 cultivars have existed over the centuries. Rose breeding firms exist in every major rose-growing country and superior new cultivars move between countries at an astonishing speed. Annually, the best cultivars for both home and commercial use are recognized and promoted by various methods, from commercial and amateur flower shows to mailed advertisements. Commercially, four major groups of rose cultivars are recognized: (1) cut flowers, (2) miniature potted flowering plants produced from stem cuttings, (3) potted flowering holiday plants produced from bare root plants, and (4) potted garden plants produced from bare root plants.

The goals of breeding programs vary, but some common objectives are disease resistance to powdery mildew, black spot, and *Botrytis;* insect resistance, particularly to the red-spotted spider mite; high flower productivity under a wide range of climatic conditions from near the Arctic to near the equator in Columbia and Ecuador at high elevation; improved flower form, size, and color; increased stem strength and length; improved postharvest characteristics; greater cold hardiness and heat resistance, particularly for the home garden; improved flower fragrance; and increased essential oil content for the perfume industry.

CUT FLOWERS

If the cut flower rose industry is to remain in northern latitudes, new cultivars with acceptable yield under the low light intensities and short durations of winter days are essential. This would reduce the dependence on supplementary high-intensity discharge (HID) lighting, which is expensive to install, maintain, and operate. Zieslin and Moe (1985) stated that only seven or eight species have been involved in the creation of the modern rose, and therefore the genes of more than 200 species could still be used.

MINIATURE POTTED FLOWERING PLANTS

Several individuals and firms in North America are breeding miniature cultivars for the amateur rose grower. However, the cultivars grown in greenhouses for 4- to 6-in. (10- to 15-cm) pot production are primarily the results of breeding programs in Denmark, the Netherlands, and Germany.

BARE ROOTED POTTED FLOWERING PLANTS

Several hybrid cultivar groups (Polyantha and Floribunda) can be forced into flower for Valentine's Day, Easter, and Mother's Day.

BARE ROOTED POTTED GARDEN PLANTS

Bare rooted garden cultivars can be forced into leaf and flower for spring garden center sales. The greenhouse forcer is faced with an enormous task of selecting from the scores of cultivars. Frequently, there are strong ties between local garden clubs and the forcer. Numerous amateur and commercial breeding programs for garden roses exist. Large shrub or "old fashion" roses are increasingly popular due to their disease resistance and low maintenance in the garden.

PROPAGATION

Seeds are used only in breeding or genetic projects. Crosses can be made at any time of the year in the greeenhouse. The seed requires scarification and stratification for rapid germination (Hartman and Kester, 1975; Semeniuk and Stuart, 1964). Six to 10 years are required from pollination to release of a new cultivar. The rate of success in producing a named seedling is only 1 in 30,000 to 40,000 seedlings. All commercially available cultivars are patented and cannot be propagated without permission. Also, *in vitro* propagation can be used and embryo rescue has been practiced for several years (Asen and Larson, 1951; Hsia and Korban, 1996).

CUT FLOWERS

Stenting, a form of grafting, has replaced traditional bud grafted plants (see next page) for most cut flower production (van de Pol and Breukelaar, 1982). Seedling rootstocks are used; a single leaf-bud scion is placed into a downward cut and held in place by a small clothespin. The union occurs within 3 weeks under fog, mist, or in high-humidity chambers under greenhouse conditions at 75°F (24°C). Grafting can also occur simultaneously with rooting of the rootstock cutting (Ohkawa, 1980, 1984). The rootstock species for cut flower production vary from location to location worldwide (J. Ferare and L. Busch, personal communications). *Rosa ×noisettiana* Thory. (synonym: *R. manetti*) rootstocks are commonly used in South America, *R. ×*'Natal Briar' in North America, *R. chinensis* L. (synonym: *R. indica major*) in southern Europe and the Mediterranean region, and *R. canina* L. in other parts of Europe. However, in Japan and parts of Europe cut flowers are grown primarily on their own roots (M. Ohkawa, personal communication).

To produce plants on their own roots, cuttings from "mature" wood or shoots with one to three nodes can be rooted. Rooting hormones can be used as can a variety of media (see Media, page 815) and rooting is rapid at 70 to 75°F (21 to 24°C). Rooting can occur in mist, fog, or high-humidity chambers, or in propagation beds or in pots. Most cultivars are patented and permission must be obtained to root cuttings. Interestingly, cut rose plants propagated from cuttings produced more flowers than similar cultivars propagated by stenting (Bredmose and Hansen, 1996).

MINIATURE POTTED FLOWERING PLANTS

Miniature flowering potted plants are exclusively propagated by single leaf-node stem cuttings. Cuttings are generally obtained from plants already in production but can also be harvested from stock plants. Cutting quality will determine the quality of the potted flowering plant 10 to 15 weeks later. The best cuttings are obtained from shoots that are produced after the second cutback or pinch, which will have three to five nodes. Cuttings are harvested from shoots with a flower bud that is large but not showing petal color. The ideal cutting is harvested from the middle of the shoot and is subtended by a five-leaflet leaf. These single-node five-leaflet cuttings root quickly; shoot elongation is rapid and uniform. Generally, 21 to 28 days after propagation, shoots will be sufficiently tall to cut back.

Usually only one to two suitable cuttings per shoot can be obtained. The upper nodes are not useful for cuttings because they produce weak shoots with few leaves below the flower bud. Flower initiation has already occurred in the axillary buds at the upper nodes of these shoots. These apical nodes frequently have only three leaflet leaves, which is an indication that they should be discarded. In addition, cuttings will wilt rapidly if harvested when not mature enough. On the other hand, nodes that have already developed axillary shoots should also be discarded. If cuttings are too mature, rooting is slow and propagation will be delayed.

The single-node cuttings are prepared so that there is a 0.75-in. (2.0-cm) stem above and below the node. Cuttings can be stored moist in plastic bags at 36 to 41°F (2 to 5°C) for up to 7 days depending on the cultivar. Some producers believe a 24-hr cold treatment is beneficial with some cultivars. Rooting hormones are not used or needed. The use of silver thiosulfate (STS) prevented leaf yellowing of cuttings but inhibited rooting (Sun and Bassuk, 1991).

Four to six cuttings per 4-in. (10-cm) pot are directly stuck into a rooting medium (see Water, page 813, and Media, page 815). Cuttings can also be propagated in plug trays and later transplanted to the final pot. Do not allow cuttings to lose turgor. Hand fogging or misting may be needed before a bench is completely planted and ready to be placed into a fog or mist chamber. Prior to this, a fungicide drench can be used (Jørgensen, 1992) (see Temperature, page 811, and Schedule and Timing, page 817).

Cuttings can be purchased from commercial propagators. Young rooted plants in plugs (liners) can be used for a shorter crop cycle. Single-node cuttings can also be grafted onto tall root stocks to create topiary rose "trees" for garden use.

BARE ROOTED POTTED FLOWERING AND GARDEN PLANTS

Rose plants are produced worldwide (B. Pemberton, personal communication). Bud grafting (T-bud) is used to propagate cultivars primarily for garden plants. Some cut flowers and potted flowering plants are still grown from dormant rootstocks, but the numbers are decreasing. To produce a grafted dormant rose bush, the axillary bud of the desired cultivar is inserted into the virus-free rootstock and secured into position by wrapping. Three to 4 weeks later the shoot above the union is partially severed (half to one-third of the way) and in another 6 weeks the aerial part of the rootstock is completely removed. One inch (2.5 cm) of stem remains above the newly developing shoot and the basal buds are removed. *Rosa* ×'Dr Huey,' *R. multiflora* Thunb. ex Murray. and *R.* ×*oderata* Andrews (Sweet) rootstocks are commonly used for garden roses (B. Pemberton, personal communication).

Cutting propagation of the rootstock in northern latitudes occurs from late October to mid-December, rooting is completed by late January or early February, and budding occurs in late March to early April. Harvesting of dormant plants and grading commences in mid-December. At this time the new shoot is cut back to 8 to 10 in. (20 to 25 cm) above the graft union.

Exposure of rose plants to short periods (4 weeks) of low temperatures of 31 to 32°F (−0.6 to 0°C) and high humidity will stimulate axillary bud activity when planted. Bare rooted plants are refrigerated and distributed to customers around the world in large waterproofed, plastic-lined corrugated cardboard boxes (Hartman and Kester, 1975; Langhans, 1987; Post, 1949; Zieslin and Moe, 1985). Stored dormant bushes should not be exposed to ethylene, which can reduce bud development, or allowed to dry out, which may kill plants, increase time to flower, and decrease flowering shoot number (Meadows and Richardson, 1983; Pemberton and Schuch, 2003).

FLOWERING CONTROL AND DORMANCY

Greenhouse roses are generally day neutral, and flowering is recurrent and occurs on a year-round basis. Flower initiation is not dependent on environment factors. Garden roses include both recurrent and nonrecurrent flowering cultivars (Zieslin and Moe, 1985). At least one rose species requires cold for dormancy release. Under low irradiance some cut flower cultivars produce fewer leaves than under high illuminance. Further, some cultivars will flower with fewer leaves under LD, making them facultative LD plants (Moe, 1970).

Floral differentiation occurs shortly after axillary buds are released from apical dominance. With cut flowers the transition from vegetative to reproductive growth occurs in 4 to 21 days, when the axillary shoots are only 1.25 to 1.50 in. (3 to 4 cm) long (Laurie and Bobula, 1938; Zieslin and Moe, 1985).

Axillary buds from the upper nodes form flower buds sooner and with fewer leaves than lower nodes (Zieslin and Byrne, 1981; Zieslin and Moe, 1985). The difference in shoot growth based on nodal position must be considered

when selecting cuttings for pot roses (see Propagation section) and when harvesting cut roses (see Pinching and Disbudding section). The speed and quality of a subsequent cut flower crop depend on the nodes remaining after the flower is harvested. If the cut is made low, the resulting axillary shoot will have more leaves and be longer (higher quality) and the time to the next harvestable stems will be longer (Byrne and Doss, 1981). The opposite occurs when the cut is high or more nodes are left because the resulting shoots will be quicker to flower but of lower quality. Further, bud selection for budding and stenting is also based on node location (Zieslin and Byrne, 1981).

Light, temperature, and carbon dioxide influence growth and development of the rose under greenhouse growing conditions (Mortensen and Moe, 1992). Numerous research papers have been published on the effect of these environmental factors. Recently, computer data recording and plant growth modeling have allowed growers to quantify and predict the effect of environmental factors on rose growth. For example, greater stem diameter and fresh and dry weights of stems, leaves, and flower buds were predicted and later measured at low day temperatures of ≤63°F (17°C) and low night temperatures of ≤57°F (14°C). However, this temperature regime delayed flowering. Increasing light increased flower stem quality (stem diameter and weight) and growth rate (Hopper and Hammer, 1991; Lieth, 1996; Passion and Lieth, 1994). Dormancy does not exist in commercial cultivars. However, placing a rose plant at 36 to 40°F (2 to 4°C) for 4 to 6 weeks will stimulate axillary bud development and adventitious (bottom breaks) shoots from stem bases (Hanan, 1979; Post, 1949; Zieslin and Moe, 1985). Any rose plant that has been field produced and harvested by the professional producer will have been cold treated prior to being shipped to the forcers.

TEMPERATURE

Roses respond dramatically to temperature. The rate of axillary bud break, shoot development, leaf unfolding, and flowering increases as the temperatures increase, all other factors equal. Excessively high temperatures increase the number of shoots that fail to produce a flower ("blind shoots") and decrease flower quality, petal number, flower stem length, and weight of the entire flowering stem. Interestingly, when temperatures are too low, blindness is also increased due to greater branching and competition for photosynthates, particularly when irradiance is low.

CUT FLOWERS

Optimal night temperature for cut roses is 60 to 62°F (16 to 17°C); day temperature ranges from 64 to 72°F (18 to 22°C) in the winter during cloudy and semi sunny days to 77°F (25°C) on sunny days (Jiao et al., 1991). Alternating night temperatures every 2 hours between 57 and 64°F (14 and 18°C) increased flower production compared to constant 64°F (18°C) while reducing energy costs (Zieslin et al., 1987). Optimum temperatures often vary with the cultivar (Langhans, 1987). In areas of the world where excessive summer heat occurs, fan and pad cooling and fogging are used to reduce temperatures; if not, flower quality will decrease (Mastalerz, 1987a; Urban, 1994). Medium temperature is also critical. Increasing the root zone temperature to 77°F (25°C) increased flower yield and stem length and the number of axillary shoots developing from the base of the plants (Brown and Ormrod, 1980; Moss and Dalgleish, 1984). If warmer media temperatures are used, nutrition must be increased accordingly.

MINIATURE POTTED FLOWERING PLANTS

The basic temperature sequence for miniature flowering potted plants is (1) 73 to 75°F (23 to 24°C) for rooting; (2) 68 to 72°F (20 to 22°C) for 7 to 10 days after rooting and prior to the first cutback; (3) 68 to 72°F (20 to 22°C) for 2 to 3 weeks of growth after cutback; (4) 66 to 72°F (19 to 22°C) for 2 to 3 weeks after the second cutback, if practiced; and (5) 64°F (18°C) for the final 3 to 4 weeks prior to flowering (Jørgensen, 1992). Avoid large increases in temperature over a short time to prevent malformed flowers (Pemberton et al., 1997). Increasing temperatures from 64 to 86°F (18 to 30°C) decreased crop time and plant height, but also decreased plant dry weight (Mortensen, 1991).

BARE ROOTED POTTED FLOWERING AND GARDEN PLANTS

Dormant plants after the appropriate cold treatment can be forced at 50 to 55°F (10 to 13°C) night temperature until axillary bud activity commences, after which time the temperature is increased to 64°F (18°C) (Heins, 1981; Post, 1949; Zieslin and Moe, 1985).

LIGHT

Roses require high light levels. Light, carbon dioxide, and temperatures interact in regard to the amount of fixed carbon. Supplemental light is essential in most northern latitudes during the winter where cut roses traditionally have been produced. Potted miniature roses and holiday potted roses for Valentine's Day should also receive supplemental lighting. Thereafter, supplemental light is not required, but can be used if days are cloudy for long durations. Shade will be required to control temperatures in the summer.

CUT FLOWERS

Tsujita (1987) reviewed the use of high-intensity supplemental lighting on cut roses, a method that is now widely used in northern latitudes (Bredmose 1993, 1996). Generally, high-pressure sodium lamps are used for 8 to 24 hr per day at 300 to 1000 fc (60 to 200 μmol $\cdot$ m^{-2} $\cdot$ s^{-1}). The duration of the lighting period is based on the season (duration and intensity of natural light), the intensity of the supplemental light (intensity $\times$ duration interaction), and cost of electricity, particularly off-peak rates. Increasing the total light integral from 17.8 to 21 mol $\cdot$ m^{-2} $\cdot$ day^{-1} in Denmark increased growth most when applied from bud break to flowering as compared to the period from flower harvest or planting to bud break (Bredmose, 1998). High-intensity supplemental lighting may not be economically useful in naturally high light areas (Hopper, 1996) and is typically not used in South America.

Light quality influences the response of rose plants to high light intensity in that decreasing the amount of blue light during the day increases stem length and dry weight (Maas and Bakx, 1995). In addition, ending the day with a 10-min period of red light increased the number of flowering shoots as compared to ending the day with a 10-min period of far-red light.

MINIATURE POTTED FLOWERING PLANTS

Supplemental or high natural light is essential for rapid rooting in the winter. A recommended light level in propagation is a constant 670 fc (134 μmol $\cdot$ m^{-2} $\cdot$ s^{-1}) 24 hr per day (Jørgensen, 1992). During production, supplement natural light with at least 350 to 500 fc (70 to 100 μmol $\cdot$ m^{-2} $\cdot$ s^{-1}) during the winter for 12 or more hours per day to produce quality plants in northern latitudes.

BARE ROOTED POTTED FLOWERING PLANTS

Supplemental lighting will result in more flowering stems per plant and bud abortion will decrease during forcing (Asaoka and Heins, 1982; Heins, 1981). For Valentine's Day, supplemental lighting is required in many locations in North America to prevent flower abortion. Supplement natural light with 250 to 300 fc (50 to 60 μmol $\cdot$ m^{-2} $\cdot$ s^{-1}) for 12 hr. Incandescent lighting did not increase the number of flowering shoots, but the number of flowers per shoot was increased (Asaoka and Heins, 1982). Shade is required when the light intensity is greater than 3000 fc (600 μmol $\cdot$ m^{-2} $\cdot$ s^{-1}).

WATER

Good-quality water must be delivered economically to the plant. At one time both cut and potted roses were hand watered. Perimeter bench-watering systems of several types are still used for cut flowers, but are quickly being replaced by constant-flow tray systems where roses are grown in rockwool or coir dust (Blom and Kerec, 2000). The water nutrient solution is captured, and the nutrient content is adjusted and recirculated (White and Holcomb, 1987).

CUT FLOWERS

The decision to irrigate has been mainly made by human judgment. Now various irrigation indicators such as tensiometers can be used to aid in the decision (Oki et al., 1996; White and Holcomb, 1987). Computer monitoring and control can replace day-to-day irrigation decisions (Lieth and Raviv, 1999). Containerized substrates are thought to improve plant growth by reducing media water tension, allowing plants to more readily take up water (Lieth and Raviv, 1999). Suboptimal water tensions of 5 to 8 kPa cause water stress, and tensions of 15 kPa or greater can cause wilting. Any period of suboptimal water tension will reduce stem length. On the other hand, media must be well aerated enough to provide sufficient oxygen.

MINIATURE POTTED FLOWERING PLANTS

The peat-based medium must not be kept too moist during rooting of the cuttings, because medium aeration is essential. Overwatering can occur when plants are cut back and the leaf canopy (transpiration) is reduced. Irrigation

should occur 1 to 2 days prior to cutback. In addition, the loss of leaf photosynthesis capacity (carbohydrates) may also be responsible for increased root injury after the cutback (Jørgensen, 1992). Excessive over- or underwatering can cause leaf yellowing, leaf abscission, and root loss (Pemberton et al., 1997). Potted flowering miniature roses are now commonly grown in ebb-and-flow benches with recirculated water (Jørgensen, 1992).

BARE ROOTED POTTED FLOWERING PLANTS

Great care must be taken to not overwater the medium, which will reduce aeration and retard new root growth. For both newly planted bare rootstocks for cut roses and recently potted holiday roses, the first few days are critical in that the canes must not dry out, which would inhibit axillary bud activity and decrease quality. Essentially, the roots are not functional until new root growth occurs. The plant is dependent on stored carbohydrates until the axillary buds begin to expand and leaves, which transpire water and conduct photosynthesis, develop. Canes must be frequently sprayed or fogged until roots are functional. Temperature and light intensity may also be reduced. Covering plants with white plastic may be practiced but excessive temperature under the plastic must be avoided and the plastic must be removed as soon as new growth is observed (Langhans, 1987).

CARBON DIOXIDE

CUT FLOWERS

An average of 1500 ppm is an acceptable CO_2 level (1000 to 2000 ppm) considering the numerous research reports, geographical locations, cultivars, and environmental conditions (Mastalerz, 1987a, b; Mattson and Widmer, 1971). While supplemental CO_2 is typically used during cool weather when greenhouses are closed, increasing CO_2 increased growth, number of bud breaks, stem diameter, and number of marketable flowers when combined with high-pressure mist evaporative cooling during the summer (Urban, 1994).

MINIATURE POTTED FLOWERING PLANTS

Carbon dioxide enrichment and supplemental lighting will ensure high-quality pot roses during the winter. Increased CO_2 levels enhance the number of flowering shoots and plant weight and also hasten flowering, but unfortunately shoot lengths are increased. Generally, 700 to 1000 ppm is an accepted CO_2 level (Clark et al., 1993; Mortensen, 1991).

BARE ROOTED POTTED FLOWERING PLANTS

Mortensen and Moe (1983) observed that with the floribunda 'Garnet,' a CO_2 level of 950 ppm increased flower shoots by 19% compared with the control plants in ambient CO_2 levels.

NUTRITION

Few crops can develop and express nutritional problems as quickly and return to normal growth as slowly as the rose (Table II-1 Rosa). Routine media and tissue testing are absolute requirements for stable production. Foliar nutrient levels for high-quality plants are listed in Chapter 6, Nutrition, Table 6-4.

CUT FLOWERS

Historically, nutrients were supplied in the form of organics such as manure, dried blood, and bone meal. Currently, nutrients are sup-

TABLE II-1 ROSA
Deficiency symptoms, remedies, and toxicity symptoms of nutrients in cut *Rosa* (White, undated).

Nutrient	Visual Deficiency Symptoms	Remedies	Toxicity
Nitrogen	Uniform light-green to yellow-green color of all leaves. Stunted growth, reduced leaf size and internodes	Ammonium nitrate, ammonium sulfate, other forms of nitrogen	500-ppm spurway test; symptoms similar to high EC: leaf necrosis and plant hardening
Phosphorus	Reduction in leaflet size and shoot growth. Leaves are gray-green with purplish tinge to the midrib	0–20–0, phosphoric acid at 7 fl oz/1000 gal (5.5 mL/100 liter) per meq of bicarbonate in water	Seldom occurs, hard and stunted growth
Potassium	Chlorotic lower foliage, smaller flowers, blind shoots, marginal chlorosis, crippled petals with necrotic leaves, reduced growth and stem length, drying up of buds	Potassium nitrate, any fertilizers with potassium	Symptoms similar to high EC
Calcium	New growth is reduced, interveinal chlorosis of young leaves, leaflets curl, calcium-boron imbalance, flower petals crinkled, deformed and poor root growth, independent of boron	Limestone, gypsum, monocalcium phosphate	High calcium will affect the pH or availability of cations before toxicity occurs
Magnesium	Reduction in shoot growth and leaflet size, interveinal chlorosis, necrotic blotches	Apply magnesium sulfate	None reported
Manganese	Interveinal chlorosis of young leaves	Reduce pH, apply manganese sulfate at 0.5 oz/100 ft^2 (1.5 g $\cdot$ m^{-2}) or 1 oz/100 gallons (7.5 g/100 liters)	Black spots on older leaves
Iron	Young leaves become chlorotic	Apply 4 oz/100 ft^2 (12.2 g $\cdot$ m^{-2}) iron chelate	Retarded growth
Copper	Youngest leaves crinkled, growing point dies	Copper sulfate at 1.0 oz/100 ft^2 (3 g $\cdot$ m^{-2})	None reported
Boron	Death of terminals on both roots and shoots, browning of the petal margins, necrosis on entire plant	Apply sodium tetraborate at 0.5 oz/100 ft^2 (1.5 g $\cdot$ m^{-2}), 1 or 2 times a year	Leaves have green islands, turn yellow, and drop

plied by liquid application in a constant-flow system when plants are growing in rockwool or coco coir or when ground beds are irrigated (Blom and Kerec, 2000). Various nutrient formulations have been devised and are reviewed by White (undated, 1987). Excellent colored plates of nutrient excesses or deficiencies are also found in these publications. Generally, the basic nutrient concentration is between 150 and 200 ppm N. Ammonium is essential for good stem elongation at a ratio of 5:1 nitrate:ammonium in the summer and 10:1 in the winter. In Israel, a 10:1 ratio is used year-round and the ammonium level is increased if there are problems with water quality or high pH (A. Halevy, personal communication). While N tissue analysis was not a dependable indicator of productivity due to variations throughout the growing season, a minimum level should be maintained (Cabrera, 2001). Minimum leaf tissue N level has traditionally been set at 3% (White, 1987), but Cabrera (2001) noted that maximum yields can occur with N levels as low as 2.4 to 2.5% in some situations. Tamimi et al. (1999) estimated the total amount of nutrients that were lost through harvesting and would need to be replaced.

MINIATURE POTTED FLOWERING PLANTS

Low EC (1.5 dS · m^{-1}) is critical and the N:P:K levels are best at 220:30:195 ppm with a constant liquid fertilizer. Jørgensen (1992) reviewed various macro- and micronutrient formulations.

BARE ROOTED POTTED FLOWERING PLANTS

Nutrient rates are similar to those used for cut flowers. High levels of nutrients cannot be used until an adequate root system is established

MEDIA

CUT FLOWERS

Plants are grown hydroponically in rockwool or coir dust with recirculatory irrigation. Nutrition is provided solely through the irrigation system. Hydroponic production is thought to increase production by improving nutrient balance, maintaining optimum root temperature, reducing soil-borne diseases, improving aeration, and increasing water availability compared with ground bed production (Blom and Kerec, 2000; Lieth and Raviv, 1999).

Successful production of roses in ground beds occurs in various media. Historically, soil was amended with various organic and inorganic materials to provide good aeration and drainage. Mulches were used during production and additional amendments were used between crops when new plants were replanted. The soil pH was amended to 5.5 to 6.0 and hopefully maintained during long-term production (White, 1987).

MINIATURE POTTED FLOWERING PLANTS

A well-drained medium must be used to facilitate excellent aeration, particularly during rooting of the cuttings. Conversely, 4-in. (10-cm) pots quickly dry during transportation and marketing and drought stress causes premature leaf drop and flower senescence. Peat-lite mixes are commonly used with a pH of 5.5 to 6.7. Dry medium is not as serious a problem for 6-in. (15-cm) holiday crops.

BARE ROOTED POTTED FLOWERING AND GARDEN PLANTS

Media requirements are the same as for miniature potted plants.

HEIGHT CONTROL
CUT FLOWERS

No height control needed.

MINIATURE POTTED FLOWERING PLANTS

Although miniature roses are genetic dwarfs, some form of height control will be needed with most cultivars to produce a proportional plant. Bonzi (paclobutrazol) is commonly used and several applications may be needed starting 14 to 21 days after the final pinch, depending on the cultivar and season (Hasek et al., 1986; Jørgensen, 1992). The Bonzi concentration may range from 16 to 60 ppm applied as a spray at 2 qt/100 ft^2 (200 mL · m^{-2}) (Jørgensen, 1992). Cultivar and pot size, such as a 4-in. (10-cm) or 2.25-in. (6-cm) pot, will determine the number of spray applications. Pobundkiewicz and Goldsberry (1989) reported that one Sumagic (uniconizole) drench of between 0.1 to 0.2 mg a.i. per 5-in. (12.5-cm) pot was adequate to control height. Adriansen (1985) noted that A-Rest (ancymidol) and B-Nine (daminozide) were marginally effective at controlling height. While a negative DIF can decrease stem elongation, the effect is not dramatic and a negative DIF for 2 hr commensing prior to sunup (DROP) is not effective (Mortensen and Moe, 1992).

BARE ROOTED POTTED FLOWERING PLANTS

Heins (1981) advised reducing the length of dormant canes to 6 to 8 in. (15 to 20 cm) and removing the dominant apical shoot once growth had commenced. These procedures will increase the total number of flowering shoots and reduce overall plant height.

Two sprays of Cycocel (chlormequat) can be used to control height. The first application (1500 ppm) is applied when shoots are 2 in. (5 cm) long and the second application 10 days later (Moe, 1970).

SPACING

CUT FLOWERS

Typically, budded plants are spaced at 1 to 1.4 ft² (0.09 to 0.13 m²) per plant and there are usually three rows across a bed (Langhans, 1987). De Hoog et al. (1999) reported using 0.9 plants/ft² (10 plants/m²). With the arching production technique (see Schedule and Timing section) 0.5 to 1.0 plants/ft² (7 to 10 plants/m²) are used (Hamrick, 2003).

MINIATURE POTTED FLOWERING PLANTS

Plants are spaced pot-to-pot from propagation until the second cutback. Afterward plants are spaced at 3 to 4.5 pots/ft² (32 to 48 pots/m²) for 4-in. (10-cm) pots and 1 to 1.5 pots/ft² (11 to 16 pots/m²) for 5- to 6.5-in. (13- to 16.5-cm) pots (Jørgensen, 1992).

BARE ROOTED POTTED FLOWERING PLANTS

The 'Garnets' cultivars are planted in a 6- to 8-in. (15- to 20-cm) pot and initially spaced pot-to-pot, but eventually spaced at 10 × 10 in. or 12 × 12 in. (25 × 25 cm or 30 × 30 cm) when growth begins (Asaoka and Heins, 1982; Heins, 1981).

BARE ROOTED POTTED GARDEN PLANTS

These plants are forced in 8- to 12-in. (21- to 30-cm) pots spaced 6 in. (15 cm) between pots.

PINCHING AND DISBUDDING

CUT FLOWERS

Pinching and harvesting of flowers are critical processes in plant management (Zieslin and Byrne, 1981). Following are five situations when pinching or pruning is considered in traditional cut rose production (Fig. II-1 Rosa). See Scheduling and Timing section for bending or arching production techniques.

1. Prior to planting dormant plants, broken roots and shoots are removed and cane height may be reduced, leaving three to four dormant axillary buds.

2. Once planted and new shoots begin to elongate, flower buds are removed at either one of two stages of growth. If the flower bud is smaller than a pea, this pinch is termed a *soft pinch;* if flower buds are larger than a pea, the pinch is termed a *hard pinch.* These new flowering shoots are removed down to the second five-leaflet leaf from the main stem, depending on the cultivar and the season. Axillary buds from a hard pinch require longer to break and form a flowering shoot; shoots from soft pinches grow more rapidly. Most cut flower growers pinch twice and prefer the soft pinch. This practice builds up the plant and establishes the basic structure or architecture of the plant

FIGURE II-1 ROSA Traditional production of *Rosa* (photo by K. Ohkawa).

from which future production is based (Langhans, 1987).

3. At the time of harvest, a decision must be made regarding where to cut the stem—leave one, two, or three nodes on the shoot or cut below the knuckle, which is the junction of an axillary shoot and the stem from which it is growing. The plants can be slowly reduced in height if the stem is cut below the knuckle. The rate and number of return shoots can be controlled by cutting above the knuckle. For example, the return shoot will be slower to break and flower and will have a longer stem with more leaves if the stem is cut at the lowest node with a five-leaflet leaf compared with cutting higher.

4. Five to 8 weeks prior to a major holiday, depending on the cultivar and production temperature, growers will sacrifice flowering shoots and pinch the developing shoots to ensure that a large number of flowers will be available at the same time for a holiday. Some producers do not practice this to maintain consistent year-round production or use it only on a limited percentage of their crop.

5. After Mother's Day and into late June when demand for cut roses declines, rose plants are severely cut back to a height of 2 to 3 ft (60 to 90 cm), particularly for older plants. The pruning can be done by hand or by electric shears.

If axillary buds form on standard roses, they are typically removed in the greenhouse while buds are immature.

MINIATURE POTTED FLOWERING PLANTS

Two cutbacks are required to produce a well-branched miniature flowering potted plant with numerous flowering stems. The first pinch is 7 days after plants are removed from propagation. The second is approximately 3 weeks later. The height of the first pinch is 1 in. (2.5 cm) above the medium level; the second pinch is made approximately 0.5 to 0.75 in. (1.2 to 2 cm) above the primary pinch. This process can be automated with the pruning bar running above the plant shoots (Jørgensen, 1992). Be sure that plants are well rooted prior to the pinch or uneven axillary shoot development will occur.

Cytokinin can be used to significantly increase branching when applied at 10 to 100 ppm (Nowak and Rudnicki, 1990; Richards and Wilkinson, 1984; Zieslin and Moe, 1985). Atrinol spray at 0.25 to 1.5 oz/gal (2 to 12 mL · L^{-1}) can also be used to encourage axillary bud activity.

BARE ROOTED POTTED FLOWERING AND GARDEN PLANTS

Canes and roots are pruned prior to planting in 6- or 7-in. (15- or 17.5-cm) pots and injured tissue is removed. Heins (1981) and Asaoka and Heins (1982) recommended that 6 to 8 in. (15 to 20 cm) of cane remain. When new growth has commenced, the dominant shoot should be removed and the remaining shoots pinched to 3 or 4 in. (7.5 to 10 cm) long. This pruning increases shoot numbers and vigor (see Height Control, page 815).

SUPPORT

Maintaining straight stems and providing support are a major concern, as well as costly and necessary with cut roses. Traditionally, rose plants are grown using at least three layers of wire with openings of 6 × 6 or 6 × 8 in. (15 × 15 or 15 × 20 cm) (Langhans, 1987). Production of cut roses using bending requires much less support. Potted and garden plants do not need support.

SCHEDULE AND TIMING

CUT FLOWERS

Cut flower harvests are frequently scheduled so that peak production coincides with major holidays. Timing of harvests is dependent on temperature, light, and date of the last pinch, cutback, or harvest. In northern latitudes the time span between a pinch or a cutback and the next harvest can be 7 to 8 weeks for Christmas and Valentine's Day, 6 to 7 weeks for Easter, and 5 to 6 weeks for Mother's Day. In addition, the position of the cut above an axillary bud can influence the rate of axillary bud elongation and flowering (see Flowering Control and Dormancy, page 811) (Langhans, 1987; Moe, 1970). Langhans (1987) developed a proposed year long timing schedule.

Traditional production methods using dormant rootstocks in ground beds were limited by the large plant size, which reduces harvesting efficiency and light penetration and increases

FIGURE II-2 ROSA Arching production of *Rosa* (photo by K. Ohkawa).

difficulty of plant maintenance. A method of rose production, known as *arching* or *bending* (Fig. II-2 Rosa), was developed to allow easy harvest and reduced plant sizes (Ohkawa and Suematsu, 1999). Although this technique was first developed in Japan, it is now commonly used around the world and has been evaluated in Canada (Blom and Kerec, 1998, 2000; Blom and Tsujita, 1996), California (Lieth and Kim, 1999), and the Netherlands (de Hoog et al., 1999).

The arching technique begins with a cutting rooted in a rockwool medium and either grafted with the desired cultivar or ungrafted on its own roots (see Propagation section). After rooting, the rockwool block is placed on a waist-high bench and plants are grown using a nutriculture system and pinched. Thirty to 40 days later the resulting shoots have a soybean size bud. These shoots are of poor quality and are not harvested. Instead the buds are removed and the shoots bent downward above the second node from the axis of shoot and main stem. If plants are grown on a bench with supports and wires, the stems can be bent down in the correct position without interfering with harvest or contacting the medium. The bent stems supply photosynthates to new shoots that develop from the basal buds.

Many of the shoots that develop from the basal buds are high quality and are harvested. The shoots are completely removed because leaving any nodes on the shoot will produce small, inferior stems. Unharvested blind or poor-quality shoots are bent downward to provide axillary buds for the next cycle of flowers. This process is repeated throughout the year and the plant height does not appreciably increase when shoots are bent, compared with the traditional method. Shoots are bent when young and gently pushed downward to prevent breaking. Bending is usually performed on cloudy days because shoots may wilt and die if bent on sunny days. After enough shoots have been bent on a new planting, the excess can be removed to make pest control easier. Dead shoots should also be removed. In some areas, stems are not bent during the winter months due to low light levels.

Bending may cause lower production than traditional systems but the stem length and weight are increased, resulting in greater numbers of high grade stems. Because plants do not have to be pruned heavily to reduce plant height, production can continue uninterrupted (Ohkawa and Suematsu, 1999). The process of bending the stems allows light to penetrate the base of the plant, which increases the quality of the resulting shoots. In addition, longer stems can be harvested because there is no need to leave two five-leaflet leaves to provide photosynthates for the axillary shoots as in traditional production systems.

Bending can also be used with rose bushes planted in traditional ground beds. Bending generally increases stem thickness and uniformity of length, allows easier harvest, and eliminates support wires. However, spider mite and *Botrytis* control can be difficult within the dense foliar canopy.

Researchers at the University of Kentucky (Anderson, 1996; Anderson and Jia, 1996a, b) have proposed another system for the production of single-stem roses from single-node cuttings. During stage 1 (propagation) cuttings are treated with a rooting compound, placed in 3-in. (8-cm) pots, and rooted under intermittent mist at a medium temperature of 95°F (35°C). During stage 2 (axillary bud break and stem development to visible pea-size flower bud) rooted cuttings are spaced at 18.6 plants/ft² (200/m²) and grown with 57 to 61°F (14 to 16°C) night temperatures and 12-hr supplemental lighting. During stage 3 (stem elongation and flower bud development) 12- to 18-in. (30- to 35-cm)-tall plants with a pea-size bud are spaced at 9.3 plants/ft² (100/m²) and grown with 57 to 61°F (14 to 16°C) night temperatures and ambient light. More than 70% of cut stems were 18 to 30 in. (46 to 75 cm) long using this method. Bredmose (1998) adapted the system in Denmark by growing the plants in rockwool cubes with ebb-and-flow irrigation and produced stem lengths ranging from 14 to 24 in. (36 to 60 cm).

MINIATURE POTTED FLOWERING PLANTS

Scheduling year-round 4-in. (10-cm) pot plant production is a challenge (Table II-2 Rosa). Growth rates vary with the season and minor temperature and light fluctuations can slow or hasten growth. Growth rates also vary with the cultivars; hence, one cultivar may need to be propagated 1 week earlier than other cultivars to have a color assortment ready for any one marketing date (Jørgensen, 1992).

BARE ROOTED POTTED FLOWERING PLANTS

The highest quality or grade of bare rootstocks (triple XXX) are needed to produce the highest number of flowering shoots and maintain uniformity. This is also true for cut flower production (Langhans, 1987). When bare roots arrive (see Propagation, page 809) keep the plants at 31 to 32°F (−0.6 to 0°C) until planting. Canes should be cut back (see Pinching and Disbudding, page 816). An older technique was to soak canes in water for 1 hr prior to planting. However, this major operation is not conducive for mechanized or automated potting.

For Valentine's Day, canes must be harvested early from the field and given 4 to 6 weeks of cooling at 36 to 40°F (2 or 4°C) either as a bare rooted or potted 6-in. (15-cm) plant (Table II-3 Rosa). On average less than 70 days will be required to flower the crop (65 to 67 days) at a forcing temperature of 68/60°F (20/16°C) day/night. Easter forcing begins in late December to early January depending on the date of Easter, and Mother's Day forcing begins in mid- to late January (Heins, 1981; Moe, 1970). Asaoka and Heins (1982) illustrated the interaction of flower bud development rate and temperature. Garden roses are forced into flower in a similar manner as bare rooted potted plants

INSECTS

Lindquist et al. (1987) reviewed insects and related pests of roses. Red spider mites, thrips, aphids, whiteflies, caterpillars, shore flies, and fungus gnats are commonly seen in rose production. Exclusion and monitoring are a priority. Chemicals should be used only on small outbreaks versus large-scale sprays. Casey and Parrella (1998) published a literature review on insect and disease control. Biological control of thrips and mites on roses is a reality when used in conjunction with biological soaps and chemicals (Smitley, 1994). These new environmentally sound techniques can be used as a marketing tool to customers (Jørgensen, 1992).

TABLE II-2 ROSA
Sample schedule for production of 4-in. (10-cm) miniature potted *Rosa*.

Cultural Step	Production Time (weeks)	Temperature °F (°C)
Propagation of single-node cutting		
	2–3	73–75 (23–24)
Growth		
	1	68–72 (20–22)
Cut back		
	2–3	68–72 (20–22)
Cut back and space, apply growth retardant as needed[a]		
	5–7	66–72 (19–22)
Flower, apply STS or BA + STS[b]		
Total	10–14[c]	64 (18)

[a]The growth retardant Bonzi is applied as a 16- to 60-ppm spray, and more than one application may be needed.
[b]Apply BA at 10 to 25 ppm when flowers begin to color.
[c]In the summer, timing may be as rapid as 10 weeks; winter, 14 weeks (Jørgensen, 1992).

TABLE II-3 ROSA

Sample schedule for production of bare root flowering potted holiday *Rosa* plants.

Cultural Step	Production Time (weeks)	Temperature °F (°C)
Plant, cut canes back leaving up to four buds or nodes/cane	2	55–62 (13–17)
Shoot emergence, remove dominant shoots when growth commences	2–3	60–68 (16–20)
Buds visible	3–5	65 (18) nights to hasten development
Flower		
Total	7–10	

Note: For Valentine's Day, HID lighting is required in northern latitudes.

DISEASES

Mildew (*Sphaerotheca pannosa* pv. *rosae*) and gray mold (*Botrytis cinerea*) are the two major disease problems. Jørgensen (1992) stated that these fungi should be considered physiological problems rather than disease problems. Environmental control can prevent the spread (Cobb et al., 1978). Exact environmental control in the greenhouse is required for both *Botrytis* and mildew. Water condensation occurs when temperatures fall below the dew point. Guttation of water along the edges of leaves also occurs. Drying must occur to prevent disease establishment. Increase the temperature 1.5 to 3°F (1 to 2°C) when the relative humidity reaches 85 to 87% and ventilate by slightly opening the vents. If the thermoscreen is closed, it should open 5% so that the humid air can escape (Jørgensen, 1992). Interestingly, Hammer and Evensen (1996) found that increasing air movement in the greenhouse increased susceptibility of the plants to *Botrytis*.

Roses are continually plagued by several other diseases. Disease research was reviewed in 1987 in *Roses, A Manual for Greenhouse Rose Production* (R.W. Langhans, editor) by Baker and Dimock on black spot, Dimock et al. on mildew, Horst on bacterial diseases and nematodes, Nelson and Nichols on root and stem diseases, Nichols and Nelson on foliar diseases, and Romaine and Horst on viruses and virus-like diseases. Research on disease and environmental interaction and control has been reported by Marois et al. (1988, 1989), Powell (1999), and Powell and De Long (1990).

CUT FLOWERS

As discussed earlier, environmental control is the primary method for avoiding mildew and *Botrytis*. Plants should be planted in a pasteurized medium.

MINIATURE POTTED FLOWERING PLANTS

Cylindrocladium scoparium, Pythium, Phytophthora, and *Peronospora* (downy mildew) may also be problems, in addition to the mildew and *Botrytis* listed earlier. *Cylindrocladium* is most common during propagation and can cause significant losses. Sanitation and environmental control are absolute necessities in pot rose production. Diseases must be addressed during all phases, from propagation and production to shipping. Disease problems can be found on both the aerial parts of the plants and the roots. Further, because cuttings are often taken from plants in production, pathogens can be carried from one crop to the next. For both *Botrytis* and mildew, chemical controls can be used when appropriate (Jørgensen, 1992).

BARE ROOTED POTTED GARDEN PLANTS

Besides the diseases already mentioned, outdoor-grown garden roses are subject to an incredible array of diseases (Horst, 1990), which mainly attack plants in the garden but can also be a problem on roses being marketed in outdoor settings. The main problems are black spot (*Diplocarpon rosae*), brown canker (*Cryptosporella umbrina*), powdery mildew (*Sphaerotheca pannosa*), and rust (*Phragmidium mucronatum*). Prompt sanitation and no overhead irrigation will help to control these diseases. Other reported diseases include verticillium wilt (*Verticillium albo-atrum* and *V. dahliae*), root rot (*Armillaria*), stem cankers and dieback (*Leptosphaeria cornothyrium, Coniothyrium fuckelii,* and *Botryosphaeria dothidea*), and leaf spot (*Cercospora* and *Pseudocercospora*) (Dreistadt, 2001).

PHYSIOLOGICAL DISORDERS

CUT FLOWERS

Petal tipburn or black petal edge is a severe blackening and marginal incurving of the outermost wrapper petal. The tapered flower form is frequently unaffected. This disorder is thought to be caused by ultraviolet light and is more prevalent in polyethylene-covered greenhouses. To reduce the severity of this disorder, use supplementary lighting during cloudy weather and maximize air movement within the canopy to reduce air to flower temperature differences (M. Raviv, personal communication).

"Bullhead" flowers are a disorder in which the flowers are not tapered at the apex, but are flatter and often darker than normal flowers. Frequently vigorous new shoots from lower buds produce bullheads. Other potential causes may also be temperatures that are too low during flower development or thrips damage. Some cultivars are more prone to producing bullheads than other. This problem is not common in potted flowering roses.

CUT FLOWERS AND MINIATURE POTTED FLOWERING PLANTS

Blind shoots occur when newly elongating axillary shoots fail to form a flower bud. This disorder is due to insufficient light or high temperatures during shoot elongation and thus the flower bud aborts. Both cut flowers and miniature potted plants have a propensity for lower axillary buds to develop into blind shoots (Zieslin and Moe, 1985). With potted plants, uneven flowering can be caused by uneven pinching, especially too high or too low; low light; or low nutrition.

BARE ROOTED POTTED GARDEN PLANTS

Dormant plants may not leaf out and grow if the plants are allowed to dry out during cold storage or during the forcing process or are exposed to ethylene. Maintain high humidity during storage and early forcing.

POSTHARVEST

CUT FLOWERS

A major concern for cut rose producers is postharvest keeping quality. Numerous factors are involved in causing and preventing poor keeping quality and these have been summarized by Durkin (1987), Durkin and Boodley (1987), Lohr and Pearson-Mims (1990), Mastalerz (1987b), Mortensen and Gislerød (1999), Nowak and Rudnicki (1990), Sacalis (1993) and Torre et al. (2001). Factors involved in maximized longevity are:

- Cultivar (cultivars vary in postharvest life)
- Optimized growth environment (proper light and temperature)
- Presence of sufficient calcium in the tissue
- Production season (flowers produced in the spring or early summer are superior to fall and winter)
- Relative humidity (increasing humidity from 75–83% to 91% during production reduced vase life)
- Correct stage of development (see below)
- Placement of stems in warm water as soon as possible
- High-quality water with an appropriate pH adjustment and with low fluoride content
- Preservatives with a carbon source (sucrose), an inhibitor of microorganisms, and an ethylene inhibitor
- Presence of light during storage [water uptake is greater with 100 to 300 fc (20 to 60 $\mu mol \cdot m^{-2} \cdot s^{-1}$) of light than in the dark]
- Minimal duration of storage and shipping
- Low storage and shipping temperature
- Recutting stems each time stems are out of water to remove air-blocked xylem tissue.

Red and pink cultivars are harvested when the calyx has reflexed below the horizontal position and one to two petals have started to unfold (Fig. II-3 Rosa). White cultivars can be harvested later; yellow cultivars sooner. Tighter buds may be harvested if cut rose flower stems are to be held in cold storage for 1 to 2 days. Stems should always be in a floral preservative solution. Cold storage should be at 32 to 34°F (0 to 1°C); water should always be warm at 73 to 77°F (23 to 25°C) when each harvesting, grading, and shipping operation occurs and the stem is recut. Humidity (80%) is also important during postharvest handling

FIGURE II-3 ROSA   *Rosa* bud ready to harvest.

to reduce transpiration and aid in maintaining turgor and preventing the tissue below the flower from collapsing. This common problem is called *neck wilt* or *bent neck* and it may be due to bacteria accumulation in the stem (van Doorn and de Witte, 1997). Tap water appears to be the origin of the bacteria, which can be reduced by using antimicrobial compounds in the water (Ohkawa et al., 1999). *Narcissus* stems also exude a mucilage that increases bacteria in the water and causes bent neck in roses if they are stored in the same water (van Doorn, 1998). Cultivars vary in sensitivity to bent neck.

Numerous floral preservatives can be purchased or formulated at the production site, wholesaler, or retail shop. Water quality greatly affects preservative performance; test several preservatives to determine the best one for each water source. Rehydration of leaves and flowers is important if stems have been out of water for any length of time. Pulsing stems with surfactants for 24 hr before storing dry improved vase life after stems were removed from storage (van Doorn et al., 1993). The recommended procedure is to recut the stems and place them in water adjusted to pH 3.0 with citric acid for 30 to 60 min. A simple formula for a floral preservative contains sugar, a biocide such as 8-hydroxyquinoline citrate (8-HQC), and citric acid as listed in Sacalis (1993). The effect of STS on cut roses has been mixed with some reports showing an increased vase life

(Liao et al., 2000; Mor et al., 1989; Reid et al., 1989) and others no effect (Ohkawa et al., 1999). Cut roses are considered to be slightly sensitive to ethylene.

MINIATURE POTTED FLOWERING PLANTS

Postharvest life is influenced by many factors such as genetics (cultivar differences); season; stage of development when harvested; culture (water stress, nutritional stress, etc.); presence of root or leaf diseases; temperature and duration of transport; and adequate light, temperature, and moisture conditions in the marketplace and home environment. High calcium in the tissue has been correlated with enhanced postharvest life (Mortensen et al., 2001; Starkey and Pedersen, 1997). Certainly, any source of ethylene from combustion engines, fruit ripening, or pathogens must be avoided. Even fumes from herbicide sacks in garden centers can cause premature flower senescence, flower bud abortion, and leaf yellowing and senescence.

Regardless, longevity will vary between series and between cultivars within any one series. For example, the postharvest life of two cultivar series with similar colors varied from 8.8 to 15.7 days after undergoing simulated transport at 46°F (8°C) and then held at 72°F (22°C) (Anonymous, 1993). Summer-grown potted roses under high temperatures and light levels last longer than winter-grown roses under low temperatures and light levels (Kyalo et al., 1996; Monteiro et al., 2001a). Monteiro et al. (2001b) related postharvest life to respiration rate and noted that cultivars with high respiration rates are best for fall/winter and those with low respiration rates are best for spring/summer. Subtle differences exist between cultivars regarding the proper stage of development for harvesting; that is, when the primary flower bud is open and axillary buds are in color versus when the primary flower is in full color and the axillary buds show color (Anonymous, 1993).

Any stress during the marketing process such as warm temperatures in the packing case, low light, or drought stress will cause premature senescence. Removing field heat and reducing the temperature prior to truck transport are both urged. Individuals involved daily in the production and marketing of potted roses will relate that high-quality plants can be sent to market and be unacceptable within 48 hr. Roses are very sensitive to low light stress;

consequently, plants should be unsleeved and placed in light at 100 fc (20 μmol $\cdot$ m^{-2} $\cdot$ s^{-1}) after being shipped.

Be certain that plants are shipped and stored at 34 to 41°F (1 to 5°C). This temperature is optimal to both decrease respiration and reduce ethylene effects (Maxie et al., 1974; Nell, 1993; Nell and Noordegraaf, 1991).

Tight-fitting plastic decorative pot wraps do not absorb leaf transpirational water and may result in free water, *Botrytis*, and leaf yellowing. Consequently, only paper sleeves or perforated plastic are recommended.

A cytokinin application can reduce leaf abscission and flower bud abortion (Clark et al., 1991; Cushman et al., 1994; Halevy and Kofranek, 1976; Nowak and Rudnicki, 1990). Preshipping sprays of 25 ppm benzyladenine (BA) or 50 ppm benzylamino (tetrahydropyranyl) purine (PBA) reduce leaf chlorosis and may increase flower life (Pemberton et al., 1997). STS sprays at 1 mM increased the longevity of flowers. Both leaf and flower longevity and quality were improved when both BA and STS were used together (Tjosvold et al., 1994). 1-methylcyclopropene (1-MCP) delayed the negative effects of exogenous ethylene including leaf, flower, and bud abscission (Müller et al., 1999; Serek et al., 1994, 1996).

KEY POINTS

- The rose is one of the world's most popular flowers and is used as a cut flower, potted flowering plant, and garden ornamental.
- Rose bushes for cut flower production and gardens are primarily graft propagated; potted flowering plants are primarily cutting propagated.
- Successful potted rose propagation requires uniform cutting selection of nodes with five-leaflet leaves from a shoot with a large flower bud not yet showing color, high humidity, and warm 73 to 75°F (23 to 24°C) temperatures.
- Commercial roses are generally day neutral.
- High light is required for high quality flowers; low light results in low plant quality and flower bud abortion.
- High temperatures increase the number of blind shoots and decrease flower quality, petal number, stem length, and weight of flowering stem.
- Axillary shoot length and thickness depend on the position of the bud on the main stem. If the shoot is cut low, the resulting axillary shoot will have more leaves and be longer (higher quality) and the time to the next harvestable stems will be longer. The opposite occurs when the cut is high or more nodes are left because the resulting shoots will be quick to flower but of lower quality.
- Cut flowers are primarily produced using the arching technique.
- Nutritional, insect, and disease problems are common.
- Postharvest care of roses is a major concern and numerous factors must be considered.

BIBLIOGRAPHY

Adriansen, E. 1985. Kemisk vækstregulering, pp. 142–162 in *Potteplanter I—Produktion, Metoder, Midler*, O.V. Christensen, A. Klougart, I.S. Pedersen, and K. Wikesjö, editors. GartnerINFO, København, Denmark. (in Danish)

Anderson, R.G. 1996. Production characteristics of high quality single-stem roses. *HortScience* 31: 597. (Abstract)

Anderson, R.G., and W. Jia. 1996a. Developmental stages of single-stem cut rose production. *HortScience* 31:654. (Abstract)

Anderson, R.G., and W. Jia. 1996b. Effect of cutting characteristics on cut stem quality of single-stem rose. *HortScience* 31:654. (Abstract)

Anonymous. 1993. 'Victory Parade' pot rose last longest. *FloraCulture International* 3(2):28.

Asaoka, M., and R.D. Heins. 1982. Influence of supplemental light and preforcing storage treatments on the forcing of 'Red Garnet' rose as a pot plant. *Journal of the American Society for Horticultural Science* 107:548–552.

Asen, S., and R.E. Larson. 1951. *Artificial Culturing of Rose Embryos*. Pennsylvania State College Progress Report Number 40.

Bailey, L.H., and E.Z. Bailey. 1976. *Rosa*, pp. 974–982 in *Hortus Third: A Concise Dictionary of Plants Cultivated in the United States and Canada*. Macmillan, New York.

Baker, K.F., and A.W. Dimock. 1987. Black spot, pp. 297–309 in *Roses, A Manual of Greenhouse Rose Production,* R.W. Langhans, editor. Roses Incorporated, Haslett, Michigan.

Blom, T.J., and D. Kerec. 1998. Rootstock/plant propagation and two canopies for harvesting using the arching technique on yield and quality of 'Kardinal' and 'Medeo' cut roses. *Roses Inc. Bulletin* Dec.:49–53.

Blom, T.J., and D. Kerec. 2000. High or low irrigation volumes on production of roses in coco coir using either a once-through or a recirculating system. *Roses Inc. Bulletin* Dec.:13–29.

Blom, T., and J. Tsujita. 1996. Bending/arching. *Roses Inc. Bulletin* Dec.:29–33.

Bredmose, N. 1993. Effects of year-round supplementary lighting on shoot development, flowering and quality of two glasshouse rose cultivars. *Scientia Horticulturae* 54:69–85.

Bredmose, N. 1997. Chronology of three physiological development phases of single-stemmed rose (*Rosa hybrida* L.) plants in response to increment in light quantum integral. *Scientia Horticulturae* 69:107–115.

Bredmose, N.B. 1998. Growth, flowering, and postharvest performance of single-stemmed rose (*Rose hybrida* L.) plants in response to light quantum integral and plant population density. *Journal of the American Society for Horticultural Science* 123:569–576.

Bredmose, N., and J. Hansen. 1996. Influence of propagation material and method on regeneration, growth and flowering of cut rose cvs. Frisco and Gabriella. *Acta Horticulturae* 424:23–28.

Brown, W.W., and D.P. Ormrod. 1980. Soil temperature effects on greenhouse roses in relation to air temperature and nutrition. *Journal of the American Society for Horticultural Science* 105:57–59.

Byrne, T.G., and R.P. Doss. 1981. Development time of 'Cara Mia' rose shoots as influenced by pruning position and parent shoot diameter. *Journal of the American Society for Horticultural Science* 106:98–100.

Cabrera, R.I. 2001. Leaf tissue analysis and nitrogen: Yield relationships in greenhouse roses. *Roses Inc. Bulletin* Mar.:33–39.

Casey, C., and M. Parrella. 1998. Literature review. *Roses Inc. Bulletin* Nov.:31–45.

Clark, D.G., J.W. Kelly, and H.B. Pemberton. 1991. Postharvest quality characteristics of cultivars of potted rose in response to holding conditions and cytokinins. *HortScience* 26:1195–1197.

Clark, D.G., J.W. Kelly, and N.C. Rajapakse. 1993. Production and postharvest characteristics of *Rosa hybrida* L. 'Meijikatar' grown in pots under carbon dioxide enrichment. *Journal of the American Society for Horticultural Science* 118:613–617.

Cobb, G.S., J.J. Hanan, and R. Baker. 1978. Environmental factors affecting rose powdery mildew in greenhouses. *HortScience* 13:464–466.

Cushman, L.C., H.B. Pemberton, and J.W. Kelly. 1994. Cultivar, flower stage, silver thiosulfate, and BA interactives affect performance of potted miniature roses. *HortScience* 29:805–808.

de Hoog, M. Warmenhoven, D. Eveleens-Clark, and N. Van Mourik. 1999. *Effects of Plant Density, Harvest Methods and Bending of Branches on the Production and Quality of Roses.* Proefstation voor Bloemisterij en Glasgroente Report 225.

Dimock, A.W., J. Tammen, L. Nichols, and P.E. Nelson. 1987. Powdery mildew, pp. 289–296 in *Roses, A Manual of Greenhouse Rose Production,* R.W. Langhans, editor. Roses Incorporated, Haslett, Michigan.

Dreistadt, S.H. 2001. *Integrated Pest Management for Floriculture and Nurseries.* University of California Division of Agriculture and Natural Resources Publication 3402.

Durkin, D.J. 1987. Post-harvest life, pp. 267–271 in *Roses, A Manual of Greenhouse Rose Production,* R.W. Langhans, editor. Roses Incorporated, Haslett, Michigan.

Durkin, D., and J. Boodley. 1987. Cutting and handling flowers, pp. 261–264 in *Roses, A Manual of Greenhouse Rose Production,* R.W. Langhans, editor. Roses Incorporated, Haslett, Michigan.

Fitch, C.M. 1977. *The Complete Book of Miniature Roses.* Hawthorn Books, New York.

Halevy, A.H., and A.M. Kofranek. 1976. The prevention of flower bud and leaf abscission in pot roses during simulated transport. *Journal of the American Society for Horticultural Science* 101:658–660.

Hammer, P.E., and K.B. Evensen. 1996. Effects of the production environment on the susceptibility of rose flowers to postharvest infections by *Botrytis cinerea*. *Journal of the American Society for Horticultural Science* 121:314–320.

Hamrick, D. 2003. *Rosa,* pp. 601–620 in *Ball Redbook,* vol. 2, 17th ed. Ball Publishing, Batavia, Illinois.

Hanan, J.J. 1979. Observation of a low temperature effect on rose. *Journal of the American Society for Horticultural Science* 104:37–40.

Hartman, H.T., and D.E. Kester. 1975. *Rosa,* pp. 611–614 in *Plant Propagation, Principles and Practices.* Prentice-Hall, Englewood Cliffs, New Jersey.

Hasek, R., R. Sciaroni, and G. Hickman. 1986. New growth regulator tested. *Greenhouse Grower* 4:52–53.

Heins, R.D. 1981. Forcing pot roses for Valentine's Day. *Florists' Review* 169(4376):14–15.

Hopper, D.A. 1996. High-pressure sodium radiation during off-peak nighttimes increases cut rose production and quality. *HortScience* 31:938–940.

Hopper, D.A., and P.A. Hammer. 1991. Regression models describing *Rosa hybrida* response to day/night temperature and photosynthetic photon flux. *Journal of the American Society for Horticultural Science* 116:609–617.

Horst, K. 1987a. Diseases caused by bacteria, pp. 343–350 in *Roses, A Manual of Greenhouse Rose Production*, R.W. Langhans, editor. Roses Incorporated, Haslett, Michigan.

Horst, R.K. 1987b. Diseases caused by nematodes, pp. 351–354 in *Roses, A Manual of Greenhouse Rose Production*, R.W. Langhans, editor. Roses Incorporated, Haslett, Michigan.

Horst, R.K. 1990. Rose, pp. 797–800 in *Westcott's Plant Disease Handbook*, 5th ed. Van Nostrand Reinhold, New York.

Hsia, C., and S.S. Korban. 1996. Organogenesis and somatic embryogenesis in callus cultures of *Rosa hybrida* and *Rosa chinensis minima*. *Plant Cell, Tissue and Organ Culture* 44:1–6.

Huxley, A., M. Griffiths, and M. Levy. 1992. *Rosa*, pp. 106–134 in *The New Royal Horticultural Society Dictionary of Gardening*, vol. 4. Stockton Press, New York.

Jiao, J., M.J. Tsujita, and B. Grodzinski. 1991. Influence of temperature on net CO_2 exchange in roses. *Canadian Journal of Plant Science* 71:235–243.

Jørgensen, E. 1992. *Growing Parade-Roses®*. Pejoe Trykcenter A/S, Hillerød, Denmark.

Kyalo, T.M., H.B. Pemberton, and J.M. Zajicek. 1996. Seasonal growing environment affects quality characteristics and postproduction longevity of potted miniature roses. *HortScience* 31:120–122.

Langhans, R.W. 1987. Planting, pp. 57–59 in *Roses, A Manual of Greenhouse Rose Production*, R.W. Langhans, editor. Roses Incorporated, Haslett, Michigan.

Laurie, A., and P.F. Bobula. 1938. A study of flowering rose shoots with reference to flower bud differentiation. *Proceedings of the American Society for Horticultural Science* 36:767–768.

Lieth, H. 1996. Modeling roses for optimum production. *GrowerTalks* 60(1):42, 44, 47, 48, 50.

Lieth, H., and S. Kim. 1999. Development of optimal rose canopy management strategies for rose growers: "Bending" versus traditional production. *Roses Inc. Bulletin* Dec.:26–40.

Lieth, H., and M. Raviv. 1999. The effect of water availability on rose productivity. *Roses Inc. Bulletin* Dec.:17–24.

Liao, L.-J., Y.-H. Lin, K.-L. Huang, W.-S. Chen, and Y.-M. Cheng. 2000. Postharvest life of cut rose flowers as affected by silver thiosulfate and sucrose. *Botanical Bulletin of Academia Sinica* 41:299–303.

Lindquist, R.K., F.F. Smith, and G.V. Johnson. 1987. Insects and related pests, pp. 355–360 in *Roses, A Manual of Greenhouse Rose Production*, R.W. Langhans, editor. Roses Incorporated, Haslett, Michigan.

Lohr, V.I., and C. H. Pearson-Mims. 1990. Damage to cut roses from fluoride in keeping solutions varies with cultivar. *HortScience* 25:215–216.

Maas, F.M., and E.J. Bakx. 1995. Effects of light on growth and flowering of *Rosa hybrida* 'Mercedes.' *Journal of the American Society for Horticultural Science* 120:571–576.

Marois, J.J., J.C. Redmond, and J.D. MacDonald. 1988. Quantification of the impact of environment on the susceptibility of *Rosa hybrida* flower to *Botrytis cinerea*. *Journal of the American Society for Horticultural Science* 113:842–845.

Marois, J.J., J.D. MacDonald, L. Tanner, S. Wagner, and J.T. English. 1989. Control of *Botrytis cinerea* on rose: Microclimate effects on disease development. *Roses Incorporated Bulletin*, Dec.:45–50.

Mastalerz, J. 1987a. Environmental factors light, temperature and carbon dioxide, pp. 147–169 in *Roses, A Manual of Greenhouse Rose Production*, R.W. Langhans, editor. Roses Incorporated, Haslett, Michigan.

Mastalerz, J. 1987b. Low temperature dry storage, pp. 273–282 in *Roses, A Manual of Greenhouse Rose Production*, R.W. Langhans, editor. Roses Incorporated, Haslett, Michigan.

Mattson, R.H., and R.E. Widmer. 1971. Year-round effects of carbon dioxide supplemented atmospheres on greenhouse rose (*Rosa hybrida*) production. *Journal of the American Society for Horticultural Science* 96:487–488.

Maxie, E.C., R.E. Hasek, and R.H. Sciaroni. 1974. Keep potted roses cool. *Flower and Nursery Report* (Cooperative Extension, University of California, Davis) Mar.:9–10.

Meadows, S.E., and D.G. Richardson. 1983. Interactive effects of ethylene concentration and storage temperature on budbreak and viability of dormant 'Viva' roses. *HortScience* 18:453–454.

Moe, R. 1970. Growth and flowering of potted roses as affected by temperature and growth retardants. *Meldinger Norges Landbrukshøgskole* 49:1–16.

Monteiro, J.A., T.A. Nell, and J.E. Barrett. 2001a. High production temperature increases postproduction flower longevity and reduces bud drop of potted, miniature roses 'Meirutral' and 'Meidanclar.' *HortScience* 36:953–954.

Monteiro, J.A., T.A. Nell, and J.E. Barrett. 2001b. Postproduction of potted miniature rose: Flower respiration and single flower longevity. *Journal of the American Society for Horticultural Science* 126:134–139.

Mor, Y., F. Johnson, and J.D. Faragher. 1989. Preserving the quality of cold-stored rose flowers with ethylene antagonists. *HortScience* 24: 640–641.

Mortensen, L.M. 1991. Effects of temperature, light and CO_2 level on growth and flowering of miniature roses. *Norwegian Journal of Agricultural Sciences* 5:295–300.

Mortensen, L.M., and H.R. Gislerød. 1999. Influence of air humidity and lighting period on growth, vase life and water relations of 14 rose cultivars. *Scientia Horticulturae* 74:1–10.

Mortensen, L.M., and R. Moe. 1992. Effects of CO_2 enrichment and different day/night temperature combinations on growth and flowering of *Rosa* L. and *Kalanchoe blossfeldiana* v. Poelln. *Scientia Horticulturae* 51:145–153.

Mortensen, L.M., and R. Moe. 1983. Growth responses of some greenhouse plants to environment. VII. Effect of CO_2 on photosynthesis and growth of roses. *Meldinger Norges Landbrukshøgskole* 62(3):1–11.

Mortensen, L.M., C.-O. Ottosen, and H.R. Gislerød. 2001. Effects of air humidity and K:Ca ratio on growth, morphology, flowering and keeping quality of pot roses. *Scientia Horticulturae* 90:131–141.

Moss, G.I., and R. Dalgleish. 1984. Increasing returns from roses with root-zone warming. *Journal of the American Society for Horticultural Science* 109:893–898.

Müller, R., B.M. Stummann, A.S. Andersen, and M. Serek. 1999. Involvement of ABA in postharvest life of miniature potted roses. *Plant Growth Regulation* 29:143–150.

Nell, T.A. 1993. *Rosa ×hybrida*, pp. 74–75 in *Potted Plants, Prolonging Shelf Performance, Postproduction Care and Handling*. Ball Publishing, Batavia, Illinois.

Nell, T.A., and C.V. Noordegraaf. 1991. Simulated transport, postproduction irradiance influence postproduction performance of potted roses. *HortScience* 26:1401–1404.

Nelson, P.E., and L.P. Nichols. 1987. Root and stem diseases, pp. 335–342 in *Roses, A Manual of Greenhouse Rose Production*, R.W. Langhans, editor. Roses Incorporated, Haslett, Michigan.

Nichols, L.P., and P.E. Nelson. 1987. Foliage diseases, pp. 311–320 in *Roses, A Manual of Greenhouse Rose Production*, R.W. Langhans, editor. Roses Incorporated, Haslett, Michigan.

Nowak, J., and R.M. Rudnicki. 1990. *Rosa hybrida* (Rose), pp. 158–159 in *Postharvest Handling and Storage of Cut Flowers, Florist Greens and Potted Plants*. Timber Press, Portland, Oregon.

Ohkawa, K. 1980. Cutting-grafts as a means to propagate greenhouse roses. *Scientia Horticulturae* 13: 191–199.

Ohkawa, K. 1984. Cutting grafts as a technique for producing started-eye rose bushes outdoors. *HortScience* 19:527–528.

Ohkawa, K., and M. Suematsu. 1999. Arching cultivation techniques for growing cut-roses. *Acta Horticulturae* 482:47–51.

Ohkawa, K., Y. Kasahara, and J.-N. Suh. 1999. Mobility and effects on vase life of silver-containing compounds in cut rose flowers. *HortScience* 34: 112–113.

Oki, L.R, J.H. Lieth, and S. Tjosvold. 1996. Reduction of run-off in greenhouse cut flower crops through automated irrigation based on soil moisture tension: Substantial improvements in rose crop productivity and quality. *FOR California Cut Flower Commission* May:7.

Passion, C.C., and J.H. Lieth. 1994. Nondestructive dry matter estimation of rose shoot leaves, stem and flower buds using regression models. *HortScience* 29:162–164.

Pemberton, H.B., and U. Schuch. 2003. Moisture loss from bare-root roses results in reduced flowering of containerized plants. *HortScience* 38:671. (Abstract)

Pemberton, H.B., J.W. Kelly, and J. Ferare. 1997. Rose, pp. 112–117 in *Tips on Growing Specialty Potted Crops*, M.L. Gasten, S.A. Carver, C.A. Irwin, and R.A. Larson, editors. Ohio Florists' Association, Columbus, Ohio.

Pinney, M.E. 1964. *The Miniature Rose Book*. D. Van Nostrand Company, New York.

Pobundkiewicz, A., and K.L. Goldsberry. 1989. Controlling the growth habit of dwarf pot roses with uniconazole (Sumagic™). *Colorado State University Research Bulletin* 471:1–2. Colorado Greenhouse Growers Association.

Post, K. 1949. *Rosa*, pp. 758–803 in *Florist Crop Production and Marketing*. Orange Judd Publishing, New York.

Powell, C.C. 1999. Some thoughts on integrated pest management (IPM) for producers of greenhouse roses. *Roses Inc. Bulletin* Mar.:41–45.

Powell, C.C., and R.E. DeLong. 1990. Studies on the chemical and environmental control of powdery mildew on greenhouse roses. *Roses Incorporated Bulletin*, Sept.:51–66.

Reid, M.S., R.Y. Evans, and L.L. Dodge. 1989. Ethylene and silver thiosulfate influence opening of cut rose flowers. *Journal of the American Society for Horticultural Science* 114:436–440.

Richards, D., and R.I. Wilkinson. 1984. Effect of manual pinching, potting-on and cytokinins on branching and flowering of *Camillia, Rhododendron*, and *Rosa*. *Scientia Horticulturae* 23: 75–83.

Romaine, C.P., and R.K. Horst. 1987. Virus and virus-like diseases, pp. 321–334 in *Roses, A Manual of*

Greenhouse Rose Production, R.W. Langhans, editor. Roses Incorporated, Haslett, Michigan.

Sacalis, J.M. 1993. Rosa hybrida, pp. 93–96 in *Cut Flowers, Prolonging Freshness*, 2nd ed., J.L. Seals, editor. Ball Publishing, Batavia, Illinois.

Semeniuk, P., and R.N. Stuart. 1964. Low temperature requirements for after-ripening of seed of *Rosa blanca*. *Proceedings of the American Society for Horticultural Science* 85:639–641.

Serek, M., E.C. Sisler, and M.S. Reid. 1994. Novel gaseous ethylene binding inhibitor prevents ethylene effects in potted flowering plants. *Journal of the American Society for Horticultural Science* 119:1230–1233.

Serek, M., E.C. Sisler, and M.S. Reid. 1996. Ethylene and the postharvest performance of miniature roses. *Acta Horticulturae* 424:145–149.

Smitley, D. 1994. Biocontrol of thrips and mites on roses. *Roses Incorporated Bulletin*, May:45–54.

Starkey, K.R., and A.R. Pedersen. 1997. Increased levels of calcium in the nutrient solution improves the postharvest life of potted roses. *Journal of the American Society for Horticultural Science* 122:863–868.

Sun, W.-Q., and N.L. Bassuk. 1991. Silver thiosulfate application influences rooting and budbreak of 'Royalty' rose cuttings. *HortScience* 26:1288–1290.

Tamimi, Y.N., D.T. Matsuyama, K.D. Ison-Takata, and R.T. Nakano. 1999. Distribution of nutrients in cut-flower roses and the quantities of biomass and nutrients removed during harvest. *HortScience* 34:251–253.

Tjosvold, S.A., M.-J. Wu, and M.S. Reid. 1994. Reduction of postproduction quality loss in potted miniature roses. *HortScience* 29:293–294.

Torre, S., T. Fjeld, and H.R. Gislerød. 2001. Effects of air humidity and K/Ca ratio in the nutrient supply on growth and postharvest characteristics of cut roses. *Scientia Horticulturae* 90:291–304.

Tsujita, M.J. 1987. High intensity supplementary radiation of roses, pp. 171–186 in *Roses, A Manual of Greenhouse Rose Production*, R.W. Langhans, editor. Roses Incorporated, Haslett, Michigan.

Urban, L. 1994. Effect of high-pressure mist and daytime continuous CO_2 enrichment on leaf diffusive conductance, CO_2 fixation and production of *Rosa hybrida* plants grown on rockwool. *Acta Horticulturae* 361:317–324.

van de Pol, P.A., and A. Breukelaar. 1982. Stenting of roses: A method for quick propagation by simultaneously cutting and grafting. *Scientia Horticulturae* 17:187–196.

van Doorn, W.G. 1998. Effects of daffodil flowers on the water relations and vase life of roses and tulips. *Journal of the American Society for Horticultural Science* 123:146–149.

van Doorn, W.G., and Y. de Witte. 1997. Sources of bacteria involved in vascular occlusion of cut rose flowers. *Journal of the American Society for Horticultural Science* 122:263–266.

van Doorn, W.G., R.R.J. Perik, and P.J.M. Belde. 1993. Effects of surfactants on the longevity of dry-stored cut flowering stems of rose, *Bouvardia* and *Astilbe*. *Postharvest Biology and Technology* 3:69–76.

White, J.W. 1987. Fertilization, pp. 87–142 in *Roses, A Manual of Greenhouse Rose Production*, R.W. Langhans, editor. Roses Incorporated, Haslett, Michigan.

White, J.W. Undated. *Greenhouse Roses, Diagnosis and Remedy of Nutritional Disorders*, pp. 1–46. Roses Incorporated, Haslett, Michigan.

White, J.W., and E.J. Holcomb. 1987. Water requirements and irrigation practices, pp. 71–86 in *Roses, A Manual of Greenhouse Rose Production*, R.W. Langhans, editor. Roses Incorporated, Haslett, Michigan.

Zieslin, N., and T. Byrne. 1981. Plant management of greenhouse roses. Flower cutting procedures. *Scientia Horticulturae* 15:179–186.

Zieslin, N., and R. Moe. 1985. *Rosa*, pp. 214–225 in *Handbook of Flowering*, vol. IV, A.H. Halevy, editor. CRC Press, Boca Raton, Florida.

Zieslin, N., E. Khayat, and Y. Mor. 1987. The response of rose plants to different night temperature regimes. *Journal of the American Society for Horticultural Science* 112:86–89.

Rumohra

INTRODUCTION

Common names: leatherleaf fern, leather fern, iron fern.

Scientific name: *Rumohra adiantiformis* (Forst. f.) Ching. (Huxley et al., 1992).

Family and related taxa: Dryopteridaceae Ching. This family contains approximately 50 genera, several of which are used as garden ornamentals.

Origin: *Rumohra adiantiformis* is widespread in tropical areas of Central and South America, South Africa, Madagascar, New Zealand, New Guinea, and Australia (Huxley et al., 1992).

Uses and current status: *Rumohra* is the most commonly used cut foliage in commercial floral arrangements. North American production is primarily in Florida. Leatherleaf is also cultivated in Europe or wild harvested worldwide in areas where it is native. Leatherleaf is mainly cultivated outdoors under shade houses. Dwarf tissue-cultured selections can be used for potted plants.

Leatherleaf fern has thick, glossy, dark-green fronds that grow up to 3 ft (90 cm) tall. Each frond consists of 7 to 15 pairs of highly dissected pinnae (primary divisions of each frond, which are similar to leaflets). The fronds originate from a thick scaly rhizome that grows horizontally at or just below the soil surface.

CULTIVARS

Named cultivars are rare; 'Capeform,' grows to 5 ft (1.5 m) tall. Select clones are available that may be suited to specific production areas. Dwarf selections such as 'Iberia' can be used for potted plants.

PROPAGATION

Leatherleaf fern is commercially propagated by rhizome divisions or clumps. Spores are rarely used for commercial production due to lengthy establishment times and great variability between plants (Henley et al., 1980). Tissue culture is possible (Amaki and Higucki, 1991).

When establishing new production beds, propagate from healthy plants of the best clones (Henley et al., 1980). Size of the propagule can range from terminal rhizome pieces 2 to 5 in. (5 to 13 cm) long to clumps 5 in. (13 cm) across. Rhizome pieces are typically used and spaced end to end in 3 or 4 rows running the length of the bed. The pieces are planted with 1 in. (2.5 cm) of soil covering them; deeper planting will delay growth and increase losses. Fronds can be retained if the rhizome pieces are going to be propagated on site but are removed if the rhizome pieces are going to be shipped. Beds established with rhizome pieces will be in full production in 2.5 to 3 years.

The use of rhizome clumps will reduce the amount of time from planting to full production to as little as 1.5 years compared with rhizome pieces. Clumps 5 in. (13 cm) across will generally have 5 to 7 fronds and at least 3 terminal buds. Larger clumps can be used if sufficient plant material is available. Clumps with soil should be positioned with the upper surface of the clump at the soil surface. Clumps without soil can be planted 0.5 in. (1.3 cm) deep. Clumps are spaced 12 × 12 to 12 × 18 in. (30 × 30 to 30 × 45 cm) apart.

FLOWER CONTROL AND DORMANCY

The fertile fronds of the leatherleaf fern are produced in the spring but are not considered in production. Dormancy is not an issue with this tropical to subtropical plant.

TEMPERATURE

Because most leatherleaf ferns are grown outdoors, precise temperature recommendations have not been developed. Fronds grow more rapidly under 86/77°F (30/25°C) day/night temperatures than under 68/59°F (20/15°C) day/night temperatures (Stamps et al., 1994). Growers are mainly concerned with preventing excessively low or high temperatures. Low temperatures can cause the most damage because immature fronds will be damaged by temperatures below 30°F (−1°C) (Henley et al., 1980).

Actual damage to the ferns will depend on plant vigor, maturity, nutritional status, and moisture and on wind and duration of cold. Growers in areas subject to possible freezes maintain temperature control systems such as sprinkler irrigation, high-pressure fog, crop covers, polyethylene coverings, and forced air heaters (Henley et al., 1980; Stamps, 1991). The use of clear plastic-lined shade houses with forced air heaters will also allow steady production of large numbers of fronds during the winter.

High temperatures are less of a concern for growers than cold temperatures but can limit production and be detrimental to workers. Air temperatures are reduced by maximizing the height of the shade houses, using coarse weave fabrics that allow air movement, rolling up sides of the houses, and using breaks in the fabric of the shade house walls (Henley et al., 1980).

LIGHT

The optimum light level for maximum frond production is 3000 to 5000 fc (600 to 1000 $\mu mol \cdot m^{-2} \cdot s^{-1}$), which is usually provided by fabric-covered houses that use 63 to 73% shade cloth (Henley et al., 1980). Higher light levels will produce low-quality fronds that are light green, thick, and curled under. Although not commonly used, production can be increased up to 15% in heated structures if the winter shade level is reduced to 47% and the summer shade level is 73% of ambient light levels. This can be accomplished by changing fabric or using two layers of shade.

Leatherleaf fern can also be grown in lathhouses or under tree canopies, typically evergreen oaks (*Quercus* spp.). Lathhouses have better air circulation and cooler temperatures, but greater construction expenses than shade houses. Production under tree canopies is less expensive to establish than shade houses but is limited by nonuniform shade, damage from falling debris, and increased difficulty in irrigation. The trees also reduce bed space, compete for nutrients, and limit equipment mobility.

WATER

Leatherleaf should not be moisture stressed because productivity will be reduced (Henley et al., 1980). However, excessive irrigation can increase the disease potential and reduce the effectiveness of pesticides. In Florida, 1 in. (2.5 cm) of water should be applied every 3 days during the summer and 0.5 in. (1.3 cm) every 4 to 7 days during the winter. Overhead sprinkler irrigation is most frequently used and can also be used for freeze control (see Temperature section). Water should have less than 600 ppm salts; water with more than 1200 ppm salts cannot be used. Water with 600 to 1200 ppm salts can be used if the soil is kept moist and frequently leached.

CARBON DIOXIDE

No data available.

NUTRITION

Liquid fertigation is most commonly used on leatherleaf fern. Although granular fertilizers are more labor intensive to apply, their application to only the beds and not the surrounding area makes them economical and nutrient efficient (Henley et al., 1980). Liquid fertigation reduces labor expenses but results in loss of fertilizer to the aisles, as well as increases weed growth. Fertilizers with a ratio of 2:1:2 or 4:1:4 are recommended in Florida on sandy soils. A 1:0:1 ratio can be used if sufficient phosphorus exists in the soil and foliage. Nitrogen should be 50% ammoniacal and 50% nitrate forms. Damage to immature fern fronds from ammonium volatilization and toxicity can occur (Schumann and Mills, 1996). Damage can be avoided by reducing ammonium-based fertilizers, acidifying irrigation water to pH 6.0 to 6.5, and irrigating with clear water immediately after application to dilute the fertilizers. Fertilizer rates for production are based on using 3000 to 5000 fc (600 to 1000 $\mu mol \cdot m^{-2} \cdot s^{-1}$) light levels (Table II-1 Rumohra). Fertilizer rates should be reduced during the winter or under low light. Reduce fertilizer rates by 25% when plants are grown using 1800 to 3000 fc (360 to 600 $\mu mol \cdot m^{-2} \cdot s^{-1}$) light (Henley et al., 1980). Minor nutrients should also be applied regularly as required. Vesicular-arbuscular mycorrhizal (VAM) fungi have been associated with leatherleaf fern but inoculation with VAM has not been commercially useful (Stamps and Johnson, 1984).

Regular soil and foliar nutrient analysis will allow growers to maximize production (Table II-2 Rumohra). Recently mature, hardened fronds that are less than 2 months beyond the cutting stage should be used for nutrient analysis (Henley et al., 1980).

MEDIA

The soil should be high in organic matter, well drained, and have a pH of 5.5 to 6.0 (Henley et

TABLE II-1 RUMOHRA

Fertilizer rates for leatherleaf fern production grown under 3000 to 5000 fc (600 to 1000 μmol · m^{-2} · s^{-1}) light (Henley et al., 1980). Actual rates used should be based on soil test results.

Element	lb/acre/month (kg/ha/month)	lb/1000 ft²/month (kg/1000 m²/month)
Nitrogen (N)	35–50 (190–265)	0.8–1.2 (19–28)
Phosphorus (P$_2$O$_5$)	15–25 (80–130)	0.3–0.6 (7–14)
Potassium (K$_2$O)	35–50 (190–265)	0.8–1.2 (19–28)
Magnesium (Mg)	4.2–12.5 (22–65)	0.1–0.3 (2.3–6.8)

TABLE II-2 RUMOHRA

Tissue nutrient levels of high-quality leatherleaf fern fronds (Henley et al., 1980).

Element	Desirable Range
Nitrogen	2.0–2.8%
Phosphorus	0.22–0.40%
Potassium	2.3–3.4%
Calcium	0.3–0.7%
Magnesium	0.2–0.4%
Iron	100–400 ppm
Manganese	40–150 ppm
Zinc	30–150 ppm
Copper	10–30 ppm
Boron	25–75 ppm

al., 1980). Soil low in organic matter can be amended with peat; incorporate dolomitic limestone, superphosphate, and micronutrients based on soil test recommendations. Beds should be 4 to 6 in. (10 to 15 cm) above the aisles and 3 to 4 ft (90 to 120 cm) wide. Beds wider than 4 ft (120 cm) increase the difficulty of harvesting for the workers and increase the likelihood of damage from stepping into the beds. Aisles should be 18 to 24 in. (45 to 60 cm) initially but will become more narrow as the rhizomes grow into the aisles. Rhizomes in the aisles can be removed for establishment of new beds (Henley et al., 1980).

HEIGHT CONTROL

Height control is not needed on this cut foliage.

SPACING

See Propagation section for initial spacing of rhizomes or clumps. Beds will fill in over time.

PINCHING AND DISBUDDING

No pinching or disbudding required.

SUPPORT

Leatherleaf fronds have thin but strong stems (stipe) that do not require support.

SCHEDULE AND TIMING

Full production of fern fronds can occur in as little as 1.5 years after planting 5-in. (13-cm) square clumps and using supplemental heat; longer establishment periods are likely (Henley et al., 1980). Beds should be replanted after several years as production declines. A well-maintained leatherleaf fernery with plastic-lined and heated structures should yield between 750,000 and 1,000,000 fronds/acre (0.4 ha). One acre includes approximately 30,000 ft² (2800 m²/ha) of bed space.

INSECTS

A number of insects can be problems on this outdoor-grown crop including caterpillars, grasshoppers, leafhoppers, leatherleaf fern borers, thrips, scale, mealybugs, and termites (Dreistadt, 2001; Henley et al., 1980; Leibee and Stamps, 1999). Several other insect-related pests include spider mites, snails, and slugs. Numerous nematode species can cause problems, of which the lesion nematode, *Pratylenchus penetrans*, is the most serious (Rhoades, 1968). However, the presence of nematodes in the soil does not always mean that damage to the ferns is occurring (Kaplan and Osborne, 1986).

DISEASES

A wide variety of disease can plague fern production including root rot from *Pythium* and *Rhizoctonia* and fungal leaf spots from *Alternaria, Ascochyta, Cercospora, Cylindrocladium,* and *Rhizoctonia* (Chase, 1982; Henley et al., 1980). In 1993 leatherleaf fern anthracnose (*Colletotrichum acutatum*) first appeared in Florida and subsequently became a major disease problem (Strandberg et al., 1997). Control of the disease depends on fungicide applications, sanitation, disease exclusion, and cultural practices. Rust (*Milesina*) and leaf galls (*Taphrina*) can also be problems; avoid overhead irrigation (Dreistadt, 2001).

PHYSIOLOGICAL DISORDERS

Because the leatherleaf fern is grown as a cut foliage, any disorders of the foliage can be serious (Henley et al., 1980). With "red edge" the leaf margins are rust to red colored. This disorder occurs most commonly in the early spring and the cause has not been ascertained. "Fern wilt" or "frond curl" is a postharvest disorder in which the frond wilts 1 to 9 days after harvest, resulting is a significantly shortened vase life compared to normal fronds (Mathur et al., 1982). The disorder is most prevalent in warm weather, July to October in Florida, when ferns are growing rapidly. The typical causes of postharvest wilting, such as pathogens and vascular blockage, are not associated with this disorder. Excessive dehydration after harvest increases the likelihood of fern wilt (Nell et al., 1983). Postharvest antitransparent frond dips had no effect on frond wilt (Nell et al., 1985).

POSTHARVEST

Only mature, dark green fronds are harvested (Henley et al., 1980). Immature fronds are easily damaged and will not have the proper postharvest life of 1 to 4 weeks. The stipes (stems) are cut as close to the rhizome as possible to avoid leaving sharp stumps that may later injure workers' hands.

Fronds are bundled into groups of 25 during harvest and should be placed in water within an hour, although the actual time may be longer (Henley et al., 1980). Prestorage water stress increases the chance of frond curl, which can occur within 1 day of harvest (Nell et al., 1985). The entire bundle can be immersed in water or the stipes can be placed in water. After hydration, fronds are packed in plastic-lined boxes and cold stored at 34 to 40°F (1 to 4°C) until shipped. Although fronds can be cold stored for up to 4 weeks, storage time should be as short as possible. Fronds can also be dipped in a preventive fungicide if long-term storage is necessary (Marousky and de Wildt, 1982).

The vase life of fronds should be 9 to 28 days, with 7 to 15 days expected (Mathur et al., 1982; Staby, 1994). Vase life varies with the season. The shortest vase life occurred with fronds that emerged June through August and were harvested September through December; the longest vase life occurred with those fronds that emerged December through March and were harvested March through June (Poole et al., 1984). Interestingly, the use of the fungicide chlorothalonil on the plants during production reduced vase life even though no visible phytotoxicity symptoms and no yield reduction occurred (Stamps and McColley, 1997)

Although pulsing fronds for 10 to 15 min with 1000 ppm 8-hydroxyquinoline citrate increased vase life, holding solution either had no effect or a negative effect on vase life (Stamps and Nell, 1986). Leatherleaf fern is not sensitive to ethylene and silver thiosulfate (STS) has no effect on vase life (Staby, 1994; Stamps and Nell, 1986).

KEY POINTS

- Leatherleaf fern (*Rumohra*) is the most commonly used cut foliage in commercial floral arrangements.
- Leatherleaf fern is cultivated in Florida and worldwide, especially in tropical areas where it is native.
- Production occurs mainly outdoors under protective shade structures. Optimum light level for maximum frond production is 3000 to 5000 fc (600 to 1000 μmol $\cdot$ m^{-2} $\cdot$ s^{-1}).

- Plants are grown in beds and are typically propagated by division.
- Numerous insects and diseases can cause problems.
- Vase life is typically 7 to 15 days.
- Fronds should be hydrated immediately after harvest and cold stored at 34 to 40°F (1 to 4°C) until shipped.

BIBLIOGRAPHY

Amaki, W., and H. Higucki. 1991. A possible propagation system of *Nephrolepis, Asplenium, Pteris, Adiantum* and *Rumohra (Arachniodes)* through tissue culture. *Acta Horticulturae* 300:237–243.

Chase, A.R. 1982. Rhizoctonia aerial blight's effects on leatherleaf ferns and pittosporums. *American Nurseryman* 156(4):75–76.

Dreistadt, S.H. 2001. *Integrated Pest Management for Floriculture and Nurseries.* University of California Division of Agriculture and Natural Resources Publication 3402.

Henley, R.W., B. Tjia, and L.L. Loadholtz. 1980. *Commercial Leatherleaf Fern Production in Florida.* Cooperative Extension Service Bulletin 191, Institute of Food and Agricultural Sciences, University of Florida.

Huxley, A., M. Griffiths, and M. Levy. 1992. *Rumohra,* pp. 147–148 in *The New Royal Horticultural Society Dictionary of Gardening,* vol. 4. Stockton Press, New York.

Kaplan, D.T., and L.S. Osborne. 1986. Plant parasitic nematodes associated with leatherleaf fern. *Journal of Nematology* 18:26–30.

Leibee, G.L., and R.H. Stamps. 1999. Biology and management of the Florida fern caterpillar. *Cut Foliage Grower* 14(1):1–4.

Marousky, F.J., and P.P.Q. de Wildt. 1982. Postharvest decay in Florida leatherleaf fern. *Plant Disease* 66:1029–1031.

Mathur, D.D., R.H. Stamps, and C.A. Conover. 1982. Postharvest wilt and yellowing of leatherleaf fern. *Proceedings of the Florida State Horticultural Society* 95:142–143.

Nell, T.A., J.E. Barrett, and R.H. Stamps. 1983. Water relations and frond curl of cut leatherleaf fern. *Journal of the American Society for Horticultural Science* 108:516–519.

Nell, T.A., C.A. Conover, J.E. Barrett, and R.T. Poole. 1985. Effects of pre- and post-harvest antitranspirant applications on vase life of leatherleaf fern. *Scientific Horticulturae* 26:225–230.

Poole, R.T., C.A. Conover, and R.H. Stamps. 1984. Vase life of leatherleaf fern harvested at various times of the year and at various frond ages. *Proceedings of the Florida State Horticultural Society* 97:266–269.

Rhoades, H.L. 1968. Pathogenicity and control of *Pratylenchus penetrans* on leatherleaf fern. *Plant Disease Reporter* 52:383–385.

Schumann, A.W., and H.A. Mills. 1996. Injury of leatherleaf fern and tomato from volatilized ammonia after fertilizer application. *Journal of Plant Nutrition* 19:573–593.

Staby, G. 1994. Leatherleaf, Leatherleaf fern, p. 52 in *Flower & Plant Care Manual.* Society of American Florists, Alexandria, Virginia.

Stamps, R.H. 1991. Cold protection of leatherleaf fern using crop covers and overhead irrigation in shadehouses. *HortScience* 26:862–865.

Stamps, R.H., and C.R. Johnson. 1984. Vesicular-arbuscular mycorrhizal inoculation and fertilizer level affect yield, morphology, chlorophyll content, water uptake and vase life of leatherleaf fern fronds. *Proceedings of the Florida State Horticultural Society* 97:264–266.

Stamps, R.H., and D.W. McColley. 1997. Chlorothalonil fungicides reduce vase life but not yield of leatherleaf fern [*Rumohra adiantiformis* (Forst.) Ching]. *HortScience* 32:1099–1101.

Stamps, R.H., and T.A. Nell. 1986. Pre- and poststorage treatment of cut leatherleaf fern fronds with floral preservatives. *Proceedings of the Florida State Horticultural Society* 99:260–263.

Stamps, R.H., T.A. Nell, and J.E. Barrett. 1994. Production temperatures influence growth and physiology of leatherleaf fern. *HortScience* 29:67–70.

Strandberg, J.O., R.H. Stamps, and D.J. Norman. 1997. *Fern Anthracnose: A Guide for Disease Management.* University of Florida Technical Bulletin 900.

Saintpaulia

INTRODUCTION

Common name: African violet.

Scientific names: *Saintpaulia ionantha* Wendl. is the commonly used scientific name, but the species *S. confusa* B.L. Burtt has also been used to develop modern cultivars (Huxley et al., 1992).

Family and related taxa: Gesneriaceae Dumort. This family includes numerous popular indoor plants. Other Gesneriaceae grown in large commercial quantities include *Achimenes*, *Sinningia*, and *Streptocarpus*.

Origin: Coastal Tanzania in eastern Africa (Bailey and Bailey, 1976).

Uses and current status: African violets have become one of the world's most popular commercial potted flowering plants (Bailey and Bailey, 1976; Strømme, 1985). Most African violets are sold in 4-in. (10-cm) pots.

African violets have a rosette habit; the ovate leaves and petioles are hairy. The flowers with five rounded petals are born on short peduncles. The peduncles are shorter than the leaves for *S. confusa* and longer for *S. ionantha* (Bailey and Bailey, 1976). The inflorescence arises from the leaf axils as the terminal meristem is always vegetative.

CULTIVARS

There are many cultivars from all over the world. Flower colors include white, red, purple, violet, blue, pink, bicolors, and even yellow. The flowers may be double and the petals may have fringed to fluted edges. Plant habits include "miniature" (genetic dwarfs), "vin-ing," and "standard" types. Leaf edging and leaf coloring have also been modified in some cultivars (Bailey and Bailey, 1976; Strømme, 1985).

PROPAGATION

Seed propagation is used only by breeders. Leaf cuttings are used commercially (Fig. II-1 Saintpaulia). The best propagation material is mature leaves from 2-month-old plants, prior to becoming reproductive. The petiole should be 0.4 to 2 in. (1 to 5 cm) long and rooting hormones are not needed (von Hentig, 1976). Leaves are placed in flats, approximately 17/ft^2 (600/m^2), which are held under high humidity (Christensson, 1986). Scott and Marston (1967) found that the rooting medium should be 75°F (24°C) and the air 64°F (18°C).

After 8 to 12 weeks, 1-in. (2.5-cm) plantlets can be harvested. Experimentally, benzylamino (tetrahydropyranyl) purine (PBA) at 100 ppm and gibberellic acid (GA$_3$) at 50 ppm sprayed together on leaf cuttings increased the number of plantlets and leaves produced during propagation (Sanderson and McGuire, 1988). For uniformity of plantlet size, some propagators carefully harvest only the largest plantlets, replant leaves, and repeat the cycle 2 weeks later for a total of three harvests. The young plants can be placed in plugs, grown for 2 to 6 weeks, and sold or transplanted into 4-in. (10-cm) pots.

In vitro propagation is used to quickly increase new cultivars or to propagate chimeras not capable of being maintained by leaf cuttings (Bilkey and Cocking, 1981; Bilkey et al., 1978; Cassells and Plunkett, 1984; Cooke, 1977; Larson, 1985; Lercari et al., 1986; Lineberger and

FIGURE II-1 SAINTPAULIA *Saintpaulia* leaves in propagation. Note development of new shoots at leaf bases.

TABLE II-I SAINTPAULIA

Effect of temperatures and irradiance levels on number of *Saintpaulia* inflorescenses and total number of flower buds per inflorescence at a constant temperature (Hildrum and Kristoffersen, 1969). Fluorescent lamps were on for 16 hr and off for 8 hr.

Light Intensity	Temperature			
	59°F (15°C)		64°F (18°C)	
	Inflorescence	Buds	Inflorescence	Buds
1200 fc (240 μmol $\cdot$ m^{-2} $\cdot$ s^{-1})	2.3	2.9	6.8	5.2
800 fc (160 μmol $\cdot$ m^{-2} $\cdot$ s^{-1})	1.4	1.9	3.6	3.5
400 fc (80 μmol $\cdot$ m^{-2} $\cdot$ s^{-1})	0.3	2.2	2.9	2.5

Druckenbrod, 1985; Peary et al., 1988; Scott and Marston, 1967; Smith and Norris, 1983; Start and Cumming, 1976; Vaquez et al., 1977).

FLOWERING CONTROL AND DORMANCY

Because flower formation occurs in the axils of leaves, environmental conditions favorable for vegetative growth will result in rapid and continuous flowering (Strømme, 1985). African violets are day-neutral plants and flowering is controlled by the total accumulated photosynthetic irradiance (Hanchey, 1955; Hildrum and Kristoffersen, 1969; Post, 1942) (Table II-1 Saintpaulia). Application of GA$_3$ can be used to increase the number of flower stalks/plant and increase flower size (Kuehny, 2001). Two 10-ppm spray applications are made 14 days apart to plants that are 4 to 5 months old; older or younger plants do not respond well.

TEMPERATURE

The optimal temperature for both day and night in the greenhouse is 69 to 79°F (21 to 26°C) (Fischer, 1991). Optimum temperature is also dependent on the light intensity and duration and stage of plant growth (see Light, next). Day temperatures above 85°F (29°C) will induce premature flowering and poor growth. Temperatures less than 65°F (18°C) will slow growth.

LIGHT

Laurie et al. (1969) and Post (1949) stated that optimum irradiance was 1000 to 1500 fc (200 to 300 μmol $\cdot$ m^{-2} $\cdot$ s^{-1}) for adult plants and 500 to 800 fc (100 to 160 μmol $\cdot$ m^{-2} $\cdot$ s^{-1}) for young vegetative plants. Floral initiation and development occurred at 500 to 1300 fc (100 to 260 μmol $\cdot$ m^{-2} $\cdot$ s^{-1}) of natural light. No flowers were initiated or developed if light levels were at or below 300 fc (60 μmol $\cdot$ m^{-2} $\cdot$ s^{-1}) (Stinson and Laurie, 1954). Plants grown under fluorescent light systems were superior to greenhouse-grown plants because leaves were heavier and darker green (Strømme, 1985). Supplementing natural daylight during winter is an accepted practice and should be used when winter light levels fall below 460 fc (90 μmol $\cdot$ m^{-2} $\cdot$ s^{-1}) for 12 hr (4 mol $\cdot$ m^{-2} $\cdot$ day^{-1}) (Brown-Faust and Heins, 1991; Strømme, 1985). High-pressure sodium and fluorescent lamps can be used (Faust and Heins, 1994). Six hours of lighting at 350 fc (70 μmol $\cdot$ m^{-2} $\cdot$ s^{-1}) or 4.5 hr at 500 fc (100 μmol $\cdot$ m^{-2} $\cdot$ s^{-1}) is adequate to ensure a minimum of 1.5 mol $\cdot$ m^{-2} $\cdot$ day^{-1}. Interestingly, *in vitro*-propagated plantlets grew best under filtered light with a reduced red:far-red light ratio and no flowering occurred on plants grown without far-red light (Hagiladi and Raviv, 1992).

Maximum flowers per plant were produced when plants were grown with fluorescent lighting of 800 to 1200 fc (160 to 240 μmol $\cdot$ m^{-2} $\cdot$ s^{-1}) for 16 hr of light at 75°F (24°C). These environmental conditions were also conducive for maximum plant weights. High temperatures of 81°F (27°C) at 1200 fc (240 μmol $\cdot$ m^{-2} $\cdot$ s^{-1}) resulted in poor growth and chlorotic, crisp, and curled leaves with necrotic spots (Hildrum and Kristoffersen, 1969). With constant 24-hr light, 8 hr should be at 64°F (18°C) and 16 hr at 75°F (24°C) at a lower light level. When using natural light, a 50% reduction in light levels is recommended from March to September and the temperature should be 70 to 75°F (21 to 24°C) (Hildrum and Kristoffersen, 1969).

Temperature					
70°F (21°C)		75°F (24°C)		81/75°F (27/24°C)[a]	
Inflorescence	Buds	Inflorescence	Buds	Inflorescence	Buds
6.0	6.8	5.1	9.1	3.5	5.5
5.8	4.8	6.6	6.9	4.5	10.0
4.9	4.6	5.3	4.7	4.1	6.6

[a]*Light/dark.*

An interaction occurs between light and temperature in regard to the number of flower buds per inflorescences and the number of inflorescences (Hildrum and Kristoffersen, 1969). Table II-1 Saintpaulia indicates that optimum conditions for one factor are not conducive for the other; for example, 1200 fc (240 μmol $\cdot$ m^{-2} $\cdot$ s^{-1}) and constant 64°F (18°C) produced the greatest number of inflorescences, while 800 fc (160 μmol $\cdot$ m^{-2} $\cdot$ s^{-1}) at 81/75°F (27/24°C) day/night temperatures produced the greatest number of flower buds per inflorescence.

WATER

Subirrigation methods such as capillary mats or ebb-and-flow are generally used and overhead watering systems avoided (Brown-Faust and Heins, 1991; Payne and Adam, 1980; Poole et al., 1986). African violets are sensitive to excessive watering and the medium should be allowed to go through a drying cycle. However, plants should not be allowed to wilt because permanent damage will occur and plants may not grow out of the damage. If water is 9 to 14°F (5 to 8°C) cooler than the leaf, the leaves develop cream-colored blotches, spots, or streaks (Fig. II-2 Saintpaulia). Water should be heated to near 79°F (26°C) to prevent spotting if surface irrigation is used (Brown-Faust and Heins, 1991; Raabe, 1957).

CARBON DIOXIDE

Plants respond favorably to supplementary CO_2. Andersen (1983) stated that 900 ppm CO_2 was adequate, while Strømme (1985) and Vogelezang (1988) stated 800 to 1000 ppm CO_2 should be used. With the use of CO_2, lower irradiance levels can be used. However, Brown-Faust and Heins (1991) stated 400 to 500 ppm

FIGURE II-2 SAINTPAULIA Cream-colored spotting, splotching, and rings due to application of cold water to *Saintpaulia* foliage.

CO_2 improved growth and increased flower bud number. At CO_2 levels higher than 500 ppm, leaves can become very brittle and easily break or crack, making shipping difficult.

NUTRITION

Saintpaulias have relatively low nutritional requirements. If the medium has been enriched or amended, no fertilizer is used the first week or until a root system is established after transplanting (Brown-Faust and Heins, 1991; Vogelezang, 1988). Recommended medium EC levels are 0.5 to 1.0 dS $\cdot$ m^{-1} with a maximum of 1.7 dS $\cdot$ m^{-1} for finished plants (Brown-Faust and Heins, 1991; Faust and Heins, 1994).

Foliar nutrient levels for high-quality plants are listed in Chapter 6, Nutrition, Table 6-4. The nutrient regimes used vary from 50 ppm N and K constant liquid fertilization to weekly applications of 200 ppm N (Brown-Faust and Heins, 1991). Various formulations and rates of slow-release encapsulated fertilizers as topdressings have been used. Few differences existed between 13–6–11 and 14–6–12 N–P–K when 3.8 to 4.5 lb/yd³ (2.25 to 2.7 kg · m⁻³) was used in the winter and 4.5 to 6.0 lb/yd³ (2.7 to 3.6 kg · m⁻³) in the summer (Payne and Adam, 1980; Poole et al., 1986).

MEDIA

The medium must be well drained and have a pH of 5.8 to 6.5. The root system of *Saintpaulia* is fine and fibrous and plants thrive in a highly organic medium. Various media can be used such as 1:1 peat:perlite (Hildrum and Kristoffersen, 1969), 100% peat (Vogelezang, 1988), and various commercial mixes (Conover and Poole, 1981). Vogelezang (1988) amended peat medium with 1.26 lb/yd³ (0.75 kg · m⁻³) superphosphate and 0.17 lb/yd³ (0.1 kg · m⁻³) micronutrient mix.

HEIGHT CONTROL

No height control needed.

SPACING

When plantlets are harvested after 12 weeks in propagation, they can be placed in 2-in. (5-cm) plug cells for 30 to 40 days, then transplanted into 4-in. (10-cm) finishing pots. They can be held pot-to-pot until leaves touch and then spaced 4 plants/ft² (43/m²).

PINCHING AND DISBUDDING

No pinching or disbudding needed.

SUPPORT

No support required.

SCHEDULE AND TIMING

In general, 12 weeks are required for plantlet production, 30 to 40 days for plantlets to develop into plugs, and 10 weeks for flowering in 4-in. (10-cm) pots (Brown-Faust and Heins, 1991). Total crop time from leaf cutting to finished plant will vary from 29 to 36 weeks.

Faust and Heins (1993, 1994) used plant growth modeling techniques to aid in scheduling and timing a crop for specific holidays. The maximum leaf unfolding rate was 0.27 leaves/day, which occurred at 77°F (25°C) and 10 mol · m⁻² · day⁻¹. As the light level decreased from 10 to 1 mol · m⁻² · day⁻¹ the optimum temperature dropped to 73°F (23°C)

and the leaf unfolding rate to 0.18. The appearance of a visible inflorescence was predicted by measuring the leaf-blade length. The days required for a bud to develop to an open flower were predicted in relation to the average daily temperature. The days from leaf emergence to first open flower ranged from 86 to 55 days as the temperature increased from 64 to 79°F (18 to 26°C). A meter based on inflorescence size was developed to aid in timing and scheduling of this crop (see Fig. II-3 Saintpaulia). Time to flower from potting of plug decreased from 64 to 59 days when root zone heating of 74 to 77°F (23.5 to 25°C) was used with an air temperature of 64 to 69°F (18 to 21°C) (Vogelezang, 1988).

INSECTS

Thrips, mealybugs, and cyclamen mites are a concern (Kimmins, 1992).

DISEASES

African violets can have problems with *Botrytis* blight, *Pythium* or *Phytophthora* crown rot, and *Rhizoctonia* root and stem rot. Powdery mildew (*Oidium*) can be a problem in the spring and tends to affect the flowers and older leaves (Horst, 1990). Bacterial blight (*Erwinia chrysanthemi*) and several viruses (impatiens necrotic spot, tobacco mosaic, and tomato spotted wilt) have also been reported (Dreistadt, 2001).

PHYSIOLOGICAL DISORDERS

Single-stem plants are preferred to multiple crown plants in North America. More multiple crown plants tend to develop when young plantlets are placed too deep into the medium and adventitious shoots develop along the stem. See Water section for leaf spotting disorder due to cold water application.

Plants with small brittle, sometime chlorotic, leaves in the center can be due to excessively high light levels, low production temperatures, or overfertilization (Hamrick, 2003). Brown centers and excessively hairy plants can be caused by water in the crown or overfertilization.

POSTHARVEST

If production schedules are too advanced, temperature can be lowered to 55 to 59°F (13 to 15°C); plants can survive at 55°F (13°C) for 3 weeks, but damage and death can occur at temperatures of 50°F (10°C) and lower (Brown-Faust and Heins, 1991). However, according to

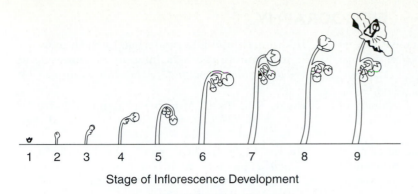

FIGURE II-3 SAINTPAULIA
Inflorescence development meter for *Saintpaulia* from buds 0.06 in. (2 mm) in size to flowering at various temperatures (Faust and Heins, 1994).

Stage of Inflorescence Development

Temp. °F (°C)	Number of Days from VB to Anthesis							
	Stage of Inflorescence Development							
	1	2	3	4	5	6	7	8
64 (18)	40	35	30	24	20	12	6	2
68 (20)	37	33	28	23	19	11	6	2
72 (22)	34	30	26	21	17	10	6	2
75 (24)	31	27	23	19	16	10	6	2
79 (26)	28	25	21	18	15	9	5	2

Tijskens et al. (1996), the optimum temperature for long-term storage was 52°F (11°C).

Light acclimatization can occur and new acclimatized leaves can develop. For example, plants grown at 1350 fc (202 μmol $\cdot$ m^{-2} $\cdot$ s^{-1}) initially ceased to flower when moved to 210 fc (32 μmol $\cdot$ m^{-2} $\cdot$ s^{-1}) but flowering commenced again after 3 months; the light was provided by fluorescent lamps for 12 hr/day (Conover and Poole, 1981). Nutrition levels had no influence on postharvest performance.

African violets are highly sensitive to ethylene with negative effects apparent from 0.05 ppm (Willumsen and Fjeld, 1995). Plants are typically harvested when five flowers are open and may be shipped at 55 to 61°F (13 to 16°C).

KEY POINTS

- African violet is one of the world's most popular potted flowering plants.
- Propagation is by leaf cuttings; seed and *in vitro* methods are primarily used by breeders.
- Mature leaves are inserted in moist medium, which should be held at 75°F (24°C).
- Plantlets form after 8 to 12 weeks.
- Plants are day neutral; flowering is controlled by temperature and light intensity.
- Optimum day and night temperatures are both 69 to 79°F (21 to 26°C).
- Water 9 to 14°F (5 to 8°C) or more cooler than the plant tissue will injure the leaves; irrigation water should be near 79°F (26°C).
- Plants die if held at 50°F (10°C) or below.
- Optimum light intensity is 800 to 1200 fc (160 to 240 μmol $\cdot$ m^{-2} $\cdot$ s^{-1}) but varies with the day length.

BIBLIOGRAPHY

Andersen, H. 1983. Development of standard growing programme for pot plants. *Acta Horticulturae* 147:131–134.

Bailey, L.H., and E.Z. Bailey. 1976. *Saintpaulia*, p. 994 in *Hortus Third: A Concise Dictionary of Plants Cultivated in the United States and Canada.* Macmillan, New York.

Bilkey, P.C., and E.C. Cocking. 1981. Increased plant vigor by *in vitro* propagation of *Saintpaulia ionantha* Wendl. from sub-epidermal tissue. *HortScience* 16:643–644.

Bilkey, P.C., B.H. McCown, and A.C. Hildebrandt. 1978. Micropropagation of African violet from petiole cross-section. *HortScience* 13:37–38.

Brown-Faust, J., and R. Heins. 1991. Cultural notes on African violets. *Greenhouse Grower* 9(2):74, 76–77.

Cassells, A.C., and A. Plunkett. 1984. Production and growth analysis of plants from leaf cuttings, and from tissue culture of disks from mature leaves and young axenic leaves of African violet (*Saintpaulia ionantha* Wendl.). *Scientia Horticulturea* 23:361–369.

Christensson, H. 1986. *Odling av Saintpaulia.* Trädgård 309, Swedish University of Agricultural Sciences Research Information Centre.

Conover, C.A., and R.T. Poole. 1981. Light acclimatization of African violet. *HortScience* 16:92–93.

Cooke, R.C. 1977. Tissue culture propagation of African violets. *HortScience* 12:549.

Dreistadt, S.H. 2001. *Integrated Pest Management for Floriculture and Nurseries.* University of California Division of Agriculture and Natural Resources Publication 3402.

Faust, J.E., and R.D. Heins. 1993. Modeling leaf development of the African violet (*Saintpaulia ionantha* Wendl.). *Journal of the American Society for Horticultural Science* 118:747–751.

Faust, J.E., and R.D. Heins. 1994. Modeling inflorescence development of the African violet (*Saintpaulia ionantha* Wendl.). *Journal of the American Society for Horticultural Science* 119:727–734.

Fischer, A.W. 1991. *Saintpaulia*, pp. 759–762 in *Ball Redbook*, 15th ed., V. Ball, editor. George J. Ball, West Chicago, Illinois.

Hagiladi, A., and M. Raviv. 1992. Modified sunlight affects growth and flowering of *Saintpaulia ionantha* H. and *Peperomia grisco-argenta* Yuncker. *HortScience* 27:999–1001.

Hamrick, D. 2003. *Saintpaulia*, pp. 625–627 in *Ball Redbook*, vol. 2, 17th ed. Ball Publishing, Batavia, Illinois.

Hanchey, R.H. 1955. Effects of fluorescent and natural light on vegetative and reproductive growth on *Saintpaulia*. *Proceedings of the American Society for Horticultural Science* 66:378–382.

Hildrum, H., and T. Kristoffersen. 1969. The effect of temperature and light intensity on flowering in *Saintpaulia ionantha*. *Acta Horticulturae* 14:249–255.

Horst, R.K. 1990. African violet, pp. 521–522 in *Westcott's Plant Disease Handbook*, 5th ed. Van Nostrand Reinhold, New York.

Huxley, A., M. Griffiths, and M. Levy. 1992. *Saintpaulia*, pp. 160–161 in *The New Royal Horticultural Society Dictionary of Gardening*, vol. 4. Stockton Press, New York.

Kimmins, R.K. 1992. *Saintpaulia ionantha*—African violet, pp. 293–296 in *Introduction to Floriculture*, R.A. Larson, editor. Academic Press, San Diego, California.

Kuehny, J. 2001. Gloxinias and other gesneriads, pp. 93–95 in *Tips on Regulating Growth of Floriculture Crops*, M.L. Gaston, L.A. Kunkle, P.S. Konjoian, and M.F. Wilt, editors. Ohio Florists' Association Services, Columbus, Ohio.

Larson, R.A. 1985. African violet chimeras: A practical use of micropropagation. *North Carolina Flower Growers Bulletin* 29(6):9–10.

Laurie, A., D.C. Kiplinger, and K.S. Nelson. 1969. African violets (*Saintpaulia ionantha*—Gesneriaceae), pp. 377–381 in *Commercial Flower Forcing.* McGraw-Hill, New York.

Lercari, B., F. Tognoni, G. Anselmo, and D. Chapel. 1986. Photocontrol of *in vitro* bud differentiation in *Saintpaulia ionantha* leaves and *Lycopersicon esculentum* cotyledons. *Physiologie Plantarum* 67:340–344.

Lineberger, R.D., and M. Druckenbrod. 1985. Chimeral nature of the pinwheel flowering African violets (*Saintpaulia*, Gesneriaceae). *American Journal of Botany* 72:1204–1212.

Payne, R.N., and S.M. Adam. 1980. Influence of rate and placement of slow release fertilizer on pot plants of African violet grown with capillary mat watering. *HortScience* 15:607–609.

Peary, J.S., R.D. Lineberger, T.J. Malinich, and M.K. Wertz. 1988. Stability of leaf variegation in *Saintpaulia ionantha* during in vitro propagation and during chimeral separation of a pinwheel flower form. *American Journal of Botany* 75:603–608.

Poole, R.T., C.A. Conner, and Y. Ozeri. 1986. Response of African violets to fertilizer source and rate. *HortScience* 21:454–455.

Post, K. 1942. Effects of day length and temperature on growth and flowering of some florist crops. *Cornell University Agriculture Experiment Station Bulletin* 787:1–10.

Post, K. 1949. *Saintpaulia*, pp. 804–805 in *Florist Crop Production and Marketing.* Orange Judd Publishing, New York.

Raabe, R.D. 1957. Physiological breakdown of chlorophyll in the Gesneriaceae. *Phytopathology* 47:28.

Sanderson, K.C., and J. McGuire. 1988. Growth regulator sprays during propagation increase African violet crowns and leaves. *HortScience* 23:1085.

Scott, M., and M.E. Marston. 1967. Effects of mist and basal temperature on the regeneration of *Saintpaulia ionantha* Wendl. from leaf cuttings. *Horticultural Research* 7:50–60.

Smith, R.H., and R.E. Norris. 1983. In vitro propagation of African violet chimeras. *HortScience* 18:436–437.

Start, N.D., and B.G. Cumming. 1976. *In vitro* propagation of *Saintpaulia ionantha*. *HortScience* 11:204–206.

Stinson, R.F., and A. Laurie. 1954. The effect of light intensity on the initiation and development of flower buds in *Saintpaulia ionantha*. *Proceedings of the American Society for Horticultural Science* 64:459–467.

Strømme, E. 1985. Gesneriaceae, pp. 48–52 in *Handbook of Flowering*, vol. III, A.H. Halevy, editor. CRC Press, Boca Raton, Florida.

Tijskens, L.M.M., M. Sloof, E.C. Wilkinson, and W.G. van Doorn. 1996. A model of the effects of temperature and time on the acceptability of potted plants stored in darkness. *Postharvest Biology and Technology* 8:293–305.

Vaquez, A.M., M.R. Davey, and K.C. Short. 1977. Organogenesis in culture of *Saintpaulia ionantha*. *Acta Horticulturae* 78:249–258.

Vogelezang, J.V.M. 1988. Effect of root-zone heating on growth flowering and keeping quality of *Saintpaulia*. *Scientia Horticulturae* 34:101–113.

von Hentig, W.U. 1976. Results of propagation with leaf cuttings of *Saintpaulia ionantha*. *Acta Horticulturae* 64:55–63.

Willumsen, K., and T. Fjeld. 1995. The sensitivity of some flowering potted plants to exogenous ethylene. *Acta Horticulturae* 405:362–367.

Schlumbergera and Hatiora

INTRODUCTION

Common names: The following species are known collectively as holiday cactus: (1) Thanksgiving cactus, (2) Christmas cactus, and (3) Easter cactus.

Scientific names: (1) *Schlumbergera truncata* (Haw.) Moran., synonym: *Zygocactus truncata*; (2) *Schlumbergera* ×*buckleyi* (Ti Moore) Tjaden. [*S. truncata* ×*S. russelliana* (Hooks.) Britt. and Rose.], synonym: *S. bridgesii*; and (3) *Hatiora gaertneri* (Reg.) Barthlott., synonym: *Rhipsalidopsis gaertneri* or *S. gaertneri* (Huxley et al., 1992).

Family and related taxa: Cactaceae Juss. The Cactaceae family contains thousands of succulent species known as cacti, which are most common in warm, dry climates; many cacti are grown as indoor and outdoor garden ornamentals.

Origin: All three holiday cactus species are from Brazil.

Uses and current status: Holiday cactus are suitable for hanging baskets (pendulous types), 4-in. (10-cm) pots (semipendulous types), or 3-in. (7.5-cm) pots (erect types) (Boyle, 1994a). All three species make colorful potted plants which adapt well in the home and reflower with modest care.

These three holiday cacti are confusing due to frequent taxonomic name changes, interspecific hybrids, and similar appearance. All three species consist of modified stems called *phylloclades*, which are flat leaflike structures that photosynthesize. *Hatiora* differ from *Schlumbergera* in that the *Hatiora* flower perianth tube is shorter, the stamens are separated, and the stigmatic lobes are spreading. Further, *Hatiora* phylloclades have shallow marginal indentations with obvious bristle-like spines, while the *Schlumbergera* do not have obvious "spines." The main difference between the Thanksgiving cactus (*S. truncata*) and the Christmas cactus

(*S.* ×*buckleyi*) is that the former has strongly toothed or pointed edges along the margins of the phylloclades; the latter has smooth-edged margins (Bailey and Bailey, 1976; Rünger and Poole, 1985; Wilkins and Rünger, 1985).

CULTIVARS

Each of the three species includes numerous cultivars, many of which are patented. Breeding continues to occur in Europe, Japan, and North America. The colors of Thanksgiving and Christmas cacti include white, rose, white and rose, salmon, salmon-pink, and violet on 2.5- to 3-in. (6.5- to 7.5-cm) long flowers (Bailey and Bailey, 1976). The Easter cactus flowers are mainly bright red, 2.5 to 3.5 in. (6.5 to 9 cm) across. Besides flower color, the time to flower from the beginning of SD, as well as "leaf" and flower form, vigor, plant habit (erect, semipendulous, or pendulous), and ethylene sensitivity vary among the species and cultivars. Intergeneric hybrids between *Schlumbergera* and *Hatiora* have been made (Boyle and Idnurm, 2003). While these hybrids currently have little commercial potential, future efforts may be more useful.

PROPAGATION

Seed propagation is used only in breeding programs (Boyle, 1994b, 2001; Boyle et al., 1995). *In vitro* culture is possible but not used commercially (Boyle and Marcotrigiano, 1997). Mature phylloclades are used commercially as cuttings. These single-stem sections are removed from vegetative stock by twisting each section 180° and separating it from the mother plant. Avoid using phylloclades from close to the medium as these are more likely to be contaminated with soil-borne pathogens than phylloclades from higher up on the plant. *Schlumbergera* cuttings can be stored 24 to 48 hr at 40°F (4°C) to enhance rooting (Boyle, 1991b, 1994a; Madsen and Madsen, 1994). Phylloclades can also be stored for up to 3 months at 50 to 59°F (10 to 15°C) and 85 to 95% relative humidity (Boyle, 1997a). *Hatiora* phylloclades can be stored for up to 6 to 8 weeks at 43 to 46°F (6 to 8°C) with constant, high humidity (J. Hansson, personal communication).

Two to four cuttings are inserted into each cell in a 60- to 72-cell tray or in a 1.5- to 2-in. (3.5- to 5-cm) pot. When direct sticking into the final container, use three segments per 3- to 4-in. (8- to 10-cm) pot, four per 4.5-in. (11-cm) pot, and seven per 6-in. (15-cm) pot (Boyle, 1997a). Well-drained medium is a requirement

and medium temperature should be held at 70 to 75°F (21 to 24°C). To maintain stem turgidity, routine fogging by hand or timed intermittent mist can be used. The medium should be kept moist, but not overwatered (Boyle, 1994a; Madsen and Madsen, 1994). Unrooted stem segments or rooted cuttings in plugs can be purchased from commercial propagators. During stock plant production and cutting propagation, use LD to encourage vegetative growth.

FLOWERING CONTROL AND DORMANCY

SCHLUMBERGERA

Schlumbergera is considered a SD plant. For rapid floral initiation, the critical night length is between 11 and 14 hr for plants grown at 70 to 72/64 to 65°F (21 to 22/18°C) day/night temperatures (Boyle, 1997b). Commercially, 13 to 16 hr or naturally long night lengths are used. At 55°F (13°C) flowering will occur at any photoperiod. As the temperature increases, the photoperiod necessary for flower initiation is shortened; at 70 to 75°F (21 to 24°C), no flowering occurs regardless of photoperiod (Roberts and Struckmeyer, 1939). Interestingly, Poole (1973) flowered plants in central Florida in the summer under 9-hr SD; 72°F (22°C) was the minimum temperature and 90°F (32°C) was the maximum tested. Under 9-hr day lengths the optimum temperature for maximum flower number is 68°F (20°C) (Erwin et al., 1990).

For floral initiation under SD, use 55 to 59°F (13 to 15°C) night temperatures. Visible buds appear in 3 to 4 weeks. After flower initiation, night temperatures can be increased to 65°F (18°C) (Boyle, 1994a; Madsen and Madsen, 1994). Once flower buds are visible, Heins et al. (1981) have shown that development is a function of temperatures ranging from 54 to 75°F (12 to 24°C) (see Table II-1 *Schlumbergera* and *Hatiora*). Night or day temperatures greater than 75°F (24°C) can result in flower abortion.

Flowering can also be accomplished through natural environmental conditions (Boyle, 1997b). In northern areas, flowering typically occurs in mid-November at 62 to 65°F (17 to 18°C) nights and in southern areas in early to mid-December. Long days can be used to delay flowering of cultivars that flower too early.

Stock plants and cuttings must be grown under LD using night interruptions of light from 2200 to 0200 HR at 5 to 10 fc (1 to 2 μmol $\cdot$ m^{-2} $\cdot$ s^{-1}). During vegetative growth use 63 to 70°F (17 to 21°C) temperature and LD. How-

TABLE II-I SCHLUMBERGERA AND HATIORA

Time to open flower for *Schlumbergera truncata* grown at various average daily temperatures based on initial flower bud length (Lange and Heins, 1992). Plants will flower faster than indicated if the following temperatures are used as night temperatures and a higher day temperature is used.

Bud Length in. (mm)	Temperature °F (°C)				
	54 (12)	59 (15)	65 (18)	70 (21)	75 (24)
	Days to Flower				
0.04 (1)	113	70	50	39	32
0.08 (2)	94	58	41	32	26
0.12 (3)	84	51	37	28	23
0.16 (4)	76	47	33	26	21
0.20 (5)	70	43	31	24	19
0.24 (6)	65	40	28	22	18
0.28 (7)	61	37	27	21	17
0.31 (8)	58	35	25	19	16
0.35 (9)	54	33	24	18	15
0.39 (10)	52	31	22	17	14
0.43 (11)	49	30	21	17	14
0.47 (12)	47	28	20	16	13
0.51 (13)	45	27	19	15	12
0.55 (14)	43	26	18	14	12
0.59 (15)	41	25	18	14	11
0.79 (20)	33	20	14	11	9
1.00 (25)	27	16	12	9	7
1.18 (30)	23	13	9	7	6
1.57 (40)	15	8	6	5	4
1.97 (50)	9	5	3	3	3
2.36 (60)	4	2	1	1	1

ever, under 9-hr day lengths the optimum temperature for phylloclade production is 86/50°F (30/10°C) day/night (Erwin et al., 1990).

HATIORA

Although *Hatiora* should be thought of as a SD/LD plant, flower induction is enhanced by 47 to 55°F (8 to 13°C) night temperatures during the SD photoperiod (Boyle, 1990, 1991a; Boyle et al., 1988; Madsen and Madsen, 1994; Wilkins and Rünger, 1985). The optimal duration of this cold treatment varies with the cultivar from 4 to 12 weeks; most cultivars require only 4 to 6 weeks. Plants flower more profusely when grown under SD prior to the cold treatment (Rohwer and Heins, 2001). The SD pretreatment is especially important if the cold treatment is only 4 weeks long. At 50°F (10°C) flower induction will occur even if plants are grown under continuous irradiation, but the flower numbers will be reduced compared with plants grown under SD. At 63°F (17°C) floral induction is low, even if plants are in SD. High

light during flower induction enhances the number of flowers initiated.

Floral development is enhanced by LD and warm temperatures after the SD and cold treatment. Long days increase the number and uniformity of flowers that will develop. Depending on the geographic location (northern Europe or southern United States), either HID lamps or incandescent lights are used. Regardless of the lamp type, light can be used from 2200 to 0200 HR as a night break or from sundown to 2200 HR as a day continuation. A 16-hr day of supplemental light at 400 fc (80 μmol · m^{-2} · s^{-1}) will ensure maximum flower numbers (Boyle, 1991a, b, 1992; Boyle et al., 1988; Madsen and Madsen, 1994; Wilkins and Rünger, 1985). The appropriate temperature for flower development is 65 to 70°F (18 to 21°C).

TEMPERATURE

SCHLUMBERGERA

Temperature and photoperiod interact for flower induction (see Flowering Control and

Dormancy). Once flowering is induced, a wide range of temperatures can be used, but never nights over 75°F (24°C) (Heins et al., 1981). However, plants grow slowly when the average daily temperature goes below 60°F (16°C) (Boyle, 1997a).

HATIORA

As with *Schlumbergera*, temperature and photoperiod interact for flower induction (see Flowering Control and Dormancy). After flower buds are visible, plants are forced at 65 to 70°F (18 to 21°C) and LD for rapid flower development (Wilkins and Rünger, 1985). Boyle (1995b) noted that forcing at 50°F (10°C) produced more flowers than at 64°F (18°C).

LIGHT

Many cultivars of both genera will develop yellow to whitish leaves if exposed to strong sunlight [greater than 3500 fc (700 μmol · m^{-2} · s^{-1})] and/or high temperature (Madsen and Madsen, 1994). However, light should not be reduced in late autumn, winter, and early spring. The optimal light level is between 1500 and 3000 fc (300 and 600 μmol · m^{-2} · s^{-1}) (Boyle, 1991b, 1994a; Madsen and Madsen, 1994). If HID lighting is used during the LD floral development phase with *Hatiora*, 16 hr at 400 fc (80μmol · m^{-2} · s^{-1}) is adequate to ensure maximum flower numbers (Boyle, 1991a).

WATER

Managing the moisture level is the primary way to control disease with *Schlumbergera* and *Hatiora*. Allow the phylloclades to dry out slightly during propagation and between irrigations. However, plants should not become severely water stressed. Heins et al. (1981) found that water stress during floral initiation reduced the number of flower buds, which counters the myth that water stress enhances floral initiation. Low EC water should be used if possible (Boyle, 1991b, 1994a; Madsen and Madsen, 1994).

CARBON DIOXIDE

No data on carbon dioxide were found.

NUTRITION

Boyle (1991b, 1994a, 1997b) stresses that the nutritional requirements for holiday cacti are modest and 150 to 200 ppm N level is adequate. Nutrient levels can be reduced by half if plants are subirrigated. Leaching should occur if medium EC is high. Adequate micronutrients must be supplied and magnesium requirements are high for these species. Media pH lower than 5.5 may induce iron and manganese toxicity (see Physiological Disorders). Foliar nutrient levels for quality plants are listed in Chapter 6, Nutrition, Table 6-4.

Routine soil testing every 4 to 6 weeks is recommended. The EC and pH can be easily monitored in the greenhouse. Fertilizer levels should be slowly decreased and eliminated 1 to 2 months prior to flower induction treatments to increase the percentage of phylloclades that will flower (Boyle, 1991b, 1994a; Madsen and Madsen, 1994; Penningsfeld, 1972).

MEDIA

Several media have been used including 92% peat and 8% calcine clay and 60% peat and 40% perlite. A pH of 5.7 to 6.5 is optimal (Boyle, 1994a; Madsen and Madsen, 1994). If medium pH drops below 5.5, iron and manganese toxicity may occur (see Physiological Disorders). Madsen and Madsen (1994) stressed that the production is long term and the medium structure must not quickly deteriorate or drainage and aeration will be reduced.

HEIGHT CONTROL

No height control required.

SPACING

Plants are kept pot-to-pot until leveling (see Pinching and Disbudding, next) occurs and flower induction treatments are started. For final spacing with 3.5-in. (9-cm) *Schlumbergera* pots, 9 to 12 plants are grown per square foot (100 to 130/m^2); with 3.5-in. (9-cm) *Hatiora* pots, 7 to 9 plants are produced per square foot (80 to 100/m^2) (Madsen and Madsen, 1994).

PINCHING AND DISBUDDING

During two occasions the phylloclades should be removed. The first is about 1 month after the end of propagation when new phylloclades are approximately 1.5 in. (4 cm) long. Typically only one new phylloclade has developed following rooting and if this one is removed, two should develop per terminal, which will increase branching. Benzyladenine (BA) sprays can dramatically increase the number of phylloclades when applied after pinching (Fig. II-1 Schlumbergera and Hatiora).

FIGURE II-1 SCHLUMBERGERA AND HATIORA Potted *Schlumbergera* plants sprayed with benzyladenine (BA) for optimum bud development.

FIGURE II-2 SCHLUMBERGERA AND HATIORA *Schlumbergera* plant after leveling has occurred and prior to placement in SD and being sprayed with benzyladenine (BA).

The second removal occurs 5 to 10 days after the start of SD. The young immature phylloclades are removed, which is known as *leveling*. Two to three mature phylloclades are left on each plant growing in a 3-in. (7.5-cm) pot, three to four per plant in a 3.5-in. (9-cm) pot, and four to five per plant in a 4-in. (10-cm) pot (Boyle, 1997a). Leveling maximizes the flower numbers to develop on a mature phylloclade and increases uniformity of flowering (Fig. II-2 Schlumbergera and Hatiora). Further, these mature phylloclades are sufficiently strong to support the weight of the flowers and less production space per pot is required because the growth is more upright. Erect growth also facilitates easier sleeving and marketing (Boyle, 1991b, 1994a; Madsen and Madsen, 1994).

SUPPORT

No support required.

SCHEDULE AND TIMING

Schlumbergera plants will initiate and develop flowers under night length of 13 to 16 hr at temperatures between 55 to 75°F (13 to 24°C) and programming for specific marketing dates is possible. Production time is 32 to 37 weeks for plants to be sold from November until March (Table II-2 Schlumbergera and Hatiora). Propagation commences in December and can continue until March. Rooted cuttings in plugs continue to be potted until April to May. Growth of new phylloclades requires 5 to 6 months after leveling. Benzyladenine (BA) sprays can dramatically increase the number of phylloclades when applied after pinching. Plants are leveled the second time 5 to 10 days after SD floral induction commences.

A BA spray of 50 to 150 ppm can also be applied 5 to 7 days after SD has commenced (or after leveling) to increase flower bud numbers (Heins et al., 1981; Ho et al., 1985; Madsen and Madsen, 1994). Adding a spreader sticker to the BA spray solution will increase effectiveness (Lang, 1997). Seven to 8 weeks are required for flowering from the beginning of SD, temperature and cultivar dependent.

In Denmark, SD treatment can commence in mid- to late July and run for 3 to 4 weeks. Flowering is rapid and occurs within 8 weeks after the start of SD at 61 to 68°F (16 to 20°C). After October floral initiation will occur naturally unless LD night interruptions are given (Madsen and Madsen, 1994) (see also Flowering Control and Dormancy).

Hatiora is similar to *Schlumbergera* in regard to timing and scheduling except date of flower is more greatly influenced by temperature. Production time is 32 to 45 weeks for sale of 3.5-in. (9-cm) pots in March and April (Table II-3). On December 1, lower the temperature to 50°F (10°C) for 8 to 10 weeks. After the cooling period, temperatures are increased and flowering occurs within 6 to 8 weeks. Level before temperatures are increased. BA at 50 ppm can also be used to increase phylloclade and flower number, but may be of reduced value if both SD and cool 65/50°F (13/10°C) day/night temperatures are used to induce flowers. If flower induction is being induced by only SD (8 to 11 hr of light) at 72/64°F (22/18°C) day/night temperatures, BA will be useful when applied 10 to 14 days after SD begin. The success of these treatments depends on the cultivar (Boyle, 1991b, 1992, 1995a; Madsen and Madsen, 1994). In many locations in the world 8 to 10 weeks of SD at 50°F (10°C) or lower

TABLE II-2 SCHLUMBERGERA AND HATIORA

Production schedule for *Schlumbergera* total production time after propagation is 32 to 37 weeks.

Cultural Step	Production Time	Temperature °F (°C)
Propagate cuttings		
	3–4 weeks	Medium: 75 (24)
Transplant rooted cuttings and space pot-to-pot		
	4 weeks	Night: 65–70 (18–21)
Level plants once or twice[a]		
	5–6 months	Night: 65 (18)
Start SD		
	5–10 days	Night: 55–59 (13–15)
Level		
	5–7 days	Night: 55–59 (13–15)[b]
Apply BA		
	7–8 weeks	Night: 59–60 (15–16)[b]
Flower[c]		Ship at 50–60 (10–16)

[a]*BA applied 5 to 7 days after each leveling.*
[b]*See Table II-1 Schlumbergera and Hatiora; never allow night temperature to go above 75°F (24°C).*
[c]*Application of STS will increase postharvest life and reduce flower abscission.*

TABLE II-3 SCHLUMBERGERA AND HATIORA

Production schedule for *Hatiora;* total time takes 35 to 45 weeks in Denmark and 32 to 36 weeks in North America.

Cultural Step	Production Time (weeks)	Temperature °F (°C)
Propagate		
	3–4 (April to May)	Medium: 75–80 (24–27)
Transplant rooted cuttings, space pot-to-pot, level if needed		
	12–18	Air: 70–85 (21–29)
Level late summer or autumn, use BA (optional)		
	As needed	Air: 70–85 (21–29)
Flower induction by SD and/or cold		
	9–14	Day: 55 (13) Night: 50 (10)
LD (16 hr)[a]		
	8–9	Day: 70–72 (20–22) Night: 65–70 (18–20)
Flower	March to May	Ship at 50–60 (10–16)

[a]*Use HID lighting under low light northern and coastal conditions and incandescent lighting in high light southern areas.*

temperatures have been completed by early December. Temperatures can then be increased and forcing can commence (Madsen and Madsen, 1994). When gibberellic acid (GA$_3$) at 5 mg/L was sprayed on 0.5- to 0.75-in. (1- to 2-cm)-long flower buds, Easter cactus flowering was accelerated by 5 days (Boyle et al., 1988). Do not apply GA$_3$ at or prior to the start of LD because that will delay flowering and reduce the number of flower buds (Boyle et al., 1994).

INSECTS

Caterpillars, fungus gnats, flower thrips, and mealybugs are problems in production. Fungus gnat larvae feed on roots and lower stem tissue, leading to disease problems. Exclusion and chemical control may be required. Constant monitoring is necessary (Boyle, 1991b, 1994a; Madsen and Madsen, 1994).

DISEASES

Cuttings should be surface disinfected with a 1:5 chlorine bleach:water solution for 5 min. Strict sanitation should be followed during propagation because the high humidity and likelihood of medium overwatering can lead to disease. Fungicidal drenches may be required. *Fusarium* is the most common disease and can cause significant losses. *Pythium, Phytophthora, Bipolaris,* and *Botrytis cinerea* and *Erwinia carotovora* can also be problems. Prevention and environmental control should be used prior to chemical control (Boyle, 1991b, 1994a; Madsen and Madsen, 1994). Other reported diseases include stem and root rot (*Rhizoctonia solani*) and tomato spotted wilt and cactus x viruses (Dreistadt, 2001).

PHYSIOLOGICAL DISORDERS

Marginal foliar chlorosis is due to excessive iron levels in the tissue (Ramirez and Lang, 1997). The long crop cycle for holiday cactus may allow iron accumulation in the tissue and warm production temperatures may accentuate iron uptake. Increase medium pH above 5.5 to reduce iron uptake. Pale green or yellow foliage may be due to high light levels, low nutrition, or root problems.

POSTHARVEST

Flower buds are highly sensitive to ethylene. Foliar sprays of silver thiosulfate (STS) (0.5 to 2.0 mM) can be used to prevent flowers and buds from abscising during shipping stress. Longevity is also increased by 20% with STS treatments. STS treatments commence when the flower buds are 0.25 in. (0.5 cm) in length (Nell, 1993; Nowak and Rudnicki, 1990; Serek and Reid, 1993). Madsen and Madsen (1994) suggested two or three weekly STS sprays prior to shipping date. 1-methylcyclopropene (1-MCP) is also effective in preventing the effects of exogenous ethylene but is generally less effective than STS (Serek and Sisler, 2001). Water stress and rapid temperature charges can also induce abscission. Plants are best shipped at 50 to 59°F (10 to 15°C) (L. Høyer, personal communication).

Schlumbergera plants are typically marketed when flower opening occurs; *Hatiora* are shipped just as flower color is showing because open flowers tend to bruise. Individual flower longevity varies from 4 to 6 days for *Schlumbergera* cultivars and from 7 to 10 days for *Hatiora* cultivars (Scott et al., 1994).

If STS is not used on *Hatiora* plants, do not ship plants with small to medium size buds (3 to 13 days from anthesis) because they are most likely to abscise (Han and Boyle, 1996). An STS application rate of 2 mM can be used, especially if the plants are to be shipped with buds less than 1 in. (2.5 cm) long (Han and Boyle, 1996). However, not all cultivars respond to STS treatments (Karle and Boyle, 1999). Plants with large buds (1 to 2 days from anthesis) will have the same flower opening rates regardless of treatment with STS. Plants will continue to flower for up to 6 weeks if properly cared for in the home. While home light intensities should be 100 fc (20 μmol · $m^{-2} \cdot s^{-1}$), plants can tolerate lower light as 97% of buds opened on plants held under either 35 or 70 fc (7 or 14 μmol · $m^{-2} \cdot s^{-1}$) (Hartley et al., 1995; Nell, 1993). Longevity varied from 31 to 40 days and, not surprisingly, holding plants at 64°F (18°C) produced the longest postharvest life compared to 70 or 75°F (21 or 24°C) (Hartley et al., 1995). Recommended storage temperature is 50 to 59°F (10 to 15°C).

KEY POINTS

- *Schlumbergera* and *Hatiora* are used as potted flowering plants or hanging basket plants.
- *Schlumbergera truncata* is known as the Thanksgiving cactus, *Schlumbergera* ×*buckleyi* the Christmas cactus, and *Hatiora gaertneri* the Easter cactus; all three are similar but the flower and leaf structure differ slightly.
- Mature phylloclades (stem segments) are used for propagation.

- *Schlumbergera* flower initiation occurs under either SD or temperatures below 55°F (13°C).
- *Hatiora* flower initiation occurs under SD and flower development is favored by LD; flower initiation is enhanced by 47 to 55°F (8 to 13°C).
- The use of BA (benzyladenine) sprays increases phylloclade number when applied after pinching (leveling) and flower bud

number when applied during the early stages of floral initiation and development.

- Allow the plants to dry slightly between irrigations, which will help control diseases.

- Plants are sensitive to ethylene and flower abscission during the marketing process and anti-ethylene agents are useful.

BIBLIOGRAPHY

Bailey, L.H., and E.Z. Bailey. 1976. *Rhipsalidopsis*, pp. 947–948; *Schlumbergera*, pp. 1018–1019 in *Hortus Third: A Concise Dictionary of Plants Cultivated in the United States and Canada*. Macmillan, New York.

Boyle, T.H. 1990. Flowering of *Rhipsalidopsis rosea* in response to temperature and photoperiod. *HortScience* 25:217–219.

Boyle, T.H. 1991a. Temperature and photoperiodic regulation of flowering in 'Crimson Giant' Easter cactus. *Journal of the American Society for Horticultural Science* 116:618–622.

Boyle, T.H. 1991b. Commercial production of Easter cactus. *Ohio Florists Association Bulletin* 743:5–6.

Boyle, T.H. 1992. Modification of plant architecture in 'Crimson Giant' Easter cactus with benzyladenine. *Journal of the American Society for Horticultural Science* 117:584–589.

Boyle, T.H. 1994a. Production of holiday cactus. *Professional Plant Growers Association News* 15(10): 15–18.

Boyle, T.H. 1994b. A simple method for extracting and cleaning seeds of *Rhipsalidopsis* and *Schlumbergera* (Cactaceae). *HortTechnology* 4:264–265.

Boyle, T.H. 1995a. BA influences flowering and dry-matter partitioning in shoots of 'Crimson Giant' Easter cactus. *HortScience* 30:289–291.

Boyle, T.H. 1995b. Flowering responses of Easter cactus clones at optimal and supraoptimal temperatures. *HortScience* 30:613–616.

Boyle, T.H. 1997a. Holiday and Easter Cactus, pp. 82–88 in *Tips on Growing Specialty Potted Crops*, M.L. Gaston, S.A. Carver, C.A. Irwin, and R.A. Larson, editors. Ohio Florists' Association, Columbus, Ohio.

Boyle, T.H. 1997b. *Schlumbergera* success tips. *GrowerTalks* 61(5):79, 84.

Boyle, T.H. 2001. Environmental control of moisture content and viability in *Schlumbergera truncata* (Cactacea) pollen. *Journal of the American Society for Horticultural Science* 126:625–630.

Boyle, T.H., and A. Idnurm. 2003. Intergeneric hybridization between *Schlumbergera* Lem. and *Hatiora* Britt. & Rose (Cactaceae). *Journal of the American Society for Horticultural Science* 128: 724–730.

Boyle, T.H., and M. Marcotrigiano. 1997. Influence of benzyladenine and gibberellic acid on organogenesis in 'Crimson Giant' Easter cactus. *Plant Growth Regulation* 22:131–136.

Boyle, T.H., D.J. Jacques, and D.P. Stimart. 1988. Influence of photoperiod and growth regulators on flowering of *Rhipsalidopsis gaertneri*. *Journal of the American Society for Horticultural Science* 113:75–78.

Boyle, T.H., M. Marcotrigiano, and S.M. Hamlin. 1994. Regulating vegetative growth and flowering with gibberellic acid in intact plants and cultured phylloclades of 'Crimson Giant' Easter cactus. *Journal of the American Society for Horticultural Science* 119:36–42.

Boyle, T.H., R. Karle, and S.S. Han. 1995. Pollen germination, pollen tube growth, fruit set, and seed development in *Schlumbergera truncata* and *S. ×buckleyi*. *Journal of the American Society for Horticultural Science* 120:313–317.

Dreistadt, S.H. 2001. *Integrated Pest Management for Floriculture and Nurseries*. University of California Division of Agriculture and Natural Resources Publication 3402.

Erwin, J., R. Heins, R. Berghage, and B. Kovanda. 1990. Temperature effects *Schlumbergera truncata* 'Madisto' flower initiation. *Acta Horticulturae* 272:97–101.

Han, S.S., and T.H. Boyle. 1996. Ethylene affects postproduction quality of Easter cactus. *Journal of the American Society for Horticultural Science* 121:1174–1178.

Hartley, G., T.A. Nell, R.T. Leonard, J.E. Barrett, and T.H. Boyle. 1995. Effect of interior light and temperature on longevity of *Rhipsalidopsis*. *Acta Horticulturae* 405:164–169.

Heins, R.D., A.M. Armitage, and W.H. Carlson. 1981. Influence of temperature, water stress and BA on vegetative and reproductive growth of *Schlumbergera truncata*. *HortScience* 16:679–680.

Ho, Y.-S., K.C. Sanderson, and J.C. Williams. 1985. Effect of chemical and photoperiod on the growth and flowering of Thanksgiving cactus. *Journal of the American Society for Horticultural Science* 110:658–662.

Huxley, A., M. Griffiths, and M. Levy. 1992. *Hatiora*, pp. 494–495, vol. 2; *Schlumbergera*, p. 232, in *The New Royal Horticultural Society Dictionary of Gardening*. Stockton Press, New York.

Karle, R., and T.H. Boyle. 1999. Relationships between floral morphology, breeding behavior, and flower longevity in Easter cactus. *Journal of the American Society for Horticultural Science* 124:296–300.

Lang, H. 1997. Looking good with holiday cactus. *Greenhouse Product News* 7(6):22, 23, 28, 29.

Lange, N., and R. Heins. 1992. How to schedule Thanksgiving cactus. *Greenhouse Grower* 10(9): 62–64.

Madsen, P., and K. Madsen. 1994. *Production Guide for Rhipsalidopsis/Schlumbergera.* Gartneriet, 207 Slettensvej, Odense N., Denmark 5270.

Nell, T.A. 1993. *Rhipsalidopsis gaertneri,* pp. 69–70; *Schlumbergera bridgesi,* pp. 78–79 in *Flowering Potted Plants, Prolonging Shelf Performance.* Ball Publishing, Batavia, Illinois.

Nowak, J., and R.M. Rudnicki. 1990. *Postharvest Handling and Storage of Cut Flowers, Florist Greens and Potted Plants.* Timber Press, Portland, Oregon.

Penningsfeld, F. 1972. Macro and micronutrient requirement of pot plants in peat. *Acta Horticulturae* 26:81–101.

Poole, R.T. 1973. Flowering of Christmas cactus during the summer. *HortScience* 8:186.

Ramirez, D., and H.L. Lang. 1997. Effect of applied iron concentration on growth and phylloclade marginal chlorosis of holiday cactus (*Schlumbergera* sp.). *Journal of the American Society for Horticultural Science* 122:438–444.

Roberts, R.N., and B.E. Struckmeyer. 1939. Further studies of the effects of temperature and other environmental factors upon the photoperiodic responses of plants. *Journal of Agricultural Research* 59:699–709.

Rohwer, C.L., and R.D. Heins. 2001. Easter cactus flowering under varied temperature, daylength, and light conditions. *HortScience* 35(3):591. (Abstract)

Rünger, W., and R.T. Poole. 1985. *Schlumbergera,* pp. 277–282 in *Handbook of Flowering,* vol. IV, A.H. Halevy, editor. CRC Press, Boca Raton, Florida.

Scott, D., T.H. Boyle, and S.S. Han. 1994. Floral development and flower longevity in *Rhipsalidopsis* and *Schlumbergera* (Cactaceae). *HortScience* 29:898–900.

Serek, M., and M.S. Reid. 1993. Anti-ethylene treatments for potted Christmas cactus—Efficacy of inhibitors of ethylene action and biosynthesis. *HortScience* 28:1180–1181.

Serek, M., and E.C. Sisler. 2001. Efficacy of inhibitors of ethylene binding in improvement of the postharvest characteristics of potted flowering plants. *Postharvest Biology and Technology* 23:161–166

Wilkins, H.F., and W. Rünger. 1985. *Rhipsalidopsis,* pp. 178–197 in *Handbook of Flowering,* vol. IV, A.H. Halevy, editor. CRC Press, Boca Raton, Florida.

Sinningia

INTRODUCTION

Common name: gloxinia.

Scientific name: *Sinningia speciosa* (Lodd.) Hiern. (Huxley et al., 1992).

Family and related taxa: Gesneriaceae Dumort. *Sinningia speciosa* is one of 40 species in the genus (Huxley et al., 1992). Other important gesneriads are the *Achimenes, Saintpaulia,* and *Streptocarpus.*

Origin: This tropical herb is native to Brazil.

Uses and current status: The modern hybrids are spectacular potted flowering plants grown for their large colorful flowers (Fig. II-1 Sinningia).

Flower colors range from pure white to violet, red, rose, pink, and deep purple and flowers may be bicolored. Double-flowered cultivars exist. The plant has a rosette growth habit with short internodes; leaves have short petioles. The blade is ovate to oblong, hairy, and dark green.

FIGURE II-I SINNINGIA   *Sinningia* potted plants.

The floral calyx is lobed, ovate, and fused to form a large tubular-bell corolla. The pedicels are 4 in. (10 cm) or more long and hold the flowers erect. Inflorescences are formed both terminally and in leaf axils. Consequently, flowering is not continuous. Plants also form tubers (Bailey and Bailey, 1976; Strømme, 1985).

CULTIVARS

Numerous seed lines are available from firms worldwide. The newer cultivars have smaller leaves and more compact growth, making them easier to ship and sell. Dwarf cultivars are available and offer three distinct advantages: less production space, 12 to 14 days shorter production time, and easier shipping (Salsedo, 1980) (see Postharvest).

Dwarf cultivars can be grown in 4-in. (10-cm) pots. Standard cultivars are grown in 5- or 6-in. (13- or 15-cm) azalea pots. Specimens can be produced in 6.5-in. (17-cm) pots. The larger the pot, the larger the final plant, regardless of genetic size potential (Love, 1985).

PROPAGATION

Propagation can be by seed, leaf-petiole cuttings, or tubers; however, the most common propagation method is by seed (Salsedo, 1980). Tissue culture has also been successful (Bigot, 1974, 1975; Johnson, 1978). Clayberg (1975) reported the genetics of various traits.

Seeds are extremely small at 340,000 seeds/oz (12,000/g) (Cummiskey, 1999). If using open flats, seed can be added to sand to aid in sowing. Seeds germinate within 10 to 12 days at 72 to 80/65 to 70°F (22 to 27/18 to 21°C) day/night temperatures and will be ready to transplant in 5 to 6 weeks. Seeds are not covered and should be kept in a fog germination chamber or under high humidity (Potter, 1962). Water carefully to avoid covering up the tiny seed. If using plugs or liners, do not allow plants to remain in small containers too long because premature flower bud formation may occur. Grow seedlings at 1500 to 3000 fc (300 to 600 μmol $\cdot$ m^{-2} $\cdot$ s^{-1}). Seedlings can be fertilized with 250 ppm N every fifth irrigation (Cummiskey, 1999).

FLOWERING CONTROL AND DORMANCY

Because flowering occurs in the leaf axils, any cultural event that enhances leaf initiation and development will enhance flowering (Strømme, 1985). Photoperiod is not effective in flowering control. Consequently, growth rate is controlled by light intensity and duration, in concert with proper temperatures (Sydnor et al., 1972). Stresses such as underwatering or high temperatures can cause premature flowering and low plant quality.

TEMPERATURE

Most growers produce gloxinia at a minimum temperature of 65°F (18°C). Various production temperatures can be found in the literature: 63 to 68°F (17 to 20°C), 64 to 70°F (18 to 21°C), 64 to 75°F or 84°F (18 to 24°C or 29°C). Rünger (1972) reported that if temperatures were lowered to 68°F (20°C) from 77°F (25°C) for 30 to 40 days, flower numbers, branching, and leaf size increased. Rünger (1972) stated that maximum growth was obtained at 77°F (25°C). Plants are tolerant to high temperatures of 84°F (29°C) (Love, 1985). Growth is slowed at 60°F (16°C) and death occurs at 50°F (10°C) (Strømme, 1985).

LIGHT

Gloxinias are produced at 2000 to 3000 fc (400 to 600 μmol $\cdot$ m^{-2} $\cdot$ s^{-1}). Proper adjustments to increase or decrease light seasonally are critical. Excessive shading delays flowering. Excess light of 3500 fc (700 μmol $\cdot$ m^{-2} $\cdot$ s^{-1}) or more decreases plant quality and causes brown spots and yellow, mottled, and hardened leaves (Cummiskey, 1999; Love, 1985; Salsedo, 1980). Shade is required when light intensities are greater than 3000 fc (600 μmol $\cdot$ m^{-2} $\cdot$ s^{-1}). Light levels of 3000 to 3500 fc (600 to 700 μmol $\cdot$ m^{-2} $\cdot$ s^{-1}) are tolerated when temperatures are cool. Reduced light also aids in temperature control.

In northern latitudes, supplementary lighting is beneficial in the winter (Salsedo, 1980; Strømme, 1985; Sydnor et al., 1972). Various sources of supplemental lighting can be used effectively including warm white fluorescent, high-pressure metal halide, high-pressure sodium, and low-pressure sodium (Grimstad, 1987). Between 300 to 670 fc (45 to 70 μmol $\cdot$ m^{-2} $\cdot$ s^{-1}) was optimal when used 24 hr/day. Low-pressure sodium lamps were the least effective.

WATER

Capillary mat, ebb-and-flow, and microtube irrigation are frequently used in commercial production. A plant with large leaves requires high volumes of water, but do not overwater (Love, 1985; Salsedo, 1980). Excessive drying may induce premature flower bud formation. Foliage damage does not occur when water is placed on the leaves unless water temperature is below 50°F (10°C) (Love, 1985). Damage appears as white to yellowish rings or spots on the foliage. If cold water is a potential problem, warm the water before irrigation.

CARBON DIOXIDE

Flowering is accelerated with CO_2 levels between 900 and 1200 ppm.

NUTRITION

When peat-based media are used, routine applications of fertilizer are required to develop deep green leaves. After seedlings are established 150 ppm N can be supplied at each irrigation by various fertilizers. Avoid excess levels of soluble salts and maintain media EC at 1.0 to 1.2 dS · m^{-1}. Avoid ammonium in the winter or use a fertilizer with a much higher nitrate than ammonium level. Dark blue-green and distorted foliage may indicate excessive ammoniacal nitrogen. Controlled-release fertilizers can also be used as a topdressing and can provide adequate nutrition (Love, 1985; Salsedo, 1980). Boron deficiency is a common problem and adequate levels of micronutrients are required (Bellardi and Bertaccini, 1990; Love, 1985). See Chapter 6, Nutrition, Table 6-4, for foliar nutrient levels.

MEDIA

Generally a medium for gloxinia will be at least 50% peat moss. Other media components can include perlite, Styrofoam, sand, calcine clay, various barks, and vermiculite. The medium should be well aerated with a pH of 5.5 to 6.0. If the medium has nutrients incorporated, routine nutritional programs need not commence for 2 to 3 weeks until the newly transplanted seedlings or plugs have established a root system (Love, 1985).

A medium can influence the plant diameter and days to flower due to its water-holding capacity, pH, and other qualities. High water-holding capacities result in large-diameter plants. The opposite is true with low water-holding capacity media (Sheehan and Tjia, 1976).

Plugs can be planted deep with the upper pair of young leaves only 1/8 to 1/4 in. (0.3 to 0.6 cm) above the media line (Cummiskey, 1999). Planting seedlings too high may cause mature plants to lean over in the pot.

HEIGHT CONTROL

Frequently, plant diameters and inflorescence heights are excessive if light intensities are too low or too much shading is used to reduce temperatures. Gloxinia plants are reported to have minimal response to various growth regulators (McDowell and Holcomb, 1983; Papenhagen, 1979). However, B-Nine (daminozide) sprays at 800 to 1250 ppm could be applied 1 to 2 weeks after transplanting or when the first leaf pair reaches the edge of the pot (Cummiskey, 1999; Kuehny, 2001; Love, 1985). A second application can be applied 1 to 2 weeks after the first. If flower buds are showing color at the time of application, petal streaking may occur. Further, Sydnor et al. (1972) found that either A-Rest (ancymidal) drenches or B-Nine sprays were effective in decreasing plant diameters and pedicel height and enhancing flower and leaf color, but flowering was delayed.

Bonzi (paclobutrazol) drenches at 4 to 8 ppm can also be used to control elongation late in the crop cycle when applied 10 weeks after transplanting (Kuehny, 2001). Bonzi sprays at 30 ppm can be applied when buds are starting to grow above the foliage. Adriansen (1985) noted that Cycocel (chlormequat) was also marginally effective on gloxinia. Dwarf cultivars are generally not treated with growth retardants.

SPACING

The most commonly sold size is in 6-in. (15-cm) azalea pots. Four-inch (10-cm) pots are used for genetic dwarfs. Spacing can be 12 × 12 in. (30 × 30 cm) for standard gloxinias and 9 × 9 to 10 × 10 in. (23 × 23 to 25 × 25 cm) for dwarf gloxinias.

PINCHING AND DISBUDDING

If the first two flower buds are removed, the remaining buds develop and reach anthesis more uniformly, and thus enhance the floral display (Love, 1985).

SUPPORT

No support needed.

SCHEDULE AND TIMING

Plants can be flowered year-round in southern latitudes (Tables II-1 and II-2 Sinningia). Generally 22 to 28 weeks are needed from seed to flower, regardless of the plant type. For this reason, most growers purchase seedlings in plugs,

TABLE II-1 SINNINGIA

Weeks to flower from potting *Sinningia* plugs when grown at a minimum 65°F (18°C) night temperature (Small, undated).

January	14
February	14
March	14
April	13
May	12
June	11
July	10
August	9
September	9
October	10
November	11
December	13

which helps cut production time to 9 to 14 weeks (Love, 1985; Small, undated). High-quality plants are also available for Thanksgiving, Christmas, or Valentine's Day when seeded in June, July, or August, respectively. Dwarf cultivars require 2 weeks less production time than standard cultivars. In northern North America, seeds are commonly germinated commencing in February and plants are sold in July and August as a summer "filler" crop (Love, 1985; Salsedo, 1980). In northern latitudes, such as in northern Europe, supplemental irradiance should be used in the winter.

INSECTS

Exclusion and constant monitoring are required for insect control (Love, 1985). Aphids, cyclamen mites, spider mites, and thrips can be problems (Love, 1985; Salsedo, 1980). Stiff, reddish-brown leaves in the center of the plant can be due to cyclamen mites.

DISEASES

Bellardi and Bertaccini (1990) summarized that fungal diseases are rare but tomato spotted wilt virus is a potentially devastating disease. Tomato spotted wilt virus infection results in spots or rings that can be chlorotic, reddish, necrotic, and green centered (Love, 1985; Salsedo, 1980). Root and crown rot (*Phytophthora cryptogaea*, *Pythium ultimum*, *Rhizoctonia solani*, and *Sclerotinia sclerotiorum*) and bud blight (*Botrytis cinerea*) can occur (Horst, 1990). Other reported diseases include crown rot (*Myrothecium roridum*), southern blight (*Sclerotium rolfsii*), and cottony rot (*Sclerotinia sclerotiorum*) (Dreistadt, 2001).

PHYSIOLOGICAL DISORDERS

Leaf margins curling inward have been associated with low temperatures of 60°F (16°C) or low nutrition (Salsedo, 1980). Leaf damage similar to that which occurs on *Saintpaulia* occurs if water with a temperature of 50°F

TABLE II-2 SINNINGIA

Sample production schedule for *Sinningia* in 6-in. (15-cm) pots.

Cultural Step	Production Time (weeks)	Temperature °F (°C)
Seeds sown		
	2–3	70 (21)
Germination complete		
	4–5	65–70 (18–21)
Transplant seedlings to plug cells		
	4–5	65–70 (18–21)
Transplant[a] cells to 6-in. (15-cm) pot, space pot-to-pot		
	2–2.5	65–70 (18–21)
First B-Nine spray 12 to 18 days after transplant		
	1–1.5	65–70 (18–21)
Second B-Nine (daminozide) spray 22 to 28 days after transplant		
	1.5	65–70 (18–21)
Space pots		
	7.5–10.5	65–70 (18–21)
Flower	22–28	

[a]*Many producers buy gloxinia plugs at this stage (see Table II-1 Sinningia).*

(10°C) or lower is splashed on the foliage (Love, 1985).

Premature flower formation on too small of plants can be due to holding plants in the plug flat too long, high light, or high temperatures (Hamrick, 2003). Dark-green foliage can be caused by too much ammoniacal nitrogen or high soluble salt levels.

POSTHARVEST

Plants are harvested when the first four to six flowers are showing color or are open. The major disadvantage of growing the standard size gloxinia is its leaf size. The plants are difficult to handle, sleeve, and ship (Salsedo, 1980). However, dwarf cultivars have reduced handling problems. Plants should be sleeved in early afternoon when the leaves are most flexible (Cummiskey, 1999). Plants have a high tolerance for ethylene (Nowak and Rudnicki, 1990). Plants cannot be shipped below 50°F (10°C) or they will die (Nell, 1993). The optimal shipping temperature is 60°F (16°C). Plants can flower for many months for the consumer if placed in a cool, well-lighted location.

KEY POINTS

- Gloxinia is used as a potted flowering plant.
- Dwarf cultivars are available that have smaller leaves and are easier to handle and ship.
- Plants are most commonly propagated by seed, but can be propagated by leaf-petiole cuttings or tubers.
- Gloxinia is day neutral.
- Recommended production night temperatures range widely from 65 to 77°F (18 to 25°C).

- Water below 50°F (10°C) injures the leaves.
- Plants are injured at 50°F (10°C) or below.
- Optimum light intensity is 2000 to 2500 fc (400 to 500 μmol $\cdot$ m^{-2} $\cdot$ s^{-1}), but varies with the day length.
- Excessive ammoniacal nitrogen results in dark blue-green and distorted foliage.
- Impatiens necrotic spot and tomato spotted wilt viruses can cause major problems.

BIBLIOGRAPHY

Adriansen, E. 1985. Kemisk vækstregulering, pp. 142–162 in *Potteplanter I—Produktion, Metoder, Midler,* O.V. Christensen, A. Klougart, I.S. Pedersen, and K. Wikesjö, editors. GartnerINFO, København, Denmark. (in Danish)

Bailey, L.H., and Bailey, E.Z. 1976. *Sinningia* Nees., pp. 1046–1047 in *Hortus Third: A Concise Dictionary of Plants Cultivated in the United States and Canada.* Macmillan, New York.

Bellardi, M.G., and A. Bertaccini. 1990. Electron microscopy of viriscent gloxinia plants. *Acta Horticulturae* 266:509–515.

Bigot, C. 1974. Obtention de plant entiers a partir de pedoncules floraux de *Gloxinia hydrida* cultives *in vitro. Zeitschrift für Pfanzenphysiologie* 73:178–183. (in French, English summary)

Bigot, C. 1975. Multiplication vegetative de *Gloxinia hybrida* a partir d'organes cultures *in vitro. Annal de l'Amelioration des Plantes* 25:337–351. (in French, English summary)

Clayberg, C.D. 1975. Genetics of corolla traits in gloxinia. *Journal of Heredity* 66:10–12.

Cummiskey, P. 1999. How we grow: Earl J. Small on gloxinias. *GrowerTalks* 62(13):44, 46, 48, 50.

Dreistadt, S.H. 2001. *Integrated Pest Management for Floriculture and Nurseries.* University of California Division of Agriculture and Natural Resources Publication 3402.

Grimstad, S.O. 1987. The effect of supplemental irradiation with different light sources on growth and flowering of gloxinia [*Sinningia speciosa* (Lodd.) Heirn]. *Scientia Horticulturae* 32:297–305.

Hamrick, D. 2003. *Sinningia,* pp. 643–645 in *Ball Redbook,* vol. 2, 17th ed. Ball Publishing, Batavia, Illinois.

Horst, R.K. 1990. Gloxinia, pp. 658–659 in *Westcott's Plant Disease Handbook,* 5th ed. Van Nostrand Reinhold, New York.

Huxley, A., M. Griffiths, and M. Levy. 1992. *Sinningia,* pp. 298–300 in *The New Royal Horticultural Society Dictionary of Gardening,* vol. 4. Stockton Press, New York.

Johnson, B.B. 1978. *In vitro* propagation of gloxinia from leaf explants. *HortScience* 13:149–150.

Kuehny, J. 2001. Gloxinias and other gesneriads, pp. 93–95 in *Tips on Regulating Growth of Floriculture Crops,* M.L. Gaston, L.A. Kunkle, P.S. Konjoian, and M.F. Wilt, editors. Ohio Florists' Association Services, Columbus, Ohio.

Love, J.W. 1985. *Commercial Gloxinia Production,* pp. 1–3. Horticulture Information Leaflet No.

539, North Carolina Agriculture Extension Service, Raleigh, North Carolina.

McDowell, J.M., and E.J. Holcomb. 1983. The effects of B-Nine and the production of gloxinia. *Pennsylvania Flower Grower* 350(8):3–4.

Nell, T.A. 1993. *Sinningia* ×*hybrida*, pp. 83–84 in *Flowering Potted Plants, Prolonging Shelf Performance*. Ball Publishing, Batavia, Illinois.

Nowak, J., and R.M. Rudnicki. 1990. *Postharvest Handling and Storage of Cut Flowers, Florist Greens, and Potted Plants*. Timber Press, Portland, Oregon.

Papenhagen, S. 1979. Durch welche Massnahmen lassen sich Kleinpflanzen van Gloxinia erzeugen? *Zier Pflanzenbau* 13:537. (in German, English summary)

Potter, C.H. 1962. Gloxinia and achimenes. *Florists' Review* 130(3358):31, 105–106.

Rünger, W. 1972. Einfluss der temperature auf das Blühen von Sinningia. *Gartenbauwissenschaft* 37:97–108. (in German)

Salsedo, C.A. 1980. Gloxinia. *Connecticut Greenhouse Newsletter* 101:8–11.

Sheehan, T.J., and B. Tjia. 1976. The effects of growing media on growth and flowering of *Gloxinia*. *Proceedings Florida State Horticultural Society* 89:319–320.

Small, E.J. Undated. *The Gloxinia Growers Manual*. E.J. Small Growers, Pinellas Park, Florida.

Strømme, E. 1985. Gesneriaceae, pp. 48–52 in *Handbook of Flowering*, vol. III, A.H. Halevy, editor. CRC Press, Boca Raton, Florida.

Sydnor, T.D., R.K. Kimmins, and R.A. Larson. 1972. The effects of light intensity and growth regulators on gloxinia. *HortScience* 7:407–408.

Solanum

INTRODUCTION

Common names: Jerusalem cherry, Christmas cherry.

Scientific name: *Solanum pseudocapsicum* L. (Huxley et al., 1992).

Family and related taxa: Solanaceae Juss. *S. pseudocapsicum* is one of approximately 1700 species in the genus, which range in habit from herbaceous herbs, vines, and shrubs to trees. Solanaceae also includes important food crops such as tomato (*Lycopersicon*) and potato (*Solanum*) and several ornamentals including *Browallia, Capsicum, Nicotiana, Petunia, Salpiglossis,* and *Schizanthus.*

Origin: This species is from the Old World and has become naturalized in the tropics and subtropics (Zone 9).

Uses and current status: Jerusalem cherry can be sold in full fruit color from October to February. Authorities believe that the plant should not be called Christmas cherries, because this name indicates a limited sales period and is most commonly available in late summer and fall (Fig. II-1 Solanum).

Jerusalem cherry has the typical *Solanum* five-lobed, star-shaped flowers that produce a round, smooth fruit ranging in color from yellow to scarlet. The 0.5- to 1-in. (1.2- to 2.5-cm) fruit does not easily abscise and the plant is a striking specimen in the home for many months with proper care (Bailey and Bailey,

FIGURE II-1 SOLANUM Fruit of *Solanum pseudocapsicum.*

1976). Jerusalem cherry can be a shrub growing up to 4 ft (1.2 m) tall. The leaves are oblong, 2 to 4 in. (5 to 10 cm) long, slightly undulating, and glossy green. As with many other Solanaceae plants, this plant was reported to be poisonous, though no known cases of illness have been reported (Kingsbury, 1967). Unfortunately, this fear has reduced its popularity.

CULTIVARS

Cultivars are available with various plant forms (spreading to treelike), fruit color, and heights. Dwarf types are available for smaller pot sizes (Bailey and Bailey, 1976).

PROPAGATION

Although Jerusalem cherry can be propagated from shoot cuttings, it is commercially propagated by seed with 12,000 seeds/oz (425/g). Seeds germinate in the light or dark at a wide temperature range of 55 to 86°F (13 to 30°C), but 73°F (23°C) is optimal (Aimone, 1985; Hammer, 1992).

FLOWERING CONTROL AND DORMANCY

No data are available regarding flowering mechanisms, but Jerusalem cherries are thought to be day neutral. When plants are in flower, they may need to be shaken one to two times per day to ensure pollination, especially when grown indoors. Wind and bees act as pollinators outdoors (Aimone, 1985).

TEMPERATURE

Plants can be grown under protection in a greenhouse or outdoors. The night temperature should be 50 to 55°F (10 to 13°C) from germination until plants are moved outdoors (for maximum flower pollination). Before the danger of frost, plants are moved into the greenhouse and held at 50°F (10°C).

LIGHT

Full light intensity is used both in the greenhouse and outdoors (Aimone, 1985; D. Bengston, personal communication).

WATER

Generally, plants require frequent irrigations. Outdoor potted plants are usually plunged into soil beds or into peat in cold frames. Because plants root into these media, pots should be turned once or twice to break roots growing outside the pot. Final root pruning should be accomplished 2 or 3 weeks prior to shipping to reduce water stress and the resulting risk of leaf and fruit abscission (Aimone, 1985; Hammer, 1992).

Do not overwater when growth slows and fruits are developing (Aimone, 1985). From personal experience, plants in the home require much water and close attention to the medium moisture level.

CARBON DIOXIDE

No data on carbon dioxide were found.

NUTRITION

Hammer (1992) stated that during periods of rapid vegetative growth, the nitrogen levels should be high. D. Bengston (personal communication) used 50 ppm N outdoors. Aimone (1985) stated 100 ppm N from 20–20–20 was sufficient and a Spurway medium ppm reading of 20 to 25 N, 4 to 6 P, 25 to 30 K was sufficient. Nutrition should be reduced as the crop matures. Anonymous (1980) also noted that high nutrition should continue while fruits are forming and then lowered in October.

MEDIA

Although a wide variety of medium types can be used from sandy-loam to peat-lite mixes, it should have enough bulk density to prevent plants from falling over, because plants in fruit are top heavy. The medium also must have sufficient water-holding capacity to preclude frequent irrigation (see Water section).

HEIGHT CONTROL

Sanderson and Martin (1974) found no growth retardants to be effective (see *Capsicum* chapter, page 375). However, Whipker (2003) reported that Cycocel (chlormequat) sprays at 400 to 1500 ppm can be used and Adriansen (1985) noted that B-Nine (daminozide) was also effective.

SPACING

Final pot spacing ranges from 6 × 6 to 8 × 8 in. (15 × 15 to 20 × 20 cm) for 4-in. pots and 10 × 10 to 12 × 12 in. (25 × 25 to 30 × 30 cm) for 6-in. pots.

PINCHING AND DISBUDDING

No pinching or disbudding is required, depending on the cultivar (Aimone, 1985). However, Hammer (1992) stated plants are pinched twice—when the young plant has developed two to three nodes and again when the resulting shoots are 2 to 3 in. (5 to 7.5 cm) long.

The art of producing topiary-type trees is described by Hammer (1992) using a series of steps including gibberellic acid (GA_3) sprays, staking, high nitrogen nutrition, lower leaf removal, and pinching. Prior to sale, a few vegetative terminal shoots may need to be removed for better fruit display.

SUPPORT

No support is needed unless topiary-type trees are grown (Hammer, 1992).

SCHEDULE AND TIMING

Seeds are direct seeded into plugs in March, April, or May and shifted into an intermediate pot size within 3 weeks. Final pot sizes vary from 4 to 8 in. (10 to 20 cm). Pot size determines propagation date (Tables II-1 and II-2 Solanum).

Plant sales begin in September and can continue into February (Aimone, 1985; D. Bengston, personal communication). In Great Britain, seed sown in mid-March produced

TABLE II-1 SOLANUM

Sample production schedule for *Solanum pseudocapsicum* (Aimone, 1985; Anonymous, 1980; D. Bengston, personal communication).

	Final Pot Size		
	8 in. (20 cm)	6 in. (15 cm)	4 to 5.5 in. (10 to 13 cm)
Sowing date[a]	March 15	April 15	May 15
Transplant date[b]	April 7[c]	May 7[c]	June 7[c]
Transplant to final pot size[b]	June 15	July 15	—
Sales date	Late October	Late October	Late October

[a] Into plugs.
[b] Do not allow to become root bound.
[c] For 8-in. (20-cm) pot production transplant first into 3-in. (8-cm) pots; for 6-in. (15-cm) pots use 2.5 in. (6 cm); and for 4- to 5.5-in. (10- to 13-cm) pots the seedings are transplanted directly into the final container.

TABLE II-2 SOLANUM

Sample production schedule for a 6-in. (15-cm) potted *Solanum pseudocapsicum* in fruit.

Cultural Step	Production Time (weeks)	Temperature °F (°C)
Seed plugs		
	1	73 (23)
Germination		
	2	50–55 (10–13)
Shift plugs to intermediate pot size[a] and space pot-to-pot		
	10	55 (13)
Shift to final pot size and space pot-to-pot or move outdoors[b]		
	9	55 (13)
Lower temperature and move indoors, if needed		
	6	50 (10)
Fruit color and market		
	Late October	
Total weeks	28	

[a] See Table II-1 Solanum.
[b] After frost.

plants in 8-in. (20-cm) pots for sale in late October. Authorities suggest a promotion for Washington's birthday in the United States. In warm climates, the plant can be used as a late autumn or early winter bedding plant (Aimone, 1985).

INSECTS

In the greenhouse, aphids, red spider mites, and mealybugs may be a problem and grasshoppers and caterpillars may occur outdoors (Aimone, 1985). Constant observation is required to prevent widespread outbreaks.

DISEASES

Outdoors, Jerusalem cherry is susceptible to numerous leaf spot diseases (*Alternari solani*, *Mycosphaerella solani*, *Ascochyta lycopersici*, *Cercospara dulcamerae*, *Phyllosticta pseudocapsici*, and *Stemphylium solani*), *Verticillium* wilt, and tomato spotted wilt virus (Horst, 1990).

PHYSIOLOGICAL DISORDERS

Edema was reported to be common in certain cultivars (Anonymous, 1980).

POSTHARVEST

In a cool home environment with moderate light, plants will last for 8 weeks. L. Høyer (personal communication) reports that this species is highly sensitive to ethylene. A 2.0 mM silver thiosulfate (STS) spray has been used to prevent ethylene damage.

KEY POINTS

- Jerusalem cherry is used as a potted plant because of the brightly colored fruit and is sold from early fall to February.
- Commercially Jerusalem cherry is seed propagated, but can be cutting propagated.
- Jerusalem cherry is considered to be day neutral.
- Plants grown under protection may need to be shaken once or twice a day to ensure pollination.
- Plants are often grown outdoors during the summer and moved inside before frost.
- Do not water stress this plant because leaves, flowers, or fruit can abscise.

BIBLIOGRAPHY

Adriansen, E. 1985. Kemisk vækstregulering, pp. 142–162 in *Potteplanter I—Produktion, Metoder, Midler*, O.V. Christensen, A. Klougart, I.S. Pedersen, and K. Wikesjö, editors. GartnerINFO, København, Denmark. (in Danish)

Aimone, T. 1985. Ornamental peppers: Genus, species: *Capsicum* species, Jerusalem cherry: Genus, species: *Solanum pseudo-capsicum*, Family: Solanaceae. *GrowerTalks*, 49(1):24.

Anonymous. 1980. *Solanum*—A colorful Christmas crop. *The Grower* 94(21):31.

Bailey, L.H., and E.Z. Bailey. 1976. *Solanum* L., pp. 1054–1056 in *Hortus Third: A Concise Dictionary of Plants Cultivated in the United States and Canada*. Macmillan, New York.

Hammer, P.A. 1992. Other flowering pot plants, pp. 483–484 in *Introduction to Floriculture*, R.A. Larson, editor. Academic Press, San Diego, California.

Horst, R.K. 1990. Jerusalem cherry, p. 695 in *Westcott's Plant Disease Handbook*, 5th ed. Van Nostrand Reinhold, New York.

Huxley, A., M. Griffiths, and M. Levy. 1992. *Solanum*, pp. 316–320 in *The New Royal Horticultural Society Dictionary of Gardening*, vol. 4. Stockton Press, New York.

Kingsbury, J.M. 1967. *Poisonous Plants of the United States and Canada*. Prentice-Hall, Englewood Cliffs, New Jersey.

Sanderson, K.C., and W.C. Martin, Jr. 1974. *Effect of Various Growth Retardants on Christmas Cherry and Christmas Pepper*. Auburn University Agricultural Experiment Station Horticulture Series, March, No. 20, Auburn, Georgia.

Whipker, B.E. 2003. Growth regulators for floricultural crops, pp. 439–448 in *2003 North Carolina Agricultural Chemicals Manual*, College of Agriculture and Life Science, North Carolina State University, Raleigh.

Solidago

FIGURE II-1 SOLIDAGO Bed of *Solidago* for cut flower production.

INTRODUCTION

Common name: goldenrod.

Scientific name: *Solidago* L. species (Huxley et al., 1992).

Family and related taxa: Compositae Giseke. This large family has many important genera including *Aster, Calendula, Callistephus, Centaurea, Chrysanthemum, Cosmos, Dahlia, Dendranthema, Echinacea, Gerbera, Helianthus, Liatris, Pericallis, Tagetes,* and *Zinnia.*

Origin: Numerous *Solidago* species are native to North America with a few species also native to Europe, Asia, the Azores, and South America (Bailey and Bailey, 1976).

Uses and current status: Goldenrods are used as a greenhouse or field-grown cut flower, both fresh and dried. Goldenrods are also occasionally sold as garden perennials (Fig. II-1 Solidago). Goldenrods are especially popular in Europe as cut flowers and garden ornamentals.

Goldenrods are long-lived plants that grow 2 to 8 ft (0.6 to 2.4 m) tall with numerous, small white to yellow flowers arranged in various types of inflorescences ranging from long, slender wands to columnar spikes to loose, open plumes (Peterson and McKenney, 1968). Goldenrods flower from midsummer to late fall. In general, plants tolerate heat, drought, and cold and are hardy from Zones 2 to 9. Contrary to popular belief, goldenrods do not cause hay fever (allergic reactions). Goldenrods produce heavy pollen, which requires transportation by insects, whereas hay fever is caused by lightweight, windblown pollen. This misconception has limited use of goldenrods in the United States. Several goldenrod species are listed as endangered in the United States, while others have become invasive weeds in Europe (Burrows, 2002).

CULTIVARS

Numerous hybrids have been created ranging in size from low-growing types suitable for perennial gardens and potted plants to taller types suitable for both cut flowers and perennial gardens (Armitage and Laushman, 2003; Burrows, 2002). Species with wand or columnar-shaped inflorescences are less likely to be recognized as goldenrods and thus may be better accepted as cut flowers in the United States. Solidaster (×*Solidaster luteus*) is a popular cut flower and thought to be a naturally occurring hybrid between *Aster ptarmicoides* and *Solidago canadensis* (Dress, 1979). Numerous cultivars of solidaster are available and are grown in a similar manner to goldenrods.

PROPAGATION

Goldenrods can be propagated from seed, shoot cuttings, or division. Seeds of some species germinate readily in 2 to 3 weeks when sown at 68 to 72°F (20 to 22°C) (Armitage and Laushman, 2003); however, other species may need to be stratified for up to 10 weeks at 40°F (4°C) (Bratcher et al., 1993). *Solidago petiolaris* germinates rapidly in 2 days after 10 weeks of stratification (Bratcher et al., 1993). Stem cuttings can be propagated from vegetative shoots and established plants can be divided every 2 to 3 years.

FLOWERING CONTROL AND DORMANCY

Although little is known about the flowering of many goldenrod species, most species examined are considered SD plants (Allard and Garner, 1940; Goodwin, 1944; Hubert, 1970; van de Krogt, 1981). Schwabe (1986) categorized the photoperiods required for flowering of several North American species in Table II-1 Solidago. At least one species, *S. canadensis* L., has been studied in detail and requires SD for flower initiation (Schwabe, 1986). Extended periods of SD, however, induce dormancy and the shorter the day length the more rapid the onset of dormancy. In nature, the LD of summer stimulate shoot elongation and vegetative growth, whereas the shorter days of late summer induce floral initiation. The continually shortening days of fall induce dormancy in preparation for the onset of winter. Under 16-hr day lengths, *S. canadensis* plants do not flower; under 14-hr day lengths plants flower normally; under 12-hr day lengths some plants flowered normally and some aborted the flowers; and under 8-hr day lengths plants went dormant so rapidly that flowering did not occur. *Solidago* can be forced in the greenhouse, but the natural photoperiods during the winter must be lengthened to 14 hr by incandescent lighting.

TEMPERATURE

After germination, seedlings and young plants can be grown at 55 to 65°F (13 to 18°C) night and 65 to 70°F (18 to 21°C) day temperatures. Some cultivars flower fastest at slightly warmer day and night temperatures (Anonymous, 1998).

LIGHT

Some goldenrod species tolerate light shade, but most species and hybrids prefer full sunlight. Supplemental lighting of approximately 450 fc (60 μmol $\cdot$ m^{-2} $\cdot$ s^{-1}) is recommended (Burrows, 2002).

WATER

Irrigate seedlings and container-grown plants as needed. Avoid overwatering cut flowers when the inflorescences are developing because that may encourage vegetative side shoots (Bartels Stek, personal communication). Slight wilting of the leaves is acceptable after flower initiation (McGrew, 1998). Established plants outdoors are highly drought tolerant, but the best growth is obtained with regular irrigation during dry periods.

CARBON DIOXIDE

No data are available on the use of supplemental CO_2 in the greenhouse.

NUTRITION

Seedlings and container-grown plants can be fertilized with 50 to 100 ppm N constant liquid fertilization. Foliar nutrient levels for high-quality plants are listed in Chapter 6, Nutrition, Table 6-4.

MEDIA

Goldenrods thrive in a wide range of media. A pH of 5.5 to 6.5 is acceptable for container and greenhouse cut flower production and 5.0 to 7.0 is common for field production. For greenhouse production the media EC should be

TABLE II-I SOLIDAGO

The photoperiodic classification for flowering of several North American *Solidago* species (Schwabe, 1986).

Photoperiod	Species
SD	*S. canadensis* var. *scabra* (Muhlenb.) Torr. & A. Gray (synonym: *S. altissima* L.)
	S. graminifolia (L.) Salisb.
	S. nemoralis Ait.
LD	*S. rugosa* Fern.
	S. sempervirens L. (one strain)
Intermediate	*S. juncea* Ait.
	S. sempervirens
	S. ulmifolia Muhlenb. ex Willd.

0.75 to 1.5 dS · m^{-1} (based on 1:2 media:water dilution) (McGrew, 1998). For retail sales, plants can be sold vegetative or flowering with one plant per quart container or one to three plants per gallon container. Outdoors, goldenrods tolerate a wide range of soil types as long as the location is well drained.

HEIGHT CONTROL

Height control of container-grown genetically dwarf plants is typically not needed. However, multiple B-Nine (daminozide) sprays at 5000 ppm, one Bonzi (paclobutrazol) spray at 80 to 100 ppm, or one Bonzi drench at 30 ppm are effective (Latimer, 2001). Cut flowers do not require plant growth regulators.

SPACING

For field cut flower production, spacing in the beds can range from 8 × 12 to 24 × 24 in. (20 × 30 to 60 × 60 cm). For greenhouse cut flower production plants are spaced at 1.5 to 2 plants/ft^2 (16 to 24 plants/m^2) if pinched and 4.5 to 5.5/ft^2 (48 to 60/m^2) if unpinched (Anonymous, 1998). Container-grown plants are typically spaced pot-to-pot until the leaves touch.

PINCHING AND DISBUDDING

Cut flowers may be grown pinched or unpinched. Plants are pinched 2 to 3 weeks after planting plugs; leave 3 to 4 leaf pairs per plant (McGrew, 1998). After harvest, plants should be cut back to the ground and all old tissue removed to stimulate new shoots to develop from the rhizome. Established plants may benefit from pinching (Armitage and Laushman,

2003). Field-grown plantings should be cut back to the ground in late fall or early spring.

Potted flowering plants are pinched one or two times (Van Zanten, personal communication). As with cut flowers plants are pinched 2 to 3 weeks after planting plugs; a second pinch can be used 2 to 3 weeks after the first pinch.

SUPPORT

Most goldenrod species need one layer of netting for cut flower production.

SCHEDULE AND TIMING

Cut flowers should be ready to harvest 12 weeks after planting plugs if pinched and 10 weeks if not pinched (Bartels Stek, personal communication). Plants are pinched 3 weeks after planting and 16-hr LD are provided for approximately 6 weeks starting at planting. For nonpinched plants, 16-hr LD are provided for 5 weeks after planting. LD lighting is discontinued when plants are 12 to 16 in. (30 to 40 cm) tall and SD is provided for flower initiation. Immediately after harvest remaining stems are cut back and plants will reflower within 10 to 12 weeks if supplied with LD for the first 5 to 6 weeks and SD thereafter. Each planting can produce up to 5 flushes of cut flowers with 3 to 4 flushes of cut flowers harvested each year. To improve stem thickness and quality, shoots should be thinned to 5.5 to 7.5 stems/ft^2 (60 to 80/m^2) with the highest quality stems produced at 5.5 stems/ft^2 (60/m^2).

Total production time for container-grown plants ranges from 29 to 40 weeks (Table II-2 Solidago). The purchase of liners or plugs from specialty propagators can reduce produc-

TABLE II-2 SOLIDAGO

Sample production schedule for *Solidago* container or field-grown cuts.

Cultural Step	Production Time	Temperature °F (°C)
Stratification (depends on species)	10 weeks	40 (4)
Germination	2–14 days	70–75 (21–24)
Growing on seedlings	2–3 weeks	70–75 (21–24)
Transplant to cell packs	9–12 weeks	60–65 (16–18)
Transplant to final container or to the field:		
Quart or gallon containers	2–3 months	60–65 (16–18)
Field	fall flowering	ambient

tion time to 8 to 13 weeks in 1-gal (3.8-L) pots. Plants in 4- to 5.5-in. (10- to 13-cm) pots can be produced in 10 weeks with one to three cuttings per pot, one pinch, 6 weeks of LD after planting, and SD to finish (Anonymous, 1998).

INSECTS

In the greenhouse, goldenrods are usually pest free, but are susceptible to aphids and whitefly infestations. Outdoors, the goldenrods are host to the larvae of numerous moths and butterflies. Late flowering goldenrods may be covered with pollen-seeking bees and other insects and care should be taken when harvesting cut flowers.

DISEASES

In the greenhouse, goldenrods are sensitive to damping-off and root rots, especially if overirrigated. Plants are also sensitive to high media EC. Outdoors, goldenrods are prone to rust (*Coleosporium asterum*), which covers the foliage and stems in late summer with rust-colored pustules (Armitage and Laushman, 2003). *Solidago* should not be planted near pine trees, which are intermediate hosts for the rust. Other rust species may also occur, including *Coleosporium delicatulum, Puccinia dioicae, P. virgae-aureae, P. grindeliae, P. stipae, Uromyces perigynius,* or *U. solidaginis* (Horst, 1990). Powdery mildew (*Ersiphe polygoni*) and numerous leaf spots (*Asteroma solidaginis, Colletotrichum solitarium, Placosphaeria havdeni,* and *Septoria*) can also be problems (Armitage and Laushman, 2003; Horst, 1990). Stem blight (*Diaporthe*) has also been reported (Dreistadt, 2001).

PHYSIOLOGICAL DISORDERS

Under the low light levels of winter or SD, flower bud abortion can occur in the greenhouse. Supplemental lighting from HID lamps should prevent this problem.

POSTHARVEST

Stems are cut when one-fourth to one-half of the florets are open. Cut flowers last 5 to 6 days in water and may be stored at 36 to 41°F (2 to 5°C) for up to 5 days (Armitage and Laushman, 2003). Leaf yellowing can be delayed by pulsing cut stems with 0.2 mM silver thiosulfate (STS) or 10 ppm benzyladenine (BA) with surfactants (Philosoph-Hadas et al., 1996). The inflorescences of many species also work well as a dried flower.

KEY POINTS

- The goldenrod has long been popular as a cut flower and garden perennial in northern Europe and is slowly gaining acceptance in North America.
- Goldenrod is not responsible for hay fever.
- Commercially, plants are propagated by seed; shoot cuttings or division can also be used.

- Most species are SD plants; however, extended periods of SD induce dormancy.
- A few species are LD plants or day neutral.
- Plants are susceptible to damping-off and root rot, especially if overirrigated.

BIBLIOGRAPHY

Allard, H.A., and W.W. Garner. 1940. *Further Observations on the Response of Various Species of Plants to Length of Day.* U.S. Department of Agriculture Technical Bulletin Number 727.

Anonymous. 1998. Solidago. *Greenhouse Management and Production* 18(6):8.

Armitage, A.M., and J.M. Laushman. 2003. *Solidago* hybrids, ×*Solidaster*, pp. 496–503 in *Specialty Cut Flowers,* 2nd ed. Timber Press, Portland, Oregon.

Bailey, L.H., and E.Z. Bailey. 1976. *Solidago,* pp. 1056–1058 in *Hortus Third: A Concise Dictionary of Plants Cultivated in the United States and Canada.* Macmillan, New York.

Bratcher, C.B., J.M. Dole, and J.C. Cole. 1993. Stratification improves seed germination of five native wildflower species. *HortScience* 28:899–901.

Burrows, R.L. 2002. Goldenrod: Plants with multi-purpose potential. *HortTechnology* 12:711–716.

Dreistadt, S.H. 2001. *Integrated Pest Management for Floriculture and Nurseries.* University of California Division of Agriculture and Natural Resources Publication 3402.

Dress, W.J. 1979. Sidelights on ×*Solidaster* [Compositae]. *Baileya* 20(4):162–165.

Goodwin, R.H. 1944. The inheritance of flowering time in a short-day species, *Solidago sempervirens* L. *Genetics* 29:503–519.

Horst, R.K. 1990. Goldenrod, p. 661 in *Westcott's Plant Disease Handbook*, 5th ed. Van Nostrand Reinhold, New York.

Hubert, S.H. 1970. Flower number, flowering time, and reproductive isolation among ten species of *Solidago* (Compositae). *Bulletin of the Torrey Botanical Club* 97:175–189.

Huxley, A., M. Griffiths, and M. Levy. 1992. *Solidago*, pp. 316–323 in *The New Royal Horticulture Society Dictionary of Gardening*, vol. 4. Stockton Press, New York.

Latimer, J. 2001. Herbaceous perennials, pp. 98–110 in *Tips on Regulating Growth of Floriculture Crops*, M.L. Gaston, L.A. Kunkle, P.S. Konjoian, and M.F. Wilt, editors. Ohio Florists' Association Services, Columbus, Ohio.

McGrew, J. 1998. *Solidago* (goldenrod), pp. 755–757 in *Ball Redbook*, 15th ed., V. Ball, editor. George J. Ball Publishing, West Chicago, Illinois.

Peterson, R.T., and M. McKenney. 1968. *A Field Guide to Wildflowers*. Houghton Mifflin, Boston.

Philosoph-Hadas, S., R. Michaeli, Y. Reuveni, and S. Meir. 1996. Benzyladenine pulsing retards leaf yellowing and improves quality of goldenrod (*Solidago canadensis*) cut flowers. *Postharvest Biology and Technology* 9:65–73.

Schwabe, W.W. 1986. *Solidago*, pp. 338–340 in *The Handbook of Flowering*, vol. V, A.H. Halevy, editor. CRC Press, Boca Raton, Florida.

van de Krogt, Th.M. 1981. *Solidago* als snijbloem de hele zomer beschikbaar. *Vakblad voor de Bloemisterij* 29:28–29. (in Dutch)

Spathiphyllum

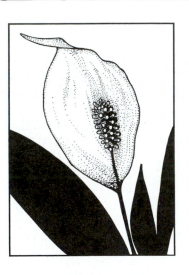

FIGURE II-I SPATHIPHYLLUM *Spathiphyllum* 'Hiho' potted plant.

INTRODUCTION

Common names: peace lily, peace flower, snowflower, spath flower, white anthurium.

Scientific names: *Spathiphyllum floribundum* (Lind. & André) N.E. Br. and *S.* hybrids. *Spathiphyllum* means *"leaflike,"* referring to the inflorescence.

Family and related taxa: Araceae Juss. Other important floricultural genera in this family include *Aglaonema, Anthurium, Arum, Caladium, Dieffenbachia, Epipremnum, Monstera, Nephthytis, Philodendron, Syngonium,* and *Zantedeschia.*

Origin: *Spathiphyllum floribundum* is native to Colombia, South America. There are 36 species within the genus, all from tropical America (Bailey, 1933; Bailey and Bailey, 1976; Huxley et al, 1992).

Uses and current status: *Spathiphyllum* is one of the few tropical foliage plants that develops an attractive inflorescence (Fig. II-1 Spathiphyllum). Further, this plant requires low light intensity and adapts well to the home or office interiorscape.

The rich green leaves are oblong, elliptical to lanceolate, and up to 6 in. (15 cm) long and 3 in. (8 cm) wide. The spath inflorescence is leaflike, white, oblong to lanceolate, and 3 in. (8 cm) long and surrounds the cream to yellow green spadix, which is the reproductive structure.

CULTIVARS

Historically, the most common cultivar was 'Mauna Loa.' This cultivar is a compact plant with deep green leaves and white, fragrant inflorescences. The cultivar 'Petite' is also popular due to its short 6-in. (15-cm) height, which make the plant suitable for small pots. Henny et al. (1991) list 26 cultivars, which are produced in Florida; several are trademarked (™), registered (®), or patented. Many cultivars are hybrids of uncertain origin.

PROPAGATION

Peace lily can be grown from seed and may require up to 9 to 15 months to produce a flowering sized plant, depending on the pot size. *In vitro*-propagated plants are more uniform than seed-propagated plants and are available year-round as a variety of named selections (Hennen and Hotchkiss, 1995; Henny, 1985; Orlikowska et al., 1995). Individual rooted microcuttings from tissue culture are more uniform than tissue-cultured clumps. However, the latter produces full plants more quickly. Watad et al. (1997) compared various micropropagation techniques.

FLOWER CONTROL AND DORMANCY

Flowering occurs mainly from January to July; few flowers are observed from August to December. In Florida, at 20° north latitude, plants are typically grown at 65 to 90°F (18 to 32°C) with light intensities of 1000 to 2500 fc (200 to 500 μmol $\cdot$ m^{-2} $\cdot$ s^{-1}). In northern Europe (Germany) at 52° north latitude, plants flower from spring to fall at production temperatures of 68 to 77°F (20 to 25°C) day and 64°F (18°C) night. In the winter, night temperatures are lowered to 61 to 64°F (16 to 18°C) (Henny, 1985). Henny (1985) stated that plants do not flower until they are 6 to 12 months old and transplanted into 6-in. (15-cm) pots. Early flowering cultivars are available.

Henny (1981a, b, 1985) and Henny and Rasmussen (1981) have researched the use of gibberellic acid (GA$_3$) to speed flower induction. A single spray to run-off of GA$_3$ (250 to 1000 ppm) resulted in flowers within 12 to 14 weeks. However, peduncle and spath malformations can occur on 15 to 20% of the inflorescences. Henny et al. (1999) compared the effects of one spray of 250 ppm GA$_3$ on 31 named and experimental cultivars; all flowered more rapidly after GA$_3$ application, within 16 weeks, while none of the untreated control plants flowered. Several cultivars produced malformed flowers.

TEMPERATURE

The optimum temperature range is 65°F (18°C) nights and up to 90°F (32°C) days. If temperatures are above 95°F (35°C) for any duration, plants develop very narrow strap-shaped leaves and have poor color and root development. Henny (1985), in a review article, stated that plants flower sooner at 77°F (25°C) than at 68°F (20°C); growth was abnormal at 86°F (30°C). Flowering is also inhibited and flowers are of poorer quality at the high temperatures. In Florida production sites, plants tolerate 45°F (7°C) where heating is not available. Frost is not an option, because plants are quickly killed (Hennen and Hotchkiss, 1995).

LIGHT

The intensity range during production can vary from 1000 to 2500 fc (200 to 500 μmol $\cdot$ m^{-2} $\cdot$ s^{-1}) depending on the cultivar. Plants produced under higher intensities are more compact and branched and the leaves tend to be lighter green in color than plants grown under lower light intensities (Hennen and Hotchkiss, 1995; Henny et al., 1991; McConnell et al., 1981).

WATER

A variety of irrigation techniques can be used in producing peace lilies, including overhead irrigation, drip tubes (Hennen and Hotchkiss, 1995), and ebb and flow (Kent and Reed, 1996). The medium must be kept evenly moist throughout production. However, do not saturate the medium (Hennen and Hotchkiss, 1995).

CARBON DIOXIDE

No data available.

NUTRITION

In commerce constant liquid fertigation and controlled-release fertilizers can be used singly or in combination. Regardless of the fertilization method, the N–P–K ratio of 3:1:2 was recommended by Henny et al. (1991) and Hennen and Hotchkiss (1995). McConnell et al. (1981) suggested 1200 lb N/acre/yr (1345 kg $\cdot$ ha^{-1} $\cdot$ yr^{-1}) of N–P–K. Henny et al. (1991) recommended 1500 lb N/acre/yr (1680 kg $\cdot$ ha^{-1} $\cdot$ yr^{-1}) which is equal to 3.5 lb N/1000 ft^2

(17 kg · m²) in the summer and 2.5 lb N/1000 ft² (12 kg · m²) in the winter. Kent and Reed (1996) recorded maximum growth at 10 mM N with ebb-and-flow irrigation. Mak and Yeh (2001) noted that 8 mM N was best with subirrigation and 16 mM N with overhead irrigation.

Hennen and Hotchkiss (1995) state that deficiencies of magnesium, iron, and sulfur are common and particularly evident when soil temperatures fall below 65°F (18°C). Broschat and Donselman (1986) give details on manganese deficiency. Daughtrey and Chase (1992) illustrated magnesium deficiency and excess fertilizer toxicity. See Chapter 6, Nutrition, Table 6-4, for foliar nutrient levels.

MEDIA

Bailey (1933) stated that a mixture of peat, fibrous loam, leaf mold, sand, and charcoal was standard. Currently, peat, perlite, and bark (1:1:1) or similar commercial premixed media are standard mixes in the southern United States. In Europe, coarse peat moss is most commonly used (Hennen and Hotchkiss, 1995). Mak and Yeh (2001) noted that a medium containing coir dust (1:1:1 coir dust:perlite:treefern) produced high-quality plants and that reduced growth and marginal necrosis occurred with an EC greater than 1.25 dS · m⁻¹ using 1:2 media:water dilutions.

HEIGHT CONTROL

None required.

SPACING

Plants can be produced in a wide array of pot sizes, from 3 to 14 in. (8 to 36 cm) in diameter (Hennen and Hotchkiss, 1995).

PINCHING AND DISBUDDING

None required. However, Henny and Fooshee (1987) found that benzyladenine (BA) stimulated basal branching, increasing the fullness of the plants. A 1000-ppm drench applied 10 to 12 weeks after transplanting was most effective and produced 6.2 axillary shoots versus 3.6 for the control. Commercially 250 to 1000 ppm BA is applied as a spray or drench. Apply after plants are established as BA can inhibit rooting development. The BA treatment could eliminate the need to plant two to three seedlings or plugs per pot to produce a full plant.

SUPPORT

None needed.

SCHEDULE AND TIMING

Production time is directly related to propagation method, size of the transplant, environmental control during production, and desired marketing size. Producers commonly use a 10- to 14-week-old *in vitro*-propagated transplant. A 3- to 5-month production time is required for a 3- to 4-in. (8- to 10-cm) pot; 7 to 9 months for a 6-in. (15-cm) pot, 11 months for an 8-in. (20-cm) pot, 10 to 12 months for a 10-in. (25-cm) pot, and 16 to 20 months for a 14-in. (36-cm) pot (Hennen and Hotchkiss, 1995). The use of GA₃ results in rapid flowering; of 31 named and experimental cultivars the earliest cultivars flowered in 9 to 10 weeks after treatment and the latest 15 to 16 weeks (Henny et al., 1999). Plants were started from *in vitro*-propagated plugs grown in 72-cell flats placed in 0.5-gal (1.9-L) pots and grown under a maximum light level of 1250 fc (250 μmol · m⁻² · s⁻¹). Plants were treated with GA₃ 12 weeks after potting; thus, crop time from planting of the plugs ranged from 21 to 28 weeks.

Seedlings can also be delivered in a variety of sizes (38 to 200 plugs/flat), which can take 9 to 15 months to produce a flowering plant (Hennen and Hotchkiss, 1995). Many small plants which are not in flower are sold as foliage plants to eliminate the extra production time and expense required for flowering. Frequently, seedlings do not flower until they are 6 months or older (Henny, 1985).

INSECTS

Henny et al. (1991) lists aphids, caterpillars, fungus gnats, mealybugs, scales, shore flies, various thrips, and whiteflies as possible insect pests. Considering the lengthy list of insect pests and potential disease problems, the authors now appreciate a well-grown, healthy spathiphyllum.

DISEASES

Cylindrocladium spathiphylii, a soil-borne fungus, is the most serious disease problem. A pasteurized medium is essential in the control of this pathogen. A medium fungicidal drenching program is often appropriate (Hennen and Hotchkiss, 1995). Daughtrey and Chase (1992) list *Erwinia* soft rot, *Myrothecium* leaf spot, and

Phytophthora leaf spot. Knauss et al. (1981) added *Colletotrichum, Pseudomonas, Cephaleuros,* and *Cercospora* to the list. Henny et al. (1991) gave detailed descriptions for many of the diseases listed previously. Dreistadt (2001) also listed *Pythium* root rot, *Rhizoctonia* aerial blight, and *Pseudomonas* and *Acremonium* soft rot.

PHYSIOLOGICAL DISORDERS

Malformed inflorescences develop at 86°F (30°C) or with the use of GA_3 (Henny, 1985).

POSTHARVEST

Plants should not be shipped below 54°F (12°C) because leaves will turn yellow. The peace lily can tolerate long-term storage or transport, up to 30 days at 55 to 61°F (13 to 16°C) and 80 to 90% relative humidity (Nowak and Rudnicki, 1990).

KEY POINTS

- Peace lily (*Spathiphyllum*) is an important indoor foliage plant grown for its glossy, dark-green leaves and white inflorescences.
- Peace lily is one of the few foliage plants to form an attractive inflorescence.
- Gibberellic acid at 250 ppm can be used to reduce time to flowering.
- Plants are grown at night temperatures of 65 to 77°F (18 to 25°C) and day temperatures up to 90°F (32°C).
- Production times range from 3 to 5 months for 3- to 4-in. (8- to 10-cm) pots to 16 to 20 months for 14-in. (36-cm) pots.

BIBLIOGRAPHY

Bailey, L.H. 1933. *Spathiphyllum,* p. 3203 in *The Standard Cyclopedia of Horticulture.* Macmillan, New York.

Bailey, L.H., and E.Z. Bailey. 1976. *Spathiphyllum,* p. 1062 in *Hortus Third: A Concise Dictionary of Plants Cultivated in the United States and Canada.* Macmillan, New York.

Broschat, T.K., and H. Donselman. 1986. Manganese deficiency symptoms in *Spathiphyllum. HortScience* 21:1234–1235.

Daughtrey, M., and A.R. Chase. 1992. *Spathiphyllum,* pp. 198–201 in *Ball Field Guide to Diseases of Greenhouse Ornamentals.* Ball Publishing, Geneva, Illinois.

Dreistadt, S.H. 2001. *Integrated Pest Management for Floriculture and Nurseries.* University of California Division of Agriculture and Natural Resources Publication 3402.

Hennen, G.R., and S.E. Hotchkiss. 1995. *Spathiphyllum:* Success for every market. *GrowerTalks* 59(10):31, 36.

Henny, R.J. 1981a. Promotion of flowering in *Spathiphyllum* 'Mauna Loa' with gibberellic acid. *HortScience* 16:554–555.

Henny, R.J. 1981b. Inducing flowering of *Spathiphyllum floribundum* (Linder & Andre) N.E. Br. with gibberellic acid (GA_3). *Proceedings of the Florida State Horticultural Society* 94:111–112.

Henny, R.J. 1985. *Spathiphyllum,* pp. 382–383 in *Handbook of Flowering,* vol IV, A.H. Halevy, editor. CRC Press, Boca Raton, Florida.

Henny, R.J., A.R. Chase, and L.S. Osborne. 1991. *Spathiphyllum.* Foliage Plant Research Note RH-91–32, Central Florida Research and Education Center, Apopka, Florida.

Henny, R.J., and W.C. Fooshee. 1987. Increasing basal shoot number in *Spathiphyllum* 'Tasson' with BA. *Foliage Digest* 10(7):5–6.

Henny, R.J., and E.M. Rasmussen. 1981. Inducing flowering of *Spathiphyllum* with gibberellic acid (GA_3). *Foliage Digest* 4(3):7–9.

Henny, R.J., D.J. Norman, and T.A. Mellich. 1999. Spathiphyllum cultivars vary in flowering response after treatment with gibberellic acid. *HortTechnology* 9:177–178.

Huxley, A., M. Griffiths, and M. Levy. 1992. *Spathiphyllum,* pp. 345–346 in *The New Royal Horticultural Society Dictionary of Gardening,* vol. 4. Stockton Press, New York.

Kent, M.W., and D.W. Reed. 1996. Nitrogen nutrition of New Guinea impatiens 'Barbados' and *Spathiphyllum* 'Petite' in a subirrigation system. *Journal of the American Society for Horticultural Science* 12:816–819.

Knauss, J.F., S.A. Alfrieri, Jr., R.B. Maylatt, and F.W. Zetter. 1981. Foliage plant diseases, pp. 351–727 in *Foliage Plant Production*, J.N. Joiner, editor. Prentice-Hall, Englewood Cliffs, New Jersey.

Mak, A.T.Y., and D.M. Yeh. 2001 Nitrogen nutrition of *Spathiphyllum* 'Sensation' grown in sphagnum peat- and coir-based media with two irrigation methods. *HortScience* 36:645–649.

McConnell, D.B., R.W. Henley, and R.L. Biamonte. 1981. Commercial foliage plants (*Spathiphyllum*), p. 590 in *Foliage Plant Production*, J.N. Joiner, editor. Prentice-Hall, Englewood Cliffs, New Jersey.

Nowak, J., and R.M. Rudnicki. 1990. *Spathiphyllum*, p. 188 in *Postharvest Handling and Storage of Cut Flowers, Florist Greens and Potted Plants*. Timber Press, Portland, Oregon.

Orlikowska, T., I. Sabala, and E. Nowak. 1995. Adventitious shoot regeneration on explants of *Anthurium, Codiaeum, Dieffenbachia, Gerbera, Rosa* and *Spathiphyllum* for breeding purposes. *Acta Horticulturae* 420:115–117.

Watad, A.A., K.G. Raghothama, M. Kochba, A. Nissim, and V. Gaba. 1997. Micropropagation of *Spathiphyllum* and *Syngonium* is facilitated by use of interfacial membrane rafts. *HortScience* 32: 307–308.

Stephanotis

FIGURE II-I STEPHANOTIS   Potted *Stephanotis* plant.

INTRODUCTION

Common names: stephanotis, Madagascar jasmine, bridal wreath, chaplet flower, waxflower.

Scientific name: *Stephanotis floribunda* (R. Br.) Brongn. (Huxley et al., 1992).

Family and related taxa: Asclepiadaceae R. Br. Other important ornamental genera in this family include *Asclepias* and *Hoya*.

Origin: *Stephanotis* includes approximately five species, all of which are climbing shrubs found in tropical Madagascar and Malaysia.

Uses and current status: The white waxy five-lobed flower is fragrant and is used individually in corsages and wedding bouquets. Vines can be trained on supports to produce potted flowering plants (Fig. II-1 Stephanotis). In frost-free areas stephanotis can be used as a landscape vine.

Vines can be 15 feet (5 m) or more in length. The leaves are opposite, elliptical, thick, 2 to 4 in. (5 to 10 cm) long, and a beautiful shiny dark green. The white flowers are 2 to 4 in. (5 to 10 cm) long and are born in an umbel inflorescence (Bailey and Bailey, 1976; Huxley et al., 1992).

CULTIVARS

There are no known cultivars. However, producers should select only the most vigorous plants for cuttings.

PROPAGATION

Bailey (1933) stated that cuttings should be made from half mature wood, which will easily root any month of the year, with spring the most common time. Hansen (1988) found little difference in the number of roots formed on cuttings from apical node 3 to the basal node 17, but axillary shoot activity was most rapid at nodes 2 to 6. In 1989, Hansen concluded that rooting was best on single-node cuttings harvested from the middle nodes and rooted at 73°F (23°C). Other temperature recommendations range from 70 to 75°F (21 to 24°C) (Bailey, 1933; Evans, 1991). At 63°F (17°C), rooting was totally suppressed.

Bailey (1933) stated cuttings were best propagated in a sand-peat mixture; Hansen (1989) used peat and Evans (1991) used sand. A 1.5-in. (4-cm) stem section was left below the node for root initiation and development (Wikesjö, 1982).

Rooting can occur under plastic tents, which are commonly used in Denmark. Maximum rooting occurs after 45 days (Wikesjö, 1982). Kano et al. (1992) used rockwool for rooting as well as CO_2 (1500 ppm) under their propagation tents. CO_2 was found to enhance rooting.

FLOWERING CONTROL AND DORMANCY

Flowering occurs at the axillary nodes. The apical meristem is always vegetative. Flowers are initiated in the leaf axillary of recently mature tissue of the elongating vines or shoots. Flowering generally does not occur on the older woody tissue. Floral initiation and development occur after a period of vigorous vegetative growth, which can be stimulated by the appropriate environmental conditions and pruning (see Pinching and Disbudding) (Evans, 1991; Kofranek, 1985; Kofranek and Criley, 1983; Kofranek and Kubota, 1981).

Under an 8-hr short-day photoperiod, limited flowering occurs at 59°F (15°C) and adequate flowering occurs at 64 to 81°F (18 to 27°C). However, under 12- or 16-hr photoperiods, plants flowered copiously at 59, 64, 70, or 81°F (15, 18, 21, or 27°C). Consequently, stephanotis is a day-neutral plant, but with a strong temperature × photoperiod interaction. Flowering occurs most readily under long days (12 to 16 hr) at warm 64 to 81°F (18 to 27°C) temperatures (Kofranek and Criley, 1983).

TEMPERATURE

For optimum production of flowers (rapidity and quality), the temperature should be between 64 and 70°F (18 to 21°C). At 59°F (15°C), flower production is low and slow and at 81°F (27°C), flower color is "greenish." Plants grown under 64 to 70°F (18 to 21°C) under a 12- or 16-hr photoperiod formed the most flower clusters and individual flowers. However, the warmer temperature, 70°F (21°C), was the more favorable for both flower cluster and individual flower numbers (Kofranek and Criley, 1983).

Interestingly, a brief exposure of plants to 59°F (15°C) from August 16 to October 15 resulted in a maximum number of individual flowers (289), but delayed flowering by 28 days compared to plants grown under a constant 70°F (21°C), which produced 221 flowers (Kofranek and Criley, 1983). The temperature drop concept was also recommended by Wikesjö (1982) in Sweden for potted flowering plants.

In Sweden the temperature was reduced from November 1 to February 1 from 65 to 55°F (18 to 13°C). After February 1, day temperatures were slowly increased for 10 days to 84°F (29°C); thereafter, the night forcing temperature was at least 65°F (18°C). Temperature drops are practical only if plants are produced in a separate greenhouse and not with other crops (Wikesjö, 1982).

Erwin and Cirhan (1991) studied the rate of leaf unfolding at various temperatures. At 86°F (30°C), the highest temperature used in the study, the rate of unfolding was still increasing. However, at 86°F (30°C), flowers were "greenish."

LIGHT

Historically, plants have been given long days as a night break or day extension using incandescent lamps during the short days of winter. In California, the natural day length plus photoperiodic lighting should equal 12 to 16 hr. It is unknown why photoperiodic incandescent light is not always effective (Kofranek, 1985). Long-day lighting responses may depend on leaf density and plant vigor (Kofranek and Kubota, 1981). Kofranek and Kubota (1981) found that long day lighting should commence by October 5 in Davis, California. A minimum of 30 fc (6 μmol $\cdot$ m^{-2} $\cdot$ s^{-1}) should be used.

Work in Europe found no differences between using a photoperiodic incandescent light intensity of 3 or 5 fc (0.6 to 1 μmol $\cdot$ m^{-2} $\cdot$ s^{-1}) (Denmark) or between fluorescent or incandescent lamps (Germany) (Jensen and Christensen, 1981; von Hentig and Heimann, 1974). Von Hentig and Heimann (1974) in Germany recommended using 4 to 5 fc (0.8 to 1 μmol $\cdot$ m^{-2} $\cdot$ s^{-1}) from October to March. The duration of lighting increased from 3 hr/night in October to 4 hr from November to February, then decreased to 3 hr in March (von Hentig and Heimann, 1974).

No scientific work has been found by the author on the use of HID photosynthetic lighting. In Minnesota, HID lighting is supplied from high-pressure sodium lamps spaced 10 ft (3.3 m) apart (Len Busch Roses, personal communication). Lighting begins in mid-August and the duration is gradually increased from 4 to 12 hr each night. Regardless, maximum photosynthetic light should be given during the summer; shade only to keep temperatures below 79°F (26°C).

WATER

Plants should be kept uniformly moist, but not wet. If plants are allowed to become water stressed (wilted) during floral initiation, low total flower production can occur and if wilting occurs later in flower development, flowers abort (Evans, 1991). Automated irrigation should be used.

CARBON DIOXIDE

Kano et al. (1992) found that CO_2 (1500 ppm) enhanced rooting. Although no data were found regarding the use of supplemental CO_2 during production, plants would likely respond well if used in conjunction with long days. In Minnesota, 1000 ppm CO_2 is used during production in situations where stephanotis are grown with rose plants in the same glasshouse (Len Busch Roses, personal communication).

NUTRITION

Growers feel nutrition should be low when plants are first being established, then increased later. Generally, 200 to 250 ppm N (constant fertigation) is considered optimum (Evans, 1991; Wikesjö, 1982). Wikesjö (1982) recommended using weekly fertigation with ammonium nitrate (100 ppm) and potassium nitrate (600 ppm). In Minnesota, medium N, P, and K test levels were kept at 120, 15, and 40 ppm, respectively, with a medium EC of 1.8 and pH of 6.0 (Len Busch Roses, personal communication).

MEDIA

Plants can be grown in any well-drained medium; however, peat-based media are most commonly used for potted plants (Wikesjö,

1982). The medium should be prepared to a depth of at least 12 in. (30 cm) and should be well drained for vines planted in ground beds for cut flower production. The pH should be 5.5 to 6.5 (Evans, 1991).

HEIGHT CONTROL

For pot plant production, Cycocel (chlormequat) and B-Nine (daminozide) sprays at 100 ppm reduced vine length and days to flower and increased flower cluster number (Evans, 1991). The authors suggest that growth retardants could also be used in cut flower production to speed flowering and increase flower cluster number.

SPACING

Europeans produce flowering stephanotis plants in 6-in. (15-cm) pots. The vines are trained on a single upright wire, which is later bent to form a wreath or trained on a wooden trellis. Potted flowering plants are given a final spacing of 9 × 9 in. (23 × 23 cm) (Wikesjö, 1982). Plants for cut flower production are spaced 3 ft (1 m) apart if grown in pots along a wall and trained on wires. Plants for cut flower production can also be planted 2 ft (60 cm) apart in 4-ft (1.3-m)-wide beds and alternated from one side of the bed to the other.

PINCHING AND DISBUDDING

Kofranek and Kubota (1981) pruned shoots that were 7/16 in. (1 cm) or less in diameter on May 1. These plants were most responsive to photoperiodic lighting, which began in October. Further, plants that were pruned in midwinter flowered with maximum production in late spring and early summer. In Minnesota, if plants are cut back in July, flower production commences again in October/November.

For cut flower production, plants are grown in ground beds for many years. Once established, plants should be cut back every 5 years (Len Busch Roses, personal communication). Vines are cut back to 3 ft (1 m). Kofranek (1985) theorizes that if the canopy becomes too thick, vine vigor decreases as photosynthetic metabolites are shunted to the older shade leaves and not to new shoots responsible for flower initiation and development. Routine soft pinching can occur at any time, which enhances flower production, reduces the time to flower of axillary buds, and reduces vine size.

SUPPORT

For cut flower production, plant vines are trained on wire trellises, which are most commonly placed along an "unused" greenhouse glass wall (see Spacing section). The maximum height of the support is 6 ft (2 m) with a total of four rows of support wires.

For potted flowering plants, 6-ft (2-m)-long strings or wires are secured overhead and used to train the vining stems (Wikesjö, 1982). The strings or wires are used to form a wreath or are secured to a trellis.

SCHEDULE AND TIMING

Flower scheduling is controlled by both long photoperiodic lighting treatments and temperature. For a potted flowering plant up to 12 months is required to produce a 6-in. (15-cm) flowering pot (Wikesjö, 1982). For cut flower production in California, plants were pruned in early May, incandescent photoperiodic lighting began in early October, and cut flower production commenced in December. Production decreased during midwinter (February), but increased in April when natural light intensity and duration increased. In Minnesota, a cutback occurred in July during periods of low cut flower demand; production commenced again in October/November (Len Busch Roses, personal communication). The time span between a visible bud and flowering is approximately 6 weeks.

INSECTS

Mealybugs, scale, spider mites, thrips, and whiteflies may be common problems if plants are not constantly observed and treated. Stephanotis is a long-term crop when produced as a cut flower and vines can be several years old. Potted plants may be up to 12 months old. Consequently, constant observation is required to prevent insect populations from increasing.

DISEASES

Sclerotinia and *Botrytis* have been reported to blemish flowers (Evans, 1991; Raabe, 1971). When irrigating, use a system that does not wet the flowers. Green et al. (1988) reported tomato spotted wilt virus in stephanotis. Crown and root rot (*Rhizoctonia*), dieback (*Glomerella cingulata*), and powdery mildew (*Oidium*) have also been reported (Dreistadt, 2001).

PHYSIOLOGICAL DISORDERS

Flowers are not pure white, but tinted green when plants are grown at 81°F (27°C) or higher.

POSTHARVEST

Individuals flowers are harvested when they are fully open or an entire cluster may be harvested when mature. Individual flowers or clusters can be placed in water, hydrated for 30 min, and then placed loose in a plastic bag. The bagged flowers can be stored for up to 1 week at 39°F (4°C) (Nowak and Rudnicki, 1990; Len Busch Roses, personal communication). No data were found on the use of floral preservatives.

Potted flowering plants are very sensitive to ethylene, which causes flower abscission. Silver thiosulfate (STS) sprays at 0.3 to 0.6 mM have been reported to increase the longevity of flowers of potted plants (Nowak and Rudnicki, 1990). Plants can be shipped at 54°F (12°C).

KEY POINTS

- The fragrant white flowers of stephanotis are the main attraction of this cut flower.
- This vine can also be trained on a support and marketed as a potted flowering plant.
- Plants are propagated from cuttings of half mature stems.

- Plants are day neutral but LD lighting is commonly used in the winter.
- Individuals flowers are harvested when they are fully open or an entire cluster may be harvested when mature.

BIBLIOGRAPHY

Bailey, L.H. 1933. *Stephanotis*, p. 3238 in *The Standard Cyclopedia of Horticulture*. Macmillan, New York.

Bailey, L.H., and E.Z. Bailey. 1976. *Stephanotis*, p. 1074 in *Hortus Third: A Concise Dictionary of* *Plants Cultivated in the United States and Canada*. Macmillan, New York.

Dreistadt, S.H. 2001. *Integrated Pest Management for Floriculture and Nurseries*. University of California

Division of Agriculture and Natural Resources Publication 3402.

Erwin, J., and C. Cirhan. 1991. Temperature effects on stephanotis leaf unfolding rate. *Minnesota Flower Growers Bulletin* 40(3):36–37.

Evans, M.R. 1991. *Stephanotis*—An alternative crop for specimen pots and hanging baskets. *Florida Ornamental Growers' Association Newsletter* Mar./Apr.:3–5.

Green, J.L., T.C. Allen, and S. Fischer. 1988. Symptoms of *Stephanotis* infected with tomato spotted wilt virus in *Ornamentals—Northwest Cooperative Extension Service*, Oregon State University, Covallis.

Hansen, J. 1988. Effect of cutting position on rooting, axillary bud break and shoot growth in *Stephanotis floribunda*. *Acta Horticulture* 226: 159–163.

Hansen, J. 1989. Influence of cutting position and temperature during rooting on adventitious root formation and axillary bud break of *Stephanotis floribunda*. *Scientific Horticulture* 40:345–354.

Huxley, A., M. Griffiths, and M. Levy. 1992. *Stephanotis*, p. 377 in *The New Royal Horticultural Science Dictionary of Gardening*, vol. 4. Stockton Press, New York.

Jensen, H.E., and O.V. Christensen. 1981. Blomsterudvikling hos *Stephanotis floribunda* som funktion af tempertur, daglengde og lysintensitet. *Nordisk Jordrugsforsknon* 63:438–439. (in Danish, English summary)

Kano, A., Y. Fukazawa, M. Aono, and K. Ohkawa. 1992. Effect of age of cuttings, propagation media, and cutting methods on rooting of *Stephanotis floribunda* Brogn. *Journal of the Japanese Society for Horticultural Science* 61:619–624. (in Japanese, English summary)

Kofranek, A.M. 1985. *Stephanotis floribunda*, pp. 393–395 in *Handbook of Flowering*, vol. IV, A.H. Halevy, editor. CRC Press, Boca Raton, Florida.

Kofranek, A.M., and R. Criley. 1983. Photoperiod and temperature effects on stephanotis flowering. *Acta Horticulture* 147:211–218.

Kofranek, A.M., and J. Kubota. 1981. The influence of pruning and of extending the photoperiod on the winter flowering of *Stephanotis floribunda*. *Acta Horticulture* 128:69–78.

Nowak, J., and R.M. Rudnicki. 1990. *Postharvest Handling and Storage of Cut Flowers, Florist Greens and Potted Plants*. Timber Press, Portland, Oregon.

Raabe, R.D. 1971. Sclerotinia blight of stephanotis flowers. *Phytopathology* 61:1524–1525.

von Hentig, W.U., and M. Heimann. 1974. *Stephanotis floribunda* (Asclepiadaceae) Stephanotis, Kranzschlinge in *Kulturkartei Zierpflanzenbau*. Paul Parey Publishing, Hamburg.

Wikesjö, K. 1982. Cultivation of the stephanotis. *Florists' Review* 170 (4409):44, 156.

Strelitzia

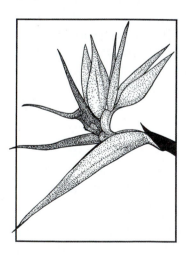

INTRODUCTION

Common names: Bird of paradise, strelitzia, crane flower, bird's tongue flower.

Scientific name: *Strelitzia reginae* Banks ex Dryand. (Huxley et al., 1992). *Strelitzia reginae* is named for Charlotte of Mecklenburg-Strelitz who became the queen of King George III of England.

Family and related taxa: Strelitziaceae (Schumann) Hutch. Two other genera in Strelitziaceae are recognized, *Ravenala* Adans. (Traveler's palm) and *Phenakospermum* Endl. In the *Strelitzia* genus, only two species are common in horticulture, *S. reginae* and *S. nicolai* Reg. & Körn, the giant bird of paradise or white bird of paradise. The species *augusta* is no longer valid and is considered a synonym for *S. alba*, a woody-stemmed, white-flowered species of the Cape Province of South Africa. The species name *angustifolia* is also not considered valid. A hybrid of *S. alba* × *S. reginae*, *S.* ×*kewensis*, is reported to be of horticultural origin.

Origin: *Strelitzia* is native to South Africa in the East London and Port Elizabeth region (latitude 27°, longitude 33–34°S). The native habitat is open forest, damp with rainfall year-round [annual total of approximately 43 in. (109 cm)], but well drained. The annual mean

FIGURE II-I STRELITZIA *Strelitzia reginae* inflorescence.

temperature is about 70°F (21°C) with a high/low range of 76/64°F (24/18°C). The native habitat of *Strelitzia* is mostly below 1000 ft (400 m) of elevation. *S. reginae* was discovered by Johann Auge, Superintendent of the Dutch East India Company gardens in CapeTown, brought into cultivation in 1772, and introduced to the Royal Gardens at Kew by Joseph Banks in 1773 (Cannon, 1953). The first record of its introduction into California is in a nursery catalog of Col. Warren of Sacramento in 1853 (Cannon, 1953).

Uses and current status: *S. reginae* is used as a cut flower and potted interior plant, while *S. nicolai* is mainly used as an interiorscape accent plant in containers or planters (Fig. II-1 Strelitzia). Both species are used in tropical, subtropical, and Mediterranean climatic regions as landscape plants. *S. reginae* is the City Flower of Los Angeles and is widely grown in California from Santa Barbara south into San Diego as a cut flower and landscape plant. The large plantings of southern California have given way to subdivisions, while production is increasing in Mexico and Hawaii. Elsewhere, large areas of production exist in the Canary Islands, Kenya, and Uganda. Formerly, *S. reginae* was grown under glass in the Netherlands, but its heat requirements, long crop time, and low productivity per unit of space contributed to cutbacks in this floricultural region. Old, twisted dry leaves of *S. reginae* are also marketed as a dried material.

CULTIVARS

'Kirstenbosch Gold,' which has been renamed 'Mandela's Gold,' has yellow-orange flowers. A similar cultivar was found in southern California and distributed in the nursery trade by Monrovia Nurseries. A form with reduced lamina is *S. reginae* var. *parvifolia*, while a form

lacking a lamina (leaves are spikelike) is *S. juncea* (van de Venter et al., 1975). The latter is also classified as a variety of *S. reginae* (Huxley et al., 1992). Selections of *S. reginae* include 'Farinosa,' with very glaucous foliage; 'Glauca,' with large, glaucous leaves; 'Humilis,' which is the same as 'Pygmaea,' with short petioles and large flowers; and 'Rutilans,' with intensely orange flowers and foliage with a red or purple midrib. Much room remains for the selection of cultivars among seed-propagated plants because there is a great variety of plant habits, inflorescence size, bract color, angle of the inflorescence to its stem, productivity, and intensity of the blue petals and orange tepals (Criley and Muruvanda, 1984).

PROPAGATION

Bird of paradise is normally propagated by division or from seed, although tissue culture is an undeveloped possibility (Ziv and Halevy, 1983). Germination of fresh seed can take 30 to 90 days, and old seed with a hardened seed coat may take 6 to 12 months. The optimum germination temperature is about 77°F (25°C). Successful experimental and commercial treatments to improve germination have included 24-hr soaks in warm water or hydrogen peroxide solutions, scarification in sulfuric acid, and treatment with ethephon or gibberellic acid (GA) (Ishihata, 1976; Jimenz Meijas and Caballero Ruano, 1990). Germination is enhanced by incubating imbibed seed in pure oxygen, but this is not practical for a grower. One practical option is a 5- to 10-min soak in concentrated sulfuric acid, followed by a rinse in water and a 24-hr soak in 50 ppm GA (Ishihata, 1976). Seedlings with five to six leaves are most efficiently field planted, but they may require up to 6 years to come into commercial levels of production.

Quality mother plants are important when using division as the propagation method to ensure quality flowers and high yields. Division of the stem mass requires considerable labor because most of the mass is at or below soil level in a dense clump. The root system is thick, fleshy, and brittle and difficult to obtain intact when digging out the divisions. Broken roots do not seem to regenerate new laterals. Divisions of two to three fans, stems with fanlike leaf arrangements, establish more readily than single divisions although the latter provides more plants from a clump. Leave four to five leaves on a fan, strip lower foliage from the stem, remove broken roots, and dust cut surfaces with a general fungicide. Although these large divisions can be planted directly to the field, higher survival is obtained by growing them in containers for 3 to 5 months and transplanting well-rooted plants to the field. Flowering is more rapid from division than from seed.

An interesting variant on propagation involves cutting a deep notch through the basal leaf sheaths just above the apical region. The apex of the stem is removed. In about 2 to 6 months several lateral shoots develop from axillary buds that can be removed with their roots. The system generates a greater number of plantlets than can develop from a single stem or from tissue culture (van de Pol and van Hell, 1988).

FLOWERING CONTROL AND DORMANCY

Seed-propagated plants that are 3 years old or younger are juvenile and do not flower. Juvenility may relate to the diameter of the basal stem because accelerating plant growth by using warm temperatures of 77°F (25°C) increased leaf and flower production (Berninger, 1981; Fransen, 1977; Noordegraaf and van der Krogt, 1976). The axillary meristem of each leaf of a mature plant is capable of producing a flower bud. However, leaf count does not equal flower count because of either flower bud abortion (Criley and Kawabata, 1984) or flower blasting (Halevy et al., 1976). Photoperiod has no effect on flowering (Halevy et al., 1976), but temperature is a major factor in flowering (Halevy et al., 1987). Weekly sprays of 50 ppm GA may enhance stem elongation, hasten flower maturation, and increase the emergence of new flower stalks within 10 weeks of the initial spray (Criley and Halevy, 1985).

True dormancy does not occur in bird of paradise, but during cold periods little leaf or flower production occurs. Flower development can take longer than a year from its initiation (van de Venter et al., 1980).

TEMPERATURE

A new leaf can be produced every 6 weeks under 81/72°F (27/22°C) or 90/81°F (32/27°C) day/night temperature regimes, while the time interval increases to 11 weeks at 63/54°F (17/12°C) (Halevy et al., 1987). Cut flowers can be harvested 8 to 9 weeks after emergence of the inflorescence bud from the leaf sheath in warm, high-light areas of Israel, but 28 weeks was recorded in South Africa for inflorescences

developing through the winter months (Halevy et al., 1987; van de Venter et al., 1980). One strategy that may shorten the juvenile phase is to grow the plants at 81°F (27°C) until they reach flowering size, then reduce the temperature to 68 to 77/63°F (20 to 25/17°C) day/night temperature for flowering. Criley and Kawabata (1984) and Halevy et al. (1987) suggested that early flower bud abortion occurs at temperatures warmer than 81°F (27°C) and cool temperatures prevent floral development, creating a seasonal flowering pattern. In field situations little temperature manipulation is possible and site selection according to temperature range is the only feasible option.

LIGHT

Although plants will flower when given 30% shade, full sunlight is preferable. Flower number is reduced under moderate and heavy shade conditions (van de Venter et al., 1980). Halevy et al. (1976) reported that bird of paradise is not responsive to photoperiod.

WATER

Established plants have a considerable tolerance to drought, but seedlings are susceptible to drought stress because their fleshy roots systems have not yet developed. In heavy soils, excessive water can cause poor aeration and rotting of the fleshy roots. In well-drained soils, 1 in. (2.5 cm) of water per week is adequate and the plants will survive on 0.5 in. (1.3 cm) of water per week. Flowering may be delayed for more favorable marketing periods by withholding water when demand for flowers is low, especially during the summer, and resuming irrigation 8 to 10 weeks before flowering is desired. This practice is used in the Canary Islands (J. Rodriguez, personal communication).

CARBON DIOXIDE

Bird of paradise is customarily grown outdoors where carbon dioxide addition is not practical.

NUTRITION

Providing a standard recommendation for fertilization of bird of paradise is complicated by the wide variety of soil, rainfall, and temperature environments in which the plants grow. Growers often throw a handful of fertilizer around the plant every 3 or 4 months with little regard to soil analysis or plant requirements. Almost all research has focused on supplying nitrogen, and recommendations range from 0.35 to 0.53 oz (10 to 15 g) per plant per month to 100 to 200 lb/acre/year (112 to 224 kg · ha^{-1} · yr^{-1}). A Hawaii extension recommendation is 1 to 1.5 lb (0.45 to 0.68 kg) of 16–16–16 fertilizer per plant every other month, but this recommendation is for a high rainfall area with a loose volcanic soil. A study of potted bird of paradise found that a 3:1:2 N:P:K ratio produced the most leaves and flowers and flower fresh weight (El-Shoura and Hosni, 1996). The foliar tissue analysis values in this experiment were 1.2 to 1.5% N, 0.5 to 0.9% P, and 2.4 to 2.9% K. Bird of paradise prefers low growing medium EC. See Chapter 6, Nutrition, Table 6-4, for foliar nutrient levels.

MEDIA

Bird of paradise grow well in a wide range of well-drained field soils from sandy to sandy clays. The medium pH should be between 5.5 and 6.5. Peat-based media have been used in pots for seedlings, but this medium is too light for older plants that become large and top heavy. Israeli experiments used a volcanic tuff for potted plants, while an Egyptian experiment found good results using a 1:3 sand:clay medium (El-Shoura and Hosni, 1996).

HEIGHT CONTROL

Bird of paradise do not require height control. No dwarf or low-growing selections exist. Periodically, old growth should be removed to open the crown of the plant for insect control.

SPACING

A minimum spacing of 5 × 7 ft (1.5 × 2.1 m) (in-row × between row) is recommended. By 5 or 6 years, even this spacing may be inadequate to get around the plants to harvest flowers. Planting density studies showed that flower production was reduced by crowding (Criley, 1984).

PINCHING AND DISBUDDING

The older leaves should be cut away after flowering to open the crown of the plant to pesticide sprays. The crowns split at or about soil level after producing 5 to 14 leaves, but removal of crowded stems is not practical in field situations. More frequently, the crown is simply divided and new plants established.

Pinching is not practiced on bird of paradise. The inflorescence is normally a single boat-shaped bract bearing up to nine flowers, but occasionally multiple inflorescences develop on one flower stalk. Because the secondary inflorescence is usually of poorer quality, it is often broken off in the field or at the packing shed. While flower designers will use stems with well-developed secondary inflorescences, packing them for shipment poses a problem because of the angle between the two inflorescences.

SUPPORT

No support is required in production of bird of paradise flowers. Flower stalks for full-sun-grown plants are strong enough without support.

SCHEDULE AND TIMING

Bird of paradise are not responsive to photoperiod. Seasonal flowering occurs in outdoor plantings in regions with extreme temperature fluctuations. No research has been conducted to manage flowering by temperature, but this may be feasible under protected conditions. Management of flowering time seems to be possible by judicious withholding and providing of irrigation (see Water section). However, the degree of control is not great.

Because cut flowers can be pulsed in sugar solutions and held in dry cold storage for up to 28 days, it is somewhat possible to provide a constant supply of flowers to market (Kofranek, 1976). *S. reginae* is grown as a foliage plant from seed with one or two plants per container, but it requires several years to flower.

INSECTS

Armored and oleander scale and mealybug insects are the principal insect problems. Mealybugs on the roots and basal stems may predispose plants to root and crown rots. Insecticides plus light oil sprays have been effective in control. Some growing areas have reported damage from ants, whiteflies, and thrips (University of Hawaii Agricultural Diagnostic Center, personal communication). The spiraling whitefly (*Aleurodiscus dispersus*) favors the leaves for their waxy coatings. Other reported insects include aphids, harlequin bugs, and crown borer (Dreistadt, 2001).

DISEASES

Root rot may be a problem in wet soils. Specific fungi that have been associated with root rots include *Phytophthora, Pythium, Rhizoctonia,*

Fusarium, and *Calonectria (Cylindrocladium)* (University of Hawaii Agricultural Diagnostic Center, personal communication). Plants can be weakened by nematodes feeding on the fleshy root system. Although a number of nematode species have been associated with damaged root systems of bird of paradise, the most important species is the burrowing nematode (*Radopholus similis*) (University of Hawaii Agricultural Diagnostic Center, personal communication). Flowers can be attacked by *Botrytis* during storage and shipment. Foliar leaf spots have been associated with *Gloeosporium, Exserohilum,* and *Phyllosticta,* while dark vascular streaking has been caused by the bacteria *Xanthomonas campestris* and *Pseudomonas solonacearum* (University of Hawaii Agricultural Diagnostic Center, personal communication). Dreistadt (2001) also reported *Armillaria* root rot and various leaf and flower spots (*Alternaria, Cercospora, Colletotrichum, Curvularia,* and *Phyllosticta*).

PHYSIOLOGICAL DISORDERS

Seasonal flower bud abortion may be due to drought stress or high temperatures at a time when the bud is about 1 to 1.5 in. (2.5 to 4 cm) long, but competition from more developed flowers cannot be ruled out as a factor (Criley and Kawabata,1984; Halevy et al., 1987; Kawabata et al., 1984). *Blasting,* the loss of an inflorescence after the stalk has elongated, also occurs, but a cause has not been identified (Halevy et al., 1976). Distorted leaves occur and represent a split in the stem. Subsequent leaves are usually normal.

POSTHARVEST

For shipping, flowers are harvested as the first orange tepals appear and before they have emerged from the bract. For local sales, harvest at the emergence of the first floret. Usually the inflorescence stalk is pulled, rather than cut, and later trimmed to the desired length in the packing shed. Occasionally stalks bearing two inflorescences are found, but these are difficult to pack and the upper inflorescence may be weak.

Flowers can be harvested in tight bud, pulsed for 2 days in a solution of 10% sucrose + 250 ppm 8-hydroxyquinoline citrate + 150 ppm citric acid, and stored at 46°F (8°C) (Halevy et al., 1978). Tight buds can be stored up to 28 days dry after being pulsed, and the vase life will still be up to 11 days if stems are placed in a forcing solution similar to the pulsing solution (Kofranek, 1976).

Flowers should not be harvested wet because *Botrytis* and other diseases can cause rot during shipment or storage. Treatment with fungicides prior to harvest or in postharvest treatments is necessary to prevent disease development.

Bird of paradise stems are usually bunched in units of 5 or 6 with the bracts all facing the same direction to facilitate packing. Inflorescences with an open floret are packed loose with a "pillow" under the necks and stems interwoven in alternating directions. Shredded paper is used to cushion the flowers.

While the inflorescences are occasionally dried, old twisted and dried foliage is more commonly used. Fresh cut foliage is also sold for its bold character.

ACKNOWLEDGMENT

The authors would like to thank Richard Criley, University of Hawaii, for writing this chapter.

KEY POINTS

- Only two species of bird of paradise are common in cultivation, *S. reginae* and *S. nicolai.*
- *S. reginae* is used as a cut flower and potted interior plant; *S. nicolai* is mainly used as an interiorscape accent plant in containers or planters.
- Bird of paradise is a day-neutral tropical plant with a juvenile period of up to 3 years when seed propagated.
- *S. reginae* is grown primarily in the field but can be greenhouse grown and *S. nicolai* is grown in a greenhouse or outdoors.

- If using greenhouses, grow plants at 81°F (27°C) until they reach flowering size, then reduce the temperature to 68 to 77/63°F (20 to 25/17°C) day/night temperature for flowering.

- Flowers are harvested as the first orange petals appear and before they have emerged from the bract. For local sales, harvest at the emergence of the first floret.

BIBLIOGRAPHY

Berninger, E. 1981. Travaux sur *Strelitzia*, pp. 67–76 in *Station Amélioration Plant Floralies, Frejus, Rapport Action.* 1977–1980. (in French)

Cannon, A.R. 1953. The status of *Strelitzia.* Unpublished paper in the library of the University of California at Los Angeles.

Criley, R.A. 1984. Yield and production of red ginger and bird-of-paradise at Waimanalo as influenced by fertilizer, planting density, and season, pp. 129–138 in *Proceedings of the 2nd Fertilizer and Ornamentals Short Course.* Hawaii Institute of Tropical Agriculture and Human Resources 01.04.85.

Criley, R.A., and A.H. Halevy. 1985. *Strelitzia reginae*, pp. 396–402 in *Handbook of Flowering*, vol. 4, A.H. Halevy, editor. CRC Press, Boca Raton, Florida.

Criley, R.A., and O. Kawabata. 1984. Development of the flower spike of bird-of-paradise and its flowering period in Hawaii. *Journal of the American Society for Horticultural Science* 109:702–706.

Criley, R.A., and Y. Muruvanda. 1984. Evaluation of plant and flower characteristics of bird of paradise (*Strelitzia reginae* Aiton) in Hawaii, pp. 91–98 in *Proceedings of the 2nd Fertilizer and Ornamentals Short Course.* Hawaii Institute of Tropical Agriculture and Human Resources 01.04.85.

Dreistadt, S.H. 2001. *Integrated Pest Management for Floriculture and Nurseries.* University of California Division of Agriculture and Natural Resources Publication 3402.

El-Shoura, H.A.S., and A.M. Hosni. 1996. Growing *Strelitzia reginae* Ait. in improved sandy growing medium under different levels of fertilization. *Annals of Agricultural Science* (Cairo) 41:973–991.

Fransen, C.M. 1977. Biedt strelitziateelt nog perspectif? *Vakblad v. Bloemistrij* 32(43):46–47.

Halevy, A.H., A.M. Kofranek, and J. Kubota. 1976. Effect of environmental conditions on flowering of *Strelitzia reginae*, Ait. *HortScience* 11:584.

Halevy, A.H., A.M. Kofranek, and S.T. Besemer. 1978. Postharvest handling methods for bird-of-paradise flowers (*Strelitzia reginae* Ait.). *Journal of the American Society for Horticultural Science* 103:165–169.

Halevy, A.H., R.A. Criley, S.T. Besemer, H.A. van de Venter, M.E. McKay, and O. Kawabata. 1987. A comparison of flowering behavior of *Strelitzia reginae* at four locations as affected by air temperature. *Acta Horticulturae* 205:89–96.

Huxley, A., M. Griffiths, and M. Levy. 1992. *Strelitzia*, pp. 386–387 in *The New Royal Horticultural Society Dictionary of Gardening*, vol. 4. Stockton Press, New York.

Ishihata, K. 1976. Studies on promoting germination and the growth of seedlings in *Strelitzia reginae* Banks. *Bulletin of the Faculty of Agricultural Kagoshima University* 26:1–15.

Jimenz Meijas, R., and M. Caballero Ruano. 1990. *Strelitzia*, pp. 527–529 in *El cultivorindustrial de plants en maceta.* Ediciiones de Horticultura, S.L. Reus, Spain.

Kawabata, O., R.A. Criley, and S.R. Oshiro. 1984. Effects of season and environment on flowering of bird of paradise in Hawaii. *Journal of the American Society for Horticultural Science* 109:706–712.

Kofranek, A.M. 1976. Opening flower buds after storage. *Acta Horticulturae* 64:231–237.

Noordegraaf, C.V., and T.M. van der Krogt. 1976. Produktie en bloei van *Strelitzia. Vakblad v. Bloemistrij* 31(49):18–19.

van de Pol, P.A., and T.F. van Hell. 1988. Vegetative propagation of *Strelitzia reginae. Acta Horticulturae* 226:581–586.

van de Venter, H.A., J.G.C. Small, and P.J. Robbertse. 1975. Notes on the distribution and comparative leaf morphology of the acaulescent species of *Strelitzia* Ait. *South African Journal of Botany* 41(1):1–16.

van de Venter, H.A., J.G.C. Small, and A.H. Halevy. 1980. Some characteristics of leaf and inflorescence production of *Strelitzia reginae* Ait. in Port Elizabeth. *South African Journal of Botany* 46:305–311.

Ziv, M., and A.H. Halevy. 1983. Control of oxidative browning and *in vitro* propagation of *Strelitzia reginae. HortScience* 18:434–436.

Streptocarpus

INTRODUCTION

Common names: streptocarpus, cape primrose.

Scientific name: *Streptocarpus* ×*hybridus* Voss. (Huxley et al., 1992).

Family and related taxa: Gesneriaceae Dumort. *S.* ×*hybridus* is the result of numerous species being hybridized over the years. *S. rexii* Lindl. and *S. johannis* Britten. are probably the major contributing species to the currently available hybrids. The genus contains approximately 132 species. Other important members of the Gesneriaceae family are *Achimenes*, *Saintpaulia*, and *Sinningia*.

Origin: Both *S. rexii* and *S. johannis* are native to the humid tropical areas of South Africa and are perennial (Bailey and Bailey, 1976; Kimmins, 1992).

Uses and current status: Although *Streptocarpus* can be grown year-round as a potted flowering plant, spring sales of 4- to 5-in. (10- to 13-cm) pots are most common. *Streptocarpus* are commonly grown in North America, Europe, and Japan.

Modern commercial hybrids have compact rosette growth; leaves are hairy and oblong. The leaves were originally 12 to 14 in. (30 to 35 cm) long but modern cultivars now have 6- to 8-in. (15- to 20-cm)-long leaves. The inflorescence is a cyme with up to six flowers, all of which are held upright on a peduncle. The funnel-formed corolla is five lobed and rounded (Fig. II-1 Streptocarpus). Flowers come in numerous shades of blue, white, or violet and bicolors (Bailey and Bailey, 1976).

CULTIVARS

Numerous cultivars have been developed through breeding (Aimone, 1985) and radiation (Broertjes, 1969; Davies and Hedley, 1975). Series with distinct vegetative characteristics and various colors are available; however, the flower size and number can vary within each series (Aimone, 1985; Kimmins, 1992). One of the main breeding goals has been to reduce leaf length and number to produce a well-balanced, symmetrical plant that is easy to sleeve and ship.

PROPAGATION

F_1 seed is used in commercial propagation (Royle, 1979). There are 900,000 to 1,000,000 seeds/oz (32,000 to 35,000/g) and a well-drained peat-lite medium is used with 70°F (21°C) temperatures. Do not cover the seeds. Germination occurs within 2 weeks under interrupted mist, in the light or the dark. Weekly fertilization with 100 ppm N from 20–20–20 fertilizer can begin when seedlings are 30 days old (Aimone, 1985). Seedlings are normally purchased from specialty propagators in various cell sizes.

Many growers buy plugs that have been asexually propagated from leaf cuttings. The midrib and base of mature leaves are removed, and the two elongate leaf blade sections are placed in a nutrient-enriched peat-lite medium. The medium is best held at 70°F (21°C) and kept moist. Roots develop within 3 weeks and

FIGURE II-1 STREPTOCARPUS   Close-up of a *Streptocarpus* flower.

20 to 30 plantlets can be harvested within 2 to 3 months (Aimone, 1985; Kimmins, 1992; Widmer and Platteter, 1975). More plantlets were produced from leaves of stock plants grown under 9-hr SD than under 15-hr LD (Yelanich, 1997). *In vitro* propagation is possible (Handro, 1983; Raman, 1977; Simmonds, 1982, 1985b).

FLOWERING CONTROL AND DORMANCY

The currently available *Streptocarpus* hybrids are considered day neutral (Widmer and Platteter, 1975). However, *S. nobilis* C.B. Clarke has been described as a SD species (Handro, 1983; Simmonds, 1982), because flowering occurred quickly under SD at 77°F (25°C); however, under LD and 77°F (25°C) plants flowered eventually. Under SD at 59°F (15°C), plants were vegetative and remained vegetative even when moved to SD at 77°F (25°C) (Simmonds, 1985a).

Widmer and Platteter (1975) found that *S. ×hybridus* plants failed to flower during the winter due to low light levels; LD as night breaks (2200 to 0200 hr) failed to significantly hasten flowering. However, under high irradiance for 15 hr, plants flowered sooner with more flowers than under a 9-hr duration. Gibberellic acid (GA_{4+7}) sprays at 100 ppm will accelerate the rate of flower development and increase flower numbers when applied 30 days after transplanting and before buds are 0.1 in. (3 mm) long (Lyons and Meyers, 1983; Lyons et al., 1985; Orvos at al., 1989).

TEMPERATURE

A night temperature of 60 to 65°F (16 to 18°C) is acceptable, with day temperatures up to 80°F (27°C); temperatures above 80°F (27°C) are detrimental (Aimone, 1985; Widmer and Platteter, 1975).

LIGHT

In late spring, summer, or early fall the light intensity should be reduced to 1000 to 2000 fc (200 to 400 μmol $\cdot$ m^{-2} $\cdot$ s^{-1}) (Aimone, 1985; Kimmins, 1992; Widmer and Platteter, 1975). Higher intensities are required for streptocarpus than for African violets (*Saintpaulia ionantha*) and plants respond to supplemental photosynthetic lighting in the winter at northern latitudes (Strømme, 1985). A minimum light intensity of 500 fc (100 μmol $\cdot$ m^{-2} $\cdot$ s^{-1}) should be maintained. High light can cause leaf injury (Heide, 1967). Use shade to control temperature and to keep the light intensity below 3000 fc (600 μmol $\cdot$ m^{-2} $\cdot$ s^{-1}) to prevent leaf burn.

WATER

Streptocarpus plants have a fine root system and can be easily overwatered and overfertilized. Medium should be moderately dry prior to being irrigated (Aimone, 1985; Kimmins, 1992).

CARBON DIOXIDE

No scientific data are available, but commercial greenhouses regularly inject supplemental CO_2 at 500 to 1000 ppm.

NUTRITION

Between 100 and 125 ppm N is used weekly or every watering, as determined by plant size or season. When in flower, fertilize every 2 weeks at 50 ppm N (Aimone, 1985; Widmer and Platteter, 1975). Do not overfertilize. Lyons et al. (1987) found that 75 or 100 ppm N produced the maximum number of plantlets from leaves in propagation and rapid foliage and flower development. Foliar nutrient levels for high-quality plants are listed in Chapter 6, Nutrition, Table 6-4.

MEDIA

Streptocarpus thrive in a light, well-drained medium. Various 1:1:1 combinations of peat moss, perlite, sand, or vermiculite have been used (Aimone, 1985; Widmer and Platteter, 1975). The pH should be adjusted to 5.5 to 6.0 (Kimmins, 1992). Lyons et al. (1987) found that a bark-based medium was acceptable.

HEIGHT CONTROL

No height control is required but the length of the leaf can be controlled by spraying A-Rest (ancymidol) at 10 to 50 ppm (Kuehny, 2001). Topflor (flurprimidol) sprays at 5 to 20 ppm can also be used (SePRO, personal communication).

SPACING

Seedlings and plantlets can be grown pot-to-pot, but space plants after 4 to 8 weeks. Do not allow the leaves to overlap because they may grow upward and appear stiff (Aimone, 1985; Widmer and Platteter, 1975). For 4-in. (10-cm)

TABLE II-1 STREPTOCARPUS

Sample production schedules for 4-in. (10-cm) *Streptocarpus* plants from seed or leaf cuttings.

Cultural Step	Production Time (weeks)	Temperature °F (°C)
Seed to Plugs:		
Germinate seed	2	70 (21)
Grow seedings	6	60–65 (16–18)
Transplant to plugs	2–4	60–65 (16–18)
Total	10–12	
Cuttings to Plugs:		
Propagate leaf cuttings	6	70 (21)
Transplant plantlets to plugs	2–4	70 (21)
Total	8–10	
Plugs to Finish:		
Transplant plugs to 4-in. (10-cm) pots, space pot-to-pot	2–5	65–70 (18–21)
Space, lower temperature	10–15	60–65 (16–18)
Flower		
Total Time:		
Seed to flower	22–32	
Cuttings to flower	20–30	

pots use a spacing of 6 × 6 in. (15 × 15 cm); for 5-in. (13-cm) pots, use a spacing of 8 × 8 in. (20 × 20 cm).

PINCHING AND DISBUDDING

No pinching or disbudding required.

SUPPORT

No support required.

SCHEDULE AND TIMING

Plants are most commonly grown in 4- or 5-in. (10- or 13-cm) azalea pots and require 4 to 7 months to finish from propagation (Table II-1 *Streptocarpus*).

INSECTS

Mealybug and thrips are the most serious and difficult-to-control insects on *Streptocarpus*. Aphids, cyclamen mites, and whiteflies can also occur (Aimone, 1985; Yelanich, 1997).

DISEASES

Crown rot (*Pythium* or *Phytophthora*) and *Botrytis* are the only two diseases reported by producers.

PHYSIOLOGICAL DISORDERS

Cold or alkaline water can cause spots on leaves.

POSTHARVEST

Plants can be shipped when one or two flowers are open. Do not ship below 50°F (10°C) or above 61°F (16°C). Retailers should unpack and place plants in high light. The plants respond to silver thiosulfate (STS) sprays (0.3 to 0.6 mM) applied 1 week prior to shipping, which will slow flower drop and prevent any potential ethylene damage (Nowak and Rudnicki, 1990). Plants are highly sensitive to ethylene (L. Høyer, personal communication).

KEY POINTS

- *Streptocarpus* is used as a potted flowering plant.
- Newer cultivars have shorter leaves and are almost rosettes; the long leaves of older cultivars make shipping difficult.
- Commercially, plants are propagated by seed or leaf cuttings; *in vitro* is possible.
- Current streptocarpus cultivars are considered day neutral; older cultivars and some species are SD plants.

- Optimum light intensity is 1000 to 2000 fc (200 to 400 μmol $\cdot$ m^{-2} $\cdot$ s^{-1}).
- Plants are sensitive to overwatering and overfertilizing.
- Do not ship at temperatures below 50°F (10°C).

BIBLIOGRAPHY

Aimone, T. 1985. Cultural notes *Streptocarpus* (Cape primrose) family: Gesneriaceae, Genus, species: *Streptocarpus hybridus. GrowerTalks* 48(11):22.

Bailey, L.H., and E.Z. Bailey. 1976. *Streptocarpus*, pp. 1079–1088 in *Hortus Third: A Concise Dictionary of Plants Cultivated in the United States and Canada.* Macmillan, New York.

Broertjes, C. 1969. Mutation breeding of *Streptocarpus. Euphytica* 18:333–339.

Davies, D.R., and C.L. Hedley. 1975. The induction by mutation of all year round flowering in *Streptocarpus. Euphytica* 24:269–275.

Handro, W. 1983. Effects of some growth regulators on *in vitro* flowering of *Streptocarpus nobilis. Plant Cell Reports* 2:133–136.

Heide, O.M. 1967. *Streptocarpus*, propagation and flowering. *Gartneryrket* 57:8–11. (in Norwegian)

Huxley, A., M. Griffiths, and M. Levy. 1992. *Streptocarpus*, pp. 388–390 in *The New Royal Horticultural Society Dictionary of Gardening*, vol. 4. Stockton Press, New York.

Kimmins, R.K. 1992. Stemless *Streptocarpus* hybrids, pp. 298–300 in *Introduction to Floriculture*, 2nd ed., R.A. Larson, editor. Academic Press, San Diego, California.

Kuehny, J. 2001. Gloxinias and other gesneriads, pp. 93–95 in *Tips on Regulating Growth of Floriculture Crops*, M.L. Gaston, L.A. Kunkle, P.S. Konjoian, and M.F. Wilt, editors. Ohio Florists' Association Services, Columbus, Ohio.

Lyons, R.E., and P. Meyers. 1983. Effects of GA$_{4+7}$ and NAA on several aspects of flowering in *Streptocarpus. HortScience* 18:457–458.

Lyons, R.E., R.E. Veilleux, and J.N. Booze-Daniels. 1985. Relationship between GA application and phyllomorph length in *Streptocarpus. Journal of the American Society for Horticultural Science* 110:647–650.

Lyons, R.E., J.N. Booze-Daniels, and R.D. Wright. 1987. Effects of nitrogen fertilization on vegetative flowering, and asexual propagation characteristics of *Streptocarpus* ×*hybridus. Journal of the American Society for Horticultural Science* 112:902–905.

Nowak, J., and R.M. Rudnicki. 1990. *Postharvest Handling and Storage of Cut Flowers, Florist Greens, and Potted Plants.* Timber Press, Portland, Oregon.

Orvos, A.R., R.E. Lyons, and R.L. Grayson. 1989. Effects of GA$_{4+7}$ on flower initiation and development and vegetative growth of *Streptocarpus* ×*hybridus* Voss. 'Hybrid Delta.' *Scientia Horticulturae* 41:131–140.

Raman, K. 1977. Rapid multiplication of *Streptocarpus* and gloxinia from *in vitro* cultured pedicel segments. *Zeitschrift für Pflanzenphysiologie* 83:411–418.

Royle, D. 1979. Streptocarpus strategy. *The Grower* 92(14):28, 30, 35.

Simmonds, J. 1982. *In vitro* flowering of leaf explants of *Streptocarpus nobilis*. The influence of culture medium components on vegetative and reproductive development. *Canadian Journal of Botany* 60:1461–1468.

Simmonds, J. 1985a. Effect of temperature on flower induction of *Streptocarpus nobilis. Plant Physiology* 77(7):110. (supplement of abstracts)

Simmonds, J. 1985b. *In vitro* propagation of leaf tissue of *Streptocarpus nobilis. Biologia Plantarium* (Praha) 27(4–5):318–324.

Strømme, E. 1985. Gesneriaceae, pp. 48–52 in *Handbook of Flowering*, vol. III, A.H. Halevy, editor. CRC Press, Boca Raton, Florida.

Widmer, R.E., and R.J. Platteter. 1975. *Streptocarpus* (Cape primrose) culture. *Minnesota State Florists Bulletin*, Aug.:3–5.

Yelanich, M. 1997. *Streptocarpus*, pp. 122–124 in *Tips on Growing Specialty Potted Crops*, M.L. Gaston, S.A. Carver, C.A. Irwin, and R.A. Larson, editors. Ohio Florists' Association, Columbus, Ohio.

Tagetes

FIGURE II-1 TAGETES Flat of *Tagetes erecta* for bedding plants.

INTRODUCTION

Common name: marigold.

Scientific names: *Tagetes* L. species. Four *Tagetes* L. species are used in commercial floriculture: *T. patula* L., the French marigold; *T. erecta* L., the African marigold; *T. lucida* Cav., the sweet-scented marigold, and *T. tenuifolia* Cav., the signet marigold (Huxley et al., 1992).

Family and related taxa: Compositae Giseke. Compositae is a large family with many important genera including *Aster, Calendula, Callistephus, Centaurea, Chrysanthemum, Cosmos, Dahlia, Dendranthema, Echinacea, Gerbera, Helianthus, Liatris, Pericallis, Solidago,* and *Zinnia*.

Origin: All 30 *Tagetes* species are native to the New World from New Mexico west into Arizona and south into Mexico and Argentina. *T. patula* originates from Mexico and Guatemala; *T. erecta* from Mexico and Central America; and both *T. lucida* and *T. tenuifolia* are from Guatemala and Mexico (Bailey and Bailey, 1976).

Uses and current status: *Tagetes patula* is primarily used as a bedding plant whose maximum height can be 1.5 ft (45 cm) with 2-in. (5-cm) flower heads. *T. erecta* can be 3 ft (90 cm) tall with 2- to 5-in. (5- to 13-cm) flower heads and is grown as a bedding plant or cut flower (Fig. II-1 Tagetes). *T. lucida* grows to 2.5 ft (76 cm) with 0.38-in. (1-cm) flower heads and *T. tenuifolia* grows to 2 ft (60 cm) with 1-in. (2.5-cm) flower heads. Both *T. lucida* and *T. tenuifolia* are more commonly used as bedding plants in Europe than in North America (Armitage, 1985; Bailey and Bailey, 1976). Interestingly, marigold petals are also used

as a coloring agent in poultry feed to obtain bright yellow egg yolks (Bosma et al., 2003).

Marigolds are herbaceous and have aromatic, pinnately divided leaves. The ray flowers may be bright yellow, orange, or red-brown (Bailey and Bailey, 1976). Some people find the aroma pleasant, while others do not.

CULTIVARS

Marigolds range in plant form from the upright, large-flowered *T. erecta* to the more branching, smaller flowered *T. patula*. Triploid hybrids between *T. erecta* and *T. patula* are shorter and more branched than *T. erecta*, but have larger flowers and greater height than *T. patula* and may be more heat tolerant than either parent (Bemis, 1998). Most commercial cultivars are double, but single forms exist with one row of ray flowers. Modern cultivars offer a wide variety of plant heights, flower sizes, plant forms, and uses. Heights can vary from 6 to 36 in. (15 to 92 cm) and flower sizes from 1 to 4 in. (2.5 to 13 cm) (Armitage, 1985; Nau, 1998). Gislerød et al. (1985) evaluated more than 100 cultivars from 18 international seed firms from North America, Europe, and Japan.

PROPAGATION

Though *T. lucida* is perennial, all commercial cultivars are treated as annuals due to frost or aesthetic reasons. Sexual propagation is difficult to automate because the seed is elongated and thin with a fuzzy tail. This tail can be removed (de-tailed) for the more important hybrids and seeds can be coated, which allows automated sowing.

There are 9000 seeds/oz (300/g). Germination is quite rapid, 2 to 3 days at 75 to 80°F (24 to 27°C). Seeds are covered and temperatures are lowered after germination to 68 to 70°F (20 to 21°C) (Ball, 1991).

For *T. patula* and *T. erecta* plug production, the following conditions are used (Ball, 1991):

Stage 1: Seed covered, 75 to 80°F (24 to 27°C), for 2 to 3 days

Stage 2: 68 to 70°F (20 to 21°C), for 5 days (*T. erecta*) or 7 days (*T. patula*)

Stage 3: 62 to 65°F (17 to 18°C), for 14 days, 100 to 150 ppm N one time/week

Stage 4: 60 to 62°F (16 to 17°C), for 7 to 10 days (*T. erecta*) or 7 to 14 days (*T. patula*), fertilize as needed.

Plugs should be ready for marketing or transplanting within 4 to 5 weeks for *T. erecta* and 5 to 6 weeks for *T. patula*. See Chapter 1, Propagation, for description of plug stages. Priming seed will shorten emergence time and increase emergence percentage (Bosma et al., 2003).

FLOWERING CONTROL AND DORMANCY

Marigolds, particularly *T. erecta*, are classified as facultative SD plants and flower more rapidly under photoperiods of less than 12.5 hr. However, responses among cultivars, hybrids, and species are varied (Tsukamoto et al., 1968). While some cultivars appear to be day neutral, flowering is delayed by LD for most cultivars. Armitage (1985) reviewed literature on photoperiod and Jacks (1982) proposed that black cloth be pulled for SD as soon as seeds are sown, not after germination. This process increased uniformity of height and flowering. Short days were required for only 2 weeks. Black cloth and SD induction should occur from April to October (Jacks, 1982). Once floral induction occurs, flower development will continue under LD. No plant growth regulators were required to produce short well-branched plants in 4-in. (10-cm) pots.

TEMPERATURE

There are temperature and photoperiod interactions. Between 70 and 75°F (21 and 24°C), *T. erecta* plants flower only under SD. Within the temperature range of 63 to 65°F (17 to 18°C), plants flower under all photoperiods. At temperatures below 60°F (16°C) growth is slow and plants become chlorotic or reddish (Post, 1949; Roberts and Struckmeyer, 1939).

During plug production, temperatures are gradually reduced after germination from 75 to 80°F (24 to 27°C) to 60 to 62°F (16 to 17°C) on specific time schedules (Ball, 1991) (see Schedule and Timing).

LIGHT

Long days are less inhibitory to flowering under high light intensities and are more inhibiting under low intensities. High light intensity increases flower development rate and flower number (Armitage, 1985; Ball, 1991; Nau, 1998).

WATER

Water stress should not occur during the early stages of plug production. Thereafter, it is a common practice to use water stress to harden plants and reduce internode elongation. However, plants used for cut flower production should not be water stressed at any time.

CARBON DIOXIDE

No data are available on supplemental carbon dioxide effects.

NUTRITION

As plants in plug production progress from the germination chamber to the greenhouse production stage, the nutritional regime should increase from 50 to 75 ppm to 100 to 150 ppm (Ball, 1991). Iron and manganese toxicity have been reported when medium pH is low (Ball, 1991; Daughtrey and Chase, 1992). Iron toxicity symptoms include chlorotic and necrotic speckling and downward curling and cupping of leaves (Albano and Miller, 2001; Albano et al., 1996). Leaf tissue iron levels should not exceed 500 ppm. Cultivars vary in susceptibility to iron toxicity (Albano and Miller, 1996). During outdoor production, sidedressing nutrients may be required as determined by rainfall and soil type. See Chapter 6, Nutrition, Table 6-4, for foliar nutrient levels.

MEDIA

Any well-drained medium is acceptable. Peatlite media are used in commercial plug production and coir-based media have also produced excellent results (Evans and Stamps,

1996). When field planted, soil should be well prepared and have excellent drainage. These beds should be soil tested and nutrient adjustments made. A pH of 6.0 to 6.5 is acceptable.

HEIGHT CONTROL

Tagetes erecta internode elongation can be controlled by A-Rest (ancymidol), B-Nine (daminozide), Bonzi (paclobutrazol), Cycocel (chlormequat), Sumagic (uniconazole), or Topflor (flurprimidol). B-Nine may delay flowering and is not effective on *T. patula* (Armitage, 1985).

A-Rest sprays at 12 ppm can be applied within a week to 10 days after sowing to the plug flat media to produce compact, well-branched plugs and subsequent bedding plants (Britten, 1999). Sumagic foliar sprays at 5 to 25 ppm can be used to control plug height without retarding subsequent growth in the final container (Davis, 1991). Bonzi sprays at 30 ppm can be applied at sowing or up 6 days later to control plug height (Barrett et al., 1999).

In the final container, A-Rest sprays can be applied at 18 to 26 ppm after transplanting or at 26 to 33 ppm on finished plants (Bell, 2001). Bonzi sprays are used at 30 to 60 ppm on *T. erecta* and at 15 to 30 ppm on *T. patula*. Cycocel sprays are applied at 800 to 1500 ppm. Sumagic sprays are applied at 10 to 20 ppm. B-Nine sprays can be applied at 2500 to 5000 ppm. Topflor sprays can be used at the rate of 20 to 60 ppm (SePRO, personal communication). Restriction of water and nutrition and lower temperatures are the primary methods to harden flats of bedding plants for marketing (Cox, 2000).

SPACING

Bedding plant flats are spaced flat-to-flat. Spacing in the garden for smaller growing cultivars varies from 10 to 12 in. (25 to 30 cm). Tall growing garden cultivars are spaced 8 to 12 in. (25 to 30 cm) between plants for background plantings or for cut flower production (Nau, 1999).

PINCHING AND DISBUDDING

No pinching or disbudding required.

SUPPORT

Only the tall growing cultivars with heights of 24 to 36 in. (61 to 92 cm) will need to be staked or provided with some form of support. Cut flower production typically uses one to two layers of netting, because the flower heads are heavy and plants may fall over.

SCHEDULE AND TIMING

Post (1949) reported 9 to 13 weeks are required for cut flower production of *T. erecta* from seed that were field planted in June or July. For bedding plant production of *T. erecta* Armitage (1985) stated that 9 to 13 weeks are required in the greenhouse. For *T. patula*, 6 to 10 weeks are required from sowing to flower in bedding flats, depending on cultivar and latitude. Time from seed to sales was 4 to 5 weeks for marigold plug production.

INSECTS

Monitor for whiteflies, aphids, spider mites, and thrips; spider mites can be especially damaging on outdoor plantings during hot summer weather. Thrips carry tomato spotted wilt virus.

DISEASES

There are a host of fungal diseases (*Botrytis*, *Fusarium*, *Phytophthora*, *Pythium*, *Verticillium*, and *Sclerotinia*), whose infections result in stem cankers, wilting, and death (Daughtrey and Chase, 1992; Forsberg, 1979; Horst, 1990; Post, 1949). *Alternaria* leaf spot frequently moves into and girdles the stem. Other leaf spots include *Ascochyta*, *Cercospora*, and *Phyllosticta* (Dreistadt, 2001). *Botrytis* can blight the large flowers during wet weather. Rust, aster yellows, and tomato spotted wilt virus have also been noted.

PHYSIOLOGICAL DISORDERS

No physiological disorders noted, but nutritional disorders can occur (see Nutrition and Temperature on p. 879).

POSTHARVEST

Plugs exhibit chilling injury at temperatures as high as 36°F (2°C). Plugs can be stored in the dark at 41°F (5°C) for 3 weeks; however, the quality of the stored plugs was improved if lights were used (Heins et al., 1994).

Cut marigold flowers are harvested when fully open. If stems are out of water for any length of time, recut the stems under water. Shipping can be for 3 days at 39°F (4°C). Flowers respond to floral preservatives. Leaves below the surface of the water must be removed. The odor of decaying marigold leaves is unpleasant (Nowak and Rudnicki, 1990).

KEY POINTS

- *Tagetes patula, T. lucida,* and *T. tenuifolia* are used as bedding plants; *T. erecta* is used as a bedding plant, cut flower, and poultry feed additive.
- All marigolds are propagated by seed.
- Marigolds are classified as facultative SD plants, although some cultivars appear to be day neutral.

- Once flowers are induced under SD, flowering will continue under LD.
- Plants are susceptible to iron toxicity, especially when the medium pH is low.
- Spider mites can be especially damaging.
- Chilling injury can occur at 36°F (2°C) or lower.

BIBLIOGRAPHY

Albano, J.P., and W.B. Miller. 1996. Marigold varieties vary in susceptibility to iron toxicity. *HortScience* 31:674. (Abstract)

Albano, J.P., and W.B. Miller. 2001. Photodegradation of FeDTPA in nutrient solutions. II. Effects on root physiology and foliar Fe and Mn levels in marigold. *HortScience* 36:317–320.

Albano, J.P., W.B. Miller, and M.C. Halbrooks. 1996. Iron toxicity stress causes bronze speckle, a specific physiological disorder of marigold (*Tagetes erecta* L.). *Journal of the American Society for Horticultural Science* 121:430–437.

Armitage, A.M. 1985. *Tagetes,* pp. 353–356 in *Handbook of Flowering,* vol. V, A.H. Halevy, editor. CRC Press, Boca Raton, Florida.

Bailey, L.H., and E.Z. Bailey. 1976. *Tagetes,* p. 1095 in *Hortus Third: A Concise Dictionary of Plants Cultivated in the United States and Canada.* Macmillan, New York.

Ball, V. 1991. Plugs—The way of the 1990s, pp. 137–153 in *Ball Redbook,* 15th ed., V. Ball, editor. Geo. J. Ball Publishing, West Chicago, Illinois.

Barrett, J.E., C.E. Wieland, T.A. Nell, and D.G. Clark. 1999. Early applications of growth regulators to bedding plants. *HortScience* 34:528. (Abstract)

Bell, M. 2001. Bedding plants and seed geraniums, pp. 54–60 in *Tips on Regulating Growth of Floriculture Crops,* M.L. Gaston, L.A. Kunkle, P.S. Konjoian, and M.F. Wilt, editors. Ohio Florists' Association Services, Columbus, Ohio.

Bemis, D. 1998. Super performance with triploid marigolds. *GrowerTalks* 63(6):14.

Bosma, T.L., K.E. Conway, J.M. Dole, and N.O. Maness. 2003. Sowing date and priming influence African marigold field emergence. *HortTechnology* 13:487–493.

Britten, A. 1999. PGRs at seeding reduce early stretch. *GrowerTalks* 63(5):46, 48.

Cox, D. 2000. Low phosphorus controls bedding plant growth. *HortScience* 35:457. (Abstract)

Daughtrey, M., and A.R. Chase. 1992. Marigold, pp. 145–147 in *Ball Field Guide to Diseases of Greenhouse Ornamentals.* Ball Publishing, Geneva, Illinois.

Davis, T.D. 1991. Post-production performance of uniconazole-treated zinnia and marigold plugs. *HortTechnology* 1:49–52.

Dreistadt, S.H. 2001. *Integrated Pest Management for Floriculture and Nurseries.* University of California Division of Agriculture and Natural Resources Publication 3402.

Evans, M.R., and R.H. Stamps. 1996. Growth of bedding plants in sphagnum peat and coir dust-based substrates. *Journal of Environmental Horticulture* 14:187–190.

Forsberg, J.L. 1979. Marigold, pp. 121–122 in *Diseases of Ornamental Plants.* Special Publication No. 3, College of Agriculture, University of Illinois, Urbana.

Gislerød, H.R., B. Litlere, and G. Skjeseth. 1985. Verdiprøving av *Tagetes,* pp. 1–7 Publication No. 333, Institute for Blomsterdyrking og Veksthusforsøk, NLK, Norway. (in Norwegian)

Heins, R., N. Lange, T.F. Wallace, Jr., and W. Carlson. 1994. *Plug Storage, Cold Storage of Plug Seedlings.* Meister Publishing, Willoughby, Ohio.

Horst, R.K. 1990. Marigold, pp. 722–723 in *Westcott's Plant Disease Handbook,* 5th ed. Van Nostrand Reinhold, New York.

Huxley, A., M. Griffiths, and M. Levy. 1992. *Tagetes,* p. 429 in *The New Royal Horticultural Society Dictionary of Gardening,* vol. 4. Stockton Press, New York.

Jacks, N.L. 1982. Create a new market with African (America) marigolds. *Bedding Plant International News* 13:10–11.

Nau, J. 1998. Marigold, pp. 763–766 in *Ball Redbook,* 16th ed., V. Ball, editor. Ball Publishing, Batavia, Illinois.

Nau, J. 1999. Marigold, pp. 662–665 in *Ball Redbook,* 15th ed., V. Ball, editor. George. J. Ball Publishing, West Chicago, Illinois.

Nowak, J., and R.M. Rudnicki. 1990. *Postharvest Handling and Storage of Cut Flowers, Florist*

Greens and Potted Plants. Timber Press, Portland, Oregon.

Post, K. 1949. *Tagetes* (Marigold), pp. 820–821 in *Florist Crop Production and Marketing*. Orange Judd Publishing, New York.

Roberts, R.H., and B.E. Struckmeyer. 1939. Further studies of the effects of temperature and other environmental factors upon photoperiodic responses of plants. *Journal of Agricultural Research* 59:699–709.

Tsukamoto, Y., H. Imanishi, and J. Yahara. 1968. Studies on the flowering of marigold. I. Photoperiodic response and its differences among strains. *Journal of the Japanese Society for Horticultural Science* 37(3):47–55.

Tulipa

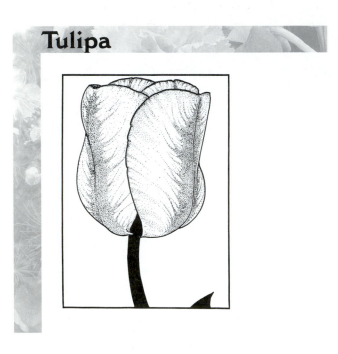

INTRODUCTION

Common names: tulip, Dutch tulip, and garden tulip for *Tulipa gesneriana* L.; candlestick tulip for *T. clusiana*, and waterlily tulip for *T. kaufmanniana*.

Scientific names: *Tulipa gesneriana* is the most important species (Huxley et al., 1992). *T. gesneriana* is divided into (1) single early, (2) double early, (3) midseason triumph, (4) midseason Darwin, and seven late flowering types: (5) singles, (6) lily-flowering, (7) fringed, (8) viridiflora (cottage), (9) Rembrandt, (10) parrot, and (11) double late (peony) types (Bailey and Bailey, 1976; Le Nard and De Hertogh, 1993).

Family and related taxa: Liliaceae Juss. Other *Tulipa* species in commerce are *T. fosteriana* Hoog ex W. Irv., *T. greigii* Reg., and many miscellaneous species (Bailey and Bailey, 1976; Le Nard and De Hertogh, 1993; Rees, 1985). The lily family is very large and contains many commercially important floriculture crops including *Allium, Alstroemeria, Brodiaea, Convallaria, Eremurus, Hyacinthus, Lachenalia, Lilium, Muscari,* and *Ornithogalum.*

Origin: The center of origin is central Asia: Siberia, Mongolia, and China. The area of greatest diversity occurs south into the Kashmir province of India and west into Afghanistan, Iran, Caucasus, and Turkey (Bailey and Bailey, 1976; Le Nard and De Hertogh, 1993; Rees, 1985). Tulip breeding was already occurring in the 12th and 13th centuries in Persia prior to the tulip being brought to western Europe in the mid–1500s. No original species is known but "gesneriana" was named for Conrad Gesner who printed the first illustration of a tulip from an Austrian garden in 1561.

Uses and current status: Tulips are important cut flowers and potted plants (Figs II-1 and II-2 Tulipa). Tulips are also grown in gardens in Zones 3 to 7. In warm climates, precooled bulbs can be planted and are discarded after flowering. Generally, the cooler the climate, the more likely tulips will perennialize. The cooler the late spring and summer, the longer the leaves can conduct photosynthesis and renew the carbohydrates of the new bulb (Armitage and Laushman, 2003).

FIGURE II-1 TULIPA Potted *Tulipa* plants.

FIGURE II-2 TULIPA 'Hamilton' *Tulipa* cut flower and garden ornamental.

The Netherlands is the primary tulip bulb producer and the largest acreages are devoted to Triumph tulips and Darwin hybrids. Forcing bulbs as cut flowers or as potted plants is an old, large, and well-established industry. Potted tulip plants are more popular than cut flowers in North America (De Hertogh, 1996; Le Nard and De Hertogh, 1993).

All tulips are herbaceous perennials with a bulb. The mature bulb consists of up to six tunicated (circular) scales attached to a basal plate, which at maturity develops a rooting primordial bulge or rooting plate. Axillary buds (one per scale) are found on the basal plate in the interior of these tunicated scales. These buds later develop into flowering scapes with leaves and various numbers of daughter bulbs. The apical (dominant) axillary bud typically forms four leaves and a terminal flower. The lowest (basipetal) leaf is the largest and is called the *wrapper leaf*. This leaf will always emerge and develop on the side of the bulb that is slightly flattened. Some species and cultivars produce more than one flower per stem. At least one new bulb, totally encased in a papery scale, forms annually.

In the 400 or more years since the tulip reached Europe and became an integral part of the Dutch culture and economy, a vast amount of literature has been developed for its field production and forcing. Tulips are one of the most researched genera in the world. In this chapter the only forcing aspects are considered. The authors also recognize Dr. A.A. De Hertogh's monumental work through the years in developing detailed forcing guidelines, which are found in the *Holland Bulb Forcer's Guide* (De Hertogh, 1996). All individuals serious about forcing *Tulipa* and other geophytes should acquire this text and *The Physiology of Flower Bulbs* (De Hertogh and Le Nard, 1993).

CULTIVARS

Thousands of cultivars have been introduced during the 400+ years of tulip cultivation in the Netherlands. Presently, hundreds of cultivars exist around the world, as do numerous flower types including singles, doubles, smooth to ruffled petal edges, rounded or pointed petals, and various degrees of flower opening. Numerous colors, other than true blue, are available. Flowers may be striped or "broken" in green, black, red, and other colors, or multicolored, frequently with different tints on the outer and inner petals. Tulips also have a wide range of flowering dates, leaf characteristics, and plant heights (De Hertogh, 1996; Buschman, undated). Cultivars vary in their ability to perennialize (Cavins and Dole, 2002).

PROPAGATION

Sexual propagation is only used to develop new cultivars in a breeding program or in a species exchange program. *In vitro* propagation is in the research stage of development (Baker et al., 1990; Le Nard and De Hertogh, 1993; Nishiuchi and Koster, 1988).

Commercially, bulb production is based on the annual development of daughter bulb offsets from the vegetative axillary buds in the axils of the tunicated scales. This occurs naturally, and the success, failure, and cost of a new cultivar rests on the rate of asexual multiplication, which is different for each cultivar. The average rate is typically two to three new bulblets annually. The time required to produce a commercial-size bulb capable of flowering varies from 2 to 3 or more years depending on cultivar and bulblet size (Rees, 1968, 1972).

FLOWERING CONTROL AND DORMANCY

Bulb circumference (size) or weight is the primary flowering control factor. Size of the apical meristem, which ultimately forms the flower, and carbohydrate reserves are also important factors. Commercially, harvested bulbs are graded and sold by bulb circumference, which also varies with the cultivar. The common bulb size sold for potted flowering plants is 4.75- to 5.5-in. (12- to 14-cm) circumference bulbs, and 4.75-in. (12-cm) circumference and larger for cut flowers. The international size or grade designation is always in 1- to 2-cm increments (De Hertogh, 1996; Le Nard and De Hertogh, 1993; Thompson and Johnston, 1974). Tulip plant growth follows natural or seasonal temperature cycles. By winter, the bulb is well rooted, with floral and leaf meristems present. Cold is required for the floral shoot to elongate and for further flower and leaf differentiation and development.

In spring, warm temperatures activate growth, resulting in rapid shoot elongation and flowering. Daughter bulb growth commences in the interior axillary buds. In late spring and early summer, the aboveground shoots mature and senesce. The new daughter bulb growth is complete and the old bulb is desiccated tissue. The new bulb appears dormant, but microscopically the reproductive and vegetative tissues and future rooting zone on the basal plate continue to differentiate and develop. Commercially, bulbs are harvested and graded in early summer. In fall after bulbs are planted, roots develop and the scape begins to elongate and emerge after the required cold has been received and spring temperatures become appropriate.

Commercially, tulips are given precise temperature treatments to program the bulb for optimum development and flowering in the shortest time span, which is accomplished with cold temperatures (see also *Crocus* chapter Flowering Control and Dormancy, page 407). Precooling at 41°F (5°C), a requirement for flowerscape elongation and flowering, increases α-amylase activity and mobilization of scale carbohydrates (Lambrechts et al., 1994). In addition, cold-treated bulbs' respiration rates are three times greater than those of non-cooled bulbs (Iwaya-Inoue and Motooka, 1996). Gibberellin (GA) levels have been unsuccessfully investigated as biochemical indicators of when bulbs have been properly cold treated (Rebers et al., 1996).

The dominant axillary bud typically initiates four vegetative leaves and then the petals, stamens, and finally the gynoecium (Le Nard and De Hertogh, 1993; Rees, 1972, 1985). It is critical that the flower primordia reach the G_3-stage of

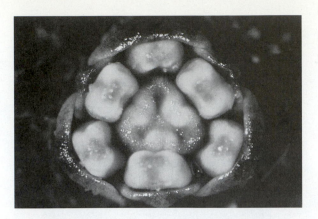

FIGURE II-3 TULIPA   G-stage of *Tulipa* bulb development. Note well-indented, three-lobed stigma (center) surrounded by anthers (inner row) and tepals (outer row).

development before bulb cooling commences. This stage is described as when the gynoecium has developed a well-indented, three-lobed stigma (De Hertogh, 1996) (Fig. II-3 Tulipa).

For the first two forcing periods of potted tulips and the first three forcing periods of cut flower tulips, the bulbs must be inspected prior to forcing for G-stage. Sample bulbs are removed from each cultivar and shipment combination, dissected, and examined to determine if the bulbs have reached G-stage. While bulbs used for these early forcing periods must be precooled as soon as possible to be sufficiently cold treated prior to the forcing date, bulbs should be held at 63°F (17°C) for 1 to 5 weeks after reaching G-stage and before precooling. This storage period is known as the *in-between temperature* and improves flower quality and uniformity of crop response to cold treatments (De Hertogh, 1996). If bulbs used for forcing schedules have not reached G-stage or cooled immediately after reaching G-stage, the flowers are not mature and the bulb does not have the capacity to perceive the cold. Consequently, the flower scape will not elongate properly and the flowers may abort or be half green and half normally pigmented. Interestingly, application of benzyladenine (BA) at 0.25% in a lanolin paste to the basal plate causes laciniated parrot-tulip-like flowers to grow on nonparrot tulips (Saniewski et al., 1997).

Flower bud abortion, floral and foliage abnormalities, and unacceptable plants may occur if bulbs are exposed to ethylene from apples or fruit in cold storage, from *Fusarium* in adjacent infected bulbs, or from heaters (De Hertogh, 1996). The effects of ethylene on tulip bulbs include gummosis, bud necrosis, flower bud blasting, and excessive splitting and cultivars vary in their sensitivity to ethylene (de Wild et al., 2002b). The anti-ethylene agent 1-methylcyclopropene (1-MCP) at 1 ppm can prevent the negative effects of ethylene (de Wild et al., 2002a).

TEMPERATURE

Cold storage facilities are called *Rooting Rooms* (see *Crocus* chapter, Flowering Control and Dormancy, page 407). To produce flowers on a certain date, specific temperature sequences are followed (see Flowering Control and Dormancy, page 883). Specific Rooting Room temperatures are maintained to accomplish specific physiological requirements in bulbs. These temperatures will result in optimal growth responses in the briefest time span to achieve flowering for a particular date.

A Rooting Room temperature of 48°F (9°C) is needed for the rooting phase (see *Crocus* chapter, Flowering Control and Dormancy, page 407). "Read" your bulbs and do not rely solely on the calendar (De Hertogh, 1996; Le Nard and De Hertogh, 1993). When bulb roots have reached the base of the pot, drop the temperature to 41°F (5°C). Tulip bulbs can develop too many roots and physically push the medium and bulbs out of the pot. The optimal temperature for both shoot elongation and continued cold treatment is 41°F (5°C). When bulb shoots have elongated 1 to 2 in. (3 to 5 cm), drop the temperature to 32 to 35°F (0 to 2°C) to prevent excessive root development and shoot elongation.

Charles-Edwards and Rees (1975) and Rees (1968, 1972, 1985) reported that the optimum temperature for floral initiation and development is between 63 and 68°F (17 and 20°C). De Hertogh (1996) suggested that bulbs be held at 63°F (17°C) after arrival and checked every 2 to 3 days until they reach G-stage. If summers are warm and hot in the Netherlands, bulbs are mature and little doubt remains that the G-stage has been reached. If summers are cool, bulbs may not have reached G-stage; however, warm or hot summers may mean small bulbs and increased incidents of *Fusarium*.

The temperature and duration of the cold temperature treatment sequence are dependent on the date the bulb will be forced into flower, the cultivar, and the final use as a potted plant or a cut flower (see Tables II-1 and II-2 Tulipa).

Cooling (precooling) commences prior to planting for schedule I and II potted tulips and for schedule I, II, and III cut flower tulips. The reasons for precooling include (1) the rooting site on the basal plate has not completely developed, hence bulbs would not root if planted; (2) less room is required for nonpotted bulbs, reducing costs; (3) the added time allows *Fusarium* to develop and infected bulbs can be discarded before planting; and (4) at this early stage nonplanted dry bulbs respond to the cold more efficiently than when planted. Precooled (PC) bulbs are shipped from the Netherlands and transported at 63°F (17°C). This temperature is appropriate for completion of floral development and for bulbs to reach G-stage.

LIGHT

Bulbs are cold treated (programmed) in the dark. Only a small amount of light is required once bulbs are removed from the rooting room for forcing. Frequently, plants from earlier forcing schedules are too short, and paper or some other material is placed over the emerging shoots to reduce light and encourage etiolation. This can also be accomplished by using heavier shade in the greenhouse. However, if the former technique is used, excessive heat trapped under the shading material may cause flower abortions. Only 1000 to 2500 fc (200 to 500 μmol $\cdot$ m^{-2} $\cdot$ s^{-1}) are needed for greenhouse forcing (De Hertogh, 1996).

Gude et al. (undated) found that tulips forced under fluorescent lights were equal or better than greenhouse forced plants when placed under 1100 fc (165 μmol $\cdot$ m^{-2} $\cdot$ s^{-1}) for a 12-hr photoperiod for potted plants, or 24-hr photoperiods for cut flowers, because stem lengths were longer.

WATER

Moisture levels of the pot must be continuously monitored while bulbs are in the rooting room, because the medium dries out even though the medium may have been thoroughly watered when bulbs were planted. Dry areas may be localized within large rooting room facilities due to lack of uniform air circulation or temperatures. Maintaining a fog of near 100% humidity in the rooting room is optimal (De Hertogh, 1996).

CARBON DIOXIDE

Supplemental CO_2 is not used.

TABLE II-1 TULIPA

Examples of two pot *Tulipa* cultivars designated by color; minimum to maximum weeks of cold treatment that bulbs can be stored for the appropriate flowering dates, type of bulb [precooled (PC) or nonprecooled (NP)] and approximate days ( ) to flower in the forcing greenhouse (modified from De Hertogh, 1996).

| Color | Appropriate Dates to Force the Cultivar | | | | | | | Weeks Cold | | |
	Jan. 1–8	Jan. 19–Feb. 7	Feb. 8–28	Mar. 1–11	Mar. 19–Apr. 2	Apr. 3–18	Apr. 19–May 5	Min.	Opt.	Max
Red:										
'Oscar'	—	—	NP(22)	NP(17)	NP(14)[a]	NP(12)[b]	—	15	16	20
Yellow:										
'Yokohama'	—	PC(26)	NP(21)	NP(19)	NP(17)[c]	NP(13)[a]	NP(11)[b]	15	17	22

[a] Use 0.25 mg a.i./pot A-Rest, if required.
[b] Use 0.50 mg a.i./pot A-Rest, if required.
[c] Use 0.125 mg a.i./pot A-Rest, if required.

TABLE II-2 TULIPA

Examples of three cut *Tulipa* cultivars designated by color; minimum to maximum weeks of cold treatment that bulbs can be stored for the appropriate flowering dates, type of bulb [precooled (PC) or nonprecooled (NP)], and the approximate days ( ) to flower in the forcing greenhouse (modified from De Hertogh, 1996).

| Color | Flower Form | Appropriate Dates to Force the Cultivar | | | | | | | Weeks Cold | | | Vase Life Days[a] |
		Jan. 3–22	Jan. 23–Feb. 2	Feb. 3–23	Feb. 24–Mar. 15	Mar. 15–Apr. 4	Apr. 5–25	Apr. 26–May 3	Min.	Opt.	Max.	
Red:												
'Ile de France'	Cup	—	—	PC(17)	NP(17)	NP(13)	NP(11)	—	16	18	21	6–7
Yellow:												
'Golden Apeldorn'	Semi-cup	—	—	PC(26)	NP(22)	NP(19)	—	—	18	20	23	3–4
Pink or Rose:												
'Gander'	Semi-cup	PC(27)	PC(23)	NP(21)	NP(17)	NP(15)	—	—	15	17	19	4–5

[a] At 70 to 75°F (21 to 23°C).

NUTRITION

Low nutrition and medium EC are acceptable. After removing the bulbs from the cooler, apply 2 lb/100 gal (2.4 g $\cdot$ L^{-1}) Ca(NO$_3$)$_2$ at each watering to reduce the potential for stem topple (De Hertogh, 1996) (see Physiological Disorders section).

MEDIA

Any medium that is well drained and lightweight is acceptable. The pH should not be acidic, nor should high levels of peat or pine bark be used because the effectiveness of A-Rest (ancymidol) drenches may be reduced for potted plant production. Do not overfill the pots; space must be left for water and application of the A-Rest solution (De Hertogh, 1996).

Hydroponic forcing of cut tulips is now more common than forcing in media (Jagers, 2000; James, 2002; Yamasaki et al., 2002). Hydroponic forcing is more automated, environmentally neutral, and cost effective. The rooting period is decreased from 16 weeks in traditional growing media to 1 to 4 weeks in water; 3 to 4 weeks is used for early crops and 1 to 2 weeks for later crops. Bulbs are placed in forcing trays designed for hydroponics and subjected to running water with an EC of 1.5 to 2.5 dS $\cdot$ m^{-1}.

HEIGHT CONTROL

A-Rest and Bonzi (paclobutrazol) are the plant growth regulators of choice. They are used as drenches and are most effective if applied within 24 hr after plants have been moved into the forcing environment (De Hertogh, 1996; Deneke and Keever, 1992). A-Rest is applied at 0.125 to 0.5 mg a.i. (1 to 4 ppm)/pot. Bonzi is typically used at three to four times the milligram rate listed for A-Rest: 0.5 to 2.0 mg a.i. (4 to 16 ppm)/pot (De Hertogh, 1996; Deneke and Keever, 1992). Soaking bulbs for 1 hr in Bonzi at 2.5 or 5 ppm was also effective in reducing height but A-Rest soaks were not effective (McDaniel, 1990). Adriansen (1985) noted that Florel (ethephon) is also effective.

For a major flowering date, it is wise to remove sample pots 10 days prior to the main crop and test applications of 0, 0.125, 0.25, and 0.50 mg a.i. A-Rest or 0, 0.50, 1.00, or 2.00 mg a.i. Bonzi/pot. Thus, a forcer can determine the appropriate concentration for that date, cultivar, and bulb source. This is particularly true for the late Easter and Mother's Day holidays,

because the shoots will have elongated in the cooler, unless temperatures were constantly maintained near freezing. Plant heights vary between years for similar forcing dates and between sources for the same cultivar.

SPACING

For potted flowering plants, plant 3 bulbs in 4-in. (10-cm) azalea pots, 6 to 7 bulbs in 6-in. (15-cm) pots, or 10 to 12 bulbs in 8-in. (20-cm) pans. The flat side of the bulb is placed facing outward and parallel to the pot's edge, the large "wrapper leaf" will emerge from the flat side and will make the potted plant more attractive. Leave the upper one-fourth of the bulb above the medium surface. Be careful during planting not to damage the emerging shoot or the basal plate. Suitable cultivars must be selected for 4-in. (10-cm) pot production. Discuss cultivar selection with a knowledgeable bulb supplier or consult De Hertogh (1996).

All plants are placed pot-to-pot both in coolers and in the greenhouse. Frequently, pallets or racks of pots are moved from cold storage to the forcing environment. For cut flower production bulbs are placed in flats or planting trays, which are usually 4 in. (10 cm) deep. Again, the upper portion of the bulb is planted above the medium (De Hertogh, 1996).

PINCHING AND DISBUDDING

No pinching or disbudding required.

SUPPORT

No support required.

SCHEDULE AND TIMING

The scheduling process begins when the correct cultivar is selected for the desired flowering date and for potted plant or cut flower use. Forcers calculate backward from flowering date to determine the days to force (date to bring into the greenhouse) and date to plant the bulb (Tables II-3 and II-4 Tulipa). The forcers must also decide on the number of weeks of cold treatment that the bulb must receive, which rooting room to use, and whether precooled or regular bulbs will be ordered (De Hertogh, 1996).

A major drawback in producing tulips, however, has been the need for cooler space. The lengthy cold treatment usually means that limited numbers of bulbs can be programmed in coolers during the high sales period from

TABLE II-3 TULIPA

Programming schedule for forcing *Tulipa* bulbs for cut flowers (modified from De Hertogh, 1996). See *Crocus* chapter, Flowering Control and Dormancy, page 407, for Rooting Room A and B temperature sequences.

Date of Desired Flowering	Date to Commence Forcing	Date to Plant Bulb	Date to Start Bulb Precooling	Rooting Room	Cold Required (weeks)
I					
Jan. 3	Dec. 10	Oct. 1–7	Aug. 23–28[a]	A	15.5
Jan.10	Dec. 17				16.5
Jan. 17	Dec. 24				17.5
II					
Jan. 23	Dec. 30	Oct. 1–7	Aug. 26–31[a]	A	17.5
Jan. 30	Jan. 7				18.5
Feb. 5	Jan. 12				19.5
IIIA					
Feb. 3	Jan. 10	Oct. 6–10	Sept. 3–7[a]	A	18
Feb. 10	Jan. 17				19
Feb. 17	Jan. 24				20
IIIB Valentine's Day					
Feb. 3	Jan. 10	Sept. 18–22	None[b]	A	16
Feb. 10	Jan. 17				17
Feb. 17	Jan. 24				18
IV					
Feb. 24	Feb. 2	Sept. 25–30	None[b]	A	18
Mar. 2	Feb. 9				19
Mar. 10	Feb. 16				20
V Early Easter					
Mar. 16	Feb. 23	Oct. 16–20	None[b]	B	18
Mar. 23	Mar. 2				19
Mar. 30	Mar. 9				20
VI Medium to late Easter					
Apr. 5	Mar. 16	Nov. 6–11	None[b]	B	18
Apr. 12	Mar. 23				19
Apr. 19	Mar. 30				20
VII Mother's Day					
Apr. 26	Apr. 6	Nov. 6–11	None[b]	B	21
May 3	Apr. 13				22

[a] Precool at 48°F (9°C); check for G-stage prior to this temperature. Store bulbs at 63°F (17°C) for 1 to 5 weeks after bulbs reach G-stage and before precooling if possible.
[b] No precooling required, hold bulbs at 63°F (17°C) until planted.

Valentine's Day to Easter. After bulbs are brought out of the cooler for Valentine's Day, there is no time to program additional bulbs for later holidays. However, a delayed potting method has been developed to reduce the amount of cooler time and space needed (Dole, 1996). With this method bulbs are still held in the cooler for the required total number of weeks of cold; however, the first portion is applied to dry unpotted bulbs (Fig. II-4 Tulipa). At 6 weeks before moving bulbs to the greenhouse for forcing, the bulbs are potted, watered, and returned to the cooler. The cooler is held at 41°F (5°C) to allow bulbs to develop roots and

TABLE II-4 TULIPA

Programming schedule for forcing *Tulipa* bulbs for potted flowering plants (modified from De Hertogh, 1996). See *Crocus* chapter, Flowering Control and Dormancy, page 407, for Rooting Room A and B temperature sequences.

Date of Desired Flowering	Date to Commence Forcing	Date to Plant Bulb	Date to Start Bulb Precooling	Rooting Room	Cold Required (weeks)
I					
Jan. 1	Dec. 10	Oct. 1–7	Aug. 26–31[a]	A	15
Jan. 8	Dec. 17				16
Jan. 15	Dec. 24				17
IIA					
Jan. 20	Dec. 30	Oct. 6–10	Sept. 1–7[a]	A	16.5
Jan. 28	Jan. 5				17.5
Feb. 5	Jan. 12				18.5
IIB					
Jan. 20	Dec. 30	Sept. 18–22	None[b]	A	14.5
Feb. 28	Jan. 5				15.5
Feb. 5	Jan. 12				16.5
III Valentine's Day					
Feb. 8	Jan. 18	Oct. 1–7	None[b]	A	15
Feb. 16	Jan. 25				16
Feb. 23	Feb. 1				17
IV					
Mar. 1	Feb. 8	Oct. 24–28	None[b]	B	15
Mar. 8	Feb. 15				16
Mar. 15	Feb. 22				17
V Early Easter					
Mar. 20	Feb. 28	Nov. 6–11	None[b]	B	16
Mar. 26	Mar. 6				17
Apr. 1	Mar. 13				18
VI Medium to late Easter					
Apr. 4	Mar. 16	Nov. 10–15	None[b]	B	18
Apr. 10	Mar. 22				19
Apr. 17	Mar. 28				20
VII Mother's Day					
Apr. 21	Apr. 1	Nov. 10–15	None[b]	B	20.5
Apr. 28	Apr. 8				21.5
May 3	Apr. 15				22.5
May 8	Apr. 22				23.5

[a]*Precool at 48°F (9°C); check for G-stage prior to this temperature. Store bulbs at 63°F (17°C) for 1 to 5 weeks after bulbs reach G-stage and before precooling if possible.*
[b]*No precooling required, hold bulbs at 63°F (17°C) until placed in Rooting Room B.*

FIGURE II-4 TULIPA 'Negritta'
Tulipa receiving 15 weeks of 41°F (5°C) supplied either dry to unpotted bulbs or moist to potted bulbs. Treatment 1 bulbs received 15 weeks moist potted cold; treatments 2, 3, 4, 5, 6, and 7 bulbs received 2, 4, 6, 8, 10, or 12 weeks dry cold, respectively; and the remaining 13, 11, 9, 7, 5, or 3 weeks moist potted cold.

shoots at the same time. Thus, a second crop can be programmed in the cooler space after the Valentine's Day crop has been moved to the greenhouse for forcing.

Cold, dry storage should not extend beyond 16 weeks or late January, after which time the bulbs must be potted and the remaining 6 weeks cold applied to bulbs in moist medium. Cooler temperatures tested for this method included 34, 37, 41, 44.5, and 48°F (1, 3, 5, 7, and 9°C) and the optimum temperature was 41°F (5°C) for both dry and moist treatments. However, temperatures cooler than 41°F (5°C) were more detrimental than temperatures greater than 41°F (5°C); flowering percentage generally decreased when temperatures were below 41°F (5°C) and shoot height increased above 41°F (5°C).

Two turns of a portion of the cooler space can be obtained by holding all or part of the bulbs intended for post–Valentine's Day sales cold and dry. As bulbs for January and Valentine's Day crops are pulled from the cooler, the cooler can be immediately refilled with potted bulbs for later forcing schedules. All bulbs must be potted by the end of January and it would probably be safest to use only the 12- to 14-cm size or larger tulip bulbs for the delayed potting method. Although optimum temperature used was 41°F (5°C), if excessive shoot or root growth is noted in the cooler, the temperature can be lowered, especially with the later forcing schedules.

INSECTS

Aphids in isolatd colonies may appear during forcing.

DISEASES

At planting, all bulbs must be inspected and discarded if infected with *Fusarium*. Planting crews must be properly trained to inspect bulbs. *Fusarium* infects the tulip bulb and can be identified by a white to tan mold growing on the outer tunic of the bulb, by soft bulbs, or by very lightweight bulbs. Infection can also be internal. All infected bulbs must be discarded. If more than 10% of the bulbs are infected with *Fusarium*, the entire lot may need to be discarded. Ethylene emanating from infected bulbs may damage noninfected bulbs.

During cold temperature programming, *Penicillium* (blue mold) may develop over the surface of the bulb above the medium level, but is usually not a serious problem. Botrytis infections may occur during forcing under high-humidity conditions with little air movement, and usually occur on the stem, which then collapses. Abortion can occur if *Botrytis* develops on the flower early in forcing. *Botrytis* can cause small circular lesions on the petals. Good air circulation and proper venting and heating are the best preventive measures (De Hertogh, 1996). A similar disease, tulip fire (*Botrytis tulipae*), can occur on tulips outdoors in which the buds are blighted, foliage blasted, and open flowers covered with spots (Horst, 1990). Diseased plant parts must be removed promptly to prevent spread of disease. Other diseases that have been reported include bulb, root and stem rot (*Pythium, Phytophthora,* and *Rhizoctonia*), bacterial soft rot (*Erwinia*), and southern wilt (*Sclerotium rolfsii*) (Dreistadt, 2001).

PHYSIOLOGICAL DISORDERS

Flower abortion during early developmental stages can be caused by a variety of conditions (Charles-Edwards and Rees, 1975). One is excessively high temperature during transport of the bulbs from the Netherlands. Ethylene exposures at any point in shipping, programming, or forcing will result in abortion or malformation of the flowers. *Fusarium* will induce ample levels of ethylene, which results in abortion or malformation of flowers (De Hertogh, 1996; Le Nard and De Hertogh, 1993; Rees, 1968). Flower abortion can also occur when immature bulbs, not at G-stage, are cold treated and due to under watering or high soluble salt levels.

Interruption of the cooling sequence with warm temperatures can cause flower bud abortion, petal malformations, increase plant height during cold storage, reduced forcing time, and shortened scape length (Liou and Miller, 2003a, b). Injury from high temperatures during cold storage is cultivar dependent with some cultivars sensitive to even 1 day of 95°F (35°C).

Stem topple occurs where the stem collapses a few inches (centimeters) below the base of the flower. This problem is related to a calcium deficiency (transport) and forcing of bulbs that have been excessively cold treated and/or forced at very high temperatures. Cultivars vary in their sensitivity to stem topple. The problem can be reduced by air circulation, which will aid in transpiration of calcium within the plant and by calcium nitrate fertilization (see Nutrition, page 887) (De Hertogh, 1996; Le Nard and De Hertogh, 1993; Rees, 1968).

POSTHARVEST

Elongation of the lower nodes on the flowering scape is controlled by endogenous GA released from the bulb as a result of cold treatment. The primary reduction of internode lengths with A-Rest occurs with the two basipetal nodes. The two basipetal nodes elongate to a greater degree than the two acropetal nodes during forcing. The elongation of the two acropetal nodes is primarily controlled by auxin from the gynoecium and occurs after sales in the home environment. Unsightly elongation of these upper nodes is accentuated by low light and warm temperatures. Currently, there is no practical method to block elongation of these upper nodes (Aung and De Hertogh, 1979; Hanks and Rees, 1980; Le Nard and De Hertogh, 1993; Rees, 1985). Ethephon at 50 ppm or ethylene may slow elongation of the uppermost two internodes, but is not used commercially (Nichols and Kofranek, 1982).

Market potted tulips when the petals begin to color. Harvest cut tulips when the petals' color intensity and development are half completed (Le Nard and De Hertogh, 1993; Nell, 1993; Nowak and Rudnicki, 1990; Sacalis, 1993). Cut flowers are harvested and stored with the bulbs attached if stems are to be stored for any duration (Fig. II-5 Tulipa). Later, bulbs are dissected and the stem broken or cut from

FIGURE II-5 TULIPA Cut *Tulipa* ready for harvest.

the basal plate. This procedure also adds 1 in. (2.5 cm) or more length to the stem. Dry storage is the preferred method for long-term cut flower storage. If the bulb is attached, store at 32 to 35°F (0 to 2°C) for 2 weeks; if not attached, 5 days is the limit. Recut the stem when removed from water for any length of time. Keep both cut and potted flowering plants as cool as possible at 32 to 35°F (0 to 2°C). At these temperatures, potted plants can be held for 1 month.

Though it has been reported that floral preservatives have little influence on vase life (Le Nard and De Hertogh, 1993; Nell, 1993; Sacalis, 1993), Nowak and Rudnicki (1990) and Pisulewski et al. (1989) reported that GA_3 enhanced longevity but caused excessive elongation. However, Ethrel (ethephon) at 10 to 25 ppm in combination with 2 to 5% sucrose and 100 ppm 8-hydroxyquinoline citrate (8-HQC) completely inhibited stem elongation without changing the positive increase GA_3 had on vase life (Pisulewski et al., 1989; Wawrzyńczak and Goszczyńska, 2000). Einert (1971, 1975) suggested that A-Rest be used in the vase solution at 25 ppm or as a 50- to 100-ppm spray to inhibit stem elongation. Benzyladenine (BA) has also been shown to slow stem elongation (Sytsema, 1971). Commercial preservatives are available that have been designed specifically for tulips (Nowak and Rudnicki, 1990). Cut *Narcissus* stems exude a mucilage that is toxic to tulips and reduces their vase life (van Doorn, 1998).

KEY POINTS

- The tulip is the most popular of the "Dutch bulb" species and has been associated with the Netherlands for more than 400 years.

- Tulip is used as a cut flower, potted flowering plant, and garden ornamental.

- Plants are propagated commercially by naturally occurring daughter bulbs; tissue culture is possible, but slow and expensive.

- Bulbs for greenhouse forcing must receive a minimum of 13 to 17 weeks of 48°F (9°C) or lower for root and shoot development.

- The initial portion of the cold treatment can be applied to the bulbs either dry and unpotted (known as precooling, PC) for early forcing dates or moist and potted (known as nonprecooled, NP) for later forcing dates.

- The final portion of the cold treatment is always applied to moist, potted bulbs.

- Bulbs must reach the G_3-stage of maturation before cooling can commence.

- With potted flowering plants, the flat side of the bulb, from which the large wrapper leaf will emerge, is placed facing outward, parallel to the pot's edge.

- After the cold treatment, plants are moved to the greenhouse and forced.

- The forcing season is divided into seven periods; recommended cultivars and forcing schedules vary with the period.

- The various forcing schedules are combined into two basic sequences known as Rooting Room A and Rooting Room B.

- Height is controlled by growth retardants, which must be applied quickly after removal from the cooler.

- *Fusarium* bulb rot is a major disease and infected bulbs produce ethylene.

- Bulbs are sensitive to ethylene, which can cause flower abortion or malformations.

- Potted plants are shipped as soon as the petals show color and cut tulips are harvested when the petals are half colored.

BIBLIOGRAPHY

Adriansen, E. 1985. Kemisk vækstregulering, pp. 142–162 in *Potteplanter I—Produktion, Metoder, Midler*, O.V. Christensen, A. Klougart, I.S. Pedersen, and K. Wikesjö, editors. Gartner-INFO, København, Denmark. (in Danish)

Armitage, A.A., and J.M. Laushman. 2003. *Tulipa*, pp. 516–522 in *Specialty Cut Flowers*, 2nd ed. Timber Press, Portland, Oregon.

Aung, L.H., and De Hertogh, A.A. 1979. Temperature regulation of growth and endogenous abscisic acid-like content of *Tulipa gesneriana L. Plant Physiology* 63:1111–1116.

Bailey, L.H., and E.Z. Bailey. 1976. *Tulipa*, pp. 1132–1134 in *Hortus Third: A Concise Dictionary of Plants Cultivated in the United States and Canada*. Macmillan, New York.

Baker, C.M., H.F. Wilkins, and P.D. Ascher. 1990. Comparisons of precultural treatments and cultural conditions of *in vitro* response of tulip. *Acta Horticulturae* 266:83–90.

Buschman, J.C.M. Undated. *Tulip Picture Book*. International Flower Bulb Centre, Hillegom, Holland.

Cavins, T.J., and J.M. Dole. 2002. Precooling, planting depth, and shade affect cut flower quality and perennialization of field-grown spring bulbs. *HortScience* 37:79–83.

Charles-Edwards, D.A., and A.R. Rees. 1975. An analysis of the growth of forced tulips. 2. Effects of low temperature treatments during development on plant structure at anthesis. *Scientia Horticulturae* 3:373–381.

De Hertogh, A.A. 1996. Tulips, pp. B1–54 in *Holland Bulb Forcer's Guide*, 5th ed. International Flower Bulb Centre, Hillegom, The Netherlands.

De Hertogh, A.A., and M. Le Nard. 1993. *Physiology of Flower Bulbs*. Elsevier, Amsterdam.

de Wild, H.P.J., H. Gude, and H.W. Peppelenbos. 2002a. Carbon dioxide and ethylene interactions in tulip bulbs. *Physiologia Plantarum* 114:320–326.

de Wild, H.P.J., H.W. Peppelenbos, M.H.G.E. Dijkema, and H. Gude. 2002b. Defining safe ethylene levels for long term storage of tulip bulbs. *Acta Horticulturae* 570:171–175.

Deneke, C.F., and G.J. Keever. 1992. Comparison of application methods of paclobutrazol for height control of potted tulips. *HortScience* 27:1329.

Dole, J.M. 1996. Spring bulb production: The delayed potting method. *Ohio Florists' Association Bulletin* 806:1, 3–4.

Dreistadt, S.H. 2001. *Integrated Pest Management for Floriculture and Nurseries*. University of California Division of Agriculture and Natural Resources Publication 3402.

Einert, A.E. 1971. Reduction in last internode elongation of cut tulips by growth retardants. *HortScience* 6:459–460.

Einert, A.E. 1975. Effects of ancymidol on vase behavior of cut tulips. *Acta Horticulturae* 41:97–101.

Gude, H., K. de Jong, and P. Vreeburg. Undated. *The Forcing of Tulip and Hyacinth under Artificial Light.* Laboratory voor Bloembollenon-derzoek, Bulb Research Center, Lisse, The Netherlands.

Hanks, G.R., and A.R. Rees. 1980. Growth substances of tulip: The activity of gibberellin-like substances in field-grown tulips from planting until flowering. *Zeitschrift für Pflanzenphysiologie* 98:213–223. (in German)

Horst, R.K. 1990. Tulip, p. 850 in *Westcott's Plant Disease Handbook,* 5th ed. Van Nostrand Reinhold, New York.

Huxley, A., M. Griffiths, and M. Levy. 1992. Tulipa, pp. 529–539 in *The New Royal Horticultural Society Dictionary of Gardening,* vol. 4. Stockton Press, New York.

Iwaya-Inoue, M., and K. Motooka. 1996. Chilling effects for normal growth of tulips bulbs estimated by MRI. *Acta Horticulturae* 440:407–412.

Jagers op Akkerhuis, F. 2000. The hydroponic revolution. *FloraCulture International* 10(12):18, 19.

James, L. 2002. Water works. *FloraCulture International* 12(4):28–34.

Lambrechts, H., F. Rook, and C. Kollöffel. 1994. Carbohydrate status of tulip bulbs during cold-induced flower stalk elongation and flowering. *Plant Physiology* 104:515–520.

Le Nard, M., and A.A. De Hertogh. 1993. *Tulipa,* pp. 617–687 in *Physiology of Flower Bulbs.* Elsevier, Amsterdam.

Liou, S.SC., and W. B. Miller. 2003. Quantifying sensitivity of tulip cultivars' susceptibility to heat. *HortScience* 38:721. (Abstract)

Liou, S.SC., and W. B. Miller. 2003. Increasing length of precooling increases susceptibility to heat injury in tulip. *HortScience* 38:753. (Abstract)

McDaniel, G.L. 1990. Postharvest height suppression of potted tulips with paclobutrazol. *HortScience* 25:212–214.

Nell, T.A. 1993. *Tulipa,* pp. 87–88 in *Flowering Potted Plants, Prolonging Shelf Performance.* Ball Publishing, Batavia, Illinois.

Nichols, R., and A.M. Kofranek. 1982. Reversal of ethylene inhibition of tulip stem elongation by silver thiosulfate. *Scientia Horticulturae* 17:71–79.

Nishiuchi, Y., and J. Koster. 1988. Difference in organogenic activity in the scale tissue culture between tulip bulbs grown at Asahikawa and bulbs grown in the Netherlands. *Journal of Hokkaido University* (Faculty of Education) (II B) 39:1–6.

Nowak, J., and R.M. Rudnicki. 1990. *Postharvest Handling and Storage of Cut Flowers, Florist Greens and Potted Plants.* Timber Press, Portland, Oregon.

Pisulewski, T.R., D.M. Goszczyńska, and R.N. Rudnicki. 1989. The influence of gibberellic acid and ethrel on cut tulips. *Acta Horticulturae* 251:115–118.

Rebers, M., E. Vermeer, E. Kregt, and L.H.W. van der Plas. 1996. Gibberellin levels are not a suitable indicator for properly cold-treated tulip bulbs. *HortScience* 31:837–838.

Rees, A.R. 1968. The initiation and growth of tulip bulbs. *Annals of Botany* 32:68–77.

Rees, A.R. 1972. Temperature, pp. 103–104 in *The Growth of Bulbs.* Academic Press, London and New York.

Rees, A.R. 1985. *Tulipa,* pp. 272–277 in *Handbook of Flowering,* vol. I. CRC Press, Boca Raton, Florida.

Sacalis, J.M. 1993. *Tulipa,* pp. 101–102 in *Cut Flowers, Prolonging Freshness,* 2nd ed., J.L. Seals, editor. Ball Publishing, Batavia, Illinois.

Saniewski, M., K. Mynett, and J. Puchalski. 1997. Formation of parrot-like flowers after treatment of non-parrot tulip bulbs with benzyladenine before flower bud development. *Acta Horticulturae* 430:107–115.

Sytsema, W. 1971. De houbdaarheid van tulpen. *Vakblad von den Bloemisterij* 26(15):8–9. (in Dutch)

Thompson, R., and R.E. Johnston. 1974. Choosing the right type of tulip bulb for forcing. *Commercial Grower* 16:234–235.

van Doorn, W.G. 1998. Effects of daffodil flowers on the water relations and vase life of roses and tulips. *Journal of the American Society for Horticultural Science* 123:146–149.

Wawrzyńczak, A., and D.M. Goszczyńska. 2000. Effect of exogenous growth regulators on quality and longevity of cut tulip flowers. *Journal of Fruit and Ornamental Plant Research* 8:87–96.

Yamasaki, A., A. Uragami, and M. Yamada. 2002. Hydroponic forcing of tulip using a nutrient film technique. *Acta Horticulturae* 570:423–427.

Viola

INTRODUCTION

Common and scientific names: *Viola odorata* L., sweet violet, garden violet, florists' violet, English violet; *V. cornuta* L. horned violet, violet; *V. tricolor* L., viola, European wild pansy, miniature pansy, field pansy, Johnny-jump-up; and *V.* ×*wittrockiana* Gams., pansy, garden pansy (Huxley et al., 1992).

Family and related taxa: Violaceae Batsch. There are approximately 500 species of *Viola*, of which most are low-growing herbaceous annuals or perennials.

Origin: Violas are widely distributed across northern and southern temperate zones. *Viola odorata* is native to a broad area of Europe, Africa, and Asia. Flowers are deep purple. *V. cornuta* has dark purple flowers and is found in the Pyrenees and Spain. *V. tricolor* is European and has become naturalized in North America. Flowers have various color combinations of yellow, purple-red, violet-blue, or white (Armitage, 1989; Bailey and Bailey, 1976).

Uses and current status: *Viola cornuta* and *V. odorata* can be classified as true violets. In this text *Viola tricolor* is called "viola" and the hybrid *V.* ×*wittrockiana* is called "pansy." Violets are planted in gardens as ground covers for early spring color and are treated as perennials. Several wildflower species are grown in the home garden, including *V. sororaria* Willd., *V. pedata* L., and *V. canadensis* L. *Viola cornuta* is also a perennial garden plant hardy from Zones 6 to 9 and is sold in garden centers.

At one time the fragrant *Viola odorata* was widely forced into flower in North America and Europe as a popular winter and early spring cut flower sold as nosegays and used in the perfume industry. Several hybrids and cultivars of *V. odorata* exist. This species has been famous in Europe for a millennium and is reported to have been sold in ancient Greece in 400 B.C.

Viola tricolor and *V.* ×*wittrockiana* hybrids are used as bedding plants and are popular for early winter and spring color (Armitage, 1989; Bailey and Bailey, 1976; Ball, 1991; Healy, 1998; Nau, 1998; Post, 1949; White, 1923). In most areas of the southern United States, they are sold in the fall, survive the winter, and commence flowering during the first warm days of late winter and early spring. In mild areas of the Deep South, Southwest, and Pacific Coast, pansies flower all winter. In some areas, pansies should be lightly mulched during the winter. In northern states and Canada, pansies are sold and planted in early spring. Pansies and violas are similarly grown in Japan and Europe. Regardless of the location, most pansies wither when hot summer weather commences and heat or water stress occurs. Newer, more cold-tolerant cultivars survive cold Minnesota winters (Zone 4) with modest protection and tolerate warm summer temperatures. Long-stemmed pansies are occasionally grown as a greenhouse cut flower.

CULTIVARS

VIOLETS

Viola cornuta flower color is commonly deep violet or purple, but white, light blue, apricot, yellow, and lilac cultivars exist. Flower size is up to 1.5 in. (4 cm) across and stems are up to 6 in. (15 cm) long. *V. odorata* cultivars have deep violet, lavender-violet, dark blue, or white flowers. Double forms also exist. Stems can be 8 to 12 in. (20 to 30 cm) long and flowers are 0.75 in. (2 cm) across (Armitage, 1989; Bailey and Bailey, 1976).

PANSIES AND VIOLAS

Hundreds of *Viola* ×*wittrockiana* cultivars are available and new releases occur annually. *V. tricolor* is sold as a novelty with its dainty 0.75-in. (2-cm) flower size. However, new hybrids are rapidly blurring the distinctions between violas and pansies. Numerous test sites across the world evaluate new releases in various climates. Cultivars have been organized into three flower size groups: (1) 1.5 to 2.5 in. (4 to 6 cm), (2) 2.5 to 3.5 in. (6 to 9 cm), and (3) 3.5 to 4.5 in. (9 to 11.5 cm). The 'Oregon Giants' pansy is used for novelty cut flower production.

PROPAGATION

VIOLETS

Violet propagation is asexual. *V. odorata* forms trailing stems, which can be made into terminal or two leaf-stem cuttings. The cuttings root easily and the leaf below the rooting medium should be removed. With both *V. cornuta* and *V. odorata* divisions can be made from established plantings, which is done from January to early March (Post, 1949; White, 1923).

PANSIES AND VIOLAS

Pansies are grown exclusively from seed and frequently reseed themselves in the home garden. There are 18,000 to 23,000 seeds/oz (635 to 800/g). Pansy germination occurs in the dark over a wide range of temperatures with the following germination results: 55% at 55°F (13°C), 48% at 60°F (16°C), 60% at 65°F (18°C), 46% at 70°F (21°C), and finally 64% at 75°F (24°C) (Cathey, 1969; Holcomb and Mastalerz, 1985). Primed seed is less sensitive to high temperatures and should be used during hot weather (Corr, 1997; Yoon et al., 1997). Violas appear to be more temperature sensitive than pansies and the night temperature should be 60°F (16°C) or less when day temperatures are above 70°F (21°C).

For plug production of pansies the following conditions are used (Ball, 1991; Styer, 1998):

Stage 1: Seed covered, 62 to 68°F (17 to 20°C), for 4 to 7 days. Keep seed uniformly moist and below 80°F (27°C).

Stage 2: 62 to 68°F (17 to 20°C), for 7 days, apply 50 ppm N once, keep media EC less than 1.0 dS · m^{-1} (saturated media extract). Maintain 1500 to 2500 fc (300 to 500 μmol · m^{-2} · s^{-1}) and reduce media moisture once radicles are present to reduce stretch.

Stage 3: 60 to 62°F (16 to 17°C), for 14 days, 100 ppm N once/week or every two to three irrigations, keep media EC less than 1.5 dS · m^{-1}. Maintain 2500 to 4000 fc (500 to 800 μmol · m^{-2} · s^{-1}) and apply plant growth regulators, if necessary. Grow dry but avoid wilting.

Stage 4: 55 to 60°F (13 to 16°C), for 14 to 21 days, fertilize as needed, keep media EC less than 1.2 dS · m^{-1}. Maintain 2500 to 4000 fc (500 to 800 μmol · m^{-2} · s^{-1}) and apply plant growth regulators, if necessary.

Plugs should be ready for marketing or transplanting within 6 to 7 weeks. See Chapter 1, Propagation, for description of plug stages.

FLOWERING CONTROL AND DORMANCY

VIOLETS

Both *V. odorata* and *V. cornuta* flowering and flower quality are influenced by photoperiod and temperature. *V. odorata* plants are vigorous in the summer (high temperatures and LD) with flowering commencing in fall (October). Few "runners" are formed during the flowering period (October to March) (Post, 1949). There are two forms of flowers: open (chasmogamous) flowers with petals during the SD of fall, winter, and early spring; and closed (cleistogamous) flowers with little petal formation during the LD of summer (Allard and Garner, 1940; Cooper and Watson, 1952). Several species' temperature interactions have been researched by Mayers (1986).

PANSIES AND VIOLAS

Long days increase flower numbers, but also increase internode length. Under SD stems are short and sturdy (Seeley, 1985). There is no apparent dormancy as pansies can flower year-round. High summer temperatures are the limiting factor, causing a decline in plant vigor.

TEMPERATURE

VIOLETS

Armitage (1989) summarized the temperature response of all *Viola*: "Plants grow best in the cool times of the year...." "Violets are cold-house crops," stated Post (1949). Preferred production temperatures are between 40 and 50°F (4 and 10°C) (Ball, 1991; Nau, 1998). Cooper and Watson (1952) noted that the flower size was greater when plants were grown at 50°F (10°C) night temperature than when grown at 40°F (4°C).

PANSIES AND VIOLAS

Plants grow best at 40 to 55°F (4 to 13°C) after plants are established with a media temperature of 45 to 50°F (7 to 10°C) (Lacy, 1999; Post, 1949). Growth is weak and internodes elongate at 60°F (16°C) or higher (Holcomb and Mastalerz, 1985; Seeley, 1985). As the temperature increased from 59°F (15°C), plant dry weight, root growth, flower size, and days to flower decreased (Faust, 2000; Niu et al., 2000). Pearson et al. (1995) also found that flower size decreased as temperature increased from 48 to 88°F (9 to 31°C), but prior to visible bud temperature did not influence final flower size. From visible bud to flower, flower development was fastest at 72°F (22°C) (Adams et al., 1997).

LIGHT

VIOLETS

Long days result in cleistogamous (closed) flowers (Mayers, 1986). Most species tolerate full sun in the garden, but grow best in shade (Armitage, 1989). In greenhouses, use heavy shade in the summer and light shade in the winter, resulting in less than 1200 fc (240 μmol · m^{-2} · s^{-1}) (Post, 1949; White, 1923).

PANSIES AND VIOLAS

Use full light, unless plugs are grown in late summer and shade is needed to reduce temperatures (Ball, 1991; Healy, 1998; Nau, 1998; Post, 1949; Seeley, 1985). Supplemental HID lighting dramatically decreases days to flower and increases flower number. Increasing the daily light integral from 4.1 to 10.6 mol · m^{-2} · day^{-1} increased plant growth, flower development rate, and flower size (Niu et al., 2000).

Long day lengths decreased time to first flower; LD were most effective when applied 2 to 6 weeks after germination (Erwin et al., 1997; Karlsson, 1996). Night interruption lighting with incandescent lamps may increase height, however (Erwin et al., 1997).

WATER

Violet and pansy plants should never be allowed to dry out.

CARBON DIOXIDE

Pansies respond to carbon dioxide levels of 1000 ppm or greater by decreasing time to flower (Kaczperski et al., 1994; Niu et al., 2000). Lower rates of 500 or 600 ppm had little effect.

NUTRITION

Moderate nutritional regimes of 100 ppm N are sufficient. Using subirrigation, optimum growth was obtained with a fertilizer EC of 1.2 to 2.0 dS · m^{-1}, and a media EC between 1.5 and 4 dS · m^{-1} as measured by the pour-through method (van Iersel, 1999; van Iersel

and Kang, 2002). Neither urea nor ammonium-based nitrogen sources should be used with this cold growing crop. Leaves may develop a blue-purple pigment at cold temperature, which may be a transitory phosphorus deficiency. Both boron and calcium deficiency cause cupping and distortion of new pansy foliage. Boron deficiency can also abort the growing tip. Boron deficiency can be caused by insufficient boron, high medium pH, or high calcium levels (Styer, 1997, 1998). Calcium deficiency can be caused by low medium pH of less than 5.5. Low medium pH can also induce iron and manganese toxicity, which causes a rusty mottling of pansy foliage. Whipker et al. (2000) described the deficiency symptoms of several nutrients on pansy. See Chapter 6, Nutrition, Table 6-4, for foliar nutrient levels.

MEDIA

Any well-drained peat-lite medium is acceptable for greenhouse production. Outdoors any soil or medium with adequate water-holding capacity is acceptable. Incorporate organic matter into the medium. The pH should be 5.5 to 6.0 (Post, 1949). Foliar chlorosis may occur if pH rises above 6.5.

HEIGHT CONTROL

VIOLETS

Growth retardants are not needed on violets.

PANSIES AND VIOLAS

No growth regulators are required if plants are produced at appropriate cool temperatures and high light; however, plants in warm southern areas may need to be treated with plant growth retardants. Sumagic (uniconazole) at 1 ppm or Bonzi (paclobutrazol) at 0.5 ppm can be sprayed on the media prior to germination to prevent early pansy stem elongation. Pansies are highly sensitive to overapplication of Bonzi and Sumagic, so measuring and application should be carefully done (Lacy, 1999). Bonzi and Sumagic sprays at 1 to 3 ppm can also be applied to finished plug flats. Wieland et al. (1997) noted that two A-Rest (ancymidol) sprays at 5 to 10 ppm were effective on pansy plugs. B-Nine (daminozide) sprays of 2500 ppm can be applied after the first true leaves appear (Lacy, 1999). Tank mixes of Cycocel (chlormequat) at 750 to 1250 ppm and B-Nine at 1250 to 2500 ppm are also effective (Kuehny et al., 2001; Lacy 1999). High rates of Cycocel can cause leaf burn (Latimer, 2000).

On finished flats Bonzi sprays at 2 to 15 ppm, Sumagic sprays at 1 to 6 ppm, A-Rest sprays at 8 to 10 ppm after transplanting or 11 to 15 ppm at finish, and B-Nine sprays at 2500 ppm are also effective (Bell, 2001; Lacy, 1999). Topflor (flurprimidol) sprays at 2.5 to 7.5 ppm can also be used (SePRO, personal communication; Whipker et al., 2003). Lower rates are recommended for less vigorous cultivars (Latimer, 2000).

Excessive stretching can also be prevented culturally by not overwatering or overfertilizing, restricting medium phosphorus level, reducing ammonium application, providing sufficient light, and providing good air movement. Height control through DIF is also effective.

SPACING

When outdoors, space violets 8 to 9 in. (20 to 23 cm) between plants in 10-in. (26-cm) rows (White, 1923). Pansy bedding flats are spaced flat-to-flat. In the garden, small flowered pansies are spaced 6 to 8 in. (15 to 20 cm) apart. The larger cultivars are spaced 8 to 10 in. (20 to 26 cm) apart (Healy, 1998; Nau, 1998).

PINCHING AND DISBUDDING

No pinching or disbudding required.

SUPPORT

No support required.

SCHEDULE AND TIMING

VIOLETS

Flowering can begin in October and progress through April under protection. Cooper and Watson (1952) noted that marketable flowers are produced 10 weeks after the start of 8-hr SD when grown at 50°F (10°C) night temperature. From spring-propagated plants, flower production can occur the following fall. Other production systems include moving plants from outdoors in late summer (White, 1923).

PANSIES AND VIOLAS

Pansy seeds are sown every month of the year (Healy, 1998). Northern pansy plug producers start seeding during the summer for fall plant sales in the region south of the 38th parallel, or Zone 6, in North America. Pansies flower all winter in Florida or southern California and flower in both the fall and late winter through spring in the southern United States. In the north, plants are grown only as an early spring crop. Seeding begins in December or January and into March for typical spring bedding plant sales, depending on the latitude. Finished flats can be produced in 13 to 14 weeks in cool climates and in 12 to 13 weeks in warm climates.

Frequently, pansies are placed in unheated cold frames or plastic hoop houses for holding and to slow growth, making it difficult to specify a production schedule. Nonstop production may require 84 to 100 days from a December or January seed date to flower in the spring.

INSECTS

Aphids, fungus gnats, shoreflies, thrips, and caterpillars can be a problem if not monitored (Baker, 2000). Post (1949) also listed a violet sawfly.

DISEASES

VIOLETS

Several leaf spot diseases (*Alternaria violae, Cercospora granuliformis, C. violae, Marssonina violae, Phyllosticta violae,* and *Septoria violae*), rusts (*Puccinia violae, P. ellisiana,* and *Ureomyces andropogonis*), and viruses occur on outdoor-grown plants (Horst, 1990). The most important disease is spot anthracnose or scab (*Sphaceloma violae*), which can cause lesions on stems and leaves (Forsberg, 1979).

PANSIES

Greenhouse-grown plants are subject to damping-off (*Pythium* and *Rhizoctonia solanii*), leaf spot (*Alternaria, Colletotrichum, Cercospora, Mycocentrospora,* and *Sphaceloma*), gray mold (*Botrytis cinerea*), petiole and stem rot (*Myrothecium*), and root and crown rot (*Fusarium oxysporum, Phytophthora, Pythium, Rhizoctonia,* or *Thielaviopsis*) (Daughtrey and Chase, 1992; Hamrick, 2003; Horst, 1990; Styer, 1997). Cottony rot (*Sclerotinia sclerotiorum*), southern wilt (*Sclerotium rolfsii*), powdery mildew (*Sphaerotheca*), downy mildew (*Peronospora violae*), and several viruses have also been reported (Dreistadt, 2001). Other diseases, including those listed for violets, attack pansies outdoors. Practice sanitation and apply preventive sprays when plants are held in long-term cold environments (Heins et al., 1994).

PHYSIOLOGICAL DISORDERS

VIOLETS

Violets develop showy open flowers under 8- to 10-hr SD, and small, closed cleistogamous types under LD of 14 to 17 hr (Cooper and Watson, 1952; Mayers, 1986).

PANSIES AND VIOLAS

Insufficient flower size on pansies can be due to high production temperatures and/or late application of growth retardants. Pansies and violas afflicted with mottled pansy syndrome exhibit elongated, twisted, and streaked leaves. Little is known about the cause of this problem, which varies greatly in severity from year to year and is accentuated by high light levels and temperatures above 85°F (29°C) when plants are young (Hamrick, 2003). High temperatures can cause upward cupping of the leaves (Faust, 2000).

Boron toxicity can also be a problem (Hamrick, 2003). Symptoms include stunted growth, small leaves, and chlorotic lower foliage with marginal necrosis.

Desiccated flowers can occur when the root ball is frozen but the air temperatures are high enough for plants to respire and transpire (Hamrick, 2003).

POSTHARVEST

Cut *Viola odorata* and *V. ×wittrockiana* flowers are harvested when the flower is almost fully open and stored in water at 34 to 41°F (1 to 5°C) for up to 7 days (Nowak and Rudnicki, 1990). Pansy plugs could be stored up to 16 weeks at 41°F (5°C) with 5 fc (1 μmol $\cdot$ m^{-2} $\cdot$ s^{-1}) or in darkness at 32 to 36°F (0 to 2°C) (Heins et al., 1994; Kaczperski and Armitage, 1992). Pansies are intermediately sensitive to ethylene gas (Rogers, 1985).

KEY POINTS

- This genus includes a number of commercially important species: pansies (*Viola ×wittrockiana*) and violas (*V. tricolor*) are grown as winter and spring bedding plants, violets (primarily *V. cornuta* and *V. odorata*) are grown as garden perennials; both violets and pansies are occasionally grown as cut flowers.

- Violets produce two types of flowers: open (chasmogamous) flowers with petals during SD and closed (cleistogamous) flowers with little petal formation during LD.

- Pansies and violas are sensitive to high temperatures and best grown at 40 to 55°F (4 to 13°C).

- Most plants will not need a growth retardant, but plants grown in warm climates areas may need one or more applications of a growth retardant.

- Excessive stretching of pansies and violas can be prevented by not overwatering or overfertilizing, restricting medium phosphorus level, reducing ammonium applications, and providing sufficient light and air movement.

BIBLIOGRAPHY

Adams, S.R., S. Pearson, and P. Hadley. 1997. The effects of temperature, photoperiod and light integral on the time to flowering of pansy cv. Universal Violet (*Viola ×wittrockiana* Gams.). *Annals of Botany* 80:107–112.

Allard, H.A., and W.W. Garner. 1940. Further observations on the response of various species of plant to the length of day. *United States Department of Agriculture Technical Bulletin* 727:1–64.

Armitage, A. 1989. *Viola*, pp. 600–608 in *Herbaceous Perennial Plants*. Varsity Press, Athens, Georgia.

Bailey, L.W., and E.Z. Bailey. 1976. *Viola*, pp. 1158–1161 in *Hortus Third, A Concise Dictionary of*

Plants Cultivated in the United States and Canada. Macmillan, New York.

Baker, J.R. 2000. Insect management, pp. 57–68 in *Pansy Production Handbook*, B.E. Whipker, P.A. Thomas, and T.J. Cavins, editors. North Carolina Commercial Flower Growers' Association, Raleigh, North Carolina.

Ball, V. 1991. Plugs—The way of the 1990s, pp. 137–153 in *Ball Redbook*, 15th ed. George J. Ball Publishing, West Chicago, Illinois.

Bell, M. 2001. Bedding plants and seed geraniums, pp. 54–60 in *Tips on Regulating Growth of Floriculture Crops*, M.L. Gaston, L.A. Kunkle,

P.S. Konjoian, and M.F. Wilt, editors. Ohio Florists' Association Services, Columbus, Ohio.

Cathey, H.M. 1969. Guidelines for the germination of annual pot plant and ornamental seeds. *Florists Review* 144(3742):21–23, 58–60; 144(3743):18–20, 52–53; 144(3744):26–28, 75–77.

Cooper, C.C., and D.P. Watson. 1952. Influence of daylength and temperature on growth of greenhouse violets. *Proceeding of the American Society for Horticultural Science* 59:549–553.

Corr, B. 1997. The ABC's of plug production. *Greenhouse Product News* 7(2):21–23.

Daughtrey, M., and A.R. Chase. 1992. Pansy, p. 148 in *Ball Field Guide of Diseases of Greenhouse Ornamentals*. Ball Publishing, Geneva, Illinois.

Dreistadt, S.H. 2001. *Integrated Pest Management for Floriculture and Nurseries*. University of California Division of Agriculture and Natural Resources Publication 3402.

Erwin, J.E., R. Warner, T. Smith, and R. Wagner. 1997. Photoperiod and temperature interact to affect *Viola ×wittrockiana* Gams. development. *HortScience* 32:466. (Abstract)

Faust, J.E. 2000. Temperature and light, pp. 20–22 in *Pansy Production Handbook*, B.E. Whipker, P.A. Thomas, and T.J. Cavins, editors. North Carolina Commercial Flower Growers' Association, Raleigh, North Carolina.

Forsberg, J.L. 1979. Pansy, Violets, pp. 126–129 in *Diseases of Ornamental Plants*. Special Publication No. 3, College of Agriculture, University of Illinois, Urbana.

Hamrick, D. 2003. *Viola*, pp. 678–684 in *Ball Redbook*, vol. 2, 17th ed. Ball Publishing, Batavia, Illinois.

Healy, W. 1998. *Viola ×wittrockiana* (Pansy), pp. 777–782 in *Ball Redbook*, 16th ed., V. Ball, editor. Ball Publishing, Batavia, Illinois.

Heins, R., N. Lange, T.F. Wallace, Jr., and W. Carlson. 1994. *Plug Storage, Cold Storage of Plug Seedlings*. Meister Publishing, Willoughby, Ohio.

Holcomb, E.J., and J.W. Mastalerz. 1985. Seeding and seedling production, pp. 87–125 in *Bedding Plants III*, 3rd ed., J.W. Mastalerz and E.J. Holcomb, editors. Pennsylvania Flower Growers, University Park, Pennsylvania.

Horst, R.K. 1990. Pansy, p. 753; Violet, pp. 859–860 in *Westcott's Plant Disease Handbook*, 5th ed. Van Nostrand Reinhold, New York.

Huxley, A., M. Griffiths, and M. Levy. 1992. Viola, pp. 665–675 in *The New Royal Horticultural Society Dictionary of Gardening*, vol. 4. Stockton Press, New York.

Kaczperski, M.P., and A.M. Armitage. 1992. Short-term storage of plug-grown bedding plant seedlings. *HortScience* 27:798–800.

Kaczperski, M.P., A.M. Armitage, and P.M. Lewis. 1994. Accelerating growth of plug-grown pansies

with carbon dioxide and light. *HortScience* 29:442. (Abstract)

Karlsson, M. 1996. Photoperiod and irradiance affect flowering in four cultivars of pansy. *HortScience* 31:681. (Abstract)

Kuehny, J.S., A. Painter, and P.C. Branch. 2001. Plug source and growth retardants affect finish size of bedding plants. *HortScience* 36:321–323.

Lacy, L. 1999. This winter, grow spring pansies. *GrowerTalks* 63(6):36, 39–40.

Latimer, J.G. 2000. Using plant growth regulators, pp. 23–25 in *Pansy Production Handbook*, B.E. Whipker, P.A. Thomas, and T.J. Cavins, editors. North Carolina Commercial Flower Growers' Association, Raleigh, North Carolina.

Mayers, A.M. 1986. *Viola odorata*, pp. 372–384 in *Handbook of Flowering*, vol. V, A.H. Halevy, editor. CRC Press, Boca Raton, Florida.

Nau, J. 1998. *Viola* (Johnny-jump-up, violet), pp. 775–776 in *Ball Redbook*, 16th ed., V. Ball, editor. Ball Publishing, Batavia, Illinois.

Niu, G., R.D. Heins, A.C. Cameron, and W.H. Carlsson. 2000. Day and night temperatures, daily light integral, and CO_2 enrichment affect growth and flower development of pansy (*Viola ×wittrockiana*). *Journal of the American Society for Horticultural Science* 125:436–441.

Nowak, J., and R.M. Rudnicki. 1990. *Postharvest Handling and Storage of Cut Flowers, Florist Greens, and Potted Plants*. Timber Press, Portland, Oregon.

Pearson, S., A. Parker, S.R. Adams, P. Hadley, and D.R. May. 1995. The effects of temperature on the flower size of pansy (*Viola ×wittrockiana* Gams.). *Journal of Horticultural Science* 70:183–190.

Post, K. 1949. *Viola tricolor* and *Viola cornuta*; *Viola odorata*, pp. 839–845 in *Florist Crop Production and Marketing*. Orange Judd Publishing, New York.

Rogers, M. 1985. Air pollution, pp. 274–314 in *Bedding Plants III*, 3rd ed., J.W. Mastalerz and E.J. Holcomb, editors. Pennsylvania Flower Growers, University Park, Pennsylvania.

Seeley, J.G. 1985. Finishing bedding plants—Effects of environmental factors: Temperature, light, carbon dioxide, growth retardants, pp. 212–244 in *Bedding Plants III*, 3rd ed., J.W. Mastalerz and E.J. Holcomb, editors. Pennsylvania Flower Growers, University Park, Pennsylvania.

Styer, R.C. 1997. Diagnosing fall pansy problems. *Greenhouse Product News* 7(8):38–40.

Styer, R.C. 1998. Producing fall pansy plugs. *GrowerTalks* 62(5):121, 126.

van Iersel, M. 1999. Fertilizer concentration affects growth and nutrient composition of subirrigated pansies. *HortScience* 34:660–663.

van Iersel, M., and J.-G. Kang. 2002. Nutrient solution concentration affects whole-plant CO_2

exchange and growth of subirrigated pansy. *Journal of the American Society for Horticultural Science* 127:423–429.

Whipker, B.E., J.L. Gibson, D.S. Pitchay, P.V. Nelson, and C.R. Campbell. 2000. Fertility management, pp. 26–38 in *Pansy Production Handbook*, B.E. Whipker, P.A. Thomas, and T.J. Cavins, editors. North Carolina Commercial Flower Growers' Association, Raleigh, North Carolina.

Whipker, B.E., I.M. McCall, B. Krug, and J.L. Gibson. 2003. Update on Topflor (flurprimidol) research: Fall pansies. *North Carolina Flower Growers' Bulletin* 48(3):10–11.

White, E.A. 1923. Violets, pp. 266–273 in *Principles of Floriculture*. Macmillan, New York.

Wieland, C.E., J.E. Barrett, C.A. Bartucka, D.G. Clark, and T.A. Nell. 1997. Growth regulator effects on development of three bedding plant plugs. *HortScience* 32:508–509. (Abstract)

Yoon, B. Y.-H., H.J. Lang, and B.G. Cobb. 1997. Priming with salt solutions improves germination of pansy seed at high temperatures. *HortScience* 32:248–250.

Zantedeschia

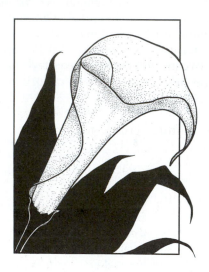

Uses and current status: Calla lilies are herbaceous perennials used as cut flowers or flowering potted plants (Figs. II-1 and II-2 Zantedeschia). They can also be used in the landscape in areas where the soil does not freeze; the plants can survive with mulch as far north as Zone 6 with temperatures of 0 to −4°F (−18 to −20°C) (B. Corr, personal communication).

The underground storage organ is thickened and fleshy and has been classified as a corm, tuber, or rhizome (Funnell, 1993). Several shoots and showy flowers develop from this storage organ. The leaves, which are entire, are born on a long petiole (Bailey and Bailey, 1976; Funnell, 1993; Harrison, 1972; Letty, 1973). The inflorescence consists of a spadix enclosed by a spathe.

FIGURE II-I ZANTEDESCHIA *Zantedeschia* 'Pershore Fantasia' garden ornamental.

INTRODUCTION

Common names: calla, calla lily, cape lily, and arum lily.

Scientific names: *Zantedeschia aethiopica* (L.) Spreng., *Z. albomaculata* (Hook.) Baill., *Z. elliotiana* (Wats.) Engl., and *Z. rehmannii* Engli. are the primary species involved in floriculture and in breeding programs (Huxley et al., 1992).

Family and related taxa: Araceae Juss. Araceae is a large family containing many important genera including *Aglaonema, Anthurium, Caladium, Dieffenbachia, Epipremnum, Monstera, Nephthytis, Philodendron, Spathiphyllum,* and *Syngonium.*

Origin: The various species are found in Cape Province, Eastern Orange Free State, Natal, Lesotho, Swaziland, Transvaal, Rhodesia, Malawi, Zambia, Angola, and into northern Nigeria (Funnell, 1993; Letty, 1973).

FIGURE II-2 ZANTEDESCHIA *Zantedeschia aethiopica* cut flower production.

CULTIVARS

Zantedeschia has seven species (Perry, 1989) and three subspecies (Bailey and Bailey, 1976; Funnell, 1993; Harrison, 1972; Letty, 1973). They fall into two types: plants with winter-appearing white spathes and evergreen leaves, or plants with variously colored summer-appearing spathes and deciduous leaves that senesce during the winter (Funnell, 1993; Kuehny, 2000; Letty, 1973).

The primary species is *Z. aethiopica* (white), which is 36 in. (100 cm) or more tall; 'Childsiana' is a dwarf selection or cultivar. *Z. aethiopica* flowers under protection or outdoors in frost-free areas from late fall into early spring (Auman, 1980; Funnell, 1993; Post, 1952). In California and other areas similar to the Cape Town climate, this species has escaped and can be seen growing in moist ditches along the road as a weed (Bailey and Bailey, 1976).

Colored species include *Z. elliotiana* (yellow to gold flowers), which is approximately 12 in. (30 cm) tall, and *Z. rehmannii* (red to pink flowers), which is 24 in. (60 cm) tall. Another colored calla known for its white spotted leaves, *Z. albomaculata* (white to pale yellow flowers with purple interior bases), is 18 in. (45 cm) tall (Bailey and Bailey, 1976; Funnell, 1993; Harrison, 1972; Letty, 1973).

Hybrids between *Z. elliotiana*, *Z. rehmannii*, and *Z. albomaculata* are commercially available, with flower colors ranging from yellow to orange and red to pink. They also exhibit various leaf patterns. Plants flower from February to April when tubers are forced in a Northern Hemisphere greenhouse. Greenhouse production with tubers from the Southern Hemisphere is from June to December.

Depending on the cultivars selected, plants can be classified as (1) true dwarfs, grown in 4- to 6-in. (10- to 15-cm) pots; (2) midrange sizes, useful for short cut flower production or large specimen pot plants; and (3) large types, mainly useful for cut flowers. The advent of new dwarf and semidwarf hybrids has renewed interest in this genus (Armitage, 1991; Auman, 1980; Corr and Widmer, 1987a; De Hertogh, 1996). Kuehny (2000) listed the cultivars and species available at the time.

PROPAGATION

Z. aethiopica is commonly propagated by division (Bailey and Bailey, 1976; Chaves des Neves and Pais, 1980a, b). *Z. elliotiana*, *Z. rehmannii*, and *Z. albomaculata* are propagated by seed from inbred hybrid lines or *in vitro*. A minimum of 2 years or two growth cycles is required from seeding in the field to sale of commercial-size tubers. About 80% of *in vitro*–propagated tubers will emerge and flower after they have been removed from culture, grown for one season, dried, stored, and properly chemically treated (Fig. II-3 Zantedeschia). However, four to five *in vitro*–propagated tubers are required to produce a sellable 4-in. (10-cm) pot and are generally too costly to be feasible. Consequently, another growth cycle in the field or under protection is required to produce a tuber with two to three growing points, which will develop an adequate sized plant in a pot (Armitage, 1991; Auman, 1980). Cohen (1981) and Chen et al. (2000) described *in vitro* techniques.

FIGURE II-3 ZANTEDESCHIA *Zantedeschia* tuber with shoots starting to elongate.

FLOWERING CONTROL AND DORMANCY

Zantedeschia aethiopica appears to have no true dormancy, because the plants will flower continuously if media temperatures are not high and moisture is supplied (Auman, 1980; Post, 1952). When night air temperatures stay above 60°F (16°C) or reach 70°F (21°C), however, flower production decreases and eventually ceases (Tjia, 1989).

In contrast, the various colored species and hybrids flower only once per year (Corr and Widmer, 1987a, b; Corr and Widmer, 1990; Funnell, 1993). It is assumed that carbohydrate reserve depletion is responsible for the limited flowering time span of these hybrids, because the tubers lose weight during the period of early growth and flowering, then increase weight later in the vegetative growth cycle. Further, gibberellic acid (GA) deficiencies may be responsible for the lack of sustained long-term production. Tubers of these colored species have separate requirements for vegetative dormancy release and for floral induction (B. Corr, personal communication).

When tubers of the colored hybrids arrive, they should be inspected and placed in dry storage at 46°F (8°C) and 70 to 80% relative humidity (De Hertogh, 1996). Storage can be up to 6 months with the optimal storage temperature of 46°F (8°C), which reduces respiration and transpiration; the cool temperature does not vernalize the tubers. Higher temperatures, for example, 55°F (13°C), can be used for short-term storage. There appears to be a maturation process as freshly harvested and immediately planted tubers will flower at the same time as tubers dry stored and then planted (Corr, 1988; Funnell, 1993) (Table II-1 Zantedeschia).

K. Funnell (personal communication) suggested that tubers should not be planted or treated with gibberellic acid until 1/8-in.- (3-mm)-long shoots are observed. This indicates that rapid growth will occur once planted.

Storage also affects many vegetative growth characteristics of the colored species. After foliar senescence of *Z. elliotiana* and *Z. rehmannii* was induced by withholding water, the tubers were harvested and then either replanted immediately or stored for 0, 3, 6, 9, or 15 weeks at 72°F (22°C). Tubers stored for 3 or more weeks had more shoots and leaves and were taller than nonstored tubers (Corr and Widmer, 1987a, b).

Partial dehydration during storage is apparently required for release of vegetative dormancy of the colored hybrids. Tubers harvested by removing the foliage with a knife, without a period of drought, were either immediately replanted or were stored dry for 6 weeks at 72°F (22°C). Tubers that were planted after 6 weeks of dry storage sprouted; those that were not stored but immediately replanted, watered, and kept at 68°F (20°C) did not sprout. The nonsprouted tubers were again harvested after 40 days, dried, stored at 72°F (22°C) for 6 weeks, and then replanted. These tubers then sprouted normally, demonstrating that vegetative dormancy was released by dry storage (Corr and Widmer, 1988).

If harvested dry tubers are immediately given a GA treatment, numerous flowers but few leaves develop; if harvested and stored for 6 weeks at 50°F (10°C), few flowers but numerous leaves develop; if stored at 50°F (10°C) and GA treated, leaf and flower emergence are rapid with numerous leaves and flowers present (Corr, 1988; Corr and Widmer, 1987b). Gibberellic acid is considered to primarily in-

TABLE II-1 ZANTEDESCHIA

The influence of storage for 0, 3, 6, 9, or 12 weeks at 59°F (15°C) on days to flower after potting of *Zantedeschia rehmannii* tubers (Corr, 1988). Note that the days in storage + days to flower are nearly equal, denoting a maturity requirement.

Storage (weeks)	Days to Flower after Potting	Total Days from Harvest to Flower (days in storage + days to flower)
0	—[a]	
3	143	21 + 143 = 164
6	116	42 + 116 = 158
9	102	63 + 102 = 165
12	83	84 + 83 = 167

[a]Failed to flower.

crease flower number and hasten flower development and emergence and, to a much lesser degree, hasten leaf development and emergence (Corr, 1988; Corr and Widmer, 1987b, 1991).

To hasten flower and leaf development and emergence, 30-min tuber soaks of 100 ppm gibberellic acid (Pro-Gibb 4%) or 75 ppm Promalin (1:1 benzyladenine:gibberellic acid) have been used. A plant pathologist should be consulted for a recommendation if a bactericide and a fungicide for disease control are to be added to the soak solution. A GA spray on the tuber rather than a soak prior to planting may be used and would forgo concern for disease spread during the soak (Funnell, 1993) and the rates should be 125 ppm Pro-Gibb 4% or 100 ppm Promalin. Regardless, tubers should be immediately planted after the plant growth regulator treatment. Thin, narrow leaf blades can develop if the GA treatment concentration is too high or the duration too long. Further, if tubers are very dry, excessive GA solution can be absorbed. Consequently, it is wise to presoak tubers in water or to spray the tubers with water to rehydrate them prior to GA treatment. Tubers are frequently pretreated by commercial suppliers (Lukens and Beckman, 1999). *Zantedeschia aethiopica* also responds to the gibberellic acid dips at 100 to 250 ppm, which adds one or two flowers (Reiser, 1998).

TEMPERATURE

Flower induction and initiation of *Z. elliotiana* and *Z. rehmannii* are not temperature dependent. All plants flowered when tubers were stored at either 41°F (5°C) or 77°F (25°C), then at 59°F (15°C), and subsequently potted and forced at either a constant 70°F (21°C) or a 70°F (21°C) day and lower night temperature (Tjia, 1989). Indeed, tissue-cultured material can be flowered year-round without special temperature treatments.

A 64 to 70/61°F (18 to 21/16°C) day/night regime is recommended for the colored hybrids; for the white *Z. aethiopica* a 64 to 70/55°F (18 to 21/13°C) day/night regime is adequate (De Hertogh, 1996). When tubers of *Z. aethiopica* were planted November 10, plants flowered in 92, 109, or 179 days when forced at 70, 60, or 50°F (21, 16, or 10°C), respectively (Post, 1936, 1952). When grown under night temperatures of 61, 55, or 50°F (16, 13, or 10°C), the colored hybrids flowered in 60, 75, or 95 days, respectively.

At constant air temperature of 59°F (15°C), *Z. rehmannii* plants flowered in 85 days; at 68°F (20°C), in 67 days. When the rooting medium was heated to 68 or 77°F (20 or 25°C) and the air temperature was 59°F (15°C), days to flower were 70 or 68 days, respectively; plants grown at 59°F (15°C) air temperature with no medium heating flowered in 85 days. Plant heights differed little at 59 to 68°F (15 to 20°C) air temperatures and 59 to 68°F (15 to 20°C) medium temperatures (Corr and Widmer, 1990).

Because of *Erwinia* disease, force the hybrids at day temperatures below 70°F (21°C), with 55 to 61°F (13 to 16°C) night temperatures. Auman (1980) recommended 70°F (21°C) on sunny and 60°F (16°C) on cloudy days with 54°F (12°C) nights.

LIGHT

Calla lily is day neutral, with no effect of photoperiod on flower production (Greene et al., 1932). Flower initiation and development occur under any condition favorable for vegetative growth (Harrison, 1972). However, plants under an 8-hr SD were shorter than the control and LD night interruption increased plant height even though fluorescent light filtered to produce an 8:1 red:far-red ratio was used (Corr and Widmer, 1990).

In areas where summer temperatures are high, decreasing light intensity to 2500 to 3500 fc (500 to 700 μmol $\cdot$ m^{-2} $\cdot$ s^{-1}) is recommended. In the fall and winter, 4000 to 4500 fc (800 to 900 μmol $\cdot$ m^{-2} $\cdot$ s^{-1}) has been suggested. Excessively high or low light intensities may reduce spathe color intensities (Corr, 1988; De Hertogh, 1996).

In Georgia, 2 years after an October planting, *Zantedeschia* 'Black Magic,' 'Pacific Pink,' 'Pink Perfection,' and 'Majestic Pink' had the highest yields in the open field compared with shaded plants. However, scape length was increased by shading (Armitage, 1991). If pricing is based on stem length, the use of a 55% shade would be wise.

WATER

One proposed method to control *Erwinia* bacterial disease problems is to plant colored calla tubers, water, and then withhold water until absolutely needed. The medium should be well drained and kept on the dry side at all times (De Hertogh, 1996; Lukens and Beckman, 1999). However, keep *Z. aethiopica* moist at all times during production.

CARBON DIOXIDE

Height and vigor will increase with supplemental CO_2; however, this may not be desired on potted flowering plants.

NUTRITION

High levels of nutrition are not important. A 100 ppm N constant liquid fertilizer program is adequate (De Hertogh, 1996; Funnell, 1993; Ohteki, 1982).

MEDIA

A well-drained medium with at least 20% porosity is recommended. A peat-lite mix is frequently used for potted flowering plants. Course peat is recommended and should be mixed with coarse perlite, fir bark, and sand (optional, for weight) (Lukens and Beckman, 1999). Less than 50% peat should be used in the fall and winter. Gypsum and lime can be added to raise the pH to 6 to 6.5.

HEIGHT CONTROL

Bonzi (paclobutrazol) has been used to control the height of taller potted plant cultivars and deepen leaf color when applied as a medium drench of 0.5 to 4 mg a.i. per pot before shoots are 1 to 2.5 in. (2.5 to 5 cm) long. A second application can be made 2 weeks later if needed (Beckman and Lukens, 1997; Lukens and Beckman, 1999). Earlier application may cause excessive stunting; later applications will be less effective. Increased rates are used when light intensities are low; reduced rates when light levels are high. If bark is used in the medium or if the medium is acidic, Bonzi drenches may be rendered inactive (Auman, 1980; Corr and Widmer, 1987a; De Hertogh, 1996; Funnell, 1993). A Sumagic (uniconazole) drench at 6 mg a.i./pot was effective (Kuehny et al., 1996). Prior to planting, tubers can be soaked in 20 ppm Bonzi for 15 min. Growth retardants are also important for postharvest height control.

SPACING

For the colored hybrids, tuber grade 1 is 2 to 2.25 in. (5 to 6 cm), grade 2 is 1.5 to 1.8 in. (4 to 4.5 cm), and grade 3 is 0.88 to 1.38 in. (2.5 to 3.5 cm) in diameter. Potting recommendations are one grade 3 tuber per 3-in. (8-cm) pot; one grade 2 tuber per 4-in. (10-cm) pot; one grade 1 or two grade 3 tubers in a 5-in. (13-cm) pot; and one grade 1, two grade 2, or three grade 3 tubers in a 6-in. (15-cm) pot. Plants can be grown pot-to-pot until leaves touch, then space according to cultivar and season.

PINCHING AND DISBUDDING

No pinching or disbudding required.

SUPPORT

No support required.

SCHEDULE AND TIMING

Domestic hybrid tubers and rhizomes in California are harvested in the fall (September to November). Plants are allowed to senesce by withholding irrigation water in late summer. After harvest the tubers are air dried (by fan) at 77 to 81°F (25 to 27°C) for 2 weeks and then moved to 50 to 54°F (10 to 12°C) at 75 to 85% humidity. Shipping commences in late November and is completed by late February. With tubers from New Zealand, the seasons are reversed (see Temperature). With *Z. rehmannii*, flowering will occur 70 to 85 days after planting from November to February and in 55 to 65 days when planted March to May (Lukens and Beckman, 1999).

Zantedeschia aethiopica, the white cut flower calla, is also sold as large specimens in 12-in. (30-cm) pots. Commercial 5- to 6-in. or 6- to 7-in. (12- to 16-cm or 16- to 18-cm) diameter tubers are used. Tubers are planted in the fall and grown in full sun. Plants will reach heights in excess of 24 to 35 in. (60 to 90 cm); flowering can commence in December and continue until summer (Auman, 1980; Bailey and Bailey, 1976). In commercial cut flower production, when plants stop flowering, they are allowed to dry down or go dormant when temperatures rise above an average of 65°F (18°C). Every 2 to 3 years, plants are divided and cleaned of old dry leaves, replanted, and watering commences in August.

INSECTS

Thrips and aphids are a problem and monitoring is required. Fungus gnat larvae can contribute to pathological problems; thrips are responsible for virus spread. With the white species, continuous selection of virus-free stock is necessary. Funnell (1993) reviewed the various disease and insect problems.

DISEASES

Within 3 days after planting, an appropriate bacteriacide and fungicide combination for bacteria and fungi should be used (Auman, 1980; Corr and Widmer, 1987a; De Hertogh, 1996; Kuehny, 2000; Lukens and Beckman, 1999). Tomato spotted wilt virus can also occur; rogue infected plants immediately (Horst, 1990).

Erwinia carotovara, a bacterial soft rot, is the major concern and is the primary reason why this plant is not more widely grown. Although most authorities believe no chemical control is reliable, preplant bulb dips of copper or other bacteriacide may be helpful (Beckman and Lukens, 1997; Kuehny et al., 1998). After unpacking tubers, Beckman and Lukens (1997) suggested storing them in well-ventilated trays at 65°F (18°C) for 3 to 7 days to allow healing of abrasions that occurred during shipping. Forcing at moderate temperatures without excessive moisture could be the major environmental technique for controlling this disease. While a 30 to 40% loss was encountered in a 70/64°F (21/18°C) day/night environment, a 5% loss occurred at 61/54°F (16/12°C) day/night environment. Consequently, if *Erwinia* is a problem, major losses can be expected if temperature control is lost in late spring. Losses from *Erwinia* can also be significant when the colored hybrid plants are grown on capillary mats. Unfortunately, a number of other diseases can also occur including root and crown rot (*Pythium, Phytophthora, Rhizoctonia, Thielaviopsis, Armillaria*), southern blight (*Sclerotium rolfsii*), leaf spots (*Coniothecium* and *Phyllosticta*), flower spot (*Alternaria alterna*), dasheen mosaic virus, and impatiens necrotic spot and tomato spotted wilt viruses (Dreistadt, 2001).

PHYSIOLOGICAL DISORDERS

If tubers are treated with excessive concentration or duration of GA, excessive leaf and flower scape elongation will occur and leaf blades will be narrow. If GA treatments are applied too soon after harvest, flowers emerge with little leaf development.

POSTHARVEST

Potted flowering colored hybrid plants could be stored at 37 to 39°F (3 to 4°C) for up to 7 days and flowers were excellent for another 8 days after the experiment was concluded. Dark storage at 39 to 54°F (4 to 12°C) cannot be tolerated for more than 1 to 2 days (Nowak and Rudnicki, 1990). Shelf life depends on the stage of floral development of *Z. aethiopica* 'Childsiana.' Plants with flowers in the "macrobud" stage stored at low light 75 fc (15 μmol $\cdot$ m^{-2} $\cdot$ s^{-1}) for 12 hr at 68°F (20°C) not only developed, but had a shelf life of 26 days. Plants stored when the flower spathe was fully open but before pollen shed had a shelf life of only 11 days (Plummer et al., 1990).

Flower stems should be cut, not pulled, and placed in a 2% sucrose solution with a disinfectant for 6 to 12 hr to prevent stem splitting or rolling (Tjia and Funnell, 1986). Harvest just before the edge of the spathe begins to turn downward. Flowers can be held at 33 to 35°F (1 to 2°C) (Nell and Reid, 2001). Flowers can be given a 12-hr pulse of 0.1 mM sucrose and stored in water at 39°F (4°C) for 1 week (Nowak and Rudnicki, 1990).

Researchers have disagreed whether calla flowers are insensitive to ethylene or whether they synthesize this gas; studies indicate ethylene is not a factor (Funnell and Downs, 1987; Post, 1952). Pais and Chaves des Neves (1982/83) have studied the greening and regreening of the senescing spathe on a hormonal basis. Ethylene had no effect on the regreening of calla flowers (Funnell and Downs, 1987).

KEY POINTS

- Calla lily is used as a cut flower, potted flowering plant, and garden ornamental.
- Plants are propagated by division of the tubers, seed, or *in vitro*.
- The white flowered *Z. aethiopica* will flower continuously as long as plants are held at near 60°F (16°C) and kept moist.
- Other species and hybrids require dormancy release by dry storage and flower only once in a season.

- A gibberellic acid (GA) treatment to the tubers applied by soaking or spraying hastens floral development and increases the number of flowers.
- Medium should be well drained and plants grown on the dry side.
- *Erwinia* is the major inhibiting factor in the production and forcing of plants.

BIBLIOGRAPHY

Armitage, A.M. 1991. Shade affects yield and stem length of field-grown cut-flower species. *HortScience* 26:1174–1176.

Auman C.W. 1980. Minor cut crops, p. 209 in *Introduction to Floriculture*, R.A. Larson, editor. Academic Press, New York.

Bailey, L.H., and E.Z. Bailey. 1976. *Zantedeschia*, p. 1181 in *Hortus Third: A Concise Dictionary of Plants Cultivated in the United States and Canada*. Macmillan, New York.

Beckman, P., and T. Lukens. 1997. Simple steps for pot calla success. *GrowerTalks* 60(12):49, 54.

Chaves des Neves, H.J., and M.S.S. Pais. 1980a. A new cytokinin from the fruits of *Zantedeschia aethiopica*. *Tetrahedron Letters* 21:4387–4390.

Chaves des Neves, H.J., and M.S.S. Pais. 1980b. Identification of a spathe regreening factor in *Zantedeschia aethiopica*. *Biomedical Biophysical Research Communication* 95:1387–1392.

Chen, J.-J., M.-C. Liu, and Y.-H. Ho. 2000. Size of *in vitro* plantlets affects subsequent tuber production of acclimated calla lily. *HortScience* 35:290–292.

Cohen, D. 1981. Micropropagation of *Zantedeschia* hybrids. *Proceedings of the International Plant Propagators Society* 31:312–317.

Corr, B.E. 1988. Factors influencing growth and flowering of *Zantedeschia elliotiana* and *Z. rehmannii*. Ph.D. thesis, University of Minnesota, St. Paul.

Corr, B.E., and R.E. Widmer. 1987a. Calla lilies: An up and coming floricultural crop. *Minnesota State Floriculture Bulletin* 36(1):6–9.

Corr, B.E., and R.E. Widmer. 1987b. Gibberellic acid increases flower number in *Zantedeschia elliotiana* and *Z. rehmannii*. *HortScience* 22:605–607.

Corr, B.E., and R.E. Widmer. 1988. Rhizome storage increases growth of *Zantedeschia elliotiana* and *Z. rehmannii*. *HortScience* 23:1001–1002.

Corr, B.E., and R.E. Widmer. 1990. Growth and flowering of *Zantedeschia elliotiana* and *Z. rehmannii*. *HortScience* 25:925–927.

Corr, B.E., and R.E. Widmer. 1991. Paclobutrazol, gibberellic acid, and rhizome size affect growth and flowering of *Zantedeschia*. *HortScience* 26:133–135.

De Hertogh, A. 1996. *Zantedeschia* (calla lily), pp. C163–172 in *Holland Bulb Forcer's Guide*, 5th ed. The International Flower Bulb Centre, Hillegom, The Netherlands.

Dreistadt, S.H. 2001. *Integrated Pest Management for Floriculture and Nurseries*. University of California Division of Agriculture and Natural Resources Publication 3402.

Funnell, K.A. 1993. Zantedeschia, pp. 683–704 in *The Physiology of Flower Bulbs*, A. De Hertogh and M. Le Nard, editors. Elsevier, Amsterdam.

Funnell, K.A., and C.G. Downs. 1987. Effect of ethylene on spathe regreening of *Zantedeschia* hybrids. *HortScience* 22:1333.

Greene, L., R. Withrow, and M. Richman. 1932. The response of greenhouse crops to electric light supplementing daylight. *Indiana Agricultural Experiment Station Bulletin* 366:20.

Harrison, R.E. 1972. *Zantedeschia* hybrids. *Journal of the Royal Horticultural Society* 97:131–132.

Horst, R.K. 1990. Zantedeschia, pp. 574–575 in *Westcott's Plant Disease Handbook*, 5th ed. Van Nostrand Reinhold, New York.

Huxley, A., M. Griffiths, and M. Levy. 1992. *Zantedeschia*, p. 734 in *The New Royal Horticultural Society Dictionary of Gardening*, vol. 4. Stockton Press, New York.

Kuehny, J.S. 2000. Calla history and culture. *HortTechnology* 10:267–274.

Kuehny, J.S., W.C. Chang, and P. Branch. 1996. Influence of plant growth regulators on postharvest quality of *Zantedeschia* and preplant treatment for preventing *Erwinia* infection. *HortScience* 31:597. (Abstract)

Kuehny, J.S., G.E. Holcomb, W.-C. Chang, and P.C. Branch. 1998. Chemical treatments to control *Erwinia* soft rot of calla rhizomes. *HortTechnoloy* 8:353–356.

Letty, C. 1973. The genus *Zantedeschia*. *Bothalia* 11:5–26.

Lukens, T., and P. Beckman. 1999. 15 must-dos for quality callas. *GrowerTalks* 63(6):48, 50–51.

Nell, T.A., and M.S. Reid. 2001. Can't take the heat. *Floral Management* 17(10):33–34.

Nowak, J., and R.M. Rudnicki. 1990. *Postharvest Handling and Storage of Cut Flowers, Florist Greens and Potted Plants*. Timber Press, Portland, Oregon.

Ohteki, T. 1982. Cut flower production—Japanese techniques—*Zantedeschia, Eucharis, Gentiana*. *Technical Bulletin*, 1:2–4. Horticultural Research Centre, Levin, New Zealand.

Pais, M.S.S., and H.J. Chaves des Neves. 1982/83. Regreening of *Zantedeschia aethiopica* Spreng. spathe induced by reapplied cytokinins. *Plant Growth Regulation* 1:233–242.

Perry, P.L. 1989. A new species of *Zantedeschia* (Araceae) from the Western Cape. *South African Journal of Botany* 55:447–451.

Plummer, J.A., T.E. Welsh, and A.M. Armitage. 1990. Stages of flower development and post production longevity of potted *Zantedeschia aethiopica* 'Childsiana.' *HortScience* 25:675–676.

Post, K. 1936. Further responses of miscellaneous plants to temperature. *Proceedings of the American Society for Horticultural Science* 34:627–629.

Post, K. 1952. *Zantedeschia* (calla), pp. 847–851 in *Florist Crop Production*. Orange Judd Publishing, New York.

Reiser, R.A. 1998. *Zantedeschia aethiopica* and *Z*. 'Green Goddess' responses to GA$_3$ and Bonzi for cut flower call lily production in Florida. *HortScience* 33:536.

Tjia, B. 1989. *Zantedeschia*, pp. 697–702 in *Handbook of Flowering*, vol. VI, A.H. Halevy, editor. CRC Press, Boca Raton, Florida.

Tjia, B., and K.A. Funnell. 1986. Postharvest studies of cut *Zantedeschia* inflorescences. *Acta Horticulturae* 181:451–459.

Zinnia

is a common and showy southwestern North American native wildflower. Compositae is a large family with many important genera including *Aster, Calendula, Callistephus, Centaurea, Chrysanthemum, Cosmos, Dahlia, Dendranthema, Echinacea, Gerbera, Helianthus, Liatris, Pericallis, Solidago,* and *Tagetes.*

Origin: Both *Z. elegans* and *Z. angustifolia* are natives of Mexico. *Z. grandiflora* Nutt. is widely distributed from Colorado and Kansas into the southwestern United States and Mexico. Use of this species in breeding efforts would be interesting because of its northern distribution (Bailey and Bailey, 1976).

Uses and current status: *Z. elegans* is grown as a bedding plant and summer specialty cut flower (Nau, 1999; Starman et al., 1995). Many cultivars of this annual plant are sold worldwide (Figs. II-1, II-2, and II-3 Zinnia). *Z. angustifolia* is grown as a bedding plant. The zinnia tolerates hot, dry, sunny environments.

INTRODUCTION

Common name: zinnia.

Scientific names: The common garden zinnia is *Z. elegans* Jacq. and most cultivars are double flowered. *Zinnia angustifolia* Kunth. has single flowers with numerous disc florets (Huxley et al., 1992). Interspecific hybrids have been listed as *Zinnia hybrida* for convenience but the name has no botanical standing.

Family and related taxa: Compositae Giseke. The genus *Zinnia* has 17 species. *Z. grandiflora*

CULTIVARS

Height varies from 0.5 to 3 ft (15 to 90 cm). Flower colors range from pure white, cream, pink, purple, peach, salmon, orange, and yellow to the brightest red. Flowers may be single or double and from 1 to 6 in. (2.5 to 15 cm) wide. Two popular series for outdoor cut flower production are 'Dahlia Blue Point' and 'Oklahoma,' which are productive all season and have moderate disease resistance and long vase life (Dole, 1996, 1997). New zinnia cultivars are

FIGURE II-I ZINNIA Interspecific hybrid *Zinnia* 'Profusion Orange' bedding plant.

FIGURE II-2 ZINNIA *Zinnia elegans* 'Oklahoma' cut flower.

FIGURE II-3 ZINNIA *Zinnia elegans* 'Benary Giant' field production for cut flowers.

released annually (Armitage and Laushman, 2003; Nau, 1999). *Z. angustifolia* is highly resistant to several diseases and is being used in breeding programs to provide similar resistance to *Z. elegans* cultivars (Boyle and Wick, 1996). New interspecific hybrids have been released with medium-sized flowers on 12-in. (30-cm)-tall plants that are resistant to mildew and heat tolerant (Nau, 1999).

PROPAGATION

The garden zinnia is a seed-propagated annual. Modern cultivars are primarily open pollinated. F_1 hybrids exist but are more expensive. There are 3000 to 6000 seeds/oz (100 to 200/g). Germination is rapid and emergence is within 3 to 5 days at a germination temperature of 80 to 85°F (27 to 29°C), 5 to 7 days at 70 to 75°F (21 to 24°C), and 10 to 14 days at 65 to 70°F (18 to 21°C).

For plug production the following conditions are used (Croft, 1998):

Stage 1: Seed lightly covered, 75 to 78°F (24 to 26°C), for 5 days

Stage 2: 65°F (18°C), 4 days, 50 to 100 ppm N one time

Stage 3: 65°F (18°C), 11 days, 100 to 150 ppm N one time/week

Stage 4: 62°F (17°C), 7 days, fertilize as needed.

Plugs should be ready for marketing or transplanting in 3 to 4 weeks (see Chapter 1, Propagation, for descriptions of stages). Be sure to transplant plugs promptly because they can stunt if left in the flat too long.

If plants are to be used as a commercial cut flower, seed can be directly sown in the field in a band, using 0.5 oz/100 ft (1.5 g/m). Sow seed about 1/4 in. (0.6 cm) deep. Plants are thinned to at least 6 to 12 in. (15 to 30 cm) between plants (Armitage and Laushman, 2003; Post, 1949). Most cut flower producers use transplants, however.

FLOWERING CONTROL AND DORMANCY

The common zinnia is a facultative SD plant in that it flowers more rapidly under SD. Post (1949) noted that the best quality zinnia flowers occur during the shortening days of late summer. Plants under photoperiods less than 12 hr flower more rapidly than plants under longer light spans. Only five SD will stimulate flowering with some cultivars. There is wide variation in cultivar response. Long days increased the number of ray flowers and flower diameters compared with plants grown under SD. For the largest flower diameters on long stems, a short-day treatment followed by LD is preferred. This process is academically interesting but not commercially used. *Zinnia angustifolia* is day neutral.

TEMPERATURE

In the greenhouse, 70°F (21°C) days and 60 to 65°F (16 to 18°C) night temperatures are optimal. Transplant seedlings into the field or use direct seeding, but direct seeding should not occur until the soil has warmed to at least 65°F (18°C) and frost danger is past.

LIGHT

Full light is a prerequisite for quality zinnias. Armitage (1983) demonstrated that high light is responsible for the zinnia's rapid change from juvenile to flowering stage; hence, delay seeding zinnia until spring. Supplemental HID lighting reduces the time from transplant to flower (Carpenter and Beck, 1973) and incandescent lighting increases stem length, which is acceptable for cut flower production (Armitage, 1985).

WATER

Water should never be a limiting factor, particularly during warm, sunny summer days.

CARBON DIOXIDE

No data are available and it is not feasible to supplement CO_2 in the field.

NUTRITION

The medium pH should be 6.3 to 6.8. Once seeds are germinated and established, constant irrigation with 100 ppm N is adequate (Armitage and Laushman, 2003). Post (1949) recommended 1200 lb/acre (1345 kg · h^{-1}) of 5–10–5 fertilizer.

MEDIA

Any medium that is well drained is acceptable. Nutrient levels should be checked and adjustments made prior to planting in the field.

HEIGHT CONTROL

Cultivars vary widely in their genetically controlled height. For cut flower production, plant growth regulators are not used. A-Rest (ancymidol) sprays at 6 ppm can be applied within a week to 10 days after sowing to the plug flat media to produce compact, well-branched plugs and subsequent bedding plants (Britten, 1999). Sumagic (uniconazole) foliar sprays at 5 to 25 ppm can be used to control plug height without retarding subsequent growth in the final container (Davis, 1991). During plug production 5000 ppm B-Nine (daminozide), 4 ppm Bonzi (paclobutrazol), or 1 ppm Sumagic can be applied during stage 1, stage 2, or stage 3 (Sawaya, 2001).

Plants in bedding flats may need up to four foliar sprays of A-Rest at 7 to 26 ppm, B-Nine at 2500 to 5000 ppm, Bonzi at 5 to 45 ppm, or Cycocel (chlormequat) at 800 to 1500 ppm (Armitage et al., 1981; Whipker, 2003). DIF is effective on zinnia (Neily et al., 1997).

SPACING

Zinnias in bedding flats are spaced flat-to-flat. Space plants 6 × 6 to 12 × 12 in. (15 ×15 to 30 × 30 cm) apart in the field or the garden (Armitage and Laushman, 2003; Post, 1949).

PINCHING AND DISBUDDING

No pinching or disbudding needed.

SUPPORT

No support is needed under normal cut flower field conditions or for bedding plant production.

SCHEDULE AND TIMING

After danger of frost, Armitage and Laushman (2003) recommended successive plantings 2 weeks apart for cut flower production. Newer cultivars may provide season-long harvests from one planting in climates with short growing seasons (Dole, 1996, 1997). Six to 8 weeks will be required for flowering depending on temperature and latitude. Some cultivars will require 9 weeks (Armitage, 1985; Armitage et al., 1981). Post (1949) stated that when grown in the greenhouse and spaced at 4 × 4 in. (10 × 10 cm), 3 months were required for a single-stem cut flower crop in the spring and 2 months in the summer. Eight to 9 weeks are required for *Zinnia elegans* and hybrid bedding plants in packs and 9 to 11 weeks in 4-in. (10-cm) pots (Nau, 1999). Add 1 to 2 weeks for *Z. angustifolia.*

INSECTS

The most common insect problem is thrips (Post, 1949); however, spider mites and aphids can also occur (Armitage and Laushman, 2003). A number of other insects can be problems outdoors including grasshoppers, bud worms, and beetles (V. Stamback, personal communication).

DISEASES

Zinnias may experience stem rot (*Phytophthora* and *Sclerotinia sclerotiorum*), head blight (*Botrytis cinerea*), leaf spot (*Cercospora zinniae*), powdery mildew (*Erysiphe cichoracearum*), blight (*Alternaria zinniae*), bacterial leaf spot (*Xanthomonas campestris*), and various viruses (Horst, 1990). These diseases may be minimized by following normal sanitation precautions. Powdery mildew is a common problem facing outdoor zinnia production, especially in mid to late summer (Armitage and Laushman, 2003; Daughtrey and Chase, 1992; Post, 1949). For cut flower production, mildew typically occurs on the lower foliage, which is normally removed during harvest. Bacterial leaf spot can be reduced by treating seeds with a 20- to 40-min chlorine bleach soak of 1:4 bleach:water. Rinse seeds, dry, and sow. Excessive treatment with bleach will injure seed.

Zinnia angustifolia is highly tolerant to powdery mildew and other diseases that commonly affect zinnias growing outdoors. However, *Z. angustifolia* can be sensitive to root rots in the greenhouse if grown too cool or too wet.

PHYSIOLOGICAL DISORDERS

Zinnias are sensitive to boron deficiency, which can cause bud blasting, and boron toxicity, which can cause distorted foliage, flower bud blasting, and proliferation of axillary shoots (Hamrick, 2003).

POSTHARVEST

Flowers should be harvested when fully open. They can be stored in water for 5 to 7 days at an average temperature of 39°F (4°C). Three common postharvest problems occur with zinnias: bent neck, petal browning, and stem rot (Arnosky and Arnosky, 2003). Bent neck may be related to overhydrating the stems, making them brittle, and can be reduced by not leaving stems in hydration solution too long. Petal browning may be due to using floral preservatives with too high of sucrose level or too cold of storage temperature, especially when stems have been harvested on hot days. Cut flowers are thought to be sensitive to storage temperatures below 39°F (4°C) (B. Hitt, personal communication). Stem rot is prevented by using clean buckets as zinnia stems are quite sensitive to microorganisms in the water. Lower leaves should be removed because they rot easily.

Flower longevity increases if a floral preservative is applied. Zinnias respond to 8-hydroxyquinoline citrate (8-HQC) at 0.25 oz/10 gal (200 mg $\cdot$ L^{-1}) and sucrose at 13.4 oz/10 gal (10 g $\cdot$ L^{-1}). Longevity can be 6 to 10 days in the home environment (Nowak and Rudnicki, 1990; Stimart et al., 1983). Zinnia are slightly sensitive to ethylene.

KEY POINTS

- *Zinnia* is used as a bedding plant or cut flower.
- Propagation is solely by seed at 70 to 75°F (21 to 24°C).
- Plants are quantitative SD plants in that flowering is most rapid under SD.

- Under LD, flower diameter and floret number are increased.
- Flower longevity is increased if a floral preservative is used.

BIBLIOGRAPHY

Armitage, A.M. 1983. Determining optimum sowing time of bedding plants for extended marketing periods. *Acta Horticulturae* 147:143–152.

Armitage, A.M. 1985. *Zinnia elegans* and *Z. angustifolia*, pp. 548–552 in *Handbook of Flowering*, vol. IV, A.H. Halevy, editor. CRC Press, Boca Raton, Florida.

Armitage, A.M., and J.M. Laushman. 2003. *Zinnia elegans*, pp. 546–551 in *Specialty Cut Flowers*, 2nd ed. Timber Press, Portland, Oregon.

Armitage, A.M., R.E. Bass, W.H. Carlson, and L.C. Ewart. 1981. Control of plant height and flowering of zinnia by photoperiod and growth retardants. *HortScience* 16:218–220.

Arnosky, P., and F. Arnosky. 2003. Mysteries of zinnia postharvest revealed. *Growing for Market* 12(9): 15–18.

Bailey, L.H., and E.Z. Bailey. 1976. *Zinnia*, p. 1184 in *Hortus Third: A Concise Dictionary of Plants Cultivated in the United States and Canada*. Macmillan, New York.

Boyle, T.H., and R.L. Wick. 1996. Responses of *Zinnia angustifolia* × *Z. violacea* backcross hybrids to three pathogens. *HortScience* 31:851–854.

Britten, A. 1999. PGRs at seeding reduce early stretch. *GrowerTalks* 63(5):46, 48.

Carpenter, W.J., and J.R. Beck. 1973. High intensity supplementary lighting of bedding plants after transplanting. *HortScience* 8:482–483.

Croft, B. 1998. Quick and easy Profusion zinnia. *GrowerTalks* 63(6):20.

Daughtrey, M., and A.R. Chase. 1992. Zinnia, pp. 211–213 in *Ball Field Guide to Diseases of Greenhouse Ornamentals*. Ball Publishing, Geneva, Illinois.

Davis, T.D. 1991. Post-production performance of uniconazole-treated zinnia and marigold plugs. *HortTechnology* 1:49–52.

Dole, J. 1996. The 1995 ASCFG National Cut Flower Trials. *The Cut Flower Quarterly* 8(1):7–13.

Dole, J. 1997. The 1996 ASCFG National Cut Flower Trials. *The Cut Flower Quarterly* 9(1):31–37.

Hamrick, D. 2003. *Zinnia*, pp. 689–692 in *Ball Redbook*, vol. 2, 17th ed. Ball Publishing, Batavia, Illinois.

Horst, R.K. 1990. Zinnia, p. 873 in *Westcott's Plant Disease Handbook*, 5th ed. Van Nostrand Reinhold, New York.

Huxley, A., M. Griffiths, and M. Levy. 1992. *Zinnia*, pp. 739–740 in *The New Royal Horticultural Society Dictionary of Gardening*, vol. 4. Stockton Press, New York.

Nau, J. 1999. *Ball Culture Guide, The Encyclopedia of Seed Germination*, 3rd ed. Ball Publishing, Batavia, Illinois.

Neily, W.G., P.R. Hicklenton, and D.N. Kristie. 1997. Temperature and developmental stage influence diurnal rhythms of stem elongation in snapdragon and zinnia. *Journal of the American Society for Horticultural Science* 122:778–783.

Nowak, J., and R.M. Rudnicki. 1990. *Postharvest Handling and Storage of Cut Flowers, Florist Greens, and Potted Plants*. Timber Press, Portland, Oregon.

Post, K. 1949. *Zinnia elegans*, pp. 851–854 in *Florist Crop Production and Marketing*. Orange Judd Publishing, New York.

Sawaya, M. 2001. Plugs, pp. 50–53 in *Tips on Regulating Growth of Floriculture Crops*, M.L. Gaston, L.A. Kunkle, P.S. Konjoian, and M.F. Wilt, editors. Ohio Florists' Association Services, Columbus, Ohio.

Starman, T.W., T.A. Cerny, and A.J. MacKenzie. 1995. Productivity and profitability of some field-grown specialty cut flowers. 30:1217–1220.

Stimart, D.P., D.J. Brown, and T. Solomos. 1983. Development of flowers and changes in carbon dioxide, ethylene and various sugars in cut *Zinnia elegans* Jacq. *Journal of the American Society for Horticultural Science* 108:651–655.

Whipker, B.E. 2003. Growth regulators for floricultural crops, pp. 439–448 in *2003 North Carolina Agricultural Chemicals Manual*, College of Agriculture and Life Science, North Carolina State University, Raleigh, North Carolina.

Part III

Part III has six general chapters that cover basic production information on hundreds of minor species. The chapters are grouped into Bedding Plants, Field-Grown Cut Flowers, Foliage Plants, Garden Perennials, Herbs, and Woody Cuts, Forced. We did not include chapters on miscellaneous potted flowering plants or greenhouse cut flowers because most species grown commercially have already been covered in individual genera chapters in Part II. Nomenclature follows the *New Royal Horticultural Society Dictionary of Gardening*.

Bedding Plants

FIGURE III-2 BEDDING PLANTS Planter with several bedding plant species.

INTRODUCTION

Numerous plant species are grown for outdoor use in commercial landscapes, public gardens, home gardens, patios, and balconies. Collectively these plants are known as bedding plants and include (1) flat-grown (packs) plants, which are primarily annual and tender perennial ornamentals and vegetables; (2) pot-grown plants, which encompass annual, tender perennial, and perennial ornamentals and vegetables; and (3) hanging baskets, which are generally limited to annual and tender perennial ornamentals (Fig. III-1 Bedding Plants). A wide variety of plants are grown as specimens in large containers as patio plants, of which one of the most popular is the tropical hibiscus, a ten-

der woody shrub. Large containers, and hanging baskets using several plant species in one container, are especially popular and are known as mixed containers, combo pots or baskets, and combination pots or baskets. (Fig. III-2 Bedding Plants).

Spring is the primary season for bedding plant sales in temperate regions (Fig. III-3 Bedding Plants). However, in frost-free climates, such as coastal California and Florida, bedding plants are sold year-round with especially strong sales from late fall through spring. Some species, such as pansy (*Viola* ×*wittrockiana*), are best grown during cool weather and are sold in the fall in warm climates or early spring

FIGURE III-I BEDDING PLANTS Greenhouse bedding plant production.

FIGURE III-3 BEDDING PLANTS Outdoor bedding plant production.

in areas with cold winters. Many cool season bedding plants tolerate light frost and some can tolerate temperatures well below freezing. Other species, such as vinca (*Catharanthus roseus*) grow best in warm weather and are typically sold in mid- to late spring after the danger of frost has passed. Most warm season bedding plants do not tolerate frost.

The majority of bedding plants are seed and cutting propagated. Many producers will propagate many species themselves and purchase the rest from specialty plug producers. Prefinished bedding plants are available as well.

Hundreds of plant species can be classified as bedding plants with numerous species being released each year by plant breeders and developers. In particular, new vegetatively propagated species have become a large portion of the bedding plant industry and continue to generate public interest in bedding plants. The lines are blurring between bedding plants and other groups of plants such as indoor foliage plants, perennials, and woody trees, shrubs, and vines. Increasingly landscapers and the general public select plants due to their color, size, and price and do not care if the plant was "supposed" to be a bedding plant. For example, many indoor foliage plants make excellent outdoor bedding plants including rex and angel wing begonias (*Begonia*), bromeliads (Bromeliaceae), spider plants (*Chlorophytum comosum*), *Pilea*, *Plectranthus*, nephthytis (*Syngonium podophyllum*), and wandering Jew (*Tradescantia*). Perennials and woody ornamentals with colorful foliage, such as *Heuchera* and *Hosta*, can also be used for one season and replaced as with other bedding plants. The right plant for the right garden location at the right price has become the guiding principle.

Many commonly used bedding plant species have already been covered in this text in separate chapters including *Begonia*, *Caladium*, *Calendula*, *Callistephus*, *Capsicum*, *Cosmos*, *Dahlia*, *Dianthus*, *Helianthus*, *Impatiens*, *Lycopersicon*, *Pelargonium*, *Petunia*, *Tagetes*, *Viola*, and *Zinnia*. In addition, see the *Garden Perennials* chapter for commonly grown perennial plant species and the *Propagation* chapter (Chapter 1) for information on seed germination of numerous species. The remainder of this chapter lists a variety of other bedding plant species with the references used listed at the end of the chapter.

ABELMOSCHUS ESCULENTUS (L.) MOENCH.

Common names: okra, gumbo.

Family: Malvaceae.

Description/uses: This 3- to 5-ft (0.9- to 1.5-m)-tall seed-propagated annual is grown for its long, upright fruit, which is used as a vegetable. Relatively few cultivars are available and they vary primarily in date of harvest and height. Plants are not frost tolerant and are sold in the spring in packs or small containers.

Temperature: Grow at 60 to 62°F (15 to 17°C). Plants do not tolerate cold weather below 54°F (12°C).

Height control: No chemical plant growth regulators can be used on this edible vegetable.

Schedule and timing: Plants will be ready for sale in 4 to 6 weeks in packs and in 8 to 9 weeks in 4-in. (10-cm) pots.

ABELMOSCHUS MOSCHATUS MEDIK.

Common names: musk mallow, annual hibiscus.

Family: Malvaceae.

Description/uses: The large, 3- to 4-in. (8- to 10-cm), white to red flowers are carried atop 12- to 15-in. (30- to 38-cm) plants. This seed-propagated, tender perennial is not frost tolerant and is grown in the spring in packs, pots, or hanging baskets.

Temperature: Grow plants at 60 to 65°F (15 to 18°C).

Height control: Cycocel (chlormequat) has been effective.

Schedule and timing: Plants will flower in the pack in 12 to 13 weeks, 4-in. (10-cm) pots in 14 to 16 weeks, and 10-in. (25-cm) hanging baskets in 17 weeks.

Comments: Plants may need to be pinched but this will increase crop time. Individual flowers remain open for only one day.

ABUTILON ×HYBRIDUM HORT.

Common names: flowering maple, Chinese lantern, abutilon.

Family: Malvaceae.

Description/uses: These charming plants are grown for their bell-shaped flowers that are available in a wide array of mostly pastel colors including white, red, peach, pink, rose, and various shades in between. These tender perennials grow up to 18 in. (45 cm) tall in temperate climates but up to 8 ft (2.4 m) tall in warm climates. The foliage resembles maples; hence, the common name flowering maple. Abutilon can be either seed or cutting propagated, is not frost tolerant, and is grown in the spring in pots or hanging baskets.

Temperature: Grow plants at 60 to 65°F (16 to 18°C).

Height control: Bonzi (paclobutrazol) (5 ppm) sprays can be used on finished plants, B-Nine (daminozide) sprays at 2500 ppm can be applied to plugs.

Schedule and timing: From seed, 4-in. (10-cm) pots will be ready in 6 to 8 weeks, 6-in. (15-cm) pots in 7 to 9 weeks, and 10-in. (25-cm) baskets in 8 to 10 weeks during the spring and summer. Add 2 weeks if growing during the fall or winter. One plant is used per 4-in. (10-cm) pot, two or three per 6-in. (15-cm) pot, and four to six per 8- to 10-in. (20- to 25-cm) hanging basket.

Comments: Grows best in partial shade in the home garden and can be kept as a house plant during the winter. Keep moist for best growth. The related species, *Abutilon megapotamicum* (Spreng.) St.-Hil. & Naudin., is a spreading version of the flowering maple and makes great hanging baskets. This cutting-propagated plant has either solid green or variegated yellow foliage and bright red and yellow flowers.

AGERATUM HOUSTONIANUM MILL.

Common names: ageratum, floss flower.

Family: Compositae.

Description/uses: This annual ornamental is grown in packs and pots. The clusters of small fuzzy-appearing flowers are available in blue, purple, white, pink, lavender, and bi-colors. Bedding cultivars grow 5 to 8 in. (13 to 20 cm) tall. Tall-growing cultivars can be used as a cut flower (see *Field-Grown Cut Flowers* chapter). Both seed and cutting-propagated cultivars are available.

Temperature: Generally grown at 60 to 65°F (15 to 18°C) night temperature, but may be grown cooler, down to 50°F (10°C).

Height control: Sprays of A-Rest (ancymidol) (7 to 26 ppm), Bonzi (5 to 45 ppm), B-Nine (2500 to 5000 ppm), Sumagic (uniconazole) (20 to 30 ppm), or Topflor (flurprimidol) (20 to 60 ppm) are effective. Grow

on the dry side and use minimal fertilizer to obtain compact rapidly flowering plants.

Schedule and timing: Seed-propagated plants will flower in the pack in 10 to 11 weeks and 4-in. (10-cm) pots in 12 to 13 weeks. Cutting-propagated plants in 4- to 6-in. (10- to 15-cm) pots are ready to sell in 5 to 6 weeks. Use one plant per 4-in. (10-cm) pot and one or two plants per 6-in. (15-cm) pot. Long days speed flowering. Cutting-propagated plants may be pinched after cuttings are established to encourage branching.

Comments: Ageratum flowers, especially those of white cultivars, may turn brown in the summer.

ALTERNANTHERA DENTATA (MOENCH) SCHEYGR. AND A. FICOIDEA (L.) R. BR.

Common names: alternanthera, Joseph's coat.

Family: Amaranthaceae.

Description/uses: *A. dentata* is grown for its dark purple foliage on plants that grow 16 to 20 in. (40 to 50 cm) tall and 2 to 3 ft (60 to 90 cm) wide. *A. ficoidea* is grown for its brilliant orange, red, yellow, maroon, or purple foliage on plants that grow up to 12 in. (30 cm) tall and 12 in. (30 cm) wide. Alternanthera can be either seed or cutting propagated. This heat-tolerant tender perennial is not frost tolerant and is grown in the spring in packs, pots, or hanging baskets.

Temperature: Grow plants at 62 to 65°F (17 to 18°C).

Height control: Bonzi (30 to 45 ppm) sprays can be used on *A. dentata*, but Cycocel will cause phytotoxicity. A-Rest sprays (35 to 132 ppm) or drenches (2 to 4 ppm) can be used on *A. ficoidea*. Alteranthera responds well to cutting back also.

Schedule and timing: From seed, plants are ready to sell in 4-in. (10-cm) pots in 8 to 10 weeks and in 6-in. (15-cm) pots in 9 to 11 weeks. From rooted cuttings, plants are ready to sell in 4-in. (10-cm) pots in 5 to 6 weeks.

Comments: Can be grown in sun to light shade in the home garden.

AMARANTHUS TRICOLOR L.

Common name: amaranthus.

Family: Amaranthaceae.

Description/uses: This seed-propagated annual is grown for its long colorful leaves, which can be red, yellow, orange, or chocolate. The upper leaves are especially colorful, while the lower leaves are usually green, maroon, or chocolate. Plants grow up to 5 ft (1.5 m) tall. Plants are not frost tolerant and are sold in the spring in packs or small containers.

Temperature: Grow at 65 to 68°F (18 to 20°C).

Height control: No information is available.

Schedule and timing: Plants show color and are ready to sell in 6 to 7 weeks in the pack and in 8 to 9 weeks in 4-in. (10-cm) pots.

Comments: Other amaranthus species are grown as field cut flowers (see *Field-Grown Cut Flowers* chapter). Staking is often required in the landscape.

ANGELONIA ANGUSTIFOLIA BENTH.

Common name: angelonia.

Family: Scrophulariaceae.

Description/uses: Loose upright spikes of striking white, pink, purple, and bicolor tubular flowers (Fig. III-4 Bedding Plants). This cutting-propagated tender perennial is hardy only to Zone 9. The plants are heat and drought tolerant. The plants are frost tolerant and are sold in the spring in pots.

Temperature: Grow at 75 to 85/65 to 70°F (24 to 29/18 to 21°C) day/night temperatures.

Height control: B-Nine (1500 to 3000 ppm) + Cycocel (750 to 1000 ppm) tank mix is effective.

FIGURE III-4 BEDDING PLANTS *Angelonia* 'Angelmist Purple Stripe.'

Schedule and timing: Four-inch (10-cm) pots will be ready in 6 to 7 weeks and 6-in. (15-cm) pots in 7 to 10 weeks. One rooted cutting is used with 4-in. (10-cm) pots and two with 6-in. (15-cm) pots. Plants are thought to be day neutral. Plants should be pinched 10 to 14 days after potting or when roots have reached the edge of the container. A second pinch can be used with pots larger than 4 in. (10 cm).

Comments: High light encourages rapid flowering, improved branching, and compact growth. It can be also grown as a cut flower in the greenhouse. Cut angelonia has a vase life of 10 to 12 days.

ARGERANTHEMUM FRUTESCENS (L.) SCHULTZ-BIP.

Common name: marguerite daisy.

Family: Compositae.

Description/uses: The white, pink, or yellow daisy-like flowers may be single with yellow centers or double. This cutting-propagated tender perennial is hardy only to Zone 9. The plants are heat and drought tolerant. The plants are frost tolerant and sold in the spring in pots.

Temperature: Grow at 65 to 75/45 to 55°F (18 to 24/7 to 13°C) day/night temperatures.

Height control: Cycocel (1000 to 1500 ppm) sprays are effective and may be reapplied every 2 weeks as required. B-Nine sprays at 1500 to 2500 ppm can also be used.

Schedule and timing: In the winter 4-in. (10-cm) pots will be ready in 8 to 9 weeks, 5-in. (13-cm) pots in 9 to 10 weeks, and 6-in. (15-cm) pots in 10 to 11 weeks. The crop will finish 2 to 3 weeks earlier in the summer. One cutting is used with 4-in. (10-cm) pots, two with 5-in. (13-cm) pots, and three with 6-in. (15-cm) pots. Plants are day neutral. Plants should be pinched 3 to 4 days after potting or when roots have reached the edge of the container.

Comments: Excessive vegetative growth can be due to high nitrogen levels, high fertilizer levels under low light, or overwatering under low light. Water stress will cause necrotic tips on leaves.

BELLIS PERENNIS L.

Common names: bellis, daisy.

Family: Compositae.

Description/uses: While technically a perennial, bellis is best treated as a cool season annual. This seed-propagated plant can be planted in the fall or spring and will flower all winter in mild climates. Plants typically die out during warm summer weather. In Europe bellis is commonly planted with tulips. The white, pink, rose, or red daisy-like flowers have yellow centers. Plants grow to 6 in. (15 cm) high and are grown in packs or small containers.

Temperature: Grow at 45 to 55°F (7 to 13°C).

Height control: None is typically required.

Schedule and timing: Plants are ready to sell green in packs in 14 to 15 weeks.

BIDENS FERULIFOLIA (JACQ.) DC.

Common names: bidens, tickseed.

Family: Compositae.

Description/uses: This heat and drought-tolerant plant is native to Mexico and the southwestern United States. It is grown for its multitude of small yellow daisy-like flowers. This tender perennial grows 5 to 15 in. (13 to 38 cm) tall and equally wide. Although bidens can be seed propagated, it is primarily cutting propagated. Bidens is not frost tolerant and is grown in the spring in pots or hanging baskets.

Temperature: Grow plants at 65 to 70°F (18 to 21°C).

Height control: B-Nine or Sumagic can be used.

Schedule and timing: From rooted cuttings, 4-in. (10-cm) pots will be ready in 4 to 6 weeks, 6-in. (15-cm) pots in 5 to 7 weeks, and 10-in. (25-cm) baskets in 8 to 10 weeks. One cutting is used per 4-in. (10-cm) pot, one or two per 6-in. (15-cm) pot, and three or four per 8- to 10-in. (20- to 25-cm) hanging basket.

Comments: Another plant with an unattractive common name—tickseed. The name *bidens* is better but not by much.

BRACHYCOME CASS. SPECIES

Common name: swan river daisy.

Family: Compositae.

Description/uses: The white, violet, or blue daisy-like flowers have yellow or black centers and are 1 in. (2.5 cm) wide. Plants grow to 10 in. (25 cm) tall. *B. iberidifolia* Benth. is an annual and is primarily seed propagated; *B. angustifolia* A.M. Cunn. ex DC., *B. multifida* DC., and *B. segmentosa* Morr. and Muell. are annuals or tender perennials and are primarily cutting propagated. Numerous hybrids exist. Brachycome is not frost tolerant and is grown in packs, pots, or hanging baskets.

Temperature: Grow at 65 to 72/55 to 60°F (18 to 22/13 to 15°C) day/night temperatures.

Height control: Usually no growth regulators are required, but A-Rest, B-Nine, and Bonzi are effective.

Schedule and timing: *B. iberidifolia* plants will flower from seed in the pack in 10 to 12 weeks, 4-in. (10-cm) pots in 12 to 14 weeks, and 10-in. hanging baskets in 14 to 16 weeks. For cutting-propagated plants in the winter, 4-in. (10-cm) pots will be ready in 7 to 9 weeks, 5-in. (13-cm) pots in 8 to 10 weeks, 6-in. (15-cm) pots in 9 to 10 weeks, 8-in. (20-cm) hanging baskets in 10 to 12 weeks, and 10-in. (25-cm) hanging baskets in 12 to 14 weeks. The crop will finish 2 to 4 weeks earlier in the spring. One plant and no pinch is used with 4- and 5-in. (10- and 13-cm) pots, one to two plants and one to two pinches with 6-in. (15-cm) pots, and two to five plants and one to two pinches with hanging baskets. Plants are day neutral.

BRACTEANTHA BRACTEATA (VENT.) A.A. ANDERBERG

Common names: strawflower golden everlasting, yellow paper daisy.

Family: Compositae.

Description/uses: This cutting-propagated annual has 1- to 2-in. (2.5- to 5-cm)-wide flowers with many papery petals. The flowers are available in white, pink, rose, purple, yellow, and orange colors. Plants grow 1.5 to 3 ft (45 to 90 cm) tall. Plants are typically grown in containers but occasionally in packs.

Temperature: Grow at 65 to 75/55 to 60°F (18 to 24/13 to 16°C) day/night temperatures.

Height control: None is generally required but Bonzi sprays at 20 to 30 ppm or Sumagic sprays at 10 to 20 ppm are effective.

Schedule and timing: Plants in 4-in. (10-cm) pots are ready to sell in 4 to 6 weeks, 6-in. (15-cm) pots are ready in 7 to 9 weeks, and 10-in. (25-cm) baskets in 10 to 12 weeks. Use one plant per 4-in. (10-cm) pot, one or two plants per 6-in. (15-cm) pot, and three to five plants per 10-in. (25-cm) basket. Pinching is rarely required.

Comments: See also the closely related *Helichrysum bracteatum*. Avoid wilting. Whiteflies and root rot can be problems. Use a pH 5.5 to 6.3 growing medium with low amounts of phosphorus.

BRASSICA OLERACEA L., ORNAMENTAL CULTIVARS

Common names: flowering cabbage, flowering kale.

Family: Cruciferae.

Description/uses: This seed-propagated biennial is grown for its rosettes of colorful young foliage, which are red, pink, or white. The older foliage is green. The plants can grow up to 24 in. (60 cm) tall but are typically removed before the plants reach that height. Cabbage types have foliage with smooth margins and kale types have deeply lobed foliage. In the warm climates plants are planted outdoors in the fall and remain until late spring. In the cool climates plants can be planted in the fall and in the spring but are not typically hardy in Zone 5 or colder. Plants are usually grown in containers but occasionally in packs.

Temperature: Grow at 55 to 59°F (13 to 14°C). Foliage color intensifies outdoors when night temperatures drop to 45 to 50°F (7 to 9°C). Plants can be retailed outdoors in the fall to enhance color. Plants are not tolerant of heat but can tolerate 20°F (–7°C).

Height control: Bonzi drenches (2 to 4 mg a.i./pot), B-Nine sprays (2500 to 5000 ppm), or Sumagic sprays (8 to 25 ppm) or drenches (0.5 to 1 mg a.i./pot) are effective. If chemical growth regulators are used, plants cannot be eaten. While the plants are edible, the leaves are generally used only for garnish.

Schedule and timing: Plants are ready to sell in the pack in 5 to 6 weeks and 6-in. (15-cm) pots are ready in 11 to 14 weeks.

Comments: Plants that overwinter will produce yellow flowers in the spring. The colorful rosettes of foliage on tall cultivars are occasionally used as field-grown fresh cuts (See *Field-Grown Cut Flowers* chapter).

BRASSICA OLERACEA L., EDIBLE CULTIVARS

Common names: cabbage, kale, broccoli, brussels sprouts, kohlrabi, cauliflower, collards. These plants are together known as cole crops.

Family: Cruciferae.

Description/uses: This seed-propagated biennial vegetable is grown in packs or small pots. Many cultivars are available for each of the following types: cabbage, kale, brussels sprouts, and collards, which are grown for their edible foliage; cauliflower and broccoli, which are grown for their flower buds; and kohlrabi, which is grown for its swollen stems. All prefer cool temperatures and are planted in the spring in cool climates and in the spring or fall in warm climates. Plants are usually grown in packs.

Temperature: Grow at 50 to 60°F (10 to 15°C). Plants can be retailed outdoors in the fall or spring. Plants are not tolerant of heat but are tolerant of frost.

Height control: None can be used on this food crop.

Schedule and timing: Plants will be ready to sell in 6 to 8 weeks in packs and in 8 to 9 weeks in 4-in. (10-cm) pots.

BROWALLIA SPECIOSA HOOK.

Common name: browallia.

Family: Solanaceae.

Description/uses: The white to blue open, star-shaped flowers are produced on 10- to 12-in. (25- to 30-cm)-long stems. This annual/tender seed-propagated perennial is not frost tolerant and is sold in the spring for summer flowering. However, plants will flower all winter in frost-free climates. Plants are grown in packs, pots, and hanging baskets and are best grown outdoors with morning sun.

Temperature: Grow plants at 60 to 65°F (15 to 18°C).

Height control: A-Rest, B-Nine, and Bonzi can be used.

Schedule and timing: Plants will flower in the pack in 14 weeks. Four-inch (10-cm) pots will be ready in 15 to 16 weeks and 10-in. (25-cm) hanging baskets in 20 to 22 weeks.

Comments: Plants are susceptible to damping-off and root rots. *B. viscosa* HBK. is also cultivated but is more heat tolerant and has smaller flowers than *B. speciosa*.

CALIBRACHOA LLAVE & LEX. HYBRIDS

Common names: calibrachoa, mini petunia.

Family: Solanaceae.

Description/uses: This cutting-propagated plant carries numerous small showy purple, pink, white, orange, and bicolor flowers. Calibrachoa is similar to the petunia (*Petu-*

nia, pp. 744) but has finer textured foliage, a more pronounced trailing habit, and greater flower numbers. The plant habit is trailing to weakly upright. This perennial is cold tolerant and hardy in Zones 9 through 11B but can take temperatures down to 15°F (−9°C) in some situations. Plants that overwinter begin flowering quite early in the spring. Plants are sold in the spring in pots and hanging baskets.

Temperature: Grow at 60 to 85/60 to 65°F (16 to 29/16 to 18°C) day/night temperatures. Cooler temperatures down to 55°F (13°C) can be used but growth will slow considerably.

Height control: While this species is typically grown as a trailing plant, plant growth regulators are sometimes used to control growth and prevent stems of neighboring containers from intertwining. B-Nine sprays at 2500 to 5000 ppm, Bonzi sprays at 20 to 50 ppm, and Sumagic sprays at 1 to 10 ppm can be used on the finished crop. Plugs can be drenched with 1 to 2 ppm Sumagic 1 to 4 days prior to planting.

Schedule and timing: Plants in 4-in. (10-cm) pots are ready to sell in 4 to 6 weeks, 6-in. (15-cm) pots are ready in 7 to 9 weeks, and 10-in. (25-cm) baskets in 9 to 11 weeks. Use one plant per 4-in. (10-cm) pot, one or two plants per 6-in. (15-cm) pot, and three to five plants per 10-in. (25-cm) basket. While typically not required, plants may be pinched at any time after establishment to increase branching and improve plant shape, but will delay marketing by 2 or more weeks. Calibrachoa is a facultative long-day plant; provide long days during propagation and production, if possible.

Comments: Maintain medium pH at 5.5 to 6.0; iron deficiency may occur at pH above 6.0. This species is quite tolerant of low medium pH.

CATHARANTHUS ROSEUS (L.) G. DON.

Common names: vinca, Madagascar periwinkle.

Family: Apocynaceae.

Description/uses: The large white, pink, rose, or red flowers are produced on upright plants with attractive shiny dark-green foliage. Numerous cultivars are now available that vary in flower color, size, and petal arrangement; growth habit; flowering time; and floriferousness. This seed-propagated

tender perennial is not frost tolerant and is sold in the spring in packs, pots, and hanging baskets.

Temperature: Night temperatures should not go below 65°F (18°C) at night; cool temperatures lead to foliage yellowing, stunting, and increased susceptibility to disease. Vinca require warmer temperatures than most bedding plants and may be best produced in a separate house.

Height control: Sprays of A-Rest (5 to 18 ppm), B-Nine (2500 to 5000 ppm), Cycocel (800 to 1500 ppm), Sumagic (1 to 3 ppm), or Topflor (2.5 to 10 ppm) are effective. Bonzi and Topflor may cause black spots on foliage.

Schedule and timing: Plants will flower in the pack in 14 to 15 weeks. Four-inch (10-cm) pots will be ready in 16 to 17 weeks and 10-in. hanging baskets in 18 to 20 weeks. Catharanthus is a day-neutral plant.

Comments: Root and crown rot can be quite destructive. Prevent it by growing at the correct temperature, using a well-drained medium, and not overwatering. *Phytophthora* is often a problem in the landscape. Plants are drought tolerant in the landscape, but are sensitive to overwatering and cool temperatures, both during production and in the landscape. Keep medium pH below 6.9 or iron deficiency may occur and keep medium EC low.

CELOSIA ARGENTEA L.

Common names: celosia, cockscomb, plume flower.

Family: Amaranthaceae.

Description/uses: This seed-propagated annual species is available in three groups: Cristata has convoluted, brainlike flower heads, Plumosa has large, feathery plumes, and Spicata has small, slender spikes. The Cristata and Plumosa groups are the most commonly grown as bedding plants, while the Spicata group is tall and less commonly used as a bedding plant. Colors for cockscomb and plume celosia tend to be very bright and range from yellow to orange to deep red. Cultivars range in height from 4 to 8 in. (10 to 20 cm) to 2 to 3 ft (60 to 90 cm) tall. Wheat celosia has a restricted color range of pale pink, pink, and pale purple. The plants are taller at 3 to 5 ft (90 to 150 cm) and much more heavily branched than the other forms of celosia. The foliage often has a purplish cast. Both flower and foliage color will deepen in cool weather.

Temperature: Grow at 65 to 68°F (18 to 20°C).

Height control: Sprays of A-Rest (7 to 26 ppm), Bonzi (4 to 45 ppm), B-Nine (2500 to 5000 ppm), Cycocel (800 to 1500 ppm), Sumagic (10 to 20 ppm), or Topflor (10 to 40 ppm) are effective.

Schedule and timing: Plants will flower in the pack in 10 to 12 weeks and 4-in. (10-cm) pots in 11 to 14 weeks. Celosia are facultative short-day plants that may flower prematurely when grown under 14-hr or shorter days. Producers may want to use long-day lighting during production.

Comments: Celosia is one of the most important field cuts for fresh and dried cut flower use (see *Field-Grown Cut Flowers* chapter). Do not allow plants to become excessively dry, root bound, or cold while in the pack. If they do, plants will not grow well in the garden.

CITRULLUS LANATUS (THUNB.) MATSUM. & NAK.

Common name: watermelon.

Family: Cucurbitaceae.

Description/uses: This annual vine is grown for its large fruit, which is available with yellow to red flesh and with or without seeds. The seed-propagated plants are not frost tolerant and are sold in the spring in small individual pots or packs with large cells.

Temperature: Grow at 65 to 70°F (18 to 21°C).

Height control: No chemical growth regulators can be used on this edible vegetable.

Schedule and timing: Plants will be ready for sale in 3 to 5 weeks.

Comments: Plants do not transplant well and should be grown in packs with large cells or in pots. The best containers are decomposable pots that can be planted directly in the soil. While growing in the pack or container, plants may become stunted if growth is checked from excessive wilting, low nutrition, or delayed transplanting. Plants may remain stunted in the garden after transplanting.

CLEOME HASSLERIANA CHODAT.

Common names: cleome, spider flower.

Family: Capparidaceae.

Description/uses: Cleome has large, terminal clusters of white, pink, rose, or violet-colored flowers on 3- to 4-ft (90- to 120-cm)-

tall plants. Each flower has four upright petals and six long threadlike stamens. This seed-propagated annual plant is not frost tolerant and is sold in the spring in packs.

Temperature: Grow plants at 60 to 70°F (15 to 21°C).

Height control: Sprays of A-Rest (7 to 26 ppm) and Cycocel (800 to 1500 ppm) are effective.

Schedule and timing: Plants are sold green in 7 to 9 weeks.

Comments: Cleome foliage is strongly scented and plants have short sharp spurs along the stems. Some cultivars may reseed in the garden.

CUCUMIS L. SPECIES

Common names: cucumber (*C. sativus* L.), cantaloupe (*C. melo* L.), muskmelon (*C. melo*). Many other *Cucumis* species are cultivated and known as melons or cucumbers.

Family: Cucurbitaceae.

Description/uses: Cucumbers are grown for their green to yellow skinned fruits, which are used as a vegetable. Cantaloupe (muskmelon) are grown for their large sweet fruit and have green to orange flesh. The length of the vine can vary from short as in "bush" cultivars to many feet (meters) long. The seed-propagated plants are not frost tolerant and are sold in the spring in small individual pots or packs with large cells (Fig. III-5 Bedding Plants). Plants are treated as annuals.

Temperature: Grow cucumbers at 60 to 62°F (15 to 17°C) and cantaloupe (muskmelon) at 65 to 70°F (18 to 21°C).

Height control: No chemical growth regulators can be used on this edible vegetable.

Schedule and timing: Plants will be ready to sell in 3 to 5 weeks.

Comments: Plants do not transplant well and should be grown in packs with large cells or in pots. The best containers are decomposable pots that can be planted directly in the soil. While growing in the pack or container, plants may become stunted if growth is checked from excessive wilting, low nutrition, or delayed transplanting. Plants may remain stunted in the garden after transplanting.

CUCURBITA L. SPECIES

Common names: winter squash (*C. maxima* Duchesne ex Lam.), pumpkin [*C. maxima*, *C.*

FIGURE III-5 BEDDING PLANTS *Cucumis* bedding plants ready for marketing.

moschata (Duchesne ex Lam.) Duchesne ex Poir], summer squash (*C. pepo* L.), zucchini (*C. pepo*).

Family: Cucurbitaceae.

Description/uses: Hundreds of cultivars of this annual vine exist that vary greatly in color, size, and shape of fruit. The length of the vine can vary from short as in "bush" cultivars to many feet (meters) long. The seed-propagated plants are not frost tolerant and are sold in the spring in small individual pots or packs with large cells.

Temperature: Grow at 62 to 65°F (17 to 18°C).

Height control: No chemical growth regulators can be used on this edible vegetable.

Schedule and timing: Plants will be ready for sale in 3 to 5 weeks.

Comments: Plants do not transplant well and should be grown in packs with large cells or in pots. The best containers are decomposable pots that can be planted directly in the soil. While in the pack or container, plants may become stunted if growth is checked from excessive wilting, low nutrition, or delayed transplanting. Plants may remain stunted in the garden after transplanting.

CUPHEA P. BROWNE.

Common names: see next column.

Family: Lythraceae.

Description/uses: Numerous cuphea species are available; most have small, narrow tubular flowers that flare open at the end. Some species have small, attractive, elliptical glossy leaves. *Cuphea hyssopifola* HBK. (Mexican heather) has numerous small lavender flowers that cover the 1- to 2-ft (30- to 60-cm)-tall plants. *C. ignea* A. DC. (cigar or firecracker plant) has bright red, black-tipped flowers on 12- to 18-in. (30- to 45-cm)-tall plants. *C. llavea* La Ll. & Lex. (bat-faced cuphea) has green tubular flowers, adorned with two scarlet petals and a dark throat, on 18- to 24-in. (45- to 60-cm)-tall plants. Most cupheas are tender perennials, not frost tolerant, and sold in the spring in pots or hanging baskets. *C. hyssopifolia* and *C. llavea* are primarily cutting propagated and *C. ignea* is primarily seed propagated.

Temperature: Grow plants at 68 to 75/60 to 65°F (20 to 24/16 to 18°C) day/night temperatures.

Height control: None is required.

Schedule and timing: In the winter 4-in. (10-cm) pots will be ready in 7 to 9 weeks, 5-in. (13-cm) pots in 8 to 10 weeks, 6-in. (15-cm) pots in 9 to 10 weeks, 8-in. (20-cm) hanging baskets in 10 to 12 weeks, and 10-in. (25-cm) hanging baskets in 12 to 14 weeks. The crop will finish 2 to 4 weeks earlier in the spring. One plant and no pinch is used with 4- and 5-in. (10- and 13-cm) pots, one or two plants and one pinch with 6-in. (15-cm) pots, and two to four plants and one to two pinches with hanging baskets. Plants are day neutral.

Comments: Several other *Cuphea* species and cultivars are available. Sudden plant death can be due to stem canker, overwatering, water stress, or high media soluble salt levels.

DIANTHUS CHINENSIS L.

Common name: dianthus.

Family: Caryophyllaceae.

Description/uses: Dianthus has large clusters of white, pink, rose, or red single or double flowers on 9- to 12-in. (23- to 30-cm)-tall plants. Many cultivars have bicolored flowers and many are mildly fragrant. Cultivars vary in flower color, plant height, heat and cold tolerance, and branching ability. This seed-propagated biennial or short-lived perennial is frost tolerant and is sold in the fall or spring in packs or pots.

Temperature: Grow at 45 to 55°F (7 to 13°C) nights.

Height control: Use sprays of A-Rest (7 to 26 ppm), Bonzi (10 to 60 ppm), B-Nine (2500 to 5000 ppm), or Cycocel (800 to 1500 ppm) can be used. Bonzi is more effective than A-Rest and Cycocel.

Schedule and timing: Plants will be ready for sale in 10 to 11 weeks as green packs; 15 to 16 weeks are needed for flowering packs or 4-in. (10-cm) pots. Long days (4-hr night interruptions) accelerate flowering and may be useful from December to March to speed flowering.

Comments: Avoid ammonium-based fertilizers. Plants do best in cool temperatures in the landscape and often disappear during the summer in warm climates. In moderate or cool climates, plants frequently overwinter. Trim plants after the first flush of flowers in the spring to encourage repeat flowering. See also Dianthus, Cut, Pot, and Sweet William chapters for information on related species.

DIASCIA LINK & OTTO. HYBRIDS

Common name: diascia.

Family: Scrophulariaceae.

Description/uses: This cutting-propagated annual/tender perennial has numerous red, pink, lavender, peach, and white flowers up to 1 in. (2.5 cm) wide. Plants grow up to 1.5 ft (45 cm) tall in a mounding or trailing habit. Plants are typically grown in containers.

Temperature: Grow at 62 to 75/52 to 60°F (17 to 24/11 to 16°C) day/night temperatures.

Height control: None is generally required if grown cool but B-Nine sprays at 3000 to 5000 ppm can be used to maintain shape.

Schedule and timing: Plants in 4-in. (10-cm) pots are ready to sell in 5 to 7 weeks, 6-in. (15-cm) pots are ready in 7 to 9 weeks, and 10-in. (25-cm) baskets in 9 to 11 weeks. Use one plant per 4-in. (10-cm) pot, one or two plants per 6-in. (15-cm) pot, and three to four plants per 10-in. (25-cm) basket. Pinching is rarely required.

Comments: Grows best in cool weather with day/night temperatures less than 90/70°F (32/21°C).

EVOLVULUS GLOMERATUS NEES. & MART.

Common name: evolvulus.

Family: Convolvulaceae.

Description/uses: This 12- to 14-in. (30- to 35-cm)-tall, procumbent plant has numerous bright blue flowers with a white eye. This cutting-propagated tender perennial is not frost tolerant and is sold in the spring in pots or hanging baskets.

Temperature: Grow plants at 68 to 75/60 to 65°F (20 to 24/16 to 18°C) day/night temperatures.

Height control: None is required.

Schedule and timing: In the winter 4-in. (10-cm) pots will be ready in 8 to 9 weeks, 5-in. (13-cm) pots in 9 to 11 weeks, 6-in. (15-cm) pots in 12 to 14 weeks, 8-in. (20-cm) hanging baskets in 10 to 12 weeks, and 10-in. (25-cm) hanging baskets in 11 to 13 weeks. The crop will finish 2 to 4 weeks earlier in the spring. One rooted cutting and one pinch is used with 4-in. (10-cm) pots, one to two rooted cuttings and one to two pinches with 5- or 6-in. (13- or 15-cm) pots, and three to four rooted cuttings and one to three pinches with hanging baskets. Evolvulus is a long-day plant.

Comments: Evolvulus is salt tolerant, allowing it to be used in coastal plantings.

FRAGARIA ×ANANASSA DUCHESNE.

Common name: strawberry.

Family: Rosaceae.

Description/uses: Although strawberries are typically planted outdoors using bare-rooted plants, seed-propagated cultivars, such as 'Sweetheart' and 'Fresca,' are available. The 8- to 12-in. (20- to 30-cm)-tall plants produce numerous small white daisy-like flowers that mature into small red fruits. This frost-tolerant perennial plant is typically sold in the spring in containers or hanging baskets. Plants will flower and produce fruit all summer long in cool climates. Plant in the fall for spring flowering in warm climates.

Temperature: Grow plants at 60 to 62°F (15 to 17°C).

Height control: No chemical growth regulators can be used on this edible plant.

Schedule and timing: Plants will be ready for sale in 9 to 10 weeks in 4-in. (10-cm) pots and in 15 to 17 weeks in hanging baskets.

Comments: Plants produce vegetative stolons, which can root in adjacent containers, making them difficult to separate. Stolons can be used for propagation, however.

GAZANIA RIGENS (L.) GAERTN.

Common names: gazania, treasure flower.

Family: Compositae.

Description/uses: This seed-propagated tender perennial is hardy only to Zone 9 and is typically grown as an annual. The large, 3- to 4-in. (8- to 10-cm)-wide, white, yellow, orange, or red flowers can be single or multicolored and grow 8- to 10-in. (20- to 25-cm)-tall rosettes of green to silvery foliage. Plants are not frost tolerant and are sold in the spring in packs, pots, or hanging baskets.

Temperature: Grow at 55 to 60°F (13 to 15°C).

Height control: None is typically required.

Schedule and timing: In cool climates plants will flower in the pack in 12 to 13 weeks, 4-in. (10-cm) pots in 14 to 15 weeks, and 10-in. hanging baskets in 16 to 17 weeks. In warm climates packs will be in flower in 10 to 11 weeks and 4-in. (10-cm) pots in 13 to 14 weeks.

Comments: Plants are susceptible to root and crown rot. Flowers close at night and during cloudy and rainy weather. Newer cultivars are less prone to flower closing.

GOMPHRENA GLOBOSA L. AND G. HAAGEANA KLOTZSCH.

Common names: globe amaranth, gomphrena.

Family: Amaranthaceae.

Description/uses: This seed-propagated annual or tender perennial produces many small round to oval-shaped flowers consisting of numerous tightly packed florets on a heavily branched plant. Of the two species being grown, *G. globosa* tends to be shorter and more heavily branched than *G. haageana*. *G. globosa* flowers are smaller than *G. haageana* and are available in white, pink, pale purple, and dark purple. *G. haageana* flowers are various shades of red and orange. Hybrids are blurring the distinctions between the two species and a greater range of colors may soon be available. *G. globosa* is most commonly used as a bedding plant due to its short and compact growth habit.

Temperature: Grow at 65 to 68°F (18 to 20°C).

Height control: Dwarf cultivars do not need growth retardants. Sprays of B-Nine (2500 to 5000 ppm) or Cycocel (800 to 1500 ppm) are effective.

Schedule and timing: Plants are ready to sell in 9 to 10 weeks in packs (green packs in 7 to 8 weeks) and 4-in. (10-cm) pots in 13 to 14 weeks.

Comments: Gomphrena is an important field-grown cut flower for fresh and dried use (see *Field-Grown Cut Flowers* chapter). Gomphrena grows well in warm weather and tolerates drought but maximum flower production occurs with irrigation.

HELICHRYSUM MILL. SPECIES

Common names: helichrysum, strawflower, everlasting.

Family: Compositae.

Description/uses: This genus includes many cultivated species. *Helichrysum bracteatum* (Vent.) Andrews cultivars have white, pink, rose, purple, yellow, and orange-colored flowers on plants that are 1.5 to 3 ft (45 to 90 cm) tall. This seed-propagated species is also used as a cut flower (see *Field-Grown Cut Flowers* chapter). Several species are available with silvery foliage. *Helichrysum thianschanicum* Reg. is a cutting-propagated tender perennial hardy to Zone 6. *H. thianschanicum* has narrow leaves and grows in an upright mound. *H. petiolare* Hilliard & B.L. Burtt. (licorice plant) is a cutting-propagated tender perennial that grows 1 to 2 ft (30 to 60 cm) tall. *H. petiolare* has leaves up to 1.4 in. (3.5 cm) wide and has an open mound to trailing habit. Although both species are grown for their silvery gray foliage, they may produce clusters of small white to yellow flowers.

Temperature: Grow at 65 to 75/55 to 62°F (18 to 24/13 to 17°C) day/night temperatures.

Height control: None is used.

Schedule and timing: *Helichrysum bracteatum* plants in packs are ready to sell in 10 to 12 weeks and 4-in. (10-cm) pots in 12 to 14 weeks. Use one plant per 4-in. (10-cm) pot. *H. petiolare* plants in 4-in. (10-cm) pots are ready to sell in 5 to 7 weeks, 6-in. (15-cm) pots in 7 to 9 weeks, and 10-in. (25-cm) baskets in 9 to 11 weeks. Use one plant per 4-in. (10-cm) pot, one or two plants per 6-in. (15-cm) pot, and three to five plants per 10-in. (25-cm) basket. *H. thianschanicum* plants in 4-in. (10-cm) pots are ready to sell in 10 to 12 weeks; 6-in. (15-cm) pots and 10-in. (25-cm) baskets are ready in 12 to 14 weeks. Use one plant per 4-in. (10-cm) pot, one or two plants per 6-in. (15-cm) pot, and three to four plants per 10-in. (25-cm) basket. Pinching is required with both species.

Comments: See also the closely related *Helichrysum bracteatum*.

HELIOTROPIUM ARBORESCENS L. (FORMERLY KNOWN AS HELIOTROPE ARBORESCENS)

Common name: heliotrope.

Family: Boraginaceae.

Description/uses: Large cluster of small fragrant purple flowers adorn the 8- to 13-in. (20- to 33-cm)-tall plants. This tender perennial is not frost tolerant and is sold in the spring in pots and packs. Heliotrope can be propagated from either seeds or cuttings.

Temperature: Grow plants at 62 to 65°F (16 to 18°C).

Height control: Compact cultivars will not need height control but taller cultivars can be sprayed with a tank mix of 1500 to 3000 ppm B-Nine + 750 to 1000 ppm Cycocel.

Schedule and timing: Non flowering seed-propagated plants will be ready in 8 to 9 weeks. Cutting-propagated plants grown in 4-in. (10-cm) pots will be ready to market in 6 to 7 weeks; 6-in. (15-cm) pots in 8 to 9 weeks, and 10-in. (25-cm) baskets in 10 to 12 weeks. Use one rooted cutting per 4-in. (10-cm) pot, one or two cuttings per 6-in. (15-cm) pot, and three to five cuttings per 10-in. (25-cm) basket.

Comments: Necrotic leaf edges may be due to water stress, high media soluble salt levels, low media pH, or iron toxicity.

HYPOESTES PHYLLOSTACHYA BAK.

Common name: polka dot plant.

Family: Acanthaceae.

Description/uses: This plant is grown for its colorful bright green leaves liberally splashed with red, pink, or white spots. These seed-propagated annuals are not frost tolerant and are sold in the spring in pots. The plants grow to 24 in. (60 cm) tall but look their best when short and compact. Flowers will form later in the season but are small and not attractive.

Temperature: Grow at 60 to 65°F (16 to 18°C).

Height control: Sprays of Cycocel (700 to 1500 ppm) or B-Nine (1000 ppm) are effective.

Schedule and timing: Plants grown in 4-in. (10-cm) pots will be ready to market in 11 to 13 weeks. Smaller and larger pot sizes can be used.

Comments: Also grown as a small potted indoor plant.

IBERIS UMBELLATA L. AND I. AMARA L.

Common name: candytuft.

Family: Cruciferae.

Description/uses: Clusters of small white, pink, rose, lilac, or red flowers are produced on 6- to 12-in. (15- to 30-cm)-tall plants. These seed-propagated annuals are not frost tolerant and are sold in the spring in packs and pots. *I. umbellata* has flat-topped inflorescences, whereas *I. amara* has elongated rounded clusters.

Temperature: Grow at 50 to 55°F (10 to 13°C).

Height control: None is generally required.

Schedule and timing: Flowers in the pack in 6 to 10 weeks.

Comments: Grows best in cool spring weather.

IMPATIENS BALSAMINA L.

Common names: balsam, garden balsam, rose balsam.

Family: Balsaminaceae.

Description/uses: This relative of the bedding impatiens and New Guinea impatiens (see individual chapters) grows 8 to 30 in. (20 to 75 cm) tall with flowers hanging down from the leaf axils. The single to double flowers are colored white, pink, lavender, purple, or bicolored. This annual is not frost tolerant and is sold in the spring in packs or pots.

Temperature: Grow plants at 60 to 62°F (15 to 17°C).

Height control: A-Rest is effective.

Schedule and timing: Flowers in the pack 9 weeks after sowing seed in the spring. Because plants often become leggy in the pack, it may be best to sell them green in 7 to 8 weeks.

Comments: Interesting plant but much less common than its flashier relatives.

IPOMOEA BATATUS (L.) POIR.

Common name: ornamental sweet potato.

Family: Convolvulaceae.

Description/uses: This ornamental version of the popular sweet potato is grown for its large burgundy, chartreuse, or pink, green, and white variegated leaves. Flowers can be produced but are usually hidden underneath the foliage. This tender cutting-propagated perennial vine is not cold tolerant and is sold in the spring in pots and hanging baskets.

Temperature: Grow plants at 60 to 65°F (15 to 18°C). Plants grow very slowly under cool temperatures. Don't start too early in the spring.

Height control: Plant size is best controlled culturally but Sumagic sprays at 10 to 15 ppm or B-Nine at 250 ppm are effective. Cut back as needed to keep plants from becoming intertwined.

Schedule and timing: Eight- to 10-in. (20- to 25-cm) pots or baskets will finish in 12 to 14 weeks when planted with three to four rooted cuttings; 4- to 6-in. (10- to 15-cm) pots will finish in 6 to 7 weeks when planted with one rooted cutting. Plants can be pinched once, 2 weeks after planting rooted cuttings.

Comments: Some cultivars are quite vigorous. One of the best plants for difficult situations outdoors such as poorly drained soil or hot, dry locations.

IRESINE HERBSTII HOOK.

Common names: bloodleaf, chicken gizzard, beefsteak plant, iresine.

Family: Amaranthaceae.

Description/uses: While originally used as an indoor foliage plant, this species has been reborn as a colorful outdoor bedding plant. It is grown for its purple or green foliage variegated with white, pink, red, or yellow. Flowers are insignificant. Spreading forms grow 6 to 8 in. (15 to 20 cm) tall and 3 to 4 ft (90 to 120 cm) wide. Upright forms grow up to 2 ft (60 cm) tall. Iresine can be either seed or cutting propagated. This tender perennial is not frost tolerant and is grown in the spring in pots or hanging baskets.

Temperature: Grow plants at 62 to 65°F (16 to 18°C).

Height control: Generally not required.

Schedule and timing: From seed, 4-in. (10-cm) pots will be ready in 9 to 11 weeks and 10-in. (25-cm) baskets in 13 to 14 weeks. From rooted cuttings, 4-in. (10-cm) pots will be ready in 6 to 8 weeks, 6-in. (15-cm) pots in 7 to 10 weeks, and 10-in. (25-cm) baskets in 9 to 12 weeks. One plant is used per 4-in. (10-cm) pot, one or two per 6-in. (15-cm) pot, and four or five per 8- to 10-in. (20- to 25-cm) hanging basket.

Comments: Can be grown in sun to partial shade in the home garden.

LACTUCA SATIVA L.

Common name: garden lettuce.

Family: Compositae.

Description/uses: This annual is grown for its large edible leaves. Many cultivars are available in headed or loose-leaf forms and with foliage that can be green to dark red/bronze. Leaf shape varies from rounded to oak-leaf shaped. Lettuce is frost tolerant and can be planted in the fall and spring. Plants are typically sold in packs.

Temperature: Grow at 55 to 58°F (13 to 14°C).

Height control: No chemical growth retardants can be used on this edible vegetable.

Schedule and timing: Plants will be ready for sale in 4 to 5 weeks in the pack and in 6 to 9 weeks in 4-in. (10-cm) pots.

Comments: Newer cultivars are more heat tolerant and less likely to bolt in the summer.

LANTANA L. SPECIES

Common names: lantana, shrub verbena.

Family: Verbenaceae.

Description/uses: Lantana has rounded clusters of small yellow, orange, red, pink, or lavender-colored flowers. Many cultivars have multicolored flower clusters with the flowers changing color as they age. *L. camara* L. tends to grow upright up to 3 ft. (90 cm) tall while *L. montevidensis* (Spreng.) Briq. is more horizontal and grows up to 18 in. (45 cm) tall. The numerous hybrid cultivars have a variety of growth habits. The foliage is fragrant. This tender woody perennial is generally not frost tolerant and is sold in the spring in packs, pots, or hanging baskets. Some cultivars are cold hardier than others and may overwinter in mild climates. All lantanas are heat and drought tolerant and perform well in hot climates.

Temperature: Grow plants at 60°F (15°C).

Height control: Several chemicals are effective including sprays of B-Nine (2500 to 5000 ppm) + Cycocel (1000 to 1500 ppm) tank mix, Florel (300 to 400 ppm), Bonzi (20 to 40 ppm), or Sumagic (10 to 20 ppm).

Schedule and timing: Softwood cuttings will root in 3 to 4 weeks. Plants in 4-in. (10-cm) pots are ready to sell in 6 to 7 weeks, 6-in. (15-cm) pots are ready in 7 to 8 weeks, and 10-in. (25-cm) baskets in 10 to 12 weeks. Use one or two plants per 4-in. (10-cm) pot, one to three plants per 6-in. (15-cm) pot, and three to six plants per 10-in. (25-cm) basket. Pinching one to several times will improve plant shape.

Comments: Lantana is an invasive plant in warm climates and has become a noxious weed in some tropical and subtropical areas. However, butterflies love lantana.

LOBELIA ERINUS L.

Common name: trailing lobelia.

Family: Campanulaceae.

Description/uses: The trailing plants produce masses of small white, lavender, blue, or purple flowers on plants that grow 3 to 6 in. (8 to 15 cm) tall. This tender perennial is not frost tolerant and is sold in the spring in packs. Both seed and cutting-propagated cultivars are available.

Temperature: Grow plants at 60°F (15°C).

Height control: None is usually required, but sprays of Bonzi (4 ppm), B-Nine (1500 to 2500 ppm), and Sumagic (1 ppm) are effective.

Schedule and timing: From seed plants will flower in the pack in 11 to 12 weeks, 4-in. (10-cm) pots in 12 to 13 weeks, and 10-in. hanging baskets in 14 to 15 weeks. Cutting-propagated plants grown in 4-in. (10-cm) pots will be ready to market in 8 to 10 weeks, 6-in. (15-cm) pots in 9 to 11 weeks, and 10-in. (25-cm) baskets in 10 to 13 weeks. Use one plant per 4-in. (10-cm) pot, two plants per 6-in. (15-cm) pot, and four to five plants per 10-in. (25-cm) basket.

Comments: Plants typically die during hot summer weather. Plantings are most spectacular in cool climates.

LOBULARIA MARITIMA (L.) DESV.

Common names: alyssum, sweet alyssum.

Family: Cruciferae.

Description/uses: This low-growing seed-propagated annual plant forms colorful mats. The short spikes of fragrant flowers are colored white, pink, red, purple, lavender, apricot, and pale yellow. The plants are frost tolerant and can be sold in the spring or fall. Plants are sold in packs or small containers.

Temperature: Grow at 50 to 55°F (10 to 13°C).

Height control: None is needed on this low-growing plant but Bonzi sprays (10 to 60 ppm) can be used.

Schedule and timing: In cool climates plants will flower in the pack in 8 to 9 weeks, 4-in. (10-cm) pots in 10 to 11 weeks, and 10-in. (25-cm) hanging baskets in 12 to 14 weeks. In warm climates plants will flower in 7 weeks in the pack and 9 weeks in 4-in. (10-cm) pots.

Comments: Plants will die during hot summer weather. Plants may reseed in the garden.

LOTUS BERTHELOTTI LOWE EX MASF.

Common names: parrot's beak, coral gem.

Family: Leguminosae.

Description/uses: The unusual orange-red to scarlet or purple pealike flowers have a long slender beak and the flowers occur in loose terminal clusters on low-growing vines. The foliage is silver gray. This tender cutting-propagated perennial is not frost tolerant and is sold in the spring in pots and hanging baskets.

Temperature: Grow plants at 50 to 60°F (10 to 16°C) nights and 65 to 75°F (18 to 24°C) days. Plants require 4 to 8 weeks of cold treatment at 40 to 45°F (4 to 7°C) for flower initiation. Once initiated, flowering will continue as long as the night temperature remains below 60°F (15°C). Plants may stop flowering during the summer but may flower again in the fall.

Height control: None is usually required.

Schedule and timing: From rooted cuttings in the spring, 4-in. (10-cm) pots will be marketable in 5 to 6 weeks, 6-in. (15-cm) pots in 6 to 7 weeks, 8-in. (20-cm) hanging baskets in 8 to 10 weeks, and 10-in. (25-cm) hanging baskets in 10 to 12 weeks. Crop time will be 1 to 2 weeks shorter during the summer. Plants grown in 6-in. (15-cm) or larger containers should be pinched; the first pinch occurs when six to eight leaves have formed and additional pinches can be made when two leaf pairs can remain.

Comments: Even, consistent irrigation is important.

MELAMPODIUM DIVARICATUM (RICH.) DC (FORMERLY KNOWN AS M. PALUDOSUM)

Common name: melampodium.

Family: Compositae.

Description/uses: The 1- to 2-in. (2.5- to 5.0-cm)-wide yellow daisy-like flowers occur on 10- to 20-in. (25- to 50-cm)-tall plants. This seed-propagated annual/tender perennial is not frost tolerant and is sold in the spring in packs or pots.

Temperature: Grow plants at 60 to 62°F (16 to 17°C).

Height control: B-Nine is effective.

Schedule and timing: Plants will flower in the pack in 7 to 8 weeks and 4-in. (10-cm) pots in 9 to 10 weeks.

Comments: This drought- and heat-tolerant species is excellent for the southern United States and other warm climates.

MIMULUS ×HYBRIDUS HORT. EX SIEBERT & VOSS.

Common name: monkey flower.

Family: Scrophulariaceae.

Description/uses: The tubular white, yellow, orange, and red flowers are produced on 8- to 12-in. (20- to 30-cm)-tall plants. The plants are not frost tolerant and are sold in the spring in packs, pots, or hanging baskets. Both seed and cutting-propagated cultivars are available with cutting-propagated cultivars most commonly grown.

Temperature: Grow plants at 55 to 60°F (13 to 16°C).

Height control: B-Nine or Cycocel sprays may be helpful.

Schedule and timing: Seed-propagated plants will flower in the pack in 8 to 9 weeks, 4-in. (10-cm) pots in 10 to 11 weeks, and 10-in. (25-cm) hanging baskets in 11 to 12 weeks. Cutting-propagated plants are ready to sell in 12 to 14 weeks, regardless of container size. Use one plant per 4-in. (10-cm) pot, one or two plants per 6-in. (15-cm) pot, and three to four plants per 10-in. (25-cm) basket. Mimulus is a long-day plant requiring day lengths of 13 hr or longer. Pinching is useful.

Comments: Plants do not tolerate water stress. In the garden mimulus does well in damp, shady to partly sunny areas.

NEMESIA STRUMOSA BENTH. IN HOOK

Common name: nemesia.

Family: Scrophulariaceae.

Description/uses: The white, rose, red, or gold tubular flowers are produced on 8- to 10-in. (20- to 25-cm)-tall plants. Cultivars with bicolored flowers are available. This annual is not frost tolerant and is sold in the spring in pots. Both seed and cutting-propagated cultivars are available.

Temperature: Grow plants at 65 to 75/55 to 60°F (18 to 24/13 to 16°C) day/night temperatures.

Height control: None is usually required but sprays of B-Nine (2500 to 3500 ppm), Sumagic (20 to 30 ppm), or Topflor (10 to 15 ppm) are effective.

Schedule and timing: Seed-propagated plants will flower in 4-in. (10-cm) pots in 13 to 15 weeks. Cutting-propagated plants in 4-in. (10-cm) pots are ready to sell in 5 to 7 weeks, 6-in. (15-cm) pots are ready in 7 to 9 weeks, and 10-in. (25-cm) baskets in 9 to 11 weeks. Use one plant per 4-in. (10-cm) pot, two to three plants per 6-in. (15-cm) pot, and three to five plants per 10-in. (25-cm) basket. Pinching can be useful to maintain shape.

Comments: Nemesia does not transplant well. Plants grow best in cool climates with low humidity.

NICOTIANA ×SANDERAE HORT. SANDER EX WILL. WATS.

Common name: flowering tobacco.

Family: Solanaceae.

Description/uses: The large, 1- to 2-in. (2.5- to 5.0-cm)-wide, tubular flowers are fragrant and produced in loose terminal inflorescences on 1- to 3-ft (30- to 90-cm)-tall plants. The flowers can be white, pink, rose, red, salmon, or lavender. This seed-propagated annual is not frost tolerant and is sold in the spring in packs or pots.

Temperature: Grow plants at 60 to 62°F (16 to 17°C).

Height control: B-Nine is effective.

Schedule and timing: Plants will flower in the pack in 9 to 10 weeks and 4-in. (10-cm) pots in 10 to 11 weeks. Flowering tobacco plants, especially older cultivars, are facultative long-day plants and flower fastest under 10-hr or longer days.

Comments: Plants may become permanently stunted if allowed to become rootbound in the plug or bedding pack.

NIEREMBERGIA HIPPOMANICA MIERS.

Common names: nierembergia, cupflower.
Family: Solanaceae.
Description/uses: The 6- to 10-in. (15- to 25-cm)-tall plants are covered with numerous small white or violet, starlike flowers. This tender perennial is typically grown as an annual and is frost tolerant. Plants are sold in the spring in packs, pots, or hanging baskets.
Temperature: Grow plants at 60 to 62°F (16 to 17°C).
Height control: None is usually required.
Schedule and timing: Plants will flower in the pack in 10 to 11 weeks, 4-in. (10-cm) pots in 12 to 13 weeks, and 10-in. (25-cm) hanging baskets in 14 to 16 weeks.
Comments: Plants may overwinter in mild climates.

OSTEOSPERMUM ECKLONIS (DC.) NORL.

Common names: African daisy, cape daisy, osteospermum.
Family: Compositae.
Description/uses: The tender perennial produces large numbers of white, pink, rose, or violet daisy-like flowers with dark centers. Some cultivars have bicolored flowers, unusually spoon-shaped petals (Fig. III-6 Bedding Plants), or petals on which the under-

side is a different color than the upperside. Cultivars with orange petals and dark centers are available. Plants grow 1 to 2 ft (30 to 60 cm) tall. This plant is not frost tolerant and is sold in the spring in pots and hanging baskets. Both seed and cutting-propagated cultivars are available with cutting-propagated cultivars most common.
Temperature: Grow plants at 65 to 72/60 to 65°F (18 to 23/16 to 18°C) day/night temperatures after propagation. Temperatures of less than 70°F (21°C) are required for flowering. Finish at 55 to 65/50 to 60°F (13 to 16/10 to 16°C) day/night temperatures.
Height control: Sprays of Bonzi (30 ppm), B-Nine (2500 ppm), Cycocel (750 ppm), or Topflor (20 to 60 ppm) can be used.
Schedule and timing: Plants are propagated from seed or cuttings. For cutting-propagated plants in the winter, 4- to 6-in. (10- to 15-cm) pots will be ready in 15 to 17 weeks and 8- to 10-in. (20- to 25-cm) hanging baskets in 16 to 18 weeks. The crop will finish 2 to 3 weeks earlier as spring advances. One plant is used per 4-in. (10-cm) pot, one or two per 5-in. (13-cm) pot, two to three per 6-in. (15-cm) pot, and three to four per 8- to 10-in. (20- to 25-cm) hanging basket. Plants should be pinched 3 weeks after planting. Plants are day neutral.
Comments: Flowers of some cultivars close at night. Plants do best in cool climates—flowering often ceases in the summer and resumes in the fall.

PENTAS LANCEOLATA (FORSSK.) DEFLERS.

Common names: pentas, star-cluster, Egyptian star-cluster.
Family: Rubiaceae.
Description/uses: Large clusters of star-shaped white, pink, rose, lavender, or red flowers are produced on 12- to 24-in. (30- to 60-cm)-tall upright plants. This tender perennial is not frost tolerant and is sold in the spring in pots or packs. Both seed and cutting-propagated cultivars are available.
Temperature: Grow plants at 62 to 65°F (17 to 18°C).
Height control: Cycocel sprays (800 to 3000 ppm) are effective.
Schedule and timing: Seed-propagated cultivars are ready for sale green in packs in 10

FIGURE III-6 BEDDING PLANTS *Osteospermum* 'Brightside Sunside Sonja.'

to 13 weeks and in 16 to 18 weeks in 4-in. (10-cm) pots. In the spring cutting-propagated, 4-in. (10-cm) pots will be ready in 5 to 6 weeks, 6-in. (15-cm) pots in 6 to 7 weeks, 8-in. (20-cm) baskets in 8 to 10 weeks, and 10-in. (25-cm) baskets in 10 to 12 weeks. The crop will finish 1 to 2 weeks earlier in the summer. One plant is used per 4- to 6-in. (10- to 15-cm) pot and three to five per 8- to 10-in. (20- to 25-cm) hanging basket. Plants should be pinched when grown in containers 6 in. (15 cm) or larger. Pentas are facultative long-day plants.

Comments: High media pH, greater than 6.5, prevents stunted growth and strapped leaves from iron toxicity. Butterflies love pentas in the garden.

PERILLA FRUTESCENS L.

Common name: perilla.

Family: Labiatae.

Description/uses: This coleus-like plant is grown for its green, bronze, or purple foliage, occasionally variegated with bright pink and white. The flowers are small and unattractive. This heat-tolerant annual grows 2 to 3 ft (60 to 90 cm) tall and 18 to 24 in. (45 to 60 cm) wide. Perilla is primarily cutting propagated, not frost tolerant, and grown in the spring in pots or large baskets.

Temperature: Grow plants at 60 to 70°F (15 to 21°C).

Height control: Sprays of B-Nine (2500 to 4000 ppm) can be used.

Schedule and timing: From rooted cuttings, 4-in. (10-cm) pots will be ready in 5 to 7 weeks, 6-in. (15-cm) pots in 6 to 8 weeks, and 10-in. (25-cm) baskets in 8 to 11 weeks. One rooted cutting is used per 4-in. (10-cm) pot, one or two per 6-in. (15-cm) pot, and three or four per 8- to 10-in. (20- to 25-cm) hanging basket.

Comments: Variegated cultivars will lose some of their color if grown in the shade in the home garden.

PHLOX DRUMMONDII HOOK.

Common name: annual phlox.

Family: Polemoniaceae.

Description/uses: This annual version of the stately perennial garden phlox also has clusters of white, pink, apricot, rose, red, or lavender flowers. Plants are only 8 to 10 in. (20 to 25 cm) tall and flower all season. This seed-propagated plant is not frost tolerant and is sold in the spring in packs and pots.

Temperature: Grow plants at 50 to 55°F (10 to 13°C).

Height control: B-Nine sprays (2500 to 5000 ppm) are effective.

Schedule and timing: Plants will flower in 10 to 11 weeks in packs and in 13 to 14 weeks in 4-in. (10-cm) pots.

PLECTRANTHUS L'HÉRIT. SPECIES AND CULTIVARS

Common name: plectranthus.

Family: Labiatae.

Description/uses: This heat and drought-tolerant group of plants is grown primarily for their dark green, silver, purple, or green variegated with yellow or white foliage. Many species have fragrant foliage and one, *P. amboinicus* (Lour.) Spreng., is known as the Cuban oregano. Although most plectranthus have small and unattractive flowers, a few species can produce a spectacular floral show. These tender perennials are either trailing or weakly upright. Most commonly cultivated species grow 8 to 16 in. (20 to 40 cm) tall and up to 3 ft (90 cm) wide. Plectranthus are primarily cutting propagated, not frost tolerant, and grown in the spring in pots or hanging baskets.

Temperature: Grow plants at 58 to 65°F (14 to 18°C).

Height control: Depending on the species, sprays of B-Nine (1500 to 2500 ppm) + Cycocel (750 to 1500 ppm) tank mix or Bonzi (5 to 20 ppm) can be used.

Schedule and timing: From rooted cuttings, 4-in. (10-cm) pots will be ready in 6 to 8 weeks, 6-in. (15-cm) pots in 7 to 10 weeks, and 10-in. (25-cm) baskets in 9 to 12 weeks. One rooted cutting is used per 4-in. (10-cm) pot, one or two per 6-in. (15-cm) pot, and three to five per 8- to 10-in. (20- to 25-cm) hanging basket. Many plectranthus species are short-day plants and flower profusely in the spring and fall.

Comments: Can be grown in sun to shade in the home garden.

FIGURE III-7 BEDDING PLANTS *Portulaca* 'Fairy Tales Cinderella.'

PORTULACA GRANDIFLORA HOOK. AND *P. OLERACEA* L.

Common names: moss rose (*P. grandiflora*), purslane (*P. oleracea*).

Family: Portulacaceae.

Description/uses: This low-growing, annual, succulent plant produces numerous 1- to 2.5-in. (2.5- to 6-cm)-wide flowers. The single or double flowers are available in a broad range of colors including white, pink, rose, red, orange, yellow, and bicolors (Fig. III-7 Bedding Plants). *P. grandiflora* has narrow leaves and is seed propagated. *P. oleracea* has rounded leaves and is primarily cutting propagated. Neither species is frost tolerant and both are sold in the spring in packs, pots, and hanging baskets.

Temperature: Grow plants at 65 to 68°F (18 to 20°C).

Height control: None is usually required for this low-growing plant. However, sprays of A-Rest (7 to 26 ppm) or Sumagic (15 to 30 ppm) are effective.

Schedule and timing: Seed-propagated plants will flower in the pack in 12 to 13 weeks in cool climates and in 8 to 9 weeks in warm climates, 4-in. (10-cm) pots in 13 to 14 weeks, and 10-in. (25-cm) hanging baskets in 13 to 14 weeks. In the spring cutting-propagated, 4-in. (10-cm) pots will be ready in 5 to 6 weeks, 6-in. (15-cm) pots in 6 to 7 weeks, 8-in. (20-cm) baskets in 8 to 10 weeks, and 10-in. (25-cm) baskets in 10 to 12 weeks. The crop will finish 1 to 2 weeks earlier in the summer. One plant is used per 4-in. (10-cm)

pot, two per 6-in. (15-cm) pot, and three to five per 8- to 10-in. (20- to 25-cm) hanging basket. Portulaca is day neutral.

Comments: Flowers close at night and during cloudy and rainy weather. Newer cultivars are more likely to stay open during cloudy weather.

SALPIGLOSSIS SINUATA RUÍZ. & PAV.

Common name: painted tongue.

Family: Solanaceae.

Description/uses: The open, bell-shaped flowers are available in many colors including red, yellow, orange, rose, and purple. Petal veins are often darker than the surrounding petal color and the throat may be yellow. The plants are not frost tolerant and are sold in the spring in packs or pots. Plants do not tolerate warm night temperatures and consequently perform best in cool climates. These annuals are seed propagated.

Temperature: Grow plants at 50 to 55°F (10 to 13°C).

Height control: Growth retardants may be required.

Schedule and timing: Green plants will be ready in the pack in 8 to 10 weeks and 4- to 5-in. (10- to 13-cm) pots in 16 to 18 weeks.

Comments: Foliage can be sticky.

SALVIA COCCINEA JUSS. EX MURRAY., S. FARINACEA BENTH., AND S. SPLENDENS SELL EX ROEM. & SCHULT.

Common names: salvia, mealy sage (*S. farinacea*), scarlet sage (*S. spendens*).

Family: Labiatae.

Description/uses: *S. splendens* has short, thick spikes of white, pink, red, purple, salmon, or bicolor flowers (Fig. III-8 Bedding Plants). *S. coccinea* has long, open spikes of white to red flowers. *S. farinacea* has long, narrow white, blue, or purple spikes. These seed-propagated annuals or tender perennials are not frost tolerant and are sold in the spring in packs and pots. Dwarf types are sold in flower in the pack and taller types are sold green in the pack.

Temperature: Grow at 70 to 75/55 to 60°F (21 to 24/13 to 15°C) day/night temperatures.

Height control: Sprays of A-Rest (10 to 26 ppm), Bonzi (5 to 60 ppm), B-Nine (2500 to

FIGURE III-8 BEDDING PLANTS *Salvia splendens* 'Vista Red.'

5000 ppm), Cycocel (800 to 1500 ppm), Sumagic (20 to 30 ppm), or Topflor (20 to 80 ppm) are effective.

Schedule and timing: *S. coccinea* and *S. splendens* plants will flower in the pack in 7 to 8 weeks. Green plants will be ready in 7 to 9 weeks and 4-in. (10-cm) pots in 11 to 13 weeks. *S. farinacea* will be ready in green packs in 8 to 9 weeks and in 4-in. (10-cm) pots in 14 to 16 weeks. Photoperiod response varies greatly with some cultivars being day neutral; others are short-day or long-day plants. Generally, photoperiod is not controlled during production.

Comments: Leaf drop occurs with stress. Avoid high medium EC. Avoid holding too long in the plug flat or plant may not root out well after transplanting. White-flowered *S. splendens* cultivars tend to readily show brown edges on the petals. Salvias are ethylene sensitive and exposure will result in flower drop. Many other salvia species are cultivated as garden perennials and cut flowers. See *Field-Grown Cut Flowers* Chapter.

SANVITALIA PROCUMBENS LAM.

Common name: sanvitalia.

Family: Compositae.

Description/uses: The small 0.5- to 0.75-in. (1.3- to 2.0-cm)-wide, orange daisy-like flowers have dark brown centers and are produced on 8- to 14-in. (20- to 36-cm)-tall plants. This annual plant is not frost tolerant and is sold in the spring in packs, pots, or hanging baskets. Plants tolerate heat and drought stress in the landscape. Both seed and cutting-propagated cultivars are available.

Temperature: Grow plants at 70 to 78/60 to 62°F (21 to 26/15 to 17°C) day/night temperatures.

Height control: Generally not required but B-Nine sprays (2500 to 3000 ppm) are effective.

Schedule and timing: Seed-propagated plants will flower in the pack in 8 to 9 weeks and 4-in. (10-cm) pots in 11 to 13 weeks. Seed-propagated plants will flower in 4-in. (10-cm) pots in 13 to 15 weeks. Cutting-propagated plants in 4-in. (10-cm) pots are ready to sell in 6 to 8 weeks, 6-in. (15-cm) pots are ready in 7 to 10 weeks, and 10-in. (25-cm) baskets in 9 to 12 weeks. Use one plant per 4-in. (10-cm) pot, two to three plants per 6-in. (15-cm) pot, and four to five plants per 10-in. (25-cm) basket. Pinching can be useful to maintain shape.

Comments: If grown cooler than indicated, root rots will be more prevalent.

SCAEVOLA AEMULA R. BR.

Common names: scaevola, fan flower.

Family: Goodeniaceae.

Description/uses: This trailing plant has short terminal spikes of white, blue, or purple flowers. The cutting-propagated plants are not frost tolerant and are sold in the spring in packs (rarely), pots, or hanging baskets.

Temperature: Grow at 75 to 80/60 to 65°F (24 to 27/16 to 18°C) day/night temperatures. Plants grow best in warm temperatures; do not start plants in the greenhouse too early in the spring because they will grow slowly until the weather warms up.

Height control: None is usually required. Bonzi drenches at 1 to 3 ppm or sprays at 20 to 40 ppm are effective. Sumagic drenches at 0.125 ppm or sprays at 30 ppm can be used. Florel sprays at 500 ppm are effective at increasing branching and may replace pinching.

Schedule and timing: Plants in 4-in. (10-cm) pots will be marketable in 8 to 9 weeks in the winter and 5 to 6 weeks in the spring; 6-in. (15-cm) pots will finish in 12 to 14 weeks in the winter and 8 to 10 weeks in the spring; 10-in. (25-cm) hanging baskets will finish in 15 to 16 weeks in the winter and 12 to

14 weeks in the spring. Plants should be pinched once. Plants are day neutral.

Comments: Excessive vegetative growth can result from excessive nitrogen, low light levels, wet medium, and overfertilization under light that is too low. Plant growth will slow significantly if grown at lower than the indicated temperatures.

SCHIZANTHUS ×WISETONENSIS HORT.

Common name: poor-man's-orchid.

Family: Solanaceae.

Description/uses: This seed-propagated annual produces numerous open, bell-shaped flowers on long spikes. The flowers are white, pink, rose, or violet with yellow throats. The plants grow 8 to 12 in. (20 to 30 cm) tall. Plants are not frost tolerant and are sold in the spring in packs and pots.

Temperature: Grow plants at 50°F (10°C).

Height control: None is usually required but A-Rest, B-Nine, Bonzi, and Sumagic are effective.

Schedule and timing: Green plants will be ready in packs in 6 to 7 weeks and 4-in. (10-cm) pots in 9 to 10 weeks.

Comments: Although beautiful, schizanthus does not tolerate heat well, which limits its use to mild climates.

SENECIO CINERARIA DC (FORMERLY KNOWN AS CINERARIA MARITIMA)

Common names: dusty miller. *Tanacetum ptarmiciflorum* is also known as dusty miller.

Family: Compositae.

Description/uses: This seed-propagated annual/biennial is grown in packs for its silvery foliage. Relatively few cultivars are available. 'Silver Dust' has deeply notched silvery foliage and grows 8 to 12 in. (20 to 30 cm) tall. 'Cirrus' and 'Silver Cloud' have less deeply notched, less gray foliage than 'Silver Dust' and grow 8 to 10 in. (20 to 25 cm) tall. 'Diamond' is similar to 'Silver Dust' but is taller, up to 15 in. (38 cm), and is less silvery.

Temperature: Grow at 70/60 to 65°F (21/15 to 18°C) day/night temperatures.

Height control: Sprays of B-Nine (2500 to 5000 ppm) or Sumagic (30 ppm) are effective.

Schedule and timing: Plants will be ready to sell in the pack in 11 to 12 weeks and 4-in. (10-cm) pots in 14 to 16 weeks.

Comments: Plants are moderately cold hardy and may survive the winter in mild climates and flower the following summer.

SOLANUM MELONGENA L.

Common name: eggplant.

Family: Solanaceae.

Description/uses: This seed-propagated annual vegetable is grown for its large white to purple fruits that hang down. The fruit varies in shape from large and round to small egg shaped to elongated. Plants grow up to 36 in. (90 cm) tall. Plants are not frost tolerant and are sold in packs in the spring.

Temperature: Grow at 60 to 62°F (16 to 17°C).

Height control: No chemical growth retardants can be used on this edible vegetable.

Schedule and timing: Plants will be ready for sale in 6 to 8 weeks in packs and in 8 to 9 weeks in 4-in. (10-cm) pots.

SOLENOSTEMON SCUTELLARIOIDES (L.) CODD. (FORMERLY COLEUS SCUTELLARIOIDES)

Common names: coleus, painted nettle.

Family: Labiatae.

Description/uses: This tender perennial is grown for its colorful foliage. Many cultivars are available in a broad range of color combinations, leaf shapes, and heights. Vegetatively-propagated "sun" coleus are more tolerant of high temperatures and high light and are slower to flower than seed-propagated cultivars. Plants are not frost tolerant and are sold in the spring in packs, pots, and hanging baskets.

Temperature: Grow at 75 to 85/60 to 75°F (24 to 29/16 to 24°C) day/night temperatures.

Height control: This fast-growing plant may need a plant growth regulator to maintain shape. Sprays of Bonzi (5 to 45 ppm), B-Nine (2500 to 5000 ppm), Cycocel (400 to 3000 ppm), Sumagic (10 or 20 ppm), or Topflor (20 to 40 ppm) are effective. A tank mix spray of B-Nine at 2500 to 4000 ppm + Cycocel at 1000 to 1500 ppm can also be used.

Schedule and timing: Seed-propagated plants will be colored and ready to sell in the pack in 9 to 12 weeks; 4-in. (10-cm) pots will be ready in 12 to 13 weeks, and 10-in. (25-cm) hanging baskets in 14 to 16 weeks. In the spring cutting-propagated, 4-in. (10-cm) pots will be ready in 4 to 5 weeks, 6-in. (15-

cm) pots in 5 to 6 weeks, 8-in. (20-cm) pots in 5 to 6 weeks, and 10-in. (25-cm) pots in 8 to 9 weeks. The crop will finish 1 to 2 weeks earlier in the summer. One plant is used per 4- to 6-in. (10- to 15-cm) pot and three to four per 8- to 10-in. (20- to 25-cm) pot. Plants should be pinched 2 weeks after transplanting when grown in containers 6 in. (15 cm) or larger. Flowering is accelerated by short days.

Comments: Foliage color varies with the light level in the landscape. Frequent deadheading is required of seed-propagated coleus in the landscape.

STROBILANTHES DYERIANUS MAST.

Common name: persian shield.

Family: Acanathaceae.

Description/uses: This tender perennial shrub is grown for its large, striking purple, silver, and green leaves. Plants grow up to 4 ft (1.2 m) tall. Plants are typically grown in containers but occasionally in packs. Spikes of small flowers occur but are not desirable.

Temperature: Grow at 75 to 80/60 to 65°F (24 to 27/16 to 18°C) day/night temperatures.

Height control: None is generally required.

Schedule and timing: Plants in 6-in. (15-cm) pots are ready to sell in 8 to 10 weeks and 10-in. (15-cm) pots are ready in 10 to 13 weeks. Use one or two plants per 6-in. (15-cm) pot and three to five plants per 10-in. (25-cm) pot. One or more pinches may be required.

Comments: Brightest color is obtained with moderate light of 3000 to 6000 fc (600 to 1200 μmol $\cdot$ m^{-2} $\cdot$ s^{-1}).

SUTERA CORDATA ROTH. AND JAMESBRITTENIA HYBRIDS KUNTZE

Common name: bacopa.

Family: Schrophulariaceae.

Description/uses: Tender procumbent perennial grown in pots or hanging baskets with small white to lavender or scarlet flowers. The plants are frost tolerant and are sold in the spring.

Temperature: Grow *Sutera* types at 65 to 75/55 to 60°F (18 to 24/13 to 16°C) day/night temperatures, but grow *Jamesbrittenia* types 5°F (3°C) warmer.

Height control: None required, but may be pinched once established in final containers.

Schedule and timing: Four-inch (10-cm) pots require 7 to 9 weeks in the winter and 5 to 6 weeks in the spring starting with a rooted plug. A 10-in. (20-cm) basket will require 10 to 12 weeks in the winter and 7 to 9 weeks in the spring starting from a rooted plug. *Sutera* is a day-neutral plant that flowers more profusely as the light intensity increases.

Comments: Foliar chlorosis from insufficient iron can occur if the media pH is too high. Inadequate flowering results from too much nitrogen or from overwatering or overfertilization under low light levels.

TANACETUM PTARMICIFLORUM (WEBB & BERTH.) SCHULTZ-BIP (FORMERLY KNOWN AS CHRYSANTHEMUM PTARMICIFLORUM)

Common name: dusty miller.

Family: Compositae.

Description/uses: Seed-propagated annual/biennial grown in packs for its woolly silvery white foliage. Relatively few cultivars are available. 'Silver Lace' has deeply notched foliage and grows 8 to 10 in. (20 to 25 cm) tall.

Temperature: Grow at 65°F (18°C) night temperatures.

Height control: Generally not required due to naturally short growth habit. If required, B-Nine and Cycocel are effective.

Schedule and timing: Plants will be ready for sale in 13 to 14 weeks in the pack and in 16 weeks in 4-in. (10-cm) pots.

Comments: Plants are moderately cold hardy and may survive the winter in mild climates and flower the following summer.

THUNBERGIA ALATA BOJER.

Common name: black-eyed susan vine.

Family: Acanthaceae.

Description/uses: This tender perennial vine has tubular flowers with white, yellow, or orange petals and a throat color ranging from light to dark brown. Plants are not frost tolerant and are sold in the spring in pots or hanging baskets. Both seed and cutting-propagated cultivars are available.

Temperature: Grow plants at 70 to 80/60 to 65°F (21 to 27/16 to 18°C) day/night temperatures. Growth will be greatly slowed if grown cooler than indicated.

Height control: None is usually required on this vine.

Schedule and timing: Seed-propagated plants will be ready in 4-in. (10-cm) pots in 8 to 9 weeks and 10-in. (25-cm) hanging baskets in 10 to 11 weeks. Seed-propagated plants will flower in 4-in. (10-cm) pots in 13 to 15 weeks. Cutting-propagated plants in 4-in. (10-cm) pots are ready to sell in 7 to 8 weeks, 6-in. (15-cm) pots are ready in 8 to 11 weeks, and 10-in. (25-cm) baskets in 10 to 12 weeks. Use one plant per 4-in. (10-cm) pot, two to three plants per 6-in. (15-cm) pot, and three to five plants per 10-in. (25-cm) basket.

Comments: Plants will stop flowering during high temperatures.

TORENIA FOURNIERI LIND. EX. FOURN.

Common names: wishbone flower, bluewings.

Family: Scrophulariaceae.

Description/uses: This plant has interesting multicolored, slightly tubular flowers with white to lavender throats edged in pink, rose, blue, or purple and a spot of yellow on the lower petal. The plants grow 6 to 8 in. (15 to 20 cm) tall. The plants are not frost tolerant and are sold in the spring in packs or pots. Both seed and cutting-propagated cultivars are available.

Temperature: Grow plants at 55 to 60°F (13 to 16°C).

Height control: None is usually required, but Bonzi is effective.

Schedule and timing: Seed-propagated plants will flower in the pack in 10 to 11 weeks and 4-in. (10-cm) pots in 13 to 15 weeks. Cutting-propagated plants in 4-in. (10-cm) pots are ready to sell in 5 to 7 weeks and 10-in. (25-cm) baskets in 8 to 12 weeks. Use one plant per 4-in. (10-cm) pot and four to five plants per 10-in. (25-cm) basket. One pinch at planting will increase branching.

Comments: Do not use Florel (ethephon) on this species. Many cultivars are not heat tolerant but newer cultivars are better suited to warm climates.

TROPAEOLUM MAJUS L.

Common name: nasturtium.

Family: Tropaeolaceae.

Description/uses: This annual ornamental is grown in packs and hanging baskets. Cultivars vary in growth habit (dwarf shrubby to viney), flower color (cream, yellow, orange, red, pink), foliage color (green, blue tinted,

variegated), and flower style (single, double). Plants are not frost tolerant and are sold in the spring. Both seed and cutting-propagated cultivars are available.

Temperature: Grow plants at 65 to 68°F (18 to 20°C).

Height control: No height control is normally required, nor should chemical growth retardants be used because the flowers are edible. For nonedible plants, Cycocel sprays (800 to 1500 ppm) are effective.

Schedule and timing: Plants will flower in the pack in 8 to 9 weeks, 4-in. (10-cm) pots in 9 to 10 weeks, and 10-in. (25-cm) hanging baskets in 10 to 11 weeks.

Comments: The flowers and leaves are edible with a peppery taste.

VERBENA ×HYBRIDA GROENL. & RUEMPL. AND V. TENERA SPRENG.

Common names: common garden verbena, florists' verbena.

Family: Verbenaceae.

Description/uses: This low-growing plant has rounded clusters of small, tubular white, pink, rose, red, lavender, or apricot-colored flowers. Flowers of some cultivars have a white eye. Plants grow 8 to 12 in. (20 to 30 cm) tall and vary in habit from rather upright to trailing. V. ×hybrida is seed propagated and V. tenera is cutting propagated. V. ×hybrida is a tender perennial and is not frost tolerant, whereas V. tenera is hardier and may overwinter. Both species are sold in the spring in packs, pots, and hanging baskets.

Temperature: Grow V. ×hybrida plants at 55 to 60°F (13 to 16°C) and V. tenera plants at 62 to 65°F (17 to 18°C) night temperatures and 70 to 80°F (21 to 27°C) day temperatures.

Height control: Sprays of Bonzi (5 to 30 ppm), B-Nine (2500 to 5000 ppm), Cycocel (800 to 1500 ppm), or Sumagic (15 to 30 ppm) are effective on V. ×hybrida. Florel sprays (500 ppm) can be used on V. tenera to increase the number of axillary shoots. A tank mix spray of B-Nine at 2500 to 3500 ppm + Cycocel at 750 to 1000 ppm can be used on V. tenera.

Schedule and timing: Seed-propagated plants will flower in the pack in 12 to 13 weeks. Generally 4-in. (10-cm) pots will be ready in 14 to 15 weeks and 10-in. (25-cm) hanging baskets in 16 to 18 weeks. In the spring cutting-propagated, 4-in. (10-cm) pots will be ready in 5 to 6 weeks, 6-in. (15-cm) pots in 6 to

7 weeks, 8-in. (20-cm) baskets in 8 to 10 weeks, and 10-in. (25-cm) baskets in 10 to 12 weeks. The crop will finish 1 to 2 weeks earlier in the summer. One plant is used per 4-in. (10-cm) pot, two per 6-in. (15-cm) pot, and three to five per 8- to 10-in. (20- to 25-cm) hanging basket. Plants should be pinched when grown in containers 6 in. (15 cm) or larger. The first pinch is made when four to six pairs of leaves can remain and subsequent pinches are made when four leaf pairs can remain. Verbena are day neutral.

Comments: *V. ×hybrida* seed tends to be difficult to germinate.

KEY POINTS

- Bedding plants include
  1. Flat-grown (packs) plants, which are primarily annual and tender perennial ornamentals and vegetables
  2. Pot-grown plants, which encompass annual, tender perennial, and perennial ornamentals and vegetables
  3. Hanging baskets, which are generally limited to annual and tender perennial ornamentals.

- Bedding plants are used in landscape plantings, vegetable and flower gardens, and in outdoor-grown hanging baskets, large pots, and other containers.
- Bedding plants can also be differentiated on the type of weather conditions under which they grow best: warm season or cool season.
- Hundreds of plant species can be classified as bedding plants with more released each year.

BIBLIOGRAPHY

Ball, V., editor. 1998. *Ball RedBook,* 16th ed. Ball Publishing, Batavia, Illinois.

Gaston, M.L., L.A. Kunkle, P.S. Konjoian, and M.F. Wilt, editors. 2001. *Tips on Regulating Growth of Floriculture Crops,* Ohio Florists' Association Services, Columbus, Ohio.

Hamrick, D. 2003. *Ball Redbook,* vol. 2, 17th ed. Ball Publishing, Batavia, Illinois.

Huxley, A., M. Griffiths, and M. Levy. 1992. *The New Royal Horticultural Society Dictionary of Gardening,* vols. 1–4. Stockton Press, New York.

Nau, J. 1993. *Ball Culture Guide, The Encyclopedia of Seed Germination,* 2nd ed. Ball Publishing, Batavia, Illinois.

Whipker, B.E. 2003. Growth regulators for floricultural crops, pp. 439–448 in *2003 North Carolina Agricultural Chemicals Manual.* College of Agriculture and Life Science, North Carolina State University, Raleigh.

Field-Grown Cut Flowers

INTRODUCTION

Commercial field-grown cut flower production encompasses an incredible array of plant materials including both fresh and dried/preserved flowers, foliage, stems, and berries. A large portion of fresh and dried cuts in North America are grown outdoors. Cuts are marketed through a variety of channels, some of which are seasonal and others are year-round. Proper selection of plant materials can allow year-round production, although harvests will be limited during the winter temperate climates. The harvest season starts with woody trees, shrubs, vines, and bulbs flowering in the early spring. Perennials and biennials begin flowering midspring in warm climates and late spring in cold climates. Annuals constitute the majority of production during the summer, supplemented with perennials and woody plants. By fall, production from annuals is decreasing, a few fall perennials are flowering, and woody plants with berries or other decorative fruits can be harvested. Woody plants with evergreen foliage or colorful stems are harvested during the winter.

Marketing channels: Due to the highly perishable nature of their product, fresh cut flower growers must develop an intensive marketing strategy. Local, niche markets are often the best choice for small growers. Niche markets include local retail florists, specialty supermarkets, or other retailers. Fifty years ago, florists grew their own product, so there was a greater variety of flowers. This is no longer the case and now florists are clamoring for fresh, hard-to-find, hard-to-ship items (L. Greer, personal communication).

Although direct marketing to consumers can offer the benefit of higher prices, this strategy requires additional time and expense. The range of possibilities for direct marketing includes farmers markets, bucket shops, pick-your-own, and subscription selling. Of these, the farmers markets option is probably the most common marketing channel.

Wholesale markets require larger volumes of flowers and growers receive lower prices per stem. The greatest benefit of wholesale is that a grower has an established market for the product and little time is spent finding individual customers. Few small to medium-sized growers sell exclusively to wholesalers, however, because of the low prices received. Growers thinking of selling to a wholesaler should visit them to see what kinds of products they offer to their customers. Because wholesalers do most of their business in the morning, they will have more time for talking with growers in the afternoon. One important point to clarify with wholesalers is transport: Will the wholesaler pick up flowers from your door, will you deliver to his door, or will you ship?

Growers may find it advantageous to develop a mixture of marketing avenues. For instance, a grower may decide to sell fresh cut flowers to retail or wholesale florists and at the farmers market. This way, growers could sell, for instance, long stems to florists and shorter stems to buyers at the farmers market. Selling at the farmers market would also increase short-term cash flow, because wholesalers usually pay their accounts only once a month.

Growers may choose to dry their crops when prices for fresh cuts fall. Drying flowers requires extra labor and storage space. These costs should be factored into the decision of whether or not it is advantageous to dry the flowers. However, dried flowers are not as perishable as fresh. Remember to make the decision to dry a crop before it is harvested—low-quality, old flowers that remain unsold from the fresh market will result in low-quality dried flowers as well. In addition, some dried flowers are harvested at different stages than when they are harvested for fresh use. For example, monarda (*Monarda*) is harvested fresh when one ring of florets has opened for maximum vase life and harvested almost fully open when drying for maximum color.

Site selection: The best locations for cut flower production are sunny and relatively flat with well-drained soil. The site should be accessible at all times, even after a heavy rainstorm, because flowers need to be harvested regardless of the weather. On the other hand, the site should have water for irrigation and postharvest requirements. Although air movement is necessary to prevent or reduce disease problems, the site should also be protected from excessive winds, which can damage the plants and flowers (see also Greenhouse Construction and Operations chapter).

Production systems: Production can be in rows spaced far enough apart for a tractor or rototiller to pass between the rows. The row system is limited to specific crops because of the difficulty of supporting the crops and of the high potential for soil and other debris to be splashed on the foliage and flowers. Consequently, most field cut production occurs in 2.5- to 4-ft (75- to 120-cm)-wide beds with two or more rows of plants within each bed. The beds should not be too wide because of the difficulty of reaching into the center during harvest. The beds are often raised 2 to 8 in. (5 to 20 cm) high to encourage drainage and allow quick drying after a rain. Beds can be mulched before planting with plastic or landscape fabric or after planting with organic materials to reduce weeds and water loss. Plastic mulch can also be used to increase soil temperature. Support can be provided by means of a plastic or wire mesh stretched between posts, usually metal T posts, spaced in pairs every 20 to 30 ft (6 to 9 m) down the bed.

The aisles should be wide enough to allow people and equipment to move between the beds without damaging the plants, which tend to grow and lean out into the aisles. If there is sufficient land, the aisles can be made wide enough to allow a small vehicle to enter, which would decrease the labor associated with carrying harvested flowers.

Soil preparation: The soil should be amended with fertilizers and organic matter prior to planting. A soil test should be collected and submitted to a lab for analysis. A local cooperative extension service office may be able to provide information on collecting and sending in soil samples. Based on the soil test results, the soil pH may need to be raised with lime or lowered with sulfur (Table III-1 Field-Grown Cut Flowers). Most crop species grow well when the soil pH is between 6.2 and 6.8, with optimum at 6.6 to 6.8. Nutrients may need to be added to raise the nutrient level up to the desired rate (Table III-2 Field-Grown Cut Flowers). Soil tests should be taken at least annually because soil pH and fertility can vary greatly between years. Inadequate nutrition will reduce yields and quality. However, excessive fertilization wastes fertilizer, may pollute the ground or surface water, and can damage plants.

Supplemental fertilizers, either organic or inorganic, may be needed later in the production season, especially in the warm climates where the growing season can be 6 months to a

TABLE III-1 FIELD-GROWN CUT FLOWERS
Rates of limestone and sulfur for altering soil pH.

Existing Soil pH	Sandy Soils		Loam Soils		Clay Soils	
	To pH 6.0	To pH 6.5	To pH 6.0	To pH 6.5	To pH 6.0	To pH 6.5
	Pounds of Limestone/100 ft^2 (kg/100 m^2) Needed to Raise Soil pH					
6.0	0.0	2.0 (10)	0.0	4.0 (20)	0.0	5.0 (10)
5.5	2.0 (10)	4.0 (20)	4.0 (20)	7.0 (35)	5.0 (25)	10.0 (20)
5.0	4.0 (20)	6.0 (30)	7.0 (35)	11.0 (55)	10.0 (50)	15.0 (75)
4.8	4.5 (22)	7.0 (35)	8.0 (40)	12.0 (60)	12.0 (60)	17.0 (85)
	Pounds of Sulfur/100 ft^2 (kg/100 m^2) Needed to Lower Soil pH					
7.5	—	1.0–1.5 (5.0–7.5)	—	1.5–2.0 (7.5–10.0)	—	2.0–2.5 (10.0–12.5)
8.0	—	2.5–3.0 (12.5–15.0)	—	3.0–4.0 (15.0–20.0)	—	4.0–5.0 (20.0–25.0)
8.5	—	4.0–5.0 (20.0–25.0)	—	5.0–6.0 (25.0–30.0)	—	6.0–7.5 (30.0–37.5)
9.0	—	5.0–7.5 (25.0–37.5)	—	—	—	—

TABLE III-2 FIELD-GROWN CUT FLOWERS
Soil test interpretation for nitrogen, phosphorus, and potassium.

Nutrient	Level in Soil	Ranking
Nitrogen	0–25 ppm	Low
	26–50 ppm	Medium
	51–80 ppm	High
Phosphorus	0–50 lb/acre (0–56 kg · ha^{-1})	Low
	51–200 lb/acre (57–225 kg · ha^{-1})	Medium
	201+ lb/acre (226+ kg · ha^{-1})	High
Potassium	0–250 lb/acre (0–280 kg · ha^{-1})	Low
	251–500 lb/acre (281–560 kg · ha^{-1})	Medium
	501+ lb/acre (561+ kg · ha^{-1})	High

year long. Supplemental fertilizers can be applied dry or as water-soluble fertilizers dissolved in water and applied through the irrigation system (fertigation). Generally, fertigation is less labor intensive once the fertilizer injector is incorporated into the irrigation system.

Unless your soil is the perfect sandy-loam, organic amendments will probably be needed. The addition of organic matter can correct many problems. It can increase the aeration and drainage of heavy clay soils or increase the nutrient and water retention of sandy soils. A variety of different sources of organic matter can be added including compost, cover crops, manures, straw, hay, silage, and wood chips. Organic matter can be applied in the fall after the fields are cleared, in the spring prior to planting, or as a mulch during production to also reduce weeds and water loss.

Manures may need to be composted or aged prior to application or applied several weeks prior to planting. Straw, hay, and wood chips may also need to be composted prior to use because they can temporarily deplete the soil of nitrogen as they decompose. If applied directly, additional nitrogen may be needed. Also, be sure that all organic matter is weed free. If you accidentally introduce one or more weed species to the farm, you may be fighting them for years.

Cover crops provide a relatively easy method to introduce large amounts of organic matter to soil. Cover crops can be planted in the fall after the annuals have been removed or in the spring after the winter annuals/biennials such as larkspur (*Consolida*) have been harvested. Cover crops can and should be planted on any areas that will remain unplanted for 4 or more weeks. The alternative is to allow the area to grow up in weeds, which will make weed con-

trol more difficult when the area is later planted. Aisles can also be planted to a low cover crop to reduce weeds. A number of legume cover crops, such as alfalfa (*Medicago sativa*), cowpeas (*Vigna unguiculata*), crimson clover (*Trifolium incarnatum*), hairy vetch (*Vicia villosa*), and Austrian winter peas (*Lathyrus hirsutus*), fix nitrogen, which is added to the soil when the cover crop is incorporated into the soil. The use of cover crops will also help break the long-term weed reproductive cycle and help retain nutrients in the short term.

Field establishment: New field plantings can be established by a variety of methods. Direct seeding can be used with species that germinate and grow rapidly. Plants with large seeds, such as sunflowers (*Helianthus*) and zinnias (*Zinnia*), do well when direct sown. Some species, such as larkspur and ammi (*Ammi*), do not transplant well and are best direct sown.

Many growers use transplants such as plugs or cell packs to establish their plantings. Transplants can be purchased ready to plant from suppliers or can be grown on site. Purchased transplants reduce the hassle of propagating your own plants, which can be especially important with some difficult-to-propagate species, such as lisianthus (*Eustoma*). However, a limited number of species, cultivars, and colors may be available and delivery is not always when the plants are needed. Transplants can be grown or purchased in a variety of plug or cell pack sizes. Small plug sizes are generally less expensive but may need to be irrigated frequently after planting in the field until they are established. In addition, small plugs will easily outgrow the flat if not planted promptly and can be difficult to irrigate properly in the greenhouse. Larger plugs are usually more expensive but establish in the field more easily and can be held in the greenhouse longer before they need to be planted. An alternative is to buy small plugs, transplant them to large cell packs, and plant in the field several weeks later.

Perennials can be established by means of transplants, divisions, or rooted cuttings. Dormant divisions can be planted soon after arrival from the supplier or held in a cooler or cool location until they can be planted. Nondormant divisions and rooted cuttings should be planted as soon as possible. Some species, such as peony (*Paeonia*), produce the greatest number of long stems when left undisturbed for many years, while other species, such as yarrow (*Achillea*), produce the best stems when divided every 2 to 4 years. Dig, divide, and replant a portion of the crop every year to make sure that your beds are always producing a high-quality crop.

A variety of species originate from bulbs, corms, tubers, or tuberous roots that can be planted. Some species are not cold hardy and the bulbs must be dug each fall and stored in a cool location over the winter until replanted in the spring, such as dahlia (*Dahlia*) or glads (*Gladiolus*) in cold climates. Other geophytic species, such as crocosmia (*Crocosmia*), can remain in the ground and be handled as for other perennials.

Although not usually cost effective, potted perennials, shrubs, vines, and trees can be purchased. A few large-sized plants can be purchased to test the species and, if successful, larger numbers of plugs, divisions, or rooted cuttings can then be purchased or propagated.

Plant spacing: Optimum plant spacing varies greatly from species to species. Plants that become large are usually planted in two rows per bed, occasionally with plants staggered, while smaller, single-harvest annuals such as plume celosia (*Celosia*) may be spaced only 4 to 6 in. (10 to 15 cm) apart with up 10 rows across a 4-ft (120-cm) bed. Generally, close spacing increases yield and profit per square foot (square meter) of bed space but decreases yield per plant and air circulation. Thus, if initial plant costs are high, a wide spacing may maximize the number of harvestable stems per plant. In addition, wide spacing increases air circulation and may prevent or reduce diseases. For some species close spacing can increase stem length, which may be particularly important with species that tend to be too short. However, close spacing does not increase stem length for all species. If the species forms a solid canopy of leaves, such as with zinnias, it is likely to respond to close spacing by growing taller. Plants such as grasses, which have an open canopy that allows light to penetrate to the crown, usually do not grow tall when spaced closer together.

Annuals are generally spaced anywhere from 4 × 4 to 18 × 18 in. (10 × 10 to 45 × 45 cm) apart. Perennial spacing ranges from 12 × 12 to 24 × 24 in. (30 × 30 to 60 × 60 cm) and woody shrubs and trees are spaced 2 to 6 ft (0.8 × 1.8 m) apart. Remember most trees, shrubs, and vines are harvested heavily enough to keep the final plant size small.

Irrigation: Cut flowers are a high-value crop and irrigation will probably be necessary, regardless of the climate. Of course, irrigation of newly planted seed beds or transplants is critical. Irrigation systems are relatively inexpensive and pay for themselves in reduced labor and increased yields and quality within a few months to a couple years. Generally, the preferred irrigation system is drip tapes. After planting, irrigation drip tapes can be laid; one to three tapes per bed are used depending on the soil type and the water requirements of the crop. With row production, one drip tape can be used per row or double row (two rows closely spaced together). Hand irrigation with a hose and nozzle is time consuming and results in high labor costs, but may be necessary for the first irrigation after planting to ensure that young plants with their small root systems receive adequate water. Overhead sprinkler irrigation is cost effective but is generally limited to when the plants are young. Overhead irrigation later in the season may splash soil on the foliage and flowers, cause lodging, and increase disease problems. Your local irrigation supplier or cooperative extension office may be able to assist in designing an effective and inexpensive irrigation system.

Weed control: Weed control is often the most time-consuming and labor-intensive component of field production. Large numbers of weeds in the production area will reduce flower quality and quantity and increase the harvesting time and cost. Weeds also make insect and disease control more difficult, increase irrigation requirements, and, of course, provide seeds for the next generation of weeds later in the season. A variety of methods are available for controlling weeds and the typical farm will use many of them.

Timing. Regardless of the weed control method, timing of the field preparation is important relative to when the foliage canopy closes. In other words, when the bed or row is covered with foliage, the light reaching the soil is reduced and weed seed germination and growth slow. If using manual weeding or cultivation, it is important for the last cultivation to occur as close to planting as possible. If the field is prepared too early in advance of planting, the weeds will begin germinating and growing quickly. Thus, you will need to begin cultivation soon after planting. However, if the crop is planted immediately after preparing the soil, then the plants will begin to grow and develop a canopy, reducing the number of times cultivation is required. The first cultivation will generally be about 10 days after transplanting or germination of direct-sown crops. Often there is not enough time to prepare a field and plant immediately. One solution to this problem is to use the stale bed method: Prepare a large area when convenient, allow weeds to sprout, and kill them immediately before planting. In this case, flame weeding (see below), herbicides (see next column), and light cultivation can be used. Do not cultivate too deeply because that might bring up new weed seeds that can germinate.

Hand weeding. Manual weeding by hand or by hoe is the age-old method of weed control. It is effective but time consuming and expensive in terms of labor costs. A small amount of manual weeding will be required in any operation such as at the end of rows or around the base of plants growing in plastic or landscape fabric. However, other methods of weed control should be used wherever possible. Regardless, a variety of hoes are available that can effectively cut and remove weeds without disturbing the roots of the cut flowers.

Mechanical cultivation. Mechanical cultivation can range from a walk-behind rototiller to a tractor-mounted cultivator. Mechanical cultivation can be used to cultivate the aisles between beds or rows of crops. The aisles must be wide enough to allow the equipment to pass without damaging plants and prevent the cultivator from being close enough to the crop roots to damage them. In addition, within rows mechanical cultivation must be done before the crop is too tall to allow the tractor to pass over the crop.

Flame weeding. With flame weeding a handheld or tractor-mounted propane burner emits a flame that is passed over the weeds. The weeds die from being seared with the high temperatures, not by being burned. Very young weed seedlings and broad-leaved weeds are easiest to kill with flame weeding. Flame weeding can be especially useful with direct seeding because the weed seedlings generally emerge first and the area can be flame-weeded prior to

emergence of the cut flower seedlings. Effective flame weeding requires an experienced operator but can be efficient and cost effective.

Herbicides. Herbicides are available in two types: (1) Preemergent herbicides kill weed seedlings as they germinate through the soil. (2) Postemergent herbicides are sprayed on the weeds and kill either the portion of the weed in direct *contact* with the herbicide or are *systemically* taken up and moved through the plant, killing the entire weed. Systemic postemergent herbicides are especially useful for controlling perennial weeds and those with underground rhizomes or storage organs. As with all chemicals, herbicides should be applied carefully so as to not poison the person applying the chemical or injure the cut flowers.

Fall and winter preparation: In the fall remove dead annuals and fallen plant material. Prune out diseased portions of perennials and woody plants. Do not cut back perennials until winter when the aboveground portions are completely dead. In the fall mulch tender perennials if necessary to protect against the cold. Mulch can also help retain soil moisture and provide organic matter. If fall and winter are dry, be sure to irrigate occasionally. On the other hand, many perennials rot easily during the winter if they are too wet.

The remainder of this chapter lists a variety of species used for field-grown cut flower production. While this list appears long, it is only a beginning; enterprising producers constantly introduce new and different species and cultivars. A number of common field-grown cuts are covered in individual chapters including *Aconitum, Anemone, Antirrhinum, Aquilegia, Asclepias, Aster, Astilbe, Calendula, Callistephus, Campanula, Capsicum, Centaurea, Clarkia, Consolida, Convallaria, Cosmos, Delphinium, Dianthus, Echinacea, Eremurus, Eustoma, Gentiana, Helianthus, Iris, Liatris, Lilium, Limonium, Matthiola, Narcissus, Ornithogalum, Paeonia, Platycodon, Solidago, Tagetes,* and *Zinnia.* Note that while some of the above chapters focus on uses other than cut field flower production, helpful information can be obtained. See also the *Woody Cuts, Forced* chapter for species that are commonly forced into flower after harvest and the *Garden Perennials* chapter for information on additional species that may be suitable as perennial cut flowers. Scientific names are based on Huxley et al. (1992) and the references used are listed at the end of the chapter.

ACHILLEA L. SPECIES

Common name: yarrow.

Family: Compositae.

Description/uses: Of the numerous yarrow species, *A. filipendulina* Lam. is one of the best with long, strong stems and excellent postharvest life. Currently, only yellow-flowered cultivars are available, including 'Coronation Gold,' 'Parker's Variety,' and 'Gold Plate.' Many other species and hybrids are available in a wide range of colors including *Achillea aegyptiaca* L., *A. millefolium* L., and *A. millefolium* ×'Taygetea.' All species are perennial, mostly in Zones 3 to 10, and used as fresh cuts; *A. filipendulina* is an excellent dried cut. Established plantings will flower from mid-June to mid-July, while new plantings may flower later in the season. Plants grow 2 to 4 ft (60 to 120 cm) tall.

Planting: Space from 12 × 12 to 12 × 18 in. (30 × 30 to 30 × 45 cm). Plants should be divided and beds replanted every 2 to 4 years. Propagate by seed, cuttings, or division.

Postharvest handling: Vase life ranges from 8 to 11 days; flowers can be cold stored 35 to 37°F (2 to 3°C) for up to 2 weeks. Be sure to strip enough of the foliage so that none is submerged in the storage or vase water. The foliage deteriorates rapidly and produces an unpleasant sulfur smell. Flowers tend to wilt readily immediately after harvest.

Comments: The foliage is scented and, as with all scents, some people find it pleasant and others do not. See also the *Garden Perennials* chapter. Flowering will be prolonged if plants are regularly harvested.

ACROCLINIUM ROSEUM HOOK. (FORMERLY *HELIPTERIUM ROSEUM*)

Common names: strawflower, everlasting, pink and white everlasting, sunray everlasting.

Family: Compositae.

Description/uses: This daisy-like annual has yellow or brown centers and white, pink, or red papery petals. The flowers are primarily used dried and the plants grow up to 20 in. (50 cm) tall.

Planting: Use 12 in. (30 cm) between plants and rows. Propagate by seed.

Postharvest handling: Cut prior to being fully open because they will continue to open after harvest. Fresh cuts should last 7 to 10 days. The flowers hold their color well when dried.

Comments: Flowers tend to open and close in response to humidity.

AGASTACHE FOENICULUM (PURSH) KUNTZE.

Common name: anise hyssop.

Family: Lamiaceae.

Description/uses: This perennial has short spikes of small white or blue florets, which are generally used fresh. The blue cultivars are generally most popular. The plant has a licorice fragrance, which may be useful in some cases. Plants grow 2 to 3 ft (60 to 90 cm) tall and are hardy in Zones 5 to 8.

Planting: Space from 9 × 9 to 12 × 12 in. (23 × 23 to 30 × 30 cm) apart. Propagate by seed.

Postharvest handling: For fresh cuts, harvest when one-half to two-thirds of the flowers are open. Vase life should be 6 to 10 days.

Comments: Many other *Agastache* species and hybrids with a wide variety of colors can be used as cut flowers. Despite wonderful colors, the flower spikes of some cultivars are not very full, relegating their use to filler flowers. *Agastache* are also favorites of hummingbirds and butterflies.

AGERATUM HOUSTONIANUM MILL.

Common names: ageratum, mist flower.

Family: Compositae.

Description/uses: This annual grows 2 to 3 ft (60 to 90 cm) tall and produces clusters of fuzzy blue, reddish purple, and white flowers. The flowers are primarily used fresh.

Planting: Space plants 9 to 12 in. (23 to 30 cm) apart. Propagate primarily by seed.

Postharvest handling: Harvest when the center floret is open (appears fuzzy) and the lateral florets are well colored. Vase life is 5 to 7 days. Cut stems do not store well.

Comments: Ageratum also works well as a greenhouse cut flower. *Ageratum houstonianum* 'Tall Blue Horizon' is one of the Association of Specialty Cut Flowers Growers' Cut Flowers of the Year. See also the *Bedding Plants* chapter.

ALLIUM L. SPECIES

Common name: ornamental onion.

Family: Liliaceae.

Description/uses: Many alliums make excellent cut flowers and range from the large flowered giant onion (*A. giganteum* Reg.) to the small flowered drumstick allium (*A. sphaerocephalon* L.). The inflorescence ranges in shape from a tight sphere of small flowers to loose open clusters; the leaves are long and narrow. Flowers are available in a broad range of colors including white, pink, rose, purple, and yellow. Alliums are perennials, some species to Zone 5, and many grow from bulbs. Alliums can be used fresh or dried and are spring flowering. Plants grow up to 1.5 to 6 ft (45 to 180 cm) tall.

Planting: Generally space 9 to 12 in. (23 to 30 cm) apart. Many species of this bulbous plant are long-lived perennials. Propagate by seed, bulblets, or division.

Postharvest handling: Harvest when one-quarter to one-half of the flowers are open for fresh use and when nearly all flowers are open for dried use. Fresh postharvest life is 10 to 14 days; some species tolerate up to 4 weeks of cold storage at 32 to 35°F (0 to 2°C) and others should not be stored at all.

Comments: The amount of onion smell varies with the species and is most noticeable during harvest.

AMARANTHUS CRUENTES L.

Common names: purple amaranth, red amaranth.

Family: Amaranthaceae.

Description/uses: This annual has dense, branched upright to drooping spikes of tiny green, orange, or red florets, which can be used fresh or dried. The foliage may also be green, orange, or red colored. Plants grow 3 to 4 ft (90 to 120 cm) tall.

Planting: Space from 10 × 10 in. (25 × 25 cm) for small varieties to 16 × 16 in. (40 × 40 cm) for tall varieties. Propagate by seed.

Postharvest handling: For fresh cuts, harvest when at least three-quarters of the flowers are open. For dried cuts, harvest when inflorescence is large, well colored, and firm, but not before it matures and produces seeds that may shatter.

Comments: Other amaranthus species such as *A. tricolor* L. are used as cut foliage brilliantly colored with crimson, maroon, yellow, and gold. *A. caudatus* (love-lies-bleeding) has long drooping, tassel-like inflorescences, which may be red or green. See also the *Bedding Plants* chapter.

AMMI MAJUS L.

Common name: false Queen Anne's lace.

Family: Umbelliferae.

Description/uses: The large umbels of tiny white flowers of this annual are used as fresh cuts. The plants grow 3 to 6.5 ft (90 to 200 cm) tall.

Planting: Plant 9 to 12 in. (23 to 30 cm) apart. Propagate by seed, which is usually planted in the fall or late winter for late spring to summer flowering. Grows best in cool weather.

Postharvest handling: Harvest when approximately 80% of the florets are open and white. Flowers will last 5 to 8 days. If harvested too young, flowers tend to wilt. If harvested too late when pollen is visible, vase life is shortened.

Comments: Sap may cause contact dermatitis and may require gloves at harvest. *A. majus* species prefer cool weather and can be too short if grown during hot weather. Grow as a winter annual in warm climates. A number of other species are known as Queen Anne's lace including the wild carrot (*Daucus carota*), which is a common roadside wildflower and occasional weed.

AMMOBIUM ALATUM R. BR.

Common names: ammobium, winged everlasting.

Family: Compositae.

Description/uses: Ammobium has open clusters of small daisy-like flowers with white petals and yellow centers. Flowers are on sturdy upright stems that have green "wings" protruding from the stem. Two cultivars are available: 'Grandiflorum,' which grows up to 36 in. (90 cm) tall, and 'Bikini,' which is 12 to 16 in. (30 to 40 cm) tall. Flowers can be used fresh or dried but are most commonly dried. This tender perennial (Zones 8 to 10) is typically treated as an annual.

Planting: Space 8 to 10 in. (20 to 25 cm) apart. Propagate by seed.

Postharvest handling: Harvest when buds are well colored but before the yellow centers are visible. Fresh cuts will last 7 to 10 days.

Comments: Flowers readily accept dye.

ARTEMISIA LUDOVICIANA NUTT.

Common names: artemisia, white sage.

Family: Compositae.

Description/uses: A perennial plant grown for its silvery foliage, which is commonly used dried but can be used fresh. Plants grow 2 to 3 ft (60 to 90 cm) tall and are hardy in Zones 4 to 9.

Planting: Space from 12 × 12 to 18 × 18 in. (30 × 30 to 45 × 45 cm). Propagate by cuttings or division.

Postharvest handling: For dried cuts, harvest when flower buds have elongated to egg shape. For fresh, harvest anytime the foliage is attractive.

Comments: This plant can be invasive and some people may be allergic to it. Having said that, however, *Artemisia* 'Silver King' was one of the Association of Specialty Cut Flower Growers' Dried Cut Flowers of the Year. Sweet annie, *Artemisia annua* L., is also popular as a dried and fresh cut filler flower.

ASTRANTIA MAJOR L.

Common name: masterwort.

Family: Umbelliferae.

Description/uses: *Astrantia* has unusual greenish white to rosy red flowers surrounded by a green or pinkish-green collar. This perennial grows 2 to 4 ft (60 to 120 cm) tall and does best in cool climates. Plants are hardy in Zones 3 to 8.

Planting: Plant 12 × 12 in. (30 × 30 cm) apart. Propagate by seed.

Postharvest handling: Harvest when the uppermost flowers are open. Flowers must be harvested at the correct stage of development; cut stems wilt if harvested too juvenile and vase life will be poor if harvested too mature. Properly harvested fresh cut flowers should last 5 to 7 days.

Comments: Plants flower the second year after planting and do not tolerate heat well. Several other *Astrantia* species are available and may be useful.

BAPTISIA AUSTRALIS (L.) R. BR.

Common name: wild blue indigo.

Family: Leguminosae.

Description/uses: *B. australis* can be used as a cut flower or foliage. The inflorescences are tall upright spikes of blue to pale purple pea-shaped flowers. The foliage is light green with a bluish cast. The flowers can also be allowed to form pods, which can be harvested, dried, and sold. This perennial grows to 4 ft (1.2 m) tall and is hardy from Zones 3 to 9.

Planting: Generally, spacing of 12 × 12 in. (30 × 30 cm) is sufficient. Propagate by seed.

Postharvest handling: Harvest when one-third of the lower florets are open but before orange pollen is visible. Vase life is 5 to 7 days. The upper florets continue to open after harvest but will be lighter in color.

Comments: Wild blue indigo is a drought-tolerant, long-lived perennial but may take up to 3 years to produce a harvest. Numerous other *Baptisia* species and hybrids are available with white, pink, lavender, or yellow flowers and should be tested.

BRASSICA OLERACEAE L.

Common names: flowering cabbage, flowering kale.

Family: Cruciferae.

Description/uses: The "flowers" of this species are the rosettes of colorful young foliage, which are red, pink, or white. The older foliage is green. The plants are grown until they reach up to 24 in. (60 cm) tall, after which time they are harvested and most of the lower foliage removed, leaving the colorful centers. Cabbage types have foliage with smooth margins and kale types have deeply notched foliage.

Planting: Plants are spaced 9 × 9 to 12 × 12 in. (23 × 23 to 30 × 30 cm) apart. Propagate by seed.

Postharvest handling: Harvest when the stems are long enough and the center leaves well colored and remove the lower foliage. The center leaves will not color well under warm temperatures.

Comments: Grows best in cool weather. See also the *Bedding Plants* chapter.

BRIZA MAXIMA L. AND B. MINOR L.

Common name: quaking grass.

Family: Gramineae.

Description/uses: *B. maxima* grows 20 to 24 in. (50 to 60 cm) tall and has large panicles of nodding spikelets. *B. minima* is similar but spikelets are smaller. Both species are annuals. Stems can be used fresh or dried.

Planting: Space plants up to 8 × 8 in. (20 × 20 cm) apart. Propagate by seed.

Postharvest handling: Harvest soon after heading. Do not delay harvest because spikelets are more prone to shattering if overmature.

Comments: All *Briza* can be dyed.

BUDDLEIA DAVIDII FRANCH.

Common names: butterfly bush, summer lilac.

Family: Loganiaceae.

Description/uses: These rapidly growing shrubs are well known for their dense spikes of small fragrant red, blue, pink, or white flowers. Many cultivars are available that vary in color, size of inflorescence, and plant height. Dwarf cultivars should be avoided. Other ´Buddleia species are available and should be tested. Production begins in mid-summer and continues until frost for either fresh or dried use. Plants grow up to 12 ft (3.6 m) tall but are usually kept much shorter by harvest or cutting back during the winter. Grows in Zones 5 to 9.

Planting: Space plants 3 ft (0.9 m) apart. Propagate by seed or cuttings. Production is usually best if *Buddleia* is treated as an herbaceous perennial and cut back to the ground each fall. In mild winters, the plants may become very large, heavily branched, and difficult to harvest if not pruned. In cold winters the plants tend to die back to the ground anyway. Requires only 2 years to reach marketable harvest size.

Postharvest handling: The short postharvest life of this species, 4 to 7 days, makes it suitable only for local markets. Recut stems under water, place stems in a floral preservative, and keep in a 40 to 45°F (4 to 7°C) cooler. Harvest when 25 to 75% of the flowers on each spike are open. Tolerates up to 2 weeks cold storage at 35 to 37°F (2 to 3°C). Flowers will maintain fragrance if dried.

Comments: This species lives up to its name and is an excellent butterfly attractant.

BUPLEURUM ROTUNDIFOLIUM L.

Common names: thorow wax, green and gold.

Family: Umbelliferae.

Description/uses: The yellow-green flowers are in small umbels subtended by smooth round leaves. This fresh cut flower is typically used as a filler flower. The perennial plants grow to 30 in. (80 cm) tall and is hardy from Zones 4 to 8.

Planting: Space plants 10 × 10 in. (25 × 25 cm) apart. Propagate by seed, cuttings, or division.

Postharvest handling: Harvest when almost all of the flowers are fully open. Flowers should last 7 to 10 days.

Comments: Unusual flower for those who want a green filler.

BUXUS SEMPERVIRENS L.

Common names: box, boxwood.

Family: Buxaceae.

Description/uses: The small dark-green glossy leaves are the main attraction of this woody shrub. Cultivars with variegated foliage are also available. Although slow-growing, established plants can provide fresh cut greens most of the year. Plants typically grow 3 to 6 ft (90 to 180 cm) tall and are hardy in Zones 5 to 10.

Planting: Space plants 3 to 5 ft (90 to 150 cm) apart. Propagate by cuttings.

Postharvest handling: Harvest stems when leaves are mature. Vase life is an astounding 6 to 8 weeks, far longer than any flowers put with it (L. Greer, personal communication).

Comments: Avoid using dwarf cultivars.

CALLICARPA AMERICANA L.

Common name: beautyberry.

Family: Verbenaceae.

Description/uses: Rich purple berries on this shrub are harvested in late fall for fresh use (Fig. III-1 Field-Grown Cut Flowers). White-fruited forms exist. The foliage is usually removed prior to sale; it may naturally abscise or it may have to be removed by hand. Plants flower on the current season's growth and plants can be cut back hard after harvest to encourage long shoots the next season. Plants grow up to 6 ft (1.8 m) tall. Plants are hardy in Zones 7 to 10.

FIGURE III-1 FIELD-GROWN CUT FLOWERS
Callicarpa americana grown for its purple fruit.

Planting: Space plants 3 ft (0.9 m) apart. Propagate by cuttings or seed.

Postharvest handling: Harvest when the basal fruit are well colored and terminal clusters are still green. Stems should be recut and immersed in hot water. Stems may then be stored at 32 to 36°F (0 to 2°C) for 2 to 4 days.

Comments: Several other beautyberry species, *C. japonica* Thunb., *C. dichotoma* (Lour.) K. Koch, and *C. bodinieri* Lév., are available, which have smaller fruit that is also quite useful. Because beautyberry fruits on the current season's growth, rigorous pruning and harvesting are required for the best production. These relatively fast-growing shrubs will reach harvestable size in 2 to 3 years.

CARTHAMUS TINCTORIUS L.

Common name: safflower.

Family: Compositae.

Description/uses: This cool season annual has large cream, yellow, gold, or orange thistle-like flowers, which can be used fresh or dried. The foliage is thick and sometimes spiney, depending on the cultivar. The plants grow 2 to 3 ft (60 to 90 cm) tall.

Planting: Space plants 9 × 9 to 12 × 12 in. (23 × 23 to 30 × 30 cm) apart. Propagate by seed.

Postharvest handling: Harvest stems when color is visible on most of the flowers and they are one-quarter to one-half open; buds do not open well after harvest. Remove most of the foliage especially if it is spiney. Fresh cuts will last up to 10 days.

Comments: Carthamus is also grown for its use as an edible oil.

CARYOPTERIS ×CLANDONENSIS A. SIMMONDS EX REHD.

Common names: blue mist spirea, bluebeard.

Family: Verbenaceae.

Description/uses: *Caryopteris* produces one of the few true blue flowers; some cultivars, however, are purple. The flowers are arranged in whorls around the stem. *Caryopteris* is a short-lived shrub hardy from Zones 4 to 9 but often freezes back to the ground in Zones 4 and 5 during severe winters. Plants grow 2 to 4 ft (60 to 120 cm) tall and the cut stems can be used fresh or dried.

Planting: Space plants 12 × 12 in. (30 × 30 cm) apart. Propagate by seed or cuttings.

Postharvest handling: Harvest when most of the whorls are showing color and the lowermost whorl of flowers is well colored or open. Delayed harvest will reduce vase life. Flowers will last 7 to 10 days; preservatives will increase vase life by 2 to 3 days. Stems can be stored for 3 to 5 days at 34 to 40°F (1 to 4°C).

Comments: The similar *C. incana* has fuller flower clusters and is more showy, but not as readily available or hardy as *C. ×clandonensis*.

CELASTRUS SCANDENS L. AND C. ORBICULATUS THUNB.

Common name: bittersweet.

Family: Celastraceae.

Description/uses: Rapidly growing, twiggy vine that produces clusters of yellow fruit capsules in the fall, which crack open to show orange to red berries. Named cultivars are available that are identified as male or female. *C. scandens*, American bittersweet, carries its fruit in large terminal clusters and is native to Zones 3 to 8 in eastern and central North America. *C. orbiculatus*, oriental bittersweet, carries its fruit in small lateral clusters and is hardy in Zones 4 to 8. The clusters of fruit of both species are harvested in the fall for fresh or dried use.

Planting: Space plants 6 ft (1.8 m) apart. Vines are vigorous. Propagate by seed or cuttings. Generally requires 2 or more years to reach harvestable size and must be trained on a trellis up to 6 ft (1.8 m) high.

Postharvest handling: Harvest fruit when fully colored. Stems have a long vase life regardless if used fresh or dried.

Comments: Male and female flowers are on separate plants. Females are desired for berries, but males are needed nearby for pollination. Plant one male to several females. Wild collection of the native *C. scandens* should be discouraged because the species is becoming scarce in some areas. However, *C. orbiculatus* is a noxious weed in many locations and should not be planted.

CELOSIA ARGENTEA L.

Common names: cockscomb (Cristata group), plume celosia (Plumosa group), wheat celosia (Spicata group).

Family: Amaranthaceae.

FIGURE III-2 FIELD-GROWN CUT FLOWERS
Celosia argentea Cristata group 'Chief.'

Description/uses: This species is available in three groups: Cristata has convoluted, brain-like flower heads (Fig. III-2 Field-Grown Cut Flowers), Plumosa has large feathery plumes, and Spicata has small, slender spikes. The Cristata and Plumosa groups are similar in production and use, while the Spicata group is sufficiently different that it is often treated separately. Colors for cockscomb and plume celosia tend to be bright, ranging from yellow to orange to deep red and the plants grow 2 to 3 ft (60 to 90 cm) tall.

Wheat celosia has a restricted color range of pale pink, pink, and pale purple. The plants are taller at 3 to 5 ft (90 to 150 cm) and much more heavily branched than the other forms of celosia. The foliage often has a purplish cast. Both flower and foliage color will deepen in cool weather.

All types of celosia can be used as a fresh or dried cut flower, which is harvested from early summer to frost. Multiple plantings of cockscomb and plume celosia are generally required for season-long production. One planting of wheat celosia will usually provide season-long production.

Planting: Plant cockscomb and plume celosia from 4 × 4 to 12 × 12 in. (10 × 10 to 30 × 30 cm) apart. Propagate by seed. For cockscomb and plume celosia, close spacings are used for single-stem production and wider spacings can be used for multiple-stem production, where the side shoots are al-

lowed to develop. Single-stem production produces the longest stems, but staggered plantings will be required for season-long harvest. Wheat celosia should be planted at 12 × 12 in. (30 × 30 cm) as the plants grow large. Celosia is a SD plant and if transplants are started too early (late winter to early spring) under natural short days, plants may initiate flowers too soon and be too short.

Postharvest handling: Vase life ranges from 6 to 9 days for plume and wheat celosias and up to 2 weeks for cockscomb celosia. Flowers can be cold stored 40 to 45°F (4 to 7°C) for 1 week. Celosia will be damaged if stored for longer than a week at temperatures less than 40°F (4°C). Harvest flowers when well colored but before seeds mature in the lower florets. If allowed to mature too far, the flowers will release seeds in the home. Dried wheat celosia tends to shatter easily.

Comments: Requires well-drained soil because plants will rot readily in water-logged soil. All celosia prefer warm weather but wheat celosia requires warm to hot weather for the best growth. This species is also grown as a bedding plant (see the *Bedding Plants* chapter).

CENTRANTHUS RUBER (L.) DC.

Common name: red valerian.

Family: Valerianaceae.

Description/uses: This short-lived perennial has clusters of small white, pink, or red flowers on 2- to 3-ft (60- to 90-cm)-tall stems. The light-green foliage is smooth. *Centranthus* is used as a fresh cut flower. Plants are hardy from Zones 5 to 8 but do not tolerate extreme temperatures well.

Planting: Space plants 12 × 12 in. (30 × 30 cm) apart. Propagate by seed.

Postharvest handling: Harvest when half of the florets are open in the cluster. Cut stems should last 7 to 10 days in preservative. Stems may be stored in water for 3 to 5 days at 40°F (4°C). Florets tend to shatter.

Comments: This species tends to reseed itself; plant with care.

CERCIS CANADENSIS L.

Common name: eastern redbud.

Family: Leguminosae.

Description/uses: Pink or white pea-shaped flowers are harvested in early spring for fresh or dried use. Redbud is a small to medium-sized tree that is drought tolerant and native to eastern and central North America in Zones 4 to 9.

Planting: When grown as a multibranched shrub, space plants 3 ft (0.9 m) apart, but when grown as large mature trees of up to 30 ft (9 m) tall, space up to 30 ft (9 m) apart. Propagate by seed or cuttings.

Postharvest handling: Vase life increased with preservatives, but does not tolerate shipping or cold storage. Harvest when 25 to 75% of flowers are open. Preservatives may enhance color.

Comments: This species is slow growing and requires 5 to 10 years to reach marketable harvest age. Western redbud, *Cercis occidentalis,* is similar to eastern redbud and native to western North America. Chinese redbud, *Cercis chinensis* Bunge., flower more profusely than North American species.

CHASMANTHIUM LATIFOLIUM (MICHX.) YATES

Common name: Northern sea oats.
Family: Gramineae.
Description/uses: This perennial grass is native to the eastern United States and northern Mexico and can be used fresh or dried. It grows to 3 ft (90 cm) tall and produces long arching panicles of flattened spikelets.
Planting: Space plants 12 × 12 in. (30 × 30 cm) apart. Propagate by seed.
Postharvest handling: Harvest soon after heading. Do not delay harvest because spikelets are more prone to shattering if overmature.
Comments: Tolerates shade well.

CHELONE OBLIQUA L.

Common name: turtlehead.
Family: Scrophulariaceae.
Description/uses: This perennial produces slightly flattened snapdragon-like flowers on 2- to 3-ft (60- to 90-cm)-tall plants. The loose spikes of pink to purple flowers are used fresh. Grows best in moist locations and with some shade in warm climates. *Chelone* is hardy to Zones 5 to 9.
Planting: Space plants 12 × 12 in. (30 × 30 cm) apart. Propagate by seed, cuttings, or division.
Postharvest handling: Harvest when the lower flowers are open.
Comments: Two other species are also available: *C. glabra* L. is slightly taller and has

creamy white flowers with a pink cast; *C. lyonii* Pursh has reddish purple flowers and is native to southeastern United States.

CIRSIUM JAPONICAUM DC.

Common name: Japanese thistle.
Family: Compositae.
Description/uses: Although *Cirsium* is a thistle, it should not be confused with its invasive weedy cousins. The pink to red flowers are carried on strong stems and used both as a fresh and a dried cut. The foliage is prickly and most of it should be removed. This perennial is hardy from Zones 3 to 7 but grows best in cool areas. Plants grow 2 to 3 ft (60 to 90 cm) tall.
Planting: Space plants 9 × 9 to 12 × 12 in. (23 × 23 to 30 × 30 cm) apart. Propagate by seed or division.
Postharvest handling: Harvest flowers when they are fully open. Stems will last 1 week in preservative.
Comments: Divide and replant every 2 to 3 years.

COREOPSIS GRANDIFLORA HOGG EX SWEET.

Common names: tickseed, coreopsis.
Family: Compositae.
Description/uses: This perennial produces loose sprays of yellow daisy-style flowers used as fresh cuts. Plants have a low rosette of foliage from which the flowering stems arise. Plants grow 1.5 to 2.5 ft (45 to 75 cm) tall and are hardy in Zones 6 to 10.
Planting: Space plants 12 × 12 in. (30 × 30 cm) apart. Propagate by seed or division.
Postharvest handling: For fresh cuts, harvest when the center flowers in the spray are fully open. Many coreopsis are prone to wilting immediately after harvest and should be thoroughly hydrated. Vase life should be 7 to 10 days.
Comments: Although the common name *tickseed* may be acceptable for wild plants, using the name *coreopsis* would probably enhance sales of fresh cut flowers. A number of other *Coreopsis* species and hybrids are available and may be useful, although many cultivars are too short. However, *Coreopsis tinctoria* Nutt. grows up to 3 ft (90 cm) tall and has numerous small yellow to orange flowers with a dark maroon ring around the center

florets. *Coreopsis* is also a popular garden ornamental (see the *Garden Perennials* chapter).

CORNUS ALBA L. AND C. STOLONIFERA MICHX. F.

Common name: redosier dogwood.

Family: Cornaceae.

Description/uses: The bright red stems can be harvested any time of the year for fresh or dried use but are most commonly harvested in the fall after the leaves have abscised. Cultivars with yellow or orange stems are available. Color is brightest on most recent growth. Cut plants back after harvest to encourage new growth. *C. alba* is native to east Asia and hardy from Zones 2 to 8. *C. stolonifera* is native to northern North America and hardy from Zones 2 to 8. Plants grow up to 10 ft (3 m) tall.

Planting: Space plants 3 ft (0.9 m) apart. Propagate by cuttings.

Postharvest handling: Stem color holds well fresh or dried.

Comments: Generally requires 2 years to a marketable harvest. Both species are exceptionally cold tolerant.

CORNUS FLORIDA L.

Common name: flowering dogwood.

Family: Cornaceae.

Description/uses: The large flowers have four bracts, which are white to red, depending on the cultivar. Many cultivars are available that vary in flower color, doubleness, flower size, and durability. Stems with flower buds can be harvested in the winter prior to opening and sold immediately prior to flower bud opening or forced into flower for sale as a flowering stem. Stems can also be cut when plants are in flower naturally outdoors. Stems bearing the bright red fruits can be harvested in the fall.

Planting: Space plants 5 to 7 ft (1.5 to 2.2 m) apart. Propagate by seed, cuttings, or grafting. While it can grow in full sun, flowering dogwood tolerates shade. In areas with low humidity and hot sunny days, shade, uniform soil moisture, and cool roots are required. Five to 10 years is required for plants to reach a harvestable size. Mature trees reach 20 ft (6 m) tall and are hardy from Zones 5 to 8.

Postharvest handling: Cut flowering stems when bracts are beginning to open but prior

to visible pollen. Floral preservatives are useful. Stems with berries can be cut as soon as berries are colored. Stems with unopened flower buds can be cut anytime after the foliage drops.

Comments: This species is native to eastern and central North America. Other species are available and should be tested.

COTINUS COGGYGRIA SCOP.

Common name: smoketree.

Family: Anacardiaceae.

Description/uses: The large plumose inflorescence is harvestable in the summer for fresh use. The fluffy inflorescence is a smoky pink to brown (hence, the common name). Cultivars are available that vary in foliage and inflorescence color. Plants are hardy from Zones 5 to 8 and grow 10 to 15 ft (3 to 4.5 m) tall.

Planting: Space plants 5 ft (1.5 m) or wider. Propagate by seed or cuttings. Generally requires 5 years to reach harvest size.

Postharvest handling: Flowers are tiny; the smoky effect is from hairs on the flower pedicels and peduncles. The hairs may change color through the season and can be harvested at any time.

Comments: *C. obovatus* Raf., American smoketree, is native to south central United States and should be tested.

CRASPEDIA GLOBOSA BENTH.

Common name: golden drumstick.

Family: Compositae.

Description/uses: This tender perennial (Zone 8) produces bright yellow spherical flowers on thin, unbranched, but strong stems. The foliage is a low-growing rosette. The stems grow up to 2 ft (60 cm) tall and are used either fresh or dried.

Planting: Space plants 10 × 12 in. (25 × 30 cm) apart. Propagate by seed.

Postharvest handling: Harvest flowers when fully colored. Flowers should last up to 10 days.

Comments: Support is useful.

CROCOSMIA ×CROCOSMIIFLORA (BURB. & DEAN) N. E. BR.

Common names: crocosmia, montbretia.

Family: Iridaceae.

FIGURE III-3 FIELD-GROWN CUT FLOWERS
Crocosmia 'Lucifer.'

Description/uses: *Crocosmia* produces long arching spikes of yellow, orange, or red flowers (Fig. III-3 Field-Grown Cut Flowers). The plants grow 2 to 4 ft (90 to 120 cm) tall and are hardy from Zones 5 to 11. The long tapered leaves are iris-like. Flowers are primarily used fresh but can be dried. Seeds pods can also be harvested.

Planting: The corms are planted 6 × 6 in. (15 × 15 cm) apart. Propagate by seed, corms, or division.

Postharvest handling: Harvest when the lowermost buds are well colored. Stems have a vase life of 7 to 10 days and can be stored for up to 4 days at 34 to 37°F (1 to 3°C). Dried storage is feasible but wet storage is preferred.

Comments: Lift, grade, clean, and store corms in the north. Divide and replant every 2 to 3 years in the south.

DICENTRA BERNH. SPECIES

Common name: bleeding heart.

Family: Fumariaceae.

Description/uses: This beautiful perennial is known for its long arching spikes of white to rose-colored heart-shaped flowers in the early spring. The foliage is gray green and fernlike. *S. eximia* (Ker-Gawl.) Torr. grows 12 to 18 in. (30 to 45 cm) tall and is hardy from Zones 3 to 9. *S. spectabilis* (L.) Lem. (old-fashioned bleeding heart) grows 2 to 3 ft (60 to 90 cm) tall and is hardy from Zones 4 to 9. Foliage usually disappears during mid- to late summer. Plants prefer moist, partly shady locations.

Planting: Space plants 12 × 12 in. (30 × 30 cm) apart. Propagate by seed or division.

Postharvest handling: Harvest when the lower one-third of flowers are fully colored and open. Vase life should be 5 to 7 days.

Comments: Cold stored crowns can be forced in the greenhouse for Valentine's Day to Mother's Day sales. Outdoors this long-lived perennial can be grown indefinitely in one location or lifted and divided every 4 to 5 years.

DIGITALIS L. SPECIES

Common name: foxglove.

Family: Scrophulariaceae.

Description/uses: The tall spikes of tubular flowers are available in many colors including white, pink, rose, yellow, and red, depending on the species being grown. *Digitalis purpurea* L. is the most commonly grown species. Named cultivars are available for several of the species. Most species are biennial or short-lived perennials. The spikes grow 2 to 4 ft (60 to 120 cm) tall from rosettes of foliage. Cold hardiness varies but is from Zones 4 to 9 for most species.

Planting: Space plants 12 × 12 to 12 × 18 in. (30 × 30 to 30 × 45 cm) apart. Propagate by seed and division.

Postharvest handling: Harvest when the lower two to three flowers are open.

Comments: *Digitalis* can be poisonous if ingested.

ECHINOPS BANNATICUS ROCHEL EX SCHRÄD.

Common name: globe thistle.

Family: Compositae.

Description/uses: The metallic blue, ball-shaped flowers are typically dried but can also be used fresh. This long-lived perennial (10+ years) is cold hardy from Zones 3 to 10. However, it does poorly in warm and humid climates. Globe thistles are adapted to a wide variety of soils and drought tolerant. Plants are seed propagated, will flower the second year after planting, and can be cut back after harvest. Plants should be allowed to remain in the ground for many years and will become more productive each year. Plant height is 2.5 to 4 ft (75 to 120 cm). Foliage is thistle-like with soft spines. Spines harden and stems become more difficult to handle when dried. Cultivars are available that vary slightly in flower color, vigor, and foliage color.

Planting: Space plants 24 × 24 in. (60 × 60 cm) apart for long-term plantings or 18 × 18 in. (45 × 45 cm) apart for shorter term plantings. Propagate by seed or division.

Postharvest handling: For fresh cut, harvest when one-half to three-quarters of the florets are open. Pollen will show if harvested when more than one-third of the florets are open. Vase life of fresh cuts is 7 to 10 days without preservatives, longer with floral preservatives. Flowers for drying are harvested when well colored but before flowers are apparent.

Comments: Globe thistle is virtually insect and disease free but can occasionally host European corn borers in corn-producing areas. *Echinops bannaticus* is one of the Association of Specialty Cut Flower Growers' Cut Flowers of the Year.

ERYNGIUM PLANUM L.

Common name: flat sea holly.

Family: Apiaceae.

Description/uses: This long-lived perennial has unusual silvery blue round inflorescences subtended by long narrow bracts, which turn metallic blue and generate slightly spiney foliage. The flowers can be used fresh or dried. Plants grow 2 to 4 ft (60 to 120 cm) tall and are hardy from Zones 3 to 8. Plants are saline tolerant.

Planting: Grow at 18 × 18 in. (45 × 45 cm) for 3 years or less, space at 24 × 24 in. (60 × 60 cm) if grown for more than 3 years. Lift and divide every 3 to 4 years. Propagate by seed, root cuttings, or division.

Postharvest handling: Harvest flowers when the entire inflorescence, including bracts, turns blue. Flower will last 10 to 12 days in water and can be cold stored at 38 to 40°F (3 to 4°C) for 7 to 10 days. Foliage tends to decline before flowers senesce and cold storage intensifies the blue color.

Comments: Some people do not like the smell of the stems. Several other *Eryngium* species can be used as cut flowers including *E. alpinum* L. (larger bracts than *E. planum*), *E. bourgatii* Gouan. (shorter than *E. planum*), *E. amethystinum* L. (shorter than *E. planum*), and *E. leavenworthia* Torr. & A. Gray. (reddish purple color).

EUONYMUS ALATUS (THUNB.) SIEB.

Common names: winged euonymus, burning bush.

Family: Celastraceae.

Description/uses: The corky, winged stems can be harvested any time for fresh or dried use. Harvest is easiest during the winter when the leaves have fallen. Stems with foliage can be harvested in the fall when the leaves are bright orange to red colored. Select cultivars with long stems and avoid dwarf, branchy cultivars. Plants grow up to 15 to 20 ft (4.5 to 6 m) tall but are usually much shorter in cultivation.

Planting: Space plants 3 to 5 ft (0.9 to 1.5 m) apart. Propagate by cuttings or seed.

Postharvest handling: If used fresh, cut, bundle, and store dry in a 35 to 40°F (2 to 4°C) cooler.

Comments: Degree of corkiness on the stems varies with the cultivars. Generally requires 5 years to a marketable harvest.

EUPATORIUM SPECIES

Common names: eupatorium, joe-pye-weed.

Family: Compositae.

Description/uses: These perennials are grown for their large clusters of fuzzy blue, reddish purple, pink, or white flowers. The flowers are used fresh. *Eupatorium maculatum* L. and *E. purpureum* L. are large plants, growing 6 to 10 ft (1.8 to 3 m) tall, and are hardy from Zones 4 to 9. *E. cannabinum* grows 3 to 4 ft (90 to 120 cm) tall, is hardy from Zones 5 to 9, and is produced for its silvery pink flowers. *Ageratina altissima* 'Chocolate' (formerly known as *Eupatorium rugosum* 'Chocolate') grows to 6 ft (1.8 m) tall, is hardy from Zones 6 to 9, and is produced as much for its brown foliage as its white flowers.

Planting: Space the large-growing species 1.5 to 2.5 ft (45 to 75 cm) apart and the smaller species 1 to 1.5 ft (30 to 45 cm) apart. Propagate by seed, cuttings, or division.

Postharvest handling: Harvest when the buds are well colored and center florets are open (fuzzy). *E. cannabinum* has a vase life of 19 to 24 days, but the other species tend to have a shorter 5- to 7-day vase life.

Comments: While several joe-pye-weeds are native to U.S. wetlands, they grow equally well in upland cultivated fields.

EUPHORBIA MARGINATA PURSH.

Common name: snow-on-the-mountain.

Family: Euphorbiaceae.

Description/uses: This late summer to fall flowering annual has large green and white variegated to entirely white bracts surrounding small flowers. The plants grow 2 to 4 ft (60 to 120 cm) tall and are heavily branched. Named cultivars such as 'Kilimanjaro' and 'Snow Top' are more uniform and whiter than the native species.

Planting: Space plants 6 × 6 to 9 × 9 in. (15 × 15 to 23 × 23 cm) apart. Propagate by seed.

Postharvest handling: Harvest when bracts are well colored but before flowers are fully open. Bracts will last 7 to 10 days. Foliage often yellows before bracts and may be best removed prior to use. Harvest while wearing gloves; sap can cause dermatitis in sensitive individuals.

Comments: This SD plant should not be planted too early in the spring when nights are long or stems will be short.

FORSYTHIA ×INTERMEDIA ZAB.

Common name: forsythia.

Family: Oleaceae.

Description/uses: Stems with the bright yellow, nodding flowers are harvested in early spring for fresh use. Numerous cultivars are available that vary in plant habit, foliage color, floriferousness, flower color, and cold hardiness. Upright, floriferous, vigorous cultivars should be selected. Plants are hardy from Zones 5 to 9, depending on the cultivar, and grow up to 6 ft (1.8 m) tall.

Planting: Space plants 3 to 5 ft (0.9 to 1.5 m) apart. Propagate by cuttings.

Postharvest handling: Harvest in the tight bud stage. Vase life should be 7 to 12 days and can be cold stored at 35 to 40°F (2 to 4°C) for 1 to several weeks.

Comments: Forsythia can be forced into flower early (see *Woody Cuts, Forced* chapter) after being harvested in the fall, cold stored, and forced. Forcing allows stems to be harvested in the fall, preventing winter injury to flower buds. Generally requires only 2 years for a marketable harvest.

GLADIOLUS CALLIANTHUS MARAIS. (FORMERLY KNOWN AS ACIDANTHERA BICOLOR)

Common name: abysinnian gladiolus.

Family: Iridaceae.

Description/uses: This species produces long spikes of fragrant, 3-in. (8-cm)-wide flowers. The white flowers have dark red or purple throats. Plants grow 3 to 4 ft (90 to 120 cm) tall and should be annually replanted even though they are hardy in Zones 7 to 10.

Planting: Space corms 3 to 4 in. (8 to 10 cm) apart. Propagate by corms.

Postharvest handling: Harvest when one flower is open. Flowers will last 5 to 11 days and can be stored for 6 to 8 days at 40 to 45°F (4 to 7°C). Preservatives should be used and stems handled upright because the tips will curve upward if stems are tilted.

Comments: See *Gladiolus* chapter for information on the commonly grown hybrids.

GOMPHRENA GLOBOSA L. AND G. HAAGEANA

Common name: globe amaranth.

Family: Amaranthaceae.

Description/uses: Of the two species being grown, *G. globosa* tends to be shorter and more heavily branched than *G. haageana* (Fig. III-4 Field-Grown Cut Flowers). *G. globosa* flowers are smaller than *G. haageana* and are available in white, pink, pale purple, and dark purple. *G. haageana* flowers are available in red and orange. Hybrids are blurring the distinctions between the two species and a greater range of colors are becoming available. Mainly used as a dried but can also be used as a fresh filler flower in mixed bouquets. One planting will provide

FIGURE III-4 FIELD-GROWN CUT FLOWERS
Gomphrena haageana 'Strawberry Fields.'

production from mid-summer to frost. Grows up to 28 in. (71 cm) tall.

Planting: Plants can be spaced 6 × 6 to 12 × 12 in. (15 × 15 to 30 × 30 cm). Propagate by seed.

Postharvest handling: Harvest when the heads are well colored and round but before the heads become elongated. If harvested too late, the lower florets will abscise after harvest. Vase life is generally 5 to 7 days and can be cold stored 35 to 40°F (2 to 4°C) for 1 week.

Comments: *Gomphrena* is a prolific producer and does very well in warm weather. *Gomphrena* tolerates drought but does best with irrigation. See also the *Bedding Plants* chapter.

GRAINS

Common names: oats (*Avena* L.), bromegrass (*Bromus* L.), barley (*Hordeum* L.), canary seed (*Phalaris canariensis* L.), foxtail millet (*Setaria* Palib.), sorghum [*Sorghum bicolor* (L.) Moench], wheat (*Triticum* L.).

Family: Gramineae.

Description/uses: The seed heads of many grains make excellent cuts, either fresh or dried, but are primarily used dried. The heads may be quite decorative and have a natural dried color of beige, green, reddish brown, dark brown, or black. Plants range in height from 16 to 60 in. (40 to 150 cm) with most species 32 to 40 in. (80 to 100 cm) tall.

Planting: Usually direct seeded at 25 to 71 lb/acre (28 to 80 kg · ha⁻¹), depending on the species grown.

Postharvest handling: The proper harvest stage varies with the species. Most species are best harvested when seed heads are full size but before seeds have matured. If harvested when seeds are mature, they may shatter when dried.

Comments: Many species are drought resistant and can be produced without irrigation. Machines are available to harvest and bunch grains.

HELICHRYSUM BRACTEATUM (VENT.) ANDREWS

Common name: strawflower.

Family: Compositae.

Description/uses: One of the staples of the dried flower industry, this annual has 1- to 2-in. (2.5- to 5-cm)-wide flowers with many papery petals. The flowers are available in white, pink, rose, purple, yellow, and orange colors. Plants grow 1.5 to 3 ft (45 to 90 cm) tall. Flowers can also be used as a fresh cut.

Planting: Space plants 10 × 10 to 12 × 12 in. (20 × 20 to 30 × 30 cm) apart. Propagate by seed.

Postharvest handling: Harvest flowers when one to two layers of petals have opened. Always harvest before the flowers are fully open because the petals will reflex after harvest, exposing the less attractive center. Fresh cut flowers will last 7 to 10 days and can be cold stored at 36 to 41°F (2 to 5°C) only if necessary.

Comments: Individual flowers can be harvested and wired by inserting a wire with a small hook at one end through the center of the flower. See also the *Bedding Plants* chapter.

HYDRANGEA L. SPECIES

Common name: hydrangea.

Family: Hydrangeaceae.

Description/uses: Large clusters of red, pink, blue, or white flowers are harvested from summer to fall and can be used fresh or dried. Many species are potential cuts and should be tried. Several of the more common species include *Hydrangea arborescens* L. (snow-on-the-mountain, treat as a herbaceous perennial, and cut back each winter, Zones 6 to 9), *H. macrophylla* (Thunb.) Ser. (bigleaf hydrangea, Zones 6 to 10; see separate chapter), *H. paniculata* Sieb. (peegee hydrangea, Zones 5 to 9) (Fig. III-5 Field-Grown Cut Flowers), and *H. quercifolia* Bartr. (oak-leaved hy-

FIGURE III-5 FIELD-GROWN CUT FLOWERS
Hydrangea paniculata grown in a shade structure.

drangea, Zones 5 to 9). *H. macrophylla* grows to 5 ft (1.5 m) tall, *H. arborescens* and *H. quercifolia* grow to 6 ft (1.8 m) tall and *H. paniculata* grows to 15 ft (45 m) tall.

Planting: Space plants 3 ft (0.9 m) apart. Propagate by cuttings or seed.

Postharvest handling: Harvest when one-half of the florets are open. Condition stems overnight in cold water with a pH of 4.0. For dried flowers, wait until flowers are papery before harvesting. Strip leaves, bunch stems, and hang in a warm, dark environment.

Comments: Most species reach harvestable size in 3 years. *H. paniculata* was selected as one of the Association of Specialty Cut Flower Growers' Cut Flowers of the Year and has white bracts, which age to green or pink.

HYPERICUM CALYCINUM L. AND H. ANDROSAEMUM L.

Common name: St. John's wort.

Family: Guttiferae.

Description/uses: This perennial or short shrub is grown primarily for its large rounded bronze to pink-bronze fruit. The bright yellow flowers can also be harvested. The foliage is dark green to blue green and develops a reddish cast in full sun. The plant grows 15 to 30 in. (38 to 75 cm) tall and is hardy in Zones 6 to 10. Plants flower mid- to late summer.

Planting: Space plants 12 × 12 to 18 × 18 in. (30 × 30 to 45 × 45 cm) apart. Propagate by cuttings or seed.

Postharvest handling: Harvest flowers when just recently opened and harvest fruit when well developed and well colored. Vase life of fruit will be 10 to 21 days.

Comments: *Hypericum* grows best in light shade but also grows well in full sun. Rust diseases can be destructive and prevent some growers from producing this species.

ILEX L. SPECIES

Common name: holly.

Family: Aquifoliaceae.

Description/uses: Branches with red, yellow, or orange berries and with or without foliage are harvested in late fall and winter for fresh use. Several species, such as *Ilex opaca* Ait. (American holly, Zones 5 to 10), *I. aquifolium* L. (English holly, Zones 6 to 10), and *I. crenata* Thunb. (Japanese holly, Zones 6 to 10),

have glossy, evergreen foliage that can be harvested during November and December for Christmas sales. Many species have foliage with spines on the margins and require care to harvest. Two commonly used deciduous species include *I. verticillata* (L.) A. Gary. (winterberry, Zones 3 to 9) and *I. decidua* Walter. (possum haw, Zones 6 to 10), both of which are used as berried branches. Numerous cultivars are available for each of the species listed and vary in fruit color, growth habit, foliage shape and color, vigor, and presence of spines. *I. opaca* and *I. aquifolium* grow to 30 ft (9 m) tall and *I. verticillata* and *I. decidua* grow to 10 ft (3 m) tall.

Planting: Depending on species, space plants 3 to 5 ft (0.9 to 1.5 m) or wider. Propagate by cuttings or seed.

Postharvest handling: Harvest when fruit are well colored. Cut stems may last up to 12 weeks in water; however, as with many species the vase life in foam will be much shorter (L. Greer, personal communication). Stems should be stored dry. Branches may be stored at 32°F (0°C) for 1 to 3 weeks in moisture-retentive boxes.

Comments: Male and female flowers are on separate plants. Females are desired for berries but males are needed nearby for pollination. Generally requires 5 years to reach harvestable size.

LAGURUS OVATUS L.

Common name: hare's tail grass.

Family: Gramineae.

Description/uses: This annual grass produces small egg-shaped woolly plumes and grows 1 to 2 ft (30 to 60 cm) tall. Although it can be used fresh, it is most commonly used dried.

Planting: Space plants 8 × 8 to 12 × 12 in. (20 × 20 to 30 × 30 cm) apart. Propagate by seed.

Postharvest handling: Harvest when plumes are fully mature. This species is shatter resistant.

Comments: The plumes are often dyed.

LATHYRUS ODORATUS L.

Common name: sweet pea.

Family: Leguminosae.

Description/uses: Although most commonly grown in a cool greenhouse or cold frame, sweet peas can also be field produced in cool climates. This annual vine is grown on trellises or strings and produces open racemes of pea-shaped flowers that are white, red, lavender, and every shade in between. Plants grow to 6 ft (1.8 m) or taller in the greenhouse but are shorter in the field. The individual clusters can be harvested or the upper 1 to 2 ft. (30 to 60 cm) of the shoot with several smaller clusters and many buds can be cut. Individual clusters are often harvested early in the season when they are long, up to 12 in. (30 cm), and shoot tips are harvested later in the season when the individual clusters are short with only a few florets each.

Planting: Space plants 4 to 6 in. (10 to 15 cm) apart in rows. Propagate by seed.

Postharvest handling: Harvest clusters when two to three flowers are showing color. Flowers are sensitive to ethylene and vase life is short, only 3 days, if not treated with an anti-ethylene agent, which increases vase life up to 6 to 9 days. Stems ship and store well if treated with an anti-ethylene agent first.

Comments: Unlike their close edible relatives, sweet peas are mildly poisonous.

LAVATERA TRIMESTRIS L.

Common name: mallow flower.

Family: Malvaceae.

Description/uses: The large 3- to 4-in. (8- to 10-cm)-diameter flowers of this annual are harvested for fresh use. The white, pink, salmon, or rose-colored flowers are carried on 2- to 2.5-ft (60- to 75-cm)-tall plants.

Planting: Space plants 12 × 12 to 24 × 24 in. (30 × 30 to 60 × 60 cm) apart. Propagate by seed.

Postharvest handling: Harvest flowers when petals are just beginning to open and before the petals are flat. Vase life is up to 7 days and cold storage is not recommended.

Comments: Plants are susceptible to many insects and diseases and grow best in cool temperatures.

LEPIDIUM SATIVUM L.

Common name: peppergrass.

Family: Cruciferae.

Description/uses: This bushy annual is grown for its open sprays of small, round seed pods that can be harvested for fresh or dried use. Plants grow up to 2 ft (60 cm) tall.

Planting: Space plants 6 × 6 to 10 × 10 in. (15 × 15 to 25 × 25 cm) apart. Propagate by seed.

Postharvest handling: Harvest when pods are fully formed.

LEUCANTHEMUM ×SUPERBUM (J. INGRAM) BERGMANS EX KENT.

Common name: shasta daisy.

Family: Compositae.

Description/uses: The shasta daisy has classic daisy flowers with white petals and yellow disc florets. Some cultivars are double. Flowers are cut for fresh use. The perennial plants grow up to 3 ft (90 cm) tall and are hardy from Zones 5 to 8.

Planting: Space from 12 × 12 to 18 × 18 in. (30 × 30 to 45 × 45 cm). Single-flowered cultivars are typically seed propagated and doubles are propagated by cuttings or division. Divide plants every 2 to 3 years.

Postharvest handling: Harvest when the petals have expanded and the first ring of inner florets are open. Vase life should be 9 to 12 days.

Comments: Plants form a slowly spreading patch, but can be short lived. Shasta daisy is also a popular garden ornamental (see the *Garden Perennials* chapter).

LOBELIA L. SPECIES

Common names: lobelia, cardinal flower (*L. cardinalis*), blue cardinal flower (*L. siphilitica*).

Family: Campanulaceae.

Description/uses: These 2- to 4-ft (60- to 120-cm)-tall perennials are known for their rich red, blue, purple, and pink flower colors. The inflorescence is a 6- to 9-in.- (15- to 23-cm)-long spike of 1- to 1.5-in. (2.5- to 4-cm)-wide flowers. Three species are available: *L. cardinalis, L. fulgens,* and *L. siphilitica;* and numerous hybrids (collectively known as *L. ×speciosa*) have been made among the species, resulting in a broad range of colors. *L. cardinalis* has scarlet flowers, green foliage, and is hardy from Zones 2 to 9. *L. fulgens* is similar to *L. cardinalis* but is cold hardy only to Zone 8. *L. siphilitica* has blue flowers, green foliage, and is hardy from Zones 4 to 9. Many of the hybrids are cold hardy from Zones 6 to 9.

Planting: Space plants 12 × 12 in. (30 × 30 cm) apart. Propagate by seed. *L. cardinalis* is native to wetlands and as such many of the hybrids prefer moist soils and partial shade in warm climates.

Postharvest handling: Harvest when one-third to one-half of the inflorescence is open. Flowers should last 7 to 10 days.

Comments: These plants tend to be short-lived perennials and can be treated as annuals.

LONAS ANNUA (L.) VINES & DRUCE

Common names: African daisy, yellow ageratum.

Family: Compositae.

Description/uses: Small clusters of yellow flowers appear on plants that are up to 20 in. (50 cm) tall. The flowers of this annual can be sold fresh or dried.

Planting: Space plants 6 × 6 in. (15 × 15 cm) apart. Propagate by seed.

Postharvest handling: Harvest when flower clusters are fully colored. Vase life is 7 to 10 days.

Comments: Not well known.

LUNARIA ANNUA L.

Common names: honesty, silver dollar.

Family: Cruciferae.

Description/uses: This biennial is grown primarily for its large round pods, which are used dried. The white, violet, or red flowers can be used fresh, but have a short vase life and tend to shatter. The plants grow to 3 ft (60 to 90 cm) tall and are hardy from Zones 3 to 8.

Planting: Space plants 12 × 12 to 10 × 18 in. (30 × 30 to 25 × 45 cm) apart. Propagate by seed.

Postharvest handling: Pods are harvested when fully mature. When dry, the two outer coverings are removed to expose the silvery, translucent inner membrane. Fresh cut vase life is 3 to 5 days.

Comments: Plants tend to reseed freely and should be planted accordingly.

LUPINUS HARTWEGII LINDL.

Common name: lupine.

Family: Leguminosae.

Description/uses: This annual is grown for its long spikes of white, blue, pink, or violet flowers and silvery green foliage. The plants grow to 3 ft (60 to 90 cm) tall and are hardy from Zones 7 to 11. Although this species can be grown outside, it does not perform well outdoors in hot, humid climates and is best

grown as a winter greenhouse crop. The cultivar 'Sunrise' has shorter spikes with fewer flowers that are blue marked with yellow and white and mildly fragrant. 'Sunrise' flowers much faster than other types but generally produces only one harvestable stem per plant.

Planting: Space plants 8 × 8 to 12 × 12 in. (20 × 20 to 30 × 30 cm) apart. Propagate by seed.

Postharvest handling: Harvest when two to four of the lower florets are open. Vase life is 7 to 9 days. Anti-ethylene agents are helpful.

Comments: Other *Lupinus* species have been grown. The genus holds much promise.

LYSIMACHIA CLETHROIDES DUBY.

Common name: gooseneck loosestrife.

Family: Primulaceae.

Description/uses: The perennial plant produces 4- to 5-in. (10- to 15-cm)-long inflorescences of small, 0.5-in. (1.5-cm)-wide white flowers. Plants grow 2 to 2.5 ft (60 to 75 cm) tall and are hardy from Zones 3 to 8. Flowers appear in late spring to midsummer.

Planting: Space plants 12 × 12 in. (30 × 30 cm) apart. Propagate by seed, cuttings, or division.

Postharvest handling: Harvest stems when the inflorescence is one-third to one-half open. Vase life is 12 days in a floral preservative but only 5 days in water. Flowers can be stored at 36 to 41°F (2 to 5°C).

MOLUCCELLA LAEVIS L.

Common name: bells-of-Ireland.

Family: Labiatae.

Description/uses: This unusual annual flower has tall spikes of large, green bell-shaped calyces that face outward. Spikes can be used fresh or dried. The small white flowers appear in the center of each "bell." The plant grows to 24 to 28 in. (60 to 70 cm) tall.

Planting: Space plants 10 × 10 in. (25 × 25 cm) apart. Propagate by seed.

Postharvest handling: Harvest stems when calyces are fully mature and remove upper leaves. If used fresh, harvest when one-third of the flowers are open. Be sure to enhance water uptake by cutting into warm, low pH water.

Comments: Grows best in cool weather; tends to flower prematurely and be too short when grown in warm weather.

MONARDA DIDYMA L. SPECIES

Common names: bee balm, bergamot, monarda.

Family: Labiatae.

Description/uses: This perennial produces large, round, terminal inflorescences of narrow tubular flowers. The flowers are available in red, rose, lavender, pink, white, and purple. Plants grow 2 to 4 ft (60 to 120 cm) tall, are hardy in Zones 4 to 9, and flower in midsummer.

Planting: Space plants 12 × 12 to 18 × 18 in. (30 × 30 to 45 × 45 cm) apart. Propagate by cuttings, division, or seed.

Postharvest handling: Harvest fresh cut flowers when one ring of florets has opened and other florets are well colored. Vase life should be 5 to 7 days. For dried flowers harvest when inflorescence is almost fully open.

Comments: Several other species native to North America can be grown. In particular, *M. fistulosa* has lavender flowers and is similar to and has been hybridized with *M. didyma*.

MYRICA L. SPECIES

Common names: bayberry (*M. pensylvanica* Lois.), wax-myrtle (*M. cerifera* L.), California bayberry (*M. californica* Cham.).

Family: Myricaceae.

Description/uses: These shrub to small trees have small fragrant, glossy, evergreen leaves and waxy berries. *M. pensylvanica* and *M. cerifera* are similar with gray berries; *M. pensylvanica* is a northern species that is hardy from Zones 2 to 8 and *M. cerifera* is a southern species that is hardy from Zones 6 to 10 and has a slightly different fragrance from *M. pensylvanica*. *Myrica californica* has large bronze-colored leaves and purple berries and is hardy from Zones 7 to 10. Berries can be harvested throughout winter and the foliage can be harvested any time for fresh use. *M. pensylvanica* grows to 10 ft (3 m) tall and *M. cerifera* and *M. californica* grow to 25 ft (7.5 m) tall.

Planting: Space plants 3 to 5 ft (0.9 to 1.5 m) apart. Propagate by seed, cuttings, or layering.

Postharvest handling: Fruit and foliage is long lasting, up to 9 weeks (L. Greer, personal communication).

Comments: It is slow growing; 5 or more years are required to reach the harvestable

stage. Male and female flowers are on separate plants. Females are desired for berries but males are needed nearby for pollination.

NANDINA DOMESTICA THUNB.

Common name: nandina.

Family: Berberidaceae.

Description/uses: This upright shrub has large compound leaves and large clusters of red to yellow berries carried on thick stems. Woody stems with large clusters of berries are harvested in the fall and early winter for fresh or dried use. Plants are hardy from Zones 5 to 10 and grow to 6 ft (1.8 m) tall.

Planting: Space plants 3 ft (0.9 m) apart. Propagate by seed or cuttings.

Postharvest handling: Cut stems when fruit are well colored.

Comments: Cultivars with compact growth habits do not fruit as well as other varieties. This species is invasive in some areas, so plant with care.

NIGELLA DAMASCENA L., N. HISPANICA L., AND N. ORIENTALIS L.

Common name: love-in-a-mist.

Family: Ranunculaceae.

Description/uses: *Nigella* have unusual appearing flowers that can be harvested for fresh use; however, it is more commonly grown for the seed pods, which can be used fresh or dried. *N. damascena* has white, blue, pink, or rose-colored flowers that mature to form round, inflated pods (Fig. III-6 Field-Grown Cut Flowers). *N. hispanica* has blue flowers, which form inflated, spider-like pods. *N. orientalis* has yellow flowers and

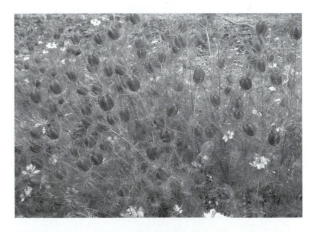

FIGURE III-6 FIELD-GROWN CUT FLOWERS
Nigella damascena grown for its interesting pods.

elongated, spikey pods. All species are annuals, have narrow, highly dissected leaves, and grow 18 to 24 in. (45 to 60 cm) tall.

Planting: Space plants 6 × 6 to 9 × 9 in. (15 × 15 to 23 × 23 cm) apart. Tight spacing encourages larger terminal flowers and fewer side branches. Propagate by seed.

Postharvest handling: Harvest fresh cut flowers when flowers are well colored but before petals have totally separated from the center. Fresh cuts will last 5 to 7 days and may be cold stored at 36 to 41°F (2 to 5°C), only if necessary. Harvest pods when fully expanded for fresh use and when firm to the touch for dried use. *N. damascena* pods should be harvested when they also have a purple-bronze color.

Comments: Tends to reseed itself, handle accordingly.

PAPAVER L. SPECIES

Common name: poppy.

Family: Papaveraceae.

Description/uses: *Papaver nudicaule* L., Iceland poppy, is grown for its large flowers, which consist of many silky petals surrounding a green to dark brown or black eye (Fig. III-7 Field-Grown Cut Flowers). Flowers are available in a broad range of colors including white, yellow, pink, orange, and red and are usually harvested for fresh use in early spring to midsummer. Plants grow to 2 ft (60 cm) tall and, al-

FIGURE III-7 FIELD-GROWN CUT FLOWERS
Papaver nudicaule.

though technically perennials, they are often treated as annuals. *P. somnifera* L., opium poppy, is an annual that has been grown for its decorative pods on plants up to 3 ft (90 cm) tall.

Planting: Space plants 12 × 12 in. (30 × 30 cm) apart. Propagate by seed.

Postharvest handling: Harvest flowers for fresh cuts when the flower petals are almost completely expanded (cup shaped). For longer postharvest life and easier shipping, buds can be harvested when the calyx is cracked and the petal color is visible. However, if buds are harvested, up to 10% will not open. Pods are harvested once they reach full size in midsummer to late fall.

Comments: *P. somnifera* L. is the source of opium and it is illegal in the United States to possess any part of the plant other than the seeds. Poppy seed is also used as a food additive.

PENSTEMON DIGITALIS NUTT.

Common name: beardtongue.

Family: Scrophulariaceae.

Description/uses: This native perennial species has loose clusters of small tube-shaped, white to pale pink flowers. In addition to the native species, the cultivar 'Husker Red' has purplish foliage. Fresh cut flowers are harvested from mid-May to mid-June. Plants grow to 30 in. (76 cm) tall and are hardy from Zones 3 to 9.

Planting: Spacing should be 12 × 12 in. (30 × 30 cm) apart and the bed should be replanted every 4 to 5 years. Propagate by seed, cuttings, and division.

Postharvest handling: Harvest when several florets are open. Vase life is excellent (9 to 10 days) and flowers can be cold stored at 35 to 37°F (2 to 3°C) for up to 3 weeks.

Comments: Flowers have glandular hairs and can be sticky. Consequently, flowers should be cut and shipped upright to prevent them from sticking to each other. The flowers have a mild fragrance and, as with all scents, some people find it pleasant and others do not. Other penstemon species and hybrids are available in many colors and should be tested, but many are quite susceptible to root and crown rots.

PHLOX PANICULATA L.

Common name: summer phlox.

Family: Polemoniaceae.

Description/uses: *P. paniculata* grows 2 to 3 ft (60 to 90 cm) tall and produces large, 6- to 10-in. (15- to 25-cm)-wide, clusters of fragrant flowers used for fresh cuts. The individual white, pink, or red flowers are 1 to 1.5 in. (2.5 to 4 cm) wide. Many cultivars are available. Plants are hardy from Zones 4 to 8.

Planting: Space plants 12 × 12 to 24 × 24 in. (30 × 30 to 60 × 60 cm) apart. Propagate by seed, cuttings, or division.

Postharvest handling: Harvest when two or more of the florets are open. Vase life is 5 to 10 days in floral preservative, which should include an anti-ethylene agent, and stems can be stored at 38°F (3°C) for 1 to 3 days.

Comments: Many *P. paniculata* cultivars are susceptible to powdery mildew, which damages foliage. Several other *Phlox* species are grown commercially including *P. maculata* L., which is slightly shorter but less susceptible to powdery mildew than *P. paniculata*. See also the *Garden Perennials* chapter.

PHYSALIS ALKEKENGI L.

Common name: Chinese lantern.

Family: Labiatae.

Description/uses: This perennial is grown for its large, orange, inflated calyces, which hang down from the stems. The tallest variety is *P. alkekengi* var. *franchetti,* which grows 24 to 32 in. (60 to 80 cm) tall and is used fresh or dried. Plants are hardy from Zones 3 to 8.

Planting: Space plants at 12 × 12 to 12 × 18 in. (30 × 30 to 30 × 45 cm) apart. Propagate by seed or division.

Postharvest handling: Harvest when the calyces are fully colored. Fresh cuts will last 2 to 3 weeks and can be cold stored at 36 to 41°F (2 to 5°C). However, *Botrytis* can be a serious issue during storage and shipping. Bunches should be air dried 1 to 2 days prior to storage or shipping. Fully dried calyces hold their color for months.

Comments: Formerly known as *P. franchetti.* Plants can be invasive.

PHYSOSTEGIA VIRGINIANA (L.) BENTH.

Common name: obedient plant.

Family: Labiatae.

Description/uses: This perennial has 8- to 12-in. (20- to 30-cm)-long spikes of 1-in. (2.5-cm)-long trumpet-like flowers used as fresh cuts. The plants grow 3 to 4 ft (90 to 120 cm) tall. Plants are hardy in Zones 3 to 9.

Planting: Space plants 12 × 12 to 18 × 18 in. (30 × 30 to 45 × 45 cm) apart. Propagate by seed, cuttings, or division.

Postharvest handling: Harvest when spikes are fully elongated and zero to four flowers are open. Later harvest will decrease vase life. Stems can last up to 14 days if properly treated with silver thiosulfate (STS) and preservatives. Stems can be stored up to 1 week at 40°F (4°C).

Comments: Plants should be replanted every 3 years to ensure tall vigorous stems. The common name is derived from the fact that individual florets can be moved around on the stem and will remain in that position.

PYRACANTHA ROEM. SPECIES

Common name: firethorn.

Family: Rosaceae.

Description/uses: The large clusters of yellow, orange, or red berries are harvested in the fall and early winter. The foliage is small and can be evergreen in mild climates. Many species can be used and one of the most common is *P. coccinea* Roem. Many cultivars of *P. coccinea* are available that vary in fruit color, growth habit, and cold hardiness. Some cultivars have resistance to powdery mildew. Plants are hardy in Zones 5 to 9 and grow up to 15 ft (3 m) tall.

Planting: Space plants 3 ft (0.9 m) apart. Propagate by seed or cuttings.

Postharvest handling: Harvest when fruit are well colored. Cuts will last 7 to 10 days.

Comments: Susceptible to fire blight. Branches can be thorny and should be harvested with care.

RHODANTHE MANGLESII LINDL. (FORMERLY *HELIPTERUM MANGLESII*)

Common name: Swan River everlasting.

Family: Compositae.

Description/uses: This daisy-like annual has yellow centers and white, pink, or rose-colored papery petals. The flowers are primarily used dried and the plants grow up to 16 in. (40 cm) tall.

Planting: Plants are spaced 12 × 12 in. (30 × 30 cm) apart. Propagate by seed.

Postharvest: Harvest when flowers are fully colored.

Comments: Petals tend to close in humid weather.

RUDBECKIA FULGIDA AIT. AND *R. HIRTA* L.

Common name: black-eyed susan.

Family: Compositae.

Description/uses: The large 3- to 9-in. (8- to 23-cm)-wide golden-yellow flowers with dark brown centers grow on 2.5- to 3.5-ft (75- to 105-cm)-tall plants. The foliage is hairy. *R. fulgida* is a perennial, flowers mid- to late summer, and is hardy in Zones 3 to 9. *R. hirta* is an annual or short-lived perennial, Zones 3 to 10, and, although the flower period is long (4 to 5 weeks), multiple plantings may be useful in warm climates for season-long harvest. Cultivars are available with double-flowered, green-centered, orange-red, or bronze-red flowers.

Planting: Space plants 12 × 12 in. (30 × 30 cm) apart. Plants are seed propagated.

Postharvest handling: Flowers should be harvested when petals have fully expanded and the first ring of inner disc florets is open. Postharvest life is up to 21 days.

Comments: *Rudbeckia hirta* 'Indian Summer' is one of the Association of Specialty Cut Flower Growers' Cut Flowers of the Year. *Rudbeckia triloba* L. (brown-eyed susan) is another excellent cut flower. This biennial to short-lived perennial grows 2 to 5 ft (60 to 150 cm) tall and is hardy from Zones 5 to 8. It produces large sprays of small golden-yellow flowers with brown to black centers.

SALIX MATSUDANA KOIDZ. 'TORTUOSA'

Common name: corkscrew willow.

Family: Salicaceae.

Description/uses: Contorted stems are harvested during dormancy (late fall, winter, early spring) for fresh or dried use. Some stems can also be harvested in early spring when the new foliage is small and just beginning to emerge from the buds. Cultivars are available with green, yellow, orange, and reddish stems. Plants are hardy from Zones 5 to 10 and grow to 30 ft (10 m) tall if not cut back.

Planting: Space plants 3 to 5 ft (0.9 to 1.5 m) apart. Plants are propagated by cuttings, which root easily.

Postharvest handling: If used fresh, cut, bundle, and store dry in a 35 to 40°F (2 to 4°C) cooler.

Comments: Plants are fast growing and harvests can often be made the second year after planting. The longest stems are produced by cutting back hard after harvesting in late winter to early spring. Plants tend to be short lived due to various diseases.

SALIX L. SPECIES

Common name: pussy willow.

Family: Salicaceae.

Description/uses: Woody stems with small, fuzzy catkins are harvested in winter to early spring for fresh or dried use. Numerous species can be used including *S. caprea* L., *S. chaenomeloides* Kimura, *S. discolor* Muhlenb., and *S. gracilistyla* Miq. The various species and cultivars differ in catkin size and color, stem color, flowering date, height, and vigor. Most species are susceptible to canker, which results in a relatively short life for a small tree. Many species are hardy in Zones 5 to 10.

Planting: Space plants 3 to 5 ft (0.9 to 1.5 m) apart. Propagate by cuttings.

Postharvest handling: Plunge stems in water after harvest and store in a 35 to 40°F (2 to 4°C) cooler. Bud scales will need to be removed. Harvest before flowers appear on the catkins. Branches can be cut in winter and forced in 7 to 10 days by placing them at 50°F (10°C).

Comments: The longest stems are obtained by cutting plants back hard after harvest and before leafing out in the spring. Plants are relatively fast growing and can often be harvested 2 to 3 years after planting.

SALVIA L. SPECIES

Common name: salvia.

Family: Labiatae.

Description/uses: *S. leucantha* Cav. is a tender perennial species (Zones 8 to 10) that grows 2 to 4 ft (60 to 120 cm) tall with long spikes of purple and white hairy flowers. *S. farinacea* Benth. is a tender perennial (Zones 8 to 11) that grows to 2 ft (60 cm) tall with short spikes of blue, purple, or white hairy flowers. *S. viridis* (formerly *S. horminum*) is also an annual species that grows to 1.5 ft (45 cm) tall with short spikes of small flowers subtended by large white, pink, or blue-colored bracts. Flowers can be used fresh or dried.

Planting: Spacing ranges from 9 × 9 in. (23 × 23 cm) for small species such as *S.*

farinacea and *S. viridis* to 12 × 12 or 12 × 18 in. (30 × 30 or 30 × 45 cm) for *S. leucantha*. *S. leucantha* is cutting propagated and *S. farinacea* and *S. viridis* are seed propagated.

Postharvest handling: Harvest when the small white flowers are visible on the lower three to four florets. Flowers of all species have a tendency to shatter and an anti-ethylene agent should be used. Fresh cuts should last up to 7 days with floral preservative and may be cold stored in water for 3 to 4 days at 35 to 40°F (2 to 4°C).

Comments: Many *Salvia* species are currently used as cut flowers and many others are suitable but not in production. See also the *Bedding Plants* and *Garden Perennials* chapters.

SCABIOSA ATROPURPUREA L., S. CAUCASIA BIEB., AND S. STELLATA L.

Common names: scabiosa, pincushion flower (*S. atropurpurea*), perennial scabiosa (*S. caucasia*), drumstick (*S. stellata*).

Family: Dipsacaceae

Description/uses: The genus *Scabiosa* includes several species useful for cut flower production. *S. atropurpurea* is an annual with 1- to 1.5-in. (2.5- to 4-cm)-wide rounded clusters of small florets. Plants grow 2 to 3 ft (60 to 90 cm) tall and the flowers are white, pink, red, or violet. *S. caucasia* is a perennial with 2- to 3-in. (5- to 8-cm)-wide clusters of flowers, the outer rows of which have large showy petals. Plants grow 2 to 2.5 ft (60 to 75 cm) tall and the flowers are white or blue. Plants are hardy from Zones 4 to 10. *S. stellata* is an annual with rounded clusters of white to light blue florets, which mature into spherical clusters of star-shaped seeds. Plants grow 2 to 2.5 ft (60 to 75 cm) tall.

Planting: Space annual species 9 × 9 to 12 × 12 in. (23 × 23 to 30 × 30 cm) apart and space *S. caucasia* 12 × 12 to 18 × 18 in. (30 × 30 to 45 × 45 cm) apart.

Postharvest handling: Harvest *S. atropurpurea* when almost fully open and *S. caucasia* when flower color is first visible. Flowers will last 6 to 8 days. Flowers can be cold stored at 36 to 41°F (2 to 5°C). *S. stellata* flowers are harvested when seeds are almost mature; late harvest will increase shattering.

Comments: *S. atropurpurea* has beautiful colors but the flowers can be tiresome to harvest because the stems tend to intertwine and it takes many stems to make a substantial bunch.

SEDUM L. SPECIES

Common name: sedum.

Family: Crassulaceae.

Description/uses: Sedums have thick succulent leaves and stems terminating in large rounded clusters of small flowers, which are used fresh. The most common species used for cut flower production are *S.* 'Autumn Joy', *S.* 'Matrona,' and *S. spectabile* [now known as *Hylotelephium spectablile* (Boreau) H. Ohba.]. The upright growing plants are 15 to 24 in. (38 to 60 cm) tall with gray green foliage and large pink to red flower clusters. Plants are hardy in Zones 3 to 9 and flower in late summer to fall.

Planting: Space plants 12 × 12 to 12 × 18 in. (30 × 30 to 30 × 45 cm) apart. Propagate by seed and cuttings.

Postharvest handling: Harvest stems when flower clusters are one-half to fully open.

Comments: See also the *Garden Perennials* chapter.

TANACETUM PARTHENIUM (L.) SCHULTZ-BIP. (FORMERLY CHRYSANTHEMUM PARTHENIUM)

Common names: feverfew, matricaria.

Family: Compositae.

Description/uses: Matricaria has numerous small white or golden yellow flowers in a cluster. Flowers can be single with white petals and yellow disk florets or heavily double and ball shaped. Flowers are cut for fresh or dried use. This short-lived perennial plant grows up to 2 ft (60 cm) tall and is hardy from Zones 6 to 10. Matricaria is often treated as an annual and replanted every year. Foliage is aromatic.

Planting: Space from 8 × 8 to 12 × 12 in. (20 × 20 to 30 × 30 cm) apart. Plants are typically seed propagated; cuttings can also be used. Matricaria are long day plants; if grown in the greenhouse during the winter, provide long days.

Postharvest handling: Harvest when the first florets are open for fresh use or when almost fully open for dried use. Vase life should be 7 to 10 days.

Comments: Plants may reseed themselves.

THALICTRUM L. SPECIES

Common name: meadow-rue.

Family: Ranunculaceae.

Description/uses: Several species of this 3- to 6-ft (0.9- to 1.8-m)-tall perennial can be grown for fresh cut flower use. The airy inflorescence consists of numerous small flowers, 0.5 to 1 in. (1 to 2.5 cm) across with white, pink, or purple sepals. Plants are hardy from Zones 4 to 8, depending on the species, and flower late spring to early summer.

Planting: Space plants at least 18 × 18 in. (45 × 45 cm) apart. Propagate by seed or division.

Postharvest handling: Harvest flowers when most of the flowers are open. Buds do not develop well after harvest. Flowers will last approximately 7 days and can be cold stored at 36 to 41°F (2 to 5°C) for up to a week only if necessary.

Comments: Plants grow best in light shade and are short lived in full sun or heavy shade. *T. delavayi* Franch. and *T. aquilegiifolium* L. are two commonly grown species.

TRACHELIUM CAERULEUM L.

Common names: trachelium, throatwort.

Family: Campanulaceae.

Description/uses: This plant produces large rounded clusters of numerous small white, pink, blue, or purple flowers. Plants grow 3 to 4 ft (90 to 120 cm) tall. Although *Trachelium* is actually a perennial (Zones 9 to 11), it is typically grown as an annual.

Planting: Space plants 9 × 9 to 18 × 18 in. (23 × 23 to 45 × 45 cm) apart. Propagate by seed.

Postharvest handling: Harvest stems when one-quarter to one-third of the inflorescence is open. Flowers will last up to 7 to 13 days and can be cold stored for a day at 40°F (4°C). Flowers last longest when treated with a hydration solution immediately after harvest to encourage water uptake.

Comments: Plants grow best in cool temperatures and perform well as a greenhouse-grown cut flower.

TRACHYMENE COERULEA GRAHAM. (FORMERLY KNOWN AS DIDISCUS CAERULEUS)

Common name: blue lace flower.

Family: Umbelliferae.

Description/uses: This annual produces many rounded clusters of small white, pink, rose, or lavender blue flowers. The flower clusters are 1.5 to 2 in. (4 to 5 cm) wide. The plants grow 2 to 2.5 ft (60 to 75 cm) tall.

Planting: Space plants 8 × 10 in. (20 × 25 cm) apart. Propagate by seed.

Postharvest handling: Harvest flowers when one or more rows of florets are open. Flowers should last 5 to 7 days.

Comments: Plants grow best in cool temperatures and perform well as a greenhouse-grown cut flower.

TRICYRTIS WALLICH. SPECIES

Common name: toad lily.

Family: Liliaceae.

Description/uses: This perennial has unusual orchid-like flowers with various combinations of white to blue flowers spotted and blotched with purple, red, or bronze. Several flowers terminate on 1- to 2.5-ft (30- to 75-cm)-stems with shiny foliage. *Tricyrtis* is used as a fresh cut. Plants are hardy in Zones 4 to 9.

Planting: Space plants 12 × 12 to 18 × 18 in. (30 × 30 to 45 × 45 cm) apart. Propagate by seed or division.

Postharvest handling: Harvest when one to two flowers are fully open.

Comments: Plants grow best in light shade. Numerous species are available. *T. sinonome* has worked well for several growers. This interesting and striking flower is certainly a plant in search of a good name—toad lily reminds one of warts and *Tricyrtis* recalls a disease. How about "orchid lily"?

TRITELEIA LAXA BENTH.

Common name: brodiaea.

Family: Liliaceae.

Description/uses: This perennial is grown for its 2- to 5-in. (5- to 13-cm)-wide clusters of deep blue tubular flowers, which are up to 1 in. (2.5 cm) long. The flower scape is a 9- to 15-in. (23- to 38-cm) leafless stalk. Flowers are used fresh. Leaves are long and narrow. Plants are hardy in Zones 6 to 9.

Planting: Plant corms 3 to 6 in. (8 to 15 cm) apart and 4 to 5 in. (10 to 13 cm) deep.

Postharvest handling: Harvest when four to six flowers are open. Flowers last 10 to 14 days and can be cold stored dry up to 4 days at 36 to 41°F (2 to 5°C).

Comments: In cold climates corms can be harvested in the fall and stored until the next spring. In moderate climates divide and re-plant periodically.

TWEEDIA CAERULEUM D. DON (FORMERLY KNOWN AS OXYPETALUM CAERULEUM)

Common names: tweedia, oxypetalum.

Family: Asclepiadaceae.

Description/uses: The sky blue flowers of this tender perennial are its main attraction and are sold as fresh cuts. The stems grow 1 to 2 ft (30 to 60 cm) tall. Plants are hardy from Zones 9 to 11.

Planting: Space plants 6 × 6 to 9 × 9 in. (15 × 15 to 23 × 23 cm) apart. Propagate by seed.

Postharvest handling: Harvest stems when six cymes are present and showing color and one or two flowers are open. Vase life will be 6 to 10 days.

Comments: Best grown under protection. Stems produce a milky sap when cut.

VACCARIA HISPANICA (MILL.) RAUSCH. (FORMERLY SAPONARIA VACCARIA)

Common name: cow cockle.

Family: Caryophyllaceae.

Description/uses: This annual has many small white to pink flowers on 20- to 28-in. (50- to 70-cm)-tall plants. Flower are harvested for fresh use.

Planting: Space plants 12 × 12 in. (30 × 30 cm) apart. Propagate by seed.

Postharvest handling: Harvest when three-quarters to almost all of the flowers are open.

Comments: Flowers quickly from seed. Sow every 1 to 2 weeks for a succession of harvests.

VERBENA BONARIENSIS L.

Common name: tall verbena.

Family: Verbenaceae.

Description/uses: This perennial produces 2- to 4-in. (5- to 10-cm)-wide clusters of small purple flowers. Plants grow to 4 ft (120 cm) tall, have relatively little foliage, and are hardy in Zones 7 to 10. They can be treated as annuals.

Planting: Space plants 12 × 12 to 20 × 20 in. (30 × 30 to 50 × 50 cm) apart. Propagate by seed.

Postharvest handling: Harvest the heads when most of the florets are open. Harvesting can be tedious because the stems become tangled. It may be best to harvest everything at once and sort out the good stems later. Florets tend to shatter but new florets will open, keeping the stem attractive. Vase life is 5 to 7 days.

Comments: This plant readily reseeds itself and can become weedy.

VERONICA LONGIFOLIA L.

Common name: ironweed.

Family: Compositae.

Description/uses: This upright perennial plant has 8- to 15-in. (20- to 38-cm)-long spikes of small blue, white, or pink flowers that are used primarily fresh. The plants grow 2 to 3 ft (60 to 90 cm) tall and flower in midsummer. Plants are hardy from Zones 4 to 8.

Planting: Space plants 12 × 12 to 12 × 18 in. (30 × 30 to 30 × 45 cm) apart. Propagate by seed, cuttings, or division.

Postharvest handling: Harvest when one-half of the flowers on the spike are open. Harvesting when stems are more mature will decrease vase life, which is normally 7 days. Although not recommended, stems can be cold stored at 36 to 41°F (2 to 5°C).

Comments: Other species such as *V. spicata* are similar and also commonly grown for cut production (see the *Garden Perennials* chapter).

VERONICASTRUM VIRGINICUM (L.) FARW.

Common name: culver's root.

Family: Scrophulariaceae.

Description/uses: This perennial has long spikes of tiny white to light blue flowers on 3- to 4-ft (90- to 120-cm)-tall plants. The plants are hardy in Zones 3 to 8.

Planting: Space plants 12 × 12 to 12 × 18 in. (30 × 30 to 30 × 45 cm) apart. Propagate by seed or division.

Postharvest handling: Harvest stems when the inflorescence is one-third open and secondary flowers are showing color. Vase life is 7 to 10 days in preservative (especially those containing 2.5 to 5% sugar). Foliage will yellow if stems are harvested too early.

Comments: Similar to *Veronica*.

VIBURNUM L. SPECIES

Common name: viburnum.

Family: Caprifoliaceae.

Description/uses: A large number of these woody shrubs to small trees can be used for their flowers, fruit, and colorful fall foliage. *V. tinus* L., Zones 7 to 10, produces 3-in. (8-cm)-wide clusters of pink buds, which open up to white flowers on stems with glossy, dark-green foliage. *V. opulus* L., Zones 2 to 10, is used for its white flower clusters, which are available as round "snowball" types or as "lacecap" types. All of the florets on snowball types are sterile, large, and showy. On lacecap types, the center florets are small and fertile and only the outer florets are large, sterile, and showy. *V. opulus* can also be grown for its bright red, soft fruit and orange-maroon fall foliage. The color of mature fruit can vary from red to purple to black, depending on the species. Species with hard, dry fruit are most useful. Some species have soft, wet fruit, which can be messy and stain clothes and tablecloths. Use the latter species carefully.

Planting: Space plants 3 to 5 ft (0.9 to 1.5 m) apart. Propagate by cuttings.

Postharvest handling: Harvest flowers when one-quarter of flowers are open and harvest fruit when well colored. *V. tinus* has a vase life of 9 to 15 days (L. Greer, personal communication).

Comments: The *Viburnum* genus has more than 150 species, many of which show potential as cuts. Species that flower early in the spring can also be forced into flower (see the *Woody Cuts, Forced,* chapter).

XERANTHEMUM ANNUUM L.

Common names: xeranthemum, immortelle.

Family: Compositae.

Description/uses: This annual grows up to 2 ft (60 cm) tall and is primarily used as a dried flower. The double flowers have papery petals. White and purple flowers hold their colors well when harvested; rose/pink flowers turn brownish when dried.

Planting: Space plants approximately 10 × 10 in. (25 × 25 cm) apart. Propagate by seed.

Postharvest handling: Cut flowers when fully open because the flowers do not continue to open after harvest. Fresh cuts last 5 to 7 days.

Comments: Can be direct seeded or grown from transplants.

ZEA MAYS L.

Common names: corn, maize.

Family: Gramineae.

Description/uses: Many cultivars of ornamental corn are available with various seed colors, including red, white, blue, and yellow and ear sizes from small (baby corn) to large. The decorative ears are primarily used dried with the outer sheath leaves attached but pulled back to form a handle.

Planting: Space plants 16 × 16 in. (40 × 40 cm) apart. Propagate by seed.

Postharvest handling: Harvest ears when husks are dry but can still be pulled back if desired. Insects and rodents are particularly fond of ornamental corn; store where protected.

Comments: If growing more than one variety, do not plant near each other because they will cross-pollinate and the ears will not come true to variety. Ornamental corn can also cross-pollinate with edible corn varieties.

KEY POINTS

- Commercial field-grown cut flower production encompasses an incredible array of plant materials including both fresh and dried/preserved flowers, foliage, stems, and berries.

- Cut flowers are marketed to the public directly through farmers markets, bucket shops, pick-your-own, or subscription selling; florists; specialty supermarkets; or wholesalers.

- The proper site for field cut flower production should be sunny, relatively flat, accessible at all times, have water for irrigation and postharvest requirements and adequate air movement.

- Cuts can be grown in rows or 2.5- to 4-ft (75- to 120-cm)-wide mounded beds with aisles wide enough to allow people and equipment to move between the beds without damaging the plants.

- The soil should be tested and amended with fertilizers and organic matter prior to planting.
- New field plantings can be established by a variety of methods including direct seeding, divisions or rooted cuttings, bulbs, corms, tubers, or tuberous roots.
- Optimum plant spacing varies greatly from species to species, ranging from only 4 × 4 in. (10 × 10 cm) for some annuals to 2 to 6 ft (0.8 × 1.8 m) apart for some woody plants.
- Cut flowers are a high-value crop and irrigation will probably be necessary, regardless of the climate; drip tape is commonly used.
- Weed control is often the most time-consuming and labor-intensive component of field production.

BIBLIOGRAPHY

Armitage, A.M., and Laushman. 2003. *Specialty Cut Flowers,* 2nd ed. Timber Press, Portland, Oregon.

Dirr, M.A. 1990. *Manual of Woody Landscape Plants: Their Identification, Ornamental Characteristics, Culture, Propagation and Uses,* 4th ed. Stipes Publishing, Champaign, Illinois.

Godwin, B.J. 1986. *Alberta Supernaturals.* Olds College, Olds Alberta, Canada.

Huxley, A., M. Griffiths, and M. Levy. 1992. *The New Royal Horticultural Society Dictionary of Gardening,* vols. 1–4. Stockton Press, New York.

Jenkins, D.F. 1991. Woody plants as cut flowers, pp. 68–74 in *Proceedings of the 4th National Conference on Specialty Cut Flowers.* Cleveland, Ohio. Association of Specialty Cut Flower Growers.

Perry, D. 1990. Woody ornamentals as cut flowers, pp. 131–137 in *Proceedings of the 3rd National Conference on Specialty Cut Flowers.* Ventura, California. Association of Specialty Cut Flower Growers.

Redman, P.B. 1994. Vase life determination and postharvest evaluation of specialty cut flowers. M.S. thesis, Oklahoma State University, Stillwater, Oklahoma.

Wyman, D. 1969. *Shrubs & Vines for American Gardens.* Macmillan, New York.

Foliage Plants

INTRODUCTION

Numerous species are grown as potted foliage plants and the list is expanding annually. Hundreds of species and cultivars are grown by home enthusiasts and are available through specialty growers. However, a limited number of species and cultivars are commercially produced on a large scale.

Tropical foliage plants are produced in a wide range of containers. Several species such as *Ardisia, Dracaena,* and *Syngonium* are propagated and grown briefly in small pots for use in dish gardens, planters, or baskets. Dish gardens, planters, or baskets may be assembled commercially and often include a small flowering plant such as *Kalanchoe* or *Saintpaulia* or a brightly colored foliage plant such as bromeliads or *Codiaeum* for extra color. Many retailers also provide an assortment of small plants that consumers can use to make their own gardens.

Large potted plants are grown for use as specimen plants for the home, business, and interiorscape. In warm climates some species are also used as outdoor landscape ornamentals.

Commercially hanging basket foliage plants can be divided into two general groups. "Soft" foliage baskets are those species, such as *Tradescantia* and *Plectranthus,* that are easily propagated, grow fast, and have relatively soft stems. "Hard" baskets are those species, such as *Epipremnum* and *Philodendron,* that have longer production times and harder stems. Although the soft baskets are easy to produce, the market is generally greater for the hard baskets.

Foliage plants can be propagated using a variety of methods. The most common are seed, cuttings, or tissue culture. Air layering and division are rarely used commercially due to time, expense, and limited material but may be used by consumers. For cutting-propagated species, stock plants or previously propagated plants are the source of cuttings. With the latter source, the shoots are removed to prune and shape plants, especially hanging basket species such as *Cissus*, *Epipremnum*, and *Philodendron*. Many growers buy rooted or unrooted cuttings, *in vitro* material, liners, or plugs propagated by specialists. Most foliage plants are grown at warm night temperatures of 65°F (18°C) or higher.

Many commonly used foliage species have already been covered in this text in separate chapters including *Anthurium*, *Begonia*, *Caladium*, *Dracaena*, *Epipremnum*, *Hedera*, *Philodendron*, and *Spathiphyllum*. Several species that are covered in the text are primarily grown as potted flowering plants, but will also grow well in the home and continue to flower if they receive proper care. These species include *Crossandra*, *Eucharis*, *Gardenia*, *Hatiora*, *Hibiscus*, *Hippeastrum*, many Orchidaceae family plants, *Saintpaulia*, *Schlumbergera*, and *Streptocarpus*. This chapter lists a variety of other tropical foliage species. Scientific names are based on Huxley et al. (1992) and the references used are listed at the end of the chapter.

ADIANTUM (L.) SPECIES

Common name: maidenhair fern.

Family: Adiantaceae.

Description/uses: The plants are grown for their airy compound foliage and sold in small 4- to 6-in. (10- to 15-cm) pots and in 6- to 12-in. (15- to 30-cm) hanging baskets with one to several plants per container. Approximately 200 species occur, of which *A. hispidulum* Sw. and *A. raddianum* C. Presl. are commonly cultivated. Several dwarf cultivars of *A. raddianum* are available.

Propagation: Small plants are propagated by spores or tissue culture and larger plants by division.

Light: Requires 1200 to 1800 fc (240 to 360 μmol $\cdot$ m^{-2} $\cdot$ s^{-1}) during production and at least 75 to 150 fc (15 to 30 μmol $\cdot$ m^{-2} $\cdot$ s^{-1}),

with 250 fc (50 μmol $\cdot$ m^{-2} $\cdot$ s^{-1}) optimum, in the home.

Comments: Wilting will cause severe frond dieback.

AESCHYNANTHUS JACK. SPECIES

Common names: lipstick vine, red bugle vine, scarlet basket vine.

Family: Gesneriaceae.

Description/uses: These vine plants are grown for their glossy foliage and interesting yellow, orange, red, or purple flowers and calyces. Two commonly grown species are *A. pulcher* (Bl.) G. Don. and *A. radicans* Jack., both of which have red flowers and red to maroon calyces. Plants are produced in 3- to 10-in. (8- to 25-cm) pots and 6- to 10-in. (15- to 25-cm) hanging baskets with several plants in each container.

Propagation: Plants are propagated by cuttings.

Light: Requires 4000 to 6000 fc (800 to 1200 μmol $\cdot$ m^{-2} $\cdot$ s^{-1}) during production and 500 to 800 fc (100 to 160 μmol $\cdot$ m^{-2} $\cdot$ s^{-1}) in the home.

Comments: Numerous other species are available and may be grown commercially. Atrimmec (dikegulac sodium) sprays can be applied at 780 to 1600 ppm to increase branching.

AGLAONEMA SCHOTT. CULTIVARS

Common name: Chinese evergreen.

Family: Araceae.

Description/uses: *Aglaonema* are grown for their elongated, variegated leaves, which are produced from short stems. 'Silver Queen' is one of the most commonly used cultivars but numerous other cultivars are available. The plants are grown in pot sizes ranging from 4 to 10 in. (10 to 25 cm) wide, with 6- to 10-in. (15- to 25-cm) pots most frequently used.

Propagation: Plants are most commonly propagated by tip cuttings; unrooted, callused, or rooted cuttings can be purchased. Use of seed, division, or stem piece cuttings is possible but rarely done.

Light: Requires 1000 to 2500 fc (200 to 500 μmol $\cdot$ m^{-2} $\cdot$ s^{-1}) in the greenhouse and 150 to 250 fc (3 to 50 μmol $\cdot$ m^{-2} $\cdot$ s^{-1}) in the home.

Comments: *Aglaonema* make excellent, long-lasting indoor plants. Six to 8 months will be required to finish a 6-in. (15-cm) pot of 'Silver Queen' starting with three to five cuttings. High media soluble salts can cause leaf tip burn.

APHELANDRA SQUARROSA NEES.

Common names: zebra plant, saffron spike.

Family: Acanthaceae.

Description/uses: The colorful zebra plant is named for its dark-green, glossy foliage boldly marked with white veins. The plants are primarily sold when the short spikes of bright yellow flowers are present. Several cultivars exist that vary in height, inflorescence, flower color, and leaf shape and color. Plants are primarily produced in 4- to 6-in. (10- to 15-cm) pots.

Propagation: Plants are propagated primarily by cuttings; tips are most commonly used but single-eye and double-eye cuttings can also be used.

Light: Requires 1000 to 1500 fc (200 to 300 μmol $\cdot$ m^{-2} $\cdot$ s^{-1}) during production and 150 to 200 fc (30 to 40 μmol $\cdot$ m^{-2} $\cdot$ s^{-1}) in the home.

Comments: Flowering plants from a single cutting can be produced in 15 to 20 weeks in a 4-in. (10-cm) pot and in 18 to 22 weeks in a 6-in. (15-cm) pot. A-Rest (ancymidol) sprays at 1 to 200 ppm or drenches at 0.5 to 5 mg a.i./pot may be useful to control height.

ARAUCARIA HETEROPHYLLA (SALISB.) FRANCO.

Common names: Norfolk Island pine, house pine.

Family: Araucariaceae

Description/uses: While not a true pine tree, the Norfolk Island pine is often treated as an indoor Christmas tree. The small needle-like leaves encircle the horizontal branches. Plants are typically grown in 4- to 10-in. (10- to 25-cm) pots with one to several plants per pot. Several cultivars exist that vary in foliage color and plant habit but are not widely available. Several other *Araucaria* species are grown commercially. In nature Norfolk Island pine grows to 20 ft (60 m) tall and is hardy to Zone 10.

Propagation: Plants are typically seed propagated but terminal cuttings or air layers can also be used.

Light: Requires 4000 to 8000 fc (800 to 1600 μmol $\cdot$ m^{-2} $\cdot$ s^{-1}) during production and 200 fc (40 μmol $\cdot$ m^{-2} $\cdot$ s^{-1}) or more in the home.

ARDISIA CRISPA (THUNB.) DC.

Common names: coral ardisia, coralberry.

Family: Myrsinaceae.

Description/uses: Coralberry is grown for its bright red berries and dark-green leaves on upright plants. The berries are readily produced even on young plants. The cultivar 'Alba' has white flowers and 'Variegata' has leaves edged in white or pink-red when young. Plants are produced in 2- to 6-in. (5- to 15-cm) pots with several seedlings in each pot.

Propagation: Plants are propagated by seed and occasionally by tip cuttings.

Light: Requires 1500 to 2000 fc (300 to 400 μmol $\cdot$ m^{-2} $\cdot$ s^{-1}) for small plants and 2000 to 3000 fc (400 to 600 μmol $\cdot$ m^{-2} $\cdot$ s^{-1}) for large plants during production and medium to high light in the home.

Comments: Tolerant of cool temperatures and can be grown outdoors in Zones 8 through 11. Plants can be sold at Christmas because of their long-lasting red berries and dark-green leaves.

ASPARAGUS (L.) SPECIES

Common name: asparagus fern.

Family: Liliaceae.

Description/uses: This genus contains approximately 300 species, many of which are cultivated, including *A. densiflorus* (Kunth) Jessop., *A. setaceus* (Kunth) Jessop., *A. virgatus* Bak., and *A. asparagoides* (L.) Druce. Numerous cultivars exist, especially for *A. densiflorus*. The plants are grown for their long arching branches with hundreds of small needle-like leaves (cladophylls). Plants are grown in 4- to 6-in. (10- to 15-cm) pots and 6- to 10-in. (15- to 25-cm) hanging baskets.

Propagation: Commercial seed propagation is used. Division is easy but limited to small numbers of plants.

Light: Requires 2000 to 4500 fc (400 to 900 μmol $\cdot$ m^{-2} $\cdot$ s^{-1}) during production and medium to high light in the home.

Comments: Asparagus ferns are also grown as outdoor bedding plants, container plants, and cut foliage. Many cultivars readily drop their needle-like leaves when brought into a low-humidity, low-light environment. The edible asparagus is *A. officinalis* L.

ASPIDISTRA ELATIOR BL.

Common name: cast-iron plant.

Family: Liliaceae.

Description/uses: This tough plant has long, dark-green, glossy leaves in a loose rosette habit. Cultivars exist that vary in leaf size and color. Plants are produced in 6- to 17-in. (15- to 43-cm) pots.

Propagation: Plants are propagated by divisions.

Light: Requires 2000 fc (400 μmol·m^{-2}·s^{-1}) during production and 50 fc (10 μmol · m^{-2} · s^{-1}) or more, with 100 to 150 fc (20 to 30 μmol · m^{-2} · s^{-1}) optimum, in the home.

Comments: Plants are cold tolerant and may be grown as an outdoor perennial in mild climates (Zones 7 through 11). The cast-iron plant is one of the most durable foliage plants, tolerating low light and neglect in the home.

ASPLENIUM NIDUS L.

Common name: bird's-nest fern.

Family: Aspleniaceae.

Description/uses: The plants are grown for their rosettes of long simple foliage and sold in small 4- to 6-in. (10- to 15-cm) pots and in 6- to 12-in. (15- to 30-cm) hanging baskets. Approximately 700 species occur, many of which are cultivated.

Propagation: Plants are propagated by spores and tissue culture.

Light: Requires 1500 to 3000 fc (300 to 600 μmol · m^{-2} · s^{-1}) during production and 75 to 150 fc (15 to 30 μmol · m^{-2} · s^{-1}), with 250 fc (50 μmol · m^{-2} · s^{-1}) optimum, in the home.

Comments: Small plants are often used as focal points in container gardens.

BROMELIACEAE JUSS.

Common names: see below.

Family: Bromeliaceae.

Description/uses: This large family has more than 2000 species, many of which are cultivated for their long-lasting colorful inflorescences and leaves. All species have rosettes of rigid leaves from 2 in. to 5 ft (5 cm to 1.5 m) across. Most species are epiphytic but some are terrestrial. One of the most important ornamental species is *Aechmea fasciata* (Lindl.) Bak., silver vase. *Ananas comosus* (L.) Merr., the pineapple, is an important food crop but some cultivars are also grown as ornamentals. Other genera commonly cultivated include *Cryptanthus* Otto & A. Dietr. (earthstars), *Guzmania* Ruíz & Pav., *Neoregelia*

L.B.Sm., *Nidularium* Lem., *Tillandsia* L., and *Vriesea* Lindl. Plants are typically sold in 4- to 6-in. (10- to 15-cm) pots. Some epiphytic species are attached to pieces of wood.

Propagation: Propagated by seeds, side or off-shoots, or tissue culture.

Light: Requires 2500 to 4000 fc (500 to 800 μmol · m^{-2} · s^{-1}) during production and medium to high light in the home. Optimum light levels will vary with the specific species grown.

Comments: Many bromeliads are epiphytic and hold water in a center ring of leaves known as the *cup*. Epiphytic bromeliads can be grown like any other potted plant, but require a well-aerated medium. Flowering can be induced by spraying mature plants with Florel (ethephon) at 2500 ppm. Individual shoots flower once then die; the offshoots will continue to grow and can be propagated. These slow-growing plants typically take 1 to 3 years to produce a salable plant. Water in the cups can allow mosquitoes to breed and cannot serve as a sole source of water.

CACTACEAE JUSS.

Common names: cactus; see also below.

Family: Cactaceae.

Description/uses: Most cactus are succulents and cactus are grown for their interesting adaptations to restrict water loss: They are low growing, rounded, and have thorns instead of leaves. Considering that approximately 1650 species of cactus are known to exist, there are a wide range of cactus from which to choose. All cactus are native to the Western Hemisphere. Some of the more popular types are the rounded *Echinocactus grusonii* Hildm. (golden barrel cactus), the tall columnar *Cereus uruguayanus* Kiesling. (column cactus), the "hairy" *Espostoa lanata* (Kunth) Britt. & Rose. (Peruvian old man cactus), and *Cephalocereus senilis* (Haw.) Schum. (Mexican old man cactus), and the flattened *Opuntia* Mill. (prickly pear). Plants are produced in pots ranging from 2 to 17 in. (5 to 43 cm) in diameter, with 3- to 4-in. (8- to 10-cm) pots being especially popular.

Propagation: Plants are propagated by seed, cuttings, offsets, or tissue culture. Grafting is also used, especially to produce brightly colored novelty cactus.

Light: Most cactus require high light, 5000 to 8000 fc (1000 to 1600 μmol · m^{-2} · s^{-1}) during production and, in the home, 500 fc (100 $\mu mol \cdot m^{-2} \cdot s^{-1}$) or more.

Comments: Because cactus are succulents, they should be irrigated thoroughly but also allowed to dry when actively growing. When cactus are not actively growing, such as during the winter, they should be irrigated only enough to prevent shriveling. The flowering control systems are known for a few species; these plants can be sold with flowers. The Easter cactus, *Hatiora,* and the Thanksgiving and Christmas cactus, *Schlumbergera,* have already been covered in a separate chapter.

CALATHEA MEY. SPECIES

Common names: see below.

Family: Marantaceae.

Description/uses: This family has more than 300 species. The plants are cultivated for their colorful variegated foliage, which can be elaborately marked on some species. The foliage originates from a crown and can form a loose rosette. Among the most commonly cultivated species are the medium-sized *C. lancifolia* Boom (rattlesnake plant), *C. louisae* Gagnep., and *C. makoyana* (E. Morr.) E. Morr. (peacock plant). Dwarf species include *C. micans* (Mathieu) Körn. and *C. undulata* Lind. & Andrè. Large species include *C. majestica* H. Kenn., *C. roseopicta* (Lindl.) Reg., *C. veithchiana* Hook., *C. warscewiczii* (Mathieu) Körn., and *C. zebrina* (Sims) Lindl. (zebra plant). *C. crocata* 'Eternal Flame' E. Morr. & Joriss. is grown for its orange flowers, which are typically insignificant in other species. Dwarf species are typically sold in 3- to 4-in. (8- to 10-cm) pots; larger species may be grown in pots up to 10 in. (25 cm) in diameter.

Propagation: Propagated by seed, tissue culture, or division.

Light: Requires 1000 to 2000 fc (200 to 400 $\mu mol \cdot m^{-2} \cdot s^{-1}$) during production and 150 to 400 fc (30 to 80 $\mu mol \cdot m^{-2} \cdot s^{-1}$) in the home.

Comments: *Calathea* can be difficult to grow. Fluoride toxicity is common and appears as a tip or marginal burn.

CHLOROPHYTUM COMOSUM (THUNB.) JACQUES

Common name: spider plant.

Family: Liliaceae.

Description/uses: Spider plants are grown for their dense clumps of long, thin leaves and arching stolons, which terminate in one to several plantlets. Plants are primarily grown in 6- to 10-in. (15- to 25-cm) hanging baskets. Several other species and cultivars are available that vary primarily in leaf variegation pattern from solid green to white or cream and green variegated.

Propagation: Plants are primarily propagated by rooting the plantlets. Seed or division could also be used.

Light: Requires 1500 to 2500 fc (300 to 500 $\mu mol \cdot m^{-2} \cdot s^{-1}$) during production and 75 to 100 fc (15 to 20 $\mu mol \cdot m^{-2} \cdot s^{-1}$), with 150 to 200 fc (30 to 40 $\mu mol \cdot m^{-2} \cdot s^{-1}$) optimum, in the home.

Comments: The tip burn common to spider plants is due to the accumulation of fluoride, boron, or sodium. Some cultivars are cold hardy and can survive outdoors in mild climates.

CISSUS L. SPECIES

Common name: grape ivy.

Family: Vitaceae.

Description/uses: *Cissus rhombifolia* Vahl is the most commonly grown species with cultivars that vary in growth habit and leaf shape. *C. antartica* Vent. is also grown. Both species are grown for their compound leaves on long vines. Plants are grown in 3- to 10-in. (8- to 25-cm) pots and 6- to 22-in. (15- to 55-cm) hanging baskets.

Propagation: Plants are propagated primarily by cuttings, usually single node, but seed can also be used.

Light: Requires 1500 to 2500 fc (300 to 500 $\mu mol \cdot m^{-2} \cdot s^{-1}$) during production and 75 to 100 fc (15 to 20 $\mu mol \cdot m^{-2} \cdot s^{-1}$), with 150 to 400 fc (30 to 80 $\mu mol \cdot m^{-2} \cdot s^{-1}$) optimum, in the home.

Comments: Plants can be damaged by high medium EC and excess watering. Atrimmec sprays can be applied at 780 to 1600 ppm to increase branching. A-Rest sprays at 10 to 200 ppm or drenches at 0.5 to 5 mg a.i./pot may be useful to control stem length.

CODIAEUM VARIEGATUM (L.) BL. VAR. *PICTUM* (LODD.) MUELL. ARG.

Common name: croton.

Family: Euphorbiaceae.

Description/uses: Crotons are grown for their leathery, brightly colored leaves on upright-growing plants. Dozens of cultivars are available that vary in foliage color (various combinations of green, yellow, orange, and red), and shape (long and thin to wide, even corkscrew), and plant habit. Plants are grown in 3- to 14-in. (8- to 35-cm) pots with one to several plants per pot.

Propagation: Plants are propagated primarily by tip cuttings. Air layering and seed can also be used.

Light: Requires 3000 to 8000 fc (600 to 1600 $\mu mol \cdot m^{-2} \cdot s^{-1}$) during production and 500 to 1000 fc (100 to 200 $\mu mol \cdot m^{-2} \cdot s^{-1}$) in the home. High light during production is essential for optimum foliage color, but low-light acclimation improves survivability once the plant has been marketed.

Comments: Commonly grown in frost-free areas as a durable shrub or hedge. Bonzi (paclobutrazol) sprays at 15 to 75 ppm and drenches at 0.05 to 0.5 mg a.i./pot may be effective at controlling height. Sumagic (uniconazole) sprays at 12 to 75 ppm are also effective.

COFFEA ARABICA L.

Common name: Arabian coffee.

Family: Rubiaceae.

Description/uses: This plant is well known as the source of coffee but also makes an attractive foliage plant due to its glossy green leaves. Older plants may flower and fruit. Plants are grown in small to medium-sized pots with several plants per pot.

Propagation: Plants are commercially propagated by seed. Stem cuttings can also be taken.

Light: Requires 4000 fc (800 $\mu mol \cdot m^{-2} \cdot s^{-1}$) during production and 400 to 500 fc (80 to 100 $\mu mol \cdot m^{-2} \cdot s^{-1}$) in the home.

Comments: In nature this plant grows on cool mountain slopes with daily cloud cover.

CORDYLINE TERMINALIS (L.) KUNTH.

Common name: ti plant.

Family: Agavaceae.

Description/uses: Ti plants are grown for their long colorful leaves on upright plants. Many cultivars are available that vary in leaf color (various combinations of green, red, and pink), shape (wide to thin), and plant habit. Plants are grown in 6- to 17-in. (15- to 43-cm) pots.

Propagation: Plants are most commonly propagated commercially by tip cuttings.

However, seed, cane cuttings, root layer tissue cultures, and air layer tissue cultures can be used.

Light: Requires 2500 to 4500 fc (500 to 900 $\mu mol \cdot m^{-2} \cdot s^{-1}$) during production and 75 to 150 fc (15 to 30 $\mu mol \cdot m^{-2} \cdot s^{-1}$) in the home.

Comments: Cordyline is susceptible to tip burn from fluoride toxicity. Individual leaves can be harvested and sold as cut greens. *Cordyline indivisa* (Forst.) Steud, is grown as an outdoor bedding plant, especially popular in mixed containers.

CRASSULA OVATA (MILL.) DRUCE.

Common names: jade plant, jade tree, dollar plant.

Family: Crassulaceae.

Description/uses: These plants have thick succulent leaves on upright branched plants. Cultivars exist that vary in growth habit and leaf shape and color (red, pink, white, green). Plants are produced in small to medium-sized pots.

Propagation: Plants are propagated by leaf bud and stem cuttings.

Light: Requires 5000 to 6000 fc (1000 to 1200 $\mu mol \cdot m^{-2} \cdot s^{-1}$) during production and 75 to 100 fc (15 to 20 $\mu mol \cdot m^{-2} \cdot s^{-1}$), with 1000 fc (200 $\mu mol \cdot m^{-2} \cdot s^{-1}$) optimum, in the home.

Comments: Drought tolerant. Plants are sometimes sold as bonzi specimens.

DAVALLIA FEJEENSIS HOOK.

Common name: rabbit's-foot fern.

Family: Davalliaceae.

Description/uses: The plants are grown for their long, compound foliage and interesting hairy rhizomes (rabbit's feet), which grow along the surface of the medium. Plants are sold in small 4- to 6-in. (10- to 15-cm) pots and in 6- to 12-in. (15- to 30-cm), preferably osmunda, hanging baskets. Approximately 40 species occur, many of which can also be cultivated.

Propagation: Small plants are propagated by spores, tissue culture, and rhizome pieces and larger plants by division.

Light: Requires 1200 to 1800 fc (240 to 360 $\mu mol \cdot m^{-2} \cdot s^{-1}$) during production and 75 to 150 fc (15 to 30 $\mu mol \cdot m^{-2} \cdot s^{-1}$), with 250 fc (50 $\mu mol \cdot m^{-2} \cdot s^{-1}$) optimum, in the home.

Comments: Foliage may yellow if allowed to dry out.

DIEFFENBACHIA SCHOTT. SPECIES

Common names: dieffenbachia, dumb cane.

Family: Araceae.

Description/uses: This important foliage plant is grown for its large green, white, and cream variegated leaves on upright plants. Coloring varies from small spots to broad splashes to primarily white or cream. Many cultivars exist and were primarily derived from *D. amoena* Bull. and/or *D. maculata* (Lodd.) Bunting. Cultivars vary in their branching potential. Plants are grown in 3- to 10-in. (8- to 25-cm) pots with one to three cuttings or liners per pot.

Propagation: Plants are propagated primarily by tissue culture. Tip and cane cuttings can also be used.

Light: Requires 1500 to 3000 fc (300 to 600 μmol $\cdot$ m^{-2} $\cdot$ s^{-1}) during production and 150 to 250 fc (30 to 50 μmol $\cdot$ m^{-2} $\cdot$ s^{-1}) light in the home.

Comments: This plant contains oxalic acid crystals, which cause swelling of the mouth and tongue, if ingested, hence the name dumb cane. Bonzi or Sumagic drenches at 0.06 to 0.5 mg a.i./pot may be effective in controlling height during production and in the retail or consumer setting.

EPISCIA MART., EMEND. WIEHLER SPECIES

Common name: episcia.

Family: Gesneriaceae.

Description/uses: These plants are grown for their textured, hairy green foliage variously marked with silver, bronze, cream, and yellow and white, yellow, orange, pink, or red tubular flowers. The low-growing plants produce runners that grow down over the edges of the containers. Of the six species, the two most important species are *E. cupreata* (Hook.) Hanst. and *E. reptans* from which many hybrids have been obtained. Plants are grown in small pots and hanging baskets.

Propagation: Plants are propagated by stem cuttings or plantlets. Division, leaf cuttings, or seed can also be used.

Light: Requires 2000 to 2500 fc (400 to 500 μmol $\cdot$ m^{-2} $\cdot$ s^{-1}) during production and 500 to 800 fc (100 to 160 μmol $\cdot$ m^{-2} $\cdot$ s^{-1}) in the home.

Comments: Cold water on the foliage will cause cream-colored spots and splotches (see related *Saintpaulia* chapter).

×FATSHEDERA LIZEI GUILL.

Common name: fatshedera.

Family: Araliaceae.

Description/uses: This plant is a hybrid derived from *Fatsia japonica* 'Moseri' × *Hedera hibernica* and is grown for its large, glossy, palmately lobed leaves on upright plants. Several cultivars are available that vary in plant habit and leaf shape and color.

Propagation: Plants are propagated by stem or tip cuttings.

Light: Requires 4000 to 6000 fc (800 to 1200 μmol $\cdot$ m^{-2} $\cdot$ s^{-1}) during production and 50 to 500 fc (10 to 100 μmol $\cdot$ m^{-2} $\cdot$ s^{-1}) in the home.

Comments: This plant is cold tolerant and can be grown outdoors in Zones 7 to 11. A-Rest sprays at 25 to 132 ppm or drenches at 0.25 to 0.5 mg a.i. (2 to 4 ppm)/6-in. (15-cm) pot can be used to control height.

FATSIA JAPONICA (THUNB.) DECNE. & PLANCH.

Common name: Japanese fatsia.

Family: Araliaceae.

Description/uses: Japanese fatsia is grown for its large, palmately lobed leaves on upright plants. Several cultivars are available that vary in leaf color and shape and plant habit. Plants are grown most commonly in 6- to 10-in. (15- to 25-cm) pots with one plant per pot.

Propagation: Plants can be propagated by seed, stem cuttings, root cuttings, or air layering. Variegated cultivars are generally propagated by stem cuttings.

Light: Requires 4000 to 6000 fc (800 to 1200 μmol $\cdot$ m^{-2} $\cdot$ s^{-1}) during production and 100 fc (20 μmol $\cdot$ m^{-2} $\cdot$ s^{-1}) or greater, with 150 to 250 fc (30 to 50 μmol $\cdot$ s^{-1} $\cdot$ m^{-2}) optimum, in the home.

Comments: Japanese fatsia is cold tolerant and can be grown outdoors in Zones 8 through 11.

FICUS BENJAMINA L. AND F. MICROPCARPA L. (FORMERLY KNOWN AS F. RETUSA)

Common names: weeping fig (*F. benjamina*), benjamin fig (*F. benjamina*), Indian laurel (*F. microcarpa*).

Family: Moraceae.

Description/uses: These popular species have numerous small green, glossy leaves on

FIGURE III-I FOLIAGE PLANTS *Ficus benjamina* with a braided trunk.

many thin woody twigs. *F. benjamina* has arching or droopy branches, whereas *F. microcarpa* is more upright. Numerous cultivars are available for all three species, which vary in leaf shape, plant habit, and white variegation. Plants are grown in a wide range of container sizes of 4 in. (10 cm) and larger.

Propagation: Plants are generally cutting propagated, but tissue culture and air layering are also commonly used.

Light: Requires 3000 to 6000 fc (600 to 1200 μmol $\cdot$ m^{-2} $\cdot$ s^{-1}) during production and 150 to 250 fc (30 to 50 μmol $\cdot$ m^{-2} $\cdot$ s^{-1}) in the home.

Comments: Braided figs are produced by intertwining the young, flexible stems of two or more plants (Fig. III-1 Foliage Plants). A variety of styles can be produced; one of the more unusual forms had a golf ball locked in a web of trunks. Postproduction leaf drop is reduced if plants are properly acclimatized under shade prior to marketing. High media soluble salt levels can cause stunting, excessive leaf drop, and wilting.

FICUS ELASTICA ROXB. EX HORNEM. AND *FICUS LYRATA* WARB.

Common names: rubber tree (*F. elastica*), fiddleleaf fig (*F. lyrata*).

Family: Moraceae.

Description/uses: Both the rubber tree and the fiddleleaf fig have large, thick, glossy leaves; the rubber tree leaves are oval and the fiddleleaf fig leaves are violin shaped. Both species are upright growing and are produced in containers 6 in. (15 cm) and larger with one or more stems per pot.

Propagation: Most plants are propagated by tissue culture. Cuttings or air layering can also be used.

Light: Requires 4000 to 6000 fc (800 to 1200 μmol $\cdot$ m^{-2} $\cdot$ s^{-1}) during production and 75 to 100 fc (15 to 20 μmol $\cdot$ m^{-2} $\cdot$ s^{-1}), with 200 fc (40 μmol $\cdot$ m^{-2} $\cdot$ s^{-1}) optimum, in the home.

Comments: Plants indoors tend to lose their lower leaves over time. Bonzi sprays at 62.5 to 125 ppm and drenches at 0.75 to 4.0 mg a.i./6-in. (15-cm) pot can be used to control the height of *F. lyrata*.

FITTONIA VERSCHAFFELTII (LEM.) COËM.

Common name: nerve plant.

Family: Acanthaceae.

Description/uses: These colorful, low-growing plants have white or reddish veins on their light green to reddish foliage. Several varieties are available that vary in leaf color. The plants are grown in small to medium-sized pots and hanging baskets.

Propagation: Plants are propagated by cuttings.

Light: Requires 1000 to 2500 fc (200 to 500 μmol $\cdot$ m^{-2} $\cdot$ s^{-1}) during production and 150 fc (30 μmol $\cdot$ m^{-2} $\cdot$ s^{-1}) or more in the home.

Comments: Insignificant flower spikes occasionally form and are best removed.

GYNURA AURANTIACA (BL.) DC.

Common names: purple passion vine, purple passion plant, purple velvet plant.

Family: Compositae.

Description/uses: This vine is grown for its green foliage heavily covered with purple hairs (Fig. III-2 Foliage Plants). The plant is produced in 4- to 6-in. (10- to 15-cm) pots and 6- to 10-in. (15- to 25-cm) hanging baskets, especially for spring holidays.

Propagation: Plants are propagated by tip cuttings.

Light: Requires 1150 fc (230 μmol $\cdot$ m^{-2} $\cdot$ s^{-1}) or less during production to remain vegetative; higher light levels can be used but may cause flowering. Generally 500 to 800 fc (100 to 160 μmol $\cdot$ m^{-2} $\cdot$ s^{-1}) should be used in the home.

FIGURE III-2 FOLIAGE PLANTS *Gynura aurantiaca.*

Comments: The yellow to orange flowers are malodorous (foul odor) and should be removed before opening. Flowering is encouraged by LD and high light levels. Plants should be grown under 8-hr SD and low light levels [1150 fc (230 μmol · m^{-2} · s^{-1})] to stay vegetative. Plants generally do not flower in the home unless given high light levels. Plants should be pinched during production to encourage branching. A-Rest sprays at 25 to 132 ppm or drenches at 0.25 to 0.5 mg a.i. (2 to 4 ppm)/6-in. (15-cm) pot can be used to control height.

HOYA CARNOSA (L. F.) R. BR.

Common name: wax plant.

Family: Asclepiadaceae.

Description/uses: A number of the 200 to 230 species of *Hoya* are cultivated for their long vines, fleshy leaves, and interesting waxy flowers. One of the most popular species is *H. carnosa* (L. f.) R. Br., which has dark-green leaves and a number of variegated cultivars with white, pink, cream, and red on the leaves. Some of the cultivars also have twisted, contorted leaves. Plants are produced in 3- to 6-in. (8- to 15-cm) pots and 5- to 10-in. (13- to 25-cm) hanging baskets with several plants per container.

Propagation: Plants are propagated by single-node or tip cuttings.

Light: Requires 1500 to 2500 fc (300 to 500 μmol · m^{-2} · s^{-1}) during production and a minimum of 125 fc (25 μmol · m^{-2} · s^{-1}) in the home.

Comments: Plants can be sold as topiary items with the vines trained around a support.

MARANTA LEUCONEURA E. MORR.

Common name: prayer plant.

Family: Marantaceae.

Description/uses: The prayer plant has a loose rosette of oblong leaves generously marked, especially along the veins, with a variety of colors including red, brown, silver, purple, and maroon. Numerous cultivars with a wide range of color patterns are available. One popular type is *M. leuconeura* var. *kerchoviana* E. Morr., the rabbit's foot plant, so named because the green leaves are marked on either side of the main vein with purplish brown spots representing rabbit tracks. Prayer plants as a group are named for the fact that the leaves fold up at night. Plants are produced in 3- to 8-in. (8- to 20-cm) pots and occasionally in hanging baskets with two or more plants per container.

Propagation: Plants are propagated by cuttings or tissue culture.

Light: Requires 1000 to 2500 fc (200 to 500 μmol · m^{-2} · s^{-1}) during production and 75 to 150 fc (15 to 30 μmol · m^{-2} · s^{-1}) in the home.

Comments: *Maranta* is closely related to *Calathea.*

MONSTERA DELICIOSA LIEBM.

Common name: Swiss cheese plant.

Family: Araceae.

Description/uses: This vine plant has large, glossy, broad leaves with perforations and splits and is similar to some philodendron species. The stem is thick. Plants are grown in medium to large pots and occasionally on totem poles.

Propagation: Plants are propagated by tip and stem cuttings. Air layers or seed can also be used.

Light: Requires 3500 to 4500 fc (700 to 900 μmol · m^{-2} · s^{-1}) during production and medium to high light in the home.

Comments: Plants have juvenile leaves, which are entire, and adult leaves, which have the characteristic perforations. A-Rest sprays at 25 to 132 ppm or drenches at 0.25 to 0.5 mg a.i. (2 to 4 ppm)/6-in. (15-cm) pot can be used to control height.

NEPHROLEPIS EXALTATA (L.) SCHOTT.

Common names: Boston fern, sword fern.

Family: Oleandraceae.

Description/uses: The plants are grown for their rosettes of long, compound foliage and sold in small 4- to 6-in. (10- to 15-cm) pots and in 6- to 12-in. (15- to 30-cm) hanging baskets. Approximately 30 species occur, of which *N. exaltata* is most commonly cultivated. Several cultivars of *N. exaltata* are available, which vary in size and leaflet (pinnae) shape and number.

Propagation: Small plants are propagated by tissue culture and stolons and larger plants by division.

Light: Requires 1500 to 3000 fc (300 to 600 μmol $\cdot$ m^{-2} $\cdot$ s^{-1}) during production and 75 to 150 fc (15 to 30 μmol $\cdot$ m^{-2} $\cdot$ s^{-1}), with 250 fc (50 μmol $\cdot$ m^{-2} $\cdot$ s^{-1}) optimum, in the home.

Comments: This species is well suited to hanging baskets and is commonly sold in the spring for patios and porches. Outdoor-grown plants can be overwintered indoors but tend to lose many leaflets. Water stress makes the foliage appear grayish.

NOLINA RECURVATA (LEM.) HENSL. (FORMERLY KNOWN AS BEAUCARNEA RECURVATA)

Common name: ponytail palm.

Family: Agavaceae.

Description/uses: This interesting plant is grown for its large swollen stem base topped by a clump of long narrow arching green leaves. Plants are produced in 6- to 14-in. (15- to 35-cm) pots with one plant per pot.

Propagation: Plants are propagated by seed.

Light: Requires 4000 to 6000 fc (800 to 1200 μmol $\cdot$ m^{-2} $\cdot$ s^{-1}) during production and 500 to 800 fc (100 to 160 μmol $\cdot$ m^{-2} $\cdot$ s^{-1}) in the home.

Comments: The strikingly swollen stem base can be quite large in old specimens.

PALMAE JUSS.

Common names: see next column.

Family: Palmae.

Description/uses: Palms are small to large trees that are grown for the upright, usually pinnately compound foliage. There are over 2700 species. The most commonly grown species are *Chamaedorea elegans* Mart. (parlor palm), *Chrysalidocarpus lutescens* (Bory) H.A. Wendl. (areca palm, yellow palm, butterfly palm, cane palm), and *Howea forsteriana* (C. Moore & F. Muell.) Becc. (kentia palm, sentry palm). Plants are sold in pots ranging in size from 3 in. (8 cm) for small seedlings up to 21 in. (53 cm) in diameter; 10- to 14-in. (25- to 35-cm) pots are most commonly used. Multiple seedlings are used in each pot.

Propagation: Commercial propagation is primarily by seed. Divisions or offsets can also be used.

Light: *Chamaedorea elegans* requires 1500 to 3000 fc (300 to 600 μmol $\cdot$ m^{-2} $\cdot$ s^{-1}) during production and 75 to 150 fc (15 to 30 μmol $\cdot$ m^{-2} $\cdot$ s^{-1}) in the home. *Chrysalidocarpus lutescens* requires 3500 to 6000 fc (700 to 1200 μmol $\cdot$ m^{-2} $\cdot$ s^{-1}) during production and 150 to 400 fc (30 to 80 μmol $\cdot$ m^{-2} $\cdot$ s^{-1}) in the home. *Howea fosteriana* requires 2500 to 6000 fc (500 to 1200 μmol $\cdot$ m^{-2} $\cdot$ s^{-1}) during production and a minimum of 50 fc (10 μmol $\cdot$ m^{-2} $\cdot$ s^{-1}), with 100 fc (20 μmol $\cdot$ m^{-2} $\cdot$ s^{-1}) or more optimum, in the home.

Comments: A wide variety of palm species can be produced. Other species commonly cultivated include *Chamaedorea erumpens* H.E. Moore. (bamboo palm), *C. seifrizii* Burret. (reed palm), *Phoenix roebelinni* O'Brien. (pygmy date palm), *P. reclinata* Jacq. (Senegal date palm), *Rhapis excelsa* (Thunb.) Henry. (lady palm), and *R. humilis* Bl. (slender lady palm). Less commonly used species are *Chamaedorea cataractarum* Mart., *C. ernesti-augusti* H.A. Wendl., *C. geonomiformis* H.A. Wendl., *C. microspadix* Burret., *C. metallica* Cook ex H.E. Moore, and *C. tepejilote* Liebm.

PEPEROMIA RUÍZ & PAV. SPECIES

Common names: peperomia; see also below.

Family: Piperaceae.

Description/uses: A number of peperomias are cultivated and most have thick, fleshy leaves variously marked with red, silver, maroon, white, cream, and yellow. Plant habit ranges from vining to loose rosettes. Several popular species are *P. argyreia* Morr., watermelon peperomia, with broad leaves striped in green and silver; *P. caperata* Yunck., emerald-ripple peperomia, with small leaves that have sunken veins; *P. clusiifolia* (Jacq.) Hook., red-edged peperomia, with oval leaves edged in red; *P. griseoargentea* Yunck., ivy-leaf peperomia, with round leaves that have sunken veins; *P. obtusifolia* (L.) Dietr., baby rubber tree, with large oval green leaves; and *P. scandens* hort., with heart-shaped leaves on a vine. Numerous cultivars exist for several of the species. These relatively small plants are grown in 2.5- to 6-in. (6- to 15-cm) pots and occasionally in hanging baskets with one to several cuttings in each container.

Propagation: Plants are propagated by stem, leaf, or single-eye stem cuttings.

Light: Requires 1500 to 3500 fc (300 to 700 μmol $\cdot$ m$^{-2} \cdot$ s^{-1}) during production and 100 to 250 fc (20 to 50 μmol $\cdot$ m$^{-2} \cdot$ s^{-1}) in the home.

Comments: Peperomias are quite sensitive to various root and crown roots; avoid overwatering. Drenches of A-Rest at 0.12 to 2 mg a.i./6-in. (15-cm) pot or Sumagic at 0.2 to 0.6 mg a.i./6-in. (15-cm) pot can be used to control the height of some *Peperomia* species.

PILEA LINDL. SPECIES

Common names: pilea; see also below.

Family: Urticaceae.

Description/uses: This genus includes a number of small to medium-sized species that are produced in 3- to 6-in. (8- to 15-cm) pots and hanging baskets. One of the most popular species is *P. cadierei* Gagnep. & Guillaum., the aluminum plant, which has glossy green and silver foliage. Other common species include *P. involucrata* (Sims) Urban., friendship plant, with coppery purple and silver leaves; *P. microphylla* (L.) Liebm., artillery plant, with a dense covering of tiny green leaves on an upright plant; and *P. nummularifolia* (Sw.) Wedd., baby tears, with numerous tiny green leaves on creeping stems.

Propagation: Plants are propagated by cuttings. Seed can also be used with some species.

Light: Requires 1500 to 3000 fc (300 to 600 μmol $\cdot$ m$^{-2} \cdot$ s^{-1}) during production and 150 to 250 fc (30 to 50 μmol $\cdot$ m$^{-2} \cdot$ s^{-1}) in the home.

Comments: The artillery plant produces abundant seeds and may become weedy in the greenhouse. A-Rest sprays at 25 to 132 ppm or drenches at 0.25 to 0.5 mg a.i. (2 to 4

ppm)/6-in. (15-cm) pot can be used to control the height of some species.

PLATYCERIUM BIFURCATUM (CAV.) C. CHR.

Common names: staghorn fern, elkhorn fern.

Family: Polypodiaceae.

Description/uses: The staghorn fern is grown for its large, broad fronds. Because it is an epiphyte, it is grown on plaques or wire baskets with sphagnum moss. Several other similar species can be grown; *P. hillii* T. Moore., the elkhorn fern, and its cultivars are commonly grown in Europe.

Propagation: Plants are propagated by spores or removal of offsets.

Light: Requires 1500 to 3000 fc (300 to 600 μmol $\cdot$ m$^{-2} \cdot$ s^{-1}) during production and 75 to 150 fc (15 to 30 μmol $\cdot$ m$^{-2} \cdot$ s^{-1}), with 250 fc (50 μmol $\cdot$ m$^{-2} \cdot$ s^{-1}) optimum, in the home.

Comments: Although difficult to water when grown on a plaque, it makes a striking plant.

PLECTRANTHUS L'HÈRIT. SPECIES

Common name: Swedish ivy.

Family: Labiatae.

Description/uses: These vine plants are grown primarily for their green to white and green foliage but they also produce loose spikes of white flowers. The most commonly grown species are *P. forsteri* Benth. (incorrectly called *P. coleoides*), *P. verticillatus* (L.f.) Druce (formerly known as *P. australis*) with glossy green or green and white leaves and *P. madagascariensis* (Pers.) Benth. with fragrant, green and white, hairy foliage. Plants are grown in 6- to 10-in. (15- to 25-cm) hanging baskets with numerous cuttings per basket.

Propagation: Plants are propagated by cuttings.

Light: Requires 3000 to 4000 fc (600 to 800 μmol $\cdot$ m$^{-2} \cdot$ s^{-1}) during production and 200 to 1000 fc (40 to 200 μmol $\cdot$ m$^{-2} \cdot$ s^{-1}) in the home.

Comments: Several species are also grown as outdoor bedding plants. Drenches of Bonzi at 0.2 to 1.0 mg a.i./6-in. (15-cm) pot or Sumagic at 0.02 to 0.8 mg a.i./6-in. (15-cm) pot can be used to control height.

POLYSCIAS FORST. & FORST. F. SPECIES (FORMERLY PART OF *ARALIA*)

Common name: aralia.

Family: Araliaceae.

Description/uses: Aralias are grown for their upright, strong stems and dark-green to variegated foliage. Commonly grown species include *Polyscias scutellaria* (Burn. f.) Fosb., the Balfour aralia, which has green and white variegated foliage; *P. guilfoylei* (Bull) L.H. Bail., wild coffee, which has dark-green foliage; and *P. fruticosa* (L.) Harms, the ming aralia, which has finely dissected foliage. Numerous cultivars of each species are available and many cultivars of uncertain origin are also available. Plants are grown in 6- to 14-in. (15- to 35-cm) pots.

Propagation: Plants are primarily propagated by tip or cane cuttings.

Light: Requires 1500 to 4500 fc (300 to 900 μmol $\cdot$ m^{-2} $\cdot$ s^{-1}) during production and 75 fc (15 μmol $\cdot$ m^{-2} $\cdot$ s^{-1}) or more in the home.

Comments: Plants can become quite leggy indoors.

PTERIS ENSIFORMIS BURM. F.

Common name: Victoria table fern.

Family: Pteridaceae.

Description/uses: The plants are grown for their rosettes of compound foliage and sold in small 4- to 6-in. (10- to 15-cm) pots and in 6- to 12-in. (15- to 30-cm) hanging baskets. Approximately 280 species occur, of which *P. ensiformis* is most commonly cultivated. Several dwarf cultivars of *P. ensiformis* are available.

Propagation: Small plants are propagated by spores or tissue culture and larger plants by division.

Light: Requires 1200 to 1800 fc (240 to 360 μmol $\cdot$ m^{-2} $\cdot$ s^{-1}) during production and 75 to 150 fc (15 to 30 μmol $\cdot$ m^{-2} $\cdot$ s^{-1}), with 250 fc (50 μmol $\cdot$ m^{-2} $\cdot$ s^{-1}) optimum, in the home.

Comments: Best grown warm, does not tolerate cool temperatures.

RADERMACHERA SINICA (HANCE) HEMSL.

Common name: China doll.

Family: Bignoniaceae.

Description/uses: This plant is grown for its large, glossy, compound leaves on upright plants. *Radermachera* is grown in 6- to 10-in. (15- to 25-cm) pots with several plants per pot.

Propagation: Plants are propagated by seed.

Light: Requires 3000 to 3500 fc (600 to 700 μmol $\cdot$ m^{-2} $\cdot$ s^{-1}) during production and 250 to 300 fc (50 to 60 μmol $\cdot$ m^{-2} $\cdot$ s^{-1}) in the home.

Comments: The leaflets drop readily if the plant is stressed.

SANSEVIERIA TRIFASCIATA HORT. EX PRAIN

Common name: snake plant.

Family: Agavaceae.

Description/uses: Many of the approximately 70 species are cultivated for their long fleshy leaves, which are often marked with gray green, white, cream, or yellow (Fig. III-3 Foliage Plants). *S. trifasciata* hort. ex. Prain. is one of the most commonly cultivated types and a number of cultivars are available. Cultivars range from short, strongly rosette forming types to open clusters of tall leaves. Plants are produced in 2.5- to 14-in. (6- to 35-cm) pots with one to several plants per pot.

Propagation: Plants are propagated by leaf cuttings, crown divisions, or rhizome cuttings.

Light: Requires 3500 to 5000 fc (700 to 1000 μmol $\cdot$ m^{-2} $\cdot$ s^{-1}) during production and 50 to 75 fc (10 to 15 μmol $\cdot$ m^{-2} $\cdot$ s^{-1}) in the home.

Comments: Snake plants are one of the most durable of foliage plants. Many cultivars are periclinal chimeras and the variegation may be lost during cutting propagation.

FIGURE III-3 FOLIAGE PLANTS *Sansevieria trifasciata* 'Laurentii.'

SCHEFFLERA FORST. & FORST. F. SPECIES

Common names: schefflera, umbrella tree [*S. actinophylla* (Endl.) Harms. (formerly known as *Brassaia actinophylla*)], dwarf schefflera [*S. arboricola* (Hayata) Hayata], and false aralia [*S. elegantissima* (formerly known as *Dizygotheca elegantissima*)].

Family: Araliaceae.

Description/uses: Scheffleras are grown for their large, glossy green, palmately compound leaves on upright plants. Umbrella tree has large broad leaflets with smooth edges. Dwarf schefflera is similar to umbrella tree but has smaller leaves and is shorter. False aralia has narrow, dark-green leaflets with serrated edges; compact forms are available but not widely used. The plant is grown in 6- to 17-in. (15- to 42-cm) pots with numerous seeds per pot. Dwarf schefflera can be grown in smaller pots of 3 to 5 in. (8 to 13 cm) and is occasionally braided with benjamin fig.

Propagation: Plants are primarily propagated by seed, but tip, stem, or single-eye cuttings or air layer may also be used.

Light: Umbrella tree and dwarf schefflera require 4000 to 6000 fc (800 to 1200 μmol $\cdot$ m^{-2} $\cdot$ s^{-1}) during production and 150 fc (30 μmol $\cdot$ m^{-2} $\cdot$ s^{-1}) or greater in the home. False aralia requires 2000 to 4000 fc (400 to 800 μmol $\cdot$ m^{-2} $\cdot$ s^{-1}) during production and 320 to 1000 fc (64 to 200 μmol $\cdot$ m^{-2} $\cdot$ s^{-1}) in the home.

Comments: The adult foliage of false aralia is large and broader lobed than the juvenile foliage. A-Rest sprays at 25 to 132 ppm, a Bonzi drench at 0.2 to 2 mg a.i./6-in. (15-cm) pot, or a Sumagic drench at 0.2 to 1 mg a.i./6-in. (15-cm) pot can be used to control height. Atrimmec sprays at 3125 ppm can be used to increase branching.

SYNGONIUM PODOPHYLLUM SCHOTT.

Common name: nephthytis.

Family: Araceae.

Description/uses: Nephthytis has large arrowhead-shaped leaves colored green, white, silver, pink, and reddish (Fig. III-4 Foliage Plants). Although this plant is a vine, juvenile plants retain a loose rosette appearance for a long time after propagation. Foliage shape changes to palmately compound as the plants become mature. Plants are produced in

FIGURE III-4 FOLIAGE PLANTS *Syngonium podophyllum* 'White Butterfly' plugs.

3- to 8-in. (8 to 20-cm) pots and 5- to 10-in. (13- to 25-cm) hanging baskets.

Propagation: Plants are propagated primarily by tissue culture. Tip or single-eye stem cuttings can also be used.

Light: Requires 1500 to 3500 fc (300 to 700 μmol $\cdot$ m^{-2} $\cdot$ s^{-1}) during production and 75 fc (15 μmol $\cdot$ m^{-2} $\cdot$ s^{-1}) or greater, with 100 to 150 fc (20 to 30 μmol $\cdot$ m^{-2} $\cdot$ s^{-1}) optimum, in the home.

Comments: Plants are excellent for shady outdoor mixed containers. A-Rest sprays at 25 to 132 ppm or drenches at 0.25 to 0.5 mg a.i. (2 to 4 ppm)/6-in. (15-cm) pot can be used to control height. Sumagic drenches at 0.02 to 0.8 mg a.i./6-in. (15-cm) pot may also be effective.

TOLMIEA MENZIESII TORR. & A. GRAY.

Common name: piggyback plant.

Family: Saxifragaceae.

Description/uses: This interesting plant has hairy, maple-leaf-shaped leaves with a plantlet at the base of every leaf blade. The leaves are arranged in an open, loose rosette. The plants are produced in small pots and hanging baskets.

Propagation: Plants are propagated from the young plantlets or by division.

Light: Requires 3500 to 4000 fc (700 to 800 μmol $\cdot$ m^{-2} $\cdot$ s^{-1}) during production and 400 to 500 fc (80 to 100 μmol $\cdot$ m^{-2} $\cdot$ s^{-1}) in the home.

Comments: This underused species is native to coastal North America from northern California to Alaska and is cold hardy in Zones 7 through 11.

TRADESCANTIA L. SPECIES

Common names: wandering Jew, inch plant.

Family: Commelinaceae.

Description/uses: These procumbent plants are popular hanging basket plants grown for their green, white, red, pink, purple, and silver foliage. One of the most popular species is *T. zebrina* hort. ex. Bosse., which has green and silver stripes on the top of the leaves and purple underneath. Other species grown include *T. cerinthoides* Kunth., with leaves smooth green above and purplish hairy below; *T. fluminensis* Vell. Conc., with green or green and white striped foliage; *T. sillamontana* Matuda., with long leaves covered in gray hairs; and *T. spathacea* Sw. with long, leaves dark green above and purple below. Numerous cultivars are available with several of the species.

Propagation: Plants are propagated by stem cuttings.

Light: Requires 3500 to 4500 fc (700 to 900 μmol $\cdot$ m^{-2} $\cdot$ s^{-1}) during production and medium to high light in the home.

Comments: This popular plant also performs well in shady outdoor mixed containers. A-Rest sprays at 25 to 132 ppm can be used to control height. Bonzi drenches at 0.5 mg a.i./6-in. (15-cm) pot may also be effective.

YUCCA ELEPHANTIPES REG.

Common name: spineless yucca.

Family: Agavaceae.

Description/uses: Yucca has an appearance similar to that of the popular dracaena with numerous long narrow green leaves on upright plants. Plants are produced in 6- to 14-in. (15- to 35-cm) pots with one to several plants per pot.

Propagation: Plants are generally propagated by tip or cane cuttings. Seed, offsets, rhizomes, or root cuttings can also be used.

Light: Requires 3500 to 4500 fc (700 to 900 μmol $\cdot$ m^{-2} $\cdot$ s^{-1}) during production and 150 fc (30 μmol $\cdot$ m^{-2} $\cdot$ s^{-1}) or more, with 250 fc (50 μmol $\cdot$ m^{-2} $\cdot$ s^{-1}) optimum, in the home.

Comments: The tips of the leaves can be pointed and sharp; handle plants carefully.

ZAMIOCULCAS ZAMIIFOLIA (LODD.) ENGL.

Common names: ZZ plant, aroid palm, arum fern, cardboard palm, emerald frond.

Family: Araceae.

Description/uses: ZZ plant has long, rigid pinnately compound leaves that arise from a thick horizontal rhizome. The leaflets are bright, shiny green and borne on thick, fleshy petioles. Plants appear similar to some cycads. Plants are produced in 4- to 10-in. (10- to 25-cm) pots with one to several plants per pot.

Propagation: Plants are generally propagated by rhizome division, leaf cuttings, or petiole cuttings.

Light: Requires 1500 to 2500 fc (300 to 500 μmol $\cdot$ m^{-2} $\cdot$ s^{-1}) during production and 25 fc (5 μmol $\cdot$ m^{-2} $\cdot$ s^{-1}) or more in the home.

Comments: A relatively new foliage plant that is exceptionally tolerant to low light, drought, and low humidity. In addition, no insects or diseases have been reported. In other words, ZZ plant is the perfect interior plant. It should be grown on the dry side during the winter.

KEY POINTS

- Numerous species are grown as potted foliage plants and the list is expanding annually.
- Foliage plants are produced in a wide range of containers, ranging from small pots for use in dish gardens, planters, or baskets to large pots used for large specimens placed in the home, business, or interiorscape.
- In warm climates some species are also used as outdoor landscape ornamentals.
- Commercially hanging basket foliage plants can be divided into two general groups: "soft" and "hard" baskets, depending on the type of plant material.
- Foliage plants can be propagated using a variety of methods, especially seed, cuttings, or tissue culture.
- For cutting-propagated species, stock plants or previously propagated plants are the source of cuttings.
- Many growers buy rooted or unrooted cuttings, *in vitro* material, liners, or plugs propagated by specialists.

BIBLIOGRAPHY

Chen, J., and R.J. Henny. 2003. ZZ: A unique tropical ornamental foliage plant. *HortTechnology* 13: 458–462.

Griffith, L.P., Jr. 1998. *Tropical Foliage Plants*. Ball Publishing, Batavia, Illinois.

Hamrick, D. 2003. *Ball Redbook*, vol. 2, 17th ed. Ball Publishing, Batavia, Illinois.

Henny, R.J. 2001. Foliage plants, pp. 83–87 in *Tips on Regulating Growth of Floriculture Crops*, M.L. Gaston, L.A. Kunkle, P.S. Konjoian, and M.F. Wilt, editors. Ohio Florists' Association Services, Columbus, Ohio.

Huxley, A., M. Griffiths, and M. Levy. 1992. *The New Royal Horticultural Society Dictionary of Gardening*, vols. 1–4. Stockton Press, New York.

Joiner, A.N., editor. 1981. *Foliage Plant Production*. Prentice Hall, Englewood Cliffs, New Jersey.

Pennisi, S.(B.)., J.J. Chen, and D. McConnell. 2003. Plant growth regulator application improves the interior performance of three dieffenbachia cultivars. *HortScience* 38:714–715. (Abstract)

Whipker, B.E. 2003. Growth regulators for floricultural crops, pp. 439–448 in *2003 North Carolina Agricultural Chemicals Manual*. College of Agriculture and Life Science, North Carolina State University, Raleigh.

Garden Perennials

INTRODUCTION

Around the world numerous plant species are grown as garden perennials. Each climate defines what a "perennial" species is for that region. Garden enthusiasts range from those who combine a few perennials with annuals to those who specialize in a specific genus and may have hundreds of species and cultivars within the genus. Increasing in popularity are specific groups of perennials used for xeriscaping, butterfly gardens, water gardens, and native plant gardens. The use of perennial species in public gardens and commercial landscapes is also increasing.

Unlike annual bedding plants, which are grown and marketed in flats or small containers, many perennial species must be grown and marketed in 1-qt (1-liter) or larger pots. Further many perennial species do not flower well in the container or, if they do flower in containers, their flowering period is short. Consequently, many perennials are sold green. Any retailer can relate the challenges of marketing plants not in flower. Even more difficult to sell are those plants that go dormant in the summer after flowering in early spring, such as *Dicentra*, leaving only bare media or a few senesced shoots. Thus, every pot sold should be labeled, preferably with a tag that has a color picture and basic culture information. Large signs displayed above or behind each plant species showing a color picture and more in-depth culture information will be quite useful. Provide as much culture information to customers as possible to help them select the species that will perform the best for them. Finally, a beautiful display garden is sure to increase sales of whichever species is in flower at the time.

Small green plants of some species can be grown in flats with up to 18 plants/flat or in 4-in. (10-cm) pots. Green plants are normally propagated during late winter or early spring and have a relatively short production time. Large flowering plants can also be produced by propagating in the summer or fall, growing in 1-qt (1-liter) or larger pots, and overwintering outdoors. However, overwintering can be expensive, time consuming, and potentially injurious to the plants in cold climates. It may be more cost effective to produce potted perennials in large containers from dormant roots or large plugs planted in late winter. Flowering pictocols have been developed for hundreds of cultivars by Michigan State University and other researchers, allowing for rapid potted flowering plant production.

Many commonly used garden perennials have already been covered in this text in separate chapters including *Aconitum, Anemone, Aquilegia, Asclepias, Aster, Astilbe, Campanula, Centaurea, Clematis, Convallaria, Crocus, Delphinium, Dendranthema, Dianthus, Echinacea, Eremurus, Gentiana, Gypsophila, Helianthus, Hyacinthus, Iris, Liatris, Lilium, Limonium, Narcissus, Ornithogalum, Oxalis, Paeonia, Platycodon, Primula, Solidago, Tulipa,* and *Zantedeschia.* Note that while the above chapters often focus on the use of these species as potted flowering plants and cut flowers, helpful information will be obtained. A number of other common garden perennials are briefly described in this chapter. Check the *Bedding Plants, Field-Grown Cut Flowers,* and *Foliage Plants* chapters also because many perennials have multiple uses. Scientific names are based on Huxley et al. (1992) and the references are listed at the end of the chapter.

ACHILLEA L. SPECIES

Common name: yarrow.

Family: Compositae.

Description/uses: Many yarrow species and hybrids are available and quite cold hardy from Zones 3 to 10. All species have many small flowers borne in flat to rounded heads atop long stems from early summer to fall. Most species spread to form a large irregular mat of fernlike foliage from which the flower stalks arise. Yarrows prefer full sun and tolerate dry conditions. *A. filipendulina* Lam. is one of the most popular with large yellow flower clusters up to 5 in. (13 cm) across. *A. millefolium* L. is available in a broad range of colors including white, pink, red, rust, and orange. Numerous other yarrow species and cultivars are also grown commercially.

Propagation: Propagate by seed, cuttings, or division.

Production: Plants of most species will flower the first year and can be flowered in 1-qt (1-liter) or larger pots. Height can be controlled by up to four spray applications of B-Nine (daminozide) at 5000 ppm each, one or more spray applications of Bonzi (paclobutrazol) at 30 to 120 ppm, or one spray application of Sumagic (uniconazole) at 15 ppm. Rates vary considerably with the species; be sure to test carefully.

Comments: The foliage has a fragrance that some people find objectionable. Yarrows are also important field-grown cut flowers (see *Field-Grown Cut Flowers* chapter).

AJUGA REPTANS L.

Common names: bugleweed, carpet bugle.

Family: Labiatae.

Description/uses: Short spikes of blue to purple flowers are carried above a mat of dark-green foliage. Some cultivars have white flowers while others have variegated foliage. This fast spreading plant prefers moist soil and is often used as a ground cover in shady areas. *Ajuga* tolerates sun in cool, moist climates. Leaves may retain their color during the winter. Plants are cold hardy from Zones 3 or 4 to 10 and flower in spring.

Propagation: Divide plants, take stem cuttings, or propagate the stolons by which it spreads.

Production: Plants can be grown in bedding plant flats or pots up to 1 gal (3.8 liter) in size. Plants will flower in the container, especially if provided with 6 wks of 41°F (5°C).

Comments: Tolerates light foot traffic.

ALCEA ROSEA L.

Common name: hollyhock.

Family: Malvaceae.

Description/uses: This biennial to short-lived perennial produces tall spikes of large, showy five-petaled flowers that may be white, pink, red, purple, yellow, or bicolored. Double-flowered cultivars exist. The plants are best grown in the background of a sunny garden and often benefit from tying or staking. The 4- to 6-ft (1.2- to 1.8-m) spikes arise from a large rosette of foliage. Dwarf cultivars are available. Plants are hardy from Zones 3 to 10.

Propagation: Propagate by seed.

Production: Plants are best produced in 1-qt (1-liter) or larger containers which should be deep to accommodate the taproot. While plants can be flowered in the container, they are typically sold green. Height can be controlled by up to four spray applications of B-Nine at 5000 ppm each, one spray application of Bonzi at 30 to 50 ppm, one drench application of Bonzi at 1.5 ppm, or one spray application of Sumagic at 15 ppm or less. However, Sumagic can result in excessive height control.

Comments: Annual cultivars are available.

ARABIS CAUCASICA SCHLDL.

Common names: rock cress, wall cress.

Family: Cruciferae.

Description/uses: *A. caucasica* is a low-growing perennial that forms a mat of gray-green foliage. The loose clusters of white to pink, fragrant flowers are carried atop 6- to 8-in. (15- to 20-cm) stems. Plants are hardy from Zones 3 to 10 and flower in the early spring. Plants perform best in full sun in cool climates and with afternoon shade in warm climates.

Propagation: Plants are propagated by seed or cuttings.

Production: Plants will flower in flats or 4-in. (10-cm) pots if started before January.

Comments: Plants are not invasive.

COREOPSIS L. SPECIES

Common name: tickseed.

Family: Compositae.

Description/uses: Two commonly grown species, *C. grandiflorum* Hogg ex Sweet. and *C. verticillata* L., have single or double yellow to orange flowers held upright on 10- to 30-in. (25- to 75-cm)-tall mounded plants. Flowers are 1.5 to 2.5 in. (4 to 6 cm) across with yellow disc florets (Fig. III-1 Garden Perennials). The foliage is dark green. Plants are hardy from Zones 3 or 4 to 9, flower early to midsummer, and have a long flowering period. Other species grown include *C. auriculata* L. with yellow flowers; *C. rosea* Nutt., which has white to red petals and yellow centers; and *C. tripteris* L., which has yellow flowers and grows to 10 ft (3 m) tall. Many durable, floriferous hybrids are available in a broad range of colors including red, pink, and rose. Most *Coreopsis* prefer sunny locations.

Propagation: Propagate from seed or cuttings. Divisions can also be used.

Production: Generally grown in 1-qt (1-liter) or larger containers. Plants will flower in the container if started early enough or overwintered. LD or cold treatment at 41°F (5°C) can be used to induce flowering of some species. Height can be controlled by up to three spray applications of B-Nine at 5000 ppm each,

FIGURE III-1 GARDEN PERENNIALS *Coreopsis* 'Sweet Dreams.'

one spray application of Bonzi at 80 to 100 ppm, one drench application of Bonzi at 5 to 10 ppm each, or one or more spray applications of Sumagic at 15 to 40 ppm.

Comments: Divide plants every 2 to 3 years. *C. verticillata* 'Moonbeam' was the 1992 Perennial Plant of the Year. *Coreopsis* are also grown as cut flowers (see *Field-Grown Cut Flowers* chapter).

GAILLARDIA ×GRANDIFLORA VAN HOUTTE.

Common name: blanket flower.

Family: Compositae.

Description/uses: This plant is a hybrid between *C. aristata* Pursh. and *C. pulchella* Foug., both of which can also be grown. The showy daisy-like flowers are 2 to 4 in. (5 to 10 cm) across and carried above 12- to 30-in. (30- to 75-cm)-tall mounded plants. The flowers are yellow, orange, bronze, or various combinations of those colors. Plants are hardy from Zones 3 to 9 and have an extended flowering period from June to frost. The foliage is hairy and light green.

Propagation: Propagate by seed, stem, or root cuttings or division. Seed is most commonly used.

Production: Produce in 4-in. (10-cm) or larger containers. Most plants will flower in the container. Cold treatment at 41°F (5°C) and LD will promote flowering of some cultivars.

Height can be controlled by up to three spray applications of B-Nine at 5000 ppm each or one spray application of Sumagic at 60 ppm.

Comments: Asexually propagated cultivars are more uniform than those grown from seed.

HEMEROCALLIS L. SPECIES

Common name: daylily.

Family: Liliaceae.

Description/uses: Daylilies are the second most important plant in the perennial plant industry (after hosta) because they are durable, have a long flowering period, grow well in many climates, and are available in an exceptionally broad array of colors. The large 2.5- to 7-in. (6- to 18-cm)-wide, six-petaled flowers (Fig. III-2 Garden Perennials) are carried atop long leafless scapes, which arise from a mound of long, narrow, arching leaves. Dwarf cultivars grow only 10 in. (25 cm) tall, while other cultivars may reach 3.5 ft (1 m). Each individual flower lasts only a day (occasionally 2 days), hence the common name, but there are many buds on each scape allowing for continuous color for several weeks. Flowering occurs from early summer to frost. The flowers are available in a dazzling array of colors due to the extensive hybridization that has occurred. Thousands of cultivars have been registered, many by private breeders. Some species and hybrids are fragrant. Plants are hardy from Zones 4 to 9 and prefer full sun.

Propagation: Most commonly propagated by division; tissue culture is also used.

Production: Grow dwarf cultivars in a 2-qt (2-liter) or larger container; 1-gal (3.8-liter)

FIGURE III-2 GARDEN PERENNIALS
Hemerocallis 'Ice Carnival.'

or larger containers will be best for large cultivars. One-year-old divisions typically do not flower the first year. Use divisions with three shoots to produce a fuller pot.

Comments: Local daylily enthusiasts can often provide guidance on choosing appropriate cultivars to grow in each region.

HEUCHERA SANGUINEA ENGELM.

Common names: coral bells, alumroot.

Family: Saxifragaceae.

Description/uses: The primary attraction of coral bells is the low 6- to 10-in. (15- to 25-cm)-tall mound of dense foliage, which can be dark green, purple, burgundy, silver, or various combinations of those colors. The long, up to 30-in. (75-cm), spikes of tiny cream to red flowers appear from early to midsummer. In warm climates the plants prefer light to moderate shade; in cool climates plants grow well in full sun. Plants are hardy in Zones 3 to 8.

Propagation: Propagate by division or seed.

Production: Typically grown in 4-in. (10-cm) to 3-qt (3-liter) pots. Plants will flower in the container but flowers are not required for sales because the leaves are so attractive. However, 10 weeks or less of 41°F (5°C) cold will promote flowering.

Comments: *H. micrantha* Douglas ex Lindl. 'Purple Palace' was the 1991 Perennial Plant of the Year.

HOSTA SPECIES

Common names: hosta, plantain lily.

Family: Liliaceae.

Description/uses: Hostas are the most important species in the perennial plant industry due to their colorful foliage, long flower spikes, and durability in shade (Fig. III-3 Garden Perennials). Thousands of species, hybrids, and cultivars are available, many of which have been bred by private breeders. The leaves vary in color from green, blue-green, to gold, often with white or yellow variegation. The rounded clumps of foliage range in size from 5 in. to 3.5 ft (13 to 105 cm) tall and from 10 in. to 9 ft (25 cm to 2.7 m) across. The 6-in.- to 6-ft (15- to 180-cm)-long flower spikes appear from midsummer to early fall. The drooping flowers are white to pale lavender. Plants are hardy from Zones 3 to 8. The cooler the climate, the more sun hostas will tolerate; morning sun is preferable.

FIGURE III-3 GARDEN PERENNIALS *Hosta* production.

Propagation: Plants are propagated primarily by division, but tissue culture is also common.

Production: Produce in 1-qt (1-liter) or larger containers. Plants will flower in the container but are generally salable without flowers. Some cultivars required 3 to 6 weeks 41°F (5°C) cold treatment to flower. Benzyladenine (BA) sprays at 3000 to 4000 ppm applied to single eye divisions will increase the number of shoots. BA can also be applied to established plants to increase shoot number.

Comments: Flower spikes and leaves can be cut and some cultivars are fragrant. Young plants may exhibit juvenile foliage that is more pointed and smoother than adult foliage; adult characteristics may take one or two growing seasons to develop. Plants are susceptible to water stress which causes necrotic leaf tips. High soluble salt levels can also cause necrotic leaf tips and edges.

IBERIS SEMPERVIRENS L.

Common names: evergreen candytuft, hardy candytuft.

Family: Cruciferae.

Description/uses: This low-growing, evergreen perennial forms compact mats 9 to 12 in. (23 to 30 cm) tall and up to 2 ft (60 cm) in diameter. The leaves are small and dark green. Short spikes of white flowers appear in early to midspring and flowering lasts up to 4 weeks. Plants are hardy from Zones 3 to 9 and prefer full sun.

Propagation: Plants are propagated by seed or cuttings.

Production: Plants are produced in 1-qt (1-liter) or larger pots and will flower in the container if propagated before January 1.

Comments: This species makes an attractive ground cover even when not in flower. Cool growing conditions may cause flowers to turn pinkish.

LAMIUM MACULATUM L.

Common name: dead nettle.

Family: Labiatae.

Description/uses: This low-growing perennial has silver and green foliage and short spikes of white, pink, or rose-colored flowers. Dead nettle can spread quickly, especially in moist areas, and grows to 12 in. (30 cm) tall when in flower. The flowers appear in early summer. Plants are hardy from Zones 3 to 8 and prefer moderate to heavy shade.

Propagation: Named cultivars should be propagated by cuttings or division. Seed can be used for the species.

Production: Plants are produced in 4-in. (10-cm) up to 1-qt (1-liter) pots. Plants will flower in the container.

Comments: This species is grown primarily for its colorful foliage.

LEUCANTHEMUM ×SUPERBUM (J. INGRAM) BERGMANS EX KENT.

Common name: shasta daisy.

Family: Compositae.

Description/uses: The shasta daisy has classic daisy flowers with white petals and yellow disc florets. Some cultivars are double. The plants are hardy from Zones 5 to 8 and prefer full sun.

Propagation: Single-flowered cultivars are typically seed propagated and doubles are propagated by cuttings or division.

Production: Plants are typically produced in 1-qt (1-liter) or larger containers. Height can be controlled by one spray application of Bonzi at 40 to 60 ppm or one application of Sumagic at 125 to 130 ppm. Five weeks of 41°F (5°C) followed by LD will encourage rapid flowering.

Comments: Plants can be short lived, lasting only 2 to 3 years. Shasta daisies are also grown as cut flowers (see *Field-Grown Cut Flowers* chapter).

LIRIOPE MUSCARI (DECNE.) L.H. BAIL. AND L. SPICATA LOUR.

Common names: liriope, lily turf.

Family: Liliaceae.

Description/uses: Liriope are grown for their evergreen, narrow upright foliage and are one of the most durable plants in the landscape. Liriope tolerate heat, drought, and salt spray. The leaves are dark green; some cultivars have leaves striped with white or cream. Spikes of small white to lavender flowers are produced in late summer. Plants grow 8 to 18 in. (20 to 45 cm) tall and tolerate full sun to shade. Light shade is preferred. *L. muscari* is used primarily in Zones 6 to 9 and the cold-hardy *L. spicata* is used in Zones 4 to 6. *L. muscari* has tuberous roots and larger flowers than *L. spicata,* which spreads by means of rhizomes.

Propagation: Propagate named cultivars by division and species by seed.

Production: Produce in 4-in. (10-cm) to 1-qt (1-liter) pots.

Comments: *Ophiopogon japonicus* (L. f.) Ker-Gawl. (mondo grass) appears similar to liriope but is finer textured and slower growing. *O. japonicus* is hardy to Zone 6 or 7.

LUPINUS POLYPHYLLUS LINDL.

Common name: lupine.

Family: Leguminosae.

Description/uses: A vigorously growing flowering lupine is a spectacular specimen with tall spikes of richly colored flowers. The spikes are densely packed with pea-shaped florets colored white, blue, pink, red, and various shades in between. Plants grow 20 to 36 in. (50 to 90 cm) tall. Plants are hardy in Zones 4 to 8 and grow best in cool climates and sunny locations. While technically a perennial, plants are short lived, typically dying out before the second spring in warm climates. Plants do not tolerate excessive heat very well. One of the most popular lupine series is the Russell Strain, which is actually a hybrid among several species including *L. polyphyllus.*

Propagation: Propagate by seed.

Production: Produce in 1-qt (1-liter) to 1-gal (3.8-liter) pots. Will flower in large containers but can also be grown green in large cell packs or 4-in. (10-cm) pots.

Comments: The famous wild flower, Texas bluebonnet, is *L. texensis.* Numerous other *Lupinus* species are cultivated and some are popular cut flowers (see *Field-Grown Cut Flowers* chapter).

PAPAVER ORIENTALE L.

Common name: oriental poppy.

Family: Papaveraceae.

Description/uses: The large, crepe-paper-textured flowers are striking, 4 to 6 in. (10 to 15 cm) across and richly colored scarlet, orange, pink, salmon, or white. At the base of each petal is a deep purple to black blotch and the multiple stamens are also purple to black. Plants grow 2 to 3 ft (60 to 90 cm) tall and flower in late spring and early summer. Plants are hardy from Zones 3 to 7 and prefer morning sun and afternoon shade. Leaves senesce and plants go dormant during the summer in July and August.

Propagation: Propagate by seed, root cuttings, or division.

Production: Produce in 1-qt (1-liter) to 1-gal (3.8-liter) pots. Cold treatment at 40 to 45°F (4 to 7°C) is required for flowering.

Comments: Many other poppy species are grown including a number of annual species. *P. nudicaule* L. (Iceland poppy) is technically a perennial but is usually treated as an annual or tender perennial. Iceland poppy prefers cool climates and the flowers are brightly colored yellow, white, pink, orange, and scarlet.

PHLOX PANICULATA L.

Common names: garden phlox, perennial phlox.

Family: Polemoniaceae.

Description/uses: *P. paniculata* is one of the most stately garden perennials. It grows 2 to 3 ft (60 to 90 cm) tall and produces large, 6- to 10-in. (15- to 25-cm)-wide, clusters of fragrant flowers (Fig. III-4 Garden Perennials). The individual white, pink, or red flowers are 1 to 1.5 in. (2.5 to 4 cm) wide. Many cultivars are available. Plants are hardy in Zones 4 to 8 and perform best in full sun.

Propagation: Propagate by division or root or stem cuttings.

Production: Produce plants in 4-in. (10-cm) to 1-qt (1-liter) pots. LD can be used to

FIGURE III-4 GARDEN PERENNIALS *Phlox paniculata* 'Miss Holland.'

induce flowering. Height can be controlled by up to two spray applications of B-Nine at 5000 ppm each; some cultivars are not responsive.

Comments: Many *P. paniculata* cultivars are susceptible to powdery mildew, which can limit their use in the landscape. Several other *Phlox* species are grown commercially including *P. subulata* L. (moss pink or creeping phlox), which is a low-growing plant that flowers in early spring. Nine weeks of 41°F (5°C) is required for flowering. Phlox also makes excellent cut flowers (see *Field-Grown Cut Flowers* chapter).

SALVIA L. SPECIES

Common names: salvia, sage.

Family: Labiatae.

Description/uses: This large genus has many useful species, hybrids, and cultivars including several annual bedding plants and many cut flowers (see *Bedding Plants* and *Field-Grown Cut Flowers* chapters). *Salvia ×superba* Stapf. (or *S. nemorosa* L., depending on the source) is one of the more popular perennial species with 6- to 10-in. (15- to 25-cm) spikes of blue, purple, white, or rose-colored tubular flowers on 12- to 30-in. (30- to 75-cm)-tall plants. Plants are hardy in Zones 4 to 8, flower in midsummer, and prefer full sun.

Propagation: Cultivars are propagated by cuttings or division. Species can be seed propagated.

Production: Produce in 4-in. (10-cm) or larger pots. Plants will flower in the container. Cold treatment and/or LD may encourage rapid flowering but often is not required. Height can be controlled by up to four spray applications of B-Nine at 5000 ppm each, one spray application of Bonzi at 40 to 60 ppm, or one spray application of B-Nine (5000 ppm) + Cycocel (chlormequat) (1500 ppm).

Comments: Numerous other species are grown and many species are hardy only to Zone 8.

SEDUM L. SPECIES

Common name: stonecrop.

Family: Crassulaceae.

Description/uses: This large and diverse genus has provided many useful garden perennials, most of which are well suited to hot, sunny, well-drained locations. Sedums have thick succulent leaves that terminate in rounded clusters of small flowers. *S. spuria* Bieb. is a low-growing, spreading plant 4 to 6 in. (10 to 15 cm) tall with green, bronze, or red foliage and white, rose, or red flowers. *S. acre* L. is also a low-growing spreading plant, only 2 to 4 in. (5 to 10 cm) tall, with yellow flowers. *S.* ×Autumn Joy, *S.* ×Matrona, and *S. spectabile* [now known as *Hylotelephium spectablile* (Boreau) H. Ohba.] are upright-growing plants, 15 to 24 in. (38 to 60 cm) tall, with gray-green foliage and large pink to red flower clusters. Plants are hardy in Zones 3 to 9 and flower in late summer to fall.

Propagation: Propagate by stem cuttings, division, or seed.

Production: Produce in 4-in. (10-cm) to 1-gal (3.8-liter) pots. Use LD for flowering. Height can be controlled by one drench of application of Bonzi at 30 ppm or one spray application of Sumagic at 15 to 30 ppm; many cultivars are unresponsive to chemical growth retardants.

Comments: Numerous other sedum species are cultivated. Some cultivars are used as cut flowers (see *Field-Grown Cut Flowers* chapter).

VERONICA SPICATA L.

Common name: spike speedwell.

Family: Scrophulariaceae.

Description/uses: This upright-growing plant has 8- to 15-in. (20- to 38-cm)-long spikes of small blue, white, or pink flowers. The plants grow 18 to 24 in. (45 to 60 cm) tall and flower in midsummer. Plants are hardy in Zones 4 to 8 and prefer full sun to light shade.

Propagation: Named cultivars can be propagated by division and cuttings. The cultivar 'Blue Bouquet' and the species can be propagated by seed.

Production: Plants can be grown in 4-in. (10-cm) pots or larger and will flower in the container. Use 6 weeks or longer of 41°F (5°C) for rapid flowering. Height can be controlled by up to four spray applications of B-Nine at 5000 ppm each, one spray application of Bonzi at 20 to 40 ppm, two spray applications of B-Nine (5000 ppm) + Cycocel (1500 ppm), or one spray application of Sumagic at 20 to 40 ppm.

Comments: Many cultivars are probably hybrids of *V. spicata* with *V. austriaca* L., *V. incana* L. (whoolly speedwell), and *V. longifolia* L. *V. repens* Clarion ex DC in Lam. & DC is also grown; it is a low-growing plant only 1.5 in. (4 cm) tall. Numerous other *Veronica* species are also grown.

KEY POINTS

- Around the world untold numbers of plant species are grown as garden perennials.
- Each climate defines what a "perennial" species is for the region.
- Many perennial species do not flower well in the container and are sold green.
- More attention must be paid to marketing perennials than bedding plants. Every pot must be labeled, much culture information should be provided, and a display garden increases sales of whichever species is in flower in the garden at the time.
- Small green plants of some species can be grown in flats and large flowering plants can be produced by propagating in the summer or fall, growing in 1-qt (1-liter) or larger pots, and overwintering outdoors.

BIBLIOGRAPHY

Armitage, A.M. 1989. *Herbaceous Perennial Plants*, 2nd ed. Stipes Publishing, Champaign, Illinois.

Armitage, A.M. 2000. *Armitage's Garden Perennials*. Timber Press, Portland, Oregon.

Cheers, G. 1999. *Botanica*. Welcome Rain Publishers, New York.

Hamrick, D. 2003. *Ball Redbook*, vol. 2, 17th ed. Ball Publishing, Batavia, Illinois.

Huxley, A., M. Griffiths, and M. Levy. 1992. *The New Royal Horticultural Society Dictionary of Gardening*, Vols. 1–4. Stockton Press, New York.

Latimer, J. 2001. Herbaceous perennials, pp. 98–110 in *Tips on Regulating Growth of Floriculture Crops*, M.L. Gaston, L.A. Kunkle, P.S. Konjoian, and M.F. Wilt, editors. Ohio Florists' Association Services, Columbus, Ohio.

Nau, J. 1996. *Ball Perennial Manual*. Ball Publishing, Batavia, Illinois.

Whipker, B.E. 2003. Growth regulators for floricultural crops, pp. 439–448 in *2003 North Carolina Agricultural Chemicals Manual*. College of Agriculture and Life Science, North Carolina State University, Raleigh.

Herbs

INTRODUCTION

Herbs are defined gastronomically or horticulturally, not botanically. The list of plant species considered to be herbs varies from region to region within a country and among countries. The difference between an herb and a spice or a medicinal plant is open for discussion. Regardless, customers expect to find herb plants and seeds in any dynamic garden center. A firm may grow only a limited selection of herbs or may specialize in herbs. For example, firms have specialized in growing fresh nasturtium (*Tropaolum majus* L.) leaves and flowers, pansy (*Viola ×wittrockiana* Gams.) flowers, and packaged herbs for grocery stores. Frequently, herbs and flowers grown for direct consumption are produced under protection without pesticides.

Herbs are used as flavorings in cooking or fresh as garnishes on various fresh foods. Herbs are aromatic and frequently have high oil content. Some herbs are also used for teas. The Labiatae Juss. (Mint) and Umbelliferae Juss. (Parsley) families are dominant in the list of herbs (Huxley et al., 1992). Herbs also are used for their ornamental value (leaf color, pattern, or texture) and many are used as edgings in the garden or sheared into a border. Cut herbs, especially various basil (*Ocimum basilicum* L.) cultivars, are frequently included in mixed bouquets to provide fragrance.

Though herbs are divided into annuals, biennials, or perennials, these classes are artificial and based on climatic location. In many sections of the world, the majority of herbs are treated as annuals because of severe winters. Several biennial and perennial species can be propagated annually and produce the required leaf canopy in one growing season. Although flowers are often of secondary interest, many herb species, including thyme (*Thymus* L. spp.), sage (*Salvia officinalis* L.), and chives (*Allium schoenoprasum* L.), can produce stunning floral displays and are very decorative in the home garden.

Herbs are typically grown in a variety of pot sizes. Combination gardens of several herb species together in a decorative pot, hanging basket, hanging bag, urn, strawberry jar, or window box are also popular. Most herb plants are sold in the spring, but some species such as rosemary (*Rosemarinus officinalis* L.) and lavender (*Lavendula augustifolia* Mill.) can also be sold during the winter holidays as potted plants in 4- to 6-in. (10- to 15-cm) pots, many of which are trimmed into various topiary shapes. Some species, such as parsley [*Petroselenium crispum* (Mill.) A.W. Hill.] and basil, are suitable for plug propagation. Generally, however, scheduling of herbs is difficult due to the wide range of propagation methods and requirements.

The following list includes the most commonly grown species (Bailey and Bailey, 1976; Long, 1998; Miller, 1985; Wilkins, 1985). Of this list, the most important commercial species include basil, chives, dill (*Anethum graveolens* L.), lavender, parsley, peppermint (*Mentha ×piperita* L.), spearmint (*Mentha spicata* L.), rosemary, sage, and thyme.

ANNUALS

Anethum graveolens L., dill (Umbelliferae). Grows to 3 ft (90 cm) tall. Germinate several seeds per pot at 70°F (21°C) and grow at 55 to 65°F (13 to 18°C).

Carthamus tinctorius L., false saffron, safflower (Compositae). Grows up to 3 ft (90 cm) tall. Germinate seed at 70°F (21°C); thereafter grow at 65 to 70°F (18 to 21°C).

Coriandium sativum L., coriander, Chinese parsley (Umbelliferae). Grows to 3 ft (90 cm) tall. Germinate four to five seeds per pot and grow at 55 to 65°F (13 to 18°C).

Ocimum basilicum L., common basil, sweet basil (Labiatae). Grows up to 2 ft (60 cm) tall. The numerous cultivars have leaf colors from green to purple and leaf edges from entire to

FIGURE III-I HERBS *Ocimum basilicum* plant ready for marketing.

highly dentated (Fig. III-1 Herbs). Heavily branched cultivars with 0.5-in. (1.5-cm) leaves can be grown as borders in herb gardens or perennial beds. Germinate seed at 70°F (21°C) and grow four plants per 4-in. (10-cm) pot at 62 to 65°F (17 to 18°C). Freshly harvested shoots and leaves are injured by 41°F (5°C) storage (Lange and Cameron, 1998). They can be stored for up to 45 days at 68°F (20°C) in 1.5% O_2 and 0% CO_2 as compared with 21% O_2 and 0.03% CO_2. Seeds can be infected with *Fusarium* and plants slowly decline as summer temperatures increase (M. Daughtry, personal communication).

Origanum majorana L., sweet marjoram, annual marjoram (Labiatae). Grows to 2 ft (60 cm) tall. Germinate seed at 70°F (21°C); produce at 55 to 65°F (13 to 18°C). The species can be propagated by cuttings also. The spreading growth habit makes this species suitable for the edges of urns, window boxes, or hanging baskets. This species is a perennial typically grown as an annual.

Pimpinella anisum L., common anise (Umbelliferae). Grows to 2 ft (60 cm) tall. Germinate seed at 70°F (21°C) and grow at 60 to 62°F (16 to 17°C).

Satureja hortensis L., summer savory (Labiatae). Grows to 18 in. (45 cm) tall. Germinate seed at 70°F (21°C) and grow at 60 to 62°F (16 to 17°C).

BIENNIALS

Carum carvi L., caraway (Umbelliferae). Seed propagated and grows to 2 ft (60 cm) tall. Plants are hardy in Zones 5 to 10.

Foeniculum vulgare Mill., fennel (Umbelliferae). Grows to 5 ft (1.5 m) tall. The several cultivars include one with bronze foliage. Germinate seed at 70°F (21°C) and grow at 55 to 60°F (13 to 16°C). Plants are hardy in Zones 5 to 10.

Petroselenium crispum (Mill.) A.W. Hill., parsley (Umbelliferae). Grows to 3 ft (90 cm) tall and has numerous cultivars. Germinate seed at 70°F (21°C) and grow four plants per pot at 60 to 65°F (16 to 18°C). Senescence of harvested leaves was retarded by storage at 41°F (5°C) in a modified atmosphere of 10% O_2 and 11% CO_2 for up to 4 months (Apeland, 1971); leaves can be stored at 32°F (0°C) but are injured at 28°F (−2°C) (Hruschka and Wang, 1979). Plants are hardy in Zones 5 to 11, but may regrow from the roots in colder climates.

Salvia sclarea L., clary (Labiatae). Seed propagated and grows to 3 ft (90 cm) tall. Several cultivars are available. Can be grown as a perennial. Plants are hardy in Zones 5 to 10.

PERENNIALS

Allium schoenoprasum L., chives (Amarylidacaeae J.St.-Hil.). Grows to 2 ft (60 cm) tall. Though a perennial this species is often grown as an annual. Germinate seed at 70°F (21°C) and grow 12 to 18 seedlings per 4-in. (10-cm) pot at 60 to 65°F (16 to 18°C), then reduce temperature. Plants are hardy in Zones 5 to 10, but may survive in colder climates with protection.

Allium tuberosum Rottl. ex Spreng., garlic, Chinese chives, Oriental garlic (Amaryllidaceae). Grows to 20 in. (50 cm) tall. Sow 12 to 18 seeds per pot. Germinate at 70°F (21°C), grow at 60 to 65°F (16 to 18°C), and finish at 50 to 55°F (10 to 13°C). Plants are hardy in Zones 7 to 11.

Aloysia triphylla (L'Hérit.) Britt., lemon verbena (Verbenaceae St.-Hil.). A shrub growing to 10 ft (3 m) tall; commonly grown in the tropics. Cuttings root with ease in September. Plants are hardy in Zones 8 to 11.

Armoracia rusticana P. Gaertnj., May. & Scherb., horseradish (Cruciferae Juss.). Grows to 15 in. (38 cm) tall. As the shoots of this deep-rooted perennial emerge from the soil, dig the root-stock and cut into 4-in. (10-cm) segments and root at 70°F (21°C). Plants are hardy in Zones 5 to 10.

Artemesia absinthium L., wormwood (Compositae). Propagate by stem cuttings at 65 to 70°F (18 to 21°C), which root with ease, or by division. Plants are hardy in Zones 4 to 10.

Artemesia dracunculus L., tarragon (Compositae). Grows to 5 ft (1.5 m) tall. Propagated by division, cuttings, or seed. After cuttings are rooted or seed are germinated at 70°F (21°C), hold and finish at 60 to 65°F (16 to 18°C). Plants are hardy in Zones 6 to 9.

Artemesia schmidtiana Maxim., silver mound (Compositae). Grows to 2 ft (60 cm) tall. Dwarf forms are available. Propagate by division or cuttings. Root three cuttings per pot at 70°F (21°C) and grow at 65 to 70°F (18 to 21°C). Plants are hardy in Zones 3 to 9.

Laurus nobiles L., bay, sweet bay, laurel (Lauraceae). Grows to 40 ft (12 m) tall. Several cultivars have leaf or growth variations. Propagate 5- to 6-in. (13- to 15-cm)-long cuttings using rooting hormones [0.3% indole-3-butyric acid (IBA)] and a medium temperature of 70°F (21°C). Mist can be used in the rooting process. Plants are hardy in Zones 7 to 10.

Lavandula augustifolia Mill., English lavender (Labiatae). Grows 2 to 3 ft (60 to 100 cm) tall. Germinate seed at 65 to 75°F (18 to 24°C) and grow at 58 to 65°F (14 to 18°C). Cuttings root with ease at 70°F (21°C). Use three plants per 3-in. (7.5-cm) pot. Six or more weeks of 41°F (5°C) are required for flowering regardless of photoperiod (Runkle et al., 1998). Plants are hardy in Zones 6 to 10.

Lavandula dentata L., French lavender (Labiatae). Grows 1 to 2 ft (30 to 60 cm) tall. Germinate seed at 65 to 75°F (18 to 24°C) and grow at 58 to 65°F (14 to 18°C). Cuttings root with ease at 70°F (21°C). Use three plants per 3-in. (7.5-cm) pot. Plants are hardy in Zones 8 to 10.

Melissa officinalis L., common bee balm, bee balm, lemon balm, sweet balm (Labiatae). Grows to 2 ft (60 cm) tall. Seed is the most rapid means of propagation. Plants are hardy in Zones 4 to 10.

Mentha ×piperita L. (*M. aquatica* L. × *M. spicata* L.), peppermint (Labiatae). Grows to 3 ft (90 cm) tall. Propagate by vegetative runners or seeds. This species can be invasive in the home garden. Germinate seed at 70 to 75°F

(21 to 24°C) and grow at 55 to 58°F (13 to 14°C). Postharvest handling of harvested leaves is similar to that for *Petroselenium*. Plants are hardy in Zones 3 to 10.

Mentha spicata L., spearmint (Labiatae). Grows to 30 in. (75 cm) tall. Propagate by vegetative shoots or seed. Root cuttings at 70°F (21°C) and grow at 60 to 65°F (16 to 18°C). This species can be invasive in the home garden. Germinate seed at 70 to 75°F (21 to 24°C) and grow at 55 to 58°F (13 to 14°C). Plants are hardy in Zones 3 to 10.

Nepeta cataria L., catnip, catmint (Labiatae). Grows to 3 ft (90 cm) tall. Propagate by cuttings. Plants are hardy in Zones 3 to 10.

Origanum vulgare spp. *hirtum* (Link) Iets. (synonym: *O. heracleoticum* L.), pot or winter marjoram, green or Greek oregano (Labiatae). Grows to 30 in. (75 cm) tall. Germinate three seeds or root three cuttings per pot at 70°F (21°C); grow and finish at 50 to 65°F (10 to 18°C). Plants are hardy in Zones 6 to 9.

Origanum vulgare L., marjoram, pot marjoram, wild marjoram, oregano (Labiatae). Grows to 30 in. (75 cm) tall. Cultivars are available. Germinate six seeds per pot at 70°F (21°C); produce at 50 to 65°F (10 to 18°C). The spreading growth habit makes this species suitable for the edges of urns, window boxes, and hanging baskets. Plants are hardy in Zones 5 to 9.

Pelargonium L'Hérit. species, scented leaved geraniums (apple, lemon, peppermint, nutmeg, and numerous other fragrances) (Geraniaceae Juss). Scented leaved geraniums are treated as annuals in cold climates. Generally cutting propagated at 70°F (21°C) and grown at 65 to 70°F (18 to 21°C). See also *Pelargonium* chapter.

Rosemarinus officinalis L., rosemary (Labiatae). Grows to 4 ft (1.2 m). Cultivars are available. Germinate seed at 70°F (21°C) and grow four to six seedlings per pot at 55 to 70°F (13 to 21°C). Three cuttings per pot can also be rooted at 70°F (21°C); grow at 60 to 65°F (16 to 18°C). Plants are hardy in Zones 6 to 11.

Salvia elegans Vahl., pineapple-scented sage (Labiatae). Grows to 3.5 ft (1.05 m) tall. Must be propagated by cuttings, which root within 2 weeks at 65°F (18°C). Plants are hardy in Zones 8 to 11.

Salvia officinalis L., common sage, garden sage (Labiatae) (Fig. III-2 Herbs). Grows to 2 ft (60 cm) tall. Various cultivars have different

FIGURE III-2 HERBS *Salvia officinalis*
'Berggarten' flat.

FIGURE III-3 HERBS *Thymus vulgaris* 'Aureus.'

leaf pigmentations, which must be propagated by cuttings. Seed-propagated cultivars are available. Root cuttings or germinate seed at 70°F (21°C); grow at 55 to 65°F (13 to 18°C). Plants are hardy in Zones 5 to 10.

Satureja montana L., winter savory (Labiatae). Grows to 12 in. (30 cm) tall. Seed propagated. Plants are hardy in Zones 6 to 10.

Teucrium chamaedrys L., germander (Labiatae). This dwarf shrub grows up to 2 ft (60 cm) tall. Root cuttings early in the spring at 70°F (21°C). Rooting is rapid, within 3 weeks. The medium must be well drained. Plants are hardy in Zones 5 to 10.

Thymus ×citriodorus (Pers.) Schreb. ex Schweig & Korte. (*T. pulegioides* L. × *T. vulgaris* L.), lemon thyme (Labiatae). This short shrub is 4 to 12 in. (10 to 30 cm) tall. Cultivars are available. Lemon thyme is propagated by 3- to 6-in. (7.5- to 15-cm) cuttings at 70°F (21°C) medium temperature. Cuttings should be made from the soft green growth; use four to six cuttings per 3-in. (7.5-

cm) pot. The spreading growth habit makes this species suitable for the edges of urns, window boxes, or hanging baskets. Plants are hardy in Zones 7 to 10.

Thymus vulgaris L., garden thyme, common thyme (Labiatae). This short shrub is 6 to 15 in. (15 to 43 cm) tall (Fig. III-3 Herbs). Cutting-propagated cultivars are available. Six to eight seeds can also be used per 3-in. (7.5-cm) pot. Seeds are germinated and cuttings are rooted at 70°F (21°C). Use five cuttings per pot. Plants are grown at 60 to 65°F (16 to 18°C) and finished at 50 to 60°F (10 to 16°C). The spreading growth habit makes this species suitable for the edges of urns, window boxes, or hanging baskets. Plants are hardy in Zones 7 to 10.

KEY POINTS

- Herbs are a small, but important segment of the bedding plant industry.
- Herbs are sold as potted plants, or leaves are harvested and sold either fresh or dried for fresh use.
- Herbs have no botanical standing but are defined horticulturally as flavorings in cooking and teas.
- Herbs are propagated by seed, cuttings, or division.

- Some of the most popular herbs are basil (*Ocimum basilicum*), chives (*Allium schoenoprasum*), dill (*Anethum graveolens*), lavender (*Lavandula augustifolia*), parsley (*Petroselenium crispum*), peppermint (*Mentha ×piperita*), spearmint (*Mentha spicata*), rosemary (*Rosemarinus officinalis*), common sage (*Salvia officinalis*), and thyme (*Thymus* spp.).
- No pesticides or plant growth regulators can be used on herbs.

Apeland, J. 1971. Factors affecting respiration and colour during storage of parsley. *Acta Horticulturae* 20:43–52.

Bailey, L.H., and E.Z. Bailey. 1976. In *Hortus Third: A Concise Dictionary of Plants Cultivated in the United States and Canada*. Macmillan, New York.

Hruschka, H.W., and C.Y. Wang. 1979. Storage and shelf life of packaged watercress, parsley, and mint. *United States Department of Agriculture Market Report* 1102:1–19.

Huxley, A., M. Griffiths, and M. Levy. 1992. In *The New Royal Horticultural Society Dictionary of Gardening*, vols. 1–4. Stockton Press, New York.

Lange, D.L., and A.C. Cameron. 1998. Controlled-atmosphere storage of sweet basil. *HortScience* 33:741–743.

Long, J. 1998. Herbs, pp. 253–271 in *Ball Redbook*, 16th ed., V. Ball, editor. Ball Publishing, Batavia, Illinois.

Miller, R.A. 1985. *The Potential of Herbs*. Acres U.S.A., Kansas City, Missouri.

Runkle, E.S., R.D. Heins, A.C. Cameron, and W.H. Carlson. 1998. Cold treatments alter the photoperiodic flowering response of some herbaceous perennial species. *HortScience* 33:508. (Abstract)

Wilkins, H. 1985. Asexually propagated bedding plants, pp. 471–502 in *Bedding Plants III*, 3rd ed. J.W. Mastalerz and E.J. Holcomb, editors. Pennsylvania Flower Growers, University Park, Pennsylvania.

Woody Cuts, Forced

INTRODUCTION

Several woody trees, shrubs, and vine plants can be grown and forced for spring flowers and foliage.

1. Flowering quince, *Chaenomeles japonica* (Thunb.) Spach. and *C. speciosa* (Sweet) Hak. (Huxley et al., 1992), forced for their white, pink, peach, or red flowers.

2. Flowering dogwood, *Cornus florida* L., forced for its large white or pink flowers.

3. Deutzia, *Deutzia gracilis* Sieb. and Zucc. and *D. scabra* Thunb., forced for their white to pink flowers.

4. Forsythia, *Forsythia ×intermedia* Zab., forced for its yellow flowers (Fig. III-1 Woody Cuts, Forced).

5. Honeysuckle, *Lonicera* L., vines and shrubs, can also be grown for their summer fruits and winter branches.

6. Magnolia, *Magnolia soulangiana* Soul.-Bod. and *M. stellata* (Sieb. and Zucc.) Maxim., grown for its large flowers, foliage, or fruits.

7. Ornamental crab apple and apple cultivars, *Malus* Mill., forced for their white, pink, or rose-colored flowers.

FIGURE III-I WOODY CUTS, FORCED
Forsythia ×intermedia flowers.

8. Mockorange, *Philadelphus coronarius* L., grown for its white, fragrant flowers.

9. Pieris, *Pieris japonica* (Thunb.) D. Don ex G. Don., grown for its interesting pendulous panicles of small white to pink flowers.

10. Ornamental flowering almond, apricot, peach, plum, and nectarine, *Prunus* L., forced for their white, pink or rose-colored, often fragrant flowers.

11. Rhododendron, *Rhododendron catawbiense* Michx. and other species and hybrids, grown for its large flower clusters.

12. Pussy willow, *Salix caprea* L., *S. discolor* L., and other species and cultivars, grown for its fuzzy white, pink, or gray catkins.

13. Spirea, *Spiraea prunifolia* Sieb. and Zucc., grown for its arching branches of white flower clusters.

14. Lilac, *Syringa vulgaris* L., grown for its well-loved sprays of fragrant flowers.

15. Cypress tree, *Taxodium distichum* (L.) Rich. (Zones 5 to 10), and larch tree, *Larix decidua* Mill. (Zones 3 to 5) or *L. laricina* (DuRoi.) K. Koch. (Zones 2 to 5), branches forced for their foliage.

16. Viburnum, *Viburnum opulus* L., branches force for their white flower clusters.

This list is not inclusive, but contains only a few of the species that can be harvested or forced and sold in commercial floriculture. Little information is available on the basic horticultural aspects of producing and forcing various spring flowering plants (Coggeshall, 1956). Much information is handed down from one generation to the next in Europe as an oral tradition where woody species production, forcing, and consumption are more prevalent than in North America. Dutch-forced *Syringa* and *Forsythia* branches are commonly exported to North America (Green, 1984).

Several characteristics are needed for a species to be forced as a spring cut, including precocious flowering, forcing ability, long postharvest life, tolerance to shipping, and ability to rehydrate, maintain turgidity, and develop the inflorescence after harvest. The production and forcing requirements for two species, lilac and forsythia, have been well documented and serve as examples for other species.

FIELD PLANT PRODUCTION

Plants are normally field produced and one of three harvesting processes is followed: (1) The entire plant is dug with an earthen ball of roots and moved into a forcing environment. The entire plant can be used as a specimen for exhibition purposes or the branches can be harvested after they have developed to the appropriate flowering stage. (2) Branches are removed from plants growing outdoors, brought into the forcing environment, and placed in appropriate forcing solutions and temperatures for flower development. (3) Branches are harvested later in the spring season at the appropriate flowering stages directly from plants in the field. Besides field production, plants can be grown in pots or containers and forced as specimens for shows or branches harvested.

For lilac the new flower buds begin to initiate and develop as the old flowers are in their final stage of senescence. Although the time of flower initiation varies with the cultivar and location, generally it commences around June 21 and is completed by late August in the Netherlands. When the upper leaf pair on the new flowering shoot has fully unfolded, one of two steps can be taken to induce early floral induction and greater flower numbers per inflorescence—plants are either root pruned or sprayed with 5900 ppm B-Nine (daminozide) in May to June (Sytsema, 1969). Some cultivars require no additional flower induction treatments. Cycocel (chlormequat) can also be used in June to replace root pruning, which is a labor-intensive process. These treatments appear to be unique for lilac (Benson, 1990; Sytsema, 1969; van den Berg, 1981).

DORMANCY

Dormancy has been well documented with both forsythia and lilac (Broertjes, 1955; Doorenbos, 1953; Rünger, 1985; Sytsema, 1962, 1969; Wilkins, 1986), but is similar for many woody species, including *Spirea* and *Weigelia* (Stimart, 1986a, b). Flower buds are fully differentiated and developed by August, but are dormant. Dormancy can be divided into three stages:

1. *Summer dormancy*, during which growth inhibitor is not found in the flower bud, but within the plant. This inhibition can frequently be controlled by removing the leaves and subjecting stems to an 86°F (30°C) 12-hr hot water bath. After the treatment in late summer, branches will immediately flower if placed in an appropriate floral preservation solution.

2. *Winter dormancy*, during which the inhibitor is within the flower bud and a natural or controlled cold temperature treatment must occur to overcome the inhibition. Some short-term cold treatments, plus hot water treatments and LD light treatments, are effective for rapid flowering during forcing. Four to 8 weeks at 41°F (5°C) are the most common optimum temperature and duration to overcome winter dormancy after late October; by December only 2 weeks of 31°F (–0.5°C) plus warm water or 30 days of cold only is required.

3. *Imposed dormancy*, during which no inhibitors are present, but growth is restricted by unfavorable natural late winter temperatures. At this time, branches will quickly flower when harvested and placed into a warm environment. Plants force with ease after January. Branches of forsythia with dormant buds can be harvested in February and held for long durations if packed dry at 32°F (0°C) for late season forcing.

FORCING TEMPERATURE

Long, 2-year-old forsythia shoots with dormant buds are harvested, after which cut stems are soaked in 82°F (28°C) water for 8 to 12 hr. The time to flower from harvest varies from 3 weeks for stems harvested in January to 2 weeks for stems harvested in February to only 1 week in March. Forcing temperatures are 59 to 64°F (15 to 18°C) at near 100% RH at low light intensities or in dark. If possible, ship at 41°F (5°C) in water or in an opening solution (Nowak and Rudnicki, 1990; Wilkins, 1986). Stems are ready for immediate marketing when buds show color. Field-grown stems can also be harvested at this stage for direct sales.

Cut branches from flowering almond, peach, plum, apricot, nectarine, cherry, and other *Prunus* species can be forced with similar holding solutions and shipping conditions as for forsythia (Coggeshall, 1956; Nowak and Rudnicki, 1990; Stimart, 1986b). All species force in 3 to 4 weeks when harvested in January and only 1 to 2 weeks in March.

For lilac, naturally cold-treated plants are lifted and moved into the forcing greenhouse. Plants should be 6 years or older and long, 1-year-old shoots are harvested. Forcing temperatures will vary according to the season and similar forcing solutions are used as for forsythia (Table III-1 Woody Cuts, Forced). After the plants are forced and branches have been removed, the remaining shoots are cut back, allowing two or three axillary buds to remain. Greenhouse temperatures are reduced and new axillary growth commences. Plants are replanted in the field when the likelihood of frost has passed. Individual plants may be decades old and can be on their own roots or on grafted rootstocks (Green, 1984).

FORCING SOLUTIONS

Numerous postharvest holding solutions have been used or proposed (Nowak and Rudnicki, 1990). The basic requirements include a water acidifier, a carbohydrate source (sucrose), an ethylene inhibitor, and a microorganism inhibitor. Sytsema-Kalkman (1991) reported that 8-HQS (hydroxyquinoline sulfate) increased water flow rate and longevity of lilac branches. Similarly, van Doorn et al. (1991) noted a similar result with 8-HQC (hydroxyquinoline citrate) and also found that 8-HQC, aminoethoxyvinylglycine (AVG), silver nitrate, and silver thiosulfate (STS) reduced ethylene syn-

TABLE III-1 WOODY CUTS, FORCED

Forcing temperatures used for lilac *(Syringa)* branches (summary from Rünger, 1985).

September	109°F (43°C) for 4 or 5 days; gradually reduce to 60°F (16°C) over 4-week forcing period
October to late November	100°F (38°C) for 4 or 5 days; gradually reduce to 60°F (16°C) over 3- to 4-week forcing period
Early December	72 to 75°F (22 to 24°C)
Late December/early January	68 to 72°F (20 to 22°C)[a]
Late January/February	64°F (18°C)[a]
Late February to end of season	61 to 64°F (16 to 18°C)[a]

[a]Branches can be soaked at 86°F (30°C) for up to 12 hr to hasten forcing.

thesis, increased water uptake, and enhanced longevity of lilac branches.

Lilac have been reported to be sensitive to ethylene, and some form of silver, such as silver nitrate or STS, to block ethylene action is recommended. If forced branches of lilac become wilted, they should be recut and placed in warm water at 110°F (43°C) (Nowak and Rudnicki, 1990). Cut stems when the first florets are open. Transport or store cut stems at 41°F (5°C) (L. Høyer, personal communication).

KEY POINTS

- Numerous species can be forced into flower or leaf for spring floral arrangements.
- The most commonly forced species are *Forsythia*, willow (*Salix*), and lilac (*Syringa*).
- The forcing of woody plants or branches into flower requires the breaking of one or more of three different types of dormancy:
summer dormancy, winter dormancy, and imposed dormancy.
- Forcing temperature and treatment vary with the time of year that branches are to be forced.
- Floral preservatives are used.

BIBLIOGRAPHY

Benson, J. 1990. Dutch production of cut lilacs. *Greenhouse Grower* 8(10):110, 113.

Broertjes, C. 1955. The forcing of *Forsythia intermedia spectabilis* Khne., pp. 1065–1071 in *Fourteenth International Horticultural Congress—1955*, vol. II, The Hague, Scheveningen, The Netherlands.

Coggeshall, R.G. 1956. Forcing woody plants for flower shows. *American Nurseryman* 103(2):7–8, 62–63.

Doorenbos, J. 1953. Orienterend onderzoek over het forceren van forsythia en rhododendron. *Mededelingen Directeur van de Tuinbouw* 16:533–543. (in Dutch, English summary)

Green, J.L. 1984. Lilac as a forced, cut flower. *Ornamentals Northwest Newsletter* 8(2):13–19.

Huxley, A., M. Griffiths, and M. Levy. 1992. *The New Royal Horticultural Society Dictionary of Gardening*, vols. 1–4. Stockton Press, New York.

Nowak, J., and R.M. Rudnicki. 1990. *Postharvest Handling and Storage of Cut Flowers, Florist Greens and Potted Plants*. Timber Press, Portland, Oregon.

Rünger, W. 1985. *Syringa vulgaris*, pp. 403–405 in *Handbook of Flowering*, vol. IV, A.H. Halevy, editor. CRC Press, Boca Raton, Florida.

Stimart, D. 1986a. *Spiraea*, pp. 341–343 in *Handbook of Flowering*, vol. V, A.H. Halevy, editor. CRC Press, Boca Raton, Florida.

Stimart, D. 1986b. *Weigelia*, pp. 385–387 in *Handbook of Flowering*, vol. V, A.H. Halevy, editor. CRC Press, Boca Raton, Florida.

Sytsema, W. 1962. Flowering of lilac on cut branches. *Mededleingen van de Landbouwhogeschool te Wageningen. Nederland* 62(2):1–57. (in Dutch, English summary)

Sytsema, W. 1969. Influence of growth retardants on flower bud initiation of lilac. *Acta Horticulturae* 14:205–207.

Sytsema-Kalkman, E.C. 1991. Post-harvest studies on *Syringa vulgaris*. *Acta Horticulturae* 298: 127–133.

van den Berg, A.J. 1981. *Concise Review of the Culture of Lilac*. Number 616, November, Advisory Agency for Horticulture, Aalsmeer-Utrecht, The Netherlands.

van Doorn, W.G., H. Harkema, and E. Otma. 1991. Is vascular blockage in stems of cut lilac flowers meditated by ethylene? *Acta Horticulturae* 298:177–181.

Wilkins, H. 1986. *Forsythia ×intermedia*, pp. 113–116 in *Handbook of Flowering*, vol. V, A.H. Halevy, editor. CRC Press, Boca Raton, Florida.

Index